חמשה חומשי תורה

תרומת צבי

The Pentateuch
T'RUMATH TZVI

חמשה חומשי תורה

תרומת צבי

מתורגם ומבואר

מאת

הגאון כמוהר״ר שמשון בן כמוהר״ר רפאל הירש
פ״פ זללה״ה

שומר משמרת הקודש בק״ק עדת ישורון בפפד״מ יע״א

לקט וערך

אפרים הלוי ארץ

תורגם מחדש לאנגלית

רייזל הירשלער

יודאיקא פרעסס

שנת **ת**רומות הרב **ש**משון רפאל הירש **נ**לקט מפירושו לפ״ק

ניו יארק

T'RUMATH TZVI

The Pentateuch
with a translation by
SAMSON RAPHAEL HIRSCH
and excerpts from
The Hirsch Commentary

Edited by
EPHRAIM ORATZ

English Translation
from the original German by
GERTRUDE HIRSCHLER

The Judaica Press, Inc.
New York • 1990

TABLE OF CONTENTS

ACKNOWLEDGMENTS

The publisher wishes to express his appreciation to the following individuals who participated in the preparation of this volume. They represent many countries of origin and reflect a broad spectrum of Jewish scholarship, but they are all united in their staunch loyalty to the Judaism expounded by Samson Raphael Hirsch.

Gertrude Hirschler, of New York City, noted translator and editor of traditional Jewish classics, whose personal and professional dedication and long-time friendship acted as a catalyst in the development of the conceptual approach that formed this work.

Rabbi Ephraim Oratz, of Jerusalem, who accomplished the formidable and challenging task of selecting the commentaries to be included in this introductory volume. Beyond this, he was a devoted, keen-eyed and sensitive editor of the whole, providing halakhic insights and stylistic suggestions and corrections, imbuing this work with the abiding imprint of his scholarship and editorial acumen.

Rabbi David Feinstein of New York City, Professor Esra Shereshevsky of Philadelphia, Pa., and Tovia (Theodor) Preschel of Brooklyn, N.Y., who gave generously of their time and knowledge.

Mr. Michael Blatt, Mrs. Neva Goldstein-Alpern, Mrs. Abigail Klein Leichman, Ms. Bonnie Goldman, of New York City, Mrs. Phyllis Bloch of London and Ms. Aida Golt of Montreal, who rendered invaluable service as copy editors and proofreaders.

Nachum Kornfeld, Avrohom Walzer and the staff of Simcha Graphic Associates, and Mr. Sam Goldman of Publishers' Bindery, who contributed unstintingly to this endeavor and whose professional expertise were always available for advice and help in the set-up and planning of this volume.

And, *achron achron chaviv*, Mr. Jacques Schwalbe of New York, whose enthusiasm, vision and generosity spurred the initiation and completion of this work.

Blessed be He Who kept us in life, preserved us and enabled us to carry this work to its conclusion.

Jack Goldman
JUDAICA PRESS

Rabbinic approbation by Rabbi Isaac Elḥanan Spektor (1817–96) to the Hebrew translation of the Hirsch Commentary on the Pentateuch begun by Rabbi Moses Zalman Aronsohn of Kovno (who, however, died before he could complete the work).

It is known among the tribes of Israel what has been achieved by that righteous man, the pious *gaon* Rabbi Samson Raphael Hirsch, of blessed memory, late head of the *beth din* of the holy congregation of Frankfurt am Main, who dedicated his strength and energy to Israel and its Torah, in order to restore the crown of the Law to its ancient glory and to lead the hearts of tens of thousands of [the people of] Israel back to our Father in Heaven. This is the man who, until his extreme old age, devoted his whole life to [the task of] winning souls for the Torah and the Testimony, to support and uphold it, with his activities—"the labors of the righteous are life-giving" [Proverbs 10:16]—as well as with his wonderful, renowned books that are irradiated by the light of the Torah and the lamp of the commandments. . . .

However, the light stored up in his books was hidden from those tens of thousands in Israel who do not know the German language. . . .

Now . . . I will offer my approbation and my blessing to my friend, the worthy R. Moses Zalman Aronsohn . . . for the great and splendid work which he has now undertaken, namely, to translate from the German language into our sacred tongue . . . the great and wonderful Commentary on the Torah . . . by the *gaon* Rabbi Samson [Raphael] Hirsch, of blessed memory.

This is the precious and much praised commentary which is indeed a crown of glory, "the beauty of Israel" [II Samuel 1:19]. It is a most honored work, done for the sake of heaven, a lovely, choice treasure to exalt the Holy Torah, to give strength and honor to the religious heritage of the community of Jacob. The many original interpretations introduced by this *gaon* and sage, who was great in knowledge and who conveyed understanding in a manner that is lucid and in conformity with reason, are invaluable. Of equally matchless value is his demonstration of the complete unity of the Written Torah and the Oral Law, which he accomplished in a truly magnificent manner. . . .

How deep are his thoughts, which reveal the wonders and the wisdom concealed in the Torah of the Lord! He removes all the alien and doubtful ideas raised by would-be scholars from generation to generation, and demonstrates that the Torah of the Lord is perfect, the word of God stands forever, and that the light of the Written Torah and the Oral Law will live for all time. . . .

Kovno, Monday, the third day of
the month of Marheshvan, 5656 (1895)

(signed) ISAAC ELḤANAN, residing in this
holy community

RABBI JACOB I. RUDERMAN
400 MT. WILSON LANE
BALTIMORE, MD. 21208

יעקב יצחק הלוי רודרמן
באלטימאר, מד.

הנה מי ימלל גבורת גדולת הגאון והצדיק הגרש"ר הירש זצ"ל אשר עוד בחייו ובדור שלפנינו העריצוהו גדולי עולם במעשיו הכבירים למען השי"ת ולמען תורתו והפליא לעשות לעמוד בפרץ ולחזק את בדק בית ישראל במדינתו באשכנז באמונה טהורה כדתה של תורה והרבה מאד השיב מעון ועוד היום השפעתו ממושכת בקרב ישראל בספריו הנכבדים אשר בחכמה יתירה השכיל להסביר יסודי עוז לדור הבא בדרך בהירה לשתול בלבם אהבת ד' ויראתו. ולכן אך למותר הוא לתת הסכמה לחיבוריו ולפירושיו כי כבר נתפרסמו לתהלה ולתפארת בכל העולם ושמו הגדול הולך לפניו ואפריון נמטייה להמתעסקים בהדפסת והפצת תורתו ובמיוחד להעורך הרב אפרים ארץ על עבודתו החשובה ולהגב' רייזל הירשלער על תרגומה החדש ולהמדפיסים יודאיקא פרעסס ונשיאם ר' יעקב דוד גאלדמאן כי מצוה גדולה עושים לזכות את הרבים באור תורתו של הגה"צ זצ"ל ויהנו רבים מאורו כי טוב.

ועכ"ז בעה"ח ביום ג' ו' לחדש ניסן שמו"ת לפ"ק.

יעקב יצחק הלוי רודרמאן
נר ישראל
ראש הישיבה

THE FOLLOWING RABBINIC APPROBATION WAS GIVEN BY THE LATE RAV HAGAON R' MOSHE FEINSTEIN, זצ"ל, TO RABBI A. J. ROSENBERG FOR THE JUDAICA PRESS' BOOKS OF THE PROPHETS SERIES. WHEN RABBI ROSENBERG COMPLETED HIS WORK ON THE HAFTAROTH AND THE FIVE MEGILLOTH, R' FEINSTEIN'S PROTRACTED ILLNESS MADE IT IMPOSSIBLE TO OBTAIN AN ADDITIONAL HASKAMAH.

RABBI MOSES FEINSTEIN
455 F. D. R. DRIVE
NEW YORK, N. Y. 10002
OREGON 7-1222

משה פיינשטיין
ר"מ תפארת ירושלים
בנוא יארק

בע"ה

הנה ידוע ומפורסם טובא בשער בת רבים ספרי הוצאת יודאיקא פרעסס על תנ"ך שכבר יצא לאור על ספרי יהושע ושמואל ועכשיו בחסדי השי"ת סדרו לדפוס ג"כ על ספר שופטים והוא כולל הפירושים המקובלים בתנ"ך הנקוב בשם מקראות גדולות ועל זה הוסיפו תרגום אנגלית שהוא השפה המדוברת במדינה זו על פסוקי תנ"ך וגם תרגום לפרש"י מלה במלה עם הוספות פירושים באנגלית הנצרכים להבנת פשוטו של קרא והכל נערך ע"י תלמידי היקר הרב הגאון ר' אברהם יוסף ראזענבערג שליט"א שהוא אומן גדול במלאכת התרגום, והרבה עמל השקיע בכל פרט ופרט בדקדוק גדול, וסידר את הכל בקצור כדי להקל על הלומדים שיוכלו לעיין בנקל ואפריון נמטיה למנהל יודאיקא פרעסס מהור"ר יעקב דוד גאלדמאן שליט"א שזכה ומזכה את הרבים בלימוד התנ"ך שמעורר לומדיה לאהבה וליראה את שמו הגדול ולהאמין בו ובעבדיו הנביאים שהוא יסוד ושורש בעבודתו יתברך ואמינא לפעלא טבא יישר ויתברכו כל העוסקים בכל ברכות התורה וחכמינו ז"ל בברוך אשר יקים את דברי התורה הזאת.

וע"ז באתי עה"ח

This edition is dedicated
in tribute to our parents
JACQUES and HANNA SCHWALBE
whose wisdom, dignity and love
guide us always

Gaby and Harold Goldblatt
Peter Schwalbe
Robert and Jane Schwalbe
Vicky and Michael Nathan

EDITOR'S FOREWORD

When Mr. Jack Goldman of Judaica Press broached the idea of an excerpted edition of Rabbi Samson Raphael Hirsch's commentary on the Torah, to introduce new readers to Hirsch's realm of thought, the task seemed an impossible one.

How does one take this matchless classic of immortal values and *excerpt* it? Which of the master's thoughts, philosophies and basic principles are to be omitted? Such intrinsic problems loomed even greater when I faced the fact that this was to be a one-volume edition.

One overriding consideration compelled me to allay my misgivings, and set forth on the venture: the importance of introducing the mind of this fearless fighter for Torah Judaism to a wider readership, and to future generations, who, remote in time and space from this genius of authentic Judaism, may otherwise never come to know him. To take part in presenting to new readers the Torah philosophies of this original thinker, ideas as relevant in our days as they were in his, outweighed the obstacles that would, of necessity, have to be conquered.

In his introduction to *Judaism Eternal*, Dayan I. Grunfeld says, "The universality of Samson Raphael Hirsch's mind, the range of his intellect and knowledge, the depth of his historic vision, the clarity of his Jewish conception are truly amazing, whilst the certainty and absoluteness of his religious conviction are awe-inspiring."

Through these excerpts, chosen with care from his magnum opus, the present volume attempts to bring the Jewry of our time to the *maor shebaTorah* (brightness of Torah) illumined by the beacon of Hirsch's unique method of Torah interpretation.

Throughout the commentary he teaches that the true understanding of Jewish life and thought can be reached only by studying it from within, by observing the facts of the Written and Oral Law. This becomes clear in his exposition of God's revelation in nature and history, in his interpretation of how language relates to individual and to national characteristics and in his historical and philosophical analysis of Jewish nationhood. The integration of Talmud and Midrash, Halakhah and Aggadah as presented by our Sages are the bases of his unique explanation of the sacrifices and of the dietary laws. This approach is fundamental in perceiving that the Jewish people has its national bond in its God and His Torah.

Man in search of truth, in search of his God, can be led to pride in a pure Torah life within the modern world as he follows Hirsch's thoughts and his proclamation of the sovereignty of Torah over every civilization. The master's world view and universal scope will lead the searching mind to the understanding of Hirsch's principle of *sich selbst begreifendes Judentum,* Judaism organically understood—a supple, resilient, vital principle that leads to spiritual self-sufficiency.

It is my fervent hope and prayer that this work will inspire the reader to delve further into the master's philosophy as developed in his full commentary and in his other writings, to achieve the purpose of להגדיל תורה ולהאדירה.

Ephraim Oratz

Written in Jerusalem
on the 27th day of Teveth 5745,
the ninety-sixth yahrzeit
of Rabbi Samson Raphael Hirsch, זצ"ל

SAMSON RAPHAEL HIRSCH: HIS LIFE AND WORK

Samson Raphael Hirsch was born in Hamburg on Sivan 24, 5568 (June 20, 1808). He died in Frankfurt am Main on Teveth 27, 5649 (December 31, 1888). A scholar, author, educator, orator, communal organizer and champion of Jewish civil and religious rights, Hirsch was the first among Orthodox rabbis to set forth in the idiom of the modern era the thesis of *Torah im derekh eretz,* traditional Jewish learning and uncompromising religious observance combined with a warm appreciation for the best of the cultural, intellectual, artistic, literary and scientific ideas contributed by the secular world for the advancement of human welfare.

Hirsch's influence has been felt not only among the Jews of Germany, in whose midst he lived and worked for all but four years of his long life, but also among Jews throughout Europe and eventually also on the American continent and in Israel.

Even during his lifetime he won the praise and confidence of spiritual leaders of Hungarian and East European Orthodoxy, many of whom initially questioned the religious trustworthiness of a rabbi who not only had acquired a thorough secular education himself but also urged such training upon other Orthodox Jews as a matter of principle. The Hungarian sage Rabbi Abraham Samuel Benjamin Schreiber (*Ketav Sofer*; 1815–71), son of the renowned Rabbi Moses Schreiber (*Hatham Sofer*; 1762–1839), was once asked whether Hirsch, who had studied at a university and was thoroughly at home in the humanities, could be accepted as a rabbinic authority in the traditional sense of the term. The *Ketav Sofer* had met Hirsch in Vienna. "I have discussed matters of religious law with [Hirsch] on many occasions, and in whatever I discussed with him he showed that he was thoroughly at home in the Talmud and in the Codes," he answered his questioner, adding somewhat wryly, "We Hungarian rabbis are lucky that he thinks we are greater *lamdanim* [Talmudic scholars] than he. If he knew, however, what a great *lamdan* he himself is, we would have no *menuḥah* from him."[1]

Rabbi Isaac Elḥanan Spektor (1817–96), founder of the great yeshiva of Kovno and spiritual leader of Russian-Lithuanian Jewry in his day, frequently corresponded with Hirsch on Jewish communal affairs and problems of Jewish law. He encouraged Rabbi Moses Zalman Aronsohn of Kovno to translate three of Hirsch's major works, the *Nineteen Letters on Judaism by Ben Uziel, Horeb* and the commentary on the Pentateuch, into Hebrew. In his rabbinic preface to the translation of the commentary on the Pentateuch (which Aronsohn, however, did not live to complete), Rabbi Spektor wrote:

> The many original interpretations introduced by this *gaon* and sage, who is great in knowledge and who conveys understanding in a manner that is lucid and in conformity with reason, are invaluable . . . how deep are his thoughts, which reveal the wonders and the wisdom concealed in the Torah of the Lord. He removes all that is alien and doubtful, demonstrating that the Torah of the Lord is perfect, the word of God stands forever.

In 1854 Hirsch, in response to arguments from the Reform movement that it was not possible to combine the theory and practice of traditional Judaism with secular educational and cultural interests, proclaimed his own joyous affirmation of Orthodox Judaism as a partner in every area of genuine human endeavor and progress:

1. Rabbi Philipp Fischer, *In seinen Spuren* [*In His Paths*] (Sarospatak, Hungary, 1922), p. 3.

Judaism is not a mere adjunct to life; it comprises all of life. To be a Jew is not a mere part, it is the sum total of our task in life. To be a Jew in synagogue and in the kitchen, in the field and the warehouse, in the office and the pulpit . . . as servant and as master, as man and as citizen . . . with the needle and the engraving tool, with the pen and the chisel—that is what it means to be a Jew. An entire life supported by the Divine idea and lived and brought to fulfillment according to the Divine will. . . .

The more the Jew is a Jew . . . the less aloof he will be from anything that is noble and good, true and upright, in art or science, in culture or education . . . the more joyfully will he devote himself to all true progress in civilization and culture—provided, that is, that he will not only not have to sacrifice his Judaism but will be able to bring it to more perfect fulfillment. He will ever desire progress, but only in alliance with religion. He will not want to accomplish anything that he cannot accomplish as a Jew. Any step which takes him away from Judaism is not for him a step forward, is not progress . . . for he does not wish to accomplish his own will on earth but labors in the service of God.[2]

This statement is perhaps one of Hirsch's most forceful assertions of his educational and cultural ideal, based on the maxim of Rabban Gamaliel III: "*Yofe talmud Torah im derekh eretz*" ("a beautiful thing is the study of Torah combined with *derekh eretz*") (*Ethics of the Fathers* 2:2).

Hirsch's interpretation of *derekh eretz* in this context is broader than the standard rendering, "a worldly occupation," which is used in most modern-language translations of the *Ethics*. Hirsch points out that *derekh eretz*, literally, "the way of the world," refers to the life that, ideally, Jews should lead jointly with the rest of humanity. God has placed upon earth all the resources needed by man in order to fulfill the destiny ordained for him by God. It is therefore the duty of every individual to acquire, to the fullest extent of his ability, the physical, intellectual and social skills by which these resources can be employed for God's purposes. Consequently, Hirsch's definition of *derekh eretz* includes not only practical training in the skills required for earning an adequate living, but also the acquisition of that true "culture"—a broad education combined with good breeding and common courtesy—which helps ensure a mutually beneficial coexistence of all men on God's earth.

In Hirsch's view, the combination of Jewish learning and observance on the one hand, and secular knowledge and culture on the other, is not a compromise reluctantly made by Orthodox Judaism with the necessities of contemporary life. It is a basic component of the Jewish *Weltanschauung*. If the Jews for centuries were estranged from secular education and culture, this estrangement was not a concomitant of traditional Judaism; it had been imposed on the Jew, by a hostile world. During the golden ages of Babylonian and Spanish Jewry, Jews had combined the best of Rabbinic learning with the finest in secular knowledge. This connection, Hirsch declared, should be restored in the modern era, for not only was secular knowledge an invaluable aid in the study of the Torah and of Rabbinic tradition, but the ability of the Jew to perform his specific tasks as a servant of God on earth was in fact dependent upon his insights into the natural, historical and social conditions under which he lived and under which his ancestors before him had survived.

2. Samson Raphael Hirsch, "Religion Allied to Progress," translated in *Judaism Eternal: Selected Essays from the Writings of Samson Raphael Hirsch*, tr. Dayan Dr. I. Grunfeld, 2 vols. (London: The Soncino Press, 1956), Vol. II, pp. 237–38.

How, asked Samson Raphael Hirsch, can we understand the sublime word pictures of world history painted by the prophets without an adequate knowledge of contemporary secular history? The Jewish youth who knows from his historical studies [the contempt for human life shown by the ancient Egyptians,] the social oppression and moral degeneration in Rome of old, the oppression and licentiousness of [ancient Greek society], understands and appreciates a thousand times better the sublime and divine character of the Sinaitic law. And as to the study of nature which is so necessary for the understanding of Jewish religious thought and practical religious life, the Talmud reproaches those who fail to undertake it with the words of Isaiah (5:12): "And the doing of God they do not contemplate and the work of His hands they do not see" (Shabbath 75a).[3]

Samson Raphael Hirsch was born into a family known for both piety and Jewish scholarship. His grandfather, Mendel Frankfurter, who adopted the surname of Hirsch, had been a disciple of the eighteenth-century Talmudist and Kabbalist Rabbi Jonathan Eybeschütz.

During his formative years, Hirsch studied with *Hakham* Isaac Jacob Bernays (1792–1849), who in 1821 had become chief rabbi of Hamburg. At the age of twenty, Hirsch left Hamburg for Mannheim, where he spent a year at the Talmudical academy of Rabbi Jacob Ettlinger (1798–1871) and received his rabbinic ordination.

In 1829 Hirsch enrolled at the University of Bonn, where he studied history, philosophy, experimental physics and classical languages. (Latin, Greek, French and English phrases occur frequently in his writings.)

In Bonn, he came into contact for the first time with the religious doubts that plagued many young Jewish intellectuals of his generation. He resolved to devote the literary and oratorical skills he had acquired at the university to the presentation of Orthodox Judaism in a style and logic that would appeal to these young searchers after truth.

In 1830, when he was only twenty-two years old, Hirsch was called away from his university studies to become Provincial Rabbi of the Grand Duchy of Oldenburg (today a part of Lower Saxony). He lived for eleven years in the city of Oldenburg, where he married and where five of his ten children were born.

In Oldenburg Hirsch wrote *Iggroth Tzafon: Neunzehn Briefe über Judentum von Ben Usiel* (*Nineteen Letters on Judaism by Ben Uziel*). This masterful exposition of Orthodox Judaism has become a classic in modern-day traditional Jewish literature.[4] Initially published in Altona in 1836 under the pseudonym Ben Uziel, it is an exchange of letters between two fictional Jewish youths, Benjamin and Naphtali. Benjamin is an intellectual, who, though originally observant, has, as a result of his secular studies and social contacts, begun to doubt the relevance of traditional Judaism in the modern era. His friend, Naphtali, a young rabbi, answers Benjamin's questions in a series of letters discussing the purpose of Judaism and the relationship of the Jews and their religion to world civilization. Proceeding from the premise that there exists a Supreme Being Who created man and rules the universe, regulating the phenomena of nature and guiding the developments of history, "Naphtali" concludes that mankind must reflect the absolute goodness and perfection of its Creator. But since God has endowed man with freedom of will, it is inevitable that man should be plagued by conflicts about right and wrong. For this reason, "Naphtali" explains, mankind was given a model community dedicated to the mission of teach-

3. I. Grunfeld, *Three Generations: The Influence of Samson Raphael Hirsch on Jewish Life and Thought* (London: 1958), pp. 15–16.

4. The *Nineteen Letters* were first translated into English by Rabbi Bernard Drachman (New York: 1899). A more recent English edition was published by Jacob Breuer, a great-grandson of Hirsch (New York: Philipp Feldheim, 1960).

ing men how to do God's will by seeking the good. This community is the people of Israel, to whom God revealed distinctive ritual and ethical laws, all of which serve to advance the ideal goodness among mankind as a whole, or to confirm Israel in its mission to mankind. These laws are embodied in the Torah, which included not only the commandments and prohibitions set forth in the Pentateuch ("Written Law") but also the entire body of Rabbinic law and tradition ("Oral Law "). Since both Laws are of Divine origin, they are not subject to change by man. In an age of emancipation, it is not Judaism but the Jews that need "reform." Jews, said Hirsch, were not in need of "progress" (the catchword of the Reformers of the day) but of spiritual elevation. If the Jews were truly to benefit from the culture of the Western world, it was imperative that they rise to the eternal ideals of Judaism instead of attempting to lower the standards of Judaism to the level of time-bound notions subject to frequent, rapid change.

The *Nineteen Letters* soon became known as the work of Hirsch and aroused keen interest among German Jews, particularly young students and intellectuals.

Two years after the *Nineteen Letters,* Hirsch published, this time under his own name, *Choreb, oder Versuche über Jissroels Pflichten in der Zerstreuung (Horeb,* or *Essays on Israel's Duties in Dispersion).* This work is an elaboration on the themes merely touched upon in the *Letters.* In *Horeb,* each of the laws of the Torah is thoroughly analyzed in terms of its place and purpose in the larger context of God's Law.

Like the Hebrew translation of the *Letters,* the Hebrew edition of *Horeb,* too, was prefaced by an enthusiastic approbation from Rabbi Elḥanan Spektor.[5]

In 1841, Hirsch assumed the chief rabbinate of the districts of Aurich and Osnabrück, in the province of Hanover. At his residence in the city of Emden, he found himself spending much of his time on administrative details. Nevertheless, he was active in educational and philanthropic endeavors, including a free loan fund which he himself organized and for which he personally solicited contributions.

In 1847 Hirsch left Germany to accept the rabbinate of the ancient Jewish community of Nikolsburg (Mikulov), Moravia. He was subsequently also named chief rabbi of Moravia and Austrian Silesia. In Nikolsburg, he urged the establishment of a traditional yeshiva but also advocated the creation of vocational schools to train Jews in agriculture and manual trades.

In the wake of the March Revolution that rocked Europe in 1848, Hirsch emerged as a vigorous fighter for Jewish civil and political rights. At the preparatory assembly for the Moravian Provincial Diet, of which, as chief rabbi, he was a member, Hirsch delivered an impassioned plea for the rights of Moravian Jewry.

When the Jews of Moravia attained their first successes in their quest for civic equality, Hirsch rejoiced, but he made it clear that no mere act of human legislation could lead to the establishment of absolute justice and equality on earth. That ideal could become a reality only if all mankind were to obey the will of God. In the specific case of the Jews, this meant the observance of all the laws set down in the Torah. Emancipation had been granted to the Jews by God's own design so that the Jews might be able to discharge their Divinely-ordained mission in the modern world. Hirsch therefore admonished the Jews of Moravia not to discard their religious heritage. As he wrote in one of his messages to his communities, what would we have achieved if, now that we have become free Jews, we were to abandon our Judaism?

In 1851 Hirsch went to Frankfurt am Main, to the pulpit which he was to occupy for the remaining thirty-seven years of his life. In Moravia, he had led a Jewish community of nearly 50,000 souls. Now he became the spiritual leader of an "Israelite Religious Association" (*Israelitische Religionsgesellschaft*), which had come into existence only two years earlier with a

5. *Horeb* was translated into English by Dayan Dr. I. Grunfeld under the title *Horeb: A Philosophy of Jewish Laws and Observances* (London: The Soncino Press, 1962).

total membership of eleven men who refused to compromise their staunch Orthodoxy in the face of a powerful Reform movement. The *Religionsgesellschaft* stood opposed to Frankfurt's government-sanctioned Jewish religious establishment, which leaned heavily toward Reform or "Liberal" Judaism. Thus, the *Religionsgesellschaft* had to maintain its synagogue and other institutions without financial assistance from the city's main Jewish community.

Despite these ideological and practical obstacles, Hirsch succeeded in expanding the *Religionsgesellschaft* into a model Orthodox community which eventually obtained government recognition as an independent religious entity and which, at the time of his death, numbered about 500 families. In addition to an imposing synagogue building, the institutions of the *Religionsgesellschaft* included a day school for boys and girls, a *mikvah*, and three ritual slaughterhouses that met the standards of uncompromising Orthodoxy.

The day school, for which Hirsch himself went from house to house, virtually begging for funds and students, has been hailed as the prototype and inspiration of the present-day Orthodox Jewish day school movement. The Hirsch school opened in 1853 with an enrollment of 84 boys and girls. By 1881 it had 600 students, and it continued to flourish until the late 1930s, when the Hitler regime put an end to all Jewish day schools in Germany. In his curriculum for the school, Hirsch put into practice his conviction that precisely because Jews must uphold the supremacy of the Torah in the midst of any given civilization, it was necessary for Jews to study the secular values of the non-Jewish world. In the primary and secondary schools of the *Religionsgesell-schaft*, non-religious subjects were not taught as a necessary evil but as a potent means of defending and advancing the cause of Orthodox Judaism in a modern age.

Hirsch fought against the reluctance of Western Jews—including many of the Orthodox—to draw public attention to their religious observances for fear of antagonizing the Gentiles or incurring ridicule from assimilationist Jews. Hirsch urged his congregants to show their Jewish allegiance proudly, also outside the home and the synagogue. He encouraged one of his wealthy, socially prominent householders to make a point of carrying his *lulav* and *ethrog* openly through the streets on his way to and from the synagogue on Sukkoth. That man could easily have afforded to buy a second palm branch and citron to keep for prayers at home, thus avoiding the necessity of carrying these religious objects through the fashionable neighborhood in which he lived. But Hirsch considered it vital for the dignity of traditional Judaism that people of known high social standing should demonstrate their own strict adherence to Jewish law in full view of the non-Jewish world.

With all his rabbinical and communal activities in Frankfurt, Hirsch continued to disseminate his thoughts in print. As early as 1854, he founded *Jeschurun*, a monthly which he published for sixteen years. In the hundreds of essays and articles which he contributed to this journal, he set forth, in the elegant German style of his time, his ideals of Jewish education and communal life, based on his interpretation of Biblical and Talmudic texts.[6]

In Frankfurt, too, he wrote the classic commentaries which have made him immortal. Between 1867 and 1878 Hirsch published, volume by volume, *Der Pentateuch, übersetzt und erläutert von Samson Raphael Hirsch* (*The Pentateuch, Translated and Explained by Samson Raphael Hirsch*). This was followed, in 1882, by *Die Psalmen, übersetzt und erläutert von Samson Raphael Hirsch* (*The Psalms, Translated and Explained by Samson Raphael Hirsch*).[7] His translation and explanation of the Daily Prayer Book appeared in 1895, the seventh year after his death.[8]

6. Many of these essays were translated by Dayan Dr. I. Grunfeld in *Judaism Eternal* (see Note 2).

7. Translated into English by Gertrude Hirschler under the title *The Psalms, Translation and Commentary by Samson Raphael Hirsch* (New York: Philipp Feldheim, 1960–1966, 1978).

8. Translated into English by the staff of the Samson Raphael Hirsch Publications Society under the title *Siddur Tefillot Yisrael: The Hirsch Siddur* (Jerusalem and New York: Philipp Feldheim, 1969). The translation of, and

Hirsch's final major written work was a defense of the Talmud against anti-Semitic slurs. In 1884, the Tsarist Russian press launched a vicious attack on Judaism and the Talmud. Fearful that this onslaught might lead to a ban on Talmudic studies throughout Russia, Rabbi Isaac Elḥanan Spektor turned to Samson Raphael Hirsch for help. Hirsch, who was then seventy-six years old, responded with a treatise entitled *Über die Beziehungen des Talmuds zum Judentum und zu der sozialen Stellung seiner Bekenner* (*On the Relations of the Talmud to Judaism and to the Social Attitude of its Adherents*), explaining the Jewish view of life on the basis of about 150 selected passages from the Talmud and the writings of Maimonides. This work was submitted to the Russian Imperial "Commission for the Solution of the Jewish Problem" and reportedly helped improve the position of the Jews in Russia at the time.

Despite failing health, Hirsch's zeal and intellect remained unimpaired until his death. His wife, the former Johanna (Hanne) Jüdel, had died in 1882 after a happy marriage of over half a century. The second part of Hirsch's commentary on the Psalms opens with a dedication to her memory. Hirsch had the satisfaction of seeing all his children—five sons and five daughters— exemplify his ideal of steadfast Orthodoxy combined with secular education and culture. Hirsch's successor as spiritual leader of the Frankfurt *Religionsgesellschaft* was his son-in-law, Rabbi Dr. Salomon Breuer (1850–1926), a native of Hungary, who had studied at the noted yeshiva of Pressburg and German universities. One of Salomon Breuer's sons, Rabbi Dr. Joseph Breuer (1882–1980), became the spiritual leader of Congregation K'hall Adath Jeshurun in New York City, which considers itself the direct spiritual heir of the *Israelitische Religionsgesellschaft* of Frankfurt am Main.

Gertrude Hirschler

commentary on, the *Ethics of the Fathers* included in the Hirsch Siddur was published also in a separate volume under the title *Chapters of the Fathers*, tr. by Gertrude Hirschler (Jerusalem and New York: Philipp Feldheim, 1967).

NOTES ON THE TRANSLATION

Samson Raphael Hirsch's commentary on the Pentateuch is the product of decades of painstaking study. Already in his youth, Hirsch had begun to take notes on Biblical passages that seemed to him particularly difficult to interpret. By the time he arrived in Frankfurt, he had accumulated sufficient material to use in his weekly lectures before his Bible study groups. As he indicates in his "Author's Preface" (see page xxiii of this volume), most of the published commentary is based on shorthand notes taken by those who attended his lectures. This may account for some unevenness of style in the commentary.

In his translation of the Biblical text, and in his commentary, Hirsch sought to interpret the Scriptural text "out of itself," as he explains in his preface, without reference to sources other than the Biblical text and Rabbinic literature. Instead of turning to comparative Semitic philology, Hirsch brought into play an etymology constructed from his original system of *Lautverwandschaften*, or "phonetic affinities," between Hebrew words and letters. It seems that Hirsch intended to publish a separate work explaining his system of "etymological investigation," but he did not live to carry out this plan.

The basic purpose of Hirsch's commentary on the Pentateuch was to demonstrate that the Written Law, as set down in the Five Books of Moses, and the Oral Law, as recorded in the Talmud, derive from the same Divine source, so that the Biblical text cannot be properly studied or understood without reference to the Mishnah and Gemara. One who studies the halakhic passages of the Hirsch commentary is afforded a sweeping view of the whole of Jewish law, Talmudic and post-Talmudic. Thus Hirsch made it clear that neither Judaism nor the Bible can be dissected into various forms and periods of development, and that every phase of Halakhah derives directly from the Pentateuchal text. Hirsch's attitude toward the Oral Law explains why rabbinical authorities who condemned other contemporary modern-language translations of the Bible gave acceptance and even praise to the translation by Samson Raphael Hirsch.

The "Hirsch Ḥumash" was widely studied by German-speaking Jews; six editions appeared before Hitler and the *Kristallnacht* pogroms put an end to organized Jewish life in Frankfurt.

Like the German original, the first complete English translation of the "Hirsch Humash," *The Pentateuch, Translated and Explained by Samson Raphael Hirsch*, was published over a period of several years. The translation of Genesis appeared in 1958; that of Deuteronomy in 1966. First published in London, these six volumes (the English rendering of Leviticus and its commentary is printed in two volumes) were republished by the Judaica Press in New York in 1971.

That English translation was the work of Hirsch's grandson Dr. Isaac Levy of London, to whom the present translator cherishes a sense of profound indebtedness. Dr. Levy, who was born and educated in England, devoted whatever time he could spare from his professional duties to the self-imposed task of disseminating among English-speaking Jews the ideals taught by his grandfather. Dr. Levy died in 1973 at the age of eighty-eight.

During the past three decades, efforts have also been made in the United States to bring the writings of Samson Raphael Hirsch to ever-widening Jewish circles. In the case of the English translations of Hirsch's other writings, this has proven relatively easy. But the complete English version of the "Hirsch Ḥumash," as already noted, consists of six volumes, totaling about 3,500 closely printed pages. It was suggested, therefore, that English-speaking readers not yet familiar with the "Hirsch Ḥumash" might welcome an introductory edition for study at home and in the synagogue.

T'rumath Tzvi: The Pentateuch with a Translation by Samson Raphael Hirsch and Excerpts from the Hirsch Commentary is an attempt to fill this need. Obviously, this volume is not intended to replace the complete Hirsch commentary in the synagogue or in the Jewish home. *T'rumath Tzvi* contains, of course, the complete text of the Pentateuch, rendered into English from Hirsch's unique German translation, which forms the basis for his commentary. The abridgments were made in Hirsch's elaborate commentaries, which, in some instances, take up several pages for one verse of text. The commentaries included in *T'rumath Tzvi* are those which, in the opinion of the editor, seem to convey most impressively the basic components of Hirsch's philosophy, or to be representative examples of the Hirschian method of exegesis, or to be indispensable to an understanding of Hirsch's translation of the Biblical text.

The task of selecting "excerpts" from Hirsch's commentary on the Pentateuch for inclusion in an introductory presentation was not taken lightly. A suggestion that Hirsch's commentaries should not be translated but merely "condensed" or epitomized was rejected. The passages of commentary included in *T'rumath Tzvi* are translations of Hirsch's own words, except that his involved sentences, typical of the ornate German of his day, have been broken up into less cumbersome structures, and lengthy passages have been divided into paragraphs for easier reading. The present translation has attempted to follow a simple, classic style which seeks to convey the sense of Hirsch's original, while at the same time making his thoughts readily accessible to the modern reader.

Paraphrasing or "editorializing" for the sake of clarity has been kept at a minimum. It was done only in isolated instances where Hirsch's German style seemed virtually untranslatable. Such paraphrases or amplifications are enclosed in square brackets to distinguish them from the direct translation.

A series of dots (. . .) indicates a partial English rendering of a paragraph; a series of asterisks (° ° °) indicates the omission of a larger section of commentary on a given verse.

All Hebrew quotations in the commentary that Hirsch did not translate are followed by English translations in square brackets. In passages where the Hebrew-English interchange interfered with the visual clarity of the text, the Hebrew was omitted altogether and replaced with its English translation.

In his original German rendering of the Biblical text, Hirsch, for reasons he explained in his commentary on Genesis 2:4, used the German *Gott* to translate all three Biblical designations for the Deity: אלהים (which denotes God in His quality of justice), יהוה (which refers to His quality of loving kindness) and יהוה אלהים (which connotes both these qualities), whereas most other translations render אלהים as "God" but יהוה as "the Lord" or "the Eternal." However, in order to underline the distinction between the concepts implicit in אלהים and יהוה, Hirsch's German translation has the word *Gott* printed in italics wherever it is used to render the Tetragrammaton or the dual designation יהוה אלהים. This mode has been followed also in the present English version.

G.H.

AUTHOR'S PREFACE

To make a contribution to the understanding of the Book of Books is in itself such a lofty aim that even a mind far more gifted than the present author's would wish to accompany his work with a few words to indicate the objectives he hoped to achieve. Without venturing even remotely to express an opinion on the success he may have attained, the author, in offering upon the spiritual altar of his people this translation and explanation of the Pentateuch, therefore wishes to preface it with a brief statement of his purpose.

The objectives were as follows:

To derive the explanation of the text from out of itself; to arrive at this explanation from the wording in all its nuances; to determine the meaning of the words from the treasure of linguistic explanations which we possess in our traditional literature; on the basis of these linguistic studies and the Halakhic and Aggadic traditions deriving from that national past from which the Biblical text has come down to us, to draw and to present the truths from which the Jewish outlook on the world and on life were formulated, and which constitute the norms of Jewish life for all time.

If the achievement of this purpose has not entirely failed; if even a small contribution has been made toward the understanding of the uniform spirit which pervades the written text of the Word of God, and toward the realization that this spirit is not part of an antiquated past, but is very much of a living present and the future aspirations of all mankind, then the author's attempts will not have been in vain.

May it be given to more talented minds to complete some day that which, considering the vastness of the task, can really never be entirely accomplished; and may God's Scripture increasingly fulfill the purpose for which the Father of all mankind has entrusted it to our hands: to sow the seeds of light and understanding for all those who would delve into it in truth and sincerity.

A detailed explanation of the system of etymological investigation on which this commentary is based must be reserved for a later date. The principle of phonetic relationships on which it rests is such a prominent characteristic of the Hebrew language, and the linguistic facts from which all the author's etymological assumptions are derived, are given in such detail, that its justification should be obvious to any thinking reader.

The commentary on Genesis, which is herewith published for the first time, originated in a series of lectures which the author delivered over a number of years, and which attentive listeners were kind enough to commit to paper. These notes were used as a basis for the present edition and could not entirely fail to influence its style.

Repetitions have purposely not been avoided so that each passage may be accompanied by the necessary explanatory material.

Some digressions refer to the commentaries on the subsequent Books of the Pentateuch, even as the commentary on Genesis as such forms the genetic foundation for the explanations on the Books that follow.

The translation and commentary on Exodus should be completed within the course of a year and, if God grants life and strength, the other Books of the Pentateuch should follow in uninterrupted sequence.

Frankfurt am Main, I Adar, 5627 [1867]

The Author

BERESHITH בראשית

[GENESIS]

—————————⟺◇⟻—————————

"The sole purpose of this entire First Book, which relates the origins of the world, of human history and of the people of Israel, is to introduce the Law of God which has been given to Israel."

—Commentary on Chapter 1, Verse 1

בראשית

BERESHITH

I 1. From the beginning did God create the heaven and the earth.
2. And this earth was once confused and

א א בְּרֵאשִׁית בָּרָא אֱלֹהִים אֵת הַשָּׁמַיִם וְאֵת
הָאָרֶץ׃ ב וְהָאָרֶץ הָיְתָה תֹהוּ וָבֹהוּ וְחֹשֶׁךְ עַל־

CHAPTER I

1. ***From the beginning did God create.*** בְּרֵאשִׁית means: "In the beginning of all existence, it was God Who created . . ." or, in the context of the rest of the verse, "It was from the very beginning that God created the heaven and the earth." In any event, the word בְּרֵאשִׁית proclaims that nothing existed prior to God's act of creation and that both heaven and earth came into existence only through Divine creation. This is the concept of יֵשׁ מֵאַיִן [creation *ex nihilo*], the basis of the conviction that the Torah seeks to build up for us. The opposing notion, i.e., that matter [did not have to be created but] was always in existence, and that the Creator therefore acts only as the molder of preexisting matter, has been the basis of pagan thinking to this very day. It is . . . a most shameful denial of all freedom of will in both God and man, which would undermine the very foundations of morality. If matter had antedated Creation, then the Creator of the Universe would not have been able to form a world that was absolutely "good," but only the best world possible within the limitations of the material given Him to shape. In that case, all evil, physical and moral, would be due to the inherent faultiness of the material available to the Creator, and not even God would be able to save the world from evil, physical or moral. Then man could be as little master over his body as God could be over the matter from which the world was made. Freedom would vanish from the earth, and all the world, including its God as well as the men who live upon it, would be propelled by a blind, immutable fate. This gloomy concept of God, the world and mankind is dispelled at the very outset with the first word of the Teaching of God. . . .

בְּרֵאשִׁית בָּרָא אֱלֹקִים ***[From the beginning did God create].*** On these words all that follows stands or falls. The substance and form of all that exists emanates from the free, almighty will of the Creator. . . .

° ° °

אֱלֹקִים ***[God].*** אלה, the root of this word, is the same as the plural of the demonstrative pronoun אֵלֶּה ["these"], a pronoun that denotes a multiplicity of things joined together into one unity. Thus, while אֵלֶּה in general points to the visible multiplicity of objects in Creation, אֱלוֹהַּ, the term denoting God, may be interpreted as describing that One Being by Whose might and will all this multiplicity is gathered into one single whole: it is through Him and their relationship to Him that all the elements in the universe become one single entity—in short, one world. Hence אֱלוֹהַּ in fact denotes the One Who is Ruler, Lawgiver and Judge over all the world in His מִדַּת הַדִּין [quality of Supreme Judge]. . . .

° ° °

This opening verse reveals to us that fundamental truth, that primal reality which basically alters our view of the world and of ourselves. This one verse would be sufficient to teach us to view the world as God's world and ourselves as God's creatures, to prepare us for the demand that we are to recognize this world and ourselves as emanations of God and hence as God's own sacred possessions, and that in this world of God we are to utilize all our energies—which also belong to Him—solely for the purpose of doing His will.

However, the Word of God is not content merely to make a general announcement, in one single verse, that it was God Who created the world. The sole purpose of this entire First Book, which relates the origins of the world, of human history and of the people of Israel, is to introduce the Law of God which has been given to Israel. For this reason the Word of God will now present to us all the individual phenomena of terrestrial diversity. It does so in order to teach us to perceive and to revere the creative, law-giving and all-governing Word of God not only in general terms but also in each and every species and group of species that exists. This should enable us to elevate ourselves to that lofty level of Jewish perception and Jewish mentality which David proclaimed in his inspired song: Since every living thing everywhere in this great universe, each in its own particular sphere and stage of development, obeys the Divine Law set for it, therefore also בָּרְכִי נַפְשִׁי אֶת ה' ["Bless the Lord, O my soul"—Psalm 104]; we, too, are to obey the Law ordained for us by God, and in this obedience to God find all the bliss of our lives and our aspirations. . . .

2. ***and this earth was.*** These words introduce a new sequence of ideas. Verse 1 has shown us heaven and earth as we see them in our own day and has proclaimed to us the one overall truth concerning them both: that it was God Who brought them into existence,

פְּנֵי תְהוֹם וְרוּחַ אֱלֹהִים מְרַחֶפֶת עַל־פְּנֵי
הַמָּיִם: ג וַיֹּאמֶר אֱלֹהִים יְהִי־אוֹר וַיְהִי־אוֹר:
ד וַיַּרְא אֱלֹהִים אֶת־הָאוֹר כִּי־טוֹב וַיַּבְדֵּל
אֱלֹהִים בֵּין הָאוֹר וּבֵין הַחֹשֶׁךְ: ה וַיִּקְרָא
אֱלֹהִים ׀ לָאוֹר יוֹם וְלַחֹשֶׁךְ קָרָא לָיְלָה וַיְהִי־
עֶרֶב וַיְהִי־בֹקֶר יוֹם אֶחָד: פ ו וַיֹּאמֶר אֱלֹהִים
יְהִי רָקִיעַ בְּתוֹךְ הַמָּיִם וִיהִי מַבְדִּיל בֵּין מָיִם

tangled, and darkness was over the turmoil, and a breath of God hovered over the
waters. 3. And God said: "Let there be
light!" And there was light. 4. God saw
the light, that it was good, and God separated the light from the darkness. 5. And
God called to the light: "Day!" and to the
darkness He called: "Night!" And it was
evening and it was morning: one day.
6. God said: "Let there be a vault in the
midst of the waters and let it separate the

in both substance and form. Now Verse 2 directs our eye back again to the earth and tells us: There was a time when this earth, on which we now behold individual objects clearly defined and distinctly set apart from one another, was תֹהוּ וָבֹהוּ ["confused and tangled"]. . . .

4. ***God saw the light, that it was good.*** This statement, along with similar statements concerning subsequent creations: וַיַּרְא אֱלֹקִים כִּי טוֹב, and at the end of His work of creation, וַיַּרְא אֱלֹקִים אֶת כָּל אֲשֶׁר עָשָׂה וְהִנֵּה טוֹב מְאֹד ["God saw the whole of what He had created and lo! it was very good"—Genesis 1:31], is intended, if we understand it correctly, to set forth one great truth: Not only the origin but also the survival of all things is directly dependent on the will and approval of God. Usually, in creations wrought by man, the work, once brought into existence, becomes a thing apart from its creator. True, he has created it, but from that point forward it continues on its own momentum. Indeed, it often escapes the control of its creator. Mortals have the power to create new things, to unleash forces or to combine them, but they are not able to control the forces they have liberated, to subdue the genii they themselves have unchained. As a result, in most instances the creation overwhelms its creator so that he is no longer master over his own work. Not so God and His world. The whole of that world, and its parts, too, not only came into existence through His almighty will but also survive only because He deems it good that this should be so. Even after He has created it, he continually examines His work and permits it to survive only as long as it meets with His approval.

° ° °

This mastery of the Creator over His creations even after they have come into existence is demonstrated at the very outset by the fact that "God separated the light from the darkness." He set clearly defined boundaries between the newly-created light and the former darkness. Both are henceforth to rule over the world and to have their impact upon it: The light is to bestir everything to its individual existence, while darkness, by temporarily eliminating stressful stimuli, is to make possible an interaction of forces that will serve to benefit and strengthen them all. Light must not operate without restraints; light and darkness each must have its own province. And again it is God, the same God Who called out into the darkness, "Light!", Who now in His almighty power intervenes between these two greatest, most significant antitheses which, by gathering all matter, molding all substance and strengthening and awakening life, are henceforth to rule over the world.

5. ***And God called.*** Wherever God gives a name to one of His creations, that name expresses the particular mission of the creation so named, as in Abraham ["father of a multitude"] or Israel ["fighter of God"] and so forth. Accordingly, light, too, should be conceived only in terms of the statement by our Sages: "God called to the light and appointed it for the tasks of day, and God called to the darkness and appointed it for the tasks of night" (Pesaḥim 2). . . .

עֶרֶב *[evening]* is the time at which outlines begin to blur, [lit.,]" to mix." בֹּקֶר [morning] connotes independence, the time at which things separate from one another and their sharp outlines emerge so that it becomes possible לְבַקֵּר, to distinguish, one thing from another . . . We are told וַיְהִי עֶרֶב וַיְהִי בֹקֶר יוֹם אֶחָד ["And it was evening and it was morning: one day"]. Day, which begins with בֹּקֶר and moves toward completion under the influence of light, is that טוֹב [good] which is the Creator's purpose. Night, which begins with עֶרֶב [evening] and moves toward completion under the impact of חֹשֶׁךְ [darkness], is merely a phase preparatory to that goal. Only when בֹּקֶר has followed עֶרֶב has the world passed one day of completed existence in the full meaning of that word.

6. . . . Before God—so His Word teaches us—withdrew the essential solvent, מַיִם ["water"], . . . from the earth by separating the dry land from the water, He lifted up part of the water and spread over the earth the רָקִיעַ, the vault that is visible to us today. It is to this vault that the earth will henceforth send up its vapors, which then, as clouds, will absorb the water and

waters from the waters." 7. God made the vault and He separated the waters which were beneath the vault from the waters which were above the vault, and it was so. 8. God called to the vault: "Sky!" And it was evening and it was morning: a second day. 9. And God said: "Let the waters from beneath the sky gather to one place, and let the dry land appear." And it was so. 10. And God called to the dry land: "Earth!" and to the gathering of the waters He called: "Seas!" And God saw that it was good. 11. And God said: "Let the earth sprout vegetation, seed-scattering plants, fruit tree[s] bearing fruit according to its species, seed-scattering above the earth." And it was so. 12. The earth brought forth vegetation, seed-scattering plants, according to its species, and tree[s] bearing fruit, seed-bearing, according to its species. And God saw that it was good. 13. And it was evening and it was morn-

לָמָּיִם: ז וַיַּעַשׂ אֱלֹהִים אֶת־הָרָקִיעַ וַיַּבְדֵּל בֵּין
הַמַּיִם אֲשֶׁר מִתַּחַת לָרָקִיעַ וּבֵין הַמַּיִם אֲשֶׁר
מֵעַל לָרָקִיעַ וַיְהִי־כֵן: ח וַיִּקְרָא אֱלֹהִים לָרָקִיעַ
שָׁמָיִם וַיְהִי־עֶרֶב וַיְהִי־בֹקֶר יוֹם שֵׁנִי: פ
ט וַיֹּאמֶר אֱלֹהִים יִקָּווּ הַמַּיִם מִתַּחַת הַשָּׁמַיִם
אֶל־מָקוֹם אֶחָד וְתֵרָאֶה הַיַּבָּשָׁה וַיְהִי־כֵן:
י וַיִּקְרָא אֱלֹהִים ׀ לַיַּבָּשָׁה אֶרֶץ וּלְמִקְוֵה הַמַּיִם
קָרָא יַמִּים וַיַּרְא אֱלֹהִים כִּי־טוֹב: יא וַיֹּאמֶר
אֱלֹהִים תַּדְשֵׁא הָאָרֶץ דֶּשֶׁא עֵשֶׂב מַזְרִיעַ זֶרַע
עֵץ פְּרִי עֹשֶׂה פְּרִי לְמִינוֹ אֲשֶׁר זַרְעוֹ־בוֹ עַל־
הָאָרֶץ וַיְהִי־כֵן: יב וַתּוֹצֵא הָאָרֶץ דֶּשֶׁא עֵשֶׂב
מַזְרִיעַ זֶרַע לְמִינֵהוּ וְעֵץ עֹשֶׂה־פְּרִי אֲשֶׁר
זַרְעוֹ־בוֹ לְמִינֵהוּ וַיַּרְא אֱלֹהִים כִּי־טוֹב:
יג וַיְהִי־עֶרֶב וַיְהִי־בֹקֶר יוֹם שְׁלִישִׁי: פ

will return it, as rain, to the parched soil and to the thirsty living things that exist upon it. Even as, initially, light penetrated the earth in diffused form but subsequently was harnessed to light-bearers to shine upon the earth from the heavenly expanse, so the water, too, is now withdrawn from the surface of the dry land, to be received again by the earth from above according to the earth's needs. It is in terms of these antitheses of giving and taking that the development of all existence on earth is presented to us. . . .

8. Even as God addressed the light as "Day!" in order to define the function of light with respect to the earth, so He now addressed the vault as "Sky!" to define its relationship to the earth. רָקִיעַ ["the vault"] is the actual "sky" as it relates to the earth. Whatever the earth receives from heaven it receives through the medium of the sky. Not even light comes down to earth in a direct, pure state; it filters down through the sky in the modified and broken form in which alone it can perform its task on earth. . . .

11–13. With this eleventh verse we first enter into the sphere of organic life. We are shown דֶּשֶׁא, the vegetation that sprouts from the soil, the seed-bearing plants, the fruit trees that produce fruit. We learn that all these countless varieties of creation are governed by one and the same law: לְמִינֵהוּ, לְמִינוֹ ["according to its species."] Each of them is to work only for its own species and to develop only within the circumscribed sphere assigned to its own kind. . . .

. . . All substances and energies must operate and develop within expressly defined limits and in clearly prescribed ways. This great law which is made so obvious to us by the infinite variety of vegetable organisms, this law which, all-powerful, all-pervading and all-embracing, rules over minute fibers and seedlings even as it does over the giant trees that reach toward the sky, and which permits each individual plant species to develop only within the limits set for it — this all-powerful law that has been proclaimed for every blade of grass no less than for the mighty cedar is known by the catchword: לְמִינוֹ ["according to its species"]. . . .

. . . Each species preserves its reproductive energies only לְמִינוֹ, for its own species, and only human caprice would force it into unnatural, that is, unlawful unions. If left to itself, each seedling will belong to its own species as exclusively as did its earliest ancestor, concerning which and concerning all of whose descendants the Creator first proclaimed His law: לְמִינוֹ ["according to its species"]. It is clear that this law which the Lawgiver of the universe implanted into organic life must be of prime importance also for our own calling, both as human beings and as Jews, for it has caused every aspect of our lives to become interwoven with Him. God's Word not only forbids us to interfere directly with this law in that it prohibits unnatural crossing: a third day.   14. God said: "Let there be a system of light-bearers upon the vault of the sky to separate day from night, and they shall serve also as signs and for festive seasons, and for cycles of days and years.   15. Let them become light-bearers upon the vault of the sky to shine upon the earth." And it was so.   16. And so it was God Who made the two great light-bearers, the great light-bearer to rule over the day and the small light-bearer to rule over the night, and the stars.   17. And so it was God Who placed them upon the vault of the sky to shine upon the earth, 18. to rule by day and by night and to separate light from darkness, and it was God Who saw that it was good so.   19. And it was evening and it was morning: a fourth

יד וַיֹּאמֶר אֱלֹהִים יְהִי מְאֹרֹת בִּרְקִיעַ הַשָּׁמַיִם לְהַבְדִּיל בֵּין הַיּוֹם וּבֵין הַלָּיְלָה וְהָיוּ לְאֹתֹת וּלְמוֹעֲדִים וּלְיָמִים וְשָׁנִים: טו וְהָיוּ לִמְאוֹרֹת בִּרְקִיעַ הַשָּׁמַיִם לְהָאִיר עַל־הָאָרֶץ וַיְהִי־כֵן: טז וַיַּעַשׂ אֱלֹהִים אֶת־שְׁנֵי הַמְּאֹרֹת הַגְּדֹלִים אֶת־הַמָּאוֹר הַגָּדֹל לְמֶמְשֶׁלֶת הַיּוֹם וְאֶת־הַמָּאוֹר הַקָּטֹן לְמֶמְשֶׁלֶת הַלַּיְלָה וְאֵת הַכּוֹכָבִים: יז וַיִּתֵּן אֹתָם אֱלֹהִים בִּרְקִיעַ הַשָּׁמָיִם לְהָאִיר עַל־הָאָרֶץ: יח וְלִמְשֹׁל בַּיּוֹם וּבַלַּיְלָה וּלְהַבְדִּיל בֵּין הָאוֹר וּבֵין הַחֹשֶׁךְ וַיַּרְא אֱלֹהִים כִּי־טוֹב: יט וַיְהִי־עֶרֶב וַיְהִי־בֹקֶר יוֹם

breedings of plant and animal species which nature has set apart from one another (cf. כִּלְאֵי בְהֵמָה and הַרְכָּבַת אִילָן and [i.e. crossbreedings of animals and fruit trees that may not be grafted onto one another]). It also controls all our relationships with the plant and animal world — sowing and planting, the use of animals in our work, the utilization of textiles derived from plants and animals for our clothing, and even the food we eat בָּשָׂר בְּחָלָב and כִּלְאֵי זְרָעִים וְכִלְאֵי כֶּרֶם, שַׁעַטְנֵז, חֲרִישָׁה בְּשׁוֹר וַחֲמוֹר) [the laws of forbidden seed mixtures, the prohibition against the use of an ox and a donkey together with the same plow, forbidden mixtures of textiles, and the separation of milk and meat]). All these laws remind us again and again of the "law of species" and of Him Who gave it.

These constant reminders are designed to admonish us to revere God as the Lawgiver also for our own species, to permit His Law to rule also over our own drives and energies, and to translate His Law into reality in all our activities. It is true that we have certain energies, drives and developmental phases in common with plants and animals. We are born, we take nourishment, we grow, we age and finally we die. Nevertheless, God has created us to be a particular, higher מִין [species] among living things because we are human beings, and among human beings He has appointed us to a particular מִין as Jews. He has set down the law of life for both man and Jew.

The Law of God does not begin only with and for the Jews. We are subject to the Law of God already by virtue of the fact that we are living creatures; only within the limits He has drawn for us can we fulfill the calling He has assigned to us. Like all other living creatures we, too, can develop our individual freedom

and independence to the fullest extent only within the framework of the Law of God. The whole Torah is nothing but the "law of species" for the human being who is a Jew. That same law which rules automatically over creatures that have no free will has been explicitly proclaimed to man and to the Jewish person so that they may accept it of their own free will, to rule over all their energies, their drives and over all the manifestations of their strength and will power. It is through this voluntary self-subordination to the Law of God that they can bring their higher מִין, the higher vocation of their species, to pure and complete realization. God needs the blade of grass as well as the cedar, the ear of corn as well as the grapes of the vine, in the household of His world, and He has given to each its own law, within which each one of them is to live its own appointed life without questioning why it is a blade of grass and not a cedar, an ear of corn and not a vine. Each leaves the planning of the world to God, gladly and loyally making its own contribution to the whole.

In the same manner God also needs in His kingdom of humanity both Jews and non-Jews. Jew and non-Jew each has been assigned his own calling and his own law, and God's sublime purpose will be attained only if each one, Jew and non-Jew, will gladly and faithfully carry out that calling and obey that law which God has set for him, and in so doing will make his own contribution to the common good as God expects him to do....

14–19. מְאֹרֹת [system of light-bearers]. אוֹר ["light"], מָאוֹר ["light-bearer"]. Until then, אוֹר, the light, had been spread over all the earth. Then וַיַּבְדֵּל, God in His almighty power separated the light from the darkness. Now that it had participated in the creation of

day. 20. God said: "Let the waters swarm
with living things which move, and let birds
fly above the earth before the vault of the
sky." 21. So it was God Who created the
great families of fish and also all the life of
every small creature which moves and with
which the waters swarmed, according to
their species, and the winged bird according
to its species, and God saw that it was good.
22. God blessed them as follows: "Be
fruitful and multiply and fill the water in
the seas, but let the birds multiply upon the
earth." 23. And it was evening and it was
morning: a fifth day. 24. God said: "Let
the earth bring forth [the] living creature
according to its species, cattle and creeping
things and animals of the land according to
their species." And it was so. 25. So it was
God Who created the animals of the land
according to their species, cattle according
to its species, and every creeping thing upon
the ground according to its species. And
God saw that it was good. 26. God said:
"Let Us make an Adam (a deputy) in a form
worthy of Us, in keeping with Our image,
and they shall exercise dominion over the
fish of the sea and the birds of the sky and

רְבִיעִי: פ כ וַיֹּאמֶר אֱלֹהִים יִשְׁרְצוּ הַמַּיִם
שֶׁרֶץ נֶפֶשׁ חַיָּה וְעוֹף יְעוֹפֵף עַל־הָאָרֶץ עַל־
פְּנֵי רְקִיעַ הַשָּׁמָיִם: כא וַיִּבְרָא אֱלֹהִים אֶת־
הַתַּנִּינִם הַגְּדֹלִים וְאֵת כָּל־נֶפֶשׁ הַחַיָּה ׀
הָרֹמֶשֶׂת אֲשֶׁר שָׁרְצוּ הַמַּיִם לְמִינֵהֶם וְאֵת
כָּל־עוֹף כָּנָף לְמִינֵהוּ וַיַּרְא אֱלֹהִים כִּי־טוֹב:
כב וַיְבָרֶךְ אֹתָם אֱלֹהִים לֵאמֹר פְּרוּ וּרְבוּ
וּמִלְאוּ אֶת־הַמַּיִם בַּיַּמִּים וְהָעוֹף יִרֶב בָּאָרֶץ:
כג וַיְהִי־עֶרֶב וַיְהִי־בֹקֶר יוֹם חֲמִישִׁי: פ
כד וַיֹּאמֶר אֱלֹהִים תּוֹצֵא הָאָרֶץ נֶפֶשׁ חַיָּה
לְמִינָהּ בְּהֵמָה וָרֶמֶשׂ וְחַיְתוֹ־אֶרֶץ לְמִינָהּ וַיְהִי־
כֵן: כה וַיַּעַשׂ אֱלֹהִים אֶת־חַיַּת הָאָרֶץ לְמִינָהּ
וְאֶת־הַבְּהֵמָה לְמִינָהּ וְאֵת כָּל־רֶמֶשׂ הָאֲדָמָה
לְמִינֵהוּ וַיַּרְא אֱלֹהִים כִּי־טוֹב: כו וַיֹּאמֶר
אֱלֹהִים נַעֲשֶׂה אָדָם בְּצַלְמֵנוּ כִּדְמוּתֵנוּ וְיִרְדּוּ
בִדְגַת הַיָּם וּבְעוֹף הַשָּׁמַיִם וּבַבְּהֵמָה וּבְכָל־

the plants, those true children of light, the light was to be harnessed to a system of light-bearers upon the vault of the heavens, from which the earth was henceforth to receive its light. . . .

20. Each of the creations of the first three days was coupled with one of the creations of the three days that followed. Not until the fourth day was the light—which had been created on the first day—assigned its light-bearers, through which alone it received in full that position in relation to the earth which it needed in order to influence terrestrial life and growth. Not until the fifth day were the expanses of water and air—created on the second day—given their living world, and only on the sixth day did the dry land—which had emerged and had been enriched with vegetation on the third day—receive its living inhabitants. The seventh day marked the beginning of a new world, a world in which man was to be educated toward God. It was once again a "first day," but on a higher level now, endowed with the spiritual light of the recognition of God. However, it was not coupled with a "fourth day," it had no "bearers"; אין לו בֶּן זוג ["it had no mate"]. Only with the creation of Israel, God's eighth work for the fashioning of the world, did this spiritual light, too, receive its bearer. As the Sages put it, יִשְׂרָאֵל יִהְיֶה בֶּן זוגֵךְ ["the Sabbath was told, 'Israel shall be your mate.'"]. . . .

26. All the other creatures are introduced by the narrative only at the moment of their actual creation. In the case of man, however, the narrative is interrupted in order to announce to the world already in existence that a "man," an "Adam," is about to be created. For this "Adam" is to enter the terrestrial world as its God-appointed ruler and master. The world is being prepared for its master's coming. It is in this sense, too, that one might interpret the use of the plural; i.e. נַעֲשֶׂה ["let *Us* make"]. The use of the *pluralis majestatis*, the royal "We" employed by human sovereigns to proclaim their will to their subjects, is probably intended to imply that in issuing his orders the sovereign is not acting from the standpoint of his personal will or his personal interests but that he conceives of himself only in terms of his people and is issuing his instructions and dispositions solely for the welfare of the larger community. Only as a representative of the community as a whole can the sovereign rule over his subjects. In the same spirit, the Creator now wishes to inform the

הָאָרֶץ וּבְכָל־הָרֶמֶשׂ הָרֹמֵשׂ עַל־הָאָרֶץ:
כז וַיִּבְרָא אֱלֹהִים | אֶת־הָאָדָם בְּצַלְמוֹ בְּצֶלֶם
אֱלֹהִים בָּרָא אֹתוֹ זָכָר וּנְקֵבָה בָּרָא אֹתָם:
כח וַיְבָרֶךְ אֹתָם אֱלֹהִים וַיֹּאמֶר לָהֶם אֱלֹהִים
פְּרוּ וּרְבוּ וּמִלְאוּ אֶת־הָאָרֶץ וְכִבְשֻׁהָ וּרְדוּ
בִּדְגַת הַיָּם וּבְעוֹף הַשָּׁמַיִם וּבְכָל־חַיָּה הָרֹמֶשֶׂת
עַל־הָאָרֶץ: כט וַיֹּאמֶר אֱלֹהִים הִנֵּה נָתַתִּי לָכֶם
אֶת־כָּל־עֵשֶׂב | זֹרֵעַ זֶרַע אֲשֶׁר עַל־פְּנֵי כָל־
הָאָרֶץ וְאֶת־כָּל־הָעֵץ אֲשֶׁר־בּוֹ פְרִי־עֵץ זֹרֵעַ
זָרַע לָכֶם יִהְיֶה לְאָכְלָה: ל וּלְכָל־חַיַּת הָאָרֶץ
וּלְכָל־עוֹף הַשָּׁמַיִם וּלְכֹל | רוֹמֵשׂ עַל־הָאָרֶץ
אֲשֶׁר־בּוֹ נֶפֶשׁ חַיָּה אֶת־כָּל־יֶרֶק עֵשֶׂב לְאָכְלָה
וַיְהִי־כֵן: לא וַיַּרְא אֱלֹהִים אֶת־כָּל־אֲשֶׁר עָשָׂה

over cattle and over all the earth and over all creeping things that creep upon the earth." 27. And God created man in an image worthy of Himself; in a form worthy of God did He create him; male and female created He them. 28. And God blessed them and God said to them: "Be fruitful and multiply and fill the earth and subdue it, and exercise your dominion over the fish of the sea, the birds of the sky and every living thing that moves upon the earth." 29. God said: "Lo! I have given you every seed-bearing plant that is upon the surface of the entire earth and every tree which has seed-bearing fruit; it shall be yours for food. 30. And to every animal of the earth and to all the birds of the sky and to everything that moves upon the earth in which there is a living spirit [I give] all green plants for food." And it was so. 31. God saw the whole of what He had

terrestrial world that its [human] master is to be appointed for its own welfare, to aid the purpose for which the world exists. . . . We have[1] interpreted the word אָדָם as deriving from the color red [אָדוֹם], the least-broken ray of the spectrum; hence, the closest manifestation of the Divine on earth. . . .

27. ***And God created man in an image worthy of Himself.*** This phrase, repeated again and again, stating that the physical form of man is worthy of God and of man's own Divinely-ordained calling, demonstrates the crucial importance which the Word of God attaches to the acknowledgment of the Divine dignity inherent in the human body. Indeed, the entire Law is based primarily not upon the hallowing of the spirit but upon the hallowing of the body. The fact that the human body, with all its drives, energies and organs, was formed by God in keeping with man's God-ordained calling, and that the human body must be kept holy and dedicated exclusively to this calling, forms the basis of all human morality. . . .

male and female created He them. Though all living creatures were created in two sexes, this fact is stressed only in the case of man in order to state the verity that both sexes, male and female, were created to be equally close to God, and equally in His image. This equality is expressed in a particularly striking manner by the transition from the singular אותו ["(did He create) him"] to the plural אותם ["(created He) them"]. The one Adam-creature, made in the image of God, has been created in two sexes which only together can effectuate the concept of "Adam" in its entirety. זָכָר ["male"] is derived from זכר, "to remember," related to the terms סכר ["to lock up"], סגר ["to close"]. The male is to be the spiritual "custodian" of tradition, both Divine and human. נְקֵבָה ["female"] is derived from נקב ["to specify" or "to intend"]. She is the "intended one." . . . Only by union with the male and by joining in his efforts does the female receive that "designation," that "purpose" and that sphere within which she can make her own contribution to the fulfillment of mankind's overall purpose. The man chooses his own calling; the woman receives her calling through the man. . . .

28. פְּרוּ ["be fruitful"] refers to marriage; וּרְבוּ ["multiply"], to the family; מִלְאוּ ["fill (the earth)"], to society; and וְכִבְשֻׁהָ ["subdue it"], to the acquisition of property. . . .

These sentences place the Divine imprint upon every aspect of family and communal life. The Word of God knows of no compartmentalization of life into God-oriented or "religious," on the one hand, and profane, untouched by things Divine, on the other. God claims all of life for His service, for the fulfillment of man's calling as "Adam." This applies, first and foremost, to family and communal life. . . .

31. ***God saw.*** God saw the whole of what He had created; He beheld the totality of His creations; He saw

[1]*Note to the English translation*: Hirsch refers to an essay in his monthly *Jeschurun* (original German, Vol. VIII. pp. 524 ff.). [G.H.]

וְהִנֵּה־טוֹב מְאֹד וַיְהִי־עֶרֶב וַיְהִי־בֹקֶר יוֹם
הַשִּׁשִּׁי: פ ב א וַיְכֻלּוּ הַשָּׁמַיִם וְהָאָרֶץ וְכָל־
צְבָאָם: ב וַיְכַל אֱלֹהִים בַּיּוֹם הַשְּׁבִיעִי מְלַאכְתּוֹ

created and lo! it was very good. And it was evening and it was morning: the sixth day.

II 1. Thus the heaven and the earth and all their host were brought to their intended completion. 2. And with the seventh day God completed His [creat-

all of His creations in harmony with one another, all centering upon the same pivotal point. The text does not read אֶת הַכֹּל אֲשֶׁר עָשָׂה ["*all* that He had created"] but כָּל אֲשֶׁר עָשָׂה ["*the whole* of what He had created"]. He saw the completeness, the harmony that united everything He had created. He considered each individual creation in relationship to the whole "and lo! it was very good." It was good even where we might not have expected it to be good, where it might appear imperfect to one who can see only its parts, not the whole. If something merely performs in accordance with our expectations, we say that it is "good," but if it exceeds our expectations, if it serves us in unexpected ways, we say that it is "very good." . . .

° ° °

. . . In the case of all the preceding days of Creation, the text reads יוֹם אֶחָד ["one day"], יוֹם שֵׁנִי ["a second day"; there was one day, a second day, a third day, a fourth day and a fifth day. But in this verse the text reads, "*the* sixth day." Clearly, then, this is the day for which all the preceding days served only as preliminaries and which was to signify the completion of everything that went before. . . .

CHAPTER II

1. וַיְכֻלּוּ ***[were brought to their intended completion.]*** The root כלה combines two connotations which at first glance seem antithetical. כלה means "to be destroyed," "to cease existing altogether." Cf. וְאַתֶּם בְּנֵי יַעֲקֹב לֹא כְלִיתֶם ["And you, sons of Jacob, have not ceased to exist"] (Malachi 3:6). But at the same time כלה implies the attainment of perfection. Cf. כָּלָה הַבַּיִת לְכָל דְּבָרָיו ["The house was complete in every respect"] (I Kings 6:38) . . . The basic connotation of כלה is to strive toward a goal or purpose. לְכָל תִּכְלָה רָאִיתִי קֵץ ["I have seen an end to every striving"] (Psalm 119:96), "there is a limit to every striving," there is no such thing as an end that justifies every means—רְחָבָה מִצְוָתְךָ מְאוֹד ["but Thy commandment is exceedingly broad in scope"] (Psalm 119:96)—except for the fulfillment of God's commandments, which is an all-embracing, all-demanding objective. Hence also כלה "to yearn for an end" and כְּלִי, anything that serves a specific purpose; e.g. a tool, an instrument, a garment, etc.

כִּלָּה, "to bring to an end," and וַיְכֻלּוּ "they were brought to the goal."

° ° °

and all their host. The fact that the Jewish nation, while at peace and encamped around the Tabernacle, was counted in terms of יוֹצְאֵי צָבָא ["who go forth to service"] and that the Levites serving in the Tabernacle were described as כָּל הַבָּא לִצְבֹא צָבָא לַעֲבֹד עֲבֹדָה בְּאֹהֶל מוֹעֵד ["every one who comes to perform communal service, to minister in the Tent of Appointed Meeting"] (Num. 4:23), and finally, that the women who came to the Tabernacle with their gifts were characterized as הַצֹּבְאֹת אֲשֶׁר צָבְאוּ פֶּתַח אֹהֶל מוֹעֵד ["the women who had gathered at the entrance of the Tent of Meeting" (Exodus 38:8)] refutes the assumption that the term צָבָא must of necessity bear the connotation of an army ready to do battle. The essential meaning of צָבָא is "host." Not every multitude gathered in one place is a "host" [in the sense of צָבָא]. This term is applicable only to a multitude that has subordinated itself to the will of one sole leader who is to command the physical and spiritual energies of all the individuals in the host and under whose orders these individuals will remain for the duration of their service. Thus a "host" becomes a "host" by virtue of the will and intelligence of its commander; a "host" is a multitude commanded by the will and intelligence of one single leader. . . .

All things created in heaven or on earth together constitute one great צָבָא, one great host rallying around its Creator and Master, its Lord and its Leader: It is He Who assigns to every creature the station where, utilizing the abilities with which it has been endowed, it is to perform its assigned task. The overall plan is within the mind of the leader. Each creature fulfills its mission to the full as long as it faithfully carries out that part of the overall plan which has been assigned to it for completion. None, great or small, stands in his station by his own authority or for himself alone. We all belong to the one great "host" of God. His is the power, the greatness, the insight, the will and the position of command; ours obedience, punctiliousness, loyalty, zeal and toil. No individual has a right to arrogance. The most that the individual can achieve is only a fraction of the whole. Yet, even the least among individuals will not be overlooked as long as he faithfully performs that which the One great Commander expects of him. His eye is upon the least of them; none is expendable or insignificant in His Divine scheme: הֲלֹא צָבָא לֶאֱנוֹשׁ עֲלֵי אָרֶץ ["Is there not a time of service for men or earth?"] (Job 7:1). כָּל יְמֵי צְבָאִי אֲיַחֵל עַד בּוֹא חֲלִיפָתִי ["I must wait all the days of my service until my relief will arrive"] (Job 14:14), until God assigns me to another station.

2. . . . Everything that God created is referred to in the text as מְלַאכְתּוֹ. This word does not denote "work" in

אֲשֶׁר עָשָׂה וַיִּשְׁבֹּת בַּיּוֹם הַשְּׁבִיעִי מִכׇּל־
מְלַאכְתּוֹ אֲשֶׁר עָשָׂה׃ ג וַיְבָרֶךְ אֱלֹהִים אֶת־יוֹם
הַשְּׁבִיעִי וַיְקַדֵּשׁ אֹתוֹ כִּי בוֹ שָׁבַת מִכׇּל־
מְלַאכְתּוֹ אֲשֶׁר־בָּרָא אֱלֹהִים לַעֲשׂוֹת׃ פ שני
ד אֵלֶּה תוֹלְדוֹת הַשָּׁמַיִם וְהָאָרֶץ בְּהִבָּרְאָם (ה׳)

ing] work that He had made and with the seventh day He ceased from all His [creating] work that He had made. 3. God blessed the seventh day and made it holy, for with it He had ceased from all His [creating] work which He, God, had created [in order] to continue shaping it. 4. These are the products of the heaven and the earth which already were set for

the sense of "labor" but in the sense of completion or accomplishment. "Labor" implies only the effort, great or small, entailed in an activity, without regard to the results of that effort. מְלָאכָה, by contrast, focuses solely upon the product, the accomplishment, the objective and the product that resulted from the activity. מְלָאכָה is simply the feminine form of מַלְאָךְ ["messenger"][2] מַלְאָךְ refers to a person; מְלָאכָה, to a thing. מַלְאָךְ is a messenger, the bearer and executor of the idea and intention of another, while מְלָאכָה is a thing that has become the bearer and executor of an idea and the intention of an intelligence. Any kind of matter to which an intelligence has given a form suited for a specified purpose, becomes, by virtue of this form, מְלָאכָה, the impersonal messenger, the subservient bearer of the idea and purpose of that intelligence. Willow branches as such, for example, have no specific purpose and may be used for a variety of purposes. But if I use them to weave a basket, then they will henceforth serve only that purpose which I have assigned to them by giving them a new form. Thus, by virtue of my having woven them to form a basket, the branches have become my personal מַלְאָךְ, my מְלָאכָה. . . .

3. ***God blessed the seventh day and made it holy.*** He conferred upon it the power to accomplish the spiritual and moral education of mankind, an educational process which He ordained as all-triumphant, not subject to disruption or mortality. Why did He do so? Because with this educational instrument for mankind He ceased from "all His [creating] work," since the purpose of this instrument is identical with the goal of the entire terrestrial world which God made, a world which, in fact, God created expressly for this goal from the very beginning.

If man, like all the other creatures on earth, had been created without a free will, then God's work would have been completed with the sixth day. But because man was created with a free will and because this freedom, though it makes him even higher than the angels, of necessity also entails the possibility of error and sin, man must be educated to recognize the truth and to do good of his own free will. Therefore, though God's work in nature had been completed, His impact on the history of mankind and on the continued shaping of nature for the sake of this educational instrument had only begun with the seventh day: מִמְּלֶאכֶת עוֹלָמוֹ שָׁבַת מִמְּלֶאכֶת צַדִּיקִים וּרְשָׁעִים לֹא שָׁבַת ["He rested from the work of creating His world, but not from the work of the wicked and the work of the righteous."] (Genesis Rabbah 11:10) The education of mankind toward the spiritual and moral level of being "Adam" was entrusted to the Sabbath. All the subsequent history of God's dispensations and revelations has no other purpose but to lead the Sabbath to victory and, as the Sages so felicitously put it, to create for the Sabbath an ever-growing number of בְּנֵי זוּג, of "mates" or "partners" to act as its "bearers."

That is why He blessed the Sabbath and made it holy, and the guarantee for the ultimate achievement of this spiritual and moral purpose of the Sabbath lies in the words אֲשֶׁר בָּרָא א׳ לַעֲשׂוֹת ["which He, God, had created (in order) to continue shaping it"], that God not merely molded the world to accommodate this purpose but indeed brought it into existence solely to this end. This repetition of אֲשֶׁר בָּרָא ["which He created"] at the end of the Sabbath charter and of the story of Creation is the granite rock upon which the whole is based. The same God Who set the spiritual and moral goals that man is to attain of his own free will also created the entire physical, material and spiritual world for this very purpose out of *His* own free will. Thus nothing in this whole world can impede the attainment of these spiritual and moral goals of mankind; indeed, there can be nothing in this world that would not accord with, or promote, the attainment of this goal. The gradual winning of mankind for all that is good and true had been God's purpose from the very beginning. Hence the realization of this goal is the one thing sure of ultimate triumph. Thus, the fact that God created the world *ex nihilo* and of His own free will is not only the cornerstone of all human verities but also, and even more so, the cornerstone of all human morality.

4. אֵלֶּה תולדות הַשָּׁמַיִם וְהָאָרֶץ בְּהִבָּרְאָם וגו׳. This cannot mean, "This is the origin of the heaven and the earth . . ." To begin with, when the word אֵלֶּה ["these"] occurs as the opening word of a sentence it generally

[2]*Note to the English translation*: מלאך is also rendered as "angel," in the sense of a "messenger" of God. [G.H.]

creation on the day when *God** made earth

(זעירא) בְּיוֹם עֲשׂוֹת יְהֹוָה אֱלֹהִים אֶרֶץ וְשָׁמָיִם׃

**Note to the English translation*: The printed English translation follows Hirsch's mode of differentiating between *Elohim* and the Tetragrammaton in his original German rendering of the Biblical text. For an explanation, see note on p. XXII and Hirsch's own commentary on this verse. [G.H.]

refers to what follows; however, we are now told nothing more about the "origin" of the heaven and the earth. Also, in Scripture, the word תּוֹלְדוֹת is not used with reference to parents, the "originators," but to the offspring, the "products" of the parents. תּוֹלְדוֹת אָדָם, תּוֹלְדוֹת נֹחַ, תּוֹלְדוֹת תֶּרַח, תּוֹלְדוֹת יִשְׁמָעֵאל — all these refer not to the "origin" or "descent" of Adam, Noah, Teraḥ, et al. but to their descendants, to the progeny whom they "produced." Finally, תּוֹלְדוֹת denotes the most natural, organic "production," while, as we have already seen, בְּרִיאָה implies creation deriving purely from the free will of God, creation *ex nihilo*—in other words, precisely the antithesis of תּוֹלְדוֹת. There could be no more infelicitous term for creation *ex nihilo* than תּוֹלְדוֹת. We must therefore interpret it in this passage as referring solely to the *products* of heaven and earth; these include all things that will take shape, *after* creation, as a result or "product" of the interaction between heaven and earth. This verse, then, is the heading for the entire series of natural phenomena which we see developing after creation. These are indeed the natural products of heaven and earth. However, the text significantly adds the word בְּהִבָּרְאָם, implying that these subsequent developments already had been inherent in the process of Creation itself. . . .

° ° °

However, the concept of God as the creating Lawgiver of nature is not sufficient in itself to help us understand and appreciate the subsequent products of heaven and earth. We are therefore given yet another datum, without which we would not be able to gain a proper understanding of all these events and phenomena. This constitutes the second half of Verse 4: בְּיוֹם עֲשׂוֹת ד׳ א׳ אֶרֶץ וְשָׁמָיִם: ["on the day when *God* made earth and heaven"]. The verb is derived from עֲשִׂיָּה ["making"], not בְּרִיאָה ["creation"]. Also, we encounter here a new designation for God: ה׳ [the Tetragrammaton]. Moreover, in this verse the earth is mentioned before heaven, whereas earlier verses consistently juxtapose the two as שָׁמַיִם וָאָרֶץ ["heaven and earth"] or, more accurately, הַשָּׁמַיִם וְהָאָרֶץ ["the heaven and the earth"]. Let us begin by acquainting ourselves with the significance of ה׳ [the Tetragrammaton]. . . .

Already our Sages would have us interpret the Tetragrammaton as describing God in terms of מִדַּת הָרַחֲמִים. [His quality of mercy or compassion], as the God of love Who manifests compassion in His Providence. Here we can already see that the translation of the Tetragrammaton as "The Eternal" is utterly inadequate. . . . "Eternal" is a metaphysical, transcendental concept that has little practical significance, certainly not in our own lives and origins. "Eternal" describes character but not behavior. The characterization of someone or something as "eternal" tells us nothing more about him or it; it does not give us the slightest indication of the manner in which that being acts. The concept "Eternal" leaves our hearts cold; it is meaningless to us and hence has nothing whatever to do with מִדַּת הָרַחֲמִים [God's quality of compassion]. The Tetragrammaton, no matter how we spell or pronounce it—the traditional spelling is the שֵׁם אַדְנוּת, which is also how we pronounce it—is not "the One Who exists" but "the One Who gives (or dispenses) existence." Also, it denotes not One Who has dispensed existence in the past but One Who is always ready to dispense new life; this, indeed, is the basic connotation of מִדַּת רַחֲמִים. God is not an "Ancient of Days," Who, after having created the world, has retired to repose within the depth of His own eternal existence. He is אֱלֹקִים חַיִּים וּמֶלֶךְ עוֹלָם ["the living God and King of the Universe"], the ever-living, ever-reigning God; He is not merely the source of the past, but also the dispenser of every moment yet to be, which He fashions in accordance with the educational needs of mankind. No matter how utterly our past conduct may have forfeited it, God in the fullness of His almighty compassion is ready at all times to grant us new life.

אֱלֹקִים [God in His quality of justice] is דַּיָּן, the Creator and Ruler of the Universe Who sets limits[3] to all things. If man had not been created, if the world did not have within it a creature endowed with freedom of will but hence also capable of straying from the right path, there would be no need for מִדַּת הָרַחֲמִים [the quality of Divine compassion] in the development of the world. All other creatures of God—except for man—move blindly in the paths assigned them at the time of their creation, without the capability of deviating from them. Without man, all the תּוֹלְדוֹת הַשָּׁמַיִם וְהָאָרֶץ would be only the products of בְּהִבָּרְאָם, products of the laws of growth and development implanted into them by the lawgiving Creator at the time of their creation. But as opposed to these creatures, man has been created with a free will; he is therefore capable of error and must be educated for his lofty calling. At this point, מִדַּת רַחֲמִים, the rule of God in the form of compassionate love, comes into play; it is in His quality of compassion that God permits man and his world to survive despite

[3] *Note to the English translation*: From דַּי, "sufficient" or "sufficing." [G.H.]

and heaven. 5. No shrub of the field was
yet on earth and the grasses of the field had
not yet grown, for *God* had not yet sent the
rain upon the earth and man was not yet
there to work the soil. 6. And vapor rose
continually from the earth and watered the
entire face of the ground. 7. And *God*
formed man, dust of the ground, and
breathed the breath of life into his counte-

ה וְכֹל ׀ שִׂיחַ הַשָּׂדֶה טֶרֶם יִהְיֶה בָאָרֶץ וְכָל־
עֵשֶׂב הַשָּׂדֶה טֶרֶם יִצְמָח כִּי לֹא הִמְטִיר יְהוָה
אֱלֹהִים עַל־הָאָרֶץ וְאָדָם אַיִן לַעֲבֹד אֶת־
הָאֲדָמָה׃ ו וְאֵד יַעֲלֶה מִן־הָאָרֶץ וְהִשְׁקָה אֶת־
כָּל־פְּנֵי הָאֲדָמָה׃ ז וַיִּיצֶר יְהוָה אֱלֹהִים אֶת־
הָאָדָם עָפָר מִן־הָאֲדָמָה וַיִּפַּח בְּאַפָּיו נִשְׁמַת

man's errors, that He leads man away from error back to the path of duty, is ready at all times to give man renewed strength for a new life and future, and shapes the תּוֹלְדוֹת שָׁמַיִם וָאָרֶץ ["products of heaven and earth"] in accordance with the educational needs of mankind.

This aspect of God's rule was already implied by לַעֲשׂוֹת in the preceding verse. In His quality of אֱלֹקִים He created heaven and earth and subjected their development to a fixed law and order. But in His quality of ה׳ [as implied in the Tetragrammaton] He intervenes in this process, constantly guiding and modifying it in accordance with His purpose, which is to educate mankind. In the physical order of things [as implicit in the concept of אֱלֹקִים] the earth is dependent on the heavens, but in the moral world order [as implicit in the concept of ה׳], for the sake of which the physical world was made, the heavens may be affected by the behavior of mankind on earth; hence, in the moral world order, the heavens may be said to be dependent on the earth. This is why, in the verses that refer to God as אֱלֹקִים, heaven is mentioned before the earth; but in this verse, in which God is described in his quality of ה׳, the earth comes before heaven.

יוֹם עֲשׂוֹת ד׳ א׳ *[the day when* **God** *made earth and heaven]* denotes the seventh day, on which God introduced the Sabbath into creation, placed His entire work of heaven and earth into the service of educating man to become "Adam" and made the survival and purpose of the world dependent on this educational process. With the creation of man, the Tetragrammaton is added to אֱלֹקִים; henceforth, there will be two factors that will shape the development of the world: a) the law of nature already set by God at the time of creation and b) God's guidance and modification *after* creation, in accordance with the conduct of man on earth at any given moment. . . . It is God in His dual capacity of ה׳ אֱלֹקִים Who guides us through history.

These are the products of the heaven and the earth which already were set for creation on the day when* God *made earth and heaven. These are the products of earth and heaven whose creation was already determined on the day when God, as ה׳ [in His quality of compassion], shaped the earth and the heavens. This verse, which serves as an introduction to the history of the world, is also a protest against the deification of nature and a rebuttal of the notion that the physical development of the world is independent of the moral conduct of mankind. The dual concept of ה׳ אֱלֹקִים opens our eyes to God's physical and moral order in the world, and to the ways of God in nature and history. . . .

5. Verse 4 was the introduction to the history of mankind; it showed us that the development of the world after its creation would depend on how man would live and conduct himself on earth. Verse 5 returns the narrative to the moment at which Creation had come to a temporary standstill, waiting to be completed by the advent of man, on whom the subsequent development of Creation would depend. At the same time it shows us that the verity expressed in general terms in the preceding verse became operative as soon as man came into the world. Also, Verse 5 shows us more specific phases in the training of man, which afford us a deeper insight into his character and help us understand his nature in relation to the lofty station and calling which was already indicated in the account of his creation as part of the series of creations.

° ° °

. . . אֲדָמָה defines the earth not as a cosmic body in the universe but in its relationship to man, as the "ground" or "soil" wedded to "Adam," as it were, and given to man as his province of activity. . . .

7. ***And* God *formed man.*** This verse sets forth the whole secret of man's nature. It is on the facts disclosed here that all our awareness of man's dignity and calling is based. It has struck many commentators that according to this verse the dignity of man lies totally in the fact that he became נֶפֶשׁ חַיָּה ["a living personality"]. Now נֶפֶשׁ חַיָּה is a characteristic that every living thing, down to the smallest insect, shares with man. However, in this verse the emphasis is not on נֶפֶשׁ חַיָּה but on וַיְהִי הָאָדָם לְנֶפֶשׁ חַיָּה, how man became a "living personality." It is not the mere fact that he became a living personality but the manner in which he became one that sets man so high above all other living creatures.

° ° °

. . . What is it that sets man apart from the animal? The individuality of the animal depends on earthly nance, and so man became a living personality. 8. And *God* planted a garden in Eden in the east and there He placed the man whom He had formed. 9. *God* caused every kind of tree to grow from the soil, delightful to the sight and good for

חַיִּ֑ים וַֽיְהִ֥י הָֽאָדָ֖ם לְנֶ֥פֶשׁ חַיָּֽה׃ ח וַיִּטַּ֞ע יְהוָ֧ה
אֱלֹהִ֛ים גַּן־בְּעֵ֖דֶן מִקֶּ֑דֶם וַיָּ֣שֶׂם שָׁ֔ם אֶת־הָֽאָדָ֖ם
אֲשֶׁ֥ר יָצָֽר׃ ט וַיַּצְמַ֞ח יְהוָ֤ה אֱלֹהִים֙ מִן־הָ֣אֲדָמָ֔ה
כָּל־עֵ֛ץ נֶחְמָ֥ד לְמַרְאֶ֖ה וְט֣וֹב לְמַאֲכָ֑ל וְעֵ֤ץ

matter; like its body, so its soul, too, came forth from the earth. Not so man. In the creation of man, only the inert substance was taken from the soil; he was turned into a living individual by the breath of God Himself. Herein lies the freedom, the immortality and, indeed, all the greatness of man. Whatever it is that gives the animal its individuality emanates from the earth and must eventually return to the earth. Not so that which makes man a "living personality." Not only man's spirit but also his vitality make him a creature higher than the animal. His vitality, too, is linked not to his body but to his spirit. It was only through the spirit that he received life, and it is to his spirit that his soul adheres. When his spirit departs from his body, the remains that are buried do not include that which was "alive" in him, for man's life is bound up with his spirit, not his body. This is why his physical survival and health do not depend on his body alone. What will kill an animal need not necessarily also cause the death of a human being, and the survival of a man cannot be predicted with the same degree of accuracy as the survival of an animal. אָדָם יֵשׁ לוֹ מַזָּל ["Man has *mazal*"]: there is something in man that defies prediction; even if all else seems to have departed, a human being can go on living by his spirit, on sheer willpower alone, for it is the spirit that also preserves life. Who would attempt to calculate the amount of time for which an unbroken human spirit could keep the body alive?

Thus, man combines within himself two essences that by their very nature are different from each other. True, one of these is indeed related to the earth. But man is not part of the earth—rather, the earth is אֲדָמָה, it has been given to man to rule. So, too, that small quantity of עָפָר מִן הָאֲדָמָה ["dust of the ground"] from which his body was formed is subject to man's control. His true living, spiritual essence is not dependent on the earth; hence, even while he is physically combined with the earthly element, he can and should exercise control over the earthly aspect of his being. That which is עָפָר ["terrestrial"] within him is of necessity not free and is therefore subject to the influences of physical factors. But the נִשְׁמַת חַיִּים ["the breath of life"] which God imparted to man with His breath and which first made man a human being elevates him beyond the forces of physical compulsion, makes him free and so elevates his body, also, into the realm of freedom.

9. ***delightful to the sight and good for food.*** One should not lose sight of the fact that in this description of the garden which was planned to cater to man's physical needs, נֶחְמָד לְמַרְאֶה, ["delightful to the sight"], the gratification of man's feeling for beauty, is put before טוֹב לְמַאֲכָל ["and good for food"], the gratification of his sense of taste and his need for nourishment. Here the esthetic element, man's feeling for beauty, receives its justification and sanctity. This seems to indicate the higher place intended for man in the scheme of Creation. The abundance of beautiful forms which we note among the creatures on our earth and the fact that—as far as we know—man is the only creature endowed with a capacity for enjoying beauty, verifies the importance which the Creator attaches to this capacity in man's spiritual and moral calling. Indeed, the beautiful forms that are scattered throughout creation, along with man's capacity for deriving pleasure from them, represent the principal means for protecting man from becoming completely brutalized. The pleasure man derives from the beauty in nature and from the beautiful forms into which God has shaped particularly the world of vegetation, represents a bridge which leads man to the stage where he is able to derive pleasure also from things and ideas of spiritual and moral beauty.

In an environment where no attention is given to harmony and beauty, man can easily run wild. The emotion that enables man to derive pleasure from order and harmony is closely akin to man's sense of order and harmony also in the sphere of ethics and morality, so much so that רע, evil, [related to רעע, "to break into pieces"] appears as something "broken," a disturbance in harmony in which the whole is no longer ruled by one uniform purpose.

° ° °

As we shall see later, the Tree of Knowledge of Good and Evil was endowed with every physical attribute designed to appeal to man's taste, imagination and intellect. His taste, his imagination and his intelligence drew man to this tree and caused him to desire its fruits as food. Nevertheless, God forbade man to eat of the fruit of this tree. In other words, partaking of this fruit was defined as being "bad" for man. This tree, then, was intended to remind man constantly of that Law on which all the purity and loftiness of his moral calling depend. Man's physical senses, his imagination and his intelligence may tell him that a certain thing is good, indeed, the very best; nevertheless, it may conflict with man's higher calling, and if man partakes of it, this may food, with the Tree of Life in the middle of the garden and also a Tree of Knowledge of Good and Evil. 10. And a river goes forth from Eden to water the garden and from there it divides and becomes four heads. 11. The name of the first is Pishon; this is the one that encompasses the whole land of Ḥavilah, where the gold is. 12. The gold of this land is good; *bedolah*° and the *shoham* stone are there. 13. The name of the second river is Giḥon; this is the one that encompasses the whole land of Cush. 14. The name of the third river is Ḥidekel°°; this is the one that flows to the east of Asshur, and the fourth river is the Euphrates. 15. *God* took the man and placed him in the Garden of Eden to work it and to guard it. 16. And *God* commanded man [saying]: "From every tree of the garden you may indeed eat, 17. but from the Tree of Knowledge of Good and Evil you must not eat, for on the

הַחַיִּים בְּתוֹךְ הַגָּן וְעֵץ הַדַּעַת טוֹב וָרָע׃
י וְנָהָר יֹצֵא מֵעֵדֶן לְהַשְׁקוֹת אֶת־הַגָּן וּמִשָּׁם
יִפָּרֵד וְהָיָה לְאַרְבָּעָה רָאשִׁים׃ יא שֵׁם הָאֶחָד
פִּישׁוֹן הוּא הַסֹּבֵב אֵת כָּל־אֶרֶץ הַחֲוִילָה
אֲשֶׁר־שָׁם הַזָּהָב׃ יב וּזֲהַב הָאָרֶץ הַהִוא טוֹב
שָׁם הַבְּדֹלַח וְאֶבֶן הַשֹּׁהַם׃ יג וְשֵׁם־הַנָּהָר הַשֵּׁנִי
גִּיחוֹן הוּא הַסּוֹבֵב אֵת כָּל־אֶרֶץ כּוּשׁ׃ יד וְשֵׁם־
הַנָּהָר הַשְּׁלִישִׁי חִדֶּקֶל הוּא הַהֹלֵךְ קִדְמַת
אַשּׁוּר וְהַנָּהָר הָרְבִיעִי הוּא פְרָת׃ טו וַיִּקַּח
יְהוָֹה אֱלֹהִים אֶת־הָאָדָם וַיַּנִּחֵהוּ בְגַן־עֵדֶן
לְעָבְדָהּ וּלְשָׁמְרָהּ׃ טז וַיְצַו יְהוָֹה אֱלֹהִים עַל־
הָאָדָם לֵאמֹר מִכֹּל עֵץ־הַגָּן אָכֹל תֹּאכֵל׃
יז וּמֵעֵץ הַדַּעַת טוֹב וָרָע לֹא תֹאכַל מִמֶּנּוּ כִּי

°*Note to the English translation*: Bdellium. [G.H.]

°°*Note to the English translation*: the river Tigris [G.H.]

be an offense that God deems deserving of death.

From this we learn that in judging what is good or evil, man must not rely on his own senses, his own imagination or his own intelligence but must look to the will of God which was revealed to him. He must accept this Divine judgment as his sole guide if he is to fulfill his purpose on earth and remain worthy of having the world shaped into a Paradise for him.

15. . . . The terms עֲבוֹדָה ["work"] and שְׁמִירָה ["guarding"] denote not merely the literal, direct "cultivation" and "care" of the soil, but also all of man's moral conduct, his conscientious endeavor to do that which is expected of him and to refrain from doing that which is forbidden. For it is by virtue of man's moral conduct and his conscientious use of the bounties of nature that nature itself receives not only aid for its development toward its purpose but also the conditions necessary for its very survival. Hence our Sages juxtapose the concepts of עֲבוֹדָה וּשְׁמִירָה [cultivation and care] with תּוֹרָה וּמִצְוֹת [Torah and the observance of the Divine commandments] which comprise the totality of man's purpose.

16–17. The prohibition set forth in Verses 16 and 17 is the starting point of man's training for his lofty, godly calling. It represents the beginning of mankind's history and it is intended to show subsequent generations the path in which they are to walk. This is not a מִצְוָה שִׂכְלִית, a "rational" prohibition. In fact, it runs counter to all the cognitive faculties with which man has been endowed: taste, imagination and intelligence. Man would never have devised such a prohibition with his own intelligence, and after this prohibition was imposed upon him he could find no other explanation for it except that it was the will of God. It is a חק ["statute"] *in optima forma.* It is also a dietary prohibition and it came down by oral communication [Oral Law], if you will, to the one who was to observe it. It was communicated to Adam for Eve and their descendants to obey. So, this one prohibition contained the following basic elements of the future Jewish law at which, in the words of the Sages, the יֵצֶר הָרַע [lit. "evil inclination"] and אוּמוֹת הָעוֹלָם ["the nations of the world"] (the judgment of our senses and of the non-Jewish world, respectively) have always taken umbrage:

מִצְוֹת לֹא תַעֲשֶׂה ["negative commandments"], חק ["statute"], מַאֲכָלוֹת אֲסוּרוֹת ["dietary prohibitions"] and תּוֹרָה שֶׁבְּעַל פֶּה ["Oral Law"].

All these aspects of the Jewish law to come were combined in this one prohibition that God proclaimed at the very outset of man's development, לָדַעַת טוֹב וָרָע, so that this prohibition should teach man to understand what he must regard as "good" and what he must reject as "evil."

Thus, the subordination of our physical nature to the Divine will as expressed by God Himself is posited

day that you will eat from it you must die."
18. *God* said: "It is not good that man
should be alone; I will make a helpmeet for
him."   19. And *God* herded together from
the ground all the animal[s] of the field and
all the birds of the sky and brought [them]
to man to see what he would call them, and
everything that man, as a living personality,
calls it,° that is its name.   20. Man gave
names to all cattle and to all the birds of
the sky and to every animal of the field,
but he found no helper fitting for a man.
21. And *God* caused unconsciousness to
fall upon the man and he slept, and He took
one of his sides and closed up the flesh in
that place.   22. Then *God* formed the side
which He had taken from the man into a
woman, and he brought her to the man.
23. And the man said: "At last this one is
it! Bone of my bone and flesh of my flesh!
This one may be called woman,°° for this

בְּיוֹם אֲכָלְךָ מִמֶּנּוּ מוֹת תָּמוּת: יח וַיֹּאמֶר יְהֹוָה
אֱלֹהִים לֹא־טוֹב הֱיוֹת הָאָדָם לְבַדּוֹ אֶעֱשֶׂה־לּוֹ
עֵזֶר כְּנֶגְדּוֹ: יט וַיִּצֶר יְהֹוָה אֱלֹהִים מִן־הָאֲדָמָה
כָּל־חַיַּת הַשָּׂדֶה וְאֵת כָּל־עוֹף הַשָּׁמַיִם וַיָּבֵא
אֶל־הָאָדָם לִרְאוֹת מַה־יִּקְרָא־לוֹ וְכֹל אֲשֶׁר
יִקְרָא־לוֹ הָאָדָם נֶפֶשׁ חַיָּה הוּא שְׁמוֹ: שלישי
כ וַיִּקְרָא הָאָדָם שֵׁמוֹת לְכָל־הַבְּהֵמָה וּלְעוֹף
הַשָּׁמַיִם וּלְכֹל חַיַּת הַשָּׂדֶה וּלְאָדָם לֹא־מָצָא
עֵזֶר כְּנֶגְדּוֹ: כא וַיַּפֵּל יְהֹוָה אֱלֹהִים | תַּרְדֵּמָה
עַל־הָאָדָם וַיִּישָׁן וַיִּקַּח אַחַת מִצַּלְעֹתָיו וַיִּסְגֹּר
בָּשָׂר תַּחְתֶּנָּה: כב וַיִּבֶן יְהֹוָה אֱלֹהִים | אֶת־
הַצֵּלָע אֲשֶׁר־לָקַח מִן־הָאָדָם לְאִשָּׁה וַיְבִאֶהָ
אֶל־הָאָדָם: כג וַיֹּאמֶר הָאָדָם זֹאת הַפַּעַם עֶצֶם
מֵעֲצָמַי וּבָשָׂר מִבְּשָׂרִי לְזֹאת יִקָּרֵא אִשָּׁה כִּי

°*Note to the English translation*: "It refers to the species. [G.H.]
°°*Note to the English translation*: In the German original

Hirsch translates אשה, "woman," as *Männin*; i.e. "she-man,"
the literal translation of the Hebrew term. [G.H.]

as a basic condition for all human morality, one inextricably bound up with man's lofty moral position
and calling. . . .

18. Before man was created, Creation came to a temporary standstill as God announced that the culmination of His work was about to appear. This was the case
now, too, before the creation of woman. The man
was already there, amidst the beauty of Paradise in full
bloom, but God did not yet say טוב, that everything was
now "good." The literal meaning of לֹא טוֹב הֱיוֹת הָאָדָם לְבַדּוֹ
is not "it is not good that man should be alone" but
"this is not good, seeing that man is alone." Everything
cannot be "good" as long as man is alone. The goal of
perfection which the terrestrial world is to attain
through man cannot be attained in full as long as man is
alone. The completion of good was not man but
woman; only woman could bring that to man and to the
world. This verity was absorbed so deeply by those
"Orientals," our "Rabbis," that they taught us: Only
through his wife can man become truly "man," only
husband and wife together can comprise "Adam." The
task is too great for either to perform alone and must
therefore be shared by another.
   And so, in order to effect the full accomplishment of
man's purpose, God created woman for the man. The
woman is to be his עֵזֶר כְּנֶגְדּוֹ, [a "help *meet*" for him].
Even a superficial glance at this term suffices to see that

it defines the true dignity of women's position. It does
not carry any implication of sexual relationship. All it
indicates is that woman was placed into the sphere of
man's activities. That was where she was needed: She
was to be עֵזֶר כְּנֶגְדּוֹ.
   עֵזֶר כְּנֶגְדּוֹ does not imply that woman is to be subordinate to man; actually, it connotes complete equality
between man and woman, on a footing of independent
parity. The woman is to stand at man's side כְּנֶגְדּוֹ, on the
same level, in a parallel position. . . .

19. קרא means "to call"; i.e., to summon another to
come to us (hence also לִקְרַאת ["to meet"], literally, to
move in the direction indicated by the position of the
other). Hence, also "to name." By naming a person or
thing, or by calling it by its name, I call it to myself or
evoke it in my mind . . .

20. Man studied the individual characteristics of
each living creature and arranged them in his mind in
accordance with his impressions. He studied the animals closest to him (בְּהֵמָה [cattle]), those least like him
(חַיָּה [undomesticated animals]) and those least submissive to him (עוֹף [birds]). But when he came to contemplate the species of "Adam" (the text reads וּלְאָדָם,
not וְלָאדם), the deputy of God on earth, created in the
image of God, he found no one that was parallel to
him, no one whom he considered capable of sharing his
great responsibility.

one was taken out of a man." 24. For this reason a man leaves his father and his mother and clings to his wife, and they become one flesh. 25. Both of them, the man and his wife, were naked and they were not ashamed.

III 1. Now the serpent was more cunning than any animal of the field that *God* had made, and it said to

מֵאִישׁ לֻקְחָה־זֹּאת׃ כד עַל־כֵּן יַעֲזָב־אִישׁ אֶת־
אָבִיו וְאֶת־אִמּוֹ וְדָבַק בְּאִשְׁתּוֹ וְהָיוּ לְבָשָׂר
אֶחָד׃ כה וַיִּהְיוּ שְׁנֵיהֶם עֲרוּמִּים הָאָדָם וְאִשְׁתּוֹ
וְלֹא יִתְבֹּשָׁשׁוּ׃ ג א וְהַנָּחָשׁ הָיָה עָרוּם מִכֹּל
חַיַּת הַשָּׂדֶה אֲשֶׁר עָשָׂה יְהוָה אֱלֹהִים וַיֹּאמֶר

24. ***For this reason.*** This means: Because, as long as man was alone, "it was not yet good," and because, once the division into two sexes had been made, it was in fact no longer possible for the man to fulfill his calling by himself, and because the woman was to be his "helpmeet" without whom he is only half a man, so that he can feel he is a complete man only if he is together with her; now, therefore, the man leaves his father and mother and unites with his wife so that, together, they may become one body.

Before the human species was divided into male and female, man's body was subordinate to one spirit, one Divine will. When male and female are reunited, they become one body as well. However, they can become "one body" only if, at the same time, they become one mind, one heart and one soul, and this in turn can come to pass only if both of them subordinate all their energies and aspirations, all their thoughts and desires, to the service of a higher will. Herein, too, lies the immense difference between the sex lives of all other living things, on the one hand, and human marriage, on the other. Other creatures are also divided into two sexes. But in their case both sexes came into being simultaneously and independently of one another. They do not need one another to fulfill their life's purpose: only for the purpose of breeding and for the time devoted to this one act do they seek and find one another. The human female, by contrast, is part of the human male; she is עֵזֶר כְּנֶגְדּוֹ. Without his wife, the male is helpless and dependent. Only the two together can form one complete human being. Life in all its aspects demands that man and woman unite. Only with reference to the human male does Scripture say that he "clings to his wife." Marriage occurs only in the human species.

Our Sages (cf. Sanhedrin 56 f.) view this verse as a basis for the laws of forbidden marriages in the Noahide code. They interpret the statement that "a man leaves his father and mother and clings to his wife" as implying that when a man chooses a wife he should remove himself from his father and mother, meaning that he should not marry a woman too closely related to him. . . . Because the wife must be the עֵזֶר ["helpmeet"] of her husband, she must be כְּנֶגְדּוֹ [lit., "against him"]. Since she is to "complete" him, she must have traits different from his. If husband and wife are close relatives, they may both have the same virtues but they may also have the same faults and thus their union would serve only to intensify their common traits, both good and bad; husband and wife would not "complete" one another. Only if husband and wife are not close relatives may we expect to find differences between man and wife that are beneficial in that they serve to shape the two partners, united, into one "complete" whole, capable of becoming "one flesh," the better and the more completely to fulfill their tasks as human beings. . . .

CHAPTER III

1. The difference between man and animal is the touchstone of human morality and at the same time the rock on which human morality can founder. It was the subtle logic of an animal that led the first man astray from his duty; today this same animal logic still serves as midwife to all human sin. The story of man's first misstep is the history also of all subsequent human error. The animal is really "like God in that it knows good from evil." Animals are endowed with an instinct; this instinct is the voice of God, the will of God as it applies to them. Hence whatever animals do in accordance with this Divine Providence within them—and they do nothing else because they can do no other—is "good," while any act from which their instinct restrains them is "evil." Animals cannot go astray because they have only their one nature whose call they can and must heed.

Not so man. Man must opt for the good and shun evil out of his own free will and sense of duty. Even when he gives his physical nature its due, he must do so not because of the stimulus of his physical appetites but out of a sense of duty. Even the most physical of his pleasures must be moral acts, performed in this spirit, of his own free will. Nowhere, and under no circumstances, may he ever be an animal. This is the reason the woman: "Even if God has said so, are you [really] not to eat from all the trees of the garden?" 2. And the woman said to the serpent: "We may eat of the fruit of the trees in the garden, 3. but regarding the fruit of the tree which is in the middle of the garden God said: 'You shall not eat from it and not touch it; lest you will die.'" 4. Thereupon the serpent said to the woman: "You will not die so soon. 5. God knows quite well that on the day you will eat from it your eyes will be opened and you will be like God, knowing what is good and what is evil." 6. When the woman saw that the tree was good for food and tempting to the sight and that the tree was a delight to contemplate, she took of its fruit and ate, and she also gave some of it to her

אֶל־הָֽאִשָּׁה אַף כִּֽי־אָמַר אֱלֹהִים לֹא תֹֽאכְלוּ
מִכֹּל עֵץ הַגָּן: ב וַתֹּאמֶר הָֽאִשָּׁה אֶל־הַנָּחָשׁ
מִפְּרִי עֵץ־הַגָּן נֹאכֵל: ג וּמִפְּרִי הָעֵץ אֲשֶׁר
בְּתוֹךְ־הַגָּן אָמַר אֱלֹהִים לֹא תֹֽאכְלוּ מִמֶּנּוּ וְלֹא
תִגְּעוּ בּוֹ פֶּן תְּמֻתוּן: ד וַיֹּאמֶר הַנָּחָשׁ אֶל־
הָאִשָּׁה לֹא־מוֹת תְּמֻתוּן: ה כִּי יֹדֵעַ אֱלֹהִים כִּי
בְּיוֹם אֲכָלְכֶם מִמֶּנּוּ וְנִפְקְחוּ עֵינֵיכֶם וִהְיִיתֶם
כֵּֽאלֹהִים יֹדְעֵי טוֹב וָרָע: ו וַתֵּרֶא הָֽאִשָּׁה כִּי
טוֹב הָעֵץ לְמַאֲכָל וְכִי תַֽאֲוָה־הוּא לָעֵינַיִם
וְנֶחְמָד הָעֵץ לְהַשְׂכִּיל וַתִּקַּח מִפִּרְיוֹ וַתֹּאכַל
וַתִּתֵּן גַּם־לְאִישָׁהּ עִמָּהּ וַיֹּאכַל: ז וַתִּפָּקַחְנָה

why man bears within him not only the quality of godliness but also the urges of his physical appetities. It is ordained that what is good and right should often seem distasteful to his physical senses, while evil should often appear attractive to him, so that he may have the opportunity, for the sake of his lofty Divine calling, to use his God-given free energy to choose good and shun evil—not because of the urgings of his appetites but in spite of them. For this reason the voice of God does not speak from within but from outside himself, to tell him what is good and evil, and it will meet resistance from man's physical appetites whenever these appetites are permitted independent expression untouched and unguided by the godly quality inherent in man. Conscience, that voice of God which was breathed into man and whose messenger, as we know, is our sense of shame, serves only to warn man in general terms to do good and shun evil. Precisely which acts are "good" and which "evil"—this he can learn only from the mouth of God speaking to him from outside himself.

Animals need only develop the physical aspects of their nature, to which their intelligence is completely subservient. But man was not placed into the terrestrial Paradise in order to satisfy his physical appetites with the delights offered there. He was called there "to work it and to guard it," in order to serve God and His world. This service is his purpose; only for its sake is he permitted to partake of the fruits of Paradise. It is enough for the animal to form all its judgments on the basis of its individual nature because the animal exists only for itself. Man, however, exists for God and for the world and must gladly sacrifice his own individuality to this higher calling. Hence, it is not from his own individual nature but from his lofty calling that he must learn what is "good" and "evil" for him. It is for this reason that he was given the tree bedecked with physical enticements. Everything in his own personal nature must tell him: "This is good." But the Word of God addressed to him has forbidden him to eat of the fruits of this tree; God has told him that to do so would be "evil." The Word of God was to be the model, the rule by which man was to differentiate between good and evil. . . . It is at this point that man first encounters animal logic in the form of its most subtle exemplification: the serpent. Even the most intelligent animal is incapable of understanding how man could possibly remain indifferent to the best, the most beautiful and appealing physical delights.

Even if God has said so. The very tone in which the serpent begins his argument shows us that this encounter is between a human being and an animal. Man has already cited God's prohibition as his reason for refusing to eat of the fruit. Now the animal replies: "Even if God has said so, does that mean that you must really obey? Is not the urge within you also the voice of God? If it were indeed 'evil' for you to partake of this fruit, why did God make the fruit so appealing and arouse within you the desire to eat it? Is this not clearly His own way of telling you that you and this pleasure were made for one another? . . . Would God create such delights and cause you to yearn for them only to forbid them to you?"

Thus spoke the serpent, and thus animal logic still speaks to us today, either in straightforward terms or in the guise of subtle sophistry, whenever an express prohibiton from God restrains man from a physical delight. Even as the serpent did then, so animal logic still distorts everything today; it permits the little that is husband, and he ate. 7. And the eyes of both of them were opened and they realized that they were naked. And they sewed together fig leaves and made themselves aprons. 8. They heard the voice of *God* withdrawing into the garden in the direction of day, and the man and his wife hid among the trees of the garden from the presence of *God*. 9. And *God* called to the man and said to him: "Where are you?" 10. He answered: "I heard Thy voice in the garden and I was afraid because I am naked and so I hid." 11. He said: "Who made you aware that you are naked? Did you eat of the tree from which I commanded you not to eat?" 12. And the man said: "The woman whom Thou [Thyself] didst put at my side, she gave me of the tree and I ate." 13. And *God* said to the woman: "What have you done?" And the woman answered: "The serpent deceived me and I ate." 14. And *God* said to the serpent: "Because you have done this, you shall be cursed more than all cattle and more than all the animals of the field; you shall crawl upon your belly and eat dust all the days of your life. 15. And I will put enmity between you and the woman, and between your seed and hers. He will strike at your head and you will strike at his heel."

עֵינֵי שְׁנֵיהֶם וַיֵּדְעוּ כִּי עֵירֻמִּם הֵם וַיִּתְפְּרוּ
עֲלֵה תְאֵנָה וַיַּעֲשׂוּ לָהֶם חֲגֹרֹת׃ ח וַיִּשְׁמְעוּ
אֶת־קוֹל יְהוָה אֱלֹהִים מִתְהַלֵּךְ בַּגָּן לְרוּחַ הַיּוֹם
וַיִּתְחַבֵּא הָאָדָם וְאִשְׁתּוֹ מִפְּנֵי יְהוָה אֱלֹהִים
בְּתוֹךְ עֵץ הַגָּן׃ ט וַיִּקְרָא יְהוָה אֱלֹהִים אֶל־
הָאָדָם וַיֹּאמֶר לוֹ אַיֶּכָּה׃ י וַיֹּאמֶר אֶת־קֹלְךָ
שָׁמַעְתִּי בַּגָּן וָאִירָא כִּי־עֵירֹם אָנֹכִי וָאֵחָבֵא׃
יא וַיֹּאמֶר מִי הִגִּיד לְךָ כִּי עֵירֹם אָתָּה הֲמִן־
הָעֵץ אֲשֶׁר צִוִּיתִיךָ לְבִלְתִּי אֲכָל־מִמֶּנּוּ אָכָלְתָּ׃
יב וַיֹּאמֶר הָאָדָם הָאִשָּׁה אֲשֶׁר נָתַתָּה עִמָּדִי
הִוא נָתְנָה־לִּי מִן־הָעֵץ וָאֹכֵל׃ יג וַיֹּאמֶר יְהוָה
אֱלֹהִים לָאִשָּׁה מַה־זֹּאת עָשִׂית וַתֹּאמֶר הָאִשָּׁה
הַנָּחָשׁ הִשִּׁיאַנִי וָאֹכֵל׃ יד וַיֹּאמֶר יְהוָה
אֱלֹהִים ׀ אֶל־הַנָּחָשׁ כִּי עָשִׂיתָ זֹּאת אָרוּר אַתָּה
מִכָּל־הַבְּהֵמָה וּמִכֹּל חַיַּת הַשָּׂדֶה עַל־גְּחֹנְךָ
תֵלֵךְ וְעָפָר תֹּאכַל כָּל־יְמֵי חַיֶּיךָ׃ טו וְאֵיבָה ׀
אָשִׁית בֵּינְךָ וּבֵין הָאִשָּׁה וּבֵין זַרְעֲךָ וּבֵין זַרְעָהּ
הוּא יְשׁוּפְךָ רֹאשׁ וְאַתָּה תְּשׁוּפֶנּוּ עָקֵב׃ ס

prohibited to eclipse the totality of what is morally permissible to us and presents God's moral law as the enemy of *all* physical pleasures.

7. The serpent was perfectly right. Their eyes were opened and they became "enlightened." But the first fact they perceived was that they were naked. If we perceive that we are naked it means that we realize we are showing something that should not be seen. This is the sense of shame, which, as we have already indicated, is rooted in man's awareness of his true calling. As long as man stands completely in the service of his God, he has no reason to feel ashamed of the physical aspects of his being. Bodily charms, too, are godly and pure as long as they are used as means to fulfill God's holy purposes. But once this relationship [between the physical and the godly self] is reversed, then we do have cause to feel ashamed of our physical attributes. For at that point a voice, closely bound up with our conscience, will stir within us to remind us that we are not meant to be animals.

° ° °

8. ***and the man and his wife hid.*** They no longer stood upright לִפְנֵי ד׳, before God, but they hid מִפְּנֵי, from His presence, because they feared it. From that time on they became aware of an increasing array of conflicts. They had already sensed the first of these, the conflict between their bodies and their spirit, and therefore they had made aprons for themselves. Immediately thereafter, they became aware of another conflict, that between themselves (who were no longer in command of their own senses, no longer pure in body and spirit) and God. They became aware that they had forfeited their unique status as human beings and therefore they hid among other living things.

14–15. . . . There is to be enmity between the serpent, on the one hand, and man (along with the cattle that attaches itself to man), on the other. As a matter of fact, of the four higher species it is only the amphibians, of which the snake is one, that are completely alien and hostile to man, cut off from man by the aversion and repugnance he feels for them.

Seen from the viewpoint of God's concern for the education of man, אֵיבָה ["enmity"], the deep loathing

16. And to the woman He said: "I will make [the pain of] your renunciation and your conceiving greater still; in renunciation will you bear children; your longing shall be for your husband and he will rule over you." 17. And to Adam He said: "Because you hearkened to the voice of your wife and ate of the tree concerning which I commanded you and said, 'You shall not eat from it,' the ground will be cursed because of you; you shall eat of it in renunciation all the days of your life. 18. Thorns and thistles shall it sprout for you and you would have to eat the grass of the field. 19. By the sweat of your countenance shall you eat bread until you return to the ground, for from it you were taken; for you are dust, and to dust you shall

טז אֶל־הָאִשָּׁה אָמַר הַרְבָּה אַרְבֶּה עִצְּבוֹנֵךְ וְהֵרֹנֵךְ בְּעֶצֶב תֵּלְדִי בָנִים וְאֶל־אִישֵׁךְ תְּשׁוּקָתֵךְ וְהוּא יִמְשָׁל־בָּךְ: ס יז וּלְאָדָם אָמַר כִּי שָׁמַעְתָּ לְקוֹל אִשְׁתֶּךָ וַתֹּאכַל מִן־הָעֵץ אֲשֶׁר צִוִּיתִיךָ לֵאמֹר לֹא תֹאכַל מִמֶּנּוּ אֲרוּרָה הָאֲדָמָה בַּעֲבוּרֶךָ בְּעִצָּבוֹן תֹּאכְלֶנָּה כֹּל יְמֵי חַיֶּיךָ: יח וְקוֹץ וְדַרְדַּר תַּצְמִיחַ לָךְ וְאָכַלְתָּ אֶת־עֵשֶׂב הַשָּׂדֶה: יט בְּזֵעַת אַפֶּיךָ תֹּאכַל לֶחֶם עַד שׁוּבְךָ אֶל־הָאֲדָמָה כִּי מִמֶּנָּה לֻקָּחְתָּ כִּי־עָפָר אַתָּה

instilled in man toward the serpent, may have been intended to make man—led astray as he was by the shrewdness of an animal—realize the full extent of the gap that separates him from the animal. At the same time it may have been meant as a constant reminder to man that there must be some other standard than that of blind instinct by which to judge whether a thing or an act is good or evil. It is only normal instinct that impels the serpent to bite man; yet, a snakebite is an evil thing for man. In the same manner something that is morally evil may gratify man's physical appetites, yet prove destructive to other, loftier aspects of his life. Therefore, man must not permit the mere dictates of his senses to tell him what is good or evil. If we may assume that henceforth the sight of a serpent is to remind man that he must fight against his lusts, then "he will strike at your head and you will strike at his heel" would imply that man has been given more power over his lusts than his lusts have over him. Man is capable of "striking at the head" of lust, while lust, at most, can catch him on his heel. . . [And] only when man is off his guard will the serpent, or lust, be able to catch him by his heel. If man is constantly alert and on guard he will be able to elude both. By the same token, man will be able to "strike at the head" of serpents, or lusts, only as long as he will not permit his physical appetites to become passions. Once he has stirred his appetites to passion pitch, he will no longer be able to resist them.

18. . . . If you would want to continue living as you did in Paradise, you would have to subsist on grass.

19. **בְּזֵעַת אַפֶּיךָ תֹּאכַל לֶחֶם** [*By the sweat of your countenance shall you eat bread*]. It is with אַפַּיִם, his

countenance, that man strives to become master over his environment and surveys his domain. Thus: It is not by the sweat of your body, your hands or even פָּנֶיךָ [your face], but בְּזֵעַת אַפֶּיךָ [by the sweat of your countenance] that you will eat your bread. That Godlike countenance of yours, the seat of your intellect, of your insights, and of all the Divine light that was intended to give expression to your dominion over the earth, will henceforth have to be used by you for obtaining your daily bread. . . .

°   °   °

One consideration . . . seems to us most significant. The only curses contained in this Divine judgment are directed at the ground and at one particular animal. God's sentence does not include a curse against man as such. There is not one syllable to suggest even the minutest change in man's lofty calling and in his ability to fulfill it. Only the external conditions in which he is to accomplish his mission have changed, and even this happened only for his own good. His mission as such, his godly calling and his God-given ability to fulfill it have remained unaltered. To this day every newborn infant springs forth from the hand of God in the same state of purity as did Adam; every child comes into the world as pure as an angel. This is one of the basic concepts in the essence of Judaism and Jewish living.

But what a miserable lie has been concocted from this historical account, a lie that undermines all the moral future of mankind! We are referring to the dogma of "original sin" against which . . . it is the duty of the Jew to protest most vigorously, with every fiber of his being. It is true that on account of the sin in the Garden of Eden all of Adam's descendants have inherited the task of living in a world that no longer smiles at

וְאֶל־עָפָר תָּשׁוּב: כ וַיִּקְרָא הָאָדָם שֵׁם אִשְׁתּוֹ
חַוָּה כִּי הִוא הָיְתָה אֵם כָּל־חָי: כא וַיַּעַשׂ יְהוָה
אֱלֹהִים לְאָדָם וּלְאִשְׁתּוֹ כָּתְנוֹת עוֹר וַיַּלְבִּשֵׁם:
פ רביעי כב וַיֹּאמֶר ׀ יְהוָה אֱלֹהִים הֵן הָאָדָם הָיָה
כְּאַחַד מִמֶּנּוּ לָדַעַת טוֹב וָרָע וְעַתָּה ׀ פֶּן־יִשְׁלַח
יָדוֹ וְלָקַח גַּם מֵעֵץ הַחַיִּים וְאָכַל וָחַי לְעֹלָם:
כג וַיְשַׁלְּחֵהוּ יְהוָה אֱלֹהִים מִגַּן־עֵדֶן לַעֲבֹד
אֶת־הָאֲדָמָה אֲשֶׁר לֻקַּח מִשָּׁם: כד וַיְגָרֶשׁ אֶת־
הָאָדָם וַיַּשְׁכֵּן מִקֶּדֶם לְגַן־עֵדֶן אֶת־הַכְּרֻבִים

return." 20. And the man called his wife
Ḥavah [Eve] because she had become the
mother of all living. 21. And *God* made
Adam and his wife garments of skins and
clothed them. 22. And *God* said: "So
man has become as one left to his own
choice, to know for himself what is good
and what is evil, and now he might stretch
out his hand and take also from the Tree of
Life and eat [from it] and live forever."
23. Therefore *God* sent him out of the
Garden of Eden to cultivate the ground
from which he was taken. 24. And He
drove out the man, and He stationed, east of
the Garden of Eden, the cherubim and the

them as once it did, but this is so only because this same sin is still being committed over and over again. However, the express purpose of the present conflict between man and the physical world and of man's resultant "training by self-denial" is to guide man toward that state of moral perfection which will pave the way for his return to a Paradise on earth. But as for the doctrine that, because of Adam's sin, all of mankind has become "sinful," that man has lost the ability to be good and is compelled to go on sinning, and that man's return to God and the restoration of Paradise on earth require something other than a revival of devotion to duty, an effort within the capacity of every human being—these are notions against which Judaism must offer its most categorical protest. Man needs no intermediary, dead or resurrected, in order to return to God. This is taught to us by all of Jewish history, which demonstrates that in subsequent generations God came as close to men of purity as He did to the first man before the latter went astray. Abraham, Moses, Isaiah, Jeremiah and others like them were able to win God's nearness simply by their pure striving to remain faithful to their duty. In Judaism, the cardinal concept of the One, free-willed God goes hand in hand with the idea that man is endowed with purity and freedom of will.

The dogma of original sin and the notion that, as a result of his sin, man has been cursed with a sinfulness that can be erased only by accepting a certain belief is a most regrettable error. Even as our past history contains no account of a Divine curse against man, so, to this day, every Jew still comes before God with the avowal נְשָׁמָה שֶׁנָּתַתָּ בִּי טְהוֹרָה הִיא ["The soul which Thou hast given me is pure"][4], and it is my task to keep it pure and to return it to Thee in its original state of purity. Moreover, our Sages (Genesis Rabbah 56) teach us that there never was an age that did not produce men of the character of Abraham, Jacob, Moses and Samuel. In every age, in every generation, man is capable of ascending to the highest level of moral and spiritual sublimity. . . .

20. חַוָּה: The *pi'el* form of חַיָּה, "one who gives life." . . . The individual dies but mankind lives on and it is through woman that man lives on in his progeny. . . .

23. It was as יהוה אלהים [in His quality of mercy] that God sent man out from the Garden of Eden. With the same love with which He initially had placed man into the Garden of Eden God now removed him from there. From the very beginning God, in His quality of mercy, had created men for one of two eventualities: either, man would manifest devotion to his duty and live in Paradise, or he would have to be trained outside of Paradise to acquire such devotion to duty.

the ground from which he was taken. The ground outside of Paradise was not a new setting for man. It was the soil upon which and for which he had been created. In Paradise he had merely been introduced to the ultimate objective, the state of bliss on earth, for which he was now to mature in the training school of self-abnegation. This is the state of complete bliss on earth, a Paradise on earth, an apperception of which all the peoples on earth have retained to this day.

24. ***to guard the way to the Tree of Life*** can mean either to guard the way to the Tree of Life so that man will not be able to find the tree, or to guard the way so that the way should not be lost to man, so that someday man may be able to return to it. The flame is not described as that of *an* ever-turning sword, but as that of *the* ever-turning sword. It seems to denote the ever-recurring affliction, namely that social affliction (חרב)

[4]*Note to the English translation*: See the daily Morning Service. [G.H.]

flame of the ever-turning sword, to guard the way to the Tree of Life.

IV 1. Adam had known his wife Havah [Eve]. She conceived and bore Kayin [Cain], and she said: "I

וְאֵת לַהַט הַחֶרֶב הַמִּתְהַפֶּכֶת לִשְׁמֹר אֶת־דֶּרֶךְ
עֵץ הַחַיִּים: ס ד א וְהָאָדָם יָדַע אֶת־חַוָּה אִשְׁתּוֹ
וַתַּהַר וַתֵּלֶד אֶת־קַיִן וַתֹּאמֶר קָנִיתִי אִישׁ אֶת־

[ruin] against which mankind, left to its own devices, would fight in vain. Thus the cherubim and the "ever-turning sword" would represent the two elements by means of which God preserves for mankind the path to the Tree of Life and guides man back to it. The cherubim would denote the hints of Divine revelation through which a chastened mankind surmises and perceives the hand of God in the course of history. These would be the positive means of instruction employed by Divine Providence for the training of mankind. Together, the sword and the cherubim, affliction and Divine revelation, guard the way to the Tree of Life. In the present context, then, the thought expressed by this verse would be: God severed His direct contacts with man, but He appointed the cherubim and the sword to preserve for man the path to the Tree of Life.

In Tanna d'be Eliyahu and Leviticus Rabbah the Sages designate this path, which is to lead to the Tree of Life, as דֶּרֶךְ אֶרֶץ, the path of culture, the path of that social wisdom which, as the result of human coexistence on earth, becomes man's first tutor and educator in his training for morality and order.

Rabbi Ishmael bar R. Nahman says: קָדְמָה דֶּרֶךְ אֶרֶץ אֶת הַתּוֹרָה הה"ד לִשְׁמוֹר אֶת דֶּרֶךְ עֵץ הַחַיִּים, דֶּרֶךְ זוֹ דֶּרֶךְ אֶרֶץ ואח"כ עֵץ הַחַיִּים זוֹ תּוֹרָה.'' דֶּרֶךְ אֶרֶץ preceded the Torah by twenty-six generations, for we are told that the cherubim and the sword were appointed to guard the path to the Tree of Life; this path is culture [דֶּרֶךְ אֶרֶץ] and only thereafter does one arrive at the Tree of Life, which is the Torah." Culture begins the education of mankind, and the Torah completes it; the Torah is human education in its consummate form. The fig leaf and the loincloth, the first possessions that man acquired in his training course, were the initial appurtenances of culture. A culture that is devoted to the service of morality constitutes the first stage of man's return to God. For us Jews, Torah and דֶּרֶךְ אֶרֶץ are one. Among Jews the perfect human being and the perfect Jew are identical concepts. In the development of mankind in general, by contrast, culture precedes Torah. The sword and the cherubim, suffering coupled with the intuitive apperception of a Higher Being, guide mankind into that path of culture which leads to the Tree of Life. That is why the Jew rejoices whenever and wherever he sees culture elevating men to the perception of truth and the cultivation of goodness. On the other hand, when culture is made subservient to sensuality, it only makes for increased corruption. However, such misuses of culture do not negate the intrinsic benefits inherent in דֶּרֶךְ אֶרֶץ. אִם אֵין דֶּרֶךְ אֶרֶץ אֵין תּוֹרָה ["Where there is no culture, there is no Torah"]. Therefore the Jew should favor all that is good and true in culture and by his personal presence and demeanor as a most cultured individual demonstrate that to be a Jew merely means to be a man raised to a higher plane. On the other hand, אִם אֵין תּוֹרָה אֵין דֶּרֶךְ אֶרֶץ ["Where there is no Torah, there is no culture"]. If culture, instead of leading to Torah, should attempt to supplant Torah, then it will not be the path to the Tree of Life but a path to corruption.

CHAPTER IV

1–2. . . . Since the verb ידע is in the past perfect[5] tense it is possible that Cain was born prior to the expulsion of his parents from Paradise, so that, in her ecstasy, his mother named him קַיִן [Cain], signifying an "acquisition" or achievement attained by her own efforts. But by the time their second son was born, the father and mother were already confronted with a world full of cares in which a child can be an additional burden. Eve's mood was not joyful when she named her second son הֶבֶל [Hevel], "Transience." . . .

° ° °

It may seem strange that in the second half of Verse 2 Hevel [Abel] is mentioned before Cain, when in fact Cain was the first-born, and indeed, Cain is mentioned first in the two verses that follow. [The explanation lies in the occupations chosen by the two brothers.] The occupation which we might have expected [both Cain and Abel] to follow most naturally would be agriculture. After all, man had been told "to cultivate the ground" in order to obtain his food. Cain did indeed take up this occupation, but Hevel turned to another field of endeavor. Hevel may have been mentioned first in order to stress this fact. . . .

Except for the fact that they followed two contrasting occupations, we are hardly told anything else about this first pair of brothers. . . .

But this occupational contrast *per se* may have been intended to suggest contrasts in character, attitudes and intellectual proclivities that subsequently were to

[5]*Note to the English translation*: The tense is indicated, too, by the fact that, as distinct from other Biblical passages, the subject, "Adam," here does not follow the predicate but precedes it. [G.H.]

have acquired a man with *God*." 2. She then bore his brother Hevel [Abel]. Hevel became a shepherd but Kayin was a tiller of the ground. 3. After some time had passed, Kayin brought an offering to *God*

יְהֹוָה: ב וַתֹּסֶף לָלֶדֶת אֶת־אָחִיו אֶת־הָבֶל
וַיְהִי־הֶבֶל רֹעֵה צֹאן וְקַיִן הָיָה עֹבֵד אֲדָמָה:
ג וַיְהִי מִקֵּץ יָמִים וַיָּבֵא קַיִן מִפְּרִי הָאֲדָמָה

assume notable dimensions also in the history of the nations on earth: namely, the contrast between agricultural and pastoral nations.

. . . Agriculture calls primarily for the use of all man's physical energies. The verdict, "by the sweat of your countenance shall you eat bread" is applicable particularly to the tiller of the soil. He becomes totally absorbed in the task of eking out a physical existence. The pride of possession and self-confidence implicit in the terms קנה, קַיִן [which relate to achievement and acquisition] are character traits more predominant in the tiller of the soil than in those who adopt other occupations. The ground that the farmer has fertilized with his own sweat becomes precious to him; since his land contains part of himself, he becomes chained to it and he "settles down" upon it. At the same time, agriculture has acted as a stimulus for all the great advances of human civilization. It has inspired many skills and inventions and the state of stationary coexistence implicit in agriculture led to the formation of society and state and to the development of law and justice. Thus, the command given to man following his banishment from Paradise "to cultivate the ground" was the most important thrust toward the subsequent development of mankind.

On the other hand, the tiller of the ground is dragged down more and more to the level of the soil he cultivates. As he bends his neck beneath the yoke of the quest for material wealth, his spirit, too, becomes bowed. His efforts may turn him into a captive; thus, they bring about the subjugation, the enslavement of one man by another. Also, the tiller of the ground will come to worship the forces of nature on whose influence the success of his crops appears so clearly dependent. *The agricultural peoples were the first to lose their pure awareness of God and of their human calling; it was in their midst that slavery and idolatry first emerged.*

Seen from this perspective, pastoral life has its advantages. The very fact that the shepherd works only with living creatures whose care stirs and preserves his humane nurturing impulses speaks in favor of his occupation. The impermanence of the shepherd's property, which owes only its care, not its very existence, to man, safeguards the shepherd from placing too much value on property and possessions. Also, sheepherding does not make as great demands on physical strength as does agriculture; it does not engage the mind to the same extent. Hence the shepherd has time to elevate his spirit toward goodness and godliness. Thus, our patriarchs, too, were shepherds, as were Moses and David.

As against the foregoing, we see the antipathy of the ancient Egyptians toward shepherds and pastoral peoples. All the outgrowths of the agricultural mentality that we have discussed before developed to a most conspicuous degree in ancient Egypt. The culture of ancient Egypt was based and structured on agriculture; its characteristic features were polytheism and an elaborate system of human enslavement. The individual was completely absorbed by his occupation, and in this process the human being *per se,* his sense of personal dignity and his freedom to shape his own life, were lost. He was born a slave to his occupation. Such concepts as God, freedom and man's likeness to God remained alive only in one tribe of shepherds: our forefathers. The politicians of ancient Egypt knew quite well what they were doing when they instilled in their own people an implacable hatred for pastoral peoples. . . .

Might not all that has been said before lead us to conclude that Hevel became a shepherd because of the kind of person he was?

By and large, it may be said that man was intended to be a tiller of the soil rather than a keeper of sheep; in fact, the people of Israel were led to agriculture by the dictates of the Torah itself. However, the Torah also took action to prevent Israel from falling victim to the aberrations that can result from agricultural pursuits and from turning landed property into an idol. The Sabbath and the Sabbatical years were instituted to testify for all time that the soil and man's energy belong not to man but to God. Such agricultural laws as כִּלְאַיִם [forbidden cross-breedings], עָרְלָה [the prohibition against eating the fruit of a tree during the tree's first three years] and שִׁכְחָה, לֶקֶט and פֵּאָה [the laws regarding the leaving of certain parts of the crop or the field to the poor][6] are constant reminders of God and admonish [the Jew] to practice humaneness and brotherly love. By means of these and other laws, the Torah resolves the difficulties inherent in maintaining an agricultural state which is to serve God and become a nation united in freedom and fraternal equality. [In agricultural societies] outside the sphere of the Torah the pure awareness of God, along with human freedom and equality, were in perpetual danger. . . .

[6]*Note to the English translation*: פאה, see Leviticus 19:9 and 23:22; שכחה, see Deuteronomy 25:19. [G.H.]

from the fruit of the ground. 4. Hevel, too, brought from the firstlings of his flock and from the best of them. And *God* turned to Hevel and his offering, 5. but to Kayin and his offering He did not turn. This distressed Kayin greatly and his countenance fell. 6. And *God* said to Kayin: "Why are you distressed and why is your countenance fallen? 7. See, whether you will use your [position of] privilege for good or not for good, for this purpose sin lies at the door and its urge is toward you, that you should master it." 8. Kayin told this to his brother Hevel. And it came to pass while they were in the field that Kayin fell upon his brother Hevel and killed him. 9. And *God* said to Kayin: "Where is Hevel, your brother?" And he replied: "I do not know. Am I my brother's keeper?" 10. And He said: "What have you done? Do you hear the voices? These are the drops of your brother's blood! They cry out to Me from

מִנְחָה לַיהוָה׃ ד וְהֶבֶל הֵבִיא גַם־הוּא מִבְּכֹרוֹת
צֹאנוֹ וּמֵחֶלְבֵהֶן וַיִּשַׁע יְהוָה אֶל־הֶבֶל וְאֶל־
מִנְחָתוֹ׃ ה וְאֶל־קַיִן וְאֶל־מִנְחָתוֹ לֹא שָׁעָה
וַיִּחַר לְקַיִן מְאֹד וַיִּפְּלוּ פָּנָיו׃ ו וַיֹּאמֶר יְהוָה
אֶל־קָיִן לָמָּה חָרָה לָךְ וְלָמָּה נָפְלוּ פָנֶיךָ׃
ז הֲלוֹא אִם־תֵּיטִיב שְׂאֵת וְאִם לֹא תֵיטִיב
לַפֶּתַח חַטָּאת רֹבֵץ וְאֵלֶיךָ תְּשׁוּקָתוֹ וְאַתָּה
תִּמְשָׁל־בּוֹ׃ ח וַיֹּאמֶר קַיִן אֶל־הֶבֶל אָחִיו וַיְהִי
בִּהְיוֹתָם בַּשָּׂדֶה וַיָּקָם קַיִן אֶל־הֶבֶל אָחִיו
וַיַּהַרְגֵהוּ׃ ט וַיֹּאמֶר יְהוָה אֶל־קַיִן אֵי הֶבֶל
אָחִיךָ וַיֹּאמֶר לֹא יָדַעְתִּי הֲשֹׁמֵר אָחִי אָנֹכִי׃
י וַיֹּאמֶר מֶה עָשִׂיתָ קוֹל דְּמֵי אָחִיךָ צֹעֲקִים

3–6. . . . This is the first time we are told of offerings being made to God. This is the place to point out two important facts. First, idolatry did not yet exist at that time. Hence, the notion that offerings [ordained in Jewish Law] can only be explained as concessions to polytheism is not supported by fact. *Sacrifices antedate polytheism.* They are as old as mankind itself; therefore, they must be natural expressions of pure human thoughts and emotions. Secondly, in this account of the very first offerings ever to be brought, we see that one offering was accepted while the other was rejected (just as, at a later date, when the first offerings were made during the consecration of the Tabernacle, the rejected offerings of the priestly youths[7] appear side by side with those [of others] that were pleasing to God.) This shows us that no absolute value was ever placed on offerings as such and *gives the lie to the notion crediting the prophets with being the first to have taught that sacrifices had only a relative value.* It is true, of course, that idolators also offered sacrifices, but then idolators also offered prayers and we would have to give up a great deal if we were to shun every practice that has been debased and misused by men of moral and spiritual corruption.

Everything depends on the spirit in which the sacrifices or prayers are offered. Two individuals may bring identical offerings and offer identical prayers and yet appear patently unequal in the eyes of God. This is made clear in connection with the first offerings ever to be brought by man to God. We are not told that God turned to the *offering* made by Hevel but not to the *offering* made by Cain; rather, the text tells us that God turned to *Hevel* and his offering but not to *Cain* and his offering. The difference lay not in the offerings as such but in the disparate personalities of the individuals who made them. God did not approve of Cain and therefore He disapproved also of Cain's offering. Hevel, on the other hand, met with God's approval and therefore his offering, too, was pleasing to God. . . .

9. . . . God's question, "Where is your brother Hevel?" and Cain's reply reflect the abject depravity of the murder and at the same time sound a most impressive warning against family discord. Everyone should know where his brother is. God's question would have been justified even if nothing had happened. And then comes the answer, "I do not know," and so forth. Cain thinks this is a perfectly legitimate excuse. It is not his business to look after his brother; he already has his hands full attending to his own affairs. In addition to reflecting a most cold-blooded egotism, the foregoing also affords us stern warning that the loveless principle, "Every man for himself" is not far distant from that malevolent hatred which impels a man to murder even the one closest to him if he feels that the latter stands in the way of his self-fulfillment.

[7]*Note to the English translation*: The reference is to the offerings of Nadab and Abihu, the sons of Aaron (Leviticus 10:1 ff.) [G.H.]

the ground. 11. And now you have already [received] your curse! [It is] from the ground which had to open its mouth to accept the spilled blood of your brother from your hand. 12. When you till the ground it will no longer yield its strength to you; you shall become restless and friendless upon the earth." 13. And Kayin said to *God:* "My sin is greater than I can bear! 14. Lo! Thou hast banished me today from the face of the ground and I am to be hidden also from Thy countenance and be restless and friendless upon the earth; why,

אֵלַי מִן־הָאֲדָמָה: יא וְעַתָּה אָרוּר אָתָּה מִן־
הָאֲדָמָה אֲשֶׁר פָּצְתָה אֶת־פִּיהָ לָקַחַת אֶת־דְּמֵי
אָחִיךָ מִיָּדֶךָ: יב כִּי תַעֲבֹד אֶת־הָאֲדָמָה לֹא־
תֹסֵף תֵּת־כֹּחָהּ לָךְ נָע וָנָד תִּהְיֶה בָאָרֶץ:
יג וַיֹּאמֶר קַיִן אֶל־יְהוָה גָּדוֹל עֲוֹנִי מִנְּשֹׂא:
יד הֵן גֵּרַשְׁתָּ אֹתִי הַיּוֹם מֵעַל פְּנֵי הָאֲדָמָה
וּמִפָּנֶיךָ אֶסָּתֵר וְהָיִיתִי נָע וָנָד בָּאָרֶץ וְהָיָה כָל־

11. אָרוּר אָתָּה ***[you have already (received) your curse!].*** There is no need for God to pass sentence upon you, for you have already been condemned in that the whole world has risen up against you. It is this cry [from the ground] that has pronounced your sentence. Note that this is the first instance in which a curse has been directed against a human being, one who has committed a crime. Earlier in the Biblical text it was the earth that received a curse for the sake of mankind's education. . . .

13–14. גָּדוֹל עֲוֹנִי מִנְּשֹׂא cannot mean, "My sin is too great for Thee to forgive," because Cain goes on to say, "Behold, Thou hast banished me . . .". He does not speak of his sin but only of his punishment. As a result, עָוֹן has been interpreted as "punishment." However, this interpretation is subject to question. In any event, עָוֹן as a rule means "sin," not "punishment." Hence, if we interpret עָוֹן as "sin," the meaning of the passage would be: "My sin is greater than I can bear. Behold, Thou hast banished me today," etc. This would give us a profound insight not only into the criminal's murky state of mind but also into Divine justice. "My sin is greater than I can bear." Thou [God] hast shown me how great my sin is, for "Thou hast banished me, Thou hast severed the bond which gave the earth to me as a human being. Also, I am not to be protected and watched over [by Thee]. And so, forsaken by the earth, by God and by man, I fear that any creature that meets me may kill me."

We see here Cain, conceived with the attitude typified by קָנִיתִי ["I have acquired"], stamped with the character of קַיִן, led to crime by קִנְאָה, selfishness goaded into envy, now realizing that he has forfeited everything by his crime. He has been made to realize the magnitude of his crime not by the thought of what he did to his brother but by what he has done to himself. He is still the same Cain; [if he were asked the same question about his brother again] he would again answer הֲשֹׁמֵר אָחִי אָנֹכִי ["Am I my brother's keeper?"]. Cain says, "My sin is too great. If I had merely murdered my brother, I could have borne it, but I did not know then that by so doing I murdered myself as well, that I have made myself אָרוּר [accursed], נָע וָנָד [restless and friendless] and that I have forfeited every claim upon the world and my fellow men."

The Torah imposes a similar sequence of penalties for manslaughter. One guilty of manslaughter becomes נָע ["restless"] in גָּלוּת [in a state of exile], even if he does not also become נָד ["friendless"]. Also, "anyone who finds me may kill me"; he must live in constant dread of the possibility that the גּוֹאֵל הַדָּם [blood advocate] will catch up with him. The law of עֶגְלָה עֲרוּפָה [concerning a murder whose perpetrator is unknown][8] may reflect a similar sequence of thoughts. In a case of a murder in which the murderer is unknown, but in which the murderer, flouting the authority of the court of justice, as it were, left his victim's body out in the open, unburied, the court must clear itself of all responsibility for the crime. It must declare that it was not even indirectly responsible for the murder by having treated transients as the people of Sodom did. Before making this declaration, the court must perform a symbolic act: by killing a "female calf that has never been worked, that has not yet pulled the yoke" and hurling it into a rough valley "which cannot be cultivated and upon which no seed can be sown," the court had to proclaim that unbridled brute force which refuses to bend beneath the yoke of the law is not tolerated among Jews, that the ground beneath such a one will become hard and stony, "it will no longer yield its strength to you!"

Thus the sin of which Cain considered himself guilty was not so much the murder of his brother but the crime which he had committed against himself. For this

[8]*Note to the English translation*: Literally, "the female calf whose neck has been broken." See Deuteronomy 21:1–9. [G.H.]

anyone who finds me may kill me!" 15. And *God* said with regard to him: "Therefore anyone who would kill Kayin: revenge is taken on him sevenfold." So *God* put a mark upon Kayin so that no one who found him should kill him. 16. And Kayin went forth from before the countenance of *God* and settled in the land of Nod, east of Eden. 17. And Kayin knew his wife, and she conceived and bore Ḥanokh [Enoch], and he became a city-builder and named the city after his son Ḥanokh. 18. To Ḥanokh was born Irad, Irad begot Meḥuyael, and Meḥiyael begot Methushael, and Methushael begot Lamekh. 19. Lemekh took to himself two wives; the name of the one was Adah and the name

מֹצְאִי יַהַרְגֵנִי: טו וַיֹּאמֶר לוֹ יְהוָה לָכֵן כָּל-
הֹרֵג קַיִן שִׁבְעָתַיִם יֻקָּם וַיָּשֶׂם יְהוָה לְקַיִן אוֹת
לְבִלְתִּי הַכּוֹת-אֹתוֹ כָּל-מֹצְאוֹ: טז וַיֵּצֵא קַיִן
מִלִּפְנֵי יְהוָה וַיֵּשֶׁב בְּאֶרֶץ-נוֹד קִדְמַת-עֵדֶן:
יז וַיֵּדַע קַיִן אֶת-אִשְׁתּוֹ וַתַּהַר וַתֵּלֶד אֶת-חֲנוֹךְ
וַיְהִי בֹּנֶה עִיר וַיִּקְרָא שֵׁם הָעִיר כְּשֵׁם בְּנוֹ
חֲנוֹךְ: יח וַיִּוָּלֵד לַחֲנוֹךְ אֶת-עִירָד וְעִירָד יָלַד
אֶת-מְחוּיָאֵל וּמְחִיָּיאֵל יָלַד אֶת-מְתוּשָׁאֵל
וּמְתוּשָׁאֵל יָלַד אֶת-לָמֶךְ: חמישי יט וַיִּקַּח-לוֹ
לֶמֶךְ שְׁתֵּי נָשִׁים שֵׁם הָאַחַת עָדָה וְשֵׁם הַשֵּׁנִית

reason he describes his act as עָוֹן, something "perverse" or "crooked." An act which leads most directly to the goal and to salvation is characterized as יָשָׁר [straight, right]. An עָוֹן is a "turning aside" not merely from the path of our duty but also from our own happiness. That is how God ordained it.

15. ויאמר לו ד׳ *[And God said with regard to him]*. Not אֵלָיו ["to him"] but לו ["*with regard* to him"]. God declared with regard to Cain that לָכֵן כָּל הֹרֵג קַיִן שִׁבְעָתַיִם יֻקָּם! ["Therefore anyone who would kill Cain! Revenge is taken on him sevenfold"] נקם is related to קום [lit., "rising"] which denotes the "raising up" of justice trampled underfoot (or the "raising up" of a person in the same condition).

The vengeance is not intended to benefit the victim, whom nothing can restore to life, but to redress the blow that has been dealt to justice. One who undertakes to avenge the right in this manner is referred to as נוקם [the avenger]. The Word of God says לֹא תִקֹּם[9]; you must not take revenge for the wrong that has been done to you, but you should help avenge the wrong done to others. Hence לָכֵן, "therefore"; i.e., because the position into which Cain has placed himself by his own doing is so unbearable, now therefore let everyone who would wish to kill Cain in order to avenge the blood of Abel hear this: Cain's punishment will be rendered seven times more severe by the fact that he will be allowed to survive. The atonement for his crime and the vengeance on behalf of Hevel will be seven times more intense than it would have been if Cain had been put to death instantly. The subject of יֻקָּם would then be Hevel, or, since he is not mentioned by name, it might be the murder: Cain's punishment represents a sevenfold atonement for his crime. . . .

[9]*Note to the English translation*: See Leviticus 19:18. [G.H.]

16. . . . Earlier, we saw the glory of God retreating from man, toward the west. Here we see a withdrawal to the east of Eden; that is, an ever-growing alienation from God. This is an attempt by man to make a life for himself on the basis of his own strength, without God.

17. The text does not read וַיִּבֶן עִיר, he "built a city" but he "became a city-builder." With him there began a new enterprise: the city. Cain had been cut off from the soil; the land no longer supported him. Thus cut off from God and his fellow men, what was there still left for him? He still had himself; he still possessed the reserve of mental energies and skills which is part of the individual personality, and this quite naturally led him to build cities. Unlike the countryside, the city is dependent on complete detachment from the soil, from agriculture. It represents an aggregate of human beings who create their existence solely by dint of human energies. In the city the products of the countryside are converted so that they may serve the purposes of men; then, art and industry place upon these products the imprint of human intelligence. The acres of the city dweller are his energies, his mind and his abilities . . . . In the countryside it is the fields that are "cultivated;" in the city, it is man . . . . It is most typical that city life began with Cain, who had been cut off from the land and thrown back upon his own resources.

18. מחויאל = מחיאל. Irad begot Meḥuyael, מחוי אל, one in whom godliness *had been blotted out;* מחי אל is one who *has blotted out* godliness. When the generation that had cast off culture was still young, it was מחויאל, a passive generation for whom godliness had been blotted out. Later, as it grew older, it became מחיאל; it actively strove to blot out godliness from others. . . .

of the other, Zillah. 20. Adah bore Yabal; he was the father of those who dwell in tents and breed cattle. 21. The name of his brother was Yubal; he was the father of all those who play the lyre and the flute. 22. As for Zillah, too, she bore Tubal-Kayin, who sharpened every instrument that cuts copper and iron. And the sister of Tubal-Kayin was Naamah. 23. And Lemekh said to his wives: "Adah and Zillah, hear my voice; O wives of Lemekh, give ear to my speech. For I have slain a man to my [own] hurt and a child to my [own] bruising. 24. If Kayin shall be avenged sevenfold, then Lemekh seven and seventy-fold!" 25. And Adam knew his wife again, and

צִלָּה׃ כ וַתֵּלֶד עָדָה אֶת־יָבָל הוּא הָיָה אֲבִי
יֹשֵׁב אֹהֶל וּמִקְנֶה׃ כא וְשֵׁם אָחִיו יוּבָל הוּא
הָיָה אֲבִי כָּל־תֹּפֵשׂ כִּנּוֹר וְעוּגָב׃ כב וְצִלָּה גַם־
הִוא יָלְדָה אֶת־תּוּבַל קַיִן לֹטֵשׁ כָּל־חֹרֵשׁ
נְחֹשֶׁת וּבַרְזֶל וַאֲחוֹת תּוּבַל־קַיִן נַעֲמָה׃ ששי
כג וַיֹּאמֶר לֶמֶךְ לְנָשָׁיו עָדָה וְצִלָּה שְׁמַעַן קוֹלִי
נְשֵׁי לֶמֶךְ הַאְזֵנָּה אִמְרָתִי כִּי אִישׁ הָרַגְתִּי
לְפִצְעִי וְיֶלֶד לְחַבֻּרָתִי׃ כד כִּי שִׁבְעָתַיִם יֻקַּם־
קַיִן וְלֶמֶךְ שִׁבְעִים וְשִׁבְעָה׃ כה וַיֵּדַע אָדָם עוֹד

22. . . . תּוּבַל. What Tubal-Cain creates is not for immediate use or enjoyment. What he creates is the *means* for all the advances of industry and the arts. What he creates is *productivity*; he creates the *tools* for industry and the arts. He is the true Tubal-Cain, the true "production" of Cain, the pride of the Cainite race. God had cut the ground from beneath Cain. It will no longer yield him its produce (יְבוּל). But now he no longer needs it. His own mind is now his field. By the production of this mechanical skill, this mighty lever for industry, landless Cain regains his ground and the countryside now brings the riches of its fields to the cities, obtaining the benefits of urban industry in return.

The sister of Tubal-Cain, on the other hand, was נַעֲמָה, from נָעִים, the adjective that primarily denotes physical beauty, things that appeal to the senses. The principal purpose of industry is utility. When the function of beauty is joined to that of utility, when "taste" is applied to industry, then we have progress. This combination as such is a step toward the re-education of man for a higher purpose. Did Naamah help her brother by adding, as her name would imply, beauty and grace to his work? Perhaps.

23. The lofty style of this speech indicates that it is a שִׁיר, a pronouncement dictated by a higher spirit. If we consider the form of this speech, if we interpret these forms of speech in their most simple, uncontrived meaning, if we remember also that a Midrash actually identifies the slain "man" as Lemekh's ancestor [Cain] and the slain "child" as his own son [Tubal-Cain], and if we view Lamekh's speech in the context of the events that preceded it, we may well interpret this speech as the last testament of a seer from the Cainite line. Lemekh had three sons, and with them he founded human civilization. What proud self-confidence should have filled the breast of this man! How greatly he should have rejoiced! But the sum total of his life's experiences had filled his soul with emotions that were the bitter reverse of what we might have expected them to be.

He says: "Listen to me, Adah and Zillah! Even if you were not the wives of Lemekh, you should listen, for what I have to say to you applies to all men. But since you are, in fact, the wives of Lemekh, the mothers of these sons, you must listen to me with double attention because my speech has double significance for you. Do you really believe that by dint of our achievements we have rehabilitated Cain and prepared a happy future for ourselves and an even happier one for our children? No! *I have not atoned for my ancestor [Cain]; I have killed him! I have also murdered the young generation and by so doing I have wounded myself most of all.*" All those aspirations of culture that stand in the service of God are sacred and beneficial. A generation inspired by this spirit keeps on building upon the godly treasure it has inherited from its ancestors; it passes on this heritage, intact and enriched, to its children, and it, too, enjoys a blessed life in the present. But whatever emanates from "Meḥuyael and Meḥiyael" from a generation among whom godliness has become extinct and which is bent solely on blotting out godliness even more diligently from the next generation, such a generation, which serves only selfish ends, can be only תּוּבַל קַיִן [a product of Cain]. It can produce only men who will fight against God with all their might. Such a generation will murder not only its ancestors but also the next generation and, in so doing, will create only pain and hurt for itself. Such a generation sacrifices both its past and its future without gaining anything for its present. . . .

she bore a son and called him Sheth, for "God has set me another seed in the place of Hevel," for Kayin had killed him.
26. And to Sheth, in turn, a son was born; he called him Enosh. It was then that man first began to proclaim in the name of *God*.

V 1. This book is of the developments of Adam. On the day that God created Adam He made him in the likeness of God. 2. Male and female did He create them, and He blessed them and called them Adam on the day that they were created. 3. Adam lived 130 years; then he

אֶת־אִשְׁתּוֹ וַתֵּלֶד בֵּן וַתִּקְרָא אֶת־שְׁמוֹ שֵׁת כִּי
שָׁת־לִי אֱלֹהִים זֶרַע אַחֵר תַּחַת הֶבֶל כִּי הֲרָגוֹ
קָיִן׃ כו וּלְשֵׁת גַּם־הוּא יֻלַּד־בֵּן וַיִּקְרָא אֶת־
שְׁמוֹ אֱנוֹשׁ אָז הוּחַל לִקְרֹא בְּשֵׁם יְהוָה׃ ס
ה א זֶה סֵפֶר תּוֹלְדֹת אָדָם בְּיוֹם בְּרֹא אֱלֹהִים
אָדָם בִּדְמוּת אֱלֹהִים עָשָׂה אֹתוֹ׃ ב זָכָר וּנְקֵבָה
בְּרָאָם וַיְבָרֶךְ אֹתָם וַיִּקְרָא אֶת־שְׁמָם אָדָם
בְּיוֹם הִבָּרְאָם׃ ג וַיְחִי אָדָם שְׁלֹשִׁים וּמְאַת

26. קרא בְּשֵׁם ה׳, literally, "call in the name of *God*"; namely, to "summon" or "invite" people in the name of God. This activity entails more than preaching about God or making proclamations about Him. Its purpose is not merely to teach or to promote the *knowledge* of God but to disseminate the *acknowledgement* of God among men; that is, devotion and submission to the will of God. It represents a summons for men to come to God and to render Him homage. Basically, then, it entails a clarification of man's relationship to God and of what God requires of man. It is in this sense that the phrase is used here and also later in the case of Abraham.

It is with the need לִקְרֹא בְּשֵׁם ה׳ ["to call in the name of *God*"] that the history of the Jewish people begins. For concomitantly with it there arises the need for an arrangement to have, in the midst of mankind, a group of men who are to preserve and to stir up the awareness of man's true calling and of man's relationship to God. It is this need that gave birth to the people of Israel, whose mission is none other than לִקְרֹא בְּשֵׁם ה׳ ["to call in the name of *God*"].

CHAPTER V

1. ***This book is of the developments of Adam.*** This verse, which introduces a new phase in the history of human education, bears a marked similarity to Verse 4 of Chapter 2: "These are the products of the heaven and the earth which already were set for creation . . .", with which the history of the world's development was introduced. That verse explained that all the natural phenomena which followed Creation were simply natural developments of the heaven and the earth, and that basically they all had their origin בְּהִבָּרְאָם, in the laws which the Creator had set for heaven and earth at the time of their creation. Similarly, in connection with the start of human history, we now learn that all the manifold phenomena occuring in mankind are merely natural outgrowths of Adam, whom God had created in His image. . . . All the history of mankind, in its lowest depths and at its loftiest peaks, the most variegated phenomena that appear in the history of humanity, they all form one whole. . . . Despite the striking contrasts that separate them, they are all merely the developments of this one Adam, who was created in the image of God. . . .

° ° °

Hence *all* men are human beings; the צֶלֶם אלק׳ ["image of God"] is never completely lost. This is the first verity that stands at the very start of mankind's history.

The second verity is that בְּיוֹם בְּרֹא אלק׳ אָדָם בִּדְמוּת אלק׳ עָשָׂה אותו ["On the day that God created Adam He made him in the likeness of God"]. Man's true pristine state was not, as some tend to think, that of a mentally and morally limited savage, bordering on the animal. At the same time, man's likeness to God is not something *supernatural*, for the sake of which man would have to sacrifice his natural, terrestrial characteristics. Neither is it something *unnatural*, which man could acquire only by culture. On the contrary, it is man's supposed "natural state" of mental and moral backwardness that is unnatural; it is a state of decadence into which man lapsed the more he forgot about the Name of ד׳. His true natural state is to be in the likeness of God; in his true natural state man is godlike in mental and moral purity, the world blossoms round about him as a paradise and he hears the voice of God moving about in the garden, for on the day that God created man, man was pure and godly, and he aspired toward God. . . .

2. ***Male and female did He create them.*** It was from the very beginning that God created "man" male and female; both sexes are equally godly, and of equal worth; neither is more in the likeness of God than the other. Together, they were blessed and *together, they were given the name "Adam."*

begot [a son] in his likeness, after his image, and he called him Sheth. 4. The days of Adam after he had begotten Sheth were 800 years and he begot sons and daughters. 5. When all the days that Adam lived were 930 years, he died. 6. Sheth lived 105 years; then he begot Enosh. 7. After he begot Enosh, Sheth lived [another] 807 years and begot sons and daughters. 8. When all the days of Sheth were 912 years, he died. 9. Enosh lived 90 years; then he begot Kenan. 10. After he begot Kenan, Enosh lived [another] 815 years and begot sons and daughters. 11. When all the days of Enosh were 905 years, he died. 12. Kenan lived 70 years; then he begot Mahalallel. 13. After he begot Mahalallel, Kenan lived [another] 840 years and begot sons and daughters. 14. When all the days of Kenan were 910 years, he died. 15. Mahalallel lived 65 years; then he begot Yered. 16. After he begot Yered, Mahalallel lived [another] 830 years and begot sons and daughters. 17. When all

שָׁנָה וַיּוֹלֶד בִּדְמוּתוֹ כְּצַלְמוֹ וַיִּקְרָא אֶת־שְׁמוֹ
שֵׁת: ד וַיִּהְיוּ יְמֵי־אָדָם אַחֲרֵי הוֹלִידוֹ אֶת־שֵׁת
שְׁמֹנֶה מֵאֹת שָׁנָה וַיּוֹלֶד בָּנִים וּבָנוֹת: ה וַיִּהְיוּ
כָּל־יְמֵי אָדָם אֲשֶׁר־חַי תְּשַׁע מֵאוֹת שָׁנָה
וּשְׁלֹשִׁים שָׁנָה וַיָּמֹת: ס ו וַיְחִי־שֵׁת חָמֵשׁ
שָׁנִים וּמְאַת שָׁנָה וַיּוֹלֶד אֶת־אֱנוֹשׁ: ז וַיְחִי־
שֵׁת אַחֲרֵי הוֹלִידוֹ אֶת־אֱנוֹשׁ שֶׁבַע שָׁנִים
וּשְׁמֹנֶה מֵאוֹת שָׁנָה וַיּוֹלֶד בָּנִים וּבָנוֹת:
ח וַיִּהְיוּ כָּל־יְמֵי־שֵׁת שְׁתֵּים עֶשְׂרֵה שָׁנָה
וּתְשַׁע מֵאוֹת שָׁנָה וַיָּמֹת: ס ט וַיְחִי אֱנוֹשׁ
תִּשְׁעִים שָׁנָה וַיּוֹלֶד אֶת־קֵינָן: י וַיְחִי אֱנוֹשׁ
אַחֲרֵי הוֹלִידוֹ אֶת־קֵינָן חֲמֵשׁ עֶשְׂרֵה שָׁנָה
וּשְׁמֹנֶה מֵאוֹת שָׁנָה וַיּוֹלֶד בָּנִים וּבָנוֹת:
יא וַיִּהְיוּ כָּל־יְמֵי אֱנוֹשׁ חָמֵשׁ שָׁנִים וּתְשַׁע
מֵאוֹת שָׁנָה וַיָּמֹת: ס יב וַיְחִי קֵינָן שִׁבְעִים
שָׁנָה וַיּוֹלֶד אֶת־מַהֲלַלְאֵל: יג וַיְחִי קֵינָן אַחֲרֵי
הוֹלִידוֹ אֶת־מַהֲלַלְאֵל אַרְבָּעִים שָׁנָה וּשְׁמֹנֶה
מֵאוֹת שָׁנָה וַיּוֹלֶד בָּנִים וּבָנוֹת: יד וַיִּהְיוּ כָּל־
יְמֵי קֵינָן עֶשֶׂר שָׁנִים וּתְשַׁע מֵאוֹת שָׁנָה וַיָּמֹת:
ס טו וַיְחִי מַהֲלַלְאֵל חָמֵשׁ שָׁנִים וְשִׁשִּׁים שָׁנָה
וַיּוֹלֶד אֶת־יָרֶד: טז וַיְחִי מַהֲלַלְאֵל אַחֲרֵי
הוֹלִידוֹ אֶת־יֶרֶד שְׁלֹשִׁים שָׁנָה וּשְׁמֹנֶה מֵאוֹת
שָׁנָה וַיּוֹלֶד בָּנִים וּבָנוֹת: יז וַיִּהְיוּ כָּל־יְמֵי

4-28. Here follows a series of generations down to Lemekh, just as in the Cainite line. Here, too, we venture to assume that each name has a special significance. The connotations of these names need not necessarily imply that the fathers of the individuals so named had the gift of prophecy or that the bearers of these names behaved in character with the connotation of their given names. For instance, Enosh himself need by no means have been אנוש [which has connotations of illness and hopelessness]. His father could very well have named the baby according to the character of the age [in which the infant had been born].

One is struck by the similarities—albeit qualified—between the names that occur in the lists of the two lines [the Cainite and the Shethite, respectively,]: Kayin and Kenan; Irad and Yered; Ḥanokh and Hanokh; Meḥiyael and Mahalallel; Methushael and Methushelaḥ; Lamekh and Lemekh. Another noteworthy point: In the Cainite line the generations show a steady moral decline (Cain, Ḥanokh, Irad, Meḥuyael, Methushael) down to Lemekh, who declares that, notwithstanding the dawn of civilization in which they participated, the generations in the final analysis were worthless. The Shethite line, on the other hand, shows a the days of Mahalalel were 895 years, he died. 18. Yered lived 162 years; then he begot Ḥanokh. 19. After he begot Ḥanokh, Yered lived [another] 800 years and begot sons and daughters. 20. When all the days of Yered were 962 years, he died. 21. Ḥanokh lived 65 years; then he begot Methushelaḥ. 22. After he begot Methushelaḥ, Ḥanokh walked with God for 300 years and begot sons and daughters. 23. All the days of Ḥanokh were 365 years. 24. Ḥanokh walked with God and [then] he was no longer there, because God had taken him. 25. Methushelaḥ lived 187 years; then he begot Lemekh. 26. After he begot Lemekh, Methushelaḥ lived [another] 782 years and begot sons and daughters. 27. When all the days of Methushelaḥ were 969 years, he died. 28. Lemekh lived 182 years; then he begot a son. 29. He called him Noaḥ, thereby to say: "Only this can give us comfort from our work and from the self-abnegating toil of our hands from the earth which *God* has cursed." 30. After he begot Noaḥ, Lemekh lived [another] 595 years and begot sons and daughters. 31. When all the days of Lemekh were 777 years, he died. 32. Noaḥ was already 500 years old when Noaḥ begot Shem, Ḥam and Yapheth.

מַהֲלַלְאֵל חָמֵשׁ וְתִשְׁעִים שָׁנָה וּשְׁמֹנֶה מֵאוֹת
שָׁנָה וַיָּמֹת: ס יח וַיְחִי־יֶרֶד שְׁתַּיִם וְשִׁשִּׁים
שָׁנָה וּמְאַת שָׁנָה וַיּוֹלֶד אֶת־חֲנוֹךְ: יט וַיְחִי־
יֶרֶד אַחֲרֵי הוֹלִידוֹ אֶת־חֲנוֹךְ שְׁמֹנֶה מֵאוֹת
שָׁנָה וַיּוֹלֶד בָּנִים וּבָנוֹת: כ וַיִּהְיוּ כָּל־יְמֵי־יֶרֶד
שְׁתַּיִם וְשִׁשִּׁים שָׁנָה וּתְשַׁע מֵאוֹת שָׁנָה וַיָּמֹת:
ס כא וַיְחִי חֲנוֹךְ חָמֵשׁ וְשִׁשִּׁים שָׁנָה וַיּוֹלֶד
אֶת־מְתוּשָׁלַח: כב וַיִּתְהַלֵּךְ חֲנוֹךְ אֶת־הָאֱלֹהִים
אַחֲרֵי הוֹלִידוֹ אֶת־מְתוּשֶׁלַח שְׁלֹשׁ מֵאוֹת שָׁנָה
וַיּוֹלֶד בָּנִים וּבָנוֹת: כג וַיְהִי כָּל־יְמֵי חֲנוֹךְ
חָמֵשׁ וְשִׁשִּׁים שָׁנָה וּשְׁלֹשׁ מֵאוֹת שָׁנָה:
כד וַיִּתְהַלֵּךְ חֲנוֹךְ אֶת־הָאֱלֹהִים וְאֵינֶנּוּ כִּי־לָקַח
אֹתוֹ אֱלֹהִים: ס שביעי כה וַיְחִי מְתוּשֶׁלַח שֶׁבַע
וּשְׁמֹנִים שָׁנָה וּמְאַת שָׁנָה וַיּוֹלֶד אֶת־לָמֶךְ:
כו וַיְחִי מְתוּשֶׁלַח אַחֲרֵי הוֹלִידוֹ אֶת־לֶמֶךְ
שְׁתַּיִם וּשְׁמוֹנִים שָׁנָה וּשְׁבַע מֵאוֹת שָׁנָה וַיּוֹלֶד
בָּנִים וּבָנוֹת: כז וַיִּהְיוּ כָּל־יְמֵי מְתוּשֶׁלַח תֵּשַׁע
וְשִׁשִּׁים שָׁנָה וּתְשַׁע מֵאוֹת שָׁנָה וַיָּמֹת: ס
כח וַיְחִי־לֶמֶךְ שְׁתַּיִם וּשְׁמֹנִים שָׁנָה וּמְאַת שָׁנָה
וַיּוֹלֶד בֵּן: כט וַיִּקְרָא אֶת־שְׁמוֹ נֹחַ לֵאמֹר זֶה
יְנַחֲמֵנוּ מִמַּעֲשֵׂנוּ וּמֵעִצְּבוֹן יָדֵינוּ מִן־הָאֲדָמָה
אֲשֶׁר אֵרְרָהּ יְהוָה: ל וַיְחִי־לֶמֶךְ אַחֲרֵי הוֹלִידוֹ
אֶת־נֹחַ חָמֵשׁ וְתִשְׁעִים שָׁנָה וַחֲמֵשׁ מֵאֹת שָׁנָה
וַיּוֹלֶד בָּנִים וּבָנוֹת: לא וַיְהִי כָּל־יְמֵי־לֶמֶךְ
שֶׁבַע וְשִׁבְעִים שָׁנָה וּשְׁבַע מֵאוֹת שָׁנָה וַיָּמֹת:
ס לב וַיְהִי־נֹחַ בֶּן־חֲמֵשׁ מֵאוֹת שָׁנָה וַיּוֹלֶד נֹחַ
אֶת־שֵׁם אֶת־חָם וְאֶת־יָפֶת:

fluctuation from worse to better and from better to worse until another Lemekh arises to proclaim, through his son, the ultimate rescue of the human race. Enosh is followed by Kenan (related to קַיִן, in any event, a tainted generation which has fallen away from God); the next generation is מַהֲלַלְאֵל, an elevation toward God; it is followed by יֶרֶד [Yered, literally, "going down"], Ḥanokh [which connotes "education for nobler things"], מְתוּ־שֶׁלַח, who "gave up the masses as lost"[10] and finally Lemekh.

[10] *Note to the English translation*: מתו as in מֵתִים, "dead," and שלח, which denotes "abandoning." [G.H.]

VI 1. It came to pass when men began to multiply on the face of the ground and daughters were born to them, 2. that the sons of the godly line saw that the daughters of men were good to look upon, and they took themselves wives from wherever they chose. 3. And *God* said: "My spirit within man will not remain the judge forever, since he is also flesh; therefore his days shall be 120 years."

ו א וַיְהִי כִּי־הֵחֵל הָאָדָם לָרֹב עַל־פְּנֵי הָאֲדָמָה
וּבָנוֹת יֻלְּדוּ לָהֶם׃ ב וַיִּרְאוּ בְנֵי־הָאֱלֹהִים אֶת־
בְּנוֹת הָאָדָם כִּי טֹבֹת הֵנָּה וַיִּקְחוּ לָהֶם נָשִׁים
מִכֹּל אֲשֶׁר בָּחָרוּ׃ ג וַיֹּאמֶר יְהוָה לֹא־יָדוֹן
רוּחִי בָאָדָם לְעֹלָם בְּשַׁגָּם הוּא בָשָׂר וְהָיוּ יָמָיו

CHAPTER VI

1–2. Here we are shown the basic cause of mankind's moral deterioration. It is the interbreeding between two distinct classes of people: "the sons of the godly line" and "the daughters of men." In the previous chapter we read the genealogies of two distinct generations. First, the Cainite line, which aspired to build its existence on earth on the basis of industry and inventions but did not take God into account. Such material aspirations *per se* are proper, but if they are pursued without God they can lead only to desolation and despair. In sharp contrast, we have the Shethite line, whose genealogy opened with repeated allusions to the Divine imprint, the power and the benediction of the pure calling that God had originally conferred upon man: אָדָם ["Adam"], דְּמוּת ["the likeness (of God)"], בְּרָכָה ["the (Divine) blessing"] and צֶלֶם ["image."].[11] Also, in view of the particular importance of what follows, the Shethite genealogy was introduced by a reference to the equality and significance of the female sex in relation to the male: "Male and female did He create them". The "daughters of men" belonged to the Cainite line, from which "godliness had been totally blotted out" (מְחוּיָאֵל). The Shethites, who had inherited the Divine stamp, were the "sons of the godly line."

We have already noted that traits of godliness, though not in sufficient strength to save all mankind, recurred over and over again in the Shethite line. That the Shethite progress toward godliness was not as sure and constant as the descent to depravity which characterized the Cainite line is attributed to the fact that the Shethites had not kept themselves pure but had intermarried with the Cainite line. We are told: *When man began to multiply* (before that time, there had been no wide selection of marital partners from among whom they could have chosen, but now that men had begun to multiply, the Shethites could have kept their line pure), *the sons of the godly line saw that the daughters of the other line were good* (probably טֹבֹת מַרְאֶה, beautiful) *to look upon* (they did not consider the lineage of the women or what offspring they could expect from women of that background; they merely looked at the women and these appealed to them). The corruption lay not in the women as such, but in their descent.

from wherever they chose. The men did not restrict their choice to daughters of "the godly line."

Some have sought to construe וַיִּקְחוּ לָהֶם נָשִׁים [literally, "they took themselves women"] as an indication that the Shethite men had been guilty of rape, of immoral conduct. However, the term לָקְחוּ אִשָּׁה in the Biblical text always denotes a marital relationship; it is, in fact, the true Hebrew expression for "contracting a marriage." The sin which, in view of what follows, must be implicit in this verse lay solely in מִכֹּל אֲשֶׁר בָּחָרוּ, the fact that they married women ["from wherever they chose"], without considering the background from which they had chosen them.

Still, the results might have been propitious if the spirit of godliness within the Shethite line had been strong enough to overcome the evil seed that the wives brought into these intermarriages. But the risk inherent in such alliances is too great ever to be justifiable. There is always the question which of the two tendencies will prevail in the offspring and whether the depravity will not increase as the interbreeding continues.

3. When this interbreeding began to assume excessive proportions, God said, "My spirit within man, the spirit which I breathed into man, was intended to be the דַּיָּן, the judge, the voice of God that judges man from within man himself." Man's soul itself is the lamp of God with which God searches into the innermost secrets of men [Proverbs 20:27]. God not only sees the actions of men but He also judges them. It was thanks to this spirit of God acting as a judge within man himself that, despite all the interbreeding, it was possible for an individual like Kenan to be followed by a man like Mahalallel; it was possible for a corrupt generation to be followed by one of lofty character. However, this "judge" within man himself is corruptible; it permits itself to be lulled to sleep. Indeed, its voice can become increasingly dulled so that, in the

[11] *Note to the English translation*: See Genesis 5:1–3. [G.H.]

4. The giants were on the earth in those days and also after that, when the sons of the godly line had already come to the daughters of men and the latter bore them children. These are the heroes of old, the men of renown. 5. When *God* saw that

מֵאָה וְעֶשְׂרִים שָׁנָה: ד הַנְּפִלִים הָיוּ בָאָרֶץ
בַּיָּמִים הָהֵם וְגַם אַחֲרֵי־כֵן אֲשֶׁר יָבֹאוּ בְּנֵי
הָאֱלֹהִים אֶל־בְּנוֹת הָאָדָם וְיָלְדוּ לָהֶם הֵמָּה
הַגִּבֹּרִים אֲשֶׁר מֵעוֹלָם אַנְשֵׁי הַשֵּׁם: פ מפטיר

course of several generations, the sensual element will become more and more active in man and eventually the judging spirit within man will abdicate its authority entirely. Not without good reason does the Law of God accord a position of such prominence to the laws of chastity and marital relations. This verse indicates to us how great the role of these laws is in keeping the spirit of God awake within man. When God saw that the sons of the godly line were choosing their marital partners indiscriminately, He said, "Now my spirit will not continue in its judicial office forever." Until that time the general moral trend, though it did not show a consistent rise, did not show a consistent decline but moved in alternately ascending and descending waves. But this state of affairs will not continue much longer. בְּשַׁגַּם הוּא בָשָׂר ["Since he, too, is flesh"]. Man's nature, too, is not altogether spiritual but also physical. Man consists not only of רוּחַ ["spirit"] but also of בָּשָׂר ["flesh"], of the spirit of God but also of a body susceptible to physical stimuli. If a man is pure, this conflict is resolved by the בָּשָׂר becoming subordinate to the רוּחַ ה׳ בָּאָדָם, but where there is constant interbreeding without attention to godliness, it may end in the opposite manner, with the flesh burying the spirit. God said that it would surely end in this manner if the present state of affairs were to be allowed to continue indefinitely. Therefore He allowed a limit of another 120 years for this conduct. That was the period for which God would permit the present state of affairs to continue [before taking action].

4. . . . In antediluvian times *nephilim* were nothing out of the ordinary. "The giants were on the earth in those days" means that "those creatures which are now gazed upon in wonderment as giants were quite common on earth in those days." In the Cainite line, in which the purely spiritual element had become extinct altogether, physical development assumed gigantic dimensions. Had the interbreeding of the two lines produced the hoped-for results, the spiritual element brought by the father to the mother would have overcome the purely physical and utilized it in its service. The issue of these unions would have been heroes of the spirit because the spirit feeds on physical energy, using up great quantities of this energy for its work. But we are told that וְגַם אַחֲרֵי כֵן, that "even after that," after the בְּנוֹת הָאָדָם had borne children to them (i.e., to the fathers descended from the godly line) and the godly element introduced into the marriage by the fathers should have prevailed in the offspring, the spiritual element was stifled by the physical. Thus the unions between these two lines bore the seeds of defection and profanation into the generation of the בְּנֵי הָאֱלֹקִים.

הֵמָּה הַגִּבֹּרִים ***[These are the heroes].*** Such were the "heroes of old" produced by these unions: they were individuals who in some instances may have surpassed their contemporaries in intellect but within whom, for the most part, the spirit was subservient to their extraordinary physical strength.

5. . . . יֵצֶר ***[imagination].*** It is unfortunate that this term is so often translated as "drive" or "impulse," as if there were some "urge" within man to "force" him to do evil. Hence, too, that bleak view of life which is at the basis of a large "religious" society, the notion of evil as a mighty force which holds man in its power and from which he can be saved only if he adopts a certain system of beliefs. So, this little word יֵצֶר was twisted into a tight cord that strangles mankind when, in fact, nothing is further away from this concept than this very word.

To begin with, the root יצר does not imply "forcing" but "forming" [or "forming an image"]. Indeed, the form יֵצֶר does not even have an active connotation; its connotation is passive. It implies not that which does the forming but that which has been formed. . . . Obviously יֵצֶר is to יוֹצֵר as "creature" is to "creator," as the work is to the one who forms it. Cf. וְיֵצֶר אָמַר לְיוֹצְרוֹ ["that the thing should say of him who made it . . ."] (Isaiah 29:16). Thus, יֵצֶר is subordinate to the יוֹצֵר just as כַּחוֹמֶר בְּיַד הַיּוֹצֵר "as clay in the potter's hands" [Jeremiah 18:6] and יֵצֶר מַחְשְׁבוֹת is the "forming" or the "imagining" of our thoughts.

Our soul is a חוֹשֵׁב, a "weaver" (the basic connotation of חשב ["to think"] is "to connect" or "combine," as in חֹשֵׁב הָאֵפוֹד "the weaving of the [priestly] ephod"). The raw material has been turned over to the soul. Every potential, good or evil, lies pliant within the soul's hands, as it were. The soul must now combine these possibilities, mold them into shapes. צורות, i.e., our thoughts, our ideals, constitute the יֵצֶר, the "image" woven by our souls. We can shape the material turned over to us into any form we wish. But at the same time God has given us the "pattern" we are expected to follow. If we follow that pattern, then all will be well. The

ה וַיַּרְא יְהוָֹה כִּי רַבָּה רָעַת הָאָדָם בָּאָרֶץ וְכָל־
יֵצֶר מַחְשְׁבֹת לִבּוֹ רַק רַע כָּל־הַיּוֹם: ו וַיִּנָּחֶם
יְהוָֹה כִּי־עָשָׂה אֶת־הָאָדָם בָּאָרֶץ וַיִּתְעַצֵּב
אֶל־לִבּוֹ: ז וַיֹּאמֶר יְהוָֹה אֶמְחֶה אֶת־הָאָדָם
אֲשֶׁר־בָּרָאתִי מֵעַל פְּנֵי הָאֲדָמָה מֵאָדָם עַד
בְּהֵמָה עַד־רֶמֶשׂ וְעַד־עוֹף הַשָּׁמָיִם כִּי נִחַמְתִּי

the evil of man was great on the earth and
that every imagination of the thoughts of his
heart was nothing but evil each day,
6. *God* was caused to alter His decision
that He had made man on earth, and He
grieved in His heart. 7. And *God*
said: "I will blot out man from the face of
the ground, from man to beast; to the creeping things, to the birds of the sky, for I have
been caused to alter My decision that I

חוֹשֵׁב ["weaver"] must have every type of thread, every color, at his disposal. He cannot dispense with any of them. Used in its proper place and in the prescribed manner, everything is good. יֵצֶר, the idea, the conception of what is within our power to achieve, does indeed spur us on to achievement, but it is we ourselves who have formed it. If the idea we have formed is a good one, then we aspire toward the good; if not, then the opposite is true.

Accordingly, this verse seeks to convey the following thought: The evil brought into the world by man was great already, at this very moment. As a consequence, all that could be expected of man in the future, of anything that still dwelt within him as a "mental image," was that "every imagination of the thoughts of his heart" would be evil, either all day long or every day. The use of the expression כָּל יֵצֶר in itself demonstrates that our text does not refer to the so-called "evil impulse." There is only one "evil impulse"; hence the form "every" could not be used to describe it. On the other hand, the word "every" can indeed be used in connection with ideas and thoughts [i.e., every idea, every thought]. Each of the ideals to which that generation of men aspired was totally devoid of good, and this tendency to aspire only to evil was the same at all times, in every aspect of their lives.

6. . . . לֵב ד׳ [the heart of *God*] denotes the most intimate expression that can be used to describe God's relationship to man. וְהָיוּ עֵינַי וְלִבִּי שָׁם כָּל הַיָּמִים ["and My eyes and My heart shall be there perpetually"— I Kings 9:3]; not only His Providence but also His love, His feeling will dwell there forever. In the context of this verse, then, לִבּוֹ ["His heart"]—speaking in anthropomorphic terms—implies that joy which God sought to gain from the mutually supportive thriving of earth and mankind (cf. יִשְׂמַח ד׳ בְּמַעֲשָׂיו "Let God rejoice in His works" [Psalms 104:31]) and which He now had to forego. Man's continued existence would have been a misfortune for the earth; for this reason וַיִּנָּחֶם, "He was caused to alter His decision," but His heart—speaking once again in anthropomorphic terms—had remained the same. He was grieved that He had to abandon His heartfelt hopes for man's continued happy existence on earth.

7. ה׳. The same mercy that had caused God to place man on earth has now caused Him to decide to destroy mankind. The depravity on earth had become so great that even the extermination [of all living things] would be an act of mercy. . . . Not earth, but פְּנֵי הָאֲדָמָה, the "face of the ground," has been given to mankind as the soil upon which it is to fulfill its calling. . . . The text does not read categorically אֶמְחֶה אֶת הָאָדָם ["I will blot out man"] but adds the modifying phrase מֵעַל פְּנֵי הָאֲדָמָה ["from the face of the ground"]. This allows for the possibility that even this destruction was a relative one only, a removal of man from the physical world. . . .

8. ***But Noaḥ found favor in the eyes of*** **God**. In a similar vein, Moses says, "So that I may know what I must do in order to continue to find favor in Thine eyes." [Exodus 33:13]. חֵן does not yet imply favor granted but only worthiness of being granted favor. . . .

° ° °

One is filled with horror at the thought that after 1,600 years of human history there should have been only one man and his family through whom God was to continue His plan for mankind. Not without reason would later generations study this phase of Divine Providence in retrospect. When David declared that God was present in all things awesome and sublime, great and beautiful, heart-stirring and glorious [Psalm 29] he concluded with the thought that ever-changing though nature and the world may appear, God's plan and His Providence remain unshaken forever. He "sat firm" even at the Time of the Flood; when all mankind perished, He remained מֶלֶךְ, King, and His מַלְכוּת ["lit., "kingdom"], His plan for the education of mankind remained firm. And even as He Himself endures throughout all change, so, too, will He permit those to have made them." 8. But Noaḥ found favor in the eyes of *God*.

כִּי עֲשִׂיתִם: ח וְנֹחַ מָצָא חֵן בְּעֵינֵי יְהוָה: פ

endure who attach themselves to Him with devotion as His people. This kind of firmness will not lead to strife; it does not disturb peace but is, in fact, the only condition under which peace is possible. ה׳ לַמַּבּוּל יָשָׁב וַיֵּשֶׁב ד׳ מֶלֶךְ לְעוֹלָם ה׳ עֹז לְעַמּוֹ יִתֵּן ד׳ יְבָרֵךְ אֶת עַמּוֹ בַשָּׁלוֹם ["God remained aloof upon His throne even at the Flood, and thus God set Himself up as king forever; to His people, however, God will grant power to be victorious over all. God will bless His people with peace"][12] (Psalm 29:10,11)

[12]*Note to the English translation*: See *The Psalms*, translation and commentary by Rabbi Samson Raphael Hirsch rendered into English by Gertrude Hirschler, Jerusalem/New York 5737/1978, The Samson Raphael Hirsch Publications Society and Feldheim Publishers, pp. 209–10 [G.H.]

The Haftarah for this Sidra may be found on page 821.

נח

NOAH

9. These are the products of Noaḥ. Noaḥ, a righteous man, was morally pure in his times: with God did Noaḥ walk. 10. And Noaḥ begot three sons, Shem, Ḥam and Japheth.

ט אֵלֶּה תּוֹלְדֹת נֹחַ נֹחַ אִישׁ צַדִּיק תָּמִים הָיָה בְּדֹרֹתָיו אֶת־הָאֱלֹהִים הִתְהַלֶּךְ־נֹחַ׃ י וַיּוֹלֶד נֹחַ שְׁלֹשָׁה בָנִים אֶת־שֵׁם אֶת־חָם וְאֶת־יָפֶת׃

9. אֵלֶּה תּוֹלְדוֹת נֹחַ ***[These are the products of Noah].*** In Chapter 2, Verse 4 the words אֵלֶּה תּוֹלְדוֹת הַשָּׁמַיִם וְהָאָרֶץ ["these are the products of the heaven and the earth"] introduced a new chain of developments in the history of the earth. In a similar vein the words אֵלֶּה תּוֹלְדוֹת נֹחַ in this verse indicate the coming of a new series of developments in the history of mankind. Mankind is about to perish. Noah, as a second Adam, is to stand at the beginning of a new generation of mankind.

The fact that the reference תּוֹלְדוֹת ["products"] is not immediately followed by an enumeration of Noah's progeny but by a description of his qualities gave our Sages the occasion to point out that, in fact, the very first of a man's "products," the very first yield of his labors, is his own character. . . . "A righteous man, morally pure": these are character traits thanks to which "Noah found favor in the eyes of God" and which God chose as seedlings for the future generation from within its ancestor-to-be.

אִישׁ ***[man].*** According to our Sages the description אִישׁ is not lightly used in the Biblical text. When the Word of God refers to someone as "a man," that individual is indeed a man, a righteous individual of proven character. What other individual had to undergo so many tests of true manly character as did Noah during the first 600 years of his life amidst the changing generations? . . .

in his times. It is significant that the word בְּדֹרֹתָיו "in his times" is stressed with תָּמִים ["morally pure"], not with צַדִּיק ["a righteous man"]. It is incomparably more difficult to remain morally pure in an age of immorality than it is to remain honest in an age of dishonesty.

Noah was an אִישׁ צַדִּיק ["a righteous man"] because of his moral purity, which in turn was rooted in the fact that הִתְהַלֶּךְ, he permitted himself to be led by the hand of God. Great men of later generations were described as having walked *before* God, as His messengers, but Noah is characterized as having walked *with* God. Foregoing all contact with his contemporaries, who ridiculed him, Noah clung fast to God, thereby becoming נֹחַ, the one through whom mankind, which at first had no prospects, won a new future.

10. Noah was already 500 years old when he sired his children. All his ancestors and contemporaries had started their families at a much earlier age. It seems highly probable that Noah had been afraid to start a family at an earlier date because he initially did not trust himself to establish a family and to be able to raise good and morally pure offspring at the time in which he lived. Only twenty years after the end [of all things] had been announced and after he had become accustomed, over a period of 500 years, to walk with God alone and in isolation, without a wife and family of his own, in order to save himself from the depravity into which the rest of mankind had fallen, did Noah finally take upon himself the risk of begetting children. The repetition of Noah's name in this verse may be intended to tell us that he took this step, too, in full awareness of his destination to become "Noah."

three sons. The ancestors of the new humanity are three in number. If, on closer consideration, it becomes clear that the names of these three individuals reflect marked differences in character and personality, this fact should be a source of great comfort to us. Different though the various races and ethnic groups of mankind may appear, we see from the names of their ancestors [who were born before the deluge] that these differences existed even prior to the Flood. The fact that God permitted these disparities to survive the Flood indicates to us that it must be part of God's plan to bring about the ultimate goal of mankind despite them, or perhaps precisely through the interaction between these differences. . . .

Let us consider these three names that show us three differing personality types even in three brothers, the sons of one אִישׁ צַדִּיק תָּמִים [man who was righteous and morally pure].

שֵׁם, literally "name," or the conception of a given object. Originally, and indeed even to this day, human wisdom basically consists in man's ability to "give names" to things; that is, to express their meaning or significance in words. שֵׁם thus implies an intellectual or spiritual activity, that of discernment, of expressing or "naming" concepts or ideas.

חָם (root: חמם ["glowing"] denotes "heat," an agitation of the passions.

יֶפֶת, from יפה, "beautiful" or "attractive." . . . [In recapitulation:] שֵׁם implies mind and spirit, חָם the

יא וַתִּשָּׁחֵת הָאָרֶץ לִפְנֵי הָאֱלֹהִים וַתִּמָּלֵא
הָאָרֶץ חָמָס: יב וַיַּרְא אֱלֹהִים אֶת־הָאָרֶץ וְהִנֵּה
נִשְׁחָתָה כִּי־הִשְׁחִית כָּל־בָּשָׂר אֶת־דַּרְכּוֹ עַל־
הָאָרֶץ: ס יג וַיֹּאמֶר אֱלֹהִים לְנֹחַ קֵץ כָּל־בָּשָׂר
בָּא לְפָנַי כִּי־מָלְאָה הָאָרֶץ חָמָס מִפְּנֵיהֶם
וְהִנְנִי מַשְׁחִיתָם אֶת־הָאָרֶץ: יד עֲשֵׂה לְךָ תֵּבַת

Yapheth. 11. And the earth was corrupt before the countenance of God and so the earth was filled with wrongdoing. 12. And God looked at the earth and lo! it was corrupt, because all flesh had corrupted its way on earth. 13. And God said to Noaḥ: "The end of all flesh has come before Me, for the earth is filled with wrongdoing because of them, and so I am about to destroy them with the earth. 14. Make

"heat" of physical lust and יֶפֶת, receptiveness to beauty. . . .

We have here, then, three distinct aspects which, together, comprise the mental and emotional life of man. In a healthy personality, all three subordinate themselves to one higher principle, and, as in the case of Noah, result in the individual's הִתְהַלֵּךְ אֶת הָאֱלֹקִים ["walking with God"], the spirit in its purest form; in תָּמִים [moral purity], the utilization of sensuality in its purest form; and in צַדִּיק [the quality of righteousness], the shaping of man's will and aspirations in their purest forms. If each of these three aspects is taken separately, then שֵׁם would be the thinker, חָם the sensualist and יֶפֶת the seeker after beauty. שֵׁם is supposed to attain a state of הִתְהַלֵּךְ אֶת ד׳ ["walking with God"]; חָם should strive לִהְיוֹת תָּמִים [to become morally pure] and יֶפֶת, instead of permitting himself to be led by the ideal of beauty, is to reach a stage where he will be guided by the ideal of goodness and become צַדִּיק [a righteous man]. (In cases where the tendency of יֶפֶת predominates, sensuality may be kept from turning into coarseness by the application of the standard of "common decency," but then such a standard, applied to the activities of everyday life, will always be a relative standard only.) . . .

These pronounced differences between national entities are not to be viewed as indicative of corruption but as character traits that were already brought into the Ark during the Flood. Hence if, side by side with nations of high intellectual or moral attainments, history shows us also nations in which fervid sensuality seems to predominate, this must not be permitted to alter our conviction that all the many races of mankind were created for one single, lofty ideal and that in due course, all of them will mature toward the goal expressed in the words וּמָלְאָה הָאָרֶץ דֵּעָה אֶת ד׳ ["and the earth will be full of the knowledge of God" —[Isaiah 11:9]

11. שחת implies "ruin" in the sense of "corruption," not "destruction." . . .

חָמָס is a "wrongdoing" which is too insidious to be caught by human justice but which, if it is committed over and over again will lead, step by step, to the ruin of one's fellow man. חָמָס is related to חֹמֶץ, "vinegar," a decay that does not come all at once; it is only step by step that wine turns into vinegar. In this verse we are told, most significantly: the earth was corrupt before the countenance of God, and so the earth was filled with wrongdoing. First came corruption of morals, sins that one might not consider capable of affecting the life of society as such. One might think that even if the young are dissolute and marriages have rotted from within, this need not prevent trade and commerce from flourishing and honest business relationships from continuing. But once the world is corrupt before God Himself, then all the institutions of human society will not be able to save that society from destruction. Society will never be filled with outright robbery, because it has penal codes and prison terms with which to protect itself from crimes such as these. However, חָמָס, underhanded dealings coupled with cunning, "wrongs" that cannot be checked by human justice but can be prevented only by moral scruples acting as their own judge before God, are indeed capable of destroying a society. And moral corruption inevitably leads to חָמָס. Once immorality has taken root, it kills the human conscience, and once that happens, a grave has been dug for the welfare of the community and of society. . . .

13. ***The end of all flesh has come before Me*** could mean, "The moral condition of all flesh has reached a state at which it demands that I put an end to it." Or, more probably, "If I do not intervene, all flesh will perish of itself; its end has already come before Me." As was already implied in connection with the concept of לְמִינֵהוּ [laws concerning the purity of species, Commentary to Gen. 1:11–13], the welfare of humanity is so inextricably linked with the concept of sexual purity that if God says, "Let the earth prosper," sexual purity is an essential prerequisite for such prosperity. . . . God says to Noah: "On account of these circumstances will I intervene and bring about destruction, but this destruction will not be annihilation; it will be, in fact, an act of rescue that this state of affairs most urgently demands."

עֲצֵי־גֹפֶר קִנִּים תַּעֲשֶׂה אֶת־הַתֵּבָה וְכָפַרְתָּ
אֹתָהּ מִבַּיִת וּמִחוּץ בַּכֹּפֶר׃ טו וְזֶה אֲשֶׁר
תַּעֲשֶׂה אֹתָהּ שְׁלֹשׁ מֵאוֹת אַמָּה אֹרֶךְ הַתֵּבָה
חֲמִשִּׁים אַמָּה רָחְבָּהּ וּשְׁלֹשִׁים אַמָּה קוֹמָתָהּ׃
טז צֹהַר ׀ תַּעֲשֶׂה לַתֵּבָה וְאֶל־אַמָּה תְּכַלֶּנָּה
מִלְמַעְלָה וּפֶתַח הַתֵּבָה בְּצִדָּהּ תָּשִׂים תַּחְתִּיִּם
שְׁנִיִּם וּשְׁלִשִׁים תַּעֲשֶׂהָ׃ יז וַאֲנִי הִנְנִי מֵבִיא
אֶת־הַמַּבּוּל מַיִם עַל־הָאָרֶץ לְשַׁחֵת כָּל־בָּשָׂר

yourself an ark of gopher wood, make the ark [to consist] of enclosures for animals and cover it inside and out with pitch. 15. This is how you shall make it: The length of the ark shall be 300 cubits, its width 50 cubits, and its height 30 cubits. 16. You shall make a light for the ark and finish it within one cubit of the top, and set the entrance to the ark in its side; with lower, second and third stories shall you make it. 17. And I—lo! I shall bring the Unsoulment° through water upon the earth, to destroy all flesh in which there is the

°*Note to the English translation*: The German expression used in Hirsch's original rendering is *Entseelung*; i.e., a deprivation of soul, life, or vitality. [G.H.]

14. תֵּבָה is a receptacle or vessel that is mentioned only in this account and in that of the rescue of the infant Moses, in which a תֵּבָה also helped a human being survive in the water by keeping him afloat. The origin of the term is obscure. . . . In any event, the ark was shaped like a box or chest, not like a boat. It was wide at the bottom, tapering toward the top, the reverse of the shape of a boat. It was not designed to cut through the waters but to ride lightly on the water's surface. . . .

16. . . . .Surely it is not without reason that the arrangements for the ark are specified in such detail, and that we are later told repeatedly that Noah did everything כֵּן, in strict accordance with the instructions he had received. God could have chosen a thousand other ways to save living things from the Flood. Such considerations as whether the size of the ark was adequate, etc., are really secondary. [What is important to remember is] that God chose one man who was to save himself, his family and the animal world for the future, but that this man would be able to do so *only* if he would do everything *exactly* in accordance with the commands he had been given. It is a basic principle in Judaism that the value of a good deed done because one is commanded by God to do so is much greater than that of a good deed performed spontaneously. Contrary to prevailing opinion, only acts performed in order to fulfill the will of God have true value. Acts performed on impulse, etc. have only uncertain, secondary significance. During the 120 years that passed between God's announcement to Noah and the actual coming of the Flood, Noah could have done so many things—he could have built a hundred arks, not just one, etc. Accordingly, what the text means to tell us is that Noah restricted himself to doing—albeit accurately and in full—that which God had commanded him to do, leaving the rest to God.

17. . . . מַבּוּל is obviously derived from the root נבל, which implies a "withering away" of vital energies in organic, animal or moral life. . . . Hence מַבּוּל is "unsoulment" as it were, and the use of this term to describe the imminent doom implies the mildest possible dimensions for the catastrophe. For everything on earth is ultimately fated to become "נבול." None of the creatures doomed to perish in the Flood would have lived forever under any circumstances. What would happen to them now, through the Flood, was simply that they would wither and die before their time. . . .

יִגְוָע (root: גוע) ["turn numb"]. Our Sages note that this expression is the one preferred for use in connection with the death of righteous men, as in the case of Abraham, Isaac and Jacob; cf. וַיִּגְוַע וַיָּמָת וַיֵּאָסֶף אֶל עַמָּיו [Gen. 25:8, 35:29 and 49:33]. Yet, here it is employed to denote the downfall of a generation such as the one that was to die in the Flood. Hardly anything could be more significant than the choice of this particular expression here. For in this verse it is not a mere mortal who pictures for himself and others all the possible horrors of the coming annihilation as we see them depicted in so many pictures or written accounts of the "Deluge." It is the merciful, compassionate Creator and Master of the Universe Himself Who informs us of what He is about to do.

Like the term מַבּוּל, so, too, the term גוע is most significant in this context. גוע is related to גוה, the root of גֵּוָה, "corporeality"; גֵּו is "body," "back"; גְּוִיָּה is a "dead body" or "corpse." גוי is a "nation" defined as a "body" in its external aspects as distinct from עָם, the "society" [or "people"] in its internal aspects. גוע denotes a gathering or collection of mass or matter. גוע would then define the moment when the body, which until that time had been conscious, feeling and responsive, turns into mere "matter," that is, into something unconscious, unfeeling and unresponsive. If such a condition precedes actual death, it will make death spirit of life, from under heaven; everything on earth shall turn numb. 18. But with you I will maintain My covenant; you will enter the ark, you, and your sons, and your wife, and your sons' wives with you. 19. And of every living thing, of all flesh, you shall take two of each into the ark, to keep them alive with you; they shall be male and female. 20. Of bird according to its species, and of cattle according to its species, of every creeping thing of the ground, according to its species; two of each sort shall come to you so that you will keep them alive. 21. As for you, take for yourself of every food that serves as nourishment and store it away, and it shall be food for you and for them." 22. Noaḥ did so: just as God had commanded him, so he did.

אֲשֶׁר־בּוֹ֙ ר֣וּחַ חַיִּ֔ים מִתַּ֖חַת הַשָּׁמָ֑יִם כֹּ֥ל אֲשֶׁר־
בָּאָ֖רֶץ יִגְוָֽע׃ יח וַהֲקִמֹתִ֥י אֶת־בְּרִיתִ֖י אִתָּ֑ךְ
וּבָאתָ֙ אֶל־הַתֵּבָ֔ה אַתָּ֕ה וּבָנֶ֛יךָ וְאִשְׁתְּךָ֥ וּנְשֵֽׁי־
בָנֶ֖יךָ אִתָּֽךְ׃ יט וּמִכָּל־הָ֠חַי מִֽכָּל־בָּשָׂ֞ר שְׁנַ֧יִם
מִכֹּ֛ל תָּבִ֥יא אֶל־הַתֵּבָ֖ה לְהַחֲיֹ֣ת אִתָּ֑ךְ זָכָ֥ר
וּנְקֵבָ֖ה יִהְיֽוּ׃ כ מֵהָע֣וֹף לְמִינֵ֗הוּ וּמִן־הַבְּהֵמָה֙
לְמִינָ֔הּ מִכֹּ֛ל רֶ֥מֶשׂ הָאֲדָמָ֖ה לְמִינֵ֑הוּ שְׁנַ֧יִם מִכֹּ֛ל
יָבֹ֥אוּ אֵלֶ֖יךָ לְהַחֲיֽוֹת׃ כא וְאַתָּ֣ה קַח־לְךָ֗ מִכָּל־
מַאֲכָל֙ אֲשֶׁ֣ר יֵֽאָכֵ֔ל וְאָסַפְתָּ֖ אֵלֶ֑יךָ וְהָיָ֥ה לְךָ֛
וְלָהֶ֖ם לְאָכְלָֽה׃ כב וַיַּ֖עַשׂ נֹ֑חַ כְּ֠כֹל אֲשֶׁ֨ר צִוָּ֥ה

painless to the dying individual. In this vein Genesis Rabbah, too, renders יִגְוָע simply as יִצְמוֹק [lit., "to shrivel"] "become numb." How could the compassionate God—to speak in anthropomorphic terms—have behaved in a more merciful manner, in what kinder way could He have announced the imminent catastrophe to those who would have to live through it and who could hardly have survived the visions of the final agony, the terror and the desperation of so many millions of creatures, than by explaining it in these terms: All flesh, everything that is conscious and capable of sensation will, in one moment, יִגְוָע turn numb and change into a mass of matter? Matter can feel no pain; what happens to it after this point is simply its reduction to the elements of which it was made. מֵתוּ, וַיִּגְוַע and וַיִּמַּח—loss of consciousness, death and disintegration—these three states will also be kept clearly distinct from one another in the historical account of the event (Genesis 7:21, 22, 23).

18. . . . A בְּרִית ["covenant"] is an arrangement which is to be carried out quite independently of, and if need be, even in opposition to, external circumstances. . . . It is absolute and unconditional. Hence, too, the establishment of a בְּרִית is denoted in Hebrew by the verb כרת, which means "to separate," "cut off" or "set apart," and the keeping of a covenant is denoted by הקים, "to maintain." . . . As a matter of fact, "covenant" is not an adequate rendering for בְּרִית, if for no other reason but that a "covenant" always implies an "agreement" between the parties concerned, whereas a בְּרִית in many instances can be entirely unilateral, as, for instance, God's בְּרִית with Noah regarding the survival of Noah and the Noahide world. . . . Perhaps nothing was more in need of a בְּרִית than the survival of Noah in the Flood.

Those few boards of the ark surely were not the true instruments of his rescue; had they been that, others could have saved themselves in the same manner. It seems that Noah was told to build the ark in keeping with the precept that one "must not rely on miracles" but must do everything possible to help himself. However, Noah's rescue and survival surely required special protection from Divine Providence; hence the בְּרִית. . . .

19. ***And of every living thing.*** The Sages interpret this as "and of everything that is viable"; i.e., whose vitality had not been sapped by the corruption that had been communicated even to the animal world. In the same vein, we are told "*they shall be* male and female," not "*you shall take* male and female." The implication is that the living things to be taken into the ark were to be males and females, still pure, untainted and uncorrupted. It seems that the repetition of לְמִינֵהוּ ["according to its species"] in Verse 20 is intended to express the same thought. The animals were to be specimens in which the characteristics of their species had remained undiluted and unadulterated, creatures that were still completely members of their own species. This untainted purity of breed in the pairs of animals to be saved is further implied in Chapter 7, Verse 2, אִישׁ וְאִשְׁתּוֹ ["the male and its mate"]. The breeds that were to be saved were uncorrupted to such a degree that, at this lofty moment, hallowed by God Himself, they were to be regarded as related to one another almost like the mates in a human marriage. After all, it must be remembered that the basic source of all the corruption on earth was that all flesh had "corrupted its way on earth," that men had become morally impure. Conversely, Noah was to be saved because he was תָּמִים [morally pure].

VII

1. And *God* said to Noaḥ: "Go into the ark, you and all your household, for I have seen you righteous before Me in this age. 2. Of every clean animal you shall take seven pairs, the male and its mate, and of animals that are not clean you shall take two each, the male and its mate. 3. Of the birds of the sky also seven pairs, male and female, to keep seed alive upon the face of all the earth. 4. For yet seven days, and I will make it rain upon the earth for forty days and forty nights and I will blot out everything in existence that I have made from off the face of the ground." 5. And Noaḥ did according to all that *God* commanded him. 6. Noaḥ was a man of 600 years when the Unsoulment through water was upon the earth. 7. And Noaḥ, his sons, his wife and his sons' wives with him, went into the ark, fleeing from the waters of Unsoulment. 8. Of clean animals, and of animals that are not clean, and of the birds, and of everything that creeps upon the ground, 9. two by two, male and female, they came to Noaḥ in the ark, as God had commanded Noaḥ. 10. It came to pass after the seven days that the waters of Unsoulment were

אִתּ֖וֹ אֱלֹהִ֑ים כֵּ֖ן עָשָֽׂה׃ שני ז א וַיֹּ֤אמֶר יְהוָה֙
לְנֹ֔חַ בֹּֽא־אַתָּ֥ה וְכָל־בֵּיתְךָ֖ אֶל־הַתֵּבָ֑ה כִּֽי־אֹתְךָ֥
רָאִ֛יתִי צַדִּ֥יק לְפָנַ֖י בַּדּ֥וֹר הַזֶּֽה׃ ב מִכֹּ֣ל ׀
הַבְּהֵמָ֣ה הַטְּהוֹרָ֗ה תִּֽקַּח־לְךָ֛ שִׁבְעָ֥ה שִׁבְעָ֖ה אִ֣ישׁ
וְאִשְׁתּ֑וֹ וּמִן־הַבְּהֵמָ֡ה אֲשֶׁר֩ לֹ֨א טְהֹרָ֥ה הִ֛וא
שְׁנַ֖יִם אִ֥ישׁ וְאִשְׁתּֽוֹ׃ ג גַּ֣ם מֵע֧וֹף הַשָּׁמַ֛יִם
שִׁבְעָ֥ה שִׁבְעָ֖ה זָכָ֣ר וּנְקֵבָ֑ה לְחַיּ֥וֹת זֶ֖רַע עַל־פְּנֵ֥י
כָל־הָאָֽרֶץ׃ ד כִּי֩ לְיָמִ֨ים ע֜וֹד שִׁבְעָ֗ה אָֽנֹכִי֙
מַמְטִ֣יר עַל־הָאָ֔רֶץ אַרְבָּעִ֣ים י֔וֹם וְאַרְבָּעִ֖ים
לָ֑יְלָה וּמָחִ֗יתִי אֶת־כָּל־הַיְקוּם֙ אֲשֶׁ֣ר עָשִׂ֔יתִי
מֵעַ֖ל פְּנֵ֥י הָאֲדָמָֽה׃ ה וַיַּ֖עַשׂ נֹ֑חַ כְּכֹ֥ל אֲשֶׁר־
צִוָּ֖הוּ יְהוָֽה׃ ו וְנֹ֕חַ בֶּן־שֵׁ֥שׁ מֵא֖וֹת שָׁנָ֑ה
וְהַמַּבּ֣וּל הָיָ֔ה מַ֖יִם עַל־הָאָֽרֶץ׃ ז וַיָּ֣בֹא נֹ֗חַ וּ֠בָנָיו
וְאִשְׁתּ֧וֹ וּנְשֵֽׁי־בָנָ֛יו אִתּ֖וֹ אֶל־הַתֵּבָ֑ה מִפְּנֵ֖י מֵ֥י
הַמַּבּֽוּל׃ ח מִן־הַבְּהֵמָה֙ הַטְּהוֹרָ֔ה וּמִ֨ן־הַבְּהֵמָ֔ה
אֲשֶׁ֥ר אֵינֶ֖נָּה טְהֹרָ֑ה וּמִ֨ן־הָע֔וֹף וְכֹ֥ל אֲשֶׁר־רֹמֵ֖שׂ
עַל־הָאֲדָמָֽה׃ ט שְׁנַ֨יִם שְׁנַ֜יִם בָּ֧אוּ אֶל־נֹ֛חַ אֶל־
הַתֵּבָ֖ה זָכָ֣ר וּנְקֵבָ֑ה כַּֽאֲשֶׁ֛ר צִוָּ֥ה אֱלֹהִ֖ים אֶת־נֹֽחַ׃
י וַיְהִ֖י לְשִׁבְעַ֣ת הַיָּמִ֑ים וּמֵ֣י הַמַּבּ֔וּל הָי֖וּ עַל־

CHAPTER VII

1. Until this point in the account of God's dealings with Noah God was referred to as אלק׳ [in His quality of justice]. We were told how God, as Creator, Lawgiver and Judge of the universe, set apart from the depraved world the one man and the animals that were to be saved because they had not participated in the general corruption. They were to be saved because they were deserving of it. . . . The events that now follow are introduced by a reference to God as ה׳ [in His quality of mercy]; this designation pertains to that aspect of God's work which mercifully educates mankind toward its goal and shapes every moment with this purpose in mind. In this manner Noah's survival becomes the cornerstone of a new future for mankind. . . .

2. . . . .This is the first mention of בְּהֵמָה טְהוֹרָה ["clean animals"]. Though men at that time did not yet use animals as food and the distinction between "clean" and "unclean" animals emerged only later, in the Law given at Sinai, God, in speaking to Noah, already classed animals as "clean" or "unclean." This means that even in those early days there must have been some reason for making such a distinction. This reason had to do with offerings, because the Noahides then, and later, were permitted to offer only clean animals as sacrifices (Zebaḥim 115a). In other words, Jews are permitted to eat only those animals that are fit to be offered as sacrifices by all men. . . .

4. . . .*forty days.* Our Sages remind us that this is also the period required for the formation of the human fetus. Thus, by its very duration, the catastrophe [of the Flood] can be interpreted in a more profound sense as the formative period of a new future. . . .

10. There now follows an exact account of all the facts in the narrative, how everything came to pass exactly as it had been announced in advance. [God's advance warning] removes the catastrophe from the realm of the blind workings of natural forces and marks it as the work of free-willed Divine Providence. In a similar vein, we will see that all the miracles which came to pass in Egypt were always announced in advance. Here we see both nature and mankind as servants of one Lord and Master. To refute the non-Jewish view according to which the so-called "Deluge" was merely the result of blind natural forces, we read

upon the earth. 11. In the six hundredth year of Noaḥ's life, in the second month, on the seventeenth day of the month, on that day all the fountains of the great deep were torn apart and the floodgates of the heavens were opened. 12. And the rain came upon the earth for forty days and forty nights. 13. On that same day Noaḥ, and Shem and Ḥam and Yapheth, the sons of Noaḥ, and Noaḥ's wife and the three wives of his sons with them, came into the ark. 14. They, and every beast according to its species, and all cattle according to their species, and every creeping thing that creeps upon the earth, according to its species, and every flying thing according to its species, every feathered animal of every kind of wing. 15. They came to Noaḥ into the ark in pairs of all flesh in which there is the spirit of life. 16. Those which entered came male and female of all flesh, as God had commanded them, and then *God* shut him in to protect him. 17. The Unsoulment was forty days upon the earth, and as the waters increased they raised the ark and it stood high above the earth. 18. Only when the waters had swelled and increased greatly over the earth did the ark move upon the surface of the waters. 19. And the waters had swelled so exceedingly high above the earth that all the high mountains which were beneath the whole sky were covered. 20. The waters had swelled fifteen cubits higher so that the

הָאָרֶץ׃ יא בִּשְׁנַת שֵׁשׁ־מֵאוֹת שָׁנָה לְחַיֵּי־נֹחַ
בַּחֹדֶשׁ הַשֵּׁנִי בְּשִׁבְעָה־עָשָׂר יוֹם לַחֹדֶשׁ בַּיּוֹם
הַזֶּה נִבְקְעוּ כָּל־מַעְיְנֹת תְּהוֹם רַבָּה וַאֲרֻבֹּת
הַשָּׁמַיִם נִפְתָּחוּ׃ יב וַיְהִי הַגֶּשֶׁם עַל־הָאָרֶץ
אַרְבָּעִים יוֹם וְאַרְבָּעִים לָיְלָה׃ יג בְּעֶצֶם הַיּוֹם
הַזֶּה בָּא נֹחַ וְשֵׁם־וְחָם וָיֶפֶת בְּנֵי־נֹחַ וְאֵשֶׁת נֹחַ
וּשְׁלֹשֶׁת נְשֵׁי־בָנָיו אִתָּם אֶל־הַתֵּבָה׃ יד הֵמָּה
וְכָל־הַחַיָּה לְמִינָהּ וְכָל־הַבְּהֵמָה לְמִינָהּ וְכָל־
הָרֶמֶשׂ הָרֹמֵשׂ עַל־הָאָרֶץ לְמִינֵהוּ וְכָל־הָעוֹף
לְמִינֵהוּ כֹּל צִפּוֹר כָּל־כָּנָף׃ טו וַיָּבֹאוּ אֶל־נֹחַ
אֶל־הַתֵּבָה שְׁנַיִם שְׁנַיִם מִכָּל־הַבָּשָׂר אֲשֶׁר־בּוֹ
רוּחַ חַיִּים׃ טז וְהַבָּאִים זָכָר וּנְקֵבָה מִכָּל־בָּשָׂר
בָּאוּ כַּאֲשֶׁר צִוָּה אֹתוֹ אֱלֹהִים וַיִּסְגֹּר יְהוָה
בַּעֲדוֹ׃ שלישי יז וַיְהִי הַמַּבּוּל אַרְבָּעִים יוֹם עַל־
הָאָרֶץ וַיִּרְבּוּ הַמַּיִם וַיִּשְׂאוּ אֶת־הַתֵּבָה וַתָּרָם
מֵעַל הָאָרֶץ׃ יח וַיִּגְבְּרוּ הַמַּיִם וַיִּרְבּוּ מְאֹד עַל־
הָאָרֶץ וַתֵּלֶךְ הַתֵּבָה עַל־פְּנֵי הַמָּיִם׃ יט וְהַמַּיִם
גָּבְרוּ מְאֹד מְאֹד עַל־הָאָרֶץ וַיְכֻסּוּ כָּל־הֶהָרִים
הַגְּבֹהִים אֲשֶׁר־תַּחַת כָּל־הַשָּׁמָיִם׃ כ חֲמֵשׁ
עֶשְׂרֵה אַמָּה מִלְמַעְלָה גָּבְרוּ הַמָּיִם וַיְכֻסּוּ

here the record and chronology of Noah, revealing two entities, both loyally obedient to the will of God: Noah on the one hand, and unreasoning nature on the other. The birds in the air, the creeping things on the ground, they all found their way to Noah "according to God's command;" they knew enough to appear at the ark, "two by two, male and female," a state of affairs certainly not typical of the ordinary course of nature. It is pointed out that the Flood, too, burst forth only at the command of God and on the day set by Him.

16. They were permitted to enter the ark only because they had come there in pairs, "male and female."

and then* God *shut him in. Noah had done everything he had been commanded to do, but this alone did not ensure his survival. He had done as he had been told, but it was ה׳, God in His intention to preserve life for the future, Who shut Noah into the ark to protect him. The verses that follow will explain what the nature of this protection was and what God did for Noah.

17–20. . . . The ark had been built, but no matter how strong it was, there was a very real danger that, in a flood that battered all other things, the ark would be dashed to pieces on the first mountaintop it struck. For this reason the ark from the very outset was in need of Divine protection. When the waters first swelled and covered the surface of the earth—we may be sure that they gushed in torrents—the ark was *raised* but it *stood still* (Verse 17). *Only after the waters had swelled to an immense level did the ark begin to move* (Verse mountains were covered. 21. All flesh that moved upon the earth turned numb, of bird and cattle and of animals of the forest and of every creeping thing that creeps upon the earth, and all people; 22. all in whose countenance there was the breath of the spirit of life, of all those that were on dry land, died. 23. And everything that stood upon the face of the ground was blotted out, from man to cattle to creeping things to the birds of the sky; they were blotted out from the earth and only Noaḥ was left, and those who were with him in the ark. 24. So the waters swelled over the earth for 150 days.

VIII

1. And God remembered Noaḥ and all the animals and all the cattle that were with him in the ark, and God caused a wind to pass over the earth, and the waters subsided. 2. The fountains of the great deep and the flood-gates of the heavens were closed, and the rain from the sky was restrained. 3. The waters receded more and more from above the earth and at the end of 150 days the waters diminished. 4. In the seventh month, on the seventeenth day of the month, the ark came to rest upon the mountains of Ararat. 5. And the waters continued to diminish until the tenth month. In the tenth month, on the first of the month, the tops of the mountains became visible. 6. And then, at the end of 40 days, it came to pass that Noaḥ opened the window of the ark that he had made, 7. and he sent forth the raven. It flew out but kept returning until the waters began to dry up from the earth. 8. Thereupon he sent off the dove from himself to see whether the waters had abated from the face of the ground. 9. But the dove found no resting place for the ball of her foot, and she returned to him in the ark, for the water was still upon the surface of all the earth. He put out his hand and took her and brought her

הֶהָרִים׃ כא וַיִּגְוַע כָּל־בָּשָׂר ׀ הָרֹמֵשׂ עַל־הָאָרֶץ
בָּעוֹף וּבַבְּהֵמָה וּבַחַיָּה וּבְכָל־הַשֶּׁרֶץ הַשֹּׁרֵץ
עַל־הָאָרֶץ וְכֹל הָאָדָם׃ כב כֹּל אֲשֶׁר נִשְׁמַת־
רוּחַ חַיִּים בְּאַפָּיו מִכֹּל אֲשֶׁר בֶּחָרָבָה מֵתוּ׃
כג וַיִּמַח אֶת־כָּל־הַיְקוּם ׀ אֲשֶׁר ׀ עַל־פְּנֵי
הָאֲדָמָה מֵאָדָם עַד־בְּהֵמָה עַד־רֶמֶשׂ וְעַד־עוֹף
הַשָּׁמַיִם וַיִּמָּחוּ מִן־הָאָרֶץ וַיִּשָּׁאֶר אַךְ־נֹחַ
וַאֲשֶׁר אִתּוֹ בַּתֵּבָה׃ כד וַיִּגְבְּרוּ הַמַּיִם עַל־הָאָרֶץ
חֲמִשִּׁים וּמְאַת יוֹם׃ ח א וַיִּזְכֹּר אֱלֹהִים אֶת־נֹחַ
וְאֵת כָּל־הַחַיָּה וְאֶת־כָּל־הַבְּהֵמָה אֲשֶׁר אִתּוֹ
בַּתֵּבָה וַיַּעֲבֵר אֱלֹהִים רוּחַ עַל־הָאָרֶץ וַיָּשֹׁכּוּ
הַמָּיִם׃ ב וַיִּסָּכְרוּ מַעְיְנֹת תְּהוֹם וַאֲרֻבֹּת
הַשָּׁמָיִם וַיִּכָּלֵא הַגֶּשֶׁם מִן־הַשָּׁמָיִם׃ ג וַיָּשֻׁבוּ
הַמַּיִם מֵעַל הָאָרֶץ הָלוֹךְ וָשׁוֹב וַיַּחְסְרוּ הַמַּיִם
מִקְצֵה חֲמִשִּׁים וּמְאַת יוֹם׃ ד וַתָּנַח הַתֵּבָה
בַּחֹדֶשׁ הַשְּׁבִיעִי בְּשִׁבְעָה־עָשָׂר יוֹם לַחֹדֶשׁ עַל
הָרֵי אֲרָרָט׃ ה וְהַמַּיִם הָיוּ הָלוֹךְ וְחָסוֹר עַד
הַחֹדֶשׁ הָעֲשִׂירִי בָּעֲשִׂירִי בְּאֶחָד לַחֹדֶשׁ נִרְאוּ
רָאשֵׁי הֶהָרִים׃ ו וַיְהִי מִקֵּץ אַרְבָּעִים יוֹם
וַיִּפְתַּח נֹחַ אֶת־חַלּוֹן הַתֵּבָה אֲשֶׁר עָשָׂה׃
ז וַיְשַׁלַּח אֶת־הָעֹרֵב וַיֵּצֵא יָצוֹא וָשׁוֹב עַד־
יְבֹשֶׁת הַמַּיִם מֵעַל הָאָרֶץ׃ ח וַיְשַׁלַּח אֶת־הַיּוֹנָה
מֵאִתּוֹ לִרְאוֹת הֲקַלּוּ הַמַּיִם מֵעַל פְּנֵי הָאֲדָמָה׃
ט וְלֹא־מָצְאָה הַיּוֹנָה מָנוֹחַ לְכַף־רַגְלָהּ וַתָּשָׁב
אֵלָיו אֶל־הַתֵּבָה כִּי מַיִם עַל־פְּנֵי כָל־הָאָרֶץ
וַיִּשְׁלַח יָדוֹ וַיִּקָּחֶהָ וַיָּבֵא אֹתָהּ אֵלָיו אֶל־

18), for by that time the water level had risen to 15 cubits above all the mountaintops (Verse 19), so that there was no more danger that the ark might founder upon one of them.

22. If it should be true that the "diluvial strata" of the geologists are the results of our "Deluge," the fact that they contain primarily fossils of land animals rather than of marine creatures could be explained by the statement in this verse that "all those that were on dry land, died"; i.e., that only land animals were caught in the Flood.

back to himself in the ark. 10. He allowed another seven days to pass and then he again sent the dove out of the ark. 11. The dove came back to him toward evening and lo! she had an olive leaf as food in her mouth. So Noaḥ knew that the waters had abated from the earth. 12. He waited yet another seven days and sent out the dove, and she did not return to him anymore. 13. At last, in the six hundred and first year, in the first month, on the first of the month, the waters were dried up from off the earth. Then Noaḥ removed the covering of the ark; he looked and lo! the face of the ground had dried up. 14. And in the second month, on the twenty-seventh day of the month, the earth was dry at last. 15. And God said to Noaḥ: 16. "Go forth from the ark, you, your wife and your sons and the wives of your sons with you. 17. Every living thing that is with you of all flesh of bird and cattle, and of every creeping thing that creeps upon the earth, let them go out with you so that they may

הַתֵּבָה: י וַיָּחֶל עוֹד שִׁבְעַת יָמִים אֲחֵרִים וַיֹּסֶף
שַׁלַּח אֶת־הַיּוֹנָה מִן־הַתֵּבָה: יא וַתָּבֹא אֵלָיו
הַיּוֹנָה לְעֵת עֶרֶב וְהִנֵּה עֲלֵה־זַיִת טָרָף בְּפִיהָ
וַיֵּדַע נֹחַ כִּי־קַלּוּ הַמַּיִם מֵעַל הָאָרֶץ: יב וַיִּיָּחֶל
עוֹד שִׁבְעַת יָמִים אֲחֵרִים וַיְשַׁלַּח אֶת־הַיּוֹנָה
וְלֹא־יָסְפָה שׁוּב־אֵלָיו עוֹד: יג וַיְהִי בְּאַחַת
וְשֵׁשׁ־מֵאוֹת שָׁנָה בָּרִאשׁוֹן בְּאֶחָד לַחֹדֶשׁ חָרְבוּ
הַמַּיִם מֵעַל הָאָרֶץ וַיָּסַר נֹחַ אֶת־מִכְסֵה הַתֵּבָה
וַיַּרְא וְהִנֵּה חָרְבוּ פְּנֵי הָאֲדָמָה: יד וּבַחֹדֶשׁ
הַשֵּׁנִי בְּשִׁבְעָה וְעֶשְׂרִים יוֹם לַחֹדֶשׁ יָבְשָׁה
הָאָרֶץ: ס רביעי טו וַיְדַבֵּר אֱלֹהִים אֶל־נֹחַ
לֵאמֹר: טז צֵא מִן־הַתֵּבָה אַתָּה וְאִשְׁתְּךָ וּבָנֶיךָ
וּנְשֵׁי־בָנֶיךָ אִתָּךְ: יז כָּל־הַחַיָּה אֲשֶׁר־אִתְּךָ
מִכָּל־בָּשָׂר בָּעוֹף וּבַבְּהֵמָה וּבְכָל־הָרֶמֶשׂ
הָרֹמֵשׂ עַל־הָאָרֶץ הוֹצֵא (היצא קרי) אִתָּךְ

CHAPTER VIII

10. . . . Noah allowed another seven days to pass, because the annihilation had come about in just the same time pattern—first seven days and then forty. Between the present that was to be destroyed and the beginning of the actual destruction there was an interval during which nothing had changed. It was during this interval that the present was allowed to expire. Perhaps a similar time pattern was now to mark the transition to the new, reshaped future. Noah became aware that God still remembered him, for the ark had come to rest and the tops of the mountains had become visible. However, Noah did not open the ark, for he believed that the flood would subside in the same manner in which it had come. That is why he waited 40 days before sending out the raven. But then he realized that there still were no habitable places on earth. He therefore assumed that, similarly to what had transpired at the onset of the flood, an interval of seven days would now have to elapse between the end of the destruction and the start of the new era. That is why he waited for another seven days to pass. Such seven-day intervals to mark the complete cessation of a former condition prior to the onset of a new condition occur also later on, in connection with the laws of טוּמְאָה וְטָהֳרָה ["uncleanness and purity"], etc.

11. . . . טָרָף *[as food].* טָרָף is not a verb [meaning "torn" or "plucked"] but a noun like טֶרֶף, meaning food that a person or an animal has seized by itself. The choice of the term in this verse is most significant. That which the animal in its non-captive state takes for nourishment by its own efforts is טֶרֶף. Cf. טֶרֶף נָתַן לִירֵאָיו ["He has given food to those who fear Him"—Psalms 111:5]: that which others must take for themselves as "prey" is received by יְרֵאִים [the God-fearing] directly from the hand of God. For a whole year the dove had been fed; it had not eaten טֶרֶף, food gained by its own efforts. The fact that this time it had remained away from the ark for a whole day was clearly a sign that "the waters had abated." The dove had already found "a resting place" for its feet. Of course, it could have been driven back to the ark by hunger. However, we are told that it returned to the ark bearing in its mouth an olive leaf —something it does not normally take as nourishment. Hence, in the view of the Sages, the bitter olive leaf in the mouth of the dove signifies this great verity: Better unfamiliar food that tastes bitter and that, under normal conditions would be unappealing, but is eaten in freedom and independence than food that is sweet but must be eaten in a position of dependency. Therefore we regard the olive leaf not as a symbol of peace but as a symbol of the value of freedom, independence, and of contentment and moderation in the midst of freedom.

move freely upon the earth and be fruitful and multiply upon the earth." 18. And Noaḥ came out, and his sons, and his wife, and the wives of his sons with him. 19. Every living thing, every creeping thing and every flying thing, everything that moves on earth according to their families went forth from the ark. 20. And Noaḥ built an altar to *God* and took of every clean animal and of every clean bird and offered an ascent offering upon the altar.

וְשָׁרְצוּ בָאָרֶץ וּפָרוּ וְרָבוּ עַל־הָאָרֶץ: יח וַיֵּצֵא
נֹחַ וּבָנָיו וְאִשְׁתּוֹ וּנְשֵׁי־בָנָיו אִתּוֹ: יט כָּל־הַחַיָּה
כָּל־הָרֶמֶשׂ וְכָל־הָעוֹף כֹּל רוֹמֵשׂ עַל־הָאָרֶץ
לְמִשְׁפְּחֹתֵיהֶם יָצְאוּ מִן־הַתֵּבָה: כ וַיִּבֶן נֹחַ
מִזְבֵּחַ לַיהוָה וַיִּקַּח מִכֹּל ׀ הַבְּהֵמָה הַטְּהֹרָה
וּמִכֹּל הָעוֹף הַטָּהֹר וַיַּעַל עֹלֹת בַּמִּזְבֵּחַ:

20. . . . For one whole year Noah had to devote all his time and energy to keeping the animals alive in the ark, and now, immediately after their deliverance, he offers them up as sacrifices! This offering is of such far-reaching significance in world history that the verses which follow—Verses 21 and 22—interpret all the subsequent development of the earth and of mankind until this day, as a result of, or perhaps in answer to, Noah's offering.

What was the significance of Noah's building an altar and offering עולות ["ascent offerings"] that it should have led to such a Divine resolve for the preservation and future development of the world? It is evident from many passages in Scripture that מִזְבֵּחַ ["altar"] denotes a man-made *elevation of the ground toward God*. . . .

It is significant to note that one of the respects in which the hallowed Jewish law differs from Noahide concepts is that the type of altar upon which we were permitted to make our offerings had to be a מִזְבֵּחַ, a *structure* built of rocks, not just מַצֵּבָה, *one rock* in its natural state. We were required to build our altars with our own hands; moreover, they could not rest on pillars or on a base. The altar had to be "connected with the ground."

The altar had to be in direct contact with the ground, to represent a continuation of the ground, as it were. Only in this manner could the altar be regarded as symbolizing *the elevation of the earth toward God by the work of human hands.* To take a single rock as an altar upon which to offer sacrifices would imply standing still on the level of nature, but a מִזְבֵּחַ in the form of a structure built by human hands expresses the concept of man seeking to work himself up, by means of his creativity, from the level of nature toward the godlike, free-willed level of humanity, from which in turn he will then aspire toward God. Thus, by *building* an altar to God upon the earth newly restored to man, Noah, as the progenitor of the future human race, consecrated that earth as the place upon which, in future, man was to pile rock upon rock, as it were, until one day all the earth would become the holy mountain of God. . . .

° ° °

מִזְבֵּחַ: root זבח, which implies a killing or a slaughter whose main purpose is not to destroy but to provide nourishment. זֶבַח actually denotes a feast. . . . Sacrifices as such are regarded as "meals," they are לֶחֶם אִשֶּׁה לד׳, food to nourish the flame of godliness on earth. The one who makes the offering sacrifices himself, as it were, in order to keep the flame of God's light shining upon the earth.

It should be pointed out, too, that Scriptural statements concerning offerings always refer to God as ה׳ [in His quality of love and mercy], never as אלקי׳ [in His quality of justice or as ruler over nature]. According to the Sages this was done on purpose in order to forestall even the slightest possibility that these offerings might be equated with the sacrifices offered by non-Jews to the blind forces of nature. At the same time the designation ה׳ [of God as the God of love] cogently refutes the blasphemous view of those who regard offerings as mere acts of killing and destruction, as spillings of blood to appease a vengeful Deity and who, in their obtuseness, now rejoice that, thank goodness, we no longer offer sacrifices in this day and age and that, thank goodness, we have already reached that stage of enlightenment where we understand that God is not served by the blood of our offerings! This view is refuted with compelling force by the fact that, in the account of Noah's building an altar to make an offering, God is designated as ה׳ [the God of love and mercy] and that the headband on the forehead of the Israelite high priest bore the inscription קֹדֶשׁ לַה׳ ["The Sanctuary is *God's*" (using the Tetragrammaton) — Exodus 28:36], to counter any distortion of the pure ideal represented by the [Jewish] concept of offerings and sacrifices.

לַה׳; it is to this aspect of Divine sovereignty that our offerings are directed, to God's rule [of love and mercy] which, indeed, is the source of all life and all future existence and which is ready at any time to grant new life, new vigor and a new future. Symbolically, one offers his own life in order to win life from God; one offers oneself up to God in order to be consecrated by God and to be elevated by Him into the sphere of a godly life on earth. This has nothing in common with

21. And *God* took note of this expression of compliance, and *God* said to Himself: "Never again will I curse the ground for the sake of man when the imagination of the heart of man is evil from his youth, nor will I ever again destroy every living thing

כא וַיָּ֣רַח יְהוָה֮ אֶת־רֵ֣יחַ הַנִּיחֹחַ֒ וַיֹּ֨אמֶר יְהוָ֜ה אֶל־לִבּ֗וֹ לֹ֣א אֹ֠סִף לְקַלֵּ֨ל ע֤וֹד אֶת־הָֽאֲדָמָה֙ בַּעֲב֣וּר הָֽאָדָ֔ם כִּ֠י יֵ֣צֶר לֵ֧ב הָאָדָ֛ם רַ֖ע מִנְּעֻרָ֑יו וְלֹֽא־אֹסִ֥ף ע֛וֹד לְהַכּ֥וֹת אֶת־כָּל־חַ֖י כַּאֲשֶׁ֥ר

bloody sacrifices to appease an irate god of vengeance. Rather, it implies a hallowing of one's every pulsebeat, one's every nervous impulse, every particle of one's muscular prowess to God and to the fulfillment of His holy will. To offer up such a sacrifice means to enter into a godly, eternal life. What one offers up is not the animal but one's own self as symbolized by the animal. When we lead an animal to the altar, place our hands upon it, slaughter it, collect its blood, sprinkle its blood upon the altar, and finally surrender its head, its legs, its breast and its carcass, etc., to the flames, it is in fact our own blood, our own mind, our own muscular strength which we symbolically offer up to godliness, surrendering ourselves completely to the all-conquering power of God's will as He has set it down for us in the Torah . . .

° ° °

By building an altar to God upon the earth restored to man and making an offering upon it, Noah consecrated the earth as the site of a man-made edifice which would strive upward to God—rock piled upon rock until at last all the earth would become a mountain of God upon which men would devote all their energies to the work of climbing steadily upward to the lofty height of their purpose, which is to serve God. . . .

21. . . . This significant passage in the text is the only place in all of Scripture where the expression רֵיחַ הַנִּיחֹחַ occurs. All other קָרְבָּנוֹת ["offerings"] are only symbolic expressions of man's fulfillment of God's will, for no one individual and no one age can fulfill all of it. Hence it can only be רֵיחַ נִיחוֹחַ [without the definite article]. Noah, however, had all of the future human race before him; hence his offering gave expression to everything that mankind as a whole, through the ages to come, would accomplish in order to give God complete satisfaction. Therefore Noah's offering was רֵיחַ הַנִּיחֹחַ, an intimation of the full compliance with God's will which God will someday receive from mankind dwelling on the earth which was restored to it and which was dedicated as an altar to God. . . .

° ° °

Whoever has truly observed children will say it is not true that youth is evil. It is not "from his youth" that "the imagination of the heart of man is evil." It is not true that man pursues evil from his youth on. In normal times there are many more mature men than young people whose hearts are turned toward evil. True, the young will do many things that are evil because they have not yet learned to subordinate themselves to "the yoke of the commandments," the command of duty. They still regard self-discipline and obedience as a yoke which, in their natural quest for independence, they seek to "shake off."

However, it is precisely in this independence of will — which is not so easily overcome and which, given the immaturity of the young, certainly takes on the form of obstinacy—that the entire morality of the future adult will be rooted.

God chose Israel not because it was the most amenable but precisely because it was the most stiff-necked of peoples. Once this obstinacy would be overcome and won over for the good (as indeed it came to pass) Israel would employ this very obstinacy for good purposes. Therefore, too, God has implanted into every human being the drive for independence so that eventually he will become persistent and steadfast in doing good. It is true that as long as the person is young this drive is expressed in attempts to shake off all restraints and in unwillingness to submit to guidance. But once their minds have matured and they realize that the rules they hitherto viewed as restrictions upon their independence will, in fact, lead them to freedom and will, indeed, secure true freedom for human nature, then it is precisely the young who will be filled with enthusiasm for the ideals of everything noble and sublime and with the high resolve to sacrifice themselves for these ideals.

Not youth but old age is the time of life when selfishness, lasciviousness, greed and that spurious "cleverness" which passes for wisdom mock at the ideals of goodness, nobleness and moral elevation as "youthful dreams."Old age, not youth, is the time when the individual, now indeed no longer a נַעַר ["youth"], learns to "conform"—but only in attitudes and behavior patterns that cater to human passions and selfishness. Normally, old age is the time when רַע [evil] reaps its true harvest. An era in which even the young deliberately aspire to evil as יֵצֶר לִבָּם, as their hearts' ideal, would demand another מַבּוּל, a second Flood in which all mankind would be destroyed. However, this would not be a normal but a most abnormal state of affairs. Hence, we are told here: "Even if the imagination of the human heart were to be evil from his youth,"

עֲשִׂיתִי׃ כב עֹד כָּל־יְמֵי הָאָרֶץ זֶרַע וְקָצִיר וְקֹר וָחֹם וְקַיִץ וָחֹרֶף וְיוֹם וָלַיְלָה לֹא יִשְׁבֹּתוּ׃

as I have done. 22. The days of the earth shall be forever; seedtime and harvest, cold and heat, summer and winter, day and night shall never cease."

even if, contrary to the natural state of affairs, the young should have set רַע [evil] as the purpose of their lives, so that nothing else but evil could be expected from such generations (for all the hopes for the future are placed in the young, not in the old) —even if such an era were to come again when God would have good reason to destroy the earth, בַּעֲבוּר הָאָדָם ["for man's own sake"], for the sake of mankind's own salvation, He still would not do it.

22. ***The days of the earth shall be forever.*** This passage is usually construed as implying that the normal rhythm of time, of day and night and of the seasons, was disrupted during the Flood, and that even as there never again will be a total annihilation of living things, so, too, there never again will be a disruption in the regular course of the seasons. This interpretation assumes that the pattern of changing seasons as we know it today was already in operation prior to the Flood. However, the traditions that have come down to us argue against this assumption. Before the Flood—according to Rabbi Isaac in Genesis Rabbah—the fields had to be cultivated only once in forty years. It was always springtime; the seasons never changed. "They enjoyed the climate (now usual) between Passover and Shevuoth (all year long)," the temperature was constant all over the earth and the continents had not yet been separated from one another, so that communications throughout the world were an easy matter. הָיוּ מְהַלְּכִין מִסּוֹף הָעוֹלָם וְעַד סוֹפוֹ לְשָׁעָה קַלָּה ["they traveled from one end of the world to the other in a brief period"]. In Genesis Rabbah the seasons of the year enumerated in this verse are explicitly characterized as an order instituted only after the Flood: מִכָּאן וְאֵילָךְ זֶרַע וְקָצִיר ["from that time on, seedtime and harvest, etc."]. Thus, when Rabbi Samuel bar Naḥman suffered from headaches due to a change in the weather, he would jokingly say, "Just see what the generation of the Flood did to us!"

The continuous sameness of climate that prevailed prior to the Flood is cited as a prime cause of the corruption which had spread all over the world. "What was responsible for their rebelling against Me? Was it not because they sowed but did not cut down; i.e. that they gave birth but did not bury (the dead)?" The phrase "they gave birth but did not bury (the dead)" implies that these antediluvian climatic conditions also caused the longevity which prevailed prior to the Flood. "From that time on, seedtime and harvest . . ." implies that the changed climatic conditions after the Flood shortened the human life span.

The assumption that the condition and position of the earth, and hence its climate, too, were different before the Flood has been borne out by the findings of geology and physical geography. The discovery of fossils described as antediluvian indicates that the pattern of seasons and climates had been entirely different prior to the Flood and that the separation and re-formation of the land masses by means of oceans, rivers, mountains and deserts date from a later era. In fact, one comment by our Sages (Berakhoth 59a) seems to attribute the Flood as such to a disturbance in the tellurian equilibrium caused by the Creator's having altered the position of the heavenly bodies: "When the Holy One, Blessed be He, wanted to bring a Flood upon the world. He took two stars from *Kimah* (Pleiades) and so brought a Flood upon the world." But quite aside from this statement it is certain our Sages did not believe that the seasonal patterns known to us today had already been operative prior to the Flood.

° ° °

It is true that the earth went through several changes even before the Flood, but these changes never occurred in a regular order. Even before the Flood, God had repeatedly brought sudden catastrophes upon the earth in order to educate mankind. Nevertheless, during the centuries immediately preceding the Flood everything was still in a state of perpetual bloom. Men were rich and grew old; they lived in luxury; חָמָס ["wrongdoing"] proliferated, inveterate רְשָׁעִים ["evil-doers"] abounded until, finally, in view of the ever-increasing moral corruption and "wrongdoing," the merciful God had no other choice but to bring about a sudden and total destruction. This, we are told, will never happen again. All the manifold changes in terrestrial phenomena which, until then, God had effected without advance warning—the alteration between bloom and decay, life and death, Edenic spring breezes and congealing cold—were henceforth to occur in a regular, unvarying rhythm. Henceforth, seedtime and harvest, cold and heat, summer and winter, day and night were to alternate on earth in a synchronized order: לֹא יִשְׁבֹּתוּ [they were never to cease]. The position and configuration of the earth were henceforth to be such that all the times of day and all the seasons of the year, all gradations of temperature and climate would be present simultaneously in various parts of the earth. When it was daytime in one part of the world it would be nighttime in another; when it was spring in one part of the world, it would be fall in another; when it was summer in one part of the world, it would be winter in

IX

1. And God blessed Noaḥ and his sons and said to them: "Be fruitful and multiply and fill the earth. 2. And the fear and the dread of you shall be upon every animal of the earth and upon every bird of the sky; of all that moves upon the ground and of all fish of the sea; into your hand are they delivered. 3. Every moving thing that lives shall be food for you; as with the green herbs have I given you all these. 4. However, you shall not eat flesh whose blood is still in its

ט א וַיְבָרֶךְ אֱלֹהִים אֶת־נֹחַ וְאֶת־בָּנָיו וַיֹּאמֶר
לָהֶם פְּרוּ וּרְבוּ וּמִלְאוּ אֶת־הָאָרֶץ׃
ב וּמוֹרַאֲכֶם וְחִתְּכֶם יִהְיֶה עַל כָּל־חַיַּת הָאָרֶץ
וְעַל כָּל־עוֹף הַשָּׁמָיִם בְּכֹל אֲשֶׁר תִּרְמֹשׂ
הָאֲדָמָה וּבְכָל־דְּגֵי הַיָּם בְּיֶדְכֶם נִתָּנוּ׃ ג כָּל־
רֶמֶשׂ אֲשֶׁר הוּא־חַי לָכֶם יִהְיֶה לְאָכְלָה כְּיֶרֶק
עֵשֶׂב נָתַתִּי לָכֶם אֶת־כֹּל׃ ד אַךְ־בָּשָׂר בְּנַפְשׁוֹ

another; when the weather in one part of the world would be hot, it would be cold in another. These are climatic patterns which men have been able to note ever since in all the lands, regions and zones of the earth.

If we dared to skim a superficial froth, as it were, from the profound depths of Divine Providence, we could say that this rearrangement of geographic and climatic phenomena was intended as a new method of educating mankind. Ever since that time, man has been in a constant state of dependence. It is no longer sufficient for him to sow his seed only once in forty years, and his efforts to eke out a livelihood are subject to interference from climatic and metereological changes.

These changes also resulted in a great diversification among individuals, with respect to degrees of both goodness and evil.

Moreover, these more pronounced and rapid changes in the conditions of life resulted in a shortening of the human life span which, very soon after the Flood, declined to the level at which it has since remained constant. . . . This curtailment of the human life span was an effective means of making certain that evil will never again gain the upper hand for an indefinite period. Not even the mightiest of despots can wield his scepter for much longer than fifty years. The shorter human life span has served to emphasize the verity that מִפִּי עוֹלְלִים וְיֹנְקִים יִסַּדְתָּ עֹז ["Out of the mouths of children and sucklings hast Thou . . . fashioned invincible might"][13] i.e., that God can build His kingdom even upon the perceptions voiced by young children. He has founded His kingdom not upon the "cleverness" of the old but upon the purity and innocence with which children still enter the world. . . . As long as evil men were able to live on earth for seven and eight centuries, this younger, better generation never had an opportunity to come into its own. But now, having curtailed the ordinary human life span, God can have one generation die off quickly and allow a new, better generation to take its place. . . .

Only when man will return to God and thus enable the earth to regain its former state of peace will the shortened life span be prolonged once more; only when all mankind will truly pay homage to God will the Edenic existence originally ordained for the earth begin again (Isaiah 65:17, 20 f.).

° ° °

This verse contains references to six seasons, three of winter and three of summer. זֶרַע ["seedtime"] is the early winter (Tishri 15 - Kislev 15); קָצִיר ["harvest"] is the early summer (Nisan 15 — Sivan 15): קֹר ["cold"] is the late winter (Shevat 15 — Nisan 15); חֹם ["heat"] is the late summer (Av 15 — Tishri 15); קַיִץ ["summer"] is midsummer (Sivan 15 — Av 15) and חֹרֶף ["winter"] is midwinter (Kislev 15 — Shevat 15) (Baba Metzia 106b).

CHAPTER IX

3. . . . The next verse sets forth the first of those dietary laws that are binding not only upon Jews but also upon all of Noahide humanity; namely, אֵבֶר מִן הַחַי [the prohibition against eating a limb torn from a living animal].

4. אַךְ בָּשָׂר בְּנַפְשׁוֹ דָמוֹ לֹא תֹאכֵלוּ ***[However, you shall not eat flesh whose blood is still in its soul].*** Clearly בְּנַפְשׁוֹ דָמוֹ ["whose blood is still in its soul"] describes an animal that is still alive. In other words, the prohibition is against eating אֵבֶר מִן הַחַי [a limb torn from a living animal].

° ° °

. . . As long as the animal is alive, נַפְשׁוֹ [its soul] is not בְּדָמוֹ [in its blood] but דָמוֹ בְּנַפְשׁוֹ, its blood is still in its soul; its blood is encompassed and dominated by its soul. Its soul is not merged in its blood; rather, its blood is merged in its soul.

° ° °

[13]*Note to the English Translation*: Psalm 8:3. See *The Psalms*, translation and commentary by Rabbi Samson Raphael Hirsch, The Samson Raphael Hirsch Publications Society and Feldheim Publishers. pp. 50–51. [G.H.]

דָּמוֹ לֹא תֹאכֵלוּ׃ ה וְאַךְ אֶת־דִּמְכֶם
לְנַפְשֹׁתֵיכֶם אֶדְרֹשׁ מִיַּד כָּל־חַיָּה אֶדְרְשֶׁנּוּ
וּמִיַּד הָאָדָם מִיַּד אִישׁ אָחִיו אֶדְרֹשׁ אֶת־נֶפֶשׁ
הָאָדָם׃ ו שֹׁפֵךְ דַּם הָאָדָם בָּאָדָם דָּמוֹ יִשָּׁפֵךְ

soul. 5. But your blood which belongs to your souls I will demand; I will demand it from the hand of every animal. But from the hand of man, from the hand of a being that is his brother, I will demand the soul of the man. 6. Whoever sheds the blood of man, by man shall his blood be

. . . The blood represents the entire body; it is the body in its liquid state, as it were. It contains all the materials that occur in the body and, as it circulates, it deposits in each part of the body the materials which belong to, and are required by, that part. Thus, the blood involves the entire organism and every part of the body is built up by, and hence dependent upon, the blood.

However, there is one element to which the blood in turn makes the entire body subservient; namely נֶפֶשׁ [the soul]. As long as the blood is subservient to נֶפֶשׁ the body is בָּשָׂר, the "messenger" or "herald"[14] of the soul. As long as the flesh, through the medium of the blood, remains subservient to the soul and the soul uses this "red cord" to bind everything together and unto itself, the organism will retain its individuality. But once this bond of the soul has been torn asunder, the organism reverts to the elements of which it is composed. Hence דָּם is only the physical "representative"[15] of the soul. It is through the blood that the soul rules the body. It is to this relationship that the Word of God refers by בְּנַפְשׁוֹ דָמוֹ, "as long as its blood is held by its soul." נֶפֶשׁ [the soul] is the individuality whose "herald" is בָּשָׂר, the body described in terms of nerves and muscles. דָּם [the blood] is the intermediary between the two. Therefore the text does not read בָּשָׂר דָּמוֹ בְנַפְשׁוֹ but בָּשָׂר בְּנַפְשׁוֹ דָמוֹ, for בָּשָׂר [the flesh] and נֶפֶשׁ [the soul] belong together, with דָּם being only the intermediary. We may eat the body of the animal only after its soul has relinquished control over its blood. The body tissues of an animal may become part of the human body, for the animal body is passive, inert, but the soul of an animal can never, and must never, become part of the human soul.

Accordingly, the Law tells us: A limb of an animal must not be eaten if it was taken from the animal while the limb was still under the control of the animal's soul. This is not on account of the blood, for once the blood has left the animal, the blood is already dead and hence is no longer the "representative" of the animal's soul. Not so the אֵבֶר מִן הַחַי, the limb torn from the animal while the animal was still alive. As part of a living animal, the limb, at the moment it was torn from the animal's body, was still completely subservient to the animal's soul and ready to obey its commands. As a result, a limb torn from a living animal still contains the unseen impact of the animal's living soul, which must not become part of the human organism. . . .

5. . . . When God declares that "I will demand" the blood that has been turned over to the human soul, He has thereby claimed our blood as His personal property and denied us the right to be master over any blood, including our own. This implies, first of all, the prohibition against suicide. . . .

6. The judicial punishments ordained by Divine law are not motivated by deterrence or revenge (the so-called *ius talionis*), despite the fact that some have attempted to infer the former motivation from the statement in Deuteronomy 13:12 ff. "and all Yisrael shall hear it and be afraid" and the latter motivation from עַיִן תַּחַת עַיִן ["compensation of eye for eye . ."] (Exodus 21:24). The notion that punishments in Jewish penal law are based on the principle of deterrence is amply refuted by the following facts: First, Jewish penal law accepts neither circumstantial evidence nor voluntary confession. Secondly, capital punishment can be administered only בְּעֵדִים וְהַתְרָאָה, on the basis of testimony from eyewitnesses who not only personally saw the accused commit the crime but had also warned the accused at the moment he was about to commit the crime, by quoting the law to him verbatim. This is a rare coincidence which anyone who commits a premeditated crime can easily evade. Finally, in most crimes involving property, including robbery, there is no punishment, not even a fine: there is only the offender's legal obligation of תַּשְׁלוּמִין, that is, to make restitution. As a matter of fact, even the passage "and all Israel shall hear, and be afraid," which the protagonists of the deterrence theory cite in their support, is a refutation of their argument. Scripture mentions only four crimes concerning the punishment of which the Law adds: Let all the people hear it and fear to commit crimes of this kind. These crimes involve עֵדִים זוֹמְמִין [false witnesses], בֵּן סוֹרֵר וּמוֹרֶה ["a son who is disobedient and recalcitrant"—Deuteronomy 21:18 ff], זָקֵן מַמְרֵה [an elder who disregarded a decision of the Sanhedrin], and מֵסִית וּמַדִּיחַ ["a seducer and instigator"].

[14]*Note to the English translation*: בָּשָׂר is flesh; לְבַשֵּׂר is "to herald" and בְּשׂוֹרָה is "message." [G.H.]

[15]*Note to the English translation*: דמה is "to resemble"; דְּמוּת is "likeness" or "image." [G.H.]

shed, for in the image of God made He man.
7. And you, be fruitful and multiply, diversify upon the earth and multiply upon

כִּי בְּצֶלֶם אֱלֹהִים עָשָׂה אֶת־הָאָדָם: ז וְאַתֶּם פְּרוּ וּרְבוּ שִׁרְצוּ בָאָרֶץ וּרְבוּ־בָהּ: ס חמישי

However, precisely these four offenses and the punishment prescribed for them seem to be anomalous. These offenses *per se*, seen in terms of their immediate effects, do not seem as execrable as they are made to appear. A מֵסִית [instigator] may merely have made an oral effort at seduction and his attempt may not have been successful. An עֵד זוֹמֵם need not necessarily have caused the death of the accused by his testimony. A זָקֵן מַמְרֵה, though guilty of an offense by his refusal to abide by the majority opinion of the Great Sanhedrin, may actually be in the right as far as his own opinion on the matter under dispute is concerned. And the בֵּן סוֹרֵר וּמוֹרֶה ["the disobedient and recalcitrant son"] is subject to the death penalty only עַל שֵׁם סוֹפוֹ [because of the possible effects of his offense]. Indeed, those guilty of any of the four offenses mentioned above are all subject to the death penalty only עַל שֵׁם סוֹפָן, in consideration of the far-reaching, pernicious effects that could result from their offense, even though, superficially seen, the misdemeanor in itself seems too light to merit the extreme penalty. But this is precisely the reason why the Law regards it as important that the entire people should be told that someone has been executed for having committed one of these particular offenses. Deterrence is the motivation not for the punishment *per se* but for the publicity given to the offense. (This is the subject of a disagreement between Rabbi Akiba and Rabbi Judah in Sanhedrin 89a). The fact that the Law requires such publicity only in the case of these four offenses proves that deterrence is generally not the motivation for punishments in Jewish Law (Sanhedrin 89a).

Similarly, the principle of "eye for eye," etc., set forth in Jewish law does not mean that punishment in Jewish law is motivated by the *ius talionis*. Tradition teaches us that this statement [in the twenty-first chapter of the Book of Exodus] merely demands the assessment of an appropriate financial indemnity, and at the same time it points out that if the law were to be interpreted literally, it could not even be enforced in an equitable manner. It is clear from the Scriptural text itself that "an eye for an eye" can mean only an adequate assessment of financial compensation. For Exodus 21:24, the verse containing the "eye for an eye" statement, is preceded by the statement (Verse 19) that שִׁבְתּוֹ יִתֵּן וְרַפֹּא יְרַפֵּא [i.e., that the victim is to receive financial compensation for the loss of his time and for the medical care he requires].

The idea expressed by the "eye for an eye" statement is the great principle that underlies the whole of Jewish penal law: A man may demand for himself only such rights as he is willing to concede also to others. If he does not respect the rights of others he forfeits the right to assert his own rights. By "making good" for the injury he has caused, he rehabilitates himself. He can do so either by accepting punishment or by making restitution, or, if this should not be feasible, by acknowledging the wrong he has done. Our Sages view every punishment as כַּפָּרָה, atonement; not "atonement for the injury done to justice" but the offender's personal act of atonement for what he has done. Even a criminal who has suffered the death penalty has a future that extends beyond the brief span of his life on earth. Having forfeited his own earthly existence in order to redress the injury he has caused, he will enter into a new existence in a regained state of purity.

כִּי בְּצֶלֶם אֱלֹקִים עָשָׂה אֶת הָאָדָם ***[for in the image of God made He man].*** This sentence, attesting to the higher, godly dignity of the human body and of human life, seems to hold the motivation for all the legal provisions cited here regarding the assignment of the animal world as food for man, the prohibition against absorbing the animal soul into the human body (אֵבֶר מִן הַחַי), the subordination of man's physical existence to God, and God's role as defender of that existence against any attack.

7. שִׁרְצוּ בָאָרֶץ וּרְבוּ בָהּ ***[diversify upon the earth and multiply upon it].*** This most significant addendum to the mission of development assigned to the Noahide world concludes the reconstitution of mankind. . . . Noahide mankind has been given the mission to spread over the entire world and, under the most diverse conditions and influences, to become men in the true sense of the word and to develop the character traits common among men. This implies a multiplying and a diversification which, as we have already seen, was God's new plan for the education of mankind in order to avert the need for total catastrophes in the future. . . .

Man thinks he is master over the earth, but in reality he himself is affected in many respects — in his thinking, his feelings, his intellect and his speech — by the soil that supports and surrounds him. This diversity in man's environment is part of the general plan. Man can be "man," he can be happy and develop all his human qualities, wherever he may live. Only no man may judge others by his *own* standards. This is why the account of man's reconstitution concludes with the command: Diversify and multiply *upon* the earth; do this *upon* the earth, *through* the earth, *with* the earth, etc.

it."   8. And God said to Noaḥ and to his sons with him: 9. "And as for Me, lo! I will establish My covenant with you and with your descendants after you,   10. and with every living soul that is with you, of the bird, of cattle, and of every animal upon the earth with you, of all that have gone forth from the ark, down to every living creature of the earth: 11. I will maintain My covenant with you that never again shall all flesh be destroyed by the waters of the Unsoulment and never again shall Unsoulment come to destroy the earth."   12. And God said: "This is the sign of the covenant which I set between Myself and you, and every living soul that is with you, for the generations of all time: 13. My bow! I have set it in the cloud and it shall now be for a sign of the covenant between Me and the earth,   14. so that, whenever I bring clouds over the earth and the bow appears in the cloud,   15. I will remember My covenant which is between Me and you and every living soul that is in all flesh, and

ח וַיֹּאמֶר אֱלֹהִים אֶל־נֹחַ וְאֶל־בָּנָיו אִתּוֹ
לֵאמֹר: ט וַאֲנִי הִנְנִי מֵקִים אֶת־בְּרִיתִי אִתְּכֶם
וְאֶת־זַרְעֲכֶם אַחֲרֵיכֶם: י וְאֵת כָּל־נֶפֶשׁ הַחַיָּה
אֲשֶׁר אִתְּכֶם בָּעוֹף בַּבְּהֵמָה וּבְכָל־חַיַּת הָאָרֶץ
אִתְּכֶם מִכֹּל יֹצְאֵי הַתֵּבָה לְכֹל חַיַּת הָאָרֶץ:
יא וַהֲקִמֹתִי אֶת־בְּרִיתִי אִתְּכֶם וְלֹא־יִכָּרֵת
כָּל־בָּשָׂר עוֹד מִמֵּי הַמַּבּוּל וְלֹא־יִהְיֶה עוֹד
מַבּוּל לְשַׁחֵת הָאָרֶץ: יב וַיֹּאמֶר אֱלֹהִים זֹאת
אוֹת־הַבְּרִית אֲשֶׁר־אֲנִי נֹתֵן בֵּינִי וּבֵינֵיכֶם וּבֵין
כָּל־נֶפֶשׁ חַיָּה אֲשֶׁר אִתְּכֶם לְדֹרֹת עוֹלָם:
יג אֶת־קַשְׁתִּי נָתַתִּי בֶּעָנָן וְהָיְתָה לְאוֹת בְּרִית
בֵּינִי וּבֵין הָאָרֶץ: יד וְהָיָה בְּעַנְנִי עָנָן עַל־
הָאָרֶץ וְנִרְאֲתָה הַקֶּשֶׁת בֶּעָנָן: טו וְזָכַרְתִּי אֶת־
בְּרִיתִי אֲשֶׁר בֵּינִי וּבֵינֵיכֶם וּבֵין כָּל־נֶפֶשׁ חַיָּה

13. *My bow! I have set it in the cloud.* It is not necessary to assume that there had been no rainbows before and to attribute the rainbow to atmospheric changes that occurred following the Flood. Just as God showed Abraham the star-studded sky and said to him "so shall your seed be" (Genesis 15:5), just as He showed Moses and Aaron the New Moon and, with the words "This renewal of the moon shall be for you . . ." (Exodus 12:2), consecrated an already existing celestial phenomenon as a symbol of Israel's spiritual and moral regeneration, and just as the seasons of the year were already in existence when God appointed them as historic and instructive memorials for Israel, so, too, the rainbow might already have been a well-known phenomenon upon the firmament when God named it as the sign of His covenant with mankind. Hence this verse may be construed as follows: Here is My bow which I placed in the clouds long ago. From now on it shall be the symbol of the covenant between Myself and yourselves.

15. We have been told about the sign and its significance. This is not subject to doubt. It only remains for us to ascertain the connection between this sign and its stated significance. Many interpretations of the rainbow have been advanced. [Some see the rainbow as] a reversed weapon, a bow with its string turned toward

the earth; hence, as a symbol of peace, implying that no more arrows will be shot from heaven at the earth. [Others perceive it] as an arc linking the earth with the sky; hence, as a bond between heaven and earth. [Still others point out that] the rainbow is the product of an interaction between light and water; thus, amidst clouds that are capable of dispensing either life or death, we behold the presence of light, a reminder that even in the midst of ominous wrath God's life-preserving mercy still endures.

But perhaps more than all the suggestions given above, the aspect that most closely approximates the rainbow's symbolic significance is the sight of the spectrum in the sky. We already have been told repeatedly that no matter what the nuances of mankind's future development, God will never again decree the destruction of the human race; indeed, these very nuances and varieties in the human personality will become the basis for mankind's future education. Now is not the rainbow simply one unified, complete ray of light in its purest form, broken up into seven colors? These colors range from the red ray, which is closest to the light, to the violet which, farthest from the light, merges into darkness. Yet they all represent light and, together, they form one complete white ray. Might this not be interpreted as expressing a thought as follows: Consider the whole infinite variety of living things,

water shall never again become an Unsoulment to destroy all flesh. 16. The bow
shall be in the cloud; I will see it and I will
remember the everlasting covenant between God and every living soul that is in all
flesh upon the earth." 17. And God said
to Noaḥ: "This is the sign of the covenant
which I have established between Myself
and all flesh that is upon the earth."
18. The sons of Noaḥ who came out of
the ark were Shem, Ḥam and Yapheth, and
Ḥam is the father of Canaan. 19. These
three were the sons of Noaḥ and from these
all the earth branched out. 20. And Noaḥ
began to be the man of the soil, and he
planted a vineyard. 21. And he drank of
the wine and became drunk, and he uncovered himself within his tent. 22. And
Ḥam, the father of Canaan, saw his father's
nakedness and told his two brothers outside.
23. And Shem and Yapheth took the
garment and laid it upon both their shoulders and, walking backward, covered their
father's nakedness; their faces were turned
backward and they did not see their father's
nakedness. 24. When Noaḥ awoke from

בְּכָל־בָּשָׂר וְלֹא־יִהְיֶה עוֹד הַמַּיִם לְמַבּוּל
לְשַׁחֵת כָּל־בָּשָׂר׃ טז וְהָיְתָה הַקֶּשֶׁת בֶּעָנָן
וּרְאִיתִיהָ לִזְכֹּר בְּרִית עוֹלָם בֵּין אֱלֹהִים וּבֵין
כָּל־נֶפֶשׁ חַיָּה בְּכָל־בָּשָׂר אֲשֶׁר עַל־הָאָרֶץ׃
יז וַיֹּאמֶר אֱלֹהִים אֶל־נֹחַ זֹאת אוֹת־הַבְּרִית
אֲשֶׁר הֲקִמֹתִי בֵּינִי וּבֵין כָּל־בָּשָׂר אֲשֶׁר עַל־
הָאָרֶץ׃ פ ששי יח וַיִּהְיוּ בְנֵי־נֹחַ הַיֹּצְאִים מִן־
הַתֵּבָה שֵׁם וְחָם וָיָפֶת וְחָם הוּא אֲבִי כְנָעַן׃
יט שְׁלֹשָׁה אֵלֶּה בְּנֵי־נֹחַ וּמֵאֵלֶּה נָפְצָה כָל־
הָאָרֶץ׃ כ וַיָּחֶל נֹחַ אִישׁ הָאֲדָמָה וַיִּטַּע כָּרֶם׃
כא וַיֵּשְׁתְּ מִן־הַיַּיִן וַיִּשְׁכָּר וַיִּתְגַּל בְּתוֹךְ אָהֳלֹה׃
כב וַיַּרְא חָם אֲבִי כְנַעַן אֵת עֶרְוַת אָבִיו וַיַּגֵּד
לִשְׁנֵי־אֶחָיו בַּחוּץ׃ כג וַיִּקַּח שֵׁם וָיֶפֶת אֶת־
הַשִּׂמְלָה וַיָּשִׂימוּ עַל־שְׁכֶם שְׁנֵיהֶם וַיֵּלְכוּ
אֲחֹרַנִּית וַיְכַסּוּ אֵת עֶרְוַת אֲבִיהֶם וּפְנֵיהֶם
אֲחֹרַנִּית וְעֶרְוַת אֲבִיהֶם לֹא רָאוּ׃ כד וַיִּיקֶץ נֹחַ

from Adam, the "red one,"[16] closest to God, to the most obscure form of life, the humblest worm, "every living soul that is in all flesh," and especially the whole spectrum of nuances in which the human element will henceforth be manifest among men, from the individual of the highest spiritual refinement to the one in whom there is only a faint, barely discernible glimmer of the Divine: God unites them all in one common bond of peace. They are all fragments of one life, all refracted emanations of the one Divine Spirit. Would this not imply that even he who is the last, the most obscure, the most distant from God, is still indeed a "son of light?" . . .

18. We have already pointed out the significance of the fact that Shem, Ḥam and Japheth were among those saved in the Ark. We have seen how important it was that, despite the differences in character which were manifest among these three even before the Flood, each of them was found worthy of being saved along with Noah. Accordingly, it is clear that such differences in character even when, in some national entities, they border on degeneration, should not keep men from being, and becoming, "human." They were all יוֹצְאֵי תֵּבָה [they had all been saved and had come out of the ark]. They were all צֶלֶם אֱלֹקִים [created in the likeness of God] and there is no man who could say to another, "You are less of a human being than I am; in fact, you cannot even be classed as a 'man.'" Because of its importance this idea is reiterated in the early part of the present chapter. . . .

19. The text repeats that all these three were the sons of one father—what is more, of a father who was צַדִּיק תָּמִים [a righteous man and morally pure]—and yet they were so different from one another. It was from these three prototypes that all the world branched out. All the variations and individualities into which mankind was henceforth to be "split up" can be traced back to these three basic character types.

24. Any sin that children commit against their parents will be punished by the manner in which their own children, in turn, will deal with them. The same rule applies to generations taken as a whole. The younger generation must stand reverently at the grave of the one that preceded it; it must take a garment, as it were, and cover the nakedness, the weakness, of its parent generation and at the same time emulate all that was noble, great and true in its forebears, adopting

[16]*Note to the English translation*: See commentary on Genesis 1:26. [G.H.]

מִיֵּינ֑וֹ וַיֵּ֕דַע אֵ֛ת אֲשֶׁר־עָ֥שָׂה ל֖וֹ בְּנ֥וֹ הַקָּטָֽן׃
כה וַיֹּ֖אמֶר אָר֣וּר כְּנָ֑עַן עֶ֥בֶד עֲבָדִ֖ים יִֽהְיֶ֥ה
לְאֶחָֽיו׃ כו וַיֹּ֕אמֶר בָּר֥וּךְ יְהוָ֖ה אֱלֹ֣הֵי שֵׁ֑ם וִיהִ֥י
כְנַ֖עַן עֶ֥בֶד לָֽמוֹ׃ כז יַ֤פְתְּ אֱלֹהִים֙ לְיֶ֔פֶת וְיִשְׁכֹּ֖ן

his wine, he learned what his youngest son had done to him, 25. and he said: "Cursed be Canaan; he shall be a servant of servants to his brothers." 26. And he said: "Blessed be *God*, the God of Shem; may Canaan become their servant. 27. God will open the emotions [of men] to Yapheth but He will dwell in the tents of

these good qualities as a precious heritage upon which to continue building its own life. Only then will the generations develop like a tree that keeps sprouting new blossoms. But if the new generation, like Ḥam, gloats over the "nakedness" of its ancestors; if it takes the shortcomings of its forebears as license to deride their great spiritual traditions; if the future generation scornfully breaks its bond with the past, then its future, too, will be only a dream and, just as they jeered at the memory of their forefathers, so, too, their own descendants will mock at them in their turn. *Ḥam will always be the father of Canaan.*

25, 26, 27. What is said in these verses may well express the most profound and far-reaching vision of the future that God ever permitted a mortal to behold or to utter. The entire history of mankind—beginning, end and middle—is summarized in these three verses.

We have already indicated our belief that the names of Noah's sons point to their personal character traits as well as to the basic traits of the national entities that will be descended from them. These names indicate the quality that would predominate in them—spiritual, physical or emotional. Here we see Shem, Ḥam and Japheth in a dual role: as individuals and as the founders of future national entities.

° ° °

26. . . . We will return later to the meaning of וִיהִי כְנַעַן עֶבֶד לָמוֹ. Here we will note only this: The fact that לָמוֹ, a plural form, is used in this verse indicates that both Shem and Canaan [who was envisioned as Shem's servant] were viewed here not as individuals but in terms of the nations that would be descended from them.

27. . . . We, who, unlike Noah, were not placed at the very beginning of history but still can look back upon a past of four thousand years, should find it easy to view, in retrospect, the impact of these divergent forces on historical personalities and entities.

The nations that have created the greatest stir in world history are those dominated by חָם [Ḥam], by that sensuality which harnesses minds and emotions to its chariot and will permit the spirit to function only as a vehicle for the physical. These are the nations that conquer and destroy, and relish what they have taken. We have seen on the proscenium of history nations representing brute force, sensuality and bestiality, almost to the exclusion of all else.

But we have also seen nations employing their energies on behalf of beauty, nations characterized by their cultivation of the arts and of esthetics. They are aware that there is a higher ideal toward which man must strive to rise from his crude state. This awareness has taught them to cloak raw physical appetites in a garb of elegance. Guided by their notions of grace and beauty, they then engage also in such intellectual and spiritual activities as poetry, music and the fine arts. All these nations that cultivate pursuits calculated to appeal to the emotions represent the character of יֶפֶת [Japheth].

However, the utilization of esthetics for the education of the uncultured is not the greatest good. A culture that affords man an ever-increasing measure of self-satisfaction as the sole standard by which to measure his life's activities but gives him no ideal outside himself, a culture that shines forth in its own light as the sole criterion for his conduct, cannot endure. Only an ideal capable of elevating man's spirit to a knowledge—and his emotions to an acknowledgement—of what is good and true can lead him toward the lofty plane of his true calling. Those nations that have contributed their share to the symposium of mankind by training the human mind and spirit to recognize truth can be said to have worked for human welfare in the spirit of Shem. . . .

יִשְׁכֹּן *[He will dwell.]* [One of the characteristic concepts] of Judaism is that of שְׁכִינָה [Shekhinah] which we read here as having been first uttered by the progenitor of the new human race. Other religions teach what man must do in order to come near to God in the *next* world. Judaism teaches us what we must do in order that God may come to us even in *this* world. Judaism teaches that עִיקַר שְׁכִינָה בַּתַּחְתּוֹנִים, God seeks, first of all, to dwell on earth among men; He says to man: וְעָשׂוּ לִי מִקְדָּשׁ וְשָׁכַנְתִּי בְּתוֹכָם ["They shall make Me a sanctuary and then I shall dwell in their midst"—Exodus 25:8]; let them make of their lives on earth a sanctuary to Me, and then I shall dwell in their midst. The task of paving the way for an age when the Kingdom of God will begin again not just in heaven but here on earth is to be the mission of Israel, the flower of the line of Shem, and this is the purpose of the Law given to Israel by God, That, too, is why the promises set

Shem, and may Canaan be a servant to them." 28. Noaḥ lived after the Unsoulment for [another] 350 years. 29. When all the days of Noaḥ were 950 years, he died.

X 1. And these are the descendants of the sons of Noaḥ — Shem, Ḥam and Yapheth. Children were born to them after the Unsoulment. 2. The sons of Yapheth: Gomer, and Magog, and Madai, and Yavan, and Tubal, and Meshekh and Tiras. 3. The sons of Gomer: Ashkenaz, and Riphath and Togarmah. 4. The sons of Yavan: Elisha, and Tarshish, Kittim and Dodanim. 5. From these the groups of nations branched out in their lands, each to its dialect, their families in their nations. 6. And the sons of Ḥam: Cush, and Mitzrayim, and Put and Canaan. 7. The sons of Cush: Seba, and Ḥavilah, and Sabtah, and Raamah and Sabtekha; and

בְּאָהֳלֵי־שֵׁם וִיהִי כְנַעַן עֶבֶד לָמוֹ: כח וַיְחִי־נֹחַ
אַחַר הַמַּבּוּל שְׁלֹשׁ מֵאוֹת שָׁנָה וַחֲמִשִּׁים שָׁנָה:
כט וַיְהִי כָּל־יְמֵי־נֹחַ תְּשַׁע מֵאוֹת שָׁנָה
וַחֲמִשִּׁים שָׁנָה וַיָּמֹת: פ י א וְאֵלֶּה תּוֹלְדֹת
בְּנֵי־נֹחַ שֵׁם חָם וָיָפֶת וַיִּוָּלְדוּ לָהֶם בָּנִים אַחַר
הַמַּבּוּל: ב בְּנֵי יֶפֶת גֹּמֶר וּמָגוֹג וּמָדַי וְיָוָן
וְתֻבָל וּמֶשֶׁךְ וְתִירָס: ג וּבְנֵי גֹּמֶר אַשְׁכְּנַז
וְרִיפַת וְתֹגַרְמָה: ד וּבְנֵי יָוָן אֱלִישָׁה וְתַרְשִׁישׁ
כִּתִּים וְדֹדָנִים: ה מֵאֵלֶּה נִפְרְדוּ אִיֵּי הַגּוֹיִם
בְּאַרְצֹתָם אִישׁ לִלְשֹׁנוֹ לְמִשְׁפְּחֹתָם בְּגוֹיֵהֶם:
ו וּבְנֵי חָם כּוּשׁ וּמִצְרַיִם וּפוּט וּכְנָעַן: ז וּבְנֵי
כוּשׁ סְבָא וַחֲוִילָה וְסַבְתָּה וְרַעְמָה וְסַבְתְּכָא

forth in this Divine Law are applicable to our lives on earth. . . . It is noteworthy that שכן denotes not only "dwelling" but also the state of being a "neighbor." Herein lies the most sublime social ideal. *In Judaism "to dwell" means to be a neighbor.* When a Jewish person chooses a dwelling place on earth he must allow his fellow man space and domain for a dwelling place also. Without his neighbor, his own existence is not a true שכן, a truly human way of living. The Jew says to his neighbor, "True, this place is narrow for me; nevertheless, I will dwell there if you will join me" (Isaiah 49:20). This conception of שְׁכִינָה [in the sense of dwelling as a neighbor] is applied also to the "dwelling" of God's glory among men on earth. God is to dwell in intimate proximity to man. However, He does not encroach in any manner upon the human sphere; He dwells among men always under the assumption that man on earth should develop entirely in accordance with his own free will. . . . The Divine becomes the שָׁכֵן [neighbor] of man, and man the שָׁכֵן of the Divine, but they never merge into one another. . . .

CHAPTER X

2. The sons of Japheth are listed first, and of these we are told the additional branches only in the case of Gomer and Javan. The latter are the most remarkable representatives of the Japheth character type and seem to typify the character of most of the peoples living in areas now known as Europe and western Asia.

5. . . . The text reads אִישׁ לִלְשֹׁנוֹ ["each *to* its dialect"], not אִישׁ בִּלְשֹׁנוֹ ["each *in* its dialect"]. The differentiation of dialects was not the cause, but the effect, of their "branching out." As a result of their numerical increase they branched out into various regions and under the impact of the soil [and the other physical realities] in [and with] which they lived, their speech underwent certain modifications. There appears to be a clear-cut difference between שָׂפָה, the term used in the account of the next development,[17] and לָשׁוֹן, the term used in the present chapter. שָׂפָה denotes "language," as in German, French, etc., while לָשׁוֹן refers to manner of speech, pronunciation or "dialect."

. . . As the descendants of Noah proliferated, it was only natural that they should spread out. They became אִיִּים [islands], spatially separated from one another. The one אֶרֶץ ["earth" or "land"] was divided into אֲרָצוֹת ["many lands"]; the one גּוֹי ["nation"] was divided into many diverse national entities, and so, since the personality of the individual can be influenced and changed by external conditions, the one language initially spoken by mankind "branched out" into various dialects. Thus the national entities separated from one another, each moving לִלְשֹׁנוֹ "to its [own] dialect." But while this differentiation of dialects acted as a means of separation to the outside and resulted in the formation of various גּוֹיִם ["nations"], it functioned internally as a strong bond, as the link between מִשְׁפְּחֹתָם בְּגוֹיֵהֶם "their families in their nations." If there are no separate entities, there can be no union. . . .

[17]*Note to the English translation*: The building of the Tower of Babel (Chapter 11). [G.H.]

וּבְנֵי רַעְמָה שְׁבָא וּדְדָן׃ ח וְכוּשׁ יָלַד אֶת־
נִמְרֹד הוּא הֵחֵל לִהְיוֹת גִּבֹּר בָּאָרֶץ׃ ט הוּא־
הָיָה גִבֹּר־צַיִד לִפְנֵי יְהוָה עַל־כֵּן יֵאָמַר כְּנִמְרֹד
גִּבּוֹר צַיִד לִפְנֵי יְהוָה׃ י וַתְּהִי רֵאשִׁית
מַמְלַכְתּוֹ בָּבֶל וְאֶרֶךְ וְאַכַּד וְכַלְנֵה בְּאֶרֶץ
שִׁנְעָר׃ יא מִן־הָאָרֶץ הַהִוא יָצָא אַשּׁוּר וַיִּבֶן
אֶת־נִינְוֵה וְאֶת־רְחֹבֹת עִיר וְאֶת־כָּלַח׃
יב וְאֶת־רֶסֶן בֵּין נִינְוֵה וּבֵין כָּלַח הִוא הָעִיר
הַגְּדֹלָה׃ יג וּמִצְרַיִם יָלַד אֶת־לוּדִים וְאֶת־
עֲנָמִים וְאֶת־לְהָבִים וְאֶת־נַפְתֻּחִים׃ יד וְאֶת־
פַּתְרֻסִים וְאֶת־כַּסְלֻחִים אֲשֶׁר יָצְאוּ מִשָּׁם
פְּלִשְׁתִּים וְאֶת־כַּפְתֹּרִים׃ ס טו וּכְנַעַן יָלַד אֶת־
צִידֹן בְּכֹרוֹ וְאֶת־חֵת׃ טז וְאֶת־הַיְבוּסִי וְאֶת־
הָאֱמֹרִי וְאֵת הַגִּרְגָּשִׁי׃ יז וְאֶת־הַחִוִּי וְאֶת־
הָעַרְקִי וְאֶת־הַסִּינִי׃ יח וְאֶת־הָאַרְוָדִי וְאֶת־
הַצְּמָרִי וְאֶת־הַחֲמָתִי וְאַחַר נָפֹצוּ מִשְׁפְּחוֹת
הַכְּנַעֲנִי׃ יט וַיְהִי גְּבוּל הַכְּנַעֲנִי מִצִּידֹן בֹּאֲכָה
גְרָרָה עַד־עַזָּה בֹּאֲכָה סְדֹמָה וַעֲמֹרָה וְאַדְמָה
וּצְבֹיִם (וצבוים קרי) עַד־לָשַׁע׃ כ אֵלֶּה בְנֵי־חָם
לְמִשְׁפְּחֹתָם לִלְשֹׁנֹתָם בְּאַרְצֹתָם בְּגוֹיֵהֶם׃ ס

the sons of Raamah: Sheba and Dedan.
8. Cush begot Nimrod; he began to be a
hero upon the earth. 9. He was a crafty
hero before *God*; hence the saying: Like
Nimrod, a crafty hero before *God*.
10. The beginning of his kingship was
Babel, and Erekh, and Akkad and Calneh,
in the land of Shinar. 11. Out of that
land Asshur went forth and built Nineveh,
and Rehoboth-ir and Calah, 12. and
Resen between Nineveh and Calah; that is
the great city. 13. Mitzrayim begot the
Ludim, the Anamim, the Lehabim and
the Naphtuhim, 14. the Pathrusim and
the Casluhim, whence the Philistines came
forth, and the Caphtorim. 15. Canaan
begot Tzidon, his first-born, and Heth;
16. the Yebusite[s], the Emorite[s] and
the Girgashite[s]; 17. the Hivvite[s],
the Arkite[s] and the Sinite[s]; 18. the
Arvadite[s], the Tzemarite[s] and the
Hamathite[s]; and afterwards, the families
of the Canaanite[s] spread out even more.
19. The border of the Canaanite[s]
extended from Tzidon toward Gerar until
Gaza; toward Sodom, Gomorrah, Admah
and Zeboiim until Lasha. 20. These are
the sons of Ham according to their families,
according to their dialects, in their lands,

8. . . . There had been גִּבּוֹרִים ["mighty ones, heroes"] even before Nimrod. We need only recall the *nephilim* (Genesis 6:4). But Nimrod began לִהְיוֹת גִּבּוֹר בָּאָרֶץ ["to be a hero upon the earth"]; he "began" to center his whole character, his vocation, his livelihood and his view of life around the idea of being a גִּבּוֹר. He was the first to introduce this mentality among the nations, which have emulated him ever since. . . .

9. . . . Although the term צַיִד [lit. "hunter"] is usually employed to denote a hunter of animals, צוד ["prey"] is frequently used to refer to the hunting and entrapment of human beings. Cf. חָמַד רָשָׁע מְצוֹד רָעִים ["The wicked desires the prey of evil men"] (Proverbs 12:12), *et al.* . . .

° ° °

גִּבּוֹר צַיִד לִפְנֵי ה׳ ***[a crafty hero before*** **God*****]***. The expression לִפְנֵי ה׳ ["before *God*"] is never used in the Bible to denote anything done against the will of God but only in connection with acts performed expressly in order to carry out His will. . . . Nimrod began to oppress his fellow men "in the name of God." He was the first to misuse the name of God, to surround brute force with the halo of Divine approval, or, rather, to demand the recognition of his might "in the name of God." In later antiquity this mentality was to assume extravagant dimensions: kings not only regarded themselves as rulers in the name of God, and "Nimrods" not only adorned themselves with the reflection of Divine majesty, but they assumed divine status themselves. Thus the descendants of Ham in particular produced pharaohs who prostrated themselves before their own images. In this way Nimrod became the prototype for all those dynastic rulers who craftily crowned themselves with the halo of pseudo-sanctity and whose power, politics and hypocrisy were characterized by the saying כְּנִמְרֹד גִּבּוֹר צַיִד לִפְנֵי ה׳ ["Like Nimrod, a crafty hero before *God*"].

11. . . . While Nimrod saw his greatness in terms of his despotic rule, Asshur measured his greatness in terms of his achievements in building cities and constructing highways leading to the cities. (*Rehoboth-ir*; [literally: "highways to the city"]). Nimrod was a conqueror; Asshur, a builder . . .

in their nations.   21. Descendants were born also to Shem, father of all the sons of Eber, the brother of Yapheth, the elder. 22. The sons of Shem: Elam and Asshur, Arpakhshad, Lud and Aram.   23. The sons of Aram: Utz, Ḥul, Gether and Mash.   24. Arpakhshad begot Shelaḥ, and Shelaḥ begot Eber.   25. Two sons were born to Eber; the name of the one was Peleg, for in his days the earth was divided° and his brother's name was Yoktan. 26. Yoktan begot Almodad and Sheleph, Ḥatzarmaveth and Yeraḥ;   27. Hadoram, Uzal and Diklah;   28. Obal, Abimael and Sheba; 29. Ophir, Ḥavilah and Yobab; all these were the sons of Yoktan.   30. Their dwelling place was from Mesha toward Sephar, to the mountains of the east. 31. These are the sons of Shem according to their families, according to their dialects, in their lands, according to their nations. 32. These are the families of the sons of Noaḥ according to their generations in their nations; and from these the nations branched out over the earth after the Unsoulment.

XI 1. The whole earth was of one language and of uniform words. 2. And it came to pass as they migrated from the east, that they found a plain in the

°*Note to the English translation*: פֶּלֶג = "part" or "section." [G.H.]

כא וּלְשֵׁם יֻלַּד גַּם־הוּא אֲבִי כָּל־בְּנֵי־עֵבֶר אֲחִי יֶפֶת הַגָּדוֹל: כב בְּנֵי שֵׁם עֵילָם וְאַשּׁוּר וְאַרְפַּכְשַׁד וְלוּד וַאֲרָם: כג וּבְנֵי אֲרָם עוּץ וְחוּל וְגֶתֶר וָמַשׁ: כד וְאַרְפַּכְשַׁד יָלַד אֶת־שָׁלַח וְשֶׁלַח יָלַד אֶת־עֵבֶר: כה וּלְעֵבֶר יֻלַּד שְׁנֵי בָנִים שֵׁם הָאֶחָד פֶּלֶג כִּי בְיָמָיו נִפְלְגָה הָאָרֶץ וְשֵׁם אָחִיו יָקְטָן: כו וְיָקְטָן יָלַד אֶת־אַלְמוֹדָד וְאֶת־שָׁלֶף וְאֶת־חֲצַרְמָוֶת וְאֶת־יָרַח: כז וְאֶת־הֲדוֹרָם וְאֶת־אוּזָל וְאֶת־דִּקְלָה: כח וְאֶת־עוֹבָל וְאֶת־אֲבִימָאֵל וְאֶת־שְׁבָא: כט וְאֶת־אוֹפִר וְאֶת־חֲוִילָה וְאֶת־יוֹבָב כָּל־אֵלֶּה בְּנֵי יָקְטָן: ל וַיְהִי מוֹשָׁבָם מִמֵּשָׁא בֹּאֲכָה סְפָרָה הַר הַקֶּדֶם: לא אֵלֶּה בְנֵי־שֵׁם לְמִשְׁפְּחֹתָם לִלְשֹׁנֹתָם בְּאַרְצֹתָם לְגוֹיֵהֶם: לב אֵלֶּה מִשְׁפְּחֹת בְּנֵי־נֹחַ לְתוֹלְדֹתָם בְּגוֹיֵהֶם וּמֵאֵלֶּה נִפְרְדוּ הַגּוֹיִם בָּאָרֶץ אַחַר הַמַּבּוּל: פ שביעי יא א וַיְהִי כָל־הָאָרֶץ שָׂפָה אֶחָת וּדְבָרִים אֲחָדִים: ב וַיְהִי בְּנָסְעָם מִקֶּדֶם וַיִּמְצְאוּ בִקְעָה בְּאֶרֶץ שִׁנְעָר

21. . . . Japheth was the elder brother [of Shem] and, in accordance with his mission, acted as Shem's herald, as it were, to make the hearts of men receptive to the teachings of Shem. It was only natural that a long time would pass before Shem was recognized as *the* גָּדוֹל ["great scholar"][18] on earth. The hearts of men are readily receptive to Japhethian arts and sciences. But as for the serene light which Shem was to carry through the world, the truth which he was to disseminate, the ideal which one must either fulfill or reject (in this respect there can be no middle course)—such concepts may have to go unrecognized for a long time to come.

[18]*Note to the English translation*: The reference is to the school of Torah conducted by Shem and his great-grandson Eber. [G.H.]

CHAPTER XI

1. . . . Almost 400 years elapsed between the Flood and the דּוֹר הַפְּלַגָּה [the generation in which "the earth was divided"], the generation in which the natural proliferation of mankind took place and the resulting modifications in dialects had ample time to evolve. Nevertheless, the language of men was still שָׂפָה אֶחָת ["one language"]; all men still spoke the same language.

. . . שָׂפָה אֶחָת *[one language]* refers to the phonetic sameness of language based on organic uniformity. דְּבָרִים אֲחָדִים ["uniform words"] refers to the uniformity in the formation of words and sentences resulting from attitudes shared in common toward things and their interrelationships. . . . In other words, the human race was still united by complete harmony, physical and spiritual, for good and for evil.

land of Shinar and settled there. 3. And they said to one another: "Come, give! Let us make bricks and burn whatever there is, for a fire;" and the bricks served them as stone and the mortar served them as clay. 4. And they said: "Come, give! Let us build ourselves a city and a tower whose

וַיֵּשְׁבוּ שָׁם: ג וַיֹּאמְרוּ אִישׁ אֶל־רֵעֵהוּ הָבָה נִלְבְּנָה לְבֵנִים וְנִשְׂרְפָה לִשְׂרֵפָה וַתְּהִי לָהֶם הַלְּבֵנָה לְאָבֶן וְהַחֵמָר הָיָה לָהֶם לַחֹמֶר:
ד וַיֹּאמְרוּ הָבָה | נִבְנֶה־לָּנוּ עִיר וּמִגְדָּל וְרֹאשׁוֹ

3. . . . הָבָה *[Come, give!]* the imperative of יהב ["give"], "give of yourself," "give of your strength." . . .

In studying this text, it is important to give attention to every detail. For while, as our Sages have noted, in the case of the Flood, the evil of which the דור המבול [the generation which lived at that time] was guilty is clearly specified, we are not explicitly told what the דור הפלגה [the generation in which the earth was divided] did to incur God's displeasure.

They "found a plain" where there was no construction material whatsoever. They wanted to settle there permanently; they wanted to see whether they might not be able to create something of their own making (this is implied by the word הָבָה). They wanted to produce "man-made" stone for building. But just as there was no construction material, so, too, there was not enough fuel to bake large quantities of bricks; hence נִשְׂרְפָה לִשְׂרֵפָה, "let us burn whatever there is." Sentences such as this one, where the object is not explicitly stated, imply a sweeping generalization. The people said, "Let us burn whatever there is, whatever we can find." And so they used bricks as stones, and mortar, which ordinarily serves the function of putty or cement, as their construction material. Normally, people in those days used stones as construction material and cemented them with clay. The stone was the חומר, the construction material, and the clay was the cement; both materials had been provided by nature. But now all the material was man-made. That which formerly had been used as חֵמָר ["mortar"] was now used as חומר ["clay"].

4. In Verse 5 we will read that ה׳ [God in His quality of mercy] came down לִרְאוֹת, in order to "see" the city and the tower that men had built for themselves. He wanted to investigate the matter before making His judgment. This means that there was nothing wrong in the act of building a city or a tower *per se.* Hence, the wrong and the resultant threat to man's moral future must have lain not in the act of building but in the purpose for which the city and the tower were to be built and in the attitude that motivated the builders. The emphasis clearly is upon the purpose as stated by the builders: נַעֲשֶׂה לָנוּ שֵׁם ["Let us make a name for ourselves"]. Who were the ones to state this purpose? It was all of mankind alive at the time. Now if mankind as a whole declares, "Let us make a name for ourselves," that declaration can be directed only against one or both of two powers: either against God, Who is above mankind, or against the individual, who is subordinate to mankind as a whole. For mankind taken as a whole has no equal. The declaration could not have implied a desire for fame after death, because the words פֶּן נָפוּץ ["lest we be scattered"] shows that the people were thinking of the immediate present. Besides, as we shall demonstrate further on, this undertaking was a project in whose construction all the generations to come were also expected to help.

In other words, all of mankind has gathered in a plain where there are no natural building materials, and the idea comes to them that they will manufacture all the needed materials by their own strength and ingenuity. The intention is to demonstrate that, if all join forces and work together, mankind can overpower nature. And so these people decide to create a structure that will serve as a perpetual reminder of the community's power over the individual.

Now it is precisely to the community that God looks: וַאֲגֻדָּתוֹ עַל אֶרֶץ יְסָדָהּ ["and He has founded His society upon the earth"—Amos 9:6]. Not without good reason did God make men so different from one another: Each individual is intended to complement the other. The individual is mortal; the powers of the individual are limited: אֵין צִבּוּר מֵת וְאֵין צִבּוּר עָנִי: [Gittin III, 45a] it is only the community that does not die and never becomes entirely impoverished. Hence all the great and noble things that endure can be created only if all forces join in a communal effort. However, the community can prosper and attain perfection only if it assumes the same attitude toward God as the individual should; that is, if it subordinates itself to God, if it uses the totality of its energies only in the service of God and if it sees its mission as nothing else but the employment of its combined forces to carry out, to the fullest possible extent, the tasks to be performed in the service of God. But at this point danger threatens. An individual will ultimately realize by himself that his powers are limited. But not so the community. For the community is indeed strong, and so it may easily come to regard itself as the purpose of its own existence, as if the individual had meaning only in terms of the communi-top shall reach to the heaven, and let us make a name for ourselves, lest we be scat-

בַשָּׁמַיִם וְנַעֲשֶׂה־לָּנוּ שֵׁם פֶּן־נָפוּץ עַל־פְּנֵי כָל־

ty, as if the community did not exist to complement the individual but the individual was to be completely absorbed by the community.

Now if the community declares, "We want to demonstrate the powers that are inherent in the community. We want to join forces so that we may establish ourselves"; if the community does not summon the individual to serve God but only to serve the community; if the community considers itself as an end instead of merely as a means toward an end, then all of mankind's moral future is compromised. The result will be that situation which is described here in almost prophetic terms: men will perceive their own powers . . . and come to believe that the community can do without God and His moral law.

"The ancients had to have stones but we are able to build even where there are no stones"; here is the creation of the idol of vacuous purpose, one which will bring no happiness but for the sake of which the individual is expected to give up his existence and the community is expected to renounce its allegiance to the moral law. Individuals, of course, will shed tears when another individual dies but when the community builds its edifice of glory the toll in human life is deemed to be of no importance. The Community says: נִשְׂרְפָה לִשְׂרֵפָה ["Let us burn whatever there is"], never mind what we destroy as long as it will aid in building the edifice of our fame. In such a state of affairs the individual will believe that he has lived long enough if he sacrifices his life for the community even if it is for a vain cause, as long as that cause will promote the fame of his community, a quest for fame which cares nothing for the cost in human life. And so חֵמָר [the mortar] becomes חֹמֶר [clay]—the means becomes an end in itself—also in spiritual and moral matters.

Our Sages teach us that this undertaking could succeed only under the leadership of Nimrod. Only a "crafty hero before God" such as Nimrod can sway men to make such a sacrifice, and not even he will succeed if he does not know how to fill others with enthusiasm for his purposes, if he does not know how to identify his own glory with that of the masses which sacrifice themselves for him. A Napoleon or an Alexander the Great knows how to win the masses for his purposes, not with promises of gold or riches but merely with a bit of ribbon to be placed into a buttonhole.

However, it would be a very dangerous error to assume that it can ever be permissible for a community to pursue any purposes other than those which have positive value and meaning when judged by the standard of the moral law. Just the opposite is true. In the case of an individual there may be, even if no justification, then at least some excuse if outside pressures beyond his control force him to deviate from the strict moral law. But there can never be such an excuse for an entire community.

In view of the foregoing, we can now understand the meaning of פֶּן נָפוּץ ["lest we be scattered"]. They were afraid that they would cease to be a community. Now what difference would that have made to them if they had viewed the community merely as an alliance to support its individual members? What cause would they have had for fear if they had regarded the community only as a means for the fulfillment of moral purposes to a greater degree than would be possible for the individual alone? If a community is what it should be, then, even if it has millions of members, it will require no artificial means to hold it together; its bonds are inherent in the consciousness of each individual member and its rallying point is God Himself. If, however, a community does not regard itself as existing for the individual, but vice versa, if it declares נַעֲשֶׂה לָנוּ שֵׁם ["Let us make a name for ourselves"], then, of course, the individual members must be compelled, or enticed by artificial methods, to submit to its command and to sacrifice themselves for it.

When the community says, נַעֲשֶׂה לָנוּ שֵׁם, when it introduces a spurious patriotism, when it unleashes that lust for glory which is regarded as a vice in an individual but as a virtue in a community, the moral mission of both community and individual is undermined. All passions have a saturation point but the lust for glory has no such limits. This is not the only instance in history where lust for glory has inspired the erection of a tower and the indiscriminate destruction of all else in order to obtain building blocks for the rearing of its own triumphs. *All of subsequent world history tells of towers of imaginary glory which Nimrods knew how to entice, or force, their nations to build.* But as for the purely human life, the simple life of ordinary men in their humble homes—of such things history has only little to relate. Such things, in the beautiful metaphor of our Sages, are recorded only by God, to be witnessed by Elijah and the Messiah, those messengers and agents of mankind's ultimate redemption.

The perverse attitude of the generation that built the tower is characterized by a pithy saying in Pirke de Rabbi Eliezer: "If a man fell at the construction site and died, they did not take it to heart, but if a brick dropped to the ground, they sat down and wept, 'From where will we be able to get another to replace it?'"

We have noted above that the construction of this tower reaching into the skies was to be an undertaking that all future generations were meant to continue.

הָאָֽרֶץ׃ ה וַיֵּ֣רֶד יְהֹוָ֔ה לִרְאֹ֥ת אֶת־הָעִ֖יר וְאֶת־
הַמִּגְדָּ֑ל אֲשֶׁ֥ר בָּנ֖וּ בְּנֵ֥י הָאָדָֽם׃ ו וַיֹּ֣אמֶר יְהֹוָ֗ה
הֵ֣ן עַ֤ם אֶחָד֙ וְשָׂפָ֤ה אַחַת֙ לְכֻלָּ֔ם וְזֶ֖ה הַחִלָּ֣ם

tered all over the earth." 5. And *God* came down to see the city and the tower which the sons of men were building. 6. And *God* said: "Lo! they are now one people and they have all one language, and this is the first thing they undertake; now

Subsequent history tells of similar edifices that were to be built higher and higher without a limit. The soil of ancient Egypt, that state which was to fall heir to those Nimrodian schemes, still bears pyramids begun by each king at the time of his accession and continued for the duration of his reign. In ancient Egypt the entire nation had been brought under the yoke to go on working without interruption on the edifices that were to commemorate the glory of its kings. These pyramids were miniature versions, as it were, of the edifice described in this account. According to our Sages it was none other than Nimrod who uttered the words נַעֲשֶׂה לָנוּ שֵׁם ["Let us make a name for ourselves"]; they construe the use of the first person plural as the *pluralis majestatis*. In reality, however, such national edifices are not truly monuments to the glory of a nation or a community but only to the glory of a tyrant who knew how to exploit the energies of his community to set a laurel wreath upon his own brow. All the history of mankind to this very day seems to represent the realization of the maxim that הַקִּנְאָה וְהַתַּאֲוָה וְהַכָּבוֹד מוֹצִיאִין אֶת הָאָדָם מִן הָעוֹלָם ["Envy, greed and thirst for honor take a man out from the world"—Sayings of the Fathers 4:28]. The antediluvian world perished because of תַּאֲוָה וְקִנְאָה [greed and envy]: נָחָשׁ [the serpent] and קַיִן [the sin of Cain], הַשְׁחָתַת דֶּרֶךְ [moral corruption] and חָמָס [wrongdoing]. Now, in the generation during which the earth was divided, the lust for glory joins this pernicious cycle.

5. While in the account of the דּוֹר הַמַּבּוּל [the generation of the Flood] God is consistently described as אֱלֹקִים [in His quality of justice and as master over nature], the story of the tower, as Naḥmanides points out, refers to Him only by the שֵׁם הויה [the Tetragrammaton; in His quality of mercy], as the One Who may suspend the laws of nature for the moral training of man. The physical and moral degeneration shown by the generation of the Flood represented a threat not only to human society but also to the order of nature as ordained by the Creator [אֱלֹקִים]. The perversion of the דּוֹר הַפְּלָגָה [the generation in which the earth was divided], by contrast, was neither physical nor, on the face of it, social in character. Peace and harmony still prevailed. But the future of mankind, which is dependent on the inalienable dignity and moral significance of each individual, had been placed in grave jeopardy by the plans of its leaders. That is why God's intervention is described as the work of ה׳, the Divine Providence that seeks to bring about the ultimate salvation of mankind.

This is the first time that the verb וַיֵּרֶד ["and He (God) came down"] occurs in Scripture. If we consider עִיקַּר שְׁכִינָה בַּתַּחְתּוֹנִים [that God seeks chiefly to dwell among men on earth, rather than in the heavens], we will note that the verb וַיֵּרֶד when used in connection with God always designates a crisis in the development of world affairs during which God's intervention prevents a widening of the gap between earth and heaven and brings the world one step closer to His goal—the day when His שְׁכִינָה will be able to dwell once more בַּתַּחְתּוֹנִים [among men on earth].

In this particular passage, however, the significance of וַיֵּרֶד is even more striking than anywhere else in the Biblical text. This community did not permit the individual to have any master other than itself. This attitude was not merely an attack on the eternal inalienable worth of the individual, a quality that is not merely conferred upon him by the worth of the community and that can never be reckoned in terms of mere bricks, not even bricks used in building the glory of the community. It was an attack also on ה׳ Himself, Who summons every individual directly to His service and precisely thereby makes every man, be he prince or slave, free and equal. ה׳ [God in His quality of mercy] will not countenance slavery. Now, at the moment when the community of mankind, instead of summoning each individual בְּשֵׁם ד׳ [in the name of *God*], substitutes its own name for that of God, וַיֵּרֶד ד׳ God comes down to earth. He does not leave the world on its own but descends "to see" the edifice that the community of mankind has been building; i.e., He comes down to earth to investigate the purpose of the structure.

6. ***And* God *said.*** Here they stand, in complete harmony. They have migrated together, and now they gather together, and as they become aware of their significance as a united community their first thought is not, "Let us glorify God; let us use our united energies for His glorification" but נַעֲשֶׂה לָנוּ שֵׁם ["Let us make a name for ourselves"]. That was the very first undertaking for which they planned to utilize their combined energies. . . . בצר means to make something unconquerable, secure from attack. Here, therefore, וְעַתָּה לֹא יִבָּצֵר מֵהֶם means that nothing will be secure from them, or beyond their reach. . . .

nothing will remain beyond their reach, whatever they already have in mind to accomplish, beyond all bounds. 7. Come, let Us go down so that their language will wither away so that the one will no longer understand the language of the other."

לַעֲשׂוֹת וְעַתָּה֙ לֹא־יִבָּצֵ֣ר מֵהֶ֔ם כֹּ֛ל אֲשֶׁ֥ר יָזְמ֖וּ לַעֲשֽׂוֹת: ז הָ֚בָה נֵֽרְדָ֔ה וְנָבְלָ֥ה שָׁ֖ם שְׂפָתָ֑ם אֲשֶׁר֙ לֹ֣א יִשְׁמְע֔וּ אִ֖ישׁ שְׂפַ֥ת רֵעֵֽהוּ: ח וַיָּ֨פֶץ יְהֹוָ֤ה

7. . . . . נָבְלָה [the "withering away"] of their language is the immediate result of יְרִידָה [God's "descent" to earth] . . .

נבל ["withering away"] is the beginning of נפל ["falling" or "dropping off"]. That which later causes the fall begins by causing a "withering away." The flower withers as soon as it has been cut off from the source of its vitality. As soon as the channels linking the flower with the source of its life shrivel up, the flower withers, and when the link has entirely ceased to be, the withered flower drops from its stem. The thought conveyed by this passage is that as soon as God comes down to earth the languages will be detached from the source which had shaped them until that time.

Until that time, we are told, mankind had שָׂפָה אַחַת and דְּבָרִים אֲחָדִים ["one language and uniform words"]. The uniformity that bound men together was not merely physical and climatic, one common organic conformity of language. There was, too, a uniformity in turn of mind and in outlook on life which preserved also דְּבָרִים אֲחָדִים, a uniform coinage of verbal expression. But such a unity of mind can survive only as long as the words uttered are not coined by the individual but derived from tradition. So long as men were in agreement about things in general and so long as their agreement enjoyed the sanction of a higher source; that is, so long as the character of the language was objective, not subjective, their language would remain based on the unchanging nature and purpose of things and not on the perspective of the individual. A language with such an objective character would create and preserve among men an agreement on views of life and of the world, and it would be the basis for all wisdom. Jurisprudence, ethics, physics and metaphysics all have the same objective: to establish what things are and what they should be; [in the ideal situation described here] all this knowledge would be set forth in the form of man's own language. . . .

If this שָׂפָה אַחַת was the "one language" in which God taught the first man to perceive things and their relationships with one another, if it comprised the terms employed by God Himself to designate these things for man and if, therefore, it contained all those perceptions that God wanted to constitute as the foundation of human wisdom, then the phrase קָרָא בְשֵׁם

ד' ["call" or "proclaim" in the name of God] may well mean simply to teach man what things really are like and what they should be like, not according to man's own subjective, arbitrary view but according to God's will for mankind. For only if we call things by their proper names will the truth remain clear and undiluted for us.

If the united community so misuses its authority that, instead of employing it to serve the treasure entrusted to it—the individuals called upon לִקְרֹא בְּשֵׁם ד' ["to proclaim in the name of God"]—it will seek to make the individual subservient not to God but only to itself, then the individual must rise up and say, "I do not recognize this community; I recognize only myself." In making this declaration, of course, he pours out the child with the bath water; he cuts himself off from the root through which he was to have absorbed all human wisdom from its Divine source, and he flings himself into a vague, uncharted subjectivity. However, given such a community, decentralization is the only way in which the individual can preserve his human qualities. This subjectiveness, this self-awareness on the part of the individual which defines things not in terms of the coercion exercised by the community but in terms of the way in which he, the individual, sees them, was the new element (described by the words אֲשֶׁר בָּלַל ד' [see Verse 9] which God awakened in the minds of men when He caused their language to disintegrate. The one would say, "Let us preserve the old order, that only those things which are within a man's purview should belong to him," while the other would say, "I do not recognize any law and order! Whatever I can seize, whatever I have, is mine," etc. Such an awakening of subjectivism would be the result of God's יְרִידָה [descent] and would complete the process of נָבְלָה [withering away].

. . . . From that time on it was such factors as obstinacy, wilfulness, mood and even passion that devised names for things—of course no longer in the uniform manner in which God formerly had defined them. And so it came to pass that men no longer understood one another. The one would give a thing a certain name for no other reason but to spite the others, for independence shows itself in a self-willed view of things, which is synonymous with a self-willed manner of naming things. We see, too, that in subsequent history every attempt at centralization has begun with an attempt to

8. And *God* scattered them from there upon the surface of all the earth, and they left off building the city. 9. Therefore He named it Babel, for there *God* had confused the language of all the earth, and from there *God* scattered them over the face of all the earth. 10. These are the descendants of Shem: Shem was 100 years old when he begot Arpakhshad two years after the Unsoulment. 11. After he begot Arpakhshad, Shem lived [another] 500 years and begot sons and daughters. 12. Arpakhshad lived 35 years; then he begot Shelaḥ. 13. After he begot Shelaḥ, Arpakhshad lived [another] 403 years and begot sons and daughters. 14. Shelaḥ lived 30 years; then he begot Eber. 15. After he begot Eber, Shelaḥ lived [another] 403 years and begot sons and daughters. 16. Eber lived 34 years; then he begot Peleg. 17. After he begot Peleg, Eber lived [another] 430 years and begot sons and daughters. 18. Peleg lived 30 years; then he begot Reu. 19. After he begot Reu, Peleg lived [another] 209 years and begot sons and daughters. 20. Reu lived 32 years; then he begot Serug. 21. After he begot Serug, Reu lived [another] 207 years and begot sons and daughters. 22. Serug lived 30 years; then he begot Naḥor. 23. After he begot Naḥor, Serug lived [another] 200 years and begot sons and daughters.

אֹתָם מִשָּׁם עַל־פְּנֵי כָל־הָאָרֶץ וַיַּחְדְּלוּ לִבְנֹת הָעִיר: ט עַל־כֵּן קָרָא שְׁמָהּ בָּבֶל כִּי־שָׁם בָּלַל יְהֹוָה שְׂפַת כָּל־הָאָרֶץ וּמִשָּׁם הֱפִיצָם יְהֹוָה עַל־פְּנֵי כָּל־הָאָרֶץ: פ י אֵלֶּה תּוֹלְדֹת שֵׁם שֵׁם בֶּן־מְאַת שָׁנָה וַיּוֹלֶד אֶת־אַרְפַּכְשָׁד שְׁנָתַיִם אַחַר הַמַּבּוּל: יא וַיְחִי־שֵׁם אַחֲרֵי הוֹלִידוֹ אֶת־אַרְפַּכְשָׁד חֲמֵשׁ מֵאוֹת שָׁנָה וַיּוֹלֶד בָּנִים וּבָנוֹת: ס יב וְאַרְפַּכְשַׁד חַי חָמֵשׁ וּשְׁלֹשִׁים שָׁנָה וַיּוֹלֶד אֶת־שָׁלַח: יג וַיְחִי אַרְפַּכְשַׁד אַחֲרֵי הוֹלִידוֹ אֶת־שֶׁלַח שָׁלֹשׁ שָׁנִים וְאַרְבַּע מֵאוֹת שָׁנָה וַיּוֹלֶד בָּנִים וּבָנוֹת: ס יד וְשֶׁלַח חַי שְׁלֹשִׁים שָׁנָה וַיּוֹלֶד אֶת־עֵבֶר: טו וַיְחִי־שֶׁלַח אַחֲרֵי הוֹלִידוֹ אֶת־עֵבֶר שָׁלֹשׁ שָׁנִים וְאַרְבַּע מֵאוֹת שָׁנָה וַיּוֹלֶד בָּנִים וּבָנוֹת: ס טז וַיְחִי־עֵבֶר אַרְבַּע וּשְׁלֹשִׁים שָׁנָה וַיּוֹלֶד אֶת־פָּלֶג: יז וַיְחִי־עֵבֶר אַחֲרֵי הוֹלִידוֹ אֶת־פֶּלֶג שְׁלֹשִׁים שָׁנָה וְאַרְבַּע מֵאוֹת שָׁנָה וַיּוֹלֶד בָּנִים וּבָנוֹת: ס יח וַיְחִי־פֶלֶג שְׁלֹשִׁים שָׁנָה וַיּוֹלֶד אֶת־רְעוּ: יט וַיְחִי־פֶלֶג אַחֲרֵי הוֹלִידוֹ אֶת־רְעוּ תֵּשַׁע שָׁנִים וּמָאתַיִם שָׁנָה וַיּוֹלֶד בָּנִים וּבָנוֹת: ס כ וַיְחִי רְעוּ שְׁתַּיִם וּשְׁלֹשִׁים שָׁנָה וַיּוֹלֶד אֶת־שְׂרוּג: כא וַיְחִי רְעוּ אַחֲרֵי הוֹלִידוֹ אֶת־שְׂרוּג שֶׁבַע שָׁנִים וּמָאתַיִם שָׁנָה וַיּוֹלֶד בָּנִים וּבָנוֹת: ס כב וַיְחִי שְׂרוּג שְׁלֹשִׁים שָׁנָה וַיּוֹלֶד אֶת־נָחוֹר: כג וַיְחִי שְׂרוּג אַחֲרֵי הוֹלִידוֹ אֶת־נָחוֹר מָאתַיִם שָׁנָה וַיּוֹלֶד בָּנִים וּבָנוֹת: ס

divest the language in question of its characteristic qualities. . . .

. . . This conflict of opinions subsequently drove men utterly apart from one another. . . .

8. Now the Word of God takes us to a small, narrow sphere in order to introduce us to the manner in which God arranges things. Out of the smallest, most insignificant beginnings, a herald and instrument is to be shaped to help promote mankind's maturing toward its ultimate goal. The chapter concludes with a genealogy beginning with Shem and ending with that simple man who, in the face of his contemporaries who had proclaimed as their guiding ideal the slogan נַעֲשֶׂה לָּנוּ שֵׁם ["Let us make ourselves a name"], would dedicate his own life, and that of the nation to be descended from him, to the principle לִקְרֹא בְּשֵׁם ה' ["to proclaim in the name of *God*"]. This is the device through which man-

24. Naḥor lived 29 years; then he begot Teraḥ. 25. After he begot Teraḥ, Naḥor lived [another] 119 years and begot sons and daughters. 26. Teraḥ lived 70 years; then he begot Abram, Naḥor and Haran. 27. These are the descendants of Teraḥ: Teraḥ begot Abram, Naḥor and Haran, and Haran begot Lot. 28. Haran died before the countenance of his father Teraḥ in the land of his birth, in Ur Casdim [Ur of the Chaldees]. 29. Abram and Naḥor took themselves wives. The name of Abram's wife was Sarai; the name of Naḥor's wife was Milcah, daughter of Haran, the father of Milcah and the father of Iscah. 30. But Sarai was barren; she had no child. 31. And Teraḥ took his son Abram, and his grandson Lot, the son of Haran, and his daughter-in-law Sarai, wife of his son Abram, and they went with them from Ur Casdim to go to the land of Canaan. But when they came to Ḥaran, they stayed there. 32. And when Teraḥ's days were 205 years, Teraḥ died in Ḥaran.

כד וַיְחִי נָחוֹר תֵּשַׁע וְעֶשְׂרִים שָׁנָה וַיּוֹלֶד
אֶת־תָּרַח׃ כה וַיְחִי נָחוֹר אַחֲרֵי הוֹלִידוֹ
אֶת־תֶּרַח תְּשַׁע־עֶשְׂרֵה שָׁנָה וּמְאַת שָׁנָה וַיּוֹלֶד
בָּנִים וּבָנוֹת׃ ס כו וַיְחִי־תֶרַח שִׁבְעִים שָׁנָה
וַיּוֹלֶד אֶת־אַבְרָם אֶת־נָחוֹר וְאֶת־הָרָן׃
כז וְאֵלֶּה תּוֹלְדֹת תֶּרַח תֶּרַח הוֹלִיד אֶת־אַבְרָם
אֶת־נָחוֹר וְאֶת־הָרָן וְהָרָן הוֹלִיד אֶת־לוֹט׃
כח וַיָּמָת הָרָן עַל־פְּנֵי תֶּרַח אָבִיו בְּאֶרֶץ
מוֹלַדְתּוֹ בְּאוּר כַּשְׂדִּים׃ מפטיר כט וַיִּקַּח אַבְרָם
וְנָחוֹר לָהֶם נָשִׁים שֵׁם אֵשֶׁת־אַבְרָם שָׂרָי וְשֵׁם
אֵשֶׁת־נָחוֹר מִלְכָּה בַּת־הָרָן אֲבִי־מִלְכָּה וַאֲבִי
יִסְכָּה׃ ל וַתְּהִי שָׂרַי עֲקָרָה אֵין לָהּ וָלָד׃
לא וַיִּקַּח תֶּרַח אֶת־אַבְרָם בְּנוֹ וְאֶת־לוֹט בֶּן־
הָרָן בֶּן־בְּנוֹ וְאֵת שָׂרַי כַּלָּתוֹ אֵשֶׁת אַבְרָם בְּנוֹ
וַיֵּצְאוּ אִתָּם מֵאוּר כַּשְׂדִּים לָלֶכֶת אַרְצָה כְּנַעַן
וַיָּבֹאוּ עַד־חָרָן וַיֵּשְׁבוּ שָׁם׃ לב וַיִּהְיוּ יְמֵי־תֶרַח
חָמֵשׁ שָׁנִים וּמָאתַיִם שָׁנָה וַיָּמָת תֶּרַח
בְּחָרָן׃ פ

kind will someday find the solution of all the problems that beset its long wanderings on earth. This man and his people, by admonition and by their personal example, were to preserve this guiding principle as a beacon for mankind so that the awareness of it might never disappear from the minds of men.

The Haftarah for this Sidra may be found on page 823.

לך לך

LEKH LEKHA

XII 1. And to Abram *God* said: "Go for yourself, out of your country, from your birthplace and from the house of your father, to the land which I shall show you. 2. I will make of you a great nation and I will bless you, and I wish

יב א וַיֹּאמֶר יְהוָה אֶל־אַבְרָם לֶךְ־לְךָ מֵאַרְצְךָ וּמִמּוֹלַדְתְּךָ וּמִבֵּית אָבִיךָ אֶל־הָאָרֶץ אֲשֶׁר אַרְאֶךָּ: ב וְאֶעֶשְׂךָ לְגוֹי גָּדוֹל וַאֲבָרֶכְךָ וַאֲגַדְּלָה

CHAPTER XII

1. לֶךְ־לְךָ *[Go for yourself]* . . . The addition of the pronoun לְךָ to the verb לֶךְ stresses the idea, "Go *for yourself*, go your own way, isolate yourself." In a similar vein we are told of Jethro, וַיֵּלֶךְ לוֹ ["and he went back to his own homeland"—Exodus 18:27]; Jethro [the father-in-law of Moses] renounced the advantages that would have accrued to him if he had cast his lot with the people of Israel. Similarly, Joshua said to the Gadites and the Reubenites, וְעַתָּה פְּנוּ וּלְכוּ לָכֶם לְאָהֳלֵיכֶם ["therefore now return and go your way to your tents"—Joshua 22:4]. "You have done your duty to the community," Joshua said to them, "and now you may go 'your own way.'" The thought conveyed by Verse 1, then, is, "Go for yourself, go your own way which will isolate you from your land, etc. and from all your previous connections."

This Divine command placed Abraham in the most emphatic contrast with the tendencies that prevailed in his day. As we have seen, the tendency of that generation which, under the slogan נַעֲשֶׂה לָנוּ שֵׁם ["Let us make ourselves a name"], began to build a tower to the glorification of man was not individualism, not the recognition of the worth and significance of the individual, but centralization, which deprived the individual of his personal worth and debased him to the status of an underling, a mere brick in the structure of what was supposed to be a representative community. This tendency gave rise to the false notion of a majority holding authority everywhere and in all things. As a result, everything that the majority in the land regarded as the greatest good automatically was considered and worshipped as such by everyone else as well.

Of course, the community should represent all that which is truly sacred and sublime, and under this assumption Judaism, too, appreciates the full significance of the individual's attaching himself to a community. However, at the outset of Jewish history we see that the principle of לֶךְ לְךָ, *"going for oneself, going one's own way," is considered even more important.* No one may say of himself, "I am as good, or as righteous, as is the fashion here nowadays." Every

individual is directly responsible to God for his personal conduct. If it becomes necessary, if the principle idolized by the majority is not the one which is truly Divine, then the individual must go "alone, his own way, with God." This conviction was set by Abraham as the starting point for his own mission and that of the people to be descended from him. . . .

How could we have survived to this day, how could we continue to survive, had we not, at the very outset, received from Abraham the courage to be a minority?

"Up-to-date Judaism!" לֶךְ לְךָ, the very first Jewish directive, constitutes the most vocal protest against that notion. Was Abraham's first stand in keeping with the spirit of his times—in the midst of the temples of Chaldea, Babylonia, Assyria, Phoenicia and ancient Egypt? In those lands the doctrine of the day was the worship of power and sensuality. The Asians worshipped pleasure, while the ancient Egyptians deified power and stifled personal freedom. Except for a few faint traces, the God-idea had almost vanished. And here, at a time when everyone else seeks to establish himself, to integrate, there arises an Abraham who is to leave his homeland, give up his rights of citizenship, become an outsider of his own free will and hurl his protest into the face of the idols worshipped by all the nations. Such conduct demands courage and a firm belief in the truth of one's inner convictions and one's awareness of God; it demands Jewish awareness, Jewish "obstinacy." This was the first situation in which Abraham had to put his calling to the test. . . .

2. *I will make of you a great nation.* Even superficially seen, it is clear from this verse that Abraham is to receive back from God everything he has given up, and indeed, in a considerably enhanced measure. By breaking away מֵאַרְצוֹ [from his country] he gives up his nationality, but God tells him that, instead of joining another nation, he himself is to become the founder of a new national entity. When he renounces מוֹלַדְתּוֹ [his birthplace], he will not have to lose the rights of citizenship which are the source of justifiable prosperity. וַאֲבָרֶכְךָ ["I will bless you"]; rather, it is directly from God that he will henceforth receive the "civil right" to prosper on earth. And when he leaves

to make your name great; you, become a blessing! 3. I wish to bless those who bless you, and whoever brings a curse upon you I will curse, and all the families of the earth shall be blessed through you." 4. So Abram went as *God* had spoken to him, and Lot went with him. And Abram was 75 years

שְׁמֶךָ וֶהְיֵה בְּרָכָה׃ ג וַאֲבָרְכָה מְבָרְכֶיךָ וּמְקַלֶּלְךָ אָאֹר וְנִבְרְכוּ בְךָ כֹּל מִשְׁפְּחֹת הָאֲדָמָה׃ ד וַיֵּלֶךְ אַבְרָם כַּאֲשֶׁר דִּבֶּר אֵלָיו יְהוָה וַיֵּלֶךְ אִתּוֹ לוֹט וְאַבְרָם בֶּן־חָמֵשׁ שָׁנִים

his own family, thus foregoing the respect and honor that is the heritage of old-established families; אֲגַדְּלָה שְׁמֶךָ ["I wish to make your name great"], he is to establish for himself a new name which will attain great renown.

Our Sages in Genesis Rabbah 39 point out that the text does not read אֲשִׂימְךָ לְגוֹי גָּדוֹל ["I will *appoint* you to be a great nation"]. We are not told that God would merely act as a patron or protector, as it were, in the development of Abraham's descendants into a nation much as Divine Providence does in the growth and prospering of other nations. The text is אֶעֶשְׂךָ, "I will *make of* you, I will *shape* you, into a great nation"; all natural conditions will be against it, so that it will be obvious for all to see that God Himself has been the creator of this nation. Seen in terms of natural conditions, the very age and previous childlessness of the man and wife who had been chosen as forebears of this future nation argued against the fulfillment of the Divine promise. Only God could make a great nation of Abraham. Hence, from the outset, the very emergence and existence of this people was to be a manifestation of God.

° ° °

On closer study, it may be seen that the sum total of Jewish history was given to Abraham *in nuce* in these first three verses. In Verse 1, לֶךְ לְךָ מֵאַרְצְךָ ["Go for yourself, out of your country"] Abraham appears merely as an individual who is told to "dare to be alone." In Verse 2, וְאֶעֶשְׂךָ לְגוֹי וגו׳ ["I will make of you a great nation"] the nation is already mentioned but not yet in the context of its relationship with the other nations. Then, in Verse 3, וַאֲבָרְכָה וגו׳ ["I will bless. . .], we see the Jewish nation in its relationship to the other nations. The blessing of Abraham is made dependent on others blessing him; indeed, it is assumed that some might wish to curse him.

It was Abraham's task to isolate himself and to walk alone with God. Next would come the creation of a nation out of this man Abraham. If it is to become apparent that the existence of this nation is a second act of creation by God in history, then this nation can become a nation only by way of גָּלוּת [exile] and גֵּרוּת [homelessness]. Had that nation already been established in a dwelling place of its own from the very beginning, its creation would not have appeared as אֶצְבַּע אֱלקי׳ ["the finger of God"] or as מַעֲשֵׂה ד׳, [an act of Divine creation].

וְאֶעֶשְׂךָ לְגוֹי גָּדוֹל ***[I will make of you a great nation]:*** These words cover the period from the days of Isaac until the Exodus from Egypt.

וַאֲבָרֶכְךָ ***[and I will bless you]:*** After that, I will plant you into a land flowing with milk and honey.

וַאֲגַדְּלָה שְׁמֶךָ ***[and I wish to make your name great]:*** We are not told אֲגַדֵּל שְׁמֶךָ ["I *will* make your name great"]. God can bless men and nations, but He can only "wish" that they will attain sufficient spiritual greatness to justify their being called "model" individuals or nations. The fulfillment of God's wish depends on whether these men or these nations will be loyal to the Law of God.

Similarly, the text does not read וְהָיִיתָ בְּרָכָה ["And you *will be* a blessing"] but וֶהְיֵה בְּרָכָה ["You, become a blessing"]. These two Hebrew words subsume all the phases of the moral mission upon whose fulfillment the fulfillment of God's own wish depends: "I wish to make your name great; therefore, you, become a blessing. I wish to make of you a nation to which the other nations need only look in order to become aware of their own task. And the task which you are to fulfill, as distinct from all other national aspirations, is: to become 'a blessing.'"

° ° °

3. וּמְקַלֶּלְךָ אָאֹר ***[and whoever brings a curse upon you I will curse]***; not אֹרְךָ אָאֹר ["and whoever curses you I will curse"]. The concept of בְּרָכָה [blessing] has two antitheses: קְלָלָה and מְאֵרָה. קלל would imply a "reduction" or "making lighter" in material things, to reduce the material wealth of a person or thing. ארר implies not merely a reduction of material wealth but also a reduction of inner strength and vitality. . . . In other words, God tells Abraham: I shall accompany you also into your life among the nations. I will bless each nation in accordance with the respect it will give to the Jewish spirit. No nation will be able to deprive you of your inner vitality, but those who will seek to restrict or stunt the physical existence of the seed of Abraham, אָאֹר, I will deprive of the inner vitality they themselves need in order to survive.

Thus, by saying that only those nations will flourish who will not only refrain from attempting to stifle the development of Abraham's principles but will actually respect and promote them, the text makes clear that the מִשְׁפְּחוֹת הָאֲדָמָה ["the families of the earth"] will be blessed "through you." The more respect they give you

וְשִׁבְעִים שָׁנָה בְּצֵאתוֹ מֵחָרָן: ה וַיִּקַּח אַבְרָם
אֶת־שָׂרַי אִשְׁתּוֹ וְאֶת־לוֹט בֶּן־אָחִיו וְאֶת־כָּל־
רְכוּשָׁם אֲשֶׁר רָכָשׁוּ וְאֶת־הַנֶּפֶשׁ אֲשֶׁר־עָשׂוּ
בְחָרָן וַיֵּצְאוּ לָלֶכֶת אַרְצָה כְּנַעַן וַיָּבֹאוּ אַרְצָה
כְּנָעַן: ו וַיַּעֲבֹר אַבְרָם בָּאָרֶץ עַד מְקוֹם שְׁכֶם
עַד אֵלוֹן מוֹרֶה וְהַכְּנַעֲנִי אָז בָּאָרֶץ: ז וַיֵּרָא
יְהוָה אֶל־אַבְרָם וַיֹּאמֶר לְזַרְעֲךָ אֶתֵּן אֶת־
הָאָרֶץ הַזֹּאת וַיִּבֶן שָׁם מִזְבֵּחַ לַיהוָה הַנִּרְאֶה

old when he left Haran. 5. Abram took his wife Sarai and his brother's son Lot and all their substance they had acquired and the souls whom they had made in Ḥaran and they left in order to go to the land of Canaan, and they came to the land of Canaan. 6. Abram passed by the land until the place of Shekhem, until the Grove of Moreh, and the Canaanite was already there in the land. 7. Then *God* appeared to Abram and said: "To your seed will I give this land." And then he built an altar to *God,* Who had appeared to him. 8. He

[Abraham and his seed] the greater the בְּרָכָה they will receive. . . .

5. . . . They left לָלֶכֶת אַרְצָה כְּנַעַן [in order to go to the land of Canaan]. God had said to Abraham: לֶךְ לְךָ, "detach yourself from your homeland," and then He had added that Abraham was to go אֶל הָאָרֶץ אֲשֶׁר אַרְאֶךָּ ["to the land which I shall show you"]. This is usually interpreted to mean "to the land to which I shall *direct* you."But אַרְאֶךָּ is never used to denote "directing." It always has the connotation of "letting someone see" or "showing" something to someone. Besides, one cannot order a person to go "to the place to which I shall direct you," for in that case he would have to wait until at least he was told in what direction he would have to proceed. Had that been God's command to Abraham, Abraham would not have known by which gate to leave Haran. Hence the positive command could only have been as follows: "Go away from this place, never mind in what direction, and move about until you come to a place where I will give you a visible sign to show you that this is the land where you are to remain." It was of his own initiative that Abraham at the very outset chose the way which led to Canaan.

If we consider the significance of this land, it should be clear to us why Abraham, and even Teraḥ before him, should have chosen to go there.

Although the land of Canaan at the time was occupied by the most corrupt tribe of the Noahides, we find living in that land also מַלְכִּי צֶדֶק מֶלֶךְ שָׁלֵם [Malki Tzedek, king of Salem], who, according to tradition, was none other than Shem. Thus, we see still living in that land the very person who had retained for himself the perception of God in its purest form. Another tradition teaches us that Mount Moriah, where Abraham was to perform the עֲקֵדָה [the "binding" of Isaac] and where later the altar of the Temple was to be built, was also the place where Noah and Abel had brought their offerings. As a matter of fact, according to the Sages, it was from there, the place of כַּפָּרָה [atonement], the constant spiritual and moral rebirth of mankind, that the dust had been taken to create the first man. In view of the foregoing, we may say that when Abraham was commanded to flee from Ur of the Chaldees because he stood there alone with his convictions and because the Chaldean kings and priestlings felt threatened by him, it was only natural that he should move toward the place where, according to the memory of men, human beings in bygone days had been closer to God than they had been in his own day . . .

6–7. Abraham "passed by" every place; he considered none of the places through which he passed as the place where he should remain, because he was waiting for the promised sign from God that would show him the place where he was to settle. . . . Then God "appeared" to Abraham [lit.: "He made Himself visible to him"] and said to him, etc. The stress here is on the fact that God appeared to Abraham. The altar, too, is described as having been built "to *God,* Who had appeared to him." For God's appearing to Abraham was the visible sign that this was indeed the land that had been chosen for the future of Abraham and his people . . .

° ° °

It was only at this place that God first appeared to Abraham, after Abraham had lived, worked and suffered for God over a period of 75 years, and after Abraham had already heard the word of God in his former homeland. The fact that it was only at this place that God actually "appeared" to Abraham was an indication to Abraham that this was the first place to which שְׁכִינָה בַּתַּחְתּוֹנִים, the Presence of God would return, a development which is, and should be, the goal and purpose of all human history. . . .

We note the following: This land of Canaan is to be the soil on which the regeneration of the human race and the return of godliness to mankind is to take place. The soil sought and chosen for this purpose was one eminently suited for this purpose, a soil upon which it

אֵלָיו: ח וַיַּעְתֵּק מִשָּׁם הָהָרָה מִקֶּדֶם לְבֵית־אֵל
וַיֵּט אָהֳלֹה בֵּית־אֵל מִיָּם וְהָעַי מִקֶּדֶם וַיִּבֶן־שָׁם
מִזְבֵּחַ לַיהוָה וַיִּקְרָא בְּשֵׁם יְהוָה: ט וַיִּסַּע

gave orders to move on from there toward the mountain to the east of Bethel, and he pitched his tent there, having Bethel on the west and Ai on the east. Then he built an altar to *God* and proclaimed in the name of *God*. 9. Abram journeyed, going on

would be possible for men living in accordance with God's will to attain the highest degree of spiritual and moral consecration. At the same time, however, it was a soil which even then, just as it was to be in later generations, was inhabited by depraved men who became more and more corrupt until they were deserving of nothing but destruction.

Hence, too, the Torah was given to us in the wilderness to teach us that the elevation of mankind is not tied to any particular time or soil. God links the return of His שְׁכִינָה to a place where human degeneracy had assumed its most blatant form. This should tell us that, though the character of a land of necessity has some effect on the character and proclivities of the nations that dwell upon it, the achievement of "nearness to God" is equally within the reach of the Lapp in Lappland and the Greek in Greece. In a land where an Abraham dwelt, murderers could live also; the same soil can bear a murderer side by side with a prophet. God's choice fell deliberately on a land seductive enough to corrupt its inhabitants so thoroughly that the very soil "spewed them out." This was the land upon which He implanted His nation, which was also not one of the most tractable of nations, one whose basic character in fact was קְשֵׁה עֹרֶף [stiff-neckedness; see Exodus 32:9 *et al.*]; He did this with the intent that if the אֵשְׁדָּת, the flame of God, would be able to win over even that people, even on that soil—as indeed it was to do—then this would be proof that there is no human nation, no matter where it dwells, that cannot be won over, by the אֵשְׁדָּת, for the אֵשְׁדָּת. The triumph of godliness was to begin with the most stubborn of nations (עַז שֶׁבְּאוּמוֹת) upon the most intractable of soils. . . .

8. The object of the verb וַיַּעְתֵּק ["He gave orders to move on"] is not expressed; it is self-evident. The object was Abraham's people. It is implied that Abraham had to exercise some energy to persuade his people to move on and to travel toward the mountain. Abraham was still searching for isolation. It was not לְךָ ["to you (Abraham)"] but לְזַרְעֲךָ ["to your seed"] that the land had been promised. Abraham's people may have felt more at home in the pleasant, fruited plain but Abraham adhered to the path of his duty, which lay in the direction of the lonely mountains, and he prevailed upon his people to follow him there.

Our Sages significantly describe the relationship of our three patriarchs to one another as follows: אַבְרָהָם קְרָאוֹ הַר, יִצְחָק שָׂדֶה, יַעֲקֹב בַּיִת ["Abraham called it a mountain; Isaac, a field, and Jacob, a home"]. Abraham considered that הַר, the mountainside, was the place where God revealed Himself, the region where men could find God. An outsider among men, Abraham was no longer able to find God within the confines of human society. If he was to follow the traces of Divine sovereignty and to rise up to God, he would have to go to the wide-open mountainside to which the traces of men's work had not yet found their way. As the story of the patriarchs unfolded, they increasingly saw the "finger of God" revealed in the course of their lives. Isaac called [his place of Divine revelation] שָׂדֶה, the field; that is, no longer the wild, open mountainside but that aspect of nature which had already been turned over to man for his nourishment. There, under conditions that had bearing upon the existence of men—though still in a material manner only—did Isaac find himself best able to discern the course of Divine Providence. (וַיִּזְרַע וגו׳ וַיִּמְצָא וגו׳ מֵאָה שְׁעָרִים "And Yitzḥak sowed in that land and in that year he reached one hundred markets. ."—Genesis 26:12). As for Jacob, he no longer considered it necessary to leave his home in order to find God: He found Him in the place where God always wants us to find him. Jacob was a family man. It was not in the mountains, nor in the plains and meadows that Jacob found God: he found Him in his own home. It was in Jacob's family life that God revealed Himself to Jacob. קְרָאוֹ בַּיִת ["he called it a home"] : the rock upon which man lays down his weary head became to him "the house of God" . . .

° ° °

וַיִּקְרָא בְּשֵׁם ד׳ *[and proclaimed in the name of* **God***]*, as opposed to a world whose whole life was guided by the slogan נַעֲשֶׂה לָּנוּ שֵׁם ["Let us make ourselves a name"].

9. Abraham kept moving south. We have already noted that Abraham did not seek out urban vicinities. He first wanted to build a firm foundation for himself and his people, and for this he felt he needed isolation. The south of Palestine was certainly not the most fruitful region of the land; the prophet Zechariah refers to the entire region south of Jerusalem as עֲרָבָה ["desert"]. In character with all the aspects of the emergence of the Jewish people—the giving of the Torah in the wilderness, the altar on Mount Ebal, Israel as the עַם קְשֵׁה עֹרֶף ["the stiff-necked people"]—the

steadily southward. ·10. There was a famine in the land, and Abram went down into Mitzrayim to sojourn there, because the famine was severe in the land. 11. And it came to pass when he was close to entering Mitzrayim that he said to his wife, Sarai: "Look, I do know that you are a beautiful woman to look upon. 12. And it will come to pass when the Mitzrites will see you, that they will say, 'This is his wife,' and they will kill me, but they will keep you alive. 13. Therefore please say that you are my sister, so that, in order for them to

אַבְרָם הָלוֹךְ וְנָסוֹעַ הַנֶּגְבָּה: פ י וַיְהִי רָעָב בָּאָרֶץ וַיֵּרֶד אַבְרָם מִצְרַיְמָה לָגוּר שָׁם כִּי־כָבֵד הָרָעָב בָּאָרֶץ: יא וַיְהִי כַּאֲשֶׁר הִקְרִיב לָבוֹא מִצְרָיְמָה וַיֹּאמֶר אֶל־שָׂרַי אִשְׁתּוֹ הִנֵּה־נָא יָדַעְתִּי כִּי אִשָּׁה יְפַת־מַרְאֶה אָתְּ: יב וְהָיָה כִּי־יִרְאוּ אֹתָךְ הַמִּצְרִים וְאָמְרוּ אִשְׁתּוֹ זֹאת וְהָרְגוּ אֹתִי וְאֹתָךְ יְחַיּוּ: יג אִמְרִי־נָא אֲחֹתִי אָתְּ לְמַעַן

spiritual metropolis of the people was set not in the north, the most prosperous region, but in the south, the most arid part of the land. The success of the Torah is not dependent on physical conditions. God says, "Out of the rock do I satisfy you with honey." And לֶךְ־לְךָ, the command given to Abraham, drew him farther and farther into the inhospitable south.

10–13. *There was a famine in the land.* With these words we come to a story that at first glance seems more than a little strange. That Abraham should have abandoned the land that had been assigned to him, instead of putting his trust in God, Who knows how to provide for men even in the midst of famine and wilderness! That he—or so, at least, it seems—should have so compromised the moral welfare of his own wife in order to save himself! Yet, even if we were not capable of explaining away the strange events in this story and even if, indeed, we would have to say with Ramban [Naḥmanides] that by his behavior toward his wife Abraham had inadvertently committed a grievous sin, indeed, that even his abandoning, at a time of famine, the land to which he had been directed was a sinful act, all this should not embarrass us. The Word of God does not seek to portray our great men as paragons of virtue; it deifies no man. It says of no one: "This is the ideal; in this man did the Divine assume human form." It does not set before us the life of any one human being as the model from whom we might learn what is good and right, and how we should conduct ourselves. When the Word of God wishes to put before us a model to emulate, it does not choose a man who is born of dust. Instead, God presents Himself as the model, saying, "Look upon Me! Emulate Me! Walk in My ways!" It gives us no occasion to say, "This must be right, because So-and-So did it." The Torah is not an "anthology of paragons." It relates events not because they are necessarily worthy of emulation but simply because they took place.

The Torah does not attempt to hide from us the faults, errors and weaknesses of our great men, and precisely thereby it places the stamp of credibility upon the happenings it relates. The fact that we are told about their faults and weaknesses does not detract from our great men; indeed, it adds to their stature and makes their life stories even more instructive. Had they all been portrayed to us as models of perfection we would have believed that they had been endowed with a higher nature not given to us to attain. Had they been presented to us free of human passions and inner conflicts, their nature would seem to us merely the result of a loftier predisposition, not a product of their personal merit, and certainly no model we could ever hope to emulate. Take, for instance the עֲנָוָה [humility] of Moses. If we did not know that he was capable also of flying into a rage, his humility would seem to us an inborn trait not within our capacity to emulate. It is precisely his outburst שִׁמְעוּ נָא הַמֹּרִים ["Hear now, you rebels . . ."—Numbers 20:10] that lends his humility its true greatness, for it shows us his humility as the product of a mighty labor of self-control and self-refinement which we should all emulate because it is within our own capacity to do so. Also, the Torah relates no sin or error without telling us also of its consequences, great or small.

Hence let us learn from our great teachers of Torah—among whom Naḥmanides certainly is one of the most outstanding—that we must never attempt to whitewash the spiritual and moral heroes of our past. They are not in need of our apologetics, nor would they tolerate such attempts on our part. אֱמֶת, truth, is the seal of our Word of God, and truthfulness is the distinctive characteristic also of all its genuinely great teachers and commentators. All this world still be true even if we were compelled to agree with the Naḥmanides that "Abraham had inadvertently committed a great sin."

But before we attempt to pass sentence [on Abraham] let us study the facts in the case more closely.

Abraham leaves Canaan after the onset of a severe famine. He does not wait to see whether God will pro-

יִיטַב־לִ֣י בַעֲבוּרֵ֔ךְ וְחָיְתָ֥ה נַפְשִׁ֖י בִּגְלָלֵֽךְ׃
שני יד וַיְהִ֕י כְּב֥וֹא אַבְרָ֖ם מִצְרָ֑יְמָה וַיִּרְא֤וּ הַמִּצְרִים֙ אֶת־הָ֣אִשָּׁ֔ה כִּֽי־יָפָ֥ה הִ֖וא מְאֹֽד׃

get to you through me, it may be well with me, and I will remain alive because of you."
14. It came to pass when Abram had come into Mitzrayim that the Mitzrites saw the woman, that she was very beautiful.

vide for him in some miraculous fashion despite the famine, but goes to Egypt in search of food. There he is threatened by another kind of peril that causes him to deny Sarah's true relationship to him, and as a result Sarah's honor is nearly compromised. Let us remind ourselves with regard to this second point that this peril must have been so dire, so unavoidable and so impossible to circumvent that Abraham considered it necessary to do the same thing also in the land of the Philistines [Genesis 20]. Had it been possible to circumvent this danger, then surely Abraham, after his experience in Egypt, would not have resorted to this same ruse a second time. As a matter of fact, we will see his son Isaac use the same subterfuge with Rebekah in a similar plight [Genesis 26].

Now of course it is easy for Naḥmanides, and for ourselves, who have already benefited from the experiences of our subsequent history, to say: Abraham should have remained in Canaan. And if he felt he had to go to Egypt, then at least he should have left everything to God once he arrived there. He who said to you [Abraham]: "This is the land" could have provided for you there in a wondrous way. God provided manna for food even in the wilderness, and מַלְאָכָיו יְצַוֶּה ["He will give His angels charge over you" — Psalms 91:11]. However, the fact that God gives special protection to those who go forth to do His will שְׁלוּחֵי מִצְוָה אֵינָן נִיזוֹקִין ["Those sent on an errand of religious duty come to no harm" —Pesaḥim 8b] was an experience Abraham and his descendants had yet to have, for Abraham did not have [the example of] another Abraham before him. Besides even if he had had such an experience it would not have exempted him from the duty of doing everything within his own power up to the limit the law allows and to put his trust in God only for the rest. Abraham could very well have argued that one must not rely on miracles.

And now for his conduct in Egypt. Could it be true that Abraham was afraid only for himself and that therefore, in order to save himself, he was ready to compromise his wife's honor? Let us listen to Abraham's own words. He says, הִנֵּה נָא יָדַעְתִּי וגו׳ ["Look, I do know that you are a beautiful woman . . ."]. The words, "I do know" imply that husband and wife must have had some conversation on that subject before. In view of all the incidents of this sort that took place in ancient Egypt and in Phoenicia we have reason to conclude —and this may not be without analogy in European countries of our own day—that in the climate of immorality which prevailed in those lands, virgins were safer than married women, especially if the virgin was also a foreigner. Regardless of whether or not Sarah was a foreigner, her honor was in danger. But had she been known as a married woman she would have been in imminent peril. In the case of a married woman one simply killed the husband and then took the wife. But in the case of a virgin traveling with her brother one worked in a more circumspect manner; one attempted to obtain the girl by trying to gain the favor of her brother. In any event, this procedure took more time and afforded a reprieve of sorts for the woman. In the meantime God could provide. . . .

It was this choice that Abraham faced as he was about to enter Mitzrayim. And it was for Sarah's sake that he decided on the latter alternative. As a married woman, she would certainly be lost, but if she were to pass as a virgin there was a chance that she might be saved.

But Sarah, unassuming woman that she was, did not believe she was in any danger. She did not consider herself beautiful. Therefore Abraham said to her, "Look, I do know that you are a beautiful woman. The Egyptians have only to see you and they will do away with me, your husband. As for you—" —so he puts it euphemistically—"they will permit you to survive." If they were to kill you also, that would not be the worst fate for you; they will keep you alive for a fate worse than death. Therefore it is better that you should say you are my sister, for in that case the Egyptians will be kind to me, in the hope that they will be able to get you by winning my favor. (As a rule בַּעֲבוּר connotes purpose and בִּגְלַל, cause). Finally, in order to overcome the last scruples of Sarah's modesty, Abraham adds, with what seems to be a note of egotism, "and then I will owe my survival to you," i.e., "If you will not do it for your own sake, then at least do it for mine." . . .

14–19. The Egyptians saw that the woman "was very beautiful." People turned to look at her, but nothing more. It seemed that Sarah might have remained unmolested, but then it had not occurred to Abraham that the king himself might become interested. If someone from among the ordinary people had taken a fancy to Sarah, he would have tried to get at her through her brother. But the king reversed the conventional order.

15. The princes of Pharaoh also saw her and praised her to Pharaoh; and the woman was taken into Pharoah's house.   16. And he showed kindness to Abram for her sake, and he now had sheep and oxen and donkeys and men servants and maidservants, she-donkeys and camels.   17. Then *God* struck Pharaoh with great plagues because of Sarai, Abram's wife.   18. And Pharaoh sent for Abram and said: "What have you done to me? Why did you not tell me that she is your wife?   19. Why did you say, 'She is my sister,' even when I took her as my wife? Well, now, here is your wife. Take her and go."   20. Pharaoh appointed men to take charge of him, and they sent away him, his wife and all that he had.

XIII   1. And Abram—he, his wife, and all that he had, and Lot with him—went out of Mitzrayim, up into the south.   2. And Abram was very rich in herds, in silver and in gold. 3. He retraced his journeys from the

טו וַיִּרְאוּ אֹתָהּ שָׂרֵי פַרְעֹה וַיְהַלְלוּ אֹתָהּ אֶל־פַּרְעֹה וַתֻּקַּח הָאִשָּׁה בֵּית פַּרְעֹה: טז וּלְאַבְרָם הֵיטִיב בַּעֲבוּרָהּ וַיְהִי־לוֹ צֹאן־וּבָקָר וַחֲמֹרִים וַעֲבָדִים וּשְׁפָחֹת וַאֲתֹנֹת וּגְמַלִּים: יז וַיְנַגַּע יְהוָה ׀ אֶת־פַּרְעֹה נְגָעִים גְּדֹלִים וְאֶת־בֵּיתוֹ עַל־דְּבַר שָׂרַי אֵשֶׁת אַבְרָם: יח וַיִּקְרָא פַרְעֹה לְאַבְרָם וַיֹּאמֶר מַה־זֹּאת עָשִׂיתָ לִּי לָמָּה לֹא־הִגַּדְתָּ לִּי כִּי אִשְׁתְּךָ הִוא: יט לָמָה אָמַרְתָּ אֲחֹתִי הִוא וָאֶקַּח אֹתָהּ לִי לְאִשָּׁה וְעַתָּה הִנֵּה אִשְׁתְּךָ קַח וָלֵךְ: כ וַיְצַו עָלָיו פַּרְעֹה אֲנָשִׁים וַיְשַׁלְּחוּ אֹתוֹ וְאֶת־אִשְׁתּוֹ וְאֶת־כָּל־אֲשֶׁר־לוֹ: יג א וַיַּעַל אַבְרָם מִמִּצְרַיִם הוּא וְאִשְׁתּוֹ וְכָל־אֲשֶׁר־לוֹ וְלוֹט עִמּוֹ הַנֶּגְבָּה: ב וְאַבְרָם כָּבֵד מְאֹד בַּמִּקְנֶה בַּכֶּסֶף וּבַזָּהָב: ג וַיֵּלֶךְ לְמַסָּעָיו

וַתֻּקַּח *[was taken]*. Sarah was first taken to the royal palace on a temporary basis. However, the king did not dare touch her yet; he hoped to gain his end in a respectable manner. He showered favors on Abraham in order to win her through him. Abraham had already received "sheep and oxen," etc. Had Sarah not been protected by the fact that she was believed to be Abraham's sister, had Pharaoh taken her at once, no time would have been permitted to pass with Abraham receiving gifts. God would have had to intervene immediately in order to save Sarah.

Is it possible that the words עַל דְּבַר שָׂרַי ["because of Sarai"] should be construed in their literal translation ["on the word of Sarai"]; i.e. to mean that Sarah had admitted to Pharaoh that she was Abraham's wife? But once having made that admission, Sarah was indeed in danger; now there was no more prospect for Pharaoh to win her in a respectable manner. Therefore Divine Providence had to intervene to save her.

Furthermore, we must reconcile two seemingly contradictory elements in Abraham's behavior. Only a little later we read of Abraham saying [to the king of Sodom]: "I have lifted up my hand toward *God* . . ." Genesis 14:22); he selflessly refuses even the most honorable offers of gifts. Could such a man really have been so base as to barter his wife's honor for ["sheep and oxen and donkeys and menservants and maidservants, she-donkeys and camels"]? . . .

The explanation is as follows: Pharaoh had tried

every possible means to win Abraham's favor. One day he sent him a fine ox, the next day a donkey, then a manservant, and so forth. Abraham did not dare refuse any of Pharaoh's gifts because had he done so he would have shattered Pharaoh's hopes and then he would have had reason to fear that the king would harm Sarah. All this is confirmed by what Pharaoh says to Abraham afterwards. He does not criticize Abraham for having passed off Sarah as his sister. His reproach was, "Why did you not tell *me* that she was your wife?" Pharaoh considered it quite natural that Abraham should have told the common people that she was his sister. But "you certainly would have had nothing to fear from *me*. Yet, you did not tell me — not even when I was ready to take her as my wife." Of course, Abraham had no answer to that question. He could not very well have told Pharaoh that he, Abraham, considered him to be no better than his people. . . .

CHAPTER XIII

1-2. Driven by famine, Abraham had temporarily given up his isolation and moved into populous Egypt where things went rather badly for him. Now he moved back to the place where a visible manifestation of God had first shown him the significance of that land for his future and the necessity for him to isolate himself for the time being. Having returned to Canaan, he resumed his work of summoning men in the name of God. . . .

south to Bethel, the place where his tent had been in the beginning, between Bethel and Ai,   4. to the place of the altar which he had erected there at first, and there Abram proclaimed in the Name of *God.*   5. And Lot also, who went with Abram, had sheep and cattle and tents.   6. And the land was not able to bear them that they might live together because their wealth was too great and they could not live together.   7. So there arose strife between the herdsmen of Abram's herds and the herdsmen of Lot's herds, and the Canaanite[s] and the Perizite[s] were already then inhabitants of the land.   8. And Abram said to Lot: "Please let there be no further discord between me and you, and hence between my herdsmen and your herdsmen, because, after all, we are kinsmen.   9. Is not the whole land open before you? Therefore, please separate yourself from me; if [you go to the] left, I will remain at the right; if [you go to the] right, I will remain at the left."   10. And Lot lifted up his eyes and saw the whole plain of the Jordan Valley, that it was well watered everywhere, before *God*

מִנֶּגֶב וְעַד־בֵּית־אֵל עַד־הַמָּקוֹם אֲשֶׁר־הָיָה שָׁם אָהֳלֹה בַּתְּחִלָּה בֵּין בֵּית־אֵל וּבֵין הָעָי: ד אֶל־מְקוֹם הַמִּזְבֵּחַ אֲשֶׁר־עָשָׂה שָׁם בָּרִאשֹׁנָה וַיִּקְרָא שָׁם אַבְרָם בְּשֵׁם יְהֹוָה: שלישי ה וְגַם־לְלוֹט הַהֹלֵךְ אֶת־אַבְרָם הָיָה צֹאן־וּבָקָר וְאֹהָלִים: ו וְלֹא־נָשָׂא אֹתָם הָאָרֶץ לָשֶׁבֶת יַחְדָּו כִּי־הָיָה רְכוּשָׁם רָב וְלֹא יָכְלוּ לָשֶׁבֶת יַחְדָּו: ז וַיְהִי־רִיב בֵּין רֹעֵי מִקְנֵה־אַבְרָם וּבֵין רֹעֵי מִקְנֵה־לוֹט וְהַכְּנַעֲנִי וְהַפְּרִזִּי אָז יֹשֵׁב בָּאָרֶץ: ח וַיֹּאמֶר אַבְרָם אֶל־לוֹט אַל־נָא תְהִי מְרִיבָה בֵּינִי וּבֵינֶךָ וּבֵין רֹעַי וּבֵין רֹעֶיךָ כִּי־אֲנָשִׁים אַחִים אֲנָחְנוּ: ט הֲלֹא כָל־הָאָרֶץ לְפָנֶיךָ הִפָּרֶד נָא מֵעָלָי אִם־הַשְּׂמֹאל וְאֵימִנָה וְאִם־הַיָּמִין וְאַשְׂמְאִילָה: י וַיִּשָּׂא־לוֹט אֶת־עֵינָיו וַיַּרְא אֶת־כָּל־כִּכַּר הַיַּרְדֵּן כִּי כֻלָּהּ מַשְׁקֶה לִפְנֵי |

---

6. ***And the land was not able to bear them that they might live together.*** Why not? It was not because they had too many herds or because there was not sufficient pastureland for both of them. If it all had been combined into one herd, one household, the land would have been sufficient. The reason why it was not sufficient was, we are told, because "their wealth was too great." Their other wealth, their "silver and gold," was too great. If two people cannot agree, if the one does not trust the other, then separate tents are needed—boxes, crates, everything separate for each of the two parties. "Because their wealth was too great and they were not congenial and could not live together," therefore they also could no longer remain on the same soil. Had their personalities been compatible, there would have been no need for separate pastures. But because the only thing that counted in Lot's enterprise was profit, while in Abraham's household attention was given also to interests of a higher level, because the two men did not put their acquisitions to the same use (it is not in the type of wealth but in the use one makes of it that differences between individuals become apparent), now therefore they could not live together. This was the reason why the land was not enough to support them both. . . .

9. מֵעָלָי *[from me],* literally, "from being next to me." Let us be completely separated from one another. Abraham must make this request in order to protect his own people from the bad example of Lot's menage. "Look!" he says to Lot, "My choice is limited. I cannot move to just any place where there happens to be surplus pastureland; I must seek isolation. But as for you—since you have dissociated yourself from my philosophy of life, you have no need to be so particular in your choice. The entire land is open to you. Regardless of whether you go to the right or to the left, I will remain here in my isolation." . . .

10–11. Lot found this argument quite logical. Indeed, it would appear that he had been waiting for just such an opportunity. The prospect of wandering through inhospitable regions could not have appealed to a man like Lot. What he sought was some rich, lush land where he would be safe from famines and crop failures, and he found what he wanted.

10. ***And Lot lifted up his eyes.*** Undeterred by considerations that would have influenced a man like Abraham, Lot allowed himself to be guided only by what appealed to his eyes. . . .

had destroyed Sodom and Gomorrah, like the garden of *God*, like the land of Mitzrayim till one comes to Tzoar. 11. And Lot chose for himself the whole plain of the Jordan valley, and Lot journeyed away from the east, and so they separated one from the other. 12. Abram remained in the land of Canaan, while Lot settled in the plain and pitched his tents as far as Sodom. 13. And the people in Sodom were wicked and dissipated; against *God*, exceedingly. 14. And *God* had said to Abram after Lot had separated from him: "Now lift up your eyes and look from the place where you are, northward and southward, eastward and westward, 15. for all the land that you see, to you will I give it, and to your seed forever. 16. I will make your seed as the dust of the earth so that if anyone can count the dust of the earth, then your seed shall also be counted. 17. Arise, therefore, go into the land, through the length of it and the breadth of it, for to you will I give it." 18. Then Abram pitched his tents and came and dwelt in the groves of Mamre, which are in Ḥebron, and there he built an altar to *God*.

XIV
1. It came to pass in the days of Amraphel, king of Shinar, Ariokh, king of Elassar, Kedorlaomer, king of Elam, and Tiddal, king of

שִׁחֵת יְהֹוָה אֶת־סְדֹם וְאֶת־עֲמֹרָה כְּגַן־יְהֹוָה
כְּאֶרֶץ מִצְרַיִם בֹּאֲכָה צֹעַר: יא וַיִּבְחַר־לוֹ לוֹט
אֵת כָּל־כִּכַּר הַיַּרְדֵּן וַיִּסַּע לוֹט מִקֶּדֶם וַיִּפָּרְדוּ
אִישׁ מֵעַל אָחִיו: יב אַבְרָם יָשַׁב בְּאֶרֶץ־כְּנָעַן
וְלוֹט יָשַׁב בְּעָרֵי הַכִּכָּר וַיֶּאֱהַל עַד־סְדֹם:
יג וְאַנְשֵׁי סְדֹם רָעִים וְחַטָּאִים לַיהֹוָה מְאֹד:
יד וַיהֹוָה אָמַר אֶל־אַבְרָם אַחֲרֵי הִפָּרֶד־לוֹט
מֵעִמּוֹ שָׂא נָא עֵינֶיךָ וּרְאֵה מִן־הַמָּקוֹם אֲשֶׁר־
אַתָּה שָׁם צָפֹנָה וָנֶגְבָּה וָקֵדְמָה וָיָמָּה: טו כִּי
אֶת־כָּל־הָאָרֶץ אֲשֶׁר־אַתָּה רֹאֶה לְךָ אֶתְּנֶנָּה
וּלְזַרְעֲךָ עַד־עוֹלָם: טז וְשַׂמְתִּי אֶת־זַרְעֲךָ
כַּעֲפַר הָאָרֶץ אֲשֶׁר | אִם־יוּכַל אִישׁ לִמְנוֹת
אֶת־עֲפַר הָאָרֶץ גַּם־זַרְעֲךָ יִמָּנֶה: יז קוּם
הִתְהַלֵּךְ בָּאָרֶץ לְאָרְכָּהּ וּלְרָחְבָּהּ כִּי לְךָ אֶתְּנֶנָּה:
יח וַיֶּאֱהַל אַבְרָם וַיָּבֹא וַיֵּשֶׁב בְּאֵלֹנֵי מַמְרֵא
אֲשֶׁר בְּחֶבְרוֹן וַיִּבֶן־שָׁם מִזְבֵּחַ לַיהֹוָה: פ
רביעי יד א וַיְהִי בִּימֵי אַמְרָפֶל מֶלֶךְ־שִׁנְעָר
אַרְיוֹךְ מֶלֶךְ אֶלָּסָר כְּדָרְלָעֹמֶר מֶלֶךְ עֵילָם

12-18. . . . Abraham persisted all the more in the state of isolation by which he had protected himself and his people from contact with the Canaanite cities. He remained only as near to human society as he had to be in order to "proclaim in the name of *God*" (קוֹרֵא בְּשֵׁם ד'). For he had just undergone the painful experience of learning that he had not been able to win and keep even his closest kinsman for himself and his mission. Only after God had encouraged him and requested him, as it were, to look beyond his isolation and to move into the bustle of the land without fear for himself and his principles did Abraham indeed enter the country and settle in Hebron.

14-15. *after Lot had separated from him.* Abraham had just gone through the bitter experience of seeing his brother's son—the second generation that would live after him and in whom Abraham, himself childless, could have placed his hopes for the continuance of his spiritual mission—depart from him and, drawn by external, material attractions, cast his lot with Sodom

and Gomorrah. It was after this experience that God told Abraham, "This land with all its abundance will not go to a man such as Lot but to you, whose foremost aspiration is not material gain. It is to you and your descendants that I will give it. You are not to go abroad as a missionary to win others for your calling. Whatever is to be yours must be sown by you yourself, begotten and reared in your own pure spirit." Jews must be born, not raised. "To you will I give it, and to your seed forever." This does not mean that they will be in physical possession of the land forever. However, it will belong to them always; they and the land will always be destined for each other, just as at this time it was given to Abraham without his ever having taken personal possession of it. . . .

CHAPTER XIV

1. This is the earliest historical record of an incident involving kings and warfare. Let us consider the conditions which the Word of God describes for us here,

Goiim. 2. They had earlier made war with Bera, king of Sodom, Birsha, king of Gomorrah, Shinab, king of Admah, Shem-ever, king of Zeboiim, and the king of Bela, which is Tzoar. 3. All of these had joined as allies in the Valley of Plowing,° which is now the Salt Sea. 4. For twelve years they had served Kedorlaomer and in the

וְתִדְעָל מֶלֶךְ גּוֹיִם: ב עָשׂוּ מִלְחָמָה אֶת־בֶּרַע
מֶלֶךְ סְדֹם וְאֶת־בִּרְשַׁע מֶלֶךְ עֲמֹרָה שִׁנְאָב ׀
מֶלֶךְ אַדְמָה וְשֶׁמְאֵבֶר מֶלֶךְ צְבֹיִּים (צבוים קרי)
וּמֶלֶךְ בֶּלַע הִיא־צֹעַר: ג כָּל־אֵלֶּה חָבְרוּ אֶל־
עֵמֶק הַשִּׂדִּים הוּא יָם הַמֶּלַח: ד שְׁתֵּים עֶשְׂרֵה

°*Note to the English translation*: Standard translations render this as "The Valley of Siddim." [G.H.]

apparently in order to give us a better understanding of the mission of Abraham and his people.

Here we see the lushest fruits of the system of government introduced by Nimrod at the dawn of world history. For the דּוֹר הַפְּלָגָה [the generation in which the earth was divided] coincided with the period of Abraham's youth. It was during this period that Nimrod proclaimed himself king. True, he is not expressly described as a king, but his activities are characterized as "the beginning of his kingship" [Chapter 10:10 above]. His way of rulership was to exploit the collective energies of his nation for his own purposes under the guise of patriotism but at the expense of his subjects. We now behold this trend in full flower. What we read here is no longer a history of nations but a story of kings—no fewer than five kings in as small an area as the Jordan valley. Here we have the beginnings of monarchy. Each city has its own king. We are told that later, in the days of Joshua, this one little land had as many as thirty-one kings. The other rulers were more formidable sovereigns, reigning over entire countries and provinces such as Shinar (Babylonia), Elam (Media) and Goiim (a name which indicates several nations, not merely one). Consider the location of the better known of these kingdoms, Babylonia and Media. They were a considerable distance away from Palestine; yet, the Palestinian kings were subject for some time to Kedorlaomer. So, we already see some sovereigns lording it over other kings.

Now let us see what form kingship, in fact, assumed in this affluent society. Each of the wealthy cities mentioned in this verse considered it necessary to have a king of its own. This may have been due to their wealth and affluence. Forms of monarchy in which kings are expected to spare their subjects the trouble of thinking for themselves occur primarily in nations where the citizens are intensely occupied with themselves. The more easy-going, the more materialistic and the more affluent a nation is, the less its people care about the idealistic interests of their community, the more will the people be ready to sacrifice their rights and their substance so that they should have no problems to worry about. Also, hardly anyone would want to be king of a nation that is poor, because people who have little to gain and nothing to lose cannot be easily frightened or enticed into obedience.

The foregoing may be the reason why in the land of Canaan, the most prosperous of regions, even the smallest community had a king of its own so that the people would be spared the need to think for themselves in the management of their communal affairs. It was for the same reason that these kings in turn agreed to become vassals to the powerful ruler of another land; they were עַבְדֵי עֲבָדִים ["servants of servants"], as their ancestor [Noah] had characterized the Ḥamite race. The kinglets gladly paid a little tribute each year as the price for peace and quiet, so that they mght be able to rule their lands and enjoy their pleasures as was considered proper for kings.

The events described in these verses are significant also from another point of view. Our Sages point out that here, on the very first page of recorded political history, we see four victorious kingdoms, and that these kingdoms are analogous to the course of world history which will culminate in the rise of four world powers destined ultimately to fall to the triumphant power of God. We find here the names of at least two countries we can readily recognize: Babylonia (Shinar) and Media (Elam). We see that even in remote antiquity two empires made military expeditions to Palestine and its environs, and we see Palestine, even then, go down in defeat.

Thus, when he first arrived in Canaan, the ancestor of what was to become the Jewish people encountered proof of the truism that affluence tends to enslave nations from within and without. We are told [Eruvin 54a] that where the text states [Exodus 32:16] חָרוּת עַל הַלּוּחוֹת ["cut right through the tablets"], we should read not חָרוּת ["cut through"] but חֵרוּת ["freedom"]. Man can be truly free in every respect only if he submits to the rule of the moral law. In Canaan, the ancestor of the Jewish people came face to face with yet another reality that concerned him more directly. His first experience in the land which had been promised to him as the future soil of his people was *famine*; the second was *war*. The land lacked the conditions conducive to thirteenth year they rebelled. 5. In the fourteenth year Kedorlaomer, and the kings who were allied with him, came; they struck down the Rephaites in Ashteroth-Karnayim, the Zuzites in Ḥam, the Emites in Shaveh Kiryatayim, 6. the Ḥorite[s] in their mountain land of Seir until the plain of Paran, which is near the wilderness. 7. Then they turned back and came to En Mishpat, which is Kadesh, and they struck down the whole field of the Amalekites, and also the Emorites, who dwell in

שָׁנָה עָבְדוּ אֶת־כְּדָרְלָעֹמֶר וּשְׁלֹשׁ־עֶשְׂרֵה שָׁנָה
מָרָדוּ׃ ה וּבְאַרְבַּע עֶשְׂרֵה שָׁנָה בָּא כְדָרְלָעֹמֶר
וְהַמְּלָכִים אֲשֶׁר אִתּוֹ וַיַּכּוּ אֶת־רְפָאִים
בְּעַשְׁתְּרֹת קַרְנַיִם וְאֶת־הַזּוּזִים בְּהָם וְאֵת
הָאֵימִים בְּשָׁוֵה קִרְיָתָיִם׃ ו וְאֶת־הַחֹרִי בְּהַרְרָם
שֵׂעִיר עַד אֵיל פָּארָן אֲשֶׁר עַל־הַמִּדְבָּר׃
ז וַיָּשֻׁבוּ וַיָּבֹאוּ אֶל־עֵין מִשְׁפָּט הִוא קָדֵשׁ וַיַּכּוּ
אֶת־כָּל־שְׂדֵה הָעֲמָלֵקִי וְגַם אֶת־הָאֱמֹרִי הַיֹּשֵׁב

material prosperity and political independence. In both respects the land of Canaan stood in stark contrast to Egypt.

Not only was the land dependent on heaven for its fertility, but similarly its political position was one of dependence; it could not offer resistance to a foreign invader. Left to its own devices, the "land of Israel" was exposed to famine and political dependence. Located at the crossroads of the world, where Europe, Asia and Africa meet, it had rarely been spared involvement in major wars. But *this was precisely the reason why it was chosen*. If, despite all these handicaps, there would have arisen in this land a nation which no invader would have dared attack (even though its borders were left open and undefended three times each year),[19] if all the מַלְכֻיּוֹת would have swept across the world and fought one another but would not have dared lift up their swords against this, the most prosperous but also the most defenseless of lands, (cf. Leviticus 26:6 וְחֶרֶב לֹא תַעֲבֹר בְּאַרְצְכֶם ["and no sword will pass through your land"]), then the nations of the world would have beheld with their own eyes the verity that this was the dwelling place of God. . . . Had this been the case, then the promise whose fulfillment still beckons to us only from the distant future would have become reality thousands of years ago. Then Zion would have shone forth as a light unto the nations, and the nations of the world would have said long ago, "We will go with you because we have seen that God is with you."

The nation of God, which dwelt in the environs of the ruins of Sodom and Gomorrah, should have seen this state of affairs as a warning that if there is no countervailing moral force, abundance and plenty are the natural enemies of freedom. This nation should have understood that it will be permitted to enjoy freedom and independence in its land only as long as it will devotedly cultivate the one element by which alone the lush abundance of "milk and honey" that usually begets weaklings can be transformed into something salutary and blessed. This element is the תּוֹרָה, the Law, which, by demanding obedience, in fact guarantees freedom and independence. Every field in the Jewish land should bear the imprint of the Law (כִּלְאַיִם), and particularly viniculture, the cultivation of the plant most symbolic of affluence, should bear most deeply engraved upon it the discipline of the Law (cf. איסור הֲנָאָה כִּלְאֵי כֶרֶם, the prohibition against "benefiting from forbidden mixtures in vineyards"). Everywhere, and at all times, let this warning be heard: Only on the basis of the Law will Israel prosper; as soon as it attempts to elude the rule of this Law, it will go to physical and social ruin.

To Abraham the war he witnessed in Canaan was one of the most impressive, if not the most impressive, experience of his life. The affluent kings had gone down in defeat and had become subordinate to Kedorlaomer. Finally, they had revolted. They must have been powerful individuals because Kedorlaomer was forced to call in allies to help him subdue them, but in the end they were beaten. And now he, Abraham, who was only one man, with his household, succeeded, with God as his ally, in overcoming this earthly king over kings. We see Abraham literally as the man who reconquered Canaan [from Kedorlaomer]. He pursues Kedorlaomer almost through the entire length of the land, from Hebron to Damascus, drives him out and liberates the country. He lives to see the Divine promise לְךָ אֶתְּנֶנָּה ["to you I shall give it"] fulfilled in the most literal manner.

Similarly, the prophets tell how the four powers will conquer everything, how they will also oppress *Eretz Yisrael*, but how Israel will overcome them all and, with God at its side, will become the conqueror of the world.

5–7. These verses afford us a brief review of the power and the prowess of these kings. They had passed through the entire eastern sector of Palestine, to the south until Edom, conquering all the territory along

[19]*Note to the English translation*: During the three Pilgrim Festivals, Passover, Shevuoth and Sukkoth. [G.H.]

Ḥatzatzon Tamar.°° 8. And the king of Sodom, the king of Gomorrah, the king of Admah, the king of Tzeboiim and the king of Bela, which is Tzoar, went forth and started a war with them in the Valley of Plowing, 9. with Kedorlaomer, king of Elam, Tiddal, king of Goiim, Amraphel, king of Shinar, Ariokh, king of Elassar — four kings against five. 10. The Valley of Plowing was full of loam pits, and the kings of Sodom and Gomorrah fled, and they fell into them; those who remained fled toward the mountains. 11. They took all the movable property from Sodom and Gomorrah and all their victuals and went. 12. They took also Lot and his movable property—[he was] the son of the brother of Abram—and they went, for he was an inhabitant of Sodom. 13. And the escapee came and brought the news to Abram, the

בְּחַצְצֹן תָּמָר׃ ח וַיֵּצֵא מֶלֶךְ־סְדֹם וּמֶלֶךְ עֲמֹרָה
וּמֶלֶךְ אַדְמָה וּמֶלֶךְ צְבֹיִים (צבוים קרי) וּמֶלֶךְ
בֶּלַע הִוא־צֹעַר וַיַּעַרְכוּ אִתָּם מִלְחָמָה בְּעֵמֶק
הַשִּׂדִּים׃ ט אֵת כְּדָרְלָעֹמֶר מֶלֶךְ עֵילָם וְתִדְעָל
מֶלֶךְ גּוֹיִם וְאַמְרָפֶל מֶלֶךְ שִׁנְעָר וְאַרְיוֹךְ מֶלֶךְ
אֶלָּסָר אַרְבָּעָה מְלָכִים אֶת־הַחֲמִשָּׁה׃ י וְעֵמֶק
הַשִּׂדִּים בֶּאֱרֹת בֶּאֱרֹת חֵמָר וַיָּנֻסוּ מֶלֶךְ־סְדֹם
וַעֲמֹרָה וַיִּפְּלוּ־שָׁמָּה וְהַנִּשְׁאָרִים הֶרָה נָּסוּ׃
יא וַיִּקְחוּ אֶת־כָּל־רְכֻשׁ סְדֹם וַעֲמֹרָה וְאֶת־כָּל־
אָכְלָם וַיֵּלֵכוּ׃ יב וַיִּקְחוּ אֶת־לוֹט וְאֶת־רְכֻשׁוֹ
בֶּן־אֲחִי אַבְרָם וַיֵּלֵכוּ וְהוּא יֹשֵׁב בִּסְדֹם׃
יג וַיָּבֹא הַפָּלִיט וַיַּגֵּד לְאַבְרָם הָעִבְרִי וְהוּא

°°*Note to the English translation*: Literally, "and also the Emorite, who dwells in Ḥatzatzon Tamar." [G.H.]

the way. Afterwards, they turned back to the north to carry out their original plan and halted when they came face to face with their true enemies.

8–10. However, the enemy kings did not wait until Kedorlaomer and his allies came but went out to meet them and attacked them. But they were quickly put to flight. The kings were the first to flee. . . . The mountains toward which they fled were to the west of the battlefield; thus, near the area where Abraham dwelt.

12. We already know from previous chapters that Lot was the son of Abraham's brother and that he lived in Sodom. Hence there must be some reason why these facts are repeated here. Lot was not originally a Sodomite. When he first arrived in Sodom he was known as the son of Abraham's brother. Had he remained what he had been, he would have been spared the fate of being taken prisoner. Even though he was caught in a war, Lot as an alien could have expected to be spared from Kedorlaomer's revenge. However, he had become an "inhabitant" of Sodom; this meant that he enjoyed the rights of Sodomite citizenship, and so he had to suffer along with the others.

Herein lies a warning to the members of Abraham's family, a warning that has been borne out by centuries of Jewish history. He who remains true to his calling and destiny as a Jew will have to make many sacrifices but, on the other hand, he will be spared much trouble because he will be borne upon כַּנְפֵי הַשְּׁכִינָה [the wings of the Divine Presence]. The ghettoes that isolated us were not only "against" the Jews; their existence also benefited those who dwelt within them. Those who lived within the ghetto walls remained safe from many evils to which those outside fell victim during the Middle Ages. To be sure, the Jews were not considered good enough to become mayors or bailiffs or to join the retinues of knights. They were not permitted to participate in tournaments and they took no part in world affairs. But neither did they have a part in the torturing, slaughtering, strangling and incineration of their fellow men. They were often the victims but never the torturers. Their hands remained innocent of human blood, and when fate caught up with the emperors and their armies, the Jews remained safe in their ghettoes. They should be happy that they were called to the proscenium of world affairs only now, when the world seems about to become more just and humane in every respect than it was in ages past. But people who indulge their physical appetites to the exclusion of all else will never learn. Lot, for one, should have learned his lesson from his experience and henceforth avoided Sodom [and everything for which Sodom stood] but when the final catastrophe struck, Lot was still there in Sodom.

13. . . . Abraham had remained the *Ivri.* This term may be interpreted as "he who came from the other side of the river" or, as Rabbi Joshua explains, "the one who stands aside," the one who stands in opposition to the rest of the world, the first "protestor," as it were. In either case, it indicates that Abraham had remained isolated in his own distinctive character and had

Hebrew, —now he dwelt in the plain of Mamre the Emorite, brother of Eshkol and of Aner, and these were the masters in a covenant with Abram. 14. When Abram heard that his kinsman had been taken captive, he led forth all those who had been born in his household and educated by him, three hundred and eighteen, and pursued [the captors] as far as Dan. 15. He divided himself against them by night, he and his servants, and he struck them down, and

שֹׁכֵן בְּאֵלֹנֵי מַמְרֵא הָאֱמֹרִי אֲחִי אֶשְׁכֹּל וַאֲחִי
עָנֵר וְהֵם בַּעֲלֵי בְרִית־אַבְרָם: יד וַיִּשְׁמַע אַבְרָם
כִּי נִשְׁבָּה אָחִיו וַיָּרֶק אֶת־חֲנִיכָיו יְלִידֵי בֵיתוֹ
שְׁמֹנָה עָשָׂר וּשְׁלֹשׁ מֵאוֹת וַיִּרְדֹּף עַד־דָּן:
טו וַיֵּחָלֵק עֲלֵיהֶם ׀ לַיְלָה הוּא וַעֲבָדָיו וַיַּכֵּם

become known and recognized for remaining thus isolated.

וְהוּא שֹׁכֵן [*now he dwelt*]. In the case of Lot, we are told וְהוּא יֹשֵׁב בִּסְדֹם ["he was *an inhabitant* of Sodom"]. יֹשֵׁב—a state of rest that entails being based on the ground, implies that the person so described has become completely integrated with the place where he now is. As in Chapter 13:7 above, וְהַכְּנַעֲנִי וְהַפְּרִזִּי אָז יֹשֵׁב בָּאָרֶץ ["and the Canaanites and the Perizites were already *inhabitants* of the land"], so we are told here that Lot יֹשֵׁב בִּסְדֹם. Of Abraham, by contrast, we are told that שֹׁכֵן בְּאֵלֹנֵי מַמְרֵא ["he *dwelt* in the plain of Mamre"]. שֹׁכֵן, [like יֹשֵׁב] denotes a state of rest; however, it does not refer to the dweller's relationship with the ground on which he lives but to his relationship with his neighbors. It implies a peaceful co-existence with one's neighbors, without, however, permitting oneself to be absorbed by them. This, as already noted in Chapter 9:27 above, is also the reason why שְׁכִינָה is the term commonly used to denote the nearness of God on earth.

In the midst of the Emorite population Abraham was not afraid to maintain his unique character traits, even if this meant having to remain a tolerated stranger among his neighbors. He was Abram from "the other side," שׁוֹכֵן, "living next to" the Emorites. He maintained a peaceful co-existence with them. Neither disturbed the other. Abraham was an outsider and merely tolerated by his neighbors; nonetheless Mamre, the lord of the region, and his kinsmen were בַּעֲלֵי בְרִית אַבְרָם ["the masters in a covenant with Abram"] [i.e., it was not Abraham who sought an alliance with Mamre and his kinsmen, but Mamre and his kinsmen, the natives, who took the initiative and made a covenant with Abraham, the stranger].

°   °   °

Abraham's conduct should serve as a model for זֶרַע אַבְרָהָם [the seed of Abraham] as long as they will be בְּאֶרֶץ לֹא לָהֶם [in a land which is not their own]. Let the Jew remain a Jew, loving peace, and in no manner attempting to disturb the conditions that prevail on alien soil. Let him, rather, develop and shape his own life as a Jew in such a way that the others will seek to draw him into their circle of friends, not the reverse. For the concept "Jew" is broader than the concept "man." Let the Jew remain simply a Jew, in the full and complete sense of the word. If he behaves in this manner, then, even though he will be only a שֹׁכֵן, [a neighbor dwelling alongside the non-Jews], he will be respected and permitted to enter into the בְּרִית [the covenant] of the nations. Abraham did not abandon his calling as a Jew in order to enter into the covenant with Mamre and his kinsmen.

14. . . . This context of the verb וַיָּרֶק ["he led forth," lit. "he 'emptied' forth," from רִיק ("empty")] may explain why until this point Abraham had so strenuously avoided close contacts with others. Abraham and Sarah had no reason to fear that they themselves might be corrupted, but Abraham had in his charge 318 חֲנִיכִים, three hundred and eighteen human souls whom he had educated, in the midst of corruption, and whom he now had to preserve for their pure human calling in which he had trained them. These people had to be protected; it was primarily for their sake that he sought isolation. They were, we are told, יְלִידֵי בֵיתוֹ ["born in his household"]; only because they were such could they become חֲנִיכָיו ["educated by him"].

Abraham had been unable to achieve this objective in the case of Lot, because the latter had come to him only as a mature man. Education must begin at birth, particularly if the purpose of that education, as was the case in Abraham's household, is to win the individual for the calling of עִבְרִי, who must perceive the rest of the world as being opposed to all he stands for. Until now, Abraham, for the sake of his חֲנִיכָיו, had kept his household from contact with the world outside; until now, חֲנִיכָיו had been contained within the confines of his household. But now, when a human life was in peril, Abraham no longer considered the danger [of corruption]. Instead, וַיָּרֶק אֶת חֲנִיכָיו, "he poured them out," all of them, and so the family of Abraham, who until then most probably had been ridiculed as recluses by men like Lot and the peoples of Sodom and Gemorrah, now sped forth to Lot's rescue. . . .

pursued them as far as Ḥobah, which is to the left of Damascus. 16. He brought back everything that had been carried off. He also brought back his brother Lot and his possessions, as well as the women and the people. 17. And the king of Sodom went out to meet him after his return from the victory over Kedorlaomer and over the kings who were with him, in the valley of Shaveh, which is the Valley of the King. 18. Malki Tzedek, king of Shalem, however, had brought out bread and wine, but then he was a priest of God the Most High. 19. He blessed him and said: "Blessed be Abram to God the Most High, Owner of heaven and earth. 20. And blessed be God the Most High, Who has delivered your enemies into your hands." And he gave him one-tenth of everything. 21. And the king of Sodom said to Abram: "Give me the souls and take the possessions for yourself." 22. But Abram said to the king of Sodom: "I have lifted up my hand toward *God*, God the Most High, Owner of heaven and earth. 23. Not from a thread to a shoelace, nor from anything that is yours will I take; you shall not say: 'I have made Abram rich.'

וַיִּרְדְּפֵם עַד־חוֹבָה אֲשֶׁר מִשְּׂמֹאל לְדַמָּשֶׂק:
טז וַיָּשֶׁב אֵת כָּל־הָרְכֻשׁ וְגַם אֶת־לוֹט אָחִיו
וּרְכֻשׁוֹ הֵשִׁיב וְגַם אֶת־הַנָּשִׁים וְאֶת־הָעָם:
יז וַיֵּצֵא מֶלֶךְ־סְדֹם לִקְרָאתוֹ אַחֲרֵי שׁוּבוֹ
מֵהַכּוֹת אֶת־כְּדָרְלָעֹמֶר וְאֶת־הַמְּלָכִים אֲשֶׁר
אִתּוֹ אֶל־עֵמֶק שָׁוֵה הוּא עֵמֶק הַמֶּלֶךְ:
יח וּמַלְכִּי־צֶדֶק מֶלֶךְ שָׁלֵם הוֹצִיא לֶחֶם וָיָיִן
וְהוּא כֹהֵן לְאֵל עֶלְיוֹן: יט וַיְבָרְכֵהוּ וַיֹּאמַר
בָּרוּךְ אַבְרָם לְאֵל עֶלְיוֹן קֹנֵה שָׁמַיִם וָאָרֶץ:
כ וּבָרוּךְ אֵל עֶלְיוֹן אֲשֶׁר־מִגֵּן צָרֶיךָ בְּיָדֶךָ
וַיִּתֶּן־לוֹ מַעֲשֵׂר מִכֹּל: חמישי כא וַיֹּאמֶר מֶלֶךְ־
סְדֹם אֶל־אַבְרָם תֶּן־לִי הַנֶּפֶשׁ וְהָרְכֻשׁ קַח־לָךְ:
כב וַיֹּאמֶר אַבְרָם אֶל־מֶלֶךְ סְדֹם הֲרִמֹתִי יָדִי
אֶל־יְהוָה אֵל עֶלְיוֹן קֹנֵה שָׁמַיִם וָאָרֶץ: כג אִם־
מִחוּט וְעַד שְׂרוֹךְ־נַעַל וְאִם־אֶקַּח מִכָּל־אֲשֶׁר־
לָךְ וְלֹא תֹאמַר אֲנִי הֶעֱשַׁרְתִּי אֶת־אַבְרָם:

17–18. These two verses show a striking contrast between two rulers. The king of Sodom, who must have felt deeply humiliated before Abraham and even more deeply indebted to him, not only failed to aid Abraham and his little band in the pursuit of the enemy but now that the victory has been won, merely goes forth to meet him. He considers that he has done Abraham sufficient honor by greeting him as an equal, as one king to another, in the "Valley of שָׁוֵה,"[20] although in fact he is about to request a favor from Abraham. A king of Sodom knows to ask favors and to make demands, but the idea that one might offer the weary victors a piece of bread to receive them or a drink of wine to refresh them is not suggested anywhere in the code of etiquette followed by the gentlemen of Sodom. Not so Malki Tzedek, king of Shalem, who had not even been involved in the incident. He has bread and wine brought out. But then he was a priest of God the Most High. Thus we see that the conception of "the God of Gods", as the Sages put it, had not yet been forgotten even among the polytheistic nations. . . .

20. . . . מַעֲשֵׂר *[one-tenth]*. This is the first mention of tithing. Tithing, or "giving *ma'aser*" is an act whereby the one whom the receiver of the tithe represents is acknowledged as the source of that which is being tithed. By giving one-tenth of the spoils of victory to Malki Tzedek, the priest of God the Most High, Abraham acknowledged "God the Most High" as the One Who granted him the victory.

° ° °

When we earn our first florin we are still capable of being moved by our good fortune; with the memory of our past poverty still fresh in our minds, we are very much aware that it is God Who has given us this florin. But our tenth, one hundredth, or one thousandth florin, and so forth, appears to us only as a natural product of the nine, or ninety-nine, or nine-hundred ninety-nine that have come before. The act of מַעֲשֵׂר is intended to remind us that the tenth, one hundredth and one thousandth florin is just as much a direct gift from הַשְׁגָּחָה פְּרָטִית [Divine Providence] as was the first florin we ever earned.

[20]*Note to the English translation*: שָׁוֵה is the Hebrew term for "equal." [G.H.]

24. Far be it from me! Only that which the people have eaten, and the portion of the men who went with me—Aner, Eshkol and Mamre—they may take their portion."

XV 1. After what has been related thus far, the word of *God* came to Abram in a vision [saying]: "Fear not, Abram, I shall remain a shield to you; your compensation shall be immeasurable." 2. And Abram said: "O *God*, my Lord, what wilt Thou give me, seeing that I go hence childless and the heir who yearns for my household is [the] Damasc[ene kin of]

כד בִּלְעָדַ֔י רַ֚ק אֲשֶׁ֣ר אָֽכְל֣וּ הַנְּעָרִ֔ים וְחֵ֙לֶק֙ הָֽאֲנָשִׁ֔ים אֲשֶׁ֥ר הָלְכ֖וּ אִתִּ֑י עָנֵר֙ אֶשְׁכֹּ֣ל וּמַמְרֵ֔א הֵ֖ם יִקְח֥וּ חֶלְקָֽם׃ ס טו א אַחַ֣ר ׀ הַדְּבָרִ֣ים הָאֵ֗לֶּה הָיָ֤ה דְבַר־יְהוָה֙ אֶל־אַבְרָ֔ם בַּֽמַּחֲזֶ֖ה לֵאמֹ֑ר אַל־תִּירָ֣א אַבְרָ֗ם אָֽנֹכִי֙ מָגֵ֣ן לָ֔ךְ שְׂכָרְךָ֖ הַרְבֵּ֥ה מְאֹֽד׃ ב וַיֹּ֣אמֶר אַבְרָ֗ם אֲדֹנָ֤י יֱהוִה֙ מַה־תִּתֶּן־לִ֔י וְאָֽנֹכִ֖י הוֹלֵ֣ךְ עֲרִירִ֑י וּבֶן־מֶ֣שֶׁק בֵּיתִ֔י

CHAPTER XV

1. . . . The phrase אַחַר הַדְּבָרִים הָאֵלֶּה [lit., "after these things"] occurs only one more time in the story of Abraham: in the introduction to the story of the עֲקֵדָה [the "binding" of Isaac, Genesis 22:1]. It means that everything we have been told about Abraham up to this point served only as an introduction to what follows. The life of Abraham may be divided into three distinct periods: 1) from לֶךְ לְךָ [Genesis 12:1 ff., where Abraham is commanded to leave his father's house and to go to the land God will show him] until בְּרִית בֵּין הַבְּתָרִים ["the covenant of the pieces," which is related in this chapter]; 2) from that point until the עֲקֵדָה, and 3) [from the "binding" of Isaac] until Abraham's death [Genesis 25:7 ff.].

The word אַחַר can denote either "after" or "other." The former connotation implies that something else has gone before; the latter is the reverse; the former, the פָּנִים ["face" or "obverse."] In other words, periods introduced by the word אַחַר represent the reverse, as it were, of what has gone before. Abraham's life until this point represented an upward trend. Starting out as one isolated individual, Abraham had become a conqueror, in fact, the spiritual conqueror of his entire generation. But that which he was yet to achieve could be accomplished only by his experiencing the "reverse" side of fortune, by going through the harsh school of suffering.

    °   °   °

The "word of God" to Abraham begins with the words: "Fear not!" It would appear that Abraham must have been in an apprehensive mood so that he was in need of encouragement.

    °   °

אַל תִּירָא *[Fear not].* That which I have to tell you will change nothing. I will continue to be your shield, and the happiness that will come to you as a result of your devotion shall be beyond measure. . . . What will now be asked of you will entail a sacrifice (hence the mood [of apprehension] which I have stirred within you), but

שְׂכָרְךָ, your compensation for this sacrifice shall be beyond measure.

The Biblical narrative has very little to say about שָׂכָר, "reward." In fact, the term hardly ever occurs again in this connotation. The good that God wants us to do is its own truest reward. Only one who thinks he has made a sacrifice will demand שָׂכָר, "compensation." The genuine Jew regards the performance of a *mitzvah* not as a sacrifice but as a personal gain: שְׂכַר מִצְוָה מִצְוָה ["the reward of a good deed is another good deed," Avoth 4:2]. In each instance, the blessings promised for a good deed are only by-products, not the purpose for which one performs that deed. It is God, not Abraham, who raises the question of "compensation." It was God Who regarded Abraham's unparalleled devotion as a sacrifice and, accordingly, describes the unbounded happiness that will eventually come to Abraham as a result of his devotion, as a "compensation beyond measure." . . .

2. אֲדֹנָי יֱהוִה is that most profound combination, even in terms of a straightforward interpretation of the Names of God, which is the overall heritage of our national awareness. It is spelled as מִדַּת הָרַחֲמִים [God in His quality of mercy] but is read like מִדַּת הַדִּין [God in His quality of justice]. Thus it teaches us that even where, on the face of it, God appears in His quality of stern justice, it must be understood as a manifestation of His love. cf. בְּרֹגֶז רַחֵם תִּזְכּוֹר ["In wrath remember compassion," Habakkuk 3:2]. His sternness is only an instrument of love by which the foundations are built for a blessed future. It is the same שֵׁם הויה except that it is read as שֵׁם אֱלֹקִים. Hence, by responding with the words אדני יהוה when God awakens within him a sense of foreboding, a fear of a gloomy, troubled future, but at the same time assures him of His continuing favor and protection, Abraham means to say: "O Thou my Lord, my Master, in Whose service I stand, and Who art stern and yet art love—I need not seek understanding, I require no explanations, for even when Thou appearest as אלק' [in Thy quality of stern justice] Thou still art ד'

Eliezer." 3. Abram thought; "Lo! to me Thou hast given no seed, and lo! the son of my house is my heir." 4. Lo! the word of *God* came to him [saying]: "This one shall not be your heir, but he who will come forth from your own inner parts shall be your heir." 5. He led him outside and said: "Look, please, toward heaven and count the stars if you are able to count them." And He said to him: "So shall your seed be." 6. And he had put all his trust in *God* and He counted this to him as a[n act of] right-

הָוּא דַּמֶּ֫שֶׂק אֱלִיעֶֽזֶר׃ ג וַיֹּ֣אמֶר אַבְרָ֔ם הֵ֣ן לִ֔י
לֹ֥א נָתַ֖תָּה זָ֑רַע וְהִנֵּ֥ה בֶן־בֵּיתִ֖י יוֹרֵ֥שׁ אֹתִֽי׃
ד וְהִנֵּ֨ה דְבַר־יְהֹוָ֤ה אֵלָיו֙ לֵאמֹ֔ר לֹ֥א יִֽירָשְׁךָ֖ זֶ֑ה
כִּי־אִם֙ אֲשֶׁ֣ר יֵצֵ֣א מִמֵּעֶ֔יךָ ה֖וּא יִֽירָשֶֽׁךָ׃
ה וַיּוֹצֵ֨א אֹת֜וֹ הַח֗וּצָה וַיֹּ֙אמֶר֙ הַבֶּט־נָ֣א
הַשָּׁמַ֗יְמָה וּסְפֹר֙ הַכּ֣וֹכָבִ֔ים אִם־תּוּכַ֖ל לִסְפֹּ֣ר
אֹתָ֑ם וַיֹּ֣אמֶר ל֔וֹ כֹּ֥ה יִהְיֶ֖ה זַרְעֶֽךָ׃ ו וְהֶאֱמִ֖ן

[the God of love]." With these words Abraham has expressed his inmost, unconditional devotion. . . .

3. . . . "True, I have יְלִידֵי בַיִת [those born in my house] but they are not יְלָדַי [they were not born to me]; they are not זַרְעִי [my seed]. I have raised them but I have not begotten them; I have acquired them but I did not receive them from Thee." Abraham does not ask God to change this situation; he merely points it out to Him: הִנֵּה, הֵן: "Behold, see whether this is as it should be. If it is right in Thine eyes, then it must be right altogether, for Thou dost practice loving-kindness even where I cannot perceive it." It is possible, indeed probable, that the verb ויאמר in this instance implies not what Abraham said, but what he thought to himself. For this reason the verse that follows does not open with ויֹּאמֶר אֵלָיו ["and *God* said to him"] but with וְהִנֵּה וגו׳ ["Lo! the word of *God*"], as if to indicate that God interrupted Abraham's thoughts.

5. . . . The trend of Abraham's thoughts is clear from the context. He had given up all hope of ever getting a child; in the natural course of events, too, he could no longer expect the joys of fatherhood. Under the impact of these emotions, he said, "Lo! whatever Thou wouldst still give me will be meaningless to me because I will depart childless from this world." Thereupon God led him out into the open and said to him, "Look, please, toward heaven." There, in the heavens, you will behold a formation of existence entirely different from that which occurs on earth. On earth we no longer see any work created *directly* by God. Everything we behold on earth today has been produced by other creatures [of God], originating not directly from the hands of God but arising and existing under conditions set by other creatures and circumstances.

Seen from the vantage point of earth, where all things originate under predetermined conditions, Abraham was entirely correct: He would have no rational basis for hoping that he might yet have children. But then God bade him look toward heaven. There, in heaven, conditions are the reverse of what they are on earth. In heaven, we behold creations which were called into existence *directly* by God, in the same pristine state as they had been when God placed them there at the time of Creation. (If we would be able, from some extra-terrestrial position, to look upon the earth as a whole, as another heavenly body, it would afford us a similar perspective.) If, therefore, a human being is to be helped visualize a form of existence brought about by the direct action of God's omnipotence, this can be done only by showing him the stars. His eyes must be directed toward heaven, to that two-fold שָׁם ["yonder"] from where a world called forth directly by God shines down upon him. "Can you possibly count these creations?" These creations which originated directly from the Creator are more numerous than the finite creatures of indirect origin upon earth. Therefore, "Abandon your astrological speculations" (Midrash), desist from your natural, earthbound speculations and open your mind instead to the concept of this starry world.

"Thus shall your people be:" of the same immediate Divine origin, just as untrammeled by natural conditions and combinations as the world of the stars above, a second act of יֵשׁ מֵאַיִן [creation *ex nihilo*].

Abraham and Sarah will have to walk the earth childless for another 30 years, their last natural prospects of parental joys will have to evaporate, these hopes of theirs must become an object of derision on earth, with Abraham and Sarah themselves unable to keep from laughing at them, כָּל הַשֹּׁמֵעַ יִצְחַק לִי ["All who will hear of this will laugh at me" (Genesis 21:6)], indeed, the whole world will have to laugh before the first child of the Divinely-ordained nation will come into the world. . . .

6. . . . We are not told here וַיַּאֲמֵן בַּה׳ [that Abraham *trusted* in God] as we are in the case of the people of Israel (וַיַּרְא יִשְׂרָאֵל וגו׳ וַיַּאֲמִינוּ בה׳ ["And Israel saw . . . and they trusted in *God*" Exodus 14:31). This would have implied that Abraham gained his אֱמוּנָה [trust] only as a result of the experiences related in the passages immediately preceding. Rather, וְהֶאֱמִן בַּד׳, ["Abraham

eous duty. 7. Thereupon He said to him:
"I am *God,* Who brought you out of Ur
Casdim to give you this land to take posses-
sion of it." 8. And he said, "My Lord,
God, whereby will I know that I am to take
possession of it?" 9. And He said to him:

בַּיהוָה וַיַּחְשְׁבֶהָ לּוֹ צְדָקָה׃ ששי ז וַיֹּאמֶר אֵלָיו
אֲנִי יְהוָה אֲשֶׁר הוֹצֵאתִיךָ מֵאוּר כַּשְׂדִּים לָתֶת
לְךָ אֶת־הָאָרֶץ הַזֹּאת לְרִשְׁתָּהּ׃ ח וַיֹּאמַר אֲדֹנָי
יֱהוִה בַּמָּה אֵדַע כִּי אִירָשֶׁנָּה׃ ט וַיֹּאמֶר אֵלָיו

had *put all his trust* in *God"*]. All of Abraham's previous life had been אֱמוּנָה. Already by using the appellation of יהוה, in addressing God, Abraham had given expression to his complete אֱמוּנָה, and this most recent insight into his own future and that of his people served only as an additional reinforcement of his אֱמוּנָה and as an added opportunity to put it into practice.

° ° °

7. In view of the fact that God introduces this momentous revelation of the future ordained for Abraham's people with an allusion to Abraham's departure from Ur Casdim, it is clear that this departure had not been an ordinary "move" from one place to another. It must have been an instance of miraculous aid from God Himself, a Divine act of deliverance even as the exodus from Egypt was to be for Abraham's descendants. Only a reference to such an extraordinary deliverance from an extraordinary peril—such as Nimrod's attempt on Abraham's life in Ur Casdim, as related by tradition—could turn Abraham's "exodus from Ur Casdim" into an experience from which the patriarch and his people would be able to draw the strength and hope to endure 400 years of *galuth* [exilic] sufferings until the "exodus from Egypt."

If this first deliverance was one from death by fire—with אוּר meaning "fire" so that this passage could be interpreted to mean, "Who brought you out of the fire of Casdim," then the peril to Israel in Egypt may be pictured allegorically as תַנּוּר עָשָׁן וְלַפִּיד אֵשׁ [15:17] a smoking, flaming furnace, implying that the ordeal which their ancestor had to endure physically in an actual furnace would be experienced in history by his descendants in the political furnace that was ancient Egypt. Thus יְצִיאַת אוּר כַּשְׂדִים [Abraham's departure from Ur Casdim] would be the prototype of יְצִיאַת מִצְרַיִם [the exodus from Egypt].

8. . . . God added to His promise one word which does not appear in the promises given by Him earlier in the narrative. The first promise (Chapter 12:7 above) had been, "To your seed will I give this land." Similarly in Chapter 13:15, "To you will I give it, and to your seed forever." Neither of these passages contains any reference to an active participation by Abraham or by his descendants in the process. But in Verse 7 the promise reads, "To give you this land *to take possession* of it." The verb לְרִשְׁתָּהּ ["to take possession of it"] so patently connotes independent action that it is used also to denote conquest and is, in fact, so used in the command (Deuteronomy 1:21) רְאֵה נָתַן ד׳ א׳ לְפָנֶיךָ אֶת הָאָרֶץ עֲלֵה רֵשׁ וגו׳ ["Lo! *God,* your God, has set the land before you; go up, take possession of it," etc.]; cf. also Deuteronomy 1:8; 9:23; 2:24, 31. Abraham is told here that God has taken him out of Ur Casdim in order to give him this land so that he, Abraham, may take possession of it as its conqueror. Abraham had just won a glorious victory over four conquering kings. He had not undertaken this campaign in response to an explicit command from God but had been impelled merely by his ordinary sense of duty. He could very well have concluded from this experience that, upheld by God's aid, he (or his descendants, if you will) was meant to conquer the Divinely-promised land in the same fashion. This is why Abraham asks, "How will I know that the proper time has come for me to conquer this land?"

Far from implying a lack of trust in God, this question in fact expresses Abraham's complete trust in Him. Even as he triumphed over the four kings, so now, too, Abraham is ready to wage the fight to conquer the land. The fact that it was God Who had promised him this land is to him sufficient assurance of victory here, too. God is אֲדֹנָיו, He is his Master, in whose service he, Abraham, lives and labors; He is also יהוה, Who dispenses favor even when He appears to be withholding it and under Whose command Abraham is therefore ready to place himself no matter what perils, struggles, anxiety and labor this might entail.

9–21. Abraham asked: בַּמָּה אֵדַע ["Whereby will I know?"], and God's answer (Verse 13) is יָדֹעַ תֵּדַע ["You shall surely know," etc.] Abraham wanted to know by what sign he would be given to understand that the time had come when, by God's decree, he was to take possession of the land.

God accedes to Abraham's request and replies: "You shall surely know that you yourself will not take possession of the land, neither will your descendants be able to do so immediately, or in the way of ever-growing prosperity. For a span of three generations they will have to live as aliens and slaves, tormented, homeless, unresisting and without freedom; only the fourth generation will return to take possession of the land. Only by that time will the moral corruption that will render the present land deserving of death reach its full measure. Those who now possess the land have yet to reach that level of corruption which will doom them; at

קְחָה לִי עֶגְלָה מְשֻׁלֶּשֶׁת וְעֵז מְשֻׁלֶּשֶׁת וְאַיִל
מְשֻׁלָּשׁ וְתֹר וְגוֹזָל׃ י וַיִּקַּח־לוֹ אֶת־כָּל־אֵלֶּה
וַיְבַתֵּר אֹתָם בַּתָּוֶךְ וַיִּתֵּן אִישׁ־בִּתְרוֹ לִקְרַאת
רֵעֵהוּ וְאֶת־הַצִּפֹּר לֹא בָתָר׃ יא וַיֵּרֶד הָעַיִט

"Bring Me three times a female calf and three times a goat and three times a ram, and a turtle-dove and a young pigeon."
10. He brought all these to Him, and He cut them in two, placing each half opposite the other, but He did not cut up the bird.
11. And the bird[s] of prey came down

the same time, those who are to possess the land in the future must experience poverty, slavery and misery in order to become sufficiently mature to take possession. You are only the one with whom the covenant has been made. You will go to your fathers in peace. Only in the fourth generation will the promise be fulfilled."

Phrased as a prediction of events to come, this announcement, made to the patriarch in answer to his question, was intended to serve his descendants as a source of courage and perseverance, of hope and confidence during the centuries of unspeakable misery in which they were to be tested and trained. It was impressed upon the patriarch not only in words but also in the form of allegorical acts and experiences—the night that never seemed to end, and the dread, followed by release and an exultant awakening—so that he might be able to communicate it all the more eloquently and forcibly to future generations. Thus God's statement beginning with יָדֹעַ תֵּדַע ["You shall surely know"] is merely an explanation of that which had already been communicated to Abraham in allegorical form, a verbal translation of the signs, acts and events that preceded it. All that now remains for us is to relate these symbolic happenings to the passages which follow.

Since the word שַׁלֵּשׁ (I Kings 18:34 ["Do it the third time"]) means to perform an act for the third time, and חוּט הַמְשֻׁלָּשׁ (Ecclesiastes 4:12) denotes a "threefold cord," the words מְשֻׁלֶּשֶׁת and מְשֻׁלָּשׁ in Verse 9 of this Pentateuchal chapter must also have a connotation of "three times"; thus, three heifers, three goats, three rams. However, the text does not read עֲגָלוֹת שָׁלֹשׁ, עִזִּים שָׁלֹשׁ וְאֵילִים שְׁלֹשָׁה "three heifers, three goats and three rams" but, literally, "three times a heifer, three times a goat, three times a ram." This is intended to convey the thought that three each of these animals constitute a group which belongs together and also that the "bringing" of these animals before God is an act to be repeated three times.

If one then links the allegorical acts with the subsequent, verbal, part of this revelation, it is clear that the dismemberment of these living creatures, with the bird of prey greedily swooping down upon the carcasses, is intended to symbolize the circumstances and the perils which have been ordained for the coming generations of Abrahamites.

If we are told, furthermore, that only the fourth generation will be redeemed; i.e., that the three preceding generations will have to endure the misery predicted in the Divine revelation to Abraham, then the symbolic connotation of the three-time presentation of these animals before God is clear: Your generations, that is, three of your future generations, will have to deliver themselves to Me [i.e., God] in terms of the qualities represented by עֶגְלָה [the heifer], עֵז [the goat], אַיִל [the ram].

וַיְבַתֵּר וגו׳ ***[and He cut them in two]***. I shall cause three of your future generations to suffer a violent death as regards their qualities symbolized by עֶגְלָה [the heifer], עֵז [the goat] and אַיִל [the ram], and shall permit only those qualities symbolized by the תּוֹר [the turtle dove] and גּוֹזָל [the young pigeon] to survive. They shall lie on the ground as carcasses of עֶגְלָה, עֵז and אַיִל [heifers, goats and rams], and the bird of prey will regard them as welcome quarry. Only due to your זְכוּת [merit], because they are your own, will you [i.e., Abraham] be able to keep them from being consumed by the bird of prey. It is quite clear that the subject of the verb וַיְבַתֵּר ["and he cut them in two"] is God, not Abraham, for it is not until Verse 11: וַיַּשֵּׁב אֹתָם אַבְרָם ["and Abram drove them away"] that Abraham occurs as the subject of that verb.

Now it remains for us to ascertain the connotation of עֶגְלָה [heifer], עֵז [goat], אַיִל [ram], תּוֹר [turtle dove] and גּוֹזָל [young pigeon] with reference to the personalities of individuals or to the character of nations.

The fact that these animal species should be considered as analogous to specific human personality types is readily apparent from no more than a superficial glance at the sacrificial laws, under which only these particular animals are permitted as offerings, and which prescribe the species and sex of animals to be offered by various personality types under given circumstances.

The species of cattle, בָּקָר, שׁוֹר, is the "working" animal, toiling in the service of its master (as distinct from חֲמוֹר, which represents the beast of burden).

The young of cattle always appear in the Biblical text as animals that must be trained for work. Accordingly, cattle in the Bible symbolize energy and efficiency. The fully developed member of the species is פָּר [the bull]; therefore, פָּר in the offerings always symbolizes the "public" personality called upon to labor in the service of God and of the community and to set an example by his endeavors. The עֶגְלָה [heifer] accordingly symbolizes energy still in its beginning or developing phases.

צאן, the species that includes sheep and goats, is the

עַל־הַפְּגָרִים וַיַּשֵּׁב אֹתָם אַבְרָם׃ יב וַיְהִי
הַשֶּׁמֶשׁ לָבוֹא וְתַרְדֵּמָה נָפְלָה עַל־אַבְרָם וְהִנֵּה
אֵימָה חֲשֵׁכָה גְדֹלָה נֹפֶלֶת עָלָיו׃ יג וַיֹּאמֶר

upon the carcasses, and Abram drove them away. 12. The sun was about to set and a deep sleep fell upon Abram; and lo! dread, a great darkness, fell upon him. 13. And

true pasture animal. Hence it is so frequently used as a metaphor for the relationship of men and nations to God. Men and nations are the sheep, the flock, and God is the shepherd. Hence, in the sacrificial code, שֶׂה [lamb] is the metaphor most generally used for Israel's national character, as in קָרְבַּן פֶּסַח [the Passover offering], תְּמִימִים [the regular offerings], etc. In the same manner כִּבְשָׂה צֹאן [ewe lamb] or שְׂעִירָה [she-goat] in the individual sin offering symbolizes the "private" personality. Within the species of צֹאן, two animal types are characterized in a distinct manner: עֵז, the goat, and אַיִל, the ram.

עֵז, as indicated by its very name (derived from עַז, "hard," "firm," "strong") is tractable only with its master. It is obstinate with all others. Thus it is the most clear-cut characterization of resistance, particularly of that manly independence which, impervious to any temptation from without or within, heeds only the command of its master in unchanging loyalty. For this reason the goat was the animal chosen for the חַטָּאת [sin offering] which is intended to counteract levity. Hence, עֵז represents the power of resistance.

אַיִל, as indicated by its very name, is the mature ram, which, because of its vigor, is the sheep in the lead of the flock. For this reason the wealthy and prominent men in a nation are designated by this term, cf. אֵילֵי הָאָרֶץ (2 Kings 24:15, Ezekiel 17:13).

אַיִל symbolizes the "man of property." For this reason it was the animal chosen for offerings intended as atonement for sins relating to property or privilege or to symbolize the installation of an individual into a position of greater privilege. Thus, אַיִל symbolizes a personage distinguished by property and privilege.

צִפּוֹר, the clean [i.e., "kosher"] bird (the "feathered animal," see Chapter 7, Verse 14 above, whose feathers are its predominant physical feature as distinct from birds of prey, which have talons to use as grasping organs and lethal weapons) is that creature which has neither strength nor power but which, nevertheless, by its ability to take wing, is able to escape man's sphere of power. Hence it symbolizes a timid, ephemeral but free form of existence for which snares are skillfully laid but which is able to avoid entrapment by means of its wings.

Hence יוֹנָה [the dove] symbolizes the existence of Israel, which is also weak and defenseless but nonetheless free, happy and secure. In the sacrificial code, e.g., קָרְבָּן עוֹלֶה וְיוֹרֵד, the "kosher" bird symbolizes that personality which has been divested of all property, power and privilege and is left only with its bare existence. Elsewhere, it symbolizes new life regained after deliverance from illness and weakness, קִנֵּי זָב וְזָבָה וְיוֹלֶדֶת וְצִפֳּרֵי מְצוֹרָע. The only bird that symbolizes in even more striking terms a state of free existence, borne upon its wings, is תּוֹר, the turtledove, the bird of passage whose return each year is the harbinger of spring (Song of Songs 2:12), as opposed to בְּנֵי יוֹנָה, [the young doves]. גּוֹזָל is the baby bird, which is still in need of maternal care and protection. Cf. עַל גּוֹזָלָיו יְרַחֵף ["... hovering over its young"] (Deuteronomy 32:11). צִפּוֹר therefore symbolizes a form of life that is weak and defenseless but that is able to save itself and to survive by "taking wing." תּוֹר וְגוֹזָל is the older generation, which, by thus taking wing, also preserves and protects its young.

Translated into verbal terms, the allegorical act קְחָה לִי עֶגְלָה מְשֻׁלֶּשֶׁת [of taking the heifers, goats, rams and turtledoves] would mean: Place yourselves at My [i.e., God's] service, either yourself [i.e., Abraham] (or, as the patriarch, the descendants who will come from you), three times with your energy, three times with your power of resistance, three times with your property and privilege and with your momentum, your ability to "take wing," which can raise both the old and the young generation to renewed life.

וַיִּקַּח לוֹ אֶת כָּל אֵלֶּה ***[He brought all these to Him].*** Abraham placed all these faculties at the service of God. וַיְבַתֵּר אֹתָם בַּתָּוֶךְ: Then He [i.e., God] cut them up; *He broke all the strength, all the resistance and all the authority in three Abrahamite generations.* וְאֶת הַצִּפּוֹר לֹא בָתָר [but He did not cut up the birds]: *Only the inner strength to take wing and to soar above misery did He allow to remain unbroken.* This simply means: You shall surely know that your descendants will be *aliens*; namely, without rights and privileges, in a land that is not theirs; this is symbolized by the dismembered אַיִל [ram]. They will become *slaves* and their energy will be broken, as symbolized by the dismemberment of the עֶגְלָה [heifer]. They *will be afflicted* and they will have to bear all this without being able to offer resistance, as symbolized by the dismembered עֵז [goat]. However, they will not be lost to deliverance: וְאֶת הַצִּפּוֹר לֹא בָתָר [He did not cut up the bird]. עַבְדוּת [slavery], גֵּרוּת [alienhood] and עִנּוּי [affliction] are to be the fate of the Abrahamites. The dismembered heifer symbolizes slavery; the dismembered goat, affliction and the dismembered ram, alienhood, the position of being without rights or soil of one's own.

וַיִּתֵּן אִישׁ בִּתְרוֹ לִקְרַאת רֵעֵהוּ ***[placing each half opposite the other].*** The parts will be juxtaposed in such a manner as to show that there will come a day when they will be joined together again. This is why the words וְאֶת

He said to Abram: "You shall surely know that your seed shall be a stranger in a land not theirs; they will serve them, and they will torment them for four hundred years. 14. But also that nation whom they shall serve do I judge, and afterwards they shall go forth with great wealth.   15. But you shall go to your fathers in peace; you shall be buried at a good old age.   16. The fourth generation will return to this place because the iniquity of the Emorites is not yet complete."   17. When the sun had set and it had become dark, lo! there was a smoking furnace, and a flaming torch which passed between these pieces.   18. On that day *God* made a covenant with Abram, as follows: To your seed have I given this land, from the river of Mitzrayim to the great river, the river Perath,° 19. the Kenite[s], the Kenizzite[s] and the Kadmonite[s],   20. the Hittite[s], the Perizzite[s] and the Rephaim,   21. the Emorite[s], the Canaanite[s], the Girgashite[s] and the Yebusite[s].

XVI 1. And Sarai, Abram's wife, had borne him no children, but she had a Mitzrite maidservant whose name was Hagar.   2. And Sarai said to Abram, "Lo! *God* has restrained me from [child]bearing; please come to my maidser-

°*Note to the English translation*: The river Euphrates. [G.H.]

לְאַבְרָם יָדֹעַ תֵּדַע כִּי־גֵר | יִהְיֶה זַרְעֲךָ בְּאֶרֶץ לֹא לָהֶם וַעֲבָדוּם וְעִנּוּ אֹתָם אַרְבַּע מֵאוֹת שָׁנָה: יד וְגַם אֶת־הַגּוֹי אֲשֶׁר יַעֲבֹדוּ דָּן אָנֹכִי וְאַחֲרֵי־כֵן יֵצְאוּ בִּרְכֻשׁ גָּדוֹל: טו וְאַתָּה תָּבוֹא אֶל־אֲבֹתֶיךָ בְּשָׁלוֹם תִּקָּבֵר בְּשֵׂיבָה טוֹבָה: טז וְדוֹר רְבִיעִי יָשׁוּבוּ הֵנָּה כִּי לֹא־שָׁלֵם עֲוֹן הָאֱמֹרִי עַד־הֵנָּה: יז וַיְהִי הַשֶּׁמֶשׁ בָּאָה וַעֲלָטָה הָיָה וְהִנֵּה תַנּוּר עָשָׁן וְלַפִּיד אֵשׁ אֲשֶׁר עָבַר בֵּין הַגְּזָרִים הָאֵלֶּה: יח בַּיּוֹם הַהוּא כָּרַת יְהֹוָה אֶת־אַבְרָם בְּרִית לֵאמֹר לְזַרְעֲךָ נָתַתִּי אֶת־הָאָרֶץ הַזֹּאת מִנְּהַר מִצְרַיִם עַד־הַנָּהָר הַגָּדֹל נְהַר־פְּרָת: יט אֶת־הַקֵּינִי וְאֶת־הַקְּנִזִּי וְאֵת הַקַּדְמֹנִי: כ וְאֶת־הַחִתִּי וְאֶת־הַפְּרִזִּי וְאֶת־הָרְפָאִים: כא וְאֶת־הָאֱמֹרִי וְאֶת־הַכְּנַעֲנִי וְאֶת־הַגִּרְגָּשִׁי וְאֶת־הַיְבוּסִי: ס טז א וְשָׂרַי אֵשֶׁת אַבְרָם לֹא יָלְדָה לוֹ וְלָהּ שִׁפְחָה מִצְרִית וּשְׁמָהּ הָגָר: ב וַתֹּאמֶר שָׂרַי אֶל־אַבְרָם הִנֵּה־נָא עֲצָרַנִי יְהֹוָה מִלֶּדֶת בֹּא־נָא אֶל־שִׁפְחָתִי אוּלַי

הַצִּפֹּר לֹא בָתָר ["But He did not cut up the bird"] are added here, to show that the unbroken power to "take wing" is the precondition for the future rejoining.

"And when the sun had gone down and it had become completely dark, lo! there was a smoking furnace and a torch": Refinement and enlightenment had come. That was the purpose for which the animals had to be cut up. Now the purification had been completed; the process of education had done its work, and hence the broken pieces could be joined together again.

°   °   °

CHAPTER XVI

1–2. In the preceding chapter we were told how Abraham uttered before God the plaintive plea, "What wilt Thou give me? I have no children and the heir

who yearns for my household is the Damascene kin of Eliezer." This shows what a great grief his childlessness must have been to Abraham. However, it is readily understandable that Sarah must have been the one most deeply hurt by her barrenness. For, as is stressed in the narrative, Sarah was אֵשֶׁת אַבְרָם, Abraham's wife in every respect; she had followed him in all his ways and had joined him in his life's path and purpose. It was an act of greatness on Abraham's part to cut himself loose from his home and from his kinsmen, but it was no less a sacrifice for Sarah. Abraham did it for the sake of God, Sarah did it for the sake of Abraham, and together they lived for the lofty calling indicated by the words אֶת הַנֶּפֶשׁ אֲשֶׁר עָשׂוּ בְחָרָן ["the souls whom they had made in Haran" — 12:5]. But the one thing which Abraham could have expected from his wife, that which every husband expects but to which Abraham attached particular significance because of his mission, Sarah vant; perhaps I shall be built up through her," and Abram gave heed to the voice of Sarai. 3. And Sarai, Abram's wife, took Hagar, the Mitzrite woman, her maidservant, after ten years had passed since Abram's settling in the land of Canaan, and she gave her to Abram, her husband, to be his wife. 4. He went to Hagar and she conceived, and when she saw that she had conceived, her mistress appeared unimportant in her eyes. 5. And Sarai said to Abram: "The wrong that I am enduring is upon you! I gave my maidservant into your bosom, and now that she sees she has conceived, I have become unimportant in her eyes. Let *God* judge between me and you." 6. And Abram said to Sarai: "Lo! your maidservant is in your hand; do to her whatever is good in your eyes." Then Sarai humbled her and she fled from before her. 7. And an angel of *God* found her by a fountain of water in the wilderness by the fountain on the way to Shur. 8. And he said: "Hagar, maidservant of Sarai! From where have you come and where are you going?" And she said: "I am fleeing from my mistress Sarai." 9. And the angel of *God* said to her: "Return to your mistress and submit yourself under her hands." 10. And the angel of *God* said to her: "I shall multiply your seed exceedingly so that it will not be possible to count it for [sheer] multitude." 11. And the angel of *God*

אִבָּנֶה מִמֶּנָּה וַיִּשְׁמַע אַבְרָם לְקוֹל שָׂרָי׃
ג וַתִּקַּח שָׂרַי ׀ אֵשֶׁת־אַבְרָם אֶת־הָגָר הַמִּצְרִית
שִׁפְחָתָהּ מִקֵּץ עֶשֶׂר שָׁנִים לְשֶׁבֶת אַבְרָם
בְּאֶרֶץ כְּנָעַן וַתִּתֵּן אֹתָהּ לְאַבְרָם אִישָׁהּ לוֹ
לְאִשָּׁה׃ ד וַיָּבֹא אֶל־הָגָר וַתַּהַר וַתֵּרֶא כִּי
הָרָתָה וַתֵּקַל גְּבִרְתָּהּ בְּעֵינֶיהָ׃ ה וַתֹּאמֶר שָׂרַי
אֶל־אַבְרָם חֲמָסִי עָלֶיךָ אָנֹכִי נָתַתִּי שִׁפְחָתִי
בְּחֵיקֶךָ וַתֵּרֶא כִּי הָרָתָה וָאֵקַל בְּעֵינֶיהָ יִשְׁפֹּט
יְהוָה בֵּינִי וּבֵינֶיךָ (נקוד על י׳ בתרא)׃ ו וַיֹּאמֶר
אַבְרָם אֶל־שָׂרַי הִנֵּה שִׁפְחָתֵךְ בְּיָדֵךְ עֲשִׂי־לָהּ
הַטּוֹב בְּעֵינָיִךְ וַתְּעַנֶּהָ שָׂרַי וַתִּבְרַח מִפָּנֶיהָ׃
ז וַיִּמְצָאָהּ מַלְאַךְ יְהוָה עַל־עֵין הַמַּיִם בַּמִּדְבָּר
עַל־הָעַיִן בְּדֶרֶךְ שׁוּר׃ ח וַיֹּאמַר הָגָר שִׁפְחַת
שָׂרַי אֵי־מִזֶּה בָאת וְאָנָה תֵלֵכִי וַתֹּאמֶר מִפְּנֵי
שָׂרַי גְּבִרְתִּי אָנֹכִי בֹּרַחַת׃ ט וַיֹּאמֶר לָהּ מַלְאַךְ
יְהוָה שׁוּבִי אֶל־גְּבִרְתֵּךְ וְהִתְעַנִּי תַּחַת יָדֶיהָ׃
י וַיֹּאמֶר לָהּ מַלְאַךְ יְהוָה הַרְבָּה אַרְבֶּה אֶת־
זַרְעֵךְ וְלֹא יִסָּפֵר מֵרֹב׃ יא וַיֹּאמֶר לָהּ מַלְאַךְ

had not been able to give him: She had been unable to bear him children. . . .

And so she said to Abraham: "God has kept me from fulfilling that purpose which God has given other women the ability to fulfill; therefore בֹּא נָא וגו׳ [please go, etc.]." Even if she herself could not present Abraham with a child to place upon his knee, she wanted to give him a child over whose rearing Abraham would have full control, with herself participating to the greatest extent possible. The word נָא in Sarah's plea suggests that Abraham was reluctant to do what she suggested. Sarah wants to do it only for his sake, but she knows that he would not do it for his own sake; hence she says אוּלַי אִבָּנֶה, "perhaps I shall be built up through this." If Abraham would not want to do it for his own sake, then let him do it for the sake of his wife because she wants it so badly.

9, 10 and 11. These are three separate statements: The first expresses a condition; the second, a promise, and the third, an instruction and a promise of a favorable outcome.

9. "Return out of your own free will and submit yourself to Sarah out of your own free will." This sacrifice on the part of Hagar is a condition for what is to follow. The son whom Hagar is to bear must be born and reared under the influence of the fact that Hagar, out of her own free will, has subordinated herself to Sarah, and under the influence of Sarah's personal guidance. But Hagar does not react to this first statement from the angel.

10. And so the angel adds: "In return for this sacrifice on your part you will become the ancestress of countless descendants." But this still is not enough for Hagar; she does not respond.

said to her: "Lo! you have conceived and you will bear a son, and you shall call him Yishmael because *God* has heard your affliction. 12. He will be a free man among men; his hand shall be against every man, and every man's hand against him; and he will take his place in the face of all his brothers." 13. And she called *God*, Who had spoken to her: "Thou art a God of seeing." For she said: "Have I looked about even here for one who might see me?" 14. Therefore He called the well, "Well

יְהֹוָה הִנָּךְ הָרָה וְיֹלַדְתְּ בֵּן וְקָרָאת שְׁמוֹ
יִשְׁמָעֵאל כִּי־שָׁמַע יְהֹוָה אֶל־עָנְיֵךְ: יב וְהוּא
יִהְיֶה פֶּרֶא אָדָם יָדוֹ בַכֹּל וְיַד כֹּל בּוֹ וְעַל־פְּנֵי
כָל־אֶחָיו יִשְׁכֹּן: יג וַתִּקְרָא שֵׁם־יְהֹוָה הַדֹּבֵר
אֵלֶיהָ אַתָּה אֵל רֳאִי כִּי אָמְרָה הֲגַם הֲלֹם
רָאִיתִי אַחֲרֵי רֹאִי: יד עַל־כֵּן קָרָא לַבְּאֵר בְּאֵר

11 and 12. Then the angel says, "Your descendants shall be the most free among all mankind." This, finally, is sufficient for Hagar. Under these terms she is ready to give in.

The basic ideal which Hagar is to instil in her son and which is to make him free is implicit in the name יִשְׁמָעֵאל, an awareness of the Divine Providence which not only watches over the deeds of men but is also concerned about their sufferings. Divine Providence weighs and judges not only the deeds of men and the conditions under which men live but also their words and their emotions. . . .

13. . . . Hagar fled. During the first stage of her flight she looked about to see whether she was being followed. She thereupon fled into the wilderness, where she felt safe. There, she had no reason to expect anyone to see her. But at this point it was brought home to her that while one could flee from men, one could never flee from God. "Until now I no longer looked about to see whether anyone saw me. But Thou art a God of seeing; Thine eye is everywhere. No one can escape from Thee."

14. . . . As a result of this incident, this well, ideally situated as a central gathering place for a Bedouin nation, at the edge of the most terrifying, desolate of wildernesses, becomes a memorial for the Arab people. The future impact of this race on the rest of mankind will derive from this one incident involving the ancestress of the Arab nation. For here she first learned that the Presence of God is not confined to any given space. . . .

This genesis of the Ishmaelite nation contains the seed of all the Ishmaelite traits which were to emerge so markedly in the future. The sensuality of Ḥam, son of Noah; Hagar's thirst for freedom; and the spirit of Abraham—these are the basic threads from which the Arab national character was woven. The Arabic nation brought forth by Abraham and Hagar is one-half Jewish. We, the Jewish people, have been assigned by God a mission with a dual aspect: 1) אֱמוּנָה, the theoretical verities which we must accept and which constitute the foundations upon which our spirit must develop and 2) The Law; the practical shaping, in harmony with these verities, of all our lives according to the dictates of the Divine will.

Seen from the theoretical aspect, the Arab nation occupies a place of great significance among men. It has developed the Abrahamite concept of God with such clarity that the monotheistic concepts in the writings of the Jewish religious philosophers have a predominant place in the philosophical treatises of Arab authors. Thus, the Arabs have the אֱמוּנָה [belief]. On the other hand, they do not have the מִצְוֹת [the commandments to put these beliefs into practice]. But it is not enough to have intellectual conceptions of God's Unity. To שְׁמַע [the command, "Hear O Yisrael"] belongs וְאָהַבְתָּ ["and you shall love God . . ."]. You must subordinate to Him, not only in theory but also in practice, all your faculties and aspirations: בְּכָל לֵב נֶפֶשׁ וּמְאוֹד. To this end it is not enough merely to have been begotten and reared by a father like Abraham; one must also have been born of a mother like Sarah. The people of Abraham were not destined to be merely messengers disseminating the theological and philosophical conceptions of God's Unity, but לִשְׁמֹר דֶּרֶךְ ד׳ לַעֲשׂוֹת צְדָקָה וּמִשְׁפָּט ["to keep the way of God, to practice dutiful benevolence"—Genesis 18:19]. All our faculties, primarily our physical energies, drives and impulses, and our bodies as a whole, must be subordinated and consecrated to this objective. Only once a man has dedicated the physical aspects of his life to this end does he begin to become a Jew. Ishmael has achieved the dedication of his intellect, which he inherited from Abraham, but he has not hallowed the physical aspects of his life—he could have inherited this latter ability only from a mother like Sarah. Wherever a Jewish

לַחַי רֹאִי הִנֵּה בֵין־קָדֵשׁ וּבֵין בָּרֶד: טו וַתֵּלֶד
הָגָר לְאַבְרָם בֵּן וַיִּקְרָא אַבְרָם שֶׁם־בְּנוֹ אֲשֶׁר־
יָלְדָה הָגָר יִשְׁמָעֵאל: טז וְאַבְרָם בֶּן־שְׁמֹנִים
שָׁנָה וְשֵׁשׁ שָׁנִים בְּלֶדֶת־הָגָר אֶת־יִשְׁמָעֵאל
לְאַבְרָם: ס יז א וַיְהִי אַבְרָם בֶּן־תִּשְׁעִים שָׁנָה
וְתֵשַׁע שָׁנִים וַיֵּרָא יְהוָה אֶל־אַבְרָם וַיֹּאמֶר
אֵלָיו אֲנִי־אֵל שַׁדַּי הִתְהַלֵּךְ לְפָנַי וֶהְיֵה תָמִים:
ב וְאֶתְּנָה בְרִיתִי בֵּינִי וּבֵינֶךָ וְאַרְבֶּה אוֹתְךָ

of the Living One Who Sees Me"; it is the one between Kadesh and Bared. 15. So Hagar bore Abram a son. Abram called his son, whom Hagar had borne, Yishmael. 16. Abram was eighty-six years old when Hagar bore Yishmael to Abram.

XVII

1. When Abram was ninety-nine years old *God* appeared to Abram and said to him: "I am אֵל שַׁדַּי; conduct yourself before Me and become complete. 2. I wish to set My covenant between Me and you, and to mul-

woman bears children, rears and nurtures them, there the physical aspects of these children's lives are consecrated to God from the very beginning. It is not without good reason that the story of Sarah and Hagar has been placed between the accounts of בְּרִית בֵּין הַבְּתָרִים ["the covenant between the pieces"] and מִילָה [the commandment of circumcision].

CHAPTER XVII

1. Now Abraham was ninety-nine years old—with a whole life behind him. He could have considered that his life was close to completion but now he learns that it is, in fact, only beginning. . . . For ninety-nine years God had guided Abraham through all the experiences meant to train him: He had Abraham accomplish all the things that He expects every pure human being to achieve. Only after that did God appear to Abraham again and say to him, אֲנִי א׳ ש׳, etc.

° ° °

הִתְהַלֵּךְ means . . . to go one's own way, not permitting oneself to be swayed by circumstances outside oneself but conducting or guiding oneself from within; i.e., הִתְהַלֵּךְ denotes a movement impelled by one's own free-willed decision and inner energy. . . .

הִתְהַלֵּךְ לְפָנַי *[conduct yourself* **before** *Me]*, not הִתְהַלֵּךְ אִתִּי [conduct yourself *with* Me]. "Conduct yourself with Me" would mean merely to permit God to guide his fate. "Conduct yourself לְפָנַי [*before* Me]" means to keep God's presence in mind at all times; that is, to look at every turn toward Him Who has set limits and boundaries to everything and Who has granted liberty only through [the discipline of] law. . . .

° ° °

One who is תָּמִים ["perfect," "whole," or "complete"] is one who takes full advantage of the limits, of the sphere, which God has assigned to him, but who never oversteps these boundaries . . .

° ° °

Accordingly, the Jewish concept of "sin" is עֲבֵרָה literally, an "overstepping" of these Divinely-set limits. Everything, including the most physical phases of our lives, is sacred and good as long as it unfolds within the limits set by God. There is nothing in man that can be regarded as absolutely good or absolutely evil. There is nothing in God's Law that commands the destruction of any human potential; the Law only directs that it be kept within specified limits. Only when these limits are overstepped (or not attained) does a human act become a sin. This is the basic character of lawfulness as Judaism sees it. "You are to conduct yourself freely within the limits set by God."

Here, too, we see the difference between Abraham the Jew and Abraham as he was before. In the Abrahamite character without the covenant the requirements of virtue are satisfied by mere good intentions. In the non-Jewish world any act can be justified by "good intentions." But in Judaism, the good intention is not enough. The good intention must be directed toward a good deed and the standard for the "goodness" of the deed is set by דַּי [lit. "it is sufficient"]; i.e., the limits established by the will and the Law of God. This verity is the basis for Judah HaLevi's *Kuzari*. Until this point, Abraham was loved and respected for his qualities of heart and character. But now something more is expected of him: lawfulness, a "free-willed subordination" of self to the law of God, in order that he may become, by his own decision, that which all other creatures are compelled to be by their natural predisposition. Thus, too, the Sages say, "At first, God gave him mastery over 243 limbs, and later over 248, the additional ones being the two legs, the two ears and the male member" (Nedarim 32b). Prior to the covenant Abraham had control over all parts of his body except for those over which ordinary human beings seldom obtain complete mastery. . . .

2. וְאֶתְּנָה בְרִיתִי וגו׳ *[I wish to set My covenant].* "Make this decision, on your own accord, to subordinate yourself to My Law, for I wish to set a sign between Myself and yourself, the בְּרִית which is to be 'absolute' as far as I and you are concerned." The

tiply you exceedingly." 3. And Abram fell upon his face and God talked with him so that he might communicate it. 4. "As for Me, lo! My covenant is now with you, and you shall become a father of the multitude of the nations. 5. And no longer shall you be called Abram, but your name shall be Abraham, for I have appointed you as father of the multitude of nations. 6. But I will make you, too, exceedingly fruitful; I will make you yourself into nations and kings shall come forth from you, 7. And I will establish My covenant between Myself and you and your descendants after you for their generations as an everlasting covenant, to be God to you and to your descendants after you. 8. And I will give to you and to your descendants after you the land of your sojourn, the entire land of Canaan as an everlasting possession, and I shall be God to them." 9. And God said to Abraham: "But you, too, must keep

בִּמְאֹד מְאֹד: ג וַיִּפֹּל אַבְרָם עַל־פָּנָיו וַיְדַבֵּר
אִתּוֹ אֱלֹהִים לֵאמֹר: ד אֲנִי הִנֵּה בְרִיתִי אִתָּךְ
וְהָיִיתָ לְאַב הֲמוֹן גּוֹיִם: ה וְלֹא־יִקָּרֵא עוֹד
אֶת־שִׁמְךָ אַבְרָם וְהָיָה שִׁמְךָ אַבְרָהָם כִּי אַב־
הֲמוֹן גּוֹיִם נְתַתִּיךָ: ו וְהִפְרֵתִי אֹתְךָ בִּמְאֹד
מְאֹד וּנְתַתִּיךָ לְגוֹיִם וּמְלָכִים מִמְּךָ יֵצֵאוּ: שביעי
ז וַהֲקִמֹתִי אֶת־בְּרִיתִי בֵּינִי וּבֵינֶךָ וּבֵין זַרְעֲךָ
אַחֲרֶיךָ לְדֹרֹתָם לִבְרִית עוֹלָם לִהְיוֹת לְךָ
לֵאלֹהִים וּלְזַרְעֲךָ אַחֲרֶיךָ: ח וְנָתַתִּי לְךָ וּלְזַרְעֲךָ
אַחֲרֶיךָ אֵת ׀ אֶרֶץ מְגֻרֶיךָ אֵת כָּל־אֶרֶץ כְּנַעַן
לַאֲחֻזַּת עוֹלָם וְהָיִיתִי לָהֶם לֵאלֹהִים: ט וַיֹּאמֶר
אֱלֹהִים אֶל־אַבְרָהָם וְאַתָּה אֶת־בְּרִיתִי תִשְׁמֹר

destiny of the Jew is not an outgrowth of natural phenomena; there cannot be such a thing as a "pragmatic history" of the Jews in the ordinary meaning of this term. In the ordinary course of nature the first Jew would never have come into being, and [even if he had] the last Jew would have ceased to exist long ago. יִצְחָק, Isaac, the very idea of whose birth would have been ridiculous and absurd in ordinary human reckoning, is the archetype of the Jewish phenomenon.

בֵּינִי וּבֵינֶךָ *[between Me and you].* "The historical existence which I am to grant you, on the one hand, and the devotion which you are to give Me, on the other, are both components of the בְּרִית, independent of all external conditions and circumstances."

° ° °

3. . . . Whereas until this point in the narrative we were told concerning Abraham's encounters with God וַיֵּרָא אֵלָיו ה׳ ["and *God* (in His quality of mercy) appeared to him"] and וְאֶתְּנָה בְרִיתִי ["I wish to set My covenant"], we are now told that וַיְדַבֵּר אִתּוֹ אֱלֹקִים ["God (in His quality of justice) talked with him"]. Initially, the decision whether or not to accept the covenant had been left to Abraham. God could only "wish" that Abraham would accept. Had Abraham not decided to accept the covenant, he would still have remained בֶּן נֹחַ [a Noahide]. But by accepting the covenant Abraham had taken upon himself an obligation toward God. Therefore God, as אֱלֹקִים, the God of justice and right, Who will not permit man to trifle with Him or with His instructions, now speaks to Abraham לֵאמֹר [literally, "to say," or "saying"]; i.e. so that Abraham should pass God's message on.

Verses 4–8 state one side of the covenant; namely, what Abraham can expect from God; Verses 9–14, the obligation accepted by Abraham and his descendants in return.

אֲנִי הִנֵּה וגו׳: "As for Me, effective as of this moment, I give you My absolute promise to be with you, and, as part of this promise, I shall cause you to become a 'father of the multitude of nations.'" . . .

8. Only then, after I have won your descendants to be My people, will I give them the land in which you sojourned as a stranger, and then I shall prove Myself to them as a God Who will guide them and guard them, and Who will provide for their needs.

9. ***But you.*** This expresses the reciprocal relation to, "As for Me" (Verse 4).

you . . . must keep. "I," said God, "will maintain My covenant regardless of circumstances, even if circumstances were to arise which could cause this covenant to collapse. However, you, too, must keep My covenant; it is incumbent upon you and upon your descendants to see to it that My covenant should not become thus endangered." This obligation devolves upon all the descendants of Abraham. They owe not only their spiritual and moral calling but also their physical and material existence solely to the fact that Abraham had assumed this obligation. Indeed, their very existence derives from this obligation! Without this covenant no

My covenant, you and your seed after you for their generations. 10. This is My covenant which you shall keep between Myself and yourselves and your descendants after you; every male among you shall be circumcised, 11. so that you shall be circumcised on the flesh of your foreskin and that this shall become as a sign of the covenant between Myself and you. 12. And at the age of eight days every male shall be circumcised among you for your generations, he that is born in the house, or acquired with money from any stranger who is not of your descendants. 13. He that is born in your house and he that is acquired with your money must indeed be circumcised, and My covenant shall be upon your flesh as an everlasting covenant. 14. An uncircumcised male who is not circumcised upon the flesh of his

אַתָּה וְזַרְעֲךָ אַחֲרֶיךָ לְדֹרֹתָם: י זֹאת בְּרִיתִי
אֲשֶׁר תִּשְׁמְרוּ בֵּינִי וּבֵינֵיכֶם וּבֵין זַרְעֲךָ אַחֲרֶיךָ
הִמּוֹל לָכֶם כָּל־זָכָר: יא וּנְמַלְתֶּם אֵת בְּשַׂר
עָרְלַתְכֶם וְהָיָה לְאוֹת בְּרִית בֵּינִי וּבֵינֵיכֶם:
יב וּבֶן־שְׁמֹנַת יָמִים יִמּוֹל לָכֶם כָּל־זָכָר
לְדֹרֹתֵיכֶם יְלִיד בָּיִת וּמִקְנַת־כֶּסֶף מִכֹּל בֶּן־נֵכָר
אֲשֶׁר לֹא מִזַּרְעֲךָ הוּא: יג הִמּוֹל ׀ יִמּוֹל יְלִיד
בֵּיתְךָ וּמִקְנַת כַּסְפֶּךָ וְהָיְתָה בְרִיתִי בִּבְשַׂרְכֶם
לִבְרִית עוֹלָם: יד וְעָרֵל ׀ זָכָר אֲשֶׁר לֹא־יִמּוֹל

such person as Isaac would have been born. Only under this condition did Abraham's descendants come into existence; only as sons of this covenant can they have breath. Therefore their very existence obligates them to keep this covenant.

10. . . . In the next verse מִילָה [circumcision] is described as אוֹת בְּרִית, a *sign* of the covenant. Thus it is to be a symbol representing the בְּרִית [covenant]; the fulfillment of the covenant must transcend the mere act of circumcision. These utterances, occurring in the first specifically Jewish law (which is a symbolic law), should be of paramount significance for the proper understanding of all similar laws to follow. This significance has a dual aspect, as follows:

In the case of commandments involving a symbolic act, not merely the perpetuation of the idea symbolized by the act but also, and indeed primarily, the actual performance of the prescribed act, is an inviolable law of God. The perpetuation of the idea can never serve as a dispensation from, or a substitute for, the performance of the act. Failure to perform the act is tantamount to denying the idea symbolized by the act. He who fails to make the sign of the covenant has in fact destroyed the covenant (Verse 14). The making of the sign itself (Verse 10) constitutes a "keeping of the covenant."

On the other hand, the performance of the act has accomplished its full purpose only if it has become an אוֹת, a symbol, if it is taken to heart as such, and if the idea which it expresses comes alive within us. Nevertheless, the performance of the act as such still represents the primary fulfillment of the Divine commandment. It is the intent of the commandment that, by performing the act, we should give expression, over and over again, to the idea as an utterance of God, thus upholding and preserving the idea and constantly reiterating and reviving it for ourselves and others.

° ° °

This body of ours should not be the master but rather מְבַשֵּׂר, בשר, the servant and herald, of the spirit. . . . An uncircumcised body does not bear the sign of subordination. By the act of cutting away the foreskin the entire body receives the stamp of subordination to the spirit which carries out the Divinely-given moral law. It is primarily upon this subordination of the body, not upon that of the spirit, that God has based His covenant. The Divine covenant of Judaism knows no splitting of the human personality in which the spirit soars up to the level of the Divine while the body is permitted to go on wallowing in the cesspool of sensuality. Rather, the covenant demands, as the primary condition for its fulfillment, the moral subordination of all corporeality. Only from a [morally] pure corporeality can a truly Divine spiritual life blossom forth.

11. . . . Not כְּרִיתָה, a "cutting off," but מִילָה, a "cutting around" or "trimming," as it were, is the fundamental concept of the Divine covenant. In the light of this covenant, celibacy and castration are no less abominable than debauchery and dissipation. To be a Jew means to make even the most corporeal aspects of life sacred to God by keeping them within the prescribed moral limits.

foreskin, his soul shall be cut off from his people; he has broken My covenant." 15. God further said to Abraham: "You shall not call your wife Sarai 'Sarai,' because her name is Sarah;   16. and I will bless her and I have already appointed for you a son from her. I will bless her, she will become nations; kings of nations shall be descended from her."   17. And Abraham fell upon his face and laughed, and he said to himself in his heart: "Shall a child be born to [a man who is] a hundred years old,

אֶת־בְּשַׂר עָרְלָתוֹ וְנִכְרְתָה הַנֶּפֶשׁ הַהִוא מֵעַמֶּיהָ אֶת־בְּרִיתִי הֵפַר: ס טו וַיֹּאמֶר אֱלֹהִים אֶל־אַבְרָהָם שָׂרַי אִשְׁתְּךָ לֹא־תִקְרָא אֶת־שְׁמָהּ שָׂרָי כִּי שָׂרָה שְׁמָהּ: טז וּבֵרַכְתִּי אֹתָהּ וְגַם נָתַתִּי מִמֶּנָּה לְךָ בֵּן וּבֵרַכְתִּיהָ וְהָיְתָה לְגוֹיִם מַלְכֵי עַמִּים מִמֶּנָּה יִהְיוּ: יז וַיִּפֹּל אַבְרָהָם עַל־פָּנָיו וַיִּצְחָק וַיֹּאמֶר בְּלִבּוֹ הַלְּבֶן מֵאָה־שָׁנָה

15. Until this point the covenant had been made only with Abraham, as it were, only the males being understood as factors in the covenant. But now Sarah is named as the second factor in the covenantal promise, Abraham's full equal in dignity and importance. Even as Abram's role in the covenant is to be placed on record by changing his name to Abraham, so, too, Sarai's equal role is to be placed on record by changing her name to Sarah.

°   °   °

. . . "You shall no longer call your wife Sarai, because her name is Sarah." She is Sarah, the moderating, tone-setting influence, who bears within her heart the most delicate feeling, the most sensitive measure for all that is right, good, beautiful, praiseworthy and holy. She applies to her own life, and judges other in terms of, this sensitive standard of justice and morality, of "decency," of that truly Divine probity, the standard of what "befits" the truly pure man regardless of time and circumstances. She no longer needs to become such a person; she already is one.

A woman who is descended from Sarah does not need an external, physical sign of the covenant. . . . By virtue of her descent from Sarah she has the propensity to subordinate herself to everything pure and godly, and she will demand the same subordination of everyone and everything that comes in contact with her. Wherever a pure "Sarah" rules as a wife and mother, nothing base will dare to come forward; she is the spirit of godliness, purity and morality. All this is most significant, since everything that follows will show quite explicitly that it is not enough to be a son of Abraham if one does not have Sarah for a mother. The father contributes the spiritual element, but the sensitivity required for measuring all things by the standard of probity and moral decency is passed on by the true, pure woman. אֵשֶׁת חַיִל [a woman of valor] like Sarah, our Sages say, is the crown of her husband. He is glorified through her; it is not she who must first receive the crown of glory from him.

16. "Even as I have blessed you so that you will be reproduced and perpetuated in your descendants, so, too, will I bless Sarah." In order to plant a nation for Himself God took not only a man who was to be perpetuated in his sons but also a woman who was to be perpetuated in her daughters. The planting of a nation of God requires not only the right fathers but also the right mothers. To this end men such as Abraham must find wives such as Sarah and must not be compelled to enter into unions with women of Hagar's kind. Accordingly, the same covenant that was made with Abraham earlier on is now reiterated explicitly as applicable also to Sarah. . . . [God says to Abraham:] Without her, I could never have made My covenant with you. . . . *She* shall become nations: *her* character shall live on in the tribes of the promised nation. . . .

17. . . . The very beginning of the Jewish people is a [historic] absurdity. Its history, its expectations, its hopes and its whole life sustained by these hopes must seem a most monstrous, ludicrous pretension if they are viewed only in natural terms, in terms of cause and effect. These things begin to make sense, indeed, they attain the highest, most justifiable importance only if one takes into account, as a basis for their evaluation, the first, supreme Cause of all, the deeply engaged, free omnipotent will and power of a free-willed almighty God.

This fact was to be brought home to our ancestors in advance and to be kept in the minds of all their descendants. That is why God delayed the planting of the seed for this nation until its ancestors had reached this "absurd" age; that is why He began to plant the fulfillment of His promise only after all human hopes for its realization had come to an end. For this was a matter of creating a nation which, with all its life and its aspirations, with its very existence, was to stand opposed to all the powers that were to emerge in world history. This nation was to be אֶצְבַּע אֱלֹקִים [lit., "a finger of God"] an indication of God in the midst of mankind. That is why, or shall Sarah, who is ninety years old, give birth?" 18. And Abraham said to God: "O that Yishmael might live before Thy countenance." 19. But God said: "Not so, [but] your wife Sarah shall bear you a son and you shall call him Yitzhak. With him will I uphold My covenant as an eternal covenant for his seed after him. 20. As for Yishmael, I have heard you. Lo! I have blessed him already and I will make him fruitful and multiply him exceedingly: he shall beget twelve princes and I shall appoint him to be a great nation. 21. But My covenant will I uphold with Yitzhak whom Sarah will bear you at this time next year." 22. When He had finished speaking to him, God went up [away] from Abraham. 23. And Abraham took his son Yishmael and all those that were born in his house and all that had been acquired with his money, all males among the members of the house of Abraham, and he circumcised the flesh of their foreskins on this selfsame day as God had said [it] to him. 24. Abraham was ninety-nine years old when he was circumcised on the flesh of his foreskin, 25. and his son Yishmael was thirteen years old when he was circumcised on the flesh of his foreskin. 26. On the selfsame

יִוָּלֵד וְאִם־שָׂרָה הֲבַת־תִּשְׁעִים שָׁנָה תֵּלֵד׃
יח וַיֹּאמֶר אַבְרָהָם אֶל־הָאֱלֹהִים לוּ יִשְׁמָעֵאל
יִחְיֶה לְפָנֶיךָ׃ יט וַיֹּאמֶר אֱלֹהִים אֲבָל שָׂרָה
אִשְׁתְּךָ יֹלֶדֶת לְךָ בֵּן וְקָרָאתָ אֶת־שְׁמוֹ יִצְחָק
וַהֲקִמֹתִי אֶת־בְּרִיתִי אִתּוֹ לִבְרִית עוֹלָם לְזַרְעוֹ
אַחֲרָיו׃ כ וּלְיִשְׁמָעֵאל שְׁמַעְתִּיךָ הִנֵּה ׀ בֵּרַכְתִּי
אֹתוֹ וְהִפְרֵיתִי אֹתוֹ וְהִרְבֵּיתִי אֹתוֹ בִּמְאֹד מְאֹד
שְׁנֵים־עָשָׂר נְשִׂיאִם יוֹלִיד וּנְתַתִּיו לְגוֹי גָּדוֹל׃
כא וְאֶת־בְּרִיתִי אָקִים אֶת־יִצְחָק אֲשֶׁר תֵּלֵד
לְךָ שָׂרָה לַמּוֹעֵד הַזֶּה בַּשָּׁנָה הָאַחֶרֶת׃ כב וַיְכַל
לְדַבֵּר אִתּוֹ וַיַּעַל אֱלֹהִים מֵעַל אַבְרָהָם׃
כג וַיִּקַּח אַבְרָהָם אֶת־יִשְׁמָעֵאל בְּנוֹ וְאֵת כָּל־
יְלִידֵי בֵיתוֹ וְאֵת כָּל־מִקְנַת כַּסְפּוֹ כָּל־זָכָר
בְּאַנְשֵׁי בֵּית אַבְרָהָם וַיָּמָל אֶת־בְּשַׂר עָרְלָתָם
בְּעֶצֶם הַיּוֹם הַזֶּה כַּאֲשֶׁר דִּבֶּר אִתּוֹ אֱלֹהִים׃
מפטיר כד וְאַבְרָהָם בֶּן־תִּשְׁעִים וָתֵשַׁע שָׁנָה
בְּהִמֹּלוֹ בְּשַׂר עָרְלָתוֹ׃ כה וְיִשְׁמָעֵאל בְּנוֹ בֶּן־
שְׁלֹשׁ עֶשְׂרֵה שָׁנָה בְּהִמֹּלוֹ אֵת בְּשַׂר עָרְלָתוֹ׃

until this very day, the Jewish people must appear to all narrow-minded deniers of God as the greatest absurdity possible. The resounding raucous laughter that has followed the Jews upon their path through history is the most cogent proof of the Divine character of this path; it does not disturb them because they were already prepared for this laughter in advance.

20. **נְשִׂיאִם** ***[princes]***. The Jewish concept of nationhood does not culminate in שָׂרִים ["rulers"] but in נְשִׂיאִים ["lit., "those who are elevated"]. Like the clouds in the heavens, they are elevated to their lofty position and are nurtured with the strength and marrow of the nation only so that these energies may eventually be turned back to fructify and strengthen the nation over which, and by which, these individuals have been elevated. The נְשִׂיאִים are bearers who in turn are upheld by that which they have been named to uphold. . . .

23. **בְּעֶצֶם** ***[self same]***; lit. "full power" . . . According to our Sages, whenever the expression בְּעֶצֶם הַיּוֹם הַזֶּה occurs in the Bible it is to be understood as meaning "in the full power of the day"; i.e., "in broad daylight." The use of this expression here would then emphasize that Abraham performed this act (by which he set himself up in sharp opposition to the rest of mankind) not in secret but openly and in full public view. Indeed, *milah* must not be performed at night but during the daytime because it is part of man's waking life. It is not a "bloody sacrifice" hallowed to the dark powers of nature which rule over the obscure aspects of life. It has no connection whatsoever with the finite sphere of man's physical relationships. Rather, it serves to consecrate man to אֵל שַׁדַּי, to Him Who controls, and reigns over, the powers of darkness which He Himself has created. It summons even man's murkiest impulses up to the shining lofty level of conscious, free-willed morality. It is not a supplement to physical birth but the octave thereof. It marks the second, higher "birthday," the entry of the child into the Divine level of free moral achievement. The physical act of birth belongs to night, מַלְאָךְ הַמְּמוּנֶּה עַל הֵרָיוֹן לַיְלָה שְׁמוֹ ["The angel appointed over pregnancy is named *Laylah* (Night)"—Niddah 16b] but *milah*, the infant's birth as a Jew, belongs to the daytime.

day Abraham and his son Yishmael were circumcised, 27. and all the members of his house, born in the house and acquired with money from strangers, were circumcised with him.

כו בְּעֶ֨צֶם֙ הַיּ֣וֹם הַזֶּ֔ה נִמּ֖וֹל אַבְרָהָ֑ם וְיִשְׁמָעֵ֖אל
בְּנֽוֹ׃ כז וְכָל־אַנְשֵׁ֤י בֵיתוֹ֙ יְלִ֣יד בָּ֔יִת וּמִקְנַת־כֶּ֖סֶף
מֵאֵ֣ת בֶּן־נֵכָ֑ר נִמֹּ֖לוּ אִתּֽוֹ׃ פ

The Haftarah for this Sidra may be found on page 825.

וירא

VAYERA

XVIII 1. And *God* appeared to him beneath the trees of Mamre, as he was sitting before the door of his tent in the heat of the day. 2. He lifted up his eyes and saw, and lo!

יח א וַיֵּרָא אֵלָיו יְהֹוָה בְּאֵלֹנֵי מַמְרֵא וְהוּא
יֹשֵׁב פֶּתַח־הָאֹהֶל כְּחֹם הַיּוֹם: ב וַיִּשָּׂא עֵינָיו

CHAPTER XVIII

1. ***And* God *appeared.*** God's presence is everywhere, but not everyone sees it. Only after an act of devotion such as Abraham had just performed did God become visible. . . .

This is the first time we see Abraham standing before God as a true נָבִיא [prophet] to whom God "reveals His secret to His servants the prophets" [Amos 3:7]. Only as the result of his *milah* had Abraham been able to attain this level. Let us consider the setting in which God revealed Himself to Abraham and ascertain the connection between this revelation and the circumstances that surrounded it.

God wanted to disclose to Abraham the imminent downfall of the most affluent and self-indulgent cities in the land that is to become the soil of the nation promised to him. It is explicitly stated that Abraham has received this disclosure solely because he is to become the ancestor of that nation. Abraham as an individual would not have needed to be told the reasons for the imminent tragic downfall of this district of flourishing cities. After all, Abraham already stood out in the sharpest contrast to the Sodomite character and philosophy of life. The very setting in which the Divine disclosure came to Abraham was proof that Abraham did not need this revelation for himself. A man who sits in front of his door in the heat of the day, looking out for weary wanderers as if he were begging them for the favor of accepting his hospitality, does not need to be informed of the terrible fate about to befall Sodom and Gomorrah as a warning lest he himself adopt the ways of these two cities. The disclosure was made to Abraham for the benefit of his descendants: The ways of Sodom and Gomorrah must not take root among the descendants of Abraham when they inherit this opulent land. Instead, the Abrahamite way must remain the inalienable heritage of Abraham's children and his children's children, so that affluence and plenty should not some day bury and destroy within them the spirit of Abraham, the spirit of service to God and love of man — in short, so that the nation of Abraham might forever maintain that opposition to the Sodomite principles of life which their ancestor had so splendidly demonstrated in his own conduct. It is for this reason that the *downfall of Sodom,* on the one hand, and *Abraham sitting in front of his tent,* on the other, have been juxtaposed in one picture before the descendants of Abraham.

Alas, to what cruel slander has Judaism, the heritage of the Abrahamites, along with its bearers, the Jews, been subjected through the ages! The "circumcised race" has been accused of regarding itself as the sole chosen people of God. We are told that the sign [of the covenant] which sets the Jews apart from all others must of necessity rob them of all cosmopolitanism, of all thought and feeling for their fellow men, turning the God of heaven and earth, the God of all human souls, into the narrow, parochial deity of their own particular spot on earth, the national god of their own tribe.

And now we are shown the first circumcised Jew. He is seated "in the grove of Mamre. . ." He is still with Abner, Eshkol and Mamre. . . . Though Abraham had been circumcised, his relationship with the non-Abrahamite world had remained unchanged. Those much-maligned rabbis of old, those most authentic spiritual heirs of Abraham, teach us that the one great concern which motivated Abraham to sit before his door, directly exposed to the burning sun, was the apprehension lest now, following his circumcision, other men might avoid him. Our Sages have pointed this out in order to impress upon the sons of Abraham, through Abraham's own example, the dictum that hospitality to wanderers is regarded as more praiseworthy than standing before the countenance of God. This is true even in the case of wanderers such as those whom Abraham might expect to receive as his guests: uncircumcised idolators (for what other people could Abraham have expected to see at this point?). And so we are shown Abraham hurrying away from God's presence in order that he may practice with these wanderers the precept of brotherly love.

Also, note the manner in which he goes about fulfilling this precept. No one could have pursued a prospect of material gain with an eagerness greater than the zeal with which Abraham seized upon this opportunity, as the first circumcised Jew, to behave humanely toward his fellow men. He arouses his wife and child, indeed, his entire household, to bustling activity. He has every-three men were standing there, turned toward him. And when he saw this, he ran from the door of his tent to meet them and bowed down to the ground,   3. and he said: "My *God*,° if indeed I have found favor in Thine eyes, pray Thee do not pass by Thy servant.   4. I beg of you, let a little water be fetched, and wash your feet, and rest beneath the tree.   5. I would fetch a morsel of bread; refresh your hearts with it, and then you may pass on, for (I ask this only) because you have passed by [the home of your] servant." They replied: "Do as you have spoken.   6. And Abraham hastened into the tent to Sarah and said: "Be quick, and of three measures of flour [get] the finest, knead it and make cakes."   7. But Abraham himself ran to the cattle and took a calf, tender and good, and gave it to the

וַיַּרְא וְהִנֵּה שְׁלֹשָׁה אֲנָשִׁים נִצָּבִים עָלָיו וַיַּרְא
וַיָּרָץ לִקְרָאתָם מִפֶּתַח הָאֹהֶל וַיִּשְׁתַּחוּ אָרְצָה:
ג וַיֹּאמַר אֲדֹנָי אִם־נָא מָצָאתִי חֵן בְּעֵינֶיךָ
אַל־נָא תַעֲבֹר מֵעַל עַבְדֶּךָ: ד יֻקַּח־נָא מְעַט־
מַיִם וְרַחֲצוּ רַגְלֵיכֶם וְהִשָּׁעֲנוּ תַּחַת הָעֵץ:
ה וְאֶקְחָה פַת־לֶחֶם וְסַעֲדוּ לִבְּכֶם אַחַר תַּעֲבֹרוּ
כִּי־עַל־כֵּן עֲבַרְתֶּם עַל־עַבְדְּכֶם וַיֹּאמְרוּ כֵּן
תַּעֲשֶׂה כַּאֲשֶׁר דִּבַּרְתָּ: ו וַיְמַהֵר אַבְרָהָם
הָאֹהֱלָה אֶל־שָׂרָה וַיֹּאמֶר מַהֲרִי שְׁלֹשׁ סְאִים
קֶמַח סֹלֶת לוּשִׁי וַעֲשִׂי עֻגוֹת: ז וְאֶל־הַבָּקָר רָץ
אַבְרָהָם וַיִּקַּח בֶּן־בָּקָר רַךְ וָטוֹב וַיִּתֵּן אֶל־

°*Note to the English translation:* Hirsch renders אֲדֹנָי here not as "my lords," but in the sense of "my God" to imply that Abraham is communicating with God even while he performs the human act of hospitality. [G.H.]

thing freshly prepared (as if he had no other refreshments at home to offer to three wanderers!), all in order to refresh the first guests who would present themselves to him following his circumcision. All the foregoing demonstrates Abraham's joy and relief that he need no longer fear remaining in isolation, and it is the merit of the Sages ז"ל that they were able to gain such a profound, genuine insight into the stirrings of Abraham's heart and mind.

This scene is presented to us immediately following the account of Abraham's *milah. The Abrahamites are to grow up in the isolation implied by circumcision; at the same time, they are to become the most humane among men.* They are to provide the most emphatic contrast to what the rest of the world represents, but at the same time they must be ever receptive to all things human. . . .

Not without reason did Abraham hasten to sit before his tent in the burning sun. If his descendants, those much-maligned Jews, have inherited anything at all from their progenitor, then it is this genius for the broad, universal love of man. No one has ever attempted to deny this fact. Wherever the hour demands open hearts, hands and homes, whenever selfless sacrifice is required for human needs (thank God, this is one spark from the teachings of Abraham that has not been struck in vain amidst mankind. It can be found also in non-Abrahamite circles), even the disparagers of Judaism turn, first of all, to the Jews.

2 and 3. . . . God revealed Himself to Abraham while he, Abraham, was engaged in practicing hospitality, in offering refreshments to his fellow men. Or perhaps Abraham proceeded to this act of hospitality at the very moment when God revealed Himself to him. [In either case] this fact of Divine revelation is of extraordinary significance in defining the true character of prophecy in Judaism. The general tendency is to place prophecy, especially our kind of prophecy, into one category with visionary excesses, augury, ecstasy and clairvoyance, etc. As a result, ecstasy is viewed as a preliminary stage of prophecy and prophecy merely as a higher phase of ecstasy. Even some of the writings of Jewish philosophers are not free of the notion that prophecy requires so-called הִתְבּוֹדְדוּת, spatial and spiritual abstraction, and physical and mental isolation. Yet, consider the gap between all this and true, authentic prophecy! Not by abstract contemplation but only through pulsating life, in active loyalty to God, can God's nearness be attained. Our kind of prophecy is not the product of a morbid imagination, of abnormal agitation; rather, it is part of life—healthy, creative, alert and cheerful—as indeed our Sages have put it: "The Divine presence rests (upon man) neither through gloom, nor through sloth, nor through frivolity, nor through levity, nor through talk, nor through idle chatter, but only through the attainment of joy derived from a precept performed" (Shabbath 30b). And even if the Word of God describes one level of prophecy in the words "mouth to mouth do I speak with him, in a vision and not in riddles" (Numbers 12:8), and another in the

הַנַּעַר וַיְמַהֵר לַעֲשׂוֹת אֹתוֹ: ח וַיִּקַּח חֶמְאָה
וְחָלָב וּבֶן־הַבָּקָר אֲשֶׁר עָשָׂה וַיִּתֵּן לִפְנֵיהֶם
וְהוּא־עֹמֵד עֲלֵיהֶם תַּחַת הָעֵץ וַיֹּאכֵלוּ:
ט וַיֹּאמְרוּ אֵלָיו (נקוד על איו) אַיֵּה שָׂרָה אִשְׁתֶּךָ
וַיֹּאמֶר הִנֵּה בָאֹהֶל: י וַיֹּאמֶר שׁוֹב אָשׁוּב אֵלֶיךָ
כָּעֵת חַיָּה וְהִנֵּה־בֵן לְשָׂרָה אִשְׁתֶּךָ וְשָׂרָה
שֹׁמַעַת פֶּתַח הָאֹהֶל וְהוּא אַחֲרָיו: יא וְאַבְרָהָם
וְשָׂרָה זְקֵנִים בָּאִים בַּיָּמִים חָדַל לִהְיוֹת לְשָׂרָה
אֹרַח כַּנָּשִׁים: יב וַתִּצְחַק שָׂרָה בְּקִרְבָּהּ לֵאמֹר
אַחֲרֵי בְלֹתִי הָיְתָה־לִּי עֶדְנָה וַאדֹנִי זָקֵן:
יג וַיֹּאמֶר יְהוָה אֶל־אַבְרָהָם לָמָּה זֶּה צָחֲקָה
שָׂרָה לֵאמֹר הַאַף אֻמְנָם אֵלֵד וַאֲנִי זָקַנְתִּי:
יד הֲיִפָּלֵא מֵיְהוָה דָּבָר לַמּוֹעֵד אָשׁוּב אֵלֶיךָ
כָּעֵת חַיָּה וּלְשָׂרָה בֵן: שני טו וַתְּכַחֵשׁ שָׂרָה ׀
לֵאמֹר לֹא צָחַקְתִּי כִּי ׀ יָרֵאָה וַיֹּאמֶר ׀ לֹא כִּי
צָחָקְתְּ: טז וַיָּקֻמוּ מִשָּׁם הָאֲנָשִׁים וַיַּשְׁקִפוּ עַל־
פְּנֵי סְדֹם וְאַבְרָהָם הֹלֵךְ עִמָּם לְשַׁלְּחָם:

lad and hurried to prepare it. 8. Then he took butter and milk and the calf that he had prepared and he set it before them. And he stood by them beneath the tree and they ate. 9. And they said to him: "Where is Sarah, your wife?" And he replied: "Inside the tent, of course." 10. Thereupon he said: "Even as this living moment [recurs] so shall I return to you, and lo! by that time Sarah, your wife, will have a son." And Sarah heard it all at the entrance of the tent but [the entrance] was behind him. 11. Abraham and Sarah were old, of advanced age, and it had long ceased to be with Sarah after the manner of women. 12. And Sarah laughed within herself: "That I shall have the greatest fulfillment now that I am already worn out! And my husband is also an old man!" 13. And *God* said to Abraham: "Why did Sarah laugh, saying, 'Should I truly give birth when I have become so old?' 14. Is there anything too wondrous for *God?* At the appointed time I shall return to you as [will] this living moment, and by that time Sarah shall have a son." 15. Sarah denied [it] and said: "I did not laugh," because she was afraid. But He said: "No, you did, in fact, laugh." 16. And the men rose up from there and looked down toward the district of Sodom; but Abraham went with them yet a while to escort them on their way.

words "I would make Myself known to him in a vision; I would speak to him in a dream" (Numbers 12:6), then there, too, dreams are solely a medium employed by God for the purpose of addressing Himself to the individual. They have nothing in common with the mental and emotional state of entranced visionaries, for God chooses as His instrument only one who is strong, wealthy, wise and humble (Nedarim 38a). We see, then, that the mental state in which Abraham becomes a נָבִיא is one of complete, practical clear-mindedness, far removed from visionary ecstasy.

16. They rose up "from there"; that is, from the feast Abraham had prepared for them, and looked in the direction of Sodom. We are already familiar with that Sodom, whose opulence seems to be indicated also by the names of its cities: סְדוֹם, "region of orchards"; עֲמֹרָה [Gomorrah]: "abundance of grain"; אַדְמָה, "mineral wealth"; צְבוֹיִם "abundance of game." But we also know of the moral depravity that prevailed there; how, in their affluence—and because of it—the people of Sodom had become רָעִים וְחַטָּאִים, loveless toward their fellow men and morally depraved to the point of brutality. Thus Sodom offered the most striking contrast to the pure, pristine environment which the three men were just preparing to leave.

The "three men" had just experienced the genesis of a nation based on two factors: (a) the hallowing of the body, with *all* its drives and proclivities, in pure moral subordination to God, as symbolized by *milah,* and (b) the practice of universal brotherly love, such as the גְּמִילוּת חֶסֶד [practical loving-kindness] which they had enjoyed at the home of Abraham. This meal, during which they had just made known the first foundations of the future nation of God, offered such a striking contrast to Sodom, it revealed such a lofty moral level as opposed to the depravity of Sodom (where they now had to go), that they "looked down upon Sodom in earnest, searching scrutiny." . . .

17. But *God* had said: "Should I keep undisclosed from Abraham that which I am doing? 18. For Abraham is to become a great and mighty nation, and through it all the nations of the earth will be blessed! 19. For I have turned My particular attention to him only so that he may bind his children and his house after him that they may keep the way of *God*, to practice dutiful benevolence, and justice, so that *God* may bring upon Abraham that which He said concerning him." 20. And *God* said: "Even if the outcry over Sodom and Gomorrah is already great, and their sin already weighs very heavily, 21. nevertheless, I will go down and see whether the cry from this outcry that has come to Me is already sufficient to incur destruction. If not, I shall recognize [from case to case]." 22. The men turned from there and went toward Sodom, but Abraham still stood before *God*. 23. And Abraham drew near and said: "Wilt Thou also sweep into ruin the righteous along with the wicked?" 24. Perhaps there are fifty righteous in the midst of the city. Wilt Thou indeed pursue them [along with the others] and not forgive the district for the sake of the fifty righteous who are within it?

יז וַיהֹוָ֣ה אָמָ֑ר הַֽמְכַסֶּ֤ה אֲנִי֙ מֵֽאַבְרָהָ֔ם אֲשֶׁ֖ר אֲנִ֥י עֹשֶֽׂה: יח וְאַ֨בְרָהָ֔ם הָי֧וֹ יִֽהְיֶ֛ה לְג֥וֹי גָּד֖וֹל וְעָצ֑וּם וְנִ֨בְרְכוּ־ב֔וֹ כֹּ֖ל גּוֹיֵ֥י הָאָֽרֶץ: יט כִּ֣י יְדַעְתִּ֗יו לְמַעַן֩ אֲשֶׁ֨ר יְצַוֶּ֜ה אֶת־בָּנָ֤יו וְאֶת־בֵּיתוֹ֙ אַֽחֲרָ֔יו וְשָֽׁמְרוּ֙ דֶּ֣רֶךְ יְהֹוָ֔ה לַֽעֲשׂ֥וֹת צְדָקָ֖ה וּמִשְׁפָּ֑ט לְמַ֗עַן הָבִ֤יא יְהֹוָה֙ עַל־אַבְרָהָ֔ם אֵ֥ת אֲשֶׁר־דִּבֶּ֖ר עָלָֽיו: כ וַיֹּ֣אמֶר יְהֹוָ֔ה זַֽעֲקַ֛ת סְדֹ֥ם וַֽעֲמֹרָ֖ה כִּי־רָ֑בָּה וְחַ֨טָּאתָ֔ם כִּ֥י כָֽבְדָ֖ה מְאֹֽד: כא אֵֽרֲדָה־נָּ֣א וְאֶרְאֶ֔ה הַכְּצַֽעֲקָתָ֛הּ הַבָּ֥אָה אֵלַ֖י עָשׂ֣וּ ׀ כָּלָ֑ה וְאִם־לֹ֖א אֵדָֽעָה: כב וַיִּפְנ֤וּ מִשָּׁם֙ הָֽאֲנָשִׁ֔ים וַיֵּֽלְכ֖וּ סְדֹ֑מָה וְאַ֨בְרָהָ֔ם עוֹדֶ֥נּוּ עֹמֵ֖ד לִפְנֵ֥י יְהֹוָֽה: כג וַיִּגַּ֥שׁ אַבְרָהָ֖ם וַיֹּאמַ֑ר הַאַ֣ף תִּסְפֶּ֔ה צַדִּ֖יק עִם־רָשָֽׁע: כד אוּלַ֛י יֵ֥שׁ חֲמִשִּׁ֥ים צַדִּיקִ֖ם בְּת֣וֹךְ הָעִ֑יר הַאַ֤ף תִּסְפֶּה֙ וְלֹֽא־תִשָּׂ֣א לַמָּק֔וֹם לְמַ֛עַן חֲמִשִּׁ֥ים הַצַּדִּיקִ֖ם אֲשֶׁ֥ר בְּקִרְבָּֽהּ:

17–19. . . . The task for which Abraham is to rear his progeny is "to keep the way of God"; to adhere to the path indicated by God and to practice acts of duty and justice. The former is a hallowed, chaste life before God modeled on the concept symbolized by *milah*; the latter, conducting oneself in a humane fashion with one's fellow men, as demonstrated by the example of Abraham. Both these concepts represent the sharpest contrast to Sodom; the former as opposed to the immorality of the חַטָּאִים [sinners] and the latter as opposed to the inhumanity of the רָעִים [wicked].

צְדָקָה וּמִשְׁפָּט ["dutiful benevolence, and justice"]: While מִשְׁפָּט [justice] denotes a benefit which a person has the right to demand from another, צְדָקָה (when used in reference to relations between man and his fellow men) designates a benefit which man as such has no right to *ask* of another, but which God has given him the right to *expect* for the simple reason that God has commanded it. מִשְׁפָּט is simple "justice"; צְדָקָה is benevolence practiced because it is a duty commanded by God. But while, as a rule, in Scripture מִשְׁפָּט is mentioned before צְדָקָה; i.e. מִשְׁפָּט וּצְדָקָה; here, very

significantly, it is צְדָקָה that occupies the foreground; i.e. לַֽעֲשׂוֹת צְדָקָה וּמִשְׁפָּט.

The rule is that מִשְׁפָּט comes first and צְדָקָה next. צְדָקָה can never atone for a violation of מִשְׁפָּט. To steal or deal dishonestly with one hand while dispensing charity with the other hand from wealth acquired by theft or in some other dishonest fashion is an abomination to the truths of Judaism. God condemns offerings made from stolen wealth: "For I, *God*, love justice; I hate robbery in offerings" (Isaiah 61:8). Only he who has clean hands may draw near to God. Hence, מִשְׁפָּט first, and צְדָקָה only thereafter.

In this verse, however, צְדָקָה is placed first, for here the order of the day is a Jewish protest against the laws and principles of life that prevailed in Sodom. Not מִשְׁפָּט, but צְדָקָה is the message of universal redemption which Abraham's household is to introduce and uphold in the world. . . . Under Sodomite law claims may be based only on achievement, not on human need. . . Begging is forbidden, and those unfortunate enough to have no money with them are imprisoned and deported. In Sodom, מִשְׁפָּט without *tzedakah* becomes perverted into cruelty and inhumanity. . . .

כה חָלִ֨לָה לְּךָ֜ מֵעֲשֹׂ֣ת ׀ כַּדָּבָ֣ר הַזֶּ֗ה לְהָמִ֤ית
צַדִּיק֙ עִם־רָשָׁ֔ע וְהָיָ֥ה כַצַּדִּ֖יק כָּרָשָׁ֑ע חָלִ֣לָה לָּ֔ךְ
הֲשֹׁפֵט֙ כָּל־הָאָ֔רֶץ לֹ֥א יַעֲשֶׂ֖ה מִשְׁפָּֽט׃
כו וַיֹּ֣אמֶר יְהוָ֔ה אִם־אֶמְצָ֥א בִסְדֹ֛ם חֲמִשִּׁ֥ים
צַדִּיקִ֖ם בְּת֣וֹךְ הָעִ֑יר וְנָשָׂ֥אתִי לְכָל־הַמָּק֖וֹם
בַּעֲבוּרָֽם׃ כז וַיַּ֥עַן אַבְרָהָ֖ם וַיֹּאמַ֑ר הִנֵּה־נָ֤א
הוֹאַ֙לְתִּי֙ לְדַבֵּ֣ר אֶל־אֲדֹנָ֔י וְאָנֹכִ֖י עָפָ֥ר וָאֵֽפֶר׃
כח א֠וּלַי יַחְסְר֞וּן חֲמִשִּׁ֤ים הַצַּדִּיקִם֙ חֲמִשָּׁ֔ה
הֲתַשְׁחִ֥ית בַּחֲמִשָּׁ֖ה אֶת־כָּל־הָעִ֑יר וַיֹּ֙אמֶר֙ לֹ֣א
אַשְׁחִ֔ית אִם־אֶמְצָ֣א שָׁ֔ם אַרְבָּעִ֖ים וַחֲמִשָּֽׁה׃
כט וַיֹּ֨סֶף ע֜וֹד לְדַבֵּ֤ר אֵלָיו֙ וַיֹּאמַ֔ר אוּלַ֛י יִמָּצְא֥וּן
שָׁ֖ם אַרְבָּעִ֑ים וַיֹּ֙אמֶר֙ לֹ֣א אֶֽעֱשֶׂ֔ה בַּעֲב֖וּר
הָאַרְבָּעִֽים׃ ל וַ֠יֹּאמֶר אַל־נָ֞א יִ֤חַר לַֽאדֹנָי֙
וַאֲדַבֵּ֔רָה אוּלַ֛י יִמָּצְא֥וּן שָׁ֖ם שְׁלֹשִׁ֑ים וַיֹּ֙אמֶר֙ לֹ֣א
אֶֽעֱשֶׂ֔ה אִם־אֶמְצָ֥א שָׁ֖ם שְׁלֹשִֽׁים׃ לא וַיֹּ֗אמֶר
הִנֵּֽה־נָ֤א הוֹאַ֙לְתִּי֙ לְדַבֵּ֣ר אֶל־אֲדֹנָ֔י אוּלַ֛י

25. To kill the righteous along with the wicked, that the righteous should be like the wicked — to do such a thing, I know, would be profanation to Thee. It would be profanation to Thee: shall the Judge of all the earth not do justice?" 26. And *God* said: "If I will find in Sodom fifty righteous in the midst of the city, I will forgive the entire district because of them." 27. But Abraham continued and said: "See, now I have begun to speak with my Lord, and I am only dust and ashes. 28. Perhaps there should lack five of the fifty righteous; wouldst Thou destroy the whole city because of the five?" And He said: "I will not destroy if I find forty-five there." 29. He continued speaking to Him and said: "Perhaps forty will be found there?" And He said: "I will not do it, because of the forty." 30. And he said: "O let it not be contrary to my Lord that I would still speak. Perhaps thirty will be found there?" And He said: "I will not do it if I find thirty there." 31. And he said: "See, I have begun to speak to my Lord; perhaps twenty

26. God replies: "If, even in a state such as Sodom, there are fifty righteous men who not only lead lives of justice and morality themselves but also stand up publicly as champions of morality, justice and humanity, then I need not spare the community merely לְמַעֲנָם, *for the sake of* the righteous individuals in Sodom. In such an eventuality it is the community itself that would be deserving of forgiveness בַּעֲבוּרָם, *because* these righteous men exist, and are being tolerated, in its midst." In this case the fact that such righteous individuals can exist, and are tolerated, in the city is proof in itself that the city has not yet descended to the lowest level of corruption.

As outlined in the תורת כֹּהֲנִים in בְּחֻקֹּתַי [Leviticus 26:3–27:34], so here, too, corruption has not yet sunk to the lowest possible level. At this stage, honesty, and upright, God-fearing men, are still only objects of derision. So long as honest men are tolerated, even officially; if they are ridiculed and insulted but not hindered in their way of life, so long as honesty and the fear of God are regarded as foolish but not yet as criminal, there is still a possibility of further deterioration. The worst has come only when people no longer merely ridicule the righteous but bare their teeth at them, and when doing good is forbidden, impeded and punished as a crime against public order. Thus, too, the sin of the Emorites had not yet been complete as long as Abraham and his household were still permitted to erect an altar in their midst to goodness and truth. So, too, Sodom will go under only after it has reached the ultimate depths of depravity.

28. . . . Abraham's descendants are destined to wander through thousands of years as a minority among men; even in their own midst, all too often, the righteous will be in the minority. Hence this insight into Divine Providence, which God in His grace has granted to Abraham, should present most vividly to the minds of his descendants the task and the significance of being such a minority.

If even only ten righteous individuals had been found in the midst of the corruption rife in Sodom and Gomorrah, God would not yet have despaired of the possibility that the entire community might mend its ways, and so He would have permitted all of them to survive for that better future. If God Himself does not despair, then man, too, must persevere and do his part, and continue, ceaselessly and confident of ultimate triumph, to stand up for the good even if the entire generation has gone astray, even if the final victory of the good will dawn only long after we are in our graves.

° ° °

will be found there?" And He said: "I will not destroy, because of the twenty." 32. And he said: "O let it not be contrary to my Lord; I would speak only this once more. Perhaps ten will be found there?" And He said: "I shall not destroy, because of the ten." 33. And *God* removed Himself when He had finished speaking with Abraham. And Abraham returned to his place.

XIX 1. The two angels came to Sodom in the evening, and Lot sat in the gate of Sodom. When Lot saw them, he rose up to meet them and bowed with his face toward the ground, 2. and he said: "Look now, my lords, I beg you turn aside into the house of your servant and stay overnight and wash your feet, then you shall arise early and go on your way." But they said: "No, we shall stay overnight in the street." 3. But when he urged them greatly they turned in to him and came to his house; he prepared a meal for them and baked cakes, and they ate. 4. But before they lay down, the men of the city, the men

יִמָּצְא֤וּן שָׁם֙ עֶשְׂרִ֔ים וַיֹּ֨אמֶר֙ לֹ֣א אַשְׁחִ֔ית בַּעֲב֖וּר הָֽעֶשְׂרִֽים: לב וַיֹּ֗אמֶר אַל־נָ֨א יִ֤חַר לַֽאדֹנָי֙ וַאֲדַבְּרָ֣ה אַךְ־הַפַּ֔עַם אוּלַ֛י יִמָּצְא֥וּן שָׁ֖ם עֲשָׂרָ֑ה וַיֹּ֨אמֶר֙ לֹ֣א אַשְׁחִ֔ית בַּעֲב֖וּר הָעֲשָׂרָֽה: לג וַיֵּ֣לֶךְ יְהֹוָ֔ה כַּאֲשֶׁ֣ר כִּלָּ֔ה לְדַבֵּ֖ר אֶל־אַבְרָהָ֑ם וְאַבְרָהָ֖ם שָׁ֥ב לִמְקֹמֽוֹ: שלישי יט א וַיָּבֹ֜אוּ שְׁנֵ֤י הַמַּלְאָכִים֙ סְדֹ֔מָה בָּעֶ֔רֶב וְל֖וֹט יֹשֵׁ֣ב בְּשַֽׁעַר־סְדֹ֑ם וַיַּרְא־לוֹט֙ וַיָּ֣קָם לִקְרָאתָ֔ם וַיִּשְׁתַּ֥חוּ אַפַּ֖יִם אָֽרְצָה: ב וַיֹּ֜אמֶר הִנֶּ֣ה נָּא־אֲדֹנַ֗י ס֣וּרוּ נָ֠א אֶל־בֵּ֨ית עַבְדְּכֶם֙ וְלִ֔ינוּ וְרַחֲצ֣וּ רַגְלֵיכֶ֔ם וְהִשְׁכַּמְתֶּ֖ם וַהֲלַכְתֶּ֣ם לְדַרְכְּכֶ֑ם וַיֹּאמְר֣וּ לֹּ֔א כִּ֥י בָרְח֖וֹב נָלִֽין: ג וַיִּפְצַר־בָּ֣ם מְאֹ֔ד וַיָּסֻ֣רוּ אֵלָ֔יו וַיָּבֹ֖אוּ אֶל־בֵּית֑וֹ וַיַּ֤עַשׂ לָהֶם֙ מִשְׁתֶּ֔ה וּמַצּ֥וֹת אָפָ֖ה וַיֹּאכֵֽלוּ: ד טֶרֶם֮ יִשְׁכָּבוּ֒ וְאַנְשֵׁ֨י הָעִ֜יר אַנְשֵׁ֤י סְדֹם֙ נָסַ֣בּוּ

CHAPTER XIX

1. ... It must certainly have been an unheard-of thing in Sodom, where strangers were not permitted to establish a home, that a stranger should have been accorded a position of such importance [as implied by Lot's privilege to "sit in the gate of Sodom"]. Lot may have been glad of this, his first opportunity to demonstrate his opposition to the very first article in the Sodomite code of laws—a prohibition against the practice of hospitality. It seems that until then, Lot, being a "smart" individual, had lain low and made no protest, so that the people of Sodom had even appointed him a judge. At any rate, we see Lot here conducting himself in Sodom according to Abraham's conception of a צַדִּיק, in that he dared to show the people an example of how they should mend their ways.

3. ... It was he who prepared the meal, he alone who baked the cakes. What a sad contrast between Lot's isolation and the cheerful bustle that unfolded at the home of Abraham whenever there was an opportunity to perform the *mitzvah* of hospitality! At Lot's home neither his wife nor any child of his participated in the *mitzvah* their husband and father sought to perform. He was left alone in his house to practice what he had learned at the home of Abraham.

4. We are told here, in explicit detail, what kind of people surrounded the home of Lot. This was not a mob of strangers; these were אַנְשֵׁי הָעִיר, residents of the city, אַנְשֵׁי סְדֹם, citizens representative of the state, who now had joined forces to confront this outrageous "attack upon the time-honored laws and prerogatives of this city."

Furthermore, we are told, the people who surrounded Lot's home were "the young" and "the old," and finally, the entire people מִקָּצֶה, "from either extreme" [lit., "from either end"]; i.e., from the lowest classes to the highest, the rabble and the קְצִינִים [officers]. Thus, the crowd outside Lot's home represented every age group and every class. This fact is of great significance when we consider the scheme of the Sodomites and its impact. The populace was already under indictment as being inhuman and immoral to the utmost degree. Now this scheme of theirs offers the conclusive evidence against them. "Bring them out to us so that we may know them" [Verse 5]. The practice of hospitality was regarded as such a great crime that an example was to be made of the strangers who had been invited by Lot as guests, so that such an attempt would never be repeated. Herein lies the inhumanity of Sodom. This abuse was to take the form of brutal debauchery. Herein lies Sodom's immorality.

However, it should be noted that the predisposition

of Sodom, had surrounded the house, both young and old, the entire people, from either extreme. 5. And they called to Lot and said to him: "Where are the men who have come to you this night? Bring them out to us so that we may know them." 6. And Lot went out to them to the entrance, but he had closed the door behind him, 7. and he said: "I beg you, my brothers, do not act so wickedly! 8. Look, please, I have two daughters, who have not yet known a man. I would rather bring them out to you so that you may do to them as you see fit; only do nothing to these men, because they have come under the shadow of my roof." 9. And they said: "Let us push up closer!" and then they said: "This one came to sojourn and already he has set himself up as a judge. Well now! We will deal even worse with you than with them!" And they pressed hard upon the man, upon Lot, and moved close to break down the door. 10. And the men put forth their hand and brought Lot into the house to them, and they closed the door. 11. And they struck blind the people who were at the entrance of the house, both small and great; they toiled in vain to find the entrance. 12. And the men said to Lot: "Whom else do you have here? Son-in-law, and your sons and daughters, and all those that belong to you in the city, take them out of this place. 13. For we are destroying this

עַל־הַבַּ֫יִת מִנַּ֫עַר וְעַד־זָקֵ֑ן כָּל־הָעָ֖ם מִקָּצֶֽה: ה וַיִּקְרְא֤וּ אֶל־לוֹט֙ וַיֹּ֣אמְרוּ ל֔וֹ אַיֵּ֧ה הָאֲנָשִׁ֛ים אֲשֶׁר־בָּ֥אוּ אֵלֶ֖יךָ הַלָּ֑יְלָה הוֹצִיאֵ֣ם אֵלֵ֔ינוּ וְנֵדְעָ֖ה אֹתָֽם: ו וַיֵּצֵ֧א אֲלֵהֶ֛ם ל֖וֹט הַפֶּ֑תְחָה וְהַדֶּ֖לֶת סָגַ֥ר אַחֲרָֽיו: ז וַיֹּאמַ֑ר אַל־נָ֥א אַחַ֖י תָּרֵֽעוּ: ח הִנֵּה־ נָ֨א לִ֜י שְׁתֵּ֣י בָנ֗וֹת אֲשֶׁ֤ר לֹא־יָֽדְעוּ֙ אִ֔ישׁ אוֹצִֽיאָה־נָּ֤א אֶתְהֶן֙ אֲלֵיכֶ֔ם וַעֲשׂ֣וּ לָהֶ֔ן כַּטּ֖וֹב בְּעֵינֵיכֶ֑ם רַ֠ק לָֽאֲנָשִׁ֤ים הָאֵל֙ אַל־תַּעֲשׂ֣וּ דָבָ֔ר כִּֽי־עַל־כֵּ֥ן בָּ֖אוּ בְּצֵ֥ל קֹֽרָתִֽי: ט וַיֹּאמְר֣וּ ׀ גֶּשׁ־ הָ֗לְאָה וַיֹּֽאמְרוּ֙ הָאֶחָ֤ד בָּֽא־לָגוּר֙ וַיִּשְׁפֹּ֣ט שָׁפ֔וֹט עַתָּ֕ה נָרַ֥ע לְךָ֖ מֵהֶ֑ם וַיִּפְצְר֨וּ בָאִ֤ישׁ בְּלוֹט֙ מְאֹ֔ד וַֽיִּגְּשׁ֖וּ לִשְׁבֹּ֥ר הַדָּֽלֶת: י וַיִּשְׁלְח֤וּ הָֽאֲנָשִׁים֙ אֶת־ יָדָ֔ם וַיָּבִ֧יאוּ אֶת־ל֛וֹט אֲלֵיהֶ֖ם הַבָּ֑יְתָה וְאֶת־ הַדֶּ֖לֶת סָגָֽרוּ: יא וְֽאֶת־הָאֲנָשִׁ֞ים אֲשֶׁר־פֶּ֣תַח הַבַּ֗יִת הִכּוּ֙ בַּסַּנְוֵרִ֔ים מִקָּטֹ֖ן וְעַד־גָּד֑וֹל וַיִּלְא֖וּ לִמְצֹ֥א הַפָּֽתַח: יב וַיֹּאמְר֨וּ הָאֲנָשִׁ֜ים אֶל־ל֗וֹט עֹ֚ד מִֽי־לְךָ֣ פֹ֔ה חָתָן֙ וּבָנֶ֣יךָ וּבְנֹתֶ֔יךָ וְכֹ֥ל אֲשֶׁר־ לְךָ֖ בָּעִ֑יר הוֹצֵ֖א מִן־הַמָּקֽוֹם: יג כִּֽי־מַשְׁחִתִ֣ים

---

to these two extremes of evil varies with age and social position. The young are generally susceptible to the influence of dissipation, but as a rule they still have human, sensitive hearts which are outraged by acts of cruelty. Similarly, the so-called lower classes derive pleasure from crude immorality, but since they themselves are victims of oppression, they always side with the underdog and revolt against any abuse of the helpless and the unfortunate. Not so the old. Of course, the old have become hardened by the experiences of life, but since they have already had their fling they will not tolerate among the younger generation excesses they themselves may have committed in their youth. Similarly, the so-called upper classes, by virtue of their position, have become hard and unfeeling toward the sufferings of the "lower classes," but they will put a stop to crude, public scandals of immorality, if not out of regard for morality, then still out of a sense of pro-

priety, which usually results from good breeding.

Hence, with a population representing all ages and classes, the execution of such an inhuman, immoral scheme would have been impossible if evil had not reached such immense proportions as it did in Sodom. Had the city not been thoroughly corrupt, the young would have joined forces with the "common folk" against inhumanity, and the old would have aided the upper classes in the preservation of public morality. But in this instance young and old, high and low, were unanimously united in the practice of the most inhuman and immoral acts, and this fact sealed the doom of the "men of Sodom."

⋄ ⋄ ⋄

9. *Well now!* If you actually dare to defend your conduct you are even more culpable, and an even greater threat to us, than they. . . .

place because the outcry concerning them has become great before the countenance of *God*; that is why *God* has sent us to destroy it." 14. And Lot went out and spoke to his sons-in-law, who had married his daughters, and said, "Arise and go out of this district because *God* will destroy the city!" And he appeared as a jester in the eyes of his sons-in-law. 15. And when the morning arose, the angels urged Lot on: "Arise, take your wife and your two daughters that are with you, for otherwise you may be swept along in the iniquity of the city." 16. And since he still lingered, the men seized him, his wife and his two daughters by the hand, since *God* took pity upon him, and they led him out and left him outside the city. 17. And when they had brought them out, he said: "Now save yourself! Do not look back! Do not stand still in all this plain! Escape to the mountain, lest you be swept away." 18. And Lot said to them: "Not so, O my Lord! 19. Lo! now, Thy servant has found favor in Thine eyes and Thou hast magnified Thy love, with which Thou hast dealt with me, in that Thou hast kept me alive. But I cannot

אֲנַחְנוּ אֶת־הַמָּקוֹם הַזֶּה כִּי־גָדְלָה צַעֲקָתָם
אֶת־פְּנֵי יְהוָה וַיְשַׁלְּחֵנוּ יְהוָה לְשַׁחֲתָהּ:
יד וַיֵּצֵא לוֹט וַיְדַבֵּר ׀ אֶל־חֲתָנָיו ׀ לֹקְחֵי בְנֹתָיו
וַיֹּאמֶר קוּמוּ צְּאוּ מִן־הַמָּקוֹם הַזֶּה כִּי־מַשְׁחִית
יְהוָה אֶת־הָעִיר וַיְהִי כִמְצַחֵק בְּעֵינֵי חֲתָנָיו:
טו וּכְמוֹ הַשַּׁחַר עָלָה וַיָּאִיצוּ הַמַּלְאָכִים בְּלוֹט
לֵאמֹר קוּם קַח אֶת־אִשְׁתְּךָ וְאֶת־שְׁתֵּי בְנֹתֶיךָ
הַנִּמְצָאֹת פֶּן־תִּסָּפֶה בַּעֲוֹן הָעִיר:
טז וַיִּתְמַהְמָהּ ׀ וַיַּחֲזִיקוּ הָאֲנָשִׁים בְּיָדוֹ וּבְיַד־
אִשְׁתּוֹ וּבְיַד שְׁתֵּי בְנֹתָיו בְּחֶמְלַת יְהוָה עָלָיו
וַיֹּצִאֻהוּ וַיַּנִּחֻהוּ מִחוּץ לָעִיר: יז וַיְהִי כְהוֹצִיאָם
אֹתָם הַחוּצָה וַיֹּאמֶר הִמָּלֵט עַל־נַפְשֶׁךָ אַל־
תַּבִּיט אַחֲרֶיךָ וְאַל־תַּעֲמֹד בְּכָל־הַכִּכָּר הָהָרָה
הִמָּלֵט פֶּן־תִּסָּפֶה: יח וַיֹּאמֶר לוֹט אֲלֵהֶם
אַל־נָא אֲדֹנָי: יט הִנֵּה־נָא מָצָא עַבְדְּךָ חֵן
בְּעֵינֶיךָ וַתַּגְדֵּל חַסְדְּךָ אֲשֶׁר עָשִׂיתָ עִמָּדִי
לְהַחֲיוֹת אֶת־נַפְשִׁי וְאָנֹכִי לֹא אוּכַל לְהִמָּלֵט

13. It is significant that throughout this account of Sodom's end God is designated as ד, in His quality of mercy. This implies that when corruption reaches such dimensions, total destruction is an act of mercy.

14. The old man goes out, in the middle of the night, to his sons-in-law, the men to whom he has entrusted his daughters, and implores them to save his daughters and themselves, but they only laugh at him as if he were a jester. Not without good reason does the text add the words "who had married his daughters" [lit., "who had taken his daughters"], to qualify the statement that these men were Lot's sons-in-law. They had indeed taken his daughters as wives, but they had not become his sons-in-law in the true sense of the word. For they were men of Sodom, so that there could be no "bond" between them and the nephew of Abraham as regarded aspirations and outlook on life. For men such as Lot there could be no true sons-in-law in Sodom, and if he had known how to win his children for himself and for his life's direction, they would not have taken husbands from among the men of Sodom.

However, as already indicated in Verse 3, Lot, though he himself had better proclivities and had even mustered the courage, at great personal risk, to stand up for the right against the entire community, was weak, and hence isolated, in his own household and in his relations with his children. A man of Abraham's caliber would never have accepted men "who had taken his daughters" but who could not have become his true sons-in-law. No daughter of Abraham would have taken a husband who would not have become wedded also to the spirit of her father's house.

Here we see a mistake which is still made in our own day, thousands of years later, in a similar fashion and under similar circumstances, and which exacts its toll today even as it did then:[21] Lot came to his sons-in-law and spoke to them of God, and they laughed at him. Yet Lot had expected more attention and consideration from his sons-in-law than he had from his own sons. It was to his sons-in-law that Lot turned first of all, and when they laughed at him, he gave up and did not even attempt to talk to his own sons. To all this, life unfortunately offers sad commentaries in our own day.

[21]*Note to the English translation*: Hirsch probably refers to the practice of permitting material and social considerations to outweigh spiritual factors in "marrying off" one's daughters. [G.H.]

escape to the mountain lest the evil reach me and I die.   20. Lo! now, this city is so near that I could flee to it, and it is a very insignificant thing. O let me escape to it; it is a very insignificant thing, and it will save my life.''   21. And He said to him: ''Lo! I have granted you consideration also in this respect, that I will not overthrow this city of which you have spoken.   22. Make haste, escape to it, for I cannot do anything until you have come there.'' This is why he called the city Tzoar.   23. The sun had risen over the earth when Lot came to Tzoar. 24. And *God* had caused sulfur and fire to rain upon Sodom and Gomorrah, from *God*, from heaven.   25. And He overthrew those cities and the entire plain and also all the inhabitants of the city and that which grew upon the ground. 26. His [i.e., Lot's] wife looked back behind him and she became a pillar of salt. 27. Abraham set out early in the morning for the place where he had stood before the countenance of *God*,   28. and he looked down toward Sodom and Gomorrah and toward all the land of the plain, and he saw, and lo! the smoke of the land rose up like the smoke from a lime kiln.   29. So it came to pass that when God destroyed the cities of the plain, God remembered Abraham and sent Lot out of the midst of the overthrow when He overthrew the cities in which Lot had settled.   30. But Lot went up out of Tzoar and dwelt upon the mountain, and his two daughters with him, because he was afraid to remain in Tzoar,

הָהָרָה פֶּן־תִּדְבָּקַנִי הָרָעָה וָמַתִּי: כ הִנֵּה־נָא הָעִיר הַזֹּאת קְרֹבָה לָנוּס שָׁמָּה וְהִוא מִצְעָר אִמָּלְטָה נָּא שָׁמָּה הֲלֹא מִצְעָר הִוא וּתְחִי נַפְשִׁי: רביעי כא וַיֹּאמֶר אֵלָיו הִנֵּה נָשָׂאתִי פָנֶיךָ גַּם לַדָּבָר הַזֶּה לְבִלְתִּי הָפְכִּי אֶת־הָעִיר אֲשֶׁר דִּבַּרְתָּ: כב מַהֵר הִמָּלֵט שָׁמָּה כִּי לֹא אוּכַל לַעֲשׂוֹת דָּבָר עַד־בֹּאֲךָ שָׁמָּה עַל־כֵּן קָרָא שֵׁם־ הָעִיר צוֹעַר: כג הַשֶּׁמֶשׁ יָצָא עַל־הָאָרֶץ וְלוֹט בָּא צֹעֲרָה: כד וַיהֹוָה הִמְטִיר עַל־סְדֹם וְעַל־ עֲמֹרָה גָּפְרִית וָאֵשׁ מֵאֵת יְהֹוָה מִן־הַשָּׁמָיִם: כה וַיַּהֲפֹךְ אֶת־הֶעָרִים הָאֵל וְאֵת כָּל־הַכִּכָּר וְאֵת כָּל־יֹשְׁבֵי הֶעָרִים וְצֶמַח הָאֲדָמָה: כו וַתַּבֵּט אִשְׁתּוֹ מֵאַחֲרָיו וַתְּהִי נְצִיב מֶלַח: כז וַיַּשְׁכֵּם אַבְרָהָם בַּבֹּקֶר אֶל־הַמָּקוֹם אֲשֶׁר־ עָמַד שָׁם אֶת־פְּנֵי יְהֹוָה: כח וַיַּשְׁקֵף עַל־פְּנֵי סְדֹם וַעֲמֹרָה וְעַל כָּל־פְּנֵי אֶרֶץ הַכִּכָּר וַיַּרְא וְהִנֵּה עָלָה קִיטֹר הָאָרֶץ כְּקִיטֹר הַכִּבְשָׁן: כט וַיְהִי בְּשַׁחֵת אֱלֹהִים אֶת־עָרֵי הַכִּכָּר וַיִּזְכֹּר אֱלֹהִים אֶת־אַבְרָהָם וַיְשַׁלַּח אֶת־לוֹט מִתּוֹךְ הַהֲפֵכָה בַּהֲפֹךְ אֶת־הֶעָרִים אֲשֶׁר־יָשַׁב בָּהֵן לוֹט: ל וַיַּעַל לוֹט מִצּוֹעַר וַיֵּשֶׁב בָּהָר וּשְׁתֵּי בְנֹתָיו עִמּוֹ כִּי יָרֵא לָשֶׁבֶת בְּצוֹעַר וַיֵּשֶׁב

---

24. *from* God, *from heaven.* Since we already have been told ד׳ הִמְטִיר וגו׳ [''and *God* had caused sulfur and fire to rain,'' etc.], the words ''from *God*, from heaven'' would seem redundant. Actually, they are of paramount significance. One who visits the Dead Sea region today and sees the sulfur springs and the volcanic terrain will interpret the destruction of these cities as an ordinary natural occurrence. The volcanic character of the terrain would explain the origins of the Dead Sea. The causes would then appear natural, without need to refer to God or to heaven. But the words ''from *God*, from heaven'' show that this view is incorrect. The destruction came ''from *God*, from heaven.'' [We are told:] You are confusing the cause with the effect. What you interpret as the cause is in reality only an effect.

You hold that the catastrophe was caused by the character of the terrain as you see it now, when in truth the present form of the terrain is only an effect of this catastrophe, an upheaval which did not originate on earth or as the result of terrestrial forces but resulted directly from God, from heaven.

The geological theories of the origins of the earth are probably based on similar errors. The visible phenomena upon which these theories are based are real, but the conclusions based upon them are false. These theories, too, confuse the causes with the effects. The phenomena which they interpret as the causes of geological upheavals are in reality only the effects of upheavals called forth by God when He formed the earth.

בַּמְּעָרָה הוּא וּשְׁתֵּי בְנֹתָיו׃ לא וַתֹּאמֶר
הַבְּכִירָה אֶל־הַצְּעִירָה אָבִינוּ זָקֵן וְאִישׁ אֵין
בָּאָרֶץ לָבוֹא עָלֵינוּ כְּדֶרֶךְ כָּל־הָאָרֶץ׃ לב לְכָה
נַשְׁקֶה אֶת־אָבִינוּ יַיִן וְנִשְׁכְּבָה עִמּוֹ וּנְחַיֶּה
מֵאָבִינוּ זָרַע׃ לג וַתַּשְׁקֶיןָ אֶת־אֲבִיהֶן יַיִן
בַּלַּיְלָה הוּא וַתָּבֹא הַבְּכִירָה וַתִּשְׁכַּב אֶת־אָבִיהָ
וְלֹא־יָדַע בְּשִׁכְבָהּ וּבְקוּמָהּ (נקוד על ו׳)׃ לד וַיְהִי
מִמָּחֳרָת וַתֹּאמֶר הַבְּכִירָה אֶל־הַצְּעִירָה הֵן־
שָׁכַבְתִּי אֶמֶשׁ אֶת־אָבִי נַשְׁקֶנּוּ יַיִן גַּם־הַלַּיְלָה
וּבֹאִי שִׁכְבִי עִמּוֹ וּנְחַיֶּה מֵאָבִינוּ זָרַע׃
לה וַתַּשְׁקֶיןָ גַּם בַּלַּיְלָה הַהוּא אֶת־אֲבִיהֶן יָיִן
וַתָּקָם הַצְּעִירָה וַתִּשְׁכַּב עִמּוֹ וְלֹא־יָדַע בְּשִׁכְבָהּ
וּבְקֻמָהּ׃ לו וַתַּהֲרֶיןָ שְׁתֵּי בְנוֹת־לוֹט מֵאֲבִיהֶן׃
לז וַתֵּלֶד הַבְּכִירָה בֵּן וַתִּקְרָא שְׁמוֹ מוֹאָב הוּא
אֲבִי־מוֹאָב עַד־הַיּוֹם׃ לח וְהַצְּעִירָה גַם־הִוא
יָלְדָה בֵּן וַתִּקְרָא שְׁמוֹ בֶּן־עַמִּי הוּא אֲבִי בְנֵי־
עַמּוֹן עַד־הַיּוֹם׃ ס כ א וַיִּסַּע מִשָּׁם אַבְרָהָם
אַרְצָה הַנֶּגֶב וַיֵּשֶׁב בֵּין־קָדֵשׁ וּבֵין שׁוּר וַיָּגָר

and so he dwelt in a cave, he and his two daughters. 31. And the elder said to the younger: "Our father is old, and there is no longer any man on earth to come to us after the manner of all the earth. 32. Come, let us give our father wine to drink and let us lie with him so that we may give life to descendants from our father." 33. And they gave their father wine to drink that night and the elder came and lay with her father, but he did not know when she lay down, nor when she arose. 34. On the next day the elder said to the younger: "Look, I lay with my father last night; let us give him wine to drink tonight also, and you go too and lie with him so that we may give life to descendants from our father." 35. And they gave their father wine to drink on this night also, and the younger arose and lay with him, but he did not know when she lay down, nor when she arose. 36. So the two daughters of Lot conceived from their father. 37. And the elder bore a son and named him Moab; he is the ancestor of Moab until this day. 38. The younger also bore a son and she named him Ben-Ami; he is the ancestor of the sons of Ammon until this day.

XX 1. Abraham journeyed forth from there to the south country and settled between Kadesh and Shur, and he stayed temporarily in Gerar.

CHAPTER XX

1. It seems that we should establish the motivations for both these moves. We have seen that, initially, Abraham considered it his duty to isolate himself and his household from the bustle of the cities. It was for this reason that he first settled in the desolate south. It was only by slow degrees that he entered into city life and finally dwelt for a long time as a highly respected friend among his confederates, Aner, Eshkol and Mamre. Now, in his declining years, we see him moving once again to the south. He settles in the region between Kadesh and Shur; that is, in the most desolate part of a most isolated region, close to the wilderness of Shur, which is known as the most barren of wastelands. At the same time he seeks a contact with city life and therefore stays temporarily in Gerar, the capital of the Philistine kings.

If we are not altogether mistaken, we might venture to say that it was the approaching birth of their son which caused Abraham and Sarah to make this odd change in residence. One such as Isaac, too, should grow up in isolation, far removed from pernicious influences. On the other hand, complete isolation, in which the youth never comes in contact with others, with people who think differently and whose aims and way of life differ from his own, is a no less dangerous mistake in education. A young person who has never seen a way of life other than that of his parents, never had an opportunity to compare it with the ways of others and never learned to appreciate the moral contrast between the two, will never learn to value, respect and hold fast to the ways his parents have taught him. He will surely fall victim to these alien influences at his very first encounter with them, even as anxiously shutting out all fresh air is the surest way of catching cold as soon as one takes his first step out of doors.

It is only proper that the son of Abraham, the future bearer of Abraham's heritage, should go from time to time into the non-Abrahamite world, there to learn

2. And Abraham said with regard to his wife, Sarah: "She is my sister." Thereupon Abimelekh, king of Gerar, sent and took Sarah. 3. And God came to Abimelekh in a dream of the night and said to him: "You shall die because of the woman you have taken, for she is the wedded wife of a man." 4. But Abimelekh had not come near her, and he said: "My God, wilt Thou slay even a righteous nation? 5. Did not he himself say to me: 'She is my sister,' and did not she, too, say to me: 'He is my brother?' In the innocence of my mind and in the purity of my hands have I done this." 6. And God said to him in the dream: "I, too, know that you did this in the innocence of your heart; therefore, I also restrained you from sinning against Me; that is why I did not permit you to touch her, even indirectly. 7. And now therefore, restore the wife of the man, because he is a prophet, so that he will pray for you and you will remain alive. But if you

בִּגְרָר: ב וַיֹּאמֶר אַבְרָהָם אֶל־שָׂרָה אִשְׁתּוֹ אֲחֹתִי הִוא וַיִּשְׁלַח אֲבִימֶלֶךְ מֶלֶךְ גְּרָר וַיִּקַּח אֶת־שָׂרָה: ג וַיָּבֹא אֱלֹהִים אֶל־אֲבִימֶלֶךְ בַּחֲלוֹם הַלָּיְלָה וַיֹּאמֶר לוֹ הִנְּךָ מֵת עַל־הָאִשָּׁה אֲשֶׁר־לָקַחְתָּ וְהִוא בְּעֻלַת בָּעַל: ד וַאֲבִימֶלֶךְ לֹא קָרַב אֵלֶיהָ וַיֹּאמַר אֲדֹנָי הֲגוֹי גַּם־צַדִּיק תַּהֲרֹג: ה הֲלֹא הוּא אָמַר־לִי אֲחֹתִי הִוא וְהִיא־גַם־הִוא אָמְרָה אָחִי הוּא בְּתָם־לְבָבִי וּבְנִקְיֹן כַּפַּי עָשִׂיתִי זֹאת: ו וַיֹּאמֶר אֵלָיו הָאֱלֹהִים בַּחֲלֹם גַּם אָנֹכִי יָדַעְתִּי כִּי בְתָם־לְבָבְךָ עָשִׂיתָ זֹּאת וָאֶחְשֹׂךְ גַּם־אָנֹכִי אוֹתְךָ מֵחֲטוֹ־לִי עַל־כֵּן לֹא־נְתַתִּיךָ לִנְגֹּעַ אֵלֶיהָ: ז וְעַתָּה הָשֵׁב אֵשֶׁת־הָאִישׁ כִּי־נָבִיא הוּא וְיִתְפַּלֵּל בַּעַדְךָ וֶחְיֵה וְאִם־אֵינְךָ

---

to take the measure of opposing ideas and to fortify himself, by practice, to preserve and uphold the way and the spirit of Abraham in a world which opposes these values. For this purpose Abraham chooses as his temporary residence the capital of a Philistine prince. In the land of the Philistines corruption does not seem to have reached the depth which it has in Canaan; hence the Philistines were not included in the destruction which precisely that corruption had brought to their Emorite neighbors.

5. בְּתָם־לְבָבִי [*In the innocence of my mind*]. I did it with heart and soul. I did not have the slightest scruples about it, nor did I see any reason for such reservations.

לֵבָב is the hub of the organism where all the threads and impulses of physical, spiritual and moral life join and from where they develop. לֵבָב denotes the entire inner process of thought; לֵב, the more marked thinking, the will, resolve, etc.

In this passage בְּתָם־לְבָבִי ["in the innocence of my mind"] etc. implies: "I had no reason whatsoever to see anything wrong in what I had done. I felt that I could devote to it all the workings of my mind, undivided, that is, undisturbed by impulses that would protest against it."

The foregoing would imply that, according to the customs of the locality at that time, it was considered permissible for kings to behave in this manner, [i.e., to take the unmarried sisters of strangers] for otherwise Abimelekh could not have said: בְּתָם־לְבָבִי . . .

7. The reasoning in this verse is difficult to follow. "Restore the wife of the man, because he is a prophet." What if he had been only a beggar? Certainly the fact that the man is a prophet could not be an adequate explanation why it was Abimelekh's duty to return the woman to him. In this connection our Sages say (Baba Kamma 92a): "Our Rabbis taught: All those fixed sums stated above specify only the payment civilly due for degradation. For regarding the hurt done to the feelings of the plaintiff, even if the offender were to bring all the rams of Nebaioth in the world, the offense would not be forgiven until he asks his pardon, as it is written, '*Now therefore, restore the wife of the man, because he is a prophet, so that he will pray for you.*' But is it only the wife of a prophet who must be returned [to her husband], whereas the wife of another man need not be returned? R. Samuel Bar Naḥmani said in the name of R. Yohanan: *Restore the man's wife* [surely applies] in every case, for as to your allegation, *Wilt Thou slay even a righteous nation? Did not he himself say to me: She is my sister, did not she, too, say to me: He is my brother?* [You should know that] *he is a prophet,* who has already taught the world that when a stranger comes to a city, he is to be questioned regarding food and drink, or regarding his wife, whether she is his wife or his sister. From this we can learn that a descendant of Noah may become liable to the death penalty if he had the opportunity to acquire instruction but failed to do so."

If we understand this passage correctly, the Sages

מֵשִׁיב דַּע כִּי־מוֹת תָּמוּת אַתָּה וְכָל־אֲשֶׁר־לָךְ:
ח וַיַּשְׁכֵּם אֲבִימֶלֶךְ בַּבֹּקֶר וַיִּקְרָא לְכָל־עֲבָדָיו
וַיְדַבֵּר אֶת־כָּל־הַדְּבָרִים הָאֵלֶּה בְּאָזְנֵיהֶם

will not restore her, know that you will surely die, you and all that are yours."
8. And Abimelekh rose early in the morning and called all his servants and told all these things in their hearing and thereupon

interpret the statement הָשֵׁב אֵשֶׁת הָאִישׁ ["restore the wife of the man"] to mean that duty demands more than just "releasing" the woman. Indeed, the text does not read הוֹצִיא אֶת הָאִשָּׁה ["release (or "bring out") the woman"] or even הָשֵׁב אֶת הָאִשָּׁה ["return the woman"] but explicitly הָשֵׁב אֵשֶׁת הָאִישׁ ["restore the wife of the man"]. This implies that Abimelekh must appease also Abraham for the wrong he has done him, indeed, conciliate Abraham to such an extent that he will even pray for him. However, this would presuppose that only Abimelekh, not Abraham, had been guilty, and that Abimelekh's citing of Abraham's and Sarah's statements in his defense was completely irrelevant.

This difficulty would be resolved by the statement "because he is a prophet." Abraham is a נָבִיא; therefore he judges the conditions and the deeds of men not in accordance with standards that vary from age to age and from place to place but in accordance with absolute laws of morality which are not subject to change. In this particular locality custom may have hallowed the immoral practice that a foreign woman is obligated to give herself to anyone among the people if she is married, and to the pleasure of the prince if she is not, and that, instead of your asking the stranger what sort of hospitality he would like to have from you, your first question to him should be: "This woman with you — is she your wife? Is she your sister?" Abraham, on the other hand, had not only known a different sort of "alien law" himself but had also taught it to others by the hospitality he himself practiced in public. It was the immoral custom prevalent in their midst which compelled Abraham to say that Sarah was not his wife, because this was the only way in which he could protect both himself and her at least against attacks from the populace.

°   °   °

This word of God to Abimelekh is of crucial significance also for all the future. This is the first time that God Himself pointed out Abraham's position to the strangers among whom Abraham lived. After all, Abimelekh and his people constituted the environment in which Isaac was to be born and to spend most of his life; also, they were to become the permanent and immediate neighbors of the people that would be descended from Abraham. This event was intended as God's warning to them: אַל תִּגְּעוּ בִמְשִׁיחָי וּבִנְבִיאַי אַל תָּרֵעוּ ["Touch not My anointed ones, and do My prophets no harm" — I Chronicles 16:22].

°   °   °

וְיִתְפַּלֵּל בַּעַדְךָ [so that he will pray for you]. Derived from פלל, "to judge," related to בלל ["to mingle"]. As we have already seen in the account of the division of mankind into language groups, בלל does not mean "to confuse," to "commingle" material which had been extant and separate before, but to introduce a new element into a mass and to create a new mass by permitting this new element to penetrate the original mass in all its parts. According to the Jewish concept this symbolizes the function of the judge. Lies and injustice divide people from one another and cause dissension among them. The judge acts to introduce the element of right, the Divine truth of things, into the disputed matter. He causes the new element to penetrate every part of the matter under dispute and, by means of the law, blends into one harmonious unit things which, without the law, would have to remain far apart from one another.

הִתְפַּלֵּל means to perform this task upon one's own person. הִתְפַּלֵּל means: *Take the element of God's truth and allow it to penetrate every aspect and relationship of our character, thus attaining for ourselves that harmonious integrity of all of life which can be gained only through God.*

Consequently, Jewish תְּפִלָּה is diametrically opposed to what is generally described as "prayer." It is not an outpouring from within, an expression of things with which the heart is already replete. (We have other terms to describe such a state: e.g., שִׂיחַ ["meditation"], תְּחִנָּה ["prayer," "supplication"], etc.) Rather, it implies an absorption and penetration of truths which come from outside oneself. If our prayer did not entail תְּפִלָּה, if "to pray," in our sense, would not be הִתְפַּלֵּל, a labor upon one's own inner self to elevate it to that level at which it can perceive the truth and make decisions in keeping with the will of God, it would make no sense to have fixed times and prescribed forms for our prayers. For [if *tefillah* were but an outpouring of our emotions] this arrangement would imply that there are certain specified times when every individual in the community is imbued with the same thoughts and the same emotions. In that case such prayers would be redundant, since thoughts and emotions which are already alive within us do not require expression, least of all expression in phrases formulated by others than ourselves. A heart that is full can always find its own ways of self-expression, except when it is so full that any expression would only detract from this fullness and the most appropriate expression is silence.

the men were very much afraid. 9. Then Abimelekh called Abraham and said to him: "What have you done to us, and with what have I sinned against you, that you have brought such a great sin upon myself and my kingdom? You have done deeds to me that should not be done." 10. Abimelekh [further] said to Abraham: "What did you see that you did this thing?" 11. And Abraham said: "Because I said: There is surely no fear of God in this place, and they will kill me on account of my wife. 12. But moreoever, the truth is that she is my sister, the daughter of my father, but not the daughter of my mother, and that is why she became my wife. 13. And when God caused me to become a wanderer from my father's house, I said to her: 'This is your kindness which you shall do to me: Wherever we will come, I beg you, say of

וַיִּירְאוּ הָאֲנָשִׁים מְאֹד׃ ט וַיִּקְרָא אֲבִימֶלֶךְ
לְאַבְרָהָם וַיֹּאמֶר לוֹ מֶה־עָשִׂיתָ לָּנוּ וּמֶה־
חָטָאתִי לָךְ כִּי־הֵבֵאתָ עָלַי וְעַל־מַמְלַכְתִּי
חֲטָאָה גְדֹלָה מַעֲשִׂים אֲשֶׁר לֹא־יֵעָשׂוּ עָשִׂיתָ
עִמָּדִי׃ י וַיֹּאמֶר אֲבִימֶלֶךְ אֶל־אַבְרָהָם מָה
רָאִיתָ כִּי עָשִׂיתָ אֶת־הַדָּבָר הַזֶּה׃ יא וַיֹּאמֶר
אַבְרָהָם כִּי אָמַרְתִּי רַק אֵין־יִרְאַת אֱלֹהִים
בַּמָּקוֹם הַזֶּה וַהֲרָגוּנִי עַל־דְּבַר אִשְׁתִּי׃ יב וְגַם־
אָמְנָה אֲחֹתִי בַת־אָבִי הִוא אַךְ לֹא בַת־אִמִּי
וַתְּהִי־לִי לְאִשָּׁה׃ יג וַיְהִי כַּאֲשֶׁר הִתְעוּ אֹתִי
אֱלֹהִים מִבֵּית אָבִי וָאֹמַר לָהּ זֶה חַסְדֵּךְ אֲשֶׁר
תַּעֲשִׂי עִמָּדִי אֶל כָּל־הַמָּקוֹם אֲשֶׁר נָבוֹא שָׁמָּה

Hence our prescribed prayers do not in themselves represent truths of which we are already assumed to be aware. Rather, they are means of awakening, reviving, confirming and preserving within us, over and over again, the perception and acceptance of these truths. Indeed, we can say that the less we feel in the mood for prayer, the greater must be our need to pray, and the greater and more redeeming must be the work upon ourselves which we are to accomplish by means of תְּפִלָּה. The absence of the mood for prayer is in itself the clearest sign that the spirit and the truths which תְּפִלָּה is intended *not* to presuppose but to *create*, bring alive and rectify within ourselves are still obscured and in need of being brought to light.

Here, then, we see God Himself sanctioning the efficacy of praying for others. This efficacy is rooted in the concept which we have already encountered in Abraham's plea on behalf of Sodom. If the one who prays is a צַדִּיק [a righteous individual], or, better still, a community, which, as the beautiful Hebrew expression has it, מִשְׁתַּתֵּף בְּצַעֲרוֹ שֶׁל חֲבֵרוֹ, identifies with the pain and sorrow of others, truly making the sorrows of others his (or its) own, then God will promise that perhaps, for the sake of this righteous individual or this righteous community, in order to spare them pain, someone who otherwise might not be worthy of such favor might be relieved of his troubles. This is certainly true here; cf. גַּם עֲנוֹשׁ לַצַּדִּיק לֹא טוֹב [Proverbs 17:26]. An upright man, a man such as Abraham, feels bitter pain whenever another man is punished, even if that other man is truly deserving of punishment.

12. "She was my sister before she became my wife. She is my sister in spirit. She was the daughter of my brother who died young, and she was raised together with me under the influence of the same parental home. So she and I became like brother and sister in mind and spirit and, as a result, she became my wife." According to the Sages, Sarah was identical with Iscah, daughter of Abraham's brother Haran, who died young and whose children, according to Genesis 11:31, apparently remained at the home of their grandfather, Teraḥ.

13. There is another interpretation, based on the fact that the subject of this sentence, אלהים, takes a predicate, הִתְעוּ, in the plural [so that אלהים could be interpreted to mean "gods" instead of "God"]: "When the gods; that is, the paganism which prevailed in my own country, drove me out of my father's house, as a wanderer (perhaps: I was forced to leave my father's house because I was considered an apostate from the beliefs of the people among whom I dwelt), I was not tolerated at my home because תּוֹעֶה מִדַּרְכֵי אֱלִילִים [I had strayed from the paths of the non-gods]."

Because of Abraham's outspoken opposition to paganism, it might have been even more dangerous for him than for anyone else to offer resistance to the immoral custom hallowed by pagan cult, so that it became all the more imperative for him to take this measure. In any event, the well-known Phoenician cult of Astarte, seen in the context of the demands made by the men of Sodom, makes such an assumption appear not so very absurd. . . .

me: 'He is my brother.'" 14. And Abimelekh took sheep and cattle, menservants and maidservants, and gave them to Abraham and returned Sarah, his wife, to him, 15. And Abimelekh said: "Look, my land is before you; settle wherever it pleases you." 16. And to Sarah he had said: "Lo! I have given your brother one thousand pieces of silver. Lo! this will serve you as a covering of the eyes for all those around you, and now you can come before everyone without disguise." 17. Abraham prayed to God, and God healed Abimelekh, his wife and his handmaids, and they gave birth; 18. For *God* had sealed up the wombs of all that belonged to the house of Abimelekh because of Sarah, the wife of Abraham.

XXI

1. And *God* had remembered Sarah, as He had said, and now *God* did for Sarah as He had spoken. 2. Sarah conceived and she bore Abraham a son for his old age, at the appointed time, which God had spoken. 3. Abraham named his son, who was born to him, whom Sarah had borne him, Yitzḥak, 4. and Abraham circumcised his son Yitzḥak at the age of eight days, as God had commanded him. 5. And Abraham was a man of one hundred years when his son Yitzḥak was born to him. 6. And Sarah said: "God has prepared laughter for me; all who will hear of this will laugh at me." 7. But she added: "Who would have said a word of that to Abraham: Sarah has nursed sons! For I have borne him a son for his old age." 8. The child grew and was weaned, and Abraham made a great feast on the day on which Yitzḥak was weaned. 9. But Sarah saw the son of Hagar, the Egyptian woman, whom she had

אָמְרִי־לִי אָחִי הוּא: יד וַיִּקַּח אֲבִימֶלֶךְ צֹאן
וּבָקָר וַעֲבָדִים וּשְׁפָחֹת וַיִּתֵּן לְאַבְרָהָם וַיָּשֶׁב לוֹ
אֵת שָׂרָה אִשְׁתּוֹ: טו וַיֹּאמֶר אֲבִימֶלֶךְ הִנֵּה
אַרְצִי לְפָנֶיךָ בַּטּוֹב בְּעֵינֶיךָ שֵׁב: טז וּלְשָׂרָה
אָמַר הִנֵּה נָתַתִּי אֶלֶף כֶּסֶף לְאָחִיךְ הִנֵּה הוּא־
לָךְ כְּסוּת עֵינַיִם לְכֹל אֲשֶׁר אִתָּךְ וְאֵת כֹּל
וְנֹכָחַת: יז וַיִּתְפַּלֵּל אַבְרָהָם אֶל־הָאֱלֹהִים
וַיִּרְפָּא אֱלֹהִים אֶת־אֲבִימֶלֶךְ וְאֶת־אִשְׁתּוֹ
וְאַמְהֹתָיו וַיֵּלֵדוּ: יח כִּי־עָצֹר עָצַר יְהֹוָה בְּעַד
כָּל־רֶחֶם לְבֵית אֲבִימֶלֶךְ עַל־דְּבַר שָׂרָה אֵשֶׁת
אַבְרָהָם: ס כא א וַיהֹוָה פָּקַד אֶת־שָׂרָה
כַּאֲשֶׁר אָמָר וַיַּעַשׂ יְהֹוָה לְשָׂרָה כַּאֲשֶׁר דִּבֵּר:
ב וַתַּהַר וַתֵּלֶד שָׂרָה לְאַבְרָהָם בֵּן לִזְקֻנָיו
לַמּוֹעֵד אֲשֶׁר־דִּבֶּר אֹתוֹ אֱלֹהִים: ג וַיִּקְרָא
אַבְרָהָם אֶת־שֶׁם־בְּנוֹ הַנּוֹלַד־לוֹ אֲשֶׁר־יָלְדָה־
לּוֹ שָׂרָה יִצְחָק: ד וַיָּמָל אַבְרָהָם אֶת־יִצְחָק בְּנוֹ
בֶּן־שְׁמֹנַת יָמִים כַּאֲשֶׁר צִוָּה אֹתוֹ אֱלֹהִים:
חמישי ה וְאַבְרָהָם בֶּן־מְאַת שָׁנָה בְּהִוָּלֶד לוֹ אֵת
יִצְחָק בְּנוֹ: ו וַתֹּאמֶר שָׂרָה צְחֹק עָשָׂה לִי
אֱלֹהִים כָּל־הַשֹּׁמֵעַ יִצְחַק־לִי: ז וַתֹּאמֶר מִי
מִלֵּל לְאַבְרָהָם הֵינִיקָה בָנִים שָׂרָה כִּי־יָלַדְתִּי
בֵן לִזְקֻנָיו: ח וַיִּגְדַּל הַיֶּלֶד וַיִּגָּמַל וַיַּעַשׂ אַבְרָהָם
מִשְׁתֶּה גָדוֹל בְּיוֹם הִגָּמֵל אֶת־יִצְחָק: ט וַתֵּרֶא
שָׂרָה אֶת־בֶּן־הָגָר הַמִּצְרִית אֲשֶׁר־יָלְדָה

16. The fact that I, the king, who did no more than attempt to approach you, have done such public penance for my attempt, and have sought to atone for it in such a generous manner, should protect you from the eyes of the people in all of my land. No one will now dare cast an improper glance at you. As a result you will no longer need to deny your true position but should be able to present yourself to everyone as the wife of Abraham.

CHAPTER XXI

9. Ishmael is described here in terms of the two character traits combined in his personality: He was the son of a Ḥamite mother but was to be born to Abraham. Sarah, who had been responsible for the birth of this child, had hoped that, if the child were given the proper training, his Ḥamite characteristics could be overcome by the Abrahamite spirit. She had hoped

לְאַבְרָהָם מְצַחֵק׃ י וַתֹּאמֶר לְאַבְרָהָם גָּרֵשׁ
הָאָמָה הַזֹּאת וְאֶת־בְּנָהּ כִּי לֹא יִירַשׁ בֶּן־
הָאָמָה הַזֹּאת עִם־בְּנִי עִם־יִצְחָק׃ יא וַיֵּרַע
הַדָּבָר מְאֹד בְּעֵינֵי אַבְרָהָם עַל אוֹדֹת בְּנוֹ׃
יב וַיֹּאמֶר אֱלֹהִים אֶל־אַבְרָהָם אַל־יֵרַע בְּעֵינֶיךָ
עַל־הַנַּעַר וְעַל־אֲמָתֶךָ כֹּל אֲשֶׁר תֹּאמַר אֵלֶיךָ
שָׂרָה שְׁמַע בְּקֹלָהּ כִּי בְיִצְחָק יִקָּרֵא לְךָ זָרַע׃
יג וְגַם אֶת־בֶּן־הָאָמָה לְגוֹי אֲשִׂימֶנּוּ כִּי זַרְעֲךָ
הוּא׃ יד וַיַּשְׁכֵּם אַבְרָהָם ׀ בַּבֹּקֶר וַיִּקַּח־לֶחֶם
וְחֵמַת מַיִם וַיִּתֵּן אֶל־הָגָר שָׂם עַל־שִׁכְמָהּ וְאֶת־
הַיֶּלֶד וַיְשַׁלְּחֶהָ וַתֵּלֶךְ וַתֵּתַע בְּמִדְבַּר בְּאֵר שָׁבַע׃
טו וַיִּכְלוּ הַמַּיִם מִן־הַחֵמֶת וַתַּשְׁלֵךְ אֶת־הַיֶּלֶד

borne to Abraham, making mockery.
10. And she said to Abraham: "Cast out this handmaid and her son, for the son of this handmaid shall not inherit together with my son Yitzḥak."
11. But the matter was very displeasing in the eyes of Abraham because of his son.
12. And God said to Abraham: "Let it not be evil in your eyes because of the lad and your handmaid; in everything that Sarah says to you, hearken to her voice, for in Yitzḥak shall seed be called for you.
13. And also of the son of the handmaid will I make a nation, for he is your seed."
14. And Abraham rose early in the morning, took bread and a skin of water and gave it to Hagar, putting it on her shoulder, and also the child, and he sent her away. She went and she lost her way in the wilderness of Beer Sheva.
15. The water from the skin came to an end and she

that, as Hagar's mistress, she would be able to neutralize Hagar's influence completely.

We already know how mistaken Sarah had been in this assumption. We have already attempted to show how the dual nature of Ishmael was preserved in his descendants. But Sarah saw this dichotomy emerge in Ishmael himself. He had absorbed just enough of Abraham's lofty ideals to view them with contempt. The world in general reacted to these ideals merely with צחוק [laughter], a gentle hint of derision. . . . But Ishmael מְצַחֵק, responded to them with outright mockery. Hence Ishmael was utterly unfit to enter upon Abraham's heritage together with Isaac.

10. ***Cast out*** is not merely a removal in space; it implies an outright "dismissal" which would put an end to all of Hagar's ties with her former home. Cf. אשה גרושה מֵאִישָׁהּ ["A woman who was divorced by her husband"—Leviticus 21:7]. . . .

° ° °

. . . Not without reason does Sarah repeat the term, הָאָמָה הַזֹּאת "this handmaid" twice. She does not mean that no son of a slave could ever join in perpetuating the heritage of her house. After all, she herself had quite expressly desired just such an arrangement and had brought it about on her own initiative. This particular handmaid, however, had proven utterly unfit for this arrangement. Therefore, "Cast out this handmaid and her son, for the son of this handmaid shall not inherit," etc. I had hoped that "I will be built by her," that Hagar's son would become *my* son, that I myself would be able to raise him for you. But Hagar's character and behavior have shattered my hopes.

12. **שְׁמַע בְּקוֹל** ***[hearken to the voice].*** True, genuine obedience is expressed by the term שְׁמַע בְּקוֹל ["hearken to the voice"], not merely by שְׁמַע בְּדָבָר ["hearken to the word"]. True obedience means to listen to the *voice* of another, not merely to his words; one is to obey because it is the other who has spoken, no matter what that other has said.

Listen to the voice of Sarah, even if the content of her words does not appeal to you. Trust her judgment. Her insights are deeper than yours, just as in general women have a more profound insight into human nature than men. In Isaac shall seed be called for you. Ishmael (Verse 13) is your seed in fact. Ishmael is a descendant of yours and may therefore have inherited many physical traits and also a few spiritual characteristics from you. But he is not worthy to be "called" your son because he can never be your spiritual heir.

בְּיִצְחָק ***[for in Yitzḥak]*** not כִּי יִצְחָק ["for Yitzḥak"]. As the Sages point out, the text does not state that seed will ripen for Abraham *because* of Isaac, but that seed will ripen for Abraham *in* Isaac. Do not grieve overly at the thought of having to eliminate one of your sons from your house. Not even all the descendants of Isaac will remain your spiritual heirs. Not even the best of trees yields only ripe fruit; if you are to obtain the pure and proper seed for the nation of God, many a seed will first have to be eliminated as unfit.

15–16. . . . Hagar's behavior is typical of her race; it reveals the primitive character of the Ḥamites. A Jewish mother would never have abandoned her child, even if all she could do for him would be to soothe him or to

threw the child under one of the shrubs,
16. and she went and sat down far over
against him, taking her distance as archers
do, for she had said: "Let me not look upon
the death of the child." Therefore she sat
down far over against him, and she raised
her voice and wept. 17. But God heard
the voice of the lad and an angel of God
called to Hagar from heaven and said to
her: "What ails you, Hagar? Do not be
afraid! For God has already heard the voice
of the lad, there where he is. 18. Arise,
pick up the lad and strengthen your hand
upon him, for I will make him a great
nation." 19. And God opened her eyes
and she saw a well of water. She went and
filled the skin with water and gave the lad to
drink. 20. God was with the lad and he
grew up. He remained in the wilderness and
became a master archer. 21. He settled in
the wilderness of Paran and his mother took
a wife for him from the land of Mitzrayim.
22. It came to pass at this time that

תַּחַת אַחַד הַשִּׂיחִם: טז וַתֵּלֶךְ וַתֵּשֶׁב לָהּ מִנֶּגֶד
הַרְחֵק כִּמְטַחֲוֵי קֶשֶׁת כִּי אָמְרָה אַל־אֶרְאֶה
בְּמוֹת הַיָּלֶד וַתֵּשֶׁב מִנֶּגֶד וַתִּשָּׂא אֶת־קֹלָהּ
וַתֵּבְךְּ: יז וַיִּשְׁמַע אֱלֹהִים אֶת־קוֹל הַנַּעַר
וַיִּקְרָא מַלְאַךְ אֱלֹהִים ׀ אֶל־הָגָר מִן־הַשָּׁמַיִם
וַיֹּאמֶר לָהּ מַה־לָּךְ הָגָר אַל־תִּירְאִי כִּי־שָׁמַע
אֱלֹהִים אֶל־קוֹל הַנַּעַר בַּאֲשֶׁר הוּא־שָׁם:
יח קוּמִי שְׂאִי אֶת־הַנַּעַר וְהַחֲזִיקִי אֶת־יָדֵךְ בּוֹ
כִּי־לְגוֹי גָּדוֹל אֲשִׂימֶנּוּ: יט וַיִּפְקַח אֱלֹהִים אֶת־
עֵינֶיהָ וַתֵּרֶא בְּאֵר מָיִם וַתֵּלֶךְ וַתְּמַלֵּא אֶת־
הַחֵמֶת מַיִם וַתַּשְׁקְ אֶת־הַנָּעַר: כ וַיְהִי אֱלֹהִים
אֶת־הַנַּעַר וַיִּגְדָּל וַיֵּשֶׁב בַּמִּדְבָּר וַיְהִי רֹבֶה
קַשָּׁת: כא וַיֵּשֶׁב בְּמִדְבַּר פָּארָן וַתִּקַּח־לוֹ אִמּוֹ
אִשָּׁה מֵאֶרֶץ מִצְרָיִם: פ ששי כב וַיְהִי בָּעֵת

ease his torment for only a millionth part of a second. To go away and do nothing because one "cannot bear to see the child's misery" betokens not compassion but the cruel egotism of a brutish character. True humanity is marked by a sense of duty capable of mastering even the strongest personal emotions; a sense of duty should make one forget his own pain and enable him to give help, even if it is nothing more than the comfort of one's compassionate presence. Hence, what follows is most significant. Although Hagar, too, was crying, it was not the voice of Hagar but "the voice of the lad" which God heard (Verse 17), for God is not moved by the tears of an egotist who cries about the sufferings of another but who makes no effort to alleviate them.

Furthermore, she throws the child away "behind one of the shrubs growing there." She does not care where the child will fall; it does not occur to her that he might fall among prickly thorns which might scratch him, so that, due to his mother's folly, needless pain would be added to his tormenting thirst. All the foregoing shows how grief caused Hagar to lose her head completely and to behave toward her child in a manner no Abrahamite woman would ever have done.

° ° °

18. "First of all, arise and pick up the lad; take him up again like a strong mother who never gives way to despair, because only then will you be worthy of God's aid. Then give him water to drink." The text reads הַחֲזִיקִי יָדֵךְ בּוֹ ["strengthen your hand upon him"], not הַחֲזִיקִי בְּיָדוֹ ["hold him fast by the hand"]: Cause your hand to keep a firm grip upon him. Be a firm support and guide to him, for I have planned a great future for him.

21. We have already indicated in our commentary to the end of Chapter 16 the clear-cut imprint which the Abrahamite heritage—though, it is true, in a one-sided manner only—has left upon the Ishmaelite Arab nation.

If we consider that, at the age of 17, Ishmael already had been removed from Abraham's influence and that the maternal, Ḥamite strain in his character became even more dominant through the influence of the Ḥamite woman, the progenitress of the future Arab nation, the fact that the Abrahamite strain is nevertheless so pronounced in the Arab nation of today must fill us with all the more admiration for the enduring, indestructible power inherent in a true Abrahamite upbringing.

22. It came to pass just at that time, after Abraham had sent away his oldest son, and the future of his house rested entirely upon the baby Isaac, who had barely been weaned, that Abimelekh, the king of the country, accompanied by his highest-ranking civil servant, came to Abraham. The two men asked Abraham to swear that he would never deal falsely with him, the king, nor with the second and third generations after him; indeed, that Abraham would remember and

Abimelekh and Phikhol, his commander, said to Abraham as follows: "God is with you in everything that you do; 23. and now swear to me here by God that you will not deal falsely with me, nor with my descendant, nor with my grandson, but according to the kindness that I have done to you, you shall do to me and to the land in which you have sojourned." 24. Abraham said: "I swear." 25. But Abraham had called Abimelekh to account with regard to the well of water which the servants of Abimelekh had violently taken away. 26. And Abimelekh said: "I had not known who did this thing; neither did you tell me, and I only heard of it today." 27. So Abraham took sheep and cattle and gave them to Abimelekh, and both of them made a covenant. 28. But Abraham set seven ewes of the flock by themselves. 29. Abimelekh said to Abraham: "What

הַהִוא וַיֹּאמֶר אֲבִימֶלֶךְ וּפִיכֹל שַׂר־צְבָאוֹ אֶל־
אַבְרָהָם לֵאמֹר אֱלֹהִים עִמְּךָ בְּכֹל אֲשֶׁר־אַתָּה
עֹשֶׂה: כג וְעַתָּה הִשָּׁבְעָה לִּי בֵאלֹהִים הֵנָּה אִם־
תִּשְׁקֹר לִי וּלְנִינִי וּלְנֶכְדִּי כַּחֶסֶד אֲשֶׁר־עָשִׂיתִי
עִמְּךָ תַּעֲשֶׂה עִמָּדִי וְעִם־הָאָרֶץ אֲשֶׁר־גַּרְתָּה
בָּהּ: כד וַיֹּאמֶר אַבְרָהָם אָנֹכִי אִשָּׁבֵעַ:
כה וְהוֹכִחַ אַבְרָהָם אֶת־אֲבִימֶלֶךְ עַל־אֹדוֹת
בְּאֵר הַמַּיִם אֲשֶׁר גָּזְלוּ עַבְדֵי אֲבִימֶלֶךְ:
כו וַיֹּאמֶר אֲבִימֶלֶךְ לֹא יָדַעְתִּי מִי עָשָׂה אֶת־
הַדָּבָר הַזֶּה וְגַם־אַתָּה לֹא־הִגַּדְתָּ לִּי וְגַם אָנֹכִי
לֹא שָׁמַעְתִּי בִּלְתִּי הַיּוֹם: כז וַיִּקַּח אַבְרָהָם צֹאן
וּבָקָר וַיִּתֵּן לַאֲבִימֶלֶךְ וַיִּכְרְתוּ שְׁנֵיהֶם בְּרִית:
כח וַיַּצֵּב אַבְרָהָם אֶת־שֶׁבַע כִּבְשֹׂת הַצֹּאן
לְבַדְּהֶן: כט וַיֹּאמֶר אֲבִימֶלֶךְ אֶל־אַבְרָהָם מָה

reward the friendship which the king and the people of his country had shown him.

Clearly Abimelekh is not addressing Abraham here as a private individual whose influence will not outlast his lifetime and who therefore would be in no position to do good or evil to any country. It is obvious that Abimelekh is thinking in terms of a future in which Abraham's descendants will be a nation in their own right and hence in a position to confront his, Abimelekh's, people either as friends or as foes. In short, this passage can be properly understood only if one assumes that Abimelekh by that time had some knowledge of the promises made [by God] to Abraham, and of Abraham's own expectations for the future, and that Abimelekh therefore wanted to secure for himself and for his country the friendship of that future nation—all on the basis of the debt of gratitude which the progenitor of that future nation owed him.

Seen from this vantage point, the proposal which the king made to Abraham בָּעֵת הַהִיא, so soon after Ishmael had been sent away, followed by the account of the crowning event in Abraham's life, assumes special significance. Ishmael is gone. Abraham is an old man who may be gathered to his fathers at any time. The future rests entirely upon an infant boy who has barely left his mother's breast. The future nation is still rocked in its cradle, as it were, but already Abraham experiences part of the fulfillment of God's promise. The king of the country has come to the cradle of the infant Isaac in order to obtain a covenant for the future,

because he expects a great nation to come from this infant.

At this point, God approaches Abraham and says to him: "Take, I beg of you, your son . . . — (22:2).Offer up to Me this only son of yours," and with him, all the future [that God has promised him].

At the same time we are shown here again what great confidence the Abrahamite kind of education must have inspired even in others, so that it is taken for granted that Abraham's children and grandchildren will respect any promise made by their ancestor. It is typical that while Abimelekh demands such a vow from Abraham, he himself does not dare to give a similar guarantee for the conduct of his own descendants. In Abimelekh's view, the mere fact that he permitted Abraham to dwell in his land—a favor which apparently was not often bestowed in those days—is sufficient justification for him to exact from Abraham a promise that would be binding also upon Abraham's descendants. It seems that Abraham, for his part, did not think it worth his while to ask, in return, for a vow that would be binding also upon the successors of Abimelekh. He must have known how little value was attached to such political covenants outside the Abrahamite world. Abraham's descendants, by contrast, once they had become a state and nation, never took lightly any agreement or alliance they contracted. As late as the period of the Second Temple, when we still enjoyed the privilege of being a state among other states, the Jewish state was noted for its faithful observance of all its contractual obligations.

is the meaning of these seven ewes which you have set by themselves?" 30. And he said: "Because you shall take the seven ewes from my hand so that this may be a witness to me that I have dug this well." 31. Therefore he named this place Beer Sheva, because there they had both sworn [an oath]. 32. Thus they made a covenant in Beer Sheva. Then Abimelekh, and Phikhol, his commander, rose up and returned to the land of the Philistines. 33. And he planted a tree in Beer Sheva, and there he proclaimed in the name of *God*, the God of the future. 34. And Abraham sojourned in the land of the Philistines many days.

XXII

1. And it came to pass after these events that God tested Abraham and said to him: "Abraham!" And he said: "Here I am!" 2. And He said: "Take, I beg of you, your son, your only son, whom you love, Yitzḥak, and get yourself to the land of Moriah and offer him up there as an offering on one of the mountains of which I will tell you." 3. And Abraham rose early in the morning and saddled his donkey and took his two

הִנֵּה שֶׁבַע כְּבָשֹׂת הָאֵלֶּה אֲשֶׁר הִצַּבְתָּ לְבַדָּנָה׃
ל וַיֹּאמֶר כִּי אֶת־שֶׁבַע כְּבָשֹׂת תִּקַּח מִיָּדִי
בַּעֲבוּר תִּהְיֶה־לִּי לְעֵדָה כִּי חָפַרְתִּי אֶת־הַבְּאֵר
הַזֹּאת׃ לא עַל־כֵּן קָרָא לַמָּקוֹם הַהוּא בְּאֵר
שָׁבַע כִּי שָׁם נִשְׁבְּעוּ שְׁנֵיהֶם׃ לב וַיִּכְרְתוּ בְרִית
בִּבְאֵר שָׁבַע וַיָּקָם אֲבִימֶלֶךְ וּפִיכֹל שַׂר־צְבָאוֹ
וַיָּשֻׁבוּ אֶל־אֶרֶץ פְּלִשְׁתִּים׃ לג וַיִּטַּע אֶשֶׁל
בִּבְאֵר שָׁבַע וַיִּקְרָא־שָׁם בְּשֵׁם יְהוָה אֵל עוֹלָם׃
לד וַיָּגָר אַבְרָהָם בְּאֶרֶץ פְּלִשְׁתִּים יָמִים רַבִּים׃
פ שביעי כב א וַיְהִי אַחַר הַדְּבָרִים הָאֵלֶּה
וְהָאֱלֹהִים נִסָּה אֶת־אַבְרָהָם וַיֹּאמֶר אֵלָיו
אַבְרָהָם וַיֹּאמֶר הִנֵּנִי׃ ב וַיֹּאמֶר קַח־נָא אֶת־
בִּנְךָ אֶת־יְחִידְךָ אֲשֶׁר־אָהַבְתָּ אֶת־יִצְחָק וְלֶךְ־
לְךָ אֶל־אֶרֶץ הַמֹּרִיָּה וְהַעֲלֵהוּ שָׁם לְעֹלָה עַל
אַחַד הֶהָרִים אֲשֶׁר אֹמַר אֵלֶיךָ׃ ג וַיַּשְׁכֵּם
אַבְרָהָם בַּבֹּקֶר וַיַּחֲבֹשׁ אֶת־חֲמֹרוֹ וַיִּקַּח אֶת־

CHAPTER XXII

1. **אחר הדברים** ***[after these events].*** As in Chapter 15:1 (see Commentary ibid.), so here, too, these words introduce a turning point, a reversal, as it were, of what has gone before. Abraham has already proclaimed God as **א׳ עולם** ["the God of the future"], Isaac has been born to him, and his elder son has been sent away for the sake of Isaac. It was **בְּיִצְחָק**, "in Yitzḥak" that the seed of the future was to be carried on. This future had been given recognition already in the present, in that the king of the country in which Abraham dwelt had made a covenant that was to be binding not only upon the lad but also upon his remote descendants. Thus the promise of the future, as represented by Isaac, had already taken root in the present. And now comes the Divine behest to Abraham to undo everything that has happened up to this point. Abraham is commanded to cut down, with his own hands, the **אֶשֶׁל** [tamarisk] which he himself has planted.

הָאלקי׳: it is that same God Who until that time had revealed Himself to Abraham and had made Isaac the culmination of Abraham's life. The term **נסה**, when used with reference to physical or moral energies, denotes "to try" or "to test"; that is, to present these energies with problems such as they had not been called upon to deal with before. Accordingly, every "trial" or "test" is a step forward, a strengthening of powers which are present in the individual but which have not yet been put to use. A cable that has already withstood the strain of carrying 50 pounds is said to have been "tested" when it is given 51 pounds to hold, but in the case of moral and spiritual powers, "testing" serves to strengthen and to enhance these energies still further.

° ° °

. . . **לֶךְ לְךָ** ***[get yourself].*** lit., "go for yourself." It was with a similar command to "go for himself," to isolate himself, attaching himself only to God, that Abraham's life began. Now it is with this same assignment, but intensified to an infinitely higher degree, that his life will reach its culmination.

. . . The very name **מוֹרִיָּה** might have indicated to Abraham that the act which now would be demanded of him was to become a **הוֹרָאָה** [teaching] for his entire people, indeed, for all mankind, so that, if Abraham's God-saturated spirit was still in need of support, this awareness certainly should have sustained him in carrying out what was now required of him.

° ° °

3. ***and took his two young men with him and Yitzḥak, his son.*** The order in which these individuals are named is not mere coincidence. Abraham waited as

שְׁנֵי נְעָרָיו אִתּוֹ וְאֵת יִצְחָק בְּנוֹ וַיְבַקַּע עֲצֵי
עֹלָה וַיָּקָם וַיֵּלֶךְ אֶל־הַמָּקוֹם אֲשֶׁר־אָמַר־לוֹ
הָאֱלֹהִים: ד בַּיּוֹם הַשְּׁלִישִׁי וַיִּשָּׂא אַבְרָהָם אֶת־
עֵינָיו וַיַּרְא אֶת־הַמָּקוֹם מֵרָחֹק: ה וַיֹּאמֶר
אַבְרָהָם אֶל־נְעָרָיו שְׁבוּ־לָכֶם פֹּה עִם־הַחֲמוֹר
וַאֲנִי וְהַנַּעַר נֵלְכָה עַד־כֹּה וְנִשְׁתַּחֲוֶה וְנָשׁוּבָה
אֲלֵיכֶם: ו וַיִּקַּח אַבְרָהָם אֶת־עֲצֵי הָעֹלָה וַיָּשֶׂם
עַל־יִצְחָק בְּנוֹ וַיִּקַּח בְּיָדוֹ אֶת־הָאֵשׁ וְאֶת־

young men with him and Yitzhak, his son. Then he split wood for the offering, rose up and went toward the place that God had told him. 4. On the third day, when Abraham lifted up his eyes, he saw the place from the distance. 5. And Abraham said to his young men: "You stay here with the donkey, and I and the lad will go yonder; we will bow down there and then return to you." 6. And Abraham took the wood for the offering and placed it upon his son Yitzhak, and took into his hand the fire and

long as possible before informing Isaac. Moreover, וַיִּקַּח אֶת שְׁנֵי נְעָרָיו אִתּוֹ ["he took his two young men with him"]. The verb וַיִּקַּח ["and he took"] does not yet refer to his journey. Only after all these actions are we told that וַיָּקָם וַיֵּלֶךְ ["Abraham rose up and went"]. He took his young men even before awakening Isaac. He wanted to spare Isaac the struggle as long as he possibly could; also, he wanted to avoid being alone with Isaac.

By that time Isaac was no longer a child; he was an independent, grown man of thirty-seven. Hence his own greatness in this event fully matched that of Abraham. Isaac had not received the order directly from God; he knew of it only from the mouth of his father as תשב"פ [an "Oral Teaching"], as it were. In the story of Adam and Eve, Eve was punished for transgressing a Divine prohibition of which she herself had known only through the mouth of Adam. In the present narrative, the first Jewish son is ready to sacrifice himself for a "tradition," as it were, which he has learned only through his father. Here, then, the seed was sown for the devotion which subsequent generations were to demonstrate for the traditions they had received from their fathers. Thus, too, our Sages ask (Sanhedrin 89b): How could, indeed how dared, Isaac give credence to such a הוֹרָאַת שָׁעָה [temporary emergency ruling suspending the law[22]] announced to him by Abraham? The answer is: הֵיכָא דְמוּחְזָק שָׁאנֵי ["When a prophet is already firmly established, it is different"]. Isaac believed his father, not on the strength of some miracle intended to authenticate Abraham's announcement, but on the strength of what he, the son, already knew concerning the character of his father. Our own devotion to the tradition of our forebears also rests on what we know of their character. Our ancestors were no more hierarchs than was Abraham. They uttered not one tradition other than the traditions for which they would also have sacrificed themselves, in the first place.

[22]*Note to the English translation*: In this case, suspending the prohibition against murder and human sacrifices. [G.H.]

No passages in all the Midrash are more moving than those in which the son states all those doubts that could well have made both Abraham and Isaac falter while on their difficult errand. Little was spoken during those three days of journeying, but there was no end of thoughts and emotions.

It seems, therefore, that by first awakening his men and keeping them with him, Abraham sought to fortify himself against being overcome by his own emotions and also avoided being alone with Isaac.

5. . . . Here, at the foot of Moriah, comes the parting of the ways between זֶרַע אַבְרָהָם, the seed of Abraham, and בְּנֵי נֹחַ, the sons of Noah. Only one within whose breast the Torah has stirred the response הִנֵּנִי ["Here I am!"] will be able, like Abraham, to abandon himself to the Divine will, with complete disregard of his own insights . . . using his energies only for the fulfillment of the will of God. The attainment of such a moral level, which outstrips even that of the angels—[as our Sages put it] "the righteous are greater than My ministering angels" — overcoming all the objections raised by one's own senses to do of one's free will that which angels are compelled to do by their harmonious nature, without need for a struggle, beckons only to those who follow in the paths lighted for them by Father Abraham. They can walk together with the בְּנֵי נֹחַ as far as Moriah, for בְּנֵי נֹחַ are also children of God. But the בְּנֵי נֹחַ can come only as far as the foot of the mountain. Further than that they cannot go.

° ° °

6. ***and so they went, both of them, together.*** This phrase will recur two more times in the present narrative. Abraham and Isaac, father and son, on an errand equally difficult for both of them, the former to make the sacrifice, the latter to be the sacrifice himself, ascending the mountain in unfaltering greatness of soul: this is the eternal example to show to all fathers and sons, to every older generation and every younger generation, of the house of Abraham, the path upon which they are to walk *together*.

the knife, and so they went, both of them, together. 7. And Yitzḥak spoke to Aḇraham, his father, and said: "My father!" And he said: "Here I am, my son." And he said: "Here is the fire and the wood—but where is the lamb for the offering?" 8. And Abraham said: "God will see for Himself the lamb for the offering, my son." And so they went, both of them, together. 9. They came to the place of which God had spoken to him, and then Aḃraham built the altar, and arranged the wood, and bound Yitzḥak, his son, and placed him on the altar upon the wood. 10. And Abraham stretched forth his hand and took the knife to slaughter his son. 11. And an angel of *God* called to him from heaven and said: "Abraham! Abraham!" He said: "Here I am!" 12. He said: "Do not stretch your hand toward the lad, nor do the slightest thing to him, for now I know that you are God-fearing and did not withhold your son, your only son, from Me." 13. And Abraham lifted up his eyes and looked, and lo! there was a ram, and after that [it was] caught in the hedge by its horns. And Abraham went and took the ram

הַמַּאֲכֶ֑לֶת וַיֵּלְכ֥וּ שְׁנֵיהֶ֖ם יַחְדָּֽו׃ ז וַיֹּ֨אמֶר יִצְחָ֜ק
אֶל־אַבְרָהָ֤ם אָבִיו֙ וַיֹּ֣אמֶר אָבִ֔י וַיֹּ֖אמֶר הִנֶּ֣נִּֽי בְנִ֑י
וַיֹּ֗אמֶר הִנֵּ֤ה הָאֵשׁ֙ וְהָ֣עֵצִ֔ים וְאַיֵּ֥ה הַשֶּׂ֖ה לְעֹלָֽה׃
ח וַיֹּ֘אמֶר֮ אַבְרָהָם֒ אֱלֹהִ֞ים יִרְאֶה־לּ֥וֹ הַשֶּׂ֛ה
לְעֹלָ֖ה בְּנִ֑י וַיֵּלְכ֥וּ שְׁנֵיהֶ֖ם יַחְדָּֽו׃ ט וַיָּבֹ֗אוּ אֶֽל־
הַמָּקוֹם֮ אֲשֶׁ֣ר אָֽמַר־ל֣וֹ הָֽאֱלֹהִים֒ וַיִּ֨בֶן שָׁ֤ם
אַבְרָהָם֙ אֶת־הַמִּזְבֵּ֔חַ וַֽיַּעֲרֹ֖ךְ אֶת־הָעֵצִ֑ים וַֽיַּעֲקֹד֙
אֶת־יִצְחָ֣ק בְּנ֔וֹ וַיָּ֤שֶׂם אֹתוֹ֙ עַל־הַמִּזְבֵּ֔חַ מִמַּ֖עַל
לָעֵצִֽים׃ י וַיִּשְׁלַ֤ח אַבְרָהָם֙ אֶת־יָד֔וֹ וַיִּקַּ֖ח אֶת־
הַֽמַּאֲכֶ֑לֶת לִשְׁחֹ֖ט אֶת־בְּנֽוֹ׃ יא וַיִּקְרָ֨א אֵלָ֜יו
מַלְאַ֤ךְ יְהוָה֙ מִן־הַשָּׁמַ֔יִם וַיֹּ֖אמֶר אַבְרָהָ֣ם ׀
אַבְרָהָ֑ם וַיֹּ֖אמֶר הִנֵּֽנִי׃ יב וַיֹּ֗אמֶר אַל־תִּשְׁלַ֤ח
יָֽדְךָ֙ אֶל־הַנַּ֔עַר וְאַל־תַּ֥עַשׂ ל֖וֹ מְא֑וּמָה כִּ֣י ׀ עַתָּ֣ה
יָדַ֗עְתִּי כִּֽי־יְרֵ֤א אֱלֹהִים֙ אַ֔תָּה וְלֹ֥א חָשַׂ֛כְתָּ אֶת־
בִּנְךָ֥ אֶת־יְחִידְךָ֖ מִמֶּֽנִּי׃ יג וַיִּשָּׂ֨א אַבְרָהָ֜ם אֶת־
עֵינָ֗יו וַיַּרְא֙ וְהִנֵּה־אַ֔יִל אַחַ֕ר נֶאֱחַ֥ז בַּסְּבַ֖ךְ
בְּקַרְנָ֑יו וַיֵּ֤לֶךְ אַבְרָהָם֙ וַיִּקַּ֣ח אֶת־הָאַ֔יִל וַיַּעֲלֵ֥הוּ

13. ***And Abraham lifted up his eyes.*** He looked around. He felt the need for an offering to symbolize the dedication, the free-willed surrender of his entire being—with hand and foot—upon the altar, which he had been prepared to make and which should be the spiritual content of the rest of his son's life and the lives of all his descendants.

Isaac had been prepared to sacrifice himself upon the altar of God and had risen from that altar to renewed life. Now he, and his children after him, were to vow to God that same spirit of self-sacrifice and to enact it in their daily lives. The life of Isaac and the lives of his children were to represent one everlasting *akedah.*[23]

The symbolic identification of the individual with the sacrifice he offers is set forth most impressively for all time in the phrase, "the ram . . . in place of his son." . . .

This is the reason why Abraham looked for an animal to express, in symbolic terms, the spirit of self-sacrifice; words were not sufficient for this purpose. And lo! there stands a ram, and אחר ["after that"], after Abraham had seen it, it got caught in the hedge and could not move. Then Abraham went and offered the ram "as an offering in place of his son." These last words which we have placed in quotation marks are a forceful refutation of the obtuse and malicious views of those narrow minds which seek to deny the symbolic significance of our offerings so that they may be able to launch into an arrogant denigration of our alleged "cult of blood sacrifices."

If our offerings had no symbolic significance, if the offering of this ram had not been intended to express, in symbolic terms, a devotion thrice higher and more meaningful in life than it would have been in the physical slaying of Isaac, then how blasphemous, how absurd, would it have been to say that the ram was offered "in place of his son!" To offer up, instead of the most cherished being for which one would gladly have suffered death oneself ten times over, an animal which one merely happened to encounter in the wilderness, so that the animal does not even represent an object of value as one's personal property! Why, that would be as if someone had generously given us a million, and we would pick up a pin we happen to see on the ground and ask our benefactor to accept at least this pin in place of his gift!

[23]*Note to the English translation*: עֲקֵדָה, a "binding up" as an offering or sacrifice. [G.H.]

לְעֹלָ֖ה תַּ֥חַת בְּנֽוֹ׃ יד וַיִּקְרָ֧א אַבְרָהָ֛ם שֵֽׁם־
הַמָּק֥וֹם הַה֖וּא יְהֹוָ֣ה ׀ יִרְאֶ֑ה אֲשֶׁר֙ יֵאָמֵ֣ר הַיּ֔וֹם
בְּהַ֥ר יְהֹוָ֖ה יֵרָאֶֽה׃ טו וַיִּקְרָ֛א מַלְאַ֥ךְ יְהֹוָ֖ה אֶל־
אַבְרָהָ֑ם שֵׁנִ֖ית מִן־הַשָּׁמָֽיִם׃ טז וַיֹּ֗אמֶר בִּ֥י
נִשְׁבַּ֖עְתִּי נְאֻם־יְהֹוָ֑ה כִּ֗י יַ֚עַן אֲשֶׁ֤ר עָשִׂ֙יתָ֙ אֶת־
הַדָּבָ֣ר הַזֶּ֔ה וְלֹ֥א חָשַׂ֖כְתָּ אֶת־בִּנְךָ֥ אֶת־יְחִידֶֽךָ׃
יז כִּֽי־בָרֵ֣ךְ אֲבָרֶכְךָ֗ וְהַרְבָּ֨ה אַרְבֶּ֤ה אֶת־זַרְעֲךָ֙
כְּכוֹכְבֵ֣י הַשָּׁמַ֔יִם וְכַח֕וֹל אֲשֶׁ֖ר עַל־שְׂפַ֣ת הַיָּ֑ם
וְיִרַ֣שׁ זַרְעֲךָ֔ אֵ֖ת שַׁ֥עַר אֹיְבָֽיו׃ יח וְהִתְבָּרְכ֣וּ
בְזַרְעֲךָ֔ כֹּ֖ל גּוֹיֵ֣ הָאָ֑רֶץ עֵ֕קֶב אֲשֶׁ֥ר שָׁמַ֖עְתָּ
בְּקֹלִֽי׃ יט וַיָּ֤שָׁב אַבְרָהָם֙ אֶל־נְעָרָ֔יו וַיָּקֻ֛מוּ

and offered it up as an offering in place of his son. 14. And Abraham named this place: *God* Sees, which today is expressed as follows: On the mountain of *God* is one seen. 15. And an angel of *God* called to Abraham a second time out of heaven, 16. and said: "By Myself have I sworn, says *God*, because you have done this thing and have not withheld from Me your son, your only son, 17. that I will bless you without fail, and without fail multiply your descendants as the stars of heaven and as the sand that is on the seashore, and your seed shall inherit the gate of its enemies. 18. And all the nations of the earth shall bless themselves through your seed, as a consequence of your having hearkened to My voice." 19. And Abraham returned to his young men; they rose up and went

14. By naming the place ד׳ יִרְאֶה ["God sees"], Abraham proclaimed the הוֹרָאָה [teaching] which the memory of the event on Mount Moriah is to proclaim to his descendants. י׳ יִרְאֶה (somewhat reminiscent of אלקים יִרְאֶה לוֹ וגו׳ ["God will see for himself the lamb," etc.]). God sees! This is how Abraham subsumes the significance of what came to pass on Mount Moriah.

° ° °

God has insight, God is able to see for us. We need have no insight into the insights of God. Neither His Law nor His Providence is in need of defense before the judgment seat of our insight, and no matter what conditions may arise on earth: ד׳ יִרְאֶה! This is the significance of the eternal offering on Mount Moriah.

17. ***and your seed shall inherit the gate of its enemies.*** . . . This can hardly imply a military conquest, because that has never been Israel's calling. Rather, it seems that it should be interpreted in the sense of, "The righteous shall inherit the earth"—[Psalm 37:29], implying that the ultimate phase of human development on earth will become the heritage of the righteous. All other powers will have vanished and right alone will prevail. The same meaning would apply in the present passage; ultimately שַׁעַר, the forum; i.e., the social and political configuration of the very nations which fought against Israel's principles, will fall to Israel; only with and through Israel will these nations acquire the blessings they had vainly striven to obtain by other means.

19. וַיֵּלְכוּ יַחְדָּיו *[they went together]*. Abraham, Isaac and his young men — all of them, together. This is the third time that יַחְדָּיו ["together"] occurs in the account of the *akedah*; it represents the final stroke of the pen in this great narrative. As distinct from יַחַד, which for the most part implies only physical simultaneity or "togetherness," יַחְדָּיו denotes rather a unity based on a spiritual, inner bond. . . .

We have read that when Abraham, accompanied by Isaac, parted from his young men at the foot of the mountain, and Abraham set out on his momentous errand with his son, he told the others, "You stay here with the donkey." For only men such as Abraham and Isaac can ascend to such heights, and we have been told repeatedly that they completed this difficult errand יַחְדָּיו, in harmony and in complete accord.

Now we are told what happened immediately after Abraham and Isaac had completed this great, indeed this greatest, achievement of theirs: They returned to their young men, and all of them—Abraham, Isaac and their young men—went to Beer Sheva יַחְדָּיו, "together." This is most typical of the spirit which had its beginnings in Abraham and Isaac. After such an upward flight to God's nearness, after such an elevation above all earthly concerns, an Abraham or an Isaac belonging to another nation would have been so full of the "I" or of the "Divine" that they would have been lost to "ordinary" earthly concerns and to "ordinary" human beings. In any other society such a "standing close to God"—even if it were only imaginary—would have engendered such arrogance in those who experienced it that they would have looked down in disdain upon all other men as "mere mortals" and avoided all contact with them.

Not so the spirit which is to be perpetuated through the example of Abraham and Isaac. After having performed the most sublime deed that can be accomplished anywhere on earth, they return to their attend-

וַיֵּלְכוּ יַחְדָּו אֶל־בְּאֵר שָׁבַע וַיֵּשֶׁב אַבְרָהָם
בִּבְאֵר שָׁבַע: פ מפטיר כ וַיְהִי אַחֲרֵי הַדְּבָרִים
הָאֵלֶּה וַיֻּגַּד לְאַבְרָהָם לֵאמֹר הִנֵּה יָלְדָה מִלְכָּה
גַם־הִוא בָּנִים לְנָחוֹר אָחִיךָ: כא אֶת־עוּץ בְּכֹרוֹ
וְאֶת־בּוּז אָחִיו וְאֶת־קְמוּאֵל אֲבִי אֲרָם: כב וְאֶת־
כֶּשֶׂד וְאֶת־חֲזוֹ וְאֶת־פִּלְדָּשׁ וְאֶת־יִדְלָף וְאֵת
בְּתוּאֵל: כג וּבְתוּאֵל יָלַד אֶת־רִבְקָה שְׁמֹנָה אֵלֶּה
יָלְדָה מִלְכָּה לְנָחוֹר אֲחִי אַבְרָהָם: כד וּפִילַגְשׁוֹ
וּשְׁמָהּ רְאוּמָה וַתֵּלֶד גַּם־הִוא אֶת־טֶבַח וְאֶת־
גַּחַם וְאֶת־תַּחַשׁ וְאֶת־מַעֲכָה: פ

together to Beer Sheva, and Abraham remained in Beer Sheva. 20. It came to pass after these events that it was told Abraham: "Behold, Milcah, too, has borne children to your brother Naḥor; 21. Utz, his first-born, and his brother Buz, and Kemuel, the father of Aram; 22. also Kessed, Ḥazo, and Pildash and Yidlaph and Bethuel." 23. And Bethuel begot Rivkah. These eight did Milcah bear to Nahor, Abraham's brother. 24. And his concubine, Reuma, had also given birth; [she bore] Tebaḥ, Gaḥam, Tahash and Maakhah.

ants whom they had left at the foot of Mount Moriah, and they walk away יַחְדָּיו, together with them. They do not feel superior to them in any respect. To the true son of Abraham no man is better than another by virtue of his calling; he sees no distinction between himself and a humble woodcutter or servant. The higher his own moral and spiritual level, the less aware is he of his own greatness. . . . Abraham and Isaac returned from the summit of Moriah as if they had done nothing out of the ordinary: וַיָּשָׁב אַבְרָהָם אֶל נְעָרָיו וַיָּקֻמוּ וַיֵּלְכוּ יַחְדָּו ["And Abraham returned to his young men; they rose up and went together"].

The Haftarah for this Sidra may be found on page 826.

חיי שרה

ḤAYYE SARAH

XXIII 1. The life of Sarah was a hundred years, and twenty years, and seven years: years of the life of Sarah. 2. And Sarah died in Kiryat Arba, which is Ḥebron, in the land of Canaan, and Abraham withdrew to mourn Sarah and to weep for her. 3. Then Abraham rose up from the presence of his dead and spoke to the sons of Ḥeth as follows: 4. "I am a stranger and an inhabitant with you; grant me burial property with you so that I may bury my dead out of my sight." 5. And the sons of Ḥeth answered Abraham, letting him know [saying]: 6. "Hear us, my lord, you are one ennobled by God in our midst. In the choicest of our sepulchers bury your dead; none of us will want to withhold his sepulcher from you to bury your dead." 7. And Abraham rose and bowed before

כג א וַיִּהְיוּ חַיֵּי שָׂרָה מֵאָה שָׁנָה וְעֶשְׂרִים שָׁנָה
וְשֶׁבַע שָׁנִים שְׁנֵי חַיֵּי שָׂרָה: ב וַתָּמָת שָׂרָה
בְּקִרְיַת אַרְבַּע הִוא חֶבְרוֹן בְּאֶרֶץ כְּנָעַן וַיָּבֹא
אַבְרָהָם לִסְפֹּד לְשָׂרָה וְלִבְכֹּתָהּ (כ׳ זעירא): ג וַיָּקָם
אַבְרָהָם מֵעַל פְּנֵי מֵתוֹ וַיְדַבֵּר אֶל־בְּנֵי־חֵת
לֵאמֹר: ד גֵּר־וְתוֹשָׁב אָנֹכִי עִמָּכֶם תְּנוּ לִי אֲחֻזַּת־
קֶבֶר עִמָּכֶם וְאֶקְבְּרָה מֵתִי מִלְּפָנָי: ה וַיַּעֲנוּ בְנֵי־
חֵת אֶת־אַבְרָהָם לֵאמֹר לוֹ: ו שְׁמָעֵנוּ | אֲדֹנִי
נְשִׂיא אֱלֹהִים אַתָּה בְּתוֹכֵנוּ בְּמִבְחַר קְבָרֵינוּ
קְבֹר אֶת־מֵתֶךָ אִישׁ מִמֶּנּוּ אֶת־קִבְרוֹ לֹא־יִכְלֶה
מִמְּךָ מִקְּבֹר מֵתֶךָ: ז וַיָּקָם אַבְרָהָם וַיִּשְׁתַּחוּ

CHAPTER XXIII

1\. . . . As is well known, the Sages present the life of Sarah in terms of three distinct age groups. If we interpret the text of the narrative in its straightforward meaning, what we are told here is not that Sarah lived 127 years, but that she lived one hundred years, twenty years and seven years. These three figures demonstrate to us the entire course of a human life: childhood, young adulthood, and finally the completed phase of old age. The life of a man who exemplified spiritual and moral perfection could not be summed up in better terms than by saying that he was old in his old age, mature in his prime, and a child in his childhood. Indeed, the Sages note: One who has truly lived takes the crowning quality of each stage of his life into the next stage. Hence also the expression בָּא בַיָּמִים; lit., "he walks *through* the days." He does not walk above or below them but passes straight through them. He retains all the spiritual and moral attainments of his past and takes them with him into the future; he does not permit his days to rob him of anything that has ever become truly "his."

Thus, Sarah took the beauty of her childhood into her mature womanhood, and she retained the innocence of a woman of twenty all the days of her life. This view of the Sages contrasts greatly with our own, and certainly not to our advantage. The Sages look for beauty not in the twenties but in childhood, and for innocence not in childhood but in young adulthood. We are accustomed to speak of "childlike innocence." It would be sad if one would have to envy children for their innocence. For innocence presupposes the possibility of guilt. Hence innocence means to have struggled with one's sensuality and one's passions and to have won the day. Only a maiden who has matured into womanhood and a youth who has ripened into manhood can justly place the wreath of innocence upon their brows. . . .

4\. אֲחֻזָּה actually means "settlement," the act of becoming "domiciled" in a place. Abraham requests more than just permission to bury his wife. He wants his wife to rest in a place that will be her permanent, everlasting possession. This is why, for the purpose of the burial, he requests, first of all, the right to acquire a piece of land as a permanent possession. For years he has dwelt in the land as a stranger; despite all his wealth he has never attempted to acquire so much as a square foot of land there. After all, his calling was to be a wanderer. But now the necessity to bury his wife makes it necessary for him, for the first time, to acquire possession of a piece of land. His wife's grave is to be the first bond that will tie him to the land, that place which will draw him to it and hold him: אֲחֻזָּה [from אחז, "to hold" or "grasp"].

the council of the land of the sons of Ḥeth, 8. and he spoke with them as follows: "If it is truly your will that I should bury my dead out of my sight, then hear me and apply on my behalf to Ephron, son of Tzohar, 9. that he may give me the cave of Makhpelah, which he has, which is situated at the end of his field; for the full price let him give it to me in your midst as a possession of a burial property." 10. Now Ephron was sitting in the midst of the sons of Ḥeth. And Ephron the Hittite answered Abraham in the hearing of the sons of Ḥeth, of all those who had come into the gate of his city, as follows: 11. "No, my lord, hear me. The field I have given you, and as for the cave that is in it, I have already given it to you; in the presence of the sons of my people I have already given it to you; bury your dead." 12. Abraham bowed down before the council of the land. 13. But he spoke to Ephron in the hearing of the council of the land as follows: "Nevertheless, even if you would—hear me; I have already laid down the money for the field; take it from me, and then I want to bury my dead there." 14. And Ephron replied to Abraham, letting him know [saying]: 15. "Hear me, my lord, a piece of land worth four hundred shekels of silver, what is that between me and you? Bury your dead." 16. And Abraham listened to Ephron and Abraham weighed out to Ephron the silver which he had named in the hearing of the sons of Heth; four hundred shekels of silver, current money with the merchant. 17. And so the field of Ephron, which was in Makhpelah, which was before Mamre, the field and the cave that was in it, all the trees that were in the field in all the surrounding terrain, was established 18. to Abraham as a possession in the presence of the sons of Ḥeth, before all those that had come into the gate of his city. 19. Only thereafter did Abraham bury his wife in the cave of the field of

לְעַם־הָאָרֶץ לִבְנֵי־חֵת: ח וַיְדַבֵּר אִתָּם לֵאמֹר
אִם־יֵשׁ אֶת־נַפְשְׁכֶם לִקְבֹּר אֶת־מֵתִי מִלְּפָנַי
שְׁמָעוּנִי וּפִגְעוּ־לִי בְּעֶפְרוֹן בֶּן־צֹחַר: ט וְיִתֶּן־לִי
אֶת־מְעָרַת הַמַּכְפֵּלָה אֲשֶׁר־לוֹ אֲשֶׁר בִּקְצֵה
שָׂדֵהוּ בְּכֶסֶף מָלֵא יִתְּנֶנָּה לִּי בְּתוֹכְכֶם לַאֲחֻזַּת־
קָבֶר: י וְעֶפְרוֹן ישֵׁב בְּתוֹךְ בְּנֵי־חֵת וַיַּעַן עֶפְרוֹן
הַחִתִּי אֶת־אַבְרָהָם בְּאָזְנֵי בְנֵי־חֵת לְכֹל בָּאֵי
שַׁעַר־עִירוֹ לֵאמֹר: יא לֹא־אֲדֹנִי שְׁמָעֵנִי הַשָּׂדֶה
נָתַתִּי לָךְ וְהַמְּעָרָה אֲשֶׁר־בּוֹ לְךָ נְתַתִּיהָ לְעֵינֵי
בְנֵי־עַמִּי נְתַתִּיהָ לָּךְ קְבֹר מֵתֶךָ: יב וַיִּשְׁתַּחוּ
אַבְרָהָם לִפְנֵי עַם־הָאָרֶץ: יג וַיְדַבֵּר אֶל־עֶפְרוֹן
בְּאָזְנֵי עַם־הָאָרֶץ לֵאמֹר אַךְ אִם־אַתָּה לוּ שְׁמָעֵנִי
נָתַתִּי כֶּסֶף הַשָּׂדֶה קַח מִמֶּנִּי וְאֶקְבְּרָה אֶת־מֵתִי
שָׁמָּה: יד וַיַּעַן עֶפְרוֹן אֶת־אַבְרָהָם לֵאמֹר לוֹ:
טו אֲדֹנִי שְׁמָעֵנִי אֶרֶץ אַרְבַּע מֵאֹת שֶׁקֶל־כֶּסֶף
בֵּינִי וּבֵינְךָ מַה־הִוא וְאֶת־מֵתְךָ קְבֹר: טז וַיִּשְׁמַע
אַבְרָהָם אֶל־עֶפְרוֹן וַיִּשְׁקֹל אַבְרָהָם לְעֶפְרֹן אֶת־
הַכֶּסֶף אֲשֶׁר דִּבֶּר בְּאָזְנֵי בְנֵי־חֵת אַרְבַּע מֵאוֹת
שֶׁקֶל כֶּסֶף עֹבֵר לַסֹּחֵר: שני יז וַיָּקָם ׀ שְׂדֵה
עֶפְרוֹן אֲשֶׁר בַּמַּכְפֵּלָה אֲשֶׁר לִפְנֵי מַמְרֵא הַשָּׂדֶה
וְהַמְּעָרָה אֲשֶׁר־בּוֹ וְכָל־הָעֵץ אֲשֶׁר בַּשָּׂדֶה אֲשֶׁר
בְּכָל־גְּבֻלוֹ סָבִיב: יח לְאַבְרָהָם לְמִקְנָה לְעֵינֵי
בְנֵי־חֵת בְּכֹל בָּאֵי שַׁעַר־עִירוֹ: יט וְאַחֲרֵי־כֵן
קָבַר אַבְרָהָם אֶת־שָׂרָה אִשְׁתּוֹ אֶל־מְעָרַת שְׂדֵה

19. ***thereafter.*** Only after the place and the area surrounding it had become his permanent possession did Abraham bury his Sarah there. Jews do not make a cult or show of their emotions. They do not rear churches or mausoleums upon their burial sites, nor do they turn their graves into gardens. On the other hand, the concept of a time limit for the preservation of cemeteries is alien to Judaism. The places where their dead rest remain sacred to them forever. That children should adorn their parents' burial places with marble

Makhpelah, before Mamre, which is Ḥebron, in the land of Canaan. 20. Thus were the field and the cave in it established for Abraham as a burial property by the sons of Ḥeth.

XXIV 1. Abraham had become old; he had come through the days,° and *God* had blessed Abraham in everything. 2. And Abraham said to his servant, the eldest of his house, who ruled over all that he had: "Place, I beg you, your hand beneath my thigh. 3. I will make you swear by *God*, the God of heaven and earth, that you will not take a wife for my son from among the daughters of the Canaanite[s] in whose midst I dwell. 4. But you shall go into my country and to my kindred and take a wife for my son, for Yitzḥak." 5. The servant said to him: "Perhaps the woman will not

הַמַּכְפֵּלָה עַל־פְּנֵי מַמְרֵא הִוא חֶבְרוֹן בְּאֶרֶץ כְּנָעַן: כ וַיָּקָם הַשָּׂדֶה וְהַמְּעָרָה אֲשֶׁר־בּוֹ לְאַבְרָהָם לַאֲחֻזַּת־קָבֶר מֵאֵת בְּנֵי־חֵת: ס כד א וְאַבְרָהָם זָקֵן בָּא בַּיָּמִים וַיהֹוָה בֵּרַךְ אֶת־אַבְרָהָם בַּכֹּל: ב וַיֹּאמֶר אַבְרָהָם אֶל־עַבְדּוֹ זְקַן בֵּיתוֹ הַמֹּשֵׁל בְּכָל־אֲשֶׁר־לוֹ שִׂים־נָא יָדְךָ תַּחַת יְרֵכִי: ג וְאַשְׁבִּיעֲךָ בַּיהֹוָה אֱלֹהֵי הַשָּׁמַיִם וֵאלֹהֵי הָאָרֶץ אֲשֶׁר לֹא־תִקַּח אִשָּׁה לִבְנִי מִבְּנוֹת הַכְּנַעֲנִי אֲשֶׁר אָנֹכִי יוֹשֵׁב בְּקִרְבּוֹ: ד כִּי אֶל־אַרְצִי וְאֶל־מוֹלַדְתִּי תֵּלֵךְ וְלָקַחְתָּ אִשָּׁה לִבְנִי לְיִצְחָק: ה וַיֹּאמֶר אֵלָיו הָעֶבֶד אוּלַי לֹא־תֹאבֶה

°*Note to the English translation:* See Hirsch's commentary on Chapter 23, Verse 1. [G.H.]

structures and everlasting flowers, only to have the grandchildren dig up the graves and, without thought or feeling, pile up their ancestors' bones in nameless heaps, is an idea utterly alien to Jews.

Two more remarks should be added here. The Jewish people has been taxed with nothing so much as their addiction to buying and selling, to doing business. Under the circumstances it is indeed odd that when our legal minds search the Scriptural texts for a passage illustrating the legal forms of purchase and sale, they can find, in all of Scripture, only two cases in point: the purchase of one grave here—שְׂדֵה עֶפְרוֹן—and the purchase of a field which a prophet—Jeremiah—was commanded to make in order to demonstrate his faith in the future at a time when the might of Babylonia was already at the gates of Jerusalem and was making ready to overrun the [Jewish] state [Jeremiah 32:6 ff.]. In other words, of the two business transactions described in Scripture, the first took place prior to the beginning, and the second just before the end, of our statehood.

The legal form used in contracting Jewish marriages is also based on the legal procedure which was employed in the purchase of the field of Ephron. Thoughtless tongues tax the Jews with "purchasing their brides." It is quite true that the Jew purchases his bride, but then she remains his own and he cherishes her as his most precious possession on earth. Fortunate we, if, on the strength of this memory, all our marriages were to be contracted at Sarah's grave, as it were, thus remaining pervaded by the spirit which was symbolized

by the marriage of Abraham and Sarah and which was given its final and lasting expression in the "purchase of the cave of Makhpelah."

CHAPTER XXIV

4. *for my son, for Yitzḥak.* Eliezer was to be guided by two considerations. "For my son": in the first place, that she should be worthy of being the wife of my son, that she would justify my hope that she will become my daughter even as he is my son. So much for the general requirements regarding her character. But it may happen that two people can be excellent characters and nevertheless incompatible. Hence "for Yitzḥak": she should be compatible also with Isaac personally.

Now Abraham refused to consider the daughters of Canaan, preferring a maiden from Aram for his son. We must remember that the Aramites were heathens, too. Therefore, the reason for Abraham's rejection of the Canaanite maidens must have been not the idolatry, but only the moral corruption that prevailed in Canaan. Paganism *per se* is a mental aberration that can be cured. Moral corruption, on the other hand, takes hold of the whole individual, in all the depths of his emotions, so that even a man such as Abraham could not hope to find among the Canaanites a chaste, morally pure and innocent maiden as a wife for his son, one who would bring with her a nobility of spirit and of morality as her most precious jewel.

want to follow me into this land. Shall I then have your son return to the land from which you came out?" 6. And Abraham said to him: "Take heed that you do not bring my son back there! 7. *God*, the God of heaven, Who took me from my father's house and from the land of my birth, Who spoke concerning me and Who swore to me as follows: 'To your seed will I give this land,' He will send His angel before you and you will take a wife for my son from there. 8. But if the woman should not be willing to follow you, then you will be free from this my oath; only do not bring my son back to that place!" 9. And the servant placed his hand beneath the thigh of Abraham, his master, and swore to him concerning this matter. 10. Thereupon the servant took ten camels from among the camels of his master, but he went [on foot] and had all the best things of his master in his hand; and so he arose and went to Aram Naharayim, to the city of Naḥor. 11. He made the camels kneel down outside the city by the well of water, at the time of evening, the time when the women who draw the water go out. 12. And he said: "O *God*, God of my master Abraham, I pray Thee, cause it to happen to me today and show kindness to my master Abraham. 13. Lo! I am standing here by the well of water, and the daughters of the townspeople come out to draw water. 14. So let it come to pass that the girl to whom I will say: 'Please tilt your

הָאִשָּׁה לָלֶכֶת אַחֲרַי אֶל־הָאָרֶץ הַזֹּאת הֶהָשֵׁב אָשִׁיב אֶת־בִּנְךָ אֶל־הָאָרֶץ אֲשֶׁר־יָצָאתָ מִשָּׁם: ו וַיֹּאמֶר אֵלָיו אַבְרָהָם הִשָּׁמֶר לְךָ פֶּן־תָּשִׁיב אֶת־בְּנִי שָׁמָּה: ז יְהֹוָה ׀ אֱלֹהֵי הַשָּׁמַיִם אֲשֶׁר לְקָחַנִי מִבֵּית אָבִי וּמֵאֶרֶץ מוֹלַדְתִּי וַאֲשֶׁר דִּבֶּר־לִי וַאֲשֶׁר נִשְׁבַּע־לִי לֵאמֹר לְזַרְעֲךָ אֶתֵּן אֶת־הָאָרֶץ הַזֹּאת הוּא יִשְׁלַח מַלְאָכוֹ לְפָנֶיךָ וְלָקַחְתָּ אִשָּׁה לִבְנִי מִשָּׁם: ח וְאִם־לֹא תֹאבֶה הָאִשָּׁה לָלֶכֶת אַחֲרֶיךָ וְנִקִּיתָ מִשְּׁבֻעָתִי זֹאת רַק אֶת־בְּנִי לֹא תָשֵׁב שָׁמָּה: ט וַיָּשֶׂם הָעֶבֶד אֶת־יָדוֹ תַּחַת יֶרֶךְ אַבְרָהָם אֲדֹנָיו וַיִּשָּׁבַע לוֹ עַל־הַדָּבָר הַזֶּה: שלישי י וַיִּקַּח הָעֶבֶד עֲשָׂרָה גְמַלִּים מִגְּמַלֵּי אֲדֹנָיו וַיֵּלֶךְ וְכָל־טוּב אֲדֹנָיו בְּיָדוֹ וַיָּקָם וַיֵּלֶךְ אֶל־אֲרַם נַהֲרַיִם אֶל־עִיר נָחוֹר: יא וַיַּבְרֵךְ הַגְּמַלִּים מִחוּץ לָעִיר אֶל־בְּאֵר הַמָּיִם לְעֵת עֶרֶב לְעֵת צֵאת הַשֹּׁאֲבֹת: יב וַיֹּאמַר ׀ יְהֹוָה אֱלֹהֵי אֲדֹנִי אַבְרָהָם הַקְרֵה־נָא לְפָנַי הַיּוֹם וַעֲשֵׂה־חֶסֶד עִם אֲדֹנִי אַבְרָהָם: יג הִנֵּה אָנֹכִי נִצָּב עַל־עֵין הַמָּיִם וּבְנוֹת אַנְשֵׁי הָעִיר יֹצְאֹת לִשְׁאֹב מָיִם: יד וְהָיָה הַנַּעֲרָ (הנערה קרי) אֲשֶׁר אֹמַר אֵלֶיהָ הַטִּי־נָא כַדֵּךְ

---

10. . . . Eliezer himself traveled on foot and bore gifts in his hands. . . . Thus he did not appear as a wealthy merchant with ten heavily-laden camels but as a heavily-laden servant who had been ordered to take his master's camels to some specified destination. Only in this manner would he truly be able to test the character of the maiden. Behavior that is truly humane when shown to a weary, heavy-laden servant may be inspired by entirely different motives when shown to a wealthy cavalier.

It goes without saying, of course, that even the most precious jewels can be transported in a chest of relatively small size.

According to our Sages, Abraham's personal camels were recognizable by the muzzles they wore to keep them from grazing on the fields of others. Thus, distinguished Jews were known not by their lack of consi-

deration, but by their special care and consideration for the property of others.

14. Our Sages (Taanith 4a) certainly do not recommend Eliezer's procedure as an ideal way of choosing a wife. Indeed, only a man such as Eliezer, one guided on his mission by the confidence of a man like Abraham that God would surely send His angel before him and lead the right girl to him, could permit himself to proceed in this fashion. . . .

The sign by which Eliezer felt he would know Isaac's destined mate is one of those character traits which to this day are typical of the descendants of Isaac and Rebekah and which we subsume under the term גְּמִילוּת חֶסֶד. It was at the home of Abraham that Eliezer had first come to know that love of man which is ever ready to lend a helping hand to another, a love that gradually

וְאֶשְׁתֶּה וְאָמְרָה שְׁתֵה וְגַם גְּמַלֶּיךָ אַשְׁקֶה אֹתָהּ
הֹכַחְתָּ לְעַבְדְּךָ לְיִצְחָק וּבָהּ אֵדַע כִּי־עָשִׂיתָ חֶסֶד
עִם־אֲדֹנִי: טו וַיְהִי־הוּא טֶרֶם כִּלָּה לְדַבֵּר וְהִנֵּה
רִבְקָה יֹצֵאת אֲשֶׁר יֻלְּדָה לִבְתוּאֵל בֶּן־מִלְכָּה
אֵשֶׁת נָחוֹר אֲחִי אַבְרָהָם וְכַדָּהּ עַל־שִׁכְמָהּ:
טז וְהַנַּעֲרָ (והנערה קרי) טֹבַת מַרְאֶה מְאֹד בְּתוּלָה
וְאִישׁ לֹא יְדָעָהּ וַתֵּרֶד הָעַיְנָה וַתְּמַלֵּא כַדָּהּ וַתָּעַל:
יז וַיָּרָץ הָעֶבֶד לִקְרָאתָהּ וַיֹּאמֶר הַגְמִיאִינִי נָא
מְעַט־מַיִם מִכַּדֵּךְ: יח וַתֹּאמֶר שְׁתֵה אֲדֹנִי וַתְּמַהֵר
וַתֹּרֶד כַּדָּהּ עַל־יָדָהּ וַתַּשְׁקֵהוּ: יט וַתְּכַל לְהַשְׁקֹתוֹ
וַתֹּאמֶר גַּם לִגְמַלֶּיךָ אֶשְׁאָב עַד אִם־כִּלּוּ לִשְׁתֹּת:
כ וַתְּמַהֵר וַתְּעַר כַּדָּהּ אֶל־הַשֹּׁקֶת וַתָּרָץ עוֹד אֶל־

pitcher so that I may drink,' and she will
say: 'Drink, and I will give your camels
drink also,' let her be the one whom Thou
hast appointed for Thy servant, Yitzḥak,
and by her I will know that Thou hast
shown kindness to my master." 15. He
had hardly finished speaking when, lo!
Rivkah came out, who had been born to
Bethuel, the son of Milcah, the wife of
Naḥor, Abraham's brother, and she had her
pitcher upon her shoulder. 16. And the
girl was exceedingly good to look upon, a
virgin, and no man had yet approached her
in a familiar way. She went down to the
well, filled her pitcher and came up.
17. And the servant ran to meet her and
said: "Let me please sip a little water from
your pitcher." 18. She replied: "Drink,
my lord!" And she hurried and let down her
pitcher upon her hand and gave him drink.
19. When she had finished giving him
drink, she said: "I will draw for your camels
also until they have finished drinking."
20. And she hurried and emptied her
pitcher into the watering trough and ran

made its way also into the non-Abrahamite world through the direct and indirect influence of the mission assigned to Abraham's progeny. Eliezer felt that this quality, an attribute typical of the home of Abraham, must also be predominant in the character of the proper wife for Isaac, and he had reason to believe that such traits of mind and spirit would still have survived only among the kinsmen of Abraham. It was on these assumptions that Eliezer based his actions.

Still, it must have been a rare quality, for otherwise Eliezer would not have considered it a sure sign.

לְעַבְדְּךָ לְיִצְחָק *[for Thy servant, Yitzḥak]*. With great delicacy Eliezer refers to Isaac as "Thy servant" instead of לַאדֹנִי ["for my master (Yitzḥak)"] or to לְבֶן אֲדֹנִי ["for the son of my master"]. The thought that Isaac himself, for whom he, Eliezer, is now seeking a wife, is עֶבֶד ד׳ [a servant of God] has impelled Eliezer to choose such a sign and at the same time to hope that God will lead the right girl to him. After all, the man for whom he is seeking a partner is a man consecrated to the service of God. Thus, the promotion of God's own purpose is dependent on whether or not Eliezer will make the right choice.

17–20. ***And the servant ran.*** It was not as Eliezer, but as "the servant," in the attitude of a servant, that he ran to meet Rebekah. He asks her for "a little water" to "sip." She, however, replies, "Drink," and addresses him as "my lord," even though he stood before her in the position of a servant. And then she proceeded, step by step, to reveal herself as that woman who, because of her Abrahamite spirit, was worthy of taking the place of Sarah. At first, as Eliezer had hoped, she said nothing about the camels. Only after she had completely quenched Eliezer's thirst did she say, "I will also draw water for your camels until they have finished drinking." Had Rebekah spoken of the camels immediately, this would have shown that she lacked one quality which characterizes the true גּוֹמֵל חֶסֶד ["doer of good"] and the true Jewish woman. She would have been a conceited prattler, one who wants to show off as a "do-gooder." But now she even goes beyond offering to give the camels a drink also (which in itself would have entailed considerable effort, for even giving one pitcherful of water to each camel would have required her to make ten trips down to the well and to draw up the bucket ten times). She says she will draw water and fill up the watering trough again and again until all the ten camels have drunk their fill. . . .

And she hurried (Verses 18 and 20): She does not hesitate and is not slow to move when she is given an opportunity to perform an act of human kindness. Note, too, that she empties into the watering trough whatever water Eliezer has left in the pitcher. She could have left it in the pitcher or poured it out on the

הַבְּאֵר לִשְׁאֹב וַתִּשְׁאַב לְכָל־גְּמַלָּיו׃ כא וְהָאִישׁ
מִשְׁתָּאֵה לָהּ מַחֲרִישׁ לָדַעַת הַהִצְלִיחַ יְהוָה דַּרְכּוֹ
אִם־לֹא׃ כב וַיְהִי כַּאֲשֶׁר כִּלּוּ הַגְּמַלִּים לִשְׁתּוֹת
וַיִּקַּח הָאִישׁ נֶזֶם זָהָב בֶּקַע מִשְׁקָלוֹ וּשְׁנֵי צְמִידִים
עַל־יָדֶיהָ עֲשָׂרָה זָהָב מִשְׁקָלָם׃ כג וַיֹּאמֶר בַּת־מִי
אַתְּ הַגִּידִי נָא לִי הֲיֵשׁ בֵּית־אָבִיךְ מָקוֹם לָנוּ
לָלִין׃ כד וַתֹּאמֶר אֵלָיו בַּת־בְּתוּאֵל אָנֹכִי בֶּן־
מִלְכָּה אֲשֶׁר יָלְדָה לְנָחוֹר׃ כה וַתֹּאמֶר אֵלָיו
גַּם־תֶּבֶן גַּם־מִסְפּוֹא רַב עִמָּנוּ גַּם־מָקוֹם לָלוּן׃
כו וַיִּקֹּד הָאִישׁ וַיִּשְׁתַּחוּ לַיהוָה׃ רביעי כז וַיֹּאמֶר
בָּרוּךְ יְהוָה אֱלֹהֵי אֲדֹנִי אַבְרָהָם אֲשֶׁר לֹא־עָזַב
חַסְדּוֹ וַאֲמִתּוֹ מֵעִם אֲדֹנִי אָנֹכִי בַּדֶּרֶךְ נָחַנִי יְהוָה
בֵּית אֲחֵי אֲדֹנִי׃ כח וַתָּרָץ הַנַּעֲרָ (הנערה קרי) וַתַּגֵּד
לְבֵית אִמָּהּ כַּדְּבָרִים הָאֵלֶּה׃ כט וּלְרִבְקָה אָח

again to the well to draw, and drew for all his camels. 21. The man kept gazing upon her in wonderment, holding his peace to know whether *God* had caused his journey to prosper or not. 22. Only after the camels had finished drinking entirely did the man take a golden nose-ring, of half a shekel weight, and two bracelets for her hands, of ten shekels weight of gold, 23. and he said: "Whose daughter are you? Tell me, please! Is there room in your father's house for us to stay overnight?" 24. And she said to him: "I am the daughter of Bethuel, a son of Milcah, who bore him to Naḥor." 25. Moreover, she said to him: "There is also plenty of straw and fodder with us, and also a place to stay overnight." 26. And the man bowed his head and prostrated himself before *God.* 27. And he said: "Blessed be *God,* the God of my master Abraham, Who has not forsaken His loving-kindness and his truth from my master! I am still on my way, but *God* has already led me to the house of my master's brothers." 28. And the girl ran and told her mother's house[hold] according to these events. 29. And Rivkah had a brother, whose name was Laban, and Laban

ground. However, the kindness which it is in the nature of the Jew to lavish upon others also makes him economical in his use of goods and energies. Precisely because he views even the most insignificant thing on earth as a means for performing a מִצְוָה, of doing one's duty, the Jew regards everything as sacred. He will not waste even an atom of energy or the tiniest drop of water. But at the same time he sets no limit to his sacrifice of strength and substance when it is for a good cause.

27. **חֶסֶד וֶאֱמֶת *[loving-kindness and truth].*** אַהֲבָה [love] is an emotion; חֶסֶד [loving-kindness] is love translated into action. אֱמֶת [truth], to some extent, serves to modify חֶסֶד. חֶסֶד וֶאֱמֶת [loving-kindness and truth] is an act of loving-kindness which is not entirely blind to the truth.

Human love is blind. It tends to accede to the wishes of the beloved without regard to the true worth of these wishes. The love of God, by contrast, is חֶסֶד וֶאֱמֶת; it grants only those wishes which tend to preserve truth and whose fulfillment will truly benefit the one who expressed them. Cf. in the story of Jacob (Genesis 47:29) [where Jacob asks his son Joseph to practice חֶסֶד וֶאֱמֶת with him and not bury him in Egypt]. Joseph's seeing to his father's burial is an act of חֶסֶד, but his compliance with his father's specification, "but do not bury me in Egypt," is אֱמֶת. Thus, too, the services which the spies promise to render to Rahab (Joshua 2:14) were acts of חֶסֶד וֶאֱמֶת, of loving-kindness modified by a specification. אֱמֶת is always the safeguard which ensures that when an act of loving-kindness is performed, truth, which is the most important thing, is not lost.

Perhaps the foregoing is relevant also here. The most cherished wish of parents is to see their children married. But if they try to accomplish this objective without regard to the most important thing (that is, if they tell themselves that "if we can't get a girl of the Abrahamite turn of mind, then we'll take one of Oner, Eshkol or Mamre, or one from Aram") then what they seek is חֶסֶד without אֱמֶת. Abraham, however, wanted חֶסֶד only coupled with אֱמֶת; God granted him both.

° ° °

29. Our Sages make a cutting remark here to the effect that there was nothing לָבָן, "white," about Laban except for his name.

ran out to the man, to the well. 30. And it came to pass when the nose-ring and the bracelets were seen upon the hands of his sister and when he heard the words of his sister Rivkah saying: "Thus did the man speak to me," that he came to the man, and lo! the latter was still standing by the camels at the well. 31. And he said: "Well, come in, you who are blessed by *God!* Why are you standing outside? I have already cleared the house and made room for your camels." 32. And the man came into the house, and he unharnessed the camels; he gave straw and fodder to the camels, and water to wash his feet and the feet of the men who were with him. 33. Food was set before him to eat, but he said: "I will not eat until I have spoken my words." And he said: "Speak." 34. He said: "I am a servant of Abraham. 35. And *God* has blessed my master exceedingly, so that he has become great. He has given him sheep and cattle, silver and gold, menservants and maidservants, camels and donkeys. 36. Sarah, my master's wife, bore my master a son when she had already grown old, and to him he has given everything he has. 37. And my master made me swear as follows: 'Do not take for my son a wife from among the

וּשְׁמוֹ לָבָן וַיָּרָץ לָבָן אֶל־הָאִישׁ הַחוּצָה אֶל־
הָעָיִן׃ ל וַיְהִי ׀ כִּרְאֹת אֶת־הַנֶּזֶם וְאֶת־הַצְּמִדִים
עַל־יְדֵי אֲחֹתוֹ וּכְשָׁמְעוֹ אֶת־דִּבְרֵי רִבְקָה אֲחֹתוֹ
לֵאמֹר כֹּה־דִבֶּר אֵלַי הָאִישׁ וַיָּבֹא אֶל־הָאִישׁ
וְהִנֵּה עֹמֵד עַל־הַגְּמַלִּים עַל־הָעָיִן׃ לא וַיֹּאמֶר
בּוֹא בְּרוּךְ יְהוָה לָמָּה תַעֲמֹד בַּחוּץ וְאָנֹכִי פִּנִּיתִי
הַבַּיִת וּמָקוֹם לַגְּמַלִּים׃ לב וַיָּבֹא הָאִישׁ הַבַּיְתָה
וַיְפַתַּח הַגְּמַלִּים וַיִּתֵּן תֶּבֶן וּמִסְפּוֹא לַגְּמַלִּים
וּמַיִם לִרְחֹץ רַגְלָיו וְרַגְלֵי הָאֲנָשִׁים אֲשֶׁר אִתּוֹ׃
לג וַיִּישַׂם (ויושם קרי) לְפָנָיו לֶאֱכֹל וַיֹּאמֶר לֹא
אֹכַל עַד אִם־דִּבַּרְתִּי דְּבָרָי וַיֹּאמֶר דַּבֵּר׃
לד וַיֹּאמַר עֶבֶד אַבְרָהָם אָנֹכִי׃ לה וַיהוָה בֵּרַךְ
אֶת־אֲדֹנִי מְאֹד וַיִּגְדָּל וַיִּתֶּן־לוֹ צֹאן וּבָקָר וְכֶסֶף
וְזָהָב וַעֲבָדִם וּשְׁפָחֹת וּגְמַלִּים וַחֲמֹרִים׃ לו וַתֵּלֶד
שָׂרָה אֵשֶׁת אֲדֹנִי בֵן לַאדֹנִי אַחֲרֵי זִקְנָתָהּ וַיִּתֶּן־
לוֹ אֶת־כָּל־אֲשֶׁר־לוֹ׃ לז וַיַּשְׁבִּעֵנִי אֲדֹנִי לֵאמֹר
לֹא־תִקַּח אִשָּׁה לִבְנִי מִבְּנוֹת הַכְּנַעֲנִי אֲשֶׁר אָנֹכִי

אֶל הָאִישׁ *[to the man].* Eliezer now no longer appears as עֶבֶד, in the role of a servant until he himself again points out that he is, indeed, a servant.

30. This passage seems strange. We already know [from Verse 29] that Laban had run out to the well, and now we are told that when he had seen the nose-ring, etc., and he had heard the words of his sister Rebekah, only then did he come, etc. It would seem that all the foregoing is a continuous narrative, and "when the nose-ring and the bracelets were seen . . ." appears to be a continuous antecedent clause to the concluding clause which follows (Verse 31). Thus: All the members of the household had seen the trinkets, but while they were busy inspecting them (the text does not read "when *he* had seen"), the sight of the gold had cast its spell on Laban. "There must be much more where this comes from! If this is what he pays for just one sip of water, imagine what he would give for food and lodging!" And so the scheming brother takes his sister aside and makes her tell him the whole story all over again. Then he rushes out to meet the man, so that no one should get there ahead of him. He expects to meet Eliezer already on the road, near his home, and is more than a little surprised that he has to run all the way to the well to find him.

When Laban arrives at the well, he is flabbergasted that a man who, according to all he has seen and heard of him, must be a Croesus scattering money right and left, should still be waiting humbly at the well with his camels, waiting to be invited. That is why Laban does not bow to Eliezer, nor does he speak courteously to him as Abraham and Lot would have done when inviting strangers. Seeing Eliezer in this humble attitude, Laban has already lost respect for him and addresses him rather brusquely: "Well, come on in! Don't be shy! Aren't you a בְּרוּךְ ד׳; a rich man, blessed with ample wealth?" This is apparent also from Verses 32 and 33.

34. [Eliezer says:] You have sensed it correctly. I am not the master. I am only the servant.

daughters of the Canaanite[s] in whose land
I dwell. 38. But you shall go to the house
of my father and to my family and take a
wife for my son.' 39. And I said to my
master: 'Perhaps the woman will not want
to follow me.' 40. And he said to me:
'*God*, before Whom I have conducted
myself, will send His angel with you and
cause your journey to prosper, so that you
will take a wife for my son from my family;
in fact, from my father's house. 41. Then
you will be free of my oath when you will
come to my family, and if they do not give
her to you, you shall be free of my oath.'
42. And so I came to the well today and I
said: 'O *God*, God of my master Abraham, if
now Thou wouldst prosper the journey
upon which I go, 43. 'behold, I am standing here at the well of water, and let it be
that the girl who comes to draw, to whom I
will say: Let me please drink a little water
from your pitcher, 44. and she will say to
me: You drink, and I will draw also for your
camels; let her be the woman whom *God*
has assigned for my master's son.'
45. And I had hardly finished speaking
thus in my heart when, lo! Rivkah came out
with her pitcher on her shoulder and she
went down to the well and drew. And I said
to her: 'Let me drink, please.' 46. And
she hurried and took down her pitcher and
said: 'Drink, and I will give your camels
drink also.' So I drank, and she gave the
camels to drink also. 47. And I asked her
and said: 'Whose daughter are you?' And
she said: 'The daughter of Bethuel, Naḥor's
son, whom Milcah bore him.' Then I put the
ring upon her nose and the bracelets upon
her hands, 48. and I bowed my head and
prostrated myself before *God* and blessed
God, the God of my master Abraham, Who
has led me on the true path to take the
daughter of my master's brother for his son.
49. And now, if you wish to deal in
loving-kindness and truth with my master,
tell me; and if not, tell me, so that I may
turn to the right, or to the left." 50. And
Laban and Bethuel answered and said:
"The matter has come forth from *God*; we
cannot speak to you, bad or good.
51. Here is Rivkah before you; take her
and go. Let her become the wife of your
master's son, as *God* has spoken."

יֹשֵׁב בְּאַרְצוֹ: לח אִם־לֹא אֶל־בֵּית־אָבִי תֵּלֵךְ
וְאֶל־מִשְׁפַּחְתִּי וְלָקַחְתָּ אִשָּׁה לִבְנִי: לט וָאֹמַר
אֶל־אֲדֹנִי אֻלַי לֹא־תֵלֵךְ הָאִשָּׁה אַחֲרָי: מ וַיֹּאמֶר
אֵלָי יְהֹוָה אֲשֶׁר־הִתְהַלַּכְתִּי לְפָנָיו יִשְׁלַח מַלְאָכוֹ
אִתָּךְ וְהִצְלִיחַ דַּרְכֶּךָ וְלָקַחְתָּ אִשָּׁה לִבְנִי
מִמִּשְׁפַּחְתִּי וּמִבֵּית אָבִי: מא אָז תִּנָּקֶה מֵאָלָתִי כִּי
תָבוֹא אֶל־מִשְׁפַּחְתִּי וְאִם־לֹא יִתְּנוּ לָךְ וְהָיִיתָ נָקִי
מֵאָלָתִי: מב וָאָבֹא הַיּוֹם אֶל־הָעָיִן וָאֹמַר יְהֹוָה
אֱלֹהֵי אֲדֹנִי אַבְרָהָם אִם־יֶשְׁךָ־נָּא מַצְלִיחַ דַּרְכִּי
אֲשֶׁר אָנֹכִי הֹלֵךְ עָלֶיהָ: מג הִנֵּה אָנֹכִי נִצָּב עַל־
עֵין הַמָּיִם וְהָיָה הָעַלְמָה הַיֹּצֵאת לִשְׁאֹב וְאָמַרְתִּי
אֵלֶיהָ הַשְׁקִינִי־נָא מְעַט־מַיִם מִכַּדֵּךְ: מד וְאָמְרָה
אֵלַי גַּם־אַתָּה שְׁתֵה וְגַם לִגְמַלֶּיךָ אֶשְׁאָב הִוא
הָאִשָּׁה אֲשֶׁר־הֹכִיחַ יְהֹוָה לְבֶן־אֲדֹנִי: מה אֲנִי
טֶרֶם אֲכַלֶּה לְדַבֵּר אֶל־לִבִּי וְהִנֵּה רִבְקָה יֹצֵאת
וְכַדָּהּ עַל־שִׁכְמָהּ וַתֵּרֶד הָעַיְנָה וַתִּשְׁאָב וָאֹמַר
אֵלֶיהָ הַשְׁקִינִי נָא: מו וַתְּמַהֵר וַתּוֹרֶד כַּדָּהּ
מֵעָלֶיהָ וַתֹּאמֶר שְׁתֵה וְגַם־גְּמַלֶּיךָ אַשְׁקֶה וָאֵשְׁתְּ
וְגַם הַגְּמַלִּים הִשְׁקָתָה: מז וָאֶשְׁאַל אֹתָהּ וָאֹמַר
בַּת־מִי אַתְּ וַתֹּאמֶר בַּת־בְּתוּאֵל בֶּן־נָחוֹר אֲשֶׁר
יָלְדָה־לּוֹ מִלְכָּה וָאָשִׂם הַנֶּזֶם עַל־אַפָּהּ
וְהַצְּמִידִים עַל־יָדֶיהָ: מח וָאֶקֹּד וָאֶשְׁתַּחֲוֶה
לַיהֹוָה וָאֲבָרֵךְ אֶת־יְהֹוָה אֱלֹהֵי אֲדֹנִי אַבְרָהָם
אֲשֶׁר הִנְחַנִי בְּדֶרֶךְ אֱמֶת לָקַחַת אֶת־בַּת־אֲחִי
אֲדֹנִי לִבְנוֹ: מט וְעַתָּה אִם־יֶשְׁכֶם עֹשִׂים חֶסֶד
וֶאֱמֶת אֶת־אֲדֹנִי הַגִּידוּ לִי וְאִם־לֹא הַגִּידוּ לִי
וְאֶפְנֶה עַל־יָמִין אוֹ עַל־שְׂמֹאל: נ וַיַּעַן לָבָן
וּבְתוּאֵל וַיֹּאמְרוּ מֵיְהֹוָה יָצָא הַדָּבָר לֹא נוּכַל
דַּבֵּר אֵלֶיךָ רַע אוֹ־טוֹב: נא הִנֵּה רִבְקָה לְפָנֶיךָ קַח
וָלֵךְ וּתְהִי אִשָּׁה לְבֶן־אֲדֹנֶיךָ כַּאֲשֶׁר דִּבֶּר יְהֹוָה:

52. And it came to pass that when the servant of Abraham heard their words, he flung himself to the ground before *God*, 53. and the servant brought forth articles of silver and of gold, and raiment, and he gave them to Rivkah, and he gave delicious fruits to her brother and her mother. 54. Then he and the men that were with him ate and drank and stayed overnight. And they arose in the morning, and he said: "Send me away to my master," 55. And her brother and her mother said: "Let the girl stay with us for a year or ten months; after that, she may go." 56. But he said to them: "Do not delay me, seeing that *God* has caused my journey to prosper; send me away so that I may go to my master." 57. And they said: "We will call the girl and ask her." 58. And they called Rivkah and said to her: "Will you go with this man?" And she replied: "I will go." 59. And they sent away their sister Rivkah and her nurse, as well as the servant of Abraham and his men, 60. And they blessed Rivkah and said to her: "Our sister! Become [the mother of] thousands of ten thousands, and may your seed inherit the gate of those that hate them." 61. And Rivkah and her maidens arose, mounted their camels and followed the man. And the servant took Rivkah and went. 62. And Yitzḥak had come home after having gone to the well of The-Living-One-Who-Sees-Me, for he lived in the land of the south.

נב וַיְהִי כַּאֲשֶׁר שָׁמַע עֶבֶד אַבְרָהָם אֶת־דִּבְרֵיהֶם
וַיִּשְׁתַּחוּ אַרְצָה לַיהוָה׃ חמישי נג וַיּוֹצֵא הָעֶבֶד
כְּלֵי־כֶסֶף וּכְלֵי זָהָב וּבְגָדִים וַיִּתֵּן לְרִבְקָה
וּמִגְדָּנֹת נָתַן לְאָחִיהָ וּלְאִמָּהּ׃ נד וַיֹּאכְלוּ וַיִּשְׁתּוּ
הוּא וְהָאֲנָשִׁים אֲשֶׁר־עִמּוֹ וַיָּלִינוּ וַיָּקוּמוּ בַבֹּקֶר
וַיֹּאמֶר שַׁלְּחֻנִי לַאדֹנִי׃ נה וַיֹּאמֶר אָחִיהָ וְאִמָּהּ
תֵּשֵׁב הַנַּעֲרָ (הנערה קרי) אִתָּנוּ יָמִים אוֹ עָשׂוֹר
אַחַר תֵּלֵךְ׃ נו וַיֹּאמֶר אֲלֵהֶם אַל־תְּאַחֲרוּ אֹתִי
וַיהוָה הִצְלִיחַ דַּרְכִּי שַׁלְּחוּנִי וְאֵלְכָה לַאדֹנִי׃
נז וַיֹּאמְרוּ נִקְרָא לַנַּעֲרָ (לנערה קרי) וְנִשְׁאֲלָה אֶת־
פִּיהָ׃ נח וַיִּקְרְאוּ לְרִבְקָה וַיֹּאמְרוּ אֵלֶיהָ הֲתֵלְכִי
עִם־הָאִישׁ הַזֶּה וַתֹּאמֶר אֵלֵךְ׃ נט וַיְשַׁלְּחוּ אֶת־
רִבְקָה אֲחֹתָם וְאֶת־מֵנִקְתָּהּ וְאֶת־עֶבֶד אַבְרָהָם
וְאֶת־אֲנָשָׁיו׃ ס וַיְבָרְכוּ אֶת־רִבְקָה וַיֹּאמְרוּ לָהּ
אֲחֹתֵנוּ אַתְּ הֲיִי לְאַלְפֵי רְבָבָה וְיִירַשׁ זַרְעֵךְ אֵת
שַׁעַר שֹׂנְאָיו׃ סא וַתָּקָם רִבְקָה וְנַעֲרֹתֶיהָ
וַתִּרְכַּבְנָה עַל־הַגְּמַלִּים וַתֵּלַכְנָה אַחֲרֵי הָאִישׁ
וַיִּקַּח הָעֶבֶד אֶת־רִבְקָה וַיֵּלַךְ׃ סב וְיִצְחָק בָּא
מִבּוֹא בְּאֵר לַחַי רֹאִי וְהוּא יוֹשֵׁב בְּאֶרֶץ הַנֶּגֶב׃

52. This is the only time that the narrative describes Eliezer as עֶבֶד אַבְרָהָם ["a servant of Abraham"]. Now that he has accomplished his errand as Abraham's servant, Eliezer feels that he is truly the servant of Abraham in the fullest sense of the word.

53. מִגְדָּנֹת ***[delicious fruits].*** There is no justification for interpreting this term as "precious things."[24] It denotes "delicious fruit," not precious gifts. מֶגֶד ["something delicious," "sweet"], from which this term is obviously derived, occurs in Scripture only in this connotation. Wherever it occurs in the Scriptural text (cf. Ezra 1:6 and II Chronicles 21:3) it comes last in an enumeration of jewels and objects of value; hence, it cannot represent the most valuable of gifts. Thus: Eliezer gave gifts of value to the young bride, sweets and compliments to her mother and her brother, and nothing at all to her father. This is significant. What a lot of nonsense had been read into the past of us Jews! In line with the principle that "nothing ever changes in the Middle East," travelers' stories and myths about the present-day customs and habits of the "Orientals" have been used as stereotypes by which to explain early Jewish life. Archaeologists tend to interpret the מהר ומתן ["marriage settlement and gifts," Genesis 34:12] as a bride price, which the bridegroom pays to the bride's parents in order to "buy" the girl. But in this "Oriental" marriage, Eliezer does not give anything to the bride's father, and the other members of the family receive only "attentions" of small value. . . .

[24]*Note to the English translation*: Standard versions render מִגְדָּנֹת as "precious things." [G.H.]

63. And Yitzḥak went out to meditate in the field at dusk and he lifted up his eyes, and lo! there were camels coming.   64. And Rivkah, too, lifted up her eyes and she saw Yitzḥak. And she let herself slip down from the camel.   65. And she said to the servant: "Who is this man there, who is walking through the field to meet us?" And the servant said: "It is my master!" And she took her veil and covered herself.   66. The servant told Yitzḥak all the things he had accomplished.   67. And Yitzḥak brought her into the tent of his mother Sarah. He married Rivkah, she became his wife, and he loved her, and only then was Yitzḥak comforted for his mother.

XXV

1. Abraham took another wife; her name was Keturah.   2. She bore him Zimran, Yokshan, Medan and Midian, and Yishbak and Shuaḥ.   3. Yokshan begot Sheba and Dedan. And the sons of Dedan were dwellers toward the plain, living in armed isolation and [in] groups of nations. 4. The sons of Midian: Ephah and Epher, Ḥanokh, Abida and Eldaah. All these were

סג וַיֵּצֵא יִצְחָק לָשׂוּחַ בַּשָּׂדֶה לִפְנוֹת עָרֶב וַיִּשָּׂא עֵינָיו וַיַּרְא וְהִנֵּה גְמַלִּים בָּאִים: סד וַתִּשָּׂא רִבְקָה אֶת-עֵינֶיהָ וַתֵּרֶא אֶת-יִצְחָק וַתִּפֹּל מֵעַל הַגָּמָל: סה וַתֹּאמֶר אֶל-הָעֶבֶד מִי-הָאִישׁ הַלָּזֶה הַהֹלֵךְ בַּשָּׂדֶה לִקְרָאתֵנוּ וַיֹּאמֶר הָעֶבֶד הוּא אֲדֹנִי וַתִּקַּח הַצָּעִיף וַתִּתְכָּס: סו וַיְסַפֵּר הָעֶבֶד לְיִצְחָק אֵת כָּל-הַדְּבָרִים אֲשֶׁר עָשָׂה: סז וַיְבִאֶהָ יִצְחָק הָאֹהֱלָה שָׂרָה אִמּוֹ וַיִּקַּח אֶת-רִבְקָה וַתְּהִי-לוֹ לְאִשָּׁה וַיֶּאֱהָבֶהָ וַיִּנָּחֵם יִצְחָק אַחֲרֵי אִמּוֹ: פ ששי כה א וַיֹּסֶף אַבְרָהָם וַיִּקַּח אִשָּׁה וּשְׁמָהּ קְטוּרָה: ב וַתֵּלֶד לוֹ אֶת-זִמְרָן וְאֶת-יָקְשָׁן וְאֶת-מְדָן וְאֶת-מִדְיָן וְאֶת-יִשְׁבָּק וְאֶת-שׁוּחַ: ג וְיָקְשָׁן יָלַד אֶת-שְׁבָא וְאֶת-דְּדָן וּבְנֵי דְדָן הָיוּ אַשּׁוּרִם וּלְטוּשִׁם וּלְאֻמִּים: ד וּבְנֵי מִדְיָן עֵיפָה וָעֵפֶר וַחֲנֹךְ וַאֲבִידָע וְאֶלְדָּעָה כָּל-אֵלֶּה בְּנֵי קְטוּרָה:

64. Undoubtedly Eliezer, all through the journey, had made a point of telling her about Isaac. This would be only natural. As a result, she recognized Isaac immediately; there is no need to think that she only had a "suspicion" [that this might be Isaac]. She may also have recognized the field from Eliezer's description, and seeing the manner in which Isaac walked straight through the field to meet them, she may have concluded that here, indeed, was the owner.

. . . Rebekah did not want to come toward Isaac riding high upon a camel's back. This, too, is significant. A haughty young lady would certainly have considered it "smart" to approach her future husband riding in state, at the head of a long train of attendants, and then to permit him to lift her gallantly from the camel's back. But especially since Isaac was moving toward her on foot she did not consider it seemly that she should ride to meet him. Also, riding on a camel seems to have been a sign of quality, and Rebekah did not want to assume the role of a grand lady when she met Isaac. This was not a premeditated, calculated act on her part (if it had been so, her modesty would only have been an act, difficult to distinguish from arrogance), but וַתִּפֹּל, she allowed herself to slip down. It all happened spontaneously, without premeditation: it

was the result of instant intuition, which proved to be correct.

67. Here again we have a character trait which, thank God, has not vanished from among the descendants of Abraham and Sarah, Isaac and Rebekah. The more she became his wife, the more he loved her. Just as this marriage of the first Jewish son, so, too, most Jewish marriages in our own day are contracted not on the basis of passion but on the strength of reason and judgment. Parents and relatives consider whether the two young people are suited to each other, and that is why their love only grows as they come to know each other better. Most non-Jewish marriages are made on the basis of what is *described* as "love." But we need only glance at "true to life" novels to see the gap which becomes apparent, in these cases, between the "love" of the partners before marriage and what happens afterwards, how dull and empty everything seems after marriage, how different from how the two partners had imagined everything before, etc. This sort of "love" is blind; each step into the future brings new disillusionment. But of the Jewish marriage it is said, "And Isaac took Rebekah . . . and she became his wife, and he loved her." Here the wedding is not the culmination but only the beginning of true love.

∴ ∴

sons of Keturah.   5. And Abraham gave all that he had to Yitzḥak.   6. But to the concubine's children whom Abraham had, Abraham gave gifts, and he sent them away, while he still lived, from his son Yitzḥak, eastward, to the land of the east.   7. And now these are the days of the years of the life of Abraham, which he lived: one hundred years and seventy years and five years.   8. Abraham expired and died in a good old age, mature and satiated, and was gathered to his people.   9. Yitzḥak and Yishmael, his sons, buried him in the cave of Makhpelah, in the field of the Hittite Ephron, son of Tzohar, which is before Mamre,   10. the field that Abraham had purchased from the sons of Ḥeth; there, Abraham and his wife Sarah were buried.   11. It came to pass after Abraham had died that God blessed his son Yitzḥak, and Yitzḥak dwelt near the well of The-Living-One-Who-Sees-Me. 12. Now these are the descendants of Yishmael, Abraham's son, whom Hagar, the Egyptian, Sarah's maidservant, had borne to Abraham.   13. These are the names of the sons of Yishmael, which names remained with their descendants: Yishmael's first-born, Nebaioth, Kedar, Abde'el and Mibsam;   14. Mishma, Dumah and Massa;   15. Haddad and Tema, Yetur, Naphish and Kedmah.   16. These are the sons of Yishmael and these are the names by their homesteads and strongholds, twelve princes according to their tribes.   17. Now these are the years of the life of Yishmael: one hundred years, thirty years and seven years; he expired and died and was gathered to his people.   18. They dwelt from Ḥavilah to Shur, that is before Mitzrayim, in the region as you go toward Asshur; before the face of all his brothers did he settle.

ה וַיִּתֵּן אַבְרָהָם אֶת־כָּל־אֲשֶׁר־לוֹ לְיִצְחָק:
ו וְלִבְנֵי הַפִּילַגְשִׁים אֲשֶׁר לְאַבְרָהָם נָתַן אַבְרָהָם מַתָּנֹת וַיְשַׁלְּחֵם מֵעַל יִצְחָק בְּנוֹ בְּעוֹדֶנּוּ חַי קֵדְמָה אֶל־אֶרֶץ קֶדֶם: ז וְאֵלֶּה יְמֵי שְׁנֵי־חַיֵּי אַבְרָהָם אֲשֶׁר־חָי מְאַת שָׁנָה וְשִׁבְעִים שָׁנָה וְחָמֵשׁ שָׁנִים: ח וַיִּגְוַע וַיָּמָת אַבְרָהָם בְּשֵׂיבָה טוֹבָה זָקֵן וְשָׂבֵעַ וַיֵּאָסֶף אֶל־עַמָּיו: ט וַיִּקְבְּרוּ אֹתוֹ יִצְחָק וְיִשְׁמָעֵאל בָּנָיו אֶל־מְעָרַת הַמַּכְפֵּלָה אֶל־שְׂדֵה עֶפְרֹן בֶּן־צֹחַר הַחִתִּי אֲשֶׁר עַל־פְּנֵי מַמְרֵא: י הַשָּׂדֶה אֲשֶׁר־קָנָה אַבְרָהָם מֵאֵת בְּנֵי־חֵת שָׁמָּה קֻבַּר אַבְרָהָם וְשָׂרָה אִשְׁתּוֹ: יא וַיְהִי אַחֲרֵי מוֹת אַבְרָהָם וַיְבָרֶךְ אֱלֹהִים אֶת־יִצְחָק בְּנוֹ וַיֵּשֶׁב יִצְחָק עִם־בְּאֵר לַחַי רֹאִי: פ שביעי יב וְאֵלֶּה תֹּלְדֹת יִשְׁמָעֵאל בֶּן־אַבְרָהָם אֲשֶׁר יָלְדָה הָגָר הַמִּצְרִית שִׁפְחַת שָׂרָה לְאַבְרָהָם: יג וְאֵלֶּה שְׁמוֹת בְּנֵי יִשְׁמָעֵאל בִּשְׁמֹתָם לְתוֹלְדֹתָם בְּכֹר יִשְׁמָעֵאל נְבָיֹת וְקֵדָר וְאַדְבְּאֵל וּמִבְשָׂם: יד וּמִשְׁמָע וְדוּמָה וּמַשָּׂא: טו חֲדַד וְתֵימָא יְטוּר נָפִישׁ וָקֵדְמָה: מפטיר טז אֵלֶּה הֵם בְּנֵי יִשְׁמָעֵאל וְאֵלֶּה שְׁמֹתָם בְּחַצְרֵיהֶם וּבְטִירֹתָם שְׁנֵים־עָשָׂר נְשִׂיאִם לְאֻמֹּתָם: יז וְאֵלֶּה שְׁנֵי חַיֵּי יִשְׁמָעֵאל מְאַת שָׁנָה וּשְׁלֹשִׁים שָׁנָה וְשֶׁבַע שָׁנִים וַיִּגְוַע וַיָּמָת וַיֵּאָסֶף אֶל־עַמָּיו: יח וַיִּשְׁכְּנוּ מֵחֲוִילָה עַד־שׁוּר אֲשֶׁר עַל־פְּנֵי מִצְרַיִם בֹּאֲכָה אַשּׁוּרָה עַל־פְּנֵי כָל־אֶחָיו נָפָל: פ

The Haftarah for this Sidra may be found on page 829.

תולדות

TOLEDOTH

19. And now these are the descendants of Yitzḥak, son of Abraham: Abraham had begotten Yitzḥak.　20. Yitzḥak was forty years old when he took Rivkah, a daughter of Bethuel the Aramite of Paddan-Aram, a sister of Laban the Aramite, to be his wife. 21. And Yitzḥak entreated *God* concerning his wife, for she was barren, and *God* was entreated by him, and Rivkah, his wife, conceived.　22. And the children moved violently against each other within her womb, and when this occurred, she said: "Why am I thus?" and she went to inquire of *God*.　23. And *God* let her know [as follows]: "Two nations [are] in your womb and two states; they will be divided from one another, starting from within you; one state shall become mightier than the other, and the mighty one shall serve the lesser." 24. And when her days to be delivered were complete, lo! there were twins in her womb.　25. The first came out red-cheeked, all over like a hairy mantle; they named him Esav.　26. After that, his brother came out, and his hand held on to the heel of Esav, and he named him Yaakov; now Yitzḥak was sixty years old when she bore them.　27. When the lads grew up, Esav was a man who understood hunting, a

כה יט וְאֵ֣לֶּה תּוֹלְדֹ֣ת יִצְחָ֖ק בֶּן־אַבְרָהָ֑ם אַבְרָהָ֖ם הוֹלִ֥יד אֶת־יִצְחָֽק: כ וַיְהִ֤י יִצְחָק֙ בֶּן־אַרְבָּעִ֣ים שָׁנָ֔ה בְּקַחְתּ֣וֹ אֶת־רִבְקָ֗ה בַּת־בְּתוּאֵל֙ הָֽאֲרַמִּ֔י מִפַּדַּ֖ן אֲרָ֑ם אֲח֛וֹת לָבָ֥ן הָאֲרַמִּ֖י ל֥וֹ לְאִשָּֽׁה: כא וַיֶּעְתַּ֨ר יִצְחָ֤ק לַֽיהֹוָה֙ לְנֹ֣כַח אִשְׁתּ֔וֹ כִּ֥י עֲקָרָ֖ה הִ֑וא וַיֵּעָ֤תֶר לוֹ֙ יְהֹוָ֔ה וַתַּ֖הַר רִבְקָ֥ה אִשְׁתּֽוֹ: כב וַיִּתְרֹֽצְצ֤וּ הַבָּנִים֙ בְּקִרְבָּ֔הּ וַתֹּ֣אמֶר אִם־כֵּ֔ן לָ֥מָּה זֶּ֖ה אָנֹ֑כִי וַתֵּ֖לֶךְ לִדְרֹ֥שׁ אֶת־יְהֹוָֽה: כג וַיֹּ֨אמֶר יְהֹוָ֜ה לָ֗הּ שְׁנֵ֤י גיים (גוים קרי) בְּבִטְנֵ֔ךְ וּשְׁנֵ֣י לְאֻמִּ֔ים מִמֵּעַ֖יִךְ יִפָּרֵ֑דוּ וּלְאֹם֙ מִלְאֹ֣ם יֶֽאֱמָ֔ץ וְרַ֖ב יַֽעֲבֹ֥ד צָעִֽיר: כד וַיִּמְלְא֥וּ יָמֶ֖יהָ לָלֶ֑דֶת וְהִנֵּ֥ה תוֹמִ֖ם בְּבִטְנָֽהּ: כה וַיֵּצֵ֤א הָרִאשׁוֹן֙ אַדְמוֹנִ֔י כֻּלּ֖וֹ כְּאַדֶּ֣רֶת שֵׂעָ֑ר וַיִּקְרְא֥וּ שְׁמ֖וֹ עֵשָֽׂו: כו וְאַֽחֲרֵי־כֵ֞ן יָצָ֣א אָחִ֗יו וְיָד֤וֹ אֹחֶ֨זֶת֙ בַּעֲקֵ֣ב עֵשָׂ֔ו וַיִּקְרָ֥א שְׁמ֖וֹ יַֽעֲקֹ֑ב וְיִצְחָ֛ק בֶּן־שִׁשִּׁ֥ים שָׁנָ֖ה בְּלֶ֥דֶת אֹתָֽם: כז וַיִּגְדְּלוּ֙ הַנְּעָרִ֔ים וַיְהִ֣י עֵשָׂ֗ו אִ֛ישׁ יֹדֵ֥עַ צַ֖יִד אִ֣ישׁ שָׂדֶ֑ה

CHAPTER XXV

20. . . . The text reminds us once again of [Rebekah's] Aramite origin and family background. Isaac was the son of Abraham, and thus it was Abraham, and Abraham alone, who had influenced him. As a result Isaac had matured to become a true son of Abraham. But Rebekah, though her good qualities are beyond dispute, was the daughter of an Aramite, born and raised in Aram, and the sister of a most pronounced Aramite type: Laban. If, according to the maxim of our Sages, most sons take after their maternal uncles, what sort of offspring could have been expected from the marriage of Isaac and Rebekah if most of them would have taken after their uncle? By means of this reminder the narrative prepares us for the conflict which arises later on. We will then not be surprised when we see an Esau appear on the scene. In fact, we will be surprised to find that, side by side with him, one like Jacob could also emerge.

21. *concerning his wife.* For twenty years Isaac had pleaded with God for the fulfillment of his wish to have children from Rebekah. He knew of the Divine promise "for in Yitzḥak shall seed be called for you"—[Genesis 21:12], and so he knew that he could expect to have children eventually. But he did have reason, particularly after waiting for so long, to wonder whether the heirs of the Abrahamite covenant could be born of a sister of Laban, no matter what her own excellent personal qualities. Therefore Isaac's entreaty referred especially to Rebekah. . . .

27. *the lads grew up.* Our Sages never hesitate to point out to us the errors and shortcomings, both great and small, of our ancestors, thereby making their life stories all the more instructive for us. . . . In regard to this passage, too, our Sages make a comment which indicates that the sharp contrast between the two grandsons of Abraham may have originated not merely in their natural tendencies but may have been caused

וְיַעֲקֹב אִישׁ תָּם יֹשֵׁב אֹהָלִים: כח וַיֶּאֱהַב יִצְחָק
אֶת־עֵשָׂו כִּי־צַיִד בְּפִיו וְרִבְקָה אֹהֶבֶת אֶת־יַעֲקֹב:
כט וַיָּזֶד יַעֲקֹב נָזִיד וַיָּבֹא עֵשָׂו מִן־הַשָּׂדֶה וְהוּא
עָיֵף: ל וַיֹּאמֶר עֵשָׂו אֶל־יַעֲקֹב הַלְעִיטֵנִי נָא מִן־
הָאָדֹם הָאָדֹם הַזֶּה כִּי עָיֵף אָנֹכִי עַל־כֵּן קָרָא־
שְׁמוֹ אֱדוֹם: לא וַיֹּאמֶר יַעֲקֹב מִכְרָה כַיּוֹם אֶת־

man of the field, and Yaakov was a single-minded man, living in tents. 28. And Yitzḥak loved Esav, because he was a hunter also with his mouth, but Rivkah loved Yaakov. 29. One day Yaakov cooked a pottage, and Esav came in from the field and he was faint. 30. And Esav said to Yaakov: "Please let me gulp down this red, red [pottage] because I am faint." Therefore he called himself Edom [i.e., the Red One].

also by mistakes in their upbringing. As long as they were little, no attention was given to the latent differences between them. Both were given the same upbringing and education. The basic tenet of education, "Train each child in accordance with his own way" [Proverbs 22:6], that each child should be educated, both as a man and as a Jew, in accordance with the tendencies latent in him and in accordance with the individuality that will result from these tendencies, was forgotten. The great task of the Jew is simple and straightforward as regards its basic content, but the modes of its fulfillment are as varied and complex as the differences in individuality and the diversity of life that result from these differences.

° ° °

For this reason each individual must be raised for the same lofty purpose but "in accordance with his own way," in keeping with the path of life to which his personal tendencies may be expected to lead him. To attempt to educate a Jacob and an Esau together, in the same classroom, in the same routines of life and in the same manner, to raise both of them for, say, a life of study and contemplation, will inevitably mean to ruin one of the two. Under such conditions a Jacob type will learn to draw with ever-growing zeal from the well of wisdom and truth, but an Esau type will hardly be able to wait for the day when he can throw away his ancient schoolbooks. At that time he will turn his back not only on his schoolbooks but also on his life's purpose, which he has been taught only in a one-sided way that has no appeal whatever to his temperament.

Had Isaac and Rebekah studied Esau's nature and asked themselves at an early stage how even an Esau, with the strength, skills and courage latent within him, could be won for endeavors in the service of God, so that the future גִּבּוֹר [mighty man] would not become גִּבּוֹר צַיִד ["a mighty hunter"] but truly a גִּבּוֹר לִפְנֵי ד' ["mighty man *before God*"], then Jacob and Esau, despite the basic differences in their tendencies, could have remained twin brothers in spirit as well as in flesh. In that case the sword of Esau could have become wedded early on to the spirit of Jacob, and who knows what a different turn all of history would have taken. But as things happened, וַיִּגְדְּלוּ הַנְּעָרִים ["the lads grew up"]: only after the lads had grown to manhood was everyone surprised to see that two brothers, from the same womb, who had enjoyed the same care, the same upbringing and the same schooling, should have grown into two such diametrical opposites [as did Jacob and Esau]. . . .

° ° °

28. Another factor which could not fail to have a pernicious effect was the difference in the feelings of the parents toward these two children. Harmony between the parents as regards the rearing of their offspring, their attitude toward, and love for, all their children, including those who are not as good as the rest (and who are in need of particular love and devotion even more than those who are physically ill): this is the cornerstone of all successful child-rearing. Incidentally, the fact that Isaac's sympathies were with Esau while Rebekah felt closer to Jacob can be attributed to the attraction of opposites.

We see Isaac, risen to new life from the sacrificial altar, withdrawing from the hurly-burly of the world, preferring to dwell near places of quiet solitude, at the well of The-Living-One-Who-Sees-Me, rather than amidst the bustling traffic of humanity. It would not be unlikely, therefore, that Esau's hearty, audacious way should have appealed to Isaac and that, perhaps, he saw in Esau the strength, which he himself lacked, to be the mainstay of his household. Rebekah, on the other hand, saw in Jacob's nature the unfolding of a life style she had never known in the home of her own parents. But while parental sympathies can be explained in this manner, parents should not permit such primeval emotions to determine their attitude toward their children.

צַיִד בְּפִיו . . . probably, the skills of hunting were also in his mouth; i.e., he practiced the skills of hunting even when he spoke. He knew how to use this art to capture his father's love. Rebekah's love for Jacob, on the other hand, came of its own. Jacob did not have to "capture" it. His personality was such that it won her love. . . .

31. And Yaakov said: "Please sell me, as this day [is clear], your birthright." 32. Esav replied: "Lo! I am going to die; of what use, then, is this birthright to me?" 33. And Yaakov said: "Swear to me as this day [is clear]." And he swore to him and sold his birthright to Yaakov. 34. And Yaakov had given Esav bread and a pottage of lentils. He ate, he drank, he rose and he went out. Thus did Esav despise his birthright.

XXVI

1. There was famine in the land, in addition to the first famine that had been in the days of Abraham. And Yitzḥak went to Abimelekh, king of the Philistines, to Gerar. 2. And *God* appeared to him and said: "Do not go down to Mitzrayim; dwell in the land of which I shall tell you. 3. Sojourn in this land and I will be with you and will bless you, for to you and to your seed will I give all these lands, and I will keep the oath which I swore to Abraham, your father. 4. I will multiply your seed as the stars of heaven and will give to your seed all these lands and through your seed all the nations of the earth shall bless themselves 5. as a consequence of Abraham's having hearkened to My voice and having guarded that which I had placed into his charge: My commandments, My statutes and My teachings." 6. Thereupon Yitzḥak remained in Gerar. 7. The people of the place asked him about his wife, but he said: "She is my sister," because he was afraid to say: "My wife," "for the people of the place could kill me because of Rivkah," for she was good to look upon. 8. But it came to pass, when he had been there a long time, that Abimelekh, king of the Philistines, looked out of a window and saw that Yitzḥak was enjoying himself with Rivkah, his wife. 9. And Abimelekh called Yitzḥak and said: "So she is your wife. Why did you say: 'She is my sister'?" And Yitzḥak replied: "Because I thought that I might die on her account." 10. And Abimelekh said: "What is this you have done to us? One of the people could easily have cohabited with your wife and you would have brought guilt upon us." 11. Therefore Abimelekh commanded all the people as follows: Whoever touches this man and his wife shall

בְּכֹרָתְךָ לִי: לב וַיֹּאמֶר עֵשָׂו הִנֵּה אָנֹכִי הוֹלֵךְ
לָמוּת וְלָמָּה־זֶּה לִי בְּכֹרָה: לג וַיֹּאמֶר יַעֲקֹב
הִשָּׁבְעָה לִּי כַּיּוֹם וַיִּשָּׁבַע לוֹ וַיִּמְכֹּר אֶת־בְּכֹרָתוֹ
לְיַעֲקֹב: לד וְיַעֲקֹב נָתַן לְעֵשָׂו לֶחֶם וּנְזִיד עֲדָשִׁים
וַיֹּאכַל וַיֵּשְׁתְּ וַיָּקָם וַיֵּלַךְ וַיִּבֶז עֵשָׂו אֶת־הַבְּכֹרָה:
פ כו א וַיְהִי רָעָב בָּאָרֶץ מִלְּבַד הָרָעָב הָרִאשׁוֹן
אֲשֶׁר הָיָה בִּימֵי אַבְרָהָם וַיֵּלֶךְ יִצְחָק אֶל־אֲבִימֶלֶךְ
מֶלֶךְ־פְּלִשְׁתִּים גְּרָרָה: ב וַיֵּרָא אֵלָיו יְהֹוָה וַיֹּאמֶר
אַל־תֵּרֵד מִצְרָיְמָה שְׁכֹן בָּאָרֶץ אֲשֶׁר אֹמַר אֵלֶיךָ:
ג גּוּר בָּאָרֶץ הַזֹּאת וְאֶהְיֶה עִמְּךָ וַאֲבָרְכֶךָּ כִּי־לְךָ
וּלְזַרְעֲךָ אֶתֵּן אֶת־כָּל־הָאֲרָצֹת הָאֵל וַהֲקִמֹתִי
אֶת־הַשְּׁבֻעָה אֲשֶׁר נִשְׁבַּעְתִּי לְאַבְרָהָם אָבִיךָ:
ד וְהִרְבֵּיתִי אֶת־זַרְעֲךָ כְּכוֹכְבֵי הַשָּׁמַיִם וְנָתַתִּי
לְזַרְעֲךָ אֵת כָּל הָאֲרָצֹת הָאֵל וְהִתְבָּרְכוּ בְזַרְעֲךָ
כֹּל גּוֹיֵי הָאָרֶץ: ה עֵקֶב אֲשֶׁר־שָׁמַע אַבְרָהָם
בְּקֹלִי וַיִּשְׁמֹר מִשְׁמַרְתִּי מִצְוֺתַי חֻקּוֹתַי וְתוֹרֹתָי:
שני ו וַיֵּשֶׁב יִצְחָק בִּגְרָר: ז וַיִּשְׁאֲלוּ אַנְשֵׁי הַמָּקוֹם
לְאִשְׁתּוֹ וַיֹּאמֶר אֲחֹתִי הִוא כִּי יָרֵא לֵאמֹר אִשְׁתִּי
פֶּן־יַהַרְגֻנִי אַנְשֵׁי הַמָּקוֹם עַל־רִבְקָה כִּי־טוֹבַת
מַרְאֶה הִוא: ח וַיְהִי כִּי אָרְכוּ־לוֹ שָׁם הַיָּמִים
וַיַּשְׁקֵף אֲבִימֶלֶךְ מֶלֶךְ פְּלִשְׁתִּים בְּעַד הַחַלּוֹן
וַיַּרְא וְהִנֵּה יִצְחָק מְצַחֵק אֵת רִבְקָה אִשְׁתּוֹ:
ט וַיִּקְרָא אֲבִימֶלֶךְ לְיִצְחָק וַיֹּאמֶר אַךְ הִנֵּה
אִשְׁתְּךָ הִוא וְאֵיךְ אָמַרְתָּ אֲחֹתִי הִוא וַיֹּאמֶר אֵלָיו
יִצְחָק כִּי אָמַרְתִּי פֶּן־אָמוּת עָלֶיהָ: י וַיֹּאמֶר
אֲבִימֶלֶךְ מַה־זֹּאת עָשִׂיתָ לָּנוּ כִּמְעַט שָׁכַב אַחַד
הָעָם אֶת־אִשְׁתֶּךָ וְהֵבֵאתָ עָלֵינוּ אָשָׁם: יא וַיְצַו
אֲבִימֶלֶךְ אֶת־כָּל־הָעָם לֵאמֹר הַנֹּגֵעַ בָּאִישׁ הַזֶּה

be put to death. 12. And Yitzhak sowed in that land and in that year he reached one hundred markets, and *God* blessed him. 13. But when the man became great and grew more and more in greatness until he became exceedingly great, 14. and he had possessions of sheep and possessions of cattle and much farmland, the Philistines became envious of him. 15. All the wells which the servants of his father had dug in the days of his father Abraham, the Philistines had stopped them up and filled them with earth. 16. And Abimelekh said to Yitzḥak: "Go away from us because you have become much too mighty for us." 17. Yitzḥak went away from there, and encamped in the Valley of Gerar and settled there. 18. And Yitzḥak dug again the wells of water which they had dug in the days of Abraham and which the Philistines had stopped up after the death of Abraham, and he called them by the names which his father had given them. 19. The servants of Yitzḥak dug in the valley and found there a well of living waters. 20. And the herdsmen of Gerar quarreled with Yitzḥak's

וּבְאִשְׁתּוֹ מוֹת יוּמָת׃ יב וַיִּזְרַע יִצְחָק בָּאָרֶץ
הַהִוא וַיִּמְצָא בַּשָּׁנָה הַהִוא מֵאָה שְׁעָרִים
וַיְבָרְכֵהוּ יְהֹוָה׃ שלישי יג וַיִּגְדַּל הָאִישׁ וַיֵּלֶךְ הָלוֹךְ
וְגָדֵל עַד כִּי־גָדַל מְאֹד׃ יד וַיְהִי־לוֹ מִקְנֵה־צֹאן
וּמִקְנֵה בָקָר וַעֲבֻדָּה רַבָּה וַיְקַנְאוּ אֹתוֹ פְּלִשְׁתִּים׃
טו וְכָל־הַבְּאֵרֹת אֲשֶׁר חָפְרוּ עַבְדֵי אָבִיו בִּימֵי
אַבְרָהָם אָבִיו סִתְּמוּם פְּלִשְׁתִּים וַיְמַלְאוּם עָפָר׃
טז וַיֹּאמֶר אֲבִימֶלֶךְ אֶל־יִצְחָק לֵךְ מֵעִמָּנוּ כִּי־
עָצַמְתָּ מִמֶּנּוּ מְאֹד׃ יז וַיֵּלֶךְ מִשָּׁם יִצְחָק וַיִּחַן
בְּנַחַל־גְּרָר וַיֵּשֶׁב שָׁם׃ יח וַיָּשָׁב יִצְחָק וַיַּחְפֹּר ׀
אֶת־בְּאֵרֹת הַמַּיִם אֲשֶׁר חָפְרוּ בִּימֵי אַבְרָהָם
אָבִיו וַיְסַתְּמוּם פְּלִשְׁתִּים אַחֲרֵי מוֹת אַבְרָהָם
וַיִּקְרָא לָהֶן שֵׁמוֹת כַּשֵּׁמֹת אֲשֶׁר־קָרָא לָהֶן אָבִיו׃
יט וַיַּחְפְּרוּ עַבְדֵי־יִצְחָק בַּנָּחַל וַיִּמְצְאוּ־שָׁם בְּאֵר
מַיִם חַיִּים׃ כ וַיָּרִיבוּ רֹעֵי גְרָר עִם־רֹעֵי יִצְחָק

CHAPTER XXVI

12. . . . In all of Scripture the term שַׁעַר is used only to denote either "gate" or "market place." Cf. II Kings 7:1 [". . . shall a measure of fine flour be sold . . . in the gate of Samaria"]. . . . Accordingly, מֵאָה שְׁעָרִים in this passage would mean "one hundred markets." The yield of Isaac's soil was not merely sufficient for his own needs; he was also in a position to bring to the market one hundred times the average quantity of produce.

and God blessed him. Therefore he became, initially, the "one blessed by *God*." Because he did not hoard his produce, but offered it for sale in the market places, those who were affected by that one year of famine benefited from his blessed harvest. As a result, they thought of him, at first, only as a man who was blessed by God.

15. . . .This קִנְאָה [envy] set into motion a train of events which marks a new phase [in Jewish history], beginning with Isaac. Abraham, despite all his riches was, like Isaac, a stranger in the midst of the nations. Yet, thanks to his personality, he gained such widespread respect that he was able to walk in their midst as "one ennobled by God" [Genesis 23:6] without stirring up envy or jealousy. Only on one occasion did Abraham become the victim of a hostile act similar to that which was perpetrated against Isaac, but that act had been promptly disavowed by no less a person than the king himself. However, with Isaac the *galuth* [the exiled state of the Jewish people] began. It was in the life of Isaac that the promise "your seed shall be a stranger" [Genesis 15:13] first became reality. Abraham still enjoyed unmixed happiness, but Isaac's serenity was already marred by envy and by hostile acts of jealousy. As for Jacob, we will see him in a position of lowly servitude. Thus history shows us three distinct positions to be occupied by the progeny of Abraham as strangers in the midst of the nations: as servants, as great figures but objects of envy, and as honored personages. In each of these three turns of fate the Divine covenant has proven a protection and a blessing, which, hence, became manifest not only as a בְּרִית עִם אַבְרָהָם, עִם יִצְחָק וְעִם יַעֲקֹב ["covenant *with* Abraham, *with* Isaac and *with* Jacob"] but as a בְּרִית אַבְרָהָם בְּרִית יִצְחָק בְּרִית יַעֲקֹב [lit., "Covenant Abraham, Covenant Yitzḥak and Covenant Yaakov"], with the names of the patriarchs understood not as the names of individuals but as designations for historic archetypes through which the various aspects of the strength of the Divine covenant have become manifest.

° ° °

herdsmen and said: "The water is ours!" Therefore he called the well Essek (Contention) because they had made a claim against his title [to the well].   21. They dug another well, but they quarreled about that also, and so he named it Sitnah (Obstruction).   22. He moved away from there and dug another well, and they did not quarrel over this one, so he named it Reḥovoth (Spaciousness) and said: "For now *God* has made room for us; now we can be fruitful in the land."   23. And he moved up from there to Beer Sheva.   24. *God* appeared to him that night and said: "I am the God of your father Abraham. Fear not, because I am with you and I will bless you and multiply your seed for the sake of My servant Abraham."   25. And he built an altar there, proclaimed in the Name of *God* and pitched his tent there, and Yitzḥak's servants dug a well there.   26. But Abimelekh had traveled to him from Gerar, and all his companions, and Phikhol, his commander.   27. And Yitzḥak said to them: "Why have you come to me, seeing that you hated me and sent me away from you?"   28. They replied: "We have seen repeatedly that *God* was with you, and so we said: 'Let there now be an oath between us, between us and you, and let us make a covenant with you,   29. so that you will do us no hurt even as we have not touched you, and even as we have done you nothing but good and have sent you away in peace. After all, you are one blessed by *God*.'"   30. He prepared a feast for them, and they ate and they drank.   31. They arose early in the morning, and swore one to the other, and Yitzḥak sent them away, and they departed from him in peace.   32. On that same day Yitzḥak's servants came to him and told him about the well which they had dug, and they said to him: "We have

לֵאמֹר לָנוּ הַמָּיִם וַיִּקְרָא שֵׁם־הַבְּאֵר עֵשֶׂק כִּי הִתְעַשְּׂקוּ עִמּוֹ: כא וַיַּחְפְּרוּ בְּאֵר אַחֶרֶת וַיָּרִיבוּ גַּם־עָלֶיהָ וַיִּקְרָא שְׁמָהּ שִׂטְנָה: כב וַיַּעְתֵּק מִשָּׁם וַיַּחְפֹּר בְּאֵר אַחֶרֶת וְלֹא רָבוּ עָלֶיהָ וַיִּקְרָא שְׁמָהּ רְחֹבוֹת וַיֹּאמֶר כִּי־עַתָּה הִרְחִיב יְהֹוָה לָנוּ וּפָרִינוּ בָאָרֶץ: רביעי כג וַיַּעַל מִשָּׁם בְּאֵר שָׁבַע: כד וַיֵּרָא אֵלָיו יְהֹוָה בַּלַּיְלָה הַהוּא וַיֹּאמֶר אָנֹכִי אֱלֹהֵי אַבְרָהָם אָבִיךָ אַל־תִּירָא כִּי־אִתְּךָ אָנֹכִי וּבֵרַכְתִּיךָ וְהִרְבֵּיתִי אֶת־זַרְעֲךָ בַּעֲבוּר אַבְרָהָם עַבְדִּי: כה וַיִּבֶן שָׁם מִזְבֵּחַ וַיִּקְרָא בְּשֵׁם יְהֹוָה וַיֶּט־שָׁם אָהֳלוֹ וַיִּכְרוּ־שָׁם עַבְדֵי־יִצְחָק בְּאֵר: כו וַאֲבִימֶלֶךְ הָלַךְ אֵלָיו מִגְּרָר וַאֲחֻזַּת מֵרֵעֵהוּ וּפִיכֹל שַׂר־צְבָאוֹ: כז וַיֹּאמֶר אֲלֵהֶם יִצְחָק מַדּוּעַ בָּאתֶם אֵלָי וְאַתֶּם שְׂנֵאתֶם אֹתִי וַתְּשַׁלְּחוּנִי מֵאִתְּכֶם: כח וַיֹּאמְרוּ רָאוֹ רָאִינוּ כִּי־הָיָה יְהֹוָה עִמָּךְ וַנֹּאמֶר תְּהִי נָא אָלָה בֵּינוֹתֵינוּ בֵּינֵינוּ וּבֵינֶךָ וְנִכְרְתָה בְרִית עִמָּךְ: כט אִם־תַּעֲשֵׂה עִמָּנוּ רָעָה כַּאֲשֶׁר לֹא נְגַעֲנוּךָ וְכַאֲשֶׁר עָשִׂינוּ עִמְּךָ רַק־טוֹב וַנְּשַׁלֵּחֲךָ בְּשָׁלוֹם אַתָּה עַתָּה בְּרוּךְ יְהֹוָה: חמישי ל וַיַּעַשׂ לָהֶם מִשְׁתֶּה וַיֹּאכְלוּ וַיִּשְׁתּוּ: לא וַיַּשְׁכִּימוּ בַבֹּקֶר וַיִּשָּׁבְעוּ אִישׁ לְאָחִיו וַיְשַׁלְּחֵם יִצְחָק וַיֵּלְכוּ מֵאִתּוֹ בְּשָׁלוֹם: לב וַיְהִי בַּיּוֹם הַהוּא וַיָּבֹאוּ עַבְדֵי יִצְחָק וַיַּגִּדוּ לוֹ עַל־אֹדוֹת הַבְּאֵר אֲשֶׁר חָפָרוּ וַיֹּאמְרוּ לוֹ מָצָאנוּ

26. This visit from Abimelekh is very significant. Though he himself has broken faith with the son of Abraham, having violated the covenant he, Abimelekh, had made with Abraham, he was anxious to obtain a covenantal oath from Isaac. For during the later and final periods of Jewish national life, too, the Jewish nation, no matter what the circumstances, was noted and grudgingly respected for its adherence to all the covenants it had ever entered upon. Typical, too, are the king's words (Verse 29), "and have sent you away in peace." The Philistines considered it a good deed on their part that they had sent him away without first robbing him of his possessions.

∘   ∘   ∘

found water." . 33. He named it Shivah; therefore the name of the city is Beer Sheva until this day.   34. When Esav was forty years old he took to wife Judith, the daughter of Beeri the Hittite and Basemath, the daughter of Elon the Hittite. 35. They were a spiritual defiance to Yitzḥak and Rivkah.

XXVII

1. It came to pass that when Yitzḥak had become old and his eyes were too dim for seeing, he called his eldest son Esav and

מָיִם: לג וַיִּקְרָא אֹתָהּ שִׁבְעָה עַל־כֵּן שֵׁם־הָעִיר בְּאֵר שֶׁבַע עַד הַיּוֹם הַזֶּה: ס לד וַיְהִי עֵשָׂו בֶּן אַרְבָּעִים שָׁנָה וַיִּקַּח אִשָּׁה אֶת־יְהוּדִית בַּת־בְּאֵרִי הַחִתִּי וְאֶת־בָּשְׂמַת בַּת־אֵילֹן הַחִתִּי: לה וַתִּהְיֶיןָ מֹרַת רוּחַ לְיִצְחָק וּלְרִבְקָה: ס כז א וַיְהִי כִּי־זָקֵן יִצְחָק וַתִּכְהֶיןָ עֵינָיו מֵרְאֹת וַיִּקְרָא אֶת־עֵשָׂו

34–35. By marrying two Hittite women, Esau proved his total unfitness to carry on the mission of Abraham. In a household run by two daughters of Ḥeth, the Abrahamite ideal was as good as dead and buried. We have seen earlier how Isaac and Rebekah considered it their duty to isolate themselves. And now, imagine the scene: While Isaac builds an altar and "proclaims in the Name of *God*," his own eldest son brings idolatry into the home of his parents. No wonder we are told that these wives were a "spiritual defiance" to Isaac and Rebekah.

CHAPTER XXVII

1. We follow the opinion of our Sages and do not consider it our task to act as apologists for great men and women, even as the Word of God itself never refrains from recording their errors and shortcomings. When Rebekah induced Jacob to deceive his father, the narrative states candidly that "Your brother came in deceit."

Rabbi Haninah (Baba Bathra 67) comments as follows on the events recorded in this chapter: "Whoever maintains that the Holy One, blessed be He, is lax in dispensing justice to His pious ones," that pious people are entitled to take liberties from time to time, "may his bowels be turned about (literally: torn out)." "God is long-suffering, but ultimately collects His due. Jacob caused Esau to break into a cry only once, and where was he punished for it? In Shushan the capital, as it is written (Esther 4:1): 'And he cried with an exceedingly loud and bitter cry' (Cf. Genesis 27:34)."

The Tanhuma states: "Three tears did Esau shed: One flowed from his right eye, one from his left, and the third he suppressed, and this one, the most bitter of them all, which he did not shed, has salted the bread of our exile with tears and made us taste the tears in full threefold measure."

On the other hand, if a calm, dispassionate study should force the conclusion that the events narrated in this chapter are not as unpleasant as they originally

seemed to be, we do not believe we would be obligated to suppress that conclusion merely in order not to appear as apologists. There still will remain enough which it will not be in our power to condone, especially not when measured by the standards of a nation which bears the honorary cognomen of יְשֻׁרוּן, meaning that it attains its objectives only by "straight" (יָשָׁר) means and that all crooked methods, no matter what their objective, must be repugnant to it.

If we attempt to understand the actions of the three principal characters in this domestic drama, then Jacob's actions are completely clear and transparent. From the very outset his mother appeals to his duty as a son to obey her orders unquestioningly (Verse 8). She does not expect that he will do it for the sake of selfish gain; indeed, she expects that as an אִישׁ תָּם he will revolt against doing such a thing. She therefore silences any objection he might have by exercising her maternal authority and citing a son's duty to obey his mother's commands. She is ready to assume full responsibility for any injustice or other negative consequences that may result from her plan. All he needs to do is to obey her. Consequently whatever Jacob did was done only in obedience to his mother's commands and the only blame which attaches to him is that he should have known that the moral law sets limits even to filial obedience: one must not practice deceit even if it is one's own mother who commands him to do so.

But what, in fact, was Rebekah's objective? Even the worst enemy of the Jews or of the Bible will want to find some reason, or, if you will, some sense, in her actions. Indeed, the more crafty such a one would like to make the Jewish matriarch appear, the less will he wish to make her seem an imbecile or a childishly stupid figure. Assuming that her intention had been nothing else but to turn the father's blessing onto the head of her beloved Jacob, what results could she conceivably have expected from this stratagem?

Regardless of the effects she might have ascribed to a father's blessing, the results inevitably would have been the very opposite of what she hoped for. Granted that said to him: "My son!" He said to him: בְּנוֹ הַגָּדֹל וַיֹּאמֶר אֵלָיו בְּנִי וַיֹּאמֶר אֵלָיו הִנֵּנִי:

the father's blessing would invoke God's own choicest blessings upon the head of the one who received it, how could Rebekah have believed that, even if she succeeded in duping the sightless, aged father, she would be able to deceive God with such a shoddy masquerade? How could she have believed that the blessing of Abraham, which God made conditional upon the practice of צְדָקָה וּמִשְׁפָּט [righteousness and justice], could be obtained from that same God by means of such trickery and deceit? Or, assuming that she had in mind some concrete advantage resulting from the paternal blessing, such as priority in matters of inheritance, should it not have been obvious to her that a blessing obtained through fraud would be null and void because it had been secured under false pretenses? It was, after all, inevitable that the deceit would be discovered. Rebekah must have known full well that even if she succeeded in carrying out this masquerade, it all would inevitably come to light as soon as Esau returned. Moreover, how clumsy was this whole act! Who but the most incredibly naive person could have been taken in by a couple of goatskins wrapped around the neck and hands? What could she possibly have hoped to achieve with all this play-acting?

The answer:

Her objective could have been precisely to put on an act! Indeed, *only if the inevitable discovery of her act had been part of Rebekah's calculations* can all her actions make any sense and appear as acts which, though they cannot be fully condoned, are understandable and, under the circumstances, even in some measure excusable.

By way of an introduction to these events we have read the account of how Esau, of his own free will, had struck a double blow at his great Abrahamite mission by marrying two Hittite women. If anything could have opened Isaac's eyes to his eldest son's utter unworthiness, this act of his certainly should have done so. Yet, we see Isaac calling his eldest son in order to bless him; that is, to appoint him as the future leader and ruler of the House of Abraham. What a "hunter with his mouth" must Esau have been, and how adept at disguising himself, if, despite his un-Abrahamite way of life, he succeeded in deceiving his father and capturing his heart!

From the particle נָא, "Lo! now, I am, after all, old," it is clear that Isaac had decided long ago to give such a blessing but that he had been kept from doing so. Perhaps Rebekah had been stalling for time, telling him over and over again; "Wait a while, there's still plenty of time. You are not all that old yet," etc., in the hope that, in the meantime, she would manage to bring about Isaac's disillusionment. But she had not succeeded in doing so. What, then, was she to do now? What

could have been her intention? Nothing except to demonstrate to him *ad hominem* that he was susceptible to deception, and how greatly he could be deceived! If even Jacob, an אִישׁ תָּם, [a "single-minded man"] could pose before him as a גִּבּוֹר צַיִד ["a mighty hunter"], how much easier would it be for Esau to pose as an אִישׁ תָּם. And in this plan—to bring about Isaac's disillusionment by this act of deception—Rebekah succeeded completely. As soon as Isaac realized that he had been tricked, he was seized with terror. As the Sages put it, he saw Gehenna opening wide before him. He saw how he had been deceived all his life. Immediately, the blindfold fell from his eyes; he composed himself quickly and, deliberately, of his own free will, he added to his blessing the words גַּם בָּרוּךְ יִהְיֶה ["He, too, shall be blessed" (Verse 33)].

Rabbi Joshua ben Levi, too, seems to have interpreted these events in this light, because he states (Genesis Rabbah ibid.): "Rebekah did not do this because she loved Jacob more than she loved Esau. She did it so that [Esau] should no longer be able to come and deceive his aged father."

A closer examination of the blessing which Isaac wanted to bestow upon Esau should help explain also the actions of Isaac. Esau himself had never expected that Isaac would want to bestow the full blessing upon him. For he immediately asks his father, "Have you not reserved a blessing for me?" Thus: If you had given me the blessing, you surely would have reserved one blessing for Jacob. Why not give that blessing to me now? Isaac accedes to this request, but by communicating to him the content of the blessing he bestowed upon Jacob, he demonstrates to Esau that this had been the only blessing appropriate for Esau. The one that had been reserved for Jacob was totally inappropriate for Esau.

Isaac's two sons represented two disparate elements in his home. Esau represented physical strength; Jacob, spiritual power. Isaac knew very well that both these tendencies would be needed if his future nation was to grow and prosper. Isaac also must have been aware of the prophecy that "the mighty one shall serve the lesser" (Chapter 25, Verse 23). But Isaac may have believed that the Abrahamite mission was destined to be carried on by Esau and Jacob in brotherly harmony, with the one complementing the other. For this reason he may have intended to give Esau a blessing of material content while reserving a private spiritual blessing for Jacob. But the blessing that had been reserved for Jacob would have been meaningless to Esau, who lacked the temperament and appreciation for this spiritual aspect of the House of Abraham. Rebekah, however, remembered from the home of Laban the impossibility of such a cleavage, and the misfortunes it

ב וַיֹּאמֶר הִנֵּה־נָא זָקַנְתִּי לֹא יָדַעְתִּי יוֹם מוֹתִי:
ג וְעַתָּה שָׂא־נָא כֵלֶיךָ תֶּלְיְךָ וְקַשְׁתֶּךָ וְצֵא הַשָּׂדֶה
וְצוּדָה לִּי צֵידָה (צַיִד קרי): ד וַעֲשֵׂה־לִי מַטְעַמִּים
כַּאֲשֶׁר אָהַבְתִּי וְהָבִיאָה לִּי וְאֹכֵלָה בַּעֲבוּר
תְּבָרֶכְךָ נַפְשִׁי בְּטֶרֶם אָמוּת: ה וְרִבְקָה שֹׁמַעַת
בְּדַבֵּר יִצְחָק אֶל־עֵשָׂו בְּנוֹ וַיֵּלֶךְ עֵשָׂו הַשָּׂדֶה
לָצוּד צַיִד לְהָבִיא: ו וְרִבְקָה אָמְרָה אֶל־יַעֲקֹב
בְּנָהּ לֵאמֹר הִנֵּה שָׁמַעְתִּי אֶת־אָבִיךָ מְדַבֵּר
אֶל־עֵשָׂו אָחִיךָ לֵאמֹר: ז הָבִיאָה לִּי צַיִד וַעֲשֵׂה־
לִי מַטְעַמִּים וְאֹכֵלָה וַאֲבָרֶכְכָה לִפְנֵי יְהֹוָה לִפְנֵי
מוֹתִי: ח וְעַתָּה בְנִי שְׁמַע בְּקֹלִי לַאֲשֶׁר אֲנִי מְצַוָּה
אֹתָךְ: ט לֶךְ־נָא אֶל־הַצֹּאן וְקַח־לִי מִשָּׁם שְׁנֵי
גְּדָיֵי עִזִּים טֹבִים וְאֶעֱשֶׂה אֹתָם מַטְעַמִּים לְאָבִיךָ
כַּאֲשֶׁר אָהֵב: י וְהֵבֵאתָ לְאָבִיךָ וְאָכָל בַּעֲבֻר אֲשֶׁר

"Here I am!" 2. He said, "Lo! now, I am, after all, old; I do not know the day of my death. 3. And now, please, take your implements, your dangler and your bow and go into the field and hunt some venison for me, 4. and prepare for me a tasty dish, such as I love, and bring it to me so that I may eat it, that my soul may bless you before I die." 5. But Rivkah listened when Yitzḥak spoke to his son Esav, and Esav went out into the field to hunt venison in order to bring it home. 6. And Rivkah had spoken to Yaakov, her son, as follows: "Lo! I have heard your father speak to your brother Esav as follows: 7. 'Please bring home for me some venison and prepare for me a tasty dish, that I may eat, so I will bless you before *God* before I die.' 8. And now, my son, hearken to my voice regarding what I command you. 9. Please go to the flock and fetch me from there two good kids of the goats so that I may make them a tasty dish for your father, as he loves it. 10. Then you will bring it to your father, that he may eat, that he may bless you before his death."

could bring. She knew from personal experience that even material things could prosper and bring true happiness only in a home pervaded by the spirit of Abraham and only through a hand guided by this spirit. She was right. She realized that any materialism without spiritual content is actually a curse and that Isaac's blessing could not be divided; it could be placed only upon the head of one of the sons. These considerations should make the actions of both parents appear understandable. Let us now turn to the details of the story.

2, 3 and 4. What could have been Isaac's motive in telling his son, whom he wanted to bless, "First prepare a nice dish for me"? . . .

. . . It was Isaac's wish to bless Esau in a manner appropriate to Esau's future vocation. He included this facet of Esau's individuality in his blessing because he hoped that Esau's natural proclivities someday would be employed successfully for moral purposes. Let him, for once, engage in the savage sport of hunting for a humane purpose. For it seems that going out to hunt in order to prepare a nourishing dish for his aged, feeble father was not a part of Esau's everyday pursuits. He derived pleasure from hunting for its own sake, from the sight of the steaming blood of his prey, from pitting his wits against the strength of the animals. But it was

not in Esau's character to engage in this sport for the purpose of providing refreshment for someone weak and ill. [So now, Isaac tells Esau:] "Please take the implements of your daily occupation, hunt some venison for me and then you, yourself, prepare tasty dishes for me. For this one time, use the implements of your savage lust for hunting in order to perform an act of human kindness to restore the strength of an old man. I want you to experience, for once, how good it feels to use one's own strength for the purpose of giving pleasure to another." This, too, was the reason why, when he gave his blessing to the son he took to be Esau, Isaac digressed from hunting to agriculture, to the "field blessed by God," to the preservation of the prosperity of the Jewish nation. The thought of such refreshment and of the blessing to be derived from this act of human kindness is expressed in the words "that my soul may bless you." Hence also Verse 5: This time Esau went hunting for the purpose of לְהָבִיא, of "bringing home" his prey.

7. The words לִפְנֵי ד׳ ["before *God*"] are a circumscription of נַפְשִׁי ["my soul"]: I want to bless you as one who is working before God; that is, as one who uses his occupation for doing good works.

11. And Yaakov said to his mother Rivkah: "Behold, Esav, my brother, is a hairy man and I am a smooth man; 12. perhaps my father will feel me and I will seem in his eyes like an impostor and I will bring a curse upon myself and not a blessing." 13. But his mother said to him: "Upon me be your curse, my son; only obey my voice and go, fetch [them] for me." 14. And he went and took and brought it to his mother: his mother prepared a tasty dish such as his father loved. 15. And Rivkah took the costly garments of Esav, her eldest son, which were with her in the house, and she put them on Yaakov, her younger son. 16. Before that, she had put the skins of the kids of the goats upon his hands and upon the smoothness of his neck, 17. and then she gave the tasty dish and the bread, which she had prepared, into the hand of Yaakov, her son. 18. So he came to his father and said: "My father!" He replied: "Here I am! Who are you, my son?" 19. And Yaakov said to his father: "I, Esav, your first-born, I have done as you told me; please arise, sit and please eat of my venison, so that your soul may bless me." 20. And Yitzḥak said to his son: "How is it that you have found [it] so quickly, my son?" He said: "Because *God*, your God, caused it to happen before me." 21. And Yitzḥak said to Yaakov: "Please come closer, so that I may feel you, my son, whether you are really my son Esav or not." 22. And Yaakov went up to his father Yitzḥak and the latter felt him and said: "The voice is the voice of Yaakov and the

יְבָרֶכְךָ֖ לִפְנֵ֥י מוֹתֽוֹ׃ יא וַיֹּ֣אמֶר יַעֲקֹ֔ב אֶל־רִבְקָ֖ה
אִמּ֑וֹ הֵ֚ן עֵשָׂ֣ו אָחִ֔י אִ֣ישׁ שָׂעִ֔ר וְאָנֹכִ֖י אִ֥ישׁ חָלָֽק׃
יב אוּלַ֤י יְמֻשֵּׁ֙נִי֙ אָבִ֔י וְהָיִ֥יתִי בְעֵינָ֖יו כִּמְתַעְתֵּ֑עַ
וְהֵבֵאתִ֥י עָלַ֛י קְלָלָ֖ה וְלֹ֥א בְרָכָֽה׃ יג וַתֹּ֤אמֶר לוֹ֙
אִמּ֔וֹ עָלַ֥י קִלְלָתְךָ֖ בְּנִ֑י אַ֛ךְ שְׁמַ֥ע בְּקֹלִ֖י וְלֵ֥ךְ קַֽח־לִֽי׃
יד וַיֵּ֙לֶךְ֙ וַיִּקַּ֔ח וַיָּבֵ֖א לְאִמּ֑וֹ וַתַּ֤עַשׂ אִמּוֹ֙ מַטְעַמִּ֔ים
כַּאֲשֶׁ֖ר אָהֵ֥ב אָבִֽיו׃ טו וַתִּקַּ֣ח רִ֠בְקָה אֶת־בִּגְדֵ֨י
עֵשָׂ֜ו בְּנָ֤הּ הַגָּדֹל֙ הַחֲמֻדֹ֔ת אֲשֶׁ֥ר אִתָּ֖הּ בַּבָּ֑יִת
וַתַּלְבֵּ֥שׁ אֶת־יַעֲקֹ֖ב בְּנָ֥הּ הַקָּטָֽן׃ טז וְאֵ֗ת עֹרֹת֙ גְּדָיֵ֣י
הָֽעִזִּ֔ים הִלְבִּ֖ישָׁה עַל־יָדָ֑יו וְעַ֖ל חֶלְקַ֥ת צַוָּארָֽיו׃
יז וַתִּתֵּ֧ן אֶת־הַמַּטְעַמִּ֛ים וְאֶת־הַלֶּ֖חֶם אֲשֶׁ֣ר
עָשָׂ֑תָה בְּיַ֖ד יַעֲקֹ֥ב בְּנָֽהּ׃ יח וַיָּבֹ֥א אֶל־אָבִ֖יו וַיֹּ֣אמֶר
אָבִ֑י וַיֹּ֣אמֶר הִנֶּ֔נִּי מִ֥י אַתָּ֖ה בְּנִֽי׃ יט וַיֹּ֨אמֶר יַעֲקֹ֜ב
אֶל־אָבִ֗יו אָנֹכִי֙ עֵשָׂ֣ו בְּכֹרֶ֔ךָ עָשִׂ֕יתִי כַּאֲשֶׁ֥ר דִּבַּ֖רְתָּ
אֵלָ֑י קֽוּם־נָ֣א שְׁבָ֗ה וְאָכְלָה֙ מִצֵּידִ֔י בַּעֲב֖וּר
תְּבָרֲכַ֥נִּי נַפְשֶֽׁךָ׃ כ וַיֹּ֤אמֶר יִצְחָק֙ אֶל־בְּנ֔וֹ מַה־זֶּ֛ה
מִהַ֥רְתָּ לִמְצֹ֖א בְּנִ֑י וַיֹּ֕אמֶר כִּ֥י הִקְרָ֛ה יְהוָ֥ה אֱלֹהֶ֖יךָ
לְפָנָֽי׃ כא וַיֹּ֤אמֶר יִצְחָק֙ אֶל־יַעֲקֹ֔ב גְּשָׁה־נָּ֣א
וַאֲמֻשְׁךָ֖ בְּנִ֑י הַאַתָּ֥ה זֶ֛ה בְּנִ֥י עֵשָׂ֖ו אִם־לֹֽא׃
כב וַיִּגַּ֧שׁ יַעֲקֹ֛ב אֶל־יִצְחָ֥ק אָבִ֖יו וַיְמֻשֵּׁ֑הוּ וַיֹּ֕אמֶר

11. In this verse, and in the passages immediately following, Rebekah is repeatedly described as אמו ["his mother"], in order to emphasize that she gave Jacob these orders because she was the mother, and that Jacob believed that it was his duty as her son to obey her commands.

12. **כִּמְתַעְתֵּעַ** ***[like an impostor]. Like*** an impostor, like one who seeks to lead another astray. The particle כ ["like"] explains everything. Jacob was not really an impostor; he did not want to deceive anyone. However, he is afraid that he will not be given a chance to explain to Isaac that he, Jacob, had done it only because he did not want to disobey his mother. He feared that his father would immediately curse him as an impostor. By thus telling Rebekah his misgivings, Jacob made it clear to her, though only in indirect terms and in a most respectful manner, how reprehensible the whole affair appeared to him and that he regarded it as detestable fraud.

15. ***which were with her in the house.*** These words provide a significant insight into Esau's married life. He did not entrust his most precious possessions to his wives [but left them with his mother].

hands are the hands of Esav." 23. He did not recognize him because his hands were hairy like the hands of his brother Esav, and so he blessed him. 24. He said: "Is it [indeed] you, my son Esav?" And he said: "I am." 25. He said: "Please bring it closer to me that I may eat of my son's venison, that my soul may bless you." He brought it closer; he ate. He brought him wine; he drank. 26. And his father Yitzḥak said to him: "Please come closer and kiss me, my son." 27. And he came closer to him and kissed him. And he smelled the smell of his clothes, and blessed him, and said: "Lo! the smell of my son is like the smell of a field which *God* has blessed. 28. So may God give you of the dew of heaven and of the fat places of the soil and an abundance of corn and new wine. 29. Peoples will serve you and nations will bow down to you. But you become a man [also] to your brothers, so that the sons of your mother may bow down to you. Then he who curses you will be cursed, and he who blesses you will be blessed." 30. It came to pass when Yitzḥak had finished blessing Yaakov and Yaakov had just gone out from the presence of his father Yitzḥak, that, his brother Esav came in from his hunting. 31. And he, too, prepared a tasty dish and brought it to his father. He said to his father: "Let my father arise and eat of his son's venison, that your soul may bless me." 32. And his father Yitzḥak said to him: "Who are you?" And he said: "I am your son, your first-born, Esav." 33. And a great terror seized Yitzḥak and he said: "Who, then, is the one who has already hunted venison and brought it to me, and I also ate of everything before you came, and I blessed him? He, too, shall be blessed." 34. When Esav heard the words of his father he cried out with an exceedingly loud and bitter cry, and then he said to his father: "Bless me also, O my father!" 35. He said: "Your brother has come with deceit and has taken away your blessing." 36. And he said: "Does he call himself Yaakov because he has already gone behind my back twice? He has taken away my birthright and now he has taken away my blessing as well!" He said: "Have you not reserved a blessing for me?"

הַקֹּל֙ ק֣וֹל יַעֲקֹ֔ב וְהַיָּדַ֖יִם יְדֵ֥י עֵשָֽׂו: כג וְלֹ֣א הִכִּיר֗וֹ כִּֽי־הָי֣וּ יָדָ֗יו כִּידֵ֛י עֵשָׂ֥ו אָחִ֖יו שְׂעִרֹ֑ת וַֽיְבָרְכֵֽהוּ: כד וַיֹּ֕אמֶר אַתָּ֥ה זֶ֖ה בְּנִ֣י עֵשָׂ֑ו וַיֹּ֖אמֶר אָֽנִי: כה וַיֹּ֗אמֶר הַגִּ֤שָׁה לִּי֙ וְאֹֽכְלָה֙ מִצֵּ֣יד בְּנִ֔י לְמַ֖עַן תְּבָֽרֶכְךָ֣ נַפְשִׁ֑י וַיַּגֶּשׁ־לוֹ֙ וַיֹּאכַ֔ל וַיָּ֧בֵא ל֦וֹ יַ֖יִן וַיֵּֽשְׁתְּ: כו וַיֹּ֥אמֶר אֵלָ֖יו יִצְחָ֣ק אָבִ֑יו גְּשָׁה־נָּ֥א וּשְׁקָה־לִּ֖י בְּנִֽי: כז וַיִּגַּשׁ֙ וַיִּשַּׁק־ל֔וֹ וַיָּ֛רַח אֶת־רֵ֥יחַ בְּגָדָ֖יו וַֽיְבָרְכֵ֑הוּ וַיֹּ֗אמֶר רְאֵה֙ רֵ֣יחַ בְּנִ֔י כְּרֵ֣יחַ שָׂדֶ֔ה אֲשֶׁ֥ר בֵּֽרְכ֖וֹ יְהֹוָֽה: ששי כח וְיִֽתֶּן־לְךָ֙ הָֽאֱלֹהִ֔ים מִטַּל֙ הַשָּׁמַ֔יִם וּמִשְׁמַנֵּ֖י הָאָ֑רֶץ וְרֹ֥ב דָּגָ֖ן וְתִירֹֽשׁ: כט יַֽעַבְד֣וּךָ עַמִּ֗ים וְיִשְׁתַּֽחֲו֤וּ (וישתחו קרי) לְךָ֙ לְאֻמִּ֔ים הֱוֵ֤ה גְבִיר֙ לְאַחֶ֔יךָ וְיִשְׁתַּֽחֲו֥וּ לְךָ֖ בְּנֵ֣י אִמֶּ֑ךָ אֹֽרְרֶ֣יךָ אָר֔וּר וּֽמְבָרֲכֶ֖יךָ בָּרֽוּךְ: ל וַיְהִ֗י כַּֽאֲשֶׁ֨ר כִּלָּ֤ה יִצְחָק֙ לְבָרֵ֣ךְ אֶֽת־יַעֲקֹ֔ב וַיְהִ֗י אַ֣ךְ יָצֹ֤א יָצָא֙ יַעֲקֹ֔ב מֵאֵ֥ת פְּנֵ֖י יִצְחָ֣ק אָבִ֑יו וְעֵשָׂ֣ו אָחִ֔יו בָּ֖א מִצֵּידֽוֹ: לא וַיַּ֤עַשׂ גַּם־הוּא֙ מַטְעַמִּ֔ים וַיָּבֵ֖א לְאָבִ֑יו וַיֹּ֣אמֶר לְאָבִ֗יו יָקֻ֤ם אָבִי֙ וְיֹאכַל֙ מִצֵּ֣יד בְּנ֔וֹ בַּֽעֲבֻ֖ר תְּבָֽרֲכַ֥נִּי נַפְשֶֽׁךָ: לב וַיֹּ֥אמֶר ל֛וֹ יִצְחָ֥ק אָבִ֖יו מִי־אָ֑תָּה וַיֹּ֕אמֶר אֲנִ֛י בִּנְךָ֥ בְכֹֽרְךָ֖ עֵשָֽׂו: לג וַיֶּֽחֱרַ֨ד יִצְחָ֣ק חֲרָדָה֮ גְּדֹלָ֣ה עַד־מְאֹד֒ וַיֹּ֡אמֶר מִֽי־אֵפ֡וֹא ה֣וּא הַצָּֽד־צַ֩יִד֩ וַיָּ֨בֵא לִ֜י וָֽאֹכַ֥ל מִכֹּ֛ל בְּטֶ֥רֶם תָּב֖וֹא וָֽאֲבָֽרֲכֵ֑הוּ גַּם־בָּר֖וּךְ יִֽהְיֶֽה: לד כִּשְׁמֹ֤עַ עֵשָׂו֙ אֶת־דִּבְרֵ֣י אָבִ֔יו וַיִּצְעַ֣ק צְעָקָ֔ה גְּדֹלָ֥ה וּמָרָ֖ה עַד־מְאֹ֑ד וַיֹּ֣אמֶר לְאָבִ֔יו בָּֽרֲכֵ֥נִי גַם־אָ֖נִי אָבִֽי: לה וַיֹּ֕אמֶר בָּ֥א אָחִ֖יךָ בְּמִרְמָ֑ה וַיִּקַּ֖ח בִּרְכָתֶֽךָ: לו וַיֹּ֡אמֶר הֲכִי֩ קָרָ֨א שְׁמ֜וֹ יַֽעֲקֹ֗ב וַֽיַּעְקְבֵ֨נִי֙ זֶ֣ה פַֽעֲמַ֔יִם אֶת־בְּכֹֽרָתִ֣י לָקָ֔ח וְהִנֵּ֥ה עַתָּ֖ה לָקַ֣ח בִּרְכָתִ֑י וַיֹּאמַ֕ר הֲלֹֽא־אָצַ֥לְתָּ לִּ֖י

37. And Yitzḥak replied and said to Esav: "See, I have made him a master to you and all his brothers have I given to him as servants, and I have sustained him with corn and new wine. And as for you—what shall I do for you, my son?" 38. And Esav said to his father: "Is this, then, the only blessing you have? Bless me, too, O my father!" And Esav lifted up his voice and wept. 39. And his father Yitzḥak answered and said to him: "Lo! the fat places of the earth will be your dwelling place, and of the dew of heaven from above; 40. you will live upon your sword and you will serve your brother; only when you will humble yourself will you loosen his yoke from your neck." 41. And Esav hated Yaakov because of the blessing with which his father had blessed him and Esav said in his heart: "Let the days of mourning for my father draw near and then I will kill my brother Yaakov." 42. The words of her eldest son Esav were told to Rivkah, and she sent and had her younger son Yaakov called and said to him: "Look, your brother Esav

בְּרָכָה: לז וַיַּעַן יִצְחָק וַיֹּאמֶר לְעֵשָׂו הֵן גְּבִיר
שַׂמְתִּיו לָךְ וְאֶת־כָּל־אֶחָיו נָתַתִּי לוֹ לַעֲבָדִים וְדָגָן
וְתִירֹשׁ סְמַכְתִּיו וּלְכָה אֵפוֹא מָה אֶעֱשֶׂה בְּנִי:
לח וַיֹּאמֶר עֵשָׂו אֶל־אָבִיו הַבְרָכָה אַחַת הִוא־לְךָ
אָבִי בָּרְכֵנִי גַם־אָנִי אָבִי וַיִּשָּׂא עֵשָׂו קֹלוֹ וַיֵּבְךְּ:
לט וַיַּעַן יִצְחָק אָבִיו וַיֹּאמֶר אֵלָיו הִנֵּה מִשְׁמַנֵּי
הָאָרֶץ יִהְיֶה מוֹשָׁבֶךָ וּמִטַּל הַשָּׁמַיִם מֵעָל:
מ וְעַל־חַרְבְּךָ תִחְיֶה וְאֶת־אָחִיךָ תַּעֲבֹד וְהָיָה
כַּאֲשֶׁר תָּרִיד וּפָרַקְתָּ עֻלּוֹ מֵעַל צַוָּארֶךָ:
מא וַיִּשְׂטֹם עֵשָׂו אֶת־יַעֲקֹב עַל־הַבְּרָכָה אֲשֶׁר
בֵּרְכוֹ אָבִיו וַיֹּאמֶר עֵשָׂו בְּלִבּוֹ יִקְרְבוּ יְמֵי אֵבֶל
אָבִי וְאַהַרְגָה אֶת־יַעֲקֹב אָחִי: מב וַיֻּגַּד לְרִבְקָה
אֶת־דִּבְרֵי עֵשָׂו בְּנָהּ הַגָּדֹל וַתִּשְׁלַח וַתִּקְרָא
לְיַעֲקֹב בְּנָהּ הַקָּטָן וַתֹּאמֶר אֵלָיו הִנֵּה עֵשָׂו אָחִיךָ

37. The words, "But you become a man [also] to your brothers" [Verse 29], which Isaac had dared utter only as a challenge when he thought that he was speaking to Esau, he now pronounces as a certainty with regard to Jacob. That Jacob will assume spiritual leadership was self-evident. And now that Isaac's eyes had been opened he awarded to Jacob—fully aware of what he was doing—also the material foundation [for leadership], as expressed in his wish "He, too, shall be blessed." For it had become clear to Isaac that all the members of the Abrahamite nation—soldiers, merchants, and so forth—had to be imbued in equal measure with the Abrahamite spirit. As a consequence, he saw that there no longer was a place for Esau in the House of Abraham.

38. [Esau wants to know:] Are there no blessings possible outside the House of Abraham?

39 and 40. Isaac does not tell Esau now, "So may God give you. . . ." [Instead, he tells him:] "You will achieve earthly wealth not under the express Providence and guidance of God but only to the extent that it lies in heaven and earth, that is, in the natural order of things. Your sword will be the creator of your destiny. You will become 'the mightier one.' You will conquer the world, but only to place all this conquered world at Jacob's feet in the end. Rome will conquer the world, only—after all its strayings through time—to place it at the feet of the triumphant ideal of Jacob-Israel. As long as you will be the ruler, as long as you will regard and exploit your every material conquest only as a stepping stone to further conquests, you will, in fact, be working only for your brother. As long as you will be רַב ['the mighty one'], רַב יַעֲבֹד צָעִיר ['the mighty one shall serve the lesser']. Only when you will 'come down' of your own free will, when you will acknowledge, of your own free will, the genius of your brother and subordinate yourself to him and to it, will you be able to emancipate yourself and stand side by side with him, on equal terms, as his brother. . . ."

42. The words "her eldest son Esav" and "her younger son Yaakov" are certainly not stressed without reason; the same applies to the words "brother of Rivkah, the mother of Yaakov and Esav" at the end of the story [Chapter 28, Verse 5]. After all these happenings, Esau was still the elder, Jacob was still the younger, and Rebekah was just as much the mother of Esau as she was of Jacob. All this fully expresses the pure and noble attitude of Rebekah and Jacob and corroborates our interpretation of this story.

If a person of base character has wronged another, he will seek all sorts of pretexts and excuses to justify his comforts himself to kill you.   43. And now, my son, hearken to my voice and arise, and flee to my brother Laban in Ḥaran. 44. You shall stay with him for some time, until the heat of your brother's wrath has subsided;   45. until your brother's anger has turned away from you, and he has forgotten what you did to him. Then I will send and have you fetched from there. For why should I be bereft of both of you in one day?"   46. And Rivkah said to Yitzḥak: "I am sick of my life because of the daughters of Ḥeth. If Yaakov takes a wife from among the daughters of Ḥeth like these, from the daughters of the land, of what use is life to me?"

XXVIII

1. And Yitzḥak called Yaakov and blessed him. He commanded him and said to him: "You shall not take a wife of the daughters of Canaan.   2. Arise, go to Paddan-Aram, to the house of Bethuel, the father of your mother, and take yourself from there a wife of the daughters of Laban, your mother's brother.   3. And God, the all-sufficing, will bless you and make you

מִתְנַחֵם לְךָ לְהָרְגֶךָ: מג וְעַתָּה בְנִי שְׁמַע בְּקֹלִי וְקוּם בְּרַח־לְךָ אֶל־לָבָן אָחִי חָרָנָה: מד וְיָשַׁבְתָּ עִמּוֹ יָמִים אֲחָדִים עַד אֲשֶׁר־תָּשׁוּב חֲמַת אָחִיךָ: מה עַד־שׁוּב אַף־אָחִיךָ מִמְּךָ וְשָׁכַח אֵת אֲשֶׁר־ עָשִׂיתָ לּוֹ וְשָׁלַחְתִּי וּלְקַחְתִּיךָ מִשָּׁם לָמָה אֶשְׁכַּל גַּם־שְׁנֵיכֶם יוֹם אֶחָד: מו וַתֹּאמֶר רִבְקָה אֶל־ יִצְחָק קַצְתִּי (ק׳ זעירא) בְחַיַּי מִפְּנֵי בְּנוֹת חֵת אִם־ לֹקֵחַ יַעֲקֹב אִשָּׁה מִבְּנוֹת־חֵת כָּאֵלֶּה מִבְּנוֹת הָאָרֶץ לָמָּה לִּי חַיִּים: כח א וַיִּקְרָא יִצְחָק אֶל־ יַעֲקֹב וַיְבָרֶךְ אֹתוֹ וַיְצַוֵּהוּ וַיֹּאמֶר לוֹ לֹא־תִקַּח אִשָּׁה מִבְּנוֹת כְּנָעַן: ב קוּם לֵךְ פַּדֶּנָה אֲרָם בֵּיתָה בְתוּאֵל אֲבִי אִמֶּךָ וְקַח־לְךָ מִשָּׁם אִשָּׁה מִבְּנוֹת לָבָן אֲחִי אִמֶּךָ: ג וְאֵל שַׁדַּי יְבָרֵךְ אֹתְךָ וְיַפְרְךָ

---

action. After they have perpetrated an injustice, ignoble souls become even more ruthless than before. But what of Rebekah and Jacob? Rebekah finds it only natural that, after what has been done to him, Esau might well be more than merely displeased. After all, Esau could never be expected to understand her motivations, much less forgive them. As for Jacob, did he ever in any manner exploit the blessing or his birthright? Never. In fact, we see Jacob definitely at a disadvantage. Jacob and Esau were twin brothers. Esau was already married when he was forty; he had brought into the house two daughters-in-law (to whom he later added a third), and he has taken a share in his father's establishment and household. Jacob, on the other hand, must leave his father's house in abject poverty, without a penny to his name, to hire himself out as a servant and to attain family status by hard labor.

It has often been pointed out as odd that Isaac, who, after all, thanks to his inheritance from Abraham and to the good fortune he attained by dint of his own efforts, had become a man of more than ordinary wealth, should have allowed his son to leave home with no possessions whatsoever except for the staff in his hand. But this state of affairs had its roots in the motives

which underlay the events related here. If, through Rebekah's instigation, Jacob had received the blessing and the birthright, it had to be made very clear that neither Jacob nor Rebekah had been guided by considerations of material advantage. After Jacob's departure, Esau should not be able to report so much as one pin missing. So this is, in fact, the most cogent testimonial to the noblemindedness of both Rebekah and Jacob. The words "the mother of Yaakov and Esav" are Rebekah's epitaph, as it were, for this is the last time she appears as an active character in the Biblical narrative. In everything she did, until the end of her life, she was the mother of both Jacob and Esau, and she always behaved as a mother to both of them.

46. Had Rebekah been an ordinary woman, surely nothing would have pleased her more than this opportunity to disclose to her husband Esau's plan to murder Jacob. In this way she could have shown to Isaac how right she had been all along, that Esau wanted to become a second Cain, and so forth. But she does not do this. Instead, she makes Jacob's journey to Paddan-Aram appear quite natural and justifiable.

fruitful and multiply you, so that you will be a gathering of nations. 4. He will give you the blessing of Abraham, to you and to your seed with you, that you may inherit the land of your alienhood which God gave to Abraham." 5. And so Yitzḥak sent away Yaakov, and he went to Paddan-Aram, to Laban, the son of Bethuel the Aramite, the brother of Rivkah, the mother of Yaakov and Esav. 6. And when Esav saw that Yitzḥak had blessed Yaakov and had sent him to Paddan-Aram to take a wife from them —that, in blessing him, he had commanded him: "You shall not take a wife of the daughters of Canaan," 7. and [that] Yaakov obeyed his father and his mother and went to Paddan-Aram; 8. then Esav saw that the daughters of Canaan were displeasing in the eyes of his father Yitzḥak. 9. And Esav went to Yishmael, and took Maḥalath, the daughter of Yishmael, the son of Abraham, sister of Nebaioth, [in addition] to his wives as his wife.

וְיַרְבֶּךָ וְהָיִיתָ לִקְהַל עַמִּים׃ ד וְיִתֶּן־לְךָ אֶת־
בִּרְכַּת אַבְרָהָם לְךָ וּלְזַרְעֲךָ אִתָּךְ לְרִשְׁתְּךָ
אֶת־אֶרֶץ מְגֻרֶיךָ אֲשֶׁר־נָתַן אֱלֹהִים לְאַבְרָהָם׃
שביעי ה וַיִּשְׁלַח יִצְחָק אֶת־יַעֲקֹב וַיֵּלֶךְ פַּדֶּנָה אֲרָם
אֶל־לָבָן בֶּן־בְּתוּאֵל הָאֲרַמִּי אֲחִי רִבְקָה אֵם
יַעֲקֹב וְעֵשָׂו׃ ו וַיַּרְא עֵשָׂו כִּי־בֵרַךְ יִצְחָק אֶת־
יַעֲקֹב וְשִׁלַּח אֹתוֹ פַּדֶּנָה אֲרָם לָקַחַת־לוֹ מִשָּׁם
אִשָּׁה בְּבָרְכוֹ אֹתוֹ וַיְצַו עָלָיו לֵאמֹר לֹא־תִקַּח
אִשָּׁה מִבְּנוֹת כְּנָעַן׃ מפטיר ז וַיִּשְׁמַע יַעֲקֹב אֶל־
אָבִיו וְאֶל־אִמּוֹ וַיֵּלֶךְ פַּדֶּנָה אֲרָם׃ ח וַיַּרְא עֵשָׂו כִּי
רָעוֹת בְּנוֹת כְּנָעַן בְּעֵינֵי יִצְחָק אָבִיו׃ ט וַיֵּלֶךְ
עֵשָׂו אֶל־יִשְׁמָעֵאל וַיִּקַּח אֶת־מָחֲלַת | בַּת־
יִשְׁמָעֵאל בֶּן־אַבְרָהָם אֲחוֹת נְבָיוֹת עַל־נָשָׁיו לוֹ
לְאִשָּׁה׃ ס

CHAPTER XXVIII

4. . . . If we compare the content of this blessing which Isaac bestowed upon Jacob [knowing now that this was indeed Jacob, not Esau], with the blessing which he had intended for Esau and which contains not so much as one allusion to the Abrahamite mission, our interpretation of this blessing would appear justified. But the whole story is epitomized in Verses 6 ff.: When Esau saw that Isaac had blessed Jacob and had sent him to Paddan-Aram, to take a wife from among the maidens there—only after Esau had seen all these things did it occur to him that his father might not be pleased with the Canaanite wives he had taken. Until this point Esau had no idea of the grief and heartache his wives had caused his parents. But now, when he first gets some idea of what is going on, what does he do? Does he send his Canaanite wives away? Not at all. We read that he took yet another [heathen] wife, in addition to the pagan wives he already had. That is how little feeling and understanding Esau had for what was really needed in the House of Abraham, thereby confirming Rebekah's judgment regarding his unfitness to take over as leader and spokesman of this family.

The Haftarah for this Sidra may be found on page 831.

ויצא

VAYETZE

10. So Yaakov went out from Beer Sheva and went toward Ḥaran. 11. And he encountered° the place and stayed there overnight because the sun had set; he took from the stones of the place, arranged them around his head and slept in this place. 12. He dreamt, and behold! a ladder, set up toward the earth, and the top of it reached to heaven, and behold! angels of God ascending and descending against

י וַיֵּצֵא יַעֲקֹב מִבְּאֵר שָׁבַע וַיֵּלֶךְ חָרָנָה׃ יא וַיִּפְגַּע
בַּמָּקוֹם וַיָּלֶן שָׁם כִּי־בָא הַשֶּׁמֶשׁ וַיִּקַּח מֵאַבְנֵי
הַמָּקוֹם וַיָּשֶׂם מְרַאֲשֹׁתָיו וַיִּשְׁכַּב בַּמָּקוֹם הַהוּא׃
יב וַיַּחֲלֹם וְהִנֵּה סֻלָּם מֻצָּב אַרְצָה וְרֹאשׁוֹ מַגִּיעַ
הַשָּׁמָיְמָה וְהִנֵּה מַלְאֲכֵי אֱלֹהִים עֹלִים וְיֹרְדִים

°*Note to the English translation*: Hirsch's original German version renders the text as "*Da traf er den Ort.*" In his commentary to this verse (which is not included in this excerpted edition) Hirsch explains, in the passive mood, "*da ward er von dem Ort betroffen,*" literally, that Jacob was "struck" or "affected" by the place. The German verbs *traf* and *betroffen* (pres: *betreffen*) both derive from *treffen*, which can denote "meeting," "encountering," "striking," "hitting" or "affecting." In order to convey Hirsch's meaning while retaining the active verb form, it was decided to render וַיִּפְגַּע into English as "encountered." [G.H.]

10. . . . If Abraham represents the root of the Jewish people and Isaac the continuation toward the trunk, then Jacob represents the true trunk. . . . For Jacob is the one who will hand to the future nation its name and destiny. We are not called "the people of Abraham" but "Israel." Thus we see Jacob, like Abraham, carrying out his own act of לֶךְ לְךָ; we see him, our next ancestor, toward whom the entire course of our history, from Abraham to Isaac, has been directed, also "going forth" in a state of isolation. But his departure takes place under completely different circumstances than that of Abraham. True, Abraham, too, left his home to go into isolation, but he did so as a householder, with his wife and retinue, with kinsmen and with wealth. In contrast, we see Jacob, impelled by circumstances, leaving home of his own accord, taking nothing at all with him. . . .

Jacob goes forth in order to establish a Jewish home, and to this end he takes with him nothing except his own person, the qualities inherent in his personality. This fact is introduced at this point in the narrative, for everything that follows is concerned solely with the establishment of that home. For Jacob was the first to declare that God must be sought, above all, within the home. He was the first to articulate the lofty concept, "the house of God," which simply means that the place within which the souls of men grow and flourish, and to which in turn man brings all that he has accomplished and transforms it into life-building activity, is the greatest and nearest place where God may be found revealed.

° ° °

12. . . . סֻלָּם, a ladder, is shown to him; i.e., it was shown to him that there was a link of communications from earth to heaven. This ladder was "set up" there; it had not come there by chance. It had been set up by a higher power. Moreover, it was set up "toward the earth"; this means that the Power and the Will which set it up are not on earth but above. The ladder was lowered from above and set down on the earth.

וְרֹאשׁוֹ מַגִּיעַ הַשָּׁמָיְמָה ***[and the top of it reached to heaven].*** Its purpose, however, is not merely to descend from heaven to earth, but to ascend from earth toward heaven. This is the first of three sets of ideas which are shown to Jacob. First, he is shown that the destiny of all of life on earth, and thus also the life of man, including his own, is not to be sought below—or, in the case of Jacob, in a journey from Beer Sheva to Haran — but should be sought above, where it has been set. Hence, all things and creatures on earth have been summoned from above to work themselves up toward a lofty, heaven-set goal. . . .

וְהִנֵּה ***[and behold].*** This word introduces a second set of ideas. . . . He sees מַלְאֲכֵי אֱלֹקִ׳, angels of God, messengers of God. . . . These messengers of God ascend the ladder in order to obtain, above, the image of what, ideally, this man should be like. They then descend and set this ideal image against the character of the man as he is in reality, so that they can "stand over against him" as a friend or as a foe, depending on how his actual character compares with the [Divinely-set] ideal. . . .

him.	13. And behold! *God* stood beside
him and said: "I am *God,* the God of your
father Abraham and the God of Yitzḥak;
the land on which you are sleeping, to you
will I give it, and to your seed.	14. And
your seed will be as the dust of the earth and
you will spread out toward the west and the
east, toward the north and the south, and
through you will all the families on earth be
blessed, and through your seed.	15. And
behold, I am with you, and I will guard you
wherever you go and I will bring you back
to this soil, for I will not leave you until I
have accomplished that which I have
promised you."	16. And Yaakov awoke
from his sleep and said: "Truly *God* is in this
place! And I did not know it!"	17. And
he was afraid and said: "How awe-inspiring
is this place! This is none other than the
house of God! And this is a gate to heaven!"
18. Yaakov rose up early in the morning
and took the stone which he had placed at
his head and set it up as a memorial stone,
and poured oil upon the top of it,	19. and
he called the name of the place Beth El, but
formerly the name of the city was
Luz.	20. And Yaakov made a vow as

בּוֹ: יג וְהִנֵּה יְהֹוָה נִצָּב עָלָיו וַיֹּאמַר אֲנִי יְהֹוָה
אֱלֹהֵי אַבְרָהָם אָבִיךָ וֵאלֹהֵי יִצְחָק הָאָרֶץ אֲשֶׁר
אַתָּה שֹׁכֵב עָלֶיהָ לְךָ אֶתְּנֶנָּה וּלְזַרְעֶךָ: יד וְהָיָה
זַרְעֲךָ כַּעֲפַר הָאָרֶץ וּפָרַצְתָּ יָמָּה וָקֵדְמָה וְצָפֹנָה
וָנֶגְבָּה וְנִבְרְכוּ בְךָ כָּל־מִשְׁפְּחֹת הָאֲדָמָה וּבְזַרְעֶךָ:
טו וְהִנֵּה אָנֹכִי עִמָּךְ וּשְׁמַרְתִּיךָ בְּכֹל אֲשֶׁר־תֵּלֵךְ
וַהֲשִׁבֹתִיךָ אֶל־הָאֲדָמָה הַזֹּאת כִּי לֹא אֶעֱזָבְךָ עַד
אֲשֶׁר אִם־עָשִׂיתִי אֵת אֲשֶׁר־דִּבַּרְתִּי לָךְ:
טז וַיִּיקַץ יַעֲקֹב מִשְּׁנָתוֹ וַיֹּאמֶר אָכֵן יֵשׁ יְהֹוָה
בַּמָּקוֹם הַזֶּה וְאָנֹכִי לֹא יָדָעְתִּי: יז וַיִּירָא וַיֹּאמַר
מַה־נּוֹרָא הַמָּקוֹם הַזֶּה אֵין זֶה כִּי אִם־בֵּית
אֱלֹהִים וְזֶה שַׁעַר הַשָּׁמָיִם: יח וַיַּשְׁכֵּם יַעֲקֹב
בַּבֹּקֶר וַיִּקַּח אֶת־הָאֶבֶן אֲשֶׁר־שָׂם מְרַאֲשֹׁתָיו
וַיָּשֶׂם אֹתָהּ מַצֵּבָה וַיִּצֹק שֶׁמֶן עַל־רֹאשָׁהּ:
יט וַיִּקְרָא אֶת־שֵׁם־הַמָּקוֹם הַהוּא בֵּית־אֵל
וְאוּלָם לוּז שֵׁם־הָעִיר לָרִאשֹׁנָה: כ וַיִּדַּר יַעֲקֹב

---

13. וְהִנֵּה: *[And behold!].* This word introduces the
third set of ideas: ד' נִצָּב עָלָיו ["God stood beside
him"]. . . . ד' stands beside him. It is ה', this Divine love
which is revealed primarily in the education of man, a
love which has in mind not only the past and the
present but which also looks and works toward the
future, a love which sees each man in terms of what he
will be in the future and if it notes within him a seed of
purity, will seek to preserve this seed and to develop it.

○	○	○

14. בְּךָ — וּבְזַרְעֶךָ (cf. לְךָ וּלְזַרְעֶךָ in the preceding verse):
"It is through you, *and* through your seed, that all the
families on earth will be blessed." . . . This is the blessing which is to come to the world through Jacob as the
father of a family and through the nation which is to
descend from him. Jacob shows us the first Jewish home
and teaches us how one can build and live a family life,
even without inherited wealth, but upheld by the blessing and the dignity of מְלָאכָה,[25] of labor, with all its

troubles, worries and cares, and still ד' נִצָּב עָלָיו ["*God*
stood beside him"], not have to do without God in one's
life. Thus: "How to live, as a family and as a nation,
upheld solely by the grace of God and in accordance
with God's will—this is what mankind is to learn from
you and from your seed."

16. וַיֹּאמֶר *[and said].* "Here, then, is God. . . . So
one need not go to heaven in search of God. Wherever a
blameless man lays down his head, there is God." This
is Jacob's first thought. And then he adds: "And to
think that I did not know this until now! I did not know
that the Glory of God seeks its dwelling place among
men here below."

20. *and will keep me.* . . . Who can count the men
who were morally pure before they "set out upon the
path to earning their daily bread and nourishment" but
who subsequently, for the sake of making a living and
attaining a position in society, denied God, sacrificed
morality and failed to consider their neighbor, not even
when it came to that most precious jewel, his personal
honor, etc. Not without cause do our Sages point out
that this "path" is beset with [temptation to commit
such sins as] evil gossip, murder, sexual immorality and

[25]*Note to the English translation:* The reference is to מַלְאָכִים
(cf. Verse 12), the "messengers" who perform the "work" of
God on earth. [G.H.]

follows: "If God will be with me and will keep me on this path upon which I am going, and will give me bread to eat and clothing to put on,   21. and I will return in peace to the house of my father: then *God* shall be God to me.   22. And this stone, which I have set as a memorial stone, shall be a house of God and all that Thou wilt give me I will tithe to Thee repeatedly."

XXIX

1. And Yaakov lifted up his feet and went to the land of the sons of the East.   2. And he looked, and behold! a well in the field, and behold! three flocks of sheep lying there by it. For out of this well they would water the flocks, and the rock which lay upon the mouth of the well was large,   3. so that all the flocks had to gather there first in order to roll away the rock from the mouth of the well and to water the sheep. And then they put the rock back into its place.   4. And Yaakov said to them: "My brothers, from where are you?" And they said: "We are from Ḥaran."   5. And he said to them: "Do you know Laban, the son of Naḥor?" And they said: "We know him."   6. And he said to them: "Are things going well with him?" And they said: "[They are going] well, and lo! his daughter Raḥel is coming with the sheep."   7. And he said: "Lo! it is still high day. It is not yet time that the property° should be gathed in. Water the sheep and go and let [them] feed."

°*Note to the English translation:* This is the literal rendering of מִקְנֶה. Standard versions render מִקְנֶה as "cattle." [G.H.]

נֶדֶר לֵאמֹר אִם־יִהְיֶה אֱלֹהִים עִמָּדִי וּשְׁמָרַנִי
בַּדֶּרֶךְ הַזֶּה אֲשֶׁר אָנֹכִי הוֹלֵךְ וְנָתַן־לִי לֶחֶם לֶאֱכֹל
וּבֶגֶד לִלְבֹּשׁ: כא וְשַׁבְתִּי בְשָׁלוֹם אֶל־בֵּית אָבִי
וְהָיָה יְהֹוָה לִי לֵאלֹהִים: כב וְהָאֶבֶן הַזֹּאת אֲשֶׁר־
שַׂמְתִּי מַצֵּבָה יִהְיֶה בֵּית אֱלֹהִים וְכֹל אֲשֶׁר תִּתֶּן־
לִי עַשֵּׂר אֲעַשְּׂרֶנּוּ לָךְ: שני כט א וַיִּשָּׂא יַעֲקֹב
רַגְלָיו וַיֵּלֶךְ אַרְצָה בְנֵי־קֶדֶם: ב וַיַּרְא וְהִנֵּה בְאֵר
בַּשָּׂדֶה וְהִנֵּה־שָׁם שְׁלֹשָׁה עֶדְרֵי־צֹאן רֹבְצִים
עָלֶיהָ כִּי מִן־הַבְּאֵר הַהִוא יַשְׁקוּ הָעֲדָרִים וְהָאֶבֶן
גְּדֹלָה עַל־פִּי הַבְּאֵר: ג וְנֶאֶסְפוּ־שָׁמָּה כָל־
הָעֲדָרִים וְגָלֲלוּ אֶת־הָאֶבֶן מֵעַל פִּי הַבְּאֵר וְהִשְׁקוּ
אֶת־הַצֹּאן וְהֵשִׁיבוּ אֶת־הָאֶבֶן עַל־פִּי הַבְּאֵר
לִמְקֹמָהּ: ד וַיֹּאמֶר לָהֶם יַעֲקֹב אַחַי מֵאַיִן אַתֶּם
וַיֹּאמְרוּ מֵחָרָן אֲנָחְנוּ: ה וַיֹּאמֶר לָהֶם הַיְדַעְתֶּם
אֶת־לָבָן בֶּן־נָחוֹר וַיֹּאמְרוּ יָדָעְנוּ: ו וַיֹּאמֶר לָהֶם
הֲשָׁלוֹם לוֹ וַיֹּאמְרוּ שָׁלוֹם וְהִנֵּה רָחֵל בִּתּוֹ בָּאָה
עִם־הַצֹּאן: ז וַיֹּאמֶר הֵן עוֹד הַיּוֹם גָּדוֹל לֹא־עֵת
הֵאָסֵף הַמִּקְנֶה הַשְׁקוּ הַצֹּאן וּלְכוּ רְעוּ:

idolatry. Jacob, who until this time has been a יוֹשֵׁב אֹהָלִים [a dweller in tents] but has now gone out into the world to seek a wife and sustenance for his future wife and family, has become so deeply aware of these dangers that, before all else, he prays to God to guard his character so that he will not lose any of his spiritual and moral blamelessness.

21. Thus, blamelessness is the first thing that the first Jew wished for himself as he went forth to set up his home. Only thereafter did he say, "and will give me . . ."; i.e., "me," implying independent sustenance, food and clothing in order to appear respectable in society (sustenance and social position). Then the third wish, which lives, and should live, within the breast of

every Jew: שָׁלוֹם, the wish for peace, and thereafter, finally, "the house of my father," which implies unchanging devotion to family.

CHAPTER XXIX

2. As a rule, the cover of a well intended for public use was made to be removed as easily as possible so that the well might be readily accessible to all. But in these parts—and this is our introduction to the character of these Arameans—people did not trust one another and no one wanted anyone else to have even the slightest advantage over him. After all, one person might draw more water from the well or drink more often from it than the others. Accordingly, the rock they had chosen

ח וַיֹּאמְרוּ לֹא נוּכַל עַד אֲשֶׁר יֵאָסְפוּ כָּל־
הָעֲדָרִים וְגָלְלוּ אֶת־הָאֶבֶן מֵעַל פִּי הַבְּאֵר
וְהִשְׁקִינוּ הַצֹּאן׃ ט עוֹדֶנּוּ מְדַבֵּר עִמָּם וְרָחֵל ׀
בָּאָה עִם־הַצֹּאן אֲשֶׁר לְאָבִיהָ כִּי רֹעָה הִוא׃
י וַיְהִי כַּאֲשֶׁר רָאָה יַעֲקֹב אֶת־רָחֵל בַּת־לָבָן אֲחִי
אִמּוֹ וְאֶת־צֹאן לָבָן אֲחִי אִמּוֹ וַיִּגַּשׁ יַעֲקֹב וַיָּגֶל
אֶת־הָאֶבֶן מֵעַל פִּי הַבְּאֵר וַיַּשְׁקְ אֶת־צֹאן לָבָן
אֲחִי אִמּוֹ׃ יא וַיִּשַּׁק יַעֲקֹב לְרָחֵל וַיִּשָּׂא אֶת־קֹלוֹ
וַיֵּבְךְּ׃ יב וַיַּגֵּד יַעֲקֹב לְרָחֵל כִּי אֲחִי אָבִיהָ הוּא
וְכִי בֶן־רִבְקָה הוּא וַתָּרָץ וַתַּגֵּד לְאָבִיהָ׃ יג וַיְהִי
כִשְׁמֹעַ לָבָן אֶת־שֵׁמַע ׀ יַעֲקֹב בֶּן־אֲחֹתוֹ וַיָּרָץ
לִקְרָאתוֹ וַיְחַבֶּק־לוֹ וַיְנַשֶּׁק־לוֹ וַיְבִיאֵהוּ אֶל־
בֵּיתוֹ וַיְסַפֵּר לְלָבָן אֵת כָּל־הַדְּבָרִים הָאֵלֶּה׃
יד וַיֹּאמֶר לוֹ לָבָן אַךְ עַצְמִי וּבְשָׂרִי אָתָּה וַיֵּשֶׁב
עִמּוֹ חֹדֶשׁ יָמִים׃ טו וַיֹּאמֶר לָבָן לְיַעֲקֹב הֲכִי־
אָחִי אַתָּה וַעֲבַדְתַּנִי חִנָּם הַגִּידָה לִּי מַה־
מַּשְׂכֻּרְתֶּךָ׃ טז וּלְלָבָן שְׁתֵּי בָנוֹת שֵׁם הַגְּדֹלָה לֵאָה

8. And they said: "We cannot do that until all the flocks have gathered together and they roll the rock from the mouth of the well; then we shall water the sheep."
9. While he was still speaking with them, there came Rahel with her father's sheep, for she was a shepherdess. 10. And it came to pass that when Yaakov saw Rahel, the daughter of Laban, his mother's brother, and the sheep of Laban, his mother's brother, that Yaakov went near and caused the rock to roll from the mouth of the well and watered the sheep of Laban, his mother's brother. 11. And Yaakov kissed Rahel, lifted up his voice and wept. 12. Thereupon Yaakov told Rahel that he was the kinsman of her father, that he was Rivkah's son, and she ran and told her father. 13. When Laban heard the news of Yaakov, his sister's son, he ran to meet him, embraced and kissed him and brought him to his house. He told Laban all these happenings. 14. And Laban said to him: "Surely, you are my bone and my flesh." And so he stayed with him for a month. 15. And Laban said to Yaakov: "Even if you are my kinsman, should you therefore serve me without compensation? Tell me, what shall your wages be?"
16. Laban had two daughters; the name of the elder was Leah, and the name of the

to cover this well was so heavy that access to the well could never be obtained by one individual alone but only by dint of combined effort.

10. . . . In this account we first learn what assets the patriarch Jacob took with him for setting up his future life. He did not have much money. His most conspicuous asset was physical strength: Jacob was a strong man. What others could accomplish only by concerted effort he was able to do alone and without strain to himself.

We would never have expected Jacob to possess such physical prowess. But at that point this strong and healthy body of his was Jacob's sole material asset. This is a treasure which cannot be overestimated; it is a significant asset for the future, one which, it should be noted, can be acquired only by a past lived in purity. It is the foundation for עוֹשֶׁר וְכָבוֹד, [the "wealth and honor"] which the Torah offers with its left hand.

The second asset we see revealed here in Jacob is his unshakable rectitude. Just like Moses, who also first found his future at a well, so Jacob, too, cannot tolerate any dereliction from duty. This is the same devotion to duty which he, Jacob, was to demonstrate so splendidly himself under the most trying conditions of servitude.

The third asset is enthusiasm for work, inspiring dexterity and activity, which enable him to lend a hand and make himself useful even where the task at hand is not his concern—a trait we would hardly have expected of this אִישׁ תָּם יוֹשֵׁב אֹהָלִים ["single-minded man, living in tents"].

Thus, Jacob appears as the true prototype of the nation whose progenitor he was to become, a nation destined to represent the most variegated material and spiritual pursuits, all with equal dignity, regarding each as equal to the other. The patriarch was so versatile that each of his sons could claim to have inherited his own particular aptitudes from his father, a man who had been equally adept at scholarship, farming and self-defense.

° ° °

younger was Raḥel. 17. Leah's eyes were tender but Raḥel was beautiful of face and beautiful to look upon. 18. Yaakov loved Raḥel and said: "I will serve you seven years for your younger daughter, Raḥel." 19. Laban said: "It is better that I give her to you than that I should give her to another man. Stay with me." 20. So Yaakov served for Raḥel seven years, but they were only a few days in his eyes because of his love for her. 21. And Yaakov said to Laban: "Give me my wife, for my [working] days are completed; I want to go to her." 22. And Laban gathered all the people of the place and prepared a feast. 23. And when it was evening, he took his daughter Leah and brought her to him, and he came to her. 24. Laban gave her his maidservant Zilpah, as a maidservant to his daughter Leah. 25. And when it was morning, behold, it was Leah! And he said to Laban: "What have you done to me? Did I not serve with you for Raḥel? Why have you deceived me?" 26. And Laban said: "It is not done in our place to give the younger before the elder. 27. Complete the wedding week of this one, and then we shall give you the other one also for the service which you will render to me for another seven years." 28. Yaakov did so, and completed the wedding week of this one, and thereupon he gave him his daughter Raḥel to wife. 29. And Laban gave to his daughter Raḥel his maidservant, Bilhah, as a maidservant for her. 30. He came also to Raḥel and he also loved Raḥel, more than Leah, and he served with him for another seven years. 31. When *God* saw that Leah was the hated one, He opened her womb, but Raḥel was barren. 32. And Leah conceived and bore a son and called him Reuben, for she had said: "*God* has looked into my affliction! Now my husband will love me." 33. She conceived again and bore a son, and she said: "*God* has heard that I am the hated one. Therefore He has given me this one also!" And she called him Shimeon. 34. She conceived again and bore a son, and she said: "Now my husband will attach himself to me! For I have borne him three sons." Therefore she called him Levi. 35. She conceived again

וְשֵׁם הַקְּטַנָּה רָחֵל: יז וְעֵינֵי לֵאָה רַכּוֹת וְרָחֵל הָיְתָה יְפַת־תֹּאַר וִיפַת מַרְאֶה: שלישי יח וַיֶּאֱהַב יַעֲקֹב אֶת־רָחֵל וַיֹּאמֶר אֶעֱבָדְךָ שֶׁבַע שָׁנִים בְּרָחֵל בִּתְּךָ הַקְּטַנָּה: יט וַיֹּאמֶר לָבָן טוֹב תִּתִּי אֹתָהּ לָךְ מִתִּתִּי אֹתָהּ לְאִישׁ אַחֵר שְׁבָה עִמָּדִי: כ וַיַּעֲבֹד יַעֲקֹב בְּרָחֵל שֶׁבַע שָׁנִים וַיִּהְיוּ בְעֵינָיו כְּיָמִים אֲחָדִים בְּאַהֲבָתוֹ אֹתָהּ: כא וַיֹּאמֶר יַעֲקֹב אֶל־לָבָן הָבָה אֶת־אִשְׁתִּי כִּי מָלְאוּ יָמָי וְאָבוֹאָה אֵלֶיהָ: כב וַיֶּאֱסֹף לָבָן אֶת־כָּל־אַנְשֵׁי הַמָּקוֹם וַיַּעַשׂ מִשְׁתֶּה: כג וַיְהִי בָעֶרֶב וַיִּקַּח אֶת־לֵאָה בִתּוֹ וַיָּבֵא אֹתָהּ אֵלָיו וַיָּבֹא אֵלֶיהָ: כד וַיִּתֵּן לָבָן לָהּ אֶת־זִלְפָּה שִׁפְחָתוֹ לְלֵאָה בִתּוֹ שִׁפְחָה: כה וַיְהִי בַבֹּקֶר וְהִנֵּה־הִוא לֵאָה וַיֹּאמֶר אֶל־לָבָן מַה־זֹּאת עָשִׂיתָ לִּי הֲלֹא בְרָחֵל עָבַדְתִּי עִמָּךְ וְלָמָּה רִמִּיתָנִי: כו וַיֹּאמֶר לָבָן לֹא־יֵעָשֶׂה כֵן בִּמְקוֹמֵנוּ לָתֵת הַצְּעִירָה לִפְנֵי הַבְּכִירָה: כז מַלֵּא שְׁבֻעַ זֹאת וְנִתְּנָה לְךָ גַּם־אֶת־זֹאת בַּעֲבֹדָה אֲשֶׁר תַּעֲבֹד עִמָּדִי עוֹד שֶׁבַע־שָׁנִים אֲחֵרוֹת: כח וַיַּעַשׂ יַעֲקֹב כֵּן וַיְמַלֵּא שְׁבֻעַ זֹאת וַיִּתֶּן־לוֹ אֶת־רָחֵל בִּתּוֹ לוֹ לְאִשָּׁה: כט וַיִּתֵּן לָבָן לְרָחֵל בִּתּוֹ אֶת־בִּלְהָה שִׁפְחָתוֹ לָהּ לְשִׁפְחָה: ל וַיָּבֹא גַּם אֶל־רָחֵל וַיֶּאֱהַב גַּם־אֶת־רָחֵל מִלֵּאָה וַיַּעֲבֹד עִמּוֹ עוֹד שֶׁבַע־שָׁנִים אֲחֵרוֹת: לא וַיַּרְא יְהֹוָה כִּי־שְׂנוּאָה לֵאָה וַיִּפְתַּח אֶת־רַחְמָהּ וְרָחֵל עֲקָרָה: לב וַתַּהַר לֵאָה וַתֵּלֶד בֵּן וַתִּקְרָא שְׁמוֹ רְאוּבֵן כִּי אָמְרָה כִּי־רָאָה יְהֹוָה בְּעָנְיִי כִּי עַתָּה יֶאֱהָבַנִי אִישִׁי: לג וַתַּהַר עוֹד וַתֵּלֶד בֵּן וַתֹּאמֶר כִּי־שָׁמַע יְהֹוָה כִּי־שְׂנוּאָה אָנֹכִי וַיִּתֶּן־לִי גַּם־אֶת־זֶה וַתִּקְרָא שְׁמוֹ שִׁמְעוֹן: לד וַתַּהַר עוֹד וַתֵּלֶד בֵּן וַתֹּאמֶר עַתָּה הַפַּעַם יִלָּוֶה אִישִׁי אֵלַי כִּי־יָלַדְתִּי לוֹ שְׁלֹשָׁה בָנִים עַל־כֵּן קָרָא־שְׁמוֹ לֵוִי: לה וַתַּהַר

and bore a son, and she said: "Now I shall give thanks to *God*." Therefore she called him Yehudah. And then she stopped bearing.

XXX 1. When Raḥel saw that she had borne Yaakov no children, Raḥel envied her sister and she said to Yaakov: "Give me children, or else I will die." 2. And Yaakov was angry with Raḥel and said: "Am I in God's place, Who has withheld from you the fruit of the womb?" 3. Thereupon she said: "Behold, my handmaid Bilhah. Come to her. Let her bear for my knees so that I, too, will be built through her." 4. And she gave him her maidservant Bilhah to wife, and Yaakov came to her, 5. Bilhah conceived and bore Yaakov a son. 6. And Raḥel said: "God has judged me and He also has heard my weeping and given me a son." Therefore she called him Dan. 7. Bilhah, Raḥel's maidservant, conceived again and bore Yaakov a second son. 8. And Rahel said: "I have fought a Divine struggle with my sister and I have prevailed." Therefore she called him Naphtali. 9. When Leah saw that she had stopped bearing she took her maidservant Zilpah and gave her to Yaakov to wife. 10. And Zilpah, Leah's maidservant, bore Yaakov a son. 11. And Leah said: "Good fortune has come," and she called him Gad. 12. Leah's maidservant, Zilpah, bore Yaakov a second son. 13. And Leah said: "I am still in my happy progress, for women have praised my progress." And she called him Asher. 14. And Reuben went in the days of the wheat harvest and found *dudaim*° in the field and brought them home to his mother Leah. Then Raḥel said to Leah: "Please give me some of your son's *dudaim*." 15. And she said to her: "Is it a small thing that you have my husband? And now you want my son's *dudaim* also!" And Raḥel said: "Well, he shall come to you this night for your son's *dudaim*." 16. When Yaakov came from the field in the evening, Leah went out to meet him

---

°*Note to the English translation:* Standard versions render דודאים as "mandrakes"; RaSHBaM (Rabbi Samuel ben Meir, 1085–1174) renders the word as "figs." [G.H.]

עוֹד וַתֵּ֣לֶד בֵּ֔ן וַתֹּ֙אמֶר֙ הַפַּ֙עַם֙ אוֹדֶ֣ה אֶת־יְהוָ֔ה עַל־כֵּ֛ן קָרְאָ֥ה שְׁמ֖וֹ יְהוּדָ֑ה וַֽתַּעֲמֹ֖ד מִלֶּֽדֶת: ל א וַתֵּ֣רֶא רָחֵ֗ל כִּ֣י לֹ֤א יָֽלְדָה֙ לְיַ֣עֲקֹ֔ב וַתְּקַנֵּ֥א רָחֵ֖ל בַּֽאֲחֹתָ֑הּ וַתֹּ֤אמֶר אֶֽל־יַעֲקֹב֙ הָֽבָה־לִּ֣י בָנִ֔ים וְאִם־אַ֖יִן מֵתָ֥ה אָנֹֽכִי: ב וַיִּֽחַר־אַ֥ף יַעֲקֹ֖ב בְּרָחֵ֑ל וַיֹּ֗אמֶר הֲתַ֤חַת אֱלֹהִים֙ אָנֹ֔כִי אֲשֶׁר־מָנַ֥ע מִמֵּ֖ךְ פְּרִי־בָֽטֶן: ג וַתֹּ֕אמֶר הִנֵּ֛ה אֲמָתִ֥י בִלְהָ֖ה בֹּ֣א אֵלֶ֑יהָ וְתֵלֵד֙ עַל־בִּרְכַּ֔י וְאִבָּנֶ֥ה גַם־אָנֹכִ֖י מִמֶּֽנָּה: ד וַתִּתֶּן־ל֛וֹ אֶת־בִּלְהָ֥ה שִׁפְחָתָ֖הּ לְאִשָּׁ֑ה וַיָּבֹ֥א אֵלֶ֖יהָ יַעֲקֹֽב: ה וַתַּ֣הַר בִּלְהָ֔ה וַתֵּ֥לֶד לְיַעֲקֹ֖ב בֵּֽן: ו וַתֹּ֤אמֶר רָחֵל֙ דָּנַ֣נִּי אֱלֹהִ֔ים וְגַם֙ שָׁמַ֣ע בְּקֹלִ֔י וַיִּתֶּן־לִ֖י בֵּ֑ן עַל־כֵּ֛ן קָרְאָ֥ה שְׁמ֖וֹ דָּֽן: ז וַתַּ֣הַר ע֗וֹד וַתֵּ֙לֶד֙ בִּלְהָ֣ה שִׁפְחַ֣ת רָחֵ֔ל בֵּ֥ן שֵׁנִ֖י לְיַֽעֲקֹֽב: ח וַתֹּ֣אמֶר רָחֵ֗ל נַפְתּוּלֵ֨י אֱלֹהִ֧ים ׀ נִפְתַּ֛לְתִּי עִם־אֲחֹתִ֖י גַּם־יָכֹ֑לְתִּי וַתִּקְרָ֥א שְׁמ֖וֹ נַפְתָּלִֽי: ט וַתֵּ֣רֶא לֵאָ֔ה כִּ֥י עָֽמְדָ֖ה מִלֶּ֑דֶת וַתִּקַּח֙ אֶת־זִלְפָּ֣ה שִׁפְחָתָ֔הּ וַתִּתֵּ֥ן אֹתָ֛הּ לְיַעֲקֹ֖ב לְאִשָּֽׁה: י וַתֵּ֗לֶד זִלְפָּ֛ה שִׁפְחַ֥ת לֵאָ֖ה לְיַעֲקֹ֥ב בֵּֽן: יא וַתֹּ֥אמֶר לֵאָ֖ה בָּ֣גָד (בא גד קרי) וַתִּקְרָ֥א אֶת־שְׁמ֖וֹ גָּֽד: יב וַתֵּ֗לֶד זִלְפָּה֙ שִׁפְחַ֣ת לֵאָ֔ה בֵּ֥ן שֵׁנִ֖י לְיַֽעֲקֹֽב: יג וַתֹּ֣אמֶר לֵאָ֔ה בְּאָשְׁרִ֕י כִּ֥י אִשְּׁר֖וּנִי בָּנ֑וֹת וַתִּקְרָ֥א אֶת־שְׁמ֖וֹ אָשֵֽׁר: רביעי יד וַיֵּ֨לֶךְ רְאוּבֵ֜ן בִּימֵ֣י קְצִיר־חִטִּ֗ים וַיִּמְצָ֤א דֽוּדָאִים֙ בַּשָּׂדֶ֔ה וַיָּבֵ֣א אֹתָ֔ם אֶל־לֵאָ֖ה אִמּ֑וֹ וַתֹּ֤אמֶר רָחֵל֙ אֶל־לֵאָ֔ה תְּנִי־נָ֣א לִ֔י מִדּֽוּדָאֵ֖י בְּנֵֽךְ: טו וַתֹּ֣אמֶר לָ֗הּ הַמְעַט֙ קַחְתֵּ֣ךְ אֶת־אִישִׁ֔י וְלָקַ֕חַת גַּ֥ם אֶת־דּֽוּדָאֵ֖י בְּנִ֑י וַתֹּ֣אמֶר רָחֵ֗ל לָכֵן֙ יִשְׁכַּ֤ב עִמָּךְ֙ הַלַּ֔יְלָה תַּ֖חַת דּֽוּדָאֵ֥י בְנֵֽךְ: טז וַיָּבֹ֨א יַעֲקֹ֤ב מִן־הַשָּׂדֶה֙ בָּעֶ֔רֶב

and said: "You must come to me because I have acquired you for my son's *dudaim*." And he slept with her that night. 17. And God hearkened to Leah; she conceived and bore Yaakov a fifth son. 18. And Leah said: "God has given me my wages because I gave my maidservant to my husband." Therefore she called him Yissakhar. 19. Leah conceived again and bore Yaakov a sixth son. 20. And Leah said: "God has apportioned me a good portion; now my husband will make his home with me, for I have borne him six sons." Therefore she called him Zebulun. 21. After that she bore him a daughter and called her Dinah. 22. And God remembered Raḥel; God hearkened to her and opened her womb. 23. She conceived and bore a son. And she said: "God has taken away my disgrace." 24. But she called him Yosef, saying: "May *God* give me yet another son!" 25. It came to pass when Raḥel had borne Yosef, that Yaakov said to Laban: "Send me away so that I may go to my place and to my country. 26. Give me my wives and my children, for whom I have served you, so I would go, for you know my service, how I have served you." 27. And Laban said to him: "May I have found favor in your eyes! I have a presentiment that *God*

וַתֵּצֵא לֵאָה לִקְרָאתוֹ וַתֹּאמֶר אֵלַי תָּבוֹא כִּי שָׂכֹר שְׂכַרְתִּיךָ בְּדוּדָאֵי בְּנִי וַיִּשְׁכַּב עִמָּהּ בַּלַּיְלָה הוּא: יז וַיִּשְׁמַע אֱלֹהִים אֶל־לֵאָה וַתַּהַר וַתֵּלֶד לְיַעֲקֹב בֵּן חֲמִישִׁי: יח וַתֹּאמֶר לֵאָה נָתַן אֱלֹהִים שְׂכָרִי אֲשֶׁר־נָתַתִּי שִׁפְחָתִי לְאִישִׁי וַתִּקְרָא שְׁמוֹ יִשָּׂשכָר: יט וַתַּהַר עוֹד לֵאָה וַתֵּלֶד בֵּן־שִׁשִּׁי לְיַעֲקֹב: כ וַתֹּאמֶר לֵאָה זְבָדַנִי אֱלֹהִים אֹתִי זֶבֶד טוֹב הַפַּעַם יִזְבְּלֵנִי אִישִׁי כִּי־יָלַדְתִּי לוֹ שִׁשָּׁה בָנִים וַתִּקְרָא אֶת־שְׁמוֹ זְבֻלוּן: כא וְאַחַר יָלְדָה בַּת וַתִּקְרָא אֶת־שְׁמָהּ דִּינָה: כב וַיִּזְכֹּר אֱלֹהִים אֶת־רָחֵל וַיִּשְׁמַע אֵלֶיהָ אֱלֹהִים וַיִּפְתַּח אֶת־רַחְמָהּ: כג וַתַּהַר וַתֵּלֶד בֵּן וַתֹּאמֶר אָסַף אֱלֹהִים אֶת־חֶרְפָּתִי: כד וַתִּקְרָא אֶת־שְׁמוֹ יוֹסֵף לֵאמֹר יֹסֵף יְהֹוָה לִי בֵּן אַחֵר: כה וַיְהִי כַּאֲשֶׁר יָלְדָה רָחֵל אֶת־יוֹסֵף וַיֹּאמֶר יַעֲקֹב אֶל־לָבָן שַׁלְּחֵנִי וְאֵלְכָה אֶל־מְקוֹמִי וּלְאַרְצִי: כו תְּנָה אֶת־נָשַׁי וְאֶת־יְלָדַי אֲשֶׁר עָבַדְתִּי אֹתְךָ בָּהֵן וְאֵלֵכָה כִּי אַתָּה יָדַעְתָּ אֶת־עֲבֹדָתִי אֲשֶׁר עֲבַדְתִּיךָ: כז וַיֹּאמֶר אֵלָיו לָבָן אִם־נָא מָצָאתִי חֵן בְּעֵינֶיךָ נִחַשְׁתִּי וַיְבָרֲכֵנִי יְהֹוָה

CHAPTER XXX

20. זבד ["portion"], related to צבט, cf. וַיִּצְבָּט לָהּ קָלִי ["and they passed to her parched corn" (Ruth 2:14)], to "mete out" or "apportion" something to another....

26. אַתָּה יָדַעְתָּ אֶת עֲבֹדָתִי אֲשֶׁר עֲבַדְתִּיךָ [*you know my service, how I have served you*]. It may well be that no other man has ever given fourteen years of such service. Jacob had worked for fourteen years not in order to provide for his wife and children but in order to earn the right to have a wife and children. He had served for fourteen years of toil in order to obtain two wives, neither of whom had a dowry. These fourteen years of service in which the national existence and family life of the house of Jacob are rooted represent a most splendid, shining gateway to that precious treasure of human achievement: Jewish family life. These fourteen years show how the Jewish husband regards his wife, and they give the lie to all the inane prattle about the Oriental-style degradation of womanhood in the Jewish marriage. At the end of fourteen years Jacob still was where he had been at the start, except that, as a result

of his toil, his cares had multiplied, for now he had four wives and twelve children to support. Yet he had for their future nothing more than he had at the time when, fourteen years earlier, he had set the memorial stone on the heath, nothing more, that is, than the treasure which could be described in terms of qualities of mind and heart, and robust physical working power.

∘ ∘ ∘

27. Laban would like to keep him as a servant, preferably for no other payment except his keep, as heretofore. Hence he now talks to Jacob like a true crafty villain who affects piety. He does not admit that he would like to keep Jacob simply because of the efficient services he has rendered him. He feels that such practical considerations would have to be paid for, and if one has gone so far as to praise such skills, they would have to be paid very well indeed. For this reason he affects extreme piety, and, just as do those today who, having cast off all genuine piety, turn to superstition and think that a superstitious belief in omens is tantamount to being "religious," Laban says to Jacob: "I don't like to let you go. There is no real reason for it,

has blessed me for your sake." 28. Then he said: "Fix your wages for me and I will gladly give it." 29. And he said to him: "You know very well how I have served you and what your property has become with me; 30. for the little that you had before I came has increased in multitude because *God* has blessed you according to my endeavor. And now, when shall I provide for my own house also?" 31. He said: "What shall I give you?" And Yaakov replied: "You shall not give me anything; if you will do this thing for me, I will feed your flock again and will keep it. 32. Today I will go through all your small cattle and will separate from them every speckled and spotted lamb and every dark lamb from among the sheep, and spotted and speckled from among the goats: this shall be my pay. 33. And in future let it testify against my attention to my duty if you will look over my pay which lies open before you: whatever is not speckled and spotted among the goats or dark among the sheep shall be counted as stolen by me." 34. Laban said: "Very well! Let it be as you have spoken." 35. On that day he separated those he-goats that were marked upon their legs and spotted and also all the speckled and spotted she-goats, everything that had even only a little white upon it, and all the dark among the sheep, and he gave them into the hands of his sons. 36. And he set three days' journey between himself

בִּגְלָלֶךְ: חמישי כח וַיֹּאמַר נָקְבָה שְׂכָרְךָ עָלַי וְאֶתֵּנָה: כט וַיֹּאמֶר אֵלָיו אַתָּה יָדַעְתָּ אֵת אֲשֶׁר עֲבַדְתִּיךָ וְאֵת אֲשֶׁר־הָיָה מִקְנְךָ אִתִּי: ל כִּי מְעַט אֲשֶׁר־הָיָה לְךָ לְפָנַי וַיִּפְרֹץ לָרֹב וַיְבָרֶךְ יְהֹוָה אֹתְךָ לְרַגְלִי וְעַתָּה מָתַי אֶעֱשֶׂה גַם־אָנֹכִי לְבֵיתִי: לא וַיֹּאמֶר מָה אֶתֶּן־לָךְ וַיֹּאמֶר יַעֲקֹב לֹא־תִתֶּן־לִי מְאוּמָה אִם־תַּעֲשֶׂה־לִּי הַדָּבָר הַזֶּה אָשׁוּבָה אֶרְעֶה צֹאנְךָ אֶשְׁמֹר: לב אֶעֱבֹר בְּכָל־צֹאנְךָ הַיּוֹם הָסֵר מִשָּׁם כָּל־שֶׂה ׀ נָקֹד וְטָלוּא וְכָל־שֶׂה־חוּם בַּכְּשָׂבִים וְטָלוּא וְנָקֹד בָּעִזִּים וְהָיָה שְׂכָרִי: לג וְעָנְתָה־בִּי צִדְקָתִי בְּיוֹם מָחָר כִּי־תָבוֹא עַל־שְׂכָרִי לְפָנֶיךָ כֹּל אֲשֶׁר־אֵינֶנּוּ נָקֹד וְטָלוּא בָּעִזִּים וְחוּם בַּכְּשָׂבִים גָּנוּב הוּא אִתִּי: לד וַיֹּאמֶר לָבָן הֵן לוּ יְהִי כִדְבָרֶךָ: לה וַיָּסַר בַּיּוֹם הַהוּא אֶת־הַתְּיָשִׁים הָעֲקֻדִּים וְהַטְּלֻאִים וְאֵת כָּל־הָעִזִּים הַנְּקֻדּוֹת וְהַטְּלֻאֹת כֹּל אֲשֶׁר־לָבָן בּוֹ וְכָל־חוּם בַּכְּשָׂבִים וַיִּתֵּן בְּיַד־בָּנָיו: לו וַיָּשֶׂם דֶּרֶךְ שְׁלֹשֶׁת

---

but I have a נִיחוּשׁ [presentiment] in this connection. It seems to me that ה', that God Whom you serve, has blessed me for your sake, because you are such a pious man. That is why I would not like to see such a pious man leave me."

Laban had hoped that this "pious" man would feel flattered by this speech and agree to stay on. But when Jacob made no reply, he saw that he would have to hold out a promise of more material rewards. "You name your wages," he said, "and I will gladly give them to you." Thereupon Jacob replied: "You know it all very well; you do not have to cite vague 'presentiments' in order to know what services I have rendered to you and how I have contributed to your prosperity. You have no need merely to surmise that God has blessed you בִּגְלָלִי, for my sake. You know that He has blessed you לְרַגְלִי, [lit., "according to my foot"], according to my ways, according to the efficiency with which I have employed

my hands and feet in your service. It is not on account of my piety that God has blessed you, but on account of my diligence. And now, don't you think the time has come when I should use some of this same diligence for building up my own household?"

o o o

31. "I do not want you to 'give' me anything." Jacob had already known by experience how deceitful Laban could be when it came to "giving" him something for his services. So Jacob now wanted Laban to "do something" for him; more specifically, he wanted him to make an arrangement whereby that which is to be Jacob's pay becomes Jacob's property from the moment of its birth, for he knew that once something had become Laban's property it would not be so easy to obtain from him, no matter how justified Jacob's claim might be.

and Yaakov, and Yaakov fed the rest of Laban's sheep.   37. And Yaakov took for himself rods of fresh aspen and of hazelnut and chestnut trees, and peeled white streaks in them by uncovering the white which was in the rods.   38. And he set the rods which he had peeled in the gutters in the watering troughs where the female animals came to drink opposite the males, and both came into heat when they came to drink. 39. And the animals came into heat opposite the rods, and the animals brought forth [young] marked upon the legs, speckled and spotted.   40. Yaakov had segregated the sheep, and he set the faces of the animals toward those which had marks upon their legs and all those dark among the animals of Laban. But he arranged separate herds for himself and did not put them to Laban's animals.   41. Whenever the animals which had been tied up came into heat, Yaakov placed the rods before the eyes of the animals in the gutters in order to bring them into heat by means of the rods. 42. But when the animals were left covered he did not place them there, and so those covered became Laban's and those banded together became Yaakov's. 43. And the man now became immensely wealthy and he had sheep in multitude, maidservants and menservants, and camels and donkeys.

XXXI

1. And he heard the words of the sons of Laban: "Yaakov has appropriated to himself everything that belongs to our father, and of that which belongs to our father he has gotten all this glory."   2. Yaakov also saw the face of Laban, and behold, he, too, was no longer toward him as he had been yesterday and the day before.   3. And *God* said to Yaakov: "Return to the land of your fathers and to your birthplace and I will be with you."   4. And Yaakov sent and called Raḥel and Leah to the field, to his sheep, 5. and he said to them: "I see your father's countenance, that it is no longer toward me as it was yesterday and the day

יָמִים בֵּינוֹ וּבֵין יַעֲקֹב וְיַעֲקֹב רֹעֶה אֶת־צֹאן לָבָן הַנּוֹתָרֹת: לז וַיִּקַּח־לוֹ יַעֲקֹב מַקַּל לִבְנֶה לַח וְלוּז וְעַרְמוֹן וַיְפַצֵּל בָּהֵן פְּצָלוֹת לְבָנוֹת מַחְשֹׂף הַלָּבָן אֲשֶׁר עַל־הַמַּקְלוֹת: לח וַיַּצֵּג אֶת־הַמַּקְלוֹת אֲשֶׁר פִּצֵּל בָּרְהָטִים בְּשִׁקֲתוֹת הַמָּיִם אֲשֶׁר תָּבֹאןָ הַצֹּאן לִשְׁתּוֹת לְנֹכַח הַצֹּאן וַיֵּחַמְנָה בְּבֹאָן לִשְׁתּוֹת: לט וַיֶּחֱמוּ הַצֹּאן אֶל־הַמַּקְלוֹת וַתֵּלַדְןָ הַצֹּאן עֲקֻדִּים נְקֻדִּים וּטְלֻאִים: מ וְהַכְּשָׂבִים הִפְרִיד יַעֲקֹב וַיִּתֵּן פְּנֵי הַצֹּאן אֶל־עָקֹד וְכָל־חוּם בְּצֹאן לָבָן וַיָּשֶׁת לוֹ עֲדָרִים לְבַדּוֹ וְלֹא שָׁתָם עַל־צֹאן לָבָן: מא וְהָיָה בְּכָל־יַחֵם הַצֹּאן הַמְקֻשָּׁרוֹת וְשָׂם יַעֲקֹב אֶת־הַמַּקְלוֹת לְעֵינֵי הַצֹּאן בָּרְהָטִים לְיַחְמֵנָּה בַּמַּקְלוֹת: מב וּבְהַעֲטִיף הַצֹּאן לֹא יָשִׂים וְהָיָה הָעֲטֻפִים לְלָבָן וְהַקְּשֻׁרִים לְיַעֲקֹב: מג וַיִּפְרֹץ הָאִישׁ מְאֹד מְאֹד וַיְהִי־לוֹ צֹאן רַבּוֹת וּשְׁפָחוֹת וַעֲבָדִים וּגְמַלִּים וַחֲמֹרִים:

לא א וַיִּשְׁמַע אֶת־דִּבְרֵי בְנֵי־לָבָן לֵאמֹר לָקַח יַעֲקֹב אֵת כָּל־אֲשֶׁר לְאָבִינוּ וּמֵאֲשֶׁר לְאָבִינוּ עָשָׂה אֵת כָּל־הַכָּבֹד הַזֶּה: ב וַיַּרְא יַעֲקֹב אֶת־פְּנֵי לָבָן וְהִנֵּה אֵינֶנּוּ עִמּוֹ כִּתְמוֹל שִׁלְשׁוֹם: ג וַיֹּאמֶר יְהֹוָה אֶל־יַעֲקֹב שׁוּב אֶל־אֶרֶץ אֲבוֹתֶיךָ וּלְמוֹלַדְתֶּךָ וְאֶהְיֶה עִמָּךְ: ד וַיִּשְׁלַח יַעֲקֹב וַיִּקְרָא לְרָחֵל וּלְלֵאָה הַשָּׂדֶה אֶל־צֹאנוֹ: ה וַיֹּאמֶר לָהֶן רֹאֶה אָנֹכִי אֶת־פְּנֵי אֲבִיכֶן כִּי־אֵינֶנּוּ אֵלַי כִּתְמֹל

CHAPTER XXXI

5. "I see from the face of your father how God has

helped me; it is solely thanks to His help that I have not fared even worse."

before, and only the God of my father has been with me.   6. But you know that I have served your father with all my strength.   7. However, your father has deceived me with promises; he changed my pay ten times and only God did not permit him to wrong me.   8. If he said: 'The speckled shall be your wages,' all the sheep bore speckled. If he said: 'Those that were marked upon their legs shall be your wages,' all the sheep bore [young with] marks upon their legs.   9. In this manner God rescued your father's property and gave it to me. 10. Now it came to pass when now the sheep came into heat, that I lifted up my eyes in a dream and saw, and lo! the bucks which mounted the sheep had marks upon their legs, were speckled and spotted. 11. And an angel of God said to me in the dream: 'Yaakov!' and I replied: 'Here I am.' 12. And he said: "Please lift up your eyes and see, all the bucks which mounted the sheep have marks upon their legs, are speckled and spotted, for I have seen everything that Laban is doing to you.   13. But I am the God of Bethel, where you anointed a memorial stone and made a vow to Me; now arise, go out of this land and return to the land of your birth.'"   14. And Raḥel and Leah answered and said to him: "Have we still a portion and inheritance in the house of our father?   15. Are we not to him as strangers, since he has sold us and has even devoured our purchase price? 16. For all the wealth which God has rescued from our father is ours and our children's. And now whatever God has said to you, do."   17. And Yaakov arose and set his children and his wives upon the camels, 18. and he led forth all his property, all the wealth which he had acquired, that which he had acquired as his property, that which he had acquired in Paddan-Aram, in order to come home to his father Yitzḥak, to the land of Canaan.   19. But Laban had gone away to shear his sheep, and Raḥel

שִׁלְשֹׁם וֵאלֹהֵי אָבִי הָיָה עִמָּדִי: ו וְאַתֵּנָה יְדַעְתֶּן כִּי בְּכָל־כֹּחִי עָבַדְתִּי אֶת־אֲבִיכֶן: ז וַאֲבִיכֶן הֵתֶל בִּי וְהֶחֱלִף אֶת־מַשְׂכֻּרְתִּי עֲשֶׂרֶת מֹנִים וְלֹא־נְתָנוֹ אֱלֹהִים לְהָרַע עִמָּדִי: ח אִם־כֹּה יֹאמַר נְקֻדִּים יִהְיֶה שְׂכָרֶךָ וְיָלְדוּ כָל־הַצֹּאן נְקֻדִּים וְאִם־כֹּה יֹאמַר עֲקֻדִּים יִהְיֶה שְׂכָרֶךָ וְיָלְדוּ כָל־הַצֹּאן עֲקֻדִּים: ט וַיַּצֵּל אֱלֹהִים אֶת־מִקְנֵה אֲבִיכֶם וַיִּתֶּן־לִי: י וַיְהִי בְּעֵת יַחֵם הַצֹּאן וָאֶשָּׂא עֵינַי וָאֵרֶא בַּחֲלוֹם וְהִנֵּה הָעַתֻּדִים הָעֹלִים עַל־הַצֹּאן עֲקֻדִּים נְקֻדִּים וּבְרֻדִּים: יא וַיֹּאמֶר אֵלַי מַלְאַךְ הָאֱלֹהִים בַּחֲלוֹם יַעֲקֹב וָאֹמַר הִנֵּנִי: יב וַיֹּאמֶר שָׂא־נָא עֵינֶיךָ וּרְאֵה כָּל־הָעַתֻּדִים הָעֹלִים עַל־הַצֹּאן עֲקֻדִּים נְקֻדִּים וּבְרֻדִּים כִּי רָאִיתִי אֵת כָּל־אֲשֶׁר לָבָן עֹשֶׂה לָּךְ: יג אָנֹכִי הָאֵל בֵּית־אֵל אֲשֶׁר מָשַׁחְתָּ שָּׁם מַצֵּבָה אֲשֶׁר נָדַרְתָּ לִּי שָׁם נֶדֶר עַתָּה קוּם צֵא מִן־הָאָרֶץ הַזֹּאת וְשׁוּב אֶל־אֶרֶץ מוֹלַדְתֶּךָ: יד וַתַּעַן רָחֵל וְלֵאָה וַתֹּאמַרְנָה לוֹ הַעוֹד לָנוּ חֵלֶק וְנַחֲלָה בְּבֵית אָבִינוּ: טו הֲלוֹא נָכְרִיּוֹת נֶחְשַׁבְנוּ לוֹ כִּי מְכָרָנוּ וַיֹּאכַל גַּם־אָכוֹל אֶת־כַּסְפֵּנוּ: טז כִּי כָל־הָעֹשֶׁר אֲשֶׁר הִצִּיל אֱלֹהִים מֵאָבִינוּ לָנוּ הוּא וּלְבָנֵינוּ וְעַתָּה כֹּל אֲשֶׁר אָמַר אֱלֹהִים אֵלֶיךָ עֲשֵׂה: ששי יז וַיָּקָם יַעֲקֹב וַיִּשָּׂא אֶת־בָּנָיו וְאֶת־נָשָׁיו עַל־הַגְּמַלִּים: יח וַיִּנְהַג אֶת־כָּל־מִקְנֵהוּ וְאֶת־כָּל־רְכֻשׁוֹ אֲשֶׁר רָכָשׁ מִקְנֵה קִנְיָנוֹ אֲשֶׁר רָכַשׁ בְּפַדַּן אֲרָם לָבוֹא אֶל־יִצְחָק אָבִיו אַרְצָה כְּנָעַן: יט וְלָבָן הָלַךְ לִגְזֹז

19 and 20. These two verses emphasize two "thefts." So, there were opportunities for theft, but the only property that was stolen were Laban's idols. Rachel stole her father's idols because, as the Sages explain, she could not bear the thought of going away and leaving her father to idolatry without any incentive to mend his ways. She therefore took those idols which were supposedly the protectors of his household. Certainly this

stole her father's idols. 20. And Yaakov stole the heart of Laban the Aramean in that he did not tell him, because he fled. 21. So he fled with all that was his; he arose and crossed the river and set his direction toward Mount Gilead. 22. On the third day it was told to Laban that Yaakov had fled. 23. And he took his companions with him and pursued him seven days' journey and he caught up with him on Mount Gilead. 24. But God came to Laban the Aramean in a dream of the night and said to him: "Take heed that you do not speak to Yaakov either good or bad." 25. Therefore, when Laban came up to Yaakov—Yaakov having pitched his tent upon the mountain, but Laban and his companions had pitched [theirs] on Mount Gilead— 26. Laban said to Yaakov: "What have you done? You have robbed my heart! You have led my daughters away like prisoners of war! 27. Why did you flee in secret and rob me? You told me nothing! Why, I would have sent you away with joy and with songs, with tabret and with harp! 28. And you did not permit me to kiss my sons and daughters! Now you see how foolishly you have acted. 29. It is within the power of my hand to do you harm, but the God of your father said to me last night as follows: 'Take heed that you do not speak to Yaakov either good or bad.' 30. Well, so you have left, because you indeed

אֶת־צֹאנוֹ וַתִּגְנֹב רָחֵל אֶת־הַתְּרָפִים אֲשֶׁר
לְאָבִיהָ: כ וַיִּגְנֹב יַעֲקֹב אֶת־לֵב לָבָן הָאֲרַמִּי עַל־
בְּלִי הִגִּיד לוֹ כִּי בֹרֵחַ הוּא: כא וַיִּבְרַח הוּא וְכָל־
אֲשֶׁר־לוֹ וַיָּקָם וַיַּעֲבֹר אֶת־הַנָּהָר וַיָּשֶׂם אֶת־פָּנָיו
הַר הַגִּלְעָד: כב וַיֻּגַּד לְלָבָן בַּיּוֹם הַשְּׁלִישִׁי כִּי
בָרַח יַעֲקֹב: כג וַיִּקַּח אֶת־אֶחָיו עִמּוֹ וַיִּרְדֹּף
אַחֲרָיו דֶּרֶךְ שִׁבְעַת יָמִים וַיַּדְבֵּק אֹתוֹ בְּהַר
הַגִּלְעָד: כד וַיָּבֹא אֱלֹהִים אֶל־לָבָן הָאֲרַמִּי בַּחֲלֹם
הַלָּיְלָה וַיֹּאמֶר לוֹ הִשָּׁמֶר לְךָ פֶּן־תְּדַבֵּר עִם־
יַעֲקֹב מִטּוֹב עַד־רָע: כה וַיַּשֵּׂג לָבָן אֶת־יַעֲקֹב
וְיַעֲקֹב תָּקַע אֶת־אָהֳלוֹ בָּהָר וְלָבָן תָּקַע אֶת־אֶחָיו
בְּהַר הַגִּלְעָד: כו וַיֹּאמֶר לָבָן לְיַעֲקֹב מֶה עָשִׂיתָ
וַתִּגְנֹב אֶת־לְבָבִי וַתְּנַהֵג אֶת־בְּנֹתַי כִּשְׁבֻיוֹת
חָרֶב: כז לָמָּה נַחְבֵּאתָ לִבְרֹחַ וַתִּגְנֹב אֹתִי וְלֹא־
הִגַּדְתָּ לִּי וָאֲשַׁלֵּחֲךָ בְּשִׂמְחָה וּבְשִׁרִים בְּתֹף
וּבְכִנּוֹר: כח וְלֹא נְטַשְׁתַּנִי לְנַשֵּׁק לְבָנַי וְלִבְנֹתָי
עַתָּה הִסְכַּלְתָּ עֲשׂוֹ: כט יֶשׁ־לְאֵל יָדִי לַעֲשׂוֹת
עִמָּכֶם רָע וֵאלֹהֵי אֲבִיכֶם אֶמֶשׁ ׀ אָמַר אֵלַי
לֵאמֹר הִשָּׁמֶר לְךָ מִדַּבֵּר עִם־יַעֲקֹב מִטּוֹב
עַד־רָע: ל וְעַתָּה הָלֹךְ הָלַכְתָּ כִּי־נִכְסֹף נִכְסַפְתָּה

theft would have to demonstrate to Laban how powerless these idols were if they could not even protect themselves. . . .

גְּנֵיבַת לֵב [lit., "stealing the heart"] is to win the good opinion of another without deserving it; to obtain the good will of another by false friendliness, kindness, favors, etc., a form of deceit which our Sages prohibit with the utmost sternness; they call it גְּנֵיבַת דַּעַת [lit., "a mental theft"] and insist that even the slightest semblance of such deception must be avoided. Jacob's גְּנֵיבַת דַּעַת lay in the fact that he did not reveal to Laban, either by a look or by an action, that he knew of the change in Laban's attitude toward him. However, Jacob had to resort to this self-control—perhaps it was even dissimulation—"in that he did not tell him" and could not have told him, because he would be able to leave Laban's home only by fleeing from it. Had he told Laban that he intended to leave his service, as he certainly would have had the right to do, then, knowing the Aramean as he did, Jacob would have had to expect that Laban would turn him out, alone and stripped of all his possessions, just as he had been when he had first arrived at Laban's house.

23. The fact that Laban took his companions with him showed that it had been Laban's intention to resort to violence. As is clear from the verses that follow, Laban in his meanness did not view Jacob's wealth as property which the latter had earned by honest toil (working power, after all, is not a tangible asset) but merely as possessions which Jacob held by the good will of his master, subject to his master's pleasure, and which Jacob could remove from his master's house only with the latter's consent.

yearned for your father's house. But why did you steal my gods?" 31. And Yaakov answered and said to Laban: "Because I was afraid, for I told myself that you might take your daughters from me by force. 32. But with whomever you will find your gods, he shall not remain alive; in the presence of our brothers discern what of yours is with me, and take it for yourself." Yaakov did not know that [it was] Raḥel [who] had stolen them. 33. And Laban came into Yaakov's tent and into Leah's tent and into the tent of the two handmaids and found nothing. And he went out of Leah's tent and came into the tent of Raḥel. 34. Now Raḥel had taken the idols and placed them into the cushion of the camel and was now sitting upon them. Laban felt about all the tent found nothing. 35. And she said to her father: "Let it not be annoying in the eyes of my lord that I cannot rise before you, because the manner of women is upon me." So he searched but did not find the idols. 36. This made Yaakov angry, and now he rose to quarrel with Laban: "What is my crime and what my sin that you pursued me? 37. You have felt all about my utensils. What have you found among of all the utensils of your house? Set it here in the presence of my brothers and yours and let them judge between the two of us. 38. For these twenty years have I been with you: your ewes and your she-goats have not miscarried and I have not eaten the rams of your flock. 39. I have not brought home to you anything torn [by other animals]: I would make restitution for it; you would claim it from my hand, whether it was stolen by day or stolen by night. 40. I was there by day when the heat consumed me, and the frost by night, and sleep was banished from my eyes. 41. This [happened] to me for twenty years at your house; I served you fourteen years for your two daughters and six years for your flock, and you changed my pay ten times. 42. Had not the God of my father and the dread of Yitzḥak at the time of the

לְבֵית אָבִיךָ לָמָּה גָנַבְתָּ אֶת־אֱלֹהָי: לא וַיַּעַן יַעֲקֹב
וַיֹּאמֶר לְלָבָן כִּי יָרֵאתִי כִּי אָמַרְתִּי פֶּן־תִּגְזֹל אֶת־
בְּנוֹתֶיךָ מֵעִמִּי: לב עִם אֲשֶׁר תִּמְצָא אֶת־אֱלֹהֶיךָ
לֹא יִחְיֶה נֶגֶד אַחֵינוּ הַכֶּר־לְךָ מָה עִמָּדִי וְקַח־לָךְ
וְלֹא־יָדַע יַעֲקֹב כִּי רָחֵל גְּנָבָתַם: לג וַיָּבֹא לָבָן
בְּאֹהֶל־יַעֲקֹב ׀ וּבְאֹהֶל לֵאָה וּבְאֹהֶל שְׁתֵּי
הָאֲמָהֹת וְלֹא מָצָא וַיֵּצֵא מֵאֹהֶל לֵאָה וַיָּבֹא
בְּאֹהֶל רָחֵל: לד וְרָחֵל לָקְחָה אֶת־הַתְּרָפִים
וַתְּשִׂמֵם בְּכַר הַגָּמָל וַתֵּשֶׁב עֲלֵיהֶם וַיְמַשֵּׁשׁ לָבָן
אֶת־כָּל־הָאֹהֶל וְלֹא מָצָא: לה וַתֹּאמֶר אֶל־אָבִיהָ
אַל־יִחַר בְּעֵינֵי אֲדֹנִי כִּי לוֹא אוּכַל לָקוּם מִפָּנֶיךָ
כִּי־דֶרֶךְ נָשִׁים לִי וַיְחַפֵּשׂ וְלֹא מָצָא אֶת־
הַתְּרָפִים: לו וַיִּחַר לְיַעֲקֹב וַיָּרֶב בְּלָבָן וַיַּעַן יַעֲקֹב
וַיֹּאמֶר לְלָבָן מַה־פִּשְׁעִי מַה חַטָּאתִי כִּי דָלַקְתָּ
אַחֲרָי: לז כִּי־מִשַּׁשְׁתָּ אֶת־כָּל־כֵּלַי מַה־מָּצָאתָ
מִכֹּל כְּלֵי־בֵיתֶךָ שִׂים כֹּה נֶגֶד אַחַי וְאַחֶיךָ
וְיוֹכִיחוּ בֵּין שְׁנֵינוּ: לח זֶה עֶשְׂרִים שָׁנָה אָנֹכִי
עִמָּךְ רְחֵלֶיךָ וְעִזֶּיךָ לֹא שִׁכֵּלוּ וְאֵילֵי צֹאנְךָ לֹא
אָכָלְתִּי: לט טְרֵפָה לֹא־הֵבֵאתִי אֵלֶיךָ אָנֹכִי
אֲחַטֶּנָּה מִיָּדִי תְּבַקְשֶׁנָּה גְּנֻבְתִי יוֹם וּגְנֻבְתִי לָיְלָה:
מ הָיִיתִי בַיּוֹם אֲכָלַנִי חֹרֶב וְקֶרַח בַּלָּיְלָה וַתִּדַּד
שְׁנָתִי מֵעֵינָי: מא זֶה־לִּי עֶשְׂרִים שָׁנָה בְּבֵיתֶךָ
עֲבַדְתִּיךָ אַרְבַּע־עֶשְׂרֵה שָׁנָה בִּשְׁתֵּי בְנֹתֶיךָ וְשֵׁשׁ
שָׁנִים בְּצֹאנֶךָ וַתַּחֲלֵף אֶת־מַשְׂכֻּרְתִּי עֲשֶׂרֶת
מֹנִים: מב לוּלֵי אֱלֹהֵי אָבִי אֱלֹהֵי אַבְרָהָם וּפַחַד

42. פַּחַד יִצְחָק *[the dread of Yitzḥak]* does not refer to God but to the terrible moment of the *akedah*, when Isaac actually sensed the knife drawn above him. This was the culmination of the moral perfection attained by

offering been at my side, you would now have sent me away empty-handed. God saw my misery and the toil of my hand, and He proved it last night." 43. And Laban answered and said to Yaakov: "The daughters are my daughters, the sons are my sons, the flocks are my flocks, and everything you see is mine—and as for my daughters, what could I do to them today, or to the sons whom they have borne? 44. And now, come, let us make a covenant, I and you, that He may remain a witness between me and you!" 45. And Yaakov took a rock and raised it high as a memorial stone, 46. And Yaakov said to his companions: "You, too, gather rocks;" and they took rocks and made a cairn, and they ate there, by the cairn. 47. Laban called it "Cairn of the Testimony" and Yaakov called it Gal-Ed, 48. for Laban said: "This cairn is witness between me and you today." Therefore he called it Gal-Ed,° 49. And also Ha-Mitzpah (The Watchpost) because he had said: "*God* will watch between me and you because we will no longer be visible to one another. 50. If you should cause my daughters to suffer or if you will take wives besides my daughters, there is, of course, no man with us, but behold: God is witness between me and you!" 51. Laban further said to Yaakov: "Behold, here is this cairn—and here, also, the memorial stone—which I have set up between myself and yourself. 52. This cairn is witness and this memorial stone is witness that I will never pass this cairn [to go] to you, and you will not pass this cairn and this memorial stone [to go] to me, for harm. 53. The God of Abraham and the God of Naḥor—the God of their father—will judge between us!" And Yaakov swore by the dread of his father Yitzḥak at the time of the offering. 54. And Yaakov prepared a meal upon the mountain and invited his companions to eat; they ate and they stayed overnight upon the mountain.

°*Note to the English translation*: Laban named the cairn in Aramaic: *Yegar-sahadutha*. *Gal-Ed* is the Hebrew for "Witness' Cairn." [G.H.]

יִצְחָק הָיָה לִי כִּי עַתָּה רֵיקָם שִׁלַּחְתָּנִי אֶת־עָנְיִי
וְאֶת־יְגִיעַ כַּפַּי רָאָה אֱלֹהִים וַיּוֹכַח אָמֶשׁ:
שביעי מג וַיַּעַן לָבָן וַיֹּאמֶר אֶל־יַעֲקֹב הַבָּנוֹת
בְּנֹתַי וְהַבָּנִים בָּנַי וְהַצֹּאן צֹאנִי וְכֹל אֲשֶׁר־אַתָּה
רֹאֶה לִי־הוּא וְלִבְנֹתַי מָה־אֶעֱשֶׂה לָאֵלֶּה הַיּוֹם אוֹ
לִבְנֵיהֶן אֲשֶׁר יָלָדוּ: מד וְעַתָּה לְכָה נִכְרְתָה בְרִית
אֲנִי וָאָתָּה וְהָיָה לְעֵד בֵּינִי וּבֵינֶךָ: מה וַיִּקַּח יַעֲקֹב
אָבֶן וַיְרִימֶהָ מַצֵּבָה: מו וַיֹּאמֶר יַעֲקֹב לְאֶחָיו
לִקְטוּ אֲבָנִים וַיִּקְחוּ אֲבָנִים וַיַּעֲשׂוּ־גָל וַיֹּאכְלוּ
שָׁם עַל־הַגָּל: מז וַיִּקְרָא־לוֹ לָבָן יְגַר שָׂהֲדוּתָא
וְיַעֲקֹב קָרָא לוֹ גַּלְעֵד: מח וַיֹּאמֶר לָבָן הַגַּל הַזֶּה
עֵד בֵּינִי וּבֵינְךָ הַיּוֹם עַל־כֵּן קָרָא־שְׁמוֹ גַּלְעֵד:
מט וְהַמִּצְפָּה אֲשֶׁר אָמַר יִצֶף יְהֹוָה בֵּינִי וּבֵינֶךָ כִּי
נִסָּתֵר אִישׁ מֵרֵעֵהוּ: נ אִם־תְּעַנֶּה אֶת־בְּנֹתַי
וְאִם־תִּקַּח נָשִׁים עַל־בְּנֹתַי אֵין אִישׁ עִמָּנוּ רְאֵה
אֱלֹהִים עֵד בֵּינִי וּבֵינֶךָ: נא וַיֹּאמֶר לָבָן לְיַעֲקֹב
הִנֵּה | הַגַּל הַזֶּה וְהִנֵּה הַמַּצֵּבָה אֲשֶׁר יָרִיתִי בֵּינִי
וּבֵינֶךָ: נב עֵד הַגַּל הַזֶּה וְעֵדָה הַמַּצֵּבָה אִם־אָנִי
לֹא־אֶעֱבֹר אֵלֶיךָ אֶת־הַגַּל הַזֶּה וְאִם־אַתָּה לֹא־
תַעֲבֹר אֵלַי אֶת־הַגַּל הַזֶּה וְאֶת־הַמַּצֵּבָה הַזֹּאת
לְרָעָה: נג אֱלֹהֵי אַבְרָהָם וֵאלֹהֵי נָחוֹר יִשְׁפְּטוּ
בֵינֵינוּ אֱלֹהֵי אֲבִיהֶם וַיִּשָּׁבַע יַעֲקֹב בְּפַחַד אָבִיו
יִצְחָק: נד וַיִּזְבַּח יַעֲקֹב זֶבַח בָּהָר וַיִּקְרָא לְאֶחָיו
לֶאֱכָל־לָחֶם וַיֹּאכְלוּ לֶחֶם וַיָּלִינוּ בָּהָר: מפטיר

Isaac. [Now Jacob says to Laban:] "Had not the God   of Abraham, and Isaac's immense merit, been at my side...."

XXXII

1. Laban rose up early in the morning and he kissed his sons and daughters and blessed them. Then Laban left and returned to his place. 2. But Yaakov had gone upon his way, and angels of God met him. 3. And when he saw them, Yaakov said: "This is a camp of God," and he called the place Maḥanayim.

לב א וַיַּשְׁכֵּ֨ם לָבָ֜ן בַּבֹּ֗קֶר וַיְנַשֵּׁ֧ק לְבָנָ֛יו
וְלִבְנוֹתָ֖יו וַיְבָ֣רֶךְ אֶתְהֶ֑ם וַיֵּ֛לֶךְ וַיָּ֥שָׁב לָבָ֖ן לִמְקֹמֽוֹ׃
ב וְיַעֲקֹ֖ב הָלַ֣ךְ לְדַרְכּ֑וֹ וַיִּפְגְּעוּ־ב֖וֹ מַלְאֲכֵ֥י
אֱלֹהִֽים׃ ג וַיֹּ֤אמֶר יַעֲקֹב֙ כַּאֲשֶׁ֣ר רָאָ֔ם מַחֲנֵ֥ה
אֱלֹהִ֖ים זֶ֑ה וַיִּקְרָ֛א שֵׁם־הַמָּק֥וֹם הַה֖וּא מַחֲנָֽיִם׃ פ

CHAPTER XXXII

2. When Jacob left his father's house twenty years earlier, וַיִּפְגַּע בַּמָּקוֹם "he met the Divine." Now, at his homecoming, it was the angels who met *him*. Twenty years earlier it had been a momentous event for him that the Divine should have appeared to him. At that moment it became clear to Jacob that it was the wish of the *shekhinah* to return to earth, so that while the angels would seek God in heaven, His glory should dwell among men on earth. Jacob was given to understand that he and his future nation were to labor with all their might to bring about this return of God's glory to earth. But now when, detached from all other circumstances, Jacob could breathe freely for the first time as [the head of] an independent family, it was the angels who viewed *his* coming as a great experience. It was a momentous experience for the angels to see such a family on earth for the first time. Jacob went quietly on his way, unaware of his own godliness and of that of his household, but the angels of God regarded their encounter with him as a momentous experience.

The Haftarah for this Sidra may be found on page 833.

וישלח

VAYISHLAḤ

ד וַיִּשְׁלַח יַעֲקֹב מַלְאָכִים לְפָנָיו אֶל־עֵשָׂו אָחִיו
אַרְצָה שֵׂעִיר שְׂדֵה אֱדוֹם׃ ה וַיְצַו אֹתָם לֵאמֹר
כֹּה תֹאמְרוּן לַאדֹנִי לְעֵשָׂו כֹּה אָמַר עַבְדְּךָ
יַעֲקֹב עִם־לָבָן גַּרְתִּי וָאֵחַר עַד־עָתָּה׃ ו וַיְהִי־לִי
שׁוֹר וַחֲמוֹר צֹאן וְעֶבֶד וְשִׁפְחָה וָאֶשְׁלְחָה
לְהַגִּיד לַאדֹנִי לִמְצֹא־חֵן בְּעֵינֶיךָ׃ ז וַיָּשֻׁבוּ
הַמַּלְאָכִים אֶל־יַעֲקֹב לֵאמֹר בָּאנוּ אֶל־אָחִיךָ
אֶל־עֵשָׂו וְגַם הֹלֵךְ לִקְרָאתְךָ וְאַרְבַּע־מֵאוֹת
אִישׁ עִמּוֹ׃ ח וַיִּירָא יַעֲקֹב מְאֹד וַיֵּצֶר לוֹ וַיַּחַץ
אֶת־הָעָם אֲשֶׁר־אִתּוֹ וְאֶת־הַצֹּאן וְאֶת־הַבָּקָר
וְהַגְּמַלִּים לִשְׁנֵי מַחֲנוֹת׃ ט וַיֹּאמֶר אִם־יָבוֹא
עֵשָׂו אֶל־הַמַּחֲנֶה הָאַחַת וְהִכָּהוּ וְהָיָה הַמַּחֲנֶה
הַנִּשְׁאָר לִפְלֵיטָה׃ י וַיֹּאמֶר יַעֲקֹב אֱלֹהֵי אָבִי
אַבְרָהָם וֵאלֹהֵי אָבִי יִצְחָק יְהוָה הָאֹמֵר אֵלַי
שׁוּב לְאַרְצְךָ וּלְמוֹלַדְתְּךָ וְאֵיטִיבָה עִמָּךְ׃
יא קָטֹנְתִּי מִכֹּל הַחֲסָדִים וּמִכָּל־הָאֱמֶת אֲשֶׁר
עָשִׂיתָ אֶת־עַבְדֶּךָ כִּי בְמַקְלִי עָבַרְתִּי אֶת־הַיַּרְדֵּן

4. Yaakov sent messengers ahead of him to his brother Esav, to the land of Seir, the fields of Edom, 5. and he commanded them as follows: "Thus shall you say to my lord, to Esav: 'Thus says your servant Yaakov: I have sojourned with Laban as a stranger and was held there until now. 6. And I have acquired oxen and donkeys, flocks and menservants and maidservants, and I have gladly sent to tell this to my lord in order to find favor in your eyes.'" 7. The messengers returned to Yaakov and said: "We came to your brother, to Esav, and moreover, he is coming to meet you, but there are four hundred men with him." 8. And Yaakov was very much afraid and was distressed. He divided the people whom he had with him, and also the flocks, the cattle and the camels, into two camps, 9. and he said: "If Esav comes to the one camp and strikes it down, then the other camp will escape." 10. Thereupon Yaakov said: "O God of my father Abraham and God of my father Yitzḥak, *God* Who says to me: 'Return to your country and to your birthplace and I will do good to you,' 11. I have become too small from all the kindnesses and all the faithfulness which Thou hast already rendered to Thy servant, for with my staff did I pass over this Yarden, and now I have become two camps.

8. . . . Even as Jacob and Esau confronted each other then, so they continue to confront one another to this day. Jacob is the family man blessed with children; hard-working, serving, weighed down by cares. Esau is the accomplished man of substance. Despite the blessing and the birthright he received, it took Jacob twenty years of toil and struggle to win that which he now brought home with him as his greatest prize, his greatest achievement: to be the independent father of a family. Others take this blessing for granted from birth, and Esau, the accomplished man of substance, already possessed it in full measure when Jacob first left home. While Jacob, by dint of his toil, achieved the happiness of building up a family life, Esau had become a political personality; he had become the leader of an army, an אלוף [general] at the head of his troops. So much for the external contrast between Jacob, who held his brother's heel when they were born, and Esau, the "man of substance."

Two opposing principles confront each other in the persons of Jacob and Esau. The struggle between them, and the outcome of this struggle, are the forces that have shaped world history. Jacob represents family life, happiness and making others happy; Esau, the glitter of political power and might. This conflict has gone on for thousands of years: Is it sufficient to be merely a human being, and does all social organization and political power have significance only as a means for attaining this lofty goal of all human endeavor, or does everything that is "human" in mankind, in home and in family life exist only in order to serve as an underpinning for such prizes as those that politics, etc., have to offer?

° ° °

12. Deliver me, I pray Thee, from the hand of my brother, from the hand of Esav, for I fear him, lest he should come and strike me down, the mother along with the children. 13. And Thou hast said it: 'I will surely do good to you so that I will make your descendants like the sand of the sea, which cannot be counted for multitude.'" 14. He stayed there that night and took of that which he had in his hands a gift for his brother Esav: 15. two hundred she-goats and twenty he-goats; two-hundred ewes and twenty rams; 16. thirty nursing camels with their young, forty cows and ten bulls; twenty she-donkeys and ten foals. 17. And he delivered them to his servants, each herd by itself, and he said to his servants: "Pass over before me and put a space between herd and herd." 18. And he commanded the first one as follows: "If my brother Esav should meet you and should ask you as follows: 'Whose are you, and where are you going, and whose are all those before you?' 19. Then you shall say: 'They belong to your servant Yaakov. It is a present sent to my lord, to Esav, and behold, he himself is behind us.'" 20. So he commanded also the second, and the third, and all those who followed the herds: "In this manner shall you speak to Esav when you meet him. 21. Say each time: Lo! your servant Yaakov is also behind us!" For he thought: "I will first appease his anger with the gift that goes before me and then I will see his countenance; perhaps he will raise my countenance." 22. So the gift passed on before him, but he himself

הַזֶּה וְעַתָּה הָיִיתִי לִשְׁנֵי מַחֲנוֹת: יב הַצִּילֵנִי נָא
מִיַּד אָחִי מִיַּד עֵשָׂו כִּי־יָרֵא אָנֹכִי אֹתוֹ פֶּן־יָבוֹא
וְהִכַּנִי אֵם עַל־בָּנִים: יג וְאַתָּה אָמַרְתָּ הֵיטֵב
אֵיטִיב עִמָּךְ וְשַׂמְתִּי אֶת־זַרְעֲךָ כְּחוֹל הַיָּם אֲשֶׁר
לֹא־יִסָּפֵר מֵרֹב: שני יד וַיָּלֶן שָׁם בַּלַּיְלָה הַהוּא
וַיִּקַּח מִן־הַבָּא בְיָדוֹ מִנְחָה לְעֵשָׂו אָחִיו:
טו עִזִּים מָאתַיִם וּתְיָשִׁים עֶשְׂרִים רְחֵלִים
מָאתַיִם וְאֵילִים עֶשְׂרִים: טז גְּמַלִּים מֵינִיקוֹת
וּבְנֵיהֶם שְׁלֹשִׁים פָּרוֹת אַרְבָּעִים וּפָרִים עֲשָׂרָה
אֲתֹנֹת עֶשְׂרִים וַעְיָרִם עֲשָׂרָה: יז וַיִּתֵּן בְּיַד־
עֲבָדָיו עֵדֶר עֵדֶר לְבַדּוֹ וַיֹּאמֶר אֶל־עֲבָדָיו עִבְרוּ
לְפָנַי וְרֶוַח תָּשִׂימוּ בֵּין עֵדֶר וּבֵין עֵדֶר: יח וַיְצַו
אֶת־הָרִאשׁוֹן לֵאמֹר כִּי יִפְגָּשְׁךָ עֵשָׂו אָחִי
וּשְׁאֵלְךָ לֵאמֹר לְמִי־אַתָּה וְאָנָה תֵלֵךְ וּלְמִי אֵלֶּה
לְפָנֶיךָ: יט וְאָמַרְתָּ לְעַבְדְּךָ לְיַעֲקֹב מִנְחָה הִוא
שְׁלוּחָה לַאדֹנִי לְעֵשָׂו וְהִנֵּה גַם־הוּא אַחֲרֵינוּ:
כ וַיְצַו גַּם אֶת הַשֵּׁנִי גַּם אֶת־הַשְּׁלִישִׁי גַּם אֶת־
כָּל־הַהֹלְכִים אַחֲרֵי הָעֲדָרִים לֵאמֹר כַּדָּבָר הַזֶּה
תְּדַבְּרוּן אֶל־עֵשָׂו בְּמֹצַאֲכֶם אֹתוֹ: כא וַאֲמַרְתֶּם
גַּם הִנֵּה עַבְדְּךָ יַעֲקֹב אַחֲרֵינוּ כִּי־אָמַר אֲכַפְּרָה
פָנָיו בַּמִּנְחָה הַהֹלֶכֶת לְפָנָי וְאַחֲרֵי־כֵן אֶרְאֶה
פָנָיו אוּלַי יִשָּׂא פָנָי: כב וַתַּעֲבֹר הַמִּנְחָה עַל־

12–13. Jacob at this point receives no answer to his cry of distress; that answer will come to him only through an experience to which all these happenings have led him.

14. Throughout the subsequent centuries of *galuth* the nation of Jacob has had to employ דורן ותפלה [presents and prayers] as means for its survival. In addition to crying to God for help, the nation had to appease Esau with gifts from its substance in order to save itself. Even so, in a similar plight, did the progenitor of this people resort to this means of self-preservation.

19ff. Jacob attached great importance to having the leader of each herd give Esau the impression that he was going to come face to face with Jacob immediately, but then, instead of finding himself face to face with Jacob, Esau should see yet another gift led up to him. Probably guided by deep psychological insight, Jacob felt that in this manner Esau's anger, which would gather force again and again in anticipation of Jacob's appearance, would be soothed each time when, instead of seeing Jacob, Esau would be presented with yet another gift of appeasement. Jacob considered this the surest way in which he could hope gradually to cool and soften Esau's wrath.

remained awake that night in the camp.
23. And he got up during that night, took
his two wives, his two maidservants and his
eleven children and passed over the ford of
the Yabbok. 24. That is, he took them
and led them across the stream and brought
across that which he had. 25. And Yaakov
was left alone, and someone wrestled with
him until the break of day. 26. He saw
that he could not prevail against him, so he
touched the upper joint of his thigh, and
the upper joint of Yaakov's thigh was dis-
located as he wrestled with him. 27. And
he said: "Let me go, for day is breaking."
But he [Yaakov] said: "I will not let you go
unless you bless me." 28. And he said:
"What is your name?" And he said: "Yaakov."
29. And he said: "Your name shall no

פָּנָיו וְהוּא לָן בַּלַּיְלָה־הַהוּא בַּמַּחֲנֶה: כג וַיָּקָם |
בַּלַּיְלָה הוּא וַיִּקַּח אֶת־שְׁתֵּי נָשָׁיו וְאֶת־שְׁתֵּי
שִׁפְחֹתָיו וְאֶת־אַחַד עָשָׂר יְלָדָיו וַיַּעֲבֹר אֵת
מַעֲבַר יַבֹּק: כד וַיִּקָּחֵם וַיַּעֲבִרֵם אֶת־הַנָּחַל וַיַּעֲבֵר
אֶת־אֲשֶׁר־לוֹ: כה וַיִּוָּתֵר יַעֲקֹב לְבַדּוֹ וַיֵּאָבֵק אִישׁ
עִמּוֹ עַד עֲלוֹת הַשָּׁחַר: כו וַיַּרְא כִּי לֹא יָכֹל לוֹ
וַיִּגַּע בְּכַף־יְרֵכוֹ וַתֵּקַע כַּף־יֶרֶךְ יַעֲקֹב בְּהֵאָבְקוֹ
עִמּוֹ: כז וַיֹּאמֶר שַׁלְּחֵנִי כִּי עָלָה הַשָּׁחַר וַיֹּאמֶר
לֹא אֲשַׁלֵּחֲךָ כִּי אִם־בֵּרַכְתָּנִי: כח וַיֹּאמֶר אֵלָיו
מַה־שְּׁמֶךָ וַיֹּאמֶר יַעֲקֹב: כט וַיֹּאמֶר לֹא יַעֲקֹב

25. According to the Sages, the dust that "whirled up" from around these two wrestlers "was a dust that rose up to the Throne of God" (Ḥullin 91a). For this struggle was the prototype of a struggle that has continued throughout history; indeed, it is the basic content of world history.

°   °   °

Jacob's experience that night was the answer to his cry of distress: As long as night prevails on earth, as long as man's consciousness is clouded, and as long as things are intermingled beyond recognition so that they cannot be understood for what they really are, Jacob will have to expect struggles and conflicts. According to the Sages, it is with שָׂרוֹ שֶׁל עֵשָׂו, the genius and spirit of Esau, armed with orb, scepter and sword, that Jacob will have to struggle until the night has gone from the earth. Jacob himself realized that his adversary was a higher being and he perpetuated this idea in the name he gave to the place.

וַיֵּאָבֵק אִישׁ עִמּוֹ [and someone wrestled with him]: It is not Jacob but his adversary who is the aggressor. Jacob fights only in self-defense.

27. . . . Jacob's adversary can fight only as long as night prevails on earth. As long as it is night he appears to be, if not the victor, then still the mightier in the struggle. But as soon as day breaks, positions are reversed, and it is Jacob who sets the terms, as it were, for the cessation of the struggle. And the condition which Jacob sets for ending the struggle, and which is therefore the sole purpose of the encounter, is the recognition that Jacob is deserving of blessing and support, not persecution, that only by paying him such recognition will the nations bring blessings also upon themselves, and only thus will the promise, "and

through you will all the families on earth be blessed, and through your seed" [Genesis 28:14] be fulfilled.

Hence, Jacob says: "All night long you have attacked me, thus implying that you regard me as an obstacle and that you must wage a ceaseless struggle in order to destroy me. But, now that day is breaking you are giving up the struggle. But I will not cease from the fight until you have accorded me recognition by blessing me." The goal of history is not that Jacob should be forced to merge into the mass of the nations, but the reverse. The nations must come to understand that precisely those principles which Jacob has championed and held aloft amidst all these struggles hold also the happiness of those nations which will adopt them as their own. The nations of their own accord should devote all their spiritual and material resources to the furtherance of these principles and indeed regard them as their sole objective.

29. . . . וַתּוּכָל [since you have prevailed;] lit., "since you have been able"]: "You have accomplished everything you wanted to achieve. I have not. I wanted to make you fall but I was unable to do so. All you wanted was not to fall, and you achieved what you wanted." This has remained the relationship between Jacob and Esau to this very day. With regard to both politics and religion Esau declares: "Outside of me there is no salvation," and he considers his own existence threatened as long as, aside from himself, there is a Jacob, as long as there is, aside from himself, yet another factor claiming its rightful share in the shaping of the world. To Israel, everything truly human is justified and inviolable; indeed, Israel declares that all things truly human will attain their greatest significance and flowering precisely if they will absorb the spirit that

longer be said to be Yaakov, but Yisrael, for you have become the commanding power before God and men, since you have prevailed." 30. Thereupon Yaakov asked and said: "Please tell me your name." But he said: "Why is it that you ask after my name?" And he blessed him there. 31. Yaakov named the place Peniel: "For I have seen the Divine face to face and my character has remained intact." 32. The sun rose for him when he passed over Penuel° and he limped upon his thigh. 33. Therefore Yisrael's sons must not eat the sinew of weakness which is on the upper joint of the thigh, to this day, because he touched the sinew of weakness at the upper joint of Yaakov's thigh.

XXXIII

1. Yaakov lifted up his eyes and

°*Note to the English translation*: Although Jacob named the place Peniel, it was later known as Penuel. Cf. I Kings 12:25: "Then Jerobeam built . . . Penuel." [G.H.]

יֵאָמֵר עוֹד שִׁמְךָ כִּי אִם־יִשְׂרָאֵל כִּי־שָׂרִיתָ עִם־
אֱלֹהִים וְעִם־אֲנָשִׁים וַתּוּכָל׃ ל וַיִּשְׁאַל יַעֲקֹב
וַיֹּאמֶר הַגִּידָה נָּא שְׁמֶךָ וַיֹּאמֶר לָמָּה זֶּה תִּשְׁאַל
לִשְׁמִי וַיְבָרֶךְ אֹתוֹ שָׁם׃ שלישי לא וַיִּקְרָא יַעֲקֹב
שֵׁם הַמָּקוֹם פְּנִיאֵל כִּי־רָאִיתִי אֱלֹהִים פָּנִים
אֶל־פָּנִים וַתִּנָּצֵל נַפְשִׁי׃ לב וַיִּזְרַח־לוֹ הַשֶּׁמֶשׁ
כַּאֲשֶׁר עָבַר אֶת־פְּנוּאֵל וְהוּא צֹלֵעַ עַל־יְרֵכוֹ׃
לג עַל־כֵּן לֹא־יֹאכְלוּ בְנֵי־יִשְׂרָאֵל אֶת־גִּיד
הַנָּשֶׁה אֲשֶׁר עַל־כַּף הַיָּרֵךְ עַד הַיּוֹם הַזֶּה כִּי נָגַע
בְּכַף־יֶרֶךְ יַעֲקֹב בְּגִיד הַנָּשֶׁה׃ לג א וַיִּשָּׂא יַעֲקֹב

Israel is to bring to them, making that spirit a reality in their own lives. The only prize for which Jacob will struggle with Esau is recognition in the form of a blessing.

° ° °

32. The Sages note that twenty years earlier, when Jacob had set out on his wanderings and he arrived at the border of his native land, the sun had set upon him. The period that followed was a dark one. Now, as he returned home, the sun rose upon him again. He had remained unbeaten, unbroken. However, he limped.

33. . . . Each time [the Children of Israel] sit down to eat, they are to be confronted by this admonition from the chronicle of their life's wanderings: that they should gladly forego the sinew, the symbol of that physical strength which was compelled to give way to Esau. They must not think that their existence and its preservation are dependent on that kind of strength. The fact that, unlike Esau, they are not armed with the sword and that they cannot even walk the earth with a firm stride, should not make them feel any less protected or less secure in their march through the ages. For Jacob-Israel, strength lies in other, higher spheres, a strength that Esau cannot sap. *If Jacob falls, he falls not because he is no match for Esau's physical power, but because he did not understand how to retain for himself the protection of his God. Conversely, if Israel stands, he stands not thanks to a firm material foundation beneath him but because his God bears him aloft upon the eagle's wing of His almighty power.* This is the message that was conveyed to Jacob and that is to be borne in the hearts and minds of all Israel forever. . . .

The Book of Genesis lists four Divinely-ordained institutions: שַׁבָּת [the Sabbath] and קֶשֶׁת [the rainbow], מִילָה [circumcision] and גִּיד הַנָּשֶׁה [the prohibition against eating the "sinew of weakness"]. The first two are of significance to all mankind; the latter two have a similar meaning in the narrower sphere of the Jewish people. The Sabbath insures the survival of the spiritual and moral calling assigned to all mankind; circumcision guarantees the survival of Israel's mission. The rainbow is the emblem of the history of mankind; the "sinew of weakness" is the emblem of Jewish history. But it is the moral action of man, and the fate ordained for man by God, that together determine the sum total of all individual and communal life on earth.

CHAPTER XXXIII

1. Jacob saw that Esau had not been disarmed by the gifts. Esau had not dismissed his troops, and so Jacob "divided," etc. Our Sages take this entire account as a guide for what our own conduct should be toward Esau and powers like him. So here, too, we learn that even though we are filled with trust in God and in His promises, we must do our part to help ourselves: אֵין סוֹמְכִין עַל הַנֵּס [One must not rely on miracles].

looked, and lo! Esav was coming, and with him four hundred men. And he divided the children among Leah, Raḥel and the two maidservants. 2. He placed the maidservants and their children foremost, Leah and her children after, and Raḥel and Yosef hindmost. 3. But he himself went ahead of them and bowed to the ground seven times, until he came close to his brother. 4. And Esav ran to meet him and embraced him, fell upon his neck and kissed him; and they wept. 5. And he lifted up his eyes and saw the women and the children, and he said: "Who are these to you?" He said: "They are the children with whom God has favored your servant." 6. And the maidservants approached, they and their children, and they bowed down. 7. Leah and her children also approached and they bowed down, and after that, Yosef and Raḥel approached and they bowed down. 8. And he said: "What is to you [the purpose of] all this camp which I have met?" He said: "To find favor in the eyes of my lord." 9. And Esav said: "I have plenty, brother; let that which you have remain yours." 10. Thereupon Yaakov said: "Please, no! If indeed I have found favor in your eyes, then take my tribute from my hand, for therefore (do I request it). I have looked up to your face as to a judge and you have accepted me with kindness. 11. Please take my blessing which was brought to you, because God has favored me with it, and then: I have everything." He pressed him, and he took it. 12. He said: "Let us now depart and go; I will keep pace with you." 13. Thereupon he replied: "My lord knows that the children are tender and that the sheep and the cattle depend on me for their growth; if they overdrive them one day, all the sheep will die. 14. Let my lord, please, pass on before his servant, and I will continue to move at my own quiet pace, in accordance with the

---

עֵינָיו וַיַּרְא וְהִנֵּה עֵשָׂו בָּא וְעִמּוֹ אַרְבַּע מֵאוֹת אִישׁ וַיַּחַץ אֶת־הַיְלָדִים עַל־לֵאָה וְעַל־רָחֵל וְעַל־ שְׁתֵּי הַשְּׁפָחוֹת: ב וַיָּשֶׂם אֶת־הַשְּׁפָחוֹת וְאֶת־ יַלְדֵיהֶן רִאשֹׁנָה וְאֶת־לֵאָה וִילָדֶיהָ אַחֲרֹנִים וְאֶת־רָחֵל וְאֶת־יוֹסֵף אַחֲרֹנִים: ג וְהוּא עָבַר לִפְנֵיהֶם וַיִּשְׁתַּחוּ אַרְצָה שֶׁבַע פְּעָמִים עַד־ גִּשְׁתּוֹ עַד־אָחִיו: ד וַיָּרָץ עֵשָׂו לִקְרָאתוֹ וַיְחַבְּקֵהוּ וַיִּפֹּל עַל־צַוָּארָו (צואריו קרי) וַיִּשָּׁקֵהוּ (נקוד על וישקהו) וַיִּבְכּוּ: ה וַיִּשָּׂא אֶת־עֵינָיו וַיַּרְא אֶת־הַנָּשִׁים וְאֶת־הַיְלָדִים וַיֹּאמֶר מִי־אֵלֶּה לָּךְ וַיֹּאמַר הַיְלָדִים אֲשֶׁר־חָנַן אֱלֹהִים אֶת־עַבְדֶּךָ: רביעי ו וַתִּגַּשְׁןָ הַשְּׁפָחוֹת הֵנָּה וְיַלְדֵיהֶן וַתִּשְׁתַּחֲוֶיןָ: ז וַתִּגַּשׁ גַּם־לֵאָה וִילָדֶיהָ וַיִּשְׁתַּחֲווּ וְאַחַר נִגַּשׁ יוֹסֵף וְרָחֵל וַיִּשְׁתַּחֲווּ: ח וַיֹּאמֶר מִי לְךָ כָּל־הַמַּחֲנֶה הַזֶּה אֲשֶׁר פָּגָשְׁתִּי וַיֹּאמֶר לִמְצֹא־חֵן בְּעֵינֵי אֲדֹנִי: ט וַיֹּאמֶר עֵשָׂו יֶשׁ־לִי רָב אָחִי יְהִי לְךָ אֲשֶׁר־לָךְ: י וַיֹּאמֶר יַעֲקֹב אַל־נָא אִם־נָא מָצָאתִי חֵן בְּעֵינֶיךָ וְלָקַחְתָּ מִנְחָתִי מִיָּדִי כִּי עַל־כֵּן רָאִיתִי פָנֶיךָ כִּרְאֹת פְּנֵי אֱלֹהִים וַתִּרְצֵנִי: יא קַח־נָא אֶת־בִּרְכָתִי אֲשֶׁר הֻבָאת לָךְ כִּי־חַנַּנִי אֱלֹהִים וְכִי יֶשׁ־לִי־כֹל וַיִּפְצַר־בּוֹ וַיִּקָּח: יב וַיֹּאמֶר נִסְעָה וְנֵלֵכָה וְאֵלְכָה לְנֶגְדֶּךָ: יג וַיֹּאמֶר אֵלָיו אֲדֹנִי יֹדֵעַ כִּי־ הַיְלָדִים רַכִּים וְהַצֹּאן וְהַבָּקָר עָלוֹת עָלָי וּדְפָקוּם יוֹם אֶחָד וָמֵתוּ כָּל־הַצֹּאן: יד יַעֲבָר־נָא אֲדֹנִי לִפְנֵי עַבְדּוֹ וַאֲנִי אֶתְנַהֲלָה לְאִטִּי לְרֶגֶל

---

4. The one little word וַיִּבְכּוּ ["and they wept"] assures us that at this point Esau was overcome by purely human emotions. A kiss can be an affected gesture; not so the tears that flow at such moments. . . .

Tears emanate from the inmost depths of the human soul. By this kiss and these tears we recognize that Esau is still a descendant of Abraham. . . .

pace of the property that goes before me, and in accordance with the pace of the children, until I come to my lord, to Seir." 15. And Esav said: "Please let me leave with you some of the people who are with me." But he said: "What purpose would that serve? May I find favor in the eyes of my lord." 16. So Esav returned on that day on his way, to Seir. 17. And Yaakov journeyed to Sukkoth and built himself a house. He built booths for his property; therefore he named the place Sukkoth. 18. Yaakov came safely to the city of Shekhem, which is situated in the land of Canaan, when he came from Paddan-Aram, and he encamped before the city. 19. He bought the part of the field where he had pitched his tent from the sons of Ḥamor, the father of Shekhem, for one hundred *kesitas*. 20. There he erected an altar as a memorial and proclaimed to himself: God is the God of Yisrael.

XXXIV

1. Dinah, the daughter of Leah, whom she had borne to Yaakov, went out to look about among the daughters of the land. 2. And Shekhem, the son of Ḥamor the Ḥivvite, the prince of the land, saw her, took her, lay with her and raped her. 3. But his soul clung to Dinah, the daughter of Yaakov; he loved the girl and spoke to the girl's heart. 4. And Shekhem spoke to his father Ḥamor as follows: "Take this girl as a wife for me." 5. Yaakov had heard that he had defiled his daughter Dinah, but his sons were with his property in the field, and Yaakov kept silent until they came home. 6. And Ḥamor, the father of Shekhem, went out to Yaakov to

הַמְּלָאכָה אֲשֶׁר־לְפָנַי וּלְרֶגֶל הַיְלָדִים עַד אֲשֶׁר־אָבֹא אֶל־אֲדֹנִי שֵׂעִירָה: טו וַיֹּאמֶר עֵשָׂו אַצִּיגָה־נָּא עִמְּךָ מִן־הָעָם אֲשֶׁר אִתִּי וַיֹּאמֶר לָמָּה זֶּה אֶמְצָא־חֵן בְּעֵינֵי אֲדֹנִי: טז וַיָּשָׁב בַּיּוֹם הַהוּא עֵשָׂו לְדַרְכּוֹ שֵׂעִירָה: יז וְיַעֲקֹב נָסַע סֻכֹּתָה וַיִּבֶן לוֹ בָּיִת וּלְמִקְנֵהוּ עָשָׂה סֻכֹּת עַל־כֵּן קָרָא שֵׁם־הַמָּקוֹם סֻכּוֹת: ס יח וַיָּבֹא יַעֲקֹב שָׁלֵם עִיר שְׁכֶם אֲשֶׁר בְּאֶרֶץ כְּנַעַן בְּבֹאוֹ מִפַּדַּן אֲרָם וַיִּחַן אֶת־פְּנֵי הָעִיר: יט וַיִּקֶן אֶת־חֶלְקַת הַשָּׂדֶה אֲשֶׁר נָטָה־שָׁם אָהֳלוֹ מִיַּד בְּנֵי־חֲמוֹר אֲבִי שְׁכֶם בְּמֵאָה קְשִׂיטָה: כ וַיַּצֶּב־שָׁם מִזְבֵּחַ וַיִּקְרָא־לוֹ אֵל אֱלֹהֵי יִשְׂרָאֵל: ס חמישי

לד א וַתֵּצֵא דִינָה בַּת־לֵאָה אֲשֶׁר יָלְדָה לְיַעֲקֹב לִרְאוֹת בִּבְנוֹת הָאָרֶץ: ב וַיַּרְא אֹתָהּ שְׁכֶם בֶּן־ חֲמוֹר הַחִוִּי נְשִׂיא הָאָרֶץ וַיִּקַּח אֹתָהּ וַיִּשְׁכַּב אֹתָהּ וַיְעַנֶּהָ: ג וַתִּדְבַּק נַפְשׁוֹ בְּדִינָה בַּת־יַעֲקֹב וַיֶּאֱהַב אֶת־הַנַּעֲרָ (הנערה קרי) וַיְדַבֵּר עַל־לֵב הַנַּעֲרָ (הנערה קרי): ד וַיֹּאמֶר שְׁכֶם אֶל־חֲמוֹר אָבִיו לֵאמֹר קַח־לִי אֶת־הַיַּלְדָּה הַזֹּאת לְאִשָּׁה: ה וְיַעֲקֹב שָׁמַע כִּי טִמֵּא אֶת־דִּינָה בִתּוֹ וּבָנָיו הָיוּ אֶת־מִקְנֵהוּ בַּשָּׂדֶה וְהֶחֱרִשׁ יַעֲקֹב עַד־בֹּאָם: ו וַיֵּצֵא חֲמוֹר אֲבִי־שְׁכֶם אֶל־יַעֲקֹב לְדַבֵּר אִתּוֹ:

---

18. שָׁלֵם *[safely]* in full, harmonious, undiminished "completeness," not only in the physical sense but also, and most important, in the moral connotation of the term, in view of the moral perils to which man is exposed when he labors to attain material independence. . . . שָׁלֵם denotes perfect harmony, particularly a complete accord between the outer and inner aspects of things. . . . True peace that is worthy of the name שָׁלוֹם, also in communal life, is not an order of things patterned on external stereotypes. It must emanate from within; it requires that there should be harmony between communal life as it actually is and the ideal of communal life as it should be.

CHAPTER XXXIV

1. *the daughter of Leah.* She was just as much a child of Leah as most of the males of the future Jewish nation. At the same time, she had been born to Jacob; so, the spirit of Jacob, too, lived within her. If she was abused, she may well have brought it upon herself by "going out" from the close circle of her family and entering into the midst of strangers. Nevertheless, she was still a "daughter of Jacob" through and through. She went forth to look about among the daughters of the land, so that she might meet the foreign girls. She was a young girl, and therefore eager to see new things.

speak with him. 7. Meanwhile, the sons of Yaakov had come home from the field as soon as they had heard it. The men were filled with sorrow and it caused them to burn fiercely [with anger] because he had committed a scandalous act against Yisrael, to lie with the daughter of Yaakov; otherwise such a thing would not have happened. 8. And Ḥamor spoke to them as follows: "The soul of my son Shekhem has a liking for your daughter. Please give her to him as a wife, 9. and intermarry with us; give us your daughters and take our daughters for yourselves. 10. And you may dwell with us; the land shall be open before you; remain, do business there, and settle there." 11. But Shekhem said to her father and to her brothers: "May I find favor in your eyes! What you will say to me I will do. 12. Impose a very large marriage settlement and gifts upon me; I will give it according to what you will say to me, and give me the girl as a wife." 13. And the sons of Yaakov replied to Shekhem and his father Ḥamor with cunning and they did all the talking, for, after all, this was the one who had dishonored their sister. 14. They said to them: "We cannot do this thing, to give our sister to a man who has a foreskin; for that is a disgrace to us. 15. However, we will be complaisant to you if you want to become like us, that every male among you will be circumcised. 16. Then we will give you our daughters and take your

ז וּבְנֵי יַעֲקֹב בָּאוּ מִן־הַשָּׂדֶה כְּשָׁמְעָם וַיִּתְעַצְּבוּ
הָאֲנָשִׁים וַיִּחַר לָהֶם מְאֹד כִּי נְבָלָה
עָשָׂה בְיִשְׂרָאֵל לִשְׁכַּב אֶת־בַּת־יַעֲקֹב וְכֵן לֹא
יֵעָשֶׂה: ח וַיְדַבֵּר חֲמוֹר אִתָּם לֵאמֹר שְׁכֶם בְּנִי
חָשְׁקָה נַפְשׁוֹ בְּבִתְּכֶם תְּנוּ נָא אֹתָהּ לוֹ לְאִשָּׁה:
ט וְהִתְחַתְּנוּ אֹתָנוּ בְּנֹתֵיכֶם תִּתְּנוּ־לָנוּ וְאֶת־
בְּנֹתֵינוּ תִּקְחוּ לָכֶם: י וְאִתָּנוּ תֵּשֵׁבוּ וְהָאָרֶץ
תִּהְיֶה לִפְנֵיכֶם שְׁבוּ וּסְחָרוּהָ וְהֵאָחֲזוּ בָּהּ:
יא וַיֹּאמֶר שְׁכֶם אֶל־אָבִיהָ וְאֶל־אַחֶיהָ אֶמְצָא־
חֵן בְּעֵינֵיכֶם וַאֲשֶׁר תֹּאמְרוּ אֵלַי אֶתֵּן: יב הַרְבּוּ
עָלַי מְאֹד מֹהַר וּמַתָּן וְאֶתְּנָה כַּאֲשֶׁר תֹּאמְרוּ
אֵלָי וּתְנוּ־לִי אֶת־הַנַּעֲרָ (הנערה קרי) לְאִשָּׁה:
יג וַיַּעֲנוּ בְנֵי־יַעֲקֹב אֶת־שְׁכֶם וְאֶת־חֲמוֹר אָבִיו
בְּמִרְמָה וַיְדַבֵּרוּ אֲשֶׁר טִמֵּא אֵת דִּינָה אֲחֹתָם:
יד וַיֹּאמְרוּ אֲלֵיהֶם לֹא נוּכַל לַעֲשׂוֹת הַדָּבָר הַזֶּה
לָתֵת אֶת־אֲחֹתֵנוּ לְאִישׁ אֲשֶׁר־לוֹ עָרְלָה כִּי־
חֶרְפָּה הִוא לָנוּ: טו אַךְ־בְּזֹאת נֵאוֹת לָכֶם אִם
תִּהְיוּ כָמֹנוּ לְהִמֹּל לָכֶם כָּל־זָכָר: טז וְנָתַנּוּ
אֶת־בְּנֹתֵינוּ לָכֶם וְאֶת־בְּנֹתֵיכֶם נִקַּח־לָנוּ

7. The men were in the grip of two distinct emotions. First, עֶצֶב ["sadness"], the pain of being forced to give up something precious, a painful sense of loss. Their pure, chaste Dinah was gone forever. Even if they were to succeed in retrieving her from the hands of Shekhem, the fact remained that they had lost her. These were their personal feelings. At the same time, the wicked deed "fired" them with anger, for Shekhem had committed נְבָלָה, a scandalous act against Israel, to defile a daughter of Jacob! . . .

From this, their first clash with the other nations, the family of Jacob learned a significant lesson: since they are weak and without any visible means of protection, they can be secure only if others will recognize their moral and spiritual nobility, through which, precisely in their material weakness, they reveal that triumphant Divine element which makes Jacob "Israel." However, in the incident related here, this human dignity had been killed in Israel, for "otherwise," i.e., had this not been so, such a thing could not have happened. He [Shekhem] would not have dared to do this to a native daughter of a full-fledged citizen. It could happen to Dinah only because she was a "Jew-girl," a בַּת יַעֲקֹב ["daughter of Jacob"].

This hurt the sons of Jacob very deeply. They had just received strict instructions to leave the mighty "sinew of the firm step" to the other nations. But they were soon to learn that there were situations, such as this one, involving the preservation of purity and morality, when one might wish it were possible to snatch the sword from Esau's hand and take it into one's own. This is the meaning of the words "and it caused them to burn fiercely."

daughters for ourselves, we will live with you and we will become one people. 17. But if you will not listen to us, to be circumcised, we will take our daughter and go." 18. Their words were found good in the eyes of Ḥamor and Shekhem, Ḥamor's son. 19. And the young man did not delay doing the thing, because he desired Yaakov's daughter, but then he was the most respected person in all his father's house. 20. And Ḥamor and his son Shekhem came to the gate of their city and they spoke to the people of their city as follows: 21. "These people are peaceable with us; let them remain in the land and do business there; for lo! the land is spacious, let it be open to them; we can take their daughters for ourselves and give our daughters to them. 22. Only on this condition will these people be complaisant to us, to remain with us to become one people: that every male among us will be circumcised, just as they are circumcised. 23. Then their property, their gain and all their animals will be ours; only let us be complaisant to them so that they will remain with us." 24. And all those who went out from the gate of his city obeyed Ḥamor and his son Shekhem, and every male was circumcised, all those who had gone out of the gate of his city. 25. It came to pass on the third day, when they were in pain, that two of the sons of

וְיָשַׁבְנוּ אִתְּכֶם וְהָיִינוּ לְעַם אֶחָד: יז וְאִם־לֹא תִשְׁמְעוּ אֵלֵינוּ לְהִמּוֹל וְלָקַחְנוּ אֶת־בִּתֵּנוּ וְהָלָכְנוּ: יח וַיִּיטְבוּ דִבְרֵיהֶם בְּעֵינֵי חֲמוֹר וּבְעֵינֵי שְׁכֶם בֶּן־חֲמוֹר: יט וְלֹא־אֵחַר הַנַּעַר לַעֲשׂוֹת הַדָּבָר כִּי חָפֵץ בְּבַת־יַעֲקֹב וְהוּא נִכְבָּד מִכֹּל בֵּית אָבִיו: כ וַיָּבֹא חֲמוֹר וּשְׁכֶם בְּנוֹ אֶל־שַׁעַר עִירָם וַיְדַבְּרוּ אֶל־אַנְשֵׁי עִירָם לֵאמֹר: כא הָאֲנָשִׁים הָאֵלֶּה שְׁלֵמִים הֵם אִתָּנוּ וְיֵשְׁבוּ בָאָרֶץ וְיִסְחֲרוּ אֹתָהּ וְהָאָרֶץ הִנֵּה רַחֲבַת־יָדַיִם לִפְנֵיהֶם אֶת־בְּנֹתָם נִקַּח־לָנוּ לְנָשִׁים וְאֶת־בְּנֹתֵינוּ נִתֵּן לָהֶם: כב אַךְ־בְּזֹאת יֵאֹתוּ לָנוּ הָאֲנָשִׁים לָשֶׁבֶת אִתָּנוּ לִהְיוֹת לְעַם אֶחָד בְּהִמּוֹל לָנוּ כָּל־זָכָר כַּאֲשֶׁר הֵם נִמֹּלִים: כג מִקְנֵהֶם וְקִנְיָנָם וְכָל־בְּהֶמְתָּם הֲלוֹא לָנוּ הֵם אַךְ נֵאוֹתָה לָהֶם וְיֵשְׁבוּ אִתָּנוּ: כד וַיִּשְׁמְעוּ אֶל־חֲמוֹר וְאֶל־שְׁכֶם בְּנוֹ כָּל־יֹצְאֵי שַׁעַר עִירוֹ וַיִּמֹּלוּ כָּל־זָכָר כָּל־יֹצְאֵי שַׁעַר עִירוֹ: כה וַיְהִי בַיּוֹם הַשְּׁלִישִׁי בִּהְיוֹתָם כֹּאֲבִים וַיִּקְחוּ

25. Here begins the account of acts which are deserving of censure and for which we are under no obligation to find an excuse. Had Simeon and Levi killed only Shekhem and Ḥamor, they could hardly have been blamed for that act. But they did not spare the unarmed, defenseless men who were at their mercy. They went even further: they looted the city. They made all the inhabitants of the place pay for a crime that had been committed by the lord of their manor, as it were. For this there can be no justification. Hence Jacob now reproaches them, saying: "You have brought me trouble by your actions. Our reputation, our good name, our honor, were as clear as crystal, but now you have disturbed that; you have brought me into bad odor even among the Canaanites and the Perizzites. In addition to doing wrong, you also acted unwisely, because we are so few in number," etc.

Their one reply, הַכְזוֹנָה וגו׳ ["Shall he treat our sister like a harlot?"] expresses the feelings that motivated

Simeon and Levi. The lord of the manor would never have taken such liberties if the maiden in question had not been a foreign, friendless "Jew-girl." This had made Simeon and Levi realize that there would be times when even the family of Jacob would have to take up the sword in defense of purity and honor. As long as men on earth will respect only that law which protects and abets violence, Jacob will have to know how to wield the sword. At this point the sons of Jacob had no desire to act prudently. They wanted to make others fear them so that no one would ever dare do such a thing to them again. Jacob's daughters would not be at the mercy of others. However, by punishing innocent people for a crime committed by the high and mighty, Jacob's sons had gone too far.

It is remarkable that the account of this incident immediately follows the story of the meeting between Jacob and Esau. There, we saw a flash of קוֹל יַעֲקֹב ["the voice of Jacob"], a spark of human emotion flare up for

שְׁנֵי־בְנֵי־יַעֲקֹב שִׁמְעוֹן וְלֵוִי אֲחֵי דִינָה אִישׁ
חַרְבּוֹ וַיָּבֹאוּ עַל־הָעִיר בֶּטַח וַיַּהַרְגוּ כָּל־זָכָר:
כו וְאֶת־חֲמוֹר וְאֶת־שְׁכֶם בְּנוֹ הָרְגוּ לְפִי־חָרֶב
וַיִּקְחוּ אֶת־דִּינָה מִבֵּית שְׁכֶם וַיֵּצֵאוּ: כז בְּנֵי
יַעֲקֹב בָּאוּ עַל־הַחֲלָלִים וַיָּבֹזּוּ הָעִיר אֲשֶׁר
טִמְּאוּ אֲחוֹתָם: כח אֶת־צֹאנָם וְאֶת־בְּקָרָם וְאֶת־
חֲמֹרֵיהֶם וְאֵת אֲשֶׁר־בָּעִיר וְאֶת־אֲשֶׁר בַּשָּׂדֶה
לָקָחוּ: כט וְאֶת־כָּל־חֵילָם וְאֶת־כָּל־טַפָּם וְאֶת־
נְשֵׁיהֶם שָׁבוּ וַיָּבֹזּוּ וְאֵת כָּל־אֲשֶׁר בַּבָּיִת:
ל וַיֹּאמֶר יַעֲקֹב אֶל־שִׁמְעוֹן וְאֶל־לֵוִי עֲכַרְתֶּם
אֹתִי לְהַבְאִישֵׁנִי בְּיֹשֵׁב הָאָרֶץ בַּכְּנַעֲנִי וּבַפְּרִזִּי
וַאֲנִי מְתֵי מִסְפָּר וְנֶאֶסְפוּ עָלַי וְהִכּוּנִי וְנִשְׁמַדְתִּי

Yaakov, Shimeon and Levi, brothers of Dinah, took each man his sword and came upon the city unawares, and killed all the males. 26. They killed Ḥamor and his son Shekhem with the sword, and they took Dinah out of Shekhem's house, and they left. 27. The sons of Yaakov came upon the slain, and plundered the city because it had defiled their sister. 28. They took their sheep, their cattle and their donkeys which were in the city and in the field, 29. and also all their wealth and all their children and their wives they took captive and plundered, and all that was in the house. 30. And Yaakov said to Shimeon and Levi: "You have brought me trouble to discredit me among the inhabitant[s] of the land, the Canaanite[s] and the Perizite[s]. And I am only few in number and they will gather together against me and strike me down, and I and my house will be

a moment in the spirit of Esau, and we recognized in this the germ of humanity which someday will develop fully even in Esau. Here we see another transient phenomenon: the sword of Esau briefly in the hands of the sons of Jacob. From this we learn, for the clarification of all future Jewish history, the following truth: If, in the course of time, we have become that people whose hands are the least bloodstained, if we have become the gentlest, the most tender-hearted of nations, this does not mean that we are weak or cowardly. The final days of our existence as a political entity demonstrated our bravery and military prowess in such an awesome manner that the most valiant of Esau's legions had to be summoned to fight us. We, too, can wield the sword; we, too, are capable of being bloodthirsty. Our gentleness and humaneness are the fruit of the education with which God has favored us by our history and by His law.

It is only the means they employed to vent their outrage that made Simeon and Levi deserving of censure. The emotions that fired Simeon and Levi, and the purpose they sought to achieve, were most sacred and justifiable. The spirit that filled them was indispensable in a family which matured into a nation as "Jacob," which had to endure the harshest blows of fate, the most abject humiliation, and which nevertheless, with resilience of spirit and nobility of heart and mind, must persevere toward a rebirth in world history, in an eternal, unparallelled march through the ages.

We will behold the aged father even on his deathbed uttering a curse upon the excessive violence employed by his sons but at the same time bestowing his praise and blessing upon the motive and the spirit which inspired their action. We will see him assign to Simeon and Levi such a position of powerlessness and dispersion within the future nation of Jacob-Israel that they would never again possess the physical or material power to perpetrate such acts of rash immoderation. However, the spiritual vigor within them, ever mindful of Israel's moral and spiritual dignity and destiny, was to remain ever present and active as a reviving, preserving and saving force within all the spheres of the nation. The same sword which Levi wielded here against a foe from without to rescue his sister's honor will be seen again later [in the incident of the Golden Calf — Exodus 32:26 ff] ruthlessly turned by the Levites against their own brethren (cf. אֶת אֶחָיו לֹא הִכִּיר וְאֶת בָּנָו לֹא יָדָע ["who did not recognize his brothers, who was not conscious of his children" —Deuteronomy 33:9] in order to save them from moral corruption.

In recapitulation, these traits, which we encounter in this first family of Jacob, here and subsequently, should also demonstrate to us what great need there must have been to harden and purify this race of men in the "iron crucible" of suffering, to refine them to a nobility of spirit qualifying them as the chosen models to be emulated by all mankind for its salvation. Not because we are the most tractable of nations, but precisely because we have been the most obstinate, inflexible race of men—עַז שֶׁבָּאוּמוֹת [Betza 25b] as our Sages put it—did God choose us as His instrument, forging us into His toughest, most enduring steel so that, by winning us over to His will, He might demonstrate the wondrous power of His providence and the wondrous strength of His Law.

destroyed." 31. And they said: "Shall he, then, treat our sister like a harlot?"

XXXV

1. And God said to Yaakov: "Arise and go up to Beth El and dwell there, and erect there an altar to the God Who appeared to you when you fled from your brother Esav." 2. Thereupon Yaakov said to his house[hold] and to all those who were with him: "Put away the foreign gods that are among you, purify yourselves and change your clothes. 3. We will arise and go up to Beth El; there I will erect an altar to the God Who answered me in the day of my distress and was with me on the way which I went." 4. They gave to Yaakov all the foreign gods that were in their hands, and the rings that were in their ears, and Yaakov buried them beneath the oak tree which is near Shekhem. 5. Then they journeyed on, and a terror of God was upon the cities that were round about them, so that they did not pursue Yaakov's sons. 6. Yaakov came to Luz, which is in the land of Canaan—this is Beth El—he, and all the people who were with him. 7. He built an altar there and called the place El-Beth El; for there the realities of Divine relationships had been revealed to him when he fled from before his brother. 8. Deborah, Rivkah's nurse, died and was buried below Beth El beneath the oak tree; he named it the Oak of Weeping. 9. God appeared to Yaakov again when he came from Paddan-Aram, and He blessed him. 10. God said to Him: "Your name is Yaakov; your name

אֲנִי וּבֵיתִי: לא וַיֹּאמְרוּ הַכְזוֹנָה יַעֲשֶׂה אֶת־
אֲחוֹתֵנוּ: פ לה א וַיֹּאמֶר אֱלֹהִים אֶל־יַעֲקֹב
קוּם עֲלֵה בֵית־אֵל וְשֶׁב־שָׁם וַעֲשֵׂה־שָׁם מִזְבֵּחַ
לָאֵל הַנִּרְאֶה אֵלֶיךָ בְּבָרְחֲךָ מִפְּנֵי עֵשָׂו אָחִיךָ:
ב וַיֹּאמֶר יַעֲקֹב אֶל־בֵּיתוֹ וְאֶל כָּל־אֲשֶׁר עִמּוֹ
הָסִרוּ אֶת־אֱלֹהֵי הַנֵּכָר אֲשֶׁר בְּתֹכְכֶם וְהִטַּהֲרוּ
וְהַחֲלִיפוּ שִׂמְלֹתֵיכֶם: ג וְנָקוּמָה וְנַעֲלֶה בֵּית־אֵל
וְאֶעֱשֶׂה־שָּׁם מִזְבֵּחַ לָאֵל הָעֹנֶה אֹתִי בְּיוֹם צָרָתִי
וַיְהִי עִמָּדִי בַּדֶּרֶךְ אֲשֶׁר הָלָכְתִּי: ד וַיִּתְּנוּ אֶל־
יַעֲקֹב אֵת כָּל־אֱלֹהֵי הַנֵּכָר אֲשֶׁר בְּיָדָם
וְאֶת־הַנְּזָמִים אֲשֶׁר בְּאָזְנֵיהֶם וַיִּטְמֹן אֹתָם יַעֲקֹב
תַּחַת הָאֵלָה אֲשֶׁר עִם־שְׁכֶם: ה וַיִּסָּעוּ וַיְהִי ׀
חִתַּת אֱלֹהִים עַל־הֶעָרִים אֲשֶׁר סְבִיבוֹתֵיהֶם
וְלֹא רָדְפוּ אַחֲרֵי בְּנֵי יַעֲקֹב: ו וַיָּבֹא יַעֲקֹב לוּזָה
אֲשֶׁר בְּאֶרֶץ כְּנַעַן הִוא בֵּית־אֵל הוּא וְכָל־הָעָם
אֲשֶׁר־עִמּוֹ: ז וַיִּבֶן שָׁם מִזְבֵּחַ וַיִּקְרָא לַמָּקוֹם
אֵל בֵּית־אֵל כִּי שָׁם נִגְלוּ אֵלָיו הָאֱלֹהִים בְּבָרְחוֹ
מִפְּנֵי אָחִיו: ח וַתָּמָת דְּבֹרָה מֵינֶקֶת רִבְקָה
וַתִּקָּבֵר מִתַּחַת לְבֵית־אֵל תַּחַת הָאַלּוֹן וַיִּקְרָא
שְׁמוֹ אַלּוֹן בָּכוּת: פ ט וַיֵּרָא אֱלֹהִים אֶל־יַעֲקֹב
עוֹד בְּבֹאוֹ מִפַּדַּן אֲרָם וַיְבָרֶךְ אֹתוֹ: י וַיֹּאמֶר־לוֹ
אֱלֹהִים שִׁמְךָ יַעֲקֹב לֹא־יִקָּרֵא שִׁמְךָ עוֹד יַעֲקֹב

CHAPTER XXXV

1. The incident related in the preceding chapter shows how Jacob's life among the inhabitants of Canaan had endangered his family. Jacob probably should not have settled in such proximity to the natives of Canaan. He should have gone, first of all, to the place where, after leaving his father's house, he had laid the cornerstone for his future and in so doing had made a vow for all his future life. Afterwards, he should have gone to the homeland which his parents and his grandparents before him had found suitable for the undisturbed development of the Abrahamite way of family life. In that place, their memory was respected and would have served to protect also Jacob and his own family. Now Jacob is instructed to go to both these places. He goes first to Beth El and then to Mamre-Kiryat Arbah-Hebron.

° ° °

2. וְהִטַּהֲרוּ וְהַחֲלִיפוּ שִׂמְלֹתֵיכֶם ***[purify yourselves and change your clothes]***. Similarly, we read in Exodus 19:14 [at the time of the giving of the Law] that וַיְקַדֵּשׁ אֶת־הָעָם וַיְכַבְּסוּ שִׂמְלֹתָם ["he (Moses) sanctified the people and they washed their clothes"]. The journey to Bethel, the place where God had been revealed to their father, was as significant for the family of Jacob as the assembly at Mount Sinai was to be for their descendants.

כִּי אִם־יִשְׂרָאֵל יִהְיֶה שְׁמֶךָ וַיִּקְרָא אֶת־שְׁמוֹ
יִשְׂרָאֵל: יא וַיֹּאמֶר לוֹ אֱלֹהִים אֲנִי אֵל שַׁדַּי
פְּרֵה וּרְבֵה גּוֹי וּקְהַל גּוֹיִם יִהְיֶה מִמֶּךָּ וּמְלָכִים
מֵחֲלָצֶיךָ יֵצֵאוּ: ששי יב וְאֶת־הָאָרֶץ אֲשֶׁר נָתַתִּי
לְאַבְרָהָם וּלְיִצְחָק לְךָ אֶתְּנֶנָּה וּלְזַרְעֲךָ אַחֲרֶיךָ
אֶתֵּן אֶת־הָאָרֶץ: יג וַיַּעַל מֵעָלָיו אֱלֹהִים בַּמָּקוֹם
אֲשֶׁר־דִּבֶּר אִתּוֹ: יד וַיַּצֵּב יַעֲקֹב מַצֵּבָה בַּמָּקוֹם
אֲשֶׁר־דִּבֶּר אִתּוֹ מַצֶּבֶת אָבֶן וַיַּסֵּךְ עָלֶיהָ נֶסֶךְ
וַיִּצֹק עָלֶיהָ שָׁמֶן: טו וַיִּקְרָא יַעֲקֹב אֶת שֵׁם
הַמָּקוֹם אֲשֶׁר דִּבֶּר אִתּוֹ שָׁם אֱלֹהִים בֵּית־אֵל:
טז וַיִּסְעוּ מִבֵּית אֵל וַיְהִי־עוֹד כִּבְרַת־הָאָרֶץ
לָבוֹא אֶפְרָתָה וַתֵּלֶד רָחֵל וַתְּקַשׁ בְּלִדְתָּהּ:
יז וַיְהִי בְהַקְשֹׁתָהּ בְּלִדְתָּהּ וַתֹּאמֶר לָהּ הַמְיַלֶּדֶת
אַל־תִּירְאִי כִּי־גַם־זֶה לָךְ בֵּן: יח וַיְהִי בְּצֵאת
נַפְשָׁהּ כִּי מֵתָה וַתִּקְרָא שְׁמוֹ בֶּן־אוֹנִי וְאָבִיו
קָרָא־לוֹ בִנְיָמִין: יט וַתָּמָת רָחֵל וַתִּקָּבֵר בְּדֶרֶךְ
אֶפְרָתָה הִוא בֵּית לָחֶם: כ וַיַּצֵּב יַעֲקֹב מַצֵּבָה
עַל־קְבֻרָתָהּ הִוא מַצֶּבֶת קְבֻרַת־רָחֵל עַד־הַיּוֹם:
כא וַיִּסַּע יִשְׂרָאֵל וַיֵּט אָהֳלֹה מֵהָלְאָה לְמִגְדַּל־

shall no more be called Yaakov, but Yisrael
shall be your name;" And He named him
Yisrael. 11. God said to him: "I am God,
the All-sufficing. Be fruitful and multiply; a
nation and a community of nations shall
come into existence from you; kings
shall come forth from your loins, 12. and
the land which I gave to Abraham and
Yitzḥak, to you will I give it, and to your
seed after you will I give the land."
13. And God went up from him at the
place where He had spoken with him.
14. And Yaakov erected a memorial at
the place where He had spoken with him, a
memorial [consisting] of one [single] rock,
and he poured a libation upon it and then
poured out oil upon it. 15. Yaakov named
the place where God had spoken with him
Beth El. 16. They journeyed from Beth
El, and there was still some way to come to
Ephrath, and Raḥel gave birth and her labor
was difficult. 17. When she had such
difficulty giving birth, the midwife said to
her: "Do not be afraid, for this one, too, is a
son for you." 18. And as her soul departed after that—for she died—she named him
Benoni. But his father named him Binyamin. 19. So Raḥel died and was buried on
the way to Ephrath, which is Bethlehem.
20. Yaakov placed a monument upon her
grave; this is the tombstone of Raḥel to
this day. 21. Yisrael journeyed on and
pitched his tent at some distance from the
Herd Tower. 22. And it came to pass

11–12. גּוֹי וּקְהַל גּוֹיִם *[a nation and a community of nations].* The nation which is to descend from him is to represent one entity to the outside world, but internally it is to be a multiplicity of elements united into one. Each tribe is to represent an ethnic individuality in its own right. The nation of Jacob, which, as "Israel," is to demonstrate to the other nations the power of God, triumphantly pervading and shaping all of mankind, should not present a one-sided image. As a model nation it should reflect the greatest possible variety of national characteristics in a microcosm. In its tribes it should represent variously the warrior nation, the merchant nation, the agricultural nation, the nation of scholars, etc. In this manner it will become clear to all the world that the consecration of human life to the covenant with the Law of God does not demand occupational restrictions, or depend on specific ethnic characteristics, but that all mankind in all its multiplicity is capable of accepting the concept of monotheism taught by Israel, and of fashioning the multiplicity of human and national individualities into one united kingdom of God. . . .

21 and 22. We have already noted[26] the spelling of אָהֳלֹה in previous passages (Genesis 9:21, 12:8 and 13:3). In each of these instances [as it is also in the present verse, the vocalization indicates that the word should be read as a masculine form, but the final consonant ה is as for the feminine; i.e., "her tent"]. This would

[26]*Note to the English translation*: The references are to the tents of Noah and Abraham. Hirsch's note to each of the three passages, in which he explains the use of this "feminine" final consonant, אָהֳלֹה, is not included in this excerpted English edition. [G.H.]

while Yisrael dwelt in this land, that Reuben went and placed his couch beside Bilhah, his father's concubine, so that Yisrael heard of it; and so the sons of Yaakov were twelve [in number]. 23. The sons of Leah: Reuben, Yaakov's first-born, and Shimeon, Levi, Yehudah, Issakhar and Zebulun. 24. The sons of Raḥel: Yosef and Binyamin. 25. The sons of Bilhah, Raḥel's maidservant: Dan and Naftali. 26. The sons of Zilpah, Leah's maidservant: Gad and Asher. These were the sons of Yaakov, that had been born to him in Paddan-Aram. 27. And Yaakov came to his father Yitzḥak, to Mamre-Kiryat Arba, which is Ḥebron, where Abraham and Yitzḥak had sojourned. 28. The days of Yitzḥak were one hundred and eighty years. 29. And Yitzḥak expired and died and was gathered to his peoples, old and sated with days, and Esav and Yaakov, his sons, buried him.

XXXVI

1. These are the descendants of Esav, that is, Edom. 2. Esav took his wives from the daughters of Canaan: Adah, a daughter of Elon the Ḥittite, and Oholibamah, a daughter of Anah, daughter of Tzibeon the Ḥivvite; 3. also Basemath, daughter of Yishmael, sister of Nebaioth. 4. Adah bore to Esav Eliphaz, and Basemath bore Reuel. 5. Oholibamah bore Yeush, Yaalam and Koraḥ. These are the sons of Esav, who were born to him in the land of Canaan. 6. Esav took his wives, his sons, his daughters and all the people of his house, his property and all his cattle and all his possessions that he had acquired in the land of Canaan, and went into an (other) land, away from his brother Yaakov, 7. for their wealth was too great for

עֵדֶר׃ כב וַיְהִי בִּשְׁכֹּן יִשְׂרָאֵל בָּאָרֶץ הַהִוא וַיֵּלֶךְ
רְאוּבֵן וַיִּשְׁכַּב אֶת־בִּלְהָה פִּילֶגֶשׁ אָבִיו וַיִּשְׁמַע
יִשְׂרָאֵל פ (פסקא באמצע פסוק) וַיִּהְיוּ בְנֵי־יַעֲקֹב
שְׁנֵים עָשָׂר׃ כג בְּנֵי לֵאָה בְּכוֹר יַעֲקֹב רְאוּבֵן
וְשִׁמְעוֹן וְלֵוִי וִיהוּדָה וְיִשָּׂשכָר וּזְבֻלוּן׃ כד בְּנֵי
רָחֵל יוֹסֵף וּבִנְיָמִן׃ כה וּבְנֵי בִלְהָה שִׁפְחַת רָחֵל
דָּן וְנַפְתָּלִי׃ כו וּבְנֵי זִלְפָּה שִׁפְחַת לֵאָה גָּד וְאָשֵׁר
אֵלֶּה בְּנֵי יַעֲקֹב אֲשֶׁר יֻלַּד־לוֹ בְּפַדַּן אֲרָם׃
כז וַיָּבֹא יַעֲקֹב אֶל־יִצְחָק אָבִיו מַמְרֵא קִרְיַת
הָאַרְבַּע הִוא חֶבְרוֹן אֲשֶׁר־גָּר־שָׁם אַבְרָהָם
וְיִצְחָק׃ כח וַיִּהְיוּ יְמֵי יִצְחָק מְאַת שָׁנָה וּשְׁמֹנִים
שָׁנָה׃ כט וַיִּגְוַע יִצְחָק וַיָּמָת וַיֵּאָסֶף אֶל־עַמָּיו
זָקֵן וּשְׂבַע יָמִים וַיִּקְבְּרוּ אֹתוֹ עֵשָׂו וְיַעֲקֹב בָּנָיו׃
פ לו א וְאֵלֶּה תֹּלְדוֹת עֵשָׂו הוּא אֱדוֹם׃ ב עֵשָׂו
לָקַח אֶת־נָשָׁיו מִבְּנוֹת כְּנָעַן אֶת־עָדָה בַּת־
אֵילוֹן הַחִתִּי וְאֶת־אָהֳלִיבָמָה בַּת־עֲנָה בַּת־
צִבְעוֹן הַחִוִּי׃ ג וְאֶת־בָּשְׂמַת בַּת־יִשְׁמָעֵאל
אֲחוֹת נְבָיוֹת׃ ד וַתֵּלֶד עָדָה לְעֵשָׂו אֶת־אֱלִיפָז
וּבָשְׂמַת יָלְדָה אֶת־רְעוּאֵל׃ ה וְאָהֳלִיבָמָה יָלְדָה
אֶת־יְעִישׁ (יעוש קרי) וְאֶת־יַעְלָם וְאֶת־קֹרַח אֵלֶּה
בְּנֵי עֵשָׂו אֲשֶׁר יֻלְּדוּ־לוֹ בְּאֶרֶץ כְּנָעַן׃ ו וַיִּקַּח
עֵשָׂו אֶת־נָשָׁיו וְאֶת־בָּנָיו וְאֶת־בְּנֹתָיו וְאֶת־כָּל־
נַפְשׁוֹת בֵּיתוֹ וְאֶת־מִקְנֵהוּ וְאֶת־כָּל־בְּהֶמְתּוֹ
וְאֵת כָּל־קִנְיָנוֹ אֲשֶׁר רָכַשׁ בְּאֶרֶץ כְּנָעַן וַיֵּלֶךְ
אֶל־אֶרֶץ מִפְּנֵי יַעֲקֹב אָחִיו׃ ז כִּי־הָיָה רְכוּשָׁם

describe the tent as the dwelling that the husband shares with his wife, where, indeed, the wife is placed into the foreground as the mistress and manager of the home. It is possible, therefore, that in the present passage, too, the form אָהֳלֹה denotes that this was the tent which Jacob formerly shared with Rachel.

Thus, the meaning of this passage would be: He pitched his tent, which he could now no longer share with Rachel, at some distance from the Herd Tower, around which his family—hence also Leah and the other wives—had encamped. As long as Rachel was alive, Jacob lived also with Leah and his other wives, but after Rachel's death he no longer lived with any of them. It may be that Reuben placed his couch into Bilhah's tent in order to induce Jacob to return to his mother, Leah. He wanted his father to understand that his sons were disturbed about his having separated himself from his family. However, Reuben did not attain his objective. Jacob continued to live apart from his wives, and the result was that the number of his sons did not increase beyond the twelve he had already fathered ["and so the sons of Jacob were twelve"].

them to dwell together, and the land of their
sojourning could not support them because
of their herds. 8. And Esav settled in the
mountainland of Seir—Esav, that is Edom.
9. Now these are the descendants of
Esav, progenitor of Edom, upon the mountainland of Seir. 10. These are the names
of the sons of Esav: Eliphaz, son of Adah,
the wife of Esav; Reuel, son of Basemath,
the wife of Esav. 11. The sons of Eliphaz
were Teman, Omar, Tzepho, Gaatham and
Kenaz. 12. Timnah was concubine to
Eliphaz, Esav's son, and she bore to Eliphaz
Amalek. These are the sons of Adah, the
wife of Esav. 13. These are the sons of
Reuel: Naḥath, Zeraḥ, Shammah and
Mizzah. These were sons of Basemath, the
wife of Esav. 14. These were sons of
Oholibamah, daughter of Anah, daughter
of Tzibeon, the wife of Esav: she bore to Esav
Yeush, Yaalam and Koraḥ. 15. These
became the chieftains of the sons of Esav.
The sons of Eliphaz, the first-born of Esav:
Chief Teman, Chief Omar, Chief Tzepho,
Chief Kenaz, 16. Chief Koraḥ, Chief
Gaatham, Chief Amalek. These were the
chieftains of Eliphaz in the land of Edom,
these the sons of Adah. 17. And these are
the sons of Reuel, Esav's son: Chief Naḥath,
Chief Zeraḥ, Chief Shammah, Chief Mizzah. These the chieftains of Reuel in the
land of Edom, these the sons of Basemath,
the wife of Esav. 18. These the sons of
Oholibamah, the wife of Esav: Chief Yeush,
Chief Yaalam, Chief Koraḥ. These the
chieftains of Oholibamah, daughter of
Anah, the wife of Esav. 19. These are the
sons of Esav, and these their chieftains,
this is Edom. 20. These are the sons of
Seir, the Ḥorite[s], the inhabitants of the
land: Lotan, Shoval, Tzibeon and Anah;
21. Dishon, Ezer and Dishan. These the
chieftains of the Ḥorite[s], sons of Seir, in
the land of Edom. 22. The sons of Lotan
were Ḥori and Hemam, Lotan's sister [was]
Timnah. 23. These the sons of Shoval:
Alvan, Manaḥath and Ebal, Shepho and
Onam. 24. These the sons of Tzibeon:
Aiah and Anah; this is the same Anah who
found the *yemim* in the wilderness when he
fed the donkeys of his father Tzibeon.
25. These the sons of Anah: Dishon; and

רַב מִשֶּׁבֶת יַחְדָּו וְלֹא יָכְלָה אֶרֶץ מְגוּרֵיהֶם
לָשֵׂאת אֹתָם מִפְּנֵי מִקְנֵיהֶם׃ ח וַיֵּשֶׁב עֵשָׂו בְּהַר
שֵׂעִיר עֵשָׂו הוּא אֱדוֹם׃ ט וְאֵלֶּה תֹּלְדוֹת עֵשָׂו
אֲבִי אֱדוֹם בְּהַר שֵׂעִיר׃ י אֵלֶּה שְׁמוֹת בְּנֵי־עֵשָׂו
אֱלִיפַז בֶּן־עָדָה אֵשֶׁת עֵשָׂו רְעוּאֵל בֶּן־בָּשְׂמַת
אֵשֶׁת עֵשָׂו׃ יא וַיִּהְיוּ בְּנֵי אֱלִיפָז תֵּימָן אוֹמָר
צְפוֹ וְגַעְתָּם וּקְנַז׃ יב וְתִמְנַע ׀ הָיְתָה פִילֶגֶשׁ
לֶאֱלִיפַז בֶּן־עֵשָׂו וַתֵּלֶד לֶאֱלִיפַז אֶת־עֲמָלֵק אֵלֶּה
בְּנֵי עָדָה אֵשֶׁת עֵשָׂו׃ יג וְאֵלֶּה בְּנֵי רְעוּאֵל נַחַת
וָזֶרַח שַׁמָּה וּמִזָּה אֵלֶּה הָיוּ בְּנֵי בָשְׂמַת אֵשֶׁת
עֵשָׂו׃ יד וְאֵלֶּה הָיוּ בְּנֵי אָהֳלִיבָמָה בַת־עֲנָה
בַּת־צִבְעוֹן אֵשֶׁת עֵשָׂו וַתֵּלֶד לְעֵשָׂו אֶת־יְעִישׁ
(יעוש קרי) וְאֶת־יַעְלָם וְאֶת־קֹרַח׃ טו אֵלֶּה
אַלּוּפֵי בְנֵי־עֵשָׂו בְּנֵי אֱלִיפַז בְּכוֹר עֵשָׂו אַלּוּף
תֵּימָן אַלּוּף אוֹמָר אַלּוּף צְפוֹ אַלּוּף קְנַז׃
טז אַלּוּף קֹרַח אַלּוּף גַּעְתָּם אַלּוּף עֲמָלֵק אֵלֶּה
אַלּוּפֵי אֱלִיפַז בְּאֶרֶץ אֱדוֹם אֵלֶּה בְּנֵי עָדָה׃
יז וְאֵלֶּה בְּנֵי רְעוּאֵל בֶּן־עֵשָׂו אַלּוּף נַחַת אַלּוּף
זֶרַח אַלּוּף שַׁמָּה אַלּוּף מִזָּה אֵלֶּה אַלּוּפֵי
רְעוּאֵל בְּאֶרֶץ אֱדוֹם אֵלֶּה בְּנֵי בָשְׂמַת אֵשֶׁת
עֵשָׂו׃ יח וְאֵלֶּה בְּנֵי אָהֳלִיבָמָה אֵשֶׁת עֵשָׂו אַלּוּף
יְעוּשׁ אַלּוּף יַעְלָם אַלּוּף קֹרַח אֵלֶּה אַלּוּפֵי
אָהֳלִיבָמָה בַּת־עֲנָה אֵשֶׁת עֵשָׂו׃ יט אֵלֶּה בְנֵי־
עֵשָׂו וְאֵלֶּה אַלּוּפֵיהֶם הוּא אֱדוֹם׃ ס שביעי
כ אֵלֶּה בְנֵי־שֵׂעִיר הַחֹרִי יֹשְׁבֵי הָאָרֶץ לוֹטָן
וְשׁוֹבָל וְצִבְעוֹן וַעֲנָה׃ כא וְדִשׁוֹן וְאֵצֶר וְדִישָׁן
אֵלֶּה אַלּוּפֵי הַחֹרִי בְּנֵי שֵׂעִיר בְּאֶרֶץ אֱדוֹם׃
כב וַיִּהְיוּ בְנֵי־לוֹטָן חֹרִי וְהֵימָם וַאֲחוֹת לוֹטָן
תִּמְנָע׃ כג וְאֵלֶּה בְּנֵי שׁוֹבָל עַלְוָן וּמָנַחַת וְעֵיבָל
שְׁפוֹ וְאוֹנָם׃ כד וְאֵלֶּה בְנֵי־צִבְעוֹן וְאַיָּה וַעֲנָה
הוּא עֲנָה אֲשֶׁר מָצָא אֶת־הַיֵּמִם בַּמִּדְבָּר בִּרְעֹתוֹ
אֶת־הַחֲמֹרִים לְצִבְעוֹן אָבִיו׃ כה וְאֵלֶּה בְנֵי־עֲנָה

Oholibamah, too, was a daughter of Anah. 26. These the sons of Dishan: Ḥemdan, Eshban, Yithran and Kheran. 27. These the sons of Ezer: Bilhan, Zaavan and Akan. 28. These the sons of Dishan: Utz and Aran. 29. These are the chieftains of the Ḥorite[s]: Chief Lotan, Chief Shoval, Chief Tzibeon, Chief Anah, 30. Chief Dishon, Chief Ezer, Chief Dishan; these are the chieftains of the Ḥorite[s] according to their chieftains in the land of Seir. 31. And these are the kings who reigned in the land of Edom before any king reigned over the sons of Yisrael: 32. Bela, son of Beor, reigned in Edom; the name of his city was Dinhabah. 33. Bela died, and Yobab, son of Zeraḥ and Bazrah, reigned in his stead. 34. Yobab died, and Ḥusham, of the land of Teman, reigned in his stead. 35. Ḥusham died, and Hadad, son of Bedad, who defeated Midian in the fields of Moab, reigned in his stead. The name of his city was Avith. 36. Hadad died, and Samlah of Masrekah reigned in his stead. 37. Samlah died, and Shaul of Reḥoboth by the river reigned in his stead. 38. Shaul died, and Baal Ḥanan, son of Akhbor, reigned in his stead. 39. Baal Ḥanan, son of Akhbor, died, and Hadar reigned in his stead. The name of his city was Pau; the name of his wife was Mehetabel, the daughter of Matred, the daughter of Me-Zahav. 40. These are the names of the chiefs of Esav according to their families, according to their places with their names: Chief Timnah, Chief Alvah, Chief Yetheth; 41. Chief Oholibamah, Chief Elah, Chief Pinon; 42. Chief Kenaz, Chief Teman, Chief Mivtzar; 43. Chief Magdiel, Chief Iram. These are the chieftains of Edom according to their dwelling-places in the land of their possession. This is Esav, the progenitor of Edom.

דִּשֹׁן וְאָהֳלִיבָמָה בַּת־עֲנָה: כו וְאֵלֶּה בְּנֵי דִישָׁן
חֶמְדָּן וְאֶשְׁבָּן וְיִתְרָן וּכְרָן: כז אֵלֶּה בְּנֵי־אֵצֶר
בִּלְהָן וְזַעֲוָן וַעֲקָן: כח אֵלֶּה בְנֵי־דִישָׁן עוּץ
וַאֲרָן: כט אֵלֶּה אַלּוּפֵי הַחֹרִי אַלּוּף לוֹטָן אַלּוּף
שׁוֹבָל אַלּוּף צִבְעוֹן אַלּוּף עֲנָה: ל אַלּוּף דִּשֹׁן
אַלּוּף אֵצֶר אַלּוּף דִּישָׁן אֵלֶּה אַלּוּפֵי הַחֹרִי
לְאַלֻּפֵיהֶם בְּאֶרֶץ שֵׂעִיר: פ לא וְאֵלֶּה הַמְּלָכִים
אֲשֶׁר מָלְכוּ בְּאֶרֶץ אֱדוֹם לִפְנֵי מְלָךְ־מֶלֶךְ לִבְנֵי
יִשְׂרָאֵל: לב וַיִּמְלֹךְ בֶּאֱדוֹם בֶּלַע בֶּן־בְּעוֹר וְשֵׁם
עִירוֹ דִּנְהָבָה: לג וַיָּמָת בָּלַע וַיִּמְלֹךְ תַּחְתָּיו יוֹבָב
בֶּן־זֶרַח מִבָּצְרָה: לד וַיָּמָת יוֹבָב וַיִּמְלֹךְ תַּחְתָּיו
חֻשָׁם מֵאֶרֶץ הַתֵּימָנִי: לה וַיָּמָת חֻשָׁם וַיִּמְלֹךְ
תַּחְתָּיו הֲדַד בֶּן־בְּדַד הַמַּכֶּה אֶת־מִדְיָן בִּשְׂדֵה
מוֹאָב וְשֵׁם עִירוֹ עֲוִית: לו וַיָּמָת הֲדָד וַיִּמְלֹךְ
תַּחְתָּיו שַׂמְלָה מִמַּשְׂרֵקָה: לז וַיָּמָת שַׂמְלָה
וַיִּמְלֹךְ תַּחְתָּיו שָׁאוּל מֵרְחֹבוֹת הַנָּהָר: לח וַיָּמָת
שָׁאוּל וַיִּמְלֹךְ תַּחְתָּיו בַּעַל חָנָן בֶּן־עַכְבּוֹר:
לט וַיָּמָת בַּעַל חָנָן בֶּן־עַכְבּוֹר וַיִּמְלֹךְ תַּחְתָּיו
הֲדַר וְשֵׁם עִירוֹ פָּעוּ וְשֵׁם אִשְׁתּוֹ מְהֵיטַבְאֵל
בַּת־מַטְרֵד בַּת מֵי זָהָב: מפטיר מ וְאֵלֶּה שְׁמוֹת
אַלּוּפֵי עֵשָׂו לְמִשְׁפְּחֹתָם לִמְקֹמֹתָם בִּשְׁמֹתָם
אַלּוּף תִּמְנָע אַלּוּף עַלְוָה אַלּוּף יְתֵת: מא אַלּוּף
אָהֳלִיבָמָה אַלּוּף אֵלָה אַלּוּף פִּינֹן: מב אַלּוּף
קְנַז אַלּוּף תֵּימָן אַלּוּף מִבְצָר: מג אַלּוּף
מַגְדִּיאֵל אַלּוּף עִירָם אֵלֶּה ׀ אַלּוּפֵי אֱדוֹם
לְמֹשְׁבֹתָם בְּאֶרֶץ אֲחֻזָּתָם הוּא עֵשָׂו אֲבִי
אֱדוֹם: פ

The Haftarah for this Sidra may be found on page 836.

וישב

VAYESHEV

לז א וישב יעקב בארץ מגורי אביו בארץ
כנען: ב אלה | תלדות יעקב יוסף בן־שבע־
עשרה שנה היה רעה את־אחיו בצאן והוא
נער את־בני בלהה ואת־בני זלפה נשי אביו
ויבא יוסף את־דבתם רעה אל־אביהם:
ג וישראל אהב את־יוסף מכל־בניו כי־בן־
זקנים הוא לו ועשה לו כתנת פסים: ד ויראו
אחיו כי־אתו אהב אביהם מכל־אחיו וישנאו
אתו ולא יכלו דברו לשלם: ה ויחלם יוסף
חלום ויגד לאחיו ויוספו עוד שנא אתו:
ו ויאמר אליהם שמעו־נא החלום הזה אשר
חלמתי: ז והנה אנחנו מאלמים אלמים בתוך

XXXVII 1. Yaakov settled down in the land of his father's sojourning, in the land of Canaan. 2. These are the descendants of Yaakov: Yosef, at the age of seventeen, being a shepherd, was with his brothers with the sheep but, being a youth, he was with the sons of Bilhah and the sons of Zilpah, his father's wives, and Yosef reported their idle talk to his father in an evil manner. 3. But Yisrael loved Yosef more than all his [other] sons, for he was to him a son of [his] old age, and he made for him an embroidered coat. 4. When the brothers saw that it was he whom their father loved more than all his brothers, they hated him and they could not speak peaceably to him. 5. And Yosef dreamed a dream and he told it to his brothers, and then they hated him all the more. 6. But he said to them: "Please listen to this dream which I have dreamed. 7. Lo! we were piling up

CHAPTER XXXVII

2. בֶּן־שְׁבַע־עֶשְׂרֵה שָׁנָה *[at the age of seventeen]* . . . Being a shepherd, he was with his brothers, tending the sheep. Only the daily chores of his calling brought him together with the brothers, the sons of Leah. However, he was also "a youth"; his life and aspirations during his formative years developed in the company of the sons of the שְׁפָחוֹת [maidservants] whom the text here describes not as his brothers but as the sons of his father's wives. Thus we see before us a youth who had grown up without a mother and without true siblings. All the others had grown up in the company of siblings and under the protection and guidance of a mother's love. Joseph, by contrast, was all alone. He had lost his mother early in life; Benjamin was still a child and hence no companion for the youth. . . .

° ° °

3. . . . It was not as "Jacob" but as "Yisrael" that he viewed Joseph as the best of his sons.

בֶּן זְקוּנִים הוּא לוֹ *[he was to him a son of (his) old age].* He saw himself living on in Joseph. He saw Joseph as heir to all his own spiritual attainments. . . .

4. **וְלֹא יָכְלוּ וגו׳** *[and they could not].* They could not abide it when he spoke to them in a friendly manner. Friends take nothing amiss from one another, but in a strained relationship each resents anything the other does, and tends to misinterpret the other's friendly overtures most of all.

5 and 6. He had a dream and told his brothers about it. When he began to confide his dream to them they wanted to hear no more of it. However, he insisted (Verse 6): "But you simply must hear this dream that I had." . . .

7 and 8. The word **וְהִנֵּה** ["and lo!"] occurs three times [in Verse 7] to emphasize three distinct points in the dream.

בְּתוֹךְ הַשָּׂדֶה ***[in the middle of the field].*** This does not mean "*in* the field" because the Hebrew form for "in the field" would be **בַּשָּׂדֶה**. Similarly, **אֲלֻמִּים** [masculine] and **אֲלֻמּוֹת** [feminine] [in Verse 7] are probably not synonymous. In Peah VI:10 a distinction is made between **אֲגוּדִים** [masculine plural form] and **אֲגוּדוֹת** [feminine plural]. Here, according to one interpretation, **אֲלוּמָה** denotes a small bundle. It seems that after the field had been completely harvested, the wheat was bound in small sheaves, **אֲלוּמוֹת**, which were then piled up to form large heaps, **אֲלוּמִים**, in the middle of the denuded field.

In other words, Joseph said to his brothers: "In my dream we were in no manner divided as we are in real life. We worked together and we wanted to pile up the sheaves in the middle of the field and lo! my sheaf arose and remained standing upright; and lo! your sheaves formed a circle around it and bowed down to my sheaf!" 8. And his brothers said to him: "Would you indeed become king over us, or perhaps rule over us already?" And they hated him all the more because of his dreams and because of his words. 9. He dreamed still another dream, and he told it to his brothers. He said: "Lo! I have had another dream, and lo! the sun and the moon and eleven stars bowed down to me." 10. He told it to his father and his brothers, and his father rebuked him and said: "What kind of dream is this that you have dreamed? Shall I, your mother and your brothers indeed come to bow to the ground before you?" 11. And his brothers envied him, and his father kept

‏הַשָּׂדֶה וְהִנֵּה קָמָה אֲלֻמָּתִי וְגַם־נִצָּבָה וְהִנֵּה תְסֻבֶּינָה אֲלֻמֹּתֵיכֶם וַתִּשְׁתַּחֲוֶיןָ לַאֲלֻמָּתִי: ח וַיֹּאמְרוּ לוֹ אֶחָיו הֲמָלֹךְ תִּמְלֹךְ עָלֵינוּ אִם־מָשׁוֹל תִּמְשֹׁל בָּנוּ וַיּוֹסִפוּ עוֹד שְׂנֹא אֹתוֹ עַל־חֲלֹמֹתָיו וְעַל־דְּבָרָיו: ט וַיַּחֲלֹם עוֹד חֲלוֹם אַחֵר וַיְסַפֵּר אֹתוֹ לְאֶחָיו וַיֹּאמֶר הִנֵּה חָלַמְתִּי חֲלוֹם עוֹד וְהִנֵּה הַשֶּׁמֶשׁ וְהַיָּרֵחַ וְאַחַד עָשָׂר כּוֹכָבִים מִשְׁתַּחֲוִים לִי: י וַיְסַפֵּר אֶל־אָבִיו וְאֶל־אֶחָיו וַיִּגְעַר־בּוֹ אָבִיו וַיֹּאמֶר לוֹ מָה הַחֲלוֹם הַזֶּה אֲשֶׁר חָלָמְתָּ הֲבוֹא נָבוֹא אֲנִי וְאִמְּךָ וְאַחֶיךָ לְהִשְׁתַּחֲוֹת לְךָ אָרְצָה: יא וַיְקַנְאוּ־בוֹ אֶחָיו וְאָבִיו שָׁמַר אֶת־‏

small sheaves to form large heaps in the middle of the field. So I, too, was prepared to contribute my own small sheaf to our common heap, but my sheaf could not be moved. It stood erect and remained so; it refused to be carried to the common heap in the center. What is more, your sheaves formed a circle around my sheaf and bowed down before my sheaf."

This is a perfect portrayal of one who has been placed into an isolated position, towering over all the others, with the others gathered around him in a gesture of obeisance. This happened against Joseph's will; he had been prepared to make his own small contribution to the whole, to let it become part of the others.

It is also interesting to note that the objects in Joseph's dream were sheaves of wheat. The brothers had never worked with wheat in any manner; they were, after all, shepherds. Their destiny to become an agricultural nation was still in the distant future. Hence, if farming was so much in Joseph's thoughts that he even dreamed about it, this could have been so only because his father, Israel, had told and taught him about the national destiny that was in store for his family. Accordingly, the brothers may have felt all the more justified in their outburst: "Do you want to become king over us some day? Or do you perhaps want to be ruler over us even now? Such notions should not occur to you even in a dream!" And so they hated him all the more, not only because of the nature of his dream but also for his impudence—as they saw it—in telling them of it.

10. At first, his brothers did not in fact interpret Joseph's dream as referring to them. But when they heard their father interpret it in this manner, they, too,

began to believe it and envied Joseph for the future that was in store for him.

11 and 12. Following Sforno, one of our most thoughtful commentators,[27] we believe it is our duty to search, if not for a justification, then at least for an explanation, of the developments that now follow. We are not dealing here with a band of robbers and murderers who would have considered it a trifling matter to commit murder for the sake of a coat. After all, Sforno rightly points out that even later, when their conscience smote them at the time of their greatest distress (Chapter 42:21), they did not blame themselves in any manner for committing a crime against Joseph but solely for their hard-heartedness which had permitted them to turn a deaf ear to his pleas. Thus they must have regarded their deed as hardhearted but not as a criminal act. We must therefore study our text closely to discern intimations of psychological explanations for the behavior of the brothers.

We are told that the discord [in the relationship between Joseph and his brothers] began with ‏קִנְאָה‏ [envy]; to this ‏שִׂנְאָה‏ [hatred] was now added. The brothers hated him because they believed they could discern his thoughts and plans from his dreams. But initially they did not fear him, because they did not believe that his dreams could ever come true. However, when they heard his second dream, which promised him not merely rulership within his own family but a position of supreme authority over all the earth, and

[27]*Note to the English translation*: Obadiah ben Jacob Sforno (1475–1550), a physician in Italy, was the author of a Bible commentary published in Venice in 1567. [G.H.]

the matter in mind. 12. Then the
brothers went away—to tend their father's
sheep in Shekhem. 13. And Yisrael said
to Yosef: "Are not your brothers tending
[the sheep] in Shekhem? Go! I will send you
to them." And he [Yosef] said to him: "I am
ready." 14. Thereupon he [Yaakov] said
to him: "Please go, see whether your
brothers are doing well, and whether the
sheep are doing well, and bring me back
word." So he sent him from the Valley of
Hebron, and he came to Shekhem. 15. A
man found him and, lo! he was wandering
about in the field. And the man asked him:
"What are you looking for?" 16. He said:
"I am looking for my brothers; please tell
me where they are tending [the sheep]."
17. "They have left here," said the man,"
for I heard them say: 'Let us go to

הַדָּבָר: שני יב וַיֵּלְכוּ אֶחָיו לִרְעוֹת אֶת־(נקוד על את)
צֹאן אֲבִיהֶם בִּשְׁכֶם: יג וַיֹּאמֶר יִשְׂרָאֵל אֶל־יוֹסֵף
הֲלוֹא אַחֶיךָ רֹעִים בִּשְׁכֶם לְכָה וְאֶשְׁלָחֲךָ אֲלֵיהֶם
וַיֹּאמֶר לוֹ הִנֵּנִי: יד וַיֹּאמֶר לוֹ לֶךְ־נָא רְאֵה אֶת־
שְׁלוֹם אַחֶיךָ וְאֶת־שְׁלוֹם הַצֹּאן וַהֲשִׁבֵנִי דָּבָר
וַיִּשְׁלָחֵהוּ מֵעֵמֶק חֶבְרוֹן וַיָּבֹא שְׁכֶמָה:
טו וַיִּמְצָאֵהוּ אִישׁ וְהִנֵּה תֹעֶה בַּשָּׂדֶה וַיִּשְׁאָלֵהוּ
הָאִישׁ לֵאמֹר מַה־תְּבַקֵּשׁ: טז וַיֹּאמֶר אֶת־אַחַי
אָנֹכִי מְבַקֵּשׁ הַגִּידָה־נָּא לִי אֵיפֹה הֵם רֹעִים:
יז וַיֹּאמֶר הָאִישׁ נָסְעוּ מִזֶּה כִּי שָׁמַעְתִּי אֹמְרִים

when they saw that their father did not take this as a mere dream but pondered over it and seemed to think that it could become reality, their feelings of קִנְאָה [envy] were stirred up again. (The literal meaning of קָנֵא ב is that one considers one's own just claims threatened by another).

We are told immediately thereafter וַיֵּלְכוּ אֶחָיו ["Then the brothers went away"]. It is significant that in the Hebrew text this statement is separated from the rest of the verse by an *ethnakhto*; i.e., "They went away!" It had been deeply impressed upon their minds that Joseph posed a threat to their rights; therefore they went away, and very far away at that. Shekhem is situated about 80 kilometers from Hebron. According to the Midrash Rabbah the two diacritical marks above the אֵת in לִרְעוֹת אֶת צֹאן ["to tend their father's sheep"] show that they only pretended to go in order to tend the sheep. In reality, they went to "tend" *themselves*; they sought to preserve their independence, which they believed to be threatened by Jacob's view of Joseph's future position.

It is significant that of all places they chose Shekhem. Shekhem was the place where they had so vigorously demonstrated their sense of family solidarity for the very first time. It was there that Simeon and Levi had uttered the memorable words: "Shall we, then, treat our sister like a harlot?" (Genesis 34:31.) Now if an entire family stands united as one man when any one of its members is threatened by a foe from without, how much more will it pull together when one of its own members arises from within to threaten the honor and the independence of all the rest! This may have been their thinking, and this is why they went to Shekhem, to the site of their original feat of fraternal solidarity. There they hoped to gain inspiration for decisions of similar import which they now considered necessary.

It is indeed true that their future would be in jeopardy if Joseph's position were to become as they had pictured it. It was, after all, not so very long ago that Nimrod had first introduced the institution of kingship. Their own cousins in Seir-Edom had already been enslaved under the whip of *alufim* [chieftains] and kings. In contrast to this type of monarchy, which reduced the individual to a mere building brick in the edifice of one man's ambition, the family of Abraham was to produce a society based on freedom and equality, in which the innate nobility and dignity of the individual would receive full recognition and in which the concept of their common mission לִשְׁמֹר דֶּרֶךְ ד׳ לַעֲשׂוֹת צְדָקָה וּמִשְׁפָּט ["to keep the way of *God,* to practice dutiful benevolence, and justice" — Genesis 18:19] would rule equally over all as the expressed will of God. But what would become of this intended future of theirs and, indeed, of the future of all mankind, if they, too, were to let themselves become enslaved to the ambitions of one man? . . . .

13. Jacob senses that there is a rift between Joseph and his brothers and he does not want it to deepen. At the same time he wants to test Joseph's feelings toward his brothers. He therefore, initially, gives Joseph no explicit instructions but merely says to him: "It is better that I should send you to their flock so that you may be with your brothers." Joseph is ready to go at once. After all, his conscience is clear. He has no ambitions to become a prince or a ruler.

נֵלְכָה דֹּתָיְנָה וַיֵּלֶךְ יוֹסֵף אַחַר אֶחָיו וַיִּמְצָאֵם
בְּדֹתָן: יח וַיִּרְאוּ אֹתוֹ מֵרָחֹק וּבְטֶרֶם יִקְרַב
אֲלֵיהֶם וַיִּתְנַכְּלוּ אֹתוֹ לַהֲמִיתוֹ: יט וַיֹּאמְרוּ אִישׁ
אֶל־אָחִיו הִנֵּה בַּעַל הַחֲלֹמוֹת הַלָּזֶה בָּא:
כ וְעַתָּה ׀ לְכוּ וְנַהַרְגֵהוּ וְנַשְׁלִכֵהוּ בְּאַחַד הַבֹּרוֹת
וְאָמַרְנוּ חַיָּה רָעָה אֲכָלָתְהוּ וְנִרְאֶה מַה־יִּהְיוּ
חֲלֹמֹתָיו: כא וַיִּשְׁמַע רְאוּבֵן וַיַּצִּלֵהוּ מִיָּדָם
וַיֹּאמֶר לֹא נַכֶּנּוּ נָפֶשׁ: כב וַיֹּאמֶר אֲלֵהֶם ׀ רְאוּבֵן
אַל־תִּשְׁפְּכוּ־דָם הַשְׁלִיכוּ אֹתוֹ אֶל־הַבּוֹר הַזֶּה
אֲשֶׁר בַּמִּדְבָּר וְיָד אַל־תִּשְׁלְחוּ־בוֹ לְמַעַן הַצִּיל
אֹתוֹ מִיָּדָם לַהֲשִׁיבוֹ אֶל־אָבִיו: שלישי כג וַיְהִי
כַּאֲשֶׁר־בָּא יוֹסֵף אֶל־אֶחָיו וַיַּפְשִׁיטוּ אֶת־יוֹסֵף
אֶת־כֻּתָּנְתּוֹ אֶת־כְּתֹנֶת הַפַּסִּים אֲשֶׁר עָלָיו:
כד וַיִּקָּחֻהוּ וַיַּשְׁלִכוּ אֹתוֹ הַבֹּרָה וְהַבּוֹר רֵק אֵין
בּוֹ מָיִם: כה וַיֵּשְׁבוּ לֶאֱכָל־לֶחֶם וַיִּשְׂאוּ עֵינֵיהֶם

Dothan.'" So Yosef went after his brothers and he found them in Dothan. 18. They saw him from afar. But before he came even closer to them, they imagined him as one plotting [against them] so that he was deserving of death. 19. They said to one another: "Behold, here comes the master of dreams! 20. Now come, let us kill him, let us throw him into one of the pits and say that a wild beast ate him. Then we shall see what will become of his dreams!" 21. Reuben heard it and rescued him from their hands. He said: "We shall not kill him." 22. Reuben said to them: "Do not spill blood; throw him into this pit that is in the wilderness, but do not lay a hand on him,"—in order that he might rescue him from their hands, to bring him back to his father. 23. And it came to pass when Yosef came to his brothers that they made him take off his coat, his embroidered coat, which was upon him; 24. and they took him and threw him into the pit. But the pit was empty; there was no water in it. 25. And afterwards when they sat down to eat they lifted up their eyes and looked;

18. . . . As Joseph came closer to them, they pictured him to themselves as the direst threat to their own most cherished and legitimate interests, so much so that לַהֲמִיתוֹ ["he was deserving of death"], they considered it permissible to put him to death. It seemed to them legitimate to kill him in self-defense.

25. **נשא עֵינַיִם** [lifting up one's eyes]. This term is never used in Scripture to denote a mere casual "looking"; it is employed only with reference to an intentional looking *at* or *toward*. When the brothers sat down to eat, their conscience gave them no peace. They kept looking in the direction of the pit.

The Ishmaelites were a tribe related to them. Now the Ishmaelites were not the sort of "traders" who would indiscriminately traffic in human beings as well as in merchandise. The brothers therefore had reason to expect that if Joseph were to be sold to the Ishmaelites he would remain with the Ishmaelites, and that after the Ishmaelites had sold their spices in Mitzrayim, they would take him with them to their homeland, Arabia. This explains why subsequently it did not occur to the brothers that Joseph might be in Egypt. This assumption would be corroborated even more firmly if—as may have been the case and as some authorities hold—the Ishmaelites had every intention of taking him home with them, and would have done so, had not Midianite traders come by in the meantime, bought Joseph from the Ishmaelites on speculation and then sold him in Egypt.

This would seem to accord with the statement in Verse 36 that the "Medanites," who were presumably identical with the Midianites, had sold Joseph in Egypt. If we are then told, nevertheless, in Verse 1 of Chapter 39, that Potiphar had purchased Joseph from the Ishmaelites who had brought him to Egypt, this would have to be understood as an indirect transaction; i.e., the sale to Potiphar had been made by the Midianites to whom the Ishmaelites had sold Joseph. In that case, the reason for naming the Ishmaelites as the first to whom Joseph passed from the hands of his brothers would be to explain why it would never have occurred to his brothers that he might be in Egypt. This assumption is by no means insignificant in the pursuance of our narrative. However, in any event, either Verse 36 of this chapter or Verse 1 of Chapter 39 would have to be interpreted figuratively, not literally. Moreover, the words מִיַּד הַיִּשְׁמְעֵאלִים ["out of the hand of the Ishmaelites" (Genesis 39:1)] would be far less likely to suggest an indirect transaction than would מָכְרוּ אֹתוֹ אֶל מִצְרָיִם [". . . had sold him to Mitzrayim" (Verse 36)], where lo! there was a caravan of Yishmaelites coming from Gilead, with their camels bearing spices, balsam and laudanum; they were going to carry these down to Mitzrayim. 26. And Yehudah said to his brothers: "What will we gain if we kill our brother and conceal his blood? 27. Come, let us sell him to the Yishmaelites, but let not our hand touch him, because he is, after all, our brother, our [own] flesh." The brothers listened to him. 28. Meanwhile Midianite men, traders, passed by, pulled and fetched Yosef out of the pit and sold Yosef to the Yishmaelites for twenty pieces of silver, and they brought Yosef to Mitzrayim. 29. When Reuben later returned to the pit and lo! Yosef was not in the pit, he rent his clothes. 30. Then he returned to his brothers and said: "The child is not here, and I—where can I go?" 31. They took Yosef's coat, slaughtered a he-goat and dipped the coat in the blood, 32. and they sent the embroidered coat and had it brought to their father and said: "We found

וַיִּרְאוּ וְהִנֵּה אֹרְחַת יִשְׁמְעֵאלִים בָּאָה מִגִּלְעָד
וּגְמַלֵּיהֶם נֹשְׂאִים נְכֹאת וּצְרִי וָלֹט הוֹלְכִים
לְהוֹרִיד מִצְרָיְמָה: כו וַיֹּאמֶר יְהוּדָה אֶל־אֶחָיו
מַה־בֶּצַע כִּי נַהֲרֹג אֶת־אָחִינוּ וְכִסִּינוּ אֶת־דָּמוֹ:
כז לְכוּ וְנִמְכְּרֶנּוּ לַיִּשְׁמְעֵאלִים וְיָדֵנוּ אַל־תְּהִי־בוֹ
כִּי־אָחִינוּ בְשָׂרֵנוּ הוּא וַיִּשְׁמְעוּ אֶחָיו:
כח וַיַּעַבְרוּ אֲנָשִׁים מִדְיָנִים סֹחֲרִים וַיִּמְשְׁכוּ
וַיַּעֲלוּ אֶת־יוֹסֵף מִן־הַבּוֹר וַיִּמְכְּרוּ אֶת־יוֹסֵף
לַיִּשְׁמְעֵאלִים בְּעֶשְׂרִים כָּסֶף וַיָּבִיאוּ אֶת־יוֹסֵף
מִצְרָיְמָה: כט וַיָּשָׁב רְאוּבֵן אֶל־הַבּוֹר וְהִנֵּה אֵין־
יוֹסֵף בַּבּוֹר וַיִּקְרַע אֶת־בְּגָדָיו: ל וַיָּשָׁב אֶל־אֶחָיו
וַיֹּאמַר הַיֶּלֶד אֵינֶנּוּ וַאֲנִי אָנָה אֲנִי־בָא: לא וַיִּקְחוּ
אֶת־כְּתֹנֶת יוֹסֵף וַיִּשְׁחֲטוּ שְׂעִיר עִזִּים וַיִּטְבְּלוּ
אֶת־הַכֻּתֹּנֶת בַּדָּם: לב וַיְשַׁלְּחוּ אֶת־כְּתֹנֶת הַפַּסִּים
וַיָּבִיאוּ אֶל־אֲבִיהֶם וַיֹּאמְרוּ זֹאת מָצָאנוּ הַכֶּר־

the particle אל, lit., "*in the direction of* Mitzrayim," instead of בְּמִצְרַיִם ["*in* Mitzrayim"], specifically expresses an indirect transaction. Finally, the text of Verse 28 explicitly states that it was not the brothers but these Midianites who had drawn Joseph up from the pit and sold him to the Ishmaelites.

In view of all the foregoing, the following interpretation of the incident would have much more to recommend it: The brothers had wanted to sell Joseph to the Ishmaelites. But in the meantime, the traders anticipated them. They pulled Joseph from the pit and sold him to the Ishmaelites. The brothers were under the impression that he was in the hands of the Ishmaelites and would go with the Ishmaelites to their homeland. They could not have known that the Ishmaelites had sold him in Egypt. Nonetheless, the blame for the sale of Joseph falls squarely upon the brothers because it was done in their spirit and they gladly permitted it to happen although they could easily have prevented it, had they so desired.

30. . . . [The words "where can I go?"] express a feeling of shame or remorse, the anticipation of a reprimand, deserved or undeserved. [Reuben says:] "I will have no place where I could be at rest, where I could hold up my head. Everyone will shun me." Why should

Reuben have had such feelings? Perhaps quite simply because he had not taken more vigorous steps to prevent what had happened. He had set out to fulfill the מִצְוָה [to save his brother's life]; however, he had failed to complete the task. But why this lack of resolve if he was, in fact, the eldest of the brothers? Perhaps he could not summon the necessary resolve because he knew that he himself was not flawless, because he was still troubled by the awareness of his own sin. Thus, his knowledge of his own weakness robbed him of the strength to take more decisive action.

There may have been yet another motive for Reuben's emotions. It was fear that had driven the brothers to commit the crime, fear that their own independence would be compromised by Joseph. And it was only natural to assume that Reuben should have felt this fear more than the others. For in Jacob's family there were, in fact, two first-born sons, Reuben and Joseph, and Joseph was the first-born of the woman whom Jacob had really wanted as his wife. Reuben would therefore naturally be the prime suspect in this evil deed, because he had the most obvious motive. That was why he had stayed aloof, and that was why he feared that everyone would now cast the first stone upon him. And indeed, subsequent events seem to have justified these apprehensions, for the primogeniture was taken away from Reuben and transferred to Joseph.

this; know now whether this is the coat of your son or not." 33. He recognized it and said: "My son's coat! A wild beast has eaten him! Yosef has been torn! Torn!" 34. And Yaakov rent his garments, put sackcloth upon his loins and kept himself in mourning for his son many days. 35. All his sons and all his daughters arose to console him, but he refused to accept consolation and he said: "For I will go down to my son, mourning, into the grave." And so his father wept for him. 36. The Medanites sold him to Mitzrayim, to Potiphar, an official at the court of Pharaoh, the chief of the cooks.

XXXVIII

1. At that time Yehudah went down from his brothers and removed himself until [he came] to a man of Adul-

נָא הַכְּתֹנֶת בִּנְךָ הִוא אִם־לֹא: לג וַיַּכִּירָהּ וַיֹּאמֶר כְּתֹנֶת בְּנִי חַיָּה רָעָה אֲכָלָתְהוּ טָרֹף טֹרַף יוֹסֵף: לד וַיִּקְרַע יַעֲקֹב שִׂמְלֹתָיו וַיָּשֶׂם שַׂק בְּמָתְנָיו וַיִּתְאַבֵּל עַל־בְּנוֹ יָמִים רַבִּים: לה וַיָּקֻמוּ כָל־בָּנָיו וְכָל־בְּנֹתָיו לְנַחֲמוֹ וַיְמָאֵן לְהִתְנַחֵם וַיֹּאמֶר כִּי־אֵרֵד אֶל־בְּנִי אָבֵל שְׁאֹלָה וַיֵּבְךְּ אֹתוֹ אָבִיו: לו וְהַמְּדָנִים מָכְרוּ אֹתוֹ אֶל־מִצְרָיִם לְפוֹטִיפַר סְרִיס פַּרְעֹה שַׂר הַטַּבָּחִים: פ רביעי לח א וַיְהִי בָּעֵת הַהִוא וַיֵּרֶד יְהוּדָה מֵאֵת אֶחָיו וַיֵּט עַד־אִישׁ

---

35. **All his sons and all his daughters.** ("His daughters" probably refers to his daughters-in-law). All of them "arose" to console him. They did not "go," or "come"; they "arose" to console him. "To arise" in order to perform an act always implies that the act is born of a resolution, an act one must bring oneself to perform. Until this point, they themselves were immersed in grief. No one feels so much grief as do those who must console a mourner. To see one's aged father inconsolable, viewing every cheerful thought as a sin, would have to move even the most hardened scoundrel to agonized remorse. He should be too distraught to offer consolation because he is in need of solace himself.

But why did none of them attempt to sprinkle soothing balm upon his father's wound by telling him: "Joseph is alive"? Because that would have been the greatest cruelty of all. In the minds of parents even a child who has been torn by wild beasts is not yet truly lost, but a child who is wicked is worse than lost. Therefore, he who would not aggravate the father's grief a thousandfold would have to keep silent until the day when Joseph would return and the joy of the reunion would mitigate in the father's mind even the crime that had been committed by his other sons. [Had they told Jacob at that time the truth about what had been done to Joseph,] Jacob would have felt as if he had lost not only one son, but ten sons at one time.

He refused לְהִתְנַחֵם ["to accept consolation," lit., "to console himself"]. (נחם see Genesis 6:6.) No one can truly console another. One can only offer him reasons for taking comfort, the mourner himself must take these reasons to heart if they are to effect a change in his

frame of mind. Jacob, however, refused even to attempt to make such a change.

כִּי אֵרֵד אֶל בְּנִי אָבֵל שְׁאֹלָה [*For I will go down to my son, mourning, into the grave*]. He did not think that his grief would kill him, but he believed that it was proper for him to mourn until he himself went to his grave. When he would be reunited with his son, Joseph must not see him in a cheerful mood. Jacob might also have felt that he had cause to blame himself for what had happened. After such a terrible misfortune those most immediately affected are apt to be called to a strict accounting by their own emotions; they will not forgive themselves for even the slightest misstep. . . . It is significant that Jacob's weeping is mentioned last of all. Jacob did not groan, nor did he cry out. The verb וַיֵּבְךְּ ["he wept"] takes the future tense. Whenever the others around him were merry, a furtive tear would appear in the father's eye.

CHAPTER XXXVIII

1. Judah's separation from his brothers may be taken as a symptom of the tension or rift that developed among the brothers because of what had been done to Joseph. These feelings of animosity were directed primarily against Judah, who, it seems, had been the most influential among the brothers and at whose suggestion, and under whose direction, the lamentable incident had taken place. In addition, we will see that Judah's own family had to pay dearly for the wrong that he had done. His wife and his son were to die before him; even more tragically, his sons died because they had done evil in the sight of God.

lam, whose name was Ḥirah. 2. Then Yehudah saw the daughter of a trader,* whose name was Shua, and he married her and came to her. 3. She conceived and bore a son; he named him Er. 4. She conceived again and bore a son; him she named Onan. 5. She bore another son and named him Shelah, and he was at Kheziv when she bore him. 6. Yehudah took for his first-born Er a wife, whose name was Tamar. 7. Er, Yehudah's first-born, was evil in the eyes of *God* and *God* caused him to die. 8. And Yehudah said to Onan: "Come to your brother's wife and fulfill [the duty of] levirate marriage with her and raise up progeny for your brother." 9. Onan knew that the progeny would not be his; hence, whenever he came to his brother's wife, he spoiled it [by spilling his seed] on the ground, in order not to give any descendants to his brother. 10. *God* was displeased with what he had done and He caused him to die also. 11. And Yehudah said to his daughter-in-law Tamar: "Remain a widow in your father's house until my son Shelah will be grown up," for he thought he might also die, like his brothers. Tamar went and remained in her father's house. 12. A long time thereafter, Shua's daughter, the wife of Yehudah, died; and Yehudah sought consolation and went up to his sheep-shearers—he and his friend Ḥirah from Adullam—to Timnah. 13. And it was told to Tamar: "See, your

עֲדֻלָּמִי וּשְׁמוֹ חִירָה: ב וַיַּרְא־שָׁם יְהוּדָה בַּת־
אִישׁ כְּנַעֲנִי וּשְׁמוֹ שׁוּעַ וַיִּקָּחֶהָ וַיָּבֹא אֵלֶיהָ:
ג וַתַּהַר וַתֵּלֶד בֵּן וַיִּקְרָא אֶת־שְׁמוֹ עֵר: ד וַתַּהַר
עוֹד וַתֵּלֶד בֵּן וַתִּקְרָא אֶת־שְׁמוֹ אוֹנָן: ה וַתֹּסֶף
עוֹד וַתֵּלֶד בֵּן וַתִּקְרָא אֶת־שְׁמוֹ שֵׁלָה וְהָיָה בִכְזִיב
בְּלִדְתָּהּ אֹתוֹ: ו וַיִּקַּח יְהוּדָה אִשָּׁה לְעֵר בְּכוֹרוֹ
וּשְׁמָהּ תָּמָר: ז וַיְהִי עֵר בְּכוֹר יְהוּדָה רַע בְּעֵינֵי
יְהוָה וַיְמִתֵהוּ יְהוָה: ח וַיֹּאמֶר יְהוּדָה לְאוֹנָן בֹּא
אֶל־אֵשֶׁת אָחִיךָ וְיַבֵּם אֹתָהּ וְהָקֵם זֶרַע לְאָחִיךָ:
ט וַיֵּדַע אוֹנָן כִּי לֹּא לוֹ יִהְיֶה הַזָּרַע וְהָיָה אִם־בָּא
אֶל־אֵשֶׁת אָחִיו וְשִׁחֵת אַרְצָה לְבִלְתִּי נְתָן־זֶרַע
לְאָחִיו: י וַיֵּרַע בְּעֵינֵי יְהוָה אֲשֶׁר עָשָׂה וַיָּמֶת
גַּם־אֹתוֹ: יא וַיֹּאמֶר יְהוּדָה לְתָמָר כַּלָּתוֹ שְׁבִי
אַלְמָנָה בֵית־אָבִיךְ עַד־יִגְדַּל שֵׁלָה בְנִי כִּי אָמַר
פֶּן־יָמוּת גַּם־הוּא כְּאֶחָיו וַתֵּלֶךְ תָּמָר וַתֵּשֶׁב בֵּית
אָבִיהָ: יב וַיִּרְבּוּ הַיָּמִים וַתָּמָת בַּת־שׁוּעַ אֵשֶׁת־
יְהוּדָה וַיִּנָּחֶם יְהוּדָה וַיַּעַל עַל־גֹּזְזֵי צֹאנוֹ הוּא
וְחִירָה רֵעֵהוּ הָעֲדֻלָּמִי תִּמְנָתָה: יג וַיֻּגַּד לְתָמָר

**Note to the English translation*: Hirsch's rendering of כנעני [Canaanite] as "trader" reflects the fact that Scripture uses the term "Canaanite" to denote a trader. (cf. Isaiah 23:8, Hosea 12:8). [G.H.]

2. Marriage derives its moral quality solely from its ultimate purpose, the begetting and rearing of children (cf. פְּרוּ וּרְבוּ ["be fruitful and multiply"]). The moral character of a marriage that fails to attain this objective is essentially incomplete. The family unit, i.e., a parental home and the branch families that emanate from it, represents a distinct branch upon the tree of mankind, as it were, a moral personality with its own character. Consequently, the death of a husband, leaving a childless widow, makes the marriage incomplete, since the marriage has then failed to attain its sublime moral purpose—the continuation of the human race in the direction set by the traits predominating in that particular family. This defect in the moral quality of the marriage can and should be made good by the marriage of the childless widow to one of the closest relatives of her deceased husband. These concepts, which reflect the splendid moral quality of marriage and the sublime moral dignity of the family, seem to form the basis of the great institution of *yibbum* [levirate marriage], which we already encounter here, in the earliest stage of the history of Jacob's family. . . .

father-in-law is going up to Timnah to
shear his sheep." 14. And she took off her
widow's garb, covered herself with a veil
and wrapped herself, and she sat at an open
lookout point which was situated on the
road to Timnah, for she had seen that
Shelah had grown up and she had not been
given to him as a wife. 15. Yehudah saw
her and took her for a harlot, for she had
covered her face. 16. He turned to her by
the road and said: "Please let me come to
you," for he did not know that she was his
daughter-in-law. And she said: "What will
you give me if you come to me?" 17. He
said: "I will send a male kid from the flock."
And she replied: "If you will give me a
pledge until you send [it]." 18. He said:
"What pledge shall I give you?" She
said: "Your signet and your cord and the staff
that you have in your hand." He gave it to
her, came to her and she conceived from
him. 19. She got up and went, removed
her veil and put on her widow's garb.
20. Yehudah sent the male kid by his friend
from Adullam to take the pledge from the
hand of the woman; but he did not find her.
21. He inquired of the people of the
place: "Where is the harlot that was at
the lookout point on the road?" They said:
"There was no harlot here." 22. He
returned to Yehudah and said: "I have not
found her, and also the men of the place
said: 'There was no harlot here.'"
23. And Yehudah said: "Let her keep it!
Otherwise we will become a laughing-
stock. After all, I did send this young kid
and you did not find her." 24. About
three months later it was reported to
Yehudah: "Your daughter-in-law Tamar
has acted the harlot, and she has also conceived by harlotry." Yehudah said: "Take
her out so that she may be burned."
25. She was taken out—but she had sent
to her father-in-law: "I have conceived
from the man to whom these belong!" She
sent him word: "Know now to whom these,
the signet and the cords and the staff,
belong." 26. Yehudah recognized them
and said: "She is more righteous than I
because I did not give her to my son
Shelah." But he did not know her again.
27. At the time of her confinement there
were twins in her womb. 28. When she

לֵאמֹר הִנֵּה חָמִיךְ עֹלֶה תִמְנָתָה לָגֹז צֹאנוֹ׃
יד וַתָּסַר בִּגְדֵי אַלְמְנוּתָהּ מֵעָלֶיהָ וַתְּכַס בַּצָּעִיף
וַתִּתְעַלָּף וַתֵּשֶׁב בְּפֶתַח עֵינַיִם אֲשֶׁר עַל־דֶּרֶךְ
תִּמְנָתָה כִּי רָאֲתָה כִּי־גָדַל שֵׁלָה וְהִוא לֹא־נִתְּנָה
לוֹ לְאִשָּׁה׃ טו וַיִּרְאֶהָ יְהוּדָה וַיַּחְשְׁבֶהָ לְזוֹנָה כִּי
כִסְּתָה פָּנֶיהָ׃ טז וַיֵּט אֵלֶיהָ אֶל־הַדֶּרֶךְ וַיֹּאמֶר
הָבָה־נָּא אָבוֹא אֵלַיִךְ כִּי לֹא יָדַע כִּי כַלָּתוֹ הִוא
וַתֹּאמֶר מַה־תִּתֶּן־לִּי כִּי תָבוֹא אֵלָי׃ יז וַיֹּאמֶר
אָנֹכִי אֲשַׁלַּח גְּדִי־עִזִּים מִן־הַצֹּאן וַתֹּאמֶר אִם־
תִּתֵּן עֵרָבוֹן עַד שָׁלְחֶךָ׃ יח וַיֹּאמֶר מָה הָעֵרָבוֹן
אֲשֶׁר אֶתֶּן־לָּךְ וַתֹּאמֶר חֹתָמְךָ וּפְתִילֶךָ וּמַטְּךָ
אֲשֶׁר בְּיָדֶךָ וַיִּתֶּן־לָהּ וַיָּבֹא אֵלֶיהָ וַתַּהַר לוֹ׃
יט וַתָּקָם וַתֵּלֶךְ וַתָּסַר צְעִיפָהּ מֵעָלֶיהָ וַתִּלְבַּשׁ
בִּגְדֵי אַלְמְנוּתָהּ׃ כ וַיִּשְׁלַח יְהוּדָה אֶת־גְּדִי
הָעִזִּים בְּיַד רֵעֵהוּ הָעֲדֻלָּמִי לָקַחַת הָעֵרָבוֹן מִיַּד
הָאִשָּׁה וְלֹא מְצָאָהּ׃ כא וַיִּשְׁאַל אֶת־אַנְשֵׁי מְקֹמָהּ
לֵאמֹר אַיֵּה הַקְּדֵשָׁה הִוא בָעֵינַיִם עַל־הַדָּרֶךְ
וַיֹּאמְרוּ לֹא־הָיְתָה בָזֶה קְדֵשָׁה׃ כב וַיָּשָׁב אֶל־
יְהוּדָה וַיֹּאמֶר לֹא מְצָאתִיהָ וְגַם אַנְשֵׁי הַמָּקוֹם
אָמְרוּ לֹא־הָיְתָה בָזֶה קְדֵשָׁה׃ כג וַיֹּאמֶר יְהוּדָה
תִּקַּח־לָהּ פֶּן נִהְיֶה לָבוּז הִנֵּה שָׁלַחְתִּי הַגְּדִי הַזֶּה
וְאַתָּה לֹא מְצָאתָהּ׃ כד וַיְהִי ׀ כְּמִשְׁלֹשׁ חֳדָשִׁים
וַיֻּגַּד לִיהוּדָה לֵאמֹר זָנְתָה תָּמָר כַּלָּתֶךָ וְגַם הִנֵּה
הָרָה לִזְנוּנִים וַיֹּאמֶר יְהוּדָה הוֹצִיאוּהָ וְתִשָּׂרֵף׃
כה הִוא מוּצֵאת וְהִיא שָׁלְחָה אֶל־חָמִיהָ לֵאמֹר
לְאִישׁ אֲשֶׁר־אֵלֶּה לּוֹ אָנֹכִי הָרָה וַתֹּאמֶר הַכֶּר־נָא
לְמִי הַחֹתֶמֶת וְהַפְּתִילִים וְהַמַּטֶּה הָאֵלֶּה׃ כו וַיַּכֵּר
יְהוּדָה וַיֹּאמֶר צָדְקָה מִמֶּנִּי כִּי־עַל־כֵּן לֹא־
נְתַתִּיהָ לְשֵׁלָה בְנִי וְלֹא־יָסַף עוֹד לְדַעְתָּהּ׃
כז וַיְהִי בְּעֵת לִדְתָּהּ וְהִנֵּה תְאוֹמִים בְּבִטְנָהּ׃

כח וַיְהִי בְלִדְתָּהּ וַיִּתֶּן־יָד וַתִּקַּח הַמְיַלֶּדֶת וַתִּקְשֹׁר
עַל־יָדוֹ שָׁנִי לֵאמֹר זֶה יָצָא רִאשֹׁנָה׃ כט וַיְהִי ׀
כְּמֵשִׁיב יָדוֹ וְהִנֵּה יָצָא אָחִיו וַתֹּאמֶר מַה־פָּרַצְתָּ
עָלֶיךָ פָּרֶץ וַיִּקְרָא שְׁמוֹ פָּרֶץ׃ ל וְאַחַר יָצָא אָחִיו
אֲשֶׁר עַל־יָדוֹ הַשָּׁנִי וַיִּקְרָא שְׁמוֹ זָרַח׃ ס חמישי
לט א וְיוֹסֵף הוּרַד מִצְרָיְמָה וַיִּקְנֵהוּ פּוֹטִיפַר
סְרִיס פַּרְעֹה שַׂר הַטַּבָּחִים אִישׁ מִצְרִי מִיַּד
הַיִּשְׁמְעֵאלִים אֲשֶׁר הוֹרִדֻהוּ שָׁמָּה׃ ב וַיְהִי יְהוָה
אֶת־יוֹסֵף וַיְהִי אִישׁ מַצְלִיחַ וַיְהִי בְּבֵית אֲדֹנָיו
הַמִּצְרִי׃ ג וַיַּרְא אֲדֹנָיו כִּי יְהוָה אִתּוֹ וְכֹל אֲשֶׁר־
הוּא עֹשֶׂה יְהוָה מַצְלִיחַ בְּיָדוֹ׃ ד וַיִּמְצָא יוֹסֵף חֵן
בְּעֵינָיו וַיְשָׁרֶת אֹתוֹ וַיַּפְקִדֵהוּ עַל־בֵּיתוֹ וְכָל־יֶשׁ־
לוֹ נָתַן בְּיָדוֹ׃ ה וַיְהִי מֵאָז הִפְקִיד אֹתוֹ בְּבֵיתוֹ
וְעַל כָּל־אֲשֶׁר יֶשׁ־לוֹ וַיְבָרֶךְ יְהוָה אֶת־בֵּית
הַמִּצְרִי בִּגְלַל יוֹסֵף וַיְהִי בִּרְכַּת יְהוָה בְּכָל־אֲשֶׁר

gave birth, one [of them] stretched out a hand and the midwife took and tied a scarlet thread upon his hand to say: "This one came out first." 29. But when he wanted to pull back his hand, his brother had come out, and she said: "What a breach you have made for yourself!" And he named him Peretz. 30. Afterwards his brother came out, [the one] who had the scarlet thread upon his hand. Him he named Zeraḥ.

XXXIX

1. Meanwhile Yosef had been brought down to Mitzrayim and Potiphar, an official at the court of Pharaoh, the chief of the cooks, a Mitzrite man, bought him out of the hand of the Yishmaelites who had brought him there. 2. And *God* was with Yosef and he became a very successful man, and he became thus in the house of his Mitzrite master. 3. When his master perceived that *God* was with him and that *God* caused everything he did to succeed in his hand, 4. Yosef found favor in his eyes so that he had to wait on him personally, and finally he set him above his house[hold] and put all that he had into his hand. 5. And it came to pass from the time that he appointed him overseer in his house and over all that he had, that *God* blessed the house of the Mitzrite on account of Yosef; the blessing of *God* was in all that he had, in

CHAPTER XXXIX

1. The narrative repeatedly stresses that Potiphar was an אִישׁ מִצְרִי [a Mitzrite man]. [Why so?] This fact would seem self-evident since, after all, we are told that he was an official at the Egyptian court, in Egypt. However, we know the contrast between the ancient Egyptians and all the other nations. We know especially of the arrogance with which the ancient Egyptians looked down on nomad peoples. The gap between the customs and lifestyle of the ancient Egyptians and those of the "Hebrew youth," as Joseph is described later on, is even wider. The word מִצְרִי [Mitzrite] in this passage points out this contrast to us and make us realize the temptations which the young man must have had to overcome in order to remain pure in an Egyptian household and under Egyptian rule, so that God deemed him worthy of His nearness. The use of this term could also indicate the enormous intelligence and skill that must have been needed for a young slave, of an Asian nomad people, purchased from the hands of Asian nomads, to gain the favor of a man such as Potiphar, an official at the royal court, and an Egyptian at that.

4. . . . Joseph became a man who accomplished everything he set out to do. . . . His master saw that "God was with him" and that God granted success to everything he undertook. This was the first manifestation of God in a Mitzrite society. In a society that attaches no value to goodness and morality there suddenly appears a young man, poor and humiliated, who, nevertheless, succeeds in everything he undertakes simply because it is he who undertakes it. Thus, suddenly, the blessed power of a pure and moral will is demonstrated. As a result, Joseph found חֵן [favor] in his master's eyes so that he promoted him to be his personal servant and subsequently appointed him overseer of his entire household. . . .

the house and upon the field. 6. He left
all that was his in Yosef's hand, and, having
him, he knew of nothing except of the bread
he ate—and Yosef was beautiful of form and
beautiful to look upon. 7. So it came to
pass, after these events, that his master's
wife cast her eyes upon Yosef and said: "Lie
with me." 8. He refused and said to his
master's wife: "Look, my master, having
me, knows of nothing that goes on in this
house, and he has put all that he has into my
hand. 9. In this house there is no one
greater than I; he has withheld from me not
the slightest thing except for you, because
you are his wife. How then should I commit
such a great wickedness and sin against
God?" 10. And it came to pass when she
talked to Yosef day after day, and he would
not listen to her, to lie with her, to be near
her, 11. and it came to pass on such a
day—he came into the house to do his work
[and] there was none of the people of the
house there in the house: 12. She caught
him by his garment and said: "Please lie
with me!" He left his garment in her hand,
fled and went outside. 13. When she saw
that he had left his garment in her hand and
had fled outside, 14. she called to the
people of her house and said to them: "See!
He has brought a Hebrew man in to us to
play games with us! He came in to me to lie
down with me, and I cried out in a loud
voice. 15. But when he heard that I cried
out in a loud voice, he left his garment next
to me, fled and went out." 16. She put
his garment next to herself until his master
came home, 17. And she spoke to him

יֶשׁ־לוֹ בַּבַּיִת וּבַשָּׂדֶה׃ ו וַיַּעֲזֹב כָּל־אֲשֶׁר־לוֹ בְּיַד
יוֹסֵף וְלֹא־יָדַע אִתּוֹ מְאוּמָה כִּי אִם־הַלֶּחֶם
אֲשֶׁר־הוּא אוֹכֵל וַיְהִי יוֹסֵף יְפֵה־תֹאַר וִיפֵה
מַרְאֶה׃ ששי ז וַיְהִי אַחַר הַדְּבָרִים הָאֵלֶּה וַתִּשָּׂא
אֵשֶׁת־אֲדֹנָיו אֶת־עֵינֶיהָ אֶל־יוֹסֵף וַתֹּאמֶר
שִׁכְבָה עִמִּי׃ ח וַיְמָאֵן ׀ וַיֹּאמֶר אֶל־אֵשֶׁת אֲדֹנָיו
הֵן אֲדֹנִי לֹא־יָדַע אִתִּי מַה־בַּבָּיִת וְכֹל אֲשֶׁר־יֶשׁ־
לוֹ נָתַן בְּיָדִי׃ ט אֵינֶנּוּ גָדוֹל בַּבַּיִת הַזֶּה מִמֶּנִּי
וְלֹא־חָשַׂךְ מִמֶּנִּי מְאוּמָה כִּי אִם־אוֹתָךְ בַּאֲשֶׁר
אַתְּ־אִשְׁתּוֹ וְאֵיךְ אֶעֱשֶׂה הָרָעָה הַגְּדֹלָה הַזֹּאת
וְחָטָאתִי לֵאלֹהִים׃ י וַיְהִי כְּדַבְּרָהּ אֶל־יוֹסֵף
יוֹם ׀ יוֹם וְלֹא־שָׁמַע אֵלֶיהָ לִשְׁכַּב אֶצְלָהּ לִהְיוֹת
עִמָּהּ׃ יא וַיְהִי כְּהַיּוֹם הַזֶּה וַיָּבֹא הַבַּיְתָה לַעֲשׂוֹת
מְלַאכְתּוֹ וְאֵין אִישׁ מֵאַנְשֵׁי הַבַּיִת שָׁם בַּבָּיִת׃
יב וַתִּתְפְּשֵׂהוּ בְּבִגְדוֹ לֵאמֹר שִׁכְבָה עִמִּי וַיַּעֲזֹב
בִּגְדוֹ בְּיָדָהּ וַיָּנָס וַיֵּצֵא הַחוּצָה׃ יג וַיְהִי כִּרְאוֹתָהּ
כִּי־עָזַב בִּגְדוֹ בְּיָדָהּ וַיָּנָס הַחוּצָה׃ יד וַתִּקְרָא
לְאַנְשֵׁי בֵיתָהּ וַתֹּאמֶר לָהֶם לֵאמֹר רְאוּ הֵבִיא לָנוּ
אִישׁ עִבְרִי לְצַחֶק בָּנוּ בָּא אֵלַי לִשְׁכַּב עִמִּי
וָאֶקְרָא בְּקוֹל גָּדוֹל׃ טו וַיְהִי כְשָׁמְעוֹ כִּי־הֲרִימֹתִי
קוֹלִי וָאֶקְרָא וַיַּעֲזֹב בִּגְדוֹ אֶצְלִי וַיָּנָס וַיֵּצֵא
הַחוּצָה׃ טז וַתַּנַּח בִּגְדוֹ אֶצְלָהּ עַד־בּוֹא אֲדֹנָיו
אֶל־בֵּיתוֹ׃ יז וַתְּדַבֵּר אֵלָיו כַּדְּבָרִים הָאֵלֶּה לֵאמֹר

6. . . .It is most significant that the remark about Joseph's beauty does not occur until the end of the description of the man. We might have expected to find this statement at the very outset to show the quality with which the unknown young man commended himself to his employer and which, in fact, is the most readily visible introduction any unknown person can bring with him. This may be significant especially as our narrative progresses. The fact that the woman who tried to seduce him was no ordinary woman must have represented a particularly great temptation for Joseph. That is why the text shows us that Joseph won the favor of his mistress primarily not with his physical beauty but because of his splendid spiritual attainments, which caused him to rise from the position of a lowly slave to become virtually his master's master. His beauty served only to intensify his impact on the woman to the point where she was overwhelmed. Hence we read in the verse that follows: אַחַר הַדְּבָרִים הָאֵלֶּה ["after these events"]. Everything that went before helped contribute to this state of affairs.

9. וְחָטָאתִי לֵאלֹקִי' *[and sin against God].* Quite aside from the wrong I would be doing to your husband it would be, like any another immoral act, a sin also against God. . . .

likewise [saying]: "The Hebrew servant whom you brought into our house came to me to mock me, 18. and when I lifted up my voice and cried out, he left his garment next to me and fled outside." 19. And when his master heard the words of his wife, who said to him: "Such things did your servant do to me," his anger broke forth; 20. and Yosef's master took him and put him into the prison, the place where the king's prisoners are kept; there he was in prison. 21. But *God* was with Yosef and turned toward him with loving-kindness; he caused him to find favor in the eyes of the chief of the prison. 22. The chief of the prison placed into Yosef's hand all the prisoners who were in the prison. Everything that they did there, he had to do. 23. The chief of the prison did not see to anything that was entrusted to him because *God* was with him [Yosef] and whatever he did, *God* caused it to succeed.

XL 1. It came to pass after these events that the butler of the king of Mitzrayim and his baker committed an offense against their master, the king of Mitzrayim. 2. And Pharaoh was angry at his two court officials, at the chief of the butlers and the chief of the bakers. 3. And he placed them into the custody of the house of the chief of the cooks in the prison, the place where Yosef, too, was imprisoned. 4. The chief of the cooks appointed Yosef to be with them; he had to

בָּא אֵלַי הָעֶבֶד הָעִבְרִי אֲשֶׁר־הֵבֵאתָ לָּנוּ לְצַחֶק בִּי: יח וַיְהִי כַּהֲרִימִי קוֹלִי וָאֶקְרָא וַיַּעֲזֹב בִּגְדוֹ אֶצְלִי וַיָּנָס הַחוּצָה: יט וַיְהִי כִשְׁמֹעַ אֲדֹנָיו אֶת־דִּבְרֵי אִשְׁתּוֹ אֲשֶׁר דִּבְּרָה אֵלָיו לֵאמֹר כַּדְּבָרִים הָאֵלֶּה עָשָׂה לִי עַבְדֶּךָ וַיִּחַר אַפּוֹ: כ וַיִּקַּח אֲדֹנֵי יוֹסֵף אֹתוֹ וַיִּתְּנֵהוּ אֶל־בֵּית הַסֹּהַר מְקוֹם אֲשֶׁר־אֲסוּרֵי (אסירי קרי) הַמֶּלֶךְ אֲסוּרִים וַיְהִי־שָׁם בְּבֵית הַסֹּהַר: כא וַיְהִי יְהֹוָה אֶת־יוֹסֵף וַיֵּט אֵלָיו חָסֶד וַיִּתֵּן חִנּוֹ בְּעֵינֵי שַׂר בֵּית־הַסֹּהַר: כב וַיִּתֵּן שַׂר בֵּית־הַסֹּהַר בְּיַד־יוֹסֵף אֵת כָּל־הָאֲסִירִם אֲשֶׁר בְּבֵית הַסֹּהַר וְאֵת כָּל־אֲשֶׁר עֹשִׂים שָׁם הוּא הָיָה עֹשֶׂה: כג אֵין | שַׂר בֵּית־הַסֹּהַר רֹאֶה אֶת־כָּל־מְאוּמָה בְּיָדוֹ בַּאֲשֶׁר יְהֹוָה אִתּוֹ וַאֲשֶׁר־הוּא עֹשֶׂה יְהֹוָה מַצְלִיחַ: פ שביעי מ א וַיְהִי אַחַר הַדְּבָרִים הָאֵלֶּה חָטְאוּ מַשְׁקֵה מֶלֶךְ־מִצְרַיִם וְהָאֹפֶה לַאֲדֹנֵיהֶם לְמֶלֶךְ מִצְרָיִם: ב וַיִּקְצֹף פַּרְעֹה עַל שְׁנֵי סָרִיסָיו עַל שַׂר הַמַּשְׁקִים וְעַל שַׂר הָאוֹפִים: ג וַיִּתֵּן אֹתָם בְּמִשְׁמַר בֵּית שַׂר הַטַּבָּחִים אֶל־בֵּית הַסֹּהַר מְקוֹם אֲשֶׁר יוֹסֵף אָסוּר שָׁם: ד וַיִּפְקֹד שַׂר הַטַּבָּחִים אֶת־יוֹסֵף

---

21. וַיֵּט אֵלָיו חָסֶד [*turned toward him with loving-kindness*]. God turned toward Joseph not the kindness of other people but His own benevolence. Joseph had reached the lowest level to which he was meant to descend. From that point on, God turned His own kindness toward him.

שַׂר בֵּית הַסֹּהַר [*the chief of the prison*]. Here we have yet another שַׂר. The more servile and enslaved a people is, the more "chiefs" it has. Anyone on a slightly higher level than the others is given the title of "chief."

CHAPTER XL

1 and 2. In Verse 1 these men are described simply as the butler and the baker. In Verse 2 they are described as the "chief of the butlers" and the "chief of the

bakers." Herein lies the irony and pettiness of such "princely" titles. The plain folk beneath him view him as a שַׂר ["a chief," literally, "prince"] but those above him look down upon him as a slave, even lower than one who sweeps the streets. His "princely" status derives solely from the fact that he has the signal honor of filling the king's goblet and of bringing him confectionery; that is, from his personal service to the king. Therefore this, the most abject of his slaves, becomes completely dependent on his master's good will. The king holds sway over the life and liberty of such "chiefs" as if they were his bondsmen. To the king they are not "chiefs," but only a baker and a butler. He is their master and if he becomes angry at them he will give them a kick with his boot and they will land in prison.

wait on them; so they remained in custody for a period of days.   5. And both of them dreamed, each one his dream in the same night, each one as [if it were] an interpretation of his dream, the butler and the baker who belonged to the king of Mitzrayim, who were imprisoned in the prison.   6. In the morning Yosef came to them and saw that they were troubled.   7. And he asked Pharaoh's court officials, who were with him in custody in his master's house: "Why were your faces sad today?"   8. They said to him: "We dreamed a dream, and there is no interpreter for it." Yosef replied to them: "Do not interpretations belong to God? Please tell [it to] me."   9. And the chief of the butlers told his dream to Yosef and said to him: "In my dream—lo! there is a vine in front of me,   10. and on the vine there are three shoots—and as soon as it buds, its blossoms bloom at once, and its clusters ripen into grapes.   11. And Pharaoh's cup is in my hand—and I took the grapes and pressed them into Pharaoh's cup, and I placed the cup upon Pharaoh's hand."   12. Yosef replied to him: "This is its interpretation: The three shoots are three days.   13. Yet another three days, and Pharaoh will number you with [the others] and restore you to your office, and you will then place Pharaoh's cup into his hand, as you did before, when you were his butler.   14. But if you will remember me when you will do well, then you will please show me kindness, you will make mention of me to Pharaoh and you will bring me out of this house,   15. for I was stolen from the land of the Hebrews and even here I have done nothing that they should have put me in the dungeon"   16. When the chief of the bakers saw that he had interpreted well, he said to Yosef: "I, too, was in my dream,

‏אֹתָם וַיְשָׁרֶת אֹתָם וַיִּהְיוּ יָמִים בְּמִשְׁמָר:‏
‏ה וַיַּחַלְמוּ חֲלוֹם שְׁנֵיהֶם אִישׁ חֲלֹמוֹ בְּלַיְלָה אֶחָד אִישׁ כְּפִתְרוֹן חֲלֹמוֹ הַמַּשְׁקֶה וְהָאֹפֶה אֲשֶׁר לְמֶלֶךְ מִצְרַיִם אֲשֶׁר אֲסוּרִים בְּבֵית הַסֹּהַר:‏
‏ו וַיָּבֹא אֲלֵיהֶם יוֹסֵף בַּבֹּקֶר וַיַּרְא אֹתָם וְהִנָּם זֹעֲפִים:‏
‏ז וַיִּשְׁאַל אֶת־סְרִיסֵי פַרְעֹה אֲשֶׁר אִתּוֹ בְמִשְׁמַר בֵּית אֲדֹנָיו לֵאמֹר מַדּוּעַ פְּנֵיכֶם רָעִים הַיּוֹם:‏
‏ח וַיֹּאמְרוּ אֵלָיו חֲלוֹם חָלַמְנוּ וּפֹתֵר אֵין אֹתוֹ וַיֹּאמֶר אֲלֵהֶם יוֹסֵף הֲלוֹא לֵאלֹהִים פִּתְרֹנִים סַפְּרוּ־נָא לִי:‏
‏ט וַיְסַפֵּר שַׂר־הַמַּשְׁקִים אֶת־חֲלֹמוֹ לְיוֹסֵף וַיֹּאמֶר לוֹ בַּחֲלוֹמִי וְהִנֵּה־גֶפֶן לְפָנָי:‏
‏י וּבַגֶּפֶן שְׁלֹשָׁה שָׂרִיגִם וְהִוא כְפֹרַחַת עָלְתָה נִצָּהּ הִבְשִׁילוּ אַשְׁכְּלֹתֶיהָ עֲנָבִים: יא וְכוֹס פַּרְעֹה בְּיָדִי וָאֶקַּח אֶת־הָעֲנָבִים וָאֶשְׂחַט אֹתָם אֶל־כּוֹס פַּרְעֹה וָאֶתֵּן אֶת־הַכּוֹס עַל־כַּף פַּרְעֹה:‏
‏יב וַיֹּאמֶר לוֹ יוֹסֵף זֶה פִּתְרֹנוֹ שְׁלֹשֶׁת הַשָּׂרִגִים שְׁלֹשֶׁת יָמִים הֵם: יג בְּעוֹד ׀ שְׁלֹשֶׁת יָמִים יִשָּׂא פַרְעֹה אֶת־רֹאשֶׁךָ וַהֲשִׁיבְךָ עַל־כַּנֶּךָ וְנָתַתָּ כוֹס־פַּרְעֹה בְּיָדוֹ כַּמִּשְׁפָּט הָרִאשׁוֹן אֲשֶׁר הָיִיתָ מַשְׁקֵהוּ: יד כִּי אִם־זְכַרְתַּנִי אִתְּךָ כַּאֲשֶׁר יִיטַב לָךְ וְעָשִׂיתָ־נָּא עִמָּדִי חָסֶד וְהִזְכַּרְתַּנִי אֶל־פַּרְעֹה וְהוֹצֵאתַנִי מִן־הַבַּיִת הַזֶּה: טו כִּי־גֻנֹּב גֻּנַּבְתִּי מֵאֶרֶץ הָעִבְרִים וְגַם־פֹּה לֹא־עָשִׂיתִי מְאוּמָה כִּי־שָׂמוּ אֹתִי בַּבּוֹר: טז וַיַּרְא שַׂר־הָאֹפִים כִּי טוֹב פָּתָר וַיֹּאמֶר אֶל־יוֹסֵף אַף־אֲנִי בַּחֲלוֹמִי‏

---

8. You say there is no one here to interpret your dreams? If dreams are worthy of interpretation, if they have any significance, then God must have sent them and then it is God, too, Who will make them understood. God is present even in this place and can have the interpretation of your dreams conveyed through the word of any man.

15. It is significant that even at this early stage in the narrative, the land is referred to as ‏אֶרֶץ הָעִבְרִים‏ ["the land of the Hebrews"], indicating that the other nations must have considered this clan so important even then that the land in which they dwelt could be described as "their land."

and lo! three baskets of select appearance are upon my head, 17. and in the top basket there are all kinds of baked foods, and the birds eat them out of the basket on my head." 18. And Yosef answered and said: "This is its interpretation: Three baskets and three days. 19. Yet another three days, and Pharaoh will lift your head from you and hang you upon a tree, and the birds will eat your flesh from off you." 20. And it came to pass on the third day, on Pharaoh's birthday, that he made a feast for all his servants and counted the chief of the butlers and the chief of the bakers among his servants. 21. He restored the chief of the butlers to his butlership and he placed the cup into Pharaoh's hand. 22. But he had the chief of the bakers hanged, as Yosef had interpreted it to them. 23. However, the chief of the butlers did not remember Yosef, and so he forgot him.

וְהִנֵּ֨ה שְׁלֹשָׁ֧ה סַלֵּ֛י חֹרִ֖י עַל־רֹאשִֽׁי: יז וּבַסַּ֣ל הָעֶלְי֗וֹן מִכֹּ֛ל מַאֲכַ֥ל פַּרְעֹ֖ה מַעֲשֵׂ֣ה אֹפֶ֑ה וְהָע֗וֹף אֹכֵ֥ל אֹתָ֛ם מִן־הַסַּ֖ל מֵעַ֥ל רֹאשִֽׁי: יח וַיַּ֨עַן יוֹסֵ֜ף וַיֹּ֗אמֶר זֶ֣ה פִּתְרֹנ֑וֹ שְׁלֹ֙שֶׁת֙ הַסַּלִּ֔ים שְׁלֹ֥שֶׁת יָמִ֖ים הֵֽם: יט בְּע֣וֹד ׀ שְׁלֹ֣שֶׁת יָמִ֗ים יִשָּׂ֤א פַרְעֹה֙ אֶת־רֹֽאשְׁךָ֙ מֵֽעָלֶ֔יךָ וְתָלָ֥ה אוֹתְךָ֖ עַל־עֵ֑ץ וְאָכַ֥ל הָע֛וֹף אֶת־בְּשָׂרְךָ֖ מֵֽעָלֶֽיךָ: מפטירכ וַיְהִ֣י ׀ בַּיּ֣וֹם הַשְּׁלִישִׁ֗י י֚וֹם הֻלֶּ֣דֶת אֶת־פַּרְעֹ֔ה וַיַּ֥עַשׂ מִשְׁתֶּ֖ה לְכָל־עֲבָדָ֑יו וַיִּשָּׂ֞א אֶת־רֹ֣אשׁ ׀ שַׂ֣ר הַמַּשְׁקִ֗ים וְאֶת־רֹ֛אשׁ שַׂ֥ר הָאֹפִ֖ים בְּת֥וֹךְ עֲבָדָֽיו: כא וַיָּ֛שֶׁב אֶת־שַׂ֥ר הַמַּשְׁקִ֖ים עַל־מַשְׁקֵ֑הוּ וַיִּתֵּ֥ן הַכּ֖וֹס עַל־כַּ֥ף פַּרְעֹֽה: כב וְאֵ֛ת שַׂ֥ר הָאֹפִ֖ים תָּלָ֑ה כַּאֲשֶׁ֥ר פָּתַ֖ר לָהֶ֥ם יוֹסֵֽף: כג וְלֹֽא־זָכַ֧ר שַׂר־הַמַּשְׁקִ֛ים אֶת־יוֹסֵ֖ף וַיִּשְׁכָּחֵֽהוּ: פ

---

23. . . . שָׁכַח means to forget because one's mind is so full of other concerns that there is no room left for anything else. The "chief of the butlers" did not think it important to keep thoughts of Joseph fresh in his mind. He was so full of the present that he forgot about Joseph.

The Haftarah for this Sidra may be found on page 838.

מקץ

MIKETZ

XLI 1. It came to pass at the end of two full years that Pharaoh had a dream, and, lo! he stood by the river deep in thought. 2. And, lo! out of the river there came seven cows, beautiful to look upon and healthy of flesh, and they went to graze in the meadow. 3. And, lo! seven other cows came out of the river after them, bad to look upon and thin of flesh, and they stood next to the cows at the river bank. 4. And the cows that were bad to look upon and thin of flesh ate up the seven cows that were beautiful to look upon and healthy of flesh; and Pharaoh awakened. 5. But he fell asleep again and had a second dream. Lo! seven ears of corn grew upon one stalk, healthy and good, 6. and, lo! seven ears, thin and blasted by the east wind, grew up after them, 7. And the thin ears swallowed up the seven healthy and full ears! Pharaoh awoke and lo! it was a dream. 8. It came to pass in the morning that his spirit was troubled; he therefore sent and called for all the hieroglyphists in Mitzrayim and all the wise men there. Pharaoh told them his dream, but none interpreted them for Pharaoh. 9. And the chief of the butlers spoke to Pharaoh as follows: "I call to mind my faults today. 10. Pharaoh was angry with his servants and placed me into the custody of the house of the chief of the cooks, me and the chief of the bakers. 11. And we had a dream in one night, I and he, each of us dreamed as if it were an interpretation of his dream. 12. There was with us a Hebrew youth, a slave of the chief of the cooks; we told [them] to him, and he interpreted our dreams; for each one he interpreted according to his dreams. 13. And just as he interpreted for us, so it happened; he had

מא א וַיְהִ֗י מִקֵּץ֙ שְׁנָתַ֣יִם יָמִ֔ים וּפַרְעֹ֖ה חֹלֵ֑ם וְהִנֵּ֖ה עֹמֵ֥ד עַל־הַיְאֹֽר: ב וְהִנֵּ֣ה מִן־הַיְאֹ֗ר עֹלֹת֙ שֶׁ֣בַע פָּר֔וֹת יְפ֥וֹת מַרְאֶ֖ה וּבְרִיאֹ֣ת בָּשָׂ֑ר וַתִּרְעֶ֖ינָה בָּאָֽחוּ: ג וְהִנֵּ֞ה שֶׁ֧בַע פָּר֣וֹת אֲחֵר֗וֹת עֹל֤וֹת אַחֲרֵיהֶן֙ מִן־הַיְאֹ֔ר רָע֥וֹת מַרְאֶ֖ה וְדַקּ֣וֹת בָּשָׂ֑ר וַֽתַּעֲמֹ֛דְנָה אֵ֥צֶל הַפָּר֖וֹת עַל־שְׂפַ֥ת הַיְאֹֽר: ד וַתֹּאכַ֣לְנָה הַפָּר֗וֹת רָע֤וֹת הַמַּרְאֶה֙ וְדַקֹּ֣ת הַבָּשָׂ֔ר אֵ֣ת שֶׁ֤בַע הַפָּרוֹת֙ יְפֹ֣ת הַמַּרְאֶ֖ה וְהַבְּרִיאֹ֑ת וַיִּיקַ֖ץ פַּרְעֹֽה: ה וַיִּישָׁ֕ן וַיַּחֲלֹ֖ם שֵׁנִ֑ית וְהִנֵּ֣ה שֶׁ֣בַע שִׁבֳּלִ֗ים עֹל֛וֹת בְּקָנֶ֥ה אֶחָ֖ד בְּרִיא֥וֹת וְטֹבֽוֹת: ו וְהִנֵּה֙ שֶׁ֣בַע שִׁבֳּלִ֔ים דַּקּ֖וֹת וּשְׁדוּפֹ֣ת קָדִ֑ים צֹמְח֖וֹת אַחֲרֵיהֶֽן: ז וַתִּבְלַ֙עְנָה֙ הַשִּׁבֳּלִ֣ים הַדַּקּ֔וֹת אֵ֚ת שֶׁ֣בַע הַשִּׁבֳּלִ֔ים הַבְּרִיא֖וֹת וְהַמְּלֵא֑וֹת וַיִּיקַ֥ץ פַּרְעֹ֖ה וְהִנֵּ֥ה חֲלֽוֹם: ח וַיְהִ֤י בַבֹּ֙קֶר֙ וַתִּפָּ֣עֶם רוּח֔וֹ וַיִּשְׁלַ֗ח וַיִּקְרָ֛א אֶת־כָּל־חַרְטֻמֵּ֥י מִצְרַ֖יִם וְאֶת־כָּל־חֲכָמֶ֑יהָ וַיְסַפֵּ֨ר פַּרְעֹ֤ה לָהֶם֙ אֶת־חֲלֹמ֔וֹ וְאֵֽין־פּוֹתֵ֥ר אוֹתָ֖ם לְפַרְעֹֽה: ט וַיְדַבֵּר֙ שַׂ֣ר הַמַּשְׁקִ֔ים אֶת־פַּרְעֹ֖ה לֵאמֹ֑ר אֶת־חֲטָאַ֕י אֲנִ֖י מַזְכִּ֥יר הַיּֽוֹם: י פַּרְעֹ֖ה קָצַ֣ף עַל־עֲבָדָ֑יו וַיִּתֵּ֨ן אֹתִ֜י בְּמִשְׁמַ֗ר בֵּ֚ית שַׂ֣ר הַטַּבָּחִ֔ים אֹתִ֕י וְאֵ֖ת שַׂ֥ר הָאֹפִֽים: יא וַנַּֽחַלְמָ֥ה חֲל֛וֹם בְּלַ֥יְלָה אֶחָ֖ד אֲנִ֣י וָה֑וּא אִ֛ישׁ כְּפִתְר֥וֹן חֲלֹמ֖וֹ חָלָֽמְנוּ: יב וְשָׁ֨ם אִתָּ֜נוּ נַ֣עַר עִבְרִ֗י עֶ֚בֶד לְשַׂ֣ר הַטַּבָּחִ֔ים וַנְּ֨סַפֶּר־ל֔וֹ וַיִּפְתָּר־לָ֖נוּ אֶת־חֲלֹמֹתֵ֑ינוּ אִ֥ישׁ כַּחֲלֹמ֖וֹ פָּתָֽר: יג וַיְהִ֛י כַּאֲשֶׁ֥ר פָּֽתַר־לָ֖נוּ כֵּ֣ן

CHAPTER XLI

8. חַרְטֻמֵּי *[hieroglyphists]* derived from חָרַט ["engraved"], those versed in the act of "engraved" hieroglyphics. These individuals, who are constantly engaged in the interpretation of symbols, would be those who could be most logically expected to interpret a dream. . . .

הָיָה אֹתִי הֵשִׁיב עַל־כַּנִּי וְאֹתוֹ תָלָה׃ יד וַיִּשְׁלַח
פַּרְעֹה וַיִּקְרָא אֶת־יוֹסֵף וַיְרִיצֻהוּ מִן־הַבּוֹר
וַיְגַלַּח וַיְחַלֵּף שִׂמְלֹתָיו וַיָּבֹא אֶל־פַּרְעֹה׃
שני טו וַיֹּאמֶר פַּרְעֹה אֶל־יוֹסֵף חֲלוֹם חָלַמְתִּי
וּפֹתֵר אֵין אֹתוֹ וַאֲנִי שָׁמַעְתִּי עָלֶיךָ לֵאמֹר
תִּשְׁמַע חֲלוֹם לִפְתֹּר אֹתוֹ׃ טז וַיַּעַן יוֹסֵף אֶת־
פַּרְעֹה לֵאמֹר בִּלְעָדָי אֱלֹהִים יַעֲנֶה אֶת־שְׁלוֹם
פַּרְעֹה׃ יז וַיְדַבֵּר פַּרְעֹה אֶל־יוֹסֵף בַּחֲלֹמִי הִנְנִי
עֹמֵד עַל־שְׂפַת הַיְאֹר׃ יח וְהִנֵּה מִן־הַיְאֹר עֹלֹת
שֶׁבַע פָּרוֹת בְּרִיאוֹת בָּשָׂר וִיפֹת תֹּאַר וַתִּרְעֶינָה
בָּאָחוּ׃ יט וְהִנֵּה שֶׁבַע־פָּרוֹת אֲחֵרוֹת עֹלוֹת
אַחֲרֵיהֶן דַּלּוֹת וְרָעוֹת תֹּאַר מְאֹד וְרַקּוֹת בָּשָׂר
לֹא־רָאִיתִי כָהֵנָּה בְּכָל־אֶרֶץ מִצְרַיִם לָרֹעַ׃
כ וַתֹּאכַלְנָה הַפָּרוֹת הָרַקּוֹת וְהָרָעוֹת אֵת שֶׁבַע
הַפָּרוֹת הָרִאשֹׁנוֹת הַבְּרִיאֹת׃ כא וַתָּבֹאנָה אֶל־
קִרְבֶּנָה וְלֹא נוֹדַע כִּי־בָאוּ אֶל־קִרְבֶּנָה וּמַרְאֵיהֶן
רַע כַּאֲשֶׁר בַּתְּחִלָּה וָאִיקָץ׃ כב וָאֵרֶא בַּחֲלֹמִי
וְהִנֵּה ׀ שֶׁבַע שִׁבֳּלִים עֹלֹת בְּקָנֶה אֶחָד מְלֵאֹת
וְטֹבוֹת׃ כג וְהִנֵּה שֶׁבַע שִׁבֳּלִים צְנֻמוֹת דַּקּוֹת
שְׁדֻפוֹת קָדִים צֹמְחוֹת אַחֲרֵיהֶם׃ כד וַתִּבְלַעְןָ
הַשִּׁבֳּלִים הַדַּקֹּת אֵת שֶׁבַע הַשִּׁבֳּלִים הַטֹּבוֹת
וָאֹמַר אֶל־הַחַרְטֻמִּים וְאֵין מַגִּיד לִי׃ כה וַיֹּאמֶר
יוֹסֵף אֶל־פַּרְעֹה חֲלוֹם פַּרְעֹה אֶחָד הוּא אֵת
אֲשֶׁר הָאֱלֹהִים עֹשֶׂה הִגִּיד לְפַרְעֹה׃ כו שֶׁבַע
פָּרֹת הַטֹּבֹת שֶׁבַע שָׁנִים הֵנָּה וְשֶׁבַע הַשִּׁבֳּלִים
הַטֹּבֹת שֶׁבַע שָׁנִים הֵנָּה חֲלוֹם אֶחָד הוּא׃
כז וְשֶׁבַע הַפָּרוֹת הָרַקּוֹת וְהָרָעֹת הָעֹלֹת אַחֲרֵיהֶן
שֶׁבַע שָׁנִים הֵנָּה וְשֶׁבַע הַשִּׁבֳּלִים הָרֵקוֹת שְׁדֻפוֹת
הַקָּדִים יִהְיוּ שֶׁבַע שְׁנֵי רָעָב׃ כח הוּא הַדָּבָר

me restored to my office and had him [the baker] hanged."
14. And Pharaoh sent and had Yosef called; they ordered him to hurry out of the prison. But [first] he shaved, changed all his clothing and [thus] came to Pharaoh.
15. And Pharaoh said to Yosef: "I had a dream and no one interprets it, but I have heard it said of you that you hear a dream in order to interpret it."
16. Yosef replied to Pharaoh: "It is not with me! May God provide an answer that will mean the peace of Pharaoh."
17. And Pharaoh said to Yosef: "In my dream—lo! I am standing there at the river bank,
18. and, lo! out of the river there came seven cows, healthy of flesh and beautiful to look upon, and they went to graze in the meadow.
19. And, lo! seven other cows came out after them, poor and very bad to look upon and meager of flesh, such as I never saw in all the land of Mitzrayim for ugliness,
20. and the thin and bad cows ate up the seven first healthy cows.
21. They came inside them, but it could not be known that they had come inside them; their appearance was as bad as before—then I awoke,
22. and I saw in my dream and, lo! seven ears grow upon one stalk, full and good—
23. and, lo! seven ears, withered, thin, blasted by the east wind, grow after them.
24. And the thin ears swallowed up the seven good ears. I have told it to the hieroglyphists but none of them knows to tell it to me."
25. And Yosef said to Pharaoh: "Pharaoh's dream is only one [dream]; what God is about to do He has announced to Pharaoh.
26. The seven good cows are seven years, and the seven good ears are seven years; it is all only one dream.
27. And the seven thin and bad cows which come after them are seven years and likewise the seven empty ears blasted by the east wind: there will be seven years of famine.
28. Thus it is as I have

15. **תִּשְׁמַע חֲלוֹם** ***[you** hear **a dream];*** not תֵּדַע ["you *know* a dream"]. [Pharoah says to Joseph:] "I have heard it said that you listen to a dream in such a manner that you are able to find its meaning from what you hear of its contents." Everything, then, depends on proper listening. Of ten people who listen to the same speech or story each person may well understand it differently; perhaps only one of them will understand it correctly.

said to Pharaoh: What God is about to do He has shown to Pharaoh. 29. Behold, there will come seven years of great plenty in all the land of Mitzrayim. 30. After this there will arise seven years of famine so that all the plenty will be forgotten in all the land of Mitzrayim and the famine will ruin the land. 31. The plenty in the land will no longer be known because of this famine that will follow it; for it will be terrible. 32. And regarding the fact that the dream was repeated to Pharaoh twice: [it is] because the thing stands ready from God and God is hastening to bring it about. 33. And now let Pharaoh seek out a judicious and wise man and set him over the land of Mitzrayim. 34. But let Pharaoh himself do this and appoint officials over the land and impose upon the land of Mitzrayim [as a tax] one-fifth during the seven years of plenty. 35. Let them hold back the food of these coming good years and let them also, under Pharaoh's hand, store up grain for food in the cities and keep it. 36. Thus the foods will remain as a reserve for the land, for the seven years of famine that will come to the land of Mitzrayim, so that the land will not perish entirely from the famine." 37. This was good in the eyes of Pharaoh and in the eyes of all his servants. 38. And Pharaoh said to his servants: "Will we be able to find a man such as this one, in whom there is the spirit of God?" 39. And to Yosef Pharaoh said: "Since God has let you know all this, there is no one as judicious and wise as you. 40. You shall be set over my house, and all my people will be organized in accordance with your word, only as regards the throne will I be greater than you." 41. Pharaoh further said to Yosef: "Look, I have set you over all the land of Mitz-

אֲשֶׁר דִּבַּרְתִּי אֶל־פַּרְעֹה אֲשֶׁר הָאֱלֹהִים עֹשֶׂה
הֶרְאָה אֶת־פַּרְעֹה׃ כט הִנֵּה שֶׁבַע שָׁנִים בָּאוֹת
שָׂבָע גָּדוֹל בְּכָל־אֶרֶץ מִצְרָיִם׃ ל וְקָמוּ שֶׁבַע שְׁנֵי
רָעָב אַחֲרֵיהֶן וְנִשְׁכַּח כָּל־הַשָּׂבָע בְּאֶרֶץ מִצְרָיִם
וְכִלָּה הָרָעָב אֶת־הָאָרֶץ׃ לא וְלֹא־יִוָּדַע הַשָּׂבָע
בָּאָרֶץ מִפְּנֵי הָרָעָב הַהוּא אַחֲרֵי־כֵן כִּי־כָבֵד הוּא
מְאֹד׃ לב וְעַל הִשָּׁנוֹת הַחֲלוֹם אֶל־פַּרְעֹה פַּעֲמָיִם
כִּי־נָכוֹן הַדָּבָר מֵעִם הָאֱלֹהִים וּמְמַהֵר הָאֱלֹהִים
לַעֲשֹׂתוֹ׃ לג וְעַתָּה יֵרֶא פַרְעֹה אִישׁ נָבוֹן וְחָכָם
וִישִׁיתֵהוּ עַל־אֶרֶץ מִצְרָיִם׃ לד יַעֲשֶׂה פַרְעֹה
וְיַפְקֵד פְּקִדִים עַל־הָאָרֶץ וְחִמֵּשׁ אֶת־אֶרֶץ
מִצְרַיִם בְּשֶׁבַע שְׁנֵי הַשָּׂבָע׃ לה וְיִקְבְּצוּ אֶת־כָּל־
אֹכֶל הַשָּׁנִים הַטֹּבוֹת הַבָּאֹת הָאֵלֶּה וְיִצְבְּרוּ־בָר
תַּחַת יַד־פַּרְעֹה אֹכֶל בֶּעָרִים וְשָׁמָרוּ׃ לו וְהָיָה
הָאֹכֶל לְפִקָּדוֹן לָאָרֶץ לְשֶׁבַע שְׁנֵי הָרָעָב אֲשֶׁר
תִּהְיֶיןָ בְּאֶרֶץ מִצְרָיִם וְלֹא־תִכָּרֵת הָאָרֶץ בָּרָעָב׃
לז וַיִּיטַב הַדָּבָר בְּעֵינֵי פַרְעֹה וּבְעֵינֵי כָּל־עֲבָדָיו׃
לח וַיֹּאמֶר פַּרְעֹה אֶל־עֲבָדָיו הֲנִמְצָא כָזֶה אִישׁ
אֲשֶׁר רוּחַ אֱלֹהִים בּוֹ׃ שלישי לט וַיֹּאמֶר פַּרְעֹה
אֶל־יוֹסֵף אַחֲרֵי הוֹדִיעַ אֱלֹהִים אוֹתְךָ אֶת־כָּל־
זֹאת אֵין־נָבוֹן וְחָכָם כָּמוֹךָ׃ מ אַתָּה תִּהְיֶה עַל־
בֵּיתִי וְעַל־פִּיךָ יִשַּׁק כָּל־עַמִּי רַק הַכִּסֵּא אֶגְדַּל
מִמֶּךָּ׃ מא וַיֹּאמֶר פַּרְעֹה אֶל־יוֹסֵף רְאֵה נָתַתִּי

40–43. . . . With his ring Pharaoh had made Joseph his מִשְׁנֶה ["double"], his *alter ego*. Pharaoh had Joseph ride in state in the chariot reserved for such an *alter ego*, and he had people call out before him: אַבְרֵךְ; literally, "I command that everyone bend the knee!" When Egypt's sovereign appeared in public, he was preceded by heralds proclaiming not "On your knees!" but אַבְרֵךְ: "I (namely, the sovereign appearing in the midst of the people) *command* that you go down on your knees!" To the true prince only a spontaneous demonstration of respect is an honor. In a sultan's view, by contrast, a voluntary demonstration of reverence is too plebeian, too egalitarian, not sufficiently servile. Under such rulers, demonstrations of homage and reverence must take place by explicit royal command. The fact that the command אַבְרֵךְ was now given in rayim."   42. Pharaoh took off his ring from his hand and placed it upon Yosef's hand, dressed him in garments of byssus and placed the golden medallion about his neck,   43. and had him ride in the chariot intended for the second after him, and they called out before him: "I command that everyone bend the knee!" And thus he set him over all the land of Mitzrayim. 44. Then Pharaoh said to Yosef: "I am Pharaoh, but without you no one in all the land of Mitzrayim shall lift his hand or his foot."   45. Pharaoh named Yosef Tzaphenath Paneaḥ, and he gave him as a wife Asenath, the daughter of Potipherah, the priest in On. Thereafter Yosef went out over the land of Mitzrayim.   46. Yosef was thirty years old when he stood before Pharaoh, the king of Mitzrayim; now Yosef went out from Pharaoh's presence and traveled through all the land of Mitzrayim. 47. The land produced by the handfuls during the seven years of plenty.   48. But he held back all the food of the seven years that were in the land of Mitzrayim, and placed food into the cities. The food of the field round about each city he placed within it.   49. Yosef piled up grain like the sand of the sea, in exceeding measure, until they ceased to count [it], for it was without number.   50. And two sons were born to Yosef before a year of famine came, whom Asenath, the daughter of Potipherah, the priest in On, had borne him.   51. Yosef named his first-born Menashe: "For God

אֹתְךָ֔ עַ֖ל כָּל־אֶ֥רֶץ מִצְרָֽיִם: מב וַיָּ֨סַר פַּרְעֹ֤ה אֶת־טַבַּעְתּוֹ֙ מֵעַ֣ל יָד֔וֹ וַיִּתֵּ֥ן אֹתָ֖הּ עַל־יַ֣ד יוֹסֵ֑ף וַיַּלְבֵּ֤שׁ אֹתוֹ֙ בִּגְדֵי־שֵׁ֔שׁ וַיָּ֛שֶׂם רְבִ֥ד הַזָּהָ֖ב עַל־צַוָּארֽוֹ: מג וַיַּרְכֵּ֣ב אֹת֗וֹ בְּמִרְכֶּ֤בֶת הַמִּשְׁנֶה֙ אֲשֶׁר־ל֔וֹ וַיִּקְרְא֥וּ לְפָנָ֖יו אַבְרֵ֑ךְ וְנָת֣וֹן אֹת֔וֹ עַ֖ל כָּל־אֶ֥רֶץ מִצְרָֽיִם: מד וַיֹּ֧אמֶר פַּרְעֹ֛ה אֶל־יוֹסֵ֖ף אֲנִ֣י פַרְעֹ֑ה וּבִלְעָדֶ֗יךָ לֹֽא־יָרִ֨ים אִ֧ישׁ אֶת־יָד֛וֹ וְאֶת־רַגְל֖וֹ בְּכָל־אֶ֥רֶץ מִצְרָֽיִם: מה וַיִּקְרָ֨א פַרְעֹ֣ה שֵׁם־יוֹסֵף֮ צָֽפְנַ֣ת פַּעְנֵחַ֒ וַיִּתֶּן־ל֣וֹ אֶת־אָֽסְנַ֗ת בַּת־פּ֥וֹטִי פֶ֛רַע כֹּהֵ֥ן אֹ֖ן לְאִשָּׁ֑ה וַיֵּצֵ֥א יוֹסֵ֖ף עַל־אֶ֥רֶץ מִצְרָֽיִם: מו וְיוֹסֵף֙ בֶּן־שְׁלֹשִׁ֣ים שָׁנָ֔ה בְּעָמְד֕וֹ לִפְנֵ֖י פַּרְעֹ֣ה מֶֽלֶךְ־מִצְרָ֑יִם וַיֵּצֵ֤א יוֹסֵף֙ מִלִּפְנֵ֣י פַרְעֹ֔ה וַיַּֽעֲבֹ֖ר בְּכָל־אֶ֥רֶץ מִצְרָֽיִם: מז וַתַּ֣עַשׂ הָאָ֔רֶץ בְּשֶׁ֖בַע שְׁנֵ֣י הַשָּׂבָ֑ע לִקְמָצִֽים: מח וַיִּקְבֹּ֞ץ אֶת־כָּל־אֹ֣כֶל ׀ שֶׁ֣בַע שָׁנִ֗ים אֲשֶׁ֤ר הָיוּ֙ בְּאֶ֣רֶץ מִצְרַ֔יִם וַיִּתֶּן־אֹ֖כֶל בֶּֽעָרִ֑ים אֹ֧כֶל שְׂדֵה־הָעִ֛יר אֲשֶׁ֥ר סְבִֽיבֹתֶ֖יהָ נָתַ֥ן בְּתוֹכָֽהּ: מט וַיִּצְבֹּ֨ר יוֹסֵ֥ף בָּ֛ר כְּח֥וֹל הַיָּ֖ם הַרְבֵּ֣ה מְאֹ֑ד עַ֛ד כִּי־חָדַ֥ל לִסְפֹּ֖ר כִּי־אֵ֥ין מִסְפָּֽר: נ וּלְיוֹסֵ֤ף יֻלַּד֙ שְׁנֵ֣י בָנִ֔ים בְּטֶ֥רֶם תָּב֖וֹא שְׁנַ֣ת הָרָעָ֑ב אֲשֶׁ֤ר יָֽלְדָה־לּוֹ֙ אָֽסְנַ֔ת בַּת־פּ֥וֹטִי פֶ֖רַע כֹּהֵ֥ן אֽוֹן: נא וַיִּקְרָ֧א יוֹסֵ֛ף אֶת־שֵׁ֥ם הַבְּכ֖וֹר מְנַשֶּׁ֑ה כִּֽי־נַשַּׁ֥נִי אֱלֹהִים֙

Joseph's name; i.e., that he commanded all to kneel before him, showed that he was to be second only to Pharaoh in every respect.

49. The plan to buy up the grain reserves of all the cities, storing them up as state property for each city, to be offered for purchase to the populace in the future, during the period of famine, also made for a rational economy. People are economical with things that cost them money. Outright gifts, given without payment, are treated with little respect.

כִּי אֵין מִסְפָּר [for it was without number]. This does not mean that the amount of grain could not be expressed in terms of numbers. There are, of course, those who would like to portray the ancients, particularly the people of the Biblical era, as childlishly inept.

It is claimed, for instance, that people in those days were not able to count beyond a certain number. This claim is not based on mature thought. For once one has terms for the numbers "one," "one hundred," "one thousand" and indeed "ten thousand," one can make any number of combinations up to infinity.... The reserves of grain that were heaped higher and higher became so great that people stopped saying, "There are so and so many bushels piled up here." The new quantities added to the already existing heaps no longer made any difference; already the day before, the total quantity had passed the limits of the human imagination.

51. נַשַּׁנִי is usually rendered as: "God has caused me to *forget* all my trouble and all my father's house." But whose heart would not turn within him at the thought

אֶת־כָּל־עֲמָלִי וְאֵת כָּל־בֵּית אָבִי׃ נב וְאֵת שֵׁם
הַשֵּׁנִי קָרָא אֶפְרָיִם כִּי־הִפְרַנִי אֱלֹהִים בְּאֶרֶץ
עָנְיִי׃ רביעי נג וַתִּכְלֶינָה שֶׁבַע שְׁנֵי הַשָּׂבָע אֲשֶׁר
הָיָה בְּאֶרֶץ מִצְרָיִם׃ נד וַתְּחִלֶּינָה שֶׁבַע שְׁנֵי
הָרָעָב לָבוֹא כַּאֲשֶׁר אָמַר יוֹסֵף וַיְהִי רָעָב בְּכָל־
הָאֲרָצוֹת וּבְכָל־אֶרֶץ מִצְרַיִם הָיָה לָחֶם׃
נה וַתִּרְעַב כָּל־אֶרֶץ מִצְרַיִם וַיִּצְעַק הָעָם אֶל־
פַּרְעֹה לַלָּחֶם וַיֹּאמֶר פַּרְעֹה לְכָל־מִצְרַיִם לְכוּ
אֶל־יוֹסֵף אֲשֶׁר־יֹאמַר לָכֶם תַּעֲשׂוּ׃ נו וְהָרָעָב
הָיָה עַל כָּל־פְּנֵי הָאָרֶץ וַיִּפְתַּח יוֹסֵף אֶת־כָּל־
אֲשֶׁר בָּהֶם וַיִּשְׁבֹּר לְמִצְרַיִם וַיֶּחֱזַק הָרָעָב בְּאֶרֶץ
מִצְרָיִם׃ נז וְכָל־הָאָרֶץ בָּאוּ מִצְרַיְמָה לִשְׁבֹּר
אֶל־יוֹסֵף כִּי־חָזַק הָרָעָב בְּכָל־הָאָרֶץ׃
מב א וַיַּרְא יַעֲקֹב כִּי יֶשׁ־שֶׁבֶר בְּמִצְרָיִם וַיֹּאמֶר
יַעֲקֹב לְבָנָיו לָמָּה תִּתְרָאוּ׃ ב וַיֹּאמֶר הִנֵּה
שָׁמַעְתִּי כִּי יֶשׁ־שֶׁבֶר בְּמִצְרָיִם רְדוּ־שָׁמָּה
וְשִׁבְרוּ־לָנוּ מִשָּׁם וְנִחְיֶה וְלֹא נָמוּת׃ ג וַיֵּרְדוּ
אֲחֵי־יוֹסֵף עֲשָׂרָה לִשְׁבֹּר בָּר מִמִּצְרָיִם׃ ד וְאֶת־
בִּנְיָמִין אֲחִי יוֹסֵף לֹא־שָׁלַח יַעֲקֹב אֶת־אֶחָיו כִּי
אָמַר פֶּן־יִקְרָאֶנּוּ אָסוֹן׃ ה וַיָּבֹאוּ בְּנֵי יִשְׂרָאֵל

has made all my trouble and all my father's house into creditors for me." 52. And he named the second Ephraim: "For God has caused me to blossom in the land of my affliction." 53. The seven years of plenty which was in the land of Mitzrayim came to an end, 54. and the seven years of famine began to come, just as Joseph had said. There was famine in all the lands, but there was bread on hand throughout the land of Mitzrayim. 55. When all the land of Mitzrayim was starving and the people cried to Pharaoh for the bread, Pharaoh said to all of Mitzrayim: "Go to Yosef; what he will say to you, do." 56. But the famine was over all the region. And Yosef opened all the storehouses and sold to the Mitzrites at retail; however, the famine kept increasing in the land of Mitzrayim. 57. And they came from all over to Mitzrayim to buy at retail, to Yosef, for the famine was severe all over.

XLII

1. Yaakov saw that there was a retail sale [of grain] in Mitzrayim, and Yaakov said to his sons: "Why are you looking at each other?" 2. For he said: "Behold, I have heard that there is a retail sale [of grain] in Mitzrayim; go down there and buy at retail for us from there so that we may survive and not die." 3. So Yosef's ten brothers went down to buy grain at retail from Mitzrayim. 4. But Yaakov did not send Yosef's brother Binyamin with the brothers, for he said: "An accident might befall him." 5. So the sons of Yisrael came to buy at

that Joseph should give his first-born son a name declaring that God had caused him to forget his aged father and all his father's family? Of course such a rendering would explain in the most plausible terms why Joseph had not concerned himself about his father all these years. It would simply mean that Joseph was a man without a heart. But fortunately נשה can have connotations other than that of "forgetting." It can also denote "being a creditor,"[28] so that נשה can be interpreted to convey the following thought: "God has turned my trouble and my family into my creditors. That which until now seemed to me misfortune and abuse God has turned into the instrument for my greatest happiness, so that I find myself deeply indebted both to my troubles and to my family." . . .

56 and 57. וַיִּשְׁבֹּר *[and sold . . . at retail].* The basic literal meaning of שבר is "to break" or "to break apart." Hence, the term in this passage denotes "retail" sales or purchases. Joseph sold to individuals only small quantities, sufficient for the immediate requirements of one household. This was the only way in which speculative buying and a cornering of the grain market could be prevented. . . .

CHAPTER XLII

5. Here they are introduced for the first time as בְּנֵי יִשְׂרָאֵל ["the sons of Yisrael"]. But then this

[28]*Note to the English translation*: נוֹשֶׁה is used throughout the Biblical text; e.g. Exodus 22:24, Deuteronomy 24:11, II Kings 4:1, Psalms 109:1 in the sense of "creditor." [E.O.]

retail among those [others] who came, for the famine was in the land of Canaan. 6. And Yosef was the governor over the land, and at the same time he was the one who sold at retail to all the population of the land. Yosef's brothers came and bowed down before him with their faces to the ground. 7. When Yosef saw his brothers, he recognized them. But he made himself a stranger to them and he spoke roughly to them and said to them: "Where do you come from?" They said: "From the land of Canaan, to buy food at retail." 8. Yosef recognized his brothers, but they did not recognize him. 9. And Yosef remembered the dreams which he had dreamed of them,

לִשְׁבֹּר בְּתוֹךְ הַבָּאִים כִּי־הָיָה הָרָעָב בְּאֶרֶץ כְּנָעַן:
ו וְיוֹסֵף הוּא הַשַּׁלִּיט עַל־הָאָרֶץ הוּא הַמַּשְׁבִּיר
לְכָל־עַם הָאָרֶץ וַיָּבֹאוּ אֲחֵי יוֹסֵף וַיִּשְׁתַּחֲווּ־לוֹ
אַפַּיִם אָרְצָה: ז וַיַּרְא יוֹסֵף אֶת־אֶחָיו וַיַּכִּרֵם
וַיִּתְנַכֵּר אֲלֵיהֶם וַיְדַבֵּר אִתָּם קָשׁוֹת וַיֹּאמֶר
אֲלֵהֶם מֵאַיִן בָּאתֶם וַיֹּאמְרוּ מֵאֶרֶץ כְּנַעַן לִשְׁבָּר־
אֹכֶל: ח וַיַּכֵּר יוֹסֵף אֶת־אֶחָיו וְהֵם לֹא הִכִּרֻהוּ:
ט וַיִּזְכֹּר יוֹסֵף אֵת הַחֲלֹמוֹת אֲשֶׁר חָלַם לָהֶם

was a moment of no small historic import. The entire future rested upon it. However, they came "among those (others) who came": they were unaware of the consequences their journey would have for future generations.

9. We must attempt to explain Joseph's behavior on the basis of the facts given in our narrative. We might have thought that, if only for his father's sake, he should have made himself known to his brothers at once, especially so since he had already recognized the hand of God in all that had befallen him and had learned to appreciate all his misfortunes, including the transgression of his brothers against him, as Divine instruments for his greatest happiness.

Also, a man of Joseph's intelligence could not have believed that he must become a slave to his dreams. If a dream has any meaning, one can leave the realization of that dream to Him Who sent it. Only considerations of compelling necessity could have caused Joseph to behave in a manner that otherwise would appear to be senseless chicanery, of which one could certainly not suspect Joseph, if not merely because of his moral character then certainly because of his intelligence, which no one can deny. If we place ourselves into Joseph's position, we might arrive at the following explanation:

If Joseph had really desired to become, and remain, a prince and nothing else but a prince in the eyes of his father and his brothers, if he really had not cared to return to his family as a son and brother, he would not have needed to resort to all these contrivances. But even after he had become a prince in Egypt, Joseph had reared his children in the spirit of the family of Jacob and eventually would request that his bones should be laid to rest in the soil of his fathers. He therefore felt that two developments would have to occur before he

could make himself known to his brothers: (a) That, if possible, he should be able to change his own opinion of his brothers, but above all, (b) that his brothers should change their opinion of him. Their feelings toward one another would have to change; otherwise they would not be able to resume their former close relationship. In that case, even if Joseph were physically restored to his family, his family would be lost to him, and he to them.

It was only natural that Joseph's view of his brothers should be prejudiced by what they had done to him, that he should remember the ruthlessness in which they had ignored his entreaties from the pit, and their father's grief. These feelings could be erased from Joseph's mind only by a proof that his brothers had had a complete change of heart. He therefore felt he would have to test his brothers to see whether they would find it in their hearts once again (and for a justifiable reason this time) to pry a son away from their father. Perhaps the real possibility of life imprisonment and the real danger that their families might be starving at home would be more convincing persuasion than any imagined threat from Joseph's supposed thirst for power.

This test was of vital import for Joseph's own feelings so that, if his brothers passed it, he would be able to banish the last drop of bitterness against them from his heart. But the second, and perhaps the most important, consideration was this: Joseph remembered his dreams, how they had caused his brothers to suspect him of lust for power and to feel threatened by him, and how these dreams had caused his brothers' suspicions to intensify into such deep-seated conviction that they would have considered it legitimate to commit even the gravest of all crimes against him because they felt they would then be acting in self-defense. If this had already been the case when Joseph went about among them in his embroidered coat, how much more would they now and he said to them: "You are spies! You have come to see the nakedness of the land." 10. They said to him: "No, my lord, your servants have come to buy food at retail, 11. and we are all sons of one man; we are honest men; your servants were never spies." 12. But he said to them: "No! You have come to see the nakedness of the land." 13. They replied: "We are twelve, your servants, brothers, the sons of one man in the land of Canaan. Behold, the youngest is still with our father today, and one [other] is gone." 14. But Yosef said to them: "This is just what I have said to you: you are spies. 15. Therefore you shall be tested: By the life of Pharaoh! You shall not go away from here unless your younger brother comes here. 16. Send one of you, and let him fetch your brother, and you remain here under arrest, so that your words may be tested whether there is truth with you. Or else, by the life of Pharaoh, you are spies!" 17. He took them into custody for three days. 18. On the third day Yosef said to them: "Do this and remain alive! I fear God. 19. If you are honest men, let one of your brothers remain under arrest in the house where you are in custody; but you go and bring home the purchase for the famine of your households, 20. and bring your younger brother to me so that your words may be verified and you will not die." And they did so. 21. And they said, one to the other: "So we are guilty after all with

וַיֹּאמֶר אֲלֵהֶם מְרַגְּלִים אַתֶּם לִרְאוֹת אֶת־עֶרְוַת הָאָרֶץ בָּאתֶם: י וַיֹּאמְרוּ אֵלָיו לֹא אֲדֹנִי וַעֲבָדֶיךָ בָּאוּ לִשְׁבָּר־אֹכֶל: יא כֻּלָּנוּ בְּנֵי אִישׁ־אֶחָד נָחְנוּ כֵּנִים אֲנַחְנוּ לֹא־הָיוּ עֲבָדֶיךָ מְרַגְּלִים: יב וַיֹּאמֶר אֲלֵהֶם לֹא כִּי־עֶרְוַת הָאָרֶץ בָּאתֶם לִרְאוֹת: יג וַיֹּאמְרוּ שְׁנֵים עָשָׂר עֲבָדֶיךָ אַחִים אֲנַחְנוּ בְּנֵי אִישׁ־אֶחָד בְּאֶרֶץ כְּנָעַן וְהִנֵּה הַקָּטֹן אֶת־אָבִינוּ הַיּוֹם וְהָאֶחָד אֵינֶנּוּ: יד וַיֹּאמֶר אֲלֵהֶם יוֹסֵף הוּא אֲשֶׁר דִּבַּרְתִּי אֲלֵכֶם לֵאמֹר מְרַגְּלִים אַתֶּם: טו בְּזֹאת תִּבָּחֵנוּ חֵי פַרְעֹה אִם־תֵּצְאוּ מִזֶּה כִּי אִם־בְּבוֹא אֲחִיכֶם הַקָּטֹן הֵנָּה: טז שִׁלְחוּ מִכֶּם אֶחָד וְיִקַּח אֶת־אֲחִיכֶם וְאַתֶּם הֵאָסְרוּ וְיִבָּחֲנוּ דִּבְרֵיכֶם הַאֱמֶת אִתְּכֶם וְאִם־לֹא חֵי פַרְעֹה כִּי מְרַגְּלִים אַתֶּם: יז וַיֶּאֱסֹף אֹתָם אֶל־מִשְׁמָר שְׁלֹשֶׁת יָמִים: יח וַיֹּאמֶר אֲלֵהֶם יוֹסֵף בַּיּוֹם הַשְּׁלִישִׁי זֹאת עֲשׂוּ וִחְיוּ אֶת־הָאֱלֹהִים אֲנִי יָרֵא: חמישי יט אִם־כֵּנִים אַתֶּם אֲחִיכֶם אֶחָד יֵאָסֵר בְּבֵית מִשְׁמַרְכֶם וְאַתֶּם לְכוּ הָבִיאוּ שֶׁבֶר רַעֲבוֹן בָּתֵּיכֶם: כ וְאֶת־אֲחִיכֶם הַקָּטֹן תָּבִיאוּ אֵלַי וְיֵאָמְנוּ דִבְרֵיכֶם וְלֹא תָמוּתוּ וַיַּעֲשׂוּ־כֵן: כא וַיֹּאמְרוּ אִישׁ אֶל־אָחִיו אֲבָל אֲשֵׁמִים אֲנַחְנוּ

have to fear him when he was not only a "king" in fact but also had cause to hate them and, in the manner of ignoble souls, to take his revenge on them!

For this reason it was imperative that the brothers should come to know Joseph's true character, and to this end it was necessary, above all, that he present himself to them in the light of his actual position of power. Until now they had known him only as a מַשְׁבִּיר [retail seller]; perhaps they had taken him for a lowly clerk taking orders from some petty official. He would therefore have to present himself to them as the שַׁלִּיט [governor]. They would have to understand that he was now in a position to do with them as he pleased. If he would then turn out to be their greatest benefactor instead, he would have reason to hope that this would cure them of all their erroneous notions about him.

Then, at the moment when he would identify himself to them as their brother Joseph, the blindfold would drop from their eyes and it would be possible for both Joseph and his brothers to forget the past and to let bygones be bygones. Only under such circumstances could Joseph hope to be truly restored as a son to his father and as a brother to his father's children.

If we are not mistaken, these same considerations were also the ones that kept Joseph from establishing contact with his father during his years of prosperity. What would Jacob's heart have won if he had regained one son but lost ten others, if henceforth he would have had to see his children divided into two bitterly warring camps? To this end all of Joseph's contrivances were essential and—as it would seem to us—entirely worthy of a man as wise as he.

regard to our brother, that we witnessed the distress of his soul when he entreated us and we did not listen! That is why this distress has come upon us!" 22. Reuben answered them: "Did I not tell you: 'Do not sin against the child?' But you would not listen. Behold, his blood is therefore now avenged." 23. They did not know that Yosef understood them, for the interpreter was between them. 24. He turned away from them and wept. Then he returned to them, spoke with them, took Shimeon from them and had him bound before their eyes. 25. Yosef gave orders, and they filled their vessels with grain, but [he gave orders] also to put back every man's money into his own sack and also to give them provision for the journey, and thus it was done for them. 26. They loaded their purchase upon their donkeys and departed from there. 27. And one of them opened his sack to give fodder to his donkey at the lodging place. And he saw the money and lo! it was at the top of his pack. 28. He said to his brothers: "My money has been returned; in fact, it is in my pack." And their hearts went out from them, and they said, frightened, to one another: "What is this that God has done to us?" 29. They came to their father Yaakov, to the land of Canaan, and told him all that had befallen them, as follows: 30. "The man, the master of the land, spoke roughly to us, and he made us out as if we were spying out the land. 31. We said to him: 'We are honest men; we were never spies. 32. We are twelve brothers, the sons of our father; one [of us] is gone and the youngest is still with our father today in the land of Canaan.' 33. There-upon the man, the master of the land, said to us: 'By this I shall know that you are honest men; leave one of your brothers with me, and take that for which your households hunger, and go away, 34. 'and bring your younger brother to me; then I will know that you are not spies, that you are honest men; I will then give your brother to you and you may do business in the land.'" 35. And it came to pass when they emptied their sacks, that, lo! each one had his [own] bundle of money in his sack! They and their father saw the bundles of money and were frightened. 36. But their father

עַל־אָחִ֔ינוּ אֲשֶׁ֨ר רָאִ֜ינוּ צָרַ֥ת נַפְשׁ֛וֹ בְּהִתְחַֽנְנ֥וֹ אֵלֵ֖ינוּ וְלֹ֣א שָׁמָ֑עְנוּ עַל־כֵּן֙ בָּ֣אָה אֵלֵ֔ינוּ הַצָּרָ֖ה הַזֹּֽאת: כב וַיַּעַן֩ רְאוּבֵ֨ן אֹתָ֜ם לֵאמֹ֗ר הֲל֨וֹא אָמַ֧רְתִּי אֲלֵיכֶ֣ם ׀ לֵאמֹ֗ר אַל־תֶּֽחֶטְא֥וּ בַיֶּ֖לֶד וְלֹ֣א שְׁמַעְתֶּ֑ם וְגַם־דָּמ֖וֹ הִנֵּ֥ה נִדְרָֽשׁ: כג וְהֵם֙ לֹ֣א יָֽדְע֔וּ כִּ֥י שֹׁמֵ֖עַ יוֹסֵ֑ף כִּ֥י הַמֵּלִ֖יץ בֵּֽינֹתָֽם: כד וַיִּסֹּ֣ב מֵֽעֲלֵיהֶם֮ וַיֵּבְךְּ֒ וַיָּ֤שָׁב אֲלֵהֶם֙ וַיְדַבֵּ֣ר אֲלֵהֶ֔ם וַיִּקַּ֤ח מֵֽאִתָּם֙ אֶת־שִׁמְע֔וֹן וַיֶּֽאֱסֹ֥ר אֹת֖וֹ לְעֵֽינֵיהֶֽם: כה וַיְצַ֣ו יוֹסֵ֗ף וַיְמַלְא֣וּ אֶת־כְּלֵיהֶם֮ בָּר֒ וּלְהָשִׁ֤יב כַּסְפֵּיהֶם֙ אִ֣ישׁ אֶל־שַׂקּ֔וֹ וְלָתֵ֥ת לָהֶ֛ם צֵדָ֖ה לַדָּ֑רֶךְ וַיַּ֥עַשׂ לָהֶ֖ם כֵּֽן: כו וַיִּשְׂא֥וּ אֶת־שִׁבְרָ֖ם עַל־חֲמֹֽרֵיהֶ֑ם וַיֵּֽלְכ֖וּ מִשָּֽׁם: כז וַיִּפְתַּ֨ח הָֽאֶחָ֜ד אֶת־שַׂקּ֗וֹ לָתֵ֥ת מִסְפּ֛וֹא לַֽחֲמֹר֖וֹ בַּמָּל֑וֹן וַיַּרְא֙ אֶת־כַּסְפּ֔וֹ וְהִנֵּה־ה֖וּא בְּפִ֥י אַמְתַּחְתּֽוֹ: כח וַיֹּ֣אמֶר אֶל־אֶחָיו֩ הוּשַׁ֨ב כַּסְפִּ֜י וְגַ֨ם הִנֵּ֤ה בְאַמְתַּחְתִּי֙ וַיֵּצֵ֣א לִבָּ֔ם וַיֶּֽחֶרְד֞וּ אִ֤ישׁ אֶל־אָחִיו֙ לֵאמֹ֔ר מַה־זֹּ֛את עָשָׂ֥ה אֱלֹהִ֖ים לָֽנוּ: כט וַיָּבֹ֛אוּ אֶל־יַֽעֲקֹ֥ב אֲבִיהֶ֖ם אַ֣רְצָה כְּנָ֑עַן וַיַּגִּ֣ידוּ ל֔וֹ אֵ֛ת כָּל־הַקֹּרֹ֥ת אֹתָ֖ם לֵאמֹֽר: ל דִּ֠בֶּר הָאִ֨ישׁ אֲדֹנֵ֥י הָאָ֛רֶץ אִתָּ֖נוּ קָשׁ֑וֹת וַיִּתֵּ֣ן אֹתָ֔נוּ כִּֽמְרַגְּלִ֖ים אֶת־הָאָֽרֶץ: לא וַנֹּ֥אמֶר אֵלָ֖יו כֵּנִ֣ים אֲנָ֑חְנוּ לֹ֥א הָיִ֖ינוּ מְרַגְּלִֽים: לב שְׁנֵים־עָשָׂ֧ר אֲנַ֛חְנוּ אַחִ֖ים בְּנֵ֣י אָבִ֑ינוּ הָֽאֶחָ֣ד אֵינֶ֔נּוּ וְהַקָּטֹ֥ן הַיּ֛וֹם אֶת־אָבִ֖ינוּ בְּאֶ֥רֶץ כְּנָֽעַן: לג וַיֹּ֣אמֶר אֵלֵ֗ינוּ הָאִישׁ֙ אֲדֹנֵ֣י הָאָ֔רֶץ בְּזֹ֣את אֵדַ֔ע כִּ֥י כֵנִ֖ים אַתֶּ֑ם אֲחִיכֶ֤ם הָֽאֶחָד֙ הַנִּ֣יחוּ אִתִּ֔י וְאֶת־רַֽעֲב֥וֹן בָּֽתֵּיכֶ֖ם קְח֥וּ וָלֵֽכוּ: לד וְ֠הָבִ֠יאוּ אֶת־אֲחִיכֶ֣ם הַקָּטֹן֮ אֵלַי֒ וְאֵֽדְעָ֗ה כִּ֣י לֹ֤א מְרַגְּלִים֙ אַתֶּ֔ם כִּ֥י כֵנִ֖ים אַתֶּ֑ם אֶת־אֲחִיכֶם֙ אֶתֵּ֣ן לָכֶ֔ם וְאֶת־הָאָ֖רֶץ תִּסְחָֽרוּ: לה וַיְהִ֗י הֵ֚ם מְרִיקִ֣ים שַׂקֵּיהֶ֔ם וְהִנֵּה־אִ֥ישׁ צְרֽוֹר־כַּסְפּ֖וֹ בְּשַׂקּ֑וֹ וַיִּרְא֞וּ אֶת־צְרֹר֧וֹת כַּסְפֵּיהֶ֛ם הֵ֥מָּה וַֽאֲבִיהֶ֖ם וַיִּירָֽאוּ: לו וַיֹּ֣אמֶר אֲלֵהֶם֮ יַֽעֲקֹ֣ב אֲבִיהֶם֒

Yaakov said to them: "You have made me childless! Yosef is gone, Shimeon is gone, and [now] you want to take Binyamin away—upon me have all these things come!" 37. And Reuben said to his father: "You can kill my two sons if I do not bring him home to you. Put him into my hands; I will bring him back to you." 38. But he said: "My son shall not go down with you, because his brother is dead and he alone is left. If an accident were to befall him on the way on which you go, you would bring down my gray head in sorrow to the grave."

XLIII

1. But the famine was severe in the land. 2. When they had used up the purchase which they had brought from Mitzrayim, their father said to them: "Please go back there; buy us a little food." 3. However, Yehudah answered him: "The man has warned us repeatedly: 'You will not see my face again if your brother is not with you.' 4. If you send our brother with us, we will gladly go down and buy you food. 5. But if you will not send him with [us] we cannot go down, because the man said to us: 'You will not see my face again if your brother is not with you.'" 6. And Yisrael said: "Why have you done this terrible

אֹתִי שִׁכַּלְתֶּם יוֹסֵף אֵינֶנּוּ וְשִׁמְעוֹן אֵינֶנּוּ וְאֶת־
בִּנְיָמִן תִּקָּחוּ עָלַי הָיוּ כֻלָּנָה: לז וַיֹּאמֶר רְאוּבֵן
אֶל־אָבִיו לֵאמֹר אֶת־שְׁנֵי בָנַי תָּמִית אִם־לֹא
אֲבִיאֶנּוּ אֵלֶיךָ תְּנָה אֹתוֹ עַל־יָדִי וַאֲנִי אֲשִׁיבֶנּוּ
אֵלֶיךָ: לח וַיֹּאמֶר לֹא־יֵרֵד בְּנִי עִמָּכֶם כִּי־אָחִיו
מֵת וְהוּא לְבַדּוֹ נִשְׁאָר וּקְרָאָהוּ אָסוֹן בַּדֶּרֶךְ אֲשֶׁר
תֵּלְכוּ־בָהּ וְהוֹרַדְתֶּם אֶת־שֵׂיבָתִי בְּיָגוֹן שְׁאוֹלָה:
מג א וְהָרָעָב כָּבֵד בָּאָרֶץ: ב וַיְהִי כַּאֲשֶׁר כִּלּוּ
לֶאֱכֹל אֶת־הַשֶּׁבֶר אֲשֶׁר הֵבִיאוּ מִמִּצְרָיִם וַיֹּאמֶר
אֲלֵיהֶם אֲבִיהֶם שֻׁבוּ שִׁבְרוּ־לָנוּ מְעַט־אֹכֶל:
ג וַיֹּאמֶר אֵלָיו יְהוּדָה לֵאמֹר הָעֵד הֵעִד בָּנוּ
הָאִישׁ לֵאמֹר לֹא־תִרְאוּ פָנַי בִּלְתִּי אֲחִיכֶם
אִתְּכֶם: ד אִם־יֶשְׁךָ מְשַׁלֵּחַ אֶת־אָחִינוּ אִתָּנוּ
נֵרְדָה וְנִשְׁבְּרָה לְךָ אֹכֶל: ה וְאִם־אֵינְךָ מְשַׁלֵּחַ לֹא
נֵרֵד כִּי־הָאִישׁ אָמַר אֵלֵינוּ לֹא־תִרְאוּ פָנַי בִּלְתִּי
אֲחִיכֶם אִתְּכֶם: ו וַיֹּאמֶר יִשְׂרָאֵל לָמָה הֲרֵעֹתֶם

36. "You cannot take it amiss of me that I will not let Benjamin go with you. I *must* not let him go. Of course I do not know the circumstances of Joseph's disappearance; I also cannot explain how Simeon was lost. Perhaps these events are not related to each other but עָלַי הָיוּ כֻלָּנָה [upon me have all these things come]: it is I who was stricken by both these misfortunes. I am bereft of both my sons."

If the same misfortune befalls a man repeatedly and under similar circumstances, then, even if he does not understand what caused these calamities, he should not place himself into a position where they are likely to recur, until he obtains an insight into the causes. He should consider the repetition of events as a סִימָן, a sign to be remembered, and protect himself against similar future occurrences until the causes have become clear to him. . . .

CHAPTER XLIII

6. וַיֹּאמֶר יִשְׂרָאֵל *[And Yisrael said].* Until this point, ever since the loss of Joseph, the narrative has referred to his father as יַעֲקֹב. For the name יַעֲקֹב signifies that depressed state of mind in which a person feels that he is dependent, failing and "limping" or lagging behind the realities of life. He feels incapable of coping with them and must therefore let himself be dragged along by them, as it were. But the true Jew feels depressed only as long as he does not know what he must do. And there are only two things that can depress a righteous Jew: 1) guilt, and 2) doubt as to where his duty lies, but not about what might happen.

As long as Jacob was in a state of doubt and felt that he must not send Benjamin to Egypt with his brothers, he is presented as יַעֲקֹב. But once he sees clearly that the peril to Benjamin's life will be no greater if he stays at home than if he will go with his brothers, Jacob pulls himself together and becomes יִשְׂרָאֵל. When the Jew realizes that it is beyond his human capacities to help himself, he is bidden: גול על ד׳ וגו׳ ["Cast (lit., "roll") the burden of your path upon God"—Psalm 37:5]: "Roll over" to God whatever is too heavy for you to bear alone. So Israel now accepts with renewed strength and courage something that will be difficult for him to do

לִי לְהַגִּיד לָאִישׁ הַעֽוֹד לָכֶם אָח: ז וַיֹּאמְרוּ שָׁאוֹל
שָֽׁאַל־הָאִישׁ לָנוּ וּלְמֽוֹלַדְתֵּנוּ לֵאמֹר הַעֽוֹד
אֲבִיכֶם חַי הֲיֵשׁ לָכֶם אָח וַנַּ֤גֶּד־לוֹ עַל־פִּי
הַדְּבָרִים הָאֵלֶּה הֲיָדוֹעַ נֵדַע כִּי יֹאמַר הוֹרִידוּ
אֶת־אֲחִיכֶם: ח וַיֹּאמֶר יְהוּדָה אֶל־יִשְׂרָאֵל אָבִיו
שִׁלְחָה הַנַּעַר אִתִּי וְנָקוּמָה וְנֵלֵכָה וְנִֽחְיֶה וְלֹא
נָמוּת גַּם־אֲנַחְנוּ גַם־אַתָּה גַּם־טַפֵּנוּ: ט אָנֹכִי
אֶֽעֶרְבֶנּוּ מִיָּדִי תְּבַקְשֶׁנּוּ אִם־לֹא הֲבִיאֹתִיו אֵלֶיךָ
וְהִצַּגְתִּיו לְפָנֶיךָ וְחָטָאתִי לְךָ כָּל־הַיָּמִים: י כִּי
לוּלֵא הִתְמַהְמָהְנוּ כִּי־עַתָּה שַׁבְנוּ זֶה פַעֲמָיִם:
יא וַיֹּאמֶר אֲלֵהֶם יִשְׂרָאֵל אֲבִיהֶם אִם־כֵּן | אֵפוֹא
זֹאת עֲשׂוּ קְחוּ מִזִּמְרַת הָאָרֶץ בִּכְלֵיכֶם וְהוֹרִידוּ
לָאִישׁ מִנְחָה מְעַט צֳרִי וּמְעַט דְּבַשׁ נְכֹאת וָלֹט
בָּטְנִים וּשְׁקֵדִים: יב וְכֶסֶף מִשְׁנֶה קְחוּ בְיֶדְכֶם
וְאֶת־הַכֶּסֶף הַמּוּשָׁב בְּפִי אַמְתְּחֹֽתֵיכֶם תָּשִׁיבוּ
בְיֶדְכֶם אוּלַי מִשְׁגֶּה הוּא: יג וְאֶת־אֲחִיכֶם קָחוּ
וְקוּמוּ שׁוּבוּ אֶל־הָאִישׁ: יד וְאֵל שַׁדַּי יִתֵּן לָכֶם
רַחֲמִים לִפְנֵי הָאִישׁ וְשִׁלַּח לָכֶם אֶת־אֲחִיכֶם
אַחֵר וְאֶת־בִּנְיָמִין וַאֲנִי כַּאֲשֶׁר שָׁכֹלְתִּי שָׁכָֽלְתִּי:
טו וַיִּקְחוּ הָאֲנָשִׁים אֶת־הַמִּנְחָה הַזֹּאת וּמִשְׁנֶה־
כֶּסֶף לָקְחוּ בְיָדָם וְאֶת־בִּנְיָמִן וַיָּקֻמוּ וַיֵּרְדוּ
מִצְרַיִם וַיַּעַמְדוּ לִפְנֵי יוֹסֵף: ששי טז וַיַּרְא יוֹסֵף
אִתָּם אֶת־בִּנְיָמִין וַיֹּאמֶר לַאֲשֶׁר עַל־בֵּיתוֹ הָבֵא
אֶת־הָאֲנָשִׁים הַבָּיְתָה וּטְבֹחַ טֶבַח וְהָכֵן כִּי אִתִּי
יֹאכְלוּ הָאֲנָשִׁים בַּֽצָּהֳרָיִם: יז וַיַּעַשׂ הָאִישׁ
כַּאֲשֶׁר אָמַר יוֹסֵף וַיָּבֵא הָאִישׁ אֶת־הָאֲנָשִׁים

thing to me, to tell the man that you have another brother?" 7. They replied: "The man repeatedly asked about us and our origin: 'Is your father still alive? Do you have another brother?' And we reported to him according to these questions. How were we to know that he would say: 'Bring down your brother?'" 8. And Yehudah said to Yisrael, his father: "Just send the lad with me and we will gladly arise and go so that we may remain alive and not die, both we, and also you and our children. 9. I will be surety for him; from my hand you shall demand him. If I do not bring him home to you and set him before you, I will have sinned against you forever. 10. For if only we had not lingered, we could have been back a second time by now." 11. And Yisrael, their father, said to them: "If that is so, what else is there to do? Do this: Take into your vessels from that of which the land boasts, and bring a gift to the man: a little balsam, a little honey, spices and laudanum, pistachio nuts and almonds. 12. And take double money in your hand, and the money that was put back at the top of your sacks, return it with your hands; perhaps it was an oversight. 13. And take your brother! Arise and go back to the man! 14. And may God, the All-Sufficing, grant you compassion before the man, so that he will let your other brother and Binyamin go. And as for me—if I must be bereft of my children, then I will be bereft." 15. The men took this gift; they also took double money with [them], and Binyamin. They arose and went down to Mitzrayim and stood before Yosef. 16. Yosef saw Binyamin with them and said to the overseer of his house: "Bring these men into the house, slaughter [animals] and prepare [the meat], for the men are to dine with me at noon." 17. The man did as Yosef had said, and the man brought the men into Yosef's house.

but that now appears to him inevitable, for it is at the point when his own capacities are no longer sufficient that the sovereignty of God begins for him, that sovereignty which was assured to him by his own name,

יִשְׂרָאֵל. He therefore makes no further complaint except to reproach his sons for having unnecessarily mentioned to the Egyptian despot that they still had a younger brother at home.

18. The men were frightened because they were brought into Yosef's house, and they said: "Because of the money which was put back into our packs we are now being brought there, that he may turn upon us, fall upon us and take us as slaves, and our beasts of burden." 19. And they stepped up to the overseer of Yosef's house and talked with him at the entrance to the house. 20. They said: "O my lord! We have already come down here once before to buy food, 21. and it came to pass when we had come to the lodging place that we opened our packs and, lo! the money of each one lay at the top of his pack; it was our own money in its weight; we have brought it back with us. 22. And we have brought down other money with us to buy food; we do not know who put our money into our packs." 23. He replied: "Peace be with you! Do not be afraid! Your God and the God of your fathers has placed a hidden treasure into your packs; your money has come to me." He also led Shimeon out to them. 24. Thereupon the man brought the men into Yosef's house, had water given [to them], they washed their feet and he also had fodder given to their donkeys. 25. They prepared the gift for Yosef's coming home at noon, for they had heard that they were to dine there. 26. When Yosef came home they brought him the gift which they had brought with them into the house and bowed down before him to the ground. 27. He inquired after their welfare and said: "Is your old father, of whom you have spoken, well? Is he still alive?" 28. They answered: "Your servant, our father, is well; he is still alive." And they bowed their heads and cast themselves down. 29. He lifted up his eyes and saw Binyamin, his brother, the son of his mother, and said: "Is this your younger brother, of whom you have told me?" He said: "May God be gracious to you, my son." 30. And Yosef hastened—for his feelings toward his brother had been stirred up and he wanted to weep—and he went into the room and wept there. 31. He washed his face, came out again, restrained himself and said: "Serve the food!" 32. They set for him by himself and for them by themselves, and also for the Mitz-

בֵּיתָה יוֹסֵף: יח וַיִּירְאוּ הָאֲנָשִׁים כִּי הוּבְאוּ בֵּית
יוֹסֵף וַיֹּאמְרוּ עַל־דְּבַר הַכֶּסֶף הַשָּׁב בְּאַמְתְּחֹתֵינוּ
בַּתְּחִלָּה אֲנַחְנוּ מוּבָאִים לְהִתְגֹּלֵל עָלֵינוּ
וּלְהִתְנַפֵּל עָלֵינוּ וְלָקַחַת אֹתָנוּ לַעֲבָדִים וְאֶת־
חֲמֹרֵינוּ: יט וַיִּגְּשׁוּ אֶל־הָאִישׁ אֲשֶׁר עַל־בֵּית
יוֹסֵף וַיְדַבְּרוּ אֵלָיו פֶּתַח הַבָּיִת: כ וַיֹּאמְרוּ בִּי
אֲדֹנִי יָרֹד יָרַדְנוּ בַּתְּחִלָּה לִשְׁבָּר־אֹכֶל: כא וַיְהִי
כִּי־בָאנוּ אֶל־הַמָּלוֹן וַנִּפְתְּחָה אֶת־אַמְתְּחֹתֵינוּ
וְהִנֵּה כֶסֶף־אִישׁ בְּפִי אַמְתַּחְתּוֹ כַּסְפֵּנוּ בְּמִשְׁקָלוֹ
וַנָּשֶׁב אֹתוֹ בְּיָדֵנוּ: כב וְכֶסֶף אַחֵר הוֹרַדְנוּ בְיָדֵנוּ
לִשְׁבָּר־אֹכֶל לֹא יָדַעְנוּ מִי־שָׂם כַּסְפֵּנוּ
בְּאַמְתְּחֹתֵינוּ: כג וַיֹּאמֶר שָׁלוֹם לָכֶם אַל־תִּירָאוּ
אֱלֹהֵיכֶם וֵאלֹהֵי אֲבִיכֶם נָתַן לָכֶם מַטְמוֹן
בְּאַמְתְּחֹתֵיכֶם כַּסְפְּכֶם בָּא אֵלָי וַיּוֹצֵא אֲלֵהֶם
אֶת־שִׁמְעוֹן: כד וַיָּבֵא הָאִישׁ אֶת־הָאֲנָשִׁים בֵּיתָה
יוֹסֵף וַיִּתֶּן־מַיִם וַיִּרְחֲצוּ רַגְלֵיהֶם וַיִּתֵּן מִסְפּוֹא
לַחֲמֹרֵיהֶם: כה וַיָּכִינוּ אֶת־הַמִּנְחָה עַד־בּוֹא
יוֹסֵף בַּצָּהֳרָיִם כִּי שָׁמְעוּ כִּי־שָׁם יֹאכְלוּ לָחֶם:
כו וַיָּבֹא יוֹסֵף הַבַּיְתָה וַיָּבִיאּוּ (א׳ דגושה) לוֹ אֶת־
הַמִּנְחָה אֲשֶׁר־בְּיָדָם הַבָּיְתָה וַיִּשְׁתַּחֲווּ־לוֹ אָרְצָה:
כז וַיִּשְׁאַל לָהֶם לְשָׁלוֹם וַיֹּאמֶר הֲשָׁלוֹם אֲבִיכֶם
הַזָּקֵן אֲשֶׁר אֲמַרְתֶּם הַעוֹדֶנּוּ חָי: כח וַיֹּאמְרוּ
שָׁלוֹם לְעַבְדְּךָ לְאָבִינוּ עוֹדֶנּוּ חָי וַיִּקְּדוּ וַיִּשְׁתַּחֲוֻ
(וישתחוו קרי): כט וַיִּשָּׂא עֵינָיו וַיַּרְא אֶת־בִּנְיָמִין
אָחִיו בֶּן־אִמּוֹ וַיֹּאמֶר הֲזֶה אֲחִיכֶם הַקָּטֹן אֲשֶׁר
אֲמַרְתֶּם אֵלָי וַיֹּאמַר אֱלֹהִים יָחְנְךָ בְּנִי: שביעי
ל וַיְמַהֵר יוֹסֵף כִּי־נִכְמְרוּ רַחֲמָיו אֶל־אָחִיו
וַיְבַקֵּשׁ לִבְכּוֹת וַיָּבֹא הַחַדְרָה וַיֵּבְךְּ שָׁמָּה:
לא וַיִּרְחַץ פָּנָיו וַיֵּצֵא וַיִּתְאַפַּק וַיֹּאמֶר שִׂימוּ
לָחֶם: לב וַיָּשִׂימוּ לוֹ לְבַדּוֹ וְלָהֶם לְבַדָּם וְלַמִּצְרִים

rites who dined with them, by themselves, because the Mitzrites could not dine with the Hebrews, for it was an abomination to the Mitzrites. 33. They sat before him, the eldest according to his age, and the younger according to his youth; and the men looked at each other in astonishment. 34. He had portions brought to them from before him, and Binyamin's portion was five times as much as any of theirs, and they drank and became intoxicated at his home.

XLIV

1. Afterwards he commanded the overseer of his house: "Fill the packs of the men with food, as much as they can carry, and place the money of each person at the top of his sack. 2. But put my goblet, the silver goblet, at the top of the sack of the youngest, and also his purchase money." He did according to the command of Yosef which the latter had uttered. 3. The morning was light and the men, they and their donkeys, had already been sent on their way. 4. They had just gone out of the city, not yet far off, but Yosef had already said to the overseer of his house: "Up! Pursue those men, and when you overtake them, say to them: 'Why have you repaid good with evil? 5. This is the one from which my master drinks, and he has a presentiment about it. You have done evil in what you have done.'" 6. He overtook them and said these words to them.

הָאֹכְלִים אִתּוֹ לְבַדָּם כִּי לֹא יוּכְלוּן הַמִּצְרִים
לֶאֱכֹל אֶת־הָעִבְרִים לֶחֶם כִּי־תוֹעֵבָה הִוא
לְמִצְרָיִם׃ לג וַיֵּשְׁבוּ לְפָנָיו הַבְּכֹר כִּבְכֹרָתוֹ
וְהַצָּעִיר כִּצְעִרָתוֹ וַיִּתְמְהוּ הָאֲנָשִׁים אִישׁ אֶל־
רֵעֵהוּ׃ לד וַיִּשָּׂא מַשְׂאֹת מֵאֵת פָּנָיו אֲלֵהֶם וַתֵּרֶב
מַשְׂאַת בִּנְיָמִן מִמַּשְׂאֹת כֻּלָּם חָמֵשׁ יָדוֹת וַיִּשְׁתּוּ
וַיִּשְׁכְּרוּ עִמּוֹ׃ מד א וַיְצַו אֶת־אֲשֶׁר עַל־בֵּיתוֹ
לֵאמֹר מַלֵּא אֶת־אַמְתְּחֹת הָאֲנָשִׁים אֹכֶל כַּאֲשֶׁר
יוּכְלוּן שְׂאֵת וְשִׂים כֶּסֶף־אִישׁ בְּפִי אַמְתַּחְתּוֹ׃
ב וְאֶת־גְּבִיעִי גְּבִיעַ הַכֶּסֶף תָּשִׂים בְּפִי אַמְתַּחַת
הַקָּטֹן וְאֵת כֶּסֶף שִׁבְרוֹ וַיַּעַשׂ כִּדְבַר יוֹסֵף אֲשֶׁר
דִּבֵּר׃ ג הַבֹּקֶר אוֹר וְהָאֲנָשִׁים שֻׁלְּחוּ הֵמָּה
וַחֲמֹרֵיהֶם׃ ד הֵם יָצְאוּ אֶת־הָעִיר לֹא הִרְחִיקוּ
וְיוֹסֵף אָמַר לַאֲשֶׁר עַל־בֵּיתוֹ קוּם רְדֹף אַחֲרֵי
הָאֲנָשִׁים וְהִשַּׂגְתָּם וְאָמַרְתָּ אֲלֵהֶם לָמָּה שִׁלַּמְתֶּם
רָעָה תַּחַת טוֹבָה׃ ה הֲלוֹא זֶה אֲשֶׁר יִשְׁתֶּה אֲדֹנִי
בּוֹ וְהוּא נַחֵשׁ יְנַחֵשׁ בּוֹ הֲרֵעֹתֶם אֲשֶׁר עֲשִׂיתֶם׃
ו וַיַּשִּׂגֵם וַיְדַבֵּר אֲלֵהֶם אֶת־הַדְּבָרִים הָאֵלֶּה׃

CHAPTER XLIV

5. . . . He attaches special importance to this goblet. It is irreplaceable because he has a נִיחוּשׁ [presentiment] about it. If he were to lose the goblet he would regard it not merely as a loss but as a calamity.

Accordingly, we read later in the narrative [Verse 15] that Joseph said to his brothers: "Did you not know that a man such as I has נִיחוּשׁ ["a presentiment" or "a belief in omens"]?" This should not be construed to mean that all those who cling to נִיחוּשׁ can cite the example of Joseph to justify their own superstitions. Joseph is speaking here as an Egyptian despot, as an Egyptian grandee, not as a son of the house of Abraham. The more highly placed a man is, the more powerful he becomes, the more superstitious will he become. We need only think of Napoleon.

The great man himself is surprised at his good fortune. An ordinary man may still have a great future in store for him. But once we have reached a point where we must admit to ourselves that we do not owe our good fortune to our own moral merits, we will easily come to ascribe it to supernatural circumstances. It is precisely because of its demoralizing effect that נִיחוּשׁ [another meaning for נִיחוּשׁ is "divination"] is forbidden. For once we begin to believe that we can promote our own good fortune by means other than merely by being good, that we have other things to fear besides doing evil, then we will be in danger of becoming evil ourselves. Then we will either neglect to do good on account of נִיחוּשׁ, or we will do evil because we will put our trust in the efficacy of נִיחוּשׁ. At this point we would no longer apply the standard of God's Law to our actions; we would no longer do that which we ought to do, because we would then believe that we have already found another way of attaining our objective.

7. They replied to him: "Why does my lord say such words? It would be profanation for your servants to do such a thing. 8. Behold, the money which we found at the top of our packs we have brought back to you from the land of Canaan; how, then, should we steal silver or gold from your master's house? 9. With whomever of your servants it will be found, he shall die! And we, too, will remain as slaves to my lord." 10. He replied: "Now, too, it is still as you say. The one with whom it will be found will remain as my slave, but you will remain free." 11. Each man quickly lowered his pack to the ground, and each man opened his pack. 12. He searched. He began with the eldest and finished with the youngest. And the goblet was found in Binyamin's pack. 13. They rent their garments; each man loaded his donkey again, and they returned to the city. 14. Yehudah and his brothers came to Yosef's house—he was still there—and they cast themselves upon the ground before him. 15. And Yosef said to them: "What deed is this that you have done? Did you not know that a man such as I believes in pre-sentiments?" 16. Yehudah replied: "What shall we say to my lord? How can we speak? How can we clear ourselves? God has found out the sin of your servants; here we are as slaves to my lord, we and also the one in whose hand the goblet was found." 17. But he said: "It would be profanation for me to do that; the man in whose hand the goblet was found shall remain my slave, but you go in peace to your father."

ז וַיֹּאמְרוּ אֵלָיו לָמָּה יְדַבֵּר אֲדֹנִי כַּדְּבָרִים הָאֵלֶּה חָלִילָה לַעֲבָדֶיךָ מֵעֲשׂוֹת כַּדָּבָר הַזֶּה: ח הֵן כֶּסֶף אֲשֶׁר מָצָאנוּ בְּפִי אַמְתְּחֹתֵינוּ הֱשִׁיבֹנוּ אֵלֶיךָ מֵאֶרֶץ כְּנָעַן וְאֵיךְ נִגְנֹב מִבֵּית אֲדֹנֶיךָ כֶּסֶף אוֹ זָהָב: ט אֲשֶׁר יִמָּצֵא אִתּוֹ מֵעֲבָדֶיךָ וָמֵת וְגַם־אֲנַחְנוּ נִהְיֶה לַאדֹנִי לַעֲבָדִים: י וַיֹּאמֶר גַּם־עַתָּה כְדִבְרֵיכֶם כֶּן־הוּא אֲשֶׁר יִמָּצֵא אִתּוֹ יִהְיֶה־לִּי עָבֶד וְאַתֶּם תִּהְיוּ נְקִיִּם: יא וַיְמַהֲרוּ וַיּוֹרִדוּ אִישׁ אֶת־אַמְתַּחְתּוֹ אָרְצָה וַיִּפְתְּחוּ אִישׁ אַמְתַּחְתּוֹ: יב וַיְחַפֵּשׂ בַּגָּדוֹל הֵחֵל וּבַקָּטֹן כִּלָּה וַיִּמָּצֵא הַגָּבִיעַ בְּאַמְתַּחַת בִּנְיָמִן: יג וַיִּקְרְעוּ שִׂמְלֹתָם וַיַּעֲמֹס אִישׁ עַל־חֲמֹרוֹ וַיָּשֻׁבוּ הָעִירָה: מפטיר יד וַיָּבֹא יְהוּדָה וְאֶחָיו בֵּיתָה יוֹסֵף וְהוּא עוֹדֶנּוּ שָׁם וַיִּפְּלוּ לְפָנָיו אָרְצָה: טו וַיֹּאמֶר לָהֶם יוֹסֵף מָה־הַמַּעֲשֶׂה הַזֶּה אֲשֶׁר עֲשִׂיתֶם הֲלוֹא יְדַעְתֶּם כִּי־נַחֵשׁ יְנַחֵשׁ אִישׁ אֲשֶׁר כָּמֹנִי: טז וַיֹּאמֶר יְהוּדָה מַה־נֹּאמַר לַאדֹנִי מַה־נְּדַבֵּר וּמַה־נִּצְטַדָּק הָאֱלֹהִים מָצָא אֶת־עֲוֹן עֲבָדֶיךָ הִנֶּנּוּ עֲבָדִים לַאדֹנִי גַּם־אֲנַחְנוּ גַּם אֲשֶׁר־נִמְצָא הַגָּבִיעַ בְּיָדוֹ: יז וַיֹּאמֶר חָלִילָה לִּי מֵעֲשׂוֹת זֹאת הָאִישׁ אֲשֶׁר נִמְצָא הַגָּבִיעַ בְּיָדוֹ הוּא יִהְיֶה־לִּי עָבֶד וְאַתֶּם עֲלוּ לְשָׁלוֹם אֶל־אֲבִיכֶם: ס

The Haftarah for this Sidra may be found on page 839.

ויגש

VAYIGGASH

18. Then Yehudah stepped up to him and said: "O my lord, let your servant speak a word into my lord's ears and let your anger not be stirred against your servant, for you are like Pharaoh. 19. My lord has asked his servants: 'Do you have a father or a[nother] brother?' 20. We said to my lord: 'We have an aged father and a young child of [his] old age, his brother is dead; he alone is left of his mother, and his father loves him.' 21. Thereupon you said to your servants: 'Bring him down to me, so that I may set my eye[s] upon him.' 22. But we said to my lord: 'The lad cannot leave his father. If he were to leave his father, he would die.' 23. You replied to your servants: 'If your youngest brother does not come down with you, you will not see my face again.' 24. And when we came up to your servant, my father, and reported my lord's words to him, 25. and our father said: 'Go there again and buy us a little food,' 26. we said: 'We cannot go down. If our youngest brother is with us, we will go down because we cannot see the face of the man again if our youngest brother is not with us.' 27. Thereupon your servant, our father, said to us: 'You know that my wife has borne me two children. 28. Of these, the one went away from me; I thought he must have been torn to pieces. I have not seen him since. 29. If you were to take this one also away from me and an accident befalls him, you will bring my gray hair down to the grave in misery.' 30. And now, if I come home to your servant, my father, and the lad is not with us, and the soul of the one is bound up with the soul of the other, 31. then it will come to pass, when he will see that the lad is not

יח וַיִּגַּשׁ אֵלָיו יְהוּדָה וַיֹּאמֶר בִּי אֲדֹנִי יְדַבֶּר־נָא
עַבְדְּךָ דָבָר בְּאׇזְנֵי אֲדֹנִי וְאַל־יִחַר אַפְּךָ בְּעַבְדֶּךָ
כִּי כָמוֹךָ כְּפַרְעֹה: יט אֲדֹנִי שָׁאַל אֶת־עֲבָדָיו
לֵאמֹר הֲיֵשׁ־לָכֶם אָב אוֹ־אָח: כ וַנֹּאמֶר אֶל־
אֲדֹנִי יֶשׁ־לָנוּ אָב זָקֵן וְיֶלֶד זְקֻנִים קָטָן וְאָחִיו מֵת
וַיִּוָּתֵר הוּא לְבַדּוֹ לְאִמּוֹ וְאָבִיו אֲהֵבוֹ: כא וַתֹּאמֶר
אֶל־עֲבָדֶיךָ הוֹרִדֻהוּ אֵלָי וְאָשִׂימָה עֵינִי עָלָיו:
כב וַנֹּאמֶר אֶל־אֲדֹנִי לֹא־יוּכַל הַנַּעַר לַעֲזֹב אֶת־
אָבִיו וְעָזַב אֶת־אָבִיו וָמֵת: כג וַתֹּאמֶר אֶל־
עֲבָדֶיךָ אִם־לֹא יֵרֵד אֲחִיכֶם הַקָּטֹן אִתְּכֶם לֹא
תֹסִפוּן לִרְאוֹת פָּנָי: כד וַיְהִי כִּי עָלִינוּ אֶל־עַבְדְּךָ
אָבִי וַנַּגֶּד־לוֹ אֵת דִּבְרֵי אֲדֹנִי: כה וַיֹּאמֶר אָבִינוּ
שֻׁבוּ שִׁבְרוּ־לָנוּ מְעַט־אֹכֶל: כו וַנֹּאמֶר לֹא נוּכַל
לָרֶדֶת אִם־יֵשׁ אָחִינוּ הַקָּטֹן אִתָּנוּ וְיָרַדְנוּ כִּי־לֹא
נוּכַל לִרְאוֹת פְּנֵי הָאִישׁ וְאָחִינוּ הַקָּטֹן אֵינֶנּוּ
אִתָּנוּ: כז וַיֹּאמֶר עַבְדְּךָ אָבִי אֵלֵינוּ אַתֶּם יְדַעְתֶּם
כִּי שְׁנַיִם יָלְדָה־לִּי אִשְׁתִּי: כח וַיֵּצֵא הָאֶחָד מֵאִתִּי
וָאֹמַר אַךְ טָרֹף טֹרָף וְלֹא רְאִיתִיו עַד־הֵנָּה:
כט וּלְקַחְתֶּם גַּם־אֶת־זֶה מֵעִם פָּנַי וְקָרָהוּ אָסוֹן
וְהוֹרַדְתֶּם אֶת־שֵׂיבָתִי בְּרָעָה שְׁאֹלָה: ל וְעַתָּה
כְּבֹאִי אֶל־עַבְדְּךָ אָבִי וְהַנַּעַר אֵינֶנּוּ אִתָּנוּ וְנַפְשׁוֹ
קְשׁוּרָה בְנַפְשׁוֹ: שני לא וְהָיָה כִּרְאוֹתוֹ כִּי־אֵין

18. ***into my lord's ears.*** This is an elegant phrase used to communicate a thought for careful consideration. [Judah says to Joseph:] "I will not appeal to your feelings but to your mind, to your intelligence. . . ."

there, that he will die, and then your servants will bring the gray head of your servant, our father, in sorrow to the grave. 32. For your servant received the lad from my father only upon his being surety [for him], and he said: 'If I do not bring him home, I will have sinned against you forever.' 33. And now, please let your servant remain as a slave to my lord in place of the lad, and let the lad go up with his brothers. 34. For how shall I come up to my father if the lad is not with me? Could I bear to see the misery that would strike my father then?''

XLV

1. Yosef could no longer restrain himself before all those who stood around him. He cried: "Everyone go away from me and go out!" And no one remained with him when Yosef made himself known to his brothers. 2. He gave his voice free rein in weeping; Mitzrayim heard it, and Pharaoh's household heard it. 3. Yosef said to his brothers: "I am Yosef; is my father still alive?" The brothers could not answer him because they were bewildered in his presence. 4. And Yosef said to his brothers: "Come closer to me!" They came closer. And he said: "I am your brother Yosef, whom you have sold into Mitzrayim. 5. And now, do not be troubled, nor let it be disturbing in your eyes that you have sold me into this place, for God sent me before you in order to preserve life. 6. For it is two years now that the famine has been on earth, and another five years will come when there will be neither plowing nor harvest. 7. And God sent me here ahead of you to establish for you a remnant in the land, to preserve it for you for your great deliverance. 8. And so it was not you who sent me here, but God! And He has appointed me as a father to Pharaoh, and master of all his house, and ruler in all the land of Mitzrayim. 9. Hurry, go up to my father and say to him: 'This is what your son Yosef said: God has appointed me master over all of Mitzrayim. Please come down to me; do not delay. 10. You will live in the land of Goshen and be close to me, you, your children, your sheep and your cattle

הַנַּעַר וָמֵת וְהוֹרִידוּ עֲבָדֶיךָ אֶת־שֵׂיבַת עַבְדְּךָ אָבִינוּ בְּיָגוֹן שְׁאֹלָה: לב כִּי עַבְדְּךָ עָרַב אֶת־הַנַּעַר מֵעִם אָבִי לֵאמֹר אִם־לֹא אֲבִיאֶנּוּ אֵלֶיךָ וְחָטָאתִי לְאָבִי כָּל־הַיָּמִים: לג וְעַתָּה יֵשֶׁב־נָא עַבְדְּךָ תַּחַת הַנַּעַר עֶבֶד לַאדֹנִי וְהַנַּעַר יַעַל עִם־אֶחָיו: לד כִּי־אֵיךְ אֶעֱלֶה אֶל־אָבִי וְהַנַּעַר אֵינֶנּוּ אִתִּי פֶּן אֶרְאֶה בָרָע אֲשֶׁר יִמְצָא אֶת־אָבִי: מה א וְלֹא־יָכֹל יוֹסֵף לְהִתְאַפֵּק לְכֹל הַנִּצָּבִים עָלָיו וַיִּקְרָא הוֹצִיאוּ כָל־אִישׁ מֵעָלָי וְלֹא־עָמַד אִישׁ אִתּוֹ בְּהִתְוַדַּע יוֹסֵף אֶל־אֶחָיו: ב וַיִּתֵּן אֶת־קֹלוֹ בִּבְכִי וַיִּשְׁמְעוּ מִצְרַיִם וַיִּשְׁמַע בֵּית פַּרְעֹה: ג וַיֹּאמֶר יוֹסֵף אֶל־אֶחָיו אֲנִי יוֹסֵף הַעוֹד אָבִי חָי וְלֹא־יָכְלוּ אֶחָיו לַעֲנוֹת אֹתוֹ כִּי נִבְהֲלוּ מִפָּנָיו: ד וַיֹּאמֶר יוֹסֵף אֶל־אֶחָיו גְּשׁוּ־נָא אֵלַי וַיִּגָּשׁוּ וַיֹּאמֶר אֲנִי יוֹסֵף אֲחִיכֶם אֲשֶׁר־מְכַרְתֶּם אֹתִי מִצְרָיְמָה: ה וְעַתָּה אַל־תֵּעָצְבוּ וְאַל־יִחַר בְּעֵינֵיכֶם כִּי־מְכַרְתֶּם אֹתִי הֵנָּה כִּי לְמִחְיָה שְׁלָחַנִי אֱלֹהִים לִפְנֵיכֶם: ו כִּי־זֶה שְׁנָתַיִם הָרָעָב בְּקֶרֶב הָאָרֶץ וְעוֹד חָמֵשׁ שָׁנִים אֲשֶׁר אֵין־חָרִישׁ וְקָצִיר: ז וַיִּשְׁלָחֵנִי אֱלֹהִים לִפְנֵיכֶם לָשׂוּם לָכֶם שְׁאֵרִית בָּאָרֶץ וּלְהַחֲיוֹת לָכֶם לִפְלֵיטָה גְּדֹלָה: שלישי ח וְעַתָּה לֹא־אַתֶּם שְׁלַחְתֶּם אֹתִי הֵנָּה כִּי הָאֱלֹהִים וַיְשִׂימֵנִי לְאָב לְפַרְעֹה וּלְאָדוֹן לְכָל־בֵּיתוֹ וּמֹשֵׁל בְּכָל־אֶרֶץ מִצְרָיִם: ט מַהֲרוּ וַעֲלוּ אֶל־אָבִי וַאֲמַרְתֶּם אֵלָיו כֹּה אָמַר בִּנְךָ יוֹסֵף שָׂמַנִי אֱלֹהִים לְאָדוֹן לְכָל־מִצְרָיִם רְדָה אֵלַי אַל־תַּעֲמֹד: י וְיָשַׁבְתָּ בְאֶרֶץ־גֹּשֶׁן וְהָיִיתָ קָרוֹב אֵלַי אַתָּה וּבָנֶיךָ וּבְנֵי בָנֶיךָ וְצֹאנְךָ וּבְקָרְךָ וְכָל־אֲשֶׁר־

and all that is yours.   11. I will fully provide for you there, for there will come yet another five years of famine, lest you, and your house and all that is yours grow poor.'   12. Behold, your eyes see it, and the eyes of my brother Binyamin, that it is my mouth that speaks to you.   13. Tell my father of all my glory in Mitzrayim, and of everything you have seen; hurry and bring my father here!"   14. He fell upon the neck of his brother Binyamin and wept, and Binyamin wept upon his neck.   15. He kissed all his brothers and wept in their embrace; afterwards his brothers, too, spoke with him.   16. The news was heard in Pharaoh's house: Yosef's brothers have come! And this pleased Pharaoh and his

לָךְ: יא וְכִלְכַּלְתִּי אֹתְךָ שָׁם כִּי־עוֹד חָמֵשׁ שָׁנִים רָעָב פֶּן־תִּוָּרֵשׁ אַתָּה וּבֵיתְךָ וְכָל־אֲשֶׁר־לָךְ: יב וְהִנֵּה עֵינֵיכֶם רֹאוֹת וְעֵינֵי אָחִי בִנְיָמִין כִּי־פִי הַמְדַבֵּר אֲלֵיכֶם: יג וְהִגַּדְתֶּם לְאָבִי אֶת־כָּל־כְּבוֹדִי בְּמִצְרַיִם וְאֵת כָּל־אֲשֶׁר רְאִיתֶם וּמִהַרְתֶּם וְהוֹרַדְתֶּם אֶת־אָבִי הֵנָּה: יד וַיִּפֹּל עַל־צַוְּארֵי בִנְיָמִן־אָחִיו וַיֵּבְךְּ וּבִנְיָמִן בָּכָה עַל־צַוָּארָיו: טו וַיְנַשֵּׁק לְכָל־אֶחָיו וַיֵּבְךְּ עֲלֵהֶם וְאַחֲרֵי כֵן דִּבְּרוּ אֶחָיו אִתּוֹ: טז וְהַקֹּל נִשְׁמַע בֵּית פַּרְעֹה לֵאמֹר בָּאוּ אֲחֵי יוֹסֵף וַיִּיטַב בְּעֵינֵי פַרְעֹה

CHAPTER XLV

11. . . . Joseph points out to his brothers again and again how this whole chain of events clearly has been the work of Divine Providence. Indeed, there is hardly another story that so cogently demonstrates the ways of Divine Providence. It is the most vivid commentary on that splendid saying of Solomonic wisdom (Proverbs 26:9), "The great Master of the Universe produces all things from their smallest beginnings. Be they physical or social, He causes them all to grow from the smallest seedling. It is He Who causes all things to be born, and therefore He has even fools and criminals in His service." Without knowing it or wishing it, even folly and sin serve His purposes. In this story the threads lie revealed; in others, they do not. But from this particular story we can learn the ways of God.

It was through the "two sela's worth of silk"—as our Sages put it (Shabbath 10b)—which Jacob used for the embroidery on Joseph's coat that the promise of the בְּרִית בֵּין הַבְּתָרִים ["covenant between the pieces" (Genesis 15:9–21)] came to be fulfilled. It is highly improbable that Jacob's family would have become a nation if they had remained in Canaan. As the family grew, they would have merged with the surrounding population. In order to become a people and not to intermingle with the other nations, they had to come into the midst of a nation whose character was completely at variance with the Jewish ethos—and that nation was Mitzrayim.

Similarly, the fanaticism that gave rise to the ghettoes was to become the most effective means in the hands of God to keep us far from the lack of culture that characterized the Middle Ages, and to have us cultivate

family solidarity and domestic happiness within our own closed circle.

In order that we should be assured a separate province in Mitzrayim as the soil for our development, a youthful scion of this family had to go there before all the others and to become "father" to Pharaoh and governor of the land. And so that no Egyptian should be able to say to the Hebrews, "You do not belong here; you were not born in this place!" the Egyptians had to leave the soil on which they had been born and they had to become strangers themselves upon the land which they were to till henceforth [Genesis 47:21].

Similarly, by the time the descendants of Jacob had begun their great migration into dispersion among the peoples of Europe, the remarkable, momentous migration of nations had already peopled virtually every part of Europe with "foreigners." Hence the expulsion order of Germanic intolerance, "Go back to Palestine, where you belong!" could be irrefutably countered by the question, "And were *your* ancestors natives of this place?"

Finally, both that first exile [i.e., the migration of Jacob and his family to Egypt] and our own last exile were the result of קִנְאָה [jealousy] and שִׂנְאַת חִנָּם [hatred without cause]. It was exile that set up the crucible of harsh fate through which all the descendants of Jacob had to pass and in which, through the training school of bitter sufferings, they were purified to make them capable of feelings for equality and brotherhood.

16. Pharaoh's servants rejoiced with Joseph and were happy that having his family in Egypt with him would now keep him permanently bound to their land. The fact that even the officials of the state did not envy him for this good fortune attests to Joseph's fine moral character.

servants. 17. Pharaoh said to Yosef: "Say to your brothers: 'Do this: Load your animals and go, come to the land of Canaan. 18. Take your father and your families and come to me! I will gladly give you the best of the land of Mitzrayim, and you shall eat the fat of the land!' 19. But you [Yosef] are [hereby] commanded [as follows]: Do this: Take yourselves wagons from the land of Mitzrayim for your children and for your wives, and carry your father and come. 20. And let your eye not be concerned about your utensils, for the best of the whole land of Mitzrayim is yours." 21. The sons of Yisrael did so. Yosef gave them wagons at Pharaoh's command, and he gave them provision for the journey. 22. He gave them all, each one of them, changes of clothing, and to Binyamin he gave three hundred pieces of silver and five changes of clothing. 23. And to his father he sent the following: ten donkeys, laden with the best [things] of Mitzrayim, and ten female donkeys, laden with grain and bread and food for his father and for the journey. 24. He sent his brothers on their way and they went, and he said to them: "Have no care on the way." 25. They went up from Mitzrayim and came to the land of Canaan to their father Yaakov. 26. They told him that Yosef was still alive and that he was ruler over the entire land of Mitzrayim. And his heart stood still because he did not believe them. 27. But when they repeated for him all the words that Yosef had spoken to them, and he saw the wagons, which Yosef had sent to carry him, the spirit of their father Yaakov revived, 28. and Yisrael said: "It is too much! Yosef, my son, is still alive! I will go there and I want to see him before I die!"

XLVI 1. And Yisrael, and all that was his, set out; he came to Beer Sheva and offered meal offer-

וּבְעֵינֵי עֲבָדָיו: יז וַיֹּאמֶר פַּרְעֹה אֶל־יוֹסֵף אֱמֹר אֶל־אַחֶיךָ זֹאת עֲשׂוּ טַעֲנוּ אֶת־בְּעִירְכֶם וּלְכוּ־בֹאוּ אַרְצָה כְּנָעַן: יח וּקְחוּ אֶת־אֲבִיכֶם וְאֶת־בָּתֵּיכֶם וּבֹאוּ אֵלָי וְאֶתְּנָה לָכֶם אֶת־טוּב אֶרֶץ מִצְרַיִם וְאִכְלוּ אֶת־חֵלֶב הָאָרֶץ: רביעי יט וְאַתָּה צֻוֵּיתָה זֹאת עֲשׂוּ קְחוּ־לָכֶם מֵאֶרֶץ מִצְרַיִם עֲגָלוֹת לְטַפְּכֶם וְלִנְשֵׁיכֶם וּנְשָׂאתֶם אֶת־אֲבִיכֶם וּבָאתֶם: כ וְעֵינְכֶם אַל־תָּחֹס עַל־כְּלֵיכֶם כִּי־טוּב כָּל־אֶרֶץ מִצְרַיִם לָכֶם הוּא: כא וַיַּעֲשׂוּ־כֵן בְּנֵי יִשְׂרָאֵל וַיִּתֵּן לָהֶם יוֹסֵף עֲגָלוֹת עַל־פִּי פַרְעֹה וַיִּתֵּן לָהֶם צֵדָה לַדָּרֶךְ: כב לְכֻלָּם נָתַן לָאִישׁ חֲלִפוֹת שְׂמָלֹת וּלְבִנְיָמִן נָתַן שְׁלֹשׁ מֵאוֹת כֶּסֶף וְחָמֵשׁ חֲלִפֹת שְׂמָלֹת: כג וּלְאָבִיו שָׁלַח כְּזֹאת עֲשָׂרָה חֲמֹרִים נֹשְׂאִים מִטּוּב מִצְרָיִם וְעֶשֶׂר אֲתֹנֹת נֹשְׂאֹת בָּר וָלֶחֶם וּמָזוֹן לְאָבִיו לַדָּרֶךְ: כד וַיְשַׁלַּח אֶת־אֶחָיו וַיֵּלֵכוּ וַיֹּאמֶר אֲלֵהֶם אַל־תִּרְגְּזוּ בַּדָּרֶךְ: כה וַיַּעֲלוּ מִמִּצְרָיִם וַיָּבֹאוּ אֶרֶץ כְּנַעַן אֶל־יַעֲקֹב אֲבִיהֶם: כו וַיַּגִּדוּ לוֹ לֵאמֹר עוֹד יוֹסֵף חַי וְכִי־הוּא מֹשֵׁל בְּכָל־אֶרֶץ מִצְרָיִם וַיָּפָג לִבּוֹ כִּי לֹא־הֶאֱמִין לָהֶם: כז וַיְדַבְּרוּ אֵלָיו אֵת כָּל־דִּבְרֵי יוֹסֵף אֲשֶׁר דִּבֶּר אֲלֵהֶם וַיַּרְא אֶת־הָעֲגָלוֹת אֲשֶׁר־שָׁלַח יוֹסֵף לָשֵׂאת אֹתוֹ וַתְּחִי רוּחַ יַעֲקֹב אֲבִיהֶם: חמישי כח וַיֹּאמֶר יִשְׂרָאֵל רַב עוֹד יוֹסֵף בְּנִי חָי אֵלְכָה וְאֶרְאֶנּוּ בְּטֶרֶם אָמוּת: מו א וַיִּסַּע יִשְׂרָאֵל וְכָל־אֲשֶׁר־לוֹ וַיָּבֹא בְּאֵרָה

CHAPTER XLVI

1. Then Israel, and all that was his, set out in a most happy frame of mind. It was the culmination of all his life, which had been so sorely tested in bitter struggles and suffering.

They traveled southward and arrived at the last frontier of Canaan, the city of Beer Sheva, which had been glorified by the memory of his fathers. Here Israel offered up זְבָחִים [meal offerings]. Nowhere else in Scripture is there mention of any of our patriarchs' having

שָׁבַע וַיִּזְבַּח זְבָחִים לֵאלֹהֵי אָבִיו יִצְחָק׃ ב וַיֹּאמֶר
אֱלֹהִים ׀ לְיִשְׂרָאֵל בְּמַרְאֹת הַלַּיְלָה וַיֹּאמֶר
יַעֲקֹב ׀ יַעֲקֹב וַיֹּאמֶר הִנֵּנִי׃ ג וַיֹּאמֶר אָנֹכִי הָאֵל
אֱלֹהֵי אָבִיךָ אַל־תִּירָא מֵרְדָה מִצְרַיְמָה כִּי־לְגוֹי
גָּדוֹל אֲשִׂימְךָ שָׁם׃ ד אָנֹכִי אֵרֵד עִמְּךָ מִצְרַיְמָה
וְאָנֹכִי אַעַלְךָ גַם־עָלֹה וְיוֹסֵף יָשִׁית יָדוֹ עַל־
עֵינֶיךָ׃ ה וַיָּקָם יַעֲקֹב מִבְּאֵר שָׁבַע וַיִּשְׂאוּ בְנֵי־
יִשְׂרָאֵל אֶת־יַעֲקֹב אֲבִיהֶם וְאֶת־טַפָּם וְאֶת־
נְשֵׁיהֶם בָּעֲגָלוֹת אֲשֶׁר־שָׁלַח פַּרְעֹה לָשֵׂאת אֹתוֹ׃
ו וַיִּקְחוּ אֶת־מִקְנֵיהֶם וְאֶת־רְכוּשָׁם אֲשֶׁר רָכְשׁוּ
בְּאֶרֶץ כְּנַעַן וַיָּבֹאוּ מִצְרָיְמָה יַעֲקֹב וְכָל־זַרְעוֹ

ings to the God of his father Yitzḥak.
2. And God spoke to *Yisrael* in visions of the night and said: "*Yaakov! Yaakov!*" He said: "Here I am."
3. He said: "I am the God, the God of your father; do not fear to go down to Mitzrayim, for I will make a great nation of you there.
4. I will go down to Mitzrayim with you, and I will also bring you back up again, and Yosef will place his hand upon your eyes."
5. And Yaakov rose up from Beer Sheva and *Yisrael*'s sons carried their father *Yaakov*, their children and their wives in the wagons that Pharaoh had sent to carry him.
6. They took their herds and their movable goods which they had acquired in the land of Canaan and they came to Mitzrayim; Yaakov and all his descendants with

offered זְבָחִים. Like all the other descendants of Noah, they offered only עולות [ascent offerings].

The עוֹלָה expresses complete personal devotion to God. זֶבַח as such is a family meal to be eaten by the householders; it consecrates the family's home and table as a temple and an altar, respectively. זְבָחִים which, as a rule, are שְׁלָמִים [peace offerings], express a loftier concept, that of "God coming into our midst." They are therefore offered in the happy awareness that wherever a family lives in harmony, is faithful to its duty and feels that it is being upheld by God, cf. אֱלֹקִ׳ בְּדוֹר צַדִּיק ["God is in the generation of the righteous" (Psalm 14:5)], there God is present. That is why the spirit of the שְׁלָמִים, the "peace offerings" of a family life blessed by God, is so typically Jewish. The concept of surrendering to God and permitting oneself to be absorbed by Him has begun to dawn also upon non-Jewish minds. But the thought that everyday life can become so thoroughly pervaded by the spirit of God that "one eats and drinks and while doing so, beholds God," that all our family rooms become temples, our tables altars, and our young men and young women priests and priestesses —this spiritualization of everyday personal life represents the unique contribution of Judaism.

The reason why Jacob-Israel at this point did not offer עולות but זְבָחִים is that now, for the first time, Jacob felt happy, joyous and "complete" [שָׁלֵם also means "complete" or "whole"] within the circle of his family. It was under the impact of this awareness and this emotion that he made a "family offering" to God. . . .

2 and 3. God said: "Do not fear to go down to Mitzrayim." Yet we are told that Jacob had been in a most happy frame of mind. Hence it must be assumed that these words from God to Jacob were preceded by something that had changed Jacob's mood to one of apprehension and anxiety so that he was in need of reassurance. The text of Verse 2 bears out this assumption. To begin with, the term used to describe the vision —"visions of the night"—reflects a serious mood. Then, the fact that God called to him יַעֲקֹב, not יִשְׂרָאֵל, was a sobering reminder, making Jacob aware of the immediate consequence of his journey down to Mitzrayim.[29] Hence Jacob replies: הִנֵּנִי ["Here I am"]: "I am ready for anything Thou wilt ordain." Thereupon God says to him: "You need have no fears. I am the God to Whom you have just made your joyous family offering. Ultimately even this journey will bring you greatness. It is in Mitzrayim that you will become the great nation of which I have spoken in My promise to you."

4. "I myself will accompany you (and your family) down to Mitzrayim, and (after you have become a nation) I will bring you back up again. And as regards you personally, you will never lose Joseph again" (Cf. Genesis 15:1).

5. Here again, significantly, there is a change in names. The family [Israel's sons] were in the happiest frame of mind. They had no premonition of the sad fate which awaited them and toward which they were now journeying. Their father, however, was filled with somber thoughts of his people's exile which he had been told to expect. Hence we read that *Israel*'s sons carried their father *Jacob*.

[29]*Note to the English translation*: The immediate consequence of the journey to Egypt would be bondage for Jacob's descendants. [G.H.]

him, 7. his sons and his sons' children with him, his daughters and his sons' daughters and all his descendants he brought with him to Mitzrayim. 8. These are the names of the sons of Yisrael, who came to Mizrayim, Yaakov and his sons. Yaakov's first-born: Reuben. 9. Reuben's sons: Ḥanokh [Enoch], Palu, Ḥetzron and Carmi. 10. Shimeon's sons: Yemuel, Yamin, Ohad, Yakhin, Tzoḥar and Shaul, son of the Canaanite woman. 11. Levi's sons: Gershon, Kehath and Merari. 12. Yehudah's sons: Er, Onan, Shelah, Peretz and Zeraḥ. Er and Onan died in the land of Canaan. The sons of Peretz were Ḥetzron and Ḥamul. 13. Yissakhar's sons: Tola, Puvah, Yov and Shimron. 14. Zebulun's sons: Sered, Elon and Yaḥle'el. 15. These are the sons of Leah, whom she bore to Yaakov in Paddan-Aram, and his daughter Dinah. All the souls of his sons and his daughters: thirty-three. 16. Gad's sons: Tzifion, Ḥaggi, Shuni and Etzbon, Eri, Arodi and Areli. 17. Asher's sons: Yimnah, Yishvah, Yishvi, Beriah and their sister Seraḥ. Beriah's sons: Ḥever and Malkiel. 18. These were the sons of Zilpah, whom Laban had given to his daughter Leah; she bore these to Yaakov: sixteen souls. 19. The sons of Raḥel, Yaakov's wife: Yosef and Binyamin. 20. To Yosef in the land of Mitzrayim were born those whom Asenath, the daughter of Potipherah, the priest in On, had borne him: Menashe and Ephraim. 21. Binyamin's sons: Bela, Bekher and Ashbel, Gera, Naaman, Eḥi and Rosh, Muppim, Ḥuppim and Ard. 22. These are the sons of Raḥel who had been born to Yaakov; all the souls: fourteen. 23. And Dan's sons: Ḥushim. 24. Naphtali's sons: Yaḥtze'el, Guni, Yetzer and Shilem. 25. These are the sons of Bilhah, whom Laban had given to his daughter Raḥel; she bore these to Yaakov;

אִתּוֹ: ז בָּנָיו וּבְנֵי בָנָיו אִתּוֹ בְּנֹתָיו וּבְנוֹת בָּנָיו וְכָל־זַרְעוֹ הֵבִיא אִתּוֹ מִצְרָיְמָה: ס ח וְאֵלֶּה שְׁמוֹת בְּנֵי־יִשְׂרָאֵל הַבָּאִים מִצְרַיְמָה יַעֲקֹב וּבָנָיו בְּכֹר יַעֲקֹב רְאוּבֵן: ט וּבְנֵי רְאוּבֵן חֲנוֹךְ וּפַלּוּא וְחֶצְרֹן וְכַרְמִי: י וּבְנֵי שִׁמְעוֹן יְמוּאֵל וְיָמִין וְאֹהַד וְיָכִין וְצֹחַר וְשָׁאוּל בֶּן־הַכְּנַעֲנִית: יא וּבְנֵי לֵוִי גֵּרְשׁוֹן קְהָת וּמְרָרִי: יב וּבְנֵי יְהוּדָה עֵר וְאוֹנָן וְשֵׁלָה וָפֶרֶץ וָזָרַח וַיָּמָת עֵר וְאוֹנָן בְּאֶרֶץ כְּנַעַן וַיִּהְיוּ בְנֵי־פֶרֶץ חֶצְרֹן וְחָמוּל: יג וּבְנֵי יִשָּׂשכָר תּוֹלָע וּפֻוָּה וְיוֹב וְשִׁמְרֹן: יד וּבְנֵי זְבֻלוּן סֶרֶד וְאֵלוֹן וְיַחְלְאֵל: טו אֵלֶּה בְּנֵי לֵאָה אֲשֶׁר יָלְדָה לְיַעֲקֹב בְּפַדַּן אֲרָם וְאֵת דִּינָה בִתּוֹ כָּל־נֶפֶשׁ בָּנָיו וּבְנוֹתָיו שְׁלֹשִׁים וְשָׁלֹשׁ: טז וּבְנֵי גָד צִפְיוֹן וְחַגִּי שׁוּנִי וְאֶצְבֹּן עֵרִי וַאֲרוֹדִי וְאַרְאֵלִי: יז וּבְנֵי אָשֵׁר יִמְנָה וְיִשְׁוָה וְיִשְׁוִי וּבְרִיעָה וְשֶׂרַח אֲחֹתָם וּבְנֵי בְרִיעָה חֶבֶר וּמַלְכִּיאֵל: יח אֵלֶּה בְּנֵי זִלְפָּה אֲשֶׁר־נָתַן לָבָן לְלֵאָה בִתּוֹ וַתֵּלֶד אֶת־אֵלֶּה לְיַעֲקֹב שֵׁשׁ עֶשְׂרֵה נָפֶשׁ: יט בְּנֵי רָחֵל אֵשֶׁת יַעֲקֹב יוֹסֵף וּבִנְיָמִן: כ וַיִּוָּלֵד לְיוֹסֵף בְּאֶרֶץ מִצְרַיִם אֲשֶׁר יָלְדָה־לּוֹ אָסְנַת בַּת־פּוֹטִי פֶרַע כֹּהֵן אֹן אֶת־מְנַשֶּׁה וְאֶת־אֶפְרָיִם: כא וּבְנֵי בִנְיָמִן בֶּלַע וָבֶכֶר וְאַשְׁבֵּל גֵּרָא וְנַעֲמָן אֵחִי וָרֹאשׁ מֻפִּים וְחֻפִּים וָאָרְדְּ: כב אֵלֶּה בְּנֵי רָחֵל אֲשֶׁר יֻלַּד לְיַעֲקֹב כָּל־נֶפֶשׁ אַרְבָּעָה עָשָׂר: כג וּבְנֵי־דָן חֻשִׁים: כד וּבְנֵי נַפְתָּלִי יַחְצְאֵל וְגוּנִי וְיֵצֶר וְשִׁלֵּם: כה אֵלֶּה בְּנֵי בִלְהָה אֲשֶׁר־נָתַן לָבָן לְרָחֵל בִּתּוֹ וַתֵּלֶד אֶת־אֵלֶּה

---

20. **וַיִּוָּלֵד לְיוֹסֵף** [To Yosef . . . were born]. Even though Joseph and his family lived in the land of Mitzrayim, surrounded by a way of life utterly alien to them, "children were born to Joseph." He did not merely beget them; they remained "his" also after they had been born. And his wife, though she was the daughter of an Egyptian priest, bore and raised them "for him" [in his spirit].

all the souls:—seven.   26. All the souls that came to Mitzrayim with Yaakov, those descended from him, not including the wives of the sons of Yaakov, all the souls: sixty-six.   27. And Yosef's sons, who were born to him in Mitzrayim: two souls; all the souls belonging to the house of Yaakov, who had come to Mitzrayim: seventy.   28. And he sent Yehudah ahead of him to Yosef so that the latter might direct him to Goshen before he [himself] arrived: so they came to the land of Goshen.   29. Yosef harnessed his chariot and went up to meet his father Yisrael, to Goshen. When he presented himself to him, he flung himself upon his neck and was still weeping upon his neck, 30. when Yisrael said to Yosef: "Now I would die, since I have seen your face that you are still alive!"   31. Yosef said to his brothers, and to his father's house: "I will go up and report to Pharaoh and say to him: 'My brothers and my father's house, who were in the land of Canaan, have come to me.   32. The men are shepherds, for they were breeders of herds; they have brought with them their sheep and their cattle and all that they have.'   33. If Pharaoh will then call you and say: 'What is your occupation?'   34. Then you, too, shall say: 'Your servants have been breeders of herds from our youth until now, both we and our

לְיַעֲקֹב כָּל־נֶפֶשׁ שִׁבְעָה: כו כָּל־הַנֶּפֶשׁ הַבָּאָה לְיַעֲקֹב מִצְרַיְמָה יֹצְאֵי יְרֵכוֹ מִלְּבַד נְשֵׁי בְנֵי־יַעֲקֹב כָּל־נֶפֶשׁ שִׁשִּׁים וָשֵׁשׁ: כז וּבְנֵי יוֹסֵף אֲשֶׁר־יֻלַּד־לוֹ בְמִצְרַיִם נֶפֶשׁ שְׁנָיִם כָּל־הַנֶּפֶשׁ לְבֵית־יַעֲקֹב הַבָּאָה מִצְרַיְמָה שִׁבְעִים: ס ששי כח וְאֶת־יְהוּדָה שָׁלַח לְפָנָיו אֶל־יוֹסֵף לְהוֹרֹת לְפָנָיו גֹּשְׁנָה וַיָּבֹאוּ אַרְצָה גֹּשֶׁן: כט וַיֶּאְסֹר יוֹסֵף מֶרְכַּבְתּוֹ וַיַּעַל לִקְרַאת־יִשְׂרָאֵל אָבִיו גֹּשְׁנָה וַיֵּרָא אֵלָיו וַיִּפֹּל עַל־צַוָּארָיו וַיֵּבְךְּ עַל־צַוָּארָיו עוֹד: ל וַיֹּאמֶר יִשְׂרָאֵל אֶל־יוֹסֵף אָמוּתָה הַפָּעַם אַחֲרֵי רְאוֹתִי אֶת־פָּנֶיךָ כִּי עוֹדְךָ חָי: לא וַיֹּאמֶר יוֹסֵף אֶל־אֶחָיו וְאֶל־בֵּית אָבִיו אֶעֱלֶה וְאַגִּידָה לְפַרְעֹה וְאֹמְרָה אֵלָיו אַחַי וּבֵית־אָבִי אֲשֶׁר בְּאֶרֶץ־כְּנַעַן בָּאוּ אֵלָי: לב וְהָאֲנָשִׁים רֹעֵי צֹאן כִּי־אַנְשֵׁי מִקְנֶה הָיוּ וְצֹאנָם וּבְקָרָם וְכָל־אֲשֶׁר לָהֶם הֵבִיאוּ: לג וְהָיָה כִּי־יִקְרָא לָכֶם פַּרְעֹה וְאָמַר מַה־מַּעֲשֵׂיכֶם: לד וַאֲמַרְתֶּם אַנְשֵׁי מִקְנֶה הָיוּ עֲבָדֶיךָ מִנְּעוּרֵינוּ וְעַד־עַתָּה גַּם־אֲנַחְנוּ גַּם־

29–30. Joseph wept. Jacob did not weep. Jacob had ceased to weep long ago but Joseph still wept. He was still weeping when Jacob was talking with him. These little details reflect a profound truth. Through all the years of Joseph's absence, Jacob had led a dull, monotonous life, weeping for Joseph. All his emotions had been spent in mourning Joseph. Joseph's life, in the meantime, had been a most eventful one. As a result, Joseph had had no time to surrender so completely to the pain of separation from his father. He was totally absorbed in the immediate present. But now, in his father's embrace, he truly felt the emotional impact of this separation and relived the twenty years that had passed. Jacob had already become Israel, but Joseph was still weeping.

33–34. In a state such as Mitzrayim, the individual was completely identified with his occupation. Indeed, it could be said that in ancient Egypt, children were not born as human beings but as artisans, peasants, soldiers,

etc. Accordingly, Pharaoh's first question to Joseph's brothers would naturally concern their occupation. They were instructed to answer Pharaoh's question candidly, to tell him the truth even though it would be unpleasant. For the undeniable loathing which the Egyptians felt for the occupation of the brothers — even as the aversion that the nations were subsequently to feel for the Jews—was to serve as the primary factor in the survival of that race which was destined to journey through the ages in isolation. Prior to the new spiritual and moral dawn of the nations, the barriers that the nations in their folly had erected to isolate the Jews served to protect the Jews from becoming infected with the barbarism and the demoralization of the men in whose midst they had to walk through the centuries. That is why Joseph made a point of disclosing that aspect of his brothers which would be most unpalatable to the Egyptians. He intended that, as a result, his brothers should be sent to dwell in a province isolated from the rest of the country.

fathers,' so that you may dwell in the land of Goshen, for every shepherd is an abomination to Mitzrayim."

XLVII

1. Yosef came and reported to Pharaoh: "My father and my brothers, their sheep and their cattle and all that is theirs have come from the land of Canaan; they are now in the land of Goshen."   2. And he took five men from among his brothers and presented them to Pharaoh.   3. Pharaoh said to his brothers: "What is your occupation?" And they said to Pharaoh: "Your servants are shepherds, both we and our fathers."   4. They also said to Pharaoh: "We have come to sojourn in the land, for there is no longer any pasture for your servants' sheep, because the famine is severe in the land of Canaan. And now, please, permit your servants to dwell in the land of Goshen."   5. Thereupon Pharaoh said to Yosef: "It is to you that your father and your brothers have come.   6. The land of Mitzrayim is open before you. Settle your father and your brothers in the best [part] of the land; let them dwell in the land of Goshen, and if you know that there are capable men among them, appoint them chief clerks over the herds which I have." 7. Yosef brought his father Yaakov and presented him to Pharaoh; Yaakov blessed Pharaoh.   8. And Pharaoh said to Yaakov: "How many are the days of the years of your life?"   9. Yaakov replied to Pharaoh: "The days of the years of my wanderings are one hundred and thirty years; the days of the years of my life have been few and unhappy, and they have not reached the days of the lives of my fathers in the days of their wanderings."   10. Then Yaakov blessed Pharaoh and went away from Pharaoh's presence.   11. Yosef settled his father and his brother and gave them a possession in the land of Mitzrayim, in the best [part] of the land, in the land of Rameses, as Pharaoh had commanded.   12. Yosef provided his father and his brothers and the entire house of his father with food according to the needs of the children.   13. But there was no food in all the land, for the famine was very severe. All the land of Mitzrayim and also the land of Canaan became weak because of the famine.   14. Yosef gathered

אֲבֹתֵינוּ בַּעֲבוּר תֵּשְׁבוּ בְּאֶרֶץ גֹּשֶׁן כִּי־תוֹעֲבַת מִצְרַיִם כָּל־רֹעֵה צֹאן: מז א וַיָּבֹא יוֹסֵף וַיַּגֵּד לְפַרְעֹה וַיֹּאמֶר אָבִי וְאַחַי וְצֹאנָם וּבְקָרָם וְכָל־אֲשֶׁר לָהֶם בָּאוּ מֵאֶרֶץ כְּנָעַן וְהִנָּם בְּאֶרֶץ גֹּשֶׁן: ב וּמִקְצֵה אֶחָיו לָקַח חֲמִשָּׁה אֲנָשִׁים וַיַּצִּגֵם לִפְנֵי פַרְעֹה: ג וַיֹּאמֶר פַּרְעֹה אֶל־אֶחָיו מַה־מַּעֲשֵׂיכֶם וַיֹּאמְרוּ אֶל־פַּרְעֹה רֹעֵה צֹאן עֲבָדֶיךָ גַּם־אֲנַחְנוּ גַּם־אֲבוֹתֵינוּ: ד וַיֹּאמְרוּ אֶל־פַּרְעֹה לָגוּר בָּאָרֶץ בָּאנוּ כִּי־אֵין מִרְעֶה לַצֹּאן אֲשֶׁר לַעֲבָדֶיךָ כִּי־כָבֵד הָרָעָב בְּאֶרֶץ כְּנָעַן וְעַתָּה יֵשְׁבוּ־נָא עֲבָדֶיךָ בְּאֶרֶץ גֹּשֶׁן: ה וַיֹּאמֶר פַּרְעֹה אֶל־יוֹסֵף לֵאמֹר אָבִיךָ וְאַחֶיךָ בָּאוּ אֵלֶיךָ: ו אֶרֶץ מִצְרַיִם לְפָנֶיךָ הִוא בְּמֵיטַב הָאָרֶץ הוֹשֵׁב אֶת־אָבִיךָ וְאֶת־אַחֶיךָ יֵשְׁבוּ בְּאֶרֶץ גֹּשֶׁן וְאִם־יָדַעְתָּ וְיֶשׁ־בָּם אַנְשֵׁי־חַיִל וְשַׂמְתָּם שָׂרֵי מִקְנֶה עַל־אֲשֶׁר־לִי: ז וַיָּבֵא יוֹסֵף אֶת־יַעֲקֹב אָבִיו וַיַּעֲמִדֵהוּ לִפְנֵי פַרְעֹה וַיְבָרֶךְ יַעֲקֹב אֶת־פַּרְעֹה: ח וַיֹּאמֶר פַּרְעֹה אֶל־יַעֲקֹב כַּמָּה יְמֵי שְׁנֵי חַיֶּיךָ: ט וַיֹּאמֶר יַעֲקֹב אֶל־פַּרְעֹה יְמֵי שְׁנֵי מְגוּרַי שְׁלֹשִׁים וּמְאַת שָׁנָה מְעַט וְרָעִים הָיוּ יְמֵי שְׁנֵי חַיַּי וְלֹא הִשִּׂיגוּ אֶת־יְמֵי שְׁנֵי חַיֵּי אֲבֹתַי בִּימֵי מְגוּרֵיהֶם: י וַיְבָרֶךְ יַעֲקֹב אֶת־פַּרְעֹה וַיֵּצֵא מִלִּפְנֵי פַרְעֹה: שביעי יא וַיּוֹשֵׁב יוֹסֵף אֶת־אָבִיו וְאֶת־אֶחָיו וַיִּתֵּן לָהֶם אֲחֻזָּה בְּאֶרֶץ מִצְרַיִם בְּמֵיטַב הָאָרֶץ בְּאֶרֶץ רַעְמְסֵס כַּאֲשֶׁר צִוָּה פַרְעֹה: יב וַיְכַלְכֵּל יוֹסֵף אֶת־אָבִיו וְאֶת־אֶחָיו וְאֵת כָּל־בֵּית אָבִיו לֶחֶם לְפִי הַטָּף: יג וְלֶחֶם אֵין בְּכָל־הָאָרֶץ כִּי־כָבֵד הָרָעָב מְאֹד וַתֵּלַהּ אֶרֶץ מִצְרַיִם וְאֶרֶץ כְּנַעַן מִפְּנֵי הָרָעָב: יד וַיְלַקֵּט יוֹסֵף

all the money on hand in the land of Mitzrayim and in the land of Canaan for the
purchase which they made; and Yosef
brought the money to Pharaoh's house.
15. When the money from the land of
Mitzrayim and from the land of Canaan had
come to an end, all Mitzrayim came to Yosef
and said: "Give us bread; why should we
die before your very eyes? For there is no
more money." 16. Yosef replied: "Bring
your herds, and I will give you [bread] for
your herds if there is no more money."
17. They brought their herds to Yosef,
and Yosef gave them bread for the horses
and for the property in sheep, in cattle, and
for the donkeys. He saw them through that
year with bread [in exchange] for all their
herds. 18. But that year, too, came to an
end and they came to him the following
year and said: "We can no longer hide from
my lord that, if the money and the property
in livestock have been forfeited to my lord,
there is nothing left for my lord except our
bodies and our land. 19. Why should we
and our land perish before your very eyes?
Purchase us and our land [in exchange] for
the bread, and then we and our land shall be
slaves to Pharaoh, and then you give us seed
that we may live and not die and that the
land may not become desolate." 20. And
Yosef purchased all the [farm] land of Mitzrayim for Pharaoh, for the Mitzrites sold,
every man, his field because the famine had
become too much for them; so the land
became Pharaoh's property. 21. And he
moved the people city by city from one end

אֶת־כָּל־הַכֶּ֫סֶף הַנִּמְצָא בְאֶרֶץ־מִצְרַ֫יִם וּבְאֶרֶץ
כְּנַ֫עַן בַּשֶּׁ֫בֶר אֲשֶׁר־הֵם שֹׁבְרִים וַיָּבֵא יוֹסֵף אֶת־
הַכֶּ֫סֶף בֵּ֫יתָה פַרְעֹה: טו וַיִּתֹּם הַכֶּ֫סֶף מֵאֶ֫רֶץ
מִצְרַ֫יִם וּמֵאֶ֫רֶץ כְּנַ֫עַן וַיָּבֹ֫אוּ כָל־מִצְרַ֫יִם אֶל־
יוֹסֵף לֵאמֹר הָ֫בָה־לָ֫נוּ לֶ֫חֶם וְלָ֫מָּה נָמ֫וּת נֶגְדֶּ֫ךָ כִּי
אָפֵס כָּ֫סֶף: טז וַיֹּ֫אמֶר יוֹסֵף הָ֫בוּ מִקְנֵיכֶם וְאֶתְּנָה
לָכֶם בְּמִקְנֵיכֶם אִם־אָפֵס כָּ֫סֶף: יז וַיָּבִ֫יאוּ אֶת־
מִקְנֵיהֶם֙ אֶל־יוֹסֵף וַיִּתֵּן לָהֶם יוֹסֵף לֶ֫חֶם בַּסּוּסִים
וּבְמִקְנֵה הַצֹּאן וּבְמִקְנֵה הַבָּקָר וּבַחֲמֹרִים
וַיְנַהֲלֵם בַּלֶּ֫חֶם בְּכָל־מִקְנֵהֶם בַּשָּׁנָה הַהִוא:
יח וַתִּתֹּם֙ הַשָּׁנָה הַהִוא וַיָּבֹ֫אוּ אֵלָיו בַּשָּׁנָה
הַשֵּׁנִית וַיֹּ֫אמְרוּ לוֹ לֹא־נְכַחֵד מֵאֲדֹנִי כִּי אִם־תַּם
הַכֶּ֫סֶף וּמִקְנֵה הַבְּהֵמָה אֶל־אֲדֹנִי לֹא נִשְׁאַר לִפְנֵי
אֲדֹנִי בִּלְתִּי אִם־גְּוִיָּתֵ֫נוּ וְאַדְמָתֵ֫נוּ: יט לָ֫מָּה נָמוּת
לְעֵינֶ֫יךָ גַּם־אֲנַ֫חְנוּ גַּם־אַדְמָתֵ֫נוּ קְנֵה־אֹתָ֫נוּ וְאֶת־
אַדְמָתֵ֫נוּ בַּלָּ֫חֶם וְנִהְיֶ֫ה אֲנַ֫חְנוּ וְאַדְמָתֵ֫נוּ עֲבָדִים
לְפַרְעֹה וְתֶן־זֶ֫רַע וְנִחְיֶה וְלֹא נָמ֫וּת וְהָאֲדָמָה לֹא
תֵשָׁם: כ וַיִּ֫קֶן יוֹסֵף אֶת־כָּל־אַדְמַת מִצְרַ֫יִם
לְפַרְעֹה כִּי־מָכְרוּ מִצְרַ֫יִם אִישׁ שָׂדֵ֫הוּ כִּי־חָזַק
עֲלֵהֶם הָרָעָב וַתְּהִי הָאָ֫רֶץ לְפַרְעֹה: כא וְאֶת־הָעָם
הֶעֱבִיר אֹתוֹ לֶעָרִים מִקְצֵה גְבוּל־מִצְרַ֫יִם וְעַד־

CHAPTER XLVII

21. לֶעָרִים does not mean "to cities," but "citywise"
or "city by city." In each instance the total population
of one city was transferred to another city. All the land
had become the property of the state, and in order to
give concrete form to this right newly acquired by the
state, all property owners in the country were ordered
to leave the land they had owned. Thus, a complete
transfer of population took place. But Joseph, wise man
that he was, mitigated the consequences of this edict by
arranging that each population entity remained
together, except that it now lived in a new location. As a
result, all the country's social and communal relationships remained the same; the change did not set off a

complete upheaval. Our Sages point to the effect which
this wholesale population transfer was bound to have
upon the new arrivals, the family of Jacob. Henceforth
no Egyptian would be able to look down upon them
with disdain as newcomers, because the Egyptians, too,
were no longer in their original homes.

It should be noted that this measure had not been
solely Joseph's invention. The people of Egypt themselves had proposed it (cf. Verse 19) and in fact had
suggested that they should become bondsmen to Pharaoh. Joseph rejected the latter suggestion, adopting
only the arrangement whereby the state purchased all
the landed property, which in the final analysis yielded
the state nothing more than revenue from a tax on
real property.

of the border of Mitzrayim to the other end.
22. Only the land of the priests did he not
purchase, for the priests had a fixed settlement from Pharaoh: They ate the portion
which Pharaoh gave them; therefore they
did not sell their land.   23. Yosef said to
the people: "Behold, I have purchased you
and your land for Pharaoh today. Here you
have seed; sow the land with it.   24. And
when it comes to the produce, you shall give
one-fifth to Pharaoh, and the remaining
four parts shall be yours as seed for your
fields, as food for you and for the members
of your houses and as food for your children."   25. They said: "You have kept us
alive! May we indeed find favor in the eyes
of my lord; we will gladly become slaves to
Pharaoh."   26. Yosef made it a law for the
land of Mitzrayim to this day. It belongs to
Pharaoh for the one-fifth. Only the land of
the priests did not become Pharaoh's property.   27. So Yisrael settled in the land of
Mitzrayim, in the land of Goshen. They
acquired property there, became fruitful
and multiplied exceedingly.

קָצֵהוּ: כב רַק אַדְמַת הַכֹּהֲנִים לֹא קָנָה כִּי חֹק
לַכֹּהֲנִים מֵאֵת פַּרְעֹה וְאָכְלוּ אֶת־חֻקָּם אֲשֶׁר נָתַן
לָהֶם פַּרְעֹה עַל־כֵּן לֹא מָכְרוּ אֶת־אַדְמָתָם:
כג וַיֹּאמֶר יוֹסֵף אֶל־הָעָם הֵן קָנִיתִי אֶתְכֶם הַיּוֹם
וְאֶת־אַדְמַתְכֶם לְפַרְעֹה הֵא־לָכֶם זֶרַע וּזְרַעְתֶּם
אֶת־הָאֲדָמָה: כד וְהָיָה בַּתְּבוּאֹת וּנְתַתֶּם
חֲמִישִׁית לְפַרְעֹה וְאַרְבַּע הַיָּדֹת יִהְיֶה לָכֶם לְזֶרַע
הַשָּׂדֶה וּלְאָכְלְכֶם וְלַאֲשֶׁר בְּבָתֵּיכֶם וְלֶאֱכֹל
לְטַפְּכֶם: מפטיר כה וַיֹּאמְרוּ הֶחֱיִתָנוּ נִמְצָא־חֵן
בְּעֵינֵי אֲדֹנִי וְהָיִינוּ עֲבָדִים לְפַרְעֹה: כו וַיָּשֶׂם
אֹתָהּ יוֹסֵף לְחֹק עַד־הַיּוֹם הַזֶּה עַל־אַדְמַת
מִצְרַיִם לְפַרְעֹה לַחֹמֶשׁ רַק אַדְמַת הַכֹּהֲנִים
לְבַדָּם לֹא הָיְתָה לְפַרְעֹה: כז וַיֵּשֶׁב יִשְׂרָאֵל בְּאֶרֶץ
מִצְרַיִם בְּאֶרֶץ גֹּשֶׁן וַיֵּאָחֲזוּ בָהּ וַיִּפְרוּ וַיִּרְבּוּ
מְאֹד:

The Haftarah for this Sidra may be found on page 841.

ויחי

VAYEḤI

28. Yaakov lived in the land of Mitzrayim for seventeen years, and the days of Yaakov, the years of his life, were one hundred and forty-seven years.   29. The days of Yisrael drew near to die, and he called for his son Yosef and said to him: "If I have indeed found favor in your eyes, then please place your hand beneath my thigh and deal with me in loving-kindness and truth: please do not bury me in Mitzrayim!   30. I will lie with my fathers, and then you shall carry me up from Mitzrayim and bury me in their burial place." He said: "I will act in accordance with your word[s]."   31. And he said: "Swear [it] to me." And he swore to

כח וַיְחִי יַעֲקֹב בְּאֶרֶץ מִצְרַיִם שְׁבַע עֶשְׂרֵה שָׁנָה וַיְהִי יְמֵי־יַעֲקֹב שְׁנֵי חַיָּיו שֶׁבַע שָׁנִים וְאַרְבָּעִים וּמְאַת שָׁנָה: כט וַיִּקְרְבוּ יְמֵי־יִשְׂרָאֵל לָמוּת וַיִּקְרָא ׀ לִבְנוֹ לְיוֹסֵף וַיֹּאמֶר לוֹ אִם־נָא מָצָאתִי חֵן בְּעֵינֶיךָ שִׂים־נָא יָדְךָ תַּחַת יְרֵכִי וְעָשִׂיתָ עִמָּדִי חֶסֶד וֶאֱמֶת אַל־נָא תִקְבְּרֵנִי בְּמִצְרָיִם: ל וְשָׁכַבְתִּי עִם־אֲבֹתַי וּנְשָׂאתַנִי מִמִּצְרַיִם וּקְבַרְתַּנִי בִּקְבֻרָתָם וַיֹּאמַר אָנֹכִי אֶעֱשֶׂה כִדְבָרֶךָ: לא וַיֹּאמֶר הִשָּׁבְעָה לִי וַיִּשָּׁבַע לוֹ וַיִּשְׁתַּחוּ

28. The portion of וַיְחִי is a direct continuation of the narrative that has gone before; it is not marked in the usual manner as a new *parashah*. Note that the seventeen years introduced by this verse were the only ones during which Jacob enjoyed a quiet, undisturbed life. If, therefore, these seventeen years, as compared to all his past years, could be regarded as the true flowering of Jacob's days on earth, one might have expected to see the account of these years highlighted by marking the opening of a new *parashah* at this point. The fact that this is not done here teaches us that though these seventeen years were indeed important in the life of Jacob as an individual, they were of lesser significance in the history of the nation. It was during the troubled, depressed period of his life, the time of testing when, in the midst of a Jacob-like existence, he had to earn the right to bear the name of Israel that Jacob acquired his eternal significance in the history of the nation. The seventeen years that now follow are merely a happy conclusion, a personal reward to Jacob for the difficult years that have gone before.

°   °   °

29. . . . Jacob knows very well that Joseph would bury his father with pomp and splendor. But he tells him: "For all your חֶסֶד [loving-kindness], please do not forget אֱמֶת [truth]. I would rather not be buried at all than be buried in Mitzrayim." The stress is on his request that he not be buried in Mitzrayim. We might have thought that the fulfillment of such a request would not be so difficult that it should require such a solemn entreaty. However, as we can deduce from the narrative that has gone before, Pharaoh and Egypt would certainly not have taken kindly to the idea of having Jacob and his family leave the land. Conse-

quently, the transfer of Jacob's remains to Canaan would not create a favorable impression; it would clearly show that Joseph's family still did not consider themselves citizens of the land, that their hearts were still in their former country.

But the motivation for Jacob's entreaty may be much more profound than that. During the seventeen years that he had lived with his family in Mitzrayim Jacob may have noted the powerful influence which הֵאָחֵז בָּהּ, the acquisition of property, literally, "allowing oneself to be bound to the land," was beginning to exercise upon his descendants. He might have seen that they had begun to regard the Nile as their Jordan, that they no longer considered their sojourn in Mitzrayim as an exile. This would be sufficient cause for Jacob's urgent insistence that they should not bury him in Mitzrayim but that they should take him back to their true homeland. It would be sufficient cause for Jacob to say to them: "You may hope and wish to live in Mitzrayim, but I do not even want to be buried there." This, too, is why he expressed this wish not as "Jacob," as an individual, but as "Israel," as the bearer of his nation's destiny, in the form of a stern reminder for that nation's future.

31. *and Yisrael bowed back toward the head of the bed.* Just as Eliezer prostrated himself before God after he had accomplished his mission, so does Jacob do at this point. Having communicated his last wishes to Joseph, he had now come to the final matter he had to put in order on earth. The head of the bed was behind his back. He had been sitting up in bed, facing the foot of his bed, and Joseph had been facing him. Thus, if Jacob bowed "toward the head of the bed," this was

him, and Yisrael bowed back toward the head of the bed.

XLVIII

1. It came to pass after these events that he sent word to Yosef: "Behold, your father is ill." He thereupon took with him his two sons, Menashe and Ephraim. 2. He had it reported to Yaakov and then had it told to him: "Behold! your son Yosef has come to you;" and Yisrael summoned his strength and sat up in bed. 3. Then Yaakov said to Yosef: "God, the All-Sufficing, appeared to me in Luz in the land of Canaan and blessed me. 4. He said to me: 'Behold, I will make you fruitful and will multiply you, and I will let you become a community of nations and will give this land to your seed after you as an everlasting possession.' 5. And now, your two sons, who were born to you in the land of Mitzrayim before I came to you, are mine: Ephraim and Menashe shall belong to me just as do Reuben and Shimeon. 6. But the children whom you beget after them shall remain yours; they shall be named in their inheritance according to the name of their brothers. 7. And I—when I came from Paddan, Raḥel died on me in the land of Canaan, on the road when there was still some way to come to Ephrath, and I buried

יִשְׂרָאֵל עַל־רֹאשׁ הַמִּטָּה. פ מח א וַיְהִי אַחֲרֵי
הַדְּבָרִים הָאֵלֶּה וַיֹּאמֶר לְיוֹסֵף הִנֵּה אָבִיךָ חֹלֶה
וַיִּקַּח אֶת־שְׁנֵי בָנָיו עִמּוֹ אֶת־מְנַשֶּׁה וְאֶת־
אֶפְרָיִם: ב וַיַּגֵּד לְיַעֲקֹב וַיֹּאמֶר הִנֵּה בִּנְךָ יוֹסֵף
בָּא אֵלֶיךָ וַיִּתְחַזֵּק יִשְׂרָאֵל וַיֵּשֶׁב עַל־הַמִּטָּה:
ג וַיֹּאמֶר יַעֲקֹב אֶל־יוֹסֵף אֵל שַׁדַּי נִרְאָה־אֵלַי
בְּלוּז בְּאֶרֶץ כְּנָעַן וַיְבָרֶךְ אֹתִי: ד וַיֹּאמֶר אֵלַי
הִנְנִי מַפְרְךָ וְהִרְבִּיתִךָ וּנְתַתִּיךָ לִקְהַל עַמִּים
וְנָתַתִּי אֶת־הָאָרֶץ הַזֹּאת לְזַרְעֲךָ אַחֲרֶיךָ אֲחֻזַּת
עוֹלָם: ה וְעַתָּה שְׁנֵי־בָנֶיךָ הַנּוֹלָדִים לְךָ בְּאֶרֶץ
מִצְרַיִם עַד־בֹּאִי אֵלֶיךָ מִצְרַיְמָה לִי־הֵם אֶפְרַיִם
וּמְנַשֶּׁה כִּרְאוּבֵן וְשִׁמְעוֹן יִהְיוּ־לִי: ו וּמוֹלַדְתְּךָ
אֲשֶׁר־הוֹלַדְתָּ אַחֲרֵיהֶם לְךָ יִהְיוּ עַל שֵׁם אֲחֵיהֶם
יִקָּרְאוּ בְּנַחֲלָתָם: ז וַאֲנִי | בְּבֹאִי מִפַּדָּן מֵתָה עָלַי
רָחֵל בְּאֶרֶץ כְּנַעַן בַּדֶּרֶךְ בְּעוֹד כִּבְרַת־אֶרֶץ לָבֹא

clearly a "bending backward." It was an act of adoration and thanksgiving to Him Who, through all his past life, had led Jacob to this goal. God had brought him to this place and to his son.

CHAPTER XLVIII

7. **מֵתָה עָלַי** ***[died on me].*** It was a blow of fate that had befallen me. This statement, in which Jacob recalls Rachel's death and burial, is usually interpreted as an attempt by Jacob to justify the importance he attaches to his being buried in Makhpelah though he himself had not buried Joseph's mother there. But if this had been Jacob's intention, we might have expected him to have made this statement during the earlier conversation in which he had made Joseph give him the promise regarding his own burial. But given the context in which the statement occurs here, it can refer only to the stipulation Jacob makes with regard to Joseph's sons. In the account of that conversation, until the moment (Verse 8) when, in his blessing to his grandsons, Jacob assigns them their position in the future of his nation, the text refers to Jacob only as Jacob, not Israel. When Joseph came to him (Verse 2), "Yisrael summoned his strength"; Jacob pulled himself together so that he might be able to view Joseph not only as his son, but also in terms of his significance in the future of the nation that will be associated with the name יִשְׂרָאֵל. It is with this in mind, too, that he pronounces his blessing on the sons of Joseph (Verse 8).

However, the privilege given to Menashe and Ephraim in that they were to be named as a double tribe in their own right derived from Jacob's personal relationship with Joseph and his sons; hence Verse 3: וַיֹּאמֶר יַעֲקֹב ["Then Yaakov said"]. The change to וַיַּרְא יִשְׂרָאֵל ["And Yisrael saw"] does not come until Verse 8. For it appears that this favor bestowed upon the sons of Joseph derived not from national considerations but from individual, personal ties which affected Jacob as Jacob, the man. During these final days of his life he recalls particularly the woman he had loved best, who in fact had been the wife of his choice, whom he had lost earliest of all and whose fate had been such that her memory was in danger of losing its proper place in the her there on the way to Ephrath, that is, Bethlehem."　　8. And Yisrael saw Yosef's sons and said: "Who are these?"　　9. Yosef replied to his father: "They are my sons, whom God has given me here." He said: "Please bring them to me so that I may bless them."　　10. Yisrael's eyes were heavy with age; he could not see. He [Yosef] brought them closer to him, and he kissed them and embraced them.　　11. And Yisrael said to Yosef: "I had not thought it possible that I would see your face, and now God has let me see even your seed."　　12. And Yosef had them step forward from [upon] his knees and threw himself upon his face to the ground.　　13. Then Yosef took both of them, Ephraim with his right hand, to Yisrael's left, and Menashe with his left hand, to Yisrael's right, and so he brought them closer to him.　　14. And Yisrael stretched out his right hand and placed it upon Ephraim's head—and he was the younger —but his left hand [was] upon Menashe's head. He guided his hands deliberately, for Menashe was the first-born.　　15. He blessed Yosef and said: "The God before Whom my fathers, Abraham and Yitzḥak, conducted themselves, the God Who has been my Shepherd for my existence until this day,　　16. the angel who has delivered me from all evil bless the lads so that my name and the name of my fathers, Abraham and Yitzḥak, may be called in them and that they may multiply like fish in the midst of the earth."　　17. When Yosef saw that his father would place his right hand upon Ephraim's head, this seemed incorrect to him; he therefore supported his father's

אֶפְרָתָה וָאֶקְבְּרֶהָ שָּׁם בְּדֶרֶךְ אֶפְרָת הִוא בֵּית
לָחֶם: ח וַיַּרְא יִשְׂרָאֵל אֶת־בְּנֵי יוֹסֵף וַיֹּאמֶר מִי־
אֵלֶּה: ט וַיֹּאמֶר יוֹסֵף אֶל־אָבִיו בָּנַי הֵם אֲשֶׁר־
נָתַן־לִי אֱלֹהִים בָּזֶה וַיֹּאמַר קָחֶם־נָא אֵלַי
וַאֲבָרֲכֵם: שני י וְעֵינֵי יִשְׂרָאֵל כָּבְדוּ מִזֹּקֶן לֹא
יוּכַל לִרְאוֹת וַיַּגֵּשׁ אֹתָם אֵלָיו וַיִּשַּׁק לָהֶם וַיְחַבֵּק
לָהֶם: יא וַיֹּאמֶר יִשְׂרָאֵל אֶל־יוֹסֵף רְאֹה פָנֶיךָ לֹא
פִלָּלְתִּי וְהִנֵּה הֶרְאָה אֹתִי אֱלֹהִים גַּם אֶת־זַרְעֶךָ:
יב וַיּוֹצֵא יוֹסֵף אֹתָם מֵעִם בִּרְכָּיו וַיִּשְׁתַּחוּ לְאַפָּיו
אָרְצָה: יג וַיִּקַּח יוֹסֵף אֶת־שְׁנֵיהֶם אֶת־אֶפְרַיִם
בִּימִינוֹ מִשְּׂמֹאל יִשְׂרָאֵל וְאֶת־מְנַשֶּׁה בִשְׂמֹאלוֹ
מִימִין יִשְׂרָאֵל וַיַּגֵּשׁ אֵלָיו: יד וַיִּשְׁלַח יִשְׂרָאֵל
אֶת־יְמִינוֹ וַיָּשֶׁת עַל־רֹאשׁ אֶפְרַיִם וְהוּא הַצָּעִיר
וְאֶת־שְׂמֹאלוֹ עַל־רֹאשׁ מְנַשֶּׁה שִׂכֵּל אֶת־יָדָיו כִּי
מְנַשֶּׁה הַבְּכוֹר: טו וַיְבָרֶךְ אֶת־יוֹסֵף וַיֹּאמַר
הָאֱלֹהִים אֲשֶׁר הִתְהַלְּכוּ אֲבֹתַי לְפָנָיו אַבְרָהָם
וְיִצְחָק הָאֱלֹהִים הָרֹעֶה אֹתִי מֵעוֹדִי עַד־הַיּוֹם
הַזֶּה: טז הַמַּלְאָךְ הַגֹּאֵל אֹתִי מִכָּל־רָע יְבָרֵךְ אֶת־
הַנְּעָרִים וְיִקָּרֵא בָהֶם שְׁמִי וְשֵׁם אֲבֹתַי אַבְרָהָם
וְיִצְחָק וְיִדְגּוּ לָרֹב בְּקֶרֶב הָאָרֶץ: שלישי יז וַיַּרְא
יוֹסֵף כִּי־יָשִׁית אָבִיו יַד־יְמִינוֹ עַל־רֹאשׁ אֶפְרַיִם
וַיֵּרַע בְּעֵינָיו וַיִּתְמֹךְ יַד־אָבִיו לְהָסִיר אֹתָהּ מֵעַל

nation's future recollections. When, in times to come, the sons of Israel will visit the tomb of their ancestors, they will find there Abraham and Sarah, Isaac and Rebekah, Jacob and Leah. But not even in death was it given to Rachel, Joseph's mother, to take her [rightful] place in the joint resting place of the patriarchs and matriarchs. And, as with the former maidservants, Bilhah and Zilpah, only two tribes will call her their mother. As a consequence, the memory of this wife of Jacob's heart, whom initially he had visualized as the true mother of his future nation, might vanish from the hearts of that very nation. For this reason it was the deep desire of Jacob's heart to raise Joseph, Rachel's

first-born son, to be the first-born of his nation, to confer upon him national primogeniture, as it were, by naming Joseph's sons as a double tribe in their own right. In this manner Jacob would be able to ensure that Rachel's memory would endure through at least one more tribe than the tribes which perpetuated the memory of Bilhah and Zilpah.

9. . . . In Verse 8 the name "Yisrael" is reintroduced. It is the progenitor of the future nation, who, uplifted by the spirit of God, now blesses his grandsons for their position in the future of that nation.

hand to remove it from Ephraim's head to the head of Menashe.   18. "Not so, my father," Yosef said to his father," for this one is the first-born; place your right hand upon his head."   19. His father refused and said: "I know it, my son, I know it; he, too, will become a tribe, he, too, will be great, but his younger brother will be greater than he, and his seed will complete the nations."   20. He blessed them on that day as follows: "With you shall Yisrael bless as follows: May God make you as Ephraim and Menashe." He put Ephraim before Menashe.   21. Thereupon Yisrael said to Yosef: "Look, I am dying, and God will be with you and bring you back to the land of your fathers.   22. Moreover, I have given you the honor to be the one over your brothers, whom I have wrested from the Emorite[s] with my sword and with my bow."

XLIX

1. Yaakov called for his sons and said: "Gather yourselves as one! I wish to tell you what

רֹאשׁ־אֶפְרַיִם עַל־רֹאשׁ מְנַשֶּׁה: יח וַיֹּאמֶר יוֹסֵף אֶל־אָבִיו לֹא־כֵן אָבִי כִּי־זֶה הַבְּכֹר שִׂים יְמִינְךָ עַל־רֹאשׁוֹ: יט וַיְמָאֵן אָבִיו וַיֹּאמֶר יָדַעְתִּי בְנִי יָדַעְתִּי גַּם־הוּא יִהְיֶה־לְּעָם וְגַם־הוּא יִגְדָּל וְאוּלָם אָחִיו הַקָּטֹן יִגְדַּל מִמֶּנּוּ וְזַרְעוֹ יִהְיֶה מְלֹא־הַגּוֹיִם: כ וַיְבָרֲכֵם בַּיּוֹם הַהוּא לֵאמוֹר בְּךָ יְבָרֵךְ יִשְׂרָאֵל לֵאמֹר יְשִׂמְךָ אֱלֹהִים כְּאֶפְרַיִם וְכִמְנַשֶּׁה וַיָּשֶׂם אֶת־אֶפְרַיִם לִפְנֵי מְנַשֶּׁה: כא וַיֹּאמֶר יִשְׂרָאֵל אֶל־יוֹסֵף הִנֵּה אָנֹכִי מֵת וְהָיָה אֱלֹהִים עִמָּכֶם וְהֵשִׁיב אֶתְכֶם אֶל־אֶרֶץ אֲבֹתֵיכֶם: כב וַאֲנִי נָתַתִּי לְךָ שְׁכֶם אַחַד עַל־אַחֶיךָ אֲשֶׁר לָקַחְתִּי מִיַּד הָאֱמֹרִי בְּחַרְבִּי וּבְקַשְׁתִּי: פ רביעי מט א וַיִּקְרָא יַעֲקֹב אֶל־בָּנָיו וַיֹּאמֶר הֵאָסְפוּ וְאַגִּידָה לָכֶם אֵת אֲשֶׁר־יִקְרָא

---

20. בַּיּוֹם הַהוּא [*on that day*]. On that day there was pronounced for the first time the בְּרָכָה [blessing] which has survived to this day upon the lips of all Jewish parents when they bless their children. . . . בְּךָ יְבָרֵךְ וגו' ["With you shall (Yisrael) bless"]: Your children shall be so greatly blessed that whenever fathers in Israel will wish to bless their children they may know of no greater blessing than to say to them: "May God make you as Ephraim and Menashe."

22. שְׁכֶם אַחַד עַל אַחֶיךָ. Since the word אַחַד is attached to שכם, שכם here cannot possibly be a proper noun, the city by that name. And even if, as is usually assumed, שכם in this passage meant "lot" or "portion," this would not explain the purpose of the word אַחַד. אַחַד never denotes only "one," but always one of two or more, one out of many. Therefore the first half of this verse cannot mean: "I have given you one portion more than to your brothers." Actually, there is no instance in Scripture of שְׁכֶם meaning "portion." Rather, שְׁכֶם denotes a "shoulder," upon which either a burden or an honor has been placed. Cf. וַתְּהִי הַמִּשְׂרָה עַל שִׁכְמוֹ ["And the government is upon his shoulder"] (Isaiah 9:5), and הֲסִירוֹתִי מִסֵּבֶל שִׁכְמוֹ ["I have removed his shoulder from the burden"] (Psalm 81:7). The literal meaning of our passage, therefore, would be: "I have given you the shoulder to be the one over your brothers." Hence the text should be interpreted: "I have given you the honor to be the one over your brothers."

. . . Jacob says to Joseph: "See, I am going to die. I do not have a great inheritance to leave you, because we are in a foreign land. God must first bring you back to our land; there you will have inheritances. Here all we have is blessings and good wishes. But whatever I have here to bequeath I herewith leave to you: the honor—and the burden—to be my successor as the head of the family, to be the first over your brothers, my children, who represent the only conquests I have made in my life and concerning whom I can make dispositions before I die. The fact that, though they were living in the midst of the Emorites, they did not become Emorites themselves, so that I can now gather all of them around me as my sons, as heirs to the name and the calling of Israel—these represent my trophies, my triumphs and victories over the Emorites."

CHAPTER XLIX

1–2. . . . At this moment Jacob did not view his sons in terms of what they had in common but in terms of the differences that divided them. Hence he now says to them: "Different though you are from one another, surrender yourselves completely to the one spirit [that unites you]. Then I will reveal to you what will befall you when time has run its course." Before the אַחֲרִית הַיָּמִים ["aftermath of days"] can come to pass, all the

אֶתְכֶם בְּאַחֲרִית הַיָּמִים׃ ב הִקָּבְצוּ וְשִׁמְעוּ בְּנֵי
יַעֲקֹב וְשִׁמְעוּ אֶל־יִשְׂרָאֵל אֲבִיכֶם׃ ג רְאוּבֵן
בְּכֹרִי אַתָּה כֹּחִי וְרֵאשִׁית אוֹנִי יֶתֶר שְׂאֵת וְיֶתֶר
עָז׃ ד פַּחַז כַּמַּיִם אַל־תּוֹתַר כִּי עָלִיתָ מִשְׁכְּבֵי
אָבִיךָ אָז חִלַּלְתָּ יְצוּעִי עָלָה׃ פ ה שִׁמְעוֹן וְלֵוִי
אַחִים כְּלֵי חָמָס מְכֵרֹתֵיהֶם׃ ו בְּסֹדָם אַל־תָּבֹא
נַפְשִׁי בִּקְהָלָם אַל־תֵּחַד כְּבֹדִי כִּי בְאַפָּם הָרְגוּ
אִישׁ וּבִרְצֹנָם עִקְּרוּ־שׁוֹר׃ ז אָרוּר אַפָּם כִּי עָז

will befall you in the aftermath of days.
2. Keep together and listen, O sons of Yaakov! And listen to your father Yisrael!
3. Reuben, you are my first-born, my strength and the first of my acquisitions, privileged in rank and privileged in power.
4. But instability like water [in you] does not permit [you] this privilege, for you have mounted your father's couch; thus you profaned the one who mounted my couch.
5. Shimeon and Levi are brothers, [but] instruments of violence are their means of acquiring gain.
6. My will must not enter into their council, my glory must not join in their assembly, for in their anger they murdered men, and they had previously lamed their ox-like strength with their friendliness.
7. A curse, therefore, upon their anger, for it is too fierce, and their

sons of Jacob's family must be imbued with one spirit. It will not come to pass until הֵאָסְפוּ [the gathering together] has become a reality. Indeed, the "aftermath of days" may not even be properly understood until that gathering has taken place; hence Jacob makes only brief allusion to the אַחֲרִית הַיָּמִים.

° ° °

הִקָּבְצוּ, הֵאָסְפוּ *[Gather yourselves . . . Keep together]*: These were the first thoughts that filled Jacob's mind when he saw his sons gathered around his deathbed. Family solidarity and a keen interest in all things of the spirit—this was Jacob's primary legacy to them all. But if a group consisting of such divergent elements is to form one entity within and also to the outside, it must have a leader. Jacob therefore now musters his sons in search of such a leader. The most natural person for this position would be the first-born son. That is why he first addresses himself to Reuben.

4. . . .Jacob says to Reuben: "You are the most precious gem in my treasure chamber, you are my strength and the first of my acquisitions. However, you are not fit to be the head of the family." The head of the family must be עַז [strong]; he must not be swayed by gentle, fawning zephyrs, nor by raging storms. He must have inner strength of character; he must not be unstable like water. . . .

5. Simeon and Levi share a character trait that should have qualified them especially as future leaders of the family: They are אַחִים [brothers]; they have a highly developed sense of fraternal solidarity which they have already demonstrated. Without any expectation of personal gain, they felt as deeply affected by a wrong done even to the least in their family as if they themselves had been the victims. . . .

6. . . . Simeon and Levi have the attitude and spirit required for leadership, but their methods are reprehensible. Therefore my will (i.e., the will of my nation) must not enter into their council. This means that the will of the nation must not be decided in their councils; their counsel must never be interpreted as a reflection of the nation's will. . . .

וּבִרְצֹנָם עִקְּרוּ שׁוֹר: *[and they had previously lamed their ox-like strength]*. This passage is more than ambiguous. שׁוֹר definitely is an ox, and עָקַר definitely means "to lame," to hamstring. But רָצוֹן predominantly implies only a friendly attitude, one of good will. . . . The sense of this verse would be: "For in their anger they murdered men. Even worse, before so doing, they had feigned good will toward their intended victims, thus paralyzing the strength which these victims, though usually peaceable, could have bravely employed to defend themselves against attack." They had lamed the strength [of Shekhem and his countrymen] by persuading them to undergo circumcision, and then had attacked them while they were in a state of physical weakness. Hence their act could not even be defended as a deed of valor.

7. . . . .Unlike Reuben, who was not sufficiently independent and lacked inner stability, Simeon and Levi were too fiercely aware of their own strength and acted ruthlessly whenever the welfare of the family as a unit was in danger.

It is most significant that at this point, where the foundations of the Jewish people are set down, a curse outrage, because it was too cruel. I will divide them in Yaakov and scatter them in Yisrael. 8. Yehudah, you are the one; to you will your brothers do homage! Your hand will sit upon the neck of your enemies. To you the sons of your father will bow. 9. Yehudah is a young, old lion; you are above base plunder, my son. He kneels down, he also rests like a lion, and who would rouse him to become a lion in full fury? 10. The scepter will not depart from Yehudah nor the law-inscribing stylus from between his feet, until his sprout, seemingly the last, and weak, will come, and then it will be to him, the one of manly strength, that the nations, dulled with age,

וְעֶבְרָתָ֖ם כִּ֣י קָשָׁ֑תָה אֲחַלְּקֵ֣ם בְּיַעֲקֹ֔ב וַאֲפִיצֵ֖ם
בְּיִשְׂרָאֵֽל׃ פ ח יְהוּדָ֗ה אַתָּה֙ יוֹד֣וּךָ אַחֶ֔יךָ יָדְךָ֖
בְּעֹ֣רֶף אֹיְבֶ֑יךָ יִשְׁתַּחֲו֥וּ לְךָ֖ בְּנֵ֥י אָבִֽיךָ׃ ט גּ֤וּר
אַרְיֵה֙ יְהוּדָ֔ה מִטֶּ֖רֶף בְּנִ֣י עָלִ֑יתָ כָּרַ֨ע רָבַ֧ץ כְּאַרְיֵ֛ה
וּכְלָבִ֖יא מִ֥י יְקִימֶֽנּוּ׃ י לֹֽא־יָס֥וּר שֵׁ֙בֶט֙ מִֽיהוּדָ֔ה
וּמְחֹקֵ֖ק מִבֵּ֣ין רַגְלָ֑יו עַ֚ד כִּֽי־יָבֹ֣א שִׁילֹ֔ה וְל֖וֹ יִקְּהַ֥ת

is laid upon any demonstration of force that runs counter to justice and morality, even if it is intended for the common good. All other states and nations have adopted the principle that any action is legitimate as long as it serves the interest of the state. Acts of cunning and violence that would be punished by ostracism or execution if practiced by an individual for selfish gain are rewarded with laurels and civic honors if they are committed for what is alleged to be the welfare of the state. The other nations assert that the laws of morality are applicable only to private affairs and that the only law recognized in politics and diplomacy is that of national self-interest. In our text, by contrast, the last will and testament upon which the Jewish people was founded pronounces a curse upon all acts of cunning and violence, even if they are committed for the most legitimate interests of the nation, and it sets down for all time the doctrine that even in public life and in the promotion of the common good not only the ends but also the means used to attain these ends must be clean.

However, it is only the אַף ["anger"] and the עֶבְרָה ["outrage"] of Simeon and Levi that are cursed. The curse is directed neither against Simeon and Levi personally, nor against their aims as such.

° ° °

8. Jacob has mustered his sons to seek out the one fit to be the leader. He has already found Reuben, Simeon and Levi unfit for the position of leadership. Now, at last, his eyes come to rest on Judah, and he says to him: "You are the one who is qualified for this task. You combine in your personality the qualities which Reuben lacks at the one extreme and Simeon and Levi at the other."

יָדְךָ בְּעֹרֶף אֹיְבֶיךָ [Your hand will sit upon the neck of your enemies]. It is not your sword but your own natural authority that will sit upon the neck of your enemies. You will not commit murder. You will not need to employ כְּלֵי חָמָס [violent methods] against your enemies. The development of your natural authority will command such respect that your enemies will turn their backs on you; they will not dare attack you and they will be glad if only you will leave them alone. And you will enjoy a position of such great superiority within your own family that your brothers will subordinate themselves to you of their own accord.

10. ***עד כי יבא שילה [until his sprout . . . will come].***[30] שִׁילֹה may be derived from שול, the outermost, lower edge, the end. Here we see Jacob, lying upon his deathbed at the time of the nation's early beginnings, when the cornerstone for that nation had barely been laid, looking down through the ages, contemplating the ultimate scion of the tribe of Judah. The word is suffixed not with the consonant ו but with the [feminine] ה, which connotes weakness. By referring to this last generation as שִׁילֹה, Jacob means to say: "The time will come when the kingdom of the House of David will be seen at its nadir, when Judah will appear not as an אֲרִי, not strong like a lion, but effeminately weak, so that it will look as if he were about to draw his last breath. Judah's might and virility will have virtually vanished. But just at this point, when the grave-diggers of world history will already have ordered a coffin to enclose Judah's remains, לוֹ יִקְּהַת עַמִּים, he will rise again in manly strength and the peoples. dulled with age, will fall to him."

יִקְּהַת, root יקה, is identical with קהה: to become dull Cf. Proverbs 30:17, the eye that mocks at לִיקְּהַת אֵם, the dullness of the aged mother. Here, then, the reference

[30]*Note to the English translation*: Rendered in standard English versions as "as long as men come to Shiloh" or "until Shiloh come." [G.H.]

עַמִּים: יא אֹסְרִי לַגֶּפֶן עִירֹה וְלַשֹּׂרֵקָה בְּנִי אֲתֹנוֹ
כִּבֵּס בַּיַּיִן לְבֻשׁוֹ וּבְדַם־עֲנָבִים סוּתֹה: יב חַכְלִילִי
עֵינַיִם מִיָּיִן וּלְבֶן־שִׁנַּיִם מֵחָלָב: פ יג זְבוּלֻן
לְחוֹף יַמִּים יִשְׁכֹּן וְהוּא לְחוֹף אֳנִיֹּת וְיַרְכָתוֹ עַל־
צִידֹן: פ יד יִשָּׂשכָר חֲמֹר גָּרֶם רֹבֵץ בֵּין
הַמִּשְׁפְּתָיִם: טו וַיַּרְא מְנֻחָה כִּי טוֹב וְאֶת־הָאָרֶץ
כִּי נָעֵמָה וַיֵּט שִׁכְמוֹ לִסְבֹּל וַיְהִי לְמַס־עֹבֵד:

will fall. 11. He ties his foal to the grapevine, the son of his she-donkey to the choice vine-branch; he has bathed his garment in wine and his mantle in the blood of grapes. 12. Eyes more sparkling than wine, teeth whiter than milk— 13. Zebulun will dwell at a bay of seas; he himself will become a harbor for ships, and his outermost border shall reach Tzidon. 14. Yissakhar, a nimble beast of burden, rests between the rows of household vessels. 15. He has seen that leisure is the good thing and the land is suited for it; he has therefore bent his shoulder to bear and has given himself to [pay] the tribute of the tiller of the soil.

is to the dullness of mankind, a dullness that comes from old age. Thus: The time will come when the Jewish spirit will appear close to death; at that point mankind, grown old and dull, having tested and experienced everything else, will sense that the time has come for a new, reviving spirit, and it is this renewed spirit which will be borne by the ultimate scion of Judah.

11. This is the manner in which Jacob visualizes מָשִׁיחַ [the Messiah]. How, indeed, does he picture him? He sees the redeemer of mankind, the conqueror of nations, riding not upon a charger but upon a young donkey. Throughout Scripture the donkey, as a beast of burden, symbolizes peaceful prosperity, the peaceful greatness of a nation, while the charger symbolizes warlike power. . . .

13. In Judah, Jacob found the person he sought: the leader and bearer of the destiny of the Jewish people unto the most distant future. Jacob reviews his other sons and briefly outlines the personal contribution that each of them will make to the future nation—until he turns again to Joseph and pauses. In Judah he found the instrument for the nation's defense. . . . Zebulun will become a tribe of traders but he will not lose himself in commercial ambitions. He will be content to have the ships of world commerce come to him, and to lean upon Tzidon. This means that the tribe of Judah will be economically dependent on Tzidon.

14. . . .מִשְׁפְּתָיִם, literally, the place where household utensils are arranged in two rows. We employ the term "hearth" to denote the household; the Hebrew language uses the expression "rows of household vessels" for the same purpose. Thus: Issakhar is a strong and nimble worker who enjoys taking his ease at his hearth. Figuratively, he is a beast of burden whose limbs show that he is willing and able to work hard, and who now takes his ease amidst the prosperity of the household which he himself has created by his labors.

15. Issakhar represents that type which is happy to work but only in such a manner and with such an attitude that his labors will make a contribution of value to the true Jewish nation. While Judah is the tribe of rulers and Zebulun the tribe of traders, Issakhar represents the true nucleus of the Jewish nation: the Jewish farmer. He does not work in order to toil without cease or to gain wealth. The Jewish man of the people does not wear himself out in his work; he works in order to gain מְנוּחָה, leisure. He is content to have Zebulun earn millions with his products; for his own part, he prefers to stay at home. He regards leisure gained by one's own labors as the greatest prize for which man should strive, for it is in leisure that man can draw himself erect, that man can "regain" himself. For this reason he bends his shoulder to bear burdens; he is content to leave the scepter to Judah and the merchantman's flag to Zebulun; he is tempted neither by the glories of battle nor by the profits of commerce. He knows other conquests and treasures that can be won and cultivated only if one has the leisure to do so. Hence, it was the tribe of Issakhar that became the nurturer of the nation's spiritual treasures.

When, after the fall of Saul, all the tribes rallied around David, thousands and hundreds of thousands came from everywhere. But Issakhar sent only two hundred, רָאשִׁים, the "heads." The others stayed at home and worked. But these delegates were יוֹדְעֵי בִינָה לָעִתִּים ["they had understanding of the times" (I Chronicles 12:32)], they brought with them בִּינָה, insight, literally, the ability to see "*between* things," the ability to recognize the interrelationships of persons and things and the results of these interactions. Issakhar attained this insight during the hours of leisure he had earned by his own labors. This insight is יוֹדֵעַ בִּינָה,

16. Dan will champion the right of his
people, as only one of the tribes of Yisrael
[can]. 17. Dan will become a serpent on
the highway, a viper on the path, which
bites the charger's heel so that the rider falls
backward. 18. For Thy help do I hope, O
God! 19. Gad, many a troop will drive
into him like a wedge, but he will drive like
a wedge into their heel. 20. Through
Asher his food will become rich, and he
will yield royal delights. 21. Naphtali, a
gazelle-like messenger, delivers eloquent
speeches. 22. Yosef was a noble, outstanding son, a noble, outstanding son
already at the source. Daughters! She, too,
strode over the wall! 23. When, therefore, [they] heaped bitter abuse upon him

ס טז דָּן יָדִין עַמּוֹ כְּאַחַד שִׁבְטֵי יִשְׂרָאֵל׃ יז יְהִי־
דָן נָחָשׁ עֲלֵי־דֶרֶךְ שְׁפִיפֹן עֲלֵי־אֹרַח הַנֹּשֵׁךְ
עִקְּבֵי־סוּס וַיִּפֹּל רֹכְבוֹ אָחוֹר׃ יח לִישׁוּעָתְךָ
קִוִּיתִי יְהוָה׃ ס חמישי יט גָּד גְּדוּד יְגוּדֶנּוּ וְהוּא יָגֻד
עָקֵב׃ ס כ מֵאָשֵׁר שְׁמֵנָה לַחְמוֹ וְהוּא יִתֵּן
מַעֲדַנֵּי־מֶלֶךְ׃ ס כא נַפְתָּלִי אַיָּלָה שְׁלֻחָה הַנֹּתֵן
אִמְרֵי־שָׁפֶר׃ ס כב בֵּן פֹּרָת יוֹסֵף בֵּן פֹּרָת עֲלֵי־
עָיִן בָּנוֹת צָעֲדָה עֲלֵי־שׁוּר׃ כג וַיְמָרְרֻהוּ וָרֹבּוּ

concrete perception; it is not sophistry but that practical understanding of the true interaction of people and things which can be derived from genuine חָכְמַת תּוֹרָה [Torah wisdom], and לְעִתִּים, from the proper appreciation of the uniqueness of a given moment in time.

. . . Such a perception of תּוֹרָה and its constant application in real life is not gained by unceasing work at one's business; it can be attained only during the hours of leisure gained by one's toil. It can therefore be attained only by a people וַיַּרְא מְנֻחָה כִּי טוֹב [which "has seen that leisure is the good thing"], which regards leisure as the true, pure profit to be obtained from work so that, as our Sages put it, [Avoth I:15] they may perceive Torah knowledge as the true end, and labor only as an incidental means toward that end. . . . Issakhar sees agriculture as the purest, surest and best suited means to this end. He therefore gave himself with enthusiasm to the burdens of tilling the soil.

° ° °

16. With Issakhar, Jacob has come to the end of the six sons of Leah. It is from her that the nucleus of the people is to be descended. Dan was the first son of the שְׁפָחוֹת, born to Jacob by one of the former maid-servants. . . . Therefore Jacob says: "Dan will champion the cause of his people as only one of the tribes of Israel can." He will not lag behind the others in any manner: he is as much as an essential component of the whole as the others. . . .

20. The importance of Gad and Dan lies in that they act as defenders of the rights of their people against enemies from without; Asher and Naphtali have traits that are brought to bear primarily on domestic affairs. . . .

21. . . . Whatever Naphtali is told to do he will carry out with dispatch. He does not act on his own initiative; he only functions as a messenger for the others. He is not creative himself but is quick to comprehend the plans adopted by others for the common good. He can be trusted to carry them out . . . and to communicate them in eloquent terms.

If our interpretation is not in error, then Gad and Dan would act as subordinate complements to Judah; Asher would perform the same function for Zebulun, and Naphtali for Issakhar.

22. . . . Joseph is בֵּן פֹּרָת, a noble son who stands alone, standing apart from his brothers by virtue of his noble character. בֵּן פֹּרָת עֲלֵי עָיִן ["a noble, outstanding son already at the source"]: He was not ennobled only of late, by virtue of his position as a minister to Pharaoh. He had shown nobility of heart and mind even when he was still a בֵּן [son], when he had not yet gone abroad, when he still stood as a son at the "source"; i.e., at home. The "source" from which Joseph had derived his nobility of spirit was certainly none other than his mother, Rachel. . . . It was from his mother that, as a child and boy, he had acquired his nobility.

בָּנוֹת: vocative: "Daughters!" or "Women!" She who had been Joseph's "source" also "strode over the wall." She, too, had not been an ordinary woman.

23–24. . . . The brothers had heaped the most bitter abuses upon Joseph. They had worked themselves into a frenzy of hatred against him. They had set him up as the target for their hatred and plotted his destruction. In order to destroy him, the owners of the arrows that had been prepared for his bow had gone so far as to sell him to Mitzrayim as a slave. However, this situation, which they themselves had created, had turned Joseph and plotted enmity, when, with deep hatred, the masters of the arrows chose him as their target,   24. his bow, nevertheless, remained serenely at rest, even when the arms of his hands were already gold-bedecked by the hands of the Power that uplifts Yaakov, which from thence shepherds the rock of Yisrael.   25. This was from the God of your father, Who will continue to help you; you will remain with the All-Sufficing, Who will continue to bless you, with blessings of heaven from above, with blessings of the flood that lies below; with blessings of breasts and of the womb. 26. These are the blessings of your father, which themselves attained strength only by reason of the blessings of my progenitors, up to that goal toward which the hills of the ages strive; they will fall upon the head of Yosef, fall upon the crown of the head of the most restrained among his brothers. 27. Binyamin will tear the wolf to pieces; he will eat a portion in the morning, but in

וַיִּשְׂטְמֻהוּ בַּעֲלֵי חִצִּים: כד וַתֵּשֶׁב בְּאֵיתָן קַשְׁתּוֹ
וַיָּפֹזּוּ זְרֹעֵי יָדָיו מִידֵי אֲבִיר יַעֲקֹב מִשָּׁם רֹעֶה
אֶבֶן יִשְׂרָאֵל: כה מֵאֵל אָבִיךָ וְיַעְזְרֶךָּ וְאֵת שַׁדַּי
וִיבָרְכֶךָּ בִּרְכֹת שָׁמַיִם מֵעָל בִּרְכֹת תְּהוֹם רֹבֶצֶת
תָּחַת בִּרְכֹת שָׁדַיִם וָרָחַם: כו בִּרְכֹת אָבִיךָ גָּבְרוּ
עַל־בִּרְכֹת הוֹרַי עַד־תַּאֲוַת גִּבְעֹת עוֹלָם תִּהְיֶיןָ
לְרֹאשׁ יוֹסֵף וּלְקָדְקֹד נְזִיר אֶחָיו: פ
ששי כז בִּנְיָמִין זְאֵב יִטְרָף בַּבֹּקֶר יֹאכַל עַד

into the master of their fate and delivered them completely into his hands. But Joseph did not take his bow from his shoulder in order to destroy his brothers with their own arrows, not even after he had attained royal power through the hand of God. Herein lies Joseph's nobility, which he had acquired by birth and through his mother's influence, and which had made him פֹּרָת עֲלֵי עָיִן ["a noble, outstanding son already at the source"], raising him so high above all others from his very birth.

26. . . . Judah and Joseph obviously represent the two focal points on which Jacob centered his prophetic vision, up to the time when the nations would grow dull with age, up to . . . "the goal toward which the hills of the ages strive," the most distant future. Indeed, throughout Scripture we see the name of Joseph coupled with that of Judah. The terms בֵּית יוֹסֵף ["house of Yosef"] and בֵּית יְהוּדָה ["house of Yehudah"] are both employed by the prophets with reference to the entire nation. And even for that still far-off future, tradition has a scion of Joseph's stand side by side with the house of Judah as a precurser and companion; מָשִׁיחַ בֶּן יוֹסֵף [Messiah the son of Yosef] and מָשִׁיחַ בֶּן דָּוִד [Messiah the son of David]. The relationship between the two is not clear because it has not been revealed to us. However, if Jacob stresses that the hopes and the blessings of that distant future will rest also upon the crown of Joseph's head even as they will rest upon

the head of Judah, he certainly does not do so without good reason.

27. It would be sad if a father, at the point of death, could find no better description of his youngest son than to characterize him as a "ravenous wolf." Note that the words used in this verse are not זְאֵב עֶרֶב ["a ravenous wolf"] or זְאֵב טוֹרֵף ["a wolf that tears (his prey) to pieces"] but זְאֵב יִטְרָף, so that זְאֵב [the wolf] may well be the object of יִטְרָף ["he will tear"]. Thus: "He [Binyamin] will tear the wolf."

If, in his last moments, Jacob speaks of a wolf, it is only because he is now taking a last look at his "flock of children." For twenty years he had to fear attacks from real wolves upon his flock of sheep. Now he sees all his children before him. He has given them his blessing; he has recognized and described the individual significance of each one of them for all time to come. And so, his final glance comes to rest upon the end of days, when the last of the world powers will be overcome. He beholds the galuth [exile] and the galuth forces against which his children will have to struggle, and he says: "It will be the smallest and the youngest among them that will repel the wolf (the eternal Amalek) from the flock of Jacob. Already early in the morning, at the outset of the nation's history, he will deal the wolf a powerful blow, but in the evening of time he will destroy the wolf completely. Indeed, Aggadic tradition has it that Amalek, the archenemy, will not be over-

וְלָעֶרֶב יְחַלֵּק שָׁלָל׃ כח כָּל־אֵלֶּה שִׁבְטֵי יִשְׂרָאֵל
שְׁנֵים עָשָׂר וְזֹאת אֲשֶׁר־דִּבֶּר לָהֶם אֲבִיהֶם וַיְבָרֶךְ
אוֹתָם אִישׁ אֲשֶׁר כְּבִרְכָתוֹ בֵּרַךְ אֹתָם׃ כט וַיְצַו
אוֹתָם וַיֹּאמֶר אֲלֵהֶם אֲנִי נֶאֱסָף אֶל־עַמִּי קִבְרוּ
אֹתִי אֶל־אֲבֹתָי אֶל־הַמְּעָרָה אֲשֶׁר בִּשְׂדֵה עֶפְרוֹן
הַחִתִּי׃ ל בַּמְּעָרָה אֲשֶׁר בִּשְׂדֵה הַמַּכְפֵּלָה אֲשֶׁר־
עַל־פְּנֵי מַמְרֵא בְּאֶרֶץ כְּנָעַן אֲשֶׁר קָנָה אַבְרָהָם
אֶת־הַשָּׂדֶה מֵאֵת עֶפְרֹן הַחִתִּי לַאֲחֻזַּת־קָבֶר׃
לא שָׁמָּה קָבְרוּ אֶת־אַבְרָהָם וְאֵת שָׂרָה אִשְׁתּוֹ
שָׁמָּה קָבְרוּ אֶת־יִצְחָק וְאֵת רִבְקָה אִשְׁתּוֹ וְשָׁמָּה
קָבַרְתִּי אֶת־לֵאָה׃ לב מִקְנֵה הַשָּׂדֶה וְהַמְּעָרָה
אֲשֶׁר־בּוֹ מֵאֵת בְּנֵי־חֵת׃ לג וַיְכַל יַעֲקֹב לְצַוֹּת
אֶת־בָּנָיו וַיֶּאֱסֹף רַגְלָיו אֶל־הַמִּטָּה וַיִּגְוַע וַיֵּאָסֶף
אֶל־עַמָּיו׃ נ א וַיִּפֹּל יוֹסֵף עַל־פְּנֵי אָבִיו וַיֵּבְךְּ
עָלָיו וַיִּשַּׁק־לוֹ׃ ב וַיְצַו יוֹסֵף אֶת־עֲבָדָיו אֶת־
הָרֹפְאִים לַחֲנֹט אֶת־אָבִיו וַיַּחַנְטוּ הָרֹפְאִים אֶת־
יִשְׂרָאֵל׃ ג וַיִּמְלְאוּ־לוֹ אַרְבָּעִים יוֹם כִּי כֵּן

the evening he will divide it as spoil." 28. All these are tribes of Yisrael, twelve, and this is what their father declared concerning them when he blessed them; he blessed them each according to what was in character with his particular blessing. 29. He commanded them and said to them: "I will be gathered away to my people; bury me among my fathers, in the cave that is in the field of Ephron the Hittite, 30. In the cave which is in the field of Makhpelah, which lies before Mamre in the land of Canaan, which field Abraham bought from Ephron the Ḥittite as a burial property. 31. There they buried Abraham and his wife Sarah; there they buried Yitzḥak and his wife Rivkah, and there I buried Leah. 32. The purchase of the field and of the cave that is in it was made from the sons of Ḥeth." 33. When Yaakov had concluded the commands to his sons, he drew his feet back into the bed, expired and was gathered to his peoples.

L 1. Then Yosef threw himself upon his father's face and wept upon him and kissed him. 2. Yosef commanded his servants, the physicians, to embalm his father, and the physicians embalmed Yisrael. 3. Forty days were fulfilled for him,

come by Judah, but by the sons of Rachel, who have the least power of all. אִם לֹא יִסְחָבוּם צְעִירֵי הַצֹּאן "the youngest of the herd will drive them off as spoil" (Jeremiah 49:20).

28. All "these" are tribes of Israel: They are twelve, no more and no less. They are not thirteen, with Joseph being counted as two tribes, nor eleven, with, say, Reuben omitted. They are all שִׁבְטֵי יִשְׂרָאֵל [tribes of Yisrael]. They are all components of the whole, part of the basic stock of Israel, twelve pillars implanted by God deep within the womb of the ages in which this nation is to mature.

All "this" is not the blessing that Jacob gave to his sons; indeed, part of it is merely a description of character traits. It merely represents their father's utterances with regard to them, the manner in which he described each in terms of his individual significance at the time when he blessed them.

But after that, he did indeed bless them, in keeping with the blessing appropriate to their individuality. After describing the individuality and significance of each of his sons, he blessed each one of them in accordance with his character sketches of them. Jacob's blessing to each one of his sons was that he should find happiness in and through his individual personality. Even those whose blessing was included in their character sketches, and perhaps they, most of all, were still in need of this special blessing so that the outwardly blessed position they attained would prove a blessing to them also in fact. For God cannot make a person happy against that person's will and without his cooperation; conversely, the genuine Jew will be able to transform even the direst plight into a source of the richest blessings.

"You must not think," the Sages say, "that because he assigned to Judah the strength of a lion, to Benjamin the boldness of a wolf, to Naphtali the swiftness of a gazelle, etc., Jacob did not include them all equally in his blessings. For this reason it is written: He blessed each according to his blessing—not אותו, him, but אותם, them all." The special blessing is the share of each one, but conversely, each individual blessing was intended to benefit them all.

יִמְלְאוּ יְמֵי הַחֲנֻטִים וַיִּבְכּוּ אֹתוֹ מִצְרַיִם שִׁבְעִים
יוֹם: ד וַיַּעַבְרוּ יְמֵי בְכִיתוֹ וַיְדַבֵּר יוֹסֵף אֶל־בֵּית
פַּרְעֹה לֵאמֹר אִם־נָא מָצָאתִי חֵן בְּעֵינֵיכֶם
דַּבְּרוּ־נָא בְּאָזְנֵי פַרְעֹה לֵאמֹר: ה אָבִי הִשְׁבִּיעַנִי
לֵאמֹר הִנֵּה אָנֹכִי מֵת בְּקִבְרִי אֲשֶׁר כָּרִיתִי לִי
בְּאֶרֶץ כְּנַעַן שָׁמָּה תִּקְבְּרֵנִי וְעַתָּה אֶעֱלֶה־נָּא
וְאֶקְבְּרָה אֶת־אָבִי וְאָשׁוּבָה: ו וַיֹּאמֶר פַּרְעֹה
עֲלֵה וּקְבֹר אֶת־אָבִיךָ כַּאֲשֶׁר הִשְׁבִּיעֶךָ: ז וַיַּעַל
יוֹסֵף לִקְבֹּר אֶת־אָבִיו וַיַּעֲלוּ אִתּוֹ כָּל־עַבְדֵי
פַרְעֹה זִקְנֵי בֵיתוֹ וְכֹל זִקְנֵי אֶרֶץ־מִצְרָיִם: ח וְכֹל
בֵּית יוֹסֵף וְאֶחָיו וּבֵית אָבִיו רַק טַפָּם וְצֹאנָם
וּבְקָרָם עָזְבוּ בְּאֶרֶץ גֹּשֶׁן: ט וַיַּעַל עִמּוֹ גַּם־רֶכֶב
גַּם־פָּרָשִׁים וַיְהִי הַמַּחֲנֶה כָּבֵד מְאֹד: י וַיָּבֹאוּ
עַד־גֹּרֶן הָאָטָד אֲשֶׁר בְּעֵבֶר הַיַּרְדֵּן וַיִּסְפְּדוּ־שָׁם
מִסְפֵּד גָּדוֹל וְכָבֵד מְאֹד וַיַּעַשׂ לְאָבִיו אֵבֶל שִׁבְעַת
יָמִים: יא וַיַּרְא יוֹשֵׁב הָאָרֶץ הַכְּנַעֲנִי אֶת־הָאֵבֶל
בְּגֹרֶן הָאָטָד וַיֹּאמְרוּ אֵבֶל־כָּבֵד זֶה לְמִצְרָיִם
עַל־כֵּן קָרָא שְׁמָהּ אָבֵל מִצְרַיִם אֲשֶׁר בְּעֵבֶר
הַיַּרְדֵּן: יב וַיַּעֲשׂוּ בָנָיו לוֹ כֵּן כַּאֲשֶׁר צִוָּם:
יג וַיִּשְׂאוּ אֹתוֹ בָנָיו אַרְצָה כְּנַעַן וַיִּקְבְּרוּ אֹתוֹ
בִּמְעָרַת שְׂדֵה הַמַּכְפֵּלָה אֲשֶׁר קָנָה אַבְרָהָם אֶת־
הַשָּׂדֶה לַאֲחֻזַּת־קֶבֶר מֵאֵת עֶפְרֹן הַחִתִּי עַל־פְּנֵי
מַמְרֵא: יד וַיָּשָׁב יוֹסֵף מִצְרַיְמָה הוּא וְאֶחָיו וְכָל־
הָעֹלִים אִתּוֹ לִקְבֹּר אֶת־אָבִיו אַחֲרֵי קָבְרוֹ אֶת־
אָבִיו: טו וַיִּרְאוּ אֲחֵי־יוֹסֵף כִּי־מֵת אֲבִיהֶם
וַיֹּאמְרוּ לוּ יִשְׂטְמֵנוּ יוֹסֵף וְהָשֵׁב יָשִׁיב לָנוּ אֵת

for such was the full time of those who were embalmed. The Mitzrites wept for him seventy days. 4. When the days of his weeping were over, Yosef said to the house-[hold] of Pharaoh as follows: "If I have indeed found favor in your eyes, then please speak in the ears of Pharaoh as follows: 5. My father made me swear as follows: 'Lo! I am dying. In my grave, which I have prepared for myself in the land of Canaan, there you shall bury me.' And now let me go up to bury my father and I shall return." 6. Thereupon Pharaoh said: "Go up and bury your father according to what he made you swear." 7. And Yosef went up to bury his father, and with him went up all the servants of Pharaoh, the elders of his house and all the elders of the land of Mitzrayim, 8. All the house of Yosef, his brothers and the house of his father; only their children, their sheep and their cattle did they leave in the land of Goshen. 9. Chariots and horsemen also went up with him; the camp was very impressive. 10. They came to the Bramble Barn beyond the Yarden and there they held a very great and impressive lamentation; he arranged a seven-day mourning period for his father. 11. The Canaanite inhabitant[s] of the land saw the mourning in the Bramble Barn and they said: "This is an impressive mourning for Mitzrayim!" Therefore he named it Mitzrayim-in-Mourning; it is beyond the Yarden. 12. Then his sons did for him as he had commanded them. 13. His sons bore him into the land of Canaan and buried him in the cave of the field of Makhpelah, which field Abraham had bought as a burial property from Ephron the Ḥittite before Mamre. 14. Yosef and his brothers and all those who had gone up with him to bury his father returned to Mitzrayim after he had buried his father. 15. Yosef's brothers saw that their father had died, and they said: "What if Yosef

CHAPTER L

15. As long as children have their father or mother, the parents are the element that holds them together. There may be slight disagreements even among the best of children, but as long as their parents are alive, each dissonance will vanish because of the love and devotion they all feel toward their parents. However, once their parents have died, the bond is loosened; the children no longer meet so frequently and they grow apart. It would have been quite a natural thing for this to happen here. The brothers "saw," they could feel that their father was gone. In such a situation, if one brother has done wrong to another, the victim must

holds a silent grudge against us after all? He might requite to us all the evil we did to him." 16. They therefore gave instruction to tell Yosef: "Your father has given instructions before his death, as follows: 17. 'Say this to Yosef: O please forgive the crime of your brothers and their sin, that they did evil to you.' And now, please grant forgiveness for the crime of the servants of the God of your father." Yosef wept when they said this to him. 18. Then his brothers also went and threw themselves down before him and said: "Here we are your slaves." 19. But Yosef said to them: "Do not be afraid! For am I in the place of God? 20. Even if you meant to do evil to me, God meant it for good, in order to bring about what is at present, in order to keep a numerous nation alive. 21. And now, do not be afraid! I will provide for you and your children." He comforted them and spoke to their hearts. 22. So Yosef lived in Mitzrayim, he and his father's house; and Yosef lived one hundred and ten years. 23. Yosef saw children of the third generation of Ephraim, also children of Makhir, the son of Menashe, were born upon Yosef's knees. 24. Yosef said to his brothers: "I am dying. And God will surely remember you again one day and bring you up from this land to the land which He swore to Abraham, Yitzhak and Yaakov." 25. And Yosef made the sons of Yisrael swear as follows: "If God will remember you again one day, then you shall bring my bones up from this place." 26. Yosef died at the age of one hundred and ten years; they embalmed him and he was placed into a coffin in Mitzrayim in accordance with his wish.

כָּל־הָרָעָ֗ה אֲשֶׁ֥ר גָּמַ֖לְנוּ אֹתֽוֹ: טז וַיְצַוּ֕וּ אֶל־יוֹסֵ֖ף לֵאמֹ֑ר אָבִ֣יךָ צִוָּ֔ה לִפְנֵ֥י מוֹת֖וֹ לֵאמֹֽר: יז כֹּֽה־תֹאמְר֣וּ לְיוֹסֵ֗ף אָ֣נָּ֡א שָׂ֣א נָ֠א פֶּ֣שַׁע אַחֶ֤יךָ וְחַטָּאתָם֙ כִּי־רָעָ֣ה גְמָל֔וּךָ וְעַתָּ֗ה שָׂ֤א נָא֙ לְפֶ֔שַׁע עַבְדֵ֖י אֱלֹהֵ֣י אָבִ֑יךָ וַיֵּ֥בְךְּ יוֹסֵ֖ף בְּדַבְּרָ֥ם אֵלָֽיו: יח וַיֵּֽלְכוּ֙ גַּם־אֶחָ֔יו וַיִּפְּל֖וּ לְפָנָ֑יו וַיֹּ֣אמְר֔וּ הִנֶּ֥נּֽוּ לְךָ֖ לַעֲבָדִֽים: יט וַיֹּ֧אמֶר אֲלֵהֶ֛ם יוֹסֵ֖ף אַל־תִּירָ֑אוּ כִּ֛י הֲתַ֥חַת אֱלֹהִ֖ים אָֽנִי: כ וְאַתֶּ֕ם חֲשַׁבְתֶּ֥ם עָלַ֖י רָעָ֑ה אֱלֹהִים֙ חֲשָׁבָ֣הּ לְטֹבָ֔ה לְמַ֗עַן עֲשֹׂ֛ה כַּיּ֥וֹם הַזֶּ֖ה לְהַחֲיֹ֥ת עַם־רָֽב: שביעי כא וְעַתָּה֙ אַל־תִּירָ֔אוּ אָנֹכִ֛י אֲכַלְכֵּ֥ל אֶתְכֶ֖ם וְאֶֽת־טַפְּכֶ֑ם וַיְנַחֵ֣ם אוֹתָ֔ם וַיְדַבֵּ֖ר עַל־לִבָּֽם: כב וַיֵּ֤שֶׁב יוֹסֵף֙ בְּמִצְרַ֔יִם ה֖וּא וּבֵ֣ית אָבִ֑יו וַיְחִ֣י יוֹסֵ֔ף מֵאָ֖ה וָעֶ֥שֶׂר שָׁנִֽים: מפטיר כג וַיַּ֤רְא יוֹסֵף֙ לְאֶפְרַ֔יִם בְּנֵ֖י שִׁלֵּשִׁ֑ים גַּ֗ם בְּנֵ֤י מָכִיר֙ בֶּן־מְנַשֶּׁ֔ה יֻלְּד֖וּ עַל־בִּרְכֵּ֥י יוֹסֵֽף: כד וַיֹּ֤אמֶר יוֹסֵף֙ אֶל־אֶחָ֔יו אָנֹכִ֖י מֵ֑ת וֵֽאלֹהִ֞ים פָּקֹ֧ד יִפְקֹ֣ד אֶתְכֶ֗ם וְהֶעֱלָ֤ה אֶתְכֶם֙ מִן־הָאָ֣רֶץ הַזֹּ֔את אֶל־הָאָ֔רֶץ אֲשֶׁ֥ר נִשְׁבַּ֛ע לְאַבְרָהָ֥ם לְיִצְחָ֖ק וּֽלְיַעֲקֹֽב: כה וַיַּשְׁבַּ֣ע יוֹסֵ֔ף אֶת־בְּנֵ֥י יִשְׂרָאֵ֖ל לֵאמֹ֑ר פָּקֹ֨ד יִפְקֹ֤ד אֱלֹהִים֙ אֶתְכֶ֔ם וְהַעֲלִתֶ֥ם אֶת־עַצְמֹתַ֖י מִזֶּֽה: כו וַיָּ֣מָת יוֹסֵ֔ף בֶּן־מֵאָ֥ה וָעֶ֖שֶׂר שָׁנִ֑ים וַיַּחַנְט֣וּ אֹת֔וֹ וַיִּ֥ישֶׂם בָּאָר֖וֹן בְּמִצְרָֽיִם: חזק

---

take particular pains to treat him with the utmost friendliness if the guilty one is not to believe that his victim wishes him ill. . . .

19. "God may judge the feelings and intentions of men. But I, a mere man, need only consider the consequences [of what was done to me], and when I consider these, I find that in fact I owe you a great debt of gratitude."

25. He made them swear it not as his brothers but as בְּנֵי יִשְׂרָאֵל [sons of Yisrael]; the promise was to be binding also upon future generations. It was not presumptuous of him to make this request of them. It was they who had originally brought him down to Mitzrayim, so he felt he had a right to impose this obligation upon them as a small token of atonement. At the same time, this obligation, along with the remains upon which they were pledged to fulfill it, symbolizes the trust with which they should look forward to their eventual permanent return to Canaan.

The Haftarah for this Sidra may be found on page 842.

SHEMOTH שמות
[EXODUS]

✦—◦◇◦—✦

"The Second Book begins the history of the Jews as a nation."

—*Commentary on Chapter 1, Verse 1*

שמות

SHEMOTH

I 1. And these are the names of the sons of Yisrael who came to Mitzrayim; every man and his household came with Yaakov. 2. Reuben, Shimeon, Levi and Yehudah. 3. Yissakhar, Zebulun and Binyamin. 4. Dan and Naphtali, Gad and Asher. 5. All the souls that descended from Yaakov were seventy souls; and Yosef was already in Mitzrayim. 6. Yosef died and all his brothers and all that generation. 7. The sons of Yisrael were fruitful by reason of numerous births; they increased most abundantly and were exceedingly strong, and the land was filled with them. 8. Now a new king rose up

א א וְאֵ֗לֶּה שְׁמוֹת֙ בְּנֵ֣י יִשְׂרָאֵ֔ל הַבָּאִ֖ים מִצְרָ֑יְמָה אֵ֣ת יַעֲקֹ֔ב אִ֥ישׁ וּבֵית֖וֹ בָּֽאוּ: ב רְאוּבֵ֣ן שִׁמְע֔וֹן לֵוִ֖י וִֽיהוּדָֽה: ג יִשָּׂשכָ֥ר זְבוּלֻ֖ן וּבְנְיָמִֽן: ד דָּ֚ן וְנַפְתָּלִ֔י גָּ֖ד וְאָשֵֽׁר: ה וַֽיְהִ֗י כָּל־נֶ֛פֶשׁ יֹצְאֵ֥י יֶ֖רֶךְ־יַעֲקֹ֑ב שִׁבְעִ֣ים נָ֑פֶשׁ וְיוֹסֵ֖ף הָיָ֥ה בְמִצְרָֽיִם: ו וַיָּ֤מָת יוֹסֵף֙ וְכָל־אֶחָ֔יו וְכֹ֖ל הַדּ֥וֹר הַהֽוּא: ז וּבְנֵ֣י יִשְׂרָאֵ֗ל פָּר֧וּ וַֽיִּשְׁרְצ֛וּ וַיִּרְבּ֥וּ וַיַּֽעַצְמ֖וּ בִּמְאֹ֣ד מְאֹ֑ד וַתִּמָּלֵ֥א הָאָ֖רֶץ אֹתָֽם: פ ח וַיָּ֥קָם

CHAPTER I

1. The Second Book begins the history of the Jews as a nation. The text makes the transition from the life stories of individuals and families to the history of the nation by recalling the names of individuals already known to us as the basic pillars of the Jewish national entity. וְאֵלֶּה, "and these are," the very same men, each a personality in his own right, from whom the Jewish nation is to spring forth: "Every man and his household came with Yaakov."

There would come a time when the corpus of the nation, dismembered by Pharaoh's assaults, would lie prone upon the ground and seem easy prey for the vultures of history (as had been shown to their ancestor [Abraham] in the prophetic vision [of the "covenant between the pieces" — Genesis 15:9–21]). But then, at God's call, that nation was to rise again "in its blood" [Ezekiel 16:6] to eternal life. At that time God would begin the upbuilding of His people not with the rooftops, as it were, but with the rocklike foundations of the home (cf. "a lamb for each parental home, a lamb for each household"—Exodus 12:3), which are based upon the mutual bonds that unite parents and their children.

We are shown here that the foundations for God's eternal nation had existed long before that time; they had only been sacked by force prior to the redemption and rehabilitation of the nation. The sons of Israel had brought these foundations with them when they journeyed down into Egypt, into that womb out of which, amidst pain and suffering, they were to be born as a nation.

אֵת יַעֲקֹב אִישׁ וּבֵיתוֹ [every man and his household came with Yaakov]. Though each one of them already had an independent household of his own, they all still cling firmly and closely to Jacob. . . . All of them together are part of the same ancient tree, but each has become an independent branch, the center of a family of his own. They are all still the children of Jacob, but now they also have children of their own. This family spirit which inspires each son to build his own household, but only as a branch of his father's house, and which enables every father to live on in his children and his children's children, forming a close, eternal bond that binds the parents to their children and the children to their parents—this is the root of Israel's eternal flowering. Herein lies the secret of the eternity of the Jewish people.

8. Unfortunately these opening sentences do not permit a conclusive identification of the prime causes of this, the earliest instance of Jew-hatred. The statement "Now a new king rose up" definitely does not imply a normal, legitimate dynastic change. The expression קוּם עַל ["rose up over"] in Scripture always indicates the violent overthrow of one ruler by another. It seems, therefore, that the old dynasty had been overthrown and that the land and people of Egypt had fallen to the power of a foreign dynasty which had invaded the country.

אֲשֶׁר לֹא יָדַע אֶת יוֹסֵף [who knew nothing of Yosef]. Had the new dynasty been an indigenous one, Joseph would not have been unknown to the new king. It is significant that the explanation given for all the Jew-hatred which followed is that the new king knew nothing of Joseph. The people—as distinct from the king—did know about Joseph and did not look askance at the Jewish province and at the Jewish

over Mitzrayim, who knew nothing of Yosef.
9. And he said to his people: "Lo! the
sons of Yisrael are a nation, too numerous
and too mighty for us. 10. Come, let us
deal cleverly with them, lest they multiply,
and then if, in the course of events, there
should be a war, they will join our enemies,
or fight against us themselves, and move up
from their land." 11. They set treasury

מֶ֥לֶךְ־חָדָ֖שׁ עַל־מִצְרָ֑יִם אֲשֶׁ֥ר לֹֽא־יָדַ֖ע אֶת־
יוֹסֵֽף׃ ט וַיֹּ֖אמֶר אֶל־עַמּ֑וֹ הִנֵּ֗ה עַ֚ם בְּנֵ֣י יִשְׂרָאֵ֔ל
רַ֥ב וְעָצ֖וּם מִמֶּֽנּוּ׃ י הָ֥בָה נִֽתְחַכְּמָ֖ה ל֑וֹ פֶּן־יִרְבֶּ֗ה
וְהָיָ֞ה כִּֽי־תִקְרֶ֤אנָה מִלְחָמָה֙ וְנוֹסַ֤ף גַּם־הוּא֙ עַל־
שֹׂ֣נְאֵ֔ינוּ וְנִלְחַם־בָּ֖נוּ וְעָלָ֥ה מִן־הָאָֽרֶץ׃

national entity that was developing there. The people considered the Jews as benefactors, not as intruders, and did not see their prosperity as a threat to their own security.

9. . . . The word מִמֶּנּוּ ["for us"] probably should be interpreted in the same sense as Abimelekh's words to Isaac (Genesis 26:16) לֵךְ מֵעִמָּנוּ כִּי עָצַמְתָּ מִמֶּנּוּ מְאֹד ["Go away from us because you have become much too mighty for us"], which means simply: "You have become too mighty for us; we cannot stand idly by while you, one individual, grow mighty, mightier by far than any other individual in our midst."

The population of ancient Egypt was divided into castes; it consisted of various national entities. So, in a similar vein, the new king of Egypt could now say: "Look at that Jewish people; they keep together like one single נֶפֶשׁ [soul]. They are becoming too mighty for us; there is not one caste among us as numerous and with such a great potential for power as they."

In broad outlines, let us note that: 1) This earliest instance of Jew-hatred was not caused by anything the Jews had done. Pharaoh was unable to charge them with any wrongdoing. Had he been able to level a specific accusation against them he would not have had to resort to חָכְמָה [dealing "cleverly" with them (Verse 10)] but could have taken overt action against them. 2) This very first instance of Jew-hatred did not arise spontaneously from amidst the people but had been fomented by the ruling circles; it was they who had to goad the people into envying the Jews. Jew-hatred was a political tool which the new ruler used in order to consolidate his own power. There is little that is new under the sun, and basically all the phenomena of history are as old as history itself. Whenever a despot sought to oppress his subjects he would throw at their mercy another people whom they could oppress in turn, so that they would not turn against him. Many anti-Jewish laws have owed their origins to such a policy.

The author of these, the very first anti-Jewish laws, may well have been motivated by similar considerations. He sought to compensate the downtrodden Egyptian people for his despotic rule by creating for their benefit a pariah caste upon which all the other castes could look down with contempt. This, he hoped, would give his oppressed subjects new self-assurance so that they would imagine themselves to be more free than the caste they had been taught to despise. Incidentally, the fact that Pharaoh could not tax the Jews with anything more serious than their fast rate of reproduction, and that he had to cite reasons of national interest to justify the harsh measures he intended to enact, is cogent proof of the social and moral probity of the Jews. . . .

10. . . . It would be difficult to understand why the possibility that the Jews might leave the land should have caused such great apprehension. After all, they had not yet been made slaves. Hence one could only assume that by this time the presence of the Jews had become so important and beneficial to the state that though the Egyptian ruler might have wished there would not be so many of them, he was afraid to see them leave altogether and in fact regarded their presence in limited numbers as both useful and necessary.

It seems more likely, then, that the words עָלָה מִן הָאָרֶץ [literally, "move up from *the* land"] do not imply an apprehension that the Jews might leave the land of Mitzrayim but fear that the Jews might move out of the province of Goshen, which had been assigned to them as "their land," and spread all over the rest of the country.

But this still would not explain why a war would be needed to set off such a development. Perhaps the king meant to express, in fact, two distinct apprehensions. One who hates another usually projects his own hostile feelings onto the object of his hatred. Pharaoh might have thought: "The Jews are our enemies and not to be trusted. If they become numerous and war should come, they will side with our enemies. But even if this does not happen, they will multiply so greatly that Goshen will no longer hold them all and they will swarm all over the land, ready to attack us." During later periods in history, a guilty conscience toward the Jews in their midst was to lead other nations also to accuse the Jews of siding with the enemies of the state—the Moors, the Turks, the French, and so forth, whichever the case might be. . . .

officials over them in order to afflict them with their° burdens. And so they built for Pharaoh storage cities, Pithom and Ramses. 12. But the more they afflicted them, the more they multiplied and spread; they became sick of everything because of the presence of the sons of Yisrael. 13. Therefore the Mitzrites made slaves of the sons of Yisrael with crushing harshness. 14. They embittered their lives by means of hard labor with clay and with bricks and with all

יא וַיָּשִׂימוּ עָלָיו שָׂרֵי מִסִּים לְמַעַן עַנֹּתוֹ בְּסִבְלֹתָם וַיִּבֶן עָרֵי מִסְכְּנוֹת לְפַרְעֹה אֶת־פִּתֹם וְאֶת־רַעַמְסֵס: יב וְכַאֲשֶׁר יְעַנּוּ אֹתוֹ כֵּן יִרְבֶּה וְכֵן יִפְרֹץ וַיָּקֻצוּ מִפְּנֵי בְּנֵי יִשְׂרָאֵל: יג וַיַּעֲבִדוּ מִצְרַיִם אֶת־בְּנֵי יִשְׂרָאֵל בְּפָרֶךְ: יד וַיְמָרְרוּ אֶת־ חַיֵּיהֶם בַּעֲבֹדָה קָשָׁה בְּחֹמֶר וּבִלְבֵנִים וּבְכָל־

°*Note to the English translation:* The literal rendering of this verse, according to Hirsch's original German translation, would be: "They [i.e., the Egyptians] set treasury officials over

it [i.e., the people] in order to afflict it with their burdens [i.e., with the burdens imposed upon the Israelites by the Egyptians]." [G.H.]

11. The Jews as a whole were regarded as a source of revenue from which the state was to make as much money as possible. The Jews were, after all, aliens, strangers in the land, who, it was argued, could be made to pay for the very air they breathed. For this reason they were placed under the jurisdiction of the treasury.

סִבְלֹתָם *[their burdens].* סבל does not denote primarily a burden imposed upon the bearer for the sole purpose of oppressing him but rather a burden in the sense of an object to be supported and cared for by its bearer. Thus the concept as such has no negative connotations. סִבְלֹתָם in this verse denote burdens imposed because they were deemed necessary for the welfare of the state. However, the text reveals the true purpose of this burden: לְמַעַן עַנֹּתוֹ ["to afflict them"]. The Jews must not be permitted to become too self-assured; therefore, ways must be found to victimize them by legal means.

    °   °   °

12. The tax imposed upon them by law did not achieve its purpose; the more the Egyptians sought to weaken the Jews, the more numerous and commanding did the Jewish presence become, so that the Egyptians literally became sick, not "of the Jews" but "of everything" because the Jews seemed to be everywhere. (The word יָקֻצוּ ["they became sick"] is accentuated by a זָקֵף גָּדוֹל, a cantillation mark that separates the word from what follows). As the *Yalkut* to Verse 7, "and the land was filled with them," puts it: "If the Egyptians went to the theater, it was full of Jews; if they went to the circus, again, the place was full of Jews."

13. Now the ill-treatment of the Jews entered a second phase. Up to this point certain burdens had been imposed upon them, ostensibly under the law of the land, because they were "foreigners." But now they were declared to be slaves. גֵּרוּת [alienhood] was followed by עַבְדוּת [enslavement] בְּפָרֶךְ ["with crush-

ing harshness"]. Elsewhere in Scripture this last-mentioned term occurs only in the form פָּרֹכֶת [the curtain that divided the Holy of Holies from the rest of the Sanctuary]; accordingly, the word בְּפָרֶךְ in the present passage would logically convey the connotation of "screening off" or "dividing." The Egyptians separated the Jews from the rest of the population, outlawing them and declaring them slaves. They set up a "partition," as it were, to isolate the Jews. The Jews were no longer to be regarded even as human beings.

In the Talmud the term פרך is used to denote "crumbling" [a division into many small pieces], cf. Ḥullin 46b נִפְרֶכֶת בְּצִפֹּרֶן ["it crumbles with the nail"]. Accordingly, our text would convey the thought that the Egyptians condemned the Jews to the status of slaves with a harshness intended to crush whatever strength the Jews might still possess.

14. . . . Now a third degree of persecution was added: "They embittered their lives." One can be a slave and be forced to perform hard labor and yet not be exposed to wanton abuse. The work assigned may be hard but still compatible with the worker's strength and ability. But here, if פרך denotes a harshness designed to crush the slave and to break his strength, we are told that the Egyptians embittered the lives of the Jews in twofold measure: they purposely assigned to the Jewish slaves tasks that would be beyond their strength. . . . In addition to this contrived harshness, which kept the slave laborer from taking pleasure in any of his work, they embittered the lives of the Jews with ingenious torments. Thus all the three phases: גֵּרוּת [alienhood], עַבְדוּת [slavery] and עִנּוּי [affliction], which had been foretold to Abraham, had become a reality in Egypt. . . . At the root of this unspeakable abuse was גֵּרוּת: the concept that an alien had no rights. The laws of Judaism concerning the rights of aliens offer the most striking contrast to the laws of other nations to this very day. . . .

manner of labor in the field; they embittered all their labors which they had made them perform, with harshness. 15. And the king of Mitzrayim spoke to the Hebrew midwives, of whom the name of the one was Shifrah and the name of the other Puah. 16. And he said: "Whenever you deliver Hebrew women, observe the laboring womb: If it is a son, you shall kill him; if it is a daughter, she may live." 17. But the midwives feared God and did not do as the king of Mitzrayim had commanded them, but they kept the [male] children alive. 18. And the king of Mitzrayim called for the midwives and said to them: "Why have you done this thing? To have kept the [male] children alive!" 19. The midwives replied to Pharaoh: "Because the Hebrew women are not like the Mitzrite women; they are lively, and they give birth even before the midwife can come to them." 20. And God dealt well with the midwives, and the people multiplied and became exceedingly strong. 21. And it came to pass, because the midwives feared God and He set up homes for them, 22. that Pharaoh commanded all his people [saying]: "Every son that is born you shall throw into the river and every daughter you shall allow to live."

II 1. And there went a man of the house of Levi and took to wife the daughter of Levi. 2. The woman became a mother and bore a son. When she saw that he was [a] good [child] she kept

עֲבֹדָה בַּשָּׂדֶה אֵת כָּל־עֲבֹדָתָם אֲשֶׁר־עָבְדוּ בָהֶם בְּפָרֶךְ: טו וַיֹּאמֶר מֶלֶךְ מִצְרַיִם לַמְיַלְּדֹת הָעִבְרִיֹּת אֲשֶׁר שֵׁם הָאַחַת שִׁפְרָה וְשֵׁם הַשֵּׁנִית פּוּעָה: טז וַיֹּאמֶר בְּיַלֶּדְכֶן אֶת־הָעִבְרִיּוֹת וּרְאִיתֶן עַל־הָאָבְנָיִם אִם־בֵּן הוּא וַהֲמִתֶּן אֹתוֹ וְאִם־בַּת הִוא וָחָיָה: יז וַתִּירֶאןָ הַמְיַלְּדֹת אֶת־הָאֱלֹהִים וְלֹא עָשׂוּ כַּאֲשֶׁר דִּבֶּר אֲלֵיהֶן מֶלֶךְ מִצְרָיִם וַתְּחַיֶּיןָ אֶת־הַיְלָדִים: שני יח וַיִּקְרָא מֶלֶךְ־מִצְרַיִם לַמְיַלְּדֹת וַיֹּאמֶר לָהֶן מַדּוּעַ עֲשִׂיתֶן הַדָּבָר הַזֶּה וַתְּחַיֶּיןָ אֶת־הַיְלָדִים: יט וַתֹּאמַרְןָ הַמְיַלְּדֹת אֶל־פַּרְעֹה כִּי לֹא כַנָּשִׁים הַמִּצְרִיֹּת הָעִבְרִיֹּת כִּי־חָיוֹת הֵנָּה בְּטֶרֶם תָּבוֹא אֲלֵהֶן הַמְיַלֶּדֶת וְיָלָדוּ: כ וַיֵּיטֶב אֱלֹהִים לַמְיַלְּדֹת וַיִּרֶב הָעָם וַיַּעַצְמוּ מְאֹד: כא וַיְהִי כִּי־ יָרְאוּ הַמְיַלְּדֹת אֶת־הָאֱלֹהִים וַיַּעַשׂ לָהֶם בָּתִּים: כב וַיְצַו פַּרְעֹה לְכָל־עַמּוֹ לֵאמֹר כָּל־הַבֵּן הַיִּלּוֹד הַיְאֹרָה תַּשְׁלִיכֻהוּ וְכָל־הַבַּת תְּחַיּוּן: פ ב א וַיֵּלֶךְ אִישׁ מִבֵּית לֵוִי וַיִּקַּח אֶת־בַּת־לֵוִי: ב וַתַּהַר הָאִשָּׁה וַתֵּלֶד בֵּן וַתֵּרֶא אֹתוֹ כִּי־טוֹב

15–16. When indirect methods failed, the king sought to accomplish his purpose by a method that would be more direct but would still be masked as cleverly as possible. . . .

21. "For them" refers to the [Jewish] people. When the king saw that, despite the law he had enacted, the Jews continued to increase in strength and numbers and to establish new families, he flew into a rage and officially ordered the extermination of all male Jewish infants.

CHAPTER II

1. . . . At a time such as this it took courage to become a father or a mother. For this reason the text does not read, "And there *was* a man of the house of Levi and he took . . ." but וַיֵּלֶךְ ["And there *went* . . ."]. The verb וַיֵּלֶךְ indicates the determination required for such a step in those days. Also, the text does not read וַיִּקַּח בַּת לֵוִי ["and took . . . *a* daughter of Levi"] but אֶת בַּת לֵוִי [". . . *the* daughter of Levi"]; i.e., a woman already predestined for this marriage. The narrative which follows indicates that when this marriage took place the couple already had a daughter and another son. This would confirm what our Sages have noted: Moses was not a child of his parents' original marriage. The man had parted from his wife following the king's decree to kill all male infants, but had then decided to return to her in order to defy that very decree.

him hidden for three months.   3. She
could not keep him hidden any longer; she
therefore took for him a little chest of
papyrus, coated it with the proper clay and
pitch, laid the child into it and then placed
it among the reeds by the banks of the river.
4. His sister placed herself at a distance
to know what would happen to him.
5. And Pharaoh's daughter came down to
bathe at the river, and her maidens walked
along the river's edge. She saw the little
chest among the reeds, sent her handmaid
there and had it fetched.   6. She opened it
and saw the child, and lo! a crying boy! She
was moved to pity for him and said: "This is
one of the Hebrews' children."   7. And
his sister said to Pharaoh's daughter: "Shall
I go and call for you a nursing woman from
among the Hebrews to nurse the child for
you?"   8. Pharaoh's daughter said to her:
"Go." And the young girl went and called
the mother of the child.   9. Pharaoh's
daughter said to her: "Take this child away
and nurse it for me; I will pay you your
wages." The woman took the child and
nursed it.   10. When the child had grown
she brought it to Pharaoh's daughter and it
became a son to her. She called him Moshe
"because," she said, "I drew him from the
water."   11. It came to pass in those days,
when Moshe had grown up, that he went
out to his brethren and looked upon their
burdens. And he saw a Mitzrite man beating
a Hebrew man, one of his brethren.
12. He turned this way and that, and
when he saw that no one was there, he
struck down the Mitzrite and hid him in the
sand.   13. On the second day he went out
and came upon two Hebrew men fighting.
He said to the one who was in the wrong:
"Why are you striking down your neighbor?"   14. He replied: "Who has made

הוּא וַתִּצְפְּנֵהוּ שְׁלֹשָׁה יְרָחִים: ג וְלֹא־יָכְלָה
עוֹד הַצְּפִינוֹ וַתִּקַּח־לוֹ תֵּבַת גֹּמֶא וַתַּחְמְרָה
בַחֵמָר וּבַזָּפֶת וַתָּשֶׂם בָּהּ אֶת־הַיֶּלֶד וַתָּשֶׂם בַּסּוּף
עַל־שְׂפַת הַיְאֹר: ד וַתֵּתַצַּב אֲחֹתוֹ מֵרָחֹק לְדֵעָה
מַה־יֵּעָשֶׂה לוֹ: ה וַתֵּרֶד בַּת־פַּרְעֹה לִרְחֹץ עַל־
הַיְאֹר וְנַעֲרֹתֶיהָ הֹלְכֹת עַל־יַד הַיְאֹר וַתֵּרֶא אֶת־
הַתֵּבָה בְּתוֹךְ הַסּוּף וַתִּשְׁלַח אֶת־אֲמָתָהּ וַתִּקָּחֶהָ:
ו וַתִּפְתַּח וַתִּרְאֵהוּ אֶת־הַיֶּלֶד וְהִנֵּה־נַעַר בֹּכֶה
וַתַּחְמֹל עָלָיו וַתֹּאמֶר מִיַּלְדֵי הָעִבְרִים זֶה:
ז וַתֹּאמֶר אֲחֹתוֹ אֶל־בַּת־פַּרְעֹה הַאֵלֵךְ וְקָרָאתִי
לָךְ אִשָּׁה מֵינֶקֶת מִן הָעִבְרִיֹּת וְתֵינִק לָךְ אֶת־
הַיָּלֶד: ח וַתֹּאמֶר־לָהּ בַּת־פַּרְעֹה לֵכִי וַתֵּלֶךְ
הָעַלְמָה וַתִּקְרָא אֶת־אֵם הַיָּלֶד: ט וַתֹּאמֶר לָהּ
בַּת־פַּרְעֹה הֵילִיכִי אֶת־הַיֶּלֶד הַזֶּה וְהֵינִקִהוּ לִי
וַאֲנִי אֶתֵּן אֶת־שְׂכָרֵךְ וַתִּקַּח הָאִשָּׁה הַיֶּלֶד
וַתְּנִיקֵהוּ: י וַיִּגְדַּל הַיֶּלֶד וַתְּבִאֵהוּ לְבַת־פַּרְעֹה
וַיְהִי־לָהּ לְבֵן וַתִּקְרָא שְׁמוֹ מֹשֶׁה וַתֹּאמֶר כִּי
מִן־הַמַּיִם מְשִׁיתִהוּ: שלישי יא וַיְהִי | בַּיָּמִים
הָהֵם וַיִּגְדַּל מֹשֶׁה וַיֵּצֵא אֶל־אֶחָיו וַיַּרְא
בְּסִבְלֹתָם וַיַּרְא אִישׁ מִצְרִי מַכֶּה אִישׁ־עִבְרִי
מֵאֶחָיו: יב וַיִּפֶן כֹּה וָכֹה וַיַּרְא כִּי־אֵין אִישׁ וַיַּךְ
אֶת־הַמִּצְרִי וַיִּטְמְנֵהוּ בַּחוֹל: יג וַיֵּצֵא בַּיּוֹם
הַשֵּׁנִי וְהִנֵּה שְׁנֵי־אֲנָשִׁים עִבְרִים נִצִּים וַיֹּאמֶר
לָרָשָׁע לָמָּה תַכֶּה רֵעֶךָ: יד וַיֹּאמֶר מִי שָׂמְךָ

---

10. . . . By giving him this name [Moshe] Pharaoh's
daughter meant to impress upon him that "as long as
he lives he must never forget that he was thrown into
the water and that I drew him up there." For this
reason his heart should always be filled with compassion for the sufferings of others and he should be ready
at all times to be a מֹשֶׁה, to "draw out" others from distress. . . .

14. The words, "Who has made you a man . . ."
reveal, even at this early stage in our history, a trait that
characterizes us to this day, one that lies at the root of
all our flaws—and our virtues—as a nation. Six
hundred thousand men cannot muster the courage to
defend their children against the minions of one non-
Jewish tyrant, but not one of them will accept the
authority of a fellow Jew. Here they will not submit to

לְאִישׁ שַׂר וְשֹׁפֵט עָלֵינוּ הַלְהָרְגֵנִי אַתָּה אֹמֵר
כַּאֲשֶׁר הָרַגְתָּ אֶת־הַמִּצְרִי וַיִּירָא מֹשֶׁה וַיֹּאמַר
אָכֵן נוֹדַע הַדָּבָר׃ טו וַיִּשְׁמַע פַּרְעֹה אֶת־הַדָּבָר
הַזֶּה וַיְבַקֵּשׁ לַהֲרֹג אֶת־מֹשֶׁה וַיִּבְרַח מֹשֶׁה מִפְּנֵי
פַרְעֹה וַיֵּשֶׁב בְּאֶרֶץ־מִדְיָן וַיֵּשֶׁב עַל־הַבְּאֵר׃
טז וּלְכֹהֵן מִדְיָן שֶׁבַע בָּנוֹת וַתָּבֹאנָה וַתִּדְלֶנָה
וַתְּמַלֶּאנָה אֶת־הָרְהָטִים לְהַשְׁקוֹת צֹאן אֲבִיהֶן׃
יז וַיָּבֹאוּ הָרֹעִים וַיְגָרְשׁוּם וַיָּקָם מֹשֶׁה וַיּוֹשִׁעָן
וַיַּשְׁקְ אֶת־צֹאנָם׃ יח וַתָּבֹאנָה אֶל־רְעוּאֵל
אֲבִיהֶן וַיֹּאמֶר מַדּוּעַ מִהַרְתֶּן בֹּא הַיּוֹם׃
יט וַתֹּאמַרְןָ אִישׁ מִצְרִי הִצִּילָנוּ מִיַּד הָרֹעִים
וְגַם־דָּלֹה דָלָה לָנוּ וַיַּשְׁקְ אֶת־הַצֹּאן׃ כ וַיֹּאמֶר
אֶל־בְּנֹתָיו וְאַיּוֹ לָמָּה זֶּה עֲזַבְתֶּן אֶת־הָאִישׁ
קִרְאֶן לוֹ וְיֹאכַל לָחֶם׃ כא וַיּוֹאֶל מֹשֶׁה לָשֶׁבֶת
אֶת־הָאִישׁ וַיִּתֵּן אֶת־צִפֹּרָה בִתּוֹ לְמֹשֶׁה׃
כב וַתֵּלֶד בֵּן וַיִּקְרָא אֶת־שְׁמוֹ גֵּרְשֹׁם כִּי אָמַר גֵּר
הָיִיתִי בְּאֶרֶץ נָכְרִיָּה׃ פ כג וַיְהִי בַיָּמִים הָרַבִּים
הָהֵם וַיָּמָת מֶלֶךְ מִצְרַיִם וַיֵּאָנְחוּ בְנֵי־יִשְׂרָאֵל

you a man, a prince and a judge over us? Do you intend to kill me as you killed the Mitzrite?" Moshe was frightened and said: "So the matter is known." 15. Pharaoh heard of this matter and sought to kill Moshe. Moshe fled from Pharaoh and settled down in the land of Midian; there he sat down near the well. 16. Now the priest of Midian had seven daughters; they came, drew water and filled the watering troughs to water their father's sheep. 17. And the shepherds came and drove them away. But Moshe stood up and helped them and watered their sheep. 18. They came to their father Reuel, and he said: "How is it that you have come home so quickly today?" 19. They answered: "A Mitzrite man rescued us from the hand of the shepherds, and he also drew all the water for us and watered the sheep." 20. He said to his daughters: "And where is he now? Why did you leave the man? Invite him so that he may have something to eat." 21. Moshe decided to remain with the man, and he gave Moshe his daughter Tzipporah. 22. She bore a son, whom he called Gershom, for he said: "I was a stranger in a foreign land." 23. It came to pass in the course of these many days that the king of Mitzrayim died, and

human authority and will regard even the most justifiable reprimand [from a fellow Jew] as a presumption, as a denial of the principle that all Jews are equal. Despite our long training in the school of exile we have not yet broken ourselves entirely of this habit. Of what intractable stuff must we have been, then, before we entered this training course! It was not the most tractable but the most intractable race of men—עַז שֶׁבָּאוּמּוֹת—that God chose for Himself. It is to this stiff-necked people that He gave His אֵשׁ דָּת, His "Law of Fire." The fiery strength of His Law was to be proven first of all by its ability to subdue this nation. We had to be pounded by harsh blows of fate to make us as tough and at the same time as pliable as steel. Pliant in our relationship with God but unbending, tough and firm against all human authority. Such stiff-neckedness can run riot and choose the wrong object. But without it, we would never have become the immortal People of the Law.

22. ***I was a stranger in a foreign land.*** The meaning of this statement is not quite clear. Where else could one be a stranger except in a foreign land? Also, Moses uses the past tense: הָיִיתִי ["I was"], when in fact Moses was still a "stranger" when he named his son Gershom. These words apparently convey the following thought: One can be a גֵּר [stranger] in a place but after a short time one comes to feel at home there, and the land is no longer נָכְרִיָּה [foreign]. By giving his first-born the name Gershom, Moses means to declare that he still does not belong in Midian. Although he is a free man in Midian, free of care and a family man in his own right, his heart is still with his people in Mitzrayim. But to express such feelings openly would imply a criticism of the land in which he now resides. Hence we can understand why he said, "I *was* a stranger" rather than, "I *am* a stranger." . . .

23. . . . We believe that the connection between the death of the king and the sighing of the people because of the bondage is obvious. As long as the individuals who first initiated so great a national outrage as the enslavement of an entire free race are still alive, there is hope that their conscience will bestir itself and will cause them to abolish the injustice which resulted

the sons of Yisrael sighed and cried out because of the bondage, and their cry for help rose up to God on account of the bondage. 24. God heard their cry of distress, and God remembered His covenant with Abraham, with Yitzḥak and with Yaakov. 25. And God saw the sons of Yisrael, and God took note of it.

III 1. Meanwhile, Moshe had been tending the sheep of his father-in-law Yithro, the priest of Midian. He led the sheep along the pastureland and came to the mountain of God, to Ḥoreb. 2. And an angel of *God* appeared to him in the heart of a fire from the midst of a thorn bush. He saw, and lo! the thorn bush

מִן־הָעֲבֹדָה וַיִּזְעָקוּ וַתַּעַל שַׁוְעָתָם אֶל־הָאֱלֹהִים מִן־הָעֲבֹדָה: כד וַיִּשְׁמַע אֱלֹהִים אֶת־נַאֲקָתָם וַיִּזְכֹּר אֱלֹהִים אֶת־בְּרִיתוֹ אֶת־אַבְרָהָם אֶת־יִצְחָק וְאֶת־יַעֲקֹב: כה וַיַּרְא אֱלֹהִים אֶת־בְּנֵי יִשְׂרָאֵל וַיֵּדַע אֱלֹהִים: ס רביעי ג א וּמֹשֶׁה הָיָה רֹעֶה אֶת־צֹאן יִתְרוֹ חֹתְנוֹ כֹּהֵן מִדְיָן וַיִּנְהַג אֶת־ הַצֹּאן אַחַר הַמִּדְבָּר וַיָּבֹא אֶל־הַר הָאֱלֹהִים חֹרֵבָה: ב וַיֵּרָא מַלְאַךְ יְהוָה אֵלָיו בְּלַבַּת־אֵשׁ מִתּוֹךְ הַסְּנֶה וַיַּרְא וְהִנֵּה הַסְּנֶה בֹּעֵר בָּאֵשׁ

from their tyranny. But once an institution, no matter how glaring the injustice that gave rise to it, has passed, along with the power of the state, into the hands of new authorities who are not aware of its origins and who accept it as a traditional, legitimate prerogative of the state, the new government will not consider that it has the right to tamper with time-honored tradition. It will presume that all the institutions of the former regime have been sanctioned by the law of the land. Then the free people who have been turned into slaves with such satanic tyranny are doomed to remain pariahs forever. This is the curse of obsolescence inherent in the time-honored institutions of a state....

When the king of Mitzrayim died, the sons of Israel saw themselves doomed to eternal slavery; hence they sighed on account of their state of bondage.... Scripture states repeatedly that their sighing and their appeals to Divine justice were מִן־הָעֲבֹדָה ["because of the bondage"]. Their sighs and their cries for help were not on account of their physical burdens or their toil. They were strong, and able to endure much; besides, there was always the possibility of a change for the better in the treatment meted out to them. What caused them to cry out was, rather, the bondage to which they felt they had been condemned for all time as the result of the king's death. They appealed to God, the Judge, because of the injustice to which they had fallen victim.

24–25. ... God turned His eyes to the present situation: He saw the outward condition of the sons of Israel, and recognized the effect that it would have upon their character. Hence He made Israel the object of His הַשְׁגָּחָה פְּרָטִית [particular Providence]. This tells us, too, that the time had now come [of which Joseph had] said "God will surely remember you" [Genesis 50:24]. Prior to this time God had not concerned Himself with them, as it were; He had permitted events to take their

natural course. Whatever had befallen them up to this point was a natural consequence of their homelessness and of the moral decadence of the nation in which they dwelled. But now God intervened, and their deliverance was as good as accomplished.

CHAPTER III

1. ... It is most significant that the redemption of the Children of Israel begins at Mount Ḥoreb, which was to be the birthplace of the Law. Thus it is clear from the outset that the sole objective of this deliverance was מַתַּן תּוֹרָה [the giving of the Law]; that is, to lead the people to the place where they were to be constituted as the People of the Law.

2. לַבַּת, from לֵבָב i.e., לֵב, the "heart," the innermost part, the "middle" of the fire. Thus the angel appeared in the "middle" of the fire and the fire in turn was in the "middle" of the thorn bush. Thus, the thorn bush was *not* enveloped by flames. Accordingly, it could not have been the intent of this phenomenon to show that here was a thorn bush which was on fire but was not consumed by the flames, thus signifying that Israel would not perish in exile. Rather, as the Sages, too, interpret it, the fire was *within* the bush and the angel was *within* the flames.... The Torah itself is nothing but אֵשׁ דָּת, a fire that fashions itself into law, retaining the power and the function of fire, as it were, in that it seeks to penetrate, purify, warm and revive us. It is a fire which we in turn are to nourish and to maintain by dedicating every phase of our lives as לֶחֶם אִשֶּׁה ד׳ "fuel for the Divine fire" on earth.

Hence, stated in broad terms, the manifestation of God within the thorn bush proclaims the following great truth: "There is no place on earth devoid of the *shekhinah*, for He spoke to Moses even from out of was on fire and the thorn bush was not consumed. 3. "I want to go over there," said Moshe, "and look at this great sight. Why does the thorn bush not burn up?" 4. When *God* saw that he had gone there to see, God called to him from the middle of the bush and said: "Moshe! Moshe!" He said: "Here I am!" 5. He said: "Do not step here! Take your shoes off your feet, for the place upon which you are standing is ground with a holy destiny." 6. He said: "I am the God of your father, the God of Abraham, the God of Yitzḥak and the God of Yaakov." And Moshe hid his face, for he was afraid to look toward God. 7. And *God* said: "I have indeed seen the affliction of My people, who are in Mitzrayim, and I have heard their cries because of their slave-drivers; for I have been aware of their sufferings. 8. Now I have come down to rescue them from the hand of Mitzrayim and to bring them up from this land to a good and spacious land, a land that can flow with milk and honey, to the place of the Canaanite, the Ḥittite, the Emorite, the Perizzite, the Ḥivvite and the Yebusite. 9. And now—lo! the cry of the sons of Yisrael has come to Me, and I have also seen the pressure which the Mitzrites are

וְהַסְּנֶה אֵינֶנּוּ אֻכָּל: ג וַיֹּאמֶר מֹשֶׁה אָסֻרָה־נָּא וְאֶרְאֶה אֶת־הַמַּרְאֶה הַגָּדֹל הַזֶּה מַדּוּעַ לֹא־יִבְעַר הַסְּנֶה: ד וַיַּרְא יְהֹוָה כִּי סָר לִרְאוֹת וַיִּקְרָא אֵלָיו אֱלֹהִים מִתּוֹךְ הַסְּנֶה וַיֹּאמֶר מֹשֶׁה מֹשֶׁה וַיֹּאמֶר הִנֵּנִי: ה וַיֹּאמֶר אַל־תִּקְרַב הֲלֹם שַׁל־נְעָלֶיךָ מֵעַל רַגְלֶיךָ כִּי הַמָּקוֹם אֲשֶׁר אַתָּה עוֹמֵד עָלָיו אַדְמַת־קֹדֶשׁ הוּא: ו וַיֹּאמֶר אָנֹכִי אֱלֹהֵי אָבִיךָ אֱלֹהֵי אַבְרָהָם אֱלֹהֵי יִצְחָק וֵאלֹהֵי יַעֲקֹב וַיַּסְתֵּר מֹשֶׁה פָּנָיו כִּי יָרֵא מֵהַבִּיט אֶל־הָאֱלֹהִים: ז וַיֹּאמֶר יְהֹוָה רָאֹה רָאִיתִי אֶת־עֳנִי עַמִּי אֲשֶׁר בְּמִצְרָיִם וְאֶת־צַעֲקָתָם שָׁמַעְתִּי מִפְּנֵי נֹגְשָׂיו כִּי יָדַעְתִּי אֶת־מַכְאֹבָיו: ח וָאֵרֵד לְהַצִּילוֹ מִיַּד מִצְרַיִם וּלְהַעֲלֹתוֹ מִן־הָאָרֶץ הַהִוא אֶל־אֶרֶץ טוֹבָה וּרְחָבָה אֶל־אֶרֶץ זָבַת חָלָב וּדְבָשׁ אֶל־מְקוֹם הַכְּנַעֲנִי וְהַחִתִּי וְהָאֱמֹרִי וְהַפְּרִזִּי וְהַחִוִּי וְהַיְבוּסִי: ט וְעַתָּה הִנֵּה צַעֲקַת בְּנֵי־יִשְׂרָאֵל בָּאָה אֵלָי וְגַם־רָאִיתִי אֶת־הַלַּחַץ

---

the thorn bush" (Numbers Rabbah 12:4). Even the humblest place is not too lowly to become the abode of the Divine Presence. All things on earth, including those that seem the least significant to man, may have the purpose and the capability to become bearers of the Divine (Exodus Rabbah).

and the thorn bush was not consumed. The destiny of all things willing to accept the Divine is not to be destroyed by the Divine but to become bound up with it; or, stated in terms of the relationship of God to the Jewish nation, "Even in Israel's present thorny state of degradation I am with him; I share his sufferings." I am with him even among the thorns (ibid.).

5. . . . "Instead of attempting to understand phenomena beyond your ken, seek to comprehend the lofty purpose of the ground upon which you are already standing and surrender yourself entirely to it." Removal of one's shoes expresses the total surrender of one's self to the significance of a given place; the act implies that one intends to derive the status and position of his own personality solely from that place, without the need for any intermediary. . . .

8. The land is "good"; it is appropriate for the intended intellectual and moral development of the people, and it is "spacious" so that the nation can grow there also in numbers. . . .

אֶרֶץ זָבַת חָלָב וּדְבָשׁ [usually rendered as "a land flowing with milk and honey"] seems to denote a land that provides this abundance not because of its natural fruitfulness but only under certain conditions. . . . Unlike Egypt, [the region that is to be the land of Israel] does not freely dispense natural bounties for its inhabitants to exploit; it is a land that can prosper only "under a special Divine Providence directed to it continuously from the beginning until the end of the year." If the land receives water, it will burst into luxuriant bloom. But it can obtain that water only from Above. It is a soil that compels those who dwell upon it to behave themselves properly. A tough nation must have a hard land.

to the place of the Canaanite. The present inhabitants of the land were corrupted by the abundance they enjoyed there, and therefore the land will disgorge them. Only if it will keep itself free from all the Canaanite abominations will Israel be able to retain this abundance for itself.

putting on them. 10. Now therefore, go; I will send you to Pharaoh, and bring My people, the sons of Yisrael, out from Mitzrayim." 11. And Moshe said to God: "Who am I that I should go to Pharaoh and that I should bring the sons of Yisrael out from Mitzrayim?" 12. He said: "Because I will be with you! Precisely this will be the sign for you that [it is] I [Who] have sent you. If you will bring the people out from Mitzrayim, [all of] you will become the servants of God upon this mountain." 13. And Moshe said to God: "Lo! when I come to the sons of Yisrael and say to them: 'The God of your fathers has sent

אֲשֶׁר מִצְרַיִם לֹחֲצִים אֹתָם: י וְעַתָּה לְכָה
וְאֶשְׁלָחֲךָ אֶל־פַּרְעֹה וְהוֹצֵא אֶת־עַמִּי בְנֵי־
יִשְׂרָאֵל מִמִּצְרָיִם: יא וַיֹּאמֶר מֹשֶׁה אֶל־
הָאֱלֹהִים מִי אָנֹכִי כִּי אֵלֵךְ אֶל־פַּרְעֹה וְכִי
אוֹצִיא אֶת־בְּנֵי יִשְׂרָאֵל מִמִּצְרָיִם: יב וַיֹּאמֶר
כִּי־אֶהְיֶה עִמָּךְ וְזֶה־לְּךָ הָאוֹת כִּי אָנֹכִי שְׁלַחְתִּיךָ
בְּהוֹצִיאֲךָ אֶת־הָעָם מִמִּצְרַיִם תַּעַבְדוּן אֶת־
הָאֱלֹהִים עַל הָהָר הַזֶּה: יג וַיֹּאמֶר מֹשֶׁה אֶל־
הָאֱלֹהִים הִנֵּה אָנֹכִי בָא אֶל־בְּנֵי יִשְׂרָאֵל
וְאָמַרְתִּי לָהֶם אֱלֹהֵי אֲבוֹתֵיכֶם שְׁלָחַנִי אֲלֵיכֶם

11. [Moses said to God:] "Thou hast set me two formidable tasks in one: I am to subdue both Pharaoh and Israel. I am to overthrow Pharaoh and to become the leader of Israel. But I feel that I possess not the slightest strength or aptitude for either of these tasks." One who is assigned such a mission might well examine himself again and again to see whether he is indeed equal to it. If it were only a matter of his personal fate, he might hazard the task, but in this case the woe and weal of an entire people were contingent upon the success of that mission. And so it was only natural that a man, particularly one such as Moses, "the humblest of all men on earth," one who truly felt within himself not even one fiber of the stuff of which successful demagogues, leaders, generals, heroes and rulers are made . . . should have recoiled from such a mission, even though the order came from God Himself. Might not the whole undertaking fail because, in his personal inadequacy, and his ineptness, he might be timid and weak in Pharaoh's presence, and would he not then only bring disaster upon disaster on his brethren? Was he not justified in asserting that he did not have the imposing, overpowering strength of personality required to transform a nation of slaves into a people of God?

12. [God's reply]: Those traits which in your view make you totally unsuited for this task are the very ones that make you best qualified to carry it out. The very fact that you sense, through and through, that you lack even the slightest aptitude to venture upon—let alone accomplish—such a mission by dint of your own human capabilities makes you the messenger best suited to carry out My mission. I need someone who is the wisest and at the same time the humblest among men. Your very inadequacy will stamp the task I intend to accomplish through you as a "sign" for all time to come that what you will achieve could be achieved only at My command and by My might. Your very inadequacy will attest to the Divine character of your mission. Without this proof, Israel's deliverance would be regarded primarily as an event in world history that glorifies the power of men. But it is not a human dominion that I seek to establish through and with you. When the deliverance has been accomplished, it is not you who will become the ruler of the people. Rather תַּעַבְדוּן ["all of you will become the servants"]; all of you, you as well as the people, shall come to this mountain as servants of God . . . and only בְּהוֹצִיאֲךָ ["if you will bring the people out"], only if a man like you will bring the people out will it be possible to fulfill the purpose of the deliverance. Only then will I be able to say: "I am *God*, your God, Who has brought you out from the land of Mitzrayim," for then you and your people will stand before Me together, all on the same level, as My servants.

And "you will become the servants of God." At that time the manifestation of God which appeared to you here and which is now sending you to deliver the people will appear to you again, here, at this same mountain (or, more accurately, *upon* this same mountain), and at that time it will be visible to all of you and will complete My acquisition of the people for My service.

13. . . . Not that Moses was in any doubt about what he should say to Pharaoh. What he sought was more detailed information concerning his mission with regard to Israel. Therefore the question: "When I come before the sons of Israel and tell them: 'The God of your fathers has sent me to you'"—a mission that serves notice of a new task, and a new relationship—"by what name shall I refer to the One Who sent me?" Accordingly, the name by which Moses is to refer to Him must afford the key to the new relationship into which the sons of Israel are now to enter with God.

. . . Our entire conception of God is based on the

וְאָמְרוּ־לִי מַה־שְּׁמוֹ מָה אֹמַר אֲלֵהֶם: יד וַיֹּאמֶר
אֱלֹהִים אֶל־מֹשֶׁה אֶהְיֶה אֲשֶׁר אֶהְיֶה וַיֹּאמֶר כֹּה
תֹאמַר לִבְנֵי יִשְׂרָאֵל אֶהְיֶה שְׁלָחַנִי אֲלֵיכֶם:
טו וַיֹּאמֶר עוֹד אֱלֹהִים אֶל־מֹשֶׁה כֹּה תֹאמַר
אֶל־בְּנֵי יִשְׂרָאֵל יְהֹוָה אֱלֹהֵי אֲבֹתֵיכֶם אֱלֹהֵי
אַבְרָהָם אֱלֹהֵי יִצְחָק וֵאלֹהֵי יַעֲקֹב שְׁלָחַנִי
אֲלֵיכֶם זֶה־שְּׁמִי לְעֹלָם וְזֶה זִכְרִי לְדֹר דֹּר: חמישי
טז לֵךְ וְאָסַפְתָּ אֶת־זִקְנֵי יִשְׂרָאֵל וְאָמַרְתָּ אֲלֵהֶם
יְהֹוָה אֱלֹהֵי אֲבֹתֵיכֶם נִרְאָה אֵלַי אֱלֹהֵי אַבְרָהָם
יִצְחָק וְיַעֲקֹב לֵאמֹר פָּקֹד פָּקַדְתִּי אֶתְכֶם וְאֶת־
הֶעָשׂוּי לָכֶם בְּמִצְרָיִם: יז וָאֹמַר אַעֲלֶה אֶתְכֶם
מֵעֳנִי מִצְרַיִם אֶל־אֶרֶץ הַכְּנַעֲנִי וְהַחִתִּי וְהָאֱמֹרִי
וְהַפְּרִזִּי וְהַחִוִּי וְהַיְבוּסִי אֶל־אֶרֶץ זָבַת חָלָב
וּדְבָשׁ: יח וְשָׁמְעוּ לְקֹלֶךָ וּבָאתָ אַתָּה וְזִקְנֵי

me to you,' then they will say to me: 'What is His name?' What shall I say to them then?" 14. Thereupon God said to Moshe: אֶהְיֶה אֲשֶׁר אֶהְיֶה [I shall be that which I wish to be]!" He said: "This is what you shall say to the sons of Yisrael: 'אֶהְיֶה has sent me to you.'" 15. And God further said to Moshe: "This is what you shall say to the sons of Yisrael: '*God,* the God of your fathers, the God of Abraham, the God of Yitzḥak and the God of Yaakov, has sent me to you.' This is My Name for the distant future and this is My memorial for every generation. 16. Go and gather the elders of Yisrael and say to them: 'God, the God of your fathers, has appeared to me, the God of Abraham, Yitzḥak and Yaakov, in order to say: I have remembered you and that which is being done to you in Mitzrayim. 17. Therefore I said: I will bring you up out from the affliction of Mitzrayim to the land of the Canaanite, the Hittite, the Emorite, the Perizzite, the Hivvite and the Yebusite, to a land that can flow with milk and honey.' 18. And they will hearken to

appellations of the Holy One, blessed be He. Everything we are meant to know about God, everything God reveals to us concerning Himself, is intended not for our eyes but for our ears. Hence the appellations by which we refer to Him will give us a concept of His attitude toward us and of our relationship with Him. . . . When Moses asks God to tell him the name to which he should refer when he informs the sons of Israel of his mission, what he actually wants to know is: What is the concept of God that he must communicate to the sons of Israel in order to transform their spirits and inspire them to decide, of their own free will, to leave the service of Pharaoh and to enter the service of God?

14. אֶהְיֶה אֲשֶׁר אֶהְיֶה ***[I shall be that which I wish to be.]*** All other beings are what they *have* to be; their existence is bound up with the will of the One Who alone can say not merely "I am," but, "I shall be that which I wish to be." This name expresses the personal, absolute and free-willed essence of God. By declaring not, "I am," but, "I shall be"; i.e., by speaking in terms of the future which is totally dependent upon His will, He has proclaimed that uniquely Jewish conception of God, an entirely new conception, which is to be made known to mankind through Israel's deliverance from Mitzrayim and which eventually will bring about the redemption of the whole world.

° ° °

16. The fact that here, and also elsewhere in Scripture, the words "the God of your fathers" are followed by the specific references "the God of Abraham," etc. is surely not without great significance. The message meant to be conveyed is fairly obvious: It is to remind us for all time to come that our relationship with God is completely independent of our outward fortunes. The fortunes of our forefathers were not all alike. Abraham prospered; Isaac reached the zenith of prosperity, but then went into a decline; Jacob seemed about to go under altogether. But God's nearness to each of them, and His covenant with each of them, remained unchanged. The same will be true in the case of their descendants throughout the ages; no matter what turns their fortunes may take, God is revealed to them in every aspect of their lives and each one may be sure of His favor.

° ° °

18. You are not to go alone. You must not create the impression in the king's mind that you are a lone fanatic or visionary; he must see that you have the entire people behind you.

הָעִבְרִיִּים ***[the Hebrews].*** This is the first time that a ruler is to be addressed in the name of the Jewish people as an entity, and this verse employs the form עִבְרִיִּים, which does not occur anywhere else in Scripture. The form used in the rest of the Biblical text is עִבְרִים.

your voice and then you and the elders of Yisrael will come to the king of Mitzrayim and you say to him: '*God*, the God of the Hebrews, has met with us, and now please let us go on a three days' journey into the wilderness and offer up a sacrifice to *God*, our God.' 19. However, I know that the king of Mitzrayim will not let you go, not even by [the threat of] a mighty hand; 20. Then I will stretch out My hand and strike down Mitzrayim with all My miracles which I will perform in its midst; after that he will send you away. 21. I shall then let Mitzrayim see that this people is worthy of favor, and so it shall come to pass that when you will go, you will not go empty-handed. 22. Then every woman shall ask of her neighbor, and of the woman living with her, articles of silver and articles of gold, and clothing, which you shall put upon your sons and daughters, and you will cause Mitzrayim to strip herself bare."

IV 1. Moshe replied and said: "But see, they will not believe me and will not hearken to my voice, because they will say: '*God* did not appear to you.'" 2. And *God* said to him: "What is that in your hand?" He said: "A staff." 3. He said: "Throw it on the ground."

יִשְׂרָאֵל אֶל־מֶלֶךְ מִצְרַיִם וַאֲמַרְתֶּם אֵלָיו יְהֹוָה
אֱלֹהֵי הָעִבְרִיִּים נִקְרָה עָלֵינוּ וְעַתָּה נֵלְכָה־נָּא
דֶּרֶךְ שְׁלֹשֶׁת יָמִים בַּמִּדְבָּר וְנִזְבְּחָה לַיהֹוָה
אֱלֹהֵינוּ׃ יט וַאֲנִי יָדַעְתִּי כִּי לֹא־יִתֵּן אֶתְכֶם מֶלֶךְ
מִצְרַיִם לַהֲלֹךְ וְלֹא בְּיָד חֲזָקָה׃ כ וְשָׁלַחְתִּי אֶת־
יָדִי וְהִכֵּיתִי אֶת־מִצְרַיִם בְּכֹל נִפְלְאֹתַי אֲשֶׁר
אֶעֱשֶׂה בְּקִרְבּוֹ וְאַחֲרֵי־כֵן יְשַׁלַּח אֶתְכֶם׃
כא וְנָתַתִּי אֶת־חֵן הָעָם־הַזֶּה בְּעֵינֵי מִצְרָיִם
וְהָיָה כִּי תֵלֵכוּן לֹא תֵלְכוּ רֵיקָם׃ כב וְשָׁאֲלָה
אִשָּׁה מִשְּׁכֶנְתָּהּ וּמִגָּרַת בֵּיתָהּ כְּלֵי־כֶסֶף וּכְלֵי
זָהָב וּשְׂמָלֹת וְשַׂמְתֶּם עַל־בְּנֵיכֶם וְעַל־בְּנֹתֵיכֶם
וְנִצַּלְתֶּם אֶת־מִצְרָיִם׃ ד א וַיַּעַן מֹשֶׁה וַיֹּאמֶר
וְהֵן לֹא־יַאֲמִינוּ לִי וְלֹא יִשְׁמְעוּ בְּקֹלִי כִּי
יֹאמְרוּ לֹא־נִרְאָה אֵלֶיךָ יְהֹוָה׃ ב וַיֹּאמֶר אֵלָיו
יְהֹוָה מַזֶּה (מה־זה קרי) בְיָדֶךָ וַיֹּאמֶר מַטֶּה׃
ג וַיֹּאמֶר הַשְׁלִיכֵהוּ אַרְצָה וַיַּשְׁלִכֵהוּ אַרְצָה

Perhaps the intention here is to place particular stress upon the character traits implicit in the name עִבְרִי, and to emphasize that these traits are not only characteristic of the nation as a whole but are reflected in every single member of this nation. As Rabbi Judah explains עִבְרִי, (Genesis Rabbah 42:13), God needed only one individual, a man of the caliber of Abraham, who had the courage to leave the whole world behind and to cross over "to the other side," alone with his God (hence the name עִבְרִי). And Abraham passed on this courage and strength of character to each and every one of his descendants.

By presenting his demands to the king on behalf of the "Ivriyim," Moses expresses the following ideas: Each and every one of us represents the entire nation; each and every one of us has the courage to represent and to uphold the mission of his people all by himself, against the rest of the world. (The prophets frequently employ the allegory of animals to describe other nations, but in most instances they depict Israel as a tree. An animal organism can be killed with one squeeze of a finger or one stab of a dagger. Not so the tree, for each of its parts is capable of surviving on its own. Even if the root of the tree is severed, one branch, one twig, even only one bud, is often sufficient to restore the plant to life and to assure its survival.)

[Moses is to say to Pharaoh]: "We are not עִבְרִים but עִבְרִיִּים. The spirit which moves me to speak lives also within the elders, within each and every member of my people, down to the last man. Our people cannot be destroyed. The spirit, the courage and the determination of the whole is reproduced in each and every one of its members. . . ."

CHAPTER IV

1. God had just told Moses that his appearance before Pharaoh would not yield immediate results. Naturally, then, Moses could assume that the apparent failure of his mission would raise doubts about the credibility of his statements. The God of Whom you speak could not have appeared to you, otherwise your words to Pharaoh would have brought results at once.

° ° °

2–5. This metamorphosis; i.e., the fact that a staff can be turned into a serpent, and then back again into a

He threw it on the ground, and it turned into a serpent and Moses fled from it. 4. And *God* said to Moshe: "Put out your hand and grasp it by its tail." He put out his hand and grasped it, and it turned into a staff in his hand. 5. "So that they may believe that *God*, the God of their fathers, appeared to you, the God of Abraham, the God of Yitzḥak and the God of Yaakov." 6. And *God* further said to him: "Please put your hand into your bosom." He put his hand into his bosom. He took it out and lo! it was leprous like snow. 7. He said: "Put your hand into your bosom again." He put his hand into his bosom again. He took it out of his bosom and lo! it had become like the rest of his flesh again. 8. "It will come to pass, if they will not believe you, nor hearken to the voice of the first sign, that they will believe the voice of this latter sign. 9. But it shall come to pass, if they will not believe even these two signs, and

וַיְהִי לְנָחָשׁ וַיָּנָס מֹשֶׁה מִפָּנָיו: ד וַיֹּאמֶר יְהֹוָה אֶל־מֹשֶׁה שְׁלַח יָדְךָ וֶאֱחֹז בִּזְנָבוֹ וַיִּשְׁלַח יָדוֹ וַיַּחֲזֶק בּוֹ וַיְהִי לְמַטֶּה בְּכַפּוֹ: ה לְמַעַן יַאֲמִינוּ כִּי־נִרְאָה אֵלֶיךָ יְהֹוָה אֱלֹהֵי אֲבֹתָם אֱלֹהֵי אַבְרָהָם אֱלֹהֵי יִצְחָק וֵאלֹהֵי יַעֲקֹב: ו וַיֹּאמֶר יְהֹוָה לוֹ עוֹד הָבֵא־נָא יָדְךָ בְּחֵיקֶךָ וַיָּבֵא יָדוֹ בְּחֵיקוֹ וַיּוֹצִאָהּ וְהִנֵּה יָדוֹ מְצֹרַעַת כַּשָּׁלֶג: ז וַיֹּאמֶר הָשֵׁב יָדְךָ אֶל־חֵיקֶךָ וַיָּשֶׁב יָדוֹ אֶל־חֵיקוֹ וַיּוֹצִאָהּ מֵחֵיקוֹ וְהִנֵּה־שָׁבָה כִּבְשָׂרוֹ: ח וְהָיָה אִם־לֹא יַאֲמִינוּ לָךְ וְלֹא יִשְׁמְעוּ לְקֹל הָאֹת הָרִאשׁוֹן וְהֶאֱמִינוּ לְקֹל הָאֹת הָאַחֲרוֹן: ט וְהָיָה אִם־לֹא יַאֲמִינוּ גַּם לִשְׁנֵי הָאֹתוֹת

staff, at will, is in itself a "sign," . . . a means of generating the conviction that a man who comes equipped with such powers is indeed the messenger of that One sole Power Which holds sway over the natural order of things and by Whose will alone the laws of nature were established and continue to operate, laws by which all things not only came into being but continue to exist. A closer examination of the text should make it clear why God should have chosen this particular sign instead of some other manifestation. God first has Moses give consideration to what it is that he is holding in his hand. . . . "Give thought to the object you are holding in your hand." . . . It is a staff. Now what, exactly, is a staff? It is the most natural symbol of man's mastery over nature. A staff has a dual function. . . . It is 1) an extension of the hand, upon which man can lean for support as he stands on the ground, and 2) an extension of man's sphere of power; it is the symbol of his authority. So the people are to be taught, through Moses, that if and when God so desires, the object upon which man leans for support and with which he wields his authority can turn into the very opposite—a serpent. To a greater or lesser degree all animals become attached to man, but amphibians, particularly snakes, feel hostility toward man, so that man flees from the serpent.

Thus [God's word to Moses is as follows:] You have been sent by the One sole God Who, if He so desires, can cause the very thing upon which man relies for support, and which serves him as an instrument for his authority, to turn against him. Conversely, if He so wishes, He can grasp something which man fears and

shuns as a foe, and place it into his hand as an unresisting support and tractable tool. This is proof that He Who sent you is indeed ה', the One upon Whose will each coming moment, every moment of the future, depends. . . . If it is His will, He can turn Pharaoh into a slave and make you a ruler; He can turn Pharaoh's staff into His own scourge, or transform Pharaoh's scourge into a staff for you.

7. The very fact that a man can make his own hand leprous by placing it "into his bosom" and then restore it to health by placing it inside his robe once again is an indication that this man has been sent by God. For this phenomenon demonstrates that not only the staff, but also the hand which holds and guides it, is subject to the control of God. . . . This incident may have been intended also to convey to the people the following message: If God wills it, then "placing one's hand into one's bosom," that is, doing nothing, can result in death. On the other hand, inactivity commanded by God (i.e. שֵׁב וְאַל תַּעֲשֶׂה ["sit still and refrain from acting"]) can bring us deliverance. Let this sign, therefore, teach the people to be patient: God knows the proper time for "placing one's hands into one's bosom" and also the proper time for taking them out again.

9. If, after these two signs, they still will not show genuine trust, you shall begin to demonstrate the ten plagues before their very eyes. You shall show them that you have been sent to lay your hand upon the land itself, that the God Who has sent you has

they will not hearken to your voice, that you shall take of the waters of the river and pour it upon the dry land, and the waters that you will take from the river will turn into blood upon the dry land." 10. And Moshe said to *God*: "O my Lord, I am not a man of speech, not from yesterday, nor from the day before, not from the [very first] time that Thou hast spoken to Thy servant, for I am heavy of speech and heavy of tongue." 11. And *God* said to him: "Who has made man's mouth, or who makes [a man] mute, or deaf, or seeing, or blind? Is it not I, *God*? 12. And now, go! I will be with your mouth and teach you what you shall say." 13. He said: "O my Lord! Please send [Thy message] through the one whom Thou wilt yet have to send." 14. Then the anger of *God* was kindled against Moshe, and He said: "Is not Aharon, your brother, the Levite? I know that *he* will gladly speak. Behold! he is coming to meet you; he will see you and he will be glad in his heart. 15. You shall speak to him and put the words in his mouth, and I will be with your mouth and with his mouth and will teach you [both] what you shall do. 16. He shall speak to the people on your behalf and it shall come to pass that he will become a mouth for you and you shall be to

הָאֵלֶּה וְלֹא יִשְׁמְעוּן לְקֹלֶךָ וְלָקַחְתָּ מִמֵּימֵי
הַיְאֹר וְשָׁפַכְתָּ הַיַּבָּשָׁה וְהָיוּ הַמַּיִם אֲשֶׁר תִּקַּח
מִן־הַיְאֹר וְהָיוּ לְדָם בַּיַּבָּשֶׁת׃ י וַיֹּאמֶר מֹשֶׁה
אֶל־יְהֹוָה בִּי אֲדֹנָי לֹא אִישׁ דְּבָרִים אָנֹכִי גַּם
מִתְּמוֹל גַּם מִשִּׁלְשֹׁם גַּם מֵאָז דַּבֶּרְךָ אֶל־עַבְדֶּךָ
כִּי כְבַד־פֶּה וּכְבַד לָשׁוֹן אָנֹכִי׃ יא וַיֹּאמֶר יְהֹוָה
אֵלָיו מִי שָׂם פֶּה לָאָדָם אוֹ מִי־יָשׂוּם אִלֵּם אוֹ
חֵרֵשׁ אוֹ פִקֵּחַ אוֹ עִוֵּר הֲלֹא אָנֹכִי יְהֹוָה׃
יב וְעַתָּה לֵךְ וְאָנֹכִי אֶהְיֶה עִם־פִּיךָ וְהוֹרֵיתִיךָ
אֲשֶׁר תְּדַבֵּר׃ יג וַיֹּאמֶר בִּי אֲדֹנָי שְׁלַח־נָא בְּיַד־
תִּשְׁלָח׃ יד וַיִּחַר־אַף יְהֹוָה בְּמֹשֶׁה וַיֹּאמֶר הֲלֹא
אַהֲרֹן אָחִיךָ הַלֵּוִי יָדַעְתִּי כִּי־דַבֵּר יְדַבֵּר הוּא
וְגַם הִנֵּה־הוּא יֹצֵא לִקְרָאתֶךָ וְרָאֲךָ וְשָׂמַח
בְּלִבּוֹ׃ טו וְדִבַּרְתָּ אֵלָיו וְשַׂמְתָּ אֶת־הַדְּבָרִים
בְּפִיו וְאָנֹכִי אֶהְיֶה עִם־פִּיךָ וְעִם־פִּיהוּ וְהוֹרֵיתִי
אֶתְכֶם אֵת אֲשֶׁר תַּעֲשׂוּן׃ טז וְדִבֶּר־הוּא לְךָ אֶל־
הָעָם וְהָיָה הוּא יִהְיֶה־לְּךָ לְפֶה וְאַתָּה תִּהְיֶה־לּוֹ

indeed the power to break the staff upon which this state has depended for support. For the river Nile is Mitzrayim's support and thus the embodiment of its power.

10. In Verse 8 we read: יִשְׁמְעוּ לְקֹול הָאוֹת ["hearken to *the voice* of the first sign"] and וְהֶאֱמִינוּ לְקוֹל הָאוֹת ["believe *the voice* of this latter sign"]. This emphasis [on "the voice"] must mean more than a mere allegorical expression for the granting or withholding of trust, for the same idea is expressed in Verse 9 without any reference to קוֹל. It seems to imply a vocal explanation which was intended to accompany these signs, to "speak" to the hearts and the minds of the people. Moses could very well have believed that such explanations would require eloquence. . . . [He says:] "I am still apprehensive; I still do not feel that I am capable of carrying out this order."

. . ."I have difficulty starting to speak, under any circumstances; besides, I have a lisp. I have no command over my tongue." It is sad when a public speaker, particularly one who seeks to sway large audiences, can elicit nothing but laughter from his listeners. . . .

11. "Is it not I, ה׳, the One Who can turn a staff into a serpent and a serpent into a staff? Could I then not also turn a stammerer into the most eloquent of orators, or conversely, an orator into a stammerer?" A stammerer was, in fact, the most fitting messenger to carry out this mission. Every word the stammerer utters is a "sign" in itself. If a man who ordinarily can only stammer is able to talk fluently without hesitation, when he speaks at God's command, then his every word will serve to accredit him as a messenger of God.

° ° °

14. This is the first time that we encounter in Scripture the term "Levite" as a description of character. [God says to Moses:] In order to be a Levite one must have strength, courage and determination. Your brother possesses all these qualities. It will not take Me long to persuade him to speak; he already has the words on the tip of his tongue. He already knows about your mission and will be happy that it was assigned to you.

him as a 'God.'   17. And you shall take
into your hand this staff, with which you are
to perform the signs."   18. Moshe went
and returned to Yether, his father-in-law,
and said to him: "I would like to go and
return to my brethren in Mitzrayim to see
whether they are still alive." Yithro said to
Moshe: "Go toward peace."   19. And *God*
said to Moshe in Midian: "Go, return to
Mitzrayim, for all the men who sought your
life have died."   20. And Moshe took his
wife and his sons, placed them on the donkey and returned to the land of Mitzrayim.
Moshe took the staff of God into his hand.
21. *God* said to Moshe: "When you go
back to Mitzrayim, see all the convincing
wonders which I have placed into your
hand; you shall perform them before Pharaoh, but I shall harden his heart and he will
not let the people go,   22. until you will
say to Pharaoh: This is what *God* has said:
'Yisrael is My son, My first-born.   23. I
have told you, let My son go so that he may
serve Me, but you have refused to let him
go. I will therefore kill your [own] son, your
[own] first-born.'"   24. And it came to

לֵאלֹהִֽים: יז וְאֶת־הַמַּטֶּ֥ה הַזֶּ֖ה תִּקַּ֣ח בְּיָדֶ֑ךָ אֲשֶׁ֥ר
תַּעֲשֶׂה־בּ֖וֹ אֶת־הָאֹתֹֽת: פ ששי יח וַיֵּ֨לֶךְ מֹשֶׁ֜ה
וַיָּ֣שָׁב ׀ אֶל־יֶ֣תֶר חֹֽתְנ֗וֹ וַיֹּ֤אמֶר לוֹ֙ אֵ֣לְכָה נָּ֗א
וְאָשׁ֨וּבָה֙ אֶל־אַחַ֣י אֲשֶׁר־בְּמִצְרַ֔יִם וְאֶרְאֶ֖ה
הַעוֹדָ֣ם חַיִּ֑ים וַיֹּ֧אמֶר יִתְר֛וֹ לְמֹשֶׁ֖ה לֵ֥ךְ לְשָׁלֽוֹם:
יט וַיֹּ֨אמֶר יְהֹוָ֤ה אֶל־מֹשֶׁה֙ בְּמִדְיָ֔ן לֵ֖ךְ שֻׁ֣ב
מִצְרָ֑יִם כִּי־מֵ֨תוּ֙ כָּל־הָ֣אֲנָשִׁ֔ים הַֽמְבַקְשִׁ֖ים אֶת־
נַפְשֶֽׁךָ: כ וַיִּקַּ֨ח מֹשֶׁ֜ה אֶת־אִשְׁתּ֣וֹ וְאֶת־בָּנָ֗יו
וַיַּרְכִּבֵם֙ עַל־הַֽחֲמֹ֔ר וַיָּ֖שָׁב אַ֣רְצָה מִצְרָ֑יִם וַיִּקַּ֥ח
מֹשֶׁ֛ה אֶת־מַטֵּ֥ה הָאֱלֹהִ֖ים בְּיָדֽוֹ: כא וַיֹּ֣אמֶר יְהֹוָ֗ה
אֶל־מֹשֶׁה֮ בְּלֶכְתְּךָ֣ לָשׁ֣וּב מִצְרַ֒יְמָה֒ רְאֵ֗ה כָּל־
הַמֹּֽפְתִים֙ אֲשֶׁר־שַׂ֣מְתִּי בְיָדֶ֔ךָ וַעֲשִׂיתָ֖ם לִפְנֵ֣י
פַרְעֹ֑ה וַאֲנִי֙ אֲחַזֵּ֣ק אֶת־לִבּ֔וֹ וְלֹ֥א יְשַׁלַּ֖ח אֶת־
הָעָֽם: כב וְאָמַרְתָּ֖ אֶל־פַּרְעֹ֑ה כֹּ֚ה אָמַ֣ר יְהֹוָ֔ה בְּנִ֥י
בְכֹרִ֖י יִשְׂרָאֵֽל: כג וָאֹמַ֣ר אֵלֶ֗יךָ שַׁלַּ֤ח אֶת־בְּנִי֙
וַיַּֽעַבְדֵ֔נִי וַתְּמָאֵ֖ן לְשַׁלְּח֑וֹ הִנֵּה֙ אָנֹכִ֣י הֹרֵ֔ג אֶת־
בִּנְךָ֖ בְּכֹרֶֽךָ: כד וַיְהִ֥י בַדֶּ֖רֶךְ בַּמָּל֑וֹן וַיִּפְגְּשֵׁ֣הוּ

21. . . . . אוֹת is a sign directed primarily to the intellect for the purpose of imparting a specific message,
but man is permitted the freedom to choose for himself
whether or not to accept the information conveyed by
this phenomenon. . . . . מוֹפֵת [a "convincing wonder"] on
the other hand, is a sign *ad hominem*, which compels
man to accept the message it seeks to convey. If, for
instance, all the potable water in Mitzrayim turns into
blood, or vermin swarm all over the body of the king,
these are מוֹפְתִים, phenomena which force themselves
upon the attention of those who experience them.
However, if any one of these signs were permitted to
persist for a longer period it would become so unbearable that the king would let you go not because he has
been persuaded [that this is the right thing to do] but
only out of fear, misery and despair. This [says God]
must not happen. I will leave the king enough strength
and courage to endure the plagues so that he eventually
will be able to persuade himself, on his own, that it is
God Who is righteous and that he and his people are
wicked. . . .

24. וַיִּפְגְּשֵׁהוּ [*God confronted him*]. The same God
Who had just sent Moses forth with a most lofty mission, which Moses was preparing to carry out, now

abruptly confronted him and considered it better that
he should die. The verses that follow make it clear why
Moses was so suddenly placed in danger of death: He
had neglected to circumcise his son. He had gone forth
to accomplish the deliverance of a people whose import
would be based solely on *milah*, and now he himself
was about to introduce into that people an uncircumcised son. God considered it better to have Moses die
than to have him set out on his mission with such an
unfortunate example for his people.

This, it seems to us, should be the interpretation of
וַיְבַקֵּשׁ. ["considered it better . . ."] [Interpreted literally
as "and *He* sought (to kill him)"], it would be a very
harsh characterization of God. God the All-Merciful
never "seeks" to "kill" a man; if it is His will that a
man should die, then that man will die. But interpreted
in the manner suggested here, this passage teaches us
the significant lesson that the plans of God cannot be
influenced by *any* human being — "the Omnipresent
has many agents (to do His will)" [Genesis Rabbah
10:6]. To God no man, not even one such as Moses, is
indispensable. This should dispose of any erroneous
notion that might have been suggested by the preceding passages, where we are told of God's strenuous
efforts to persuade Moses to accept His mission. God is

pass on the way, at the lodging place, that *God* confronted him and considered it better that he should die. 25. And Tzipporah took a fragment of rock, cut off her son's foreskin and cast it at his feet and she said: "Because you have become wedded to the death sentence [lit., "you have become a bridegroom of blood"] on my account." 26. So it [i.e., the danger] withdrew from him, and she said: "Wedded to the death penalty for all [future] circumcisions!" 27. *God* said to Aharon: "Go toward the wilderness to meet Moshe." He went, met him at the mountain of God, and kissed him. 28. Moshe told Aharon all the words of *God* with which He had sent him, and all the signs which he had instructed him [to perform]. 29. Moshe and Aharon went and they gathered all the elders of the sons of Yisrael. 30. And Aharon uttered the words which *God* had spoken to Moshe, and he performed the signs before the eyes of the people. 31. The people trusted; they heard that *God* had remembered the sons of

יְהֹוָה וַיְבַקֵּשׁ הֲמִיתוֹ: כה וַתִּקַּח צִפֹּרָה צֹר
וַתִּכְרֹת אֶת־עָרְלַת בְּנָהּ וַתַּגַּע לְרַגְלָיו וַתֹּאמֶר
כִּי חֲתַן־דָּמִים אַתָּה לִי: כו וַיִּרֶף מִמֶּנּוּ אָז
אָמְרָה חֲתַן דָּמִים לַמּוּלֹת: פ כז וַיֹּאמֶר יְהֹוָה
אֶל־אַהֲרֹן לֵךְ לִקְרַאת מֹשֶׁה הַמִּדְבָּרָה וַיֵּלֶךְ
וַיִּפְגְּשֵׁהוּ בְּהַר הָאֱלֹהִים וַיִּשַּׁק־לוֹ: כח וַיַּגֵּד
מֹשֶׁה לְאַהֲרֹן אֵת כָּל־דִּבְרֵי יְהֹוָה אֲשֶׁר שְׁלָחוֹ
וְאֵת כָּל־הָאֹתֹת אֲשֶׁר צִוָּהוּ: כט וַיֵּלֶךְ מֹשֶׁה
וְאַהֲרֹן וַיַּאַסְפוּ אֶת־כָּל־זִקְנֵי בְּנֵי יִשְׂרָאֵל:
ל וַיְדַבֵּר אַהֲרֹן אֵת כָּל־הַדְּבָרִים אֲשֶׁר־דִּבֶּר
יְהֹוָה אֶל־מֹשֶׁה וַיַּעַשׂ הָאֹתֹת לְעֵינֵי הָעָם:
לא וַיַּאֲמֵן הָעָם וַיִּשְׁמְעוּ כִּי־פָקַד יְהֹוָה אֶת־בְּנֵי

---

not indulgent toward mistakes made by His messengers, not even if it is a man like Moses. On the contrary, God says: "I will be sanctified by those near to Me" [Leviticus 10:3]. This is made very clear at this point in the narrative [at the very outset of Moses' mission.]

25. [In a lengthy homily on this verse, Hirsch suggests that the person at whose feet the foreskin was cast and to whom Tzipporah then addressed herself was not (as some authorities assume) her newly circumcised son but her husband, Moses. She felt that she was to blame for the threat to Moses' life because she had kept him from carrying out the Divine command to have their son circumcised. Hirsch cites a statement by Rabbi Eliezer of Modai in the Mekhilta to Parshath Yithro (Exodus 18:1–20:23) to the effect that Yithro had agreed to have Tzipporah marry Moses only under the condition that the first son of this union should remain a heathen and not be circumcised. Also, Hirsch points out that Tzipporah, not being of Jewish origin, may have been naturally reluctant to see her son undergo the pain and the dangers of circumcision. In either case, Moses may have stalled for time, waiting for an opportune moment to carry out the Divine command. Seeing her husband on the point of death, Tzipporah suspected that this was God's punishment for Moses' failure to circumcise their son. She therefore quickly circumcised her son with her own hands, cast the boy's foreskin at

her husband's feet and said to him, as Hirsch puts it: "I have done this because you have become a 'bridegroom of death' on my account. I am to blame, for I held you back from performing this duty. Because of your love for me, you did not press the issue; so you took upon yourself a mortal sin on my account, and this is how you became wedded to the death sentence, i.e., marked for death."]

26. [According to Hirsch, Tzipporah felt that this incident would ensure the observance of circumcision for all time to come. If even a man like Moses, who had just been charged with a Divine mission, nearly lost his life for failing to circumcise his son, what Jew in future would dare be guilty of the same neglect?]

31. וַיַּאֲמֵן [trusted]. The proper translation of the Hebrew אֱמוּנָה is not "belief." "Belief" suggests a lack of firm conviction. One does not sacrifice one's life and substance for that which one merely "believes." האמין denotes more than such "belief." It means to acknowledge that which has been told us as אמן, as that firm foundation upon which we rely and to which we cling. It is to guide and educate us. To Israel, the Divine Providence to which it gives its אֱמוּנָה is the fixed foundation, true beyond all doubt, for every aspect of life. It accepts as true only that which accords with this one criterion of truth. . . .

יִשְׂרָאֵל וְכִי רָאָה אֶת־עָנְיָם וַיִּקְּדוּ וַיִּשְׁתַּחֲווּ׃
שביעי ה א וְאַחַר בָּאוּ מֹשֶׁה וְאַהֲרֹן וַיֹּאמְרוּ
אֶל־פַּרְעֹה כֹּה־אָמַר יְהוָה אֱלֹהֵי יִשְׂרָאֵל שַׁלַּח
אֶת־עַמִּי וְיָחֹגּוּ לִי בַּמִּדְבָּר׃ ב וַיֹּאמֶר פַּרְעֹה מִי
יְהוָה אֲשֶׁר אֶשְׁמַע בְּקֹלוֹ לְשַׁלַּח אֶת־יִשְׂרָאֵל
לֹא יָדַעְתִּי אֶת־יְהוָה וְגַם אֶת־יִשְׂרָאֵל לֹא
אֲשַׁלֵּחַ׃ ג וַיֹּאמְרוּ אֱלֹהֵי הָעִבְרִים נִקְרָא עָלֵינוּ
נֵלֲכָה־נָּא דֶּרֶךְ שְׁלֹשֶׁת יָמִים בַּמִּדְבָּר וְנִזְבְּחָה
לַיהוָה אֱלֹהֵינוּ פֶּן־יִפְגָּעֵנוּ בַּדֶּבֶר אוֹ בֶחָרֶב׃
ד וַיֹּאמֶר אֲלֵהֶם מֶלֶךְ מִצְרַיִם לָמָּה מֹשֶׁה
וְאַהֲרֹן תַּפְרִיעוּ אֶת־הָעָם מִמַּעֲשָׂיו לְכוּ

Yisrael and that He had seen their affliction; they bowed their heads and cast themselves down.

V 1. Afterwards Moshe and Aharon came and said to Pharaoh: "This is what *God*, the God of Yisrael, has said: 'Let My people go so that they may celebrate a festival for Me in the wilderness.'" 2. Pharaoh replied: "Who is *God* that I should hearken to His voice to let Yisrael go? I do not know *God* and, moreover, I will not let Yisrael go." 3. Thereupon they said: "The God of the Hebrews has been proclaimed over us. Please let us go on a three days' journey into the wilderness and offer sacrifices to *God*, our God. Otherwise He may strike us with the plague or with the sword." 4. And the king of Mitzrayim said to them: "Why do you, Moshe and Aharon, want to make the people break

CHAPTER V

2. The Pharaohs, as we have come to know them by now, were as subtle and astute in their speech and actions as any ruler of our own day. [Pharaoh says to Moses and Aaron:] You have come to me in the name of your God Whom you say I must obey by giving away that which belongs to me. I do not know of such a God. And if you say that you are speaking in the name of your people, perhaps as part of some great mission which this God will assign to you at some future date, then I say to you: Even this would not be enough to persuade me to relinquish, even temporarily, what belongs to me.

3. [In reply to Pharaoh's negative response] Moses and Aaron now reformulated their request in terms of Pharaoh's point of view, and in his own language: "Even if you do not know ד׳, you will at least understand us if we speak of the 'God of the Hebrews.' Like the Egyptians, we, too, have a God of our own, and if, by reason of that higher imperative that rules over gods and men alike, He makes an appearance in the visible world, this must be, as you surely know, a matter of grave concern, and He must be appeased. If this is not done, we may be stricken with the plague and with the sword, and then not only we, but you and your people, too, would suffer. So, for your own sake—since after all, you, too, fear the wrath of the gods—permit us to celebrate our festival."

4. Until this point the ruler has spoken in his own name, as Pharaoh. Now he speaks as a king and addresses himself to Moses and Aaron candidly, man to man. "I know all about you old men! 'Celebrate festivals,' 'Divine revelation,' indeed! You know very well that I know—and I know that you know it, too—that all this talk is intended only for the masses. Among men like you and me, religion and worship are merely a matter of politics. You know very well that I know it: all these demands of yours are intended only to cut the people loose from the bonds of their work. Until now the people have known nothing except that the law of the land is binding upon them, and that hard labor is the natural station to which they were born. Why should you want to put other ideas into their heads? Why suggest to them that there are times when they do not have to work? That is simply not worthy of venerable men such as you, O Moses and Aaron."

Pharaoh chooses his words with great care. He is careful not to speak of סְבָלוֹת ["burdens"] when he describes the position of the people. Moses and Aaron, the aristocrats, the men of exalted station, can be said to be weighed down by "burdens" and "cares." The Egyptians, too, as we shall see [in Verse 5], are described as coping with the "burdens" of their occupations. But the yoke of the slave labor beneath which the Hebrews are groaning is merely מַעֲשָׂיו [their "work"], their natural employment, the only kind appropriate to them.

לְכוּ לְסִבְלֹתֵיכֶם ***[Go (back) to the burdens of your calling].*** Go back to those concerns which are part of your legitimate calling. Rabble-rousing is not your business.

loose from their work? Go [back] to the burdens of your calling.''   5. Finally Pharaoh
said: "See, the population of the land has
now increased, and you want them to take a
holiday from the burdens of their calling!''
6. On that same day Pharaoh commanded the officers in charge of the people, and
their taskmasters, as follows: 7. "You
shall no longer give the people straw to
prepare bricks as you did yesterday and the
day before. Let them go and gather for
themselves stubble for straw.   8. And you
shall impose upon them the [same] quota of
bricks that they made yesterday and the day
before; you shall not reduce it. For they are
lazy; that is why they cry: 'We want to go!
We want to offer sacrifices to our God!'
9. The work must weigh heavily upon
the men so that they may be fully occupied
with it and not dabble in useless things.''
10. The officers in charge of the people
and their taskmasters went out and said to
the people: "This is what Pharaoh has said:
'I will not give you straw.   11. Go yourselves, get yourselves straw wherever you
can find it, because none of your work will
be reduced.'''   12. And the people scattered all over the land of Mitzrayim to look

לְסִבְלֹתֵיכֶם: ה וַיֹּאמֶר פַּרְעֹה הֵן־רַבִּים עַתָּה
עַם הָאָרֶץ וְהִשְׁבַּתֶּם אֹתָם מִסִּבְלֹתָם: ו וַיְצַו
פַּרְעֹה בַּיּוֹם הַהוּא אֶת־הַנֹּגְשִׂים בָּעָם וְאֶת־
שֹׁטְרָיו לֵאמֹר: ז לֹא תֹאסִפוּן לָתֵת תֶּבֶן לָעָם
לִלְבֹּן הַלְּבֵנִים כִּתְמוֹל שִׁלְשֹׁם הֵם יֵלְכוּ וְקֹשְׁשׁוּ
לָהֶם תֶּבֶן: ח וְאֶת־מַתְכֹּנֶת הַלְּבֵנִים אֲשֶׁר הֵם
עֹשִׂים תְּמוֹל שִׁלְשֹׁם תָּשִׂימוּ עֲלֵיהֶם לֹא תִגְרְעוּ
מִמֶּנּוּ כִּי־נִרְפִּים הֵם עַל־כֵּן הֵם צֹעֲקִים לֵאמֹר
נֵלְכָה נִזְבְּחָה לֵאלֹהֵינוּ: ט תִּכְבַּד הָעֲבֹדָה עַל־
הָאֲנָשִׁים וְיַעֲשׂוּ־בָהּ וְאַל־יִשְׁעוּ בְּדִבְרֵי־שָׁקֶר:
י וַיֵּצְאוּ נֹגְשֵׂי הָעָם וְשֹׁטְרָיו וַיֹּאמְרוּ אֶל־הָעָם
לֵאמֹר כֹּה אָמַר פַּרְעֹה אֵינֶנִּי נֹתֵן לָכֶם תֶּבֶן:
יא אַתֶּם לְכוּ קְחוּ לָכֶם תֶּבֶן מֵאֲשֶׁר תִּמְצָאוּ כִּי
אֵין נִגְרָע מֵעֲבֹדַתְכֶם דָּבָר: יב וַיָּפֶץ הָעָם בְּכָל־

---

5. . . . The term עַם הָאָרֶץ [rendered here as "the
population of the land"] does not refer to the "mob" or
the "common people." Originally, it had no such
pejorative connotations. In Leviticus 4:27 it refers to
the entire Jewish nation with the exception of its ruler.
In Leviticus 20:4 it actually denotes the representatives
of the nation charged with safeguarding and implementing the nation's laws. Hence, in this passage, too,
עַם הָאָרֶץ is probably not intended to refer to the Hebrew
slave caste but to the true inhabitants of the country,
the Egyptians.

Pharaoh says: "See, the population of Egypt has
grown so much that the state can survive only if each
and every one of its subjects works diligently and
unceasingly at his occupation. It is this, the Egyptian
population, that upholds the might of our country.
Compared to these intellectual and technical activities,
the menial tasks that the Hebrews perform are mere
child's play. Now see how impolitic your demands are,
and what a threat to our state! You are demanding a
whole week's holiday for the Hebrews. This will give
our own growing, hard-working Egyptian population
the very natural notion that they, too, would like to

have a 'Sabbatical week'—or perhaps even several
weeks of no work. And that would paralyze the state
completely. Why, it might even cause its downfall! This
I will not and cannot permit. הֵן: Look—this never
occurred to you, did it?''

9. *The work must weigh heavily.* Pharaoh says: "I
am not doing this out of barbarism or out of selfish
motivations. We must see to it that we train these Jews.
They must be made to work hard so that they will come
to regard this work as their natural employment. They
must learn to be productive and practical.''

they may be fully occupied. They must no longer
theorize, meditate and dream.

and not dabble. Their minds must no longer be occupied with impractical, useless things. "Spirit," "God,"
"religion," "the fear of God"—all these are impractical
notions that render the Jews useless to the state.

12 and 13. וַיָּפֶץ [*And (the people) scattered*]. The
verb is in the active mood. Like the authors of so many
anti-Jewish laws in ages to come, Pharaoh, too, asked
for the impossible. One who is kept busy looking for

for stubble instead of straw. 13. But the officers in charge pressed them and said: "Complete your work, the daily fixed amount each day as it was when you still received your straw." 14. And the task-masters of the sons of Yisrael whom Pharaoh's officers in charge had set over them were beaten, with the words: "Why have you not completed your fixed amount of brickmaking both yesterday and today, as you did yesterday and the day before that?" 15. The taskmasters of the sons of Yisrael came and cried to Pharaoh: "Why are you doing this to your slaves? 16. Straw is not given to your slaves, and they tell us: 'Make bricks!' So your slaves are struck down and your people must sin against us." 17. He said: "You are lazy! Lazy! That is why you say: 'We want to go! We want to offer sacri-fices to *God!*' 18. And now go, do your work, and straw will not be given to you, and you must deliver your quota of bricks!" 19. And the taskmasters of the sons of Yisrael found themselves in the unhappy position of having to say: "You must not reduce any of [the amount of] your bricks. The daily quota each day!" 20. When they came away from Pharaoh, they stepped up to Moshe and Aharon, who stood waiting for them, 21. and they said to them: "May *God* look down upon you and judge,

אֶרֶץ מִצְרַיִם לְקֹשֵׁשׁ קַשׁ לַתֶּבֶן: יג וְהַנֹּגְשִׂים אָצִים לֵאמֹר כַּלּוּ מַעֲשֵׂיכֶם דְּבַר־יוֹם בְּיוֹמוֹ כַּאֲשֶׁר בִּהְיוֹת הַתֶּבֶן: יד וַיֻּכּוּ שֹׁטְרֵי בְּנֵי יִשְׂרָאֵל אֲשֶׁר־שָׂמוּ עֲלֵהֶם נֹגְשֵׂי פַרְעֹה לֵאמֹר מַדּוּעַ לֹא כִלִּיתֶם חָקְכֶם לִלְבֹּן כִּתְמוֹל שִׁלְשֹׁם גַּם־תְּמוֹל גַּם־הַיּוֹם: טו וַיָּבֹאוּ שֹׁטְרֵי בְּנֵי יִשְׂרָאֵל וַיִּצְעֲקוּ אֶל־פַּרְעֹה לֵאמֹר לָמָּה תַעֲשֶׂה כֹה לַעֲבָדֶיךָ: טז תֶּבֶן אֵין נִתָּן לַעֲבָדֶיךָ וּלְבֵנִים אֹמְרִים לָנוּ עֲשׂוּ וְהִנֵּה עֲבָדֶיךָ מֻכִּים וְחָטָאת עַמֶּךָ: יז וַיֹּאמֶר נִרְפִּים אַתֶּם נִרְפִּים עַל־כֵּן אַתֶּם אֹמְרִים נֵלְכָה נִזְבְּחָה לַיהֹוָה: יח וְעַתָּה לְכוּ עִבְדוּ וְתֶבֶן לֹא־יִנָּתֵן לָכֶם וְתֹכֶן לְבֵנִים תִּתֵּנוּ: יט וַיִּרְאוּ שֹׁטְרֵי בְנֵי־יִשְׂרָאֵל אֹתָם בְּרָע לֵאמֹר לֹא־תִגְרְעוּ מִלִּבְנֵיכֶם דְּבַר־יוֹם בְּיוֹמוֹ: כ וַיִּפְגְּעוּ אֶת־מֹשֶׁה וְאֶת־אַהֲרֹן נִצָּבִים לִקְרָאתָם בְּצֵאתָם מֵאֵת פַּרְעֹה: כא וַיֹּאמְרוּ אֲלֵהֶם יֵרֶא יְהֹוָה עֲלֵיכֶם וְיִשְׁפֹּט אֲשֶׁר

straw cannot, at the same time, make bricks, and vice versa. The people therefore chose the only way out: some of them were sent all over the land to search for straw, while others made the bricks. But this was not what Pharaoh wanted. The administrators had to insist that each individual deliver his personal daily quota of bricks as before. . . .

16. Your hapless people, who are flogging us by your orders, are sinning against us by so doing. But they are not to blame; they do it only because you have ordered them to do so.

21. These men had taken upon their own backs the lashes intended for their brethren. They thus became the prototypes of those noble individuals of all the centuries of *galuth* to come, who, as the "Jew elders" of their communities, were to go through fire and water for their tortured fellow Jews. One cannot blame the taskmasters if, after such encounters [as those described

in these passages], they lost their confidence in the mis-sion of Moses and Aaron.

באש [literally, "stink"] refers to the disgust aroused in us by anything that exudes a foul odor. God has so implanted in man the joy of life and pleasure in living things that human beings feel a natural revulsion against anything dead, decayed or putrid. Hence [a form of] באש is used in general to denote the arousal of disgust. If we are aware that we have done wrong to another person, then we sense that this other person must consider us morally rotten and that we have become disgusting (נִבְאַשׁ) to him. The word is related to בוש, "to be ashamed"; i.e. to feel that one has become morally foul himself. Shame is that feeling of revulsion which God has implanted in us against any "foulness" in our own character, a feeling that gives us no peace until we have rid ourselves of our moral "foulness."

Here we read הִבְאַשְׁתֶּם אֶת רֵיחֵנוּ ["you have brought us into foul odor"]: "You have made our existence a malodorous thing in the eyes of Pharaoh and his ser-

because you have brought us into foul odor
in the eyes of Pharaoh and his servant,
putting a sword in their hand to kill us!"
22. And Moshe returned to *God* and said,
"My Lord! For what purpose hast Thou
made misfortune the lot of this people?
Why didst Thou send me [of all men]?
23. And ever since I came to Pharaoh to
speak in Thy Name, he has abused the
people even more, and Thou hast not
rescued Thy people even from this?"

VI   1. And *God* said to Moshe:
"Now you will see what I will
do to Pharaoh; for by a strong hand will he
let them go. Indeed, by a strong hand will
he drive them out of his land!"

הַבְאַשְׁתֶּם אֶת־רֵיחֵנוּ בְּעֵינֵי פַרְעֹה וּבְעֵינֵי
עֲבָדָיו לָתֶת־חֶרֶב בְּיָדָם לְהָרְגֵנוּ: מפטיר כב וַיָּשָׁב
מֹשֶׁה אֶל־יְהֹוָה וַיֹּאמַר אֲדֹנָי לָמָה הֲרֵעֹתָה לָעָם
הַזֶּה לָמָּה זֶּה שְׁלַחְתָּנִי: כג וּמֵאָז בָּאתִי אֶל־
פַּרְעֹה לְדַבֵּר בִּשְׁמֶךָ הֵרַע לָעָם הַזֶּה וְהַצֵּל לֹא־
הִצַּלְתָּ אֶת־עַמֶּךָ: ו א וַיֹּאמֶר יְהֹוָה אֶל־מֹשֶׁה
עַתָּה תִרְאֶה אֲשֶׁר אֶעֱשֶׂה לְפַרְעֹה כִּי בְיָד חֲזָקָה
יְשַׁלְּחֵם וּבְיָד חֲזָקָה יְגָרְשֵׁם מֵאַרְצוֹ: ס

---

vants"; i.e., Pharaoh and his servants will henceforth
regard us as individuals to be shunned because they
will regard us as "foul" in every respect—moral,
social and practical. Until now they abused us, but
because of the benefits they derived from us, they (like
the Pharaohs of future generations) considered our
survival to be in the best interests of the state. But now
that you have stirred up notions of liberation in our
midst we appear to them as individuals who are of no
value to the state, who shirk their duties, who ask for
time off from work, and so you have supplied them with
reasons for wanting to destroy us.

22–23. . . . Let us picture to ourselves the feelings of
Moses at this point. His mission had been a complete
failure. Pharaoh had become even more hard-hearted
and had added insult to injury. The people looked upon
Moses and Aaron as swindlers or, at best, as the dupes
of others. Moses himself lost confidence; he would not
have been Moses if he had not felt that what had happened only served to justify his mistrust in his own
capabilities. Perhaps, he may have thought, he had not
gone about his mission in the proper manner. What

man would not despair of himself when he sees six
hundred thousand other innocent human beings beaten
black and blue and cast into utter despair because of
something he has done?

CHAPTER VI

1. עַתָּה *[Now]*. This is just the moment for which I
had been waiting. Precisely this sense of utter helplessness and despair had to come. It had to become clear
that human efforts and conventional representations to
Pharaoh would be of no avail. Moses and Aaron had to
face the representatives of the people speechless and
exposed in all their ineffectuality before redemption, as
a work of God, could begin. At this point even the last
pretense that natural expedients were available had
vanished, and it was evident that Moses was only
an instrument of God and redemption only the work
of God.

יָד חֲזָקָה *[a strong hand]*. The supreme power of God,
which none can withstand, is to become apparent in
this act of redemption. Hence Moses and Aaron could
not be spared this moment of despair.

° ° °

The Haftarah for this Sidra may be found on page 843.

ואַרא

VAERA

2. God spoke to Moshe and said to him: "I am 'ד, 3. [and was so] even when I appeared to Abraham, Yitzḥak and Yaakov as the All-sufficing God but had not become known to them as that which My Name 'ד implies. 4. And I have also established My covenant with them, to give them the land of Canaan, the land of their sojourning as strangers, where they sojourned, 5. and I have also heard the cry of distress of the sons of Yisrael, whom the Mitzrites are holding in bondage,

ב וַיְדַבֵּר אֱלֹהִים אֶל־מֹשֶׁה וַיֹּאמֶר אֵלָיו אֲנִי יְהֹוָה: ג וָאֵרָא אֶל־אַבְרָהָם אֶל־יִצְחָק וְאֶל־יַעֲקֹב בְּאֵל שַׁדָּי וּשְׁמִי יְהֹוָה לֹא נוֹדַעְתִּי לָהֶם: ד וְגַם הֲקִמֹתִי אֶת־בְּרִיתִי אִתָּם לָתֵת לָהֶם אֶת־אֶרֶץ כְּנָעַן אֵת אֶרֶץ מְגֻרֵיהֶם אֲשֶׁר־גָּרוּ בָהּ: ה וְגַם | אֲנִי שָׁמַעְתִּי אֶת־נַאֲקַת בְּנֵי יִשְׂרָאֵל אֲשֶׁר מִצְרַיִם מַעֲבִדִים אֹתָם וָאֶזְכֹּר

2. *I am 'ד.* These two short words contain the complete answer to Moses' cry of despair. In the previous verse Moses had received the first soothing reply. What follows is an elaboration of God's answer.

אֱלֹקִים is the invisible One Who reigns in the visible world [אֵלֶּה = "these"]. He is the unseen Guide of all the events that have transpired until this point. Until now, all the despair, the insults, the misery and the distress [which Israel had had to suffer] had sprung from natural circumstances that God had permitted to develop. These had been the natural results of Egypt's corruption and might as against Israel's weakness and helplessness. But now "*I am 'ה Who brings new things into being:*" I am the One Who exercises His will independently of and, indeed, despite, existing realities. With this factor a completely new world is to arise amidst mankind, one that will be independent of all the conditions upon which the phenomena of world history had been dependent thus far.

3. This completely new manifestation of God had, in fact, been prepared from the very beginning of history. All the paths of history have led up to this moment. [God says:] "I was already 'ה when I appeared to Abraham, Isaac and Jacob only as אל שדי and had not yet permitted My intended sovereignty as 'ה to become manifest to them in their own lives. You are wondering why things have become worse and worse for you, and why even your mission thus far has served only to push your misery to the utmost limits. But do you not see that, in fact, your entire history up to this point has been a downhill road? Abraham was the 'prince of God' among the nations, but then came Jacob, the unfortunate, hard-working servant who had to toil in order to get himself a wife and then was forced to perform additional labor in order to keep her. You know that I

could just as easily have had your fortunes rise steadily, without interruption. Instead of making Abraham wait until the one hundredth year of his life before giving him a son, I could have permitted him to have a family by the time he was seventy, and I could have permitted his progeny to grow into a people upon their own native soil in happy, favorable circumstances. But then this nation would never have become 'the people of God,' the people who are to reveal God in His quality of 'ה. Then this people, too, like all the other nations, would have been rooted solely in the world of things that can be seen and touched; like them, they would have had only physical foundations and would have understood their greatness and might only in terms of physical size and strength, aspiring to spiritual and moral attainments only as long as these would have been compatible with, and beneficial to, their material ambitions.

"But this people is not to be like the other nations. Unlike the others, this nation is to be founded solely upon God and upon the free-willed moral fulfillment of His will, and to derive even its earthly substance and foundations only from that God and from these endeavors."

Remember that the concept of a free-willed, almighty God and of a humanity made free by that God had vanished from the earth; men and nations had become chained to materialism in both theory and practice. Through the emergence of the nation of Abraham this concept was to be revived and mankind freed from the bonds of materialism. That is why this nation had to begin where the other nations had left off. It had to despair of itself, to lie prone, about to perish in its own blood, and it could rise to nationhood only through the Creator's call, so that, by its very existence as a nation, this nation should proclaim to the other nations that אֲנִי ד'!

and I have remembered My covenant.
6. Therefore say to the sons of Yisrael: I
am 'ד! I will bring you out from succumbing
under the burdens of Mitzrayim, I will
rescue you from their bondage, I will redeem
you with an outstretched arm and with
great judgments.   7. I will take you to
Myself as a people and I will be a God to
you; you will come to know that I am 'ד,
your God, Who brings you out from succumbing under the burdens of Mitzrayim.
8. And then I will bring you into the land
concerning which I raised My hand, to give
it to Abraham, Yitzḥak and Yaakov, and I
shall give it to you as a heritage, I, 'ד!"
9. Moshe spoke thus to the sons of Yis-

אֶת־בְּרִיתִֽי: ו לָכֵן אֱמֹר לִבְנֵֽי־יִשְׂרָאֵל אֲנִי
יְהֹוָה וְהוֹצֵאתִי אֶתְכֶם מִתַּחַת סִבְלֹת מִצְרַיִם
וְהִצַּלְתִּי אֶתְכֶם מֵעֲבֹדָתָם וְגָאַלְתִּי אֶתְכֶם
בִּזְרוֹעַ נְטוּיָה וּבִשְׁפָטִים גְּדֹלִים: ז וְלָקַחְתִּי
אֶתְכֶם לִי לְעָם וְהָיִיתִי לָכֶם לֵאלֹהִים וִידַעְתֶּם
כִּי אֲנִי יְהֹוָה אֱלֹהֵיכֶם הַמּוֹצִיא אֶתְכֶם מִתַּחַת
סִבְלוֹת מִצְרָֽיִם: ח וְהֵבֵאתִי אֶתְכֶם אֶל־הָאָרֶץ
אֲשֶׁר נָשָׂאתִי אֶת־יָדִי לָתֵת אֹתָהּ לְאַבְרָהָם
לְיִצְחָק וּלְיַעֲקֹב וְנָתַתִּי אֹתָהּ לָכֶם מוֹרָשָׁה אֲנִי
יְהֹוָֽה: ט וַיְדַבֵּר מֹשֶׁה כֵּן אֶל־בְּנֵי יִשְׂרָאֵל וְלֹא

---

6. . . . [Here follow] אַרְבַּע לְשׁוֹנוֹת שֶׁל גְּאוּלָה ["the four
expressions of redemption"]: The work of redemption
will become manifest in four distinct phases, which
must be appreciated properly for a due understanding
of all that follows. . . .

○   ○   ○

וְהוֹצֵאתִי אֶתְכֶם מִתַּחַת וגו' [I will bring you out from
succumbing under the burdens]. Not: "I will smash
your burdens so that you may rise up under your own
power." No, I will permit your burdens to remain
intact, but I will take you up and bring you out from
beneath them. Your own role in your deliverance will
be completely passive.

וְהִצַּלְתִּי וגו' [I will rescue you]. The Mitzrites have
enclosed your necks in stocks so that you cannot get
out. But I do not intend that you should get out under
your own power. It is My purpose to demonstrate
that I have the power to rescue you from burdens that
defy your efforts to save yourselves. Mitzrayim is holding you fast as a chattel without a will of your own: I
will strike Mitzrayim upon its arm so that it will be
forced to let you go.

וְגָאַלְתִּי [I will redeem you]. You do not have one
kindred soul in Egypt that would feel personally hurt
by abuses to which you are being subjected. Therefore I
Myself shall step in as your kinsman. He who touches
any one of My children inflicts pain also upon Me.
Through Me you will regain your rights and your
independence. הציל implies rescue from an impending
danger; גאל denotes redemption from a process of
destruction that has already begun. . . .

Under Jewish law the גּוֹאֵל ["redeemer" or "advocate"] steps in when his kinsman has been forced by
destitution to sell his inheritance or his person; that is,
when the latter has already become legally enslaved or
unpropertied. This is to be God's relationship to us. . . .

7. וְלָקַחְתִּי [I will take you]. Once you have been
raised up, when you will be free and aware once more

of your human rights, I will take you to Myself as My
people. As soon as you are free you will become
My people! You will become My people, without a
land, without territory of your own, solely by virtue of
the fact that you belong to Me!

לִי לְעָם [to Myself as a people]. These few words
are the first statement of Israel's destiny. They express
the quality that makes Judaism so unique. People have
thoughtlessly placed what is so inappropriately
described as "the Jewish religion" into the category of
religions in general, as one religion among many others,
only to find to their amazement that this "religion"
includes many elements other than those ordinarily
regarded as part of "religion." לִי לְעָם: Israel is to be a
people unto God. This statement alone already makes it
clear that Judaism, as established by God, is not a
"religion" at all. True, Judaism embraces also elements
generally characterized as "religion," but the concept
of Judaism is completely different and infinitely broader. In "religion," God has only temples, churches,
priests, congregations, etc. Nations are subject only to
kings, governments, etc.; they are founded on the concept of statehood, not on religion and God. In Judaism,
however, God has established not a church but a
nation, and every aspect of that nation's life is to be
founded upon Him. It is as a nation, not as a
mere religious sect, that Israel is His. . . .

8. [And then I will bring you]. Israel is to be
fully constituted as a nation before it receives a land of
its own. Its existence as a nation is therefore not contingent upon whether it possesses a land of its own.
Indeed, whether or not it will possess a land of its own
will depend on whether it will faithfully discharge its
task as a nation.

מוֹרָשָׁה [heritage]. It was already given to your forefathers in spirit. You will be given this land only
because you are their heirs.

rael, but they did not hearken to Moshe because of impatience and because of harsh bondage. 10. And *God* spoke to Moshe [saying]: 11. "Go there, tell it to Pharaoh, king of Mitzrayim, that he should send out the sons of Yisrael from his land!" 12. And Moshe spoke before God [saying]: "See, the sons of Yisrael did not hearken to me; how, then, will Pharaoh hearken to me, who am of unpliant lips?" 13. Thereupon *God* spoke to Moshe and to Aharon and commanded them concerning the sons of Yisrael and concerning Pharaoh, king of Mitzrayim, to bring the sons of Yisrael out from Mitzrayim. 14. These are the heads of their fathers' houses. The sons of Reuben, Yisrael's first-born: Ḥanokh, Palu, Ḥetzron and Carmi. These are the families of Reuben. 15. Shimeon's sons: Yemuel, Yamin, Ohad, Yakhin, Tzoḥar and Shaul, son of the Canaanite woman. These are the families of Shimeon. 16. And these are the names of Levi's sons in the order of their birth: Gershon, Kehath and Merari. The years of Levi's life: One hundred thirty-seven years. 17. Gershon's sons: Livni and Shimei, according to their families. 18. Kehath's sons: Amram, Yitzhar, Ḥebron and Uzziel. The years of Kehath's life: One hundred thirty-three years. 19. Merari's sons: Maḥli and Mushi. These are the families of Levi according to their descent. 20. Amram took himself his aunt Yokhebed to wife and she bore him Aharon and Moshe. The years of Amram's life: One hundred thirty-seven years. 21. Yitzhar's sons: Koraḥ, Nepheg and Zikhri. 22. Uzziel's sons: Mishael, Eltzaphan and Sithri. 23. Aharon took himself Elisheba, daughter of Amminadab, sister of Naḥshon, to wife; she bore him Nadab and Abihu, Eleazar and Ithamar. 24. Koraḥ's sons: Assir, Elkanah and Abiassaph; these are the families of the Koraḥite branch. 25. Eleazar, son of Aharon, took himself one of the daughters of Putiel to wife; she bore him Pinḥas; these are the heads of the Levites' fathers' houses according to their families. 26. These are Aharon and Moshe, to whom *God* said: "Bring out the sons of Yisrael from the land of Mitzrayim according to their hosts." 27. These are

שָׁמְעוּ אֶל־מֹשֶׁה מִקֹּצֶר רוּחַ וּמֵעֲבֹדָה קָשָׁה: פ
י וַיְדַבֵּר יְהֹוָה אֶל־מֹשֶׁה לֵּאמֹר: יא בֹּא דַבֵּר אֶל־פַּרְעֹה מֶלֶךְ מִצְרָיִם וִישַׁלַּח אֶת־בְּנֵי־יִשְׂרָאֵל מֵאַרְצוֹ: יב וַיְדַבֵּר מֹשֶׁה לִפְנֵי יְהֹוָה לֵּאמֹר הֵן בְּנֵי־יִשְׂרָאֵל לֹא־שָׁמְעוּ אֵלַי וְאֵיךְ יִשְׁמָעֵנִי פַרְעֹה וַאֲנִי עֲרַל שְׂפָתָיִם: פ יג וַיְדַבֵּר יְהֹוָה אֶל־מֹשֶׁה וְאֶל־אַהֲרֹן וַיְצַוֵּם אֶל־בְּנֵי יִשְׂרָאֵל וְאֶל־פַּרְעֹה מֶלֶךְ מִצְרָיִם לְהוֹצִיא אֶת־בְּנֵי־יִשְׂרָאֵל מֵאֶרֶץ מִצְרָיִם: ס שני יד אֵלֶּה רָאשֵׁי בֵית־אֲבֹתָם בְּנֵי רְאוּבֵן בְּכֹר יִשְׂרָאֵל חֲנוֹךְ וּפַלּוּא חֶצְרֹן וְכַרְמִי אֵלֶּה מִשְׁפְּחֹת רְאוּבֵן: טו וּבְנֵי שִׁמְעוֹן יְמוּאֵל וְיָמִין וְאֹהַד וְיָכִין וְצֹחַר וְשָׁאוּל בֶּן־הַכְּנַעֲנִית אֵלֶּה מִשְׁפְּחֹת שִׁמְעוֹן: טז וְאֵלֶּה שְׁמוֹת בְּנֵי־לֵוִי לְתֹלְדֹתָם גֵּרְשׁוֹן וּקְהָת וּמְרָרִי וּשְׁנֵי חַיֵּי לֵוִי שֶׁבַע וּשְׁלֹשִׁים וּמְאַת שָׁנָה: יז בְּנֵי גֵרְשׁוֹן לִבְנִי וְשִׁמְעִי לְמִשְׁפְּחֹתָם: יח וּבְנֵי קְהָת עַמְרָם וְיִצְהָר וְחֶבְרוֹן וְעֻזִּיאֵל וּשְׁנֵי חַיֵּי קְהָת שָׁלֹשׁ וּשְׁלֹשִׁים וּמְאַת שָׁנָה: יט וּבְנֵי מְרָרִי מַחְלִי וּמוּשִׁי אֵלֶּה מִשְׁפְּחֹת הַלֵּוִי לְתֹלְדֹתָם: כ וַיִּקַּח עַמְרָם אֶת־יוֹכֶבֶד דֹּדָתוֹ לוֹ לְאִשָּׁה וַתֵּלֶד לוֹ אֶת־אַהֲרֹן וְאֶת־מֹשֶׁה וּשְׁנֵי חַיֵּי עַמְרָם שֶׁבַע וּשְׁלֹשִׁים וּמְאַת שָׁנָה: כא וּבְנֵי יִצְהָר קֹרַח וָנֶפֶג וְזִכְרִי: כב וּבְנֵי עֻזִּיאֵל מִישָׁאֵל וְאֶלְצָפָן וְסִתְרִי: כג וַיִּקַּח אַהֲרֹן אֶת־אֱלִישֶׁבַע בַּת־עַמִּינָדָב אֲחוֹת נַחְשׁוֹן לוֹ לְאִשָּׁה וַתֵּלֶד לוֹ אֶת־נָדָב וְאֶת־אֲבִיהוּא אֶת־אֶלְעָזָר וְאֶת־אִיתָמָר: כד וּבְנֵי קֹרַח אַסִּיר וְאֶלְקָנָה וַאֲבִיאָסָף אֵלֶּה מִשְׁפְּחֹת הַקָּרְחִי: כה וְאֶלְעָזָר בֶּן־אַהֲרֹן לָקַח לוֹ מִבְּנוֹת פּוּטִיאֵל לוֹ לְאִשָּׁה וַתֵּלֶד לוֹ אֶת־פִּינְחָס אֵלֶּה רָאשֵׁי אֲבוֹת הַלְוִיִּם לְמִשְׁפְּחֹתָם: כו הוּא אַהֲרֹן וּמֹשֶׁה אֲשֶׁר אָמַר יְהֹוָה לָהֶם הוֹצִיאוּ אֶת־בְּנֵי יִשְׂרָאֵל מֵאֶרֶץ מִצְרַיִם עַל־צִבְאֹתָם: כז הֵם הַמְדַבְּרִים אֶל־פַּרְעֹה מֶלֶךְ

the ones who spoke to Pharaoh, king of Mitzrayim, to bring out the sons of Yisrael from Mitzrayim; these are Moshe and Aharon. 28. This was on the day upon which *God* spoke to Moshe in the land of Mitzrayim. 29. When *God* spoke to Moshe [saying]: "I, *God!* Speak to Pharaoh, king of Mitzrayim, everything that I will say to you," 30. Moshe said before *God*: "Look, I am of unpliant lips; how will Pharaoh hearken to me?"

VII 1. Thereupon *God* said to Moshe: "Lo! I have appointed you as a god for Pharaoh, and your brother Aharon will be your prophet. 2. You shall utter everything that I command you, and your brother Aharon will utter it to Pharaoh, that he may let the sons of Yisrael go out of his land. 3. But I will harden Pharaoh's heart and will give many signs and convincing acts from Me in the land of Mitzrayim. 4. Pharaoh will not hearken to you; then I will turn My might against Mitzrayim and I shall bring out My hosts, My people, the sons of Yisrael, from the land of Mitzrayim, with great judgments. 5. The Mitzrites will become aware that I am *God*, when I stretch out My hand over Mitzrayim and bring the sons of Yisrael out from their midst." 6. Moshe and Aharon did this. As *God* had commanded them, so did they do. 7. And Moshe was eighty years old, and Aharon eighty-

מִצְרַיִם לְהוֹצִיא אֶת־בְּנֵי־יִשְׂרָאֵל מִמִּצְרָיִם הוּא מֹשֶׁה וְאַהֲרֹן: כח וַיְהִי בְּיוֹם דִּבֶּר יְהֹוָה אֶל־מֹשֶׁה בְּאֶרֶץ מִצְרָיִם: ס שלישי כט וַיְדַבֵּר יְהֹוָה אֶל־מֹשֶׁה לֵּאמֹר אֲנִי יְהֹוָה דַּבֵּר אֶל־פַּרְעֹה מֶלֶךְ מִצְרַיִם אֵת כָּל־אֲשֶׁר אֲנִי דֹבֵר אֵלֶיךָ: ל וַיֹּאמֶר מֹשֶׁה לִפְנֵי יְהֹוָה הֵן אֲנִי עֲרַל שְׂפָתַיִם וְאֵיךְ יִשְׁמַע אֵלַי פַּרְעֹה: פ

ז א וַיֹּאמֶר יְהֹוָה אֶל־מֹשֶׁה רְאֵה נְתַתִּיךָ אֱלֹהִים לְפַרְעֹה וְאַהֲרֹן אָחִיךָ יִהְיֶה נְבִיאֶךָ: ב אַתָּה תְדַבֵּר אֵת כָּל־אֲשֶׁר אֲצַוֶּךָּ וְאַהֲרֹן אָחִיךָ יְדַבֵּר אֶל־פַּרְעֹה וְשִׁלַּח אֶת־בְּנֵי־יִשְׂרָאֵל מֵאַרְצוֹ: ג וַאֲנִי אַקְשֶׁה אֶת־לֵב פַּרְעֹה וְהִרְבֵּיתִי אֶת־אֹתֹתַי וְאֶת־מוֹפְתַי בְּאֶרֶץ מִצְרָיִם: ד וְלֹא־יִשְׁמַע אֲלֵכֶם פַּרְעֹה וְנָתַתִּי אֶת־יָדִי בְּמִצְרָיִם וְהוֹצֵאתִי אֶת־צִבְאֹתַי אֶת־עַמִּי בְנֵי־יִשְׂרָאֵל מֵאֶרֶץ מִצְרַיִם בִּשְׁפָטִים גְּדֹלִים: ה וְיָדְעוּ מִצְרַיִם כִּי־אֲנִי יְהֹוָה בִּנְטֹתִי אֶת־יָדִי עַל־מִצְרָיִם וְהוֹצֵאתִי אֶת־בְּנֵי־יִשְׂרָאֵל מִתּוֹכָם: ו וַיַּעַשׂ מֹשֶׁה וְאַהֲרֹן כַּאֲשֶׁר צִוָּה יְהֹוָה אֹתָם כֵּן עָשׂוּ: ז וּמֹשֶׁה בֶּן־שְׁמֹנִים שָׁנָה

CHAPTER VII

1. *... and your brother Aharon will be your prophet.* "As a prophet is to Me, so shall Aharon be to you." This characterization is of paramount significance in the background of true Jewish prophecy. As surely as Moses and Aaron act here as two separate individuals, with Moses giving the directions and orders which Aaron is to carry out and pass on, so certain it is that the concept of prophecy which has God speak not *to* the prophet but *from within* the prophet is false. To this day there are those who, denying the concept of true Divine revelation, permit words and appearances to stand but in fact reduce the prophet to a mere inspired poet or lawgiver prophesying while in a state of exaltation or ecstasy. The true prophet stands *face to face* with God, as Aaron does here with Moses. Consequently, נָבִיא is a passive concept.... The proph-

et is used by God as a "wellspring" through which He, God, reveals His word. The prophet is not the author but only the transmitter of the words he utters.

3. אַקְשֶׁה *[I will harden].* We find in the Scriptural text three nuances [referring to Pharaoh's attitude]: קָשֶׁה, כָּבֵד and חָזָק.

קָשֶׁה means to be altogether "hard," not to absorb any impressions, to allow everything that happens to pass one by without permitting it to leave an impact.

כָּבֵד [lit., "heavy"], difficult to move, unmoved. One may receive an impression but there is still a wide gap between receiving an impression and permitting oneself to be influenced by it; however, this gap can be bridged, though it entails effort.

חָזָק [lit., "strong"], solid, but deliberately resisting any influence aimed at making him pliant [i.e., obdurate]....

וְאַהֲרֹן בֶּן־שָׁלֹשׁ וּשְׁמֹנִים שָׁנָה בְּדַבְּרָם אֶל־
פַּרְעֹה: פ רביעי ח וַיֹּאמֶר יְהוָה אֶל־מֹשֶׁה וְאֶל־
אַהֲרֹן לֵאמֹר: ט כִּי יְדַבֵּר אֲלֵכֶם פַּרְעֹה לֵאמֹר
תְּנוּ לָכֶם מוֹפֵת וְאָמַרְתָּ אֶל־אַהֲרֹן קַח אֶת־
מַטְּךָ וְהַשְׁלֵךְ לִפְנֵי־פַרְעֹה יְהִי לְתַנִּין: י וַיָּבֹא
מֹשֶׁה וְאַהֲרֹן אֶל־פַּרְעֹה וַיַּעֲשׂוּ כֵן כַּאֲשֶׁר צִוָּה
יְהוָה וַיַּשְׁלֵךְ אַהֲרֹן אֶת־מַטֵּהוּ לִפְנֵי פַרְעֹה
וְלִפְנֵי עֲבָדָיו וַיְהִי לְתַנִּין: יא וַיִּקְרָא גַּם־פַּרְעֹה
לַחֲכָמִים וְלַמְכַשְּׁפִים וַיַּעֲשׂוּ גַם־הֵם חַרְטֻמֵּי
מִצְרַיִם בְּלַהֲטֵיהֶם כֵּן: יב וַיַּשְׁלִיכוּ אִישׁ מַטֵּהוּ
וַיִּהְיוּ לְתַנִּינִם וַיִּבְלַע מַטֵּה־אַהֲרֹן אֶת־מַטֹּתָם:
יג וַיֶּחֱזַק לֵב פַּרְעֹה וְלֹא שָׁמַע אֲלֵהֶם כַּאֲשֶׁר
דִּבֶּר יְהוָה: ס יד וַיֹּאמֶר יְהוָה אֶל־מֹשֶׁה כָּבֵד
לֵב פַּרְעֹה מֵאֵן לְשַׁלַּח הָעָם: טו לֵךְ אֶל־פַּרְעֹה
בַּבֹּקֶר הִנֵּה יֹצֵא הַמַּיְמָה וְנִצַּבְתָּ לִקְרָאתוֹ

three years old, when they spoke to Pharaoh. 8. God *said* to Moshe and Aharon: 9. "When Pharaoh will speak to you [saying]: 'Prove yourselves!' then you shall say to Aharon: 'Take your staff and throw it down before Pharaoh'; it will turn into a crocodile." 10. Thereupon Moshe and Aharon came to Pharaoh and they did as *God* had commanded them. Aharon threw down his staff before Pharaoh and before his servants, and it turned into a crocodile. 11. But Pharaoh also called for the wise men and the magicians, and they, too, the hieroglyphists of Mitzrayim, did likewise with their sleight of hand. 12. Each one of them threw down his staff and they turned into crocodiles. But Aharon's staff swallowed up their staffs. 13. Pharaoh's heart remained stubborn and he did not hearken to them, just as *God* had spoken. 14. And *God* said to Moshe: "Pharaoh's heart is difficult to move; he refuses to let the people go. 15. Go to Pharaoh in the morning; lo! he goes out to the water, so you shall stand where you will meet him on the

9. . . . תַּנִּין is not a serpent but a huge animal that lives in the water, an aquatic monster. . . . Pharaoh himself is described in Ezekiel 29:3 as הַתַּנִּים הַגָּדוֹל הָרוֹבֵץ בְּתוֹךְ יְאֹרָיו ["the great crocodile that lies in the midst of his rivers"], the monster that exists by the grace of the river gods. The sign described in this verse is meant to tell Pharaoh: "You and your gods are merely the staff in My hand." We therefore assume that תַּנִּין in this verse denotes a crocodile.

15. הִנֵּה *[lo!]* This is the hour at which he usually makes his daily visits to the river Nile. This river is indeed the origin of Egypt's existence. Only due to the Nile could such a fertile region be developed in the midst of a desert. The continued existence and prosperity of the land was [considered to be] dependent upon the good will of the gods of the Nile. It was no wonder, therefore, that the king of the country came to the river every morning to pay his respects.

[God tells Moses:] "Now you present yourself there, too, in such a manner that Pharaoh will see that you have been waiting for him, that he will meet you before he gets to his river."

We have now come to the beginning of the account of the עֶשֶׂר מַכּוֹת [Ten Plagues]. Let us attempt to summarize them. As early an authority as Rabbi Judah arranged the plagues into three distinct groups [by their Hebrew initials, as a mnemonic aid]: ד׳צ׳ך, ע׳ד׳ש ב׳א׳ח׳ב: It is clear that this arrangement follows the narrative itself. The first two plagues in each group are preceded by a distinct warning; the third in each group; i.e. כִּנִּים [vermin], שְׁחִין [boils or blisters] and חֹשֶׁךְ [darkness], strike without advance warning. The third plague in each group comes as a punishment to the Egyptians for their failure to respond properly to the two plagues that went before.

On closer study one notes that these three groups of plagues are closely linked to the three basic aspects of the Egyptian *galuth* that were to be liquidated by the redemption. גֵּרוּת [alienhood], עַבְדוּת [slavery] and עִנּוּי [affliction] —these were the components of the fate inflicted upon the Israelites by Egypt's sinful acts against them; these same conditions were now to be brought also upon the Egyptians to impress upon them how wrong they had been to abuse this hapless people, and to make them feel upon their own flesh the bitterness of the affliction they had brought upon their victims.

דָּם [blood], עָרוֹב ["beasts of the wilderness"] and בָּרָד [hail] demonstrated to the Egyptians that they themselves were only גֵּרִים [aliens] in their own land and hence hardly in a position to outlaw Israel as גֵּרִים. צְפַרְדֵּעַ [frogs], דֶּבֶר [the plague] and אַרְבֶּה [locusts] showed them how illusory were the notions that had made them feel bank of the river, and take into your hand the staff which was turned into a serpent, 16. and you shall say to him: '*God,* the

עַל־שְׂפַת הַיְאֹר וְהַמַּטֶּה אֲשֶׁר־נֶהְפַּךְ לְנָחָשׁ תִּקַּח בְּיָדֶךָ׃ טו וְאָמַרְתָּ אֵלָיו יְהֹוָה אֱלֹהֵי

superior to the people whom they had reduced to the status of עֲבָדִים [slaves]. Finally, כִּנִּים [vermin], שְׁחִין [boils or blisters] and חֹשֶׁךְ [darkness] were the afflictions that made the Egyptians feel what it meant to have to submit to a systematic regime of עִנּוּי [affliction]. מַכַּת בְּכוֹרוֹת [the killing of the first-born] finally concludes the series and brings about [Israel's] redemption.

In recapitulation, the plagues are grouped as follows:

עִנּוּי [afflictions]	עַבְדוּת [slavery]	גֵּרוּת [alienhood]
כִּנִּים [vermin]	צְפַרְדֵּעַ [frogs]	דָּם [blood]
שְׁחִין [boils or blisters]	דֶּבֶר [plague]	עָרוֹב [beasts of the wilderness]
חֹשֶׁךְ [darkness]	אַרְבֶּה [locusts]	בָּרָד [hail]

מַכַּת בְּכוֹרוֹת [the killing of the first-born]

Each of these three groups of plagues was intended to cure the Egyptians of the delusion that they had the right to inflict גֵּרוּת [alienhood], עַבְדוּת [slavery] and עִנּוּי [affliction] upon the Israelites. ד׳צ׳ך [blood, frogs and vermin] were to accomplish this purpose by demonstrating the power of God over *water* and *land*; ע׳ד׳ש ["beasts of the wilderness," the plague and boils or blisters], by demonstrating the power of God over the *inhabitants* who lived upon the land; and ב׳א׳ח [hail, locusts and darkness], by demonstrating the power of God over the *atmosphere* that surrounded both the land and the people who lived upon it.

דָּם [blood], עָרֹב ["beasts of the wilderness"] plus בָּרָד [hail] = גֵּרוּת [alienhood]. A גֵּר [alien] is one whose continued sojourn in a place is dependent upon the will and the tolerance of another. Mitzrayim's self-assurance was founded upon its river; that is why it felt more arrogant upon its own soil than any other national entity: it considered itself independent even of the heavens. The Egyptians said: לִי יְאוֹרִי וַאֲנִי עֲשִׂיתִנִי ["My river is mine and I have created it" . . . Ezekiel 29:3]. By inflicting upon them מַכַּת דָּם [the turning of the Nile into blood] God said to them: "*Your river is (not yours but) Mine.*" If I will it, your river will not only dry up but will bring you decay instead of blessings and prosperity, and it will vomit you out. You yourselves are only גֵּרִים [aliens] upon this land; you will stay there only as long as it is My will that you do so.

With עָרוֹב ["the beasts of the wilderness"] He showed them that it was only thanks to His own interdict that the beasts of the wilderness make room upon the soil for man. God needs only to say the word and the barrier between man and beast will fall. Then man will no longer be safe even in his own home, and the beasts will avoid only the area inhabited by those humans whom the Egyptians now regard as strangers with no legal rights.

Finally, by sending בָּרָד [hail], God showed the Egyptians, to their stark terror, that no more than a nod from above was needed to cause a total upheaval in the climatic conditions of the land. Egypt has little precipitation. Whatever moisture it receives comes from the Nile. That was why the Egyptians had never seen hail before. Now, suddenly, they see a drastic change in their atmospheric environment, and the first hailstorm they had ever witnessed comes as an ominous warning that they may suddenly find themselves living under completely changed climatic conditions. This, too, is why the impending hailstorm was announced to them by the words "This time I will send all of My plagues into your heart" [Exodus 9:14].

צְפַרְדֵּעַ [frogs], דֶּבֶר [the plague] plus אַרְבֶּה [locusts] = עַבְדוּת [slavery]. A master who feels that he is superior to his slaves is laboring under a dual delusion: first, that he belongs to a superior species and second, that he is superior by virtue of his power and wealth. צְפַרְדֵּעַ, the frogs, the most timid creatures, which as a rule hide from man in the marshes and among the reeds, now emerge from their hiding places, boldly invade the habitations of man, impudently hopping even upon the bodies of the rulers of the land, thus ridding the high and mighty of their notions of superiority by showing that even the smallest and lowliest creatures have lost all respect for them.

Then דֶּבֶר [the plague] strikes, killing their horses (Egypt's pride and renown), their donkeys and their camels (the beasts of burden that bear their possessions), and the cattle and sheep (that represent their true wealth).

And then come אַרְבֶּה [the locusts], finishing off whatever produce has survived the hailstorm.

כִּנִּים [vermin], שְׁחִין [boils or blisters] and חֹשֶׁךְ [darkness] = עִנּוּי [affliction]. Now the Egyptians learned what it meant to lead a life filled with torment, pain and want. This lesson took the form of physical pain and torment, the כִּנִּים, the שְׁחִין, and the three days of hunger which the חֹשֶׁךְ brought upon Egypt. God does not need chains or cages to imprison men. He imprisons them in the darkness of night so that, not daring to move from wherever they happen to be when the darkness strikes, they remain rooted to the spot and go without food until He gives them light again.

° ° °

God of the Hebrews, has sent me to you to
say to you: Let My people go, so that they
may serve Me in the wilderness, and lo! you
have not hearkened to me thus far.
17. This is what *God* has said: By this you
shall know that I am *God*. Lo! I will strike
the water which is in the river with the staff
that I have in my hand, and it will be turned
into blood.   18. The fish in the river will
die, the river will become putrid and the
Mitzrites will give up drinking water from
the river.''   19. *God* said to Moshe: "Say
to Aharon: 'Take your staff and stretch out
your hand over the waters of Mitzrayim,
over their rivers, over their streams, their
ponds and on every gathering of their
waters so that they will turn into blood; so
there will be blood in all the land of Mitzrayim, even in vessels of wood and stone.'''
20. Moshe and Aharon did so, as *God* had
commanded them; he waved the staff and
struck the water that was in the river, before
the eyes of Pharaoh and his servants; and all
the water that was in the river was turned
into blood.   21. And the fish in the river
died so that the river became putrid and the
Mitzrites could not drink water from the
river; the blood was in all the land of Mitzrayim.   22. The hieroglyphists of Mitzrayim did the same with their secret arts;
and Pharaoh's heart remained stubborn and
he did not hearken to them, just as *God* had
said.   23. Pharaoh turned and went home
and did not take even this to heart.
24. All the Mitzrites dug around the river
for water to drink, for they could not drink
from the waters of the river.   25. Seven
full days passed after *God* had struck the
river.   26. And *God* said to Moshe: "Go to
Pharaoh and say to him: 'This is what *God*
has said: Let My people go, so that they
may serve Me!   27. If you refuse to let
them go, lo! I will strike all your territory
with frogs.   28. The river will swarm with
frogs; they will go up and come into your
house, into your bedchamber and upon
your bed! And into the house of your servants and among your people, into your
ovens and into your kneading troughs.
29. Indeed, the frogs will crawl upon you
and upon your people and all your servants.'''

הָעִבְרִים שְׁלָחַנִי אֵלֶיךָ לֵאמֹר שַׁלַּח אֶת־עַמִּי
וַיַּעַבְדֻנִי בַּמִּדְבָּר וְהִנֵּה לֹא־שָׁמַעְתָּ עַד־כֹּה:
יז כֹּה אָמַר יְהֹוָה בְּזֹאת תֵּדַע כִּי אֲנִי יְהֹוָה
הִנֵּה אָנֹכִי מַכֶּה ׀ בַּמַּטֶּה אֲשֶׁר־בְּיָדִי עַל־הַמַּיִם
אֲשֶׁר בַּיְאֹר וְנֶהֶפְכוּ לְדָם: יח וְהַדָּגָה אֲשֶׁר־
בַּיְאֹר תָּמוּת וּבָאַשׁ הַיְאֹר וְנִלְאוּ מִצְרַיִם
לִשְׁתּוֹת מַיִם מִן־הַיְאֹר: ס יט וַיֹּאמֶר יְהֹוָה
אֶל־מֹשֶׁה אֱמֹר אֶל־אַהֲרֹן קַח מַטְּךָ וּנְטֵה־יָדְךָ
עַל־מֵימֵי מִצְרַיִם עַל־נַהֲרֹתָם ׀ עַל־יְאֹרֵיהֶם
וְעַל־אַגְמֵיהֶם וְעַל כָּל־מִקְוֵה מֵימֵיהֶם וְיִהְיוּ־
דָם וְהָיָה דָם בְּכָל־אֶרֶץ מִצְרַיִם וּבָעֵצִים
וּבָאֲבָנִים: כ וַיַּעֲשׂוּ־כֵן מֹשֶׁה וְאַהֲרֹן כַּאֲשֶׁר ׀
צִוָּה יְהֹוָה וַיָּרֶם בַּמַּטֶּה וַיַּךְ אֶת־הַמַּיִם אֲשֶׁר
בַּיְאֹר לְעֵינֵי פַרְעֹה וּלְעֵינֵי עֲבָדָיו וַיֵּהָפְכוּ כָּל־
הַמַּיִם אֲשֶׁר־בַּיְאֹר לְדָם: כא וְהַדָּגָה אֲשֶׁר־
בַּיְאֹר מֵתָה וַיִּבְאַשׁ הַיְאֹר וְלֹא־יָכְלוּ מִצְרַיִם
לִשְׁתּוֹת מַיִם מִן־הַיְאֹר וַיְהִי הַדָּם בְּכָל־אֶרֶץ
מִצְרָיִם: כב וַיַּעֲשׂוּ־כֵן חַרְטֻמֵּי מִצְרַיִם
בְּלָטֵיהֶם וַיֶּחֱזַק לֵב־פַּרְעֹה וְלֹא־שָׁמַע אֲלֵהֶם
כַּאֲשֶׁר דִּבֶּר יְהֹוָה: כג וַיִּפֶן פַּרְעֹה וַיָּבֹא אֶל־
בֵּיתוֹ וְלֹא־שָׁת לִבּוֹ גַּם־לָזֹאת: כד וַיַּחְפְּרוּ כָל־
מִצְרַיִם סְבִיבֹת הַיְאֹר מַיִם לִשְׁתּוֹת כִּי לֹא
יָכְלוּ לִשְׁתֹּת מִמֵּימֵי הַיְאֹר: כה וַיִּמָּלֵא שִׁבְעַת
יָמִים אַחֲרֵי הַכּוֹת־יְהֹוָה אֶת־הַיְאֹר: פ
כו וַיֹּאמֶר יְהֹוָה אֶל־מֹשֶׁה בֹּא אֶל־פַּרְעֹה
וְאָמַרְתָּ אֵלָיו כֹּה אָמַר יְהֹוָה שַׁלַּח אֶת־עַמִּי
וְיַעַבְדֻנִי: כז וְאִם־מָאֵן אַתָּה לְשַׁלֵּחַ הִנֵּה אָנֹכִי
נֹגֵף אֶת־כָּל־גְּבוּלְךָ בַּצְפַרְדְּעִים: כח וְשָׁרַץ
הַיְאֹר צְפַרְדְּעִים וְעָלוּ וּבָאוּ בְּבֵיתֶךָ וּבַחֲדַר
מִשְׁכָּבְךָ וְעַל־מִטָּתֶךָ וּבְבֵית עֲבָדֶיךָ וּבְעַמֶּךָ
וּבְתַנּוּרֶיךָ וּבְמִשְׁאֲרוֹתֶיךָ: כט וּבְכָה וּבְעַמְּךָ

VIII 1. *God* said to Moshe: "Say to Aharon: 'Stretch out your hand with your staff over the rivers, over the streams and over the ponds and make frogs come up over the land of Mitzrayim.'" 2. And Aharon stretched out his hand over the waters of Mitzrayim, and the frog[s] came up and covered the land of Mitzrayim. 3. The hieroglyphists did likewise with their secret arts—and they brought the frogs upon the land of Mitzrayim. 4. And Pharaoh sent for Moshe and Aharon and said: "Entreat *God* to make the frogs depart from me and my people, and I will gladly let the people go so that they may offer sacrifices to *God*." 5. Thereupon Moshe replied to Pharaoh: "Seek a glory for yourself over me. For what time shall I entreat for you, for your servants and for your people, that the frogs should be destroyed from you and your houses? They shall remain only in the river." 6. He said: "For tomorrow." He replied: "[Let it be] as you have spoken, so that you may know that there is no one equal to *God*, our God. 7. The frogs will depart from you and from your houses, and from your servants and from your people; they will remain only in the river." 8. And Moshe and Aharon went away from Pharaoh, and Moshe cried out to *God* concerning the word regarding the frogs, which he had stated to Pharaoh. 9. *God*

וּבְכָל־עֲבָדֶ֖יךָ יַעֲל֥וּ הַֽצְפַרְדְּעִֽים׃ ח א וַיֹּ֣אמֶר
יְהוָה֮ אֶל־מֹשֶׁה֒ אֱמֹ֣ר אֶֽל־אַהֲרֹ֗ן נְטֵ֤ה אֶת־יָֽדְךָ֙
בְּמַטֶּ֔ךָ עַל־הַנְּהָרֹת֙ עַל־הַיְאֹרִ֣ים וְעַל־הָאֲגַמִּ֔ים
וְהַ֥עַל אֶת־הַֽצְפַרְדְּעִ֖ים עַל־אֶ֥רֶץ מִצְרָֽיִם׃ וַיֵּ֤ט
אַהֲרֹן֙ אֶת־יָד֔וֹ עַ֖ל מֵימֵ֣י מִצְרָ֑יִם וַתַּ֙עַל֙
הַֽצְפַרְדֵּ֔עַ וַתְּכַ֖ס אֶת־אֶ֥רֶץ מִצְרָֽיִם׃ ג וַיַּעֲשׂוּ־כֵ֥ן
הַֽחַרְטֻמִּ֖ים בְּלָטֵיהֶ֑ם וַיַּעֲל֥וּ אֶת־הַֽצְפַרְדְּעִ֖ים
עַל־אֶ֥רֶץ מִצְרָֽיִם׃ ד וַיִּקְרָ֨א פַרְעֹ֜ה לְמֹשֶׁ֣ה
וּֽלְאַהֲרֹ֗ן וַיֹּ֙אמֶר֙ הַעְתִּ֣ירוּ אֶל־יְהוָ֔ה וְיָסֵר֙
הַֽצְפַרְדְּעִ֔ים מִמֶּ֖נִּי וּמֵֽעַמִּ֑י וַאֲשַׁלְּחָה֙ אֶת־הָעָ֔ם
וְיִזְבְּח֖וּ לַֽיהוָֽה׃ ה וַיֹּ֨אמֶר מֹשֶׁ֣ה לְפַרְעֹה֮
הִתְפָּאֵ֣ר עָלַי֒ לְמָתַ֣י ׀ אַעְתִּ֣יר לְךָ֗ וְלַעֲבָדֶ֙יךָ֙
וּֽלְעַמְּךָ֔ לְהַכְרִית֙ הַֽצְפַרְדְּעִ֔ים מִמְּךָ֖ וּמִבָּתֶּ֑יךָ רַ֥ק
בַּיְאֹ֖ר תִּשָּׁאַֽרְנָה׃ ו וַיֹּ֖אמֶר לְמָחָ֑ר וַיֹּ֙אמֶר֙
כִּדְבָ֣רְךָ֔ לְמַ֣עַן תֵּדַ֔ע כִּי־אֵ֖ין כַּיהוָ֥ה אֱלֹהֵֽינוּ׃
חמישי ז וְסָר֣וּ הַֽצְפַרְדְּעִ֗ים מִמְּךָ֙ וּמִבָּ֣תֶּ֔יךָ
וּמֵעֲבָדֶ֖יךָ וּמֵעַמֶּ֑ךָ רַ֥ק בַּיְאֹ֖ר תִּשָּׁאַֽרְנָה׃ ח וַיֵּצֵ֛א
מֹשֶׁ֥ה וְאַהֲרֹ֖ן מֵעִ֣ם פַּרְעֹ֑ה וַיִּצְעַ֤ק מֹשֶׁה֙ אֶל־
יְהוָ֔ה עַל־דְּבַ֥ר הַֽצְפַרְדְּעִ֖ים אֲשֶׁר־שָׂ֥ם לְפַרְעֹֽה׃

CHAPTER VIII

3. . . . On closer consideration, the role of the hieroglyphists in this narrative seems strange. If indeed they were such masters of their art, they should have used their power to free the land from the plagues, not to increase them. Could they have thought that there were too few frogs about? As a matter of fact, it appears that, contrary to the conventional interpretation, their efforts in the case of each plague were directed toward the elimination of that plague. The words וַיַּעֲשׂוּ וגו׳ לְהוֹצִיא אֶת הַכִּנִּים וְלֹא יָכֹלוּ (Verse 14) clearly mean: "They did . . . to make the vermin go away, but they were unable to do so." It seems that the statement וַיַּעֲשׂוּ כֵן ["they also did thus"] has been interpreted—erroneously it would seem to us—as referring in each case to the *results* achieved by Moses and Aaron. It seems to us that, in fact, it refers only to the *means*, that is, the motions of hands and staff, which Aaron was commanded to make before the plague struck. It was these motions that the hieroglyphists mimicked because they believed that by doing so they would immediately counteract the plague. That the word כֵּן ["the same"] refers to these motions is quite clear from Verse 14. For in Verse 13 we are told also concerning Moses and Aaron: וַיַּעֲשׂוּ כֵן ["They did thus"], and this statement is immediately followed by an explanation of what Aaron did; i.e. וַיֵּט אַהֲרֹן וגו׳ ["Aharon stretched out," etc.].

Accordingly, the interpretation of Verse 3 would be: Aaron had stretched out his hand over the waters of Mitzrayim. The hieroglyphists made similar motions in order to counteract the effects of Aaron's motions, but the result was the opposite of what they had wanted to achieve. וַיַּעֲלוּ אֶת הַצְפַרְדְּעִים וגו׳ ["and they brought the frogs . . ."]: They only succeeded in bringing even more frogs upon the land of Mitzrayim. . . .

did according to the word of Moshe. The frogs died out of the houses, the courtyards and the fields.　10. They gathered them together in heaps and the land stank. 11. But when Pharaoh saw that relief had come and that his heart had regained obduracy, he did not hearken to them; [it was] as *God* had foretold it.　12. And *God* said to Moshe: "Say to Aharon: 'Stretch out your staff and strike the dust of the land,' and it will turn into vermin in all the land of Mitzrayim."　13. They did thus. Aharon stretched out his hand with his staff and struck the dust of the land, and there was vermin on man and on beast; all the dust of the land had become vermin in all the land of Mitzrayim.　14. The hieroglyphists also did thus with their secret arts to make the vermin go away but they could not do it. The vermin remained on man and on beast. 15. And the hieroglyphists said to Pharaoh: "This is a finger of God." But Pharaoh's heart remained obdurate and he did not hearken to them, just as *God* had said. 16. *God* said to Moshe: "Rise up early in the morning and place yourself before Pharaoh; lo! he goes out to the water, and say to him: 'This is what God has said: Let My people go, so that they may serve Me. 17. For if you will not let My people go, I shall let loose the beast[s] of the wilderness upon you and upon your servants and upon your people and into your homes; the houses of Mitzrayim will be full of the beast[s] of the wilderness and so will be even the ground on which they are. 18. But the land of Goshen, upon which My people stand, I shall miraculously set apart on that day so that no beast of the wilderness will come here, so that you may know that I, *God*, am in the midst of the earth.　19. I will set redemption between My people and your people. This sign shall take place tomorrow.'"　20. *God* did so; beasts of the wilderness came in heavy numbers into the house of Pharaoh and into the house of his servants, and in all the land of Mitzrayim the land was going to ruin

ט וַיַּ֣עַשׂ יְהֹוָ֔ה כִּדְבַ֖ר מֹשֶׁ֑ה וַיָּמֻ֙תוּ֙ הַֽצְפַרְדְּעִ֔ים מִן־הַבָּתִּ֥ים מִן־הַחֲצֵרֹ֖ת וּמִן־הַשָּׂדֹֽת: י וַיִּצְבְּר֥וּ אֹתָ֖ם חֳמָרִ֣ם חֳמָרִ֑ם וַתִּבְאַ֖שׁ הָאָֽרֶץ: יא וַיַּ֣רְא פַּרְעֹ֗ה כִּ֤י הָֽיְתָה֙ הָֽרְוָחָ֔ה וְהַכְבֵּד֙ אֶת־לִבּ֔וֹ וְלֹ֥א שָׁמַ֖ע אֲלֵהֶ֑ם כַּֽאֲשֶׁ֖ר דִּבֶּ֥ר יְהֹוָֽה: ס יב וַיֹּ֣אמֶר יְהֹוָה֮ אֶל־מֹשֶׁה֒ אֱמֹר֙ אֶֽל־אַֽהֲרֹ֔ן נְטֵ֣ה אֶֽת־מַטְּךָ֔ וְהַ֖ךְ אֶת־עֲפַ֣ר הָאָ֑רֶץ וְהָיָ֥ה לְכִנִּ֖ם בְּכָל־אֶ֥רֶץ מִצְרָֽיִם: יג וַיַּֽעֲשׂוּ־כֵ֗ן וַיֵּט֩ אַֽהֲרֹ֨ן אֶת־יָד֤וֹ בְמַטֵּ֨הוּ֙ וַיַּךְ֙ אֶת־עֲפַ֣ר הָאָ֔רֶץ וַתְּהִי֙ הַכִּנָּ֔ם בָּֽאָדָ֖ם וּבַבְּהֵמָ֑ה כָּל־עֲפַ֥ר הָאָ֛רֶץ הָיָ֥ה כִנִּ֖ים בְּכָל־אֶ֥רֶץ מִצְרָֽיִם: יד וַיַּֽעֲשׂוּ־כֵ֨ן הַֽחַרְטֻמִּ֧ים בְּלָֽטֵיהֶ֛ם לְהוֹצִ֥יא אֶת־הַכִּנִּ֖ים וְלֹ֣א יָכֹ֑לוּ וַתְּהִי֙ הַכִּנָּ֔ם בָּֽאָדָ֖ם וּבַבְּהֵמָֽה: טו וַיֹּֽאמְר֤וּ הַֽחַרְטֻמִּם֙ אֶל־פַּרְעֹ֔ה אֶצְבַּ֥ע אֱלֹהִ֖ים הִ֑וא וַיֶּֽחֱזַ֤ק לֵֽב־פַּרְעֹה֙ וְלֹֽא־שָׁמַ֣ע אֲלֵהֶ֔ם כַּֽאֲשֶׁ֖ר דִּבֶּ֥ר יְהֹוָֽה: ס טז וַיֹּ֨אמֶר יְהֹוָ֜ה אֶל־מֹשֶׁ֗ה הַשְׁכֵּ֤ם בַּבֹּ֨קֶר֙ וְהִתְיַצֵּב֙ לִפְנֵ֣י פַרְעֹ֔ה הִנֵּ֖ה יוֹצֵ֣א הַמָּ֑יְמָה וְאָֽמַרְתָּ֣ אֵלָ֗יו כֹּ֚ה אָמַ֣ר יְהֹוָ֔ה שַׁלַּ֥ח עַמִּ֖י וְיַֽעַבְדֻֽנִי: יז כִּ֣י אִם־אֵֽינְךָ֣ מְשַׁלֵּ֘חַ֘ אֶת־עַמִּי֒ הִנְנִי֩ מַשְׁלִ֨יחַ בְּךָ֜ וּבַֽעֲבָדֶ֤יךָ וּבְעַמְּךָ֙ וּבְבָתֶּ֨יךָ֙ אֶת־הֶ֣עָרֹ֔ב וּמָ֣לְא֗וּ בָּתֵּ֤י מִצְרַ֨יִם֙ אֶת־הֶ֣עָרֹ֔ב וְגַ֥ם הָֽאֲדָמָ֖ה אֲשֶׁר־הֵ֥ם עָלֶֽיהָ: יח וְהִפְלֵיתִי֩ בַיּ֨וֹם הַה֜וּא אֶת־אֶ֣רֶץ גֹּ֗שֶׁן אֲשֶׁ֤ר עַמִּי֙ עֹמֵ֣ד עָלֶ֔יהָ לְבִלְתִּ֥י הֱיֽוֹת־שָׁ֖ם עָרֹ֑ב לְמַ֣עַן תֵּדַ֔ע כִּ֥י אֲנִ֥י יְהֹוָ֖ה בְּקֶ֥רֶב הָאָֽרֶץ: ששי יט וְשַׂמְתִּ֣י פְדֻ֔ת בֵּ֥ין עַמִּ֖י וּבֵ֣ין עַמֶּ֑ךָ לְמָחָ֥ר יִֽהְיֶ֖ה הָאֹ֥ת הַזֶּֽה: כ וַיַּ֤עַשׂ יְהֹוָה֙ כֵּ֔ן וַיָּבֹא֙ עָרֹ֣ב כָּבֵ֔ד בֵּ֖יתָה פַרְעֹ֑ה וּבֵ֣ית עֲבָדָ֑יו וּבְכָל־אֶ֧רֶץ מִצְרַ֛יִם תִּשָּׁחֵ֥ת הָאָֽרֶץ

14–15. ... After they had tried three times and failed each time, they humbly admitted: אֶצְבַּע אֱלֹקִ' הִיא

["This is a finger of God"] and they do not appear again in the narrative. ...

because of the beast[s] of the wilderness.
21. And Pharaoh called to Moshe and
Aharon and said: "Go, offer sacrifices to
your God in the land." 22. Moshe replied:
"It is not possible to do that, because what
we offer up to *God*, our God, is Mitzrayim's
abomination; see, could we offer up that
which Mitzrayim abominates before their
eyes and not have them stone us? 23. We
will make a three days' journey into the
wilderness and offer sacrifices to *God*, our
God, as He will tell us." 24. Thereupon
Pharaoh replied: "I will let you go, and you
shall offer sacrifices to *God*, your God, in the
wilderness; only do not go too far away;
entreat for me!" 25. And Moshe said: "See,
when I go away from you I will entreat *God*,
and the beast[s] of the wilderness will
depart from Pharaoh, from his servants and
from his people tomorrow. Only let Pharaoh
not tease anymore, in not letting the people
go after all, to offer sacrifices to *God*."
26. Moshe went away from Pharaoh and
entreated *God*. 27. And *God* did according to the word of Moshe. He made the
beast[s] of the wilderness depart from
Pharaoh, from his servants and from his
people; not one remained. 28. But this
time, too, Pharaoh made his heart obdurate
and did not let the people go.

IX

1. And *God* said to Moshe: "Go
to Pharaoh and speak to him
[saying]: 'This is what *God*, the God of the
Hebrews, has said: Let My people go, so
that they may serve Me. 2. For if you
refuse to let them go and will still hold them
as your property, 3. then, lo! the hand of
God will be upon your property that you
have in the field, upon the horses, upon the
donkeys, the camels, upon the cattle and
upon the sheep in a very severe plague.
4. And *God* will make a miraculously
sharp division between the property of Yisrael and the property of Mitzrayim; not the
least of what belongs to the sons of Yisrael
will die. 5. *God* has set a fixed time.
Tomorrow *God* will fulfill this word in the
land.'" 6. *God* fulfilled this word the
next day; all the property of Mitzrayim
died, but of all the property of the sons of
Yisrael not one died. 7. And Pharaoh sent
and lo! of all the property of Yisrael not one
had died; nevertheless, Pharaoh's heart

מִפְּנֵי הֶעָרֹב: כא וַיִּקְרָא פַרְעֹה אֶל־מֹשֶׁה
וּלְאַהֲרֹן וַיֹּאמֶר לְכוּ זִבְחוּ לֵאלֹהֵיכֶם בָּאָרֶץ:
כב וַיֹּאמֶר מֹשֶׁה לֹא נָכוֹן לַעֲשׂוֹת כֵּן כִּי
תּוֹעֲבַת מִצְרַיִם נִזְבַּח לַיהֹוָה אֱלֹהֵינוּ הֵן נִזְבַּח
אֶת־תּוֹעֲבַת מִצְרַיִם לְעֵינֵיהֶם וְלֹא יִסְקְלֻנוּ:
כג דֶּרֶךְ שְׁלֹשֶׁת יָמִים נֵלֵךְ בַּמִּדְבָּר וְזָבַחְנוּ
לַיהֹוָה אֱלֹהֵינוּ כַּאֲשֶׁר יֹאמַר אֵלֵינוּ: כד וַיֹּאמֶר
פַּרְעֹה אָנֹכִי אֲשַׁלַּח אֶתְכֶם וּזְבַחְתֶּם לַיהֹוָה
אֱלֹהֵיכֶם בַּמִּדְבָּר רַק הַרְחֵק לֹא־תַרְחִיקוּ
לָלֶכֶת הַעְתִּירוּ בַּעֲדִי: כה וַיֹּאמֶר מֹשֶׁה הִנֵּה
אָנֹכִי יוֹצֵא מֵעִמָּךְ וְהַעְתַּרְתִּי אֶל־יְהֹוָה וְסָר
הֶעָרֹב מִפַּרְעֹה מֵעֲבָדָיו וּמֵעַמּוֹ מָחָר רַק
אַל־יֹסֵף פַּרְעֹה הָתֵל לְבִלְתִּי שַׁלַּח אֶת־הָעָם
לִזְבֹּחַ לַיהֹוָה: כו וַיֵּצֵא מֹשֶׁה מֵעִם פַּרְעֹה
וַיֶּעְתַּר אֶל־יְהֹוָה: כז וַיַּעַשׂ יְהֹוָה כִּדְבַר מֹשֶׁה
וַיָּסַר הֶעָרֹב מִפַּרְעֹה מֵעֲבָדָיו וּמֵעַמּוֹ לֹא
נִשְׁאַר אֶחָד: כח וַיַּכְבֵּד פַּרְעֹה אֶת־לִבּוֹ גַּם
בַּפַּעַם הַזֹּאת וְלֹא שִׁלַּח אֶת־הָעָם: פ
ט א וַיֹּאמֶר יְהֹוָה אֶל־מֹשֶׁה בֹּא אֶל־פַּרְעֹה
וְדִבַּרְתָּ אֵלָיו כֹּה־אָמַר יְהֹוָה אֱלֹהֵי הָעִבְרִים
שַׁלַּח אֶת־עַמִּי וְיַעַבְדֻנִי: ב כִּי אִם־מָאֵן אַתָּה
לְשַׁלֵּחַ וְעוֹדְךָ מַחֲזִיק בָּם: ג הִנֵּה יַד־יְהֹוָה
הוֹיָה בְּמִקְנְךָ אֲשֶׁר בַּשָּׂדֶה בַּסּוּסִים בַּחֲמֹרִים
בַּגְּמַלִּים בַּבָּקָר וּבַצֹּאן דֶּבֶר כָּבֵד מְאֹד:
ד וְהִפְלָה יְהֹוָה בֵּין מִקְנֵה יִשְׂרָאֵל וּבֵין מִקְנֵה
מִצְרָיִם וְלֹא יָמוּת מִכָּל־לִבְנֵי יִשְׂרָאֵל דָּבָר:
ה וַיָּשֶׂם יְהֹוָה מוֹעֵד לֵאמֹר מָחָר יַעֲשֶׂה יְהֹוָה
הַדָּבָר הַזֶּה בָּאָרֶץ: ו וַיַּעַשׂ יְהֹוָה אֶת־הַדָּבָר
הַזֶּה מִמָּחֳרָת וַיָּמָת כֹּל מִקְנֵה מִצְרָיִם וּמִמִּקְנֵה
בְנֵי־יִשְׂרָאֵל לֹא־מֵת אֶחָד: ז וַיִּשְׁלַח פַּרְעֹה
וְהִנֵּה לֹא־מֵת מִמִּקְנֵה יִשְׂרָאֵל עַד־אֶחָד וַיִּכְבַּד

remained immovable and he did not let the
people go.　　8. Thereupon *God* said to
Moshe and to Aharon: "Take both your
hands full of soot from a lime-kiln and let
Moshe throw it toward heaven before
Pharaoh's eyes.　　9. It shall become dust
over all the land of Mitzrayim and it will
turn into a rash breaking out in blisters on
man and beast in all the land of Mitzrayim."
10. They took soot from the lime-kiln
and placed themselves before Pharaoh.
Moshe threw it toward heaven, and then an
inflammatory rash of blisters was over
man and beast.　　11. The hieroglyphists
could not stand up before Moshe because of
the rash, for the rash was upon the
hieroglyphists and upon all of Mitzrayim.
12. But *God* let Pharaoh's heart be
obdurate and he did not hearken to them,
just as *God* had said to Moshe.　　13. And
God said to Moshe: "Rise up early in the
morning and place yourself before Pharaoh
and say to him: 'This is what *God*, the God
of the Hebrews, has said: Let My people go,
so that they may serve Me.　　14. For this
time I will send all of My plagues into your
heart, to your servants and to your people,
so that you may know that there is none like
Me on all the earth.　　15. For by now I
could have stretched out My hand, I could
have stricken you and your people with the
plague, and you would have been annihilated from the earth,　　16. but for this very
reason I have permitted you to stand, in
order to let you see My strength, and thus to
tell My Name all over the earth.　　17. You
still exalt yourself very high above My
people, not letting them go—　18. lo!
tomorrow, at about this time, I will cause a
very severe hail to rain down, such as there
has never been in Mitzrayim, even if you go
back to the day when it was founded from
small beginnings, until now.　　19. And
now send, let your property and everything
that you have in the field[s] take refuge, for
every man and beast that will be found in
the field and will not be brought home, the
hail will come down upon them and they
will die.'"　　20. Now whoever feared the
word of *God* among Pharaoh's servants
made his servants and his property flee into
the houses.　　21. But whoever did not take
the word of *God* to heart left his servants

לֵ֣ב פַּרְעֹ֔ה וְלֹ֥א שִׁלַּ֖ח אֶת־הָעָֽם: פ ח וַיֹּ֣אמֶר
יְהֹוָ֗ה אֶל־מֹשֶׁה֙ וְאֶֽל־אַהֲרֹ֔ן קְח֤וּ לָכֶם֙ מְלֹ֣א
חׇפְנֵיכֶ֔ם פִּ֖יחַ כִּבְשָׁ֑ן וּזְרָק֧וֹ מֹשֶׁ֛ה הַשָּׁמַ֖יְמָה
לְעֵינֵ֥י פַרְעֹֽה: ט וְהָיָ֣ה לְאָבָ֔ק עַ֖ל כׇּל־אֶ֣רֶץ
מִצְרָ֑יִם וְהָיָ֨ה עַל־הָאָדָ֜ם וְעַל־הַבְּהֵמָ֗ה לִשְׁחִ֥ין
פֹּרֵ֛חַ אֲבַעְבֻּעֹ֖ת בְּכׇל־אֶ֥רֶץ מִצְרָֽיִם: י וַיִּקְח֞וּ
אֶת־פִּ֣יחַ הַכִּבְשָׁ֗ן וַיַּֽעַמְדוּ֙ לִפְנֵ֣י פַרְעֹ֔ה וַיִּזְרֹ֥ק
אֹת֛וֹ מֹשֶׁ֖ה הַשָּׁמָ֑יְמָה וַיְהִ֗י שְׁחִין֙ אֲבַעְבֻּעֹ֔ת
פֹּרֵ֕חַ בָּֽאָדָ֖ם וּבַבְּהֵמָֽה: יא וְלֹֽא־יָכְל֣וּ הַֽחַרְטֻמִּ֗ים
לַֽעֲמֹ֛ד לִפְנֵ֥י מֹשֶׁ֖ה מִפְּנֵ֣י הַשְּׁחִ֑ין כִּֽי־הָיָ֣ה
הַשְּׁחִ֔ין בַּֽחַרְטֻמִּ֖ם וּבְכׇל־מִצְרָֽיִם: יב וַיְחַזֵּ֤ק
יְהֹוָה֙ אֶת־לֵ֣ב פַּרְעֹ֔ה וְלֹ֥א שָׁמַ֖ע אֲלֵהֶ֑ם כַּֽאֲשֶׁ֛ר
דִּבֶּ֥ר יְהֹוָ֖ה אֶל־מֹשֶֽׁה: ס יג וַיֹּ֤אמֶר יְהֹוָה֙ אֶל־
מֹשֶׁ֔ה הַשְׁכֵּ֣ם בַּבֹּ֔קֶר וְהִתְיַצֵּ֖ב לִפְנֵ֣י פַרְעֹ֑ה
וְאָֽמַרְתָּ֣ אֵלָ֗יו כֹּֽה־אָמַ֤ר יְהֹוָה֙ אֱלֹהֵ֣י הָֽעִבְרִ֔ים
שַׁלַּ֥ח אֶת־עַמִּ֖י וְיַֽעַבְדֻֽנִי: יד כִּ֣י | בַּפַּ֣עַם הַזֹּ֗את
אֲנִ֨י שֹׁלֵ֜חַ אֶת־כׇּל־מַגֵּֽפֹתַי֙ אֶל־לִבְּךָ֔ וּבַֽעֲבָדֶ֖יךָ
וּבְעַמֶּ֑ךָ בַּֽעֲב֣וּר תֵּדַ֔ע כִּ֛י אֵ֥ין כָּמֹ֖נִי בְּכׇל־הָאָֽרֶץ:
טו כִּ֤י עַתָּה֙ שָׁלַ֣חְתִּי אֶת־יָדִ֔י וָאַ֥ךְ אֽוֹתְךָ֛ וְאֶת־
עַמְּךָ֖ בַּדָּ֑בֶר וַתִּכָּחֵ֖ד מִן־הָאָֽרֶץ: טז וְאוּלָ֗ם
בַּֽעֲב֥וּר זֹאת֙ הֶֽעֱמַדְתִּ֔יךָ בַּֽעֲב֖וּר הַרְאֹֽתְךָ֣ אֶת־
כֹּחִ֑י וּלְמַ֛עַן סַפֵּ֥ר שְׁמִ֖י בְּכׇל־הָאָֽרֶץ:
שביעי יז עֽוֹדְךָ֖ מִסְתּוֹלֵ֣ל בְּעַמִּ֑י לְבִלְתִּ֖י שַׁלְּחָֽם:
יח הִנְנִ֤י מַמְטִיר֙ כָּעֵ֣ת מָחָ֔ר בָּרָ֖ד כָּבֵ֣ד מְאֹ֑ד
אֲשֶׁ֨ר לֹֽא־הָיָ֤ה כָמֹ֨הוּ֙ בְּמִצְרַ֔יִם לְמִן־הַיּ֥וֹם
הִוָּֽסְדָ֖ה וְעַד־עָֽתָּה: יט וְעַתָּ֗ה שְׁלַ֤ח הָעֵז֙ אֶת־
מִקְנְךָ֔ וְאֵ֛ת כׇּל־אֲשֶׁ֥ר לְךָ֖ בַּשָּׂדֶ֑ה כׇּל־הָֽאָדָ֣ם
וְהַבְּהֵמָ֗ה אֲשֶׁר־יִמָּצֵ֤א בַשָּׂדֶה֙ וְלֹ֣א יֵֽאָסֵ֣ף
הַבַּ֔יְתָה וְיָרַ֧ד עֲלֵהֶ֛ם הַבָּרָ֖ד וָמֵֽתוּ: כ הַיָּרֵא֙ אֶת־
דְּבַ֣ר יְהֹוָ֔ה מֵֽעַבְדֵ֖י פַּרְעֹ֑ה הֵנִ֛יס אֶת־עֲבָדָ֖יו
וְאֶת־מִקְנֵ֖הוּ אֶל־הַבָּתִּֽים: כא וַֽאֲשֶׁ֥ר לֹא־שָׂ֛ם
לִבּ֖וֹ אֶל־דְּבַ֣ר יְהֹוָ֑ה וַֽיַּֽעֲזֹ֥ב אֶת־עֲבָדָ֖יו וְאֶת־

and his property in the field[s]. 22. And *God* said to Moshe: "Stretch out your hand toward the sky so that there will be hail upon all the land of Mitzrayim, upon man and beast and upon every herb of the field in the land of Mitzrayim." 23. Moshe stretched his staff toward the sky, and *God* had already sent thunder and hail, and continuous fire ran down to the ground. *God* caused hail to rain upon the land of Mitzrayim. 24. There was hail, and fire self-contained in the midst of the hail. It was very severe; the like had never been in all the land of Mitzrayim since it had become a nation. 25. In all the land of Mitzrayim the hail struck down everything that was in the field[s], from man to beast. The hail struck down every herb of the field and shattered every tree of the field. 26. Only in the land of Goshen, where the sons of Yisrael were, was there no hail. 27. And Pharaoh sent and called for Moshe and Aharon and said to them: "Now I have sinned; *God* is the righteous One, and I and my people, we are the guilty ones. 28. Entreat *God!* He is the Master, that He should let this God-proclaiming thunder and hail be no more, then I will gladly let you go, and you shall no longer stay." 29. Moshe replied to him: "As soon as I have gone out from the city I will spread out my hands to *God*; the thunderclaps will cease and the hail will be no more, so that you may know that the earth is *God*'s. 30. But as for you and your servants, I know that you are still far from fearing *God*. 31. For though the flax and the barley were struck down because the barley was already upon the straw and the flax was on the stalk, 32. neither the wheat nor the spelt was struck down because they ripen late." 33. Moshe went away from Pha-

מִקְנֵהוּ בַּשָּׂדֶה: פ כב וַיֹּאמֶר יְהֹוָה אֶל־מֹשֶׁה
נְטֵה אֶת־יָדְךָ עַל־הַשָּׁמַיִם וִיהִי בָרָד בְּכָל־אֶרֶץ
מִצְרָיִם עַל־הָאָדָם וְעַל־הַבְּהֵמָה וְעַל כָּל־עֵשֶׂב
הַשָּׂדֶה בְּאֶרֶץ מִצְרָיִם: כג וַיֵּט מֹשֶׁה אֶת־מַטֵּהוּ
עַל־הַשָּׁמַיִם וַיהֹוָה נָתַן קֹלֹת וּבָרָד וַתִּהֲלַךְ־אֵשׁ
אַרְצָה וַיַּמְטֵר יְהֹוָה בָּרָד עַל־אֶרֶץ מִצְרָיִם:
כד וַיְהִי בָרָד וְאֵשׁ מִתְלַקַּחַת בְּתוֹךְ הַבָּרָד כָּבֵד
מְאֹד אֲשֶׁר לֹא־הָיָה כָמֹהוּ בְּכָל־אֶרֶץ מִצְרַיִם
מֵאָז הָיְתָה לְגוֹי: כה וַיַּךְ הַבָּרָד בְּכָל־אֶרֶץ
מִצְרַיִם אֵת כָּל־אֲשֶׁר בַּשָּׂדֶה מֵאָדָם וְעַד־
בְּהֵמָה וְאֵת כָּל־עֵשֶׂב הַשָּׂדֶה הִכָּה הַבָּרָד וְאֶת־
כָּל־עֵץ הַשָּׂדֶה שִׁבֵּר: כו רַק בְּאֶרֶץ גֹּשֶׁן אֲשֶׁר־
שָׁם בְּנֵי יִשְׂרָאֵל לֹא הָיָה בָּרָד: כז וַיִּשְׁלַח
פַּרְעֹה וַיִּקְרָא לְמֹשֶׁה וּלְאַהֲרֹן וַיֹּאמֶר אֲלֵהֶם
חָטָאתִי הַפָּעַם יְהֹוָה הַצַּדִּיק וַאֲנִי וְעַמִּי
הָרְשָׁעִים: כח הַעְתִּירוּ אֶל־יְהֹוָה וְרַב מִהְיֹת
קֹלֹת אֱלֹהִים וּבָרָד וַאֲשַׁלְּחָה אֶתְכֶם וְלֹא
תֹסִפוּן לַעֲמֹד: כט וַיֹּאמֶר אֵלָיו מֹשֶׁה כְּצֵאתִי
אֶת־הָעִיר אֶפְרֹשׂ אֶת־כַּפַּי אֶל־יְהֹוָה הַקֹּלוֹת
יֶחְדָּלוּן וְהַבָּרָד לֹא יִהְיֶה־עוֹד לְמַעַן תֵּדַע כִּי
לַיהֹוָה הָאָרֶץ: ל וְאַתָּה וַעֲבָדֶיךָ יָדַעְתִּי כִּי טֶרֶם
תִּירְאוּן מִפְּנֵי יְהֹוָה אֱלֹהִים: לא וְהַפִּשְׁתָּה
וְהַשְּׂעֹרָה נֻכָּתָה כִּי הַשְּׂעֹרָה אָבִיב וְהַפִּשְׁתָּה
גִּבְעֹל: לב וְהַחִטָּה וְהַכֻּסֶּמֶת לֹא נֻכּוּ כִּי אֲפִילֹת
הֵנָּה: מפטיר לג וַיֵּצֵא מֹשֶׁה מֵעִם פַּרְעֹה אֶת־

CHAPTER IX

24. מִתְלַקַּחַת [***self-contained,*** lit., "(fire that) grasped itself"]: The fire remained self-contained within the hailstorm, otherwise it would have caused the hailstones to melt.

27. [Pharaoh says:] "That which I have learned now has made me realize that God is in the right and we are in the wrong. Now I have seen that it is God Who is master over the land, and not we, and that we are therefore doing wrong if we act toward strangers as if we were the masters of the land." Pharaoh responded only to the effects of power; only under the stupendous impact of this plague did he finally begin to sense the infinite power of the God of the Hebrews.

° ° °

הָעִיר֙ וַיִּפְרֹ֥שׂ כַּפָּ֖יו אֶל־יְהוָ֑ה וַיַּחְדְּל֤וּ הַקֹּלוֹת֙
וְהַבָּרָ֔ד וּמָטָ֖ר לֹא־נִתַּ֥ךְ אָֽרְצָה׃ לד וַיַּ֣רְא פַּרְעֹ֗ה
כִּֽי־חָדַ֨ל הַמָּטָ֧ר וְהַבָּרָ֛ד וְהַקֹּלֹ֖ת וַיֹּ֣סֶף לַחֲטֹ֑א
וַיַּכְבֵּ֥ד לִבּ֖וֹ ה֥וּא וַעֲבָדָֽיו׃ לה וַיֶּֽחֱזַק֙ לֵ֣ב פַּרְעֹ֔ה
וְלֹ֥א שִׁלַּ֖ח אֶת־בְּנֵ֣י יִשְׂרָאֵ֑ל כַּאֲשֶׁ֛ר דִּבֶּ֥ר יְהוָ֖ה
בְּיַד־מֹשֶֽׁה׃ פ

raoh, out of the city, and spread out his
hands toward *God,* and the thunderclaps
and the hail ceased, neither did rain pour
down upon the ground.
34. When Pharaoh saw that the rain and the hail and the
thunder had ceased, he continued to sin and
made his heart immovable, he and his servants.
35. Pharaoh's heart remained
obdurate and he did not let the sons of
Yisrael go, as *God* had spoken through
Moshe.

The Haftarah for this Sidra may be found on page 847.

בא

BO

י א וַיֹּאמֶר יְהוָה אֶל־מֹשֶׁה בֹּא אֶל־פַּרְעֹה כִּי־
אֲנִי הִכְבַּדְתִּי אֶת־לִבּוֹ וְאֶת־לֵב עֲבָדָיו לְמַעַן
שִׁתִי אֹתֹתַי אֵלֶּה בְּקִרְבּוֹ: ב וּלְמַעַן תְּסַפֵּר
בְּאָזְנֵי בִנְךָ וּבֶן־בִּנְךָ אֵת אֲשֶׁר הִתְעַלַּלְתִּי
בְּמִצְרַיִם וְאֶת־אֹתֹתַי אֲשֶׁר־שַׂמְתִּי בָם וִידַעְתֶּם
כִּי־אֲנִי יְהוָה: ג וַיָּבֹא מֹשֶׁה וְאַהֲרֹן אֶל־פַּרְעֹה
וַיֹּאמְרוּ אֵלָיו כֹּה־אָמַר יְהוָה אֱלֹהֵי הָעִבְרִים
עַד־מָתַי מֵאַנְתָּ לֵעָנֹת מִפָּנָי שַׁלַּח עַמִּי
וְיַעַבְדֻנִי: ד כִּי אִם־מָאֵן אַתָּה לְשַׁלֵּחַ אֶת־עַמִּי
הִנְנִי מֵבִיא מָחָר אַרְבֶּה בִּגְבֻלֶךָ: ה וְכִסָּה אֶת־
עֵין הָאָרֶץ וְלֹא יוּכַל לִרְאֹת אֶת־הָאָרֶץ וְאָכַל ׀
אֶת־יֶתֶר הַפְּלֵטָה הַנִּשְׁאֶרֶת לָכֶם מִן־הַבָּרָד
וְאָכַל אֶת־כָּל־הָעֵץ הַצֹּמֵחַ לָכֶם מִן־הַשָּׂדֶה:
ו וּמָלְאוּ בָתֶּיךָ וּבָתֵּי כָל־עֲבָדֶיךָ וּבָתֵּי כָל־
מִצְרַיִם אֲשֶׁר לֹא־רָאוּ אֲבֹתֶיךָ וַאֲבוֹת אֲבֹתֶיךָ

X 1. And *God* said to Moshe: "Go in to Pharaoh, for I have let his heart and the heart of his servants be unmoved in order to set up these My signs in his midst, 2. and so that you may tell in the ears of your son and your son's son the succession of acts in which I have revealed Myself upon Mitzrayim, and My signs that I have established among them, so that you may recognize that I am *God.*" 3. And Moshe and Aharon went to Pharaoh and said to him: "Thus *God,* the God of the Hebrews, has spoken: 'How long will you refuse to humble yourself before My countenance? Let My people go so that they may serve Me! 4. For if you will refuse to let My people go, then, lo! I will bring locusts into your territory tomorrow. 5. It [the locust plague] will cover the eye of the earth so that it [the eye] will not be able to see the earth, and it [the plague] will eat up the remnant of what has been saved, that has remained to you from the hail; it will eat up every tree that grows for you from the field. 6. Your house and the houses of all your servants and the houses of all Mitzrites will be filled, in a manner that neither your fathers nor your fathers' fathers have seen

CHAPTER X

1. As in all the plagues linked with עַבְדוּת [slavery]; i.e., the frogs and the plague, which have already struck Egypt, so, too, in the case of the final plague in the עַבְדוּת group, Moses is told: "Go to Pharaoh," seek out Pharaoh in his palace, in the midst of his royal splendor. The purpose of these particular plagues, after all, was to make Pharaoh aware that even if the river and the soil, the land and all its lush natural wealth were to remain unchanged, it was only at the pleasure of God that he would be permitted to possess and to enjoy all this abundance. If, in his pride of ownership, Pharaoh will consider himself authorized to rob strangers in his land of their freedom and independence in payment for allowing them the privilege of enjoying even a small part of his wealth, and if he will think he has a right to enslave them, then God will know how to destroy all this abundance. God will then send into Pharaoh's kingdom a new breed of "strangers," one that will be capable of devouring all his wealth before his very eyes, down to the last shred.

I have let his heart . . . be unmoved. By not destroying his wealth all at once but leaving his most precious possessions intact in each instance, particularly in the hailstorm, I left Pharaoh something to which he could cling. And since I spared him, until the very last, the most grievous blow of all, the destruction of Egypt's agricultural wealth, he could still have doubts about the true extent of My power. He could still delude himself that the true foundation of Egypt's might and wealth was under the protection of a power beyond my reach. My purpose in proceeding in this manner was to impress the stamp of My dominion and majesty on each of the things, one after the other, that support man's existence and power on earth. I did this in order to set up "My signs in his midst," in that proud and mighty land of Egypt.

since the day that they were on earth, until this day.'" Thereupon he turned and went away from Pharaoh.   7. And Pharaoh's servants said to him: "How long shall this man be a snare for us? Let the men go and serve *God,* their God! Do you not yet realize that Mitzrayim is lost?"   8. Moshe and Aharon were brought to Pharaoh again and he said to them: "Go, serve *God,* your God; but who are the ones that are to go?" 9. Moshe replied: "We will go with our young and with our old, with our sons and with our daughters, with our sheep and with our cattle, for we have a festival of *God.*" 10. And he said to them: "So may *God* be with you, as I will let you and your children go! See, your face is turned toward evil! 11. Not so, go, please, [those of] you [who are] men, and serve *God,* for this is, after all, what you desire." And he drove them out from before Pharaoh's presence. 12. And *God* said to Moshe: "Stretch out your hand over the land of Mitzrayim against the locust [plague] so that it may come up over the land of Mitzrayim. It will eat up all the herbage of the land, everything that the hail has left over."   13. And Moshe stretched out his staff over the land of Mitzrayim, and *God* had already brought an east wind upon the earth, all day and all night. Morning came and the east wind had picked up the locust[s].   14. The locust [plague] came upon the entire land of Mitzrayim and descended upon the entire territory of Mitzrayim. It was exceedingly severe; thus, there never had been such a locust [plague] like this before, and there will not be one like it after.   15. It covered the eye of the entire land, the land became dark, and it ate up all the herbage of the

מִיּוֹם הֱיוֹתָם עַל־הָאֲדָמָה עַד הַיּוֹם הַזֶּה וַיִּפֶן וַיֵּצֵא מֵעִם פַּרְעֹה: ז וַיֹּאמְרוּ עַבְדֵי פַרְעֹה אֵלָיו עַד־מָתַי יִהְיֶה זֶה לָנוּ לְמוֹקֵשׁ שַׁלַּח אֶת־הָאֲנָשִׁים וְיַעַבְדוּ אֶת־יְהֹוָה אֱלֹהֵיהֶם הֲטֶרֶם תֵּדַע כִּי אָבְדָה מִצְרָיִם: ח וַיּוּשַׁב אֶת־מֹשֶׁה וְאֶת־אַהֲרֹן אֶל־פַּרְעֹה וַיֹּאמֶר אֲלֵהֶם לְכוּ עִבְדוּ אֶת־יְהֹוָה אֱלֹהֵיכֶם מִי וָמִי הַהֹלְכִים: ט וַיֹּאמֶר מֹשֶׁה בִּנְעָרֵינוּ וּבִזְקֵנֵינוּ נֵלֵךְ בְּבָנֵינוּ וּבִבְנוֹתֵנוּ בְּצֹאנֵנוּ וּבִבְקָרֵנוּ נֵלֵךְ כִּי חַג־יְהֹוָה לָנוּ: י וַיֹּאמֶר אֲלֵהֶם יְהִי כֵן יְהֹוָה עִמָּכֶם כַּאֲשֶׁר אֲשַׁלַּח אֶתְכֶם וְאֶת־טַפְּכֶם רְאוּ כִּי רָעָה נֶגֶד פְּנֵיכֶם: יא לֹא כֵן לְכוּ־נָא הַגְּבָרִים וְעִבְדוּ אֶת־יְהֹוָה כִּי אֹתָהּ אַתֶּם מְבַקְשִׁים וַיְגָרֶשׁ אֹתָם מֵאֵת פְּנֵי פַרְעֹה: ס שני יב וַיֹּאמֶר יְהֹוָה אֶל־מֹשֶׁה נְטֵה יָדְךָ עַל־אֶרֶץ מִצְרַיִם בָּאַרְבֶּה וְיַעַל עַל־אֶרֶץ מִצְרָיִם וְיֹאכַל אֶת־כָּל־עֵשֶׂב הָאָרֶץ אֵת כָּל־אֲשֶׁר הִשְׁאִיר הַבָּרָד: יג וַיֵּט מֹשֶׁה אֶת־מַטֵּהוּ עַל־אֶרֶץ מִצְרַיִם וַיהֹוָה נִהַג רוּחַ־קָדִים בָּאָרֶץ כָּל־הַיּוֹם הַהוּא וְכָל־הַלָּיְלָה הַבֹּקֶר הָיָה וְרוּחַ הַקָּדִים נָשָׂא אֶת־הָאַרְבֶּה: יד וַיַּעַל הָאַרְבֶּה עַל כָּל־אֶרֶץ מִצְרַיִם וַיָּנַח בְּכֹל גְּבוּל מִצְרָיִם כָּבֵד מְאֹד לְפָנָיו לֹא־הָיָה כֵן אַרְבֶּה כָּמֹהוּ וְאַחֲרָיו לֹא יִהְיֶה־כֵּן: טו וַיְכַס אֶת־עֵין כָּל־הָאָרֶץ וַתֶּחְשַׁךְ הָאָרֶץ וַיֹּאכַל אֶת־כָּל־עֵשֶׂב

---

7. לְמוֹקֵשׁ [*a snare*]. Moses had been quite candid with Pharaoh's servants. How, then, could they refer to him as a מוֹקֵשׁ ["snare"]? Actually, the use of this epithet only confirms our interpretation of what has gone before. Had God sent only one plague and allowed that one plague to persist until the Egyptians had let Israel go, Israel would have gone free long before. But this did not happen. Each of the plagues was only a partial one, ceasing each time Pharaoh

begged to have it stop. However, each of these plagues was followed by yet another calamity designed to make God's power felt in ever-increasing intensity and awesomeness. From the Egyptian point of view such a demonstration of God's might upon Egypt, followed by periodic lulls that emboldened Pharaoh to revert to his old obduracy, making Pharaoh's heart immovable, could be construed only as a "snare."

land and all the fruit of the tree[s] that the hail had left over. Not a green thing remained on the tree[s] and on the herbage of the field in all the land of Mitzrayim. 16. And Pharaoh sent for Moshe and Aharon in haste and said: "I have sinned against *God,* your God, and against you. 17. And now, please forgive my sin again only this once, and let the entreaty break through to *God,* your God, so that He may only take away this death from me." 18. He went away from Pharaoh and entreated *God.* 19. *God* again brought a very strong west wind; it picked up the locust[s] and plunged [them] into the Sea of Reeds; not one locust remained in all the territory of Mitzrayim. 20. In this manner *God* made Pharaoh's heart obdurate again, and he did not let the sons of Yisrael go. 21. And *God* said to Moshe: "Stretch out your hand toward the sky, and there will be darkness over the land of Mitzrayim and the darkness will make [the people of Mitzrayim] grope." 22. Moshe stretched out his hand toward the sky and there was an all-enveloping darkness in all the land of Mitzrayim for three days. 23. They did not see one another and no one rose up from his place for three days. But all the sons of Yisrael had light in their dwellings. 24. And Pharaoh sent for Moshe and said: "Go, serve *God,* only your sheep and your cattle shall remain behind; let your children also go with you," 25. And Moshe replied: "You yourself must place meal offerings and ascent offerings into our hands so that we may offer them to *God,* our God. 26. And our property must also go with us, not one hoof may remain behind,

הָאָ֗רֶץ וְאֵת֙ כָּל־פְּרִ֣י הָעֵ֔ץ אֲשֶׁ֥ר הוֹתִ֖יר הַבָּרָ֑ד וְלֹא־נוֹתַ֨ר כָּל־יֶ֧רֶק בָּעֵ֛ץ וּבְעֵ֥שֶׂב הַשָּׂדֶ֖ה בְּכָל־אֶ֥רֶץ מִצְרָֽיִם: טז וַיְמַהֵ֣ר פַּרְעֹ֔ה לִקְרֹ֖א לְמֹשֶׁ֣ה וּֽלְאַהֲרֹ֑ן וַיֹּ֗אמֶר חָטָ֛אתִי לַֽיהוָ֥ה אֱלֹֽהֵיכֶ֖ם וְלָכֶֽם: יז וְעַתָּ֗ה שָׂ֣א נָ֤א חַטָּאתִי֙ אַ֣ךְ הַפַּ֔עַם וְהַעְתִּ֖ירוּ לַֽיהוָ֣ה אֱלֹֽהֵיכֶ֑ם וְיָסֵר֙ מֵֽעָלַ֔י רַ֖ק אֶת־הַמָּ֥וֶת הַזֶּֽה: יח וַיֵּצֵ֖א מֵעִ֣ם פַּרְעֹ֑ה וַיֶּעְתַּ֖ר אֶל־יְהוָֽה: יט וַיַּֽהֲפֹ֨ךְ יְהוָ֤ה רֽוּחַ־יָם֙ חָזָ֣ק מְאֹ֔ד וַיִּשָּׂא֙ אֶת־הָ֣אַרְבֶּ֔ה וַיִּתְקָעֵ֖הוּ יָ֣מָּה סּ֑וּף לֹ֤א נִשְׁאַר֙ אַרְבֶּ֣ה אֶחָ֔ד בְּכֹ֖ל גְּב֥וּל מִצְרָֽיִם: כ וַיְחַזֵּ֥ק יְהוָ֖ה אֶת־לֵ֣ב פַּרְעֹ֑ה וְלֹ֥א שִׁלַּ֖ח אֶת־בְּנֵ֥י יִשְׂרָאֵֽל: פ כא וַיֹּ֨אמֶר יְהוָ֜ה אֶל־מֹשֶׁ֗ה נְטֵ֤ה יָֽדְךָ֙ עַל־הַשָּׁמַ֔יִם וִ֥יהִי חֹ֖שֶׁךְ עַל־אֶ֣רֶץ מִצְרָ֑יִם וְיָמֵ֖שׁ חֹֽשֶׁךְ: כב וַיֵּ֥ט מֹשֶׁ֛ה אֶת־יָד֖וֹ עַל־הַשָּׁמָ֑יִם וַיְהִ֧י חֹֽשֶׁךְ־אֲפֵלָ֛ה בְּכָל־אֶ֥רֶץ מִצְרַ֖יִם שְׁלֹ֥שֶׁת יָמִֽים: כג לֹֽא־רָא֞וּ אִ֣ישׁ אֶת־אָחִ֗יו וְלֹא־קָ֛מוּ אִ֥ישׁ מִתַּחְתָּ֖יו שְׁלֹ֣שֶׁת יָמִ֑ים וּֽלְכָל־בְּנֵ֧י יִשְׂרָאֵ֛ל הָ֥יָה א֖וֹר בְּמֽוֹשְׁבֹתָֽם: שלישי כד וַיִּקְרָ֨א פַרְעֹ֜ה אֶל־מֹשֶׁ֗ה וַיֹּ֨אמֶר֙ לְכוּ֙ עִבְד֣וּ אֶת־יְהוָ֔ה רַ֛ק צֹאנְכֶ֥ם וּבְקַרְכֶ֖ם יֻצָּ֑ג גַּֽם־טַפְּכֶ֖ם יֵלֵ֥ךְ עִמָּכֶֽם: כה וַיֹּ֣אמֶר מֹשֶׁ֔ה גַּם־אַתָּ֛ה תִּתֵּ֥ן בְּיָדֵ֖נוּ זְבָחִ֣ים וְעֹלֹ֑ת וְעָשִׂ֖ינוּ לַֽיהוָ֥ה אֱלֹהֵֽינוּ: כו וְגַם־מִקְנֵ֙נוּ֙ יֵלֵ֣ךְ

---

17. **this death.** At last Pharaoh realizes that the destruction of Egypt's agricultural wealth is tantamount to the country's ruin. If the locusts remain and deposit their larvae upon the land, future harvests, too, will be doomed.

21. Darkness is the final plague in the עֹנִי [affliction] group. The "alienhood" and "slavery" plagues [see pp. 236–37] in this third and final group had the most powerful impact of all in that the hail and the locusts threatened to destroy the entire land of Egypt as well as

all the personal wealth of its citizens. In a similar manner the third and final plague in the "affliction" group was the most all-encompassing in the group in that it seized the whole individual in its grip, cutting him off from all his fellow men and from all his possessions so that he could move neither his hands nor his feet to obtain the necessities of life. This was עֹנִי [affliction] in the literal sense of the word. All the Egyptians were forced to go hungry for three days because the darkness chained them to the places where they happened to be when the plague struck.

for we must take of it, in order to serve *God,* our God; we do not know with what we will have to serve *God* until we come there." 27. *God* let Pharaoh's heart become obdurate and he would not consent to let them go. 28. Pharaoh replied to him: "Go away from me! Take heed, do not come before my face, for as soon as you will come before my face again, you shall die!" 29. Thereupon Moshe said: "You have spoken well; I will not come before your face again."

XI   1. For *God* said to Moshe: "I will bring yet one more plague upon Pharaoh and upon Mitzrayim; after that, he will send you away from here; when he does send you away he will drive you out completely, with force. 2. Please speak in the ears of the people, that each man may ask from his friend and each woman from her friend articles of silver and gold." 3. And *God* let Mitzrayim see that the people was worthy of favor; the man Moshe, too, was very great in the land of Mitzrayim, in the eyes of the servants of

עַמָּ֫נוּ לֹא תִשָּׁאֵר פַּרְסָ֔ה כִּי מִמֶּ֫נּוּ נִקַּח לַעֲבֹד֙ אֶת־יְהֹוָה אֱלֹהֵ֫ינוּ וַאֲנַ֫חְנוּ לֹא־נֵדַ֗ע מַה־נַּעֲבֹד֙ אֶת־יְהֹוָ֔ה עַד־בֹּאֵ֫נוּ שָׁמָּה: כז וַיְחַזֵּ֣ק יְהֹוָה֙ אֶת־לֵ֣ב פַּרְעֹ֔ה וְלֹ֥א אָבָ֖ה לְשַׁלְּחָֽם: כח וַיֹּֽאמֶר־ ל֤וֹ פַרְעֹה֙ לֵ֣ךְ מֵֽעָלָ֔י הִשָּׁ֣מֶר לְךָ֗ אַל־תֹּ֫סֶף רְא֣וֹת פָּנַ֔י כִּ֗י בְּי֛וֹם רְאֹתְךָ֥ פָנַ֖י תָּמֽוּת: כט וַיֹּ֣אמֶר מֹשֶׁ֔ה כֵּ֣ן דִּבַּ֑רְתָּ לֹא־אֹסִ֥ף ע֖וֹד רְא֥וֹת פָּנֶֽיךָ: פ יא א וַיֹּ֤אמֶר יְהֹוָה֙ אֶל־מֹשֶׁ֔ה ע֣וֹד נֶ֤גַע אֶחָד֙ אָבִ֤יא עַל־פַּרְעֹה֙ וְעַל־מִצְרַ֔יִם אַֽחֲרֵי־כֵ֕ן יְשַׁלַּ֥ח אֶתְכֶ֖ם מִזֶּ֑ה כְּשַׁלְּחוֹ֙ כָּלָ֔ה גָּרֵ֛שׁ יְגָרֵ֥שׁ אֶתְכֶ֖ם מִזֶּֽה: ב דַּבֶּר־נָ֖א בְּאָזְנֵ֣י הָעָ֑ם וְיִשְׁאֲל֣וּ ׀ אִ֣ישׁ ׀ מֵאֵ֣ת רֵעֵ֗הוּ וְאִשָּׁה֙ מֵאֵ֣ת רְעוּתָ֔הּ כְּלֵי־כֶ֖סֶף וּכְלֵ֥י זָהָֽב: ג וַיִּתֵּ֧ן יְהֹוָ֛ה אֶת־חֵ֥ן הָעָ֖ם בְּעֵינֵ֣י מִצְרָ֑יִם גַּ֣ם ׀ הָאִ֣ישׁ מֹשֶׁ֗ה גָּד֤וֹל מְאֹד֙ בְּאֶ֣רֶץ

CHAPTER XI

2 and 3. דַּבֶּר נָא [*Please speak*]. נָא always implies a degree of reluctance on the part of the person to whom the request is addressed. Cf. Genesis 12:13: אִמְרִי נָא ["Please say," etc., where Abraham asks Sarah to say to the Egyptians that she is his sister]. The Children of Israel had just given the most cogent proof of their true moral worth. For three days their oppressors, blinded and rooted to the spot by darkness, had been completely at their mercy. For three days all the possessions of the Egyptians had lain unprotected in their homes. But no Jew took advantage of this opportunity for revenge; no Jew touched an Egyptian or even the least of his possessions. It was at this moment, when sight was restored to the Egyptians and they found all their possessions untouched where they had left them, that God caused the Egyptians to comprehend the moral greatness of this people. This realization at last overcame the antipathy the Egyptians had felt for the Hebrews, and, even more than all the miracles he had performed, the moral greatness of his people made also Moses, as a man, great in the eyes of the Egyptians.

Moses and the people of Israel might well have been reluctant to compromise this moral victory by making such requests of the Egyptians as God now commanded

them to make. However, it was the will of God that His people should not leave the land empty-handed. The previous generations of the Children of Israel, having spent their lives in slavery, had not been able to acquire even the most modest possessions. For this reason God now desired to have His people lay the groundwork for their future prosperity, which was to be acquired and consecrated by them as a result of the fact that those who hitherto had despised Israel now recognized its moral greatness. Hence the use of נָא [in God's request to Moses and the Children of Israel].

Moreover, time was growing short. Only twelve hours were left until noon the next day. Therefore דַּבֶּר נָא בְּאָזְנֵי הָעָם ["Please speak in the ears of the people"]: Persuade them, urge them to take this step. Thus, even as Moses stood before Pharaoh and Pharaoh was threatening him with death, his people were already preparing for their departure, and he and they together won their greatest moral victory over their erstwhile enslavers and oppressors in that the latter, acknowledging Israel's greatness, now felt impelled to be generous and to make some amends, however slight, for their past behavior. This response on the part of the Egyptians teaches us the lofty moral significance of God's promise [to Abraham]: "And afterwards they shall go forth with great wealth" [Genesis 15:14].

Pharaoh and in the eyes of the people.
4. Therefore Moshe continued: "This is
what *God* has said: 'When the night will
divide itself again, I will step forth into the
midst of Mitzrayim,   5. and every first-
born in the land of Mitzrayim shall die,
from the first-born of Pharaoh who sits
upon his throne, to the first-born of the
slave girl who stands behind the mill, and
all the first-born of the cattle.'   6. Then
there will be a great cry throughout the land
of Mitzrayim such as there has never been
before and there will never be again.
7. But against any of the sons of Yisrael,
from man to beast, not a dog will move its
tongue, so that you may recognize that *God*
makes a miraculous distinction between
Mitzrayim and Yisrael.   8. Then all these
servants of yours will come down to me and
throw themselves at my feet, saying:
'Leave, you and all the people who follow
you!' and after that I will go out!" He went
away from Pharaoh in hot anger.   9. *God*
said to Moshe: "Pharaoh will not hearken to
you, so that My instructive miracles may be
multiplied in the land of Mitzrayim."
10. And Moshe and Aharon had performed all these instructive miracles before
Pharaoh, and *God* had let Pharaoh's heart
be obdurate so that he did not let the sons of
Yisrael go from his land.

XII   1. And *God* said to Moshe
and Aharon in the land of
Mitzrayim as follows: 2. "This renewal of
the moon shall be for you a beginning
of new moons; it shall be for you the first

מִצְרַיִם בְּעֵינֵי עַבְדֵי־פַרְעֹה וּבְעֵינֵי הָעָם: ס
רביעי ד וַיֹּאמֶר מֹשֶׁה כֹּה אָמַר יְהוָה כַּחֲצֹת
הַלַּיְלָה אֲנִי יוֹצֵא בְּתוֹךְ מִצְרָיִם: ה וּמֵת כָּל־
בְּכוֹר בְּאֶרֶץ מִצְרַיִם מִבְּכוֹר פַּרְעֹה הַיֹּשֵׁב עַל־
כִּסְאוֹ עַד בְּכוֹר הַשִּׁפְחָה אֲשֶׁר אַחַר הָרֵחָיִם
וְכֹל בְּכוֹר בְּהֵמָה: ו וְהָיְתָה צְעָקָה גְדֹלָה בְּכָל־
אֶרֶץ מִצְרָיִם אֲשֶׁר כָּמֹהוּ לֹא נִהְיָתָה וְכָמֹהוּ
לֹא תֹסִף: ז וּלְכֹל | בְּנֵי יִשְׂרָאֵל לֹא יֶחֱרַץ־כֶּלֶב
לְשֹׁנוֹ לְמֵאִישׁ וְעַד־בְּהֵמָה לְמַעַן תֵּדְעוּן אֲשֶׁר
יַפְלֶה יְהוָה בֵּין מִצְרַיִם וּבֵין יִשְׂרָאֵל: ח וְיָרְדוּ
כָל־עֲבָדֶיךָ אֵלֶּה אֵלַי וְהִשְׁתַּחֲווּ־לִי לֵאמֹר צֵא
אַתָּה וְכָל־הָעָם אֲשֶׁר־בְּרַגְלֶיךָ וְאַחֲרֵי־כֵן אֵצֵא
וַיֵּצֵא מֵעִם־פַּרְעֹה בָּחֳרִי־אָף: ס ט וַיֹּאמֶר
יְהוָה אֶל־מֹשֶׁה לֹא־יִשְׁמַע אֲלֵיכֶם פַּרְעֹה
לְמַעַן רְבוֹת מוֹפְתַי בְּאֶרֶץ מִצְרָיִם: י וּמֹשֶׁה
וְאַהֲרֹן עָשׂוּ אֶת־כָּל־הַמֹּפְתִים הָאֵלֶּה לִפְנֵי
פַרְעֹה וַיְחַזֵּק יְהוָה אֶת־לֵב פַּרְעֹה וְלֹא־שִׁלַּח
אֶת־בְּנֵי־יִשְׂרָאֵל מֵאַרְצוֹ: ס יב א וַיֹּאמֶר יְהוָה
אֶל־מֹשֶׁה וְאֶל־אַהֲרֹן בְּאֶרֶץ מִצְרַיִם לֵאמֹר:
ב הַחֹדֶשׁ הַזֶּה לָכֶם רֹאשׁ חֳדָשִׁים רִאשׁוֹן הוּא

---

9 and 10. These last two verses bring the narrative
back to the point at which God's miraculous acts had
not yet achieved their purpose and the ultimate deliverance had not yet been announced. Following the
account of the entire series of signs and convincing
deeds that revealed God to the Egyptians, and the
impact of these acts upon Pharaoh and his people,
the scene shifts back to the Jewish people, and the narrative now records the preparations they made for the
night of their deliverance. The story goes back in time
to the period between the end of the locust plague and
the onset of the darkness. At long last Pharaoh had felt
compelled to admit: "I have sinned against *God*, your
God, and against you" [10:16]. But as soon as the plague
had ceased, the better impulses vanished once again

from Pharaoh's heart. He persisted in his old stubbornness and refused to let the people go.

CHAPTER XII

1 and 2. After the earth had been restored to mankind, God called Noah to turn his eyes from the earth
and look toward heaven, and He showed him the rainbow; saying: "This is the sign of the covenant"
(Genesis 9:17): Let this henceforth be the sign of My
covenant with the earth of mankind, to which I have
just granted a new future.

Similarly, now, in Egypt, at the threshold of the new
future to be given to the Jewish people, God called
forth Moses and Aaron, showed them the silver crescent

among the months of the year. 3. Speak to the whole community of Yisrael [saying]:

לָכֶם לְחָדְשֵׁי הַשָּׁנָה׃ ג דַּבְּרוּ אֶל־כָּל־עֲדַת

of the new moon, and said: "This renewal of the moon shall be for you a beginning of new moons" (literally, "a beginning of renewals"), and the month which begins with this new moon shall be for you the first of the months of the year." This verse contains two distinct commandments: (1) That the beginning of each month is to be established by a physical viewing of the new moon, and (2) that the order of the months of the year is to begin with Nisan, the month of our deliverance.

° ° °

It is to this directive (i.e. that the date for the beginning of each new month is to be established by the nation as a whole) that the commandment אֵלֶּה מוֹעֲדֵי ד׳ מִקְרָאֵי קֹדֶשׁ אֲשֶׁר תִּקְרְאוּ אֹתָם בְּמוֹעֲדָם ["These are *God's* appointed times for meeting, convocations to the Sanctuary, which you must proclaim at the time appointed for them" (Leviticus 23:4)] refers. It seems to us that all these provisions are based on the concept of מוֹעֵד [coming together]. For ראש חֹדֶשׁ [the New Moon], too, is described as a מוֹעֵד, and indeed, we shall see that ראש חֹדֶשׁ as such represents the overall concept of מוֹעֵד, though, unlike the other *mo'adim*, it has no specific historic or seasonal associations. . . .

מוֹעֵד . . . denotes a place . . . or a time designated for a meeting. In this passage, מוֹעֵד has the latter connotation. מוֹעֲדִים are times or seasons designated for our meeting with God. Explained in human terms, this meeting is to be a voluntary act for both parties. It is not to be a matter of a master *summoning* his servants into his presence. It is God Who wishes that His people should come to Him. That is why He specifies only in general terms the time of their coming to Him; He allows them a certain latitude within which they themselves may set the exact date for the meeting, so that the time of the meeting will be by mutual choice. Note: It is to be by mutual choice! If the beginnings of our months, and hence also the festivals associated with them, were to be tied inextricably to the astronomical phases of the planets, so that, for instance, the lunar cycle would automatically determine the *mo'ed* and the *mo'adim*, then we and our God Himself, as it were, would appear bound to the blind, unchanging cycle of nature. In that case, our *mo'ed* of the New Moon, in particular, could be cited as a persuasive argument in favor of nature worship.

But this is precisely what it should not be. Indeed, this dangerous illusion that so readily suggests itself must be countered with all deliberate firmness. It is not the physical "coming together" of the moon and the sun and the renewed irradiation of the former by the latter that produces the beginning of the month; it is not this natural phenomenon that the New Moon should celebrate. The physical phenomenon is to serve us only as a symbolic reminder: Every time that the moon reunites with the sun and receives new light from it, God wants His people to find their way back to Him and receive new irradiation from His light, no matter where they may be or through what periods of darkness they may have to pass in their path through history. Thus, the reunion of the moon with the sun is to serve as a model and occasion for our own rebirth. *Mo'ed* literally means a "joining together."

Hence, it is neither the astronomical cycle nor astronomical calculations, but only we ourselves, through the representatives of our community, that are to create our "חֹדֶשׁ" and set the date for our מוֹעֵד, our meeting with God. Hence the provision in Jewish Law: מִצְוָה לְקַדֵּשׁ ע״פ רְאִיָּה. ["the commandment to sanctify (the New Moon) entails the actual viewing (of the moon)"]. Objective astronomical data are not sufficient; subjective perception, too, is required. . . .

° ° °

"This renewal of the moon shall be *for you* a beginning of renewals." This means, your perception of the renewal of the moon shall cause you, also, to renew yourselves; it is through this perception that you are to set your own periods of renewal. The text does not read הַחֹדֶשׁ הַזֶּה ראש חֳדָשִׁים ["This renewal of the moon shall be a beginning of new moons"] but הַחֹדֶשׁ הַזֶּה לָכֶם ראש חֳדָשִׁים ["This renewal of the moon shall be *for you* a beginning of new moons"]. What we are to establish is not an astronomical cycle of months but monthly renewals for ourselves. . . .

° ° °

In the land of Egypt, the land of the most stubborn paganism, where pagan torpidity reached into the social structure of the state itself, creating the fetters of the caste system, in that land did God call forth the future leaders of His people, show them the sickle of the moon struggling to emerge from darkness into renewed light, and say to them: "This is to be the model for your own conduct! Even as the moon renews itself by the law of nature, so you, too, should renew yourselves, but of your own free will. Each time the new moon appears, it shall remind you to effect your own free-willed renewal. And as I renew you, and you renew yourselves, you shall move, like the moon, through the darkened skies of the nations and, wherever you go, proclaim the message of חִידּוּשׁ [renewal], the teaching of God, the free-willed Creator of all things, Who makes men free. Through Him alone can man become truly free in both body and soul.". . .

° ° °

3–6. . . . "I will take you to Myself as a people." [6:7] This is what God declared as the positive object of

On the tenth of this month they shall take each [man] for himself a lamb for each parental home, a lamb for each house[hold]. 4. And if the house[hold] should be too small for one lamb, then he and his neighbor, who is close to his house, shall take one according to the added number of souls; according to each one's eating shall you make your count for the lamb. 5. It shall be to you a complete lamb, a male of the first year; you may take it from the sheep or from the goats. 6. It shall be to you for

יִשְׂרָאֵל לֵאמֹר בֶּעָשֹׂר לַחֹדֶשׁ הַזֶּה וְיִקְחוּ לָהֶם
אִישׁ שֶׂה לְבֵית־אָבֹת שֶׂה לַבָּיִת: ד וְאִם־יִמְעַט
הַבַּיִת מִהְיוֹת מִשֶּׂה וְלָקַח הוּא וּשְׁכֵנוֹ הַקָּרֹב
אֶל־בֵּיתוֹ בְּמִכְסַת נְפָשֹׁת אִישׁ לְפִי אָכְלוֹ
תָּכֹסּוּ עַל־הַשֶּׂה: ה שֶׂה תָמִים זָכָר בֶּן־שָׁנָה
יִהְיֶה לָכֶם מִן־הַכְּבָשִׂים וּמִן־הָעִזִּים תִּקָּחוּ:

the *geulah* [redemption] from Egypt. Stated in the idiom of our own day, what God wanted to create was not an "ecclesiastical congregation" to worship Him, but a people, a nation, a society. The outgrowth of this redemption was to be a state whose existence as a society would be wholly rooted in God, built and shaped by Him, and consecrated to Him. And it was with the קָרְבַּן פֶּסַח [Pesaḥ offering] that God laid the foundations for this new structure.

Let us see, then, how God went about building such a state.

The human beings with whom He built it were once slaves. As such, they had no identity, no property and no families. עֶבֶד גּוּפוֹ קָנוּי לְרַבּוֹ ["A slave's body is owned by his master" (Kiddushin 16a)]; עֶבֶד אֵין לוֹ חַיִּים ["A slave has no pedigree" (Kiddushin 69a)]; עֶבֶד מַה שֶּׁקָּנָה ; עֶבֶד קָנָה רַבּוֹ ["Whatever a slave owns, his master owns" (Pesaḥim 88b)]. By saying to them: "They shall *take* each *man* for *himself*," God, in full view of their masters (on the tenth day of Nisan, one day before the darkness came), conferred upon these slaves personalities and property of their own. By His decree that an individual could "take" one lamb, and hence slaughter it, also for several other individuals, which meant that one individual was authorized to act also on behalf of one or more others in both civil and religious matters, God declared that all were equal before Him and before His Law. This concept is expressed by the Talmudic dictum שְׁלוּחוֹ שֶׁל אָדָם כְּמוֹתוֹ ["A man's agent is as himself"] (Kiddushin, 41, 42). However, since the law employs the word אִישׁ ["man"], the implication is that the exercise of such legal authority presupposes the individuals having reached a certain age of maturity: אִישׁ זוֹכֶה וְאֵין קָטָן זוֹכֶה ["A man is authorized, but a minor is not authorized"] (ibid).

Having taken up these individuals and having conferred upon them personal independence and legal prerogatives, God as the State-builder now gathers them, first of all, into family units. These familial ties are both ascending and descending. *Ascending*: the ties that bind children to their parents, uniting even the married children, who already have children of their

own, around the grandfather and the great-grandfather in a בֵּית אָבוֹת [parental home]. *Descending*: the ties that bind parents to their children, permitting the children to establish homes of their own in which they will live again for, and in, their own offspring even as their parents had lived for them and will continue to live on through them. But in this state structure, even ascending familial ties are to be based on free will, not on compulsion. By virtue of the provision "and if the household should be too small. . . ," the Law allows for self-determination in the formation of household units: "One may not slaughter (the Passover lamb) on behalf of one's adult son or daughter, or on behalf of his Hebrew slave, male or female, or on behalf of one's wife, without their explicit consent" (Pesaḥim 88a).

The law that confers upon the individual personal independence, equality, freedom and the right to own property, and the ties of blood kinship and free choice by which individuals gather into separate households — this is the foundation of the state built by God. However, the law functions also as a dividing element, placing individuals and households firmly upon their own feet and securing them against intrusion from the outside. What, then, is the bond that, in the Jewish state, should bind one household to another so that the individual families will join to form one society? Is it to be, as in other state-building systems, considerations of necessity, of mutual need, of weakness that should wrench the individual from selfish isolation and suggest to him that his concern for his own welfare should make him concerned about his neighbor's welfare also? True, the Divine system of state-building is also based on mutual need, but it is a need springing from abundance, a need to do one's duty [by one's neighbor]. "If the household should be too small. . ." Such is the law that is to build the Jewish state. It is not the poor that need the rich, but the rich that need the poor. Let him whose own household is too small to take in the blessings God has bestowed upon him seek out his neighbor, so that this neighbor may supply him with additional souls to benefit from his abundance and thus help him fulfill his duty. God can provide for the poor without

6 וְהָיָה לָכֶם לְמִשְׁמֶרֶת עַד אַרְבָּעָה עָשָׂר יוֹם
לַחֹדֶשׁ הַזֶּה וְשָׁחֲטוּ אֹתוֹ כֹּל קְהַל עֲדַת־
יִשְׂרָאֵל בֵּין הָעַרְבָּיִם: 7 וְלָקְחוּ מִן־הַדָּם וְנָתְנוּ
עַל־שְׁתֵּי הַמְּזוּזֹת וְעַל־הַמַּשְׁקוֹף עַל הַבָּתִּים

safekeeping until the fourteenth day of this month; afterwards the whole assembly of the community of Yisrael shall slaughter it between the two evenings.
7. And they shall take of the blood and put it upon the two doorposts and upon the lintel, upon the houses in which they are to

the help of the rich. But without the poor the rich cannot fulfill their life's purpose. In the state built by God, it is not considerations of personal need but a sense of duty, מְצָוָה, that should join one household to another, uniting the individual entities into one national community. Only such a concrete society, secured by מִשְׁפָּט [justice] and linked by צְדָקָה [righteousness] will give rise to a formal national structure, which, with its leaders, will become קְהַל עֲדַת יִשְׂרָאֵל [an "assembly of the community of Yisrael"].

Israel is the national entity. עֵדָה [the community] denotes the independent constituents who are responsible for the fulfillment of the nation's mission. קָהָל [the assembly] denotes the authorities that perform the functions of administration and leadership.

At this moment of emergence into a new life, each individual, each household, each family, and the entire community, as a whole and in its individual parts, is to see itself in its relationship to God as שֶׂה [a lamb]; each constituent must dedicate himself completely to the task of being צֹאן מַרְעִיתוֹ [the flock of His pasture], conceive of God as his Shepherd, as the רוֹעֵה יִשְׂרָאֵל, and place himself under His guidance and direction. From the moment at which God assumed His position as our Leader, the concept of God as our Shepherd and of ourselves as His flock became the most comprehensive and lasting view of our relationship toward God and God's relationship toward us.

כֶּבֶשׂ אֶחָד בַּבֹּקֶר ["one sheep in the morning"] and כֶּבֶשׂ אֶחָד בֵּין הָעַרְבָּיִם ["one sheep between the two evenings"]. These instructions symbolize the manner in which Israel henceforth was to present and dedicate itself to its God at the waxing and waning of each day; they represent nothing else but a continuation and reiteration of that moment when Israel first set out upon its path through history as שֶׂה [a lamb], submitting to the leadership of God, the רוֹעֵה יִשְׂרָאֵל [Shepherd of Israel], cf. נוֹהֵג כַּצֹּאן יוֹסֵף ["Thou Who leadest Yosef like a flock"] (Psalms 80:2).

It should be noted, however, that the Jewish "lamb" is not a meek, sad creature that bears the troubles of the world upon its shoulders and allows itself to be led to the slaughter without putting up resistance. It is שֶׂה תָמִים זָכָר בֶּן שָׁנָה יִהְיֶה לָכֶם ["a whole, unblemished lamb, a male of the first year"]: It is to express the ideas of our character candidly, without distortion, with manly vigor and the freshness of eternal youth. The flock of God is to be perfect, standing upon its own feet. At the same time it must remain forever young, never regard itself as having outgrown God's guidance.

We may consider our social position in terms of either כֶּבֶשׂ [a sheep] or עֵז [a goat]. Cf. "You may take it from the sheep or from the goats." As long as the individual remains within the צֹאן [flock], he may choose to be either a "sheep" or a "goat." The latter, עֵז, shows greater independence toward the outside than does the sheep. Hence עֵז implies resistance. The goat takes on an outward posture of defiance, showing its horns to every stranger. But in his relationship to his keeper he is as obedient and pliant as the sheep.

תָּמִים ["complete," "whole," "unblemished"] implies the unreserved devotion of the entire personality, in all its aspects; it is a basic qualification for any קָרְבָּן, any "coming closer"[1] to God, even as the basic prerequisite for the covenant of Abraham is "conduct yourself before Me and become complete" [Genesis 17:1].

בֵּין הָעַרְבָּיִם *[between the two evenings]*. Between the two "comminglings of day and night"; the one in which night already mingles with daytime, and the other in which daytime is still intermingled with night; the one in which the day begins to wane, and the other in which the last rays of daylight depart. This is the time span between the moment at which the sun has already passed its zenith and the moment of actual nightfall. This means, the entire afternoon of the fourteenth day of Nisan; i.e., the point of separation between the fourteenth day of Nisan, which was still part of the era of slavery, and the fifteenth, which did not begin until nightfall but which in fact already "dawned" during the afternoon of the fourteenth and was to bring deliverance and freedom. Israel was to prepare itself for this moment, which was to mark the beginning of deliverance to the outside ("and I will redeem you with an outstretched arm") and of election within ("and I shall take you to Me as a people"), by presenting itself for its election as the "sheep of His flock," prepared in every respect to submit to God's guidance, and by expressing symbolically through the act of שְׁחִיטָה [the slaughter of the Passover lamb] its own readiness to give up every aspect of its former existence.

[1]*Note to the English translation*: קָרְבָּן = "offering" or "sacrifice," from קרב "to come near." [G.H.]

eat it. 8. Then they shall eat the meat during that night, roasted with fire, and unleavened bread; with bitter herbs shall

אֲשֶׁר־יֹאכְלוּ אֹתוֹ בָּהֶם: ח וְאָכְלוּ אֶת־הַבָּשָׂר בַּלַּיְלָה הַזֶּה צְלִי־אֵשׁ וּמַצּוֹת עַל־מְרֹרִים

7 and 8. However, the act of giving up all of one's former existence before God as symbolized by the slaughter of the animal offering is not to be equated with self-destruction. Rather, it is a basic requirement for the attainment of a higher level of existence through God. The blood that is shed is immediately taken up and received for this new and loftier level of existence. This is true particularly in the case of the Passover offering; the Passover lamb is slaughtered solely for the purpose of being enjoyed as food by the individuals who, by offering it, have symbolically presented themselves to God and given themselves up entirely to Him. In none of the other offerings is the act of eating as essential as in the case of the Passover lamb (Cf. Pesaḥim 78b, f.). Only in connection with the Passover lamb are we told, "Its only purpose is to be eaten" (Pesaḥim 76b).

To become free and independent—does this mean anything else but to have the free use and enjoyment of one's own personality? To be permitted to spend all of oneself, to use all one's physical energies and mental abilities, for his own purposes: this is the very essence of independence. This is what establishes the ego in its full personal worth and confers upon the individual his physical and spiritual self as his personal domain over which he alone may rule. This, so we believe, is the reason why particularly in the case of the Passover offering it is so important that the flesh of the animal offering must be eaten by the same individuals to whom the animal had belonged; that is, by the individuals whose self-sacrifice the offering was to represent. The Passover offering symbolizes the independence to be gained by giving oneself up to God; it represents the gaining of one's own self which, until that time, had been absorbed and lost in the personality of the master whom the slave had served. Hence we are told also in connection with this offering: "A slaughtering not performed for those assigned to partake of it and not performed for the purpose of personal consumption is invalid under the Law." A slaughtering "not performed for those assigned to partake of it" would imply outright enslavement, and "not for the purpose of personal consumption" would imply an act of self-immolation made without regaining an independent personality of one's own.

However, the components from which God sought to build up His people were not to be free and independent *individuals* but, as we have already noted, free and independent *households*, formed on the basis of blood ties or of free personal choice. Only within the framework of the family, formed by the free will of its members, can the individual mature so that he will be able to derive enjoyment from his own personality. This thought is to be expressed symbolically by having the blood of the lamb taken up and put upon the מְזוּזוֹת [doorposts] and מַשְׁקוֹף [lintel] of the house within which the lamb is to be consumed by the same people who offered it.

The text reads עַל שְׁתֵּי הַמְּזוּזוֹת וְעַל הַמַּשְׁקוֹף עַל הַבָּתִּים וגו׳ ["the two doorposts and upon the lintel, upon the houses"]; the מְזוּזוֹת [doorposts] and the מַשְׁקוֹף [lintel] represent the entire house. The function of the house is a dual one, social and physical: first, to separate its occupants from the rest of human society, and secondly, to protect its occupants from the elements of nature. The former function is performed by the walls; the latter, by the roof. The function of separation is symbolized by the two doorposts; that of protection, by the lintel, the beam above the door which suggests the roof in that it "looks down from above."

When the slave becomes a person in his own right, a father and a son in a family of his own, he receives from God מְזוּזוֹת וּמַשְׁקוֹף: legal protection from the invasion of his privacy by other individuals, and physical protection from the elements of nature. But in order to attain this Divine protection, he must first place all of his existence, past and present, at the command of God as his Shepherd, and devote to God his entire personality which he is to enjoy within the framework of Divine guidance and protection. All this is symbolized by putting some of the blood of the lamb upon the doorposts and upon the lintel of the house within which the lamb is to be consumed. It is not the walls that protect the individual from the violence of other individuals, nor is it the roof that shelters him from the hostile elements of nature. It is God Who protects those ready to give themselves to Him.

Then they shall eat the meat. On this night that will make them free, they themselves are to benefit, once again, from the personality they have offered up; however, they must eat the lamb that symbolizes their offering in the following manner: roasted directly over fire, and with unleavened bread and bitter herbs.

The explanation of the מַצּוֹת [matzoth] and מְרוֹרִים [bitter herbs] is obvious: When the Children of Israel left Egypt, their oppressors did not permit them sufficient time to wait for their dough to rise, and so they had to take it with them as מַצּוֹת, in the unleavened state. Throughout their enslavement, too, they were never given time to let their dough leaven; driven by the taskmaster's whip and the breathless rush of unremitting toil, they could bake their bread only in utmost haste. Thus, מַצּוֹת is literally the bread of slaves; indeed, we describe it as the "bread of dependence, which our

יֹאכְלֻהוּ: ט אַל־תֹּאכְלוּ מִמֶּנּוּ נָא וּבָשֵׁל מְבֻשָּׁל
בַּמָּיִם כִּי אִם־צְלִי־אֵשׁ רֹאשׁוֹ עַל־כְּרָעָיו וְעַל־
קִרְבּוֹ: י וְלֹא־תוֹתִירוּ מִמֶּנּוּ עַד־בֹּקֶר וְהַנֹּתָר
מִמֶּנּוּ עַד־בֹּקֶר בָּאֵשׁ תִּשְׂרֹפוּ: יא וְכָכָה תֹּאכְלוּ
אֹתוֹ מָתְנֵיכֶם חֲגֻרִים נַעֲלֵיכֶם בְּרַגְלֵיכֶם
וּמַקֶּלְכֶם בְּיֶדְכֶם וַאֲכַלְתֶּם אֹתוֹ בְּחִפָּזוֹן פֶּסַח
הוּא לַיהוָה: יב וְעָבַרְתִּי בְאֶרֶץ־מִצְרַיִם בַּלַּיְלָה
הַזֶּה וְהִכֵּיתִי כָל־בְּכוֹר בְּאֶרֶץ מִצְרַיִם מֵאָדָם
וְעַד־בְּהֵמָה וּבְכָל־אֱלֹהֵי מִצְרַיִם אֶעֱשֶׂה
שְׁפָטִים אֲנִי יְהוָה: יג וְהָיָה הַדָּם לָכֶם לְאֹת עַל
הַבָּתִּים אֲשֶׁר אַתֶּם שָׁם וְרָאִיתִי אֶת־הַדָּם
וּפָסַחְתִּי עֲלֵכֶם וְלֹא־יִהְיֶה בָכֶם נֶגֶף לְמַשְׁחִית
בְּהַכֹּתִי בְּאֶרֶץ מִצְרָיִם: יד וְהָיָה הַיּוֹם הַזֶּה
לָכֶם לְזִכָּרוֹן וְחַגֹּתֶם אֹתוֹ חַג לַיהוָה לְדֹרֹתֵיכֶם
חֻקַּת עוֹלָם תְּחָגֻּהוּ: טו שִׁבְעַת יָמִים מַצּוֹת

they eat it. 9. You shall not eat it half-done and also not cooked in water as is usual; in no other way but roasted with fire, the head with the legs and the entrails. 10. And you shall not leave any of it over until the morning, and any of it that will remain until the morning you shall burn in fire. 11. And this is how you shall eat it: With your loins girded, your shoes upon your feet and your staff in your hand; you shall eat it in haste; it is a Pesaḥ intended for *God*. 12. I will pass through the land of Mitzrayim on that night and I will kill every first-born in the land of Mitzrayim, from man to beast, and I will perform acts of judgment upon all the gods of Mitzrayim, I, *God*. 13. Then the blood shall serve as a sign for you upon the houses in which you are; I will see the blood and will pass over you, and no fatal blow shall strike you while I strike in the land of Mitzrayim. 14. This day shall remain for you as a memorial and you shall celebrate it as a festival consecrated to *God*; you shall celebrate it for your descendants as an everlasting statute. 15. Seven days you shall eat only unleavened bread; however, on that first day

forefathers ate in Egypt." Hence it clearly symbolizes enslavement.

It is obvious, too, that the מְרוֹרִים ["bitter herbs"] allude to the fact that the Egyptians embittered the lives of our ancestors. Thus, they symbolize the affliction, the torment with which the Egyptians embittered the lives of the Children of Israel.

Now if מַצּוֹת and מָרוֹר symbolize two of the three aspects of the Egyptian *galuth* which we already know, it does not seem too far-fetched to suggest that the lamb, roasted in fire, symbolizes the third element, that of גֵּרוּת [alienhood]. Without a foundation, without firm ground beneath its feet, suspended in midair—not roasted in a pot but suspended on a spit—this is the manner in which the קָרְבַּן פֶּסַח [Passover offering] must be prepared for our consumption. Without a foundation, without firm ground beneath one's feet—this is a literal description of the state of גֵּרוּת [alienhood] in which this people, now rising to freedom and independence, was to mature for its destiny. Thus, conversely, in a later era, when Judah was threatened with exile once again, those who believed they could resist the fate ordained for them said of Jerusalem (Ezekiel 11:3): "This city is the caldron and we are the meat"; i.e., "Jerusalem is our natural, permanent base which cannot be removed from beneath our feet and upon which we will attain the perfection ordained for us." But then they are informed that they cannot escape exile: ". . . This city shall not be your caldron" (11:11). Accordingly, at the moment of freedom regained, the specifications צְלִי אֵשׁ וּמַצּוֹת עַל מְרוֹרִים ["roasted with fire, and unleavened bread; with bitter herbs"] symbolically bid the Children of Israel to recall גֵּרוּת, עַבְדוּת וְעִנּוּי [alienhood, slavery and affliction], the three primary aspects of Egyptian oppression, to make them aware that, even at the moment of their deliverance, the oppression still lay heavily upon them. They were still slaves under Egyptian domination, and it was God, and God alone, Who could and did give them their freedom.

15. . . . We have already stated our interpretation of מַצָּה [the unleavened bread] as a symbol of slavery, of social dependence. חָמֵץ [leaven] is the antithesis of מַצָּה; it is therefore the symbol of social independence. The day of Passover is to serve us "as a memorial" [Verse 14], recalling to us anew each year the moment at which we received our freedom and independence, so that we may never forget the manner in which these gifts were bestowed upon us. Therefore the day which brings us our rise to freedom and independence intro-

you shall clear away all leaven from your
houses, for whoever eats anything leavened,
that soul shall be cut off from Yisrael, from
the first day until the seventh day.
16. And on the first day there shall be for
you a convocation to the Sanctuary and on
the seventh day a convocation to the Sanctuary; no [creating] work may be done on
them; however, that which can serve as food
for all men, only that may be done for you.
17. And you shall keep [watch over] the
[cakes of] unleavened bread, for on this very
day I brought your hosts out from the land
of Mitzrayim, and thus you shall keep this
day for your descendants as an everlasting
statute.   18. In the first [month], on the
fourteenth day of the month, in the evening, you shall eat unleavened bread; until
the twenty-first day of the month, in the
evening.   19. Seven days no leaven shall
be found in your houses; for whoever eats
anything containing *hametz*, that soul shall
be cut off from the community of Yisrael, whether he has come from abroad
or whether he is a native of the land.
20. Whatever contains *hametz* you must
not eat; you shall eat *matzoth* in all your
dwelling places."   21. Then Moshe called

תֹּאכֵ֔לוּ אַ֚ךְ בַּיּ֣וֹם הָרִאשׁ֔וֹן תַּשְׁבִּ֖יתוּ שְּׂאֹ֑ר
מִבָּתֵּיכֶ֗ם כִּ֣י ׀ כָּל־אֹכֵ֣ל חָמֵ֗ץ וְנִכְרְתָ֞ה הַנֶּ֤פֶשׁ
הַהִוא֙ מִיִּשְׂרָאֵ֔ל מִיּ֥וֹם הָרִאשֹׁ֖ן עַד־י֥וֹם
הַשְּׁבִעִֽי: טז וּבַיּ֤וֹם הָרִאשׁוֹן֙ מִקְרָא־קֹ֔דֶשׁ
וּבַיּוֹם֙ הַשְּׁבִיעִ֔י מִֽקְרָא־קֹ֖דֶשׁ יִהְיֶ֣ה לָכֶ֑ם כָּל־
מְלָאכָה֙ לֹא־יֵעָשֶׂ֣ה בָהֶ֔ם אַ֣ךְ אֲשֶׁ֧ר יֵאָכֵ֣ל לְכָל־
נֶ֗פֶשׁ ה֥וּא לְבַדּ֖וֹ יֵעָשֶׂ֥ה לָכֶֽם: יז וּשְׁמַרְתֶּם֮ אֶת־
הַמַּצּוֹת֒ כִּ֗י בְּעֶ֙צֶם֙ הַיּ֣וֹם הַזֶּ֔ה הוֹצֵ֥אתִי אֶת־
צִבְאֽוֹתֵיכֶ֖ם מֵאֶ֣רֶץ מִצְרָ֑יִם וּשְׁמַרְתֶּ֞ם אֶת־הַיּ֤וֹם
הַזֶּה֙ לְדֹרֹֽתֵיכֶ֔ם חֻקַּ֖ת עוֹלָֽם: יח בָּֽרִאשֹׁ֗ן
בְּאַרְבָּעָ֣ה עָשָׂ֥ר י֙וֹם֙ לַחֹ֔דֶשׁ בָּעֶ֖רֶב תֹּאכְל֣וּ מַצֹּ֑ת
עַ֠ד י֣וֹם הָאֶחָ֧ד וְעֶשְׂרִ֛ים לַחֹ֖דֶשׁ בָּעָֽרֶב:
יט שִׁבְעַ֣ת יָמִ֔ים שְׂאֹ֕ר לֹ֥א יִמָּצֵ֖א בְּבָתֵּיכֶ֑ם כִּ֣י ׀
כָּל־אֹכֵ֣ל מַחְמֶ֗צֶת וְנִכְרְתָ֞ה הַנֶּ֤פֶשׁ הַהִוא֙ מֵעֲדַ֣ת
יִשְׂרָאֵ֔ל בַּגֵּ֖ר וּבְאֶזְרַ֥ח הָאָֽרֶץ: כ כָּל־מַחְמֶ֖צֶת
לֹ֣א תֹאכֵ֑לוּ בְּכֹל֙ מֽוֹשְׁבֹ֣תֵיכֶ֔ם תֹּאכְל֖וּ מַצּֽוֹת: פ
חמישי כא וַיִּקְרָ֥א מֹשֶׁ֛ה לְכָל־זִקְנֵ֥י יִשְׂרָאֵ֖ל

duces a whole cycle of days, not with the sign of
freedom but with the removal of the symbol of
independence.

For a complete cycle of seven days we must not
permit ourselves to partake of the bread of independence. Indeed, on the very day we attained personal
independence and the right to property of our own, as
symbolized by the words וְיִקְחוּ לָהֶם אִישׁ ... לַבָּיִת ["they
shall *take* each [*man*] ... for each *household*"], we
must, on our own accord, clear out from all our homes
that specific symbol of social independence, and for the
seven days that follow we are not permitted to nourish
ourselves with the bread of independence. In this way
we are to remind ourselves, in symbolic terms, that at
the moment of our emergence to freedom and independence we had not yet possessed even a trace of independence or of ability to achieve independence (as symbolized by שְׂאֹר [leaven]). We still had neither freedom nor
power, and it was only the free commanding power of
God that made us free and independent. Therefore,
anyone who, during those seven days that commemorate our rise to freedom, אוֹכֵל כְּזַיִת חָמֵץ ["eats a quantity
of *hametz* equivalent to the size of an olive"], partakes
of the bread of independence in any quantity sufficient

for the preservation of life (i.e., of the personality),
thereby denies the Divine origin of our freedom and
asserts that it was achieved by man [without the aid of
God]. But by so doing, he departs from the foundation
of Israel's past and thereby also has cut himself off from
a future as part of the people of Israel.

o   o   o

16. ... [In Scripture] a cycle of seven days always
represents a time span within which a new or revived
level is attained. Whenever such a seven-day cycle is
devoted to a *mo'ed*, this means that the ideas and
attitudes that are to emerge with the phase of revival on
the first day are to attain the peak of clarity and force
on the seventh day. Then, having attained this elevation and vitality, we are to return to everyday life in
order to put these ideas into practice. Hence it is on the
first day, and again on the seventh, that this "convocation to God and to His Sanctuary" attains its full
impact. On the first day, the idea to be revived is to be
brought home to us in full force; on the seventh, we
should have assimilated this idea completely so that
we may take it with us as we return to everyday life.

o   o   o

וַיֹּאמֶר אֲלֵהֶם מִשְׁכוּ וּקְחוּ לָכֶם צֹאן
לְמִשְׁפְּחֹתֵיכֶם וְשַׁחֲטוּ הַפָּסַח׃ כב וּלְקַחְתֶּם
אֲגֻדַּת אֵזוֹב וּטְבַלְתֶּם בַּדָּם אֲשֶׁר־בַּסַּף וְהִגַּעְתֶּם
אֶל־הַמַּשְׁקוֹף וְאֶל־שְׁתֵּי הַמְּזוּזֹת מִן־הַדָּם
אֲשֶׁר בַּסָּף וְאַתֶּם לֹא תֵצְאוּ אִישׁ מִפֶּתַח־בֵּיתוֹ
עַד־בֹּקֶר׃ כג וְעָבַר יְהוָה לִנְגֹּף אֶת־מִצְרַיִם
וְרָאָה אֶת־הַדָּם עַל־הַמַּשְׁקוֹף וְעַל שְׁתֵּי
הַמְּזוּזֹת וּפָסַח יְהוָה עַל־הַפֶּתַח וְלֹא יִתֵּן
הַמַּשְׁחִית לָבֹא אֶל־בָּתֵּיכֶם לִנְגֹּף׃ כד וּשְׁמַרְתֶּם
אֶת־הַדָּבָר הַזֶּה לְחָק־לְךָ וּלְבָנֶיךָ עַד־עוֹלָם׃
כה וְהָיָה כִּי־תָבֹאוּ אֶל־הָאָרֶץ אֲשֶׁר יִתֵּן יְהוָה
לָכֶם כַּאֲשֶׁר דִּבֵּר וּשְׁמַרְתֶּם אֶת־הָעֲבֹדָה
הַזֹּאת׃ כו וְהָיָה כִּי־יֹאמְרוּ אֲלֵיכֶם בְּנֵיכֶם מָה
הָעֲבֹדָה הַזֹּאת לָכֶם׃ כז וַאֲמַרְתֶּם זֶבַח־פֶּסַח
הוּא לַיהוָה אֲשֶׁר פָּסַח עַל־בָּתֵּי בְנֵי־יִשְׂרָאֵל
בְּמִצְרַיִם בְּנָגְפּוֹ אֶת־מִצְרַיִם וְאֶת־בָּתֵּינוּ הִצִּיל
וַיִּקֹּד הָעָם וַיִּשְׁתַּחֲווּ׃ כח וַיֵּלְכוּ וַיַּעֲשׂוּ בְּנֵי

all the elders of Yisrael and said to them: "Go out and take for yourselves sheep for your families and slaughter the *Pesaḥ* [offering]. 22. Take a bunch of hyssop, dip it into the blood that is in the basin, and touch the lintel and the two doorposts with some of the blood that is in the basin; but as for yourselves, none of you shall go out from his house until the morning. 23. And *God* will pass through in order to strike Mitzrayim, and He will see the blood upon the lintel and upon the two doorposts, and *God* will pause as He passes over the entrance and will not permit that which destroys to enter your houses to deal you a mortal blow. 24. You shall keep this word so that it may be a statute for you and your children forever. 25. And it shall come to pass that when you come to the land which *God* will give you as He has said, so you shall keep this service. 26. And it shall come to pass that when your sons will say to you; 'What is this service to you?' 27. you shall say: 'It is a meal of a deliverance performed through a pausing pass-over, consecrated to *God*, Who paused as He passed over the houses of the sons of Yisrael in Mitzrayim when He struck Mitzrayim mortally and rescued our houses!" And the people bowed and cast themselves down. 28. The sons of Yisrael went and did as *God* had com-

22. This very first law offers us a concrete example of תשבע״פ [the Oral Law]. We read here how Moses communicated orally to the elders of his people details for the observance of a law which had not been included in the utterance of God as recorded in the written text. The utterances of God as recorded in the Biblical text gave only the broad outlines of the law; more detailed instructions were left for oral communication to Moses, who in turn conveyed them to the people, again by word of mouth.

° ° °

27. וַאֲמַרְתֶּם וגו׳ *[you shall say]*. The text reads simply ["You shall say"], not וַאֲמַרְתֶּם לָהֶם ["You shall say *to them*"], as it does later in וְהִגַּדְתָּ לְבִנְךָ ["You shall tell to your child" 13:8], וְאָמַרְתָּ אֵלָיו ["and you shall say *to him*"]. The Word of God does not expect that a generation mired in materialistic alienation from God will mend its ways as the result of simple instruction. Such results can be expected only from personal examples of earnest, enthusiastic compliance with the Law.

Do not heed the disdainful protests of a generation which, ossified in materialism, no longer understands the meaning and the spirit of God-ordained practices. Proclaim it so that anyone who wishes to hear may hear it: that even to this day it is still זֶבַח פֶּסַח הוּא לַד׳ ["a meal of deliverance. . ."], a meal intended to lead us from death to life, that for the people of Israel life and liberty are still dependent on the conditions which initially had brought them these gifts, and that therefore this עֲבוֹדָה, this repeated symbolic entry into the service of God, is and shall forever remain an act of the highest, most positive significance. . . .

28. ***The sons of Yisrael went and did . . . so did they do.*** Moses and Aaron faithfully transmitted the command of God to the Children of Israel, who in turn accepted it and carried it out faithfully. Thus, Israel's conduct completely accorded with God's command. This, incidentally, shows how from the very outset the Law could be observed solely on the basis of oral transmission. For of the 600,000 individuals who were

manded Moshe and Aharon; so did they do.
29. It came to pass in the middle of the
night that *God* struck down every first-born
in the land of Mitzrayim, from the first-
born of Pharaoh who sits upon his throne,
to the first-born of the captive [woman] in
the dungeon, and all the first-born of the
cattle.   30. And Pharaoh arose in the
night, he, all his servants and all of Mitzrayim, and there was a great cry in
Mitzrayim, for there was no house where
there was not one dead.   31. And he called
Moshe and Aharon during the night and
said: "Arise, go away from among my
people, you as well as the sons of Yisrael;
and go, serve *God*, as you have spoken.
32. Take also your sheep and also your
cattle, as you have spoken, and go—and
bless me also."   33. Mitzrayim used force
upon the people to send them out from the
land in haste, for they said: "We are all
dead men!"   34. The people picked up
their dough before it was leavened, their
kneading troughs being bound up in their
clothes upon their shoulders.   35. The
sons of Yisrael had done according to the
word of Moshe and had asked of Mitzrayim
silver and golden articles, and garments,
36. and *God* let Mitzrayim see that the
people was worthy of favor, they anticipated
their requests and stripped Mitzrayim bare.
37. The sons of Yisrael set out from
Ramses to Sukkoth, about six times one
hundred thousand men on foot, not counting the children.   38. A great mixed
multitude also went up with them,
and sheep and cattle, a very considerable
herd.   39. They baked the dough that
they had brought out from Mitzrayim into
unleavened cakes, for it was not leavened;
for they had been driven out of Mitzrayim
and could not linger, and they had not even
prepared   provisions   for   themselves.
40. Now the manner in which the sons of
Yisrael dwelled in Mitzrayim had lasted
four hundred and thirty years.   41. And it
came to pass at the end of four hundred and

יִשְׂרָאֵ֑ל כַּאֲשֶׁ֨ר צִוָּ֧ה יְהֹוָ֛ה אֶת־מֹשֶׁ֥ה וְאַהֲרֹ֖ן כֵּ֥ן
עָשֽׂוּ׃ ס ששי כט וַיְהִ֣י ׀ בַּחֲצִ֣י הַלַּ֗יְלָה וַֽיהֹוָה֮
הִכָּ֣ה כָל־בְּכוֹר֮ בְּאֶ֣רֶץ מִצְרַ֒יִם֒ מִבְּכֹ֤ר פַּרְעֹה֙
הַיֹּשֵׁ֣ב עַל־כִּסְא֔וֹ עַ֚ד בְּכ֣וֹר הַשְּׁבִ֔י אֲשֶׁ֖ר בְּבֵ֣ית
הַבּ֑וֹר וְכֹ֖ל בְּכ֥וֹר בְּהֵמָֽה׃ ל וַיָּ֨קׇם פַּרְעֹ֜ה לַ֗יְלָה
ה֤וּא וְכׇל־עֲבָדָיו֙ וְכׇל־מִצְרַ֔יִם וַתְּהִ֛י צְעָקָ֥ה
גְדֹלָ֖ה בְּמִצְרָ֑יִם כִּֽי־אֵ֣ין בַּ֔יִת אֲשֶׁ֥ר אֵֽין־שָׁ֖ם
מֵֽת׃ לא וַיִּקְרָא֩ לְמֹשֶׁ֨ה וּֽלְאַהֲרֹ֜ן לַ֗יְלָה וַיֹּ֙אמֶר֙
ק֤וּמוּ צְּאוּ֙ מִתּ֣וֹךְ עַמִּ֔י גַּם־אַתֶּ֖ם גַּם־בְּנֵ֣י
יִשְׂרָאֵ֑ל וּלְכ֛וּ עִבְד֥וּ אֶת־יְהֹוָ֖ה כְּדַבֶּרְכֶֽם׃
לב גַּם־צֹאנְכֶ֨ם גַּם־בְּקַרְכֶ֥ם קְח֛וּ כַּאֲשֶׁ֥ר דִּבַּרְתֶּ֖ם
וָלֵ֑כוּ וּבֵֽרַכְתֶּ֖ם גַּם־אֹתִֽי׃ לג וַתֶּחֱזַ֤ק מִצְרַ֙יִם֙ עַל־
הָעָ֔ם לְמַהֵ֖ר לְשַׁלְּחָ֣ם מִן־הָאָ֑רֶץ כִּ֥י אָמְר֖וּ כֻּלָּ֥נוּ
מֵתִֽים׃ לד וַיִּשָּׂ֥א הָעָ֛ם אֶת־בְּצֵק֖וֹ טֶ֣רֶם יֶחְמָ֑ץ
מִשְׁאֲרֹתָ֛ם צְרֻרֹ֥ת בְּשִׂמְלֹתָ֖ם עַל־שִׁכְמָֽם׃
לה וּבְנֵֽי־יִשְׂרָאֵ֥ל עָשׂ֖וּ כִּדְבַ֣ר מֹשֶׁ֑ה וַֽיִּשְׁאֲלוּ֙
מִמִּצְרַ֔יִם כְּלֵי־כֶ֛סֶף וּכְלֵ֥י זָהָ֖ב וּשְׂמָלֹֽת׃
לו וַֽיהֹוָ֞ה נָתַ֨ן אֶת־חֵ֥ן הָעָ֛ם בְּעֵינֵ֥י מִצְרַ֖יִם
וַיַּשְׁאִל֑וּם וַֽיְנַצְּל֖וּ אֶת־מִצְרָֽיִם׃ פ לז וַיִּסְע֧וּ
בְנֵֽי־יִשְׂרָאֵ֛ל מֵרַעְמְסֵ֖ס סֻכֹּ֑תָה כְּשֵׁשׁ־מֵא֨וֹת
אֶ֧לֶף רַגְלִ֛י הַגְּבָרִ֖ים לְבַ֥ד מִטָּֽף׃ לח וְגַם־עֵ֥רֶב
רַ֖ב עָלָ֣ה אִתָּ֑ם וְצֹ֣אן וּבָקָ֔ר מִקְנֶ֖ה כָּבֵ֥ד מְאֹֽד׃
לט וַיֹּאפ֨וּ אֶת־הַבָּצֵ֜ק אֲשֶׁ֨ר הוֹצִ֧יאוּ מִמִּצְרַ֛יִם
עֻגֹ֥ת מַצּ֖וֹת כִּ֣י לֹ֣א חָמֵ֑ץ כִּֽי־גֹרְשׁ֣וּ מִמִּצְרַ֗יִם
וְלֹ֤א יָֽכְלוּ֙ לְהִתְמַהְמֵ֔הַּ וְגַם־צֵדָ֖ה לֹא־עָשׂ֥וּ
לָהֶֽם׃ מ וּמוֹשַׁב֙ בְּנֵ֣י יִשְׂרָאֵ֔ל אֲשֶׁ֥ר יָשְׁב֖וּ
בְּמִצְרָ֑יִם שְׁלֹשִׁ֣ים שָׁנָ֔ה וְאַרְבַּ֥ע מֵא֖וֹת שָׁנָֽה׃
מא וַיְהִ֗י מִקֵּץ֙ שְׁלֹשִׁ֣ים שָׁנָ֔ה וְאַרְבַּ֥ע מֵא֖וֹת

obliged to make the Passover offering, only the elders
had received the command directly from Moses. All the
others received it only through a chain of intermedia-
ries. But despite this indirect method of transmission,

the manner in which the Children of Israel carried out
the command accorded completely with the command
as originally communicated to Moses and Aaron
by God.

thirty years, on that very day, it came to pass that all the hosts of *God* went out from the land of Mitzrayim.   42. It was a night of abundant, solicitious [vigil-]keeping for *God*, to bring them out from the land of Mitzrayim. This night remains for all the sons of Yisrael an abundant, painstaking [vigil-] keeping to *God* for their descendants.   43. *God* said to Moshe and Aharon: "This is the requirement for the Pesaḥ [offering]: No son of alien values may eat of it.   44. And every man's servant who was acquired for money you must circumcise; then he may eat of it.   45. One who is not a full citizen or a hired hand may not eat of it.   46. It must be eaten in one house; you may not take any of the meat out of the house and you may not break any of its bones.   47. The entire community of Yisrael shall make it.   48. And if a stranger sojourns with you and wishes to make a Pesaḥ [offering] to *God*, then all his males must be circumcised; then he may come

שָׁנָה וַיְהִי בְּעֶ֫צֶם הַיּוֹם הַזֶּה יָצְא֥וּ כָּל־צִבְא֖וֹת יְהֹוָ֖ה מֵאֶ֥רֶץ מִצְרָֽיִם: מב לֵ֣יל שִׁמֻּרִ֥ים הוּא֙ לַֽיהֹוָ֔ה לְהוֹצִיאָ֖ם מֵאֶ֣רֶץ מִצְרָ֑יִם הֽוּא־הַלַּ֤יְלָה הַזֶּה֙ לַֽיהֹוָ֔ה שִׁמֻּרִ֖ים לְכָל־בְּנֵ֥י יִשְׂרָאֵ֖ל לְדֹרֹתָֽם: פ מג וַיֹּ֤אמֶר יְהֹוָה֙ אֶל־מֹשֶׁ֣ה וְאַֽהֲרֹ֔ן זֹ֖את חֻקַּ֣ת הַפָּ֑סַח כָּל־בֶּן־נֵכָ֖ר לֹא־יֹ֥אכַל בּֽוֹ: מד וְכָל־עֶ֥בֶד אִ֖ישׁ מִקְנַת־כָּ֑סֶף וּמַלְתָּ֣ה אֹת֔וֹ אָ֖ז יֹ֥אכַל בּֽוֹ: מה תּוֹשָׁ֥ב וְשָׂכִ֖יר לֹא־יֹ֥אכַל בּֽוֹ: מו בְּבַ֤יִת אֶחָד֙ יֵֽאָכֵ֔ל לֹֽא־תוֹצִ֧יא מִן־הַבַּ֛יִת מִן־הַבָּשָׂ֖ר ח֑וּצָה וְעֶ֖צֶם לֹ֥א תִשְׁבְּרוּ־בֽוֹ: מז כָּל־עֲדַ֥ת יִשְׂרָאֵ֖ל יַֽעֲשׂ֥וּ אֹתֽוֹ: מח וְכִֽי־יָג֨וּר אִתְּךָ֜ גֵּ֗ר וְעָ֤שָׂה פֶ֨סַח֙ לַֽיהֹוָ֔ה הִמּ֧וֹל ל֣וֹ כָל־זָכָ֗ר וְאָז֙ יִקְרַ֣ב לַֽעֲשֹׂת֔וֹ

---

43. ***This is the requirement of the Pesaḥ (offering).*** This law concerning the Passover offering now proceeds to list the personal qualifications for membership in a Jewish household. The members of a Jewish household must belong to the Jewish national covenant of God by virtue of their personal conduct, and their bodies must bear the Divinely-ordained symbol of that covenant. For even as God wishes to view the Jewish community only in terms of its constituent households, so, too, He wishes to perceive each Jewish household only in terms of the community to which it belongs. The individual home is not meant to be an isolated unit, responsible only for itself. Each home is to serve as a nursery in which the nation's collective spirit is to be nurtured and its mission carried out. Hence only one who is part of the Jewish nation may be part of a Jewish household. However, the mission of this nation is so great and variegated that every home, by virtue of its individuality, shaped by the character, tendencies, abilities and positions of its members, can contribute its own unique segment to the spectrum of the nation's development. Thus the nation's mission will be accomplished in its entirety through the concerted efforts of all the individual units toward one common goal.

48. Already when the Jewish nation was first constituted it was specified that membership in this nation was not to be restricted to the descendants of Abraham who had been delivered in Egypt, or to their posterity.

The events that transpired [in Jewish history] from the days of Abraham until the deliverance from Egypt had in fact been intended for the benefit of all mankind. Any man can make this past his own and join the circle of those that were redeemed. Membership in the constituted state of God is dependent neither on birth nor on descent; the only factors that apply here are the personal qualities the individual bears within himself, those qualities that make him a human being. One who is born a Jew forfeits his title if he becomes a בֶּן נֵכָר ["son of alien values"], if he becomes a pagan, estranged from Judaism. Conversely, one who was born a pagan can attain full equality with native members of the Jewish nation as soon as he enrolls himself and his family into the Jewish covenant of God. The Jewish state grants citizenship with all the pertinent civil rights . . . even to an individual who does not become a Jew as long as he subscribes to the obligations emanating from his vocation as a human being and thus becomes a גֵּר תּוֹשָׁב [lit., "a sojourning stranger"].

A גֵּר צֶדֶק [lit., "righteous stranger"], an individual who has actually become a Jew, may make the Passover offering on his own behalf and on behalf of his family despite the fact that his forefathers had not been among those that went forth from Egypt, because it was also for him that the forefathers of the Jewish nation suffered [in Egypt] and then received their freedom from the hand of God. As implied in Verse 27, the Passover offering is not to be regarded as part of the past; it is not near to make it and shall be like a native of the land. No uncircumcised person may eat of it. 49. There shall be one and the same Teaching for the native and for the stranger who dwells in your midst." 50. All the sons of Yisrael did it; even as *God* had commanded Moshe and Aharon, so did they do. 51. It came to pass on that very day when *God* brought the sons of Yisrael out from the land of Mitzrayim by their groups of hosts,

XIII

1. that *God* spoke to Moshe as follows: 2. "Sanctify to Me every first-born, whatever opens the womb among the sons of Yisrael, both of man and of beast; it is Mine." 3. And Moshe said to the people: "Remember this day on which you went out from Mitzrayim, out from the house of bondage, that by strength of hand did *God* bring you out from here, and for this reason no leaven shall be eaten. 4. Today you are going out, in the month of the standing grain! 5. And it shall be when *God* will bring you to the land of the Canaanite and of the Ḥittite, of the Emorite, the Ḥivvite and the Yebusite, which he swore to your fathers to give to you, a land flowing with milk and honey, then you shall observe this service in this month. 6. Then you shall eat unleavened bread seven days, and then, on the seventh day, there shall be a festival consecrated to *God*. 7. Unleavened bread

וְהָיָה כְּאֶזְרַח הָאָרֶץ וְכָל־עָרֵל לֹא־יֹאכַל בּוֹ׃
מט תּוֹרָה אַחַת יִהְיֶה לָאֶזְרָח וְלַגֵּר הַגָּר
בְּתוֹכְכֶם׃ נ וַיַּעֲשׂוּ כָּל־בְּנֵי יִשְׂרָאֵל כַּאֲשֶׁר צִוָּה
יְהֹוָה אֶת־מֹשֶׁה וְאֶת־אַהֲרֹן כֵּן עָשׂוּ׃ ס נא וַיְהִי
בְּעֶצֶם הַיּוֹם הַזֶּה הוֹצִיא יְהֹוָה אֶת־בְּנֵי יִשְׂרָאֵל
מֵאֶרֶץ מִצְרַיִם עַל־צִבְאֹתָם׃ פ שביעי
יג א וַיְדַבֵּר יְהֹוָה אֶל־מֹשֶׁה לֵּאמֹר׃ ב קַדֶּשׁ־לִי
כָל־בְּכוֹר פֶּטֶר כָּל־רֶחֶם בִּבְנֵי יִשְׂרָאֵל בָּאָדָם
וּבַבְּהֵמָה לִי הוּא׃ ג וַיֹּאמֶר מֹשֶׁה אֶל־הָעָם
זָכוֹר אֶת־הַיּוֹם הַזֶּה אֲשֶׁר יְצָאתֶם מִמִּצְרַיִם
מִבֵּית עֲבָדִים כִּי בְּחֹזֶק יָד הוֹצִיא יְהֹוָה אֶתְכֶם
מִזֶּה וְלֹא יֵאָכֵל חָמֵץ׃ ד הַיּוֹם אַתֶּם יֹצְאִים
בְּחֹדֶשׁ הָאָבִיב׃ ה וְהָיָה כִי־יְבִיאֲךָ יְהֹוָה
אֶל־אֶרֶץ הַכְּנַעֲנִי וְהַחִתִּי וְהָאֱמֹרִי וְהַחִוִּי
וְהַיְבוּסִי אֲשֶׁר נִשְׁבַּע לַאֲבֹתֶיךָ לָתֶת לָךְ אֶרֶץ
זָבַת חָלָב וּדְבָשׁ וְעָבַדְתָּ אֶת־הָעֲבֹדָה הַזֹּאת
בַּחֹדֶשׁ הַזֶּה׃ ו שִׁבְעַת יָמִים תֹּאכַל מַצֹּת
וּבַיּוֹם הַשְּׁבִיעִי חַג לַיהֹוָה׃ ז מַצּוֹת יֵאָכֵל אֶת

merely an observance commemorating the days of old. It is the symbol of a process, ever-recurring and ever-progressing, for the upbuilding of all the present and all the future upon the ancient foundations created by the Exodus from Egypt, for all time to come.

° ° °

CHAPTER XIII

1. As with the law set forth in Verses 21 ff. of Chapter 12, so this second law, too, provides a striking example of the Oral Law. Just as in the case of that first law, so here, too, we are told not only God's direct utterance to Moses but also the words in which Moses transmitted this law to the people. The sentence that reports to us the word of God to Moses contains only the brief statement, "Sanctify to Me every first-born. . . ." Moses' communication of God's law to the people contains statements and detailed instructions that do not appear in the report of the words God uttered to Moses. If, as will be the case in all the subsequent laws, we had not also been told the words in which Moses transmitted the law to the people, only the simple general statement, "Sanctify to Me every first-born . . ." would have come down to us as a written law. In that case all the details contained in Moses' instructions to the people, such as those concerning the *matzoth*, the duty to retell the story of the Exodus, the commandment to put on *tefillin*, and particularly the specifications for the observance of the laws relating to the sanctification of the first-born as set down in Verses 11 ff., would have been left to the Oral Law and would have come down to us only by word of mouth. As a consequence, these two initial laws afford us an instructive example of the manner in which God, the Giver of the Law, wished to have the revelation of His will brought home to us.

shall be eaten these seven days and no
leaven shall be seen with you in all your
territory. 8. And then you shall tell to
your child on that day: 'It is because of this
that *God* acted for me when I came out
from Mitzrayim.' 9. And this shall be for
you a sign upon your hand and a memorial
between your eyes—so that the Teaching of
God shall be the content of your mouth—
that with a strong hand did *God* bring you
out from Mitzrayim. 10. And you shall
keep this statute at its appointed time from
year to year. 11. And now it shall be
when *God* will bring you into the land of the
Canaanite, as He swore to you and to your
fathers, and He will have given it to you,
12. then you shall bring to *God* all that
opens the womb, and every firstling of a
beast that will belong to you, the males shall
be brought to *God*. 13. Every firstling of

שִׁבְעַת הַיָּמִים וְלֹא־יֵרָאֶה לְךָ חָמֵץ וְלֹא־יֵרָאֶה
לְךָ שְׂאֹר בְּכָל־גְּבֻלֶךָ: ח וְהִגַּדְתָּ לְבִנְךָ בַּיּוֹם
הַהוּא לֵאמֹר בַּעֲבוּר זֶה עָשָׂה יְהֹוָה לִי בְּצֵאתִי
מִמִּצְרָיִם: ט וְהָיָה לְךָ לְאוֹת עַל־יָדְךָ וּלְזִכָּרוֹן
בֵּין עֵינֶיךָ לְמַעַן תִּהְיֶה תּוֹרַת יְהֹוָה בְּפִיךָ כִּי
בְּיָד חֲזָקָה הוֹצִאֲךָ יְהֹוָה מִמִּצְרָיִם: י וְשָׁמַרְתָּ
אֶת־הַחֻקָּה הַזֹּאת לְמוֹעֲדָהּ מִיָּמִים יָמִימָה: פ
יא וְהָיָה כִּי־יְבִאֲךָ יְהֹוָה אֶל־אֶרֶץ הַכְּנַעֲנִי
כַּאֲשֶׁר נִשְׁבַּע לְךָ וְלַאֲבֹתֶיךָ וּנְתָנָהּ לָךְ:
יב וְהַעֲבַרְתָּ כָל־פֶּטֶר־רֶחֶם לַיהֹוָה וְכָל־פֶּטֶר ׀
שֶׁגֶר בְּהֵמָה אֲשֶׁר יִהְיֶה לְךָ הַזְּכָרִים לַיהֹוָה:

8. ***And then you shall tell.*** As already noted at the outset, it is here, where we are told of the festival that is to mark the upbuilding of the Jewish households, an upbuilding to be performed over and over again upon the foundation laid by the deliverance from Egypt, that we also learn the basic function of Jewish education. Not merely through unspoken habituation, nor even through mere moralizing, should our children be led to the faithful observance of God's Law. We must show them the way by our personal example and at the same time awaken their hearts and minds by explaining to them what it is we are doing, so that they may learn to practice the *mitzvoth* with intelligence and awareness and that their enthusiasm for the task of Judaism should appeal to their intellect [as well as to their emotions].

It is because of this. It is because of these practices, because of all these acts that you see me perform now. When I went forth from slavery to freedom there was only one contribution I could make toward the attainment of this freedom: to take upon myself the observance of these commandments as an obligation for all time. My acceptance of this obligation was the sole reason for my deliverance, and my fulfillment of it the sole purpose of my redemption. It was God Who did everything else for me. From this you can understand the incalculable significance of these practices. It is upon them that all of our existence, based on God and dependent upon Him, rests.

9. . . . The remembrance of this deliverance should not be a mere memorial celebration. The fact that you owe all of your present freedom solely to the strong hand of God, that you therefore belong to Him with all your being, shall become the hallmark of all your actions, a paramount consideration in all your thinking, so that every word you utter—since it is in the spoken word that all of man's thoughts and desires find expression—will emanate from the Law of God and you will then become a herald of God's Law. . . .

° ° °

so that the Teaching of* God *shall be the content of your mouth. It is to the living word, not to the dead letter, that the teaching of God has been entrusted. Cf. ". . . to carry it out with your mouth and with your heart" (Deuteronomy 30:14); "And I have put My words into your mouth" (Isaiah 51:16) and "and My word which I have put into your mouth" (ibid. 59:21). Not only so that we may teach it to others but also that we may study it ourselves are we directed not to the mere written word but also to the words that have been entrusted to our mouths. Thus we are told most significantly: "This Book of the Teaching shall not depart from your mouth" (Joshua 1:8). The purpose of the written word of the Torah is to call to your mind over and over again that which was entrusted to your mouth. The intention is that even one studying by himself should enunciate aloud the Word of God as he reads it so that he may impress God's Teaching upon his mind by means of the living word. Every individual is a herald of the Torah for himself first and foremost; it is through his own mouth that the Torah is to make its way into his soul.

a donkey you shall redeem with a lamb; if you do not redeem it, you must kill it with a blow on the back of its neck; you must also redeem all the first-born of men among your sons. 14. And if in time to come your son will ask you: 'What is this?' Then you shall say to him: 'By strength of hand did *God* bring us out from Mitzrayim, from the house of bondage.' 15. It came to pass when Pharaoh was [too] stubborn to let us go, that *God* struck down every first-born in the land of Mitzrayim, from the first-born of man to the first-born of beast. Therefore I offer up to *God* all that opens the womb, the males, and I redeem every first-born of my sons.' 16. And it shall be a sign also upon your hand and an ornament for your brow between your eyes, that by strength of hand did *God* bring us out from Mitzrayim.

יג וְכָל־פֶּ֤טֶר חֲמֹר֙ תִּפְדֶּ֣ה בְשֶׂ֔ה וְאִם־לֹ֥א תִפְדֶּ֖ה
וַעֲרַפְתּ֑וֹ וְכֹ֨ל בְּכ֥וֹר אָדָ֛ם בְּבָנֶ֖יךָ תִּפְדֶּֽה׃ מפטיר
יד וְהָיָ֞ה כִּֽי־יִשְׁאָלְךָ֥ בִנְךָ֛ מָחָ֖ר לֵאמֹ֣ר מַה־זֹּ֑את
וְאָמַרְתָּ֣ אֵלָ֔יו בְּחֹ֣זֶק יָ֔ד הוֹצִיאָ֧נוּ יְהוָ֛ה מִמִּצְרַ֖יִם
מִבֵּ֥ית עֲבָדִֽים׃ טו וַיְהִ֗י כִּֽי־הִקְשָׁ֣ה פַרְעֹה֮
לְשַׁלְּחֵ֒נוּ֒ וַיַּהֲרֹ֨ג יְהוָ֤ה כָּל־בְּכוֹר֙ בְּאֶ֣רֶץ מִצְרַ֔יִם
מִבְּכֹ֥ר אָדָ֖ם וְעַד־בְּכ֣וֹר בְּהֵמָ֑ה עַל־כֵּ֞ן אֲנִ֣י זֹבֵ֗חַ
לַֽיהוָ֗ה כָּל־פֶּ֤טֶר רֶ֙חֶם֙ הַזְּכָרִ֔ים וְכָל־בְּכ֥וֹר בָּנַ֖י
אֶפְדֶּֽה׃ טז וְהָיָ֤ה לְאוֹת֙ עַל־יָ֣דְכָ֔ה וּלְטוֹטָפֹ֖ת בֵּ֣ין
עֵינֶ֑יךָ כִּ֚י בְּחֹ֣זֶק יָ֔ד הוֹצִיאָ֥נוּ יְהוָ֖ה מִמִּצְרָֽיִם׃ ס

The Haftarah for this Sidra may be found on page 849.

בשלח

BESHALLAH

17. Now when Pharaoh had let the people go, God did not lead them by way of the land of the Philistines, because that was near, for God said: "The people might reconsider when they see war before them and turn back to Mitzrayim." 18. God made the people take a roundabout path; that is, the way into the wilderness to the Sea of Reeds, and the sons of Yisrael went out from the land of Mitzrayim [well] armed. 19. Moshe took with him the bones of Yosef, for he had bound the sons of Yisrael by an oath: "God will surely remember you: then you shall take my bones from here with you." 20. They took their journey from Sukkoth and camped in Etham at the edge of the wilderness, 21. and *God* went before them by day in a pillar of cloud to guide them on their way, and by night in a pillar of fire to give them light, so that they could go by day and by night. 22. The pillar of cloud by day, and the pillar of fire by night, did not depart from before the people.

XIV 1. And *God* spoke to Moshe [saying]: 2. "Speak to the sons of Yisrael that they turn back and camp before Pi HaHiroth, between Migdol and the sea; facing the Baal Tzefon, opposite him, shall you camp by the sea. 3. [Then] Pharaoh will say concerning the sons of Yisrael: 'They are trapped in the land! The wilderness has closed in around them!' 4. So I will let the heart of Pharaoh become obdurate, so that he will pursue

יז וַיְהִ֗י בְּשַׁלַּ֣ח פַּרְעֹה֮ אֶת־הָעָם֒ וְלֹא־נָחָ֣ם אֱלֹהִ֗ים דֶּ֚רֶךְ אֶ֣רֶץ פְּלִשְׁתִּ֔ים כִּ֥י קָר֖וֹב ה֑וּא כִּ֣י ׀ אָמַ֣ר אֱלֹהִ֗ים פֶּֽן־יִנָּחֵ֥ם הָעָ֛ם בִּרְאֹתָ֥ם מִלְחָמָ֖ה וְשָׁ֥בוּ מִצְרָֽיְמָה: יח וַיַּסֵּ֨ב אֱלֹהִ֧ים ׀ אֶת־הָעָ֛ם דֶּ֥רֶךְ הַמִּדְבָּ֖ר יַם־ס֑וּף וַחֲמֻשִׁ֛ים עָל֥וּ בְנֵֽי־יִשְׂרָאֵ֖ל מֵאֶ֥רֶץ מִצְרָֽיִם: יט וַיִּקַּ֥ח מֹשֶׁ֛ה אֶת־עַצְמ֥וֹת יוֹסֵ֖ף עִמּ֑וֹ כִּי֩ הַשְׁבֵּ֨עַ הִשְׁבִּ֜יעַ אֶת־בְּנֵ֤י יִשְׂרָאֵל֙ לֵאמֹ֔ר פָּקֹ֨ד יִפְקֹ֤ד אֱלֹהִים֙ אֶתְכֶ֔ם וְהַעֲלִיתֶ֧ם אֶת־עַצְמֹתַ֛י מִזֶּ֖ה אִתְּכֶֽם: כ וַיִּסְע֖וּ מִסֻּכֹּ֑ת וַיַּחֲנ֣וּ בְאֵתָ֔ם בִּקְצֵ֖ה הַמִּדְבָּֽר: כא וַֽיהֹוָ֡ה הֹלֵךְ֩ לִפְנֵיהֶ֨ם יוֹמָ֜ם בְּעַמּ֤וּד עָנָן֙ לַנְחֹתָ֣ם הַדֶּ֔רֶךְ וְלַ֛יְלָה בְּעַמּ֥וּד אֵ֖שׁ לְהָאִ֣יר לָהֶ֑ם לָלֶ֖כֶת יוֹמָ֥ם וָלָֽיְלָה: כב לֹֽא־יָמִ֞ישׁ עַמּ֤וּד הֶֽעָנָן֙ יוֹמָ֔ם וְעַמּ֥וּד הָאֵ֖שׁ לָ֑יְלָה לִפְנֵ֖י הָעָֽם: פ יד א וַיְדַבֵּ֥ר יְהֹוָ֖ה אֶל־מֹשֶׁ֥ה לֵּאמֹֽר: ב דַּבֵּר֘ אֶל־בְּנֵ֣י יִשְׂרָאֵל֒ וְיָשֻׁ֗בוּ וְיַחֲנוּ֙ לִפְנֵי֙ פִּ֣י הַֽחִירֹ֔ת בֵּ֥ין מִגְדֹּ֖ל וּבֵ֣ין הַיָּ֑ם לִפְנֵי֙ בַּ֣עַל צְפֹ֔ן נִכְח֥וֹ תַחֲנ֖וּ עַל־הַיָּֽם: ג וְאָמַ֤ר פַּרְעֹה֙ לִבְנֵ֣י יִשְׂרָאֵ֔ל נְבֻכִ֥ים הֵ֖ם בָּאָ֑רֶץ סָגַ֥ר עֲלֵיהֶ֖ם הַמִּדְבָּֽר: ד וְחִזַּקְתִּ֣י אֶת־לֵֽב־פַּרְעֹה֘

17–18. . . . The object of the establishment of the Jewish nation was that, among all the nations of the world that develop their national lives under the guidance of God but do not know it, there should enter one nation that is fully aware of God. A national life of this quality requires that one must activate one's own strength, to the fullest extent of human ability, on behalf of the goals set by God and that one must then entrust the success of these efforts to the help of God, which has been promised for every act performed in loyal obedience to Him. However, [the Children of Israel] were not yet ready for such a way of life. They were not yet aware that God's direct Providence for those who faithfully obey His commandments was capable not only of saving them from destruction but also of ensuring their survival day by day, no matter what might befall. They had yet to be educated toward this awareness by means of extraordinary experiences. This was the purpose of Israel's wanderings through the wilderness; this was the significance of the march upon which God now caused the Children of Israel to set out.

them and that, even as I wish it, I shall be
recognized in all the impact of My greatness
upon Pharaoh and upon all his host. Mitzrayim shall come to know that I am *God*."
They did so.   5. It was told to the king of
Mitzrayim that the people had fled, and the
minds of Pharaoh and his servants were
changed regarding the people, and they
said: "What have we done that we have let
Yisrael go from our service?"   6. He
harnessed his chariot and took his people
with him.   7. He took six hundred chariots
with chosen crews and all the chariots of
Mitzrayim and commanders over them all.
8. *God* caused the heart of Pharaoh, the
king of Mitzrayim, to be obdurate so that he
pursued the sons of Yisrael again, though
the sons of Yisrael had gone out with a high
hand.   9. The Mitzrites pursued them, all
the horses of Pharaoh's chariots, his horsemen and his army, and overtook them
camping by the sea, besides Pi HaḤiroth,
facing the Baal Tzefon.   10. Pharaoh
made [his army] draw closer, and the sons of
Yisrael lifted up their eyes and lo! Mitzrayim is marching after them! And they
became greatly frightened, and the sons of
Yisrael cried out to *God*.   11. And they
said to Moshe: "Is it for lack of graves in
Mitzrayim that you brought us here, to die
in the wilderness? What have you done to us
to take us out from Mitzrayim?   12. Is this
not the word that we already spoke to you in
Mitzrayim: 'Leave us alone; we would
rather serve Mitzrayim!'—For it is better for
us to serve Mitzrayim than to die in the
wilderness."   13. Thereupon Moshe said
to the people: "Do not be afraid! Stand firm
and see the salvation of *God*, which He will

וְרָדַף אַחֲרֵיהֶם וְאִכָּבְדָה בְּפַרְעֹה וּבְכָל־חֵילוֹ
וְיָדְעוּ מִצְרַיִם כִּי־אֲנִי יְהֹוָה וַיַּעֲשׂוּ־כֵן: ה וַיֻּגַּד
לְמֶלֶךְ מִצְרַיִם כִּי בָרַח הָעָם וַיֵּהָפֵךְ לְבַב פַּרְעֹה
וַעֲבָדָיו אֶל־הָעָם וַיֹּאמְרוּ מַה־זֹּאת עָשִׂינוּ כִּי־
שִׁלַּחְנוּ אֶת־יִשְׂרָאֵל מֵעָבְדֵנוּ: ו וַיֶּאְסֹר אֶת־
רִכְבּוֹ וְאֶת־עַמּוֹ לָקַח עִמּוֹ: ז וַיִּקַּח שֵׁשׁ־מֵאוֹת
רֶכֶב בָּחוּר וְכֹל רֶכֶב מִצְרָיִם וְשָׁלִשִׁם עַל־כֻּלּוֹ:
ח וַיְחַזֵּק יְהֹוָה אֶת־לֵב פַּרְעֹה מֶלֶךְ מִצְרַיִם
וַיִּרְדֹּף אַחֲרֵי בְּנֵי יִשְׂרָאֵל וּבְנֵי יִשְׂרָאֵל יֹצְאִים
בְּיָד רָמָה: שני ט וַיִּרְדְּפוּ מִצְרַיִם אַחֲרֵיהֶם
וַיַּשִּׂיגוּ אוֹתָם חֹנִים עַל־הַיָּם כָּל־סוּס רֶכֶב
פַּרְעֹה וּפָרָשָׁיו וְחֵילוֹ עַל־פִּי הַחִירֹת לִפְנֵי בַּעַל
צְפֹן: י וּפַרְעֹה הִקְרִיב וַיִּשְׂאוּ בְנֵי־יִשְׂרָאֵל אֶת־
עֵינֵיהֶם וְהִנֵּה מִצְרַיִם נֹסֵעַ אַחֲרֵיהֶם וַיִּירְאוּ
מְאֹד וַיִּצְעֲקוּ בְנֵי־יִשְׂרָאֵל אֶל־יְהֹוָה:
יא וַיֹּאמְרוּ אֶל־מֹשֶׁה הֲמִבְּלִי אֵין־קְבָרִים
בְּמִצְרַיִם לְקַחְתָּנוּ לָמוּת בַּמִּדְבָּר מַה־זֹּאת
עָשִׂיתָ לָּנוּ לְהוֹצִיאָנוּ מִמִּצְרָיִם: יב הֲלֹא־זֶה
הַדָּבָר אֲשֶׁר דִּבַּרְנוּ אֵלֶיךָ בְמִצְרַיִם לֵאמֹר חֲדַל
מִמֶּנּוּ וְנַעַבְדָה אֶת־מִצְרָיִם כִּי טוֹב לָנוּ עֲבֹד
אֶת־מִצְרַיִם מִמֻּתֵנוּ בַּמִּדְבָּר: יג וַיֹּאמֶר מֹשֶׁה
אֶל־הָעָם אַל־תִּירָאוּ הִתְיַצְּבוּ וּרְאוּ אֶת־יְשׁוּעַת
יְהֹוָה אֲשֶׁר־יַעֲשֶׂה לָכֶם הַיּוֹם כִּי אֲשֶׁר רְאִיתֶם

CHAPTER XIV

11. They began to have doubts concerning the mission of Moses. In view of their situation, seen from their
point of view, it is easy to account for their misgivings.
How could they have assumed so unquestioningly that
God would lead them to their goal in such an extraordinary manner, unprecedented in history, in a manner running counter to all natural assumptions? As
Judah HaLevi points out in his *Kuzari,* these persistent
doubts in fact constituted an important documentation

for the authenticity of Moses' mission. Moses was dealing with a people whose minds were clear and lucid,
not befogged by fanciful notions, a nation that was not
easily taken in. If, then, ultimately, this nation willingly
gave itself through the centuries to do battle with the
whole world and to accept martyrdom for the sake of
"the teaching of that man Moses," this alone is cogent
proof that the impact of the events which transpired
won that nation over to an unshakeable belief in the
authenticity of the mission of "that man Moses."...

work for you today; for the Mitzrites whom you have seen today, you shall see them again no more, forever.   14. *God* will fight for you, but you must remain silent."
15. And *God* said to Moshe: "Why do you cry out to Me? Speak to the sons of Yisrael that they go forward.   16. And you lift up your staff and stretch out your hand over the sea and split it, so that the sons of Yisrael shall go into the midst of the sea on dry ground.   17. And I — behold! I shall let the heart of Mitzrayim be stubborn. They will go after them and [then] in accordance with My purpose I shall be recognized in the impact of My greatness upon Pharaoh and upon all his host, despite his chariots and his horsemen.   18. Let Mitzrayim itself recognize that I am *God*, in that I shall show Myself to Pharaoh in the impact of My greatness despite his chariots and his horsemen."   19. Then the angel of God that went before the camp of Yisrael moved and went behind them. The pillar of cloud also moved away from them and placed itself behind them.   20. It came between the camp of Mitzrayim and the camp of Yisrael, and so the cloud and the darkness, too, were there, while He illuminated the night. The one did not come near the other all that night.   21. And Moshe stretched out his hand over the sea, and *God* led the sea by a strong east wind all that night and made the sea dry land; the waters were split.   22. The sons of Yisrael entered into the sea on dry ground, and the waters were for them a wall on their right and on their left.   23. The Mitzrites pursued them and went after them, all the horses of Pharaoh, his chariots and his horsemen, into the sea. 24. It came to pass during the morning watch that *God* looked down upon the camp of Mitzrayim through a pillar of fire and cloud and put the camp of Mitzrayim to confusion.   25. He took off the wheels of his chariots and drove it° heavily. And Mitz-

°*Note to the English translation:* "It" is interpreted as a collective pronoun, referring to the Egyptian encampment. [G.H.]

אֶת־מִצְרַיִם הַיּוֹם לֹא תֹסִפוּ לִרְאֹתָם עוֹד עַד־עוֹלָם: יד יְהֹוָה יִלָּחֵם לָכֶם וְאַתֶּם תַּחֲרִשׁוּן: פ
שלישי טו וַיֹּאמֶר יְהֹוָה אֶל־מֹשֶׁה מַה־תִּצְעַק אֵלָי דַּבֵּר אֶל־בְּנֵי־יִשְׂרָאֵל וְיִסָּעוּ: טז וְאַתָּה הָרֵם אֶת־מַטְּךָ וּנְטֵה אֶת־יָדְךָ עַל־הַיָּם וּבְקָעֵהוּ וְיָבֹאוּ בְנֵי־יִשְׂרָאֵל בְּתוֹךְ הַיָּם בַּיַּבָּשָׁה: יז וַאֲנִי הִנְנִי מְחַזֵּק אֶת־לֵב מִצְרַיִם וְיָבֹאוּ אַחֲרֵיהֶם וְאִכָּבְדָה בְּפַרְעֹה וּבְכָל־חֵילוֹ בְּרִכְבּוֹ וּבְפָרָשָׁיו: יח וְיָדְעוּ מִצְרַיִם כִּי־אֲנִי יְהֹוָה בְּהִכָּבְדִי בְּפַרְעֹה בְּרִכְבּוֹ וּבְפָרָשָׁיו: יט וַיִּסַּע מַלְאַךְ הָאֱלֹהִים הַהֹלֵךְ לִפְנֵי מַחֲנֵה יִשְׂרָאֵל וַיֵּלֶךְ מֵאַחֲרֵיהֶם וַיִּסַּע עַמּוּד הֶעָנָן מִפְּנֵיהֶם וַיַּעֲמֹד מֵאַחֲרֵיהֶם: כ וַיָּבֹא בֵּין | מַחֲנֵה מִצְרַיִם וּבֵין מַחֲנֵה יִשְׂרָאֵל וַיְהִי הֶעָנָן וְהַחֹשֶׁךְ וַיָּאֶר אֶת־הַלָּיְלָה וְלֹא־קָרַב זֶה אֶל־זֶה כָּל־הַלָּיְלָה: כא וַיֵּט מֹשֶׁה אֶת־יָדוֹ עַל־הַיָּם וַיּוֹלֶךְ יְהֹוָה | אֶת־הַיָּם בְּרוּחַ קָדִים עַזָּה כָּל־הַלַּיְלָה וַיָּשֶׂם אֶת־הַיָּם לֶחָרָבָה וַיִּבָּקְעוּ הַמָּיִם: כב וַיָּבֹאוּ בְנֵי־יִשְׂרָאֵל בְּתוֹךְ הַיָּם בַּיַּבָּשָׁה וְהַמַּיִם לָהֶם חוֹמָה מִימִינָם וּמִשְּׂמֹאלָם: כג וַיִּרְדְּפוּ מִצְרַיִם וַיָּבֹאוּ אַחֲרֵיהֶם כֹּל סוּס פַּרְעֹה רִכְבּוֹ וּפָרָשָׁיו אֶל־תּוֹךְ הַיָּם: כד וַיְהִי בְּאַשְׁמֹרֶת הַבֹּקֶר וַיַּשְׁקֵף יְהֹוָה אֶל־מַחֲנֵה מִצְרַיִם בְּעַמּוּד אֵשׁ וְעָנָן וַיָּהָם אֵת מַחֲנֵה מִצְרָיִם: כה וַיָּסַר אֵת אֹפַן מַרְכְּבֹתָיו

---

19. The sea was to retreat not before an angel of God but before human beings who put their trust in Him.

20. Because the cloud interposed itself between the two camps, the camp of the Egyptians remained in darkness even while God illuminated the camp of Israel with the pillar of fire.

rayim said: "Let me flee from before Yisrael because *God* is fighting for them against Mitzrayim." 26. And *God* said to Moshe: "Stretch out your hand over the sea, and the waters will come back over Mitzrayim, over its chariots and its horsemen." 27. Moshe stretched out his hand over the sea, and at the turn of morning the sea returned to its original position, the Mitzrites fled toward it and *God* spilled Mitzrayim into the sea. 28. So the waters came back for all the hosts of Pharaoh that had come into the sea after them, and they covered the chariots and the horsemen, so that not even one of them was left. 29. And the sons of Yisrael walked upon dry ground in the midst of the sea, and the waters were for them a wall on their right and on their left. 30. Thus did *God* save Yisrael on that day from the hand of Mitzrayim, and Yisrael saw Mitzrayim dead upon the seashore. 31. And when Yisrael saw the great hand which *God* had used upon Mitzrayim, the people feared *God* and they trusted in *God* and in His servant Moshe.

XV 1. Then Moshe and the sons of Yisrael sang this song to *God*; they said: "I would sing to *God,* how exalted, exalted He has been; the horse and its rider has He thrown into the sea. 2. *God* is my victory and song; this was my salvation. Henceforth this will be my

וַיְנַהֲגֵהוּ בִּכְבֵדֻת וַיֹּאמֶר מִצְרַיִם אָנוּסָה מִפְּנֵי יִשְׂרָאֵל כִּי יְהֹוָה נִלְחָם לָהֶם בְּמִצְרָיִם: פ רביעי כו וַיֹּאמֶר יְהֹוָה אֶל־מֹשֶׁה נְטֵה אֶת־יָדְךָ עַל־הַיָּם וְיָשֻׁבוּ הַמַּיִם עַל־מִצְרַיִם עַל־רִכְבּוֹ וְעַל־פָּרָשָׁיו: כז וַיֵּט מֹשֶׁה אֶת־יָדוֹ עַל־הַיָּם וַיָּשָׁב הַיָּם לִפְנוֹת בֹּקֶר לְאֵיתָנוֹ וּמִצְרַיִם נָסִים לִקְרָאתוֹ וַיְנַעֵר יְהֹוָה אֶת־מִצְרַיִם בְּתוֹךְ הַיָּם: כח וַיָּשֻׁבוּ הַמַּיִם וַיְכַסּוּ אֶת־הָרֶכֶב וְאֶת־הַפָּרָשִׁים לְכֹל חֵיל פַּרְעֹה הַבָּאִים אַחֲרֵיהֶם בַּיָּם לֹא־נִשְׁאַר בָּהֶם עַד־אֶחָד: כט וּבְנֵי יִשְׂרָאֵל הָלְכוּ בַיַּבָּשָׁה בְּתוֹךְ הַיָּם וְהַמַּיִם לָהֶם חֹמָה מִימִינָם וּמִשְּׂמֹאלָם: ל וַיּוֹשַׁע יְהֹוָה בַּיּוֹם הַהוּא אֶת־יִשְׂרָאֵל מִיַּד מִצְרָיִם וַיַּרְא יִשְׂרָאֵל אֶת־מִצְרַיִם מֵת עַל־שְׂפַת הַיָּם: לא וַיַּרְא יִשְׂרָאֵל אֶת־הַיָּד הַגְּדֹלָה אֲשֶׁר עָשָׂה יְהֹוָה בְּמִצְרַיִם וַיִּירְאוּ הָעָם אֶת־יְהֹוָה וַיַּאֲמִינוּ בַּיהֹוָה וּבְמֹשֶׁה עַבְדּוֹ: פ טו א אָז יָשִׁיר־מֹשֶׁה וּבְנֵי יִשְׂרָאֵל אֶת־הַשִּׁירָה הַזֹּאת לַיהֹוָה וַיֹּאמְרוּ לֵאמֹר אָשִׁירָה לַיהֹוָה כִּי־גָאֹה גָּאָה סוּס וְרֹכְבוֹ רָמָה בַיָּם: ב עָזִּי וְזִמְרָת יָהּ וַיְהִי־לִי לִישׁוּעָה

---

31. יִרְאָה [fear] and אֱמוּנָה [trust]: These are the two basic attitudes toward God that are to remain alive and awake forever in the heart and mind of the Jew. There is only One Whom we must fear and trust at the same time, and that is God, the One sole God, Who is as loving as He is just and as just as He is loving, and Whose almighty power is equally unlimited whether He practices loving-kindness or metes out justice. To reveal and to teach all three: His justice, which is to be feared at all times; His loving-kindness, which is to be trustingly awaited at all times, and His almighty power, commanding freely over all things, in which He can practice loving-kindness and justice simul-taneously—this constitutes the eternal significance of the moment of redemption, unique in its greatness, when the once-enslaved nation, now forever free, saw the colossus of Egypt stretched out dead at its feet. But even as it gave eternal proof of the almighty power in which the hand of God practices both loving-kindness and justice, so, too, this moment is everlasting testi-

mony to the veracity of His servant Moses. The hand of Moses had been raised over the sea and it was through the hand of Moses that God led Egypt to its death and Israel toward the path that led to life and freedom.

CHAPTER XV

1. אָשִׁירָה *[I would sing]* to God in order to glorify Him, to spread the knowledge of Him, how infinitely exalted He has shown Himself to be through the event we witnessed in this place.

the horse and its rider. He has thrown into the sea that mighty army which we had feared so greatly, and it was He, and He alone, Who acted in this event.

אָשִׁירָה: I would like to sing. I would like to find words that are worthy of Him and that would express my emotions. . . .

2. זֶה אֵלִי *[Henceforth this will be my God]*. Even as I have perceived Him here as the One Who alone

זֶ֤ה אֵלִי֙ וְאַנְוֵ֔הוּ אֱלֹהֵ֥י אָבִ֖י וַאֲרֹמְמֶֽנְהוּ׃ ג יְהֹוָ֖ה
אִ֣ישׁ מִלְחָמָ֑ה יְהֹוָ֖ה שְׁמֽוֹ׃ ד מַרְכְּבֹ֥ת פַּרְעֹ֛ה
וְחֵיל֖וֹ יָרָ֣ה בַיָּ֑ם וּמִבְחַ֣ר שָֽׁלִשָׁ֔יו טֻבְּע֖וּ בְיַם־
סֽוּף׃ ה תְּהֹמֹ֖ת יְכַסְיֻ֑מוּ יָרְד֥וּ בִמְצוֹלֹ֖ת כְּמוֹ־
אָֽבֶן׃ ו יְמִֽינְךָ֣ יְהֹוָ֔ה נֶאְדָּרִ֖י בַּכֹּ֑חַ יְמִֽינְךָ֥ יְהֹוָ֖ה
תִּרְעַ֥ץ אוֹיֵֽב׃ ז וּבְרֹ֥ב גְּאוֹנְךָ֖ תַּהֲרֹ֣ס קָמֶ֑יךָ
תְּשַׁלַּח֙ חֲרֹ֣נְךָ֔ יֹאכְלֵ֖מוֹ כַּקַּֽשׁ׃ ח וּבְר֤וּחַ אַפֶּ֙יךָ֙
נֶ֣עֶרְמוּ מַ֔יִם נִצְּב֥וּ כְמוֹ־נֵ֖ד נֹזְלִ֑ים קָֽפְא֥וּ תְהֹמֹ֖ת
בְּלֶב־יָֽם׃ ט אָמַ֥ר אוֹיֵ֛ב אֶרְדֹּ֥ף אַשִּׂ֖יג אֲחַלֵּ֣ק
שָׁלָ֑ל תִּמְלָאֵ֣מוֹ נַפְשִׁ֔י אָרִ֣יק חַרְבִּ֔י תּֽוֹרִישֵׁ֖מוֹ
יָדִֽי׃ י נָשַׁ֥פְתָּ בְרֽוּחֲךָ֖ כִּסָּ֣מוֹ יָ֑ם צָֽלֲלוּ֙ כַּֽעוֹפֶ֔רֶת
בְּמַ֖יִם אַדִּירִֽים׃ יא מִֽי־כָמֹ֤כָה בָּֽאֵלִם֙ יְהֹוָ֔ה מִ֖י

God; to Him would I be a habitation. He was already my father's God; I would raise Him higher still'. 3. *God* is a man of war; *God* is His Name. 4. Pharaoh's chariots and his hosts has He hurled into the sea, and the chosen among his captains were drowned in the Sea of Reeds. 5. The deeps cover them now; they went down into the shadowy depths like a stone. 6. Thy right hand, O *God,* which has shown itself uniquely mighty in this [display of] force, Thy right hand, O *God,* shall henceforth seize each foe with fright. 7. In the abundance of Thy majesty Thou smashest those that rise up against Thee; hadst Thou not restrained Thy wrath, it would have consumed them like stubble! 8. And at the blast of Thy insistence waters indeed piled up; the floods stood back timidly like a wall, for the deeps were congealed in the heart of the sea! 9. And therefore the enemy said: 'I will pursue; I will overtake; I will divide the spoils. My lust shall be satisfied upon them. I will draw my sword; my hand will reconquer them!' 10. And then Thou didst blow with Thy wind; the sea covered them; they sank shadow-deep like lead into mighty, surging waters. 11. Who is like Thee among the gods, O *God?* Who, like

shapes my fate and my inner life, so shall I in the future, place all my life, within and without, at His command, to have Him guide and shape it—only one who thus commits himself to God can claim Him as "his" God—and He shall be, in the literal sense of the word, the Power that moves me.

To Him would I be a habitation. I shall offer myself to Him as a habitation; all my life and all my being shall become a temple to His glorification, a place in which He will be revealed. This is the natural effect of זֶה אֵלִי ["Henceforth this will be my God"].

. . . ***He was already my father's God; I would raise Him higher still.*** He has already proven Himself as the God of my fathers; even my fathers recognized Him as such and passed this knowledge to me. But I shall endeavor to add still more to the recognition of His greatness and His sovereignty. These words outline the mission of every subsequent generation in Israel: to continue to disseminate the knowledge of God, and allegiance to Him, in ever-growing intensity.

3. Herewith begins the expression of the new knowledge of God derived from this experience: ד׳, as the Creator of a new and better future for mankind, is a "man of war" in that He overcomes every power in human society that would withstand His plan for this better future.

God *is His Name*. This is inherent in His very Name by which He has proclaimed Himself to us. The path to salvation which brings good from God must lead over the destruction of evil.

4. **יָרָה בַיָּם *[has He hurled into the sea].*** ירה does not simply mean "to throw"; it means "to hurl" something at a particular target. Hence it is the term customarily employed in connection with the shooting of arrows. . . . God's manner of waging war is the opposite of warfare as practiced by man. When man wages war, he hurls the missile at his foe, but when God does battle, He hurls His foe at the missile.

° ° °

11. . . . Any song of praise to God that does not stir up the fear of Him, let alone a song that seeks to be a substitute for the fear of God, is blasphemy. The expression נוֹרָא תְהִלֹּת ["Feared in songs proclaiming (Thy

כָּמֹכָה נֶאְדָּר בַּקֹּדֶשׁ נוֹרָא תְהִלֹּת עֹשֵׂה־פֶלֶא:
יב נָטִיתָ יְמִינְךָ תִּבְלָעֵמוֹ אָרֶץ: יג נָחִיתָ בְחַסְדְּךָ
עַם־זוּ גָּאָלְתָּ נֵהַלְתָּ בְעָזְּךָ אֶל־נְוֵה קָדְשֶׁךָ:
יד שָׁמְעוּ עַמִּים יִרְגָּזוּן חִיל אָחַז יֹשְׁבֵי פְּלָשֶׁת:
טו אָז נִבְהֲלוּ אַלּוּפֵי אֱדוֹם אֵילֵי מוֹאָב יֹאחֲזֵמוֹ
רָעַד נָמֹגוּ כֹּל יֹשְׁבֵי כְנָעַן: טז תִּפֹּל עֲלֵיהֶם
אֵימָתָה וָפַחַד בִּגְדֹל זְרוֹעֲךָ יִדְּמוּ כָּאָבֶן עַד
יַעֲבֹר עַמְּךָ יְהוָה עַד־יַעֲבֹר עַם־זוּ קָנִיתָ:
יז תְּבִאֵמוֹ וְתִטָּעֵמוֹ בְּהַר נַחֲלָתְךָ מָכוֹן לְשִׁבְתְּךָ

Thee, uniquely mighty in holiness? Feared in songs proclaiming [Thy mighty] acts, Doer of Wonders! 12. Thou stretchest out Thy right hand—the earth swallows them. 13. But in Thy loving-kindness Thou hast led to the goal the people that Thou hast redeemed; with Thy might, which none can withstand, Thou hast guided them to Thy holy habitation. 14. Peoples have already heard and tremble; pang-like fear had already seized the inhabitants of Pelesheth. 15. But now the generals of Edom became dismayed; trembling seizes the mighty of Moab; all the inhabitants of Canaan are melted away. 16. Terror and dread fall upon them— when Thine arm proves great, they fall silent as a stone; until Thy people pass over, O *God,* until this people passes over which Thou hast acquired. 17. Thou bringest them home, Thou plantest them in the mountain of Thine inheritance, the place prepared for Thy habitation, which Thou,

mighty) acts''] remains the strict standard for all the "songs of worship" that have been composed on earth since the "song at the shores of the sea" and that, consciously or unconsciously, have been patterned upon it. תְּהִלּוֹת [lit., "songs proclaiming (mighty) acts"] connote objective perceptions of God; יִרְאָה [fear] denotes the subjective impact of these perceptions upon us.

° ° °

13. Verses 3 to 7 and 8 to 12 view the event as having revealed God in His awesome greatness and might, overcoming all other forces, political and physical. Verses 13 to 17 show how this same event revealed God in His almighty love which He brought into play as He guided and built the nation. The first two sets of four verses were dedicated to יִרְאָה [the fear of God]; the four verses that follow are dedicated to אֱמוּנָה [trust in Him]. Since Verse 14 names the Philistines as the first nation to be struck down by fate, and Verse 15 (introduced by the word אָז ["But now"]) names Edom and Moab, it would seem that Verses 13 and 14 refer to the initial impact of the Exodus from Egypt, while Verses 15 ff. refer to the repercussions of Israel's passage through the Red Sea. When God first delivered His people and led them out of Egypt in order to have them take possession of Eretz Yisrael, the inhabitants of Philistia were the first to be seized with terror because they felt the most naturally threatened, cf. "by way of the land of the Philistines, because that was near"—(Exodus 13:17). But now that God has directed the people to pass through the wilderness, across the Red Sea and along its shoreline, so that they will first enter the land from the southeast, it is Edom and Moab, the border nations on that side, that feel threatened.

נָחִיתָ *[Thou hast led].* Until this point the theme of the song was what God did to Egypt; now the theme shifts to what God did for Israel. The term נחה connotes "leading to the goal." The word נהל is always employed to denote the "leading" or "guiding" of a weak object with due consideration for its weakness. . . . Hence: In Thy loving-kindness Thou didst not only save this people but didst also undertake to guide them to their goal. In Thy might, which none can withstand, Thou couldst have led them directly to their destination; i.e., to the habitation of Thy holiness. But out of consideration for the fact that they were still weak and immature, Thou didst guide them upon a path which they had the capacity to follow. (cf. 13:17: וְלֹא נָחָם אֱלֹקִים וגו׳). Israel's deliverance from slavery and abuse in Egypt was first and foremost an act of Divine justice, but the care and guidance God gave to the Children of Israel afterwards was an act of חֶסֶד, pure loving-kindness, of loving solicitude for the welfare of another. The goal to be attained was the possession not of a fruitful land but of a land that was to be the habitation of God's absolute sovereignty. (Cf. זֶה אֵלִי וְאַנְוֵהוּ [Verse 2: "Henceforth this will be my God, to Him would I be a habitation"].)

O *God*, hast secured, the Sanctuary, O God, which Thy hands have established. 18. *God* will reign in all eternity." 19. For the horse of Pharaoh with his chariot and with his riders came into the sea, and *God* brought back the waters of the sea over them and the sons of Yisrael walked on dry ground in the midst of the sea. 20. Miriam the prophetess, the sister of Aharon, took the timbrel in her hand, and all the women went out after her with timbrels and with dances. 21. And Miriam answered them: "Sing to *God*, how exalted, exalted He has been; the horse and its rider has He thrown into the sea." 22. Moshe made Yisrael journey forth from the Sea of Reeds and they went out into the wilderness of Shur. They went three days in the wilderness and found no water. 23. They came to Marah and could not drink of the waters of Marah because they were bitter; therefore it [i.e., the nation] called the place Marah [Bitterness]. 24. The people murmured against Moshe and said: "What shall we drink?" 25. He cried out to *God*, and *God* instructed him [concerning] a [piece of] wood; he threw it into the waters and the waters became sweet. There He established law and [social] ordinance for him, and there it tested them. 26. He said: "If you will only hearken to the voice of *God*, your God, and will do that which is upright in His eyes, and you will give ear to His commandments and will keep all His statutes, then I will not inflict upon you any of the sickness[es] which I have inflicted upon Mitzrayim, for I, *God*, am your Healer." 27. They came to Elim and there were twelve springs of water and seventy date palms; they camped there by the water.

פָּעַ֣לְתָּ יְהוָ֑ה מִקְּדָ֕שׁ אֲדֹנָ֖י כּוֹנְנ֥וּ יָדֶֽיךָ׃ יח יְהוָ֥ה ׀
יִמְלֹ֖ךְ לְעֹלָ֥ם וָעֶֽד׃ יט כִּ֣י בָא֩ ס֨וּס פַּרְעֹ֜ה בְּרִכְבּ֤וֹ
וּבְפָרָשָׁיו֙ בַּיָּ֔ם וַיָּ֧שֶׁב יְהוָ֛ה עֲלֵהֶ֖ם אֶת־מֵ֣י הַיָּ֑ם
וּבְנֵ֧י יִשְׂרָאֵ֛ל הָלְכ֥וּ בַיַּבָּשָׁ֖ה בְּת֥וֹךְ הַיָּֽם׃ פ
כ וַתִּקַּח֩ מִרְיָ֨ם הַנְּבִיאָ֜ה אֲח֧וֹת אַהֲרֹ֛ן אֶת־הַתֹּ֖ף
בְּיָדָ֑הּ וַתֵּצֶ֤אןָ כָל־הַנָּשִׁים֙ אַחֲרֶ֔יהָ בְּתֻפִּ֖ים
וּבִמְחֹלֹֽת׃ כא וַתַּ֥עַן לָהֶ֖ם מִרְיָ֑ם שִׁ֤ירוּ לַֽיהוָה֙
כִּֽי־גָאֹ֣ה גָּאָ֔ה ס֥וּס וְרֹכְב֖וֹ רָמָ֥ה בַיָּֽם׃ ס כב וַיַּסַּ֨ע
מֹשֶׁ֤ה אֶת־יִשְׂרָאֵל֙ מִיַּם־ס֔וּף וַיֵּצְא֖וּ אֶל־מִדְבַּר־
שׁ֑וּר וַיֵּלְכ֧וּ שְׁלֹֽשֶׁת־יָמִ֛ים בַּמִּדְבָּ֖ר וְלֹא־מָ֥צְאוּ
מָֽיִם׃ כג וַיָּבֹ֣אוּ מָרָ֔תָה וְלֹ֣א יָֽכְל֗וּ לִשְׁתֹּ֥ת מַ֙יִם֙
מִמָּרָ֔ה כִּ֥י מָרִ֖ים הֵ֑ם עַל־כֵּ֥ן קָֽרָא־שְׁמָ֖הּ מָרָֽה׃
כד וַיִּלֹּ֧נוּ הָעָ֛ם עַל־מֹשֶׁ֥ה לֵּאמֹ֖ר מַה־נִּשְׁתֶּֽה׃
כה וַיִּצְעַ֣ק אֶל־יְהוָ֗ה וַיּוֹרֵ֤הוּ יְהוָה֙ עֵ֔ץ וַיַּשְׁלֵךְ֙
אֶל־הַמַּ֔יִם וַֽיִּמְתְּק֖וּ הַמָּ֑יִם שָׁ֣ם שָׂ֥ם ל֛וֹ חֹ֥ק
וּמִשְׁפָּ֖ט וְשָׁ֥ם נִסָּֽהוּ׃ כו וַיֹּאמֶר֩ אִם־שָׁמ֨וֹעַ
תִּשְׁמַ֜ע לְק֣וֹל ׀ יְהוָ֣ה אֱלֹהֶ֗יךָ וְהַיָּשָׁ֤ר בְּעֵינָיו֙
תַּעֲשֶׂ֔ה וְהַֽאֲזַנְתָּ֙ לְמִצְוֺתָ֔יו וְשָׁמַרְתָּ֖ כָּל־חֻקָּ֑יו
כָּֽל־הַמַּחֲלָ֞ה אֲשֶׁר־שַׂ֤מְתִּי בְמִצְרַ֙יִם֙ לֹא־אָשִׂ֣ים
עָלֶ֔יךָ כִּ֛י אֲנִ֥י יְהוָ֖ה רֹפְאֶֽךָ׃ ס חמישי כז וַיָּבֹ֣אוּ
אֵילִ֔מָה וְשָׁ֗ם שְׁתֵּ֥ים עֶשְׂרֵ֛ה עֵינֹ֥ת מַ֖יִם
וְשִׁבְעִ֣ים תְּמָרִ֑ים וַיַּֽחֲנוּ־שָׁ֖ם עַל־הַמָּֽיִם׃

17. . . . Moses and Israel see themselves as the servants and instruments of God's great future of salvation, for which He has now laid the foundations by revealing to the world His unique mighty reign of justice and loving-kindness. For this reason the song concludes with a glimpse into the remote future: "*God will reign in all eternity.*": This can mean not only that God will reign through all the future; i.e., even as we perceived His almighty sovereignty here at the shore of the sea, so, too, He will continue to reign forever, but also that at some time in a future that is still far distant but nonetheless sure to come, God will become King over all mankind. . . .

25. . . . There God gave to the nation the fundamentals of His Law and there the nation tested them; i.e., the sweetening of the bitter waters taught the nation to know the power inherent in faithful compliance with the will of God.

XVI 1. They took their journey from Elim and they came, the whole community of the sons of Yisrael, to the wilderness of Sin, which is between Elim and Sinai, on the fifteenth day of the second month after their departure from Mitzrayim. 2. And the whole community of the sons of Yisrael murmured against Moshe and Aharon in the wilderness. 3. And sons of Yisrael said to them: "Would that we had died by the hand of *God* in the land of Mitzrayim while we sat by the meat pot, while we ate our fill of bread; for you have brought us out into this wilderness to have this whole multitude die of hunger." 4. But *God* said to Moshe:

טז א וַיִּסְעוּ מֵאֵילִם וַיָּבֹאוּ כָּל־עֲדַת בְּנֵי־
יִשְׂרָאֵל אֶל־מִדְבַּר־סִין אֲשֶׁר בֵּין־אֵילִם וּבֵין
סִינָי בַּחֲמִשָּׁה עָשָׂר יוֹם לַחֹדֶשׁ הַשֵּׁנִי לְצֵאתָם
מֵאֶרֶץ מִצְרָיִם: ב וַיִּלִּינוּ (וילונו קרי) כָּל־עֲדַת
בְּנֵי־יִשְׂרָאֵל עַל־מֹשֶׁה וְעַל־אַהֲרֹן בַּמִּדְבָּר:
ג וַיֹּאמְרוּ אֲלֵהֶם בְּנֵי יִשְׂרָאֵל מִי־יִתֵּן מוּתֵנוּ
בְיַד־יְהוָה בְּאֶרֶץ מִצְרַיִם בְּשִׁבְתֵּנוּ עַל־סִיר
הַבָּשָׂר בְּאָכְלֵנוּ לֶחֶם לָשֹׂבַע כִּי־הוֹצֵאתֶם אֹתָנוּ
אֶל־הַמִּדְבָּר הַזֶּה לְהָמִית אֶת־כָּל־הַקָּהָל הַזֶּה
בָּרָעָב: ס ד וַיֹּאמֶר יְהוָה אֶל־מֹשֶׁה הִנְנִי

CHAPTER XVI

2. . . . The memory of the miracles of deliverance and rescue in Mitzrayim and at the sea, along with the basic instructive experience at Marah—all these vanish before the specter of starvation that now threatens their wives and children. Here, too, the adage applies that "it is more difficult to provide man's daily sustenance than it is to split the Red Sea." The threat of starvation, real or imagined, can cause man to waver in his principles, silence all his better resolves, and as long as the individual is not freed, not from his cares about his material sustenance but from the crushing impact of these cares, there will be no chance for a complete realization of the Law of God. But the individual can rid himself of this specter only if he becomes thoroughly imbued with the awareness that this, the first among all human cares, the worry about one's material sustenance, does not rest upon him alone, not even primarily upon his shoulders only. He must realize that to this end, also, man can and should do only his part; namely, that which God expects him to contribute toward the achievement of this objective. As for the success of his endeavors, he must leave that to God Who has made every single human soul and every household with all its hungry members, great and small, the object of His ever-watchful, almighty, caring love. Man must understand that, in general, he must regard his work for his sustenance not as a right but as a duty.

As long as man is not aware of these truths, as long as he feels that with his limited powers he is fettered to the yoke of toil for the daily bread that ensures his own survival and that of his loved ones, this anxiety will know no bounds. In that case, worry about his sustenance can turn any man's world into a wilderness, not only while he is in a true wilderness but even when he dwells in the midst of a society in which there is an abundance of wealth—but also of competition. Then his anxiety can make him believe that he must secure sustenance not only for the next day but also for his whole future, and for the future of his children, grandchildren and great-grandchildren. As a result, a tireless, and hence ruthless, striving to conquer ever-increasing portions of the world's wealth for himself and for his family will seem to him a necessity which soon will leave him little time for the pursuit of other aims and purposes.

It is for this reason that God led the future nation of His Law into a true wilderness, bare of all the necessities of life. There He first made them feel all the anxiety of a present devoid of nourishment and of a future without visible prospects of sustenance. There, He caused them to experience in their own lives, both for themselves and for all their future generations, the ruthlessness to which such a situation, even if it is only temporary, can lead a man. As we can surmise from the verse that follows, this entire generation had been totally unaccustomed to worry about their sustenance. While they were slaves it had been in the interest of their masters to provide for the sustenance of their bondsmen, even as one sees to the survival and maintenance of one's working animals and beasts of burden. Only after they had come into the wilderness did the entire community of Israel begin to murmur against Moses and Aaron.

3. בְּנֵי יִשְׂרָאֵל *[sons of Yisrael].* Certain individuals, the most impudent in the community, gave expression to the genuine mood of disaffection by openly voicing reproaches and accusations against Moses and Aaron. . . .

"See, I am about to have bread rain down from heaven for you. The people will go out and gather the daily [requirement] each day, so that I may test them whether they will walk in My Teaching or not. 5. And it shall come to pass on the sixth day, that they will prepare that which they bring home, and then it will be twice as much as [that which] they gather day by day." 6. And Moshe and Aharon said to all the sons of Yisrael: "When evening comes, you will recognize that it was *God* Who brought you out from the land of Mitzrayim, 7. and in the morning you will see the glory of *God*, even though He has heard your murmuring against *God*. But we—who are we that you should foment murmuring against us?" 8. And Moshe said: "If *God* gives you meat to eat in the evening, and bread in the morning to fill you up, if *God* has heard your murmuring that you foment against Him—what, then, are we? Your murmuring is not against us, but against *God*." 9. Thereupon Moshe said to Aharon: "Tell the whole community of the sons of Yisrael: 'Come near before *God*, for He has heard your murmuring.'" 10. And it came to pass while Aharon spoke to the whole community of the sons of Yisrael and they turned toward the wilderness that lo! the glory of *God* appeared in the cloud. 11. And *God* spoke to Moshe: [saying]: 12. "I have heard the murmuring of the sons of Yisrael. Speak to them [saying]: 'Between the two evenings you shall eat meat and in the morning you shall have your fill of bread, and you shall recognize that I, *God*, am your God.'" 13. And it came to pass in the evening that the *s'lav* came up and covered the camp, and in the

מַמְטִיר לָכֶם לֶחֶם מִן־הַשָּׁמָיִם וְיָצָא הָעָם
וְלָקְטוּ דְּבַר־יוֹם בְּיוֹמוֹ לְמַעַן אֲנַסֶּנּוּ הֲיֵלֵךְ
בְּתוֹרָתִי אִם־לֹא׃ ה וְהָיָה בַּיּוֹם הַשִּׁשִּׁי וְהֵכִינוּ
אֵת אֲשֶׁר־יָבִיאוּ וְהָיָה מִשְׁנֶה עַל אֲשֶׁר־יִלְקְטוּ
יוֹם | יוֹם׃ ו וַיֹּאמֶר מֹשֶׁה וְאַהֲרֹן אֶל־כָּל־בְּנֵי
יִשְׂרָאֵל עֶרֶב וִידַעְתֶּם כִּי יְהוָה הוֹצִיא אֶתְכֶם
מֵאֶרֶץ מִצְרָיִם׃ ז וּבֹקֶר וּרְאִיתֶם אֶת־כְּבוֹד
יְהוָה בְּשָׁמְעוֹ אֶת־תְּלֻנֹּתֵיכֶם עַל־יְהוָה וְנַחְנוּ
מָה כִּי תַלּוֹנוּ (תלינו קרי) עָלֵינוּ׃ ח וַיֹּאמֶר מֹשֶׁה
בְּתֵת יְהוָה לָכֶם בָּעֶרֶב בָּשָׂר לֶאֱכֹל וְלֶחֶם
בַּבֹּקֶר לִשְׂבֹּעַ בִּשְׁמֹעַ יְהוָה אֶת־תְּלֻנֹּתֵיכֶם
אֲשֶׁר־אַתֶּם מַלִּינִם עָלָיו וְנַחְנוּ מָה לֹא־עָלֵינוּ
תְלֻנֹּתֵיכֶם כִּי עַל־יְהוָה׃ ט וַיֹּאמֶר מֹשֶׁה אֶל־
אַהֲרֹן אֱמֹר אֶל־כָּל־עֲדַת בְּנֵי יִשְׂרָאֵל קִרְבוּ
לִפְנֵי יְהוָה כִּי שָׁמַע אֵת תְּלֻנֹּתֵיכֶם׃ י וַיְהִי
כְּדַבֵּר אַהֲרֹן אֶל־כָּל־עֲדַת בְּנֵי־יִשְׂרָאֵל וַיִּפְנוּ
אֶל־הַמִּדְבָּר וְהִנֵּה כְּבוֹד יְהוָה נִרְאָה בֶּעָנָן׃ פ
ששי יא וַיְדַבֵּר יְהוָה אֶל־מֹשֶׁה לֵּאמֹר׃
יב שָׁמַעְתִּי אֶת־תְּלוּנֹּת בְּנֵי יִשְׂרָאֵל דַּבֵּר אֲלֵהֶם
לֵאמֹר בֵּין הָעַרְבַּיִם תֹּאכְלוּ בָשָׂר וּבַבֹּקֶר
תִּשְׂבְּעוּ־לָחֶם וִידַעְתֶּם כִּי אֲנִי יְהוָה אֱלֹהֵיכֶם׃
יג וַיְהִי בָעֶרֶב וַתַּעַל הַשְּׂלָו וַתְּכַס אֶת־הַמַּחֲנֶה

4. ***whether they will walk in My Teaching.*** The observance of My Law is dependent on My finding men for whom it is enough to know that their wives and children have sufficient sustenance from one day to the next, and who are content to enjoy each day in happiness and good cheer, to do their duty for today and to leave the care for tomorrow to Him Who gave them the present day and its sustenance, and Who will give them also the next day and its required sustenance. Only such unreserved trust in God will safeguard the observance of His Law against violations caused by anxiety about material hardship, real or imagined. He who has not learned to trust God for the next day will worry so much about the prospects of years to come that he will ultimately be led astray from God and from His Law. Hence the great saying of [the Tannaite] Rabbi Eleazar of Modi'in: "He Who has created the day will also create the sustenance for it," and "He who has enough to eat for today but says: 'What will I have to eat tomorrow?' is among those who have little trust in God."

13. In Yoma 75b the Gemarah enumerates four kinds

morning there was a layer of dew around the camp.   14. The layer of dew went up and lo! there was on the surface of the wilderness something fine, completely without a husk, fine as the hoarfrost upon the ground.   15. The sons of Yisrael saw it and they said to one another: "It is a gift (Heb.: *man*)." For they did not know what it was. But Moshe said to them: "It is the bread that *God* has given you for food.   16. This is what *God* has commanded: Let each man gather of it according to the need of his nourishment; one *omer* a head, according to the number of your souls let each one take for the members of his tent."   17. The sons of Yisrael did so; they gathered, some more and some less.   18. But when they measured it with the *omer* he who had gathered much had nothing left over, and he who had gathered little did not have too little; each one had gathered according to the need of his nourishment.   19. Moshe said to them: "Let no one leave any of it over until the morning."   20. But some did not hearken to Moshe and left of it until the morning. And it came alive with worms and grew putrid; Moshe was angry with them.   21. So they gathered it each morning, every man according to the need of his nourishment; when the sun grew hot, it melted.   22. And it came to pass on the sixth day that they had gathered a double portion of bread, two *omers* for each one; all the princes of the community came and reported it to Moshe.   23. And he said to them: "This is what *God* has already spoken; tomorrow is a cessation of [creating] work to celebrate the Sabbath, holy to *God*. Bake whatever you wish to bake, cook what-

וּבַבֹּקֶר הָיְתָה שִׁכְבַת הַטָּל סָבִיב לַמַּחֲנֶה: יד וַתַּעַל שִׁכְבַת הַטָּל וְהִנֵּה עַל־פְּנֵי הַמִּדְבָּר דַּק מְחֻסְפָּס דַּק כַּכְּפֹר עַל־הָאָרֶץ: טו וַיִּרְאוּ בְנֵי־יִשְׂרָאֵל וַיֹּאמְרוּ אִישׁ אֶל־אָחִיו מָן הוּא כִּי לֹא יָדְעוּ מַה־הוּא וַיֹּאמֶר מֹשֶׁה אֲלֵהֶם הוּא הַלֶּחֶם אֲשֶׁר נָתַן יְהֹוָה לָכֶם לְאָכְלָה: טז זֶה הַדָּבָר אֲשֶׁר צִוָּה יְהֹוָה לִקְטוּ מִמֶּנּוּ אִישׁ לְפִי אָכְלוֹ עֹמֶר לַגֻּלְגֹּלֶת מִסְפַּר נַפְשֹׁתֵיכֶם אִישׁ לַאֲשֶׁר בְּאָהֳלוֹ תִּקָּחוּ: יז וַיַּעֲשׂוּ־כֵן בְּנֵי יִשְׂרָאֵל וַיִּלְקְטוּ הַמַּרְבֶּה וְהַמַּמְעִיט: יח וַיָּמֹדּוּ בָעֹמֶר וְלֹא הֶעְדִּיף הַמַּרְבֶּה וְהַמַּמְעִיט לֹא הֶחְסִיר אִישׁ לְפִי־אָכְלוֹ לָקָטוּ: יט וַיֹּאמֶר מֹשֶׁה אֲלֵהֶם אִישׁ אַל־יוֹתֵר מִמֶּנּוּ עַד־בֹּקֶר: כ וְלֹא־שָׁמְעוּ אֶל־מֹשֶׁה וַיּוֹתִרוּ אֲנָשִׁים מִמֶּנּוּ עַד־בֹּקֶר וַיָּרֻם תּוֹלָעִים וַיִּבְאַשׁ וַיִּקְצֹף עֲלֵהֶם מֹשֶׁה: כא וַיִּלְקְטוּ אֹתוֹ בַּבֹּקֶר בַּבֹּקֶר אִישׁ כְּפִי אָכְלוֹ וְחַם הַשֶּׁמֶשׁ וְנָמָס: כב וַיְהִי | בַּיּוֹם הַשִּׁשִּׁי לָקְטוּ לֶחֶם מִשְׁנֶה שְׁנֵי הָעֹמֶר לָאֶחָד וַיָּבֹאוּ כָּל־נְשִׂיאֵי הָעֵדָה וַיַּגִּידוּ לְמֹשֶׁה: כג וַיֹּאמֶר אֲלֵהֶם הוּא אֲשֶׁר דִּבֶּר יְהֹוָה שַׁבָּתוֹן שַׁבַּת־קֹדֶשׁ לַיהֹוָה מָחָר אֵת אֲשֶׁר־תֹּאפוּ אֵפוּ וְאֵת

of *s'lav*, including **פְּסְיוֹנִי**, probably pheasants. *S'lav* is described as the most insignificant of the species and as an exceptionally fat bird. *S'lav* is thought to be a kind of quail. . . .

16–21. Thus, at the very outset the experiences of the Children of Israel during the six days of gathering *manna*, and the Jewish philosophy of procuring one's sustenance as established by these experiences, teach us most important lessons for all time to come. Laziness, avarice, stinginess and pettiness are punished while

diligence, contentment, good cheer and trust in God are rewarded.

23. . . . The seventh day as a memorial to God's creation of the world and to His sovereignty over it had been known ever since the seventh day of the world's existence. Perhaps that day had even borne the name of Sabbath from that time on, as the Sabbath of God, as the day כִּי בוֹ שָׁבַת מִכָּל מְלַאכְתּוֹ [Genesis 2:3] on which God withdrew His creating hand from the world He had made and henceforth allowed the world to stand in the

ever you wish to cook; and everything that is left over store up for yourselves to be kept until the morning."   24. They let it remain until the morning, as Moshe had commanded, and it did not become putrid and there was no worm in it.   25. And Moshe said: "Eat it today! For today is a Sabbath to *God!* Today you will not find it in the field!   26. Six days shall you gather it, but on the seventh day it is the Sabbath, on which there will be none."   27. Nevertheless, some of the people went out to gather on the seventh day, but they found none.   28. Thereupon *God* said to Moshe: "How long will you refuse to

אֲשֶׁר־תְּבַשֵּׁלוּ בַּשֵּׁלוּ וְאֵת כָּל־הָעֹדֵף הַנִּיחוּ לָכֶם לְמִשְׁמֶרֶת עַד־הַבֹּקֶר: כד וַיַּנִּיחוּ אֹתוֹ עַד־הַבֹּקֶר כַּאֲשֶׁר צִוָּה מֹשֶׁה וְלֹא הִבְאִישׁ וְרִמָּה לֹא־הָיְתָה בּוֹ: כה וַיֹּאמֶר מֹשֶׁה אִכְלֻהוּ הַיּוֹם כִּי־שַׁבָּת הַיּוֹם לַיהֹוָה הַיּוֹם לֹא תִמְצָאֻהוּ בַּשָּׂדֶה: כו שֵׁשֶׁת יָמִים תִּלְקְטֻהוּ וּבַיּוֹם הַשְּׁבִיעִי שַׁבָּת לֹא יִהְיֶה־בּוֹ: כז וַיְהִי בַּיּוֹם הַשְּׁבִיעִי יָצְאוּ מִן־הָעָם לִלְקֹט וְלֹא מָצָאוּ: ס כח וַיֹּאמֶר יְהֹוָה אֶל־מֹשֶׁה עַד־אָנָה מֵאַנְתֶּם

---

degree of completion He had bestowed upon it. . . . The very fact that, ever since that day, there has been a Sabbath in Creation, that we have not seen any new creations emerge since that time, and that the world which He created had attained one goal of its creation, reveals God irrefutably as the free-willed Creator of the world. Until this point both the day and its name might have served to keep the awareness of God alive and vibrant among the sons of Abraham. However, the Sabbath of God at this stage had not yet become the Sabbath of man; the awareness of God had not yet found expression in the form of a symbolic act of homage, nor had this symbolic act of homage yielded a conclusion regarding man's place in the world and his relationship to God. Both these things are accomplished at this juncture by the introduction of the Sabbath among the Jewish people and by the hallowing of the Sabbath through the individual. The Sabbath as such had come into existence long before, but the שַׁבָּתוֹן, the idea that the individual, too, is to celebrate the Sabbath by ceasing from all work is a new development. Hence the emphasis upon the Sabbath at this point.

    °   °   °

25. *Eat it today! For today is a Sabbath to* **God!** On other days the Children of Israel were permitted to eat only that which they had acquired on the same day by dint of their toil. But on the Sabbath they could eat food for which they had not worked on that same day. For inactivity on the Sabbath is not self-chosen indolence, which is culpable, but a rest commanded by God, sacred to Him and therefore endowed with the same high positive value as any activity commanded by God. At the same time this command turns the very act of eating on the Sabbath into a מִצְוָה, an act which is commanded by God and directed toward Him, but which at the same time gladdens man even as it ennobles him.

The command that man is to submit to the direction of God in his search for sustenance is not intended to stunt his existence on earth; on the contrary, it is meant to enhance his enjoyment of earthly life, elevating even his physical pleasures into the sphere of morally free, God-serving acts, so that he will feel close to God even while he enjoys physical pleasures. The elevation of man's physical pleasures to the level of God-serving acts, dedicated to God, constitutes one of the most striking features distinguishing the Jewish conception of God from all others. In other religions the thought of the power of the gods is disheartening; a happy smile is likely to incur the wrath of the deity. The Jewish concept of God's power, by contrast, is a cheering one; sustained by it, puny man can struggle to his feet. By entering into the service of this power, man with all his weakness gains a share, as it were, in that power. That power gives meaning and protection to his humble existence on earth; he becomes joyously aware that his great God takes pleasure in the happiness of His little creature.

Hence also the significance of the third Sabbath meal. God's purpose in forbidding us to acquire and prepare food on the Sabbath is not to spoil our lives but to endow this work and this enjoyment with true human dignity by making them both subordinate to the will of God. Such a mentality and its acquisition are capable of lifting man unharmed above all the sufferings that God, in His educational Providence, would impose upon the Jewish people, upon the individual and upon the political and social world as a whole, in order to pave the way for such a mentality and in order to cleanse and purify them all. . . .

28. He who goes forth to seek his sustenance on the Sabbath in contravention of God's will thereby denies that his sustenance is given him by God. He demonstrates a belief that he is able to obtain the sustenance

keep My commandments and My teachings? 29. See that *God* has given you the Sabbath; that is why He gives you bread for two days on the sixth day. Let everyone remain where he is; let no one go out from his place on the seventh day!'' 30. And the people ceased from all activity on the seventh day. 31. The house of Yisrael called it *manna*; it was white like the seed of *gad* and its taste was like [that of] the finest flour with honey. 32. Moshe said: ''This is what *God* has commanded: Let one *omer*ful of it be preserved for your descendants so that they may see the bread which I fed you in the wilderness when I brought you out from the land of Mitzrayim.'' 33. But to Aharon Moshe said: ''Take a cooling-jar and put into it an *omer*ful of *manna* and set it down before *God* to be kept for your descendants.'' 34. As *God* had commanded Moshe, Aharon set it down before the Testimony, to be kept. 35. The sons of Yisrael ate the *manna* forty years until they came to an inhabited land; they ate the *manna* until they came to the border of the land of Canaan. 36. The *omer* is one-tenth of an *ephah*.

לִשְׁמֹ֥ר מִצְוֺתַ֖י וְתוֹרֹתָֽי: כט רְא֗וּ כִּֽי־יְהֹוָה֘ נָתַ֣ן לָכֶ֣ם הַשַּׁבָּת֒ עַל־כֵּ֠ן ה֣וּא נֹתֵ֥ן לָכֶ֛ם בַּיּ֥וֹם הַשִּׁשִּׁ֖י לֶ֣חֶם יוֹמָ֑יִם שְׁב֣וּ ׀ אִ֣ישׁ תַּחְתָּ֗יו אַל־יֵ֥צֵא אִ֛ישׁ מִמְּקֹמ֖וֹ בַּיּ֥וֹם הַשְּׁבִיעִֽי: ל וַיִּשְׁבְּת֥וּ הָעָ֖ם בַּיּ֥וֹם הַשְּׁבִעִֽי: לא וַיִּקְרְא֧וּ בֵֽית־יִשְׂרָאֵ֛ל אֶת־שְׁמ֖וֹ מָ֑ן וְה֗וּא כְּזֶ֤רַע גַּד֙ לָבָ֔ן וְטַעְמ֖וֹ כְּצַפִּיחִ֥ת בִּדְבָֽשׁ: לב וַיֹּ֣אמֶר מֹשֶׁ֗ה זֶ֤ה הַדָּבָר֙ אֲשֶׁ֣ר צִוָּ֣ה יְהֹוָ֔ה מְלֹ֤א הָעֹ֨מֶר֙ מִמֶּ֔נּוּ לְמִשְׁמֶ֖רֶת לְדֹרֹֽתֵיכֶ֑ם לְמַ֣עַן ׀ יִרְא֣וּ אֶת־הַלֶּ֗חֶם אֲשֶׁ֨ר הֶֽאֱכַ֤לְתִּי אֶתְכֶם֙ בַּמִּדְבָּ֔ר בְּהוֹצִיאִ֥י אֶתְכֶ֖ם מֵאֶ֥רֶץ מִצְרָֽיִם: לג וַיֹּ֨אמֶר מֹשֶׁ֜ה אֶֽל־אַהֲרֹ֗ן קַ֚ח צִנְצֶ֣נֶת אַחַ֔ת וְתֶן־שָׁ֥מָּה מְלֹֽא־הָעֹ֖מֶר מָ֑ן וְהַנַּ֤ח אֹתוֹ֙ לִפְנֵ֣י יְהֹוָ֔ה לְמִשְׁמֶ֖רֶת לְדֹרֹֽתֵיכֶֽם: לד כַּאֲשֶׁ֛ר צִוָּ֥ה יְהֹוָ֖ה אֶל־מֹשֶׁ֑ה וַיַּנִּיחֵ֧הוּ אַהֲרֹ֛ן לִפְנֵ֥י הָעֵדֻ֖ת לְמִשְׁמָֽרֶת: לה וּבְנֵ֣י יִשְׂרָאֵ֗ל אָֽכְל֤וּ אֶת־הַמָּן֙ אַרְבָּעִ֣ים שָׁנָ֔ה עַד־בֹּאָ֖ם אֶל־אֶ֣רֶץ נוֹשָׁ֑בֶת אֶת־הַמָּן֙ אָֽכְל֔וּ עַד־בֹּאָ֕ם אֶל־קְצֵ֖ה אֶ֥רֶץ כְּנָֽעַן: לו וְהָעֹ֕מֶר עֲשִׂרִ֥ית

---

he needs without any reference to, and even in contradiction with, the will of God. And so he declares that he obtains his sustenance not at the pleasure of God but solely through his own efforts and through ordinary means, subject only to the laws of nature. He believes that he has only to seek in order to find, only to find in order to possess, only to possess in order to be happy, and that none of these endeavors—seeking, finding and possessing—is dependent upon God. Hence a Jew who goes forth to seek his sustenance on the Sabbath thereby turns his back entirely upon God and upon compliance with His will; he places himself on his own and breaks the bond between himself and all of God's Law. Thus we are told: ''How long will you refuse to keep My commandments and My teachings?'' The violation of the Sabbath demonstrates a refusal to heed all of God's commandments and teachings. Like all symbolic commandments, the observance of the Sabbath is a מִצְוָה [commandment] as well as a תּוֹרָה [teaching]. It requires the performance of, or the abstention from, specified acts (מִצְוָה) in order to illustrate a given truth and to impress it upon the mind and spirit (תּוֹרָה). . . .

32. The command to preserve one *omer*ful of *manna* was intended to make it clear to the generation of the

wilderness that someday their wanderings in the wilderness would come to an end and that they eventually would be able to obtain their sustenance under normal conditions. However, even under normal conditions, they and their descendants were to preserve the spirit inculcated into them by their *manna* diet, and they were to regard the לֶחֶם [bread], טֶרֶף [food] and צֵידָה [provisions], the sustenance obtained from society and from the physical world by struggle and by hunting,[2] solely as מָן, as a gift ''granted and apportioned'' by God. That is the reason why the jar in which the *manna* was preserved was to be stored לִפְנֵי הָעֵדוּת [''before the Testimony''], together with the tablets testifying that the Law was a gift of God. God, Who gave the Law, also gives the sustenance that preserves life so that this Law may be observed. Conversely, it is God, the Source of all sustenance, Who has also given the Law defining the manner in which the life to be maintained by this sustenance is to be conducted. Both these facts must be kept in mind together; they are complementary.

[2]*Note to the English translation:* לחם = to wage war; טֶרֶף = prey; צַיִד = hunting. [G.H.]

XVII

1. The whole community of the sons of Yisrael journeyed from the wilderness of Sin according to their journeys at *God*'s behest; they camped in Refidim, and there was no water for the people to drink.　2. And the people quarreled with Moshe and they said: "Give us water that we may drink!" Moshe said to them: "Why do you quarrel with me? Why do you put *God* to the test?"　3. But when the people there became thirsty for water, the people murmured against Moshe, and it [i.e., the people] said: "Why have you brought us up out from Mitzrayim, to make me and my children and my herds die of thirst?"　4. Moshe cried out to *God*: "What shall I do to this people? Yet a little more and they will stone me."　5. And *God* said to Moshe: "Pass ahead of the people and take with you [some] of the elders of Yisrael; and your staff, with which you struck the river, take [it] in your hand and go.　6. Lo! I will stand before you there upon the rock in Ḥoreb; you will strike the rock and then water will come out of it and the people will drink." Moshe did so before the eyes of the elders of Yisrael.　7. He called the place Testing-and-Quarreling because of the quarreling of the sons of Yisrael and because they had put *God* to the test, saying: "Is *God* in our midst or not?"

הָאֵיפָה הוּא: פ שביעי יז א וַיִּסְעוּ כָּל־עֲדַת
בְּנֵי־יִשְׂרָאֵל מִמִּדְבַּר־סִין לְמַסְעֵיהֶם עַל־פִּי
יְהֹוָה וַיַּחֲנוּ בִּרְפִידִים וְאֵין מַיִם לִשְׁתֹּת הָעָם:
ב וַיָּרֶב הָעָם עִם־מֹשֶׁה וַיֹּאמְרוּ תְּנוּ־לָנוּ מַיִם
וְנִשְׁתֶּה וַיֹּאמֶר לָהֶם מֹשֶׁה מַה־תְּרִיבוּן עִמָּדִי
מַה־תְּנַסּוּן אֶת־יְהֹוָה: ג וַיִּצְמָא שָׁם הָעָם לַמַּיִם
וַיָּלֶן הָעָם עַל־מֹשֶׁה וַיֹּאמֶר לָמָּה זֶּה הֶעֱלִיתָנוּ
מִמִּצְרַיִם לְהָמִית אֹתִי וְאֶת־בָּנַי וְאֶת־מִקְנַי
בַּצָּמָא: ד וַיִּצְעַק מֹשֶׁה אֶל־יְהֹוָה לֵאמֹר מָה
אֶעֱשֶׂה לָעָם הַזֶּה עוֹד מְעַט וּסְקָלֻנִי: ה וַיֹּאמֶר
יְהֹוָה אֶל־מֹשֶׁה עֲבֹר לִפְנֵי הָעָם וְקַח אִתְּךָ
מִזִּקְנֵי יִשְׂרָאֵל וּמַטְּךָ אֲשֶׁר הִכִּיתָ בּוֹ אֶת־הַיְאֹר
קַח בְּיָדְךָ וְהָלָכְתָּ: ו הִנְנִי עֹמֵד לְפָנֶיךָ שָּׁם |
עַל־הַצּוּר בְּחֹרֵב וְהִכִּיתָ בַצּוּר וְיָצְאוּ מִמֶּנּוּ
מַיִם וְשָׁתָה הָעָם וַיַּעַשׂ כֵּן מֹשֶׁה לְעֵינֵי זִקְנֵי
יִשְׂרָאֵל: ז וַיִּקְרָא שֵׁם הַמָּקוֹם מַסָּה וּמְרִיבָה
עַל־רִיב | בְּנֵי יִשְׂרָאֵל וְעַל נַסֹּתָם אֶת־יְהֹוָה
לֵאמֹר הֲיֵשׁ יְהֹוָה בְּקִרְבֵּנוּ אִם־אָיִן: פ ח וַיָּבֹא

CHAPTER XVII

7. . . . In Refidim it was still a mixture of suspicion and lack of courage that made the people want to be certain of help before exposing themselves to danger. Their question "Is *God* in our midst or not?" expresses not so much doubt concerning God's almighty power as uncertainty whether He is indeed "in our midst"; whether His wonder-working almighty power is present also among mankind and whether He indeed concerns Himself with the wants and needs of men. The conceptions of nature, God and man current in that generation were diametrically opposed to the truth that was to be realized in and through Israel. Nature was regarded as an absolute force bound for all time by the laws of blind, immutable necessity. The deities themselves were considered bound by these all-compelling laws of nature, and man, too, was deemed to be completely under the dual dominion of the blind powers of both nature and the gods.

As a consequence, the step toward the recognition of nature as a force freely created and freely dominated by one, almighty, unfettered God, the recognition of God as the sole personal, free and almighty Creator, Regulator and absolute Ruler of the universe, and above all, the realization that this personal, free-willed Creator had created man as a free-willed personality, who, as first among the servants of God, was to be raised by and through this free-willed Ruler of the universe above the blind forces of nature—all this was indeed a giant step forward, and the opposition from the rest of the world was overwhelming. Consequently, it should really not surprise us that these basic concepts of all Jewish thought and action should have taken root in the spirit of that first people of God only little by little, and that all the momentous events of Jewish history now about to begin were necessary in order to make this truth our inalienable possession for all time.

8. Amalek came and fought with Yisrael
in Refidim.   9. And Moshe said to Yehoshua: "Choose men for us and go out, fight
with Amalek. Tomorrow I will stand on the
top of the hill, with the staff of God in my
hand."   10. Yehoshua did as Moshe had
said to him, to fight with Amalek. Moshe,
Aharon and Ḥur had gone up to the top of
the hill.   11. And it came to pass, when
Moshe held up his hand, that Yisrael prevailed, but when he allowed his hand to
rest, Amalek prevailed.   12. The hands of
Moshe became heavy; and they took a stone
and placed it under him, and he sat upon it.
Aharon and Ḥur supported his hands, the
one on the one side and the other on the
other side; so his hands remained an expression of trust until the sun went down.
13. Yehoshua weakened Amalek and his
people with the edge of the sword.
14. *God* said to Moshe: "Write this as a
memorial in the book, and put it also in the
ears of Yehoshua, that I will completely blot
out the remembrance of Amalek from under
the heavens."   15. And Moshe built an
altar and called it *God*-Is-My-Banner.
16. He said this; for the sovereignty of the
throne of God means war for *God* against
Amalek from generation to generation.

עֲמָלֵק וַיִּלָּחֶם עִם־יִשְׂרָאֵל בִּרְפִידִם: ט וַיֹּאמֶר
מֹשֶׁה אֶל־יְהוֹשֻׁעַ בְּחַר־לָנוּ אֲנָשִׁים וְצֵא הִלָּחֵם
בַּעֲמָלֵק מָחָר אָנֹכִי נִצָּב עַל־רֹאשׁ הַגִּבְעָה
וּמַטֵּה הָאֱלֹהִים בְּיָדִי: י וַיַּעַשׂ יְהוֹשֻׁעַ כַּאֲשֶׁר
אָמַר־לוֹ מֹשֶׁה לְהִלָּחֵם בַּעֲמָלֵק וּמֹשֶׁה אַהֲרֹן
וְחוּר עָלוּ רֹאשׁ הַגִּבְעָה: יא וְהָיָה כַּאֲשֶׁר יָרִים
מֹשֶׁה יָדוֹ וְגָבַר יִשְׂרָאֵל וְכַאֲשֶׁר יָנִיחַ יָדוֹ וְגָבַר
עֲמָלֵק: יב וִידֵי מֹשֶׁה כְּבֵדִים וַיִּקְחוּ־אֶבֶן
וַיָּשִׂימוּ תַחְתָּיו וַיֵּשֶׁב עָלֶיהָ וְאַהֲרֹן וְחוּר תָּמְכוּ
בְיָדָיו מִזֶּה אֶחָד וּמִזֶּה אֶחָד וַיְהִי יָדָיו אֱמוּנָה
עַד־בֹּא הַשָּׁמֶשׁ: יג וַיַּחֲלֹשׁ יְהוֹשֻׁעַ אֶת־עֲמָלֵק
וְאֶת־עַמּוֹ לְפִי־חָרֶב: פ מפטיר יד וַיֹּאמֶר יְהֹוָה
אֶל־מֹשֶׁה כְּתֹב זֹאת זִכָּרוֹן בַּסֵּפֶר וְשִׂים בְּאָזְנֵי
יְהוֹשֻׁעַ כִּי־מָחֹה אֶמְחֶה אֶת־זֵכֶר עֲמָלֵק מִתַּחַת
הַשָּׁמָיִם: טו וַיִּבֶן מֹשֶׁה מִזְבֵּחַ וַיִּקְרָא שְׁמוֹ
יְהֹוָה ׀ נִסִּי: טז וַיֹּאמֶר כִּי־יָד עַל־כֵּס יָהּ
מִלְחָמָה לַיהֹוָה בַּעֲמָלֵק מִדֹּר דֹּר: פ

8–16. All the phenomena which Israel, destined to
become the nation of God, had witnessed in the wilderness thus far—Marah, the quail, the *manna*, the
Sabbath, the water from the rock—had taught the people what its future place would be in the world of
nature. These experiences demonstrated to the people
of Israel the independence they would gain from the
forces of nature simply by subjecting themselves to
the will of the One God. But there was yet one experience left for them to undergo during those weeks of
preparation for receiving the Law; they had yet to learn
the position of the future nation of God as a nation
among other nations; its position in relation to the
forces operative among men and to man's future use of
force. This experience was to come to the Children of
Israel while they were still in Refidim, and the instrument by which they would be taught this lesson was
Amalek.

    In an earlier age, the evil spirit of Esau attacked
Jacob, the ancestor of the Children of Israel, at night as

Jacob was on his way toward personal independence.
This event caused Jacob to experience in his personal
life a foretaste of the struggle that the children of Esau
would force upon his sons during the centuries of darkness in the history of the nations, and then the ultimate
victory that would proclaim God's almighty power.
Similarly, the nation descended from Esau's grandson,
Amalek, was now to be the first, and the only, nation
that, without any threat or provocation from Israel,
would hurl itself upon the Children of Israel as they
marched toward national independence. . . .

9–12. Attacked by Amalek, Israel is compelled to
assume the risks of battle. However, it is not the sword
of Israel but the staff of Moses that defeats Amalek. It is
not a magic power inherent in the staff but the אֱמוּנָה,
Israel's clinging trust in God, as demonstrated by the
uplifted hand of Moses, that achieves this victory.

                    ∘   ∘   ∘

The Haftarah for this Sidra may be found on page 850.

XVIII

1. Yithro, priest in Midian, Moshe's father-in-law, heard of all that God had done for Moshe and for his people Yisrael, that *God* had brought Yisrael out from Mitzrayim. 2. And Yithro, Moshe's father-in-law, took Moshe's wife, Tzipporah, who had been sent home [earlier], 3. and her two sons, of whom one was named Gershom, because he had said: "I have been a stranger in a foreign land," 4. and the [name of the] other [was] Eliezer: "For the God of my father was my Help and rescued me from the sword of Pharaoh." 5. Yithro, Moshe's father-in-law, came with his sons and his wife to Moshe into the wilderness, where he had camped, as far as the mountain of God. 6. He sent word to Moshe: "I, your father-in-law, Yithro, am coming to you, and your wife and her two sons with her." 7. And Moshe went out to meet his father-in-law; he bowed down and kissed him; they inquired about each other's welfare and went into the tent. 8. Moshe told his father-in-law all that *God* had done to Pharaoh and to Mitzrayim because of Yisrael; all the hardships that had come upon them on the way, and how *God* had rescued them. 9. Yithro rejoiced at all the good that *God* had done for Yisrael in that He had rescued them from the hand of Mitzrayim, 10. and Yithro said: "Blessed be *God*, Who has rescued you from the hand of Mitzrayim and from the hand of Pharaoh, Who has rescued the people from the yoke of the hand of Mitzrayim. 11. Now I have realized that *God* is greater than all the gods; for I recognized Him precisely in the evil that they plotted against them." 12. Yithro, Moshe's father-in-law, consecrated to God an ascent offering and meal offerings, and Aharon, and all the elders of Yisrael, came to eat with Moshe's father-in-law before God. 13. On the next day Moshe sat to judge the people, and the people stood around Moshe from morning until the evening. 14. Moshe's father-in-law saw all that he was doing for the people and he

יח א וַיִּשְׁמַ֞ע יִתְר֨וֹ כֹהֵ֤ן מִדְיָן֙ חֹתֵ֣ן מֹשֶׁ֔ה אֵת֩ כָּל־אֲשֶׁ֨ר עָשָׂ֤ה אֱלֹהִים֙ לְמֹשֶׁ֔ה וּלְיִשְׂרָאֵ֖ל עַמּ֑וֹ כִּֽי־הוֹצִ֧יא יְהֹוָ֛ה אֶת־יִשְׂרָאֵ֖ל מִמִּצְרָֽיִם׃ ב וַיִּקַּ֗ח יִתְרוֹ֙ חֹתֵ֣ן מֹשֶׁ֔ה אֶת־צִפֹּרָ֖ה אֵ֣שֶׁת מֹשֶׁ֑ה אַחַ֖ר שִׁלּוּחֶֽיהָ׃ ג וְאֵ֖ת שְׁנֵ֣י בָנֶ֑יהָ אֲשֶׁ֨ר שֵׁ֤ם הָֽאֶחָד֙ גֵּֽרְשֹׁ֔ם כִּ֣י אָמַ֔ר גֵּ֣ר הָיִ֔יתִי בְּאֶ֖רֶץ נָכְרִיָּֽה׃ ד וְשֵׁ֥ם הָֽאֶחָ֖ד אֱלִיעֶ֑זֶר כִּֽי־אֱלֹהֵ֤י אָבִי֙ בְּעֶזְרִ֔י וַיַּצִּלֵ֖נִי מֵחֶ֥רֶב פַּרְעֹֽה׃ ה וַיָּבֹ֞א יִתְר֨וֹ חֹתֵ֥ן מֹשֶׁ֛ה וּבָנָ֥יו וְאִשְׁתּ֖וֹ אֶל־מֹשֶׁ֑ה אֶל־הַמִּדְבָּ֗ר אֲשֶׁר־ה֛וּא חֹנֶ֥ה שָׁ֖ם הַ֥ר הָאֱלֹהִֽים׃ ו וַיֹּ֙אמֶר֙ אֶל־מֹשֶׁ֔ה אֲנִ֛י חֹתֶנְךָ֥ יִתְר֖וֹ בָּ֣א אֵלֶ֑יךָ וְאִ֨שְׁתְּךָ֔ וּשְׁנֵ֥י בָנֶ֖יהָ עִמָּֽהּ׃ ז וַיֵּצֵ֨א מֹשֶׁ֜ה לִקְרַ֣את חֹֽתְנ֗וֹ וַיִּשְׁתַּ֙חוּ֙ וַיִּשַּׁק־ל֔וֹ וַיִּשְׁאֲל֥וּ אִישׁ־לְרֵעֵ֖הוּ לְשָׁל֑וֹם וַיָּבֹ֖אוּ הָאֹֽהֱלָה׃ ח וַיְסַפֵּ֤ר מֹשֶׁה֙ לְחֹ֣תְנ֔וֹ אֵת֩ כָּל־אֲשֶׁ֨ר עָשָׂ֤ה יְהֹוָה֙ לְפַרְעֹ֣ה וּלְמִצְרַ֔יִם עַ֖ל אוֹדֹ֣ת יִשְׂרָאֵ֑ל אֵ֤ת כָּל־הַתְּלָאָה֙ אֲשֶׁ֣ר מְצָאָ֣תַם בַּדֶּ֔רֶךְ וַיַּצִּלֵ֖ם יְהֹוָֽה׃ ט וַיִּ֣חַדְּ יִתְר֔וֹ עַ֚ל כָּל־הַטּוֹבָ֔ה אֲשֶׁר־עָשָׂ֥ה יְהֹוָ֖ה לְיִשְׂרָאֵ֑ל אֲשֶׁ֥ר הִצִּיל֖וֹ מִיַּ֥ד מִצְרָֽיִם׃ י וַיֹּ֙אמֶר֙ יִתְר֔וֹ בָּר֣וּךְ יְהֹוָ֔ה אֲשֶׁ֨ר הִצִּ֥יל אֶתְכֶ֛ם מִיַּ֥ד מִצְרַ֖יִם וּמִיַּ֣ד פַּרְעֹ֑ה אֲשֶׁ֤ר הִצִּיל֙ אֶת־הָעָ֔ם מִתַּ֖חַת יַד־מִצְרָֽיִם׃ יא עַתָּ֣ה יָדַ֔עְתִּי כִּֽי־גָד֥וֹל יְהֹוָ֖ה מִכָּל־הָאֱלֹהִ֑ים כִּ֣י בַדָּבָ֔ר אֲשֶׁ֥ר זָד֖וּ עֲלֵיהֶֽם׃ יב וַיִּקַּ֞ח יִתְר֨וֹ חֹתֵ֤ן מֹשֶׁה֙ עֹלָ֣ה וּזְבָחִ֖ים לֵֽאלֹהִ֑ים וַיָּבֹ֨א אַֽהֲרֹ֜ן וְכֹ֣ל ׀ זִקְנֵ֣י יִשְׂרָאֵ֗ל לֶֽאֱכָל־לֶ֛חֶם עִם־חֹתֵ֥ן מֹשֶׁ֖ה לִפְנֵ֥י הָאֱלֹהִֽים׃ שני יג וַיְהִי֙ מִֽמָּחֳרָ֔ת וַיֵּ֥שֶׁב מֹשֶׁ֖ה לִשְׁפֹּ֣ט אֶת־הָעָ֑ם וַיַּֽעֲמֹ֤ד הָעָם֙ עַל־מֹשֶׁ֔ה מִן־הַבֹּ֖קֶר עַד־הָעָֽרֶב׃ יד וַיַּרְא֙ חֹתֵ֣ן מֹשֶׁ֔ה אֵ֛ת כָּל־אֲשֶׁר־ה֥וּא עֹשֶׂ֖ה

לָעָם וַיֹּאמֶר מָה־הַדָּבָר הַזֶּה אֲשֶׁר אַתָּה עֹשֶׂה
לָעָם מַדּוּעַ אַתָּה יוֹשֵׁב לְבַדֶּךָ וְכָל־הָעָם נִצָּב
עָלֶיךָ מִן־בֹּקֶר עַד־עָרֶב: טו וַיֹּאמֶר מֹשֶׁה
לְחֹתְנוֹ כִּי־יָבֹא אֵלַי הָעָם לִדְרֹשׁ אֱלֹהִים:
טז כִּי־יִהְיֶה לָהֶם דָּבָר בָּא אֵלַי וְשָׁפַטְתִּי בֵּין
אִישׁ וּבֵין רֵעֵהוּ וְהוֹדַעְתִּי אֶת־חֻקֵּי הָאֱלֹהִים
וְאֶת־תּוֹרֹתָיו: יז וַיֹּאמֶר חֹתֵן מֹשֶׁה אֵלָיו לֹא־
טוֹב הַדָּבָר אֲשֶׁר אַתָּה עֹשֶׂה: יח נָבֹל תִּבֹּל
גַּם־אַתָּה גַּם־הָעָם הַזֶּה אֲשֶׁר עִמָּךְ כִּי־כָבֵד
מִמְּךָ הַדָּבָר לֹא־תוּכַל עֲשֹׂהוּ לְבַדֶּךָ: יט עַתָּה
שְׁמַע בְּקֹלִי אִיעָצְךָ וִיהִי אֱלֹהִים עִמָּךְ הֱיֵה
אַתָּה לָעָם מוּל הָאֱלֹהִים וְהֵבֵאתָ אַתָּה אֶת־
הַדְּבָרִים אֶל־הָאֱלֹהִים: כ וְהִזְהַרְתָּה אֶתְהֶם
אֶת־הַחֻקִּים וְאֶת־הַתּוֹרֹת וְהוֹדַעְתָּ לָהֶם אֶת־
הַדֶּרֶךְ יֵלְכוּ בָהּ וְאֶת־הַמַּעֲשֶׂה אֲשֶׁר יַעֲשׂוּן:
כא וְאַתָּה תֶחֱזֶה מִכָּל־הָעָם אַנְשֵׁי־חַיִל יִרְאֵי
אֱלֹהִים אַנְשֵׁי אֱמֶת שֹׂנְאֵי בָצַע וְשַׂמְתָּ עֲלֵהֶם
שָׂרֵי אֲלָפִים שָׂרֵי מֵאוֹת שָׂרֵי חֲמִשִּׁים וְשָׂרֵי
עֲשָׂרֹת: כב וְשָׁפְטוּ אֶת־הָעָם בְּכָל־עֵת וְהָיָה
כָּל־הַדָּבָר הַגָּדֹל יָבִיאוּ אֵלֶיךָ וְכָל־הַדָּבָר הַקָּטֹן
יִשְׁפְּטוּ־הֵם וְהָקֵל מֵעָלֶיךָ וְנָשְׂאוּ אִתָּךְ: כג אִם
אֶת־הַדָּבָר הַזֶּה תַּעֲשֶׂה וְצִוְּךָ אֱלֹהִים וְיָכָלְתָּ
עֲמֹד וְגַם כָּל־הָעָם הַזֶּה עַל־מְקֹמוֹ יָבֹא
בְשָׁלוֹם: שלישי כד וַיִּשְׁמַע מֹשֶׁה לְקוֹל חֹתְנוֹ
וַיַּעַשׂ כֹּל אֲשֶׁר אָמָר: כה וַיִּבְחַר מֹשֶׁה אַנְשֵׁי־

said: "What is this you are doing for the people? Why are you sitting alone and all the people are standing around you from morning until the evening?" 15. Moshe replied to his father-in-law: "The people come to me to seek God. 16. Whenever they have a concern, they come to me. I must judge between a man and his neighbor. I must make known to them the statutes of God and His teachings." 17. Moshe's father-in-law said to him: "What you are doing is not good. 18. You will surely become weary, you, as well as this people that is with you, for this thing is too difficult for you. You cannot carry it out all alone. 19. Now, hearken to my voice; I will give you advice, and God will be with you: You be for the people before God and you bring the concerns to God, 20. and you must also clarify to them the statutes and the teachings, and make known to them the way in which they must go, and the acts they are to perform. 21. But you must seek out from all the people men of ability, God-fearing men of truth who hate improper gain, and place over them princes out of thousands, princes out of hundreds, princes out of fifties and princes out of tens. 22. And let these judge the people at all times, and let it be thus, that they shall bring every great matter to you, but they shall judge every small matter. Make the burden easier for yourself and let them bear it with you. 23. If you will do this, then God can give you His commands and you will be able to endure, and all this people, too, each one of them will come in peace to the place rightfully due him." 24. Moshe hearkened to the voice of his father-in-law and did all that he had said. 25. Moshe chose the most capable men out of all

CHAPTER XVIII

13–15. . . . They came to Moses, or, as we will now learn, to the men who acted as his deputies, לִדְרֹשׁ אֱלֹקִים ["to seek God," or "to inquire of God"]. דְּרֹשׁ אֱלֹקִים means to seek instruction and help from God. Thus, the term would encompass the relationship which all our activities and all our lives should have toward God, a relationship which we must maintain if God is indeed to be *our* God. . . . The years of their wandering through the wilderness were indeed the great training period for the Jewish people. The task of the Jewish people through all the centuries to come would be to spread the knowledge of the Teaching of God among all the classes of the people; that is why the people now stood around Moses from morning until night, and Verse 15 states their purpose in general terms: "They come to me לִדְרֹשׁ אֱלֹקִים [to seek God]."

Yisrael and he named them heads over the people: princes out of thousands, princes out of hundreds, princes out of fifties and princes out of tens. 26. These had to judge the people at all times; a difficult matter they brought to Moshe, but every small matter they decided themselves. 27. Moshe let his father-in-law depart and he went back to his [own] homeland.

XIX

1. On the third New Moon after the departure of the sons of Yisrael from the land of Mitzrayim, on that same day did they come into the wilderness of Sinai. 2. They departed from Refidim, came into the wilderness of Sinai, camped in the wilderness, and Yisrael camped there, opposite the mountain. 3. But Moshe had gone up toward God, and *God* called to him from the mountain: "Thus shall you speak to the house of Yaakov and tell the sons of Yisrael: 4. You have seen what I have done to Mitzrayim, while I lifted you up on eagle's wings and brought you to Myself. 5. And now, if you will earnestly hearken to My voice and will keep My covenant, then you must belong to Me exclusively, more than all the nations, for all the earth is Mine. 6. But you shall be to me a kingdom of priests and a holy nation! These are the words that you shall speak to the sons of Yisrael." 7. Moshe came, summoned the elders of

חַ֫יִל מִכָּל־יִשְׂרָאֵל וַיִּתֵּן אֹתָם רָאשִׁים עַל־הָעָם
שָׂרֵי אֲלָפִים שָׂרֵי מֵא֔וֹת שָׂרֵי חֲמִשִּׁים וְשָׂרֵי
עֲשָׂרֹת: כו וְשָׁפְט֣וּ אֶת־הָעָ֖ם בְּכָל־עֵ֑ת אֶת־
הַדָּבָ֤ר הַקָּשֶׁה֙ יְבִיא֣וּן אֶל־מֹשֶׁ֔ה וְכָל־הַדָּבָ֥ר
הַקָּטֹ֖ן יִשְׁפּוּט֥וּ הֵ֑ם: כז וַיְשַׁלַּ֥ח מֹשֶׁ֖ה אֶת־חֹֽתְנ֑וֹ
וַיֵּ֥לֶךְ ל֖וֹ אֶל־אַרְצֽוֹ: פ רביעי **יט א** בַּחֹ֙דֶשׁ֙
הַשְּׁלִישִׁ֔י לְצֵ֥את בְּנֵֽי־יִשְׂרָאֵ֖ל מֵאֶ֣רֶץ מִצְרָ֑יִם
בַּיּ֣וֹם הַזֶּ֔ה בָּ֖אוּ מִדְבַּ֥ר סִינָֽי: ב וַיִּסְע֣וּ מֵרְפִידִ֗ים
וַיָּבֹ֙אוּ֙ מִדְבַּ֣ר סִינַ֔י וַֽיַּחֲנ֖וּ בַּמִּדְבָּ֑ר וַיִּֽחַן־שָׁ֥ם
יִשְׂרָאֵ֖ל נֶ֥גֶד הָהָֽר: ג וּמֹשֶׁ֥ה עָלָ֖ה אֶל־הָֽאֱלֹהִ֑ים
וַיִּקְרָ֙א אֵלָ֤יו יְהֹוָה֙ מִן־הָהָ֣ר לֵאמֹ֔ר כֹּ֤ה תֹאמַר֙
לְבֵ֣ית יַעֲקֹ֔ב וְתַגֵּ֖יד לִבְנֵ֥י יִשְׂרָאֵֽל: ד אַתֶּ֣ם
רְאִיתֶ֔ם אֲשֶׁ֥ר עָשִׂ֖יתִי לְמִצְרָ֑יִם וָאֶשָּׂ֤א אֶתְכֶם֙
עַל־כַּנְפֵ֣י נְשָׁרִ֔ים וָאָבִ֥א אֶתְכֶ֖ם אֵלָֽי: ה וְעַתָּ֗ה
אִם־שָׁמ֤וֹעַ תִּשְׁמְעוּ֙ בְּקֹלִ֔י וּשְׁמַרְתֶּ֖ם אֶת־בְּרִיתִ֑י
וִהְיִ֤יתֶם לִי֙ סְגֻלָּה֙ מִכָּל־הָ֣עַמִּ֔ים כִּי־לִ֖י כָּל־
הָאָֽרֶץ: ו וְאַתֶּ֧ם תִּֽהְיוּ־לִ֛י מַמְלֶ֥כֶת כֹּהֲנִ֖ים וְג֣וֹי
קָד֑וֹשׁ אֵ֚לֶּה הַדְּבָרִ֔ים אֲשֶׁ֥ר תְּדַבֵּ֖ר אֶל־בְּנֵ֥י
יִשְׂרָאֵֽל: חמישי ז וַיָּבֹ֣א מֹשֶׁ֔ה וַיִּקְרָ֖א לְזִקְנֵ֣י הָעָ֑ם

CHAPTER XIX

1-2. . . . When they arrived at this destination, facing Mount Sinai, all other considerations vanished from their minds. It was as "Yisrael" that they camped opposite the mountain. By thus pitching their tents opposite the mountain they signified that they had placed themselves at God's command and were awaiting further instructions from Him. This fact would justify the assumption that all their outbursts of weak-spiritedness and dissatisfaction up to this point had been caused more by doubts concerning the authenticity of the mission of Moses and Aaron than by a faltering of their trust in God Himself. Hence, we can readily understand the significance of the words uttered by God through Jeremiah: "Go and shout it in the ears of Jerusalem. This is what *God* has said: I remember for you the devotion of your youth, the love of your bridal

days, when you went after Me into the wilderness, into a land that was not sown" (Jeremiah 2:2).

5. . . . סְגֻלָּה denotes an "exclusive" possession to which no one else except its owner is entitled, and which has no relationship to anyone except its owner. Hence by employing this expression to define our relationship with Him, God basically demands that we must belong to Him, completely and exclusively, with every aspect of our nature, with all our being and with all our aspirations. He asks of us to make all our existence and all our aspirations dependent upon Him alone, to allow Him to shape them all and to permit nothing and no one else to direct our lives or to influence our actions.

כִּי לִי כָּל הָאָרֶץ *[for all the earth is Mine]*. The relationship into which you are to enter with Me is in fact nothing exceptional; it is merely to begin the restoration of that normal relationship which all the earth should really have with Me. . . .

the people and placed before them all these words that *God* had commanded him. 8. All the people answered with one voice and said: "All that *God* has spoken we will do." Moshe brought the words of the people back to *God*. 9. Thereupon *God* said to Moshe: "Behold, I am coming to you in a thickening of the cloud so that the people may hear when I speak with you, and then they will also trust you forever." Moshe held out the words of the people toward *God*. 10. And *God* said to Moshe: "Go to the people and sanctify them today and tomorrow and have them wash their garments. 11. Let them be ready for the third day, for on the third day *God* will descend before the eyes of all the people

וַיָּשֶׂם לִפְנֵיהֶם אֵת כָּל־הַדְּבָרִים הָאֵלֶּה אֲשֶׁר
צִוָּהוּ יְהוָה׃ ח וַיַּעֲנוּ כָל־הָעָם יַחְדָּו וַיֹּאמְרוּ כֹּל
אֲשֶׁר־דִּבֶּר יְהוָה נַעֲשֶׂה וַיָּשֶׁב מֹשֶׁה אֶת־דִּבְרֵי
הָעָם אֶל־יְהוָה׃ ט וַיֹּאמֶר יְהוָה אֶל־מֹשֶׁה הִנֵּה
אָנֹכִי בָּא אֵלֶיךָ בְּעַב הֶעָנָן בַּעֲבוּר יִשְׁמַע הָעָם
בְּדַבְּרִי עִמָּךְ וְגַם־בְּךָ יַאֲמִינוּ לְעוֹלָם וַיַּגֵּד מֹשֶׁה
אֶת־דִּבְרֵי הָעָם אֶל־יְהוָה׃ י וַיֹּאמֶר יְהוָה אֶל־
מֹשֶׁה לֵךְ אֶל־הָעָם וְקִדַּשְׁתָּם הַיּוֹם וּמָחָר
וְכִבְּסוּ שִׂמְלֹתָם׃ יא וְהָיוּ נְכֹנִים לַיּוֹם הַשְּׁלִישִׁי
כִּי ׀ בַּיּוֹם הַשְּׁלִשִׁי יֵרֵד יְהוָה לְעֵינֵי כָל־הָעָם

9. . . . **וַיַּגֵּד** *[held out . . . toward].* Since we have already been told in Verse 8 that Moses had reported [lit., "brought back"] the words of the people to God, **וַיַּגֵּד** in this verse can denote only a repetition of these words. By repeating these words Moses wanted to show that the people had already declared themselves unanimously and completely ready to carry out all the laws which God would give them. By so doing, they had also proclaimed their unreserved trust in Moses as the bearer of these laws. Therefore Moses felt that perhaps such an overwhelming display [i.e., God coming in a cloud to speak with Moses so that the people might hear] was not needed to substantiate and ensure their trust in him. We have therefore presumed to translate **וַיַּגֵּד** here in a literal manner: Moses "held out" the words of the people "toward" God.[3]

10–13. . . . Jewish Law is the only system of laws that did not emanate from the people whose constitution it was intended to be. Judaism is the only "religion" that did not originate from the human beings who find in it the spiritual basis for their lives. It is precisely this "objective" quality of Jewish Law and of the Jewish "religion" that makes them both unique, setting them apart clearly and explicitly from all else on earth that goes by the name of law or religion. It makes Jewish Law the sole cultural factor in mankind that may be considered the activator and culmination of every other manifestation of progress, while in itself, as the given absolute ideal, the Law remains above all manifestations of human progress. All other "religions" and codes of law have originated only in the human minds of a given era; they merely express the conceptions of God, of human destiny, and of their relationship to God and to one another held by a given society at a specified period in history. Hence all these man-made religions and codes, like all other aspects of human civilization—science, art and folkways — are subject to change with the passing of time. For by their very nature and origin they are nothing but expressions of levels reached by civilization at various stages in human development.

Not so the Jewish "religion" and Jewish Law. They do not stem from beliefs held by human beings at one period or another. They do not represent time-bound human concepts of God, of things human and Divine. They are God-given; they contain ideas that, by the will of God, should mold the concepts of men for all time with regard to God and to things Divine, but above all with regard to man and human affairs. From the very outset the Law of God stood in opposition to the people in whose midst it was to make its first appearance on earth. It was to prove its power first of all upon this people, who opposed it because they were "a stiff-necked people." But precisely the resistance which this Law encountered among the people in whose midst it obtained its first dwelling place on earth is the most convincing proof of the Divine origin of this Law, a law which did not arise from *within* the people but came *to* the people from the outside and required centuries of struggle to win this people for itself so that they would become bearers of the Laws of God through the ages.

To make known, in the most self-evident, categorical terms possible, the uniqueness which so fundamentally characterized the nature and origin of this Law from its

[3]*Note to the English translation*: The German term used by Hirsch is *entgegenhalten. Entgegen* can mean either "toward" or "against." The Hebrew **וַיַּגֵּד** is related to **נֶגֶד**, "against." [G.H.]

upon Mount Sinai. 12. Set boundaries around the people and say to them: 'Be careful not to ascend the mountain or even to touch a part of it! Whoever touches the mountain shall be put to death. 13. Let no hand touch it! For he shall be stoned to death, or only thrown down, whether it be beast or man, it shall not live.' When the horn of dismissal will sound a long-drawn-out blast, they may ascend the mountain again." 14. Moshe went down from the mountain to the people, he sanctified the people, and they washed their garments. 15. And he said to the people: "Keep yourselves in readiness for three days; do not come near a woman." 16. And it came to pass on the third day, when it was morning, that there were thunderbolts and flashes of lightning and a heavy cloud upon the mountain and an exceedingly loud *shofar* blast. All the people who were in the camp trembled. 17. Moshe led the people out of the camp toward God; they stood upright at the foot of the mountain. 18. Mount Sinai was all in smoke because *God* had descended upon it in fire. Its smoke went up like the smoke of a lime-kiln and the entire mountain shook violently. 19. And while the *shofar* blast continued and grew louder, Moshe spoke and God answered him aloud. 20. *God* descended upon Mount Sinai, to the top of the mountain, and *God* called Moshe to the top of the mountain, and Moshe went up. 21. And *God* said to Moshe: "Go down, warn the people that they must not break through

עַל־הַר סִינָי: יב וְהִגְבַּלְתָּ אֶת־הָעָם סָבִיב לֵאמֹר הִשָּׁמְרוּ לָכֶם עֲלוֹת בָּהָר וּנְגֹעַ בְּקָצֵהוּ כָּל־הַנֹּגֵעַ בָּהָר מוֹת יוּמָת: יג לֹא־תִגַּע בּוֹ יָד כִּי־סָקוֹל יִסָּקֵל אוֹ־יָרֹה יִיָּרֶה אִם־בְּהֵמָה אִם־אִישׁ לֹא יִחְיֶה בִּמְשֹׁךְ הַיֹּבֵל הֵמָּה יַעֲלוּ בָהָר: יד וַיֵּרֶד מֹשֶׁה מִן־הָהָר אֶל־הָעָם וַיְקַדֵּשׁ אֶת־הָעָם וַיְכַבְּסוּ שִׂמְלֹתָם: טו וַיֹּאמֶר אֶל־הָעָם הֱיוּ נְכֹנִים לִשְׁלֹשֶׁת יָמִים אַל־תִּגְּשׁוּ אֶל־אִשָּׁה: טז וַיְהִי בַיּוֹם הַשְּׁלִישִׁי בִּהְיֹת הַבֹּקֶר וַיְהִי קֹלֹת וּבְרָקִים וְעָנָן כָּבֵד עַל־הָהָר וְקֹל שֹׁפָר חָזָק מְאֹד וַיֶּחֱרַד כָּל־הָעָם אֲשֶׁר בַּמַּחֲנֶה: יז וַיּוֹצֵא מֹשֶׁה אֶת־הָעָם לִקְרַאת הָאֱלֹהִים מִן־הַמַּחֲנֶה וַיִּתְיַצְּבוּ בְּתַחְתִּית הָהָר: יח וְהַר סִינַי עָשַׁן כֻּלּוֹ מִפְּנֵי אֲשֶׁר יָרַד עָלָיו יְהֹוָה בָּאֵשׁ וַיַּעַל עֲשָׁנוֹ כְּעֶשֶׁן הַכִּבְשָׁן וַיֶּחֱרַד כָּל־הָהָר מְאֹד: יט וַיְהִי קוֹל הַשֹּׁפָר הוֹלֵךְ וְחָזֵק מְאֹד מֹשֶׁה יְדַבֵּר וְהָאֱלֹהִים יַעֲנֶנּוּ בְקוֹל: ששי כ וַיֵּרֶד יְהֹוָה עַל־הַר סִינַי אֶל־רֹאשׁ הָהָר וַיִּקְרָא יְהֹוָה לְמֹשֶׁה אֶל־רֹאשׁ הָהָר וַיַּעַל מֹשֶׁה: כא וַיֹּאמֶר יְהֹוָה אֶל־מֹשֶׁה רֵד הָעֵד בָּעָם פֶּן־יֶהֶרְסוּ אֶל־

first entrance into the world—this seems to be the purpose of the preparations and arrangements noted in the Scriptural text. The Law is about to come to the people. Its arrival is to be anticipated over a period of three days. In order to be found worthy even of awaiting this Law, the people must sanctify their bodies and their garments; that is, they must make themselves worthy of the Law by becoming aware, symbolically, of the rebirth of their lives, without and within, which the Law is to bring about. In their present state they are not yet ready to receive the Law. Only a resolve ultimately to become what they should be will make them worthy of receiving the Law. The distinction between the people about to receive the Law, and the source from which they are to receive it, is underscored also in terms of physical separation. The place from which the

people are to receive the Law is to be very clearly set apart from them. It is to be elevated into the realm of the extraterrestrial. No man, and not even a beast, may set foot upon that place, or even touch it. Any living thing that sets foot upon it must be put to death. Only when the giving of the Law has been completed is the place to be restored to the terrestrial sphere and both man and beast will be free once more to walk upon it. Until that time, the people are to be warned off and restrained by a barrier. All this is done in order to make clear that this Law originates from a source outside the earth and outside mankind.

20–25. . . . Moses himself was to stand below, with the people, at the moment when God would address toward *God* in order to see: many of them might fall.   22. And the priests also who come near to *God* should think to sanctify themselves, for *God* could send destruction upon them."   23. Moshe replied to *God*: "The people cannot go up to Mount Sinai, for Thou hast warned us: 'Set boundaries around the mountain and sanctify it!'"   24. And *God* said to him: "Go down, and come up again, you, and Aharon with you. But the priests and the people must not break through to go up to *God*, for He could send destruction among them."   25. Moshe went down to the people and told it to them.

XX 1. And God spoke all these words [saying]:   2. "I, *ד',* shall be your God, I, Who brought you out from the land of Mitzrayim, from the house of slaves.   3. You shall not have another god before My Presence!   4. Do not make yourself [a representation] in the form of an image, nor in the form of any [other] likeness, [of] that which is in heaven above, that

יְהֹוָה לִרְאוֹת וְנָפַל מִמֶּנּוּ רָב: כב וְגַם הַכֹּהֲנִים הַנִּגָּשִׁים אֶל־יְהֹוָה יִתְקַדָּשׁוּ פֶּן־יִפְרֹץ בָּהֶם יְהֹוָה: כג וַיֹּאמֶר מֹשֶׁה אֶל־יְהֹוָה לֹא־יוּכַל הָעָם לַעֲלֹת אֶל־הַר סִינָי כִּי־אַתָּה הַעֵדֹתָה בָּנוּ לֵאמֹר הַגְבֵּל אֶת־הָהָר וְקִדַּשְׁתּוֹ: כד וַיֹּאמֶר אֵלָיו יְהֹוָה לֶךְ־רֵד וְעָלִיתָ אַתָּה וְאַהֲרֹן עִמָּךְ וְהַכֹּהֲנִים וְהָעָם אַל־יֶהֶרְסוּ לַעֲלֹת אֶל־יְהֹוָה פֶּן־יִפְרָץ־בָּם: כה וַיֵּרֶד מֹשֶׁה אֶל־הָעָם וַיֹּאמֶר אֲלֵהֶם: ס כ א וַיְדַבֵּר אֱלֹהִים אֵת כָּל־הַדְּבָרִים הָאֵלֶּה לֵאמֹר: ס (בצבור קורין בטעם העליון תמצא בסוף הספר)° ב אָנֹכִי יְהֹוָה אֱלֹהֶיךָ אֲשֶׁר הוֹצֵאתִיךָ מֵאֶרֶץ מִצְרַיִם מִבֵּית עֲבָדִים: ג לֹא־יִהְיֶה לְךָ אֱלֹהִים אֲחֵרִים עַל־פָּנָי: ד לֹא־תַעֲשֶׂה לְךָ פֶסֶל וְכָל־תְּמוּנָה אֲשֶׁר בַּשָּׁמַיִם מִמַּעַל וַאֲשֶׁר בָּאָרֶץ

° For *Ta'am Ha'elyon* see page 1057.

Israel from above. Moses went down to the people and spoke to them (Verse 25) and then God uttered the words that follow (Chapter 20:1 ff). The Law was not only to be proclaimed by Moses; it was to be addressed to Moses even as it was to the rest of the people.

CHAPTER XX

2. ... Since this verse is formulated not as a declaration but as a מִצְוָה, a commandment, it does not mean, "'I, *ד',* am your God," but, "I, *ד', shall be* your God." In this manner it postulates as the basis for our relationship to God that demand which our Sages describe as קַבָּלַת עוֹל מַלְכוּת שָׁמַיִם ["accepting the yoke of the Kingdom of Heaven"].

the land of Mitzrayim. The state and the land which held us enchained represented the epitome of human statecraft based on human power and on the full range of natural forces harnessed in the service of human might. By breaking the might of men and disrupting the forces of nature, transforming or destroying them according to His will, passing judgment on human perversity and nature worship, smashing tyranny and raising up the downtrodden innocent, saving them and fulfilling His promise; in short, by shaping the destinies of men and intervening directly in earthly affairs, by delivering us and bringing us out

from the land of Mitzrayim, God in His almighty loving and righteous sovereignty has inscribed Himself forever upon our consciousness. He Who could say to us אֲשֶׁר הוֹצֵאתִיךָ מֵאֶרֶץ מִצְרַיִם ["Who brought you out from the land of Mitzrayim"] is the One Whom we are to acknowledge as the sole Guide of our fate for all time.

3. לֹא יִהְיֶה לְךָ [lit., "There shall not be for you"] is the first implication of the basic statement אָנֹכִי ["I, *ד',* shall be. . ."], and it is a negative one. As will be specifically explained in Verse 5, the acknowledgement of God excludes the worship of any other being. If God is indeed God, then any other deity is by definition a "non-god." ... This refutes the perverse notion of שִׁתּוּף ["partnership"], which, though not denying the existence of God, believes that another deity can be placed at His side and forgets that to place another deity at the side of God is tantamount to doing away with the concept of God altogether. (See *Sefer Mitzvoth Gadol*, Negative Precepts, 1).[4]

[4]*Note to the English translation*: This work by the thirteenth-century French scholar and Tosafist R. Moses ben Jacob of Coucy, first published sometime prior to 1480, includes, in effect, the essence of the Oral Law, divided into two parts: Positive Precepts and Negative Precepts. It is based on Moses Maimonides' *Mishne Torah*. [G.H.]

מִתַּחַת וַאֲשֶׁר בַּמַּיִם מִתַּחַת לָאָרֶץ: ה לֹא־
תִשְׁתַּחֲוֶה לָהֶם וְלֹא תָעָבְדֵם כִּי אָנֹכִי יְהוָֹה
אֱלֹהֶיךָ אֵל קַנָּא פֹּקֵד עֲוֹן אָבֹת עַל־בָּנִים עַל־
שִׁלֵּשִׁים וְעַל־רִבֵּעִים לְשֹׂנְאָי: ו וְעֹשֶׂה חֶסֶד
לַאֲלָפִים לְאֹהֲבַי וּלְשֹׁמְרֵי מִצְוֹתָי: ס ז לֹא
תִשָּׂא אֶת־שֵׁם־יְהוָֹה אֱלֹהֶיךָ לַשָּׁוְא כִּי לֹא יְנַקֶּה
יְהוָֹה אֵת אֲשֶׁר־יִשָּׂא אֶת־שְׁמוֹ לַשָּׁוְא: פ
ח זָכוֹר אֶת־יוֹם הַשַּׁבָּת לְקַדְּשׁוֹ: ט שֵׁשֶׁת יָמִים
תַּעֲבֹד וְעָשִׂיתָ כָּל־מְלַאכְתֶּךָ: י וְיוֹם הַשְּׁבִיעִי

which is on earth below, or that which is in the water deep below the earth. 5. Do not cast yourself down before them and do not serve them, for I, ד׳, your God, am a God Who demands His exclusive right; I remember the sin of parents for [their] children, for the third and fourth generation, for those who hate Me. 6. And I practice loving-kindness upon thousands, upon those who love Me and those who keep My commandments. 7. Do not take upon yourself the Name of ד׳, your God, in vain, for *God* will not hold guiltless one who takes His Name upon himself in vain. 8. Remember the Sabbath day to sanctify it. 9. Six days shall you serve and do all your [creating] work, 10. and the seventh

7. "Taking the Name" seems to be a conceptual circumlocution for הַשְׁבֻעָה [an oath]. . . . An oath in the Name of God implies that we seek to prove the veracity of our word and the honesty of our actions by subordinating our entire future to God's power of deciding over our fate. Hence, conversely, perjury represents the most contemptuous denial of God. . . .

for* God *will not hold guiltless. This utterance of God makes taking an oath tantamount to staking all of one's future on earth upon the veracity of one's oath or upon his intention to do what he has vowed to do. Our Sages teach us (Shavuoth 39a) that when God declared on Mount Sinai that He would not hold guiltless one who took His Name in vain, the whole earth trembled. For by virtue of these words the entire world was summoned to execute God's sentence upon the words of any man who makes a vow and then breaks it.

8. **אָנֹכִי *[I, ד׳, shall be . . .]*** commands us to acknowledge God in positive terms as the Pilot of our destinies and as the Guide of all our actions. The second commandment **לֹא יִהְיֶה לְךָ** ["You shall not have. . ."] states the negative implication of this acknowledgement in that it excludes allegiance to any other being. The third commandment **לֹא תִשָּׂא** ["Do not take upon yourself. . ."] makes this acknowledgement of God the basis of all human relationships, because the earnestness of our acknowledgment of God, as expressed by the oath, which is an appeal to the presence and the sovereign rule of God in all human relationships, is actually the mainstay of the political structure of human society. Also, this commandment warns us—again in negative terms—not to treat this acknowledgement of God with levity. The fourth commandment **זָכוֹר** ["Remember the Sabbath day. . ."] now recalls to us the ancient memorial which God had established when He first appointed man as His representative "servant and guard" over the world He had created. He instituted this memorial in order to secure man's acknowledgement of God, because the downward course of mankind's history was caused solely by man's forgetting God, thus necessitating the election of Israel as God's herald to lead the world upward once again.

° ° °

9. **תַּעֲבֹד *[shall you serve].*** You shall not conceive of your dominion over the world, as expressed in your work, as a function of autocratic rule on your part. You are to regard it as a "service" to the Kingdom of God, which you perform for Him and, by His command, for the world into which He has placed you to serve it and to keep it. By appropriating, transforming and altering the resources of the world, you are to raise this world from the sphere of blind physical compulsion into the realm of purposeful, freely-chosen morality, serving God of its own free will. It is in this spirit **וְעָשִׂיתָ כָּל מְלַאכְתֶּךָ**, that you are to do all your creating work. We have already (in our commentary on Genesis 2:2) defined the concept of **מְלָאכָה**. Even as **מַלְאָךְ** ["messenger"] is a personal being who carries out the will and the orders of his superior, so **מְלָאכָה** denotes anything impersonal made subservient to the will and the orders of a superior intelligence, in this case, man. **עֲשִׂיַּת מְלָאכָה** means to transform a substance, or an object, into our **מַלְאָךְ**; i.e., to impose upon it a permanent state which will henceforth make it fit to serve a purpose conceived and desired by ourselves, to carry out our will and our purposes. Every act subsumed under **עֲשִׂיַּת מְלָאכָה** [the performance of "creating" work] is a function of our dominion over the things of the terrestrial world. But **תַּעֲבֹד**, you are to exercise this dominion only as an act of "service."

day is a Sabbath to *God*, your God. On it you shall not perform any kind of [creating] work, you, nor your son, nor your daughter, nor your manservant, nor your handmaid, nor your livestock, nor your stranger who is

שַׁבָּת לַיהֹוָה אֱלֹהֶיךָ לֹא־תַעֲשֶׂה כָל־מְלָאכָה אַתָּה ׀ וּבִנְךָ וּבִתֶּךָ עַבְדְּךָ וַאֲמָתְךָ וּבְהֶמְתֶּךָ

10. . . . לֹא תַעֲשֶׂה כָל מְלָאכָה *[you shall not perform any kind of (creating) work].* The translation of לֹא תַעֲשֶׂה כָל מְלָאכָה simply as "you shall not do any kind of work" has distorted the entire concept of the Sabbath and subverted the laws of Sabbath observance. When Jews first began to denounce the oath of allegiance they had taken at Sinai to "bring life into line with the Law" and replaced it with the slogan, "bring the Law into line with life," the great law of the Sabbath, which forms the basis of all Jewish life, was also to be "reinterpreted" in order to make it "conform with the demands of life." Without troubling in the least to investigate whether such a reinterpretation could be derived from the Law, or whether the Law, in fact, admitted of such a reinterpretation, the Sabbath was declared to be a day of physical rest, which would allow man greater freedom to turn his spirit toward God. Accordingly, the מְלָאכָה that is prohibited on the Sabbath was interpreted to mean "work," which was then defined, quite correctly—or at least half-correctly, because there also is such a thing as mental work—as any activity involving physical exertion. It was explained that only activities entailing physical exertion were forbidden on the Sabbath. Light physical activities, or tasks performed for purposes of intellectual activity, on the other hand, were not forbidden. And so the so-called "reconciliation of the Law with the demands of life" was accomplished.

But in fact the Law does not indicate anywhere by so much as one syllable that the true essence of Sabbath observance requires something beyond the cessation of all מְלָאכָה, something which שְׁבִיתָה [cessation] serves only as a means to fulfill. Throughout the Law, observance of the Sabbath is defined as שְׁבִיתָה מִמְּלָאכָה [cessation of *all* activities classed as "creation"] and the desecration of the Sabbath as עֲשִׂיַּת מְלָאכָה [the performance of מְלָאכָה]. We are told [Exodus 31:14] that anyone who performs a מְלָאכָה on the Sabbath is to be put to death, and he is to be "uprooted," etc. We are not told that this punishment applies to one who does not go to the synagogue on the Sabbath or who does not listen to the sermon, etc. It applies only to one who has performed a מְלָאכָה on the Sabbath. Those who apprehended the poor man caught gathering brushwood on the Sabbath (Numbers 15:32–36) and who brought him to trial did not first inquire whether he had already "given the Sabbath its due" by attending services or by listening to the sermon, or whether, perhaps, he had gathered the wood because he wanted to use it for preparing his Sabbath meal. The fact was that he had gathered brushwood; this meant that he had gathered products of nature, removed them from their native soil and taken possession of them. Or perhaps he had gathered the wood from רְשׁוּת הָרַבִּים [an area defined by the law as "public property"] and then carried it אַרְבַּע אַמּוֹת [for a distance of four cubits or more]. In other words, he had performed a מְלָאכָה [an activity involving tasks classed as "creation"], and this was an offense sufficient to make him subject to the death penalty.

Also, note that physical exertion is not one of the basic criteria of מְלָאכָה. The term occurs almost 200 times in Scripture, and among these there is not one single instance of the word being used to denote strenuous activity. Likewise, the slave labor performed by the Children of Israel in Egypt is never described as מְלָאכָה. Rather, it appears that throughout Scripture, the term מְלָאכָה—as we have also come to understand from the etymological defintion of מַלְאָךְ—indicates not activities entailing a greater or lesser degree of physical exertion but solely activities connected with the intelligent "carrying out" of an intention. Hence, even if we did not know the definitions of מְלָאכָה offered by the Oral Law, the simple meaning of the term, and the hundredfold evidence supplied by the manner in which it is used in Scripture, would be sufficient to have us say: לֹא תַעֲשֶׂה כָל מְלָאכָה means, "You shall not perform any kind of activity involving tasks classed as 'creation.'" You must not carry out your intentions on any substance or object; you must not shape any substance or object in order to make it an idea, or a purpose, of yours. Stated in general terms: You must not produce or create anything. Indeed, were it not for the detailed instructions in the Oral Law, we might be led to carry this concept further still and to interpret it in even more comprehensive terms, construing מְלָאכָה as any activity entailing any "carrying out" of our intentions upon a substance or object. It is precisely the Oral Law that teaches us to interpret the concept in a more precise, literal manner as עֲשִׂיַּת מְלָאכָה, any activity that turns a substance into מְלָאכָה, our impersonal "messenger" for carrying out our intentions; in other words, an activity involving "construction" or "production." . . . It is true that activities in the category of physical exertion and workday toil are also forbidden on the Sabbath, but these prohibitions do not emanate from the concepts of אִיסּוּר מְלָאכָה.

° ° °

within your gates,   11. for [in] six days *God* formed the heaven and the earth, the sea and all that is in them, [even] when He rested on the seventh day; therefore *God* blessed the Sabbath day when He hallowed it.   12. Honor your father and your mother so that your days may be long upon the soil which *God*, your God, is giving you. 13. You shall not murder; you shall not commit adultery; you shall not steal; you shall not testify as a false witness against your neighbor.   14. You shall not covet your neighbor's house; you shall not covet

וְגֵרְךָ֖ אֲשֶׁ֣ר בִּשְׁעָרֶ֑יךָ: יא כִּ֣י שֵֽׁשֶׁת־יָמִים֩ עָשָׂ֨ה יְהֹוָ֜ה אֶת־הַשָּׁמַ֣יִם וְאֶת־הָאָ֗רֶץ אֶת־הַיָּם֙ וְאֶת־כָּל־אֲשֶׁר־בָּ֔ם וַיָּ֖נַח בַּיּ֣וֹם הַשְּׁבִיעִ֑י עַל־כֵּ֗ן בֵּרַ֧ךְ יְהֹוָ֛ה אֶת־י֥וֹם הַשַּׁבָּ֖ת וַֽיְקַדְּשֵֽׁהוּ: ס יב כַּבֵּ֥ד אֶת־אָבִ֖יךָ וְאֶת־אִמֶּ֑ךָ לְמַ֙עַן֙ יַֽאֲרִכ֣וּן יָמֶ֔יךָ עַ֚ל הָֽאֲדָמָ֔ה אֲשֶׁר־יְהֹוָ֥ה אֱלֹהֶ֖יךָ נֹתֵ֥ן לָֽךְ: ס יג לֹ֖א תִּרְצָֽח: ס לֹ֖א תִּנְאָֽף: ס לֹ֖א תִּגְנֹֽב: ס לֹֽא־תַֽעֲנֶ֥ה בְרֵֽעֲךָ֖ עֵ֥ד שָֽׁקֶר: ס יד לֹ֤א תַחְמֹד֙ בֵּ֣ית רֵעֶ֔ךָ ס

11. Thus, for six days you shall exercise, in the service of God, your dominion over the things of your world which He conferred upon you. You shall utilize them for your own purposes and, like a creator, modify them for these purposes. You are to shape them all into servants of your might. But the seventh day is to put a stop to all these activities of yours; on it you are to desist (שבת) from your creating, in order to render homage to ד׳ as your God. . . .

       ○   ○   ○

12. . . . The exodus from Egypt and the giving of the Law: these two basic facts in the history of the Jewish people that form the foundation for our allegiance to God as the Ruler of our destinies and the Guide for our lives are historic truths. However, our knowledge and acknowledgement of historic truths depend on our having a tradition. The maintenance of that tradition in turn requires parents who will faithfully transmit it to their children, and children who are willing to accept it from the hands of their parents. Thus, the survival of the great Divine institution that is Judaism rests entirely upon the obedience of children toward their parents, both in theory and in practice, and the honor given to one's father and mother is the basic condition for the eternity of the Jewish nation. Through the father and the mother God gives the child more than merely his physical existence. Parents in fact represent the tie that binds the child to the past of the Jewish people and that enables the child to be a Jewish man or woman. It is they who are to hand down to the child the traditions of Judaism through instruction, custom and training. The child is to receive from their hands both Jewish history and Jewish Law so that eventually he in turn will be able to pass them on to his own children. Just as he looks up to his parents, so shall his own children someday look up to him. Without this tie the chain of generations is broken, the past of the Jewish people is lost to the future, and the Jewish nation will cease to exist. It is this significant function that gives Jewish parents their prominent place in the Decalogue, so that

the Law of God tells us: "Honor your father and your mother so that your days may be long upon the soil which *God*, your God, gives to you."

       ○   ○   ○

13. . . . The five commandments that now follow proclaim the implications of our knowledge and acknowledgement of God for our lives as members of human society. If God is the one sole Ruler of man's destinies, and if He is to be the sole Guide of all the deeds of men, then each and every one of your fellow men, too, must be considered equally under His care in every aspect of his destinies, and the eye of God will be upon any action you take against your fellow man. It is by the will of God that each of your fellow men has been placed where he is beside you. It is through God that each man becomes a human being and, like yourself, endowed with human rights hallowed by God. All that is his — his life, his marriage, his freedom, his happiness, his honor, his possessions—has been sanctified to him by God Himself. Therefore you must not murder him, you must not destroy his marriage, you must not deprive him of his freedom, you must not encroach upon his personal happiness and honor by giving false testimony against him. Indeed, you must not even allow yourself to covet anything that is part of your neighbor's household, and this includes anything he calls his own during his life on earth.

       ○   ○   ○

14. . . . If we consider the order in which these basic principles were set forth, it would seem to us to express yet another truth that seems to be of no small significance for the fundamental concepts of God's Law. The first half [of the fundamental Ten Commandments] begins with אָֽנֹכִי ["I, ד׳, shall be your God"] and ends with כַּבֵּד ["Honor your father and your mother"]. The second half begins with לֹא תִּרְצָח ["You shall not murder"] and ends with לֹא תַחְמֹד ["You shall not covet"]. Thus, the demand that we acknowledge God opens with a demand imposed upon the intellect: "I, ד׳, shall be your God" and "You shall not have another

your neighbor's wife, his manservant, his handmaid, his ox, his donkey, or anything else that belongs to your neighbor." 15. And all the people saw the voices and the flames and the call of the *shofar* and the mountain smoking; the people saw and trembled and stood afar off. 16. And they said to Moshe: "You speak to us; we will listen. But let not God speak with us, for we might die." 17. And Moshe said to the people: "Do not be afraid, for God came in this manner in order to test you and in order that His fear should remain before you so that you will not sin." 18. The people remained afar off, and Moshe had drawn near to the opaque darkness where God had appeared. 19. And *God* said to Moshe: "This is what you shall say to the sons of Yisrael: You have seen that I have talked with you from heaven; 20. do not make [a representation of] anything [that is] with Me; you shall not make yourselves gods of silver and gods of gold. 21. You shall make for Me an altar of earth and you shall make your ascent offerings, and your peace offerings, and offer your sheep and your

לֹֽא־תַחְמֹ֞ד אֵ֣שֶׁת רֵעֶ֗ךָ וְעַבְדּ֤וֹ וַאֲמָתוֹ֙ וְשׁוֹר֣וֹ וַחֲמֹר֔וֹ וְכֹ֖ל אֲשֶׁ֥ר לְרֵעֶֽךָ׃ פ שביעי טו וְכָל־הָעָם֩ רֹאִ֨ים אֶת־הַקּוֹלֹ֜ת וְאֶת־הַלַּפִּידִ֗ם וְאֵת֙ ק֣וֹל הַשֹּׁפָ֔ר וְאֶת־הָהָ֖ר עָשֵׁ֑ן וַיַּ֤רְא הָעָם֙ וַיָּנֻ֔עוּ וַיַּֽעַמְד֖וּ מֵֽרָחֹֽק׃ טז וַיֹּֽאמְרוּ֙ אֶל־מֹשֶׁ֔ה דַּבֵּר־אַתָּ֥ה עִמָּ֖נוּ וְנִשְׁמָ֑עָה וְאַל־יְדַבֵּ֥ר עִמָּ֛נוּ אֱלֹהִ֖ים פֶּן־נָמֽוּת׃ יז וַיֹּ֨אמֶר מֹשֶׁ֣ה אֶל־הָעָם֮ אַל־תִּירָאוּ֒ כִּ֗י לְבַֽעֲבוּר֙ נַסּ֣וֹת אֶתְכֶ֔ם בָּ֖א הָאֱלֹהִ֑ים וּבַעֲב֗וּר תִּהְיֶ֧ה יִרְאָת֛וֹ עַל־פְּנֵיכֶ֖ם לְבִלְתִּ֥י תֶחֱטָֽאוּ׃ יח וַיַּֽעֲמֹ֥ד הָעָ֖ם מֵֽרָחֹ֑ק וּמֹשֶׁה֙ נִגַּ֣שׁ אֶל־הָ֣עֲרָפֶ֔ל אֲשֶׁר־שָׁ֖ם הָאֱלֹהִֽים׃ ס מפטיר יט וַיֹּ֤אמֶר יְהֹוָה֙ אֶל־מֹשֶׁ֔ה כֹּ֥ה תֹאמַ֖ר אֶל־בְּנֵ֣י יִשְׂרָאֵ֑ל אַתֶּ֣ם רְאִיתֶ֔ם כִּ֚י מִן־הַשָּׁמַ֔יִם דִּבַּ֖רְתִּי עִמָּכֶֽם׃ כ לֹ֥א תַעֲשׂ֖וּן אִתִּ֑י אֱלֹ֤הֵי כֶ֙סֶף֙ וֵֽאלֹהֵ֣י זָהָ֔ב לֹ֥א תַעֲשׂ֖וּ לָכֶֽם׃ כא מִזְבַּ֣ח אֲדָמָה֮ תַּֽעֲשֶׂה־לִּי֒ וְזָבַחְתָּ֣ עָלָ֗יו אֶת־עֹלֹתֶ֙יךָ֙ וְאֶת־שְׁלָמֶ֔יךָ אֶת־צֹֽאנְךָ֖ וְאֶת־

god. . . ." However, it is not enough to acknowledge God in theory; we must express our acknowledgement of God also in practice by exercising control over our words ("Do not take upon yourself the Name of God . . . in vain"), our actions ("Remember the Sabbath day. . .") and our family lives ("Honor your father and your mother"). The social legislation begins with demands upon both our actions and our words ("You shall not murder; you shall not commit adultery; you shall not steal; you shall not testify as a false witness . . ."). However, it is not enough to control our words and deeds; the Law demands that we exercise control also over our spirit and our attitudes ("You shall not covet. . .").

°   °   °

19–23. These five verses contain the most significant and momentous implications of our direct relationship with God, which the people as a whole, and every individual separately, experienced through the revelation on Mount Sinai.

They saw that God had spoken directly with each and every one of them. Thus they realized that no intermediary is needed to have God come near to us. This realization should banish from our midst for all time any attempt to make a representation of anything to place at His side, even if that representation were

only intended to bring God to our minds. Whenever God wishes to make Himself and His personal Providence apparent to us, it will be in the form of His blessing that we will perceive His personal nearness. It is not through a physical representation but through His workings that we are to perceive God and become certain of His Presence.

We will indeed have symbols in our midst—symbolic representations, objects and acts. However—and herein lies the crucial difference between Jewish symbolism and all other symbolisms—our symbols are to represent not what man requires in order to realize God, but what God requires in order to have man realize what it is that God demands of a true human being.

20. לֹא תַעֲשׂוּן אִתִּי [*do not make . . . with Me*]. Do not fashion anything to place it next to Me. Whatever you human beings will fashion according to your own ideas in order to represent the supernatural for yourselves will always turn out to be אֱלֹהֵי כֶסֶף וגו׳, ["gods of silver," etc.], idols. Men use symbols to represent the Divine to themselves; you must not do this. . . . Even those representations which I Myself have commanded you to make must be limited to the specifications I have established. . . .

בְּקָרֶךָ בְּכָל־הַמָּקוֹם אֲשֶׁר אַזְכִּיר אֶת־שְׁמִי
אָבוֹא אֵלֶיךָ וּבֵרַכְתִּיךָ׃ כב וְאִם־מִזְבַּח אֲבָנִים
תַּעֲשֶׂה־לִּי לֹא־תִבְנֶה אֶתְהֶן גָּזִית כִּי חַרְבְּךָ
הֵנַפְתָּ עָלֶיהָ וַתְּחַלְלֶהָ׃ כג וְלֹא־תַעֲלֶה בְמַעֲלֹת
עַל־מִזְבְּחִי אֲשֶׁר לֹא־תִגָּלֶה עֶרְוָתְךָ עָלָיו׃ פ

cattle upon it; at every palce where I would have My Name remembered I will come to you and bless you.
22. And if some day you will make for Me an altar of stones, you shall not build it out of cut stones; for if you have wielded your sword over one [of the stones], you will have desecrated it.
23. And you shall not ascend to My altar with steps so that your nakedness will not be exposed upon it."

The Haftarah for this Sidra may be found on page 854.

משפטים

MISHPATIM

XXI 1. Now these are the [social] ordinances which you are to set forth to them in detail. 2. If you purchase a Hebrew servant, he shall

כא א וְאֵ֙לֶּה֙ הַמִּשְׁפָּטִ֔ים אֲשֶׁ֥ר תָּשִׂ֖ים לִפְנֵיהֶֽם׃
ב כִּ֤י תִקְנֶה֙ עֶ֣בֶד עִבְרִ֔י שֵׁ֥שׁ שָׁנִ֖ים יַעֲבֹ֑ד

CHAPTER XXI

2. ***If you purchase a Hebrew servant.*** To the unprejudiced mind nothing can demonstrate the authenticity of the Oral Law as cogently as these two first sections, Verses 2–6 and 7–11, with which the "Mosaic legislation" begins. This is to be the civil and criminal code of a nation; it is to set forth the principles and provisions of right and humanity that are to regulate human relationships within a state. As might be expected, the first title deals with personal rights. But with what does this title begin? With laws applicable if a man sells another man, and if a man sells his own daughter as a slave! What an unthinkable monstrosity this would be if this "document" would indeed be the sole "book of law" for the Jewish people, if it, and it alone, were to be the primary source of "Jewish social law"! These are indeed exceptional situations, and one could reasonably have expected to find a mass of other laws and legal principles stated and decided, discussed, specified and explained before the Law could even turn to such bizarre cases. And yet it is precisely with these statements, which in fact would seem to negate the concept of personal freedom by accepting limitations on this, the most sacred of human rights, that the law begins!

However, all this will appear in an altogether different light if we understand that this "book" is not the primary source of Jewish Law, if we realize that the primary source of the Law is that legal tradition which has been kept alive by the living word, with the "book" serving only as an aid to memory and a resource for resolving cases of doubt. Consider, as is confirmed by the text itself, that by the time Moses, immediately before his death, turned over this book to the people, the Law had already been handed down to them and impressed upon them over a period of forty years. Given these facts, it will be readily understandable how it came about that precisely the exceptional cases should have been recorded at the very outset: This was done in order to remind us all the more forcefully of the ordinary principles of social justice.

We will then understand that in fact the "book" does not record legal principles at all, but primarily individual, concrete cases in point. And it does so in such an instructive manner that we can easily derive from these cases the principles that were entrusted to the living spirit of the people. In general, the language used in this "book" was so skillfully chosen that in many instances one unusual term, one altered construction, or the position of one word or even one letter, and so forth, can imply a whole train of legal concepts. This book was not intended as a primary source of the Law. It was meant for those who were already well-versed in the Law, to use only as a means of retaining and of reviving, over and over again, the knowledge that they had already committed to memory. It was intended as a teaching aid for teachers of the Law, as a reference to confirm the Oral Law, so that the attentive student should find it easy, with the aid of the written text before him, to reproduce in his mind, over and over again, the knowledge he received by word of mouth.

The relationship between תּוֹרָה שֶׁבִּכְתָב [the Written Teaching] and תּוֹרָה שֶׁבְּעַל פֶּה [The Oral Law] is the same as that between brief written notes taken on a detailed scientific lecture, and the lecture itself. Students of a discipline who have attended the lecture require only their brief notes to recall the entire lecture at any time. They often find that a word, a question mark, an exclamation mark, a period, or the underscoring of a word is sufficient for this purpose. But for those who did not attend the instructor's lecture these notes would be of no use whatsoever. If they were to attempt to reconstruct the entire lecture solely from these notes, they would of necessity make many errors. Words, marks, etc., that serve the students who listened to the lecture as most instructive guiding stars for the retention of the truths expounded by the lecturer appear completely meaningless to the uninitiated. The noninitiate who will attempt to use these same notes in order to construct (as opposed to *reconstruct*) for himself the lecture he did not attend and could not have understood will only dismiss the fine points of the Law as baseless mental gymnastics and idle speculations leading nowhere.

° ° °

If you purchase a Hebrew servant: The Oral Law teaches us that the matter under discussion here is the case described in Exodus 22:2, where it is stated that a thief who lacks the means to make restitution for what he has stolen must be sold in order to indemnify his victim ("if he has nothing, then he shall be sold for his theft"). Such a sale can be effected only in order to serve for six years; but in the seventh he shall go out free, for nothing.   3. If he entered service only by himself, he shall also leave by himself; if he is a married man, his wife shall leave with him. 4. If his master gives him a wife, and she bears him sons or daughters, the woman and her children shall remain with her master, and he shall leave by himself.   5. But if the servant shall say repeatedly: "I have grown to love my master, my wife and my children; I do not want to go out free," 6. then his master shall bring him to the judges, and shall bring him to the gate or to the doorpost, and his master shall pierce his

וּבַשְּׁבִעֵת יֵצֵא לַחׇפְשִׁי חִנָּם: ג אִם־בְּגַפּוֹ יָבֹא בְּגַפּוֹ יֵצֵא אִם־בַּעַל אִשָּׁה הוּא וְיָצְאָה אִשְׁתּוֹ עִמּוֹ: ד אִם־אֲדֹנָיו יִתֶּן־לוֹ אִשָּׁה וְיָלְדָה־לּוֹ בָנִים אוֹ בָנוֹת הָאִשָּׁה וִילָדֶיהָ תִּהְיֶה לַאדֹנֶיהָ וְהוּא יֵצֵא בְגַפּוֹ: ה וְאִם־אָמֹר יֹאמַר הָעֶבֶד אָהַבְתִּי אֶת־אֲדֹנִי אֶת־אִשְׁתִּי וְאֶת־בָּנָי לֹא אֵצֵא חׇפְשִׁי: ו וְהִגִּישׁוֹ אֲדֹנָיו אֶל־הָאֱלֹהִים וְהִגִּישׁוֹ אֶל־הַדֶּלֶת אוֹ אֶל־הַמְּזוּזָה וְרָצַע אֲדֹנָיו

make restitution for the value of the actual theft, not in order to raise the double indemnity stipulated in 22:3 as a penalty. Also, this means of making restitution is applicable only if the thief is a male, not a female. The written text does not read simply אִם אֵין לוֹ וְנִמְכַּר ["if he has nothing, then he shall be sold"] but adds the qualifying word בִּגְנֵבָתוֹ ["for this theft"] [to show that a thief could be sold only in order to make restitution for the property he has stolen]. And the fact that the text reads not simply בִּגְנֵבָה ["for *the* theft"] but בִּגְנֵבָתוֹ ["for *his* theft"] indicates that females found guilty of theft are excluded from this provision. A situation in which someone voluntarily sells himself as a slave out of dire poverty is treated in Leviticus 25:39 f. ("If your brother becomes impoverished and sells himself to you.") For this reason, too, we are told only here, in the case of a thief, כִּי תִקְנֶה עֶבֶד עִבְרִי ["If you purchase a Hebrew servant"]. The law has already declared him an עֶבֶד before you have purchased him; you can purchase him only from the court of law. At the same time, however, as the Mekhilta notes, he must remain in your eyes an עִבְרִי, a fellow citizen; the law refers to him as an עֶבֶד only because it has no other option but to describe him in these terms.

     º   º   º

6. . . . If we consider this law, which the Word of God has placed at the beginning of its social legislation [in the preceding verses], we shall see that there is hardly another law as eminently suited as this one to afford us an insight into the purpose of the Divine institutions of social justice and to show us how fundamentally different the character of Jewish Law is from all other legal systems. We have here [in the case of a thief] *the one sole instance* in which the Law of God imposes loss of freedom as a punishment (though we shall see that in fact even this is not to be construed as a punishment). And in what manner is this punishment to be carried out? The law specifies that the offender must be placed

with a family, just as we today might place a juvenile delinquent into a family environment. Note, too, the precautions which the law enumerates for this procedure in order not to crush the offender's self-respect, so that, despite the degradation he has brought upon himself, he may still feel that he is treated and respected as a brother, capable of earning and giving love! *Note how the law makes sure that he can retain his contact with his family, and how it sees to it that his family should not suffer distress because of his offense!* Even as it deprives the offender of his freedom and thus of the ability to provide for his loved ones, the law imposes the responsibility for their care upon those who benefit from his labors for the duration of his servitude.

Prison sentences, with all the attendant despair and moral debasement behind prison bars, with all the woe and misery that imprisonment inflicts upon the prisoner's wife and children, are unknown in God's Law. Where God's Law holds sway, prisons as an abode for criminals do not exist. Jewish Law provides only for detention pending trial, and even this can happen only in accordance with a judicial procedure set down in detail. Such a detention can be of short duration only, and circumstantial evidence is inadmissible.

But even this solitary case in which the Law decrees loss of freedom as the consequence of a crime cannot be construed as a "punishment." The purpose of this law cannot be punishment because it sentences the thief to six years' servitude only with the object of making restitution for the actual value of the theft but not with the object of raising the fine (double restitution) imposed as a punishment for the offense. Hence loss of freedom is merely a consequence of the offender's legal obligation to make restitution for the theft he committed. Restitution is not to be made by the offender as a punishment for his offense; it is merely a way of canceling the effects of the crime that endure as long as the unlawful or felonious damage done to the victim's property has ear with an awl, and then he shall serve him forever.   7. If a man sells his daughter to be a handmaid, she shall not leave as male servants leave.   8. If she is not pleasing in the eyes of her master who has provisionally designated her for marriage to him, he must arrange to have her redeemed; he does not have the right to sell her into a circle that will remain alien to her, seeing that he has dealt with her in an unfatherly manner. 9. But if he designates her for marriage to his son, he shall deal with her according to the rights of daughters;   10. if he takes for himself another [wife], he may not diminish

אֶת־אָזְנוֹ בַּמַּרְצֵעַ וַעֲבָדוֹ לְעֹלָם׃ ס ז וְכִי־יִמְכֹּר אִישׁ אֶת־בִּתּוֹ לְאָמָה לֹא תֵצֵא כְּצֵאת הָעֲבָדִים׃ ח אִם־רָעָה בְּעֵינֵי אֲדֹנֶיהָ אֲשֶׁר־לֹא (לוֹ קרי) יְעָדָהּ וְהֶפְדָּהּ לְעַם נָכְרִי לֹא־יִמְשֹׁל לְמָכְרָהּ בְּבִגְדוֹ־בָהּ׃ ט וְאִם־לִבְנוֹ יִיעָדֶנָּה כְּמִשְׁפַּט הַבָּנוֹת יַעֲשֶׂה־לָּהּ׃ י אִם־אַחֶרֶת יִקַּח־לוֹ שְׁאֵרָהּ

not been redressed. Even if he has not been sentenced by a court of law, anyone who steals the property of another automatically becomes liable to pay for it with his personal assets; i.e., his working capacity. Hence there is only one question still in need of an answer: Why does the court assess damages in terms of the offender's working capacity only in cases of outright theft and not also in every other case in which an individual is liable to make restitution for damage he has caused but does not have the means to make such restitution? This limitation is probably motivated by the consideration that theft is the most obvious expression of contempt for the sanctity of personal property, particularly when an owner considers his property safe because he trustingly assumes that everyone respects the property rights of others. . . . Man's position in the world begins with the concept of property ownership, and it is his respect for the property of others that makes a man truly human. We can see, then, why it is only in the case of theft that the obligation to make restitution is imposed upon every aspect of the offender's person.

However, this sentence to servitude is so inextricably linked only with the offender's obligation to make restitution, and the law is so very far from seeking to impose servitude as a punishment, and so respectful of the sanctity of personal freedom, that the court of law may effect the sale of a thief only if the value of the property he has stolen is equal to, or in excess of, the value of his working capacity. For only in this case is the offender automatically liable to pay the consequences of his act with every aspect of his person. If the value of his working capacity is in excess of the value of the stolen property, the court [may impound his labor to pay for the value of the theft but it] has no right to sell him, for if it did so, it would be guilty of infringing, as it were, upon a part of the offender's person that is not liable to loss of freedom (Kiddushin 18a). Incidentally, accord-

ing to the Mekhilta, the victim of the theft has the right to waive restitution derived from the sale of the thief and to content himself with a signed promise from the thief to pay restitution as soon as his material circumstances improve.

.   .   .

7. . . . All that we have learned from the literature of our nation concerning the position of respect which Judaism accords to women, the relationship of parents to their children, and the considerations that must guide parents in finding suitable marriage partners for their offspring permits us to conclude without hesitation that if a Jewish man sells his young daughter in this manner to be a maidservant, or perhaps to become her master's wife, only the most bitter, compelling necessity could have driven him to do so. He must have sold all his house and home, even his last shirt, before he is permitted to take such a step (Kiddushin 20a, Maimonides, *Hilkhoth Avadim* IV, 2).

.   .   .

10. This is the only passage in which the Written Law discusses a man's obligations toward his wife. In order to delineate מִשְׁפַּט הַבָּנוֹת, the basic marital rights of the daughters of its people, it chooses as a case in point a woman from the very lowest rung of the social ladder, a pauper's daughter, the child of a man who has already sold the last shirt off his back and who now, in order to save himself and his child from starvation, has sold her as a maidservant. Then the girl, scorned by her master and perhaps already the victim of his abuse, becomes the wife of her master's son. Once this has happened, the law makes her an equal of the woman who comes to marriage from freedom and affluence, and it proclaims the great maxim: Not by one hair's breadth may the treatment of the one be different from that accorded to the other!

כְּסוּתָהּ וְעֹנָתָהּ לֹא יִגְרָע: יא וְאִם־שְׁלָשׁ־אֵלֶּה
לֹא יַעֲשֶׂה לָהּ וְיָצְאָה חִנָּם אֵין
כָּסֶף: ס יב מַכֵּה אִישׁ וָמֵת מוֹת יוּמָת:
יג וַאֲשֶׁר לֹא צָדָה וְהָאֱלֹהִים אִנָּה לְיָדוֹ וְשַׂמְתִּי
לְךָ מָקוֹם אֲשֶׁר יָנוּס שָׁמָּה: ס יד וְכִי־יָזִד אִישׁ
עַל־רֵעֵהוּ לְהָרְגוֹ בְעָרְמָה מֵעִם מִזְבְּחִי תִּקָּחֶנּוּ
לָמוּת: ס טו וּמַכֵּה אָבִיו וְאִמּוֹ מוֹת יוּמָת: ס
טז וְגֹנֵב אִישׁ וּמְכָרוֹ וְנִמְצָא בְיָדוֹ מוֹת
יוּמָת: ס יז וּמְקַלֵּל אָבִיו וְאִמּוֹ מוֹת יוּמָת: ס
יח וְכִי־יְרִיבֻן אֲנָשִׁים וְהִכָּה־אִישׁ אֶת־רֵעֵהוּ

her food, her clothing or her conjugal rights.
11. If he does not arrange any of these
three for her, she shall go out for nothing,
without repayment of money. 12. One
who strikes a man so that he dies
shall be put to death. 13. But if it had not
been his aim to do so, but God placed him
into his hand, then I shall appoint for you a
place to which he may flee. 14. But if one
deliberately plots against another, to kill
him with premeditation, then you must take
him away [even] from My altar that he may
die. 15. Also one who strikes his father or
his mother shall be put to death. 16. And
one who steals a man and sells him, and he
was found in his hand, he shall be put to
death. 17. And one who curses his father
or his mother shall be put to death. 18. If
men are engaged in a quarrel, and one of
them strikes the other with a stone or with

11. . . . Crime and poverty—these are the two factors that in ordinary social life tend to reduce to the zero point the respect due a man's personal dignity. But the Law has taken a criminal and a child of abject poverty and set them both as cases in point at the very beginning of its social legislation. By so doing, it demonstrates to us its concept of the respect due to human dignity and the manner in which it seeks to safeguard this right down to the very lowest rung of society.

Verses 12–32 contain laws referring to personal rights: Verses 12–17 deal with crimes against human life and against situations considered tantamount to life itself. Verses 18–26 deal with offenses against the well-being of the body; i.e., injuries and damage to health. Verses 27–32 deal with bodily injury and loss of life inflicted by animals.

° ° °

15. In order to denote a fatal blow, the verb הַכָּאָה ["to strike"] must be followed by וָמֵת ["and he dies"]. The verb הַכָּאָה alone does not indicate that the victim died as the result of the attack. (The Halakhah teaches that even if his victim died, the offender can be put to death only if his act produced a visible injury.) Hence, if this verse is read in context with Verse 12, the law is seen to be as follows: וָמֵת וגו׳ וּמַכֵּה אָבִיו וגו׳: One who strikes another person so that the victim dies incurs the death penalty. But one who strikes his father or his mother incurs the death penalty even if the [visible] injury which he dealt his parent was not fatal in itself.

16. Just as in the preceding verse, the "partial killing," that is, the physical wounding of one's own father and mother, is declared tantamount to actual murder and thus classed as a capital offense, so, too, the Law now teaches us that personal freedom is a possession the theft of which amounts to "social murder" and is therefore punishable by death. However, a kidnapper is subject to the death penalty only if the victim is found in the kidnapper's possession and, as Deuteronomy 24:7 adds, "and he has availed himself of his services and has sold him"; in other words, if he has treated him as if he were an object, a "thing." . . .

17. Kidnapping is the actual destruction of the victim's personal dignity. But in the case of one's own father and mother, קְלָלָה, the mere verbal expression of the child's wish that they should be destroyed, is a capital crime. This is so even if the parent thus cursed is no longer alive.

° ° °

18. . . . רִיב ["quarrel"] primarily denotes a verbal dispute as distinct from וְכִי יִנָּצוּ ["if men fight. . ."] in Verse 22, which primarily implies a physical struggle. . . . We are therefore told in this verse וְכִי יְרִיבֻן ["If men are engaged in a quarrel"], with the final *nun* added for emphasis, to declare that the quarrel in this case was only verbal. The two parties had no intention of doing one another physical harm; the physical blow may have been struck under the impact of strong emotion. But this in no way mitigates the offender's liability to make restitution to his victim, for the purpose of restitution is not to punish the offender but to redress, as much as possible, the damage that was done. Therefore, too, since a monetary indemnity is not punishment for the

his fist, and it is not fatal, but he is confined to his bed, 19. if he rises [again] and walks about with his former support, the one who struck him shall go free; he shall pay him only for the loss of his time and shall provide for his cure. 20. If a person strikes his manservant or handmaid to discipline [him or her] and he [or she] dies under his hand, he [i.e., the victim] shall be avenged. 21. However, if he survives for a day or two, he shall not be avenged, because he is his property. 22. If men fight [with one another] and hit a pregnant woman so that her [unborn] children escape, but no fatality ensues, he shall be fined, if the woman's husband demands that such [fine] be imposed, and he shall pay it as the judges determine. 23. But if a fatality ensues, you must give life for life. 24. Compensation of eye for eye; compensation of tooth for tooth; compensation of hand for hand; compensation of foot

בְּאֶבֶן אוֹ בְאֶגְרֹף וְלֹא יָמוּת וְנָפַל לְמִשְׁכָּב׃
יט אִם־יָקוּם וְהִתְהַלֵּךְ בַּחוּץ עַל־מִשְׁעַנְתּוֹ
וְנִקָּה הַמַּכֶּה רַק שִׁבְתּוֹ יִתֵּן וְרַפֹּא יְרַפֵּא׃ ס שני
כ וְכִי־יַכֶּה אִישׁ אֶת־עַבְדּוֹ אוֹ אֶת־אֲמָתוֹ
בַּשֵּׁבֶט וּמֵת תַּחַת יָדוֹ נָקֹם יִנָּקֵם׃ כא אַךְ אִם־
יוֹם אוֹ יוֹמַיִם יַעֲמֹד לֹא יֻקַּם כִּי כַסְפּוֹ הוּא׃ ס
כב וְכִי־יִנָּצוּ אֲנָשִׁים וְנָגְפוּ אִשָּׁה הָרָה וְיָצְאוּ
יְלָדֶיהָ וְלֹא יִהְיֶה אָסוֹן עָנוֹשׁ יֵעָנֵשׁ כַּאֲשֶׁר
יָשִׁית עָלָיו בַּעַל הָאִשָּׁה וְנָתַן בִּפְלִלִים׃
כג וְאִם־אָסוֹן יִהְיֶה וְנָתַתָּה נֶפֶשׁ תַּחַת נָפֶשׁ׃
כד עַיִן תַּחַת עַיִן שֵׁן תַּחַת שֵׁן יָד תַּחַת יָד רֶגֶל

wrong that was done, but restitution for the damage sustained by the victim, this restitution can never really be complete in cases where the victim suffered bodily injury; particularly, it can never make up for the pain of the victim's personal hurt. Therefore the offender remains guilty in the eyes of God even after he has paid his indemnity in full, and he can make atonement for his act only by first obtaining forgiveness from his victim.

° ° °

19. עַל מִשְׁעַנְתּוֹ in this context cannot possibly denote a staff or a crutch.[5] For if the victim was previously able to walk unaided and now has become lame as the result of his injury, compensation for the loss of his time and for his medical expenses cannot in any manner be deemed adequate restitution. Nor can מִשְׁעַנְתּוֹ be construed as referring to a staff or crutch needed by the victim during his convalescence, for as long as the effects of his injury persist, the law could not declare that "the one who struck him shall go free." מִשְׁעַנְתּוֹ denotes the support to which the victim was normally accustomed prior to his injury. Hence it implies his complete recovery; i.e., that he is able to walk again as he did before he was injured.

° ° °

וְרַפֹּא יְרַפֵּא *[and shall provide for his cure]*. The insistence implied by the repetition of the verb form is intended to refute the erroneous conception that resorting to medical aid shows a lack of trust in God. Cf. "Whence it can be derived that authorization was granted (by God) to the physicians to heal" (Baba Kamma 85a). The Law takes it for granted that the victim will seek medical aid. Indeed, as noted in תוספות ibid., the Law insists that the patient seek medical help not only for bodily injury, as in this instance, but also for other illnesses.

[5]*Note to the English translation*: Standard translations of the Pentateuch render עַל מִשְׁעַנְתּוֹ as "upon his staff." [G.H.]

23. . . . וְנָתַתָּה נֶפֶשׁ תַּחַת נָפֶשׁ *[you must give life for life]*. Only in the case of a murder—meaning that the actual person who would be entitled to compensation has been destroyed—must the punishment be carried out on the physical person of the criminal. But even here, as we have already noted, the expression וְנָתַתָּה ["you must give"] makes it clear that the punishment is in fact intended as a form of restitution except that in place of the physical person of the victim, who would have had the first claim for restitution, there is the "ideal person" of law, justice and human dignity whose claim must be satisfied. . . .

° ° °

24 and 25. . . . עַיִן תַּחַת עַיִן וגו׳ [lit., "An eye for an eye," etc.]: Baba Kamma 83b points out the moral absurdity of interpreting this law literally; i.e., that one who puts out the eye of another must have his own eye put out, etc. What if, for instance, a one-eyed man put out one eye of a man who had two healthy eyes, is punished by having his own one eye put out and then

תַּחַת רָגֶל׃ כה כְּוִיָּה תַּחַת כְּוִיָּה פֶּצַע תַּחַת פָּצַע
חַבּוּרָה תַּחַת חַבּוּרָה׃ ס כו וְכִי־יַכֶּה אִישׁ אֶת־
עֵין עַבְדּוֹ אוֹ־אֶת־עֵין אֲמָתוֹ וְשִׁחֲתָהּ לַחָפְשִׁי
יְשַׁלְּחֶנּוּ תַּחַת עֵינוֹ׃ כז וְאִם־שֵׁן עַבְדּוֹ אוֹ־שֵׁן
אֲמָתוֹ יַפִּיל לַחָפְשִׁי יְשַׁלְּחֶנּוּ תַּחַת שִׁנּוֹ׃ פ
כח וְכִי־יִגַּח שׁוֹר אֶת־אִישׁ אוֹ אֶת־אִשָּׁה וָמֵת
סָקוֹל יִסָּקֵל הַשּׁוֹר וְלֹא יֵאָכֵל אֶת־בְּשָׂרוֹ וּבַעַל
הַשּׁוֹר נָקִי׃ כט וְאִם שׁוֹר נַגָּח הוּא מִתְּמֹל
שִׁלְשֹׁם וְהוּעַד בִּבְעָלָיו וְלֹא יִשְׁמְרֶנּוּ וְהֵמִית
אִישׁ אוֹ אִשָּׁה הַשּׁוֹר יִסָּקֵל וְגַם־בְּעָלָיו יוּמָת׃
ל אִם־כֹּפֶר יוּשַׁת עָלָיו וְנָתַן פִּדְיֹן נַפְשׁוֹ כְּכֹל
אֲשֶׁר־יוּשַׁת עָלָיו׃ לא אוֹ־בֵן יִגָּח אוֹ־בַת יִגָּח
כַּמִּשְׁפָּט הַזֶּה יֵעָשֶׂה לּוֹ׃ לב אִם־עֶבֶד יִגַּח
הַשּׁוֹר אוֹ אָמָה כֶּסֶף ׀ שְׁלֹשִׁים שְׁקָלִים יִתֵּן
לַאדֹנָיו וְהַשּׁוֹר יִסָּקֵל׃ ס לג וְכִי־יִפְתַּח אִישׁ
בּוֹר אוֹ כִּי־יִכְרֶה אִישׁ בֹּר וְלֹא יְכַסֶּנּוּ וְנָפַל־

for foot. 25. Compensation of burn for burn; compensation of wound for wound; compensation of bruise for bruise. 26. If a person strikes the eye of his manservant or the eye of his handmaid and destroys it, he shall set him free as compensation for his eye. 27. And if he knocks out the tooth of his manservant or the tooth of his handmaid, he shall set him free as compensation for his tooth. 28. If an ox gores a man or a woman so that he [or she] dies, the ox shall be stoned to death and its flesh may not be eaten, but the owner of the ox goes free. 29. But if it is a goring ox in that it already had gored yesterday and the day before, and this has been attested to its owner but he did not keep it in thereafter, and it kills a man or a woman, the ox shall be stoned to death and its owner, too, is liable to [the] death penalty. 30. If an atonement fine is imposed upon him, he must give for the redemption of his person whatever is imposed upon him. 31. Also if it gores a boy or a girl, he shall be dealt with in accordance with this [social] ordinance. 32. If an ox gores a manservant or a handmaid, he [i.e., the owner] shall give his [i.e., the servant's] master thirty shekels, but the ox must be stoned to death. 33. If a person opens a pit, or if a person prepares a pit and does not cover it, and an ox or a

dies as a result? In that case his punishment would not be just, since he would then lose his life for an offense which caused his victim only the loss of one of two bodily organs [with the other still left intact]. Moreover . . . the provisions set forth in Verse 18 and 19 above, according to which victims of injuries requiring bed rest and medical attention must be indemnified for the loss of their time and for their medical care, rule out the interpretation of (lit.) "an eye for an eye," etc., "a wound for a wound," etc. as *ius talionis*, for if a similar injury were to be inflicted on the offender, the latter would require bed rest and medical attention himself. From these objective considerations alone it should be clear that the Halakhah's explanation of monetary restitution as the only form of compensation intended by Biblical law for such cases is the sole interpretation conformable to the spirit of the Biblical text. Moreover, a closer consideration of the word תַּחַת ["for"; i.e. "instead of"], upon which in fact this entire legal concept is based, will reveal that this interpretation is also the one most faithful to the letter of the text.

° ° °

In the vast majority of instances where the word תַּחַת occurs in Scripture it indicates compensation rather than punishment, so that עַיִן תַּחַת עַיִן [lit., "an eye for an eye"], etc. simply means that the offender must "replace" an eye, or any other organ, which he has destroyed; i.e., he must compensate his victim, whose eye he has put out, by giving him a new eye, etc. But putting out the offender's eye would in no way restore the eye which he caused his victim to lose. Since no human being can literally restore the eye of another *in natura*, this law can only mean that he must render full monetary compensation for the lost eye.

° ° °

33. . . . כִּי יִפְתַּח *[If (a person) opens]* refers to an already existing pit; so does כִּי יִכְרֶה ["if (a person) prepares. . ."]. This is probably the reason why the text employs a form of the verb כרה rather than of חפר. חפר would denote only "digging"; כרה, however, denotes not only "digging" but also "preparing" or "arranging." The verb יִכְרֶה is therefore best suited to connote an *alteration* in the character of an already existing pit.

donkey falls into it, 34. then the owner of the pit must make restitution; he must restore the full value [of the animal] to its owner; however, the dead [animal] shall remain the property of the latter. 35. If one man's ox gores the ox of his neighbor so that it dies, they shall sell the live ox and

שָׁמָּה שׁוֹר אוֹ חֲמוֹר: לד בַּעַל הַבּוֹר יְשַׁלֵּם
כֶּסֶף יָשִׁיב לִבְעָלָיו וְהַמֵּת יִהְיֶה־לּוֹ: ס לה וְכִי־
יִגֹּף שׁוֹר־אִישׁ אֶת־שׁוֹר רֵעֵהוּ וָמֵת וּמָכְרוּ

The repetition of the word אִישׁ ["a person"] conveys the legal concept that if anything is done to alter the character of a pit, then even if the pit was the work of several persons the liability for damage caused by the alteration is placed upon the last individual to contribute to the alteration. . . .

° ° °

34. . . . בּוֹר is the classic example (אָב [lit., "father-type"]) of an inanimate property or product that causes damage while it is in a stationary position. Thus, a potsherd or any other object thrown out onto a public highway where it can cause injury to an animal or a person is תּוֹלְדָה דְבוֹר; it is in the category subsumed under the heading בּוֹר. However, in order to be regarded as an object causing damage while in a stationary position, the dangerous object need not have been purposely thrown out onto a public highway. It comes into this category even if it was merely left in a position where, under ordinary circumstances, it could be expected to roll, fall or be blown onto the public highway. Once this has happened, it can cause damage there even while it is in a stationary position; e.g. (Baba Kamma 3b): "Rocks, knives, or any other objects that someone placed upon a roof and that were blown into the street, where they caused damage after having come to rest." If they cause damage while they are still in the process of falling, they belong to the category subsumed under the heading אֵשׁ ["fire"] (22:5). Incidentally, in the category of בּוֹר, restitution is payable only in the case of living creatures that are threatened directly by the object; i.e., only in the case of those that cannot be expected to be careful where they are walking (e.g., children or young animals, or older persons, and animals walking in the dark).

It is an essential requirement of Jewish "piety," a basic character trait of the true *hassid,* to dispose of broken needles, or of any other objects that could possibly cause injury, only in a place where they will cause no harm. "He who would be pious must (in the first place) carry out all the laws in the Order of Torts" (Baba Kamma 30a).

35. . . . As soon as an object, animate or inanimate, comes into the legal custody of an individual, that individual becomes responsible for all the actions of this property and for the consequences of these actions. Fundamentally, a man's property is only an extension of his body. Hence, even as a man's mind is responsible for the actions of his body, so, too, when a man, who is endowed with intelligence, acquires an object that has no intelligence of its own, he automatically becomes the object's guardian, as it were, and becomes responsible for all its actions, as we have already seen in Verses 33 and 34 under the heading of בּוֹר with regard to inanimate property.

However, a man is responsible only for those actions of his property which may reasonably be expected from that property by virtue of its nature and which he is therefore under obligation to prevent. It is not in the normal nature of an ox to gore; i.e., to do damage intentionally, out of pure viciousness. In this respect an ox is תָּם [lit. "innocent"], or, as expressed in Baba Kamma 15a, "Ordinary oxen can control themselves not to gore"; i.e., in this respect oxen are not in need of restraint. As a consequence, if an ox does damage, the law does not hold its owner liable for compensation. However, in the interest of safe traffic in the public domain the owner of the animal is made liable to a fine so that he should restrain his ox to make sure that it will do no damage, not even by acts which as a rule are not expected of oxen. Had the law imposed full compensation for such damage, it might have, in fact, increased the threat to traffic on public highways because it might have encouraged the owners of potential victims to drive their animals along the highways without a care, or even deliberately to create situations in which the animals would sustain injury, knowing that they, the owners, would be legally entitled to full compensation.

That is why, in such cases, the law imposes a penalty on both the owner of the live ox and the owner of the dead ox. By so doing, the law forces both owners to exercise precautions which alone will ensure the safety of all traffic on public highways. When two animals meet on a public highway, the law places them both under the joint guardianship of their owners, as it were, thus linking both owners in a temporary community of interests which forms the basis for the rights of open traffic. For this reason the two owners appear also in the text as joint owners of both the animals, with both owners equally liable for damage in which both of them divide the money received for it and they shall also divide the dead [ox]. 36. Or if it is now recognized that it is a goring ox, in that it had already gored yesterday and the day before, and its owner did not keep it in thereafter, then the owner must pay full compensation, ox for ox, but the dead [animal] remains his property. 37. If a man steals an ox or a sheep and then slaughters or sells it, he shall pay five oxen as compensation for the ox and four sheep as compensation for the sheep.

XXII

1. If the thief is discovered in the act of breaking in and he is struck so that he dies, there shall be no blood guilt on his account. 2. If the sun has risen upon him, there shall be blood guilt on his account. He is obligated to make restitution; if he has nothing, then he shall be sold for his theft. 3. However, if the stolen article is found in his possession, then, whether it be an ox, or a donkey, or a sheep, he shall pay compensation for it, that is, double [compensation for full value. 4. If a person allows a field or a vineyard to be damaged by

אֶת־הַשּׁוֹר הַחַי֙ וְחָצ֣וּ אֶת־כַּסְפּ֔וֹ וְגַ֥ם אֶת־הַמֵּ֖ת
יֶחֱצֽוּן׃ לו א֣וֹ נוֹדַ֗ע כִּ֠י שׁ֣וֹר נַגָּ֥ח הוּא֙ מִתְּמ֣וֹל
שִׁלְשֹׁ֔ם וְלֹ֥א יִשְׁמְרֶ֖נּוּ בְּעָלָ֑יו שַׁלֵּ֨ם יְשַׁלֵּ֥ם שׁוֹר֙
תַּ֣חַת הַשּׁ֔וֹר וְהַמֵּ֖ת יִֽהְיֶה־לּֽוֹ׃ ס לז כִּ֤י יִגְנֹֽב־
אִישׁ֙ שׁ֣וֹר אוֹ־שֶׂ֔ה וּטְבָח֖וֹ א֣וֹ מְכָר֑וֹ חֲמִשָּׁ֣ה
בָקָ֗ר יְשַׁלֵּם֙ תַּ֣חַת הַשּׁ֔וֹר וְאַרְבַּע־צֹ֖אן תַּ֥חַת
הַשֶּֽׂה׃ כב א אִם־בַּמַּחְתֶּ֛רֶת יִמָּצֵ֥א הַגַּנָּ֖ב וְהֻכָּ֣ה
וָמֵ֑ת אֵ֥ין ל֖וֹ דָּמִֽים׃ ב אִם־זָֽרְחָ֥ה הַשֶּׁ֛מֶשׁ עָלָ֖יו
דָּמִ֣ים ל֑וֹ שַׁלֵּ֣ם יְשַׁלֵּ֔ם אִם־אֵ֣ין ל֔וֹ וְנִמְכַּ֖ר
בִּגְנֵבָתֽוֹ׃ ג אִם־הִמָּצֵ֨א תִמָּצֵ֤א בְיָדוֹ֙ הַגְּנֵבָ֔ה
מִשּׁ֥וֹר עַד־חֲמ֖וֹר עַד־שֶׂ֑ה חַיִּ֑ים שְׁנַ֖יִם יְשַׁלֵּֽם׃ ס
שלישי ד כִּ֤י יַבְעֶר־אִישׁ֙ שָׂדֶ֣ה אוֹ־כֶ֔רֶם וְשִׁלַּח֙

share the blame. It is for this reason, too, that the claim of the plaintiff in such a case of injury to his animal cannot exceed the actual value of the animal that did the damage. The purpose of the preventive measure is simply to safeguard the joint interests of the owners of both animals, attacker and victim, in order to prevent accidents to either. . . .

36. . . . From the wording of the text [Verse 35] ["If one man's ox gores the ox of his neighbor"] tradition has derived the important legal principle, "(this means) the ox of his neighbor, not an ox that was consecrated to the Sanctuary" (Baba Kamma 6b). **תוספות** ibid., enlarging on the theme, states that no compensation of any form is to be imposed on damage caused to sacred objects or holy places by the failure of an individual to restrain an animal or to guard other property that might be expected to cause damage, or on damage perpetrated directly upon these sacred objects or holy places by an individual. Restitution can be made only for damage done to non-sacred property, not for property consecrated to God. Whether the intent of this law is to tell the one responsible for the damage that "in causing this damage you have not hurt God but only yourself," or to convey the thought that God does not wish the hand of a mere human lifted to act as advocate for His property, or to point out that in such a case any material restitution would only serve to blur the true significance of the crime (that violence was done to the idea symbolized by the damaged object)—in any event, one fact remains: That as far as this law is concerned, a person could have smashed the holy Ark of the Covenant, rent the holy Curtain, destroyed the Temple vessels and indeed all the treasures of the Temple, and yet there would have been no judge on earth authorized to make him pay so much as one penny in damages.

This state of affairs is certainly unique among all the world's legal systems, and we cannot help pointing out that already this one fact proves most cogently that Jewish Law is not the work of men, much less the product of a priestly hierarchy (to which so many would like to attribute Jewish Law). Priests or hierarchs would have branded the perpetrators of such a sacrilege as criminals guilty of a most flagrant offense and would have directed the secular officials of the government to serve first and foremost as protectors and avengers of their treasures. Only when sacred objects are put to a profane use, and particularly if this is done erroneously, must compensation be paid for the damage done.

livestock, either by letting his livestock run loose, or by letting his livestock graze in the field of another, he shall make restitution with the best of his own field and the best of his own vineyard. 5. If a fire goes out [of control] and spreads through thorns, so that stacks of grain, or standing grain, or the field, are consumed, then the one who kindled the fire shall make full restitution. 6. If a man gives to his neighbor money or articles for safekeeping, and it is claimed that it was stolen from the man's house, then, if the thief is found, he must make double restitution. 7. If the thief is not found, then he [i.e., the bailee], being the master of the house, shall place himself close to God, provided that he has not stretched out his hand over his neighbor's property. 8. (In the case of any charge, whether it involves an ox, a donkey, a sheep, a garment, or any lost property of which he says that this is it, the word of both parties shall come up as far as God); if judges then find him guilty, he shall make double restitution to his neighbor. 9. If a man gives his neighbor a donkey, or an ox, or a sheep, or any other animal to look after, and it dies or is broken or is carried off without eyewitnesses, 10. then there shall be an oath of God between them, provided that he has not stretched out his hand over his neighbor's property; and the owner must

אֶת־בְּעִירֹה (בעירו קרי) וּבִעֵר בִּשְׂדֵה אַחֵר מֵיטַב שָׂדֵהוּ וּמֵיטַב כַּרְמוֹ יְשַׁלֵּם: ס ה כִּי־תֵצֵא אֵשׁ וּמָצְאָה קֹצִים וְנֶאֱכַל גָּדִישׁ אוֹ הַקָּמָה אוֹ הַשָּׂדֶה שַׁלֵּם יְשַׁלֵּם הַמַּבְעִר אֶת־הַבְּעֵרָה: ס ו כִּי־יִתֵּן אִישׁ אֶל־רֵעֵהוּ כֶּסֶף אוֹ־כֵלִים לִשְׁמֹר וְגֻנַּב מִבֵּית הָאִישׁ אִם־יִמָּצֵא הַגַּנָּב יְשַׁלֵּם שְׁנָיִם: ז אִם־לֹא יִמָּצֵא הַגַּנָּב וְנִקְרַב בַּעַל־הַבַּיִת אֶל־הָאֱלֹהִים אִם־לֹא שָׁלַח יָדוֹ בִּמְלֶאכֶת רֵעֵהוּ: ח עַל־כָּל־דְּבַר־פֶּשַׁע עַל־שׁוֹר עַל־חֲמוֹר עַל־שֶׂה עַל־שַׂלְמָה עַל־כָּל־אֲבֵדָה אֲשֶׁר יֹאמַר כִּי־הוּא זֶה עַד הָאֱלֹהִים יָבֹא דְּבַר־שְׁנֵיהֶם אֲשֶׁר יַרְשִׁיעֻן אֱלֹהִים יְשַׁלֵּם שְׁנַיִם לְרֵעֵהוּ: ס ט כִּי־יִתֵּן אִישׁ אֶל־רֵעֵהוּ חֲמוֹר אוֹ־שׁוֹר אוֹ־שֶׂה וְכָל־בְּהֵמָה לִשְׁמֹר וּמֵת אוֹ־נִשְׁבַּר אוֹ־נִשְׁבָּה אֵין רֹאֶה: י שְׁבֻעַת יְהֹוָה תִּהְיֶה בֵּין שְׁנֵיהֶם אִם־לֹא שָׁלַח יָדוֹ בִּמְלֶאכֶת

CHAPTER XXII

6. With Verses 6 to 14 we arrive at a discussion of the responsibilities resulting from obligations undertaken voluntarily. These cases are categorized according to four distinct legal relationships, שׁוֹמֵר חִנָּם, שׁוֹמֵר שָׂכָר, שׂוֹכֵר, שׁוֹאֵל: the unpaid custodian of the property of another, the paid custodian of the property of another, the lessee of the property of another, and the borrower of the property of another. The problems cited in the Biblical text as cases in point for a discussion of these relationships, and the legal provisions set forth in these verses, embody significant principles of civil law.

∘ ∘ ∘

7. *shall place himself close to God.* The bailee, in his capacity as master of the house, shall place himself close to God; i.e., he must take an oath before the court

of law to clear himself with regard to his conduct toward the article placed into his house for safekeeping. If he follows this procedure he is not obligated to make restitution, provided אִם לֹא שָׁלַח that he himself has indeed not already, prior to the purported theft, "stretched out his hand" over the property entrusted to his care; i.e., he had no intention of using the article for his own purposes. For even if he does no more than conceive an intention to appropriate such an article for his own use, his relationship to the article entrusted to his care ceases to be that of שׁוֹמֵר [custodian] and becomes that of גַּזְלָן [robber or embezzler]. In that case he automatically becomes responsible for whatever may have happened to the article under his care, including its theft by another, so that he must make restitution to the owner for his loss.

∘ ∘ ∘

accept it [i.e., the oath]; he [i.e., the bailee] does not have to make restitution. 11. But if it was stolen from him in any manner, he must make restitution to its owner. 12. But if it was torn to pieces in any manner, he shall present the case with evidence: he does not have to make restitution for the torn [animal]. 13. If a man borrows [something] from another, and it is broken or it dies; then, if its owner is not with it, he [i.e., the borrower] must make full restitution for it. 14. But if its owner was with it, he [i.e., the bailee] does not have to make restitution. If the article was rented, it is covered by its rental fee. 15. If a man seduces a virgin who is not betrothed to a man, and he lies with her, he shall acquire her as his wife. 16. But if her father refuses to give her to him, he shall weigh out to him silver in the amount [customarily] paid as dowry for virgins. 17. You shall not permit a sorceress to live. 18. Whoever lies with an animal shall be put to death. 19. Whoever offers sacrifices to the gods—except to *God* alone—shall be cut off by being destroyed. 20. But you shall not grieve a stranger

רֵעֵהוּ וְלָקַח בְּעָלָיו וְלֹא יְשַׁלֵּם: יא וְאִם־גָּנֹב יִגָּנֵב מֵעִמּוֹ יְשַׁלֵּם לִבְעָלָיו: יב אִם־טָרֹף יִטָּרֵף יְבִאֵהוּ עֵד הַטְּרֵפָה לֹא יְשַׁלֵּם: פ יג וְכִי־יִשְׁאַל אִישׁ מֵעִם רֵעֵהוּ וְנִשְׁבַּר אוֹ־מֵת בְּעָלָיו אֵין עִמּוֹ שַׁלֵּם יְשַׁלֵּם: יד אִם־בְּעָלָיו עִמּוֹ לֹא יְשַׁלֵּם אִם־שָׂכִיר הוּא בָּא בִּשְׂכָרוֹ: ס טו וְכִי־יְפַתֶּה אִישׁ בְּתוּלָה אֲשֶׁר לֹא־אֹרָשָׂה וְשָׁכַב עִמָּהּ מָהֹר יִמְהָרֶנָּה לּוֹ לְאִשָּׁה: טז אִם־מָאֵן יְמָאֵן אָבִיהָ לְתִתָּהּ לוֹ כֶּסֶף יִשְׁקֹל כְּמֹהַר הַבְּתוּלֹת: ס יז מְכַשֵּׁפָה לֹא תְחַיֶּה: יח כָּל־שֹׁכֵב עִם־בְּהֵמָה מוֹת יוּמָת: ס יט זֹבֵחַ לָאֱלֹהִים יָחֳרָם בִּלְתִּי לַיהֹוָה לְבַדּוֹ: כ וְגֵר לֹא־תוֹנֶה וְלֹא

13. . . . It appears that in its provisions regarding the "four kinds of custodians," the Law sought to underscore the full extent of the responsibility automatically assumed by anyone entering such a legal relationship. For the relationship designated as that of שׁוֹמֵר [custodian] is subject to so-called "voluntary jurisdiction," in which the responsibilities entailed are determined by free mutual agreement. The law of the "four kinds of custodians" in particular is the basis for all social interrelationships. The concept of שׁוֹמֵר in a broader sense is operative in all social relationships, up to and including the person of the sovereign. All these instances represent practical expressions of mutual trust and exchanges of services. To him who is scrupulous about dealing justly and fairly with others, the Law here delineates in categorical terms the obligations and responsibilities he automatically assumes even when he undertakes to render a service voluntarily and without pay, as in that of שׁוֹמֵר חִנָּם [unpaid custodian]. . . .

20. The commandment "But you shall not grieve a stranger," etc. is closely linked with the thought expressed in the commandment that precedes it. In Verse 19 we are given to understand that even one who

was born a Jew and is of the purest, unimpeachable Jewish descent forfeits his existence as part of the Jewish community as soon as he departs, in the slightest degree, from the pure basic Jewish conception of God. In contrast to the foregoing, we are now told that one who was born a heathen is entitled to full equality among Jews under Jewish Law from the moment he joins the Jewish fold by accepting the Jewish concept of God. The juxtaposition of these two verses sets down the significant principle, frequently reiterated in Scripture, that personal and civil rights, and personal worth, are not dependent on descent, place of birth or property ownership — indeed, that they are independent of any external, incidental factor which bears no relationship to the individual's true character. These rights are determined solely by the individual's moral and spiritual qualities. This principle is further safeguarded against violation by the explanation "because you (yourselves) were strangers in the land of Mitzrayim." For it seems that the meaning of this verse is not equivalent to that of Chapter 23 Verse 9: ". . . for you know the feelings of a stranger because. . ." Rather, Verse 20 tells us in categorical terms: All your misfortunes in Mitzrayim were caused by the fact that you who has come over to you, or oppress him, because you [yourselves] were strangers in the land of Mitzrayim.   21. You shall not let any widow or orphan feel their dependent state.   22. Woe [to you] if you, too, should let them feel their dependent state! For if they must cry out to Me, I will certainly hear their cry,   23. and then My anger will grow hot, and I will let you die by the sword, and then your wives will become widows and your children orphans!   24. If you lend money to My people, to the poor man who is with you, you shall not behave toward him like a creditor; you shall not impose interest upon him.   25. If you, in any way whatsoever, take your neighbor's garment as a pledge, return it to him by sunset,   26. for this alone is his covering; it is his garment for his body. With what shall he sleep? If he will cry out to Me, I will hear, because I am merciful.   27. You shall not curse a judge and you shall not curse a prince of your people.   28. You must not alter the [prescribed] order of the offerings from the abundance of your harvest and from your wine press; you shall

תְלָחָצֶנּוּ כִּי־גֵרִים הֱיִיתֶם בְּאֶרֶץ מִצְרָיִם:
כא כָּל־אַלְמָנָה וְיָתוֹם לֹא תְעַנּוּן: כב אִם־עַנֵּה
תְעַנֶּה אֹתוֹ כִּי אִם־צָעֹק יִצְעַק אֵלַי שָׁמֹעַ
אֶשְׁמַע צַעֲקָתוֹ: כג וְחָרָה אַפִּי וְהָרַגְתִּי אֶתְכֶם
בֶּחָרֶב וְהָיוּ נְשֵׁיכֶם אַלְמָנוֹת וּבְנֵיכֶם
יְתֹמִים: פ כד אִם־כֶּסֶף ׀ תַּלְוֶה אֶת־עַמִּי אֶת־
הֶעָנִי עִמָּךְ לֹא־תִהְיֶה לוֹ כְּנֹשֶׁה לֹא־תְשִׂימוּן
עָלָיו נֶשֶׁךְ: כה אִם־חָבֹל תַּחְבֹּל שַׂלְמַת רֵעֶךָ
עַד־בֹּא הַשֶּׁמֶשׁ תְּשִׁיבֶנּוּ לוֹ: כו כִּי הִוא כְסוּתֹה
(כסותו קרי) לְבַדָּהּ הִוא שִׂמְלָתוֹ לְעֹרוֹ בַּמֶּה יִשְׁכָּב
וְהָיָה כִּי־יִצְעַק אֵלַי וְשָׁמַעְתִּי כִּי־חַנּוּן אָנִי: ס
(חצי הספר בפסוקים) רביעי כז אֱלֹהִים לֹא תְקַלֵּל
וְנָשִׂיא בְעַמְּךָ לֹא תָאֹר: כח מְלֵאָתְךָ וְדִמְעֲךָ לֹא

---

were foreigners there, and that as such, in the view of the other nations, you had no right to land, honor or existence there, so that anyone could deal with you as he chose. Because you were aliens, you were outlawed in Mitzrayim; this was the cause of your עַבְדוּת and עִנּוּי [enslavement and affliction]. Therefore we are warned: See to it that when you have a state of your own you do not make the rights of any foreigner in your midst dependent upon anything other than the pure human quality inherent in every person. As soon as you abridge this basic human right you open the door to all the abominations of tyranny and abuse that were practiced in the land of Egypt.

° ° °

24. ... His money is to be regarded as belonging also to God. It is therefore, in fact, your duty to make a loan to him. The borrower is not to be viewed merely as an individual, but should be regarded as an integral part of the community of God, which God seeks to have built upon the magic power of duty. When God first conferred upon the slaves in Egypt the right to own property by virtue of their status as human beings, He cemented these individuals into a community not by the force of sheer personal need but by the bond of duty that binds them together as members of one society. It is not the less affluent man who should have to turn to

his more prosperous brother for help; no, it is the duty of the more fortunate individual to seek out a neighbor who could benefit from his abundance. The rich need the poor much more, and in a much higher sense, then the poor need the rich. All that the poor man can get from the rich is assistance for his material needs. But for the rich man, the poor are in fact the means that enable him to carry out his sublime spiritual and moral task of paying to God that tribute He expects in return for every penny He has bestowed upon us. By enabling us to become property owners, God has reserved for Himself the right to enlist our property in His service. The prime beneficiary in this arrangement is to be "His people," the society to be created through the spirit of His Law. This is the spirit of *tzedakah,* the Jewish concept of righteousness as a matter of duty, which to this day is responsible for the miraculous survival of the Jews as a nation and which finds its most potent expression in our obligation to lend money to those in need of it. This is also the spirit to which any claim to interest must yield.

The obligation to lend money [to fellow Jews] without interest is a rock in that granite foundation upon which the society of the Jewish people is based. . . .

° ° °

תְאַחֵ֑ר בְּכ֥וֹר בָּנֶ֖יךָ תִּתֶּן־לִֽי׃ כט כֵּן־תַּעֲשֶׂ֥ה
לְשֹׁרְךָ֖ לְצֹאנֶ֑ךָ שִׁבְעַ֤ת יָמִים֙ יִהְיֶ֣ה עִם־אִמּ֔וֹ
בַּיּ֥וֹם הַשְּׁמִינִ֖י תִּתְּנוֹ־לִֽי׃ ל וְאַנְשֵׁי־קֹ֖דֶשׁ תִּהְי֣וּן
לִ֑י וּבָשָׂ֨ר בַּשָּׂדֶ֤ה טְרֵפָה֙ לֹ֣א תֹאכֵ֔לוּ לַכֶּ֖לֶב
תַּשְׁלִכ֥וּן אֹתֽוֹ׃ ס כג א לֹ֥א תִשָּׂ֖א שֵׁ֣מַע שָׁ֑וְא
אַל־תָּ֤שֶׁת יָֽדְךָ֙ עִם־רָשָׁ֔ע לִהְיֹ֖ת עֵ֥ד חָמָֽס׃ ב לֹא־
תִהְיֶ֥ה אַחֲרֵֽי־רַבִּ֖ים לְרָעֹ֑ת וְלֹא־תַעֲנֶ֣ה עַל־רִ֗ב
לִנְטֹ֛ת אַחֲרֵ֥י רַבִּ֖ים לְהַטֹּֽת׃ ג וְדָ֕ל לֹ֥א תֶהְדַּ֖ר

give the first-born of your sons to Me. 29. You shall do likewise with your ox, with your small livestock. Seven days it shall remain with its mother; on the eighth day you can give it to Me. 30. And you shall be to Me men of a holy calling. You shall not eat meat that was torn off by beasts in the field for [their] food; you shall throw it to the dog[s].

XXIII

1. Do not accept false testimony. Do not place your power upon the side of a wicked man so that he should become a witness committing an outrage [against justice]. 2. Do not follow a simple majority in passing sentence of punishment, and where there is a difference of opinion do not vote in a manner that one should change his mind in order to make the verdict that of the majority. 3. And you shall not favor even a poor man, who has been brought

30. The term used here is not אֲנָשִׁים קְדוֹשִׁים ["holy men"], but אַנְשֵׁי קֹדֶשׁ, men who belong to a holy calling. Abstaining from eating טְרֵפָה [lit., "torn off"] meat alone does not make one קָדוֹשׁ ["holy"], but it makes it easier for him to achieve personal sanctity. The eating of טְרֵפָה meat blocks our path to the attainment of our sacred calling. He who eats טְרֵפָה will find it more difficult to ascend to the moral and spiritual level that all of us are bidden to attain. The words "and you shall be to Me men of a holy calling" as an explanation introducing the prohibition against טְרֵפָה meat represent the first of the dietary laws given at Mount Sinai. They refute all the explanations proposed by those seeking to abrogate the dietary laws; i.e., that they were based on nutritional considerations, climatic necessities, time-bound conditions, and so forth. Not the promotion of our physical health but the promotion of our moral and spiritual fitness and purity, our קְדוּשָׁה [holiness], our becoming and remaining receptive to everything godly and pure—that is the expressly stated purpose the Lawgiver seeks to attain through these laws. This is clearly set forth not only here but also in other Scriptural passages—Leviticus 11, Leviticus 20:25 f. and Deuteronomy 14:21, where these laws are discussed in greater detail.

° ° °

At a cursory glance the laws contained in this portion, Verses 27–30, may seem unconnected. But closer consideration will show that they all emanate from one common idea, with each law representing another aspect of putting that idea into practice. Verses 20–26 safeguard the legal basis for the full equality of all citizens of the state before the Law. They also insure our awareness of the dictates of social law and justice. Neither birth, nor origin, nor personal fate or fortunes should be permitted to make a difference in our legal and human obligations toward our fellow men. A stranger, an orphan, a widow, a poor man must not be slighted in any manner. At the same time Verse 27 f. specifies the respect and recognition due within this society, based on full personal and civil equality, to those whom God has appointed to serve and work directly or indirectly on behalf of the Law and its sanctity among His people. The categories of individuals and institutions listed in this connection are the judge and the prince (Verse 27), the Temple, the priests and the Levites (Verse 28), who must not only be given respect in general terms but whose exact rank must be recognized in the observance of the order prescribed for the offerings due them. It is pointed out that similar distinctions of rank must be observed also within one's own family, even among one's animals, in the form of primogeniture (Verses 28 and 29), that, in fact, the Jewish community as a whole and in all its parts (תִּהְיוּן ["you shall be"]) has been exalted above (but actually for the benefit of) the rest of mankind to a sacred calling (Verse 30), and that this exalted calling of ours must find expression even in the food we eat. Our diet must be exalted above the physical and animal world which is compelled to follow blindly the laws of nature. לַכֶּלֶב תַּשְׁלִיכוּן אותו ["You shall throw it to the dog(s)"].

CHAPTER XXIII

3. וְדָל *[a poor man]*. Scripture employs three distinct

בְּרִיבוֹ: ס ד כִּי תִפְגַּע שׁוֹר אֹיִבְךָ אוֹ חֲמֹרוֹ
תֹּעֶה הָשֵׁב תְּשִׁיבֶנּוּ לוֹ: ס ה כִּי־תִרְאֶה חֲמוֹר
שֹׂנַאֲךָ רֹבֵץ תַּחַת מַשָּׂאוֹ וְחָדַלְתָּ מֵעֲזֹב לוֹ עָזֹב
תַּעֲזֹב עִמּוֹ: ס חמישי ו לֹא תַטֶּה מִשְׁפַּט אֶבְיֹנְךָ
בְּרִיבוֹ: ז מִדְּבַר־שֶׁקֶר תִּרְחָק וְנָקִי וְצַדִּיק אַל־
תַּהֲרֹג כִּי לֹא־אַצְדִּיק רָשָׁע: ח וְשֹׁחַד לֹא תִקָּח
כִּי הַשֹּׁחַד יְעַוֵּר פִּקְחִים וִיסַלֵּף דִּבְרֵי צַדִּיקִים:
ט וְגֵר לֹא תִלְחָץ וְאַתֶּם יְדַעְתֶּם אֶת־נֶפֶשׁ הַגֵּר

low, by showing him greater honor in his lawsuit [than to his opponent]. 4. If you encounter the ox of your enemy, or his donkey, straying, you shall take it back to him each time. 5. If you see the donkey of one who hates you lying under its load, you shall not permit yourself to leave it to him; instead, you shall let all else go and hasten to his aid. 6. Do not twist the judgment of your poor man in his favor in his lawsuit. 7. Keep distant from a word of falsehood, and do not execute one who is innocent or one who has been acquitted, for I will not acquit one who is guilty. 8. And you shall not accept bribery, for bribery blinds the clear-sighted and causes the words of the righteous to falter. 9. And you shall not impose restrictions upon a stranger—for you know the feelings of a

expressions to denote poverty: דַּל, עָנִי, אֶבְיוֹן. . . . דַּל is one who has been brought low. עָנִי denotes one who is dependent on others for his subsistence. אֶבְיוֹן denotes one whose will is dependent upon the wishes of others. הָדָר is an outward show of honor and respect (cf. Leviticus 19:32). There is nothing more comforting to one who has "come down in the world" than to feel that he is still treated with the same respect that was accorded him in better days. There is nothing more in character with the spirit of this law than to demonstrate that the esteem and respect we accord to another person do not rise or fall with his fortunes. It would seem that there is no greater extrajudicial *mitzvah* than to show respect for the poor man who has come down in the world.

Nevertheless, we are told, when such a poor man comes before you with an opponent to settle a lawsuit, you must treat both parties alike even in your outward manner toward them. Not even in your outward behavior, guided by the most humane considerations, are you permitted to give preference to the poorer of the two litigants.

7. ***Keep distant from a word of falsehood.*** This is the most significant statement concerning the functions of a judge. In general terms, it commands the judge to avoid anything that might create even the slightest possibility of a miscarriage of justice by the court. . . . This passage implies a number of most significant obligations not only for the judge but also for the litigants and the witnesses.

° ° °

8. שֹׁחַד [bribe], probably related to שחט [slaughter] and שחת [destruction, ruin]. These etymological similarities indicate the basic connotation of the term: bribery undermines the spiritual and moral vitality of another. A bribe kills the spiritual and moral strength of the one who accepts it. The spiritual strength that qualifies a man to act as a judge is פקח, clear-sightedness, which enables him to perceive the relevant facts and laws in the proper light. The term for moral strength is צֶדֶק, justice, which makes a man recognize and utter only that which is just and right. A bribe blinds even one who is ordinarily clearsighted; without his being aware of it, the bribe prejudices his view and he can no longer be objective. . . . Once he accepts a bribe, even a fair-minded judge who wants justice to be done will not announce his verdict with the proper firmness and categorical impartiality. His eye will become clouded and he will falter when he speaks. As Rava[6] so aptly puts it, he cannot help becoming חַד, "one," with the party from whom he accepted the bribe. Therefore the Hebrew term for bribery is שֹׁחַד: it causes the judge to identify with the party who bribed him. . . . A Jewish judge must feel that he can be completely impartial; otherwise he must disqualify himself (See Kethuboth 105, 106 and Shulḥan Arukh, Ḥoshen Mishpat 9). . . .

9. This verse obviously harks back to Verse 20 of the preceding chapter, resuming the train of thought in order to develop from it a new series of laws. Verse 20 of

[6] *Note to the English translation*: Babylonian *Amora* active in the middle of the fourth century. He served for some time as head of the academy of Pumbeditha. [G.H.]

stranger because you [yourselves] were strangers in the land of Mitzrayim. 10. And six years you shall sow your land and gather in its produce, 11. but throughout the seventh year you shall let it go and abandon it so that the poor in your midst may be able to eat [from] it, and whatever they leave over can be eaten by the beast[s] of the field; you shall deal likewise with your vineyard [and with] your olive tree. 12. Six days shall you do all your tasks and on the seventh day you shall cease from work, so that your ox and your donkey may rest, and that the son of your handmaid and the stranger may recover. 13. And with regard to all that which I have said to you, you shall place yourselves into your own keeping; you shall not make

כִּי־גֵרִים הֱיִיתֶם בְּאֶרֶץ מִצְרָיִם׃ י וְשֵׁשׁ שָׁנִים
תִּזְרַע אֶת־אַרְצֶךָ וְאָסַפְתָּ אֶת־תְּבוּאָתָהּ׃
יא וְהַשְּׁבִיעִת תִּשְׁמְטֶנָּה וּנְטַשְׁתָּהּ וְאָכְלוּ אֶבְיֹנֵי
עַמֶּךָ וְיִתְרָם תֹּאכַל חַיַּת הַשָּׂדֶה כֵּן־תַּעֲשֶׂה
לְכַרְמְךָ לְזֵיתֶךָ׃ יב שֵׁשֶׁת יָמִים תַּעֲשֶׂה מַעֲשֶׂיךָ
וּבַיּוֹם הַשְּׁבִיעִי תִּשְׁבֹּת לְמַעַן יָנוּחַ שׁוֹרְךָ
וַחֲמֹרֶךָ וְיִנָּפֵשׁ בֶּן־אֲמָתְךָ וְהַגֵּר׃ יג וּבְכֹל אֲשֶׁר־
אָמַרְתִּי אֲלֵיכֶם תִּשָּׁמֵרוּ וְשֵׁם אֱלֹהִים אֲחֵרִים

Chapter 22 introduced the Divine sanction of the dual principle upon which the society in the Jewish state is to be founded: The complete equality of all before the Law but, at the same time, consideration and humanity toward any member of that society who is in need of help. The laws beginning with that verse and ending with Verse 9 of the present chapter contain solely the implications of this principle for the implementation of justice based on equality and for the molding of society on foundations of humanity. Verse 9 now once again underscores the principle of equality and humanity as it should be implemented particularly in the guarantee of unabridged justice and considerate treatment for all foreigners in the Jewish state. (The treatment accorded by a state to the aliens living within its jurisdiction is the most accurate indication of the extent to which justice and humanity prevail in that state.)

In this spirit the Law now introduces a series of institutions which are only outlined here in general terms but which, aside from the specific truths each of them is intended to convey, all have one feature in common: By virtue of their inmost essence they nurture the spirit of equality and humanity in the nation by training the members of that nation to regard themselves, too, as aliens upon the land and soil of God. Thus these institutions guide the people away from an overrating of material possessions, which is the root of all injustice and inhumanity on earth, and toward that just, and therefore loftier, appreciation of all the spiritual and moral values that make man truly human, that postulate the equality of all men and foster mutual love between man and his fellow man. . . .

10 and 11. שְׁמִיטָה: For six years you shall treat your

land as your property, but throughout each seventh year "you shall let it go," literally, you shall let the ground slip from your hand. You must neither plow it nor sow it, but abandon it. You must leave alone whatever grows upon it during the year; you must not treat it as your property. The poor among your people, who at all other times are dependent upon your good will, shall now be able to enjoy the produce of your land undisturbed, without first having to ask your permission. And whatever they leave over shall be left for the beasts of the field. . . .

This Sabbatical year is the great act by which an entire nation proclaims God as the one, sole true Owner and Master of the land, humbly placing the land at His feet and not exercising its rights of ownership for one whole year. By so doing, the nation proclaims that it, too, is in fact a nation of "strangers and aliens" on its own soil, dwelling upon it only at the pleasure of God. Then the arrogance that causes men, boasting of the soil they call their own, to act brutally and unfeelingly toward the unpropertied, melts away, yielding place to love for the stranger, the poor, and even for animals, as creatures of God entitled to dwell upon God's soil, which they all share in common.

13. וּבְכֹל אֲשֶׁר אָמַרְתִּי וגו׳. This cannot mean "guard yourselves *from* violating any of the prohibitions I have imposed upon you." For in that case the wording would have to be מִכֹּל אֲשֶׁר וגו׳ ["*from* all that. . ."]. The sense of וּבְכֹל אֲשֶׁר וגו׳ [lit., "*in* all that. . ."] clearly is: you shall guard yourselves; i.e., place yourselves into your own keeping, *with regard to* all the commandments and prohibitions that I have given to you. You shall frame for yourselves laws and resolutions that will keep you from violating My words. My Law tells you what is right and

לֹ֥א תַזְכִּ֖ירוּ לֹ֥א יִשָּׁמַ֖ע עַל־פִּֽיךָ׃ יד שָׁלֹ֣שׁ
רְגָלִ֔ים תָּחֹ֥ג לִ֖י בַּשָּׁנָֽה׃ טו אֶת־חַ֣ג הַמַּצּוֹת֮
תִּשְׁמֹר֒ שִׁבְעַ֣ת יָ֠מִים תֹּאכַ֨ל מַצּ֜וֹת כַּאֲשֶׁ֣ר
צִוִּיתִ֗ךָ לְמוֹעֵד֙ חֹ֣דֶשׁ הָֽאָבִ֔יב כִּי־ב֖וֹ יָצָ֣אתָ

mention of the name of other gods; you must not cause it to be heard. 14. You shall celebrate three pilgrimage festivals for Me each year. 15. The Festival of Unleavened Bread you shall keep; seven days you shall eat unleavened bread, as I have commanded you, at the appointed meeting time of the month of the standing grain; for

what is wrong and enumerates your tasks and obligations. What I now expect of you is that you will be sufficiently conscientious to devise precautions of your own to ensure that My commandments will be carried out and My prohibitions observed.

With this verse we are given the momentous commandment "to place a fence around the Law" and to ensure its observance, to formulate גְּזֵרוֹת ["decrees"] (גְּדָרִים [guards against trangressing the Law;], סְיָגִים ["hedges," or preventive measures]) and תַּקָּנוֹת ["positive enactments," regulations that supplement the laws of the Torah]. Only thanks to the scrupulous observance of these measures has the Law of God been preserved to this day. . . .

The Law proceeds to cite one example of what is meant by the obligation to "place a fence around the Law." The example it has chosen is the very first prohibition in the Decalogue: the prohibition against idolatry. One who worships idols trangresses this prohibition. Of course, merely to mention the name of an idol or to cause another person to mention it is certainly not tantamount to practicing idolatry. Nevertheless, we are commanded to refrain not only from mentioning the name of the idol ourselves but also from having others mention it. The purpose of this self-imposed control is to guard ourselves against actually practicing idolatry. This is a most significant example of how one should avoid not only sin itself but even any act that might border on evil or might be conducive to sin.

° ° °

14. . . . ***You shall celebrate three pilgrimage festivals for Me each year.*** This means, literally: Each year you shall undertake three pilgrimages in order to form a circle [חוג] around Me. . . . In this manner the nation as a whole will rally around My Sanctuary which they all cherish in common, so that every single member of that nation will regard himself as part of this great circle. As we shall see shortly, these "pilgrimage festivals" occur at the seasons when the most important agricultural work must be performed. Consequently, to leave one's field at such seasons in order to present oneself to God at His Sanctuary as a son and servant of His Law, to leave one's house and home in order to appear before God in the Sanctuary at a time of the most pressing material cares, represents a great and sacrificing acknowledgement of God that must melt the icy bonds of materialism from the heart of every Jew. In the Sanctuary of God he learns to see himself as only one member of a great circle that has joined together to uphold one common mission. As a result, at a time that would most urgently demand his presence at home to see to his personal welfare, there is stirred within him a feeling of national unity, which, by its inspiring force, banishes the curse of egotism from the heart of the Jewish person.

15. ***and My Presence shall not be beheld.*** And when you come before My Presence "you shall not come empty-handed." When you leave your house and home in order to come before My Presence you shall not do so under the impression that the Temple is a thing apart from your house and home, that the things of heaven and of the spirit belong to the Temple while earthly affairs and material concerns belong to the home. You must not think that the Temple provides you with "food" for your "spirit and your emotions," the better to be able to devote yourselves to the gratification of your body and of your senses at home, and that you worship at the Temple only so that your conscience may be at ease when you devote your house and home to the most materialistic egotism and to the most egotistic materialism. Not so! When we appear before God we are to bring with us our material possessions. We must present ourselves along with זֶבַח וּנְסָכִים, עוֹלָה וּמִנְחָה ["ascent offering, homage offering, meal offering and libation"] (Leviticus 23:37). We are to place ourselves at God's service with every facet of our personality, with all our possessions: food (as symbolized by סֹלֶת, "fine flour"), health (as symbolized by שֶׁמֶן, "oil"] and joy (as symbolized by יַיִן, "wine") and have them all receive the sanctity that can be gained in the Temple.

The three festival offerings that every Jew is commanded to make correspond to the three aspects of our festivals: רֶגֶל ["pilgrimage"], personal presence in the Sanctuary of the Law; חַג, coming together [in a "circle"] with all the other members of our nation and מוֹעֵד, "meeting" with God. . . . The עוֹלַת רְאִיָּה [the pilgrimage offering] corresponds to רֶגֶל; the שַׁלְמֵי חֲגִיגָה [the festival offering] to חַג; and the שַׁלְמֵי שִׂמְחָה [offerings of rejoicing] to מוֹעֵד. The last-named group of offerings is associated with the joyous awareness of God's presence within the circle of our own family, which exalts the in it you came out from Mitzrayim and My Presence shall not be beheld with empty hands. 16. And the Festival of the Harvest, of the first fruits of your labors that you sow in the field, and the Festival of Ingathering, when the year has come to an end, when you gather in your labors from the field. 17. Three times each year shall all your male[s] appear before the Presence of *God*, the Lord. 18. Do not sacrifice the blood of My meal offering with leavened bread, and do not allow the fat of My festival offering to remain overnight until the morning. 19. You shall bring the first of the first fruits of your soil into the House of *God*, your God; do not cook the flesh of an animal in its mother's milk. 20. Lo! I send a messenger before you to safeguard you on the way and to bring you to the place which I have prepared. 21. Beware of him and obey him; do not permit any bitter words against him! Because he cannot pardon your disobedience, since he bears My Name within himself. 22. Rather, obey, obey him and do all that I will say;

מִמִּצְרָיִם וְלֹא־יֵרָאוּ פָנַי רֵיקָם: טז וְחַג הַקָּצִיר בִּכּוּרֵי מַעֲשֶׂיךָ אֲשֶׁר תִּזְרַע בַּשָּׂדֶה וְחַג הָאָסִף בְּצֵאת הַשָּׁנָה בְּאָסְפְּךָ אֶת־מַעֲשֶׂיךָ מִן־הַשָּׂדֶה: יז שָׁלֹשׁ פְּעָמִים בַּשָּׁנָה יֵרָאֶה כָּל־זְכוּרְךָ אֶל־פְּנֵי הָאָדֹן | יְהֹוָה: יח לֹא־תִזְבַּח עַל־חָמֵץ דַּם־זִבְחִי וְלֹא־יָלִין חֵלֶב־חַגִּי עַד־בֹּקֶר: יט רֵאשִׁית בִּכּוּרֵי אַדְמָתְךָ תָּבִיא בֵּית יְהֹוָה אֱלֹהֶיךָ לֹא־תְבַשֵּׁל גְּדִי בַּחֲלֵב אִמּוֹ: פ ששי כ הִנֵּה אָנֹכִי שֹׁלֵחַ מַלְאָךְ לְפָנֶיךָ לִשְׁמָרְךָ בַּדָּרֶךְ וְלַהֲבִיאֲךָ אֶל־הַמָּקוֹם אֲשֶׁר הֲכִנֹתִי: כא הִשָּׁמֶר מִפָּנָיו וּשְׁמַע בְּקֹלוֹ אַל־תַּמֵּר בּוֹ כִּי לֹא יִשָּׂא לְפִשְׁעֲכֶם כִּי שְׁמִי בְּקִרְבּוֹ: כב כִּי אִם־שָׁמֹעַ תִּשְׁמַע בְּקֹלוֹ וְעָשִׂיתָ כֹּל אֲשֶׁר אֲדַבֵּר וְאָיַבְתִּי

home to the position of Temple, transforms the family table into an altar, and makes all the members of our household priests and priestesses, serving with their lives to fulfill the mission assigned to us by God.

20f. The verses that follow are linked with the preceding passages in various ways. The last part of the *mishpatim* from Verse 20 of the preceding chapter until the end of that chapter concerns itself primarily with the equality of all before the Law, and with the mutual obligations of the inhabitants of the future state to be ruled by the Law of God, obligations deriving from the fact that the land belongs to God. These passages also mention the weekly Sabbaths and the institution of the Sabbatical year, and the three annual pilgrimage festivals in the spring, summer and fall, along with the laws pertaining to their observance, which are intended to make us aware that everything belongs to God and to cultivate within us the spirit of justice and brotherhood.

These ideas are now amplified by the following thoughts:

1) The people of Israel did not obtain the soil of this state, which is to be founded upon the Law of God, as a result of their own prowess. The soil was entrusted to them by God solely because they subordinated themselves obediently to His will.

2) This loyal obedience toward the Law of God will also be the only means of ensuring their material prosperity in the land. This thought is expressed, again and again, in terms of both the nation and its individual members, by the pilgrimages [lit., "ascents"] in the spring, summer and fall, and by Israel's act of laying its first fruits at the feet of this Law.

3) Therefore the people of Israel must not permit their contacts with the previous occupants of the land (which will be ceded to them only little by little) to delude them into the heathen notion, diametrically opposed to Judaism, that material prosperity is not dependent upon observance of the laws of morality, and that the forces of nature must be worshipped as sources of material prosperity.

4) Not a trace of these idolatrous delusions may be tolerated in this state, which is to be founded upon the Law of God. Hence, if the social legislation of this state, based on the principle of equality for all, is to find expression primarily in the equality accorded to the "stranger" before the Law, it can find such expression only under the condition that the "stranger" has ceased to worship idols.

° ° °

then I will be an enemy to your enemies and oppress your oppressors. 23. Now when My messenger will go before you and will bring you to the Emorite, the Ḥittite, the Perizite, the Canaanite, the Ḥivvite and the Yebusite, and I will destroy them one by one, 24. you shall not cast yourselves down before their gods and not serve them and not act in accordance with their doings; rather, you shall tear them down and break their memorial stones to pieces. 25. And you shall serve *God*, your God, and He will bless your bread and your waters, and I will banish sickness from your midst. 26. There will be no woman who miscarries and no barren woman in your land; I will let the number of your days become full. 27. I will send the terror of My might before you and I will throw into utter confusion all the population into whose midst you will enter; I will make all your enemies turn their necks toward you. 28. I will send the hornet[s] before you and they will drive out the Ḥivvite, the Canaanite and the Hittite from before you. 29. I will not drive them out before you in a single year, for the land could become desolate and the beast[s] of the field could become too many for you. 30. I will drive them out from before you little by little, until you have increased and can occupy the land. 31. I will set your border from the Sea of Reeds to the Philistine Sea, and from the wilderness to the river; for I will place the inhabitants of the land under your sway and you will drive them out from before you. 32. You shall not make a covenant with them and their gods. 33. They shall not remain as residents in your land so that they will not bring you to sin against Me; for you will serve their gods; for it will become a trap for you.

אֶת־אֹיְבֶ֔יךָ וְצַרְתִּ֖י אֶת־צֹרְרֶֽיךָ׃ כג כִּֽי־יֵלֵ֣ךְ מַלְאָכִי֮ לְפָנֶיךָ֒ וֶהֱבִֽיאֲךָ֗ אֶל־הָ֣אֱמֹרִי֙ וְהַ֣חִתִּ֔י וְהַפְּרִזִּי֙ וְהַֽכְּנַעֲנִ֔י הַחִוִּ֖י וְהַיְבוּסִ֑י וְהִכְחַדְתִּֽיו׃ כד לֹֽא־תִשְׁתַּחֲוֶ֤ה לֵאלֹֽהֵיהֶם֙ וְלֹ֣א תָֽעָבְדֵ֔ם וְלֹ֥א תַעֲשֶׂ֖ה כְּמַעֲשֵׂיהֶ֑ם כִּ֤י הָרֵס֙ תְּהָ֣רְסֵ֔ם וְשַׁבֵּ֥ר תְּשַׁבֵּ֖ר מַצֵּבֹתֵיהֶֽם׃ כה וַעֲבַדְתֶּ֗ם אֵ֚ת יְהֹוָ֣ה אֱלֹֽהֵיכֶ֔ם וּבֵרַ֥ךְ אֶֽת־לַחְמְךָ֖ וְאֶת־מֵימֶ֑יךָ וַהֲסִרֹתִ֥י מַחֲלָ֖ה מִקִּרְבֶּֽךָ׃ ס שביעי כו לֹ֥א תִהְיֶ֛ה מְשַׁכֵּלָ֥ה וַעֲקָרָ֖ה בְּאַרְצֶ֑ךָ אֶת־מִסְפַּ֥ר יָמֶ֖יךָ אֲמַלֵּֽא׃ כז אֶת־אֵֽימָתִי֙ אֲשַׁלַּ֣ח לְפָנֶ֔יךָ וְהַמֹּתִי֙ אֶת־כׇּל־הָעָ֔ם אֲשֶׁ֥ר תָּבֹ֖א בָּהֶ֑ם וְנָתַתִּ֧י אֶת־כׇּל־אֹֽיְבֶ֛יךָ אֵלֶ֖יךָ עֹֽרֶף׃ כח וְשָׁלַחְתִּ֥י אֶת־הַצִּרְעָ֖ה לְפָנֶ֑יךָ וְגֵרְשָׁ֗ה אֶת־הַחִוִּ֛י אֶת־הַֽכְּנַעֲנִ֥י וְאֶת־הַֽחִתִּ֖י מִלְּפָנֶֽיךָ׃ כט לֹ֧א אֲגָרְשֶׁ֛נּוּ מִפָּנֶ֖יךָ בְּשָׁנָ֣ה אֶחָ֑ת פֶּן־תִּהְיֶ֤ה הָאָ֙רֶץ֙ שְׁמָמָ֔ה וְרַבָּ֥ה עָלֶ֖יךָ חַיַּ֥ת הַשָּׂדֶֽה׃ ל מְעַ֥ט מְעַ֛ט אֲגָרְשֶׁ֖נּוּ מִפָּנֶ֑יךָ עַ֚ד אֲשֶׁ֣ר תִּפְרֶ֔ה וְנָחַלְתָּ֖ אֶת־הָאָֽרֶץ׃ לא וְשַׁתִּ֣י אֶת־גְּבֻֽלְךָ֗ מִיַּם־סוּף֙ וְעַד־יָ֣ם פְּלִשְׁתִּ֔ים וּמִמִּדְבָּ֖ר עַד־הַנָּהָ֑ר כִּ֣י ׀ אֶתֵּ֣ן בְּיֶדְכֶ֗ם אֵ֚ת יֹשְׁבֵ֣י הָאָ֔רֶץ וְגֵרַשְׁתָּ֖מוֹ מִפָּנֶֽיךָ׃ לב לֹֽא־תִכְרֹ֥ת לָהֶ֛ם וְלֵאלֹֽהֵיהֶ֖ם בְּרִֽית׃ לג לֹ֤א יֵֽשְׁבוּ֙ בְּאַרְצְךָ֔ פֶּן־יַחֲטִ֥יאוּ אֹֽתְךָ֖ לִ֑י כִּ֤י תַֽעֲבֹד֙ אֶת־אֱלֹ֣הֵיהֶ֔ם כִּֽי־יִהְיֶ֥ה לְךָ֖ לְמוֹקֵֽשׁ׃ פ

---

33. *for it will become a trap for you.* If they will remain in the land without renouncing idolatry, this will become a snare for you. You must not believe that you have already risen to such heights of purity that you no longer need to fear the nearness of impurity and falsehood and that, by your contact with these deluded peoples, you will be able to elevate them to the plane of your own ideals of truth instead of their dragging you down to their delusions. Only in isolation will you be able to grow strong enough ultimately to accomplish the spiritual conquest of these nations. Until you have attained that level, your contacts with them will become a trap for you.

XXIV

1. And to Moshe He had said: "Go up to *God*, you and Aharon, Nadab and Abihu, and seventy from among the elders of Yisrael, and bow down at a distance. 2. But only Moshe shall draw nearer to *God*; they shall not draw nearer, and the people shall not go up with him at all." 3. And Moshe came and told the people all the words of *God* and all the [social] ordinances. And the entire people answered with one voice and said: "All the words that *God* has spoken we will do." 4. Thereupon Moshe wrote down all the words of *God*. He arose early in the morning, built an altar at the foot of the mountain and twelve memorial stones for the twelve tribes of Yisrael. 5. And he sent the youths of the sons of Yisrael; they brought ascent offerings and they offered to *God* steers as meal-of-peace offerings. 6. And Moshe took half of the blood and set it [aside] in the basin[s], and the other half of the blood he dashed against the altar. 7. He took the Book of the Covenant and read it to the people. And they said: "All that *God* has spoken we will do and hear." 8. And Moshe took the blood, poured it out toward the people and said: "Behold the blood of the covenant that *God* has made with you regarding all these words." 9. Thereupon Moshe and Aharon, Nadab and Abihu, and seventy from among the elders of Yisrael went up. 10. And they saw Yisrael's God—and at His feet something like the forming of a sapphire brick, and [it was] like the essence of heaven in

כד א וְאֶל־מֹשֶׁה אָמַר עֲלֵה אֶל־יְהֹוָה אַתָּה וְאַהֲרֹן נָדָב וַאֲבִיהוּא וְשִׁבְעִים מִזִּקְנֵי יִשְׂרָאֵל וְהִשְׁתַּחֲוִיתֶם מֵרָחֹק: ב וְנִגַּשׁ מֹשֶׁה לְבַדּוֹ אֶל־יְהֹוָה וְהֵם לֹא יִגָּשׁוּ וְהָעָם לֹא יַעֲלוּ עִמּוֹ: ג וַיָּבֹא מֹשֶׁה וַיְסַפֵּר לָעָם אֵת כָּל־דִּבְרֵי יְהֹוָה וְאֵת כָּל־הַמִּשְׁפָּטִים וַיַּעַן כָּל־הָעָם קוֹל אֶחָד וַיֹּאמְרוּ כָּל־הַדְּבָרִים אֲשֶׁר־דִּבֶּר יְהֹוָה נַעֲשֶׂה: ד וַיִּכְתֹּב מֹשֶׁה אֵת כָּל־דִּבְרֵי יְהֹוָה וַיַּשְׁכֵּם בַּבֹּקֶר וַיִּבֶן מִזְבֵּחַ תַּחַת הָהָר וּשְׁתֵּים עֶשְׂרֵה מַצֵּבָה לִשְׁנֵים עָשָׂר שִׁבְטֵי יִשְׂרָאֵל: ה וַיִּשְׁלַח אֶת־נַעֲרֵי בְּנֵי יִשְׂרָאֵל וַיַּעֲלוּ עֹלֹת וַיִּזְבְּחוּ זְבָחִים שְׁלָמִים לַיהֹוָה פָּרִים: ו וַיִּקַּח מֹשֶׁה חֲצִי הַדָּם וַיָּשֶׂם בָּאַגָּנֹת וַחֲצִי הַדָּם זָרַק עַל־הַמִּזְבֵּחַ: ז וַיִּקַּח סֵפֶר הַבְּרִית וַיִּקְרָא בְּאָזְנֵי הָעָם וַיֹּאמְרוּ כֹּל אֲשֶׁר־דִּבֶּר יְהֹוָה נַעֲשֶׂה וְנִשְׁמָע: ח וַיִּקַּח מֹשֶׁה אֶת־הַדָּם וַיִּזְרֹק עַל־הָעָם וַיֹּאמֶר הִנֵּה דַם־הַבְּרִית אֲשֶׁר כָּרַת יְהֹוָה עִמָּכֶם עַל כָּל־הַדְּבָרִים הָאֵלֶּה: ט וַיַּעַל מֹשֶׁה וְאַהֲרֹן נָדָב וַאֲבִיהוּא וְשִׁבְעִים מִזִּקְנֵי יִשְׂרָאֵל: י וַיִּרְאוּ אֵת אֱלֹהֵי יִשְׂרָאֵל וְתַחַת רַגְלָיו כְּמַעֲשֵׂה לִבְנַת הַסַּפִּיר וּכְעֶצֶם הַשָּׁמַיִם לָטֹהַר:

CHAPTER XXIV

10. Who would be so presumptuous as to attempt to describe such a vision in exact detail? Given the wording of the text, we would presume to make the following comment: Since we are told explicitly (Exodus 33:20): "You cannot see My Countenance, for man shall not see Me and live!" and since it is stated just as explicitly (Deuteronomy 4:12 and 15) with regard to this revelation on Mount Sinai that no physical form was seen when God spoke to us from out of the fire at Horeb, the words "and they saw—Yisrael's God—"can refer only to the vision through which God announced His Presence. Or, and this seems to us more probable, this passage is to be construed in a similar manner as "I

have seen this people and lo! it is a stiff-necked people" (Exodus 32:9) and "I beheld the earth and lo! it was waste and void, and the heavens, and their light has gone" (Jeremiah 4:23). In both these passages it is not the people, the earth or the heavens but their condition that is seen in the vision. Hence the meaning of these verses can only be: "I saw that the people was stiff-necked, that the earth was waste and that the light of the heavens was gone." In a similar vein, the statement "And they saw." . . . might mean only: "They saw at the feet of the God of Israel something like the formation of a sapphire brick," etc.

°   °   °   °

purity.   11. But He did not send forth His
hand toward those sons of Yisrael that were
farther off; they had a vision of God within
themselves, and they ate and drank.
12. And *God* said to Moshe: "Come up to
Me, to the mountain, and remain there. I
will give you the tablets of stone, the Teaching and the commandments, which I have
written in order to teach them."   13. And
Moshe and his servant Yehoshua arose
and Moshe went up to the mountain of God.
14. But to the elders he had said: "Stay
and wait for us here until we return to
you. Behold, Aharon and Hur are with you;
whoever has a case to present, let him go to
them."   15. When Moshe ascended the
mountain, the cloud enveloped the mountain.   16. The glory of *God* rested upon
Mount Sinai and the cloud enveloped it six
days. On the seventh day He called out to
Moshe from amidst the cloud.   17. And
the appearance of the glory of *God* was like
a consuming fire on the top of the mountain
before the eyes of the sons of Yisrael.
18. Moshe entered into the midst of the
cloud and ascended the mountain, and
Moshe remained upon the mountain for
forty days and forty nights.

יא וְאֶל־אֲצִילֵי בְּנֵי יִשְׂרָאֵל לֹא שָׁלַח יָדוֹ וַיֶּחֱזוּ
אֶת־הָאֱלֹהִים וַיֹּאכְלוּ וַיִּשְׁתּוּ: ס יב וַיֹּאמֶר
יְהֹוָה אֶל־מֹשֶׁה עֲלֵה אֵלַי הָהָרָה וֶהְיֵה־שָׁם
וְאֶתְּנָה לְךָ אֶת־לֻחֹת הָאֶבֶן וְהַתּוֹרָה וְהַמִּצְוָה
אֲשֶׁר כָּתַבְתִּי לְהוֹרֹתָם: יג וַיָּקָם מֹשֶׁה וִיהוֹשֻׁעַ
מְשָׁרְתוֹ וַיַּעַל מֹשֶׁה אֶל־הַר הָאֱלֹהִים: יד וְאֶל־
הַזְּקֵנִים אָמַר שְׁבוּ־לָנוּ בָזֶה עַד אֲשֶׁר־נָשׁוּב
אֲלֵיכֶם וְהִנֵּה אַהֲרֹן וְחוּר עִמָּכֶם מִי־בַעַל
דְּבָרִים יִגַּשׁ אֲלֵהֶם: טו וַיַּעַל מֹשֶׁה אֶל־הָהָר
וַיְכַס הֶעָנָן אֶת־הָהָר: מפטיר טז וַיִּשְׁכֹּן כְּבוֹד־
יְהֹוָה עַל־הַר סִינַי וַיְכַסֵּהוּ הֶעָנָן שֵׁשֶׁת יָמִים
וַיִּקְרָא אֶל־מֹשֶׁה בַּיּוֹם הַשְּׁבִיעִי מִתּוֹךְ הֶעָנָן:
יז וּמַרְאֵה כְּבוֹד יְהֹוָה כְּאֵשׁ אֹכֶלֶת בְּרֹאשׁ הָהָר
לְעֵינֵי בְּנֵי יִשְׂרָאֵל: יח וַיָּבֹא מֹשֶׁה בְּתוֹךְ הֶעָנָן
וַיַּעַל אֶל־הָהָר וַיְהִי מֹשֶׁה בָּהָר אַרְבָּעִים יוֹם
וְאַרְבָּעִים לָיְלָה: פ

12. . . . We are told (Chapter 31:18) at the end of the
account of Moses' sojourn atop Mount Sinai: "He gave
Moshe two tablets of the Testimony, tablets of stone,
written with the finger of God."

which I have written in order to teach them. The
Written Law is only a teaching aid intended as a refer-
ence source to facilitate the retention of the actual
Torah Law, which was to be taught by word of mouth.

The Haftarah for this Sidra may be found on page 855.

XXV 1. *God* spoke to Moshe [saying]: 2. Speak to the sons of Yisrael that they accept for Me an uplifted donation. From every man whose heart moves him to make a free-will gift you shall accept My uplifted donation. 3. This is the uplifted donation that you are to accept from them: gold and silver and copper; 4. sky-blue wool, purple and scarlet wool, byssus and goats' hair; 5. rams' skins dyed red, *tahash* skins and *shittim* wood; 6. oil for the lighting, spices for the anointing oil and for the spicy incense; 7. *shoham* stones and stones to be set for the *ephod* and the breastplate. 8. They shall make Me a sanctuary and

כה א וַיְדַבֵּ֥ר יְהֹוָ֖ה אֶל־מֹשֶׁ֥ה לֵּאמֹֽר: ב דַּבֵּ֞ר
אֶל־בְּנֵ֣י יִשְׂרָאֵ֗ל וְיִקְחוּ־לִ֖י תְּרוּמָ֑ה מֵאֵ֤ת כָּל־
אִישׁ֙ אֲשֶׁ֣ר יִדְּבֶ֣נּוּ לִבּ֔וֹ תִּקְח֖וּ אֶת־תְּרֽוּמָתִֽי:
ג וְזֹאת֙ הַתְּרוּמָ֔ה אֲשֶׁ֥ר תִּקְח֖וּ מֵאִתָּ֑ם זָהָ֥ב
וָכֶ֖סֶף וּנְחֹֽשֶׁת: ד וּתְכֵ֧לֶת וְאַרְגָּמָ֛ן וְתוֹלַ֥עַת שָׁנִ֖י
וְשֵׁ֥שׁ וְעִזִּֽים: ה וְעֹרֹ֨ת אֵילִ֧ם מְאָדָּמִ֛ים וְעֹרֹ֥ת
תְּחָשִׁ֖ים וַעֲצֵ֥י שִׁטִּֽים: ו שֶׁ֖מֶן לַמָּאֹ֑ר בְּשָׂמִים֙
לְשֶׁ֣מֶן הַמִּשְׁחָ֔ה וְלִקְטֹ֖רֶת הַסַּמִּֽים: ז אַבְנֵי־
שֹׁ֕הַם וְאַבְנֵ֖י מִלֻּאִ֑ים לָאֵפֹ֖ד וְלַחֹֽשֶׁן: ח וְעָ֥שׂוּ לִ֖י

CHAPTER XXV

2. **that they accept for Me.** The gift should not be given directly to God; rather, the gift of each individual should be made to the community for God's purposes. This implies that it is not the individual but the community that is to set up the institutions dedicated to God's purposes, and it is not for the individual donors but for the community as a whole that these institutions are to be established.

תְּרוּמָה *[uplifted donation]* derived from רוּם, "to be exalted," "lifted up"; hence, "to lift out"; i.e., to set apart for a higher purpose. יִדְּבֶנּוּ ["whose heart moves him to make a free-will gift," from the root], נדב, "to move (someone) to make a free-will gift." The connotation is one of complete spontaneity.

8. **They shall make Me a sanctuary. . . .** In our essay entitled *Grundlinien einer jüdischen Symbolik*[7] [originally] published in the *Jeschurun* [periodical] we have traced in considerable detail the symbolic significance of the Tabernacle in general, and that of the materials used for its construction in particular. We would therefore refer our readers to that study, upon which the notes that follow are based.

[7]*Note to the English translation*: This essay, "A Basic Outline of Jewish Symbolism," appears in an English translation in *Timeless Torah: An Anthology of the Writings of Samson Raphael Hirsch*, ed. Jacob Breuer, New York, 1957, published for the Samson Raphael Hirsch Publications Society by Philipp Feldheim, Inc., pp. 303–419. [G.H.]

"I will dwell in your midst" is specified in our text as a direct result of "They shall make Me a sanctuary." Hence the symbolic function of the מִקְדָּשׁ [sanctuary] can be only to express that collective task upon whose fulfillment the promised presence of the *Shekhinah* in Israel's midst depends. The statement "They shall make a sanctuary for Me and then I will dwell in their midst" thus seems to imply two distinct concepts that are to be symbolized by the structure of the Tabernacle and its furnishings. These concepts are מִקְדָּשׁ [Sanctuary] and מִשְׁכָּן [Dwelling Place]. מִקְדָּשׁ denotes the mission that we are to discharge for God; מִשְׁכָּן expresses the fulfillment of the promise made to us by God in return for our discharging that mission. This mission is epitomized in מִקְדָּשׁ: We are to consecrate all of our lives, both public and private, to the fulfillment of God's Law. The promise implied in מִשְׁכָּן is simply the protection and blessing to be provided by the Divine Presence and demonstrated in the flourishing of our outer and inner lives. The Sanctuary is to be מִקְדָּשׁ, the place of our consecration; מִשְׁכָּן, the dwelling place of God's Presence. This is the place where we are to seek, and to attain, our own consecration and the Presence of God. Our consecration; i.e., the mutual covenantal relationship between God and Israel, established through the giving of the Law (by God) and its acceptance (by Israel) is to be the context within which the significance of the Sanctuary as a whole and in its parts is to be sought and found. Hence this chapter, in which the construction of the Sanctuary is described, is a logical sequel to the preceding chapter, which contains the principal features of the Law and of the covenant made on the foundations of that Law.

Seen from this vantage point, the materials to be donated for the construction of the מִשְׁכָּן־מִקְדָּשׁ [Sanctuary–Dwelling Place] symbolize the elements by means of which we are to perform this consecration and which, at the same time, are to proclaim the blessed Presence of God. For it is in fact from God Himself that we first received the objects with which we symbolize our consecration. By dedicating them to the Sanctuary we will receive them back with a twofold blessing, even as Jacob said when he laid the original cornerstone for the very first House of God (Genesis 28:22): "And all that Thou wilt give me I will tithe to Thee repeatedly." King David set forth the same thought in even more precise terms when preparations were made for the construction of the First Temple (I Chronicles 29:14): "All things come from Thee, and it is from Thine own that we have given to Thee," and we have just been reminded of this idea in even more comprehensive terseness by Moses' act of pouring out one-half of the blood of the covenantal offering in front of the altar and the other half in front of the assembled people (Chapter 24, Verses 6 and 8).

In our discussions [of Jewish symbolism] we have shown how the Biblical text has chosen metals, because of their hardness, as the most appropriate metaphors for firmness and strength (cf. Jeremiah 1:18, Job 6:12, and Isaiah 48:4.) Because of the value attached to metals, Scripture employs them as symbols of the value attached to qualities of the spirit (cf. Proverbs 2:10, Psalms 19:11, and Job 28). But it is especially because of their metallurgical properties that Scripture cites metals as the most striking symbols of all that is good and true, in "alloys" of various degrees with evil and falsehood, and as a metaphor for the process of "testing" and "refinement" associated with truth and morality. (Cf. Job 23:10; Zekhariah 13:9; Malakhi 3:3; Proverbs 17:3; Isaiah 48:10; Proverbs 25:4, 10:20 and 26:23; Jeremiah 6:29 and 30; Psalms 119:119; Ezekiel 22:18; Isaiah 1:22, and Daniel 2:32–33). In all these Scriptural passages metals symbolize varying degrees of moral truth and purity. Copper symbolizes baseness, or nature still in its unrefined state. Silver denotes a more advanced stage at which the object is still in need of purification but has clearly become amenable to refinement. Gold, which primarily occurs in unalloyed form and can withstand the most rigorous tests, is taken as the symbol of the purest, most genuine form of moral nobleness and true constancy.

Metals combine maximal ductility with maximal firmness. When softened by fire and beaten with a hammer while still soft, they can be given any desired shape, but once they have received that shape they retain it so firmly that it can be destroyed only by superior force. Hence metals symbolize to us the character trait we should activate in our obedience to the dictates of duty and particularly to the will of God as it has been revealed to us. Indeed, the Word of God is described as a "hammer" and a "fire": "Is not

My Word like fire . . . and like a hammer that breaks the rock to pieces?" (Jeremiah 23:29). Consequently, metals, more than any other substance in nature, present themselves as the most fitting symbol of what our moral attitude should be toward our calling.

Thus, seen in accordance with their respective metallurgical properties, copper represents nature in its still unrefined state; silver, nature capable of being improved by refinement; and gold, the pristine and most genuine, and hence the most perfect, form of goodness and purity.

[In our study] we have shown in detail how clothing in general expresses the nature and character of the wearer. The nature of man has two aspects: vegetative and animal. The vegetative aspect includes nourishment and sex life, with all the stimuli and impulses, efforts and pleasures emanating from these. The animal aspect encompasses life with all its vital faculties of perception, volition and aspirations. We have demonstrated how in the laws pertaining to *tzitzith* [fringes] and *shaatnez* [forbidden mixtures of wool and flax], wool as a dress material represents the animal aspect of human nature, while flax symbolizes its vegetative aspect.

Hence the only textiles that were accepted for use in the construction of the Sanctuary were wool and flax: "sky-blue wool, purple and scarlet wool," and "byssus," a fine yellow flax, each of which was further categorized in terms of its colors: white, blue and two distinct shades of red.

שֵׁשׁ [*byssus*], flax, which represents the vegetative aspect of human nature, is white, which, as we have explained [in our study], is the color of purity. In the Law, moral purity refers primarily to the forces inherent in this aspect of human nature. Corruption in matters of diet and sex life constitutes a most serious stain upon the purity of man's character. Purity is the character trait that engenders the degree of refinement demanded by God precisely for the vegetative aspect of human nature.

Even as wool, which symbolizes the animal aspect of human nature, is itself of animal origin, so the dyes specified for the wool in Verse 4—blue, purple and scarlet—are also derived from the animal kingdom. Of the two shades of red listed in this verse, שָׁנִי [scarlet] is the paler and אַרְגָּמָן [purple] the more noble, so that if red, as the color of blood, symbolizes life itself, then שָׁנִי would refer to the subordinate, animal level of life, while אַרְגָּמָן would denote the higher, or "human" stage. Indeed, the Biblical text refers to man as אָדָם, literally, "the red one" *par excellence*, life in its highest form.

תְּכֵלֶת ["sky-blue"] is the color that points to the "limitations" of our horizon, to the invisible realm of the Divine that is beyond our physical ken. When used as a dye for our garments, this color therefore represents the godly things that were revealed to us, God's covenant with man, the symbol of the godly element

then I will dwell in their midst. 9. Just as
I show you the [plans for] the fashioning of
the Dwelling Place and the fashioning of all
its furnishings, so, too, shall you make it also
in future. 10. They shall make an ark of
shittim wood, two and one-half cubits long,
one cubit and a half wide, and one cubit and
a half high. 11. Cover it with pure gold;

מִקְדָּשׁ וְשָׁכַנְתִּי בְּתוֹכָם׃ ט כְּכֹל אֲשֶׁר אֲנִי
מַרְאֶה אוֹתְךָ אֵת תַּבְנִית הַמִּשְׁכָּן וְאֵת תַּבְנִית
כָּל־כֵּלָיו וְכֵן תַּעֲשׂוּ׃ ס י וְעָשׂוּ אֲרוֹן עֲצֵי
שִׁטִּים אַמָּתַיִם וָחֵצִי אָרְכּוֹ וְאַמָּה וָחֵצִי רָחְבּוֹ
וְאַמָּה וָחֵצִי קֹמָתוֹ׃ יא וְצִפִּיתָ אֹתוֹ זָהָב טָהוֹר

that unites with the pure human character and penetrates it, thus shaping every aspect of the individual's life.

Hence, שֵׁשׁ [byssus] represents the vegetative element; שָׁנִי [the scarlet wool], the animal; אַרְגָּמָן [the purple wool], the human, and תְּכֵלֶת [the sky-blue wool], the Divine element in man. So we are all the components of human nature listed in their ascending order.

עִזִּים *[goats' hair]*, which is used only for making sacks, or mourning and penitential garb [sackcloth], is a material that affords the wearer protection and repels would-be attackers.

עֲצֵי שִׁטִּים [shittim *wood*]. עֵץ, the tree, in general symbolizes progressive growth and development. אֶרֶז, the cedar, of which שִׁטָּה is one among ten varieties, represents, in addition, the characteristic of greatness and strength. Thus, the *shittim* wood to be employed in the construction of the Sanctuary and its furnishings symbolizes, in general terms, a development that is firm, consistent, vigorous and progressive.

The materials listed in Verses 3–5 are linked together with a copulative *vav*. Together, they represent that material from which the actual framework of the Tabernacle, and its furnishings, are to be made. Verse 7 lists the precious stones required for the priestly vestments. In this manner the priests, along with their vestments, become essential components of the Sanctuary itself. They are among the "vessels of the Sanctuary," as Maimonides aptly classifies them in his *Yad Hazakah* and as we shall also note in our discussion of the sacrificial laws. It is odd that Verse 6 should make mention also of the oil to be used for lighting and of spices for the anointing oil and for incense. שֶׁמֶן הַמִּשְׁחָה [the anointing oil] is not part of the מִקְדָּשׁ in the literal sense. However, its inclusion among the other furnishings of the Sanctuary can be explained by the fact that this oil plays an essential role in the consecration of the Sanctuary and its furnishings; only by virtue of their anointment are these objects vested with their symbolic meaning.

Still, the oil for lighting and the incense seem to belong only to the materials needed for the *service* in the Sanctuary, along with the flour required for the showbreads, the wood for the fire upon the altar, the lambs for the daily offerings, etc. It is therefore noteworthy that these substances should have been enumerated among the gifts needed for the actual *construction* of the Sanctuary. Note, however, that, as we shall demonstrate further on, the light in the Sanctuary is intended to symbolize man's spiritual life, which is to be stimulated by the Law and which we are to employ in the service of the Law, and that קְטֹרֶת ["the spicy incense"] symbolizes the flowering ideal inherent in every act of consecration to God. Both together, then, symbolize the complete subordination of the human self for the purpose of obtaining God's approval. Thus, the fact that these substances are mentioned at this point is intended to teach us, already in the appeal for free-will gifts to be used in the construction of the Sanctuary, that the final product of this effort is the attainment of the two ultimate goals of all human existence: enlightenment for man's spirit and Divine approval for his acts. Listed between the oil for lighting and the oil for the incense are the spices to be used in the preparation of the anointing oil which is to exalt the Sanctuary, as a thing inviolate and God-given, to a position of dominance over the spirit and the deeds of man. The hallowing of these goals is an essential requirement for the development of the human spirit and of behavior patterns pleasing in the eyes of God.

° ° °

11. ***Cover it.*** Receptivity and the vital capacity for development must be combined with firmness, iron persistence and constancy with respect to all that is good and noble, true and genuine. The wood must be joined by metal; the tree, by gold. The acceptance of the Law of God necessitates an ability to develop but it requires also firmness, a noble firmness to be demonstrated both within and without. Cf. "You shall cover it inside and outside." The Ark consisted of three receptacles: one inner and one outer receptacle, each made of gold, and in between these a receptacle made of *shittim* wood. Be true and firm in every aspect of your life, both within and without, noble and true, free from all dross, resistant to all change and corruption: this is the condition, these the golden boundaries within which your life is to unfold, growing by stages, like the tree, from within the Law. You are to remain proof against all evil and receptive to all that is good. זָהָב and עֵץ [the gold and the cedar tree], the former symbolizing מִצְוֹת לֹא תַעֲשֶׂה [the observance of the negative commandments,

you shall cover it inside and outside, and make a gold rim all around, extending above its top,   12. and cast four golden rings for it and place them upon its four foot-corners, two rings upon its one side and two rings upon its other side. 13. And make poles of *shittim* wood and cover them with gold,   14. and place the poles into the rings on the sides of the ark, to carry the ark with them.   15. The poles shall remain in the rings of the ark; they shall never depart from it.   16. Then you will put into the ark the Testimony which I will give you.   17. And make a cover of pure gold, two and one-half cubits long, one cubit and a half wide.   18. And make two cherubim of gold; you shall make them hammered out of the two ends of the cover.   19. Make one cherub out of the one end and the other cherub out of the other end; out of one piece with the cover shall you make the cherubim at both its ends.   20. The cherubim shall spread their wings upward, shielding the cover with their wings, and their faces shall be [turned] toward one another; the faces of the cherubim shall be turned toward the cover. 21. You shall put the cover on top of the ark, and into the ark you shall put the Testimony which I will give you.   22. There I will meet with you at appointed times, and I will speak with you from above the cover, from between the two cherubim that are upon the Ark of the Testimony, concerning all the things that I shall command you for the sons of Yisrael.   23. And make a table of *shittim* wood, two cubits long and one cubit wide, and one cubit and a half high. 24. And cover it with pure gold and make for it a gold rim all around.   25. Make for it a border of a handbreadth all around and a gold rim all around upon its border. 26. And make for it four golden rings and put the rings upon the four corners that form its four legs.   27. The rings shall be

מִבַּ֖יִת וּמִח֑וּץ תְּצַפֶּ֑נּוּ וְעָשִׂ֧יתָ עָלָ֛יו זֵ֥ר זָהָ֖ב סָבִֽיב: יב וְיָצַ֣קְתָּ לּ֗וֹ אַרְבַּע֙ טַבְּעֹ֣ת זָהָ֔ב וְנָ֣תַתָּ֔ה עַ֖ל אַרְבַּ֣ע פַּעֲמֹתָ֑יו וּשְׁתֵּ֣י טַבָּעֹ֗ת עַל־צַלְעוֹ֙ הָֽאֶחָ֔ת וּשְׁתֵּי֙ טַבָּעֹ֔ת עַל־צַלְע֖וֹ הַשֵּׁנִֽית: יג וְעָשִׂ֥יתָ בַדֵּ֖י עֲצֵ֣י שִׁטִּ֑ים וְצִפִּיתָ֥ אֹתָ֖ם זָהָֽב: יד וְהֵֽבֵאתָ֤ אֶת־הַבַּדִּים֙ בַּטַּבָּעֹ֔ת עַ֖ל צַלְעֹ֣ת הָֽאָרֹ֑ן לָשֵׂ֥את אֶת־הָֽאָרֹ֖ן בָּהֶֽם: טו בְּטַבְּעֹת֙ הָֽאָרֹ֔ן יִהְי֖וּ הַבַּדִּ֑ים לֹ֥א יָסֻ֖רוּ מִמֶּֽנּוּ: טז וְנָֽתַתָּ֖ אֶל־הָֽאָרֹ֑ן אֵ֚ת הָֽעֵדֻ֔ת אֲשֶׁ֥ר אֶתֵּ֖ן אֵלֶֽיךָ: שני יז וְעָשִׂ֥יתָ כַפֹּ֖רֶת זָהָ֣ב טָה֑וֹר אַמָּתַ֤יִם וָחֵ֨צִי֙ אָרְכָּ֔הּ וְאַמָּ֥ה וָחֵ֖צִי רָחְבָּֽהּ: יח וְעָשִׂ֛יתָ שְׁנַ֥יִם כְּרֻבִ֖ים זָהָ֑ב מִקְשָׁה֙ תַּֽעֲשֶׂ֣ה אֹתָ֔ם מִשְּׁנֵ֖י קְצ֥וֹת הַכַּפֹּֽרֶת: יט וַֽעֲשֵׂ֞ה כְּר֤וּב אֶחָד֙ מִקָּצָ֣ה מִזֶּ֔ה וּכְרוּב־אֶחָ֥ד מִקָּצָ֖ה מִזֶּ֑ה מִן־הַכַּפֹּ֛רֶת תַּֽעֲשׂ֥וּ אֶת־הַכְּרֻבִ֖ים עַל־שְׁנֵ֥י קְצוֹתָֽיו: כ וְהָי֣וּ הַכְּרֻבִים֩ פֹּֽרְשֵׂ֨י כְנָפַ֜יִם לְמַ֗עְלָה סֹֽכְכִ֤ים בְּכַנְפֵיהֶם֙ עַל־הַכַּפֹּ֔רֶת וּפְנֵיהֶ֖ם אִ֣ישׁ אֶל־אָחִ֑יו אֶל־הַכַּפֹּ֔רֶת יִֽהְי֖וּ פְּנֵ֥י הַכְּרֻבִֽים: כא וְנָֽתַתָּ֧ אֶת־הַכַּפֹּ֛רֶת עַל־הָֽאָרֹ֖ן מִלְמָ֑עְלָה וְאֶל־הָ֣אָרֹ֔ן תִּתֵּן֙ אֶת־הָ֣עֵדֻ֔ת אֲשֶׁ֥ר אֶתֵּ֖ן אֵלֶֽיךָ: כב וְנֽוֹעַדְתִּ֣י לְךָ֮ שָׁם֒ וְדִבַּרְתִּ֨י אִתְּךָ֜ מֵעַ֣ל הַכַּפֹּ֗רֶת מִבֵּין֙ שְׁנֵ֣י הַכְּרֻבִ֔ים אֲשֶׁ֖ר עַל־אֲר֣וֹן הָֽעֵדֻ֑ת אֵ֣ת כָּל־אֲשֶׁ֧ר אֲצַוֶּ֛ה אֽוֹתְךָ֖ אֶל־בְּנֵ֥י יִשְׂרָאֵֽל: פ כג וְעָשִׂ֥יתָ שֻׁלְחָ֖ן עֲצֵ֣י שִׁטִּ֑ים אַמָּתַ֤יִם אָרְכּוֹ֙ וְאַמָּ֣ה רָחְבּ֔וֹ וְאַמָּ֥ה וָחֵ֖צִי קֹֽמָתֽוֹ: כד וְצִפִּיתָ֥ אֹת֖וֹ זָהָ֣ב טָה֑וֹר וְעָשִׂ֥יתָ לּ֛וֹ זֵ֥ר זָהָ֖ב סָבִֽיב: כה וְעָשִׂ֨יתָ לּ֤וֹ מִסְגֶּ֨רֶת֙ טֹ֣פַח סָבִ֔יב וְעָשִׂ֧יתָ זֵר־זָהָ֛ב לְמִסְגַּרְתּ֖וֹ סָבִֽיב: כו וְעָשִׂ֣יתָ לּ֗וֹ אַרְבַּע֙ טַבְּעֹ֣ת זָהָ֔ב וְנָֽתַתָּ֙ אֶת־הַטַּבָּעֹ֔ת עַ֚ל אַרְבַּ֣ע הַפֵּאֹ֔ת אֲשֶׁ֖ר לְאַרְבַּ֥ע רַגְלָֽיו:

---

or prohibitions] and the latter מִצְוֹת עֲשֵׂה [the observance of the positive commandments]: these are the two aspects of the character that qualifies Israel as a vessel for the Law of God. ∘   ∘   ∘

17–20. . . . In this manner אָרוֹן וְכַפֹּרֶת [the Ark and its

cover] are to symbolize the task וְעָשׂוּ לִי מִקְדָּשׁ [''They shall make Me a sanctuary''], and the כְּרוּבִים [the cherubim], the result of the task accomplished; i.e., וְשָׁכַנְתִּי בְּתוֹכָם [''and then I will dwell in their midst''].

∘   ∘   ∘

adjacent to the border as holders for the poles, to carry the table. 28. Make the poles of *shittim* wood and cover them with gold; with them the table will be carried. 29. And make its dishes, its spoons, its supports and its purification tubes with which it will be covered; of pure gold shall you make them. 30. And upon this table you shall place the Bread of the Countenance before My Countenance at all times. 31. And make a menorah of pure gold; the menorah, its base and its shaft shall be made hammered out of one piece; its cups, its knobs and its flowers shall be made of one piece with it. 32. And six branches shall go out from its sides; three branches of the menorah from its one side and three branches of the menorah from its other side. 33. Three cups shaped like almond blossoms in one branch, with a knob and a flower, and three cups shaped like almond blossoms on the other branch, with a knob and a flower, and so for [all] the six branches that go out from the menorah. 34. Upon the menorah itself shall be four cups, shaped like almond blossoms, with its knobs and its flowers. 35. One knob under the two branches that go out from it, and one knob under the [second] set of two branches that go out from it, and one knob under the [third] set of two branches that go out from it; and so for [all] the six branches that go out from the menorah. 36. Their knobs and their branches shall be of one piece with it; the whole of it hammered out of one piece of pure gold. 37. And you shall make its lamps seven in number. Whoever kindles the lamps shall have them shine toward it [i.e., toward the shaft]. 38. Its tongs and its charcoal pans shall also be made of pure gold. 39. One shall make it of one *kikkar* of pure gold, together with all

כז לְעֻמַּת֙ הַמִּסְגֶּ֔רֶת תִּהְיֶ֖יןָ הַטַּבָּעֹ֑ת לְבָתִּ֣ים לְבַדִּ֔ים לָשֵׂ֖את אֶת־הַשֻּׁלְחָֽן: כח וְעָשִׂ֥יתָ אֶת־ הַבַּדִּ֖ים עֲצֵ֣י שִׁטִּ֑ים וְצִפִּיתָ֤ אֹתָם֙ זָהָ֔ב וְנִשָּׂא־בָ֖ם אֶת־הַשֻּׁלְחָֽן: כט וְעָשִׂ֤יתָ קְּעָֽרֹתָיו֙ וְכַפֹּתָ֔יו וּקְשׂוֹתָיו֙ וּמְנַקִּיֹּתָ֔יו אֲשֶׁ֥ר יֻסַּ֖ךְ בָּהֵ֑ן זָהָ֥ב טָה֖וֹר תַּעֲשֶׂ֥ה אֹתָֽם: ל וְנָתַתָּ֧ עַל־הַשֻּׁלְחָ֛ן לֶ֥חֶם פָּנִ֖ים לְפָנַ֥י תָּמִֽיד: פ שלישי לא וְעָשִׂ֥יתָ מְנֹרַ֖ת זָהָ֣ב טָה֑וֹר מִקְשָׁ֞ה תֵּעָשֶׂ֤ה הַמְּנוֹרָה֙ יְרֵכָ֣הּ וְקָנָ֔הּ גְּבִיעֶ֛יהָ כַּפְתֹּרֶ֥יהָ וּפְרָחֶ֖יהָ מִמֶּ֥נָּה יִהְיֽוּ: לב וְשִׁשָּׁ֣ה קָנִ֔ים יֹצְאִ֖ים מִצִּדֶּ֑יהָ שְׁלֹשָׁ֣ה ׀ קְנֵ֣י מְנֹרָ֗ה מִצִּדָּהּ֙ הָֽאֶחָ֔ד וּשְׁלֹשָׁה֙ קְנֵ֣י מְנֹרָ֔ה מִצִּדָּ֖הּ הַשֵּׁנִֽי: לג שְׁלֹשָׁ֣ה גְ֠בִעִים מְֽשֻׁקָּדִ֞ים בַּקָּנֶ֣ה הָאֶחָד֮ כַּפְתֹּ֣ר וָפֶ֒רַח֒ וּשְׁלֹשָׁ֣ה גְבִעִ֗ים מְשֻׁקָּדִ֛ים בַּקָּנֶ֥ה הָאֶחָ֖ד כַּפְתֹּ֣ר וָפָ֑רַח כֵּ֚ן לְשֵׁ֣שֶׁת הַקָּנִ֔ים הַיֹּצְאִ֖ים מִן־ הַמְּנֹרָֽה: לד וּבַמְּנֹרָ֖ה אַרְבָּעָ֣ה גְבִעִ֑ים מְשֻׁקָּדִ֔ים כַּפְתֹּרֶ֖יהָ וּפְרָחֶֽיהָ: לה וְכַפְתֹּ֡ר תַּ֣חַת שְׁנֵי֩ הַקָּנִ֨ים מִמֶּ֜נָּה וְכַפְתֹּ֗ר תַּ֚חַת שְׁנֵ֣י הַקָּנִ֔ים מִמֶּ֑נָּה וְכַפְתֹּ֕ר תַּֽחַת־שְׁנֵ֥י הַקָּנִ֖ים מִמֶּ֑נָּה לְשֵׁ֙שֶׁת֙ הַקָּנִ֔ים הַיֹּצְאִ֖ים מִן־הַמְּנֹרָֽה: לו כַּפְתֹּרֵיהֶ֥ם וּקְנֹתָ֖ם מִמֶּ֣נָּה יִהְי֑וּ כֻּלָּ֛הּ מִקְשָׁ֥ה אַחַ֖ת זָהָ֥ב טָהֽוֹר: לז וְעָשִׂ֥יתָ אֶת־נֵרֹתֶ֖יהָ שִׁבְעָ֑ה וְהֶעֱלָה֙ אֶת־ נֵ֣רֹתֶ֔יהָ וְהֵאִ֖יר עַל־עֵ֥בֶר פָּנֶֽיהָ: לח וּמַלְקָחֶ֥יהָ וּמַחְתֹּתֶ֖יהָ זָהָ֥ב טָהֽוֹר: לט כִּכַּ֛ר זָהָ֥ב טָה֖וֹר

---

30. you shall place. And you shall place upon this table the Bread of the Countenance before My Countenance at all times. Only for such a table, and only if it is placed upon such a table, will your bread become לֶחֶם הַפָּנִים, "Bread of the Countenance," earned and eaten before the countenance of God; granted, protected and blessed by His Presence.

39. ... If we inquire into the significance of the

menorah within the Sanctuary of God's Law, the answer at first glance would seem quite obvious. The menorah with its burning lights, we would assume, expresses its symbolic significance through the light which it disseminates, and we should consider it self-evident that the light, in turn, represents understanding. In that case nothing would be easier than to interpret the menorah, particularly in view of its position opposite the table and in front of the Ark of God's Law, as symbolizing that spiritual understanding which, together with the table—the symbol of material prosperity—would indicate the results of a Jewish national life emanating from, and eternally consecrated to, the Law of God.

However, a more thoroughgoing study, based on the Scriptural text, may give rise to justifiable doubts as to whether the answer is indeed as obvious as all that.

°   °   °

If we gather all the facts regarding the significance of the menorah in the concepts of Judaism which have been placed before us in numerous cases in point, then "knowledge and understanding" would represent only part, indeed only one aspect, of the symbolic significance of light in the Holy Scriptures.

°   °   °

We would feel justified in interpreting the menorah in the Sanctuary as a symbol of the spirit, more specifically, of the dual aspects of the human spirit: theory and practice, cognition and volition, perception and the will to practical action.

Fortunately the Word of God itself offers us clear support for our explanation.

Zekhariah was the messenger of God to Zerubbabel, the leader who was to build upon the ruins of the former Jewish state the foundations for a new Jewish national life, a task in which he encountered obstacles at every turn. Zekhariah was shown the menorah with its seven lights. When he asked the angel who had brought him the word from God to explain to him the meaning of this vision, the angel retorted: "Do you not know what these mean?" When the prophet replied: "No, my lord," the angel said to him: "This is the word of God to be conveyed to Zerubbabel: Not by armed might, nor by physical force, but by My spirit, says the Lord of Hosts" (Zekhariah 4:6). This is proof that it is the spirit, or more accurately, the spirit of God, which is represented by the menorah with the seven lamps, and that this symbolic connotation should be so self-evident that the angel's retort to Zekhariah: "Do you not know what these mean?" implies a reproach of sorts, criticizing the prophet for feeling that he needed a special explanation in order to understand this symbolic vision.

Note also that when Zerubbabel is advised that he will be able to accomplish his mission only by and through the spirit of God, the "spirit" appears not merely as a mental phenomenon but also as a medium for practical action. For the word of God was communicated to Zerubbabel as the leader, not as the teacher, of the people. It was not his task to *teach* them the will of God, but to *recognize* it and *to carry it out*. He had been entrusted with the task of laying a cornerstone for an edifice toward the completion of which "all the fullness of Divine Providence" was directed.

Moreover, the Word of God itself has described to us elsewhere the nature and the content of that spirit. In Isaiah 11:2, in connection with the shoot that is to come

forth from the stock of Jesse, we are told וְנָחָה עָלָיו רוּחַ ד׳ ["and the spirit of God shall rest upon it"] and the text proceeds at once to explain the spirit of God as רוּחַ חָכְמָה וּבִינָה, רוּחַ עֵצָה וּגְבוּרָה, רוּחַ דַּעַת וְיִרְאַת ד׳,— the spirit of wisdom and understanding, the spirit of counsel *and* strength, the spirit of knowledge *and* of the fear of God. This would seem to confirm beyond doubt that the spirit which God regards as His spirit and which, as Zekhariah has informed us, is symbolized by the menorah, is not a spirit of mere theoretical knowledge and perception but one that imparts understanding and practical action at the same time.

מְנוֹרָה [The Menorah]

Now if the light that is borne by the menorah symbolizes the spirit of understanding and action that is bestowed by God upon man, what is the relationship of this menorah to the light that it bears?

If we picture the menorah to ourselves in terms of its physical form, then its base which bears one flower, and its shaft and its branches with their cups shaped like almond blossoms, their knobs and flowers, clearly create the impression of a tree which, shooting upward from its root stock, grows up to become the bearer of this light.

If, at the same time, we consider that the menorah was the sole object in the Sanctuary to be made entirely of metal, and, what is more, of gold, we can readily see that, by virtue of the substance from which it was fashioned, it was meant to symbolize firmness, perseverance and immutability, but that its form implied growth and development. Thus, the two aspects of the menorah, substance and form, would represent the growth and development of qualities of firmness, perseverance and endurance that are to remain unchanged for all time.

Hence the menorah by its very appearance forms the complete antithesis of the concept symbolized by the table. The table is fashioned predominantly of wood. Wood represents a constant process of development; it derives its appointed limits, its support, its firmness and its endurance only from its form and its accessories. The table thus symbolizes the material aspects of life which, by their very nature, are subject to changes inherent in the phenomena of germination and growth, blossoming, ripening and, eventually, death and decay. Only in the Sanctuary of God does the table, through the spirit and the ordinances of God's Law, receive its set limits, its firmness, endurance and eternal meaning.

As opposed to the table, we then see the menorah. Made of gold through and through, it symbolizes precisely that unchanging firmness and timelessness which, as indicated by its form, is to blossom and develop in the Sanctuary of God through the spirit of God's Law. But as for man, the only firm, immutable and eternal element within him is the Divine element, which dwells within him and of which we become aware when we come to know what the truth is and when we are moved by the will to put this awareness into practice by doing good. These elements of cognition and volition in man, along with the objects of his actions; i.e., goodness and truth, are eternal and immutable, subject to neither modification nor alteration in the course of his life. True, the godliness of the mature man appears infinitely richer than that which was latent within his breast when he was a child. Nevertheless, essentially, the godliness that was latent within the child is fully equal, both in quality and purity, to those godly qualities that attained full development only after the child had matured to manhood. Only the outward manifestations of that godliness give an appearance of differences in degree. Similarly, the simplest truths and the most commonplace acts of goodness are not one whit less genuine or good than the most sublime truths and the most unique manifestations of goodness.

Anything that is genuinely good and true is good and true indeed; that is all. There can be no question of "more" or "less." In the development of physical things, any higher form can grow only at the expense of a lower form. Lower forms must die off so that higher, more elaborate forms may emerge. Hence, in the physical world anything that is higher or more elaborate than what has gone before represents a negation of the lower forms that have preceded it. Every form of life has a grave for a cradle; like the phoenix, each form of life arises from the ashes of earlier forms and generations. Not so the things of the spirit. Goodness and truth never lose any of their validity or justification. Whatever is good and true remains so for all time. Higher manifestations of goodness and truth represent not a negation but only a fuller realization of all the goodness and truth that have gone before. Not even the oldest of men can deny the virtues that were his when he was a child. Indeed, the virtues of his maturity are merely the fruits of those earlier virtues, now realized under more comprehensive circumstances than they could have been in the narrower context of childhood. The most complex system of the most sublime, momentous verities cannot do without the simplest truths that served as their starting point. Indeed, that firm and inviolable stock of simple truths from which it evolved is the basis for the existence of the most far-reaching of verities. In the final analysis, any form of truth, no matter how elaborate, is nothing but the substance—restated and realized in more sophisticated terms—of elements already inherent in basic truths that have always existed, albeit undeveloped and veiled from the conscious mind.

Accordingly, the "tree" that symbolizes the recognition and the practical implementation of what is good and true is a "tree" wrought from gold, from its roots to its flowers, golden in its every part and at every stage of its development. (Like gold, it is equally pure, genuine and good in all its parts and at every level of its growth.)

Moreover, in its highest form of completion, from its roots to its flowers, it is indivisible, not composed piecemeal from various parts. It is all of one piece. In short, it is a tree as represented for us by the menorah of pure gold, which must be hammered from one piece, and "its base and its shaft . . . its cups, its knobs and its flowers shall be made of one piece with it." This tree is symbolized by a menorah in its highest form of perfection, wrought with a base, shaft, branches, cups, knobs and flowers, all hammered out of one piece, of pure gold through and through.

Now let us examine the individual parts of the menorah. First of all, the seven lamps that it bears tell us that the spirit nurtured here is not one-sided (as would be implied if there were only one lamp). Rather, this spirit embraces a great diversity of aspects that we recognize at once not as mere diversity but as a comprehensive totality of spiritual cognition and moral volition. If we consider the lamps more closely, we will see that, in addition to this diversity, they symbolize also the concept of sublime harmony and unity. We see the middle lamp with its light shining upward, or straight ahead. At the same time, the lights from both sides, right and left, shine toward that central light in such a manner that the three lamps on the right side turn their light toward the left and the three lamps at the left turn their light toward the right, so that all of them together turn their lights toward the one light in the center, with all the seven lights forming one perfect unity. Thus the central light becomes the ultimate goal toward which all the other lights of the menorah must strive; or, phrased in different terms, the spot toward which that one central lamp casts its light is the goal common also to all the other lights of the menorah.

Moreover, these lamps are borne by seven branches. But this does not mean that each lamp has its own distinctive base and shaft. No, all of them have one base in common; one root, one shaft serves to support them all. Indeed, a more detailed study shows, as indicated also by the specifications contained in the Word of God, that the shaft upon which the central lamp rests and which rises straight upward from the root stock, is the true central menorah, the trunk, as it were, from which the other six branches extend in pairs on either side, but only from a level above the center of the trunk. The text repeatedly draws our attention to the fact that these six branches emanate from the shaft in the center. Thus the central light is not only the ultimate goal that serves to unite all the other lights but also the starting point from which all the other lights emanate. They all go forth from one shaft in the center and they all strive toward the one central light at the top of the shaft. Thus we must conceive of the seven lights not simply as seven individual lights, but as one light plus six lights, as one single entity from which six lights come forth and within which, at the same time, all six must reunite.

Our study of the symbolism of *milah* and

יַעֲשֶׂה אֹתָהּ אֵת כָּל־הַכֵּלִים הָאֵלֶּה: מ וּרְאֵה
וַעֲשֵׂה בְּתַבְנִיתָם אֲשֶׁר־אַתָּה מָרְאֶה בָּהָר: ס

these utensils. 40. See that you make them according to the form that will be shown to you upon the mountain.

tzitzith . . . in the 1858 volume of *Jeschurun* has already shown that the number six is the symbol of the physical world of creation, and, in this connection, that the number one, the seventh, symbolizes the One supernatural Being that stands outside the physical world, yet keeps in close touch with it. It symbolizes the One sole God and the godly elements that emanate from Him. We would therefore have to conceive of the one central shaft with its central lamp as the spirit of cognition and volition that aspires toward God, as the spirit that strives to recognize God and to serve Him. The six branches and their six lamps, on the other hand, symbolize those spiritual aspirations of understanding and will to practical implementation that are turned toward the material world. But then it is the one central shaft itself that branches out into those six lamps; all the lateral branches emanate from the same shaft and at the same time their six lights all turn toward the one light in the center. This teaches us that the spirit of the theoretical knowledge and practical service of God to be cultivated in God's Sanctuary is not an abstraction, an isolating agent that turns away from the knowledge and the practical aspirations of this world. Rather, it is a spirit that in fact comes into full play within those theoretical and practical aspirations which are aware of this world and which work for its upbuilding. Precisely by virtue of this fact, all the theoretical and practical aspirations directed toward the world, its perceptions and its demands, cease to be estranged, or "turned aside," from God, or from the theoretical knowledge and practical service of God. On the contrary, it is precisely cognition and volition turned *toward* God that gives these perceptions their one starting point and their ultimate goal, and that purifies and hallows them. All the sciences and all moral action begin and end with God. All that is truly spiritual and ethical has only one base, one root and one goal: God is its beginning, God its end; תְּחִלַּת חָכְמָה יִרְאַת ד׳ ["the beginning of all wisdom is the fear of God"] and רֵאשִׁית חָכְמָה יִרְאַת ד׳ ["the first fruit of all wisdom is the fear of God"]. The fear of God is the beginning, and also the flower, of all wisdom.

First of all, the text of the Word of God stresses this distinction between the one central shaft—which is the actual menorah—and the six lateral branches. "And make a menorah of pure gold . . . and six branches shall go out from its sides" [Verse 31]. At the same time the text repeatedly distinguishes between the lateral branches on the basis of the fact that they extend from one or the other of the two sides of the shaft: "Three branches of the menorah from its one side and three branches of the menorah from its other side" [Verse 32]. It further defines this distinction by showing that of these six branches, two branches each project from the same place on the menorah, directly above one and the same knob. "One knob under the two branches that go out from it," etc. As a result, the central (seventh) light, which is directed solely toward God, presents a dual, contradictory phenomenon in that it also dominates the material world (as symbolized by the number six). By turning its light toward the physical world, it engenders a dichotomy, but this is reconciled by the harmonious reunion of all the lateral lights at their central point of origin.

Now we have already noted above how רוּחַ, the spirit, which is symbolized by the light of the menorah in the Temple, should be understood as that which perceives, or that which grants perception, and as that which moves or which makes movement possible. In the case of man, this dichotomy takes the form of cognition and volition. We have seen that spiritual perception and moral volition [the knowledge of what is good and the will to act upon this knowledge] are the two phases in which the presence of this spirit is demonstrated. Already these facts would seem sufficient justification for our viewing the two sides of the menorah as symbolizing this duality of spiritual knowledge and moral action. Both of these are so united and inseparable in their origin and actuality that the one of necessity presupposes the existence of the other. True morality; i.e., the free-willed practical implementation of that which has been recognized in theory as good, presupposes cognition, an activity of the mind. For otherwise the good deed would be an unconscious act performed instinctively, not out of free-willed morality. By the same token, however, the mere act of recognizing what is good presupposes a moral will to translate that good into action, for it demands that one's cognitive faculties should be turned, by one's own free will, toward that objective which has been recognized as "good." But then every conscious directing of one's faculties toward some desired end is in itself an activity arising from moral volition. Thus, essentially, the spirit inherent in man has theoretical knowledge and practical volition at the same time, and it is only our abstract perceptions that interpret the one as a manifestation of theoretical cognition and the other as a demonstration of practical will, depending on whether the objective of the endeavor is mental activity or practical action. This difference lies in the result, not in the source, of the activity. At their root, both are in fact one, and they strive to come together again in their goals. Any perception of truth has value only if it is directed toward the practical implementation of what is good, if it ultimately leads to the performance of a good deed. On the other hand, a good deed must always be accomplished in the awareness of truth. Only from the perception of truth can the good deed derive its motivation and the assurance that it really represents a genuine value.

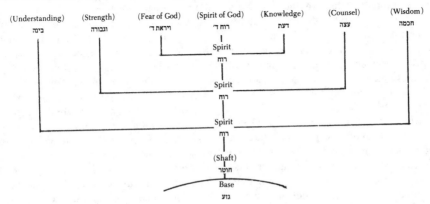

This is exactly as it is in the menorah, where the pairs of lateral branches emanate from one and the same point on the central shaft and where, once they have reached the level of the top of the shaft, they turn their lights toward one another—thus, at the same time, toward the central point that is common to them both. But if now, as is the case here, this central point symbolizes the "seventh"; that is, the spirit which aspires to God and which is nurtured and fostered in the Sanctuary, we will understand all the more readily how it is that in this central point all theoretical perception, and all volition translated into practical action, originate from one common root and then unite for the purpose of one common lofty goal. For we can recognize this root stock of our spiritual life, which aspires toward God, only in that spirit which seizes, fills, revives and completes both mind and heart with the same pristine power and strength, a spirit which the sacred text describes as יִרְאַת ד׳ ["the fear of God"]. For the fear of God represents the highest degree of cognition, which at the same time, and immediately, engenders morality in its highest form. It is the spirit in which the perception of the loftiest truth is wed with the accomplishment of the greatest good. . . .

The explanation given in Zekhariah 4:6 regarding the significance of the menorah as a symbol of the רוּחַ ד׳ [spirit of God] guides us toward the comments in Isaiah 11:2 with regard to a more precise definition of the Spirit of God. There the spirit of God resting upon man is described in its most sublime form. Already at first glance it becomes evident that this spirit develops in two distinct dimensions, חָכְמָה, עֵצָה, דַּעַת [wisdom, counsel and knowledge] on the one hand, and בִּינָה, גְבוּרָה, יִרְאָה [understanding, strength and fear of God], on the other; i.e., theory and practice, knowledge and action, thus confirming what we have already seen from the definition of "spirit" in Scripture. If we examine this verse from Isaiah more closely, we will note that it is surprisingly consistent with all that we have learned about the construction of the menorah, a consistency so striking that we cannot help thinking that this verse is, in fact, simply a verbal expression of the symbolism of the menorah.

"And the spirit of God shall rest upon it, the spirit of wisdom and understanding, the spirit of counsel and strength, the spirit of knowledge and of the fear of God." Here we see the spirit defined in its totality but unfolding through six components. These six components are arranged in two pairs each, with each pair having one common bearer, for the wording is not רוּחַ חָכְמָה וְרוּחַ בִּינָה וגו׳ ["the spirit of wisdom *and the spirit of* understanding," etc.] but רוּחַ חָכְמָה וּבִינָה וגו׳ ["the spirit of wisdom and understanding," etc.]

This is the complete picture of the menorah of gold, with six branches going out from its sides, three from one side and three from the other side, one knob under the two branches and one knob under the (second set of) two branches and one knob under the (third set of) two branches and so for (all) the six branches that emanate from the menorah. Indeed, the verse in Isaiah continues, וַהֲרִיחוֹ בְּיִרְאַת ד׳ ["and he shall be enlivened by the fear of God"], which, given the etymology of the word הֲרִיחוֹ, can mean nothing else but to permeate or to imbue another with a spirit. Thus, after the spirit of God, coming to rest upon the shoot from the stock of Jesse, is described in its sevenfold aspect, one of these seven aspects is singled out as the root and medium of all this spiritualization, just as in the case of the seven lights of the menorah there was one light from which all the other lights were kindled and which was tended at the end of each day. Indeed, to make the analogy complete, the bearer of the spirit of God, with its seven emanations, is represented as a shoot growing from a root stock, upon which rests the one spirit of God with the six branches that go forth from it. Thus, if we review this passage in its context (see above), we should have a complete picture of the ideas expressed in symbolic terms by the menorah. . . .

° ° °

XXVI

1. And you shall make the Dwelling Place from ten tapestries out of byssus twisted into six-ply thread, sky-blue, purple and scarlet wool; with cherubim of weaver's work shall you make them. 2. The length of one tapestry [shall be] twenty-eight cubits and the width four cubits, thus [shall be] one tapestry, and all the tapestries shall have the same measurements. 3. Five of these tapestries shall be joined to one another and [the other] five tapestries shall be joined to one another. 4. And you shall make loops of sky-blue wool on the edge of the one tapestry that is outermost in the first set, and make the same on the edge of the tapestry that is outermost in the second set. 5. Place fifty loops upon the one tapestry and fifty loops upon the edge of the tapestry that corresponds to the second set; the loops shall be opposite one another. 6. And make fifty gold clasps and join the tapestries to one another with the clasps, so that the Dwelling Place will become one whole. 7. Also make tapestries of goats' hair for the tent over the Dwelling Place; eleven tapestries shall you make them. 8. The length of one tapestry [shall be] thirty cubits and the width four cubits, thus [shall be] one tapestry. And all eleven tapestries shall have the same measurements. 9. You shall join [the first] five of these tapestries by themselves and [the] six [other] tapestries by themselves, and you shall double over the sixth tapestry over the front side of the tent. 10. And place fifty loops upon the edge of the one outermost tapestry in the first set and fifty loops on the edge of the outermost tapestry in the second set. 11. And make fifty copper clasps and put the clasps into the loops: thus you shall join the tent together so that it will become one. 12. The overhanging length that remains of the tapestries of the tent; that is, the half-tapestry that remains over, shall hang over the back of the Dwelling Place. 13. One cubit on the one side, and another cubit on the other side of that which remains over in the length of the tapestries of the tent shall hang on the sides of the Dwelling Place on this side and on the other side, to cover it. 14. Also make a covering for the tent of

כו א וְאֶת־הַמִּשְׁכָּן תַּעֲשֶׂה עֶשֶׂר יְרִיעֹת שֵׁשׁ מָשְׁזָר וּתְכֵלֶת וְאַרְגָּמָן וְתֹלַעַת שָׁנִי כְּרֻבִים מַעֲשֵׂה חֹשֵׁב תַּעֲשֶׂה אֹתָם: ב אֹרֶךְ ׀ הַיְרִיעָה הָאַחַת שְׁמֹנֶה וְעֶשְׂרִים בָּאַמָּה וְרֹחַב אַרְבַּע בָּאַמָּה הַיְרִיעָה הָאֶחָת מִדָּה אַחַת לְכָל־הַיְרִיעֹת: ג חֲמֵשׁ הַיְרִיעֹת תִּהְיֶיןָ חֹבְרֹת אִשָּׁה אֶל־אֲחֹתָהּ וְחָמֵשׁ יְרִיעֹת חֹבְרֹת אִשָּׁה אֶל־אֲחֹתָהּ: ד וְעָשִׂיתָ לֻלְאֹת תְּכֵלֶת עַל שְׂפַת הַיְרִיעָה הָאֶחָת מִקָּצָה בַּחֹבָרֶת וְכֵן תַּעֲשֶׂה בִּשְׂפַת הַיְרִיעָה הַקִּיצוֹנָה בַּמַּחְבֶּרֶת הַשֵּׁנִית: ה חֲמִשִּׁים לֻלָאֹת תַּעֲשֶׂה בַּיְרִיעָה הָאֶחָת וַחֲמִשִּׁים לֻלָאֹת תַּעֲשֶׂה בִּקְצֵה הַיְרִיעָה אֲשֶׁר בַּמַּחְבֶּרֶת הַשֵּׁנִית מַקְבִּילֹת הַלֻּלָאֹת אִשָּׁה אֶל־אֲחֹתָהּ: ו וְעָשִׂיתָ חֲמִשִּׁים קַרְסֵי זָהָב וְחִבַּרְתָּ אֶת־הַיְרִיעֹת אִשָּׁה אֶל־אֲחֹתָהּ בַּקְּרָסִים וְהָיָה הַמִּשְׁכָּן אֶחָד: ז וְעָשִׂיתָ יְרִיעֹת עִזִּים לְאֹהֶל עַל־הַמִּשְׁכָּן עַשְׁתֵּי־עֶשְׂרֵה יְרִיעֹת תַּעֲשֶׂה אֹתָם: ח אֹרֶךְ ׀ הַיְרִיעָה הָאַחַת שְׁלֹשִׁים בָּאַמָּה וְרֹחַב אַרְבַּע בָּאַמָּה הַיְרִיעָה הָאֶחָת מִדָּה אַחַת לְעַשְׁתֵּי עֶשְׂרֵה יְרִיעֹת: ט וְחִבַּרְתָּ אֶת־חֲמֵשׁ הַיְרִיעֹת לְבָד וְאֶת־שֵׁשׁ הַיְרִיעֹת לְבָד וְכָפַלְתָּ אֶת־הַיְרִיעָה הַשִּׁשִּׁית אֶל־מוּל פְּנֵי הָאֹהֶל: י וְעָשִׂיתָ חֲמִשִּׁים לֻלָאֹת עַל שְׂפַת הַיְרִיעָה הָאֶחָת הַקִּיצֹנָה בַּחֹבָרֶת וַחֲמִשִּׁים לֻלָאֹת עַל שְׂפַת הַיְרִיעָה הַחֹבֶרֶת הַשֵּׁנִית: יא וְעָשִׂיתָ קַרְסֵי נְחֹשֶׁת חֲמִשִּׁים וְהֵבֵאתָ אֶת־הַקְּרָסִים בַּלֻּלָאֹת וְחִבַּרְתָּ אֶת־הָאֹהֶל וְהָיָה אֶחָד: יב וְסֶרַח הָעֹדֵף בִּירִיעֹת הָאֹהֶל חֲצִי הַיְרִיעָה הָעֹדֶפֶת תִּסְרַח עַל אֲחֹרֵי הַמִּשְׁכָּן: יג וְהָאַמָּה מִזֶּה וְהָאַמָּה מִזֶּה בָּעֹדֵף בְּאֹרֶךְ יְרִיעֹת הָאֹהֶל יִהְיֶה סָרוּחַ עַל־צִדֵּי הַמִּשְׁכָּן מִזֶּה וּמִזֶּה לְכַסֹּתוֹ: יד וְעָשִׂיתָ מִכְסֶה לָאֹהֶל עֹרֹת אֵילִם

rams' skins dyed red and a covering of *tahash* skins above. 15. And make the beams for the Dwelling Place from *shittim* wood, standing upright. 16. Ten cubits [shall be] the length of the beam and one cubit and a half the width of each beam. 17. Two tenons [shall be] in each beam, mortised one against the other; thus you shall make in all the beams of the Dwelling Place. 18. And you shall make these beams for the Dwelling Place twenty beams for the south side, on the right. 19. And you shall make forty silver sockets under the twenty beams, two sockets under the one beam for its two tenons and two sockets under another beam for its two tenons. 20. And for the second wall of the Dwelling Place, on the north side, twenty beams, 21. and their forty sockets of silver, two sockets under the one beam and two sockets under the one [other] beam. 22. And for the rear side of the Dwelling Place, to the west, you shall make six beams, 23. and you shall make two beams at the corners of the Dwelling Place in the rear. 24. They shall be joined together exactly below, and at the top border they shall be joined together in one ring; so shall it be for both of them; they shall be on both the corners. 25. So there shall be eight beams and their silver sockets, sixteen sockets; two sockets under one beam and two sockets under one [other] beam. 26. And make bars of *shittim* wood, five for the beams of the one wall of the Dwelling Place, 27. and five bars for the beams of the second wall of the Dwelling Place, and five bars for the beams of the wall of the Dwelling Place for the rear part, westward. 28. The middle bar, on the inside of the beams, shall pass through them from one end to the other. 29. You shall cover the beams with gold; you shall make their rings of gold as holders for the bars, and cover also the bars with gold. 30. And you shall put up the Dwelling Place according to the

מֵאָדָּמִים וּמִכְסֵה עֹרֹת תְּחָשִׁים מִלְמָעְלָה: פ
רביעי טו וְעָשִׂיתָ אֶת־הַקְּרָשִׁים לַמִּשְׁכָּן עֲצֵי
שִׁטִּים עֹמְדִים: טז עֶשֶׂר אַמּוֹת אֹרֶךְ הַקָּרֶשׁ
וְאַמָּה וַחֲצִי הָאַמָּה רֹחַב הַקֶּרֶשׁ הָאֶחָד: יז שְׁתֵּי
יָדוֹת לַקֶּרֶשׁ הָאֶחָד מְשֻׁלָּבֹת אִשָּׁה אֶל־אֲחֹתָהּ
כֵּן תַּעֲשֶׂה לְכֹל קַרְשֵׁי הַמִּשְׁכָּן: יח וְעָשִׂיתָ אֶת־
הַקְּרָשִׁים לַמִּשְׁכָּן עֶשְׂרִים קֶרֶשׁ לִפְאַת נֶגְבָּה
תֵימָנָה: יט וְאַרְבָּעִים אַדְנֵי־כֶסֶף תַּעֲשֶׂה תַּחַת
עֶשְׂרִים הַקָּרֶשׁ שְׁנֵי אֲדָנִים תַּחַת־הַקֶּרֶשׁ הָאֶחָד
לִשְׁתֵּי יְדֹתָיו וּשְׁנֵי אֲדָנִים תַּחַת־הַקֶּרֶשׁ הָאֶחָד
לִשְׁתֵּי יְדֹתָיו: כ וּלְצֶלַע הַמִּשְׁכָּן הַשֵּׁנִית לִפְאַת
צָפוֹן עֶשְׂרִים קָרֶשׁ: כא וְאַרְבָּעִים אַדְנֵיהֶם
כָּסֶף שְׁנֵי אֲדָנִים תַּחַת הַקֶּרֶשׁ הָאֶחָד וּשְׁנֵי
אֲדָנִים תַּחַת הַקֶּרֶשׁ הָאֶחָד: כב וּלְיַרְכְּתֵי
הַמִּשְׁכָּן יָמָּה תַּעֲשֶׂה שִׁשָּׁה קְרָשִׁים: כג וּשְׁנֵי
קְרָשִׁים תַּעֲשֶׂה לִמְקֻצְעֹת הַמִּשְׁכָּן בַּיַּרְכָתָיִם:
כד וְיִהְיוּ תֹאֲמִם מִלְּמַטָּה וְיַחְדָּו יִהְיוּ תַמִּים
עַל־רֹאשׁוֹ אֶל־הַטַּבַּעַת הָאֶחָת כֵּן יִהְיֶה
לִשְׁנֵיהֶם לִשְׁנֵי הַמִּקְצֹעֹת יִהְיוּ: כה וְהָיוּ שְׁמֹנָה
קְרָשִׁים וְאַדְנֵיהֶם כֶּסֶף שִׁשָּׁה עָשָׂר אֲדָנִים שְׁנֵי
אֲדָנִים תַּחַת הַקֶּרֶשׁ הָאֶחָד וּשְׁנֵי אֲדָנִים תַּחַת
הַקֶּרֶשׁ הָאֶחָד: כו וְעָשִׂיתָ בְרִיחִם עֲצֵי שִׁטִּים
חֲמִשָּׁה לְקַרְשֵׁי צֶלַע־הַמִּשְׁכָּן הָאֶחָד:
כז וַחֲמִשָּׁה בְרִיחִם לְקַרְשֵׁי צֶלַע־הַמִּשְׁכָּן
הַשֵּׁנִית וַחֲמִשָּׁה בְרִיחִם לְקַרְשֵׁי צֶלַע הַמִּשְׁכָּן
לַיַּרְכָתַיִם יָמָּה: כח וְהַבְּרִיחַ הַתִּיכֹן בְּתוֹךְ
הַקְּרָשִׁים מַבְרִחַ מִן־הַקָּצֶה אֶל־הַקָּצֶה:
כט וְאֶת־הַקְּרָשִׁים תְּצַפֶּה זָהָב וְאֶת־טַבְּעֹתֵיהֶם
תַּעֲשֶׂה זָהָב בָּתִּים לַבְּרִיחִם וְצִפִּיתָ אֶת־
הַבְּרִיחִם זָהָב: ל וַהֲקֵמֹתָ אֶת־הַמִּשְׁכָּן כְּמִשְׁפָּטוֹ

CHAPTER XXVI

14. . . . We are told [Shabbath 28a] that תַּחַשׁ is an animal that was available only to Moses and that it is

not certain whether it belonged to the species of בְּהֵמָה טְהוֹרָה [a kosher and domesticated animal of the cattle species] or whether it was חַיָּה טְהוֹרָה [undomesticated but kosher]. In any event, it was a kosher animal. . . .

manner that was shown you upon the mountain. 31. Furthermore, make a dividing curtain of sky-blue, purple and scarlet wool and out of byssus twisted into six-ply thread; it shall be made woven in a cherubim design. 32. And you shall hang it upon four pillars of *shittim* wood covered with gold, their hooks [being] of gold, on four silver sockets. 33. You shall place the dividing curtain underneath the clasps, and you shall bring there, inside the dividing curtain, the Ark of the Testimony; let the dividing curtain thus divide between the Holy Place and the Holy of Holies. 34. And you shall place the cover upon the Ark of the Testimony in the Holy of Holies. 35. And you shall place the table outside the dividing curtain and the menorah outside the table on the side of the Dwelling Place, toward the south, and you shall place the table on the north side. 36. And you shall make a protective curtain for the entrance to the tent, of sky-blue, purple and scarlet wool, and of byssus twisted into six-ply thread, embroidery

אֲשֶׁ֥ר הָרְאֵ֖יתָ בָּהָֽר׃ ס חמישי לא וְעָשִׂ֣יתָ פָרֹ֗כֶת תְּכֵ֧לֶת וְאַרְגָּמָ֛ן וְתוֹלַ֥עַת שָׁנִ֖י וְשֵׁ֣שׁ מׇשְׁזָ֑ר מַעֲשֵׂ֥ה חֹשֵׁ֛ב יַעֲשֶׂ֥ה אֹתָ֖הּ כְּרֻבִֽים׃ לב וְנָתַתָּ֣ה אֹתָ֗הּ עַל־אַרְבָּעָה֙ עַמּוּדֵ֣י שִׁטִּ֔ים מְצֻפִּ֣ים זָהָ֗ב וָוֵיהֶ֣ם זָהָ֔ב עַל־אַרְבָּעָ֖ה אַדְנֵי־כָֽסֶף׃ לג וְנָתַתָּ֣ה אֶת־הַפָּרֹ֘כֶת֮ תַּ֣חַת הַקְּרָסִים֒ וְהֵבֵאתָ֣ שָׁ֗מָּה מִבֵּ֣ית לַפָּרֹ֔כֶת אֵ֖ת אֲר֣וֹן הָעֵד֑וּת וְהִבְדִּילָ֤ה הַפָּרֹ֙כֶת֙ לָכֶ֔ם בֵּ֣ין הַקֹּ֔דֶשׁ וּבֵ֖ין קֹ֥דֶשׁ הַקֳּדָשִֽׁים׃ לד וְנָתַתָּ֙ אֶת־הַכַּפֹּ֔רֶת עַ֚ל אֲר֣וֹן הָעֵדֻ֔ת בְּקֹ֖דֶשׁ הַקֳּדָשִֽׁים׃ לה וְשַׂמְתָּ֤ אֶת־הַשֻּׁלְחָן֙ מִח֣וּץ לַפָּרֹ֔כֶת וְאֶת־הַמְּנֹרָה֙ נֹ֣כַח הַשֻּׁלְחָ֔ן עַ֛ל צֶ֥לַע הַמִּשְׁכָּ֖ן תֵּימָ֑נָה וְהַ֨שֻּׁלְחָ֔ן תִּתֵּ֖ן עַל־צֶ֥לַע צָפֽוֹן׃ לו וְעָשִׂ֤יתָ מָסָךְ֙ לְפֶ֣תַח הָאֹ֔הֶל תְּכֵ֧לֶת וְאַרְגָּמָ֛ן וְתוֹלַ֥עַת שָׁנִ֖י וְשֵׁ֣שׁ מׇשְׁזָ֑ר מַעֲשֵׂ֖ה רֹקֵֽם׃

36. . . . Unless we are mistaken, the beams of cedarwood that surround the Sanctuary symbolize the tribes of the Jewish nation, who have accepted the Law and its spiritual and material ideals of national life for realization in their midst. This is what Ezekiel refers to as the עֵץ יוֹסֵף [tree of Joseph] and the עֵץ יְהוּדָה [tree of Judah], etc. (Ezekiel 37:15 ff.)[8] These, too, are the trees that שְׁתוּלִים בְּבֵית ד׳ בְּחַצְרוֹת אֱלֹקֵינוּ יַפְרִיחוּ ["planted in the House of God, shall flourish in the forecourts of our God"] (Psalm 92:14), trees that, "planted in the House of God, bring their blossoms to fruition in the totality of life surrounding the House of God." These are the tribes of the people of whom their first leader sang, "Thou bringest them home, Thou plantest them in the mountain of Thine inheritance, the place prepared for Thy habitation which Thou, O *God*, hast secured, the Sanctuary, O *God*, which Thy hands have established" (Exodus 15:17). These are the "tents of Jacob, the dwelling places of Israel" that the alien seer viewed,

"like gardens by the river, like *ahol* trees that *God* has planted, like cedars by the waters; the water flows from *His* buckets and it is *His* seed that is at the abundant flow" (Numbers 24:5-7). This is the "vine that God transplanted to this place from Mitzrayim, having driven out the nations, and planted it," the tree whose shade covered whole mountains and whose branches were cedars of God (Psalm 80:9 and 11). These are trees planted by God of which we read in the pages of the Prophets and which will ultimately become perfected for the glorification of God; מַטַּע ד׳ לְהִתְפָּאֵר ["the planting of God, wherein He might glory"] (Isaiah 61:3).

. . . The beams have a dual significance. To the outside, they were seen as being held together by four bars on each side. On the inside, unseen from without, they were all joined into one united whole by one single bar (Verses 26-29). The tribes of the people of Jacob-Israel had four matriarchs [i.e., Jacob's four wives] and one patriarch [i.e., Jacob]. Each of the matriarchs is symbolized by one bar that unites the people from within through the bond of common ancestry. On the other hand, to the outside, the tribes are symbolically arranged in four groups according to physical, maternal descent. But even as they are all descended from one father, so the vocation of Jacob-Israel which they all inherited from that father, and the Jacob-Israel spirit which they inherited from him along with that voca-

[8]*Note to the English translation*: Ezekiel is directed to take a stick and to write upon it, "For Judah, and for the Children of Israel, his companions," and then to take another stick and write upon it, "For Joseph, the stick of Ephraim and of all the house of Israel his companions," and to join the two sticks together so that they "may become one in your hand." [G.H.]

work. 37. And make for the protective curtain five pillars of *shittim* wood and cover them with gold; their hooks [shall be] of gold, and cast for them five copper sockets.

XXVII

1. And you shall make the altar of *shittim* wood, five cubits long and five cubits wide; the altar shall be square, and three cubits high. 2. You shall make protrusions on its four corners; its elevated corners shall be made of one piece with it, and you shall cover it with copper. 3. And make its pots to clear away its ashes, its shovels and its sprinkling basins, its forks and its pans; you shall make all its utensils of copper. 4. And make for it a grating of copper net and make four copper rings on the net upon its four corners, 5. and place it under the ledge of the altar, downward, so that the net may extend downward until the middle of the altar. 6. And make poles for the altar, poles of *shittim* wood, and cover them with copper. 7. And its poles shall be placed into the rings, and the poles shall be on the two sides of the altar in carrying it. 8. Make it hollow, out of planks; as it was shown you upon the mountain, so shall they make [it]. 9. And make the forecourt of the Dwelling Place: for the south side on the right there shall be hangings for the forecourt of byssus twisted into six-ply thread, one hundred cubits long for one side. 10. And its pillars [shall be] twenty, its sockets twenty of copper; the hooks of the pillars and their bands [shall be] of silver. 11. Likewise for the length of the north side, hangings of one hundred (cubits) in length; its pillars [shall be] twenty and their sockets twenty, of copper; the hooks of the pillars and their bands [shall be] of silver. 12. The width of the forecourt on the west side shall be hangings of fifty cubits; their pillars [shall be] ten and their sockets

לז וְעָשִׂיתָ לַמָּסָךְ חֲמִשָּׁה עַמּוּדֵי שִׁטִּים וְצִפִּיתָ
אֹתָם זָהָב וָוֵיהֶם זָהָב וְיָצַקְתָּ לָהֶם חֲמִשָּׁה אַדְנֵי
נְחֹשֶׁת: ס ששי כז א וְעָשִׂיתָ אֶת־הַמִּזְבֵּחַ עֲצֵי
שִׁטִּים חָמֵשׁ אַמּוֹת אֹרֶךְ וְחָמֵשׁ אַמּוֹת רֹחַב
רָבוּעַ יִהְיֶה הַמִּזְבֵּחַ וְשָׁלֹשׁ אַמּוֹת קֹמָתוֹ:
ב וְעָשִׂיתָ קַרְנֹתָיו עַל אַרְבַּע פִּנֹּתָיו מִמֶּנּוּ
תִּהְיֶיןָ קַרְנֹתָיו וְצִפִּיתָ אֹתוֹ נְחֹשֶׁת: ג וְעָשִׂיתָ
סִּירֹתָיו לְדַשְּׁנוֹ וְיָעָיו וּמִזְרְקֹתָיו וּמִזְלְגֹתָיו
וּמַחְתֹּתָיו לְכָל־כֵּלָיו תַּעֲשֶׂה נְחֹשֶׁת: ד וְעָשִׂיתָ
לּוֹ מִכְבָּר מַעֲשֵׂה רֶשֶׁת נְחֹשֶׁת וְעָשִׂיתָ עַל־
הָרֶשֶׁת אַרְבַּע טַבְּעֹת נְחֹשֶׁת עַל אַרְבַּע קְצוֹתָיו:
ה וְנָתַתָּה אֹתָהּ תַּחַת כַּרְכֹּב הַמִּזְבֵּחַ מִלְּמָטָּה
וְהָיְתָה הָרֶשֶׁת עַד חֲצִי הַמִּזְבֵּחַ: ו וְעָשִׂיתָ בַדִּים
לַמִּזְבֵּחַ בַּדֵּי עֲצֵי שִׁטִּים וְצִפִּיתָ אֹתָם נְחֹשֶׁת:
ז וְהוּבָא אֶת־בַּדָּיו בַּטַּבָּעֹת וְהָיוּ הַבַּדִּים
עַל־שְׁתֵּי צַלְעֹת הַמִּזְבֵּחַ בִּשְׂאֵת אֹתוֹ: ח נְבוּב
לֻחֹת תַּעֲשֶׂה אֹתוֹ כַּאֲשֶׁר הֶרְאָה אֹתְךָ בָּהָר כֵּן
יַעֲשׂוּ: ס שביעי ט וְעָשִׂיתָ אֵת חֲצַר הַמִּשְׁכָּן
לִפְאַת נֶגֶב־תֵּימָנָה קְלָעִים לֶחָצֵר שֵׁשׁ מָשְׁזָר
מֵאָה בָאַמָּה אֹרֶךְ לַפֵּאָה הָאֶחָת: י וְעַמֻּדָיו
עֶשְׂרִים וְאַדְנֵיהֶם עֶשְׂרִים נְחֹשֶׁת וָוֵי הָעַמֻּדִים
וַחֲשֻׁקֵיהֶם כָּסֶף: יא וְכֵן לִפְאַת צָפוֹן בָּאֹרֶךְ
קְלָעִים מֵאָה אֹרֶךְ וְעַמֻּדָו (ועמדיו קרי) עֶשְׂרִים
וְאַדְנֵיהֶם עֶשְׂרִים נְחֹשֶׁת וָוֵי הָעַמֻּדִים
וַחֲשֻׁקֵיהֶם כָּסֶף: יב וְרֹחַב הֶחָצֵר לִפְאַת־יָם
קְלָעִים חֲמִשִּׁים אַמָּה עַמֻּדֵיהֶם עֲשָׂרָה וְאַדְנֵיהֶם

tion, form "the middle bar, on the inside of the beams," that inner bar which holds all the tribes, in their various individual characteristics, together as שִׁבְטֵי ד׳ [the tribes of *God*] in one wondrous united whole. One spirit and one power, one aspiration and one strength lives and operates within them all and holds them united as brothers forever around the Sanctuary of God, which belongs to them all.

° ° °

עֲשָׂרָה: יג וְרֹחַב הֶחָצֵר לִפְאַת קֵדְמָה מִזְרָחָה
חֲמִשִּׁים אַמָּה: יד וַחֲמֵשׁ עֶשְׂרֵה אַמָּה קְלָעִים
לַכָּתֵף עַמֻּדֵיהֶם שְׁלֹשָׁה וְאַדְנֵיהֶם שְׁלֹשָׁה:
טו וְלַכָּתֵף הַשֵּׁנִית חֲמֵשׁ עֶשְׂרֵה קְלָעִים
עַמֻּדֵיהֶם שְׁלֹשָׁה וְאַדְנֵיהֶם שְׁלֹשָׁה: טז וּלְשַׁעַר
הֶחָצֵר מָסָךְ ׀ עֶשְׂרִים אַמָּה תְּכֵלֶת וְאַרְגָּמָן
וְתוֹלַעַת שָׁנִי וְשֵׁשׁ מָשְׁזָר מַעֲשֵׂה רֹקֵם עַמֻּדֵיהֶם
אַרְבָּעָה וְאַדְנֵיהֶם אַרְבָּעָה: מפטיר יז כָּל־עַמּוּדֵי
הֶחָצֵר סָבִיב מְחֻשָּׁקִים כֶּסֶף וָוֵיהֶם כָּסֶף
וְאַדְנֵיהֶם נְחֹשֶׁת: יח אֹרֶךְ הֶחָצֵר מֵאָה בָאַמָּה
וְרֹחַב ׀ חֲמִשִּׁים בַּחֲמִשִּׁים וְקֹמָה חָמֵשׁ אַמּוֹת
שֵׁשׁ מָשְׁזָר וְאַדְנֵיהֶם נְחֹשֶׁת: יט לְכֹל כְּלֵי
הַמִּשְׁכָּן בְּכֹל עֲבֹדָתוֹ וְכָל־יְתֵדֹתָיו וְכָל־יִתְדֹת
הֶחָצֵר נְחֹשֶׁת: ס

ten. 13. The width of the forecourt at the front to the east shall be fifty cubits. 14. The hangings for the one side shall be fifteen cubits; their pillars [shall be] three and their sockets three. 15. And on the other side there shall be fifteen hangings; their pillars [shall be] three and their sockets three. 16. At the gate of the forecourt there shall be a protective curtain of twenty cubits, of sky-blue, purple and scarlet wool and of byssus twisted into six-ply thread, embroidery work; their pillars [shall be] four and their sockets four. 17. All the pillars of the forecourt [shall be] banded with silver all around; their hooks [shall be] of silver but their sockets [shall be] of copper. 18. The length of the forecourt: one hundred cubits; the free width: fifty by fifty; the height: five cubits, byssus twisted into six-ply thread; and their sockets [shall be] of copper. 19. All the utensils of the Dwelling Place for all its services, and its stakes and the stakes of the forecourt shall be of copper.

CHAPTER XXVII

18. . . . חָצֵר *[The Forecourt]*

Let us picture for ourselves the forecourt that surrounds the Sanctuary. It was formed of white hangings of byssus, [a fine linen] woven with six-ply thread. These hangings were hung from pillars that stood on copper sockets; they were encircled by silver bands and held the hangings by silver hooks. This arrangement is closely related to the symbolism of the forecourt and the altar from which the forecourt derives its significance. Like the altar, so, too, the surroundings amidst which it is set announce to us that we are standing in a forecourt of purification. The basic impression we receive is one of whiteness, particularly white byssus, a fine white linen. This conveys to us the concept of טָהֳרָה, purity, and primarily as טָהֳרָה in the vegetative aspects of human nature: man's dietary habits and his sexual behavior. This is the very first stage of purity to which we are to aspire. The character of this aspiration is purely negative; we are to keep away from everything unholy, from anything that would spoil human nature for its sacred vocation. This is the prerequisite for any progress in a positive direction. This physical representation of the purity required of us bears—both in the strength of the threads with which it is woven and by virtue of its name, שֵׁשׁ—the number six, which symbolizes creature life, the material world. The great task of self-discipline to which the forecourt of the Sanctuary calls us, as it were, is not superhuman; it does not call for an elevation beyond the capacities of the human nature with which we were created. It is the Creator of that very same human nature Who now summons us there. He does not require of us anything for which He did not give us natural proclivities and capacities. In fact, it is precisely for this purity that He created us; only through such purity can we truly demonstrate the godly nature of our being with which He created us. The basic concept of humanity is moral freedom, and the first expression of this is purity.

The pillars of the forecourt stand on copper sockets, but they are encircled by silver bands and topped by silver hooks. The walls of the Sanctuary stand on silver sockets but they are topped with gold. From copper to silver to gold: this is the order of progress from crude nature, by a process of purification, to immutable, genuine perfection. The level to which the forecourt symbolically aspires is the basis upon which the whole Sanctuary stands and which offers us the noblest degree of perfection. The manner in which the metals to be used were specified and allocated indicates the step-by-step progression symbolized by the chambers of the Sanctuary.

° ° °

The Haftarah for this Sidra may be found on page 857.

20. And you shall command the sons of Yisrael that they take for you pure olive oil, pressed, for lighting, to make light spring up continually: 21. in the Tent of Appointed Meeting, outside the dividing curtain that is in front of the Testimony, shall Aharon and his sons tend it before *God* from evening to morning; [it shall be] an everlasting statute for their generations: from the sons of Yisrael.

XXVIII 1. And furthermore, have your brother Aharon and his sons with him come closer to you from among the sons of Yisrael so that he may serve Me as a priest: Aharon, Nadab and Abihu, Eleazar and Ithamar, as the sons of Aharon. 2. And make holy garments for your brother Aharon, for honor and distinction. 3. And you speak to all the wise men whose hearts I have filled with the spirit of wisdom, that they make Aharon's garments to sanctify him, that he may serve Me as a priest. 4. These are the

כ וְאַתָּה תְּצַוֶּה | אֶת־בְּנֵי יִשְׂרָאֵל וְיִקְחוּ אֵלֶיךָ שֶׁמֶן זַיִת זָךְ כָּתִית לַמָּאוֹר לְהַעֲלֹת נֵר תָּמִיד: כא בְּאֹהֶל מוֹעֵד מִחוּץ לַפָּרֹכֶת אֲשֶׁר עַל־הָעֵדֻת יַעֲרֹךְ אֹתוֹ אַהֲרֹן וּבָנָיו מֵעֶרֶב עַד־בֹּקֶר לִפְנֵי יְהֹוָה חֻקַּת עוֹלָם לְדֹרֹתָם מֵאֵת בְּנֵי יִשְׂרָאֵל: ס כח א וְאַתָּה הַקְרֵב אֵלֶיךָ אֶת־אַהֲרֹן אָחִיךָ וְאֶת־בָּנָיו אִתּוֹ מִתּוֹךְ בְּנֵי יִשְׂרָאֵל לְכַהֲנוֹ־לִי אַהֲרֹן נָדָב וַאֲבִיהוּא אֶלְעָזָר וְאִיתָמָר בְּנֵי אַהֲרֹן: ב וְעָשִׂיתָ בִגְדֵי־קֹדֶשׁ לְאַהֲרֹן אָחִיךָ לְכָבוֹד וּלְתִפְאָרֶת: ג וְאַתָּה תְּדַבֵּר אֶל־כָּל־חַכְמֵי־לֵב אֲשֶׁר מִלֵּאתִיו רוּחַ חָכְמָה וְעָשׂוּ אֶת־בִּגְדֵי אַהֲרֹן לְקַדְּשׁוֹ לְכַהֲנוֹ־לִי: ד וְאֵלֶּה

20. . . . *And you shall command the sons of Yisrael.* You [Moses], as the transmitter of the Law, the study of which, as an obligation for all time to come, is to be symbolized by the care of this light: תְּצַוֶּה, put it before them as their particular duty. The Gemarah notes that the term תְּצַוֶּה is used wherever the intention is to place special emphasis on a commandment that is effective immediately and for all generations to come, particularly when it comes to sacrificing material values for spiritual and ideal purposes whose profit is not immediately apparent. . . .

to make light spring up. This term for kindling lights is used only in connection with the care of the menorah. It precisely describes the task of the keepers of the flame; i.e., to hold the kindling flame against the wick to be kindled until the wick "continues burning on its own." The task of the Torah teacher is to render his services unnecessary. His task is not to keep the "laity" forever dependent upon him. This is meant as an admonition to both teachers and students that they should be patient and persevering.

21. . . . *outside the dividing curtain that is in front of the Testimony.* This admonition is reiterated in

Leviticus 24:3: "Outside the dividing curtain of the Testimony." Even as the human mind turns toward the תּוֹרָה and seeks enlightenment from the תּוֹרָה, it must be kept aware at all times that man stands "outside the תּוֹרָה": The Law was given to man; it is not a product of the human spirit. Man is to draw, and to increase, his enlightenment from and through the Law, but he must never introduce his own light into the area of the Law to "amend" or "reform" it. He must always be aware of the cherubim that descend to screen off the Law and to protect it. Should the need arise, these cherubim will guard this Law against any intellectual trend which, misjudging its proper place, would deny the inviolability of the Law of God, and against arrogant men who, instead of sitting as disciples at the feet of God's Law, would presume to act as its masters.

CHAPTER XXVIII

1. . . . *come closer to you.* Aaron attains his dignity by virtue of the fact that he has been singled out from the rest of the nation to be placed closer to you [Moses], for your work on behalf of the nation; he has been assigned a role in helping carry out your mission.

garments that they shall make: a breastplate, an *ephod* and a robe, and a tunic of checker work, a turban and a sash; they shall make them as holy garments for your brother Aharon and for his sons so that he may serve Me as a priest. 5. They shall take the gold, the sky-blue, the purple and the scarlet wool and the byssus, 6. and they shall make the *ephod* of gold, sky-blue and purple wool, scarlet wool and byssus twisted into six-ply thread, weaver's work. 7. It shall have attached two connected shoulder pieces at both its corners and be entirely connected. 8. The band for its belt shall be woven together with it: gold, sky-blue, purple wool, scarlet wool and byssus twisted into six-ply thread. 9. Then take two *shoham* stones and engrave upon them the names of the sons of Yisrael. 10. Six of their names on the one stone and the names of the remaining six on the second stone, according to their birth. 11. With the work of an engraver of gems, like the engravings of a signet, shall you engrave the two stones according to the names of the sons of Yisrael; you shall make them enclosed in gold settings. 12. And you shall put the two stones upon the shoulder pieces of the *ephod* as stones of remembrance for the sons of Yisrael; Aharon shall bear their names before *God* upon his two shoulders as a remembrance. 13. Also make settings of gold, 14. and two chains of pure gold, as chains shall you make them, attached at the edges after the manner of cables, and you shall place the cable chains upon the settings. 15. And make a breastplate of judgment, of woven material; you shall make it like the work of the *ephod*; of gold, sky-blue and purple wool, scarlet wool, and byssus twisted into six-ply thread shall you make it. 16. Let it be foursquare [and] double; one span shall be its length and one span its width. 17. And you shall set into it settings of stones, four rows of stones. One row: *odem*, *pitdah* and *barekketh*; thus shall the one row be. 18. The second row: *nofekh*, *sapir* and *yahalom*. 19. The third row: *leshem*, *shevo* and *ahlamah*. 20. And the fourth row: *tarshish*, *shoham* and *yashpheh*; they shall be enclosed in gold in their settings. 21. The stones shall be according

הַבְּגָדִ֜ים אֲשֶׁ֣ר יַעֲשׂ֗וּ חֹ֤שֶׁן וְאֵפוֹד֙ וּמְעִ֔יל
וּכְתֹ֥נֶת תַּשְׁבֵּ֖ץ מִצְנֶ֣פֶת וְאַבְנֵ֑ט וְעָשׂ֨וּ בִגְדֵי־
קֹ֜דֶשׁ לְאַהֲרֹ֥ן אָחִ֛יךָ וּלְבָנָ֖יו לְכַהֲנוֹ־לִֽי׃ ה וְהֵם֙
יִקְח֣וּ אֶת־הַזָּהָ֔ב וְאֶת־הַתְּכֵ֖לֶת וְאֶת־הָֽאַרְגָּמָ֑ן
וְאֶת־תּוֹלַ֥עַת הַשָּׁנִ֖י וְאֶת־הַשֵּֽׁשׁ׃ פ ו וְעָשׂ֖וּ אֶת־
הָאֵפֹ֑ד זָהָ֡ב תְּכֵ֨לֶת וְאַרְגָּמָ֜ן תּוֹלַ֧עַת שָׁנִ֛י וְשֵׁ֥שׁ
מָשְׁזָ֖ר מַעֲשֵׂ֥ה חֹשֵֽׁב׃ ז שְׁתֵּ֧י כְתֵפֹ֣ת חֹֽבְרֹ֗ת
יִהְיֶה־לּ֛וֹ אֶל־שְׁנֵ֥י קְצוֹתָ֖יו וְחֻבָּֽר׃ ח וְחֵ֤שֶׁב
אֲפֻדָּתוֹ֙ אֲשֶׁ֣ר עָלָ֔יו כְּמַעֲשֵׂ֖הוּ מִמֶּ֣נּוּ יִהְיֶ֑ה זָהָ֗ב
תְּכֵ֧לֶת וְאַרְגָּמָ֛ן וְתוֹלַ֥עַת שָׁנִ֖י וְשֵׁ֥שׁ מָשְׁזָֽר׃
ט וְלָ֣קַחְתָּ֔ אֶת־שְׁתֵּ֖י אַבְנֵי־שֹׁ֑הַם וּפִתַּחְתָּ֣
עֲלֵיהֶ֔ם שְׁמ֖וֹת בְּנֵ֥י יִשְׂרָאֵֽל׃ י שִׁשָּׁה֙ מִשְּׁמֹתָ֔ם
עַ֖ל הָאֶ֣בֶן הָאֶחָ֑ת וְאֶת־שְׁמ֞וֹת הַשִּׁשָּׁ֧ה הַנּוֹתָרִ֛ים
עַל־הָאֶ֥בֶן הַשֵּׁנִ֖ית כְּתוֹלְדֹתָֽם׃ יא מַעֲשֵׂ֣ה חָרַשׁ֮
אֶבֶן֒ פִּתּוּחֵ֣י חֹתָ֗ם תְּפַתַּח֙ אֶת־שְׁתֵּ֣י הָאֲבָנִ֔ים
עַל־שְׁמֹ֖ת בְּנֵ֣י יִשְׂרָאֵ֑ל מֻסַבֹּ֛ת מִשְׁבְּצ֥וֹת זָהָ֖ב
תַּעֲשֶׂ֥ה אֹתָֽם׃ יב וְשַׂמְתָּ֞ אֶת־שְׁתֵּ֣י הָאֲבָנִ֗ים עַ֚ל
כִּתְפֹ֣ת הָאֵפֹ֔ד אַבְנֵ֥י זִכָּרֹ֖ן לִבְנֵ֣י יִשְׂרָאֵ֑ל וְנָשָׂא֩
אַהֲרֹ֨ן אֶת־שְׁמוֹתָ֜ם לִפְנֵ֧י יְהוָ֛ה עַל־שְׁתֵּ֥י כְתֵפָ֖יו
לְזִכָּרֹֽן׃ ס שני יג וְעָשִׂ֥יתָ מִשְׁבְּצֹ֖ת זָהָֽב׃ יד וּשְׁתֵּ֤י
שַׁרְשְׁרֹת֙ זָהָ֣ב טָה֔וֹר מִגְבָּלֹ֛ת תַּעֲשֶׂ֥ה אֹתָ֖ם
מַעֲשֵׂ֣ה עֲבֹ֑ת וְנָתַתָּ֛ה אֶת־שַׁרְשְׁרֹ֥ת הָעֲבֹתֹ֖ת עַל־
הַמִּשְׁבְּצֹֽת׃ ס טו וְעָשִׂ֜יתָ חֹ֤שֶׁן מִשְׁפָּט֙ מַעֲשֵׂ֣ה
חֹשֵׁ֔ב כְּמַעֲשֵׂ֥ה אֵפֹ֖ד תַּעֲשֶׂ֑נּוּ זָ֠הָב תְּכֵ֨לֶת וְאַרְגָּמָ֜ן
וְתוֹלַ֧עַת שָׁנִ֛י וְשֵׁ֥שׁ מָשְׁזָ֖ר תַּעֲשֶׂ֥ה אֹתֽוֹ׃
טז רָב֛וּעַ יִהְיֶ֖ה כָּפ֑וּל זֶ֥רֶת אָרְכּ֖וֹ וְזֶ֥רֶת רָחְבּֽוֹ׃
יז וּמִלֵּאתָ֥ בוֹ֙ מִלֻּ֣אַת אֶ֔בֶן אַרְבָּעָ֖ה טוּרִ֣ים אָ֑בֶן
ט֗וּר אֹ֤דֶם פִּטְדָה֙ וּבָרֶ֔קֶת הַטּ֖וּר הָאֶחָֽד׃
יח וְהַטּ֖וּר הַשֵּׁנִ֑י נֹ֥פֶךְ סַפִּ֖יר וְיָהֲלֹֽם׃ יט וְהַטּ֖וּר
הַשְּׁלִישִׁ֑י לֶ֥שֶׁם שְׁב֖וֹ וְאַחְלָֽמָה׃ כ וְהַטּוּר֙
הָֽרְבִיעִ֔י תַּרְשִׁ֥ישׁ וְשֹׁ֖הַם וְיָשְׁפֵ֑ה מְשֻׁבָּצִ֥ים זָהָ֛ב
יִהְי֖וּ בְּמִלּוּאֹתָֽם׃ כא וְהָאֲבָנִ֡ים תִּהְיֶ֜יןָ עַל־שְׁמֹ֤ת

to the names of the sons of Yisrael, twelve, according to their names; like the engraving of a signet, every one according to his name shall they be for twelve tribes. 22. And you shall make upon the breastplate cable-like chains at the edges, of pure gold. 23. You shall make for the breastplate two golden rings and you shall place the two rings on the two corners of the breastplate, 24. and you shall place the two golden cables on the two rings, at the corners of the breastplate. 25. And you shall place the two ends of the two cables upon the two settings and place these upon the shoulder pieces of the *ephod,* on its front part. 26. You shall make two golden rings and place them on the two corners of the breastplate on its lower edge, which is turned toward the side of the *ephod,* inward. 27. You shall also make two golden rings and place them on the two shoulder pieces of the *ephod,* underneath, on its front part, close to its coupling above the band of the *ephod,* 28. and they shall bind the breastplate by its rings to the rings of the *ephod* with a thread of sky-blue, so that it may be upon the band of the *ephod* and the breastplate will not move from the *ephod.* 29. Thus shall Aharon bear the names of the sons of Yisrael with the breastplate of judgment over his heart when he goes into the Sanctuary, as a remembrance before *God* at all times. 30. You shall place the *Urim* and *Thummim* into the breastplate of judgment so that they will be over Aharon's heart when he comes before *God.* Let Aharon bear the judgment of the sons of Yisrael over his heart before *God* at all times. 31. And make the robe of the *ephod* all of sky-blue wool. 32. The opening at its top shall be turned inward; the opening shall have a woven border all around it. It shall be like the opening of a coat of mail so that it shall not be torn. 33. And you shall make upon its bottom hems pomegranates of sky-blue, purple and scarlet wool, round about its bottom hems, and golden bells between them round about. 34. A golden bell and a pomegranate, a golden bell and a pomegranate, upon the bottom hems of the robe round about. 35. Aharon shall wear it when he performs the service; its sound shall be

בְּנֵי־יִשְׂרָאֵל שְׁתֵּים עֶשְׂרֵה עַל־שְׁמֹתָם פִּתּוּחֵי
חוֹתָם אִישׁ עַל־שְׁמוֹ תִּהְיֶיןָ לִשְׁנֵי עָשָׂר שָׁבֶט:
כב וְעָשִׂיתָ עַל־הַחֹשֶׁן שַׁרְשֹׁת גַּבְלֻת מַעֲשֵׂה
עֲבֹת זָהָב טָהוֹר: כג וְעָשִׂיתָ עַל־הַחֹשֶׁן שְׁתֵּי
טַבְּעוֹת זָהָב וְנָתַתָּ אֶת־שְׁתֵּי הַטַּבָּעוֹת עַל־שְׁנֵי
קְצוֹת הַחֹשֶׁן: כד וְנָתַתָּה אֶת־שְׁתֵּי עֲבֹתֹת הַזָּהָב
עַל־שְׁתֵּי הַטַּבָּעֹת אֶל־קְצוֹת הַחֹשֶׁן: כה וְאֵת
שְׁתֵּי קְצוֹת שְׁתֵּי הָעֲבֹתֹת תִּתֵּן עַל־שְׁתֵּי
הַמִּשְׁבְּצוֹת וְנָתַתָּה עַל־כִּתְפוֹת הָאֵפֹד אֶל־מוּל
פָּנָיו: כו וְעָשִׂיתָ שְׁתֵּי טַבְּעוֹת זָהָב וְשַׂמְתָּ אֹתָם
עַל־שְׁנֵי קְצוֹת הַחֹשֶׁן עַל־שְׂפָתוֹ אֲשֶׁר אֶל־עֵבֶר
הָאֵפוֹד בָּיְתָה: כז וְעָשִׂיתָ שְׁתֵּי טַבְּעוֹת זָהָב
וְנָתַתָּה אֹתָם עַל־שְׁתֵּי כִתְפוֹת הָאֵפוֹד מִלְּמַטָּה
מִמּוּל פָּנָיו לְעֻמַּת מַחְבַּרְתּוֹ מִמַּעַל לְחֵשֶׁב
הָאֵפוֹד: כח וְיִרְכְּסוּ אֶת־הַחֹשֶׁן מִטַּבְּעֹתָו
(מטבעתיו קרי) אֶל־טַבְּעֹת הָאֵפוֹד בִּפְתִיל תְּכֵלֶת
לִהְיוֹת עַל־חֵשֶׁב הָאֵפוֹד וְלֹא־יִזַּח הַחֹשֶׁן מֵעַל
הָאֵפוֹד: כט וְנָשָׂא אַהֲרֹן אֶת־שְׁמוֹת בְּנֵי־
יִשְׂרָאֵל בְּחֹשֶׁן הַמִּשְׁפָּט עַל־לִבּוֹ בְּבֹאוֹ אֶל־
הַקֹּדֶשׁ לְזִכָּרֹן לִפְנֵי־יְהוָה תָּמִיד: ל וְנָתַתָּ אֶל־
חֹשֶׁן הַמִּשְׁפָּט אֶת־הָאוּרִים וְאֶת־הַתֻּמִּים וְהָיוּ
עַל־לֵב אַהֲרֹן בְּבֹאוֹ לִפְנֵי יְהוָה וְנָשָׂא אַהֲרֹן
אֶת־מִשְׁפַּט בְּנֵי־יִשְׂרָאֵל עַל־לִבּוֹ לִפְנֵי יְהוָה
תָּמִיד: ס שלישי לא וְעָשִׂיתָ אֶת־מְעִיל הָאֵפוֹד
כְּלִיל תְּכֵלֶת: לב וְהָיָה פִי־רֹאשׁוֹ בְּתוֹכוֹ שָׂפָה
יִהְיֶה לְפִיו סָבִיב מַעֲשֵׂה אֹרֵג כְּפִי תַחְרָא יִהְיֶה־
לּוֹ לֹא יִקָּרֵעַ: לג וְעָשִׂיתָ עַל־שׁוּלָיו רִמֹּנֵי תְּכֵלֶת
וְאַרְגָּמָן וְתוֹלַעַת שָׁנִי עַל־שׁוּלָיו סָבִיב וּפַעֲמֹנֵי
זָהָב בְּתוֹכָם סָבִיב: לד פַּעֲמֹן זָהָב וְרִמּוֹן פַּעֲמֹן
זָהָב וְרִמּוֹן עַל־שׁוּלֵי הַמְּעִיל סָבִיב: לה וְהָיָה

עַל־אַהֲרֹן לְשָׁרֵת וְנִשְׁמַע קוֹלוֹ בְּבֹאוֹ אֶל־
הַקֹּדֶשׁ לִפְנֵי יְהוָה וּבְצֵאתוֹ וְלֹא יָמוּת׃ ס
לו וְעָשִׂיתָ צִּיץ זָהָב טָהוֹר וּפִתַּחְתָּ עָלָיו פִּתּוּחֵי
חֹתָם קֹדֶשׁ לַיהוָה׃ לז וְשַׂמְתָּ אֹתוֹ עַל־פְּתִיל
תְּכֵלֶת וְהָיָה עַל־הַמִּצְנָפֶת אֶל־מוּל פְּנֵי־
הַמִּצְנֶפֶת יִהְיֶה׃ לח וְהָיָה עַל־מֵצַח אַהֲרֹן וְנָשָׂא
אַהֲרֹן אֶת־עֲוֺן הַקֳּדָשִׁים אֲשֶׁר יַקְדִּישׁוּ בְּנֵי
יִשְׂרָאֵל לְכָל־מַתְּנֹת קָדְשֵׁיהֶם וְהָיָה עַל־מִצְחוֹ
תָּמִיד לְרָצוֹן לָהֶם לִפְנֵי יְהוָה׃ לט וְשִׁבַּצְתָּ
הַכְּתֹנֶת שֵׁשׁ וְעָשִׂיתָ מִצְנֶפֶת שֵׁשׁ וְאַבְנֵט תַּעֲשֶׂה
מַעֲשֵׂה רֹקֵם׃ מ וְלִבְנֵי אַהֲרֹן תַּעֲשֶׂה כֻתֳּנֹת
וְעָשִׂיתָ לָהֶם אַבְנֵטִים וּמִגְבָּעוֹת תַּעֲשֶׂה לָהֶם
לְכָבוֹד וּלְתִפְאָרֶת׃ מא וְהִלְבַּשְׁתָּ אֹתָם אֶת־
אַהֲרֹן אָחִיךָ וְאֶת־בָּנָיו אִתּוֹ וּמָשַׁחְתָּ אֹתָם
וּמִלֵּאתָ אֶת־יָדָם וְקִדַּשְׁתָּ אֹתָם וְכִהֲנוּ־לִי׃
מב וַעֲשֵׂה לָהֶם מִכְנְסֵי־בָד לְכַסּוֹת בְּשַׂר עֶרְוָה
מִמָּתְנַיִם וְעַד־יְרֵכַיִם יִהְיוּ׃ מג וְהָיוּ עַל־אַהֲרֹן

heard when he goes into the Sanctuary before *God* and when he goes out, so that he will not die. 36. And also make a showplate of pure gold and engrave upon it like the engraving of a signet: "The Sanctuary is *God*'s." 37. And you shall fasten it upon a thread of sky-blue wool and it shall go over the turban, but it shall be upon the front side of the turban. 38. It shall be upon Aharon's forehead, and thus Aharon shall lift away the crookedness of the holy things that the sons of Yisrael sanctify to the Sanctuary, with reference to all their holy gifts. It shall be upon his forehead at all times for them to express their will before the Presence of *God*. 39. You shall make the tunic of checker work, of byssus, and you shall make a turban of byssus; but the sash you shall make of embroidery work. 40. For Aharon's sons, make tunics and sashes, and make them high turbans for honor and distinction. 41. With these you shall clothe your brother Aharon and his sons along with him; anoint them and invest them with full authority and sanctify them so that they may serve Me as priests. 42. Make for them also linen breeches to cover [their] nakedness; they shall reach from the loins down to the thighs. 43. They shall cover Aharon and his sons

42 and 43. בִּגְדֵי כְּהוּנָּה *[The Priestly Garments]*

. . . The significance of the priestly garments should be evident from the instructions set forth in the concluding verses of this chapter. There, we are told that the character of priesthood, and thus also the validity of the sacrificial service, is so dependent upon the priestly garments and upon every prescribed detail connected with them—we are told that these instructions shall be "a statute forever"—that without these garments the priest is regarded as a "stranger" and the dictum that "the stranger that comes near (the Sanctuary) shall die" (Numbers 18:7) will apply to him also. (See Maimonides, *Mishne Torah, Hilkhoth K'lei HaMikdash* 10:4).

The fact that the priestly garments must be supplied and owned by the nation makes it clear to us why only a *kohen* dressed in these garments can be regarded as a priest at all. Only in this attire does he come forward as the servant of the nation for the Sanctuary of the Law. Only in this manner does the ritual he performs become that service which the nation was commanded to render to the Sanctuary of the Law of God. Only thus can the ideas to be expressed by the ritual attain the character of a duty commanded by the Law God gave to the nation. Only thus will the ritual act become a symbol of obedience put into practice by devotion to the will of God as it has been revealed in the Law, an adequate compliance with the requirements upon whose fulfillment God's nearness depends, a way of coming closer to God oneself and bringing others nearer to Him also.

Without these garments [executed in accordance with the Law] the *kohen* is merely an ordinary individual and his ritual act takes on the character of personal predilection, thus producing the very reverse of the attitude that the Sanctuary is basically intended to foster. Let us point out here quite candidly that without these garments, the individual personality of the officiating priest stands "naked" and, with all the failings and shortcomings that can afflict even the best among us, he may all too easily present a most defective version of the ideal which the sacrifices should symbolize when they enter into the Tent of Appointed Meeting, or when they go up to the altar to serve in the Sanctuary, so they will not bear iniquity and die. It shall be a statute forever for him and for his descendants after him.

XXIX

1. And this is what you shall do for them to sanctify them, to serve Me as priests: take a young bull and two rams, without blemish. 2. And matzoth bread and matzoth cakes kneaded with oil, and thin matzoth brushed with oil; out of fine wheat flour shall you

וְעַל־בָּנָיו בְּבֹאָם ׀ אֶל־אֹהֶל מוֹעֵד אוֹ בְגִשְׁתָּם
אֶל־הַמִּזְבֵּחַ לְשָׁרֵת בַּקֹּדֶשׁ וְלֹא־יִשְׂאוּ עָוֺן וָמֵתוּ
חֻקַּת עוֹלָם לוֹ וּלְזַרְעוֹ אַחֲרָיו׃ ס רביעי
כט א וְזֶה הַדָּבָר אֲשֶׁר תַּעֲשֶׂה לָהֶם לְקַדֵּשׁ
אֹתָם לְכַהֵן לִי לְקַח פַּר אֶחָד בֶּן־בָּקָר וְאֵילִם
שְׁנַיִם תְּמִימִם׃ ב וְלֶחֶם מַצּוֹת וְחַלֹּת מַצֹּת
בְּלוּלֹת בַּשֶּׁמֶן וּרְקִיקֵי מַצּוֹת מְשֻׁחִים בַּשָּׁמֶן

as being in accordance with the Law of God. In this vein Hosea castigates (4:8) the unworthiness of the priests in his day: "They eat the sin offering of My people and lift up the soul of My people to their own sin," or "by eating the sin offering they present their own sinful lives as an example for My people to follow."

But when he is clothed in his priestly garments, the priest presents himself not in terms of the personality he actually has as an individual but in terms of the character he should have in accordance with the requirements of the Law of God. By the very act of donning the priestly garments for his service in the Sanctuary he then makes both himself and those about him aware that as a person he is still inadequate when it comes to complying with the demands symbolized by the Sanctuary.

... Viewed in objective terms, too, the origins of clothing have a place of great importance in the moral education of mankind; consequently, clothing has acquired great moral significance in its own right. Clothing was first given to man by the Father of mankind when He sent His children out from Paradise into the training school of toil and renunciation, with all its attendant dangers that man might stray and thus descend to the level of the beast. Clothing *per se* is a reminder of man's moral calling; it is the first and most conspicuous feature that characterizes a creature as a human being.

° ° °

The character and form of the Urim and Thummim have remained a mystery. However, the etymology of these terms implies "enlightenment" and "perfection," respectively; אוֹר in the form of אור denotes not merely light but also the warming and, in fact, overwhelmingly consuming power of fire. תּוּמִּים is the plural form of תּוֹם, "perfection." The plural form אוּרִים וְתוּמִּים implies a multiplicity of objects that have the property or the effect of purifying and quickening the spirit and promoting moral perfection. The only objects we know that answer to this description are the words of God, the תּוֹרוֹת [teachings] and מִצְוֹת [commandments] which, emanating as they do from the Source of supreme knowledge and perfection, are intended to wield, and are capable of wielding, the greatest possible spiritual and moral influence upon us. The Torah, which is kept in the Ark of the Covenant, becomes אוּרִים and תּוּמִּים within the breast of the individual Jew and within the heart of the Jewish nation. The nation's representative, the high priest, bears the Urim and Thumim "over his heart" as a treasure to be preserved, and the knowledge of what is true and good, to be derived from the Word of God, becomes a מִשְׁפַּט בְּנֵי יִשְׂרָאֵל ["judgment of the Sons of Yisrael"]; ... that which is appropriate to Israel, consistent with its calling, that which it should expect, and to which it should aspire, in keeping with its vocation.

Inasmuch as this מִשְׁפַּט בְּנֵי יִשְׂרָאֵל can be ascertained only through the Urim and Thummim, this means that Israel's aims and aspirations must be shaped only under the influence of the Urim and Thummim; i.e., Israel may have no other desires or aspirations than those that accord with the standard of what is "true and good," as set forth in the Word of God. Thus "Let Aharon bear the judgment of the sons of Yisrael over his heart before *God* at all times" [Verse 30] would simply mean: Let Aaron bear Israel's concerns, its wishes and its aspirations over his heart before God at all times.

° ° °

If we visualize the progressive stages of moral perfection symbolized by the בִּגְדֵי כְהוּנָּה, they appear to be three in number. The breeches and the tunic, symbolizing freedom from all moral and social wrong, correspond to the ideal of צֶדֶק, justice which is basically rooted in a negative concept. The robe, which symbolizes the dedication of the whole man to the dictates of duty, corresponds to צְדָקָה [righteousness]. And the *ephod*, which symbolizes the devotion of all man's resources and faculties to serve as instruments for the fulfillment of God's purposes, corresponds to חֶסֶד [loving-kindness].

prepare them.   3. Place them upon a
basket and bring them in the basket along
with the bull and the two rams.   4. And
you shall have Aharon and his sons come
closer to the entrance of the Tent of
Appointed Meeting, and bathe them in
water.   5. Then you shall take the garments and clothe Aharon with the tunic,
with the *ephod* robe, with the *ephod* and
the breastplate, and you shall gird it for him
with the band of the *ephod*.   6. You shall
place the turban upon his head and place
the diadem of the Sanctuary upon the turban,   7. take the anointing oil and pour it
upon his head and anoint him.   8. Then
you shall have his sons come closer and
clothe them with tunics.   9. And you shall
gird them, Aharon and his sons, with sashes
and wind high turbans for them; in this
manner the priesthood will become their
eternal due and so you will invest Aharon
and his sons with full authority.   10. You
shall then bring the bull to the front of the
Tent of Appointed Meeting and Aharon and
his sons shall lean their hands upon the
head of the bull.   11. You shall then
slaughter the bull before *God,* in front of the
entrance of the Tent of Appointed Meeting.
12. Take [some] of the blood of the bull
and place it at the elevated corners of the
altar with your finger, but you shall pour
out all the [remaining] blood upon the
base of the altar.   13. You shall then take
all the fat that covers the entrails, and the
diaphragm with the liver, also the two kidneys and the fat that is upon them, and give
it to rise up in smoke upon the altar.
14. But the meat of the bull, its hide and
its dung you shall burn in fire outside the
camp; it is an offering that clears [him who
brings it] of sin.   15. You shall then take
the one ram, and Aharon and his sons shall
lean their hands upon the head of the ram.
16. You shall slaughter the ram, take its
blood and dash it round about upon
the altar.   17. As for the ram itself, you
shall divide it into its parts, wash its entrails
and its legs and put them with its parts
and with its head,   18. and you shall give
the entire ram to rise up in smoke upon the
altar; it is an ascent offering made to *God;* it
is an expression of compliance, a fire offering to *God.*   19. And you shall take the

סֹ֣לֶת חִטִּ֑ים תַּעֲשֶׂ֖ה אֹתָֽם: ג וְנָתַתָּ֤ אוֹתָם֙
עַל־סַ֣ל אֶחָ֔ד וְהִקְרַבְתָּ֥ אֹתָ֖ם בַּסָּ֑ל וְאֶת־הַפָּ֔ר
וְאֵ֖ת שְׁנֵ֥י הָאֵילִֽם: ד וְאֶת־אַהֲרֹ֤ן וְאֶת־בָּנָיו֙
תַּקְרִ֔יב אֶל־פֶּ֖תַח אֹ֣הֶל מוֹעֵ֑ד וְרָחַצְתָּ֥ אֹתָ֖ם
בַּמָּֽיִם: ה וְלָקַחְתָּ֣ אֶת־הַבְּגָדִ֗ים וְהִלְבַּשְׁתָּ֤ אֶת־
אַהֲרֹן֙ אֶת־הַכֻּתֹּ֔נֶת וְאֵת֙ מְעִ֣יל הָאֵפֹ֔ד וְאֶת־
הָ֣אֵפֹ֔ד וְאֶת־הַחֹ֑שֶׁן וְאָפַדְתָּ֣ ל֔וֹ בְּחֵ֖שֶׁב הָאֵפֹֽד:
ו וְשַׂמְתָּ֥ הַמִּצְנֶ֖פֶת עַל־רֹאשׁ֑וֹ וְנָתַתָּ֛ אֶת־נֵ֥זֶר
הַקֹּ֖דֶשׁ עַל־הַמִּצְנָֽפֶת: ז וְלָֽקַחְתָּ֙ אֶת־שֶׁ֣מֶן
הַמִּשְׁחָ֔ה וְיָצַקְתָּ֖ עַל־רֹאשׁ֑וֹ וּמָשַׁחְתָּ֖ אֹתֽוֹ:
ח וְאֶת־בָּנָ֖יו תַּקְרִ֑יב וְהִלְבַּשְׁתָּ֖ם כֻּתֳּנֹֽת:
ט וְחָגַרְתָּ֩ אֹתָ֨ם אַבְנֵ֜ט אַהֲרֹ֣ן וּבָנָ֗יו וְחָבַשְׁתָּ֤
לָהֶם֙ מִגְבָּעֹ֔ת וְהָיְתָ֥ה לָהֶ֛ם כְּהֻנָּ֖ה לְחֻקַּ֣ת עוֹלָ֑ם
וּמִלֵּאתָ֥ יַֽד־אַהֲרֹ֖ן וְיַד־בָּנָֽיו: י וְהִקְרַבְתָּ֙ אֶת־
הַפָּ֔ר לִפְנֵ֖י אֹ֣הֶל מוֹעֵ֑ד וְסָמַ֨ךְ אַהֲרֹ֧ן וּבָנָ֛יו אֶת־
יְדֵיהֶ֖ם עַל־רֹ֥אשׁ הַפָּֽר: יא וְשָׁחַטְתָּ֥ אֶת־הַפָּ֖ר
לִפְנֵ֣י יְהֹוָ֑ה פֶּ֖תַח אֹ֥הֶל מוֹעֵֽד: יב וְלָֽקַחְתָּ֙ מִדַּ֣ם
הַפָּ֔ר וְנָתַתָּ֛ה עַל־קַרְנֹ֥ת הַמִּזְבֵּ֖חַ בְּאֶצְבָּעֶ֑ךָ וְאֶת־
כָּל־הַדָּ֣ם תִּשְׁפֹּ֔ךְ אֶל־יְס֖וֹד הַמִּזְבֵּֽחַ: יג וְלָֽקַחְתָּ֗
אֶת־כָּל־הַחֵ֘לֶב֮ הַֽמְכַסֶּ֣ה אֶת־הַקֶּ֒רֶב֒ וְאֵ֗ת הַיֹּתֶ֨רֶת֙
עַל־הַכָּבֵ֔ד וְאֵת֙ שְׁתֵּ֣י הַכְּלָיֹ֔ת וְאֶת־הַחֵ֖לֶב אֲשֶׁ֣ר
עֲלֵיהֶ֑ן וְהִקְטַרְתָּ֖ הַמִּזְבֵּֽחָה: יד וְאֶת־בְּשַׂ֤ר הַפָּר֙
וְאֶת־עֹר֣וֹ וְאֶת־פִּרְשׁ֔וֹ תִּשְׂרֹ֣ף בָּאֵ֔שׁ מִח֖וּץ
לַֽמַּחֲנֶ֑ה חַטָּ֖את הֽוּא: טו וְאֶת־הָאַ֥יִל הָֽאֶחָ֖ד
תִּקָּ֑ח וְסָ֨מְכ֜וּ אַהֲרֹ֧ן וּבָנָ֛יו אֶת־יְדֵיהֶ֖ם עַל־רֹ֥אשׁ
הָאָֽיִל: טז וְשָׁחַטְתָּ֖ אֶת־הָאָ֑יִל וְלָֽקַחְתָּ֙ אֶת־דָּמ֔וֹ
וְזָֽרַקְתָּ֥ עַל־הַמִּזְבֵּ֖חַ סָבִֽיב: יז וְאֶ֨ת־הָאַ֔יִל תְּנַתֵּ֖חַ
לִנְתָחָ֑יו וְרָֽחַצְתָּ֤ קִרְבּ֙וֹ וּכְרָעָ֔יו וְנָתַתָּ֥ עַל־נְתָחָ֖יו
וְעַל־רֹאשֽׁוֹ: יח וְהִקְטַרְתָּ֤   אֶת־כָּל־הָאַ֨יִל֙
הַמִּזְבֵּ֔חָה עֹלָ֥ה ה֖וּא לַֽיהֹוָ֑ה רֵ֣יחַ נִיח֔וֹחַ אִשֶּׁ֥ה
לַֽיהֹוָ֖ה הֽוּא: חמישי יט וְלָֽקַחְתָּ֙ אֵ֚ת הָאַ֣יִל הַשֵּׁנִ֔י

second ram and Aharon and his sons shall lean their hands upon the head of the ram. 20. You shall slaughter the ram, take [some] of its blood and place it upon the right earlobe of Aharon and upon the right earlobe[s] of his sons, also upon the thumb of their right hands and upon the big toe of their right foot and dash the blood round about upon the altar. 21. You shall then take [some] of the blood that is upon the altar and [some] of the anointing oil, and sprinkle it upon Aharon and upon his garments, upon his sons and upon the garments of his sons with him; thus he will become holy along with his garments, and his sons and their garments with him. 22. And you shall take from the ram the fat and the tailpiece and the fat that covers the entrails, the diaphragm of the liver, the two kidneys along with the fat that is upon them, and the right thigh—for it is a ram of investiture— 23. and one loaf of bread, one loaf of oil bread and one thin wafer from the basket of *matzoth* that stands before *God*, 24. and you shall place it all upon the hands of Aharon and upon the hands of his sons, and wave them as a wave offering before *God*. 25. You shall then take them from their hands and give them to the altar to rise up in smoke on the ascent offering; it is an expression of compliance before *God*; it is a fire offering to *God*. 26. And you shall take the breast of the ram of investiture which is Aharon's, and wave it as a wave offering before *God*; it will then become your portion. 27. Thus shall you sanctify the breast of the wave offering and the thigh of the uplifted donation, which were waved and lifted up, of the ram of investiture, of that which is Aharon's and of that which is his sons'. 28. And so it shall remain for Aharon and his sons as a perpetual due from the sons of Yisrael; for it is an uplifted donation, and it shall remain an uplifted donation from the sons of Yisrael of their peace offerings; it is an uplifted donation to God. 29. But as for the garments of the Sanctuary that are now Aharon's, they shall remain also for his sons after him, so that they may be anointed and invested with full authority through them. 30. Seven days shall the son who will be priest in his place

וְסָמַ֨ךְ אַהֲרֹ֤ן וּבָנָיו֙ אֶת־יְדֵיהֶ֔ם עַל־רֹ֥אשׁ הָאָֽיִל:

כ וְשָׁחַטְתָּ֣ אֶת־הָאַ֔יִל וְלָקַחְתָּ֙ מִדָּמ֔וֹ וְנָתַתָּ֛ה עַל־תְּנ֤וּךְ אֹ֨זֶן֙ אַהֲרֹ֔ן וְעַל־תְּנ֛וּךְ אֹ֥זֶן בָּנָיו֙ הַיְמָנִ֔ית וְעַל־בֹּ֤הֶן יָדָם֙ הַיְמָנִ֔ית וְעַל־בֹּ֥הֶן רַגְלָ֖ם הַיְמָנִ֑ית וְזָרַקְתָּ֧ אֶת־הַדָּ֛ם עַל־הַמִּזְבֵּ֖חַ סָבִֽיב:

כא וְלָקַחְתָּ֞ מִן־הַדָּ֨ם אֲשֶׁ֥ר עַל־הַמִּזְבֵּ֘חַ֘ וּמִשֶּׁ֣מֶן הַמִּשְׁחָ֒ה֒ וְהִזֵּיתָ֤ עַל־אַהֲרֹן֙ וְעַל־בְּגָדָ֔יו וְעַל־בָּנָ֛יו וְעַל־בִּגְדֵ֥י בָנָ֖יו אִתּ֑וֹ וְקָדַ֥שׁ הוּא֙ וּבְגָדָ֔יו וּבָנָ֛יו וּבִגְדֵ֥י בָנָ֖יו אִתּֽוֹ:

כב וְלָקַחְתָּ֣ מִן־הָ֠אַ֠יִל הַחֵ֨לֶב וְהָֽאַלְיָ֜ה וְאֶת־הַחֵ֣לֶב ׀ הַֽמְכַסֶּ֣ה אֶת־הַקֶּ֗רֶב וְאֵ֨ת יֹתֶ֤רֶת הַכָּבֵד֙ וְאֵ֣ת ׀ שְׁתֵּ֣י הַכְּלָיֹ֗ת וְאֶת־הַחֵ֨לֶב֙ אֲשֶׁ֣ר עֲלֵהֶ֔ן וְאֵ֖ת שׁ֣וֹק הַיָּמִ֑ין כִּ֛י אֵ֥יל מִלֻּאִ֖ים הֽוּא:

כג וְכִכַּ֨ר לֶ֜חֶם אַחַ֗ת וְחַלַּ֨ת לֶ֤חֶם שֶׁ֨מֶן֙ אַחַ֔ת וְרָקִ֖יק אֶחָ֑ד מִסַּל֙ הַמַּצּ֔וֹת אֲשֶׁ֖ר לִפְנֵ֥י יְהוָֽה:

כד וְשַׂמְתָּ֣ הַכֹּ֔ל עַ֚ל כַּפֵּ֣י אַהֲרֹ֔ן וְעַ֖ל כַּפֵּ֣י בָנָ֑יו וְהֵנַפְתָּ֥ אֹתָ֛ם תְּנוּפָ֖ה לִפְנֵ֥י יְהוָֽה:

כה וְלָקַחְתָּ֤ אֹתָם֙ מִיָּדָ֔ם וְהִקְטַרְתָּ֥ הַמִּזְבֵּ֖חָה עַל־הָֽעֹלָ֑ה לְרֵ֤יחַ נִיחֹ֨וחַ֙ לִפְנֵ֣י יְהוָ֔ה אִשֶּׁ֥ה ה֖וּא לַֽיהוָֽה:

כו וְלָקַחְתָּ֣ אֶת־הֶֽחָזֶ֗ה מֵאֵ֤יל הַמִּלֻּאִים֙ אֲשֶׁ֣ר לְאַהֲרֹ֔ן וְהֵנַפְתָּ֥ אֹת֛וֹ תְּנוּפָ֖ה לִפְנֵ֣י יְהוָ֑ה וְהָיָ֥ה לְךָ֖ לְמָנָֽה:

כז וְקִדַּשְׁתָּ֞ אֵ֣ת ׀ חֲזֵ֣ה הַתְּנוּפָ֗ה וְאֵת֙ שׁ֣וֹק הַתְּרוּמָ֔ה אֲשֶׁ֥ר הוּנַ֖ף וַאֲשֶׁ֣ר הוּרָ֑ם מֵאֵיל֙ הַמִּלֻּאִ֔ים מֵאֲשֶׁ֥ר לְאַהֲרֹ֖ן וּמֵאֲשֶׁ֥ר לְבָנָֽיו:

כח וְהָיָה֩ לְאַהֲרֹ֨ן וּלְבָנָ֜יו לְחָק־עוֹלָ֗ם מֵאֵת֙ בְּנֵ֣י יִשְׂרָאֵ֔ל כִּ֥י תְרוּמָ֖ה ה֑וּא וּתְרוּמָ֞ה יִהְיֶ֨ה מֵאֵ֤ת בְּנֵֽי־יִשְׂרָאֵל֙ מִזִּבְחֵ֣י שַׁלְמֵיהֶ֔ם תְּרֽוּמָתָ֖ם לַֽיהוָֽה:

כט וּבִגְדֵ֤י הַקֹּ֨דֶשׁ֙ אֲשֶׁ֣ר לְאַהֲרֹ֔ן יִהְי֥וּ לְבָנָ֖יו אַחֲרָ֑יו לְמָשְׁחָ֣ה בָהֶ֔ם וּלְמַלֵּא־בָ֖ם אֶת־יָדָֽם:

ל שִׁבְעַ֣ת יָמִ֗ים יִלְבָּשָׁ֧ם הַכֹּהֵ֛ן תַּחְתָּ֖יו מִבָּנָ֑יו

put them on; that is, he who is to enter the Tent of Appointed Meeting to serve in the Sanctuary. 31. You shall take the ram of investiture and cook its meat in a holy place. 32. Aharon and his sons shall eat the meat of the ram, and the bread that is in the basket, in front of the entrance of the Tent of Appointed Meeting. 33. They shall now eat these very things with which atonement has been effected before, in order to invest them with full authority, to sanctify them; but a stranger shall not eat of them, because they are a sacred thing. 34. If any of the meat of investiture or of the bread is left over until the next morning, you shall burn what is left over in fire; it shall not be eaten, because it is a sacred thing. 35. Thus, exactly as I have commanded, shall you do for Aharon and his sons; seven days you shall repeat their investiture, 36. and every day you shall offer a bull as an offering that clears [him who brings it] of sin, in addition to these atonement offerings; at the same time you purge the altar of sin by performing atonement upon it, and you shall anoint it, in order to sanctify it. 37. Seven days shall you perform atonement upon the altar and sanctify it. Henceforth the altar shall be a holy of holies.

אֲשֶׁר יָבֹא אֶל־אֹהֶל מוֹעֵד לְשָׁרֵת בַּקֹּדֶשׁ׃
לא וְאֵת אֵיל הַמִּלֻּאִים תִּקָּח וּבִשַּׁלְתָּ אֶת־בְּשָׂרוֹ
בְּמָקֹם קָדֹשׁ׃ לב וְאָכַל אַהֲרֹן וּבָנָיו אֶת־בְּשַׂר
הָאַיִל וְאֶת־הַלֶּחֶם אֲשֶׁר בַּסָּל פֶּתַח אֹהֶל מוֹעֵד׃
לג וְאָכְלוּ אֹתָם אֲשֶׁר כֻּפַּר בָּהֶם לְמַלֵּא אֶת־
יָדָם לְקַדֵּשׁ אֹתָם וְזָר לֹא־יֹאכַל כִּי־קֹדֶשׁ הֵם׃
לד וְאִם־יִוָּתֵר מִבְּשַׂר הַמִּלֻּאִים וּמִן־הַלֶּחֶם עַד־
הַבֹּקֶר וְשָׂרַפְתָּ אֶת־הַנּוֹתָר בָּאֵשׁ לֹא יֵאָכֵל כִּי־
קֹדֶשׁ הוּא׃ לה וְעָשִׂיתָ לְאַהֲרֹן וּלְבָנָיו כָּכָה
כְּכֹל אֲשֶׁר־צִוִּיתִי אֹתָכָה שִׁבְעַת יָמִים תְּמַלֵּא
יָדָם׃ לו וּפַר חַטָּאת תַּעֲשֶׂה לַיּוֹם עַל־הַכִּפֻּרִים
וְחִטֵּאתָ עַל־הַמִּזְבֵּחַ בְּכַפֶּרְךָ עָלָיו וּמָשַׁחְתָּ אֹתוֹ
לְקַדְּשׁוֹ׃ לז שִׁבְעַת יָמִים תְּכַפֵּר עַל־הַמִּזְבֵּחַ
וְקִדַּשְׁתָּ אֹתוֹ וְהָיָה הַמִּזְבֵּחַ קֹדֶשׁ קָדָשִׁים כָּל־

CHAPTER XXIX

30. . . . ***Seven days.*** The consecration and investiture of the first high priest was to be repeated daily for seven days. The investiture of every future high priest was to be performed in the same manner. Nothing is more indicative of the symbolic character and the profound significance of the high priest's garments and that of the entire מִלֻּאִים [investiture] of the high priest than the fact that the ceremony was to be repeated on seven consecutive days. Every day, for seven days, the high priests were to saturate themselves with all the conceptual meaning and profundity of these rites.

° ° °

37. וְהָיָה הַמִּזְבֵּחַ קֹדֶשׁ קָדָשִׁים כָּל הַנֹּגֵעַ וגו׳ [*Henceforth the altar shall be a holy of holies. Whatever touches . . .*]. קֹדֶשׁ קָדָשִׁים ["holy of holies"]. We doubt that this expression is to be interpreted simply as a hyperbole. עֶבֶד עֲבָדִים is "a slave to slaves," מֶלֶךְ מְלָכִים is "a king over kings," שְׁמֵי הַשָּׁמַיִם ["heaven of heavens"] is a higher sphere of heaven compared to which the heavens visible to us bear the same relationship as does our earth to the heavens that our eyes can behold. Thus, it is the "heaven of *our* heavens." Similarly, then, קֹדֶשׁ קָדָשִׁים ["holy of holies"] would be a sacred thing from which all other sacred things derive their sanctity.

° ° °

Nothing serves more directly to sanctify man's actions than does the altar. It is situated directly in front of the entrance to the Sanctuary, directly opposite the Ark of the Law and the Holy of Holies. It is the visible outgrowth of the Law that rests unseen in the Holy of Holies. It constitutes the true center of the area in front of, and around, the Sanctuary, and by virtue of the fire of the Law that burns upon it, the altar reminds us in symbolic terms that devotion to the Law of God is a prerequisite for entry into the Sanctuary. This is the reason why it is called מִזְבַּח הָעוֹלָה ["altar of ascent"]. Its function is based entirely upon the concept of the sanctification of man's acts; hence it is קֹדֶשׁ קָדָשִׁים ["a holy of holies"].

° ° °

הַנֹּגֵעַ בַּמִּזְבֵּחַ יִקְדָּשׁ: ס ששי לח וְזֶה אֲשֶׁר
תַּעֲשֶׂה עַל־הַמִּזְבֵּחַ כְּבָשִׂים בְּנֵי־שָׁנָה שְׁנַיִם

Whatever touches the altar will remain holy. 38. And this is what you shall offer upon the altar: yearling sheep, two, day by

38. The preceding verse concludes the instructions for the construction and consecration of the Sanctuary and for the consecration and investiture of the priests. However, the establishment and consecration of the Temple and the consecration of the priests in themselves do not bring the Presence of God to the people as promised in Verse 8 of Chapter 25: "They shall make Me a sanctuary and then I will dwell in their midst." This objective can be attained only by means of daily self-dedication on the part of the people, as expressed in symbolic terms by the priests, to the ideals of the Jewish calling symbolized by the Sanctuary. Only such dedication will transform the מִקְדָּשׁ [Sanctuary] into the Dwelling Place of the שְׁכִינָה [Presence of God]. This is the content of Verses 38 to 46, which describe the purpose to be realized through the erection of the Sanctuary. The establishment of the Temple alone does not achieve this purpose for all time; the Temple affords only a possibility to attain this end. The goal is attained only when the Sanctuary receives life and effect through the constant acts of self-dedication performed by the people, through the life-rhythm of the nation, as it were. This thought is symbolized by the *tamid* offerings, and that is why the discussion of the daily offerings immediately follows that of the dedication and consecration of the Sanctuary and of the priests.

° ° °

yearling sheep. At the hour of its birth as a nation, Israel stood before God as a "sheep of His flock." Indeed, it attained its existence as a nation only by thus entrusting its destiny to God as its Shepherd for all time. And that which it vowed to do at the great, solemn hour of its birth it shall carry out for the duration of its existence. Israel must never think that it has outgrown the leadership of its Shepherd. It must remain young forever. In its relationship with God it is to remain forever as it was in the first year of its existence, to stand before Him forever as the "yearling sheep of His flock." . . .

° ° °

. . . The day, יוֹם, the time of "standing erect" as an independent entity, is flanked on either side by night. It is in its ascendant phase from night until high noon, and on the decline from noon to night. The entire physical world in which man lives—and thus also his physical existence and all that he requires for the physical foundations of his work and attainments on earth—is governed by this cycle of waxing and waning. But the waxing and waning of daylight, the waxing and waning of fortune, the waxing and waning of all life on earth—they all are part of one order instituted by the One sole God. They are in the keeping of the One sole Shepherd of Life, and therefore both the waxing and the waning—be it of day, of fortune or of life itself—summon us to one and the same mission, to one and the same destiny.

It is as the same "sheep of God's pasture," with the same tributes of homage to God, "sustenance, prosperity and joy," that Israel faces both the waxing and the waning, and acknowledges the oneness of its God by acknowledging the oneness of its own calling and its joy of life. . . .

For this reason it is on the northwestern side of the Sanctuary that Israel offers its daily morning sacrifice, so that the rays of the rising sun may fall upon the offering from the east, while its daily evening sacrifice is performed on the northeastern side so that the rays of the setting sun may fall upon the offering from the west: Israel is to face both sunrise and sunset in the same unaltered spirit.

° ° °

According to Maimonides (*Hilkhoth T'midim u-Musafim*, 1:4), the lamb of the *tamid* offering was not bound but was only held down by hand upon the altar by its front and hind legs. The Gemarah (Tamid 31b) offers a curious explanation for this requirement: If the lamb were to be bound to the altar, this would be following in the ways of the heathens. *Ravad* [R. Abraham ben David of Posquières] and also Maimonides *ibid.* seem to read this as [following in the ways of the] אֶפִּיקוֹרְסִין [Epicureans] instead of עַמִּים [the nations]. (However, in his commentary on the Mishnah, Maimonides, too, reads the text as שלא יַחְקוּ לְאוּמוֹת ["lest they follow in the ways of the (heathen) nations"]). We are not told what pagan or un-Jewish ways or ideas were to be countered by not binding the lamb upon the altar. We have already noted in Exodus 12:5 the contrast between the "lamb" of Jewish symbolism and the "lamb" of another, non-Jewish view. The lamb in Jewish thought symbolizes the ever joyful, manly, unblemished creature in the vigor of eternal youth, finding its strength and its life's content precisely by entrusting itself freely to the guidance of its Shepherd. Contrast this with that other view, which sees the lamb as a symbol of passive suffering and martyrdom and which regards this death-directed resignation as the ideal of life's purpose. We would be very much inclined to say that it is this un-Jewish perception of the lamb that our law is intended to counteract. Not as a lamb bound hand and foot but as a free, vital creature does Israel entrust itself, of its own free will, to the guidance and leadership of its day, continually. 39. The one sheep you shall offer in the morning and the other sheep you shall offer between the two evenings. 40. And one tenth of fine flour, thoroughly mixed with a full quarter of a *hin* of pressed oil, and as a libation one quarter of a *hin* of wine: [this is] for the one sheep. 41. The other sheep you shall offer between the two evenings; you shall offer it like the homage offering of the morning and its libation, as an expression of compliance, a fire offering to *God*. 42. It shall be a continual ascent offering for your descendants, at the entrance of the Tent of Appointed Meeting before *God*, where I will appoint meetings with you, to speak with you there. 43. There I will set [times for] Myself to meet with the sons of Yisrael, and so it will be sanctified by My glory. 44. I will sanctify the Tent of Appointed Meeting and the altar, and I will sanctify Aharon and his sons to serve Me as priests. 45. I will dwell in the midst of the sons of Yisrael and I will be their God. 46. They will experience it that I, *God*, am their God, who brought them out from the land of Mitzrayim in order to dwell in their midst, I, *God*, their God.

לַיּ֖וֹם תָּמִֽיד׃ לט אֶת־הַכֶּ֥בֶשׂ הָאֶחָ֖ד תַּעֲשֶׂ֣ה
בַבֹּ֑קֶר וְאֵת֙ הַכֶּ֣בֶשׂ הַשֵּׁנִ֔י תַּעֲשֶׂ֖ה בֵּ֥ין הָעַרְבָּֽיִם׃
מ וְעִשָּׂרֹ֨ן סֹ֜לֶת בָּל֨וּל בְּשֶׁ֤מֶן כָּתִית֙ רֶ֣בַע הַהִ֔ין
וְנֵ֕סֶךְ רְבִיעִ֥ת הַהִ֖ין יָ֑יִן לַכֶּ֖בֶשׂ הָאֶחָֽד׃ מא וְאֵת֙
הַכֶּ֣בֶשׂ הַשֵּׁנִ֔י תַּעֲשֶׂ֖ה בֵּ֣ין הָעַרְבָּ֑יִם כְּמִנְחַ֨ת
הַבֹּ֤קֶר וּכְנִסְכָּהּ֙ תַּעֲשֶׂה־לָּ֔הּ לְרֵ֣יחַ נִיחֹ֔חַ אִשֶּׁ֖ה
לַיהֹוָֽה׃ מב עֹלַ֤ת תָּמִיד֙ לְדֹרֹ֣תֵיכֶ֔ם פֶּ֥תַח אֹֽהֶל־
מוֹעֵ֖ד לִפְנֵ֣י יְהֹוָ֑ה אֲשֶׁ֨ר אִוָּעֵ֤ד לָכֶם֙ שָׁ֔מָּה לְדַבֵּ֥ר
אֵלֶ֖יךָ שָֽׁם׃ מג וְנֹעַדְתִּ֥י שָׁ֖מָּה לִבְנֵ֣י יִשְׂרָאֵ֑ל
וְנִקְדַּ֖שׁ בִּכְבֹדִֽי׃ מד וְקִדַּשְׁתִּ֛י אֶת־אֹ֥הֶל מוֹעֵ֖ד
וְאֶת־הַמִּזְבֵּ֑חַ וְאֶת־אַהֲרֹ֧ן וְאֶת־בָּנָ֛יו אֲקַדֵּ֖שׁ
לְכַהֵ֥ן לִֽי׃ מה וְשָׁ֣כַנְתִּ֔י בְּת֖וֹךְ בְּנֵ֣י יִשְׂרָאֵ֑ל
וְהָיִ֥יתִי לָהֶ֖ם לֵאלֹהִֽים׃ מו וְיָֽדְע֗וּ כִּ֣י אֲנִ֤י יְהֹוָה֙
אֱלֹ֣הֵיהֶ֔ם אֲשֶׁ֨ר הוֹצֵ֧אתִי אֹתָ֛ם מֵאֶ֥רֶץ מִצְרַ֖יִם
לְשָׁכְנִ֣י בְתוֹכָ֑ם אֲנִ֖י יְהֹוָ֥ה אֱלֹהֵיהֶֽם׃ פ שביעי

Shepherd, and only in this giving of itself does it truly find life and freedom.

° ° °

42. ***at the entrance of the Tent of Appointed Meeting before* God.** Only by standing ready to fulfill the Law can we stand before God.

שָׁמָּה ***[where].*** There, in the place where the Testimony of His Law abides, God sets a time for us to meet with Him. It is there that He waits for us. Hence, if we expect God to come to us, it is there that we must appear with our ascent offering as a token of our eternal devotion to God and to His Law.

אִוָּעֵד לָכֶם שָׁמָּה לְדַבֵּר אֵלֶיךָ שָׁם ***[where I will appoint meetings with you (*plural*) to speak with you (*singular*) there].*** It is not the personality of Moses but only the devotion of the nation that will secure God's nearness. It is to the nation that God comes when He speaks with Moses.

43 and 44. All the consecrations and sanctifications that have been described above are only symbolic acts. The Sanctuary becomes holy only by virtue of the presence of God's glory, with which God places the stamp of His approval upon the works and deeds of man.

45. The presence of the glory of God in the Temple in turn is merely a proof of His presence in the midst of that nation of which He wishes to be the God; i.e., the One Who decides its destinies and guides its actions.

46. This special presence of God in the midst of the nation will not be a mere abstraction. They will experience this nearness in practical terms. The whole tenor of their lives, physical and spiritual, will prove to them the nearness of God, even as He Himself declared that wherever He wishes His Name to be remembered; i.e., wherever He wishes that men should recognize and acknowledge that "God is there," He will come to us and bless us. It is in His blessing of our material existence that we are to experience the Presence of God. "At every place where I would have My Name remembered I will come to you and bless you." (Exodus 20:21, see commentary *ibid.*)

XXX

1. Make an altar, for burning incense; of *shittim* wood shall you make it. 2. One cubit shall be its length and one cubit its width; it shall be square, and two cubits its height; its elevated corners shall be of one piece with it. 3. You shall cover it with pure gold, its top, its walls round about and its elevated corners; and you shall make a golden rim around it. 4. Make two golden rings for it underneath its rim on its two sides, that is, on its two opposite sides shall you make them, so that they may serve as holders for poles with which to carry it. 5. You shall make the poles of *shittim* wood and cover them with gold. 6. And you shall place it in front of the dividing curtain that is upon the Ark of the Testimony; in front of the cover that lies upon the Testimony where I have set [times for] Myself to meet with you. 7. Aharon shall make incense of sweet spices go up in smoke upon it, and every morning when he sets the lights in order he shall make it go up in smoke. 8. And when Aharon kindles the lights between the two evenings he shall make it go up in smoke: a continual incense before *God* for your descendants. 9. You shall offer no alien incense, make no ascent offering or homage offering upon it and you shall pour no libation upon it. 10. Once a year Aharon shall make atonement upon its elevated corners; with the blood of the offering that clears [him who brings it] of sin, of the atonements, he shall effect atonement upon it once a year for your descendants; it is a holy of holies to *God*.

ל א וְעָשִׂיתָ מִזְבֵּחַ מִקְטַר קְטֹרֶת עֲצֵי שִׁטִּים
תַּעֲשֶׂה אֹתוֹ: ב אַמָּה אָרְכּוֹ וְאַמָּה רָחְבּוֹ רָבוּעַ
יִהְיֶה וְאַמָּתַיִם קֹמָתוֹ מִמֶּנּוּ קַרְנֹתָיו: ג וְצִפִּיתָ
אֹתוֹ זָהָב טָהוֹר אֶת־גַּגּוֹ וְאֶת־קִירֹתָיו סָבִיב
וְאֶת־קַרְנֹתָיו וְעָשִׂיתָ לּוֹ זֵר זָהָב סָבִיב: ד וּשְׁתֵּי
טַבְּעֹת זָהָב תַּעֲשֶׂה־לּוֹ ׀ מִתַּחַת לְזֵרוֹ עַל שְׁתֵּי
צַלְעֹתָיו תַּעֲשֶׂה עַל־שְׁנֵי צִדָּיו וְהָיָה לְבָתִּים
לְבַדִּים לָשֵׂאת אֹתוֹ בָּהֵמָּה: ה וְעָשִׂיתָ אֶת־
הַבַּדִּים עֲצֵי שִׁטִּים וְצִפִּיתָ אֹתָם זָהָב: ו וְנָתַתָּה
אֹתוֹ לִפְנֵי הַפָּרֹכֶת אֲשֶׁר עַל־אֲרֹן הָעֵדֻת לִפְנֵי
הַכַּפֹּרֶת אֲשֶׁר עַל־הָעֵדֻת אֲשֶׁר אִוָּעֵד לְךָ שָׁמָּה:
ז וְהִקְטִיר עָלָיו אַהֲרֹן קְטֹרֶת סַמִּים בַּבֹּקֶר
בַּבֹּקֶר בְּהֵיטִיבוֹ אֶת־הַנֵּרֹת יַקְטִירֶנָּה: מפטיר
ח וּבְהַעֲלֹת אַהֲרֹן אֶת־הַנֵּרֹת בֵּין הָעַרְבַּיִם
יַקְטִירֶנָּה קְטֹרֶת תָּמִיד לִפְנֵי יְהֹוָה לְדֹרֹתֵיכֶם:
ט לֹא־תַעֲלוּ עָלָיו קְטֹרֶת זָרָה וְעֹלָה וּמִנְחָה
וְנֵסֶךְ לֹא תִסְּכוּ עָלָיו: י וְכִפֶּר אַהֲרֹן עַל־
קַרְנֹתָיו אַחַת בַּשָּׁנָה מִדַּם חַטַּאת הַכִּפֻּרִים
אַחַת בַּשָּׁנָה יְכַפֵּר עָלָיו לְדֹרֹתֵיכֶם קֹדֶשׁ־
קָדָשִׁים הוּא לַיהֹוָה: פ

The Haftarah for this Sidra may be found on page 859.

כי תשא

KI THISSA

11. *God* spoke to Moshe [saying]:
12. "When you take the sum of the sons
of Yisrael according to their numbered ones,
let each one of them give to *God* an atonement for his person when they are numbered; then there will be no dying among
them when they are numbered. 13. This
they shall give, each one that passes over to
those numbered: half a shekel according to
the weight of the Sanctuary—twenty *gerahs*
equal one shekel—half of such a shekel to
God as an uplifted donation. 14. Indeed,

יא וַיְדַבֵּר יְהֹוָה אֶל־מֹשֶׁה לֵּאמֹר: יב כִּי תִשָּׂא
אֶת־רֹאשׁ בְּנֵי־יִשְׂרָאֵל לִפְקֻדֵיהֶם וְנָתְנוּ אִישׁ
כֹּפֶר נַפְשׁוֹ לַיהֹוָה בִּפְקֹד אֹתָם וְלֹא־יִהְיֶה בָהֶם
נֶגֶף בִּפְקֹד אֹתָם: יג זֶה | יִתְּנוּ כָּל־הָעֹבֵר עַל־
הַפְּקֻדִים מַחֲצִית הַשֶּׁקֶל בְּשֶׁקֶל הַקֹּדֶשׁ עֶשְׂרִים
גֵּרָה הַשֶּׁקֶל מַחֲצִית הַשֶּׁקֶל תְּרוּמָה לַיהֹוָה:

CHAPTER XXX

11. **God** ***spoke to Moshe.*** The section from Verse 1 of Chapter 25 until the present verse is one continuous Divine oration, commanding the establishment and sanctification of the Temple and of the priests. The Divine oration that now follows outlines the relationship that is to exist between the nation and the Sanctuary. From the very outset we were taught that Temple and nation are not to be considered as two separate entities. The Sanhedrin was to have its place next to the altar, and the altar was to bring justice, peace and morality to the life of the nation. Therefore the basic features of the life to be developed by the nation were set forth prior to the instructions for the building of the Temple. In the same spirit, now that these instructions have been completed, the shekel law is given as a constant reminder to the people that nation and Temple are one. Here, a great Jewish truth is proclaimed: The Sanctuary of the Temple is not an institution which, once established for all time, is left for the priests to manage. The Sanctuary cannot achieve its purpose without the ever-vigorous, ever-vital participation of the nation as a whole. By the same token, the significance of each and every member of the nation, and that of the nation as a whole, consists solely in the contribution made by each, a contribution enabling the Sanctuary, which, after all, is nothing but the Sanctuary of the nation's Law, to achieve its purpose.

13. ***This they shall give.*** Not with the sum of his concrete accomplishments but with the symbolic expression of what he knows to be his duty shall each one come near to God at the moment when he is to "pass" from the ranks of the uncounted into the ranks of those that have been counted. There is no greater distinction and no greater bliss than to be among those who have been counted for and by God, to take one's place on God's roster even though one be in the most humble circumstances, and even in the most transient moment of life on earth, to be counted as a member of the hosts of God. Only after having become aware of the full extent of his duty and after having resolved to perform it fully can one pass from the nondescript crowd of the selfish multitudes into the ennobled circle of those who have been counted by God, and attain the blissful awareness that he is now among those whom God has numbered among His own.

However, the contribution required of each individual is symbolized by מַחֲצִית הַשֶּׁקֶל, [not one whole shekel but only] one half-shekel. Viewed objectively, not even the most complete and perfect contribution of any one individual can accomplish the whole of the work that must be done. The effort of any individual can be only a fragment of the whole. An equally selfless sacrifice of his brother is required in order to produce the whole. In fact, it is not expected of any one individual to accomplish the entire task. לא עָלֶיךָ הַמְּלָאכָה לִגְמוֹר ["It is not expected of you to complete the entire task . . ." (Avoth 2:21)]. But the individual is indeed expected to make his personal contribution to the whole, weighed by the standard of the Sanctuary. One shekel was equivalent to 20 *gerahs*, of which the individual was expected to contribute ten; thus, viewed subjectively, one rounded whole. Let it be his whole contribution as far as he is concerned. Let him weigh it out with scrupulous accuracy, no matter how small a fraction his own contribution represents in relation to the whole of the task to be accomplished. Let him leave nothing undone, let him not withold any effort, any talent, any ability that could help promote the welfare of the whole. Although you are not expected to complete the entire task, "you are not free to desist from it" (Avoth 2:21). Let his half-shekel comprise a complete unit by the standard of the Sanctuary.

each one that passes over to the numbered ones, from the age of twenty upward, shall give an uplifted donation to *God*. 15. The rich shall not give more and the poor not less than half a shekel, with which to give the uplifted donation to *God*, to effect atonement for your souls. 16. You shall take the money of atonements from the sons of Yisrael and use it for the service of the Tent of Appointed Meeting; it shall be a remembrance for the sons of Yisrael before *God*, to effect atonement for your souls." 17. *God* spoke to Moshe [saying]: 18. "Make a basin of copper and its base of copper for washing; place it between the Tent of Appointed Meeting and the altar and put water into it. 19. Aharon and his sons shall wash their hands and their feet from it. 20. When they go into the Tent of Appointed Meeting they shall wash them with water, so that they will not die, or when they go up to the altar to serve, to make a fire offering rise up in smoke to *God*, 21. they shall wash their hands and feet, so that they will not die; this shall be for them a statute forever, for him and for his children, for their descendants." 22. *God* spoke to Moshe [saying]: 23. "And [as for] you, take yourself spices of the finest sort: of pure myrrh five hundred; of spicy cinnamon two half-portions of two hundred

יד כֹּל הָעֹבֵר עַל־הַפְּקֻדִים מִבֶּן עֶשְׂרִים שָׁנָה וָמָעְלָה יִתֵּן תְּרוּמַת יְהֹוָה: טו הֶעָשִׁיר לֹא־יַרְבֶּה וְהַדַּל לֹא יַמְעִיט מִמַּחֲצִית הַשָּׁקֶל לָתֵת אֶת־תְּרוּמַת יְהֹוָה לְכַפֵּר עַל־נַפְשֹׁתֵיכֶם: טז וְלָקַחְתָּ אֶת־כֶּסֶף הַכִּפֻּרִים מֵאֵת בְּנֵי יִשְׂרָאֵל וְנָתַתָּ אֹתוֹ עַל־עֲבֹדַת אֹהֶל מוֹעֵד וְהָיָה לִבְנֵי יִשְׂרָאֵל לְזִכָּרוֹן לִפְנֵי יְהֹוָה לְכַפֵּר עַל־נַפְשֹׁתֵיכֶם: פ יז וַיְדַבֵּר יְהֹוָה אֶל־מֹשֶׁה לֵּאמֹר: יח וְעָשִׂיתָ כִּיּוֹר נְחֹשֶׁת וְכַנּוֹ נְחֹשֶׁת לְרָחְצָה וְנָתַתָּ אֹתוֹ בֵּין־אֹהֶל מוֹעֵד וּבֵין הַמִּזְבֵּחַ וְנָתַתָּ שָׁמָּה מָיִם: יט וְרָחֲצוּ אַהֲרֹן וּבָנָיו מִמֶּנּוּ אֶת־יְדֵיהֶם וְאֶת־רַגְלֵיהֶם: כ בְּבֹאָם אֶל־אֹהֶל מוֹעֵד יִרְחֲצוּ־מַיִם וְלֹא יָמֻתוּ אוֹ בְגִשְׁתָּם אֶל־הַמִּזְבֵּחַ לְשָׁרֵת לְהַקְטִיר אִשֶּׁה לַיהֹוָה: כא וְרָחֲצוּ יְדֵיהֶם וְרַגְלֵיהֶם וְלֹא יָמֻתוּ וְהָיְתָה לָהֶם חָק־עוֹלָם לוֹ וּלְזַרְעוֹ לְדֹרֹתָם: פ כב וַיְדַבֵּר יְהֹוָה אֶל־מֹשֶׁה לֵּאמֹר: כג וְאַתָּה קַח־לְךָ בְּשָׂמִים רֹאשׁ מָר־דְּרוֹר חֲמֵשׁ מֵאוֹת וְקִנְּמָן־בֶּשֶׂם מַחֲצִיתוֹ

---

15. . . . The rich shall not give more and the poor not less. This equality of rich and poor expresses the symbolic character of the contribution fixed at one half-shekel. If the rich man and the poor man each contributes his share, if each accomplishes the whole of what is required of him, then the hundreds and the thousands of the rich weigh no more upon God's scales than the tens and the ones of the poor, and the tens and the ones of the poor will be equal in every respect to the hundreds and the thousands of the rich. The rich man can give no more than half a shekel; the poor man is not permitted to give more. God and His Sanctuary do not weigh the absolute quantity of the contribution but judge the gift only in terms of its relation to the total abilities and resources of the donor. Anyone who employs the sum total of his abilities and resources bestowed upon him to serve God and to promote the purposes of His Sanctuary has thereby placed his own מַחֲצִית הַשָּׁקֶל [half-shekel] as his required symbolic contribution upon the altar of God.

18. כִּיּוֹר *[The Basin]*

. . . The laws pertaining to the כִּיּוֹר [basin] are to remind the officiating priests at all times that when they enter the Sanctuary on behalf of the nation they do not do so because their personal conduct has already been sanctified by their day-to-day lives. Their importance as priests is only symbolic in that they represent the sanctification of life required by the Law of God.

21. this shall be for them a statute forever. Literally: This shall be a duty payable by the priests to the Sanctuary forever. By sanctifying their hands and their feet the priests acknowledge the supreme spiritual authority of the Sanctuary. Not by their own personal merit but only by virtue of the requirements of the Sanctuary that they symbolically represent are they deemed worthy of entering the Sanctuary as its servants. . . .

חֲמִשִּׁים וּמָאתָיִם וּקְנֵה־בֹשֶׂם חֲמִשִּׁים
וּמָאתָיִם׃ כד וְקִדָּה חֲמֵשׁ מֵאוֹת בְּשֶׁקֶל הַקֹּדֶשׁ
וְשֶׁמֶן זַיִת הִין׃ כה וְעָשִׂיתָ אֹתוֹ שֶׁמֶן מִשְׁחַת־
קֹדֶשׁ רֹקַח מִרְקַחַת מַעֲשֵׂה רֹקֵחַ שֶׁמֶן מִשְׁחַת־
קֹדֶשׁ יִהְיֶה׃ כו וּמָשַׁחְתָּ בוֹ אֶת־אֹהֶל מוֹעֵד
וְאֵת אֲרוֹן הָעֵדֻת׃ כז וְאֶת־הַשֻּׁלְחָן וְאֶת־כָּל־
כֵּלָיו וְאֶת־הַמְּנֹרָה וְאֶת־כֵּלֶיהָ וְאֵת מִזְבַּח
הַקְּטֹרֶת׃ כח וְאֶת־מִזְבַּח הָעֹלָה וְאֶת־כָּל־כֵּלָיו
וְאֶת־הַכִּיֹּר וְאֶת־כַּנּוֹ׃ כט וְקִדַּשְׁתָּ אֹתָם וְהָיוּ
קֹדֶשׁ קָדָשִׁים כָּל־הַנֹּגֵעַ בָּהֶם יִקְדָּשׁ׃ ל וְאֶת־
אַהֲרֹן וְאֶת־בָּנָיו תִּמְשָׁח וְקִדַּשְׁתָּ אֹתָם לְכַהֵן
לִי׃ לא וְאֶל־בְּנֵי יִשְׂרָאֵל תְּדַבֵּר לֵאמֹר שֶׁמֶן
מִשְׁחַת־קֹדֶשׁ יִהְיֶה זֶה לִי לְדֹרֹתֵיכֶם׃ לב עַל־
בְּשַׂר אָדָם לֹא יִיסָךְ וּבְמַתְכֻּנְתּוֹ לֹא תַעֲשׂוּ
כָּמֹהוּ קֹדֶשׁ הוּא קֹדֶשׁ יִהְיֶה לָכֶם׃ לג אִישׁ
אֲשֶׁר יִרְקַח כָּמֹהוּ וַאֲשֶׁר יִתֵּן מִמֶּנּוּ עַל־זָר
וְנִכְרַת מֵעַמָּיו׃ ס לד וַיֹּאמֶר יְהֹוָה אֶל־מֹשֶׁה
קַח־לְךָ סַמִּים נָטָף ׀ וּשְׁחֵלֶת וְחֶלְבְּנָה סַמִּים
וּלְבֹנָה זַכָּה בַּד בְּבַד יִהְיֶה׃ לה וְעָשִׂיתָ אֹתָהּ
קְטֹרֶת רֹקַח מַעֲשֵׂה רוֹקֵחַ מְמֻלָּח טָהוֹר קֹדֶשׁ׃
לו וְשָׁחַקְתָּ מִמֶּנָּה הָדֵק וְנָתַתָּה מִמֶּנָּה לִפְנֵי
הָעֵדֻת בְּאֹהֶל מוֹעֵד אֲשֶׁר אִוָּעֵד לְךָ שָׁמָּה קֹדֶשׁ
קָדָשִׁים תִּהְיֶה לָכֶם׃ לז וְהַקְּטֹרֶת אֲשֶׁר תַּעֲשֶׂה
בְּמַתְכֻּנְתָּהּ לֹא תַעֲשׂוּ לָכֶם קֹדֶשׁ תִּהְיֶה לְךָ
לַיהֹוָה׃ לח אִישׁ אֲשֶׁר־יַעֲשֶׂה כָמוֹהָ לְהָרִיחַ בָּהּ
וְנִכְרַת מֵעַמָּיו׃ ס לא א וַיְדַבֵּר יְהֹוָה אֶל־
מֹשֶׁה לֵּאמֹר׃ ב רְאֵה קָרָאתִי בְשֵׁם בְּצַלְאֵל בֶּן־

and fifty each; of fragrant cane, two
hundred and fifty, 24. and of cassia five
hundred shekels [according to the shekels]
of the Sanctuary, and of olive oil one *hin*.
25. You shall make this into an oil of holy
anointment, a perfume compound after the
art of the perfumer; it shall be an oil of holy
anointment. 26. And you shall anoint
with it the Tent of Appointed Meeting and
the Ark of the Testimony, 27. the table
and all its utensils, the menorah and all its
utensils and the altar of incense, 28. the
altar of the ascent offering and all its utensils,
the basin and its base. 29. And you shall
sanctify them so that they become a holy of
holies; whatever touches them shall become
holy. 30. You shall also anoint Aharon and
his sons, and sanctify them, to serve Me as
priests. 31. And to the sons of Yisrael you
shall speak [saying]: This shall be oil of a holy
anointment to Me for your descendants.
32. It shall not be poured upon the flesh of
a man, and you shall not make a formula like
it; it is a holy thing; it shall be a holy thing to
you." 33. Whoever compounds anything
like it or puts any of it on a stranger shall be
uprooted from among his people. 34. *God*
said to Moshe: "Take yourself spices such as
balsam sap, onycha and galbanum; these
fragrances and pure frankincense; each shall
remain separate for itself. 35. And you
shall make it into an incense, a perfume compound after the art of the perfumer, well
blended, pure, holy. 36. And you shall
grind some of it very finely and set it before
the Testimony in the Tent of Appointed
Meeting, which I have appointed for meeting with you there; it shall be to you a holy of
holies. 37. And this incense which you prepare, you shall not make for yourselves
according to its specified formula; it shall be
holy to you for *God*. 38. Whoever prepares anything equal to it, to smell [its
fragrance], shall be uprooted from among his
people.

XXXI

1. *God* spoke to Moshe
[saying]: 2. "See, I
have called by name Bezalel, the son of Uri,

CHAPTER XXXI

1. The preceding chapter concludes the instructions for the construction of the Sanctuary. All that was still left to do was to charge the craftsmen who were to carry out the instructions, and to introduce the one object which was not to be made by human hands but would be given by God, the object for which human hands had erected the entire Sanctuary as a dwelling place: the Testimony of the Law. Both these events,

the son of Ḥur, of the tribe of Yehudah,
3. since I have filled him with the spirit
of God, with wisdom, with insight and with
knowledge and with [talent for] all manner
of craftsmanship, 4. to combine ideas, to
work them out in gold, in silver and in
copper, 5. to execute them in the cutting
of stones for setting and in the carving of
wood, in every manner of craftsmanship.
6. And, likewise, behold, I have placed at
his side Oholiab, the son of Aḥisamakh, of
the tribe of Dan, and I have put wisdom into
the heart of every one that is wise-hearted;
they will make everything that I have commanded you: 7. The Tent of Appointed
Meeting and the Ark for the Testimony, as
well as the cover that shall be upon it, and
all the utensils of the Tent, 8. and the
table and its utensils, and the pure menorah
and all its utensils, and the altar of incense,
9. the altar for the ascent offering and all
its utensils, the basin and its base, 10. the
garments of distinction and the garments of
the Sanctuary for Aharon the priest, and
the garments of his sons for the priestly
service, 11. the anointing oil and the
incense of spices for the Sanctuary; in complete accordance with everything I have
commanded you will they make it.
12. *God* said to Moshe: 13. "But [as
for] you, utter it to the sons of Yisrael: Only
keep My Sabbaths! For it is a sign between
Me and you for your descendants, that you

אוּרִי בֶן־חוּר לְמַטֵּה יְהוּדָה: ג וָאֲמַלֵּא אֹתוֹ
רוּחַ אֱלֹהִים בְּחָכְמָה וּבִתְבוּנָה וּבְדַעַת וּבְכָל־
מְלָאכָה: ד לַחְשֹׁב מַחֲשָׁבֹת לַעֲשׂוֹת בַּזָּהָב
וּבַכֶּסֶף וּבַנְּחֹשֶׁת: ה וּבַחֲרֹשֶׁת אֶבֶן לְמַלֹּאת
וּבַחֲרֹשֶׁת עֵץ לַעֲשׂוֹת בְּכָל־מְלָאכָה: ו וַאֲנִי
הִנֵּה נָתַתִּי אִתּוֹ אֵת אָהֳלִיאָב בֶּן־אֲחִיסָמָךְ
לְמַטֵּה־דָן וּבְלֵב כָּל־חֲכַם־לֵב נָתַתִּי חָכְמָה
וְעָשׂוּ אֵת כָּל־אֲשֶׁר צִוִּיתִךָ: ז אֵת | אֹהֶל מוֹעֵד
וְאֶת־הָאָרֹן לָעֵדֻת וְאֶת־הַכַּפֹּרֶת אֲשֶׁר עָלָיו
וְאֵת כָּל־כְּלֵי הָאֹהֶל: ח וְאֶת־הַשֻּׁלְחָן וְאֶת־כֵּלָיו
וְאֶת־הַמְּנֹרָה הַטְּהֹרָה וְאֶת־כָּל־כֵּלֶיהָ וְאֵת
מִזְבַּח הַקְּטֹרֶת: ט וְאֶת־מִזְבַּח הָעֹלָה וְאֶת־כָּל־
כֵּלָיו וְאֶת־הַכִּיּוֹר וְאֶת־כַּנּוֹ: י וְאֵת בִּגְדֵי הַשְּׂרָד
וְאֶת־בִּגְדֵי הַקֹּדֶשׁ לְאַהֲרֹן הַכֹּהֵן וְאֶת־בִּגְדֵי בָנָיו
לְכַהֵן: יא וְאֵת שֶׁמֶן הַמִּשְׁחָה וְאֶת־קְטֹרֶת
הַסַּמִּים לַקֹּדֶשׁ כְּכֹל אֲשֶׁר־צִוִּיתִךָ יַעֲשׂוּ: פ
יב וַיֹּאמֶר יְהוָה אֶל־מֹשֶׁה לֵּאמֹר: יג וְאַתָּה
דַּבֵּר אֶל־בְּנֵי יִשְׂרָאֵל לֵאמֹר אַךְ אֶת־שַׁבְּתֹתַי
תִּשְׁמֹרוּ כִּי אוֹת הִוא בֵּינִי וּבֵינֵיכֶם לְדֹרֹתֵיכֶם

the charge to the craftsmen and the presentation of the Testimony, are described in the chapter that now begins.

3. . . . .The fact that these sublime spiritual attributes are ascribed to Bezalel makes it clear that the work to be produced is not to be merely a work of art in the ordinary sense of the term but one in which every part is to have symbolic significance, and that the ideas which are to be expressed in and through this work must remain ever present in the minds of the craftsmen to guide their thoughts and intentions as they execute it.

12. **God *said.*** This statement does not introduce a new law. The law of Sabbath observance had already been given before. Here this law merely receives additional dimensions, specifically in relation to the commandments pertaining to the construction of the Sanctuary, which were given in the preceding passages. It is probably for this reason that it is written: וַיֹּאמֶר ד׳ וגו׳ ["*God* said"] and not, as in other proclamations of laws valid for all time, וַיְדַבֵּר ["and (*God*) spoke"]. God gave the instructions for the construction of the Sanctuary; now He states the relationship between these commandments and the observance of the Sabbath.

13. ***Only keep My Sabbaths!*** With these words שְׁמִירַת שַׁבָּת [Sabbath observance] is given priority over the commandment to build the Sanctuary; even the construction work on the Dwelling Place must defer to the Sabbath. This is the first time in Scripture that a form of the term שְׁמִירָה ["to keep"] is used with reference to the Sabbath. This idea is repeated three times in the present chapter (Verses 13, 14 and 16), making it

may know that I, *God*, sanctify you. 14. Therefore keep the Sabbath, for it is a sacred thing for you. Those who desecrate it shall be put to death, for whoever performs [creating] work upon it, that soul will be uprooted from the midst of its society. 15. Six days shall [creating] work be done, but the seventh day is a Sabbath to be observed by cessation from [creating work], a sanctity belonging to *God*; whoever performs [creating] work on the Sabbath day shall be put to death. 16. Thus shall the sons of Yisrael keep the Sabbath, to realize the Sabbath for their descendants as an everlasting covenant. 17. It is a sign between Me and the sons of Yisrael forever, that for six days *God* created the heaven and

לָדַ֕עַת כִּ֛י אֲנִ֥י יְהוָ֖ה מְקַדִּשְׁכֶֽם׃
יד וּשְׁמַרְתֶּם֙ אֶת־הַשַּׁבָּ֔ת כִּ֛י קֹ֥דֶשׁ הִ֖וא לָכֶ֑ם מְחַֽלְלֶ֙יהָ֙ מ֣וֹת יוּמָ֔ת כִּ֗י כָּל־הָעֹשֶׂ֥ה בָהּ֙ מְלָאכָ֔ה וְנִכְרְתָ֛ה הַנֶּ֥פֶשׁ הַהִ֖וא מִקֶּ֥רֶב עַמֶּֽיהָ׃
טו שֵׁ֣שֶׁת יָמִים֮ יֵעָשֶׂ֣ה מְלָאכָה֒ וּבַיּ֣וֹם הַשְּׁבִיעִ֗י שַׁבַּ֧ת שַׁבָּת֛וֹן קֹ֖דֶשׁ לַיהוָ֑ה כָּל־הָעֹשֶׂ֧ה מְלָאכָ֛ה בְּי֥וֹם הַשַּׁבָּ֖ת מ֥וֹת יוּמָֽת׃
טז וְשָׁמְר֥וּ בְנֵֽי־יִשְׂרָאֵ֖ל אֶת־הַשַּׁבָּ֑ת לַעֲשׂ֧וֹת אֶת־הַשַּׁבָּ֛ת לְדֹרֹתָ֖ם בְּרִ֥ית עוֹלָֽם׃
יז בֵּינִ֗י וּבֵין֙ בְּנֵ֣י יִשְׂרָאֵ֔ל א֥וֹת הִ֖וא לְעֹלָ֑ם כִּי־שֵׁ֣שֶׁת יָמִ֗ים עָשָׂ֤ה יְהוָה֙ אֶת־הַשָּׁמַ֣יִם וְאֶת־

clear that the Sabbath and its observance constitute the basic purport of this chapter. The use of this term teaches us to view the Sabbath as a precious possession given to us and entrusted to our keeping, and that we have certain duties as its שׁוֹמְרִים [keepers]. We are not to be פּוֹשֵׁעַ [to transgress (the Sabbath)]; we are not to be שׁוֹלֵחַ יָד against it [we are not to violate it]; we must never lose sight of it, nor tamper with it according to our own ideas. Instead, we are to be most scrupulous and vigilant to avoid anything that might harm the sacred treasure entrusted to our care. . . .

The reference here is not to the Sabbath in general but to שַׁבְּתוֹתַי ["*My* Sabbaths"]: each and every Sabbath that enters into history is commended anew to our keeping as a Divine sanctity in its own right; each Sabbath day reminds us anew of our obligation toward it and demands of us that we devote every effort to our duty as its keepers. . . . The Sabbath is not defended here against violation by some personal profane activity or by ordinary occupational pursuits. It is safeguarded from violation by an activity that is in fact devoted to the most sublime, sacred purposes of God and of the nation: the erection of the Temple, which is intended to attain God's nearness. Thus, the Sabbath observance which is required of us with respect to other endeavors, less sacred than this one, is impressed upon us with redoubled impact.

כִּי אוֹת הִוא ***[For it is a sign]*** Since the Sabbath in this verse takes the plural form; i.e., שַׁבְּתוֹתַי ["My Sabbaths"], the word הִיא ["it"] cannot refer to the Sabbath day but can refer only to the שְׁמִירָה [the keeping or observance of the Sabbath] which has been commanded to us. Thus the cessation from all *melakhah* ["creating work"] on the Sabbath has been elevated to become אוֹת ["a sign"], a symbol with implications of mutuality for the relationship between God and Israel.

בֵּינִי וּבֵינֵיכֶם ***[between Me and you]***. It is by this sign that God recognizes us and that we, in turn, acknowledge God in accordance with the ideals which it symbolizes. . . .

17. In Verse 13 שְׁמִירָה [the keeping of the Sabbath], the cessation of "creating work" on that day, was designated as אוֹת ["a sign"]. Here this designation is conferred upon the day itself. The Sabbath day as such is a memorial to God's free-willed creation of the world, and our cessation from "creating work" on that day, in turn, is a memorial to us, reminding us to acknowledge the Creator as our Master and keeping us aware that He has called us to His service. . . .

The Sabbath is the memorial of our relationship to God, while the Temple is a memorial of our position with regard to His Law. It is obvious that the construction of the Temple must defer to the observance of the Sabbath, for the Temple as such presupposes the observance of the Sabbath. On the other hand, the Sabbath defers to פִּקּוּחַ נֶפֶשׁ, the saving of a human life. Cf. פִּקּוּחַ נֶפֶשׁ דוֹחֶה שַׁבָּת ["The saving of a life suspends the laws of Sabbath observance"]. This principle is applied also to other commandments. Thus, we are told, "Keep My statutes and My [social] ordinances which man must carry out and through which he gains life (Leviticus 18:5): So that he will live and not die, through them." Also "for it is a sacred thing to you (Exodus 31:14): It has been handed over to you, but you have not been handed over to it." The purpose of the Sabbath is to sanctify you; hence, its observance must not endanger your lives.

"Thus shall the sons of Yisrael keep the Sabbath" (Exodus 31:16): "[Let him] violate one Sabbath so that he may be able to keep many more Sabbaths." The Sabbath needs living men to keep it; hence it is the earth and ceased to create upon the seventh day, when He withdrew into His own essence." 18. When He had finished speaking with him on Mount Sinai, He gave Moshe two tablets of the Testimony, tablets of stone, written with the finger of God.

XXXII

1. When the people saw that Moshe did not fulfill their expectation that he would come down from the mountain, the people gathered against Aharon, and they said to

הָאָ֔רֶץ וּבַיּוֹם֙ הַשְּׁבִיעִ֔י שָׁבַ֖ת וַיִּנָּפַֽשׁ׃ ס שני
יח וַיִּתֵּ֣ן אֶל־מֹשֶׁ֗ה כְּכַלֹּתוֹ֙ לְדַבֵּ֤ר אִתּוֹ֙ בְּהַ֣ר
סִינַ֔י שְׁנֵ֖י לֻחֹ֣ת הָעֵדֻ֑ת לֻחֹ֣ת אֶ֔בֶן כְּתֻבִ֖ים
בְּאֶצְבַּ֥ע אֱלֹהִֽים׃ לב א וַיַּ֣רְא הָעָ֔ם כִּֽי־בֹשֵׁ֥שׁ
מֹשֶׁ֖ה לָרֶ֣דֶת מִן־הָהָ֑ר וַיִּקָּהֵ֨ל הָעָ֜ם עַֽל־אַהֲרֹ֗ן

---

permissible to violate a Sabbath for the sake of one whose life is in danger so that he may live to keep many more Sabbaths (Yoma 85b). By preserving the life of a keeper of the Sabbath you preserve the Sabbath itself; when the life of a Sabbath observer is in danger, the future observance of the Sabbath itself is imperiled.

CHAPTER XXXII

1. Upon the mountain, the instructions for the construction of the Sanctuary of the Law and the presentation of the Testimony of the Law had brought the revelation to that point where the Law was to find a home in the midst of the nation. From this dwelling place, as that nation's very soul, it was to imbue the nation as a whole and the individuals that comprised it with the spirit of their Divinely-ordained vocation, which was to win for the nation the Presence of God in its midst, as promised [in Chap. 25:8]: "They shall make Me a sanctuary and then I will dwell in their midst."

But even while all this was transpiring on Mount Sinai events were taking place in the camp below that served to underline most cogently . . . the gap between reality as reflected by the mentality of the nation, and the ideals set forth in the Law which the nation was to receive. The fact that this nation could not tolerate the absence of their leader Moses for forty days and that, so soon after the flashes of lightning amidst which they were commanded: "Do not make yourself . . . an image" the Children of Israel should have been capable of making for themselves a "golden calf" showed that the nation was still remote from the truths and requirements of the Law of God.

This makes it obvious that such a Law could not possibly be construed as a product of its own time. It cannot possibly be a law which, like all other religions and codes of law, had come forth from amidst the people itself at a given period in its history. At the same time, these events show us the Law in its absolute character—absolute by virtue of its Divine origin and in its inevitable destiny to gain a dwelling place among men and to become effective on earth. At the moment

when this Law first entered into the world, the unworthiness of the nation that was meant to be the first to receive it on earth made it obvious that one of the two would have to go: either the Law or the entire generation of the nation for whom it had been intended. The decision was instantaneous: that entire generation would have to go and a new generation would have to be created that would be ready and able to accept the Law. Until that point the Law would bide its time.

God's statement to Moses, "I will annihilate them, and I will make you into a great nation" (Verse 10); i.e., that the nation which had been established in order to receive the Law should be destroyed, while Moses and the Law would be assured of a different kind of future, demonstrates from the very outset the absolute character of the destiny ordained for the Law, a destiny guaranteed and promoted by God Himself. This Law will never have to accommodate itself to changing times; on the contrary, any given period is entitled to a present and a future only as long as it accommodates itself to the requirements of this Law. The Law was the absolute destiny of the Jewish nation, but the generation in the wilderness was still infinitely far away from that goal. If, then, this Law, with its ideal requirements unchanged, was, nevertheless, able to enter into the midst of the nation at that point in its history, this could not have happened merely to the end that the nation should be permitted to alter it in accordance with changing times; i.e., to suit the nation's convenience. Rather, it was the nation that would have to undergo changes until such time as it had worked its way up to the moral and spiritual level of this Law.

In recapitulation: as soon as this Law entered into the midst of the nation over whom it was meant to reign supreme, the "golden calf" incident presented it with its first challenge. The Law was to demonstrate its Divine power by training this nation to recognize it and then to set up its Sanctuary first and foremost as a place of atonement, a place where the nation would undergo ceaseless training for a better, purer future.

Before the Sanctuary of the Law was erected, the

him: "Arise, make us gods who shall go before us, because this man Moshe, who brought us up from the land of Mitzrayim, we do not know what has happened to him." 2. Aharon said to them: "Take off the golden rings that are in the ears of your wives, your sons and your daughters, and bring them to me." 3. Thereupon the

וַיֹּאמְרוּ אֵלָיו קוּם ׀ עֲשֵׂה־לָנוּ אֱלֹהִים אֲשֶׁר יֵלְכוּ לְפָנֵינוּ כִּי־זֶה ׀ מֹשֶׁה הָאִישׁ אֲשֶׁר הֶעֱלָנוּ מֵאֶרֶץ מִצְרַיִם לֹא יָדַעְנוּ מֶה־הָיָה לוֹ: ב וַיֹּאמֶר אֲלֵהֶם אַהֲרֹן פָּרְקוּ נִזְמֵי הַזָּהָב אֲשֶׁר בְּאָזְנֵי נְשֵׁיכֶם בְּנֵיכֶם וּבְנֹתֵיכֶם וְהָבִיאוּ אֵלָי:

nation and the priests had to be made aware of their need for atonement.

make us gods who shall go before us, because this man Moshe... The explanation of the purpose of these gods "who shall go before us" and the rationalization "because this man Moshe," etc., make it clear that this was not a lapse into idolatry in the sense of an ordinary defection from God. What the people wanted Aaron to make was an object to replace not God but Moses. The people believed that Moses had met with some accident, that he had died, and so they demanded from Aaron that he make for them a new "Moses" whom they could never lose. But the fact that they pinned their hopes for the future upon the existence of Moses, and their notion that man could, might and indeed should, make a "Moses figure" for himself— these are notions totally at variance with the basic Jewish concept of God and the mutual relationship between God and man that already had been made clear to the Children of Israel by God's warning: "I have talked with you from heaven; do not make (a representation of) anything (that is) with Me..." (Exodus 20:19-20; see commentary *ibid.*).

They who said to Aaron: "Arise, make us gods who shall go before us, because this man Moshe, who brought us out from the land of Mitzrayim, we do not know what has happened to him," were caught up in a pagan delusion of subjectivism. They saw Moses not as an instrument of God's will, chosen and sent on God's initiative, but as a human being who, by virtue of his own personality, towered over ordinary human nature and had become divine. Therefore, they thought that Moses could influence the will of God and that Moses' existence could assure them God's protection. In their view it was not God Who had brought them out of Egypt through Moses, but Moses who had caused God to perform this work of deliverance. They did not see the Divine laws and ordinances that had come to them through Moses as things that would remain with them even after the mortal who had communicated them to the Children of Israel was no longer there; they did not regard the Law as their inalienable bond with God and as their inalienable guarantee of Divine protection. Instead, they considered the personality of Moses, a

man who was close to God, as the vital link in their connection with God. Only as long as Moses was alive could they be certain of God's protection. They believed that the relationship between Moses and God had been initiated not by God but by Moses; hence, they reasoned, if Moses was no longer alive they could, and indeed must, take some action on their own in order to bind the Deity to themselves. They had not yet completely absorbed the Jewish concept that man had direct access to God, without the need for any intermediary, as long as he conducted himself in accordance with God's will. Or perhaps the fear that henceforth they would have to wander through the wilderness without a leader to guide them caused them to doubt this truth.

2-4. ... It is worth our while to consider why Aaron, who had been given a free hand in the choice of the form to be cast, should have chosen the figure of a calf. It has been suggested that the calf was supposed to represent Apis, the sacred bull of the ancient Egyptians. However, the Egyptian Apis was not a man-made idol but a live bull of specified shape and with specified markings on its hide. Moreover, why should Aaron have chosen precisely the figure of an animal that was worshipped as the supreme deity in the land where his people had once dwelled?

Aaron's choice of this particular form shows precisely that it was not intended to represent Apis or anything else meant to resemble the sacred bull. We have already noted on several occasions—this has been borne out in our study of the sacrificial ritual—that in the symbolism of offerings in Judaism the genuses of פַּר [bullock], שׁוֹר [ox] and בָּקָר [cattle], all of which are the servants of man in his labors, symbolically represent strength employed in the service of a higher being. This is the reason for Aaron's choice of a calf: On the one hand, he sought to satisfy the demands of the people who did not really seek another God but merely a new "Moses," and on the other hand he sought to confine the aberration of the people to the limits of semi-idolatry. To this end no other figure would have been as well suited as that of a bovine animal which does not represent a commanding power but only a servile tool. Also, by choosing from this category not a bull but only entire people took off the golden rings that were in their ears and brought them to Aharon.   4. He took it from their hand, fashioned it with an engraving tool and so made it into a calf of cast metal; thereupon they said: "These are your gods, O Yisrael, who have brought you up from the land of Mitzrayim!"   5. When Aharon saw this, he built an altar before himself and Aharon proclaimed and said: "Tomorrow shall be a festival to *God*."   6. But on the next day they arose early and made ascent offerings, and brought meal-of-peace offerings, and

ג וַיִּתְפָּרְקוּ כָּל־הָעָם אֶת־נִזְמֵי הַזָּהָב אֲשֶׁר בְּאָזְנֵיהֶם וַיָּבִיאוּ אֶל־אַהֲרֹן: ד וַיִּקַּח מִיָּדָם וַיָּצַר אֹתוֹ בַּחֶרֶט וַיַּעֲשֵׂהוּ עֵגֶל מַסֵּכָה וַיֹּאמְרוּ אֵלֶּה אֱלֹהֶיךָ יִשְׂרָאֵל אֲשֶׁר הֶעֱלוּךָ מֵאֶרֶץ מִצְרָיִם: ה וַיַּרְא אַהֲרֹן וַיִּבֶן מִזְבֵּחַ לְפָנָיו וַיִּקְרָא אַהֲרֹן וַיֹּאמַר חַג לַיהֹוָה מָחָר: ו וַיַּשְׁכִּימוּ מִמָּחֳרָת וַיַּעֲלוּ עֹלֹת וַיַּגִּשׁוּ שְׁלָמִים

---

a calf, Aaron endeavored to represent even this servile tool only in its least potent dimension.

°   °   °

5. *When Aharon saw this.* Aaron saw that the aberration had already crossed the narrow gap between seeing the figure as a divine intermediary and regarding it as a deity in its own right. He therefore wanted to put a stop to this aberration by calling for an act of positive homage to the One sole God. Also, he wanted to gain time by setting the festival for the next day only. He built the altar לְפָנָיו, in front of *himself*, not in front of the calf. The fact that Aaron's name is repeated twice in this verse implies that he made this proclamation to counter the utterance of the people and that he put all his own energy into this effort.

6. Verse 8 makes it clear that Aaron's intention had been thwarted in that the offerings were made not to God but to the calf. The fact that the verb וַיֵּשֶׁב ["sat down"] introduces "the people" as a new nominative implies that not all the people participated in the actual sacrifices. Only their spokesmen and ringleaders went to that extreme. However, the people did join in the sacrificial feast and in the attendant merrymaking.

It is significant that this merrymaking should be characterized as צַחֵק [lit., "to laugh"]. In Scripture the use of a form of the verb צחק always implies a denigration of the target of the merrymaking; it expresses the merrymaker's feeling of superiority over something which in fact is serious, great, lofty or noble. When one makes an offering to the One God and to His Law in accordance with that Law, he thereby shows that he is subordinating himself, "offering himself up," as it were, to God and to the dictates of His holy, sanctifying moral Law. Such an offering entails an act of homage to something lofty, great and noble that towers high above man and invites him to aspire to its own high level. In contrast, heathen sacrifices brought to a god of one's own making spring from base sub-

jectivism and thus inspire subjectivism also in the individual who offers them. Such a sacrifice does not imply any offering of self on the part of the individual. What he attempts to do is use the sacrifice as a means to make the supposed master of his fate comply with his personal wishes. He thinks that by means of his sacrifice he can appease the wrath or overcome the indifference of this divine power. By offering this sacrifice he has placed fetters not upon his personal wishes but upon the deity he worships. Paganism and its sacrificial rites represent not only a demoralizing idealization of physical things but are also the complete antithesis of the Jewish concept of "offering." The immediate outgrowths of these rites are dissolution and licentiousness; the heathen sacrifice is likely to "unleash" the individual, as it were. צחק, too, implies an unleashing of sensuality. As the term itself indicates, it is not dissipation born of momentary passion but a more deliberate kind of licentiousness—an attempt to demonstrate the invalidity of the restraints of morality, to mock the moral law by canonizing immorality.

Thus, at the very moment when God's moral law was to enter into its midst and win a sanctuary on earth as the sole bond and guarantee of the link between God and Israel, the Jewish people learned from its own experience, and for all time to come, that even the slightest deviation from exclusive allegiance to the One sole God, the adoption of any heathen cult, no matter what its form, inevitably results in a negation of the law of morality given to Israel. At the same time the first high priest of the Jewish people, on the eve of his induction into office, learned for his own person and for all the future that a Jewish priest must not try to be "smart," that the truths of God are not of his own making. They are not his to compromise; he cannot give up a part of them in order to save the rest. The Teaching of God is inscribed upon a granite rock. One can accept it, or one can reject it; but no priest can alter so much as one iota of it.

the people sat down to eat and to drink, and they arose to behave wantonly. 7. And *God* spoke to Moshe: "Go, go down, for your people that you have brought up from the land of Mitzrayim has become corrupt. 8. They have turned aside very quickly from the path that I have commanded them; they have made themselves a calf of cast metal! And then they cast themselves down before it, offered sacrifices to it, and said: "These are your gods, O Yisrael, who have brought you up from the land of Mitzrayim. 9. And *God* said to Moshe: "I have seen this people and lo! it is a stiff-necked people. 10. Now therefore leave it to Me, and My anger will grow hot against them so that I will annihilate them, and I will make you into a great nation."
11. Thereupon Moshe made supplication before *God*, his God, and said: "For what purpose, O *God*, shall Thy anger grow hot against Thy people which Thou hast brought out from the land of Mitzrayim with great power and with a strong hand? 12. Why should the Mitzrites say: 'He brought them out with evil intent, to kill them in the mountains and to annihilate them from the surface of the earth'? Retreat from the heat of Thine anger and let Thyself be moved to change thy intent regarding the evil intended for Thy people. 13. Remember Abraham, Yitzhak and Yisrael, Thy servants, to whom Thou didst swear by Thine own Name and to whom Thou didst say: 'I will multiply your descendants like the stars of heaven, and all this land of which I said that I would give to your descendants, they shall keep it as their possession forever.'" 14. Thereupon *God* let Himself be moved to change His intent regarding the evil He had said He would do to His people. 15. Now Moshe turned and went down from the mountain with the

וַיֵּ֤שֶׁב הָעָם֙ לֶאֱכֹ֣ל וְשָׁת֔וֹ וַיָּקֻ֖מוּ לְצַחֵֽק: פ
ז וַיְדַבֵּ֥ר יְהֹוָ֖ה אֶל־מֹשֶׁ֑ה לֶךְ־רֵ֕ד כִּ֚י שִׁחֵ֣ת עַמְּךָ֔
אֲשֶׁ֥ר הֶעֱלֵ֖יתָ מֵאֶ֥רֶץ מִצְרָֽיִם: ח סָ֣רוּ מַהֵ֗ר מִן־
הַדֶּ֨רֶךְ֙ אֲשֶׁ֣ר צִוִּיתִ֔ם עָשׂ֣וּ לָהֶ֔ם עֵ֖גֶל מַסֵּכָ֑ה
וַיִּֽשְׁתַּחֲווּ־ל֗וֹ וַיִּזְבְּחוּ־ל֔וֹ וַיֹּ֣אמְר֔וּ אֵ֣לֶּה אֱלֹהֶ֣יךָ
יִשְׂרָאֵ֔ל אֲשֶׁ֥ר הֶעֱל֖וּךָ מֵאֶ֥רֶץ מִצְרָֽיִם: ט וַיֹּ֥אמֶר
יְהֹוָ֖ה אֶל־מֹשֶׁ֑ה רָאִ֙יתִי֙ אֶת־הָעָ֣ם הַזֶּ֔ה וְהִנֵּ֥ה
עַם־קְשֵׁה־עֹ֖רֶף הֽוּא: י וְעַתָּה֙ הַנִּ֣יחָה לִּ֔י וְיִֽחַר־
אַפִּ֥י בָהֶ֖ם וַאֲכַלֵּ֑ם וְאֶֽעֱשֶׂ֥ה אֽוֹתְךָ֖ לְג֥וֹי גָּדֽוֹל:
יא וַיְחַ֣ל מֹשֶׁ֔ה אֶת־פְּנֵ֖י יְהֹוָ֣ה אֱלֹהָ֑יו וַיֹּ֗אמֶר
לָמָ֤ה יְהֹוָה֙ יֶחֱרֶ֤ה אַפְּךָ֙ בְּעַמֶּ֔ךָ אֲשֶׁ֤ר הוֹצֵ֙אתָ֙
מֵאֶ֣רֶץ מִצְרַ֔יִם בְּכֹ֥חַ גָּד֖וֹל וּבְיָ֥ד חֲזָקָֽה: יב לָ֠מָּה
יֹאמְר֨וּ מִצְרַ֜יִם לֵאמֹ֗ר בְּרָעָ֤ה הֽוֹצִיאָם֙ לַהֲרֹ֤ג
אֹתָם֙ בֶּֽהָרִ֔ים וּ֨לְכַלֹּתָ֔ם מֵעַ֖ל פְּנֵ֣י הָֽאֲדָמָ֑ה שׁ֚וּב
מֵחֲר֣וֹן אַפֶּ֔ךָ וְהִנָּחֵ֥ם עַל־הָרָעָ֖ה לְעַמֶּֽךָ: יג זְכֹ֡ר
לְאַבְרָהָם֩ לְיִצְחָ֨ק וּלְיִשְׂרָאֵ֜ל עֲבָדֶ֗יךָ אֲשֶׁ֨ר
נִשְׁבַּ֣עְתָּ לָהֶם֮ בָּךְ֒ וַתְּדַבֵּ֣ר אֲלֵהֶ֔ם אַרְבֶּה֙ אֶת־
זַרְעֲכֶ֔ם כְּכוֹכְבֵ֖י הַשָּׁמָ֑יִם וְכָל־הָאָ֨רֶץ הַזֹּ֜את
אֲשֶׁ֣ר אָמַ֗רְתִּי אֶתֵּן֙ לְזַרְעֲכֶ֔ם וְנָחֲל֖וּ לְעֹלָֽם:
יד וַיִּנָּ֖חֶם יְהֹוָ֑ה עַל־הָ֣רָעָ֔ה אֲשֶׁ֥ר דִּבֶּ֖ר לַעֲשׂ֥וֹת
לְעַמּֽוֹ: פ טו וַיִּ֜פֶן וַיֵּ֤רֶד מֹשֶׁה֙ מִן־הָהָ֔ר וּשְׁנֵ֣י

---

10. ... If you leave it to Me, if you will not intercede in its behalf, the nation will be left to its own devices. If no element will emerge from within the nation to help it mend its ways and to lead it away from apostasy, there will be no alternative but that it will have to be destroyed. However, My original intention and the promise I intend to fulfill through Israel will not be lost, for you are still here. I will make you be a second Abraham and will raise the promised "great nation" from your progeny, since, after all, you, too, are of the seed of Abraham.

two tablets of the Testimony in his hand, tablets inscribed upon both their sides; on the one side and on the other side were they inscribed.   16. And the tablets are a work of God and the writing is a writing of God cut right through the tablets.   17. When Yehoshua heard the voice of the people in the noise of its exuberance, he said to Moshe: "There is a sound of war in the camp!"   18. But the latter said: "[It is] not a voice that announces a victory, nor a sound that announces a defeat; a voice that strikes us down do I hear."   19. And it came to pass when he had come closer to the camp and he saw the calf and the dances, that Moshe's anger grew hot and he threw the tablets out of his joined hands and shattered them at the foot of the mountain. 20. Then he took the calf which they had made, burned it in fire, ground it to fine

לֻחֹת הָעֵדֻת בְּיָדוֹ לֻחֹת כְּתֻבִים מִשְּׁנֵי עֶבְרֵיהֶם מִזֶּה וּמִזֶּה הֵם כְּתֻבִים: טז וְהַלֻּחֹת מַעֲשֵׂה אֱלֹהִים הֵמָּה וְהַמִּכְתָּב מִכְתַּב אֱלֹהִים הוּא חָרוּת עַל־הַלֻּחֹת: יז וַיִּשְׁמַע יְהוֹשֻׁעַ אֶת־קוֹל הָעָם בְּרֵעֹה וַיֹּאמֶר אֶל־מֹשֶׁה קוֹל מִלְחָמָה בַּמַּחֲנֶה: יח וַיֹּאמֶר אֵין קוֹל עֲנוֹת גְּבוּרָה וְאֵין קוֹל עֲנוֹת חֲלוּשָׁה קוֹל עַנּוֹת אָנֹכִי שֹׁמֵעַ: יט וַיְהִי כַּאֲשֶׁר קָרַב אֶל־הַמַּחֲנֶה וַיַּרְא אֶת־הָעֵגֶל וּמְחֹלֹת וַיִּחַר־אַף מֹשֶׁה וַיַּשְׁלֵךְ מִיָּדָו אֶת־הַלֻּחֹת וַיְשַׁבֵּר אֹתָם תַּחַת הָהָר: כ וַיִּקַּח אֶת־הָעֵגֶל אֲשֶׁר עָשׂוּ וַיִּשְׂרֹף בָּאֵשׁ וַיִּטְחַן עַד

15 and 16. Following the events described in the preceding verses, Moses descended from the mountain to perform the task which he himself had recognized as necessary and which had been hallowed, indeed suggested, by God Himself: to quell the treason perpetrated against the cause of God, and to do it in such a manner as to save the future of the nation. Moses went down in order to wage the fight so that a place for the Law of God might yet be established in the midst of the nation. Therefore, he went down "with the two tablets of the Testimony in his hand." Like Phinehas, he went down as a zealot in behalf of God and the action he took was not taken in accordance with express instructions from God. It was Moses' own action performed in the spirit of God.

19. So long as pagan delusions, no matter what their form, are based merely on intellectual error and remain confined to the mind, there is always hope that error may give way to enlightenment and delusion to truth, and that those afflicted by such notions may readily revert to better ways. Not so, however, once the pagan delusion has passed from the limits of intellectual error to the stage where it has poisoned morality and where unleashed excesses of immorality are openly worshipped upon the altar of error. In that case sensuality will cling to the root that offers it such welcome nourishment, and as easy as it is to teach better ways to those who have merely gone astray, so difficult will it be to improve and instruct those whose morals have already been corrupted.

As long as Moses knew only that a calf had been

made and that it was worshipped, he still hoped that he would succeed in his effort to prepare a pure dwelling place for God's Law among the people. He therefore took the Testimony of the Law with him when he descended from the mountain. But when he actually saw the calf and the dancing, he realized that the pagan error had already borne its usual fruit, the unleashing of sensuality. At that point he realized that a new nation would have to be established for this Law. So, without hesitation, with both his hands—יָדָו implies the plural element in the singular—he threw down the tablets and broke them to pieces, thus expressing in no uncertain terms the idea that this people was unworthy of the Law and not fit to receive it. . . .

20. Moses' first act was to make the people aware, by some concrete action, that the god of their delusion was utter nothingness. He not only destroyed the calf idol but ordered each and every member of his nation to assist physically in the total destruction of its god. The people had to drink up their god, as it were. That upon which they had pinned their hopes for physical survival and security had to be put out of existence within their own bodies. That which had been about to dig a grave for their physical purity now had to find its own grave within their physical being. To such expressive teaching devices does a Moses resort. The fact that no one lifted a finger to save his god from the hands of this man Moses and that no one refused to drink the dust of his idol was the first sign of repentance among the people and at the same time proof that a more vigorous stance

אֲשֶׁר־דָּק וַיִּזֶר עַל־פְּנֵי הַמַּיִם וַיַּשְׁק אֶת־בְּנֵי
יִשְׂרָאֵל: כא וַיֹּאמֶר מֹשֶׁה אֶל־אַהֲרֹן מֶה־עָשָׂה
לְךָ הָעָם הַזֶּה כִּי־הֵבֵאתָ עָלָיו חֲטָאָה גְדֹלָה:
כב וַיֹּאמֶר אַהֲרֹן אַל־יִחַר אַף אֲדֹנִי אַתָּה יָדַעְתָּ
אֶת־הָעָם כִּי בְרָע הוּא: כג וַיֹּאמְרוּ לִי עֲשֵׂה־
לָנוּ אֱלֹהִים אֲשֶׁר יֵלְכוּ לְפָנֵינוּ כִּי־זֶה ׀ מֹשֶׁה
הָאִישׁ אֲשֶׁר הֶעֱלָנוּ מֵאֶרֶץ מִצְרַיִם לֹא יָדַעְנוּ
מֶה־הָיָה לוֹ: כד וָאֹמַר לָהֶם לְמִי זָהָב הִתְפָּרָקוּ
וַיִּתְּנוּ־לִי וָאַשְׁלִכֵהוּ בָאֵשׁ וַיֵּצֵא הָעֵגֶל הַזֶּה:
כה וַיַּרְא מֹשֶׁה אֶת־הָעָם כִּי פָרֻעַ הוּא כִּי־
פְרָעֹה אַהֲרֹן לְשִׁמְצָה בְּקָמֵיהֶם: כו וַיַּעֲמֹד
מֹשֶׁה בְּשַׁעַר הַמַּחֲנֶה וַיֹּאמֶר מִי לַיהוָה אֵלָי
וַיֵּאָסְפוּ אֵלָיו כָּל־בְּנֵי לֵוִי: כז וַיֹּאמֶר לָהֶם כֹּה־
אָמַר יְהוָה אֱלֹהֵי יִשְׂרָאֵל שִׂימוּ אִישׁ־חַרְבּוֹ
עַל־יְרֵכוֹ עִבְרוּ וָשׁוּבוּ מִשַּׁעַר לָשַׁעַר בַּמַּחֲנֶה

powder, scattered it upon the water and gave the sons of Yisrael to drink of it.
21. Now Moshe said to Aharon: "What did this people do to you that you permitted such a great sin to come upon them?"
22. Aharon replied: "Let not my lord's anger grow hot! You know the people when they are in [the grip of] evil.
23. They said to me: 'Make us gods who shall go before us, because this man Moshe, who brought us up from the land of Mitzrayim, we do not know what has become of him.'
24. When I said to them: 'Who has gold?' they had already taken it off and gave it to me; I threw it into the fire and so this calf came out."
25. And Moshe saw the people, that it was unrestrained, that Aharon had left it in its moral weakness, without restraints, to the degree of utter irresolution in the midst of those of them who rose up against the Law.
26. And Moshe stood in the gate of the camp and said: "Whoever is *God*'s, [let him come] to me!" And all the sons of Levi gathered around him.
27. He said to them: "Thus says *God*, the God of Yisrael: Let every man place his sword upon his thigh and pass back and forth from one gate to the other in the

before the act might have prevented the people from going astray.

° ° °

21. The first and most urgent order of the day was to demonstrate the ineffectuality of the idol by physically destroying it. This act prepared the ground for the people to come back to their senses. Only after that does Moses address himself to Aaron. The total lack of resistance to his destruction of the calf idol showed what vigorous action could have accomplished among the people. Therefore Moses' question to Aaron was all the more insistent: "What force did this people use against you that you had to let them have their way and persist in their error? . . ."

22–24. This reply truly reveals Aaron's greatness. He says nothing in his own defense; he keeps silent about the extenuating circumstances of which we already know and which would have mitigated his guilt. . . . He voluntarily accepts almost all the blame for what has happened and accuses himself of a gross lack of spirit. "You know what these people are like when they are in the grip of evil. You know how impetuously they can act when they are in the grip of passion." This is all that Aaron has to say in his own defense. "For this reason I did not even attempt to oppose them but acceded to their request at once."

Compare Aaron's watered-down version: "They said to me: Make us gods. . ." with the Scriptural account of what really happened: "The people gathered against Aharon, and they said to him: "Arise, make us gods. . . ." He then continues: "I threw their gold into the fire" (in order to melt it down, he explains, but he says nothing of the wearisome work he had to do after that). "It was in this way, because of my weak-kneed acquiescence, that the calf came into being."

25. From this report Moses realized that the voice of truth and duty had all but disappeared from among the people. . . . But this lack of restraint had come about only because Aaron had not exerted his vigor to bring the voice of truth and duty to bear upon the people. He had failed to champion the ideals that should have served as restraints to control their will and their actions. Instead, he had left the people completely to their own devices. Note the use of the feminine פְּרָעֹה instead of the masculine פרעו. The feminine gender emphasizes the weakness of the nation. . . .

וְהִרְג֧וּ אִֽישׁ־אֶת־אָחִ֛יו וְאִ֥ישׁ אֶת־רֵעֵ֖הוּ וְאִ֥ישׁ
אֶת־קְרֹבֽוֹ׃ כח וַיַּֽעֲשׂ֥וּ בְנֵֽי־לֵוִ֖י כִּדְבַ֣ר מֹשֶׁ֑ה
וַיִּפֹּ֤ל מִן־הָעָם֙ בַּיּ֣וֹם הַה֔וּא כִּשְׁלֹ֥שֶׁת אַלְפֵ֖י
אִֽישׁ׃ כט וַיֹּ֣אמֶר מֹשֶׁ֗ה מִלְא֨וּ יֶדְכֶ֤ם הַיּוֹם֙
לַֽיהֹוָ֔ה כִּ֛י אִ֥ישׁ בִּבְנ֖וֹ וּבְאָחִ֑יו וְלָתֵ֧ת עֲלֵיכֶ֛ם
הַיּ֖וֹם בְּרָכָֽה׃ ל וַֽיְהִי֙ מִֽמָּחֳרָ֔ת וַיֹּ֥אמֶר מֹשֶׁה֙
אֶל־הָעָ֔ם אַתֶּ֥ם חֲטָאתֶ֖ם חֲטָאָ֣ה גְדֹלָ֑ה וְעַתָּה֙
אֶֽעֱלֶ֣ה אֶל־יְהֹוָ֔ה אוּלַ֥י אֲכַפְּרָ֖ה בְּעַ֥ד חַטַּאתְכֶֽם׃
לא וַיָּ֧שָׁב מֹשֶׁ֛ה אֶל־יְהֹוָ֖ה וַיֹּאמַ֑ר אָ֣נָּ֗א חָטָ֞א
הָעָ֤ם הַזֶּה֙ חֲטָאָ֣ה גְדֹלָ֔ה וַיַּֽעֲשׂ֥וּ לָהֶ֖ם אֱלֹהֵ֥י זָהָֽב׃
לב וְעַתָּ֖ה אִם־תִּשָּׂ֣א חַטָּאתָ֑ם וְאִם־אַ֕יִן מְחֵ֣נִי נָ֔א
מִֽסִּפְרְךָ֖ אֲשֶׁ֥ר כָּתָֽבְתָּ׃ לג וַיֹּ֥אמֶר יְהֹוָ֖ה אֶל־
מֹשֶׁ֑ה מִ֚י אֲשֶׁ֣ר חָֽטָא־לִ֔י אֶמְחֶ֖נּוּ מִסִּפְרִֽי׃
לד וְעַתָּ֞ה לֵ֣ךְ ׀ נְחֵ֣ה אֶת־הָעָ֗ם אֶ֤ל אֲשֶׁר־דִּבַּ֨רְתִּי֙
לָ֔ךְ הִנֵּ֥ה מַלְאָכִ֖י יֵלֵ֣ךְ לְפָנֶ֑יךָ וּבְי֣וֹם פָּקְדִ֔י
וּפָקַדְתִּ֥י עֲלֵהֶ֖ם חַטָּאתָֽם׃ לה וַיִּגֹּ֥ף יְהֹוָ֖ה אֶת־
הָעָ֑ם עַ֚ל אֲשֶׁ֣ר עָשׂ֣וּ אֶת־הָעֵ֔גֶל אֲשֶׁ֥ר עָשָׂ֖ה
אַֽהֲרֹֽן׃ ס לג א וַיְדַבֵּ֨ר יְהֹוָ֤ה אֶל־מֹשֶׁה֙ לֵ֣ךְ עֲלֵ֣ה
מִזֶּ֔ה אַתָּ֣ה וְהָעָ֔ם אֲשֶׁ֥ר הֶֽעֱלִ֖יתָ מֵאֶ֣רֶץ מִצְרָ֑יִם
אֶל־הָאָ֗רֶץ אֲשֶׁ֣ר נִ֠שְׁבַּ֠עְתִּי לְאַבְרָהָ֨ם לְיִצְחָ֤ק
וּֽלְיַעֲקֹב֙ לֵאמֹ֔ר לְזַרְעֲךָ֖ אֶתְּנֶֽנָּה׃ ב וְשָֽׁלַחְתִּ֣י
לְפָנֶ֖יךָ מַלְאָ֑ךְ וְגֵֽרַשְׁתִּ֗י אֶת־הַֽכְּנַעֲנִי֙ הָֽאֱמֹרִ֔י

camp, and let every man kill his brother, every man his friend, every man his kinsman." 28. The sons of Levi did according to the word of Moshe; on that day there fell from among the people some three thousand men. 29. And Moshe said: "Assume full authority for yourselves on behalf of *God*—for let each man remain against his son and against his brother—so that He may bestow a blessing upon you this day." 30. It came to pass on the next day that Moshe said to the people: "You have committed a great sin. And now I will go up to *God*; perhaps I will be able to obtain atonement for your sin." 31. And Moshe returned to *God* and said: "Oh! This people has committed a great sin by making themselves gods of gold. 32. And now, if Thou wilt forgive their sin—but if not, then please blot me out from Thy book, which Thou hast written." 33. And *God* said to Moshe: "Whoever has sinned against Me, him I will blot out from My book! 34. And now go, lead the people to the place of which I have spoken to you. Behold, My angel will go before you. But on the day when I remember, I will remember their sin, against them." 35. Then God struck the people with sudden death because they made the calf that Aharon had made.

XXXIII

1. *God* spoke to Moshe: "Depart! Go up from here, you and the people that you brought up from the land of Mitzrayim, to the land that I swore to Abraham, Yitzḥak and Yaakov as follows: To your descendants will I give it 2. —I will send an angel before you and drive out the Canaanite, the Emorite, the Ḥittite and the Perizzite, the

29. After they had completed the act that saved the Law, Moses said to them: "Remain that which you have begun to be today." Constitute yourselves as "zealots" and champions of the Law of God. You need no special appointment or call to do this. Whenever the Law is treated with scorn, every individual is called upon to act as champion and preserver of the Law. The duty and responsibility incumbent on each one in this regard constitutes his letter of appointment. Indeed, the less "official" their action, the more significant and effective it will be, and the more deeply will it impress everyone with the spirit that should be alive within them all.

let each man remain against his son and against his brother. However, only he who is capable of defending the Law even against his own next of kin can act as champion of the Law against the whole community. He can demand of others only such conduct as he would expect also from his own closest kin. . . .

Ḥivvite and the Yebusite— 3. to a land
flowing with milk and honey; for I will no longer go on in your midst because you are a stiff-necked people, lest I destroy you on the way."
4. When the people heard this
evil word they immersed themselves in mourning and no one put on his ornament.
5. And *God* said to Moshe: "Say to the sons of Yisrael: You are a stiff-necked people; if I were to go on in your midst for one moment longer, I would destroy you; but now leave off your ornament, so that I may know what to do with you."
6. So the
sons of Yisrael, on their own, stripped themselves of their ornament from Mount Ḥoreb.
7. And Moshe was to take the tent and pitch it for himself outside the camp, at a distance from the camp, and call it the Tent of Appointed Meeting; whoever sought *God* was to go out to the Tent of Appointed Meeting, which was outside the camp.
8. So it came to pass, whenever Moshe went out to the tent, that all the people would rise, and every man would remain standing at the entrance of his tent, and so they would look after Moshe until he had gone into the tent.
9. And then it came to
pass when Moshe had gone into the tent

וְהַחִתִּי וְהַפְּרִזִּי הַחִוִּי וְהַיְבוּסִי: ג אֶל־אֶרֶץ זָבַת
חָלָב וּדְבָשׁ כִּי לֹא אֶעֱלֶה בְּקִרְבְּךָ כִּי עַם־קְשֵׁה־
עֹרֶף אַתָּה פֶּן־אֲכֶלְךָ בַּדָּרֶךְ: ד וַיִּשְׁמַע הָעָם
אֶת־הַדָּבָר הָרָע הַזֶּה וַיִּתְאַבָּלוּ וְלֹא־שָׁתוּ אִישׁ
עֶדְיוֹ עָלָיו: ה וַיֹּאמֶר יְהֹוָה אֶל־מֹשֶׁה אֱמֹר אֶל־
בְּנֵי־יִשְׂרָאֵל אַתֶּם עַם־קְשֵׁה־עֹרֶף רֶגַע אֶחָד
אֶעֱלֶה בְקִרְבְּךָ וְכִלִּיתִיךָ וְעַתָּה הוֹרֵד עֶדְיְךָ
מֵעָלֶיךָ וְאֵדְעָה מָה אֶעֱשֶׂה־לָּךְ: ו וַיִּתְנַצְּלוּ בְנֵי־
יִשְׂרָאֵל אֶת־עֶדְיָם מֵהַר חוֹרֵב: ז וּמֹשֶׁה יִקַּח
אֶת־הָאֹהֶל וְנָטָה־לוֹ ׀ מִחוּץ לַמַּחֲנֶה הַרְחֵק
מִן־הַמַּחֲנֶה וְקָרָא לוֹ אֹהֶל מוֹעֵד וְהָיָה כָּל־
מְבַקֵּשׁ יְהֹוָה יֵצֵא אֶל־אֹהֶל מוֹעֵד אֲשֶׁר מִחוּץ
לַמַּחֲנֶה: ח וְהָיָה כְּצֵאת מֹשֶׁה אֶל־הָאֹהֶל יָקוּמוּ
כָּל־הָעָם וְנִצְּבוּ אִישׁ פֶּתַח אָהֳלוֹ וְהִבִּיטוּ אַחֲרֵי
מֹשֶׁה עַד־בֹּאוֹ הָאֹהֱלָה: ט וְהָיָה כְּבֹא מֹשֶׁה

CHAPTER XXXIII

4. ***. . . and no one put on his ornament.*** We are not told what kind of ornament this was. But it is clear from the context that it was an ornament in the literal sense of the term, one that could be put on and taken off. If one interprets the words מֵהַר חוֹרֵב ["from Mount Horeb"] to mean that they obtained this ornament on Mount Horeb, it must have been not simply jewelry, but an ornament of a special kind.

We would venture the following suggestion: There is only one object that has been described for us as the national ornament of the Jewish people; namely, טוֹטָפוֹת, the "ornament for the brow" mentioned in Exodus 13:16. Ezekiel 24:17 refers to it as פְּאֵר; i.e., "ornament," without additional qualifications, and it is taken off as a sign of mourning. Should we not, then, consider the "ornament" mentioned in this verse as identical with this, the sole national ornament of the Jewish people? These are the תְּפִלִּין which they received immediately upon their departure from Mitzrayim.

The words קַדֶּשׁ ["Sanctify to Me . . ."] (Exodus 13:2) and וְהָיָה כִּי יְבִיאֲךָ ["And now it shall be when (*God*) will bring you . . ."] (Exodus 13:11) informed every Jewish male of his calling to be consecrated to God. With these words the arm and the head of each Jewish male were consecrated for their sacred vocation, one that was to be imparted to the Children of Israel in more explicit detail only at Mount Horeb. And at Mount Horeb, too, they first became aware that they were not adequate to the vocation that had been assigned to them with their departure from Mitzrayim. Was it, then, not only natural that this realization of their spiritual and moral immaturity should have grieved them sufficiently to keep them from putting on their תְּפִלִּין? . . .

If this ornament was indeed the תְּפִלִּין, which God Himself had commanded them to put on, they had to have Divine sanction also for leaving it off. In that case it is not at all redundant for the text to stress, by means of these repeated statements, that, even before God had commanded them to do so, they had left off their ornament on their own initiative, out of a feeling of unworthiness. For the fact that they had divested themselves of their ornament on their own gave this act its true significance: it expressed their realization that they had sinned.

9–11. Neither God Himself nor anything Divine

that the pillar of cloud would descend and stand at the entrance of the tent, and then He would speak with Moshe. 10. All the people saw the pillar of cloud standing at the entrance of the tent; all the people rose and every man cast himself down at the entrance of his tent. 11. *God* spoke to Moshe face to face, as a man would speak to his companion; [afterwards,] when he returned to the camp, his young servant Yehoshua, the son of Nun, would not depart from the tent. 12. Moshe said to *God*: "See, Thou sayest to me: 'Lead this people on!' But Thou didst not let me know what Thou wilt send with me. And Thou hast said: 'I have recognized you by name and you have also attained worthiness of favor in Mine eyes.' 13. And now, if I have attained worthiness of favor in Thine eyes, enable me, I pray, to recognize the unity [of purpose] in the diversity of Thy ways, so that I may know Thee, so that I may continue to attain worthiness of favor in Thine eyes; and consider, too, that this nation is, after all, Thy people." 14. He said: "My Countenance itself will go, and I will comply with your request. 15. And he said to Him: "If Thy Countenance itself will not go [with us], do not let us go on

הָאֹהֱלָה יֵרֵד עַמּוּד הֶעָנָן וְעָמַד פֶּתַח הָאֹהֶל וְדִבֶּר עִם־מֹשֶׁה: י וְרָאָה כָל־הָעָם אֶת־עַמּוּד הֶעָנָן עֹמֵד פֶּתַח הָאֹהֶל וְקָם כָּל־הָעָם וְהִשְׁתַּחֲווּ אִישׁ פֶּתַח אָהֳלוֹ: יא וְדִבֶּר יְהֹוָה אֶל־מֹשֶׁה פָּנִים אֶל־פָּנִים כַּאֲשֶׁר יְדַבֵּר אִישׁ אֶל־רֵעֵהוּ וְשָׁב אֶל־הַמַּחֲנֶה וּמְשָׁרְתוֹ יְהוֹשֻׁעַ בִּן־נוּן נַעַר לֹא יָמִישׁ מִתּוֹךְ הָאֹהֶל: פ שלישי יב וַיֹּאמֶר מֹשֶׁה אֶל־יְהֹוָה רְאֵה אַתָּה אֹמֵר אֵלַי הַעַל אֶת־הָעָם הַזֶּה וְאַתָּה לֹא הוֹדַעְתַּנִי אֵת אֲשֶׁר־תִּשְׁלַח עִמִּי וְאַתָּה אָמַרְתָּ יְדַעְתִּיךָ בְשֵׁם וְגַם־מָצָאתָ חֵן בְּעֵינָי: יג וְעַתָּה אִם־נָא מָצָאתִי חֵן בְּעֵינֶיךָ הוֹדִעֵנִי נָא אֶת־דְּרָכֶךָ וְאֵדָעֲךָ לְמַעַן אֶמְצָא־חֵן בְּעֵינֶיךָ וּרְאֵה כִּי עַמְּךָ הַגּוֹי הַזֶּה: יד וַיֹּאמַר פָּנַי יֵלֵכוּ וַהֲנִחֹתִי לָךְ: טו וַיֹּאמֶר אֵלָיו אִם־אֵין פָּנֶיךָ הֹלְכִים אַל־

dwelt within this tent. It was the tent in which Moses lived. That is why his servant always remained inside. Joshua was there as a נַעַר [youth], one who had yet to become a man. The Presence of God did not seek him out there. Only when Moses came into the tent did the cloud that heralded God's Presence descend. . . .

12. Nowhere must any translation or explanation of the Word of God tread more carefully than with the contents of Verses 12 to 23. For these passages lead us to the outer limits of man's knowledge of God. The area that lies beyond these limits is indicated to us precisely in order to show us the spheres we cannot reach with the [finite] measure of knowledge granted us for our life on earth. How, then, in any attempt of ours to understand and interpret these passages, should we not be filled with trepidation lest we overshoot the mark of truth and go beyond the bounds of what the text was meant to convey? . . .

13. *And now.* And now, if I am to be able to lead this people through the immediate future according to my own insight, I need a dimension of knowledge that I still lack. I must be able to recognize דְּרָכֶךָ וגו׳. The text

reads neither דַּרְכְּךָ ["Thy way"], nor דְּרָכֶיךָ ["Thy ways"], but דְּרָכֶךָ. This form [combining both singular and plural] indicates that God's ways are manifold but that they all have one single purpose.

[Moses says] "I still lack the understanding of how, in all the diversity of Thy ways, Thou pursuest only one purpose also in this instance. Clearly, there has been a change in the leadership of the people. Yet Thou hast not given up Thy original plan for Thy people and surely Thou pursuest Thy original purpose, albeit by other ways. But I am still in need of this insight, to know the one purpose inherent in the diversity of Thy ways."

so that I may know Thee. So that my view of Thy intentions may remain clear.

so that I may continue to attain worthiness of favor. So that I may continue to prove myself worthy of Thy favor, that I may justify the trust Thou hast placed in me and discharge the mission Thou hast assigned to me, a mission that can be nothing else but to lead this people in accordance with Thy intentions. . . .

15 and 16. . . . If the Word of God is to be transmitted to all mankind, there must be a messenger of God

from here. 16. For how else will it then be known that I have attained worthiness of favor in Thine eyes, I and Thy people? Is it not in that Thou goest with us? Then we, I and Thy people, will be miraculously distinguished from every other nation which is on the face of the earth." 17. And *God* said to Moshe: "I shall fulfill also this word which you have spoken, for you have attained worthiness of favor in Mine eyes, since I have recognized you by name." 18. And he said: "Let me, I pray, behold Thy glory!" 19. He said: "I will let all My goodness pass before your face; I will proclaim *God* by name before you; I will favor whomever I will favor, and I will have compassion upon whomever I will have compassion." 20. He said: "You cannot see My Countenance, for man shall

תַּעֲלֵנוּ מִזֶּה: טז וּבַמֶּה | יִוָּדַע אֵפוֹא כִּי־מָצָאתִי
חֵן בְּעֵינֶיךָ אֲנִי וְעַמֶּךָ הֲלוֹא בְּלֶכְתְּךָ עִמָּנוּ
וְנִפְלֵינוּ אֲנִי וְעַמְּךָ מִכָּל־הָעָם אֲשֶׁר עַל־פְּנֵי
הָאֲדָמָה: פ רביעי יז וַיֹּאמֶר יְהוָה אֶל־מֹשֶׁה גַּם
אֶת־הַדָּבָר הַזֶּה אֲשֶׁר דִּבַּרְתָּ אֶעֱשֶׂה כִּי־מָצָאתָ
חֵן בְּעֵינַי וָאֵדָעֲךָ בְּשֵׁם: יח וַיֹּאמַר הַרְאֵנִי נָא
אֶת־כְּבֹדֶךָ: יט וַיֹּאמֶר אֲנִי אַעֲבִיר כָּל־טוּבִי
עַל־פָּנֶיךָ וְקָרָאתִי בְשֵׁם יְהוָה לְפָנֶיךָ וְחַנֹּתִי
אֶת־אֲשֶׁר אָחֹן וְרִחַמְתִּי אֶת־אֲשֶׁר אֲרַחֵם:
כ וַיֹּאמֶר לֹא תוּכַל לִרְאֹת אֶת־פָּנָי כִּי לֹא־

and a people of God. Israel's history, which reveals the workings of God, is the essential instrument for implanting into mankind the Law which was revealed by God.

18. . . . [Moses'] first request was that he might be given an understanding of the ways of God so that he might attain an understanding of God Himself. "Enable me, I pray, to recognize the one purpose in all the diversity of Thy ways, so that I may know Thee."

Moses' second request is on a higher level. He now seeks to obtain a direct perception of God from which an understanding of His ways would naturally follow. The perception he now seeks is on a higher level, that of intuition: It is now הַרְאֵנִי ["let me behold"], not הודיעֵנִי ["teach me"]. The relationship between these two concepts is the same as that between רְאִיָּה [sight, direct perception] and יְדִיעָה [knowledge].

19 and 20. Moses receives the answer to his request in two verses, 19 and 20. In Verse 19 he is told what part of his request will be granted; in Verse 20, what part will have to be denied him. Intuitive knowledge, that higher level of cognition, will be granted him.

I will let all My goodness pass before your face; I will proclaim. He will perceive not only words but also visual phenomena, and while he is shown that which he is to behold, he will hear words that will explain to him the meaning of what he is beholding. However, that which he is to behold is merely that to which his first request referred: the ways of God, diverse but always directed toward one single purpose. This unity of purpose, this basic principle that is realized in every aspect of God's ways, even as the spectrum of seven colors unites to form one single ray of [white] light, is טובִי ["My goodness"]. טוב ד׳, the "goodness" of God, as in חַטאות נְעורַי וגו׳ לְמַעַן טוּבְךָ ד׳ ["Remember not the sins of my youth . . . according to Thy loving-kindness remember Thou me, for the sake of Thy goodness. . ."] (Psalm 25:7).

טוב, "good," is essentially a relative concept. It denotes that which is consistent with well-being. But this well-being is conditional upon the character of the object whose well-being is to be promoted. By letting כָּל טוּבוֹ [all His goodness] pass before Moses, God intended that Moses should perceive all the diversity of the phenomena which demonstrate the one consistent goodness of God to all His creatures, particularly man. The diversity of human nature, resulting from the moral freedom with which man is endowed, necessitates the same diversity in the ways of God that are intended to train him for his own well-being. In every instance it is the same well-being and the same goodness. The ordinary eye sees only a multitude of ways which often appear to be mutually contradictory. But the eye of Moses is not only to surmise, imagine and comprehend the sublimely harmonious unity of purpose inherent in all this diversity: he is to behold it: אַעֲבִיר כָּל טוּבִי עַל פָּנֶיךָ ["I will let all My goodness pass before you"].

Simultaneously, God will explain to him, in words, that which he will behold; וְקָרָאתִי בְשֵׁם ד׳ לְפָנֶיךָ ["I will proclaim *God* by name before you"]. This turn of phrase could be interpreted in the same sense as we interpret the phrase קָרָא בְּשֵׁם ד׳ ["to call in the name of *God*"], in the story of Abraham, *et al.* God will teach Moses how to put into words that which he is to behold, so that he will be able to proclaim God to men in the not see Me and live." 21. And *God* said: "Behold, there is one vantage point* next to

יִרְאַנִי הָאָדָם וָחָי: כא וַיֹּאמֶר יְהֹוָה הִנֵּה מָקוֹם

**Note to the English translation:* In his German translation, Hirsch renders מָקוֹם lit., "place," as *Standpunkt*, lit. "standpoint." [G.H.]

language of human beings. Indeed, in Rosh HaShanah 17b the fulfillment of this promise (Exodus 34:5) is described as follows: "Rabbi Yohanan said: Were it not written in the text, it would be impossible for one to say such a thing; this verse teaches us that the Holy One, blessed be He, drew His *tallith* over His head like the reader of a congregation and showed Moses the order of prayer."

God taught Moses the way in which men are to make Him known among themselves. . . . The interpretation here is: . . . I will let all the diverse manifestations of My consistent goodness pass before your eye so that you may perceive them, and I will bring every nuance of this diversity to your understanding by proclaiming to you a name for God which reflects that particular attribute.

וְחַנֹּתִי וגו׳ ***[I will favor].*** I will practice חֲנִינָה [favor] and רַחֲמִים [compassion] before your very eyes. I will make you see the various forms in which My חֲנִינָה and רַחֲמִים are demonstrated, depending on the character traits of the individual to whom I grant them. I will show you not only how My consistent goodness is manifest in the diverse demonstrations of My רַחֲמִים, חֲנִינָה, etc., but also how even these varied manifestations differ according to the personalities of the individuals who are to receive them. You will come to know the individualized character of My Providence.

This individualized character of Divine Providence —the fact that the forms of God's חֵן [favor] vary according to the personality of אֶת אֲשֶׁר יָחוֹן [whoever He will favor] and that the forms of His רַחֲמִים [compassion], too, are adapted to the personality of אֶת אֲשֶׁר יְרַחֵם [upon whomever He will have compassion] — is precisely what eludes the insight of mortal men. If need be, man is capable of comprehending such things in general terms, but the individual aspects of these phenomena remain a secret before him. This is why we are so prone to error in judging the "ways of God"; we tend to forget that when it seems to us that צַדִּיק וְרַע לוֹ ["this man is righteous, yet things go badly with him"], while רָשָׁע וְטוֹב לוֹ ["that man is evil, yet things go well with him"], we may be mistaken in our judgment of who is really a צַדִּיק and who a רָשָׁע, and also that we are in no position to be certain whether, in a given case, טוֹב לוֹ or רַע לוֹ [things do indeed go badly or well with an individual]. For only a most profound insight into the individuality of a human being would enable us to determine what in truth may be רַע or טוֹב ["evil" or "good"] for him.

Seen from this point of view, either of the two following interpretations may be acceptable: That of Rabbi Yosi (Berakhoth 7a), according to which Moses was shown the answer to this vexing question, or that of Rabbi Meir (ibid.), according to which the answer remained a mystery even to Moses. Even if, as implied by the words "I will favor whomever I will favor. . . ," God permitted him to behold the answer to this mystery by concrete demonstrations of the individualized aspects of His Providence, the limited human insight of even such an individual as Moses was not sufficient to judge every instance of Divine Providence by that standard.

° ° °

The promise which was made to Moses in this verse and the fulfillment of which is described in 34:6 was simply a response to Moses' first request: "Enable me, I pray, to recognize the one purpose in the diversity of Thy ways." This is clear from Psalm 103:7 and 8, "He makes known His ways to Moses . . . that God is full of compassion . . . and ready to be gracious," referring to the revelation which was granted to Moses and which is described in Exodus 34:6.

Verse 20 gives the reason why the request [made by Moses in Verse 18] was denied him; namely, that it is beyond the limits set for man's cognitive capacity while he is on earth.

21. ***And* God *said.*** We could almost say that the answers in the two preceding verses take the form of a didactic synthesis. First, there is the positive response; only then comes the negative response, accompanied by an explanation of why Moses' request must be denied. Both responses are offered separately, in two distinct explanations. "And *God* said": God adds, by way of an explanation, "Behold, there is one vantage point next to Me." If we understand these words correctly, they would indicate most meaningfully not only the pinnacle but also the limits set for the human mind. "You are not to behold God Himself, but you are to view the earth and earthly concerns, men and human affairs, from the standpoint of God." This is the highest goal attainable to man here below, and hence the only goal to which he may aspire.

there is one vantage point next to Me. There is only one vantage point set as the highest goal for even the greatest human intellect. Even for a man such as Moses there is only one vantage point: not to look up from earth to God in order to attain a vision of God and of things Divine, but to be uplifted by God, to stand "next

Me; stand upon the rock.   22. When My glory will then pass by, I will shelter you in the cleft of the rock and I will cover you with My hand until I have passed by. 23. Then I will take away My hand, and you will look after Me; My face shall not be seen.''

XXXIV

1. And *God* said to Moshe: ''Hew for yourself two tablets of stones like the first ones; I will write upon the tablets the words that were on the first tablets, which you broke.   2. Be prepared for the morning, and in the morning you will ascend Mount Sinai and stand waiting for Me upon the summit of the mountain.   3. No man shall ascend with you, neither shall any man be seen anywhere on the mountain, neither shall the sheep and the cattle graze facing this mountain.''   4. He hewed two tablets of stones like the first ones, and Moshe arose early in the morning and ascended Mount Sinai as *God* had commanded him, and he took two tablets of stones into his hand.   5. And *God* descended in the cloud and placed Himself next to him there, and He proclaimed *God* by name.   6. And *God* passed by before him and proclaimed: ''*God* always remains *God*, exercising power, loving His creation and ready to

אֹתִי וְנִצַּבְתָּ עַל־הַצּוּר: כב וְהָיָה בַּעֲבֹר כְּבֹדִי וְשַׂמְתִּיךָ בְּנִקְרַת הַצּוּר וְשַׂכֹּתִי כַפִּי עָלֶיךָ עַד־ עָבְרִי: כג וַהֲסִרֹתִי אֶת־כַּפִּי וְרָאִיתָ אֶת־אֲחֹרָי וּפָנַי לֹא יֵרָאוּ: פ חמישי לד א וַיֹּאמֶר יְהֹוָה אֶל־מֹשֶׁה פְּסָל־לְךָ שְׁנֵי־לֻחֹת אֲבָנִים כָּרִאשֹׁנִים וְכָתַבְתִּי עַל־הַלֻּחֹת אֶת־הַדְּבָרִים אֲשֶׁר הָיוּ עַל־הַלֻּחֹת הָרִאשֹׁנִים אֲשֶׁר שִׁבַּרְתָּ: ב וֶהְיֵה נָכוֹן לַבֹּקֶר וְעָלִיתָ בַבֹּקֶר אֶל־הַר סִינַי וְנִצַּבְתָּ לִי שָׁם עַל־רֹאשׁ הָהָר: ג וְאִישׁ לֹא־יַעֲלֶה עִמָּךְ וְגַם־אִישׁ אַל־יֵרָא בְּכָל־הָהָר גַּם־הַצֹּאן וְהַבָּקָר אַל־יִרְעוּ אֶל־מוּל הָהָר הַהוּא: ד וַיִּפְסֹל שְׁנֵי־ לֻחֹת אֲבָנִים כָּרִאשֹׁנִים וַיַּשְׁכֵּם מֹשֶׁה בַבֹּקֶר וַיַּעַל אֶל־הַר סִינַי כַּאֲשֶׁר צִוָּה יְהֹוָה אֹתוֹ וַיִּקַּח בְּיָדוֹ שְׁנֵי לֻחֹת אֲבָנִים: ה וַיֵּרֶד יְהֹוָה בֶּעָנָן וַיִּתְיַצֵּב עִמּוֹ שָׁם וַיִּקְרָא בְשֵׁם יְהֹוָה: ו וַיַּעֲבֹר יְהֹוָה עַל־פָּנָיו וַיִּקְרָא יְהֹוָה | יְהֹוָה אֵל רַחוּם

---

to Him,'' to look upon man and human concerns from the standpoint of God; to understand and to judge man and all things human from the lofty vantage point of God. ''The vantage point for your beholding is not *before* Me or *toward* Me; it is *next* to Me. You shall stand upon the rock so that, from this lofty vantage point, you may look upon the earth as it is under the power of Divine Providence.''

23. **אַחֲרָי** *[after Me]*. You will not see Me at work; you can and shall see only the traces of Myself and My Providence.

CHAPTER XXXIV

1. The condition for the restoration of God's original intimate relationship with Israel is that we must accept again in our midst His Law as the only intermediary in this relationship. Since the people has broken the Law, the people must now hand to God the blank tablets, with the humble request that the old Law be inscribed

upon the new tablets by the finger of God. Our transgressions do not in any way alter the contents of the Law of God. God will not reform the Law to accommodate our weaknesses. The Law that we scorned stands unaltered, awaiting our return to give it our unqualified allegiance. . . .

    ∘   ∘   ∘

6 and 7. **And God *passed by before him and proclaimed.*** This is the fulfillment of the promise given in 33:19: ''I will let all My goodness pass before your face and I will proclaim *God* by name before you,'' see commentary ibid.

''Enable me, I pray, to recognize the one purpose in the diversity of Thy ways'': This was the content of Moses' first request, which was granted, and it was to be granted him on the second, higher level of cognition referred to in his second request, **הַרְאֵנִי** [''Let me behold, I pray. . .''] as well as on the first level, **הוֹדִיעֵנִי** [Please enable me to recognize. . .].

God accedes to his request on both levels. **וַיַּעֲבֹר** [God's passing before Moses] is God's response to **הַרְאֵנִי** [Moses' request to be permitted to behold God's glory]

וְחַנּוּן אֶרֶךְ אַפַּיִם וְרַב־חֶסֶד וֶאֱמֶת׃ ז נֹצֵר (נ׳
רבתי) חֶסֶד לָאֲלָפִים נֹשֵׂא עָוֹן וָפֶשַׁע וְחַטָּאָה
וְנַקֵּה לֹא יְנַקֶּה פֹּקֵד ׀ עֲוֹן אָבוֹת עַל־בָּנִים
וְעַל־בְּנֵי בָנִים עַל־שִׁלֵּשִׁים וְעַל־רִבֵּעִים׃
ח וַיְמַהֵר מֹשֶׁה וַיִּקֹּד אַרְצָה וַיִּשְׁתָּחוּ׃ ט וַיֹּאמֶר
אִם־נָא מָצָאתִי חֵן בְּעֵינֶיךָ אֲדֹנָי יֵלֶךְ־נָא אֲדֹנָי
בְּקִרְבֵּנוּ כִּי עַם־קְשֵׁה־עֹרֶף הוּא וְסָלַחְתָּ לַעֲוֹנֵנוּ
וּלְחַטָּאתֵנוּ וּנְחַלְתָּנוּ׃ ששי י וַיֹּאמֶר הִנֵּה אָנֹכִי
כֹּרֵת בְּרִית נֶגֶד כָּל־עַמְּךָ אֶעֱשֶׂה נִפְלָאֹת אֲשֶׁר
לֹא־נִבְרְאוּ בְכָל־הָאָרֶץ וּבְכָל־הַגּוֹיִם וְרָאָה כָל־
הָעָם אֲשֶׁר־אַתָּה בְקִרְבּוֹ אֶת־מַעֲשֵׂה יְהוָה כִּי־
נוֹרָא הוּא אֲשֶׁר אֲנִי עֹשֶׂה עִמָּךְ׃ יא שְׁמָר־לְךָ
אֵת אֲשֶׁר אָנֹכִי מְצַוְּךָ הַיּוֹם הִנְנִי גֹרֵשׁ מִפָּנֶיךָ

bestow favor, long-suffering and abundant in loving-kindness and truth, 7. preserving loving-kindness for the thousandth [generation], lifting away crookedness and rebellion and levity; yet He remits nothing. He remembers the crookedness of parents for the children and children's children, to the third and fourth generation." 8. And Moshe made haste, bowed his head to the ground and cast himself down, 9. and he said: "If I have attained worthiness of favor in Thine eyes, my Lord, then, I pray, let my Lord go in our midst; because it is a stiff-necked people, Thou wilt forgive our crookedness and our levity and thus secure us as Thy possession forever." 10. Thereupon He said: "Lo! I will make a covenant; I will perform miracles in the presence of all your people such as have not been brought forth upon all the earth and among all the nations; all the people in whose midst you are shall see the work of *God,* how awe-inspiring it is, that which I will do with you. 11. Keep carefully that which I command you today; lo! I will drive out from

and וַיִּקְרָא [His proclamation] responds to הוֹדִיעֵנִי [Moses' request to be taught the one purpose in all the diversity of God's ways].

Moses' search for the one purpose in all the diversity of God's ways was set off by the serious incident [of the golden calf], in which God had caused Moses to experience God's workings in a diversity of manifestations. Moses now sought the unifying factor that underlay all these manifestations of Divine Providence. . . . Moses searched for the one purpose in all this diversity. He dared seek to comprehend this unity of purpose at its true source, by a direct view of the personal Deity, from which he believed he might gain insight into the one purpose of all God's workings. This *a priori* perception of God's ways was denied him. However, he was to be permitted to view the unity of God's purpose in all the diversity of His ways, and to behold the diversity that emanates from this unity of purpose. This is now demonstrated physically for Moses to see and explained verbally for Him to understand. Exactly what he saw is not made known to us, but we do have a record of the words, the "names" by which the phenomena he beheld were explained to him.

10. . . .With these words God assures Moses that He will support Moses' activities in the midst of the people by successes and happenings that will be miracles, obviously direct creations of God, because they will be completely unrelated to the ordinary physical laws of cause and effect.

such as have not been brought forth upon all the earth and among all the nations. Events without precedent or parallel anywhere in the realm of nature or in the history of nations.

As a result, the "mission of Moses" will be revealed as a phenomenon unique in time and space, thus confirming for all time the uniqueness, the Divine character and the inviolability (נוֹרָא [awe-inspiring character]) of the Law of God that Moses brought [down from Mount Sinai]. . . . It was to be brought home to the people for all time that the "mission of Moses" was בְּרִיאָה, a "creation" of God in the midst of the history of mankind, and that as such it was different from all other phenomena in history. It is in no way comparable to anything classed as "religion," "law," etc. that has emerged among the nations in the past or will develop in the future.

The "mission of Moses" is addressed first of all to Israel, and that mission must now confirm the Divine absoluteness of its conquering power by winning over this, the most stiff-necked among nations.

before you the Emorite and the Canaanite, the Hittite and the Perizzite, the Hivvite and the Yebusite. 12. For your own sake, take heed that you do not make a covenant with the inhabitant[s] of the land into which you will come, so that it will not become a snare in your midst. 13. For you shall destroy their altars and break their memorial stones, and cut down his sacred trees. 14. For you shall not cast yourself down before another god, because *God*, Whose Name is exclusive [of all others], is a God Who demands His exclusive right. 15. If you were to make a covenant with the inhabitant[s] of the land, they would go astray after their gods, they would offer sacrifices to their gods, and one of them **would invite you and you would eat of his meal,** 16. and you would take of his daughters for your sons; then his daughters would go astray after their gods and would lead your sons also to apostasy and to cast themselves down before their gods. 17. You shall not make yourself gods

אֶת־הָאֱמֹרִי֙ וְהַֽכְּנַעֲנִ֔י וְהַֽחִתִּי֙ וְהַפְּרִזִּ֔י וְהַֽחִוִּ֖י וְהַיְבוּסִֽי׃ יב הִשָּׁ֣מֶר לְךָ֗ פֶּן־תִּכְרֹ֤ת בְּרִית֙ לְיוֹשֵׁ֣ב הָאָ֔רֶץ אֲשֶׁ֥ר אַתָּ֖ה בָּ֣א עָלֶ֑יהָ פֶּן־יִהְיֶ֥ה לְמוֹקֵ֖שׁ בְּקִרְבֶּֽךָ׃ יג כִּ֤י אֶת־מִזְבְּחֹתָם֙ תִּתֹּצ֔וּן וְאֶת־מַצֵּבֹתָ֖ם תְּשַׁבֵּר֑וּן וְאֶת־אֲשֵׁרָ֖יו תִּכְרֹתֽוּן׃ יד כִּ֛י לֹ֥א תִֽשְׁתַּחֲוֶ֖ה לְאֵ֣ל אַחֵ֑ר (ר׳ רבתי) כִּ֤י יְהֹוָה֙ קַנָּ֣א שְׁמ֔וֹ אֵ֥ל קַנָּ֖א הֽוּא׃ טו פֶּן־תִּכְרֹ֥ת בְּרִ֖ית לְיוֹשֵׁ֣ב הָאָ֑רֶץ וְזָנ֣וּ ׀ אַחֲרֵ֣י אֱלֹֽהֵיהֶ֗ם וְזָבְחוּ֙ לֵֽאלֹ֣הֵיהֶ֔ם וְקָרָ֣א לְךָ֔ וְאָֽכַלְתָּ֖ מִזִּבְחֽוֹ׃ טז וְלָֽקַחְתָּ֥ מִבְּנֹתָ֖יו לְבָנֶ֑יךָ וְזָנ֣וּ בְנֹתָ֗יו אַֽחֲרֵי֙ אֱלֹ֣הֵיהֶ֔ן וְהִזְנוּ֙ אֶת־בָּנֶ֔יךָ אַֽחֲרֵ֖י אֱלֹֽהֵיהֶֽן׃ יז אֱלֹהֵ֥י מַסֵּכָ֖ה לֹ֥א

15 and 16. The use of a form of the verb זנה [which is usually employed in Scripture to denote marital infidelity] with reference to the idolatry practiced by the other nations shows that the relationship which God seeks to have with mankind and which mankind should have with Him is conceived in terms of the intimacy that Israel associates with marriage. The other nations, too, should be wed spiritually to God in everlasting faithfulness; hence their idolatry is an act of infidelity to God. . . .

17. The laws immediately preceding this verse, as well as the ones that now follow, were already stated earlier as the conclusion of the מִשְׁפָּטִים, the basic principles of social legislation. There, they stressed these institutions as the instruments to stimulate and foster for all time adherence to the Law as such, particularly the concept that all the citizens of the state are equal before the Law of God. At this point, where the Law which the people almost forfeited is reiterated, these principles are restated particularly to underscore their contrast with the notions of paganism and with that particular pagan delusion which nearly caused the people to lose its individuality and its Law.

"Make us gods. . ." (Exodus 32:1): This cry was born of the notion that man could, and indeed must, fashion for himself some sort of deity, a divine object, even if it be only to serve as an agent to embody the relationship

of God to man as man's Guardian and Guide; as if man could have no direct relationship with God but could, or must, resort to means other than the faithful observance of His Law in order to secure His protection!

This law and all the laws that follow refute this delusion. They set up the personality of man in direct proximity to God and show that it is neither nature, nor anything else in the world around him, that brings man near to God, but that it is in fact through man that nature and all the world around him are to be elevated to a covenantal relationship with God.

Hence, first, Verse 17: "You shall not make yourself gods of cast metal!" You shall not make an image of a god for yourself; you shall not labor under the delusion that you must capture the Divine for yourself by means of an image. It is you who must raise yourself up to your God by arranging all your life as a human being in accordance with His will.

Next comes Verse 18: "The Festival of Unleavened Bread you shall keep. . . ." When springtime beckons, when summer causes your fruits to ripen, when autumn brings you your harvest, it is not nature and her gifts that you must celebrate. Instead, it is the springtime of your own person that you must celebrate in the spring, the maturing of your person in the summer, and the attainment of your completion as a person in the fall. The manifestations of nature's annual cycle do not summon you to worship in nature's temple. Rather, at of cast metal!   18. The Festival of Unleavened Bread you shall keep; seven days you shall eat unleavened bread which I have commanded you, at the appointed meeting time of the month of the standing grain; for in the month of the standing grain did you go out from Mitzrayim.   19. All that opens the womb is Mine, and all your property shall have the remembrance of its dependent state consecrated by the male first-born of ox or sheep.   20. The firstling of a donkey you shall redeem with a lamb; if you do not redeem it, you must kill it by a blow on the back of the neck; you must also redeem all the first-born among your sons, and My Countenance must not be beheld empty-handed.   21. Six days you shall create, serving, but on the seventh day you shall cease from your work; at ploughing time and at harvest time you shall cease from your work.   22. And you shall mark the festival of the first fruit of the wheat cutting for yourself as a Festival of Weeks, and a festival of harvest at the turn of the year.   23. Three times each year shall all your male[s] appear directly before the Countenance of the Lord, *God*, the God of Yisrael.   24. Even [though] I drive out

תַּעֲשֶׂה־לָּךְ: יח אֶת־חַג הַמַּצּוֹת תִּשְׁמֹר שִׁבְעַת יָמִים תֹּאכַל מַצּוֹת אֲשֶׁר צִוִּיתִךָ לְמוֹעֵד חֹדֶשׁ הָאָבִיב כִּי בְּחֹדֶשׁ הָאָבִיב יָצָאתָ מִמִּצְרָיִם: יט כָּל־פֶּטֶר רֶחֶם לִי וְכָל־מִקְנְךָ תִּזָּכָר פֶּטֶר שׁוֹר וָשֶׂה: כ וּפֶטֶר חֲמוֹר תִּפְדֶּה בְשֶׂה וְאִם־לֹא תִפְדֶּה וַעֲרַפְתּוֹ כֹּל בְּכוֹר בָּנֶיךָ תִּפְדֶּה וְלֹא־ יֵרָאוּ פָנַי רֵיקָם: כא שֵׁשֶׁת יָמִים תַּעֲבֹד וּבַיּוֹם הַשְּׁבִיעִי תִּשְׁבֹּת בֶּחָרִישׁ וּבַקָּצִיר תִּשְׁבֹּת: כב וְחַג שָׁבֻעֹת תַּעֲשֶׂה לְךָ בִּכּוּרֵי קְצִיר חִטִּים וְחַג הָאָסִיף תְּקוּפַת הַשָּׁנָה: כג שָׁלֹשׁ פְּעָמִים בַּשָּׁנָה יֵרָאֶה כָּל־זְכוּרְךָ אֶת־פְּנֵי הָאָדֹן | יְהֹוָה אֱלֹהֵי יִשְׂרָאֵל: כד כִּי־אוֹרִישׁ גּוֹיִם מִפָּנֶיךָ

each stage of nature in the annual cycle you shall hasten from the realm of nature up to, and into, the Temple of the One sole Being Who is the Lord of nature even as He is your own Lord, Who means more to you and is even nearer to you than He is to nature. He, to Whose Temple you should hasten, is "*God*, the God of Israel." He did not set you up in one static position as He did nature; instead, He remains close to you at all times, guiding, leading, protecting, shaping and blessing every moment of your life. By paying your tribute of allegiance to His Law in the Temple you will win for yourself and for your land His protection against all enemies.

This contrast between the Jewish festivals and pagan notions is stated also in Pesaḥim 118a: "One who despises the Festivals is as though he were practicing idolatry, for it is written: 'You shall not make yourself gods of cast metal,' which is followed by 'The Festival of Unleavened Bread you shall keep.'"

21. In Chapter 23:10 above, at the conclusion of the basic outline of social legislation, certain institutions are described in terms of their relevance to the principles of

equality and brotherhood upon which all these laws are based. First among these institutions are the weekly Sabbath day and the Sabbatical year, שַׁבָּת and שְׁבִיעִית. These are the most eloquent and continuous proclamations of God as the One sole Owner of the land and of all the world; it follows naturally that all the citizens of the land and all men on earth are equal before the Law.

In the present section, where the Law is given to Israel again, the same institutions are named, but this time they are discussed specifically in terms of their contrast to pagan notions. Here the point of departure is the exodus from Mitzrayim, the great event that demonstrates God's immediate nearness to man. The institution of the Sabbath is also relevant here.

Six days you shall create, serving. Only in serving do you dominate the world. Only by subordinating yourself and all your abilities directly to God can you become master of your world. The earth will submit only to that work of yours which is done in the service of God. By ceasing from your work on the Sabbath you express the significance of your work as an act of homage to God. . . .

nations from before you and will make your
territory wide, no one will covet your land if
you go up, to appear directly before the
Countenance of *God*, your God, three times
each year. 25. But you shall not slaughter
the blood of My meal offering together with
leaven, and the meal of the Pesaḥ offering
shall not remain overnight until the morning. 26. You shall bring home into the
House of *God*, your God, the first of the first
fruits of your soil; you shall not cook a
young in the milk of its mother." 27. *God*
said to Moshe: "Write down these words for
yourself, for according to the living content
of these words have I made a covenant with
you and with Yisrael." 28. Forty days and
forty nights he was there with *God*; he did
not eat bread and did not drink water, and
he wrote upon the tablets the words of the
Covenant, the Ten Words. 29. And it
came to pass when Moshe came down from
Mount Sinai, and the two tablets of the
Testimony were in the hand of Moshe, when
he came down from the mountain—and
Moshe did not know that the skin of his face
had become radiant while He spoke with
him—30. that Aharon and all the sons of
Yisrael saw Moshe and lo! the skin of his
face had become radiant, and they were
afraid to come near him. 31. But Moshe
called to them, and Aharon and all the
princes in the community returned to him,
and Moshe spoke with them. 32. Afterwards all the sons of Yisrael, too, came up to
him, and he commanded them everything
[about] which *God* had spoken with him
on Mount Sinai. 33. When Moshe had
finished talking with them he placed a
covering over his face. 34. When Moshe
went in before *God*, in order to speak with
Him, he took off the covering until he went
out again; then he went out and spoke to
the sons of Yisrael that which had been
commanded to him. 35. Then the sons of

וְהִרְחַבְתִּי֙ אֶת־גְּבֻלֶ֔ךָ וְלֹא־יַחְמֹ֥ד אִ֖ישׁ אֶת־
אַרְצְךָ֔ בַּעֲלֹֽתְךָ֗ לֵרָאוֹת֙ אֶת־פְּנֵי֙ יְהֹוָ֣ה אֱלֹהֶ֔יךָ
שָׁלֹ֥שׁ פְּעָמִ֖ים בַּשָּׁנָֽה: כה לֹא־תִשְׁחַ֥ט עַל־חָמֵ֖ץ
דַּם־זִבְחִ֑י וְלֹא־יָלִ֣ין לַבֹּ֔קֶר זֶ֖בַח חַ֥ג הַפָּֽסַח:
כו רֵאשִׁ֗ית בִּכּוּרֵי֙ אַדְמָ֣תְךָ֔ תָּבִ֕יא בֵּ֖ית יְהֹוָ֣ה
אֱלֹהֶ֑יךָ לֹא־תְבַשֵּׁ֥ל גְּדִ֖י בַּחֲלֵ֥ב אִמּֽוֹ: פ שביעי
כז וַיֹּ֤אמֶר יְהֹוָה֙ אֶל־מֹשֶׁ֔ה כְּתָב־לְךָ֖ אֶת־
הַדְּבָרִ֣ים הָאֵ֑לֶּה כִּ֞י עַל־פִּ֣י | הַדְּבָרִ֣ים הָאֵ֗לֶּה
כָּרַ֧תִּי אִתְּךָ֛ בְּרִ֖ית וְאֶת־יִשְׂרָאֵֽל: כח וַיְהִי־שָׁ֣ם
עִם־יְהֹוָ֗ה אַרְבָּעִ֥ים יוֹם֙ וְאַרְבָּעִ֣ים לַ֔יְלָה לֶ֚חֶם
לֹ֣א אָכַ֔ל וּמַ֖יִם לֹ֣א שָׁתָ֑ה וַיִּכְתֹּ֣ב עַל־הַלֻּחֹ֗ת אֵ֚ת
דִּבְרֵ֣י הַבְּרִ֔ית עֲשֶׂ֖רֶת הַדְּבָרִֽים: כט וַיְהִ֗י בְּרֶ֤דֶת
מֹשֶׁה֙ מֵהַ֣ר סִינַ֔י וּשְׁנֵ֞י לֻחֹ֤ת הָעֵדֻת֙ בְּיַד־מֹשֶׁ֔ה
בְּרִדְתּ֖וֹ מִן־הָהָ֑ר וּמֹשֶׁ֣ה לֹֽא־יָדַ֗ע כִּ֤י קָרַן֙ ע֣וֹר
פָּנָ֔יו בְּדַבְּר֖וֹ אִתּֽוֹ: ל וַיַּ֨רְא אַהֲרֹ֜ן וְכָל־בְּנֵ֤י
יִשְׂרָאֵל֙ אֶת־מֹשֶׁ֔ה וְהִנֵּ֥ה קָרַ֖ן ע֣וֹר פָּנָ֑יו וַיִּֽירְא֖וּ
מִגֶּ֥שֶׁת אֵלָֽיו: לא וַיִּקְרָ֤א אֲלֵהֶם֙ מֹשֶׁ֔ה וַיָּשֻׁ֧בוּ
אֵלָ֛יו אַהֲרֹ֥ן וְכָל־הַנְּשִׂאִ֖ים בָּעֵדָ֑ה וַיְדַבֵּ֥ר מֹשֶׁ֖ה
אֲלֵהֶֽם: לב וְאַחֲרֵי־כֵ֥ן נִגְּשׁ֖וּ כָּל־בְּנֵ֣י יִשְׂרָאֵ֑ל
וַיְצַוֵּ֕ם אֵת֩ כָּל־אֲשֶׁ֨ר דִּבֶּ֧ר יְהֹוָ֛ה אִתּ֖וֹ בְּהַ֥ר סִינָֽי:
מפטיר לג וַיְכַ֣ל מֹשֶׁ֔ה מִדַּבֵּ֖ר אִתָּ֑ם וַיִּתֵּ֥ן עַל־פָּנָ֖יו
מַסְוֶֽה: לד וּבְבֹ֨א מֹשֶׁ֜ה לִפְנֵ֤י יְהֹוָה֙ לְדַבֵּ֣ר אִתּ֔וֹ
יָסִ֥יר אֶת־הַמַּסְוֶ֖ה עַד־צֵאת֑וֹ וְיָצָ֗א וְדִבֶּר֙ אֶל־
בְּנֵ֣י יִשְׂרָאֵ֔ל אֵ֖ת אֲשֶׁ֥ר יְצֻוֶּֽה: לה וְרָא֤וּ בְנֵֽי־

---

26. This whole section, again, closes with two verses
of all-embracing significance: Every ear of grain in the
fields, every fruit on the trees of your land, ripens for
the Law of God in the Temple. Even when you eat,
your godly human qualities shall not descend to the
physical and sensual aspects of your being. Rather, you
shall elevate all the physical and sensual aspects of your
life so that you will become truly human. Nature is not
the intermediary between God and yourself; it is you
who are the intermediary between nature and God. . . .

Yisrael saw Moshe's face, that the skin of Moshe's face had become radiant; but then Moshe placed the covering over his face again until he went in again to speak with Him.

יִשְׂרָאֵל אֶת־פְּנֵי מֹשֶׁה כִּי קָרַן עוֹר פְּנֵי מֹשֶׁה וְהֵשִׁיב מֹשֶׁה אֶת־הַמַּסְוֶה עַל־פָּנָיו עַד־בֹּאוֹ לְדַבֵּר אִתּוֹ: ס

The Haftarah for this Sidra may be found on page 860.

ויקהל

VAYAKHEL

XXXV 1. Moshe had the whole community of the sons of Yisrael assemble, and he said to them: "These are the objects which *God* commanded that they be made. 2. For six days shall [creating] work be done, but on the seventh day there shall be to you a sanctity, a Sabbath to be observed for *God* by cessation from work; whoever performs [an act of creating] work on it shall be put to death. 3. You shall kindle no fire in all your habitations on the Sabbath day." 4. Moshe said to the whole community of the sons of Yisrael: "This is what *God* has commanded. 5. Take from among yourselves an uplifted donation to *God*; let each one, moved by his heart, bring it; the uplifted donation to *God* of gold, silver and copper, 6. of sky-blue, purple and scarlet wool, of byssus and goats' hair; 7. of rams' skins dyed red, *taḥash* skins and *shittim* wood; 8. of oil for lighting and

לה א וַיַּקְהֵל מֹשֶׁה אֶת־כָּל־עֲדַת בְּנֵי יִשְׂרָאֵל
וַיֹּאמֶר אֲלֵהֶם אֵלֶּה הַדְּבָרִים אֲשֶׁר־צִוָּה יְהוָה
לַעֲשֹׂת אֹתָם׃ ב שֵׁשֶׁת יָמִים תֵּעָשֶׂה מְלָאכָה
וּבַיּוֹם הַשְּׁבִיעִי יִהְיֶה לָכֶם קֹדֶשׁ שַׁבַּת שַׁבָּתוֹן
לַיהוָה כָּל־הָעֹשֶׂה בוֹ מְלָאכָה יוּמָת׃ ג לֹא־
תְבַעֲרוּ אֵשׁ בְּכֹל מֹשְׁבֹתֵיכֶם בְּיוֹם הַשַּׁבָּת׃ פ
ד וַיֹּאמֶר מֹשֶׁה אֶל־כָּל־עֲדַת בְּנֵי־יִשְׂרָאֵל
לֵאמֹר זֶה הַדָּבָר אֲשֶׁר־צִוָּה יְהוָה לֵאמֹר׃
ה קְחוּ מֵאִתְּכֶם תְּרוּמָה לַיהוָה כֹּל נְדִיב לִבּוֹ
יְבִיאֶהָ אֵת תְּרוּמַת יְהוָה זָהָב וָכֶסֶף וּנְחֹשֶׁת׃
ו וּתְכֵלֶת וְאַרְגָּמָן וְתוֹלַעַת שָׁנִי וְשֵׁשׁ וְעִזִּים׃
ז וְעֹרֹת אֵילִם מְאָדָּמִים וְעֹרֹת תְּחָשִׁים וַעֲצֵי
שִׁטִּים׃ ח וְשֶׁמֶן לַמָּאוֹר וּבְשָׂמִים לְשֶׁמֶן

CHAPTER XXXV

1. Now that the Testimony of the Law, the pledge of God's special Presence in the midst of the people, had been given to Israel once again, the erection of a dwelling place for this Testimony had again become relevant. The grim events described previously, which had jeopardized the realization of this task, are of the most far-reaching significance for the task as such, for the Sanctuary and the purpose for which the Sanctuary is to be erected. The construction of the Sanctuary was to take place under the impact of a completely new experience. The people and the priests had come to realize how weak and imperfect they still were, how much they still needed to work upon themselves incessantly and how greatly they were in need of uplift and atonement. Moreover, they had come to know God in all the severity of His judgment, but also in all the fullness of His grace. They had experienced all the nuances of our relationship with God, from the feeling of utter rejection by God up to the height of Divine favor regained. The Sanctuary to be constructed was to become the place from which the ideal of their vocation would shine forth forever to individual and community alike. It was to be the place where, at any stage of error and weakness, they would find renewed strength to work their way up again and to persevere on the high level of their vocation, and where they would find God's help and blessing for both objectives. Thus, the experience that had been recorded forever in the history of the nation between the time it had been commanded to build its very first Sanctuary, and the actual execution of that command, is documentary proof that it is possible at any stage of error to return, and to regain the favor of God.

But the most significant element in this experience which preceded the construction of the first Sanctuary is as follows: The nation had committed the most serious crime in its history thus far, and yet it had been able to regain the greatest demonstration of Divine favor without having a temple and without making any offerings. If any more proof were needed that a temple and offerings in themselves do not secure God's favor but are intended only as guides to show how God's favor can be won, then such proof is most cogently offered by this experience, which preceded the construction of the first Sanctuary and which has become so inextricably woven into Israel's history.

° ° °

spices for the anointing oil and for the spicy incense, 9. and of *shoham* stones and stones to be set for the *ephod* and the breastplate. 10. and every wise-hearted man among you, let them come and make everything that *God* commanded; 11. the Dwelling Place and its tent and its covering; its clasps and its beams, its bars, pillars and sockets; 12. the Ark and its poles, the cover, and the dividing curtain of the covering; 13. the table along with its poles and all its utensils and the showbread; 14. the menorah for lighting along with its utensils and lights, and the oil for lighting; 15. the incense altar along with its poles, the anointing oil and the spicy incense, and the protective curtain for the door for the entrance to the Dwelling Place; 16. the altar for the ascent offering along with its copper grating, its poles and all its utensils; the basin and its base; 17. the hangings of the forecourt, its pillars and its sockets, and the protective curtain for the gate of the forecourt; 18. the stakes of the Dwelling Place, the stakes of the forecourt and their ropes, 19. the garments of distinction for service in the Sanctuary; the garments of the Sanctuary for Aharon the priest and the garments of his sons for the priestly service." 20. The whole community of the sons of Yisrael departed from the assembly before Moshe. 21. And thereupon there came everyone whose heart had lifted him up and everyone whose spirit had moved him; they brought the uplifted donation to *God* for the work of the Tent of Appointed Meeting and for everything that was required for it, as well as for the garments of the Sanctuary. 22. The men came, along with the women, all, moved by their hearts: they brought brooches, nose-rings, rings and buckles, all kinds of golden objects, and everyone who had assigned an offering of gold to *God*; 23. and also everyone with whom there was found sky-blue, purple and scarlet wool, byssus and goats' hair, rams' skins dyed red and *taḥash* skins, brought them. 24. Also everyone who had made an uplifted donation of silver and copper brought therein the uplifted donation to *God*, and also every-

הַמִּשְׁחָה וְלִקְטֹרֶת הַסַּמִּים׃ ט וְאַבְנֵי־שֹׁהַם
וְאַבְנֵי מִלֻּאִים לָאֵפוֹד וְלַחֹשֶׁן׃ י וְכָל־חֲכַם־לֵב
בָּכֶם יָבֹאוּ וְיַעֲשׂוּ אֵת כָּל־אֲשֶׁר צִוָּה יְהוָה׃
יא אֶת־הַמִּשְׁכָּן אֶת־אָהֳלוֹ וְאֶת־מִכְסֵהוּ אֶת־
קְרָסָיו וְאֶת־קְרָשָׁיו אֶת־בְּרִחָו (בריחיו קרי) אֶת־
עַמֻּדָיו וְאֶת־אֲדָנָיו׃ יב אֶת־הָאָרֹן וְאֶת־בַּדָּיו
אֶת־הַכַּפֹּרֶת וְאֵת פָּרֹכֶת הַמָּסָךְ׃ יג אֶת־הַשֻּׁלְחָן
וְאֶת־בַּדָּיו וְאֶת־כָּל־כֵּלָיו וְאֵת לֶחֶם הַפָּנִים׃
יד וְאֶת־מְנֹרַת הַמָּאוֹר וְאֶת־כֵּלֶיהָ וְאֶת־נֵרֹתֶיהָ
וְאֵת שֶׁמֶן הַמָּאוֹר׃ טו וְאֶת־מִזְבַּח הַקְּטֹרֶת
וְאֶת־בַּדָּיו וְאֵת שֶׁמֶן הַמִּשְׁחָה וְאֵת קְטֹרֶת
הַסַּמִּים וְאֶת־מָסַךְ הַפֶּתַח לְפֶתַח הַמִּשְׁכָּן׃
טז אֵת ׀ מִזְבַּח הָעֹלָה וְאֶת־מִכְבַּר הַנְּחֹשֶׁת
אֲשֶׁר־לוֹ אֶת־בַּדָּיו וְאֶת־כָּל־כֵּלָיו אֶת־הַכִּיֹּר
וְאֶת־כַּנּוֹ׃ יז אֵת קַלְעֵי הֶחָצֵר אֶת־עַמֻּדָיו וְאֶת־
אֲדָנֶיהָ וְאֵת מָסַךְ שַׁעַר הֶחָצֵר׃ יח אֶת־יִתְדֹת
הַמִּשְׁכָּן וְאֶת־יִתְדֹת הֶחָצֵר וְאֶת־מֵיתְרֵיהֶם׃
יט אֶת־בִּגְדֵי הַשְּׂרָד לְשָׁרֵת בַּקֹּדֶשׁ אֶת־בִּגְדֵי
הַקֹּדֶשׁ לְאַהֲרֹן הַכֹּהֵן וְאֶת־בִּגְדֵי בָנָיו לְכַהֵן׃
כ וַיֵּצְאוּ כָּל־עֲדַת בְּנֵי־יִשְׂרָאֵל מִלִּפְנֵי מֹשֶׁה׃
שני כא וַיָּבֹאוּ כָּל־אִישׁ אֲשֶׁר־נְשָׂאוֹ לִבּוֹ וְכֹל
אֲשֶׁר נָדְבָה רוּחוֹ אֹתוֹ הֵבִיאוּ אֶת־תְּרוּמַת
יְהוָה לִמְלֶאכֶת אֹהֶל מוֹעֵד וּלְכָל־עֲבֹדָתוֹ
וּלְבִגְדֵי הַקֹּדֶשׁ׃ כב וַיָּבֹאוּ הָאֲנָשִׁים עַל־הַנָּשִׁים
כֹּל ׀ נְדִיב לֵב הֵבִיאוּ חָח וָנֶזֶם וְטַבַּעַת וְכוּמָז
כָּל־כְּלִי זָהָב וְכָל־אִישׁ אֲשֶׁר הֵנִיף תְּנוּפַת זָהָב
לַיהוָה׃ כג וְכָל־אִישׁ אֲשֶׁר־נִמְצָא אִתּוֹ תְּכֵלֶת
וְאַרְגָּמָן וְתוֹלַעַת שָׁנִי וְשֵׁשׁ וְעִזִּים וְעֹרֹת אֵילִם
מְאָדָּמִים וְעֹרֹת תְּחָשִׁים הֵבִיאוּ׃ כד כָּל־מֵרִים
תְּרוּמַת כֶּסֶף וּנְחֹשֶׁת הֵבִיאוּ אֵת תְּרוּמַת יְהוָה

one with whom there was found *shittim* wood for all the work of the task to be accomplished, brought it.   25. All the wise-hearted women spun with their own hands and brought in the form of spun yarn the sky-blue and purple wool, the scarlet wool and the byssus.   26. And all the women whose hearts had uplifted them in wisdom spun the goats' hair.   27. And the princes brought the *shoham* stones and the stones to be set for the *ephod* and the breastplate,   28. the spices and the oil for lighting and for the anointing oil and for the spicy incense.   29. Every man and every woman whose heart had moved them to contribute to the whole work that *God* had commanded through Moshe should be done, brought, as sons of Yisrael, a gift, of their own free will, to *God*. 30. And Moshe said to the sons of Yisrael: "See, *God* has called by name Bezalel, the son of Uri, the son of Ḥur, of the tribe of Yehudah,   31. since He has filled him with the spirit of God, with wisdom, with insight and with knowledge and with [talent for] all manner of craftsmanship, 32. and to combine ideas, to work them out in gold, in silver and in copper;   33. to execute them in the cutting of stones for setting and in the carving of wood, in every manner of craftsmanship.   34. And He has also put into his heart the ability to teach; both he and Oholiab, the son of Aḥisamakh, of the tribe of Dan.   35. He has filled them with wisdom of heart, to execute all manner of work, of an engraver, weaver and embroiderer in sky-blue and purple wool, in scarlet wool and in byssus, and of the weaver; they execute all manner of work and combine ideas.

XXXVI

1. Bezalel and Oholiab and every wise-hearted man into whom *God* had put wisdom and insight for knowledgeable execution shall execute all the work required for the service in the Sanctuary in accordance with all that *God* has commanded."   2. And Moshe called Bezalel and Oholiab and every wise-hearted man into whom *God* had put wisdom, everyone whom his heart had uplifted, to approach the work, to execute it.   3. And they received from Moshe all the uplifted dona-

וְכֹל אֲשֶׁר־נִמְצָא אִתּוֹ עֲצֵי שִׁטִּים לְכָל־מְלֶאכֶת הָעֲבֹדָה הֵבִיאוּ: כה וְכָל־אִשָּׁה חַכְמַת־לֵב בְּיָדֶיהָ טָווּ וַיָּבִיאוּ מַטְוֶה אֶת־הַתְּכֵלֶת וְאֶת־הָאַרְגָּמָן אֶת־תּוֹלַעַת הַשָּׁנִי וְאֶת־הַשֵּׁשׁ: כו וְכָל־הַנָּשִׁים אֲשֶׁר נָשָׂא לִבָּן אֹתָנָה בְּחָכְמָה טָווּ אֶת־הָעִזִּים: כז וְהַנְּשִׂאִם הֵבִיאוּ אֵת אַבְנֵי הַשֹּׁהַם וְאֵת אַבְנֵי הַמִּלֻּאִים לָאֵפוֹד וְלַחֹשֶׁן: כח וְאֶת־הַבֹּשֶׂם וְאֶת־הַשָּׁמֶן לְמָאוֹר וּלְשֶׁמֶן הַמִּשְׁחָה וְלִקְטֹרֶת הַסַּמִּים: כט כָּל־אִישׁ וְאִשָּׁה אֲשֶׁר נָדַב לִבָּם אֹתָם לְהָבִיא לְכָל־הַמְּלָאכָה אֲשֶׁר צִוָּה יְהוָה לַעֲשׂוֹת בְּיַד־מֹשֶׁה הֵבִיאוּ בְנֵי־ יִשְׂרָאֵל נְדָבָה לַיהוָה: פ שלישי (שני כשהן מחוברין)

ל וַיֹּאמֶר מֹשֶׁה אֶל־בְּנֵי יִשְׂרָאֵל רְאוּ קָרָא יְהוָה בְּשֵׁם בְּצַלְאֵל בֶּן־אוּרִי בֶן־חוּר לְמַטֵּה יְהוּדָה: לא וַיְמַלֵּא אֹתוֹ רוּחַ אֱלֹהִים בְּחָכְמָה בִּתְבוּנָה וּבְדַעַת וּבְכָל־מְלָאכָה: לב וְלַחְשֹׁב מַחֲשָׁבֹת לַעֲשֹׂת בַּזָּהָב וּבַכֶּסֶף וּבַנְּחֹשֶׁת: לג וּבַחֲרֹשֶׁת אֶבֶן לְמַלֹּאת וּבַחֲרֹשֶׁת עֵץ לַעֲשׂוֹת בְּכָל־מְלֶאכֶת מַחֲשָׁבֶת: לד וּלְהוֹרֹת נָתַן בְּלִבּוֹ הוּא וְאָהֳלִיאָב בֶּן־אֲחִיסָמָךְ לְמַטֵּה־ דָן: לה מִלֵּא אֹתָם חָכְמַת־לֵב לַעֲשׂוֹת כָּל־ מְלֶאכֶת חָרָשׁ וְחֹשֵׁב וְרֹקֵם בַּתְּכֵלֶת וּבָאַרְגָּמָן בְּתוֹלַעַת הַשָּׁנִי וּבַשֵּׁשׁ וְאֹרֵג עֹשֵׂי כָּל־מְלָאכָה וְחֹשְׁבֵי מַחֲשָׁבֹת: לו א וְעָשָׂה בְצַלְאֵל וְאָהֳלִיאָב וְכֹל אִישׁ חֲכַם־לֵב אֲשֶׁר נָתַן יְהוָה חָכְמָה וּתְבוּנָה בָּהֵמָּה לָדַעַת לַעֲשֹׂת אֶת־כָּל־ מְלֶאכֶת עֲבֹדַת הַקֹּדֶשׁ לְכֹל אֲשֶׁר־צִוָּה יְהוָה: ב וַיִּקְרָא מֹשֶׁה אֶל־בְּצַלְאֵל וְאֶל־אָהֳלִיאָב וְאֶל כָּל־אִישׁ חֲכַם־לֵב אֲשֶׁר נָתַן יְהוָה חָכְמָה בְּלִבּוֹ כֹּל אֲשֶׁר נְשָׂאוֹ לִבּוֹ לְקָרְבָה אֶל־הַמְּלָאכָה לַעֲשֹׂת אֹתָהּ: ג וַיִּקְחוּ מִלִּפְנֵי מֹשֶׁה אֵת כָּל־

tion, which the sons of Yisrael had brought for the work required for the service in the Sanctuary, in order to execute it; they were still bringing him gifts, of their own free will, every morning. 4. And all the wise men came, who executed all the work of the Sanctuary, each one from his work which they executed, 5. and they said to Moshe: "The people are bringing too much, more than enough for the service required for the work that *God* has commanded to execute." 6. And Moshe gave orders and they caused it to be proclaimed throughout the camp: "Let no man or woman create any more work for the uplifted donation of the Sanctuary." Then the people restrained themselves from bringing. 7. The work was enough for them for all the work to execute it, and there was even more [left over]. 8. All the wise-hearted among those who executed the work made the Dwelling Place out of ten tapestries of byssus twisted into six-ply thread, and of sky-blue, purple and

הַתְּרוּמָה אֲשֶׁר הֵבִיאוּ בְּנֵי יִשְׂרָאֵל לִמְלֶאכֶת
עֲבֹדַת הַקֹּדֶשׁ לַעֲשֹׂת אֹתָהּ וְהֵם הֵבִיאוּ אֵלָיו
עוֹד נְדָבָה בַּבֹּקֶר בַּבֹּקֶר׃ ד וַיָּבֹאוּ כָּל־הַחֲכָמִים
הָעֹשִׂים אֵת כָּל־מְלֶאכֶת הַקֹּדֶשׁ אִישׁ־אִישׁ
מִמְּלַאכְתּוֹ אֲשֶׁר־הֵמָּה עֹשִׂים׃ ה וַיֹּאמְרוּ אֶל־
מֹשֶׁה לֵּאמֹר מַרְבִּים הָעָם לְהָבִיא מִדֵּי הָעֲבֹדָה
לַמְּלָאכָה אֲשֶׁר־צִוָּה יְהוָה לַעֲשֹׂת אֹתָהּ׃ ו וַיְצַו
מֹשֶׁה וַיַּעֲבִירוּ קוֹל בַּמַּחֲנֶה לֵאמֹר אִישׁ וְאִשָּׁה
אַל־יַעֲשׂוּ־עוֹד מְלָאכָה לִתְרוּמַת הַקֹּדֶשׁ וַיִּכָּלֵא
הָעָם מֵהָבִיא׃ ז וְהַמְּלָאכָה הָיְתָה דַיָּם לְכָל־
הַמְּלָאכָה לַעֲשׂוֹת אֹתָהּ וְהוֹתֵר׃ ס רביעי
ח וַיַּעֲשׂוּ כָל־חֲכַם־לֵב בְּעֹשֵׂי הַמְּלָאכָה אֶת־
הַמִּשְׁכָּן עֶשֶׂר יְרִיעֹת שֵׁשׁ מָשְׁזָר וּתְכֵלֶת

CHAPTER XXXVI

8 ff. Let us bear in mind that the entire Sanctuary, in all its individual components, was intended to have symbolic meaning, but that not one object in the Sanctuary could be vested with symbolic meaning unless it was deliberately planned and manufactured with this purpose in mind. Let us further bear in mind that even in the case of script, which one might think cannot possibly have anything but symbolic significance, its symbolic value, when used for a sacred purpose, depends on the intent of the scribe who executes it. Thus, in the writing of a סֵפֶר תּוֹרָה [Scroll of the Law], the intention of the scribe is so essential that the Scroll is considered as having קְדוּשַּׁת סֵפֶר תּוֹרָה [the sanctity required for a Scroll of the Law] only if it was written לְשֵׁם קְדוּשַּׁת סֵפֶר תּוֹרָה [with the intent that it should be a sacred Scroll of the Law]. Whenever the scribe writes down the Name of God, he must enunciate each time that it is now his intention to write these letters for the purpose of setting down the Name of God, לְשֵׁם קְדוּשַּׁת הַשֵּׁם. The sanctity of these letters is so completely determined by the attitude of the scribe who writes them down that a Torah Scroll written by a heretic—a man whose attitude when he wrote out the Name of God may be assumed to have been contrary to the Divine truth [inherent in the Torah], so that one might even say he did the work לְשֵׁם עֲבוֹדָה זָרָה ([for the purpose of idol worship])—must be burned. (See Shulḥan Arukh, Yoreh Deah 274:1, 276:2 and 281:1).

Let us bear in mind that, since the objects of the Sanctuary—ark, table, menorah, hangings, curtains, tapestries, garments, etc.,—were in fact everyday objects, their sacred character depended entirely on whether the artisans who made them were mindful of the symbolic significance of the object they were manufacturing.

In view of all the foregoing, it should be readily understandable why the steps in the construction of the Sanctuary are reiterated in such detail in Chapters 36:8 to 39:32, why Verses 33 to 43 in Chapter 39 again enumerate all the individual articles as they were delivered to Moses and why Chapter 40 retells the construction of the Sanctuary in all its particulars; in short, why Scripture did not consider it sufficient to say at this point:

"The artisans and craftsmen executed all the work according to the instructions they had been given, they brought the articles to Moses, and Moses then constructed the Sanctuary as he had been commanded to do."

If we are not mistaken, these detailed repetitions of facts already set forth in previous chapters are intended to let us know that the craftsmen and Moses were constantly mindful of the sacred and symbolic purpose of each object not only during the manufacturing process scarlet wool, out of cherubim of weaver's work did he make them. 9. The length of one tapestry was twenty-eight cubits and the width four cubits; thus [was] one curtain; all the tapestries had the same measurements. 10. He joined five tapestries one to the other and [the other] five tapestries to one another. 11. He made loops of sky-blue wool on the edge of the one tapestry that was at the end of the coupling and he made the same on the edge of the tapestry that was at the other end of the coupling. 12. He placed fifty loops upon the one tapestry, and fifty loops upon the edge of the tapestry that was on the other coupling; the loops were opposite one another. 13. He made fifty gold clasps and joined the tapestries to one another with the clasps, so that the Dwelling Place became one whole. 14. He made tapestries of goats' hair as a tent over the Dwelling Place; eleven tapestries did he make them. 15. The length of the one tapestry was thirty cubits and the width of the one tapestry four cubits. All eleven tapestries had the same measurements. 16. He joined [the first] five of the tapestries by themselves, and [the] six [other] tapestries by themselves; 17. and he placed fifty loops upon the edge of the outermost tapestry [in the coupling] and fifty loops upon the edge of the other tapestry connecting with it. 18. He made fifty copper clasps to join the tent together so that it should become one. 19. He made a covering for the tent of rams' skins dyed red and a covering of *taḥash* skins above that. 20. He made the beams for the Dwelling Place from *shittim* wood, standing upright, 21. ten cubits [was] the length of the beam and one cubit and a half the width of each beam. 22. Two tenons upon each beam, mortised one against the other; thus did he make upon all the beams of the Dwelling Place. 23. He made these

וְאַרְגָּמָן וְתוֹלַעַת שָׁנִי כְּרֻבִים מַעֲשֵׂה חֹשֵׁב
עָשָׂה אֹתָם: ט אֹרֶךְ הַיְרִיעָה הָאַחַת שְׁמֹנֶה
וְעֶשְׂרִים בָּאַמָּה וְרֹחַב אַרְבַּע בָּאַמָּה הַיְרִיעָה
הָאֶחָת מִדָּה אַחַת לְכָל־הַיְרִיעֹת: י וַיְחַבֵּר אֶת־
חֲמֵשׁ הַיְרִיעֹת אַחַת אֶל־אֶחָת וְחָמֵשׁ יְרִיעֹת
חִבַּר אַחַת אֶל־אֶחָת: יא וַיַּעַשׂ לֻלְאֹת תְּכֵלֶת עַל
שְׂפַת הַיְרִיעָה הָאֶחָת מִקָּצָה בַּמַּחְבָּרֶת כֵּן עָשָׂה
בִּשְׂפַת הַיְרִיעָה הַקִּיצוֹנָה בַּמַּחְבֶּרֶת הַשֵּׁנִית:
יב חֲמִשִּׁים לֻלָאֹת עָשָׂה בַּיְרִיעָה הָאֶחָת
וַחֲמִשִּׁים לֻלָאֹת עָשָׂה בִּקְצֵה הַיְרִיעָה אֲשֶׁר
בַּמַּחְבֶּרֶת הַשֵּׁנִית מַקְבִּילֹת הַלֻּלָאֹת אַחַת אֶל־
אֶחָת: יג וַיַּעַשׂ חֲמִשִּׁים קַרְסֵי זָהָב וַיְחַבֵּר אֶת־
הַיְרִיעֹת אַחַת אֶל־אַחַת בַּקְּרָסִים וַיְהִי הַמִּשְׁכָּן
אֶחָד: פ יד וַיַּעַשׂ יְרִיעֹת עִזִּים לְאֹהֶל עַל־
הַמִּשְׁכָּן עַשְׁתֵּי־עֶשְׂרֵה יְרִיעֹת עָשָׂה אֹתָם:
טו אֹרֶךְ הַיְרִיעָה הָאַחַת שְׁלֹשִׁים בָּאַמָּה וְאַרְבַּע
אַמּוֹת רֹחַב הַיְרִיעָה הָאֶחָת מִדָּה אַחַת לְעַשְׁתֵּי
עֶשְׂרֵה יְרִיעֹת: טז וַיְחַבֵּר אֶת־חֲמֵשׁ הַיְרִיעֹת
לְבָד וְאֶת־שֵׁשׁ הַיְרִיעֹת לְבָד: יז וַיַּעַשׂ לֻלָאֹת
חֲמִשִּׁים עַל שְׂפַת הַיְרִיעָה הַקִּיצֹנָה בַּמַּחְבָּרֶת
וַחֲמִשִּׁים לֻלָאֹת עָשָׂה עַל־שְׂפַת הַיְרִיעָה
הַחֹבֶרֶת הַשֵּׁנִית: יח וַיַּעַשׂ קַרְסֵי נְחֹשֶׁת חֲמִשִּׁים
לְחַבֵּר אֶת־הָאֹהֶל לִהְיֹת אֶחָד: יט וַיַּעַשׂ מִכְסֶה
לָאֹהֶל עֹרֹת אֵילִם מְאָדָּמִים וּמִכְסֵה עֹרֹת
תְּחָשִׁים מִלְמָעְלָה: ס חמישי כ וַיַּעַשׂ אֶת־
הַקְּרָשִׁים לַמִּשְׁכָּן עֲצֵי שִׁטִּים עֹמְדִים: כא עֶשֶׂר
אַמֹּת אֹרֶךְ הַקָּרֶשׁ וְאַמָּה וַחֲצִי הָאַמָּה רֹחַב
הַקֶּרֶשׁ הָאֶחָד: כב שְׁתֵּי יָדֹת לַקֶּרֶשׁ הָאֶחָד
מְשֻׁלָּבֹת אַחַת אֶל־אֶחָת כֵּן עָשָׂה לְכֹל קַרְשֵׁי
הַמִּשְׁכָּן: כג וַיַּעַשׂ אֶת־הַקְּרָשִׁים לַמִּשְׁכָּן

but also while the finished products were delivered and set up in their places, so that all these objects were manufactured, handled and assembled in a spirit consistent with their purpose. In this way the sacred character and significance of the objects were confirmed by the spirit in which they were manufactured.

° ° °

beams for the Dwelling Place: twenty beams for the south side, on the right, 24. and he made forty silver sockets under the twenty beams, two sockets under the one beam for its two tenons and two sockets under another beam for its two tenons. 25. And for the second wall of the Dwelling Place, on the north side, twenty beams, 26. and their forty silver sockets, two sockets under the one beam and two sockets under another beam. 27. And for the rear side of the Dwelling Place, to the west, he made six beams, 28. and he made two beams at the corners of the Dwelling Place in the rear. 29. They were to be joined together exactly below, and at the top they were to be joined together in one ring; so he made them on both the corners. 30. So there were eight beams and their silver sockets, sixteen sockets; two sockets each under one beam. 31. He made bars of *shittim* wood, five for the beams of the one wall of the Dwelling Place, 32. and five bars for the beams of the second wall of the Dwelling Place, and five bars for the beams of the Dwelling Place for the rear part, westward. 33. He made the middle bar on the inside of the beams, to lock them from one end to the other. 34. He covered the beams with gold; he made their rings of gold as holders for the bars, and he covered also the bars with gold. 35. He made the dividing curtain of sky-blue, purple and scarlet wool and out of byssus twisted into six-ply thread; he made it woven in a cherubim design. 36. And he made for it four pillars of *shittim* wood and covered them with gold, their hooks [being] of gold, and he cast for them four silver sockets. 37. He made a protective curtain for the entrance to the Tent, of sky-blue, purple and scarlet wool and byssus twisted into six-ply thread, embroidery work. 38. Its pillars were five [in number], and their hooks, and he made the covers of their capitals and their bands of gold, but their five sockets he made of copper.

XXXVII

1. Bezalel himself made the Ark of *shittim* wood, two and one-half cubits long, one cubit and a half wide, and one cubit and a half high. 2. He covered it inside and outside with pure gold and

עֶשְׂרִים קְרָשִׁים לִפְאַת נֶגֶב תֵּימָנָה: כד וְאַרְבָּעִים אַדְנֵי־כֶסֶף עָשָׂה תַּחַת עֶשְׂרִים הַקְּרָשִׁים שְׁנֵי אֲדָנִים תַּחַת־הַקֶּרֶשׁ הָאֶחָד לִשְׁתֵּי יְדֹתָיו וּשְׁנֵי אֲדָנִים תַּחַת־הַקֶּרֶשׁ הָאֶחָד לִשְׁתֵּי יְדֹתָיו: כה וּלְצֶלַע הַמִּשְׁכָּן הַשֵּׁנִית לִפְאַת צָפוֹן עָשָׂה עֶשְׂרִים קְרָשִׁים: כו וְאַרְבָּעִים אַדְנֵיהֶם כָּסֶף שְׁנֵי אֲדָנִים תַּחַת הַקֶּרֶשׁ הָאֶחָד וּשְׁנֵי אֲדָנִים תַּחַת הַקֶּרֶשׁ הָאֶחָד: כז וּלְיַרְכְּתֵי הַמִּשְׁכָּן יָמָּה עָשָׂה שִׁשָּׁה קְרָשִׁים: כח וּשְׁנֵי קְרָשִׁים עָשָׂה לִמְקֻצְעֹת הַמִּשְׁכָּן בַּיַּרְכָתָיִם: כט וְהָיוּ תוֹאֲמִם מִלְּמַטָּה וְיַחְדָּו יִהְיוּ תַמִּים אֶל־רֹאשׁוֹ אֶל־הַטַּבַּעַת הָאֶחָת כֵּן עָשָׂה לִשְׁנֵיהֶם לִשְׁנֵי הַמִּקְצֹעֹת: ל וְהָיוּ שְׁמֹנָה קְרָשִׁים וְאַדְנֵיהֶם כֶּסֶף שִׁשָּׁה עָשָׂר אֲדָנִים שְׁנֵי אֲדָנִים שְׁנֵי אֲדָנִים תַּחַת הַקֶּרֶשׁ הָאֶחָד: לא וַיַּעַשׂ בְּרִיחֵי עֲצֵי שִׁטִּים חֲמִשָּׁה לְקַרְשֵׁי צֶלַע־הַמִּשְׁכָּן הָאֶחָת: לב וַחֲמִשָּׁה בְרִיחִם לְקַרְשֵׁי צֶלַע־הַמִּשְׁכָּן הַשֵּׁנִית וַחֲמִשָּׁה בְרִיחִם לְקַרְשֵׁי הַמִּשְׁכָּן לַיַּרְכָתַיִם יָמָּה: לג וַיַּעַשׂ אֶת־הַבְּרִיחַ הַתִּיכֹן לִבְרֹחַ בְּתוֹךְ הַקְּרָשִׁים מִן־הַקָּצֶה אֶל־הַקָּצֶה: לד וְאֶת־הַקְּרָשִׁים צִפָּה זָהָב וְאֶת־טַבְּעֹתָם עָשָׂה זָהָב בָּתִּים לַבְּרִיחִם וַיְצַף אֶת־הַבְּרִיחִם זָהָב: לה וַיַּעַשׂ אֶת־הַפָּרֹכֶת תְּכֵלֶת וְאַרְגָּמָן וְתוֹלַעַת שָׁנִי וְשֵׁשׁ מָשְׁזָר מַעֲשֵׂה חֹשֵׁב עָשָׂה אֹתָהּ כְּרֻבִים: לו וַיַּעַשׂ לָהּ אַרְבָּעָה עַמּוּדֵי שִׁטִּים וַיְצַפֵּם זָהָב וָוֵיהֶם זָהָב וַיִּצֹק לָהֶם אַרְבָּעָה אַדְנֵי־כָסֶף: לז וַיַּעַשׂ מָסָךְ לְפֶתַח הָאֹהֶל תְּכֵלֶת וְאַרְגָּמָן וְתוֹלַעַת שָׁנִי וְשֵׁשׁ מָשְׁזָר מַעֲשֵׂה רֹקֵם: לח וְאֶת־עַמּוּדָיו חֲמִשָּׁה וְאֶת־וָוֵיהֶם וְצִפָּה רָאשֵׁיהֶם וַחֲשֻׁקֵיהֶם זָהָב וְאַדְנֵיהֶם חֲמִשָּׁה נְחֹשֶׁת: פ לז א וַיַּעַשׂ בְּצַלְאֵל אֶת־הָאָרֹן עֲצֵי שִׁטִּים אַמָּתַיִם וָחֵצִי אָרְכּוֹ וְאַמָּה וָחֵצִי רָחְבּוֹ וְאַמָּה וָחֵצִי קֹמָתוֹ: ב וַיְצַפֵּהוּ זָהָב טָהוֹר מִבַּיִת וּמִחוּץ וַיַּעַשׂ לוֹ

made for it a gold rim all around. 3. He cast four golden rings for it at its four corners, two rings upon its one side and two rings upon its other side. 4. He made poles of *shittim* wood and covered them with gold, 5. and placed the poles into the rings on the sides of the Ark, so that the Ark could be carried with them. 6. He made a cover of pure gold, two and one-half cubits long, one cubit and a half wide. 7. He made two cherubim of gold; he made them hammered out of the two ends of the cover. 8. One cherub out of the one end and the other cherub out of the other end; out of one piece with the cover did he make the cherubim at both its ends. 9. The cherubim were [made] with their wings spread upward, shielding the cover with their wings, and their faces were [turned] toward one another; the faces of the cherubim were turned toward the cover. 10. He made a table of *shittim* wood, two cubits long, one cubit wide and one cubit and a half high. 11. He covered it with pure gold and made for it a gold rim all around. 12. He made for it a border of a handbreadth all around and he made a gold rim all around upon its border. 13. And he cast for it four golden rings and put the rings upon the four corners that form its four legs. 14. The rings were adjacent to the border, as holders for the poles, to carry the table. 15. He made the poles of *shittim* wood and covered them with gold, to carry the table. 16. He made the utensils which belonged to the table, its dishes, its spoons, its purification tubes and the supports with which it is covered, of pure gold. 17. He made the menorah of pure gold, the menorah, its base and its shaft hammered out of one piece; its cups, its knobs and its flowers were made of one piece with it. 18. Six branches went out from its sides; three branches of the menorah from its one side and three branches of the menorah from its other side. 19. Three cups shaped like almond blossoms on the one branch, [with a] knob and a flower, and three cups shaped like almond blossoms on the other branch, [with a] knob and a flower, and so for [all] the six branches that went out from the menorah.

זֵר זָהָב סָבִיב׃ ג וַיִּצֹק לוֹ אַרְבַּע טַבְּעֹת זָהָב עַל
אַרְבַּע פַּעֲמֹתָיו וּשְׁתֵּי טַבָּעֹת עַל־צַלְעוֹ הָאֶחָת
וּשְׁתֵּי טַבָּעֹת עַל־צַלְעוֹ הַשֵּׁנִית׃ ד וַיַּעַשׂ בַּדֵּי
עֲצֵי שִׁטִּים וַיְצַף אֹתָם זָהָב׃ ה וַיָּבֵא אֶת־
הַבַּדִּים בַּטַּבָּעֹת עַל צַלְעֹת הָאָרֹן לָשֵׂאת אֶת־
הָאָרֹן׃ ו וַיַּעַשׂ כַּפֹּרֶת זָהָב טָהוֹר אַמָּתַיִם וָחֵצִי
אָרְכָּהּ וְאַמָּה וָחֵצִי רָחְבָּהּ׃ ז וַיַּעַשׂ שְׁנֵי כְרֻבִים
זָהָב מִקְשָׁה עָשָׂה אֹתָם מִשְּׁנֵי קְצוֹת הַכַּפֹּרֶת׃
ח כְּרוּב אֶחָד מִקָּצָה מִזֶּה וּכְרוּב־אֶחָד מִקָּצָה
מִזֶּה מִן־הַכַּפֹּרֶת עָשָׂה אֶת־הַכְּרֻבִים מִשְּׁנֵי
קְצוֹוֹתָו (קצותיו קרי)׃ ט וַיִּהְיוּ הַכְּרֻבִים פֹּרְשֵׂי
כְנָפַיִם לְמַעְלָה סֹכְכִים בְּכַנְפֵיהֶם עַל־הַכַּפֹּרֶת
וּפְנֵיהֶם אִישׁ אֶל־אָחִיו אֶל־הַכַּפֹּרֶת הָיוּ פְּנֵי
הַכְּרֻבִים׃ פ י וַיַּעַשׂ אֶת־הַשֻּׁלְחָן עֲצֵי שִׁטִּים
אַמָּתַיִם אָרְכּוֹ וְאַמָּה רָחְבּוֹ וְאַמָּה וָחֵצִי קֹמָתוֹ׃
יא וַיְצַף אֹתוֹ זָהָב טָהוֹר וַיַּעַשׂ לוֹ זֵר זָהָב
סָבִיב׃ יב וַיַּעַשׂ לוֹ מִסְגֶּרֶת טֹפַח סָבִיב וַיַּעַשׂ
זֵר־זָהָב לְמִסְגַּרְתּוֹ סָבִיב׃ יג וַיִּצֹק לוֹ אַרְבַּע
טַבְּעֹת זָהָב וַיִּתֵּן אֶת־הַטַּבָּעֹת עַל אַרְבַּע הַפֵּאֹת
אֲשֶׁר לְאַרְבַּע רַגְלָיו׃ יד לְעֻמַּת הַמִּסְגֶּרֶת הָיוּ
הַטַּבָּעֹת בָּתִּים לַבַּדִּים לָשֵׂאת אֶת־הַשֻּׁלְחָן׃
טו וַיַּעַשׂ אֶת־הַבַּדִּים עֲצֵי שִׁטִּים וַיְצַף אֹתָם
זָהָב לָשֵׂאת אֶת־הַשֻּׁלְחָן׃ טז וַיַּעַשׂ אֶת־הַכֵּלִים ׀
אֲשֶׁר עַל־הַשֻּׁלְחָן אֶת־קְעָרֹתָיו וְאֶת־כַּפֹּתָיו
וְאֵת מְנַקִּיֹּתָיו וְאֶת־הַקְּשָׂוֹת אֲשֶׁר יֻסַּךְ בָּהֵן זָהָב
טָהוֹר׃ פ ששי (שלישי כשהן מחוברין) יז וַיַּעַשׂ אֶת־
הַמְּנֹרָה זָהָב טָהוֹר מִקְשָׁה עָשָׂה אֶת־הַמְּנֹרָה
יְרֵכָהּ וְקָנָהּ גְּבִיעֶיהָ כַּפְתֹּרֶיהָ וּפְרָחֶיהָ מִמֶּנָּה
הָיוּ׃ יח וְשִׁשָּׁה קָנִים יֹצְאִים מִצִּדֶּיהָ שְׁלֹשָׁה ׀
קְנֵי מְנֹרָה מִצִּדָּהּ הָאֶחָד וּשְׁלֹשָׁה קְנֵי מְנֹרָה
מִצִּדָּהּ הַשֵּׁנִי׃ יט שְׁלֹשָׁה גְבִעִים מְשֻׁקָּדִים בַּקָּנֶה
הָאֶחָד כַּפְתֹּר וָפֶרַח וּשְׁלֹשָׁה גְבִעִים מְשֻׁקָּדִים
בְּקָנֶה אֶחָד כַּפְתֹּר וָפָרַח כֵּן לְשֵׁשֶׁת הַקָּנִים
הַיֹּצְאִים מִן־הַמְּנֹרָה׃ כ וּבַמְּנֹרָה אַרְבָּעָה

20. Upon the menorah itself four cups, shaped like almond blossoms, [with] its knobs and its flowers. 21. One knob under the two branches that went out from it, and one knob under the [second set of] two branches that went out from it, and one knob under the [third set of] two branches that went out from it; and so for [all] the six branches that went out from it [the menorah]. 22. Their knobs and their branches were of one piece with it; the whole [of it] was hammered out of one piece of pure gold. 23. He made its lamps seven in number, and its tongs and its charcoal pans of pure gold. 24. He made it and all its utensils of one *kikkar* of pure gold. 25. He made the altar for burning incense of *shittim* wood, one cubit long and one cubit wide, square, and two cubits high; its elevated corners were [made] of one piece with it. 26. He covered it with pure gold, its top, its walls round about and its elevated corners, and he made a golden ring for it round about. 27. He made two golden rings for it underneath its rim on its two sides; that is, on its two opposite sides, so that they serve[d] as holders for poles with which to carry it. 28. He made the poles of *shittim* wood and covered them with gold. 29. He made the anointing oil as a sacred thing and the pure spicy incense after the art of the perfumer.

XXXVIII

1. He made the altar for the ascent offering of *shittim* wood, five cubits long and five cubits wide; square, and three cubits high. 2. He made its elevated corners on its four corners; its elevated corners were made of one piece with it, and he covered it with copper. 3. He made all the utensils of the altar: the pots, the shovels, the sprinkling basins, the forks and the pans; he made all its utensils of copper. 4. He made for the altar a grating of copper net under its ledge, to extend halfway down the altar. 5. He cast four rings on the net upon its four corners, as holders for the poles. 6. He made the poles of *shittim* wood and covered them with copper. 7. He placed the poles into the rings on the sides of the altar, to carry it with them; he made it hol-

גְּבִעִים מְשֻׁקָּדִים כַּפְתֹּרֶיהָ וּפְרָחֶיהָ: כא וְכַפְתֹּר תַּחַת שְׁנֵי הַקָּנִים מִמֶּנָּה וְכַפְתֹּר תַּחַת שְׁנֵי הַקָּנִים מִמֶּנָּה וְכַפְתֹּר תַּחַת־שְׁנֵי הַקָּנִים מִמֶּנָּה לְשֵׁשֶׁת הַקָּנִים הַיֹּצְאִים מִמֶּנָּה: כב כַּפְתֹּרֵיהֶם וּקְנֹתָם מִמֶּנָּה הָיוּ כֻּלָּהּ מִקְשָׁה אַחַת זָהָב טָהוֹר: כג וַיַּעַשׂ אֶת־נֵרֹתֶיהָ שִׁבְעָה וּמַלְקָחֶיהָ וּמַחְתֹּתֶיהָ זָהָב טָהוֹר: כד כִּכָּר זָהָב טָהוֹר עָשָׂה אֹתָהּ וְאֵת כָּל־כֵּלֶיהָ: פ כה וַיַּעַשׂ אֶת־מִזְבַּח הַקְּטֹרֶת עֲצֵי שִׁטִּים אַמָּה אָרְכּוֹ וְאַמָּה רָחְבּוֹ רָבוּעַ וְאַמָּתַיִם קֹמָתוֹ מִמֶּנּוּ הָיוּ קַרְנֹתָיו: כו וַיְצַף אֹתוֹ זָהָב טָהוֹר אֶת־גַּגּוֹ וְאֶת־קִירֹתָיו סָבִיב וְאֶת־קַרְנֹתָיו וַיַּעַשׂ לוֹ זֵר זָהָב סָבִיב: כז וּשְׁתֵּי טַבְּעֹת זָהָב עָשָׂה־לוֹ מִתַּחַת לְזֵרוֹ עַל שְׁתֵּי צַלְעֹתָיו עַל שְׁנֵי צִדָּיו לְבָתִּים לְבַדִּים לָשֵׂאת אֹתוֹ בָּהֶם: כח וַיַּעַשׂ אֶת־הַבַּדִּים עֲצֵי שִׁטִּים וַיְצַף אֹתָם זָהָב: כט וַיַּעַשׂ אֶת־שֶׁמֶן הַמִּשְׁחָה קֹדֶשׁ וְאֶת־קְטֹרֶת הַסַּמִּים טָהוֹר מַעֲשֵׂה רֹקֵחַ: ס שביעי (רביעי כשהן מחוברין)

לח א וַיַּעַשׂ אֶת־מִזְבַּח הָעֹלָה עֲצֵי שִׁטִּים חָמֵשׁ אַמּוֹת אָרְכּוֹ וְחָמֵשׁ־אַמּוֹת רָחְבּוֹ רָבוּעַ וְשָׁלֹשׁ אַמּוֹת קֹמָתוֹ: ב וַיַּעַשׂ קַרְנֹתָיו עַל אַרְבַּע פִּנֹּתָיו מִמֶּנּוּ הָיוּ קַרְנֹתָיו וַיְצַף אֹתוֹ נְחֹשֶׁת: ג וַיַּעַשׂ אֶת־כָּל־כְּלֵי הַמִּזְבֵּחַ אֶת־הַסִּירֹת וְאֶת־הַיָּעִים וְאֶת־הַמִּזְרָקֹת אֶת־הַמִּזְלָגֹת וְאֶת־הַמַּחְתֹּת כָּל־כֵּלָיו עָשָׂה נְחֹשֶׁת: ד וַיַּעַשׂ לַמִּזְבֵּחַ מִכְבָּר מַעֲשֵׂה רֶשֶׁת נְחֹשֶׁת תַּחַת כַּרְכֻּבּוֹ מִלְּמַטָּה עַד־חֶצְיוֹ: ה וַיִּצֹק אַרְבַּע טַבָּעֹת בְּאַרְבַּע הַקְּצָוֹת לְמִכְבַּר הַנְּחֹשֶׁת בָּתִּים לַבַּדִּים: ו וַיַּעַשׂ אֶת־הַבַּדִּים עֲצֵי שִׁטִּים וַיְצַף אֹתָם נְחֹשֶׁת: ז וַיָּבֵא אֶת־הַבַּדִּים בַּטַּבָּעֹת עַל צַלְעֹת הַמִּזְבֵּחַ לָשֵׂאת אֹתוֹ בָּהֶם נְבוּב לֻחֹת

low, out of planks. 8. He made the basin of copper and its base of copper, from the mirrors of the women who had gathered at the entrance of the Tent of Appointed Meeting. 9. He made the forecourt: for the south side on the right, hangings for the forecourt, of byssus twisted into six-ply thread, one hundred cubits long; 10. its pillars twenty and its sockets twenty of copper; the hooks of the pillars and their bands of silver. 11. For the north side, one hundred cubits, their pillars twenty and their sockets twenty of copper; the hooks of the pillars and their bands of silver. 12. For the west side, hangings of fifty cubits; their pillars ten and their sockets ten, the hooks of the pillars and their bands of silver. 13. The front side, to the east, was fifty cubits. 14. The hangings for the one side [were] fifteen cubits, their pillars three and their sockets three. 15. And on the other side, on either side of the gate to the forecourt [there were] hangings of fiteen cubits, their pillars three and their sockets three. 16. All the hangings of the forecourt round about of byssus twisted into six-ply thread. 17. The sockets of the pillars [were made] of copper, the hooks of the pillars and their bands of silver, also the covering of their capitals [was made] of silver; they, all the pillars of the forecourt, were banded with silver. 18. The protective curtain of the gate to the forecourt [was] of embroidery work of sky-blue, purple and scarlet wool and of byssus twisted into six-ply thread; namely, twenty cubits long, and the height in the width was five cubits, corresponding to the hangings of the forecourt. 19. Their pillars [were] four and their sockets four, of copper; their hooks [were] of silver and the covering of their capitals and their bands [were made] of silver. 20. All the stakes for the Dwelling Place and for the forecourt all around [were made] of copper.

עָשָׂה אֹתוֹ: ס ח וַיַּעַשׂ אֵת הַכִּיּוֹר נְחֹשֶׁת וְאֵת
כַּנּוֹ נְחֹשֶׁת בְּמַרְאֹת הַצֹּבְאֹת אֲשֶׁר צָבְאוּ פֶּתַח
אֹהֶל מוֹעֵד: ס ט וַיַּעַשׂ אֶת־הֶחָצֵר לִפְאַת ׀ נֶגֶב
תֵּימָנָה קַלְעֵי הֶחָצֵר שֵׁשׁ מָשְׁזָר מֵאָה בָּאַמָּה:
י עַמּוּדֵיהֶם עֶשְׂרִים וְאַדְנֵיהֶם עֶשְׂרִים נְחֹשֶׁת
וָוֵי הָעַמּוּדִים וַחֲשֻׁקֵיהֶם כָּסֶף: יא וְלִפְאַת צָפוֹן
מֵאָה בָאַמָּה עַמּוּדֵיהֶם עֶשְׂרִים וְאַדְנֵיהֶם
עֶשְׂרִים נְחֹשֶׁת וָוֵי הָעַמּוּדִים וַחֲשֻׁקֵיהֶם כָּסֶף:
יב וְלִפְאַת־יָם קְלָעִים חֲמִשִּׁים בָּאַמָּה
עַמּוּדֵיהֶם עֲשָׂרָה וְאַדְנֵיהֶם עֲשָׂרָה וָוֵי הָעַמֻּדִים
וַחֲשׁוּקֵיהֶם כָּסֶף: יג וְלִפְאַת קֵדְמָה מִזְרָחָה
חֲמִשִּׁים אַמָּה: יד קְלָעִים חֲמֵשׁ־עֶשְׂרֵה אַמָּה
אֶל־הַכָּתֵף עַמּוּדֵיהֶם שְׁלֹשָׁה וְאַדְנֵיהֶם שְׁלֹשָׁה:
טו וְלַכָּתֵף הַשֵּׁנִית מִזֶּה וּמִזֶּה לְשַׁעַר הֶחָצֵר
קְלָעִים חֲמֵשׁ עֶשְׂרֵה אַמָּה עַמֻּדֵיהֶם שְׁלֹשָׁה
וְאַדְנֵיהֶם שְׁלֹשָׁה: טז כָּל־קַלְעֵי הֶחָצֵר סָבִיב
שֵׁשׁ מָשְׁזָר: יז וְהָאֲדָנִים לָעַמֻּדִים נְחֹשֶׁת וָוֵי
הָעַמּוּדִים וַחֲשׁוּקֵיהֶם כֶּסֶף וְצִפּוּי רָאשֵׁיהֶם
כָּסֶף וְהֵם מְחֻשָּׁקִים כֶּסֶף כֹּל עַמֻּדֵי הֶחָצֵר:
מפטיר יח וּמָסַךְ שַׁעַר הֶחָצֵר מַעֲשֵׂה רֹקֵם תְּכֵלֶת
וְאַרְגָּמָן וְתוֹלַעַת שָׁנִי וְשֵׁשׁ מָשְׁזָר וְעֶשְׂרִים
אַמָּה אֹרֶךְ וְקוֹמָה בְרֹחַב חָמֵשׁ אַמּוֹת לְעֻמַּת
קַלְעֵי הֶחָצֵר: יט וְעַמֻּדֵיהֶם אַרְבָּעָה וְאַדְנֵיהֶם
אַרְבָּעָה נְחֹשֶׁת וָוֵיהֶם כֶּסֶף וְצִפּוּי רָאשֵׁיהֶם
וַחֲשֻׁקֵיהֶם כָּסֶף: כ וְכָל־הַיְתֵדֹת לַמִּשְׁכָּן וְלֶחָצֵר
סָבִיב נְחֹשֶׁת: ס

The Haftarah for this Sidra may be found on page 863

פקודי

PEKUDE

21. These are the accounts of the Dwelling Place of the Testimony, which were drawn up by command of Moshe; this was the work of the Levites under the direction of Ithamar, son of Aharon the priest. 22. Bezalel, son of Uri, son of Ḥur, of the tribe of Yehudah, had made all that *God* had commanded Moshe. 23. With him was Oholiab, son of Aḥisamakh, of the tribe of Dan, sculptor and weaver, and embroiderer in sky-blue, purple and scarlet wool and in byssus. 24. All the gold that had been used for the work was in all the work of the Sanctuary; the donated gold was twenty-nine *kikkars*, seven hundred and thirty shekels, reckoned by the [standard] weight of the Sanctuary. 25. The silver of the community census was one hundred *kikkars* and one thousand seven hundred and seventy-five shekels, reckoned by the [standard] weight of the Sanctuary. 26. One *bekka* per head; that is, half a shekel according to the shekel of the Sanctuary for each one who passed over to the numbered ones, from the age of twenty upward, for six times one hundred thousand, three thousand five hundred and fifty. 27. One hundred *kikkars* of this silver was used for casting the sockets for the Sanctuary and the sockets for the dividing curtain; one hundred sockets from one hundred *kikkars*, one *kikkar* for each socket. 28. And the one thousand seven hundred and seventy-five [shekels] he used for making hooks for the pillars; he covered their capitals with it and made bands for them. 29. The copper of the donation was seventy *kikkars* and two thousand four hundred shekels. 30. From that he made the sockets for the entrance to the Tent of Appointed Meeting, the copper altar, the copper grating upon it, and all the utensils of the altar, 31. and the sockets for the forecourt round about and the sockets for the gate to the forecourt, all the stakes for the Dwelling Place and all the stakes for the forecourt round about.

כא אֵ֣לֶּה פְקוּדֵ֤י הַמִּשְׁכָּן֙ מִשְׁכַּ֣ן הָעֵדֻ֔ת אֲשֶׁ֥ר
פֻּקַּ֖ד עַל־פִּ֣י מֹשֶׁ֑ה עֲבֹדַת֙ הַלְוִיִּ֔ם בְּיַד֙ אִֽיתָמָ֔ר
בֶּֽן־אַהֲרֹ֖ן הַכֹּהֵֽן׃ כב וּבְצַלְאֵ֛ל בֶּן־אוּרִ֥י בֶן־ח֖וּר
לְמַטֵּ֣ה יְהוּדָ֑ה עָשָׂ֕ה אֵ֛ת כָּל־אֲשֶׁר־צִוָּ֥ה יְהוָ֖ה
אֶת־מֹשֶֽׁה׃ כג וְאִתּ֗וֹ אָהֳלִיאָ֛ב בֶּן־אֲחִיסָמָ֖ךְ
לְמַטֵּה־דָ֑ן חָרָ֖שׁ וְחֹשֵׁ֑ב וְרֹקֵ֗ם בַּתְּכֵ֙לֶת֙ וּבָֽאַרְגָּמָ֔ן
וּבְתוֹלַ֥עַת הַשָּׁנִ֖י וּבַשֵּֽׁשׁ׃ ס כד כָּל־הַזָּהָ֗ב הֶֽעָשׂוּי֙
לַמְּלָאכָ֔ה בְּכֹ֖ל מְלֶ֣אכֶת הַקֹּ֑דֶשׁ וַיְהִ֣י ׀ זְהַ֣ב
הַתְּנוּפָ֗ה תֵּ֤שַׁע וְעֶשְׂרִים֙ כִּכָּ֔ר וּשְׁבַ֨ע מֵא֤וֹת
וּשְׁלֹשִׁים֙ שֶׁ֔קֶל בְּשֶׁ֖קֶל הַקֹּֽדֶשׁ׃ כה וְכֶ֛סֶף פְּקוּדֵ֥י
הָעֵדָ֖ה מְאַ֣ת כִּכָּ֑ר וְ֠אֶלֶף וּשְׁבַ֨ע מֵא֜וֹת וַחֲמִשָּׁ֧ה
וְשִׁבְעִ֛ים שֶׁ֖קֶל בְּשֶׁ֥קֶל הַקֹּֽדֶשׁ׃ כו בֶּ֚קַע לַגֻּלְגֹּ֔לֶת
מַחֲצִ֥ית הַשֶּׁ֖קֶל בְּשֶׁ֣קֶל הַקֹּ֑דֶשׁ לְכֹ֡ל הָעֹבֵר֩ עַל־
הַפְּקֻדִ֜ים מִבֶּ֨ן עֶשְׂרִ֤ים שָׁנָה֙ וָמַ֔עְלָה לְשֵׁשׁ־
מֵא֥וֹת אֶ֙לֶף֙ וּשְׁלֹ֣שֶׁת אֲלָפִ֔ים וַחֲמֵ֥שׁ מֵא֖וֹת
וַחֲמִשִּֽׁים׃ כז וַיְהִ֗י מְאַת֙ כִּכַּ֣ר הַכֶּ֔סֶף לָצֶ֗קֶת אֵ֚ת
אַדְנֵ֣י הַקֹּ֔דֶשׁ וְאֵ֖ת אַדְנֵ֣י הַפָּרֹ֑כֶת מְאַ֧ת אֲדָנִ֛ים
לִמְאַ֥ת הַכִּכָּ֖ר כִּכָּ֥ר לָאָֽדֶן׃ כח וְאֶת־הָאֶ֜לֶף וּשְׁבַ֣ע
הַמֵּא֗וֹת וַחֲמִשָּׁה֙ וְשִׁבְעִ֔ים עָשָׂ֥ה וָוִ֖ים לָֽעַמּוּדִ֑ים
וְצִפָּ֥ה רָאשֵׁיהֶ֖ם וְחִשַּׁ֥ק אֹתָֽם׃ כט וּנְחֹ֥שֶׁת
הַתְּנוּפָ֖ה שִׁבְעִ֣ים כִּכָּ֑ר וְאַלְפַּ֥יִם וְאַרְבַּע־מֵא֖וֹת
שָֽׁקֶל׃ ל וַיַּ֣עַשׂ בָּ֗הּ אֶת־אַדְנֵי֙ פֶּ֚תַח אֹ֣הֶל מוֹעֵ֔ד
וְאֵת֙ מִזְבַּ֣ח הַנְּחֹ֔שֶׁת וְאֶת־מִכְבַּ֥ר הַנְּחֹ֖שֶׁת אֲשֶׁר־
ל֑וֹ וְאֵ֖ת כָּל־כְּלֵ֥י הַמִּזְבֵּֽחַ׃ לא וְאֶת־אַדְנֵ֤י הֶחָצֵר֙
סָבִ֔יב וְאֶת־אַדְנֵ֖י שַׁ֣עַר הֶחָצֵ֑ר וְאֵ֨ת כָּל־יִתְדֹ֧ת
הַמִּשְׁכָּ֛ן וְאֶת־כָּל־יִתְדֹ֥ת הֶחָצֵ֖ר סָבִֽיב׃

XXXIX

1. From the sky-blue, purple and scarlet wool they made garments of distinction for the service in the Sanctuary; that is, they made the garments of the Sanctuary which were intended for Aharon, as *God* had commanded Moshe. 2. He made the *ephod* of gold, sky blue, purple and scarlet wool and byssus twisted into six-ply thread. 3. They beat out the sheets of gold and he cut threads out of them, to work them into the sky-blue, into the purple and scarlet and into the byssus, [this was] weaver's work. 4. They attached to it connected shoulder pieces at its two corners so that it was joined together. 5. The band for its belt was woven from out of itself, of the same kind of work, of gold, sky-blue, purple and scarlet wool and byssus twisted into six-ply thread, as *God* had commanded Moshe. 6. They made the *shoham* stones surrounded by golden settings, like the engravings of a signet, engraved according to the names of the sons of Yisrael. 7. He put them upon the shoulder pieces of the *ephod* as stones of remembrance for the sons of Yisrael, as *God* had commanded Moshe. 8. He made the breastplate of woven material like the work of the *ephod*, of gold, sky-blue, purple and scarlet wool and byssus twisted into six-ply thread. 9. It was foursquare; they made the breastplate double, one span long and one span wide, double. 10. They set into it four rows of stones. One row: *odem, pitdah* and *barekketh*; thus was the one row. 11. The second row: *nofekh, sapir* and *yahalom*. 12. The third row: *leshem, shevo* and *aḥlamah*. 13. And the fourth row: *tarshish, shoham* and *yashpheh*, enclosed in gold frames in their settings. 14. The stones [were] according to the names of the sons of Yisrael, twelve, according to their names; like the engraving of a signet, every one according to his name for the twelve tribes. 15. They made upon the breastplate cable-like chains at the edges, of pure gold. 16. They made two golden settings and two golden rings and placed the two rings on the two corners of the breastplate. 17. They placed the two golden

לט א וּמִן־הַתְּכֵלֶת וְהָאַרְגָּמָן וְתוֹלַעַת הַשָּׁנִי
עָשׂוּ בִגְדֵי־שְׂרָד לְשָׁרֵת בַּקֹּדֶשׁ וַיַּעֲשׂוּ אֶת־
בִּגְדֵי הַקֹּדֶשׁ אֲשֶׁר לְאַהֲרֹן כַּאֲשֶׁר צִוָּה יְהֹוָה
אֶת־מֹשֶׁה׃ פ שני (חמישי כשהן מחוברין) ב וַיַּעַשׂ אֶת־
הָאֵפֹד זָהָב תְּכֵלֶת וְאַרְגָּמָן וְתוֹלַעַת שָׁנִי וְשֵׁשׁ
מָשְׁזָר׃ ג וַיְרַקְּעוּ אֶת־פַּחֵי הַזָּהָב וְקִצֵּץ פְּתִילִם
לַעֲשׂוֹת בְּתוֹךְ הַתְּכֵלֶת וּבְתוֹךְ הָאַרְגָּמָן וּבְתוֹךְ
תּוֹלַעַת הַשָּׁנִי וּבְתוֹךְ הַשֵּׁשׁ מַעֲשֵׂה חֹשֵׁב׃
ד כְּתֵפֹת עָשׂוּ־לוֹ חֹבְרֹת עַל־שְׁנֵי קְצוֹתָו
(קצותיו קרי) חֻבָּר׃ ה וְחֵשֶׁב אֲפֻדָּתוֹ אֲשֶׁר עָלָיו
מִמֶּנּוּ הוּא כְּמַעֲשֵׂהוּ זָהָב תְּכֵלֶת וְאַרְגָּמָן
וְתוֹלַעַת שָׁנִי וְשֵׁשׁ מָשְׁזָר כַּאֲשֶׁר צִוָּה יְהֹוָה
אֶת־מֹשֶׁה׃ ס ו וַיַּעֲשׂוּ אֶת־אַבְנֵי הַשֹּׁהַם
מֻסַבֹּת מִשְׁבְּצֹת זָהָב מְפֻתָּחֹת פִּתּוּחֵי חוֹתָם
עַל־שְׁמוֹת בְּנֵי יִשְׂרָאֵל׃ ז וַיָּשֶׂם אֹתָם עַל
כִּתְפֹת הָאֵפֹד אַבְנֵי זִכָּרוֹן לִבְנֵי יִשְׂרָאֵל כַּאֲשֶׁר
צִוָּה יְהֹוָה אֶת־מֹשֶׁה׃ פ ח וַיַּעַשׂ אֶת־הַחֹשֶׁן
מַעֲשֵׂה חֹשֵׁב כְּמַעֲשֵׂה אֵפֹד זָהָב תְּכֵלֶת וְאַרְגָּמָן
וְתוֹלַעַת שָׁנִי וְשֵׁשׁ מָשְׁזָר׃ ט רָבוּעַ הָיָה כָּפוּל
עָשׂוּ אֶת־הַחֹשֶׁן זֶרֶת אָרְכּוֹ וְזֶרֶת רָחְבּוֹ כָּפוּל׃
י וַיְמַלְאוּ־בוֹ אַרְבָּעָה טוּרֵי אָבֶן טוּר אֹדֶם
פִּטְדָה וּבָרֶקֶת הַטּוּר הָאֶחָד׃ יא וְהַטּוּר הַשֵּׁנִי
נֹפֶךְ סַפִּיר וְיָהֲלֹם׃ יב וְהַטּוּר הַשְּׁלִישִׁי לֶשֶׁם
שְׁבוֹ וְאַחְלָמָה׃ יג וְהַטּוּר הָרְבִיעִי תַּרְשִׁישׁ
שֹׁהַם וְיָשְׁפֵה מוּסַבֹּת מִשְׁבְּצֹת זָהָב בְּמִלֻּאֹתָם׃
יד וְהָאֲבָנִים עַל־שְׁמֹת בְּנֵי־יִשְׂרָאֵל הֵנָּה שְׁתֵּים
עֶשְׂרֵה עַל־שְׁמֹתָם פִּתּוּחֵי חֹתָם אִישׁ עַל־שְׁמוֹ
לִשְׁנֵים עָשָׂר שָׁבֶט׃ טו וַיַּעֲשׂוּ עַל־הַחֹשֶׁן
שַׁרְשְׁרֹת גַּבְלֻת מַעֲשֵׂה עֲבֹת זָהָב טָהוֹר׃
טז וַיַּעֲשׂוּ שְׁתֵּי מִשְׁבְּצֹת זָהָב וּשְׁתֵּי טַבְּעֹת זָהָב
וַיִּתְּנוּ אֶת־שְׁתֵּי הַטַּבָּעֹת עַל־שְׁנֵי קְצוֹת הַחֹשֶׁן׃
יז וַיִּתְּנוּ שְׁתֵּי הָעֲבֹתֹת הַזָּהָב עַל־שְׁתֵּי הַטַּבָּעֹת

cables on the two rings, at the corners of the breastplate. 18. They placed the two ends of the two cables upon the two settings and placed these upon the shoulder pieces of the *ephod,* on its front part. 19. They made two golden rings and placed them on the two corners of the breastplate on its lower edge, which [was] turned toward the side of the *ephod,* inward. 20. They furthermore made two golden rings and placed them upon the two shoulder pieces of the *ephod,* underneath, on its front part, close to its coupling above the band of the *ephod.* 21. And they bound the breastplate by its rings to the rings of the *ephod* with a thread of sky-blue, so that it might stay upon the band of the *ephod* and the breastplate might not move from the *ephod,* as *God* had commanded Moshe. 22. He made the robe of the *ephod* of woven work, all of sky-blue wool. 23. The opening of the robe was turned inward, like the opening of a coat of mail; its opening had a woven border all around it that it should not be torn. 24. They made upon the bottom hems of the robe pomegranates of twisted sky-blue, purple and scarlet wool. 25. They made bells of pure gold and placed the bells between the pomegranates, round about between the pomegranates, upon the bottom hems of the robe. 26. A bell and a pomegranate, a bell and a pomegranate each upon the bottom hems of the robe round about, for performing the service, as *God* has commanded Moshe. 27. They made the tunics of byssus of woven work for Aharon and for his sons. 28. The turban of byssus and the ornament of the high turbans of byssus, and the linen breeches of byssus twisted into six-ply thread. 29. The sash of byssus twisted into six-ply thread, sky-blue, purple and scarlet wool, embroiderer's work, as *God* had commanded Moshe. 30. They made the showplate, the diadem of the Sanctuary, of pure gold and inscribed upon it like the script in the engraving of a signet: "The Sanctuary is *God's.*" 31. They placed upon it a thread of sky-blue wool, to go over the turban from above, as *God* had commanded Moshe. 32. All the work to be

עַל־קְצ֣וֹת הַחֹ֑שֶׁן: יח וְאֵ֨ת שְׁתֵּ֜י קְצ֣וֹת שְׁתֵּ֣י הָעֲבֹתֹ֗ת נָֽתְנ֖וּ עַל־שְׁתֵּ֣י הַֽמִּשְׁבְּצֹ֑ת וַֽיִּתְּנֻ֛ם עַל־כִּתְפֹ֥ת הָאֵפֹ֖ד אֶל־מ֥וּל פָּנָֽיו: יט וַֽיַּעֲשׂ֗וּ שְׁתֵּי֙ טַבְּעֹ֣ת זָהָ֔ב וַיָּשִׂ֕ימוּ עַל־שְׁנֵ֖י קְצ֣וֹת הַחֹ֑שֶׁן עַל־שְׂפָת֕וֹ אֲשֶׁ֛ר אֶל־עֵ֥בֶר הָאֵפֹ֖ד בָּֽיְתָה: כ וַֽיַּעֲשׂוּ֮ שְׁתֵּ֣י טַבְּעֹ֣ת זָהָב֒ וַֽיִּתְּנֻ֞ם עַל־שְׁתֵּ֣י כִתְפֹ֣ת הָאֵפֹ֗ד מִלְמַ֙טָּה֙ מִמּ֣וּל פָּנָ֔יו לְעֻמַּ֖ת מַחְבַּרְתּ֑וֹ מִמַּ֕עַל לְחֵ֖שֶׁב הָאֵפֹֽד: כא וַיִּרְכְּס֣וּ אֶת־הַחֹ֡שֶׁן מִטַּבְּעֹתָיו֩ אֶל־טַבְּעֹ֨ת הָאֵפֹ֜ד בִּפְתִ֣יל תְּכֵ֗לֶת לִֽהְיֹת֙ עַל־חֵ֣שֶׁב הָאֵפֹ֔ד וְלֹֽא־יִזַּ֥ח הַחֹ֖שֶׁן מֵעַ֣ל הָאֵפֹ֑ד כַּֽאֲשֶׁ֛ר צִוָּ֥ה יְהֹוָ֖ה אֶת־מֹשֶֽׁה: פ שלישי

(ששי כשהן מחוברין) כב וַיַּ֛עַשׂ אֶת־מְעִ֥יל הָאֵפֹ֖ד מַֽעֲשֵׂ֣ה אֹרֵ֑ג כְּלִ֖יל תְּכֵֽלֶת: כג וּפִֽי־הַמְּעִ֥יל בְּתוֹכ֖וֹ כְּפִ֣י תַחְרָ֑א שָׂפָ֥ה לְפִ֛יו סָבִ֖יב לֹ֥א יִקָּרֵֽעַ: כד וַֽיַּעֲשׂוּ֙ עַל־שׁוּלֵ֣י הַמְּעִ֔יל רִמּוֹנֵ֕י תְּכֵ֥לֶת וְאַרְגָּמָ֖ן וְתוֹלַ֣עַת שָׁנִ֣י מָשְׁזָֽר: כה וַיַּעֲשׂ֥וּ פַֽעֲמֹנֵ֖י זָהָ֣ב טָה֑וֹר וַיִּתְּנ֨וּ אֶת־הַפַּֽעֲמֹנִ֜ים בְּת֣וֹךְ הָֽרִמֹּנִ֗ים עַל־שׁוּלֵ֤י הַמְּעִיל֙ סָבִ֔יב בְּת֖וֹךְ הָֽרִמֹּנִֽים: כו פַּֽעֲמֹ֤ן וְרִמֹּן֙ פַּֽעֲמֹ֣ן וְרִמֹּ֔ן עַל־שׁוּלֵ֥י הַמְּעִ֖יל סָבִ֑יב לְשָׁרֵ֕ת כַּֽאֲשֶׁ֛ר צִוָּ֥ה יְהֹוָ֖ה אֶת־מֹשֶֽׁה: ס כז וַֽיַּעֲשׂ֤וּ אֶת־הַכָּתְנֹת֙ שֵׁ֣שׁ מַֽעֲשֵׂ֣ה אֹרֵ֔ג לְאַֽהֲרֹ֖ן וּלְבָנָֽיו: כח וְאֵת֙ הַמִּצְנֶ֣פֶת שֵׁ֔שׁ וְאֶת־פַּֽאֲרֵ֥י הַמִּגְבָּעֹ֖ת שֵׁ֑שׁ וְאֶת־מִכְנְסֵ֥י הַבָּ֖ד שֵׁ֥שׁ מָשְׁזָֽר: כט וְאֶת־הָֽאַבְנֵ֞ט שֵׁ֣שׁ מָשְׁזָ֗ר וּתְכֵ֧לֶת וְאַרְגָּמָ֛ן וְתוֹלַ֥עַת שָׁנִ֖י מַֽעֲשֵׂ֣ה רֹקֵ֑ם כַּֽאֲשֶׁ֛ר צִוָּ֥ה יְהֹוָ֖ה אֶת־מֹשֶֽׁה: ס ל וַֽיַּעֲשׂ֛וּ אֶת־צִ֥יץ נֵֽזֶר־הַקֹּ֖דֶשׁ זָהָ֣ב טָה֑וֹר וַיִּכְתְּב֣וּ עָלָ֗יו מִכְתַּב֙ פִּתּוּחֵ֣י חוֹתָ֔ם קֹ֖דֶשׁ לַֽיהֹוָֽה: לא וַיִּתְּנ֤וּ עָלָיו֙ פְּתִ֣יל תְּכֵ֔לֶת לָתֵ֥ת עַל־הַמִּצְנֶ֖פֶת מִלְמָ֑עְלָה כַּֽאֲשֶׁ֛ר צִוָּ֥ה יְהֹוָ֖ה אֶת־מֹשֶֽׁה: ס לב וַתֵּ֕כֶל כָּל־עֲבֹדַ֕ת מִשְׁכַּ֖ן אֹ֥הֶל

accomplished for the Dwelling Place of the Tent of Appointed Meeting was completed; the sons of Yisrael had done it; entirely as *God* had commanded Moshe, so they did. 33. Now they brought the Dwelling Place to Moshe, the tent and all its utensils, its clasps, its beams, its bars, its pillars and its sockets; 34. the covering of rams' skins dyed red, the covering of *tahash* skins, and the covering dividing curtain; 35. the Ark of the Testimony and its poles and the cover; 36. the table and all its utensils and the showbread; 37. the pure menorah, its lamps, the lamps to be set in order and all its utensils, and the oil for the lighting; 38. the golden altar, the anointing oil and the spicy incense, and also the curtain for the entrance to the tent; 39. the copper altar and the copper grating that belonged to its poles and all its utensils; the basin and its base; 40. the hangings of the forecourt, its pillars and its sockets, and the covering for the gate to the forecourt, its cables and its stakes and all the utensils required for the service at the Dwelling Place for the Tent of Appointed Meeting; 41. the garments of distinction for service in the Sanctuary; the garments of the Sanctuary for Aharon the priest and the garments of his sons for priestly service. 42. In accordance with all that *God* had commanded Moshe, so did the sons of Yisrael accomplish all the work that had been set for them. 43. Moshe saw the entire work and lo! they had accomplished it; as

מוֹעֵד וַיַּעֲשׂוּ בְּנֵי יִשְׂרָאֵל כְּכֹל אֲשֶׁר צִוָּה יְהוָה
אֶת־מֹשֶׁה כֵּן עָשׂוּ: פ רביעי לג וַיָּבִיאוּ אֶת־
הַמִּשְׁכָּן אֶל־מֹשֶׁה אֶת־הָאֹהֶל וְאֶת־כָּל־כֵּלָיו
קְרָסָיו קְרָשָׁיו בְּרִיחָו (בריחיו קרי) וְעַמֻּדָיו וַאֲדָנָיו:
לד וְאֶת־מִכְסֵה עוֹרֹת הָאֵילִם הַמְאָדָּמִים וְאֶת־
מִכְסֵה עֹרֹת הַתְּחָשִׁים וְאֵת פָּרֹכֶת הַמָּסָךְ:
לה אֶת־אֲרוֹן הָעֵדֻת וְאֶת־בַּדָּיו וְאֵת הַכַּפֹּרֶת:
לו אֶת־הַשֻּׁלְחָן אֶת־כָּל־כֵּלָיו וְאֵת לֶחֶם הַפָּנִים:
לז אֶת־הַמְּנֹרָה הַטְּהֹרָה אֶת־נֵרֹתֶיהָ נֵרֹת
הַמַּעֲרָכָה וְאֶת־כָּל־כֵּלֶיהָ וְאֵת שֶׁמֶן הַמָּאוֹר:
לח וְאֵת מִזְבַּח הַזָּהָב וְאֵת שֶׁמֶן הַמִּשְׁחָה וְאֵת
קְטֹרֶת הַסַּמִּים וְאֵת מָסַךְ פֶּתַח הָאֹהֶל: לט אֵת ׀
מִזְבַּח הַנְּחֹשֶׁת וְאֶת־מִכְבַּר הַנְּחֹשֶׁת אֲשֶׁר־לוֹ
אֶת־בַּדָּיו וְאֶת־כָּל־כֵּלָיו אֶת־הַכִּיֹּר וְאֶת־כַּנּוֹ:
מ אֵת קַלְעֵי הֶחָצֵר אֶת־עַמֻּדֶיהָ וְאֶת־אֲדָנֶיהָ
וְאֶת־הַמָּסָךְ לְשַׁעַר הֶחָצֵר אֶת־מֵיתָרָיו
וִיתֵדֹתֶיהָ וְאֵת כָּל־כְּלֵי עֲבֹדַת הַמִּשְׁכָּן לְאֹהֶל
מוֹעֵד: מא אֶת־בִּגְדֵי הַשְּׂרָד לְשָׁרֵת בַּקֹּדֶשׁ אֶת־
בִּגְדֵי הַקֹּדֶשׁ לְאַהֲרֹן הַכֹּהֵן וְאֶת־בִּגְדֵי בָנָיו
לְכַהֵן: מב כְּכֹל אֲשֶׁר־צִוָּה יְהוָה אֶת־מֹשֶׁה כֵּן
עָשׂוּ בְּנֵי יִשְׂרָאֵל אֵת כָּל־הָעֲבֹדָה: מג וַיַּרְא
מֹשֶׁה אֶת־כָּל־הַמְּלָאכָה וְהִנֵּה עָשׂוּ אֹתָהּ

CHAPTER XXXIX

43. ***Moshe saw . . . and lo! they had accomplished it; as* God *had commanded, so had they done.*** Moses inspected all the work that had been completed, and he noted that the work bore two distinct characteristics: First, עָשׂוּ אוֹתָהּ, it was *they* who had done it; every part, from the smallest to the largest, expressed their whole personality, their devotion, their spontaneous enthusiasm and the strength and the energies of the entire nation. Secondly, כַּאֲשֶׁר צִוָּה כֵּן עָשׂוּ, "as *God* had commanded, so had they done." Their zeal and enthusiasm. in its sum total as well as in its every detail, had been subordinated completely to the commands of God. There had been no attempt on the part of any craftsman to bring his own ideas and his own individuality to bear upon the work by making additions or omissions. Rather, each and every one of the craftsmen had considered it his supreme accomplishment to execute obediently, and with scrupulous care and precision, not his own idea but the ideas and the commandments of God. This free-willed, joyous obedience, this freedom in obedience and this obedience in freedom, which makes one most happily aware of one's own strength precisely by subordinating one's personality completely to the will of God—these constitute the most important characteristic of sublime moral perfection in the deeds of the Jewish person. This is what characterizes a human being as עֶבֶד ד׳ [a servant of God].

The hope that this characteristic may remain impressed forever upon the conduct of the Jew is expressed in the final verse of the Prayer of Moses

God had commanded, so had they done; and Moshe blessed them.

XL 1. *God* spoke to Moshe [saying]: 2. "On the first day of the New Moon, on the first of the month, you shall set up the Dwelling Place of the Tent of Appointed Meeting. 3. You shall place there the Ark of the Testimony, and you shall spread the dividing curtain over the Ark; 4. you shall bring in the table and set it in order; you shall bring in the menorah and kindle its lamps. 5. You shall place the golden altar for burning incense before the Ark of the Testimony and fasten the protective curtain at the entrance of the Dwelling Place. 6. You shall place the altar of the ascent offering[s] in front of the entrance to the Dwelling Place of the Tent of Appointed Meeting. 7. You shall place the basin between the Tent of Appointed Meeting and the altar, and put water into it. 8. And you shall put up the forecourt round about, and set up the protective curtain for the gate to the forecourt. 9. You shall take the anointing oil and anoint the Dwelling Place and everything that is in it, and you shall sanctify it and all its utensils; thus it will become a holy thing. 10. You shall anoint the altar for the ascent offering[s] and all its utensils; you shall sanctify the altar; thus the altar will become a holy of holies. 11. You shall anoint the basin and its base and sanctify it. 12. You shall have Aharon and his sons come near the entrance of the Tent of Appointed Meeting and you shall bathe them in water; 13. you shall clothe Aharon with the garments of the

כַּאֲשֶׁ֛ר צִוָּ֥ה יְהֹוָ֖ה כֵּ֣ן עָשׂ֑וּ וַיְבָ֣רֶךְ אֹתָ֔ם מֹשֶֽׁה: פ חמישי (שביעי כשהן מחוברין) מ א וַיְדַבֵּ֥ר יְהֹוָ֖ה אֶל־מֹשֶׁ֥ה לֵּאמֹֽר: ב בְּיוֹם־הַחֹ֥דֶשׁ הָרִאשׁ֖וֹן בְּאֶחָ֣ד לַחֹ֑דֶשׁ תָּקִ֕ים אֶת־מִשְׁכַּ֖ן אֹ֥הֶל מוֹעֵֽד: ג וְשַׂמְתָּ֣ שָׁ֔ם אֵ֖ת אֲר֣וֹן הָעֵד֑וּת וְסַכֹּתָ֥ עַל־הָֽאָרֹ֖ן אֶת־הַפָּרֹֽכֶת: ד וְהֵבֵאתָ֣ אֶת־הַשֻּׁלְחָ֔ן וְעָרַכְתָּ֖ אֶת־עֶרְכּ֑וֹ וְהֵבֵאתָ֙ אֶת־הַמְּנֹרָ֔ה וְהַעֲלֵיתָ֖ אֶת־נֵרֹתֶֽיהָ: ה וְנָתַתָּ֞ה אֶת־מִזְבַּ֣ח הַזָּהָ֗ב לִקְטֹ֙רֶת֙ לִפְנֵ֖י אֲר֣וֹן הָעֵדֻ֑ת וְשַׂמְתָּ֛ אֶת־מָסַ֥ךְ הַפֶּ֖תַח לַמִּשְׁכָּֽן: ו וְנָתַתָּ֕ה אֵ֖ת מִזְבַּ֣ח הָעֹלָ֑ה לִפְנֵ֕י פֶּ֖תַח מִשְׁכַּ֥ן אֹֽהֶל־מוֹעֵֽד: ז וְנָֽתַתָּ֙ אֶת־הַכִּיֹּ֔ר בֵּֽין־אֹ֥הֶל מוֹעֵ֖ד וּבֵ֣ין הַמִּזְבֵּ֑חַ וְנָתַתָּ֥ שָׁ֖ם מָֽיִם: ח וְשַׂמְתָּ֥ אֶת־הֶחָצֵ֖ר סָבִ֑יב וְנָֽתַתָּ֔ אֶת־מָסַ֖ךְ שַׁ֥עַר הֶחָצֵֽר: ט וְלָֽקַחְתָּ֙ אֶת־שֶׁ֣מֶן הַמִּשְׁחָ֔ה וּמָֽשַׁחְתָּ֥ אֶת־הַמִּשְׁכָּ֖ן וְאֶת־כָּל־אֲשֶׁר־בּ֑וֹ וְקִדַּשְׁתָּ֥ אֹת֛וֹ וְאֶת־כָּל־כֵּלָ֖יו וְהָ֥יָה קֹֽדֶשׁ: י וּמָֽשַׁחְתָּ֛ אֶת־מִזְבַּ֥ח הָעֹלָ֖ה וְאֶת־כָּל־כֵּלָ֑יו וְקִדַּשְׁתָּ֙ אֶת־הַמִּזְבֵּ֔חַ וְהָיָ֥ה הַמִּזְבֵּ֖חַ קֹ֥דֶשׁ קָֽדָשִֽׁים: יא וּמָֽשַׁחְתָּ֥ אֶת־הַכִּיֹּ֖ר וְאֶת־כַּנּ֑וֹ וְקִדַּשְׁתָּ֖ אֹתֽוֹ: יב וְהִקְרַבְתָּ֤ אֶת־אַֽהֲרֹן֙ וְאֶת־בָּנָ֔יו אֶל־פֶּ֖תַח אֹ֣הֶל מוֹעֵ֑ד וְרָֽחַצְתָּ֥ אֹתָ֖ם בַּמָּֽיִם: יג וְהִלְבַּשְׁתָּ֙ אֶת־אַֽהֲרֹ֔ן אֵ֖ת בִּגְדֵ֥י הַקֹּ֑דֶשׁ

(Psalm 90:17) as his most fervent wish for the future of his people, and our Sages accordingly note it in connection with this Scriptural verse as the content of Moses' blessing. That *tefillah* concludes with the words: "May Thy work become manifest to Thy servants and may Thy glory remain with their children! May the bliss of our God, our Lord, remain our lot; establish Thou the work of our hands upon us, and [as for] the work of our hands, establish Thou it!" מַעֲשֵׂה יָדֵינוּ כּוֹנְנָה עָלֵינוּ ["establish Thou the work of our hands upon us"]: that is freedom, and וּמַעֲשֵׂה יָדֵינוּ כּוֹנְנֵהוּ ["(as for) the work of our hands, establish Thou it!"]: that is obedience. Only

both of these together, in intimate union, can confer upon us the bliss which God prepares for us if we dedicate ourselves to Him as our "Lord."

The present verse: "Moshe saw the entire work and lo! they had accomplished it; as *God* had commanded, so had they done; and Moshe blessed them" is the source from which those thoughts in Moses' *tefillah* emanated. Hence the Sages say: "*And Moshe blessed them*: He said to them: May it be the will (of God) that the *Shekhinah* may rest upon the work of your hands, and may the bliss of *God*, our God, be upon us," etc. (Midrash Tanḥuma-Pekude 11).

Sanctuary, anoint him and sanctify him so that he may serve Me as a priest 14. and have his sons come here and clothe them with tunics,   15. and anoint them, as you anointed their father, so that they may serve Me as priests. And this shall be so that their anointment shall remain for them an everlasting priesthood for their descendants."   16. Moshe did it; according to all that *God* had commanded him, so did he do.   17. It came to pass in the first month, in the second year, on the first day of the month, that the Dwelling Place was set up.   18. Moshe set up the Dwelling Place, placed its sockets, put up its beams, put in its bars and set up its pillars.   19. He spread the tent over the Dwelling Place and placed the tent covering above it, as *God* had commanded Moshe.   20. He took and placed the Testimony into the Ark, put the poles upon the Ark and put the cover on top of the Ark.   21. He brought the Ark into the Dwelling Place and fastened the covering dividing curtain so that it formed a protective covering before the Ark of the Testimony, as *God* had commanded Moshe. 22. He placed the table into the Tent of Appointed Meeting at the side of the Dwelling Place, on the north side, outside the dividing curtain.   23. He set out upon it an arrangement of bread before *God*, as *God* had commanded Moshe. 24. He placed the menorah into the Tent of Appointed Meeting, opposite the table, at the side of the Dwelling Place, on the south side.   25. He kindled the lamps before *God*, as *God* had commanded Moshe.   26. He placed the golden altar into the Tent of Appointed Meeting in front of the dividing curtain.   27. He let the spicy incense go up in smoke upon it, as *God* had commanded Moshe.   28. He fastened the protective cover for the entrance of the Dwelling Place.   29. He placed the altar for ascent offering[s] in front of the entrance to the Dwelling Place of the Tent of Appointed Meeting; and caused the ascent offering and the homage offering to go up upon it, as *God* had commanded Moshe.   30. He placed the basin between the Tent of Appointed Meeting and the altar, and put water into it for

וּמָשַׁחְתָּ אֹתוֹ וְקִדַּשְׁתָּ אֹתוֹ וְכִהֵן לִי: יד וְאֶת־
בָּנָיו תַּקְרִיב וְהִלְבַּשְׁתָּ אֹתָם כֻּתֳּנֹת: טו וּמָשַׁחְתָּ
אֹתָם כַּאֲשֶׁר מָשַׁחְתָּ אֶת־אֲבִיהֶם וְכִהֲנוּ לִי
וְהָיְתָה לִהְיֹת לָהֶם מָשְׁחָתָם לִכְהֻנַּת עוֹלָם
לְדֹרֹתָם: טז וַיַּעַשׂ מֹשֶׁה כְּכֹל אֲשֶׁר צִוָּה יְהֹוָה
אֹתוֹ כֵּן עָשָׂה: ס ששי יז וַיְהִי בַּחֹדֶשׁ הָרִאשׁוֹן
בַּשָּׁנָה הַשֵּׁנִית בְּאֶחָד לַחֹדֶשׁ הוּקַם הַמִּשְׁכָּן:
יח וַיָּקֶם מֹשֶׁה אֶת־הַמִּשְׁכָּן וַיִּתֵּן אֶת־אֲדָנָיו
וַיָּשֶׂם אֶת־קְרָשָׁיו וַיִּתֵּן אֶת־בְּרִיחָיו וַיָּקֶם אֶת־
עַמּוּדָיו: יט וַיִּפְרֹשׂ אֶת־הָאֹהֶל עַל־הַמִּשְׁכָּן
וַיָּשֶׂם אֶת־מִכְסֵה הָאֹהֶל עָלָיו מִלְמָעְלָה כַּאֲשֶׁר
צִוָּה יְהֹוָה אֶת־מֹשֶׁה: ס כ וַיִּקַּח וַיִּתֵּן אֶת־
הָעֵדֻת אֶל־הָאָרֹן וַיָּשֶׂם אֶת־הַבַּדִּים עַל־הָאָרֹן
וַיִּתֵּן אֶת־הַכַּפֹּרֶת עַל־הָאָרֹן מִלְמָעְלָה:
כא וַיָּבֵא אֶת־הָאָרֹן אֶל־הַמִּשְׁכָּן וַיָּשֶׂם אֵת
פָּרֹכֶת הַמָּסָךְ וַיָּסֶךְ עַל אֲרוֹן הָעֵדוּת כַּאֲשֶׁר
צִוָּה יְהֹוָה אֶת־מֹשֶׁה: ס כב וַיִּתֵּן אֶת־הַשֻּׁלְחָן
בְּאֹהֶל מוֹעֵד עַל יֶרֶךְ הַמִּשְׁכָּן צָפֹנָה מִחוּץ
לַפָּרֹכֶת: כג וַיַּעֲרֹךְ עָלָיו עֵרֶךְ לֶחֶם לִפְנֵי יְהֹוָה
כַּאֲשֶׁר צִוָּה יְהֹוָה אֶת־מֹשֶׁה: ס כד וַיָּשֶׂם אֶת־
הַמְּנֹרָה בְּאֹהֶל מוֹעֵד נֹכַח הַשֻּׁלְחָן עַל יֶרֶךְ
הַמִּשְׁכָּן נֶגְבָּה: כה וַיַּעַל הַנֵּרֹת לִפְנֵי יְהֹוָה
כַּאֲשֶׁר צִוָּה יְהֹוָה אֶת־מֹשֶׁה: ס כו וַיָּשֶׂם אֶת־
מִזְבַּח הַזָּהָב בְּאֹהֶל מוֹעֵד לִפְנֵי הַפָּרֹכֶת:
כז וַיַּקְטֵר עָלָיו קְטֹרֶת סַמִּים כַּאֲשֶׁר צִוָּה יְהֹוָה
אֶת־מֹשֶׁה: ס שביעי כח וַיָּשֶׂם אֶת־מָסַךְ הַפֶּתַח
לַמִּשְׁכָּן: כט וְאֵת מִזְבַּח הָעֹלָה שָׂם פֶּתַח מִשְׁכַּן
אֹהֶל־מוֹעֵד וַיַּעַל עָלָיו אֶת־הָעֹלָה וְאֶת־הַמִּנְחָה
כַּאֲשֶׁר צִוָּה יְהֹוָה אֶת־מֹשֶׁה: ס ל וַיָּשֶׂם אֶת־
הַכִּיֹּר בֵּין־אֹהֶל מוֹעֵד וּבֵין הַמִּזְבֵּחַ וַיִּתֵּן שָׁמָּה

washing. 31. Moshe, Aharon and his sons washed their hands and their feet from it. 32. Whenever they went into the Tent of Appointed Meeting and when they went near to the altar they had to wash them, as *God* had commanded Moshe. 33. He set up the forecourt round about the Dwelling Place and the altar, put up the protective curtain at the entrance to the forecourt, and Moshe completed the work. 34. And the cloud covered the Tent of Appointed Meeting, and the glory of *God* filled the Dwelling Place. 35. Moshe was not able to enter the Tent of Appointed Meeting, because the cloud rested upon it and the glory of *God* filled the Dwelling Place. 36. If the cloud rose up from over the Dwelling Place, the sons of Yisrael set out in all their journeys. 37. If the cloud did not rise up, they did not set out until the day that it rose. 38. For the cloud of *God* was upon the Dwelling Place by day, and there was fire inside it by night, before the eyes of the entire House of Yisrael in all their journeys.

מַ֖יִם לְרָחְצָ֑ה: לֹא וְרָחֲצ֛וּ מִמֶּ֖נּוּ מֹשֶׁ֥ה וְאַהֲרֹ֖ן
וּבָנָ֑יו אֶת־יְדֵיהֶ֖ם וְאֶת־רַגְלֵיהֶֽם: לֹב בְּבֹאָ֣ם אֶל־
אֹ֤הֶל מוֹעֵד֙ וּבְקָרְבָתָ֣ם אֶל־הַמִּזְבֵּ֔חַ יִרְחָ֑צוּ
כַּאֲשֶׁ֛ר צִוָּ֥ה יְהֹוָ֖ה אֶת־מֹשֶֽׁה: ס לֹג וַיָּ֣קֶם אֶת־
הֶֽחָצֵ֗ר סָבִיב֙ לַמִּשְׁכָּ֣ן וְלַמִּזְבֵּ֔חַ וַיִּתֵּ֕ן אֶת־מָסַ֖ךְ
שַׁ֣עַר הֶחָצֵ֑ר וַיְכַ֥ל מֹשֶׁ֖ה אֶת־הַמְּלָאכָֽה: פ מפטיר
לֹד וַיְכַ֥ס הֶעָנָ֖ן אֶת־אֹ֣הֶל מוֹעֵ֑ד וּכְב֣וֹד יְהֹוָ֔ה
מָלֵ֖א אֶת־הַמִּשְׁכָּֽן: לֹה וְלֹא־יָכֹ֣ל מֹשֶׁה֮ לָבוֹא֒
אֶל־אֹ֣הֶל מוֹעֵ֑ד כִּֽי־שָׁכַ֥ן עָלָ֖יו הֶעָנָ֑ן וּכְב֣וֹד
יְהֹוָ֔ה מָלֵ֖א אֶת־הַמִּשְׁכָּֽן: לֹו וּבְהֵעָל֤וֹת הֶֽעָנָן֙
מֵעַ֣ל הַמִּשְׁכָּ֔ן יִסְע֖וּ בְּנֵ֣י יִשְׂרָאֵ֑ל בְּכֹ֖ל מַסְעֵיהֶֽם:
לֹז וְאִם־לֹ֥א יֵעָלֶ֖ה הֶעָנָ֑ן וְלֹ֣א יִסְע֔וּ עַד־י֖וֹם
הֵעָלֹתֽוֹ: לֹח כִּי֩ עֲנַ֨ן יְהֹוָ֤ה עַֽל־הַמִּשְׁכָּן֙ יוֹמָ֔ם
וְאֵ֕שׁ תִּהְיֶ֥ה לַ֖יְלָה בּ֑וֹ לְעֵינֵ֥י כָל־בֵּֽית־יִשְׂרָאֵ֖ל
בְּכָל־מַסְעֵיהֶֽם:
חֲזַק

The Haftarah for this Sidra may be found on page 866.

VAYIKRA* ויקרא
[LEVITICUS]

———————◆◇◆———————

"This entire Third Book consists of instructions telling us how to meet the requirements represented by the Sanctuary of the Law; how to lead hallowed lives as individuals and as a nation, an endeavor to be expressed in symbolic terms by our offerings and in practice by our conduct."

—*Commentary on Chapter 27, Verse 1*

Note: In order to avoid confusion and misunderstanding, the expression טהור and טמא in Leviticus have been rendered into English as follows: With reference to animals or seeds: "Clean" and "unclean," respectively. With reference to persons, places, garments, objects and leprous marks: "Pure" and "unclean," respectively.

[G.H. and E.O.]

ויקרא

VAYIKRA

א א וַיִּקְרָ֖א (א זעירא) אֶל־מֹשֶׁ֑ה וַיְדַבֵּ֤ר יְהֹוָה֙ אֵלָ֔יו
מֵאֹ֥הֶל מוֹעֵ֖ד לֵאמֹֽר׃ ב דַּבֵּ֞ר אֶל־בְּנֵ֤י יִשְׂרָאֵל֙
וְאָמַרְתָּ֣ אֲלֵהֶ֔ם אָדָ֗ם כִּֽי־יַקְרִ֥יב מִכֶּ֛ם קָרְבָּ֖ן

I 1. And He called to Moshe and *God* spoke to him from the Tent of Appointed Meeting [saying]: 2. Articulate this to the sons of Yisrael and explain it to them: If any man from among you would bring near an offering to *God*, you

CHAPTER I

1. **וַיִּקְרָא אֶל מֹשֶׁה וַיְדַבֵּר ה׳ אֵלָיו** ***[Lit., "And-there-called to Moshe and-there-said* God *to him"].*** If the Hebrew text had been וַיִּקְרָא ה׳ אֶל מֹשֶׁה וַיְדַבֵּר אֵלָיו [in the usual Hebrew syntax, with the subject, "God," placed between the two predicates וַיִּקְרָא and וַיְדַבֵּר], the call to Moses would have appeared as an act independent of God's speaking to him It would then have been a simple, straightforward statement meaning that God had called Moses to him in order to speak with him. However, the structure of this sentence [with the subject, "God," not *separating* the two predicates, וַיִּקְרָא and וַיְדַבֵּר, but *following* them] indicates a more profound meaning. God's call is described as an act that was an integral part of His speaking with Moses and in fact defined the manner in which the speaking was done. The word to be communicated to Moses was prefaced by a call to Moses.

This formulation of the text was apparently intended to make it clear that when God spoke with Moses it was indeed the word of God addressed to Moses by God Himself. The intention probably was to forestall those deliberate misrepresentations which so delight in changing the Divine Revelation to Moses into something emanating from within Moses himself, thus equating the Revelation with the delusion of so-called mantic ecstasy arising from within the man himself. Such an interpretation, of course, would reduce "Judaism" or "the Jewish religion" to the level of other religious phenomena in the history of mankind, presenting Judaism as merely another "phase in the development of the human spirit."

But this is not true. We are told in Exodus 33:11 that God spoke with Moses "as a man would speak tc his companion." The word of one man to another, the speech passing from one man to another, emanates solely from the spirit and the will of the speaker and in no wise from the spirit of the one to whom the speech is addressed. Therefore the word of the speaker cannot in any manner be interpreted as a product also of the mind of him who hears the speech. So, too, the word of God to Moses came purely and solely from God. It did not come from within Moses. It came to Moses from without, calling him away, as it were, from his own thought processes so that he might listen attentively to what God wished to say to him. Thus, the fact that the call from God came directly before God's words to Moses refutes the notion that these words were preceded by some process taking place within Moses himself. It characterizes God alone as the speaker and Moses merely as the listener. The word of God to Moses was in no manner a phenomenon initiated or evoked by Moses, not even a development Moses could have surmised in advance; it came to Moses as a historic event from without.

2. **קָרְבָּן** ***[offering].*** It is truly regrettable that we have no word [in Western languages] that would adequately convey the concept inherent in the Hebrew term קָרְבָּן. Unfortunately, the German term *Opfer*[1] which, in fact, as seen from its Latin source, *offero*, simply means "offering," has come to imply that he who makes the "sacrifice" is giving up something and destroying it to his own detriment. But this notion is altogether foreign and indeed totally contrary to the character and the connotation of the Hebrew term קָרְבָּן. Not even the concept inherent in the term "offering" adequately conveys the significance of קָרְבָּן. For the concept of "offering" or "presenting" implies that the one to whom the gift is "presented" has a desire, a wish or a need to be gratified by the gift. The concept implicit in קָרְבָּן has no relevance whatsoever to such notions. Scripture never employs the term קָרְבָּן to denote a "present" or a "gift." Indeed, Scripture uses it exclusively with reference to man's relationship with God, and it can be understood only in the connotation implicit in its root, קרב. For קרב means "to approach,"

[1]*Note to the English translation*: For lack of a better German word, Hirsch in his German translation and commentary found himself compelled to use the term *Opfer*, which has the clear connotation of "sacrifice." The English word "offering" much more closely approximates the concept of קָרְבָּן. [G.H.]

shall bring near your offering from the livestock species, from cattle and from small livestock. 3. If his offering is an ascent offering of the cattle species, then male, without blemish* shall he bring it near, to the entrance of the Tent of Appointed Meet-

לַיהוָ֑ה מִן־הַבְּהֵמָ֗ה מִן־הַבָּקָר֙ וּמִן־הַצֹּ֔אן תַּקְרִ֖יבוּ אֶת־קָרְבַּנְכֶֽם׃ ג אִם־עֹלָ֤ה קָרְבָּנוֹ֙ מִן־הַבָּקָ֔ר זָכָ֥ר תָּמִ֖ים יַקְרִיבֶ֑נּוּ אֶל־פֶּ֜תַח אֹ֤הֶל מוֹעֵד֙

*Note to the English translation: Throughout his German translation of Leviticus, Hirsch renders תָּמִים as *ganz*, lit., "whole," to convey the meaning of "entire," "without blemish." [G.H.]

to "come closer" or "near." Thus, it implies attaining a "close" relationship with another. This in turn makes it clear that the act of הַקְרָבָה [bringing near] implies the attainment of a place in a higher sphere of life.

Thus, too, the concept of קָרְבָּן negates the notion of "sacrifice" as an act of destruction or renunciation. Moreover, it indicates that the קָרְבָּן is intended not to satisfy the desire of the one to whom it is "brought near," but to fulfill a need of the מַקְרִיב, the one who makes the קָרְבָּן. It is the desire of the מַקְרִיב that something of his should enter into a closer, intimate relationship with God. This is his קָרְבָּן, and the act by which the מַקְרִיב is to attain this closer relationship with God is termed הַקְרָבָה [bringing near]. The purpose of the קָרְבָּן is to seek קִרְבַת אֱלֹקִים, the nearness of God. Cf. קִרְבַת אֱלֹקִים יֶחְפָּצוּן ["They delight in the nearness of God"] (Isaiah 58:2). It is this nearness of God which the Jew regards as the highest, indeed the only attainable, good. Cf. קִרְבַת אֱלֹקִים לִי טוֹב — ["God's nearness is my good"] (Psalm 73:28). Without God's nearness, he feels "beast-like" (ibid., Verse 22), stripped of all those qualities which elevate him to the destiny of a human being and whose values he regards as the sole standard against which to measure his own outlook on life and his own concept of human happiness—concepts that become clear to him when he enters the halls of God's Sanctuary. Cf. "Until I entered the Sanctuaries of God and learned to look for their end"] (ibid., Verse 17). . . .

קָרְבָּן לה׳ *[an offering to God]*. R. Yosi notes in *Torath Kohanim*[2] ibid.: "Wherever there is [in Scripture] a discussion of the offerings, the Tetragrammaton is employed with reference to God in order to give the scorners of the Law no opportunity to degrade the truth of Judaism to the level of pagan delusion."

When Scripture discusses the offerings, God does not characterize Himself as אֱלֹקִים, for there He does not wish to be conceived in terms of the retributive, inexorable quality of His justice, as a deity that takes pleasure in sacrifices, one that, according to blasphemous pagan delusion, is a God of vengeance, accepting an animal's death struggle as a substitute for a forfeited human life. In the context of the offerings, He would rather be viewed as ה׳, the loving God, Who, in the full power of His almighty love, is ready at all times to grant new life and a new future. Not killing but revival, rebirth, moral and spiritual resurrection, an entry and eternal re-entry into an ever loftier, purer life, a regaining of strength to live such a life, a strength to be drawn from the never-failing source of love eternal—that is the concept on which the offerings in Judaism are based. That which dies upon the altar is only that which is moribund also in human life. That which is consumed upon the altar is only that which is transitory as long as it is far from God but which, once it is brought near to God, meets with His approval and so comes into its rightful portion of eternal life. The designation ה׳, which is used in Scripture only in connection with offerings that are made to God by Jews, demolishes all the drivel of the scorners of the Law who would equate the majesty of the Jewish laws pertaining to offerings with a "bloody sacrificial cult," with the intention of dragging down what they call "Mosaic" Judaism from the eternal lofty spheres of its Divine truth to the baseness of a long-outworn heathen notion.

° ° °

3. **עוֹלָה** ***[an ascent offering].*** The usual translation of עוֹלָה as a "burnt offering"; i.e., meaning that the offering "goes up completely in flames" has only a tenuous basis in the root of the term, which is עלה [to ascend]. . . . If we examine the designations for the other offerings: חַטָּאת [offering that clears (him who brings it) of sin], אָשָׁם [guilt offering], שְׁלָמִים [peace offering], תּוֹדָה [offering of thanksgiving] and מִנְחָה [homage or meal offering], we see that each denotes the occasion or purpose of the offering without indicating the procedure it entails.

And so we believe that עוֹלָה, too, should be understood [not in terms of its ritual] but as a statement of its purpose; i.e., it is an offering that originates in the desire and striving לַעֲלוֹת [to ascend]. . . . עוֹלָה arises from the individual's awareness that he is in need of making greater strides toward goodness and godliness and that he is capable of doing so. . . . In any event, the עוֹלָה is offered in the awareness that one has failed to

[2]*Note to the English translation*: *Torath Kohanim*, or *Sifra*, is a Halakhic Midrash on the Book of Leviticus, a Midrashic commentary interpreting the Book of Leviticus, chapter by chapter and verse by verse. [G.H.]

ing shall he bring it near, to express his striving before *God*. 4. He shall lean his hand upon the head of the ascent offering; thus it will be accepted as being in accordance with the Divine will, to effect atonement for him. 5. He shall then slaughter the animal of the cattle species before *God*, and Aharon's sons, the priests, shall bring the blood nearer and dash the blood round about upon the altar which is at the entrance to the Tent of Appointed Meeting. 6. He shall skin the ascent offering and cut it up into its parts. 7. And the sons of Aharon the priest shall put fire upon the altar and arrange [logs of] wood upon the fire. 8. Sons of Aharon, the priests, shall arrange the parts, the head and the loose fat upon the [logs of] wood that are upon the fire that is upon the altar. 9. He shall wash its entrails and its legs in water, and the priest shall give all [of it] to the altar to go up in smoke as an ascent offering, an offering made by fire as

יַקְרִיב אֹתוֹ לִרְצֹנוֹ לִפְנֵי יְהוָֹה׃ ד וְסָמַךְ יָדוֹ עַל
רֹאשׁ הָעֹלָה וְנִרְצָה לוֹ לְכַפֵּר עָלָיו׃ ה וְשָׁחַט
אֶת־בֶּן הַבָּקָר לִפְנֵי יְהוָֹה וְהִקְרִיבוּ בְּנֵי אַהֲרֹן
הַכֹּהֲנִים אֶת־הַדָּם וְזָרְקוּ אֶת־הַדָּם עַל־הַמִּזְבֵּחַ
סָבִיב אֲשֶׁר־פֶּתַח אֹהֶל מוֹעֵד׃ ו וְהִפְשִׁיט אֶת־
הָעֹלָה וְנִתַּח אֹתָהּ לִנְתָחֶיהָ׃ ז וְנָתְנוּ בְּנֵי אַהֲרֹן
הַכֹּהֵן אֵשׁ עַל־הַמִּזְבֵּחַ וְעָרְכוּ עֵצִים עַל־הָאֵשׁ׃
ח וְעָרְכוּ בְּנֵי אַהֲרֹן הַכֹּהֲנִים אֵת הַנְּתָחִים אֶת־
הָרֹאשׁ וְאֶת־הַפָּדֶר עַל־הָעֵצִים אֲשֶׁר עַל־הָאֵשׁ
אֲשֶׁר עַל־הַמִּזְבֵּחַ׃ ט וְקִרְבּוֹ וּכְרָעָיו יִרְחַץ
בַּמַּיִם וְהִקְטִיר הַכֹּהֵן אֶת־הַכֹּל הַמִּזְבֵּחָה עֹלָה

perform certain duties and that he should guard against such neglect in the future. Each duty performed is a positive step forward, an elevation of one's own moral level toward the ideal of perfection, another step toward that moral elevation which brings one closer to God. . . .

° ° °

without blemish . . . shall he bring it. Malakhi (Chapter 1, Verses 8 ff.) lashes out at those who would offer up the blind, the lame and the sick to God. He declares that this is a degradation of the Name and the altar of God. He charges the priests with having promoted these acts of degradation by their teachings. "And you profane it" (Verse 12) "by saying that the table of God is polluted, and that its fruit, and its food, is contemptible" (Verse 7). You desecrate the altar; in your speeches you represent the table of God as something generally disdained and God's harvest as something of which no one would wish to partake.

Clearly, the prophet's criticism of the priests in this passage is that, instead of representing God and His Sanctuary as the greatest good, entitled to the best, the most vigorous, the most vital and the strongest that is within man to offer, they reduce the Sanctuary to the level of a hospital or a home for incurables built for the wrecks of humanity, where only those come for whom there is no other place in the world and who must therefore be satisfied with the crumbs from the table of humanity. "Try to present this to your pasha," the prophet angrily cries out, "and see whether he will give you a gracious reception!" [Verse 8].

This is the same charge that Hosea (10:5) hurls at the priestlings of the kingdom of Israel: If the people grieve over themselves, the priestlings will rejoice. The priestlings and their minions exploit the grief and the misfortunes of their "believers." It is not the vigorous and the joyful who flock to their halls. Only the blind and the lame, the sick and the weak make their way to these altars. They see religion not as the ruler over a vigorous, throbbing life of action, filled with the joy of living, but only as the comforter of the suffering and the underprivileged. But the God Whom Israel is to bear aloft through history as the God of all mankind is not so; neither is His Temple. The Sanctuary of His Law demands the total, unreserved and uncurtailed dedication of human life. In return for this dedication, it promises its adherents a life of vitality in which even death and grief lose their sting. Therefore, just as the priests who serve at the altar of Israel's Law must be free of all wounds and physical blemishes, so too—and indeed even more so—must the animals by whose offering man celebrates his entry into, and his progress toward the covenant of God's nearness upon the altar of His Law, be free of injury and blemish, full of vigor and without a flaw.

° ° °

9\. ***. . . an ascent offering, an offering made by fire as an expression of compliance, to*** **God.** This is an

an expression of compliance, to *God*.
10. And even if his offering is from the
small livestock, from the sheep or from the
goats, as an ascent offering, male, without
blemish, shall he bring it near.　　11. He
shall slaughter it at the back of the altar,
northward, before *God*, and the sons of
Aharon, the priests, shall dash its blood
round about the altar.　　12. He shall cut it
up into its parts, with its head and its loose
fat and the priest shall arrange them for the
[logs of] wood that are upon the fire that is
upon the altar.　　13. And he shall wash
the entrails and the feet in water, and the
priest shall bring all [of it] near and give it
to the altar to go up in smoke; it is an
ascent offering, an offering made by fire as
an expression of compliance, to *God*.
14. And if his offering to *God* is an
ascent offering of birds, he shall bring near
his offering from the turtle-doves or from
the young of the pigeon.　　15. And the
priest shall bring it nearer to the altar,
pinch off its head and give it to the altar to
go up in smoke, while its blood shall be
pressed out upon the wall of the altar.
16. He shall remove its crop with its
feathers and throw it beside the altar, eastward, to the place of the ashes.　　17. He
shall split it apart by its wings, but without
dividing it completely in half, and the
priest shall give it to the altar to go up in
smoke, upon the [logs of] wood that are
upon the fire; it is an ascent offering, an
offering made by fire as an expression of
compliance, to *God*.

אִשֵּׁה רֵיחַ־נִיחֹ֖וחַ לַיהֹוָֽה: ס י וְאִם־מִן־הַצֹּ֨אן
קָרְבָּנ֜וֹ מִן־הַכְּשָׂבִ֛ים א֥וֹ מִן־הָעִזִּ֖ים לְעֹלָ֑ה זָכָ֥ר
תָּמִ֖ים יַקְרִיבֶֽנּוּ: יא וְשָׁחַ֨ט אֹת֜וֹ עַ֣ל יֶ֤רֶךְ הַמִּזְבֵּ֙חַ֙
צָפֹ֔נָה לִפְנֵ֖י יְהֹוָ֑ה וְזָרְק֡וּ בְּנֵי֩ אַהֲרֹ֨ן הַכֹּֽהֲנִ֧ים
אֶת־דָּמ֛וֹ עַל־הַמִּזְבֵּ֖חַ סָבִֽיב: יב וְנִתַּ֤ח אֹתוֹ֙
לִנְתָחָ֔יו וְאֶת־רֹאשׁ֖וֹ וְאֶת־פִּדְר֑וֹ וְעָרַ֤ךְ הַכֹּהֵן֙
אֹתָ֔ם עַל־הָֽעֵצִים֙ אֲשֶׁ֣ר עַל־הָאֵ֔שׁ אֲשֶׁ֖ר עַל־
הַמִּזְבֵּֽחַ: יג וְהַקֶּ֥רֶב וְהַכְּרָעַ֖יִם יִרְחַ֣ץ בַּמָּ֑יִם
וְהִקְרִ֨יב הַכֹּהֵ֤ן אֶת־הַכֹּל֙ וְהִקְטִ֣יר הַמִּזְבֵּ֔חָה עֹלָ֣ה
ה֗וּא אִשֵּׁ֛ה רֵ֥יחַ נִיחֹ֖חַ לַיהֹוָֽה: פ שני יד וְאִ֣ם מִן־
הָע֗וֹף עֹלָ֛ה קָרְבָּנ֖וֹ לַֽיהֹוָ֑ה וְהִקְרִ֣יב מִן־הַתֹּרִ֗ים
א֥וֹ מִן־בְּנֵ֛י הַיּוֹנָ֖ה אֶת־קָרְבָּנֽוֹ: טו וְהִקְרִיב֤וֹ
הַכֹּהֵן֙ אֶל־הַמִּזְבֵּ֔חַ וּמָלַק֙ אֶת־רֹאשׁ֔וֹ וְהִקְטִ֖יר
הַמִּזְבֵּ֑חָה וְנִמְצָ֣ה דָמ֔וֹ עַ֖ל קִ֥יר הַמִּזְבֵּֽחַ:
טז וְהֵסִ֤יר אֶת־מֻרְאָתוֹ֙ בְּנֹֽצָתָ֔הּ וְהִשְׁלִ֣יךְ אֹתָ֗הּ
אֵ֤צֶל הַמִּזְבֵּ֙חַ֙ קֵ֔דְמָה אֶל־מְק֖וֹם הַדָּֽשֶׁן: יז וְשִׁסַּ֨ע
אֹת֣וֹ בִכְנָפָיו֮ לֹ֣א יַבְדִּיל֒ וְהִקְטִ֨יר אֹת֤וֹ הַכֹּהֵן֙
הַמִּזְבֵּ֔חָה עַל־הָעֵצִ֖ים אֲשֶׁ֣ר עַל־הָאֵ֑שׁ עֹלָ֣ה ה֗וּא

---

apposition to הַכֹּל ["all (of it)"]. He must place all of it
upon the altar to go up in smoke as an עֹלָה, etc. . . . .

　　　　° ° °

10–13. . . . Offerings brought from צֹאן [the small
livestock] symbolize the personality of the individual in
terms of his fate, which is dependent upon the guidance
of God. They symbolically represent the individual as a
member of the flock of God. Offerings from the בָּקָר
[cattle] species, on the other hand, symbolize the
individual's personality in terms of the practical tasks
assigned to him, in his function as a worker in the
cultivation of God's own field. Thus, each of these two
categories of offerings symbolizes one of the two phases

which, together, comprise the sum total of human life.
　　Accordingly, it is readily understandable why עֹולַת
בָּקָר [the ascent offering from the cattle species] and עֹולַת
צֹאן [the ascent offering from the small livestock],
though both subject to the same laws in every respect,
must be discussed in two separate sections of Scripture.
But we also see that the two complement one another;
this fact is implicit in the copulative *vav* at the opening
of the section dealing with the צֹאן.

עַל־הָעֵצִים [*for the (logs of) wood*]. For the purpose of
placing the parts upon the logs of wood; this would
imply the principle according to which the parts should
be arrayed. . . .

אִשֵּׁה רֵיחַ נִיחֹחַ לַיהוָה׃ ס ב א וְנֶפֶשׁ כִּי־
תַקְרִיב קָרְבַּן מִנְחָה לַיהוָה סֹלֶת יִהְיֶה קָרְבָּנוֹ
וְיָצַק עָלֶיהָ שֶׁמֶן וְנָתַן עָלֶיהָ לְבֹנָה׃ ב וֶהֱבִיאָהּ
אֶל־בְּנֵי אַהֲרֹן הַכֹּהֲנִים וְקָמַץ מִשָּׁם מְלֹא קֻמְצוֹ
מִסָּלְתָּהּ וּמִשַּׁמְנָהּ עַל כָּל־לְבֹנָתָהּ וְהִקְטִיר
הַכֹּהֵן אֶת־אַזְכָּרָתָהּ הַמִּזְבֵּחָה אִשֵּׁה רֵיחַ נִיחֹחַ
לַיהוָה׃ ג וְהַנּוֹתֶרֶת מִן־הַמִּנְחָה לְאַהֲרֹן וּלְבָנָיו
קֹדֶשׁ קָדָשִׁים מֵאִשֵּׁי יְהוָה׃ ס ד וְכִי תַקְרִב
קָרְבַּן מִנְחָה מַאֲפֵה תַנּוּר סֹלֶת חַלּוֹת מַצֹּת
בְּלוּלֹת בַּשֶּׁמֶן וּרְקִיקֵי מַצּוֹת מְשֻׁחִים בַּשָּׁמֶן׃ ס
ה וְאִם־מִנְחָה עַל־הַמַּחֲבַת קָרְבָּנֶךָ סֹלֶת בְּלוּלָה
בַשֶּׁמֶן מַצָּה תִהְיֶה׃ ו פָּתוֹת אֹתָהּ פִּתִּים וְיָצַקְתָּ
עָלֶיהָ שָׁמֶן מִנְחָה הִוא׃ ס שלישי ז וְאִם־מִנְחַת
מַרְחֶשֶׁת קָרְבָּנֶךָ סֹלֶת בַּשֶּׁמֶן תֵּעָשֶׂה׃ ח וְהֵבֵאתָ
אֶת־הַמִּנְחָה אֲשֶׁר יֵעָשֶׂה מֵאֵלֶּה לַיהוָה

II 1. A person who would bring near a homage offering to *God*, his offering shall be of fine wheat flour; he shall pour oil upon it and place frankincense upon it. 2. And he shall bring it to the sons of Aharon, the priests, of whom one shall take out his handful of its flour and of its oil, along with all its incense; and the priest shall give its memorial portion to the altar to go up in smoke, as an offering made by fire, an expression of compliance, to *God*. 3. The rest of the homage offering shall fall to Aharon and his sons, a holy of holies from the fire offerings to *God*. 4. And if you would bring near a homage offering that is baked in an oven, then let it be fine wheat flour mixed with oil in the form of *matzah* loaves or of thin *matzah* wafers brushed with oil. 5. And if your offering is a homage offering [fried] upon a pan, then let it be fine wheat flour mixed with oil, *matzah*. 6. You shall break it* into pieces and you shall pour oil upon it; it is a homage offering. 7. And if your offering is a homage offering prepared in a deep pot, let it be prepared from fine wheat flour in oil. 8. You shall bring to *God* the homage offering that is prepared from these

Note to the English translation: Hirsch, literally, "One shall break it . . . and you shall pour . . ." [G.H.]

CHAPTER II

8\. . . . Although the act of הַגָּשָׁה [bringing up] is not essential to the validity of the offering, it is one of the acts that can be performed only by a כֹּהֵן [priest] in his official capacity as a כֹּהֵן. Hence it must be an element of basic significance in the concept of the *minḥah* [homage] offering.

We read in I Kings 5:1: "And Solomon ruled over all the kingdoms from the River to the land of the Philistines . . . . they brought near offerings of homage and served Solomon all the days of his life." Thus הַגָּשָׁה is that act through which the offering becomes an act of homage; it is a presentation, an act of placing an offering at the disposal of the one for whom it is intended. And so the הַגָּשָׁה in the homage offering should have the same connotation. . . . The priest . . . symbolically acknowledges the fact that it is to God alone that we owe all the material comforts of life: nourishment, prosperity and the physical satisfaction to be gained from both of these, and that we must therefore subordinate all these resources to the spirit emanating from His Law. This indicates the frame of mind in which we are expected to carry out the acts of taking out the handful of flour, etc., placing it into a vessel, placing the offering upon the altar to let it go up in smoke and finally having the priests consume the offering.

If, by these acts, we symbolically allow the Sanctuary of God's Law to take out a handful of our material wealth, to be used for His purposes; if we thereby consecrate a portion of our material resources and all of our joy of living to the cultivation of Godliness on earth, thus indicating our resolve to place into the fire of God's altar also the resources related to our physical existence and comforts; if we are prepared to derive our own joy of life solely from the awareness that we are pleasing to God; indeed, if God's rejoicing in us will be our own sole source of joy; if the fact that the priests partake of the gift then teaches us that such a surrender of our material resources to God does not imply a renunciation of all our worldly goods and pleasures but only that these benefits are meant to be enjoyed in a manner befitting priests, in the spirit of the Law of God, turning the very act of [ingredients]; one brings them near to the priest, who [in turn] shall bring it up to the altar. 9. The priest shall lift out its memorial portion from the homage offering and give it to the altar to go up in smoke as an offering made by fire as an expression of compliance, to *God*. 10. The rest of the homage offering shall fall to Aharon and his sons, a holy of holies from the fire offerings, of *God*. 11. Any homage offering that you bring near to *God* must not be prepared fermented, for you must not allow anything leavened or any fruit honey at all to go up in smoke as a fire offering to *God*. 12. You shall bring these near to *God* as an offering of first fruits, but they

וְהִקְרִיבָהּ אֶל־הַכֹּהֵן וְהִגִּישָׁהּ אֶל־הַמִּזְבֵּחַ:
ט וְהֵרִים הַכֹּהֵן מִן־הַמִּנְחָה אֶת־אַזְכָּרָתָהּ
וְהִקְטִיר הַמִּזְבֵּחָה אִשֵּׁה רֵיחַ נִיחֹחַ לַיהוָֹה:
י וְהַנּוֹתֶרֶת מִן־הַמִּנְחָה לְאַהֲרֹן וּלְבָנָיו קֹדֶשׁ
קָדָשִׁים מֵאִשֵּׁי יְהוָֹה: יא כָּל־הַמִּנְחָה אֲשֶׁר
תַּקְרִיבוּ לַיהוָֹה לֹא תֵעָשֶׂה חָמֵץ כִּי כָל־שְׂאֹר
וְכָל־דְּבַשׁ לֹא־תַקְטִירוּ מִמֶּנּוּ אִשֶּׁה לַיהוָֹה:
יב קָרְבַּן רֵאשִׁית תַּקְרִיבוּ אֹתָם לַיהוָֹה וְאֶל־

enjoyment into a *mitzvah*, a free-willed act of moral service to God—then the act of הַגָּשָׁה will indeed have taught us to conceive of this dedication of our physical existence to God's approval not as an act to be performed at our discretion, above and beyond the call of duty, but as nothing more than the discharge of an obligation we owe to God with every fiber of our being. . . . Even our greatest act of self-dedication to God is nothing more than the fulfillment of our most elementary duty toward Him. . . . From the foregoing, we can also understand why the act of הַגָּשָׁה is performed only with those *menaḥoth* of which part is offered upon the altar.

We further note that while in all the laws that precede and follow, the text uses the impersonal third person singular to address the individual who makes the offering, it changes to the second person singular in the case of the *minḥah* offering, Verses 6–8, and perhaps already in Verse 5. The reason for this peculiarity might be as follows: In the case of all the other offerings, it is only the person himself (דָּם = נֶפֶשׁ) [the blood representing the soul of life] who seeks to attain nearness to God by means of his קָרְבָּן. In other words, the person is still considered far away from God; that is why he is addressed in impersonal terms. In the case of *minḥah*, by contrast, the person who makes the offering already feels that his personality has come near to God; hence he feels that he must now bring near to God also the material aspects of his physical life. Thus, the person now stands before God and symbolically places at His feet the good things that symbolize his material resources. Hence the form of address is now in the [more intimate] second person singular. . . .

11 and 12. . . . שְׂאוֹר *[leavened].* As we have already set forth in our notes to Exodus 12:8, the symbolic significance of חָמֵץ [leavened bread] and מַצָּה [unleavened bread] is a historical one. מַצָּה symbolizes a state of political dependence, a situation in which we have lost the power to command freely over our time. This is tantamount to a loss of command over our physical energies. It is a sign of servitude. By contrast, שְׂאוֹר [leaven] and חָמֵץ symbolize independence and the power to be master over ourselves.

Israel's original bread was מַצָּה. Had Israel been left to its own devices, the "bread of servitude" would never have left its hands. Each year when we celebrate the festival commemorating our deliverance from Egypt, the מַצָּה displaces the שְׂאוֹר and the חָמֵץ from our homes; reminding us anew each year that we did not obtain freedom and independence through our own power but can have it only as a perpetual gift of God's favor. So, too, the symbolic reminders of this fact are never absent from His Sanctuary, opposite the altar of His Law. The bread we place upon the altar of God as a symbol of our homage must always be *matzah*. We received the bread of freedom from His hands only under the condition that we leave the service of Pharaoh in order to enter into the service of God forever. The *matzah* in our hands symbolizes the foundation upon which rests our relationship to God and to His Law. It is true that freedom from all other servitude, complete political independence in the midst of mankind, is the reward that has been promised us for עֲבוֹדַת ד׳, for our complete submission to the will of the One God. On שָׁבוּעוֹת, the festival which commemorates the giving of His Law and which is also יוֹם הַבִּכּוּרִים, the festival on which we begin to place our first fruits before God, acknowledging that "I have come to the land that *God* swore to our fathers to give to us" (Deuteronomy 26:3), that God has kept His word regarding the Promised Land, Israel comes before God with two loaves of leavened bread. This is the bread of freedom and independence, symbolically acknowledging that Israel enjoys freedom and independence only in return for submitting to the Law of God.

must not come upon the altar as an expression of compliance. 13. And any homage offering that you bring near you shall season with salt, and do not allow salt, the covenant of your God, to be lacking from your homage offering; with anything that you offer, you shall offer salt. 14. If you bring near to *God* a homage offering of first fruits, it shall be brought as soon as it ripens on the stalk; roasted in fire, the kernels still freshly shucked from the ears; thus shall you bring near the homage offering of your first fruits. 15. You shall put oil upon it and place frankincense upon it; it is a homage offering. 16. The priest shall give its memorial portion from the meal made of its kernel, and its oil, along with all its frankincense, to go up in smoke as a fire offering, to *God*.

III 1. And if a meal of peace is his offering, if he brings it near from the cattle, whether male or female, he

הַמִּזְבֵּחַ לֹא־יַעֲלוּ לְרֵיחַ נִיחֹחַ: יג וְכָל־קָרְבַּן
מִנְחָתְךָ בַּמֶּלַח תִּמְלָח וְלֹא תַשְׁבִּית מֶלַח בְּרִית
אֱלֹהֶיךָ מֵעַל מִנְחָתֶךָ עַל כָּל־קָרְבָּנְךָ תַּקְרִיב
מֶלַח: ס יד וְאִם־תַּקְרִיב מִנְחַת בִּכּוּרִים לַיהוָה
אָבִיב קָלוּי בָּאֵשׁ גֶּרֶשׂ כַּרְמֶל תַּקְרִיב אֵת מִנְחַת
בִּכּוּרֶיךָ: טו וְנָתַתָּ עָלֶיהָ שֶׁמֶן וְשַׂמְתָּ עָלֶיהָ
לְבֹנָה מִנְחָה הִוא: טז וְהִקְטִיר הַכֹּהֵן אֶת־
אַזְכָּרָתָהּ מִגִּרְשָׂהּ וּמִשַּׁמְנָהּ עַל כָּל־לְבֹנָתָהּ
אִשֶּׁה לַיהוָה: פ רביעי ג א וְאִם־זֶבַח שְׁלָמִים
קָרְבָּנוֹ אִם מִן־הַבָּקָר הוּא מַקְרִיב אִם־זָכָר

However, this is done only once a year. Only on the day that commemorates the giving of the Law must Israel, as a consequence of its observance of the Law, bring before God the bread of its political independence; a fruit, as it were, ripened upon the tree of the Law. But these loaves must not come upon the altar as an expression of the desire to be pleasing to God. They must not be brought to the altar as אִשֶּׁה [a fire offering] to nourish the fire of God as a symbolic expression of our desire to be pleasing to Him. That which we are to place upon the altar as a fire offering, as an expression of the desire to be pleasing to God, is merely that which was already ours heretofore, without giving up anything in return, possessions with which we part only now in order to devote them to God for the furtherance of His will on earth.

שְׂאוֹר, חָמֵץ ["leaven," "leavened bread"]: Political independence, by contrast, is a gift concerning which we must always remember we do not possess even a trace of it by virtue of our own power. It is ours only as long as we submit completely to the Law of God. It is a gift we can obtain by conducting ourselves in the manner symbolized by the fire offering that expresses our desire to be pleasing to God, but it cannot itself be offered up to God as אִשֶּׁה רֵיחַ נִיחוֹחַ because it is not a possession that could be ours without the nearness of God.

דְּבַשׁ ***[fruit honey].*** The foregoing should also make clear to us why דְּבַשׁ cannot be used as a fire offering. דְּבַשׁ, מְתִיקַת פְּרִי [lit., "the sweetness in fruit"] is a product of the soil that specifically symbolizes the value of landed property for man. It is that ingredient which nature has expressly prepared for a man's immediate enjoyment. As a by-product of the fruits of trees, it is eminently suited to symbolize land ownership. But the ownership of its land, like freedom and political independence, is an asset which Israel does not owe to its own strength and to which it is not entitled by virtue of its own power. Israel can win and retain possession of its land, or its political independence, only by obeying the Law of God. That is why the festival of the Giving of the Law marks the beginning of the season at which the first fruits of the soil, primarily the first fruits of the trees, are to be brought up to God, into the Sanctuary of His Law, and handed over to the priest to be placed upon the altar with the declaration: "I have given evidence this day to *God,* your God, that I have come to the land that *God* swore to our fathers to give to them" (Deuteronomy 26:3). But again, "they must not be placed upon the altar as an expression of the desire to be pleasing to God." The land we possess is not inherently our own so that we would be in a position to part with it in order to demonstrate our devotion to God's Law. It, too, is a treasure we can win only by our devotion to that Law.

° ° °

CHAPTER III

1. שְׁלָמִים ***[a meal of peace].*** שָׁלֵם implies a state of completeness, of perfection. When used with reference to a human being it denotes a state in which the person does not feel a gap in any aspect of his life; he feels that

shall bring it near without blemish before *God.* 2. He shall lean his hand upon the head of his offering, and he shall slaughter it at the entrance to the Tent of Appointed

אִם־נְקֵבָה תָמִים יַקְרִיבֶנּוּ לִפְנֵי יְהֹוָה: ב וְסָמַךְ יָדוֹ עַל־רֹאשׁ קָרְבָּנוֹ וּשְׁחָטוֹ פֶּתַח אֹהֶל מוֹעֵד

he lacks for nothing. Cf. וַיָּבֹא יַעֲקֹב שָׁלֵם ["Yaakov came safe by..."] (Genesis 33:18). Thus, שָׁלֵם is a relative concept; primarily, it describes an object in relation to all its parts, and a person in relation to the circumstances and surroundings in which he lives. However, the term is used in Scripture also, though only on rare occasions, to define the state of these circumstances and surroundings in relation to an individual who becomes שָׁלֵם through them. Cf. הָאֲנָשִׁים הָאֵלֶּה שְׁלֵמִים הֵם אִתָּנוּ ["These people are peaceable with us"] (Genesis 34:21); i.e., the relationship of these people toward us is such that they will not cause us to suffer any "gap" or loss.

שָׁלוֹם is that state of affairs in which no component of a person or thing detracts from any of the others but in which, rather, each component is complemented in and through all the others.... שָׁלוֹם is not mere superficial coexistence but an organic agreement and interaction among all the parts of the whole. Thus, שְׁלָמִים are offerings that emanate from the feeling that one is שָׁלֵם [in a state of peace].... קָרְבַּן שְׁלָמִים [the meal-of-peace offering] symbolizes a quest for the nearness of God based on the fact that the person who makes the offering feels completely at peace, that he does not feel he lacks for anything. The only thing he still needs to crown his good is the nearness of God, and this he now symbolically seeks to attain through his offering. שְׁלָמִים epitomize the Jewish philosophy of life. Not grief but joy is to form the eternal bridge to God; the highest form of Divine service is to enjoy one's existence on earth before the countenance of God. To seek God even if, and precisely because, one does not seek any particular favors from Him, not even to give thanks to Him for some extraordinary good fortune—this is the concept on which the שְׁלָמִים offerings are based.

The fact that שְׁלָמִים are intended to reflect a state of mind in which the person who offers them feels neither hurt nor bereft naturally results in the law that "one who is in a state of *aninut* must not make offerings"; i.e., one is not permitted to make an offering in the Temple on the day when he has lost a close relative (spouse, parent, brother or sister) by death, when he is an אוֹנֵן, in a state of deep mourning. This law was set forth primarily in connection with שְׁלָמִים: "He shall offer שְׁלָמִים when he feels at peace with himself, not when he is in deep mourning," but it is applicable also to all other offerings—even the Passover offering if he happens to be an אוֹנֵן at the midnight hour of the day on

which the offering must be made (Zebaḥim 99b and 100a). The sense of שָׁלוֹם [peace] from which the שְׁלָמִים emanate and which the שְׁלָמִים are intended to express must not be lacking from any offering made to God! We are told: שְׁלָמִים קָרְבָּנוֹ—"His offering should be *shelamim*"; i.e., all the offerings he brings, he shall bring when he is "whole" (*shalem*) [Zebaḥim 99b]. One must not cross the threshold of God's Sanctuary while one's heart is torn with grief; only a spirit completely at peace and reconciled with its lot can find its way to God's nearness.

Other religions view it as their greatest triumph if they can help their adherents overcome grief and sorrow, if they can give them comfort in the sorrows of life. But in Judaism sorrow must be overcome *before* one enters the Sanctuary; this is, in fact, a precondition for the impact of God's Sanctuary upon the Jew. The purpose of the Sanctuary is not to offer us comfort in sorrow but to give us the strength and determination to serve God with gladness through practical action. Calm courage to face whatever life may bring: this is the atmosphere that fills the halls of the Sanctuary. The Sanctuary of God is the Sanctuary of His Law.

if ... from the cattle. One who feels שָׁלֵם may see himself [symbolically] as בָּקָר, [cattle], with his mission in life to labor in the service of God, or as צֹאן [a "smaller animal" or a part of a "flock"], who accepts his fate as part of God's guidance. If the latter, he may see himself as כֶּבֶשׂ [a sheep], trusting God implicitly as the Shepherd of his life, and/or as עֵז [a goat], aware that he has the strength to resist any influence that may seek to lure him away from God's guidance. Depending on the image that corresponds most closely to his self-image, he is then to choose his offering from among the בָּקָר or (cf. Verses 6 and 12) the צֹאן. The offering may be either male or female, depending on whether the person sees his position in life as one of independence or one of dependence. For a person can feel שָׁלֵם even if he is in a dependent position. Jewish Law recognizes the position of an עֶבֶד [lit., "servant," a Hebrew slave] who would not want to exchange his condition of servitude for one of freedom and independence because "he fares well with you" (Deuteronomy 15:16). But no matter what his position, his offering must be "without blemish." It is as a "whole" person, with his entire being, that he must come before the one sole Guide of his action and Leader of his destinies.

Meeting, and Aharon's sons, the priests, shall dash the blood round about upon the altar.   3. And he shall bring near from the meal of peace a fire offering to *God*; the fat that covers the entrails and all the fat that is attached to the entrails;   4. also the two kidneys and the fat that is attached to them, that is along the flanks; also the diaphragm upon the liver; he must remove it together with the kidneys.   5. And sons of Aharon shall give it to the altar to go up in smoke, upon the ascent offering that is upon the [logs of] wood which are upon the fire; [it is] an offering made by fire as an expression of compliance, to *God*. 6. If his meal-of-peace offering to *God* is from the small livestock, he shall bring it near, male or female, without blemish. 7. If it is a sheep that he brings near as his offering, then he [himself] must bring it near before *God*.   8. And he shall lean his hand upon the head of the offering, and he shall slaughter it in front of the Tent of Appointed Meeting, and sons of Aharon shall dash its blood round about upon the altar.   9. He shall then bring, of the meal of peace, as a fire offering before *God*, its fat; he shall remove the entire tailpiece up to the backbone, and the fat that covers the entrails and all the fat that is attached to the entrails.   10. Also the two kidneys and the fat that is attached to them, that is along the flanks; also the diaphragm upon the liver; he must remove it together with the kidneys.   11. And the priest shall place it upon the altar to go up in smoke, an offering to be made to *God* by placing it into the fire.   12. And if a goat is his offering, he shall bring it near before *God*.   13. And he shall lean his hand upon its head, and he shall slaughter it in front of the Tent of

וְזָרְק֡וּ בְּנֵי֩ אַהֲרֹ֨ן הַכֹּהֲנִ֧ים אֶת־הַדָּ֛ם עַל־הַמִּזְבֵּ֖חַ
סָבִ֑יב: ג וְהִקְרִיב֙ מִזֶּ֣בַח הַשְּׁלָמִ֔ים אִשֶּׁ֖ה לַֽיהֹוָ֑ה
אֶת־הַחֵ֙לֶב֙ הַֽמְכַסֶּ֣ה אֶת־הַקֶּ֔רֶב וְאֵת֙ כָּל־הַחֵ֔לֶב
אֲשֶׁ֖ר עַל־הַקֶּֽרֶב: ד וְאֵת֙ שְׁתֵּ֣י הַכְּלָיֹ֔ת וְאֶת־
הַחֵ֙לֶב֙ אֲשֶׁ֣ר עֲלֵהֶ֔ן אֲשֶׁ֖ר עַל־הַכְּסָלִ֑ים וְאֶת־
הַיֹּתֶ֙רֶת֙ עַל־הַכָּבֵ֔ד עַל־הַכְּלָיֹ֖ות יְסִירֶֽנָּה:
ה וְהִקְטִ֣ירוּ אֹתֹ֩ו בְנֵֽי־אַהֲרֹ֨ן הַמִּזְבֵּ֜חָה עַל־
הָעֹלָ֗ה אֲשֶׁ֤ר עַל־הָֽעֵצִים֙ אֲשֶׁ֣ר עַל־הָאֵ֔שׁ אִשֵּׁ֛ה
רֵ֥יחַ נִיחֹ֖חַ לַֽיהֹוָֽה: פ ו וְאִם־מִן־הַצֹּאן֙ קָרְבָּנֹ֜ו
לְזֶ֧בַח שְׁלָמִ֛ים לַיהֹוָ֑ה זָכָר֙ אֹ֣ו נְקֵבָ֔ה תָּמִ֖ים
יַקְרִיבֶֽנּוּ: ז אִם־כֶּ֥שֶׂב הֽוּא־מַקְרִ֖יב אֶת־קָרְבָּנֹ֑ו
וְהִקְרִ֥יב אֹתֹ֖ו לִפְנֵ֥י יְהֹוָֽה: ח וְסָמַ֤ךְ אֶת־יָדֹו֙ עַל־
רֹ֣אשׁ קָרְבָּנֹ֔ו וְשָׁחַ֣ט אֹתֹ֔ו לִפְנֵ֖י אֹ֣הֶל מֹועֵ֑ד
וְ֠זָרְק֠וּ בְּנֵ֨י אַהֲרֹ֧ן אֶת־דָּמֹ֛ו עַל־הַמִּזְבֵּ֖חַ סָבִֽיב:
ט וְהִקְרִ֞יב מִזֶּ֣בַח הַשְּׁלָמִ֗ים אִשֶּׁה֙ לַֽיהֹוָ֔ה חֶלְבֹּו֙
הָֽאַלְיָ֣ה תְמִימָ֔ה לְעֻמַּ֥ת הֶֽעָצֶ֖ה יְסִירֶ֑נָּה וְאֶת־
הַחֵ֙לֶב֙ הַֽמְכַסֶּ֣ה אֶת־הַקֶּ֔רֶב וְאֵת֙ כָּל־הַחֵ֔לֶב אֲשֶׁ֖ר
עַל־הַקֶּֽרֶב: י וְאֵת֙ שְׁתֵּ֣י הַכְּלָיֹ֔ת וְאֶת־הַחֵ֙לֶב֙
אֲשֶׁ֣ר עֲלֵהֶ֔ן אֲשֶׁ֖ר עַל־הַכְּסָלִ֑ים וְאֶת־הַיֹּתֶ֙רֶת֙
עַל־הַכָּבֵ֔ד עַל־הַכְּלָיֹ֖ת יְסִירֶֽנָּה: יא וְהִקְטִירֹ֥ו
הַכֹּהֵ֖ן הַמִּזְבֵּ֑חָה לֶ֥חֶם אִשֶּׁ֖ה לַֽיהֹוָֽה: פ יב וְאִם־
עֵ֖ז קָרְבָּנֹ֑ו וְהִקְרִיבֹ֖ו לִפְנֵ֥י יְהֹוָֽה: יג וְסָמַ֤ךְ אֶת־
יָדֹו֙ עַל־רֹאשֹׁ֔ו וְשָׁחַ֣ט אֹתֹ֔ו לִפְנֵ֖י אֹ֣הֶל מֹועֵ֑ד

11. . . . We believe we can understand why, the concept of לֶחֶם which, as we shall see in Chapter 21, applies to all the offerings made upon the altar, is expressed in the present chapter primarily in connection with the שְׁלָמִים. שְׁלָמִים are those offerings that seek to symbolize God's presence in all our happy life on earth. It is this offering which, by virtue of the procedure it entails (including the pleasure of eating the meat at home),

transforms the family table into an altar, the home into a temple, and elevates the members of the household to the position of priests and priestesses. A prerequisite to this end is the ideal symbolized by לֶחֶם: any way of life on earth that wishes to enjoy God's Presence must make itself worthy of that Presence by the goals it sets for itself and by the means that it uses to attain these goals. . . .

וְזָרְקוּ בְּנֵי אַהֲרֹן אֶת־דָּמוֹ עַל־הַמִּזְבֵּחַ סָבִיב׃
יד וְהִקְרִיב מִמֶּנּוּ קָרְבָּנוֹ אִשֶּׁה לַיהוָה אֶת־
הַחֵלֶב הַמְכַסֶּה אֶת־הַקֶּרֶב וְאֵת כָּל־הַחֵלֶב אֲשֶׁר
עַל־הַקֶּרֶב׃ טו וְאֵת שְׁתֵּי הַכְּלָיֹת וְאֶת־הַחֵלֶב
אֲשֶׁר עֲלֵהֶן אֲשֶׁר עַל־הַכְּסָלִים וְאֶת־הַיֹּתֶרֶת
עַל־הַכָּבֵד עַל־הַכְּלָיוֹת יְסִירֶנָּה׃ טז וְהִקְטִירָם
הַכֹּהֵן הַמִּזְבֵּחָה לֶחֶם אִשֶּׁה לְרֵיחַ נִיחֹחַ כָּל־חֵלֶב
לַיהוָה׃ יז חֻקַּת עוֹלָם לְדֹרֹתֵיכֶם בְּכֹל

Appointed Meeting, and sons of Aharon shall dash its blood round about upon the altar.
14. He shall then bring near his offering from it as a fire offering to *God*: the fat that covers the entrails and all the fat that is attached to the entrails.
15. Also the two kidneys and the fat that is attached to them, that is along the flanks; also the diaphragm upon the liver; he must remove it together with the kidneys.
16. The priest shall give it to go up in smoke upon the altar as an offering made by fire as an expression of compliance; all the fat belongs to *God*.
17. It shall be an everlasting statute for your descendants in all your

17. ***It shall be an everlasting statute.*** The details of the law concerning חֵלֶב [the suet or hard fat that must not be eaten] follow in Chapter 7, Verses 23 ff. At this point the reference to the prohibition against eating hard fat and blood is appended to the words "all the fat belongs to *God*" in the preceding verse, to indicate that this prohibition is linked to the role of the fat and the blood in the offering, and also to stress that though the use of these substances in the offerings is limited to certain stated times and to a certain place, the prohibition against eating חֵלֶב דָּם [the hard fat and blood] remains valid "for your descendants in all your dwelling places." The prohibition remains in force regardless of whether the Temple is in existence or not, and not only בְּאֶרֶץ [in the Land (of Israel)] but also בְּחוּצָה לָאָרֶץ [outside the Land (of Israel)]. . . . *Torath Kohanim* ibid. states: "*An everlasting statute*: For the Everlasting House. *For your descendants*: This is binding upon all future generations. *In all your dwelling places*: Both in the Land (of Israel) and outside the Land (of Israel)."

The words חֻקַּת עוֹלָם ["an everlasting statute"] continue the train of thought begun with the final words of the preceding verse, כָּל חֵלֶב לה׳ ["all the fat belongs to *God*"], to indicate that all the חֵלֶב of the animals offered up to God belongs to Him, and that this holds true not only in the מִשְׁכָּן [the Dwelling Place that was built in the wilderness] but also in the place that shall remain for all time the Sanctuary of God, the one place where the offerings may be made: the בֵּית הַמִּקְדָּשׁ [the Temple], which, therefore, is termed בֵּית עוֹלָמִים [the Everlasting House]. The text then continues logically with the statement ". . . for your descendants in all your dwelling places: You shall not eat any fat. . ."; i.e., that no חֵלֶב and no דָּם may be eaten לְדוֹרוֹתֵיכֶם [by any of your descendants] בְּכָל מוֹשְׁבוֹתֵיכֶם [no matter where you may dwell]. For even as the Temple is called the "Everlasting House," so, too, the laws concerning the offerings have been given to us as "an everlasting statute." This means that the sacrificial laws and all the laws deriving from them are binding upon us for all time.

The destruction of the Temple and our exile from our land are only temporary situations that temporarily prevent us from observing these laws. For the time being, we lack the conditions under which we are expected and permitted to observe the laws pertaining to the offerings. But this does not mean that the laws and the consequences deriving from them have been abolished, just as little as the commandment to "honor your father" ceases to be binding upon a child whose parent happens to be temporarily absent, or as the law "and you shall teach them (i.e., the laws of the Torah) to your children" is irrelevant to an individual who does not yet have children of his own. So, too, the laws prohibiting the consumption of חֵלֶב דָּם [hard fat and blood], which we are to observe "for your descendants in all your dwelling places," and the duties connected with the service in the Temple and with the offerings, are binding upon us even today, in the literal sense. Each time we refrain from eating blood or חֵלֶב [hard fat] we attest to the perpetual validity of the sacrificial laws, reaffirm the ultimate restoration of the offerings in the Temple, and lodge the most effective protest against any attempt to justify efforts at so-called "reform" with the claim that the sacrificial laws are obsolete and were abrogated long ago.

The connection between the prohibition against eating חֵלֶב and the sacrificial laws is made particularly obvious by the fact that, according to Chapter 7:25, this prohibition applies only to animals of the cattle species which may be used as offerings; i.e., oxen, sheep, and goats. It is not applicable in the case of undomesticated animals and birds. But the prohibition against eating blood, which is linked with the offerings, just as is the prohibition against eating חֵלֶב [hard fat], is not confined to animals fit for use as offerings but is applicable also to undomesticated animals and birds—indeed, to all dwelling places: You shall not eat any fat, nor any blood.

מוֹשְׁבֹתֵיכֶם כָּל־חֵלֶב וְכָל־דָּם לֹא תֹאכֵלוּ: פ

IV 1. *God* spoke to Moshe [saying]: 2. Speak to the sons of Yisrael [saying]: If a person inadvertently sins regarding some of all the things which *God* has commanded that they shall not be done, and he commits any one of them; 3. if the anointed priest sins so as to bring guilt upon the people, he shall bring near for his sin which he has commit-

חמישי ד א וַיְדַבֵּר יְהוָה אֶל־מֹשֶׁה לֵּאמֹר:
ב דַּבֵּר אֶל־בְּנֵי יִשְׂרָאֵל לֵאמֹר נֶפֶשׁ כִּי־תֶחֱטָא
בִשְׁגָגָה מִכֹּל מִצְוֹת יְהוָה אֲשֶׁר לֹא תֵעָשֶׂינָה
וְעָשָׂה מֵאַחַת מֵהֵנָּה: ג אִם הַכֹּהֵן הַמָּשִׁיחַ
יֶחֱטָא לְאַשְׁמַת הָעָם וְהִקְרִיב עַל חַטָּאתוֹ אֲשֶׁר

warm-blooded animals. Therefore, the prohibition against eating blood must be based on considerations over and beyond those associated with the offerings.

The fact that the prohibition against eating חֵלֶב [hard fat] and דָּם [blood] is linked in this verse with the animal offerings would indicate an underlying thought as follows: Blood and the [hard] fat known as חֵלֶב are the two substances upon which the animal organism is founded. The animal's whole being is concentrated in its blood; cf. הַדָּם הוּא הַנָּפֶשׁ ["the blood, it is the soul" (Deuteronomy 12:23). The [hard] fat known as חֵלֶב is the final product of the animal's organic life. . . . Thus, in the case of an animal offering, the blood of the animal may be interpreted as representing man's personality, while the animal's חֵלֶב stands for man's self-serving aims. However, in reality, the animal ego can never become a human personality, nor is man ever permitted to make the self-serving aims of animals his own. Precisely because, in the ritual of the offerings, the hard fat and the blood of the animal both [symbolically] represent aspects of the human personality, they must never physically become part of the human body, so that our self-image should not be based on our equating human nature in any manner with the nature of animals. . . .

CHAPTER IV

2. נֶפֶשׁ כִּי תֶחֱטָא וגו׳ וְעָשָׂה וגו׳ *[If a person inadvertently sins . . . and he commits . . .].* נֶפֶשׁ, the soul, is the true core of the human personality that manifests itself in the human will and spirit and to whose control and guidance the body with its organs and energies has been subordinated. In order to perform these functions of control and guidance in accordance with the will of God, the נֶפֶשׁ in turn must submit to the "fire" of the Law of God, allowing itself to be tempered at all times by the light and the warmth of the Law. If the body is subordinated to the soul, and the soul is subordinated to God, then all of man's activities, spiritual and physical, will be conducted in the service of God. In that case, if man uses his body, which serves him, for the exercise of his own free will, he will do only that which is also the will of God. However, if the נֶפֶשׁ resists the enlightenment and stimulation offered by the fire of the Law of God (this is the basic, literal meaning of חָטָא)[3] . . . then there is the danger that the organs and the energies of the body, which should be permitted to function only within the limits hallowed by the will of God, will act contrary to His will. The offering through which a soul, having strayed from the sphere of God's will (which should be the focal point of all man's actions), now seeks to regain the nearness of God on which the purity of its active life depends and which it should never have left, is called קָרְבַּן חַטָּאת ["an offering that clears (him who brings it) of sin"].

3. ***he shall bring near for his sin which he has committed.*** The expression לְאַשְׁמַת הָעָם ["so as to bring guilt upon the people"] defines a sin which was committed inadvertently by the כֹּהֵן הַמָּשִׁיחַ ["anointed priest"; i.e., the high priest] and for which atonement is to be made by means of the חַטָּאת [offering that clears (him who brings it) of sin], in the same manner as it defines an error committed by the entire nation; namely, as a practical violation of God's Law caused by an intellectual error. It entails theoretical ignorance of the Law together with error in practice. But the added phrase חַטָּאתוֹ אֲשֶׁר חָטָא ["his sin which he has committed"] makes it clear that a teaching set forth by the כֹּהֵן הַמָּשִׁיחַ can bring guilt upon the entire nation only if he himself has committed a sin inadvertently, as a result of his own erroneous interpretation of the Law. It does not apply if his erroneous teaching caused only others than himself, even the entire Jewish community, to commit a sin. (Horayoth 6b)

[3] *Note to the English translation:* In his commentary on Genesis 39:9, which is not included in this excerpted edition, Hirsch suggests a relationship between חטא (sin) and the verb חתה (to take out) which is used in the Mishnah (Yoma IV:4) in connection with "taking out coals from a pan." Hirsch suggests that חטא therefore implies the removal of something from the place where it belongs, hence, withdrawing our personality from that Divine "fire" which should serve to pervade, revive and purify us. [G.H.]

ted, one young bull, without blemish,   חָטָא פַּר בֶּן־בָּקָר תָּמִים לַיהוָה לְחַטָּאת:

This legal limitation draws a sharp line of distinction between the functions of the high priest and those of the Supreme Court of Law; i.e., the Sanhedrin. In Judaism neither the priest nor even the high priest wields personal authority by virtue of his priestly office. His priesthood alone does not qualify him to be an interpreter of the Law. His word as a priest does not have binding authority. Only in the Temple does the priest symbolically represent the unity that should exist between the Supreme Court of Law and the Jewish community, the ideal of a nation led by the spirit of the Law of God. The priest's teachings are binding only upon himself; only with regard to the laws of the Temple service הוֹרָאַת כֹּהֵן מָשִׁיחַ לְעַצְמוֹ כְּהוֹרָאַת בֵּית דִּין לַצִּבּוּר ["is the teaching of the anointed priest to himself tantamount to a ruling handed down by the Supreme Court of Law to the community"] and hence liable to the same atonement before God. In everyday life, in the midst of his people, the position of the high priest in relation to the Law of God is no different from that of the lowliest woodcutter. The only difference is that a high priest cannot use an offering to effect atonement for an ordinary sin which he has committed inadvertently.

The foregoing demolishes all the notions of a Jewish "hierarchy" that seek to characterize the Jewish priesthood as the epitome of hierarchical arrogance. This assumption, which has passed from mouth to mouth as indisputable fact, has been utterly discredited both by the theory of Jewish Law and the facts of Jewish history. Nowhere in all the millennia of Jewish history do we see a priest exercising a significant influence on the development of his community by virtue of his priestly office. By far the overwhelming majority of the men who have had an impact on the life of the Jewish nation as its leaders and teachers were not priests, and those among them who happened to be priests wielded their authority not by virtue of their priestly position but thanks to their personal qualities that would have opened the nation's hearts and minds to them even if they had not been of Aharonide stock.

Hence, if in Deuteronomy 17:9 the appeal to the highest authority in the Law is expressed by the statement: "And you shall come to the priests, the Levites, and to the judge," this is explained by *Sifri* in a manner consistent with what we have said here: If there happen to be among the Aharonides and the Levites individuals who are qualified to serve on the Sanhedrin, it is a מִצְוָה [virtuous act] to have such Aharonides and Levites, too, serve on the Sanhedrin. But this does not mean that the Sanhedrin can exercise authority only if it includes priests and Levites, and certainly not that the Sanhedrin must consist of priests to the exclusion of all others. "It is a *mitzvah* that the Sanhedrin should include priests and Levites, but the Sanhedrin is legally qualified even if it has no priests and no Levites among its members."

On the other hand, according to Sanhedrin 14b, the juxtaposition of the highest court of law with the priesthood implies that the Sanhedrin is fully competent to act only when and if the priests are exercising their functions in the Temple. In like manner, the exercise of the Sanhedrin's supreme authority was limited in space in that the Sanhedrin was permitted to meet only in the Temple area: מְלַמֵּד שֶׁהַמָּקוֹם גּוֹרֵם ["This teaches us that venue was a determining factor (in the authority of the Sanhedrin)"]. In Judaism, justice was not seen as a separate area of political and national expediency but as an emanation of the same will of God Who caused His altar to be built for His Law and Who commanded that the fulfillment of His will be represented symbolically in His Sanctuary by the offerings given to the fire of His Law. The function of the Sanhedrin was to bring about the realization, in practical life, of the ideals that the priest taught in symbolic terms in the Sanctuary. The function of the priest and that of the Sanhedrin each was עֲבוֹדַת ד' [Divine service] in its own right.

True, the Word of God expects that their functions in the Sanctuary of the Law and their position in the midst of the nation, without the security of personal landed property, should cause the priests, and indeed the entire tribe of Levi, to view God Himself as their inheritance and to become men imbued with the knowledge and spirit of the Torah. Those who will "place incense for Thy perception and whole offerings upon Thy altar" [Deuteronomy 33:10] should also be the ones who "teach Thy [social] ordinances to Yaakov and Thy Teaching to Yisrael" [ibid.]; or, in the words of Malakhi, the last of the prophets, exhorting the corrupt priests of his day, "the priest's lips should keep knowledge and they should seek the Law at his mouth" (Malakhi 2:7). Nonetheless, the functions expected of the priest in Judaism, both in theory and practice, were confined to setting a personal example: Only by his personal conduct was he to teach, to exhort, to reprove, and to lead men back to God and to one another ["The law of truth was in his mouth and unrighteousness was not found upon his lips; he walked with Me in peace and uprightness and turned many away from iniquity"] (ibid. 2:6). It was not one of the functions of priesthood to wield the authority of the Law and compel obedience to it. The Gemarah (Sanhedrin 6b), referring to this verse of Malakhi, draws a sharp distinction between the functions of the Sanhedrin and those of the priests: "The principle of Moses is: The Law must cut through the mountain. That of Aaron: Love peace and pursue

ד וְהֵבִיא אֶת־הַפָּר אֶל־פֶּתַח אֹהֶל מוֹעֵד לִפְנֵי
יְהוָה וְסָמַךְ אֶת־יָדוֹ עַל־רֹאשׁ הַפָּר וְשָׁחַט אֶת־
הַפָּר לִפְנֵי יְהוָה: ה וְלָקַח הַכֹּהֵן הַמָּשִׁיחַ מִדַּם
הַפָּר וְהֵבִיא אֹתוֹ אֶל־אֹהֶל מוֹעֵד: ו וְטָבַל הַכֹּהֵן
אֶת־אֶצְבָּעוֹ בַּדָּם וְהִזָּה מִן־הַדָּם שֶׁבַע פְּעָמִים
לִפְנֵי יְהוָה אֶת־פְּנֵי פָּרֹכֶת הַקֹּדֶשׁ: ז וְנָתַן הַכֹּהֵן
מִן־הַדָּם עַל־קַרְנוֹת מִזְבַּח קְטֹרֶת הַסַּמִּים לִפְנֵי

to *God* as an offering for the sin. 4. He shall bring the bull to the entrance of the Tent of Appointed Meeting before *God*, lean his hand upon the head of the bull and slaughter the bull before *God*. 5. The anointed priest shall then take [some] of the bull's blood and bring it into the Tent of Appointed Meeting. 6. The priest shall dip his finger into this blood and sprinkle [some] of this blood seven times before *God* toward the dividing curtain of the Sanctuary. 7. Then the priest shall put [some] of the blood upon the elevated corners of the altar of spicy incense before

peace and make peace between man and man." . . . At any rate, we nowhere find even the slightest hint in Jewish history of a Jewish high priest who served as a prototype for the authority of a "pope." The Urim and Thummim were indeed pronouncements of God, but they were used only in very few national undertakings, and even in those cases merely to ascertain whether the undertaking in question was, or was not, in accordance with the will of God.

If we consider that the "bull of the anointed priest" must be offered only "for his sin which he has committed," only for a transgression committed by the priest himself due to an error on his part in interpreting the Law, then it is clear that the function of the Jewish high priest is simply so to live that his conduct should serve as an example to others of how the Law should be understood and observed. The function of the Sanhedrin is to teach the nation the ideals it is to fulfill; that of the high priest is to exemplify these ideals by his personal life. He should be an expert whom one can consult on teachings of the Law, but primarily he is to use his knowledge of the Law for arranging his own life so that it may serve as an example for others to emulate. For this reason, too, our high priest had to be a "complete" person; he had to be married and a family man in order to be able to function in every respect as a model man and citizen in the midst of his people. Our high priests were not permitted to remain unmarried.

פַּר בֶּן בָּקָר [one young bull]. His offering is to be פַּר, the subservient working animal, for he makes his offering not as a private individual but as a servant appointed to labor in the field of God. (In Judaism, "God's acre" is not the graveyard but the arena of active life). He must view his transgression in terms of his position as an "anointed priest" and must consciously resolve to be true to this calling in the future. Symbolically, he comes to the entrance of God's sanctuary as פַּר [a bull that works in the field], as one who,

by leading a life consistent with his functions in the Sanctuary of God's Law, is to open the hearts and minds of God's people so that they may receive the seeds of light and life from the Law of God. He comes, symbolically, as a פַּר בֶּן בָּקָר. According to *Torath Kohanim*, פַּר denotes a mature animal, while בֶּן בָּקָר denotes the animal in its immaturity. Thus, the combination פַּר בֶּן בָּקָר means "a young bull"; i.e., a bull in the first stage of its maturity, an animal in its third year (See also Rosh HaShanah 10a). Even as the nation should always remain "a yearling," appearing before God in eternal youth, even as one of the direst apprehensions voiced in the Word of God is that the community's relationship to God might grow "old" and stale; cf. "and you have grown old in the land" (Deuteronomy 4:25), and even as the Torah seeks to stir us up anew each day to face the tasks of life with renewed vigor and enthusiasm, so, too, though they may be mature, those who serve and uphold the people of God should remain "young" forever, constantly experiencing their vocation anew in all its greatness. They must never grow "old," too well-established, in their office. For precisely when they feel well settled in their office do they run the danger of committing the kind of sin for which the atonement is described in this passage. The study of the Law and its practical fulfillment over a period of many years may easily lead us into a set routine and make us believe that we no longer need to refer, with ever-new devotion, to the wellsprings of God's Law before each step we take in our everyday lives, making certain that our conduct accords with the demands of God's Law. Hence, in his offering, the anointed priest who "has sinned himself because he has misinterpreted the Law" and therefore "erred in practice," must present himself symbolically to God as a פַּר בֶּן בָּקָר, signifying his undertaking to rid himself of the illusion that he is "well-established" in the knowledge and observance of the Law.

יְהֹוָה אֲשֶׁר בְּאֹהֶל מוֹעֵד וְאֵת ׀ כָּל־דַּם הַפָּר
יִשְׁפֹּךְ אֶל־יְסוֹד מִזְבַּח הָעֹלָה אֲשֶׁר־פֶּתַח אֹהֶל
מוֹעֵד׃ ח וְאֶת־כָּל־חֵלֶב פַּר הַחַטָּאת יָרִים מִמֶּנּוּ
אֶת־הַחֵלֶב הַמְכַסֶּה עַל־הַקֶּרֶב וְאֵת כָּל־הַחֵלֶב
אֲשֶׁר עַל־הַקֶּרֶב׃ ט וְאֵת שְׁתֵּי הַכְּלָיֹת וְאֶת־
הַחֵלֶב אֲשֶׁר עֲלֵיהֶן אֲשֶׁר עַל־הַכְּסָלִים וְאֶת־
הַיֹּתֶרֶת עַל־הַכָּבֵד עַל־הַכְּלָיוֹת יְסִירֶנָּה׃
י כַּאֲשֶׁר יוּרַם מִשּׁוֹר זֶבַח הַשְּׁלָמִים וְהִקְטִירָם
הַכֹּהֵן עַל מִזְבַּח הָעֹלָה׃ יא וְאֶת־עוֹר הַפָּר
וְאֶת־כָּל־בְּשָׂרוֹ עַל־רֹאשׁוֹ וְעַל־כְּרָעָיו וְקִרְבּוֹ
וּפִרְשׁוֹ׃ יב וְהוֹצִיא אֶת־כָּל־הַפָּר אֶל־מִחוּץ
לַמַּחֲנֶה אֶל־מָקוֹם טָהוֹר אֶל־שֶׁפֶךְ הַדֶּשֶׁן וְשָׂרַף
אֹתוֹ עַל־עֵצִים בָּאֵשׁ עַל־שֶׁפֶךְ הַדֶּשֶׁן יִשָּׂרֵף׃ פ
יג וְאִם כָּל־עֲדַת יִשְׂרָאֵל יִשְׁגּוּ וְנֶעְלַם דָּבָר
מֵעֵינֵי הַקָּהָל וְעָשׂוּ אַחַת מִכָּל־מִצְוֺת יְהֹוָה
אֲשֶׁר לֹא־תֵעָשֶׂינָה וְאָשֵׁמוּ׃ יד וְנוֹדְעָה הַחַטָּאת
אֲשֶׁר חָטְאוּ עָלֶיהָ וְהִקְרִיבוּ הַקָּהָל פַּר בֶּן־בָּקָר
לְחַטָּאת וְהֵבִיאוּ אֹתוֹ לִפְנֵי אֹהֶל מוֹעֵד׃

God, which is in the Tent of Appointed Meeting; but he shall pour all the [remaining] blood of the bull into the base of the altar of ascent offering which is next to the entrance to the Tent of Appointed Meeting.
8. He shall lift out from it all the fat of the bull, [the] offering that clears [him who brings it] of sin, the fat that covers the entrails and all the fat that is attached to the entrails. 9. Also the two kidneys and the fat that is attached to them, that is along the flanks; also the diaphragm upon the liver; he must remove it together with the kidneys, 10. just as it was lifted off the ox of the meal of peace; and the priest shall give them to go up in smoke upon the altar of ascent offering. 11. But the skin of the bull, and all its flesh, along with its head and its legs, along with its entrails and its dung, 12. he shall take out the whole bull to a pure place outside the camp, where the ashes are poured out, and burn it on [logs of] wood with fire; where the ashes are poured out shall it be burned. 13. And if the entire council of Yisrael sins inadvertently, and something is hidden from the community, and they commit one of all the things concerning which *God* has commanded that they shall not be done, and they have thus incurred guilt, 14. and the sin that they have committed has become known, then the community shall bring near a young bull as an offering for the sin and they shall bring it before the Tent of

13. כָּל עֲדַת יִשְׂרָאֵל ***[the entire council of Yisrael]***. As a rule, Scripture, in referring to adult Jewish males as a whole, uses the collective expression עֲדַת בְּנֵי יִשְׂרָאֵל, the community formed by all the sons of Yisrael. Only in Chapter 12 of Exodus, where the initial establishment of the nation is described, have we thus far repeatedly noted the term עֲדַת יִשְׂרָאֵל used to characterize the community as such; i.e., as a multitude united by virtue of a common destiny inherent in their name, יִשְׂרָאֵל. In two later instances in Scripture will we find the term עֲדַת יִשְׂרָאֵל with reference to this national entity: once, where, in order to counter Koraḥ's effrontery, the intention is to stress the privileged status already assigned to the Levites over and beyond that of the rest of the community, in which initially all were equal by virtue of their common destiny (Numbers 16:9), and again where, prior to the demands of the tribes of Reuben and Gad for preferential treatment, we are told that the whole nation had equal title to the conquered territory (Numbers 32:4). Everywhere else in Scripture the collective term used to describe the nation is always עֲדַת בְּנֵי יִשְׂרָאֵל. In the present passage the term עֲדַת יִשְׂרָאֵל is used to refer to the סַנְהֶדְרִין, בֵּית דִּין הַגָּדוֹל, the Supreme Court of the Law, the Sanhedrin, which is charged with the task of seeing to it that Israel remains faithful in the discharge of its tasks as a nation. Similarly, in Numbers 35:24 and 25 the supreme criminal court with powers of life and death is simply called הָעֵדָה. The fact that in the present verse the reference is specifically to the Supreme Council that stands at the helm of the whole nation, is indicated by the apposition of the word יִשְׂרָאֵל, עֲדַת יִשְׂרָאֵל, which denotes the 71-member Sanhedrin.

• • •

טו וְסָמְכוּ זִקְנֵי הָעֵדָה אֶת־יְדֵיהֶם עַל־רֹאשׁ
הַפָּר לִפְנֵי יְהוָה וְשָׁחַט אֶת־הַפָּר לִפְנֵי יְהוָה׃
טז וְהֵבִיא הַכֹּהֵן הַמָּשִׁיחַ מִדַּם הַפָּר אֶל־אֹהֶל
מוֹעֵד׃ יז וְטָבַל הַכֹּהֵן אֶצְבָּעוֹ מִן־הַדָּם וְהִזָּה
שֶׁבַע פְּעָמִים לִפְנֵי יְהוָה אֶת־פְּנֵי הַפָּרֹכֶת׃
יח וּמִן־הַדָּם יִתֵּן ׀ עַל־קַרְנֹת הַמִּזְבֵּחַ אֲשֶׁר
לִפְנֵי יְהוָה אֲשֶׁר בְּאֹהֶל מוֹעֵד וְאֵת כָּל־הַדָּם
יִשְׁפֹּךְ אֶל־יְסוֹד מִזְבַּח הָעֹלָה אֲשֶׁר־פֶּתַח אֹהֶל
מוֹעֵד׃ יט וְאֵת כָּל־חֶלְבּוֹ יָרִים מִמֶּנּוּ וְהִקְטִיר
הַמִּזְבֵּחָה׃ כ וְעָשָׂה לַפָּר כַּאֲשֶׁר עָשָׂה לְפַר
הַחַטָּאת כֵּן יַעֲשֶׂה־לּוֹ וְכִפֶּר עֲלֵהֶם הַכֹּהֵן וְנִסְלַח
לָהֶם׃ כא וְהוֹצִיא אֶת־הַפָּר אֶל־מִחוּץ לַמַּחֲנֶה
וְשָׂרַף אֹתוֹ כַּאֲשֶׁר שָׂרַף אֵת הַפָּר הָרִאשׁוֹן
חַטַּאת הַקָּהָל הוּא׃ פ כב אֲשֶׁר נָשִׂיא יֶחֱטָא
וְעָשָׂה אַחַת מִכָּל־מִצְוֺת יְהוָה אֱלֹהָיו אֲשֶׁר לֹא־

Appointed Meeting. 15. The elders of the council shall lean their hand upon the head of the bull before *God,* and the bull shall be slaughtered before *God.* 16. The anointed priest shall bring [some] of the blood of the bull into the Tent of Appointed Meeting, 17. and the priest shall bedaub his finger [by immersion] with [some] of the blood and sprinkle [it] seven times before *God* toward the dividing curtain. 18. He shall place [some] of the blood upon the elevated corners of the altar which stands before *God,* in the Tent of Appointed Meeting; but he shall pour all the [remaining] blood into the base of the altar of ascent offering, which is next to the entrance to the Tent of Appointed Meeting. 19. He shall lift out all its fat from it and place it upon the altar to go up in smoke. 20. And he shall do with this bull as he did with the bull of the [priest's] offering that clears [him who brings it] of sin, exactly so shall he do with it. The priest will effect atonement for them and they will be forgiven. 21. One shall take out the bull [to a place] outside the camp and burn it, even as one burned the first bull; it is an offering that clears the community of sin. 22. But if a prince commits a sin and inadvertently does one of the things concerning which *God,* his God, has commanded that they shall not be

22. In the two preceding cases of transgression, the one requiring the offering of a young bull by the "anointed priest" and the other requiring the offering of a bull for "something hidden from the community," the atonement to be made is for a sin committed by the entire nation, because the sin committed by the "anointed priest" brings guilt also upon the entire people. Both types of transgression have in common the characteristic that they are not merely practical transgressions but acts committed as the result of theoretical errors made by the two highest authorities competent in the knowledge of the Law: the anointed high priest who may be consulted in matters of law and the supreme court of law; i.e., the Sanhedrin.

The verses that follow deal with two other types of sin offering: the sin offering to be made by the ruler of the nation and the sin offering to be made by an individual. Both these cases involve practical acts of transgression pure and simple, transgressions committed in error not resulting from a theoretical misinterpretation of the law. Hence atonement in the case of both must be made as for purely personal errors. . . .

According to Horayoth 11a, the apposition of the words מִצְוֺת ד׳ אֱלֹקָיו ["... which *God,* his God, has commanded..."] defines the נָשִׂיא [prince] whose transgression is discussed here as that of a person who has none above him except God. He is not merely one of the tribal rulers but the ruler who stands at the head of the entire nation, the king, of whom, in a similar vein, it is said in Deuteronomy 17:19: "That he may learn to fear *God,* his God. . . ."

The grouping of these portions dealing with the offerings that clear him who brings them of sin assigns to the king the key role in the practical fulfillment of the Law, even as it assigns to the high priest the key role in the knowledge and dissemination of the Law. This grouping implies that the king must be the first in the nation to obey the Law. But the fact that his חַטָּאת

done, then he has incurred guilt. 23. Or if his sin which he has committed was made known to him, he shall bring as his offering a buck from the goat species, male, without blemish. 24. And he shall lean his hand upon the head of the he-goat and slaughter it at the place where the ascent offering is slaughtered, before *God*; it is an offering that clears [him who brings it] of sin. 25. The priest shall take with his finger [some] of the blood of the offering that clears [him who brings it] of sin and place it upon the elevated corners of the altar of ascent offering; he shall then pour [the remainder of] its blood into the base of the altar of ascent offering. 26. He shall give all its fat to the altar to go up in smoke, as with the fat of the meal-of-peace offering; the priest will effect atonement for him for his sin and he will be forgiven. 27. And if any person from among the people of the land inadvertently sins by doing one of the things concerning which *God* commanded that they shall not be done, he has incurred guilt. 28. Or if his sin which he has committed was made known to him, then he shall bring as his offering a she-goat, from the goat species, without blemish, female, for the sin which he has committed. 29. He shall lean his hand upon the head of the offering that clears [him who brings it] of sin, and he shall slaughter the offering that clears [him who brings it] of sin at the place of the ascent offering. 30. The priest shall take [some] of its blood with his finger and place it upon the elevated corners of the altar of ascent offering, and he shall then

תֵעָשֶׂינָה בִּשְׁגָגָה וְאָשֵׁם׃ כג אוֹ־הוֹדַע אֵלָיו
חַטָּאתוֹ אֲשֶׁר חָטָא בָּהּ וְהֵבִיא אֶת־קָרְבָּנוֹ
שְׂעִיר עִזִּים זָכָר תָּמִים׃ כד וְסָמַךְ יָדוֹ עַל־רֹאשׁ
הַשָּׂעִיר וְשָׁחַט אֹתוֹ בִּמְקוֹם אֲשֶׁר־יִשְׁחַט אֶת־
הָעֹלָה לִפְנֵי יְהוָה חַטָּאת הוּא׃ כה וְלָקַח הַכֹּהֵן
מִדַּם הַחַטָּאת בְּאֶצְבָּעוֹ וְנָתַן עַל־קַרְנֹת מִזְבַּח
הָעֹלָה וְאֶת־דָּמוֹ יִשְׁפֹּךְ אֶל־יְסוֹד מִזְבַּח הָעֹלָה׃
כו וְאֶת־כָּל־חֶלְבּוֹ יַקְטִיר הַמִּזְבֵּחָה כְּחֵלֶב זֶבַח
הַשְּׁלָמִים וְכִפֶּר עָלָיו הַכֹּהֵן מֵחַטָּאתוֹ וְנִסְלַח
לוֹ׃ פ ששי כז וְאִם־נֶפֶשׁ אַחַת תֶּחֱטָא בִשְׁגָגָה
מֵעַם הָאָרֶץ בַּעֲשֹׂתָהּ אַחַת מִמִּצְוֹת יְהוָה אֲשֶׁר
לֹא־תֵעָשֶׂינָה וְאָשֵׁם׃ כח אוֹ הוֹדַע אֵלָיו חַטָּאתוֹ
אֲשֶׁר חָטָא וְהֵבִיא קָרְבָּנוֹ שְׂעִירַת עִזִּים תְּמִימָה
נְקֵבָה עַל־חַטָּאתוֹ אֲשֶׁר חָטָא׃ כט וְסָמַךְ אֶת־
יָדוֹ עַל רֹאשׁ הַחַטָּאת וְשָׁחַט אֶת־הַחַטָּאת
בִּמְקוֹם הָעֹלָה׃ ל וְלָקַח הַכֹּהֵן מִדָּמָהּ בְּאֶצְבָּעוֹ
וְנָתַן עַל־קַרְנֹת מִזְבַּח הָעֹלָה וְאֶת־כָּל־דָּמָהּ

does not stress an error in the teaching of the Law indicates that his position as king does not include the function of interpreting the Law. Like any other individual among his people, he must turn to the court of law to learn what is "right" according to the Law. He is merely the first individual among other individuals. As distinct from transgressions committed by the high priest, or transgressions committed by the entire nation as the result of a decision by the supreme court—acts referred to by the words אַשְׁמַת הָעָם (Verse 3), וְאָשֵׁמוּ (Verse 13) and חַטַּאת הַקָּהָל (Verse 21)—we are told with regard to any transgression committed by the king that any sin he commits jeopardizes only his personal future. No matter how highly he has been placed above the nation by virtue of the position of power assigned to him, he must stand alone before God to answer for his sins, just as the humblest citizen. This can be seen from the statement of R. Yoḥanan ben Zakkai concerning a ruler who commits a sin: "Fortunate the generation whose ruler seeks atonement by making an offering for the wrong he has committed in error! How must the conscience of the ordinary citizen be stirred by the conscientious conduct of the king, and if he is so deeply affected by a transgression he has committed in error, how much more deeply will he be affected if he has been guilty of an intentional sin."

pour all [the remainder of] its blood into the base of the altar. 31. He shall remove all its fat, even as the fat was removed from the meal-of-peace offering, and the priest shall give it to go up in smoke to the altar as an expression of compliance, to *God*; the priest will effect atonement for him and he will be forgiven. 32. If he brings a sheep as his offering for an offering that clears [him who brings it] of sin, then he shall bring it, female, without blemish. 33. He shall lean his hand upon the head of the offering that clears [him who brings it] of sin, and one slaughters it (the female sheep) as an offering that clears [him who brings it] of sin, at the place where the ascent offering is slaughtered. 34. The priest shall take [some] of the blood of the offering that clears [him who brings it] of sin with his finger and place it upon the elevated corners of the altar of ascent offering, and he shall then pour all [the remainder of] its blood into the base of the altar. 35. He shall remove all its fat, even as the fat of the sheep of the meal-of-peace offering is to be removed, and the priest shall give it to go up in smoke, to the altar, to the fire offerings, to *God*; the priest will effect atonement for him for his sin and he will be forgiven.

V 1. And if a person sins and hears the demand that he take an oath, and he is a witness—having seen or known [something]—so that, if he does not testify, he shall bear his iniquity; 2. or if a person touches some unclean object, be it the carcass of an unclean animal, or the carcass of unclean livestock, or the carcass of an unclean small creature, and it escapes his notice, but he is unclean and [therefore] guilty; 3. or if he touches the uncleanness of a human being, whatever the unclean state of that by which he has become unclean, and it escapes his notice, but he has discovered it, and therefore he incurs guilt; 4. or if a person swears, uttering [it] with his lips, to deny or to grant something, with regard to anything that a man may utter in an oath, and it has escaped his notice, and he has now discovered it, and he incurs guilt regarding one of these; 5. then it shall be that if he incurs guilt regarding one of these, he shall

יִשְׁפֹּךְ אֶל־יְסוֹד הַמִּזְבֵּחַ׃ לא וְאֶת־כָּל־חֶלְבָּהּ
יָסִיר כַּאֲשֶׁר הוּסַר חֵלֶב מֵעַל זֶבַח הַשְּׁלָמִים
וְהִקְטִיר הַכֹּהֵן הַמִּזְבֵּחָה לְרֵיחַ נִיחֹחַ לַיהוָה
וְכִפֶּר עָלָיו הַכֹּהֵן וְנִסְלַח לוֹ׃ פ לב וְאִם־כֶּבֶשׂ
יָבִיא קָרְבָּנוֹ לְחַטָּאת נְקֵבָה תְמִימָה יְבִיאֶנָּה׃
לג וְסָמַךְ אֶת־יָדוֹ עַל רֹאשׁ הַחַטָּאת וְשָׁחַט
אֹתָהּ לְחַטָּאת בִּמְקוֹם אֲשֶׁר יִשְׁחַט אֶת־הָעֹלָה׃
לד וְלָקַח הַכֹּהֵן מִדַּם הַחַטָּאת בְּאֶצְבָּעוֹ וְנָתַן
עַל־קַרְנֹת מִזְבַּח הָעֹלָה וְאֶת־כָּל־דָּמָהּ יִשְׁפֹּךְ
אֶל־יְסוֹד הַמִּזְבֵּחַ׃ לה וְאֶת־כָּל־חֶלְבָּהּ יָסִיר
כַּאֲשֶׁר יוּסַר חֵלֶב־הַכֶּשֶׂב מִזֶּבַח הַשְּׁלָמִים
וְהִקְטִיר הַכֹּהֵן אֹתָם הַמִּזְבֵּחָה עַל אִשֵּׁי יְהוָה
וְכִפֶּר עָלָיו הַכֹּהֵן עַל־חַטָּאתוֹ אֲשֶׁר־חָטָא
וְנִסְלַח לוֹ׃ פ ה א וְנֶפֶשׁ כִּי־תֶחֱטָא וְשָׁמְעָה
קוֹל אָלָה וְהוּא עֵד אוֹ רָאָה אוֹ יָדָע אִם־לוֹא
יַגִּיד וְנָשָׂא עֲוֺנוֹ׃ ב אוֹ נֶפֶשׁ אֲשֶׁר תִּגַּע בְּכָל־
דָּבָר טָמֵא אוֹ בְנִבְלַת חַיָּה טְמֵאָה אוֹ בְּנִבְלַת
בְּהֵמָה טְמֵאָה אוֹ בְּנִבְלַת שֶׁרֶץ טָמֵא וְנֶעְלַם
מִמֶּנּוּ וְהוּא טָמֵא וְאָשֵׁם׃ ג אוֹ כִי יִגַּע בְּטֻמְאַת
אָדָם לְכֹל טֻמְאָתוֹ אֲשֶׁר יִטְמָא בָּהּ וְנֶעְלַם מִמֶּנּוּ
וְהוּא יָדַע וְאָשֵׁם׃ ד אוֹ נֶפֶשׁ כִּי תִשָּׁבַע לְבַטֵּא
בִשְׂפָתַיִם לְהָרַע ׀ אוֹ לְהֵיטִיב לְכֹל אֲשֶׁר יְבַטֵּא
הָאָדָם בִּשְׁבֻעָה וְנֶעְלַם מִמֶּנּוּ וְהוּא־יָדַע וְאָשֵׁם
לְאַחַת מֵאֵלֶּה׃ ה וְהָיָה כִי־יֶאְשַׁם לְאַחַת מֵאֵלֶּה

acknowledge to himself that regarding which he has sinned,   6. and he shall bring to God as an expression of his guilt, regarding the sin which he committed, a female from the small livestock, a female sheep or a female of the goat species as an offering that clears [him who brings it] of sin, and the priest will effect atonement for him from his sin.   7. And if his means are not sufficient for a sheep, he shall bring as an expression of his sin which he has committed, two turtle-doves or two young pigeons to God, one as an offering that clears [him who brings it] of sin and one as an ascent offering.   8. He shall bring them to the priest and the latter shall bring near first the one intended as an offering that clears [him who brings it] of sin; he shall pinch off its head near its neck without severing it completely,   9. and he shall sprinkle [some] of the blood of the offering that clears [him who brings it] of sin upon the wall of the altar but what remains of the blood shall be pressed out into the base of the altar: it is an offering that clears [him who brings it] of sin. 10. And he shall offer the second as an ascent offering as prescribed; the priest will effect atonement for him for his sin which

וְהִתְוַדָּה אֲשֶׁר חָטָא עָלֶיהָ: ו וְהֵבִיא אֶת־אֲשָׁמוֹ לַיהֹוָה עַל חַטָּאתוֹ אֲשֶׁר חָטָא נְקֵבָה מִן־הַצֹּאן כִּשְׂבָּה אוֹ־שְׂעִירַת עִזִּים לְחַטָּאת וְכִפֶּר עָלָיו הַכֹּהֵן מֵחַטָּאתוֹ: ז וְאִם־לֹא תַגִּיעַ יָדוֹ דֵּי שֶׂה וְהֵבִיא אֶת־אֲשָׁמוֹ אֲשֶׁר חָטָא שְׁתֵּי תֹרִים אוֹ־שְׁנֵי בְנֵי־יוֹנָה לַיהֹוָה אֶחָד לְחַטָּאת וְאֶחָד לְעֹלָה: ח וְהֵבִיא אֹתָם אֶל־הַכֹּהֵן וְהִקְרִיב אֶת־אֲשֶׁר לַחַטָּאת רִאשׁוֹנָה וּמָלַק אֶת־רֹאשׁוֹ מִמּוּל עָרְפּוֹ וְלֹא יַבְדִּיל: ט וְהִזָּה מִדַּם הַחַטָּאת עַל קִיר הַמִּזְבֵּחַ וְהַנִּשְׁאָר בַּדָּם יִמָּצֵה אֶל־יְסוֹד הַמִּזְבֵּחַ חַטָּאת הוּא: י וְאֶת־הַשֵּׁנִי יַעֲשֶׂה עֹלָה כַּמִּשְׁפָּט וְכִפֶּר עָלָיו הַכֹּהֵן מֵחַטָּאתוֹ אֲשֶׁר־

CHAPTER V

5. וְהִתְוַדָּה [he shall acknowledge to himself]. It is most significant that Scripture almost always uses the reflexive form, הִתְוַדָּה, to denote a confession of guilt. The sinner is not expected to "make confession" to another man, and certainly not to God, Who, in any event, does not need our "confession" in order to know that we have sinned. It is to himself that the sinner must admit that he has sinned. Indeed, such an admission of guilt to oneself is the very first, indispensable step toward mending one's ways, a solemn resolution that is in fact a prerequisite for his sin offering. For the offering as such presupposes the earnest resolve of תְּשׁוּבָה [repentance]; the "sin offering" is only an outward expression of this resolve. Without this resolve, the offering is meaningless. . . .

The first step toward a resolve of תְּשׁוּבָה is self-knowledge, free of all delusion, so that one sees clearly where and how he has sinned. As long as the mind is caught up in self-deception that cloaks reality, the sinner cannot be expected in future to conduct his life in a truly punctilious manner. Nor is it sufficient

that "he shall acknowledge to himself that he has sinned"; that he admit to himself in general terms that he has done wrong. He must admit the specific thing "regarding which he has sinned." He must have in mind specifically that thing with regard to which the transgression occurred. Only then will he be able to avoid committing a similar sin in future. Such a confession; lit., "acknowledgment," had to be made whenever a person brought a sin offering, a guilt offering or an ascent offering; it was uttered at the moment when the person placed his hand upon his offering (Yoma 33). The concept of וְהִתְוַדָּה is so far removed from the popular notion of "confession," and the admission of guilt to one's own self is so much the only acceptable way to repentance, that Judaism regards a confession of one's sins to another human being as a mistake rather than as a virtuous act. Judaism regards such a disclosure of sins that involve only our relationship with God, and need be known only to Him, as an improper exposure of a shame that the truly repentant sinner should keep quietly within his heart (Berakhoth 34 and Yoma 56). . . .

he has committed and he will be forgiven.
11. And if his means are not sufficient
for two turtle-doves or two young pigeons,
he shall bring, as an expression of
his coming near [to *God*] again, for that
regarding which he sinned, one-tenth of
an *ephah* of fine flour as an offering that
clears [him who brings it] of sin; he shall
put no oil upon it and place no incense
upon it, for it is an offering that clears [him
who brings it] of sin.   12. He shall bring
it to the priest, and the priest shall take out
his handful, its memorial portion, and give
it to the altar to go up in smoke upon the
fire offerings to *God*; it is an offering
that clears [him who brings it] of sin.
13. The priest will effect atonement for
him for his sin which he has committed

חָטָא וְנִסְלַח לוֹ: ס שביעי יא וְאִם־לֹא תַשִּׂיג
יָדוֹ לִשְׁתֵּי תֹרִים אוֹ לִשְׁנֵי בְנֵי־יוֹנָה וְהֵבִיא אֶת־
קׇרְבָּנוֹ אֲשֶׁר חָטָא עֲשִׂירִת הָאֵפָה סֹלֶת לְחַטָּאת
לֹא־יָשִׂים עָלֶיהָ שֶׁמֶן וְלֹא־יִתֵּן עָלֶיהָ לְבֹנָה כִּי
חַטָּאת הִוא: יב וֶהֱבִיאָהּ אֶל־הַכֹּהֵן וְקָמַץ
הַכֹּהֵן ׀ מִמֶּנָּה מְלוֹא קֻמְצוֹ אֶת־אַזְכָּרָתָהּ
וְהִקְטִיר הַמִּזְבֵּחָה עַל אִשֵּׁי יְהֹוָה חַטָּאת הִוא:
יג וְכִפֶּר עָלָיו הַכֹּהֵן עַל־חַטָּאתוֹ אֲשֶׁר־חָטָא

13. . . . If we consider the spheres in which the sins
[named in Verses 1, 2, 3 and 4]—all of them liable to
קָרְבַּן עוֹלָה וְיוֹרֵד, lit., "an offering on an ascending and
descending scale,"[4]—occur, we will note that שְׁמִיעַת
הַקּוֹל [being requested to testify under oath as a witness
when one is in a position to do so (and then failing to
testify)] impinges upon the relationship of the individual to society and upon the principle of justice upon
which society is founded; טוּמְאַת מִקְדָּשׁ וְקׇדָשָׁיו [defilement
of the Sanctuary or one of its holy things][5] relates to the
principle of moral freedom, upon which God's Sanctuary is founded, and שְׁבוּעַת בִּטּוּי [a vow that is explicitly
articulated] relates to the human spirit and to the truthfulness of thought and will that should be its basic
principle. All three transgressions may be subsumed
under the concept of *truth*: the truth of justice, the
truth of morality and the truth inherent in the human
spirit. These truths are to be interpreted not as matters
of social or personal expediency but as postulates set
forth by God for every נֶפֶשׁ ["person"; lit. "soul"] in
Israel to govern his relationship to society, to the Sanctuary of the Law, to himself and to God. These are
awarenesses that make the נֶפֶשׁ a Jewish personality.
Anyone who denies or ignores them will be held
accountable by God.

[4]*Note to the English translation*: In his notes to Verse 1 of
this chapter, which are not included in this excerpted edition,
Hirsch explains the קָרְבַּן עוֹלָה וְיוֹרֵד as an offering
that is variable according to the means of the individual who
must bring it. [G.H.]

[5] *Note to the English translation*: In his notes on Verse 2,
which are not included in this excerpted edition, Hirsch points
out that the sin named in this verse is liable to an
offering only if the sinner was aware that his transgression
involved the defilement of the Sanctuary or one of the "holy
things" within it. [G.H.]

שְׁמִיעַת הַקּוֹל [being requested to testify under oath as a
witness] shows the Jewish individual his place in
society. It makes him aware that God is the Guarantor
of that society and of the justice and right upon which it
is founded, and that God has called upon every
member of society to serve the welfare of all the others
to whom He has given the knowledge and the living
Word that hold society together. From among all our
other duties as members of society, it singles out, as the
one obligation of paramount significance in man's justice toward his fellow men, our duty to be truthful in
giving testimony. Any man may invoke the Name of
God, even out of court, in order to call upon another to
do his duty and testify in court on his behalf. If the
person thus called upon has knowledge that would put
him into a position to testify but he denies that he has
this knowledge, then, even though he has neither sworn
nor responded with "Amen" when asked to swear that
he has no such knowledge, he has committed perjury
not only against his fellow man but also against God,
the Defender of the rights of his fellow man, and
against the veracity of his own knowledge. Man's
awareness of the truth of justice emanates from God
Himself.

טוּמְאַת מִקְדָּשׁ וְקׇדָשָׁיו [a defilement of the Sanctuary and
its holy things] confronts the Jew with the Sanctuary of
the Law and its holy things, which derive their sanctity
solely from the fact that man has been endowed with
freedom of will. Also, it confronts him with טוּמְאָה, the
lack of moral freedom proclaimed by the phenomenon
of death. It speaks to him as follows: Let not the mortality of physical life rob you of the awareness, or even
cause you to doubt, that your moral life, which is near
to God, is free and unhampered by the restraints of
death. The Sanctuary of the Law, which God has established for you, and its holy things, which He Himself

מֵאַחַת מֵאֵלֶּה וְנִסְלַח לוֹ וְהָיְתָה לַכֹּהֵן כַּמִּנְחָה: ס יד וַיְדַבֵּר יְהֹוָה אֶל־מֹשֶׁה לֵּאמֹר: טו נֶפֶשׁ כִּי־תִמְעֹל מַעַל וְחָטְאָה בִּשְׁגָגָה	and he will be forgiven. And it shall belong to the priest, like the homage offering. 14. *God* spoke to Moshe [saying]: 15. If a person commits a breach of trust and thoughtlessly trespasses against any of

presented to you, represent God's guarantee to you that your moral awareness is founded on truth. With this truth, these holy things step into the midst of your narrow physical surroundings and summon the free-willed moral aspect of your personality to enter, of its own free will, into the service of God.

Both spheres, טוּמְאָה [uncleanness], which represents bondage to physical forces, and טָהֳרָה [purity], your complete freedom of will in moral and spiritual matters, are basic facts of life. Both emanate from God, the One Creator of physical nature and moral life. Only when these two are intermingled do they become falsehood. You belong to both spheres, but beware of entering into the one while even a breath of the other is upon you. Physically you are not free, but morally you have freedom, and for as long as you will live, God Himself has wedded your physical faculties, which are bound by the constraints of nature, with the rule of your Godlike free moral energy in order that you may serve the Sanctuary of His Law. Physical truths are applicable only to physical existence. Your existence as a human being extends beyond the sphere of the purely physical. God, Who is free, has ennobled your existence with a breath of Godlike freedom of will, and in that realm the physical laws of matter and energy have no validity. Do not allow anyone to tell you that the knowledge you were taught by your teacher, the teachings of טָהֳרָה, the purity with which alone you may enter into the Sanctuary and partake of its קָדָשִׁים [holy things], are all mere fairy tales; that the concept of man's duty to choose between טוּמְאָה and טָהֳרָה . . . is a myth. Rather, let this knowledge that you were taught by your teacher guide you through the vicissitudes of life. Do not deny the sacred truth of moral freedom of will by seeking to enter the Sanctuary of God and to enjoy its holy things while your mind is filled with thoughts of טוּמְאָה stirred by your contact with death. Always keep in mind the parting of the ways between קְדוּשָׁה [holiness] and טוּמְאָה. Remember that the verity of moral and spiritual freedom within man's consciousness emanates from God.

שְׁבוּעַת בִּטּוּי [a vow that is explicitly articulated] confronts the inner self of the Jew with God and speaks to him as follows: See, all your inner spiritual self, with all its thoughts and aspirations, belongs to God. He is aware even of the most insignificant creation of your mind, the slightest stirrings of your will. He perceives every thought you express, each resolve you frame. He will not have you trifle with thoughts once you have expressed them and with resolutions once you have made them. You are free to call upon Him as the Guarantor of your word or of your intentions even in matters that otherwise would seem utterly insignificant. But once you have thus called upon Him to act as your Guarantor, even if the matter does not affect the interests of anyone but yourself, and then your word is not true, or you fail to carry out your resolve, heaven and earth will be the messengers of His judgment against you, even for the most insignificant word or resolution you may have uttered in His Name and then have failed to carry out. The truth inherent in the human spirit as expressed in the thoughts and aspirations of man emanates from God.

Justice, upon which human society is founded; moral freedom of will, upon which the Sanctuary of the Law is built; and truth, the foundation of the human intellect with its capacity for thought and volition—all these, confirmed and championed by God Himself, represent the soil upon which Jewish life blossoms. The Jew cannot dispense with even one of them, if he is not to become untrue to his destiny. If he has violated any of these basic principles—even if he did so, to some extent, without being aware of it—then the Law will see to it that everyone, down to the humblest member of the Jewish nation, is made aware of how, by ignoring even one of these principles, he has crossed the threshold into isolation. The Law will then make everyone aware that God expects every Jew, even the humblest among them, to act as a guarantor of justice in society, of morality within the Sanctuary and of truth within the human spirit. He who committed the transgression will be spared from isolation only if he acknowledges to himself, in all their sacred inviolable reality, the principles against which he has sinned, and if, by resolving to be more mindful of his duty in future (as expressed in symbolic terms by his offering), he will regain God's nearness upon the altar in the Sanctuary of His Law.

° ° °

15. **נֶפֶשׁ כִּי תִמְעֹל מַעַל** ***[If a person commits a breach of trust].*** **מַעַל** is related to **מְעִיל**, the Hebrew term for the robe of the high priest; in the same manner **בגד**, "to be faithless," is related to **בֶּגֶד**, the Hebrew term for "garment." Here we have an excellent example of the harmonious logic on which the roots of Hebrew words are based. **בֶּגֶד** is the "garment" worn by human beings, and **בגד** means to be "faithless" in ordinary human affairs. **מְעִיל** is the "robe" worn by the high priest, and **מעל** means to commit a breach of trust in sacred, priestly matters. Clearly **בגד** implies a promise that turned out to be nothing but a "garment," and **מעל** refers to an act

מִקָּדְשֵׁי יְהֹוָה וְהֵבִיא אֶת־אֲשָׁמוֹ לַיהֹוָה אַיִל
תָּמִים מִן־הַצֹּאן בְּעֶרְכְּךָ כֶּסֶף־שְׁקָלִים בְּשֶׁקֶל־
הַקֹּדֶשׁ לְאָשָׁם: טז וְאֵת אֲשֶׁר חָטָא מִן־הַקֹּדֶשׁ
יְשַׁלֵּם וְאֶת־חֲמִישִׁתוֹ יוֹסֵף עָלָיו וְנָתַן אֹתוֹ
לַכֹּהֵן וְהַכֹּהֵן יְכַפֵּר עָלָיו בְּאֵיל הָאָשָׁם וְנִסְלַח
לוֹ: פ יז וְאִם־נֶפֶשׁ כִּי תֶחֱטָא וְעָשְׂתָה אַחַת
מִכָּל־מִצְוֹת יְהֹוָה אֲשֶׁר לֹא תֵעָשֶׂינָה וְלֹא־יָדַע
וְאָשֵׁם וְנָשָׂא עֲוֹנוֹ: יח וְהֵבִיא אַיִל תָּמִים מִן־
הַצֹּאן בְּעֶרְכְּךָ לְאָשָׁם אֶל־הַכֹּהֵן וְכִפֶּר עָלָיו
הַכֹּהֵן עַל שִׁגְגָתוֹ אֲשֶׁר־שָׁגָג וְהוּא לֹא־יָדַע
וְנִסְלַח לוֹ: יט אָשָׁם הוּא אָשֹׁם אָשַׁם לַיהֹוָה: פ
כ וַיְדַבֵּר יְהֹוָה אֶל־מֹשֶׁה לֵּאמֹר: כא נֶפֶשׁ כִּי
תֶחֱטָא וּמָעֲלָה מַעַל בַּיהֹוָה וְכִחֵשׁ בַּעֲמִיתוֹ
בְּפִקָּדוֹן אוֹ־בִתְשׂוּמֶת יָד אוֹ בְגָזֵל אוֹ עָשַׁק
אֶת־עֲמִיתוֹ: כב אוֹ־מָצָא אֲבֵדָה וְכִחֶשׁ בָּהּ
וְנִשְׁבַּע עַל־שָׁקֶר עַל־אַחַת מִכֹּל אֲשֶׁר־יַעֲשֶׂה
הָאָדָם לַחֲטֹא בָהֵנָּה: כג וְהָיָה כִּי־יֶחֱטָא וְאָשֵׁם
וְהֵשִׁיב אֶת־הַגְּזֵלָה אֲשֶׁר גָּזָל אוֹ אֶת־הָעֹשֶׁק
אֲשֶׁר עָשָׁק אוֹ אֶת־הַפִּקָּדוֹן אֲשֶׁר הָפְקַד אִתּוֹ
אוֹ אֶת־הָאֲבֵדָה אֲשֶׁר מָצָא: מפטיר כד אוֹ מִכֹּל
אֲשֶׁר־יִשָּׁבַע עָלָיו לַשֶּׁקֶר וְשִׁלַּם אֹתוֹ בְּרֹאשׁוֹ
וַחֲמִשִׁתָיו יֹסֵף עָלָיו לַאֲשֶׁר הוּא לוֹ יִתְּנֶנּוּ בְּיוֹם

the holy things of *God*, he shall bring to *God*, as an expression of his guilt, one ram, without blemish, selected from among the sheep, according to your valuation of silver shekels, according to the shekel of the Sanctuary, as a guilt offering. 16. And he shall make restitution for that which he has trespassed against the holy thing, and shall add to it one-fifth and give it to the priest; the priest will effect atonement for him with the ram of the guilt [offering] and he will be forgiven. 17. And a person who sins and commits one of all these acts concerning which *God* has commanded that they shall not be done, but he is not certain, yet he has incurred guilt and must bear his iniquity, 18. he shall bring one ram, without blemish, from among the sheep, according to your valuation, as a guilt offering, to the priest. The priest will effect atonement for him for his act of negligence which he has committed and concerning which he is still uncertain, and he will be forgiven. 19. It is a guilt offering. He is surely guilty before *God*. 20. *God* spoke to Moshe [saying]: 21. If a person sins and commits a breach of trust against *God* by making a denial to his neighbor with regard to an article that was entrusted to him, or a loan, or an object taken by robbery, or he has withheld something from his neighbor, 22. or he has found a lost article and denies it, and has sworn to a lie regarding anything of that which a man may do to sin in this respect, 23. then it shall be, if he knows that he has sinned and that he has incurred guilt, that he shall restore that which he took by robbery, or that which he withheld, or that which was entrusted to him for safekeeping, or the lost article which he has found, 24. or anything else concerning which he has sworn to a lie; he shall pay for it in capital, equivalent to its value, and shall add one-fifth to it. He shall give it to the one whose rightful due it is, on the

that was committed beneath the "robe" or "cloak" of priestly office. בֶּגֶד, the garment worn by an individual, implies that the wearer is indeed a human being. If someone puts his trust in me as a human being and I betray that trust, then I have shown myself to be merely the "outer garment" of a human being. I am clad in the trappings of a human being, but it is only a disguise. . . .

אַשְׁמָתוֹ׃ כה וְאֶת־אֲשָׁמוֹ יָבִיא לַיהוָה אַיִל
תָּמִים מִן־הַצֹּאן בְּעֶרְכְּךָ לְאָשָׁם אֶל־הַכֹּהֵן׃
כו וְכִפֶּר עָלָיו הַכֹּהֵן לִפְנֵי יְהוָה וְנִסְלַח לוֹ עַל־
אַחַת מִכֹּל אֲשֶׁר־יַעֲשֶׂה לְאַשְׁמָה בָהּ׃ פ

day on which he acknowledges his guilt. 25. But as for his guilt offering he shall bring it to *God*, a ram in unblemished condition from among the sheep, according to your valuation, as a guilt offering, to the priest. 26. The priest will effect atonement for him before *God* and he will be forgiven regarding [any] one of all the things which he has done to incur guilt through them.

20–26. . . . ***If a person sins and commits a breach of trust against* God.** Any dishonest act in relations between man and man is regarded as a breach of trust against God. As is stated in *Torath Kohanim*, God is the unseen Third Party Who is present wherever and whenever one man has dealings with another, even if no other witnesses are on hand. God Himself is the Guarantor for honest dealings between men. If, therefore, this Guarantor is invoked as a witness when any factor in these dealings has been disavowed, it is not merely an act of ordinary בְּגִידָה [faithlessness]. For in this case the offender has pledged his priestly character, his relationship to God, as surety for his honesty, and if this invocation of God was only sham and pretense, then the aptest designation that can be applied to such a transgression is מְעִילָה (See commentary on Verse 15).

• • •

25. . . . Of all the laws deriving from those noted above we will single out two typical ones for closer consideration. These seem to be interrelated, and they appear to have an essential bearing on our proper understanding of what our attitude should be toward the Law of God. We are referring to the legal dictum that if a sacred object has been misused unintentionally, it becomes profane, whereas if the misuse was deliberate, the object retains its sacred character. Moreover, as is noted in *Torath Kohanim*, a "doubtful" transgression is even more in need of atonement than a clear-cut transgression. In the case of סָפֵק [a "doubtful" transgression] a standard valuation is set for the offering, whereas in the case of וַדַּאי [a clear-cut transgression] a nominal value is deemed sufficient (Zebaḥim 48a).

It is not deliberate desecration but only indifference that the Sanctuary of Judaism need fear from its children! This seems to be the thought expressed by the dictum that "if the misuse was unintentional, the object becomes profane, whereas if the misuse was deliberate, the object does not become profane." When the act of desecration was deliberate, the sacred object retains its inviolable sanctity, for the very fact that it was singled out for deliberate violation only proves that it is indeed holy. On the other hand, שְׁגָגָה, indifference, a thoughtless act of desecration committed because one has forgotten the sacred character of the object and what our conduct toward it should be—this would dig the grave for the holiness of the Sanctuary, because its throne, from which it is meant to direct and penetrate our lives, is founded solely upon the awareness of those who profess allegiance to it.

• • •

The Haftarah for this Sidra may be found on page 868.

צו

TZAV

VI 1. *God* spoke to Moshe [saying]: 2. Command Aharon and his sons as follows: This is the teaching with regard to the ascent offering: It is an ascent offering upon the place where the offerings are burned upon the altar all night until the morning, when the fire of the altar shall be rekindled upon it.

ו א וַיְדַבֵּר יְהוָה אֶל־מֹשֶׁה לֵּאמֹר׃ ב צַו אֶת־
אַהֲרֹן וְאֶת־בָּנָיו לֵאמֹר זֹאת תּוֹרַת הָעֹלָה הִוא
הָעֹלָה עַל מוֹקְדָה (מ זעירא) עַל־הַמִּזְבֵּחַ כָּל־
הַלַּיְלָה עַד־הַבֹּקֶר וְאֵשׁ הַמִּזְבֵּחַ תּוּקַד בּוֹ׃

CHAPTER VI

2. ***This is the teaching with regard to the ascent offering.*** These supplementary instructions to the priests regarding the manner in which they are to handle the offerings turned over to them begin with the laws applicable to the time span during which the Sanctuary of the Temple is given over exclusively to the priests but is closed to the rest of the nation: the hours of night.

° ° °

Night—לַיְלָה, the time when things are "commingled," when man, too, reverts to the bondage of physical forces, brings the heathen mind closer to its gods. At night the heathen believes he feels the power of the gods that hold him in bondage along with all other creatures. Conversely, he perceives יום, the day, the time of "standing erect,"[6] when man becomes aware of himself and resumes the struggle to subdue the physical world, as the time when man must take up anew the struggle against the gods.

By virtue of the Word of God, the position of Judaism is the direct antithesis to these notions. The Jew need not wait until night in order to feel the power of his God. He stands near to his God particularly when his mind is clear and when he is in the midst of his endeavors to subdue the world. He regards the lucidity of his clear mind, the energy of his free will and the results of his creative endeavors, indeed, all of his free personality that achieves its highest potential during his daily activities, as a gift from his Creator, the One sole God. By breathing into him a tiny spark from the infinite fullness of His own spirit that fills the world with His thoughts, from His own holy, unfettered will, from His own creative power that freely dominates the world which He Himself freely created, God has raised man high to Himself beyond the bonds of the physical world. God has thereby elevated man, made in God's image, to become a free personality, ruling freely over the world in the service of God and God's purposes. Precisely by implementing this power in his daily personal life does man fulfill the will of his God; only in this manner, uplifted and encouraged by God Himself, can man render his service to God in this world.

The heathen mentality sees daytime as the period when mortals must do battle against the might of the gods. To the Jews day is the time for action, for achievements in the service of God and for His approval. Hence in the Sanctuary of Judaism it is not night that drags day with it into the grave of mortality, but day that raises night with it into the eternity of a life of nearness to God. Physical nature is not the intermediary between the Jew and his God; man's personality stands high above physical nature and in direct proximity to God. For this reason it was in the wilderness, where man has nothing and no one but himself, that God came near to Israel. It was there that God established with Israel the covenant of His Law. It was there, in the wilderness, where man has nothing to offer to his God except himself, nothing but that which he bears within his own personality, that God first commanded Israel to make the offerings of its devotion to Him.

An unfettered personality that subordinates its thoughts, its aspirations and its achievements to God of its own free will: such is the personality to which God's command was addressed and which is a prerequisite for the offerings made to Him. "This is the teaching for the ascent offering, for the homage offering, for the offering that clears (him who brings it) of sin, and for the guilt offering; and for the offering of investiture and for the meal-of-peace offering, which *God* had already commanded to Moses on Mount Sinai on the day He made it obligatory for the sons of Yisrael to bring near their offerings to *God*, in the wilderness of Sinai" [Leviticus 7:37].

° ° °

4. . . . The law stated here, i.e. that the place where

[6]*Note to the English translation:* In his commentary on Genesis 1:5, which is not included in this excerpted edition, Hirsch explains that the noun יום [day] is related to the verb קום [to arise]. [G.H.]

3. The priest shall put his linen garments and his linen breeches upon his body and shall take up the ashes into which the fire has consumed the ascent offering upon the altar, and shall put them down at the side of the altar. 4. He shall then take off his garments and clothe himself in other garments and take the ashes out of the camp to a pure place. 5. And the fire for the altar shall be kindled upon it; it must not go out. Early in the morning the priest shall lay upon it [logs of] wood to burn [there]; he shall arrange the ascent offering upon it and shall make the fat parts of the peace offering go up in smoke on it. 6. Fire shall constantly be kindled upon the altar, where it must never go out. 7. And this is the teaching of the homage offering: Aharon's sons shall bring it near before *God* in front of the altar. 8. He shall take out from it his handful of the fine flour of the homage offering and of its oil, along with all the frankincense that is upon the homage offering, and he shall give its memorial portion to the altar to go up in smoke, as an expression of compliance, to *God*. 9. Whatever is left of it Aharon and his sons shall eat; it shall be eaten as *matzoth* in a holy place, in the forecourt of the Tent of Appointed

ג וְלָבַשׁ הַכֹּהֵן מִדּוֹ בַד וּמִכְנְסֵי־בַד יִלְבַּשׁ עַל־
בְּשָׂרוֹ וְהֵרִים אֶת־הַדֶּשֶׁן אֲשֶׁר תֹּאכַל הָאֵשׁ אֶת־
הָעֹלָה עַל־הַמִּזְבֵּחַ וְשָׂמוֹ אֵצֶל הַמִּזְבֵּחַ׃ ד וּפָשַׁט
אֶת־בְּגָדָיו וְלָבַשׁ בְּגָדִים אֲחֵרִים וְהוֹצִיא אֶת־
הַדֶּשֶׁן אֶל־מִחוּץ לַמַּחֲנֶה אֶל־מָקוֹם טָהוֹר׃
ה וְהָאֵשׁ עַל־הַמִּזְבֵּחַ תּוּקַד־בּוֹ לֹא תִכְבֶּה וּבִעֵר
עָלֶיהָ הַכֹּהֵן עֵצִים בַּבֹּקֶר בַּבֹּקֶר וְעָרַךְ עָלֶיהָ
הָעֹלָה וְהִקְטִיר עָלֶיהָ חֶלְבֵי הַשְּׁלָמִים׃ ו אֵשׁ
תָּמִיד תּוּקַד עַל־הַמִּזְבֵּחַ לֹא תִכְבֶּה׃ ס ז וְזֹאת
תּוֹרַת הַמִּנְחָה הַקְרֵב אֹתָהּ בְּנֵי־אַהֲרֹן לִפְנֵי
יְהוָה אֶל־פְּנֵי הַמִּזְבֵּחַ׃ ח וְהֵרִים מִמֶּנּוּ בְּקֻמְצוֹ
מִסֹּלֶת הַמִּנְחָה וּמִשַּׁמְנָהּ וְאֵת כָּל־הַלְּבֹנָה אֲשֶׁר
עַל־הַמִּנְחָה וְהִקְטִיר הַמִּזְבֵּחַ רֵיחַ נִיחֹחַ
אַזְכָּרָתָהּ לַיהוָה׃ ט וְהַנּוֹתֶרֶת מִמֶּנָּה יֹאכְלוּ
אַהֲרֹן וּבָנָיו מַצּוֹת תֵּאָכֵל בְּמָקוֹם קָדֹשׁ בַּחֲצַר

the offerings are burned must be cleared of all traces of the preceding day's offerings, that the place must be made ready for the service of the following day . . . is in all probability itself a part of the sacrificial service. (See *Mishneh LaMelekh*[7] to Maimonides, *Hilkhoth T'midim U'Musaphim*, 2:10). While the "taking up" of the ashes is meant to introduce the new day's service in terms of what was accomplished on the preceding day, as a permanent reminder of these past accomplishments, the removal of the ashes from the camp conveys the thought that, at the same time, the Jewish nation must begin its task anew each day. The start of every new day summons us to set out upon our task with full, renewed devotion as if we had never accomplished anything before. The memory of yesterday's accomplishments must not detract from the energy with which we must do our duty today. Thoughts of what has already been accomplished can spell death to what has yet to be done. Woe to him who rests upon his laurels in smug complacency, who does not begin the work of each new day with new, complete devotion as if it were the very first day of his life's work.

and take the ashes out. Every trace of yesterday's devotion is to be removed from the place upon the altar where the offerings were burned so that the next day's service may be begun on completely untouched ground, as it were. In light of the above, the law that the priests must wear humble, worn garb when they handle the products of the past day's functions, when they remove, and probably also "take up" the ashes, may be seen in its full significance. The past must recede into the background; it must not clothe us in pride as we set out upon the new task to which every new day summons us.

[7]*Note to the English translation: Mishneh LaMelekh* is a commentary on Maimonides' *Yad Hahazakah*. It was edited by Rabbi Yaakov Culi (1689–1732) from the writings of his teacher, Rabbi Yehuda Rosanes (1658–1727), chief rabbi of Constantinople. [G.H.]

° ° °

Meeting shall they eat it. 10. It must not be baked fermented; I have given it as their portion from the fire offerings made to Me; it is a holy of holies, like the offering that clears [him who brings it] of sin, and like the guilt offering. 11. Every male among the sons of Aharon may eat it; it is an everlasting due for your descendants from the fire offerings to *God*; everything that touches them shall become holy. 12. *God* spoke to Moshe [saying]: 13. This is the offering of Aharon and his sons which they shall bring near to *God*, each one on the day he was consecrated; one-tenth of an *ephah* of fine flour as a perpetual homage offering, half of it in the morning and half of it in the evening. 14. It shall be prepared upon a pan in oil; you shall bring it boiled to softness, baked variously after the manner of the homage offering that is to be broken into pieces shall you bring it near as an expression of compliance, to *God*. 15. The priest who will be anointed from among his sons in his place shall do it. It shall be given as an everlasting tribute to *God* to go up entirely in smoke. 16. Every homage offering of a priest, then, must be made [i.e., burned] in its entirety; it must not be eaten. 17. *God* spoke to Moshe [saying]: 18. Speak to Aharon and to his sons [saying]: This is the teaching of the offering that clears [him who brings it] of sin. At the place where the ascent offering is slaughtered shall the offering that clears [him who brings it] of sin also be slaughtered before

אֹהֶל־מוֹעֵד יֹאכְלוּהָ: י לֹא תֵאָפֶה חָמֵץ חֶלְקָם
נָתַתִּי אֹתָהּ מֵאִשָּׁי קֹדֶשׁ קָדָשִׁים הִוא כַּחַטָּאת
וְכָאָשָׁם: יא כָּל־זָכָר בִּבְנֵי אַהֲרֹן יֹאכְלֶנָּה חָק־
עוֹלָם לְדֹרֹתֵיכֶם מֵאִשֵּׁי יְהוָה כֹּל אֲשֶׁר־יִגַּע
בָּהֶם יִקְדָּשׁ: פ שני יב וַיְדַבֵּר יְהוָה אֶל־מֹשֶׁה
לֵּאמֹר: יג זֶה קָרְבַּן אַהֲרֹן וּבָנָיו אֲשֶׁר־יַקְרִיבוּ
לַיהוָה בְּיוֹם הִמָּשַׁח אֹתוֹ עֲשִׂירִת הָאֵפָה סֹלֶת
מִנְחָה תָּמִיד מַחֲצִיתָהּ בַּבֹּקֶר וּמַחֲצִיתָהּ בָּעָרֶב:
יד עַל־מַחֲבַת בַּשֶּׁמֶן תֵּעָשֶׂה מֻרְבֶּכֶת תְּבִיאֶנָּה
תֻּפִינֵי מִנְחַת פִּתִּים תַּקְרִיב רֵיחַ־נִיחֹחַ לַיהוָה:
טו וְהַכֹּהֵן הַמָּשִׁיחַ תַּחְתָּיו מִבָּנָיו יַעֲשֶׂה אֹתָהּ
חָק־עוֹלָם לַיהוָה כָּלִיל תָּקְטָר: טז וְכָל־מִנְחַת
כֹּהֵן כָּלִיל תִּהְיֶה לֹא תֵאָכֵל: פ יז וַיְדַבֵּר יְהוָה
אֶל־מֹשֶׁה לֵּאמֹר: יח דַּבֵּר אֶל־אַהֲרֹן וְאֶל־בָּנָיו
לֵאמֹר זֹאת תּוֹרַת הַחַטָּאת בִּמְקוֹם אֲשֶׁר
תִּשָּׁחֵט הָעֹלָה תִּשָּׁחֵט הַחַטָּאת לִפְנֵי יְהוָה קֹדֶשׁ

15. . . . The priest was to remember at all times that he must not perform the duties of his office for the sake of the material benefits it affords but that he must consider these benefits only as inevitable prerequisites for his physical existence, which he must dedicate entirely to the Divine purposes of his office. The Jewish priest saw his service as the sole purpose of his existence. However, he must not permit his functions to be bound up with his physical existence but must, instead, devote all his physical existence to the functions of his office.

16. ***Every homage offering of a priest, then, must be made in its entirety; it must not be eaten.*** Every individual member of the nation is expected to place all his material possessions at the feet of God, as it were, and then to permit the Sanctuary of the Law to take out its "handful," in order to "nourish" the Divine purpose on earth. It is this willingness to devote a part of his possessions to God's Sanctuary that makes a man a Jew. It also commends his material existence to God's remembrance and care and makes his own joy of living dependent on God's approval of his conduct. But in the case of the priest, not only part, but all of his existence, including all the material aspects of his life and prosperity, must be spent to serve God's purposes on earth. By his own exemplary conduct . . . he is to "prepare" (as is implied by the term *kohen* [from הָכֵן, "to prepare"]) a place for holiness on earth. There must be nothing unpriestly or unholy in him. Therefore, when he takes into the Sanctuary his "sustenance," his "prosperity" and his "comfort," as symbolized by his *minḥah* offering, he does not merely place a "memorial portion" of it upon God's altar but must allow all of it to be consumed by the fire of godliness on earth.

God; it is a holy of holies. 19. The priest whose function it is to offer it as an offering that clears [him who brings it] of sin shall eat it; in a holy place shall it be eaten, in the forecourt of the Tent of Appointed Meeting. 20. Anything that touches its flesh shall become holy, and if any of its blood splashes on a garment, you shall wash that on which it is splashed, in a holy place. 21. And an earthenware vessel in which it was cooked must be broken, but if it was cooked in a copper vessel, it shall be scoured and rinsed in water. 22. Every male among the priests shall eat it; it is a holy of holies. 23. Every offering that clears [him who brings it] of sin, of which any of the blood is brought into the Tent of Appointed Meeting in order to effect atonement in the Sanctuary, must not be eaten; it must be burned in fire.

VII 1. And this is the teaching with regard to the guilt offering: it is a holy of holies. 2. In the place where they slaughter the ascent offering they shall also slaughter the guilt offering, and he shall dash its blood round about upon the altar. 3. He shall bring near all of its fat, the tailpiece and the fat that covers the entrails, 4. the two kidneys and the fat that is attached to them, that is along the flanks; also the diaphragm upon the liver; he must remove it together with the kidneys. 5. The priest shall give them to the altar to go up in smoke, a fire offering to *God*: It is a guilt offering. 6. Every male among the priests shall eat of it. In a holy place shall it be eaten: it is a holy of holies. 7. As is the offering that clears [him who brings it] of sin, so is the guilt offering; one law applies for [both of] them: the priest who is to effect atonement with it, it shall be his. 8. And [as for] the priest who brings any man's ascent offering, the skin of the ascent offering that he has brought near shall belong to the priest; it shall be his. 9. Also every homage offering that is baked in the oven, and every one that is prepared in a deep pot and upon a pan shall belong to the priest who brings it near; it shall be his. 10. And likewise every homage offering, be it mixed with oil or dry, it shall belong to all sons of Aharon, one as well as another. 11. And this is

קָדָשִׁים הִוא: יט הַכֹּהֵן הַמְחַטֵּא אֹתָהּ יֹאכְלֶנָּה
בְּמָקוֹם קָדֹשׁ תֵּאָכֵל בַּחֲצַר אֹהֶל מוֹעֵד: כ כֹּל
אֲשֶׁר־יִגַּע בִּבְשָׂרָהּ יִקְדָּשׁ וַאֲשֶׁר יִזֶּה מִדָּמָהּ עַל־
הַבֶּגֶד אֲשֶׁר יִזֶּה עָלֶיהָ תְּכַבֵּס בְּמָקוֹם קָדֹשׁ:
כא וּכְלִי־חֶרֶשׂ אֲשֶׁר תְּבֻשַּׁל־בּוֹ יִשָּׁבֵר וְאִם־
בִּכְלִי נְחֹשֶׁת בֻּשָּׁלָה וּמֹרַק וְשֻׁטַּף בַּמָּיִם:
כב כָּל־זָכָר בַּכֹּהֲנִים יֹאכַל אֹתָהּ קֹדֶשׁ קָדָשִׁים
הִוא: כג וְכָל־חַטָּאת אֲשֶׁר יוּבָא מִדָּמָהּ אֶל־
אֹהֶל מוֹעֵד לְכַפֵּר בַּקֹּדֶשׁ לֹא תֵאָכֵל בָּאֵשׁ
תִּשָּׂרֵף: פ ז א וְזֹאת תּוֹרַת הָאָשָׁם קֹדֶשׁ
קָדָשִׁים הוּא: ב בִּמְקוֹם אֲשֶׁר יִשְׁחֲטוּ אֶת־
הָעֹלָה יִשְׁחֲטוּ אֶת־הָאָשָׁם וְאֶת־דָּמוֹ יִזְרֹק עַל־
הַמִּזְבֵּחַ סָבִיב: ג וְאֵת כָּל־חֶלְבּוֹ יַקְרִיב מִמֶּנּוּ
אֵת הָאַלְיָה וְאֶת־הַחֵלֶב הַמְכַסֶּה אֶת־הַקֶּרֶב:
ד וְאֵת שְׁתֵּי הַכְּלָיֹת וְאֶת־הַחֵלֶב אֲשֶׁר עֲלֵיהֶן
אֲשֶׁר עַל־הַכְּסָלִים וְאֶת־הַיֹּתֶרֶת עַל־הַכָּבֵד עַל־
הַכְּלָיֹת יְסִירֶנָּה: ה וְהִקְטִיר אֹתָם הַכֹּהֵן
הַמִּזְבֵּחָה אִשֶּׁה לַיהוָה אָשָׁם הוּא: ו כָּל־זָכָר
בַּכֹּהֲנִים יֹאכְלֶנּוּ בְּמָקוֹם קָדוֹשׁ יֵאָכֵל קֹדֶשׁ
קָדָשִׁים הוּא: ז כַּחַטָּאת כָּאָשָׁם תּוֹרָה אַחַת
לָהֶם הַכֹּהֵן אֲשֶׁר יְכַפֶּר־בּוֹ לוֹ יִהְיֶה: ח וְהַכֹּהֵן
הַמַּקְרִיב אֶת־עֹלַת אִישׁ עוֹר הָעֹלָה אֲשֶׁר
הִקְרִיב לַכֹּהֵן לוֹ יִהְיֶה: ט וְכָל־מִנְחָה אֲשֶׁר
תֵּאָפֶה בַּתַּנּוּר וְכָל־נַעֲשָׂה בַמַּרְחֶשֶׁת וְעַל־
מַחֲבַת לַכֹּהֵן הַמַּקְרִיב אֹתָהּ לוֹ תִהְיֶה: י וְכָל־
מִנְחָה בְלוּלָה־בַשֶּׁמֶן וַחֲרֵבָה לְכָל־בְּנֵי אַהֲרֹן
תִּהְיֶה אִישׁ כְּאָחִיו: פ שלישי יא וְזֹאת תּוֹרַת

the teaching of the meal-of-peace offering which he brings near to *God*.   12. If he offers it by reason of thanksgiving, he shall bring near with the offering of thanksgiving, *matzah* loaves mixed with oil and thin *matzah* wafers brushed with oil, and loaves of bread made from fine flour boiled to softness, mixed with oil.   13. He shall bring his offering together with loaves of leavened bread, together with his meal-of-peace offering of thanksgiving.   14. He shall bring from it one out of each offering as an uplifted donation to *God*; it shall belong to the priest who dashes the blood of the peace offering [upon the altar].   15. And the flesh of his meal-of-peace offering of thanksgiving shall be eaten on the day it is offered; he must not leave any of it until the morning.   16. But if his meal offering is [occasioned by] a vow or a free-will offering, it shall be eaten on the day it is brought near as an offering, and on the next day whatever is left of it may be eaten also.   17. But whatever is left of the flesh of the meal offering shall be burned in fire on the third day.   18. And if any of the flesh of his meal-of-peace offering should be eaten on the third day, it will not be accepted for him who offers it as being in accordance with the Divine will. It will not be credited to him. It shall be an abominable thing. The person who eats [any] of it shall bear his iniquity.   19. Also the flesh that touches any unclean thing shall not be eaten; it shall be burned in fire. As for the

זֶבַח הַשְּׁלָמִים אֲשֶׁר יַקְרִיב לַיהֹוָה: יב אִם עַל־
תּוֹדָה יַקְרִיבֶנּוּ וְהִקְרִיב | עַל־זֶבַח הַתּוֹדָה חַלּוֹת
מַצּוֹת בְּלוּלֹת בַּשֶּׁמֶן וּרְקִיקֵי מַצּוֹת מְשֻׁחִים
בַּשָּׁמֶן וְסֹלֶת מֻרְבֶּכֶת חַלֹּת בְּלוּלֹת בַּשָּׁמֶן:
יג עַל־חַלֹּת לֶחֶם חָמֵץ יַקְרִיב קָרְבָּנוֹ עַל־זֶבַח
תּוֹדַת שְׁלָמָיו: יד וְהִקְרִיב מִמֶּנּוּ אֶחָד מִכָּל־
קָרְבָּן תְּרוּמָה לַיהֹוָה לַכֹּהֵן הַזֹּרֵק אֶת־דַּם
הַשְּׁלָמִים לוֹ יִהְיֶה: טו וּבְשַׂר זֶבַח תּוֹדַת שְׁלָמָיו
בְּיוֹם קָרְבָּנוֹ יֵאָכֵל לֹא־יַנִּיחַ מִמֶּנּוּ עַד־בֹּקֶר:
טז וְאִם־נֶדֶר | אוֹ נְדָבָה זֶבַח קָרְבָּנוֹ בְּיוֹם
הַקְרִיבוֹ אֶת־זִבְחוֹ יֵאָכֵל וּמִמָּחֳרָת וְהַנּוֹתָר
מִמֶּנּוּ יֵאָכֵל: יז וְהַנּוֹתָר מִבְּשַׂר הַזָּבַח בַּיּוֹם
הַשְּׁלִישִׁי בָּאֵשׁ יִשָּׂרֵף: יח וְאִם הֵאָכֹל יֵאָכֵל
מִבְּשַׂר־זֶבַח שְׁלָמָיו בַּיּוֹם הַשְּׁלִישִׁי לֹא יֵרָצֶה
הַמַּקְרִיב אֹתוֹ לֹא יֵחָשֵׁב לוֹ פִּגּוּל יִהְיֶה וְהַנֶּפֶשׁ
הָאֹכֶלֶת מִמֶּנּוּ עֲוֺנָהּ תִּשָּׂא: יט וְהַבָּשָׂר אֲשֶׁר יִגַּע
בְּכָל־טָמֵא לֹא יֵאָכֵל בָּאֵשׁ יִשָּׂרֵף וְהַבָּשָׂר כָּל־

CHAPTER VII

12–14. *If he offers it by reason of thanksgiving*. In Chapter 3 we have already learned about the שְׁלָמִים [peace] offering. We believe we may define this offering as the symbolic expression of a personality which feels that it is in a state of שָׁלֵם [completeness], that it lacks for nothing and which seeks the nearness of God in and with this state of being "at peace." What is presented to us now is a special type of שְׁלָמִים offering, one occasioned by a situation in which the individual's state of שָׁלֵם had been threatened and regained.

Thus Psalm 107 names אַרְבָּעָה צְרִיכִין לְהוֹדוֹת, four types of individuals who are duty bound to give thanks to God in public: Those who were saved from the wilder-

ness, those who were freed from prison, those who have recovered from an illness and those who were rescued from the perils of the sea. These people are to avow their thanks to God for His loving-kindness and to acknowledge among men the miracles He performed; they are to make offerings of thanksgiving and to recount with rejoicing what God did for them. Clearly the phrase, "If he offers it by reason of thanksgiving," which refers to the teaching with regard to the peace offering, characterizes תּוֹדָה [the offering of thanksgiving] as belonging to the category of שְׁלָמִים [meal-of-peace offerings]. For this reason we are given here only the requirements unique to the תּוֹדָה; all the other requirements for שְׁלָמִים are applicable also to the תּוֹדָה.

∘   ∘   ∘

flesh, any person who is pure may eat of it. 20. But the person who eats of the flesh of the meal-of-peace offering that is *God's*, and his uncleanness is upon him, that person shall be uprooted from among his people. 21. A person who touches anything unclean, the uncleanness of a human being, an unclean animal, or some unclean creeping thing, and he eats of the flesh of the meal-of-peace offering that is *God's*, that person shall be uprooted from among his people. 22. *God* spoke to Moshe [saying]: 23. Speak to the sons of Yisrael [saying]: You shall not eat any fat of oxen, sheep or goats. 24. And the fat of an animal that has died of itself and the fat of that which was seized to be devoured may be used for any other purpose, but for [both] these reasons you must not eat it. 25. For whoever eats the fat of an animal of which a fire offering can be brought near to *God*, that person who eats it shall be uprooted from among his people. 26. And you shall eat no kind of blood in all your dwelling places, whether it be of bird or of livestock. 27. Any person who eats any kind of blood, that person shall be uprooted from among his people. 28. *God* spoke to Moshe [saying]: 29. Speak to the sons of Yisrael [saying]: He who brings a meal-of-peace offering near to *God* shall bring to *God* his offering from his meal-of-peace offering.

טָה֖וֹר יֹאכַ֥ל בָּשָֽׂר׃ כ וְהַנֶּ֜פֶשׁ אֲשֶׁר־תֹּאכַ֣ל בָּשָׂ֗ר מִזֶּ֤בַח הַשְּׁלָמִים֙ אֲשֶׁ֣ר לַֽיהֹוָ֔ה וְטֻמְאָת֖וֹ עָלָ֑יו וְנִכְרְתָ֛ה הַנֶּ֥פֶשׁ הַהִ֖וא מֵֽעַמֶּֽיהָ׃ כא וְנֶ֜פֶשׁ כִּֽי־תִגַּ֣ע בְּכָל־טָמֵ֗א בְּטֻמְאַ֤ת אָדָם֙ א֣וֹ ׀ בִּבְהֵמָ֣ה טְמֵאָ֗ה א֚וֹ בְּכָל־שֶׁ֣קֶץ טָמֵ֔א וְאָכַ֛ל מִבְּשַׂר־זֶ֥בַח הַשְּׁלָמִ֖ים אֲשֶׁ֣ר לַֽיהֹוָ֑ה וְנִכְרְתָ֛ה הַנֶּ֥פֶשׁ הַהִ֖וא מֵֽעַמֶּֽיהָ׃ כב וַיְדַבֵּ֥ר יְהֹוָ֖ה אֶל־מֹשֶׁ֥ה לֵּאמֹֽר׃ כג דַּבֵּ֞ר אֶל־בְּנֵ֤י יִשְׂרָאֵל֙ לֵאמֹ֔ר כָּל־חֵ֜לֶב שׁ֥וֹר וְכֶ֛שֶׂב וָעֵ֖ז לֹ֥א תֹאכֵֽלוּ׃ כד וְחֵ֤לֶב נְבֵלָה֙ וְחֵ֣לֶב טְרֵפָ֔ה יֵעָשֶׂ֖ה לְכָל־מְלָאכָ֑ה וְאָכֹ֖ל לֹ֥א תֹֽאכְלֻֽהוּ׃ כה כִּ֚י כָּל־אֹכֵ֣ל חֵ֔לֶב מִן־הַבְּהֵמָ֔ה אֲשֶׁ֨ר יַקְרִ֥יב מִמֶּ֛נָּה אִשֶּׁ֖ה לַֽיהֹוָ֑ה וְנִכְרְתָ֛ה הַנֶּ֥פֶשׁ הָאֹכֶ֖לֶת מֵֽעַמֶּֽיהָ׃ כו וְכָל־דָּם֙ לֹ֣א תֹֽאכְל֔וּ בְּכֹ֖ל מֽוֹשְׁבֹתֵיכֶ֑ם לָע֖וֹף וְלַבְּהֵמָֽה׃ כז כָּל־נֶ֖פֶשׁ אֲשֶׁר־תֹּאכַ֣ל כָּל־דָּ֑ם וְנִכְרְתָ֛ה הַנֶּ֥פֶשׁ הַהִ֖וא מֵֽעַמֶּֽיהָ׃ פ כח וַיְדַבֵּ֥ר יְהֹוָ֖ה אֶל־מֹשֶׁ֥ה לֵּאמֹֽר׃ כט דַּבֵּ֞ר אֶל־בְּנֵ֤י יִשְׂרָאֵל֙ לֵאמֹ֔ר הַמַּקְרִ֛יב אֶת־זֶ֥בַח שְׁלָמָ֖יו לַֽיהֹוָ֑ה יָבִ֤יא אֶת־קָרְבָּנוֹ֙ לַֽיהֹוָ֔ה מִזֶּ֖בַח שְׁלָמָֽיו׃

19–21. . . . It is obvious that טוּמְאָה is a "lack of freedom." Its transmission to a human being who has been called to moral freedom can be set off by any natural phenomenon in which organic life succumbs to a physical force. The most striking example of such a phenomenon, of course, is a dead body. . . .

טָמֵא would be that which has given up its freedom of vital, independent existence (in Aramaic טַמְיָא actually denotes the bone of a dead body); the symbolic connotation would be anything that tends to destroy the moral freedom and independence of him who comes in contact with it. . . .

26. . . . The words "in all your dwelling places" make it clear that, just as in the prohibition against eating חֵלֶב [hard fat], the blood of animals fit for use as offerings is not the only forbidden blood. Moreover, the

words "whether it be of bird or of livestock" extends the prohibition to include all higher mammals, בְּהֵמָה וְחַיָּה [livestock and undomesticated animals] and all birds.

29. *He who brings.* This teaching with regard to the wave offering and the offering of breast and thigh clearly stresses the significance of זֶבַח as a "meal" offering. The thought conveyed here is as follows: He who wishes to bring near to God the meal that symbolizes the peace he enjoys must bring his offering from that meal; i.e., he must make God a participant, as it were, in his meal. His enjoyment of the peace that has been given him must not have only a negative quality in that it is free of selfish motivations, but also a positive effect in that he channels the enjoyment of his happiness into action for the promotion of God's purposes.

30. His [own] hands shall bring the fire offerings to *God*; the fat upon the breast, he [himself] shall bring it, [and] the breast, in order to perform with it a waving before *God*.   31. The priest shall give the fat to the altar to go up in smoke and the breast shall then belong to Aharon and his sons.   32. And the right thigh you shall give as an uplifted donation to the priest from your meal-of-peace offerings.   33. One among the sons of Aharon who brings near the blood of the peace offering and the fat, he shall have the right thigh as a portion.   34. For I have taken the breast of the wave [offering] and the thigh of the uplifted donation from the sons of Yisrael from their meal-of-peace offerings and I have given them to Aharon the priest and to his sons as an everlasting due from the sons of Yisrael.   35. This is the consecration of

ל יָדָיו תְּבִיאֶ֫ינָה אֵת אִשֵּׁי יְהֹוָה אֶת־הַחֵ֫לֶב עַל־
הֶֽחָזֶה יְבִיאֶ֫נּוּ אֵת הֶֽחָזֶה לְהָנִיף אֹתוֹ תְּנוּפָה
לִפְנֵי יְהֹוָה: לא וְהִקְטִיר הַכֹּהֵן אֶת־הַחֵ֫לֶב
הַמִּזְבֵּ֫חָה וְהָיָה הֶֽחָזֶה לְאַהֲרֹן וּלְבָנָיו: לב וְאֵת
שׁוֹק הַיָּמִין תִּתְּנוּ תְרוּמָה לַכֹּהֵן מִזִּבְחֵי
שַׁלְמֵיכֶם: לג הַמַּקְרִיב אֶת־דַּם הַשְּׁלָמִים וְאֶת־
הַחֵ֫לֶב מִבְּנֵי אַהֲרֹן לוֹ תִהְיֶה שׁוֹק הַיָּמִין לְמָנָה:
לד כִּי אֶת־חֲזֵה הַתְּנוּפָה וְאֵת | שׁוֹק הַתְּרוּמָה
לָקַ֫חְתִּי מֵאֵת בְּנֵי־יִשְׂרָאֵל מִזִּבְחֵי שַׁלְמֵיהֶם
וָאֶתֵּן אֹתָם לְאַהֲרֹן הַכֹּהֵן וּלְבָנָיו לְחָק־עוֹלָם
מֵאֵת בְּנֵי יִשְׂרָאֵל: לה זֹאת מִשְׁחַת אַהֲרֹן

32. . . . The breast symbolically represents all of man's thoughts and aspirations; hence, on the one hand, the moral and spiritual source of all human accomplishments achieved in moral freedom of will, and on the other hand, that aspect of the human character which forms the true basis of the priest's functions. For all our thoughts and aspirations should come into flower beneath the radiance of God's Law, which is represented by the priest. If, with all the moral energy of our free will, we will devote all the aspirations of our lives, and all our impulses directed toward the attainment of these aspirations, to become "nourishment for godliness on earth," as symbolically taught by the burning of the soft parts of the offering upon the altar, then this act in itself represents a fruit, as it were, of our thoughts and aspirations, which has ripened only thanks to the Law of God that is to be nurtured by the priest. When we offer up the soft parts of the peace offering that reflects our personal happiness, it is only logical that the priest should receive the breast. It is our symbolic acknowledgment that, if the outlook and the aims of life symbolized by the offering of the soft parts form the true core of our personal happiness, then we owe this mentality and its implementation in our lives to the Law of God, which was entrusted to the priests.

The thigh, on the other hand, is a symbolic expression of physical strength and forward movement. . . . As such, it symbolizes all the concrete power and strength of man, which seem to derive from the influence of the priestly functions no more than do the riches of the soil — although there, also, for each stage of the harvest, a symbolic donation must be made to the priest in the form of first fruits, uplifted donations and חַלָּה (one

kernel is sufficient to fulfill the requirements of this law) in order to acknowledge that the blessings of material prosperity, too, derive from the Law of God, which is represented by the priest, and to remind us that even the blessings of material prosperity should be used first of all to promote the knowledge of God's Law which the priest represents.

Scripture for the most part refers to this symbolic acknowledgement and reminder as תְּרוּמָה. It is a "lifting up" of material things for godly, moral and spiritual purposes. If, therefore, the individual who feels happy and content offers the right thigh of the meal-of-peace offering as a תְּרוּמָה [uplifted donation] to the priest, he does so with the same twofold intent: To symbolize his acknowledgment that his material happiness and prosperity are based only on the moral foundation of God's Law which is represented by the priest, and to pledge, symbolically, that he will permit the strength of his thigh, the physical power afforded him by his good fortune, to serve only for the support and implementation of the Law of God which the priest represents. Hence the difference between the concepts implicit in the donation of the חָזֶה [breast] and that of the שׁוֹק [thigh] to the priest. It is logical that he should receive the חָזֶה, but he receives the שׁוֹק only as an "uplifted donation." Hence . . . throughout Scripture, the terms חֲזֵה הַתְּנוּפָה ["the breast of the wave (offering)"] and שׁוֹק הַתְּרוּמָה ["the thigh of the uplifted donation"], although in fact, both motions, תְּנוּפָה [waving] and תְּרוּמָה [lifting], are performed in the case of both.

35. **This is the consecration of Aharon.** This gift of the breast and thigh from the nation's meal-of-peace

Aharon and the consecration of his sons from the fire offerings to *God*, on the day on which He caused them to come nearer to serve *God* as priests. 36. It is this that *God* commanded on the day He consecrated them, that it shall be given them by the sons of Yisrael: an everlasting statute for their descendants. 37. This is the teaching for the ascent offering, for the homage offering, for the offering that clears [him who brings it] of sin and for the guilt offering; and for the offering of investiture and for the meal-of-peace offering, 38. which *God* had already commanded to Moshe on Mount Sinai, on the day He made it obligatory for the sons of Yisrael to bring near their offerings to *God*, in the wilderness of Sinai.

VIII

1. *God* spoke to Moshe [saying]: 2. "Take Aharon and his sons with him, and the garments and the anointing oil; the bull of the offering that clears [him who brings it] of sin and the two rams and the basket of *matzoth*, 3. and gather the entire community together at the entrance of the Tent of Appointed Meeting." 4. Moshe did as *God* had commanded him and the community gathered at the entrance of the Tent of Appointed Meeting. 5. And Moshe said to the community: "This is the utterance which *God* has commanded

וּמִשְׁחַ֣ת בָּנָ֗יו מֵאִשֵּׁ֤י יְהֹוָה֙ בְּיוֹם֙ הִקְרִ֣יב אֹתָ֔ם לְכַהֵ֖ן לַֽיהֹוָֽה: לו אֲשֶׁר֩ צִוָּ֨ה יְהֹוָ֜ה לָתֵ֣ת לָהֶ֗ם בְּיוֹם֙ מָשְׁח֣וֹ אֹתָ֔ם מֵאֵ֖ת בְּנֵ֣י יִשְׂרָאֵ֑ל חֻקַּ֥ת עוֹלָ֖ם לְדֹֽרֹתָֽם: לז זֹ֣את הַתּוֹרָ֗ה לָֽעֹלָה֙ לַמִּנְחָ֔ה וְלַֽחַטָּ֖את וְלָֽאָשָׁ֑ם וְלַ֨מִּלּוּאִ֔ים וּלְזֶ֖בַח הַשְּׁלָמִֽים: לח אֲשֶׁ֨ר צִוָּ֧ה יְהֹוָ֛ה אֶת־מֹשֶׁ֖ה בְּהַ֣ר סִינָ֑י בְּי֗וֹם צַוֺּתוֹ֙ אֶת־בְּנֵ֣י יִשְׂרָאֵ֔ל לְהַקְרִ֥יב אֶת־קָרְבְּנֵיהֶ֖ם לַֽיהֹוָ֑ה בְּמִדְבַּ֖ר סִינָֽי: פ רביעי ח א וַיְדַבֵּ֥ר יְהֹוָ֖ה אֶל־מֹשֶׁ֥ה לֵּאמֹֽר: ב קַ֤ח אֶֽת־אַהֲרֹן֙ וְאֶת־בָּנָ֣יו אִתּ֔וֹ וְאֵת֙ הַבְּגָדִ֔ים וְאֵ֖ת שֶׁ֣מֶן הַמִּשְׁחָ֑ה וְאֵ֣ת ׀ פַּ֣ר הַֽחַטָּ֗את וְאֵת֙ שְׁנֵ֣י הָֽאֵילִ֔ים וְאֵ֖ת סַ֥ל הַמַּצּֽוֹת: ג וְאֵ֥ת כָּל־הָֽעֵדָ֖ה הַקְהֵ֑ל אֶל־פֶּ֖תַח אֹ֥הֶל מוֹעֵֽד: ד וַיַּ֣עַשׂ מֹשֶׁ֔ה כַּֽאֲשֶׁ֛ר צִוָּ֥ה יְהֹוָ֖ה אֹת֑וֹ וַתִּקָּהֵל֙ הָֽעֵדָ֔ה אֶל־פֶּ֖תַח אֹ֥הֶל מוֹעֵֽד: ה וַיֹּ֥אמֶר מֹשֶׁ֖ה אֶל־הָֽעֵדָ֑ה זֶ֣ה הַדָּבָ֔ר אֲשֶׁר־צִוָּ֥ה יְהֹוָ֖ה לַֽעֲשֽׂוֹת:

---

offerings represents a constant renewal of the original consecration of the priests. The gift reminds the priest that he should view the nation's "breast," i.e., the nation's thoughts and aspirations, as the true sphere of his functions, that he should regard the nation's strength, as symbolized by the thigh, as the support and implementor of his teachings, and that the climate in which the seeds of the teachings of his Sanctuary will thrive is not one of contrition and gloom but one of good cheer, of vibrant joy in the awareness of a life lived in the presence of God. At the same time, the gift to the priest should remind the nation that, although the priest makes no direct, tangible contribution to the nation's prosperity, the prosperity of every single member of the nation is derived from the spiritual treasure of God that has been entrusted to the priest. A man's happiness and prosperity have a firm foundation only if his "breast" belongs to the Law of God, and they have meaning and value only if he will use also his "thigh," the concrete power of his position, for the safe-

guarding and realization of the Law of God that is nurtured by the priest.

○   ○

37–38. *which God had already commanded to Moshe.* The laws concerning the offerings which were proclaimed here "from the Tent of Appointed Meeting" (Leviticus 1:1) had already been set forth to Moses on Mount Sinai along with all the other laws, of which these form a basic, integral part. They are neither a transient concession made to a generation still under the influence of paganism, nor do they constitute a separate chapter of magic mystery. They are מִצְוָה, law, like all the rest of the Law. Their purpose is to educate the nation for the ideals of the Law and to preserve the nation through the Law. For this reason they were already given on Mount Sinai along with all the other laws. They were reiterated from the Tent of the Appointed Meeting after the erection of the Sanctuary only because they represented institutions explicitly associated with the Sanctuary.

to be carried out." 6. Thereupon Moshe made Aharon and his sons come nearer, bathed them in water, 7. put upon him the tunic, girded him with the sash, clothed him with the robe, put upon him the *ephod*, girded him with the band of the *ephod* and encircled him with it. 8. He placed the breastplate upon him and put the Urim and the Thummim into the breastplate. 9. He placed the turban upon his head and upon the turban, in front, he placed the golden showplate, the diadem of the Sanctuary, as *God* had commanded Moshe. 10. Then Moshe took the anointing oil and anointed the Dwelling Place and all that was within it, and sanctified them. 11. He sprinkled [some] of it upon the altar seven times and anointed the altar and all its utensils, and the basin and its base, to sanctify them. 12. He poured [some] of the anointing oil upon Aharon's head and anointed him, to sanctify him. 13. And Moshe made Aharon's sons draw nearer, clothed them with the tunics, girded them with a sash and bound tall turbans upon them, as *God* had commanded Moshe. 14. He then brought closer the bull of the offering that clears [him who brings it] of sin; Aharon and his sons leaned their hands upon the head of the bull of the offering that clears [him who brings it] of sin. 15. He slaughtered [it] and Moshe took the blood and placed [some] of it with his finger upon the elevated corners of the altar round about and purged the altar of sin; and he poured the [rest of the] blood into the base of the altar and sanctified the altar so that atonement could be effected upon it. 16. He took all the fat that is attached to the entrails, the diaphragm of the liver and the two kidneys along with their fat, and Moshe gave it to the altar to go up in smoke. 17. But the bull, along with its skin, its flesh and its dung, he burned in fire outside the camp, as *God* had commanded Moshe. 18. He thereupon brought near the ram of the ascent offering, and Aharon and his sons leaned their hands upon the head of the ram. 19. He slaughtered [it] and Moshe dashed the blood round about upon the altar. 20. And he cut up the ram into its parts,

ו וַיַּקְרֵב מֹשֶׁה אֶת־אַהֲרֹן וְאֶת־בָּנָיו וַיִּרְחַץ אֹתָם בַּמָּיִם: ז וַיִּתֵּן עָלָיו אֶת־הַכֻּתֹּנֶת וַיַּחְגֹּר אֹתוֹ בָּאַבְנֵט וַיַּלְבֵּשׁ אֹתוֹ אֶת־הַמְּעִיל וַיִּתֵּן עָלָיו אֶת־הָאֵפֹד וַיַּחְגֹּר אֹתוֹ בְּחֵשֶׁב הָאֵפֹד וַיֶּאְפֹּד לוֹ בּוֹ: ח וַיָּשֶׂם עָלָיו אֶת־הַחֹשֶׁן וַיִּתֵּן אֶל־הַחֹשֶׁן אֶת־הָאוּרִים וְאֶת־הַתֻּמִּים: ט וַיָּשֶׂם אֶת־הַמִּצְנֶפֶת עַל־רֹאשׁוֹ וַיָּשֶׂם עַל־הַמִּצְנֶפֶת אֶל־מוּל פָּנָיו אֵת צִיץ הַזָּהָב נֵזֶר הַקֹּדֶשׁ כַּאֲשֶׁר צִוָּה יְהֹוָה אֶת־מֹשֶׁה: י וַיִּקַּח מֹשֶׁה אֶת־שֶׁמֶן הַמִּשְׁחָה וַיִּמְשַׁח אֶת־הַמִּשְׁכָּן וְאֶת־כָּל־אֲשֶׁר־בּוֹ וַיְקַדֵּשׁ אֹתָם: יא וַיַּז מִמֶּנּוּ עַל־הַמִּזְבֵּחַ שֶׁבַע פְּעָמִים וַיִּמְשַׁח אֶת־הַמִּזְבֵּחַ וְאֶת־כָּל־כֵּלָיו וְאֶת־הַכִּיֹּר וְאֶת־כַּנּוֹ לְקַדְּשָׁם: יב וַיִּצֹק מִשֶּׁמֶן הַמִּשְׁחָה עַל רֹאשׁ אַהֲרֹן וַיִּמְשַׁח אֹתוֹ לְקַדְּשׁוֹ: יג וַיַּקְרֵב מֹשֶׁה אֶת־בְּנֵי אַהֲרֹן וַיַּלְבִּשֵׁם כֻּתֳּנֹת וַיַּחְגֹּר אֹתָם אַבְנֵט וַיַּחֲבֹשׁ לָהֶם מִגְבָּעוֹת כַּאֲשֶׁר צִוָּה יְהֹוָה אֶת־מֹשֶׁה: חמישי יד וַיַּגֵּשׁ אֵת פַּר הַחַטָּאת וַיִּסְמֹךְ אַהֲרֹן וּבָנָיו אֶת־יְדֵיהֶם עַל־רֹאשׁ פַּר הַחַטָּאת: טו וַיִּשְׁחָט וַיִּקַּח מֹשֶׁה אֶת־הַדָּם וַיִּתֵּן עַל־קַרְנוֹת הַמִּזְבֵּחַ סָבִיב בְּאֶצְבָּעוֹ וַיְחַטֵּא אֶת־הַמִּזְבֵּחַ וְאֶת־הַדָּם יָצַק אֶל־יְסוֹד הַמִּזְבֵּחַ וַיְקַדְּשֵׁהוּ לְכַפֵּר עָלָיו: טז וַיִּקַּח אֶת־כָּל־הַחֵלֶב אֲשֶׁר עַל־הַקֶּרֶב וְאֵת יֹתֶרֶת הַכָּבֵד וְאֶת־שְׁתֵּי הַכְּלָיֹת וְאֶת־חֶלְבְּהֶן וַיַּקְטֵר מֹשֶׁה הַמִּזְבֵּחָה: יז וְאֶת־הַפָּר וְאֶת־עֹרוֹ וְאֶת־בְּשָׂרוֹ וְאֶת־פִּרְשׁוֹ שָׂרַף בָּאֵשׁ מִחוּץ לַמַּחֲנֶה כַּאֲשֶׁר צִוָּה יְהֹוָה אֶת־מֹשֶׁה: יח וַיַּקְרֵב אֵת אֵיל הָעֹלָה וַיִּסְמְכוּ אַהֲרֹן וּבָנָיו אֶת־יְדֵיהֶם עַל־רֹאשׁ הָאָיִל: יט וַיִּשְׁחָט וַיִּזְרֹק מֹשֶׁה אֶת־הַדָּם עַל־הַמִּזְבֵּחַ סָבִיב: כ וְאֶת־הָאַיִל נִתַּח לִנְתָחָיו

and Moshe gave the head, the parts and the fat to go up in smoke. 21. He washed the entrails and the legs in water, and Moshe gave the entire ram to the altar to go up in smoke. It is an ascent offering to express compliance; it is a fire offering to *God*, as *God* had commanded Moshe. 22. He then brought near the second ram, the ram of investiture, and Aharon and his sons leaned their hands upon the head of the ram. 23. He slaughtered [it], and Moshe took [some] of its blood and placed it upon the right earlobe of Aharon, upon the thumb of his right hand and upon the big toe of his right foot. 24. He then made the sons of Aharon draw closer, and Moshe placed [some] of the blood upon their right earlobes, upon the thumbs of their right hands and upon the big toes of their right feet, and Moshe dashed the blood round about upon the altar. 25. He took the fat, the tailpiece and all the fat that is attached to the entrails, the diaphragm of the liver, and the two kidneys along with their fat, and the right thigh; 26. he took from the basket of *matzoth* that stood before *God* one *matzah* loaf, one loaf of oil bread, and one thin wafer and placed it upon the fat parts and upon the right thigh, 27. and put it all upon the hands of Aharon and upon the hands of his sons, and he waved them as a wave [offering] before *God*. 28. Moshe then took them from their hands and gave them to the altar to go up in smoke, upon the ascent offering; they are offerings of investiture, to express compliance; it is a fire offering to *God*. 29. Moshe then took the breast, waved it as a wave [offering] before *God*. This was Moshe's portion of the ram of investiture, as *God* had commanded Moshe. 30. Last of all, Moshe took [some] of the anointing oil and of the blood that was upon the altar and sprinkled it upon Aharon, upon his garments, upon his sons and upon the garments of his sons, and he sanctified Aharon, his garments, his sons and the garments of his sons with him. 31. Then Moshe said to Aharon and to his sons: "Cook the flesh at the entrance of the Tent of Appointed Meeting and there you shall eat it and the bread that is in the basket of the investiture

וַיַּקְטֵ֤ר מֹשֶׁה֙ אֶת־הָרֹ֔אשׁ וְאֶת־הַנְּתָחִ֖ים וְאֶת־הַפָּֽדֶר: כא וְאֶת־הַקֶּ֤רֶב וְאֶת־הַכְּרָעַ֖יִם רָחַ֣ץ בַּמָּ֑יִם וַיַּקְטֵר֩ מֹשֶׁ֨ה אֶת־כָּל־הָאַ֜יִל הַמִּזְבֵּ֗חָה עֹלָ֨ה ה֤וּא לְרֵֽיחַ־נִיחֹ֙חַ֙ אִשֶּׁ֥ה הוּא֙ לַֽיהֹוָ֔ה כַּאֲשֶׁ֛ר צִוָּ֥ה יְהֹוָ֖ה אֶת־מֹשֶֽׁה: ששי כב וַיַּקְרֵב֙ אֶת־הָאַ֣יִל הַשֵּׁנִ֔י אֵ֖יל הַמִּלֻּאִ֑ים וַֽיִּסְמְכ֞וּ אַהֲרֹ֧ן וּבָנָ֛יו אֶת־יְדֵיהֶ֖ם עַל־רֹ֥אשׁ הָאָֽיִל: כג וַיִּשְׁחָ֓ט | וַיִּקַּ֤ח מֹשֶׁה֙ מִדָּמ֔וֹ וַיִּתֵּ֛ן עַל־תְּנ֥וּךְ אֹֽזֶן־אַהֲרֹ֖ן הַיְמָנִ֑ית וְעַל־בֹּ֤הֶן יָדוֹ֙ הַיְמָנִ֔ית וְעַל־בֹּ֥הֶן רַגְל֖וֹ הַיְמָנִֽית: כד וַיַּקְרֵ֞ב אֶת־בְּנֵ֣י אַהֲרֹ֗ן וַיִּתֵּ֨ן מֹשֶׁ֤ה מִן־הַדָּם֙ עַל־תְּנ֤וּךְ אָזְנָם֙ הַיְמָנִ֔ית וְעַל־בֹּ֤הֶן יָדָם֙ הַיְמָנִ֔ית וְעַל־בֹּ֥הֶן רַגְלָ֖ם הַיְמָנִ֑ית וַיִּזְרֹ֨ק מֹשֶׁ֧ה אֶת־הַדָּ֛ם עַל־הַמִּזְבֵּ֖חַ סָבִֽיב: כה וַיִּקַּ֞ח אֶת־הַחֵ֣לֶב וְאֶת־הָ֣אַלְיָ֗ה וְאֶֽת־כָּל־הַחֵ֘לֶב֮ אֲשֶׁ֣ר עַל־הַקֶּ֒רֶב֒ וְאֵת֙ יֹתֶ֣רֶת הַכָּבֵ֔ד וְאֶת־שְׁתֵּ֥י הַכְּלָיֹ֖ת וְאֶת־חֶלְבְּהֶ֑ן וְאֵ֖ת שׁ֥וֹק הַיָּמִֽין: כו וּמִסַּ֣ל הַמַּצּ֗וֹת אֲשֶׁר֮ | לִפְנֵ֣י יְהֹוָה֒ לָקַ֞ח חַלַּ֤ת מַצָּ֨ה אַחַ֜ת וְֽחַלַּ֨ת לֶ֥חֶם שֶׁ֛מֶן אַחַ֖ת וְרָקִ֣יק אֶחָ֑ד וַיָּ֙שֶׂם֙ עַל־הַ֣חֲלָבִ֔ים וְעַ֖ל שׁ֥וֹק הַיָּמִֽין: כז וַיִּתֵּ֣ן אֶת־הַכֹּ֗ל עַ֚ל כַּפֵּ֣י אַהֲרֹ֔ן וְעַ֖ל כַּפֵּ֣י בָנָ֑יו וַיָּ֧נֶף אֹתָ֛ם תְּנוּפָ֖ה לִפְנֵ֥י יְהֹוָֽה: כח וַיִּקַּ֨ח מֹשֶׁ֤ה אֹתָם֙ מֵעַ֣ל כַּפֵּיהֶ֔ם וַיַּקְטֵ֥ר הַמִּזְבֵּ֖חָה עַל־הָעֹלָ֑ה מִלֻּאִ֥ים הֵם֙ לְרֵ֣יחַ נִיחֹ֔חַ אִשֶּׁ֥ה ה֖וּא לַֽיהֹוָֽה: כט וַיִּקַּ֤ח מֹשֶׁה֙ אֶת־הֶ֣חָזֶ֔ה וַיְנִיפֵ֥הוּ תְנוּפָ֖ה לִפְנֵ֣י יְהֹוָ֑ה מֵאֵ֣יל הַמִּלֻּאִ֗ים לְמֹשֶׁ֤ה הָיָה֙ לְמָנָ֔ה כַּאֲשֶׁ֛ר צִוָּ֥ה יְהֹוָ֖ה אֶת־מֹשֶֽׁה: שביעי ל וַיִּקַּ֨ח מֹשֶׁ֜ה מִשֶּׁ֣מֶן הַמִּשְׁחָ֗ה וּמִן־הַדָּם֮ אֲשֶׁ֣ר עַל־הַמִּזְבֵּ֒חַ֒ וַיַּ֤ז עַֽל־אַהֲרֹן֙ עַל־בְּגָדָ֔יו וְעַל־בָּנָ֕יו וְעַל־בִּגְדֵ֥י בָנָ֖יו אִתּ֑וֹ וַיְקַדֵּ֤שׁ אֶֽת־אַהֲרֹן֙ אֶת־בְּגָדָ֔יו וְאֶת־בָּנָ֛יו וְאֶת־בִּגְדֵ֥י בָנָ֖יו אִתּֽוֹ: לא וַיֹּ֨אמֶר מֹשֶׁ֜ה אֶל־אַהֲרֹ֣ן וְאֶל־בָּנָ֗יו בַּשְּׁל֤וּ אֶת־הַבָּשָׂר֙ פֶּ֚תַח אֹ֣הֶל מוֹעֵ֔ד וְשָׁם֙ תֹּאכְל֣וּ אֹת֔וֹ וְאֶ֨ת־הַלֶּ֔חֶם אֲשֶׁ֖ר בְּסַ֣ל הַמִּלֻּאִ֑ים כַּאֲשֶׁ֣ר צִוֵּ֔יתִי

offerings, even as I transmitted the commandment; Aharon and his sons shall eat it. 32. Whatever is left of the flesh and the bread you shall burn in fire. 33. And you shall not remove yourselves from the entrance of the Tent of Appointed Meeting for seven days until the day on which the days of your investiture are completed; for He shall perform your investiture for seven days. 34. As He has done this day, so has *God* commanded to do repeatedly in order to effect atonement for you. 35. You shall remain in the entrance of the Tent of Appointed Meeting day and night for seven days, and you shall keep the charge of *God*, so that you will not die, for so it was commanded to me." 36. Aharon and his sons carried out all the utterances which *God* had commanded through Moshe.

לֵאמֹר אַהֲרֹן וּבָנָיו יֹאכְלֻהוּ׃ לב וְהַנּוֹתָר בַּבָּשָׂר
וּבַלָּחֶם בָּאֵשׁ תִּשְׂרֹפוּ׃ מפטיר לג וּמִפֶּתַח אֹהֶל
מוֹעֵד לֹא תֵצְאוּ שִׁבְעַת יָמִים עַד יוֹם מְלֹאת
יְמֵי מִלֻּאֵיכֶם כִּי שִׁבְעַת יָמִים יְמַלֵּא אֶת־יֶדְכֶם׃
לד כַּאֲשֶׁר עָשָׂה בַּיּוֹם הַזֶּה צִוָּה יְהוָה לַעֲשֹׂת
לְכַפֵּר עֲלֵיכֶם׃ לה וּפֶתַח אֹהֶל מוֹעֵד תֵּשְׁבוּ
יוֹמָם וָלַיְלָה שִׁבְעַת יָמִים וּשְׁמַרְתֶּם אֶת־
מִשְׁמֶרֶת יְהוָה וְלֹא תָמוּתוּ כִּי־כֵן צֻוֵּיתִי׃
לו וַיַּעַשׂ אַהֲרֹן וּבָנָיו אֵת כָּל־הַדְּבָרִים אֲשֶׁר־
צִוָּה יְהוָה בְּיַד־מֹשֶׁה׃ ס

The Haftarah for this Sidra may be found on page 870.

שמיני

SHEMINI

IX 1. And it came to pass on the eighth day that Moshe called Aharon and his sons and the elders of Yisrael, 2. and he said to Aharon: "Take for yourself a calf born of cattle as an offering that clears [him who brings it] of sin and a ram as an ascent offering, without blemish, and bring them nearer before *God*. 3. And to the sons of Yisrael you shall speak [saying]: 'Take a he-goat for an offering that clears [him who brings it] of sin, and a calf and a sheep, one year old, without blemish, for an ascent offering. 4. And an ox and a ram for a peace offering, to perform a meal-offering before *God*, a homage offering mixed with oil, for today *God* will appear to you.'" 5. They took that which Moshe had commanded to the Tent of Appointed Meeting; the entire community drew nearer and they stood before *God*. 6. And Moshe said: "This word that *God* has commanded, carry it out, and then the

ט א וַיְהִי בַּיּוֹם הַשְּׁמִינִי קָרָא מֹשֶׁה לְאַהֲרֹן וּלְבָנָיו וּלְזִקְנֵי יִשְׂרָאֵל: ב וַיֹּאמֶר אֶל־אַהֲרֹן קַח־לְךָ עֵגֶל בֶּן־בָּקָר לְחַטָּאת וְאַיִל לְעֹלָה תְּמִימִם וְהַקְרֵב לִפְנֵי יְהֹוָה: ג וְאֶל־בְּנֵי יִשְׂרָאֵל תְּדַבֵּר לֵאמֹר קְחוּ שְׂעִיר־עִזִּים לְחַטָּאת וְעֵגֶל וָכֶבֶשׂ בְּנֵי־שָׁנָה תְּמִימִם לְעֹלָה: ד וְשׁוֹר וָאַיִל לִשְׁלָמִים לִזְבֹּחַ לִפְנֵי יְהֹוָה וּמִנְחָה בְּלוּלָה בַשָּׁמֶן כִּי הַיּוֹם יְהֹוָה נִרְאָה אֲלֵיכֶם: ה וַיִּקְחוּ אֵת אֲשֶׁר צִוָּה מֹשֶׁה אֶל־פְּנֵי אֹהֶל מוֹעֵד וַיִּקְרְבוּ כָּל־הָעֵדָה וַיַּעַמְדוּ לִפְנֵי יְהֹוָה: ו וַיֹּאמֶר מֹשֶׁה זֶה הַדָּבָר אֲשֶׁר־צִוָּה יְהֹוָה תַּעֲשׂוּ וְיֵרָא

CHAPTER IX

1. *And it came to pass on the eighth day.* In our article on circumcision in [the monthly] *Jeschurun*, Volume 5, pp. 14 ff., we have explained the symbolic significance of the eighth day after the completion of seven consecutive days. We stated there that such a counting of seven days symbolizes the conclusion of a phase that is past, with the eighth day representing a new beginning, on a higher level than what has gone before. It is the beginning of a higher "octave," as it were. Here, too, the seven consecutive days which the priests spent before the entrance of the Tent of Appointed Meeting symbolize the close of the personal, individual phase of the lives of the men who have been called to priestly service. On the eighth day they enter into the new, loftier phase of a life consecrated to God and to the nation.

6. *This word that God has commanded, carry it out.* As *Korban Aharon*[8] notes to *Torath Kohanim*, this

[8]*Note to the English translation: Korban Aharon is a commentary on Torath Kohanim by Aharon Ibn Hayyim, first printed in Venice in 1609 under the author's personal supervision.* [G.H.]

oration, which was addressed to the entire nation, cannot refer to the physical performance of the offering. For the nation had already performed all the physical acts required of it for this purpose. Therefore *Torath Kohanim* adds the following explanation to the words "And Moshe said: 'This word that *God* has commanded'": "Moshe said to Israel: Remove that evil impulse from your hearts and be, all of you, together, united in fear and united in one resolve to serve before the Omnipresent. Even as He is unique in the world, so shall your service be unique before Him, as it is written; 'And circumcise the foreskin of your hearts. Wherefore? Because I am *God*, your God'; He is the God of Gods and the Lord of Lords. Do this and the glory of *God* will reveal itself to you."

If we are not mistaken, this explanation in *Torath Kohanim* understands זֶה הַדָּבָר ["this word"] to define all the rituals of the offerings specified here as one single act; i.e., these acts which we are required to perform express one דָּבָר, one single utterance of God. The one common purpose of all the requirements set forth to us symbolically in the rites of the offerings is not to leave any room in our hearts for "that evil impulse," that uncontrolled animal sensuality which is symbolized by the animal we present before God as an offering. Rather, as expressed by the acts entailed in

אֲלֵיכֶם כְּבוֹד יְהֹוָה: ז וַיֹּאמֶר מֹשֶׁה אֶל־אַהֲרֹן
קְרַב אֶל־הַמִּזְבֵּחַ וַעֲשֵׂה אֶת־חַטָּאתְךָ וְאֶת־
עֹלָתֶךָ וְכַפֵּר בַּעַדְךָ וּבְעַד הָעָם וַעֲשֵׂה אֶת־קָרְבַּן
הָעָם וְכַפֵּר בַּעֲדָם כַּאֲשֶׁר צִוָּה יְהֹוָה: ח וַיִּקְרַב
אַהֲרֹן אֶל־הַמִּזְבֵּחַ וַיִּשְׁחַט אֶת־עֵגֶל הַחַטָּאת
אֲשֶׁר־לוֹ: ט וַיַּקְרִבוּ בְּנֵי אַהֲרֹן אֶת־הַדָּם אֵלָיו
וַיִּטְבֹּל אֶצְבָּעוֹ בַּדָּם וַיִּתֵּן עַל־קַרְנוֹת הַמִּזְבֵּחַ
וְאֶת־הַדָּם יָצַק אֶל־יְסוֹד הַמִּזְבֵּחַ: י וְאֶת־הַחֵלֶב
וְאֶת־הַכְּלָיֹת וְאֶת־הַיֹּתֶרֶת מִן־הַכָּבֵד מִן־
הַחַטָּאת הִקְטִיר הַמִּזְבֵּחָה כַּאֲשֶׁר צִוָּה יְהֹוָה
אֶת־מֹשֶׁה: יא וְאֶת־הַבָּשָׂר וְאֶת־הָעוֹר שָׂרַף
בָּאֵשׁ מִחוּץ לַמַּחֲנֶה: יב וַיִּשְׁחַט אֶת־הָעֹלָה
וַיַּמְצִאוּ בְּנֵי אַהֲרֹן אֵלָיו אֶת־הַדָּם וַיִּזְרְקֵהוּ עַל־
הַמִּזְבֵּחַ סָבִיב: יג וְאֶת־הָעֹלָה הִמְצִיאוּ אֵלָיו

glory of *God* will reveal itself to you."
7. And Moshe said to Aharon: "Draw
nearer to the altar and perform your
offering that clears [him who brings it] of
sin, and your ascent offering, and effect
atonement for yourself and for the people,
and then perform the offering of the people
and effect atonement for them, as *God* has
commanded." 8. And Aharon drew near-
er to the altar and slaughtered the calf of the
offering that clears [him who brings it] of sin
that was his. 9. The sons of Aharon
brought the blood near to him, he dipped
his finger into the blood and placed it upon
the elevated corners of the altar and he
poured the [remainder of the] blood toward
the base of the altar. 10. The fat and the
kidneys along with the diaphragm of the
liver of the offering that clears [him who
brings it] of sin he gave to the altar to go up
in smoke, as *God* had commanded Moshe.
11. But the flesh and the skin he burned
in fire outside the camp. 12. He then
slaughtered the ascent offering; the sons of
Aharon presented the blood to him and he
dashed it round about upon the altar.
13. They had presented to him the ascent

slaughtering the animal, giving the animal to the altar, sprinkling the animal's blood upon the altar and allowing the animal's carcass to go up in smoke, we are to subordinate our sensuous impulses to the energy of our moral will, mastering, guiding and hallowing them in such a manner that the fear of God will guard us from error and that we will form only one resolve; that is, to serve God in accordance with our duty (as symbolized by the ascent offering).

And just as here the community symbolically presents itself before God by means of one single offering, so, in general, the thought of the One sole God, to Whom each and every one of us, every single member of the community, stands in the same relation, should engender within us not only inner harmony reconciling the dichotomous nature of our individual selves, but also equality and unity to weld the national entity together, as it is stated in Deuteronomy 10:16 and 17 with regard to the individual: "Circumcise the עָרְלָה, the foreskin of your heart (place your sensuality within firm bounds) by means of the fear of God, as symbolized by the act of the offering that clears [him who brings it] of sin, and no longer allow yourselves to be stiff-necked (do good joyously and willingly, resolve to serve the Omnipresent, as symbolized by the act of the ascent offering), for your God is the God of Gods (He alone holds all your existence in His hands) and Lord of Lords (consciously or unconsciously, voluntarily or by force, all things serve Him)."

Clearly the thought expressed by this statement is that the harmony which should rule one's life's service to God, in that one shuns every act forbidden by God and carries out all that He has commanded, is a logical outgrowth of the unity and uniqueness of God Himself. "Do this," *Torath Kohanim* concludes. If you devote yourselves, one and all, to God, translating into reality the ideal symbolized by the offerings God has commanded, then "the glory of *God* will reveal itself to you." The united devotion with which the entire community goes forth to meet God will cause the glory of God in turn to come forth to meet you. By a visible demonstration of its entry into your midst, it will translate into reality the objective of the erection of the Sanctuary: "And they shall make Me a Sanctuary and I will dwell in their midst."

We believe that this passage in *Torath Kohanim* contains the idea basic to all the offerings and to the symbolic significance of all the rituals associated with them.

° ° °

לִנְתָחֶיהָ וְאֶת־הָרֹאשׁ וַיַּקְטֵר עַל־הַמִּזְבֵּחַ׃
יד וַיִּרְחַץ אֶת־הַקֶּרֶב וְאֶת־הַכְּרָעָיִם וַיַּקְטֵר עַל־
הָעֹלָה הַמִּזְבֵּחָה׃ טו וַיַּקְרֵב אֵת קָרְבַּן הָעָם וַיִּקַּח
אֶת־שְׂעִיר הַחַטָּאת אֲשֶׁר לָעָם וַיִּשְׁחָטֵהוּ
וַיְחַטְּאֵהוּ כָּרִאשׁוֹן׃ טז וַיַּקְרֵב אֶת־הָעֹלָה
וַיַּעֲשֶׂהָ כַּמִּשְׁפָּט׃ שני יז וַיַּקְרֵב אֶת־הַמִּנְחָה
וַיְמַלֵּא כַפּוֹ מִמֶּנָּה וַיַּקְטֵר עַל־הַמִּזְבֵּחַ מִלְּבַד
עֹלַת הַבֹּקֶר׃ יח וַיִּשְׁחַט אֶת־הַשּׁוֹר וְאֶת־הָאַיִל
זֶבַח הַשְּׁלָמִים אֲשֶׁר לָעָם וַיַּמְצִאוּ בְּנֵי אַהֲרֹן
אֶת־הַדָּם אֵלָיו וַיִּזְרְקֵהוּ עַל־הַמִּזְבֵּחַ סָבִיב׃
יט וְאֶת־הַחֲלָבִים מִן־הַשּׁוֹר וּמִן־הָאַיִל הָאַלְיָה
וְהַמְכַסֶּה וְהַכְּלָיֹת וְיֹתֶרֶת הַכָּבֵד׃ כ וַיָּשִׂימוּ
אֶת־הַחֲלָבִים עַל־הֶחָזוֹת וַיַּקְטֵר הַחֲלָבִים
הַמִּזְבֵּחָה׃ כא וְאֵת הֶחָזוֹת וְאֵת שׁוֹק הַיָּמִין
הֵנִיף אַהֲרֹן תְּנוּפָה לִפְנֵי יְהוָֹה כַּאֲשֶׁר צִוָּה
מֹשֶׁה׃ כב וַיִּשָּׂא אַהֲרֹן אֶת־יָדָו (ידיו קרי) אֶל־הָעָם
וַיְבָרְכֵם וַיֵּרֶד מֵעֲשֹׂת הַחַטָּאת וְהָעֹלָה
וְהַשְּׁלָמִים׃ כג וַיָּבֹא מֹשֶׁה וְאַהֲרֹן אֶל־אֹהֶל
מוֹעֵד וַיֵּצְאוּ וַיְבָרְכוּ אֶת־הָעָם וַיֵּרָא כְבוֹד־
יְהוָֹה אֶל־כָּל־הָעָם׃ שלישי כד וַתֵּצֵא אֵשׁ מִלִּפְנֵי
יְהוָֹה וַתֹּאכַל עַל־הַמִּזְבֵּחַ אֶת־הָעֹלָה וְאֶת־
הַחֲלָבִים וַיַּרְא כָּל־הָעָם וַיָּרֹנּוּ וַיִּפְּלוּ עַל־

offering in its parts, and the head, and he let it go up in smoke upon the altar.
14. He then washed the entrails and the feet and gave them to go up in smoke upon the ascent offering on the altar.
15. Thereupon he brought near the offering of the people, took the he-goat of the offering that clears [him who brings it] of sin that was the people's, slaughtered it and offered it as an offering that clears [him who brings it] of sin, like the first one.
16. He brought near the ascent offering and offered it as prescribed.
17. He brought near the homage offering, filled his hand from it and let it go up in smoke upon the altar, in addition to the morning's ascent offering.
18. He then slaughtered the ox and the ram, the meal-of-peace offering that was the people's; the sons of Aharon presented the blood to him and he dashed it round about upon the altar.
19. Also the fat parts of the ox, and the tailpiece of the ram, the membrane and the kidneys and the diaphragm of the liver.
20. They placed the fat parts upon the breast pieces; he gave the fat parts to the altar to go up in smoke.
21. But Aharon had [already] waved the breast pieces and the right thigh in a wave [offering] before *God*, as Moshe had commanded.
22. And Aharon lifted up his hands toward the people and blessed them and then he came down from performing the offering that clears [him who brings it] of sin, the ascent offering and the peace offering.
23. Thereupon Moshe and Aharon went into the Tent of Appointed Meeting; they came out again, blessed the people—and the glory of *God* revealed itself to all the people.
24. Fire went forth from before *God* and consumed the ascent offering and the fat parts upon the altar; the people saw [it] and shouted for joy and they fell upon their faces.

21 and 22. בִּרְכַּת כֹּהֲנִים . . . [the priestly blessing] is not an independent act that stands on its own. The blessings pronounced in it can be attained only as a result of conduct symbolically expressed by the עֲבוֹדָה [the service at which the offerings are made] that has gone before. Hence the בִּרְכַּת כֹּהֲנִים must be recited immediately following the עֲבוֹדָה.

וַיִּשָּׂא אַהֲרֹן אֶת יָדָו *[And Aharon lifted up his hands].* בִּנְשִׂיאַת כַּפַּיִם ["With his hands uplifted in the (priestly) blessing"] (Sotah 38a). The hands of our priests do not possess any inherent power to bestow blessings; this is probably the reason why the word יָדָו is spelled חָסֵר, in an "incomplete" manner [without the *yod* between the *daled* and the *vav*]. All that the hand of the priest can and should do is point heavenward to God Who has promised the blessing. . . .

X 1. And Aharon's sons, Nadab and Abihu, each took his pan, put fire into them and placed incense upon it, and they brought near before *God* strange fire which He had not commanded them.

פְּנֵיהֶם׃ י א וַיִּקְחוּ בְנֵי־אַהֲרֹן נָדָב וַאֲבִיהוּא
אִישׁ מַחְתָּתוֹ וַיִּתְּנוּ בָהֵן אֵשׁ וַיָּשִׂימוּ עָלֶיהָ
קְטֹרֶת וַיַּקְרִיבוּ לִפְנֵי יְהוָה אֵשׁ זָרָה אֲשֶׁר לֹא

CHAPTER X

1. We have already indicated elsewhere (Genesis 4:3) that in the very first Scriptural reference to offerings, and again each time Scripture introduces a new kind of offering, it is impressively shown that while one offering was accepted, another was rejected. Thus, from the very outset, the Scriptural text demolishes the blasphemous delusion in which our present-day "reformers" so delight. The "realization" that the offerings have only relative significance, they claim, did not come until the days of the Prophets, who had advanced beyond the "primitive" stage of the Pentateuch. But this claim is cogently refuted by the fact that Cain's offering was rejected while that of Abel was accepted, and by the warnings repeatedly addressed to King Solomon during the construction and following the completion of his splendid Temple (I Kings 6:12 and 13, and 9:3–9). These two Scriptural portions loudly proclaim that the value of the Sanctuary and of the offerings to be made there is dependent on how attentive we are to our duties. The death of the youths of priestly stock who were consumed by the fire of God because of the offerings they had made, when that same fire, at the same time, had accepted the offerings of the nation to express God's approval, and indeed to demonstrate God's presence in the midst of the nation, is a most eloquent protest against any misinterpretation of the value of offerings. At the same time it is an even more solemn warning against allowing personal whims to determine our "cultic" relationship with God.

And Aharon's sons . . . each took. "The sons of Aharon did not give the proper respect to Aharon. Nadab and Abihu did not take counsel with Moshe; each man took his own pan, each went forth on his own, not even taking counsel with one another." Thus *Torath Kohanim* points out how the wording of the text stresses the arrogance with which these youths had behaved. The text does not read: "And Nadab and Abihu took pans and put strange fire into them." It states at the very outset that they were "Aharon's sons"; i.e., it stresses their filial relationship to Aaron. Then come the words אִישׁ ["each"] and מַחְתָּתוֹ ["his pan"]. All these words describe the conceit that had taken hold of their minds and show that both Nadab and Abihu were alike in this respect. Both Nadab and Abihu were sons of Aaron. Yet they did not consult with their father before acting. Or perhaps they believed that precisely because they were the sons of Aaron they were under no obligation to seek advice from anyone else. In fact, they were only "Nadab and Abihu," individual members of the nation, but they did not seek advice from the leader of their nation. Or perhaps they were so greatly taken with their own sense of self-worth as individuals that they felt sufficient unto themselves. Indeed, איש וגו׳, each man followed his own impulse. They did not consult even with one another!

To be sure, their intention was praiseworthy. Even after their sin God Himself refers to them as "those near to Me." *Torath Kohanim* describes their intention as follows: "But in their joy, when they beheld a new fire, they wished to add one love to another." But the fact that, at their moment of greatest delight, when God's Oneness was demonstrated to the entire nation, they could feel the urge to make a separate offering on their own shows that they were not imbued with the spirit that Judaism requires of its priests. In Judaism, the priest is completely identified with the nation. His position is in no way set apart from his nation; only within and through his nation does he have standing before God. Hence, the very fact that the two youths presumed to "come near" to make such an offering bespeaks sinful arrogance.

Moreover, the offering *per se* was illegal in every respect. The twofold illegality of their act is pointed out in *Torath Kohanim* to Leviticus 16:1 on the basis of two distinct Scriptural statements: "It was because of their drawing near before *God* that they died" (Leviticus 16:1) and "But Nadab and Abihu died before *God* when they brought near strange fire" (Numbers 3:4). Not only their attitude, their "drawing near," but also their offering as such could be regarded as sinful. Not only the pans but also the fire and the incense were illegal, because all the utensils employed in the service had to be both the property of the entire community and holy. (See Maimonides, *K'lei HaMikdash* 8:7; *Beth HaB'ḥirah* 1:20). Only if he uses the utensils of his nation's Sanctuary when he makes his offering can the individual, and his offering with him, enter into the sphere of the Sanctuary of the nation's Law. Only thus can he give himself up entirely to the demands of this Sanctuary, to the exclusion of all personal caprice. But the pans of Nadab and Abihu were מַחְתָּתוֹ; each of the two men used his own pan. Not in the spirit of self-abnegation, not with the utensils of the Sanctuary, but with their own utensils, did they come before God.

put fire into them. Rabbi Akiba defines this more precisely in *Torath Kohanim*: "Strange fire: From their own hearths." They offered incense not to the fire of the altar, as prescribed for the daily incense offering

צִוָּה אֹתָם: ב וַתֵּצֵא אֵשׁ מִלִּפְנֵי יְהוָה וַתֹּאכַל
אוֹתָם וַיָּמֻתוּ לִפְנֵי יְהוָה: ג וַיֹּאמֶר מֹשֶׁה אֶל־
אַהֲרֹן הוּא אֲשֶׁר־דִּבֶּר יְהוָה ׀ לֵאמֹר בִּקְרֹבַי
אֶקָּדֵשׁ וְעַל־פְּנֵי כָל־הָעָם אֶכָּבֵד וַיִּדֹּם אַהֲרֹן:
ד וַיִּקְרָא מֹשֶׁה אֶל־מִישָׁאֵל וְאֶל אֶלְצָפָן בְּנֵי
עֻזִּיאֵל דֹּד אַהֲרֹן וַיֹּאמֶר אֲלֵהֶם קִרְבוּ שְׂאוּ אֶת־

2. Then fire went forth from before *God* and consumed them, and they died before *God*. 3. And Moshe said to Aharon: "This is what *God* spoke, [saying]: 'I will be sanctified by those near to Me and thus I will be honored by all the people.'" And Aharon was silent. 4. And Moshe called Mishael and Eltzaphan, sons of Aharon's uncle, Uzziel, and said to them: "Draw

and the incense offering of Yom Kippur, not to the "fire of the Law" which demands the devotion of the entire community, from the highest to the humblest in the nation, but to fire from their own hearths.

Now as to the incense itself. The incense offering was the only offering that could never be presented as a free-will offering, neither by the community nor by any individual. It could be performed only as prescribed by the Law: by the community as a daily offering and by the high priest only on Yom Kippur (Menaḥoth 50a and b). We believe we are justified in interpreting the incense offering as a symbolic expression of our complete absorption in the endeavor to gain God's approval, of our giving ourselves completely as an expression of compliance to God. (See Exodus 30f. and 34f.). The idea symbolized by this offering, then, is the goal set by God as the absolute ideal of His requirements. But if this idea were to be expressed by one's own choice; i.e., as a free-will offering, it would be gross presumption on our part [because this would imply that we feel we have already reached the goal set for us by God].

Above and beyond all else, however, the Word of God describing this ill-fated offering stresses that it was one which God had not commanded Aaron's sons to make. Even if the individual phases of the offering as such had not been illegal (and we have seen that they were indeed unlawful) the mere fact that this offering had not been expressly commanded by God would have been sufficient to make it forbidden. Offerings made in the Sanctuary of the Law are not subject to personal preference. Even the free-will offerings, which are voluntary, must comply strictly with specified forms and qualifications. For the nearness of God and the approach to God, both of which are symbolically sought through the קָרְבָּן [offering], can be found only through obedience to, and compliance with, the will of God; through complete personal submission to God's will.

This is only one of the points where Judaism and paganism come to a sharp parting of the ways. The pagan sees his sacrifice as an attempt to make his deity subservient to his will. In Judaism, by contrast, the offering expresses the idea that the one who brings the offering seeks to place himself in the service of God. The purpose of his offering is to make him subservient to the fulfillment of God's will. Hence all offerings in Judaism represent statements of God's demands; he who makes the offering symbolically demonstrates that he has adopted these demands as the standards for his own future conduct. Hence, offerings of one's own devising would be a subversion of that very truth that is to attain dominion over man precisely by means of the offering he makes; it would be tantamount to erecting a pedestal of glory to personal caprice where obedience should be enthroned to the exclusion of all else. Now we understand the reason for the death of the two priestly youths. Their death at the moment when God's own Sanctuary was consecrated is a most solemn warning for all future priests who will serve in that Sanctuary. It bars every trace of personal choice and caprice from the precincts of God's Sanctuary, which is to be nothing else but the Sanctuary of His Law. In Judaism the priest must demonstrate his efficacy not by inventing novelties for the Divine service but by carrying out what God Himself has commanded.

3. ***I will be sanctified.*** [God says:] "The more a person stands out from among his people as a teacher and leader in relation to Me, the less will I show indulgence for his errors. Even by having him die I demonstrate that My will is absolute and that not even —indeed, least of all—those nearest to Me, the highest before Me, may permit themselves the slightest deviation from it. This will make the entire nation realize the full, solemn import of the obedience they owe Me." Seen in this light, these words of God should be sufficient consolation for Aaron, so that the text can indeed state: "And Aharon was silent." Had his sons not been close to God, allowance might have been made for their aberration, and the Heavenly decree that overtook them might not have come to them as a warning of such solemn import for the entire nation. In sharpest divergence from the modern view, which regards intellectual attainments as a license for moral laxity and tends to make allowances for violators of God's moral law if they happen to be men of intellect, Judaism postulates that the higher the intellect, the greater must be the moral demands placed upon it. . . .

∘ ∘ ∘

nearer and carry your brethren from before
the Sanctuary, out of the camp." 5. They
drew nearer and carried them out in their
tunics, out of the camp, as Moshe had
spoken. 6. Moshe said to Aharon and to
his sons, Eleazar and Ithamar: "Do not let
your heads remain unshorn and do not
make a rent in your garments, lest you die
and lest He be angry with the entire
community; but your brethren, the entire
House of Yisrael, shall bewail the burning
that *God* has kindled. 7. And do not
move away from the entrance of the Tent of
Appointed Meeting, lest you die, for the oil
of *God*'s consecration is upon you." They
did according to Moshe's word. 8. *God*
spoke to Aharon [saying]: 9. "Drink no
wine or strong drink, you and your sons who
stand by you, when you go into the Tent of
Appointed Meeting, so that you will not die;
[this is] an everlasting statute for your
descendants. 10. And this is also in order
to differentiate between the sanctified and
the unsanctified, and between unclean
and pure, 11. and to teach the sons of
Yisrael all the laws that *God* has uttered for
them through Moshe." 12. Moshe spoke
to Aharon and to his surviving sons Eleazar
and Ithamar [saying]: "Take that homage
offering which is left over from the fire
offerings of *God* and eat it as *matzoth* beside
the altar, for it is a holy of holies. 13. Eat
it in a holy place, for this is your [due] and
your sons' due from the fire offerings of
God, for so I was commanded. 14. And
you shall eat the breast of the wave [offer-
ing] and the thigh of the uplifted donation
in a pure place, you and your sons and your
daughters with you; for they have been
given as your due and your sons' due from
the meal-of-peace offerings of the sons
of Yisrael. 15. Let them bring the thigh
of the uplifted donation and the breast of
the wave [offering] upon the fire offerings
of the fat parts in order to make a wave

אֲחִיכֶם מֵאֵת פְּנֵי־הַקֹּדֶשׁ אֶל־מִחוּץ לַמַּחֲנֶה:
ה וַיִּקְרְבוּ וַיִּשָּׂאֻם בְּכֻתֳּנֹתָם אֶל־מִחוּץ לַמַּחֲנֶה
כַּאֲשֶׁר דִּבֶּר מֹשֶׁה: ו וַיֹּאמֶר מֹשֶׁה אֶל־אַהֲרֹן
וּלְאֶלְעָזָר וּלְאִיתָמָר ׀ בָּנָיו רָאשֵׁיכֶם אַל־
תִּפְרָעוּ ׀ וּבִגְדֵיכֶם לֹא־תִפְרֹמוּ וְלֹא תָמֻתוּ וְעַל
כָּל־הָעֵדָה יִקְצֹף וַאֲחֵיכֶם כָּל־בֵּית יִשְׂרָאֵל יִבְכּוּ
אֶת־הַשְּׂרֵפָה אֲשֶׁר שָׂרַף יְהֹוָה: ז וּמִפֶּתַח אֹהֶל
מוֹעֵד לֹא תֵצְאוּ פֶּן־תָּמֻתוּ כִּי־שֶׁמֶן מִשְׁחַת
יְהֹוָה עֲלֵיכֶם וַיַּעֲשׂוּ כִּדְבַר מֹשֶׁה: פ ח וַיְדַבֵּר
יְהֹוָה אֶל־אַהֲרֹן לֵאמֹר: ט יַיִן וְשֵׁכָר אַל־תֵּשְׁתְּ ׀
אַתָּה ׀ וּבָנֶיךָ אִתָּךְ בְּבֹאֲכֶם אֶל־אֹהֶל מוֹעֵד וְלֹא
תָמֻתוּ חֻקַּת עוֹלָם לְדֹרֹתֵיכֶם: י וּלְהַבְדִּיל בֵּין
הַקֹּדֶשׁ וּבֵין הַחֹל וּבֵין הַטָּמֵא וּבֵין הַטָּהוֹר:
יא וּלְהוֹרֹת אֶת־בְּנֵי יִשְׂרָאֵל אֵת כָּל־הַחֻקִּים
אֲשֶׁר דִּבֶּר יְהֹוָה אֲלֵיהֶם בְּיַד־מֹשֶׁה: פ רביעי
יב וַיְדַבֵּר מֹשֶׁה אֶל־אַהֲרֹן וְאֶל אֶלְעָזָר וְאֶל־
אִיתָמָר ׀ בָּנָיו הַנּוֹתָרִים קְחוּ אֶת־הַמִּנְחָה
הַנּוֹתֶרֶת מֵאִשֵּׁי יְהֹוָה וְאִכְלוּהָ מַצּוֹת אֵצֶל
הַמִּזְבֵּחַ כִּי קֹדֶשׁ קָדָשִׁים הִוא: יג וַאֲכַלְתֶּם אֹתָהּ
בְּמָקוֹם קָדוֹשׁ כִּי חָקְךָ וְחָק־בָּנֶיךָ הִוא מֵאִשֵּׁי
יְהֹוָה כִּי־כֵן צֻוֵּיתִי: יד וְאֵת חֲזֵה הַתְּנוּפָה וְאֵת ׀
שׁוֹק הַתְּרוּמָה תֹּאכְלוּ בְּמָקוֹם טָהוֹר אַתָּה
וּבָנֶיךָ וּבְנֹתֶיךָ אִתָּךְ כִּי־חָקְךָ וְחָק־בָּנֶיךָ נִתְּנוּ
מִזִּבְחֵי שַׁלְמֵי בְּנֵי יִשְׂרָאֵל: טו שׁוֹק הַתְּרוּמָה
וַחֲזֵה הַתְּנוּפָה עַל אִשֵּׁי הַחֲלָבִים יָבִיאוּ לְהָנִיף

---

6. **lest He be angry with the entire community.** Cf.
Leviticus 4:3: "If the anointed priest sins so as to bring
guilt upon the people." If the spiritual elite of the
nation, especially when they are called upon to represent the national entity in its ideal state of unity
before God, commit a sin deserving of death, and
if death then snatches them from their activities on
behalf of the nation, their sin is the sin of the entire
nation and their death a national calamity. "Your
death," Moses says, would be "a time of wrath for the
entire congregation." . . .

[offering] before *God,* and it shall be an eternal due for you and for your sons who stand by you, as *God* has commanded." 16. Moshe inquired [in detail] about the he-goat of the offering that clears [him who brings it] of sin, and lo! it had [already] been burned. And he was angry with Eleazar and Ithamar, the surviving sons of Aharon, and he said: 17. "Why did you not eat the offering that clears [him who brings it] of sin in the place of the Sanctuary, seeing that it is a holy of holies, and that He gave it to you precisely in order to lift away the sin of the congregation, to effect atonement for them before God? 18. See, its blood was not brought into the interior of the Sanctuary; you should have eaten it in a holy place, as I had commanded." 19. And Aharon said to Moshe: "See, today they brought near their offering that cleared [him who brings it] of sin, and their ascent offering, to *God,* and then such befell me. If I had eaten today offerings that clear [him who brings them] of sin, would that have been what is right in the eyes of *God?*" 20. When Moshe heard this, it was right in his eyes.

XI 1. *God* spoke to Moshe and to Aharon, in order to say to them: 2. Speak to the sons of Yisrael [saying]:

תְּנוּפָה לִפְנֵי יְהֹוָה וְהָיָה לְךָ וּלְבָנֶיךָ אִתְּךָ לְחָק־
עוֹלָם כַּאֲשֶׁר צִוָּה יְהֹוָה: חמישי טז וְאֵת ׀ שְׂעִיר
הַחַטָּאת דָּרֹשׁ דָּרַשׁ מֹשֶׁה וְהִנֵּה שֹׂרָף וַיִּקְצֹף
עַל־אֶלְעָזָר וְעַל־אִיתָמָר בְּנֵי אַהֲרֹן הַנּוֹתָרִם
לֵאמֹר: יז מַדּוּעַ לֹא־אֲכַלְתֶּם אֶת־הַחַטָּאת
בִּמְקוֹם הַקֹּדֶשׁ כִּי קֹדֶשׁ קָדָשִׁים הִוא וְאֹתָהּ ׀
נָתַן לָכֶם לָשֵׂאת אֶת־עֲוֹן הָעֵדָה לְכַפֵּר עֲלֵיהֶם
לִפְנֵי יְהֹוָה: יח הֵן לֹא־הוּבָא אֶת־דָּמָהּ אֶל־
הַקֹּדֶשׁ פְּנִימָה אָכוֹל תֹּאכְלוּ אֹתָהּ בַּקֹּדֶשׁ
כַּאֲשֶׁר צִוֵּיתִי: יט וַיְדַבֵּר אַהֲרֹן אֶל־מֹשֶׁה הֵן
הַיּוֹם הִקְרִיבוּ אֶת־חַטָּאתָם וְאֶת־עֹלָתָם לִפְנֵי
יְהֹוָה וַתִּקְרֶאנָה אֹתִי כָּאֵלֶּה וְאָכַלְתִּי חַטָּאת
הַיּוֹם הַיִּיטַב בְּעֵינֵי יְהֹוָה: כ וַיִּשְׁמַע מֹשֶׁה
וַיִּיטַב בְּעֵינָיו: פ ששי יא א וַיְדַבֵּר יְהֹוָה אֶל־
מֹשֶׁה וְאֶל־אַהֲרֹן לֵאמֹר אֲלֵהֶם: ב דַּבְּרוּ אֶל־בְּנֵי

CHAPTER XI

1. The entire preceding chapter is closely tied to the dietary laws that form the content of the present chapter. It shows how sentiment can misguide even individuals worthy of the priesthood and lead them to commit errors punishable by death. Accordingly it warns both the priests in the Sanctuary and the teachers of the Law that when they are called to serve the Sanctuary and the Law they must deny themselves pleasures which are ordinarily permitted but which could impair the clarity of mind and emotion they need on these occasions. Finally, it teaches them that the Sanctuary of God's Law views precisely the sanctification of physical pleasures as the culmination of the sanctification of life emanating from the Law, and that the Sanctuary requires the "meal eaten by the priests in the area where the offering was made" as a final act needed to complete the atonement effected by the "sin offering." All this already suggests that the nourishment we enjoy must not be regarded as irrelevant to our spiritual and

moral calling and to the discharge of the task that has been assigned to us as a "kingdom of priests and a holy nation."

In keeping with this trend of thought initiated by the contents of the preceding chapter, the present chapter at its very outset declares the unique, momentous significance the Lawgiver attaches to the dietary laws about to be set forth. The very fact that not only Moses but also Aaron ["*God* spoke to Moshe and to Aharon"] was summoned to receive this law attests to the special importance of its contents. . . . The contents of this law were imparted first of all to Moses and Aaron for them to take to heart in particular because of their position before the Law within the nation. Both Moses, as the transmitter and teacher of the Law, and Aaron, as the educator of the nation toward the realization of the Law, have a role of unique significance with regard to this Law so that their activities on behalf of the nation may achieve the desired results. The roles of both Moses and Aaron—the former, to work for the nation's intellect and for its knowledge of the Law; the latter, to mold the

This, if it is viable, is what you may eat of all the animals that live upon the land:
3. Whatever forms a hoof and cleaves it completely into two hooves and at the same time chews the cud among the animals, this you may eat.
4. But this you may not eat from among those that chew the cud and that are thus hoofed: The camel, because it chews the cud but does not form the proper hoof; it is unclean to you.
5. And the rabbit, because it chews the cud but does not form a hoof; it is unclean to you.
6. And the hare, because it chews the cud but does not form a hoof; it is unclean to you.
7. And the pig, because it forms a hoof and cleaves the hoof completely but does not chew the cud; it is unclean to you.
8. You shall not eat of their flesh and not touch their carcasses; they are unclean to you.
9. This you may eat of all that lives in the water: whatever has fins and scales in the water, in seas and in rivers, these you may eat.
10. But whatever does not have fins and scales in seas and in rivers, of all small creatures of the water and of all animal life that lives in the water; they are an abomination to you.
11. And they shall be an abomination to you, you shall not eat of their flesh, and their bodies removed from their habitat you shall hold in abomination.
12. Whatever has neither fins nor scales in the water, that is an abomination to you.
13. And these you shall hold in abomination from among the fowl; they shall not be eaten; they are an abomination: the *nesher,* the *peres* and the *azniyah*;
14. the *da'ah* and the *ayah* according to its species;
15. any *orev* according to its species;
16. the *bath ha-yaanah,* the *taḥmas,* the *shahaf* and the *netz* according to its species;
17. the *kos,* the *shalakh* and the *yanshuf*;
18. the *tinshemeth,* the *kaath* and the *raḥam*;
19. the *hasidah,* the *anafah* according to its species, the *dukhiphath* and the *atalef.*
20. Any winged creeping thing that goes upon four legs is an abomination to you.
21. Only this may you eat of all the winged creeping

יִשְׂרָאֵל לֵאמֹר זֹאת הַחַיָּה אֲשֶׁר תֹּאכְלוּ מִכָּל־
הַבְּהֵמָה אֲשֶׁר עַל־הָאָרֶץ: ג כֹּל | מַפְרֶסֶת
פַּרְסָה וְשֹׁסַעַת שֶׁסַע פְּרָסֹת מַעֲלַת גֵּרָה בַּבְּהֵמָה
אֹתָהּ תֹּאכֵלוּ: ד אַךְ אֶת־זֶה לֹא תֹאכְלוּ מִמַּעֲלֵי
הַגֵּרָה וּמִמַּפְרִסֵי הַפַּרְסָה אֶת־הַגָּמָל כִּי־מַעֲלֵה
גֵרָה הוּא וּפַרְסָה אֵינֶנּוּ מַפְרִיס טָמֵא הוּא לָכֶם:
ה וְאֶת־הַשָּׁפָן כִּי־מַעֲלֵה גֵרָה הוּא וּפַרְסָה לֹא
יַפְרִיס טָמֵא הוּא לָכֶם: ו וְאֶת־הָאַרְנֶבֶת כִּי־
מַעֲלַת גֵּרָה הִוא וּפַרְסָה לֹא הִפְרִיסָה טְמֵאָה
הִוא לָכֶם: ז וְאֶת־הַחֲזִיר כִּי־מַפְרִיס פַּרְסָה הוּא
וְשֹׁסַע שֶׁסַע פַּרְסָה וְהוּא גֵּרָה לֹא־יִגָּר טָמֵא
הוּא לָכֶם: ח מִבְּשָׂרָם לֹא תֹאכֵלוּ וּבְנִבְלָתָם לֹא
תִגָּעוּ טְמֵאִים הֵם לָכֶם: ט אֶת־זֶה תֹּאכְלוּ מִכֹּל
אֲשֶׁר בַּמָּיִם כֹּל אֲשֶׁר־לוֹ סְנַפִּיר וְקַשְׂקֶשֶׂת
בַּמַּיִם בַּיַּמִּים וּבַנְּחָלִים אֹתָם תֹּאכֵלוּ: י וְכֹל
אֲשֶׁר אֵין־לוֹ סְנַפִּיר וְקַשְׂקֶשֶׂת בַּיַּמִּים וּבַנְּחָלִים
מִכֹּל שֶׁרֶץ הַמַּיִם וּמִכֹּל נֶפֶשׁ הַחַיָּה אֲשֶׁר בַּמָּיִם
שֶׁקֶץ הֵם לָכֶם: יא וְשֶׁקֶץ יִהְיוּ לָכֶם מִבְּשָׂרָם לֹא
תֹאכֵלוּ וְאֶת־נִבְלָתָם תְּשַׁקֵּצוּ: יב כֹּל אֲשֶׁר אֵין־
לוֹ סְנַפִּיר וְקַשְׂקֶשֶׂת בַּמָּיִם שֶׁקֶץ הוּא לָכֶם:
יג וְאֶת־אֵלֶּה תְּשַׁקְּצוּ מִן־הָעוֹף לֹא יֵאָכְלוּ
שֶׁקֶץ הֵם אֶת־הַנֶּשֶׁר וְאֶת־הַפֶּרֶס וְאֵת הָעָזְנִיָּה:
יד וְאֶת־הַדָּאָה וְאֶת־הָאַיָּה לְמִינָהּ: טו אֵת כָּל־
עֹרֵב לְמִינוֹ: טז וְאֵת בַּת הַיַּעֲנָה וְאֶת־הַתַּחְמָס
וְאֶת־הַשָּׁחַף וְאֶת־הַנֵּץ לְמִינֵהוּ: יז וְאֶת־הַכּוֹס
וְאֶת־הַשָּׁלָךְ וְאֶת־הַיַּנְשׁוּף: יח וְאֶת־הַתִּנְשֶׁמֶת
וְאֶת־הַקָּאָת וְאֶת־הָרָחָם: יט וְאֵת הַחֲסִידָה
הָאֲנָפָה לְמִינָהּ וְאֶת־הַדּוּכִיפַת וְאֶת־הָעֲטַלֵּף:
כ כֹּל שֶׁרֶץ הָעוֹף הַהֹלֵךְ עַל־אַרְבַּע שֶׁקֶץ הוּא
לָכֶם: כא אַךְ אֶת־זֶה תֹּאכְלוּ מִכֹּל שֶׁרֶץ הָעוֹף

nation's will and spirit—are dependent primarily upon the faithfulness with which the nation will observe the laws given here to Moses and Aaron, to be inculcated by them into the nation. . . .

things that go upon four legs; those that
have jointed legs above their feet, to hop
with them upon the earth; 22. these of
them you may eat: the *arbeh* according to
its species; the *salam* according to its species; the *hargol* according to its species and
the *hagav* according to its species.
23. Every winged creeping thing that has
four legs is an abomination to you.
24. And concerning these you shall regard
yourselves as unclean; whoever touches
their carcass shall remain unclean until
evening, 25. and whoever carries [any
part] of their carcass shall wash his
garments and remain unclean until evening.
26. Concerning any animal that has
hooves but does not cleave them and does
not chew the cud; they are unclean to you;
whatever touches them shall be unclean.
27. And also whatever goes upon its paws
among all animals that go upon four legs,
they are unclean to you; whoever touches
their carcass shall remain unclean until
evening. 28. And whoever carries their
carcass shall wash his garments and remain
unclean until evening; they are unclean
to you. 29. And this is what is unclean to
you among the creeping things that creep
upon the earth: the weasel, the mouse and
the toad according to its species, 30. the
hedgehog, the *koah*, the lizard, the *homet*
and the mole. 31. These are those that
are unclean to you among all creeping
things; whoever touches them when they
are dead shall be unclean until evening.
32. And everything upon which any part
of them falls when they are dead—of any
wooden utensils, or a garment, or articles of
leather, or a sack, any utensil with which
[creating] work is done—shall be put into
water, remain unclean until evening and
then be pure. 33. And any earthen vessel
into whose cavity any part of them falls,
whatever is within its cavity becomes unclean, and you shall break it. 34. Of any
food that is [usually] eaten, that on which
water comes, becomes unclean when this
happens, and so, too, any beverage that is
[usually] drunk, in any vessel, becomes
unclean. 35. And whatever upon which
any part of their carcass falls becomes
unclean, even an oven and a hearth must be
demolished; they are unclean and only as

הַהֹלֵךְ עַל־אַרְבַּע אֲשֶׁר־לֹא (לו קרי) כְרָעַיִם
מִמַּעַל לְרַגְלָיו לְנַתֵּר בָּהֵן עַל־הָאָרֶץ: כב אֶת־
אֵלֶּה מֵהֶם תֹּאכֵלוּ אֶת־הָאַרְבֶּה לְמִינוֹ וְאֶת־
הַסָּלְעָם לְמִינֵהוּ וְאֶת־הַחַרְגֹּל לְמִינֵהוּ וְאֶת־
הֶחָגָב לְמִינֵהוּ: כג וְכֹל שֶׁרֶץ הָעוֹף אֲשֶׁר־לוֹ
אַרְבַּע רַגְלָיִם שֶׁקֶץ הוּא לָכֶם: כד וּלְאֵלֶּה
תִּטַּמָּאוּ כָּל־הַנֹּגֵעַ בְּנִבְלָתָם יִטְמָא עַד־הָעָרֶב:
כה וְכָל־הַנֹּשֵׂא מִנִּבְלָתָם יְכַבֵּס בְּגָדָיו וְטָמֵא
עַד־הָעָרֶב: כו לְכָל־הַבְּהֵמָה אֲשֶׁר הִוא מַפְרֶסֶת
פַּרְסָה וְשֶׁסַע אֵינֶנָּה שֹׁסַעַת וְגֵרָה אֵינֶנָּה
מַעֲלָה טְמֵאִים הֵם לָכֶם כָּל־הַנֹּגֵעַ בָּהֶם יִטְמָא:
כז וְכֹל הוֹלֵךְ עַל־כַּפָּיו בְּכָל־הַחַיָּה הַהֹלֶכֶת
עַל־אַרְבַּע טְמֵאִים הֵם לָכֶם כָּל־הַנֹּגֵעַ בְּנִבְלָתָם
יִטְמָא עַד־הָעָרֶב: כח וְהַנֹּשֵׂא אֶת־נִבְלָתָם יְכַבֵּס
בְּגָדָיו וְטָמֵא עַד־הָעָרֶב טְמֵאִים הֵמָּה לָכֶם: ס
כט וְזֶה לָכֶם הַטָּמֵא בַּשֶּׁרֶץ הַשֹּׁרֵץ עַל־הָאָרֶץ
הַחֹלֶד וְהָעַכְבָּר וְהַצָּב לְמִינֵהוּ: ל וְהָאֲנָקָה
וְהַכֹּחַ וְהַלְּטָאָה וְהַחֹמֶט וְהַתִּנְשָׁמֶת: לא אֵלֶּה
הַטְּמֵאִים לָכֶם בְּכָל־הַשָּׁרֶץ כָּל־הַנֹּגֵעַ בָּהֶם
בְּמֹתָם יִטְמָא עַד־הָעָרֶב: לב וְכֹל אֲשֶׁר־יִפֹּל
עָלָיו מֵהֶם בְּמֹתָם יִטְמָא מִכָּל־כְּלִי־עֵץ אוֹ
בֶגֶד אוֹ־עוֹר אוֹ שָׂק כָּל־כְּלִי אֲשֶׁר־יֵעָשֶׂה
מְלָאכָה בָּהֶם בַּמַּיִם יוּבָא וְטָמֵא עַד־הָעֶרֶב
וְטָהֵר: שביעי לג וְכָל־כְּלִי־חֶרֶשׂ אֲשֶׁר־יִפֹּל מֵהֶם
אֶל־תּוֹכוֹ כֹּל אֲשֶׁר בְּתוֹכוֹ יִטְמָא וְאֹתוֹ תִשְׁבֹּרוּ:
לד מִכָּל־הָאֹכֶל אֲשֶׁר יֵאָכֵל אֲשֶׁר יָבוֹא עָלָיו
מַיִם יִטְמָא וְכָל־מַשְׁקֶה אֲשֶׁר יִשָּׁתֶה בְּכָל־כְּלִי
יִטְמָא: לה וְכֹל אֲשֶׁר־יִפֹּל מִנִּבְלָתָם עָלָיו
יִטְמָא תַּנּוּר וְכִירַיִם יֻתָּץ טְמֵאִים הֵם וּטְמֵאִים

unclean may they serve you.   36. But a spring and a cistern, a gathering of water, remains clean; however, anything that touches their carcass, even there, becomes unclean.   37. And if [any part] of their carcass falls upon any sowing seed which is to be sown, it [i.e., the seed] is clean.   38. But if water has been put on [such] seeds and [any part] of their carcass falls upon it, it is unclean to you.   39. And if any animal permitted for you to eat dies, he that touches its carcass shall be unclean until evening.   40. Whoever eats of its carcass must wash his garments and is unclean until evening; even one who only carries its carcass must wash his garments and is unclean until evening.   41. And every creeping thing that creeps upon the earth, it is an abomination; it shall not be eaten.   42. Whatever goes upon the belly and whatever goes upon four legs, to whatever has many legs, of any creeping thing that creeps upon the earth, you shall not eat them because they are an abomination. 43. Do not make your souls an abomination with all the creeping things that creep, and do not make yourselves unclean with them; you would go under entirely on their account.   44. For I, *God*, am your God; therefore sanctify yourselves and then you will become holy, for I am holy, and do not make your souls unclean with all the creeping things that move upon the earth. 45. For I, *God*, am He Who leads you up from out of the land of Mitzrayim, to be God to you; therefore be holy, for I am holy. 46. This is the teaching with regard to

יִהְי֣וּ לָכֶ֑ם: לו אַ֣ךְ מַעְיָ֣ן וּב֛וֹר מִקְוֵה־מַ֖יִם יִהְיֶ֣ה טָה֑וֹר וְנֹגֵ֥עַ בְּנִבְלָתָ֖ם יִטְמָֽא: לז וְכִ֤י יִפֹּל֙ מִנִּבְלָתָ֔ם עַ֖ל כָּל־זֶ֥רַע זֵר֖וּעַ אֲשֶׁ֣ר יִזָּרֵ֑עַ טָה֖וֹר הֽוּא: לח וְכִ֤י יֻתַּן־מַ֨יִם֙ עַל־זֶ֔רַע וְנָפַ֥ל מִנִּבְלָתָ֖ם עָלָ֑יו טָמֵ֥א ה֖וּא לָכֶֽם: ס לט וְכִ֤י יָמוּת֙ מִן־הַבְּהֵמָ֗ה אֲשֶׁר־הִ֨יא לָכֶ֤ם לְאָכְלָ֔ה הַנֹּגֵ֥עַ בְּנִבְלָתָ֖הּ יִטְמָ֥א עַד־הָעָֽרֶב: מ וְהָֽאֹכֵל֙ מִנִּבְלָתָ֔הּ יְכַבֵּ֣ס בְּגָדָ֔יו וְטָמֵ֖א עַד־הָעָ֑רֶב וְהַנֹּשֵׂא֙ אֶת־נִבְלָתָ֔הּ יְכַבֵּ֥ס בְּגָדָ֖יו וְטָמֵ֥א עַד־הָעָֽרֶב: מא וְכָל־הַשֶּׁ֖רֶץ הַשֹּׁרֵ֣ץ עַל־הָאָ֑רֶץ שֶׁ֥קֶץ ה֖וּא לֹ֥א יֵֽאָכֵֽל: מב כֹּל֩ הוֹלֵ֨ךְ עַל־גָּח֜וֹן (וי"ו דגחון חצי התורה באותיות והוי"ו רבתי) וְכֹ֣ל ׀ הוֹלֵ֣ךְ עַל־אַרְבַּ֗ע עַ֚ד כָּל־מַרְבֵּ֣ה רַגְלַ֔יִם לְכָל־הַשֶּׁ֖רֶץ הַשֹּׁרֵ֣ץ עַל־הָאָ֑רֶץ לֹ֥א תֹֽאכְל֖וּם כִּי־שֶׁ֥קֶץ הֵֽם: מג אַל־תְּשַׁקְּצוּ֙ אֶת־נַ֨פְשֹׁ֣תֵיכֶ֔ם בְּכָל־הַשֶּׁ֖רֶץ הַשֹּׁרֵ֑ץ וְלֹ֤א תִטַּמְּאוּ֙ בָּהֶ֔ם וְנִטְמֵתֶ֖ם בָּֽם: מד כִּ֣י אֲנִ֣י יְהֹוָה֮ אֱלֹֽהֵיכֶם֒ וְהִתְקַדִּשְׁתֶּם֙ וִהְיִיתֶ֣ם קְדֹשִׁ֔ים כִּ֥י קָד֖וֹשׁ אָ֑נִי וְלֹ֤א תְטַמְּאוּ֙ אֶת־נַפְשֹׁ֣תֵיכֶ֔ם בְּכָל־הַשֶּׁ֖רֶץ הָֽרֹמֵ֥שׂ עַל־הָאָֽרֶץ: מפטיר מה כִּ֣י ׀ אֲנִ֣י יְהֹוָ֗ה הַֽמַּעֲלֶ֤ה אֶתְכֶם֙ מֵאֶ֣רֶץ מִצְרַ֔יִם לִהְיֹ֥ת לָכֶ֖ם לֵֽאלֹהִ֑ים וִהְיִיתֶ֣ם קְדֹשִׁ֔ים כִּ֥י קָד֖וֹשׁ אָֽנִי: מו זֹ֣את תּוֹרַ֣ת

---

35. and only as unclean may they serve you. In their unclean state they may be used for profane purposes; i.e., where there is no contact with the Sanctuary and its holy things. . . .

     °   °   °

46 and 47. . . . All the things that are said about the "dietary regulations" of the Mosaic law in order to justify the assertion that these laws were intended only for a certain time and for certain places are refuted by the straightforward text of the Law itself. These laws are not intended to preserve the health of our bodies but to ensure the mental and moral health of our spiritual personality. They are meant to guard the sensual

aspects of our personality from unrestrained animal passion and to keep our moral and spiritual willpower from becoming dulled and unresponsive. They seek to impress upon us that the basic prerequisite for our ability to discharge our spiritual and moral task is that we keep our physical bodies within that narrow path of purity which will make them both vital and receptive and thus obedient, efficient instruments and servants to the godly and moral spiritual aspect of our personalities. . . .

     °   °   °

Let us try, tnen, to ascertain the ideas that seem to be conveyed by the laws of טומאה [uncleanness or impurity] contained in this chapter. The categories of

הַבְּהֵמָה֙ וְהָע֔וֹף וְכֹל֙ נֶ֣פֶשׁ הַֽחַיָּ֔ה הָֽרֹמֶ֖שֶׂת בַּמָּ֑יִם

the animal and the bird and every living thing that moves in the water, and for every

uncleanness set forth in the present chapter are those of טומאת מגע [uncleanness caused by physical contact with an unclean thing]. Uncleanness resulting from the physical condition of living human beings is not discussed here but only in the following chapter. In the present chapter we have טומאת נבלה and שֶׁרֶץ, uncleanness resulting from contact with the carcasses of all larger mammals and eight smaller animal species. . . .

We have already had occasion repeatedly to note how the dead body of a human being calls attention to a fact most apt to foster the pernicious delusion that is called טוּמְאָה [uncleanness]: The corpse represents a human being that has succumbed completely to the power of physical forces. But the corpse we see before us is not the real human being. Man's true being cannot be touched by the power of physical forces. It departed before the body, which was only its earthly shell, could become forfeit to the leaden laws of earth's natural forces. Indeed, all the time that this true, vital human being, with his free-willed, self-determining godly nature, was present in the body that has now succumbed to the forces of nature, that body had been freed from subservience to mere physical forces and had been uplifted, with all its capacities for action and also for pleasure, into the realm of freedom, there to perform, of its own free will, the moral task of its life. In short, death really begins only with death. As long as there is life, man, endowed with emotions, with intelligence and with the ability to plan and to act, is able to dominate and control, guide and employ the physical aspects of his body, with all its inherent powers, drives and faculties, in godly, free self-determination, within the limits, and for the discharge, of the duties commanded by the moral law. In the face of the phenomena of death that preach the frailty of man and the power of physical forces, all these truths must be impressed, over and over again, upon the conscious mind of the living person so that he may remain constantly aware of his upright, free position in the midst of the physical world and, in proud awareness of his own vital freedom, remain forearmed against all those materialist notions that draw their wisdom from post-mortem examinations and whose teachings would stifle all morality.

° ° °

Susceptibility to טוּמְאָה is limited to articles actually used by men for specific purposes, and even there only to certain types of articles. This limitation seems to be based on the idea that טוּמְאָה is not a physical condition attaching to physical properties of the articles or materials involved. Rather, טוּמְאָה is an abstract concept to be negated in all phases of human life, and utensils do represent such phases: a chest is an object in which to keep one's material possessions; a tool is an article with which creative work can be performed; a pot is a vessel in which food can be prepared for nourishment and pleasure, etc. Since כֵּלִים [utensils or vessels] thus appear as symbols of specific aspects of human life, the concept of טוּמְאָה does not apply to all כֵּלִים indiscriminately but only to those singled out as representing the most significant phases of human life which the laws relating to טוּמְאָה seek to express in symbolic terms.

Precisely this selection and clear-cut limitation of objects to which these laws apply tend to preserve the conceptual and symbolic significance of the whole, because sharp delineation and maximum precision in definition are basic prerequisites for anything chosen to symbolize an abstract concept. Thus, in the case of the צִיצִית [fringes], which serve as reminders of the moral sanctification inherent in human clothing, the garments specified as requiring צִיצִית are those made of wool or flax because these are the materials most commonly used for clothing. (See Numbers 15:37 ff.). In the case of the מְזוּזָה, which expresses the consecration of the home as the place where the Word of God is to attain its truest realization, the מְזוּזָה is not commanded for every room but only for such rooms which, by their spaciousness and arrangement, best symbolize the concept of "home." Likewise, in the case of אִיסוּר מְלָאכָה [the prohibition against carrying out "creating" work] on the Sabbath, the activities singled out to represent the truths symbolized by that prohibition are those that most significantly demonstrate man's constructive power over matter. Again, in the same spirit, in the case of the truth to be symbolized by אִיסוּר בָּשָׂר בְּחָלָב [the prohibition against eating meat and milk together], the law is stated only in terms of the meat and milk of "clean"; i.e., kosher animals, because these are man's principal source of nourishment. Undomesticated animals and fowl are not mentioned. Again, this very choice ensures to all these and similar laws that symbolic character which expresses abstract ideas and which therefore requires, above all, sharp and clear-cut definitions.

So, too, in the laws of טוּמְאָה we find a deliberate selection of articles used by men in everyday life, and we note that susceptibility to טוּמְאָה is limited to articles that most eminently symbolize the various activities complementing the human personality. Moreover, in each category selected, טוּמְאָה is associated only with specific features that characterize these articles in their relation to everyday life.

° ° °

Accordingly, these laws specify three distinct categories of utensils or vessels.

First, utensils made of wood or of any other animal

creature that creeps upon the earth, 47. to differentiate between the unclean and the clean, and between the living [things] that may be eaten and the living [things] that shall not be eaten.

וּלְכָל־נֶ֣פֶשׁ הַֽשֹּׁרֶ֔צֶת עַל־הָאָֽרֶץ׃ מז לְהַבְדִּ֕יל בֵּ֥ין הַטָּמֵ֖א וּבֵ֣ין הַטָּהֹ֑ר וּבֵ֤ין הַֽחַיָּה֙ הַֽנֶּאֱכֶ֔לֶת וּבֵין֙ הַֽחַיָּ֔ה אֲשֶׁ֖ר לֹ֥א תֵאָכֵֽל׃ פ

or vegetable material. Most typically, these articles are used to make clothing for man and portable containers for his possessions. . . . This category of utensils symbolically represents man as part of society and as the active utilizer of his possessions. . . .

Second, metal utensils. The outstanding feature of utensils in this category is that they are used as tools. . . .

Third, earthenware utensils. . . . We conceive of earthenware utensils as vessels intended for the preservation and preparation of foods. These vessels, then, symbolically represent man in his food-getting activities.

We may sum up the ideas expressed by the laws regarding unclean utensils or vessels as follows: They admonish us to remove our lives as citizens in human society, the manner in which we handle our possessions and our activities of work and pleasure, from the sphere of purely physical accomplishment, and to employ our energies to keep these abilities free from all moral impurity so that we may utilize our energies, in morally free self-determination, to accomplish the objectives set for us by the Sanctuary and its holy things.

Foods and beverages. These are self-explanatory. They are the things from which man derives nourishment and pleasure. Here, again, we see the category of "foods" limited only to matter clearly associated with the idea of "food." The category of beverages lists only seven liquids—water, milk, wine, etc.—that are generally associated with the idea of "beverage." Only these liquids are susceptible to uncleanness.

°   °   °

טְבִילָה [immersion in water]. . . . By immersing his entire body into such water [i.e., water gathered in a depression in the ground], making complete and direct contact with that element, without anything intervening between it and himself, he completely severs every link with the sphere of טוּמְאָה. He leaves the stage of humanity, as it were, and returns temporarily to the elemental world in order to begin a new life of "cleanness" or purity. It is, symbolically, an act of rebirth. . . .

The Haftarah for this Sidra may be found on page 872.

תזריע

THAZRIA

XII

1. *God* spoke to Moshe [saying]:   2. Speak to the sons of Yisrael [saying]: If a woman has matured a human seed and gives birth to a male [child], she shall be unclean for seven days; just as in the days of her separation during her period shall she be unclean.   3. And on the eighth day the flesh of his foreskin shall be circumcised.   4. And she shall remain in the blood of purification for thirty-three days; she shall touch no sanctified thing and not come into the Sanctuary until the days of her purity are complete.   5. But if she gives birth to a female [child], she shall be unclean for two weeks just as at her time of separation and remain upon the blood of purification for sixty-six days.   6. And when the days of her purity are completed, for a son or for a daughter, she shall bring a sheep still in its first year for an ascent offering, and a young pigeon or a turtle-dove for an offering that clears [him who brings it] of sin, to the entrance of the Tent of Appointed Meeting, to the

יב א וַיְדַבֵּ֥ר יְהֹוָ֖ה אֶל־מֹשֶׁ֥ה לֵּאמֹֽר: ב דַּבֵּ֞ר אֶל־
בְּנֵ֤י יִשְׂרָאֵל֙ לֵאמֹ֔ר אִשָּׁה֙ כִּ֣י תַזְרִ֔יעַ וְיָלְדָ֖ה זָכָ֑ר
וְטָֽמְאָה֙ שִׁבְעַ֣ת יָמִ֔ים כִּימֵ֛י נִדַּ֥ת דְּוֺתָ֖הּ תִּטְמָֽא:
ג וּבַיּ֖וֹם הַשְּׁמִינִ֑י יִמּ֖וֹל בְּשַׂ֥ר עָרְלָתֽוֹ:
ד וּשְׁלֹשִׁ֣ים יוֹם֙ וּשְׁלֹ֣שֶׁת יָמִ֔ים תֵּשֵׁ֖ב בִּדְמֵ֣י
טׇהֳרָ֑ה בְּכׇל־קֹ֣דֶשׁ לֹֽא־תִגָּ֗ע וְאֶל־הַמִּקְדָּשׁ֙ לֹ֣א
תָבֹ֔א עַד־מְלֹ֖את יְמֵ֥י טׇהֳרָֽהּ: ה וְאִם־נְקֵבָ֣ה תֵלֵ֔ד
וְטָֽמְאָ֥ה שְׁבֻעַ֖יִם כְּנִדָּתָ֑הּ וְשִׁשִּׁ֥ים יוֹם֙ וְשֵׁ֣שֶׁת
יָמִ֔ים תֵּשֵׁ֖ב עַל־דְּמֵ֥י טׇהֳרָֽה: ו וּבִמְלֹ֣את ׀ יְמֵ֣י
טׇהֳרָ֗הּ לְבֵן֮ א֣וֹ לְבַת֒ תָּבִ֞יא כֶּ֤בֶשׂ בֶּן־שְׁנָתוֹ֙ לְעֹלָ֔ה
וּבֶן־יוֹנָ֥ה אוֹ־תֹ֖ר לְחַטָּ֑את אֶל־פֶּ֥תַח אֹֽהֶל־מוֹעֵ֖ד

CHAPTER XII

4–5. . . . In the case of a woman who has given birth to a female child the period of טומְאָה [uncleanness] and "pure days" is twice as long as that applicable when the child is male. The "two weeks just as in her time of separation" seem to imply that this cycle is to be viewed as a twofold one: The mother must observe one week of "uncleanness" and thirty-three "pure" days after giving birth to a son. This she does for herself. When she gives birth to a daughter, she must observe the same period twice, once for herself and once for her girl-child, to take the place of what would have been *milah*, had the infant been a boy.

As we have pointed out in connection with the chapter on *milah* (Genesis 17:15 ff.), one of the basic traits of the Jewish woman, as a true daughter of Sarah, is her willingness to subordinate herself, of her own free will, to that "measure" of morality of which the male is constantly reminded by the *milah* on his flesh. Now the laws of טומְאָה [uncleanness] and טׇהֳרָה [cleanness or purity] to be observed by women appear to serve as equally forceful aids in training the woman for purity of character. The day when the father performs *milah*, the first duty a man must perform for his son, should imbue the father with the sacred resolve to "raise his son to walk in moral strength before God, the God of the Law," and to serve his son, by his own conduct, as a model for such a way of life. Similarly, the fact that the woman's path to purity following the birth of a daughter is twice as long as after the birth of a son certainly should serve to impress the mother with all the solemnity and grandeur of her own task to become teacher, guide and model for the Jewish woman of the future. After all, the mother's influence in molding the moral standards of her daughters is twice as great as her influence on the moral development of her sons. With sons, the main thrust of their training comes from the father, to whom they can look as a model for their own future male role. With daughters, on the other hand, the mother is not only their role model but also the molder of their character, so that after the birth of each daughter she will do well to prepare herself with redoubled intensity, both for her own sake and for the sake of her newborn daughter, in order that they both may ascend the lofty path of purity and morality to the heights of God's own ideal of holiness.

∘   ∘   ∘

priest.   7. He shall bring it near before *God* and effect atonement for her, and so she will be purified from the source of her blood. This is the teaching with regard to one who gives birth, be it to a male or to a female [child].   8. But if her means are not sufficient to defray [the cost of] a sheep, she shall take two turtle-doves or two young pigeons, one for an ascent offering and one for an offering that clears [him who brings it] of sin; the priest will effect atonement for her and she shall be pure.

XIII
1. *God* spoke to Moshe and to Aharon [saying]:
2. If a man has on the skin of his flesh a very white spot, or one that is nearly so, or one that is shiny white, and it forms a leprous mark in the skin of his flesh, then

אֶל־הַכֹּהֵן: ז וְהִקְרִיבוֹ לִפְנֵי יְהֹוָה וְכִפֶּר עָלֶיהָ וְטָהֲרָה מִמְּקֹר דָּמֶיהָ זֹאת תּוֹרַת הַיֹּלֶדֶת לַזָּכָר אוֹ לַנְּקֵבָה: ח וְאִם־לֹא תִמְצָא יָדָהּ דֵּי שֶׂה וְלָקְחָה שְׁתֵּי־תֹרִים אוֹ שְׁנֵי בְּנֵי יוֹנָה אֶחָד לְעֹלָה וְאֶחָד לְחַטָּאת וְכִפֶּר עָלֶיהָ הַכֹּהֵן וְטָהֵרָה: פ יג א וַיְדַבֵּר יְהֹוָה אֶל־מֹשֶׁה וְאֶל־אַהֲרֹן לֵאמֹר: ב אָדָם כִּי־יִהְיֶה בְעוֹר־בְּשָׂרוֹ שְׂאֵת אוֹ־סַפַּחַת אוֹ בַהֶרֶת וְהָיָה בְעוֹר־בְּשָׂרוֹ לְנֶגַע

CHAPTER XIII

נְגָעִים *[Leprous Marks]*

No part of God's Law has had to serve so prominently to explode the illusion about the "sanitary purposes of Mosaic legislation" as has this chapter, which deals with נְגָעִים [leprous "marks" or "afflictions"]. On the face of it, there are facts stated in this chapter that would seem to foster such an illusion. After all, it obviously deals with diseases, more specifically with a disease that appears to be contagious. Those affected must be quarantined. Why should that be done if not in order to prevent contagion? All this was sufficient to label these laws as "sanitary regulations" and the priests who administered them as medicine men or physicians. And if, out of the whole register of human diseases, only this one disease, "leprosy," was singled out for police regulations, then, it is claimed, the reason obviously is that this was the one horrible disease from which the Jews suffered most of all, and then there must be some foundation to Tacitus' fairy tale that the Jews were expelled from Egypt because they were carriers of leprosy!

Now let us examine these laws in their salient details to see whether there is even a tenuous justification for classing them as "sanitary regulations."

Let us study the facts. True leprosy, שְׁחִין, in itself, is not מְטַמֵּא [It cannot render a person unclean]. Even the "malignant" leprosy, the "boil[s] of Mitzrayim of which you cannot be cured" (Deuteronomy 28:27 and 35) cannot possibly render a person unclean because, as we see in Verse 18 of the present chapter, the question of an "unclean mark" can arise only after the "leprosy" has begun to heal and healthy skin has already formed over the affected area. Moreover, if the "leprosy" has

erupted over the person's entire body, "from his head to his feet" (Verses 12 and 13), he becomes טָהוֹר [pure]. The "health theorists" interpret this to mean that a violent attack of the disease, affecting the entire body, was a sign of impending recovery. Yet, precisely in the description of "the skin disease of Egypt of which you cannot be cured," the disease is portrayed in its most horrible manifestations, as extending [Deuteronomy 28:35] "from the sole of your foot to the crown of your head." Certainly this last fact, if nothing else, should have given those theorists pause.

Let us continue. In Verses 10, 15, 16 and 17 we are told several times that the appearance of healthy flesh on the diseased spot is a sign of טוּמְאָה [uncleanness], but that if this healthy flesh disappears and the leprous mark breaks out again on that spot, טָהֳרָה [purity] sets in once more. Verse 12 does not demand a microscopic examination of all the body's creases, but only an examination "as far as the eyes of the priest see," of those parts of the body which are directly visible to the eye of the כֹּהֵן. In Chapter 14, Verse 36, the priest is explicitly commanded to have everything removed from the house of the affected person prior to the examination so that if the priest should have to pronounce the person טָמֵא [unclean] all the articles in the house should not become unclean along with the "patient" (Leviticus 14:36). [If the purpose of the "patient's" isolation were indeed to prevent contagion] would it not be a strange "sanitary" procedure to have all garments, beds, household utensils, etc. that might be carrying the infection removed from the house before the inspection in order to safeguard their owner from material loss in case the patient is declared "unclean"?

Moreover, tradition in general deduces, from what

he shall be brought to Aharon, the priest, or to one of his sons, the priests, 3. and the priest shall look at the mark in the skin of the flesh, [and] the hair on the mark has turned white, and the color of the mark is deeper than the skin of his flesh, then it is a leprous mark; the priest must see it and pronounce it unclean. 4. But if it is a shiny white spot in the skin of his flesh, even if its color is not so much deeper than the skin, and the hair has not turned white, then

צָרָעַת וְהוּבָא אֶל־אַהֲרֹן הַכֹּהֵן אוֹ אֶל־אַחַד
מִבָּנָיו הַכֹּהֲנִים: ג וְרָאָה הַכֹּהֵן אֶת־הַנֶּגַע
בְּעוֹר־הַבָּשָׂר וְשֵׂעָר בַּנֶּגַע הָפַךְ | לָבָן וּמַרְאֵה
הַנֶּגַע עָמֹק מֵעוֹר בְּשָׂרוֹ נֶגַע צָרַעַת הוּא וְרָאָהוּ
הַכֹּהֵן וְטִמֵּא אֹתוֹ: ד וְאִם־בַּהֶרֶת לְבָנָה הִוא
בְּעוֹר בְּשָׂרוֹ וְעָמֹק אֵין־מַרְאֶהָ מִן־הָעוֹר
וּשְׂעָרָה לֹא־הָפַךְ לָבָן וְהִסְגִּיר הַכֹּהֵן אֶת־הַנֶּגַע

has just been said, that the "public health physicians" in priestly garb must be very considerate and lenient in every respect [always ready to give the benefit of the doubt in questionable cases]. If this טָמֵא declaration and the isolation of the affected person had been intended to prevent physical contagion, such leniency in dealing with so "dangerous" and "revolting" a disease as "leprosy" would be utterly senseless.

Furthermore, where, and when, would such public health examinations and quarantine be more appropriate than at seasons when masses of people gather in one place and "lepers" mingling unhindered with the crowds could infect entire families, indeed, the entire nation? Yet, precisely at those seasons the priests were ordered to hold their "leprosy" examinations in abeyance. No examinations for leprous marks were made during the week of a wedding, and not even during the pilgrim festival seasons, when the entire nation streamed into the city of God's Sanctuary, and also never on Sabbaths or festivals. . . . Note, moreover, that in Jerusalem, of all places, leprous marks on houses were not considered of any consequence (see Commentary on Chapter 14:34). Furthermore . . . [there is the general rule that] any doubtful case of leprosy is pronounced "pure" unless proven otherwise. All this bespeaks a far more lenient attitude than that generally applied in the case of other Scriptural prohibitions. If the laws of "leprosy" had been based on sanitary and health considerations, then especially in the case of leprous marks the law would have had to be particularly strict, in keeping with the legal principle that "regulations concerning danger to human life are more stringent than ritual prohibitions" (Ḥullin 10a).

Note also that . . . in cases where there is absolute certainty that a mark has characteristics that render a person טָמֵא, but there is doubt as to which of two marks on the person's body is the one that is טָמֵא, the person affected cannot be pronounced unclean.

Moreover . . . the מְצוֹרָע ["leper"] had to be expelled only from cities that had been surrounded by a wall at the time the Israelites first took possession of the land (even if those walls had been taken down at a later period). The "leper" was permitted to move about freely in the open countryside and in all towns and cities that were unwalled, or around which walls had been built only after the arrival of the Israelites. There was no police quarantine in those places to protect the people from infection supposedly spread by "lepers." The only cases of "leprosy" that had to be removed from all inhabited places were those involving garments! Also, note that all the "leprosy" laws were applicable only to those inhabitants of the land who were Jews. A non-Jew did not become unclean from any kind of mark; if he had a mark he did not have to be examined, he did not have to be kept in isolation, and if he converted to Judaism any mark that had already been present on his body prior to his conversion was disregarded. . . . Similarly, none of these laws was applicable to leprous marks on houses or clothing owned by non-Jews. . . .

These and similar considerations make it quite inconceivable that this chapter deals with sanitary regulations or preventive measures against disease, or that we should regard our כֹּהֲנִים (whom, by the way, we do not see described anywhere in this chapter as administering medicines or other cures) as public functionaries charged with ministering to the nation's "department of health."

° ° °

Therefore, any interpretation of the laws pertaining to *nega'im* as "sanitary regulations" must be categorically dismissed as myth, pure and simple. . . .

° ° °

If we consider the נְגָעִים laws in their totality, we will see them as a most splendid institution of the most direct Divine Providence that watches over, and educates, each and every individual. We see how in the Jewish state, based upon the Law of God, social sins and misdemeanors are brought out into the open, to be punished and corrected. Under the systems, such sins as arrogance, falsehood, avarice and slander escape the authority of human tribunals, but in the Jewish state governed by God's Law, God Himself appears as the

the priest shall have the [person with the] mark confined for seven days. 5. And the priest then looks at him on the seventh day, and lo! the mark is still there, it has remained the same shade, and moreover, the mark has not spread in the skin, then the priest shall have him remain confined for another seven days. 6. And the priest shall look at him on the seventh day for a second time, and lo! the mark has become darker and the mark has not spread in the skin, then the priest must declare him pure; it is merely a mark resembling leprosy; he must wash his garments and he is then pure. 7. But if the mark resembling leprosy spreads in the skin after it has been shown to the priest to be pronounced pure, it shall be shown to the priest again, 8. and the priest then looks, and lo! the mark resembling leprosy has spread in the skin, then the priest shall pronounce him unclean; it is leprosy. 9. If a leprous mark appears on a person, he shall be brought to the priest, 10. and the priest then looks, and lo! it is a very white spot in the skin, and the hair has turned white; and likewise if there is an area of healthy flesh in the very white [spot], 11. then it is an old leprosy in the skin of his flesh; the priest must pronounce him unclean; he does not need to keep him confined, for he is unclean. 12. But if the leprosy then breaks out further in the skin and the leprosy covers all the skin that is susceptible to the mark, from his head to his feet, as far as the eyes of the priest see, 13. and the priest looks, and lo! the leprosy has covered his whole body; then he must pronounce the mark pure. It has all turned white; therefore he is pure. 14. But on that day on which healthy flesh appears on him again he becomes unclean. 15. The priest shall look at the healthy flesh and must pronounce him unclean. The healthy flesh is unclean; it is leprosy. 16. Or if the healthy flesh turns white again, he shall come to the priest. 17. The priest looks at him, and lo! the

שִׁבְעַת יָמִים: ה וְרָאָהוּ הַכֹּהֵן בַּיּוֹם הַשְּׁבִיעִי
וְהִנֵּה הַנֶּגַע עָמַד בְּעֵינָיו לֹא־פָשָׂה הַנֶּגַע בָּעוֹר
וְהִסְגִּירוֹ הַכֹּהֵן שִׁבְעַת יָמִים שֵׁנִית: שני ו וְרָאָה
הַכֹּהֵן אֹתוֹ בַּיּוֹם הַשְּׁבִיעִי שֵׁנִית וְהִנֵּה כֵּהָה
הַנֶּגַע וְלֹא־פָשָׂה הַנֶּגַע בָּעוֹר וְטִהֲרוֹ הַכֹּהֵן
מִסְפַּחַת הִוא וְכִבֶּס בְּגָדָיו וְטָהֵר: ז וְאִם־פָּשֹׂה
תִפְשֶׂה הַמִּסְפַּחַת בָּעוֹר אַחֲרֵי הֵרָאֹתוֹ אֶל־
הַכֹּהֵן לְטָהֳרָתוֹ וְנִרְאָה שֵׁנִית אֶל־הַכֹּהֵן:
ח וְרָאָה הַכֹּהֵן וְהִנֵּה פָּשְׂתָה הַמִּסְפַּחַת בָּעוֹר
וְטִמְּאוֹ הַכֹּהֵן צָרַעַת הִוא: פ ט נֶגַע צָרַעַת כִּי
תִהְיֶה בְּאָדָם וְהוּבָא אֶל־הַכֹּהֵן: י וְרָאָה הַכֹּהֵן
וְהִנֵּה שְׂאֵת־לְבָנָה בָּעוֹר וְהִיא הָפְכָה שֵׂעָר לָבָן
וּמִחְיַת בָּשָׂר חַי בַּשְׂאֵת: יא צָרַעַת נוֹשֶׁנֶת הִוא
בְּעוֹר בְּשָׂרוֹ וְטִמְּאוֹ הַכֹּהֵן לֹא יַסְגִּרֶנּוּ כִּי טָמֵא
הוּא: יב וְאִם־פָּרוֹחַ תִּפְרַח הַצָּרַעַת בָּעוֹר
וְכִסְּתָה הַצָּרַעַת אֵת כָּל־עוֹר הַנֶּגַע מֵרֹאשׁוֹ
וְעַד־רַגְלָיו לְכָל־מַרְאֵה עֵינֵי הַכֹּהֵן: יג וְרָאָה
הַכֹּהֵן וְהִנֵּה כִסְּתָה הַצָּרַעַת אֶת־כָּל־בְּשָׂרוֹ
וְטִהַר אֶת־הַנֶּגַע כֻּלּוֹ הָפַךְ לָבָן טָהוֹר הוּא:
יד וּבְיוֹם הֵרָאוֹת בּוֹ בָּשָׂר חַי יִטְמָא: טו וְרָאָה
הַכֹּהֵן אֶת־הַבָּשָׂר הַחַי וְטִמְּאוֹ הַבָּשָׂר הַחַי טָמֵא
הוּא צָרַעַת הוּא: טז אוֹ כִי יָשׁוּב הַבָּשָׂר הַחַי
וְנֶהְפַּךְ לְלָבָן וּבָא אֶל־הַכֹּהֵן: יז וְרָאָהוּ הַכֹּהֵן

accuser and as the witness for the prosecution. Thus, *Torath Kohanim* comments on Chapter 14, Verse 35: "*He who owns the house shall come and inform the priest saying.* Saying: The priest shall say to him words of reproof: My son, leprous marks come only as a result of such sins as evil gossip, etc."

mark has turned white, then the priest must pronounce the mark pure; he is pure. 18. And [as for] flesh on whose skin there is a boil and it has healed, 19. but there is on the place of the boil a very white or shiny white spot intermingled with red, it must be shown to the priest, 20. and the priest looks, and lo! its color is lower than the skin and its hair has turned white; then the priest must pronounce him unclean. It is a leprous mark that has broken out on the boil. 21. But if the priest looks at it, and lo! there is no white hair upon it, and even if it is not so much lower than the skin, but is darker, then the priest must keep him confined for seven days. 22. If it has then spread further in the skin, the priest must pronounce him unclean; it is a [leprous] mark. 23. But if the shiny white spot has remained where it was, it has not spread, then it is a scar from the boil; the priest must pronounce him pure. 24. Or [as for] flesh in whose skin there is a burn caused by fire and the spot where the burn has healed is shiny white intermingled with red, or pure white, 25. and the priest looks at it, and lo! there is hair that has turned white in the shiny white [spot], and its color is deeper than the skin; then it is leprosy. It has broken out in the burn. The priest must pronounce him unclean; it is leprosy. 26. But if the priest looks at it, and lo! there is no white hair in the shiny white [spot], even if it is not so much lower than the skin, but is darker, then the priest must keep him confined for seven days. 27. And the priest looks at him on the seventh day; if it has then spread further in the skin, the priest must pronounce him unclean; it is a leprous mark. 28. But if the shiny white [spot] has remained where it was, it has not spread in the skin, and likewise if it is darker, then it is a very white [spot] due to the burn; the priest must pronounce him pure, for it is the scar of the burn. 29. And a man or a woman on whom there is a mark on the head or on the beard, 30. and the priest looks at the mark, and lo! its color is deeper than the skin and there is short, golden hair upon it, then the priest must pronounce him unclean; it is an alopecia, a leprosy of the head or of the beard. 31. But if the priest looks

וְהִנֵּה נֶהְפַּךְ הַנֶּגַע לְלָבָן וְטִהַר הַכֹּהֵן אֶת־הַנֶּגַע
טָהוֹר הוּא: פ שלישי יח וּבָשָׂר כִּי־יִהְיֶה בוֹ־
בְעֹרוֹ שְׁחִין וְנִרְפָּא: יט וְהָיָה בִּמְקוֹם הַשְּׁחִין
שְׂאֵת לְבָנָה אוֹ בַהֶרֶת לְבָנָה אֲדַמְדָּמֶת וְנִרְאָה
אֶל־הַכֹּהֵן: כ וְרָאָה הַכֹּהֵן וְהִנֵּה מַרְאֶהָ שָׁפָל
מִן־הָעוֹר וּשְׂעָרָהּ הָפַךְ לָבָן וְטִמְּאוֹ הַכֹּהֵן נֶגַע־
צָרַעַת הִוא בַּשְּׁחִין פָּרָחָה: כא וְאִם ׀ יִרְאֶנָּה
הַכֹּהֵן וְהִנֵּה אֵין־בָּהּ שֵׂעָר לָבָן וּשְׁפָלָה אֵינֶנָּה
מִן־הָעוֹר וְהִיא כֵהָה וְהִסְגִּירוֹ הַכֹּהֵן שִׁבְעַת
יָמִים: כב וְאִם־פָּשֹׂה תִפְשֶׂה בָּעוֹר וְטִמֵּא הַכֹּהֵן
אֹתוֹ נֶגַע הִוא: כג וְאִם־תַּחְתֶּיהָ תַּעֲמֹד הַבַּהֶרֶת
לֹא פָשָׂתָה צָרֶבֶת הַשְּׁחִין הִוא וְטִהֲרוֹ הַכֹּהֵן: ס
רביעי (שני כשהן מחוברין) כד אוֹ בָשָׂר כִּי־יִהְיֶה בְעֹרוֹ
מִכְוַת־אֵשׁ וְהָיְתָה מִחְיַת הַמִּכְוָה בַּהֶרֶת לְבָנָה
אֲדַמְדֶּמֶת אוֹ לְבָנָה: כה וְרָאָה אֹתָהּ הַכֹּהֵן וְהִנֵּה
נֶהְפַּךְ שֵׂעָר לָבָן בַּבַּהֶרֶת וּמַרְאֶהָ עָמֹק מִן־הָעוֹר
צָרַעַת הִוא בַּמִּכְוָה פָּרָחָה וְטִמֵּא אֹתוֹ הַכֹּהֵן
נֶגַע צָרַעַת הִוא: כו וְאִם ׀ יִרְאֶנָּה הַכֹּהֵן וְהִנֵּה
אֵין־בַּבַּהֶרֶת שֵׂעָר לָבָן וּשְׁפָלָה אֵינֶנָּה מִן־הָעוֹר
וְהִוא כֵהָה וְהִסְגִּירוֹ הַכֹּהֵן שִׁבְעַת יָמִים:
כז וְרָאָהוּ הַכֹּהֵן בַּיּוֹם הַשְּׁבִיעִי אִם־פָּשֹׂה
תִפְשֶׂה בָּעוֹר וְטִמֵּא הַכֹּהֵן אֹתוֹ נֶגַע צָרַעַת
הִוא: כח וְאִם־תַּחְתֶּיהָ תַעֲמֹד הַבַּהֶרֶת לֹא־
פָשְׂתָה בָעוֹר וְהִוא כֵהָה שְׂאֵת הַמִּכְוָה הִוא
וְטִהֲרוֹ הַכֹּהֵן כִּי־צָרֶבֶת הַמִּכְוָה הִוא: פ
חמישי כט וְאִישׁ אוֹ אִשָּׁה כִּי־יִהְיֶה בוֹ נָגַע
בְּרֹאשׁ אוֹ בְזָקָן: ל וְרָאָה הַכֹּהֵן אֶת־הַנֶּגַע וְהִנֵּה
מַרְאֵהוּ עָמֹק מִן־הָעוֹר וּבוֹ שֵׂעָר צָהֹב דָּק
וְטִמֵּא אֹתוֹ הַכֹּהֵן נֶתֶק הוּא צָרַעַת הָרֹאשׁ אוֹ
הַזָּקָן הוּא: לא וְכִי־יִרְאֶה הַכֹּהֵן אֶת־נֶגַע הַנֶּתֶק

at the alopecia mark, and lo! its color is not
deeper than the skin and there is no black
hair upon it, then the priest shall keep the
[person with the] alopecia mark confined for
seven days. 32. On the seventh day the
priest shall look at the mark, and lo! [if] the
alopecia has not spread, and also no golden
hair has grown upon it and the color of the
alopecia is not deeper than the skin;
33. then he shall shave himself, but he
shall not shave off the alopecia and the
priest shall keep the [person with the]
alopecia confined again for seven days.
34. And the priest looks at the alopecia
on the seventh day, and lo! the alopecia has
not spread in the skin, and its color is not
deeper than the skin, then the priest must
pronounce him pure; he must wash his garments and shall be pure. 35. But if the
alopecia has spread in the skin even after it
was pronounced pure, 36. and the priest
looks at him, and lo! the alopecia has spread
in the skin, then the priest need not look for
golden hair; he is unclean. 37. But if the
appearance of the alopecia remained
unchanged and black hair has grown upon
it, then the alopecia has healed; he is pure
and the priest must pronounce him pure.
38. If a man or a woman has shiny spots
on the skin of their flesh, [and] the spots are
shiny white, 39. and the priest looks, and
lo! there are shiny spots on the skin of their
flesh but [they are] dull white, then it is only
a shininess that has broken out on the skin;
he is pure. 40. And anyone whose head
has become bald, it is [merely] an occipital
baldness; he is pure. 41. If his head
becomes bald on the front side, it is [merely]
a frontal baldness; he is pure. 42. But if a
white mark intermingled with red appears
on the occipital baldness or on the frontal
baldness, then it is a leprosy breaking out on
his occipital baldness or on his frontal baldness. 43. If the priest looks at him, and
lo! the very white [color] of the mark is
white intermingled with red, on his occipital
baldness or on his frontal baldness, similar
to the leprous color on the skin of the
flesh, 44. then he is a leprous man, he is
unclean; the priest must pronounce him unclean. He has his mark on his head.
45. But every leper to whom the mark
attaches, his garments shall be rent, his

וְהִנֵּ֤ה אֵין־מַרְאֵ֙הוּ֙ עָמֹ֣ק מִן־הָע֔וֹר וְשֵׂעָ֥ר שָׁחֹ֖ר
אֵ֣ין בּ֑וֹ וְהִסְגִּ֧יר הַכֹּהֵ֛ן אֶת־נֶ֥גַע הַנֶּ֖תֶק שִׁבְעַ֥ת
יָמִֽים׃ לב וְרָאָ֨ה הַכֹּהֵ֣ן אֶת־הַנֶּגַע֮ בַּיּ֣וֹם הַשְּׁבִיעִי֒
וְהִנֵּה֙ לֹא־פָשָׂ֣ה הַנֶּ֔תֶק וְלֹא־הָ֥יָה ב֖וֹ שֵׂעָ֣ר צָהֹ֑ב
וּמַרְאֵ֣ה הַנֶּ֔תֶק אֵ֥ין עָמֹ֖ק מִן־הָעֽוֹר׃ לג וְהִתְגַּלָּ֔ח
(ג׳ רבתי) וְאֶת־הַנֶּ֖תֶק לֹ֣א יְגַלֵּ֑חַ וְהִסְגִּ֨יר הַכֹּהֵ֧ן אֶת־
הַנֶּ֛תֶק שִׁבְעַ֥ת יָמִ֖ים שֵׁנִֽית׃ לד וְרָאָה֩ הַכֹּהֵ֨ן אֶת־
הַנֶּ֜תֶק בַּיּ֣וֹם הַשְּׁבִיעִ֗י וְ֠הִנֵּה לֹא־פָשָׂ֤ה הַנֶּ֙תֶק֙
בָּע֔וֹר וּמַרְאֵ֕הוּ אֵינֶ֥נּוּ עָמֹ֖ק מִן־הָע֑וֹר וְטִהַ֤ר אֹתוֹ֙
הַכֹּהֵ֔ן וְכִבֶּ֥ס בְּגָדָ֖יו וְטָהֵֽר׃ לה וְאִם־פָּשֹׂ֥ה יִפְשֶׂ֛ה
הַנֶּ֖תֶק בָּע֑וֹר אַחֲרֵ֖י טָהֳרָתֽוֹ׃ לו וְרָאָ֙הוּ֙ הַכֹּהֵ֔ן
וְהִנֵּ֛ה פָּשָׂ֥ה הַנֶּ֖תֶק בָּע֑וֹר לֹֽא־יְבַקֵּ֧ר הַכֹּהֵ֛ן לַשֵּׂעָ֥ר
הַצָּהֹ֖ב טָמֵ֥א הֽוּא׃ לז וְאִם־בְּעֵינָ֞יו עָמַ֣ד הַנֶּ֗תֶק
וְשֵׂעָ֨ר שָׁחֹ֧ר צָֽמַח־בּ֛וֹ נִרְפָּ֥א הַנֶּ֖תֶק טָה֣וֹר ה֑וּא
וְטִהֲר֖וֹ הַכֹּהֵֽן׃ ס לח וְאִ֕ישׁ אֽוֹ־אִשָּׁ֕ה כִּֽי־יִהְיֶ֥ה
בְעוֹר־בְּשָׂרָ֖ם בֶּהָרֹ֑ת בֶּהָרֹ֖ת לְבָנֹֽת׃ לט וְרָאָ֣ה
הַכֹּהֵ֗ן וְהִנֵּ֛ה בְעוֹר־בְּשָׂרָ֥ם בֶּהָרֹ֖ת כֵּה֣וֹת לְבָנֹ֑ת
בֹּ֥הַק ה֛וּא פָּרַ֥ח בָּע֖וֹר טָה֥וֹר הֽוּא׃ ס ששי (שלישי
כשהן מחוברין) מ וְאִ֕ישׁ כִּ֥י יִמָּרֵ֖ט רֹאשׁ֑וֹ קֵרֵ֥חַ ה֖וּא
טָה֥וֹר הֽוּא׃ מא וְאִם֙ מִפְּאַ֣ת פָּנָ֔יו יִמָּרֵ֖ט רֹאשׁ֑וֹ
גִּבֵּ֥חַ ה֖וּא טָה֥וֹר הֽוּא׃ מב וְכִֽי־יִהְיֶ֤ה בַקָּרַ֙חַת֙ א֣וֹ
בַגַּבַּ֔חַת נֶ֖גַע לָבָ֣ן אֲדַמְדָּ֑ם צָרַ֤עַת פֹּרַ֙חַת֙ ה֔וא
בְּקָרַחְתּ֖וֹ א֥וֹ בְגַבַּחְתּֽוֹ׃ מג וְרָאָ֨ה אֹת֜וֹ הַכֹּהֵ֗ן
וְהִנֵּ֤ה שְׂאֵֽת־הַנֶּ֙גַע֙ לְבָנָ֣ה אֲדַמְדֶּ֔מֶת בְּקָרַחְתּ֖וֹ א֣וֹ
בְגַבַּחְתּ֑וֹ כְּמַרְאֵ֥ה צָרַ֖עַת ע֥וֹר בָּשָֽׂר׃ מד אִישׁ־
צָר֥וּעַ ה֖וּא טָמֵ֣א ה֑וּא טַמֵּ֧א יְטַמְּאֶ֛נּוּ הַכֹּהֵ֖ן
בְּרֹאשׁ֥וֹ נִגְעֽוֹ׃ מה וְהַצָּר֜וּעַ אֲשֶׁר־בּ֣וֹ הַנֶּ֗גַע
בְּגָדָ֞יו יִהְי֣וּ פְרֻמִ֗ים וְרֹאשׁוֹ֙ יִהְיֶ֣ה פָר֔וּעַ וְעַל־

head shall remain unshorn, he shall cover himself down to his upper lip, and he shall call out: "Unclean! Unclean!" 46. All the days, as long as the mark is upon him, he shall be unclean; he is unclean. He shall remain in isolation, outside the camp shall his place be. 47. And [as for the] garment in which there is a leprous mark, in a woolen garment or a linen garment, 48. whether it is in the warp or the woof [thread], of flax or of wool, or on a skin, or on anything made of skin, 49. and the mark is dark green or dark red, in the garment or on the skin, or in the warp or the woof [thread], or on any utensil made of skin, then it is a leprous mark and must be shown to the priest. 50. If the priest sees the mark, he must keep [the article with] the mark confined for seven days. 51. And if he sees the mark on the day, that the mark has spread in the garment, or in the warp or the woof [thread] or on the skin, whatever the use for which the skin may have been manufactured, so the mark is a malignant leprosy; it is unclean. 52. He shall burn the garment or the warp and woof [thread] of wool or of flax or the entire vessel of skin in which the mark is, for it is a malignant leprosy; it shall be burned in fire. 53. But if the priest sees, and lo! the mark has not spread in the garment, or in the warp or woof [thread] or in any utensil of skin, 54. then the priest shall command that they wash that upon which the mark is, and he shall keep [the article with] it confined for another seven days. 55. If the priest sees, after the mark was washed, and lo! the mark has not changed its color, and the mark has not spread; then it is unclean. You shall burn it in fire, it is a pitting whether it is on a worn or on a downy place. 56. But if the priest sees, and lo! the mark has become paler after it was washed, he shall tear it out of the garment, or of the skin, or of the warp or woof [thread]. 57. And if it appears again in the garment or in the warp or the woof [thread] or on any utensil of skin, it is a recurrent [condition]; you shall burn in fire that on which the mark is. 58. But the garment, or the warp or the woof [thread], or any skin utensil which you wash and the mark disappears from it, it shall be washed a

שָׂפָם יַעְטֶה וְטָמֵא | טָמֵא יִקְרָא: מו כָּל־יְמֵי
אֲשֶׁר הַנֶּגַע בּוֹ יִטְמָא טָמֵא הוּא בָּדָד יֵשֵׁב
מִחוּץ לַמַּחֲנֶה מוֹשָׁבוֹ: ס מז וְהַבֶּגֶד כִּי־יִהְיֶה
בוֹ נֶגַע צָרָעַת בְּבֶגֶד צֶמֶר אוֹ בְּבֶגֶד פִּשְׁתִּים:
מח אוֹ בִשְׁתִי אוֹ בְעֵרֶב לַפִּשְׁתִּים וְלַצָּמֶר אוֹ
בְעוֹר אוֹ בְּכָל־מְלֶאכֶת עוֹר: מט וְהָיָה הַנֶּגַע
יְרַקְרַק | אוֹ אֲדַמְדָּם בַּבֶּגֶד אוֹ בָעוֹר אוֹ־בַשְּׁתִי
אוֹ־בָעֵרֶב אוֹ בְכָל־כְּלִי־עוֹר נֶגַע צָרַעַת הוּא
וְהָרְאָה אֶת־הַכֹּהֵן: נ וְרָאָה הַכֹּהֵן אֶת־הַנָּגַע
וְהִסְגִּיר אֶת־הַנֶּגַע שִׁבְעַת יָמִים: נא וְרָאָה אֶת־
הַנֶּגַע בַּיּוֹם הַשְּׁבִיעִי כִּי־פָשָׂה הַנֶּגַע בַּבֶּגֶד אוֹ־
בַשְּׁתִי אוֹ־בָעֵרֶב אוֹ בָעוֹר לְכֹל אֲשֶׁר־יֵעָשֶׂה
הָעוֹר לִמְלָאכָה צָרַעַת מַמְאֶרֶת הַנֶּגַע טָמֵא
הוּא: נב וְשָׂרַף אֶת־הַבֶּגֶד אוֹ אֶת־הַשְּׁתִי | אוֹ
אֶת־הָעֵרֶב בַּצֶּמֶר אוֹ בַפִּשְׁתִּים אוֹ אֶת־כָּל־כְּלִי
הָעוֹר אֲשֶׁר־יִהְיֶה בוֹ הַנָּגַע כִּי־צָרַעַת מַמְאֶרֶת
הִוא בָּאֵשׁ תִּשָּׂרֵף: נג וְאִם יִרְאֶה הַכֹּהֵן וְהִנֵּה
לֹא־פָשָׂה הַנֶּגַע בַּבֶּגֶד אוֹ בַשְּׁתִי אוֹ בָעֵרֶב אוֹ
בְּכָל־כְּלִי־עוֹר: נד וְצִוָּה הַכֹּהֵן וְכִבְּסוּ אֵת
אֲשֶׁר־בּוֹ הַנָּגַע וְהִסְגִּירוֹ שִׁבְעַת־יָמִים שֵׁנִית:
שביעי (רביעי כשהן מחוברין) נה וְרָאָה הַכֹּהֵן אַחֲרֵי |
הֻכַּבֵּס אֶת־הַנֶּגַע וְהִנֵּה לֹא־הָפַךְ הַנֶּגַע אֶת־עֵינוֹ
וְהַנֶּגַע לֹא־פָשָׂה טָמֵא הוּא בָּאֵשׁ תִּשְׂרְפֶנּוּ
פְּחֶתֶת הִוא בְּקָרַחְתּוֹ אוֹ בְגַבַּחְתּוֹ: נו וְאִם רָאָה
הַכֹּהֵן וְהִנֵּה כֵּהָה הַנֶּגַע אַחֲרֵי הֻכַּבֵּס אֹתוֹ וְקָרַע
אֹתוֹ מִן־הַבֶּגֶד אוֹ מִן־הָעוֹר אוֹ מִן־הַשְּׁתִי אוֹ
מִן־הָעֵרֶב: מפטיר נז וְאִם־תֵּרָאֶה עוֹד בַּבֶּגֶד אוֹ־
בַשְּׁתִי אוֹ־בָעֵרֶב אוֹ בְכָל־כְּלִי־עוֹר פֹּרַחַת הִוא
בָּאֵשׁ תִּשְׂרְפֶנּוּ אֵת אֲשֶׁר־בּוֹ הַנָּגַע: נח וְהַבֶּגֶד
אוֹ־הַשְּׁתִי אוֹ־הָעֵרֶב אוֹ־כָל־כְּלִי הָעוֹר אֲשֶׁר
תְּכַבֵּס וְסָר מֵהֶם הַנָּגַע וְכֻבַּס שֵׁנִית וְטָהֵר:

second time and shall be pure. 59. This is the teaching with regard to the leprous mark of the wool or linen garment, or of the warp or woof [thread] or of any skin utensil, to pronounce it pure or to pronounce it unclean.

נט זֹ֠את תּוֹרַ֨ת נֶֽגַע־צָרַ֜עַת בֶּ֥גֶד הַצֶּ֣מֶר ׀ א֣וֹ הַפִּשְׁתִּ֗ים א֤וֹ הַשְּׁתִי֙ א֣וֹ הָעֵ֔רֶב א֖וֹ כָּל־כְּלִי־ע֑וֹר לְטַהֲר֖וֹ א֥וֹ לְטַמְּאֽוֹ׃ פ

The Haftarah for this Sidra may be found on page 875.

XIV

1. *God* spoke to Moshe [saying]: 2. Let this be the teaching with regard to the leper on the day of his becoming pure; he shall be brought to the priest. 3. The priest shall go out, outside the camp, and the priest shall look, and lo! the mark of leprosy is healed from the leper, 4. then the priest shall command to take for him who purifies himself two living, clean° birds and a piece of cedar wood and scarlet wool and hyssop. 5. The priest shall command to slaughter the one bird in an earthen vessel over living water. 6. As for the living bird, he himself shall take it, and the piece of cedar wood with the scarlet wool and the hyssop, and shall dip them, together with the living bird, into the blood of the slaughtered bird over the living water, 7. and he shall sprinkle [it] upon him who purifies himself from the leprosy, seven times, and he will be purified, and he shall let the living bird fly away into the [open] field. 8. The one who purifies himself shall wash his garments, shave off all his hair, bathe in water and become pure, and after that he may come into the camp, but he must remain outside his tent for seven days. 9. On the seventh day he shall shave off all his hair: his head, his beard, his eyebrows, he shall shave off all his hair, and wash his garments, bathe his body in water and become pure. 10. On the eighth day

° *Note to the English translation*: i.e., kosher birds. [G.H.]

יד א וַיְדַבֵּ֣ר יְהֹוָ֔ה אֶל־מֹשֶׁ֥ה לֵּאמֹֽר: ב זֹ֤את תִּֽהְיֶה֙ תּוֹרַ֣ת הַמְּצֹרָ֔ע בְּי֖וֹם טׇהֳרָת֑וֹ וְהוּבָ֖א אֶל־הַכֹּהֵֽן: ג וְיָצָא֙ הַכֹּהֵ֔ן אֶל־מִח֖וּץ לַֽמַּחֲנֶ֑ה וְרָאָה֙ הַכֹּהֵ֔ן וְהִנֵּ֛ה נִרְפָּ֥א נֶֽגַע־הַצָּרַ֖עַת מִן־הַצָּרֽוּעַ: ד וְצִוָּה֙ הַכֹּהֵ֔ן וְלָקַ֣ח לַמִּטַּהֵ֗ר שְׁתֵּֽי־צׇפֳּרִ֛ים חַיּ֥וֹת טְהֹר֖וֹת וְעֵ֣ץ אֶ֑רֶז וּשְׁנִ֥י תוֹלַ֖עַת וְאֵזֹֽב: ה וְצִוָּה֙ הַכֹּהֵ֔ן וְשָׁחַ֖ט אֶת־הַצִּפֹּ֣ר הָאֶחָ֑ת אֶל־כְּלִי־חֶ֖רֶשׂ עַל־מַ֥יִם חַיִּֽים: ו אֶת־הַצִּפֹּ֤ר הַֽחַיָּה֙ יִקַּ֣ח אֹתָ֔הּ וְאֶת־עֵ֥ץ הָאֶ֖רֶז וְאֶת־שְׁנִ֣י הַתּוֹלַ֑עַת וְאֶת־הָֽאֵזֹ֗ב וְטָבַ֣ל אוֹתָ֣ם וְאֵ֣ת ׀ הַצִּפֹּ֣ר הַֽחַיָּ֗ה בְּדַם֙ הַצִּפֹּ֣ר הַשְּׁחֻטָ֔ה עַ֖ל הַמַּ֥יִם הַֽחַיִּֽים: ז וְהִזָּ֗ה עַ֧ל הַמִּטַּהֵ֛ר מִן־הַצָּרַ֖עַת שֶׁ֣בַע פְּעָמִ֑ים וְטִ֣הֲר֔וֹ וְשִׁלַּ֥ח אֶת־הַצִּפֹּ֛ר הַֽחַיָּ֖ה עַל־פְּנֵ֥י הַשָּׂדֶֽה: ח וְכִבֶּס֩ הַמִּטַּהֵ֨ר אֶת־בְּגָדָ֜יו וְגִלַּ֣ח אֶת־כׇּל־שְׂעָר֗וֹ וְרָחַ֤ץ בַּמַּ֙יִם֙ וְטָהֵ֔ר וְאַחַ֖ר יָב֣וֹא אֶל־הַֽמַּחֲנֶ֑ה וְיָשַׁ֛ב מִח֥וּץ לְאׇהֳל֖וֹ שִׁבְעַ֥ת יָמִֽים: ט וְהָיָה֩ בַיּ֨וֹם הַשְּׁבִיעִ֜י יְגַלַּ֣ח אֶת־כׇּל־שְׂעָר֗וֹ אֶת־רֹאשׁ֤וֹ וְאֶת־זְקָנוֹ֙ וְאֵת֙ גַּבֹּ֣ת עֵינָ֔יו וְאֶת־כׇּל־שְׂעָר֖וֹ יְגַלֵּ֑חַ וְכִבֶּ֣ס אֶת־בְּגָדָ֗יו וְרָחַ֧ץ אֶת־בְּשָׂר֛וֹ בַּמַּ֖יִם וְטָהֵֽר: י וּבַיּ֣וֹם

CHAPTER XIV

6. . . . Cedar tree and hyssop, the greatest and the smallest manifestations of plant life, together, represent the entire range of vegetable life (Cf. I Kings 5:13) [". . . from the cedar that is in Lebanon to the hyssop that springs out from the wall"], even as wool dyed with the blood of worms, a mammal's product combined with the blood of the lowliest creeping thing, symbolizes the entire range of animal life. All three— cedar wood, wool and hyssop—bound together with the red thread into one single unit, symbolize the complete range of organic life as manifest in the flora and fauna of the open field, where the "leper" was condemned to dwell because of his anti-social, reprehensible conduct. To them is added the "free" bird, which has not been killed, to symbolize the animal that lives without self-restraint, blindly following its instincts. Its way of life makes it part and parcel of plant and animal nature. A sevenfold gap separates this animal from the "everlasting" life that is to be gained by the morally free-willed control of one's animal instincts (this is symbolically expressed by the blood of the pigeon slaughtered over living water) and that is to be realized in the communal life of the moral human being. The sprinkling of the blood, seven times, is meant as a symbolic admonition to him who was banished into the community of plant and animal life that he must now exert sevenfold energy to bridge this gap before he can be pronounced pure and ready for re-entry into the community of men. . . .

∘ ∘ ∘

he shall take two sheep without blemish and
a yearling ewe without blemish, and three
tenths of fine flour, for a homage offering
mixed with oil, and one *log* of oil.
11. And the priest who effects the purification shall place the one who is purifying
himself, along with these, before *God* in the
entrance to the Tent of Appointed Meeting.
12. The priest shall take the one sheep
and bring it near as a guilt offering, and the
log of oil, and wave them as a wave [offer-
ing] before *God*.   13. And he shall
slaughter the sheep in the place where he
slaughters the offering that clears [him who
brings it] of sin and the ascent offering, in
the place of the Sanctuary; for like the offering that clears [him who brings it] of sin, the
guilt offering, too, belongs to the priest; it is
a holy of holies.   14. Then the priest shall
take up [some] of the blood of the guilt
offering, and the priest shall put [it] upon
the right earlobe of him who is purifying
himself, and upon the thumb of his right
hand and upon the big toe of his right foot.
15. And the priest shall take [some] of the
log of oil and pour it into the priest's left
palm.   16. The priest shall bedaub his
right index finger with the oil that is in his
left palm and shall sprinkle [some] of the oil
with his index finger seven times before
God;   17. and of the rest of the oil that is
in his palm, the priest shall put upon the
right earlobe of him who is purifying himself, and upon the thumb of his right hand
and upon the big toe of his right foot, upon
the blood from the guilt offering.   18. And
what is left over from the oil that is in the
priest's palm he shall put upon the head of
the one who is purifying himself and the
priest will effect atonement for him before

הַשְּׁמִינִי יִקַּח שְׁנֵי־כְבָשִׂים תְּמִימִם וְכַבְשָׂה
אַחַת בַּת־שְׁנָתָהּ תְּמִימָה וּשְׁלֹשָׁה עֶשְׂרֹנִים סֹלֶת
מִנְחָה בְּלוּלָה בַשֶּׁמֶן וְלֹג אֶחָד שָׁמֶן: יא וְהֶעֱמִיד
הַכֹּהֵן הַמְטַהֵר אֵת הָאִישׁ הַמִּטַּהֵר וְאֹתָם לִפְנֵי
יְהֹוָה פֶּתַח אֹהֶל מוֹעֵד: יב וְלָקַח הַכֹּהֵן אֶת־
הַכֶּבֶשׂ הָאֶחָד וְהִקְרִיב אֹתוֹ לְאָשָׁם וְאֶת־לֹג
הַשָּׁמֶן וְהֵנִיף אֹתָם תְּנוּפָה לִפְנֵי יְהֹוָה: שני
יג וְשָׁחַט אֶת־הַכֶּבֶשׂ בִּמְקוֹם אֲשֶׁר יִשְׁחַט אֶת־
הַחַטָּאת וְאֶת־הָעֹלָה בִּמְקוֹם הַקֹּדֶשׁ כִּי כַּחַטָּאת
הָאָשָׁם הוּא לַכֹּהֵן קֹדֶשׁ קָדָשִׁים הוּא: יד וְלָקַח
הַכֹּהֵן מִדַּם הָאָשָׁם וְנָתַן הַכֹּהֵן עַל־תְּנוּךְ אֹזֶן
הַמִּטַּהֵר הַיְמָנִית וְעַל־בֹּהֶן יָדוֹ הַיְמָנִית וְעַל־
בֹּהֶן רַגְלוֹ הַיְמָנִית: טו וְלָקַח הַכֹּהֵן מִלֹּג הַשֶּׁמֶן
וְיָצַק עַל־כַּף הַכֹּהֵן הַשְּׂמָאלִית: טז וְטָבַל הַכֹּהֵן
אֶת־אֶצְבָּעוֹ הַיְמָנִית מִן־הַשֶּׁמֶן אֲשֶׁר עַל־כַּפּוֹ
הַשְּׂמָאלִית וְהִזָּה מִן־הַשֶּׁמֶן בְּאֶצְבָּעוֹ שֶׁבַע
פְּעָמִים לִפְנֵי יְהֹוָה: יז וּמִיֶּתֶר הַשֶּׁמֶן אֲשֶׁר עַל־
כַּפּוֹ יִתֵּן הַכֹּהֵן עַל־תְּנוּךְ אֹזֶן הַמִּטַּהֵר הַיְמָנִית
וְעַל־בֹּהֶן יָדוֹ הַיְמָנִית וְעַל־בֹּהֶן רַגְלוֹ הַיְמָנִית
עַל דַּם הָאָשָׁם: יח וְהַנּוֹתָר בַּשֶּׁמֶן אֲשֶׁר עַל־כַּף
הַכֹּהֵן יִתֵּן עַל־רֹאשׁ הַמִּטַּהֵר וְכִפֶּר עָלָיו הַכֹּהֵן

18. . . . This entire procedure—the seven-time
sprinkling of the oil in the direction of the Holy of
Holies, the placing of the oil upon the earlobe, the
thumb and the big toe of the one to be purified, and
then the act of pouring the rest of the oil from the *log*
upon his head, while the rest of the *log* of oil is given to
the priests for their personal consumption (Verse
13)—symbolically sets forth a great truth for the one
who has now recovered from his נְגָעִים disease and who
is about to be readmitted to the ambiance of the Sanctuary: *His physical well-being is completely dependent*

on his spiritual and moral health. He must pledge, in
advance, and with ever-new resolve, every particle of
the health and strength he hopes to receive from God
(as symbolized by שֶׁבַע הַזָּיוֹת [the seven sprinklings]) to
the realization of the Law of God in קֹדֶשׁ קָדָשִׁים, the
Sanctuary. He must carry out this self-dedication
primarily by the use of his senses, by his ability to
imbibe ideas (as symbolized by his ear), by the deeds he
is to accomplish (as symbolized by his thumb) and by
his striving for possessions and attainments (symbolized
by his big toe). He must activate his every thought and

God. 19. The priest shall then make the offering that clears [him who brings it] of sin and he will effect for the one who is purifying himself atonement for his uncleanness; then he shall slaughter the ascent offering. 20. And the priest shall lift the ascent offering and the homage offering onto the altar; the priest will effect atonement for him and he becomes pure. 21. And if he is poor, so that his means are not sufficient, he shall take a sheep for a guilt offering to be waved, to effect atonement for him, and one tenth of fine flour mixed with oil for a homage offering, and one *log* of oil. 22. Also two turtle-doves or two young pigeons for such as his means suffice. The one shall be an offering that clears [him who brings it] of sin; the other, an ascent offering. 23. He shall bring them on the eighth day for his purification, to the priest,

לִפְנֵי יְהֹוָה: יט וְעָשָׂה הַכֹּהֵן אֶת־הַחַטָּאת וְכִפֶּר עַל־הַמִּטַּהֵר מִטֻּמְאָתוֹ וְאַחַר יִשְׁחַט אֶת־הָעֹלָה: כ וְהֶעֱלָה הַכֹּהֵן אֶת־הָעֹלָה וְאֶת־הַמִּנְחָה הַמִּזְבֵּחָה וְכִפֶּר עָלָיו הַכֹּהֵן וְטָהֵר: ס שלישי
(חמישי כשהן מחוברין) כא וְאִם־דַּל הוּא וְאֵין יָדוֹ מַשֶּׂגֶת וְלָקַח כֶּבֶשׂ אֶחָד אָשָׁם לִתְנוּפָה לְכַפֵּר עָלָיו וְעִשָּׂרוֹן סֹלֶת אֶחָד בָּלוּל בַּשֶּׁמֶן לְמִנְחָה וְלֹג שָׁמֶן: כב וּשְׁתֵּי תֹרִים אוֹ שְׁנֵי בְּנֵי יוֹנָה אֲשֶׁר תַּשִּׂיג יָדוֹ וְהָיָה אֶחָד חַטָּאת וְהָאֶחָד עֹלָה: כג וְהֵבִיא אֹתָם בַּיּוֹם הַשְּׁמִינִי לְטָהֳרָתוֹ אֶל־

action with such devotion that it will absorb all the intellectual and spiritual aspects of his personality (as symbolized by his head).

Only if he behaves in this manner will he become hallowed in both body and spirit, a dedicated servant of the Law. And only if he becomes such a "priestly" individual may he hope to receive the health and strength he desires.

and the priest will effect atonement for him before God. With reference to the offering that clears [him who brings it] of sin, which is mentioned in the next verse, we are told, "and he will effect for the one who is purifying himself atonement for his uncleanness." With reference to the ascent offering we are told [Verse 20], "the priest will effect atonement for him and he becomes pure." By means of the guilt offering and the *log* of oil that is part of the ritual, and the offerings performed with these things, one atones for the social sins that have incurred him God's displeasure as manifested by his leprous affliction. This procedure seeks to impress upon him who performs it all the basic truths of a life of Jewish social justice before God. With that, his past sins are erased and he must now, and in all the future, behave as a Jew, a righteous member of society before God under the dominion of God's Law.

19–20. However, social justice is only one aspect of the Jew's mission. Only if he adheres to all the standards set by God's moral law (as symbolically taught by חַטָּאת [the offering that clears him who brings it of sin]) and unceasingly carries out all the duties commanded him by God (as expressed by the symbolic pledge of the עוֹלָה [ascent offering]) can he become a complete Jew.

Indeed, these observances may be likened to the one true root and trunk of the plant of God that is the Jewish people; it is they that engender true Jewish social justice as their fruit and flower. If Jewish justice and Jewish humanity were observed as things apart from all the other Divine laws whose devoted and punctilious observance God demands, it would be only a fragment of a so-called "Judaism" which would never be allowed to win the day in history.

The אֲשַׁם מְצוֹרָע [leper's guilt offering] must be based on a חַטָּאת [offering that clears (him who brings it) of sin] and an עוֹלָה [ascent offering]. By his חַטָּאת the "leper" must symbolically foreswear all his lack of moral self-determination, and by his עוֹלָה he must pledge his morally free-willed devotion to all that which God has declared to be good, so that he may become pure and that the finger of God need never touch him again as a sign of God's displeasure and banish him from the ambiance of Jewish life that develops around the Sanctuary of God's Law.

21–31. ***And if he is poor.*** Even if he is poor, his guilt offering is the same as that of anyone else. The social duty of justice and brotherhood is the same for both rich and poor; social position is not a factor when a man is judged for social sins of the type to be atoned for by the "leper's" guilt offering. Only the tenor of life as such varies with the station into which the individual has been placed, and each station in life calls for the testing of other phases of moral strength. Therefore, although the guilt offering and the one *log* of oil are the same for all "lepers," rich and poor alike, nevertheless, to the entrance to the Tent of Appointed Meeting before *God*. 24. The priest shall take the sheep of the guilt offering and the *log* of oil and the priest shall wave them as a wave [offering] before *God*. 25. He shall slaughter the sheep of the guilt offering, and the priest shall take [some] of the blood of the guilt offering and put [it] upon the right earlobe of the one who is purifying himself, and upon the thumb of his right hand, and upon the big toe of his right foot. 26. The priest shall pour [some] of the oil into the priest's left palm; 27. the priest shall sprinkle with his right index finger from the oil in his left palm seven times before *God*. 28. The priest shall put [some] of the oil that is in his palm upon the right earlobe of the one who is purifying himself, and upon the thumb of his right hand, and upon the big toe of his right foot, upon the place of the blood from the guilt offering. 29. And what is left over from the oil that is in the priest's palm he shall put upon the head of the one who is purifying himself, in order to effect atonement for him before *God*. 30. He shall then offer the one of the turtle-doves, or of the young pigeons, for such as his means suffice; 31. that for which his means suffice, the one for an offering that clears [him who brings it] of sin, and the other for an ascent offering along with the homage offering; and the priest will effect for the one who is purifying himself atonement before *God*. 32. This is the teaching with regard to one on whom there is a leprous mark, whose means do not suffice in his purification. 33. *God* spoke to Moshe and Aharon [saying]: 34. When you come into the land of Canaan, which I give to you as a possession, and I shall cause a leprous mark to develop on a house of the land of your possession, 35. he who owns the house shall come and inform the priest [saying]: "It seems to me as if there were a mark on the house." 36. And the priest shall command that they empty the house before the priest comes to look at the mark, so that everything in the house will not

הַכֹּהֵ֑ן אֶל־פֶּ֥תַח אֹֽהֶל־מוֹעֵ֖ד לִפְנֵ֥י יְהֹוָֽה׃
כד וְלָקַ֥ח הַכֹּהֵ֛ן אֶת־כֶּ֥בֶשׂ הָאָשָׁ֖ם וְאֶת־לֹ֣ג
הַשָּׁ֑מֶן וְהֵנִ֨יף אֹתָ֥ם הַכֹּהֵ֛ן תְּנוּפָ֖ה לִפְנֵ֥י יְהֹוָֽה׃
כה וְשָׁחַט֮ אֶת־כֶּ֣בֶשׂ הָאָשָׁם֒ וְלָקַ֣ח הַכֹּהֵ֗ן מִדַּ֣ם
הָֽאָשָׁ֔ם וְנָתַ֛ן עַל־תְּנ֥וּךְ אֹֽזֶן־הַמִּטַּהֵ֖ר הַיְמָנִ֑ית
וְעַל־בֹּ֣הֶן יָד֔וֹ הַיְמָנִ֔ית וְעַל־בֹּ֥הֶן רַגְל֖וֹ הַיְמָנִֽית׃
כו וּמִן־הַשֶּׁ֖מֶן יִצֹ֣ק הַכֹּהֵ֑ן עַל־כַּ֥ף הַכֹּהֵ֖ן
הַשְּׂמָאלִֽית׃ כז וְהִזָּ֤ה הַכֹּהֵן֙ בְּאֶצְבָּע֣וֹ הַיְמָנִ֔ית
מִן־הַשֶּׁ֕מֶן אֲשֶׁ֖ר עַל־כַּפּ֣וֹ הַשְּׂמָאלִ֑ית שֶׁ֥בַע
פְּעָמִ֖ים לִפְנֵ֥י יְהֹוָֽה׃ כח וְנָתַ֨ן הַכֹּהֵ֜ן מִן־הַשֶּׁ֣מֶן ׀
אֲשֶׁ֣ר עַל־כַּפּ֗וֹ עַל־תְּנ֞וּךְ אֹ֤זֶן הַמִּטַּהֵר֙ הַיְמָנִ֔ית
וְעַל־בֹּ֤הֶן יָדוֹ֙ הַיְמָנִ֔ית וְעַל־בֹּ֥הֶן רַגְל֖וֹ הַיְמָנִ֑ית
עַל־מְק֖וֹם דַּ֥ם הָאָשָֽׁם׃ כט וְהַנּוֹתָ֗ר מִן־הַשֶּׁ֙מֶן֙
אֲשֶׁר֙ עַל־כַּ֣ף הַכֹּהֵ֔ן יִתֵּ֖ן עַל־רֹ֣אשׁ הַמִּטַּהֵ֑ר
לְכַפֵּ֥ר עָלָ֖יו לִפְנֵ֥י יְהֹוָֽה׃ ל וְעָשָׂ֤ה אֶת־הָֽאֶחָד֙
מִן־הַתֹּרִ֔ים א֖וֹ מִן־בְּנֵ֣י הַיּוֹנָ֑ה מֵאֲשֶׁ֥ר תַּשִּׂ֖יג יָדֽוֹ׃
לא אֵ֣ת אֲשֶׁר־תַּשִּׂ֞יג יָד֗וֹ אֶת־הָאֶחָ֥ד חַטָּ֛את
וְאֶת־הָאֶחָ֥ד עֹלָ֖ה עַל־הַמִּנְחָ֑ה וְכִפֶּ֧ר הַכֹּהֵ֛ן עַ֥ל
הַמִּטַּהֵ֖ר לִפְנֵ֥י יְהֹוָֽה׃ לב זֹ֣את תּוֹרַ֔ת אֲשֶׁר־בּ֖וֹ
נֶ֣גַע צָרָ֑עַת אֲשֶׁ֛ר לֹא־תַשִּׂ֥יג יָד֖וֹ בְּטָהֳרָתֽוֹ׃ פ
רביעי (ששי כשהן מחוברין) לג וַיְדַבֵּ֣ר יְהֹוָ֔ה אֶל־מֹשֶׁ֥ה
וְאֶל־אַהֲרֹ֖ן לֵאמֹֽר׃ לד כִּ֤י תָבֹ֙אוּ֙ אֶל־אֶ֣רֶץ כְּנַ֔עַן
אֲשֶׁ֥ר אֲנִ֛י נֹתֵ֥ן לָכֶ֖ם לַאֲחֻזָּ֑ה וְנָתַתִּי֙ נֶ֣גַע צָרַ֔עַת
בְּבֵ֖ית אֶ֥רֶץ אֲחֻזַּתְכֶֽם׃ לה וּבָא֙ אֲשֶׁר־ל֣וֹ הַבַּ֔יִת
וְהִגִּ֥יד לַכֹּהֵ֖ן לֵאמֹ֑ר כְּנֶ֕גַע נִרְאָ֥ה לִ֖י בַּבָּֽיִת׃
לו וְצִוָּ֨ה הַכֹּהֵ֜ן וּפִנּ֣וּ אֶת־הַבַּ֗יִת בְּטֶ֨רֶם יָבֹ֤א
הַכֹּהֵן֙ לִרְא֣וֹת אֶת־הַנֶּ֔גַע וְלֹ֥א יִטְמָ֖א כָּל־אֲשֶׁ֣ר

just as in the case of the offering on an ascending and descending scale, the poor leper uses birds both for the offering that clears [him who brings it] of sin and for the ascent offering.

become unclean, and [only] afterwards shall the priest come to look at the house. 37. If he sees the mark, and lo! the mark is upon the walls of the house, penetrating stains, dark green or dark red, and they appear to be below [the surface of] the wall, 38. then the priest shall go out of the house to the entrance of the house and pronounce the house locked up for seven days. 39. If the priest returns on the seventh day and looks, and lo! the mark has spread on the walls of the house, 40. then the priest shall order that they remove the stones on which the mark is and throw them away outside the city into an unclean place. 41. And he shall have the house scraped inside round about, and they shall pour out the earth they have scraped off outside the city into an unclean place. 42. They shall then take other stones and put them into the place of those stones, and he shall take other earth and face the house with it. 43. If the mark comes again and breaks out on the house after he has removed the stones and after the house has been scraped and after it has been refaced, 44. and the priest comes and he looks, and lo! the mark has spread on the house, then this is a malignant mark on the house; it is unclean. 45. He shall demolish the house, its stones, its wood, and all the earth of the house and shall take it away outside the city, to an unclean place. 46. Anyone who comes into the house all the days that he has pronounced it locked up shall be unclean until evening. 47. But anyone who has lain down in the house must wash his garments; also anyone who eats in the house must wash his garments. 48. But if the priest comes again and looks, and lo! the mark has not spread in the house after the house was refaced, then he must pronounce the house pure because the mark has healed. 49. In order to clear the house of sin, he shall take two birds and one piece of cedar wood, scarlet wool and hyssop, 50. and he shall slaughter the one bird in an earthen vessel over living water. 51. He shall then take the piece of cedar wood, the hyssop and the scarlet wool and the living bird, dip them in the blood of the slaughtered bird and into the living water and sprinkle [it] toward the house seven times. 52. He shall clear the

בַּבָּ֑יִת וְאַ֥חַר כֵּ֛ן יָבֹ֥א הַכֹּהֵ֖ן לִרְא֥וֹת אֶת־הַבָּֽיִת׃
לז וְרָאָ֣ה אֶת־הַנֶּ֗גַע וְהִנֵּ֤ה הַנֶּ֙גַע֙ בְּקִירֹ֣ת הַבַּ֔יִת
שְׁקַֽעֲרוּרֹת֙ יְרַקְרַקֹּ֔ת א֖וֹ אֲדַמְדַּמֹּ֑ת וּמַרְאֵיהֶ֥ן
שָׁפָ֖ל מִן־הַקִּֽיר׃ לח וְיָצָ֧א הַכֹּהֵ֛ן מִן־הַבַּ֖יִת אֶל־
פֶּ֣תַח הַבָּ֑יִת וְהִסְגִּ֥יר אֶת־הַבַּ֖יִת שִׁבְעַ֥ת יָמִֽים׃
לט וְשָׁ֥ב הַכֹּהֵ֖ן בַּיּ֣וֹם הַשְּׁבִיעִ֑י וְרָאָ֕ה וְהִנֵּ֛ה פָּשָׂ֥ה
הַנֶּ֖גַע בְּקִירֹ֥ת הַבָּֽיִת׃ מ וְצִוָּה֙ הַכֹּהֵ֔ן וְחִלְּצוּ֙ אֶת־
הָ֣אֲבָנִ֔ים אֲשֶׁ֥ר בָּהֵ֖ן הַנָּ֑גַע וְהִשְׁלִ֤יכוּ אֶתְהֶן֙ אֶל־
מִח֣וּץ לָעִ֔יר אֶל־מָק֖וֹם טָמֵֽא׃ מא וְאֶת־הַבַּ֛יִת
יַקְצִ֥עַ מִבַּ֖יִת סָבִ֑יב וְשָֽׁפְכ֗וּ אֶת־הֶֽעָפָר֙ אֲשֶׁ֣ר
הִקְצ֔וּ אֶל־מִח֣וּץ לָעִ֔יר אֶל־מָק֖וֹם טָמֵֽא׃
מב וְלָֽקְחוּ֙ אֲבָנִ֣ים אֲחֵר֔וֹת וְהֵבִ֖יאוּ אֶל־תַּ֣חַת
הָאֲבָנִ֑ים וְעָפָ֥ר אַחֵ֛ר יִקַּ֖ח וְטָ֥ח אֶת־הַבָּֽיִת׃
מג וְאִם־יָשׁ֤וּב הַנֶּ֙גַע֙ וּפָרַ֣ח בַּבַּ֔יִת אַחַ֖ר חִלֵּ֣ץ
אֶת־הָאֲבָנִ֑ים וְאַחֲרֵ֛י הִקְצ֥וֹת אֶת־הַבַּ֖יִת וְאַחֲרֵ֥י
הִטּֽוֹחַ׃ מד וּבָא֙ הַכֹּהֵ֔ן וְרָאָ֕ה וְהִנֵּ֛ה פָּשָׂ֥ה הַנֶּ֖גַע
בַּבָּ֑יִת צָרַ֨עַת מַמְאֶ֥רֶת הִ֛וא בַּבַּ֖יִת טָמֵ֥א הֽוּא׃
מה וְנָתַ֣ץ אֶת־הַבַּ֗יִת אֶת־אֲבָנָיו֙ וְאֶת־עֵצָ֔יו וְאֵ֖ת
כָּל־עֲפַ֣ר הַבָּ֑יִת וְהוֹצִיא֙ אֶל־מִח֣וּץ לָעִ֔יר אֶל־
מָק֖וֹם טָמֵֽא׃ מו וְהַבָּא֙ אֶל־הַבַּ֔יִת כָּל־יְמֵ֖י הִסְגִּ֣יר
אֹת֑וֹ יִטְמָ֖א עַד־הָעָֽרֶב׃ מז וְהַשֹּׁכֵ֣ב בַּבַּ֔יִת יְכַבֵּ֖ס
אֶת־בְּגָדָ֑יו וְהָאֹכֵ֣ל בַּבַּ֔יִת יְכַבֵּ֖ס אֶת־בְּגָדָֽיו׃
מח וְאִם־בֹּ֨א יָבֹ֜א הַכֹּהֵ֗ן וְרָאָה֙ וְהִנֵּ֙ה לֹא־פָשָׂ֤ה
הַנֶּ֙גַע֙ בַּבַּ֔יִת אַחֲרֵ֖י הִטֹּ֣חַ אֶת־הַבָּ֑יִת וְטִהַ֤ר הַכֹּהֵן֙
אֶת־הַבַּ֔יִת כִּ֥י נִרְפָּ֖א הַנָּֽגַע׃ מט וְלָקַ֛ח לְחַטֵּ֥א
אֶת־הַבַּ֖יִת שְׁתֵּ֣י צִפֳּרִ֑ים וְעֵ֣ץ אֶ֔רֶז וּשְׁנִ֥י תוֹלַ֖עַת
וְאֵזֹֽב׃ נ וְשָׁחַ֖ט אֶת־הַצִּפֹּ֣ר הָאֶחָ֑ת אֶל־כְּלִי־
חֶ֖רֶשׂ עַל־מַ֥יִם חַיִּֽים׃ נא וְלָקַ֣ח אֶת־עֵֽץ־הָ֠אֶרֶז
וְאֶת־הָאֵזֹ֨ב וְאֵ֜ת ׀ שְׁנִ֣י הַתּוֹלַ֗עַת וְאֵת֙ הַצִּפֹּ֣ר
הַחַיָּ֔ה וְטָבַ֣ל אֹתָ֗ם בְּדַם֙ הַצִּפֹּ֣ר הַשְּׁחוּטָ֔ה וּבַמַּ֖יִם
הַחַיִּ֑ים וְהִזָּ֥ה אֶל־הַבַּ֖יִת שֶׁ֥בַע פְּעָמִֽים׃ נב וְחִטֵּ֣א

אֶת־הַבַּ֖יִת בְּדַם֙ הַצִּפּ֔וֹר וּבַמַּ֖יִם הַחַיִּ֑ים וּבַצִּפֹּ֣ר

house of sin with the blood of the bird and
with the living water and with the living
bird, the piece of cedar wood and the scarlet
wool,   53. and he shall let the living bird
fly out of the city into the [open] field; in
this manner he shall effect atonement for
the house, and it is pure.   54. This is the
teaching for all leprous marks and for
alopecia,   55. for the leprous marks of the
garment and for the house,   56. for
the very white and the near-white and for

הַחַיָּ֔ה וּבְעֵ֥ץ הָאֶ֖רֶז וּבָאֵזֹ֥ב וּבִשְׁנִ֖י הַתּוֹלָֽעַת:
נג וְשִׁלַּ֞ח אֶת־הַצִּפֹּ֧ר הַחַיָּ֛ה אֶל־מִח֥וּץ לָעִ֖יר
אֶל־פְּנֵ֣י הַשָּׂדֶ֑ה וְכִפֶּ֥ר עַל־הַבַּ֖יִת וְטָהֵֽר:
חמישי נד זֹ֖את הַתּוֹרָ֑ה לְכָל־נֶ֥גַע הַצָּרַ֖עַת וְלַנָּֽתֶק:
נה וּלְצָרַ֥עַת הַבֶּ֖גֶד וְלַבָּֽיִת: נו וְלַשְׂאֵ֥ת וְלַסַּפַּ֖חַת

52–53. . . . The fact that the laws concerning leprous marks on houses, just like those applicable to leprous marks on humans and on clothing, have nothing whatever to do with sanitary precautions, and that the sole purpose of the leprous marks is to serve as a warning of God's displeasure over moral errors, is evident not only from the characteristics all these symptoms have in common but also from the laws that apply to each of these symptoms separately. Thus, first of all, the laws apply only in the Land of Israel and even there they came into force only after the land had been divided into individual holdings; i.e., they must be observed only with regard to houses that can be categorically classed as private dwellings. These provisions clearly show that the leprous mark does not refer to the building as such but to the person of its owner, that the affliction is "addressed" to him, as it were. What is affected by the leprous affliction is not the house but the household, the life of the individual as distinct from the life of the community, a separation symbolically represented by the private dwelling. For this reason the mark is regarded as a leprous mark only if it appears on the walls of the house, the elements that close off the house, and even then only if the mark is directly on the material of which the wall was constructed; i.e., stone, wood or plaster. Furthermore, a house can become unclean from a leprous mark only if it is constructed in a normal manner; it must be a structure with four walls and must be made neither of building bricks nor of marble. All these specifications are intended to provide the clarity of definition desirable for any symbol, to make it clear that there is no other purpose or motivation behind these laws and to direct attention to the one basic concept that the law intends to stress; in this case, the concept of the house as the place of human domesticity.

Of all the social sins that generally provoke leprous marks as signs of Divine displeasure the Sages single out one in particular to which leprous marks on houses are addressed first and foremost: the egotism that makes a man refuse to render brotherly services to his fellow man, the selfishness that makes an individual view his house as his alone, that Sodomite principle which perverts the principle of private property: "What I have is mine and what you have is yours." He forgets that the law that separates the property of one person from that of others exists side by side with an obligation that is no less binding: that of brotherly love. צְדָקָה [righteousness] must be added to צֶדֶק [right] if the society is to be a Jewish national entity before God and if the private existence of each household within it is to be justified and maintained. Therefore, in the Land of Israel, on the soil of God's Law, leprous afflictions serve to pass sentence upon such a barren loveless concept of right, and the proclamation of that sentence begins at the moment when that same Law confers its sanction upon private property rights by dividing the land among individual owners.

According to the Sages, the passage introducing this section: "When you come into the land of Canaan, which I give to you as a possession, and I shall cause a leprous mark to develop on a house of the land of your possession, he who owns the house shall come and inform the priest (saying): 'It seems to me as if there were a mark on the house'" (Verses 34–35) conveys the following profound thought: Beginning with the moment when you take possession of property in the land which I will give you, I will send the touch of My finger upon the houses you own so that he who has taken possession of the house *for himself only* will be forced to come to the priest and say, "It seems to me as if the finger of God were pointing at this house."

The various possible developments in "leprosy" on a house—the condition remaining stable, the spread or disappearance of the symptoms, their recurrence or non-recurrence, until finally the house is either demolished or pronounced pure—are to be interpreted in the same manner as the leprous mark in humans. In either case, changes in physical condition are intended as admonitions, warning, reprieves or periods of grace addressed to the person who owns the affected house. . . .

•   •   •

the shiny white [spots], 57. to teach as to the day when it is to be pronounced unclean, and on the day when it is to be pronounced pure; this is the teaching with regard to leprosy.

XV

1. *God* spoke to Moshe and to Aharon [saying]: 2. Speak to the sons of Yisrael and say to them: If any man suffers from a discharge from his organ, his discharge is unclean. 3. This shall be his state of uncleanness caused by his discharge—whether his organ runs with his discharge or whether his organ is closed up by his discharge, in any event, it renders him unclean. 4. Any bed on which one suffering from a discharge lies becomes unclean and any object on which he sits becomes unclean. 5. And whoever touches his bed must wash his garments, bathe in water and remains unclean until evening; 6. one who sits on the object on which one suffering from a discharge sits, must wash his garments, bathe in water and remains unclean until evening; 7. and one who touches the body of one suffering from a discharge must wash his garments, bathe in water and remains unclean until evening. 8. Even if one who suffers from a discharge [only] spits upon one who is pure, the latter must wash his garments, bathe in water and remains unclean until evening. 9. Any riding gear upon which one suffering from a discharge rides becomes unclean. 10. And whoever touches anything that is under him shall be unclean until evening. But one who carries them must wash his garments, bathe in water and remains unclean until evening. 11. And whoever one suffering from a discharge touches, without having rinsed his hands, must wash his garments, bathe in water and remains unclean until evening. 12. An earthen vessel which one suffering from a discharge touches shall be broken, and any wooden vessel must be rinsed in water. 13. And when one who suffered from a discharge becomes pure from his discharge, he must count for himself seven days for his purification and wash his garments. He shall bathe his body in living water and become pure. 14. On the eighth day he shall take for himself two turtle-doves or two young pigeons, come

וְלַבֶּהָֽרֶת׃ נז לְהוֹרֹת בְּיוֹם הַטָּמֵא וּבְיוֹם הַטָּהֹר
זֹאת תּוֹרַת הַצָּרָֽעַת׃ פ טו א וַיְדַבֵּר יְהוָה אֶל־
מֹשֶׁה וְאֶל־אַהֲרֹן לֵאמֹֽר׃ ב דַּבְּרוּ אֶל־בְּנֵי
יִשְׂרָאֵל וַאֲמַרְתֶּם אֲלֵהֶם אִישׁ אִישׁ כִּי יִהְיֶה זָב
מִבְּשָׂרוֹ זוֹבוֹ טָמֵא הֽוּא׃ ג וְזֹאת תִּהְיֶה טֻמְאָתוֹ
בְּזוֹבוֹ רָר בְּשָׂרוֹ אֶת־זוֹבוֹ אוֹ־הֶחְתִּים בְּשָׂרוֹ
מִזּוֹבוֹ טֻמְאָתוֹ הִֽוא׃ ד כָּל־הַמִּשְׁכָּב אֲשֶׁר יִשְׁכַּב
עָלָיו הַזָּב יִטְמָא וְכָל־הַכְּלִי אֲשֶׁר־יֵשֵׁב עָלָיו
יִטְמָֽא׃ ה וְאִישׁ אֲשֶׁר יִגַּע בְּמִשְׁכָּבוֹ יְכַבֵּס בְּגָדָיו
וְרָחַץ בַּמַּיִם וְטָמֵא עַד־הָעָֽרֶב׃ ו וְהַיֹּשֵׁב עַל־
הַכְּלִי אֲשֶׁר־יֵשֵׁב עָלָיו הַזָּב יְכַבֵּס בְּגָדָיו וְרָחַץ
בַּמַּיִם וְטָמֵא עַד־הָעָֽרֶב׃ ז וְהַנֹּגֵעַ בִּבְשַׂר הַזָּב
יְכַבֵּס בְּגָדָיו וְרָחַץ בַּמַּיִם וְטָמֵא עַד־הָעָֽרֶב׃
ח וְכִי־יָרֹק הַזָּב בַּטָּהוֹר וְכִבֶּס בְּגָדָיו וְרָחַץ
בַּמַּיִם וְטָמֵא עַד־הָעָֽרֶב׃ ט וְכָל־הַמֶּרְכָּב אֲשֶׁר
יִרְכַּב עָלָיו הַזָּב יִטְמָֽא׃ י וְכָל־הַנֹּגֵעַ בְּכֹל אֲשֶׁר
יִהְיֶה תַחְתָּיו יִטְמָא עַד־הָעָרֶב וְהַנּוֹשֵׂא אוֹתָם
יְכַבֵּס בְּגָדָיו וְרָחַץ בַּמַּיִם וְטָמֵא עַד־הָעָֽרֶב׃
יא וְכֹל אֲשֶׁר יִגַּע־בּוֹ הַזָּב וְיָדָיו לֹא־שָׁטַף
בַּמָּיִם וְכִבֶּס בְּגָדָיו וְרָחַץ בַּמַּיִם וְטָמֵא עַד־
הָעָֽרֶב׃ יב וּכְלִי־חֶרֶשׂ אֲשֶׁר־יִגַּע־בּוֹ הַזָּב יִשָּׁבֵר
וְכָל־כְּלִי־עֵץ יִשָּׁטֵף בַּמָּֽיִם׃ יג וְכִי־יִטְהַר הַזָּב
מִזּוֹבוֹ וְסָפַר לוֹ שִׁבְעַת יָמִים לְטָהֳרָתוֹ וְכִבֶּס
בְּגָדָיו וְרָחַץ בְּשָׂרוֹ בְּמַיִם חַיִּים וְטָהֵֽר׃ יד וּבַיּוֹם
הַשְּׁמִינִי יִקַּח־לוֹ שְׁתֵּי תֹרִים אוֹ שְׁנֵי בְּנֵי יוֹנָה

before *God* to the entrance of the Tent of Appointed Meeting, and give them to the priest.   15. The priest offers them, the one as an offering that clears [him who brings it] of sin, the other as an ascent offering, and the priest will effect atonement for him before *God* for his discharge.   16. But a man who has a discharge of semen must bathe all his flesh in the water and remains unclean until evening.   17. And any garment and any skin on which the semen comes must be washed in the water and remains unclean until evening.   18. And [as for] a woman with whom a man cohabits and he has a discharge of semen—they must [both] bathe in the water and remain unclean until evening.   19. And if a woman has her discharge, and her discharge in her body is blood, she shall remain seven days in her separation, and anything she touches becomes unclean until evening. 20. And anything upon which she lies during her [period of] separation becomes unclean, and anything on which she sits becomes unclean.   21. Whoever touches her bed must wash his garments, bathe in water and remains unclean until evening. 22. Whoever touches any article on which she sits must wash his garments, bathe in water and remains unclean until evening. 23. And so, too, if he is upon the bed or upon the article on which she sits, if he only touches it, he becomes unclean until evening.   24. And if a man cohabits with her, her separation shall be upon him and he becomes unclean for seven days; any bed on which he lies down becomes unclean. 25. And a woman who has a discharge of blood for a number of days during a time that is not part of her [period of] separation —or if, after having passed her [period of] separation, she has a discharge again, then all the days of the discharge of her uncleanness shall be as in the days of her [period of] separation; she is unclean.   26. Any bed on which she lies on any day of her discharge shall be for her like the bed of her [period of] separation, and any article on which she sits shall be unclean like the uncleanness of her [period of] separation. 27. And whoever comes near to [i.e., touches] them becomes unclean; he must wash his garments, bathe in water and

וּבָ֣א ׀ לִפְנֵ֤י יְהֹוָה֙ אֶל־פֶּ֙תַח֙ אֹ֣הֶל מוֹעֵ֔ד וּנְתָנָ֖ם אֶל־הַכֹּהֵֽן: טו וְעָשָׂ֤ה אֹתָם֙ הַכֹּהֵ֔ן אֶחָ֣ד חַטָּ֔את וְהָאֶחָ֖ד עֹלָ֑ה וְכִפֶּ֨ר עָלָ֧יו הַכֹּהֵ֛ן לִפְנֵ֥י יְהֹוָ֖ה מִזּוֹבֽוֹ: ס ששי (שביעי כשהן מחוברין) טז וְאִ֕ישׁ כִּֽי־תֵצֵ֥א מִמֶּ֖נּוּ שִׁכְבַת־זָ֑רַע וְרָחַ֥ץ בַּמַּ֛יִם אֶת־כָּל־בְּשָׂר֖וֹ וְטָמֵ֥א עַד־הָעָֽרֶב: יז וְכָל־בֶּ֣גֶד וְכָל־ע֗וֹר אֲשֶׁר־יִהְיֶ֥ה עָלָ֛יו שִׁכְבַת־זָ֖רַע וְכֻבַּ֣ס בַּמַּ֑יִם וְטָמֵ֖א עַד־הָעָֽרֶב: יח וְאִשָּׁ֕ה אֲשֶׁ֨ר יִשְׁכַּ֥ב אִ֛ישׁ אֹתָ֖הּ שִׁכְבַת־זָ֑רַע וְרָחֲצ֣וּ בַמַּ֔יִם וְטָמְא֖וּ עַד־הָעָֽרֶב: פ יט וְאִשָּׁה֙ כִּֽי־תִהְיֶ֣ה זָבָ֔ה דָּ֛ם יִהְיֶ֥ה זֹבָ֖הּ בִּבְשָׂרָ֑הּ שִׁבְעַ֤ת יָמִים֙ תִּהְיֶ֣ה בְנִדָּתָ֔הּ וְכָל־הַנֹּגֵ֥עַ בָּ֖הּ יִטְמָ֥א עַד־הָעָֽרֶב: כ וְכֹל֩ אֲשֶׁ֨ר תִּשְׁכַּ֥ב עָלָ֛יו בְּנִדָּתָ֖הּ יִטְמָ֑א וְכֹ֛ל אֲשֶׁר־תֵּשֵׁ֥ב עָלָ֖יו יִטְמָֽא: כא וְכָל־הַנֹּגֵ֖עַ בְּמִשְׁכָּבָ֑הּ יְכַבֵּ֧ס בְּגָדָ֛יו וְרָחַ֥ץ בַּמַּ֖יִם וְטָמֵ֥א עַד־הָעָֽרֶב: כב וְכָל־הַנֹּגֵ֔עַ בְּכָל־כְּלִ֖י אֲשֶׁר־תֵּשֵׁ֣ב עָלָ֑יו יְכַבֵּ֧ס בְּגָדָ֛יו וְרָחַ֥ץ בַּמַּ֖יִם וְטָמֵ֥א עַד־הָעָֽרֶב: כג וְאִ֨ם עַל־הַמִּשְׁכָּ֜ב ה֗וּא א֤וֹ עַל־הַכְּלִי֙ אֲשֶׁר־הִ֣וא יֹשֶׁ֣בֶת עָלָ֔יו בְּנָגְעוֹ־ב֖וֹ יִטְמָ֥א עַד־הָעָֽרֶב: כד וְאִ֡ם שָׁכֹב֩ יִשְׁכַּ֨ב אִ֜ישׁ אֹתָ֗הּ וּתְהִ֤י נִדָּתָהּ֙ עָלָ֔יו וְטָמֵ֖א שִׁבְעַ֣ת יָמִ֑ים וְכָל־הַמִּשְׁכָּ֛ב אֲשֶׁר־יִשְׁכַּ֥ב עָלָ֖יו יִטְמָֽא: ס כה וְאִשָּׁ֡ה כִּֽי־יָזוּב֩ ז֨וֹב דָּמָ֜הּ יָמִ֣ים רַבִּ֗ים בְּלֹא֙ עֶת־נִדָּתָ֔הּ א֥וֹ כִֽי־תָז֖וּב עַל־נִדָּתָ֑הּ כָּל־יְמֵ֞י ז֣וֹב טֻמְאָתָ֗הּ כִּימֵ֧י נִדָּתָ֛הּ תִּהְיֶ֖ה טְמֵאָ֥ה הִֽוא: כו כָּל־הַמִּשְׁכָּ֞ב אֲשֶׁר־תִּשְׁכַּ֤ב עָלָיו֙ כָּל־יְמֵ֣י זוֹבָ֔הּ כְּמִשְׁכַּ֥ב נִדָּתָ֖הּ יִֽהְיֶה־לָּ֑הּ וְכָֽל־הַכְּלִי֙ אֲשֶׁ֣ר תֵּשֵׁ֣ב עָלָ֔יו טָמֵ֣א יִהְיֶ֔ה כְּטֻמְאַ֖ת נִדָּתָֽהּ: כז וְכָל־הַנּוֹגֵ֥עַ בָּ֖ם יִטְמָ֑א וְכִבֶּ֧ס בְּגָדָ֛יו וְרָחַ֥ץ

remains unclean until evening. 28. And
when she has become pure from her discharge, she shall count for herself seven
days and after that she becomes pure.
29. On the eighth day she shall take for
herself two turtle-doves or two young
pigeons and bring them to the priest to the
entrance of the Tent of Appointed Meeting.
30. The priest shall offer the one as an
offering that clears [him who brings it] of sin
and the other as an ascent offering, and the
priest will effect atonement for her before
God for the discharge of her uncleanness.
31. Teach the sons of Yisrael to keep
away from their uncleanness so that they

בַּמַּיִם וְטָמֵא עַד־הָעָרֶב׃ כח וְאִם־טָהֲרָה מִזּוֹבָהּ
וְסָפְרָה לָּהּ שִׁבְעַת יָמִים וְאַחַר תִּטְהָר׃ שביעי
כט וּבַיּוֹם הַשְּׁמִינִי תִּקַּח־לָהּ שְׁתֵּי תֹרִים אוֹ
שְׁנֵי בְּנֵי יוֹנָה וְהֵבִיאָה אוֹתָם אֶל־הַכֹּהֵן אֶל־
פֶּתַח אֹהֶל מוֹעֵד׃ ל וְעָשָׂה הַכֹּהֵן אֶת־הָאֶחָד
חַטָּאת וְאֶת־הָאֶחָד עֹלָה וְכִפֶּר עָלֶיהָ הַכֹּהֵן
לִפְנֵי יְהוָה מִזּוֹב טֻמְאָתָהּ׃ מפטיר לא וְהִזַּרְתֶּם
אֶת־בְּנֵי־יִשְׂרָאֵל מִטֻּמְאָתָם וְלֹא יָמֻתוּ

CHAPTER XV

31. . . . This commandment commends the observance of the laws of טוּמְאָה to the nation's scrupulous self-discipline in much the same manner as the duty of "keeping" or "observing" calls for self-discipline in Israel's attitude toward the entire Law. This law demands not only the avoidance of טוּמְאָה that already exists but also the avoidance of proximity to it in time and space where it is likely to occur (Mo'ed Katan 5a and Niddah 63b).

However, this commandment to keep away from טוּמְאָה is not addressed directly to the nation: the text does not say, "And the sons of Yisrael shall keep away from their uncleanness." The command is addressed, instead, to Moses and Aaron, who are assigned the task of teaching and training the nation so that it will keep away from טוּמְאָה. For the mission of Moses and Aaron—to spread the theoretical knowledge and practical observance of the Law and to labor constantly at training the nation for this purpose—is basically and entirely dependent on the assumption that the nation will be aware at all times of the concepts of טוּמְאָה and טָהֳרָה.

For this reason, too, the law is motivated by the statement "so that they will not die because of their uncleanness by making My Dwelling Place, which is in their midst, unclean." The observance of each and every one of the laws of טוּמְאָה places each and every member of the nation, from the most exalted to the lowliest, into a direct relationship to the Sanctuary of the Law, to the Dwelling Place of God through which God wishes to demonstrate His immediate presence in the nation's midst. Every law relating to טוּמְאָה proclaims to every member of the nation that this Sanctuary of God seeks its place not with "Moses and Aaron," not among the intellectual and priestly elite of the nation, but "in their midst," in the midst of the sons of Israel, and that the first prerequisite for all moral ennoblement is the free-willed elevation of one's self beyond the bonds of טוּמְאָה. God has set up the Dwelling Place of His Law, which He describes as His own Dwelling Place, with all its requirements that can be fulfilled only on the basis of purity; i.e., of free-willed morality, in the midst of His people. This shows that these laws do not presume a Utopian, superhuman state that does not exist on earth. We are told in Verse 16 of the next chapter that the Sanctuary "has its place among them in the midst of their defilements." Also, *Torath Kohanim* to the present verse notes: "*By making My Dwelling Place, which is in their midst, unclean*: The Divine Presence is in their midst even when they are unclean." God was very much aware of man's sensual nature and of all the various stimuli that can tempt him to give up his moral freedom. But it is precisely in the light of this טוּמְאָה aspect of human nature that He gave the Law as a condition for His שְׁכִינָה, for being שָׁכֵן [lit., "a neighbor"], standing "beside" human nature in all its phases. He did so in order that the Law, with the power of its flame that gives both light and life, should stir up the other aspect of human nature, the godliness that is destined to reign supreme, so that it may guide man to free-willed mastery over anything within him that is fettered to physical bonds and lead him to elevate all the phases of his life, including the most physical ones, to become free-willed, moral, God-serving acts, toward the goal of ultimate moral triumph.

But this means, too, that this particular nation was given a free choice between two alternatives: Either it will allow the Law to train it for the purity that the Law demands, in which case the nation will gain eternal life, close to God, even here below, or else the nation will perish in, and by reason of, its טוּמְאָה, for if it persists in its טוּמְאָה, which stands opposed to God's Dwelling Place in its midst, it obscures and distorts the ideal of purity symbolized by the Sanctuary of God.

will not die because of their uncleanness by making My Dwelling Place, which is in their midst, unclean.   32. This is the teaching with regard to one who suffers from a discharge and with regard to one who had a discharge of semen that has made him unclean;   33. with regard to the menstruating woman in her [period of] separation and with regard to one who develops a discharge, be it a male or a female, and for the man who cohabits with a woman who is unclean.

בְּטֻמְאָתָם בְּטַמְּאָם אֶת־מִשְׁכָּנִי אֲשֶׁר בְּתוֹכָם: לב זֹאת תּוֹרַת הַזָּב וַאֲשֶׁר תֵּצֵא מִמֶּנּוּ שִׁכְבַת־זֶרַע לְטָמְאָה־בָהּ: לג וְהַדָּוָה בְּנִדָּתָהּ וְהַזָּב אֶת־זוֹבוֹ לַזָּכָר וְלַנְּקֵבָה וּלְאִישׁ אֲשֶׁר יִשְׁכַּב עִם־טְמֵאָה: פ

---

33. . . . Precisely the sublimest aspects of man's spiritual and moral future that must develop in an atmosphere of moral freedom—marriage, the home, the family, upon whose moral character the survival of the state, too, depends—are based on physiological processes which, to a greater or lesser extent, belong to the physical, unfree aspect of human nature. Therefore it is all the more imperative that these processes should be rescued and raised into the sphere of moral freedom, and that man should be warned against the delusion that there is no such thing as moral freedom of choice. That which becomes apparent with such decisive clarity in childbirth, so obviously a physiological process, holds true for relations between the sexes in general. It would seem that the states of uncleanness that set in even as a result of such normal processes and phenomena are intended to make man aware, and to keep him aware, that notwithstanding physiological bonds which cannot be denied, moral freedom is guaranteed by the Sanctuary of God's Law, and that only allegiance to this Law, to be demonstrated even in the most sensuous aspects of human nature, can open the portals to God's Sanctuary, permitting man to draw near to the sanctities of God.

    o   o   o

The Haftarah for this Sidra may be found on page 877.

אחרי מות

AḤARE MOTH

טז א וַיְדַבֵּר יְהוָה אֶל־מֹשֶׁה אַחֲרֵי מוֹת שְׁנֵי
בְּנֵי אַהֲרֹן בְּקָרְבָתָם לִפְנֵי־יְהוָה וַיָּמֻתוּ׃
ב וַיֹּאמֶר יְהוָה אֶל־מֹשֶׁה דַּבֵּר אֶל־אַהֲרֹן אָחִיךָ
וְאַל־יָבֹא בְכָל־עֵת אֶל־הַקֹּדֶשׁ מִבֵּית לַפָּרֹכֶת
אֶל־פְּנֵי הַכַּפֹּרֶת אֲשֶׁר עַל־הָאָרֹן וְלֹא יָמוּת כִּי
בֶּעָנָן אֵרָאֶה עַל־הַכַּפֹּרֶת׃ ג בְּזֹאת יָבֹא אַהֲרֹן
אֶל־הַקֹּדֶשׁ בְּפַר בֶּן־בָּקָר לְחַטָּאת וְאַיִל לְעֹלָה׃

XVI 1. And *God* spoke [as follows] to Moshe after the death of the two sons of Aharon: "It was because of their drawing near before *God* that they died." 2. And *God* said to Moshe: Speak to your brother Aharon that he not come into the Sanctuary at all times, nor behind the dividing curtain, nor before the cover that is upon the Ark, so that he may not die, for through the cloud shall I be looked upon, above the cover. 3. With these shall Aharon come into the Sanctuary: with one young bull for an offering that clears [him who brings it] of sin and one ram

CHAPTER XVI

1. ***It was because of their drawing near before* God *that they died.*** The cause of their death was that they dared to draw so near to God. The subjective aspect of their sin, "drawing near (to God)," lay in their overweening estimation of themselves, which caused them to misunderstand the loftiness of the Jewish ideal and to fail to recognize their own inadequacy. That is why they died (see notes to Chapter 10:1).

2. . . . The Holy of Holies with the Testimony of the Law in its gold-covered wooden Ark beneath the golden cover upon which were the cherubim, the dividing curtain hanging in front of the Ark to protect it and to set it apart from the rest of the Sanctuary, the Sanctuary with the golden menorah, the gold-covered wooden Table, and the gold-covered wooden altar—all these, as we have already explained in our notes to the relevant portions in the Book of Exodus, symbolize the Law, and the Jewish national life that develops from it, in the ideal state of perfection. They embody the one ultimate goal which was set for us and toward which we all must eternally strive.

If we enter these precincts and perform rituals in them at the times and in the manner we have been commanded to do so, the very fact that we carry out these acts in obedience to Divine *command* symbolically demonstrates that we have subordinated ourselves to the way of life and norms of conduct set for us in the Sanctuary. No matter how far removed the life of one who enters the Sanctuary and performs rituals there—or the life of one who does it on his behalf—may still be from the ideal symbolized by the Holy of Holies and the Sanctuary, the fact remains that he has been *commanded,* by these acts, symbolically to pledge allegiance anew to these ideals for his future life and conduct. This renewed pledge is meant to make him aware how far from perfection his present life and conduct still are. On the other hand, one who enters these precincts and performs rituals there only whenever he decides to do so is guilty of gross presumption because he thereby implies that he has already attained these ideals both in theory and practice. Such conceit would subvert the very purpose of these ideals and hence also the future of the one who labors under the illusion that his life already accords with the standards set by God's Law. The court, the forecourt of the Sanctuary, on the other hand, with its altar for ascent offerings, and the basin, symbolically represents the "antechambers to the sanctuary of life's ideals." Anyone entering that area and performing rituals there symbolically demonstrates his preparedness to work upon himself so that he may become fit to strive toward the lofty ideals set by God.

3. ***With these shall Aharon come.*** Aaron shall enter the Sanctuary with the symbols intended to make him aware of his official functions: The bull symbolizes his role as a "worker upon the field of God, upon the purpose of the Jew's life." The specification that the animal must be פַּר בֶּן בָּקָר [a young bull] should remind him to maintain his original devotion to his priestly service, a devotion that must remain forever "young," undulled by routine or smugness. When he enters the Sanctuary he must be aware of his personal purpose before God and His Law. . . .

However, he must present the animal as an offering that clears (him who brings it) of sin, thus symbolically demonstrating that he has not come with a sense of achievement, with pride in having accomplished his life's mission, but that he is fully aware of how much he personally is still in need of atonement because of the for an ascent offering.   4. He shall clothe himself with the linen tunic of the Sanctuary, and linen breeches shall be upon his body [before], and he shall gird himself with his linen sash, and he shall bind his head with a linen turban; these are garments of the Sanctuary. He shall bathe his body in water and put them on.   5. And from the community of the sons of Yisrael he shall take two he-goats for an offering [that clears him who brings it] of sin and a ram for an ascent offering.   6. And Aharon shall bring near the bull of the offering that clears [him who brings it] of sin, and effect atone-

ד כְּתֹנֶת־בַּד קֹדֶשׁ יִלְבָּשׁ וּמִכְנְסֵי־בַד יִהְיוּ עַל־בְּשָׂרוֹ וּבְאַבְנֵט בַּד יַחְגֹּר וּבְמִצְנֶפֶת בַּד יִצְנֹף בִּגְדֵי־קֹדֶשׁ הֵם וְרָחַץ בַּמַּיִם אֶת־בְּשָׂרוֹ וּלְבֵשָׁם: ה וּמֵאֵת עֲדַת בְּנֵי יִשְׂרָאֵל יִקַּח שְׁנֵי־שְׂעִירֵי עִזִּים לְחַטָּאת וְאַיִל אֶחָד לְעֹלָה: ו וְהִקְרִיב אַהֲרֹן אֶת־פַּר הַחַטָּאת אֲשֶׁר־לוֹ וְכִפֶּר בַּעֲדוֹ

wide gap that still separates him from the fulfillment of his mission. Also, he must bring with him a ram as an ascent offering. When he enters the Sanctuary he must be filled with the same spirit that inspired him at the time of his investiture, fully aware of his position as a "lead ram of God's own flock," leading all the rest. However, he must not think of his position in terms of the privileges it entails, as expressed symbolically by the "ram of investiture," but in terms of what is expected of one in his position: to wield his influence as a leader and guide, leading all the others onward and upward in an unceasing ascent toward the supreme ideal of all that is good and noble, the moral ideal set by the Law.

בְּזֹאת [With these], not filled with a purpose he has set for himself according to his own preferences, but with a symbol of the goal set for him [by the Law of God] "shall Aharon come into the Sanctuary."

4. ... Before all else, he shall put on white garments ... garments in the color of purity. ...

He shall bathe his body in water and put them on. Before he may clothe his body even with these, the humblest garments of his functions in the Sanctuary, he must perform the act of immersion, thus symbolically removing his flesh from all uncleanness, and allowing it to revert to its pristine purity (see notes on Leviticus 11:46–47) so that he may recognize, clearly and without any illusions, the gap that still exists between the realities of his own life, on the one hand, and the fulfillment of even the most elementary standards set by the Sanctuary, on the other.

o   o   o

5. *And from the community of the sons of Yisrael.* However, when he appears in the Sanctuary before God, Aaron must bring with him not only offerings that symbolize his own relationship to God and His Law but also offerings that symbolize the relationship of the entire nation to God and the Torah. For in Judaism the

priest is in no manner an intermediary between God and the people. The priest and the people both enjoy the same direct ties with God and His Law and with the mission that the Law has set for each. The priest is to exercise the function symbolized by the bull; he is to work at cultivating the hearts and minds of the people, God's own field, for the purposes of God and His Law. The position of the people is symbolized by the he-goat, submissive only to the leadership of God, stubbornly resisting all influences alien to godliness, and persistent in his devotion to God's guidance and in the fulfillment of God's Law. Therefore, the people are equal to the priest in that the functions of both are symbolized by the ram. What the priest should be to the nation, the nation should be to the rest of mankind: a "lead ram," as it were, striding steadily forward and upward at the head of all mankind, the flock of God, leading the way to the fulfillment of all that is noble and good.

o   o   o

6. ... The basic connotation of כַּפָּרָה [atonement] is a "burial" of the past. It is the supreme act of God's absolute, free Almighty power, which alone can suspend the laws of cause and effect, laws which, after all, He Himself has instituted. He effects כַּפָּרָה so that the sins of the past and their consequences should not mar the individual's future material and spiritual life and that even a shadowed moral past can be followed by a future of purity and happiness. כַּפָּרָה holds out the promise of such a "burial" of the past to anyone who sincerely and firmly resolves henceforth to devote his entire being loyally and steadfastly to his duty as commanded by God and as symbolically pledged by the presentation of the blood of the offering. Every offering, along with the rituals prescribed in connection with it, symbolizes life as it should have been lived in the past, and life as it must be lived in the future if it is to meet with God's approval. The basic condition for attaining כַּפָּרָה is a solemn pledge henceforth to trans-

וּבְעַ֣ד בֵּית֑וֹ׃ ז וְלָקַ֖ח אֶת־שְׁנֵ֣י הַשְּׂעִירִ֑ם וְהֶעֱמִ֤יד
אֹתָם֙ לִפְנֵ֣י יְהוָ֔ה פֶּ֖תַח אֹ֥הֶל מוֹעֵֽד׃ ח וְנָתַ֧ן
אַהֲרֹ֛ן עַל־שְׁנֵ֥י הַשְּׂעִירִ֖ם גֹּרָל֑וֹת גּוֹרָ֤ל אֶחָד֙
לַֽיהוָ֔ה וְגוֹרָ֥ל אֶחָ֖ד לַעֲזָאזֵֽל׃ ט וְהִקְרִ֤יב אַהֲרֹן֙
אֶת־הַשָּׂעִ֔יר אֲשֶׁ֨ר עָלָ֥ה עָלָ֛יו הַגּוֹרָ֖ל לַיהוָ֑ה
וְעָשָׂ֖הוּ חַטָּֽאת׃ י וְהַשָּׂעִ֗יר אֲשֶׁר֩ עָלָ֨ה עָלָ֤יו
הַגּוֹרָל֙ לַעֲזָאזֵ֔ל יָֽעֳמַד־חַ֛י לִפְנֵ֥י יְהוָ֖ה לְכַפֵּ֣ר

ment for himself and for his house.
7. He shall then take the two he-goats and place them before *God* in the entrance of the Tent of Appointed Meeting.
8. Aharon shall place two lots upon the two he-goats; one lot "for *God*" and one lot "for Azazel."
9. Aharon shall bring near the he-goat that has the lot "for *God*" and designate it as an offering that clears [him who brings it] of sin.
10. But the he-goat that has the lot "for Azazel" shall remain standing alive before *God*, in the hope of effecting atone-

late this ideal into reality in one's own life. Hence "The meaning of the blood is: It is with the soul that one effects atonement."

However, a basic prerequisite for the fulfillment of this pledge—indeed, a criterion for the sincerity of the pledge—is that the more a shadowed moral past needs to be "buried" by the absolute omnipotence of Divine grace, the more it must remain *unburied* in the consciousness of the person concerned. It must remain alive within his mind, bare of all illusions and self-deception, forever. This is the meaning of the Jewish concept of וִדּוּי [confession]. It does not imply a "confession" to another man, or even to God; it is essentially, as indicated by the reflexive form of the term הִתְוַדָּה, an "acknowledgment (or admission) to oneself" that one has done wrong, which should silence any attempt by the "defender" within us to put a good face on the wrong we have done or to find an excuse for it. Only if we have the courage to look at our past wrongdoings with the same critical openness as they are viewed by the eye of God will we be sure to carry out our resolve to be faithful to our duty in future. A genuine admission to oneself that "I have sinned" will preclude a future relapse into sin. All genuine self-criticism includes self-knowledge, not only for the realization that we *should* have behaved differently but also that we *could* have behaved differently. Such an acknowledgment of one's moral freedom of will is capable of rejecting any excuse for present or future failings.

and for his house. Judaism cannot conceive of a high priest without a "house"; i.e. a high priest who is celibate, who has no wife. The man who is to represent the nation's moral ideal in the Sanctuary of God's Law and who is to walk before the nation in everyday life as a model for its moral progress and upward striving must embody in his own person the life of a man in the entirety of its moral purpose. Marriage, the basis of all moral development and the foundation of the nation's moral welfare, must not be missing from his life. The high priest's wife was such an essential part of the high priest's representative functions in the Sanctuary that if she died on Yom Kippur before he had performed the main service of Yom Kippur, he was not permitted to perform it (Yoma 13). In order to be able to officiate on Yom Kippur, the high priest must have a wife.

10. . . . Clearly, we have here a description of two creatures which at the outset are identical in every respect but which come to a complete parting of the ways once they arrive at the threshold of the Sanctuary. They are both identical in appearance, size, and monetary value. Both were purchased at the same time. Both are placed in the same manner "before *God* in the entrance of the Tent of Appointed Meeting." The lot marked "for *God*" or that "for Azazel" could fall upon either one of them. The chances of becoming the one or the other are the same for each. Indeed, each of the two can only become that which it will become because it could just as well have become the other. But the lot does not determine anything except such [an animal] as is fit for God, and at that point the two creatures come to a parting of the ways. The one marked "for *God*" is killed by שְׁחִיטָה [slaughter] with the knife of the Sanctuary; afterwards, however, it is taken up in the vessel of the Sanctuary and is brought into the Holy of Holies, close to that most holy place where the ideal of a life lived completely in accordance with Jewish Law attains perfection as the bearer of godliness on earth. The he-goat marked "for Azazel" is not touched by the knife of the Sanctuary; it does not suffer death by שְׁחִיטָה, it remains alive, untouched and unchanged, in its original vital self, before God at the entrance of the Sanctuary. However, it is not permitted inside. Instead, it is sent away from the precincts of the Sanctuary, away from the place of human habitation, out into the wilderness, there to end, in utter desolation, the self-centered life which it saved when it turned its back on the Sanctuary.

Nevertheless, both these he-goats represent חַטָּאת [offerings that clear (him who brings them) of sin]. Therefore, both must symbolize the same concept of חַטָּאת, only seen from two contrasting vantage points. We therefore believe we are not in error if we assume that, whereas חַטָּאת usually symbolizes life as it should

עָלָיו לְשַׁלַּח אֹתוֹ לַעֲזָאזֵל הַמִּדְבָּרָה: יא וְהִקְרִיב

ment upon it, to send it as "for Azazel" into the wilderness. 11. And Aharon shall

have been lived in the past and as it should be lived in future, we see here the reverse side of the coin: life as it should never have been lived in the past, a life that we vow shall also have no place in our future. In this sense, each and every one of us is a "he-goat," as it were. Each and every one of us has powers of resistance, the ability to oppose with firmness any demands made on our will. Whether or not our life will be morally worthy depends on the use to which we put this power. We can utilize it in the service of God; we can become "God's own he-goat," as it were, by offering firm resistance to any enticements and considerations, from within or without, that would lure us away from God and from His holy will and to have us forfeit our close attachment to God. Or we can use it in obstinate refusal to obey God and to comply with the demands of His holy moral law. We can turn against Him the powers of resistance which He Himself bestowed upon us and supinely give ourselves up to that sensuality and to those enticements which God meant to have us fight with the powers of resistance He bestowed upon us.

Here, this surrender to the power of sensuality, in contrast to attachment to God and obedience to His moral law, is described by the term לַעֲזָאזֵל. The most straightforward, natural interpretation of the word עֲזָאזֵל would be to explain it as עַז אָזַל: עַז, the kind of headstrong "goat-like" obstinacy which is אָזַל, which has no future and which, precisely by imagining itself to be עַז [strong], digs its own grave. עֲזָאזֵל symbolizes sensuality practiced as a matter of principle, which God does not wish to accord any place in the destinies of man.

A *boraitha* in Yoma 67b interprets the word as עזז אל or עזאל, which should convey the same thought. It is that strength which is comformable to the nature and purposes of the non-human forces of nature to which the Creator has assigned only one possible direction, from which they are not permitted, and therefore not enabled, to deviate; forces which must blindly obey their Creator and Master by following the dictates of their nature with all the firmness and determination inherent in their instincts. Such is the lot and the destiny of the unfree, elemental, organic world.

But man has been assigned another, higher purpose, and only when he practices this other, higher calling does he become a man and prove himself worthy of being human. For ה', the One sole, free, almighty God, stands high above the sphere of the forces which He has created to be ruled and bound by His laws of nature and which are strong and firm only in and through their unchanging performance of His will. But He has sent down to earth an emanation of His own unique, free essence, of His free-willed power, freely ruling over these natural forces. Into the midst of these forces without number, He has placed one creature as spirit of His spirit, breath of His breath, clothed him in an earthly shell and said to him: "Be 'Adam'; be a likeness of Me, be a God in miniature, in and over the little world that I have assigned to you along with your physical shell. You shall have freedom from My freedom; you shall have power from My power, which controls the forces of nature. There are forces and impulses at work within your shell, your portion of the terrestrial world, which operate also in the rest of the elemental, organic world from which they are derived. If they are left uncontrolled, these forces, as in the other creations, will travel with compelling determination along the path inherent in their nature, and they will derive satisfaction from so doing. But you are free; you have freedom from My freedom, power from My power, which controls the forces of nature. You have spirit from My spirit and so are capable of perceiving My will, and you are to use that freedom and that power to master your own world of inner forces and impulses with a strong hand, guiding them with your free-willed energy to make them all subservient to the Law of My will. By thus controlling the forces and impulses within yourself, you will attain high rank, close to Me and above all others, the only free creature amidst a world of forces and impulses without a will of their own."

Implicit in the concept of freedom, however, is the possibility that one may choose to disobey the Divine will. The ability to sin and the enticements of the senses are not consequences of human degeneration. Indeed, without the ability to sin and to yield to temptation, man would not even be human. Man's whole majesty and dignity derive from the fact that he has the ability to sin; he is the only creature that has been given an opportunity to disobey the will of God. In the sphere of the primitive organic world there is no sin, but hence also no virtue, no morality. And if that human sensuality which runs counter to God's will were not attractive to man, if man derived gratification and comfort only from using his faculties in a manner willed by God, if he perceived all evil as bitter and all good as sweet, if he were not capable of resisting God just as he is not capable of resisting the urges and enticements of his senses, if he did not have the capacity to be a שָׂעִיר לַעֲזָאזֵל [he-goat for Azazel] just as well as a שָׂעִיר לה' [he-goat for God], then God's Law would operate in him, too, with the same compelling force that it exerts on all the other unfree creatures of His creation which are kept on the path ordained for them solely by the fact that only this path satisfies them and that they are by nature

אַהֲרֹן אֶת־פַּר הַחַטָּאת אֲשֶׁר־לוֹ וְכִפֶּר בַּעֲדוֹ
וּבְעַד בֵּיתוֹ וְשָׁחַט אֶת־פַּר הַחַטָּאת אֲשֶׁר־לוֹ׃
יב וְלָקַח מְלֹא־הַמַּחְתָּה גַּחֲלֵי־אֵשׁ מֵעַל הַמִּזְבֵּחַ
מִלִּפְנֵי יְהוָה וּמְלֹא חָפְנָיו קְטֹרֶת סַמִּים דַּקָּה
וְהֵבִיא מִבֵּית לַפָּרֹכֶת׃ יג וְנָתַן אֶת־הַקְּטֹרֶת עַל־
הָאֵשׁ לִפְנֵי יְהוָה וְכִסָּה ׀ עֲנַן הַקְּטֹרֶת אֶת־
הַכַּפֹּרֶת אֲשֶׁר עַל־הָעֵדוּת וְלֹא יָמוּת׃ יד וְלָקַח
מִדַּם הַפָּר וְהִזָּה בְאֶצְבָּעוֹ עַל־פְּנֵי הַכַּפֹּרֶת
קֵדְמָה וְלִפְנֵי הַכַּפֹּרֶת יַזֶּה שֶׁבַע־פְּעָמִים מִן־
הַדָּם בְּאֶצְבָּעוֹ׃ טו וְשָׁחַט אֶת־שְׂעִיר הַחַטָּאת

again bring near the bull, of the offering that clears [him who brings it] of sin, that is his, and strive for atonement for himself and for his house, and he shall slaughter the bull of the offering that clears [him who brings it] of sin, that is his.
12. He shall then take down the pan full of burning coals from the altar, from the side that is toward *God*, and his handfuls of finely-ground incense, and he shall then bring it beyond the dividing curtain.
13. He shall then place the incense upon the fire before *God*, so that the cloud of the incense covers the cover that is upon the Testimony, and that he will not die.
14. He shall then take [some] of the blood of the bull and sprinkle it with his finger upon the surface of the cover facing east, and in front of the cover he shall sprinkle [some] of the blood with his finger, seven times.
15. He shall then slaughter the he-goat of the offering that clears [him

repelled or unaffected by temptations to deviate from that path.

Thus, all of us are placed into the entrance of His Sanctuary, without distinction, [to decide] between ד׳ and עֲזָאזֵל, between God and the powers of our senses. Inside, in the Holy of Holies, is the Law of His will, waiting for us. It is in the light of His Law that we must make our decision. It can be לד׳, for God. We can decide in His favor, mustering all the powers of resistance given us to withstand anything that would snatch us from our vocation, so that we may become close to God, belong to Him and become like Him in our free-willed performance of His will, in our free-willed realization of all that is good and pure. In that case we will come into the forecourt of the Sanctuary of His Law, cheerfully ready to give up, beneath the sharp cut of Divine sanctification, the selfish animal aspects of our sensuality. Thus we will secure admission to His Sanctuary and attain His nearness even with the physical and sensual aspects of our lives, as long as we use them to fulfill His holy will on earth. On the other hand, we may decide לַעֲזָאזֵל [in favor of Azazel]. Standing at the entrance of the Sanctuary, confronted by the demands which God's Law places upon us, we may elect to use our powers of resistance to turn our backs upon these demands. We can refuse to give up our self-willed sensual life, to offer up our sensuality beneath the cut of the willpower given us in order that we may sanctify the will of God's Law. There, at the entrance of the Sanctuary, in full view of His Law, we can elect to maintain our self-willed sensual life without subjecting it to any controls. But if we do this, we turn ourselves over to עֲזָאזֵל, to the uncontrolled forces of a sensuality that has a place neither in the Sanctuary nor in the individual or national life which is to flourish in the ambiance of this Sanctuary beneath the radiance of God's Law. Such a sensuality belongs only in the wilderness, where free-willed human self-control does not act to elevate the terrestrial world into the sphere of Divine freedom.

This choice is not made for any of us in advance. Physical appearance, physical stature, financial status, higher or lower social standing, greater or lesser affluence, even the circumstances under which we are called upon to make our choice—none of these have a compelling influence on our decision. Respected or obscure, great or humble, rich or poor, today or tomorrow, no matter what his powers or possessions—anyone can become either לד׳ or לַעֲזָאזֵל at any time. Indeed, a decision לד׳ [in favor of God] has value and meaning only if, at the same point, the individual could have chosen לַעֲזָאזֵל instead. Conversely, a decision לַעֲזָאזֵל [in favor of Azazel] is unworthy of man only because at that point he could have chosen, instead, to become and remain true to God and to cleave to Him. Indeed, the very enticements of עֲזָאזֵל should have led him to God, for without these temptations he could never have become the free-willed son and servant of God, of the free-willed Holy One. Sensuality has been given to man not that it should control him but in order that he should control and guide it. Cf. Genesis 4:7: "Its urge is toward you that you should master it."

° ° °

who brings it] of sin, that is the people's, and shall bring its blood inside beyond the dividing curtain, and he shall do with its blood as he did with the blood of the bull; he shall sprinkle it upon the cover and in front of the cover. 16. And thus he will effect atonement for the Sanctuary from the defilements of the sons of Yisrael and from their offenses with regard to all their aberrations, and he shall do likewise for the Tent of Appointed Meeting, which has its place among them in the midst of their defilements. 17. But no man shall be in the Tent of Appointed Meeting when he goes in to effect atonement in the Sanctuary, until he comes out and has effected atonement for himself and for his house and for the entire community of Yisrael. 18. He shall then go out to the altar that stands before *God* and effect atonement upon it. That is, he shall take [some] of the blood of the bull and of the blood of the he-goat and place it upon the elevated corners of the altar round about. 19. And he shall sprinkle [some] of the blood upon it with his finger seven times and cleanse it and sanctify it from the defilements of the sons of Yisrael. 20. After he has thus made atonement for the Sanctuary, the Tent of Appointed Meeting and the altar, he shall bring near the live he-goat, 21. Aharon shall lean both his hands together upon the head of the live he-goat and acknowledge to himself upon it all the iniquities of the sons of Yisrael and all their offenses with regard to all their aberrations, and shall put them upon the head of the he-goat and send it into the wilderness by a man prepared long in advance for this purpose. 22. The he-goat shall bear upon itself all their iniquities, away to a precipitous ground that is cut off, and from there he shall send the he-goat down into the wilderness. 23. And Aharon shall come once more into the Tent of Appointed Meeting; after that, he shall take off the

אֲשֶׁר לָעָם וְהֵבִיא אֶת־דָּמוֹ אֶל־מִבֵּית לַפָּרֹכֶת
וְעָשָׂה אֶת־דָּמוֹ כַּאֲשֶׁר עָשָׂה לְדַם הַפָּר וְהִזָּה
אֹתוֹ עַל־הַכַּפֹּרֶת וְלִפְנֵי הַכַּפֹּרֶת: טז וְכִפֶּר עַל־
הַקֹּדֶשׁ מִטֻּמְאֹת בְּנֵי יִשְׂרָאֵל וּמִפִּשְׁעֵיהֶם לְכָל־
חַטֹּאתָם וְכֵן יַעֲשֶׂה לְאֹהֶל מוֹעֵד הַשֹּׁכֵן אִתָּם
בְּתוֹךְ טֻמְאֹתָם: יז וְכָל־אָדָם לֹא־יִהְיֶה | בְּאֹהֶל
מוֹעֵד בְּבֹאוֹ לְכַפֵּר בַּקֹּדֶשׁ עַד־צֵאתוֹ וְכִפֶּר
בַּעֲדוֹ וּבְעַד בֵּיתוֹ וּבְעַד כָּל־קְהַל יִשְׂרָאֵל: שני
יח וְיָצָא אֶל־הַמִּזְבֵּחַ אֲשֶׁר לִפְנֵי־יְהֹוָה וְכִפֶּר
עָלָיו וְלָקַח מִדַּם הַפָּר וּמִדַּם הַשָּׂעִיר וְנָתַן עַל־
קַרְנוֹת הַמִּזְבֵּחַ סָבִיב: יט וְהִזָּה עָלָיו מִן־הַדָּם
בְּאֶצְבָּעוֹ שֶׁבַע פְּעָמִים וְטִהֲרוֹ וְקִדְּשׁוֹ מִטֻּמְאֹת
בְּנֵי יִשְׂרָאֵל: כ וְכִלָּה מִכַּפֵּר אֶת־הַקֹּדֶשׁ וְאֶת־
אֹהֶל מוֹעֵד וְאֶת־הַמִּזְבֵּחַ וְהִקְרִיב אֶת־הַשָּׂעִיר
הֶחָי: כא וְסָמַךְ אַהֲרֹן אֶת־שְׁתֵּי יָדָו (ידיו קרי) עַל־
רֹאשׁ הַשָּׂעִיר הַחַי וְהִתְוַדָּה עָלָיו אֶת־כָּל־עֲוֹנֹת
בְּנֵי יִשְׂרָאֵל וְאֶת־כָּל־פִּשְׁעֵיהֶם לְכָל־חַטֹּאתָם
וְנָתַן אֹתָם עַל־רֹאשׁ הַשָּׂעִיר וְשִׁלַּח בְּיַד־אִישׁ
עִתִּי הַמִּדְבָּרָה: כב וְנָשָׂא הַשָּׂעִיר עָלָיו אֶת־כָּל־
עֲוֹנֹתָם אֶל־אֶרֶץ גְּזֵרָה וְשִׁלַּח אֶת־הַשָּׂעִיר
בַּמִּדְבָּר: כג וּבָא אַהֲרֹן אֶל־אֹהֶל מוֹעֵד וּפָשַׁט

21. עָוֺן . . . [iniquity] is a deviation from the one true, "straight" path that was committed deliberately but only as the result of surrender to passion. פֶּשַׁע is an act of rebellion, an act committed out of contempt for the Law of God, not *although*, but precisely *because* that act is forbidden. חֵטְא ["sin," aberration] denotes a wrong done because one has forgotten the Law. . . .

22. . . . The term *gezerah* denotes something that is "cut off" (Yoma 67b), a place where the ground is abruptly "cut off," a steep ground, falling precipitously to an abyss where the wilderness begins. . . .

linen garments which he had put on again when he went into the Sanctuary, and he shall leave them there.   24. But before that he shall bathe his body in water in a holy place and put on his garments, go out and make his ascent offering, the ascent offering of the people, and he shall effect atonement for himself and for the people. 25. And he shall give the fat of the offering that clears [him who brings it] of sin to the altar to go up in smoke.   26. The one who sends away the he-goat as Azazel's must wash his garments and bathe his body in water; afterwards he shall come back into the camp.   27. But as for the bull of the offering that clears [him who brings it] of sin and the he-goat of the offering that clears [him who brings it] of sin, whose blood was brought in to effect atonement in the Sanctuary, he shall have [them] taken out, outside the camp, and they shall burn their skin, their flesh and their dung in fire. 28. And the one who burns them must wash his garments and bathe his body in water; afterwards he shall come back into the camp.   29. Let it be a statute for you forever: in the seventh month, on the tenth of the month, you shall starve your vital energies and do no manner of [creating] work, the native-born and the stranger who has come into your midst from abroad. 30. For on this day it shall bring atonement upon you, to purify you, before *God*

אֶת־בִּגְדֵי הַבָּד אֲשֶׁר לָבַשׁ בְּבֹאוֹ אֶל־הַקֹּדֶשׁ וְהִנִּיחָם שָׁם: כד וְרָחַץ אֶת־בְּשָׂרוֹ בַמַּיִם בְּמָקוֹם קָדוֹשׁ וְלָבַשׁ אֶת־בְּגָדָיו וְיָצָא וְעָשָׂה אֶת־עֹלָתוֹ וְאֶת־עֹלַת הָעָם וְכִפֶּר בַּעֲדוֹ וּבְעַד הָעָם: שלישי (שני כשהן מחוברין) כה וְאֵת חֵלֶב הַחַטָּאת יַקְטִיר הַמִּזְבֵּחָה: כו וְהַמְשַׁלֵּחַ אֶת־הַשָּׂעִיר לַעֲזָאזֵל יְכַבֵּס בְּגָדָיו וְרָחַץ אֶת־בְּשָׂרוֹ בַּמָּיִם וְאַחֲרֵי־כֵן יָבוֹא אֶל־הַמַּחֲנֶה: כז וְאֵת פַּר הַחַטָּאת וְאֵת ׀ שְׂעִיר הַחַטָּאת אֲשֶׁר הוּבָא אֶת־דָּמָם לְכַפֵּר בַּקֹּדֶשׁ יוֹצִיא אֶל־מִחוּץ לַמַּחֲנֶה וְשָׂרְפוּ בָאֵשׁ אֶת־עֹרֹתָם וְאֶת־בְּשָׂרָם וְאֶת־פִּרְשָׁם: כח וְהַשֹּׂרֵף אֹתָם יְכַבֵּס בְּגָדָיו וְרָחַץ אֶת־בְּשָׂרוֹ בַּמָּיִם וְאַחֲרֵי־כֵן יָבוֹא אֶל־הַמַּחֲנֶה: כט וְהָיְתָה לָכֶם לְחֻקַּת עוֹלָם בַּחֹדֶשׁ הַשְּׁבִיעִי בֶּעָשׂוֹר לַחֹדֶשׁ תְּעַנּוּ אֶת־נַפְשֹׁתֵיכֶם וְכָל־מְלָאכָה לֹא תַעֲשׂוּ הָאֶזְרָח וְהַגֵּר הַגָּר בְּתוֹכְכֶם: ל כִּי־בַיּוֹם הַזֶּה יְכַפֵּר עֲלֵיכֶם לְטַהֵר אֶתְכֶם

---

30. *For on this day ... it shall bring atonement upon you.* The subject of יְכַפֵּר ["it shall bring atonement upon you"] can only be עֲשׂוֹר לַחֹדֶשׁ, the tenth day of Tishri mentioned in the preceding verse.... The motivation for the prohibition against every "creating" type of activity and the starving of one's vital energies on Yom Kippur is the atonement and the purity to be attained by means of that day. יוֹם כִּפּוּר is to bring us כַּפָּרָה [atonement]; it is, literally, to "cover us" against the consequences of past sin.

The immediate effect of this כַּפָּרָה is "to purify you," the regaining of one's moral freedom that is disturbed by every sin committed. The effect of every sin upon the sinner is twofold: misfortune without and defilement within. Were it not for the wondrous almighty intervention of God's grace, then, in a world of God built upon truth and right, any sin would cause the destruction of the sinner, and each sin would make the once-pure soul increasingly well-versed in wrongdoing and prone to additional sin. Increased familiarity with sin is a visible punishment that often does not come until long afterwards; increasing proneness to sin is the immediate, destructive effect on one's inner life. "The wages of sin are (additional) sin."

Life about us and life within us both develop in accordance with certain unchanging laws. The only One for Whom these laws are not immutable is the One Whose free, almighty will first instituted them and Who maintains them in force, but Who also has promised man to be ready at all times, with His free, almighty will, to institute an entirely new future for his life within and without, regardless of the kind of future for which men may have sown the seeds in the past. Thus, God has proclaimed Himself not only as אֱלֹקִים, Who instituted the laws that regulate the world, but also as ד׳, through Whom not only all that exists was

shall you become pure of all your aberrations.   31. It is for you a Sabbath to be
observed by cessation from all activity, and
you shall starve your vital energies as a
statute forever.   32. But also the priest
who will be anointed and invested to perform priestly duties in his father's place
shall effect atonement, and he shall clothe
himself with the linen garments, the garments of the Sanctuary.   33. He shall
effect atonement for the holy place of
the Sanctuary, and he shall effect atonement for the Tent of Appointed Meeting
and the altar, and he shall effect atonement

מִכֹּל חַטֹּאתֵיכֶם לִפְנֵי יְהוָֹה תִּטְהָרוּ׃ לֹא שַׁבַּת
שַׁבָּתוֹן הִיא לָכֶם וְעִנִּיתֶם אֶת־נַפְשֹׁתֵיכֶם חֻקַּת
עוֹלָם׃ לב וְכִפֶּר הַכֹּהֵן אֲשֶׁר־יִמְשַׁח אֹתוֹ וַאֲשֶׁר
יְמַלֵּא אֶת־יָדוֹ לְכַהֵן תַּחַת אָבִיו וְלָבַשׁ אֶת־בִּגְדֵי
הַבָּד בִּגְדֵי הַקֹּדֶשׁ׃ לג וְכִפֶּר אֶת־מִקְדַּשׁ הַקֹּדֶשׁ
וְאֶת־אֹהֶל מוֹעֵד וְאֶת־הַמִּזְבֵּחַ יְכַפֵּר וְעַל

created in the past but on Whose free almighty will the
future, too, depends, and Who, with the love He exercises in training mankind, is ready to have a new future
begin for any man at any time.

Hence, too, the momentous statement of כַּפָּרָה:
"Before *God* shall you become pure of all your aberrations." Whatever your past may have been, no matter
where and how you may have strayed, before ד', *God*,
Who owns and dispenses all the future, you can and
shall rise up to a new future of purity. Before Him, and
by Him, will you be delivered from the seeds of misfortune that you, with your sins, have deposited into the
womb of the future, and from the moral bondage in
which you have been entrapped because of your sins.
You shall rise again before God with a new spirit and a
new heart, with a new, pure mind receptive once again
to all things godly, joyously going out toward all that is
good and pure.

The prohibition against every "creating" type of
activity, and the starving of one's vital energies, with
which we are expected to observe יוֹם כִּפּוּר, symbolically
accord with the winning of a new future before God
through a twofold gift: כַּפָּרָה and טָהֳרָה, protection for life
without and rebirth to purity within. On the Sabbath
our cessation from all "creating" activity makes us
aware that we are not naturally entitled to be masters
over the world. Similarly, the prohibition against
engaging in "creating" activity on יוֹם כִּפּוּר expresses our
awareness that we have forfeited the right conferred
upon all creatures: that of sustaining ourselves physically by taking nourishment. Both of these observances
together symbolically express our avowal that, by
reason of our past failings, we have forfeited the
right to the pleasures of physical existence and to the
satisfactions of creative life, and that without the intervention of God's grace we would have to cease living.
The former, the prohibition against engaging in "creat-

ing" activity, is the symbolic confession that accords
with the atonement to be attained. By sinning against
the world around us and misusing our position of power
in nature and human society . . . we have broken the
bond by which the Creator's Word placed His terrestrial world at man's feet. Hence, we have forfeited the
blessings necessary for growth and prosperity, blessings
that the King of man's world has promised for every
honest endeavor in the struggle for existence. Both
nature and society, outraged by our actions, have
turned against us, and only the atonement that can be
attained from and before God can restore us to our
former position of power and prosperity in the midst of
nature and society.

Starving one's vital energies, on the other hand,
symbolizes the confession that accords with the purity
we seek to regain. By yielding to the enticements of physical pleasures that had been given us
solely in order to serve God's purposes for the world, we
have divested our physical existence of its moral character, its purity; we have abandoned our moral freedom,
fallen to the bondage of sensuality and thereby forfeited the basis for a continued existence worthy of human
beings. "Before *God* shall you become pure"; only
before God, the pure original Source of all freedom and
of all pure moral strength, can we be freed from the
bonds of this sensuality and can we be reborn and rise
anew to purity.

In this context, Rabbi Akiba declares: "Fortunate are
you, O Israel! Before whom do you become pure, and
who is it that makes you pure? Is it your Father in
Heaven, as it is said (Ezekiel 36:25), 'And I will sprinkle
clear water upon you and you shall be pure.' And it is
further said, 'The source of Israel's purity is God; even
as the wellspring of water purifies the unclean, so does
God make Israel pure'" (Yoma 85b).

· · ·

הַכֹּהֲנִ֛ים וְעַל־כָּל־עַ֥ם הַקָּהָ֖ל יְכַפֵּֽר׃ לד וְהָֽיְתָה־
זֹּ֨את לָכֶ֜ם לְחֻקַּ֣ת עוֹלָ֗ם לְכַפֵּ֞ר עַל־בְּנֵ֤י יִשְׂרָאֵל֙
מִכָּל־חַטֹּאתָ֔ם אַחַ֖ת בַּשָּׁנָ֑ה וַיַּ֕עַשׂ כַּאֲשֶׁ֛ר צִוָּ֥ה
יְהֹוָ֖ה אֶת־מֹשֶֽׁה׃ פ רביעי יז א וַיְדַבֵּ֥ר יְהֹוָ֖ה אֶל־
מֹשֶׁ֥ה לֵּאמֹֽר׃ ב דַּבֵּ֨ר אֶֽל־אַהֲרֹ֜ן וְאֶל־בָּנָ֗יו וְאֶל֙
כָּל־בְּנֵ֣י יִשְׂרָאֵ֔ל וְאָמַרְתָּ֖ אֲלֵיהֶ֑ם זֶ֣ה הַדָּבָ֔ר
אֲשֶׁר־צִוָּ֥ה יְהֹוָ֖ה לֵאמֹֽר׃ ג אִ֥ישׁ אִישׁ֙ מִבֵּ֣ית
יִשְׂרָאֵ֔ל אֲשֶׁ֨ר יִשְׁחַ֜ט שׁ֥וֹר אוֹ־כֶ֛שֶׂב אוֹ־עֵ֖ז
בַּֽמַּחֲנֶ֑ה א֚וֹ אֲשֶׁ֣ר יִשְׁחָ֔ט מִח֖וּץ לַֽמַּחֲנֶֽה׃ ד וְאֶל־
פֶּ֜תַח אֹ֤הֶל מוֹעֵד֙ לֹ֣א הֱבִיאוֹ֔ לְהַקְרִ֤יב קָרְבָּן֙
לַֽיהֹוָ֔ה לִפְנֵ֖י מִשְׁכַּ֣ן יְהֹוָ֑ה דָּ֣ם יֵחָשֵׁ֞ב לָאִ֤ישׁ
הַהוּא֙ דָּ֣ם שָׁפָ֔ךְ וְנִכְרַ֛ת הָאִ֥ישׁ הַה֖וּא מִקֶּ֥רֶב
עַמּֽוֹ׃ ה לְמַ֡עַן אֲשֶׁר֩ יָבִ֨יאוּ בְּנֵ֜י יִשְׂרָאֵ֗ל אֶֽת־
זִבְחֵיהֶם֮ אֲשֶׁ֣ר הֵ֣ם זֹבְחִים֮ עַל־פְּנֵ֣י הַשָּׂדֶה֒
וֶהֱבִיאֻ֣ם לַֽיהֹוָ֗ה אֶל־פֶּ֛תַח אֹ֥הֶל מוֹעֵ֖ד אֶל־הַכֹּהֵ֑ן
וְזָבְח֞וּ זִבְחֵ֧י שְׁלָמִ֛ים לַֽיהֹוָ֖ה אוֹתָֽם׃ ו וְזָרַ֨ק

for the priests and for all the people of the congregation. 34. And let this remain a statute for you forever, to effect atonement for the sons of Yisrael from all their aberrations, once each year. And he did as *God* had commanded Moshe.

XVII

1. *God* spoke to Moshe [saying]: 2. Speak to Aharon and to his sons and to all the sons of Yisrael and say to them: This is the word which *God* has commanded: 3. Anyone, *anyone* of the house of Yisrael who slaughters as an offering an ox, or a sheep, or a goat, in the camp, or who slaughters them [for this purpose] outside the camp, 4. and he has not brought it to the entrance of the Tent of Appointed Meeting, to bring it near as an offering to *God* before the Dwelling Place of *God*, it shall be counted for that man as blood; he has shed blood and that man shall be uprooted from the midst of his people, 5. to the end that the sons of Yisrael will bring in their slaughtered meal offerings which they slaughter in the open field, and bring them to *God* to the entrance of the Tent of Appointed Meeting, to the priest, and offer them to *God* as a meal-of-peace offering. 6. And the priest

CHAPTER XVII

1 and 2. The underlying thought of the preceding chapter was to warn us against that error in which, failing to recognize the lofty ideal of moral perfection, and, at the same time, the imperfection of what we have actually attained, we would overlook the gap that still separates us from meriting God's nearness. This error would lead us, as it did the young priests [Nadab and Abihu], to hail the elation of one solemn moment as proof that we have already reached perfection. We would then fail to realize that not fleeting moments of exaltation, blocking out mundane concerns, but only godliness in everyday life, demonstrated by assiduous attention to our duties toward God in every phase of our lives, can lead us to the lofty level of God's nearness as symbolized by Mount Moriah. For this reason it is stated in Chapter 16 that if we would step across the threshold of the Holy of Holies, we must first subject our past lives to careful scrutiny. Standing before the ideal of life that shines forth from the Holy of Holies of the Law, we are bidden to strip ourselves of the illusion that we have already attained a measure of greatness, and to draw near to the Sanctuary with no other emotion except renewed determination to strive continually toward the lofty goal that has been set for us.

The sense of the present chapter, conversely, is to warn us against erring in the opposite direction, against seeking to divest ourselves of the nobility of moral human dignity, against turning our backs upon the moral ideal of humanity to which God Himself attests in His Sanctuary, and against dismissing this ideal as spurious presumption. For if that were our attitude, we would view as the basis of man's position not his relationship with God but his kinship with the animal world and we could look not to the fulfillment of God's moral law but only to the gratification of animal appetites as the goal of man's existence.

Both these errors, overweening conceit on the one hand and self-deprecation to the animal level on the other, would bar us from a true understanding of what we should be and how we should conduct ourselves, and keep us from fulfilling our calling. The preceding chapter, which warns us against arrogance, was addressed primarily to Aaron. The present chapter, which is intended to keep us aware of our moral human dignity, is addressed to all classes of the nation.

shall dash the blood against the altar of *God* in the entrance of the Tent of Appointed Meeting and shall cause the fat to go up in smoke as an expression of compliance to *God*, 7. so that they will no longer slaughter their meal offerings for the he-goats after which, straying from Me, they follow. This shall be an everlasting statute for [all] their descendants. 8. And you shall also say to them: Anyone, *anyone* of the house of Yisrael or of the stranger who will have come into their midst from abroad, who offers an ascent offering or a meal offering, 9. and does not bring it to the entrance of the Tent of Appointed Meeting, to make it to *God*, that man shall be uprooted from among his people. 10. And [as for] anyone, *anyone* of the house of Yisrael or of the stranger who has

הַכֹּהֵ֤ן אֶת־הַדָּם֙ עַל־מִזְבַּ֣ח יְהֹוָ֔ה פֶּ֖תַח אֹ֣הֶל
מוֹעֵ֑ד וְהִקְטִ֣יר הַחֵ֔לֶב לְרֵ֥יחַ נִיחֹ֖חַ לַיהֹוָֽה׃
ז וְלֹא־יִזְבְּח֥וּ עוֹד֙ אֶת־זִבְחֵיהֶ֔ם לַשְּׂעִירִ֕ם אֲשֶׁ֛ר
הֵ֥ם זֹנִ֖ים אַחֲרֵיהֶ֑ם חֻקַּ֥ת עוֹלָ֛ם תִּֽהְיֶה־זֹּ֥את לָהֶ֖ם
לְדֹרֹתָֽם׃ חמישי (שלישי כשהן מחוברין) ח וַאֲלֵהֶ֣ם
תֹּאמַ֔ר אִ֥ישׁ אִישׁ֙ מִבֵּ֣ית יִשְׂרָאֵ֔ל וּמִן־הַגֵּ֖ר
אֲשֶׁר־יָג֣וּר בְּתוֹכָ֑ם אֲשֶׁר־יַעֲלֶ֥ה עֹלָ֖ה אוֹ־זָֽבַח׃
ט וְאֶל־פֶּ֜תַח אֹ֤הֶל מוֹעֵד֙ לֹ֣א יְבִיאֶ֔נּוּ לַעֲשׂ֥וֹת
אֹת֖וֹ לַיהֹוָ֑ה וְנִכְרַ֛ת הָאִ֥ישׁ הַה֖וּא מֵעַמָּֽיו׃
י וְאִ֨ישׁ אִ֜ישׁ מִבֵּ֣ית יִשְׂרָאֵ֗ל וּמִן־הַגֵּר֙ הַגָּ֣ר

7. ***so that they will no longer slaughter their meal offerings for the he-goats.*** The preceding chapter speaks of a he-goat symbolizing a sensuous animality which gratifies its instincts in complete unrestraint and which therefore belongs in the wilderness, not to human society, which is based upon the Sanctuary of God's moral law. In Isaiah, too, cf. 13:21: "And the he-goats shall dance there" and 34:14: "and the he-goat shall cry to his fellow," he-goats typify the unrestraint of the woods and the wilderness. Hence there is no greater contrast to the ideal of the moral law which God gave to man, and by allegiance to which man can come close to God, than "the he-goats of the field." A man who makes his offering, which is meant to symbolize his personality, not "to *God* at the entrance of the Tent of Appointed Meeting, to the priest" in order to come close to God, to the Sanctuary of His Law, as the servant of the Law which God instituted for man as a means and condition for attaining His nearness, but to "the he-goats in the open field," thereby states that he has set as his ideal that animality which gratifies its instincts without restraint. He thereby denies that man has a godly character as a specific trait distinguishing man from the animal. Along with the materialists of our own day and of all the other eras in history, he considers animal sensuality the be-all and end-all of human destiny, thereby tearing up the last fibers by which he was rooted in his humanity, which is God's own.

Such a man shall be "uprooted from the midst of his people," because he has committed an act of spiritual homicide. "It shall be counted for that man as blood; he has shed blood" (Verse 4). For when the Word of God (Genesis 9:6, see commentary ibid.) permitted the killing of animals but, by contrast, stamped homicide as the gravest of all crimes, it cited as its motivation the respect due to the image of God in man. Since man was created in the image of God, his nature is entirely different from, and high above, that of the animal. Therefore one who takes an offering meant to symbolize the human personality and, instead, turns it . . . into a symbol of animality is guilty of so grave a violation of the image of God in which man was created that "it shall be counted for that man as blood; he has shed blood"!

° ° °

8 and 9. ***And you shall also say to them.*** God says to Moses: You have just warned the priests and all the members of the nation against erroneous notions about God. But now tell them that in order to be a Jew it is not enough merely to bear the true conception of God within one's heart. The relationship of the Jew with God is directly dependent on the Torah, so that denying the Torah is tantamount to denying the existence of God, and both transgressions are subject to the same severe punishment: the transgressor shall be uprooted from the base of his nationhood.

10–12. . . . We have already noted in Leviticus 3:17 and 7:26, 27 the prohibition against eating blood. In each of these instances it is joined to the prohibition against eating hard fat in connection with animal offerings. In the present verses the prohibition against eating blood is reiterated alone and in a particularly impressive manner. . . . The blood, which is present throughout the body, is the visible messenger of the

בְּתוֹכָ֔ם אֲשֶׁ֥ר יֹאכַ֖ל כָּל־דָּ֑ם וְנָתַתִּ֣י פָנַ֗י בַּנֶּ֙פֶשׁ֙
הָאֹכֶ֣לֶת אֶת־הַדָּ֔ם וְהִכְרַתִּ֥י אֹתָ֖הּ מִקֶּ֥רֶב עַמָּֽהּ׃
יא כִּ֣י־נֶ֣פֶשׁ הַבָּשָׂר֮ בַּדָּ֣ם הִוא֒ וַאֲנִ֞י נְתַתִּ֤יו לָכֶם֙
עַל־הַמִּזְבֵּ֔חַ לְכַפֵּ֖ר עַל־נַפְשֹׁתֵיכֶ֑ם כִּֽי־הַדָּ֥ם ה֖וּא
בַּנֶּ֥פֶשׁ יְכַפֵּֽר׃ יב עַל־כֵּ֤ן אָמַ֙רְתִּי֙ לִבְנֵ֣י יִשְׂרָאֵ֔ל
כָּל־נֶ֥פֶשׁ מִכֶּ֖ם לֹא־תֹ֣אכַל דָּ֑ם וְהַגֵּ֛ר הַגָּ֥ר
בְּתוֹכְכֶ֖ם לֹא־יֹ֥אכַל דָּֽם׃ יג וְאִ֨ישׁ אִ֜ישׁ מִבְּנֵ֣י
יִשְׂרָאֵ֗ל וּמִן־הַגֵּר֙ הַגָּ֣ר בְּתוֹכָ֔ם אֲשֶׁ֨ר יָצ֜וּד צֵ֥יד
חַיָּ֛ה אוֹ־ע֖וֹף אֲשֶׁ֣ר יֵאָכֵ֑ל וְשָׁפַךְ֙ אֶת־דָּמ֔וֹ וְכִסָּ֖הוּ
בֶּעָפָֽר׃ יד כִּֽי־נֶ֣פֶשׁ כָּל־בָּשָׂ֗ר דָּמ֣וֹ בְנַפְשׁוֹ֮ הוּא֒
וָאֹמַר֙ לִבְנֵ֣י יִשְׂרָאֵ֔ל דַּ֥ם כָּל־בָּשָׂ֖ר לֹ֣א תֹאכֵ֑לוּ כִּ֣י
נֶ֤פֶשׁ כָּל־בָּשָׂר֙ דָּמ֣וֹ הִ֔וא כָּל־אֹכְלָ֖יו יִכָּרֵֽת׃
טו וְכָל־נֶ֗פֶשׁ אֲשֶׁ֨ר תֹּאכַ֤ל נְבֵלָה֙ וּטְרֵפָ֔ה בָּֽאֶזְרָ֖ח
וּבַגֵּ֑ר וְכִבֶּ֨ס בְּגָדָ֜יו וְרָחַ֥ץ בַּמַּ֛יִם וְטָמֵ֥א עַד־הָעֶ֖רֶב
וְטָהֵֽר׃ טז וְאִם֙ לֹ֣א יְכַבֵּ֔ס וּבְשָׂר֖וֹ לֹ֣א יִרְחָ֑ץ
וְנָשָׂ֖א עֲוֺנֽוֹ׃ פ יח א וַיְדַבֵּ֥ר יְהוָ֖ה אֶל־מֹשֶׁ֥ה

come into their midst, who eats any blood, I will set My Countenance against that soul which eats blood and shall cause it to be uprooted from the midst of its people.
11. For the soul of the flesh is present in the blood, and therefore I have given it to you [to be placed upon] the altar, to effect atonement for your souls, for the meaning of the blood is: It is with the soul that one effects atonement.
12. Therefore I have said to the sons of Yisrael: No soul of you shall eat blood, and the stranger who has come into your midst shall not eat blood.
13. And anyone, *anyone* of the sons of Yisrael and of the stranger who has entered into their midst, who has made a catch of any game or bird that may be eaten, he must pour out its blood and cover it with dust of the earth.
14. For the soul of all flesh is its blood, which is ruled by its soul, wherefore I said to the sons of Yisrael: You shall not eat blood of any flesh because the soul of all flesh is its blood; whoever eats it shall be uprooted.
15. And any soul that eats anything that died of itself or that was torn, whether he be among the native-born or among the strangers, he must wash his garments, bathe in water, remains unclean until evening and then becomes pure.
16. If he does not wash [his garments] and does not bathe his body, he must bear his iniquity.

XVIII

1. *God* spoke to Moshe [saying]:
2. Speak to

soul, which is also present throughout the body and controls the body but cannot be seen. It is indeed fitting, therefore, that the blood, as the visible substance representing the soul, should be used in the offerings to symbolize the elevation and devotion of the soul to God, and the soul's steadfast adherence to Him.

° ° °

The character of the blood and its close relationship to the soul make it fitting that the blood of an animal should serve as the symbolic expression of the soul of a man. But precisely for this reason, the physical absorption of the blood into the human body, which is the physical aspect of the human soul, is forbidden. The purpose of this prohibition seems to be not only to counteract the pernicious illusion—which might be encouraged by the symbolism inherent in the offerings—that the animal soul is identical with the soul of a human being, but also to avert a physical threat to the spiritual character of man. The solemnity of the warning in Verse 10: "I will set My Countenance against that soul which eats blood," etc., and also the urgency of the warning uttered again and again in the Book of Deuteronomy (12:23–25): "Only remain firm not to eat the blood". . . "do not eat the soul with the flesh" and "Do not eat it! So that it may go well with you," etc., would indicate that the consumption of animal blood could so endanger a human being, or at least so corrupt his nature, that it could prevent him from attaining the moral level of the Jew's human calling as set forth in the Law of God.

° ° °

CHAPTER XVIII

1. . . . The cornerstone of individual morality and of the civilization and prosperity of nations is the exercise

the sons of Yisrael and say to them: I, *God*,
am your God. 3. After the doings of the
land of Mitzrayim, where you dwelled, you
shall not do, and after the doings of the land
of Canaan, where I am bringing you, you
shall not do, and you shall not walk in their
statutes. 4. Practice My [social] ordi-

לֵאמֹר: ב דַּבֵּר אֶל־בְּנֵי יִשְׂרָאֵל וְאָמַרְתָּ אֲלֵהֶם
אֲנִי יְהוָה אֱלֹהֵיכֶם: ג כְּמַעֲשֵׂה אֶרֶץ־מִצְרַיִם
אֲשֶׁר יְשַׁבְתֶּם־בָּהּ לֹא תַעֲשׂוּ וּכְמַעֲשֵׂה אֶרֶץ־
כְּנַעַן אֲשֶׁר אֲנִי מֵבִיא אֶתְכֶם שָׁמָּה לֹא תַעֲשׂוּ
וּבְחֻקֹּתֵיהֶם לֹא תֵלֵכוּ: ד אֶת־מִשְׁפָּטַי תַּעֲשׂוּ

and maintenance of morally free-willed control over animal sensuality so that the latter may work in the service of God. The most powerful aspect of animal sensuality is sex life, which is to be controlled by the Divine laws set forth in the present chapter and introduced by Verses 1–4.

2. ***Speak . . . and say.*** Speak to them and explain to them in detail the great significance of these three words: אֲנִי ד׳ אֱלֹקֵיכֶם ["I, *God*, am your God"]. The entire Law was prefaced with the words אָנֹכִי ד׳ אֱלֹקֶיךָ ["I am *God*, your God"]. This basic premise of Judaism is set forth here again in the preamble to the laws concerning sex life, thus showing the solemn import of what will follow. These words constitute the basic assumption of Jewish life, just as *milah*, symbolizing mastery over the carnal aspects of human nature, was set down as the cornerstone of the Jewish covenant with God. Also, in keeping with the seriousness of the subject, the personal pronoun in the present verse is not אָנֹכִי but אֲנִי. אֲנִי denotes that Personality, which, if necessary, can set itself up against the whole world and also against your ego; ד׳ upon Whom every future moment of your life and development depends and Who alone is able and willing to train you for the salvation that is your goal. This One is אֱלֹקֵיכֶם; He is your Creator, Lawgiver and Judge. Even as you received your personal existence and your nationhood from Him, so, too, you are to accept from Him, and from Him alone, the laws governing your development and the use to which you are to put the existence given you.

3. "The doings of the land of Mitzrayim" and "the doings of the land of Canaan" seem to refer to the social behavior patterns that characterized human relationships in Mitzrayim and Canaan. "Walking in their statutes" refers to the private behavior patterns typical of personal and family life in these countries. The social behavior patterns are regulated by legislation; private conduct is governed not so much by law as by norms that custom and usage have hallowed. The social aspects of human interaction reflect a nation's concepts of law and statehood. As a rule, the motives and principles—pure and honest, or otherwise—from which these patterns of conduct are derived are transparently clear and can be discerned from the conditions they are intended to regulate and from the purposes they are meant to achieve. On the other hand, the individual aspects of personal and family life, and also the ethos that characterizes a nation as one entity, are usually shaped by more or less vague notions concerning the relationship of individuals and nations to the supernatural.

Mostly, the supernatural is regarded as an inimical force seeking to block the aspirations of men and nations. Efforts to secure the favor of supernatural forces, or at least to make certain that they will not interfere in men's endeavors, then become a purpose and a consideration on behalf of which norms for personal behavior, worship of the deities and securing the favor of the gods evolve and become firmly imbedded in the lives of men and nations. The social behavior patterns are the מִשְׁפָּטִים ["(social) ordinances"] of the nations; the institutions of personal and family behavior are their חוקות ["statutes"]. In the ancient Egyptian state the former had smothered all human dignity and freedom; in Canaan the latter had sanctioned moral excesses descending to the lowest depths of bestial depravity. Even as corruption and wrongdoing in the antediluvian world joined together to cause destruction, and even as the confederation of Sodomite cities buried in the bed of the Dead Sea had been "wicked" and "sinful" at the same time, so, too, "social ordinances" and "statutes" always interact [for good or for evil]. Immorality in personal life and brutality in social relations always go hand in hand. Only a family life built on chastity can produce a nation that will champion justice and loving-kindness, and only in a free nation built on the pillars of justice and duty can the heavenly blossom of pure human morality ripen into full flower. In a slave society, the individual, too, must lose his moral freedom.

This is the reason why the preamble to the laws regulating sex life and the moral basis of the family makes reference to the social and moral corruption that predominated in Mitzrayim and Canaan, and we are told: Do not permit the example of Mitzrayim and Canaan to mold your social and moral life. Do not take your social ordinances and your statutes from Mitzrayim and Canaan. Rather, "Practice My (social) ordinances and keep My statutes," etc.

° ° °

4 and 5. וָחַי בָּהֶם *[through which he gains life]*. The

וְאֶת־חֻקֹּתַי תִּשְׁמְרוּ לָלֶכֶת בָּהֶם אֲנִי יְהֹוָה
אֱלֹהֵיכֶם׃ ה וּשְׁמַרְתֶּם אֶת־חֻקֹּתַי וְאֶת־מִשְׁפָּטַי
אֲשֶׁר יַעֲשֶׂה אֹתָם הָאָדָם וָחַי בָּהֶם אֲנִי יְהֹוָה׃ ס
ששי ו אִישׁ אִישׁ אֶל־כָּל־שְׁאֵר בְּשָׂרוֹ לֹא

nances and keep My statutes in order to walk in them; I, *God*, am your God.
5. Keep My statutes and My [social] ordinances, which man must carry out and through which he gains life; I, *God*.
6. No one, *no one* of you shall approach

gain to be derived from observing these laws is nothing more and nothing less than וָחַי, life elevated to the highest potency.

° ° °

6. . . . לֹא תִקְרְבוּ *[No (one . . . of you) shall approach]* (second person plural, male gender): Even though this entire chapter is formulated in terms of the male, the prohibitions it contains are addressed equally to both sexes and both men and women are punishable in the same degree if they transgress any of them (*Torath Kohanim*).

לְגַלּוֹת עֶרְוָה ***[to uncover (their) nakedness].*** Any sexual relationship that is forbidden by the Creator and therefore cannot be sanctioned as a moral act in the service of God is nothing but naked bestiality. Hence the Law uses the expression גִּלּוּי עֲרָיוֹת [uncovering of nakedness] as a general term for all forbidden sexual unions. . . .

When God led the first woman to the first man He did so in order that their union, based on free-willed morality (as opposed to the blind physical urges of the animal), might serve Him as a pillar on which to build all of human development—marriage, the family and society. Hence, even as He declared the primary purpose of the wife to be her husband's helpmeet, He stated as His very first requirement for the morality of human marriage: "For this reason a man leaves his father and mother and clings to his wife, and they become one flesh" (Genesis 2:24, see commentary ibid.), thereby indicating that if the lofty moral purpose of human marriage is to be attained, the male must not take a wife from among his closest kin.

This is God's law of לְמִינֵהוּ [the separation of species] for the human race, a law which plants and animals follow blindly and unchangingly because of His utterance at the time of their creation, but which His Adam, His man, the one creature endowed with moral freedom, was meant to hear directly from Him so that he might obey it of his own free will. The moral and social disintegration of the antediluvian world set in when men first began to choose their mates not in accordance with God's will but in accordance with their personal caprice. "They took themselves wives from wherever they chose" (Genesis 6:2). This state of affairs deadened the Divine spirit in man and sent mankind to its grave.

In order to produce a priestly nation and a holy people in the midst of a generation of men that had gone astray morally and socially, but that He wished to save, the Father of Mankind drew even narrower limits for the marital choices open to this nation. Narrower still were the limits He set for the marital choices of the priests within that priestly nation (Leviticus 29). Human gardeners and geneticists seeking to improve plant and animal breeds will certainly not leave the dispersion of seeds to chance or permit males and females of a species to mate at random. They will not permit seeds to mingle indiscriminately under uncontrolled conditions. Why, then, should anyone not consider it necessary to heed the mating laws proclaimed by the Father and Educator of the human species, when the task to be accomplished is to win the noblest flower from earthly matter, earthly creatures made in the image of God—in short, to produce creatures that are truly human?

It is certain that the reasons for His laws relating to mate selection are to be found deep within the very source of human nature that is beyond man's understanding. These reasons are clear only to Him Who can already see the finished creation at its beginning and Who has woven, and still weaves, the mysterious bond that unites heavenly spirits with earthly bodies.

In our commentary on Genesis 2:5 we did not attempt to discuss these motives; all we presumed to do was to make speculative suggestions regarding the physiological consequences that might result from violations of these laws. Here, however, where Scripture deals in greater detail with forbidden unions between close relatives; where, indeed, the Law moves beyond the concept of blood relationships and prohibits certain unions even when two families are linked only by קִידּוּשִׁין [betrothal] (i.e., from the moment when a man and a woman are betrothed to one another by the act of קִידּוּשִׁין, certain relatives on either side become forbidden as marriage partners for one another), it appears proper to discuss not only the profound physiological impact of marriage and family life but also the moral and social factors they entail. Let us, then, set forth a few suggestions also in this connection.

Not the least of the considerations which elevate acts that otherwise would be עֶרְוָה, crude animal behavior, to the sphere of *mitzvoth* that sanctify man should be the fact that the physical union of husband and wife immediately lays the foundation for the purest, closest, strongest and mightiest spiritual merger of two hearts and minds. It becomes the soil for that blossoming any kin of his flesh to uncover [their] nakedness; I, *God*. 7. The nakedness of your father and the nakedness of your mother you shall not uncover. She is your mother; you must not uncover her nakedness. 8. The nakedness of your father's wife you shall not uncover; it is your father's nakedness. 9. The nakedness of your sister, [be it] the daughter of your father or the daughter of your mother, whether born in the house or outside, their nakedness you

תִקְרְב֖וּ לְגַלּ֣וֹת עֶרְוָ֑ה אֲנִ֖י יְהוָֽה׃ ס ז עֶרְוַ֥ת
אָבִ֛יךָ וְעֶרְוַ֥ת אִמְּךָ֖ לֹ֣א תְגַלֵּ֑ה אִמְּךָ֙ הִ֔וא לֹ֥א
תְגַלֶּ֖ה עֶרְוָתָֽהּ׃ ס ח עֶרְוַ֥ת אֵֽשֶׁת־אָבִ֖יךָ לֹ֣א
תְגַלֵּ֑ה עֶרְוַ֥ת אָבִ֖יךָ הִֽוא׃ ס ט עֶרְוַ֨ת אֲחוֹתְךָ֤
בַת־אָבִ֙יךָ֙ א֣וֹ בַת־אִמֶּ֔ךָ מוֹלֶ֣דֶת בַּ֔יִת א֖וֹ מוֹלֶ֣דֶת

which the blessing recited in our marriage service proclaims as "love, harmony, peace and companionship" and which is the moral essence of that sublime, unique conjugal love extolled by Judaism in the hymn to the love between man and woman, and between God and Israel, as "stronger than death, one which all the floods of fate cannot quench." In short, the command that the man must cling to his wife loses every semblance of עֶרְוָה sensuality and becomes invested instead with the most sublime moral consecration, provided that it truly effects that wonder of all wonders upon which the true happiness of families and nations alike is based; that "the two become one flesh."

Therefore, the less the husband and wife were linked before marriage by bonds of mutual attachment and affection, or of familial love, the more that strongest of all bonds of love between the mates begins only with marriage, the more will even the sexual aspect of marriage become a basic factor in the moral sphere of a happy marriage, imbued and maintained throughout by love, and will itself become elevated into the realm of pure morality.

However, where the bonds of nature have already linked hearts and minds in parental, fraternal, filial or other familial ties—and the more pure and genuine the moral influence exercised by family ties in God's priestly nation, the stronger and more far-reaching will be the pull of familial affection—there marriage will have only a little love to add. Love will have been there before, and marriage will add almost nothing more than the sexual element, which descends to the level of עֶרְוָה [nakedness] if it exists only by itself and does not create the wonder of a loving union between the two partners.

And then again, parental, fraternal, filial and familial love, and the purpose and influence of these loves, are a thing apart from conjugal love and the purpose of marriage. They themselves are such formidable independent factors, and the family life to be attained under God's Law depends so greatly upon their pure interaction, that the Law of God could never tolerate the displacement of any one of them. A man's mother cannot become his wife without ceasing to be his mother, a man's sister cannot become his wife without ceasing to be his sister, a man's aunt cannot become his wife without ceasing to be his aunt, and so forth. A sexual union between a man and such blood relatives whom he can never marry would be nothing but crude עֶרְוָה and the Law of God proclaims: "She is your mother; you must not uncover her nakedness," "she is your sister; you must not uncover her nakedness."

We certainly do not think that with these suggestions we have even touched upon, let alone exhausted, the true motivation behind these laws. However, we believe we may point out that, even in our own limited insight and within those moral and social spheres accessible to our insight, we can indeed see that the observance of these laws, or failure to observe them, yields consequences that are clearly discernible and of profound significance.

All the forbidden marriages enumerated in this chapter are forbidden in such categorical terms that a marriage between the parties concerned is not only legally prohibited but in fact impossible. Any קידושין performed for them is legally null and void. Such marriages are therefore subsumed under the concept of עֶרְוָה [nakedness]. The sexual intercourse in itself is nothing but עֶרְוָה. Only in the case of a woman in her period of menstrual impurity (Verse 19) are קידושין תופסין [is the marriage valid], because approaching a woman in this condition for sexual intercourse is forbidden only temporarily (Yebamoth 49a and b; Kiddushin 67, 68).

No one . . . of you shall approach . . . to uncover (their) nakedness. Any personal advances that might lead to גִּלּוּי עֲרָיוֹת [sexual intercourse] with these relatives must be avoided.

9. ***whether born in the house or outside.*** "Whether your father is told, 'Keep her,' or whether your father is told, 'Let her go.'" (Yebamoth 23a). Regardless of whether or not the mother belongs to the father's house; i.e., regardless of whether or not the sister was born in wedlock.

חוּץ לֹא תְגַלֶּה עֶרְוָתָן: ס י עֶרְוַת בַּת־בִּנְךָ אוֹ
בַת־בִּתְּךָ לֹא תְגַלֶּה עֶרְוָתָן כִּי עֶרְוָתְךָ הֵנָּה: ס
יא עֶרְוַת בַּת־אֵשֶׁת אָבִיךָ מוֹלֶדֶת אָבִיךָ אֲחוֹתְךָ
הִוא לֹא תְגַלֶּה עֶרְוָתָהּ: ס יב עֶרְוַת אֲחוֹת־
אָבִיךָ לֹא תְגַלֵּה שְׁאֵר אָבִיךָ הִוא: ס יג עֶרְוַת
אֲחוֹת־אִמְּךָ לֹא תְגַלֵּה כִּי־שְׁאֵר אִמְּךָ הִוא: ס
יד עֶרְוַת אֲחִי־אָבִיךָ לֹא תְגַלֵּה אֶל־אִשְׁתּוֹ לֹא
תִקְרָב דֹּדָתְךָ הִוא: ס טו עֶרְוַת כַּלָּתְךָ לֹא תְגַלֵּה
אֵשֶׁת בִּנְךָ הִוא לֹא תְגַלֶּה עֶרְוָתָהּ: ס טז עֶרְוַת
אֵשֶׁת־אָחִיךָ לֹא תְגַלֵּה עֶרְוַת אָחִיךָ הִוא: ס
יז עֶרְוַת אִשָּׁה וּבִתָּהּ לֹא תְגַלֵּה אֶת־בַּת־בְּנָהּ
וְאֶת־בַּת־בִּתָּהּ לֹא תִקַּח לְגַלּוֹת עֶרְוָתָהּ שַׁאֲרָה
הֵנָּה זִמָּה הִוא: יח וְאִשָּׁה אֶל־אֲחֹתָהּ לֹא תִקָּח
לִצְרֹר לְגַלּוֹת עֶרְוָתָהּ עָלֶיהָ בְּחַיֶּיהָ: יט וְאֶל־
אִשָּׁה בְּנִדַּת טֻמְאָתָהּ לֹא תִקְרַב לְגַלּוֹת עֶרְוָתָהּ:
כ וְאֶל־אֵשֶׁת עֲמִיתְךָ לֹא־תִתֵּן שְׁכָבְתְּךָ לְזָרַע
לְטָמְאָה־בָהּ: כא וּמִזַּרְעֲךָ לֹא־תִתֵּן לְהַעֲבִיר

shall not uncover. 10. The nakedness of your son's daughter, or of your daughter's daughter, you shall not uncover their nakedness, for they are your nakedness. 11. The nakedness of the daughter of your father's wife, born to your father—she is your sister; you shall not uncover her nakedness. 12. The nakedness of your father's sister you shall not uncover; she is your father's [close] relative. 13. The nakedness of your mother's sister you shall not uncover, for she is your mother's [close] relative. 14. The nakedness of your father's brother you shall not uncover; you shall not approach his wife; she is your aunt. 15. The nakedness of your daughter-in-law you shall not uncover; she is your son's wife; you must not uncover her nakedness. 16. The nakedness of your brother's wife you must not uncover; it is your brother's nakedness. 17. The nakedness of a woman and her daughter you shall not uncover; you shall not take her son's daughter or her daughter's daughter, to uncover her nakedness; they are [close] relatives; it is lewdness. 18. And you shall not take a woman along with her sister, to join them together, to uncover her nakedness beside the other in her lifetime. 19. And you shall not approach a woman during the separation period of her uncleanness, to uncover her nakedness. 20. And you shall not place next to your neighbor's wife your bed that is for procreation, to lose your purity through her. 21. And you shall not give any of your progeny to pass it

21. . . . The position of the prohibition "and you shall not give any of your progeny. . ." in the enumeration of sexual laws is [most] significant. Verse 20 concludes the list of sexual aberrations that could result in the birth of offspring, זֶרַע, progeny, literally "seed" for humanity. We believe that the word לְזָרַע ["for procreation"] in the last of these prohibitions is meant to remind us of the lofty moral goal of man's sex life. This is logically followed by the prohibition against sacrificing one's offspring to the Molekh. The underlying logic is as follows: Even as your children are not to be the products of blind physical urges but should be begotten in a moral manner, so, too, their lives and their fate should not be given over to the random workings of a blind physical force. Even as they were produced under the protection of God's Law, so, too, their lives and fortunes belong to Divine protection and guidance, which seeks man's moral development for his own future happiness.

Regarding your children, God says: אֲנִי ד׳ ["I, *God*"]; it is to Me, the God of grace and compassion, Who brings man's future to its moral fulfillment, that your children belong. It is for Me that you must educate every child of yours; it is to Me that you must turn over every child of yours. You must guide each one of your offspring in My ways and then leave it to Me to guide each one in his own way, toward his personal happiness and toward the fulfillment of his life's purpose. "You to the Molekh, and you shall not desecrate the name of your God; I, *God.*   22. And you shall not cohabit with a male as one cohabits with a woman; it is an abomination.   23. And you shall not place your bed next to an animal [in such a manner as] to defile yourself thereby; and a woman shall not stand before an animal for copulation; it is dehumanizing.   24. Do not defile yourselves with any of this! For through this did the people whom I send away from before you become defiled. 25. Thus the land was defiled, and I visited its iniquities upon it, and the land vomited out its inhabitants.   26. Therefore keep My statutes and My [social] ordinances, and do not do any of these abominations, neither the native-born nor the one who has entered into your midst as a stranger, 27. —for the people of the land who went before you did all these abominations, and thus the land became defiled— 28. so that the land will not vomit you out when you defile it, as it vomited out the nation that went before you.   29. For whoever

לַמֹּ֔לֶךְ וְלֹ֥א תְחַלֵּ֛ל אֶת־שֵׁ֥ם אֱלֹהֶ֖יךָ אֲנִ֥י יְהֹוָֽה: שביעי (רביעי כשהן מחוברין) כב וְאֶ֨ת־זָכָ֔ר לֹ֥א תִשְׁכַּ֖ב מִשְׁכְּבֵ֣י אִשָּׁ֑ה תּוֹעֵבָ֖ה הִֽוא: כג וּבְכׇל־בְּהֵמָ֛ה לֹא־תִתֵּ֥ן שְׁכׇבְתְּךָ֖ לְטׇמְאָה־בָ֑הּ וְאִשָּׁ֗ה לֹֽא־תַעֲמֹ֞ד לִפְנֵ֧י בְהֵמָ֛ה לְרִבְעָ֖הּ תֶּ֥בֶל הֽוּא: כד אַל־תִּֽטַּמְּא֖וּ בְּכׇל־אֵ֑לֶּה כִּ֤י בְכׇל־אֵ֨לֶּה֙ נִטְמְא֣וּ הַגּוֹיִ֔ם אֲשֶׁר־אֲנִ֥י מְשַׁלֵּ֖חַ מִפְּנֵיכֶֽם: כה וַתִּטְמָ֣א הָאָ֔רֶץ וָאֶפְקֹ֥ד עֲוֺנָ֖הּ עָלֶ֑יהָ וַתָּקִ֥א הָאָ֖רֶץ אֶת־יֹשְׁבֶֽיהָ: כו וּשְׁמַרְתֶּ֣ם אַתֶּ֗ם אֶת־חֻקֹּתַי֙ וְאֶת־מִשְׁפָּטַ֔י וְלֹ֣א תַעֲשׂ֔וּ מִכֹּ֥ל הַתּוֹעֵבֹ֖ת הָאֵ֑לֶּה הָֽאֶזְרָ֔ח וְהַגֵּ֖ר הַגָּ֥ר בְּתוֹכְכֶֽם: כז כִּ֚י אֶת־כׇּל־הַתּוֹעֵבֹ֣ת הָאֵ֔ל עָשׂ֥וּ אַנְשֵֽׁי־הָאָ֖רֶץ אֲשֶׁ֣ר לִפְנֵיכֶ֑ם וַתִּטְמָ֖א הָאָֽרֶץ: מפטיר כח וְלֹֽא־תָקִ֤יא הָאָ֨רֶץ֙ אֶתְכֶ֔ם בְּטַֽמַּאֲכֶ֖ם אֹתָ֑הּ כַּאֲשֶׁ֥ר קָאָ֛ה אֶת־הַגּ֖וֹי אֲשֶׁ֥ר לִפְנֵיכֶֽם:

shall not give any of your progeny to pass it to the Molekh, and you shall not desecrate the name of your God; I, *God.*''

24-28. . . . Just as the people is "the people of God," so its land, too, is "the land of God." . . . From the time that Abraham was chosen, and the land was chosen for him, the land has never meekly endured corruption in those who dwelt upon it. The flowering of the land is dependent on the moral flowering of the people which the land has brought forth, nourishing them with its fruit and enriching them with its treasures. All that stirs within the womb of this earth, all that is produced by this earth, all that absorbs dew and rain beneath its skies and is invigorated and brought to maturity by the sunlight above it—all this is subject to the Law God gave to man. It is for the fulfillment of God's will by men of moral purity that each seed germinates, each flower blooms, each fruit ripens. For this purpose alone does the sun shine and the dew provide life-giving moisture. All of physical life in this land shall attain its own perfection as the bearer of a nation of perfect, free-willed morality.

Hence, if the society that lives in this land subverts the purpose of its existence by social and moral corruption, the land, too, loses the reason for its existence.

Therefore a nation that is socially and morally corrupt can have no future on the soil of this land. For it is with the vital forces of this land of God, liberated through the muscles and sinews of its human inhabitants, that the nation has perpetrated its crimes against the Law of God. In other words, God's own strength and resources have been misused and squandered for the aberrations and immoral excesses of men. Through the טֻמְאָה [uncleanness] of its inhabitants, the land, too, becomes טָמֵא [defiled] and the crimes of its inhabitants become its crimes. As long as sin and excesses of immorality remain confined to individuals while the nation as a whole continues to maintain, champion and enforce God's Law, the individual who transgresses the Law is eliminated from that society by the sentence of God or man, and the nation will continue to grow and prosper on the land because it adheres to God. But once sin and excesses of immorality become the rule rather than the exception, if society finds excuses for them and, indeed, gives them sanction so that they become national institutions, then the human society which has thus set itself against God's moral law has set itself also against the soil that is sacred to this law, and in that case the land will vomit out that society even as any organism will reject an element that has become incompatible with it.

o   o   o

does any of these abominations, the souls that do them shall be uprooted from the midst of their people. 30. Therefore keep that which has been given by Me to you for keeping, so that none of the abominable statutes that were practiced before you will be done, so that you will not become defiled through them; I, *God*, your God.

כט כִּי כָּל־אֲשֶׁר יַעֲשֶׂה מִכֹּל הַתּוֹעֵבֹת הָאֵלֶּה
וְנִכְרְתוּ הַנְּפָשׁוֹת הָעֹשֹׂת מִקֶּרֶב עַמָּם׃
ל וּשְׁמַרְתֶּם אֶת־מִשְׁמַרְתִּי לְבִלְתִּי עֲשׂוֹת
מֵחֻקּוֹת הַתּוֹעֵבֹת אֲשֶׁר נַעֲשׂוּ לִפְנֵיכֶם וְלֹא
תִטַּמְּאוּ בָּהֶם אֲנִי יְהֹוָה אֱלֹהֵיכֶם׃ פ

30. **וּשְׁמַרְתֶּם אֶת מִשְׁמַרְתִּי לְבִלְתִּי עֲשׂוֹת וגו׳** ***[Therefore keep that which has been given by Me to you for keeping, so that none . . . will be done].*** **מִשְׁמַרְתִּי** is the "charge" God gave us to keep His Law. The Law is a treasure entrusted to us. Each one of us is its **שׁוֹמֵר**, its appointed keeper or guardian, and we must guard it, first of all, from ourselves. We must protect it from being violated by our own transgressions, intentional or unintentional. We are not told, "Therefore keep that which has been given by Me to you for keeping, *and you will not do* any of the abominable statutes. . ." but "Therefore keep that which has been given by Me to you for keeping, so that *none of the abominable statutes . . . will be done*." Clearly, this means: Guard the Law that I have placed into your keeping in such a manner that you will not come to transgress it. And this, in turn, obviously means: Do not refrain only from actual violations of the Law but also from any act that might lead you to violate the Law. Or, as it is stated in Yebamoth 21a and Moed Katan 5a: **עֲשׂוּ מִשְׁמֶרֶת לְמִשְׁמַרְתִּי**: Let the keeping of the Law as such be the purpose of your guarding; i.e., keep away from yourselves anything that might cause you to neglect your duty to guard the Law against violation.

This means that we are urged to be most punctilious to shun not only any act forbidden by the Law but also any act that, because of its similarity to, or other association with, a forbidden act, could bring us to commit the violation itself. This is the Jewish concept of punctilious observance which is subsumed under the Rabbinic terms **גָּדֵר** ["fence"], and **סְיָג** ["hedge"], "making a fence, or a hedge, around the law," and which is expressed by the formula: "Keep away from anything that is morally evil and also from anything that resembles it," or, as is stated in Shabbath 13a: "Take a circuitous route, O Nazirite; do not come close to the vineyard." One who is forbidden to drink wine, as, for instance, a Nazirite, is warned to keep away from vineyards.

Thus, when the Sages, in their profound insight into human nature and into the practical aspects of observing the Law, were led to enact such **גְּזֵרוֹת**, dispositions, in order to safeguard the observance of the laws, they were simply enacting into law precautions which any sensible, conscientious Jew concerned about the observance of God's Law should adopt on his own as a habit to govern his personal life. (Cf. Exodus 23:13 and Leviticus 19:2). The duty to safeguard the observance of the Law has given rise to such "fences" particularly in connection with the laws relating to forbidden sexual relationships that are set down in this section. The "fences" relevant to these laws are known as **שְׁנִיּוֹת** [second degree], and they refer to marriages forbidden **מִדְּרַבָּנָן** [by Rabbinic law] because the familial ties between the parties concerned resemble kinship ties which, under Biblical law, preclude marriage so that the former degree of kinship can easily be confused with the latter. (See Yebamoth 21).

of the abominable statutes. Sexual excesses among the Canaanite population had not only ceased to be considered as abominations but had, in fact, become sanctioned by custom and religious cult. They had become "statutes," or "institutions." As stated in Isaiah 24:5: They have changed the law into its opposite; i.e., they have elevated immorality to become law.

The Haftarah for this Sidra may be found on page 879.

קדושים

KEDOSHIM

XIX 1. *God* spoke to Moshe [saying]: 2. Speak to the entire community of the sons of Yisrael and say to them: You shall be holy, for I, *God,*

יט א וַיְדַבֵּר יְהוָה אֶל־מֹשֶׁה לֵּאמֹר: ב דַּבֵּר
אֶל־כָּל־עֲדַת בְּנֵי־יִשְׂרָאֵל וְאָמַרְתָּ אֲלֵהֶם
קְדֹשִׁים תִּהְיוּ כִּי קָדוֹשׁ אֲנִי יְהוָה אֱלֹהֵיכֶם:

CHAPTER XIX

1. וַיִּקְרָא, צַו, שְׁמִינִי, תַּזְרִיעַ, מְצוֹרָע, אַחֲרֵי מוֹת, קְדֹשִׁים! [This sequence of weekly portions is significant]. If the moral ideal of life to be achieved through the Word of God resting beneath the wings of the cherubim is to be translated into living reality, as symbolically represented by the Dwelling Place and the offerings discussed in the portions ot וַיִּקְרָא [Leviticus 1:1 through 5:26] and צַו [Leviticus 6:1 through 8:36], men must first be produced, nurtured and educated under the laws concerning forbidden foods, impurity and forbidden sexual relationships set forth in the portions from שְׁמִינִי [Leviticus 9:1 through 11:47] to אַחֲרֵי מוֹת [Leviticus 16:1 through 18:30]. Only then can they be told: "You shall be holy because I, *God*, your God, am holy."

Here, in direct connection with the preceding chapter on the laws of forbidden sexual relationships, we are given pithy aphorisms outlining the character of a hallowed Jewish life. They are the fundamentals for the מִשְׁפָּטִים [(social) ordinances] that govern a communal life flourishing under the Law of God. These fundamentals were already pointed out in the introduction to the laws concerning forbidden sexual relationships, in connection with the statutes, and allusion is made to them over and over again in subsequent parts of Leviticus (18:4, 5, 26; 19:37 and 20:22) in order to make clear that the justice, selflessness and brotherly love which God requires man to practice and on which alone man's true happiness is founded can be translated into reality only by a people whose existence is firmly rooted in these statutes. . . .

If we consider that the major portion of the laws contained in Chapter 19 has already been set forth elsewhere, we are probably not in error if we assume that while the preceding chapter set forth the negative aspects of Jewish law as contrasted with the "abominable statutes" of a Canaanite world, the present chapter sketches the positive aspects of a society that can be built only upon the Divinely-given foundation of a morally pure sex life. This is why the present chapter opens with the command to honor one's father and mother, the cornerstone of all society and of all human civilization. Note that in Verse 3 the mother is mentioned before the father. Only where a man has taken to himself the right wife in a Divinely-sanctioned marriage will the children have a true mother, the very first prerequisite for true moral and spiritual humanness. Only such conditions can produce that Jewish relationship between children and their parents, the soul of that family life, in which children will flourish toward God and in which all the seeds of social virtue will be effectively nurtured from the cradle on. . . .

2. ***You shall be holy.*** This admonition to strive for absolute human perfection is addressed to each and every member of the nation as an individual. No station in life, no sex, no age, no state of personal fortune is excluded from this call to strive for the heights of absolute morality, nor is the call addressed to any one individual apart from all others. We must all be קְדוֹשִׁים, "holy."

. . . קְדוּשָׁה [holiness] results when a morally free human being has complete dominion over all his energies and inclinations and over the enticements and tendencies associated with these, and places them into the service of God's will. Such dominion over one's self, the greatest skill in man's power to practice, does not consist in neglecting, stunting, suppressing or destroying any human drive or faculty. No potential or impulse given to man, from the most spiritual to the most sensual, is good or bad in itself. Each has been given to him for beneficial purposes in order to accomplish the will of God on earth. God's Law has set for each a positive purpose and negative limits. Anything employed in the service of this God-appointed purpose and within the limits drawn by God is holy and good. Only where man's strengths and inclinations are turned away from this purpose and practiced outside these limits do coarseness and evil begin.

However, as in any activity, virtuosity in this, the highest skill in human morality, can be attained only through practice, through the use of one's moral free will to gain dominion over existing personal propensities. But these exercises are not to be performed in the sphere of the expressly forbidden, where any slip would result in wrongdoing. Moral resolve must be tested and strengthened within the sphere of the permitted. By exercising one's powers of self-restraint in conduct that is permitted but nonetheless related to what is forbid-your God, am holy. 3. You shall reverence every man his mother and his father and keep My Sabbaths; I, *God,* your God. 4. Do not turn to the gods that deny and do not make yourselves molten deities; I, *God,* your God. 5. And when you slaughter a meal-of-peace offering for *God,* slaughter it as an expression of your [own] will. 6. On the day that you slaughter it shall it be eaten and also on the next day; anything that is left over until the third day shall be burned in fire. 7. If it was intended to be eaten on the third day it is a rejected thing; it is not considered to be in accordance with the Divine will. 8. Whoever eats it must bear his iniquity, for he has desecrated the Sanctuary of *God*; that soul shall be uprooted from among its

ג אִישׁ אִמּוֹ וְאָבִיו תִּירָאוּ וְאֶת־שַׁבְּתֹתַי
תִּשְׁמֹרוּ אֲנִי יְהוָה אֱלֹהֵיכֶם: ד אַל־תִּפְנוּ אֶל־
הָאֱלִילִם וֵאלֹהֵי מַסֵּכָה לֹא תַעֲשׂוּ לָכֶם אֲנִי
יְהוָה אֱלֹהֵיכֶם: ה וְכִי תִזְבְּחוּ זֶבַח שְׁלָמִים
לַיהוָה לִרְצֹנְכֶם תִּזְבָּחֻהוּ: ו בְּיוֹם זִבְחֲכֶם יֵאָכֵל
וּמִמָּחֳרָת וְהַנּוֹתָר עַד־יוֹם הַשְּׁלִישִׁי בָּאֵשׁ
יִשָּׂרֵף: ז וְאִם הֵאָכֹל יֵאָכֵל בַּיּוֹם הַשְּׁלִישִׁי פִּגּוּל
הוּא לֹא יֵרָצֶה: ח וְאֹכְלָיו עֲוֺנוֹ יִשָּׂא כִּי־אֶת־
קֹדֶשׁ יְהוָה חִלֵּל וְנִכְרְתָה הַנֶּפֶשׁ הַהִוא מֵעַמֶּיהָ:

den, man is to gain mastery over his inclinations and thus make all his powers and potential subservient to the pure fulfillment of God's will.

This is the training course through which everyone is required to pass, each according to his personal peculiarities, quietly, in a manner known only to himself, working upon his inner self. It is a task which the Sages call abstinence, and for which the Gemarah (Yebamoth 20a) gives the formula: "Achieve personal sanctity within the realm of that which is permitted to you." Abstinence is not yet holiness, but it is a first step toward it, as Rabbi Phinehas ben Yair teaches in his "ascending steps" toward moral perfection set down in Avodah Zarah 20b.

° ° °

The pillars of our sanctification consist of three basic principles: the respect due to one's parents and to the Sabbath (Verse 3), the purity of our awareness of God (Verse 4) and the purity and social productivity of our relationships with Him (Verses 5–10).

3. . . . In this passage the Sabbath is perceived as the source and foundation of the calling of the Jewish people and as the epitome of God's Law, even as it is the eternal, most eloquent symbol of our allegiance to God in all our activities in the physical world and in human society. Only when a Jewish child sees his parents observe the Sabbath will he learn, from their example, to place himself and his own world at God's feet; only then will his obedience to his parents lead him to obey God. Honoring one's father and mother is the living "Sabbath" for the children, and the Sabbath is the spiritual father and mother to parent and child alike. Both the Sabbath and his parents educate the Jewish individual toward godliness. . . .

5–8. ***And when you slaughter.*** If, therefore, we make meal-of-peace offerings in a mood of unclouded happiness, we should not be motivated in any way by the pagan notion that this free-will offering must be made in order to appease a deity who envies our undisturbed bliss. The offering is made not to satisfy a need of God's but to satisfy our own need. "Slaughter it as an expression of your [own] will": Our offering is to be a symbolic pledge of our own firm resolve (Cf. Leviticus 1:3).

° ° °

It is most significant that the meal-of-peace offerings and the related laws concerning what to do with what is left over, and concerning the "rejected thing"; i.e., the prohibition against eating anything left over on the third day, are discussed as the third fundamental law at the very outset of the chapter on holiness. This shows most clearly that in Judaism the sanctity of life is just as remote from a "mortification of the flesh" as it is from unrestrained self-abandonment to physical appetites. Respect for one's parents and the observance of the Sabbath are the educators for a life of sanctity; the basis for such a life is a clear and pure conception of God.

"Meal-of-peace offerings:" The spiritualization and moralization also of our sensual pleasures, so that even the everyday table of our happy, joyous family life becomes an altar of God and we ourselves turn our eyes to God even when we eat—such is the blossom of the Jewish sanctification of personal life, which, in turn, if it is genuine, must immediately yield, as its fruit in communal life, the fulfillment of our duty to love our fellow men as our brothers. . . .

people.   9. And when you reap the harvest of your land you shall not wholly harvest the corner of your field and you shall
not gather the gleanings of your harvest;
10. and you shall not pluck the unripe
grapes from your vineyard and not gather
up the fallen berries of your vineyard; you
shall leave them for the poor man and for
the stranger; I, *God*, your God.   11. You
shall not steal and you shall not deny [a
rightful claim] and you shall not tell lies one
against the other;   12. and you shall not
swear falsely by My Name, for you would
profane the name of your God; I, *God*.
13. Do not withhold that which is due to
your neighbor and do not rob him; the
wages earned by a day laborer shall not
remain overnight with you until the morn-

ט וּבְקֻצְרְכֶם אֶת־קְצִיר אַרְצְכֶם לֹא תְכַלֶּה
פְּאַת שָׂדְךָ לִקְצֹר וְלֶקֶט קְצִירְךָ לֹא תְלַקֵּט:
י וְכַרְמְךָ לֹא תְעוֹלֵל וּפֶרֶט כַּרְמְךָ לֹא תְלַקֵּט
לֶעָנִי וְלַגֵּר תַּעֲזֹב אֹתָם אֲנִי יְהֹוָה אֱלֹהֵיכֶם:
יא לֹא תִּגְנֹבוּ וְלֹא־תְכַחֲשׁוּ וְלֹא־תְשַׁקְּרוּ אִישׁ
בַּעֲמִיתוֹ: יב וְלֹא־תִשָּׁבְעוּ בִשְׁמִי לַשָּׁקֶר וְחִלַּלְתָּ
אֶת־שֵׁם אֱלֹהֶיךָ אֲנִי יְהֹוָה: יג לֹא־תַעֲשֹׁק אֶת־
רֵעֲךָ וְלֹא תִגְזֹל לֹא־תָלִין פְּעֻלַּת שָׂכִיר אִתְּךָ

---

10. The obligation to leave for the poor the "gleanings," "forgotten sheaves" and "corners of the field"
devolves upon everyone who owns a field, regardless of
his economic situation. Even if he himself is poor, other
needy individuals are entitled to these leavings from his
field (Ḥullin 131a and b).

Note that according to Scriptural law there is no legal
minimum measure for the corner of the field left to the
poor. Consequently, the owner of the field has discharged his obligation even if he has left only a minus-
cule amount. It is therefore clear that these laws were
not intended explicitly for the purpose of assuring the
upkeep of the poor. For a poor man, too, is obligated
under the Law to leave the "gleanings," "forgotten
sheaves," "corners" and unripe grapes from his own
field and vineyard to other poor people. Obviously,
then, these laws have another motivation. At the time
of reaping, when the owner of the field, surveying what
nature has done for him and what he is now about to
take home as his harvest, proudly utters the momentous
statement, "This is mine," these laws come to remind
every member of the national entity—and require him
to acknowledge this by practical action—that anyone
who has possessions is obligated to care for the needy.
The laws regarding the "corners of the field" and the
unripe grapes serve to remind him that his field and his
vineyard did not yield their produce for him alone, and
the laws regarding the "gleanings" and the "single
grapes" fallen off during the cutting impress upon him
that his hand is not to work for himself alone, and that
in the holy state governed by the Law of God the care
of the "poor and the unpropertied stranger" is not a
matter to be left to personal feelings of sympathy, or to
apprehension lest the poor, in desperation, may threat-
en the land of the propertied. The care of the poor is not
to be left to personal sentiment or expedience. It is
something that the poor have a right to expect and that
the propertied are obligated to give under the Law of
God, Who says to everyone, "I, *God*, your God"; thereby assuring each and every one equally of His personal
consideration, encompassing all with equal love and
bestowing upon all equal rights, declaring that, in the
same measure, all are duty-bound to give others equal
rights and equal love. Thus the law unites them all to
form a society holy to God, held together by respect for
the rights and the duties inherent in the giving and
acceptance of brotherly love.

*   *   *

11 and 12. The basic principles set forth in the preceding verses are followed by several verses from the
social tenets of the nation that is to be sacred to
God. . . .

You shall not steal. You must not let the cunning that
seeks unfair advantage over others guide you in your
business and social dealings, for that would be גְּנֵיבָה
[theft] in the broader sense of the term. גַּנָּב [thief] is
related to כנף [to hide or cover up]. The basic characteristics of theft are stealth and illegality. Hence, whenever a person takes even as little as one *perutah* or one
penny from another and appropriates it for himself
without the other's knowledge, it is a theft in the eyes
of God, a violation of His commandment, "You shall
not steal." . . .

*   *   *

ing.   14. Do not curse a deaf man and do not place a stumbling block before a blind man, and fear your God; I, *God.*   15. Do not do wrong in judgment. Do not give special consideration to one who has been brought low and do not give a great man preferential treatment out of respect; judge your neighbor in accordance with justice. 16. Do not go about as a talebearer among your people; do not stand idly by the

עַד־בֹּקֶר: יד לֹא־תְקַלֵּל חֵרֵשׁ וְלִפְנֵי עִוֵּר לֹא תִתֵּן מִכְשֹׁל וְיָרֵאתָ מֵּאֱלֹהֶיךָ אֲנִי יְהֹוָה: שני (חמישי כשהן מחוברין) טו לֹא־תַעֲשׂוּ עָוֶל בַּמִּשְׁפָּט לֹא־תִשָּׂא פְנֵי־דָל וְלֹא תֶהְדַּר פְּנֵי גָדוֹל בְּצֶדֶק תִּשְׁפֹּט עֲמִיתֶךָ: טז לֹא־תֵלֵךְ רָכִיל בְּעַמֶּיךָ לֹא

14. The preceding verses instruct us to refrain from harming another individual by doing damage to his property for selfish gain. The two verses that follow instruct us to refrain also from injuring others in the widest application of this concept.

To begin with: "Do not curse. . . ." Though words alone may have no power, it is forbidden to express, even if only in speech, the wish that another may lose his happiness. For a curse expresses malice which only lack of power prevents from bringing about the destruction of another. The prohibition "do not curse" is a global one. The qualification "a deaf man" constitutes not a limitation but an extension of this prohibition. It is forbidden to curse another even if he does not hear it and the curse cannot hurt his feelings or upset him (Shevuoth 36a; Maimonides, *Hilkhoth Sanhedrin* 26:1). It is prohibited even to utter a curse against oneself (ibid.).

The prohibition "and do not place a stumbling block before a blind man" is of most far-reaching import. It cautions us against any careless word or act that could in any manner endanger the material or moral welfare of another. The term "a blind man" refers not only to one who is physically blind, but also to one who is intellectually or morally "blind," say, one "blinded" by strong emotion. Hence, this prohibition does not apply merely to the literal placing of, say, a rock in the path of one who cannot see.

The following, too, are guilty of transgressing this law: (1) One who, when asked for advice, intentionally gives the wrong advice (*Torath Kohanim*); (2) One who provides the means or paves the way for wrongdoing; e.g., one who hands a glass of wine to a Nazirite (Pesaḥim 22b), or sells [to another Jew] material, or a garment, of which he knows—though the purchaser does not—that it contains a forbidden mixture of wool and linen so that he causes another to commit a sin unknowingly (ibid., 55b); (3) One who actively or passively abets or furthers wrongdoing on the part of others (Maimonides, *Hilkhoth Rotzeaḥ* 12:14); (4) One who provokes another to anger so that this other forgets himself in his rage; e.g., when a father provokes his adult son (Mo'ed Katan 17a and Kiddush-

in 32a). Each of the foregoing cases in point constitutes a transgression of the prohibition [against "placing a stumbling block before a blind man"] under which every aspect of our neighbor's material and spiritual welfare has been entrusted to our care. We must permit our fellow men to benefit from our caution, insight and circumspection so that they will not incur material or spiritual harm through any fault of ours.

and fear your God; I, **God.** With regard to all these matters we are to feel that we will be judged not by men in a human court of law but by the all-knowing, all-seeing eye of God Himself, Whose omnipresence teaches us to keep stringent watch over ourselves and to be candid critics of our own conduct.

15 and 16. The dicta set down in these two verses caution us against misusing our authority and against being remiss in our duty when the happiness and personal dignity of others have been entrusted to our hands.

    ∘   ∘   ∘

judge your neighbor in accordance with justice. This is a positive complement to what has gone before. . . . This impartial conception of justice which is to be derived from the Law of God shall guide the judge at all times. Because it is the antithesis of the עָוֶל [wrong] that is forbidden in the first part of Verse 15, he must make justice his sole consideration in his judgments without regard to the social position or other personal circumstances of the parties in the case. He must measure those standing before him with the yardstick of right and make his decision by this standard alone. He must look upon each party before him as his neighbor, one who has the same rights as he himself. All those to be judged by him stand on the same level; all of them, without exception, have an equal claim to justice. Hence the admonition (Shevuoth 30a) to the judge that he must treat both parties with equal courtesy also during the actual court hearing, "not to permit one to sit while the other must stand, or one to speak as long as he likes while telling the other to 'make it short.'"

    ∘   ∘   ∘

blood of your neighbor; I, *God.*   17. Do
not hate your brother in your heart. Rebuke
your neighbor again and again but do not
take sin upon yourself because of it.
18. Do not take revenge nor bear a

תַּעֲמֹד עַל־דַּם רֵעֶךָ אֲנִי יְהֹוָה: יז לֹא־תִשְׂנָא
אֶת־אָחִיךָ בִּלְבָבֶךָ הוֹכֵחַ תּוֹכִיחַ אֶת־עֲמִיתֶךָ
וְלֹא־תִשָּׂא עָלָיו חֵטְא: יח לֹא־תִקֹּם וְלֹא־תִטֹּר

17. **Do not hate.** The laws in Verses 11 to 16 deal
with our behavior toward our fellow men in general and
teach us that we must not permit our words and actions
to be influenced in any manner by selfish motivations,
by indifference to the welfare of others, and certainly
not by malice. Rather, mindful of God's constant
presence, we must measure all our deeds by the standard of veracity, integrity, punctiliousness and brotherliness that God has set for us and expects us to follow
because we are His. . . .

Rebuke . . . again and again. In the vast majority
of cases where it occurs in Scripture, the word הוֹכִיחַ
denotes making someone aware of an unpleasant fact
about himself, to explain to him that he has been guilty
of an intellectual error (as in Job 9:33), or that he has
strayed from the path of morality (as in most other
Scriptural passages where the term occurs). The latter
kind of rebuke may be administered either directly by
verbal statements, as in Isaiah 29:21 and elsewhere, or
indirectly, by means of sufferings, as in Proverbs 3:13
and elsewhere. . . .

In this verse we are told: Do not hate your brother in
your heart, but take him to task, make him realize what
he has done. This command imposes upon us the noble
duty, if we feel we have been wronged or insulted by
another, to forget the matter completely and not permit
it to affect our attitude toward him in any manner, or, if
we feel we cannot do this, not to allow sinister hatred to
smoulder in our hearts but to speak out to him
candidly in order to give him an opportunity to justify
his conduct or to make amends for it. Bearing a grudge
in silence bespeaks an ignoble character. The *Tanhuma*
to Genesis 39:4 makes such a reference to Absalom, of
whom it is written in II Samuel 13:22: "And Absalom
spoke to Amnon neither bad nor good because Absalom
hated Amnon."

At the same time, however, the commandment הוֹכֵחַ
תּוֹכִיחַ ["rebuke . . . again and again"] implies that every
member of the Jewish community has the duty not to
remain silent when he sees a fellow Jew commit a sin,
be it great or small, but must do his part, by remonstrat-
ing with him, again and again, . . . so that the sinner
may, if possible, gain insight into his conduct and mend
his ways (Baba Metzia 31a). According to the Gemarah
(ibid.) this obligation is applicable to any human relationship; indeed, in such situations it is even permissible for a disciple to remonstrate with his teacher;
according to Arakhin 16b one remains duty bound to
rebuke his erring neighbor until the latter rejects the

rebuke by abusing him or even striking him. The
Gemarah states (Shabbath 54b) that anyone who could
have prevented members of his own household, his
fellow citizens, or the entire world from doing wrong,
but has failed to do so, is considered an accomplice in
their guilt. Even if his own conduct is exemplary and
blameless he is the first to be condemned if he has not
done his share to help his contemporaries mend their
ways (ibid., 55a). If this commandment, which is based
on the principle that all Jews bear collective responsibility for the fulfillment of God's Law by every individual
Jew, were actually observed in everyday life, it would
transform the moral aspect of the entire world. . . .

•   •   •

18. **and love your neighbor's welfare as (if it were)
your own; I, God.** This is the maxim that must guide
all our social behavior in thought, word and deed. The
noblest fundamental attitude toward God and man is
אַהֲבָה, "love." . . .

The term לְרֵעֲךָ [lit., "*to* your neighbor"] does not
refer to your neighbor's person but to everything that
pertains to his person, the circumstances that determine
his station in life on earth for better or for worse. It is
this, his woe or weal, that we should love as if it were
our own. We are to rejoice in his happiness as if it were
our own, grieve over his sorrow as if it were our own,
assist as eagerly in advancing his welfare as if we were
working to advance our own, and keep trouble away
from him as if we ourselves were threatened by it. This
is a requirement that we can and must fulfill even
toward an individual who is downright repugnant to us,
for this requirement of love is not dependent on our
neighbor's person or on his personality traits. . . . No
one may view the prosperity of another as an obstacle to
his own well-being or the downfall of another as an aid
to his own growth, and no one may rejoice in his own
flowering as long as his neighbor's life remains blight-
ed. . . .

The Sages (Nedarim 65b) cite this verse not only as a
principle of altruistic love for one's fellow man in
general but also, repeatedly, as an injunction to deal
humanely even with a criminal who has been condemned to death (Sanhedrin 52a et al.): "*Love your
neighbor as yourself*: This implies: Choose an easy
death for him," and as an admonition to married
couples to keep away from sensual impressions that
might diminish their conjugal affection (Kiddushin 41a
et al.)

grudge against the sons of your people and
love your neighbor's welfare as [if it were]

אֶת־בְּנֵי עַמֶּךָ וְאָהַבְתָּ לְרֵעֲךָ כָּמוֹךָ אֲנִי יְהֹוָה:

Hillel's dictum, "Do not do to your neighbor that which would be hateful to you," is well known. It was his response to the request of a heathen to teach him the Law in the briefest terms possible. "This is the entire Law. Everything else is only its explanation; now go and study it," Hillel added. "This is the entire Torah, while the rest is its explanation; go and learn it" (Shabbath 31a). Hillel's statement is simply a negative version of that which our text, "and love. . .," sets forth as a positive commandment. "The command to do nothing to your neighbor that would be hateful to you" proclaims the complete equality of all men as the guiding principle for all our actions; it appeals to us to regard the woe and weal of all others as if it were our own and transforms egotism and self-love into respect and love for our neighbor, teaching us to love and respect each fellow man as our full equal. If we interpret the term חֲבֵרְךָ as including not only our fellow men but also all our other fellow creatures, Hillel's statement indeed sums up the content of the whole Law, which, after all, is simply the teaching to shun anything that would be inimical to our own life's happiness or to that of all the other creatures which enjoy existence in this world along with us. But of course the Law does not leave it to the subjective, limited views and vague emotions of man to decide what is inimical to our own welfare and to that of our fellow creatures; it has given us for this purpose a standard revealed by the wisdom and insight of God. This is what Hillel called "its explanation"; this is the commentary on the statement which is to be derived from the Law. Thus, Rashi ibid.: "Only by studying the rest of the Torah can we find out what is truly hateful to us."

Of course, if one interprets Hillel's dictum simply as, "Do not do to others what you would not want others to do to you" and transforms this wise adage into a maxim of practical expediency: "If you do not want others to do you harm, you must also not harm them, for violence begets violence and wrong begets wrong; therefore, he who does not wish to be wronged himself must also do no wrong to others," then, of course, one has not only failed to convey the true content of our Divine Law but has not even set forth a lesson in "ethics." In that case one has taught only expediency and elevated calculating selfishness to be the guiding principle for all of human conduct.

At the same time precisely this section of our text cogently demonstrates that Hillel's words, "This is the entire Law. Everything else is only its explanation; now go and study it," should not be interpreted as a mere figure of speech, but should be understood as a profound statement regarding the nature of God's Law.

From the commandment "Love your neighbor's welfare as (if it were) your own," the text proceeds directly to the commandment: "You must not mix animal species by crossbreeding, you must not sow your field with a mixture of seeds, and a garment made of a shaatnez mixture must not come upon you," and it does so without a transition, as if this were a continuation of the same theme, setting forth the two laws in the same sequence as "Do not place a stumbling block before a blind man" (Verse 14) and "Do not do wrong in judgment" (Verse 15), and "Do not go about as a talebearer" (Verse 16) and "Do not hate your brother in your heart" (Verse 17). Indeed, the fact that this group of laws and the law concerning a betrothed female slave which follows (Verse 20) conclude the first part of the laws given us to sanctify our social ethics seems to indicate that there is a mutually explanatory and complementary relationship between these categories of laws which, at first glance, seem completely unrelated.

This connection becomes readily apparent in a twofold aspect. The teachings of integrity and uprightness, veracity and good faith, punctiliousness, circumspection, fairness, consideration for (and preservation of) the welfare of others in both word and action, the suppression of all hatred and of all lust for revenge—in short, the most godly element in man, a willingness to forget completely whatever wrong one may have suffered, the sum total of the duty to sanctify our social relationships—all this is subsumed in the teaching of the universal and equal love we are to show our fellow men. All these requirements for the sanctification of our lives as members of society bear the official sanction of God's own seal: "I, God." This makes it clear that these teachings have nothing to do with selfish considerations or expediency. They were set down simply as logical results of any true awareness of God. We honor God; therefore we honor also everything that lives and breathes because it is godly and belongs to God. God is holy; therefore we, too, must exercise our ability and our calling to be "holy"; i.e., to be truly human in moral freedom and to emulate God in truth, justice and loving-kindness. All living things are godly because they come from God, and man has a higher calling because he, too, comes from God—these two basic concepts of the sacred human calling conferred upon the Jew lead us out from the narrower sphere of mankind, teaching us to respect the Divine order also in the world outside human society, so that precisely in this larger world, which bears everywhere the stamp and the imprint of God's Law, "I, God," we should become aware also of our own higher station accorded us by your own; I, *God*. 19. Keep My statutes; you must not mix animal species by crossbreeding, you must not sow your field with a mixture of seeds, and a garment made of a

יט אֶת־חֻקֹּתַי֮ תִּשְׁמֹרוּ֒ בְּהֶמְתְּךָ֙ לֹא־תַרְבִּ֣יעַ
כִּלְאַ֔יִם שָׂדְךָ֖ לֹא־תִזְרַ֣ע כִּלְאָ֑יִם וּבֶ֤גֶד כִּלְאַ֙יִם֙

God. These are the truths symbolized by the group of laws that now follows.

19. . . . If we consider the prohibitions set down together in this verse: the prohibitions against the crossbreeding of animals and plants, against the sowing of mixtures of seeds and against the wearing of garments made from a specific mixture of materials, all of which are prefaced by the general statement, "Keep My statutes," it is obvious that the crossbreeding of animals and the crossbreeding of plants actually constitute human encroachments upon the Divine laws of Creation in that man forces plant and animal species that by nature are "closed" to one another to unite in unnatural couplings.

However, the sowing of mixtures of seeds does not in fact involve an unnatural coupling of species. Planting different species of seeds side by side does not interfere with the development of the original species, and in fact it is not even forbidden to sow two different species of seeds side by side as long as there is a visible separation between them when they sprout above the ground. Clearly, then, the prohibition against the sowing of mixtures of seeds goes beyond forbidding man to interfere actively with the Divinely-ordained separation of species. When he works with the vegetable kingdom, man is to be reminded of the law of לְמִינֵהוּ [the Divine law of the separation of species], which still dominates plant life with creative omnipotence. Man is to be made aware of God also as the Lawgiver of nature, whose lawgiving did not begin with or for the Jews alone, or even for mankind as a whole, but Who rules over all the active and formative forces in nature and to Whom even the tiniest seedling and the smallest fiber of all organic life yields obedience with undeviating loyalty.

From there, the Law logically proceeds to mixtures of materials in garments which constitute even less of an interference with God's law of nature than the sowing of mixtures of seeds. If the impressive admonition "Keep My statutes" is made to apply also to this prohibition, then its purpose, too, can only be to remind man of the world's great Lawgiver and of His great law of לְמִינֵהוּ, which has divided the infinite variety of living things into separate species, assigning to each its own specific purpose and its own physical form appropriate to this purpose, a law which applies also to man and which he must therefore keep in mind even when he puts on his clothes.

We have already had occasion repeatedly to point out the profound moral significance of man's clothing, how the Law views clothing as a distinguishing mark that separates man from animals, and to demonstrate the message to man which is inherent in the historic origin of his clothing (Genesis 3:21): Be "man," remain human, do not walk in the ways of beasts! This admonition is further stressed for the calling of the Jew by the commandment to wear *tzitzith* (Numbers 15:37). See the article on *tzitzith* in [the monthly] *Jeschurun*, Vol. V. Also . . . the Law regards only wool and flax or linen as materials specifically suited for clothing; hence, whenever garments or clothes are mentioned without any further qualification, the reference can be only to garments made from one of these two materials. Keeping apart the species of seeds when he tills his soil should remind the thinking man of the great law of the separation of species, and thereby also of the One sole all-commanding Lawgiver of the world. It should admonish him to subordinate also his own activities to the Law of God, and not to be the only creature in all of God's great universe to scorn His Law. In the same manner, the act of keeping apart the two materials used specifically for man's clothing should remind man of the One Who enacted the law of the separation of species and it should thus spur man on to fulfill his moral calling for which his clothing helps prepare the ground. Particularly, it is to remind the Jew that by observing God's Law that was made known[9] to him he does not isolate himself from the rest of Creation but is merely taking his proper place among all the other creatures that obey the Law of God. All the creatures around him attain existence, life, growth, achievement and increase only by their devoted loyalty to the law of לְמִינוֹ which God proclaimed for their species. The Jew, too, received from God the law of לְמִינוֹ applicable to him, the law which establishes his calling as a human being in the midst of all other living things, and as a Jew in the midst of mankind. Only by fulfilling the Torah, the law of לְמִינוֹ which God instituted for the Jew, can one whom God made a Jew by birth accomplish the purpose assigned to him. If he fails to do so, then, as our Sages put it, "even a gnat is greater than you."

° ° °

We have already explained in our commentary on the law of בָּשָׂר בְּחָלָב [the separation of meat and milk]

[9]*Note to the English translation*: In contrast to the other creatures, which must follow this law blindly, without the freedom of conscious choice to do so. [G.H.]

shaatnez mixture must not come upon you.
20. And if a man cohabits with a woman
and has a discharge of seed, and she is a
slave betrothed to another man, and she has
not yet been entirely redeemed or has not
yet been given her freedom, then she shall
be disciplined; [however] they shall not be
put to death because she has not yet been
freed.   21. But he shall bring to *God* his
guilt offering to the entrance of the Tent of
Appointed Meeting in [the form of] a ram of
guilt offering.   22. The priest shall effect
atonement for him with the ram of the guilt
offering before *God* because of the sin which
he has committed, and he will be forgiven
for the sin which he has committed.
23. And when you come into the land
and plant any tree bearing fruit for food,
you shall be restricted regarding the use of
its fruit for a period during which it shall be
withdrawn from your use. For three years it
shall be restricted to you [but] only as
regards use; it shall not be enjoyed.
24. Then, in the fourth year, all its fruit
shall become holy for the purpose of prais-
ing the work of *God,*   25. and only in the
fifth year shall you eat its fruit so that
henceforth it shall add to its yield for you; I,
God, your God.   26. Do not eat with the

שַׁעַטְנֵ֕ז לֹ֥א יַעֲלֶ֖ה עָלֶֽיךָ׃ כ וְ֠אִישׁ כִּֽי־יִשְׁכַּ֨ב אֶת־
אִשָּׁ֜ה שִׁכְבַת־זֶ֗רַע וְהִ֤וא שִׁפְחָה֙ נֶחֱרֶ֣פֶת לְאִ֔ישׁ
וְהָפְדֵּה֙ לֹ֣א נִפְדָּ֔תָה א֥וֹ חֻפְשָׁ֖ה לֹ֣א נִתַּן־לָ֑הּ
בִּקֹּ֧רֶת תִּֽהְיֶ֛ה לֹ֥א יוּמְת֖וּ כִּי־לֹ֥א חֻפָּֽשָׁה׃
כא וְהֵבִ֤יא אֶת־אֲשָׁמוֹ֙ לַֽיהֹוָ֔ה אֶל־פֶּ֖תַח אֹ֣הֶל
מוֹעֵ֑ד אֵ֖יל אָשָֽׁם׃ כב וְכִפֶּר֩ עָלָ֨יו הַכֹּהֵ֜ן בְּאֵ֣יל
הָֽאָשָׁם֙ לִפְנֵ֣י יְהֹוָ֔ה עַל־חַטָּאת֖וֹ אֲשֶׁ֣ר חָטָ֑א
וְנִסְלַ֣ח ל֔וֹ מֵֽחַטָּאת֖וֹ אֲשֶׁ֥ר חָטָֽא׃ פ שלישי
כג וְכִֽי־תָבֹ֣אוּ אֶל־הָאָ֗רֶץ וּנְטַעְתֶּם֙ כָּל־עֵ֣ץ
מַֽאֲכָ֔ל וַעֲרַלְתֶּ֥ם עָרְלָת֖וֹ אֶת־פִּרְי֑וֹ שָׁלֹ֣שׁ שָׁנִ֗ים
יִהְיֶ֥ה לָכֶ֛ם עֲרֵלִ֖ים לֹ֥א יֵֽאָכֵֽל׃ כד וּבַשָּׁנָה֙
הָֽרְבִיעִ֔ת יִהְיֶ֖ה כָּל־פִּרְי֑וֹ קֹ֥דֶשׁ הִלּוּלִ֖ים לַֽיהֹוָֽה׃
כה וּבַשָּׁנָ֣ה הַֽחֲמִישִׁ֗ת תֹּֽאכְלוּ֙ אֶת־פִּרְי֔וֹ לְהוֹסִ֥יף
לָכֶ֖ם תְּבֽוּאָת֑וֹ אֲנִ֖י יְהֹוָ֥ה אֱלֹֽהֵיכֶֽם׃ כו לֹ֣א

(Exodus 23:19)[10] that, just as in the animal organism,
so, too, in the human organism, there are present two
distinct elements: the vegetative (nourishment and
reproduction) and the animal (perception and motion).
However, man is distinguished from the animal by
virtue of the relationship between these two elements
in him as distinct from the animal. In the animal
organism the components of the animal element—
perception, sensation and motion—are completely subservient to the vegetative, the physical drives related to
food-getting and reproduction. In man, on the other
hand, the vegetative element is meant to be subordinate to the animal element, which in turn is meant to
be subordinate to the human element, to the intelligent, perceptive and free-willed spirit, and thereby also
to God and to His holy will. Man represents a pyramid
pointing upward to God, while the animal represents a
self-contained sphere. In the animal, the animal and
vegetative elements are closely intertwined. Stated in
symbolic terms, if we take wool as symbolizing the
animal element and flax as symbolizing the vegetative
element, we could say that in the animal the "wool"
and the "flax" are one and inseparable. In man,
however, the animal element—thought and willpower—is not meant to incline toward the vegetative
element; it should not be closely linked with the drives
of hunger and sex. In man the "wool" and the "flax,"
as it were, must remain apart, with each kept contained
within its own realm. The animal element should draw
man not downward to vegetative sensuality but upward
to the pinnacle of humanity, the perceptive and godly
free-willed human spirit, ennobling him so that he may
accomplish the purposes sacred to God. And so the
spirit of God within man is to elevate everything within
him, including the animal and vegetative elements,
toward the nearness of God, whose שְׁכִינָה [Presence]
descends toward man in accordance with the extent to
which man, with his whole being, strives toward God in
moral sanctity.

---

[10]*Note to the English translation*: This portion of Hirsch's
commentary is not included in this excerpted edition. [G.H.]

∘   ∘   ∘

blood; do not consult omens and auspicious times. 27. You shall not round off the corner[s] of your hair upon your head and you shall not shave off the corner[s] of your beard. 28. And you shall not make a wound in your flesh for one who has died nor put a tattoo upon yourselves; I, *God.*

תֹאכְלוּ עַל־הַדָּם לֹא תְנַחֲשׁוּ וְלֹא תְעוֹנֵנוּ׃
כז לֹא תַקִּפוּ פְּאַת רֹאשְׁכֶם וְלֹא תַשְׁחִית אֵת
פְּאַת זְקָנֶךָ׃ כח וְשֶׂרֶט לָנֶפֶשׁ לֹא תִתְּנוּ
בִּבְשַׂרְכֶם וּכְתֹבֶת קַעֲקַע לֹא תִתְּנוּ בָּכֶם אֲנִי

26. . . . Deuteronomy 18:10 cites the prohibition against consulting an astrologer or a consulter of omens together with a prohibition against consulting a soothsayer or sorcerer, etc., and stresses the destructive effect of such aberrations on our relationship with God. Here, these errors are cited together with the commandment, "Do not eat with the blood," in order to emphasize the threat which all three aberrations pose to the lofty moral character of man. The prohibition, "Do not eat with the blood," relates to the morally free human being in the activity that is closest to the purely physical aspect of his existence, that of eating, and it teaches us to separate even this activity—and thus all of man's character—from הַדָּם [the blood], from the impact of a physically fettered animal existence.

do not consult omens and auspicious times. This prohibition is in fact only a logical result of the separation discussed above. The former prohibition applies to the gratification of our physical appetites in the same manner as the latter relates to our conduct. Only one who "eats with the blood," who, by his manner of eating, puts himself on a level with the animal, and who sees himself only as an animal when he satisfies his physical appetites, may also be an astrologer or an enchanter, since he believes that anything he does, or refrains from doing, and all his hopes and fears for the future, and indeed, his entire being, are subject to the rule of a blind physical-mechanical force that governs the world. Not so one who does not "eat with the blood," one who remains human and a morally free-willed servant of God even while he eats. His awareness of the moral ideal set for his nature raises him high above the limits of the notion that would bury the world in a welter of obscure physical and mechanical interactions. He will place himself, and whatever he does, or refrains from doing, at the clear command of God's moral law, not of mechanical-physical forces but of the loving, caring and righteous rule of Divine Providence. Neither cats nor serpents, neither ravens' croaks nor falling sticks, neither today nor tomorrow will hold terrors for him. He will know only one fear: the fear of sin, and only one source of trust: the observance of the *mitzvoth.* All his worldly wisdom lies in his awareness of his duty—"one who walks in integrity will walk in safety"—and he will make a sharp distinction between the physical laws of nature given to the physical world and the free unfettered Divine sovereignty under which God has placed man by giving him moral freedom.

° ° °

28. שֶׂרֶט is any kind of wound, even a scratch, made by the hand alone or with an instrument . . . .

° ° °

Let us examine [the prohibition in this verse] more closely. The text does not read "and you shall not make a wound" but "and you shall not make a wound *in your flesh.*" Hence it seems that the Law frowns not so much upon the *act* of making a wound as it does upon the "wound in your flesh" that *results* from the act. We therefore believe that the intent of this law is something more than a prohibition against inflicting physical wounds upon ourselves as an expression of grief over the loss of a loved one.

The motivation for making a wound in our flesh, an act forbidden to mourners, might appear similar to that of rending one's garments as a sign of mourning, which is expressly commanded on the death of a close relative. [But there is a basic difference between these two symbols of mourning.] The rent made in the mourner's garment symbolizes the "rent" which the death of the departed has made in the survivor's closest surroundings, in the world about him. A wound made in the survivor's flesh, however, would imply that the death of a loved one has caused a breakdown also in our physical selves—and this must not happen. No matter how dear and precious the departed was to us, no matter how much he meant to us, the end of his existence must not be permitted to end, or even to diminish, the value and meaning of our own lives. Every man's life has an importance all its own in his direct relationship with God. Every fiber of our physical existence, every spark of energy and every minute of life which God has given us belongs to Him. As long as He commands us to be here, we must not deliberately impair our own strength but must persevere in His service with all our might as individual personalities sacred to Him. In fact, the loss of one who meant a great deal to us must spur us on to redoubled vital energy so that we may help fill the gap which death has left in the service of God's work.

However, the connection between making "a wound in your flesh for one who has died" and inflicting a

29. You shall not profane your daughter, leading her astray to practice unchastity, so

יְהוָה׃ כט אַל־תְּחַלֵּל אֶת־בִּתְּךָ לְהַזְנוֹתָהּ וְלֹא־

wound upon one's flesh as an idolatrous practice pointed out in Makkoth 21a suggests the possibility that this prohibition was intended also to counteract a pagan concept which, despite the disappearance of the so-called pagan nations, has not yet altogether left the minds of men. According to one such heathen notion, death was a power inimical to life, one that took pleasure in seeing men waste away. The survivors inflicted wounds on themselves, mutilated their bodies and even offered human sacrifices in order to pay homage to those dark forces that thirsted after human life. They believed that by such acts they could protect themselves and others who were still alive. The truths and perceptions of Judaism reject such ideas.

אֲנִי ד׳ *[I, God]*. Death and life come from one and the same loving hand, both are in the service of the One sole living and life-giving God. Death leads only from one life to another, from being "here" to being "there." "Here" and "there"—both are in the same realm of the One God of life and love. That the survivors should go on living is no less His will than was the death of the departed. Making a wound in your flesh, self-mutilation in mourning for the dead, throwing away your own life, or even only a fragment of your life, as it were, after the departed, is not an act of homage but a crime against the hand that led your departed brother to his death, for this same hand has willed that you should go on living, living for its service until it calls you away also; every fiber of your physical being is sacred to it. Therefore, "You shall not make a wound in your flesh for one who has died . . . I, *God.*"

° ° °

Reviewing the six distinct ideas included in the above group of laws, we note that the last four are an elaboration of the first two, and that all of them together serve as a constant reminder of two fundamental truths: that man has been endowed with moral dignity and that his whole existence and his fate are dependent on God alone. The prohibition "Do not eat with the blood" is further elaborated upon in the prohibition "You shall not round off the corners of the hair upon your head" and "You shall not shave off the corners of your beard": Man's body is to bear a visible mark demonstrating his higher moral calling. In like manner, the prohibitions against self-mutilation and tattooing one's flesh emanate logically from the prohibition against consulting omens and auspicious times, which bids us subordinate our fate to God.

These two truths, our moral calling, along with the fact that our prosperity, or lack of prosperity, is determined by whether or not we fulfill this calling, are impressively reaffirmed in the admonition that now follows: "You shall not profane your daughter. . . ."

29. The prohibitions relating to rounding off the corners of the hair upon one's head and to shaving off the corners of one's beard apply to the human body, where they are intended to symbolize the body's higher moral purpose. They are addressed primarily to the male sex, because both nature and the Law assume that the female is innately endowed with a greater measure of chastity and modesty [than the male] and hence not in need of such explicit physical reminders. In general, it is not woman but the corruption of the male that threatens morality. As long as the Law can preserve the morality of the male, the chastity innate in the female sex will keep woman within the bounds of modesty and decency.

This expectation, which was already implied in the preceding laws, now finds its most significant expression in Verse 29. God says to the Jewish father: "You shall not profane your daughter, leading her astray to practice unchastity." . . . The use of the words "You shall not profane" implies the assumption that the daughters of the Jewish nation are "holy" unless they are led astray by an outside influence. The daughters of the Jewish nation are "holy" with regard to chastity and morality. If they become morally corrupt, it is the sons of the Jewish people—the fathers, the men—that are to blame. Read in the context of the laws set forth in the preceding verses, the thought expressed here is as follows: Keep the physical aspects of your bodies holy, if only for the sake of your daughters. If your daughters' morals are corrupted, a heavy burden of guilt will rest upon the fathers because of the example they have set by their own conduct. Thus (cf. Leviticus 21:9) immoral behavior on the part of a priest's daughter reflects upon her father, the priest: "She profanes her father."

For this reason the punishment of an immoral woman (Deuteronomy 22:21) must be carried out at "the gate of her father's house" and Hosea (4:14) says: "I will not punish your daughters when they become immoral, nor your daughters-in-law when they commit adultery, for they themselves consort with whores and offer sacrifices with harlots; a society that does not consider the consequences of its behavior brings about its own punishment."

° ° °

so that the land will not break faith with you. The earth as an astronomical body may have various telluric and cosmic functions of its own. But the land, the surface of the earth, which bears the earth's fruit, is *adamah*, wedded to the human race [*adam*]. If men

that the land will not break faith with you
and the land will [not] be filled with lewdness. 30. Keep My Sabbaths and fear
My Sanctuary; I, *God.* 31. Do not turn to
the *oboth* and the *yiddonim*; do not let
yourself be robbed by them of your purity;
I, *God,* your God. 32. Stand up before a
hoary head and honor the face of one
matured in wisdom, and fear your God; I,
God. 33. And if a stranger comes into
your midst, from abroad, in your land, you
shall not grieve him. 34. The stranger
who has come into your midst from abroad
shall be to you like a native-born of you,
you shall love him as yourself, for you were
strangers in the land of Mitzrayim; I, *God,*

תִזְנֶה הָאָרֶץ וּמָלְאָה הָאָרֶץ זִמָּה׃ ל אֶת־שַׁבְּתֹתַי
תִּשְׁמֹרוּ וּמִקְדָּשִׁי תִּירָאוּ אֲנִי יְהוָה׃ לא אַל־
תִּפְנוּ אֶל־הָאֹבֹת וְאֶל־הַיִּדְּעֹנִים אַל־תְּבַקְשׁוּ
לְטָמְאָה בָהֶם אֲנִי יְהוָה אֱלֹהֵיכֶם׃ לב מִפְּנֵי
שֵׂיבָה תָּקוּם וְהָדַרְתָּ פְּנֵי זָקֵן וְיָרֵאתָ מֵּאֱלֹהֶיךָ
אֲנִי יְהוָה׃ ס רביעי (ששי כשהן מחוברין) לג וְכִי־יָגוּר
אִתְּךָ גֵּר בְּאַרְצְכֶם לֹא תוֹנוּ אֹתוֹ׃ לד כְּאֶזְרָח
מִכֶּם יִהְיֶה לָכֶם הַגֵּר ׀ הַגָּר אִתְּכֶם וְאָהַבְתָּ לוֹ
כָּמוֹךָ כִּי־גֵרִים הֱיִיתֶם בְּאֶרֶץ מִצְרָיִם אֲנִי יְהוָה

break faith with the land by engaging in immoral behavior, the land will break faith with them. If men trifle with the land's most precious product, the seed and the fruit of man, then the seeds and the fruits in the womb of the land, too, will fail, atrophy and deteriorate. "They break faith as regards their fruit: Rabbi Judah says: Behold, he says, 'And you have polluted the land with your harlotries and your wickedness.' Therefore the showers have been witheld and there has been no late rain" (*Torath Kohanim,* Jeremiah 3:2 and 3).

° ° °

33–34. אִתְּךָ, בְּאַרְצְכֶם . . . *[into your* (sing.) *midst . . . in your* (plu.) *land].* The change from the singular אִתְּךָ to the plural form בְּאַרְצְכֶם teaches that the singular form אִתְּךָ refers to the nation as a whole. He is to be regarded as a גֵּר [stranger] only after he has officially joined the nation, after his conversion has taken place before a body officially representing the nation, before a High Court of three (Kiddushin 46b).

בְּאַרְצְכֶם *[in your land].* He is now a "stranger" in the land that belongs to *all* of you, a land of which every part is already owned by a native, a land in which, under the provisions of the Jubilee laws, he can, under ordinary circumstances, never obtain true, permanent possession of landed property, so that he remains forever a man without land of his own in your land.

you shall not grieve him. In Exodus [22:20] we were told, "You shall not grieve a stranger." There the form of address was in the second person singular. The state as an entity was warned not to grieve the stranger but to accord him rights and obligations equal to those of the native-born. Here the form of address is in the second person plural; each and every member of the national entity is commanded not to let him feel he is a stranger in their dealings with him, not even by words that might hurt his feelings (Baba Metzia 59b). Rather, make him feel "like a native-born of you": Either, "like a native-born of yours"; i.e., one of your own, or "a native-born from among you"; i.e., one actually descended from you, one born in your land. In any event, this commandment implies complete equality of status and treatment, not only under the law but also in your attitude toward the stranger and in the acts of loving-kindness which you are duty bound to perform for him. The commandment, "you shall love him as yourself," with regard to the stranger, is based on the same principle as the commandment, "love your neighbor's welfare as (if it were) your own," with regard to everyone else in the nation of Israel (see commentary on Verse 18).

for you were strangers in the land of Mitzrayim. You yourselves experienced the harshness in which a land can lose itself when it refuses to recognize the human rights of foreigners. Your misfortune in Mitzrayim was that you were גֵּרִים ["strangers"]; this led to your עַבְדוּת ["enslavement"] and to your עִנּוּי ["affliction"]. Therefore the constitution of your own land is based upon the principle that all inhabitants of the land, natives and immigrants alike, are equal before the law in every respect (Exodus 22:20). However, the hallowing of your lives in theory and practice to which you must aspire demands something more: you must accord the stranger full equality with his native-born brother also in your attitude and your good will. In fact, by the love you show to one who has come from abroad to live in your midst you demonstrate the idea, "I, *God,* your God"; that you truly acknowledge God as your God and that for His sake you will sincerely embrace all His children with genuine brotherly love. The love and respect you give to the stranger is the true test of your fear and love of God.

your God.   35. Do no wrong in judgment—in measures of length, of weight and of volume.   36. You shall have just scales, just weights, a just *ephah* and a just *hin*; I, *God*, your God, Who brought you out from the land of Miztrayim.   37. Therefore keep all My statutes and all my [social] ordinances and fulfill them; I, *God*.

XX   1. *God* spoke to Moshe [saying]:   2. "But to the sons of

אֱלֹהֵיכֶם: לה לֹא־תַעֲשׂוּ עָוֶל בַּמִּשְׁפָּט בַּמִּדָּה
בַּמִּשְׁקָל וּבַמְּשׂוּרָה: לו מֹאזְנֵי צֶדֶק אַבְנֵי־צֶדֶק
אֵיפַת צֶדֶק וְהִין צֶדֶק יִהְיֶה לָכֶם אֲנִי יְהֹוָה
אֱלֹהֵיכֶם אֲשֶׁר־הוֹצֵאתִי אֶתְכֶם מֵאֶרֶץ מִצְרָיִם:
לז וּשְׁמַרְתֶּם אֶת־כָּל־חֻקֹּתַי וְאֶת־כָּל־מִשְׁפָּטַי
וַעֲשִׂיתֶם אֹתָם אֲנִי יְהֹוָה: פ חמישי כ א וַיְדַבֵּר
יְהֹוָה אֶל־מֹשֶׁה לֵּאמֹר: ב וְאֶל־בְּנֵי יִשְׂרָאֵל

35–36. . . . The abuse of mutual trust to which this passage refers does not refer to acts of outright fraud already committed. Using dishonest weights and measures in buying and selling, or having honest weights and measures but using them in a fraudulent manner, is robbery and theft pure and simple, and should not have been left for discussion only at the conclusion of a chapter on the hallowing of human life. "The merciful God need not have written about just weights in this place." The prohibition stated here with regard to weights and measures calls us to account, even before a fraud has actually been perpetrated, for any act of ours which would make it possible for our neighbor to be cheated, or even for any failure on our part to prevent his being cheated. The Law insists that we must not even keep in our possession an imperfect weight or measure; it forbids us to be slipshod in measuring or weighing out materials as long as there is even the slightest chance that these might be bought or sold. It commands us not only to exercise the utmost care in the manufacture of weights and measures but also to be most punctilious about keeping them in good condition and repair. We are to guard our scales, weights and measures most zealously against any changes due to wear and tear or to deposits of foreign matter from prolonged use, or, in the case of instruments for measuring length, against changes due to fluctuations in temperature. All these and other matters relevant to various kinds of measuring instruments, materials to be measured, wholesale and retail transactions, household purchases, etc., are taught in explicit detail by the Halakhah in Baba Bathra 88a and b ff. . . .

. . . The laws pertaining to just weights and measures are placed (Baba Bathra 88b) on a level with those concerning forbidden sexual relationships. In fact, the punishments for transgressions of the former are even more severe than those instituted for violations of the latter: "Punishments for (using or owning) unjust measures are more severe than those for engaging in forbidden sexual relationships." Hence, if the laws concerning forbidden sexual relationships form the basis of personal morality and family life, the laws concerning honest weights and measures constitute the

basis of honesty and morality in public life. The Law does not frown upon dishonest weights and measures only after they have been used in a fraudulent act (which, as we have already noted, would be classed as common theft). Rather, it views the possession of measures and the act of measuring as legal acts in themselves, so that every measure owned, and any material measured out by a Jew, becomes a Jewish act of honesty, symbolic of the Jew's respect for justice and fairness. In this manner the Law sets up the right, *per se*, in its most absolute form, as a sanctum to be kept inviolate by every Jew and seeks to make the sense of justice, respect for justice, and honesty in general a basic character trait of the Jewish nation.

     °   °   °

This entire chapter on the Jewish hallowing of life, then, concludes with the two great basic principles which are to uphold the Divinely-established Jewish state as distinct from other states that are based solely on national self-interest. These principles to be brought to full fruition in the Jewish state are: (1) Love and respect for one's fellow men, to be demonstrated most cogently by granting the stranger true equality with the native-born in the law of the Jewish state and also in the love and respect accorded him by the society which makes up that state (Verses 33 and 34), and (2) Respect for law and justice, expressed in that honesty of weights and measures which in turn is an expression of homage to God.

CHAPTER XX

1. We have already stated in our introductory notes to the preceding chapter that this, Chapter 20, is clearly a continuation of Chapter 18, completing the laws regarding עֲרָיוֹת [forbidden sexual relationships] that were begun there. Chapter 18 lists the prohibitions; Chapter 20 now sets forth the penalties for transgressing them—the death penalty to be imposed by the Court of Law, and כָּרֵת, the Divine decree that the transgressor is to be "uprooted" from the midst of his people. In Chapter 18 the laws concerning עֲרָיוֹת are followed by Verse 21, the prohibition against offering

Yisrael you shall say: Anyone, *anyone* from among the sons of Yisrael or from among the strangers who have entered into Yisrael from abroad, who gives of his progeny to the Molekh, shall be put to death; the community of the people of the land shall stone him.   3. And I, too, will set My Countenance against that man and will cause him to be uprooted from the midst of his people, because he has given of his progeny to the Molekh in order to rob My Sanctuary of its purity and to profane My holy Name. 4. But if the community of the people of the land withdraw their eyes from that man when he gives of his progeny to the Molekh, so that they do not put him to death,

תֹּאמַר֒ אִ֣ישׁ אִישׁ֩ מִבְּנֵ֨י יִשְׂרָאֵ֜ל וּמִן־הַגֵּ֣ר ׀ הַגָּ֣ר
בְּיִשְׂרָאֵ֗ל אֲשֶׁ֨ר יִתֵּ֤ן מִזַּרְעוֹ֙ לַמֹּ֔לֶךְ מ֥וֹת יוּמָ֑ת עַ֥ם
הָאָ֖רֶץ יִרְגְּמֻ֥הוּ בָאָֽבֶן: ג וַאֲנִ֞י אֶתֵּ֤ן אֶת־פָּנַי֙
בָּאִ֣ישׁ הַה֔וּא וְהִכְרַתִּ֥י אֹת֖וֹ מִקֶּ֣רֶב עַמּ֑וֹ כִּ֣י
מִזַּרְעוֹ֙ נָתַ֣ן לַמֹּ֔לֶךְ לְמַ֗עַן טַמֵּא֙ אֶת־מִקְדָּשִׁ֔י
וּלְחַלֵּ֖ל אֶת־שֵׁ֥ם קָדְשִֽׁי: ד וְאִ֡ם הַעְלֵ֣ם יַעְלִימוּ֩
עַ֨ם הָאָ֜רֶץ אֶת־עֵֽינֵיהֶ֗ם מִן־הָאִ֤ישׁ הַהוּא֙ בְּתִתּ֣וֹ
מִזַּרְעוֹ֙ לַמֹּ֔לֶךְ לְבִלְתִּ֖י הָמִ֣ית אֹת֑וֹ: ה וְשַׂמְתִּ֨י

---

sacrifices to the Molekh. In Chapter 20 the penal code for עֲרָיוֹת is introduced with the penalty for making offerings to the Molekh. Between these two chapters comes Chapter 19, which discusses the Jewish manner of hallowing life. Before the death and כָּרֵת penalties are pronounced for transgressions involving עֲרָיוֹת, and the national entity (through its representative authorities, the courts of law) is commanded to implement the death penalty, we are shown the significance of these laws for the mission of the nation as a whole and of all its individual members. It is impressed upon us that the hallowing of all our lives, individual and national, depends on our observance of the laws relating to עֲרָיוֹת. Only a nation whose sons and daughters are products of a family life regulated by the prohibitions against עֲרָיוֹת can be told, "You shall be holy." Only such a nation can be expected to carry out this command and all its corollaries as set down in this chapter, which outlines the principles of a physical and spiritual life, both as individuals and as a nation, hallowed to God. This sequence demonstrates how every transgression of the laws relating to עֲרָיוֹת strikes at the very nerve of the moral future of individual and nation alike. It makes us understand the law in all its serious import, in that this law makes the transgressors against the עֲרָיוֹת prohibitions subject either to the death penalty imposed by the court of law or to the penalty of כָּרֵת, denying the transgressor the right to continued existence in the midst of the nation and making it the duty of the nation itself to impose and implement the first of these two penalties.

2. ... *who gives of his progeny to the Molekh.* We have already indicated in our notes on Chapter 18, Verse 21, the import of this crime and its connection with the prohibitions against עֲרָיוֹת. [We said there that] this transgression implies belief in the notion that the

human family, particularly its children. is subject to the rule of a blind force of fate (מֹלֶךְ)[11] which is inimical to human happiness, an impersonal power to which some children must be sacrificed in order to save the rest. The belief in a fate-ordaining power other than God, a power that must be worshipped by sacrificing to it our most precious possessions, our children, is a blasphemous delusion because it denies that our children belong to God and that they have moral significance as the "seed" of mankind meant to mature under God's care and for His purposes. This in turn constitutes a denial of the basic Divinely-ordained morality of our sex life; therefore the penal code relevant to עֲרָיוֹת opens with the imposition of the death penalty for making sacrifices to the Molekh. To give one's progeny to the Molekh is tantamount in principle to both idol worship and forbidden sexual relationships.

⁎   ⁎   ⁎

3. As we have pointed out in our notes to Chapter 18, Verse 21, the worship of the Molekh, though it does not constitute a desertion of God for outright idolatry, implies the belief that there exists, in addition to God, side by side with Him, another fate-ordaining power that is inimical to man and must therefore be feared and appeased. Therefore we can readily see the reason for God's stern utterance against this aberration.

⁎   ⁎   ⁎

[11]*Note to the English translation*: In his note to Leviticus 18:21, which is not included in this excerpted edition, Hirsch explains that the term "Molekh" is not meant to convey the idea of a specific deity. The form is not a substantive but an abstract concept and thus denotes not a specific ruler or king but the act of "ruling" or "governing" in general. Hence the Molekh is that impersonal force of fate which, in the pagan view, even the gods were powerless to change or to control. [G.H.]

5. then I will set My Countenance against that man and against his family and will cause him to be uprooted, along with all those who stray after him, to give themselves over to the Molekh instead of Me, from the midst of their people.   6. And the person who turns to the *oboth* and the *yiddonim* to stray after them, I will set My Countenance against that person and will cause him to be uprooted from the midst of his people.   7. Keep yourselves holy, and you will be holy, for I, *God*, am your God. 8. Therefore keep watch over My statutes and carry them out; I, *God*, am He Who leads you to holiness.   9. For anyone, *anyone* who curses his father or his mother shall be put to death; he has cursed his father or his mother; his blood falls back upon him.°
10. And one who commits adultery with the wife of a[nother] man, who commits adultery with his neighbor's wife, he, the transgressor, and the adulteress, shall be put to death.   11. And one who cohabits with his father's wife has uncovered his father's

אֲנִי אֶת־פָּנַי בָּאִישׁ הַהוּא וּבְמִשְׁפַּחְתּוֹ וְהִכְרַתִּי
אֹתוֹ וְאֵת ׀ כָּל־הַזֹּנִים אַחֲרָיו לִזְנוֹת אַחֲרֵי
הַמֹּלֶךְ מִקֶּרֶב עַמָּם: ו וְהַנֶּפֶשׁ אֲשֶׁר תִּפְנֶה אֶל־
הָאֹבֹת וְאֶל־הַיִּדְּעֹנִים לִזְנֹת אַחֲרֵיהֶם וְנָתַתִּי
אֶת־פָּנַי בַּנֶּפֶשׁ הַהִוא וְהִכְרַתִּי אֹתוֹ מִקֶּרֶב עַמּוֹ:
ז וְהִתְקַדִּשְׁתֶּם וִהְיִיתֶם קְדֹשִׁים כִּי אֲנִי יְהֹוָה
אֱלֹהֵיכֶם: ששי (שביעי כשהן מחוברין) ח וּשְׁמַרְתֶּם
אֶת־חֻקֹּתַי וַעֲשִׂיתֶם אֹתָם אֲנִי יְהֹוָה מְקַדִּשְׁכֶם:
ט כִּי־אִישׁ אִישׁ אֲשֶׁר יְקַלֵּל אֶת־אָבִיו וְאֶת־
אִמּוֹ מוֹת יוּמָת אָבִיו וְאִמּוֹ קִלֵּל דָּמָיו בּוֹ:
י וְאִישׁ אֲשֶׁר יִנְאַף אֶת־אֵשֶׁת אִישׁ אֲשֶׁר יִנְאַף
אֶת־אֵשֶׁת רֵעֵהוּ מוֹת־יוּמַת הַנֹּאֵף וְהַנֹּאָפֶת:
יא וְאִישׁ אֲשֶׁר יִשְׁכַּב אֶת־אֵשֶׁת אָבִיו עֶרְוַת

°*Note to the English translation*: In a note to Verse 2 of this chapter, which is not included in this excerpted edition, Hirsch explains "his blood falls back upon him" as meaning that he will be isolated, "rebuffed," as it were, by the soil that once upheld him as it does all other living things. [G.H.]

---

7. **Keep yourselves holy.** "This refers to the holiness of keeping away from idol worship" (*Torath Kohanim*). This law does not refer to the sanctity of all the commandments, that holiness after which we are to strive in the observance of all the commandments in general and which was already mentioned in [Verse 2 of] the previous chapter: "You shall be holy." Rather, it refers specifically to that holiness which is to be sought and attained by keeping away from every form of idolatry, as indicated in the prohibitions against making child sacrifices to the Molekh and consulting *oboth* and *yiddonim*. The concept קָדוֹשׁ [holy] in the purest sense of the term, and thus as an attribute of God, encompasses not only absolute freedom of will but also absolute freedom of existence; hence, eternity. Cf. Sanhedrin 92a on Isaiah 4:13: "*And it shall come to pass that he who is left in Zion and he who remains in Jerusalem shall be called 'holy,'* etc.: Even as the Holy One endures forever, so shall they endure forever."

In the present verse, too, the term קָדוֹשׁ may have both these implications. The preceding verses made reference to the delusions reflected by the belief in the Molekh and in *ob* and *yiddoni*.

These verses are now followed by an admonition:

Keep yourselves free of all pagan ideas, stay aloof from all fear of the dark powers that exist only in the minds of men. Be above believing in them. Keep yourselves completely free to do My will. By thus making your will and spirit free, you will make your existence free also, and by subordinating yourselves entirely to Me you will be holy and beyond the reach of any other power, because I, 'ה, upon Whose signal every moment of the future depends, am אֱלֹקֵיכֶם; I am as much the Ruler of your destinies as I am the Guide of your actions.

9. . . . The relationship of children to their parents and the institution of marriage, these two indispensable fundamentals of all human and social development, are mentioned (Verses 9 and 10) at the outset of the section listing the severe penalties for violations of the sexual laws. By appointing the judicial arm of the Jewish state as the guardian of these laws, the Law of God makes it clear to us that the transgressors who by their conduct undermine the influence of parents and the institution of marriage, these two fundamental conditions for all human development, will not be permitted to survive.

     •   •   •

nakedness; both of them shall be put to
death; their blood falls back upon them.
12. And one who cohabits with his
daughter-in-law, both of them shall be put
to death; they have committed a dehumanizing act; their blood falls back upon
them. 13. And if a man cohabits with a
male as with a woman, both of them have
done an abominable thing; they shall be put
to death; their blood falls back upon them.
14. And one who takes a woman and
[also] her mother, it is lewd sensuality, they
shall be burned with fire, he and they, and
lewd sensuality shall not be permitted to
exist in your midst. 15. And one who lies
with an animal shall be put to death, and
you shall kill the animal also. 16. And [as
for] a woman who approaches an animal to
copulate with her, you shall put the woman
and the animal to death; their blood falls
back upon them. 17. And one who takes
his sister—his father's daughter or his
mother's daughter—and he sees her nakedness and she sees his nakedness, it is an act
of sinful abandon;° they shall be uprooted
before the eyes of their fellow citizens;
he has uncovered his sister's nakedness; he
must bear his iniquity. 18. And one who
cohabits with a woman while she is menstruating and he uncovers her nakedness—
even if he has only uncovered her source
and she, too, has uncovered the source of
her bleeding,—both of them shall be
uprooted from the midst of their people.
19. And you shall not uncover the nakedness of your mother's sister or your father's
sister. Even if one only uncovers the nakedness of his blood relation, they [both] will
have to bear their iniquity. 20. And one
who cohabits with his aunt has uncovered
his uncle's nakedness; they must bear their

אָבִיו גִּלָּה מוֹת־יוּמְתוּ שְׁנֵיהֶם דְּמֵיהֶם בָּם׃
יב וְאִישׁ אֲשֶׁר יִשְׁכַּב אֶת־כַּלָּתוֹ מוֹת יוּמְתוּ
שְׁנֵיהֶם תֶּבֶל עָשׂוּ דְּמֵיהֶם בָּם׃ יג וְאִישׁ אֲשֶׁר
יִשְׁכַּב אֶת־זָכָר מִשְׁכְּבֵי אִשָּׁה תּוֹעֵבָה עָשׂוּ
שְׁנֵיהֶם מוֹת יוּמָתוּ דְּמֵיהֶם בָּם׃ יד וְאִישׁ אֲשֶׁר
יִקַּח אֶת־אִשָּׁה וְאֶת־אִמָּהּ זִמָּה הִוא בָּאֵשׁ
יִשְׂרְפוּ אֹתוֹ וְאֶתְהֶן וְלֹא־תִהְיֶה זִמָּה בְּתוֹכְכֶם׃
טו וְאִישׁ אֲשֶׁר יִתֵּן שְׁכָבְתּוֹ בִּבְהֵמָה מוֹת יוּמָת
וְאֶת־הַבְּהֵמָה תַּהֲרֹגוּ׃ טז וְאִשָּׁה אֲשֶׁר תִּקְרַב
אֶל־כָּל־בְּהֵמָה לְרִבְעָה אֹתָהּ וְהָרַגְתָּ אֶת־הָאִשָּׁה
וְאֶת־הַבְּהֵמָה מוֹת יוּמָתוּ דְּמֵיהֶם בָּם׃ יז וְאִישׁ
אֲשֶׁר־יִקַּח אֶת־אֲחֹתוֹ בַּת־אָבִיו אוֹ־בַת־אִמּוֹ
וְרָאָה אֶת־עֶרְוָתָהּ וְהִיא תִרְאֶה אֶת־עֶרְוָתוֹ
חֶסֶד הוּא וְנִכְרְתוּ לְעֵינֵי בְּנֵי עַמָּם עֶרְוַת אֲחֹתוֹ
גִּלָּה עֲוֺנוֹ יִשָּׂא׃ יח וְאִישׁ אֲשֶׁר־יִשְׁכַּב אֶת־אִשָּׁה
דָּוָה וְגִלָּה אֶת־עֶרְוָתָהּ אֶת־מְקֹרָהּ הֶעֱרָה וְהִוא
גִּלְּתָה אֶת־מְקוֹר דָּמֶיהָ וְנִכְרְתוּ שְׁנֵיהֶם מִקֶּרֶב
עַמָּם׃ יט וְעֶרְוַת אֲחוֹת אִמְּךָ וַאֲחוֹת אָבִיךָ לֹא
תְגַלֵּה כִּי אֶת־שְׁאֵרוֹ הֶעֱרָה עֲוֺנָם יִשָּׂאוּ׃
כ וְאִישׁ אֲשֶׁר יִשְׁכַּב אֶת־דֹּדָתוֹ עֶרְוַת דֹּדוֹ גִּלָּה

° *Note to the English translation*: Hirsch explains here, and also in a note on Genesis 47:29, that the term חֶסֶד is generally used to denote an act of giving up one's person for a good purpose, but that in this case it implies a sinful "giving up"; i.e., an act of abandon. [G.H.]

18. . . . Here the law forbidding sexual relations with a נִדָּה [menstruating woman] directly follows the prohibition against incestuous relations between a brother and sister. Perhaps this sequence is intended to indicate that there are periods in a Jewish marriage during which husband and wife may live together only as brother and sister. Far from encroaching upon the intimacy of marriage, this relationship can in fact make the intimacy even closer and elevate it to ever loftier spiritual and moral levels.

° ° °

חֶטְאָם יִשָּׂאוּ עֲרִירִים יָמֻתוּ׃ כא וְאִישׁ אֲשֶׁר
יִקַּח אֶת־אֵשֶׁת אָחִיו נִדָּה הִוא עֶרְוַת אָחִיו גִּלָּה
עֲרִירִים יִהְיוּ׃ כב וּשְׁמַרְתֶּם אֶת־כָּל־חֻקֹּתַי
וְאֶת־כָּל־מִשְׁפָּטַי וַעֲשִׂיתֶם אֹתָם וְלֹא־תָקִיא
אֶתְכֶם הָאָרֶץ אֲשֶׁר אֲנִי מֵבִיא אֶתְכֶם שָׁמָּה
לָשֶׁבֶת בָּהּ׃ שביעי כג וְלֹא תֵלְכוּ בְּחֻקֹּת הַגּוֹי
אֲשֶׁר־אֲנִי מְשַׁלֵּחַ מִפְּנֵיכֶם כִּי אֶת־כָּל־אֵלֶּה
עָשׂוּ וָאָקֻץ בָּם׃ כד וָאֹמַר לָכֶם אַתֶּם תִּירְשׁוּ
אֶת־אַדְמָתָם וַאֲנִי אֶתְּנֶנָּה לָכֶם לָרֶשֶׁת אֹתָהּ
אֶרֶץ זָבַת חָלָב וּדְבָשׁ אֲנִי יְהוָה אֱלֹהֵיכֶם אֲשֶׁר־
הִבְדַּלְתִּי אֶתְכֶם מִן־הָעַמִּים׃ מפטיר כה וְהִבְדַּלְתֶּם
בֵּין־הַבְּהֵמָה הַטְּהֹרָה לַטְּמֵאָה וּבֵין־הָעוֹף
הַטָּמֵא לַטָּהֹר וְלֹא־תְשַׁקְּצוּ אֶת־נַפְשֹׁתֵיכֶם
בַּבְּהֵמָה וּבָעוֹף וּבְכֹל אֲשֶׁר תִּרְמֹשׂ הָאֲדָמָה
אֲשֶׁר־הִבְדַּלְתִּי לָכֶם לְטַמֵּא׃ כו וִהְיִיתֶם לִי
קְדֹשִׁים כִּי קָדוֹשׁ אֲנִי יְהוָה וָאַבְדִּל אֶתְכֶם מִן־
הָעַמִּים לִהְיוֹת לִי׃ כז וְאִישׁ אוֹ־אִשָּׁה כִּי־יִהְיֶה

iniquity; they will die childless. 21. And one who takes his brother's wife, as long as she must be avoided by him, has uncovered his brother's nakedness; they will remain childless. 22. Therefore keep all My statutes and all My [social] ordinances and carry them out, so that the land to which I bring you in order that you may dwell there shall not vomit you out. 23. And do not walk in the statutes of the [native] population which I am sending away from before you, for they did all these things and therefore I abhorred them, 24. and I said to you: You are fit to take possession of their land and I shall give it to you, to possess it, as a land overflowing with milk and honey, I, *God*, your God, Who has set you apart from among the peoples. 25. Make a distinction between clean animals and unclean, and between the unclean fowl and the clean, and do not make your souls abominable through animals and birds and through anything that creeps upon the ground, that which I have set apart from you as unclean. 26. And remain holy to Me, for I, *God*, am holy and it is you whom I have set apart from among the peoples to be Mine. 27. But if there shall be among the

22–24. Just as in the opening and closing verses (2–5 and 24–30, respectively) of Chapter 18, which contains the laws regulating sexual relations, so here, too, at the conclusion of the penal code relating to transgressions of these laws, which also concludes the entire section on the regulation and hallowing of the individual's moral life (beginning with Chapter 11), the Word of God summons us once again to keep and to carry out all of God's laws and to preserve the Divinely-ordained social institutions. . . . It reminds us that our observance of these laws is not only indispensable to the nation's prosperity and to its continued happy existence in its own land but also the very purpose of our chosenhood. As is explained in Chapter 12 of *Torath Kohanim,* "the Land of Israel is not like other lands; it does not tolerate inhabitants who are sinful." The land rejects them as it would a substance it cannot assimilate. The corrupt Canaanites, the original population of the land, were not given the land as their permanent possession; they are only its temporary keepers until you come (*ibid.*, Chapter 9). But you shall come "that you may dwell there . . . to posses it," to take possession of it as your property and to reside there permanently (*ibid.*). Therefore "do not walk in the statutes of the (native) population," take heed not to imitate their institutions or their customs. You are given this warning with every moment that you live in this land, for all the acts which I have forbidden you are precisely those which so utterly corrupted the peoples who were there before you that "therefore I abhorred them"; they came to be completely at variance with My will and they became abhorrent to Me.

And I said to you: You are fit to take possession. It is you whom I called to live in this land, for by preserving the morality of your family life even while you dwelt in the midst of a nation degenerate much like the natives of Canaan, you have shown that you are capable of carrying out the moral mission upon which your permanent possession of the land depends.

. . . I, God, your God, Who has set you apart. Of course there is an immense gap between the spiritual and moral grandeur which I expect of you and the depravity to which the nations around you have descended (*ibid.*).

27. The warning against consulting the pseudo-wisdom of an *ob* or *yiddoni* recurs three times in the portion of קְדֹשִׁים [Leviticus 19:1 through 20:27]. In

men or women an *ob* or a *yiddoni,* they shall be put to death; they shall be stoned; their blood falls back upon them."

בָהֶם אֻוֹב אֽוֹ יִדְּעֹנִי מֽוֹת יוּמָתוּ בָּאֶבֶן יִרְגְּמוּ אֹתָם דְּמֵיהֶם בָּם׃ פ

19:31 it is formulated as a prohibition and in 20:6 it specifies the penalty of כָּרֵת. In the present verse, which concludes the portion, this offense is declared subject to the penalty of סְקִילָה [death by stoning]. It seems, therefore, that the Law of God sees as the greatest threat to its survival and observance in our midst the possibility that its clear dictates and promises, emanating from the highest level of understanding, power, wisdom, justice and goodness might be confused with the oracles of an illusory pseudo-science that crops up again and again in various guises. Adherents and practitioners of these superstitious notions claim the ability to pry the mysteries of life and living things from the dead, utilizing the phenomena of a fettered material world that ends in death and decay in order to interpret the purpose and the fate of man, who is near to God and should be aware of his immortality.

Thus, too, it became the task of Isaiah (8:16 through 9:1) to guard the Testimony of the Divine promise and to confirm the Law through disciples who seek their knowledge only from God. "Bind up the Testimony, seek the Teaching among My disciples": Isaiah considered it his duty to have the people see him, his children and his disciples, whom God had set up as "signs and instructive evidence," in stark contrast with the *oboth* and *yiddonim,* who speak only "stutteringly and in riddles," and who, according to the custom of the [pagan] nations, consult "the dead on behalf of the living." The prophet declares on behalf of the Law, and on behalf of the Divine promise contained in the Testimony, that the *oboth* and *yiddonim* formulate their words in the guise of Divine messages; cf. "Surely they will speak according to this word" (8:20). However, he emphasizes that, because they are born of darkness, these words do not bear the light of truth and cannot promise a dawn of fulfillment, "where there is no light." They may be able to delude suffering mankind temporarily, but disillusionment sets in all too soon. The people will "curse by its king and its God" and "they turn their faces upward," they will search for something higher. However, the people of the true, authentic Word of God has always succeeded in struggling from darkness to light and has always been able to perceive the rays of the coming dawn, even in the darkest shadow of death: "Those who walked in darkness see a great light; they who dwelt in the land of the shadow of death, upon them has the light shone."

The Haftarah for this Sidra may be found on page 881.

אמור

EMOR

XXI 1. *God* said to Moshe: "Now declare this to the priests, the sons of Aharon. Say to them: He may not defile himself for any person among his people. 2. Only for his spouse,° who is close to him, for his mother,

כא א וַיֹּאמֶר יְהֹוָה אֶל־מֹשֶׁה אֱמֹר אֶל־הַכֹּהֲנִים
בְּנֵי אַהֲרֹן וְאָמַרְתָּ אֲלֵהֶם לְנֶפֶשׁ לֹא־יִטַּמָּא
בְּעַמָּיו: ב כִּי אִם־לִשְׁאֵרוֹ הַקָּרֹב אֵלָיו לְאִמּוֹ

°*Note to the English translation*: Hirsch explains that שְׁאֵר, literally, "the remainder," means one's "complement," which specifically refers to one's wife. (Commentary on this verse and on Genesis 19:1 is not included in this excerpted edition.) [G.H.]

CHAPTER XXI

1. The entire section of laws beginning with Chapter 11, down to the present chapter, deals with the hallowing of the Jewish individual and shows the ways in which capability for such personal holiness may be attained. It outlines the content of this hallowing of life, showing how it encompasses every aspect of physical, spiritual, individual and communal life. The chapter that now follows deals with the special manner in which the priests in Judaism are to hallow their lives. It opens with the words: אֱמוֹר אֶל הַכֹּהֲנִים בְּנֵי אַהֲרֹן וְאָמַרְתָּ ["Now declare this to the priests, the sons of Aharon. Say to them. . ."]. Since the word וְאָמַרְתָּ וגו׳ ["Say. . ."] begins a new sentence, a new speech and its contents, the words אֱמוֹר אֶל הַכֹּהֲנִים בְּנֵי אַהֲרֹן ["Now declare this to the priests, the sons of Aharon. . ."] must also introduce a new, separate oration. They are not to be equated with the usual form: דַּבֵּר אֶל בְּנֵי יִשְׂרָאֵל וְאָמַרְתָּ אֲלֵיהֶם ["Speak to the sons of Yisrael and say to them"], where דַּבֵּר denotes the thought subsumed in concise terms, the law stated in general terms, while וְאָמַרְתָּ implies the explanation of the law in detail, appealing to both mind and heart.

דבר differs from אמר as "speaking" does from "telling." "Speaking," in general, means to put ideas into words, regardless of whether or not the listener accepts them. "Telling," on the other hand, always implies "communication." One can speak to oneself, but one cannot communicate anything to oneself. So it is with דבר and אמר. While דַּבֵּר denotes the concise statement of an idea, אֱמֹר implies the instilling of the idea into the mind and spirit of another—hence, the thorough explanation and elaboration of the idea. Therefore, in the parlance of Jewish Law, דבר is always the concise statement of the law as given to us in תּוֹרָה שֶׁבִּכְתָב [the Written Law], while אמר indicates the complete explanation that has been handed down to us through תּוֹרָה שֶׁבְּעַל פֶּה [the Oral Law]. Hence אָמוֹרָא is the "interpreter" and אָמוֹרָאִים are the "interpreters" of the Law; they are the successors of the תַּנָּאִים, whose skill lay in שנה (literally, "saying a second time," "repeating"), handing down that which they themselves had received. For this reason we speak of עֲשֶׂרֶת הַדִּבְּרוֹת [the Ten Commandments (of the Written Law)] and עֲשָׂרָה מַאֲמָרוֹת [the ten Divine injunctions of Creation in Aboth 5:1]. The word of Creation is אֲמִירָה because it immediately materializes in the object to which it is addressed. The word of the Law, on the other hand, is דִּבּוּר; the fact that it has been pronounced does not necessarily mean that it will be automatically accepted and fulfilled.

In this section, the meaning implicit in אֱמֹר applies to the entire sentence, which revolves around אֲמִירָה: אֱמֹר וגו׳ וְאָמַרְתָּ וגו׳ וַיֹּאמֶר וגו׳. All the ideas that are put down here in terse sentences were explained by God to Moses in detail, and their meaning and content must likewise be communicated to the ones whom the Law addresses so that they may understand it and take it to heart. Therefore the words, "Now declare this to the priests, the sons of Aharon," must have been intended to express an independent idea, which can hardly be anything other than as follows: Declare this to the priests because they are sons of Aharon. Explain to them how their priesthood derives from their Aharonide descent. Make them aware of this, and let them always remember that they do not owe their priestly office to personal merit but solely to their birth. In Judaism, priesthood is a function imposed by birth, a task to which one is born and which he is raised to discharge so that when he has grown to manhood, it will absorb his whole life. Therefore, even as the כֹּהֲנִים are to view themselves as בְּנֵי אַהֲרֹן, so they should see their children, too, as future כֹּהֲנִים, and raise them in and for the functions they are to perform as members of their tribe. This is stressed by the expression הַכֹּהֲנִים בְּנֵי אַהֲרֹן which occurs only in this one Scriptural verse. The form used everywhere else in Scripture is בְּנֵי אַהֲרֹן הַכֹּהֲנִים ["The sons of Aharon, the priests"]. . . .

his father, his son, his daughter and his brother; 3. and also for his virgin sister, who is still close to him, who has not yet belonged to a man, for her he has to defile himself. 4. A married man must not defile himself among his people for a marriage that was profanation for him. 5. They shall not make a bald spot on their head, nor shall they shave off the corner[s] of their beard and they shall not make a wound in their flesh. 6. They shall be holy to their God and shall not profane the Name of their God, for what they bring near becomes an offering of their God by being given over to the fire of *God*; therefore they [themselves] are to be a sanctuary. 7. They shall not marry a harlot or a profaned woman, and they shall not marry a woman who was divorced by her husband, for it (the tribe of Aharon) is holy to its God. 8. And you shall exhort him to be holy, for it is the offering of your God that he

וּלְאָבִיו וְלִבְנוֹ וּלְבִתּוֹ וּלְאָחִיו: ג וְלַאֲחֹתוֹ
הַבְּתוּלָה הַקְּרוֹבָה אֵלָיו אֲשֶׁר לֹא־הָיְתָה לְאִישׁ
לָהּ יִטַּמָּא: ד לֹא יִטַּמָּא בַּעַל בְּעַמָּיו לְהֵחַלּוֹ:
ה לֹא־יִקְרְחָה (יקרחו קרי) קָרְחָה בְּרֹאשָׁם וּפְאַת
זְקָנָם לֹא יְגַלֵּחוּ וּבִבְשָׂרָם לֹא יִשְׂרְטוּ שָׂרָטֶת:
ו קְדֹשִׁים יִהְיוּ לֵאלֹהֵיהֶם וְלֹא יְחַלְּלוּ שֵׁם
אֱלֹהֵיהֶם כִּי אֶת־אִשֵּׁי יְהוָה לֶחֶם אֱלֹהֵיהֶם הֵם
מַקְרִיבִם וְהָיוּ קֹדֶשׁ: ז אִשָּׁה זֹנָה וַחֲלָלָה לֹא
יִקָּחוּ וְאִשָּׁה גְּרוּשָׁה מֵאִישָׁהּ לֹא יִקָּחוּ כִּי־קָדֹשׁ
הוּא לֵאלֹהָיו: ח וְקִדַּשְׁתּוֹ כִּי־אֶת־לֶחֶם אֱלֹהֶיךָ

5. . . . Pagans, both ancient and modern, have a predilection for associating religion and religious matters with death and thoughts of death. For them the kingdom of God begins only where man ends. They view death and dying as the true manifestations of their deity, whom they see as a god of death, not of life; a god that kills and never revives, that sends death and its forerunners, sickness and affliction, so that men, realizing the might of their god and their own impotence, may fear him. For this reason they set up their shrines near graves and the place of their priests is prominently near the dead. Death and mourning are the most fertile soil for the dissemination of their religion, and it seems that in their view, the presence, on their own flesh, of a mark of death, a symbol of death's power to conquer all of life, would be a sign of religiosity *par excellence* and, above all, the most essential attribute of the priest and his office.

Not so the priests in Judaism, because the Jewish concept of God and the Jewish religion are not so. The God Whose Name assigns the priest his place among the Jewish people is a God of life. His most exalted manifestation is not the power of death that crushes strength and vitality but the power of life that enables man to exercise free will and to be immortal. Judaism teaches us not how to die but how to live so that, even in life, we may overcome death, lack of freedom, the enslavement to physical things and moral weakness. Judaism teaches us how to spend every moment of a life marked by moral freedom, thought, aspirations, creativity and achievement, along with the enjoyment of physical pleasures, as one more moment in life's constant service to the everlasting God. This is the teaching to which God has dedicated His Sanctuary and for whose service He has consecrated the כֹּהֲנִים, the guardians of the basis and "direction" (Hebrew: כֹּהֵן [priest] = כון [direction]) of the people's life.

When death summons the other members of his people to perform the final acts of loving-kindness for the physical shell of a נֶפֶשׁ [soul] that has been called home to God, the כֹּהֲנֵי ה׳ ["priests of *God*"] must stay away in order to keep aloft the banner of life beside the dead body, to make certain that the concept of life; i.e., the thought that man has been endowed with moral freedom, that he is godly and not subject to the physical forces that seek to crush moral freedom, is not overshadowed by thoughts of death. Only when the realities of life require even the priest to perform his final duty as a husband, son, father or brother for the shell of a departed נֶפֶשׁ, or the presence of an abandoned body makes it necessary for him to take the place of the father or brother of the deceased, does his priestly function yield to his calling as a human being and as a member of a family. In such cases he is not only permitted but in fact commanded to have the necessary contact with the dead body. Under all other circumstances, however, priests must stay away from the bodies of the dead.

° ° °

הוּא מַקְרִיב קָדֹשׁ יִהְיֶה־לָּךְ כִּי קָדוֹשׁ אֲנִי יְהֹוָה
מְקַדִּשְׁכֶם: ט וּבַת אִישׁ כֹּהֵן כִּי תֵחֵל לִזְנוֹת
אֶת־אָבִיהָ הִיא מְחַלֶּלֶת בָּאֵשׁ תִּשָּׂרֵף: ס
י וְהַכֹּהֵן הַגָּדוֹל מֵאֶחָיו אֲשֶׁר־יוּצַק עַל־רֹאשׁוֹ |
שֶׁמֶן הַמִּשְׁחָה וּמִלֵּא אֶת־יָדוֹ לִלְבֹּשׁ אֶת־
הַבְּגָדִים אֶת־רֹאשׁוֹ לֹא יִפְרָע וּבְגָדָיו לֹא יִפְרֹם:
יא וְעַל כָּל־נַפְשֹׁת מֵת לֹא יָבֹא לְאָבִיו וּלְאִמּוֹ
לֹא יִטַּמָּא: יב וּמִן־הַמִּקְדָּשׁ לֹא יֵצֵא וְלֹא יְחַלֵּל

brings near; he shall be holy also to you, for I, *God*, Who summons you to holiness, am holy. 9. And if the daughter of a man who is a priest profanes herself by acting the harlot, she profanes her father; she shall be burned. 10. But the priest who is the greatest among his brethren, upon whose head the anointing oil shall be poured and who has been authorized to clothe himself with the garments, shall not allow the hair of his head to grow wild and shall not rend his garments, 11. and he shall not go to any persons that lie there as corpses (or, to any parts of a corpse that represent the personality); he may defile himself neither for his father nor for his mother. 12. And he must not go out of the Sanctuary so as

10–12. *. . . the priest who is the greatest among his brethren.* The reference is to that priest who towers over all the other priests, who is to represent priesthood on its highest positive level, and who, therefore, as taught in Yoma 18a, should be greater than all the others in both physical and spiritual qualities and should enjoy a position of social independence even before he is anointed to the office of high priest. His independence is considered so important that if he should not possess the material means needed to insure it, "they must make him great from what belongs to his brethren"; i.e., the other priests, whose leader he is, must provide him with means from their own wealth to make him economically independent.

upon whose head the anointing oil shall be poured. He has received his personal consecration with the anointing oil from the Sanhedrin, the supreme representative body of the nation, and he has been authorized to wear the high priestly garments so that he may represent the symbolic expression of the highest moral ideal which Israel is to translate into reality. Such a man has ceased to be an ordinary individual; he must now perceive and value also his personal relationships primarily from the standpoint of the ideals of the nation, ideals which should be in his mind so vividly that, if he must give personal expression to them, they will override any personal mood or emotion that could interfere with them.

The ideal of the nation does not know death, "the community never dies," and under this concept of the "eternal whole," every individual who is part of the community and has lived for the community has a share in this immortality even here below. With every pure fiber of his life on earth lived in faithfulness [to the Law] he will remain interwoven forever with the eternal essence of the community, and the impact of his own personal nobility will make him immortal on earth even after the physical shell in which he visibly walked among his people has become dust. And he who has lost his wife, and with her his "home," who has lost parents, children, brothers or sisters and, with them, his "family" that upheld him and that was upheld by him in turn, will find his home and family again in the national entity to which he belongs. There he will find the basis for his existence and creativity which he can never lose, the eternal ambiance for his life and his work. But above all, the Name of God, in Whose Sanctuary he serves and which he bears upon his forehead, will raise him to those great heights of thought and emotion in which all of existence, with its many vicissitudes, becomes a path of life forever serene in God, a path leading not from the cradle to the grave, not from existence to non-existence, but from life to life, from eternity to eternity.

⋅   ⋅   ⋅

This does not mean that human emotions should be alien to him, that he should allow the loss of his closest kin to pass him by without touching his heart. . . . [When he loses a close relative] he does become an אוֹנֵן[12] and therefore, though he is permitted to perform the priestly service entailed in the offerings, he is not allowed to partake of the offerings. Cf. "The *onen* may make offerings though he must not partake of them" (Horayoth 12b). . . . While he must not give symbolic expression to the gap left in his personal world by rending his garments in a conspicuous place "on top,"

[12]*Note to the English translation:* The mourner between the time of the death and the funeral. During this period he is exempt from performing certain religious functions and duties. [G.H.]

not to profane the Sanctuary of his God, for the crown of his God's anointing oil is upon him; I, *God*. 13. And he shall marry a woman in her virginity; 14. a widow or a divorced woman, or a profaned woman, or a harlot, he shall not marry any of these but he shall marry a virgin from among his people, 15. and he shall not profane his progeny among his people, for I, *God*, make him holy." 16. *God* spoke to Moshe [saying]: 17. "Speak to Aharon [saying]: Anyone among your progeny for all the future who has a bodily blemish shall not approach to bring near an offering to his God. 18. For any man who has a bodily blemish shall not approach: a blind man, or a lame man, or one whose nose is flat or whose hips are not equal, 19. or a man with a broken foot or a broken hand, 20. or one with overhanging eyebrows, or one with a film or a mixture [the white of the eye encroaching upon the pupil], or with a dry or moist scurf, or an injury of the testicle; 21. no man of the progeny of Aharon the priest who has a bodily blemish may approach to bring near the offerings to the fire of *God*; as long as he has a bodily blemish he may not approach to bring an offering to his God. 22. An offering to his God from the most holy of holies and from the holy things he may eat, 23. but he must not go in to the dividing curtain and he must not approach the altar, because he has a bodily blemish; he shall not profane My holy things, for I, *God*, make them holy." 24. Moshe articulated this to Aharon and his sons, and to all the sons of Yisrael.

אֵת מִקְדַּשׁ אֱלֹהָיו כִּי נֵזֶר שֶׁמֶן מִשְׁחַת אֱלֹהָיו
עָלָיו אֲנִי יְהוָה׃ יג וְהוּא אִשָּׁה בִבְתוּלֶיהָ יִקָּח׃
יד אַלְמָנָה וּגְרוּשָׁה וַחֲלָלָה זֹנָה אֶת־אֵלֶּה לֹא
יִקָּח כִּי אִם־בְּתוּלָה מֵעַמָּיו יִקַּח אִשָּׁה׃ טו וְלֹא־
יְחַלֵּל זַרְעוֹ בְּעַמָּיו כִּי אֲנִי יְהוָה מְקַדְּשׁוֹ׃ פ שני
טז וַיְדַבֵּר יְהוָה אֶל־מֹשֶׁה לֵּאמֹר׃ יז דַּבֵּר אֶל־
אַהֲרֹן לֵאמֹר אִישׁ מִזַּרְעֲךָ לְדֹרֹתָם אֲשֶׁר יִהְיֶה
בוֹ מוּם לֹא יִקְרַב לְהַקְרִיב לֶחֶם אֱלֹהָיו׃ יח כִּי
כָל־אִישׁ אֲשֶׁר־בּוֹ מוּם לֹא יִקְרָב אִישׁ עִוֵּר אוֹ
פִסֵּחַ אוֹ חָרֻם אוֹ שָׂרוּעַ׃ יט אוֹ אִישׁ אֲשֶׁר־יִהְיֶה
בוֹ שֶׁבֶר רָגֶל אוֹ שֶׁבֶר יָד׃ כ אוֹ־גִבֵּן אוֹ־דַק אוֹ
תְּבַלֻּל בְּעֵינוֹ אוֹ גָרָב אוֹ יַלֶּפֶת אוֹ מְרוֹחַ אָשֶׁךְ׃
כא כָּל־אִישׁ אֲשֶׁר־בּוֹ מוּם מִזֶּרַע אַהֲרֹן הַכֹּהֵן
לֹא יִגַּשׁ לְהַקְרִיב אֶת־אִשֵּׁי יְהוָה מוּם בּוֹ אֵת
לֶחֶם אֱלֹהָיו לֹא יִגַּשׁ לְהַקְרִיב׃ כב לֶחֶם אֱלֹהָיו
מִקָּדְשֵׁי הַקֳּדָשִׁים וּמִן־הַקֳּדָשִׁים יֹאכֵל׃ כג אַךְ
אֶל־הַפָּרֹכֶת לֹא יָבֹא וְאֶל־הַמִּזְבֵּחַ לֹא יִגַּשׁ כִּי־
מוּם בּוֹ וְלֹא יְחַלֵּל אֶת־מִקְדָּשַׁי כִּי אֲנִי יְהוָה
מְקַדְּשָׁם׃ כד וַיְדַבֵּר מֹשֶׁה אֶל־אַהֲרֹן וְאֶל־בָּנָיו

at his neck, above the breast, he does make a rent "below," at the hem (ibid.). Although he cannot join the funeral procession ("he must not follow immediately behind the bier"), he must follow it from some distance until it has reached the gate of the city so that he enters each street on the route of the procession directly after the cortege has gone on to the next street. Cf. "(He must not walk immediately behind the bier) but when they disappear he may show himself, and when they appear, he must be hidden. In this way he may go with them as far as the entrance of the gate of the city" (Sanhedrin 18a).

But even while he feels in his heart the pain that death has brought him, in the midst of these thoughts of death, he must demonstrate all the more eloquently the power and the joy of life that emanate from God even amidst life's bitterness—a concept taught by that Sanctuary whose first servant he is.

• • •

XXII

1. *God* spoke to Moshe [saying]: 2. "Speak to Aharon and his sons that they withdraw from the holy things of the sons of Yisrael and that they do not profane My holy Name, which they hallow for Me; I, *God*. 3. Declare to them: For your descendants, anyone of all your progeny who comes near to the holy things which the sons of Yisrael sanctify to God while his uncleanness is upon him, that person shall be uprooted from before My Countenance; I, *God*. 4. Anyone, *anyone* from the progeny of Aharon who is leprous or has a discharge may not eat any of the holy things until he has become pure. And one who touches anyone who has become unclean from [contact with] a dead body, or who has had a discharge of seed, 5. or one who has touched any creeping thing that is unclean for him, or a person who is unclean for him, with regard to any of his unclean states, 6. the person who touches any of these things shall remain unclean until the evening and may not eat of any of the holy things as long as he has not bathed his body in water. 7. And when the sun has set and he has become pure, only then may he eat of the holy things, for it is food that has been assigned to him. 8. He must not eat anything that has died of itself or that has been torn, to become unclean by it; I, *God*. 9. They are to keep what I have entrusted to them and they must not burden themselves with sin thereby, lest they die if they were to profane it; it is I, *God*, Who makes them holy. 10. And no stranger shall eat any holy thing; one who sojourns with a priest or is hired by him must not eat any holy thing. 11. But if a priest acquires a person as his property, that one may eat of it, also one born in his house; these may eat of the food assigned to him, 12. but the daughter of a priest, if she is married to an outsider [i.e., non-priest], she must not eat of the uplifted donations of holy things. 13. But if the daughter of a priest becomes a widow or a divorcée and she has no children and returns to her father's house as in her youth, she may eat of the food assigned to her father, but no outsider [i.e., non-priest] may eat of it. 14. But if one inadvertently eats a holy thing he must add

וְאֶל־כָּל־בְּנֵי יִשְׂרָאֵל: פ כב א וַיְדַבֵּר יְהֹוָה
אֶל־מֹשֶׁה לֵּאמֹר: ב דַּבֵּר אֶל־אַהֲרֹן וְאֶל־בָּנָיו
וְיִנָּזְרוּ מִקָּדְשֵׁי בְנֵי־יִשְׂרָאֵל וְלֹא יְחַלְּלוּ אֶת־שֵׁם
קָדְשִׁי אֲשֶׁר הֵם מַקְדִּשִׁים לִי אֲנִי יְהֹוָה: ג אֱמֹר
אֲלֵהֶם לְדֹרֹתֵיכֶם כָּל־אִישׁ ׀ אֲשֶׁר־יִקְרַב מִכָּל־
זַרְעֲכֶם אֶל־הַקֳּדָשִׁים אֲשֶׁר יַקְדִּישׁוּ בְנֵי־
יִשְׂרָאֵל לַיהֹוָה וְטֻמְאָתוֹ עָלָיו וְנִכְרְתָה הַנֶּפֶשׁ
הַהִוא מִלְּפָנַי אֲנִי יְהֹוָה: ד אִישׁ אִישׁ מִזֶּרַע
אַהֲרֹן וְהוּא צָרוּעַ אוֹ זָב בַּקֳּדָשִׁים לֹא יֹאכַל עַד
אֲשֶׁר יִטְהָר וְהַנֹּגֵעַ בְּכָל־טְמֵא־נֶפֶשׁ אוֹ אִישׁ
אֲשֶׁר־תֵּצֵא מִמֶּנּוּ שִׁכְבַת־זָרַע: ה אוֹ־אִישׁ אֲשֶׁר
יִגַּע בְּכָל־שֶׁרֶץ אֲשֶׁר יִטְמָא־לוֹ אוֹ בְאָדָם אֲשֶׁר
יִטְמָא־לוֹ לְכֹל טֻמְאָתוֹ: ו נֶפֶשׁ אֲשֶׁר תִּגַּע־בּוֹ
וְטָמְאָה עַד־הָעָרֶב וְלֹא יֹאכַל מִן־הַקֳּדָשִׁים כִּי
אִם־רָחַץ בְּשָׂרוֹ בַּמָּיִם: ז וּבָא הַשֶּׁמֶשׁ וְטָהֵר
וְאַחַר יֹאכַל מִן־הַקֳּדָשִׁים כִּי לַחְמוֹ הוּא:
ח נְבֵלָה וּטְרֵפָה לֹא יֹאכַל לְטָמְאָה־בָהּ אֲנִי
יְהֹוָה: ט וְשָׁמְרוּ אֶת־מִשְׁמַרְתִּי וְלֹא־יִשְׂאוּ עָלָיו
חֵטְא וּמֵתוּ בוֹ כִּי יְחַלְּלֻהוּ אֲנִי יְהֹוָה מְקַדְּשָׁם:
י וְכָל־זָר לֹא־יֹאכַל קֹדֶשׁ תּוֹשַׁב כֹּהֵן וְשָׂכִיר
לֹא־יֹאכַל קֹדֶשׁ: יא וְכֹהֵן כִּי־יִקְנֶה נֶפֶשׁ קִנְיַן
כַּסְפּוֹ הוּא יֹאכַל בּוֹ וִילִיד בֵּיתוֹ הֵם יֹאכְלוּ
בְלַחְמוֹ: יב וּבַת־כֹּהֵן כִּי תִהְיֶה לְאִישׁ זָר הִוא
בִּתְרוּמַת הַקֳּדָשִׁים לֹא תֹאכֵל: יג וּבַת־כֹּהֵן כִּי
תִהְיֶה אַלְמָנָה וּגְרוּשָׁה וְזֶרַע אֵין לָהּ וְשָׁבָה אֶל־
בֵּית אָבִיהָ כִּנְעוּרֶיהָ מִלֶּחֶם אָבִיהָ תֹּאכֵל וְכָל־
זָר לֹא־יֹאכַל בּוֹ: יד וְאִישׁ כִּי־יֹאכַל קֹדֶשׁ

one fifth of it and give the holy thing to the priest. 15. They shall not profane the holy things of the sons of Yisrael which they must lift up to *God*, 16. for they would burden themselves with an iniquity if they were to eat their holy things; for I, *God*, make them holy." 17. *God* spoke to Moshe [saying]: 18. "Speak to Aharon and to his sons and to all the sons of Yisrael and say to them: Anyone, *anyone* of the house of Yisrael and of those who have entered into Yisrael from abroad who wishes to bring near his offering for all their vows and all their free-will offerings that they wish to bring near to *God* as an ascent offering, 19. as an expression of your will, it must be without blemish, male, from the cattle, from the sheep or from the goats. 20. Anything with a blemish you shall not bring near, for it shall not serve you as an expression of [your] will. 21. And if anyone brings near to *God* a meal-of-peace offering as a pledge or a free-will offering, from the cattle or from small livestock, it shall be without blemish as an expression of [your] will; no blemish shall come upon it. 22. Blind or broken, or scratched, or with a wart, or with a dry or moist scurf, these you shall not bring near to *God*, and you shall not place any of them upon the altar as a fire offering to *God*. 23. And if an ox or a lamb has an overgrown limb or a clubfoot, you can make it as a free-will offering, but it shall not serve you as a vow to express [your] will. 24. And anything that has been crushed or mangled, torn off or cut off you shall not bring near to *God* and you shall also not do such a thing in your land. 25. Also from the hand of a foreigner shall you not bring the offering of your God, not from any of these, because they bear

בִּשְׁגָגָה וְיָסַף חֲמִשִׁיתוֹ עָלָיו וְנָתַן לַכֹּהֵן אֶת־
הַקֹּדֶשׁ׃ טו וְלֹא יְחַלְּלוּ אֶת־קָדְשֵׁי בְּנֵי יִשְׂרָאֵל
אֵת אֲשֶׁר־יָרִימוּ לַיהֹוָה׃ טז וְהִשִּׂיאוּ אוֹתָם עֲוֺן
אַשְׁמָה בְּאָכְלָם אֶת־קָדְשֵׁיהֶם כִּי אֲנִי יְהֹוָה
מְקַדְּשָׁם׃ פ שלישי יז וַיְדַבֵּר יְהֹוָה אֶל־מֹשֶׁה
לֵּאמֹר׃ יח דַּבֵּר אֶל־אַהֲרֹן וְאֶל־בָּנָיו וְאֶל כָּל־
בְּנֵי יִשְׂרָאֵל וְאָמַרְתָּ אֲלֵהֶם אִישׁ אִישׁ מִבֵּית
יִשְׂרָאֵל וּמִן־הַגֵּר בְּיִשְׂרָאֵל אֲשֶׁר יַקְרִיב קָרְבָּנוֹ
לְכָל־נִדְרֵיהֶם וּלְכָל־נִדְבוֹתָם אֲשֶׁר־יַקְרִיבוּ
לַיהֹוָה לְעֹלָה׃ יט לִרְצֹנְכֶם תָּמִים זָכָר בַּבָּקָר
בַּכְּשָׂבִים וּבָעִזִּים׃ כ כֹּל אֲשֶׁר־בּוֹ מוּם לֹא
תַקְרִיבוּ כִּי־לֹא לְרָצוֹן יִהְיֶה לָכֶם׃ כא וְאִישׁ
כִּי־יַקְרִיב זֶבַח־שְׁלָמִים לַיהֹוָה לְפַלֵּא־נֶדֶר אוֹ
לִנְדָבָה בַּבָּקָר אוֹ בַצֹּאן תָּמִים יִהְיֶה לְרָצוֹן כָּל־
מוּם לֹא יִהְיֶה־בּוֹ׃ כב עַוֶּרֶת אוֹ שָׁבוּר אוֹ־
חָרוּץ אוֹ־יַבֶּלֶת אוֹ גָרָב אוֹ יַלֶּפֶת לֹא־תַקְרִיבוּ
אֵלֶּה לַיהֹוָה וְאִשֶּׁה לֹא־תִתְּנוּ מֵהֶם עַל־הַמִּזְבֵּחַ
לַיהֹוָה׃ כג וְשׁוֹר וָשֶׂה שָׂרוּעַ וְקָלוּט נְדָבָה
תַּעֲשֶׂה אֹתוֹ וּלְנֵדֶר לֹא יֵרָצֶה׃ כד וּמָעוּךְ וְכָתוּת
וְנָתוּק וְכָרוּת לֹא תַקְרִיבוּ לַיהֹוָה וּבְאַרְצְכֶם לֹא
תַעֲשׂוּ׃ כה וּמִיַּד בֶּן־נֵכָר לֹא תַקְרִיבוּ אֶת־לֶחֶם
אֱלֹהֵיכֶם מִכָּל־אֵלֶּה כִּי מָשְׁחָתָם בָּהֶם מוּם בָּם

CHAPTER XXII

17. Verses 16–24 of the preceding chapter declared "physical wholeness," freedom from bodily blemishes, as an essential qualification for a priest who serves in the Sanctuary. The verses that now follow set the same qualification for animal offerings, a qualification already stated in the opening chapters on offerings (תָּמִים = "whole," "without blemish,"), and give more detailed specifications.

24. ***crushed or mangled.*** The text refers to injuries or mutilations of the animal's genital organs.

in your land. The prohibition against peforming any kind of castration on a human being or on an animal is a duty related to the body of an individual; it therefore has no relevance to the country in which the individual lives, and is applicable both inside and outside the Land of Israel. . . .

their corruption in the blemish that is upon them; they cannot serve you as an expression of [your] will." 26. *God* spoke to Moshe [saying]: 27. "If an ox, or a sheep, or a goat is born, it shall be under its mother seven days, and from the eighth day and thereafter it can serve as an expression of will, to bring near as a fire offering to *God*, 28. and [as for] an ox or a sheep, you shall not slaughter it and its young on the same day. 29. And if you slaughter a meal-of-thanksgiving offering to *God*, you shall slaughter it as an expression of your will. 30. It shall be eaten on the same day; you shall not leave any of it until the [next] morning; I, *God*. 31. Keep My commandments and carry them out; I, *God*. 32. And do not profane My holy Name but let Me be sanctified in the midst of the sons of Yisrael; I, *God*, make you holy,

לֹא יֵרָצוּ לָכֶם: ס כו וַיְדַבֵּר יְהֹוָה אֶל־מֹשֶׁה לֵּאמֹר: כז שׁוֹר אוֹ־כֶשֶׂב אוֹ־עֵז כִּי יִוָּלֵד וְהָיָה שִׁבְעַת יָמִים תַּחַת אִמּוֹ וּמִיּוֹם הַשְּׁמִינִי וָהָלְאָה יֵרָצֶה לְקָרְבַּן אִשֶּׁה לַיהֹוָה: כח וְשׁוֹר אוֹ־שֶׂה אֹתוֹ וְאֶת־בְּנוֹ לֹא תִשְׁחֲטוּ בְּיוֹם אֶחָד: כט וְכִי־תִזְבְּחוּ זֶבַח־תּוֹדָה לַיהֹוָה לִרְצֹנְכֶם תִּזְבָּחוּ: ל בַּיּוֹם הַהוּא יֵאָכֵל לֹא־תוֹתִירוּ מִמֶּנּוּ עַד־בֹּקֶר אֲנִי יְהֹוָה: לא וּשְׁמַרְתֶּם מִצְוֹתַי וַעֲשִׂיתֶם אֹתָם אֲנִי יְהֹוָה: לב וְלֹא תְחַלְּלוּ אֶת־שֵׁם קָדְשִׁי וְנִקְדַּשְׁתִּי בְּתוֹךְ בְּנֵי יִשְׂרָאֵל אֲנִי יְהֹוָה

28. *an ox or a sheep.* The Law prohibits the slaughtering of the female of a kosher animal and its young on the same day. . . .

. . . We believe we may venture the assumption that this is the one aspect of animal life that shows the beginning of a faint resemblance to the human character. Egotism, love and concern for self, is the powerful drive that motivates all animal life. The sacrifice of self for the existence of another creature and devoted care for its welfare, as manifested in the animal's mother love when the animal bears and nurtures its young, is the first move of the animal's character toward that selflessness which, in human love, represents the godliest trait in the human character. This trace of humanity in the animal's character must not be blurred; indeed, it must be emphasized with particular care in our treatment of those animals which, as our offerings, are intended to symbolize a moral ideal toward which man should strive.

It is this inherent trace of humanity that qualifies the animal to fill this symbolic function, and the fact that the Law gives it such explicit consideration makes it clear that animal offerings in Judaism are intended solely for the promotion of human morality, in sharp contrast with the pagan concept, which views the sacrificial rituals as killings performed to please the gods.

       o   o   o

29-30. . . . The thanksgiving that God, the God of true Judaism, expects from the person He has blessed consists not in self-destructive, immoral and uncontrolled revelry in earthly pleasures but in the gladsome enjoyment of the happiness He has granted him, or

saved and preserved for him. However, that enjoyment must be kept within the bounds of morality and precisely thereby is elevated to become a hallowed, God-serving fulfillment of life.

32. *And do not profane My holy Name.* By erecting the Sanctuary of His Law in our midst so that His Name might have its Presence there, God has appointed us, with every aspect of our lives as individuals and as a nation, to uphold His Name. He declared us and all that is ours as His possession, and has set in our midst the proclamation of His will, instructing us how to prove ourselves and all that is ours as His own, and how to do justice to the Name we bear.

The Name of God which we bear is to be holy, the supreme Absolute in our midst. At the same time it is to act as the universal stimulus which, by its power, binds, preserves, bestirs us and all that is ours to do our duty in the service of God. Each time we refuse to devote so much as one impulse of our nature, one stimulus of our aspirations, one fiber of our being, one fragment of our possessions, to the fulfillment of His holy will, we are מְחַלֵּל אֶל שֵׁם קָדְשׁוֹ [we profane His holy Name]. We cause the Name, which to us should be our supreme, most holy, absolute good, the sole justification for our lives and possessions, which should hold total sway over us and over all that is ours, to become חָלָל, a "lifeless, powerless shell." In this manner we desecrate His Name, and to the extent that others become aware of our sin against the Law of God, our invidious example becomes propaganda to demonstrate the impotence of the Name of God that rests upon us. By our sin we imply that one can call himself a Jew, and

33. Who brings you out from the land of Mitzrayim, to be a God to you; I, *God*."

מְקַדִּשְׁכֶם: לג הַמּוֹצִיא אֶתְכֶם מֵאֶרֶץ מִצְרַיִם
לִהְיוֹת לָכֶם לֵאלֹהִים אֲנִי יְהוָה: פ רביעי

XXIII

1. *God* spoke to Moshe [saying]: 2. "Speak

כג א וַיְדַבֵּר יְהוָה אֶל־מֹשֶׁה לֵּאמֹר: ב דַּבֵּר

be regarded as such, even if he abandons the obedience to God implicit in this Name as worth nothing compared to the first opportunity for sensual gratification, for personal pleasure or for material profit. Such a sin on our part would imply the notion that one can call himself a Jew, and be regarded as such, even if he does not regard the will of God as the absolute, and his own will as only conditional, but sets up his own will as the absolute idol to which the will of God, impotent and dependent, must give way.

Also, the more an individual stands out as an "upholder of the Name of God" by virtue of his knowledge of the Word of God and his personal standing in the nation, the more imperative is it that he heed the command, "Do not profane My holy Name." In his case, even his slightest deviation, or semblance of deviation, from veracity and integrity, from morality and godly living, from the justice, goodness and loving-kindness which the Law demands, will become a gross act of חִלּוּל הַשֵּׁם (Yoma 86a). The ever-recurring dictum that an individual of high moral and spiritual attainments is required to be more punctilious than others in his conduct shows the manner in which the great intellects of the Jewish people have always perceived their position in relation to the moral law and how far removed they were from the deplorable notion that each rung of intellectual greatness attained represented one more dispensation from observing the moral law. On the contrary, "Let Me be sanctified in the midst of the sons of Yisrael"; God and His holy will are to be perceived and obeyed as the supreme, all-surpassing, all-commanding sanctum in every aspect of Jewish life. Moreover—as is taught and pledged in symbolic terms by every offering we make—we are to offer up our very lifeblood, all our urges and aspirations, the energies of our bodies, our nourishment, prosperity and joy of living, upon the altar of God for the fulfillment of His will. This ideal is to become a concrete reality in the life of every single one of us, for our own perfection and as an example to be followed "in the midst of the sons of Yisrael," by everyone else who has a part in the mission of Judaism.

° ° °

The ideal expressed by the words," "Let Me be sanctified in the midst of the sons of Yisrael," in the text of the Law, is to be kept alive symbolically by the nation's daily offerings, with the rise and fall of every new day, and brought to the nation's consciousness again and again as the supreme object of its mission. In a similar manner, by composing and arranging the order of the synagogue service to parallel the ritual of the offerings in the Temple, did the men of the Great Assembly, those true fathers of our nation, set the pronouncement, וְנִקְדַּשְׁתִּי וגו׳ ["and let Me be sanctified. . ."], and the pledge to fulfill it—the quintessence of the entire service of the offerings—as the focus for our national assemblies at Divine services (i.e., any gathering of at least ten adult males); to find ever-recurring verbal expression in the *Kaddish* and the *Kedushah* (Berakhoth 21b).

CHAPTER XXIII

1. . . . The subject of this chapter is the chronological order of the festivals in the annual cycle, the "system" or "order," as it is called in *Sifrei* to Deuteronomy 16:1. Here are set forth, in detail, the specifications for the particular commandments relating to the observances that express the unique significance of each festival. . . .

° ° °

All the festival observances discussed here have one concept in common with the Temple and with the ritual of its offerings. The laws regarding these were essentially concluded with the group of laws set forth in the preceding chapter. We are referring to the concept of מוֹעֵד (see Exodus ibid.). That which the Temple represents in space, the festivals represent in time. The purpose of both is to effect our union with God. The purpose of the Temple is to set up the Law of God as the eternal center of our spatial world. Its message is: This is where you can find your way to God. The festival cycle singles out certain seasons fixed in time by Divine Revelation. Its message is: These were the days on which God was near to you in the past. Each year, when they recur, God expects to meet you in renewed reunion. But the Temple and the festivals are different from one another as space is different from time. Even as space represents the concept of constancy, so the Sanctuary of God in space concerns itself with the mutual relationship between that which is forever godly; i.e., the Law of God, and that which is forever human; i.e., the nature of man. And even as time represents the concept of the everlasting cycle of natural phenomena, so the Divine sancta in time concern themselves with the Divine element manifest in the changes of the seasons: the revelation of God in nature and history and the human element in time; i.e., our relationship, as individuals and as a nation, to nature and history.

° ° °

to the sons of Yisrael and say to them: *God*'s appointed times for meeting, which you shall proclaim as convocations to the Sanctuary: these are My appointed times for meeting. 3. Six days shall [creating] work be done and on the seventh day the Sabbath

אֶל־בְּנֵ֤י יִשְׂרָאֵל֙ וְאָמַרְתָּ֣ אֲלֵהֶ֔ם מוֹעֲדֵ֣י יְהֹוָ֔ה
אֲשֶׁר־תִּקְרְא֥וּ אֹתָ֖ם מִקְרָאֵ֣י קֹ֑דֶשׁ אֵ֖לֶּה הֵ֥ם
מוֹעֲדָֽי׃ ג שֵׁ֣שֶׁת יָמִים֮ תֵּעָשֶׂ֣ה מְלָאכָה֒ וּבַיּ֣וֹם

The most outstanding characteristic of a man's independence is that he has the freedom to use his time as he sees fit, without any restrictions imposed upon him from the outside. One who can call his time his own is truly free. One who has a claim on the time of another is his master. In Egypt we could not call even one minute our own, and the lack of this right to use our time for our own purposes marked us as slaves even at the moment of our deliverance and made the *matzah* the symbol of our bondage. By making a claim on our time and reserving certain days and weeks of our annual cycle for His purposes, God proclaims Himself as our master, and the fact that we place our time at His disposal becomes the most eloquent proof of our subordination to God into which we have passed from our subordination to men and which in fact has made us forever free. However, this relation of ours to God is to be perceived not only as that of a servant to his master but also as that of a child to his father. This thought is set forth most significantly in the verse that follows and that introduces the laws governing the sancta of God in time.

2. . . . A season assigned by God as a מוֹעֵד [an appointed time] becomes a מוֹעֵד ד׳ [a time of meeting with *God*], solely by virtue of the fact that the nation has proclaimed it as a מִקְרָא קֹדֶשׁ ["convocation to its Sanctuary"]. This sets forth the great principle which we have already discussed in connection with the sanctification of the New Moon (Exodus ibid.): The days of the Jewish New Moon and the Jewish festivals are not fixed astronomically in such a manner that the arrival of the proper astronomical point in time would automatically hallow that day as a New Moon or as a festival. The astronomical lunar and solar seasons for both have been set only to provide the occasion for which, and in conjunction with which, the New Moons and festivals of the Jewish nation should be fixed and sanctified as מוֹעֲדֵי ד׳, seasons when Israel is to meet with God.

By virtue of this principle our New Moons and our festivals that come in the spring, summer and autumn are divested of any resemblance to pagan cults of sun or moon worship, and the seasons set aside for the meetings between God and Israel are elevated from the bondage of the master-servant relationship to the love between Father and child; they become seasons of meeting derived from a mutual choice founded on mutual love and yearning. Here, at the outset, we are informed that the fixing of the annual cycle of festivals, which sets the beginning of each festival for the appropriate season of the year, is to be dependent upon a decision and proclamation made by the representatives of the nation.

° ° °

. . . The חֹדֶשׁ הָאָבִיב [month of spring; i.e., Passover]; the חַג הַקָּצִיר בִּכּוּרֵי מַעֲשֶׂיךָ, "festival when you gather in the first fruits of your activities"; i.e., Shevuoth, and חַג הָאָסִיף [the festival of the harvest; i.e., Sukkoth] are no more spring, summer or autumn festivals to glorify nature as an act of sun worship than the Jewish New Moon celebration is a cultic festival to worship the moon. Even as the renewal of the moon is only an occasion for celebrating the renewal of our own selves, so, too, the Jewish festivals that come in the spring, summer and autumn are מִקְרָאֵי קֹדֶשׁ ["convocations to the Sanctuary"]. They literally call us away from nature around us, away from field, forest and meadow and summon us upward into the Sanctuary of God's moral law. They represent a loud and clear protest against pagan nature worship. The fruits of our soil and of our trees do not ripen and our granaries are not filled by the grace of a solar power that determines the coming of spring, summer and autumn. No, it is the sovereignty of God, judging our loyalty or disloyalty to the will of His Law as set down in His Sanctuary, that decides whether or not our springtimes will be blessed with blossoms, our summers with ripe fruits and our autumns with abundance. Only if, of our own free will, we subordinate all our moral and social conduct to the light and the fire of the Law which He has given to us, allowing it to awaken, develop and fashion us even as the seeds of plant and fruit awaken, develop and take shape beneath the light and the fire of the law He has given to nature, only if we effect a moral blossoming, development and maturation within ourselves, will He grant blossoms to our meadows, ripeness to our fruit and abundance to our granaries, even as it is said in His Word again and again: "If you will walk in My statutes and keep My commandments and carry them out, I will give your rains in their season; the earth will yield its produce and the tree of the field will yield its fruit. Your threshing season will extend until the vintage and the vintage will extend until the sowing time. You will eat your bread until you are satisfied and you will dwell securely in your land" (Leviticus 26:3–5 et al.).

of cessation from [creating] work is a convocation to the Sanctuary; you may not perform any [creating] work then; it is a Sabbath to *God* in all your dwelling places. 4. These are *God*'s appointed times for meeting, convocations to the Sanctuary, which you must proclaim at the time appointed for them. 5. In the first month, on the fourteenth of the month, between the two evenings, is the Pesaḥ to *God*. 6. And on the fifteenth of that month is the festival of *matzoth* dedicated to *God*; for seven days you shall eat only unleavened bread. 7. On the first day there shall be for you a convocation to the Sanctuary; you must not do any service work. 8. And you shall bring near to *God* for seven days a fire offering; on the seventh day is a convocation to the Sanctuary; you must not do any service work." 9. *God* spoke to Moshe [saying]: 10. "Speak to the sons of Yisrael and say to them: When you come to the land which I give you and you reap its harvest, you shall bring the *omer* of your first reaping to the priest, 11. and he shall wave the *omer* before *God* as an expression of your will; on the day after that Sabbath shall the priest wave it. 12. And on the day when you wave the *omer* you shall offer an unblemished yearling sheep as an ascent offering to *God*. 13. And its homage offering, two tenths of fine wheat flour mixed with oil, a fire offering to *God*, as an expression of compliance, and its wine libation one fourth of a *hin*. 14. And you shall not eat bread, parched flour and green

הַשְּׁבִיעִי שַׁבַּת שַׁבָּתוֹן מִקְרָא־קֹדֶשׁ כָּל־מְלָאכָה לֹא תַעֲשׂוּ שַׁבָּת הִוא לַיהֹוָה בְּכֹל מוֹשְׁבֹתֵיכֶם: פ ד אֵלֶּה מוֹעֲדֵי יְהֹוָה מִקְרָאֵי קֹדֶשׁ אֲשֶׁר־תִּקְרְאוּ אֹתָם בְּמוֹעֲדָם: ה בַּחֹדֶשׁ הָרִאשׁוֹן בְּאַרְבָּעָה עָשָׂר לַחֹדֶשׁ בֵּין הָעַרְבָּיִם פֶּסַח לַיהֹוָה: ו וּבַחֲמִשָּׁה עָשָׂר יוֹם לַחֹדֶשׁ הַזֶּה חַג הַמַּצּוֹת לַיהֹוָה שִׁבְעַת יָמִים מַצּוֹת תֹּאכֵלוּ: ז בַּיּוֹם הָרִאשׁוֹן מִקְרָא־קֹדֶשׁ יִהְיֶה לָכֶם כָּל־מְלֶאכֶת עֲבֹדָה לֹא תַעֲשׂוּ: ח וְהִקְרַבְתֶּם אִשֶּׁה לַיהֹוָה שִׁבְעַת יָמִים בַּיּוֹם הַשְּׁבִיעִי מִקְרָא־קֹדֶשׁ כָּל־מְלֶאכֶת עֲבֹדָה לֹא תַעֲשׂוּ: פ ט וַיְדַבֵּר יְהֹוָה אֶל־מֹשֶׁה לֵּאמֹר: י דַּבֵּר אֶל־בְּנֵי יִשְׂרָאֵל וְאָמַרְתָּ אֲלֵהֶם כִּי־תָבֹאוּ אֶל־הָאָרֶץ אֲשֶׁר אֲנִי נֹתֵן לָכֶם וּקְצַרְתֶּם אֶת־קְצִירָהּ וַהֲבֵאתֶם אֶת־עֹמֶר רֵאשִׁית קְצִירְכֶם אֶל־הַכֹּהֵן: יא וְהֵנִיף אֶת־הָעֹמֶר לִפְנֵי יְהֹוָה לִרְצֹנְכֶם מִמָּחֳרַת הַשַּׁבָּת יְנִיפֶנּוּ הַכֹּהֵן: יב וַעֲשִׂיתֶם בְּיוֹם הֲנִיפְכֶם אֶת־הָעֹמֶר כֶּבֶשׂ תָּמִים בֶּן־שְׁנָתוֹ לְעֹלָה לַיהֹוָה: יג וּמִנְחָתוֹ שְׁנֵי עֶשְׂרֹנִים סֹלֶת בְּלוּלָה בַשֶּׁמֶן אִשֶּׁה לַיהֹוָה רֵיחַ נִיחֹחַ וְנִסְכֹּה (ונסכו קרי) יַיִן רְבִיעִת הַהִין: יד וְלֶחֶם וְקָלִי וְכַרְמֶל לֹא תֹאכְלוּ

---

3. שַׁבָּת הִוא לַד׳ *[(It) is a Sabbath to* **God***]*. The Sabbath is not intended as a day to satisfy man's need for rest, but as one for rendering homage to God. Its שְׁבִיתָה ["cessation from creating work"] is an expression of this homage.

it is a Sabbath to **God.** It is given, fixed and hallowed by God, and the very fact that its claim was thus fixed, independently of human choice, makes its observance a universal homage offering to God. "It is a Sabbath to *God* in all your dwelling places," and as such it comes to us no matter where and how widely we may be scattered. In the case of all the other מוֹעֲדִים [appointed

seasons], the Law refers us to our character as a nation; they are fixed by the representatives of the nation and hence point to the geographic center of our national life. The sanctity of the Sabbath, by contrast, antedates the emergence of the nation and hence does not require the nation as an intermediary. In the case of the Sabbath, man is called upon as an individual to do homage to his Creator, Who is also the Creator of the universe. Wherever he may be in God's world, the Sabbath comes to him and summons him to resign from his position of dominion and offer up "his" world in order to pay homage to the true Ruler of the universe. . . .

ears until that day, until you have made the offering of your God; an everlasting statute for your descendants in all your dwelling places.　15. And you shall count for yourselves from the day after that Sabbath, from the day of your bringing the wave offering of the *omer*; it shall be seven complete Sabbaths.　16. Until the day after the seventh Sabbath you shall count fifty days, and then you shall bring a new homage offering near to *God*.　17. You shall bring from your dwelling places two loaves of bread as a wave [offering], made of two tenths; they shall be of fine wheat flour; they shall be baked as leavened bread; they are the first fruits for *God*.　18. And you shall bring near, with the bread, seven sheep, without blemish, one year old, and one young bull and two rams. They shall be an ascent offering to *God*, and their homage offering and their libations; a fire offering of an expression of compliance, to *God*. 19. And you shall offer one he-goat as an offering that clears [him who brings it] of sin

עַד־עֶ֙צֶם֙ הַיּ֣וֹם הַזֶּ֔ה עַ֚ד הֲבִֽיאֲכֶ֔ם אֶת־קׇרְבַּ֖ן אֱלֹהֵיכֶ֑ם חֻקַּ֤ת עוֹלָם֙ לְדֹרֹ֣תֵיכֶ֔ם בְּכֹ֖ל מֹשְׁבֹֽתֵיכֶֽם׃ ס טו וּסְפַרְתֶּ֤ם לָכֶם֙ מִמׇּחֳרַ֣ת הַשַּׁבָּ֔ת מִיּוֹם֙ הֲבִ֣יאֲכֶ֔ם אֶת־עֹ֖מֶר הַתְּנוּפָ֑ה שֶׁ֥בַע שַׁבָּת֖וֹת תְּמִימֹ֥ת תִּהְיֶֽינָה׃ טז עַ֣ד מִֽמׇּחֳרַ֤ת הַשַּׁבָּת֙ הַשְּׁבִיעִ֔ת תִּסְפְּר֖וּ חֲמִשִּׁ֣ים י֑וֹם וְהִקְרַבְתֶּ֛ם מִנְחָ֥ה חֲדָשָׁ֖ה לַיהֹוָֽה׃ יז מִמּֽוֹשְׁבֹ֨תֵיכֶ֜ם תָּבִ֣יאּוּ ׀ לֶ֣חֶם תְּנוּפָ֗ה שְׁתַּ֙יִם֙ שְׁנֵ֣י עֶשְׂרֹנִ֔ים סֹ֣לֶת תִּהְיֶ֔ינָה חָמֵ֖ץ תֵּאָפֶ֑ינָה בִּכּוּרִ֖ים לַֽיהֹוָֽה׃ יח וְהִקְרַבְתֶּ֣ם עַל־הַלֶּ֗חֶם שִׁבְעַ֤ת כְּבָשִׂים֙ תְּמִימִם֙ בְּנֵ֣י שָׁנָ֔ה וּפַ֧ר בֶּן־בָּקָ֛ר אֶחָ֖ד וְאֵילִ֣ם שְׁנָ֑יִם יִהְי֤וּ עֹלָה֙ לַֽיהֹוָ֔ה וּמִנְחָתָם֙ וְנִסְכֵּיהֶ֔ם אִשֵּׁ֥ה רֵֽיחַ־נִיחֹ֖חַ לַֽיהֹוָֽה׃ יט וַעֲשִׂיתֶ֛ם שְׂעִיר־עִזִּ֥ים אֶחָ֖ד לְחַטָּ֑את וּשְׁנֵ֣י

16. . . . Aside from the sevenfold effect which the Sabbath is intended to have during these seven weeks, the period of forty-nine and fifty days which passes and is completed within these seven Sabbaths must have a significance of its own. The counting of days—more specifically, of seven-day periods—is already known to us from such Scriptural laws as those concerning the man or woman who suffers from a [genital] discharge (Leviticus 15:13 and 28), and in general, we know the seven-day periods in the laws of uncleanness and purity as periods during which the individual strives to bring his uncleanness to a close so that, on the eighth day, he may enter into a state of purity.

Thus, a sevenfold counting of seven-day periods; that is, a counting of forty-nine days, in order to be able to enter into a new state on the fiftieth day, would symbolize the consummate elimination of uncleanness; i.e., of bondage to our senses, and the fiftieth day would mark our final entry into purity; i.e., into the realm of moral freedom. Even as the fiftieth year marked the re-establishment of the Jewish state on the basis of social freedom throughout the land, so the fiftieth day of the *omer* is to mark moral freedom as that attainment which is indispensable to political freedom and independence. It is essential for that climate in which, along with the freedom and independence granted to it by God, the nation will be capable of receiving from the

hands of God also His Law. We were able to obtain political freedom as a gift of God's grace without any effort on our part, but we can acquire moral freedom only through sevenfold intensive work upon ourselves.

If we consider, in light of the above, that the idea symbolized by the fiftieth day; i.e., the day immediately following the period of seven times seven days, closely resembles the concept represented by the eighth day of the *milah*. . . and if we juxtapose the counting of Sabbath weeks and the counting of days until the fiftieth day, we will perceive both the Sabbath weeks and the fiftieth day as emanations of the two institutions, the Sabbath and *milah*, with which God wished to lay the foundations for Israel as the people of the Law. The homage to God in nature and history, the resulting subordination of man and his place in the world to the service of God, as taught by the Sabbath, and the struggle for moral purity through the free-willed subordination of the flesh to God's moral law, as required by *milah*—these are the two historic factors which were implanted into the nation long before it was constituted as the people of the Law of God and which are to be brought to mind anew each year, through the counting of the days and weeks of the *omer* until the Day of the Receiving of the Law, as elementary prerequisites for our lofty mission.

•　•　•　•

and two yearling sheep as a meal-of-peace offering.   20. And the priest shall wave these together with the bread of the first fruits as a wave [offering] before *God*, together with two sheep. They shall be holy to *God*, and through Him [they shall belong] to the priest.   21. And you shall make a proclamation on that very day, it shall be to you a convocation to the Sanctuary; you must not do any service work; an everlasting statute in all your dwelling places for your descendants.   22. And when you reap the harvest of your land you shall not completely remove the corner of your field when you reap, and you shall not gather the gleanings of your harvest; you shall leave them for the poor man and for the stranger; I, *God*, your God.''   23. *God* spoke to Moshe [saying]:   24. "Speak to the sons of Yisrael [saying]: In the seventh month, on the first day of the month, there shall be for you cessation from work, a retrospection of *teruah*, a convocation to the Sanctuary.   25. You must not do any service work, and you shall bring near a fire offering to *God*."   26. *God* spoke to Moshe [saying]:   27. "Only on the tenth of this seventh month is the day of atonements; it shall be for you a convocation to the Sanctuary; and you shall starve your vital energies and you shall bring near a fire offering to *God*.   28. And you must not do any [creating] work on that day, for it is a day of atonements, to effect atonement for you before *God*, your God.   29. For any soul that is not made to starve on that same day shall be uprooted from among its people,   30. and any person that does any

כְּבָשִׂים בְּנֵי שָׁנָה לְזֶבַח שְׁלָמִים: כ וְהֵנִיף הַכֹּהֵן ׀ אֹתָם עַל לֶחֶם הַבִּכֻּרִים תְּנוּפָה לִפְנֵי יְהוָה עַל־שְׁנֵי כְּבָשִׂים קֹדֶשׁ יִהְיוּ לַיהוָה לַכֹּהֵן: כא וּקְרָאתֶם בְּעֶצֶם ׀ הַיּוֹם הַזֶּה מִקְרָא־קֹדֶשׁ יִהְיֶה לָכֶם כָּל־מְלֶאכֶת עֲבֹדָה לֹא תַעֲשׂוּ חֻקַּת עוֹלָם בְּכָל־מוֹשְׁבֹתֵיכֶם לְדֹרֹתֵיכֶם: כב וּבְקֻצְרְכֶם אֶת־קְצִיר אַרְצְכֶם לֹא־תְכַלֶּה פְּאַת שָׂדְךָ בְּקֻצְרֶךָ וְלֶקֶט קְצִירְךָ לֹא תְלַקֵּט לֶעָנִי וְלַגֵּר תַּעֲזֹב אֹתָם אֲנִי יְהוָה אֱלֹהֵיכֶם: פ

חמישי כג וַיְדַבֵּר יְהוָה אֶל־מֹשֶׁה לֵּאמֹר: כד דַּבֵּר אֶל־בְּנֵי יִשְׂרָאֵל לֵאמֹר בַּחֹדֶשׁ הַשְּׁבִיעִי בְּאֶחָד לַחֹדֶשׁ יִהְיֶה לָכֶם שַׁבָּתוֹן זִכְרוֹן תְּרוּעָה מִקְרָא־קֹדֶשׁ: כה כָּל־מְלֶאכֶת עֲבֹדָה לֹא תַעֲשׂוּ וְהִקְרַבְתֶּם אִשֶּׁה לַיהוָה: ס כו וַיְדַבֵּר יְהוָה אֶל־מֹשֶׁה לֵּאמֹר: כז אַךְ בֶּעָשׂוֹר לַחֹדֶשׁ הַשְּׁבִיעִי הַזֶּה יוֹם הַכִּפֻּרִים הוּא מִקְרָא־קֹדֶשׁ יִהְיֶה לָכֶם וְעִנִּיתֶם אֶת־נַפְשֹׁתֵיכֶם וְהִקְרַבְתֶּם אִשֶּׁה לַיהוָה: כח וְכָל־מְלָאכָה לֹא תַעֲשׂוּ בְּעֶצֶם הַיּוֹם הַזֶּה כִּי יוֹם כִּפֻּרִים הוּא לְכַפֵּר עֲלֵיכֶם לִפְנֵי יְהוָה אֱלֹהֵיכֶם: כט כִּי כָל־הַנֶּפֶשׁ אֲשֶׁר לֹא־תְעֻנֶּה בְּעֶצֶם הַיּוֹם הַזֶּה וְנִכְרְתָה מֵעַמֶּיהָ: ל וְכָל־

---

24. . . . In the annual cycle of our festivals, רֹאשׁ הַשָּׁנָה, the beginning of the year for our life on earth, is the day of self-examination on which we are summoned to review all the aspects of our lives on earth, to see how far they accord with our timeless mission as Jews, which was given to us on the first day of Nissan. We are to draw up a balance sheet, as it were, of what we are now as against the eternal standard of what we should be.

28. . . . On the first tenth day of Tishri in its history, Israel did not yet have the Temple and the offerings; nevertheless, that day enabled Israel to rise from the depths of depravity and to find its God and His forgiv-

ing grace again. So, too, Israel may be certain of atonement, and of the gift of atonement derived from that day, even while there is no Temple and there are no offerings. No other offering—no "vicarious sacrifice"—is needed for this purpose. All that was done in the Temple and upon the altar on Yom Kippur, and will be done again on that day in times to come, the entire Temple Service of the day, is merely a symbolic expression of what every Jew must do in actuality outside the Temple, within himself, and the tenth day of Tishri remains for Israel יוֹם כִּפּוּרִים: "It is a day of atonements, to effect atonement for you before *God*, your God."

manner of [creating] work on that same day, I shall cause that soul to be destroyed from the midst of its people. 31. You must not do any [creating] work; an everlasting statute for your descendants, in all your dwelling places. 32. It is for you a Sabbath to be observed by cessation from activity, and you shall starve your vital energies; on the ninth of the month, in the evening, from evening to evening, you shall observe your Sabbath." 33. *God* spoke to Moshe [saying]; 34. "Speak to the sons of Yisrael [saying]: On the fifteenth day of this seventh month is the Festival of Huts, seven days dedicated to God. 35. On the first day [shall be a] convocation to the Sanctuary; you must not do any service work. 36. Seven days you shall bring near a fire offering to *God*; on the eighth day there

הַנֶּפֶשׁ אֲשֶׁר תַּעֲשֶׂה כָּל־מְלָאכָה בְּעֶצֶם הַיּוֹם הַזֶּה וְהַאֲבַדְתִּי אֶת־הַנֶּפֶשׁ הַהִוא מִקֶּרֶב עַמָּהּ: לֹא כָּל־מְלָאכָה לֹא תַעֲשׂוּ חֻקַּת עוֹלָם לְדֹרֹתֵיכֶם בְּכֹל מֹשְׁבֹתֵיכֶם: לב שַׁבַּת שַׁבָּתוֹן הוּא לָכֶם וְעִנִּיתֶם אֶת־נַפְשֹׁתֵיכֶם בְּתִשְׁעָה לַחֹדֶשׁ בָּעֶרֶב מֵעֶרֶב עַד־עֶרֶב תִּשְׁבְּתוּ שַׁבַּתְּכֶם: פ ששי לג וַיְדַבֵּר יְהוָֹה אֶל־מֹשֶׁה לֵּאמֹר: לד דַּבֵּר אֶל־בְּנֵי יִשְׂרָאֵל לֵאמֹר בַּחֲמִשָּׁה עָשָׂר יוֹם לַחֹדֶשׁ הַשְּׁבִיעִי הַזֶּה חַג הַסֻּכּוֹת שִׁבְעַת יָמִים לַיהוָֹה: לה בַּיּוֹם הָרִאשׁוֹן מִקְרָא־קֹדֶשׁ כָּל־מְלֶאכֶת עֲבֹדָה לֹא תַעֲשׂוּ: לו שִׁבְעַת יָמִים תַּקְרִיבוּ אִשֶּׁה לַיהוָֹה בַּיּוֹם הַשְּׁמִינִי

---

36. עֲצֶרֶת הִיא [*a gathering up, for preservation*]. . . The word עצר is clearly related to אצר [collect, store up], אזר [gird up], אסר [bind], עשר [to gather up wealth], and עזר [aid], all of which denote a "holding together" and "concentration." . . . We believe we are therefore not in error if we interpret עֲצֶרֶת as a day which is not intended for the communication of new truths for us to accept and assimilate, but which has as its function to keep us before God's Presence for yet a while longer (this would be implicit also in the idea of עֲצִירָה מִמְּלָאכָה [withdrawal from the "creating" type of activity]) so that we may fix in our memories the perceptions we have already gained, to have them remain with us forever and not lose them amidst the vicissitudes of everyday life.

This idea would accord entirely with the purpose of the last day of a festival. For seven days we have saturated ourselves with all the truths that the fact of the Exodus from Egypt has granted and guaranteed to the consciousness of the Jew. The seventh day is עֲצֶרֶת, a gathering up of all the spiritual "treasures" we have collected during the festival in the presence of God, so that they may be preserved for us and that we may be truly enriched by them as we return to the everyday life which begins again at the end of the seventh day. The function of עֲצֶרֶת is accomplished if we allow all our spiritual gains from the festival to pass in review before us once again and firmly resolve not to permit the work and turmoil of life to rob us of what we have thus won.

Herein lies the twofold connotation of עצר: to "abide"[13] with God and to "hold fast" to the spiritual

acquisitions we have made in His presence. Basically, these connotations are one and the same. The function of עֲצֶרֶת is to preserve for us everything we have gained and thus also to preserve us for God. Now if the seventh day of Sukkoth were designated as עֲצֶרֶת, the task of recapitulating and preserving would apply only to the truths taught by the festival of Sukkoth. But in the case of Sukkoth, עֲצֶרֶת comes on the eighth day. It thus functions as a *mo'ed* in its own right, and so the idea of "abiding," "retaining" and "holding fast" before God appears here as a concept independent of Sukkoth: it is intended to conclude not only the festival series of the seventh month but also that of the entire Jewish calendar cycle. The purpose of שְׁמִינִי עֲצֶרֶת, then, would be to have us gather up all the perceptions and resolves brought to us by the *mo'adim* of the entire year, and to have us resolve to "abide" before God, and to "retain" and "hold fast" our new spiritual gains, impressing them so deeply upon our hearts that they will remain our inalienable possession throughout the year of everyday life to which we are about to return and that, thus enriched, we will "abide and remain with God" no matter what the coming year may hold in store for us.

Sifrei to Numbers 29:35, too, interprets עֲצֶרֶת as implying the task of "abiding and remaining with God," and links this idea with the law that, in general, any offering made in the Temple is subject to the requirement to "remain overnight"; i.e., that no one who brings an offering to the Temple may leave Jerusalem, the periphery of the Temple, immediately thereafter, as if the act of making the offering alone had been enough to accomplish the purpose for which the offering was ordained. Anyone who has entered the Sanctuary of God with his offering must remain in the vicinity of the Temple at least until the next morning so

---

[13]*Note to the English translation*: Accordingly, Hirsch renders עֲצֶרֶת in Numbers 29:35 as "a festival of abiding." [G.H.]

shall be for you [a] convocation to the Sanctuary and you shall bring near a fire offering to *God*; it shall be a gathering up, for preservation; you must not do any service work. 37. These are *God's* appointed times for meeting, which you shall proclaim as convocations to the Sanctuary, to bring near to *God* a fire offering, ascent offering and homage offering, meal offering and libation, each in accordance with its own day, 38. apart from the Sabbaths of *God,* and apart from your obligatory offerings and apart from all your vows and apart from all your free-will offerings which you have to give to *God.* 39. Only on the fifteenth day of the seventh month, when you gather in the produce of the land, you shall celebrate the festival of *God* for seven days; on the first day shall be a cessation from work and on the eighth day shall be a cessation from work. 40. And you shall take for yourselves on the first day the fruit of the tree of beauty, leaves of palm branches and

מִקְרָא־קֹ֫דֶשׁ יִהְיֶה לָכֶ֔ם וְהִקְרַבְתֶּ֥ם אִשֶּׁ֖ה לַיהֹוָ֑ה
עֲצֶ֣רֶת הִ֔וא כָּל־מְלֶ֥אכֶת עֲבֹדָ֖ה לֹ֥א תַעֲשֽׂוּ׃
לז אֵ֚לֶּה מוֹעֲדֵ֣י יְהֹוָ֔ה אֲשֶׁר־תִּקְרְא֥וּ אֹתָ֖ם
מִקְרָאֵ֣י קֹ֑דֶשׁ לְהַקְרִ֨יב אִשֶּׁ֜ה לַיהֹוָ֗ה עֹלָ֤ה וּמִנְחָה֙
זֶ֣בַח וּנְסָכִ֔ים דְּבַר־י֖וֹם בְּיוֹמֽוֹ׃ לח מִלְּבַ֖ד שַׁבְּתֹ֣ת
יְהֹוָ֑ה וּמִלְּבַ֣ד מַתְּנֽוֹתֵיכֶ֗ם וּמִלְּבַד֙ כָּל־נִדְרֵיכֶ֔ם
וּמִלְּבַד֙ כָּל־נִדְבֹֽתֵיכֶ֔ם אֲשֶׁ֥ר תִּתְּנ֖וּ לַיהֹוָֽה׃
לט אַ֡ךְ בַּחֲמִשָּׁה֩ עָשָׂ֨ר י֜וֹם לַחֹ֣דֶשׁ הַשְּׁבִיעִ֗י
בְּאָסְפְּכֶם֙ אֶת־תְּבוּאַ֣ת הָאָ֔רֶץ תָּחֹ֥גּוּ אֶת־חַג־
יְהֹוָ֖ה שִׁבְעַ֣ת יָמִ֑ים בַּיּ֤וֹם הָֽרִאשׁוֹן֙ שַׁבָּת֔וֹן וּבַיּ֥וֹם
הַשְּׁמִינִ֖י שַׁבָּתֽוֹן׃ מ וּלְקַחְתֶּ֨ם לָכֶ֜ם בַּיּ֣וֹם
הָרִאשׁ֗וֹן פְּרִ֨י עֵ֤ץ הָדָר֙ כַּפֹּ֣ת תְּמָרִ֔ים וַעֲנַ֥ף

---

that he may gather up his impressions of the Sanctuary to retain and to take home with him (see commentary on Deuteronomy 16:7). But in the case of this particular *mo'ed*, the act of עֲצִירָה [retention], which as a rule entails only an overnight stay, becomes a *mo'ed* in its own right, an עֲצֶרֶת, a special festival of "abiding" [with God].

40. And you shall take for yourselves on the first day. The tenth day of Tishri, with its demand "and you shall starve [וְעִנִּיתֶם] your vital energies, found us עֲנִיִּים, poor, indeed the most deprived of all, having acknowledged to ourselves before God that we had forfeited our right to the nourishment required for our existence and survival. This realization and our acknowledgement of it before God brought us כַּפָּרָה; it "covered over," as it were, all the things from our past that had deprived us of our right to a future, and now we have been called to a new existence, to renewed survival as members of the eternal nation around God.

Now, seven days are dedicated to the awareness of our renewed right to survival, the antithesis of excision and destruction from the midst of one's people. On the first of these seven days, that same God Who on the tenth day of Tishri had commanded us: "And you shall starve your vital energies," tells us, "Take for yourselves. . . ." With these words, He informs us that He has conferred upon us once again the right, indeed the duty, to stretch forth our hands to grasp the good things of His earth, to attain thereby, in contrast to the fate of "starvation of vital energies" represented by יוֹם כִּפּוּר,

the most precious treasure of earthly existence— indeed, as far as we know, of all existence: "rejoicing in the presence of God": "And you shall take for yourselves . . . and rejoice before *God,* your God. . .'"

The seven-day period of national rejoicing with the gifts of God in the Sanctuary of the Law presupposes that each and every one within the nation's borders has partaken of nature's bounty on the first day of the festival. The nation as an entity cannot rejoice before God in its prosperity before His Law unless everyone, everywhere, has an opportunity to achieve economic independence by honest means—not by theft and not by borrowing the property of another. The invitation וּלְקַחְתֶּם לָכֶם ["and you shall take for yourselves. . ."], addressed on the very first day to each and everyone within the nation's borders, must precede the command, "and rejoice before *God,* your God, for seven days."

But true, genuine joy of living, undisturbed and unperturbable, no matter how brilliant and splendid, is not to be sought in the upbuilding and development of the individual personality. Only if the individual, with all his personal life and aspirations, will give himself completely to the common task of the national entity, to translate the Law of God into reality; only if, with all his personal life and strivings, whatever his social position, he will seek to be nothing but a building block in the one great edifice whose blueprint is the Law and whose Architect is God—only then, whether he is subservient like the willow, lustrous like the myrtle, serene

עֵץ־עָבֹת וְעַרְבֵי־נָחַל וּשְׂמַחְתֶּם לִפְנֵי יְהוָה
אֱלֹהֵיכֶם שִׁבְעַת יָמִים: מא וְחַגֹּתֶם אֹתוֹ חַג
לַיהוָה שִׁבְעַת יָמִים בַּשָּׁנָה חֻקַּת עוֹלָם
לְדֹרֹתֵיכֶם בַּחֹדֶשׁ הַשְּׁבִיעִי תָּחֹגּוּ אֹתוֹ:
מב בַּסֻּכֹּת תֵּשְׁבוּ שִׁבְעַת יָמִים כָּל־הָאֶזְרָח
בְּיִשְׂרָאֵל יֵשְׁבוּ בַּסֻּכֹּת: מג לְמַעַן יֵדְעוּ דֹרֹתֵיכֶם
כִּי בַסֻּכּוֹת הוֹשַׁבְתִּי אֶת־בְּנֵי יִשְׂרָאֵל בְּהוֹצִיאִי

myrtle branch[es] and willows of the brook, and rejoice before *God*, your God, for seven days. 41. You shall celebrate it as a festival of *God* seven days in the year, an everlasting statute for your descendants; in the seventh month shall you celebrate it. 42. You shall dwell in the huts for seven days; all who are native-born in Yisrael shall dwell in the huts. 43. So that your descendants may know that I made the sons of Yisrael dwell in the huts when I brought

and quietly fruitful like the palm tree, or crowned with fame and accomplishments like the "fruit of beauty," will he attain the gift of complete, lasting and perpetual rejoicing before God. . . .

° ° °

43. . . . The purpose of their experience in the wilderness was to free the Children of Israel from overrating and worshipping the human skills and ingenuity used in "bread getting." The message to be conveyed by the *sukkah* to us and to future generations is the story of a wilderness filled with God's providence and loving care, a "wilderness made habitable by God's care and providence," of Israel's "happy, contented sojourn in the shelter of the wilderness." הַסֻּכּוֹת [the huts], which are recalled by our own *sukkoth*, may be interpreted, as various authorities suggest (Sukkah 11b), as עֲנָנֵי כָבוֹד [the "clouds of glory"], the clouds that heralded God's presence and beneath whose protecting cover God sheltered our ancestors in the wilderness, or they may be construed as huts in the literal sense, built by our ancestors themselves in the wilderness. But in either interpretation our *sukkoth* should recall to us the sojourn of our ancestors in the wilderness and all the lessons this historical experience should teach us.

The term "wilderness" implies the absence of all the supports usually provided by nature and human ingenuity for man's survival. One who enters a wilderness has moved beyond the reach of the protection afforded by nature and human power, and he can survive only with the aid of God. The legal requirement for the סְכָךְ, the covering for our *sukkoth*, is that it must be entirely cut off from nature and untouched by such human skills as would ordinarily mark the produce of the earth, which acts as our caring, nurturing mother. The material must be made of products of the soil, but it must not be "attached" to the soil (so that whoever seeks shelter beneath it would thereby entrust himself to the protective strength of terrestrial nature), nor may it be made from materials susceptible to ritual uncleanness, materials such as fruits and vessels which already bear the imprint of human dominion. Thus the coverings of our *sukkah* must either have the characteristics of עֲנָנֵי כָבוֹד, ["the clouds of glory"], in that the latter, too, had their origin in the ground (אֵד יַעֲלֶה מִן הָאָרֶץ ["vapor rose continually from the earth"—Gen. 2:6]) but they were marked neither by the power of the soil nor by the strength of man, or else they must literally recall the huts of the wilderness; i.e., bringing to mind the wilderness, in that they have support neither from nature nor from man. The coverings must not be products of the threshing floor or of the wine press which normally give man "nourishment and pleasure," but must be "the refuse of the threshing floor or of the wine press," refuse that is usually discarded because it has no food value and does not afford pleasure (Sukkah 11b and 12a). They are improvisations; they do not represent normal conditions but bear the imprint of an improvised dwelling, of a temporary situation.

God did not wish us to walk in His laws in order to give us the precarious existence of wanderers in the wilderness, devoid of all pleasure, art and beauty. God's intention was "to bring us into a good land, a land of streams of water, where springs and billows gush from hills and flatlands, into a land yielding wheat and barley, wine and figs and pomegranates, olives and dates, a land where one can eat bread without stinting himself, where nothing is lacking, where the rocks yield iron and the mountains copper." But lest we "eat and be satisfied, build beautiful houses and live in them, multiply sheep and cattle, silver and gold, and all our possessions, and then become arrogant and forget God, and say in our hearts: 'It is my strength and the power of my hands that have gotten me all this wealth,'" we must, once each year, precisely during the harvest season, go back in time to the complete antithesis of our present lives: to the life we led in the wilderness, where there are no gushing springs, no ripening fields, no verdant trees; where there is no harvest to gather in, no splendid buildings and no trade or commerce to multiply silver and gold, but where, nevertheless, we lived for forty years with our wives and children, without a care, lacking for nothing because we lived under God's protection and by His Word.

By leaving our permanent dwelling place, our fine homes, and sojourning happily beneath the thatch that them out from the land of Mitzrayim; I, *God,* your God."   44. Moshe proclaimed *God's* appointed times for meeting to the sons of Yisrael.

XXIV

1. *God* spoke to Moshe [saying]:   2. "Command the sons of Yisrael that they take for you pure olive oil, pressed, for light, to make light spring up continually.   3. Aharon shall set it out before *God* continually from evening to morning outside the dividing curtain of the Testimony in the Tent of Appointed Meeting; an everlasting statute for your generations.   4. He shall set out the lamps upon the pure menorah, before *God,* continually.   5. And you shall take fine wheat flour and bake it into twelve loaves. Each loaf shall be of two tenths. 6. And you shall set them up in two stacks, six in each stack, upon the pure Table, before *God.*   7. And you shall add to each stack pure frankincense; this shall be the memorial portion for the bread, a fire offering to *God.*   8. He shall set it out Sabbath by Sabbath, continually, before

אוֹתָם מֵאֶרֶץ מִצְרַיִם אֲנִי יְהֹוָה אֱלֹהֵיכֶם: מד וַיְדַבֵּר מֹשֶׁה אֶת־מֹעֲדֵי יְהֹוָה אֶל־בְּנֵי יִשְׂרָאֵל: פ שביעי כד א וַיְדַבֵּר יְהֹוָה אֶל־מֹשֶׁה לֵּאמֹר: ב צַו אֶת־בְּנֵי יִשְׂרָאֵל וְיִקְחוּ אֵלֶיךָ שֶׁמֶן זַיִת זָךְ כָּתִית לַמָּאוֹר לְהַעֲלֹת נֵר תָּמִיד: ג מִחוּץ לְפָרֹכֶת הָעֵדֻת בְּאֹהֶל מוֹעֵד יַעֲרֹךְ אֹתוֹ אַהֲרֹן מֵעֶרֶב עַד־בֹּקֶר לִפְנֵי יְהֹוָה תָּמִיד חֻקַּת עוֹלָם לְדֹרֹתֵיכֶם: ד עַל הַמְּנֹרָה הַטְּהֹרָה יַעֲרֹךְ אֶת־הַנֵּרוֹת לִפְנֵי יְהֹוָה תָּמִיד: פ ה וְלָקַחְתָּ סֹלֶת וְאָפִיתָ אֹתָהּ שְׁתֵּים עֶשְׂרֵה חַלּוֹת שְׁנֵי עֶשְׂרֹנִים יִהְיֶה הַחַלָּה הָאֶחָת: ו וְשַׂמְתָּ אוֹתָם שְׁתַּיִם מַעֲרָכוֹת שֵׁשׁ הַמַּעֲרָכֶת עַל הַשֻּׁלְחָן הַטָּהֹר לִפְנֵי יְהֹוָה: ז וְנָתַתָּ עַל־הַמַּעֲרֶכֶת לְבֹנָה זַכָּה וְהָיְתָה לַלֶּחֶם לְאַזְכָּרָה אִשֶּׁה לַיהֹוָה: ח בְּיוֹם הַשַּׁבָּת בְּיוֹם הַשַּׁבָּת יַעַרְכֶנּוּ לִפְנֵי יְהֹוָה

covers our *sukkah,* without support from the powers of man and nature, we are to throw off our slavish dependence on the protectio.. afforded by nature and human ingenuity, and to repeat anew each year to ourselves and to our children the ancient lesson that our forty years in the wilderness have taught us for all time to come: The Jew, the genuine Jew, "all who are native-born in Israel," every individual who is rooted with mind and heart in the nation of Israel, "shall dwell in the huts", they must be prepared at any time, if need be, to forego the shelter and defense afforded by the powers of man and nature and, if God so wills it, move even into the wilderness without fear and trepidation, dwelling in the shelter of the wilderness "as happily and free from care as one would in a house in the city," trusting in God's care and protection even there. "It is not by bread alone that man can make a life for himself, but that man can live by everything that comes from the mouth of *God"* [Deuteronomy 8:3]. Human life is sustained not by "bread" alone, by the product and symbol of nature wed to human ingenuity. Each utterance of the will of God, each Divinely-appointed institution is capable of keeping man alive. Even normal urban life, with all the amenities afforded by its combinations of natural forces and human ingenuity for the protection and defense of human survival, can sustain and nourish us only as long

as this is permitted and desired by the will of God (Cf. Exodus, Chapter 16).

o   o   o

CHAPTER XXIV

8. *Sabbath by Sabbath.* The Sabbath is the day on which every Jew, by ceasing from all "creating" activity, from all work designed to wrest a livelihood and prosperity from nature and society, places himself, his world and his striving after sustenance at the feet of God, the Creator and Master of the world. On that day, the Jewish community, through its representative, the priest, places its "bread" and its "incense" upon the Table in the Sanctuary of God's Law, to "express before God at all times" the idea that although—as the Sabbath teaches us—God, as the Creator and Master of the whole world, is the Master and Father of all mankind, the fate of Israel is the special object of His providence, which for Israel has taken the form of a unique, everlasting covenant. It is in this everlasting covenant that the institution of the "show bread" and its place at the conclusion of the laws relating to the *mo'adim* culminates.

The truths for which the foundations were first laid with the Exodus from Egypt, the Giving of the Law and the atonement following the incident of the Golden

תָּמִ֑יד מֵאֵ֥ת בְּנֵֽי־יִשְׂרָאֵ֖ל בְּרִ֥ית עוֹלָֽם: ט וְהָֽיְתָה֙
לְאַהֲרֹ֣ן וּלְבָנָ֔יו וַאֲכָלֻ֖הוּ בְּמָק֣וֹם קָדֹ֑שׁ כִּ֡י קֹ֩דֶשׁ֩
קָֽדָשִׁ֨ים ה֥וּא ל֛וֹ מֵאִשֵּׁ֥י יְהוָֹ֖ה חָק־עוֹלָֽם: ס
י וַיֵּצֵא֙ בֶּן־אִשָּׁ֣ה יִשְׂרְאֵלִ֔ית וְהוּא֙ בֶּן־אִ֣ישׁ
מִצְרִ֔י בְּת֖וֹךְ בְּנֵ֣י יִשְׂרָאֵ֑ל וַיִּנָּצוּ֙ בַּֽמַּחֲנֶ֔ה בֶּ֚ן
הַיִּשְׂרְאֵלִ֔ית וְאִ֖ישׁ הַיִּשְׂרְאֵלִֽי: יא וַ֠יִּקֹּב בֶּן־
הָֽאִשָּׁ֨ה הַיִּשְׂרְאֵלִ֤ית אֶת־הַשֵּׁם֙ וַיְקַלֵּ֔ל וַיָּבִ֥יאוּ

God; for the sons of Yisrael as an everlasting covenant.
9. But it shall be for Aharon and his sons, and they shall eat it in a holy place, for as a holy of holies is it [given] to him from the fire offerings of *God* as an everlasting due."
10. And the son of a Yisraelite woman—however, he was the son of a Mitzrite man—went out into the midst of the sons of Yisrael, and the son of the Yisraelite woman and a man who was a Yisraelite got into a quarrel in the camp.
11. The son of the Yisraelite woman pronounced the Name of God in full and blasphemed, and they brought him to.

Calf and the miraculous survival of the Children of Israel in the wilderness as symbolized by the *sukkah*—truths revived in the nation's memory again and again each year through the *mo'adim*, are nothing but the basic factors in the eternal covenant that God made with Israel through His acts. This covenant is manifest at all times in the care and guidance which God devotes to Israel's destinies. Israel, in turn, acknowledges this covenantal providence and symbolically demonstrates what should be its attitude toward the covenant: a complete subordination of its destinies to God's care and guidance. This symbolic demonstration is effected with the bread that is to be placed before God at all times by the sons of Israel. This bread is called "show bread," but lit., "bread of the Countenance"; it is the bread toward which God turns His Countenance, as it were, with particular attention. It is the bread symbolizing God's unique providence and sovereignty. Tradition teaches that even as the ever-watchful care extended by God to the [spiritual] "light of Israel" was demonstrated also physically by the fact that the light of the westernmost lamp on the menorah never went out, so, too, the fact that the show bread remained fresh all week long was a physical sign of the care that God constantly lavishes upon Israel's material welfare. "A great miracle was performed with the show bread, for when it was removed it was as (fresh as it had been when) it was set out" (Menaḥoth 29a).

10. ***And the son . . . went out into the midst of the sons of Yisrael.*** He stepped out of the bounds within which he belonged, and went out into the midst of the Children of Israel, where he did not belong. . . . According to *Torath Kohanim*, "in the camp" means that he injected himself into the affairs of the camp and that this was the cause of the quarrel. The trouble arose not from a claim on his part that he was a Jew [which would have been legitimate] but from his claim that he had a place "in the camp" of the nation. This claim was not justifiable under the Law because membership in a tribe was determined by family ties, which in turn were determined by paternal descent. Cf. "each man . . . next to his standard, each designated with the insignia of their fathers' houses" (Numbers 2:2). This particular man claimed the right, on the basis of his maternal descent, to camp with the tribe of Dan. But even though he himself was a Jew by birth (or could have become a Jew by converting to Judaism), he could not be counted as a member of this tribe because his father was a non-Jew. Therefore his opponent's objections were fully justified. . . .

This is a concrete example of the effect of "moral purity" on an individual's legal and social status under Jewish Law. The significance of these two principles in the life of the Jewish nation is symbolically represented by the Table to which the preceding verses made reference.

11. ***The name of his mother.*** At that time she was the only woman in Israel to commit such a sin; that is why she achieved the sad distinction of having her name recorded on a page of God's eternal Scripture. However, her name is mentioned only after the reference to her son's crime, for this crime showed the sad consequences of her own moral transgression. Without her sin, such an explosion of un-Jewish depravity could never have occurred among the people of Israel. Only her transgression with the non-Jewish man could have planted the seed for so great a crime in Israel's midst. Amidst the horror evoked by the son's crime it became clear that the original guilt lay with his mother, Shelomith. . . . It seems that the son of the Mitzrite man blasphemed the God of Israel because that God had founded His nation and its laws upon ideals of moral purity which were utterly incompatible

Moshe. The name of his mother was
Shelomith, daughter of Divri, of the tribe of
Dan.   12. They placed him into custody
so that they might receive an explanation
according to the utterance of *God*.
13. And *God* spoke to Moshe [saying]:
14. "Take the blasphemer out of the
camp, and let all those who heard it lean
their hands upon his head and let the whole
community stone him to death.   15. And
you shall speak to the sons of Yisrael [say-
ing]: Anyone, *anyone* who blasphemes his
God must bear his sin.   16. And one who
[in blaspheming] pronounces the Name
'God' in full shall be put to death; the whole
community must pelt him with stones to
stone him to death; one who has entered
from abroad as well as the native-born; if he
[in blaspheming] pronounces the Name of
God in full, he shall be put to death.
17. And if one strikes down a human
being, he shall be put to death.   18. But
one who strikes down an animal creature
must make compensation for it, a creature
as compensation for a creature.   19. And
if one inflicts an injury upon his neighbor,
then as he has done, so shall be done to him.

אֹתוֹ אֶל־מֹשֶׁה וְשֵׁם אִמּוֹ שְׁלֹמִית בַּת־דִּבְרִי
לְמַטֵּה־דָן: יב וַיַּנִּיחֻהוּ בַּמִּשְׁמָר לִפְרֹשׁ לָהֶם
עַל־פִּי יְהֹוָה: פ יג וַיְדַבֵּר יְהֹוָה אֶל־מֹשֶׁה
לֵּאמֹר: יד הוֹצֵא אֶת־הַמְקַלֵּל אֶל־מִחוּץ
לַמַּחֲנֶה וְסָמְכוּ כָל־הַשֹּׁמְעִים אֶת־יְדֵיהֶם עַל־
רֹאשׁוֹ וְרָגְמוּ אֹתוֹ כָּל־הָעֵדָה: טו וְאֶל־בְּנֵי
יִשְׂרָאֵל תְּדַבֵּר לֵאמֹר אִישׁ אִישׁ כִּי־יְקַלֵּל
אֱלֹהָיו וְנָשָׂא חֶטְאוֹ: טז וְנֹקֵב שֵׁם־יְהֹוָה מוֹת
יוּמָת רָגוֹם יִרְגְּמוּ־בוֹ כָּל־הָעֵדָה כַּגֵּר כָּאֶזְרָח
בְּנָקְבוֹ־שֵׁם יוּמָת: יז וְאִישׁ כִּי יַכֶּה כָּל־נֶפֶשׁ
אָדָם מוֹת יוּמָת: יח וּמַכֵּה נֶפֶשׁ־בְּהֵמָה
יְשַׁלְּמֶנָּה נֶפֶשׁ תַּחַת נָפֶשׁ: יט וְאִישׁ כִּי־יִתֵּן מוּם
בַּעֲמִיתוֹ כַּאֲשֶׁר עָשָׂה כֵּן יֵעָשֶׂה לּוֹ: כ שֶׁבֶר

with the corruptness of his own Egyptian origin and
which he perceived as obstacles to the fulfillment of his
desire.

    14. *Take the blasphemer out.* According to Sanhed-
rin 42b, the execution site had to be located "outside
the three camps," outside the "camp of Israel"; i.e.,
beyond the city limits. Even as the seat of the court of
law itself was beyond the city limits, the execution site
had to be outside the court area, indeed, some distance
away from the seat of the court, "so that the court
should not appear to be murderously inclined";
i.e., so it should not appear as if the court considered
the executioner's sword as its most important attribute.

    As was clearly demonstrated in [our] essay on the role
of evidence in Jewish criminal law (*Jeschurun*, Vol. 12,
p. 143 ff), the basic function of the court of law was not
to hand down death sentences but to find legitimate
reasons for acquitting the accused. The mere fact that
the accusing witnesses appeared at the court and gave
their testimony implied a proposed verdict of "guilty."
It was then the task of the court to examine the evidence and, if possible, to find extenuating circumstances in favor of the accused. Another reason given
(ibid.) for having the execution site some distance away

from the courthouse was "so that there might be a
possibility for deliverance"; so that, due to the distance
between the two places, enough time could elapse
between the pronouncement of the sentence and its
execution (according to the letter of the law, the execution had to take place immediately after the sentenc-
ing) to find some new evidence that could invalidate
the death sentence. As the condemned man was led out
of the courthouse on the way to the execution site, a
man stood at the gate of the courthouse with a signal
flag in his hand, and a mounted messenger was waiting
within sight of this man. If one of the judges believed
he had found new evidence in favor of the accused, that
man would wave his flag and the mounted messenger
would gallop off to the execution site to stop the proceedings. Indeed, even if the accused himself, on the
way to the execution site, declared that he had additional evidence in his own defense, he had to be taken
back to the courthouse, once, or twice, or even four or
five times, "providing that there is substance to his
assertions"; i.e., if, in the opinion of the two legal
experts who had to escort him to the execution site
(precisely for this eventuality), there was some basis, no
matter how tenuous, for his assertion that he was innocent (ibid. 42b and 43a).

20. Compensation of a fracture for a fracture, compensation of an eye for an eye, compensation of a tooth for a tooth, even as he inflicts an injury upon a man, so it shall be given by him. 21. One who strikes

תַּחַת שֶׁבֶר ֽעַיִן תַּחַת עַיִן שֵׁן תַּחַת שֵׁן כַּאֲשֶׁר יִתֵּן מוּם בָּאָדָם כֵּן יִנָּתֶן בּוֹ: מפטיר כא וּמַכֵּה

21. . . . In our notes to Exodus 21:23 we have already explained in detail the legal principle of תנא דבי חזקיה[14] and its applications, and have noted how the Jewish concept of justice upholds the matchless dignity of a human life. Jewish Law makes a sharp distinction between the value of a human life and that of an animal. Let us review the personal and property laws given here. It is clear that they, too, derive from this legal axiom, which differentiates between an animal and a human being. A distinction is made between נֶפֶשׁ אָדָם [lit., "a human soul"] and נֶפֶשׁ בְּהֵמָה ["an animal creature"; lit., "an animal soul"]. The Law regards נֶפֶשׁ אָדָם as a *person* and נֶפֶשׁ בְּהֵמָה as a *thing*. The slaying of a נֶפֶשׁ אָדָם can be treated only as a crime against the person of the victim. The unique dignity inherent in a human being is an object for which there can be no monetary compensation. The only possible restitution for such an offense against the grandeur of human life is to deprive the murderer of his own existence on earth. The slaying of נֶפֶשׁ בְּהֵמָה [an animal], on the other hand, is regarded under the Law only as a crime against its owner. Although "pity for all living things" is considered a Biblical commandment . . . so that the slaying of an animal is regarded as a sin against God, one who slays an ownerless animal is not subject to trial and punishment by judges on earth. With regard to an injury inflicted on a part or organ of the human body, the law views these parts as "possessions" and "tools" of the נֶפֶשׁ אָדָם. Accordingly, an injury inflicted on the body of a human being is considered a crime not only against the *person* of the victim but also against his *property*. Where it is possible to make adequate monetary compensation and the physical damage is insignificant, the law emphasizes the crime against the victim's person and imposes the sentence of lashes.

All these principles and their underlying legal concepts have already been set forth in the *mishpatim*, the basic outline of Jewish social and civil law, which is likewise founded on the dignity of the human personality. In the presentation, however, they are linked with one legal concept that is placed above them all, so that they must be interpreted as logical outgrowths of the truth acknowledged by this one concept. As a result, that truth emerges as the concept basic to all law and justice and as the indispensable prerequisite for the human personality on which all human rights are dependent.

This primary concept of all law, that indispensable foundation for all human rights, is nothing less than the concept of a personal God.

Remove the personal God from this world and you have also banished justice from the world and reduced the concept of right and wrong to mere fiction. The claims of justice can be satisfied only by free will. Therefore, one who denies the existence of free will must not speak to us of law and justice. If he is not to be guilty of sham and delusion, he can speak only in terms of power, of the impact of physical, mechanical or organic forces. The concept of law and justice, right and wrong, simply does not exist for him. But if the world, and hence also man, does not have a free-willed Creator, Who has endowed man, the noblest of His creatures on earth, with spirit from His spirit, thus giving him a portion of His own freedom of will, and if there is no free-willed supernatural Creator of the Universe, so that man is nothing but a physical product of a physical world fettered by the physical laws of nature—then from where should that physical product of a physical world obtain moral freedom? If God is not free, if God does not have complete and absolute freedom of will, how could man have freedom of will, and how could one, then, think in terms of right and wrong?

Furthermore, just as the concept of right and wrong, and its corollary of moral freedom, too, is inconceivable without a free-willed God, so, too, the concept of a personal God is indispensable to the concept of the human personality. For a "personality" is nothing else than a being capable of making his own choices in matters of right and wrong; it is moral freedom embodied in the person of an individual. But if such an individual personality is not inherent to an absolute degree in God Himself; if there is no personal, supernatural Creator of the Universe Who has endowed man, His noblest creature on earth, with spirit from His spirit and said to him: "Be free! Make your own choices!"; if nothing exists but this material world, and if man, too, is merely one of the many products of that material world, then man, too, is merely a "thing," and if the world consists only of "things," then there can be no freedom and no free-willed personality. The differences between the "things" in this world are then only quantitative, not qualitative, and all things in this world are only playthings and products of impersonal forces bound by the laws of nature. In that case the

[14]*Note to the English translation*: This section of Hirsch's commentary is not included in this excerpted edition. [G.H.]

בְהֵמָ֖ה יְשַׁלְּמֶ֑נָּה וּמַכֵּ֥ה אָדָ֖ם יוּמָֽת׃ כב מִשְׁפַּ֤ט
אֶחָד֙ יִהְיֶ֣ה לָכֶ֔ם כַּגֵּ֥ר כָּאֶזְרָ֖ח יִהְיֶ֑ה כִּ֛י אֲנִ֥י יְהוָ֖ה
אֱלֹהֵיכֶֽם׃ כג וַיְדַבֵּ֣ר מֹשֶׁה֮ אֶל־בְּנֵ֣י יִשְׂרָאֵל֒
וַיּוֹצִ֣יאוּ אֶת־הַֽמְקַלֵּ֗ל אֶל־מִחוּץ֙ לַֽמַּחֲנֶ֔ה וַיִּרְגְּמ֥וּ
אֹת֖וֹ אָ֑בֶן וּבְנֵֽי־יִשְׂרָאֵ֣ל עָשׂ֔וּ כַּאֲשֶׁ֛ר צִוָּ֥ה יְהוָ֖ה
אֶת־מֹשֶֽׁה׃ פ

down an animal must pay for it, and one who strikes down a man shall be put to death. 22. You shall have one [standard of] right for him who has entered from abroad and for the native-born, for I, *God*, am your God." 23. Moshe spoke to the sons of Yisrael, and they took the blasphemer out of the camp and stoned him to death; the sons of Yisrael did as *God* had commanded Moshe.

plant is merely a more sophisticated crystalline form, the animal merely a more sophisticated form of plant life, and man only a more sophisticated species of animal. In such a world of "things" there could be no differences in kind; man would have no unique dignity, and there would be no such thing as a human "personality."

Hence, even as the very first legal axiom in the Pentateuch (Genesis 9:5, 6) bases the unique personal dignity of human life (as against the life of animals) on the concept of man created in the image of God, so, here, the list of crimes against the human personality is prefaced by the account of a sin against the Personality of God, namely, pronouncing the Name of God in a blasphemous manner. Thus, God introduces Himself into the Law He gave to men on earth, setting up His own Personality as the foundation for all law and for the legal concept of the personality of man. For this reason only one guilty of having pronounced the Tetragrammaton is subject to the death penalty, because only this Name is a descriptive expression of the Personality of God.

22. Even as the Personality of God is the basis for all law and all human dignity, so, too, it is the foundation for complete equality in law and justice. "One [standard of] right," etc. One and the same standard shall be applicable to all the procedures by which justice is administered. There shall be an equal standard for all in such matters as qualifications for witnesses (the testimony of close relatives is unacceptable) and establishing the veracity of witnesses, no matter whether the case involves persons or property (Sanhedrin 28a and 32a). In other words, equal rights "for him who has entered from abroad and for the native-born," for He Who declared, "I am *God*" is the God of them all.

The Haftarah for this Sidra may be found on page 883.

בהר

BEHAR

XXV 1. *God* spoke to Moshe on Mount Sinai [saying]: 2. Speak to the sons of Yisrael and say to them: When you come into the land which I give you, the land shall observe a Sabbath to *God*. 3. Six years you shall sow your field and six years you shall prune your vineyard

כה א וַיְדַבֵּר יְהוָה אֶל־מֹשֶׁה בְּהַר סִינַי לֵאמֹר׃
ב דַּבֵּר אֶל־בְּנֵי יִשְׂרָאֵל וְאָמַרְתָּ אֲלֵהֶם כִּי
תָבֹאוּ אֶל־הָאָרֶץ אֲשֶׁר אֲנִי נֹתֵן לָכֶם וְשָׁבְתָה
הָאָרֶץ שַׁבָּת לַיהוָה׃ ג שֵׁשׁ שָׁנִים תִּזְרַע שָׂדֶךָ
וְשֵׁשׁ שָׁנִים תִּזְמֹר כַּרְמֶךָ וְאָסַפְתָּ אֶת־תְּבוּאָתָהּ׃

CHAPTER XXV

1. The concluding verses of the preceding chapter placed God (the source of all justice) and the Personality of God (the foundation for all the laws governing the rights of men and pertaining to the things men mark out as their property) at the head of the laws of personal and property rights. The present chapter deals with the narrower sphere of Jewish agrarian law. Here, God is proclaimed as the one rightful Lord and Owner of the land of the Jews, of the Jewish person and of Jewish property, and this one legal premise becomes the basis for a detailed code of agrarian, personal and property laws. שְׁבִיעִית [the Sabbatical year], יוֹבֵל [the Jubilee year], the institution of גְּאוּלָּה [lit., "redemption"], relating to the purchase of land, houses and servants, and the law relating to רִבִּית [interest] are simply logical outgrowths of the premise that these things belong to God and that God has the sole legitimate claim to them all.

These laws are introduced by the statement "*God* spoke to Moshe on Mount Sinai . . .," to which *Torath Kohanim* gives the following explanation: Why does Scripture make a point of telling us that the laws of the Sabbatical year were given to us on Mount Sinai? Were not all the other laws, too, given there? It is only to teach us that, even as the laws relating to the Sabbatical year were revealed on Mount Sinai complete with their explanations, so all the other laws, too, were revealed on Mount Sinai not only in their basic text but with all their detailed explanations. We believe that this emphasis on the Sinaitic origin not only of the laws but also of their relevant details, and the fact that this remark is made in connection with the laws of the Sabbatical year, may be directly linked to the case of the blasphemer of God's Name described in the preceding chapter. For that incident involved a law which had been given on Mount Sinai only in general outlines; the generalizations and details for its implementation were so obviously lacking that when it first became necessary to invoke this law in practice, inquiry had to be made of God concerning the procedure to be followed: "They placed him into custody so that they might receive an explanation according to the utterance of *God*" (Leviticus 24:12). What a law! And what a Subject, particularly when compared with the legislation of the Sabbatical year and with the subject to which that legislation applies! The transgression described in Chapter 24 is the grossest crime conceivable, and the Subject of the crime is indeed the only One completely independent of time and space, present everywhere and at all times, so that He can be sinned against at any time and in any place. One might therefore ask: If even a law such as this one concerning blasphemy was set forth on Mount Sinai only in such vague terms that its details had to be ascertained from God when the necessity for its implementation first arose, why should one expect that such laws as those concerning the Sabbatical year should have been set forth on Mount Sinai with all their generalizations and details? After all, at the time when the Law was first given, and indeed for many years thereafter, the laws of the Sabbatical year could not even be applied to their intended object, the land of the Jews. Later, too, the object of these laws [the land] would not be available for hundreds, perhaps even thousands of years.

It would seem that the Law here gives us the answer to this question. It does so by stressing, precisely in connection with the laws regarding the Sabbatical and Jubilee years immediately following the account of the sinful "invocation of God's Name," that although, in the case of the blasphemer, detailed instructions for the implementation of the law had to be sought from God when they were needed, the details of all the other laws, including those applicable only to specified times and places, such as those of the Sabbatical year, etc., had indeed been communicated to Moses already on Mount Sinai. . . .

2. ***the land shall observe a Sabbath to* God.** What שַׁבַּת בְּרֵאשִׁית, the seventh day of Creation, is to the earth, the seventh year shall be to the land. The former is a day of homage to God as the Creator and Master of the world; the latter, a year of homage to God as the Owner and Master of the land. . . .

and gather in its produce, 4. but in the seventh year there shall be a Sabbath observed by cessation from work for the land, a Sabbath to *God*; you shall not sow your field nor prune your vineyard. 5. You shall not harvest the aftergrowth of your harvest and not gather in the grapes from a vine left untended; there shall be a year of cessation from work for the land. 6. But the Sabbath [produce] of the land shall be permitted for you as food, for yourself and for your servant and for your handmaid, also for your hired worker and your tenant who sojourn with you. 7. And for your cattle, as well as for your animal[s] that are in your land shall all its produce be for food. 8. And you shall count for yourself seven Sabbath years, seven times seven years, and the days of the seven Sabbath years shall be for you forty-nine years. 9. Then you shall have the *teruah* of the *shofar* go forth in the seventh month, on the tenth of the month; on the Day of Atonements you shall have *shofar* sounds go forth throughout your land. 10. And you shall sanctify the fiftieth year, and you shall proclaim liberty in the land to all its inhabitants. It shall be a [year of] homebringing

ד וּבַשָּׁנָה הַשְּׁבִיעִת שַׁבַּת שַׁבָּתוֹן יִהְיֶה לָאָרֶץ
שַׁבָּת לַיהוָה שָׂדְךָ לֹא תִזְרָע וְכַרְמְךָ לֹא תִזְמֹר׃
ה אֵת סְפִיחַ קְצִירְךָ לֹא תִקְצוֹר וְאֶת־עִנְּבֵי
נְזִירֶךָ לֹא תִבְצֹר שְׁנַת שַׁבָּתוֹן יִהְיֶה לָאָרֶץ׃
ו וְהָיְתָה שַׁבַּת הָאָרֶץ לָכֶם לְאָכְלָה לְךָ וּלְעַבְדְּךָ
וְלַאֲמָתֶךָ וְלִשְׂכִירְךָ וּלְתוֹשָׁבְךָ הַגָּרִים עִמָּךְ׃
ז וְלִבְהֶמְתְּךָ וְלַחַיָּה אֲשֶׁר בְּאַרְצֶךָ תִּהְיֶה כָל־
תְּבוּאָתָהּ לֶאֱכֹל׃ ס ח וְסָפַרְתָּ לְךָ שֶׁבַע שַׁבְּתֹת
שָׁנִים שֶׁבַע שָׁנִים שֶׁבַע פְּעָמִים וְהָיוּ לְךָ יְמֵי
שֶׁבַע שַׁבְּתֹת הַשָּׁנִים תֵּשַׁע וְאַרְבָּעִים שָׁנָה׃
ט וְהַעֲבַרְתָּ שׁוֹפַר תְּרוּעָה בַּחֹדֶשׁ הַשְּׁבִעִי
בֶּעָשׂוֹר לַחֹדֶשׁ בְּיוֹם הַכִּפֻּרִים תַּעֲבִירוּ שׁוֹפָר
בְּכָל־אַרְצְכֶם׃ י וְקִדַּשְׁתֶּם אֵת שְׁנַת הַחֲמִשִּׁים
שָׁנָה וּקְרָאתֶם דְּרוֹר בָּאָרֶץ לְכָל־יֹשְׁבֶיהָ יוֹבֵל

4. ***a Sabbath to* God.** Scripture states repeatedly that the Sabbatical year of the land is a Sabbath לד׳, intended as an expression of homage to God, not, as might be supposed, as a year during which the land is allowed to lie fallow merely in order to improve the soil.

° ° °

5. . . . If we visualize the practical implementation of the law concerning שְׁבִיעִית [the Sabbatical year], we will understand that it constitutes a most splendid overt act of homage performed by an entire nation for one whole year in fields, in gardens and meadows. The observance of the Sabbatical year places the nation's land at the feet of God, as it were, as its one rightful Owner and Master. The people see themselves merely as tolerated residents and tenants of the land, which belongs to God. Stripped of all authority and pride of ownership, they retreat before God to a level equal to that of the poorest among men and the beasts of the field.

10. **יוֹבֵל הִיא תִּהְיֶה לָכֶם. . .** ***[It shall be a (year of) homebringing . . . to you].*** יבל in its active causative inflection means, "to bring." It implies an act of bringing that is appropriate, such as the bringing of a person to a place where it is right for him to be, or of a thing to the person who rightly should have it. . . . Thus יְבוּל is the produce of the soil; i.e., that which the soil "brings home" to its owner. . . . יוֹבֵל is, literally, "one who brings," one who brings people or things "home," restoring them to their proper place and order. For this reason the horn with which the Shepherd calls His flock home is called שׁוֹפְרוֹת הַיּוֹבְלִים [the *shofar* of *yovels*] (Joshua 6:4 f), קֶרֶן הַיּוֹבֵל [horn of *yovel*] (ibid. 8). The *yovel* tones sounded around the walls of Jericho, the first of the cities to be taken over by the Children of Israel in the land of the Jews, were a summons calling upon the city to surrender, or, if you will, to "come home" to its rightful owner. The collapse of the walls of Jericho was the response to this summons. . . . In these passages, יוֹבֵל denotes not only the horn but also the "home-calling" signal sounded by the horn. . . .

The text reads יוֹבֵל הִיא תִּהְיֶה לָכֶם. This form occurs again in Verses 11 and 12. The use of both words, הִיא and תִּהְיֶה, in these verses makes it clear that *yovel* refers not only to the observances associated with the fiftieth year but also to the year as such. The fiftieth year is to be one of restitution and reclamation, a year of restoring and returning; in short, a *yovel* year, and this is the reason why we should observe it as such. We would presume to believe that this gives the *yovel* year a con-

and shall be to you as such, and each one of
you shall return to his landed property and
each one of you shall return to his family.
11. It is a [year of] homebringing, the
fiftieth year shall this be to you; and you
shall not sow, nor harvest its aftergrowths,

הִוא תִּהְיֶה לָכֶם וְשַׁבְתֶּם אִישׁ אֶל־אֲחֻזָּתוֹ וְאִישׁ
אֶל־מִשְׁפַּחְתּוֹ תָּשֻׁבוּ: יא יוֹבֵל הִוא שְׁנַת
הַחֲמִשִּׁים שָׁנָה תִּהְיֶה לָכֶם לֹא תִזְרָעוּ וְלֹא

notation of restitution and reclamation beyond the mere release of persons and restitution of property that we ourselves are to effect. The atonement of יוֹם הַכִּפֻּרִים each year should bring about the moral rebirth of the individual with all its healing and restorative effects on the outer and inner life of the individual, as a miraculous gift from God's almighty grace. This gift of regeneration entails, and is conditional upon, our duty to starve our vital energies and to observe the prohibition against engaging in "creating" work on that day. The יוֹם הַכִּפֻּרִים of the *yovel* year is to effect also a social and political rebirth of the nation, with all its healing and restorative effects on the nation's domestic and external affairs, as a miraculous gift from the almighty grace of God.

The evils that beset the inner life of society due to social class differences and the unequal distribution of property, with the resultant sharp contrasts between opulence and misery, independence and dependence, etc., and the precarious situations that afflict nations in the course of their political relationships with other nations—all these are to be atoned for and erased by the *yovel*. By the grace of God, the nation is to be restored to the social health and political freedom with which it began its life as a nation founded on the Law of God. Israel is to progress in this freedom and independence, within and without, which God bestows upon it again and again, from *yovel* to *yovel*, until it reaches that ideal state in which it will become a bright and shining national entity in the midst of the nations. Then all the other nations will be drawn to it in order to learn from it the Divinely-established institutions which alone will guarantee freedom, justice and everlasting peace on earth (Isaiah 2:1 f; see also 2:18 and 19). However, if such a political rebirth of the nation is to be obtained from God, then Israel, too, must do its part; it must perform the two splendid acts of restitution and regeneration which it is within human power to accomplish: the release of the land and the release of slaves, and both of these must be proclaimed not as humanitarian or political measures but by תְּקִיעַת שׁוֹפָר [the blast of the *shofar*], as being performed in the name of God, as a legal consequence of His sovereignty and of his rights as the original Owner of all things.

יוֹבֵל הִיא תִּהְיֶה לָכֶם: It is a *yovel* of God, but it must be proclaimed and observed as such also by ourselves. The relationship between the *yovel* that is to be observed by man and the *yovel* that man can expect to be granted by God in return is expressed in negative terms in Jeremiah 34:17, where the consequences of man's failure to observe the *yovel* are set forth: "Therefore thus says *God*: You have not hearkened to Me to proclaim liberty, every man to his brother, and every man to his neighbor; behold, I proclaim for you a liberty, says *God*, to the sword, to the pestilence and to the famine, and I will make you a horror to all the kingdoms of the earth." Masters who fail to "release" or "dismiss" their slaves in that year will themselves be "released" or "dismissed" by God. They will be left to their own devices; they will no longer have God as their Master, to act as their Defender. From this it follows that by observing the *yovel* year we demonstrate our wish to remain in the service of God, Who will then grant us, His servants, independence, protection and prosperity, defending us against the forces of man and nature as exemplified by the sword, the pestilence and the famine. The fact that, as it seems to us from the foregoing, the regenerative effect of the *yovel* goes beyond the mere restitution of property and the release of slaves which we are to perform, and becomes a political atonement, a political rebirth to be obtained from God, puts the significance of the counting of the seven *shemitoth* into its proper light as a forty-nine-year period climaxing in a fiftieth year. . . .

This would also explain why the institution of the *yovel* can be observed only as long as the entire nation dwells in its land in accordance with the original tribal divisions in the provinces assigned to them. The Word of God repeatedly refers to the settling of the Children of Israel in the land intended for it as a "planting," and we have already noted in connection with Genesis 35:11[15] the profound, significant impact of the character differences between the twelve tribes, as set forth by their patriarch in his farewell blessing (Genesis 49), on Israel's mission in the world. Consequently, too, we can understand why each tribe was originally "implanted," by God's explicit intent and under His direct guidance, into its own special sector of the land, and that the presence of the entire nation in its land, and the presence of each tribe in that part of the land best suited for the development of its unique characteristics, are by no means irrelevant to the attainment of the ultimate goal of national perfection to be promoted by the institution of *yovel*.

• • •

[15]*Note to the English translation*: This passage is not included in this excerpted edition. [G.H.]

nor shall you gather the grapes that were
left upon their vines untended.   12. For it
is a [year of] homebringing; it shall be a
holy thing to you; you shall eat its produce
from the field.   13. In this year of homebringing every one of you shall return
to his landed property.   14. And if you
now transact a sale to your neighbor, or
acquire anything from the hand of your
neighbor, you shall not grieve one another.
15. According to the number of years
that have passed since the [last] *yovel* shall
you buy from your neighbor; according to
the number of years or produce [until the
next *yovel*] shall he sell to you. 16. According to the multitude of years [still to run
before the *yovel*] shall you raise the purchase price, and according to the fewness of
years [still to run before the *yovel*] shall you
lower the purchase price, for a [given]
number of crops does he sell to you.
17. And   you   shall   not   grieve   one
another, and you shall fear your God, for I,
God, am your God.   18. Carry out My
statutes and observe and carry out My
[social] ordinances; then you will be sustained by the land in security.   19. The
land will yield its fruit and you will eat until

תִּקְצְרוּ֙ אֶת־סְפִיחֶ֔יהָ וְלֹ֥א תִבְצְר֖וּ אֶת־נְזִרֶ֑יהָ
יב כִּ֤י יוֹבֵל֙ הִ֔וא קֹ֖דֶשׁ תִּהְיֶ֣ה לָכֶ֑ם מִן־הַ֨שָּׂדֶ֔ה
תֹּאכְל֖וּ אֶת־תְּבֽוּאָתָֽהּ׃ יג בִּשְׁנַ֥ת הַיּוֹבֵ֖ל הַזֹּ֑את
תָּשֻׁ֕בוּ אִ֖ישׁ אֶל־אֲחֻזָּתֽוֹ׃ שני יד וְכִי־תִמְכְּר֤וּ
מִמְכָּר֙ לַֽעֲמִיתֶ֔ךָ א֥וֹ קָנֹ֖ה מִיַּ֣ד עֲמִיתֶ֑ךָ אַל־תּוֹנ֖וּ
אִ֥ישׁ אֶת־אָחִֽיו׃ טו בְּמִסְפַּ֤ר שָׁנִים֙ אַחַ֣ר הַיּוֹבֵ֔ל
תִּקְנֶ֖ה מֵאֵ֣ת עֲמִיתֶ֑ךָ בְּמִסְפַּ֥ר שְׁנֵֽי־תְבוּאֹ֖ת
יִמְכָּר־לָֽךְ׃ טז לְפִ֣י ׀ רֹ֣ב הַשָּׁנִ֗ים תַּרְבֶּה֙ מִקְנָת֔וֹ
וּלְפִי֙ מְעֹ֣ט הַשָּׁנִ֔ים תַּמְעִ֖יט מִקְנָת֑וֹ כִּ֚י מִסְפַּ֣ר
תְּבוּאֹ֔ת ה֥וּא מֹכֵ֖ר לָֽךְ׃ יז וְלֹ֤א תוֹנוּ֙ אִ֣ישׁ אֶת־
עֲמִית֔וֹ וְיָרֵ֖אתָ מֵֽאֱלֹהֶ֑יךָ כִּ֛י אֲנִ֥י יְהֹוָ֖ה אֱלֹֽהֵיכֶֽם׃
יח וַֽעֲשִׂיתֶם֙ אֶת־חֻקֹּתַ֔י וְאֶת־מִשְׁפָּטַ֥י תִּשְׁמְר֖וּ
וַֽעֲשִׂיתֶ֣ם אֹתָ֑ם וִֽישַׁבְתֶּ֥ם עַל־הָאָ֖רֶץ לָבֶֽטַח׃ שלישי
‏(שני כשהן מחוברין) יט וְנָֽתְנָ֤ה הָאָ֨רֶץ֙ פִּרְיָ֔הּ וַֽאֲכַלְתֶּ֖ם

•   •   •

14. . . . The words "and if you now transact a sale"
in this verse are primarily a logical consequence of "in
this year of homebringing. . ." (Verse 13), which refers
to the restoration of landed property in the *yovel* year to
its original owner (a return which, incidentally, in
accordance with the concept discussed in our notes
above, is understood not as the return of the property to
its original owner, but as the return of the owner to his
original property). The commandment in Verse 14
intends to revise the conception of the sale of landed
property in accordance with the spirit of the *yovel* by
pronouncing a general admonition against unfair
business dealings: "You shall   not   grieve   one
another." . . .

•   •   •

17. וְלֹא תוֹנוּ וגו' וְיָרֵאתָ וגו' כִּי וגו' אֱלֹקֵיכֶם [*And you*
(plu.) *shall not grieve one another, and you* (sing.)
shall fear . . ., for I, God, am your God]. This warning
is addressed to all the members of the nation: They are
not to "grieve" one another, and each individual
member of the nation shall fear his God. Each member
of the nation should keep in mind that God's eye and
ear are directed toward each and every person and that
He is equally the God of all his brethren. This state-

ment delineates the most immediate effect of the institutions of *shemittah* and *yovel* upon the communal life
of the individuals who dwell together in the land.
Shemittah and *yovel* introduce the concept of God into
all the business transactions of man, and make it clear
that all men live and work together on the one soil of
God, in the one land of God, where God is the Master
and Owner of all property and where, exercising His
rights of ownership, He expects us to pay Him homage
in all our transactions. The obvious corollary to this
idea; i.e., that all of communal life takes place before
the eye of God, is that God is present not only in the
Temple but also in the midst of all business and commerce transacted by the members of the nation. He will
support and bless these transactions in His land and
upon His soil, and all the individuals involved in them,
only if they bring happiness and prosperity to all; if no
one "grieves" the other; if no one abuses the position
he has attained on God's soil, or the breath he draws in
God's land, to cheat or "grieve" another, and if that
one basic truth of all truths, אֲנִי ד' אֱלֹקֵיכֶם ["I am *God,*
your God"], with all its consequences, becomes
permanently imbedded in every phase of our lives, both
as individuals and as a nation.

you are satisfied, and you will live in security, sustained by it. 20. And if you will say: "What shall we eat in the seventh year? For, see, we must not sow and must not gather that which grows for our home harvest." 21. Then I will command My blessing upon you in the sixth year; it will make its produce for the three years. 22. You will sow during the eighth year and eat of the old produce; until the ninth year, when its produce comes in, you will eat old produce. 23. And the land shall not be sold in perpetuity, for the land is Mine; for you are only strangers and tenants with Me. 24. And you shall grant a redemption for the land in all the land of your possession. 25. If your brother becomes impoverished and sells some of his landed property, then his advocate,* who is closest to him, shall come and redeem that which his brother has sold. 26. And one who has no advocate, but his own hand has accomplished it and he has attained [assets] sufficient to redeem it, 27. he shall calculate the number of years for which the land has been sold and shall return the overplus to the man to whom he sold it, and he shall return to his landed property. 28. But if his own hand has not attained [assets] sufficient to get it back, then what he has sold shall remain in the hand of the purchaser until the *yovel* year; in the *yovel* it shall go out and he shall return to his landed property. 29. But if one sells a dwelling house in a walled city, [the time of] its redemption shall be until the end of one year after its sale; [the time of] its redemption shall be one full year. 30. But if he has not redeemed it within one full year, the house in a city legally considered as walled shall belong to the purchaser in perpetuity for his descendants; it shall not go out in the *yovel*. 31. Houses in unwalled, open localities shall be considered like the field of the land; it shall therefore be redeemable and it shall go out in the *yovel*. 32. And as for the cities of the Levites, the houses of the cities of their landed property, the Levites shall have the right of redemption at any time. 33. And the same applies to that which he has to redeem from the Levites. A house or a city of their landed property shall go out again in the *yovel*, for

לָשֹׂבַע וִישַׁבְתֶּם לָבֶטַח עָלֶיהָ: כ וְכִי תֹאמְרוּ
מַה־נֹּאכַל בַּשָּׁנָה הַשְּׁבִיעִת הֵן לֹא נִזְרָע וְלֹא
נֶאֱסֹף אֶת־תְּבוּאָתֵנוּ: כא וְצִוִּיתִי אֶת־בִּרְכָתִי
לָכֶם בַּשָּׁנָה הַשִּׁשִּׁית וְעָשָׂת אֶת־הַתְּבוּאָה
לִשְׁלֹשׁ הַשָּׁנִים: כב וּזְרַעְתֶּם אֵת הַשָּׁנָה הַשְּׁמִינִת
וַאֲכַלְתֶּם מִן־הַתְּבוּאָה יָשָׁן עַד ׀ הַשָּׁנָה
הַתְּשִׁיעִת עַד־בּוֹא תְּבוּאָתָהּ תֹּאכְלוּ יָשָׁן:
כג וְהָאָרֶץ לֹא תִמָּכֵר לִצְמִתֻת כִּי־לִי הָאָרֶץ כִּי־
גֵרִים וְתוֹשָׁבִים אַתֶּם עִמָּדִי: כד וּבְכֹל אֶרֶץ
אֲחֻזַּתְכֶם גְּאֻלָּה תִּתְּנוּ לָאָרֶץ: פ רביעי כה כִּי־
יָמוּךְ אָחִיךָ וּמָכַר מֵאֲחֻזָּתוֹ וּבָא גֹאֲלוֹ הַקָּרֹב
אֵלָיו וְגָאַל אֵת מִמְכַּר אָחִיו: כו וְאִישׁ כִּי לֹא
יִהְיֶה־לּוֹ גֹּאֵל וְהִשִּׂיגָה יָדוֹ וּמָצָא כְּדֵי גְאֻלָּתוֹ:
כז וְחִשַּׁב אֶת־שְׁנֵי מִמְכָּרוֹ וְהֵשִׁיב אֶת־הָעֹדֵף
לָאִישׁ אֲשֶׁר מָכַר־לוֹ וְשָׁב לַאֲחֻזָּתוֹ: כח וְאִם
לֹא־מָצְאָה יָדוֹ דֵּי הָשִׁיב לוֹ וְהָיָה מִמְכָּרוֹ בְּיַד
הַקֹּנֶה אֹתוֹ עַד שְׁנַת הַיּוֹבֵל וְיָצָא בַּיֹּבֵל וְשָׁב
לַאֲחֻזָּתוֹ: ס חמישי (שלישי כשהן מחוברין) כט וְאִישׁ
כִּי־יִמְכֹּר בֵּית־מוֹשַׁב עִיר חוֹמָה וְהָיְתָה גְּאֻלָּתוֹ
עַד־תֹּם שְׁנַת מִמְכָּרוֹ יָמִים תִּהְיֶה גְאֻלָּתוֹ:
ל וְאִם לֹא־יִגָּאֵל עַד־מְלֹאת לוֹ שָׁנָה תְמִימָה
וְקָם הַבַּיִת אֲשֶׁר־בָּעִיר אֲשֶׁר־לא (לו קרי) חֹמָה
לַצְּמִיתֻת לַקֹּנֶה אֹתוֹ לְדֹרֹתָיו לֹא יֵצֵא בַּיֹּבֵל:
לא וּבָתֵּי הַחֲצֵרִים אֲשֶׁר אֵין־לָהֶם חֹמָה סָבִיב
עַל־שְׂדֵה הָאָרֶץ יֵחָשֵׁב גְּאֻלָּה תִּהְיֶה־לּוֹ וּבַיֹּבֵל
יֵצֵא: לב וְעָרֵי הַלְוִיִּם בָּתֵּי עָרֵי אֲחֻזָּתָם גְּאֻלַּת
עוֹלָם תִּהְיֶה לַלְוִיִּם: לג וַאֲשֶׁר יִגְאַל מִן־הַלְוִיִּם
וְיָצָא מִמְכַּר־בַּיִת וְעִיר אֲחֻזָּתוֹ בַּיֹּבֵל כִּי בָתֵּי

***Note to the English translation*: In his original German rendering of this text, Hirsch translates the Hebrew גֹּאֵל as *Annehmer,* lit one who "takes up" the cause of a person or thing; i.e., "advocate." [G.H.]

the houses of the cities of the Levites are their property in the midst of the sons of Yisrael. 34. And the open country on the outskirts of their cities must not be sold

עָרֵ֣י הַלְוִיִּ֗ם הִ֚וא אֲחֻזָּתָ֔ם בְּת֖וֹךְ בְּנֵ֥י יִשְׂרָאֵֽל׃
לד וּֽשְׂדֵ֛ה מִגְרַ֥שׁ עָרֵיהֶ֖ם לֹ֣א יִמָּכֵ֑ר כִּֽי־אֲחֻזַּ֥ת

34. . . . We have already indicated . . . the profound significance of the institution of *yovel* as the national *Yom Kippur*, the purpose of which it is to restore and regenerate the social and political life of the nation. The Law itself has shown, by its prohibitions (Verses 15–17) against "grieving" one's neighbor, how the concept of God's supreme sovereignty over land and people, which the *yovel* injects into every transaction conducted among the people, should engender punctilious respect for the rights of others in both word and deed.

Let us note a few of the most conspicuous effects of the various provisions of the *yovel* law on the national economy of the Jewish people. Obviously, the periodic reversion of all landed property to its original owner has the effect of maintaining the original distribution of the land according to tribal and familial divisions, which was such an important factor in the intended development of the nation and on which, in fact, the efficacy of the *yovel* was dependent. The provision in Verse 34 that the open rural areas on the outskirts of the Levite cities must not be sold, as well as the distinction made between houses in unwalled, open localities and houses in walled cities, and the limitations of the latter definition to include only cities that had walls from the time of Joshua ben Nun, perpetuates the division of the land in one more respect which, it seems to us, has an influence of no mean significance on the development and character of the nation. We are referring to the relationship between city and countryside. It is clear that the purpose of these regulations was to maintain the Land of Israel as primarily one of "city dwellers engaged in tilling the soil," and to prevent the expansion of the cities into metropolises detached from the surrounding countryside. The cities already in existence must not expand beyond their original area at the expense of arable soil; indeed, they must not even fill up the open spaces within their limits, and no farmland may be converted into urban acreage. If the cities become overcrowded, new cities may be built, but only on land that has never been used for agricultural purposes. Thus, Joshua (17:5) advised the sons of Joseph to build cities in clearings in the mountain woodlands. Moreover, the law under which, like the land itself, the houses in unwalled cities not cut off from arable land could not be sold in perpetuity, but had to revert, in the *yovel* year, to their original owner or the latter's heirs, had the effect that, on the whole, city and countryside remained linked as family properties. As a result, every field and every vineyard normally would be owned by an individual who also owned a house in the nearest city. Thus the purpose of this momentous, sweeping legislation was to encourage a combination of the city dweller's intelligence and ingenuity with the simple life of the countryside. Only cities with walls were detached from the countryside that surrounded them. Houses in walled cities, unlike those in localities without walls, *could* be sold in perpetuity. Hence, in these cities, a population could develop without ties to the surrounding arable land, an urban population compelled to make its living from commerce and industry. However, such a course of development was restricted to cities around which walls had been built—and which had thus been detached from the surrounding countryside—before the Israelites had settled and built houses in them ("First a wall was built around the city and then it was settled"). Localities that originally had been without walls were not permitted to lose their character even if, at a later date, walls were built around them for purposes of protection ("First the city was settled and then a wall was built around it"). And these localities could be detached from arable property as houses within walled cities only if the cities had already been surrounded by a wall from the days of Joshua. As a result, the growth of an urban life completely detached from agriculture was restricted to localities whose number was permanently fixed and could not be increased. A state whose population is, and remains, settled primarily in moderate-sized country towns is protected not only from peasant dullness and stultification but to an equal extent also from the extremes of urban luxury and proletarianism.

No less striking is the effect of the automatic reversion of all landed property to its original owner or his heirs during the *yovel* year. It is an effective way of preventing the rise of an economic system in which some families must live in perpetual poverty while huge tracts of land remain in the hands of a privileged few. A powerful class of large landowners living in the midst of a landless and therefore pauperized class can never arise or survive in a country where in every fiftieth year the land as a whole reverts to its original owners, with the richest returning to his original patrimonial property and the poorest getting back the field that had been his inheritance.

Between *yovel* years, too, the Law protects the temporarily impoverished from the avarice of the rich; for this purpose it has set up the great institution of *geulah* [lit., "redemption"]. No impoverished landowner can ever be victimized by unscrupulous real estate speculators in a land where, after two years, the original seller, or his close kinsman, has the right to buy back his property by repaying only the amount for

עוֹלָם הוּא לָהֶם: ס לה וְכִי־יָמוּךְ אָחִיךָ וּמָטָה
יָדוֹ עִמָּךְ וְהֶחֱזַקְתָּ בּוֹ גֵּר וְתוֹשָׁב וָחַי עִמָּךְ:
לו אַל־תִּקַּח מֵאִתּוֹ נֶשֶׁךְ וְתַרְבִּית וְיָרֵאתָ

away, for it is their possession for all time.
35. And if your brother becomes impoverished and his hand wavers beside you, then you shall support him, even the stranger who has become only a sojourner, so that he may live with you.
36. But you must not take any interest or increase from him, and you must fear your God, and your

which it was originally sold and is entitled to deduct even from that price the benefit for the years during which it was in the purchaser's possession. The less a purchaser has paid for a piece of landed property, the less can he be sure of keeping it for a longer period, and the easier will it be for the seller, the original owner, to raise the amount required for its repurchase (or for his close kinsman to decide to redeem the property on his behalf). A wealthy man wishing to purchase the field of an impoverished landowner and to keep it as his property for as long as possible will be careful not to haggle for a low purchase price, since he knows that under the Law the only way he can make it difficult for the original owner to repurchase his land is to pay him a high price for it.

At the same time the Law seeks to make certain that fields and houses are not rashly sold for cash. Since the Law does not favor real estate transactions in general and seems to consider any sale of landed property as justifiable only in cases of dire necessity (cf. Verse 25, "If your brother becomes impoverished"), even one in financial straits will not quickly decide to sell his inherited property, for he knows that he will be permitted to buy it back only after two years and even then he can do so only if his circumstances have improved. Once he has sold his land, he can repurchase it in the near future only by dint of redoubled diligence and industry because he may not redeem his property by selling other property, or with borrowed funds, but only with newly-earned money. Also, he cannot repurchase only part of the land at a time; he must be in a position to buy it back in full. . . .

Characteristically, on the other hand, the Law leaves open a possibility for reversals of the transactions described above. It recognizes as valid a sale not made out of necessity, in the same manner . . . that it recognizes eventualities in which a sale may remain in force beyond the *yovel*. As regards such cases, the Law limits itself to indicating its disapproval, for it relies on the self-judging punctiliousness of the individual, and on the climate of public opinion created thereby, to ensure the observance of its institutions. It is therefore willing to countenance exceptions in a variety of family situations, taking it for granted that the force of public opinion will be sufficiently strong to keep such exceptions well within bounds.

We are not quite clear about the significance of property redemption by close relatives. It seems that this is to be done primarily in the kinsman's own interest, or in the interest of the whole family, so that the property should not pass out of the family's hands even temporarily. It seems that the seller himself does not derive any direct advantage from such a transaction. Nevertheless, the kinsman [or "advocate"] is described here as his גּוֹאֵל [lit., "redeemer"], which implies that the repurchase transacted by this kinsman will bring the seller some advantage, some relief or "redemption" from his distress. It may be that custom went beyond the bare requirements of the Law, as indeed we see, for instance in Ruth 4:5, that according to custom the kinsman who "redeemed" the field of a deceased relative also was obligated to marry the widow and to provide for her.

36. . . . We have already discussed in detail (to Exodus 22:24) the concept on which the prohibition against taking interest from a fellow Jew is based. We have shown there that Jewish Law definitely does not regard charging interest on loans *per se* as illegal or morally wrong. If it did, it would not also have prohibited, with equal emphasis, the paying of interest by the borrower, and the prohibition against charging interest would not have been restricted to loan transactions among Jews. Rather, not charging—or paying—interest in loan transactions among Jews is a splendid act of homage to God, expressing our recognition of Him as the Master and Owner also of our movable possessions even as the release of the land and the institution of *yovel* demonstrate our acknowledgement of His dominion and control over our landed property.

It is clear, too, that the law as set forth in this verse appears as a continuation and logical consequence of the *yovel* institution. For the land and the soil are the source of all the nation's wealth, and all its movable possessions are, first and foremost, products of agricultural prosperity (cf. Verse 38) . . . and even as the gratuitous return of all purchased land in the *yovel* year is an act performed in the land of the Jews to proclaim God as the Master and original Owner of the land of the Jews, so, too, the fact that we are willing to lend our movable possessions without interest is intended to proclaim God throughout Jewish society as the Master and original Owner of our movable assets.

brother's life shall be bound up with you. 37. You must not give him your money at

מֵאֱלֹהֶ֑יךָ וְחֵ֥י אָחִ֖יךָ עִמָּֽךְ׃ לז אֶ֨ת־כַּסְפְּךָ֔ לֹֽא־

If we were the true owners of our money, and if the loans we grant would be acts deriving entirely from our own free will, then perhaps any interest we would charge after the return of the principal would be neither נֶשֶׁךְ [interest] from the viewpoint of the borrower nor תַּרְבִּית [increase] from our own vantage point as lenders. After all, the borrower may have made earnings with our money (it is precisely to such a loan, to be used for business purposes, that our text in Verse 35 refers). The interest he would pay us would then not constitute a "bite" [the literal meaning of נֶשֶׁךְ]; it would not be a deduction from his own assets. It would be only part of the fruit which our capital yielded while it was in the borrower's hands. By the same token, it would not represent an "increase" in our own capital. After all, seen from the business point of view, we were under no obligation to lend him any of our money. The capital could have borne fruit just as well in our hands; we might have made earnings with it. Hence the interest would not constitute an "increase" in our assets; it would be only compensation, and perhaps only partial compensation at that, for the "increase" we may have lost by lending out the principal.

This is the non-Jewish view of loans and interest. One argument against this view, of course, is its demand that the interest must be paid in any case, even if the borrower has made no earnings with the loan or has, in fact, incurred losses with it. The interest is payable even if it is just as clear that if the capital had remained with the lender, it would have lain idle or would have been lost. At any rate, no matter what the circumstances, the principal must be repaid, and interest, too, is payable, so that the money lent must be regarded as a usable object and the interest as a "rental" paid by the debtor for its "hire."

The Jewish point of view is completely different. Judaism teaches us that our money is not our own; it is ours only under certain conditions. The One Who is truly entitled to exercise control over our money is God. It is He Who commands us to place some of the assets, which are His but which happen to be in our hands, into the hands of our brother, to enable him not merely to obtain the necessities of life, but also to help him maintain and continue his business activities. God's behest is that, in return for the obligation the borrower has assumed to reimburse us with an equal amount of money at a given time, the money, which until then was our money, becomes the borrower's at the moment it passes from our hands into his.

Thus, the money with which the borrower does business is not ours at all, but his own. His earnings from it will be a product of his own work with his own money, and will therefore be entirely his own. If we were to demand any part of these earnings from him, we would be taking נֶשֶׁךְ; we would be taking "a bite," as it were, from his personal assets. At the same time, it would represent תַּרְבִּית ["an increase"] in our assets. It would not be a compensation for earnings we could have made with the principal, for we had no right to withhold the loan from the borrower in order to use the money for our own business, seeing that it is God, the true Owner of all things, Who has placed the money at the disposal of another. Therefore, even if the borrower has made earnings with the principal or if the lender could have made earnings with it, any interest charged or paid on the loan would be נֶשֶׁךְ and תַּרְבִּית.

Here we have the great impact of the Jewish concept of צְדָקָה, which is indisputably part of צֶדֶק, that which is just and right: what in the eyes of the giver would seem to be an act of loving-kindness is, in the eyes of God, no more than the repayment of a legal debt. . . . And so the following logic evolves: If God is the Owner of all that we have and this thought is to find expression in the social relationship between man and his fellow man, then any interest charged or paid on loans, though legitimate *per se*, becomes נֶשֶׁךְ and תַּרְבִּית, and a loan extended without interest becomes the greatest sacrifice on our part by which we are to seal our homage to God. Therefore, the Law stresses the prohibition not only against charging but also against paying interest and forbids both practices with equal emphasis. By forbidding נֶשֶׁךְ, the Law demands our acknowledgment that while our money is in the hands of the borrower it ceases to be ours, and by forbidding תַּרְבִּית it proclaims that before God's tribunal our act of granting the loan is nothing but our duty, which we could not evade before God and for which we have no right to expect any reward or compensation.

For this reason the Law immediately follows the prohibition against נֶשֶׁךְ and תַּרְבִּית with the words, "And you must fear your God." "Fear of God" is the true motivation for the prohibition against charging interest, against a business transaction that would be entirely justifiable from both the human and the social point of view—if God were left out of the equation. It is because you recognize God as "your God," as the Ruler of your destinies and the Guide of your actions, that you are forbidden to charge interest. The intended effect of this prohibition is that "your brother's life shall be bound up with you." We have already indicated what a far-reaching beneficial effect the prohibition against interest was meant to have on the nation's economy (Exodus

תִּתֵּ֥ן ל֖וֹ בְּנֶ֑שֶׁךְ וּבְמַרְבִּ֖ית לֹא־תִתֵּ֥ן אָכְלֶֽךָ׃
לח אֲנִ֗י יְהוָה֙ אֱלֹ֣הֵיכֶ֔ם אֲשֶׁר־הוֹצֵ֥אתִי אֶתְכֶ֖ם
מֵאֶ֣רֶץ מִצְרָ֑יִם לָתֵ֤ת לָכֶם֙ אֶת־אֶ֣רֶץ כְּנַ֔עַן לִהְי֥וֹת
לָכֶ֖ם לֵאלֹהִֽים׃ ס ששי (רביעי כשהן מחוברין) לט וְכִֽי־
יָמ֥וּךְ אָחִ֛יךָ עִמָּ֖ךְ וְנִמְכַּר־לָ֑ךְ לֹא־תַעֲבֹ֥ד בּ֖וֹ
עֲבֹ֥דַת עָֽבֶד׃ מ כְּשָׂכִ֥יר כְּתוֹשָׁ֖ב יִהְיֶ֣ה עִמָּ֑ךְ עַד־
שְׁנַ֥ת הַיֹּבֵ֖ל יַעֲבֹ֥ד עִמָּֽךְ׃ מא וְיָצָא֙ מֵֽעִמָּ֔ךְ ה֖וּא
וּבָנָ֣יו עִמּ֑וֹ וְשָׁב֙ אֶל־מִשְׁפַּחְתּ֔וֹ וְאֶל־אֲחֻזַּ֥ת

interest and you must not give him your food for increase. 38. I, *God*, am your God, Who brought you out from the land of Mitzrayim to give you the land of Canaan, to be God to you. 39. And if your brother becomes impoverished beside you and sells himself to you, you shall not work him like a [bond]servant. 40. He shall be like a day laborer, like a sojourner with you; he shall serve with you until the *yovel* year. 41. Then he shall go out from you, he and his children with him; he shall then return to his family and return also to the

22:24).[16] It complements the effects of the *yovel* institution, to which the prohibition against interest, in a wider sense, also belongs. All these beneficial effects on the nation's welfare are subsumed in the statement "and your brother's life shall be bound up with you." We are not told here, as we are in Verse 35, וְחַי וגו׳, "that your brother may live with you," which would make it your duty to concern yourself merely with keeping your brother alive—but וְחֵי אָחִיךָ עִמָּךְ. חֵי is the *stat. constr.* of חַיִּים, just as מֵי is that of מַיִם. . . . In the present verse חֵי is a noun [not a verb]. Hence, the thought expressed in Verse 36 is as follows: The life of your brother is bound up with you; i.e., all his future, and whether or not he will fulfill his life's purpose, is closely bound up with you and with the purpose of your own life. You do not exist for yourself alone, nor is it for yourself alone that you acquire wealth. To be sure, you must, first of all, provide for yourself so that you may acquire the means to accomplish your life's mission that God has assigned to you. But it is part of your life's mission to acquire also the means for helping your brother (who is bound up with you as part of the society in which you live) accomplish his own life's mission as well. Whatever you acquire you acquire also for him. His life is bound up with you and with what is yours. It is this עִם [with] that makes you עַם [a people]. And since it is not communist coercion, nor the tax authorities of a government on earth, nor the specter of a Red revolution, but solely a sense of duty dictated by your fear of God that ties this bond of mutual support, free-willed but nonetheless (or perhaps precisely therefore) so eternally strong, we have here the practical realization of the words God uttered when He chose us: "I will take you to Myself as a people" (Exodus 6:7), for it is the pure awareness of God that shapes such a society and such a nation.

° ° °

39. ***And if your brother becomes impoverished beside you.*** This is a logical continuation of the *yovel* laws. After discussing the "redeeming" effect of the *yovel* in transactions involving landed property and movable assets, the chapter now concludes with the effect of the *yovel* on the personal rights of the individual. Under the impact of the *yovel* we find introduced an institution that appears to be the last resort for the poor. Before turning to this final desperate effort to escape destitution, the Law referred the impoverished individual to the brotherly aid of his compatriots. This is not political communism. However, it lays the foundation for a moral communism, as it were, which does not give the individual the right to demand, but certainly the right to expect that, motivated solely by a sense of duty born of the fear of God alone, the affluent will readily make their capital available to those threatened by pauperization, to support and sustain them without fee or interest. . . .

41. . . . The institution of עֶבֶד עִבְרִי [the Hebrew slave or bondservant] is the last recourse for a family mired in destitution which until that point has struggled in vain to preserve its economic independence. Now the breadwinner of the family has no asset left but his own capacity for work, and perhaps also that of his family. . . . It is with this skill that he and his family temporarily enter the household of a well-to-do individual who, in return for the use of his bondservant's labor, not only assumes the obligation to provide for the servant's family while its breadwinner is in his service but also remains duty bound to treat him as a fellow man and brother. In this manner the unfortunate man is protected from misery and starvation, and when he has completed his period of service he may go out and use his accumulated savings in an attempt to build up a new, independent existence.

[16]*Note to the English translation*: This part of Hirsch's commentary on Exodus 22:24 is not included in this excerpted edition. [G.H.]

landed property of his fathers.   42. For they are My [bond]servants, whom I brought out from the land of Mitzrayim; they shall not be sold as [bond]servants are sold.   43. You must not rule over him with harshness, and you shall fear your God. 44. But [bond]servants and handmaids who will remain yours from among the nations that live round about you, from among them you may acquire [bond]servants and handmaids.   45. And also from among the descendants of those who sojourn in your midst as strangers, from among them you may acquire, and from among their families who are with you, which they have begotten in your land, so that they become your permanent property. 46. You make them an inheritance for your children after you. You shall keep them as [bond]servants always, but as for your brothers, the sons of Yisrael, you must not rule, one over the other, with harshness. 47. And if the hand of a stranger who has become a sojourner with you has acquired means, and your brother becomes impoverished beside him, and he sells himself to a stranger sojourning in your midst or even to the breadwinner of a family of strangers, 48. then, after he has sold himself, he shall be redeemed; one of his brethren shall redeem him.   49. His uncle or the son of his uncle shall redeem him, or one of his blood relations, of his family, shall redeem him, or if his own hand has acquired means, he shall redeem himself.   50. He shall make a reckoning with the one who purchased him, from the year he sold himself to him, until the *yovel* year, and the money

אֲבֹתָיו יָשׁוּב: מב כִּי־עֲבָדַי הֵם אֲשֶׁר־הוֹצֵאתִי אֹתָם מֵאֶרֶץ מִצְרָיִם לֹא יִמָּכְרוּ מִמְכֶּרֶת עָבֶד: מג לֹא־תִרְדֶּה בוֹ בְּפָרֶךְ וְיָרֵאתָ מֵאֱלֹהֶיךָ: מד וְעַבְדְּךָ וַאֲמָתְךָ אֲשֶׁר יִהְיוּ־לָךְ מֵאֵת הַגּוֹיִם אֲשֶׁר סְבִיבֹתֵיכֶם מֵהֶם תִּקְנוּ עֶבֶד וְאָמָה: מה וְגַם מִבְּנֵי הַתּוֹשָׁבִים הַגָּרִים עִמָּכֶם מֵהֶם תִּקְנוּ וּמִמִּשְׁפַּחְתָּם אֲשֶׁר עִמָּכֶם אֲשֶׁר הוֹלִידוּ בְּאַרְצְכֶם וְהָיוּ לָכֶם לַאֲחֻזָּה: מו וְהִתְנַחַלְתֶּם אֹתָם לִבְנֵיכֶם אַחֲרֵיכֶם לָרֶשֶׁת אֲחֻזָּה לְעֹלָם בָּהֶם תַּעֲבֹדוּ וּבְאַחֵיכֶם בְּנֵי־יִשְׂרָאֵל אִישׁ בְּאָחִיו לֹא־תִרְדֶּה בוֹ בְּפָרֶךְ: ס שביעי מז וְכִי תַשִּׂיג יַד גֵּר וְתוֹשָׁב עִמָּךְ וּמָךְ אָחִיךָ עִמּוֹ וְנִמְכַּר לְגֵר תּוֹשָׁב עִמָּךְ אוֹ לְעֵקֶר מִשְׁפַּחַת גֵּר: מח אַחֲרֵי נִמְכַּר גְּאֻלָּה תִּהְיֶה־לּוֹ אֶחָד מֵאֶחָיו יִגְאָלֶנּוּ: מט אוֹ־דֹדוֹ אוֹ בֶן־דֹּדוֹ יִגְאָלֶנּוּ אוֹ־מִשְּׁאֵר בְּשָׂרוֹ מִמִּשְׁפַּחְתּוֹ יִגְאָלֶנּוּ אוֹ־הִשִּׂיגָה יָדוֹ וְנִגְאָל: נ וְחִשַּׁב עִם־קֹנֵהוּ מִשְּׁנַת הִמָּכְרוֹ לוֹ עַד שְׁנַת הַיֹּבֵל וְהָיָה כֶּסֶף מִמְכָּרוֹ בְּמִסְפַּר

If a *yovel* occurs while he is in service, he is released and regains not only his personal freedom but also any land he has inherited as his patrimony, land from which, provided God blesses his industry and perseverance, he and his family will be able to achieve economic independence. Of course the implementation of this institution presupposes that the nation's life will be based on justice and humanity, ruled through and through by the ideal of duty, as it can be only in a Divinely-ordained state governed by the Law of God. That is why this institution, too, can be invoked only in

a completely independent Jewish state; cf. "The Law concerning the Hebrew bondservant applies only when the *yovel* law applies" (Arakhin 29a).

42. *For they are My [bond]servants.* Subordination to God excludes subservience to any other master. Entering into the service of God makes man truly free.

they shall not be sold as [bond]servants are sold. According to *Torath Kohanim*, the Hebrew slave or bondservant must not be sold in the manner that slaves are sold; i.e., at public auction, etc.

from his sale shall be divided into the number of years; it shall be in his case according to the time of a hired worker. 51. If there are still many years [until the *yovel*] he must return the price of his redemption accordingly out of the money for which he was purchased. 52. And if only a few years are left until the *yovel*, he must charge him with it. He must pay his redemption money according to the years he still would have to serve. 53. He shall be to him [the same] as one hired from year to year; he shall not rule over him with harshness before your eyes. 54. If he is not redeemed by any of these, he shall go out in the *yovel* year, he and his children with him. 55. For to Me the sons of Yisrael are [bond]servants; they are My [bond]servants; I Who brought them out from the land of Mitzrayim, I, *God*, their God.

XXVI 1. Do not make gods for yourselves, and do not set up an image or a memorial stone or put up a marker anywhere in your land to cast yourselves down upon it; I, *God*, your

שָׁנִים כִּימֵי שָׂכִיר יִהְיֶה עִמּוֹ: נא אִם־עוֹד רַבּוֹת בַּשָּׁנִים לְפִיהֶן יָשִׁיב גְּאֻלָּתוֹ מִכֶּסֶף מִקְנָתוֹ: נב וְאִם־מְעַט נִשְׁאַר בַּשָּׁנִים עַד־שְׁנַת הַיֹּבֵל וְחִשַּׁב־לוֹ כְּפִי שָׁנָיו יָשִׁיב אֶת־גְּאֻלָּתוֹ: נג כִּשְׂכִיר שָׁנָה בְּשָׁנָה יִהְיֶה עִמּוֹ לֹא־יִרְדֶּנּוּ בְּפֶרֶךְ לְעֵינֶיךָ: נד וְאִם־לֹא יִגָּאֵל בְּאֵלֶּה וְיָצָא בִּשְׁנַת הַיֹּבֵל הוּא וּבָנָיו עִמּוֹ: מפטיר נה כִּי־לִי בְנֵי־יִשְׂרָאֵל עֲבָדִים עֲבָדַי הֵם אֲשֶׁר־הוֹצֵאתִי אוֹתָם מֵאֶרֶץ מִצְרָיִם אֲנִי יְהֹוָה אֱלֹהֵיכֶם: כו א לֹא־תַעֲשׂוּ לָכֶם אֱלִילִם וּפֶסֶל וּמַצֵּבָה לֹא־תָקִימוּ לָכֶם וְאֶבֶן מַשְׂכִּית לֹא תִתְּנוּ בְּאַרְצְכֶם לְהִשְׁתַּחֲוֹת עָלֶיהָ כִּי אֲנִי יְהֹוָה

---

55. *For to Me the sons of Yisrael are [bond]servants.* Here again, at the conclusion of the laws relating to personal freedom, the text states the premise upon which the inalienable personal liberty of the sons of Israel is based: Israel's subordination to God, which is founded on Israel's deliverance from Egypt and which precludes subservience to anyone or anything else. The fact that God Himself is his master raises the servant of God above any other condition of servitude and makes it impossible for him to accept the yoke of any other master. As *Torath Kohanim* ibid. puts it, [God says]: "My deed of purchase came first; therefore I have first priority." Every fiber of your being, every ounce of your strength is Mine; therefore you cannot enter into the bondage of another. Jewish Law is so consistent in impressing upon every Jew the inalienable character of personal freedom that, as a rule, it does not even regard the daily contract of a hired day laborer as irrevocable and the day laborer may break it at any time during the day: "The worker can withdraw from it even in the middle of the day."

CHAPTER XXVI

1 and 2. . . . Wherever you may be, it is My Sabbaths that will make you aware of Me and of My sovereignty and will win you for Myself. And the place

that is to sanctify all of your lives in order to win My Presence is the Sanctuary of My Law. Therefore, "Keep My Sabbaths and fear My Sanctuary; I, *God*."

We are to keep ourselves aware of God not by means of an image, or a memorial stone. It is the Sabbaths of God, the Sabbath of Creation and the Sabbaths of the land, שַׁבָּת, שְׁמִיטָה, and יוֹבֵל [the fiftieth year], which, by governing and shaping our private and public lives and by ordaining great acts of personal sacrifice, make the acknowledgment of God a reality in our lives; also the מוֹעֲדִים, the Sabbaths of God in the wider sense of the term, the times of meeting set so that we may remember His workings—these represent our sign, our covenant and our time of meeting. These symbols are not carved from lifeless stone. They are the symbols of recognition, covenant and remembrance woven from the vital tissue of our active lives, enabling us to perceive God and His sovereignty not merely as facts in themselves but in terms of their immediate impact on our everyday lives. By bidding us to subordinate and consecrate all our lives to Him, they make it possible for us to "meet" with Him wherever we may be.

God does not desire "a marker anywhere in your land to cast yourselves down upon it"; He does not wish to have you worship Him by casting yourselves down before Him at any place that pleases you, no matter

God.   2. Keep My Sabbaths and fear My
Sanctuary; I, *God*.

אֱלֹהֵיכֶם: ב אֶת־שַׁבְּתֹתַי תִּשְׁמֹרוּ וּמִקְדָּשִׁי
תִּירָאוּ אֲנִי יְהוָה: פ

how fervent your devotion. He has placed His Law
between Himself and ourselves and we can pay Him
homage only by paying homage to His Law. Only by
casting ourselves down before His Law do we cast ourselves down before Him. For this reason the only spot
on earth that may be marked by stones set in the
ground as the place where we may cast ourselves down
before Him in complete devotion is the Sanctuary
which He Himself established for His Law on Mount
Moriah-Zion. And because, anywhere else on earth, we
may prostrate ourselves before God only on ground *not*
especially marked by a stone for this purpose, the whole
wide world becomes simply one great orbit around that
one central point which God Himself has consecrated
for the Testimony of His Law and which remains consecrated as such even while it lies in ruins (cf. "The
throne of Thy glory, on high from the beginning"—
Jeremiah 17:12)—and wherever we cast ourselves down
before God we do so only in the thought of His Law.

Moreover, it is not the physical movement symbolizing our unreserved subordination to the Law of His
Sanctuary, but "reverence" (cf. "and fear My Sanctuary"), the earnestness of attitude that accompanies us
wherever we may be, that will keep before us at all
times, wherever we may be, the solemn requirement
that we must let ourselves be sanctified out of that
sacred center, fulfilling the lofty ideal of our life's purpose as set down there. This attitude will spur us on to a
personal and public life of such quality that we will be
able to contemplate this ideal without having to blush
in shame, a life that will not desecrate this sanctuary of
our life's ideal. Only such a "fear of God's Sanctuary"
will truly make the Sanctuary of God's Law a lofty
spiritual center which, at all times and wherever we
may be, will draw us all with mighty bonds toward
itself and thus toward God. It is this reverence . . . that,
by causing us to look up into the eye of God, which is
always upon us, will bring us directly into
God's Presence, to the Source of all the seeds of protection and blessings that the commandments of His Law
scatter upon the field of our life.

God says: אֲנִי ד׳ ["I, *God*"]. Do not spend your energies on efforts to influence Me. It is My nature that I
am ready at all times to bestow blessings and loving-
kindness. But it is your task to make yourselves worthy
and fit to receive these blessings by observing My
Laws. The Sanctuary of *God* and the Sabbaths of *God*,
the Sanctuary of the Law in space, with its role in the
hallowing of our moral lives, and the Divine sancta in
time, with their effects on our spiritual and social lives
— these comprise the sum total of all the laws that form
the content of this third Book of God's Law, from the
opening chapter until this point.

The Haftarah for this Sidra may be found on page 885.

בחקתי

BEḤUKKOTHAI

3. If you will walk in My statutes and
keep My commandments and carry them
out, 4. I will give your rains in their
season; the earth will yield its produce and
the tree of the field will yield its fruit.
5. Your threshing season will extend until
the vintage, and the vintage will extend
until the sowing time. You will eat your
bread until you are satisfied and you will
dwell securely in your land. 6. I will give
peace in the land, you will lie down and
nothing will disturb your rest. I will make
wild beasts disappear from the land and
no sword will pass through your land.
7. If you pursue your enemies, they will
fall to the sword before you. 8. Five of
you will pursue one hundred, and one
hundred of you will pursue ten thousand,
and your enemies will fall to the sword
before you. 9. And I will turn to you and
make you fruitful and multiply you, and I
will maintain My covenant with you.
10. You will eat old produce from the
previous year and you will clear out the old
because of the new. 11. I will set My
Presence among you, and My soul will not
reject you. 12. I will walk among you and
will show Myself your God, and you will be
a people to Me. 13. I, *God*, your God,
Who brought you out from the land of
Mitzrayim so that you should not remain
[bond]servants to them; at that time I also
broke the bars of your yoke and taught you
to walk upright. 14. But if you will not

ג אִם־בְּחֻקֹּתַי תֵּלֵכוּ וְאֶת־מִצְוֺתַי תִּשְׁמְרוּ
וַעֲשִׂיתֶם אֹתָם׃ ד וְנָתַתִּי גִשְׁמֵיכֶם בְּעִתָּם וְנָתְנָה
הָאָרֶץ יְבוּלָהּ וְעֵץ הַשָּׂדֶה יִתֵּן פִּרְיוֹ׃ ה וְהִשִּׂיג
לָכֶם דַּיִשׁ אֶת־בָּצִיר וּבָצִיר יַשִּׂיג אֶת־זָרַע
וַאֲכַלְתֶּם לַחְמְכֶם לָשֹׂבַע וִישַׁבְתֶּם לָבֶטַח
בְּאַרְצְכֶם׃ שני ו וְנָתַתִּי שָׁלוֹם בָּאָרֶץ וּשְׁכַבְתֶּם
וְאֵין מַחֲרִיד וְהִשְׁבַּתִּי חַיָּה רָעָה מִן־הָאָרֶץ
וְחֶרֶב לֹא־תַעֲבֹר בְּאַרְצְכֶם׃ ז וּרְדַפְתֶּם אֶת־
אֹיְבֵיכֶם וְנָפְלוּ לִפְנֵיכֶם לֶחָרֶב׃ ח וְרָדְפוּ מִכֶּם
חֲמִשָּׁה מֵאָה וּמֵאָה מִכֶּם רְבָבָה יִרְדֹּפוּ וְנָפְלוּ
אֹיְבֵיכֶם לִפְנֵיכֶם לֶחָרֶב׃ ט וּפָנִיתִי אֲלֵיכֶם
וְהִפְרֵיתִי אֶתְכֶם וְהִרְבֵּיתִי אֶתְכֶם וַהֲקִימֹתִי אֶת־
בְּרִיתִי אִתְּכֶם׃ שלישי (חמישי כשהן מחוברין)
י וַאֲכַלְתֶּם יָשָׁן נוֹשָׁן וְיָשָׁן מִפְּנֵי חָדָשׁ תּוֹצִיאוּ׃
יא וְנָתַתִּי מִשְׁכָּנִי בְּתוֹכְכֶם וְלֹא־תִגְעַל נַפְשִׁי
אֶתְכֶם׃ יב וְהִתְהַלַּכְתִּי בְּתוֹכְכֶם וְהָיִיתִי לָכֶם
לֵאלֹהִים וְאַתֶּם תִּהְיוּ־לִי לְעָם׃ יג אֲנִי יְהֹוָה
אֱלֹהֵיכֶם אֲשֶׁר הוֹצֵאתִי אֶתְכֶם מֵאֶרֶץ מִצְרַיִם
מִהְיֹת לָהֶם עֲבָדִים וָאֶשְׁבֹּר מֹטֹת עֻלְּכֶם וָאוֹלֵךְ
אֶתְכֶם קוֹמְמִיּוּת׃ פ יד וְאִם־לֹא תִשְׁמְעוּ לִי

3. Verses 9–12 of the preceding chapter showed how our observance of the *yovel* laws and the resulting subordination of all the material and social affairs of the nation-state to God will bring God Himself to reshape these affairs so as to promote prosperity and regeneration. . . . It was indicated also in Verses 18 and 19 that our observance of the God-given moral laws and social ordinances will bring about a material, social and political flowering of the nation, thus demonstrating the special care lavished upon that nation by Divine Providence.

Now, Verses 3–13 picture in bold strokes the happiness and prosperity that will come if the nation observes the Law of God; conversely, Verses 14 ff. describe the ruin that will come upon the nation if it should fail to carry out God's Law.

° ° °

6. ***I will give peace in the land.*** As a result of the atmosphere of contentment and harmony within the population and of the people's mutual joy in one another, such as can blossom only on the soil of God's Law beneath the light of His blessing, the nation's communal life will be blessed with tranquillity. . . .

hearken to Me and will not carry out all these commandments, 15. and if you will despise My statutes and if your soul will reject My [social] ordinances so that all My commandments will not be carried out, so

וְלֹ֣א תַֽעֲשׂ֔וּ אֵ֥ת כָּל־הַמִּצְוֺ֖ת הָאֵֽלֶּה׃ טו וְאִם־
בְּחֻקֹּתַ֣י תִּמְאָ֔סוּ וְאִ֥ם אֶת־מִשְׁפָּטַ֖י תִּגְעַ֣ל
נַפְשְׁכֶ֑ם לְבִלְתִּ֤י עֲשׂוֹת֙ אֶת־כָּל־מִצְוֺתַ֔י לְהַפְרְכֶ֖ם

14. וְאִם לֹא תִשְׁמְעוּ לִי *[But if you will not hearken to Me].* שמע אֶל, and שמע לְקול and שמע בְּקול definitely mean "to heed," "to obey," but in just as many instances in Scripture . . . שמע לְ־ has the connotation of "hearkening" or "listening" to another. . . . Since the words that follow ["and you will not carry out. . ."] would already imply failure to *obey* the Word of God, the words וְאִם לֹא תִשְׁמְעוּ לִי ["but if you will not hearken to Me"] would connote failure to *listen* to the Word of God, showing that forsaking the Law in practice begins with neglect to study the laws of God in theory. We find a similar interpretation in *Torath Kohanim* ibid. The consequence of this sin in theory will be disobedience in practice. וְלֹא תַעֲשׂוּ וגו׳. כָּל שֶׁאֵינוֹ לוֹמֵד אֵינוֹ עוֹשֶׂה ["*And will not carry out*: One who does not study will not observe."]

15. ***and if you will despise My statutes.*** The process of defection continues. Once you have lost the theoretical knowledge and understanding of the laws and, no matter what the reason, have ceased to observe the laws in practice, your conscience will give you no peace until, in order to justify your behavior, you will be able to rationalize your disobedience as "progress," to look down upon loyalty to the Law as an outworn idea. For even if you have lost your theoretical knowledge of the Law and the Law has ceased to be a factor in your daily life, its power to shape and rule life still becomes apparent to you from the lives of contemporaries who do adhere to it. As a result, every such loyal adherent of the Law becomes a mute reproach to the defector until he has convinced himself that he is superior to the others and has taught himself to look down with contempt upon the Law and those who obey it.

This sort of "self-training" becomes particularly easy in relation to the חוקות, those Divine statutes which set limits to the sensual aspects of our lives and which, to those who no longer observe the Law, seem to obstruct the happiness and stunt the lives of observant contemporaries. More than with any other laws of God, the hallowing moral effect of these particular laws can be understood only by those who observe them faithfully, and the defectors, who consider that they have "liberated" themselves from such "silly restraints," find these laws the easiest to dismiss with contempt. And so the defection from the Law that began with ignorance progresses to outright contempt for the Law. "One who does not study and does not observe the Law will come to despise those who observe it" (*Torath Kohanim*).

and if your soul will reject My [social] ordinances. The process of defection continues. Unable to rise to the realization that loyalty to the Law is the product of pure inner conviction and free-willed, enthusiastic devotion to God and to His Law, the defectors seek a superficial explanation for the persistence of their contemporaries in observing the Law. They find the answer in the institutions of Jewish communal life that are all based on the theoretical knowledge and practical observance of the Law. These are institutions that presuppose the cultivation and practice of the Law and have created a family and community life—and at one time also a political life—which made the study and observance of the Law the most important concern of all classes in Jewish society. The defectors therefore now turn in fierce hatred against these Jewish communal institutions and, above all, against the *ḥakhamim* [the Sages], the upholders and guardians of these institutions. They view them as the "misfortune" of their race, and the contempt they feel for those of their brethren who continue to be loyal to the Law turns into hatred for the spiritual upholders and guardians of the institutions of Jewish Law. "One who does not study and does not observe the Law and despises those who observe it will come to hate the Sages" (*Torath Kohanim*).

so that all My commandments will not be carried out. The process of defection continues. Up to this point the defector did not go beyond becoming estranged from the Law himself and hating and despising the Law and those who observe and guard it. But once he has conceived such deep feelings of inner opposition to the Law he will not stop there. When the opportunity arises, his opposition will turn into fanatical intolerance toward any observance of the Law. That which the defector does not respect must not be respected by anyone else; what he no longer observes must also not be observed by others. And so he declares war on the Law and obstructs its observance wherever and in whatever way he can. Of course, he is sure that he will win the day and persuades himself that he is in fact performing a good deed that will benefit all mankind. He tells himself, too, that in fighting against the survival of the Law he is not really fighting against God and His holy will. In his eyes that against which he fights cannot be the Law of God; therefore he labels Revelation as a myth, Moses and the Prophets as impostors, and those who transmitted the Law from Sinai as dupes and deceivers. Inasmuch as he has set the disappearance of Jewish observances ("so that all My commandments will not be carried out") as the goal of his fanatical struggle, he must cease to view these laws that you will break My covenant, 16. then I also will do the same to you; I will bring upon you consternation that produces prostration and fever that cause the eyes to pine away and fill the spirit with grief. You will then sow your seed in vain; your enemies will eat it. 17. And I will set My Countenance against you; you will be beaten before your enemies. Those that hate you will rule over you and you will flee even when no one pursues you. 18. And if, even at this point, you will not hearken to Me, I will continue to chastise you, seven times for your sins. 19. I will break the pride of your power, and I will make your heavens be like iron and your land like copper. 20. Your strength will be spent in vain; your land will no longer yield its produce and the tree of the land will no longer yield its fruit. 21. And if you walk with Me [only] by

אֶת־בְּרִיתִי: טז אַף־אֲנִי אֶעֱשֶׂה־זֹּאת לָכֶם וְהִפְקַדְתִּי עֲלֵיכֶם בֶּהָלָה אֶת־הַשַּׁחֶפֶת וְאֶת־הַקַּדַּחַת מְכַלּוֹת עֵינַיִם וּמְדִיבֹת נָפֶשׁ וּזְרַעְתֶּם לָרִיק זַרְעֲכֶם וַאֲכָלֻהוּ אֹיְבֵיכֶם: יז וְנָתַתִּי פָנַי בָּכֶם וְנִגַּפְתֶּם לִפְנֵי אֹיְבֵיכֶם וְרָדוּ בָכֶם שֹׂנְאֵיכֶם וְנַסְתֶּם וְאֵין־רֹדֵף אֶתְכֶם: יח וְאִם־עַד־אֵלֶּה לֹא תִשְׁמְעוּ לִי וְיָסַפְתִּי לְיַסְּרָה אֶתְכֶם שֶׁבַע עַל־חַטֹּאתֵיכֶם: יט וְשָׁבַרְתִּי אֶת־גְּאוֹן עֻזְּכֶם וְנָתַתִּי אֶת־שְׁמֵיכֶם כַּבַּרְזֶל וְאֶת־אַרְצְכֶם כַּנְּחֻשָׁה: כ וְתַם לָרִיק כֹּחֲכֶם וְלֹא־תִתֵּן אַרְצְכֶם אֶת־יְבוּלָהּ וְעֵץ הָאָרֶץ לֹא יִתֵּן פִּרְיוֹ: כא וְאִם־תֵּלְכוּ

as "My laws," the laws of God, and, as *Torath Kohanim* describes this next step in the process of defection: "One who does not study and does not observe the Law and despises those who observe it and hates the Sages will eventually not permit others to observe it, and if he does not study and does not observe the Law and despises those who observe it and hates the Sages and does not permit others to observe it, the end will be that he will deny the validity of the commandments that were given on Mount Sinai."

However, the process of defection does not stop even here. There still remains one final step: "So that you will break My covenant," to break the last slender thread that still binds the defector to the covenant of God. According to *Torath Kohanim*, this is כְּפִירָה בְּעִיקָּר, [the denial of the fundamental truth]; the defector ends by denying the existence of God. Once he has started on the slippery path of defection it is inevitable that he should arrive at this final stage. As long as any thought of God still lingers in his heart, as long as there is still room in his soul for some concept, no matter how nebulous, of God, his conscience will give him no peace, for if there is even a possibility that God exists, then the idea of Revelation is not entirely inadmissible. If he is to attain peace of mind, night must descend completely upon his spirit, the last glimmering spark of his awareness of God must be stamped out and the last thread that could lead him back to the covenant broken. In order to find this supposed peace of mind he must rudely stamp out this last spark and break this last thread, and "one who has all these character traits will come to deny the fundamental truth" (*Torath Kohanim*).

17. **And I will set My Countenance against you.** My Countenance, which was always turned toward you, will turn against you. When you pursue your marauding neighbors, it is you (as contrasted to the promise in Verses 7 and 8) who will be beaten.

Those that hate you will rule over you. You will fall under the sway of "those that hate you"; i.e., the neighboring nations that envied your former prosperity and that came to hate you because of your way of life, so completely opposed to their own. Then, in your state of political dependence, and as a result of your defection from My laws, you will become so timid that "you will flee even when no one pursues you," you will suspect danger and hostility even where there are none.

Torath Kohanim interprets שֹׂנְאֵיכֶם ["those that hate you"] to denote enemies from without, as opposed to אֹיְבֵיכֶם, foes within.... Political disaster from without will set off fragmentation within. There will arise, from amidst the people, enemies of the Jewish way of life who will blame Israel's political disaster not on those who defected from the Law but on those still faithful to its tenets. They will promise the people emancipation from the political yoke imposed on them by the other nations if only they will emancipate themselves completely from the "yoke" of God's Law. These enemies from within will make themselves the tools of the enemies from without, and this inner fragmentation will serve only to increase the misery inflicted upon Israel by its foes.

21. וְאִם תֵּלְכוּ עִמִּי קֶרִי [And if you walk with Me (only) by chance]. קֶרִי, derived from קרה ["to happen"] denotes anything that happens without our intention or

chance and will not resolve to hearken to Me, I will add yet another blow for you, seven times according to your sins. 22. And I will let the wild beast[s] of the field loose against you so that they will rob you of your children, destroy your cattle and reduce your numbers; and your highways will be desolate.   23. And if, despite these things, you will not be corrected for Me by chastisement, and you will walk with Me [only] by chance, 24. then I, too, will walk with you [only] by chance and I will also strike you seven times for your sins.   25. I will bring upon you an avenging sword to avenge the covenant, and you will gather in your cities. Then I will send pestilence into your midst and you will deliver yourselves up into the hand of the enemy. 26. When I break your staff of bread, ten women will bake your bread in one oven and bring back your bread by weight; you will eat but you will not be satisfied. 27. And if, nevertheless, you will not hearken to Me and will walk with me [only] by chance,   28. I will walk with you in the [random] fury of chance and I, too, will chastise you seven-fold because of your sins.   29. You will eat the flesh of your sons, and the flesh of your daughters will you eat,   30. and I will cause your high places to be destroyed and cause your images of the sun to be cut off, and I will place your remains beside the remains of your monstrous gods, and My soul will reject you.   31. I will give your cities to be smashed and will make your sanctuaries desolate, and will no longer accept your offerings as an expression of compliance.   32. And I Myself will make the land desolate and your enemies who settle there will become desolate upon it.

עַמִּי קֶ֫רִי וְלֹא תֹאבוּ לִשְׁמֹעַ לִי וְיָסַפְתִּי עֲלֵיכֶם מַכָּה שֶׁ֫בַע כְּחַטֹּאתֵיכֶם: כב וְהִשְׁלַחְתִּי בָכֶם אֶת־חַיַּת הַשָּׂדֶה וְשִׁכְּלָה אֶתְכֶם וְהִכְרִיתָה אֶת־בְּהֶמְתְּכֶם וְהִמְעִיטָה אֶתְכֶם וְנָשַׁ֫מּוּ דַּרְכֵיכֶם: כג וְאִם־בְּאֵ֫לֶּה לֹא תִוָּסְרוּ לִי וַהֲלַכְתֶּם עִמִּי קֶ֫רִי: כד וְהָלַכְתִּי אַף־אֲנִי עִמָּכֶם בְּקֶ֫רִי וְהִכֵּיתִי אֶתְכֶם גַּם־אָ֫נִי שֶׁ֫בַע עַל־חַטֹּאתֵיכֶם: כה וְהֵבֵאתִי עֲלֵיכֶם חֶ֫רֶב נֹקֶ֫מֶת נְקַם־בְּרִית וְנֶאֱסַפְתֶּם אֶל־עָרֵיכֶם וְשִׁלַּחְתִּי דֶ֫בֶר בְּתוֹכְכֶם וְנִתַּתֶּם בְּיַד־אוֹיֵב: כו בְּשִׁבְרִי לָכֶם מַטֵּה־לֶ֫חֶם וְאָפוּ עֶ֫שֶׂר נָשִׁים לַחְמְכֶם בְּתַנּוּר אֶחָד וְהֵשִׁ֫יבוּ לַחְמְכֶם בַּמִּשְׁקָל וַאֲכַלְתֶּם וְלֹא תִשְׂבָּ֫עוּ: ס כז וְאִם־בְּזֹאת לֹא תִשְׁמְעוּ לִי וַהֲלַכְתֶּם עִמִּי בְּקֶ֫רִי: כח וְהָלַכְתִּי עִמָּכֶם בַּחֲמַת־קֶ֫רִי וְיִסַּרְתִּי אֶתְכֶם אַף־אָ֫נִי שֶׁ֫בַע עַל־חַטֹּאתֵיכֶם: כט וַאֲכַלְתֶּם בְּשַׂר בְּנֵיכֶם וּבְשַׂר בְּנֹתֵיכֶם תֹּאכֵלוּ: ל וְהִשְׁמַדְתִּי אֶת־בָּמֹתֵיכֶם וְהִכְרַתִּי אֶת־חַמָּנֵיכֶם וְנָתַתִּי אֶת־פִּגְרֵיכֶם עַל־פִּגְרֵי גִּלּוּלֵיכֶם וְגָעֲלָה נַפְשִׁי אֶתְכֶם: לא וְנָתַתִּי אֶת־עָרֵיכֶם חָרְבָּה וַהֲשִׁמּוֹתִי אֶת־מִקְדְּשֵׁיכֶם וְלֹא אָרִיחַ בְּרֵיחַ נִיחֹחֲכֶם: לב וַהֲשִׁמֹּתִי אֲנִי אֶת־הָאָ֫רֶץ וְשָׁמְמוּ עָלֶ֫יהָ אֹיְבֵיכֶם הַיֹּשְׁבִים בָּהּ:

planning. ... Your going with Me is only קֶ֫רִי. The fact that you happen to be conducting yourself in accordance with My will is the result of pure chance. It was not your intention, your resolve—your very first resolve before all others, as it should have been—to obey Me and to do what is in accordance with My will. Perhaps you are now no longer opposed to My will as a matter of principle, but My will is still a matter of indifference to you. You allow entirely different considerations to determine your way of life and leave it to chance whether or not this makes you conduct yourself in accordance with My will.

and will not resolve to hearken to Me. You have not resolved to ascertain My will before all else. ...

28. ... If even such experiences of war, resulting in your being conquered by a world power that wields the sword to avenge My covenant with man, will not be sufficient to teach you how utterly impotent you are without God's protection and to make you resolve to return to My Law, I will make you experience the same disaster once again in all its savage fury. This random fury of events, the unrestrained ruthless fury shown by a conqueror toward a weak, defenseless nation, is חֲמַת קֶ֫רִי.

33. And as for you, I will scatter you among the nations and will draw the sword behind you; and your land will remain desolate and your cities will remain in ruins. 34. Then the land will have its satisfaction from its Sabbaths; as long as it is desolate and you are in the land of your enemies, the land will observe a Sabbath and satisfy its Sabbath years. 35. As long as it is desolate it will observe a Sabbath, the Sabbath that it did not have during your Sabbath years, when you dwelt in it. 36. And as for those of you who will remain, I will bring despair into their hearts in the lands of their enemies; the sound of a driven leaf will put them to flight; they will flee as one flees from the sword; they will fall even though no one pursues them. 37. They will stumble over one another as if it were before the sword, and there is not [even] a pursuer, and you will not have the strength to stand up before your enemies. 38. You will become lost among the nations, and the land of your enemies will devour you, 39. but those of you who will remain will rot away because of their iniquity in the lands of your enemies, and they will rot away also because of the iniquities of their parents which are still with them, 40. until they will acknowledge to themselves their iniquity and the iniquity of

לג וְאֶתְכֶם אֱזָרֶה בַגּוֹיִם וַהֲרִיקֹתִי אַחֲרֵיכֶם
חָרֶב וְהָיְתָה אַרְצְכֶם שְׁמָמָה וְעָרֵיכֶם יִהְיוּ
חָרְבָּה: לד אָז תִּרְצֶה הָאָרֶץ אֶת־שַׁבְּתֹתֶיהָ כֹּל
יְמֵי הָשַּׁמָּה וְאַתֶּם בְּאֶרֶץ אֹיְבֵיכֶם אָז תִּשְׁבַּת
הָאָרֶץ וְהִרְצָת אֶת־שַׁבְּתֹתֶיהָ: לה כָּל־יְמֵי
הָשַּׁמָּה תִּשְׁבֹּת אֵת אֲשֶׁר לֹא־שָׁבְתָה
בְּשַׁבְּתֹתֵיכֶם בְּשִׁבְתְּכֶם עָלֶיהָ: לו וְהַנִּשְׁאָרִים
בָּכֶם וְהֵבֵאתִי מֹרֶךְ בִּלְבָבָם בְּאַרְצֹת אֹיְבֵיהֶם
וְרָדַף אֹתָם קוֹל עָלֶה נִדָּף וְנָסוּ מְנֻסַת־חֶרֶב
וְנָפְלוּ וְאֵין רֹדֵף: לז וְכָשְׁלוּ אִישׁ־בְּאָחִיו
כְּמִפְּנֵי־חֶרֶב וְרֹדֵף אָיִן וְלֹא־תִהְיֶה לָכֶם תְּקוּמָה
לִפְנֵי אֹיְבֵיכֶם: לח וַאֲבַדְתֶּם בַּגּוֹיִם וְאָכְלָה
אֶתְכֶם אֶרֶץ אֹיְבֵיכֶם: לט וְהַנִּשְׁאָרִים בָּכֶם יִמַּקּוּ
בַּעֲוֹנָם בְּאַרְצֹת אֹיְבֵיכֶם וְאַף בַּעֲוֹנֹת אֲבֹתָם
אִתָּם יִמָּקּוּ: מ וְהִתְוַדּוּ אֶת־עֲוֹנָם וְאֶת־עֲוֹן
אֲבֹתָם בְּמַעֲלָם אֲשֶׁר מָעֲלוּ־בִי וְאַף אֲשֶׁר־הָלְכוּ

39–41. _but those of you who will remain... until they will acknowledge to themselves... And I, too, will walk with them._ As for those who will survive these harassments of the initial period of their exile, their future in exile will be determined by their conception and implementation of their mission in exile. Their life in exile will take either one of two courses, as follows:

_(1)_ Even the impact of their disaster has not yet put the survivors into the proper frame of mind before God. Instead of making them more observant of the Law, exile will loosen even more the ties that bound them to the Law of God. They will view exile as a dispensation from the obligations imposed upon them by the Law.... Living under conditions suited for anything but the observance of God's laws, conditions which, in fact, are basically adverse to such observances, they will argue that the Law was intended for observance only in _Eretz Yisrael._ They will persuade themselves that as long as they live on alien soil, amidst alien and indeed hostile conditions, the duty of self-preservation affords

at least an excuse for their defection from the Law of God.... [However,] this added and continued defection from the Law of God will serve only to vitiate the one principle of survival that could have molded them, even in exile, into a vital nation and brought them a material and spiritual flowering unique to _galuth_ life and based on the Law. Without this principle of survival, the _galuth_ will become their grave and "they will rot away because of their iniquity." Instead of attaining "life," as they had hoped to do, by casting off the traits that made them unique, they will "rot away" because of their sin.

until they will acknowledge to themselves. This state of affairs will continue until they will realize that their deliberate defection in exile and their continued indifference to the observance of the Law has brought them not life but decay—spiritual, moral and social ruin....

     •   •   •

_(2)_ אוֹ אָז _[Or then, perhaps]._ Or perhaps the

עִמִּי בְּקֶרִי: מא אַף־אֲנִי אֵלֵךְ עִמָּם בְּקֶרִי
וְהֵבֵאתִי אֹתָם בְּאֶרֶץ אֹיְבֵיהֶם אוֹ־אָז יִכָּנַע
לְבָבָם הֶעָרֵל וְאָז יִרְצוּ אֶת־עֲוֹנָם: מב וְזָכַרְתִּי
אֶת־בְּרִיתִי יַעֲקוֹב וְאַף אֶת־בְּרִיתִי יִצְחָק וְאַף
אֶת־בְּרִיתִי אַבְרָהָם אֶזְכֹּר וְהָאָרֶץ אֶזְכֹּר:
מג וְהָאָרֶץ תֵּעָזֵב מֵהֶם וְתִרֶץ אֶת־שַׁבְּתֹתֶיהָ
בָּהְשַׁמָּה מֵהֶם וְהֵם יִרְצוּ אֶת־עֲוֹנָם יַעַן וּבְיַעַן

their parents with which they committed perfidy against Me, and also that they walked with Me [only] by chance.
41. And I, too, will walk with them [only] by chance and will bring them to their home in the land of their enemies. Or then, perhaps, their unyielding heart will bow and then they will satisfy the debt of their iniquity.
42. Then I shall remember My covenant "Yaakov," and also My covenant "Yitzḥak," and I shall remember also My covenant "Abraham," and I will remember the land.
43. And the land, left behind by them, will be satisfied by its Sabbaths as long as it

second alternative will come to pass. Instead of continuing in the sinful ways of their forefathers, and augmenting them with new sins born of exile, אָז then, after all the crushing blows of the initial period of exile, the hearts of "those of you who will remain," those who survive this period, will not "rot away in sins old and new," but will become bowed down. They will bow down to God, they will cease to be "uncircumcised" before God; they will give up their recalcitrance. . . . וְאָז, and then, instead of waiting until the end of time, "they will satisfy the debt of their iniquity." They will willingly bear all their future fate in exile and gladly accomplish their mission in exile as a means of atoning for their past sins, thus satisfying themselves and paying the debt they have incurred with their transgressions. If this happens, their *galuth* will gain an entirely different aspect. Instead of becoming a grave, a place of decay, exile will turn into a habitat for a new fulfillment of Israel's God-ordained mission, fruitful soil for a *galuth* life directed toward God, and bound up with Him, a new life whose entire purpose and content is that "they will satisfy the debt of their iniquity." . . .

42. . . . ***Then I shall remember My covenant "Yaakov."*** Then I will fulfill the promise I made in My covenant as symbolized by the life of Jacob. I will be with them through all the long, long nights of their *galuth* and will transform even the darkest night of their exile into a shining revelation of Divine Providence. In both life and death they will shine in the dark night of the nations as stars of self-sacrificing dedication to the spiritual and moral mission of all mankind.

And when they have suffered enough, when, though beset by adversity, they will have inscribed their loyalty to the Law with their heart's blood upon the pages of martyrdom in world history, then I will remember "also My covenant 'Isaac.'"

Then they will not have lived and bled in vain among the nations. The example they will set will enlighten the spirit of the nations, making the nations gentler. And with the dawn of the morning of the nations, the dark midnight of Israel's *galuth* will come to an end. The exiles will be able to breathe more freely and to come into full flower on soil which, until then, had been alien to them. During the period symbolized by the life of Jacob, they had to endure hatred. Now, in this next phase, their life will resemble the history of Isaac. They will be rebuffed by the nations that will envy them (see Genesis 26:14 and 16) and they will have to pass the next phase of their training in *galuth* which, given their nature, will surely not be easy for them. In the midst of growing prosperity, living among nations that will alternate between humaneness and envy in their treatment of them, they will have to preserve their unique character even as did Isaac. They will have to employ all their resources, ampler and less restricted than before, to attain even greater loyalty to the Law for a more perfect and many-sided elaboration of their own mission in *galuth,* in utter disregard of the envy of the nations that will still keep them isolated from the rest of the world.

If they pass this second test in exile, the test whether they will remain loyal to the Law even in the midst of prosperity, then "I shall remember also My covenant 'Abraham.'" The sun that shone upon Abraham will shine upon them even in exile. Like Abraham, they will build their altars to God and to His Law in the midst of the other nations. Like Abraham, too, they will bring to the nations all the goodness and truth of the Law of God that had been entrusted to Israel for the salvation of all mankind. They will translate these truths into reality among the nations and for the nations in such a manner that Israel will be tolerated and respected not even though, but precisely *because,* they are the people of the covenant of Abraham, because they understand in theory and also observe in practice the Law of God for the salvation of mankind. . . .

43. **יַעַן וּבְיַעַן** ***[all in accordance with, and by that which accords].*** The fate decreed for them in exile will

lies desolate without them, and they shall satisfy the debt of their iniquity—all in accordance with, and by that which accords with, [the fact] that they despised My [social] ordinances and their soul rejected My statutes, 44. and yet for all that, even by their being in the land of their enemies, I have not despised them and not rejected them in order to destroy them, to break My covenant with them, for I, *God*, am still their God, 45. and I will remember for them the covenant of those that came before [them], whom, after all, I brought out from Mitzrayim before the eyes of the nations, to prove Myself to them as God; I, *God*. 46. These are the statutes, the [social] ordinances and the teachings which *God* has

בְּמִשְׁפָּטַי מָאָסוּ וְאֶת־חֻקֹּתַי גָּעֲלָה נַפְשָׁם: מד וְאַף־גַּם־זֹאת בִּהְיוֹתָם בְּאֶרֶץ אֹיְבֵיהֶם לֹא־מְאַסְתִּים וְלֹא־גְעַלְתִּים לְכַלֹּתָם לְהָפֵר בְּרִיתִי אִתָּם כִּי אֲנִי יְהֹוָה אֱלֹהֵיהֶם: מה וְזָכַרְתִּי לָהֶם בְּרִית רִאשֹׁנִים אֲשֶׁר הוֹצֵאתִי־אֹתָם מֵאֶרֶץ מִצְרַיִם לְעֵינֵי הַגּוֹיִם לִהְיוֹת לָהֶם לֵאלֹהִים אֲנִי יְהֹוָה: מו אֵלֶּה הַחֻקִּים וְהַמִּשְׁפָּטִים וְהַתּוֹרֹת אֲשֶׁר נָתַן יְהֹוָה בֵּינוֹ וּבֵין בְּנֵי יִשְׂרָאֵל בְּהַר סִינַי

be in direct relationship to their sins. They will have to atone for their iniquities by exercising virtues representing the exact opposite of their sins. The sin which weighs heavily upon them as a debt for which they must make atonement is that "they despised My [social] ordinances." Despising the God-given social ordinances, they believed they could build and maintain their social and political life as a nation on the basis of other values. Moreover, "their soul rejected My statutes." They felt that the laws of God which placed moral restraints upon the sensual aspects of their lives thwarted them in their quest for personal happiness and stunted their lives, and therefore they rejected them. As a result of the first of these two sins, their social and political life as a nation would be shattered for centuries. They would have to dwell, for centuries, as an outlawed entity in alien lands, barred from all the blessings derived from the protection of the law, and deemed worthy only of oppression and harsh treatment. As a result of their second sin, their personal happiness would be curtailed for centuries and their share in the joys and pleasures of life severely restricted.

And even as their punishment would be in accordance with their sin, so their atonement, too, would have to consist in acts that accorded with their transgression. They had given first place to social advantage, to personal gain and pleasure, and made the Law of God and its requirements secondary to these ambitions. The atonement for this sin must take the form of a corresponding virtue. They will be forced to live for centuries amidst personal and objective conditions under which almost every observance of the laws of God will entail the sacrifice of one of life's pleasures or the renunciation of a human right. Under these circumstances the Law of God will indeed appear to be, as the prophet (Ezekiel 20:25) put it, "statutes that are not

good" and "[social] ordinances by which you shall not live." For centuries they will suffer misery and despair, imprisonment and martyrdom, for their loyalty to the Law. All they will need to do in order to rid themselves and their children of this misery, and to enable them to share in the happiness and honors the nations have to offer, is to declare with one word their renunciation of the Law of God. But this is the one word they may never utter. They must willingly mount the scaffold with the Law of God in their arms; they must cheerfully build their humble abodes, marry, raise children, live out their lives and finally die—all in the observance of God's Law. At all times and wherever they may be, no matter what the sacrifices and hardships, the persecution and the misery they will bring upon themselves and their children by so doing, they must look upon the observance of God's Law by themselves and by their children as the one vital consideration to which all other considerations, including material prosperity and social position, must yield place as secondary factors, to be regarded with indifference. In order to atone for their former indifference to the observance of the Law, they will now have to become indifferent to the promotion of their personal happiness, and thus "satisfy the debt of their iniquity" יַעַן וּבְיַעַן, by acts that accord with their sin. יַעַן וּבְיַעַן: the sufferings decreed for them will be in accordance with their sin, and the proper atonement for their sin shall be that they will remain loyal to the Law even in the midst of these sufferings.

◦   ◦

46. *These are the statutes.* This concluding verse refers to all the laws of God governing morals, safeguarding social justice and edifying minds and hearts, from the time of the giving of the Law to this point. The text refers to these laws, and thus to all the laws of

set between Himself and the sons of Yisrael on Mount Sinai in the hand of Moshe.

XXVII   1. *God* spoke to Moshe [saying]: 2. Speak to the sons of Yisrael and say to them: If a person utters his particular resolve in the form of a vow in your valuation of souls for *God*, 3. then your valuation for males shall be from the age of twenty years to the age of sixty years, and for this your valuation shall be fifty shekels of silver according to the weight of the Sanctuary. 4. If it is a female, your valuation shall be thirty shekels. 5. And if it is from the age of five years to the age of twenty years, then your valuation for a male shall be twenty shekels and for a female, ten shekels. 6. And if it is from the age of one month to the age of five years, then your valuation for a male shall be five shekels of silver and for a female, three shekels of silver. 7. And if it is from the age of sixty years and above, if it is a male, your valuation shall be fifteen shekels, and for a female, ten shekels. 8. But if he is too poor for your valuation, he shall present him before the priest and the priest shall set his valuation; according to the means of him who made the vow shall the priest set his

בְּיַד־מֹשֶׁה: פ   רביעי   (ששי כשהן מחוברין)

כז א וַיְדַבֵּר יְהֹוָה אֶל־מֹשֶׁה לֵּאמֹר: ב דַּבֵּר אֶל־בְּנֵי יִשְׂרָאֵל וְאָמַרְתָּ אֲלֵהֶם אִישׁ כִּי יַפְלִא נֶדֶר בְּעֶרְכְּךָ נְפָשֹׁת לַיהֹוָה: ג וְהָיָה עֶרְכְּךָ הַזָּכָר מִבֶּן עֶשְׂרִים שָׁנָה וְעַד בֶּן־שִׁשִּׁים שָׁנָה וְהָיָה עֶרְכְּךָ חֲמִשִּׁים שֶׁקֶל כֶּסֶף בְּשֶׁקֶל הַקֹּדֶשׁ: ד וְאִם־נְקֵבָה הִוא וְהָיָה עֶרְכְּךָ שְׁלֹשִׁים שָׁקֶל: ה וְאִם מִבֶּן־חָמֵשׁ שָׁנִים וְעַד בֶּן־עֶשְׂרִים שָׁנָה וְהָיָה עֶרְכְּךָ הַזָּכָר עֶשְׂרִים שְׁקָלִים וְלַנְּקֵבָה עֲשֶׂרֶת שְׁקָלִים: ו וְאִם מִבֶּן־חֹדֶשׁ וְעַד בֶּן־חָמֵשׁ שָׁנִים וְהָיָה עֶרְכְּךָ הַזָּכָר חֲמִשָּׁה שְׁקָלִים כָּסֶף וְלַנְּקֵבָה עֶרְכְּךָ שְׁלֹשֶׁת שְׁקָלִים כָּסֶף: ז וְאִם מִבֶּן־שִׁשִּׁים שָׁנָה וָמַעְלָה אִם־זָכָר וְהָיָה עֶרְכְּךָ חֲמִשָּׁה עָשָׂר שָׁקֶל וְלַנְּקֵבָה עֲשָׂרָה שְׁקָלִים: ח וְאִם־מָךְ הוּא מֵעֶרְכֶּךָ וְהֶעֱמִידוֹ לִפְנֵי הַכֹּהֵן וְהֶעֱרִיךְ אֹתוֹ הַכֹּהֵן עַל־פִּי אֲשֶׁר תַּשִּׂיג יַד הַנֹּדֵר יַעֲרִיכֶנּוּ הַכֹּהֵן: ס ט וְאִם־

God, as laws that God has set between Himself and the sons of Israel. These laws are the only connecting link between ourselves and God, the sole determining factor in our relations with Him. For us there is no other intermediary, no other way to God than through His Law, even as the concluding admonition has taught us: "If you will walk in My statutes." Our nearness to God, and thus also our weal and ill, are determined solely by whether or not we observe these laws. Moreover, all the statutes, social ordinances and teachings, not merely the "Ten Commandments," were given by God at Mount Sinai at the same time and are therefore of equal importance and value. Furthermore, the Law given at Mount Sinai includes not only what is explicitly set down in this text but also the many details and instructions regarding its observance which were imparted to Moses, which "remained in his hand" after the material in this text had been recorded and which Moses can pass on only by word of mouth.

on Mount Sinai in the hand of Moshe. "This teaches us that the (entire) Torah, including its general rules and all its details, was placed into the hands of Moses at Mount Sinai" (*Torath Kohanim*).

CHAPTER XXVII

1. This entire Third Book consists of instructions telling us how to meet the requirements represented by the Sanctuary of the Law; how to lead hallowed lives as individuals and as a nation, an endeavor to be expressed in symbolic terms by our offerings and in practice by our conduct. By way of recapitulation, the preceding chapter states that the חוקים [statutes], מִשְׁפָּטִים [(social) ordinances] and תורות [teachings], which tell us what we must do in order to hallow our lives as individuals and as a nation, are the sole covenantal intermediary between ourselves and God and the only means for assuring our welfare.

The concluding chapter, which begins here, deals with free-willed donations to the Sanctuary; i.e., with the procedure to be followed if an individual should feel the need or the desire to make to the Sanctuary a voluntary gift of an object, or of its equivalent value, in order to demonstrate his special interest in the Sanctuary or to express the thought that the object he wishes to donate has a special relationship to the Sanctuary. . . .

בְּהֵמָה אֲשֶׁר יַקְרִיבוּ מִמֶּנָּה קָרְבָּן לַיהֹוָה כֹּל
אֲשֶׁר יִתֵּן מִמֶּנּוּ לַיהֹוָה יִהְיֶה־קֹּדֶשׁ׃ י לֹא
יַחֲלִיפֶנּוּ וְלֹא־יָמִיר אֹתוֹ טוֹב בְּרָע אוֹ־רַע
בְּטוֹב וְאִם־הָמֵר יָמִיר בְּהֵמָה בִּבְהֵמָה וְהָיָה־
הוּא וּתְמוּרָתוֹ יִהְיֶה־קֹּדֶשׁ׃ יא וְאִם כָּל־בְּהֵמָה
טְמֵאָה אֲשֶׁר לֹא־יַקְרִיבוּ מִמֶּנָּה קָרְבָּן לַיהֹוָה
וְהֶעֱמִיד אֶת־הַבְּהֵמָה לִפְנֵי הַכֹּהֵן׃ יב וְהֶעֱרִיךְ
הַכֹּהֵן אֹתָהּ בֵּין טוֹב וּבֵין רָע כְּעֶרְכְּךָ הַכֹּהֵן כֵּן
יִהְיֶה׃ יג וְאִם־גָּאֹל יִגְאָלֶנָּה וְיָסַף חֲמִישִׁתוֹ עַל־
עֶרְכֶּךָ׃ יד וְאִישׁ כִּי־יַקְדִּשׁ אֶת־בֵּיתוֹ קֹדֶשׁ
לַיהֹוָה וְהֶעֱרִיכוֹ הַכֹּהֵן בֵּין טוֹב וּבֵין רָע כַּאֲשֶׁר
יַעֲרִיךְ אֹתוֹ הַכֹּהֵן כֵּן יָקוּם׃ טו וְאִם־הַמַּקְדִּישׁ
יִגְאַל אֶת־בֵּיתוֹ וְיָסַף חֲמִישִׁית כֶּסֶף־עֶרְכְּךָ
עָלָיו וְהָיָה לוֹ׃ חמישי (שביעי כשהן מחוברין) טז וְאִם ׀
מִשְּׂדֵה אֲחֻזָּתוֹ יַקְדִּישׁ אִישׁ לַיהֹוָה וְהָיָה עֶרְכְּךָ
לְפִי זַרְעוֹ זֶרַע חֹמֶר שְׂעֹרִים בַּחֲמִשִּׁים שֶׁקֶל
כָּסֶף׃ יז אִם־מִשְּׁנַת הַיֹּבֵל יַקְדִּישׁ שָׂדֵהוּ כְּעֶרְכְּךָ
יָקוּם׃ יח וְאִם־אַחַר הַיֹּבֵל יַקְדִּישׁ שָׂדֵהוּ וְחִשַּׁב־
לוֹ הַכֹּהֵן אֶת־הַכֶּסֶף עַל־פִּי הַשָּׁנִים הַנּוֹתָרֹת עַד
שְׁנַת הַיֹּבֵל וְנִגְרַע מֵעֶרְכֶּךָ׃ יט וְאִם־גָּאֹל יִגְאַל
אֶת־הַשָּׂדֶה הַמַּקְדִּישׁ אֹתוֹ וְיָסַף חֲמִשִׁית כֶּסֶף־

valuation. 9. And if it is an animal of which an offering can be made to *God*, then anything that one has given of it to *God* shall remain holy. 10. He shall not alter it or exchange it, good for bad or bad for good. No matter how he exchanges animal for animal, both it and that for which he has exchanged it shall be holy. 11. But if it is an animal that has become unfit, so that none of it can be offered to *God*, one shall present the animal before the priest, 12. and the priest shall set its valuation, whether it is good or bad, as the priest sets its valuation for you, so shall it be. 13. If he himself redeems it, he shall add one fifth to your valuation. 14. And if a person consecrates his house to *God* as a holy thing, the priest shall set its valuation, whether it is good or bad, as the priest sets its valuation, so shall it stand. 15. But if the one who has consecrated it will redeem his house himself, he shall add one fifth of your valuation and then it shall be his again. 16. If a person consecrates to *God* part of the field of his inherited property, your valuation shall be according to the measure of its seed [needed to sow it], one *homer* of barley seed for fifty shekels of silver. 17. If he consecrates his field immediately after the *yovel* year, it shall stand according to this, your valuation, 18. but if he consecrates his field [later] after the *yovel*, the priest shall set the valuation for him according to the years still remaining until the [next] *yovel* year, and its value shall be deducted accordingly from your valuation. 19. And whenever he who has consecrated the field redeems it, he shall add one fifth of your valuation, and then it shall revert to him.

14 and 15. . . . In Judaism, "canonical law" does not in any manner endow objects consecrated by a human being with permanent mystical or sacramental qualities. In Jewish Law, הֶקְדֵּשׁ, a "holy thing," is merely a "legal person." Its property rights are no greater than those of a private "legal person" that has not been consecrated. Indeed, it lacks many of the rights conferred upon the latter. In Judaism, הֶקְדֵּשׁ can only acquire that status which an authorized, legitimate owner and proprietor confers upon it. A consecration made illegally, or even in error, is not recognized as a consecration. Cf. "A consecration made in error is not recognized as a consecration" (Nazir 31b). By making provisions, as it does, for פִּדְיוֹן, the "redemption" of any "holy thing," the Law shows how far removed the Jewish conception of consecration is from the notion that a verbal declaration can endow an object with permanent magic, sacramental properties. In every instance the "holiness" is inherent in a deliberate, conscious thought; it lies not in the object but in the idea, which is therefore transferable from one object to another. . . .

° ° °

20. But if he does not redeem the field or one has already sold the field to another, it cannot be redeemed anymore. 21. In that case the field, when it goes out in the *yovel*, shall become a holy thing to *God*, like a field that has been placed under a vow of interdiction; the right of its ownership shall then be the priest's. 22. But if it is a field he has bought, one that is not part of the field of his inherited property, that he consecrates to *God*, 23. then the priest shall assess for him the amount of your valuation until the [next] *yovel* year, and on that day he shall give your valuation as a holy thing to *God*. 24. In the *yovel* year the field shall revert to the one from whom he bought it; that is, to the one who inherited the land as his property. 25. Any valuation of yours shall be according to the shekel of the Sanctuary, twenty *gerahs* shall the shekel be. 26. But as for a firstling, which, as a firstling of animals, belongs to *God*, no one may consecrate it, whether it is an ox or a sheep, it belongs to *God*. 27. But whatever one consecrates of an unclean animal must be redeemed according to your valuation and one fifth must be added to it. If it is not redeemed it shall be sold according to your valuation. 28. But any [thing made subject to a] vow of interdiction that a person has vowed to *God* as an interdicted thing from anything that is his, from among men and animals and from the field of his inherited property shall neither be sold nor redeemed.

עֶרְכְּךָ֛ עָלָ֖יו וְקָ֥ם לֽוֹ׃ כ וְאִם־לֹ֤א יִגְאַל֙ אֶת־
הַשָּׂדֶ֔ה וְאִם־מָכַ֥ר אֶת־הַשָּׂדֶ֖ה לְאִ֣ישׁ אַחֵ֑ר
לֹֽא־יִגָּאֵ֖ל עֽוֹד׃ כא וְהָיָ֨ה הַשָּׂדֶ֜ה בְּצֵאת֣וֹ בַיֹּבֵ֗ל
קֹ֛דֶשׁ לַֽיהוָ֖ה כִּשְׂדֵ֣ה הַחֵ֑רֶם לַכֹּהֵ֖ן תִּהְיֶ֥ה אֲחֻזָּתֽוֹ׃
ששי כב וְאִם֙ אֶת־שְׂדֵ֣ה מִקְנָת֔וֹ אֲשֶׁ֕ר לֹ֖א מִשְּׂדֵ֣ה
אֲחֻזָּת֑וֹ יַקְדִּ֖ישׁ לַֽיהוָֽה׃ כג וְחִשַּׁב־ל֣וֹ הַכֹּהֵ֗ן אֵ֚ת
מִכְסַ֣ת הָֽעֶרְכְּךָ֔ עַ֖ד שְׁנַ֣ת הַיֹּבֵ֑ל וְנָתַ֤ן אֶת־הָֽעֶרְכְּךָ֙
בַּיּ֣וֹם הַה֔וּא קֹ֖דֶשׁ לַֽיהוָֽה׃ כד בִּשְׁנַ֤ת הַיּוֹבֵל֙
יָשׁ֣וּב הַשָּׂדֶ֔ה לַאֲשֶׁ֥ר קָנָ֖הוּ מֵאִתּ֑וֹ לַאֲשֶׁר־ל֖וֹ
אֲחֻזַּ֥ת הָאָֽרֶץ׃ כה וְכָ֨ל־עֶרְכְּךָ֔ יִהְיֶ֖ה בְּשֶׁ֣קֶל
הַקֹּ֑דֶשׁ עֶשְׂרִ֥ים גֵּרָ֖ה יִהְיֶ֥ה הַשָּֽׁקֶל׃ כו אַךְ־בְּכ֞וֹר
אֲשֶׁ֨ר יְבֻכַּ֤ר לַֽיהוָה֙ בִּבְהֵמָ֔ה לֹֽא־יַקְדִּ֥ישׁ אִ֖ישׁ
אֹת֑וֹ אִם־שׁ֣וֹר אִם־שֶׂ֔ה לַֽיהוָ֖ה הֽוּא׃ כז וְאִ֨ם
בַּבְּהֵמָ֤ה הַטְּמֵאָה֙ וּפָדָ֣ה בְעֶרְכֶּ֔ךָ וְיָסַ֥ף חֲמִשִׁת֖וֹ
עָלָ֑יו וְאִם־לֹ֥א יִגָּאֵ֖ל וְנִמְכַּ֥ר בְּעֶרְכֶּֽךָ׃ כח אַ֣ךְ כָּל־
חֵ֡רֶם אֲשֶׁ֣ר יַחֲרִם֩ אִ֨ישׁ לַֽיהוָ֜ה מִכָּל־אֲשֶׁר־ל֗וֹ
מֵאָדָ֤ם וּבְהֵמָה֙ וּמִשְּׂדֵ֣ה אֲחֻזָּת֔וֹ לֹ֥א יִמָּכֵ֖ר וְלֹ֣א

20–21. . . . In Judaism the priests have no right to identify with the Sanctuary and the Temple; the priest can derive no personal advantages from donations made to support the purposes of the Temple. Only in a symbolic manner do the priests appear as sustainers and representatives of the ideal represented by the Temple. They are entitled only to certain specified prerogatives, derived from the Table of God, as it were. In every other respect, the relationship of the priest to the Temple is no different from that of any "layman."

28. . . . Our text reads מִכָּל אֲשֶׁר לוֹ מֵאָדָם וגו׳ וּמִשְּׂדֵה וגו׳ ["*from* anything that is his, *from* among men . . . and *from* the field. . ."], not אֲשֶׁר לוֹ אָדָם וגו׳ וּשְׂדֵה וגו׳ ["all that is his, man . . . and the field. . ."]. According to Arakhin 28a this law assumes that a person will consecrate, by a vow of interdiction, only part of his property, never all of it, not even all that he owns of one category of property; e.g., all his sheep, all his cattle, etc. In fact, the Law sternly censures one who would deprive himself of all his possessions—even only of all that he has of one kind—to consecrate them to God. Jewish "canonical law" regards it not as a virtue but as a sin to divest oneself of all his possessions to further the purposes sacred to the Temple. Indeed, the Law states that a man does not even have the right to divest himself of his property in such a manner. The Law thereby indicates that you serve God best by using the possessions He has given you for the purpose of developing and enhancing human life on earth in accordance with His will.

יִגָּאֵל כָּל־חֵרֶם קֹדֶשׁ־קָדָשִׁים הוּא לַיהוָה׃
שביעי כט כָּל־חֵרֶם אֲשֶׁר יָחֳרַם מִן־הָאָדָם לֹא
יִפָּדֶה מוֹת יוּמָת׃ ל וְכָל־מַעְשַׂר הָאָרֶץ מִזֶּרַע
הָאָרֶץ מִפְּרִי הָעֵץ לַיהוָה הוּא קֹדֶשׁ לַיהוָה׃
לא וְאִם־גָּאֹל יִגְאַל אִישׁ מִמַּעַשְׂרוֹ חֲמִשִׁיתוֹ
יֹסֵף עָלָיו׃ מפטיר לב וְכָל־מַעְשַׂר בָּקָר וָצֹאן כֹּל
אֲשֶׁר־יַעֲבֹר תַּחַת הַשָּׁבֶט הָעֲשִׂירִי יִהְיֶה־קֹּדֶשׁ
לַיהוָה׃ לג לֹא יְבַקֵּר בֵּין־טוֹב לָרַע וְלֹא יְמִירֶנּוּ
וְאִם־הָמֵר יְמִירֶנּוּ וְהָיָה־הוּא וּתְמוּרָתוֹ יִהְיֶה־
קֹּדֶשׁ לֹא יִגָּאֵל׃ לד אֵלֶּה הַמִּצְוֹת אֲשֶׁר צִוָּה
יְהוָה אֶת־מֹשֶׁה אֶל־בְּנֵי יִשְׂרָאֵל בְּהַר סִינָי׃

חזק

Anything made subject to a vow of interdiction is a holy of holies to *God*.
29. But one who has incurred interdiction from the midst of men cannot be redeemed; he must be put to death.
30. Every tithe of the seeds of the land, of the fruit of the tree, is *God*'s; it is holy to *God*.
31. Whenever a person redeems part of his tithe, he must add one fifth of it.
32. All tithes of cattle or sheep, anything that passes beneath the staff, shall be holy to *God*.
33. He shall make no distinction between good and bad [quality] and he shall not exchange it. If he exchanges it, no matter how it is done, both it and that for which he has exchanged it shall be holy. It must not be redeemed.
34. These are the commandments which *God* commanded Moshe for the sons of Yisrael on Mount Sinai.

33. . . . The "Jewish priestly code" concludes with a discussion of two holy things: מַעֲשֵׂר שֵׁנִי ["the second tithe"] and מַעְשַׂר בְּהֵמָה ["the tithe of an animal"]. Under these laws the enjoyment of life's pleasures, kept within the bounds of morality, becomes in itself a godly act, with every home becoming an abode of God and every table an altar. Every Jewish man and woman is then consecrated as a priest or priestess without the need for any priestly rite, and they themselves may partake of the things hallowed to God. The "priestly code" of Judaism proclaims that the ultimate purpose of all sacred institutions and priestly functions is to imbue the entire people and its national life with the spirit of holiness and with that quality of priestly life and conduct which alone can transform the Sanctuary into an abode of God and which must be perceived by the priest as the sole purpose of his priestly calling.

° ° °

34. ***These are the commandments.*** The preceding chapter, too, ended in Verse 46 with a similar, though not identical conclusion regarding all the laws that went before. Nevertheless, these words are repeated here, at the conclusion of the "priestly code," to show that this chapter, too, which deals with the consecration of holy things to the Sanctuary and with the valuation of holy things for this purpose, is part of the Law of God.

The laws concerning objects vowed as gifts to the Temple, which form the content of this chapter, show that these donations are left to the free will of the individual and are therefore not part of the laws which were characterized at the conclusion of the preceding chapter as the purpose of the bond between God and ourselves. Nevertheless, these laws represent commandments given by God to Moses at Mount Sinai for Israel along with all the other laws. Hence, though it is not compulsory to make them, these pledges are just as much subject to the specifications of God's Law as are any of our other day-to-day activities.

The Haftarah for this Sidra may be found on page 887.

BAMIDBAR במדבר
[NUMBERS]

———————⟨⟩———————

"This Fourth Book resumes the factual narrative. It shows us the relationship of the nation of Israel, as it actually is, to the ideal of its calling as outlined in the Third Book."

—Commentary on Chapter 1, Verse 1

במדבר

BAMIDBAR

I 1. *God* spoke to Moshe in the wilderness of Sinai in the Tent of Appointed Meeting, on the first day of the second month in the second year of their exodus from the land of Mitzrayim [saying]: 2. "Take the total count of the entire community of the sons of Yisrael according to their families, according to their fathers'

א א וַיְדַבֵּ֨ר יְהֹוָ֧ה אֶל־מֹשֶׁ֛ה בְּמִדְבַּ֥ר סִינַ֖י בְּאֹ֣הֶל מוֹעֵ֑ד בְּאֶחָד֩ לַחֹ֨דֶשׁ הַשֵּׁנִ֜י בַּשָּׁנָ֣ה הַשֵּׁנִ֗ית לְצֵאתָ֛ם מֵאֶ֥רֶץ מִצְרַ֖יִם לֵאמֹֽר: ב שְׂא֗וּ אֶת־רֹאשׁ֙ כׇּל־עֲדַ֣ת בְּנֵֽי־יִשְׂרָאֵ֔ל לְמִשְׁפְּחֹתָ֖ם לְבֵ֥ית

CHAPTER I

1. The Second Book [Exodus] concludes with an account of the construction of the Sanctuary of the Law. The entire Third Book [Leviticus] is then devoted to the standards which this Sanctuary sets for Israel—in symbolic terms, by the offerings, and in practical terms, by the laws that sanctify every aspect of daily life. Thus an outline is presented of the ideal to be translated into reality by every individual member of the nation as well as by the nation as a whole. The concluding chapter of Leviticus deals with free-will offerings pledged to the Sanctuary, setting legal specifications to guide one who might feel the need to express his personal relationship to the Sanctuary by a symbolic consecration of his own person or by the dedication of personal property to the Sanctuary.

Now this Fourth Book resumes the factual narrative. It shows us the relationship of the nation of Israel, as it actually is, to the ideal of its calling as outlined in the Third Book. It opens with the command to take a census of the nation as עֵדָה; i.e., a "congregation" or "community" united by and for its collective vocation. The nation is to be counted in terms of its individual components. A census of this nature makes it clear to the authorized spokesmen of the nation that the community cannot exist as an abstract idea but can have true being only in terms of the totality of its components. At the same time, each member of the community is made aware that he personally "counts" as an important constituent of this totality, and that the task to be performed by the nation as a whole requires every one of its members to remain true to his duty and purposefully devoted to the vocation he shares with all the others.

The Third Book concludes with a numbering of the nation's herds in terms of groups and flocks, by their owners, for the purpose of consecrating these creatures to God. The Fourth Book now opens with the command to have the nation, too, numbered as the flock of God, as it were, for its Shepherd, in accordance with its Divinely-ordained familial and tribal groupings. As

with the animals, so the individual members of the nation, too, now pass, one by one, beneath the staff of their Shepherd so that each one, in his own right, may be counted as a member of God's flock.

בְּמִדְבַּר סִינַי *[in the wilderness of Sinai]*. The choice of the wilderness as the place for this census is proof positive that the purpose of this census could have been neither economic nor political—because economics and politics have no relevance to life in the wilderness. Rather, the addition of the words סִינַי ["Sinai"] and אֹהֶל מוֹעֵד ["Tent of Appointed Meeting"] makes it clear at once that this census was to be made in the service of the Law which had been given at Mount Sinai, and to which homage is to be paid in the אֹהֶל מוֹעֵד. First, the Children of Israel had received the Law at Mount Sinai. Then, on the first day of the month of Nisan following their aberration with the golden calf, the Testimony of the Law, having been given to them a second time as a pledge that the nation had been reinstated into God's covenant, received a dwelling place symbolizing its ideals. Now, on the first day of the month of Iyar, all the tribes, the families and the male members of the nation, were to be numbered and to rally around the Law as its guardians and keepers.

2. . . . Each tribe and each family, each with its own unique personality and its own character traits, must join with all the others in carrying out the mission it shares in common with all the rest of the House of Israel, and in rearing and training future generations so that they, too, may employ their inherited traits for the fulfillment of the task assigned to the nation. That is why the hundreds and thousands of members of the House of Israel do not come to the nation as an unorganized multitude but "according to their families, according to their fathers' house"; i.e., as family groups which in turn are grouped according to the tribes to which they belong. . . . In censuses, גֻּלְגֹּלֶת; lit., "skull," is used as a unit representing the concrete, physically present individual. The "head" would be the most logical means for counting an assembled mass of people. Judaism, however, counts not the heads, but . . . the half-shekels that are paid for each head.

[513]

house, counting the names, all males, for each head. 3. From twenty years old and upward, each one who goes forth into communal service in Yisrael, you shall number them according to their serving divisions, you and Aharon. 4. And along-side you there shall be one man for each tribe, each one the head of his fathers' house. 5. These are the names of the men who shall stand alongside you: For Reuben: Elitzur, son of Sh'deur. 6. For Shimeon: Shelumiel, son of Tzurishaddai. 7. For Yehudah: Naḥshon, son of Amminadab. 8. For Yissakhar: Nethanel, son of Tzuar. 9. For Zebulun: Eliab, son of Ḥelon. 10. For the sons of Joseph: for Ephraim, Elishama, son of Ammihud; for Menashe, Gamliel, son of Pedahtzur. 11. For Binyamin: Abidan, son of Gideoni. 12. For Dan: Aḥiezer, son of Ammishaddai. 13. For Asher: Pagiel, son of Okhran. 14. For Gad: Eliassaph, son of Deuel. 15. For Naphtali: Aḥira, son of Enan." 16. These are the ones called from the community, princes of the tribes of their fathers; they are heads of the thousands of Yisrael. 17. Moshe took, and [so did] Aharon, these men, who had been designated by name, 18. and they assembled the entire community on the first day of the second month, and they declared themselves by their births in their families, according to the house of their fathers, numbering the names from twenty years old and upward, for each head. 19. Even as *God* had commanded Moshe, so did he number them in the wilderness of Sinai. 20. There were the sons of Reuben, the firstborn of Yisrael, their births according to their families according to the house of their fathers, numbering the names, for each

אֲבֹתָ֔ם בְּמִסְפַּ֣ר שֵׁמ֔וֹת כָּל־זָכָ֖ר לְגֻלְגְּלֹתָֽם׃
ג מִבֶּ֨ן עֶשְׂרִ֤ים שָׁנָה֙ וָמַ֔עְלָה כָּל־יֹצֵ֥א צָבָ֖א
בְּיִשְׂרָאֵ֑ל תִּפְקְד֥וּ אֹתָ֛ם לְצִבְאֹתָ֖ם אַתָּ֥ה וְאַהֲרֹֽן׃
ד וְאִתְּכֶ֣ם יִהְי֔וּ אִ֥ישׁ אִ֖ישׁ לַמַּטֶּ֑ה אִ֛ישׁ רֹ֥אשׁ
לְבֵית־אֲבֹתָ֖יו הֽוּא׃ ה וְאֵ֙לֶּה֙ שְׁמ֣וֹת הָֽאֲנָשִׁ֔ים
אֲשֶׁ֥ר יַֽעַמְד֖וּ אִתְּכֶ֑ם לִרְאוּבֵ֕ן אֱלִיצ֖וּר בֶּן־
שְׁדֵיאֽוּר׃ ו לְשִׁמְע֕וֹן שְׁלֻמִיאֵ֖ל בֶּן־צוּרִֽישַׁדָּֽי׃
ז לִֽיהוּדָ֕ה נַחְשׁ֖וֹן בֶּן־עַמִּֽינָדָֽב׃ ח לְיִ֨שָּׂשכָ֔ר
נְתַנְאֵ֖ל בֶּן־צוּעָֽר׃ ט לִזְבוּלֻ֕ן אֱלִיאָ֖ב בֶּן־חֵלֹֽן׃
י לִבְנֵ֣י יוֹסֵ֔ף לְאֶפְרַ֕יִם אֱלִישָׁמָ֖ע בֶּן־עַמִּיה֑וּד
לִמְנַשֶּׁ֕ה גַּֽמְלִיאֵ֖ל בֶּן־פְּדָהצֽוּר׃ יא לְבִ֨נְיָמִ֔ן
אֲבִידָ֖ן בֶּן־גִּדְעֹנִֽי׃ יב לְדָ֕ן אֲחִיעֶ֖זֶר בֶּן־עַמִּֽישַׁדָּֽי׃
יג לְאָשֵׁ֕ר פַּגְעִיאֵ֖ל בֶּן־עָכְרָֽן׃ יד לְגָ֕ד אֶלְיָסָ֖ף
בֶּן־דְּעוּאֵֽל׃ טו לְנַ֨פְתָּלִ֔י אֲחִירַ֖ע בֶּן־עֵינָֽן׃
טז אֵ֚לֶּה קְרִיאֵ֣י (קרואי קרי) הָֽעֵדָ֔ה נְשִׂיאֵ֖י מַטּ֣וֹת
אֲבוֹתָ֑ם רָאשֵׁ֛י אַלְפֵ֥י יִשְׂרָאֵ֖ל הֵֽם׃ יז וַיִּקַּ֥ח מֹשֶׁ֖ה
וְאַהֲרֹ֑ן אֵ֚ת הָאֲנָשִׁ֣ים הָאֵ֔לֶּה אֲשֶׁ֥ר נִקְּב֖וּ בְּשֵׁמֽוֹת׃
יח וְאֵ֨ת כָּל־הָעֵדָ֜ה הִקְהִ֗ילוּ בְּאֶחָד֙ לַחֹ֣דֶשׁ הַשֵּׁנִ֔י
וַיִּתְיַֽלְד֥וּ עַל־מִשְׁפְּחֹתָ֖ם לְבֵ֣ית אֲבֹתָ֑ם בְּמִסְפַּ֣ר
שֵׁמ֗וֹת מִבֶּ֨ן עֶשְׂרִ֥ים שָׁנָ֛ה וָמַ֖עְלָה לְגֻלְגְּלֹתָֽם׃
יט כַּאֲשֶׁ֛ר צִוָּ֥ה יְהוָ֖ה אֶת־מֹשֶׁ֑ה וַֽיִּפְקְדֵ֖ם בְּמִדְבַּ֥ר
סִינָֽי׃ ס שני כ וַיִּהְי֤וּ בְנֵֽי־רְאוּבֵן֙ בְּכֹ֣ר יִשְׂרָאֵ֔ל
תּֽוֹלְדֹתָ֥ם לְמִשְׁפְּחֹתָ֖ם לְבֵ֣ית אֲבֹתָ֑ם בְּמִסְפַּ֣ר

3. ***From twenty years old and upward, each one who goes forth into communal service in Yisrael.*** The term צָבָא in Scripture does not necessarily, or even primarily, denote an army, or service in an armed "host." In Numbers 4:3, כָּל בָּא לַצָּבָא לַעֲשׂוֹת מְלָאכָה בְּאֹהֶל מוֹעֵד ["each one who comes to communal service to do (sacred) work in the Tent of Appointed Meeting"]; ibid., Verse 23 לִצְבֹא צָבָא לַעֲבֹד וגו׳ ["who comes to perform communal service, to minister. . ."], and also elsewhere in Scripture, it refers to the service performed by the Levites in the Tabernacle. Verses 24 and 14 in Chapter 8, too, prove that צָבָא denotes any group of individuals united for communal service under the orders of a higher authority, or the service to be performed by such individuals. In the present verse, too, צָבָא need not necessarily have the connotation of armed service. Rather, it would denote anyone under obligation to come forth from his private life and perform communal services whenever this is needed; hence, anyone on whom the community can rely upon to attend to its interests. . . .

head, all males from twenty years old and upward, each one who goes forth into communal service: 21. Their numbered ones of the tribe of Reuben: forty-six thousand five hundred. 22. To the sons of Shimeon, their births according to their families according to the house of their fathers; also his numbered ones, numbering the names, for each head, all males from twenty years old and upward, each one who goes forth into communal service: 23. Their numbered ones of the tribe of Shimeon: fifty-nine thousand three hundred. 24. To the sons of Gad, their births according to their families according to the house of their fathers; numbering the names from twenty years old and upward, each one who goes forth into communal service: 25. Their numbered ones of the tribe of Gad: forty-five thousand six hundred and fifty. 26. To the sons of Yehudah, their births according to their families according to the house of their fathers; numbering the names from twenty years old and upward, each one who goes forth into communal service: 27. Their numbered ones of the tribe of Yehudah: seventy-four thousand six hundred. 28. To the sons of Yissakhar, their births according to their families according to the house of their fathers; numbering the names from twenty years old and upward, each one who goes forth into communal service: 29. Their numbered ones of the tribe of Yissakhar: fifty-four thousand four hundred. 30. To the sons of Zebulun, their births according to their families according to the house of their fathers; numbering the names from twenty years old and upward, each one who goes forth into communal service: 31. Their numbered ones of the tribe of Zebulun: fifty-seven thousand four hundred. 32. To the sons of Yosef, to the sons of Ephraim, their births according to the house of their fathers; numbering the names from twenty years old and upward, each one who goes forth into communal service: 33. Their numbered ones of the tribe of Ephraim: forty thousand five hundred. 34. To the sons of Menashe, their births according to their families according to the house of their fathers; numbering the names from twenty

שְׁמוֹת לְגֻלְגְּלֹתָם כָּל־זָכָר מִבֶּן עֶשְׂרִים שָׁנָה
וָמַעְלָה כֹּל יֹצֵא צָבָא: כא פְּקֻדֵיהֶם לְמַטֵּה
רְאוּבֵן שִׁשָּׁה וְאַרְבָּעִים אֶלֶף וַחֲמֵשׁ מֵאוֹת: פ
כב לִבְנֵי שִׁמְעוֹן תּוֹלְדֹתָם לְמִשְׁפְּחֹתָם לְבֵית
אֲבֹתָם פְּקֻדָיו בְּמִסְפַּר שֵׁמוֹת לְגֻלְגְּלֹתָם כָּל־
זָכָר מִבֶּן עֶשְׂרִים שָׁנָה וָמַעְלָה כֹּל יֹצֵא צָבָא:
כג פְּקֻדֵיהֶם לְמַטֵּה שִׁמְעוֹן תִּשְׁעָה וַחֲמִשִּׁים
אֶלֶף וּשְׁלֹשׁ מֵאוֹת: פ כד לִבְנֵי גָד תּוֹלְדֹתָם
לְמִשְׁפְּחֹתָם לְבֵית אֲבֹתָם בְּמִסְפַּר שֵׁמוֹת מִבֶּן
עֶשְׂרִים שָׁנָה וָמַעְלָה כֹּל יֹצֵא צָבָא:
כה פְּקֻדֵיהֶם לְמַטֵּה גָד חֲמִשָּׁה וְאַרְבָּעִים אֶלֶף
וְשֵׁשׁ מֵאוֹת וַחֲמִשִּׁים: פ כו לִבְנֵי יְהוּדָה
תּוֹלְדֹתָם לְמִשְׁפְּחֹתָם לְבֵית אֲבֹתָם בְּמִסְפַּר
שֵׁמֹת מִבֶּן עֶשְׂרִים שָׁנָה וָמַעְלָה כֹּל יֹצֵא צָבָא:
כז פְּקֻדֵיהֶם לְמַטֵּה יְהוּדָה אַרְבָּעָה וְשִׁבְעִים
אֶלֶף וְשֵׁשׁ מֵאוֹת: פ כח לִבְנֵי יִשָּׂשכָר תּוֹלְדֹתָם
לְמִשְׁפְּחֹתָם לְבֵית אֲבֹתָם בְּמִסְפַּר שֵׁמֹת מִבֶּן
עֶשְׂרִים שָׁנָה וָמַעְלָה כֹּל יֹצֵא צָבָא:
כט פְּקֻדֵיהֶם לְמַטֵּה יִשָּׂשכָר אַרְבָּעָה וַחֲמִשִּׁים
אֶלֶף וְאַרְבַּע מֵאוֹת: פ ל לִבְנֵי זְבוּלֻן תּוֹלְדֹתָם
לְמִשְׁפְּחֹתָם לְבֵית אֲבֹתָם בְּמִסְפַּר שֵׁמֹת מִבֶּן
עֶשְׂרִים שָׁנָה וָמַעְלָה כֹּל יֹצֵא צָבָא:
לא פְּקֻדֵיהֶם לְמַטֵּה זְבוּלֻן שִׁבְעָה וַחֲמִשִּׁים אֶלֶף
וְאַרְבַּע מֵאוֹת: פ לב לִבְנֵי יוֹסֵף לִבְנֵי אֶפְרַיִם
תּוֹלְדֹתָם לְמִשְׁפְּחֹתָם לְבֵית אֲבֹתָם בְּמִסְפַּר
שֵׁמֹת מִבֶּן עֶשְׂרִים שָׁנָה וָמַעְלָה כֹּל יֹצֵא צָבָא:
לג פְּקֻדֵיהֶם לְמַטֵּה אֶפְרָיִם אַרְבָּעִים אֶלֶף
וַחֲמֵשׁ מֵאוֹת: פ לד לִבְנֵי מְנַשֶּׁה תּוֹלְדֹתָם
לְמִשְׁפְּחֹתָם לְבֵית אֲבֹתָם בְּמִסְפַּר שֵׁמוֹת מִבֶּן

years old and upward, each one who goes forth into communal service: 35. Their numbered ones of the tribe of Menashe: thirty-two thousand two hundred. 36. To the sons of Binyamin, their births according to their families according to the house of their fathers; numbering the names from twenty years old and upward, each one who goes forth into communal service: 37. Their numbered ones of the tribe of Binyamin: thirty-five thousand four hundred. 38. To the sons of Dan, their births according to their families according to the house of their fathers; numbering the names from twenty years old and upward, each one who goes forth into communal service: 39. Their numbered ones of the tribe of Dan: sixty-two thousand seven hundred. 40. To the sons of Asher, their births according to their families according to the house of their fathers; numbering the names from twenty years old and upward, each one who goes forth into communal service: 41. Their numbered ones of the tribe of Asher: forty-one thousand five hundred. 42. Lastly, the sons of Naphtali, their births according to their families according to the house of their fathers; numbering the names from twenty years old and upward, each one who goes forth into communal service: 43. Their numbered ones of the tribe of Naphtali: fifty-three thousand four hundred. 44. These were the numberings that Moshe counted, and [so did] Aharon and the twelve princes of Yisrael. They were one man each for his fathers' house. 45. All the numberings of the sons of Yisrael were according to their fathers' house, from twenty years old and upward, each one who goes forth into communal service in Yisrael. 46. All their numbered ones were six hundred and three thousand five hundred and fifty. 47. But the Levites according to the tribe of their fathers were not allowed to number themselves among them. 48. For *God* spoke to Moshe [saying]: 49. "Only the tribe of

עֶשְׂרִים שָׁנָהֹ וָמַ֫עְלָה כֹּל יֹצֵא צָבָא: לה פְּקֻדֵיהֶם לְמַטֵּה מְנַשֶּׁה שְׁנַ֫יִם וּשְׁלֹשִׁים אֶ֫לֶף וּמָאתָֽיִם: פ לו לִבְנֵי בִנְיָמִן֮ תּוֹלְדֹתָם לְמִשְׁפְּחֹתָם לְבֵית אֲבֹתָ֒ם בְּמִסְפַּר שֵׁמֹת מִבֶּן עֶשְׂרִים שָׁנָה֙ וָמַ֫עְלָה כֹּל יֹצֵא צָבָֽא: לז פְּקֻדֵיהֶם לְמַטֵּה בִנְיָמִן חֲמִשָּׁה וּשְׁלֹשִׁים אֶ֫לֶף וְאַרְבַּע מֵאֽוֹת: פ לח לִבְנֵי דָן֮ תּוֹלְדֹתָם לְמִשְׁפְּחֹתָם לְבֵית אֲבֹתָ֒ם בְּמִסְפַּר שֵׁמֹת מִבֶּן עֶשְׂרִים שָׁנָה֙ וָמַ֫עְלָה כֹּל יֹצֵא צָבָֽא: לט פְּקֻדֵיהֶם לְמַטֵּה דָן שְׁנַ֫יִם וְשִׁשִּׁים אֶ֫לֶף וּשְׁבַע מֵאֽוֹת: פ מ לִבְנֵי אָשֵׁר֮ תּוֹלְדֹתָם לְמִשְׁפְּחֹתָם לְבֵית אֲבֹתָ֒ם בְּמִסְפַּר שֵׁמֹת מִבֶּן עֶשְׂרִים שָׁנָה֙ וָמַ֫עְלָה כֹּל יֹצֵא צָבָֽא: מא פְּקֻדֵיהֶם לְמַטֵּה אָשֵׁר אֶחָד וְאַרְבָּעִים אֶ֫לֶף וַחֲמֵשׁ מֵאֽוֹת: פ מב בְּנֵי נַפְתָּלִי֮ תּוֹלְדֹתָם לְמִשְׁפְּחֹתָם לְבֵית אֲבֹתָ֒ם בְּמִסְפַּר שֵׁמֹת מִבֶּן עֶשְׂרִים שָׁנָה֙ וָמַ֫עְלָה כֹּל יֹצֵא צָבָֽא: מג פְּקֻדֵיהֶם לְמַטֵּה נַפְתָּלִי שְׁלֹשָׁה וַחֲמִשִּׁים אֶ֫לֶף וְאַרְבַּע מֵאֽוֹת: פ מד אֵ֫לֶּה הַפְּקֻדִים אֲשֶׁר֩ פָּקַד מֹשֶׁה וְאַהֲרֹן וּנְשִׂיאֵי יִשְׂרָאֵל שְׁנֵים עָשָׂר אִישׁ אִישׁ־אֶחָד לְבֵית־אֲבֹתָיו הָיֽוּ: מה וַיִּהְיוּ כָּל־פְּקוּדֵי בְנֵי־יִשְׂרָאֵל לְבֵית אֲבֹתָם מִבֶּן עֶשְׂרִים שָׁנָה וָמַ֫עְלָה כָּל־יֹצֵא צָבָא בְּיִשְׂרָאֵֽל: מו וַיִּֽהְיוּ כָּל־הַפְּקֻדִים שֵׁשׁ־מֵאוֹת אֶ֫לֶף וּשְׁלֹשֶׁת אֲלָפִים וַחֲמֵשׁ מֵאוֹת וַחֲמִשִּֽׁים: מז וְהַלְוִיִּם לְמַטֵּה אֲבֹתָם לֹא הָתְפָּֽקְדוּ בְּתוֹכָֽם: פ מח וַיְדַבֵּר יְהֹוָה אֶל־מֹשֶׁה לֵּאמֹֽר: מט אַ֫ךְ אֶת־

---

48. ... At the very first defection from the Law, when the people, failing to understand the "given" character of this Law, set about to make for themselves a divine "Moses figure," there was one tribe that remained faithful to God and to His Law, defending the inviolability of the Law against the rest of the nation, even against their own kin. As guardians of this Law, too, the tribe of Levi remained apart from the rest

Levi you shall not number and you shall not take up their total number among the sons of Yisrael. 50. And you shall appoint the Levites over the Dwelling Place of the Testimony, over all its utensils and over all that belongs to it; they are to carry the Dwelling Place and all its utensils and they are to minister to it, and they shall camp around the Dwelling Place. 51. When the Dwelling Place journeys forth, the Levites are to take it down, and when the Dwelling Place comes to rest, the Levites are to set it up; any outsider who comes near is liable to the death penalty. 52. The sons of Yisrael shall camp, each man near his own camp and each one near his own standard, according to their serving divisions. 53. But the Levites shall camp around the Dwelling Place of the Testimony so that no wrath shall come upon the community of the sons of Yisrael and the Levites shall keep the charge of the Dwelling Place of the Testimony." 54. The sons of Yisrael did so; according to all that *God* had commanded Moshe, thus did they do.

II

1. *God* spoke to Moshe and Aharon [saying]: 2. "Every man shall camp next to his standard, each designated with the insignia of their fathers' house, [so] shall the sons of Yisrael camp; they shall camp at some distance around the Tent of Appointed Meeting. 3. Those camping in the front, toward the east: the standard of the camp of Yehudah according to their serving divisions and the prince of the sons of Yehudah: Naḥshon, son of Amminadab. 4. His division and their

מַטֵּה לֵוִי לֹא תִפְקֹד וְאֶת־רֹאשָׁם לֹא תִשָּׂא
בְּתוֹךְ בְּנֵי יִשְׂרָאֵל: נ וְאַתָּה הַפְקֵד אֶת־הַלְוִיִּם
עַל־מִשְׁכַּן הָעֵדֻת וְעַל כָּל־כֵּלָיו וְעַל כָּל־אֲשֶׁר־
לוֹ הֵמָּה יִשְׂאוּ אֶת־הַמִּשְׁכָּן וְאֶת־כָּל־כֵּלָיו וְהֵם
יְשָׁרְתֻהוּ וְסָבִיב לַמִּשְׁכָּן יַחֲנוּ: נא וּבִנְסֹעַ
הַמִּשְׁכָּן יוֹרִידוּ אֹתוֹ הַלְוִיִּם וּבַחֲנֹת הַמִּשְׁכָּן
יָקִימוּ אֹתוֹ הַלְוִיִּם וְהַזָּר הַקָּרֵב יוּמָת: נב וְחָנוּ
בְּנֵי יִשְׂרָאֵל אִישׁ עַל־מַחֲנֵהוּ וְאִישׁ עַל־דִּגְלוֹ
לְצִבְאֹתָם: נג וְהַלְוִיִּם יַחֲנוּ סָבִיב לְמִשְׁכַּן הָעֵדֻת
וְלֹא־יִהְיֶה קֶצֶף עַל־עֲדַת בְּנֵי יִשְׂרָאֵל וְשָׁמְרוּ
הַלְוִיִּם אֶת־מִשְׁמֶרֶת מִשְׁכַּן הָעֵדוּת: נד וַיַּעֲשׂוּ
בְּנֵי יִשְׂרָאֵל כְּכֹל אֲשֶׁר צִוָּה יְהוָה אֶת־מֹשֶׁה כֵּן
עָשׂוּ: פ שלישי ב א וַיְדַבֵּר יְהוָה אֶל־מֹשֶׁה וְאֶל־
אַהֲרֹן לֵאמֹר: ב אִישׁ עַל־דִּגְלוֹ בְאֹתֹת לְבֵית
אֲבֹתָם יַחֲנוּ בְּנֵי יִשְׂרָאֵל מִנֶּגֶד סָבִיב לְאֹהֶל־
מוֹעֵד יַחֲנוּ: ג וְהַחֹנִים קֵדְמָה מִזְרָחָה דֶּגֶל
מַחֲנֵה יְהוּדָה לְצִבְאֹתָם וְנָשִׂיא לִבְנֵי יְהוּדָה
נַחְשׁוֹן בֶּן־עַמִּינָדָב: ד וּצְבָאוֹ וּפְקֻדֵיהֶם אַרְבָּעָה

of the nation. They did not belong to the "community," but solely to the "Testimony" that was to be preserved as the living force reigning supreme over the community. For this reason, as already stated in the previous verse, and as will be explained in greater detail in the verses that follow, the tribe of Levi was not numbered "amongst the sons of Yisrael."...

50. ***And you shall appoint.*** Even as they are to cultivate and defend the Law in their personal lives, so, too, the care and the guardianship of the Sanctuary of the Law is now to be assigned to them. Their care of the Sanctuary entails acting as bearers of the Sanctuary and its utensils when the nation is on the march and reassembling the Sanctuary when the nation sets up camp.

they are to minister to it. Their guardianship of the Sanctuary is expressed in physical terms by their camping around it in order to protect and defend it.

CHAPTER II

1. At the end of the preceding chapter the command was given in general terms to group the Children of Israel into separate camps, with the Levites and the Dwelling Place of the Testimony encamped apart from the rest. This command will now be discussed in detail....

numbered ones: seventy-four thousand six hundred. 5. Those camping next to him: the tribe of Issakhar; and the prince of the sons of Issakhar: Nethanel, son of Tzuar. 6. His division and its numbered ones: fifty-four thousand four hundred. 7. The tribe of Zebulun; and the prince of the sons of Zebulun: Eliab, son of Ḥelon. 8. His division and its numbered ones: fifty-seven thousand four hundred. 9. All the numbered ones belonging to the camp of Yehudah: one hundred eighty-six thousand four hundred according to their serving divisions; they shall journey forth first. 10. The standard of the camp of Reuben, toward the south, according to their serving divisions; and the prince of the sons of Reuben: Elitzur, son of Sh'deur. 11. His division; and its numbered ones: forty-six thousand five hundred. 12. Those camping next to him: the tribe of Shimeon; and the prince of the sons of Shimeon: Shelumiel, son of Tzurishaddai. 13. His division and their numbered ones: fifty-nine thousand three hundred. 14. And the tribe of Gad; and the prince of the sons of Gad: Eliassaph, son of Reuel. 15. His division and their numbered ones: forty-five thousand six hundred and fifty. 16. All the numbered ones belonging to the camp of Reuben: one hundred fifty-one thousand four hundred and fifty according to their serving divisions; they shall journey forth second. 17. Then the Tent of Appointed Meeting shall journey forth, the camp of the Levites in the midst of the camp; even as they camp, so shall they journey, every one in his position, according to their standards. 18. The standard of the camp of Ephraim according to their serving divisions toward the west; and the prince of the sons of Ephraim: Elishama, son of Ammihud. 19. His division and their numbered ones: forty thousand five hundred. 20. Next to him the tribe of Menashe; and the prince of the sons of Menashe: Gamliel, son of Pedahtzur. 21. His division and their numbered ones: thirty-two thousand two hundred. 22. And the tribe of Binyamin; and the prince of the tribe of Binyamin: Abidan, son of Gideoni. 23. His division and their numbered ones: thirty-five thousand four hundred. 24. All the num-

וְשִׁבְעִים אֶלֶף וְשֵׁשׁ מֵאוֹת: ה וְהַחֹנִים עָלָיו מַטֵּה יִשָּׂשׂכָר וְנָשִׂיא לִבְנֵי יִשָּׂשׂכָר נְתַנְאֵל בֶּן־צוּעָר: ו וּצְבָאוֹ וּפְקֻדָיו אַרְבָּעָה וַחֲמִשִּׁים אֶלֶף וְאַרְבַּע מֵאוֹת: ז מַטֵּה זְבוּלֻן וְנָשִׂיא לִבְנֵי זְבוּלֻן אֱלִיאָב בֶּן־חֵלֹן: ח וּצְבָאוֹ וּפְקֻדָיו שִׁבְעָה וַחֲמִשִּׁים אֶלֶף וְאַרְבַּע מֵאוֹת: ט כָּל־הַפְּקֻדִים לְמַחֲנֵה יְהוּדָה מְאַת אֶלֶף וּשְׁמֹנִים אֶלֶף וְשֵׁשֶׁת־אֲלָפִים וְאַרְבַּע־מֵאוֹת לְצִבְאֹתָם רִאשֹׁנָה יִסָּעוּ: ס י דֶּגֶל מַחֲנֵה רְאוּבֵן תֵּימָנָה לְצִבְאֹתָם וְנָשִׂיא לִבְנֵי רְאוּבֵן אֱלִיצוּר בֶּן־שְׁדֵיאוּר: יא וּצְבָאוֹ וּפְקֻדָיו שִׁשָּׁה וְאַרְבָּעִים אֶלֶף וַחֲמֵשׁ מֵאוֹת: יב וְהַחוֹנִם עָלָיו מַטֵּה שִׁמְעוֹן וְנָשִׂיא לִבְנֵי שִׁמְעוֹן שְׁלֻמִיאֵל בֶּן־צוּרִישַׁדָּי: יג וּצְבָאוֹ וּפְקֻדֵיהֶם תִּשְׁעָה וַחֲמִשִּׁים אֶלֶף וּשְׁלֹשׁ מֵאוֹת: יד וּמַטֵּה גָּד וְנָשִׂיא לִבְנֵי גָד אֶלְיָסָף בֶּן־רְעוּאֵל: טו וּצְבָאוֹ וּפְקֻדֵיהֶם חֲמִשָּׁה וְאַרְבָּעִים אֶלֶף וְשֵׁשׁ מֵאוֹת וַחֲמִשִּׁים: טז כָּל־הַפְּקֻדִים לְמַחֲנֵה רְאוּבֵן מְאַת אֶלֶף וְאֶחָד וַחֲמִשִּׁים אֶלֶף וְאַרְבַּע־מֵאוֹת וַחֲמִשִּׁים לְצִבְאֹתָם וּשְׁנִיִּם יִסָּעוּ: ס יז וְנָסַע אֹהֶל־מוֹעֵד מַחֲנֵה הַלְוִיִּם בְּתוֹךְ הַמַּחֲנֹת כַּאֲשֶׁר יַחֲנוּ כֵּן יִסָּעוּ אִישׁ עַל־יָדוֹ לְדִגְלֵיהֶם: ס יח דֶּגֶל מַחֲנֵה אֶפְרַיִם לְצִבְאֹתָם יָמָּה וְנָשִׂיא לִבְנֵי אֶפְרַיִם אֱלִישָׁמָע בֶּן־עַמִּיהוּד: יט וּצְבָאוֹ וּפְקֻדֵיהֶם אַרְבָּעִים אֶלֶף וַחֲמֵשׁ מֵאוֹת: כ וְעָלָיו מַטֵּה מְנַשֶּׁה וְנָשִׂיא לִבְנֵי מְנַשֶּׁה גַּמְלִיאֵל בֶּן־פְּדָהצוּר: כא וּצְבָאוֹ וּפְקֻדֵיהֶם שְׁנַיִם וּשְׁלֹשִׁים אֶלֶף וּמָאתָיִם: כב וּמַטֵּה בִּנְיָמִן וְנָשִׂיא לִבְנֵי בִנְיָמִן אֲבִידָן בֶּן־גִּדְעֹנִי: כג וּצְבָאוֹ וּפְקֻדֵיהֶם חֲמִשָּׁה וּשְׁלֹשִׁים אֶלֶף וְאַרְבַּע מֵאוֹת: כד כָּל־

bered ones belonging to the camp of
Ephraim: one hundred eight thousand one
hundred according to their serving divisions; they shall journey forth third.
25. The standard of the camp of Dan to
the north according to their serving divisions; and the prince of the sons
of Dan: Aḥiezer, son of Ammishaddai.
26. His division and their numbered
ones: sixty-two thousand seven hundred.
27. Those camping next to him: the tribe
of Asher; and the prince of the sons of
Asher: Pagiel, son of Okhran.   28. His
division and their numbered ones: forty-
one thousand five hundred.   29. And the
tribe of Naphtali; and the prince of the sons
of Naphtali: Aḥira, son of Enan. 30. His
division and their numbered ones: fifty-
three thousand four hundred.   31. All the
numbered ones belonging to the tribe of
Dan: one hundred fifty-seven thousand six
hundred; they shall journey forth last,
according to their standards." 32. These
are the numbered ones of the sons of Yisrael
according to their fathers' houses. All the
numbered ones of the camps according to
their serving divisions: six hundred three
thousand five hundred and fifty. 33. The
Levites were not caused to number themselves among the sons of Yisrael, [it was] as
God had commanded Moshe.   34. The
sons of Yisrael did so. According to all that
God had commanded Moshe, so did they

הַפְּקֻדִים לְמַחֲנֵה אֶפְרַיִם מְאַת אֶלֶף וּשְׁמֹנַת־
אֲלָפִים וּמֵאָה לְצִבְאֹתָם וּשְׁלִשִׁים יִסָּעוּ: ס
כה דֶּגֶל מַחֲנֵה דָן צָפֹנָה לְצִבְאֹתָם וְנָשִׂיא לִבְנֵי
דָן אֲחִיעֶזֶר בֶּן־עַמִּישַׁדָּי: כו וּצְבָאוֹ וּפְקֻדֵיהֶם
שְׁנַיִם וְשִׁשִּׁים אֶלֶף וּשְׁבַע מֵאוֹת: כז וְהַחֹנִים
עָלָיו מַטֵּה אָשֵׁר וְנָשִׂיא לִבְנֵי אָשֵׁר פַּגְעִיאֵל בֶּן־
עָכְרָן: כח וּצְבָאוֹ וּפְקֻדֵיהֶם אֶחָד וְאַרְבָּעִים
אֶלֶף וַחֲמֵשׁ מֵאוֹת: כט וּמַטֵּה נַפְתָּלִי וְנָשִׂיא
לִבְנֵי נַפְתָּלִי אֲחִירַע בֶּן־עֵינָן: ל וּצְבָאוֹ
וּפְקֻדֵיהֶם שְׁלֹשָׁה וַחֲמִשִּׁים אֶלֶף וְאַרְבַּע מֵאוֹת:
לא כָּל־הַפְּקֻדִים לְמַחֲנֵה דָן מְאַת אֶלֶף וְשִׁבְעָה
וַחֲמִשִּׁים אֶלֶף וְשֵׁשׁ מֵאוֹת לָאַחֲרֹנָה יִסְעוּ
לְדִגְלֵיהֶם: פ לב אֵלֶּה פְּקוּדֵי בְנֵי־יִשְׂרָאֵל לְבֵית
אֲבֹתָם כָּל־פְּקוּדֵי הַמַּחֲנֹת לְצִבְאֹתָם שֵׁשׁ־
מֵאוֹת אֶלֶף וּשְׁלֹשֶׁת אֲלָפִים וַחֲמֵשׁ מֵאוֹת
וַחֲמִשִּׁים: לג וְהַלְוִיִּם לֹא הָתְפָּקְדוּ בְּתוֹךְ בְּנֵי
יִשְׂרָאֵל כַּאֲשֶׁר צִוָּה יְהֹוָה אֶת־מֹשֶׁה: לד וַיַּעֲשׂוּ
בְּנֵי יִשְׂרָאֵל כְּכֹל אֲשֶׁר־צִוָּה יְהֹוָה אֶת־מֹשֶׁה

---

34. **The sons of Yisrael did so.** If we picture for ourselves the grouping of the Jewish people according to
camps as directed in these verses, we will see, in the
front, to the east, beneath the standard of Judah,
the tribes of Judah, Issakhar and Zebulun. At right,
toward the south, beneath the standard of Reuben, are
the tribes of Reuben, Shimeon and Gad. At the left,
toward the north, beneath the standard of Dan, are the
tribes of Dan, Asher and Naphtali. In the rear, facing
Judah and beneath the standard of Ephraim, are the
tribes of Ephraim, Menashe and Binyamin.

Each of the three tribes that form the camp of Judah,
leading the march through the wilderness, has been
characterized in both material and spiritual terms. The
patriarch [Jacob] on his deathbed (Genesis 49:8-10)
already visualized Judah as the tribe leading all the rest,
with the scepter, which symbolizes the authority of the
ruler, and the stylus, with which the law is recorded.
Issakhar was the tribe of agriculture, with sufficient

leisure also to cultivate learning (ibid., Verses 14-15).
Zebulun (ibid., Verse 13) was the tribe of commerce; at
the same time, according to the Song of Deborah
(Judges 5:14), the sons of Zebulun were to be "those
who wield the writer's staff"; i.e., cultivators of literature. Thus, the camp of Judah, which traveled in the
lead, united all the essential attributes upon which
the material and spiritual welfare of the nation depended: the scepter and the law, agriculture and
scholarship, commerce and literature.

These two groups, symbolizing specified spiritual
and material attributes, combined in the lead camp, are
divided into two subordinate camps, which follow the
main camp on either side. Reuben, Shimeon and Gad
comprise the nation's right hand, as it were. Reuben,
the first-born, is endowed with ample intellectual gifts
and with a keen sense of justice, but also with softness
of character, which makes him incapable of acting as
the leader of the nation. Assigned to flank him are

camp next to their standards, and so did they journey, each one according to his families, according to his fathers' house.

III 1. And these were the descendants of Aharon and Moshe on the day that *God* spoke with Moshe on Mount Sinai. 2. These are the names of the sons of Aharon: Nadab the first-born and Abihu, Eleazar and Ithamar. 3. These are the names of the sons of Aharon, those who were anointed as priests, who were invested with full authority to minister as priests. 4. But Nadab and Abihu died before *God* when they brought near strange fire before *God* in the wilderness of Sinai, and they had no sons, and so only Eleazar and Ithamar remained to minister as priests before the countenance of Aharon, their father. 5. *God* spoke to Moshe [saying]: 6. "Let the tribe of Levi come near, and place it before Aharon the priest; they shall minister to him, 7. and they shall keep his charge and the charge of the entire community before the Tent of

כֵּן־חָנוּ לְדִגְלֵיהֶם וְכֵן נָסָעוּ אִישׁ לְמִשְׁפְּחֹתָיו עַל־בֵּית אֲבֹתָיו: פ רביעי ג א וְאֵלֶּה תּוֹלְדֹת אַהֲרֹן וּמֹשֶׁה בְּיוֹם דִּבֶּר יְהֹוָה אֶת־מֹשֶׁה בְּהַר סִינָי: ב וְאֵלֶּה שְׁמוֹת בְּנֵי־אַהֲרֹן הַבְּכֹר ׀ נָדָב וַאֲבִיהוּא אֶלְעָזָר וְאִיתָמָר: ג אֵלֶּה שְׁמוֹת בְּנֵי אַהֲרֹן הַכֹּהֲנִים הַמְּשֻׁחִים אֲשֶׁר־מִלֵּא יָדָם לְכַהֵן: ד וַיָּמָת נָדָב וַאֲבִיהוּא לִפְנֵי יְהֹוָה בְּהַקְרִבָם אֵשׁ זָרָה לִפְנֵי יְהֹוָה בְּמִדְבַּר סִינַי וּבָנִים לֹא־הָיוּ לָהֶם וַיְכַהֵן אֶלְעָזָר וְאִיתָמָר עַל־פְּנֵי אַהֲרֹן אֲבִיהֶם: פ ה וַיְדַבֵּר יְהֹוָה אֶל־מֹשֶׁה לֵּאמֹר: ו הַקְרֵב אֶת־מַטֵּה לֵוִי וְהַעֲמַדְתָּ אֹתוֹ לִפְנֵי אַהֲרֹן הַכֹּהֵן וְשֵׁרְתוּ אֹתוֹ: ז וְשָׁמְרוּ אֶת־מִשְׁמַרְתּוֹ וְאֶת־מִשְׁמֶרֶת כָּל־הָעֵדָה לִפְנֵי אֹהֶל

Shimeon, the swift, impulsive avenger of personal honor, and Gad, as sharp as an arrowhead to strike back against unprovoked attacks (see Genesis 49:3–7 and 19). Thus we have, marching at the right hand of Judah, tribal entities symbolizing the courage to fend off insults and attacks, but all under the egis of gentle mercy.

Marching at Judah's left hand were Dan, symbol of adroit cunning (ibid., Verses 16, 17); Asher, representing refinement of taste (ibid., Verse 20, cf. Yoma 76b חמרא וריחני פקחין ["Wine and aromatic spices made me wise"]), and Naphtali (ibid., Verse 21), symbolizing eloquence. Thus, while the standard of Judah implies a tendency to seek power, there was to be a splendid unfolding of spiritual attainments beneath the standard of Dan.

The symbolism of the tribes of Ephraim, Menashe and Binyamin, which camped to the west, facing the eastern sector of the camp of Judah, beneath the standard of Ephraim, is not as clear as that of the other tribes. Actually, Ephraim and Menashe together represent the tribe of Joseph. But what Jacob said on his deathbed with regard to Joseph (Genesis 49:22 f.) referred to Joseph personally more than to the tribe that was to be descended from him. What Jacob said (ibid., 48:19) concerning Ephraim and Menashe indicates an unfolding of power, particularly in the case of Ephraim, about whom Jacob predicted that he would become very great and that his descendants "would complete the

(other) nations," which we believe we may interpret to mean that the tribe of Ephraim would serve as an armor reinforcing the defenses of the other tribes. Thus, in the case of Ephraim, we probably will have to think symbolically in terms of valor which, for the sake of the nation's well-being, should take up its position facing the camp of Judah in the lead. Judah is to be in the east, and Ephraim in the west. Thus, too, the Song of Assaph (Psalm 80, Verses 2, 3) sees Israel's salvation as depending upon the achievements of "Joseph," and Assaph prays: "O Shepherd of Israel, incline Thine ear! Thou Who leadest Joseph like a flock, O Thou Who art enthroned among the cherubim, shine forth, before Ephraim and Binyamin and Menashe, stir up Thy omnipotence and come to our aid for Thine own sake." When, later in our history, the house of Joseph, instead of seeking to complement Judah, came into conflict with the latter and usurped its role of leadership, when Joseph planted his "standard" not behind Judah but at the head of the nation, it spelled the nation's downfall. Itself estranged from the Testimony of the Law and from its Dwelling Place, the house of Joseph perished, dragging down to ruin with it the ten-twelfths of the nation that had joined it. . . .

CHAPTER III

7. *to perform the service of the Dwelling Place.* The Levites have been charged by the priests and by

Appointed Meeting, to perform the service of the Dwelling Place. 8. They are to be in charge of all the utensils of the Tent of Appointed Meeting and to keep the charge of the sons of Yisrael to perform the service of the Dwelling Place. 9. You shall give the Levites to Aharon and to his sons; they shall be given, [indeed] given to him from among the sons of Yisrael. 10. You shall appoint Aharon and his sons that they may keep [watch over] their priesthood; any outsider who comes near becomes liable to the death penalty." 11. *God* spoke to Moshe [saying]: 12. "As for Me, lo! I have taken the Levites from amidst the sons of Yisrael in place of every first-born, the opening of a mother's womb, from among the sons of Yisrael, and the Levites shall be Mine. 13. For all that is first-born is Mine; on the day I struck down all the first-born in the land of Mitzrayim, I sanctified for Myself all that is first-born in Yisrael from man to beast; Mine they shall remain; I, *God*." 14. *God* spoke to Moshe in the wilderness of Sinai [saying]: 15. "Number the sons of Levi according to their

מוֹעֵד לַעֲבֹד אֶת־עֲבֹדַת הַמִּשְׁכָּן: ח וְשָׁמְרוּ אֶת־כָּל־כְּלֵי אֹהֶל מוֹעֵד וְאֶת־מִשְׁמֶרֶת בְּנֵי יִשְׂרָאֵל לַעֲבֹד אֶת־עֲבֹדַת הַמִּשְׁכָּן: ט וְנָתַתָּה אֶת־הַלְוִיִּם לְאַהֲרֹן וּלְבָנָיו נְתוּנִם נְתוּנִם הֵמָּה לוֹ מֵאֵת בְּנֵי יִשְׂרָאֵל: י וְאֶת־אַהֲרֹן וְאֶת־בָּנָיו תִּפְקֹד וְשָׁמְרוּ אֶת־כְּהֻנָּתָם וְהַזָּר הַקָּרֵב יוּמָת: פ יא וַיְדַבֵּר יְהֹוָה אֶל־מֹשֶׁה לֵּאמֹר: יב וַאֲנִי הִנֵּה לָקַחְתִּי אֶת־הַלְוִיִּם מִתּוֹךְ בְּנֵי יִשְׂרָאֵל תַּחַת כָּל־בְּכוֹר פֶּטֶר רֶחֶם מִבְּנֵי יִשְׂרָאֵל וְהָיוּ לִי הַלְוִיִּם: יג כִּי לִי כָּל־בְּכוֹר בְּיוֹם הַכֹּתִי כָל־בְּכוֹר בְּאֶרֶץ מִצְרַיִם הִקְדַּשְׁתִּי לִי כָל־בְּכוֹר בְּיִשְׂרָאֵל מֵאָדָם עַד־בְּהֵמָה לִי יִהְיוּ אֲנִי יְהֹוָה: פ חמישי יד וַיְדַבֵּר יְהֹוָה אֶל־מֹשֶׁה בְּמִדְבַּר סִינַי לֵאמֹר: טו פְּקֹד אֶת־בְּנֵי לֵוִי לְבֵית

the entire community to perform the service of the Dwelling Place of the Testimony. They serve the Sanctuary on behalf of Aharon and on behalf of the entire community.

9. **You shall give.** Even though the Levites must perform their functions in the name of the priests and in the name of the entire people, this does not imply by any means that they are to be appointed by the authority or by the will emanating from the priests or from the community. Rather, God tells Moses, "*you shall give.*" Thus God Himself is acting here through Moses. It is by the command of God, to be carried out by Moses, that the functions of standing guard over the Sanctuary and of ministering to it—duties incumbent upon the community and upon the priests on the community's behalf—are to be turned over to the Levites. Moses is to "give" the Levites, from among the people, or as members of the people, to the priests for this purpose. Aside from this specific purpose and aside from the duties implicit in this Divine command, therefore, the priests have no authority whatsoever over the Levites. The Levites have been "given, [indeed] given" to Aaron. The position of the Levites in relation to the priests does not result from any inherent superiority of the priests over the Levites; also, the relationship between the two does not transcend the limits of the

purposes for which this Divine command was given to the priests.

11. The position of the Levites in relation to the community, on the one hand, and to the priests, on the other, has just been defined as based on a command emanating directly from God. The verses that follow will discuss this command in detail and explain the resultant special relationship of the Levites to God.

13. **For all that is first-born is Mine.** (Cf. Exodus 13:15). "Mine they shall remain": The transfer of the functions in the Sanctuary from the first-born to the Levites does not imply that the first-born are no longer to be consecrated to God. Despite this transfer of functions, they remain sanctified to God. The only prerogative they no longer have is the function of representing the entire nation in the Sanctuary. Their function within their own families; i.e., their role in expressing the entire family's subordination to God, continues, as does their obligation to consecrate their clean animals and the first-born of their donkeys, symbolizing the subordination of the family's sustenance and its possessions to God. . . . The consecration of the first-born has no physical significance. Its significance is solely moral; hence its paramount importance to the nation. . . .

fathers' house, according to their families; every male from one month old and upward shall you number them." 16. Moshe numbered them according to the utterance of *God,* as he had been commanded. 17. These were the sons of Levi, by their names: Gershon, Kehath and Merari; 18. and these the names of the sons of Gershon according to their families: Livni and Shimm'i. 19. The sons of Kehath according to their families: Amram, Yitzhar, Ḥebron and Uzziel. 20. The sons of Merari according to their families: Maḥli and Mushi. These are the families of the Levites according to their fathers' houses. 21. Of Gershon: The family of the Livnite branch and the family of the Shimm'ite branch. These are the families of the Gershonite house. 22. Their numberings were carried out according to the number of all males from one month old and upward. Their numbered ones were seven thousand five hundred. 23. The families of the Gershonite house shall camp behind the Dwelling Place, to the west. 24. The prince of the fathers' house of the Gershonite house [was] Eliassaph, son of Lael. 25. The charge of the sons of Gershon in

אֲבֹתָ֖ם לְמִשְׁפְּחֹתָ֑ם כָּל־זָכָ֛ר מִבֶּן־חֹ֥דֶשׁ וָמַ֖עְלָה
תִּפְקְדֵֽם׃ טז וַיִּפְקֹ֥ד אֹתָ֛ם מֹשֶׁ֖ה עַל־פִּ֣י יְהוָ֑ה
כַּאֲשֶׁ֖ר צֻוָּֽה׃ יז וַיִּֽהְיוּ־אֵ֥לֶּה בְנֵֽי־לֵוִ֖י בִּשְׁמֹתָ֑ם
גֵּֽרְשׁ֕וֹן וּקְהָ֖ת וּמְרָרִֽי׃ יח וְאֵ֛לֶּה שְׁמ֥וֹת בְּנֵֽי־
גֵרְשׁ֖וֹן לְמִשְׁפְּחֹתָ֑ם לִבְנִ֖י וְשִׁמְעִֽי׃ יט וּבְנֵ֥י קְהָ֖ת
לְמִשְׁפְּחֹתָ֑ם עַמְרָ֣ם וְיִצְהָ֔ר חֶבְר֖וֹן וְעֻזִּיאֵֽל׃
כ וּבְנֵ֧י מְרָרִ֛י לְמִשְׁפְּחֹתָ֖ם מַחְלִ֣י וּמוּשִׁ֑י אֵ֥לֶּה
הֵ֛ם מִשְׁפְּחֹ֥ת הַלֵּוִ֖י לְבֵ֥ית אֲבֹתָֽם׃ כא לְגֵ֣רְשׁ֔וֹן
מִשְׁפַּ֙חַת֙ הַלִּבְנִ֔י וּמִשְׁפַּ֖חַת הַשִּׁמְעִ֑י אֵ֣לֶּה הֵ֔ם
מִשְׁפְּחֹ֖ת הַגֵּרְשֻׁנִּֽי׃ כב פְּקֻדֵיהֶם֙ בְּמִסְפַּ֣ר כָּל־
זָכָ֔ר מִבֶּן־חֹ֖דֶשׁ וָמָ֑עְלָה פְּקֻדֵיהֶ֕ם שִׁבְעַ֥ת אֲלָפִ֖ים
וַחֲמֵ֥שׁ מֵאֽוֹת׃ כג מִשְׁפְּחֹ֖ת הַגֵּרְשֻׁנִּ֑י אַחֲרֵ֧י
הַמִּשְׁכָּ֛ן יַחֲנ֖וּ יָֽמָּה׃ כד וּנְשִׂ֥יא בֵית־אָ֖ב לַגֵּרְשֻׁנִּ֑י
אֶלְיָסָ֖ף בֶּן־לָאֵֽל׃ כה וּמִשְׁמֶ֤רֶת בְּנֵֽי־גֵרְשׁוֹן֙

15. ***Number***. The tribe of Levi represents the entire House of Israel in microcosm in that, like the House of Israel, it, too, is divided into groupings. The sons of Jacob formed tribes according to "fathers' houses" and their sons in turn formed family branches, so that the nation was divided into tribes (Reuben, Shimeon, Levi, etc.), after the sons of Jacob, and these tribes in turn were divided into the Ḥanokhites and the Paluites (see Chapter 26, Verses 5 ff.), after the sons of these sons. In the same manner, Levi's three sons, Gershon, Kehath and Merari, formed three "fathers' houses" of Levites, with their sons, Livni, Shimm'i, etc., forming the families of the Levites.

from one month old and upward shall you number them. The fact that the Levites are to be numbered from earliest infancy; i.e., from the age at which they can be said to have proven their viability, would seem to indicate that their Levite vocation entails more than the mere performance of the tasks for the Sanctuary enumerated in this text. Their caretaking and guarding functions while the Sanctuary is at rest and while it is traveling can be only a logical outgrowth and practical expression of the ideal concepts inherent in their calling. For (as will be seen in Chapter 4) they must be numbered again when they actually enter their service, and this they can do only after they have reached the age of thirty. Hence the fact that their first numbering takes place when they are still children must imply that they have a calling over and beyond this practical service, a purpose which they may perhaps be qualified to serve already at an earlier age but for which, nonetheless, the individual requires training from earliest childhood and boyhood onward. As a matter of fact, we know that the Levites were meant to function not merely as keepers and guardians of the physical Dwelling Place of the Law, represented in wood and gold, in byssus and purple, but also as keepers and guardians, disseminators and defenders of the Law itself, and of its observance. In this way they served to promote the realization, in the nation's life, of the ideals of the nation's mission implicit in the Dwelling Place of the Law that was entrusted to their physical care. (See Moses' blessing of the tribe of Levi, Deuteronomy 33:9–11). This vocation, common to all Levites, is incumbent upon every male Levite from the first month of his life onward, and his training for it must begin when he first becomes aware of his surroundings.

the Tent of Appointed Meeting is the Dwelling Place and the Tent, its cover and the protective curtain of the entrance of the Tent of Appointed Meeting; 26. the hangings of the forecourt and the protective curtain of the entrance of the forecourt, which is round about the Dwelling Place and the altar, and its ropes, for all its prerequisites. 27. Of Kehath: The family of the Amramite branch, the family of the Yitzharite branch, the family of the Ḥebronite branch and the family of the Uzzielite branch. These are the families of the Kehathite house. 28. According to the number of all males from one month old and upward: eight thousand six hundred, keepers of the charge of the Sanctuary. 29. The families of the sons of Kehath shall camp at the side of the Dwelling Place, to the south. 30. The prince of the fathers' house of the families of the Kehathite house: Elitzaphan, son of Uzziel. 31. Their charge: the Ark, the Table, the menorah and the altars, and the utensils of the Sanctuary with which one ministers, and the protective curtain and all its prerequisites. 32. The prince of the princes of the Levites: Eleazar, son of Aharon the priest. He was appointed over the keepers of the charge of the Sanctuary. 33. Of Merari: The family of the Maḥlite branch, and the family of the Mushite branch; these [are] the families of the Merarite house. 34. Their numbered ones according to the number of all males from one month old and upward: six thousand two hundred. 35. The prince of the fathers' house of the Merarite branch: Tzuriel, son of Aviḥayil; they shall camp at the side of the Dwelling Place, to the north. 36. The appointment of the charge of the sons of the Merarite branch, [being] the beams of the Dwelling Place, its bars, its pillars and its sockets, its utensils and all its prerequisites. 37. Also the pillars of the forecourt round about, and their sockets, their stakes and their ropes. 38. But those who are to camp in front of the Dwelling Place, to the east, [are] Moshe and Aharon and his sons, keeping the charge of the entire Sanctuary as the charge of the sons of Yisrael. Any outsider who comes near is liable to the death penalty. 39. All the numbered ones of the

בְּאֹהֶל מוֹעֵד הַמִּשְׁכָּן וְהָאֹהֶל מִכְסֵהוּ וּמָסַךְ
פֶּתַח אֹהֶל מוֹעֵד: כו וְקַלְעֵי הֶחָצֵר וְאֶת־מָסַךְ
פֶּתַח הֶחָצֵר אֲשֶׁר עַל־הַמִּשְׁכָּן וְעַל־הַמִּזְבֵּחַ
סָבִיב וְאֵת מֵיתָרָיו לְכֹל עֲבֹדָתוֹ: ס כז וְלִקְהָת
מִשְׁפַּחַת הָעַמְרָמִי וּמִשְׁפַּחַת הַיִּצְהָרִי וּמִשְׁפַּחַת
הַחֶבְרֹנִי וּמִשְׁפַּחַת הָעָזִּיאֵלִי אֵלֶּה הֵם מִשְׁפְּחֹת
הַקְּהָתִי: כח בְּמִסְפַּר כָּל־זָכָר מִבֶּן־חֹדֶשׁ וָמָעְלָה
שְׁמֹנַת אֲלָפִים וְשֵׁשׁ מֵאוֹת שֹׁמְרֵי מִשְׁמֶרֶת
הַקֹּדֶשׁ: כט מִשְׁפְּחֹת בְּנֵי־קְהָת יַחֲנוּ עַל יֶרֶךְ
הַמִּשְׁכָּן תֵּימָנָה: ל וּנְשִׂיא בֵית־אָב לְמִשְׁפְּחֹת
הַקְּהָתִי אֱלִיצָפָן בֶּן־עֻזִּיאֵל: לא וּמִשְׁמַרְתָּם
הָאָרֹן וְהַשֻּׁלְחָן וְהַמְּנֹרָה וְהַמִּזְבְּחֹת וּכְלֵי הַקֹּדֶשׁ
אֲשֶׁר יְשָׁרְתוּ בָּהֶם וְהַמָּסָךְ וְכֹל עֲבֹדָתוֹ:
לב וּנְשִׂיא נְשִׂיאֵי הַלֵּוִי אֶלְעָזָר בֶּן־אַהֲרֹן הַכֹּהֵן
פְּקֻדַּת שֹׁמְרֵי מִשְׁמֶרֶת הַקֹּדֶשׁ: לג לִמְרָרִי
מִשְׁפַּחַת הַמַּחְלִי וּמִשְׁפַּחַת הַמּוּשִׁי אֵלֶּה הֵם
מִשְׁפְּחֹת מְרָרִי: לד וּפְקֻדֵיהֶם בְּמִסְפַּר כָּל־זָכָר
מִבֶּן־חֹדֶשׁ וָמָעְלָה שֵׁשֶׁת אֲלָפִים וּמָאתָיִם:
לה וּנְשִׂיא בֵית־אָב לְמִשְׁפְּחֹת מְרָרִי צוּרִיאֵל
בֶּן־אֲבִיחָיִל עַל יֶרֶךְ הַמִּשְׁכָּן יַחֲנוּ צָפֹנָה:
לו וּפְקֻדַּת מִשְׁמֶרֶת בְּנֵי מְרָרִי קַרְשֵׁי הַמִּשְׁכָּן
וּבְרִיחָיו וְעַמֻּדָיו וַאֲדָנָיו וְכָל־כֵּלָיו וְכֹל עֲבֹדָתוֹ:
לז וְעַמֻּדֵי הֶחָצֵר סָבִיב וְאַדְנֵיהֶם וִיתֵדֹתָם
וּמֵיתְרֵיהֶם: לח וְהַחֹנִים לִפְנֵי הַמִּשְׁכָּן קֵדְמָה
לִפְנֵי אֹהֶל־מוֹעֵד ׀ מִזְרָחָה מֹשֶׁה ׀ וְאַהֲרֹן וּבָנָיו
שֹׁמְרִים מִשְׁמֶרֶת הַמִּקְדָּשׁ לְמִשְׁמֶרֶת בְּנֵי
יִשְׂרָאֵל וְהַזָּר הַקָּרֵב יוּמָת: לט כָּל־פְּקוּדֵי

Levites, whom Moshe numbered, and [so did] Aharon, according to the utterance of *God*, according to their families, all males from one month old and upward: twenty-two thousand. 40. *God* said to Moshe: "Number all the male first-born of the sons of Yisrael from one month old and upward, and take the number of their names. 41. And take the Levites for Me—I, *God*—instead of every first-born among the sons of Yisrael, and the livestock of the Levites instead of every first-born among the livestock of the sons of Yisrael." 42. And Moshe numbered, as *God* had commanded him, all the first-born among the sons of Yisrael. 43. All the male first-born according to the number of names from one month old and upward according to their numbered ones were: Twenty-two thousand two hundred seventy-three. 44. *God* spoke to Moshe [saying]: 45. "Take the Levites instead of all the first-born among the sons of Yisrael and the livestock of the Levites instead of their livestock; so the Levites shall be Mine, I, *God*. 46. But as regards the redemption of the two hundred seventy-three of the first-born of the sons of Yisrael who are over and above the [number of the] Levites, 47. you shall take five shekels per head, according to the shekel of the Sanctuary you shall take [them], twenty *gerahs* to the shekel, 48. and you shall give the money to Aharon and his sons as a redemption for those [first-born] who are over and above [the number of Levites]." 49. Moshe took the redemption money from those who were over and above [the number of] those who were redeemed through the Levites. 50. From the first-born of the sons of Yisrael did he take the money, one thousand three hundred sixty-five according to the shekel of the Sanctuary. 51. And Moshe gave the redemption money to Aharon and his sons according to the utterance of *God*, as *God* had commanded Moshe.

IV

1. *God* spoke to Moshe and Aharon [saying]: 2. "Take

הַלְוִיִּם אֲשֶׁר פָּקַד מֹשֶׁה וְאַהֲרֹן עַל־פִּי יְהוָה
לְמִשְׁפְּחֹתָם כָּל־זָכָר מִבֶּן־חֹדֶשׁ וָמַעְלָה שְׁנַיִם
וְעֶשְׂרִים אָלֶף: ס ששי מ וַיֹּאמֶר יְהוָה אֶל־מֹשֶׁה
פְּקֹד כָּל־בְּכֹר זָכָר לִבְנֵי יִשְׂרָאֵל מִבֶּן־חֹדֶשׁ
וָמָעְלָה וְשָׂא אֵת מִסְפַּר שְׁמֹתָם: מא וְלָקַחְתָּ
אֶת־הַלְוִיִּם לִי אֲנִי יְהוָה תַּחַת כָּל־בְּכֹר בִּבְנֵי
יִשְׂרָאֵל וְאֵת בֶּהֱמַת הַלְוִיִּם תַּחַת כָּל־בְּכוֹר
בְּבֶהֱמַת בְּנֵי יִשְׂרָאֵל: מב וַיִּפְקֹד מֹשֶׁה כַּאֲשֶׁר
צִוָּה יְהוָה אֹתוֹ אֶת־כָּל־בְּכוֹר בִּבְנֵי יִשְׂרָאֵל:
מג וַיְהִי כָל־בְּכוֹר זָכָר בְּמִסְפַּר שֵׁמֹת מִבֶּן־
חֹדֶשׁ וָמַעְלָה לִפְקֻדֵיהֶם שְׁנַיִם וְעֶשְׂרִים אֶלֶף
שְׁלֹשָׁה וְשִׁבְעִים וּמָאתָיִם: פ מד וַיְדַבֵּר יְהוָה
אֶל־מֹשֶׁה לֵּאמֹר: מה קַח אֶת־הַלְוִיִּם תַּחַת כָּל־
בְּכוֹר בִּבְנֵי יִשְׂרָאֵל וְאֶת־בֶּהֱמַת הַלְוִיִּם תַּחַת
בְּהֶמְתָּם וְהָיוּ־לִי הַלְוִיִּם אֲנִי יְהוָה: מו וְאֵת
פְּדוּיֵי הַשְּׁלֹשָׁה וְהַשִּׁבְעִים וְהַמָּאתַיִם הָעֹדְפִים
עַל־הַלְוִיִּם מִבְּכוֹר בְּנֵי יִשְׂרָאֵל: מז וְלָקַחְתָּ
חֲמֵשֶׁת חֲמֵשֶׁת שְׁקָלִים לַגֻּלְגֹּלֶת בְּשֶׁקֶל הַקֹּדֶשׁ
תִּקָּח עֶשְׂרִים גֵּרָה הַשָּׁקֶל: מח וְנָתַתָּה הַכֶּסֶף
לְאַהֲרֹן וּלְבָנָיו פְּדוּיֵי הָעֹדְפִים בָּהֶם: מט וַיִּקַּח
מֹשֶׁה אֵת כֶּסֶף הַפִּדְיוֹם מֵאֵת הָעֹדְפִים עַל
פְּדוּיֵי הַלְוִיִּם: נ מֵאֵת בְּכוֹר בְּנֵי יִשְׂרָאֵל לָקַח
אֶת־הַכָּסֶף חֲמִשָּׁה וְשִׁשִּׁים וּשְׁלֹשׁ מֵאוֹת וָאֶלֶף
בְּשֶׁקֶל הַקֹּדֶשׁ: נא וַיִּתֵּן מֹשֶׁה אֶת־כֶּסֶף הַפְּדֻיִם
לְאַהֲרֹן וּלְבָנָיו עַל־פִּי יְהוָה כַּאֲשֶׁר צִוָּה יְהוָה
אֶת־מֹשֶׁה: פ שביעי ד א וַיְדַבֵּר יְהוָה אֶל־מֹשֶׁה

CHAPTER IV

1. In the preceding chapter the command was given to number all those destined for the Levite vocation. The order was applicable to all Levites from one month old and upward. Now follows the numbering of those Levites who were liable to active duty in the carrying

the total count of the sons of Kehath from among the sons of Levi according to their families, according to their fathers' house, 3. from thirty years old and upward until fifty years old, each one who comes to communal service, to do [sacred] work in the Tent of Appointed Meeting.   4. This is the service of the sons of Kehath in the Tent of Appointed Meeting; [it is] the Holy of Holies.   5. And Aharon and his sons shall come when the camp journeys forth, and they shall take off the protective curtain and cover the Ark of the Testimony with it. 6. They shall place upon this a cover of *taḥash* skin and shall spread over it a cloth entirely of sky-blue wool and adjust its [carrying] poles.   7. And upon the Table of the Countenance they shall spread a cloth of sky-blue wool and shall place upon it the dishes, the spoons, the purification tubes and the supports of the covering, and the continual bread shall be upon it.   8. Over this they shall spread a cloth of crimson wool and cover it with a cover of *taḥash* skin and insert its [carrying] poles.   9. They shall then take a cloth of sky-blue wool and cover the menorah of the light and its lamps, its tongs and its pans and also all its oil vessels with which they minister to it. 10. They shall place it [i.e., the menorah] and all its utensils into a cover of *taḥash* skins and they shall place it upon the carrying frame.   11. Over the golden altar they shall spread a cloth of sky-blue wool and cover it with a cover of *taḥash* skin and insert its [carrying] poles.   12. They shall then take all the utensils of ministry with which they minister in the Sanctuary, place them into a cloth of sky-blue wool and cover them with a cover of *taḥash* skin, and they shall place them upon the carrying frame.   13. They shall clear the altar of ashes and spread over it a cloth of purple wool,   14. and shall place upon it all its utensils with which they minister upon it: the pans, the forks, the shovels, the bowls for dashing [the blood of the animal offerings], all the utensils of the altar; they shall

וְאֶל־אַהֲרֹן לֵאמֹר: ב נָשֹׂא אֶת־רֹאשׁ בְּנֵי קְהָת מִתּוֹךְ בְּנֵי לֵוִי לְמִשְׁפְּחֹתָם לְבֵית אֲבֹתָם: ג מִבֶּן שְׁלֹשִׁים שָׁנָה וָמַעְלָה וְעַד בֶּן־חֲמִשִּׁים שָׁנָה כָּל־בָּא לַצָּבָא לַעֲשׂוֹת מְלָאכָה בְּאֹהֶל מוֹעֵד: ד זֹאת עֲבֹדַת בְּנֵי־קְהָת בְּאֹהֶל מוֹעֵד קֹדֶשׁ הַקֳּדָשִׁים: ה וּבָא אַהֲרֹן וּבָנָיו בִּנְסֹעַ הַמַּחֲנֶה וְהוֹרִדוּ אֵת פָּרֹכֶת הַמָּסָךְ וְכִסּוּ־בָהּ אֵת אֲרֹן הָעֵדֻת: ו וְנָתְנוּ עָלָיו כְּסוּי עוֹר תַּחַשׁ וּפָרְשׂוּ בֶגֶד־כְּלִיל תְּכֵלֶת מִלְמָעְלָה וְשָׂמוּ בַּדָּיו: ז וְעַל שֻׁלְחַן הַפָּנִים יִפְרְשׂוּ בֶּגֶד תְּכֵלֶת וְנָתְנוּ עָלָיו אֶת־הַקְּעָרֹת וְאֶת־הַכַּפֹּת וְאֶת־הַמְּנַקִּיֹּת וְאֵת קְשׂוֹת הַנָּסֶךְ וְלֶחֶם הַתָּמִיד עָלָיו יִהְיֶה: ח וּפָרְשׂוּ עֲלֵיהֶם בֶּגֶד תּוֹלַעַת שָׁנִי וְכִסּוּ אֹתוֹ בְּמִכְסֵה עוֹר תָּחַשׁ וְשָׂמוּ אֶת־בַּדָּיו: ט וְלָקְחוּ בֶגֶד תְּכֵלֶת וְכִסּוּ אֶת־מְנֹרַת הַמָּאוֹר וְאֶת־נֵרֹתֶיהָ וְאֶת־מַלְקָחֶיהָ וְאֶת־מַחְתֹּתֶיהָ וְאֵת כָּל־כְּלֵי שַׁמְנָהּ אֲשֶׁר יְשָׁרְתוּ־לָהּ בָּהֶם: י וְנָתְנוּ אֹתָהּ וְאֶת־כָּל־כֵּלֶיהָ אֶל־מִכְסֵה עוֹר תָּחַשׁ וְנָתְנוּ עַל־הַמּוֹט: יא וְעַל מִזְבַּח הַזָּהָב יִפְרְשׂוּ בֶּגֶד תְּכֵלֶת וְכִסּוּ אֹתוֹ בְּמִכְסֵה עוֹר תָּחַשׁ וְשָׂמוּ אֶת־בַּדָּיו: יב וְלָקְחוּ אֶת־כָּל־כְּלֵי הַשָּׁרֵת אֲשֶׁר יְשָׁרְתוּ־בָם בַּקֹּדֶשׁ וְנָתְנוּ אֶל־בֶּגֶד תְּכֵלֶת וְכִסּוּ אוֹתָם בְּמִכְסֵה עוֹר תָּחַשׁ וְנָתְנוּ עַל־הַמּוֹט: יג וְדִשְּׁנוּ אֶת־הַמִּזְבֵּחַ וּפָרְשׂוּ עָלָיו בֶּגֶד אַרְגָּמָן: יד וְנָתְנוּ עָלָיו אֶת־כָּל־כֵּלָיו אֲשֶׁר יְשָׁרְתוּ עָלָיו בָּהֶם אֶת־הַמַּחְתֹּת אֶת־הַמִּזְלָגֹת וְאֶת־הַיָּעִים וְאֶת־הַמִּזְרָקֹת כֹּל כְּלֵי הַמִּזְבֵּחַ וּפָרְשׂוּ עָלָיו

and safeguarding of the Sanctuary during its wanderings, along with more detailed instructions regarding the duties assigned in this connection to each of the Levite "houses." . . .

spread over this a cover of *taḥash* skin and insert its [carrying] poles. 15. When Aharon and his sons have finished covering the holy [objects] and all the utensils of the Sanctuary when the camp journeys forth —only after that shall the sons of Kehath come to carry [them] so that they will not touch the holy [objects] and die. These constitute the burden to be carried by the sons of Kehath for the Tent of Appointed Meeting. 16. But the responsibility of Eleazar, the son of Aharon the priest, is the oil for the light, the spicy incense, the homage gift of the daily offering and the anointing oil; the responsibility for the entire Dwelling Place and its entire contents of holy [objects] and its utensils." 17. *God* spoke to Moshe and Aharon [saying]: 18. "Do not permit the tribe of the Kehathite families to become extinct from among the Levites. 19. You shall do this for them so that they will live and not die when they approach the Holy of Holies: Aharon and his sons shall come and set them, every single one [separately], to his service and to his burden. 20. They shall not go in to see when the holy [objects] are completely wrapped, and die."

כְּסוּי עוֹר תַּחַשׁ וְשָׂמוּ בַדָּיו: טו וְכִלָּה אַהֲרֹן־
וּבָנָיו לְכַסֹּת אֶת־הַקֹּדֶשׁ וְאֶת־כָּל־כְּלֵי הַקֹּדֶשׁ
בִּנְסֹעַ הַמַּחֲנֶה וְאַחֲרֵי־כֵן יָבֹאוּ בְנֵי־קְהָת
לָשֵׂאת וְלֹא־יִגְּעוּ אֶל־הַקֹּדֶשׁ וָמֵתוּ אֵלֶּה מַשָּׂא
בְנֵי־קְהָת בְּאֹהֶל מוֹעֵד: טז וּפְקֻדַּת אֶלְעָזָר ׀ בֶּן־
אַהֲרֹן הַכֹּהֵן שֶׁמֶן הַמָּאוֹר וּקְטֹרֶת הַסַּמִּים
וּמִנְחַת הַתָּמִיד וְשֶׁמֶן הַמִּשְׁחָה פְּקֻדַּת כָּל־
הַמִּשְׁכָּן וְכָל־אֲשֶׁר־בּוֹ בְּקֹדֶשׁ וּבְכֵלָיו: פ
מפטיר יז וַיְדַבֵּר יְהֹוָה אֶל־מֹשֶׁה וְאֶל־אַהֲרֹן
לֵאמֹר: יח אַל־תַּכְרִיתוּ אֶת־שֵׁבֶט מִשְׁפְּחֹת
הַקְּהָתִי מִתּוֹךְ הַלְוִיִּם: יט וְזֹאת ׀ עֲשׂוּ לָהֶם וְחָיוּ
וְלֹא יָמֻתוּ בְּגִשְׁתָּם אֶת־קֹדֶשׁ הַקֳּדָשִׁים אַהֲרֹן
וּבָנָיו יָבֹאוּ וְשָׂמוּ אוֹתָם אִישׁ אִישׁ עַל־עֲבֹדָתוֹ
וְאֶל־מַשָּׂאוֹ: כ וְלֹא־יָבֹאוּ לִרְאוֹת כְּבַלַּע אֶת־
הַקֹּדֶשׁ וָמֵתוּ: פ

17. **וַיְדַבֵּר** *[God] spoke.* In the preceding verses the command was given that the Kehathites were to be handed the sacred objects to carry only after these objects had been completely covered, so that the bearers would have no direct physical contact with them. Now we are told that the Kehathites must not even be present while the covering is done. They must not see these sacred objects while they are still in the process of being covered. If we are not in error, the intent of this prohibition is that the sacred things should remain to their bearers ideational concepts, not objects of physical perception, so that these individuals should be inspired all the more by the ideals the objects represent. The spiritual contemplation of the sacred objects entrusted to the care of the Kehathites would seem to be an essential aspect of their duties, and a physical perception of these objects while they are being covered would distract the Kehathites from their spiritual contemplation and thereby in effect desecrate the objects themselves.

The Haftarah for this Sidra may be found on page 888.

נשא

NASO

כא וַיְדַבֵּר יְהוָה אֶל־מֹשֶׁה לֵּאמֹר: כב נָשֹׂא אֶת־
רֹאשׁ בְּנֵי גֵרְשׁוֹן גַּם־הֵם לְבֵית אֲבֹתָם
לְמִשְׁפְּחֹתָם: כג מִבֶּן שְׁלֹשִׁים שָׁנָה וָמַעְלָה עַד
בֶּן־חֲמִשִּׁים שָׁנָה תִּפְקֹד אוֹתָם כָּל־הַבָּא לִצְבֹא
צָבָא לַעֲבֹד עֲבֹדָה בְּאֹהֶל מוֹעֵד: כד זֹאת עֲבֹדַת
מִשְׁפְּחֹת הַגֵּרְשֻׁנִּי לַעֲבֹד וּלְמַשָּׂא: כה וְנָשְׂאוּ
אֶת־יְרִיעֹת הַמִּשְׁכָּן וְאֶת־אֹהֶל מוֹעֵד מִכְסֵהוּ
וּמִכְסֵה הַתַּחַשׁ אֲשֶׁר־עָלָיו מִלְמָעְלָה וְאֶת־מָסַךְ
פֶּתַח אֹהֶל מוֹעֵד: כו וְאֵת קַלְעֵי הֶחָצֵר וְאֶת־
מָסַךְ ׀ פֶּתַח ׀ שַׁעַר הֶחָצֵר אֲשֶׁר עַל־הַמִּשְׁכָּן
וְעַל־הַמִּזְבֵּחַ סָבִיב וְאֵת מֵיתְרֵיהֶם וְאֶת־כָּל־כְּלֵי
עֲבֹדָתָם וְאֵת כָּל־אֲשֶׁר יֵעָשֶׂה לָהֶם וְעָבָדוּ:
כז עַל־פִּי אַהֲרֹן וּבָנָיו תִּהְיֶה כָּל־עֲבֹדַת בְּנֵי
הַגֵּרְשֻׁנִּי לְכָל־מַשָּׂאָם וּלְכֹל עֲבֹדָתָם וּפְקַדְתֶּם
עֲלֵהֶם בְּמִשְׁמֶרֶת אֵת כָּל־מַשָּׂאָם: כח זֹאת
עֲבֹדַת מִשְׁפְּחֹת בְּנֵי הַגֵּרְשֻׁנִּי בְּאֹהֶל מוֹעֵד
וּמִשְׁמַרְתָּם בְּיַד אִיתָמָר בֶּן־אַהֲרֹן הַכֹּהֵן: ס
כט בְּנֵי מְרָרִי לְמִשְׁפְּחֹתָם לְבֵית־אֲבֹתָם תִּפְקֹד
אֹתָם: ל מִבֶּן שְׁלֹשִׁים שָׁנָה וָמַעְלָה וְעַד בֶּן־
חֲמִשִּׁים שָׁנָה תִּפְקְדֵם כָּל־הַבָּא לַצָּבָא לַעֲבֹד
אֶת־עֲבֹדַת אֹהֶל מוֹעֵד: לא וְזֹאת מִשְׁמֶרֶת
מַשָּׂאָם לְכָל־עֲבֹדָתָם בְּאֹהֶל מוֹעֵד קַרְשֵׁי
הַמִּשְׁכָּן וּבְרִיחָיו וְעַמּוּדָיו וַאֲדָנָיו: לב וְעַמּוּדֵי
הֶחָצֵר סָבִיב וְאַדְנֵיהֶם וִיתֵדֹתָם וּמֵיתְרֵיהֶם
לְכָל־כְּלֵיהֶם וּלְכֹל עֲבֹדָתָם וּבְשֵׁמֹת תִּפְקְדוּ

21 *God* spoke to Moshe [saying]:
22. "Take also the total count of the sons of Gershon, according to their fathers' house, according to their families.
23. From thirty years old and upward until fifty years old shall you number them, every one who comes to perform communal service, to minister at the Tent of Appointed Meeting.
24. This is the service of the families of the Gershonite house to minister and to carry:
25. They shall carry the tapestries of the Dwelling Place; and the Tent of Appointed Meeting, its covering and the covering of *taḥash* skin which is above it; and also the protective curtain of the entrance to the Tent of Appointed Meeting;
26. the hangings of the forecourt; the protective curtain of the gate of the forecourt, which is round about the Dwelling Place and around the altar, their ropes and all the utensils of ministry—and in whatever must be done for these objects they shall serve.
27. According to the utterance of Aharon and his sons shall all the service of the entire Gershonite house be with regard to everything they have to carry and to serve. Everything that they have to carry you must appoint for them, along with the duty to take charge of them.
28. This is the service of the sons of the Gershonite house for the Tent of Appointed Meeting, and their charge shall be under the direction of Ithamar, son of Aharon the priest.
29. As for the sons of Merari, you shall number them according to their families, according to their fathers' houses.
30. From thirty years old and upward until fifty years old shall you number them, every one who comes to communal service, to perform the service for the Tent of Appointed Meeting.
31. And this is the charge of their burden for all their service at the Tent of Appointed Meeting: the beams of the Dwelling Place, its bars, pillars and sockets;
32. the pillars of the forecourt round about, their sockets, stakes and ropes, along with all their utensils and all that is required for their service—and [you shall refer to these objects] by their name when

you turn over the utensils to their charge in carrying. 33. This is the service of the families of the sons of Merari for all their service at the Tent of Appointed Meeting, under the direction of Ithamar, son of Aharon the priest." 34. And Moshe and Aharon and the princes of the community numbered the sons of the Kehathite house according to their families and according to their fathers' houses, 35. from thirty years old and upward until fifty years old, every one who comes to communal service, to the service at the Tent of Appointed Meeting. 36. The numbered ones according to their families were two thousand seven hundred and fifty. 37. These are the numbered ones of the families of the Kehathite house, every one ministering at the Tent of Appointed Meeting, whom Moshe and Aharon numbered, according to the utterance of *God* through Moshe. 38. And the numbered ones of the sons of Gershon according to their families and according to their fathers' house, 39. from thirty years old and upward until fifty years old, every one who comes to communal service, to the service at the Tent of Appointed Meeting. 40. Their numbered ones according to their families, according to their fathers' house, were two thousand six hundred and thirty. 41. These are the numbered ones of the families of the sons of Gershon, every one ministering at the Tent of Appointed Meeting, whom Moshe and Aharon numbered, according to the utterance of *God*. 42. And the numbered ones of the families of the sons of Merari according to their families and according to their fathers' house, 43. from thirty years old and upward until fifty years old, every one who comes to communal service, to the service at the Tent of Appointed Meeting. 44. Their numbered ones according to their families were three thousand two hundred. 45. These are the numbered ones of the families of the sons of Merari, whom Moshe and Aharon numbered, according to the utterance of *God* through Moshe. 46. All the numbered ones, whom Moshe and Aharon and the princes of Yisrael had numbered of the Levites according to their families and according to their

אֶת־כְּלֵי מִשְׁמֶרֶת מַשָּׂאָם׃ לג זֹאת עֲבֹדַת
מִשְׁפְּחֹת בְּנֵי מְרָרִי לְכָל־עֲבֹדָתָם בְּאֹהֶל מוֹעֵד
בְּיַד אִיתָמָר בֶּן־אַהֲרֹן הַכֹּהֵן׃ לד וַיִּפְקֹד מֹשֶׁה
וְאַהֲרֹן וּנְשִׂיאֵי הָעֵדָה אֶת־בְּנֵי הַקְּהָתִי
לְמִשְׁפְּחֹתָם וּלְבֵית אֲבֹתָם׃ לה מִבֶּן שְׁלֹשִׁים
שָׁנָה וָמַעְלָה וְעַד בֶּן־חֲמִשִּׁים שָׁנָה כָּל־הַבָּא
לַצָּבָא לַעֲבֹדָה בְּאֹהֶל מוֹעֵד׃ לו וַיִּהְיוּ פְקֻדֵיהֶם
לְמִשְׁפְּחֹתָם אַלְפַּיִם שְׁבַע מֵאוֹת וַחֲמִשִּׁים׃
לז אֵלֶּה פְקוּדֵי מִשְׁפְּחֹת הַקְּהָתִי כָּל־הָעֹבֵד
בְּאֹהֶל מוֹעֵד אֲשֶׁר פָּקַד מֹשֶׁה וְאַהֲרֹן עַל־פִּי
יְהוָה בְּיַד־מֹשֶׁה׃ ס שני לח וּפְקוּדֵי בְּנֵי גֵרְשׁוֹן
לְמִשְׁפְּחוֹתָם וּלְבֵית אֲבֹתָם׃ לט מִבֶּן שְׁלֹשִׁים
שָׁנָה וָמַעְלָה וְעַד בֶּן־חֲמִשִּׁים שָׁנָה כָּל־הַבָּא
לַצָּבָא לַעֲבֹדָה בְּאֹהֶל מוֹעֵד׃ מ וַיִּהְיוּ פְּקֻדֵיהֶם
לְמִשְׁפְּחֹתָם לְבֵית אֲבֹתָם אַלְפַּיִם וְשֵׁשׁ מֵאוֹת
וּשְׁלֹשִׁים׃ מא אֵלֶּה פְקוּדֵי מִשְׁפְּחֹת בְּנֵי גֵרְשׁוֹן
כָּל־הָעֹבֵד בְּאֹהֶל מוֹעֵד אֲשֶׁר פָּקַד מֹשֶׁה וְאַהֲרֹן
עַל־פִּי יְהוָה׃ מב וּפְקוּדֵי מִשְׁפְּחֹת בְּנֵי מְרָרִי
לְמִשְׁפְּחֹתָם לְבֵית אֲבֹתָם׃ מג מִבֶּן שְׁלֹשִׁים שָׁנָה
וָמַעְלָה וְעַד בֶּן־חֲמִשִּׁים שָׁנָה כָּל־הַבָּא לַצָּבָא
לַעֲבֹדָה בְּאֹהֶל מוֹעֵד׃ מד וַיִּהְיוּ פְקֻדֵיהֶם
לְמִשְׁפְּחֹתָם שְׁלֹשֶׁת אֲלָפִים וּמָאתָיִם׃ מה אֵלֶּה
פְקוּדֵי מִשְׁפְּחֹת בְּנֵי מְרָרִי אֲשֶׁר פָּקַד מֹשֶׁה
וְאַהֲרֹן עַל־פִּי יְהוָה בְּיַד־מֹשֶׁה׃ מו כָּל־הַפְּקֻדִים
אֲשֶׁר פָּקַד מֹשֶׁה וְאַהֲרֹן וּנְשִׂיאֵי יִשְׂרָאֵל אֶת־

fathers' house, 47. from thirty years old and upward until fifty years old, every one who comes to perform the service of the service and the service of carrying burdens for the Tent of Appointed Meeting. 48. Their numbered ones were eight thousand five hundred and eighty, 49. according to the utterance of *God*: He had appointed each one [separately] through Moshe with regard to his service and his carrying, and they were His numbered ones, since *God* had commanded it to Moshe.

V 1. *God* spoke to Moshe [saying]: 2. "Command the sons of Yisrael that they send away from the camp every leper and everyone with a discharge and everyone who has become unclean [by contact] with a [dead] person. 3. Both male and female shall you send away, outside the camp shall you send them, and they shall not divest their camps of purity, in whose midst I dwell." 4. The sons of Yisrael did so, they sent them away outside the camp; as *God* had spoken to Moshe, so did the sons of Yisrael do. 5. *God* spoke to Moshe [saying]: 6. "Speak to the sons of Yisrael [saying]: If a man or a woman shall commit a sin from among all the sins of man, one [of] committing a breach of trust against *God*, and that person has incurred guilt. 7. They must acknowledge to themselves the sin that they committed, and he must then make restitution for the object

הַלְוִיִּ֑ם לְמִשְׁפְּחֹתָ֖ם וּלְבֵ֥ית אֲבֹתָֽם׃ מז מִבֶּ֨ן
שְׁלֹשִׁ֥ים שָׁנָה֙ וָמַ֔עְלָה וְעַ֖ד בֶּן־חֲמִשִּׁ֣ים שָׁנָ֑ה כָּל־
הַבָּ֗א לַעֲבֹ֨ד עֲבֹדַ֧ת עֲבֹדָ֛ה וַעֲבֹדַ֥ת מַשָּׂ֖א בְּאֹ֥הֶל
מוֹעֵֽד׃ מח וַיִּהְי֖וּ פְּקֻדֵיהֶ֑ם שְׁמֹנַ֣ת אֲלָפִ֔ים וַחֲמֵ֥שׁ
מֵא֖וֹת וּשְׁמֹנִֽים׃ מט עַל־פִּ֨י יְהוָ֜ה פָּקַ֤ד אוֹתָם֙
בְּיַד־מֹשֶׁ֔ה אִ֥ישׁ אִ֛ישׁ עַל־עֲבֹדָת֖וֹ וְעַל־מַשָּׂא֑וֹ
וּפְקֻדָ֕יו אֲשֶׁר־צִוָּ֥ה יְהוָ֖ה אֶת־מֹשֶֽׁה׃ פ שלישי
ה א וַיְדַבֵּ֥ר יְהוָ֖ה אֶל־מֹשֶׁ֥ה לֵּאמֹֽר׃ ב צַ֚ו אֶת־
בְּנֵ֣י יִשְׂרָאֵ֔ל וִישַׁלְּחוּ֙ מִן־הַֽמַּחֲנֶ֔ה כָּל־צָר֖וּעַ
וְכָל־זָ֑ב וְכֹ֖ל טָמֵ֥א לָנָֽפֶשׁ׃ ג מִזָּכָ֤ר עַד־נְקֵבָה֙
תְּשַׁלֵּ֔חוּ אֶל־מִח֥וּץ לַֽמַּחֲנֶ֖ה תְּשַׁלְּח֑וּם וְלֹ֤א
יְטַמְּאוּ֙ אֶת־מַ֣חֲנֵיהֶ֔ם אֲשֶׁ֥ר אֲנִ֖י שֹׁכֵ֥ן בְּתוֹכָֽם׃
ד וַיַּֽעֲשׂוּ־כֵן֙ בְּנֵ֣י יִשְׂרָאֵ֔ל וַיְשַׁלְּח֣וּ אוֹתָ֔ם אֶל־
מִח֖וּץ לַֽמַּחֲנֶ֑ה כַּאֲשֶׁ֨ר דִּבֶּ֤ר יְהוָה֙ אֶל־מֹשֶׁ֔ה כֵּ֥ן
עָשׂ֖וּ בְּנֵ֥י יִשְׂרָאֵֽל׃ פ ה וַיְדַבֵּ֥ר יְהוָ֖ה אֶל־מֹשֶׁ֥ה
לֵּאמֹֽר׃ ו דַּבֵּר֮ אֶל־בְּנֵ֣י יִשְׂרָאֵל֒ אִ֣ישׁ אֽוֹ־אִשָּׁ֗ה
כִּ֤י יַעֲשׂוּ֙ מִכָּל־חַטֹּ֣את הָֽאָדָ֔ם לִמְעֹ֥ל מַ֖עַל
בַּֽיהוָ֑ה וְאָֽשְׁמָ֖ה הַנֶּ֥פֶשׁ הַהִֽוא׃ ז וְהִתְוַדּ֗וּ אֶֽת־
חַטָּאתָם֮ אֲשֶׁ֣ר עָשׂוּ֒ וְהֵשִׁ֤יב אֶת־אֲשָׁמוֹ֙ בְּרֹאשׁ֔וֹ

CHAPTER V

5. **God *spoke*.** There now follow three categories of laws; namely גֶּזֶל הַגֵּר [laws pertaining to a breach of trust for which no restitution can be made to the wronged party, because he has died and has no legal heirs since he was a proselyte]; סוֹטָה [laws pertaining to the wife suspected of adultery] and נָזִיר [laws pertaining to the *nazir*]. All these laws are closely linked to the three spheres of Jewish nationhood: יִשְׂרָאֵל [Israel], לְוִיָּה [the Levite vocation] and שְׁכִינָה [the Dwelling Place of the Divine Presence] discussed earlier, and also to the physical removal, from these three spheres, of צָרוּעַ [the leper], זָב [one suffering from a genital discharge] and טָמֵא [one defiled by contact with a dead body].

The ideas taught symbolically by the physical removal of specified categories of unclean persons from the three spheres of Jewish nationhood are introduced into the realities of everyday life by the laws concerning גֶּזֶל הַגֵּר, סוֹטָה and נָזִיר. גֶּזֶל הַגֵּר [a breach of trust for which no restitution can be made to the wronged party, because he has died and has no legal heirs since he was a proselyte] parallels the law that all lepers must be sent away from the Israelite camp; this concept demonstrates the presence of God in all the social relationships in the nation as a whole. סוֹטָה [the laws pertaining to the wife suspected of adultery] parallel the law that one suffering from a genital discharge must be sent away from the Levite camp; they demonstrate the presence of God in the sexual aspects of family life. נָזִיר [the laws pertaining to the *nazir*] parallel the law that anyone defiled by contact with a dead person must be sent away from the camp of the Divine Presence; they show the presence of God in the personal life of each individual who aspires to moral freedom. . . .

וַחֲמִישִׁתוֹ יֹסֵף עָלָיו וְנָתַן לַאֲשֶׁר אָשַׁם לוֹ׃
ח וְאִם־אֵין לָאִישׁ גֹּאֵל לְהָשִׁיב הָאָשָׁם אֵלָיו
הָאָשָׁם הַמּוּשָׁב לַיהוָה לַכֹּהֵן מִלְּבַד אֵיל
הַכִּפֻּרִים אֲשֶׁר יְכַפֶּר־בּוֹ עָלָיו׃ ט וְכָל־תְּרוּמָה
לְכָל־קָדְשֵׁי בְנֵי־יִשְׂרָאֵל אֲשֶׁר־יַקְרִיבוּ לַכֹּהֵן לוֹ
יִהְיֶה׃ י וְאִישׁ אֶת־קֳדָשָׁיו לוֹ יִהְיוּ אִישׁ אֲשֶׁר־
יִתֵּן לַכֹּהֵן לוֹ יִהְיֶה׃ פ רביעי יא וַיְדַבֵּר יְהוָה אֶל־
מֹשֶׁה לֵּאמֹר׃ יב דַּבֵּר אֶל־בְּנֵי יִשְׂרָאֵל וְאָמַרְתָּ
אֲלֵהֶם אִישׁ אִישׁ כִּי־תִשְׂטֶה אִשְׁתּוֹ וּמָעֲלָה בוֹ
מָעַל׃ יג וְשָׁכַב אִישׁ אֹתָהּ שִׁכְבַת־זֶרַע וְנֶעְלַם
מֵעֵינֵי אִישָׁהּ וְנִסְתְּרָה וְהִיא נִטְמָאָה וְעֵד אֵין
בָּהּ וְהִוא לֹא נִתְפָּשָׂה׃ יד וְעָבַר עָלָיו רוּחַ־
קִנְאָה וְקִנֵּא אֶת־אִשְׁתּוֹ וְהִוא נִטְמָאָה אוֹ־עָבַר
עָלָיו רוּחַ־קִנְאָה וְקִנֵּא אֶת־אִשְׁתּוֹ וְהִיא לֹא

of his guilt in its [full] capital value and add to it one fifth, and give it to the one with regard to whom he has been guilty.
8. But if a man has no legal heir to whom restitution could be made for the object of the guilt, then the object of guilt for which restitution is made to *God* shall be the priest's, except for the ram of the atonements with which atonement is effected for him.
9. Also any uplifted donation with regard to all the holy things of the sons of Yisrael, which they bring to the priest to be nearer to *God* shall be his.
10. But [as for] every man's holy things, they are his; only that which a man gives to the priest shall be his [i.e., the priest's]."
11. *God* spoke to Moshe [saying]:
12. "Speak to the sons of Yisrael and say to them: Any man whose wife strays from the right path and commits a breach of trust against him,
13. and a man has lain with her carnally, but it has remained hidden from her husband and she went to a secret place so that she has forfeited her purity; then no complete testimony is required against her; all that matters is that she was not forced.
14. But if the spirit has come over him that he must maintain his [marital] claim, and he has warned his wife, but she may nevertheless have forfeited her purity, or there has come over him the spirit to maintain his [marital] claim, and he has warned his wife, but she may not have forfeited her

12. **אִישׁ אִישׁ כִּי תִשְׂטֶה אִשְׁתּוֹ** ***[Any man whose wife strays].*** שטה is to turn aside from a given path. . . . Here, too, the verb denotes a straying or deviation from the prescribed path of morality. In Chaldean, שטה denotes straying from the path of rationality; i.e., a mental aberration, insanity. The Sages equate the two concepts: "A person does not commit a transgression unless a spirit of folly enters into him" (Sotah 3a). Any moral lapse is also a mental abberation; moral and logical truth are synonymous and no man sins unless he has first lost the true perspective of things.

and commits a breach of trust against him. Since in 5:6 the expression "committing a breach of trust against *God*" implies that social relationships between man and his fellow man are sacred also to God, the use of the word מְעִילָה here to describe a wife's infidelity makes it clear that the relationship between husband and wife, too, is sacred to God. Therefore, in the following verse and further on, the wife's act that has made her unfit for continuing her marriage to her husband is referred to by the expression "so that she has forfeited her purity."

Marriage is a קדש [holy thing]; therefore, the appropriate moral conduct in marriage; i.e., marital fidelity, is טָהֳרָה [purity] (Verse 28). Its antithesis is טוּמְאָה [moral uncleanness]. Hence, if the wife becomes forbidden to her husband as a marital partner, it is said of her that וְהִיא נִטְמָאָה ["she has forfeited her purity"], even as the condition of טוּמְאָה in other areas also debars the unclean individual from the Sanctuary and from holy things. The conduct of the wife described here, in Verse 12, is not yet outright adultery; however, it does imply a reprehensible deviation on the wife's part from the path of chastity and morality that characterizes the Jewish wife, so that her husband has had just cause to warn her about her conduct (Verse 14).

purity, 15. then the man shall bring his
wife to the priest and he shall bring her
offering for her: one tenth of an *ephah* of
barley meal; he shall not pour oil upon it
and shall not place frankincense upon it, for
it is a gift symbolizing that he subordinates
the maintaining of his (marital) claim to
God; it is a gift symbolizing that he subordinates the remembrance to God, to recall a
sin. 16. The priest shall have her come
nearer and have her stand before *God*.
17. And the priest shall take holy water in
an earthen vessel, and [some] of the dust
from the ground that is on the floor of the
Dwelling Place shall the priest take and
place it in the water. 18. And the priest
shall have the woman stand before *God*
again and he shall uncover the woman's
head and place upon her hands the
gift symbolizing that her husband subordinates the remembrance [to *God*]; it is a
gift symbolizing that he subordinates the
maintaining of his [marital] claim [to *God*],
and in the priest's hand shall be the curse-
bearing waters of bitternesses. 19. The

נִטְמָאָה: טו וְהֵבִיא הָאִישׁ אֶת־אִשְׁתּוֹ אֶל־הַכֹּהֵן
וְהֵבִיא אֶת־קָרְבָּנָהּ עָלֶיהָ עֲשִׂירִת הָאֵיפָה קֶמַח
שְׂעֹרִים לֹא־יִצֹק עָלָיו שֶׁמֶן וְלֹא־יִתֵּן עָלָיו
לְבֹנָה כִּי־מִנְחַת קְנָאֹת הוּא מִנְחַת זִכָּרוֹן
מַזְכֶּרֶת עָוֹן: טז וְהִקְרִיב אֹתָהּ הַכֹּהֵן וְהֶעֱמִדָהּ
לִפְנֵי יְהוָה: יז וְלָקַח הַכֹּהֵן מַיִם קְדֹשִׁים בִּכְלִי־
חָרֶשׂ וּמִן־הֶעָפָר אֲשֶׁר יִהְיֶה בְּקַרְקַע הַמִּשְׁכָּן
יִקַּח הַכֹּהֵן וְנָתַן אֶל־הַמָּיִם: יח וְהֶעֱמִיד הַכֹּהֵן
אֶת־הָאִשָּׁה לִפְנֵי יְהוָה וּפָרַע אֶת־רֹאשׁ הָאִשָּׁה
וְנָתַן עַל־כַּפֶּיהָ אֵת מִנְחַת הַזִּכָּרוֹן מִנְחַת קְנָאֹת
הִוא וּבְיַד הַכֹּהֵן יִהְיוּ מֵי הַמָּרִים הַמְאָרְרִים:

15. קְנָאֹת ***[the maintaining of his (marital) claim].*** The husband seeks to maintain his legal claim upon his wife. If she is still legally his, he wants her to remain his in fact also. This intention is already made clear by the fact that he brings her before God, as it were, for the final verdict. If he had wanted to dissolve the marriage, there would be no need for him to take this action. Under the Law, she is already אָסוּר [forbidden] to him; therefore, if he wishes to keep her he must turn to God for הֶיתֵּר [legal dispensation to do so]. . . .

18. ***And the priest shall have the woman stand before* God.** We have already read in Verse 16 that "he shall have her stand before *God*." The repetition here indicates that she was repeatedly led back and forth in order to prolong the procedure, giving her time to confess (Sotah 8a).

and he shall uncover the woman's head. A chaste wife wears a covering on her head to "prevent" or "restrain" her hair from being seen by others. For this reason the Hebrew term used here for uncovering the hair on her head is פָּרַע, literally, "to free." In addition, according to Sotah 7a, a rent must be made in the neckline of her dress, which is then tied into place over her bosom with a bast ribbon, and the uncovering of her hair is given additional emphasis by undoing her braids and allowing her hair to hang loose. Such an uncovering of a married woman's hair is repugnant to any chaste Jewish wife. Ketuboth 72a notes in connection with this passage: "This is a warning to the daughters of Israel that they shall not go forth with their heads uncovered." The daughters of Israel are forbidden to appear in public with their hair uncovered. If a married woman uncovers her hair it is עֶרְוָה [nakedness] in the literal sense of the term, and in cases such as the one described in this passage it is intended to expose the woman as wanting in Jewish modesty. The head covering that hides the woman's hair is an external symbol of her marital fidelity. A woman who by her conduct has forsaken the path of chastity is no longer worthy of this diadem of צְנִיעוּת [modesty], the basic trait that typifies Jewish womanhood. By removing the covering from her head, the priest gives physical expression to the blame that attaches to her.

It must be remembered that, though there is still a question—now in the process of being decided—whether she has actually committed adultery and has thereby incurred טוּמְאָה [impurity], it is already a proven fact that, by straying from the path of modesty (cf. Verse 20), the woman gave her husband cause to warn her and then disregarded his warning by going to a secret place with the man involved. Therefore, in any event, she is guilty, at the very least, of levity.

• • •

יט וְהִשְׁבִּ֨יעַ אֹתָ֜הּ הַכֹּהֵ֗ן וְאָמַ֤ר אֶל־הָֽאִשָּׁה֙ אִם־
לֹ֨א שָׁכַ֥ב אִישׁ֙ אֹתָ֔ךְ וְאִם־לֹ֥א שָׂטִ֛ית טֻמְאָ֖ה
תַּ֣חַת אִישֵׁ֑ךְ הִנָּקִ֕י מִמֵּ֛י הַמָּרִ֥ים הַֽמְאָרְרִ֖ים
הָאֵֽלֶּה: כ וְאַ֗תְּ כִּ֥י שָׂטִ֛ית תַּ֥חַת אִישֵׁ֖ךְ וְכִ֣י
נִטְמֵ֑את וַיִּתֵּ֨ן אִ֥ישׁ בָּךְ֙ אֶת־שְׁכָבְתּ֔וֹ מִֽבַּלְעֲדֵ֖י
אִישֵֽׁךְ: כא וְהִשְׁבִּ֨יעַ הַכֹּהֵ֥ן אֶֽת־הָאִשָּׁה֮ בִּשְׁבֻעַ֣ת
הָאָלָה֒ וְאָמַ֤ר הַכֹּהֵן֙ לָֽאִשָּׁ֔ה יִתֵּ֨ן יְהוָ֥ה אוֹתָ֛ךְ
לְאָלָ֥ה וְלִשְׁבֻעָ֖ה בְּת֣וֹךְ עַמֵּ֑ךְ בְּתֵ֨ת יְהוָ֤ה אֶת־
יְרֵכֵךְ֙ נֹפֶ֔לֶת וְאֶת־בִּטְנֵ֖ךְ צָבָֽה: כב וּ֠בָאוּ הַמַּ֨יִם
הַמְאָרְרִ֤ים הָאֵ֙לֶּה֙ בְּמֵעַ֔יִךְ לַצְבּ֥וֹת בֶּ֖טֶן וְלַנְפִּ֣ל
יָרֵ֑ךְ וְאָמְרָ֥ה הָאִשָּׁ֖ה אָמֵ֥ן ׀ אָמֵֽן: כג וְ֠כָתַב אֶת־
הָאָלֹ֥ת הָאֵ֛לֶּה הַכֹּהֵ֖ן בַּסֵּ֑פֶר וּמָחָ֖ה אֶל־מֵ֥י
הַמָּרִֽים: כד וְהִשְׁקָה֙ אֶת־הָ֣אִשָּׁ֔ה אֶת־מֵ֥י הַמָּרִ֖ים
הַמְאָרְרִ֑ים וּבָ֥אוּ בָ֛הּ הַמַּ֥יִם הַמְאָרְרִ֖ים לְמָרִֽים:
כה וְלָקַ֤ח הַכֹּהֵן֙ מִיַּ֣ד הָֽאִשָּׁ֔ה אֵ֖ת מִנְחַ֣ת הַקְּנָאֹ֑ת

priest shall adjure her and shall say to the woman: "If no man has lain with you and if you have not strayed in your relationship to your husband so as to forfeit your purity, then you shall remain untouched by the waters of these curse-bearing bitternesses.
20. But if you have strayed in your relationship to your husband and have forfeited your purity in that a man other than your husband has lain with you—"
21. at this point the priest shall adjure the woman with an oath of the curse and the priest shall say to the woman: "Thus may *God* make you into a curse-word and an oath among your people, in that God will cause your thigh to fall away and your belly to swell,
22. and these curse-bearing waters shall enter into your bowels and cause your belly to swell and your thigh to fall away," and the woman shall say: "Amen, Amen."
23. The priest shall then write these curses upon a piece of parchment and shall blot them in the waters of bitternesses,
24. and he shall make the woman drink the curse-bearing waters of bitternesses, and the curse-bearing waters shall enter into her as bitternesses.
25. The priest shall then take from the woman the gift symbolizing [her husband's]

22. ***and the woman shall say: "Amen, Amen."*** . . . By responding with "Amen" to an oath pronounced by another, one signifies that he confirms this oath with all of his own being; it is as if he himself took the oath. The response of אָמֵן confirms the idea implicit in the oath, the concept of the vow; . . . that the one thus responding has subordinated all of his own being to the might and judgment of God and has made this subordination of self the one immovable foundation that will uphold and shape all his future life. Cf. "If one responds 'Amen' to an oath it is as if he had uttered that oath with his own mouth" (Shevuoth 29b); "Amen implies oaths, the acceptance of words and the confirmation of words" (ibid. 36a). Thus, by responding with "Amen," the woman takes upon herself the priest's adjuration in its entirety, the simple oath without the אָלָה ["curse-word"] (Verse 19) as well as the oath linked with אָלָה (Verse 21). . . .

25. ***The priest shall then take . . . and he shall wave . . . and bring it nearer.*** "And he shall wave": The movements associated with the "wave offering" and the "uplifted donation," "to and fro, up and down.". . .

Heaven and earth and all that dwell on earth are hereby summoned to function as witnesses to this act and to participate in the vindication of the woman's morality. It is toward them that the *minḥah* vindicating the marriage is turned in the presence of God.

Thereafter וְהִקְרִיב וגו׳ ["he shall bring it nearer"]; it is given to the altar that sanctifies the Law on the southwestern side, at the side of the Sanctuary symbolically consecrated to the spiritual life to be derived from the Law. Thus the verdict now sought from God is sought not from the viewpoint of this one marriage alone, but in the name of heaven and earth, in the name of all of human society and in the name of the Jewish spiritual life to be achieved through the Law, all of which have an equal share in maintaining the morality of womanhood. It is the woman and the priest who together (cf. Leviticus 7:30 and Sotah 19a) perform the act introducing the plea for the Divine verdict—the woman in her endeavor to prove her innocence, and the priest in his endeavor to safeguard the sanctity of marriage as demanded by the Sanctuary of the Law.

subordination of the maintaining of [his] claim and he shall wave the gift of subordination before *God* and bring it nearer to the altar.   26. The priest shall then scoop out the memorial portion of the gift of subordination and give it to the altar to go up in smoke. Only after that can he make the woman drink the waters.   27. He shall give her the waters to drink, and then it shall come to pass that if she has forfeited her purity by committing a breach of trust against her husband, the curse-bearing waters will enter her and become bitter ones; her belly will swell and her thigh will fall away and the woman will become a curse-word among her people.   28. But if the woman has not forfeited her purity and is still pure, she will remain untouched by it and, in fact, she will be blessed with offspring.   29. This is the teaching concerning the maintaining of [the husband's marital] claim if a woman strays in her relationship to her husband and has forfeited her purity.   30. Or if the spirit has come over him that he must maintain his [marital] claim and he has warned his wife, and he has the woman stand before *God* and the priest shall implement all this teaching upon her.   31. If the man is free

וְהֵנִיף אֶת־הַמִּנְחָה לִפְנֵי יְהֹוָה וְהִקְרִיב אֹתָהּ אֶל־הַמִּזְבֵּחַ: כו וְקָמַץ הַכֹּהֵן מִן־הַמִּנְחָה אֶת־אַזְכָּרָתָהּ וְהִקְטִיר הַמִּזְבֵּחָה וְאַחַר יַשְׁקֶה אֶת־הָאִשָּׁה אֶת־הַמָּיִם: כז וְהִשְׁקָהּ אֶת־הַמַּיִם וְהָיְתָה אִם־נִטְמְאָה וַתִּמְעֹל מַעַל בְּאִישָׁהּ וּבָאוּ בָהּ הַמַּיִם הַמְאָרְרִים לְמָרִים וְצָבְתָה בִטְנָהּ וְנָפְלָה יְרֵכָהּ וְהָיְתָה הָאִשָּׁה לְאָלָה בְּקֶרֶב עַמָּהּ: כח וְאִם־לֹא נִטְמְאָה הָאִשָּׁה וּטְהֹרָה הִוא וְנִקְּתָה וְנִזְרְעָה זָרַע: כט זֹאת תּוֹרַת הַקְּנָאֹת אֲשֶׁר תִּשְׂטֶה אִשָּׁה תַּחַת אִישָׁהּ וְנִטְמָאָה: ל אוֹ אִישׁ אֲשֶׁר תַּעֲבֹר עָלָיו רוּחַ קִנְאָה וְקִנֵּא אֶת־אִשְׁתּוֹ וְהֶעֱמִיד אֶת־הָאִשָּׁה לִפְנֵי יְהֹוָה וְעָשָׂה לָהּ הַכֹּהֵן אֵת כָּל־הַתּוֹרָה הַזֹּאת: לא וְנִקָּה

31. *If the man is free of iniquity.* A man can expect a Divine verdict regarding his wife's moral status only if, at the time he submits the question of her guilt or innocence to God, he knows that he himself is innocent of all sexual crimes and misdemeanors. If he himself has violated the laws of sexual purity, if (1) he has continued his relationship with his wife even after she had become forbidden to him (Verse 14), because he had warned her, but she, nevertheless, had gone away to a secret place with the man under suspicion; or (2) if ever, from the time he has come of age with regard to his observance of God's Law, he has transgressed any of the laws of chastity, even only by turning an indulgent blind eye to sexual excesses committed by members of his family, he has no right to make his wife drink the *sotah* potion. . . . God's laws of morality do not give men greater license for sexual irregularities than they do to women.

    °   °   °

[This whole law shows] that God is present in every Jewish marriage, that He directs His special attention not only to the marital fidelity of the wife but also to

that of the husband, and that sexual morality is the basis of all moral and spiritual happiness, so that even for this alone a direct appeal may be made to the all-seeing Presence of God. Thus, the legal institution with respect to the *sotah* is simply a practical manifestation, in the nation's day-to-day life, of that basic truth which is symbolically taught and kept before the eyes of the people by the fact that a man or woman suffering from a genital discharge is banished from the Levite camp. The law according to which a man or woman suffering from a [genital] discharge must be sent away from the Levite camp marks sexual purity as the first prerequisite for all spiritual self-elevation toward God, and the giving of the bitter waters to a wife suspected of adultery characterizes the sexual purity of family life as the most urgent concern of Divine Providence. The Biblical portion stating the laws pertaining to the wife suspected of adultery relates to the law concerning the banishment from the Levite camp of any male or female suffering from a genital discharge in the same way that the passage dealing with a "breach of trust" (where no restitution can be made to the wronged party

הָאִ֖ישׁ מֵעָוֹ֑ן וְהָאִשָּׁ֣ה הַהִ֔וא תִּשָּׂ֖א אֶת־עֲוֺנָֽהּ׃ פ
ו א וַיְדַבֵּ֥ר יְהֹוָ֖ה אֶל־מֹשֶׁ֥ה לֵּאמֹֽר׃ ב דַּבֵּ֞ר אֶל־
בְּנֵ֤י יִשְׂרָאֵל֙ וְאָמַרְתָּ֣ אֲלֵהֶ֔ם אִ֣ישׁ אֽוֹ־אִשָּׁ֗ה כִּ֤י
יַפְלִא֙ לִנְדֹּר֙ נֶ֣דֶר נָזִ֔יר לְהַזִּ֖יר לַיהֹוָֽה׃ ג מִיַּ֤יִן
וְשֵׁכָר֙ יַזִּ֔יר חֹ֥מֶץ יַ֛יִן וְחֹ֥מֶץ שֵׁכָ֖ר לֹ֣א יִשְׁתֶּ֑ה
וְכָל־מִשְׁרַ֤ת עֲנָבִים֙ לֹ֣א יִשְׁתֶּ֔ה וַעֲנָבִ֛ים לַחִ֥ים
וִיבֵשִׁ֖ים לֹ֥א יֹאכֵֽל׃ ד כֹּ֖ל יְמֵ֣י נִזְר֑וֹ מִכֹּל֩ אֲשֶׁ֨ר
יֵעָשֶׂ֜ה מִגֶּ֣פֶן הַיַּ֗יִן מֵחַרְצַנִּ֛ים וְעַד־זָ֖ג לֹ֥א יֹאכֵֽל׃
ה כָּל־יְמֵי֙ נֶ֣דֶר נִזְר֔וֹ תַּ֖עַר לֹא־יַעֲבֹ֣ר עַל־רֹאשׁ֑וֹ

of iniquity, the woman must bear her iniquity.

VI 1. *God* spoke to Moshe [saying]: 2. "Speak to the sons of Yisrael and say to them: When anyone, man or woman, makes the express resolve to take the vow of a *nazir*, to fulfill the task of a *nazir* for *God*, 3. then he must fulfill his *nazir*ship, abstaining from weak and strong wine; he shall not drink vinegar from weak [wine] or vinegar from strong wine; he shall not drink any [liquid] in which grapes were steeped and he shall not eat grapes, fresh or dried. 4. All the days of his *nazir*ship he shall not eat anything prepared from the wine-producing grapevine, from [its] seeds to [its] skin. 5. All the days of his *nazir* vow no razor shall come upon his head, until

because he has died and has no legal heirs since he was a proselyte) relates to the law concerning the banishment of lepers from the Israelite camp.

CHAPTER VI

1. What now follows is the portion of laws relating to the *nazir* which parallel the laws relating to the banishment, from the camp of the Divine Presence, of anyone defiled by physical contact with a dead body.

2. ***makes the express resolve.*** נָזִיר (Leviticus 22:2 and Zeḥariah 7:3) is to "withdraw" or "abstain" from something. Hence, in view of the abstention from wine commanded to the *nazir* (Verse 3) it would be most natural to interpret נָזִיר as an "abstainer" or "abstemious person." However, the fact that the *nazir* is forbidden to partake not only of wine and grapes, but even of wine vinegar and of the seeds and skins of grapes—restrictions that do not seem to entail great personal sacrifice—already suggests that the concept of נָזִיר must be broader than that of mere abstinence. Moreover, the fact that a *nazir*'s physical contact with a dead body, even if it happens without, or against, his will (Verse 9), completely invalidates the period he has already spent in fulfilling his *nazir* vow, whereas his partaking of wine does not have this effect, should indicate that though "abstention from wine" is indeed one of the obligations of a *nazir*, no less than avoiding physical contact with a dead body and letting his hair grow, it does not by any means constitute the whole definition of the *nazir*, or even the outstanding characteristic of one. Hence a *nazir* is not primarily an "abstainer." A thoughtful study of Verses 4–6 and then, by way of recapitulation, of Verse 8, will make it clear that even all the three obligations mentioned in connection with the *nazir* do not exhaust the concept of *nazir*ship; they are merely external manifestations advertising the fact that the person concerned has taken the *nazir* vow.

The concept of *nazir*ship is to be defined in terms of the statement in Verse 8, that all the days of his *nazir*ship "he is holy to *God*." The "three activities forbidden to the *nazir*: Defiling himself (by contact with a dead body), shaving his hair and partaking of grape products" (Nazir 34a) are only logical consequences of this holiness. Indeed, in Amos 2:11 we see *nezirim* put in one class with prophets and the presence of both in Israel's midst is stressed as a sign of special Divine favor. If we consider that the form נזר is used (in Leviticus 25:5 and 11) to characterize vines left untended; i.e., left to grow on their own during the Sabbatical and Jubilee years, then we will understand that in any event נָזִיר does not refer to one who keeps away from something, but one *from* whom, or *from* which, *others* must keep away or be kept apart.

The term נֵזֶר denotes the royal circlet that marks its wearer as a person "set apart" from all others and therefore kept at a distance from them. In a similar vein נזר here denotes a discipline of life and aspirations which raises him who has voluntarily vowed to adopt it above and beyond his contemporaries in whose midst he lives and sets him the task of being completely "holy to his God," of belonging exclusively to God with all his being and with all his aspirations. He seeks to draw around himself a נֵזֶר, a circle, as it were, within which God alone is permitted. The Hebrew term for such an act of drawing a circle around oneself for the sake of God, meaning to go into isolation with and for God, is לְהַזִּיר לד׳, and one who has become isolated in this manner is a נָזִיר. Note, however, that this does not imply physical isolation, a hermit's life in the wilderness, but a mental and spiritual isolation with God even while one remains an active part of everyday life.

the days are completed in which he took upon himself to fulfill the task of *nazir*ship for *God*, it [i.e., his head] shall be holy in that he shall allow the hair of his head to grow free.   6. All the days of his *nazir* task to be fulfilled for *God* he must not come near to the person of one who has died. 7. Not even with regard to his father and his mother, his brother and his sister—even with regard to these he must not defile himself when they have died, because the circlet of his God is upon his head.   8. All the days of his *nazir*ship he is holy to *God*. 9. And if someone dies very suddenly beside him, and this deprives his *nazir* head of its purity, he shall shave his head on the day he regains his purity; on the seventh day shall he shave it.   10. And on the eighth day he shall bring two turtle-doves or two young pigeons to the priest to the entrance of the Tent of Appointed Meeting. 11. The priest shall offer the one as an offering that clears [him who brings it] of sin and the other as an ascent offering, and he shall effect atonement for him for that which he sinned concerning the person, and he shall hallow his head again on that day. 12. He shall then fulfill for *God* the *nazir* task during the days of his *nazir*ship, but he shall bring a sheep in its first year as a guilt offering; the previous days become void because his *nazir*ship had lost its purity. 13. But this is the teaching concerning the *nazir*: On the day when his *nazir* days are completed, he shall take himself to the entrance of the Tent of Appointed Meeting, 14. and he shall bring near his offering to *God*: one sheep in its first year, without blemish, for an ascent offering; and one female sheep in its first year, without blemish, for an offering that clears [him who brings it] of sin, and one ram, without blemish, for a peace offering.   15. And one basket of *matzoth* from fine wheat flour, cakes mixed with oil and thin *matzoth* brushed with oil, and their homage offerings and their libations.   16. And the priest shall bring [it] near to *God* and shall make his offering that clears [him who brings it] of sin and his ascent offering. 17. And he shall make the ram for a meal-of-peace offering to *God* for the basket of *matzoth*, and the priest shall make

עַד־מְלֹאת הַיָּמִם אֲשֶׁר־יַזִּיר לַיהֹוָה קָדֹשׁ יִהְיֶה גַּדֵּל פֶּרַע שְׂעַר רֹאשׁוֹ: ו כָּל־יְמֵי הַזִּירוֹ לַיהֹוָה עַל־נֶפֶשׁ מֵת לֹא יָבֹא: ז לְאָבִיו וּלְאִמּוֹ לְאָחִיו וּלְאַחֹתוֹ לֹא־יִטַּמָּא לָהֶם בְּמֹתָם כִּי נֵזֶר אֱלֹהָיו עַל־רֹאשׁוֹ: ח כָּל יְמֵי נִזְרוֹ קָדֹשׁ הוּא לַיהֹוָה: ט וְכִי־יָמוּת מֵת עָלָיו בְּפֶתַע פִּתְאֹם וְטִמֵּא רֹאשׁ נִזְרוֹ וְגִלַּח רֹאשׁוֹ בְּיוֹם טָהֳרָתוֹ בַּיּוֹם הַשְּׁבִיעִי יְגַלְּחֶנּוּ: י וּבַיּוֹם הַשְּׁמִינִי יָבֹא שְׁתֵּי תֹרִים אוֹ שְׁנֵי בְּנֵי יוֹנָה אֶל־הַכֹּהֵן אֶל־פֶּתַח אֹהֶל מוֹעֵד: יא וְעָשָׂה הַכֹּהֵן אֶחָד לְחַטָּאת וְאֶחָד לְעֹלָה וְכִפֶּר עָלָיו מֵאֲשֶׁר חָטָא עַל־הַנָּפֶשׁ וְקִדַּשׁ אֶת־רֹאשׁוֹ בַּיּוֹם הַהוּא: יב וְהִזִּיר לַיהֹוָה אֶת־יְמֵי נִזְרוֹ וְהֵבִיא כֶּבֶשׂ בֶּן־שְׁנָתוֹ לְאָשָׁם וְהַיָּמִים הָרִאשֹׁנִים יִפְּלוּ כִּי טָמֵא נִזְרוֹ: יג וְזֹאת תּוֹרַת הַנָּזִיר בְּיוֹם מְלֹאת יְמֵי נִזְרוֹ יָבִיא אֹתוֹ אֶל־פֶּתַח אֹהֶל מוֹעֵד: יד וְהִקְרִיב אֶת־קָרְבָּנוֹ לַיהֹוָה כֶּבֶשׂ בֶּן־שְׁנָתוֹ תָמִים אֶחָד לְעֹלָה וְכַבְשָׂה אַחַת בַּת־שְׁנָתָהּ תְּמִימָה לְחַטָּאת וְאַיִל־אֶחָד תָּמִים לִשְׁלָמִים: טו וְסַל מַצּוֹת סֹלֶת חַלֹּת בְּלוּלֹת בַּשֶּׁמֶן וּרְקִיקֵי מַצּוֹת מְשֻׁחִים בַּשָּׁמֶן וּמִנְחָתָם וְנִסְכֵּיהֶם: טז וְהִקְרִיב הַכֹּהֵן לִפְנֵי יְהֹוָה וְעָשָׂה אֶת־חַטָּאתוֹ וְאֶת־עֹלָתוֹ: יז וְאֶת־הָאַיִל יַעֲשֶׂה זֶבַח שְׁלָמִים לַיהֹוָה עַל סַל הַמַּצּוֹת

his homage offering and his libation.
18. And the *nazir* shall shave his *nazir*
head at the opened Tent of Appointed
Meeting and he shall take the hair from his
nazir head and place it upon the fire that is
underneath the meal-of-peace.   19. The
priest shall then take the cooked foreleg of
the ram and one *matzah* cake from the
basket and one thin *matzah*, and then place
it upon the hands of the *nazir*, after he has
shaved his *nazir* head.   20. And the priest
shall wave them in a waving before *God*; as
a holy thing, it is the priest's, along with the
breast of the wave [offering] and the thigh
of the uplifted donation; after that, the *nazir*
may drink wine.   21. This is the teaching
concerning the *nazir* who vowed his offering
to *God* for his *nazir*ship, in addition to
anything that his means make possible;
according to his vow which he has vowed,
thus shall he do in addition to that which is
prescribed for his *nazir*ship.   22. *God*
spoke to Moshe [saying]:   23. "Speak to
Aharon and to his sons [as follows]: Thus
shall you bless the sons of Yisrael — this is to

וְעָשָׂה֩ הַכֹּהֵ֨ן אֶת־מִנְחָת֜וֹ וְאֶת־נִסְכּֽוֹ: יח וְגִלַּ֣ח
הַנָּזִ֗יר פֶּ֛תַח אֹ֥הֶל מוֹעֵ֖ד אֶת־רֹ֣אשׁ נִזְר֑וֹ וְלָקַ֗ח
אֶת־שְׂעַ֤ר רֹ֣אשׁ נִזְרוֹ֙ וְנָתַן֙ עַל־הָאֵ֔שׁ אֲשֶׁר־תַּ֖חַת
זֶ֥בַח הַשְּׁלָמִֽים: יט וְלָקַ֨ח הַכֹּהֵ֜ן אֶת־הַזְּרֹ֣עַ
בְּשֵׁלָה֮ מִן־הָאַיִל֒ וְֽחַלַּ֨ת מַצָּ֤ה אַחַת֙ מִן־הַסַּ֔ל
וּרְקִ֖יק מַצָּ֣ה אֶחָ֑ד וְנָתַן֙ עַל־כַּפֵּ֣י הַנָּזִ֔יר אַחַ֖ר
הִֽתְגַּלְּח֥וֹ אֶת־נִזְרֽוֹ: כ וְהֵנִ֨יף אוֹתָ֥ם הַכֹּהֵ֣ן ׀
תְּנוּפָה֮ לִפְנֵ֣י יְהֹוָה֒ קֹ֤דֶשׁ הוּא֙ לַכֹּהֵ֔ן עַ֚ל חֲזֵ֣ה
הַתְּנוּפָ֔ה וְעַ֖ל שׁ֣וֹק הַתְּרוּמָ֑ה וְאַחַ֛ר יִשְׁתֶּ֥ה הַנָּזִ֖יר
יָֽיִן: כא זֹ֣את תּוֹרַ֣ת הַנָּזִיר֮ אֲשֶׁ֣ר יִדֹּר֒ קָרְבָּנ֤וֹ
לַֽיהֹוָה֙ עַל־נִזְר֔וֹ מִלְּבַ֖ד אֲשֶׁר־תַּשִּׂ֣יג יָד֑וֹ כְּפִ֣י
נִדְרוֹ֙ אֲשֶׁ֣ר יִדֹּ֔ר כֵּ֣ן יַֽעֲשֶׂ֔ה עַ֖ל תּוֹרַ֥ת נִזְרֽוֹ: פ
כב וַיְדַבֵּ֥ר יְהֹוָ֖ה אֶל־מֹשֶׁ֥ה לֵּאמֹֽר: כג דַּבֵּ֤ר אֶל־
אַֽהֲרֹן֙ וְאֶל־בָּנָ֣יו לֵאמֹ֔ר כֹּ֥ה תְבָֽרְכ֖וּ אֶת־בְּנֵ֣י

---

21. . . . If we consider this whole institution of *nazir*-
ship, we will see that it represents a legal permission, as
it were, for any individual member of the nation striving toward spiritual and moral ennoblement to elevate
himself temporarily to a position akin to that of the
priest or, indeed, of the high priest, in which his striving toward God is symbolized essentially by his keeping
away from defilement through physical contact with a
dead body. This obviously parallels the laws relating to
the banishment, from the camp of the Divine Presence,
of anyone defiled by physical contact with a dead body.

The three portions dealing with a breach of trust
(where no restitution can be made to the wronged party,
because he has died and has no legal heirs since he was
a proselyte), the wife suspected of adultery and the
nazir, seen in connection with the preceding portion
dealing with categories of unclean persons to be sent
away from the three camps of Jewish nationhood, yield
the following parallel concepts:

The law that all lepers must be sent away from the
Israelite camp is introduced into everyday life through
the laws in the portion relating to a breach of trust for
which no restitution can be made to the wronged party,
because he has died and has no legal heirs since he was
a proselyte. This is the legal institution that proclaims
the presence of God in the social relationships of the
nation.

The law that one suffering from a genital discharge
must be sent away from the Levite camp is introduced
into everyday life through the laws in the portion relating to the wife suspected of adultery. This is the legal
institution that proclaims the presence of God in the
sexual purity of the *family*.

The law that anyone defiled by contact with a dead
person must be sent away from the camp of the Divine
Presence is introduced into everyday life through the
portion relating to the *nazir*. This is the legal institution
that proclaims the Divine Presence for every *individual*
who aspires toward God in spiritual and moral self-
consecration.

All these three legal institutions impress upon
society, family and individual the stamp of Divine
consecration.

23. *Speak to Aharon.* The function of blessing the
sons of Israel is not an authorization conferred upon
the descendants of Aaron, but a duty assigned to them.
The Priestly Blessing does not emanate from the personal benevolence of the priests, but constitutes part of
their service in the Sanctuary. It is defined in Deuteronomy 10:8 as standing "before *God* in order to serve
Him and to bless with His Name." Similarly, ibid. 21:5:
"because it is they whom *God*, your God, has chosen to
serve Him and to pronounce blessing[s] in the name of
God." Consequently, בִּרְכַּת כֹּהֲנִים [the Priestly Blessing]

יִשְׂרָאֵ֑ל אָמ֖וֹר לָהֶֽם: ס כד יְבָרֶכְךָ֥ יְהֹוָ֖ה

וְיִשְׁמְרֶֽךָ: ס כה יָאֵ֨ר יְהֹוָ֧ה ׀ פָּנָ֛יו אֵלֶ֖יךָ

וִֽיחֻנֶּֽךָּ: ס כו יִשָּׂ֨א יְהֹוָ֤ה ׀ פָּנָיו֙ אֵלֶ֔יךָ וְיָשֵׂ֥ם לְךָ֖

שָׁלֽוֹם: ס כז וְשָׂמ֥וּ אֶת־שְׁמִ֖י עַל־בְּנֵ֣י יִשְׂרָאֵ֑ל

וַאֲנִ֖י אֲבָרֲכֵֽם: ס חמישי ז א וַיְהִ֡י בְּיוֹם֩ כַּלּ֨וֹת

מֹשֶׁ֜ה לְהָקִ֣ים אֶת־הַמִּשְׁכָּ֗ן וַיִּמְשַׁ֨ח אֹת֜וֹ וַיְקַדֵּ֤שׁ

אֹתוֹ֙ וְאֶת־כָּל־כֵּלָ֔יו וְאֶת־הַמִּזְבֵּ֖חַ וְאֶת־כָּל־כֵּלָ֑יו

וַיִּמְשָׁחֵ֖ם וַיְקַדֵּ֥שׁ אֹתָֽם: ב וַיַּקְרִ֙יבוּ֙ נְשִׂיאֵ֣י

יִשְׂרָאֵ֔ל רָאשֵׁ֖י בֵּ֣ית אֲבֹתָ֑ם הֵ֚ם נְשִׂיאֵ֣י הַמַּטֹּ֔ת

הֵ֥ם הָעֹמְדִ֖ים עַל־הַפְּקֻדִֽים: ג וַיָּבִ֣יאוּ אֶת־

קָרְבָּנָ֞ם לִפְנֵ֣י יְהֹוָ֗ה שֵׁשׁ־עֶגְלֹ֥ת צָב֙ וּשְׁנֵ֣י־עָשָׂ֣ר

be said to them — 24. 'May *God* bless you and keep you. 25. May *God* illuminate His Countenance for you and favor you. 26. May *God* lift up His Countenance toward you and establish peace for you.' 27. They shall place My Name upon the sons of Yisrael; and as for Me, I shall bless them."

VII 1. It came to pass even on the day when Moshe had finished setting up the Dwelling Place, when he had anointed it and sanctified it and its utensils, the altar and all its utensils, when he had anointed and sanctified them all together, 2. that the princes of Yisrael, the heads of their fathers' house brought near—these were the princes of the tribes, the same ones who had then superintended the numberings— 3. and brought their offering before *God*: six covered wagons and twelve

---

is part of the Divine service and is intimately linked with it. The priest literally "stands" in an attitude of service before God and it is by God's command that he pronounces the blessing along with the Name of God. For this reason the כֹּהֲנִים [priests] were to pronounce the blessing only at the conclusion of the communal offerings. . . . In our religious services today, also, the בִּרְכַּת כֹּהֲנִים [priestly blessing] can be recited only following the עֲבוֹדָה[1]. . . . There are no magic powers inherent in the priest himself or in the blessing he pronounces. The attitude of the one who pronounces it is an essential part of the blessing; indeed, it is his attitude that turns the formula he recites into a blessing (see Verse 27). . . .

24. May God bless you. The verse beginning with יְבָרֶכְךָ ["May *God* bless you"] concludes with וְיִשְׁמְרֶךָ ["and keep you"]. Therefore the blessing pronounced here presumably refers primarily to possessions in regard to which—even after they have been granted us—we are in need of [Divine] "keeping" or "watching," so that they may be preserved for us, that our ownership of them will bring us true happiness. . . . Thus the first verse of the blessing refers to the prospering of all our personal and material possessions and their protection from anything that might harm them.

25. May God illuminate His Countenance for you.

[1]*Note to the English translation*: In our present-day liturgy, the paragraph beginning with רְצֵה ["Be pleased . . . with Thy people Israel and with their prayer. . ."] refers to Israel's prayers and offerings. [G.H.]

This would mean: May God reveal to you the objectives of His sovereignty and His purposes that He means to have fulfilled through you—the former through the words of His prophets, the latter through the Word of His Law—

and favor you. May He favor you with the intellectual and spiritual abilities to understand the revelations granted to you in תּוֹרָה [the Law] and in נְבוּאָה [prophecy] and to perceive from these His work in history and your own tasks in life. . . .

*   *   *

26. May God lift up His Countenance toward you. It is you whom God has made the object of His sovereignty.

and establish peace for you. It may appear as if your efforts that are directed toward God and God alone, and the sovereignty of God that seems to be directed solely toward you, will make you out of step with all the others and completely isolate you from them. But in reality it is only for you that God "establishes peace," only for you has He assured consummate, imperturbable harmony. If only you will be a true, genuine servant of God with all your body and soul, so that God will be able to see in you the fulfillment of His ultimate purposes, then all those around you who are sensitive and thoughtful will recognize you as that element which makes their own lives whole, spurs them on to good endeavors and sustains them in existence. Every breath drawn by an individual who truly serves God will elicit a responsive chord from the universe around him.

oxen, one wagon each for two princes and one ox for each one. They brought them near in front of the Dwelling Place. 4. Then *God* spoke to Moshe [saying]: 5. "Take it from them; they shall remain in order to serve for the service of the Tent of Appointed Meeting, and you shall give them to the Levites, to each man according to his service." 6. And Moshe took the wagons and the oxen and gave them to the Levites. 7. Two of the wagons and four of the oxen he gave to the sons of Gershon according to their service, 8. and four of the wagons and eight of the oxen he gave to the sons of Merari; according to their service under the direction of Ithamar, son of Aharon the priest. 9. He did not give any to the sons of Kehath because the service of the Sanctuary devolved upon them; they had to carry [the holy things] upon their shoulders. 10. Thereupon the princes brought near the dedication [offering] of the altar, on the day it was anointed; the princes brought near their offering before the altar. 11. And *God* said to Moshe: "One prince each on a [given] day, one prince each on a [given] day shall they bring near their offering for the dedication of the altar." 12. And the one who brought near his offering on the first day was Naḥshon, son of Amminadab of the tribe of Yehudah. 13. And his offering was: one silver dish one hundred and thirty in weight, one silver sprinkling basin° seventy shekels by the weight [standard] of the Sanctuary, both filled with fine wheat flour mixed with oil for a homage offering. 14. One spoon

בָּקָ֗ר עֲגָלָ֞ה עַל־שְׁנֵ֤י הַנְּשִׂאִים֙ וְשׁ֣וֹר לְאֶחָ֔ד וַיַּקְרִ֥יבוּ אוֹתָ֖ם לִפְנֵ֥י הַמִּשְׁכָּֽן׃ ד וַיֹּ֥אמֶר יְהֹוָ֖ה אֶל־מֹשֶׁ֥ה לֵּאמֹֽר׃ ה קַ֚ח מֵֽאִתָּ֔ם וְהָי֕וּ לַֽעֲבֹ֕ד אֶת־עֲבֹדַ֖ת אֹ֣הֶל מוֹעֵ֑ד וְנָֽתַתָּ֤ה אוֹתָם֙ אֶל־הַֽלְוִיִּ֔ם אִ֖ישׁ כְּפִ֥י עֲבֹֽדָתֽוֹ׃ ו וַיִּקַּ֣ח מֹשֶׁ֔ה אֶת־הָֽעֲגָלֹ֖ת וְאֶת־הַבָּקָ֑ר וַיִּתֵּ֥ן אוֹתָ֖ם אֶל־הַֽלְוִיִּֽם׃ ז אֵ֣ת ׀ שְׁתֵּ֣י הָֽעֲגָלֹ֗ת וְאֵת֙ אַרְבַּ֣עַת הַבָּקָ֔ר נָתַ֖ן לִבְנֵ֣י גֵֽרְשׁ֑וֹן כְּפִ֖י עֲבֹֽדָתָֽם׃ ח וְאֵ֣ת ׀ אַרְבַּ֣ע הָֽעֲגָלֹ֗ת וְאֵת֙ שְׁמֹנַ֣ת הַבָּקָ֔ר נָתַ֖ן לִבְנֵ֣י מְרָרִ֑י כְּפִי֙ עֲבֹ֣דָתָ֔ם בְּיַד֙ אִֽיתָמָ֔ר בֶּֽן־אַֽהֲרֹ֖ן הַכֹּהֵֽן׃ ט וְלִבְנֵ֥י קְהָ֖ת לֹ֣א נָתָ֑ן כִּֽי־עֲבֹדַ֤ת הַקֹּ֨דֶשׁ֙ עֲלֵהֶ֔ם בַּכָּתֵ֖ף יִשָּֽׂאוּ׃ י וַיַּקְרִ֣יבוּ הַנְּשִׂאִ֗ים אֵ֚ת חֲנֻכַּ֣ת הַמִּזְבֵּ֔חַ בְּי֖וֹם הִמָּשַׁ֣ח אֹת֑וֹ וַיַּקְרִ֧יבוּ הַנְּשִׂיאִ֛ם אֶת־קָרְבָּנָ֖ם לִפְנֵ֥י הַמִּזְבֵּֽחַ׃ יא וַיֹּ֥אמֶר יְהֹוָ֖ה אֶל־מֹשֶׁ֑ה נָשִׂ֨יא אֶחָ֜ד לַיּ֗וֹם נָשִׂ֤יא אֶחָד֙ לַיּ֔וֹם יַקְרִ֨יבוּ֙ אֶת־קָרְבָּנָ֔ם לַֽחֲנֻכַּ֖ת הַמִּזְבֵּֽחַ׃ ס יב וַיְהִ֗י הַמַּקְרִ֛יב בַּיּ֥וֹם הָֽרִאשׁ֖וֹן אֶת־קָרְבָּנ֑וֹ נַחְשׁ֥וֹן בֶּן־עַמִּֽינָדָ֖ב לְמַטֵּ֥ה יְהוּדָֽה׃ יג וְקָרְבָּנ֞וֹ קַֽעֲרַת־כֶּ֣סֶף אַחַ֗ת שְׁלֹשִׁ֣ים וּמֵאָה֮ מִשְׁקָלָהּ֒ מִזְרָ֤ק אֶחָד֙ כֶּ֔סֶף שִׁבְעִ֥ים שֶׁ֖קֶל בְּשֶׁ֣קֶל הַקֹּ֑דֶשׁ שְׁנֵיהֶ֣ם ׀ מְלֵאִ֗ים סֹ֛לֶת בְּלוּלָ֥ה בַשֶּׁ֖מֶן לְמִנְחָֽה׃ יד כַּ֤ף אַחַת֙ עֲשָׂרָ֣ה

° *Note to the English translation*: In his commentary on this verse, which is not included in this excerpted edition, Hirsch explains that this was the basin (see also Exodus 27:3)

from which the blood of the animal offerings was dashed upon the altar. [G.H.]

CHAPTER VII

10. *the princes brought near their offering before the altar.* They brought it, all of them together, simultaneously, thus symbolically demonstrating the equality of the tribes they represented and their unanimity in their attitude toward the Sanctuary of the Law.

11. *And God said.* However, God commanded that

each tribal prince should be assigned his own particular day on which to make his offering; for each tribe represents a unique configuration of social characteristics, which, if purified, pervaded with the spirit of the Law and employed for putting the Law's requirements into practice, will enable each tribe to make its own contribution to the accomplishment of the mission assigned to the nation as a whole.

[weighing] ten shekels of gold, filled with incense.   15. One young bull, one ram, one sheep in its first year for an ascent offering.   16. One male goat for an offering that clears [him who brings it] of sin.   17. And for the meal-of-peace offering: two oxen, five rams, five bucks, five yearling sheep. This [was] the offering of Naḥshon, son of Amminadab.   18. On the second day Nethanel, son of Tzuar, prince of Yissakhar, brought near — 19. he brought near his offering: one silver dish one hundred and thirty in weight, one silver sprinkling basin seventy shekels by the weight [standard] of the Sanctuary, both filled with fine wheat flour mixed with oil for a homage offering.   20. One spoon [weighing] ten shekels of gold, filled with incense.   21. One young bull, one ram, one sheep in its first year for an ascent offering.   22. One male goat for an offering that clears [him who brings it] of sin.   23. And for the meal-of-peace offering: two oxen, five rams, five bucks, five yearling sheep. This [was] the offering of Nethanel, son of Tzuar.   24. On the third day the prince of the son of Zebulun: Eliab, son of Ḥelon.   25. His offering: one silver dish one hundred and thirty in weight, one silver sprinkling basin seventy shekels by the weight [standard] of the Sanctuary, both filled with fine wheat flour mixed with oil for a homage offering.   26. One spoon [weighing] ten shekels of gold, filled with incense.   27. One young bull, one ram, one sheep in its first year for an ascent offering.   28. One male goat for an offering that clears [him who brings it] of sin.   29. And for the meal-of-peace offering: two oxen, five rams, five bucks, five yearling sheep. This [was] the offering of Eliab, son of Ḥelon.   30. On the fourth day, the prince of the sons of Reuben: Elitzur, son of Sh'deur.   31. His offering: one silver dish one hundred and thirty in weight, one silver sprinkling basin seventy shekels by the weight [standard] of the Sanctuary, both filled with fine wheat flour mixed with oil for a homage offering.   32. One spoon [weighing] ten shekels of gold, filled with incense.   33. One young bull, one ram, one sheep in its first year for an ascent offering.   34. One male goat for an offering

זָהָב מְלֵאָה קְטֹרֶת: טו פַּר אֶחָד בֶּן־בָּקָר אַיִל אֶחָד כֶּבֶשׂ־אֶחָד בֶּן־שְׁנָתוֹ לְעֹלָה: טז שְׂעִיר־עִזִּים אֶחָד לְחַטָּאת: יז וּלְזֶבַח הַשְּׁלָמִים בָּקָר שְׁנַיִם אֵילִם חֲמִשָּׁה עַתּוּדִים חֲמִשָּׁה כְּבָשִׂים בְּנֵי־שָׁנָה חֲמִשָּׁה זֶה קָרְבַּן נַחְשׁוֹן בֶּן־עַמִּינָדָב: פ יח בַּיּוֹם הַשֵּׁנִי הִקְרִיב נְתַנְאֵל בֶּן־צוּעָר נְשִׂיא יִשָּׂשכָר: יט הִקְרִב אֶת־קָרְבָּנוֹ קַעֲרַת־כֶּסֶף אַחַת שְׁלֹשִׁים וּמֵאָה מִשְׁקָלָהּ מִזְרָק אֶחָד כֶּסֶף שִׁבְעִים שֶׁקֶל בְּשֶׁקֶל הַקֹּדֶשׁ שְׁנֵיהֶם ׀ מְלֵאִים סֹלֶת בְּלוּלָה בַשֶּׁמֶן לְמִנְחָה: כ כַּף אַחַת עֲשָׂרָה זָהָב מְלֵאָה קְטֹרֶת: כא פַּר אֶחָד בֶּן־בָּקָר אַיִל אֶחָד כֶּבֶשׂ־אֶחָד בֶּן־שְׁנָתוֹ לְעֹלָה: כב שְׂעִיר־עִזִּים אֶחָד לְחַטָּאת: כג וּלְזֶבַח הַשְּׁלָמִים בָּקָר שְׁנַיִם אֵילִם חֲמִשָּׁה עַתֻּדִים חֲמִשָּׁה כְּבָשִׂים בְּנֵי־שָׁנָה חֲמִשָּׁה זֶה קָרְבַּן נְתַנְאֵל בֶּן־צוּעָר: פ כד בַּיּוֹם הַשְּׁלִישִׁי נָשִׂיא לִבְנֵי זְבוּלֻן אֱלִיאָב בֶּן־חֵלֹן: כה קָרְבָּנוֹ קַעֲרַת־כֶּסֶף אַחַת שְׁלֹשִׁים וּמֵאָה מִשְׁקָלָהּ מִזְרָק אֶחָד כֶּסֶף שִׁבְעִים שֶׁקֶל בְּשֶׁקֶל הַקֹּדֶשׁ שְׁנֵיהֶם ׀ מְלֵאִים סֹלֶת בְּלוּלָה בַשֶּׁמֶן לְמִנְחָה: כו כַּף אַחַת עֲשָׂרָה זָהָב מְלֵאָה קְטֹרֶת: כז פַּר אֶחָד בֶּן־בָּקָר אַיִל אֶחָד כֶּבֶשׂ־אֶחָד בֶּן־שְׁנָתוֹ לְעֹלָה: כח שְׂעִיר־עִזִּים אֶחָד לְחַטָּאת: כט וּלְזֶבַח הַשְּׁלָמִים בָּקָר שְׁנַיִם אֵילִם חֲמִשָּׁה עַתֻּדִים חֲמִשָּׁה כְּבָשִׂים בְּנֵי־שָׁנָה חֲמִשָּׁה זֶה קָרְבַּן אֱלִיאָב בֶּן־חֵלֹן: פ ל בַּיּוֹם הָרְבִיעִי נָשִׂיא לִבְנֵי רְאוּבֵן אֱלִיצוּר בֶּן־שְׁדֵיאוּר: לא קָרְבָּנוֹ קַעֲרַת־כֶּסֶף אַחַת שְׁלֹשִׁים וּמֵאָה מִשְׁקָלָהּ מִזְרָק אֶחָד כֶּסֶף שִׁבְעִים שֶׁקֶל בְּשֶׁקֶל הַקֹּדֶשׁ שְׁנֵיהֶם ׀ מְלֵאִים סֹלֶת בְּלוּלָה בַשֶּׁמֶן לְמִנְחָה: לב כַּף אַחַת עֲשָׂרָה זָהָב מְלֵאָה קְטֹרֶת: לג פַּר אֶחָד בֶּן־בָּקָר אַיִל אֶחָד כֶּבֶשׂ־אֶחָד בֶּן־שְׁנָתוֹ לְעֹלָה: לד שְׂעִיר־עִזִּים אֶחָד לְחַטָּאת:

that clears [him who brings it] of sin.
35. And for the meal-of-peace offering:
two oxen, five rams, five bucks, five yearling
sheep. This [was] the offering of Elitzur, son
of Sh'deur. 36. On the fifth day the
prince of the sons of Shimeon: Shelumiel,
son of Tzurishaddai. 37. His offering: one
silver dish one hundred and thirty in
weight, one silver sprinkling basin seventy
shekels by the weight [standard] of the
Sanctuary, both filled with fine wheat flour
mixed with oil for a homage offering.
38. One spoon [weighing] ten shekels of
gold, filled with incense. 39. One young
bull, one ram, one sheep in its first year for
an ascent offering. 40. One male goat
for an offering that clears [him who brings
it] of sin. 41. And for the meal-of-peace
offering: two oxen, five rams, five bucks,
five yearling sheep. This [was] the offering
of Shelumiel, son of Tzurishaddai.
42. On the sixth day the prince of the
sons of Gad: Eliassaph, son of Deuel.
43. His offering: one silver dish one
hundred and thirty in weight, one silver
sprinkling basin seventy shekels by the
weight [standard] of the Sanctuary, both
filled with fine wheat flour mixed with oil
for a homage offering. 44. One spoon
[weighing] ten shekels of gold, filled with
incense. 45. One young bull, one ram,
one sheep in its first year for an ascent offering. 46. One male goat for an offering
that clears [him who brings it] of sin
47. And for the meal-of-peace offering:
two oxen, five rams, five bucks, five yearling
sheep. This [was] the offering of Eliassaph,
son of Deuel. 48. On the seventh day the
prince of the sons of Ephraim: Elishama,
son of Ammihud. 49. His offering: one
silver dish one hundred and thirty in
weight, one silver sprinkling basin seventy
shekels by the weight [standard] of the
Sanctuary, both filled with fine wheat flour
mixed with oil for a homage offering.
50. One spoon [weighing] ten shekels of
gold, filled with incense. 51. One young
bull, one ram, one sheep in its first year
for an ascent offering. 52. One male
goat for an offering that clears [him
who brings it] of sin. 53. And for the
meal-of-peace offering: two oxen, five
rams, five bucks, five yearling sheep.

לה וּלְזֶ֣בַח הַשְּׁלָמִים֮ בָּקָ֣ר שְׁנַ֒יִם֒ אֵילִ֤ם חֲמִשָּׁה֙
עַתֻּדִ֣ים חֲמִשָּׁ֔ה כְּבָשִׂ֥ים בְּנֵֽי־שָׁנָ֖ה חֲמִשָּׁ֑ה זֶ֛ה
קָרְבַּ֥ן אֱלִיצ֖וּר בֶּן־שְׁדֵיאֽוּר: פ לו בַּיּוֹם֙
הַֽחֲמִישִׁ֔י נָשִׂ֖יא לִבְנֵ֣י שִׁמְע֑וֹן שְׁלֻֽמִיאֵ֖ל בֶּן־
צוּרִֽישַׁדָּֽי: לז קָרְבָּנ֞וֹ קַֽעֲרַת־כֶּ֣סֶף אַחַ֗ת שְׁלֹשִׁ֣ים
וּמֵאָה֙ מִשְׁקָלָ֔הּ מִזְרָ֤ק אֶחָד֙ כֶּ֔סֶף שִׁבְעִ֥ים שֶׁ֖קֶל
בְּשֶׁ֣קֶל הַקֹּ֑דֶשׁ שְׁנֵיהֶ֣ם ׀ מְלֵאִ֗ים סֹ֛לֶת בְּלוּלָ֥ה
בַשֶּׁ֖מֶן לְמִנְחָֽה: לח כַּ֥ף אַחַ֛ת עֲשָׂרָ֥ה זָהָ֖ב מְלֵאָ֥ה
קְטֹֽרֶת: לט פַּ֣ר אֶחָ֞ד בֶּן־בָּקָ֗ר אַ֧יִל אֶחָ֛ד כֶּֽבֶשׂ־
אֶחָ֥ד בֶּן־שְׁנָת֖וֹ לְעֹלָֽה: מ שְׂעִיר־עִזִּ֥ים אֶחָ֖ד
לְחַטָּֽאת: מא וּלְזֶ֣בַח הַשְּׁלָמִים֮ בָּקָ֣ר שְׁנַ֒יִם֒ אֵילִ֤ם
חֲמִשָּׁה֙ עַתֻּדִ֣ים חֲמִשָּׁ֔ה כְּבָשִׂ֥ים בְּנֵֽי־שָׁנָ֖ה
חֲמִשָּׁ֑ה זֶ֛ה קָרְבַּ֥ן שְׁלֻֽמִיאֵ֖ל בֶּן־צוּרִֽישַׁדָּֽי: פ
ששי מב בַּיּוֹם֙ הַשִּׁשִּׁ֔י נָשִׂ֖יא לִבְנֵ֣י גָ֑ד אֶלְיָסָ֖ף בֶּן־
דְּעוּאֵֽל: מג קָרְבָּנ֞וֹ קַֽעֲרַת־כֶּ֣סֶף אַחַ֗ת שְׁלֹשִׁ֣ים
וּמֵאָה֙ מִשְׁקָלָ֔הּ מִזְרָ֤ק אֶחָד֙ כֶּ֔סֶף שִׁבְעִ֥ים שֶׁ֖קֶל
בְּשֶׁ֣קֶל הַקֹּ֑דֶשׁ שְׁנֵיהֶ֣ם ׀ מְלֵאִ֗ים סֹ֛לֶת בְּלוּלָ֥ה
בַשֶּׁ֖מֶן לְמִנְחָֽה: מד כַּ֥ף אַחַ֛ת עֲשָׂרָ֥ה זָהָ֖ב מְלֵאָ֥ה
קְטֹֽרֶת: מה פַּ֣ר אֶחָ֞ד בֶּן־בָּקָ֗ר אַ֧יִל אֶחָ֛ד כֶּֽבֶשׂ־
אֶחָ֥ד בֶּן־שְׁנָת֖וֹ לְעֹלָֽה: מו שְׂעִיר־עִזִּ֥ים אֶחָ֖ד
לְחַטָּֽאת: מז וּלְזֶ֣בַח הַשְּׁלָמִים֮ בָּקָ֣ר שְׁנַ֒יִם֒ אֵילִ֤ם
חֲמִשָּׁה֙ עַתֻּדִ֣ים חֲמִשָּׁ֔ה כְּבָשִׂ֥ים בְּנֵֽי־שָׁנָ֖ה
חֲמִשָּׁ֑ה זֶ֛ה קָרְבַּ֥ן אֶלְיָסָ֖ף בֶּן־דְּעוּאֵֽל: פ
מח בַּיּוֹם֙ הַשְּׁבִיעִ֔י נָשִׂ֖יא לִבְנֵ֣י אֶפְרָ֑יִם אֱלִֽישָׁמָ֖ע
בֶּן־עַמִּיהֽוּד: מט קָרְבָּנ֞וֹ קַֽעֲרַת־כֶּ֣סֶף אַחַ֗ת
שְׁלֹשִׁ֣ים וּמֵאָה֙ מִשְׁקָלָ֔הּ מִזְרָ֤ק אֶחָד֙ כֶּ֔סֶף
שִׁבְעִ֥ים שֶׁ֖קֶל בְּשֶׁ֣קֶל הַקֹּ֑דֶשׁ שְׁנֵיהֶ֣ם ׀ מְלֵאִ֗ים
סֹ֛לֶת בְּלוּלָ֥ה בַשֶּׁ֖מֶן לְמִנְחָֽה: נ כַּ֥ף אַחַ֛ת עֲשָׂרָ֥ה
זָהָ֖ב מְלֵאָ֥ה קְטֹֽרֶת: נא פַּ֣ר אֶחָ֞ד בֶּן־בָּקָ֗ר אַ֧יִל
אֶחָ֛ד כֶּֽבֶשׂ־אֶחָ֥ד בֶּן־שְׁנָת֖וֹ לְעֹלָֽה: נב שְׂעִיר־
עִזִּ֥ים אֶחָ֖ד לְחַטָּֽאת: נג וּלְזֶ֣בַח הַשְּׁלָמִים֮ בָּקָ֣ר
שְׁנַ֒יִם֒ אֵילִ֤ם חֲמִשָּׁה֙ עַתֻּדִ֣ים חֲמִשָּׁ֔ה כְּבָשִׂ֥ים

This [was] the offering of Elishama, son of Ammihud. 54. On the eighth day the prince of the sons of Menashe: Gamliel, son of Pedahtzur. 55. His offering: one silver dish one hundred and thirty in weight, one silver sprinkling basin seventy shekels by the weight [standard] of the Sanctuary, both filled with fine wheat flour mixed with oil for a homage offering. 56. One spoon [weighing] ten shekels of gold, filled with incense. 57. One young bull, one ram, one sheep in its first year for an ascent offering. 58. One male goat for an offering that clears [him who brings it] of sin. 59. And for the meal-of-peace offering: two oxen, five rams, five bucks, five yearling sheep. This [was] the offering of Gamliel, son of Pedahtzur. 60. On the ninth day the prince of the sons of Binyamin: Abidan, son of Gideoni. 61. His offering: one silver dish one hundred and thirty in weight, one silver sprinkling basin seventy shekels by the weight [standard] of the Sanctuary, both filled with fine wheat flour mixed with oil for a homage offering. 62. One spoon [weighing] ten shekels of gold, filled with incense. 63. One young bull, one ram, one sheep in its first year for an ascent offering. 64. One male goat for an offering that clears [him who brings it] of sin. 65. And for the meal-of-peace offering: two oxen, five rams, five bucks, five yearling sheep. This [was] the offering of Abidan, son of Gideoni. 66. On the tenth day the prince of the sons of Dan: Aḥiezer, son of Ammishaddai. 67. His offering: one silver dish one hundred and thirty in weight, one silver sprinkling basin seventy shekels by the weight [standard] of the Sanctuary, both filled with fine wheat flour mixed with oil for a homage offering. 68. One spoon [weighing] ten shekels of gold, filled with incense. 69. One young bull, one ram, one sheep in its first year for an ascent offering. 70. One male goat for an offering that clears [him who brings it] of sin. 71. And for the meal-of-peace offering: two oxen, five rams, five bucks, five yearling sheep. This [was] the offering of Aḥiezer, son of Ammishaddai. 72. On the eleventh day the prince of the sons of Asher: Pagiel, son of Okhran. 73. His offering: one silver dish one hundred and

בְּנֵי־שָׁנָה חֲמִשָּׁה זֶה קָרְבַּן אֱלִישָׁמָע בֶּן־
עַמִּיהוּד: פ נד בַּיּוֹם הַשְּׁמִינִי נָשִׂיא לִבְנֵי
מְנַשֶּׁה גַּמְלִיאֵל בֶּן־פְּדָהצוּר: נה קָרְבָּנוֹ קַעֲרַת־
כֶּסֶף אַחַת שְׁלֹשִׁים וּמֵאָה מִשְׁקָלָהּ מִזְרָק אֶחָד
כֶּסֶף שִׁבְעִים שֶׁקֶל בְּשֶׁקֶל הַקֹּדֶשׁ שְׁנֵיהֶם ׀
מְלֵאִים סֹלֶת בְּלוּלָה בַשֶּׁמֶן לְמִנְחָה: נו כַּף אַחַת
עֲשָׂרָה זָהָב מְלֵאָה קְטֹרֶת: נז פַּר אֶחָד בֶּן־בָּקָר
אַיִל אֶחָד כֶּבֶשׂ־אֶחָד בֶּן־שְׁנָתוֹ לְעֹלָה:
נח שְׂעִיר־עִזִּים אֶחָד לְחַטָּאת: נט וּלְזֶבַח
הַשְּׁלָמִים בָּקָר שְׁנַיִם אֵילִם חֲמִשָּׁה עַתֻּדִים
חֲמִשָּׁה כְּבָשִׂים בְּנֵי־שָׁנָה חֲמִשָּׁה זֶה קָרְבַּן
גַּמְלִיאֵל בֶּן־פְּדָהצוּר: פ ס בַּיּוֹם הַתְּשִׁיעִי
נָשִׂיא לִבְנֵי בִנְיָמִן אֲבִידָן בֶּן־גִּדְעֹנִי: סא קָרְבָּנוֹ
קַעֲרַת־כֶּסֶף אַחַת שְׁלֹשִׁים וּמֵאָה מִשְׁקָלָהּ
מִזְרָק אֶחָד כֶּסֶף שִׁבְעִים שֶׁקֶל בְּשֶׁקֶל הַקֹּדֶשׁ
שְׁנֵיהֶם ׀ מְלֵאִים סֹלֶת בְּלוּלָה בַשֶּׁמֶן לְמִנְחָה:
סב כַּף אַחַת עֲשָׂרָה זָהָב מְלֵאָה קְטֹרֶת: סג פַּר
אֶחָד בֶּן־בָּקָר אַיִל אֶחָד כֶּבֶשׂ־אֶחָד בֶּן־שְׁנָתוֹ
לְעֹלָה: סד שְׂעִיר־עִזִּים אֶחָד לְחַטָּאת:
סה וּלְזֶבַח הַשְּׁלָמִים בָּקָר שְׁנַיִם אֵילִם חֲמִשָּׁה
עַתֻּדִים חֲמִשָּׁה כְּבָשִׂים בְּנֵי־שָׁנָה חֲמִשָּׁה זֶה
קָרְבַּן אֲבִידָן בֶּן־גִּדְעֹנִי: פ סו בַּיּוֹם הָעֲשִׂירִי
נָשִׂיא לִבְנֵי דָן אֲחִיעֶזֶר בֶּן־עַמִּישַׁדָּי: סז קָרְבָּנוֹ
קַעֲרַת־כֶּסֶף אַחַת שְׁלֹשִׁים וּמֵאָה מִשְׁקָלָהּ
מִזְרָק אֶחָד כֶּסֶף שִׁבְעִים שֶׁקֶל בְּשֶׁקֶל הַקֹּדֶשׁ
שְׁנֵיהֶם ׀ מְלֵאִים סֹלֶת בְּלוּלָה בַשֶּׁמֶן לְמִנְחָה:
סח כַּף אַחַת עֲשָׂרָה זָהָב מְלֵאָה קְטֹרֶת: סט פַּר
אֶחָד בֶּן־בָּקָר אַיִל אֶחָד כֶּבֶשׂ־אֶחָד בֶּן־שְׁנָתוֹ
לְעֹלָה: ע שְׂעִיר־עִזִּים אֶחָד לְחַטָּאת: עא וּלְזֶבַח
הַשְּׁלָמִים בָּקָר שְׁנַיִם אֵילִם חֲמִשָּׁה עַתֻּדִים
חֲמִשָּׁה כְּבָשִׂים בְּנֵי־שָׁנָה חֲמִשָּׁה זֶה קָרְבַּן
אֲחִיעֶזֶר בֶּן־עַמִּישַׁדָּי: פ שביעי עב בְּיוֹם עַשְׁתֵּי
עָשָׂר יוֹם נָשִׂיא לִבְנֵי אָשֵׁר פַּגְעִיאֵל בֶּן־עָכְרָן:
עג קָרְבָּנוֹ קַעֲרַת־כֶּסֶף אַחַת שְׁלֹשִׁים וּמֵאָה

thirty in weight, one silver sprinkling basin seventy shekels by the weight [standard] of the Sanctuary, both filled with fine wheat flour mixed with oil for a homage offering. 74. One spoon [weighing] ten shekels of gold, filled with incense. 75. One young bull, one ram, one sheep in its first year for an ascent offering. 76. One male goat for an offering that clears [him who brings it] of sin. 77. And for the meal-of-peace offering: two oxen, five rams, five bucks, five yearling sheep. This [was] the offering of Pagiel, son of Okhran. 78. On the twelfth day the prince of the sons of Naphtali: Aḥira, son of Enan. 79. His offering: one silver dish one hundred and thirty in weight, one silver sprinkling basin seventy shekels by the weight [standard] of the Sanctuary, both filled with fine wheat flour mixed with oil for a homage offering. 80. One spoon [weighing] ten shekels of gold, filled with incense. 81. One young bull, one ram, one sheep in its first year for an ascent offering. 82. One male goat for an offering that clears [him who brings it] of sin. 83. And for the meal-of-peace offering: two oxen, five rams, five bucks, five yearling sheep. This [was] the offering of Aḥira, son of Enan. 84. This [was] the dedication [offering] of the altar, on the day it was anointed by the princes of Israel: twelve silver dishes, twelve sprinkling basins, twelve gold spoons. 85. Each dish [weighing] one hundred and thirty in silver and each sprinkling basin seventy; all the silver of the vessels: two thousand four hundred by the weight [standard] of the Sanctuary. 86. Twelve gold spoons filled with incense, each spoon [weighing] ten by the weight [standard] of the Sanctuary; all the gold of the spoons [amounted to] one hundred and twenty. 87. All the oxen for the ascent offering: twelve bulls, the rams twelve, the yearling sheep twelve along with their homage offering, and the male goats for an offering that clears [him who brings it] of sin, twelve. 88. And all the

מִשְׁקָלָהּ מִזְרָק אֶחָד כֶּסֶף שִׁבְעִים שֶׁקֶל בְּשֶׁקֶל הַקֹּדֶשׁ שְׁנֵיהֶם ׀ מְלֵאִים סֹלֶת בְּלוּלָה בַשֶּׁמֶן לְמִנְחָה: עד כַּף אַחַת עֲשָׂרָה זָהָב מְלֵאָה קְטֹרֶת: עה פַּר אֶחָד בֶּן־בָּקָר אַיִל אֶחָד כֶּבֶשׂ־אֶחָד בֶּן־שְׁנָתוֹ לְעֹלָה: עו שְׂעִיר־עִזִּים אֶחָד לְחַטָּאת: עז וּלְזֶבַח הַשְּׁלָמִים בָּקָר שְׁנַיִם אֵילִם חֲמִשָּׁה עַתֻּדִים חֲמִשָּׁה כְּבָשִׂים בְּנֵי־שָׁנָה חֲמִשָּׁה זֶה קָרְבַּן פַּגְעִיאֵל בֶּן־עָכְרָן: פ עח בְּיוֹם שְׁנֵים עָשָׂר יוֹם נָשִׂיא לִבְנֵי נַפְתָּלִי אֲחִירַע בֶּן־עֵינָן: עט קָרְבָּנוֹ קַעֲרַת־כֶּסֶף אַחַת שְׁלֹשִׁים וּמֵאָה מִשְׁקָלָהּ מִזְרָק אֶחָד כֶּסֶף שִׁבְעִים שֶׁקֶל בְּשֶׁקֶל הַקֹּדֶשׁ שְׁנֵיהֶם ׀ מְלֵאִים סֹלֶת בְּלוּלָה בַשֶּׁמֶן לְמִנְחָה: פ כַּף אַחַת עֲשָׂרָה זָהָב מְלֵאָה קְטֹרֶת: פא פַּר אֶחָד בֶּן־בָּקָר אַיִל אֶחָד כֶּבֶשׂ־אֶחָד בֶּן־שְׁנָתוֹ לְעֹלָה: פב שְׂעִיר־עִזִּים אֶחָד לְחַטָּאת: פג וּלְזֶבַח הַשְּׁלָמִים בָּקָר שְׁנַיִם אֵילִם חֲמִשָּׁה עַתֻּדִים חֲמִשָּׁה כְּבָשִׂים בְּנֵי־שָׁנָה חֲמִשָּׁה זֶה קָרְבַּן אֲחִירַע בֶּן־עֵינָן: פ פד זֹאת ׀ חֲנֻכַּת הַמִּזְבֵּחַ בְּיוֹם הִמָּשַׁח אֹתוֹ מֵאֵת נְשִׂיאֵי יִשְׂרָאֵל קַעֲרֹת כֶּסֶף שְׁתֵּים עֶשְׂרֵה מִזְרְקֵי־כֶסֶף שְׁנֵים עָשָׂר כַּפּוֹת זָהָב שְׁתֵּים עֶשְׂרֵה: פה שְׁלֹשִׁים וּמֵאָה הַקְּעָרָה הָאַחַת כֶּסֶף וְשִׁבְעִים הַמִּזְרָק הָאֶחָד כֹּל כֶּסֶף הַכֵּלִים אַלְפַּיִם וְאַרְבַּע־מֵאוֹת בְּשֶׁקֶל הַקֹּדֶשׁ: פו כַּפּוֹת זָהָב שְׁתֵּים־עֶשְׂרֵה מְלֵאֹת קְטֹרֶת עֲשָׂרָה עֲשָׂרָה הַכַּף בְּשֶׁקֶל הַקֹּדֶשׁ כָּל־זְהַב הַכַּפּוֹת עֶשְׂרִים וּמֵאָה: מפטיר פז כָּל־הַבָּקָר לָעֹלָה שְׁנֵים עָשָׂר פָּרִים אֵילִם שְׁנֵים־עָשָׂר כְּבָשִׂים בְּנֵי־שָׁנָה שְׁנֵים עָשָׂר וּמִנְחָתָם וּשְׂעִירֵי עִזִּים שְׁנֵים עָשָׂר לְחַטָּאת: פח וְכֹל

---

84. *This [was] the dedication [offering].* This recapitulation expresses the complete equality and unanimity of the princes of Israel in the attitude of their tribes toward the Sanctuary and toward all that pertained to it, as demonstrated by the dedication (offering) upon the altar.

cattle for the meal-of-peace offering: twenty-four bulls, the rams sixty, the bucks sixty, the yearling sheep sixty. This [was] the dedication [offering] of the altar after it had been anointed.   89. And when Moshe went into the Tent of Appointed Meeting to speak with Him, he heard the voice speaking to him from above the cover which was upon the Ark of the Testimony, from between the two cherubim; thus did He speak to him.

בָּקָ֑ר ׀ זֶ֣בַח הַשְּׁלָמִים֮ עֶשְׂרִ֣ים וְאַרְבָּעָה֒ פָּרִ֨ים אֵילִ֤ם שִׁשִּׁים֙ עַתֻּדִ֣ים שִׁשִּׁ֔ים כְּבָשִׂ֥ים בְּנֵי־שָׁנָ֖ה שִׁשִּׁ֑ים זֹ֚את חֲנֻכַּ֣ת הַמִּזְבֵּ֔חַ אַחֲרֵ֖י הִמָּשַׁ֥ח אֹתֽוֹ׃

פט וּבְבֹ֨א מֹשֶׁ֜ה אֶל־אֹ֣הֶל מוֹעֵד֮ לְדַבֵּ֣ר אִתּוֹ֒ וַיִּשְׁמַ֨ע אֶת־הַקּ֜וֹל מִדַּבֵּ֣ר אֵלָ֗יו מֵעַ֤ל הַכַּפֹּ֙רֶת֙ אֲשֶׁר֙ עַל־אֲרֹ֣ן הָעֵדֻ֔ת מִבֵּ֖ין שְׁנֵ֣י הַכְּרֻבִ֑ים וַיְדַבֵּ֖ר אֵלָֽיו׃ פ

The Haftarah for this Sidra may be found on page 890.

בהעלותך

BEHA'ALOTHEKHA

VIII 1. *God* spoke to Moshe [saying]: 2. "Speak to Aharon and say to him: 'When you light up the lights, the seven lights shall shine toward the [center of] the menorah.'" 3. Aharon did so; he lit up its lights toward the [center of] the menorah, as *God* had commanded Moshe. 4. And this is the workmanship of the menorah: hammered out of one piece of gold, to its rootstock, to its blossom, it is beaten work. Like the vision that *God* had let Moshe behold, so had he made the menorah. 5. *God* spoke to Moshe [saying]: 6. "Take the Levites from the midst of the sons of Yisrael and purify them. 7. Thus shall you do with them to purify them: sprinkle upon them waters that clear of sin. They shall then have a razor pass over all their flesh; they shall rinse their garments and purify themselves. 8. They shall then take a young bull and its homage offering, fine wheat flour mixed with oil, and you shall take a second young bull for an offering that

ח א וַיְדַבֵּר יְהוָה אֶל־מֹשֶׁה לֵּאמֹר׃ ב דַּבֵּר
אֶל־אַהֲרֹן וְאָמַרְתָּ אֵלָיו בְּהַעֲלֹתְךָ אֶת־הַנֵּרֹת
אֶל־מוּל פְּנֵי הַמְּנוֹרָה יָאִירוּ שִׁבְעַת הַנֵּרוֹת׃
ג וַיַּעַשׂ כֵּן אַהֲרֹן אֶל־מוּל פְּנֵי הַמְּנוֹרָה הֶעֱלָה
נֵרֹתֶיהָ כַּאֲשֶׁר צִוָּה יְהוָה אֶת־מֹשֶׁה׃ ד וְזֶה
מַעֲשֵׂה הַמְּנֹרָה מִקְשָׁה זָהָב עַד־יְרֵכָהּ עַד־
פִּרְחָהּ מִקְשָׁה הִוא כַּמַּרְאֶה אֲשֶׁר הֶרְאָה יְהוָה
אֶת־מֹשֶׁה כֵּן עָשָׂה אֶת־הַמְּנֹרָה׃ פ ה וַיְדַבֵּר
יְהוָה אֶל־מֹשֶׁה לֵּאמֹר׃ ו קַח אֶת־הַלְוִיִּם מִתּוֹךְ
בְּנֵי יִשְׂרָאֵל וְטִהַרְתָּ אֹתָם׃ ז וְכֹה־תַעֲשֶׂה לָהֶם
לְטַהֲרָם הַזֵּה עֲלֵיהֶם מֵי חַטָּאת וְהֶעֱבִירוּ תַעַר
עַל־כָּל־בְּשָׂרָם וְכִבְּסוּ בִגְדֵיהֶם וְהִטֶּהָרוּ׃
ח וְלָקְחוּ פַּר בֶּן־בָּקָר וּמִנְחָתוֹ סֹלֶת בְּלוּלָה
בַשָּׁמֶן וּפַר־שֵׁנִי בֶן־בָּקָר תִּקַּח לְחַטָּאת׃

CHAPTER VIII

1. In this portion the narrative turns back to the development of those redeemed from Mitzrayim toward the goal of becoming the nation of God. This narrative was broken off following Chapter 34 of the Book of Exodus, which dealt with the renewal of the Covenant after the people had atoned for their sin with the golden calf. The purpose of this interruption was to set down—in the account of the erection of the Sanctuary of the Law, and through the legislation forming the content of the entire Third Book and of the beginning of the Fourth Book up to this point—the ideal for which Israel was to become the people of God. However, Israel would have to be trained for that ideal over hundreds, indeed thousands of years that were to extend beyond our own present day. . . .

Precisely the paradox that there should have been such a wide gap between Israel as it was at the time of the Giving of the Law, on the one hand, and the Law and its assumptions and requirements, on the other, a gap that could be bridged only over a span of centuries, should be the most eloquent proof that this Law is indeed of Divine origin and should mark it as a unique phenomenon in the history of mankind. All other codes of law were predicated on conditions that prevailed at the time of their origin. This Law is the only one to have set itself up as the supreme goal of human development on earth; it still awaits a generation sufficiently mature at last to translate its ideals into reality.

The transition to the continuation of this developmental history is made by a reiteration of the instructions given to the priests for the care of the lights of the *menorah*, the account of the induction of the Levites into their service for the Sanctuary of the Law in the midst of the nation, and the revival of the nation's self-awareness as the people of God through the establishment of Israel's vocation, to be reconfirmed anew each year by the Passover offering. And finally there is Israel's departure, the resumption of its march, from the mountain on which the Law had been given, a march that in the natural course of events should have led them directly to the Promised Land, where this people was to put that Law into practice for all time to come. Then—at Verses 35 and 36 of Chapter 10—there is another break in the narrative and we are led down into the midst of the camp of the nation to see how much training and maturation this nation still required in order to fulfill the lofty aims that had been set for it.

clears [him who brings it] of sin.   9. You
shall have the Levites come near before the
Tent of Appointed Meeting and you shall
assemble the whole community of the sons
of Yisrael,   10. and you shall have the
Levites come near before *God,* and the sons
of Yisrael shall lean their hands upon the
Levites.   11. Aharon shall then perform
with the Levites a waving before *God* for
the sons of Yisrael; in this manner they shall
be consecrated to do the service of *God.*
12. And the Levites shall lean their hands
upon the heads of the bulls, and you shall
make the one as an offering that clears [him
who brings it] of sin, and the other as an
ascent offering, to *God,* to effect atonement
for the Levites.   13. You shall then have
the Levites stand before Aharon and his
sons and you shall perform with them a
waving before *God.*   14. Thus shall you
set apart the Levites from out of the midst of
the sons of Yisrael, and the Levites shall
become Mine.   15. Thereafter the Levites
shall come to do the service at the Tent of
Appointed Meeting; it is for this purpose
that you shall purify them and for this purpose shall you perform a waving with them.
16. For they are given, [indeed] given to
Me from out of the midst of the sons of Yisrael, in place of the opening of every
mother's womb, the first-born of all the
sons of Yisrael, have I taken them for
Myself.   17. For every first-born among
the sons of Yisrael among men and among
beast became Mine; on the day I struck
every first-born in the land of Mitzrayim
I sanctified them for Myself.   18. Now I
have taken the Levites in place of every
first-born among the sons of Yisrael.
19. And I have given the Levites to
Aharon and to his sons from out of the midst
of the sons of Yisrael to do the service of the
sons of Yisrael at the Tent of Appointed
Meeting and to effect atonement for the
sons of Yisrael. Thus there shall be no
[sudden] death among the sons of Yisrael
when the sons of Yisrael approach the Sanctuary."   20. Moshe, Aharon and the whole
community of the sons of Yisrael did with
the Levites according to all that which *God*
had commanded Moshe regarding the
Levites; thus did the sons of Yisrael do with
them.   21. The Levites cleared them-

ט וְהִקְרַבְתָּ֣ אֶת־הַלְוִיִּ֔ם לִפְנֵ֖י אֹ֣הֶל מוֹעֵ֑ד
וְהִ֨קְהַלְתָּ֔ אֶת־כָּל־עֲדַ֖ת בְּנֵ֥י יִשְׂרָאֵֽל: י וְהִקְרַבְתָּ֥
אֶת־הַלְוִיִּ֖ם לִפְנֵ֣י יְהוָ֑ה וְסָמְכ֧וּ בְנֵֽי־יִשְׂרָאֵ֛ל אֶת־
יְדֵיהֶ֖ם עַל־הַלְוִיִּֽם: יא וְהֵנִיף֩ אַהֲרֹ֨ן אֶת־הַלְוִיִּ֤ם
תְּנוּפָה֙ לִפְנֵ֣י יְהוָ֔ה מֵאֵ֖ת בְּנֵ֣י יִשְׂרָאֵ֑ל וְהָי֕וּ לַעֲבֹ֖ד
אֶת־עֲבֹדַ֥ת יְהוָֽה: יב וְהַלְוִיִּם֙ יִסְמְכ֣וּ אֶת־יְדֵיהֶ֔ם
עַ֖ל רֹ֣אשׁ הַפָּרִ֑ים וַ֠עֲשֵׂ֠ה אֶת־הָאֶחָ֨ד חַטָּ֜את
וְאֶת־הָאֶחָ֤ד עֹלָה֙ לַֽיהוָ֔ה לְכַפֵּ֖ר עַל־הַלְוִיִּֽם:
יג וְהַֽעֲמַדְתָּ֙ אֶת־הַלְוִיִּ֔ם לִפְנֵ֥י אַהֲרֹ֖ן וְלִפְנֵ֣י בָנָ֑יו
וְהֵנַפְתָּ֥ אֹתָ֛ם תְּנוּפָ֖ה לַֽיהוָֽה: יד וְהִבְדַּלְתָּ֙ אֶת־
הַלְוִיִּ֔ם מִתּ֖וֹךְ בְּנֵ֣י יִשְׂרָאֵ֑ל וְהָ֥יוּ לִ֖י הַלְוִיִּֽם: שני
טו וְאַֽחֲרֵי־כֵ֗ן יָבֹ֨אוּ֙ הַלְוִיִּ֔ם לַעֲבֹ֖ד אֶת־אֹ֣הֶל
מוֹעֵ֑ד וְטִֽהַרְתָּ֣ אֹתָ֔ם וְהֵנַפְתָּ֥ אֹתָ֖ם תְּנוּפָֽה: טז כִּי֩
נְתֻנִ֨ים נְתֻנִ֥ים הֵ֨מָּה֙ לִ֔י מִתּ֖וֹךְ בְּנֵ֣י יִשְׂרָאֵ֑ל תַּ֣חַת
פִּטְרַ֣ת כָּל־רֶ֠חֶם בְּכ֨וֹר כֹּל֙ מִבְּנֵ֣י יִשְׂרָאֵ֔ל לָקַ֥חְתִּי
אֹתָ֖ם לִֽי: יז כִּ֣י לִ֤י כָל־בְּכוֹר֙ בִּבְנֵ֣י יִשְׂרָאֵ֔ל
בָּאָדָ֖ם וּבַבְּהֵמָ֑ה בְּי֗וֹם הַכֹּתִ֤י כָל־בְּכוֹר֙ בְּאֶ֣רֶץ
מִצְרַ֔יִם הִקְדַּ֥שְׁתִּי אֹתָ֖ם לִֽי: יח וָאֶקַּ֖ח אֶת־הַלְוִיִּ֑ם
תַּ֥חַת כָּל־בְּכ֖וֹר בִּבְנֵ֥י יִשְׂרָאֵֽל: יט וָאֶתְּנָ֨ה אֶת־
הַלְוִיִּ֜ם נְתֻנִ֣ים ׀ לְאַהֲרֹ֣ן וּלְבָנָ֗יו מִתּוֹךְ֘ בְּנֵ֣י
יִשְׂרָאֵל֒ לַעֲבֹ֞ד אֶת־עֲבֹדַ֤ת בְּנֵֽי־יִשְׂרָאֵל֙ בְּאֹ֣הֶל
מוֹעֵ֔ד וּלְכַפֵּ֖ר עַל־בְּנֵ֣י יִשְׂרָאֵ֑ל וְלֹ֨א יִהְיֶ֜ה בִּבְנֵ֤י
יִשְׂרָאֵל֙ נֶ֔גֶף בְּגֶ֥שֶׁת בְּנֵֽי־יִשְׂרָאֵ֖ל אֶל־הַקֹּֽדֶשׁ:
כ וַיַּ֨עַשׂ מֹשֶׁ֤ה וְאַהֲרֹן֙ וְכָל־עֲדַ֣ת בְּנֵֽי־יִשְׂרָאֵ֔ל
לַלְוִיִּ֑ם כְּ֠כֹ֠ל אֲשֶׁר־צִוָּ֨ה יְהוָ֤ה אֶת־מֹשֶׁה֙ לַלְוִיִּ֔ם
כֵּן־עָשׂ֥וּ לָהֶ֖ם בְּנֵ֥י יִשְׂרָאֵֽל: כא וַיִּֽתְחַטְּא֣וּ הַלְוִיִּ֗ם

selves of sin and rinsed their garments, and Aharon performed with them a waving before *God*, and Aharon effected atonement for them, to purify them.   22. Afterwards the Levites came to do their service at the Tent of Appointed Meeting before Aharon and before his sons; as *God* had commanded Moshe with regard to the Levites, thus did they do with them.   23. *God* spoke to Moshe [saying]:   24. "This is what pertains to the Levites: From twenty-five years old and upward he shall come to perform communal service in the service of the Tent of Appointed Meeting,   25. and after the age of fifty years he shall retire from the public performance of the service and need no longer do service.   26. He shall serve with his brethren to keep watch at the Tent of Appointed Meeting but he shall no longer do service. Thus shall you do with the Levites concerning the obligations of their office.

IX   1. *God* spoke to Moshe in the wilderness of Sinai in the second year after their exodus from the land of Mitzrayim, in the first month [saying]: 2. "Let the sons of Yisrael make the Pesaḥ [offering] at its appointed season. 3. On the fourteenth day of this month, between the two evenings, you shall make it at its appointed season. According to all its laws and all the regulations pertaining to it shall you make it."   4. And Moshe spoke to the sons of Yisrael that they might make the Pesaḥ [offering],   5. and they made the Pesaḥ [offering] in the first month, on the fourteenth day of the month, between the two evenings, in the wilderness of Sinai; in accordance with all that *God* had commanded Moshe, thus did the sons of Yisrael do.   6. But there were [some] men who were unclean by [contact with] the person of a man, and therefore they could not make the Pesaḥ [offering] on that day,   7. and these men said to him: "We are unclean by [contact with] the person of a man; why should we stand back so as not to bring near the offering of *God* at its appointed season in the midst of the sons of Yisrael?" 8. And Moshe said to them: "Wait; I wish to hear what *God* will command with regard to you."   9. And *God* spoke to Moshe [saying]:   10. "Speak to the sons of

וַיְכַבְּסוּ בִּגְדֵיהֶם וַיָּנֶף אַהֲרֹן אֹתָם תְּנוּפָה לִפְנֵי יְהוָה וַיְכַפֵּר עֲלֵיהֶם אַהֲרֹן לְטַהֲרָם: כב וְאַחֲרֵי־ כֵן בָּאוּ הַלְוִיִּם לַעֲבֹד אֶת־עֲבֹדָתָם בְּאֹהֶל מוֹעֵד לִפְנֵי אַהֲרֹן וְלִפְנֵי בָנָיו כַּאֲשֶׁר צִוָּה יְהוָה אֶת־ מֹשֶׁה עַל־הַלְוִיִּם כֵּן עָשׂוּ לָהֶם: ס כג וַיְדַבֵּר יְהוָה אֶל־מֹשֶׁה לֵּאמֹר: כד זֹאת אֲשֶׁר לַלְוִיִּם מִבֶּן חָמֵשׁ וְעֶשְׂרִים שָׁנָה וָמַעְלָה יָבוֹא לִצְבֹא צָבָא בַּעֲבֹדַת אֹהֶל מוֹעֵד: כה וּמִבֶּן חֲמִשִּׁים שָׁנָה יָשׁוּב מִצְּבָא הָעֲבֹדָה וְלֹא יַעֲבֹד עוֹד: כו וְשֵׁרֵת אֶת־אֶחָיו בְּאֹהֶל מוֹעֵד לִשְׁמֹר מִשְׁמֶרֶת וַעֲבֹדָה לֹא יַעֲבֹד כָּכָה תַּעֲשֶׂה לַלְוִיִּם בְּמִשְׁמְרֹתָם: פ שלישי ט א וַיְדַבֵּר יְהוָה אֶל־ מֹשֶׁה בְמִדְבַּר־סִינַי בַּשָּׁנָה הַשֵּׁנִית לְצֵאתָם מֵאֶרֶץ מִצְרַיִם בַּחֹדֶשׁ הָרִאשׁוֹן לֵאמֹר: ב וְיַעֲשׂוּ בְנֵי־יִשְׂרָאֵל אֶת־הַפָּסַח בְּמוֹעֲדוֹ: ג בְּאַרְבָּעָה עָשָׂר־יוֹם בַּחֹדֶשׁ הַזֶּה בֵּין הָעַרְבַּיִם תַּעֲשׂוּ אֹתוֹ בְּמֹעֲדוֹ כְּכָל־חֻקֹּתָיו וּכְכָל־ מִשְׁפָּטָיו תַּעֲשׂוּ אֹתוֹ: ד וַיְדַבֵּר מֹשֶׁה אֶל־בְּנֵי יִשְׂרָאֵל לַעֲשֹׂת הַפָּסַח: ה וַיַּעֲשׂוּ אֶת־הַפֶּסַח בָּרִאשׁוֹן בְּאַרְבָּעָה עָשָׂר יוֹם לַחֹדֶשׁ בֵּין הָעַרְבַּיִם בְּמִדְבַּר סִינָי כְּכֹל אֲשֶׁר צִוָּה יְהוָה אֶת־מֹשֶׁה כֵּן עָשׂוּ בְּנֵי יִשְׂרָאֵל: ו וַיְהִי אֲנָשִׁים אֲשֶׁר הָיוּ טְמֵאִים לְנֶפֶשׁ אָדָם וְלֹא־יָכְלוּ לַעֲשֹׂת־הַפֶּסַח בַּיּוֹם הַהוּא וַיִּקְרְבוּ לִפְנֵי מֹשֶׁה וְלִפְנֵי אַהֲרֹן בַּיּוֹם הַהוּא: ז וַיֹּאמְרוּ הָאֲנָשִׁים הָהֵמָּה אֵלָיו אֲנַחְנוּ טְמֵאִים לְנֶפֶשׁ אָדָם לָמָּה נִגָּרַע לְבִלְתִּי הַקְרִיב אֶת־קָרְבַּן יְהוָה בְּמֹעֲדוֹ בְּתוֹךְ בְּנֵי יִשְׂרָאֵל: ח וַיֹּאמֶר אֲלֵהֶם מֹשֶׁה עִמְדוּ וְאֶשְׁמְעָה מַה־יְצַוֶּה יְהוָה לָכֶם: פ ט וַיְדַבֵּר יְהוָה אֶל־מֹשֶׁה לֵּאמֹר: י דַּבֵּר אֶל־בְּנֵי יִשְׂרָאֵל

Yisrael [saying]: If anyone will be unclean by [contact with] a person or will be on a distant journey—among you or among your descendants—and he must make the Pesah offering to *God*, 11. they shall make it in the second month on the fourteenth day between the two evenings; with *matzoth* and bitter herbs shall they eat it. 12. They shall not leave any of it until the morning and not break any of its bones; according to all the law of the Pesaḥ offering shall they make it. 13. But one who is pure and was not on a journey and neglects to make the Pesah offering, that person shall be uprooted from among his people; that same man, if he has not brought near the offering of *God* at its appointed season, must bear his sin. 14. And if someone from outside will have entered among you, he must make the Pesaḥ offering to *God* according to the law of the Pesaḥ offering and according to the regulations pertaining to it, thus shall he make it. There shall be one and the same law for him who has entered from outside and the native-born of the land." 15. And on the day that the Dwelling Place was erected, the cloud covered the Dwelling Place in the direction of the Tent of the Testimony, and in the evening there was above the Dwelling Place a fire-like glow until the morning. 16. Thus it was always; the cloud covered it, and [there was] a fire-like glow at night. 17. And only when the cloud rose from the Tent did the sons of Yisrael journey forth; and at the place where the cloud settled, there did the sons of Yisrael encamp. 18. According to the utterance of *God* did the sons of Yisrael journey forth and according to the utterance of *God* did they camp; as long as the cloud rested upon the Dwelling Place did they remain encamped.

לֵאמֹ֑ר אִ֣ישׁ אִ֣ישׁ כִּֽי־יִהְיֶ֣ה טָמֵ֣א ׀ לָנֶ֡פֶשׁ א֩וֹ
בְדֶ֨רֶךְ רְחֹקָ֜ה (נקוד על ה) לָכֶ֗ם א֚וֹ לְדֹרֹ֣תֵיכֶ֔ם
וְעָ֥שָׂה פֶ֖סַח לַיהוָֽה׃ יא בַּחֹ֨דֶשׁ הַשֵּׁנִ֜י בְּאַרְבָּעָ֨ה
עָשָׂ֥ר י֛וֹם בֵּ֥ין הָעַרְבַּ֖יִם יַעֲשׂ֣וּ אֹת֑וֹ עַל־מַצּ֥וֹת
וּמְרֹרִ֖ים יֹאכְלֻֽהוּ׃ יב לֹֽא־יַשְׁאִ֤ירוּ מִמֶּ֙נּוּ֙ עַד־
בֹּ֔קֶר וְעֶ֖צֶם לֹ֣א יִשְׁבְּרוּ־ב֑וֹ כְּכָל־חֻקַּ֥ת הַפֶּ֖סַח
יַעֲשׂ֥וּ אֹתֽוֹ׃ יג וְהָאִ֡ישׁ אֲשֶׁר־הוּא֩ טָה֨וֹר וּבְדֶ֜רֶךְ
לֹא־הָיָ֗ה וְחָדַל֙ לַעֲשׂ֣וֹת הַפֶּ֔סַח וְנִכְרְתָ֛ה הַנֶּ֥פֶשׁ
הַהִ֖וא מֵעַמֶּ֑יהָ כִּ֣י ׀ קָרְבַּ֣ן יְהוָ֗ה לֹ֤א הִקְרִיב֙
בְּמֹ֣עֲד֔וֹ חֶטְא֥וֹ יִשָּׂ֖א הָאִ֥ישׁ הַהֽוּא׃ יד וְכִֽי־יָג֨וּר
אִתְּכֶ֜ם גֵּ֗ר וְעָ֤שָׂה פֶ֙סַח֙ לַֽיהוָ֔ה כְּחֻקַּ֥ת הַפֶּ֛סַח
וּכְמִשְׁפָּט֖וֹ כֵּ֣ן יַעֲשֶׂ֑ה חֻקָּ֤ה אַחַת֙ יִהְיֶ֣ה לָכֶ֔ם וְלַגֵּ֖ר
וּלְאֶזְרַ֥ח הָאָֽרֶץ׃ ס רביעי טו וּבְיוֹם֙ הָקִ֣ים אֶת־
הַמִּשְׁכָּ֔ן כִּסָּ֤ה הֶעָנָן֙ אֶת־הַמִּשְׁכָּ֔ן לְאֹ֖הֶל הָעֵדֻ֑ת
וּבָעֶ֜רֶב יִהְיֶ֧ה עַל־הַמִּשְׁכָּ֛ן כְּמַרְאֵה־אֵ֖שׁ עַד־
בֹּֽקֶר׃ טז כֵּ֚ן יִהְיֶ֣ה תָמִ֔יד הֶעָנָ֖ן יְכַסֶּ֑נּוּ וּמַרְאֵה־
אֵ֖שׁ לָֽיְלָה׃ יז וּלְפִ֞י הֵעָלֹ֤ת הֶֽעָנָן֙ מֵעַ֣ל הָאֹ֔הֶל
וְאַ֣חֲרֵי כֵ֔ן יִסְע֖וּ בְּנֵ֣י יִשְׂרָאֵ֑ל וּבִמְק֗וֹם אֲשֶׁ֤ר
יִשְׁכָּן־שָׁם֙ הֶֽעָנָ֔ן שָׁ֥ם יַחֲנ֖וּ בְּנֵ֥י יִשְׂרָאֵֽל׃ יח עַל־
פִּ֣י יְהוָ֗ה יִסְעוּ֙ בְּנֵ֣י יִשְׂרָאֵ֔ל וְעַל־פִּ֥י יְהוָ֖ה יַחֲנ֑וּ
כָּל־יְמֵ֗י אֲשֶׁ֨ר יִשְׁכֹּ֧ן הֶעָנָ֛ן עַל־הַמִּשְׁכָּ֖ן יַחֲנֽוּ׃

CHAPTER IX

16–23. The cloud represented the shepherd's crook, as it were, by means of which God, the Shepherd of Israel, made His will known to the people He was leading: where and when they were to pitch camp, and when and in what direction they were to journey forth. And we are told here that the will and purpose of His guidance seemed unpredictable indeed to those who were to be led by it. There were times when they had to stay in one place for a long period; at other times, they were allowed to remain at rest for a few days only. Some of their rest periods lasted only one night, or one day and one night, and then again there were times when they had to remain encamped for a whole month, or even a year. Nahmanides notes that since they never

19. Even when the cloud remained over the Dwelling Place for many days, the sons of Yisrael kept that which had been given to them by God to keep and they did not journey forth.   20. It happened sometimes that the cloud remained upon the Dwelling Place for only a few days; according to the utterance of God did they camp, and according to the utterance of God did they journey forth.   21. It also happened sometimes that the cloud remained [only] from evening until morning, and the cloud rose in the morning and they journeyed forth; or [it might be] for a day and a night, and [then] the cloud rose and they journeyed forth.   22. Or [it might be] two days, or a year; when the cloud remained over the Dwelling Place for a long time and rested upon it, the sons of Yisrael remained encamped and did not journey forth; when it rose, they journeyed forth.   23. Accord-

יט וּבְהַאֲרִיךְ הֶעָנָן עַל־הַמִּשְׁכָּן יָמִים רַבִּים וְשָׁמְרוּ בְנֵי־יִשְׂרָאֵל אֶת־מִשְׁמֶרֶת יְהֹוָה וְלֹא יִסָּעוּ: כ וְיֵשׁ אֲשֶׁר יִהְיֶה הֶעָנָן יָמִים מִסְפָּר עַל־הַמִּשְׁכָּן עַל־פִּי יְהֹוָה יַחֲנוּ וְעַל־פִּי יְהֹוָה יִסָּעוּ: כא וְיֵשׁ אֲשֶׁר יִהְיֶה הֶעָנָן מֵעֶרֶב עַד־בֹּקֶר וְנַעֲלָה הֶעָנָן בַּבֹּקֶר וְנָסָעוּ אוֹ יוֹמָם וָלַיְלָה וְנַעֲלָה הֶעָנָן וְנָסָעוּ: כב אוֹ־יֹמַיִם אוֹ־חֹדֶשׁ אוֹ־יָמִים בְּהַאֲרִיךְ הֶעָנָן עַל־הַמִּשְׁכָּן לִשְׁכֹּן עָלָיו יַחֲנוּ בְנֵי־יִשְׂרָאֵל וְלֹא יִסָּעוּ וּבְהֵעָלֹתוֹ יִסָּעוּ: כג עַל־

had advance indication of how long each rest period would be, it sometimes happened that they made all the arrangements for encampment, only to find themselves compelled, just a few hours later, to pull up stakes and resume their journey, following the movement of the cloud.

Such was the training school of our wanderings through the wilderness in which we should have learned for all time to follow God's guidance with devotion and trust, no matter how incomprehensible it may seem to us, whether He commands us to leave a place just when we have become attached to it, or to remain in a position we find most untoward. During that period we should have learned always to do, gladly and cheerfully, whatever God commands; happy at all times beneath the shepherd's crook of His guidance; content in our own proven loyal obedience; ready to subordinate our own life's plan to God and to follow His direction, even if it leads to goals we do not know, along paths we do not understand; to remain in our place with patience and endurance, or to move on with never-failing courage.

However, on closer consideration of the narrative in Verses 17–22, describing the exercises with which God sought to train the people whom He seeks to guide for all time, it would seem that the primary function of these exercises was not so much to subject the people to the stresses of prolonged wanderings as it was to teach them patience and endurance over long periods of rest. We are given no details about the wanderings and their duration, but we are told repeatedly, and in very definite terms, about the endurance shown by the Children

of Israel during long periods of rest. In Verse 17 we read, "Only when . . . did the sons of Yisrael journey forth"; they journeyed forth only after—not before—the cloud rose up. And in Verse 18, after we were already told before, "According to the utterance of God did the sons of Yisrael journey forth, and according to the utterance of God did they camp," the text repeats, "so long as the cloud rested . . . did they remain encamped." Finally, in Verse 19, the fact that Israel did not journey forth even when the cloud stood still for many days is described as a special observance of God's command, a special proof of Israel's obedience to Him.

It is clear, then, that particular stress is placed on Israel's endurance and patience. This is all the more understandable if one considers the inhospitability of the wilderness, and particularly the fact that the people were fully aware that the wilderness did not represent the end of their wanderings. They knew that their destination lay not in the wilderness but elsewhere. Therefore every stop they made in the wilderness, particularly the stop preceding the fateful decree that ordained for them forty years of wandering, served only to keep them away from what they knew to be their final destination. Herein lay the exercise in that virtue of quiet, serene resignation and trusting patience, which the nation guided by God was to need more than all else in its *galuth* wanderings through what the prophet calls "the wilderness of the nations," through so many centuries in the future, and concerning the purpose of which the prophet says so significantly, "although it tarry, wait for it" (Habbakuk 2:3).

ing to the utterance of *God* did they camp and according to the utterance of *God* did they journey forth; that which had been given to them by *God* to keep they kept, according to the utterance of *God* through Moshe.

X 1. *God* spoke to Moshe [saying]: 2. "Make yourself two silver trumpets, hammered of one piece shall you make them, and they shall serve you to call the community together and to cause the camps to journey forth. 3. When they will blow with them, the whole community shall be ordered to you to the entrance of the Tent of Appointed Meeting. 4. But if they blow [only] with one [of them], the princes will be ordered to you, the heads of the thousands of Yisrael. 5. And if you blow a *teruah*, the camps that camp to the east shall journey forth. 6. And if you blow a *teruah* a second time, the camps that camp to the south shall journey forth; they shall blow *teruah* for their journeyings forth. 7. When the assembly of the community is to be assembled, you shall blow, but do not blow a *teruah*. 8. Aharon's sons, the priests, shall blow with the trumpets; they shall remain for you an everlasting statute for your descendants. 9. And if you will come into war in your land against the oppressor that oppresses you, then you shall blow *teruoth* with the trumpets and you will be remembered before *God*, your God, and you will be delivered from your enemies. 10. And on the day of your rejoicing, and in your festive seasons, and at the beginning of your months you shall blow with the trumpets over your ascent offerings and

פִּי יְהֹוָה֙ יַחֲנ֔וּ וְעַל־פִּ֥י יְהֹוָ֖ה יִסָּ֑עוּ אֶת־מִשְׁמֶ֤רֶת יְהֹוָה֙ שָׁמָ֔רוּ עַל־פִּ֥י יְהֹוָ֖ה בְּיַד־מֹשֶֽׁה׃ פ י א וַיְדַבֵּ֥ר יְהֹוָ֖ה אֶל־מֹשֶׁ֥ה לֵּאמֹֽר׃ ב עֲשֵׂ֣ה לְךָ֗ שְׁתֵּי֙ חֲצֽוֹצְרֹ֣ת כֶּ֔סֶף מִקְשָׁ֖ה תַּעֲשֶׂ֣ה אֹתָ֑ם וְהָי֤וּ לְךָ֙ לְמִקְרָ֣א הָֽעֵדָ֔ה וּלְמַסַּ֖ע אֶת־הַֽמַּחֲנֽוֹת׃ ג וְתָקְע֖וּ בָּהֵ֑ן וְנֽוֹעֲד֤וּ אֵלֶ֨יךָ֙ כׇּל־הָ֣עֵדָ֔ה אֶל־פֶּ֖תַח אֹ֥הֶל מוֹעֵֽד׃ ד וְאִם־בְּאַחַ֖ת יִתְקָ֑עוּ וְנֽוֹעֲד֤וּ אֵלֶ֨יךָ֙ הַנְּשִׂיאִ֔ים רָאשֵׁ֖י אַלְפֵ֥י יִשְׂרָאֵֽל׃ ה וּתְקַעְתֶּ֖ם תְּרוּעָ֑ה וְנָֽסְעוּ֙ הַֽמַּחֲנ֔וֹת הַחֹנִ֖ים קֵֽדְמָה׃ ו וּתְקַעְתֶּ֤ם תְּרוּעָה֙ שֵׁנִ֔ית וְנָֽסְעוּ֙ הַֽמַּחֲנ֔וֹת הַחֹנִ֖ים תֵּימָ֑נָה תְּרוּעָ֥ה יִתְקְע֖וּ לְמַסְעֵיהֶֽם׃ ז וּבְהַקְהִ֖יל אֶת־הַקָּהָ֑ל תִּתְקְע֖וּ וְלֹ֥א תָרִֽיעוּ׃ ח וּבְנֵ֤י אַֽהֲרֹן֙ הַכֹּ֣הֲנִ֔ים יִתְקְע֖וּ בַּֽחֲצֹֽצְר֑וֹת וְהָי֥וּ לָכֶ֛ם לְחֻקַּ֥ת עוֹלָ֖ם לְדֹרֹֽתֵיכֶֽם׃ ט וְכִֽי־תָבֹ֨אוּ מִלְחָמָ֜ה בְּאַרְצְכֶ֗ם עַל־הַצַּר֙ הַצֹּרֵ֣ר אֶתְכֶ֔ם וַהֲרֵֽעֹתֶ֖ם בַּחֲצֹֽצְרֹ֑ת וְנִזְכַּרְתֶּ֗ם לִפְנֵי֙ יְהֹוָ֣ה אֱלֹֽהֵיכֶ֔ם וְנֽוֹשַׁעְתֶּ֖ם מֵאֹֽיְבֵיכֶֽם׃ י וּבְי֨וֹם שִׂמְחַתְכֶ֥ם וּֽבְמֽוֹעֲדֵיכֶם֮ וּבְרָאשֵׁ֣י חׇדְשֵׁיכֶם֒ וּתְקַעְתֶּ֣ם בַּחֲצֹֽצְרֹ֗ת עַ֚ל עֹלֹ֣תֵיכֶ֔ם וְעַ֖ל זִבְחֵ֣י

CHAPTER X

10. . . . Let us note at the outset that שִׂמְחָה need not necessarily denote a mood of elation set off by a happy event, but that it may be used just as well with reference to the inner mood of serenity and good cheer which should, in fact, be the keynote of our whole existence. Such passages as Psalms 4:8, 90:14, 97:11, 100:2 and 104:34; Ecclesiastes 3:12, 9:7 and 11:9; Proverbs 5:18, 13:9, 23:24 and 25, should be sufficient evidence of this.

And certainly this should apply to the nation as a whole, with which this text is concerned; the immortal nation that is to know neither death nor total destitu-

tion. . . . It should surely apply also to the Divine Dwelling Place of the Sanctuary of the Law, at whose threshold death and mourning must be left behind; where, beneath the bright light of God's Presence, only the joy of duty performed, only the serenity of rejoicing in God, born of a cheerful sense of duty, can flourish before God; where the concept that joy is in its true abode becomes reality and where everyone receives the call to "serve *God* with rejoicing." Here, any ordinary day could rightly be described as a day of rejoicing, so that this term is used in the present verse only in contrast to the day of oppression described in the preceding verse, which refers to the trouble and

שַׁלְמֵיכֶם וְהָיוּ לָכֶם לְזִכָּרוֹן לִפְנֵי אֱלֹהֵיכֶם אֲנִי
יְהֹוָה אֱלֹהֵיכֶם: פ חמישי יא וַיְהִי בַּשָּׁנָה הַשֵּׁנִית
בַּחֹדֶשׁ הַשֵּׁנִי בְּעֶשְׂרִים בַּחֹדֶשׁ נַעֲלָה הֶעָנָן מֵעַל
מִשְׁכַּן הָעֵדֻת: יב וַיִּסְעוּ בְנֵי־יִשְׂרָאֵל לְמַסְעֵיהֶם
מִמִּדְבַּר סִינָי וַיִּשְׁכֹּן הֶעָנָן בְּמִדְבַּר פָּארָן:
יג וַיִּסְעוּ בָּרִאשֹׁנָה עַל־פִּי יְהֹוָה בְּיַד־מֹשֶׁה:
יד וַיִּסַּע דֶּגֶל מַחֲנֵה בְנֵי־יְהוּדָה בָּרִאשֹׁנָה
לְצִבְאֹתָם וְעַל־צְבָאוֹ נַחְשׁוֹן בֶּן־עַמִּינָדָב:
טו וְעַל־צְבָא מַטֵּה בְּנֵי יִשָּׂשכָר נְתַנְאֵל בֶּן־
צוּעָר: טז וְעַל־צְבָא מַטֵּה בְּנֵי זְבוּלֻן אֱלִיאָב בֶּן־
חֵלֹן: יז וְהוּרַד הַמִּשְׁכָּן וְנָסְעוּ בְנֵי־גֵרְשׁוֹן וּבְנֵי

over your meal-of-peace offerings, and they
shall become for you a remembrance before
your God; I, *God*, your God." 11. It came
to pass in the second year, in the second
month, on the twentieth [day] of the month,
that the cloud rose from its dwelling over
the Dwelling Place of the Testimony.
12. Then the sons of Yisrael journeyed
forth upon their journeys out of the wilderness of Sinai, and the cloud came to rest in
the wilderness of Paran. 13. This was the
first time that they journeyed according to
the order imparted by *God* through Moshe.
14. The standard of the camp of the sons
of Yehudah journeyed forth first according
to their serving divisions, and over its division was Naḥshon, son of Amminadab.
15. And over the division of the tribe of
the sons of Yissakhar [was] Nethanel, son
of Tzuar. 16. And over the division of the
tribe of the sons of Zebulun [was] Eliab, son
of Ḥelon. 17. When the Dwelling Place

oppression that befall the nation because God has forsaken it. Hence the words, "on the day of your rejoicing," may very well refer to the continual offerings that are made every day, while the Sabbath offerings may be included in the "festive seasons." For particularly with regard to the special offerings characterizing that day, the שַׁבָּת is included in the general concept of מוֹעֵד, even as, according to Pesaḥim 77a, the concluding verse (39) of Numbers 29: "These you shall make to *God* at your seasons of appointed meeting" refers to all the communal offerings, the offerings for which a fixed day has been instituted, so that it would include also the additional offerings of the Sabbath. . . .

However, if, by virtue of our awareness of God that accompanies its every moment, any ordinary day not clouded by distinct sorrow becomes a day of rejoicing, then a day such as the Sabbath, dedicated exclusively to this same conception of God that infuses the breath of שִׂמְחָה also into the work and striving of all the other days of the week, should certainly be designated particularly and especially as *the* "day of our rejoicing." No matter what the state of mind in which the Sabbath may find us—be it in a mood of "full flowering," or in a "withered" state of sadness, or deep in contemplation, meditating upon the mysteries of life, "with the full sound and with the plaintive tone, in meditation upon the harp" (Psalm 92:4)—the thoughts bestirred by each Sabbath, namely, that we live and work in a world of God, together with other creatures of God, in the midst of all the other works of God, will always move us to exclaim, "Thou hast given me joy in Thy work, O *God*; I will exult in the work of Thy hands" (Psalm 92:4); or, in the words of our Sabbath prayer, יִשְׂמְחוּ בְמַלְכוּתְךָ שׁוֹמְרֵי שַׁבָּת ["Let those who keep the Sabbath rejoice in Thy kingdom"]. . . .

Thus, the Law means to tell us: On days of joyous God-awareness, at seasons when special memories invite us to communion with God, on days that summon us to renew ourselves, we are to express our joy of life and the consecration of our daily activities to strive after God's nearness. We are to do this symbolically by means of the ascent offerings, as in the continual daily offerings and additional offerings, and by means of the communal meal-of-peace offerings, as in the lambs offered on Shevuoth. On all these occasions we are to call upon God, by תְּקִיעָה [sounding the trumpets], to look down upon the pledges of our devotion in our search for the nearness of God bestirred by that particular season, calling Him to come near to us, even as we ourselves, heeding His call, strive after His nearness. Thus the sounding of the trumpets over the communal offerings is Israel's call to God to come to us. It expresses, literally, the concept of קָרְבָּן ["offering," lit., "bringing near"]; and our upward striving toward God, even as we call upon Him to descend to us, translates into reality that ideal which transforms these offerings into offerings for appointed seasons—the Sabbath offerings and the continual daily offerings are also מוֹעֲדִים—and thus into moments of union between Israel and God.

° ° °

was taken down, the sons of Gershon and the sons of Merari, the bearers of the Dwelling Place, journeyed forth.   18. Then the standard of the camp of Reuben journeyed forth according to their serving divisions, and over its division [was] Elitzur, son of Sh'deur.   19. And over the division of the tribe of the sons of Shimeon [was] Shelumiel, son of Tzurishaddai.   20. And over the division of the tribe of the sons of Gad [was] Eliassaph, son of Deuel. 21. Then the Kehathites, the bearers of the Sanctuary, journeyed forth first, so that the Dwelling Place would be set up by the time they arrived.   22. Thereafter the standard of the camp of Ephraim journeyed forth according to their serving divisions, and over its division [was] Elishama, son of Ammihud.   23. And over the division of the tribe of the sons of Menashe [was] Gamliel, son of Pedahtzur.   24. And over the division of the tribe of the sons of Binyamin [was] Abidan, son of Gideoni. 25. Then the standard of the camp of the sons of Dan journeyed forth, as the rear guard of all the camps according to their serving divisions, and over its division [was] Aḥiezer, son of Ammishaddai.   26. And over the division of the tribe of the sons of Asher [was] Pagiel, son of Okhran. 27. And over the division of the tribe of the sons of Naphtali [was] Aḥira, son of Enan.   28. Thus were the marching orders of the sons of Yisrael according to their serving divisions, and now they journeyed forth.   29. Moshe said to Ḥobab, son of Reuel the Midianite, father-in-law of Moshe: "We are journeying to the place of which *God* said: 'I will give it to you.' Please come with us and we will do good with you, for *God* has promised good concerning Yisrael."   30. Then he said to him: "I will not go; I will rather go to my [own] land and to my birthplace." 31. But he said: "Please do not leave us! For I am asking this because you are familiar with the places of our camping in the wilderness and you can serve us as eyes. 32. If you go with us, it shall be that the same good that *God* in His goodness will do for us, we will do for you."   33. So they journeyed forth from the mountain of *God* a journey of three days, and the Ark of the

מְרָרִי נֹשְׂאֵי הַמִּשְׁכָּן: יח וְנָסַע דֶּגֶל מַחֲנֵה רְאוּבֵן לְצִבְאֹתָם וְעַל־צְבָאוֹ אֱלִיצוּר בֶּן־ שְׁדֵיאוּר: יט וְעַל־צְבָא מַטֵּה בְּנֵי שִׁמְעוֹן שְׁלֻמִיאֵל בֶּן־צוּרִישַׁדָּי: כ וְעַל־צְבָא מַטֵּה בְּנֵי־ גָד אֶלְיָסָף בֶּן־דְּעוּאֵל: כא וְנָסְעוּ הַקְּהָתִים נֹשְׂאֵי הַמִּקְדָּשׁ וְהֵקִימוּ אֶת־הַמִּשְׁכָּן עַד־בֹּאָם: כב וְנָסַע דֶּגֶל מַחֲנֵה בְנֵי־אֶפְרַיִם לְצִבְאֹתָם וְעַל־ צְבָאוֹ אֱלִישָׁמָע בֶּן־עַמִּיהוּד: כג וְעַל־צְבָא מַטֵּה בְּנֵי מְנַשֶּׁה גַּמְלִיאֵל בֶּן־פְּדָהצוּר: כד וְעַל־צְבָא מַטֵּה בְּנֵי בִנְיָמִן אֲבִידָן בֶּן־גִּדְעוֹנִי: כה וְנָסַע דֶּגֶל מַחֲנֵה בְנֵי־דָן מְאַסֵּף לְכָל־הַמַּחֲנֹת לְצִבְאֹתָם וְעַל־צְבָאוֹ אֲחִיעֶזֶר בֶּן־עַמִּישַׁדָּי: כו וְעַל־צְבָא מַטֵּה בְּנֵי אָשֵׁר פַּגְעִיאֵל בֶּן־עָכְרָן: כז וְעַל־צְבָא מַטֵּה בְּנֵי נַפְתָּלִי אֲחִירַע בֶּן־עֵינָן: כח אֵלֶּה מַסְעֵי בְנֵי־יִשְׂרָאֵל לְצִבְאֹתָם וַיִּסָּעוּ: ס כט וַיֹּאמֶר מֹשֶׁה לְחֹבָב בֶּן־רְעוּאֵל הַמִּדְיָנִי חֹתֵן מֹשֶׁה נֹסְעִים ׀ אֲנַחְנוּ אֶל־הַמָּקוֹם אֲשֶׁר אָמַר יְהוָה אֹתוֹ אֶתֵּן לָכֶם לְכָה אִתָּנוּ וְהֵטַבְנוּ לָךְ כִּי־ יְהוָה דִּבֶּר־טוֹב עַל־יִשְׂרָאֵל: ל וַיֹּאמֶר אֵלָיו לֹא אֵלֵךְ כִּי אִם־אֶל־אַרְצִי וְאֶל־מוֹלַדְתִּי אֵלֵךְ: לא וַיֹּאמֶר אַל־נָא תַּעֲזֹב אֹתָנוּ כִּי ׀ עַל־כֵּן יָדַעְתָּ חֲנֹתֵנוּ בַּמִּדְבָּר וְהָיִיתָ לָּנוּ לְעֵינָיִם: לב וְהָיָה כִּי־ תֵלֵךְ עִמָּנוּ וְהָיָה ׀ הַטּוֹב הַהוּא אֲשֶׁר יֵיטִיב יְהוָה עִמָּנוּ וְהֵטַבְנוּ לָךְ: לג וַיִּסְעוּ מֵהַר יְהוָה דֶּרֶךְ שְׁלֹשֶׁת יָמִים וַאֲרוֹן בְּרִית־יְהוָה נֹסֵעַ

Covenant of *God* traveled ahead of them a three days' journey to seek out rest for them.
34. And the cloud of *God* was over them by day when they journeyed forth from the camp.
35. It came to pass when the Ark journeyed forth that Moshe said: "Arise, O *God,* so that Thine enemies may be scattered and those that hate Thee flee from before Thy Countenance."
36. And when it gently came to rest, he said: "Return, O

לִפְנֵיהֶם דֶּרֶךְ שְׁלֹשֶׁת יָמִים לָתוּר לָהֶם מְנוּחָה׃
לד וַעֲנַן יְהוָה עֲלֵיהֶם יוֹמָם בְּנָסְעָם מִן־
הַמַּחֲנֶה׃ ס ששי ׆ לה וַיְהִי בִּנְסֹעַ הָאָרֹן וַיֹּאמֶר
מֹשֶׁה קוּמָה ׀ יְהוָה וְיָפֻצוּ אֹיְבֶיךָ וְיָנֻסוּ
מְשַׂנְאֶיךָ מִפָּנֶיךָ׃ לו וּבְנֻחֹה יֹאמַר שׁוּבָה יְהוָה

33. . . . Throughout this three-day journey they saw before their eyes the Ark of God's Covenant, traveling ahead of them and seeking out for them, as it were, an appropriate resting place. This constant sight certainly could maintain in them the cheerfulness and good courage that comes from the awareness that one is walking in the ways of God, even as the cloud of God that hovered above them and moved with them when they journeyed forth could assure them of God's constant protection on their way.

35–36. ***It came to pass when the Ark journeyed forth.*** We have already noted by way of an introduction in our commentary on Chapter 8, Verse 1, that this portion resumes, and continues, the history of the people of Israel, the narrative that was interrupted to relate Israel's sin with the golden calf and the renewal of Israel's covenantal relationship with God, in the thirty-fourth chapter of Exodus. If that nation had already attained the lofty level required for the realization of the ideals inherent in the Law whose promulgation had now been completed at Mount Sinai, all of its subsequent history would have been completely different, and less complicated. Israel's path away from the mountain of God would then have led it directly into the Land of God. Israel's faithful observance of this Law in the Land would then have elevated the Jewish Sanctuary of the Law and the Jewish people of the Law to become a light of God, sending its rays far out among the nations of the world—a destiny which at present beckons to us only from the distant end of days. In that case, like Israel's history, so, too, the history of all mankind would have taken a different course.

However, the nation had not yet reached the lofty level of its calling. In the very next verse we will be taken into the midst of Israel's camp and shown a series of aberrations that eventually stamped that entire generation as unworthy of entering the Land of the Law. We are shown that, as a result, the promised gift of the Land to Israel as a permanent possession had to be deferred for centuries, that Israel would have to undergo a history of training for its vocation (Psalm 126:27), and that even this process of training in the Land could not begin before all that generation had died out and a new generation had grown up.

Consequently, Verse 34 marks one of the most significant phases, a true turning point, in Jewish history, so much so, that this thirty-fourth verse of Chapter 10 is regarded as the concluding verse of one book. Chapter 11, which follows, is considered the beginning of a new book, with the two verses—35 and 36 of Chapter 10—in between interpreted as comprising an important book by themselves. That is the reason, also, why these two verses are placed in the text within two inverted letters *nun*, corresponding, perhaps, to brackets in modern usage. Hence, there are, in fact, not five Books of Moses—but seven (Shabbath 115b and 116a and Mishnah Yadayim III).

The text reads: "When the Ark journeyed forth . . . Moshe said: 'Arise,'" etc., and "when it gently came to rest, he said: 'Return,'" etc. When the Ark journeyed forth, Moses invited it, as it were, to journey forth, and when it came to rest, he called upon it to come to rest. Now we know that when the Ark journeyed forth, and also when it came to rest, it did not act at the behest of Moses. Yet, Moses accompanied both processes with an express invitation from himself, as if what had already come to pass had, in fact, not yet occurred. Obviously, then, Moses' invitation is an expression of the highest, fullest, most perfect and joyous acquiescence in the will of God, in which every decree of God's will is welcomed as if it were one's own. It is the most splendid manifestation of Rabban Gamliel's adage, "Do His will as if it were your own" (Aboth II:4). Here, too, the implication is that Moses' will was in perfect harmony with the will of God. This utterly selfless acquiescence in, and self-identification with, the will of God, stands in the crassest contrast to the mood and the attitude that still characterized Moses' contemporaries, as will be shown by the events about to be related. It represents that height of complete moral and spiritual permeation with God-awareness [which characterized Moses but] which will not characterize the nation as a whole until the end of days, and on which depends the attainment of the goal of all history, an objective for which Israel and its Law are to lay the groundwork.

God, to the myriads of the thousands of Yisrael."

XI 1. But the people were as if in mourning over themselves; they were evil in the ears of *God*. *God* heard it, His anger was kindled and *God*'s fire broke out against them and devoured at one edge of the camp. 2. And the people cried out to Moshe; Moshe prayed to *God* and the fire died down. 3. He called the name of that place Taberah because the fire of *God* had broken out against them. 4. But the rabble whom they had taken up into their midst had worked themselves into a lust and then the sons of Yisrael, too, began to weep again and said: "Would that someone gave us meat to eat! 5. We still remember the fish we used to eat in Mitzrayim at no cost; the cucumbers and the melons, the leeks and the onions and the garlic, 6. and now our soul is dried out, without anything; we have nothing except this *manna* before our eyes." 7. And yet the *manna* was like the seed of *gad* and its luster was as the appearance of crystal! 8. The people roamed about and gathered [it], and they ground it in mills and crushed it in mortars; they cooked it in a pot or made it into cakes, and its taste was like that of an oil-cake. 9. When the dew fell upon the camp during the night, the *manna* fell upon it. 10. Moshe heard the people weeping within their families, each one at the entrance of his tent. *God*'s wrath was

רְבֲב֖וֹת אַלְפֵ֥י יִשְׂרָאֵֽל׃ ׆ פ יא א וַיְהִ֤י הָעָם֙
כְּמִתְאֹ֣נְנִ֔ים רַ֖ע בְּאָזְנֵ֣י יְהֹוָ֑ה וַיִּשְׁמַ֤ע יְהֹוָה֙ וַיִּ֣חַר
אַפּ֔וֹ וַתִּבְעַר־בָּם֙ אֵ֣שׁ יְהֹוָ֔ה וַתֹּ֖אכַל בִּקְצֵ֥ה
הַֽמַּחֲנֶֽה׃ ב וַיִּצְעַ֥ק הָעָ֖ם אֶל־מֹשֶׁ֑ה וַיִּתְפַּלֵּ֤ל מֹשֶׁה֙
אֶל־יְהֹוָ֔ה וַתִּשְׁקַ֖ע הָאֵֽשׁ׃ ג וַיִּקְרָ֛א שֵֽׁם־הַמָּק֥וֹם
הַה֖וּא תַּבְעֵרָ֑ה כִּֽי־בָעֲרָ֥ה בָ֖ם אֵ֥שׁ יְהֹוָֽה׃
ד וְהָֽאסַפְסֻף֙ אֲשֶׁ֣ר בְּקִרְבּ֔וֹ הִתְאַוּ֖וּ תַּאֲוָ֑ה וַיָּשֻׁ֣בוּ
וַיִּבְכּ֗וּ גַּ֚ם בְּנֵ֣י יִשְׂרָאֵ֔ל וַיֹּ֣אמְר֔וּ מִ֥י יַאֲכִלֵ֖נוּ בָּשָֽׂר׃
ה זָכַ֙רְנוּ֙ אֶת־הַדָּגָ֔ה אֲשֶׁר־נֹאכַ֥ל בְּמִצְרַ֖יִם חִנָּ֑ם
אֵ֣ת הַקִּשֻּׁאִ֗ים וְאֵת֙ הָֽאֲבַטִּחִ֔ים וְאֶת־הֶחָצִ֥יר
וְאֶת־הַבְּצָלִ֖ים וְאֶת־הַשּׁוּמִֽים׃ ו וְעַתָּ֛ה נַפְשֵׁ֥נוּ
יְבֵשָׁ֖ה אֵ֣ין כֹּ֑ל בִּלְתִּ֖י אֶל־הַמָּ֥ן עֵינֵֽינוּ׃ ז וְהַמָּ֕ן
כִּזְרַע־גַּ֖ד ה֑וּא וְעֵינ֖וֹ כְּעֵ֥ין הַבְּדֹֽלַח׃ ח שָׁ֩טוּ֩ הָעָ֨ם
וְלָֽקְט֜וּ וְטָחֲנ֣וּ בָרֵחַ֗יִם א֤וֹ דָכוּ֙ בַּמְּדֹכָ֔ה וּבִשְּׁלוּ֙
בַּפָּר֔וּר וְעָשׂ֥וּ אֹת֖וֹ עֻג֑וֹת וְהָיָ֣ה טַעְמ֔וֹ כְּטַ֖עַם
לְשַׁ֥ד הַשָּֽׁמֶן׃ ט וּבְרֶ֧דֶת הַטַּ֛ל עַל־הַֽמַּחֲנֶ֖ה לָ֑יְלָה
יֵרֵ֥ד הַמָּ֖ן עָלָֽיו׃ י וַיִּשְׁמַ֨ע מֹשֶׁ֜ה אֶת־הָעָ֗ם בֹּכֶה֙
לְמִשְׁפְּחֹתָ֔יו אִ֖ישׁ לְפֶ֣תַח אָהֳל֑וֹ וַיִּֽחַר־אַ֤ף יְהֹוָה֙

The lack of this quality in the nation brought about the great turning point in Israel's history that suggests that these particular words of Moses, set down for us here in writing, were intended to be a dividing interpolation between two distinct books of Jewish history.

° ° °

CHAPTER XI

1. Even when the dispensations of Divine Providence led through wilderness and wastelands, Moses cheerfully accepted them, then and for all time to come, with utterly selfless devotion, gladly merging his own will with that of God. By so doing, he demonstrated that God-pervaded attitude and philosophy of life which should have been common to all the members of the nation. However, that nation was still far removed from such a state of spiritual and moral perfection. In contrast to Moses, the people were "as if in mourning over themselves." The people behaved as if they had gone into mourning over themselves. The cloud of God above them and the Ark of God's Covenant traveling before them only made them feel utterly cut off from the rest of the world, its manifestations and its conditions of life. They did not consider themselves adequately compensated for [this supposed isolation] by the unique bond that tied them to God, by the nearness of God, by the presence of the Sanctuary of God in their midst, by their Divine calling and by their Divinely-promised destiny, toward which they were moving. All these values were still worthless and meaningless in Israel's eyes. The people did not yet see them as symbols of a much loftier, happier mode of life. And so the people felt as if they had been buried alive and they mourned over themselves. . . .

kindled greatly, and it was evil in the eyes of
Moshe. 11. And Moshe said to *God*:
"Why hast Thou ordered such evil for Thy
servant—and why have I not found favor in
Thine eyes—to place the burden of this
entire people upon me? 12. Have I been
pregnant with this entire people, or have I
begotten them, that Thou shouldst say to
me: Carry them in your bosom, as a male
nurse carries the suckling infant, up to the
land that Thou hast sworn to their ancestors? 13. From where should I have meat
to give to all this people? For they weep to
me and say: 'Please give us meat so that we
may eat.' 14. I am not able to carry this
entire people because it is too heavy for me.
15. And if Thou wilt deal with me in this
manner, withdrawing from me, then rather
let me die at once, if I have found favor in
Thine eyes, and do not let me see my misfortune." 16. And *God* said to Moshe:

מְאֹד וּבְעֵינֵי מֹשֶׁה רָע: יא וַיֹּאמֶר מֹשֶׁה אֶל־
יְהֹוָה לָמָה הֲרֵעֹתָ לְעַבְדֶּךָ וְלָמָּה לֹא־מָצָתִי חֵן
בְּעֵינֶיךָ לָשׂוּם אֶת־מַשָּׂא כָּל־הָעָם הַזֶּה עָלָי:
יב הֶאָנֹכִי הָרִיתִי אֵת כָּל־הָעָם הַזֶּה אִם־אָנֹכִי
יְלִדְתִּיהוּ כִּי־תֹאמַר אֵלַי שָׂאֵהוּ בְחֵיקֶךָ כַּאֲשֶׁר
יִשָּׂא הָאֹמֵן אֶת־הַיֹּנֵק עַל הָאֲדָמָה אֲשֶׁר
נִשְׁבַּעְתָּ לַאֲבֹתָיו: יג מֵאַיִן לִי בָּשָׂר לָתֵת לְכָל־
הָעָם הַזֶּה כִּי־יִבְכּוּ עָלַי לֵאמֹר תְּנָה־לָּנוּ בָשָׂר
וְנֹאכֵלָה: יד לֹא־אוּכַל אָנֹכִי לְבַדִּי לָשֵׂאת אֶת־
כָּל־הָעָם הַזֶּה כִּי כָבֵד מִמֶּנִּי: טו וְאִם־כָּכָה ׀
אַתְּ־עֹשֶׂה לִּי הָרְגֵנִי נָא הָרֹג אִם־מָצָאתִי חֵן
בְּעֵינֶיךָ וְאַל־אֶרְאֶה בְּרָעָתִי: פ טז וַיֹּאמֶר יְהֹוָה

---

10. and it was evil in the eyes of Moshe. To Moses
this was an indication that his mission had been a complete failure. He had been sent to win this nation for
the supreme ideal of moral and spiritual perfection, and
here they were, crying because they had to do without leeks and onions!

11. לָמָה הֲרֵעֹתָ *[Why hast Thou ordered such evil]*.
From the very outset I felt that I was not adequate to
this mission. Now this mission has become my misfortune. Yet, I would gladly bear it if I could see that
others would derive some benefit from it. But it seems
that the entire people will perish on account of my
ineptitude, and so all my sufferings have gone for nothing. . . . I urgently requested the favor not to be
entrusted with this lofty mission because I did not feel
capable of carrying it out. Should not my own misgivings about my talents have been sufficient reason for
Thee to grant my request? Is not confidence in one's
own abilities the first prerequisite for the mission
of leading a nation, and was not, therefore, my lack of
confidence in my own skills sufficient proof that I am
truly not fit for this task? Why, then, hast Thou refused
my request? . . .

12. Have I been pregnant. If a father and mother
are not adequate to the task of educating their children,
it is a misfortune for the parents as well as for the children. But that would be one of the natural concomi-
tants of parenthood. . . . Besides, the biological bond
between parent and child engenders in the child a
natural love, respect and trust for his parents, which

will make the parents' task of educating him considerably easier. But I am not the natural educator of this
people. It was Thou Who didst choose me to be their
educator, and, alas, Thy choice fell on a man who has
neither the eloquence, nor the imposing personality,
nor any of the other skills needed to influence and to
win the respect of a whole nation.

13. From where should I have meat. They know
very well that they are asking me for something quite
beyond my power to give them. . . . Their demands
have no other purpose but to torment the man whom
they regard as the guide of their destinies. Had he been
the right man for the task, he would long ago have won
from them such love and respect that they would never
have permitted themselves to victimize him with such
cravings.

        ◦   ◦   ◦

14. I am not able. I cannot carry out by myself
the task Thou hast assigned to me. I lack not only the
required ability to influence others but even the skill to
acquire this ability. I am only half the right man for this
task. I can receive Thy Law, and I can teach it to others,
but I am not capable of training for Thee a people to
observe this Law. I cannot function as a master over the
spirit of this people, to mold and educate it in a manner
conducive to this end (Cf. Exodus 3:11).

16. from among the elders of Yisrael. Even before
that time, indeed, from the very beginnings of Israel's
history as a nation, Israel had זְקֵנִים, "elders," who had

אֶל־מֹשֶׁה אֶסְפָה־לִּי שִׁבְעִים אִישׁ מִזִּקְנֵי
יִשְׂרָאֵל אֲשֶׁר יָדַעְתָּ כִּי־הֵם זִקְנֵי הָעָם וְשֹׁטְרָיו
וְלָקַחְתָּ אֹתָם אֶל־אֹהֶל מוֹעֵד וְהִתְיַצְּבוּ שָׁם
עִמָּךְ׃ יז וְיָרַדְתִּי וְדִבַּרְתִּי עִמְּךָ שָׁם וְאָצַלְתִּי מִן־
הָרוּחַ אֲשֶׁר עָלֶיךָ וְשַׂמְתִּי עֲלֵיהֶם וְנָשְׂאוּ אִתְּךָ
בְּמַשָּׂא הָעָם וְלֹא־תִשָּׂא אַתָּה לְבַדֶּךָ׃ יח וְאֶל־
הָעָם תֹּאמַר הִתְקַדְּשׁוּ לְמָחָר וַאֲכַלְתֶּם בָּשָׂר כִּי
בְּכִיתֶם בְּאָזְנֵי יְהוָה לֵאמֹר מִי יַאֲכִלֵנוּ בָּשָׂר
כִּי־טוֹב לָנוּ בְּמִצְרָיִם וְנָתַן יְהוָה לָכֶם בָּשָׂר
וַאֲכַלְתֶּם׃ יט לֹא יוֹם אֶחָד תֹּאכְלוּן וְלֹא יוֹמָיִם
וְלֹא ׀ חֲמִשָּׁה יָמִים וְלֹא עֲשָׂרָה יָמִים וְלֹא
עֶשְׂרִים יוֹם׃ כ עַד ׀ חֹדֶשׁ יָמִים עַד אֲשֶׁר־יֵצֵא
מֵאַפְּכֶם וְהָיָה לָכֶם לְזָרָא יַעַן כִּי־מְאַסְתֶּם אֶת־
יְהוָה אֲשֶׁר בְּקִרְבְּכֶם וַתִּבְכּוּ לְפָנָיו לֵאמֹר לָמָּה
זֶּה יָצָאנוּ מִמִּצְרָיִם׃ כא וַיֹּאמֶר מֹשֶׁה שֵׁשׁ־
מֵאוֹת אֶלֶף רַגְלִי הָעָם אֲשֶׁר אָנֹכִי בְּקִרְבּוֹ
וְאַתָּה אָמַרְתָּ בָּשָׂר אֶתֵּן לָהֶם וְאָכְלוּ חֹדֶשׁ
יָמִים׃ כב הֲצֹאן וּבָקָר יִשָּׁחֵט לָהֶם וּמָצָא לָהֶם
אִם אֶת־כָּל־דְּגֵי הַיָּם יֵאָסֵף לָהֶם וּמָצָא לָהֶם׃ פ
כג וַיֹּאמֶר יְהוָה אֶל־מֹשֶׁה הֲיַד יְהוָה תִּקְצָר

"Gather for Me seventy men from among the elders of Yisrael [of] whom you know that they are the elders of the people and its overseers, and take them to the Tent of Appointed Meeting and have them stand there with you.
17. I will descend and will speak with you there and will keep back [part] of the spirit that has come upon you and put it upon them. They will then bear the burden of the people with you and you will not have to bear it alone.
18. And to the people you shall say: Hold yourselves in readiness for tomorrow, and you shall eat meat, for you have wept before the ears of *God* and said: Would that someone gave us meat to eat! For we were better off in Mitzrayim. Therefore *God* will give you meat to eat.
19. You shall have [meat] to eat not for one day and not for two days, not for five days and not for ten days and not for twenty days;
20. until a full month, until it comes out of your nostrils and will make you nauseated, because you have rejected *God,* Who dwells in your midst, and have wept before Him, saying: Why did we ever go out from Mitzrayim?"
21. Then Moshe said: "The people in whose midst I am are six times one hundred thousand men on foot, and Thou sayest I shall give them meat so that they may have to eat for a whole month!
22. Shall sheep and cattle be slaughtered for them so that it may be enough for them, or shall all the fish of the sea be gathered so that it may be enough for them?"
23. And *God* said to Moshe: "Will the hand of *God* not suffice?

occupied a position of prominence and authority among the people (see Exodus 3:16 and the chapter following, and Leviticus 9:1). As we shall now learn, they even performed an official function: these elders acted as "overseers" to monitor the conduct of the people. As a result of the natural, spontaneous trust the people had come to have in them, the elders even then were able to exert considerable influence upon the people. Their position was similar to that of fathers and mothers, a position that Moses complained (Verse 12) he lacked. Of these individuals, seventy were now to be chosen to collaborate with Moses in his educational endeavors; this assignment is to be conferred upon them publicly by God Himself.

° ° °

23. . . . Note that the appointment of the seventy elders to assist Moses in leading the nation constituted the basis for the future Sanhedrin (Sanhedrin 2a and 16b); which, through all the centuries of the most varied dispensations of God, was to lead the people and to act as the messenger of God's word long after Moses had departed this world, when there would be no more obvious miracles from Divine Providence to support the realization of God's word.

In light of the foregoing, it can be seen that the nature of the event about to be narrated, the fact that Moses himself did not expect it to happen when he was about to address the people, and the fact that it occurred within the framework of natural conditions (only now these conditions had been channeled by God

You shall see at once whether My word will come to pass for you or not." 24. Moshe went out and told the words of *God* to the people. He then gathered seventy men from among the elders of the people and had them stand round about the Tent. 25. And *God* descended in the cloud and spoke with him and held back some of the spirit that came upon him and placed a shadow of it upon the seventy men [who had been] appointed as elders. And it came to pass that when the spirit had come to rest upon them, they uttered words of prophecy such as they never did again. 26. But two men remained behind in the camp; the name of the one [was] Eldad and the name of the second, Medad; the spirit came to rest also upon them. They were among those who had been registered but they had not gone out to the Tent. They uttered words of prophecy in the camp. 27. And the lad ran and reported it to Moshe and said: "Eldad and Medad are uttering words of prophecy in the camp." 28. And Yehoshua, son of Nun, the attendant of Moshe from his youth, replied and said: "My lord Moshe, restrain them." 29. And Moshe

עַתָּה תִרְאֶה הֲיִקְרְךָ דְבָרִי אִם־לֹא: כד וַיֵּצֵא
מֹשֶׁה וַיְדַבֵּר אֶל־הָעָם אֵת דִּבְרֵי יְהֹוָה וַיֶּאֱסֹף
שִׁבְעִים אִישׁ מִזִּקְנֵי הָעָם וַיַּעֲמֵד אֹתָם סְבִיבֹת
הָאֹהֶל: כה וַיֵּרֶד יְהֹוָה ׀ בֶּעָנָן וַיְדַבֵּר אֵלָיו וַיָּאצֶל
מִן־הָרוּחַ אֲשֶׁר עָלָיו וַיִּתֵּן עַל־שִׁבְעִים אִישׁ
הַזְּקֵנִים וַיְהִי כְּנוֹחַ עֲלֵיהֶם הָרוּחַ וַיִּתְנַבְּאוּ וְלֹא
יָסָפוּ: כו וַיִּשָּׁאֲרוּ שְׁנֵי־אֲנָשִׁים ׀ בַּמַּחֲנֶה שֵׁם
הָאֶחָד ׀ אֶלְדָּד וְשֵׁם הַשֵּׁנִי מֵידָד וַתָּנַח עֲלֵהֶם
הָרוּחַ וְהֵמָּה בַּכְּתֻבִים וְלֹא יָצְאוּ הָאֹהֱלָה
וַיִּתְנַבְּאוּ בַּמַּחֲנֶה: כז וַיָּרָץ הַנַּעַר וַיַּגֵּד לְמֹשֶׁה
וַיֹּאמַר אֶלְדָּד וּמֵידָד מִתְנַבְּאִים בַּמַּחֲנֶה:
כח וַיַּעַן יְהוֹשֻׁעַ בִּן־נוּן מְשָׁרֵת מֹשֶׁה מִבְּחֻרָיו
וַיֹּאמַר אֲדֹנִי מֹשֶׁה כְּלָאֵם: כט וַיֹּאמֶר לוֹ מֹשֶׁה

toward the fulfillment of His purposes), all were closely related to the appointment of the elders. The circumstances that surrounded this event will also explain why the appointment of the elders had to precede it, when, in fact, the event was intended only to satisfy an immediate, temporary need. Whenever, in years to come, they would have to champion the Word of God under circumstances that, in human reckoning, did not seem to favor the realization of the Word they championed, the future זְקֵנִים [elders] of the Jewish people would be able to look back for moral support upon that initial moment, upon the events surrounding the appointment of the very first זְקֵנִים [elders] of the Jewish people. These historic memories should always serve to reassure these men that, as long as the message they represent and convey is indeed the Word of God, then, even if the heavens do not literally descend upon the earth, they can safely entrust themselves to the unseen Providence of God, Who knows how to arrange circumstances even within the framework of natural causality (though this may be beyond the understanding of human shortsightedness) in order to promote the realization of His Word. The very first event in which they were asked to participate gave our זְקֵנִים a firm foundation of confidence for all their future endeavors.

25. *And* God *descended . . . and spoke with him.* The text does not tell us the words that God uttered to Moses on this occasion. Was this omission, perhaps, intended to make clear to all future Sanhedrins that not everything God said to Moses is recorded in Scripture? Was this meant to remind them that the field of competence for which they had been appointed at that moment was the Oral Law, that Word of God which was to remain unwritten, handed down only by word of mouth? . . .

such as they never did again. Only at this moment of their appointment were they found worthy of a portion of the Divine spirit that had come upon Moses. To prove that they had indeed been called to their function, they were permitted at this moment to be one with Moses and thus to regard every word addressed by God to Moses as addressed to them also, and their task would be to see that it is carried out.

28. *My lord Moshe, restrain them.* Joshua regarded the behavior of Eldad and Medad as an infringement on the authority of Moses, as a violation of his prerogatives. The chosen elders had been granted a portion of the spirit of prophecy only from the spirit that rested upon Moses, but Eldad and Medad had come forward on their own initiative.

said to him: "Are you jealous for my sake? Would that the entire people of *God* were prophets, so that *God* would place His spirit upon them." 30. And Moshe withdrew into the camp, he and the elders of Yisrael. 31. But a wind went forth from *God* and drove quails up from the sea and let them down upon the camp, [the distance of] about one day's journey in one direction and one day's journey in the other direction round about the camp, and about two cubits above the ground. 32. And the people arose all that day and all the night and all the next day, and they gathered the quails. The one who had gathered the least gathered ten *homers* and they spread them out round about the camp. 34. The meat was still between their teeth, not yet chewed, and the anger of *God* broke out against the people, and *God* struck the people a heavy blow. 34. He called the name of this place [Kibroth Hataavah] Graves of Lust, for there they had buried the people who had lusted. 35. From the Graves of Lust the people journeyed to Ḥatzeroth, and they stayed at Ḥatzeroth.

XII 1. And Miriam and Aharon spoke against Moshe regarding the "dark-skinned woman" whom he had married, for he had [indeed] married a "dark-skinned woman." 2. They said: "Has *God* indeed spoken only with Moshe? Has He not also spoken to us?" And *God*

הַמְקַנֵּא אַתָּה לִי וּמִי יִתֵּן כָּל־עַם יְהֹוָה נְבִיאִים כִּי־יִתֵּן יְהֹוָה אֶת־רוּחוֹ עֲלֵיהֶם: שביעי ל וַיֵּאָסֵף מֹשֶׁה אֶל־הַמַּחֲנֶה הוּא וְזִקְנֵי יִשְׂרָאֵל: לא וְרוּחַ נָסַע ׀ מֵאֵת יְהֹוָה וַיָּגָז שַׂלְוִים מִן־הַיָּם וַיִּטֹּשׁ עַל־הַמַּחֲנֶה כְּדֶרֶךְ יוֹם כֹּה וּכְדֶרֶךְ יוֹם כֹּה סְבִיבוֹת הַמַּחֲנֶה וּכְאַמָּתַיִם עַל־פְּנֵי הָאָרֶץ: לב וַיָּקָם הָעָם כָּל־הַיּוֹם הַהוּא וְכָל־הַלַּיְלָה וְכֹל ׀ יוֹם הַמׇּחֳרָת וַיַּאַסְפוּ אֶת־הַשְּׂלָו הַמַּמְעִיט אָסַף עֲשָׂרָה חֳמָרִים וַיִּשְׁטְחוּ לָהֶם שָׁטוֹחַ סְבִיבוֹת הַמַּחֲנֶה: לג הַבָּשָׂר עוֹדֶנּוּ בֵּין שִׁנֵּיהֶם טֶרֶם יִכָּרֵת וְאַף יְהֹוָה חָרָה בָעָם וַיַּךְ יְהֹוָה בָּעָם מַכָּה רַבָּה מְאֹד: לד וַיִּקְרָא אֶת־שֵׁם־הַמָּקוֹם הַהוּא קִבְרוֹת הַתַּאֲוָה כִּי־שָׁם קָבְרוּ אֶת־הָעָם הַמִּתְאַוִּים: לה מִקִּבְרוֹת הַתַּאֲוָה נָסְעוּ הָעָם חֲצֵרוֹת וַיִּהְיוּ בַּחֲצֵרוֹת: פ יב א וַתְּדַבֵּר מִרְיָם וְאַהֲרֹן בְּמֹשֶׁה עַל־אֹדוֹת הָאִשָּׁה הַכֻּשִׁית אֲשֶׁר לָקָח כִּי־אִשָּׁה כֻשִׁית לָקָח: ב וַיֹּאמְרוּ הֲרַק אַךְ־בְּמֹשֶׁה דִּבֶּר יְהֹוָה הֲלֹא גַּם־בָּנוּ דִבֵּר וַיִּשְׁמַע

29. *Are you jealous for my sake?* Do you feel that you must speak up for my rights? Do you think that the behavior of Eldad and Medad infringes on my authority so that you feel you must defend my rights? . . .

The conduct of Eldad and Medad at the moment the elders were chosen to serve as the first Sanhedrin, and Moses' remarks on that occasion, are of profound significance for all the successors of this Jewish "Assembly of Elders" for all time to come. We are shown here that the appointment of certain individuals to act as the supreme spiritual authority in Israel did not imply that one group of individuals had obtained a spiritual monopoly in Israel. Moreover, we see that endowment with the Divine spirit is not dependent on any special "office" or "vocation." The humblest in the nation may be deemed just as worthy of a portion of the Divine spirit as the foremost holder of the most exalted office.

At the same time, Moses' reply to Joshua will always serve to remind all those who will ever be called to act as guides and teachers in Israel that the ideal goal of their endeavors must be to render their own services superfluous. All the classes of the nation must attain such a lofty spiritual level that teachers and guides will no longer be needed. And indeed, the spiritual heirs of these "elders" have been true inheritors of the spirit of Moses: they have understood that their supreme task is to spread the Torah in Israel, to construct the broadest possible foundation among the people for an understanding of God's Law, and they have proclaimed the command "raise up many disciples" (Aboth 1:1) as the first maxim to be followed by all future spiritual leaders of their people. With his words "Are you jealous for my sake?" our own Moses effectively eliminated the foundations for a division between "clergy" and "laity" among true Israelites for all time to come. . . .

heard it. 3. And the man Moshe was extremely humble, more than all the men who live on the face of the earth. 4. And *God* suddenly said to Moshe, to Aharon and to Miriam: "Go out, all three of you, to the Tent of Appointed Meeting." All three of them went out. 5. Then *God* descended in a pillar of cloud and He stood at the entrance of the Tent. He called Aharon and Miriam, and both of them went out. 6. He said: "Hear, now, My words; if he were your prophet, then *God*—I—would make Myself known to him in a vision; I would speak to him in a dream. 7. Not so is My servant Moshe; he is trusted in all My house. 8. Mouth to mouth do I speak with him, in a vision and not in riddles, and he beholds the image of *God*; why, then, were you not afraid to speak against My servant, against Moshe?" 9. The anger of *God* was kindled against them and He went. 10. But when the cloud had departed from the Tent, Miriam was leprous as snow. And Aharon turned to Miriam and lo! she was a leper. 11. And Aharon said to Moshe: "O my lord, do not count it as a grave sin against us what we have done thoughtlessly and what we have sinned. 12. Let her not remain like a corpse! For since she came forth from your mother's womb, it would be [as if] half of your [own] flesh had been consumed." 13. And Moshe cried to *God*: "O God! Do heal her, I beseech Thee!" 14. And *God* said to Moshe: "If her father had spat in her presence, would she not have been ashamed for seven days? Let her be confined outside the camp for seven days and afterwards she shall be taken in again." 15. And Miriam was confined outside the camp for seven days, and the people did not journey on until Miriam had been taken in again. 16. Afterwards the people journeyed

יְהֹוָה: ג וְהָאִישׁ מֹשֶׁה עָנָו מְאֹד מִכֹּל הָאָדָם
אֲשֶׁר עַל־פְּנֵי הָאֲדָמָה: ס ד וַיֹּאמֶר יְהֹוָה
פִּתְאֹם אֶל־מֹשֶׁה וְאֶל־אַהֲרֹן וְאֶל־מִרְיָם צְאוּ
שְׁלָשְׁתְּכֶם אֶל־אֹהֶל מוֹעֵד וַיֵּצְאוּ שְׁלָשְׁתָּם:
ה וַיֵּרֶד יְהֹוָה בְּעַמּוּד עָנָן וַיַּעֲמֹד פֶּתַח הָאֹהֶל
וַיִּקְרָא אַהֲרֹן וּמִרְיָם וַיֵּצְאוּ שְׁנֵיהֶם: ו וַיֹּאמֶר
שִׁמְעוּ־נָא דְבָרָי אִם־יִהְיֶה נְבִיאֲכֶם יְהֹוָה
בַּמַּרְאָה אֵלָיו אֶתְוַדָּע בַּחֲלוֹם אֲדַבֶּר־בּוֹ: ז לֹא־
כֵן עַבְדִּי מֹשֶׁה בְּכָל־בֵּיתִי נֶאֱמָן הוּא: ח פֶּה
אֶל־פֶּה אֲדַבֶּר־בּוֹ וּמַרְאֶה וְלֹא בְחִידֹת וּתְמֻנַת
יְהֹוָה יַבִּיט וּמַדּוּעַ לֹא יְרֵאתֶם לְדַבֵּר בְּעַבְדִּי
בְמֹשֶׁה: ט וַיִּחַר־אַף יְהֹוָה בָּם וַיֵּלַךְ: י וְהֶעָנָן
סָר מֵעַל הָאֹהֶל וְהִנֵּה מִרְיָם מְצֹרַעַת כַּשָּׁלֶג וַיִּפֶן
אַהֲרֹן אֶל־מִרְיָם וְהִנֵּה מְצֹרָעַת: יא וַיֹּאמֶר
אַהֲרֹן אֶל־מֹשֶׁה בִּי אֲדֹנִי אַל־נָא תָשֵׁת עָלֵינוּ
חַטָּאת אֲשֶׁר נוֹאַלְנוּ וַאֲשֶׁר חָטָאנוּ: יב אַל־נָא
תְהִי כַּמֵּת אֲשֶׁר בְּצֵאתוֹ מֵרֶחֶם אִמּוֹ וַיֵּאָכֵל חֲצִי
בְשָׂרוֹ: יג וַיִּצְעַק מֹשֶׁה אֶל־יְהֹוָה לֵאמֹר אֵל נָא
רְפָא נָא לָהּ: פ מפטיר יד וַיֹּאמֶר יְהֹוָה אֶל־מֹשֶׁה
וְאָבִיהָ יָרֹק יָרַק בְּפָנֶיהָ הֲלֹא תִכָּלֵם שִׁבְעַת
יָמִים תִּסָּגֵר שִׁבְעַת יָמִים מִחוּץ לַמַּחֲנֶה וְאַחַר
תֵּאָסֵף: טו וַתִּסָּגֵר מִרְיָם מִחוּץ לַמַּחֲנֶה שִׁבְעַת
יָמִים וְהָעָם לֹא נָסַע עַד הֵאָסֵף מִרְיָם:

CHAPTER XII

6. *if he were your prophet.* If he, Moses, were "your" prophet; i.e., if he were the kind of prophet you thought him to be. Or: If Moses were a prophet like yourselves, if he were merely a prophet from among your own. . . .

16. If we look back upon the events that stand out particularly in this weekly portion, we see them, and their central figures, showing many degrees of endowment with the Divine spirit and of relationship to the Divine. First we see Moses and the nation as a whole (10:35–36), then Moses, Aaron, Miriam and the other prophets (12:4 ff). Might there not be a profound

from Ḥatzeroth and they camped in the wilderness of Paran.

טז וְאַחַר נָסְעוּ הָעָם מֵחֲצֵרוֹת וַיַּחֲנוּ בְּמִדְבַּר פָּארָן: פ

underlying link between the contents of this portion and the menorah, the "Tree of Light," which symbol-izes the spiritual development of Judaism and to which reference is made at the beginning of this portion?

The Haftarah for this Sidra may be found on page 892.

שלח לך

SHELAḤ LEKHA

XIII 1. *God* spoke to Moshe [saying]: 2. "Send out men for yourself to explore the land of Canaan, which I am giving to the sons of Yisrael. You shall send out one man each for every tribe of his fathers; each an outstanding person in their midst." 3. And Moshe sent them out from the wilderness of Paran according to the command of *God*, they were all of them men, heads of the sons of Yisrael. 4. And these were their names: For the tribe of Reuben, Shammua, son of Zakkur; 5. for the tribe of Shimeon, Shaphat, son of Ḥori; 6. for the tribe of Yehudah, Caleb, son of Yefunneh; 7. for the tribe of Yissakhar, Yigal, son of Yosef; 8. for the tribe of Ephraim, Hoshea, son of Nun; 9. for the tribe of Binyamin, Palti, son of Raphu; 10. for the tribe of Zebulun, Gaddiel, son of Sodi; 11. for the tribe of Yosef, [of] the tribe of Menashe, Gaddi, son of Susi; 12. for the tribe of Dan, Amiel, son of Gemali; 13. for the tribe of Asher, Sethur, son of Michael; 14. for the tribe of Naphtali, Naḥbi, son of Vafsi; 15. for the tribe of Gad, Ge'uel, son of Makhi. 16. These are the names of the men whom Moshe sent out to explore the land. And Moshe called Hoshea, son of Nun, "Yehoshua." 17. Moshe sent them out to explore the land of Canaan and he said to them: "Go up here in the south and

יג א וַיְדַבֵּר יְהוָה אֶל־מֹשֶׁה לֵּאמֹר: ב שְׁלַח־
לְךָ אֲנָשִׁים וְיָתֻרוּ אֶת־אֶרֶץ כְּנַעַן אֲשֶׁר־אֲנִי נֹתֵן
לִבְנֵי יִשְׂרָאֵל אִישׁ אֶחָד אִישׁ אֶחָד לְמַטֵּה
אֲבֹתָיו תִּשְׁלָחוּ כֹּל נָשִׂיא בָהֶם: ג וַיִּשְׁלַח אֹתָם
מֹשֶׁה מִמִּדְבַּר פָּארָן עַל־פִּי יְהוָה כֻּלָּם אֲנָשִׁים
רָאשֵׁי בְנֵי־יִשְׂרָאֵל הֵמָּה: ד וְאֵלֶּה שְׁמוֹתָם
לְמַטֵּה רְאוּבֵן שַׁמּוּעַ בֶּן־זַכּוּר: ה לְמַטֵּה שִׁמְעוֹן
שָׁפָט בֶּן־חוֹרִי: ו לְמַטֵּה יְהוּדָה כָּלֵב בֶּן־יְפֻנֶּה:
ז לְמַטֵּה יִשָּׂשכָר יִגְאָל בֶּן־יוֹסֵף: ח לְמַטֵּה
אֶפְרָיִם הוֹשֵׁעַ בִּן־נוּן: ט לְמַטֵּה בִנְיָמִן פַּלְטִי
בֶּן־רָפוּא: י לְמַטֵּה זְבוּלֻן גַּדִּיאֵל בֶּן־סוֹדִי:
יא לְמַטֵּה יוֹסֵף לְמַטֵּה מְנַשֶּׁה גַּדִּי בֶּן־סוּסִי:
יב לְמַטֵּה דָן עַמִּיאֵל בֶּן־גְּמַלִּי: יג לְמַטֵּה אָשֵׁר
סְתוּר בֶּן־מִיכָאֵל: יד לְמַטֵּה נַפְתָּלִי נַחְבִּי בֶּן
וָפְסִי: טו לְמַטֵּה גָד גְּאוּאֵל בֶּן־מָכִי: טז אֵלֶּה
שְׁמוֹת הָאֲנָשִׁים אֲשֶׁר־שָׁלַח מֹשֶׁה לָתוּר אֶת־
הָאָרֶץ וַיִּקְרָא מֹשֶׁה לְהוֹשֵׁעַ בִּן־נוּן יְהוֹשֻׁעַ:
יז וַיִּשְׁלַח אֹתָם מֹשֶׁה לָתוּר אֶת־אֶרֶץ כְּנָעַן
וַיֹּאמֶר אֲלֵהֶם עֲלוּ זֶה בַּנֶּגֶב וַעֲלִיתֶם אֶת־הָהָר:

CHAPTER XIII

2. ***each an outstanding person in their midst.*** The accentuation[2] shows that the word **נָשִׂיא** is a predicate defining **כֹּל**; i.e., "let every man [of those sent out] be a **נָשִׂיא** among the others in his tribe." These were not to be the "princes of the tribes of their fathers," to whom reference is made in 1:4 and 16 as "the head of his fathers' house" and; "princes of the tribes of their fathers," respectively; individuals who were at the head of each tribe and were explicitly defined as such in 7:2. Rather, they were to be, each one of them, **נָשִׂיא בָהֶם** ["outstanding in their midst"]. They were to be **בָּהֶם** ["in their midst"]; not at the head of the people but in the midst of them, individuals who, though not in positions of leadership, stood out from all the rest by virtue of their character and ability. . . .

16. ***And Moshe called Hoshea, son of Nun, "Yehoshua."*** With this change of name Moshe hinted at a truth that Yehoshua was to remember always and that his companions, too, were to remember each time they addressed him by his new name, as they went about fulfilling their mission. **הוֹשֵׁעַ**, He Who has always helped us in the past, is also **יְהוֹשֻׁעַ**, He Who will bring about our salvation in the future. Indeed, **יְהוֹשֻׁעַ**: God represents all our wealth, all our power, the sum total of our aspirations; without Him, all these things have no meaning.

[2] *Note to the English translation*: The word **כל** has a separating accent. [G.H.]

ascend the mountain, 18. and look at the land, what it is like, and at the people that dwell upon it: whether they are strong or weak, whether they are few or many, 19. and what the land is like in which they dwell: whether it is good or bad, and what the cities are like in which they dwell: whether [they are] in open or in fortified places. 20. And what the soil is like: whether it is fat or lean, whether there is woodland in it or not—and take courage and take [some] of the fruit of the land." The season was the season when the first grapes become ripe. 21. They went up and explored the land from the wilderness of Tzin to Reḥob, toward Ḥamath. 22. They went up in the south and came as one man as far as Ḥebron; [and] there were Aḥiman, Sheshai and Talmai, the offspring of Anak. And Ḥebron had been built in seven years, long before Tzoan Mitzrayim. 23. They came as far as the Valley of Grapes and cut down from there one vine and one cluster of grapes, and they carried it between two [of them] upon a carrying-pole, and [they] also [took some] of the pomegranates and of the figs. 24. This place was called Valley of Grapes because of the cluster of grapes that the sons of Yisrael had cut from there. 25. They returned from the exploration of the land at the end of forty days. 26. They went, and they came to Moshe and to Aharon and to the entire community

יח וּרְאִיתֶ֛ם אֶת־הָאָ֖רֶץ מַה־הִ֑וא וְאֶת־הָעָ֣ם הַיֹּשֵׁ֣ב עָלֶ֗יהָ הֶחָזָ֥ק הוּא֙ הֲרָפֶ֔ה הַמְעַ֥ט ה֖וּא אִם־רָֽב: יט וּמָ֣ה הָאָ֗רֶץ אֲשֶׁר־הוּא֙ יֹשֵׁ֣ב בָּ֔הּ הֲטוֹבָ֥ה הִ֖וא אִם־רָעָ֑ה וּמָ֣ה הֶֽעָרִ֗ים אֲשֶׁר־הוּא֙ יוֹשֵׁ֣ב בָּהֵ֔נָּה הַבְּמַֽחֲנִ֖ים אִ֥ם בְּמִבְצָרִֽים: כ וּמָ֣ה הָ֠אָ֠רֶץ הַשְּׁמֵנָ֨ה הִ֜וא אִם־רָזָ֗ה הֲיֵֽשׁ־בָּ֥הּ עֵץ֙ אִם־אַ֔יִן וְהִ֨תְחַזַּקְתֶּ֔ם וּלְקַחְתֶּ֖ם מִפְּרִ֣י הָאָ֑רֶץ וְהַ֨יָּמִ֔ים יְמֵ֖י בִּכּוּרֵ֥י עֲנָבִֽים: שני כא וַֽיַּעֲל֖וּ וַיָּתֻ֣רוּ אֶת־הָאָ֑רֶץ מִמִּדְבַּר־צִ֥ן עַד־רְחֹ֖ב לְבֹ֥א חֲמָֽת: כב וַיַּֽעֲל֣וּ בַנֶּ֘גֶב֮ וַיָּבֹ֣א עַד־חֶבְרוֹן֒ וְשָׁ֤ם אֲחִימָ֣ן שֵׁשַׁ֣י וְתַלְמַ֔י יְלִידֵ֖י הָֽעֲנָ֑ק וְחֶבְר֗וֹן שֶׁ֤בַע שָׁנִים֙ נִבְנְתָ֔ה לִפְנֵ֖י צֹ֥עַן מִצְרָֽיִם: כג וַיָּבֹ֜אוּ עַד־נַ֣חַל אֶשְׁכֹּ֗ל וַיִּכְרְת֨וּ מִשָּׁ֤ם זְמוֹרָה֙ וְאֶשְׁכּ֤וֹל עֲנָבִים֙ אֶחָ֔ד וַיִּשָּׂאֻ֥הוּ בַמּ֖וֹט בִּשְׁנָ֑יִם וּמִן־הָרִמֹּנִ֖ים וּמִן־הַתְּאֵנִֽים: כד לַמָּק֣וֹם הַה֔וּא קָרָ֖א נַ֣חַל אֶשְׁכּ֑וֹל עַ֚ל אֹד֣וֹת הָאֶשְׁכּ֔וֹל אֲשֶׁר־כָּֽרְת֥וּ מִשָּׁ֖ם בְּנֵ֥י יִשְׂרָאֵֽל: כה וַיָּשֻׁ֖בוּ מִתּ֣וּר הָאָ֑רֶץ מִקֵּ֖ץ אַרְבָּעִ֥ים יֽוֹם: כו וַיֵּֽלְכ֡וּ וַיָּבֹאוּ֩ אֶל־מֹשֶׁ֨ה וְאֶֽל־אַֽהֲרֹ֜ן וְאֶל־כָּל־

19. **and what the land is like in which they dwell.** This question refers to the quality of the land as a place where human beings dwell. The question in Verse 18 relates to "the people that dwell upon it." The inhabitants of the land are viewed apart from the soil; i.e., in terms of the manner in which they developed *upon* that land. In the present verse, on the other hand, the question is, "and what the land is like *in* which they dwell." The people are considered within the context of the land, amidst all the influences brought to bear upon them by the quality of the land. What is the value of this land as a seedbed for the development of a nation?

whether it is good or bad. Is this land "good" or "bad" in this respect? Will it serve to promote the spiritual and moral growth of the nation, or hinder it? In this connection, we would call to mind the saying of our

Sages, "The very air of the Land of Israel makes people wise" (Baba Bathra 158b). . . .

26. **They went and they came.** On their way back they had decided that they would not go directly to Moses and Aaron with their report, but would first report their findings to the entire nation. This showed their evil intentions. Had their intentions been good, they would have made their report first to Moses and Aaron and sought their advice and instructions before going any further. But this is precisely what they did not want to do. They believed that they, and the nation, would be best served if they would set themselves up in opposition to Moses. Their report therefore took the form of an accusation against Moses and Aaron in the presence of the entire nation; they appealed to the people to save themselves from the ruin that would

of the sons of Yisrael, to the wilderness of Paran toward Kadesh, and brought back word to them and to the entire community and showed them the fruit of the land. 27. They told him and said: "We came into the land where you sent us, and it is indeed flowing with milk and honey, and this is its fruit. 28. But the people that dwell in the land are too strong, and the cities are exceedingly great fortresses, and we also saw offspring of Anak there. 29. Amalek dwells in the land of the south, the Ḥittite[s], and the Yebusite[s] and the Amorite[s] in the mountains, and the Canaanite[s] dwell by the sea and on the banks of the Jordan." 30. Then Caleb quieted the people for Moshe and said: "We can indeed go up and take possession of it, for we are truly able to do so." 31. But the men who had gone up with him said: "We cannot go up against this people because they are too strong for us." 32. And now they brought calumny, concerning the land they had explored, to the sons of Yisrael, as follows: "The land through which we passed, to explore it, is a land that destroys its inhabitants, and the entire population that we saw are big in stature. 33. We saw giants there, the sons of Anak, descendants of the giants. We were in our own eyes like grasshoppers, and so, too, were we in their eyes."

XIV 1. Then the entire community lifted up their voice and gave it free rein, and the people wept all through that night. 2. Then all the sons of Yisrael murmured against Moshe and against Aharon, and the entire community said to them: "Would that we had died in the land of Mitzrayim, or in this wilderness—would that we had died there! 3. Why is *God* bringing us to this land to fall by the sword? Our wives and our children will become prey! Truly it would be better for us to return to Mitzrayim." 4. And they said to one another: "Let us appoint a leader and go back to Mitzrayim." 5. Then Moshe and Aharon fell upon their faces before the whole assembly of the

עֲדַת בְּנֵי־יִשְׂרָאֵל אֶל־מִדְבַּר פָּארָן קָדֵשָׁה
וַיָּשִׁיבוּ אֹתָם דָּבָר וְאֶת־כָּל־הָעֵדָה וַיַּרְאוּם אֶת־
פְּרִי הָאָרֶץ: כז וַיְסַפְּרוּ־לוֹ וַיֹּאמְרוּ בָּאנוּ אֶל־
הָאָרֶץ אֲשֶׁר שְׁלַחְתָּנוּ וְגַם זָבַת חָלָב וּדְבַשׁ הִוא
וְזֶה־פִּרְיָהּ: כח אֶפֶס כִּי־עַז הָעָם הַיֹּשֵׁב בָּאָרֶץ
וְהֶעָרִים בְּצֻרוֹת גְּדֹלֹת מְאֹד וְגַם־יְלִדֵי הָעֲנָק
רָאִינוּ שָׁם: כט עֲמָלֵק יוֹשֵׁב בְּאֶרֶץ הַנֶּגֶב וְהַחִתִּי
וְהַיְבוּסִי וְהָאֱמֹרִי יוֹשֵׁב בָּהָר וְהַכְּנַעֲנִי יֹשֵׁב
עַל־הַיָּם וְעַל יַד הַיַּרְדֵּן: ל וַיַּהַס כָּלֵב אֶת־הָעָם
אֶל־מֹשֶׁה וַיֹּאמֶר עָלֹה נַעֲלֶה וְיָרַשְׁנוּ אֹתָהּ כִּי־
יָכוֹל נוּכַל לָהּ: לא וְהָאֲנָשִׁים אֲשֶׁר־עָלוּ עִמּוֹ
אָמְרוּ לֹא נוּכַל לַעֲלוֹת אֶל־הָעָם כִּי־חָזָק הוּא
מִמֶּנּוּ: לב וַיֹּצִיאוּ דִּבַּת הָאָרֶץ אֲשֶׁר תָּרוּ אֹתָהּ
אֶל־בְּנֵי יִשְׂרָאֵל לֵאמֹר הָאָרֶץ אֲשֶׁר עָבַרְנוּ בָהּ
לָתוּר אֹתָהּ אֶרֶץ אֹכֶלֶת יוֹשְׁבֶיהָ הִוא וְכָל־הָעָם
אֲשֶׁר־רָאִינוּ בְתוֹכָהּ אַנְשֵׁי מִדּוֹת: לג וְשָׁם
רָאִינוּ אֶת־הַנְּפִילִים בְּנֵי עֲנָק מִן־הַנְּפִלִים וַנְּהִי
בְעֵינֵינוּ כַּחֲגָבִים וְכֵן הָיִינוּ בְּעֵינֵיהֶם:
יד א וַתִּשָּׂא כָּל־הָעֵדָה וַיִּתְּנוּ אֶת־קוֹלָם וַיִּבְכּוּ
הָעָם בַּלַּיְלָה הַהוּא: ב וַיִּלֹּנוּ עַל־מֹשֶׁה וְעַל־
אַהֲרֹן כֹּל בְּנֵי יִשְׂרָאֵל וַיֹּאמְרוּ אֲלֵהֶם כָּל־הָעֵדָה
לוּ־מַתְנוּ בְּאֶרֶץ מִצְרַיִם אוֹ בַּמִּדְבָּר הַזֶּה לוּ־
מָתְנוּ: ג וְלָמָה יְהוָה מֵבִיא אֹתָנוּ אֶל־הָאָרֶץ
הַזֹּאת לִנְפֹּל בַּחֶרֶב נָשֵׁינוּ וְטַפֵּנוּ יִהְיוּ לָבַז
הֲלוֹא טוֹב לָנוּ שׁוּב מִצְרָיְמָה: ד וַיֹּאמְרוּ אִישׁ
אֶל־אָחִיו נִתְּנָה רֹאשׁ וְנָשׁוּבָה מִצְרָיְמָה:
ה וַיִּפֹּל מֹשֶׁה וְאַהֲרֹן עַל־פְּנֵיהֶם לִפְנֵי כָּל־קְהַל

surely come upon them if the plans of Moses and Aaron would materialize. . . .

CHAPTER XIV

5. ***Then Moshe and Aharon fell upon their faces.***

community of the sons of Yisrael. 6. But Yehoshua, son of Nun, and Caleb, son of Yefunneh, of those who had explored the land, had rent their garments. 7. And they said to the entire community of the sons of Yisrael: "The land through which we passed, to explore it, is an exceedingly good land. 8. If *God* is pleased with us, He will bring us into this land and give it to us, a land truly flowing with milk and honey. 9. Only do not rebel against *God!* And as for you, you [of all people] should not fear the people of this land, for they are our bread! Their shade has departed from them, because *God* is with us; do not fear them." 10. The entire community spoke of stoning them to death, when the glory of *God* appeared in the Tent of Appointed Meeting to all the sons of Yisrael. 11. And *God* said to Moshe: "How long will this people mock Me? And how long will they put no trust in Me, despite all the signs that I have performed in their midst? 12. I will strike them with pestilence and drive them out of existence and I will make you into a greater, mightier nation than they are." 13. And Moshe said to *God*: "When the Mitzrites will hear this— for, after all, it is with Thy might that Thou hast brought out this people from their midst— 14. and they will say to the inhabitants of this land—they, too, have already heard that Thou, O *God*, dwellest in the midst of this people, that Thou, O *God*,

עֲדַת בְּנֵי יִשְׂרָאֵל: ו וִיהוֹשֻׁעַ בִּן־נוּן וְכָלֵב בֶּן־יְפֻנֶּה מִן־הַתָּרִים אֶת־הָאָרֶץ קָרְעוּ בִּגְדֵיהֶם: ז וַיֹּאמְרוּ אֶל־כָּל־עֲדַת בְּנֵי־יִשְׂרָאֵל לֵאמֹר הָאָרֶץ אֲשֶׁר עָבַרְנוּ בָהּ לָתוּר אֹתָהּ טוֹבָה הָאָרֶץ מְאֹד מְאֹד: שלישי ח אִם־חָפֵץ בָּנוּ יְהוָה וְהֵבִיא אֹתָנוּ אֶל־הָאָרֶץ הַזֹּאת וּנְתָנָהּ לָנוּ אֶרֶץ אֲשֶׁר־הִוא זָבַת חָלָב וּדְבָשׁ: ט אַךְ בַּיהוָה אַל־תִּמְרֹדוּ וְאַתֶּם אַל־תִּירְאוּ אֶת־עַם הָאָרֶץ כִּי לַחְמֵנוּ הֵם סָר צִלָּם מֵעֲלֵיהֶם וַיהוָה אִתָּנוּ אַל־תִּירָאֻם: י וַיֹּאמְרוּ כָּל־הָעֵדָה לִרְגּוֹם אֹתָם בָּאֲבָנִים וּכְבוֹד יְהוָה נִרְאָה בְּאֹהֶל מוֹעֵד אֶל־כָּל־בְּנֵי יִשְׂרָאֵל: פ יא וַיֹּאמֶר יְהוָה אֶל־מֹשֶׁה עַד־אָנָה יְנַאֲצֻנִי הָעָם הַזֶּה וְעַד־אָנָה לֹא־יַאֲמִינוּ בִי בְּכֹל הָאֹתוֹת אֲשֶׁר עָשִׂיתִי בְּקִרְבּוֹ: יב אַכֶּנּוּ בַדֶּבֶר וְאוֹרִשֶׁנּוּ וְאֶעֱשֶׂה אֹתְךָ לְגוֹי־גָּדוֹל וְעָצוּם מִמֶּנּוּ: יג וַיֹּאמֶר מֹשֶׁה אֶל־יְהוָה וְשָׁמְעוּ מִצְרַיִם כִּי־הֶעֱלִיתָ בְכֹחֲךָ אֶת־הָעָם הַזֶּה מִקִּרְבּוֹ: יד וְאָמְרוּ אֶל־יוֹשֵׁב הָאָרֶץ הַזֹּאת שָׁמְעוּ כִּי־אַתָּה יְהוָה בְּקֶרֶב הָעָם הַזֶּה אֲשֶׁר־

By saying, "Let us appoint a leader," as stated in the preceding verse, the people had served notice on Moses and Aaron that they would no longer follow their orders. Moses and Aaron took this to mean that their mission was at an end. They cast themselves down "before the whole assembly of the community. . . ."

קְהַל עֲדַת is the assembly to which the leadership of the community had been entrusted; i.e., the elders (see Exodus 12:6). By thus casting themselves down before these elders, Moses and Aaron implied that the leadership of the people had now reverted to the elders. Since the people had refused them obedience, Moses and Aaron wished to demonstrate that their authority was at an end and that there was nothing more they could do for the people.

9. **And as for you.** These words sum up all the spiri-

tual greatness, moral nobility, God-ordained vocation and nearness to God's covenant associated with Israel's past and with its foreordained future. Even if these people are the most terrifying giants, with fortresses of solid granite, *you* should not be afraid of them. Knowing your spiritual and moral strength, in and with God, they should melt away. You should be ashamed to fear them. . . .

Their shade has departed from them. They exist only as long as they remain hidden in the shade, as long as they are unnoticed. But when we enter into their midst, God, with His truth and His right, which bring salvation to mankind, will enter along with us. Before the brilliance of this truth, their shade will vanish. Their depravity will stand fully exposed, and they will be judged and destroyed because of their corruption. Therefore, do not fear them.

art seen eye to eye, that Thy cloud rests over them, and Thou goest before them in a pillar of cloud by day and in a pillar of fire by night— 15. now if Thou wilt kill this people as one man, then these nations that have heard this news of Thee will say: 16. 'It is beyond the capacity of *God* to bring these people into the land that He has sworn to them. That is why He slaughtered them in the wilderness.' 17. And now do let the power of my Lord be great, as Thou didst once utter it: 18. '*God*, long-suffering and abundant in loving-kindness, lifting away crookedness and rebellion, yet He remits nothing; He remembers the crookedness of parents for the children, to the third and fourth generation.' 19. Forgive, I beseech thee, the crookedness of this people according to the greatness of Thy loving-kindness and even as Thou hast extended forbearance to this people from Mitzrayim even until now." 20. And *God*

עַ֫יִן בְּעַ֫יִן נִרְאָ֣ה ׀ אַתָּ֣ה יְהֹוָ֗ה וַעֲנָֽנְךָ֙ עֹמֵ֣ד עֲלֵהֶ֔ם וּבְעַמֻּ֣ד עָנָ֗ן אַתָּ֞ה הֹלֵ֤ךְ לִפְנֵיהֶם֙ יוֹמָ֔ם וּבְעַמּ֥וּד אֵ֖שׁ לָֽיְלָה׃ טו וְהֵמַתָּ֛ה אֶת־הָעָ֥ם הַזֶּ֖ה כְּאִ֣ישׁ אֶחָ֑ד וְאָֽמְרוּ֙ הַגּוֹיִ֔ם אֲשֶׁר־שָֽׁמְע֥וּ אֶת־שִׁמְעֲךָ֖ לֵאמֹֽר׃ טז מִבִּלְתִּ֞י יְכֹ֣לֶת יְהֹוָ֗ה לְהָבִיא֙ אֶת־הָעָ֣ם הַזֶּ֔ה אֶל־הָאָ֖רֶץ אֲשֶׁר־נִשְׁבַּ֣ע לָהֶ֑ם וַיִּשְׁחָטֵ֖ם בַּמִּדְבָּֽר׃ יז וְעַתָּ֖ה (י רבתי) יִגְדַּל־נָ֣א כֹּ֣חַ אֲדֹנָ֑י כַּֽאֲשֶׁ֥ר דִּבַּ֖רְתָּ לֵאמֹֽר׃ יח יְהֹוָ֗ה אֶ֤רֶךְ אַפַּ֨יִם֙ וְרַב־חֶ֔סֶד נֹשֵׂ֥א עָוֺ֖ן וָפָ֑שַׁע וְנַקֵּה֙ לֹ֣א יְנַקֶּ֔ה פֹּקֵ֞ד עֲוֺ֤ן אָבוֹת֙ עַל־בָּנִ֔ים עַל־שִׁלֵּשִׁ֖ים וְעַל־רִבֵּעִֽים׃ יט סְלַֽח־נָ֗א לַֽעֲוֺ֛ן הָעָ֥ם הַזֶּ֖ה כְּגֹ֣דֶל חַסְדֶּ֑ךָ וְכַֽאֲשֶׁ֤ר נָשָׂ֨אתָה֙ לָעָ֣ם הַזֶּ֔ה מִמִּצְרַ֖יִם וְעַד־הֵֽנָּה׃ כ וַיֹּ֣אמֶר יְהֹוָ֔ה

15. . . . The words "as one man" clearly indicate that if the fathers who had become unworthy of the land would die off gradually, in the natural course of events, and only their children would enter the land, this would not have an adverse effect on the recognition of God among the nations. Only a mass dying such as God had announced and as a result of which God's promise would not be fulfilled until centuries hence could give rise to such a misconception [i.e., that God was not capable of bringing the people into their land].

18. **God,** *long-suffering.* Moses stresses those qualities of God's sovereignty to which he would appeal particularly at this point. The most prominent of these is אֶרֶךְ אַפַּיִם, God's long-suffering patience in awaiting the satisfaction of His just demands. Instead of the instantaneous annihilation they would in fact deserve, God in this attribute gives the people time, very much time, to come to their senses, to mend their ways, to rise again from their fall and to regain what they had forfeited in their folly.

רַב חֶסֶד is His abundance of loving-kindness. He does not withhold His love but has an ample store of loving-kindness, which he bestows again and again, and which He is ready to continue bestowing even for a thousandth time after it had been forfeited on nine hundred ninety-nine previous occasions.

נֹשֵׂא עָוֺן וָפֶשַׁע literally means the "lifting away" of the onus of crookedness and rebellion from one who has left the straight path knowingly, but motivated solely by passion, or even from one who is engaged in open

rebellion against the Law of God, so that he will not be buried beneath this burden. And finally, there is that profound greatness of love in God's sovereignty which always views the present in terms of the future, every man in terms of his children and children's children, and every generation in terms of its posterity. Since He seeks to cleanse all men, all generations and all eras in history to save them from moral ruin, He will not allow even the slightest unrepented sin to go unpunished; yet, He will extend the opportunity for repentance over many generations and over long periods of time. Before passing sentence upon a man, He will look upon that man's great-grandson, still unborn, who might come to his senses and ascend again to that high level of morality from which his ancestor—in error, or perhaps deliberately—has fallen. "Yet He remits nothing; He remembers the crookedness of parents for the children, to the third and fourth generation."

20. **And God** *said: "I have forgiven, in accordance with your word."* For precisely the reasons cited by Moses, God had already decided beforehand to forgive them. The punishment He announced to Moses in Verse 12 was merely a description of the punishment that would be indicated for the defection of this people, were it not for these Divine considerations. Also, it was intended to help Moses gain an insight into the nature of God's sovereignty, at the same time giving him an opportunity to demonstrate his own consummate selflessness. Moses does not harbor the slightest bitterness against the people whose rebellion had been directed

said: "I have forgiven, in accordance with your word.   21. However, as surely as I live, and as surely as the whole earth will be full of the glory of *God*,   22. all the men who have seen My glory and My signs that I performed in Mitzrayim and in the wilderness, and who have nevertheless put Me to the test these ten times and still did not listen to My voice,   23. they shall not see the land that I swore to their fathers, and all those whose mock Me shall not see it.   24. But as for My servant Caleb, because there was a different spirit with him, and [because], following Me, he fulfilled his duty, him I will bring into the land into which he went, and he will leave it to his descendants.   25. The Amalekite[s] and the Canaanite[s] dwell in the valley; tomorrow you shall turn and journey into the wilderness toward the Sea of Reeds." 26. And *God* spoke to Moshe and Aharon [saying]:   27. "How long will this community be permitted to stir up revolt against Me? I have heard the murmurings of the sons of Yisrael, which they make in order to stir up revolt against Me.   28. Say to

סָלַ֖חְתִּי כִּדְבָרֶֽךָ׃ כא וְאוּלָ֖ם חַי־אָ֑נִי וְיִמָּלֵ֥א כְבֽוֹד־יְהֹוָ֖ה אֶת־כָּל־הָאָֽרֶץ׃ כב כִּ֣י כָל־הָ֣אֲנָשִׁ֗ים הָרֹאִ֤ים אֶת־כְּבֹדִי֙ וְאֶת־אֹ֣תֹתַ֔י אֲשֶׁר־עָשִׂ֥יתִי בְמִצְרַ֖יִם וּבַמִּדְבָּ֑ר וַיְנַסּ֣וּ אֹתִ֗י זֶ֚ה עֶ֣שֶׂר פְּעָמִ֔ים וְלֹ֥א שָׁמְע֖וּ בְּקוֹלִֽי׃ כג אִם־יִרְאוּ֙ אֶת־הָאָ֔רֶץ אֲשֶׁ֥ר נִשְׁבַּ֖עְתִּי לַאֲבֹתָ֑ם וְכָל־מְנַאֲצַ֖י לֹ֥א יִרְאֽוּהָ׃ כד וְעַבְדִּ֣י כָלֵ֗ב עֵ֣קֶב הָֽיְתָ֞ה ר֤וּחַ אַחֶ֙רֶת֙ עִמּ֔וֹ וַיְמַלֵּ֖א אַחֲרָ֑י וַהֲבִֽיאֹתִ֗יו אֶל־הָאָ֙רֶץ֙ אֲשֶׁר־בָּ֣א שָׁ֔מָּה וְזַרְע֖וֹ יוֹרִשֶֽׁנָּה׃ כה וְהָֽעֲמָלֵקִ֥י וְהַֽכְּנַעֲנִ֖י יוֹשֵׁ֣ב בָּעֵ֑מֶק מָחָ֗ר פְּנ֤וּ וּסְע֤וּ לָכֶ֛ם הַמִּדְבָּ֖ר דֶּ֥רֶךְ יַם־סֽוּף׃ פ רביעי כו וַיְדַבֵּ֣ר יְהֹוָ֔ה אֶל־מֹשֶׁ֥ה וְאֶֽל־אַהֲרֹ֖ן לֵאמֹֽר׃ כז עַד־מָתַ֗י לָעֵדָ֤ה הָֽרָעָה֙ הַזֹּ֔את אֲשֶׁ֛ר הֵ֥מָּה מַלִּינִ֖ים עָלָ֑י אֶת־תְּלֻנּוֹת֙ בְּנֵ֣י יִשְׂרָאֵ֔ל אֲשֶׁ֛ר הֵ֥מָּה מַלִּינִ֖ים עָלַ֖י שָׁמָֽעְתִּי׃ כח אֱמֹ֣ר

---

primarily against him, nor was he tempted in the least by the brilliant prospect of becoming a second Abraham, the Patriarch of a new people of God! Only such an utterly selfless character will be privileged to attain so profound a perception of God's sovereignty, a level of human insight so high that it comes close to the insight of God. Only a person of this character will be enabled to obtain that clear objectivity, unclouded by subjective considerations, which this insight presupposes. . . .

22–23. *and all those who mock Me shall not see it.* Psalm 106:24–27 looks back upon this episode in our history with these words: "They rejected the lovely land; they did not trust His word; they murmured in their tents; they did not hearken to the voice of *God*; then He lifted up His hand with regard to them, that He would cause them to fall in the wilderness, and that He would cast out their descendants among the nations and scatter them in the lands." This passage would indicate that Israel's loss of its land and its dispersion among the nations were foretold at the same time as it was decreed that the generation that had gone forth from Egypt would die in the wilderness. It would seem that the words, "all those who mock Me

shall not see it," announce Israel's future banishment from the land (see Naḥmanides ibid.).

If the children will fall back into the same blindness that lost their forefathers the right to enter the land of God's Law, they, too, will not be permitted to remain in possession of the land. We may well say that the Divine attribute of אֶרֶךְ אַפַּיִם, thanks to which the immature generation was spared the fate of mass annihilation, and the sons they themselves had begotten and reared were led into the land, extended into all the subsequent centuries of the training plan introduced at that point. In this plan, Divine Providence envisioned that its purposes would be fully realized only in a future beyond our own present day. For the generation reared by the generation of the wilderness, which had been reserved the right to enter the Promised Land, had in no manner attained the full mature phase of its calling. Its two periods of statehood in the land, and its two exiles, the second of which has lasted into our own day, are nothing but a pedagogical process conducted by God in His attribute of אֶרֶךְ אַפַּיִם, in order to train us for our spiritual and moral vocation. The time when Israel will be pure, perfect and ever devoted in its observance of God's Law is still far in the future even today. The words, "and all those who mock Me shall not see it," indicate the course of our subsequent history.

them: As surely as I live—thus is it said by *God*—even as you have spoken before My ears, so will I do to you.   29. Your corpses will fall in the wilderness and all your numbered ones at all your numberings from twenty years old and upward, those who brought you to revolt against Me. 30. You shall not come into the land concerning which I lifted up My hand to have you settle there to dwell, except for Caleb, son of Yefunneh, and Yehoshua, son of Nun.   31. Your children, of whom you said that they would become prey, them I will bring in; they will come to know the land that you have scorned.   32. But as for you, your corpses will fall in this wilderness, 33. and your sons shall wander about in the wilderness for forty years and shall bear your defection until the last of your corpses has fallen in the wilderness. 34. According to the number of days in which you explored the land, forty days, for every day one year, you shall bear your iniquities: forty years, and you shall come to know [the consequences of] refusing Me.   35. I, *God*, have spoken it. This I will do to all this evil community that gathered together against Me: in this wilderness they shall meet their end and there they shall die."   36. But [as for] the men whom Moshe sent out to explore the land and who returned and incited the whole community against him by bringing calumny concerning the land: 37. the[se] men who brought the evil calumny against the land died by sudden death before *God*.   38. But Yehoshua, son of Nun, and Caleb, son of Yefunneh, remained alive from among those men who had gone to explore the land.   39. Moshe spoke these words to all the sons of Yisrael, and the people mourned greatly.   40. And they rose up early in the morning and went up to the top of the mountain, thereby saying: "We are ready to go up in that place which *God* has described, for we have sinned."   41. And Moshe said: "Why do you now transgress the command of *God*? This will not succeed.   42. Do not go up, for *God* is not in your midst. Do not be struck down before your enemies! 43. For the Amalekite[s] and the Canaanite[s] are there before you; you will fall by the sword! For since you have

אֲלֵהֶ֗ם חַי־אָ֕נִי נְאֻם־יְהֹוָ֑ה אִם־לֹ֣א כַּֽאֲשֶׁ֧ר דִּבַּרְתֶּ֛ם בְּאָזְנָ֖י כֵּ֥ן אֶעֱשֶׂ֥ה לָכֶֽם: כט בַּמִּדְבָּ֣ר הַזֶּ֩ה יִפְּל֨וּ פִגְרֵיכֶ֜ם וְכָל־פְּקֻֽדֵיכֶם֙ לְכָל־מִסְפַּרְכֶ֔ם מִבֶּ֛ן עֶשְׂרִ֥ים שָׁנָ֖ה וָמָ֑עְלָה אֲשֶׁ֥ר הֲלִֽינֹתֶ֖ם עָלָֽי: ל אִם־אַתֶּם֙ תָּבֹ֣אוּ אֶל־הָאָ֔רֶץ אֲשֶׁ֤ר נָשָׂ֨אתִי֙ אֶת־יָדִ֔י לְשַׁכֵּ֥ן אֶתְכֶ֖ם בָּ֑הּ כִּ֚י אִם־כָּלֵ֣ב בֶּן־יְפֻנֶּ֔ה וִֽיהוֹשֻׁ֖עַ בִּן־נֽוּן: לא וְטַ֨פְּכֶ֔ם אֲשֶׁ֥ר אֲמַרְתֶּ֖ם לָבַ֣ז יִהְיֶ֑ה וְהֵבֵיאתִ֣י אֹתָ֔ם וְיָֽדְעוּ֙ אֶת־הָאָ֔רֶץ אֲשֶׁ֥ר מְאַסְתֶּ֖ם בָּֽהּ: לב וּפִגְרֵיכֶ֖ם אַתֶּ֑ם יִפְּל֖וּ בַּמִּדְבָּ֥ר הַזֶּֽה: לג וּֽבְנֵיכֶ֗ם יִֽהְי֤וּ רֹעִים֙ בַּמִּדְבָּר֙ אַרְבָּעִ֣ים שָׁנָ֔ה וְנָֽשְׂא֖וּ אֶת־זְנֽוּתֵיכֶ֑ם עַד־תֹּ֥ם פִּגְרֵיכֶ֖ם בַּמִּדְבָּֽר: לד בְּמִסְפַּ֨ר הַיָּמִ֜ים אֲשֶׁר־תַּרְתֶּ֣ם אֶת־הָאָ֗רֶץ אַרְבָּעִ֣ים יוֹם֙ י֣וֹם לַשָּׁנָ֞ה י֤וֹם לַשָּׁנָה֙ תִּשְׂא֣וּ אֶת־עֲוֹֽנֹֽתֵיכֶ֗ם אַרְבָּעִ֣ים שָׁנָ֑ה וִֽידַעְתֶּ֖ם אֶת־תְּנֽוּאָתִֽי: לה אֲנִ֣י יְהֹוָה֮ דִּבַּ֒רְתִּי֒ אִם־לֹ֣א ׀ זֹ֣את אֶֽעֱשֶׂ֗ה לְכָל־הָֽעֵדָ֤ה הָֽרָעָה֙ הַזֹּ֔את הַנּֽוֹעָדִ֖ים עָלָ֑י בַּמִּדְבָּ֥ר הַזֶּ֛ה יִתַּ֖מּוּ וְשָׁ֥ם יָמֻֽתוּ: לו וְהָ֣אֲנָשִׁ֔ים אֲשֶׁר־שָׁלַ֥ח מֹשֶׁ֖ה לָת֣וּר אֶת־הָאָ֑רֶץ וַיָּשֻׁ֗בוּ (וילינו קרי) וַיִּלּוֹנוּ עָלָיו֙ אֶת־כָּל־הָ֣עֵדָ֔ה לְהוֹצִ֥יא דִבָּ֖ה עַל־הָאָֽרֶץ: לז וַיָּמֻ֨תוּ֙ הָֽאֲנָשִׁ֔ים מֽוֹצִאֵ֥י דִבַּת־הָאָ֖רֶץ רָעָ֑ה בַּמַּגֵּפָ֖ה לִפְנֵ֥י יְהֹוָֽה: לח וִֽיהוֹשֻׁ֣עַ בִּן־נ֔וּן וְכָלֵ֖ב בֶּן־יְפֻנֶּ֑ה חָי֗וּ מִן־הָֽאֲנָשִׁ֣ים הָהֵ֔ם הַהֹֽלְכִ֖ים לָת֥וּר אֶת־הָאָֽרֶץ: לט וַיְדַבֵּ֤ר מֹשֶׁה֙ אֶת־הַדְּבָרִ֣ים הָאֵ֔לֶּה אֶל־כָּל־בְּנֵ֖י יִשְׂרָאֵ֑ל וַיִּֽתְאַבְּל֥וּ הָעָ֖ם מְאֹֽד: מ וַיַּשְׁכִּ֣מוּ בַבֹּ֔קֶר וַיַּֽעֲל֥וּ אֶל־רֹאשׁ־הָהָ֖ר לֵאמֹ֑ר הִנֶּ֗נּוּ וְעָלִ֛ינוּ אֶל־הַמָּק֛וֹם אֲשֶׁר־אָמַ֥ר יְהֹוָ֖ה כִּ֥י חָטָֽאנוּ: מא וַיֹּ֣אמֶר מֹשֶׁ֔ה לָ֥מָּה זֶּ֛ה אַתֶּ֥ם עֹֽבְרִ֖ים אֶת־פִּ֣י יְהֹוָ֑ה וְהִ֖וא לֹ֥א תִצְלָֽח: מב אַֽל־תַּֽעֲל֔וּ כִּ֛י אֵ֥ין יְהֹוָ֖ה בְּקִרְבְּכֶ֑ם וְלֹא֙ תִּנָּ֣גְפ֔וּ לִפְנֵ֖י אֹֽיְבֵיכֶֽם: מג כִּ֣י הָֽעֲמָֽלֵקִ֞י וְהַכְּנַֽעֲנִ֥י שָׁם֙ לִפְנֵיכֶ֔ם וּנְפַלְתֶּ֖ם

shrunk back from following *God*, *God* will not be with you."   44. They insisted on going up to the top of the mountain, but the Ark of the Covenant of *God* and Moshe did not depart from the camp. 45. And the Amalekite[s] and the Canaanite[s] who dwelt on that mountain came down and they struck them and crushed them all the way to Ḥormah.

XV   1. *God* spoke to Moshe [saying]:   2. "Speak to the sons of Yisrael and say to them: When you come into the land of your habitations that I am giving you,   3. and you will make a fire offering, an ascent offering or a meal offering to *God*, for a vow, or in free-will dedication, or in your festive seasons, to make for *God* an expression of compliance from cattle or sheep,   4. then one who brings his offering near to *God* shall at the same time bring a homage offering; fine flour, one tenth, mixed with one-quarter of a *hin* of oil.   5. And wine for a libation, one-quarter of a *hin* with the ascent offering or for the meal offering; thus [shall it be] for one sheep.   6. Or for a ram you shall make a homage offering: fine flour, two tenths, mixed with one-third of a *hin* of oil. 7. And wine for a libation, one-third of a *hin* shall you bring near to *God* as an expression of compliance.   8. And if you prepare an animal of the cattle species as an ascent offering or a meal offering to *God*, as a vow or as a peace offering,   9. he must make, along with the animal of the cattle species, a homage offering: fine flour, three tenths, mixed with half a *hin* of oil.   10. And you shall bring near wine for a libation, half a *hin*; it is a fire offering to *God* as an expression of compliance.   11. Thus shall be done for every ox or for every ram, or for the lamb among the sheep or goats.   12. Thus shall you do, in accordance with the number [of offerings] you make, one for each, according to their number.   13. Every native-born can do these things also in this fashion, to bring near to *God* a fire offering as an expression of compliance.   14. And if an outsider enters among you from abroad, or whoever shall enter into your midst among your descendants, and he makes a fire offering to *God* as an expression of compliance, as you do it, thus shall he do.

בְּחֶ֑רֶב כִּֽי־עַל־כֵּ֤ן שַׁבְתֶּם֙ מֵאַחֲרֵ֣י יְהֹוָ֔ה וְלֹא־יִהְיֶ֥ה יְהֹוָ֖ה עִמָּכֶֽם: מד וַיַּעְפִּ֕לוּ לַעֲל֖וֹת אֶל־רֹ֣אשׁ הָהָ֑ר וַאֲר֤וֹן בְּרִית־יְהֹוָה֙ וּמֹשֶׁ֔ה לֹא־מָ֖שׁוּ מִקֶּ֥רֶב הַֽמַּחֲנֶֽה: מה וַיֵּ֤רֶד הָעֲמָלֵקִי֙ וְהַֽכְּנַעֲנִ֔י הַיֹּשֵׁ֖ב בָּהָ֣ר הַה֑וּא וַיַּכּ֥וּם וַֽיַּכְּת֖וּם עַד־הַֽחׇרְמָֽה: פ

טו א וַיְדַבֵּ֥ר יְהֹוָ֖ה אֶל־מֹשֶׁ֥ה לֵּאמֹֽר: ב דַּבֵּר֙ אֶל־בְּנֵ֣י יִשְׂרָאֵ֔ל וְאָמַרְתָּ֖ אֲלֵהֶ֑ם כִּ֣י תָבֹ֗אוּ אֶל־אֶ֙רֶץ֙ מוֹשְׁבֹ֣תֵיכֶ֔ם אֲשֶׁ֥ר אֲנִ֖י נֹתֵ֥ן לָכֶֽם: ג וַעֲשִׂיתֶ֨ם אִשֶּׁ֤ה לַֽיהֹוָה֙ עֹלָ֣ה אוֹ־זֶ֔בַח לְפַלֵּא־נֶ֙דֶר֙ א֣וֹ בִנְדָבָ֔ה א֖וֹ בְּמֹעֲדֵיכֶ֑ם לַעֲשׂ֞וֹת רֵ֤יחַ נִיחֹ֙חַ֙ לַֽיהֹוָ֔ה מִן־הַבָּקָ֖ר א֥וֹ מִן־הַצֹּֽאן: ד וְהִקְרִ֛יב הַמַּקְרִ֥יב קׇרְבָּנ֖וֹ לַֽיהֹוָ֑ה מִנְחָה֙ סֹ֣לֶת עִשָּׂר֔וֹן בָּל֕וּל בִּרְבִעִ֥ית הַהִ֖ין שָֽׁמֶן: ה וְיַ֤יִן לַנֶּ֙סֶךְ֙ רְבִיעִ֣ית הַהִ֔ין תַּעֲשֶׂ֥ה עַל־הָעֹלָ֖ה א֣וֹ לַזָּ֑בַח לַכֶּ֖בֶשׂ הָאֶחָֽד: ו א֤וֹ לָאַ֙יִל֙ תַּעֲשֶׂ֣ה מִנְחָ֔ה סֹ֖לֶת שְׁנֵ֣י עֶשְׂרֹנִ֑ים בְּלוּלָ֥ה בַשֶּׁ֖מֶן שְׁלִשִׁ֥ית הַהִֽין: ז וְיַ֥יִן לַנֶּ֖סֶךְ שְׁלִשִׁ֣ית הַהִ֑ין תַּקְרִ֥יב רֵֽיחַ־נִיחֹ֖חַ לַֽיהֹוָֽה: חמישי ח וְכִֽי־תַעֲשֶׂ֥ה בֶן־בָּקָ֖ר עֹלָ֣ה אוֹ־זָ֑בַח לְפַלֵּא־נֶ֛דֶר אֽוֹ־שְׁלָמִ֖ים לַֽיהֹוָֽה: ט וְהִקְרִ֤יב עַל־בֶּן־הַבָּקָר֙ מִנְחָ֔ה סֹ֖לֶת שְׁלֹשָׁ֣ה עֶשְׂרֹנִ֑ים בָּל֥וּל בַּשֶּׁ֖מֶן חֲצִ֥י הַהִֽין: י וְיַ֛יִן תַּקְרִ֥יב לַנֶּ֖סֶךְ חֲצִ֣י הַהִ֑ין אִשֵּׁ֥ה רֵֽיחַ־נִיחֹ֖חַ לַֽיהֹוָֽה: יא כָּ֣כָה יֵעָשֶׂ֗ה לַשּׁוֹר֙ הָֽאֶחָ֔ד א֖וֹ לָאַ֣יִל הָאֶחָ֑ד אֽוֹ־לַשֶּׂ֥ה בַכְּבָשִׂ֖ים א֥וֹ בָֽעִזִּֽים: יב כַּמִּסְפָּ֖ר אֲשֶׁ֣ר תַּעֲשׂ֑וּ כָּ֚כָה תַּעֲשׂ֣וּ לָאֶחָ֔ד כְּמִסְפָּרָֽם: יג כׇּל־הָאֶזְרָ֥ח יַעֲשֶׂה־כָּ֖כָה אֶת־אֵ֑לֶּה לְהַקְרִ֛יב אִשֵּׁ֥ה רֵֽיחַ־נִיחֹ֖חַ לַֽיהֹוָֽה: יד וְכִֽי־יָגוּר֩ אִתְּכֶ֨ם גֵּ֜ר א֤וֹ אֲשֶֽׁר־בְּתֽוֹכְכֶם֙ לְדֹרֹ֣תֵיכֶ֔ם וְעָשָׂ֛ה אִשֵּׁ֥ה רֵֽיחַ־נִיחֹ֖חַ לַֽיהֹוָ֑ה כַּאֲשֶׁ֥ר תַּעֲשׂ֖וּ כֵּ֥ן יַעֲשֶֽׂה: טו הַקָּהָ֕ל חֻקָּ֥ה

15. O assembly! There shall be one and the same statute for you and for the outsider who has entered from abroad. It is an everlasting statute for your descendants: The outsider who has entered from abroad shall be equal with you before *God*. 16. There shall be one Teaching and one [standard of] right for you and for the outsider who has entered among you from abroad." 17. *God* spoke to Moshe [saying]: 18. "Speak to the sons of Yisrael and say to them: When you come into the land to which I am bringing you, 19. then it shall be: when you eat of the bread of the land, you shall lift out an uplifted donation for *God*. 20. As the first portion from your kneading troughs you shall lift out a cake of bread as an uplifted donation. Like the uplifted donation from your threshing floor, so shall you lift up this one. 21. From the first portion from your kneading troughs shall you give to *God* an uplifted donation for your descendants. 22. And if one day you should fall into the error that you need no longer observe all these commandments that *God* uttered to Moshe— 23. all that which *God* has commanded you, from the day that *God* gave His commandments and onward to your descendants— 24. then it shall be, if by the eyes of the community an act of inadvertence has been committed, then the entire community shall prepare

אַחַת לָכֶם וְלַגֵּר הַגָּר חֻקַּת עוֹלָם לְדֹרֹתֵיכֶם
כָּכֶם כַּגֵּר יִהְיֶה לִפְנֵי יְהֹוָה: טז תּוֹרָה אַחַת
וּמִשְׁפָּט אֶחָד יִהְיֶה לָכֶם וְלַגֵּר הַגָּר אִתְּכֶם: פ
ששי יז וַיְדַבֵּר יְהֹוָה אֶל־מֹשֶׁה לֵּאמֹר: יח דַּבֵּר
אֶל־בְּנֵי יִשְׂרָאֵל וְאָמַרְתָּ אֲלֵהֶם בְּבֹאֲכֶם אֶל־
הָאָרֶץ אֲשֶׁר אֲנִי מֵבִיא אֶתְכֶם שָׁמָּה: יט וְהָיָה
בַּאֲכָלְכֶם מִלֶּחֶם הָאָרֶץ תָּרִימוּ תְרוּמָה לַיהֹוָה:
כ רֵאשִׁית עֲרִסֹתֵכֶם חַלָּה תָּרִימוּ תְרוּמָה
כִּתְרוּמַת גֹּרֶן כֵּן תָּרִימוּ אֹתָהּ: כא מֵרֵאשִׁית
עֲרִסֹתֵיכֶם תִּתְּנוּ לַיהֹוָה תְּרוּמָה לְדֹרֹתֵיכֶם: ס
כב וְכִי תִשְׁגּוּ וְלֹא תַעֲשׂוּ אֵת כָּל־הַמִּצְוֹת הָאֵלֶּה
אֲשֶׁר־דִּבֶּר יְהֹוָה אֶל־מֹשֶׁה: כג אֵת כָּל־אֲשֶׁר
צִוָּה יְהֹוָה אֲלֵיכֶם בְּיַד־מֹשֶׁה מִן־הַיּוֹם אֲשֶׁר
צִוָּה יְהֹוָה וָהָלְאָה לְדֹרֹתֵיכֶם: כד וְהָיָה אִם
מֵעֵינֵי הָעֵדָה נֶעֶשְׂתָה לִשְׁגָגָה וְעָשׂוּ כָל־הָעֵדָה

CHAPTER XV

20. ***Like the uplifted donation from your threshing floor.*** Even as the threshing floor reminds us of the abundance with which God has blessed our fields, so the kneading trough represents the prosperity He has bestowed upon our households. And just as the owner may not partake of the produce laid up on his threshing floor without previously having made the gift of the תְּרוּמָה גְדוֹלָה ["great uplifted donation"] to the כֹּהֵן [priest], to symbolize his awareness that he owes his abundant harvest only to God (for which reason he must make a homage offering to the Sanctuary of the Law as represented by the priests), so this awareness and this reminder come to him with renewed impact when he prepares his daily bread for himself and for his loved ones and considers the particular care which God extends to every household and to every soul within it. . . .

22. . . . Our relationship to God and to His commandments is defined as a consistent one, which does not permit any choices or fine distinctions. It does not accommodate the illusion that one can give up concepts that are "specifically Jewish," retaining only what is "universal" from the Noaḥide point of view—as if one could dispense with the Mosaic Law and construct for oneself a so-called "prophetic" code to observe. For us there is no alternative. It is a choice of "either—or": Either one is a full Jew, observing the entire Law, or one has turned completely away from God. Not without good reason does God in this verse equate defection from Himself with defection from His Law; or, more accurately, defection from His Law with defection from Himself, euphemistically describing idolatry as a defection from His Law. The sole link He recognizes between Himself and ourselves is the one of loyal adherence to His Law. . . .

° ° °

24. ***the eyes of the community.*** Namely, the "intel-

פַּר בֶּן־בָּקָר אֶחָד לְעֹלָה לְרֵיחַ נִיחֹחַ לַיהוָה
וּמִנְחָתוֹ וְנִסְכּוֹ כַּמִּשְׁפָּט וּשְׂעִיר־עִזִּים אֶחָד
לְחַטָּת (חסר א'): כה וְכִפֶּר הַכֹּהֵן עַל־כָּל־עֲדַת בְּנֵי
יִשְׂרָאֵל וְנִסְלַח לָהֶם כִּי־שְׁגָגָה הִוא וְהֵם הֵבִיאוּ
אֶת־קָרְבָּנָם אִשֶּׁה לַיהוָה וְחַטָּאתָם לִפְנֵי יְהוָה
עַל־שִׁגְגָתָם: כו וְנִסְלַח לְכָל־עֲדַת בְּנֵי יִשְׂרָאֵל
וְלַגֵּר הַגָּר בְּתוֹכָם כִּי לְכָל־הָעָם בִּשְׁגָגָה: שביעי
כז וְאִם־נֶפֶשׁ אַחַת תֶּחֱטָא בִשְׁגָגָה וְהִקְרִיבָה עֵז
בַּת־שְׁנָתָהּ לְחַטָּאת: כח וְכִפֶּר הַכֹּהֵן עַל־הַנֶּפֶשׁ
הַשֹּׁגֶגֶת בְּחֶטְאָה בִשְׁגָגָה לִפְנֵי יְהוָה לְכַפֵּר עָלָיו
וְנִסְלַח לוֹ: כט הָאֶזְרָח בִּבְנֵי יִשְׂרָאֵל וְלַגֵּר הַגָּר
בְּתוֹכָם תּוֹרָה אַחַת יִהְיֶה לָכֶם לָעֹשֶׂה בִּשְׁגָגָה:
ל וְהַנֶּפֶשׁ אֲשֶׁר־תַּעֲשֶׂה ׀ בְּיָד רָמָה מִן־הָאֶזְרָח
וּמִן־הַגֵּר אֶת־יְהוָה הוּא מְגַדֵּף וְנִכְרְתָה הַנֶּפֶשׁ
הַהִוא מִקֶּרֶב עַמָּהּ: לא כִּי דְבַר־יְהוָה בָּזָה וְאֶת־

one young bull each for an ascent offering as
an expression of compliance to *God*, and its
homage offering and its libation according
to regulation, and one male goat as an offering that clears [him who brings it] of sin.
25. The priest shall effect atonement for
the entire community of Yisrael and they
will be forgiven, for it is an act of inadvertence, and they have renewed their nearness
by bringing a fire offering to *God*, and their
sin offering that clears [him who brings it] of
sin, before *God* for their inadvertence.
26. The entire community of the sons of
Yisrael and he who has entered into their
midst from abroad shall be forgiven,
because the entire people has acted in
inadvertence. 27. And if a person sins
inadvertently, he shall bring a female goat
in its first year as an offering that clears [him
who brings it] of sin. 28. And the priest
shall effect atonement before *God* for the
person who was inadvertent in that he
sinned inadvertently, and he shall be forgiven. 29. [As for both] the native-born
among the sons of Yisrael and one who
entered into their midst from abroad, there
shall be one Teaching for one who committed anything inadvertently. 30. But as for
the person who does this with an uplifted
hand, either among the native-born or one
who has entered from abroad, he has
blasphemed *God* by so doing, and that soul
shall be uprooted from the midst of its
people, 31. for he has scorned a word of

ligence" of the nation. It is represented by the great Sanhedrin. If, then, this supreme authority of the Law erroneously (as the result of a theoretical error; cf. Verse 22) declares an act of idolatry as permissible and, as a consequence, "an act of inadvertence has been committed"; i.e., this theoretical error has given rise to a sin in practice. . . .

31. . . . Hence also the statement in Sanhedrin 99a, to the effect that one who denies that the Law was revealed by God—even if he accepts the entire תּוֹרָה as Divine except for only one verse that he attributes to Moses, not to God, or even if he denies the Divine origin of only one nuance expressed in one law, or the hermeneutic validity of only one קַל וָחוֹמֶר[3] or one גְּזֵרָה שָׁוָה[4]—is classed as a scorner of the Law, as expressed in this verse by the words, "he has scorned a word of *God*."

Not without good reason does this portion open with the concept of Divine revelation in all its components, which includes תּוֹרָה שֶׁבִּכְתָב [the Written Law], תּוֹרָה שֶׁבְּעַל פֶּה [the Oral Law], pre-Mosaic law; i.e., laws given to Adam, Noaḥ and to the Patriarchs, and post-Mosaic utterances; i.e., the words of the Prophets. Concerning one who denies even as much as one דָּבָר [word] of these דִּבְרֵי ד׳ [words of God], or one מִצְוָה [commandment] of these commandments of God, the Law says: "For he

[3]*Note to the English translation*: A legal inference drawn from a minor premise to a major one. [G.H.]

[4]*Note to the English translation*: An inference, from a similarity of words or phrases occurring in two passages, that the idea expressed in the one passage is applicable also to the other. [G.H.]

מִצְוָתוֹ הֵפַר הִכָּרֵת ׀ תִּכָּרֵת הַנֶּפֶשׁ הַהִוא עֲוֺנָה
בָהּ: פ לב וַיִּהְיוּ בְנֵי־יִשְׂרָאֵל בַּמִּדְבָּר וַיִּמְצְאוּ
אִישׁ מְקֹשֵׁשׁ עֵצִים בְּיוֹם הַשַּׁבָּת: לג וַיַּקְרִיבוּ
אֹתוֹ הַמֹּצְאִים אֹתוֹ מְקֹשֵׁשׁ עֵצִים אֶל־מֹשֶׁה
וְאֶל־אַהֲרֹן וְאֶל כָּל־הָעֵדָה: לד וַיַּנִּיחוּ אֹתוֹ
בַּמִּשְׁמָר כִּי לֹא פֹרַשׁ מַה־יֵּעָשֶׂה לוֹ: ס
לה וַיֹּאמֶר יְהוָה אֶל־מֹשֶׁה מוֹת יוּמַת הָאִישׁ
רָגוֹם אֹתוֹ בָאֲבָנִים כָּל־הָעֵדָה מִחוּץ לַמַּחֲנֶה:
לו וַיֹּצִיאוּ אֹתוֹ כָּל־הָעֵדָה אֶל־מִחוּץ לַמַּחֲנֶה
וַיִּרְגְּמוּ אֹתוֹ בָּאֲבָנִים וַיָּמֹת כַּאֲשֶׁר צִוָּה יְהוָה
אֶת־מֹשֶׁה: פ מפטיר לז וַיֹּאמֶר יְהוָה אֶל־מֹשֶׁה
לֵּאמֹר: לח דַּבֵּר אֶל־בְּנֵי יִשְׂרָאֵל וְאָמַרְתָּ אֲלֵהֶם
וְעָשׂוּ לָהֶם צִיצִת עַל־כַּנְפֵי בִגְדֵיהֶם לְדֹרֹתָם
וְנָתְנוּ עַל־צִיצִת הַכָּנָף פְּתִיל תְּכֵלֶת: לט וְהָיָה
לָכֶם לְצִיצִת וּרְאִיתֶם אֹתוֹ וּזְכַרְתֶּם אֶת־כָּל־
מִצְוֹת יְהוָה וַעֲשִׂיתֶם אֹתָם וְלֹא־תָתוּרוּ אַחֲרֵי

God; he has nullified a commandment of His; that soul shall be uprooted; its iniquity shall turn against it." 32. [While] the sons of Yisrael were in the wilderness, they discovered a man gathering sticks on the Sabbath day. 33. Then those that had discovered him gathering sticks brought him to Moshe, to Aharon and to the entire community. 34. They placed him into custody because it had not been explained what should be done with him. 35. And *God* said to Moshe: "The man shall be executed; let the entire community stone him with stones outside the camp." 36. The entire community led him outside the camp and they stoned him with stones so that he died, as *God* had commanded Moshe. 37. And *God* said to Moshe: 38. "Speak to the sons of Yisrael and say it to them so that they will make themselves fringes upon the corners of their garments, for [the generations of] their descendants, and they shall place upon the fringes of the corner a thread of sky-blue wool. 39. And this shall be fringes for you, so that you may see them and remember all the commandments of *God* and carry them out, and not go exploring after your

has scorned a word of *God*; he has nullified a commandment of His."

° ° °

32. . . . There is one *mitzvah* by which God has designated the performance of a specific act, or rather, refraining from a specific act, as symbolically demonstrating that we acknowledge Him and that we pay Him homage as the master over our destinies and over our actions. Accordingly, the observance of this *mitzvah* constitutes an act of allegiance to God; conversely, refusal to observe it implies a denial that God is indeed the master over our destinies and over our actions. For this reason, a refusal to observe this *mitzvah* is subject to the penalties of "excision" (being "uprooted" from the midst of the people of Israel) and death by stoning, no less than idolatry or blasphemy. This *mitzvah* is שַׁבָּת [the observance of the Sabbath]. Inasmuch as the Sabbath puts a halt to our labors by explicit command of God, this cessation from "creating" work on our part implies that we place all our actions, along with the world in which we live, at the feet of God. Our refraining from "creating" work on the Sabbath is a dual act of homage to God's sovereignty. Conversely, the performance of any such activity on the Sabbath is equivalent to a double denial of God's dominion. So there is a close link between the concrete instance of a חילול שַׁבָּת [violation of the Sabbath] that will now be related, and the laws and events set forth in the preceding verses.

We now see these same בְּנֵי יִשְׂרָאֵל [sons of Israel], that same community, that same people whom, at the opening of this portion, we saw in full rebellion against God and against His direction, becoming loyal to God once again. And though, for this present generation, they have been doomed to wander through the wilderness, without any hope of arriving at their destination, we see them aware once again of their duty and now earnestly defending their loyalty to God and to His Law even against their own kinsmen. Compared with the incident of blasphemy described in Leviticus 24:10 ff., the opening phrase, "(While) the sons of Yisrael were in the wilderness," along with the wording of this entire report, indicates particular emphasis on the initiative exercised by the entire nation on this occasion. . . .

° ° °

own heart and after your own eyes [and] following them, become unfaithful to Me. 40. In order that you may remember and carry out all My commandments and remain holy to your God. 41. I, *God*, your God, Who brought you out from the land

לְבַבְכֶם֙ וְאַחֲרֵ֣י עֵֽינֵיכֶ֔ם אֲשֶׁר־אַתֶּ֥ם זֹנִ֖ים אַחֲרֵיהֶֽם: מ לְמַ֣עַן תִּזְכְּר֔וּ וַעֲשִׂיתֶ֖ם אֶת־כָּל־מִצְוֺתָ֑י וִהְיִיתֶ֥ם קְדֹשִׁ֖ים לֵאלֹֽהֵיכֶֽם: מא אֲנִ֞י יְהֹוָ֣ה אֱלֹֽהֵיכֶ֗ם אֲשֶׁ֨ר הוֹצֵ֤אתִי אֶתְכֶם֙ מֵאֶ֣רֶץ

41. . . . If we consider what the text of the Law itself has to say (Verses 39–41) concerning the significance and purpose of these *tzitzith* threads upon our garments, we will see that there is no room for ambiguity. Quite clearly the *tzitzith* are intended to serve as reminders, which, by calling our attention to the Law of God and our commitment to it, should guard us against erroneous notions that could induce us to forsake God and our duty. The *tzitzith* are meant to keep us loyal and dedicated to our vocation as human beings and as Jews.

The only question still to be explored is the connection between the visible means that the Law has chosen as our reminders, and the ideas of which we are to be reminded. We believe that, at the outset, we may say that even as the *milah* upon our bodies, the *tefillin* on arm and forehead and the *mezuzah* in our homes are intended to sanctify the body, the hand, the head and the house, respectively, upon which they have been placed as symbols; thus consecrating our bodies and our homes for their Divinely-ordained purpose; so, too, the *tzitzith* on our garments are intended to sanctify our clothing by symbolically consecrating it for the purpose God has decreed for it. . . .

According to its historical origin (Genesis 3:7 and 21), the relation of our clothing to our moral calling as human beings is very close indeed. The error which preceded [the giving of the first garments to Adam and Eve] and from which our clothing was meant to guard us in future is not merely related, or similar, to the errors cited in Verse 39 but is, in fact, so identical with the latter that we believe the association could hardly be more cogent. We need only recall the statement in Genesis 3:6, "When the woman saw that the tree was good for food and tempting for the sight and that the tree was a delight to contemplate," to understand that men came to disregard the commandments of God because they "went about after their own heart and after their own eyes" and regarded as "good" anything that, in the judgment of their greedy eye and their mental quest for bodily gratification, seemed conducive to the satisfaction of their physical desires.

By thus following the dictates of their eyes and their hearts, they descended to the primitive intelligence of animals, which, of course, are guided solely by the stimuli of heart and eye in choosing what to pursue and what to avoid. Man, by contrast, must heed the voice of God within him, which, among other things, has taught

him modesty, to cover his animal nakedness. This dictate of modesty was reconfirmed and hallowed for men by the clothing that God gave them when He sent them away from Paradise. The purpose of his clothing was to have man remember at all times that his calling was different from and higher than that of the animal, and that man, having been given the ability to reason, must submit to the dictates of a higher authority with regard to what is "good" and "evil."

In light of the foregoing, the admonition inherent in man's clothing, translated into words, can be none other, and no more cogent, than this: "So that you may remember all the commandments of *God* and carry them out, and not go about after your own heart and after your own eyes, (and) following them, become unfaithful to Me." Thus, as "fringes sprouting from the garment," the *tzitzith* in themselves symbolize the call to translate into reality the admonition inherent in man's clothing.

It must be added here that man's clothing has a dual significance. It is בֶּגֶד; by "covering over" the animal aspects of the human body, it is intended to demonstrate that man has been endowed with a moral character. But it also acts as כְּסוּת, a protective cover against the elements of the physical world.

At the moment when his moral weakness made it necessary for man to have clothing in order to remind him of his moral calling, God, in His guiding love, drove man out of the harmonious, pleasant Paradise of nature into the raw, hostile ambiance of an earth offering only thorns and thistles. And so man needed clothing also to protect him while he performed the mission common to all mankind under the most diverse climatic conditions. The *tzitzith* commandment, referring to clothing as בֶּגֶד, as a "covering over" of the physical body, reads: "so that they will make themselves fringes upon the corners of their garments (בְּגְדֵיהֶם) for [the generations of] their descendants," thus declaring that we must discharge our mission as Jews among men unconditionally, for all time, and independently of changing times; i.e., לְדֹרֹתָם ["for the generations of their descendants"]. Similarly, the same commandment, referring to clothing as כְּסוּת, a protective cover, is formulated [in Deuteronomy 22:12] in the words, "Make yourself twisted threads on the four corners of your garment with which you cover yourself (כְּסוּתְךָ)," thereby declaring that we must discharge our mission as Jews among men no matter where on earth we may

מִצְרַ֔יִם לִהְי֥וֹת לָכֶ֖ם לֵאלֹהִ֑ים אֲנִ֖י יְהוָ֥ה אֱלֹהֵיכֶֽם׃ פ

of Mitzrayim to be God to you; I, *God*, your God."

dwell and irrespective of changing climatic and natural conditions. No matter where, and into what isolation, you may have to migrate, wherever you may go—to אַרְבַּע כַּנְפוֹת,[5] to all the "four corners" of the world, north or south, east or west—you are to wear upon your body the same reminder of the one mission which remains constant and which you must discharge no matter where you go. . . . Neither time nor place can undo so much as one thread from this bond of your duty; לְדֹרֹתָם, in every age, and בְּאַרְבַּע כַּנְפוֹת ["in the four corners"] of the earth, in every place, your existence as a human being must be identical with your calling as a Jew.

° ° °

If we now look back on the entire weekly portion of שְׁלַח לְךָ, which concludes with the *tzitzith* commandment, it immediately becomes evident that this commandment is closely linked with the incident relating to the מְרַגְּלִים [scouts]. . . .

The מְרַגְּלִים had been sent out, as repeatedly stated, לָתוּר אֶת הָאָרֶץ ["to explore the land"]. By failing to discharge their mission as תָּרִים [explorers], they came to defect openly from God and dragged the people along with them into their own fateful error. And now, at the conclusion of the narrative, the institution of *tzitzith* comes to admonish us each day and at every hour לֹא תָתוּרוּ, not to "go exploring after your own heart and after your own eyes (and) following them, become unfaithful to Me."

. . . Only because they had wandered about after their own hearts and after their own eyes did they completely forget the concept of God as the One Who directed their actions and guided their destinies. Thus, notwithstanding their moral relationship to God, they shrunk in their own minds to the size and impotence of grasshoppers, while the land and its inhabitants, despite the moral depravity of both, grew in their minds to gigantic dimensions, too big for them to overcome. That which God condemned came to seem "good" in their eyes, while that which God Himself had promised them seemed "evil." And as a result of this perverted judgment, the gate of the promised, reborn Paradise clanged shut before them, even as that same perversion had caused the first men on earth to lose their Paradise.

° ° °

[5]*Note to the English translation*: The term אַרְבַּע כַּנְפוֹת refers to the four-cornered garment to which the *tzitzith* are attached. [G.H.]

The Haftarah for this Sidra may be found on page 893.

קרח

KORAḤ

XVI 1. Koraḥ presumed—[he was] the son of Yitzhar, son of Kehath, son of Levi—and [so did] Dathan and Abiram, sons of Eliab, and On, son of Peleth, sons of Reuben, 2. and they rose up before Moshe; and so, too, [did] men from [among] the sons of Yisrael—two hundred and fifty—princes of the community, representatives of the assembly, men of renown. 3. When these had assembled themselves against Moshe and Aharon, they said to them: "You take too much upon yourselves, for the entire community, they all are holy and *God* is in their midst. And why do you lift yourselves up above the community of *God?*" 4. Moshe heard [it] and he fell upon his face.

טז א וַיִּקַּח קֹרַח בֶּן־יִצְהָר בֶּן־קְהָת בֶּן־לֵוִי
וְדָתָן וַאֲבִירָם בְּנֵי אֱלִיאָב וְאוֹן בֶּן־פֶּלֶת בְּנֵי
רְאוּבֵן׃ ב וַיָּקֻמוּ לִפְנֵי מֹשֶׁה וַאֲנָשִׁים מִבְּנֵי־
יִשְׂרָאֵל חֲמִשִּׁים וּמָאתָיִם נְשִׂיאֵי עֵדָה קְרִאֵי
מוֹעֵד אַנְשֵׁי־שֵׁם׃ ג וַיִּקָּהֲלוּ עַל־מֹשֶׁה וְעַל־
אַהֲרֹן וַיֹּאמְרוּ אֲלֵהֶם רַב־לָכֶם כִּי כָל־הָעֵדָה
כֻּלָּם קְדֹשִׁים וּבְתוֹכָם יְהוָה וּמַדּוּעַ תִּתְנַשְּׂאוּ
עַל־קְהַל יְהוָה׃ ד וַיִּשְׁמַע מֹשֶׁה וַיִּפֹּל עַל־פָּנָיו׃

CHAPTER XVI

1. The weekly portion of שְׁלַח לְךָ dealt with the rebellion against God; the weekly portion of קֹרַח tells of the rebellion against Moses. . . . Koraḥ arrogated to himself the right to question Moses and Aaron regarding their position in the nation. The fact that this idea is expressed by the word לְקִיחָה [a form of "taking"] indicates that Koraḥ was motivated by selfish considerations; he did it for his own advantage, and the form in which he posed the questions, as a spokesman for the interests of the community, was nothing but sham and pretense.

2. ***and they rose up before Moshe.*** The peculiar order in which the participants in the uprising are introduced in the narrative seems to indicate the degree of their involvement. Koraḥ appears as the instigator of the incident; hence Verse 1 opens with the words וַיִּקַּח קֹרַח ["Koraḥ presumed"]. Dathan, Abiram and On then joined him as additional agitators. These four men came before Moses; "they rose up. . ." after they had won over another 250 men from among the people, who "assembled . . .," a mob of rebels supporting the four ringleaders.

3. ***these had assembled themselves. . .they said.*** Koraḥ, Dathan and Abiram came before Moses, and after the 250 men whom they had incited to support them in their reproaches and demands had gathered *en masse,* Koraḥ and his companions, claiming to be spokesmen of the entire group, said: "You take too much upon yourselves. . . ."

4. ***Moshe heard [it].*** Moses heard, or rather, he understood the aim and the motivation of the claims and accusations made against him. It was a denial of the Divine character of his mission, motivated not by an erroneous notion that would have responded to correction, but by self-seeking jealousy which, under the pretense of representing the public interest, seeks only the satisfaction of its own selfish ambitions. . . .

° ° °

A true, authentic messenger of God—and none more so than one like Moses—will surely be the first and the most willing to admit that he is unworthy of his task and to beseech God to choose as His herald someone worthier, better and more capable. But if, despite his protests, God has sent him and none other as the one most worthy and qualified to bear His message, who would dare to come before him and ask him: "Why do you lift yourself up above the community of *God?*" The use of the expression "you lift yourself up" constitutes a denial that God has sent him; it implies that Moses is a fraud and that his mission is a lie.

Therefore "Moshe heard [it] and he fell upon his face." The truth of a statement presented as a fact can be confirmed only by another fact, not by reasoning. Reasoning can suggest an assumption, in terms of probability or necessity, but it can never establish a fact. The veracity of a messenger can be confirmed only by the one who sent him; so, too, the authenticity of Moses' mission can be confirmed only by God Himself. For this reason Moses does not utter a word to counter Koraḥ's accusations. If God would not consider it

5. And he spoke to Koraḥ and to his company [saying]: "Let morning come and then *God* will make known who is His, and who is the holy one, so that He will allow him to come near to Him. Whoever He will chose, He will allow him to come near to Him. 6. Do this: Take your fire pans, Korah and all his company, 7. place fire into them and lay incense upon them tomorrow before *God,* and then it shall be [that] the man whom *God* will choose, he is the holy one. You want too much, O sons of Levi." 8. And Moshe said to Koraḥ: "Hear now, O sons of Levi! 9. Is it too little for you that the God of Yisrael has set you apart from the community of Yisrael, to have you come near to Him to do the service of the Dwelling Place of God and to stand before the community to minister before them? 10. And since He has thus brought you and all your brothers, the sons of Levi with you, near to Him, will you now seek the priesthood also? 11. Therefore you and all your company, you are the ones who have assembled against *God.* But as for Aharon, what is he that you should stir up rebellion against

ה וַיְדַבֵּ֨ר אֶל־קֹ֜רַח וְאֶֽל־כָּל־עֲדָתוֹ֮ לֵאמֹר֒ בֹּ֣קֶר וְיֹדַ֧ע יְהֹוָ֛ה אֶת־אֲשֶׁר־ל֖וֹ וְאֶת־הַקָּד֑וֹשׁ וְהִקְרִ֣יב אֵלָ֔יו וְאֵ֛ת אֲשֶׁ֥ר יִבְחַר־בּ֖וֹ יַקְרִ֥יב אֵלָֽיו: ו זֹ֖את עֲשׂ֑וּ קְחוּ־לָכֶ֣ם מַחְתּ֔וֹת קֹ֖רַח וְכָל־עֲדָתֽוֹ: ז וּתְנ֣וּ בָהֵ֣ן ׀ אֵ֗שׁ וְשִׂ֤ימוּ עֲלֵיהֶן֙ קְטֹ֙רֶת֙ לִפְנֵ֣י יְהֹוָ֔ה מָחָ֑ר וְהָיָ֗ה הָאִ֛ישׁ אֲשֶׁר־יִבְחַ֥ר יְהֹוָ֖ה ה֣וּא הַקָּד֑וֹשׁ רַב־לָכֶ֖ם בְּנֵ֥י לֵוִֽי: ח וַיֹּ֥אמֶר מֹשֶׁ֖ה אֶל־קֹ֑רַח שִׁמְעוּ־נָ֖א בְּנֵ֥י לֵוִֽי: ט הַמְעַ֣ט מִכֶּ֗ם כִּֽי־הִבְדִּיל֩ אֱלֹהֵ֨י יִשְׂרָאֵ֤ל אֶתְכֶם֙ מֵֽעֲדַ֣ת יִשְׂרָאֵ֔ל לְהַקְרִ֥יב אֶתְכֶ֖ם אֵלָ֑יו לַֽעֲבֹ֕ד אֶת־עֲבֹדַ֖ת מִשְׁכַּ֣ן יְהֹוָ֑ה וְלַֽעֲמֹ֞ד לִפְנֵ֧י הָֽעֵדָ֛ה לְשָֽׁרְתָֽם: י וַיַּקְרֵב֙ אֹֽתְךָ֔ וְאֶת־כָּל־אַחֶ֥יךָ בְנֵֽי־לֵוִ֖י אִתָּ֑ךְ וּבִקַּשְׁתֶּ֖ם גַּם־כְּהֻנָּֽה: יא לָכֵ֗ן אַתָּה֙ וְכָל־עֲדָ֣תְךָ֔ הַנֹּֽעָדִ֖ים עַל־יְהֹוָ֑ה וְאַֽהֲרֹ֣ן מַה־ה֔וּא כִּ֥י תַלִּ֖ונוּ (תלינו קרי)

---

proper to refute Koraḥ's words by reconfirming the authenticity of Moses' mission, then his mission was indeed at an end, and so "he fell upon his face."

    ○   ○   ○

5. . . . Since the verdict of necessity would mean the destruction of the rebels, they were to be given time to come to their senses, particularly in the quiet and seclusion of the night, when everyone is relegated to the company of his family and to communion with himself, and thus removed from the influence of companions that could lead him astray. At the same time, Moses wanted to utilize this time to remonstrate with those who had gone astray, as will be seen from what now follows. . . .

6–7. Moses had seen through Koraḥ. Koraḥ's rebellion had been motivated solely by jealousy of the priestly honors conferred upon the tribe of Aaron while the other Levite families had been ignored. In order to wipe out this distinction, and perhaps even to have himself and his descendants elected to the priesthood by popular vote, Koraḥ explained his rebellion as motivated by his belief that all were equally entitled to these prerogatives, and he suggested that the elevation of Aaron to his position had not come from God.

Very well, then, if they were really convinced that their claim was justified, let Koraḥ and his company dare to put it to the test by performing before God a function permitted only to the high priest. The supreme function of the high priest is to make the incense offering, the symbolic expression of complete devotion to the work of complying with God's will. Let them act upon their claim by performing this function and so submit the issue to Divine resolution. However, Moses warned them that this was an act of presumption fraught with danger, not only for all the other tribes represented by the 250 men but also for the Levites, whose position already brought them close to the Sanctuary and as whose representative Koraḥ wanted to be accepted. Hence, "You want too much, O sons of Levi."

8–11. . . . It seems that Dathan and Abiram, on the other hand, did not particularly care for the priesthood or its prerogatives. . . . However, it seems that they regarded Moses' political position as an obstacle to their ambitions, and they probably joined Koraḥ under the assumption that once the people's trust in the Divine origin of Moses' mission had been undermined, his position in the nation would be destroyed also.

    ○   ○   ○

him?" 12. Thereupon Moshe sent to call
Dathan and Abiram, sons of Eliab. But they
said: "We will not come up. 13. Is it too
little that you brought us out from a land
flowing with milk and honey to let us perish
in the wilderness, that you now would also
set yourself up as a despot over us?
14. Moreover, you certainly have not
brought us into a land flowing with milk
and honey merely by giving us an inheritance
of field and vineyard. Will you put out the
eyes of these people? We will not go up."
15. This hurt Moshe exceedingly, and he
said to *God*: "Do not turn to their homage
offering! I did not take [so much as] a
donkey from any one of them, neither have
I hurt any one of them." 16. And Moshe
said to Koraḥ: "Then you and your whole
company shall be before *God*, you, and
they, and also Aharon, tomorrow, 17. and
let each one of you take his pan and place
incense upon it and let each one bring near
his pan before *God*, two hundred and fifty
pans, and you also, and Aharon, each one his
pan." 18. And each man indeed took his
pan, placed fire upon it, and they stationed
themselves at the entrance of the Tent of
Appointed Meeting, along with Moshe and
Aharon. 19. But Koraḥ assembled the
entire community against them to the

עָלָֽיו׃ יב וַיִּשְׁלַ֣ח מֹשֶׁ֔ה לִקְרֹ֛א לְדָתָ֥ן וְלַאֲבִירָ֖ם
בְּנֵ֣י אֱלִיאָ֑ב וַיֹּֽאמְר֖וּ לֹ֥א נַעֲלֶֽה׃ יג הַמְעַ֗ט כִּ֤י
הֶֽעֱלִיתָ֙נוּ֙ מֵאֶ֨רֶץ זָבַ֤ת חָלָב֙ וּדְבַ֔שׁ לַהֲמִיתֵ֖נוּ
בַּמִּדְבָּ֑ר כִּֽי־תִשְׂתָּרֵ֥ר עָלֵ֖ינוּ גַּם־הִשְׂתָּרֵֽר׃ שני
יד אַ֡ף לֹ֣א אֶל־אֶ֩רֶץ֩ זָבַ֨ת חָלָ֤ב וּדְבַשׁ֙ הֲבִ֣יאֹתָ֔נוּ
וַתִּתֶּן־לָ֕נוּ נַחֲלַ֖ת שָׂדֶ֣ה וָכָ֑רֶם הַעֵינֵ֞י הָאֲנָשִׁ֥ים
הָהֵ֛ם תְּנַקֵּ֖ר לֹ֥א נַעֲלֶֽה׃ טו וַיִּ֤חַר לְמֹשֶׁה֙ מְאֹ֔ד
וַיֹּ֙אמֶר֙ אֶל־יְהוָ֔ה אַל־תֵּ֖פֶן אֶל־מִנְחָתָ֑ם לֹ֠א
חֲמ֨וֹר אֶחָ֤ד מֵהֶם֙ נָשָׂ֔אתִי וְלֹ֥א הֲרֵעֹ֖תִי אֶת־אַחַ֥ד
מֵהֶֽם׃ טז וַיֹּ֤אמֶר מֹשֶׁה֙ אֶל־קֹ֔רַח אַתָּה֙ וְכָל־
עֲדָ֣תְךָ֔ הֱי֖וּ לִפְנֵ֣י יְהוָ֑ה אַתָּ֥ה וָהֵ֛ם וְאַהֲרֹ֖ן מָחָֽר׃
יז וּקְח֣וּ ׀ אִ֣ישׁ מַחְתָּת֗וֹ וּנְתַתֶּ֤ם עֲלֵיהֶם֙ קְטֹ֔רֶת
וְהִקְרַבְתֶּ֞ם לִפְנֵ֤י יְהוָה֙ אִ֣ישׁ מַחְתָּת֔וֹ חֲמִשִּׁ֥ים
וּמָאתַ֖יִם מַחְתֹּ֑ת וְאַתָּ֥ה וְאַהֲרֹ֖ן אִ֥ישׁ מַחְתָּתֽוֹ׃
יח וַיִּקְח֞וּ אִ֣ישׁ מַחְתָּת֗וֹ וַיִּתְּנ֤וּ עֲלֵיהֶם֙ אֵ֔שׁ
וַיָּשִׂ֥ימוּ עֲלֵיהֶ֖ם קְטֹ֑רֶת וַיַּֽעַמְדוּ֙ פֶּ֚תַח אֹ֣הֶל מוֹעֵ֔ד
וּמֹשֶׁ֖ה וְאַהֲרֹֽן׃ יט וַיַּקְהֵ֨ל עֲלֵיהֶ֥ם קֹ֙רַח֙ אֶת־כָּל־

12. ***Thereupon Moshe sent.*** We have already noted that Dathan and Abiram seem to have formed a faction of their own within Koraḥ's conspiracy. Koraḥ's rebellion was primarily against Aaron's position as a priest; it was aimed only indirectly against the authority of Moses, the source and support of Aaron's priesthood. Dathan and Abiram, on the other hand, had rebelled specifically against Moses; their aim was to remove Moses from his position of political leadership. It was their common hostility—direct and indirect—against Moses that united the two factions. This was the reason why Moses wanted to speak to Dathan and Abiram separately from the others, but they replied: "We will not come up."... We will not go up to the "master"! We will not take orders from him; it is presumptuous of him to summon us into his presence as if he were greater than we; he has no right to give us any orders.

15. ***This hurt Moshe exceedingly.*** Literally, "this burned Moshe exceedingly." It hurt him deeply that anyone would dare suggest that he had exploited his position to commit arbitrary acts. . . .

I did not take [so much as] a donkey from any one of them. If I had blemished my character even by the slightest demonstration of self-interest or despotism, they would have a right not merely to doubt, but frankly to deny, that God sent me. . . . But I do not deserve the accusation that I undermined the people's confidence in my mission by willful acts of despotism. Not only have I never given my burden to any of the people—not even to any of their beasts of burden—to bear, but I also have never knowingly or willingly hurt any of them.

° ° °

19. ***But Koraḥ assembled.*** Koraḥ was so sure of himself, he must have forgotten so completely the relationship to God put in question here that, even at the moment of this fateful decision, he summoned the entire nation to take part in his dispute and to witness what he felt certain would be his triumph. It must have been his intention to impose his will by sheer force of numbers, without waiting for Divine intervention. In any event, this rebellious gathering was directed

entrance of the Tent of Appointed Meeting —then the glory of *God* appeared to the entire community. 20. And *God* spoke to Moshe and Aharon [saying]: 21. "Separate yourselves from the midst of this community so that I may destroy them instantly." 22. And they fell upon their faces and said: "O God, God of the spirits of all flesh! If one man sins, wilt Thou be angry with the whole community?" 23. And *God* spoke to Moshe [saying]: 24. "Speak to the community [saying]: Raise yourselves up, away from the environs of the dwelling place of Koraḥ, Dathan and Abiram." 25. And Moshe arose and went to Dathan and Abiram; the elders of Yisrael followed him. 26. And he spoke to the community [saying]: "Depart, I beseech you, from near the tents of those wicked people and do not touch anything that is theirs, lest you perish along with them in all their sins." 27. And they raised themselves up, away from near the dwelling place of Koraḥ, Dathan and Abiram, from every side. But Dathan and Abiram stepped out and stood upright at the entrance of their tents, with their wives, and their children, and their little ones. 28. And Moshe said: "By this you shall know that *God* has sent me to do all these deeds and [that I have] not [done them] of my own mind. 29. If these [men] will die as all men die, and if a fate like that of all men will be visited upon them, then *God* has not sent me. 30. But if *God* will create an entirely new thing, and the earth

הָעֵדָה אֶל־פֶּתַח אֹהֶל מוֹעֵד וַיֵּרָא כְּבוֹד־יְהֹוָה אֶל־כָּל־הָעֵדָה: ס שלישי כ וַיְדַבֵּר יְהֹוָה אֶל־מֹשֶׁה וְאֶל־אַהֲרֹן לֵאמֹר: כא הִבָּדְלוּ מִתּוֹךְ הָעֵדָה הַזֹּאת וַאֲכַלֶּה אֹתָם כְּרָגַע: כב וַיִּפְּלוּ עַל־פְּנֵיהֶם וַיֹּאמְרוּ אֵל אֱלֹהֵי הָרוּחֹת לְכָל־בָּשָׂר הָאִישׁ אֶחָד יֶחֱטָא וְעַל כָּל־הָעֵדָה תִּקְצֹף: ס כג וַיְדַבֵּר יְהֹוָה אֶל־מֹשֶׁה לֵּאמֹר: כד דַּבֵּר אֶל־הָעֵדָה לֵאמֹר הֵעָלוּ מִסָּבִיב לְמִשְׁכַּן־קֹרַח דָּתָן וַאֲבִירָם: כה וַיָּקָם מֹשֶׁה וַיֵּלֶךְ אֶל־דָּתָן וַאֲבִירָם וַיֵּלְכוּ אַחֲרָיו זִקְנֵי יִשְׂרָאֵל: כו וַיְדַבֵּר אֶל־הָעֵדָה לֵאמֹר סוּרוּ נָא מֵעַל אָהֳלֵי הָאֲנָשִׁים הָרְשָׁעִים הָאֵלֶּה וְאַל־תִּגְּעוּ בְּכָל־אֲשֶׁר לָהֶם פֶּן־תִּסָּפוּ בְּכָל־חַטֹּאתָם: כז וַיֵּעָלוּ מֵעַל מִשְׁכַּן־קֹרַח דָּתָן וַאֲבִירָם מִסָּבִיב וְדָתָן וַאֲבִירָם יָצְאוּ נִצָּבִים פֶּתַח אָהֳלֵיהֶם וּנְשֵׁיהֶם וּבְנֵיהֶם וְטַפָּם: כח וַיֹּאמֶר מֹשֶׁה בְּזֹאת תֵּדְעוּן כִּי־יְהֹוָה שְׁלָחַנִי לַעֲשׂוֹת אֵת כָּל־הַמַּעֲשִׂים הָאֵלֶּה כִּי־לֹא מִלִּבִּי: כט אִם־כְּמוֹת כָּל־הָאָדָם יְמֻתוּן אֵלֶּה וּפְקֻדַּת כָּל־הָאָדָם יִפָּקֵד עֲלֵיהֶם לֹא יְהֹוָה שְׁלָחָנִי: ל וְאִם־בְּרִיאָה יִבְרָא יְהֹוָה וּפָצְתָה הָאֲדָמָה

against Moses and Aaron: hence all those who came demonstrated by their presence that they sided with Koraḥ.

22. *O God, God of the spirits of all flesh.* Thou knowest how easily the masses can be talked into error by the oratory and the misrepresentations of a man of superior intellect such as Koraḥ, who has hitherto enjoyed the complete trust of the masses. As a rule, when a mob turns to crime, the ones really to blame are only a handful of agitators who stand above the rest. If human authorities then intervene, it often happens that only these masses, who have been duped, are made to suffer, while the individuals who misled them in the first place and are therefore the ones truly to

blame, go free. But Thou, "God, God of the spirits of all flesh," being the Almighty Power, art capable of reaching those whom Thou knowest to be guilty, and as "the God of the spirits of all flesh," Thou knowest how to determine who is truly guilty.

If one man sins. "Consequently, it must be known to Thee that only Koraḥ is to blame; it would seem that the people, who were led astray by him, should receive Thy clemency." We have already noted on several previous occasions how, by evoking such intercessions from him on behalf of others, God helped Moses gain insight into the motives of His workings, thus elevating his mind to think along the lines of Divine Providence, as it were.

will open its mouth and swallow them up with all that is theirs, so that they go down into the grave alive, then you will know that [it is] these people [who] have scorned *God*." 31. And it came to pass when he had finished uttering all these words that the ground under them split; 32. the earth opened its mouth and swallowed them up and their houses and all the men who belonged to Koraḥ, and all the property. 33. They and all that was theirs went down into the grave alive, and the earth closed over them and they vanished from the midst of the community. 34. All of Yisrael who had been round about them fled at their cries, for they thought: "The earth could swallow us up also." 35. But a fire had gone out from *God* and it consumed the two hundred and fifty men who had offered the incense.

XVII

1. *God* spoke to Moshe [saying]: 2. "Say to Eleazar, the son of Aharon the priest, that he shall lift the pans out from the conflagration, but you shall throw away the fire, for they have become holy. 3. The very pans of those who became sinners against their own persons, let them be made into thin beaten plates as an overlay for the altar; for since they brought them before *God*, they have become holy and shall remain as a sign for the sons of Yisrael." 4. Eleazar the priest took the copper pans which those that were burned had brought near, and they were beaten thin as an overlay for the altar; 5. as a memorial for the sons of Yisrael, so that no stranger who is not a descendant of Aharon will draw near to make incense go up in smoke before *God*, and he will not fare like Koraḥ and his company, as *God* had told him through Moshe. 6. On the next day the whole community of the sons of Yisrael murmured against Moshe and Aharon and said: "You have caused the death of the people of *God*." 7. And it came to pass as the community assembled against Moshe and Aharon that they turned toward the Tent of Appointed Meeting, and lo! the cloud had covered it, and the glory of *God* appeared. 8. Moshe and Aharon came to the front of the Tent of Appointed Meeting. 9. And *God* spoke to Moshe [saying]:

אֶת־פִּ֗יהָ וּבָלְעָ֤ה אֹתָם֙ וְאֶת־כָּל־אֲשֶׁ֣ר לָהֶ֔ם וְיָרְד֥וּ חַיִּ֖ים שְׁאֹ֑לָה וִֽידַעְתֶּ֕ם כִּ֧י נִֽאֲצ֛וּ הָאֲנָשִׁ֥ים הָאֵ֖לֶּה אֶת־יְהֹוָֽה: לא וַיְהִי֙ כְּכַלֹּת֔וֹ לְדַבֵּ֕ר אֵ֥ת כָּל־הַדְּבָרִ֖ים הָאֵ֑לֶּה וַתִּבָּקַ֛ע הָֽאֲדָמָ֖ה אֲשֶׁ֥ר תַּחְתֵּיהֶֽם: לב וַתִּפְתַּ֤ח הָאָ֨רֶץ֙ אֶת־פִּ֔יהָ וַתִּבְלַ֥ע אֹתָ֖ם וְאֶת־בָּֽתֵּיהֶ֑ם וְאֵ֤ת כָּל־הָֽאָדָם֙ אֲשֶׁ֣ר לְקֹ֔רַח וְאֵ֖ת כָּל־הָֽרְכֽוּשׁ: לג וַיֵּ֨רְד֜וּ הֵ֣ם וְכָל־אֲשֶׁ֥ר לָהֶ֛ם חַיִּ֖ים שְׁאֹ֑לָה וַתְּכַ֤ס עֲלֵיהֶם֙ הָאָ֔רֶץ וַיֹּֽאבְד֖וּ מִתּ֥וֹךְ הַקָּהָֽל: לד וְכָל־יִשְׂרָאֵ֗ל אֲשֶׁ֛ר סְבִֽיבֹֽתֵיהֶ֖ם נָ֣סוּ לְקֹלָ֑ם כִּ֣י אָֽמְר֔וּ פֶּן־תִּבְלָעֵ֖נוּ הָאָֽרֶץ: לה וְאֵ֥שׁ יָֽצְאָ֖ה מֵאֵ֣ת יְהֹוָ֑ה וַתֹּ֗אכַל אֵ֣ת הַֽחֲמִשִּׁ֤ים וּמָאתַ֨יִם֙ אִ֔ישׁ מַקְרִיבֵ֖י הַקְּטֹֽרֶת: ס יז א וַיְדַבֵּ֥ר יְהֹוָ֖ה אֶל־מֹשֶׁ֥ה לֵּאמֹֽר: ב אֱמֹ֨ר אֶל־אֶלְעָזָ֜ר בֶּן־אַֽהֲרֹ֣ן הַכֹּהֵ֗ן וְיָרֵ֤ם אֶת־הַמַּחְתֹּת֙ מִבֵּ֣ין הַשְּׂרֵפָ֔ה וְאֶת־הָאֵ֖שׁ זְרֵה־הָ֑לְאָה כִּ֖י קָדֵֽשׁוּ: ג אֵ֡ת מַחְתּוֹת֩ הַֽחַטָּאִ֨ים הָאֵ֜לֶּה בְּנַפְשֹׁתָ֗ם וְעָשׂ֨וּ אֹתָ֜ם רִקֻּעֵ֤י פַחִים֙ צִפּ֣וּי לַמִּזְבֵּ֔חַ כִּֽי־הִקְרִיב֥וּם לִפְנֵֽי־יְהֹוָ֖ה וַיִּקְדָּ֑שׁוּ וְיִֽהְי֥וּ לְא֖וֹת לִבְנֵ֥י יִשְׂרָאֵֽל: ד וַיִּקַּ֞ח אֶלְעָזָ֣ר הַכֹּהֵ֗ן אֵ֚ת מַחְתּ֣וֹת הַנְּחֹ֔שֶׁת אֲשֶׁ֥ר הִקְרִ֖יבוּ הַשְּׂרֻפִ֑ים וַיְרַקְּע֖וּם צִפּ֥וּי לַמִּזְבֵּֽחַ: ה זִכָּר֞וֹן לִבְנֵ֣י יִשְׂרָאֵ֗ל לְ֠מַ֠עַן אֲשֶׁ֨ר לֹֽא־יִקְרַ֜ב אִ֣ישׁ זָ֗ר אֲ֠שֶׁ֠ר לֹ֣א מִזֶּ֤רַע אַֽהֲרֹן֙ ה֔וּא לְהַקְטִ֣יר קְטֹ֔רֶת לִפְנֵ֖י יְהֹוָ֑ה וְלֹֽא־יִֽהְיֶ֤ה כְקֹ֨רַח֙ וְכַ֣עֲדָת֔וֹ כַּֽאֲשֶׁ֨ר דִּבֶּ֧ר יְהֹוָ֛ה בְּיַד־מֹשֶׁ֖ה לֽוֹ: פ ו וַיִּלֹּ֜נוּ כָּל־עֲדַ֤ת בְּנֵֽי־יִשְׂרָאֵל֙ מִֽמָּחֳרָ֔ת עַל־מֹשֶׁ֥ה וְעַל־אַֽהֲרֹ֖ן לֵאמֹ֑ר אַתֶּ֥ם הֲמִתֶּ֖ם אֶת־עַ֥ם יְהֹוָֽה: ז וַיְהִ֗י בְּהִקָּהֵ֤ל הָֽעֵדָה֙ עַל־מֹשֶׁ֣ה וְעַל־אַֽהֲרֹ֔ן וַיִּפְנוּ֙ אֶל־אֹ֣הֶל מוֹעֵ֔ד וְהִנֵּ֥ה כִסָּ֖הוּ הֶֽעָנָ֑ן וַיֵּרָ֖א כְּב֥וֹד יְהֹוָֽה: ח וַיָּבֹ֤א מֹשֶׁה֙ וְאַֽהֲרֹ֔ן אֶל־פְּנֵ֖י אֹ֥הֶל מוֹעֵֽד: ס רביעי ט וַיְדַבֵּ֥ר יְהֹוָ֖ה אֶל־מֹשֶׁ֥ה לֵּאמֹֽר: י הֵרֹ֗מּוּ

10. "Lift yourselves up from the midst of this community so that I may destroy them instantly." But they fell upon their faces. 11. And Moshe said to Aharon: "Take the pan and place upon it fire from the altar and add incense to it and take it quickly to the community and effect atonement for them, because the anger has already gone forth from *God*; the plague has begun." 12. Aharon took as Moshe had spoken and ran into the midst of the community, and lo! the plague had begun among the people. He placed the incense there and effected atonement for the people. 13. And he stood between the dying and the living, and the plague was checked. 14. Those that died by the plague were fourteen thousand seven hundred, in addition to those that had died because of the matter of Koraḥ. 15. Aharon returned to Moshe, to the entrance of the Tent of Appointed Meeting, and the plague was checked. 16. And *God* spoke to Moshe [saying]: 17. "Speak to the sons of Yisrael and take from them one staff for each father's house, from all their princes of the house of their fathers, twelve staffs, and inscribe the name of each one upon his staff. 18. And you shall write the name of Aharon upon the staff of Levi, for there shall be one staff for the head of the house of their fathers. 19. And you shall lay them down in the Tent of Appointed Meeting, in front of the Testimony, where I have set a time to meet with you. 20. And it shall come to pass that the man whom I will choose, his staff will blossom. Thus will I calm down—turning [them] away from Me—the murmuring

מִתּוֹךְ הָעֵדָה הַזֹּאת וַאֲכַלֶּה אֹתָם כְּרָגַע וַיִּפְּלוּ
עַל־פְּנֵיהֶם׃ יא וַיֹּאמֶר מֹשֶׁה אֶל־אַהֲרֹן קַח אֶת־
הַמַּחְתָּה וְתֶן־עָלֶיהָ אֵשׁ מֵעַל הַמִּזְבֵּחַ וְשִׂים
קְטֹרֶת וְהוֹלֵךְ מְהֵרָה אֶל־הָעֵדָה וְכַפֵּר עֲלֵיהֶם
כִּי־יָצָא הַקֶּצֶף מִלִּפְנֵי יְהוָֹה הֵחֵל הַנָּגֶף׃
יב וַיִּקַּח אַהֲרֹן כַּאֲשֶׁר ׀ דִּבֶּר מֹשֶׁה וַיָּרָץ
אֶל־תּוֹךְ הַקָּהָל וְהִנֵּה הֵחֵל הַנֶּגֶף בָּעָם וַיִּתֵּן אֶת־
הַקְּטֹרֶת וַיְכַפֵּר עַל־הָעָם׃ יג וַיַּעֲמֹד בֵּין־הַמֵּתִים
וּבֵין הַחַיִּים וַתֵּעָצַר הַמַּגֵּפָה׃ יד וַיִּהְיוּ הַמֵּתִים
בַּמַּגֵּפָה אַרְבָּעָה עָשָׂר אֶלֶף וּשְׁבַע מֵאוֹת מִלְּבַד
הַמֵּתִים עַל־דְּבַר־קֹרַח׃ טו וַיָּשָׁב אַהֲרֹן אֶל־
מֹשֶׁה אֶל־פֶּתַח אֹהֶל מוֹעֵד וְהַמַּגֵּפָה נֶעֱצָרָה׃ פ
חמישי טז וַיְדַבֵּר יְהוָֹה אֶל־מֹשֶׁה לֵּאמֹר׃ יז דַּבֵּר ׀
אֶל־בְּנֵי יִשְׂרָאֵל וְקַח מֵאִתָּם מַטֶּה מַטֶּה לְבֵית
אָב מֵאֵת כָּל־נְשִׂיאֵהֶם לְבֵית אֲבֹתָם שְׁנֵים עָשָׂר
מַטּוֹת אִישׁ אֶת־שְׁמוֹ תִּכְתֹּב עַל־מַטֵּהוּ׃ יח וְאֵת
שֵׁם אַהֲרֹן תִּכְתֹּב עַל־מַטֵּה לֵוִי כִּי מַטֶּה אֶחָד
לְרֹאשׁ בֵּית אֲבוֹתָם׃ יט וְהִנַּחְתָּם בְּאֹהֶל מוֹעֵד
לִפְנֵי הָעֵדוּת אֲשֶׁר אִוָּעֵד לָכֶם שָׁמָּה׃ כ וְהָיָה
הָאִישׁ אֲשֶׁר אֶבְחַר־בּוֹ מַטֵּהוּ יִפְרָח וַהֲשִׁכֹּתִי

CHAPTER XVII

17. ***Speak to***. Because they "branched off" from one common stem, the tribes of the Jewish people are called מַטּוֹת, literally, "branches," so that מטות is the most appropriate term in this context. However, since each tribe transmitted to its posterity its own unique traits within the ethos of the nation of which they all were a part, each tribe represented a separate בֵּית אָב ["father's house"] within the overall בֵּית יִשְׂרָאֵל ["House of Israel"]. Therefore, the word מטות describes the tribes in terms of the character traits they all hold in common, while בָּתֵּי אָבוֹת refers to them in terms of their specific tribal characteristics.

The fact that here the twelve בָּתֵּי אָבוֹת of the Jewish people are to be represented by twelve מַטּוֹת suggests the question whether, no matter what the differences between them, all the tribes should be considered equal to all the others with regard to the matter about to be decided, since, after all, they do hold certain basic traits in common; or whether, regardless of the traits they all hold in common, they should *not* be considered as equals because each tribe has unique traits that set it apart from all the others.

complaints of the sons of Yisrael which they stir up against you." 21. And Moshe spoke to the sons of Yisrael, and all their princes gave him one staff apiece, one for each prince of their fathers' houses, [all together] twelve staffs. And the staff of Aharon was among their staffs. 22. And Moshe laid down the staffs before *God* in the Tent of the Testimony. 23. And it came to pass on the next day, when Moshe came to the Tent of the Testimony, that lo! Aharon's staff from the house of Levi had blossomed. It had put forth a bud and sprouted twigs and bore ripe almonds. 24. Moshe brought out all the staffs from their place before *God* to all the sons of Yisrael. Each man saw and took his [own] staff. 25. And *God* said to Moshe: "Put Aharon's staff back again in front of the Testimony to be kept there as a sign for men of disobedience so that it may put an end to their murmuring complaints—that were turned away by Me—and they will not die." 26. Moshe did so; as *God* had commanded him, so did he do. 27. And the sons of Yisrael said to Moshe: "So then we are about to die, we are lost, we are all lost! 28. Whoever comes near, whoever comes too near to the Dwelling Place of *God*, dies—are we then altogether given to die?"

XVIII 1. And *God* said to Aharon: "You and your sons, and your father's house with you, you must bear the iniquity against the Sanctuary, and you and your sons with you must bear the iniquity against your priesthood. 2. But also your brothers, the branch of Levi, the tribe of your father—let them come near along with you; they shall join with you and minister to you while you and your sons with you keep watch before the Tent of the Testimony. 3. They are to keep your charge and the charge of the entire Tent, but they must not come near

מֵעָלַי אֶת־תְּלֻנּוֹת בְּנֵי יִשְׂרָאֵל אֲשֶׁר הֵם מַלִּינִם עֲלֵיכֶם: כא וַיְדַבֵּר מֹשֶׁה אֶל־בְּנֵי יִשְׂרָאֵל וַיִּתְּנוּ אֵלָיו ׀ כָּל־נְשִׂיאֵיהֶם מַטֶּה לְנָשִׂיא אֶחָד מַטֶּה לְנָשִׂיא אֶחָד לְבֵית אֲבֹתָם שְׁנֵים עָשָׂר מַטּוֹת וּמַטֵּה אַהֲרֹן בְּתוֹךְ מַטּוֹתָם: כב וַיַּנַּח מֹשֶׁה אֶת־ הַמַּטֹּת לִפְנֵי יְהֹוָה בְּאֹהֶל הָעֵדֻת: כג וַיְהִי מִמָּחֳרָת וַיָּבֹא מֹשֶׁה אֶל־אֹהֶל הָעֵדוּת וְהִנֵּה פָּרַח מַטֵּה־אַהֲרֹן לְבֵית לֵוִי וַיֹּצֵא פֶרַח וַיָּצֵץ צִיץ וַיִּגְמֹל שְׁקֵדִים: כד וַיֹּצֵא מֹשֶׁה אֶת־כָּל־ הַמַּטֹּת מִלִּפְנֵי יְהֹוָה אֶל־כָּל־בְּנֵי יִשְׂרָאֵל וַיִּרְאוּ וַיִּקְחוּ אִישׁ מַטֵּהוּ: פ ששי כה וַיֹּאמֶר יְהֹוָה אֶל־ מֹשֶׁה הָשֵׁב אֶת־מַטֵּה אַהֲרֹן לִפְנֵי הָעֵדוּת לְמִשְׁמֶרֶת לְאוֹת לִבְנֵי־מֶרִי וּתְכַל תְּלוּנֹּתָם מֵעָלַי וְלֹא יָמֻתוּ: כו וַיַּעַשׂ מֹשֶׁה כַּאֲשֶׁר צִוָּה יְהֹוָה אֹתוֹ כֵּן עָשָׂה: פ כז וַיֹּאמְרוּ בְּנֵי יִשְׂרָאֵל אֶל־מֹשֶׁה לֵאמֹר הֵן גָּוַעְנוּ אָבַדְנוּ כֻּלָּנוּ אָבָדְנוּ: כח כֹּל הַקָּרֵב ׀ הַקָּרֵב אֶל־מִשְׁכַּן יְהֹוָה יָמוּת הַאִם תַּמְנוּ לִגְוֹעַ: ס יח א וַיֹּאמֶר יְהֹוָה אֶל־ אַהֲרֹן אַתָּה וּבָנֶיךָ וּבֵית־אָבִיךָ אִתָּךְ תִּשְׂאוּ אֶת־ עֲוֹן הַמִּקְדָּשׁ וְאַתָּה וּבָנֶיךָ אִתָּךְ תִּשְׂאוּ אֶת־עֲוֹן כְּהֻנַּתְכֶם: ב וְגַם אֶת־אַחֶיךָ מַטֵּה לֵוִי שֵׁבֶט אָבִיךָ הַקְרֵב אִתָּךְ וְיִלָּווּ עָלֶיךָ וִישָׁרְתוּךָ וְאַתָּה וּבָנֶיךָ אִתָּךְ לִפְנֵי אֹהֶל הָעֵדֻת: ג וְשָׁמְרוּ מִשְׁמַרְתְּךָ וּמִשְׁמֶרֶת כָּל־הָאֹהֶל אַךְ אֶל־כְּלֵי

CHAPTER XVIII

1. ***And God said.*** This is not a new law. It is only an elaboration on a situation already existing in accordance with God's command. The significance of this situation must be explained to the people in order to set their minds at ease. It is not the people who need to feel

threatened by the Sanctuary because of a thoughtless act or careless error on their part. It is Aaron, his family and his tribe—all those appointed to serve in and for the Sanctuary—who bear a responsibility they can discharge only by unceasing vigilance and attention to their duty. . . .

· · ·

הַקֹּדֶשׁ וְאֶל־הַמִּזְבֵּחַ לֹא יִקְרָבוּ וְלֹא־יָמֻתוּ
גַם־הֵם גַּם־אַתֶּם׃ ד וְנִלְווּ עָלֶיךָ וְשָׁמְרוּ אֶת־
מִשְׁמֶרֶת אֹהֶל מוֹעֵד לְכֹל עֲבֹדַת הָאֹהֶל וְזָר
לֹא־יִקְרַב אֲלֵיכֶם׃ ה וּשְׁמַרְתֶּם אֵת מִשְׁמֶרֶת
הַקֹּדֶשׁ וְאֵת מִשְׁמֶרֶת הַמִּזְבֵּחַ וְלֹא־יִהְיֶה עוֹד
קֶצֶף עַל־בְּנֵי יִשְׂרָאֵל׃ ו וַאֲנִי הִנֵּה לָקַחְתִּי אֶת־
אֲחֵיכֶם הַלְוִיִּם מִתּוֹךְ בְּנֵי יִשְׂרָאֵל לָכֶם מַתָּנָה

the utensils of the Sanctuary or to the altar so that they will not die, neither they nor you.
4. They shall join you and keep the charge of the Tent of Appointed Meeting with regard to all the service of the Tent, and no stranger shall come near to you.
5. Keep the charge of the Sanctuary and the charge of the altar; then anger shall come no more upon the sons of Yisrael.
6. I, lo! I have taken your brothers, the Levites, from out of the midst of the sons of Yisrael, to you are they given as a gift for

6–7. **ואני וגו׳** *[I, lo! I].* In conclusion, the text declares once again that the exclusive authorization conferred upon the Levites and the Aaronides to perform the service in and for the Sanctuary derives from God alone. This declaration should obviate any presumptuousness or conceit on the part of those authorized to perform these functions. At the same time, it reconfirms the absolute godliness not only of the service, but also of those who perform that service, and of the Law to which the whole Sanctuary is dedicated and with which the entire service is linked.

ואני *[I].* the choice of these individuals derives from Me [God]; "Lo! I have taken. . .": the Levites have taken a completely passive role in their selection; they only carry out a decree which God ordained for them. . . .

The specific עֲבוֹדָה [service] performed by the priests is characterized as עֲבוֹדַת מַתָּנָה ["a service of free-willed giving"], a service characterized by the making of gifts and the giving of oneself. All the acts to be performed in the Sanctuary center on the concept of "giving gifts and giving of oneself." While the מִקְדָּשׁ [Sanctuary] with its אָרוֹן [Ark], שׁוּלְחָן [altar] and מְנוֹרָה [menorah] symbolizes all that we have *received* from God through the Law and for the sake of the Law, the purpose of the עֲבוֹדָה [service] that takes place in the מִקְדָּשׁ is to teach us to *give* ourselves and our God-given possessions to God and to His Law. . . . The purpose of כְּהֻנָּה [priesthood]; i.e., that the priests are to teach themselves and the rest of the people the "direction"[6] that God has set down for our lives, is nothing but עֲבוֹדַת מַתָּנָה, a service conducive to the dedication of oneself to God. . . .

Now follows a most significant statement: "I am giving you your priesthood for a service of free-willed giving": God wants to "give" to us our free-willed giving of ourselves. If we understand this correctly, [a gift] certainly denotes an act motivated entirely by our own free will. Hence, the giving of ourselves and of our possessions to God should be an act emanating from the deepest wellsprings of our moral freedom of will.

At the same time, as regards both its motivation and the manner in which it is to be performed, this free-willed act of giving to God must not in any manner be guided by personal whim. It must conform with strict standards; it must be nothing else but an act of completely free-willed obedience on our part—עֲבוֹדַת מַתָּנָה, an act of completely free-willed dedication to the fulfillment of life's purpose as set down in the Law of God. We must keep in mind not only that the things we give, namely, the possessions we call our own, are in fact the possessions of God, so that we are merely giving back to God that which we have received from Him (cf. "And of Thine own have we given Thee"—I Chronicles 29:14), but also that the very fact of our giving, and the quantity, quality and purpose of our gift, symbolize our obedience to a Divine dictate. Thus, in truth, our מַתָּנָה becomes a נְתִינָה [act of giving] from God, an act accomplished by God's will through the medium of our own free-willed obedience.

This free-willed obedience to the will of God is the basis of Judaism. It rejects the mere inner impulse of "piety" or "devoutness" that seeks expression and gratification in self-devised practices, presumed to be "pleasing to God," and calls these a "Divine service." God has told the Jew what is "good" and what God requires of him (Micah 6:8). His עֲבוֹדָה, his Divine service, consists in "serving God," in obedience, in the faithful performance of God's expressed will. The most sacred object in the Jewish Holy of Holies is the Law of God, which in turn regulates the acts that symbolize the Jew's devotion to the Law. The individuals who perform these acts are Divinely-appointed servants of this Law and of its Sanctuary. They accept, in the name of God and of His Law, the tokens of our free-willed devotion to the dictates set down in the Law. And the fact that the Aaronides were appointed, to the exclusion of all others, to perform the עֲבוֹדַת מַתָּנָה in the Sanc-

[6]*Note to the English translation*: The reference is to Hirsch's view that "direction" is related to כֹּהֵן, "priest." Hirsch's detailed explanation, in his commentary on Genesis 14:17–18, is not included in this excerpted edition. [G.H.].

God's purposes, to perform the service of the Tent of Appointed Meeting. 7. But you and your sons with you must attend to your priesthood, with regard to everything pertaining to the altar and to anything behind the cloth partition you are to do the service; I am giving you your priesthood for a service of free-willed giving; the stranger that comes near shall die." 8. *God* spoke to Aharon: "And I, lo! I have given you the charge of My uplifted donations; [this applies] also to all the holy things of the sons of Yisrael. I have given them to you as a consecration, and to your sons, as an everlasting due. 9. This shall be yours from the holy of holies reserved from the fire: everything that they bring near, their every homage offering, and their every offering that clears [him who brings it] of sin, and their every guilt offering that they return to Me, a holy of holies shall it be to you and to your sons. 10. In the holiness of holy things must you eat it; every male may eat it; it shall be a holy thing to you. 11. And this shall be for you as an uplifted donation from their gift, from all the [wave] offerings of the sons of Yisrael have I given them to you and to your sons and to your daughters with you as an everlasting due. Every one in your house who is [ritually] pure may eat it. 12. All the best of the oil and all the best of the new wine and of the grain, the first of that which

נְתֻנִים֙ לַֽיהֹוָ֔ה לַֽעֲבֹ֕ד אֶת־עֲבֹדַ֖ת אֹ֥הֶל מוֹעֵֽד: ז וְאַתָּ֣ה וּבָנֶ֣יךָ אִתְּךָ֡ תִּשְׁמְר֣וּ אֶת־כְּהֻנַּתְכֶ֡ם לְכָל־דְּבַ֣ר הַמִּזְבֵּ֩חַ֩ וּלְמִבֵּ֨ית לַפָּרֹ֜כֶת וַֽעֲבַדְתֶּ֗ם עֲבֹדַ֤ת מַתָּנָה֙ אֶתֵּ֣ן אֶת־כְּהֻנַּתְכֶ֔ם וְהַזָּ֥ר הַקָּרֵ֖ב יוּמָֽת: פ ח וַיְדַבֵּ֣ר יְהֹוָה֮ אֶֽל־אַהֲרֹן֒ וַֽאֲנִ֞י הִנֵּ֧ה נָתַ֣תִּי לְךָ֗ אֶת־מִשְׁמֶ֖רֶת תְּרֽוּמֹתָ֑י לְכָל־קָדְשֵׁ֣י בְנֵֽי־יִשְׂרָאֵ֗ל לְךָ֧ נְתַתִּ֛ים לְמָשְׁחָ֥ה וּלְבָנֶ֖יךָ לְחָק־ עוֹלָֽם: ט זֶֽה־יִֽהְיֶ֥ה לְךָ֛ מִקֹּ֥דֶשׁ הַקֳּדָשִׁ֖ים מִן־הָאֵ֑שׁ כָּל־קָ֠רְבָּנָ֠ם לְֽכָל־מִנְחָתָ֞ם וּלְכָל־חַטָּאתָ֗ם וּלְכָל־ אֲשָׁמָם֙ אֲשֶׁ֣ר יָשִׁ֣יבוּ לִ֔י קֹ֥דֶשׁ קָֽדָשִׁ֛ים לְךָ֥ ה֖וּא וּלְבָנֶֽיךָ: י בְּקֹ֥דֶשׁ הַקֳּדָשִׁ֖ים תֹּֽאכְלֶ֑נּוּ כָּל־זָכָר֙ יֹאכַ֣ל אֹת֔וֹ קֹ֖דֶשׁ יִֽהְיֶה־לָּֽךְ: יא וְזֶה־לְּךָ֞ תְּרוּמַ֣ת מַתָּנָ֗ם לְכָל־תְּנוּפֹת֮ בְּנֵ֣י יִשְׂרָאֵל֒ לְךָ֣ נְתַתִּ֗ים וּלְבָנֶ֧יךָ וְלִבְנֹתֶ֛יךָ אִתְּךָ֖ לְחָק־עוֹלָ֑ם כָּל־טָה֥וֹר בְּבֵֽיתְךָ֖ יֹאכַ֥ל אֹתֽוֹ: יב כֹּ֚ל חֵ֣לֶב יִצְהָ֔ר וְכָל־חֵ֖לֶב תִּיר֣וֹשׁ וְדָגָ֑ן רֵֽאשִׁיתָ֛ם אֲשֶׁר־יִתְּנ֥וּ לַֽיהֹוָ֖ה לְךָ֥

---

tuary of the Law, imparts to the Law itself and to its Sanctuary the final stamp of Divine origin, showing that the fulfillment of our lives must be identical with the fulfillment of God's will.

Basically, Koraḥ's statement, "the entire community, they are all holy and *God* is in their midst," with which he proclaimed his uprising against the appointment of the Aaronides as priests, was a denial of the Divine origin of Moses' mission and of the Law transmitted by him. Koraḥ sought to replace the Law with the personal, subjective wishes of the individual. In his view, the individual needed only to follow his inner stirrings of "holiness" in order to obtain God's nearness and approval.

As opposed to such subjectivism, which would undermine the whole of Judaism, the Word of God concludes with the words: "I am giving you your priesthood for a service of free-willed giving; the stranger that comes

near shall die." And the comment in Sanhedrin 84a to this statement is—מִיתָה בִּידֵי שָׁמַיִם [that such a person will be punished by "death at the hand of Heaven"].

10. *In the holiness of holy things.* As already specified in Leviticus 6:9 and 19 and 7:6 with regard to the מִנְחָה [homage offering], the חַטָּאת [offering that clears (him who brings it) of sin] and the אָשָׁם [guilt offering], this must be eaten not in the Holy of Holies but in the עֲזָרָה, the area of the Sanctuary set aside as the place where the "holy things" are to be eaten. In this verse קֹדֶשׁ (as in שַׁבַּת קֹדֶשׁ ["holy Sabbath"] and אַדְמַת קֹדֶשׁ ["holy ground"]) may perhaps not mean "sanctuary" but "holiness"; i.e., these offerings must be eaten in the holiest manner as befits holy things; this also means, as stated in the passage just cited, that they may be eaten only in the עֲזָרָה. . . .

they give to God, to you have I given them.
13. The first fruit of all that is in their
land, that they bring to God, shall be yours;
every one in your house who is [ritually]
pure may eat it.   14. Whatever has been
placed under a vow of interdiction in Yisrael
shall be yours.   15. Whatever opens the
mother's womb of any creature that is
brought near to God, among men and
among livestock, shall be yours; however,
you must redeem the first-born of man and
you shall also redeem the first-born of an
unclean animal.   16. And you shall perform its redemption from the age of one
month according to your valuation, silver,
five shekels of the shekel of the Sanctuary—
the same is twenty *gerahs*.   17. However,
the first-born of an ox, or the first-born of a
sheep, or the first-born of a goat you shall
not redeem; they are a holy thing; you
shall dash their blood onto the altar, and
you shall give its fat to go up in smoke as a fire
offering, as an expression of compliance, to
God.   18. But their flesh shall be yours;
like the breast of the wave [offering] and the
right thigh, it shall be yours.   19. All the
uplifted donations from the holy things that
the sons of Yisrael lift up to God I have
given to you and your sons and your
daughters with you, as an everlasting due. It
is a covenant of everlasting salt before God
for you and for your descendants with you."
20. God furthermore said to Aharon:
"You shall receive no inheritance in their
land and you shall not have any portion
among them. I [Myself] am your portion
and your inheritance in the midst of the sons
of Yisrael.   21. But to the sons of Levi, lo!
I have given all the tithes in Yisrael as an
inheritance, as a compensation for their
service which they perform in the service of
the Tent of Appointed Meeting,   22. so
that the sons of Yisrael shall no longer come
near to the Tent of Appointed Meeting to
incur a sin deserving of death.   23. As for
the Levite, he must perform the service of
the Tent of Appointed Meeting, and they

נְתַתִּֽים: יג בִּכּוּרֵ֞י כָּל־אֲשֶׁ֤ר בְּאַרְצָם֙ אֲשֶׁר־
יָבִ֥יאוּ לַֽיהֹוָ֖ה לְךָ֣ יִֽהְיֶ֑ה כָּל־טָה֥וֹר בְּבֵֽיתְךָ֖
יֹֽאכְלֶֽנּוּ: יד כָּל־חֵ֥רֶם בְּיִשְׂרָאֵ֖ל לְךָ֥ יִֽהְיֶֽה: טו כָּל־
פֶּ֣טֶר רֶ֠חֶם לְֽכָל־בָּשָׂ֞ר אֲשֶׁר־יַקְרִ֧יבוּ לַֽיהֹוָ֛ה
בָּֽאָדָ֥ם וּבַבְּהֵמָ֖ה יִֽהְיֶה־לָּ֑ךְ אַ֣ךְ ׀ פָּדֹ֣ה תִפְדֶּ֗ה אֵ֚ת
בְּכ֣וֹר הָֽאָדָ֔ם וְאֵ֛ת בְּכֽוֹר־הַבְּהֵמָ֥ה הַטְּמֵאָ֖ה
תִּפְדֶּֽה: טז וּפְדוּיָו֙ מִבֶּן־חֹ֣דֶשׁ תִּפְדֶּ֔ה בְּעֶ֨רְכְּךָ֜
כֶּ֣סֶף חֲמֵ֤שֶׁת שְׁקָלִים֙ בְּשֶׁ֣קֶל הַקֹּ֔דֶשׁ עֶשְׂרִ֥ים גֵּרָ֖ה
הֽוּא: יז אַ֣ךְ בְּכֽוֹר־שׁ֡וֹר אֽוֹ־בְכ֨וֹר כֶּ֜שֶׂב אֽוֹ־
בְכ֥וֹר עֵ֛ז לֹ֥א תִפְדֶּ֖ה קֹ֣דֶשׁ הֵ֑ם אֶת־דָּמָ֞ם תִּזְרֹ֤ק
עַל־הַמִּזְבֵּ֨חַ֙ וְאֶת־חֶלְבָּ֣ם תַּקְטִ֔יר אִשֶּׁ֛ה לְרֵ֥יחַ
נִיחֹ֖חַ לַֽיהֹוָֽה: יח וּבְשָׂרָ֖ם יִֽהְיֶה־לָּ֑ךְ כַּֽחֲזֵ֧ה
הַתְּנוּפָ֛ה וּכְשׁ֥וֹק הַיָּמִ֖ין לְךָ֥ יִֽהְיֶֽה: יט כֹּ֣ל ׀
תְּרוּמֹ֣ת הַקֳּדָשִׁ֗ים אֲשֶׁ֨ר יָרִ֤ימוּ בְנֵֽי־יִשְׂרָאֵל֙
לַֽיהֹוָ֔ה נָתַ֣תִּֽי לְךָ֗ וּלְבָנֶ֧יךָ וְלִבְנֹתֶ֛יךָ אִתְּךָ֖ לְחָק־
עוֹלָ֑ם בְּרִית֩ מֶ֨לַח עוֹלָ֥ם הִוא֙ לִפְנֵ֣י יְהֹוָ֔ה לְךָ֖
וּלְזַרְעֲךָ֥ אִתָּֽךְ: כ וַיֹּ֨אמֶר יְהֹוָ֜ה אֶֽל־אַהֲרֹ֗ן
בְּאַרְצָם֙ לֹ֣א תִנְחָ֔ל וְחֵ֕לֶק לֹֽא־יִֽהְיֶ֥ה לְךָ֖ בְּתוֹכָ֑ם
אֲנִ֤י חֶלְקְךָ֙ וְנַֽחֲלָ֣תְךָ֔ בְּת֖וֹךְ בְּנֵ֥י יִשְׂרָאֵֽל: ס
שביעי כא וְלִבְנֵ֣י לֵוִ֔י הִנֵּ֥ה נָתַ֛תִּי כָּל־מַֽעֲשֵׂ֥ר
בְּיִשְׂרָאֵ֖ל לְנַֽחֲלָ֑ה חֵ֣לֶף עֲבֹֽדָתָ֗ם אֲשֶׁר־הֵ֣ם
עֹֽבְדִ֔ים אֶת־עֲבֹדַ֖ת אֹ֥הֶל מוֹעֵֽד: כב וְלֹֽא־יִקְרְב֥וּ
ע֛וֹד בְּנֵ֥י יִשְׂרָאֵ֖ל אֶל־אֹ֣הֶל מוֹעֵ֑ד לָשֵׂ֥את חֵ֖טְא
לָמֽוּת: כג וְעָבַ֨ד הַלֵּוִ֜י ה֗וּא אֶת־עֲבֹדַת֙ אֹ֣הֶל

---

23. *As for the Levite, he must perform.* A Levite
receives compensation for the service he performs, but
he cannot evade this service by waiving his compensation. He must perform it even if he receives no tithe,
which is always a possibility, since no Levite has a
direct personal claim on any tithe and the distribution
of the tithe is entirely subject to the wishes of the one
who is obligated to give it. . . .

must bear their iniquity. [It is] an everlasting statute for your descendants, but they shall receive no inheritance in the midst of the sons of Yisrael.   24. For the tithe of the sons of Yisrael, which they lift up to *God* as an uplifted donation, have I given to the Levites as an inheritance. For this reason I have declared concerning them that they shall have no inheritance in the midst of the sons of Yisrael."   25. *God* spoke to Moshe [saying]:   26. "But speak to the Levites and say to them: When you take from the sons of Yisrael the tithe which I have given to you from them as your inheritance, you shall lift from it as *God*'s uplifted donation one tenth of the tithe.   27. And your uplifted donation shall be regarded by you as the grain from the threshing floor and the fullness of the wine press.   28. Thus you, too, shall lift out an uplifted donation from all of your tithes which you receive from the sons of Yisrael, and you shall then give *God*'s uplifted donation to Aharon the priest.   29. From all that is given you, you shall lift out *God*'s every uplifted donation, of all the best of it, that part of it which is to be sanctified.   30. And furthermore say to them: When you lift out its best part from it, this is to be regarded as Levite property even as the produce of the threshing floor and the produce of the wine press. 31. You may eat it at any place, you and your households; for it is your wages, a compensation for your service in the Tent of Appointed Meeting.   32. Do not incur sin concerning it when you lift out its best part from it, and do not desecrate the holy things of the sons of Yisrael, so that you will not die."

מוֹעֵד וְהֵם יִשְׂאוּ עֲוֺנָם חֻקַּת עוֹלָם לְדֹרֹתֵיכֶם וּבְתוֹךְ בְּנֵי יִשְׂרָאֵל לֹא יִנְחֲלוּ נַחֲלָה: כד כִּי אֶת־מַעְשַׂר בְּנֵי־יִשְׂרָאֵל אֲשֶׁר יָרִימוּ לַיהֹוָה תְּרוּמָה נָתַתִּי לַלְוִיִּם לְנַחֲלָה עַל־כֵּן אָמַרְתִּי לָהֶם בְּתוֹךְ בְּנֵי יִשְׂרָאֵל לֹא יִנְחֲלוּ נַחֲלָה: פ כה וַיְדַבֵּר יְהֹוָה אֶל־מֹשֶׁה לֵּאמֹר: כו וְאֶל־הַלְוִיִּם תְּדַבֵּר וְאָמַרְתָּ אֲלֵהֶם כִּי־תִקְחוּ מֵאֵת בְּנֵי־יִשְׂרָאֵל אֶת־הַמַּעֲשֵׂר אֲשֶׁר נָתַתִּי לָכֶם מֵאִתָּם בְּנַחֲלַתְכֶם וַהֲרֵמֹתֶם מִמֶּנּוּ תְּרוּמַת יְהֹוָה מַעֲשֵׂר מִן־הַמַּעֲשֵׂר: כז וְנֶחְשַׁב לָכֶם תְּרוּמַתְכֶם כַּדָּגָן מִן־הַגֹּרֶן וְכַמְלֵאָה מִן־הַיָּקֶב: כח כֵּן תָּרִימוּ גַם־אַתֶּם תְּרוּמַת יְהֹוָה מִכֹּל מַעְשְׂרֹתֵיכֶם אֲשֶׁר תִּקְחוּ מֵאֵת בְּנֵי יִשְׂרָאֵל וּנְתַתֶּם מִמֶּנּוּ אֶת־תְּרוּמַת יְהֹוָה לְאַהֲרֹן הַכֹּהֵן: כט מִכֹּל מַתְּנֹתֵיכֶם תָּרִימוּ אֵת כָּל־תְּרוּמַת יְהֹוָה מִכָּל־חֶלְבּוֹ אֶת־מִקְדְּשׁוֹ מִמֶּנּוּ: מפטיר ל וְאָמַרְתָּ אֲלֵהֶם בַּהֲרִימְכֶם אֶת־חֶלְבּוֹ מִמֶּנּוּ וְנֶחְשַׁב לַלְוִיִּם כִּתְבוּאַת גֹּרֶן וְכִתְבוּאַת יָקֶב: לא וַאֲכַלְתֶּם אֹתוֹ בְּכָל־מָקוֹם אַתֶּם וּבֵיתְכֶם כִּי־שָׂכָר הוּא לָכֶם חֵלֶף עֲבֹדַתְכֶם בְּאֹהֶל מוֹעֵד: לב וְלֹא־תִשְׂאוּ עָלָיו חֵטְא בַּהֲרִימְכֶם אֶת־חֶלְבּוֹ מִמֶּנּוּ וְאֶת־קָדְשֵׁי בְנֵי־יִשְׂרָאֵל לֹא תְחַלְּלוּ וְלֹא תָמוּתוּ: פ

The Levite must perform this service even during periods such as the Sabbatical year and the *yovel*, when all produce is considered ownerless and hence not subject to tithing, so that no tithe is distributed (*Sifre*). But though his claim to tithes is thus conditional, his duty to serve is unconditional.

and they must bear their iniquity. It must be remembered, too, that this service entails grave responsibilities (Verse 3), "but they shall receive no inheritance in the midst of the sons of Yisrael." The tithe is due them as compensation for services they must render to the community as a whole, but they must renounce all claims to inherit any part of the nation's land. Thus, the material position of the Levites is by no means a privileged one, and as a consequence, Scripture repeatedly commends the tribe of Levi to the charity and the good will of the nation (Deuteronomy 12:12 and 18:19); indeed, Scripture classes the Levites in this respect with the stranger, the orphan and the widow (ibid. 26:11–13).

The Haftarah for this Sidra may be found on page 895.

חקת

ḤUKKATH

XIX 1. *God* spoke to Moshe and Aharon [saying]: 2. "This is a basic statute of the Teaching that *God* has commanded: Speak to the sons of Yisrael that they take for you a completely red cow on which there is no blemish and on which no yoke has ever come. 3. And you shall give it to Eleazar the priest; he shall take it out, outside the camp, and he shall slaughter it before his countenance. 4. And Eleazar the priest shall take [some] of its blood with his finger and sprinkle [some of] its blood toward the front of the Tent of Appointed Meeting, seven times. 5. The cow shall thereafter be burned before his eyes; its skin, its flesh, its blood, along with its dung, shall be burned. 6. And the priest shall take a piece of cedar wood and hyssop and scarlet wool and he shall throw it into the burning of the cow. 7. And the priest shall rinse his garments and he shall bathe his flesh in water, and only thereafter may he come into the camp. However, the priest shall remain unclean until the evening. 8. Also the

יט א וַיְדַבֵּר יְהֹוָה אֶל־מֹשֶׁה וְאֶל־אַהֲרֹן לֵאמֹר׃
ב זֹאת חֻקַּת הַתּוֹרָה אֲשֶׁר־צִוָּה יְהֹוָה לֵאמֹר
דַּבֵּר ׀ אֶל־בְּנֵי יִשְׂרָאֵל וְיִקְחוּ אֵלֶיךָ פָרָה אֲדֻמָּה
תְּמִימָה אֲשֶׁר אֵין־בָּהּ מוּם אֲשֶׁר לֹא־עָלָה
עָלֶיהָ עֹל׃ ג וּנְתַתֶּם אֹתָהּ אֶל־אֶלְעָזָר הַכֹּהֵן
וְהוֹצִיא אֹתָהּ אֶל־מִחוּץ לַמַּחֲנֶה וְשָׁחַט אֹתָהּ
לְפָנָיו׃ ד וְלָקַח אֶלְעָזָר הַכֹּהֵן מִדָּמָהּ בְּאֶצְבָּעוֹ
וְהִזָּה אֶל־נֹכַח פְּנֵי אֹהֶל־מוֹעֵד מִדָּמָהּ שֶׁבַע
פְּעָמִים׃ ה וְשָׂרַף אֶת־הַפָּרָה לְעֵינָיו אֶת־עֹרָהּ
וְאֶת־בְּשָׂרָהּ וְאֶת־דָּמָהּ עַל־פִּרְשָׁהּ יִשְׂרֹף׃
ו וְלָקַח הַכֹּהֵן עֵץ אֶרֶז וְאֵזוֹב וּשְׁנִי תוֹלָעַת
וְהִשְׁלִיךְ אֶל־תּוֹךְ שְׂרֵפַת הַפָּרָה׃ ז וְכִבֶּס בְּגָדָיו
הַכֹּהֵן וְרָחַץ בְּשָׂרוֹ בַּמַּיִם וְאַחַר יָבֹא אֶל־
הַמַּחֲנֶה וְטָמֵא הַכֹּהֵן עַד־הָעָרֶב׃ ח וְהַשֹּׂרֵף

CHAPTER XIX

1. . . . This mode of address to Moses and Aaron indicates the great importance of the subject matter that follows, both for the understanding of the Law in theory and for the education of the people to observe the Law in practice.

2. ***This is a basic statute of the Teaching.*** This turn of phrase occurs in only one other place in Scripture: in Numbers 31:21, as an introduction to the discussion of the purification and immersion of utensils captured from the Midianites.

These legal institutions and the institution of the פָּרָה אֲדֻמָּה [red cow] described in the verses that follow have in common the function of restoring purity; the former relate to the purification of eating, cooking and food-keeping utensils for the sake of the purity of the human body; the function of the latter, the red cow, is to purify man for the purpose of preserving the purity of holy things. Both institutions constitute elements basic to the entire Law; the provisions relevant to them are essential to the observance of the Law as such. If we had no means of restoring the ritual purity of our vessels or utensils, or of restoring the purity of our persons after defilement through contact with a dead body, which cannot be avoided in life, then it would be impossible for us to observe the Law as such. As a consequence, both these legal institutions are classed as "basic statutes of the Teaching"; i.e., directives that are basic to the observance of the Law.

And if now, as we shall see and as can already be understood at first glance, the institution of the פָּרָה אֲדֻמָּה is the clearest public proclamation of טָהֳרָה [ritual purity], this is indeed the fundamental concept of moral freedom of will on which the entire Law is based. Then one can grasp all the more thoroughly the reason for the categorical tone of the words that introduce these laws—זאת חֻקַּת הַתּוֹרָה ["This is a basic statute of the Teaching"]. In Menaḥoth 19a it is stated in connection with the term חֻקָּה that each and every part of the regulations of the פָּרָה אֲדֻמָּה institution that now follow is basic to the validity of the entire Law. "Wherever Scripture says *hukkah* [in connection with any regulations], it does so in order to indicate the indispensability [of those regulations]." . . .

one who burns it shall rinse his garments in
water and bathe his flesh in water and shall
remain unclean until the evening. 9. A
man who is [ritually] pure shall then gather
up the ashes of the cow and lay them down
outside the camp in a pure place. It
shall remain for the sons of Yisrael to be
kept as a water of separation; it is an offering that clears [him who brings it] of sin.
10. And the one who gathers the ashes of
the cow shall rinse his garments and shall
remain unclean until the evening. And this
shall be—for the sons of Yisrael and for the
stranger who has entered into their midst—
as an everlasting statute. 11. One who
touches the corpse of any human soul
becomes unclean for seven days. 12. He
must purify himself with it [i.e., the water]
on the third day and on the seventh day so
that he may become pure. If he does not
purify himself on the third day and on the
seventh day he will not become pure.
13. One who, by [touching] a corpse,
comes into contact with the soul of man,
which is subject to death, and does not
purify himself, has brought uncleanness to
the Dwelling Place of *God*; so, that soul
shall be uprooted from Yisrael. If the water
of separation was not dashed upon him, he
shall remain unclean; his uncleanness is
permanent upon him. 14. Now this is the

אֹתָהּ יְכַבֵּס בְּגָדָיו בַּמַּיִם וְרָחַץ בְּשָׂרוֹ בַּמָּיִם
וְטָמֵא עַד־הָעָרֶב: ט וְאָסַף ׀ אִישׁ טָהוֹר אֵת
אֵפֶר הַפָּרָה וְהִנִּיחַ מִחוּץ לַמַּחֲנֶה בְּמָקוֹם טָהוֹר
וְהָיְתָה לַעֲדַת בְּנֵי־יִשְׂרָאֵל לְמִשְׁמֶרֶת לְמֵי נִדָּה
חַטָּאת הִוא: י וְכִבֶּס הָאֹסֵף אֶת־אֵפֶר הַפָּרָה
אֶת־בְּגָדָיו וְטָמֵא עַד־הָעָרֶב וְהָיְתָה לִבְנֵי
יִשְׂרָאֵל וְלַגֵּר הַגָּר בְּתוֹכָם לְחֻקַּת עוֹלָם:
יא הַנֹּגֵעַ בְּמֵת לְכָל־נֶפֶשׁ אָדָם וְטָמֵא שִׁבְעַת
יָמִים: יב הוּא יִתְחַטָּא־בוֹ בַּיּוֹם הַשְּׁלִישִׁי וּבַיּוֹם
הַשְּׁבִיעִי יִטְהָר וְאִם־לֹא יִתְחַטָּא בַּיּוֹם הַשְּׁלִישִׁי
וּבַיּוֹם הַשְּׁבִיעִי לֹא יִטְהָר: יג כָּל־הַנֹּגֵעַ בְּמֵת
בְּנֶפֶשׁ הָאָדָם אֲשֶׁר־יָמוּת וְלֹא יִתְחַטָּא אֶת־
מִשְׁכַּן יְהוָה טִמֵּא וְנִכְרְתָה הַנֶּפֶשׁ הַהִוא
מִיִּשְׂרָאֵל כִּי מֵי נִדָּה לֹא־זֹרַק עָלָיו טָמֵא יִהְיֶה
עוֹד טֻמְאָתוֹ בוֹ: יד זֹאת הַתּוֹרָה אָדָם כִּי־יָמוּת

9. ***to be kept as a water of separation,*** נִדָּה (cf. notes on Leviticus 12:2). In Leviticus the term נִדָּה designates a condition that necessitates a temporary separation, and that terminates after a period of seven days and an act of ritual immersion. Similarly, the term נִדָּה is used in the present verse to denote a separation from all קֹדֶשׁ [holy things], necessitated by defilement through contact with a dead body, except that in this case the immersion must be preceded by a sprinkling with the מַיִם חַיִּים ["living waters"] and with the ashes of the cow. This mixture of the ashes of the cow and מַיִם חַיִּים is called מֵי נִדָּה ["water of separation"]. . . .

10. . . . The legal institution of פָּרָה אֲדֻמָּה [the red cow] may be divided into two distinct parts: the preparation of the אֵפֶר הַפָּרָה [ashes of the cow] and the use of these ashes for the purification of one who has become unclean through contact with a dead body. The discussion of the preparation of the ashes ends with the words, "and the one who gathers the ashes . . . shall rinse. . . ." The application of the ashes is described in the verses that follow.

Both parts, Verse 10 and Verse 21, respectively, conclude with statements to the effect that "this shall be for the sons of Yisrael. . . as an everlasting statute," and וְהָיְתָה לָהֶם לְחֻקַּת עוֹלָם ["It shall remain for them an everlasting statute"]. This pronouncement occurs in only three other places in Scripture: in connection with the observance of Yom Kippur (Leviticus 16:19 and 34) and in connection with the laws concerning the trumpets to be sounded by the כֹּהֲנִים [priests] (Numbers 10:8). In these passages, then, the dictum וְהָיְתָה לָכֶם לְחֻקַּת עוֹלָם ["and it shall remain for you an everlasting statute"] proclaims the principle of כַּפָּרָה [atonement] and the fundamental tenet that all authority is based on the Law and that all hopes for Israel's salvation are dependent on Israel's recognition of the Law as an everlasting norm for Israel. In the same manner, the concept of the פָּרָה אֲדֻמָּה implies a basic principle of Jewish life, to which the repetition of the dictum, "It shall remain for them, etc." lends sanction for all time to come. . . .

Teaching: If a person dies in a tent, then all that comes into the tent, and all that is in the tent, shall be unclean for seven days.
15. And every open vessel that does not have a cover bound to it shall be unclean.
16. And all that which, in the open field, comes into contact with one who was slain by the sword, or with a dead body, or with a human bone, or with a grave, shall be unclean for seven days.
17. And they shall take for the unclean person [some] of the ashes from the burning of the offering that clears [him who brings it] of sin, and he shall place upon them living water in a vessel.
18. And a man who is [ritually] pure shall take hyssop and dip it into the water and shall sprinkle [it] upon the tent and upon all the persons who were there, and upon the who one touched the bone or the one slain, or the dead body, or the grave.
19. The [ritually] pure person shall sprinkle upon the unclean person on the third day and on the seventh day and shall purify him on the seventh day; he shall wash his garments and bathe in water and shall become pure in the evening.
20. But one who becomes unclean and does not clear himself of sin, that soul shall be uprooted from the midst of the community, for he has defiled the Sanctuary of *God*; water of separation has not been dashed upon him; he is unclean.
21. It shall remain for them an everlasting statute. One who sprinkles water of separation for another purpose has to wash his garments, and one who touches water of separation shall remain unclean until the evening.
22. Also anything that the unclean per-

בְּאֹ֔הֶל כָּל־הַבָּ֤א אֶל־הָאֹ֙הֶל֙ וְכָל־אֲשֶׁ֣ר בָּאֹ֔הֶל
יִטְמָ֖א שִׁבְעַ֥ת יָמִֽים׃ טו וְכֹל֙ כְּלִ֣י פָת֔וּחַ אֲשֶׁ֛ר
אֵין־צָמִ֥יד פָּתִ֖יל עָלָ֑יו טָמֵ֖א הֽוּא׃ טז וְכֹ֨ל אֲשֶׁר־
יִגַּ֜ע עַל־פְּנֵ֣י הַשָּׂדֶ֗ה בַּֽחֲלַל־חֶ֙רֶב֙ א֣וֹ בְמֵ֔ת אֽוֹ־
בְעֶ֥צֶם אָדָ֖ם א֣וֹ בְקָ֑בֶר יִטְמָ֖א שִׁבְעַ֥ת יָמִֽים׃
יז וְלָֽקְחוּ֙ לַטָּמֵ֔א מֵֽעֲפַ֖ר שְׂרֵפַ֣ת הַֽחַטָּ֑את וְנָתַ֥ן
עָלָ֛יו מַ֥יִם חַיִּ֖ים אֶל־כֶּֽלִי׃ שני יח וְלָקַ֨ח אֵז֜וֹב
וְטָבַ֣ל בַּמַּ֘יִם֮ אִ֣ישׁ טָהוֹר֒ וְהִזָּ֤ה עַל־הָאֹ֙הֶל֙ וְעַל־
כָּל־הַכֵּלִ֔ים וְעַל־הַנְּפָשׁ֖וֹת אֲשֶׁ֣ר הָֽיוּ־שָׁ֑ם וְעַל־
הַנֹּגֵ֗עַ בַּעֶ֙צֶם֙ א֣וֹ בֶֽחָלָ֔ל א֥וֹ בַמֵּ֖ת א֥וֹ בַקָּֽבֶר׃
יט וְהִזָּ֣ה הַטָּהֹ֗ר עַל־הַטָּמֵ֔א בַּיּ֥וֹם הַשְּׁלִישִׁ֖י
וּבַיּ֣וֹם הַשְּׁבִיעִ֑י וְחִטְּאוֹ֙ בַּיּ֣וֹם הַשְּׁבִיעִ֔י וְכִבֶּ֧ס
בְּגָדָ֛יו וְרָחַ֥ץ בַּמַּ֖יִם וְטָהֵ֥ר בָּעָֽרֶב׃ כ וְאִ֤ישׁ אֲשֶׁר־
יִטְמָא֙ וְלֹ֣א יִתְחַטָּ֔א וְנִכְרְתָ֛ה הַנֶּ֥פֶשׁ הַהִ֖וא מִתּ֣וֹךְ
הַקָּהָ֑ל כִּי֩ אֶת־מִקְדַּ֨שׁ יְהֹוָ֜ה טִמֵּ֗א מֵ֥י נִדָּ֛ה לֹא־
זֹרַ֥ק עָלָ֖יו טָמֵ֥א הֽוּא׃ כא וְהָֽיְתָ֥ה לָהֶ֖ם לְחֻקַּ֣ת
עוֹלָ֑ם וּמַזֵּ֤ה מֵֽי־הַנִּדָּה֙ יְכַבֵּ֣ס בְּגָדָ֔יו וְהַנֹּגֵ֙עַ֙ בְּמֵ֣י
הַנִּדָּ֔ה יִטְמָ֖א עַד־הָעָֽרֶב׃ כב וְכֹ֥ל אֲשֶׁר־יִגַּע־בּ֛וֹ

17. . . . The term מַיִם חַיִּים ["living water"] implies water from springs that rarely dry up and that have not undergone any chemical changes; that is, it excludes warm springs and springs that contain salt (Parah 8:9). . . .

21. ***It shall remain for them an everlasting statute.*** This law has remained in force to this day. Since we all have become defiled by contact with a dead body at one time or another and cannot obtain purification because we do not have the ashes of the red cow, anyone who sets foot on the actual Temple site on Mount Moriah is subject to the penalty of "excision," being cut off from his people. The fact that the Temple was destroyed does not mean that the site of the Temple has lost its sanctity. "The initial sanctification hallowed it for its own time and for all time to come" (Maimonides, *Hilkhoth Beth HaBeḥirah* 6, 14; however, see RaBaD ibid.).

22. . . . If we consider the laws set forth here concerning the red cow and defilement through contact with a dead body, and attempt to ascertain the ideas they express, we believe we must, first of all, be clear about the concept in terms of which the Law itself bids us to perceive the institution of the red cow. This is the

son touches becomes unclean and also the הַטָּמֵא יִטְמָא וְהַנֶּפֶשׁ הַנֹּגַעַת תִּטְמָא עַד־

concept of חַטָּאת, by which the Law defines it and which forms the basis for its detailed provisions.

חַטָּאת, literally, a clearing away of sin, a cancellation of sin and of sinning in general, is a concept that belongs exclusively to the sphere of morality. The institution of the red cow, the basic statute of the Teaching, forms the fundamental institution of the entire teaching of defilement through contact with a dead body, which in turn represents the principal category of the whole teaching relating to [ritual] uncleanness. If, therefore, the Law refers to its institution of פָּרָה אֲדֻמָּה as חַטָּאת, it thereby indicates to us in most categorical terms that we must look to morality as that conceptual sphere where we will find the meaning of the laws of טוּמְאָה and טָהֳרָה in general and the institution of פָּרָה אֲדֻמָּה in particular.

At the same time the foregoing should confirm for us in no uncertain terms the perspective from which we have already sought to understand the laws of טוּמְאָה and טָהֳרָה discussed earlier. We advanced the opinion that freedom of will in matters of morality is the first and indispensable condition for that hallowing of our lives after which the Law of God commands us to strive. It seemed to us that this first and most basic of all truths according to which we are to fashion our lives is threatened by the fact that all men must die, and by the physical sight of a human corpse. For these realities would tell the superficial, limited human intelligence that all things in the universe, including man, are dominated by the forces of nature. Now if death were to mean that the *whole* man has died, if the dead body lying before us, overwhelmed by the compelling forces of nature, represented all that there is to man, then man, even during his lifetime, would be no different from any other living thing. He would be under the spell of a universally compelling necessity. If all this were indeed so, then this physical "must" would not leave room for any moral "thou shalt." Then moral freedom of will would be an illusion, and the entire God-given moral law, with its demands for a totally free-willed dedication of all one's existence and aspirations, to the fire of the Sanctuary that gives light, warmth, life and happiness by shaping and purifying man's existence, would be inconceivable. . . .

Over against this we have the laws of טוּמְאָה and טָהֳרָה, as presented in the Book of Leviticus. These laws confront the demoralizing illusion of physical non-freedom with the Divine guarantee that man does indeed have freedom of will in matters of morality. Throughout our lives, whenever the energy of moral awareness is threatened by reminders of bondage to physical forces, the Law seeks to accomplish this purpose by reminding us of the concept of טָהֳרָה, that there is no lack of freedom in matters of morality, as we have already noted in the details of טוּמְאָה and טָהֳרָה presented in the pertinent laws.

At this point, this same טוּמְאָה and טָהֳרָה legislation seeks to proclaim the great concept of חַטָּאת publicly, in the presence of the entire nation, through the nation's priestly representatives, in full view of the Sanctuary of its Law. It does so through a most significant act: by setting forth, as the moral basis for all the life of this nation, the truth that man can become, and remain, free of sin.

Such is the meaning of this particular חַטָּאת, this symbolic "clearing of sin" that must be performed outside the Sanctuary. It is not to be equated with the sin offerings that are made in the Sanctuary for the purpose of cleansing one particular individual from one particular sin by an act symbolizing his vow to remain faithful to his duty henceforth. Rather, it is a public demonstration that it is indeed possible to be free of sin, that man is indeed capable of controlling himself in the face of any physical temptation. It is a proclamation in general terms that man is endowed with moral willpower.

However, when the Law proclaims this freedom to man, it does not ignore those areas in which he has no freedom. It demonstrates to him his freedom in moral matters within the context of those physical aspects of life that lack freedom. It does not teach him to turn a blind eye to that aspect of human nature which is bound to physical elements. It shows man in all the contrasting aspects of his nature: mortal and eternal, fettered and free, physical and moral. By placing him, with all this duality of his nature, before the one sole Sanctuary of the Law of His One sole God, the only Being with absolute freedom, the Law elevates man with all his nature, both physical transience and moral immortality, into the free, everlasting kingdom of that One sole Being and says to him: "Be not misled by the sight of corpses and of death; become free, become immortal, not despite, but along with, all those aspects of your existence that are mortal and physically fettered. Remain the immortal master over your mortal body; remain pure and, in the midst of טוּמְאָה, preserve your own טָהֳרָה. . . ."

° ° °

"And he shall sprinkle . . . on the third day and on the seventh day" (Verse 19). The מֵי חַטָּאת [lit., "water that clears of sin"] symbolizes the transient yet nonetheless intimate tie between the organic material element and the immortal godly element. In this manner it expresses the concept of "man." In the same manner the sprinkling, an act intended to raise this pure concept of humanity from obfuscation back to

הָעֶרֶב: פ כ א וַיָּבֹאוּ בְנֵי־יִשְׂרָאֵל כָּל־הָעֵדָה
מִדְבַּר־צִן בַּחֹדֶשׁ הָרִאשׁוֹן וַיֵּשֶׁב הָעָם בְּקָדֵשׁ

person who touches him shall be unclean until the evening."

XX 1. The sons of Yisrael, the entire community, came into the wilderness of Tzin in the first month, and the people settled down in Kadesh, and

clear awareness, is also a dual act, dedicated to both these elements of human nature. The awareness that one has freedom of will in matters of morality and thus is capable of subordinating himself freely, with the whole of his being, to the Law of God, must form the constant basis for the organic and physical aspect no less than for the Divine and spiritual aspect of life. The gratification of one's physical urges, hunger and sex, which is part of organic life, must be subjected of one's own free will to the guidance of God's Law, no less than the thoughts, aspirations and accomplishments in which the spiritual and divine aspect of man unfolds. Both require free-willed devotion to the directives of the Teaching and the Law of God. Hence, before the one defiled through contact with a dead body can return to טָהֳרָה [purity] by the act of טְבִילָה [immersion] following his טוּמְאָה [unclean] period, the basic teaching that man has freedom of will must be brought home not only to the spiritual, godly aspect but also to the organic, physical aspect of human nature. This is done by the act of sprinkling, which must be performed on the third day and again on the seventh.

We have already pointed out in our commentary on Genesis 1:11–13 how, on the third day of Creation, the physical-organic world came into being with the imprint of the Divine law of לְמִינוֹ [species]. Therefore, the third day can bear the seal of physical, organic life submitting to the Law of God even as the seventh day presents itself as the day when man, with his Godlike powers of mastering the material world, places his use of these powers under the dominion of God. For this reason, the act of sprinkling on the third day has been given to man as a physical, organic creature, while that of the seventh day has been given to him as a spritual, Godlike being. The hallowing of the spirit and of the mind cannot be achieved without the hallowing of the body, so much so that on whatever day the first act of sprinkling may be performed, even if it is done after the third day, that day is always counted as the third day, and four days must be allowed to pass before the second sprinkling, the sprinkling of the seventh day, can be performed. But the idea that the sprinkling with מֵי חַטָּאת has reference to Creation, thus endowing the sprinkling days with their special character, seems all the less far-fetched because, as we seem to have recognized, this dust and living water upon the vessel precisely symbolizes man in his genesis at the time of Creation

In recapitulation, then, the first sprinkling, that of the third day, paves the way for the physical, bodily purification of man. The second, that of the seventh day, prepares man for the purification of his spiritual, godly aspect. Hence, before man as a whole, or human nature in its entirety, can rise again to full purity, the sprinkling and immersion of man and of his vessels must be performed.

° ° °

CHAPTER XX

1. ***and Miriam died there and was buried there.*** Miriam died there; and there, too, she was buried. She had completed her mission on earth. Her grave in Kadesh might show future generations that she did not leave this world until the next generation was ready to enter into the future that had been promised to them. During Israel's long wanderings, filled with so many sad experiences, it was the women who were least implicated in the frequent incidents of defection born of despair. It was the women who did the most to preserve serene trust and persevering devotion to God. This, according to *Midrash Rabbah* Numbers 27:1, was the reason why the women were not included in the decree under which the entire old generation had to die out before the nation could enter the Promised Land. As a result, the women, as grandmothers and mothers, were able to go with the new generation when it entered the Promised Land for its new future, and to bring with them into that new future their personal recollections of their past in Egypt and of the momentous events they had witnessed in the wilderness under the protection and guidance of God. Thus they were given the opportunity to inspire their grandchildren and great-grandchildren with the spirit of the God-revealing experiences they themselves had witnessed. The fact that these Jewish women were so deeply and thoroughly imbued with the Jewish spirit may be ascribed in no small part to Miriam, who set them a shining example as a prophetess. . . .

It is not without good cause that this chapter which, in such terse, austere terms, reports the deaths of Moses' siblings, Miriam and Aaron, is preceded by the momentous chapter concerning פָּרָה אֲדֻמָּה [the red cow], which teaches the Jewish concept of immortality. That chapter is in itself a most thoughtful introduction to the death of Miriam and Aaron. It declares that whatever in

וַתָּמָת שָׁם מִרְיָם וַתִּקָּבֵר שָׁם: ב וְלֹא־הָיָה מַיִם
לָעֵדָה וַיִּקָּהֲלוּ עַל־מֹשֶׁה וְעַל־אַהֲרֹן: ג וַיָּרֶב
הָעָם עִם־מֹשֶׁה וַיֹּאמְרוּ לֵאמֹר וְלוּ גָוַעְנוּ בִּגְוַע
אַחֵינוּ לִפְנֵי יְהֹוָה: ד וְלָמָה הֲבֵאתֶם אֶת־קְהַל
יְהֹוָה אֶל־הַמִּדְבָּר הַזֶּה לָמוּת שָׁם אֲנַחְנוּ
וּבְעִירֵנוּ: ה וְלָמָה הֶעֱלִיתֻנוּ מִמִּצְרַיִם לְהָבִיא
אֹתָנוּ אֶל־הַמָּקוֹם הָרָע הַזֶּה לֹא | מְקוֹם זֶרַע
וּתְאֵנָה וְגֶפֶן וְרִמּוֹן וּמַיִם אַיִן לִשְׁתּוֹת: ו וַיָּבֹא
מֹשֶׁה וְאַהֲרֹן מִפְּנֵי הַקָּהָל אֶל־פֶּתַח אֹהֶל מוֹעֵד
וַיִּפְּלוּ עַל־פְּנֵיהֶם וַיֵּרָא כְבוֹד־יְהֹוָה אֲלֵיהֶם: פ
שלישי (שני כשהן מחוברין) ז וַיְדַבֵּר יְהֹוָה אֶל־מֹשֶׁה
לֵּאמֹר: ח קַח אֶת־הַמַּטֶּה וְהַקְהֵל אֶת־הָעֵדָה
אַתָּה וְאַהֲרֹן אָחִיךָ וְדִבַּרְתֶּם אֶל־הַסֶּלַע
לְעֵינֵיהֶם וְנָתַן מֵימָיו וְהוֹצֵאתָ לָהֶם מַיִם מִן־

Miriam died there and was buried there.
2. And there was no water for the
community, and they assembled against
Moshe and Aharon. 3. The people contended with Moshe and said: "Would that
we had perished when our brothers perished
before *God!* 4. Why did you bring the
community of *God* into this wilderness, that
we and our animals should die there?
5. For what purpose have you brought
us up from Mitzrayim? In order to bring us
to this evil place? This is not a place of seed,
or of figs, or of wine, or of pomegranates.
There is not even water to drink!"
6. And Moshe and Aharon withdrew
from the assembly to the entrance of the
Tent of Appointed Meeting and fell upon
their faces. And the glory of *God* appeared
to them. 7. And *God* spoke to Moshe
[saying]: 8. "Take the staff and assemble
the community, you and your brother
Aharon, and speak to the rock before their
eyes that it may give forth its water; then
you will bring forth water to them from out

Miriam was indeed Miriam, and whatever in Aaron was indeed Aaron, did not die when Miriam and Aaron died. Even while their work on earth lives on in all the future generations of their people, their true essence returned from earthly transience to eternity, to God, the first Source of all life. The Sages (Moed Katan 28a) teach: "Why is the account of Miriam's death placed next to the [laws concerning the] red cow? To inform you that even as the red cow afforded atonement, so does the death of the righteous afford atonement [for the living they have left behind]." This may well indicate that, even as the institution of the פָּרָה אֲדֻמָּה teaches that the Divine aspect of human nature is immortal and hence endowed with free will, the death of the righteous, too, teaches us these truths. For one must truly be spiritually blind if he does not perceive the death of a righteous man as the most eloquent sermon in immortality; if he regards that which now lies before him inert, already marked by the traces of decay, as the same being that only a short time before had employed its mind and aspirations in spiritual strength and in the power of moral freedom of will; or if he considers the dead body of a righteous man as anything more than an empty husk, cast aside by the one who has departed hence.

2. ***. . . and there was no water for the community.*** The sequence in the narrative implies that if the Children of Israel, until that time, had been able to enjoy the water from the Well of Ḥoreb, this was due to the merits of Miriam. What Miriam's unobtrusive activities had meant for the moral future of the nation, and what a great loss her death was to the nation as a whole, can be seen from the fact that the Well of Ḥoreb dried up immediately after her passing.

4. ***Why did you bring. . .?*** This cannot have been the will of God. This was your doing, and, by so doing, you committed treachery against the community of God. . . .

5. ***For what purpose have you brought us. . .?*** The period for which it was decreed that we should wander through the wilderness has come to an end. We should already be entering the flourishing land that was promised to us, a land that in this spring season should be resplendent with all the beauty of seed and fruit. What a contrast this is to the place where we are now, where there is not even water for us to drink! This cannot be the will of God; this can be only your doing.

8. ***Take the staff.*** We note that Moses had not taken the staff in his hand since the victory over Amalek (Exodus 17:9). As we can see from Verse 9 in the present chapter, the staff had been placed "before God"; i.e., into the Sanctuary, next to the Ark of the Testimony. The staff of God held in the hands of Moses identified Moses as the one sent by God. Whenever Moses moved that staff of God, whenever he inclined it

of the rock and you will give the community and their animals to drink." 9. And Moshe took the staff that had been laid down before *God*, as He had commanded him. 10. And Moshe and Aharon assembled the community before the rock. And he said to them: "Hear now, you rebels! Shall we bring forth water for you out of this rock?" 11. And Moshe raised his hand and he struck the rock with his staff twice,

הַסֶּ֑לַע וְהִשְׁקִיתָ֥ אֶת־הָעֵדָ֖ה וְאֶת־בְּעִירָֽם׃
ט וַיִּקַּ֥ח מֹשֶׁ֛ה אֶת־הַמַּטֶּ֖ה מִלִּפְנֵ֣י יְהוָ֑ה כַּאֲשֶׁ֖ר
צִוָּֽהוּ׃ י וַיַּקְהִ֜לוּ מֹשֶׁ֧ה וְאַהֲרֹ֛ן אֶת־הַקָּהָ֖ל אֶל־
פְּנֵ֣י הַסָּ֑לַע וַיֹּ֣אמֶר לָהֶ֗ם שִׁמְעוּ־נָא֙ הַמֹּרִ֔ים
הֲמִן־הַסֶּ֣לַע הַזֶּ֔ה נוֹצִ֥יא לָכֶ֖ם מָֽיִם׃ יא וַיָּ֨רֶם מֹשֶׁ֜ה
אֶת־יָד֗וֹ וַיַּ֧ךְ אֶת־הַסֶּ֛לַע בְּמַטֵּ֖הוּ פַּעֲמָ֑יִם וַיֵּצְאוּ֙

or struck a blow with it prior to an event of which advance warning had been given, this meant that the event about to occur would be the result of an instantaneous, direct intervention by God. The people had accused Moses and Aaron of having betrayed their Divine mission. It could not have been in accordance with God's will, they said, that they had been brought to this waterless place; it was through the malevolence of Moses and Aaron that they had come to this pass. It could not have been God's will that they should die of thirst. "Take the staff," God now said to Moses. "Show them that you are still My messenger, that you have never, not even for one moment, ceased to be in My service."

and assemble the community. In the name of your Divine mission, as manifested by the staff in your hand, assemble this "community (of the future), and speak to the rock before their eyes," but do not use the staff.

לְעֵינֵיהֶם ***[before their eyes].*** In the presence of the entire people, you are to use only words to call upon the rock to give forth מֵימָיו ["its water"], that water which is already contained within it. If you were to strike the rock with your staff, as in Exodus 17:6, it would give the impression that the water was coming forth as the result of a new Divine intervention provoked by the people's uproar. And precisely this was not to be. The people should be given to understand that it was not Moses and Aaron but God Who had brought them to this place, and if His cloud had therefore directed them to set up camp in this place, it would not require a rebellion on their part to make God give them water. God had already seen to it in advance that the water they needed should be present in this place, and that one word from Moses and Aaron to the rock would be sufficient to have the rock give forth the water God had already placed within it, in readiness for them. "Then you will bring forth . . . and you will give . . . to drink." Their need, which cannot be denied, will be satisfied not by a new miracle performed by God but simply by a word from you.

This manner of obtaining water from the rock would have convinced the people what a great wrong they had done in accusing Moses and Aaron of having led them to this waterless place against the will of God. If the waters had gushed forth only after a blow of the staff upon the rock, it would still have left room for the assumption that originally the people had indeed been led into the wilderness of Tzin because of the whims of Moses and Aaron, that they had been justified in revolting, and that only this revolt and their distress had caused God to take pity upon them and to perform a miracle for them. But if the people had received their water by a mere word from the mouth of Moses, they would have learned that under God's guidance they could banish all care and be certain of receiving the right help at the right time—even without the staff of Moses. . . .

10 and 11. ***And Moshe and Aharon assembled . . . And he said . . . And Moshe raised.*** May we presume to explore the impulses that could have influenced the emotions of one such as Moses, that most faithful servant of God, of whom God Himself once said that "he is faithful in all My house"; impulses that could have distracted him, for even one moment in his life, from carrying out his mission adequately?

If we may presume to do so, then our conjecture would be as follows: In accordance with God's command, Moses removed the staff from the Sanctuary, where it had lain for almost forty years, and took it into his own hand, and it was with this symbol of his Divine mission that he gathered his people. But when he realized that even now, after forty years, it was still necessary for him to lift up his staff to prove the authenticity of his mission, just as he had been compelled to do almost forty years earlier (Exodus 4:1–15, 17), he was bitterly grieved by the thought that after all he had done during those forty years he had not yet won the trust and confidence of his people. In the bitterness of these emotions he forgot what he had been commanded to do and, instead of speaking calmly to the rock, he addressed words of angry reproach to the people and then, in the heat of passion, "he raised his hand . . . and struck. . . ." He struck the rock, whereupon water gushed forth from it in abundance and quenched the thirst of the people and their animals.

Shall we bring forth water for you out of this rock? We believe that this question should be interpreted as

מַ֥יִם רַבִּ֖ים וַתֵּ֥שְׁתְּ הָעֵדָ֖ה וּבְעִירָֽם׃ ס יב וַיֹּ֣אמֶר
יְהֹוָה֮ אֶל־מֹשֶׁ֣ה וְאֶל־אַהֲרֹן֒ יַ֚עַן לֹא־הֶאֱמַנְתֶּ֣ם
בִּ֔י לְהַ֨קְדִּישֵׁ֔נִי לְעֵינֵ֖י בְּנֵ֣י יִשְׂרָאֵ֑ל לָכֵ֗ן לֹ֤א
תָבִ֙יאוּ֙ אֶת־הַקָּהָ֣ל הַזֶּ֔ה אֶל־הָאָ֖רֶץ אֲשֶׁר־נָתַ֥תִּי
לָהֶֽם׃ יג הֵ֚מָּה מֵ֣י מְרִיבָ֔ה אֲשֶׁר־רָב֥וּ בְנֵֽי־
יִשְׂרָאֵ֖ל אֶת־יְהֹוָ֑ה וַיִּקָּדֵ֖שׁ בָּֽם׃ ס רביעי יד וַיִּשְׁלַ֨ח

and water came forth abundantly, and the community and their animals drank.
12. And *God* said to Moshe and Aharon: "Because you did not hold fast to Me, to sanctify Me before the eyes of the sons of Yisrael, therefore you shall not bring this community into the land that I have given them."
13. These are the waters of contention where the sons of Yisrael contended with *God* and He showed Himself in His

follows: Is it *we* who shall bring forth water for you out of this rock? You have raised the accusation that it was we [Moses and Aaron] who brought you "to this wilderness," "to this evil place," where "there is not even any water to drink." Very well, then, if at a mere word from us, this very rock before which you are now standing should give you the water you need, will you then cease your rebellion? Will you then understand at last that wherever you have gone, it was not we, but God, that led you there? With these words alone, Moses had not yet exceeded the bounds of the command he had received. By their content, these words would have been proper preparation for what was now to take place "before their eyes," to teach them what they needed to know. Moses' error consisted only in the fact that he uttered these words in a passion that also impelled him to raise the staff with a violent motion and to strike the rock with it.

12. ***Because you did not hold fast to Me, to sanctify Me.*** In interpreting the events that have occurred up to this point, we have ventured the assumption that Moses' anger sprang from his bitter feeling that all the work he had done for the people until then had been in vain; that the attitude of the people toward him was still one of "rebels," one of intractability, impervious to any argument to change their minds. Such anger on the part of Moses would imply that he had permitted his own personality to come to the fore, and this was not in keeping with his character, for he should have relegated his own personality to the background in the face of his awareness that he was the messenger of God. A man such as Moses—and this is probably the most difficult of all tests—should never have permitted himself to lose his patience as long as God Himself remained patient. In light of all the foregoing, one could not deny that Moses, even if only for a fleeting moment, must have doubted the ultimate success of his own Divine mission and the possibility of ultimately winning the entire nation for the accomplishment of its vocation on earth. If these assumptions on our part are not completely erroneous, should not all these facts, taken together, be construed as a momentary faltering of that אֱמוּנָה [trust] which could hold fast to God and believe in His intentions, no matter how perverse their manifestations might appear; and which should prove itself most of all where one apparent failure might tempt even God's messenger to doubt the authenticity of his own mission? A messenger of God should never cease to be aware of God as the decisive Absolute Whom nothing can keep from accomplishing His will and His purposes. Therefore, no matter what befalls, he must emulate the angels that sanctify God, covering their eyes and their feet, employing their winged might only to accomplish their mission as messengers of God. Such behavior could be construed as the greatest possible קידוש השם [sanctification of the Divine Name] in the midst of the people for whom God's message is intended. Should not then the words לא הֶאֱמַנְתֶּם בִּי לְהַקְדִּישֵׁנִי ["you did not hold fast to Me, to sanctify Me"] strike at the very heart of the error that Moses had committed in losing his patience and giving in to his anger?

But then who could presume to complete the unspoken link between the words יַעַן ["because"] and לָכֵן ["therefore"], which motivate God's sentence? Or who could presume to define in exact terms the error that made Aaron appear before God as no less guilty and deserving of punishment than Moses? In any event, we have presented here in all its momentous significance the fact that because of one small and so easily understandable moment of weakness in אֱמוּנָה, the leaders of the nation, standing at the borders of the Promised Land, had to suffer the same fate as that meted out to the generation of the wilderness whom they had led and who had been sentenced to die in the wilderness because they had lacked אֱמוּנָה all the time. Now the grave of the leaders beside those of all the others who had had to die in the wilderness will bear eternal witness to the justice of God's sovereignty, upon whose scale even the slightest error of men close to Him, hallowed by their Divine service, weighs as heavily as the most heinous crime of ordinary mortals. Precisely by making even Moses and Aaron expendable for further progress in the accomplishment of His purposes on earth, God demonstrates the קְדוּשָׁה [sanctity] of His absolute greatness, whose objectives are not dependent on any outside factor and to which even men like Moses and Aaron are not indispensable. . . .

holiness through them.   14. And Moshe sent messengers from Kadesh to the king of Edom: "Thus says your brother Yisrael to you: You have learned about all the trouble that we have encountered.   15. Our fathers went down to Mitzrayim, and we remained in Mitzrayim for a long time, but the Mitzrites did evil to us and to our fathers.   16. Then we cried to *God* and He heard our voice; He sent His messenger and led us out of Mitzrayim. Now we are in Kadesh, a city on the border of your territory.   17. Please let us pass through your land; we will not pass through field or through vineyard; we will not drink water from the wells; we will go by the king's highway; we will not turn aside to the right or to the left until we have passed through your territory."   18. Then Edom sent word to him: "You shall not pass through me, or else I will come out to meet you with the sword."   19. The sons of Yisrael sent word to him in return: "We will go up by the high road and if we should drink from your waters, I or my livestock, then I will pay their purchase price—[I will do] nothing else whatsoever; only let me pass through with my feet."   20. Then he sent word: "You shall not pass through." And Edom went out to meet him with a massive complement of men and with enormous power.   21. Thus Edom refused to permit Yisrael to pass through his territory and Yisrael turned aside from it.   22. They journeyed forth from Kadesh, and the sons of Yisrael, the whole community, came to Mount Hor.   23. And *God* said to Moshe and to Aharon on Mount Hor, on the border of the land of Edom: 24. "Aharon shall be gathered to his people, because he shall not enter into the land that I have given to the sons of Yisrael, because you have acted contrary to My word with regard to the

מֹשֶׁה מַלְאָכִים מִקָּדֵשׁ אֶל־מֶלֶךְ אֱדוֹם כֹּה אָמַר
אָחִיךָ יִשְׂרָאֵל אַתָּה יָדַעְתָּ אֵת כָּל־הַתְּלָאָה אֲשֶׁר
מְצָאָתְנוּ: טו וַיֵּרְדוּ אֲבֹתֵינוּ מִצְרַיְמָה וַנֵּשֶׁב
בְּמִצְרַיִם יָמִים רַבִּים וַיָּרֵעוּ לָנוּ מִצְרַיִם
וְלַאֲבֹתֵינוּ: טז וַנִּצְעַק אֶל־יְהֹוָה וַיִּשְׁמַע קֹלֵנוּ
וַיִּשְׁלַח מַלְאָךְ וַיֹּצִאֵנוּ מִמִּצְרָיִם וְהִנֵּה אֲנַחְנוּ
בְקָדֵשׁ עִיר קְצֵה גְבוּלֶךָ: יז נַעְבְּרָה־נָּא בְאַרְצֶךָ
לֹא נַעֲבֹר בְּשָׂדֶה וּבְכֶרֶם וְלֹא נִשְׁתֶּה מֵי בְאֵר
דֶּרֶךְ הַמֶּלֶךְ נֵלֵךְ לֹא נִטֶּה יָמִין וּשְׂמֹאול (יתיר
וא"ו) עַד אֲשֶׁר־נַעֲבֹר גְּבֻלֶךָ: יח וַיֹּאמֶר אֵלָיו
אֱדוֹם לֹא תַעֲבֹר בִּי פֶּן־בַּחֶרֶב אֵצֵא לִקְרָאתֶךָ:
יט וַיֹּאמְרוּ אֵלָיו בְּנֵי־יִשְׂרָאֵל בַּמְסִלָּה נַעֲלֶה
וְאִם־מֵימֶיךָ נִשְׁתֶּה אֲנִי וּמִקְנַי וְנָתַתִּי מִכְרָם רַק
אֵין־דָּבָר בְּרַגְלַי אֶעֱבֹרָה: כ וַיֹּאמֶר לֹא תַעֲבֹר
וַיֵּצֵא אֱדוֹם לִקְרָאתוֹ בְּעַם כָּבֵד וּבְיָד חֲזָקָה:
כא וַיְמָאֵן | אֱדוֹם נְתֹן אֶת־יִשְׂרָאֵל עֲבֹר בִּגְבֻלוֹ
וַיֵּט יִשְׂרָאֵל מֵעָלָיו: פ חמישי (שלישי כשהן מחוברין)
כב וַיִּסְעוּ מִקָּדֵשׁ וַיָּבֹאוּ בְנֵי־יִשְׂרָאֵל כָּל־הָעֵדָה
הֹר הָהָר: כג וַיֹּאמֶר יְהֹוָה אֶל־מֹשֶׁה וְאֶל־אַהֲרֹן
בְּהֹר הָהָר עַל־גְּבוּל אֶרֶץ־אֱדוֹם לֵאמֹר:
כד יֵאָסֵף אַהֲרֹן אֶל־עַמָּיו כִּי לֹא יָבֹא אֶל־
הָאָרֶץ אֲשֶׁר נָתַתִּי לִבְנֵי יִשְׂרָאֵל עַל אֲשֶׁר

---

14. *And Moshe sent.* Undeterred by the fate decreed for him, that he himself was to be denied the prospect of arriving at the destination he had made such great efforts to reach, Moses was determined to continue carrying out his mission with vigor for as long as God would permit him to live in the midst of his people. . . .

17. *we will not drink water from the wells.* We will not touch any private property. "The king's highway" is a highway constructed by the "king"; i.e., by the nation, a public highway, one that is not private property, perhaps not even the property of a local community.

waters of contention.   25. Take Aharon
and his son Eleazar and bring them up to
Mount Hor,   26. and divest Aharon of
his garments, and invest his son Eleazar with
them; and Aharon shall be gathered up and
die there."   27. And Moshe did as *God*
had commanded him. They went up Mount
Hor before the eyes of the entire community.   28. Moshe divested Aharon of
his garments and invested his son Eleazar
with them, and Aharon died there on the
top of the mountain. Moshe and Eleazar
descended from the mountain.   29. And
the entire community saw that Aharon was
dead and the entire house of Yisrael wept
for Aharon thirty days.

XXI   1. The Canaanite king
Arad, who dwelt in the
south, heard that Yisrael was coming by the
way of the scouts; he made war on Yisrael
and took some of them captive.   2. Then
Yisrael vowed a vow to *God* and said: "If
Thou wilt deliver this people into my hand,
then I will place an interdiction upon their
cities."   3. *God* hearkened to the voice of
Yisrael and delivered up the Canaanite[s].
It° then placed an interdiction upon them
and upon their cities. It therefore called the
place Ḥormah.°°   4. They journeyed
from Mount Hor toward the Red Sea, in

° *Note to the English translation*: "It" refers to the
nation of Israel. Hirsch explains this from the grammar
of the text, in his commentary on Verses 2 and 3, which
is not included in this excerpted edition. [G.H.]
°°From *herem*, meaning "interdiction," "ban."

מְרִיתֶם אֶת־פִּי לְמֵי מְרִיבָה: כה קַח אֶת־אַהֲרֹן
וְאֶת־אֶלְעָזָר בְּנוֹ וְהַעַל אֹתָם הֹר הָהָר:
כו וְהַפְשֵׁט אֶת־אַהֲרֹן אֶת־בְּגָדָיו וְהִלְבַּשְׁתָּם
אֶת־אֶלְעָזָר בְּנוֹ וְאַהֲרֹן יֵאָסֵף וּמֵת שָׁם:
כז וַיַּעַשׂ מֹשֶׁה כַּאֲשֶׁר צִוָּה יְהוָה וַיַּעֲלוּ אֶל־הֹר
הָהָר לְעֵינֵי כָּל־הָעֵדָה: כח וַיַּפְשֵׁט מֹשֶׁה אֶת־
אַהֲרֹן אֶת־בְּגָדָיו וַיַּלְבֵּשׁ אֹתָם אֶת־אֶלְעָזָר בְּנוֹ
וַיָּמָת אַהֲרֹן שָׁם בְּרֹאשׁ הָהָר וַיֵּרֶד מֹשֶׁה
וְאֶלְעָזָר מִן־הָהָר: כט וַיִּרְאוּ כָּל־הָעֵדָה כִּי גָוַע
אַהֲרֹן וַיִּבְכּוּ אֶת־אַהֲרֹן שְׁלֹשִׁים יוֹם כֹּל בֵּית
יִשְׂרָאֵל: ס כא א וַיִּשְׁמַע הַכְּנַעֲנִי מֶלֶךְ־עֲרָד
יֹשֵׁב הַנֶּגֶב כִּי בָּא יִשְׂרָאֵל דֶּרֶךְ הָאֲתָרִים וַיִּלָּחֶם
בְּיִשְׂרָאֵל וַיִּשְׁבְּ ׀ מִמֶּנּוּ שֶׁבִי: ב וַיִּדַּר יִשְׂרָאֵל
נֶדֶר לַיהוָה וַיֹּאמַר אִם־נָתֹן תִּתֵּן אֶת־הָעָם הַזֶּה
בְּיָדִי וְהַחֲרַמְתִּי אֶת־עָרֵיהֶם: ג וַיִּשְׁמַע יְהוָה
בְּקוֹל יִשְׂרָאֵל וַיִּתֵּן אֶת־הַכְּנַעֲנִי וַיַּחֲרֵם אֶתְהֶם
וְאֶת־עָרֵיהֶם וַיִּקְרָא שֵׁם־הַמָּקוֹם חָרְמָה: פ
ד וַיִּסְעוּ מֵהֹר הָהָר דֶּרֶךְ יַם־סוּף לִסְבֹב

26. and divest … and invest. By this act Eleazar
was inducted as high priest in place of Aaron (cf.
Exodus 29:29). Before his own death, Aaron was given
the satisfaction of seeing himself live on in the person of
his son.

29. And the entire community saw. Our Sages
(Taanith 9a) teach that even as, after the death of
Miriam, the loss to the nation became manifest by the
drying up of the well, so, too, the death of Aaron
became "visible" to the nation by a physical manifestation. With Aaron's death, the cloud which until then
had protectively enveloped the people and had gone
before them in their wanderings through the wilderness,
departed from them. Cf. "The clouds of glory depart-

ed." Their resultant state of defenselessness immediately encouraged the Canaanite king who dwelled in the
region to launch an attack against them. . . .

**and the entire house of Yisrael wept for Aharon
thirty days.** Only a few days earlier this same people
had heaped the gravest and most unjust accusations
upon the man whom they now mourned so
deeply and universally (Verse 2 ff.). This deep mourning
for Aaron, so soon after the accusations they had
leveled against him, would indicate that the revolts
that had troubled the lives of Aaron and Moses had
been, in fact, only passing incidents of unrest, brought
about by transient moods of despair. Basically, in its
normal state, the nation knew and appreciated the
merits of its leaders.

אֶת־אֶרֶץ אֱדוֹם וַתִּקְצַר נֶפֶשׁ־הָעָם בַּדָּרֶךְ׃
ה וַיְדַבֵּר הָעָם בֵּאלֹהִים וּבְמֹשֶׁה לָמָה הֶעֱלִיתֻנוּ
מִמִּצְרַיִם לָמוּת בַּמִּדְבָּר כִּי אֵין לֶחֶם וְאֵין מַיִם
וְנַפְשֵׁנוּ קָצָה בַּלֶּחֶם הַקְּלֹקֵל׃ ו וַיְשַׁלַּח יְהוָה
בָּעָם אֵת הַנְּחָשִׁים הַשְּׂרָפִים וַיְנַשְּׁכוּ אֶת־הָעָם
וַיָּמָת עַם־רָב מִיִּשְׂרָאֵל׃ ז וַיָּבֹא הָעָם אֶל־מֹשֶׁה
וַיֹּאמְרוּ חָטָאנוּ כִּי־דִבַּרְנוּ בַיהוָה וָבָךְ הִתְפַּלֵּל
אֶל־יְהוָה וְיָסֵר מֵעָלֵינוּ אֶת־הַנָּחָשׁ וַיִּתְפַּלֵּל
מֹשֶׁה בְּעַד הָעָם׃ ח וַיֹּאמֶר יְהוָה אֶל־מֹשֶׁה

order to bypass the land of Edom, and the people became impatient along the way.
5. And the people spoke against God and against Moshe: "Why have you brought us up from Mitzrayim to die in the wilderness? For we have no bread and no water, and our soul is sick of this unsubstantial nourishment."
6. And *God* sent the venomous snakes against the people; they bit the people and many people of Yisrael died.
7. And the people came to Moshe and said: "We have sinned because we have spoken against *God* and against you. Pray to *God* that He may turn away the snakes from us." And Moshe prayed for the people.
8. And *God* said to Moshe: "Make your-

CHAPTER XXI

4. וַתִּקְצַר נֶפֶשׁ הָעָם בַּדָּרֶךְ ***[and the people became impatient along the way].*** Cf. Exodus 6:9, מִקֹּצֶר רוּחַ [lit., "short spirit"], and thus here also קֹצֶר נֶפֶשׁ [lit., "short soul"], is probably the antithesis of אֶרֶךְ אַפַּיִם [long-suffering, slow to anger], and would denote impatience; i.e., that רוּחַ [the spirit] and נֶפֶשׁ [the soul] are not sufficiently long-suffering to wait patiently for the goal they desire. Here, in particular, the נֶפֶשׁ, the vital spirits that strive forward, were not adequate to bear with patience the troubles of the long journey, mindful of the goal they were to reach. But they had no specific unfulfilled needs that would have given them cause for dissatisfaction.

5. ***And the people spoke against God.*** Their discontent turned also directly against God. Now they did not merely doubt the authenticity of Moses' mission, but they were dissatisfied with the guidance of God Himself.

Why have you brought us up. [The second person plural refers to] God and Moses.

to die in the wilderness. If we continue in this way we will never reach our goal but will end our days in the wilderness, always under the same utterly abnormal conditions.

For we have no bread and no water. This cannot mean that they lacked the nourishment they needed in order to survive, for they themselves hasten to add that they do have "nourishment," lit., "bread." What they miss is the kind of food and drink people normally have. The nourishment with which they had been provided by miracle, without any effort on their own part, had become monotonous to them. God's special Providence, which they had experienced each day for a period of forty years, had become to them a routine matter, and their discontent caused them to denigrate the nutritive value of the *manna* God had given them. They called it "unsubstantial nourishment"; according to the *Pesikta*, a light, easily digestible food, so easily digested that, according to the *Midrash Shoḥer Tov,*[7] it was completely absorbed and used entirely to renew the body's tissues. "It was absorbed entirely by the 248 parts of the body" (Yoma 75b). In their discontent they saw this excellent nutritive quality as something detrimental; they claimed that the food was not substantial enough for them.

6. Not נְחָשִׁים שְׂרָפִים ["venomous snakes"] but הַנְּחָשִׁים הַשְּׂרָפִים ["*the* venomous snakes"]. These venomous snakes had always existed in the wilderness. However, until that time, God, in His Providence, had kept them away from the people. But now God removed this restraint and the snakes of the wilderness reverted to their natural habits, to which the people then fell victim. Thus, too, Moses, in Deuteronomy 8:15, when speaking of the wilderness through which God's wondrous might had permitted the Children of Israel to pass unscathed, referred to God as the One "Who led you in the great and terrible wilderness, where there were snakes, *saraf* and scorpions, thirst. . . ." Thus, "venomous snakes" are as much a natural phenomenon of the wilderness as "thirst.". . .

8. ***And God said . . . and it shall come to pass that anyone who is bitten.*** The sole purpose of the snakebites was to make the people see the perils that dogged them at every turn in the wilderness and realize that it

[7]*Note to the English Translation*: Midrash on the Book of Psalms. [G.H.]

self a venomous snake and place it upon a
tall pole and it shall come to pass that
anyone who is bitten, let him look upon it
and he will live." 9. And Moshe made a
copper snake and placed it upon the tall
pole, and it came to pass that if a snake had
bitten a man, he would look upon the
copper snake and live. 10. The sons of
Yisrael journeyed on and camped in Oboth.
11. They journeyed from Oboth and
camped in the wastelands of the transitions
in the wilderness that lies before Moab,
toward sunrise. 12. From there they
journeyed and camped in the basin of
Zared. 13. From there they journeyed
and camped on the side of the Arnon, which
is in the wilderness that comes out of the
territory of the Emorite[s]. For the Arnon
forms the border of Moab, between Moab
and the Emorites. 14. Therefore it is said
in the Book of the Wars of *God*: "Vaheb in
Suphah, and the streams that form the
Arnon. 15. And the pouring forth of the
streams that made a turn to give living
space to Ar and then clings to the territory
of Moab." 16. From there toward the
well. This is the well of which *God* had said
to Moshe: "Gather the people; I will give
them water." 17. It was then that Yisrael
sang this song: "Rise again, O well, sing
responsively to it. 18. You are the well
that was dug by princes, that the nobles of
the people carved out with the stylus of the
Law upon their staffs!" And from the wilderness it [the well] was given again as a gift.

עֲשֵׂה לְךָ שָׂרָף וְשִׂים אֹתוֹ עַל־נֵס וְהָיָה כָּל־
הַנָּשׁוּךְ וְרָאָה אֹתוֹ וָחָי: ט וַיַּעַשׂ מֹשֶׁה נְחַשׁ
נְחֹשֶׁת וַיְשִׂמֵהוּ עַל־הַנֵּס וְהָיָה אִם־נָשַׁךְ הַנָּחָשׁ
אֶת־אִישׁ וְהִבִּיט אֶל־נְחַשׁ הַנְּחֹשֶׁת וָחָי: ששי
י וַיִּסְעוּ בְּנֵי יִשְׂרָאֵל וַיַּחֲנוּ בְּאֹבֹת: יא וַיִּסְעוּ
מֵאֹבֹת וַיַּחֲנוּ בְּעִיֵּי הָעֲבָרִים בַּמִּדְבָּר אֲשֶׁר עַל־
פְּנֵי מוֹאָב מִמִּזְרַח הַשָּׁמֶשׁ: יב מִשָּׁם נָסָעוּ וַיַּחֲנוּ
בְּנַחַל זָרֶד: יג מִשָּׁם נָסָעוּ וַיַּחֲנוּ מֵעֵבֶר אַרְנוֹן
אֲשֶׁר בַּמִּדְבָּר הַיֹּצֵא מִגְּבֻל הָאֱמֹרִי כִּי אַרְנוֹן
גְּבוּל מוֹאָב בֵּין מוֹאָב וּבֵין הָאֱמֹרִי: יד עַל־כֵּן
יֵאָמַר בְּסֵפֶר מִלְחֲמֹת יְהֹוָה אֶת־וָהֵב בְּסוּפָה
וְאֶת־הַנְּחָלִים אַרְנוֹן: טו וְאֶשֶׁד הַנְּחָלִים אֲשֶׁר
נָטָה לְשֶׁבֶת עָר וְנִשְׁעַן לִגְבוּל מוֹאָב: טז וּמִשָּׁם
בְּאֵרָה הִוא הַבְּאֵר אֲשֶׁר אָמַר יְהֹוָה לְמֹשֶׁה אֱסֹף
אֶת־הָעָם וְאֶתְּנָה לָהֶם מָיִם: ס יז אָז יָשִׁיר
יִשְׂרָאֵל אֶת־הַשִּׁירָה הַזֹּאת עֲלִי בְאֵר עֱנוּ־לָהּ:
יח בְּאֵר חֲפָרוּהָ שָׂרִים כָּרוּהָ נְדִיבֵי הָעָם
בִּמְחֹקֵק בְּמִשְׁעֲנֹתָם וּמִמִּדְבָּר מַתָּנָה:

was only God's miraculous power that had kept these
perils away from them, so far away that they did not
even have an idea that such things existed. Anyone
who was bitten must fix the image of the snake firmly in
his mind so that it should always remain before him,
even after God, in the power of His grace,
would keep the snakes away from him once more. In
this manner the victim will remain aware of the existence of the perils through which God's special protection guides us safely every day and at all times without
our even knowing it, perils that demonstrate to us how
each breath of our lives is a new gift of God's goodness
and might. Nothing is more suited to reconcile us with
everyday disappointments that could so easily incite us
to impatience, nothing can more cogently infuse into
our every moment the exaltation of God-given salvation and the bliss of newly-granted existence, than to

consider the precipice along whose narrow rim runs the
path of all our lives, a precipice which the kindly hand
of God screens from our view, lest we become dizzy, and
the precipice past which God bears us in His power and
goodness as on eagles' wings. Nothing would be more
conducive to this purpose than to consider the
venomous snakes which lurk upon our path unseen and
which only God's almighty Providence knows how to
render harmless. Hence the "ingrates," as our Sages
call them, are to be punished by God's removing the
protective screen which until that time had hidden the
venomous fangs of the snakes in the wilderness and
rendered them harmless. For this reason, the remedy
for anyone bitten by a snake was that he must fix in his
mind the image of the snake to remember for all time.
It shall come to pass that "anyone who is bitten, let him
look upon it and he will live."

19. And from the renewed gift, a stream of God, and from the stream of God up to the high places, 20. and from the high places into the valley which is in the field of Moab, up to the summit of the high places and now looks out upon the face of the wasteland. 21. And Yisrael sent messengers to Siḥon, king of the Emorites [saying]: 22. "Let me pass through your land; we will not turn aside into field or into vineyard; we will not drink water from the wells; we will go by the king's highway until we have passed through your territory." 23. But Siḥon did not permit Yisrael to pass through his territory. Siḥon gathered all his people and went out to meet Yisrael, toward the wilderness, and he came to Yahatz and attacked Yisrael. 24. And Yisrael struck him down with the edge of the sword, took possession of his land from the Arnon to the Yabbok, as far as the sons of Ammon, for this territory of the sons of Ammon was firm. 25. Yisrael took all these cities and Yisrael settled in all the cities of the Emorites, in Ḥeshbon and in all its daughter cities. 26. For Ḥeshbon was then a city of Siḥon, king of the Emorite[s]. He had overcome the earlier king of Moab with war and taken his entire land out of his hand as far as the Arnon. 27. Therefore the makers of parables say: "Just go to Ḥeshbon! It has now been rebuilt as the city of Siḥon and reestablished. 28. For then fire went forth from Ḥeshbon, a flame from the citadel of Siḥon; it consumed Ar of Moab, ruler of the heights of Arnon. 29. Woe to you, O Moab! You are lost, O people of Kemosh! He has given his sons as fugitives and his daughters into captivity to Siḥon, king of the Emorites. 30. And we overthrew them; Ḥeshbon has perished as far as Dibbon; we laid waste as far as Nofaḥ that reaches to Medva." 31. Yisrael settled in the land of the Emorites. 32. But Moshe sent to reconnoiter Yaazer, and they captured its daughter cities and he drove out the Emorite[s] that lived there. 33. They then turned and went up by the way of Bashan, and Og, king of the Bashan, went out to meet them, he and all his people, for war, to Edrei. 34. And *God*

יט וּמִמַּתָּנָה נַחֲלִיאֵל וּמִנַּחֲלִיאֵל בָּמוֹת:
כ וּמִבָּמוֹת הַגַּיְא אֲשֶׁר בִּשְׂדֵה מוֹאָב רֹאשׁ
הַפִּסְגָּה וְנִשְׁקָפָה עַל־פְּנֵי הַיְשִׁימֹן: פ שביעי (רביעי
כשהן מחוברין) כא וַיִּשְׁלַח יִשְׂרָאֵל מַלְאָכִים אֶל־
סִיחֹן מֶלֶךְ־הָאֱמֹרִי לֵאמֹר: כב אֶעְבְּרָה בְאַרְצֶךָ
לֹא נִטֶּה בְּשָׂדֶה וּבְכֶרֶם לֹא נִשְׁתֶּה מֵי בְאֵר
בְּדֶרֶךְ הַמֶּלֶךְ נֵלֵךְ עַד אֲשֶׁר־נַעֲבֹר גְּבֻלֶךָ:
כג וְלֹא־נָתַן סִיחֹן אֶת־יִשְׂרָאֵל עֲבֹר בִּגְבֻלוֹ
וַיֶּאֱסֹף סִיחֹן אֶת־כָּל־עַמּוֹ וַיֵּצֵא לִקְרַאת
יִשְׂרָאֵל הַמִּדְבָּרָה וַיָּבֹא יָהְצָה וַיִּלָּחֶם בְּיִשְׂרָאֵל:
כד וַיַּכֵּהוּ יִשְׂרָאֵל לְפִי־חָרֶב וַיִּירַשׁ אֶת־אַרְצוֹ
מֵאַרְנֹן עַד־יַבֹּק עַד־בְּנֵי עַמּוֹן כִּי עַז גְּבוּל בְּנֵי
עַמּוֹן: כה וַיִּקַּח יִשְׂרָאֵל אֵת כָּל־הֶעָרִים הָאֵלֶּה
וַיֵּשֶׁב יִשְׂרָאֵל בְּכָל־עָרֵי הָאֱמֹרִי בְּחֶשְׁבּוֹן
וּבְכָל־בְּנֹתֶיהָ: כו כִּי חֶשְׁבּוֹן עִיר סִיחֹן מֶלֶךְ
הָאֱמֹרִי הִוא וְהוּא נִלְחַם בְּמֶלֶךְ מוֹאָב הָרִאשׁוֹן
וַיִּקַּח אֶת־כָּל־אַרְצוֹ מִיָּדוֹ עַד־אַרְנֹן: כז עַל־כֵּן
יֹאמְרוּ הַמֹּשְׁלִים בֹּאוּ חֶשְׁבּוֹן תִּבָּנֶה וְתִכּוֹנֵן
עִיר סִיחוֹן: כח כִּי־אֵשׁ יָצְאָה מֵחֶשְׁבּוֹן לֶהָבָה
מִקִּרְיַת סִיחֹן אָכְלָה עָר מוֹאָב בַּעֲלֵי בָּמוֹת
אַרְנֹן: כט אוֹי־לְךָ מוֹאָב אָבַדְתָּ עַם־כְּמוֹשׁ נָתַן
בָּנָיו פְּלֵיטִם וּבְנֹתָיו בַּשְּׁבִית לְמֶלֶךְ אֱמֹרִי
סִיחוֹן: ל וַנִּירָם אָבַד חֶשְׁבּוֹן עַד־דִּיבֹן וַנַּשִּׁים
עַד־נֹפַח אֲשֶׁר עַד־מֵידְבָא: לא וַיֵּשֶׁב יִשְׂרָאֵל
בְּאֶרֶץ הָאֱמֹרִי: לב וַיִּשְׁלַח מֹשֶׁה לְרַגֵּל אֶת־יַעְזֵר
וַיִּלְכְּדוּ בְּנֹתֶיהָ וַיִּירֶשׁ (ויורש קרי) אֶת־הָאֱמֹרִי
אֲשֶׁר־שָׁם: לג וַיִּפְנוּ וַיַּעֲלוּ דֶּרֶךְ הַבָּשָׁן וַיֵּצֵא
עוֹג מֶלֶךְ־הַבָּשָׁן לִקְרָאתָם הוּא וְכָל־עַמּוֹ
לַמִּלְחָמָה אֶדְרֶעִי: מפטיר לד וַיֹּאמֶר יְהֹוָה אֶל־

said to Moshe: "Do not be afraid of him, for I have delivered him and all his people and his land into your hand; do to him as you have done to Siḥon, king of the Emorite[s] who resided in Ḥeshbon." 35. They struck him and his sons and all his people, so that none of them was left, and they took possession of his land.

XXII 1. Thereupon the sons of Yisrael journeyed on and camped in the wastelands of Moab, on the other side of the Yarden of Jericho.

מֹשֶׁה֙ אַל־תִּירָ֣א אֹת֔וֹ כִּ֣י בְיָדְךָ֞ נָתַ֧תִּי אֹת֛וֹ וְאֶת־
כָּל־עַמּ֖וֹ וְאֶת־אַרְצ֑וֹ וְעָשִׂ֣יתָ לּ֗וֹ כַּאֲשֶׁ֤ר עָשִׂ֙יתָ֙
לְסִיחֹן֙ מֶ֣לֶךְ הָֽאֱמֹרִ֔י אֲשֶׁ֥ר יוֹשֵׁ֖ב בְּחֶשְׁבּֽוֹן׃
לה וַיַּכּ֨וּ אֹת֤וֹ וְאֶת־בָּנָיו֙ וְאֶת־כָּל־עַמּ֔וֹ עַד־בִּלְתִּ֥י
הִשְׁאִֽיר־ל֖וֹ שָׂרִ֑יד וַיִּֽירְשׁ֖וּ אֶת־אַרְצֽוֹ׃
כב א וַיִּסְע֖וּ בְּנֵ֣י יִשְׂרָאֵ֑ל וַֽיַּחֲנוּ֙ בְּעַֽרְב֣וֹת מוֹאָ֔ב
מֵעֵ֖בֶר לְיַרְדֵּ֥ן יְרֵחֽוֹ׃ ס

The Haftarah for this Sidra may be found on page 898.

בלק

BALAK

2. When Balak, son of Tzippor, saw all that Yisrael had done to the Emorites— 3. and Moab became terrified of the people because they were so powerful, and everything had become loathsome to Moab because of the presence of the sons of Yisrael, 4. and Moab had already sent word to the elders of Midian: "Now this united multitude will lick up all that is around us just as the ox licks up the herbs of

ב וַיַּרְא בָּלָק בֶּן־צִפּוֹר אֵת כָּל־אֲשֶׁר־עָשָׂה
יִשְׂרָאֵל לָאֱמֹרִי׃ ג וַיָּגָר מוֹאָב מִפְּנֵי הָעָם מְאֹד
כִּי רַב־הוּא וַיָּקָץ מוֹאָב מִפְּנֵי בְּנֵי יִשְׂרָאֵל׃
ד וַיֹּאמֶר מוֹאָב אֶל־זִקְנֵי מִדְיָן עַתָּה יְלַחֲכוּ
הַקָּהָל אֶת־כָּל־סְבִיבֹתֵינוּ כִּלְחֹךְ הַשּׁוֹר אֵת יֶרֶק

CHAPTER XXII

3. וַיָּגָר מוֹאָב *[and Moab became terrified].* In the preceding verse, Balak is described merely as an individual, not as the king of Moab. Therefore, "Moab" in this verse cannot be identical with its king, Balak. Rather, the words "and Moab became terrified" continue the description of what Balak had seen. He had seen the defeat of Siḥon and Og, and also the impact of these events on Moab; namely, that "Moab became terrified" and "everything had become loathsome to Moab." The Moabites were seized with such terror that they became unstable, as if the ground had been cut from beneath their feet (see Genesis 37:1). As the *Midrash Rabbah* so aptly puts it, the Moabites already saw themselves as גָּרִים [strangers] in their own land. They felt as if the land were no longer theirs; they already visualized it as being in the hands of Israel, and this terror "of the people because they were so powerful" seized them; they feared Israel as a people that had proven overwhelmingly mighty. . . .

4. ***and Moab had already sent word to the elders of Midian.*** This fear had already driven them to take action. Moab—the people of Moab, ignoring their king—had sent a message to the elders of the people of Midian, not to the Midianite kings (of whom there were five [Numbers 31:8]), telling them of their apprehensions. Since Siḥon and Og, the mightiest kings of their time, had proven utterly ineffectual in the face of Israel, the popular belief in the power of kings as defenders of the independence of their peoples had been severely shaken, and messengers went back and forth from nation to nation, ignoring the kings, with the nations inviting one another to take counsel and to take action together. The message ran as follows: ". . . As naturally and effortlessly as the ox licks up grass as food with his tongue, so, too, with the same ease, we will all become the prey of this קָהָל [united multitude]." They purposely did not refer to Israel as עַם [a people] or גוֹי [a nation]. They still did not regard Israel as a duly constituted nation because Israel still had no land of its own, which in the popular mind was an indispensable prerequisite for nationhood. They regarded Israel as a קָהָל, a community united by some factor unknown to them.

all that is around us. They will lick up not only us, opposite whom they are now encamped and who are the most immediately threatened by them, but also all the territories around us. . . .

And yet Balak, son of Tzippor, was king for Moab at that time. The term used in Scripture for "king *of* Moab" is always מֶלֶךְ מוֹאָב, *never* מֶלֶךְ לְמוֹאָב, as in the present verse. Consequently, the term מֶלֶךְ לְמוֹאָב would denote the position of king that someone has, or should have, as far as the land and people of Moab are concerned. Thus, בָּלָק בֶּן צִפּוֹר מֶלֶךְ לְמוֹאָב וגו׳ means: Balak had the calling and the position of king as far as Moab was concerned. In conjunction with the words that went before, the statement, "and yet Balak, son of Tzippor, was king *for* Moab at that time," implies that the Moabite people should have discussed their apprehensions with him, the king, before communicating them to anyone else. After all, it was precisely for times such as these that the king was expected to function as a king. When the people in their terror completely ignored his role of king, so that at a time such as this he saw that he was merely Balak, son of Tzippor (as he is called in Verse 2), not מֶלֶךְ מוֹאָב [king of Moab], he realized the full seriousness of the situation, and this realization motivated all his subsequent actions. Israel's mere presence and the wondrous victories already won by the Israelites had worked such a spell on his people that the Moabites had lost all their trust in the ordinary powers of nations and their rulers and did not expect the military prowess of their king to have any effect on Israel. No matter whether Balak himself shared this belief in magic powers or whether, the field." And yet Balak, son of Tzippor, was king for Moab at that time — 5. and he sent messengers to Balaam, son of Beor, to Pethor (which lies on the river in the land of his fellow citizens) in order to invite him to come to him; they shall tell him: "Lo! A people has come out from Mitzrayim. Lo! It has already covered the eye of the earth, and now it has settled opposite me. 6. And now, please come; curse the people for me, because they are too mighty for me; perhaps I will then be able to bring it about that we will deal them a blow, and I will drive them out of the land, for I know that whoever you bless is blessed, and whoever you curse is cursed." 7. And the elders of Moab and the elders of Midian went with magic charms in their hands, came to Balaam and uttered to him the words of Balak. 8. And he said to them: "Spend the night here, and then I will give you an answer as *God* will speak to me." And the princes of Moab remained with Balaam. 9. And *God* came to Balaam and said: "Who are these people with you?" 10. Balaam said to God: "Balak, son of Tzippor, king of Moab, has sent [a message] to me: 11. Lo! This is the people that came out of Mitzrayim and already covers the eye of the earth; now, please come and curse them for me; perhaps I will then be

הַשָּׂדֶה וּבָלָק בֶּן־צִפּוֹר מֶלֶךְ לְמוֹאָב בָּעֵת הַהִוא: ה וַיִּשְׁלַח מַלְאָכִים אֶל־בִּלְעָם בֶּן־בְּעוֹר פְּתוֹרָה אֲשֶׁר עַל־הַנָּהָר אֶרֶץ בְּנֵי־עַמּוֹ לִקְרֹא־לוֹ לֵאמֹר הִנֵּה עַם יָצָא מִמִּצְרַיִם הִנֵּה כִסָּה אֶת־עֵין הָאָרֶץ וְהוּא יֹשֵׁב מִמֻּלִי: ו וְעַתָּה לְכָה־נָּא אָרָה־לִּי אֶת־הָעָם הַזֶּה כִּי־עָצוּם הוּא מִמֶּנִּי אוּלַי אוּכַל נַכֶּה־בּוֹ וַאֲגָרְשֶׁנּוּ מִן־הָאָרֶץ כִּי יָדַעְתִּי אֵת אֲשֶׁר־תְּבָרֵךְ מְבֹרָךְ וַאֲשֶׁר תָּאֹר יוּאָר: ז וַיֵּלְכוּ זִקְנֵי מוֹאָב וְזִקְנֵי מִדְיָן וּקְסָמִים בְּיָדָם וַיָּבֹאוּ אֶל־בִּלְעָם וַיְדַבְּרוּ אֵלָיו דִּבְרֵי בָלָק: ח וַיֹּאמֶר אֲלֵיהֶם לִינוּ פֹה הַלַּיְלָה וַהֲשִׁבֹתִי אֶתְכֶם דָּבָר כַּאֲשֶׁר יְדַבֵּר יְהֹוָה אֵלָי וַיֵּשְׁבוּ שָׂרֵי־מוֹאָב עִם־בִּלְעָם: ט וַיָּבֹא אֱלֹהִים אֶל־בִּלְעָם וַיֹּאמֶר מִי הָאֲנָשִׁים הָאֵלֶּה עִמָּךְ: י וַיֹּאמֶר בִּלְעָם אֶל־הָאֱלֹהִים בָּלָק בֶּן־צִפֹּר מֶלֶךְ מוֹאָב שָׁלַח אֵלָי: יא הִנֵּה הָעָם הַיֹּצֵא מִמִּצְרַיִם וַיְכַס אֶת־עֵין הָאָרֶץ עַתָּה לְכָה קָבָה

as it would appear (Verse 7), he himself had been initiated into the secret tricks of the art; this spell, or the conception of it in the minds of the people, had to be broken by some higher or equally mysterious power before Balak could dare to lead his people into battle against Israel, or before he could even hope to succeed in doing so.

5. *And he sent messengers.* He therefore sent messengers to Aram in the Euphrates region, to the ancestral homeland of this dreaded miracle-working people, to the place where the cradle of their ancestors had stood. . . .

Lo! A people. The repetition of the word הִנֵּה ["lo!"] indicates that the words "a people has come out from Mitzrayim" represent a separate thought for Balaam to consider. The fact that "a people has come out from Mitzrayim," that a multitude of human beings which previously had been completely submerged both politically and socially in the power and nationhood of Egypt should have been able to go forth from there to

freedom and independence as a people welded into one social entity, marks this people as a unique phenomenon. Hence, it is to the cause of this uniqueness that you, Balaam, must give your full attention if you wish to help me attain my purposes. . . .

7. *the elders of Moab and the elders of Midian.* Balak chose as his emissaries not courtiers of high rank who were distant from the people but, in keeping with the purpose of his mission, individuals who were close to the people and who enjoyed their confidence; individuals whom the people respected as its זְקֵנִים, its counselors. After all, it must have been important to him that this event should gain the greatest possible amount of publicity among the people. "The elders of Midian," with whom the people had already taken counsel before (Verse 4), attached themselves to this mission.

with magic charms in their hands. Perhaps it was part of the superstition that whoever sought the counsel of an oracle had to donate some of his own possessions for this purpose.

לִ֔י אֹת֑וֹ אוּלַ֥י אוּכַ֛ל לְהִלָּ֥חֶם בּ֖וֹ וְגֵרַשְׁתִּֽיו׃
יב וַיֹּ֤אמֶר אֱלֹהִים֙ אֶל־בִּלְעָ֔ם לֹ֥א תֵלֵ֖ךְ עִמָּהֶ֑ם
לֹ֤א תָאֹר֙ אֶת־הָעָ֔ם כִּ֥י בָר֖וּךְ הֽוּא׃ שני יג וַיָּ֤קָם
בִּלְעָם֙ בַּבֹּ֔קֶר וַיֹּ֙אמֶר֙ אֶל־שָׂרֵ֣י בָלָ֔ק לְכ֖וּ אֶל־
אַרְצְכֶ֑ם כִּ֚י מֵאֵ֣ן יְהוָ֔ה לְתִתִּ֖י לַהֲלֹ֥ךְ עִמָּכֶֽם׃
יד וַיָּק֙וּמוּ֙ שָׂרֵ֣י מוֹאָ֔ב וַיָּבֹ֖אוּ אֶל־בָּלָ֑ק וַיֹּ֣אמְר֔וּ
מֵאֵ֥ן בִּלְעָ֖ם הֲלֹ֥ךְ עִמָּֽנוּ׃ טו וַיֹּ֥סֶף ע֖וֹד בָּלָ֑ק שְׁלֹ֣חַ
שָׂרִ֔ים רַבִּ֥ים וְנִכְבָּדִ֖ים מֵאֵֽלֶּה׃ טז וַיָּבֹ֖אוּ אֶל־
בִּלְעָ֑ם וַיֹּ֣אמְרוּ ל֗וֹ כֹּ֤ה אָמַר֙ בָּלָ֣ק בֶּן־צִפּ֔וֹר
אַל־נָ֥א תִמָּנַ֖ע מֵהֲלֹ֥ךְ אֵלָֽי׃ יז כִּֽי־כַבֵּ֤ד אֲכַבֶּדְךָ֙
מְאֹ֔ד וְכֹ֛ל אֲשֶׁר־תֹּאמַ֥ר אֵלַ֖י אֶֽעֱשֶׂ֑ה וּלְכָה־נָּא֙
קָֽבָה־לִּ֔י אֵ֖ת הָעָ֥ם הַזֶּֽה׃ יח וַיַּ֣עַן בִּלְעָ֗ם וַיֹּ֙אמֶר֙
אֶל־עַבְדֵ֣י בָלָ֔ק אִם־יִתֶּן־לִ֥י בָלָ֛ק מְלֹ֥א בֵית֖וֹ
כֶּ֣סֶף וְזָהָ֑ב לֹ֣א אוּכַ֗ל לַעֲבֹר֙ אֶת־פִּי֙ יְהוָ֣ה אֱלֹהָ֔י
לַעֲשׂ֥וֹת קְטַנָּ֖ה א֥וֹ גְדוֹלָֽה׃ יט וְעַתָּ֗ה שְׁב֨וּ נָ֥א בָזֶ֛ה
גַּם־אַתֶּ֖ם הַלָּ֑יְלָה וְאֵ֣דְעָ֔ה מַה־יֹּסֵ֥ף יְהוָ֖ה דַּבֵּ֥ר
עִמִּֽי׃ כ וַיָּבֹ֨א אֱלֹהִ֥ים ׀ אֶל־בִּלְעָם֮ לַ֒יְלָה֒ וַיֹּ֣אמֶר
ל֗וֹ אִם־לִקְרֹ֤א לְךָ֙ בָּ֣אוּ הָאֲנָשִׁ֔ים ק֖וּם לֵ֣ךְ אִתָּ֑ם

able to wage war against them and will drive them out." 12. And God said to Balaam: "Do not go with them! You will not curse the people, for they are blessed." 13. Balaam arose in the morning and said to the princes of Balak: "Go to your land, because *God* has refused to permit me to go with you." 14. And the princes of Moab set out and came to Balak and said: "Balaam has refused to go with us." 15. But Balak still persisted; he sent princes, a large number and higher in rank than the former. 16. They came to Balaam and said to him: "Thus says Balak, son of Tzippor: Please do not refuse to come to me. 17. For I will honor you beyond all measure, and whatever you will say I will do; and please come, curse this people for me." 18. And Balaam replied and said to the servants of Balak: "Even if Balak were to give me his house full of silver and gold, I cannot go beyond the utterance of *God,* my God, to do anything small or great. 19. And now, you, too, please remain here this night; I will find out what else *God* will utter to me." 20. And God came to Balaam at night and said to him: "If the men have come to invite you, then arise and go with them; however, the

12. ***You will not curse.*** "Do not go with them, because you will not be able to accomplish the purpose of your mission. You will not curse this people. Even if you should wish to do so, I will prevent it, because this people is blessed. The element that makes this people a nation is precisely the purpose which I have determined to promote with My sovereignty. . . ." If Balaam had been a true prophet, he would have faithfully conveyed this utterance of God to Balak's emissaries, and the purpose of God's intervention would have been accomplished without all the events narrated in the following episode. And in that case, Balak, Moab and Midian, instead of having to fear Israel's conquering might, would have had an opportunity to become acquainted with the moral factor inherent in this nation to which God had promised His blessing, and they would have been able to befriend Israel for their own benefit. However. . . .

13. ***Balaam arose.*** Balaam tells them nothing about the second part of God's utterance, the essential element in God's warning. He speaks only in general terms of a refusal on the part of God, "because *God* has refused," implying that he, Balaam, would have liked to curse the people. However, "*God* has refused to permit me to go with you." God does not consider it fitting that one like myself should go with people like yourselves. After all, they were only "elders of Moab," not "princes of Moab"; they were men from among the common people, not true princes.

18. . . . He treated the true princes of the highest rank as if they had been slaves. This showed the true character of the man: He was condescending to the lowly and arrogant toward the high and the mighty.

Even if Balak were to give me his house. This statement, too, shows Balaam's character. As much as he seeks honor, he values money even more. Balak's message did not contain any reference to a monetary reward; it had mentioned only honors beyond all measure and the king's readiness to comply with all of Balaam's wishes. But Balaam immediately translates honor into cash, or he says that even if he were to receive the highest possible monetary reward, etc. Thus, too, our Sages (Aboth 5:22), describing the character of Balaam, place his avarice, נֶפֶשׁ רְחָבָה, side by side with his haughty spirit, רוּחַ גְּבוֹהָה.

word that I will speak to you, that you must do." 21. And Balaam arose in the morning, saddled his she-donkey and went with the princes of Moab. 22. And the anger of *God* was awakened because he had proceeded toward his own purpose in this manner, and an angel of *God* placed himself in the way to hinder him. And here he was riding on his she-donkey and two of his attendants were with him. 23. The she-donkey saw the angel of *God* standing in the way with his sword drawn in his hand, and the she-donkey turned aside from the way and went into the field. Then Balaam struck the she-donkey to get her back upon the way. 24. And the angel of *God* placed himself in a footpath of the vineyards; there was a fence on one side and a fence on the other. 25. The she-donkey saw the angel of *God* and she pressed up against the wall and also pressed Balaam's foot against the wall; and he struck her again. 26. The angel continued to go ahead and placed himself in a narrow place where there was no way to turn aside either to the right or to the left. 27. When the she-donkey saw the angel of *God*, she lay down under Balaam, and Balaam's anger was stirred up and he struck the she-donkey with the staff. 28. And *God* opened the mouth of the she-donkey and she said to Balaam: "What

וְאַ֤ךְ אֶת־הַדָּבָ֛ר אֲשֶׁר־אֲדַבֵּ֥ר אֵלֶ֖יךָ אֹת֥וֹ תַעֲשֶֽׂה: שלישי כא וַיָּ֤קָם בִּלְעָם֙ בַּבֹּ֔קֶר וַֽיַּחֲבֹ֖שׁ אֶת־אֲתֹנ֑וֹ וַיֵּ֖לֶךְ עִם־שָׂרֵ֥י מוֹאָֽב: כב וַיִּֽחַר־אַ֣ף אֱלֹהִים֮ כִּֽי־הוֹלֵ֣ךְ הוּא֒ וַיִּתְיַצֵּ֞ב מַלְאַ֧ךְ יְהֹוָ֛ה בַּדֶּ֖רֶךְ לְשָׂטָ֣ן ל֑וֹ וְהוּא֙ רֹכֵ֣ב עַל־אֲתֹנ֔וֹ וּשְׁנֵ֥י נְעָרָ֖יו עִמּֽוֹ: כג וַתֵּ֣רֶא הָאָתוֹן֩ אֶת־מַלְאַ֨ךְ יְהֹוָ֜ה נִצָּ֣ב בַּדֶּ֗רֶךְ וְחַרְבּ֤וֹ שְׁלוּפָה֙ בְּיָד֔וֹ וַתֵּ֤ט הָֽאָתוֹן֙ מִן־הַדֶּ֔רֶךְ וַתֵּ֖לֶךְ בַּשָּׂדֶ֑ה וַיַּ֤ךְ בִּלְעָם֙ אֶת־הָ֣אָת֔וֹן לְהַטֹּתָ֖הּ הַדָּֽרֶךְ: כד וַֽיַּעֲמֹד֙ מַלְאַ֣ךְ יְהֹוָ֔ה בְּמִשְׁע֖וֹל הַכְּרָמִ֑ים גָּדֵ֥ר מִזֶּ֖ה וְגָדֵ֥ר מִזֶּֽה: כה וַתֵּ֣רֶא הָאָת֣וֹן אֶת־מַלְאַ֣ךְ יְהֹוָ֗ה וַתִּלָּחֵץ֙ אֶל־הַקִּ֔יר וַתִּלְחַ֛ץ אֶת־רֶ֥גֶל בִּלְעָ֖ם אֶל־הַקִּ֑יר וַיֹּ֖סֶף לְהַכֹּתָֽהּ: כו וַיּ֥וֹסֶף מַלְאַךְ־יְהֹוָ֖ה עֲב֑וֹר וַֽיַּעֲמֹד֙ בְּמָק֣וֹם צָ֔ר אֲשֶׁ֛ר אֵֽין־דֶּ֥רֶךְ לִנְט֖וֹת יָמִ֥ין וּשְׂמֹֽאול: כז וַתֵּ֤רֶא הָֽאָתוֹן֙ אֶת־מַלְאַ֣ךְ יְהֹוָ֔ה וַתִּרְבַּ֖ץ תַּ֣חַת בִּלְעָ֑ם וַיִּֽחַר־אַ֣ף בִּלְעָ֔ם וַיַּ֥ךְ אֶת־הָאָת֖וֹן בַּמַּקֵּֽל: כח וַיִּפְתַּ֥ח יְהֹוָ֖ה אֶת־פִּ֣י הָאָת֑וֹן וַתֹּ֥אמֶר לְבִלְעָם֙

22. . . . The angel, unseen by him, had already placed himself on the road to block his path, but Balaam still rode proudly on "his" beast of burden, with two of "his" attendants to wait on him. Surely, the royal deputation that had been sent to call for him must have brought a proper mount for him, along with a sufficient number of attendants to wait on him. Yet, in his arrogance, Balaam indulged in the luxury of riding on his own animal which, like the gentleman he considered himself to be, he had skillfully saddled that morning [cf. Verse 21], and he permitted only his own men—two of them, to be exact—to wait on him. All this conceit and arrogance toward God and man had to be broken during Balaam's journey so that he could offer himself to Balak as the obedient instrument of the words of God.

Balaam is out to alter God's own plan for the world, but he is even blinder than his beast of burden. He seeks to overcome God's resistance, but finds that he must accommodate himself to the wishes of his beast of

burden. He wants to bring about the ruin of a whole nation with his words, but finds himself forced to concede that his rage is impotent even when directed against a mere animal. He would strut before lords and princes, but finds that he has become a laughing stock among his own attendants.

. . .

28. **And God opened.** When the mind of a man who was given the ability to utter words of superior intelligence becomes unhinged by passion or base cupidity, he becomes unworthy of the mental abilities granted him. At that moment God will make it possible even for an animal, under the stress of unjustified abuse, to utter words like a human being. By so doing, God prepares the man of superior oratorical skill—no matter how unworthy he himself may be of this talent and no matter how much he may have misused it—for the moment when he will have to use his gift of speech as a vehicle for the word of God and when—albeit reluc-

have I done to you that you have struck me these three times?" 29. And Balaam said to the she-donkey: "Because you have acted willfully against me! If only I had a sword in my hand I would have killed you!" 30. And the she-donkey said to Balaam: "Am I not your she-donkey on which you have ridden ever since you have been in existence, until this day? Have I ever been in the habit of doing this to you?" And he answered: "No." 31. And *God* unveiled the eyes of Balaam and he saw the angel of *God* standing in the way with his sword drawn in his hand. And he bowed down and threw himself upon his face. 32. But the angel of *God* said to him: "Why have you struck your she-donkey these three times? Lo! I have come out to hinder you, for the way was too abruptly contrary to me, 33. and the she-donkey saw me and turned aside before me these three times. Perhaps she turned aside from fear of me. For otherwise I would have killed you also but I would have let her live." 34. And Balaam said to the angel of *God*: "I have sinned, for I did not know that you stood in the way against me. And now, if it is displeasing in your eyes, I will gladly go back." 35. But the angel of *God* said to Balaam: "Go with the men, but the word that I will speak to you, that you must speak." And Balaam went with the princes of Balak. 36. When Balak heard that Balaam was coming, he went to meet him as far as the city of Moab, which is situated on the border of Arnon, which is at the extreme end of the territory. 37. And Balak said to Balaam: "Have I not sent to you befittingly to invite you? Why did you not come to me? Do you really think that I cannot pay you [due] honor?" 38. Balaam replied to Balak: "Lo! Now I have come to you; will I be able to say anything at all? The word that God will put into my mouth, that I will have to speak." 39. Thereupon Balaam went with Balak and they came to the City of Thoroughfares. 40. Balak slaughtered

מֶה־עָשִׂיתִי לְךָ כִּי הִכִּיתַנִי זֶה שָׁלֹשׁ רְגָלִים:
כט וַיֹּאמֶר בִּלְעָם לָאָתוֹן כִּי הִתְעַלַּלְתְּ בִּי לוּ
יֶשׁ־חֶרֶב בְּיָדִי כִּי עַתָּה הֲרַגְתִּיךְ: ל וַתֹּאמֶר
הָאָתוֹן אֶל־בִּלְעָם הֲלוֹא אָנֹכִי אֲתֹנְךָ אֲשֶׁר־
רָכַבְתָּ עָלַי מֵעוֹדְךָ עַד־הַיּוֹם הַזֶּה הַהַסְכֵּן
הִסְכַּנְתִּי לַעֲשׂוֹת לְךָ כֹּה וַיֹּאמֶר לֹא: לא וַיְגַל
יְהֹוָה אֶת־עֵינֵי בִלְעָם וַיַּרְא אֶת־מַלְאַךְ יְהֹוָה
נִצָּב בַּדֶּרֶךְ וְחַרְבּוֹ שְׁלֻפָה בְּיָדוֹ וַיִּקֹּד וַיִּשְׁתַּחוּ
לְאַפָּיו: לב וַיֹּאמֶר אֵלָיו מַלְאַךְ יְהֹוָה עַל־מָה
הִכִּיתָ אֶת־אֲתֹנְךָ זֶה שָׁלוֹשׁ רְגָלִים הִנֵּה אָנֹכִי
יָצָאתִי לְשָׂטָן כִּי־יָרַט הַדֶּרֶךְ לְנֶגְדִּי: לג וַתִּרְאַנִי
הָאָתוֹן וַתֵּט לְפָנַי זֶה שָׁלֹשׁ רְגָלִים אוּלַי נָטְתָה
מִפָּנַי כִּי עַתָּה גַּם־אֹתְכָה הָרַגְתִּי וְאוֹתָהּ
הֶחֱיֵיתִי: לד וַיֹּאמֶר בִּלְעָם אֶל־מַלְאַךְ יְהֹוָה
חָטָאתִי כִּי לֹא יָדַעְתִּי כִּי אַתָּה נִצָּב לִקְרָאתִי
בַּדָּרֶךְ וְעַתָּה אִם־רַע בְּעֵינֶיךָ אָשׁוּבָה לִּי:
לה וַיֹּאמֶר מַלְאַךְ יְהֹוָה אֶל־בִּלְעָם לֵךְ עִם־
הָאֲנָשִׁים וְאֶפֶס אֶת־הַדָּבָר אֲשֶׁר־אֲדַבֵּר אֵלֶיךָ
אֹתוֹ תְדַבֵּר וַיֵּלֶךְ בִּלְעָם עִם־שָׂרֵי בָלָק:
לו וַיִּשְׁמַע בָּלָק כִּי בָא בִלְעָם וַיֵּצֵא לִקְרָאתוֹ
אֶל־עִיר מוֹאָב אֲשֶׁר עַל־גְּבוּל אַרְנֹן אֲשֶׁר
בִּקְצֵה הַגְּבוּל: לז וַיֹּאמֶר בָּלָק אֶל־בִּלְעָם הֲלֹא
שָׁלֹחַ שָׁלַחְתִּי אֵלֶיךָ לִקְרֹא־לָךְ לָמָּה לֹא־הָלַכְתָּ
אֵלָי הַאֻמְנָם לֹא אוּכַל כַּבְּדֶךָ: לח וַיֹּאמֶר בִּלְעָם
אֶל־בָּלָק הִנֵּה־בָאתִי אֵלֶיךָ עַתָּה הֲיָכֹל אוּכַל
דַּבֵּר מְאוּמָה הַדָּבָר אֲשֶׁר יָשִׂים אֱלֹהִים בְּפִי
אֹתוֹ אֲדַבֵּר: רביעי (ששי כשהן מחוברין) לט וַיֵּלֶךְ
בִּלְעָם עִם־בָּלָק וַיָּבֹאוּ קִרְיַת חֻצוֹת: מ וַיִּזְבַּח

---

tantly—he will be forced to lend his mouth to proclaim the truths of God. He who can make an animal speak can use the mouth of even one such as Balaam as an instrument to proclaim His word. . . .

34. *And now, if it is displeasing.* And so, at last, Balaam had attained that meekness and humility toward God which he should have felt from the very outset, and which was necessary for the mission he is now to accomplish.

cattle and sheep and sent this for Balaam and for the princes who were with him. 41. In the morning Balak took Balaam and led him up to the high places of Baal. From there he saw a part of the people.

XXIII

1. And Balaam said to Balak: "Build me seven altars here and prepare for me here seven bulls and seven rams." 2. And Balak did as Balaam had spoken, and Balak and Balaam offered one bull and one ram on each altar as an ascent offering. 3. And Balaam said to Balak: "Place yourself here next to your ascent offering. I will go there; perhaps *God* will bring it about that He will come to meet me and whatever He will let me see I will give you word of it." And he went to the elevation. 4. God brought it about for Balaam, and the latter said to Him: "I have prepared the seven altars and have offered bulls and rams upon the altar as an ascent offering." 5. And *God* put a word into Balaam's mouth and He said: "Return to Balak and thus shall you speak." 6. He returned to him, and lo! He was still standing next to his ascent offering, he and all the princes of Moab. 7. And he took up his parable and said: "From Aram has Balak, king of Moab, brought me, from the mountains of the East: 'Go, curse Yaakov for me, and go, cast anger upon Yisrael.' 8. Can I make a hole into what God has not hollowed? What can I strike with anger when *God* has not been angry? 9. For I see it from the top of the rocks, and I behold it from the hills; this is a

בָּלָק בָּקָר וָצֹאן וַיְשַׁלַּח לְבִלְעָם וְלַשָּׂרִים אֲשֶׁר
אִתּוֹ: מא וַיְהִי בַבֹּקֶר וַיִּקַּח בָּלָק אֶת־בִּלְעָם
וַיַּעֲלֵהוּ בָּמוֹת בָּעַל וַיַּרְא מִשָּׁם קְצֵה הָעָם:
כג א וַיֹּאמֶר בִּלְעָם אֶל־בָּלָק בְּנֵה־לִי בָזֶה
שִׁבְעָה מִזְבְּחֹת וְהָכֵן לִי בָּזֶה שִׁבְעָה פָרִים
וְשִׁבְעָה אֵילִים: ב וַיַּעַשׂ בָּלָק כַּאֲשֶׁר דִּבֶּר
בִּלְעָם וַיַּעַל בָּלָק וּבִלְעָם פַּר וָאַיִל בַּמִּזְבֵּחַ:
ג וַיֹּאמֶר בִּלְעָם לְבָלָק הִתְיַצֵּב עַל־עֹלָתֶךָ
וְאֵלְכָה אוּלַי יִקָּרֶה יְהוָה לִקְרָאתִי וּדְבַר מַה־
יַּרְאֵנִי וְהִגַּדְתִּי לָךְ וַיֵּלֶךְ שֶׁפִי: ד וַיִּקָּר אֱלֹהִים
אֶל־בִּלְעָם וַיֹּאמֶר אֵלָיו אֶת־שִׁבְעַת הַמִּזְבְּחֹת
עָרַכְתִּי וָאַעַל פַּר וָאַיִל בַּמִּזְבֵּחַ: ה וַיָּשֶׂם יְהוָה
דָּבָר בְּפִי בִלְעָם וַיֹּאמֶר שׁוּב אֶל־בָּלָק וְכֹה
תְדַבֵּר: ו וַיָּשָׁב אֵלָיו וְהִנֵּה נִצָּב עַל־עֹלָתוֹ הוּא
וְכָל־שָׂרֵי מוֹאָב: ז וַיִּשָּׂא מְשָׁלוֹ וַיֹּאמַר מִן־
אֲרָם יַנְחֵנִי בָלָק מֶלֶךְ־מוֹאָב מֵהַרְרֵי־קֶדֶם לְכָה
אָרָה־לִּי יַעֲקֹב וּלְכָה זֹעֲמָה יִשְׂרָאֵל: ח מָה אֶקֹּב
לֹא קַבֹּה אֵל וּמָה אֶזְעֹם לֹא זָעַם יְהוָה: ט כִּי־
מֵרֹאשׁ צֻרִים אֶרְאֶנּוּ וּמִגְּבָעוֹת אֲשׁוּרֶנּוּ הֶן־עָם

CHAPTER XXIII

9. ***For I see it from the top of the rocks.*** When I look at it from the vantage point of a high place I see it as if it were close by. From the perspective of a low lookout point it appears to be still far away. Even as distances seem to shrink from the perspective of a high lookout point, so does time. Surveyed in comprehensive terms, from a higher perspective encompassing centuries of world history, events that seem distant when viewed from the vantage point of the present day appear clustered together. The verb שור [beholding] denotes a broad vision that enables one to see that which is still concealed from others. Balaam says: I see this people in terms of its future, which, though not close at hand, does not appear all that distant when viewed in the overall perspective of time. This is the future in which this people will attain the ideal for which it was created (Cf. Numbers 24:17).

this is a people that will dwell apart. It will dwell in a circumscribed territory where, without engaging in much traffic with other nations, it will live for the accomplishment of its own "inner" national mission as עָם, as a people that forms a community: it will not strive for greatness [merely] as another גוי [nation] among גוים [nations]. It will not seek to impress other national entities [merely] with its power as a nation.

לְבָדָד יִשְׁכֹּן וּבַגּוֹיִם לֹא יִתְחַשָּׁב: י מִי מָנָה
עֲפַר יַעֲקֹב וּמִסְפָּר אֶת־רֹבַע יִשְׂרָאֵל תָּמֹת
נַפְשִׁי מוֹת יְשָׁרִים וּתְהִי אַחֲרִיתִי כָּמֹהוּ:
יא וַיֹּאמֶר בָּלָק אֶל־בִּלְעָם מֶה עָשִׂיתָ לִי לָקֹב
אֹיְבַי לְקַחְתִּיךָ וְהִנֵּה בֵּרַכְתָּ בָרֵךְ: יב וַיַּעַן וַיֹּאמַר
הֲלֹא אֵת אֲשֶׁר יָשִׂים יְהוָה בְּפִי אֹתוֹ אֶשְׁמֹר
לְדַבֵּר: חמישי יג וַיֹּאמֶר אֵלָיו בָּלָק לְךָ־נָּא אִתִּי
אֶל־מָקוֹם אַחֵר אֲשֶׁר תִּרְאֶנּוּ מִשָּׁם אֶפֶס קָצֵהוּ
תִרְאֶה וְכֻלּוֹ לֹא תִרְאֶה וְקָבְנוֹ־לִי מִשָּׁם:
יד וַיִּקָּחֵהוּ שְׂדֵה צֹפִים אֶל־רֹאשׁ הַפִּסְגָּה וַיִּבֶן

people that will dwell apart and not count itself among the nations. 10. Who would count the dust of Yaakov and the number of the creature births of Yisrael? I myself would die the death of the straightforward and let my end be like his!" 11. And Balak said to Balaam: "What have you done to me? I have fetched you to execrate my enemies but now you have, in fact, blessed them!" 12. But he answered: "Truly, I must be careful to utter that which *God* puts into my mouth." 13. And Balak said to him: "Come with me to another place from where you will be able to see them. But you will see only a part of them; you will not see them all, and execrate them for me from there." 14. He took him to the Field of Seers, to the top of the elevation. He

10. ***Who would count the dust of Yaakov.*** You, Balak, see this nation in terms of its numerical size, in terms of the number of warriors it can muster. In your estimation this nation is too big for you, and you think that if you could diminish that aspect of its existence you would be able to defeat it. In short, you believe you could strike at its innermost essence if you could utter a curse against its physical growth. However, "Who would count the dust of Yaakov?" Who would count the creature products of this nation of God? The structure of other nations may be determined by their number of "bodies"; therefore, other nations may view a potential enemy's numerical increase as a cause for alarm and his numerical decrease as a reason for hope. It is not so with the people of Jacob-Israel. Whether they appear as "Jacob," small in numbers, or as "Israel," numerous and growing, does not alter their significance. Their importance, their woe or weal, is not determined by that aspect of their existence which is עָפָר [dust] and which can increase or decrease physically, after the manner of animals. . . . They need not fear even physical death, for not even death can affect their true essence. "I myself would die. . . ." I would like to die as they will. I would like to know that my own death will be like theirs. Their death is more blessed than our lives because these people are יְשָׁרִים [straightforward], because they measure up to the purpose for which men were created human, and because they strive toward that ideal in a "straight," undeviating line.

° ° °

13 and 14. First Balak led Balaam up to בָּמוֹת הַבַּעַל ["the high places of Baal"]. Now he took him to שְׂדֵה צוֹפִים ["the Field of Seers"]. And when, there, too, he found his aims thwarted and turned into the opposite of what he had intended, he made one more attempt on רֹאשׁ הַפְּעוֹר ["the Peak of Peor"] (Verse 28). If we compare the names of the three locations mentioned in the narrative and the utterances Balak was forced to hear at each location in reply to his request, it would seem that Balak took Balaam from each one of these locations to the next in order to have him test various vantage points or perspectives from which the people might be cursed. Each time one of his attempts failed, Balak arranged for a change in the vantage point from which Balaam was to view the Children of Israel.

בַּעַל [Baal], צוֹפִים [the Seers] and פְּעוֹר [Peor]: These would seem to symbolize the mightiest among the powers which, in the view of one like Balak, could decide the woe or weal of nations.

בַּעַל. Baal appears as the most universally worshipped Canaanite deity, the supreme "force of nature" that influenced physical growth and material prosperity. . . . In Balak's view, the first prerequisite for a nation's survival was that it must have the favor of "Baal," the natural force that could decide over growth and decay. By taking Balaam to the high places of Baal, he posed to him the question: Where does this nation stand in the favor of the divine power that can grant or withhold material prosperity? Could not its growth be impeded from that perspective? Balaam answered this question in the negative because the magnitude which is implied by the concepts of עָפָר ["dust"] and רְבִיעָה ["copulation"], and which supposedly thrives under the influence of Baal, is not in any manner a precondition for the survival of the Jewish nation.

Balak's reaction to Balaam's reply was to take him to שְׂדֵה צוֹפִים, the "Field of Seers and Watchmen," and there he led him to the top of the elevation. It seemed built seven altars and offered one bull and one ram as an ascent offering on each altar. 15. And he said to Balak: "Place yourself here next to your ascent offering, and I will submit myself there to what will be brought about." 16. And *God* directed Himself to Balaam and put a word into his mouth and said: "Return to Balak and thus shall you speak." 17. He came to him and found him standing next to his ascent offering, and the princes of Moab with him. And Balak said to him: "What has *God* spoken?" 18. And he took up his parable and said: "Arise, O Balak, and hear; incline your ear to me, you, whom Tzippor calls his son. 19. God is not a man that He should play false, a son of Adam that He should change His mind. Should He indeed make a promise and not do it, or speak and not uphold it? 20. Lo! It is a blessing that I have received. He has blessed; I will not change it. 21. He has perceived no misuse of power in Yaakov; therefore He has seen no misfortune in Yisrael; *God*, his God, is with him and homage to the King is

שִׁבְעָה מִזְבְּחֹת וַיַּעַל פָּר וָאַיִל בַּמִּזְבֵּחַ: טו וַיֹּאמֶר אֶל־בָּלָק הִתְיַצֵּב כֹּה עַל־עֹלָתֶךָ וְאָנֹכִי אִקָּרֶה כֹּה: טז וַיִּקָּר יְהֹוָה אֶל־בִּלְעָם וַיָּשֶׂם דָּבָר בְּפִיו וַיֹּאמֶר שׁוּב אֶל־בָּלָק וְכֹה תְדַבֵּר: יז וַיָּבֹא אֵלָיו וְהִנּוֹ נִצָּב עַל־עֹלָתוֹ וְשָׂרֵי מוֹאָב אִתּוֹ וַיֹּאמֶר לוֹ בָּלָק מַה־דִּבֶּר יְהֹוָה: יח וַיִּשָּׂא מְשָׁלוֹ וַיֹּאמַר קוּם בָּלָק וּשֲׁמָע הַאֲזִינָה עָדַי בְּנוֹ צִפֹּר: יט לֹא אִישׁ אֵל וִיכַזֵּב וּבֶן־אָדָם וְיִתְנֶחָם הַהוּא אָמַר וְלֹא יַעֲשֶׂה וְדִבֶּר וְלֹא יְקִימֶנָּה: כ הִנֵּה בָרֵךְ לָקָחְתִּי וּבֵרֵךְ וְלֹא אֲשִׁיבֶנָּה: כא לֹא־הִבִּיט אָוֶן בְּיַעֲקֹב וְלֹא־רָאָה עָמָל בְּיִשְׂרָאֵל יְהֹוָה אֱלֹהָיו עִמּוֹ וּתְרוּעַת מֶלֶךְ

to Balak that another precondition for the survival of a nation was its intelligence, as demonstrated by the presence in its midst of an intellectual elite with insight into the counsel of the gods; individuals who could look into the future and who, as "seers and watchmen," could predict the future, and control and shape events to come. By taking Balaam to this location, Balak posed to him the question: Does this nation have intellectual gifts that can decide and control the fate of nations by insight, prudence, foresight and magic powers? Seen from the perspective of "seers and watchmen," might not this people have a weak spot that could be exploited to undermine its future? Once again Balak built seven altars and, by means of the ascent offerings of bulls and rams, he symbolically addressed the same question to the One sole unseen Deity on high that rules over the actions and the destinies of mortals.

18. And he took up his parable. Balak had asked Balaam to find a vulnerable spot in the nation from the perspective of "seers" and of "watchmen."

Thereupon Balaam utters his "words of rulership,"[8] saying, "Arise, O Balak," etc. You have inquired whether this people has an intellectual elite that can come close to the gods. . . .

21. וּתְרוּעַת מֶלֶךְ בּוֹ [*and homage to the King is within him*]. תְּרוּעָה is a stirring note [of the trumpet and the *shofar*]; it also implies deep inner emotion, the mood of "quivering awe" which this note serves to express and awaken in the hearts of men. . . . When used with reference to God, it connotes a mood of abject homage and submission, engendered by an overwhelming awareness of God's greatness. Hence, we are told here: God is *with* Israel, and there is no room *within* Israel for anything but a mood of "homage to the King." Israel pays homage to God as the King; all of its inner being is pervaded by this mood. This turn of phrase can also imply a cause-and-effect relationship: God is *with* Israel because the mood of "homage to the King" is *within* Israel.

---

[8] *Note to the English translation*: In the original German, Hirsch uses a German term of his own devising, *Herrschwort* (which we have rendered as "words of rulership"), perhaps to indicate the linguistic relationship between the Hebrew מָשָׁל (parable) and מָשַׁל (rule). In German, the connotations would seem more felicitous than in English; the German term for "ruler" is *Herrscher*, and the German for speaking roughly or peremptorily to a person is *anherrschen*. [G.H.]

within him. 22. The God Who brought them out from Mitzrayim, He is to him like the ascending power of *re'em.* 23. For no divination is needed in Yaakov, nor magic in Yisrael. At this very moment it is told to Yaakov and Yisrael what God has wrought here. 24. Lo! As a people united he arises like a leopard, and he lifts himself up like a lion that does not lie down until he has devoured prey and drunk the blood of the slain." 25. And Balak said to Balaam: "[If] you are not to execrate them, [then] you should also not bless them." 26. But Balaam answered and said to Balak: "Have I not spoken to you and said: All that *God* will speak, that must I do?" 27. And Balak said to Balaam: "Pray come, I will take you to yet another place; perhaps it will be right in the eyes of God that you should execrate them for me from there." 28. Balak took Balaam to the Peak of Peor,

בּוֹ: כב אֵל מוֹצִיאָם מִמִּצְרָיִם כְּתוֹעֲפֹת רְאֵם
לוֹ: כג כִּי לֹא־נַחַשׁ בְּיַעֲקֹב וְלֹא־קֶסֶם בְּיִשְׂרָאֵל
כָּעֵת יֵאָמֵר לְיַעֲקֹב וּלְיִשְׂרָאֵל מַה־פָּעַל אֵל:
כד הֶן־עָם כְּלָבִיא יָקוּם וְכַאֲרִי יִתְנַשָּׂא לֹא
יִשְׁכַּב עַד־יֹאכַל טֶרֶף וְדַם־חֲלָלִים יִשְׁתֶּה:
כה וַיֹּאמֶר בָּלָק אֶל־בִּלְעָם גַּם־קֹב לֹא תִקֳּבֶנּוּ
גַּם־בָּרֵךְ לֹא תְבָרְכֶנּוּ: כו וַיַּעַן בִּלְעָם וַיֹּאמֶר
אֶל־בָּלָק הֲלֹא דִּבַּרְתִּי אֵלֶיךָ לֵאמֹר כֹּל אֲשֶׁר־
יְדַבֵּר יְהֹוָה אֹתוֹ אֶעֱשֶׂה: ששי (שביעי כשהן מחוברין)
כז וַיֹּאמֶר בָּלָק אֶל־בִּלְעָם לְכָה־נָּא אֶקָּחֲךָ אֶל־
מָקוֹם אַחֵר אוּלַי יִישַׁר בְּעֵינֵי הָאֱלֹהִים וְקַבֹּתוֹ
לִי מִשָּׁם: כח וַיִּקַּח בָּלָק אֶת־בִּלְעָם רֹאשׁ

22. ***The God Who brought them out.*** In Mitzrayim they were still a loosely-knit, suppressed multitude, and it was as such a multitude, unable to help themselves, that God brought them out of Mitzrayim and made them into one united nation. The God Who thus brought about their liberation without their aid is the same God Who, again without their aid, will lead them on to the full glory of power and independence. This awareness lends them an impetus toward power as awesome as [the horns of] the *re'em* [wild ox]. But Israel does not have to strive for this power on his own; he need not apply his own physical and spiritual strength to this end—because God hands it to him, ready and complete. It is God's will that this nation should be great and mighty. All He requires of the nation is "homage to the King," to be demonstrated by its keeping away from any misuse of the powers granted to it by God. . . .

23. ***For no divination is needed.*** Jacob-Israel does not need the wisdom of seers whom you seek among this people and on whose existence you believe you can base your own prediction of this nation's future. Jacob-Israel does not need a wisdom that gropes in the dark with occult "divinations" and that claims the ability to sway the fates, by means of magic, in accordance with its own wishes. Jacob-Israel does not need these methods, which exploit man's feelings of helplessness and impotence. It is not to "divinations" that Jacob hearkens in his distress; it is not to "magic arts" that Israel owes his greatness. At this very moment, while we are talking together and becoming aware that, before God, we are utterly powerless to initiate any action against this nation of God, that nation is already receiving the revelation of what God has wrought here with us. They are told this so that they should understand it not only when they are in the position of "Jacob," but also so that they never forget it when they are in the [powerful] position of "Israel."

Instead of the paltry devices of divination and magic employed by the obscure wisdom of our seers, Jacob-Israel receives the bright, clear word of God without first having to inquire after it.

° ° °

28. It became clear to Balak that Israel was vulnerable neither from the physical, material aspect, as symbolized by the high places of Baal, nor from the spiritual and godly aspect, as symbolized by the Field of Seers. However, a nation may be blessed with every conceivable material and spiritual gift and still hasten headlong to its ruin. Providence may shower upon it all the treasures, all the physical and spiritual wealth that heaven affords, and yet that nation may bear within itself a worm devouring it from within so that all its prosperity will be turned into adversity, and it will ultimately become not only unworthy but also incapable of receiving and retaining God's blessings. This worm is called immorality; it is the shameless surrender to dissolute sensualism.

Hence, after Balak has had Balaam look in vain from the high places of Baal and the Field of Seers for weak points in the nation of Israel, he says to him: "Please come. . .," I will make one more attempt; please come with me and let me show you the nation from yet which looks out upon the wasteland. 29. And Balaam said to Balak: "Build me seven altars here, and prepare for me here seven bulls and seven rams." 30. Balak did as Balaam had spoken, and he offered one bull and one ram on each altar as an ascent offering.

XXIV 1. But Balaam saw now that in the eyes of *God* it was right only to bless Yisrael; therefore he did not go, as at other times, to meet divinations, but set his face toward the wilderness. 2. When Balaam lifted up his eyes and saw Yisrael camping according to its tribes, the spirit of God came upon him, 3. and he took up his parable and said: "Thus speaks Balaam, whom Beor calls his son; thus speaks the man whose eye has been opened. 4. He speaks, hearing the utterances of God, [he] who beholds that which שׁדי permits to behold; [he] who has fallen down, yet has his eye unveiled: 5. How good are your tents, O Yaakov, your dwelling places, O Yisrael! 6. Like brooks are they turned, like gardens by the

הַפְּעוֹר הַנִּשְׁקָף עַל־פְּנֵי הַיְשִׁימֹן: כט וַיֹּאמֶר
בִּלְעָם אֶל־בָּלָק בְּנֵה־לִי בָזֶה שִׁבְעָה מִזְבְּחֹת
וְהָכֵן לִי בָּזֶה שִׁבְעָה פָרִים וְשִׁבְעָה אֵילִם:
ל וַיַּעַשׂ בָּלָק כַּאֲשֶׁר אָמַר בִּלְעָם וַיַּעַל פָּר וָאַיִל
בַּמִּזְבֵּחַ: כד א וַיַּרְא בִּלְעָם כִּי טוֹב בְּעֵינֵי יְהֹוָה
לְבָרֵךְ אֶת־יִשְׂרָאֵל וְלֹא־הָלַךְ כְּפַעַם־בְּפַעַם
לִקְרַאת נְחָשִׁים וַיָּשֶׁת אֶל־הַמִּדְבָּר פָּנָיו:
ב וַיִּשָּׂא בִלְעָם אֶת־עֵינָיו וַיַּרְא אֶת־יִשְׂרָאֵל
שֹׁכֵן לִשְׁבָטָיו וַתְּהִי עָלָיו רוּחַ אֱלֹהִים: ג וַיִּשָּׂא
מְשָׁלוֹ וַיֹּאמַר נְאֻם בִּלְעָם בְּנוֹ בְעֹר וּנְאֻם הַגֶּבֶר
שְׁתֻם הָעָיִן: ד נְאֻם שֹׁמֵעַ אִמְרֵי־אֵל אֲשֶׁר מַחֲזֵה
שַׁדַּי יֶחֱזֶה נֹפֵל וּגְלוּי עֵינָיִם: ה מַה־טֹּבוּ אֹהָלֶיךָ
יַעֲקֹב מִשְׁכְּנֹתֶיךָ יִשְׂרָאֵל: ו כִּנְחָלִים נִטָּיוּ כְּגַנֹּת

---

another aspect. Perhaps if you see them from that new vantage point, God Himself will permit you to curse them. And so he took him to the peak of "shamelessness deified," which looks down on wastelands. Peor denotes a cult that presents the most bestial aspects of human physicality to the gods as an act of worship, thereby saying to man: "Why do you prate of modesty and of a higher moral calling when your own body tells you that you are no better and have no higher calling than any beast, and that, in fact, you have no cause to be ashamed of this before the gods?" Thus, by taking Balaam to the Peak of Peor, Balak put to him the question: What is the attitude of this nation toward modesty and sexual morality, on which the strength and prosperity of all nations ultimately depends?

o   o   o

CHAPTER XXIV

2. **When Balaam lifted up his eyes.** But when he lifted up his eyes and saw Israel encamped according to its tribes, grouped by households and families, he saw with his own eyes the answer to Balak's question, and "the spirit of God came upon him." Now he was no longer, as he had been in the first two instances, the unwilling organ for the words which God had put into

his mouth; whatever he will say henceforth he will utter in the pure spirit of prophecy.

5 and 6. **How good.** Balak's question to Balaam was: "What view do you have of this nation from the vantage point of the Peak of Peor? What is its attitude toward modesty and morality in sexual relations?" The camp "according to its tribes" that he now beholds, the "tents of Yaakov," the "dwelling places of Yisrael" that make it possible for every child to know who his father is, the fact that households, families and tribes are grouped according to paternal descent . . . these are the criteria by which the sexual morality of this people could be judged.

. . . How good, how very much in accord with the ideal of morality and with the true welfare of a people, are your "houses," be they the transient tents of "Jacob" during his wanderings, or the proud, more permanent dwelling places of "Israel." The homes of Israel's families . . . are like brooks that carry the blessings of abundance, and like gardens that are themselves richly blessed. Like a brook, each household and each family branch causes the blessings of material prosperity and spiritual and moral welfare to descend upon every future generation. At the same time, each is in itself a "garden of humanity," blessed with material, intellectual and moral abundance. Each is a brook unto river; like *ahol* trees that *God* has planted, like cedars beside the waters.   7. The water flows from *His* buckets, and it is *His* seed that is at the abundant flow. Therefore his king shall be higher than Agag, and his kingdom shall be exalted.   8. The God Who brought him out from Mitzrayim is to him as the ascending power of *re'em*. He [i.e., Yisrael] devours nations because they are His [i.e., God's] enemies, and he drains the marrow from their bones, and as His arrows does he wound them.   9. When he kneels, he rests like a lion and like a leopard—who would dare rouse him! Those who bless you are the blessed, and those who curse you are themselves laden with the curse."   10. Then Balak's anger was stirred against Balaam and he struck his

עֲלֵי נָהָר כַּאֲהָלִים נָטַע יְהֹוָה כַּאֲרָזִים עֲלֵי־
מָיִם: ז יִזַּל־מַיִם מִדָּלְיָו וְזַרְעוֹ בְּמַיִם רַבִּים
וְיָרֹם מֵאֲגַג מַלְכּוֹ וְתִנַּשֵּׂא מַלְכֻתוֹ: ח אֵל
מוֹצִיאוֹ מִמִּצְרַיִם כְּתוֹעֲפֹת רְאֵם לוֹ יֹאכַל גּוֹיִם
צָרָיו וְעַצְמֹתֵיהֶם יְגָרֵם וְחִצָּיו יִמְחָץ: ט כָּרַע
שָׁכַב כַּאֲרִי וּכְלָבִיא מִי יְקִימֶנּוּ מְבָרֲכֶיךָ בָרוּךְ
וְאֹרֲרֶיךָ אָרוּר: י וַיִּחַר־אַף בָּלָק אֶל־בִּלְעָם

itself, running its own particular course independently of all the others, but each one causes its attainments to flow, as it were, into the one river they all share in common. At the same time each is a garden that owes its abundance of fruit and flowers to one and the same river. . . .

7. . . . The secret that confers the character of "goodness" upon the tents and dwelling places of Jacob-Israel and that makes all the life unfolding within them such a "garden of mankind," bestowing blessings upon others and itself blessed in turn, lies precisely in the morality of this people. It lies in the complete sanctity and hallowing of family and sex life, which, immune to every taint of the vulgarity symbolized by Peor, regards the strength inherent in man's seed as most intimately linked with God and sacred to Him alone. According to this view, every human seed can be sown and planted only by God and only in accordance with His directions, at the wellsprings of His Teaching and His Law, to glorify Him and to implement His will on earth. All these truths are imparted to the onlooker by the sight of the tents and dwelling places of Jacob-Israel grouped by household, familial and tribal units around the Sanctuary of God's Law, which they all cherish in common. It is precisely from this morality in the most intimate aspects of sex in family life that the people of Israel derives its triumphant strength and invincibility against every foe from without. . . .

8. **The God Who brought him out**. This sexual morality, this freedom from גִּלּוּי עֲרָיוֹת [immorality] and from all the lewdness symbolized by Peor, represented the hereditary patent of nobility held by all the sons and daughters of Israel even in Egypt. It was this

unanimity in their attitude toward sexual morality that formed a strong bond, which united them even in Egypt, when they still lacked all the external prerequisites of nationhood. The God Who delivered them because of their basic moral character is also the One Who will continue to lend them this mighty impetus to power, because it is through them that His moral law will regain its rightful place among men. They will defeat other nations, or, rather, God will cause other nations to vanish before them, because these nations are "His arrows"; they are the enemies of His moral law and contest its place on earth. Indeed, it is repeatedly pointed out in the chapter on עֲרָיוֹת (Leviticus, Chapter 18) that the inhabitants of Canaan were doomed by God because of their excesses of immorality.

9. . . . Once again Balaam looks down upon Israel and now he utters the momentous words, "Those who bless you . . .," the same sublime words that God spoke when He first chose Abraham (Genesis 12:3) and that Isaac reiterated when he blessed Jacob (ibid. 27:29). . . . "All those who bless you"; i.e., those who respect the principles for which you stand and who will help promote them are the ones who will be blessed. They are the ones who may expect blessings and prosperity from God; indeed, they are the only ones who will have a future under God's sovereignty. Conversely, "those who curse you"; i.e., those who are hostile toward the principles that are brought to mankind's consciousness through you, and those who hope for your downfall so that the values for which you stand may be destroyed along with you, "are themselves laden with the curse"; they will bear the curse within themselves. They are the ones whom God has doomed to destruction and who have no future on God's earth.

hands together. And Balak said to Balaam: "I have called you to execrate my enemies and now you have blessed them these three times. 11. Now run away to your place! I thought I would show you great honor, but lo! *God* has held you back from honor." 12. And Balaam said to Balak: "Have I not spoken it to your messengers whom you sent to me: 13. Even if Balak were to give me his house full of silver and gold, I cannot go beyond the utterance of *God*, to do good or evil out of my own mind; that which *God* will speak I will have to speak. 14. And now I go to my people. Come, I will give you a piece of advice. What this people will do to your people will be only in the end of days." 15. And he took up his parable and said: "Thus speaks Balaam, whom Beor calls his son; thus speaks the man whose eye has been opened. 16. He speaks, hearing the utterance of *God*, and recognizing the thoughts of the Most High. That which שדי permits to be beheld, he beholds—[he] who has fallen down, yet has his eye unveiled. 17. I see it, but not now; I behold it, but it is not near. A star has set out on its way from Yaakov, and a scepter has arisen from Yisrael that strikes the hinges of Moab and breaks down the walls of all the sons of Seth. 18. And Edom shall pass over to a master, to a master over Seir, his enemies, and Yisrael shall grow in might. 19. He shall rule from out of Yaakov and this shall cause the last [remnant] to be lost from the cities." 20. He saw Amalek and took up his parable and said: "Amalek is the first among the nations—until he will be one lost." 21. And he saw the Kenite[s] and took up his parable and said: "Let your seat remain very firm and build your nest in the rock, 22. for if Kayin is laid waste, to what place would Asshur carry you off!" 23. And he took up his parable and said: "Alas! Who shall survive since God has founded him? 24. Ships shall come from the coast of the Kittites and weaken Asshur and weaken Eber and he, too—until

וַיִּסְפֹּ֖ק אֶת־כַּפָּ֑יו וַיֹּ֨אמֶר בָּלָ֜ק אֶל־בִּלְעָ֗ם לָקֹ֤ב
אֹֽיְבַי֙ קְרָאתִ֔יךָ וְהִנֵּה֙ בֵּרַ֣כְתָּ בָרֵ֔ךְ זֶ֖ה שָׁלֹ֥שׁ
פְּעָמִֽים׃ יא וְעַתָּ֖ה בְּרַח־לְךָ֣ אֶל־מְקוֹמֶ֑ךָ אָמַ֙רְתִּי֙
כַּבֵּ֣ד אֲכַבֶּדְךָ֔ וְהִנֵּ֛ה מְנָעֲךָ֥ יְהֹוָ֖ה מִכָּבֽוֹד׃
יב וַיֹּ֥אמֶר בִּלְעָ֖ם אֶל־בָּלָ֑ק הֲלֹ֗א גַּ֚ם אֶל־
מַלְאָכֶ֛יךָ אֲשֶׁר־שָׁלַ֥חְתָּ אֵלַ֖י דִּבַּ֥רְתִּי לֵאמֹֽר׃
יג אִם־יִתֶּן־לִ֨י בָלָ֜ק מְלֹ֣א בֵיתוֹ֮ כֶּ֣סֶף וְזָהָב֒ לֹ֣א
אוּכַ֗ל לַעֲבֹר֙ אֶת־פִּ֣י יְהֹוָ֔ה לַעֲשׂ֥וֹת טוֹבָ֛ה א֥וֹ
רָעָ֖ה מִלִּבִּ֑י אֲשֶׁר־יְדַבֵּ֥ר יְהֹוָ֖ה אֹת֥וֹ אֲדַבֵּֽר׃ שביעי
יד וְעַתָּ֕ה הִנְנִ֥י הוֹלֵ֖ךְ לְעַמִּ֑י לְכָה֙ אִיעָ֣צְךָ֔ אֲשֶׁ֨ר
יַעֲשֶׂ֜ה הָעָ֥ם הַזֶּ֛ה לְעַמְּךָ֖ בְּאַחֲרִ֥ית הַיָּמִֽים׃
טו וַיִּשָּׂ֥א מְשָׁל֖וֹ וַיֹּאמַ֑ר נְאֻ֤ם בִּלְעָם֙ בְּנ֣וֹ בְעֹ֔ר
וּנְאֻ֥ם הַגֶּ֖בֶר שְׁתֻ֥ם הָעָֽיִן׃ טז נְאֻ֗ם שֹׁמֵ֙עַ֙ אִמְרֵי־
אֵ֔ל וְיֹדֵ֖עַ דַּ֣עַת עֶלְי֑וֹן מַחֲזֵ֤ה שַׁדַּי֙ יֶֽחֱזֶ֔ה נֹפֵ֖ל
וּגְל֥וּי עֵינָֽיִם׃ יז אֶרְאֶ֙נּוּ֙ וְלֹ֣א עַתָּ֔ה אֲשׁוּרֶ֖נּוּ וְלֹ֣א
קָר֑וֹב דָּרַ֨ךְ כּוֹכָ֜ב מִֽיַּעֲקֹ֗ב וְקָ֥ם שֵׁ֙בֶט֙ מִיִּשְׂרָאֵ֔ל
וּמָחַץ֙ פַּאֲתֵ֣י מוֹאָ֔ב וְקַרְקַ֖ר כׇּל־בְּנֵי־שֵֽׁת׃
יח וְהָיָ֨ה אֱד֜וֹם יְרֵשָׁ֗ה וְהָיָ֧ה יְרֵשָׁ֛ה שֵׂעִ֖יר אֹיְבָ֑יו
וְיִשְׂרָאֵ֖ל עֹ֥שֶׂה חָֽיִל׃ יט וְיֵ֖רְדְּ מִֽיַּעֲקֹ֑ב וְהֶאֱבִ֥יד
שָׂרִ֖יד מֵעִֽיר׃ כ וַיַּרְא֙ אֶת־עֲמָלֵ֔ק וַיִּשָּׂ֥א מְשָׁל֖וֹ
וַיֹּאמַ֑ר רֵאשִׁ֤ית גּוֹיִם֙ עֲמָלֵ֔ק וְאַחֲרִית֖וֹ עֲדֵ֥י
אֹבֵֽד׃ כא וַיַּרְא֙ אֶת־הַקֵּינִ֔י וַיִּשָּׂ֥א מְשָׁל֖וֹ וַיֹּאמַ֑ר
אֵיתָן֙ מֽוֹשָׁבֶ֔ךָ וְשִׂ֥ים בַּסֶּ֖לַע קִנֶּֽךָ׃ כב כִּ֥י אִם־
יִהְיֶ֖ה לְבָ֣עֵֽר קָ֑יִן עַד־מָ֖ה אַשּׁ֥וּר תִּשְׁבֶּֽךָּ׃ כג וַיִּשָּׂ֥א
מְשָׁל֖וֹ וַיֹּאמַ֑ר א֕וֹי מִ֥י יִחְיֶ֖ה מִשֻּׂמ֥וֹ אֵֽל׃ כד וְצִים֙
מִיַּ֣ד כִּתִּ֔ים וְעִנּ֥וּ אַשּׁ֖וּר וְעִנּוּ־עֵ֑בֶר וְגַם־ה֖וּא עֲדֵ֥י

20. ***until he will be one lost.*** He goes on his way until he becomes אֹבֵד, one completely lost. Even his memory will vanish from the minds of men.

he will be one lost."   25. Thereupon Balaam arose, went, and returned to his place, and Balak, too, went on his way.

XXV 1. Yisrael' had settled in Shittim, and the people began to defect in immorality to the daughters of Moab.   2. They invited the people to the sacrificial feasts of their gods; the people ate with [them], and they bowed to their gods.   3. And Yisrael attached itself to the Baal Peor and the anger of *God* was stirred against Yisrael.   4. And *God* said to Moshe: "Take all the heads of the people and hang them [i.e., the guilty]

אָבֵד: כה וַיָּקָם בִּלְעָם וַיֵּלֶךְ וַיָּשָׁב לִמְקֹמוֹ וְגַם־
בָּלָק הָלַךְ לְדַרְכּוֹ: פ כה א וַיֵּשֶׁב יִשְׂרָאֵל
בַּשִּׁטִּים וַיָּחֶל הָעָם לִזְנוֹת אֶל־בְּנוֹת מוֹאָב:
ב וַתִּקְרֶאןָ לָעָם לְזִבְחֵי אֱלֹהֵיהֶן וַיֹּאכַל הָעָם
וַיִּשְׁתַּחֲווּ לֵאלֹהֵיהֶן: ג וַיִּצָּמֶד יִשְׂרָאֵל לְבַעַל
פְּעוֹר וַיִּחַר־אַף יְהוָֹה בְּיִשְׂרָאֵל: ד וַיֹּאמֶר יְהוָֹה
אֶל־מֹשֶׁה קַח אֶת־כָּל־רָאשֵׁי הָעָם וְהוֹקַע

CHAPTER XXV

1. Neither the sword nor the curse of a foe from without can cause Israel's downfall. Only Israel can bring destruction upon itself by defecting from God and His Law. . . .

2. **They invited.** The women whom they had seduced invited them to their sacrificial feasts and finally induced them to prostrate themselves before their Peor deities, in whose cult moral depravity was not considered a sin but an act of surrender and homage to the power of the gods.

3. . . . There was also a בַּעַל פְּעוֹר, a god of shamelessness, who was worshipped by giving brazen prominence to the most bestial aspects of human life. . . . The cult of Peor is a manifestation of the type of Darwinism that glories in man's descent to the level of the beast, where, stripping himself of his Divinely-given nobility, he comes to regard himself as merely a higher species of animal.

and the anger. But by so doing, Israel abrogated the very first prerequisite for its future existence before God.

4. **And God said.** In the Law of God, criminal justice is based entirely on the process of indictment. Under Jewish law the court has no authority to act on its own initiative as long as no criminal charges have been made. However, such indictments are not made by a public prosecutor; under Jewish law the entire nation acts as the prosecutor through its male members who are legally of age. When an individual is about to commit a crime, two men from among the people must warn him, informing him what law he would violate and to what punishment he would then be liable. If, despite these warnings, he commits the crime, these same two men who warned him must apprehend him, produce him physically before the judges and, in the

name of the Law, demand that he receive the punishment due him. . . . Hence, if there were no witnesses to bring the guilty party to court, the judges had no legal authority to perform their judicial functions.

Now in this widespread open defection from the Law, no men from among the people intervened to warn the criminals of the authority of the Law and, after the deed had been done, no men intervened to seize the guilty parties and bring them before their lawful judges, to put a stop to these outrages. Therefore, everyone who stood by idly while these acts were committed became an accessory to the crime, and so the entire nation was responsible for what had happened. For this reason we were told "and the anger of *God* was stirred against Yisrael," and for this reason, too, God conferred upon Moses, by the legal device of an "emergency provision," temporary authority (and thus also the obligation) to act as a judge in this exceptional situation.

Take all the heads of the people. This refers to the "judges of Yisrael" to whom reference is made in the next verse. The command קַח וגו׳ ["take . . ."] corresponds entirely to the event described in Numbers 1:17: "Moshe took and (so did) Aharon, these men . . .", telling us how certain individuals were coopted by Moses and Aaron to assist in the performance of an official function that Moses and Aaron had been commanded to carry out. Moses is to act here, too, as the supreme legal authority, as the personification of the Sanhedrin. He was to coopt all the "heads of the people," the "princes over the thousands," etc., who had been appointed as judges (Deuteronomy 1:15, 16), to assist him in inflicting upon all those who participated in the worship of פְּעוֹר the penalty of סְקִילָה [death by stoning] that the Law ordains for an idol worshipper. In the case of one who was guilty of blasphemy or idol worship this punishment entailed תְּלִיָּה, a momentary "hanging" of the criminal's body after his execution (Sanhedrin 46b). . . .

. . .

for *God* in the presence of the sun, and then the anger of *God* that has been stirred will turn away from Yisrael."   5. And Moshe said to the judges of Yisrael: "Let each one execute those men turned over to him who attached themselves to Baal Peor." 6. And lo! There came a man from among the sons of Yisrael and brought the Midianite woman before the eyes of Moshe and the eyes of the whole community of the sons of Yisrael, and the latter wept at the entrance of the Tent of Appointed Meeting. 7. Pinḥas, son of Eleazar, son of Aharon the priest, saw it, arose from the midst of the community, took a spear in his hand, 8. followed the man of Yisrael into the alcove and ran both of them through—the man of Yisrael and ·the woman through her belly—and the dying was stopped from among the sons of Yisrael. 9. But those who lost their lives in the death were twenty-four thousand.

אוֹתָם לַיהֹוָה נֶגֶד הַשֶּׁמֶשׁ וְיָשֹׁב חֲרוֹן אַף־יְהֹוָה מִיִּשְׂרָאֵל: ה וַיֹּאמֶר מֹשֶׁה אֶל־שֹׁפְטֵי יִשְׂרָאֵל הִרְגוּ אִישׁ אֲנָשָׁיו הַנִּצְמָדִים לְבַעַל פְּעוֹר: ו וְהִנֵּה אִישׁ מִבְּנֵי יִשְׂרָאֵל בָּא וַיַּקְרֵב אֶל־אֶחָיו אֶת־הַמִּדְיָנִית לְעֵינֵי מֹשֶׁה וּלְעֵינֵי כָּל־עֲדַת בְּנֵי־יִשְׂרָאֵל וְהֵמָּה בֹכִים פֶּתַח אֹהֶל מוֹעֵד: מפטיר ז וַיַּרְא פִּינְחָס בֶּן־אֶלְעָזָר בֶּן־אַהֲרֹן הַכֹּהֵן וַיָּקָם מִתּוֹךְ הָעֵדָה וַיִּקַּח רֹמַח בְּיָדוֹ: ח וַיָּבֹא אַחַר אִישׁ־יִשְׂרָאֵל אֶל־הַקֻּבָּה וַיִּדְקֹר אֶת־שְׁנֵיהֶם אֵת אִישׁ יִשְׂרָאֵל וְאֶת־הָאִשָּׁה אֶל־קֳבָתָהּ וַתֵּעָצַר הַמַּגֵּפָה מֵעַל בְּנֵי יִשְׂרָאֵל: ט וַיִּהְיוּ הַמֵּתִים בַּמַּגֵּפָה אַרְבָּעָה וְעֶשְׂרִים אָלֶף: פ

---

6. . . . We learn from Verse 14 that this man was one of the tribal princes. However, in the present verse he is identified merely as "a man from among the sons of Yisrael," probably so that what follows should be interpreted purely from the perspective of his being a "Jewish individual." Surely his crime must appear all the more serious because he was a prince and should therefore have served as a model of moral purity. Surely, too, the act of Phineḥas must appear all the more significant since the person whom he put to death in order to avenge the insult dealt to the Law was above his own rank and station. All this may well explain why the ranks of both the man and the woman are given in Verses 14 and 15, respectively. Yet it is equally certain that the crime that was committed and avenged in this incident was regarded as so grave not simply because the individual who committed it was a prince. What makes the act appear so reprehensible is that it was committed by a "Jewish man." An אִישׁ מִבְּנֵי יִשְׂרָאֵל ["man from among the sons of Yisrael"] had flouted God, His Law and Israel with the Midianite woman and, having been caught *in flagrante delicto*, became liable to punishment at the hands of the zealous adherents of God, of His Law and of יִשְׂרָאֵל. Cf. "As for one who cohabits with an Aramite woman, the zealous may put him to death" (Sanhedrin 82a).

9. *twenty-four thousand.* In the incident of the golden calf only three thousand died. Even if one assumes that, in addition to these, other guilty individuals also fell victim to sudden death, it would seem that the number that died in the Baal Peor incident still must have been substantially larger. Thus we can see that joining in the rites of a pagan cult in which dissolution is openly sanctioned as an act of worship has much more far-reaching consequences than a mere temporary metaphysical aberration into idolatry.

The Haftarah for this Sidra may be found on page 900.

פינחס

PINḤAS

10. *God* spoke to Moshe [saying]:
11. "Pinḥas, son of Eleazar, son of Aharon
the priest, has turned My anger away from
the sons of Yisrael by bringing My rights
to bear in their midst, so that I did not
destroy the sons of Yisrael by bringing
My rights to bear. 12. Therefore proclaim it: Lo! I shall give to him My
covenant: Peace. 13. And there shall be
to him and to his descendants after him a
covenant of everlasting priesthood because
he brought to bear the rights of his God and
effected atonement for the sons of Yisrael."
14. The name of the slain man of Yisrael,
who was slain along with the Midianite
woman, was Zimri, son of Salu, a prince of a
father's house of the Shimeonite tribe.
15. And the name of the slain Midianite
woman [was] Cozbi, daughter of Tzur; he
was the head of the peoples of a father's
house in Midian. 16. *God* spoke to Moshe
[saying]: 17. "The Midianites are to be
treated as enemies and you shall strike
them, 18. for they treat you as enemies
with the same tricks that they perpetrated
against you in the matter of Peor and at the
same time in the matter of Cozbi, the

י וַיְדַבֵּ֥ר יְהֹוָ֖ה אֶל־מֹשֶׁ֥ה לֵּאמֹֽר׃ יא פִּֽינְחָ֨ס בֶּן־
אֶלְעָזָ֜ר בֶּן־אַהֲרֹ֣ן הַכֹּהֵ֗ן הֵשִׁ֤יב אֶת־חֲמָתִי֙ מֵעַ֣ל
בְּנֵֽי־יִשְׂרָאֵ֔ל בְּקַנְא֥וֹ אֶת־קִנְאָתִ֖י בְּתוֹכָ֑ם וְלֹא־
כִלִּ֥יתִי אֶת־בְּנֵֽי־יִשְׂרָאֵ֖ל בְּקִנְאָתִֽי׃ יב לָכֵ֖ן אֱמֹ֑ר
הִנְנִ֨י נֹתֵ֥ן ל֛וֹ אֶת־בְּרִיתִ֖י שָׁלֽוֹם׃ יג וְהָ֤יְתָה לּוֹ֙
וּלְזַרְע֣וֹ אַחֲרָ֔יו בְּרִ֖ית כְּהֻנַּ֣ת עוֹלָ֑ם תַּ֗חַת אֲשֶׁ֤ר
קִנֵּא֙ לֵֽאלֹהָ֔יו וַיְכַפֵּ֖ר עַל־בְּנֵ֥י יִשְׂרָאֵֽל׃ יד וְשֵׁ֠ם
אִ֨ישׁ יִשְׂרָאֵ֜ל הַמֻּכֶּ֗ה אֲשֶׁ֤ר הֻכָּה֙ אֶת־הַמִּדְיָנִ֔ית
זִמְרִ֖י בֶּן־סָל֑וּא נְשִׂ֥יא בֵֽית־אָ֖ב לַשִּׁמְעֹנִֽי׃
טו וְשֵׁ֨ם הָאִשָּׁ֧ה הַמֻּכָּ֛ה הַמִּדְיָנִ֖ית כָּזְבִּ֣י בַת־צ֑וּר
רֹ֣אשׁ אֻמּ֥וֹת בֵּֽית־אָ֛ב בְּמִדְיָ֖ן הֽוּא׃ פ טז וַיְדַבֵּ֥ר
יְהֹוָ֖ה אֶל־מֹשֶׁ֥ה לֵּאמֹֽר׃ יז צָר֖וֹר אֶת־הַמִּדְיָנִ֑ים
וְהִכִּיתֶ֖ם אוֹתָֽם׃ יח כִּ֣י צֹרְרִ֥ים הֵם֙ לָכֶ֔ם
בְּנִכְלֵיהֶ֛ם אֲשֶׁר־נִכְּל֥וּ לָכֶ֖ם עַל־דְּבַ֣ר פְּע֑וֹר

12. שָׁלוֹם . . . [Peace], the most complete harmony of all the conditions on earth among one another and with God, is declared to be a בְּרִית [covenant]. . . . Here God places the responsibility for the realization of the supreme harmony of peace on precisely those individuals whose actions a thoughtless world, anxious to mask its passivity and negligence as "love of peace," would brand and condemn as "disturbances of the peace." Peace is a precious thing for which one may sacrifice all of one's own rights and possessions, but never the rights of others and never those values that God has declared to be good and true. There can be true peace among men only if all men are at peace with God. Hence anyone who wages war on the enemies of what is good and true in the eyes of God is a champion of the בְּרִית שָׁלוֹם [covenant of peace] on earth even while he is engaged in war. Conversely, one who, for the sake of what he considers to be the preservation of peace with his fellow men, cedes the field without protest to individuals who are truly in conflict with God, actually makes common cause with the enemies of the בְּרִית שָׁלוֹם on earth. What saved the people was not the passivity of the masses, nor even the idle tears of sorrow shed at the entrance to the Tent of Appointed Meeting. It was the valiant act of Phineḥas that saved the people and restored to them their peace with God and His Law, thus also restoring to them the foundation for their own true inner peace. . . .

° ° °

14. ***The name of the slain man of Yisrael.*** (Cf. Verse 6). . . . The exalted rank of the man against whom Phineḥas had arisen makes Phineḥas' act of devotion appear even greater. He gave no thought to the harm that might come to him personally as a result of his act. He forgot everything except the cause of God. . . .

15. ***And the name of the slain Midianite woman.*** Not even the consideration that his act might bring the hostility of the Midianites upon his entire nation could keep Phineḥas from taking action when the task at hand was to preserve the very soul of the nation, its loyalty to God and to His Law. . . .

daughter of the Midianite prince, their sister, who was slain on the day of the plague that had come because of Peor."

XXVI

1. It came to pass after the plague: *God* said to Moshe and to Eleazar, son of Aharon the priest [saying]: 2. "Take the total count of the entire community of the sons of Yisrael from twenty years old and upward, according to their fathers' houses, every one who goes forth into communal service in Yisrael." 3. And Moshe and Eleazar the priest proclaimed them in the wastelands of Moab near the Yarden of Jericho [saying]: 4. From twenty years old and upward, as *God* had commanded Moshe and the sons of Yisrael who had gone out of the land of Mitzrayim. 5. Reuben, first-born of Yisrael: The sons of Reuben: Ḥanokh, the family of the Ḥanokhite branch; of Palu, the family of the Paluite branch; 6. of Ḥetzron, the family of the Ḥetzronite branch; of Carmi, the family of the Carmite branch; 7. these are the families of the Reubenite tribe. Their numbered ones were forty-three thousand seven hundred and thirty. 8. The sons of Palu: Eliab, 9. and the sons of Eliab: Nemuel, Dathan and Abiram. These are Dathan and Abiram, who had been designated by the community, who had incited strife against Moshe and Aharon with the community of Koraḥ when they incited strife against *God*. 10. And the earth opened its mouth and swallowed them and Koraḥ, when the community died, when the fire devoured the two hundred and fifty men; then they became a sign [of admonition]. 11. But the sons of Koraḥ did not die. 12. The sons of Shimeon according to their families: of Nemuel, the family of the Nemuelite

וְעַל־דְּבַר כָּזְבִּי בַת־נְשִׂיא מִדְיָן אֲחֹתָם הַמֻּכָּה
בְיוֹם־הַמַּגֵּפָה עַל־דְּבַר פְּעוֹר׃ כו א וַיְהִי אַחֲרֵי
הַמַּגֵּפָה (פסקא באמצע פסוק) פ וַיֹּאמֶר יְהֹוָה אֶל־
מֹשֶׁה וְאֶל אֶלְעָזָר בֶּן־אַהֲרֹן הַכֹּהֵן לֵאמֹר׃
ב שְׂאוּ אֶת־רֹאשׁ ׀ כָּל־עֲדַת בְּנֵי־יִשְׂרָאֵל מִבֶּן
עֶשְׂרִים שָׁנָה וָמַעְלָה לְבֵית אֲבֹתָם כָּל־יֹצֵא
צָבָא בְּיִשְׂרָאֵל׃ ג וַיְדַבֵּר מֹשֶׁה וְאֶלְעָזָר הַכֹּהֵן
אֹתָם בְּעַרְבֹת מוֹאָב עַל־יַרְדֵּן יְרֵחוֹ לֵאמֹר׃
ד מִבֶּן עֶשְׂרִים שָׁנָה וָמָעְלָה כַּאֲשֶׁר צִוָּה יְהֹוָה
אֶת־מֹשֶׁה וּבְנֵי יִשְׂרָאֵל הַיֹּצְאִים מֵאֶרֶץ מִצְרָיִם׃
שני ה רְאוּבֵן בְּכוֹר יִשְׂרָאֵל בְּנֵי רְאוּבֵן חֲנוֹךְ
מִשְׁפַּחַת הַחֲנֹכִי לְפַלּוּא מִשְׁפַּחַת הַפַּלֻּאִי׃
ו לְחֶצְרֹן מִשְׁפַּחַת הַחֶצְרוֹנִי לְכַרְמִי מִשְׁפַּחַת
הַכַּרְמִי׃ ז אֵלֶּה מִשְׁפְּחֹת הָרְאוּבֵנִי וַיִּהְיוּ
פְקֻדֵיהֶם שְׁלֹשָׁה וְאַרְבָּעִים אֶלֶף וּשְׁבַע מֵאוֹת
וּשְׁלֹשִׁים׃ ח וּבְנֵי פַלּוּא אֱלִיאָב׃ ט וּבְנֵי אֱלִיאָב
נְמוּאֵל וְדָתָן וַאֲבִירָם הוּא־דָתָן וַאֲבִירָם קְרוּאֵי
(קריאי קרי) הָעֵדָה אֲשֶׁר הִצּוּ עַל־מֹשֶׁה וְעַל־
אַהֲרֹן בַּעֲדַת־קֹרַח בְּהַצֹּתָם עַל־יְהֹוָה׃ י וַתִּפְתַּח
הָאָרֶץ אֶת־פִּיהָ וַתִּבְלַע אֹתָם וְאֶת־קֹרַח בְּמוֹת
הָעֵדָה בַּאֲכֹל הָאֵשׁ אֵת חֲמִשִּׁים וּמָאתַיִם אִישׁ
וַיִּהְיוּ לְנֵס׃ יא וּבְנֵי־קֹרַח לֹא־מֵתוּ׃ ס יב בְּנֵי
שִׁמְעוֹן לְמִשְׁפְּחֹתָם לִנְמוּאֵל מִשְׁפַּחַת הַנְּמוּאֵלִי

CHAPTER XXVI

1\. . . . Once all those corrupted by the sexual rites of Peor worship had died, the people of Israel could shine forth once more in their hereditary distinction of sexual purity, even as the Moabite prophet had beheld them before they had been seduced into Peor worship. This was most cogently demonstrated by every subsequent census taken of the people, and this was the reason why a new census was taken after the plague. The fact that every single member of the nation could still be counted "according to his family and his father's house," as had been done forty years earlier, following the exodus from Egypt, proved that there could be no doubt concerning the paternity of any child in Israel and that the orgy of Peor worship had been only an isolated, exceptional aberration in Israel's history. . . .

branch; of Yamin, the family of the Yaminite branch; of Yakhin, the family of the Yakhinite branch;   13. of Zeraḥ, the family of the Zeraḥite branch; of Shaul, the family of the Shaulite branch;   14. these [are the] families of the Shimeonite tribe: twenty-two thousand two hundred. 15. The sons of Gad according to their families: of Tzefon, the family of the Tzefonite branch; of Ḥaggi, the family of the Ḥaggite branch; of Shuni, the family of the Shunite branch;   16. of Ozni, the family of the Oznite branch; of Eri, the family of the Erite branch;   17. of Arad, the family of the Aradite branch; of Areli, the family of the Arelite branch; 18. these [are the] families of the sons of Gad according to their numbered ones: forty thousand five hundred.   19. The sons of Yehudah: Er and Onan; Er and Onan died in the land of Canaan. 20. There were the sons of Yehudah according to their families: Of Shelah, the family of the Shelanite branch; of Peretz, the family of the Partzite branch; of Zeraḥ, the family of the Zeraḥite branch. 21. And the sons of Peretz were: Of Ḥetzron, the family of the Ḥetzronite branch; of Ḥamul, the family of the Ḥamulite branch.   22. These [are the] families of Yehudah according to their numbered ones: seventy-six thousand five hundred.   23. The sons of Yissakhar according to their families: Tola, the family of the Tola'ite branch; of Puvah, the family of the Punite branch;   24. of Yashuv, the family of the Yashuvite branch; of Shimron, the family of the Shimronite branch; 25. these [are the] families of Yissakhar according to their numbered ones: sixty-four thousand three hundred.   26. The sons of Zebulun according to their families: of Sered, the family of the Sardite branch; of Elon, the family of the Elonite branch; of Yaḥle'el, the family of the Yaḥle'elite branch;   27. these [are] the families of the Zebulunite tribe according to their numbered ones: sixty thousand five hundred.   28. The sons of Yosef according to their families: Menashe and Ephraim. 29. The sons of Menashe: of Makhir, the familiy of the Makhirite branch; and Makhir begat Gilead, and from Gilead

לְיָמִין מִשְׁפַּחַת הַיָּמִינִי לְיָכִין מִשְׁפַּחַת הַיָּכִינִי: יג לְזֶרַח מִשְׁפַּחַת הַזַּרְחִי לְשָׁאוּל מִשְׁפַּחַת הַשָּׁאוּלִי: יד אֵלֶּה מִשְׁפְּחֹת הַשִּׁמְעֹנִי שְׁנַיִם וְעֶשְׂרִים אֶלֶף וּמָאתָיִם: ס טו בְּנֵי גָד לְמִשְׁפְּחֹתָם לִצְפוֹן מִשְׁפַּחַת הַצְּפוֹנִי לְחַגִּי מִשְׁפַּחַת הַחַגִּי לְשׁוּנִי מִשְׁפַּחַת הַשּׁוּנִי: טז לְאָזְנִי מִשְׁפַּחַת הָאָזְנִי לְעֵרִי מִשְׁפַּחַת הָעֵרִי: יז לַאֲרוֹד מִשְׁפַּחַת הָאֲרוֹדִי לְאַרְאֵלִי מִשְׁפַּחַת הָאַרְאֵלִי: יח אֵלֶּה מִשְׁפְּחֹת בְּנֵי־גָד לִפְקֻדֵיהֶם אַרְבָּעִים אֶלֶף וַחֲמֵשׁ מֵאוֹת: ס יט בְּנֵי יְהוּדָה עֵר וְאוֹנָן וַיָּמָת עֵר וְאוֹנָן בְּאֶרֶץ כְּנָעַן: כ וַיִּהְיוּ בְנֵי־יְהוּדָה לְמִשְׁפְּחֹתָם לְשֵׁלָה מִשְׁפַּחַת הַשֵּׁלָנִי לְפֶרֶץ מִשְׁפַּחַת הַפַּרְצִי לְזֶרַח מִשְׁפַּחַת הַזַּרְחִי: כא וַיִּהְיוּ בְנֵי־פֶרֶץ לְחֶצְרֹן מִשְׁפַּחַת הַחֶצְרֹנִי לְחָמוּל מִשְׁפַּחַת הֶחָמוּלִי: כב אֵלֶּה מִשְׁפְּחֹת יְהוּדָה לִפְקֻדֵיהֶם שִׁשָּׁה וְשִׁבְעִים אֶלֶף וַחֲמֵשׁ מֵאוֹת: ס כג בְּנֵי יִשָּׂשכָר לְמִשְׁפְּחֹתָם תּוֹלָע מִשְׁפַּחַת הַתּוֹלָעִי לְפֻוָּה מִשְׁפַּחַת הַפּוּנִי: כד לְיָשׁוּב מִשְׁפַּחַת הַיָּשֻׁבִי לְשִׁמְרֹן מִשְׁפַּחַת הַשִּׁמְרֹנִי: כה אֵלֶּה מִשְׁפְּחֹת יִשָּׂשכָר לִפְקֻדֵיהֶם אַרְבָּעָה וְשִׁשִּׁים אֶלֶף וּשְׁלֹשׁ מֵאוֹת: ס כו בְּנֵי זְבוּלֻן לְמִשְׁפְּחֹתָם לְסֶרֶד מִשְׁפַּחַת הַסַּרְדִּי לְאֵלוֹן מִשְׁפַּחַת הָאֵלֹנִי לְיַחְלְאֵל מִשְׁפַּחַת הַיַּחְלְאֵלִי: כז אֵלֶּה מִשְׁפְּחֹת הַזְּבוּלֹנִי לִפְקֻדֵיהֶם שִׁשִּׁים אֶלֶף וַחֲמֵשׁ מֵאוֹת: ס כח בְּנֵי יוֹסֵף לְמִשְׁפְּחֹתָם מְנַשֶּׁה וְאֶפְרָיִם: כט בְּנֵי מְנַשֶּׁה לְמָכִיר מִשְׁפַּחַת הַמָּכִירִי וּמָכִיר הוֹלִיד אֶת־

[came] the family of the Gileadite branch.
30. These [are] the sons of Gilead:
Iyezer; the family of the Iyezerite branch; of
Ḥelek, the family of the Ḥelekite branch;
31. and Asriel, the family of the Asrielite
branch; and Shekhem, the family of the
Shikhmite branch; 32. and Shemida, the
family of the Shemidaite branch; and
Ḥefer, the family of the Ḥeferite branch.
33. Tzelopheḥad, son of Ḥefer, had no
sons, only daughters, and the name[s] of the
daughters of Tzelopheḥad were: Maḥlah,
Noa, Ḥoglah, Milkah and Thirtzah.
34. These [are] the families of Menashe:
their numbered ones were fifty-two thousand seven hundred. 35. These [are] the
sons of Ephraim according to their families:
of Shuthelaḥ, the family of the Shuthelaḥite
branch; of Bekher, the family of the
Bakhrite branch; of Taḥan, the family of the
Taḥanite branch. 36. And the sons of
Shuthelaḥ: of Eran, the family of the
Eranite branch. 37. These [are] the
families of the sons of Ephraim according to
their numbered ones: thirty-two thousand
five hundred; these [are] the sons of Yosef
according to their families. 38. The sons
of Binyamin according to their families;
of Bela, the family of the Belaite branch; of
Ashbel, the family of the Ashbelite branch;
of Aḥiram, the family of the Aḥiramite
branch; 39. of Shefufam, the family of
the Shufamite branch; of Ḥufam, the family
of the Ḥufamite branch. 40. The sons of
Bela were Ard and Na'aman; the family
of the Ardite branch; of Na'aman, the family
of the Na'amite branch. 41. These [are]
the sons of Binyamin according to their
families, and their numbered ones: forty-
five thousand six hundred. 42. These
[are] the sons of Dan according to their
families; of Shuḥam, the family of the
Shuḥamite branch; these [are] the families
of Dan according to their families. 43. All
the families of the Shuḥamite branch
according to their numbered ones: sixty-
four thousand four hundred. 44. The
sons of Asher according to their families: of
Yimnah, the family of the Yimnite branch;
of Yishvi, the family of the Yishvite branch;
of Beriah, the family of the Beriite
branch. 45. Of the sons of Beriah, of

גִּלְעָד לְגִלְעָד מִשְׁפַּחַת הַגִּלְעָדִי: ל אֵלֶּה בְּנֵי
גִלְעָד אִיעֶזֶר מִשְׁפַּחַת הָאִיעֶזְרִי לְחֵלֶק מִשְׁפַּחַת
הַחֶלְקִי: לא וְאַשְׂרִיאֵל מִשְׁפַּחַת הָאַשְׂרְאֵלִי
וְשֶׁכֶם מִשְׁפַּחַת הַשִּׁכְמִי: לב וּשְׁמִידָע מִשְׁפַּחַת
הַשְּׁמִידָעִי וְחֵפֶר מִשְׁפַּחַת הַחֶפְרִי: לג וּצְלָפְחָד
בֶּן־חֵפֶר לֹא־הָיוּ לוֹ בָּנִים כִּי אִם־בָּנוֹת וְשֵׁם
בְּנוֹת צְלָפְחָד מַחְלָה וְנֹעָה חָגְלָה מִלְכָּה וְתִרְצָה:
לד אֵלֶּה מִשְׁפְּחֹת מְנַשֶּׁה וּפְקֻדֵיהֶם שְׁנַיִם
וַחֲמִשִּׁים אֶלֶף וּשְׁבַע מֵאוֹת: ס לה אֵלֶּה בְנֵי־
אֶפְרַיִם לְמִשְׁפְּחֹתָם לְשׁוּתֶלַח מִשְׁפַּחַת
הַשֻּׁתַלְחִי לְבֶכֶר מִשְׁפַּחַת הַבַּכְרִי לְתַחַן מִשְׁפַּחַת
הַתַּחֲנִי: לו וְאֵלֶּה בְּנֵי שׁוּתָלַח לְעֵרָן מִשְׁפַּחַת
הָעֵרָנִי: לז אֵלֶּה מִשְׁפְּחֹת בְּנֵי־אֶפְרַיִם
לִפְקֻדֵיהֶם שְׁנַיִם וּשְׁלֹשִׁים אֶלֶף וַחֲמֵשׁ מֵאוֹת
אֵלֶּה בְנֵי־יוֹסֵף לְמִשְׁפְּחֹתָם: ס לח בְּנֵי בִנְיָמִן
לְמִשְׁפְּחֹתָם לְבֶלַע מִשְׁפַּחַת הַבַּלְעִי לְאַשְׁבֵּל
מִשְׁפַּחַת הָאַשְׁבֵּלִי לַאֲחִירָם מִשְׁפַּחַת
הָאֲחִירָמִי: לט לִשְׁפוּפָם מִשְׁפַּחַת הַשּׁוּפָמִי
לְחוּפָם מִשְׁפַּחַת הַחוּפָמִי: מ וַיִּהְיוּ בְנֵי־בֶלַע
אַרְדְּ וְנַעֲמָן מִשְׁפַּחַת הָאַרְדִּי לְנַעֲמָן מִשְׁפַּחַת
הַנַּעֲמִי: מא אֵלֶּה בְנֵי־בִנְיָמִן לְמִשְׁפְּחֹתָם
וּפְקֻדֵיהֶם חֲמִשָּׁה וְאַרְבָּעִים אֶלֶף וְשֵׁשׁ
מֵאוֹת: ס מב אֵלֶּה בְנֵי־דָן לְמִשְׁפְּחֹתָם לְשׁוּחָם
מִשְׁפַּחַת הַשּׁוּחָמִי אֵלֶּה מִשְׁפְּחֹת דָּן
לְמִשְׁפְּחֹתָם: מג כָּל־מִשְׁפְּחֹת הַשּׁוּחָמִי
לִפְקֻדֵיהֶם אַרְבָּעָה וְשִׁשִּׁים אֶלֶף וְאַרְבַּע
מֵאוֹת: ס מד בְּנֵי אָשֵׁר לְמִשְׁפְּחֹתָם לְיִמְנָה
מִשְׁפַּחַת הַיִּמְנָה לְיִשְׁוִי מִשְׁפַּחַת הַיִּשְׁוִי
לִבְרִיעָה מִשְׁפַּחַת הַבְּרִיעִי: מה לִבְנֵי בְרִיעָה

לְחֵבֶר מִשְׁפַּחַת הַחֶבְרִי לְמַלְכִּיאֵל מִשְׁפַּחַת
הַמַּלְכִּיאֵלִי: מו וְשֵׁם בַּת־אָשֵׁר שָׂרַח: מז אֵלֶּה
מִשְׁפְּחֹת בְּנֵי־אָשֵׁר לִפְקֻדֵיהֶם שְׁלֹשָׁה וַחֲמִשִּׁים
אֶלֶף וְאַרְבַּע מֵאוֹת: ס מח בְּנֵי נַפְתָּלִי
לְמִשְׁפְּחֹתָם לְיַחְצְאֵל מִשְׁפַּחַת הַיַּחְצְאֵלִי לְגוּנִי
מִשְׁפַּחַת הַגּוּנִי: מט לְיֵצֶר מִשְׁפַּחַת הַיִּצְרִי
לְשִׁלֵּם מִשְׁפַּחַת הַשִּׁלֵּמִי: נ אֵלֶּה מִשְׁפְּחֹת
נַפְתָּלִי לְמִשְׁפְּחֹתָם וּפְקֻדֵיהֶם חֲמִשָּׁה וְאַרְבָּעִים
אֶלֶף וְאַרְבַּע מֵאוֹת: נא אֵלֶּה פְּקוּדֵי בְּנֵי יִשְׂרָאֵל
שֵׁשׁ־מֵאוֹת אֶלֶף וָאָלֶף שְׁבַע מֵאוֹת
וּשְׁלֹשִׁים: פ שלישי נב וַיְדַבֵּר יְהוָה אֶל־מֹשֶׁה
לֵּאמֹר: נג לָאֵלֶּה תֵּחָלֵק הָאָרֶץ בְּנַחֲלָה בְּמִסְפַּר
שֵׁמוֹת: נד לָרַב תַּרְבֶּה נַחֲלָתוֹ וְלַמְעַט תַּמְעִיט
נַחֲלָתוֹ אִישׁ לְפִי פְקֻדָיו יֻתַּן נַחֲלָתוֹ: נה אַךְ־
בְּגוֹרָל יֵחָלֵק אֶת־הָאָרֶץ לִשְׁמוֹת מַטּוֹת־אֲבֹתָם

Ḥever, the family of the Ḥevrite branch; of
Malkiel, the family of the Malkielite branch.
46. And the name of one daughter of
Asher was Seraḥ. 47. These [are] the
families of the sons of Asher according to
their numbered ones: fifty-three thousand
four hundred. 48. The sons of Naphtali
according to their families; from Yaḥtze'el,
the family of the Yaḥtze'elite branch; of
Guni, the family of the Gunite branch;
49. of Yetzer, the family of the Yitzrite
branch; of Shillem, the family of the
Shillemite branch. 50. These [are] the
families of Naphtali according to their
families. And their numbered ones: forty-
five thousand four hundred. 51. These
numbered ones of the sons of Yisrael were:
six hundred and one thousand, seven
hundred and thirty. 52. *God* spoke to
Moshe [saying]: 53. "To these shall the
land be apportioned as an inheritance
according to the number of the names.
54. To the numerous you shall give a
large inheritance and to the few a small
inheritance; to each according to his
numbered ones shall his inheritance be
given. 55. Only by lot shall the land be
divided; according to the names of the

55. . . . If we examine more closely the system by which the land was to be apportioned, we will note that the land was treated as the estate left by the generation immediately preceding that which went forth from Egypt. Each of the fathers of those who went forth from Egypt was assigned a portion of the Promised Land equivalent to the number of his grandsons twenty years of age and older who would enter the land. This estate could be inherited only by those of the sons who were more than twenty years old at the time they left Egypt; these sons in turn could bequeath the land to those of their own sons who would be more than twenty years old at the time they entered the Land.

It seems that the intention was to perpetuate in the land register of the Jewish nation two distinct truths:

First, whatever God promises is so certain of fulfillment that it must be regarded as an accomplished fact even before it has come to pass. Not only those who have already been delivered in fact, but even the members of the generation that still languishes beneath the Egyptian yoke, are regarded as the owners of the land promised them by God, with legal rights assigned to their descendants accordingly. This is the reason why Eretz Yisrael is regarded as מוּחְזָק, property already owned in fact by the fathers, not merely as רָאוּי, property to which they are entitled under the law. As a consequence, the legal rights of the first-born, too, were applicable in the apportionment of the land (Numbers 27:6 and Deuteronomy 21:17).

The greatest and most precious acquisitions of parents and grandparents are children and grandchildren that prove themselves loyal and true to their heritage. Such progeny bears witness to the merits of its forebears and atones for their shortcomings. Even as, according to one interpretation, Jacob regarded his sons as "conquests" he had won from the Emorites, as the trophies of his life, as it were, so we see here that good and honest children and grandchildren are considered a credit to their fathers and grandfathers. Notwithstanding all the trials devised by Egypt to break the spirit of the Children of Israel, more than 600,000 able-bodied men were worthy of redemption and stood ready to submit to God's guidance. And again, notwithstanding all the aberrations and the attrition in the wilderness, more than 600,000 were found to be deserving of the land, the soil and the Law of God, and Moses was able to say to them: "And you who cling to *God*, your God, are all of you still alive today." All this was due to the spirit

יִנְחָלוּ: נו עַל־פִּי הַגּוֹרָל תֵּחָלֵק נַחֲלָתוֹ בֵּין רַב
לִמְעָט: ס נז וְאֵלֶּה פְקוּדֵי הַלֵּוִי לְמִשְׁפְּחֹתָם
לְגֵרְשׁוֹן מִשְׁפַּחַת הַגֵּרְשֻׁנִּי לִקְהָת מִשְׁפַּחַת
הַקְּהָתִי לִמְרָרִי מִשְׁפַּחַת הַמְּרָרִי: נח אֵלֶּה ׀
מִשְׁפְּחֹת לֵוִי מִשְׁפַּחַת הַלִּבְנִי מִשְׁפַּחַת הַחֶבְרֹנִי
מִשְׁפַּחַת הַמַּחְלִי מִשְׁפַּחַת הַמּוּשִׁי מִשְׁפַּחַת
הַקָּרְחִי וּקְהָת הוֹלִד אֶת־עַמְרָם: נט וְשֵׁם ׀ אֵשֶׁת
עַמְרָם יוֹכֶבֶד בַּת־לֵוִי אֲשֶׁר יָלְדָה אֹתָהּ לְלֵוִי
בְּמִצְרָיִם וַתֵּלֶד לְעַמְרָם אֶת־אַהֲרֹן וְאֶת־מֹשֶׁה
וְאֵת מִרְיָם אֲחֹתָם: ס וַיִּוָּלֵד לְאַהֲרֹן אֶת־
נָדָב וְאֶת־אֲבִיהוּא אֶת־אֶלְעָזָר וְאֶת־אִיתָמָר:
סא וַיָּמָת נָדָב וַאֲבִיהוּא בְּהַקְרִיבָם אֵשׁ־זָרָה
לִפְנֵי יְהוָה: סב וַיִּהְיוּ פְקֻדֵיהֶם שְׁלֹשָׁה וְעֶשְׂרִים
אֶלֶף כָּל־זָכָר מִבֶּן־חֹדֶשׁ וָמָעְלָה כִּי ׀ לֹא
הָתְפָּקְדוּ בְּתוֹךְ בְּנֵי יִשְׂרָאֵל כִּי לֹא־נִתַּן לָהֶם

tribes of their fathers shall they receive it as a possession.
56. According to lot shall their inheritance be apportioned to them, with due regard for whether they are many or few."
57. And these are the numbered ones of the Levite tribe according to their families: of Gershon, the family of the Gershonite branch; of Kehath, the family of the Kehathite branch; of Merari, the family of the Merarite branch.
58. These [are] the Levite families: the family of the Livnite branch, the family of the Ḥebronite branch, the family of the Maḥlite branch, the family of the Mushite branch, the family of the Koraḥite branch. And Kehath had begotten Amram.
59. The name of Amram's wife was Yokhebed, daughter of Levi, whom she had borne to Levi in Mitzrayim. The former bore to Amram Aharon and Moshe and their sister Miriam.
60. To Aharon were born Nadab and Abihu, Eleazar and Ithamar.
61. But Nadab and Abihu died when they brought near strange fire before *God.*
62. Their numbered ones were twenty-three thousand, all males from one month old upward; for they were not caused to number themselves among the sons of Yisrael, for no inheritance had been given

which the ancestors nurtured in their children even in the midst of Egyptian slavery. Each plot of God's land that the grandchildren received, these grandchildren then humbly placed, in spirit, at the feet of their grandfathers, as their conquest, which they, the grandchildren, would in turn receive as their inheritance only after their fathers had died. "I will cite you a parable," the Sages say (Baba Bathra 117a). "It is similar to two brothers who are priests and live in the same city, one of them having only one son, while the other has two. They go to the shed where the produce is stored in order to receive their priestly portion. The one who sends his one son receives one portion. The other, who has two sons, receives two portions, but all that they have received they take home to their aged father, of whose household they still consider themselves members and for the sake of whose merits the grandsons were given their donated portions, and then they divided the whole amount equally."

The fact that, although they were deemed worthy in their own right of taking possession of the Land of God, the sons were given the land only as the heirs of their fathers and as the bearers of their names, proves that, notwithstanding the error that had cost their fathers the right to enter the land, these same fathers, during thirty-eight years of wandering in the wilderness, had implanted the right spirit in the new generation. And the fact that, of this new generation, more than 600,000 individuals were found worthy of entering the land under God's guidance, proves that the fathers had understood how to atone for their own sins through their children, so that, as the Sages put it, the generation of the wilderness had been, after all, a generation of understanding (*Midrash Rabbah* Chap. 19). Indeed, as noted in Sanhedrin 110b, the words of the prophet Jeremiah (2:2) recall with love the generation of the wilderness: "Go and proclaim it in the ears of Jerusalem as follows: I have remembered for you the lovingkindness of your youth, the love of the days of your betrothal, when you went after Me into the wilderness, into a land that was not sown." To this the Sages note: "The fact that others came into the land on account of the merit (of that generation) shows how great must have been the merit of that generation itself." Thus, on the whole, despite repeated lapses, the image of Israel wandering through the wilderness is a worthy one.

to them among the sons of Yisrael.
63. These are the ones numbered by
Moshe and by Eleazar the priest, who
numbered the sons of Yisrael in the wastelands of Moab, on the Yarden of Jericho.
64. Among these there was not one man
from those who had been numbered by
Moshe and by Aharon the priest, whom the
sons of Yisrael had numbered in the wilderness of Sinai; 65. for *God* had decreed
concerning them: "They shall die in the
wilderness!" Therefore none of them was
left except Caleb, son of Yefunneh, and
Yehoshua, son of Nun.

XXVII

1. And the daughters
of Tzelopheḥad, son
of Ḥefer, son of Gilead, son of Makhir,
son of Menashe of the families of Menashe,
the son of Yosef, came near—and these were
the names of his daughters: Maḥlah, Noa
and Ḥoglah, Milkah and Thirtzah—
2. and they placed themselves before
Moshe, before Eleazar the priest, before the
princes and the entire community in the
entrance of the Tent of Appointed Meeting,
and they said: 3. "Our father died in the
wilderness; he was not among the company
that banded together against *God*; he was
not among Koraḥ's allies, but he died
because of his own sin, and he had no sons.
4. Now why should the name of our
father disappear from the midst of his
family just because he did not have a son?
Please give us a possession among the
brothers of our father." 5. Moshe
brought their legitimate claim before *God*.
6. And *God* said to Moshe: 7. "The
daughters of Tzelopheḥad speak justly;
certainly you shall give them, according to
the legal right of males, a hereditary

נַחֲלָה בְּתוֹךְ בְּנֵי יִשְׂרָאֵל: סג אֵלֶּה פְּקוּדֵי מֹשֶׁה
וְאֶלְעָזָר הַכֹּהֵן אֲשֶׁר פָּקְדוּ אֶת־בְּנֵי יִשְׂרָאֵל
בְּעַרְבֹת מוֹאָב עַל יַרְדֵּן יְרֵחוֹ: סד וּבְאֵלֶּה לֹא־
הָיָה אִישׁ מִפְּקוּדֵי מֹשֶׁה וְאַהֲרֹן הַכֹּהֵן אֲשֶׁר
פָּקְדוּ אֶת־בְּנֵי יִשְׂרָאֵל בְּמִדְבַּר סִינָי: סה כִּי־
אָמַר יְהוָֹה לָהֶם מוֹת יָמֻתוּ בַּמִּדְבָּר וְלֹא־נוֹתַר
מֵהֶם אִישׁ כִּי אִם־כָּלֵב בֶּן־יְפֻנֶּה וִיהוֹשֻׁעַ בִּן־
נוּן: ס כז א וַתִּקְרַבְנָה בְּנוֹת צְלָפְחָד בֶּן־חֵפֶר
בֶּן־גִּלְעָד בֶּן־מָכִיר בֶּן־מְנַשֶּׁה לְמִשְׁפְּחֹת מְנַשֶּׁה
בֶן־יוֹסֵף וְאֵלֶּה שְׁמוֹת בְּנֹתָיו מַחְלָה נֹעָה וְחָגְלָה
וּמִלְכָּה וְתִרְצָה: ב וַתַּעֲמֹדְנָה לִפְנֵי מֹשֶׁה וְלִפְנֵי
אֶלְעָזָר הַכֹּהֵן וְלִפְנֵי הַנְּשִׂיאִם וְכָל־הָעֵדָה פֶּתַח
אֹהֶל־מוֹעֵד לֵאמֹר: ג אָבִינוּ מֵת בַּמִּדְבָּר וְהוּא
לֹא־הָיָה בְּתוֹךְ הָעֵדָה הַנּוֹעָדִים עַל־יְהוָֹה בַּעֲדַת־
קֹרַח כִּי־בְחֶטְאוֹ מֵת וּבָנִים לֹא־הָיוּ לוֹ: ד לָמָּה
יִגָּרַע שֵׁם־אָבִינוּ מִתּוֹךְ מִשְׁפַּחְתּוֹ כִּי אֵין לוֹ בֵּן
תְּנָה־לָּנוּ אֲחֻזָּה בְּתוֹךְ אֲחֵי אָבִינוּ: ה וַיַּקְרֵב
מֹשֶׁה אֶת־מִשְׁפָּטָן (נ רבתי) לִפְנֵי יְהוָֹה: פ
רביעי ו וַיֹּאמֶר יְהוָֹה אֶל־מֹשֶׁה לֵּאמֹר: ז כֵּן בְּנוֹת
צְלָפְחָד דֹּבְרֹת נָתֹן תִּתֵּן לָהֶם אֲחֻזַּת נַחֲלָה

CHAPTER XXVII

3. . . . The Sages note that the daughters of Tzelopheḥad were familiar with the Law and endowed with penetrating minds. The Sages could have arrived at this conclusion only from the manner in which these women presented their case, stating all the facts pertinent to their claim and not uttering one word too much. . . .

6. ***And* God *said to Moshe*.** The fact that the legal provisions which now follow are introduced with וַיֹּאמֶר ["and (*God*) *said*"], not with וַיְדַבֵּר ["And (*God*) *spoke*"], makes it appear that this is not a new set of laws but an elaboration of a canon already given before. . . . It is also not improbable that the reason for the prominent emphasis on the suffix *nun* in מִשְׁפָּטָן ["their claim"] in the preceding verse is to indicate that Moses was already thoroughly familiar with the laws of inheritance in general and that he had to seek a decision only in this specific case. . . .

possession among the brothers of their father and you shall cause their father's inheritance to pass to them. 8. And to the sons of Yisrael you shall say: If a man dies and he has no son, then you shall cause his inheritance to pass to his daughter. 9. If he has no daughter, you shall give his inheritance to his brothers. 10. If he has no brothers, then you shall give his inheritance to his father's brothers. 11. If his father has no brothers, you shall give his inheritance to his kin that is closest to him from among his family and that one shall inherit it. This shall remain for Yisrael as a legal norm, as *God* had commanded Moshe." 12. And *God* said to Moshe: "Go to this Mountain of Transitions and look at the land that I have given to the sons of Yisrael. 13. And when you have seen it, you, too, shall be gathered to your people, even as your brother Aharon was gathered; 14. as you acted against My words in the wilderness of Tzin, during the contention of the community, [when you were] to sanctify Me before their eyes by means of the water. These are the waters of contention at Kadesh in the wilderness of Tzin." 15. And Moshe

בְּתוֹךְ אֲחֵי אֲבִיהֶם וְהַעֲבַרְתָּ אֶת־נַחֲלַת אֲבִיהֶן לָהֶן: ח וְאֶל־בְּנֵי יִשְׂרָאֵל תְּדַבֵּר לֵאמֹר אִישׁ כִּי־יָמוּת וּבֵן אֵין לוֹ וְהַעֲבַרְתֶּם אֶת־נַחֲלָתוֹ לְבִתּוֹ: ט וְאִם־אֵין לוֹ בַּת וּנְתַתֶּם אֶת־נַחֲלָתוֹ לְאֶחָיו: י וְאִם־אֵין לוֹ אַחִים וּנְתַתֶּם אֶת־נַחֲלָתוֹ לַאֲחֵי אָבִיו: יא וְאִם־אֵין אַחִים לְאָבִיו וּנְתַתֶּם אֶת־נַחֲלָתוֹ לִשְׁאֵרוֹ הַקָּרֹב אֵלָיו מִמִּשְׁפַּחְתּוֹ וְיָרַשׁ אֹתָהּ וְהָיְתָה לִבְנֵי יִשְׂרָאֵל לְחֻקַּת מִשְׁפָּט כַּאֲשֶׁר צִוָּה יְהֹוָה אֶת־מֹשֶׁה: פ יב וַיֹּאמֶר יְהֹוָה אֶל־מֹשֶׁה עֲלֵה אֶל־הַר הָעֲבָרִים הַזֶּה וּרְאֵה אֶת־הָאָרֶץ אֲשֶׁר נָתַתִּי לִבְנֵי יִשְׂרָאֵל: יג וְרָאִיתָה אֹתָהּ וְנֶאֱסַפְתָּ אֶל־עַמֶּיךָ גַּם־אָתָּה כַּאֲשֶׁר נֶאֱסַף אַהֲרֹן אָחִיךָ: יד כַּאֲשֶׁר מְרִיתֶם פִּי בְּמִדְבַּר־צִן בִּמְרִיבַת הָעֵדָה לְהַקְדִּישֵׁנִי בַמַּיִם לְעֵינֵיהֶם הֵם מֵי־מְרִיבַת קָדֵשׁ מִדְבַּר־צִן: ס טו וַיְדַבֵּר מֹשֶׁה

12. **And** [God] **said.** This is not yet the command to Moses to ascend the mountain. That command only comes later (Deuteronomy 32:48). Here these words serve only to explain what has gone before and to give the reason for what follows. The passage immediately preceding the present verse concludes the instructions for the apportionment of the land. This is logically followed by a statement to the effect that Moses himself would not be permitted to enter the land. His activities on earth are to end with his viewing of the land from a distance.

The mission of Moses was to lead the people to the Land of the Law, to prepare them for their occupancy of the land and for fulfilling their mission there. But Moses is to have no personal part in the realization of Israel's mission. He is to die not in the land to which he was to lead the nation but only within sight of that land. This announcement did not come as a surprise to Moses. He had known of this Divine decree ever since the incident at Kadesh. However, he was now to be informed in no uncertain terms that he had indeed come to the end of his earthly pilgrimage, so that he might have an opportunity to accomplish, on his own initiative, everything he would wish to see accomplished before his departure. Particularly, the

appointment of his successor was to appear as the desire of his own faithful heart, and he himself should be able to appoint and install the man who would take his place.

Mountain of Transitions; i.e., the mountain that must be passed before crossing from one bank of the Jordan to the other, in order to enter the land.

14. ... Perhaps the intent of this verse is to juxtapose two factors: the transgression of Moses and Aaron and the decree that both of them would have to die within sight of the land for which they had yearned so long. Their transgression was that they had frustrated an intention of God, and they must now atone for it by having their own long-cherished goal denied them.

° ° °

15. וַיְדַבֵּר וגו׳ לֵאמֹר [*And Moshe spoke ... saying*]. This form of introduction indicates that what follows is not so much a request on the part of Moses, but his statement of a disposition he considered to be of immediate urgency now that he knew he was about to die. He dared couch his speech in these terms because this matter concerned not his personal happiness but the future welfare of his people. ...

spoke to *God* [saying]: 16. "Let *God*, the God of the spirits of all flesh, appoint a man over the community 17. who will go out before them and who will come in before them, and who will lead them out and who will bring them in, so that the community of *God* should not be like sheep that have no shepherd." 18. And *God* said to Moshe: "Take yourself Yehoshua, son of Nun, a man in whom there is spirit, and lean your hand upon him, 19. and present him to Eleazar the priest and to the entire community, and charge him before their eyes. 20. You will thus place [some] of your [own] prestige upon him, so that the entire community of the sons of Yisrael will obey him. 21. But he shall stand before Eleazar the priest, and the latter shall make inquiry on his behalf through the judgment of the Urim before *God*. According to its utterance shall they go out, and according to its utterance shall they go in; he and all the

אֶל־יְהֹוָ֖ה לֵאמֹֽר׃ טז יִפְקֹ֣ד יְהֹוָ֔ה אֱלֹהֵ֥י הָרוּחֹ֖ת
לְכָל־בָּשָׂ֑ר אִ֖ישׁ עַל־הָעֵדָֽה׃ יז אֲשֶׁר־יֵצֵ֣א
לִפְנֵיהֶ֗ם וַאֲשֶׁ֤ר יָבֹא֙ לִפְנֵיהֶ֔ם וַאֲשֶׁ֥ר יוֹצִיאֵ֖ם
וַאֲשֶׁ֣ר יְבִיאֵ֑ם וְלֹ֤א תִהְיֶה֙ עֲדַ֣ת יְהֹוָ֔ה כַּצֹּ֕אן אֲשֶׁ֥ר
אֵין־לָהֶ֖ם רֹעֶֽה׃ יח וַיֹּ֨אמֶר יְהֹוָ֜ה אֶל־מֹשֶׁ֗ה
קַח־לְךָ֙ אֶת־יְהוֹשֻׁ֣עַ בִּן־נ֔וּן אִ֖ישׁ אֲשֶׁר־ר֣וּחַ בּ֑וֹ
וְסָמַכְתָּ֥ אֶת־יָדְךָ֖ עָלָֽיו׃ יט וְהַֽעֲמַדְתָּ֣ אֹת֗וֹ לִפְנֵי֙
אֶלְעָזָ֣ר הַכֹּהֵ֔ן וְלִפְנֵ֖י כָּל־הָעֵדָ֑ה וְצִוִּיתָ֥ה אֹת֖וֹ
לְעֵינֵיהֶֽם׃ כ וְנָתַתָּ֥ה מֵהוֹדְךָ֖ עָלָ֑יו לְמַ֣עַן יִשְׁמְע֔וּ
כָּל־עֲדַ֖ת בְּנֵ֥י יִשְׂרָאֵֽל׃ כא וְלִפְנֵ֨י אֶלְעָזָ֤ר הַכֹּהֵן֙
יַעֲמֹ֔ד וְשָׁ֥אַל ל֛וֹ בְּמִשְׁפַּ֥ט הָאוּרִ֖ים לִפְנֵ֣י יְהֹוָ֑ה
עַל־פִּ֨יו יֵצְא֜וּ וְעַל־פִּ֣יו יָבֹ֗אוּ ה֛וּא וְכָל־בְּנֵֽי־

16. . . . God is "the God of the spirits of all flesh" in a dual sense: It is through Him that all flesh receives its spirit, and it is also through Him that this spirit remains within all flesh. He places the spirit into the physical body and, for as long as it is meant to remain combined with this earthly substance, He keeps it there, protects it and strengthens it, endowing it with talents and with the ability to grow and develop. Thus He is much nearer to every spirit during its life on earth than He will be to it when the soul, at the end of its pilgrimage on earth, is stored away in the "covenant of life," along with all the other ingathered souls, for a new future. . . . God, Who, as "the God of the spirits of all flesh," knows and watches over all the souls He has placed into human bodies on earth, will also know how to find the right man to take the place of Moses. Therefore, let God Himself appoint Moses' successor. For even if Moses and Aaron are no longer required . . . someone else will be needed to carry out the Divine mission that is now about to become reality.

17. ***who will go out before them.*** "Go out . . . and come in before . . ." does not by any means connote merely the leading of troops into battle. . . . A man is required "who will go out before them and who will come in before them," one who will "go before" the people as an example for them to emulate in their own lives, both personal and public, "and who will lead them out and who will bring them in"; one who, particularly by his own personal example but also by his influence, will be able to bring the people to fulfill all their obligations, both public and personal, in accordance with the dictates of duty. . . .

18. **איש אשר רוח בו** ***[a man in whom there is spirit].*** When used in the connotation of "wind," רוח denotes a force that is invisible and can be recognized only by its effect as an active, moving power. When used with reference to a man, it connotes the human faculties of perception and volition. . . . This spiritual and moral force is present in every human being. Hence, if we are told here, nevertheless, that Joshua is well suited to be Moses' successor because he is "a man in whom there is spirit," the intention can only be to emphasize Joshua's qualifications, even as we would use the expression "a man of spirit" to describe one who possesses this quality in an eminent degree. . . . In Deuteronomy 34:9 we read: "Yehoshua, son of Nun, was filled with the spirit of wisdom, for Moshe had laid his hands upon him. . . ." Once he had been appointed successor to Moses, his natural talent of רוח was further enhanced; his רוח [spirit] became רוח חָכְמָה ["the spirit of wisdom"] and filled him completely.

° ° °

21. ***But he shall stand before Eleazar the priest.*** He is not to be appointed as an autocratic ruler. In all matters that concern the nation as a whole, where the question is not one of clear-cut right and wrong to be decided in accordance with the revealed Law, but one of whether or not an overall plan will serve the purpose for

sons of Yisrael with him and the entire community." 22. Moshe did as *God* had commanded him. He took Yehoshua and presented him to Eleazar the priest and to the entire community, 23. and he leaned his hands upon him and charged him, as *God* had commanded through Moshe.

XXVIII

1. God spoke to Moshe [saying]: 2. Command the sons of Yisrael and say to them: That which is to be brought near to Me as My offering, for My fire offerings, the expressions of compliance due to Me, you shall keep, to bring near to Me in its season of appointed meeting. 3. And then say to them: This is the fire offering that you shall bring near to *God*: two yearling sheep without blemish, two per day, as a continual ascent offering. 4. The sheep you shall offer, that is, only one, in the morning—the second you shall offer between the two evenings— 5. and the one tenth of an *ephah* of fine flour as a homage offering, mixed with one-quarter of a *hin* of oil obtained by pressing. 6. A continual

יִשְׂרָאֵל אִתּוֹ וְכָל־הָעֵדָה: כב וַיַּעַשׂ מֹשֶׁה כַּאֲשֶׁר
צִוָּה יְהֹוָה אֹתוֹ וַיִּקַּח אֶת־יְהוֹשֻׁעַ וַיַּעֲמִדֵהוּ
לִפְנֵי אֶלְעָזָר הַכֹּהֵן וְלִפְנֵי כָּל־הָעֵדָה: כג וַיִּסְמֹךְ
אֶת־יָדָיו עָלָיו וַיְצַוֵּהוּ כַּאֲשֶׁר דִּבֶּר יְהֹוָה בְּיַד־
מֹשֶׁה: פ חמישי כח א וַיְדַבֵּר יְהֹוָה אֶל־מֹשֶׁה
לֵּאמֹר: ב צַו אֶת־בְּנֵי יִשְׂרָאֵל וְאָמַרְתָּ אֲלֵהֶם
אֶת־קָרְבָּנִי לַחְמִי לְאִשַּׁי רֵיחַ נִיחֹחִי תִּשְׁמְרוּ
לְהַקְרִיב לִי בְּמוֹעֲדוֹ: ג וְאָמַרְתָּ לָהֶם זֶה הָאִשֶּׁה
אֲשֶׁר תַּקְרִיבוּ לַיהֹוָה כְּבָשִׂים בְּנֵי־שָׁנָה תְמִימִם
שְׁנַיִם לַיּוֹם עֹלָה תָמִיד: ד אֶת־הַכֶּבֶשׂ אֶחָד
תַּעֲשֶׂה בַבֹּקֶר וְאֵת הַכֶּבֶשׂ הַשֵּׁנִי תַּעֲשֶׂה בֵּין
הָעַרְבָּיִם: ה וַעֲשִׂירִית הָאֵיפָה סֹלֶת לְמִנְחָה
בְּלוּלָה בְּשֶׁמֶן כָּתִית רְבִיעִת הַהִין: ו עֹלַת תָּמִיד

---

which it was intended, the leader is to ascertain the utterance of God by consulting the Urim that rest upon the breast of the high priest, who represents the Sanctuary of the Law to the nation. The leader must then abide by the decision that will be communicated to him....

But he shall stand before ... and ... make inquiry on his behalf. Eleazar will make inquiry on his behalf before God to ascertain the judgment of the Urim....

CHAPTER XXVIII

1. The preceding chapter tells of the arrangements made, on the recommendation of Moses, so that after his death, which was now close at hand, the community of God should not remain without a leader to serve as a model for private and public life; a leader who, through his personal influence, would guide and keep the individual and communal life of the nation in the paths marked by God.

The intended effect of the offerings that were compulsory for the nation as such, the communal offerings, the continual offerings and the additional offerings, respectively, which are described in the verses that follow, is to make certain that the nation and its leaders will never lose sight of their calling; that they will always keep in mind Israel's eternal mission and its relationship to God, as indicated by God's special guidance of their destinies and by His commandments, and that they will remember these things at all times.

The offerings mentioned here are eloquent symbolic expressions of these relationships, and of the attitudes and resolves that they are meant to engender within the nation. Thus they serve to reinforce the provision made by the appointment of Joshua for the continuation of God's work upon the people that Moses had begun. That is also why the description of these offerings logically follows the account of Joshua's appointment. It can be said that at the time of his departure Moses was to hand over to Joshua and also to the communal offerings, as it were, the work of God which until then had been entrusted to his own care.

The chapters that deal with the communal offerings represent, in the true sense, the conclusion of the actual code of laws. ... These offerings are discussed only in the "Book of Wanderings through the Wilderness," indeed only at the end of that book, because it required the experiences of forty years in the wilderness to make us aware of ourselves as a nation, and to make us feel the need for constant reminders of our relationship to God and of the attitudes and resolves on our part that this relationship demands of us.

ascent offering that is made on Mount Sinai, as an expression of compliance, for *God*, a fire offering;   7. and its libation, the quarter of a *hin* for the one sheep, in the Sanctuary, to pour out a libation of strong wine before *God*;   8. and the second sheep you shall offer between the two evenings, like the homage offering of the morning and its libation shall you offer to *God* as a fire offering to express compliance. 9. And on the Sabbath day two yearling sheep without blemish and two tenths of fine flour as a homage offering, mixed with oil, and its libation.   10. The ascent offering of the Sabbath on its Sabbath, over and above the continual ascent offering and its libation.   11. And at the beginnings of your months you shall bring near to *God* an ascent offering: two young bulls and one ram, seven yearling sheep without blemish. 12. Three tenths of fine flour as a homage offering, mixed with oil, for each bull; two tenths of fine flour as a homage offering mixed with oil for the one ram,   13. and one tenth of fine flour each as a homage offering, mixed with oil, for each sheep; an ascent offering as an expression of compliance, to *God*, as a fire offering. 14. And their libations: half a *hin* for each bull, one third of a *hin* for the ram and one quarter of a *hin* for each sheep, [of] wine. This [is] the ascent offering of the New Moon on its New Moon for the months of the year.   15. And one he-goat, as an offering that clears [him who brings it] of sin, to *God,* over and above the continual ascent offering shall it be made, and its libation. 16. And in the first month, on the fourteenth day of the month, is a Pesaḥ dedicated to *God.*   17. And on the fifteenth day of that month is a festival: matzoth shall be eaten for seven days.

הֵעָשָׂיָה בְּהַר סִינַי לְרֵיחַ נִיחֹחַ אִשֶּׁה לַיהֹוָה: ז וְנִסְכּוֹ רְבִיעִת הַהִין לַכֶּבֶשׂ הָאֶחָד בַּקֹּדֶשׁ הַסֵּךְ נֶסֶךְ שֵׁכָר לַיהֹוָה: ח וְאֵת הַכֶּבֶשׂ הַשֵּׁנִי תַּעֲשֶׂה בֵּין הָעַרְבָּיִם כְּמִנְחַת הַבֹּקֶר וּכְנִסְכּוֹ תַּעֲשֶׂה אִשֵּׁה רֵיחַ נִיחֹחַ לַיהֹוָה: פ ט וּבְיוֹם הַשַּׁבָּת שְׁנֵי־כְבָשִׂים בְּנֵי־שָׁנָה תְּמִימִם וּשְׁנֵי עֶשְׂרֹנִים סֹלֶת מִנְחָה בְּלוּלָה בַשֶּׁמֶן וְנִסְכּוֹ: י עֹלַת שַׁבַּת בְּשַׁבַּתּוֹ עַל־עֹלַת הַתָּמִיד וְנִסְכָּהּ: פ יא וּבְרָאשֵׁי חָדְשֵׁיכֶם תַּקְרִיבוּ עֹלָה לַיהֹוָה פָּרִים בְּנֵי־בָקָר שְׁנַיִם וְאַיִל אֶחָד כְּבָשִׂים בְּנֵי־שָׁנָה שִׁבְעָה תְּמִימִם: יב וּשְׁלֹשָׁה עֶשְׂרֹנִים סֹלֶת מִנְחָה בְּלוּלָה בַשֶּׁמֶן לַפָּר הָאֶחָד וּשְׁנֵי עֶשְׂרֹנִים סֹלֶת מִנְחָה בְּלוּלָה בַשֶּׁמֶן לָאַיִל הָאֶחָד: יג וְעִשָּׂרֹן עִשָּׂרוֹן סֹלֶת מִנְחָה בְּלוּלָה בַשֶּׁמֶן לַכֶּבֶשׂ הָאֶחָד עֹלָה רֵיחַ נִיחֹחַ אִשֶּׁה לַיהֹוָה: יד וְנִסְכֵּיהֶם חֲצִי הַהִין יִהְיֶה לַפָּר וּשְׁלִישִׁת הַהִין לָאַיִל וּרְבִיעִת הַהִין לַכֶּבֶשׂ יָיִן זֹאת עֹלַת חֹדֶשׁ בְּחָדְשׁוֹ לְחָדְשֵׁי הַשָּׁנָה: טו וּשְׂעִיר עִזִּים אֶחָד לְחַטָּאת לַיהֹוָה עַל־עֹלַת הַתָּמִיד יֵעָשֶׂה וְנִסְכּוֹ: פ ששי טז וּבַחֹדֶשׁ הָרִאשׁוֹן בְּאַרְבָּעָה עָשָׂר יוֹם לַחֹדֶשׁ פֶּסַח לַיהֹוָה: יז וּבַחֲמִשָּׁה עָשָׂר יוֹם לַחֹדֶשׁ הַזֶּה חָג שִׁבְעַת יָמִים מַצּוֹת

---

6. We have already noted in connection with Exodus 27:1–8⁹ that in the Book of Ezekiel [43:15] the altar is called הַרְאֵל, ''the mountain of God.'' In view of this fact, and in light of Psalm 68:18—ד' בָּם סִינַי בַּקֹּדֶשׁ [''my Lord is now among them, Sinai in the Sanctuary''] we have

stated our assumption that in the present verse the term הַר סִינַי [''Mount Sinai''] refers to the altar. The altar in the Sanctuary, with its fire, represents Mount Sinai with the ''consuming fire'' on its summit. . . . Thus the *tamid* [continual] offering symbolizes the everlasting daily renewal of the vow נַעֲשֶׂה וְנִשְׁמַע [''we shall do and we shall hear''], with which the nation responded to the revelation of the Law on Mount Sinai and first entered into the covenant of the Law. . . .

⁹*Note to the English translation*: This note is not included in this excerpted edition. [G.H.]

18. On the first day is a convocation to the Sanctuary; you must not do any service work.   19. And you shall bring near to *God* a fire offering as an ascent offering: two young bulls, one ram and seven yearling sheep; without blemish shall they be to you. 20. And their homage offering: fine flour mixed with oil; you shall make three tenths for the ram.   21. You shall make one tenth for each sheep; likewise for [all] the seven sheep.   22. And one buck as an offering that clears [him who brings it] of sin, to effect atonement for you.   23. Apart from the ascent offering of the morning, which is for a continual ascent offering, shall you make these.   24. Like these you shall make daily, for seven days, an offering to *God* as a fire offering to express compliance; it shall be made over and above the continual ascent offering and its libation. 25. On the seventh day there shall be for you a convocation to the Sanctuary; you must not do any service work.   26. And on the day of first fruits, when you bring near to *God* a new homage offering, on your Festival of Weeks, there shall be for you a convocation to the Sanctuary; you must not do any service work.   27. And you shall bring near to *God*, as an ascent offering to express compliance, two young bulls, one ram, seven yearling sheep.   28. And their homage offering: fine flour mixed with oil, three tenths for each bull; two tenths for the one ram.   29. One tenth each for every sheep; likewise for [all] the seven sheep. 30. One buck of the goat species, to effect atonement for you.   31. Apart from the continual ascent offering and its homage offering shall you make them—without blemish shall they be to you—and their libations.

XXIX   1. And in the seventh month, on the first of the month, there shall be for you a convocation to the Sanctuary; you must not do any service work. It shall be to you a day of impressive sound.   2. And you shall make as an ascent offering to *God*, as an expression of compliance: one young bull; one ram; yearling sheep, seven, without blemish.   3. And their homage offering: fine flour mixed with oil, three tenths for the bull, two tenths for the ram   4. and one

יֹאכֵל: יח בַּיּוֹם הָרִאשׁוֹן מִקְרָא־קֹדֶשׁ כָּל־מְלֶאכֶת עֲבֹדָה לֹא תַעֲשׂוּ: יט וְהִקְרַבְתֶּם אִשֶּׁה עֹלָה לַיהֹוָה פָּרִים בְּנֵי־בָקָר שְׁנַיִם וְאַיִל אֶחָד וְשִׁבְעָה כְבָשִׂים בְּנֵי שָׁנָה תְּמִימִם יִהְיוּ לָכֶם: כ וּמִנְחָתָם סֹלֶת בְּלוּלָה בַשָּׁמֶן שְׁלֹשָׁה עֶשְׂרֹנִים לַפָּר וּשְׁנֵי עֶשְׂרֹנִים לָאַיִל תַּעֲשׂוּ: כא עִשָּׂרוֹן עִשָּׂרוֹן תַּעֲשֶׂה לַכֶּבֶשׂ הָאֶחָד לְשִׁבְעַת הַכְּבָשִׂים: כב וּשְׂעִיר חַטָּאת אֶחָד לְכַפֵּר עֲלֵיכֶם: כג מִלְּבַד עֹלַת הַבֹּקֶר אֲשֶׁר לְעֹלַת הַתָּמִיד תַּעֲשׂוּ אֶת־אֵלֶּה: כד כָּאֵלֶּה תַּעֲשׂוּ לַיּוֹם שִׁבְעַת יָמִים לֶחֶם אִשֵּׁה רֵיחַ־נִיחֹחַ לַיהֹוָה עַל־עוֹלַת הַתָּמִיד יֵעָשֶׂה וְנִסְכּוֹ: כה וּבַיּוֹם הַשְּׁבִיעִי מִקְרָא־קֹדֶשׁ יִהְיֶה לָכֶם כָּל־מְלֶאכֶת עֲבֹדָה לֹא תַעֲשׂוּ: פ כו וּבְיוֹם הַבִּכּוּרִים בְּהַקְרִיבְכֶם מִנְחָה חֲדָשָׁה לַיהֹוָה בְּשָׁבֻעֹתֵיכֶם מִקְרָא־קֹדֶשׁ יִהְיֶה לָכֶם כָּל־מְלֶאכֶת עֲבֹדָה לֹא תַעֲשׂוּ: כז וְהִקְרַבְתֶּם עוֹלָה לְרֵיחַ נִיחֹחַ לַיהֹוָה פָּרִים בְּנֵי־בָקָר שְׁנַיִם אַיִל אֶחָד שִׁבְעָה כְבָשִׂים בְּנֵי שָׁנָה: כח וּמִנְחָתָם סֹלֶת בְּלוּלָה בַשֶּׁמֶן שְׁלֹשָׁה עֶשְׂרֹנִים לַפָּר הָאֶחָד שְׁנֵי עֶשְׂרֹנִים לָאַיִל הָאֶחָד: כט עִשָּׂרוֹן עִשָּׂרוֹן לַכֶּבֶשׂ הָאֶחָד לְשִׁבְעַת הַכְּבָשִׂים: ל שְׂעִיר עִזִּים אֶחָד לְכַפֵּר עֲלֵיכֶם: לא מִלְּבַד עֹלַת הַתָּמִיד וּמִנְחָתוֹ תַּעֲשׂוּ תְּמִימִם יִהְיוּ־לָכֶם וְנִסְכֵּיהֶם: פ כט א וּבַחֹדֶשׁ הַשְּׁבִיעִי בְּאֶחָד לַחֹדֶשׁ מִקְרָא־קֹדֶשׁ יִהְיֶה לָכֶם כָּל־מְלֶאכֶת עֲבֹדָה לֹא תַעֲשׂוּ יוֹם תְּרוּעָה יִהְיֶה לָכֶם: ב וַעֲשִׂיתֶם עֹלָה לְרֵיחַ נִיחֹחַ לַיהֹוָה פַּר בֶּן־בָּקָר אֶחָד אַיִל אֶחָד כְּבָשִׂים בְּנֵי־שָׁנָה שִׁבְעָה תְּמִימִם: ג וּמִנְחָתָם סֹלֶת בְּלוּלָה בַשֶּׁמֶן שְׁלֹשָׁה עֶשְׂרֹנִים לַפָּר שְׁנֵי עֶשְׂרֹנִים לָאָיִל: ד וְעִשָּׂרוֹן

tenth for each sheep; likewise for [all] the
seven sheep. 5. One buck of the goat
species as an offering that clears [him who
brings it] of sin, to effect atonement for
you. 6. Apart from the New Moon ascent
offering and its homage offering and the
continual ascent offering and its homage
offering, and their libations according to
their regulation, as an expression of compliance, to *God*, a fire offering. 7. And on
the tenth [day] of that seventh month there
shall be for you a convocation to the Sanctuary, and you shall let your souls starve;
you must do no manner of work. 8. And
you shall bring to *God* as an ascent offering,
to express compliance: one young bull, one
ram, seven yearling sheep, without blemish
shall they be to you. 9. And their homage
offering: fine flour mixed with oil, three
tenths for the bull, two tenths for the one
ram. 10. One tenth each for every sheep;
likewise for [all] the seven sheep. 11. One
buck of the goat species as an offering that
clears [him who brings it] of sin, apart
from the sin offering of the atonements, the
continual ascent offering and its homage
offering, and their libations. 12. And on the
fifteenth day of the seventh month there
shall be for you a convocation to the Sanctuary; you must not do any service work,
and you shall celebrate a festival to *God* for
seven days. 13. And you shall bring near
an ascent offering, a fire offering, to express
compliance, to *God*: thirteen young bulls,
two rams, fourteen yearling sheep; they
shall be without blemish. 14. And their
homage offering: fine flour mixed with oil,
three tenths for each bull of the thirteen
bulls, two tenths for each ram of the two
rams, 15. and one tenth each for every
sheep of the fourteen sheep. 16. And one
buck of the goat species as an offering that
clears [him who brings it] of sin; apart from
the continual ascent offering, its homage
offering and its libation. 17. And on the
second day: twelve young bulls, two rams,
fourteen yearling sheep without blemish.
18. And their homage offering and their
libations for the bulls, for the rams and for
the sheep, according to their number, as
prescribed. 19. And one buck of the goat
species as an offering that clears [him who
brings it] of sin, apart from the continual

אֶחָד לַכֶּבֶשׂ הָאֶחָד לְשִׁבְעַת הַכְּבָשִׂים׃
ה וּשְׂעִיר־עִזִּים אֶחָד חַטָּאת לְכַפֵּר עֲלֵיכֶם׃
ו מִלְּבַד עֹלַת הַחֹדֶשׁ וּמִנְחָתָהּ וְעֹלַת הַתָּמִיד
וּמִנְחָתָהּ וְנִסְכֵּיהֶם כְּמִשְׁפָּטָם לְרֵיחַ נִיחֹחַ אִשֶּׁה
לַיהוָה׃ ס ז וּבֶעָשׂוֹר לַחֹדֶשׁ הַשְּׁבִיעִי הַזֶּה
מִקְרָא־קֹדֶשׁ יִהְיֶה לָכֶם וְעִנִּיתֶם אֶת־נַפְשֹׁתֵיכֶם
כָּל־מְלָאכָה לֹא תַעֲשׂוּ׃ ח וְהִקְרַבְתֶּם עֹלָה
לַיהוָה רֵיחַ נִיחֹחַ פַּר בֶּן־בָּקָר אֶחָד אַיִל אֶחָד
כְּבָשִׂים בְּנֵי־שָׁנָה שִׁבְעָה תְּמִימִם יִהְיוּ לָכֶם׃
ט וּמִנְחָתָם סֹלֶת בְּלוּלָה בַשָּׁמֶן שְׁלֹשָׁה
עֶשְׂרֹנִים לַפָּר שְׁנֵי עֶשְׂרֹנִים לָאַיִל הָאֶחָד׃
י עִשָּׂרוֹן עִשָּׂרוֹן לַכֶּבֶשׂ הָאֶחָד לְשִׁבְעַת
הַכְּבָשִׂים׃ יא שְׂעִיר־עִזִּים אֶחָד חַטָּאת מִלְּבַד
חַטַּאת הַכִּפֻּרִים וְעֹלַת הַתָּמִיד וּמִנְחָתָהּ
וְנִסְכֵּיהֶם׃ ס שביעי יב וּבַחֲמִשָּׁה עָשָׂר יוֹם
לַחֹדֶשׁ הַשְּׁבִיעִי מִקְרָא־קֹדֶשׁ יִהְיֶה לָכֶם כָּל־
מְלֶאכֶת עֲבֹדָה לֹא תַעֲשׂוּ וְחַגֹּתֶם חַג לַיהוָה
שִׁבְעַת יָמִים׃ יג וְהִקְרַבְתֶּם עֹלָה אִשֵּׁה רֵיחַ
נִיחֹחַ לַיהוָה פָּרִים בְּנֵי־בָקָר שְׁלֹשָׁה עָשָׂר אֵילִם
שְׁנָיִם כְּבָשִׂים בְּנֵי־שָׁנָה אַרְבָּעָה עָשָׂר תְּמִימִם
יִהְיוּ׃ יד וּמִנְחָתָם סֹלֶת בְּלוּלָה בַשָּׁמֶן שְׁלֹשָׁה
עֶשְׂרֹנִים לַפָּר הָאֶחָד לִשְׁלֹשָׁה עָשָׂר פָּרִים שְׁנֵי
עֶשְׂרֹנִים לָאַיִל הָאֶחָד לִשְׁנֵי הָאֵילִם׃ טו וְעִשָּׂרוֹן
(נקוד על ו בתרא) עִשָּׂרוֹן לַכֶּבֶשׂ הָאֶחָד לְאַרְבָּעָה
עָשָׂר כְּבָשִׂים׃ טז וּשְׂעִיר־עִזִּים אֶחָד חַטָּאת
מִלְּבַד עֹלַת הַתָּמִיד מִנְחָתָהּ וְנִסְכָּהּ׃ ס יז וּבַיּוֹם
הַשֵּׁנִי פָּרִים בְּנֵי־בָקָר שְׁנֵים עָשָׂר אֵילִם שְׁנָיִם
כְּבָשִׂים בְּנֵי־שָׁנָה אַרְבָּעָה עָשָׂר תְּמִימִם׃
יח וּמִנְחָתָם וְנִסְכֵּיהֶם לַפָּרִים לָאֵילִם וְלַכְּבָשִׂים
בְּמִסְפָּרָם כַּמִּשְׁפָּט׃ יט וּשְׂעִיר־עִזִּים אֶחָד
חַטָּאת מִלְּבַד עֹלַת הַתָּמִיד וּמִנְחָתָהּ וְנִסְכֵּיהֶם׃

ascent offering and its homage offering and their libations. 20. And on the third day: eleven bulls, two rams, fourteen yearling sheep without blemish.   21. And their homage offering and their libations for the bulls, for the rams and for the sheep, according to their number, as prescribed. 22. And one buck to clear [him who offers it] of sin, apart from the continual ascent offering and its homage offering and its libation.   23. And on the fourth day: ten bulls, two rams, fourteen yearling sheep without blemish,   24. their homage offering and their libations for the bulls, for the rams and for the sheep, according to their number, as prescribed.   25. And one buck of the goat species as an offering that clears [him who brings it] of sin, apart from the continual ascent offering, its homage offering and its libation.   26. And on the fifth day: nine bulls, two rams, fourteen yearling sheep without blemish. 27. And their homage offering and their libations for the bulls, for the rams and for the sheep, according to their number, as prescribed 28. And one buck to clear [him who offers it] of sin, apart from the continual ascent offering, its homage offering and its libation.   29. And on the sixth day: eight bulls, two rams, fourteen yearling sheep without blemish. 30. And their homage offering and their libations for the bulls, for the rams and for the sheep, according to their number, as prescribed.   31. And one buck to clear [him who offers it] of sin, apart from the continual ascent offering, its homage offering and its libations. 32. And on the seventh day: seven bulls, two rams, fourteen yearling sheep without blemish.   33. And their homage offering and their libations for the bulls, for the rams and for the sheep, according to their numbers, as prescribed regarding them. 34. And one buck to clear [him who offers it] of sin, apart from the continual ascent offering, its homage offering and its libation.   35. On the eighth day there shall be for you a festival of abiding; you must not do any service work, 36. and you shall bring near an ascent offering, a fire offering to express compliance, to *God*: one bull, one ram, seven yearling sheep without blemish. 37. Their homage offering and

כ וּבַיּוֹם הַשְּׁלִישִׁי פָּרִים עַשְׁתֵּי־עָשָׂר אֵילִם שְׁנָיִם כְּבָשִׂים בְּנֵי־שָׁנָה אַרְבָּעָה עָשָׂר תְּמִימִם: כא וּמִנְחָתָם וְנִסְכֵּיהֶם לַפָּרִים לָאֵילִם וְלַכְּבָשִׂים בְּמִסְפָּרָם כַּמִּשְׁפָּט: כב וּשְׂעִיר חַטָּאת אֶחָד מִלְּבַד עֹלַת הַתָּמִיד וּמִנְחָתָהּ וְנִסְכָּהּ: ס

כג וּבַיּוֹם הָרְבִיעִי פָּרִים עֲשָׂרָה אֵילִם שְׁנָיִם כְּבָשִׂים בְּנֵי־שָׁנָה אַרְבָּעָה עָשָׂר תְּמִימִם: כד מִנְחָתָם וְנִסְכֵּיהֶם לַפָּרִים לָאֵילִם וְלַכְּבָשִׂים בְּמִסְפָּרָם כַּמִּשְׁפָּט: כה וּשְׂעִיר־עִזִּים אֶחָד חַטָּאת מִלְּבַד עֹלַת הַתָּמִיד מִנְחָתָהּ וְנִסְכָּהּ: ס

כו וּבַיּוֹם הַחֲמִישִׁי פָּרִים תִּשְׁעָה אֵילִם שְׁנָיִם כְּבָשִׂים בְּנֵי־שָׁנָה אַרְבָּעָה עָשָׂר תְּמִימִם: כז וּמִנְחָתָם וְנִסְכֵּיהֶם לַפָּרִים לָאֵילִם וְלַכְּבָשִׂים בְּמִסְפָּרָם כַּמִּשְׁפָּט: כח וּשְׂעִיר חַטָּאת אֶחָד מִלְּבַד עֹלַת הַתָּמִיד וּמִנְחָתָהּ וְנִסְכָּהּ: ס

כט וּבַיּוֹם הַשִּׁשִּׁי פָּרִים שְׁמֹנָה אֵילִם שְׁנָיִם כְּבָשִׂים בְּנֵי־שָׁנָה אַרְבָּעָה עָשָׂר תְּמִימִם: ל וּמִנְחָתָם וְנִסְכֵּיהֶם לַפָּרִים לָאֵילִם וְלַכְּבָשִׂים בְּמִסְפָּרָם כַּמִּשְׁפָּט: לא וּשְׂעִיר חַטָּאת אֶחָד מִלְּבַד עֹלַת הַתָּמִיד מִנְחָתָהּ וּנְסָכֶיהָ: ס

לב וּבַיּוֹם הַשְּׁבִיעִי פָּרִים שִׁבְעָה אֵילִם שְׁנָיִם כְּבָשִׂים בְּנֵי־שָׁנָה אַרְבָּעָה עָשָׂר תְּמִימִם: לג וּמִנְחָתָם וְנִסְכֵּהֶם לַפָּרִים לָאֵילִם וְלַכְּבָשִׂים בְּמִסְפָּרָם כְּמִשְׁפָּטָם: לד וּשְׂעִיר חַטָּאת אֶחָד מִלְּבַד עֹלַת הַתָּמִיד מִנְחָתָהּ וְנִסְכָּהּ: ס מפטיר

לה בַּיּוֹם הַשְּׁמִינִי עֲצֶרֶת תִּהְיֶה לָכֶם כָּל־מְלֶאכֶת עֲבֹדָה לֹא תַעֲשׂוּ: לו וְהִקְרַבְתֶּם עֹלָה אִשֵּׁה רֵיחַ נִיחֹחַ לַיהֹוָה פַּר אֶחָד אַיִל אֶחָד כְּבָשִׂים בְּנֵי־שָׁנָה שִׁבְעָה תְּמִימִם: לז מִנְחָתָם

their libations for the bull, for the ram and for the sheep, according to their number, as prescribed. 38. And one buck that clears [him who offers it] of sin, apart from the continual ascent offering and its homage offering and its libation. 39. These you shall make to *God* at your seasons of appointed meeting, apart from your vows and your dedications, your ascent offerings and your homage offerings, your libations and your peace offerings.

XXX   1. Moshe explained to the sons of Yisrael all that which *God* had commanded Moshe.

וְנִסְכֵּיהֶם לַפָּר לָאַיִל וְלַכְּבָשִׂים בְּמִסְפָּרָם כַּמִּשְׁפָּט: לח וּשְׂעִיר חַטָּאת אֶחָד מִלְּבַד עֹלַת הַתָּמִיד וּמִנְחָתָהּ וְנִסְכָּהּ: לט אֵלֶּה תַּעֲשׂוּ לַיהוָה בְּמוֹעֲדֵיכֶם לְבַד מִנִּדְרֵיכֶם וְנִדְבֹתֵיכֶם לְעֹלֹתֵיכֶם וּלְמִנְחֹתֵיכֶם וּלְנִסְכֵּיכֶם וּלְשַׁלְמֵיכֶם: ל א וַיֹּאמֶר מֹשֶׁה אֶל־בְּנֵי יִשְׂרָאֵל כְּכֹל אֲשֶׁר־צִוָּה יְהוָה אֶת־מֹשֶׁה: פ

CHAPTER XXX

1. *Moshe explained.* The regulations pertaining to the festival offerings comprise the final chapter of the actual Law. What follows now is only the chapter pertaining to vows. It contains the sanctions and the limitations relating to acts that were not commanded or forbidden to us by God but that we ourselves have resolved to perform, or to abstain from performing. The principles set down in this chapter form the basis for those legal provisions and established customs, תַּקָּנוֹת and מִנְהָגִים, which emanate from the arrangements made by the community, and from the community's practical life, and which serve to regulate and ensure the realization of the laws of God according to the special requirements of local conditions.

We therefore believe that the words, "Moshe explained to the sons of Yisrael all that which *God* had commanded Moshe," form a concluding sentence referring to all the laws that have gone before. If we are not mistaken, the words וַיֹּאמֶר וגו׳ כְּכֹל וגו׳ ["(Moshe) explained . . . all that . . ."] are not used anywhere else in Scripture to report that Moses had communicated to the people a specific law he had received. What is characteristic here is the expression וַיֹּאמֶר which, as a rule, is used in Scripture to denote the explanation of something already known, but particularly the expression כְּכֹל, which indicates that the communication goes beyond the mere promulgation of a law in that it also includes the "how," the manner in which that law should be interpreted. Thus [the form כ] is used else-

where in Scripture only for reporting *how* a law was observed in practice; cf. וַיַּעֲשׂוּ בְּנֵי יִשְׂרָאֵל כְּכֹל אֲשֶׁר צִוָּה ד׳ אֶת מֹשֶׁה כֵּן עָשׂוּ ["The sons of Yisrael did so; according to all that *God* had commanded Moshe, thus did they do"] (Numbers 1:54), and many other Scriptural passages, where the intention is to say that the people did not merely observe a particular command in general terms but that they carried it out in all its minute details, in the manner in which it was meant to be carried out.

Hence, the literal rendering of the present verse would be: "Moses explained to the sons of Israel the 'how' of all that which God had commanded Moses." Placed at the conclusion of all the laws given up to this point, these words mean to tell us that the people were not merely told the terse sentences in which the law is set down here in writing, but that Moses explained to them orally each law in terms of the modality of its contents. We believe there is only one other instance in Scripture where the expression כְּכֹל is used in connection with the communication of a law (in Deuteronomy 1:3): וַיְהִי וגו׳ דִּבֶּר מֹשֶׁה אֶל בְּנֵי יִשְׂרָאֵל כְּכֹל אֲשֶׁר צִוָּה ד׳ אֹתוֹ אֲלֵיהֶם ["It came to pass . . . that Moshe uttered it again to the sons of Yisrael, how *God* had commanded him everything for them"]. There, too, the expression clearly refers to the entire Law that Moses reiterated (דבר) before his death, not merely in terse sentences but in terms of the entire "how" pertaining to its contents. It had already been communicated to the people previously in terse form and detail. Now both modes of communication were reiterated.

The Haftarah for this Sidra may be found on page 902.

מטות

MATTOTH

2. And Moshe spoke to the heads of the tribes of the sons of Yisrael [saying]: "This is the word that *God* has commanded: 3. If a man vows a vow to *God*, or swears an oath to bind a bond for his will, he must not permit his word to remain unfulfilled; he shall do whatever has come forth from his mouth.   4. But [as for] a woman, if she vows a vow to *God* and binds [herself] a bond in her father's house in her youth,   5. and her father hears her vow and her bond which she bound for her will, and her father remains silent, then all her vows shall stand, and every bond that she has bound for her will shall stand. 6. But if her father obstructed her on the day he heard it, none of her vows and her bonds that she bound for her will shall stand. *God* will forgive her, because her father has obstructed her.   7. And if she belongs in any way to a man and has [taken] upon herself a vow or an utterance of her lips that she has bound for her will, 8. and her man heard it and remained silent for her on the day he heard it, then her vows shall stand, and her bonds she has

ב וַיְדַבֵּר מֹשֶׁה אֶל־רָאשֵׁי הַמַּטּוֹת לִבְנֵי יִשְׂרָאֵל לֵאמֹר זֶה הַדָּבָר אֲשֶׁר צִוָּה יְהֹוָה: ג אִישׁ כִּי־יִדֹּר נֶדֶר לַיהֹוָה אוֹ־הִשָּׁבַע שְׁבֻעָה לֶאְסֹר אִסָּר עַל־נַפְשׁוֹ לֹא יַחֵל דְּבָרוֹ כְּכָל־הַיֹּצֵא מִפִּיו יַעֲשֶׂה: ד וְאִשָּׁה כִּי־תִדֹּר נֶדֶר לַיהֹוָה וְאָסְרָה אִסָּר בְּבֵית אָבִיהָ בִּנְעֻרֶיהָ: ה וְשָׁמַע אָבִיהָ אֶת־נִדְרָהּ וֶאֱסָרָהּ אֲשֶׁר אָסְרָה עַל־נַפְשָׁהּ וְהֶחֱרִישׁ לָהּ אָבִיהָ וְקָמוּ כָּל־נְדָרֶיהָ וְכָל־אִסָּר אֲשֶׁר־אָסְרָה עַל־נַפְשָׁהּ יָקוּם: ו וְאִם־הֵנִיא אָבִיהָ אֹתָהּ בְּיוֹם שָׁמְעוֹ כָּל־נְדָרֶיהָ וֶאֱסָרֶיהָ אֲשֶׁר־אָסְרָה עַל־נַפְשָׁהּ לֹא יָקוּם וַיהֹוָה יִסְלַח־לָהּ כִּי־הֵנִיא אָבִיהָ אֹתָהּ: ז וְאִם־הָיוֹ תִהְיֶה לְאִישׁ וּנְדָרֶיהָ עָלֶיהָ אוֹ מִבְטָא שְׂפָתֶיהָ אֲשֶׁר אָסְרָה עַל־נַפְשָׁהּ: ח וְשָׁמַע אִישָׁהּ בְּיוֹם שָׁמְעוֹ וְהֶחֱרִישׁ לָהּ וְקָמוּ נְדָרֶיהָ וֶאֱסָרֶהָ אֲשֶׁר־אָסְרָה

2. *And Moshe spoke.* Here, however, we have a new pronouncement. It opens the sphere of what we have called "voluntary" [or self-imposed] legislation. The laws concerning these self-imposed obligations are given here in the form of an appendix, as it were, to the actual laws whose observance in both theory and practice forms the basis for the sanction conferred upon obligations voluntarily assumed. The intent of the regulations that now follow is to make it possible for individuals, for communities and for the entire nation to establish for themselves permanent norms that will ensure the faithful observance of the actual Law. So it is not without cause that this chapter in the Law is addressed particularly to the princes, who, significantly, are described here as "heads of tribes." We have already noted in Chapter 1 how the word מַטֶּה [lit., "staff" or "stalk"] defines each tribe as a "branch" of the larger whole, with each branch working, through its own unique characteristics, to carry out the mission shared in common by the entire nation. It was the task of the רָאשֵׁי הַמַּטּוֹת [heads of the tribes] to guide and to preserve the customs and usages that arose from the individual characteristics of each "branch," and to see to it that the laws, the activities and the aspirations they all shared in common should persevere in a manner conducive to the fulfillment of the mission assigned to the nation as a whole. The one indispensable means for achieving this end, of bringing about the development of the nation as a whole, and of every form of communal life, in this direction, is the acknowledgment that all the self-imposed obligations to which the laws that follow refer are endowed with binding force; cf. Verse 3: "He must not permit his word to remain unfulfilled." Such vows must be regarded as inviolable. At the same time, the heads of the tribes are entrusted with the task, if need be, of annulling such vows in an effective manner. These individuals function as family counselors and spiritual advisors, coming from among the people themselves. It is for this reason, too, that the laws pertaining to vows are addressed, in the first place, to the רָאשֵׁי הַמַּטּוֹת.

• • •

עַל־נַפְשָׁהּ יָקֻמוּ׃ ט וְאִם בְּיוֹם שְׁמֹעַ אִישָׁהּ
יָנִיא אוֹתָהּ וְהֵפֵר אֶת־נִדְרָהּ אֲשֶׁר עָלֶיהָ וְאֵת
מִבְטָא שְׂפָתֶיהָ אֲשֶׁר אָסְרָה עַל־נַפְשָׁהּ וַיהוָה
יִסְלַח־לָהּ׃ י וְנֵדֶר אַלְמָנָה וּגְרוּשָׁה כֹּל אֲשֶׁר־
אָסְרָה עַל־נַפְשָׁהּ יָקוּם עָלֶיהָ׃ יא וְאִם־בֵּית
אִישָׁהּ נָדָרָה אוֹ־אָסְרָה אִסָּר עַל־נַפְשָׁהּ
בִּשְׁבֻעָה׃ יב וְשָׁמַע אִישָׁהּ וְהֶחֱרִשׁ לָהּ לֹא הֵנִיא
אֹתָהּ וְקָמוּ כָּל־נְדָרֶיהָ וְכָל־אִסָּר אֲשֶׁר־אָסְרָה
עַל־נַפְשָׁהּ יָקוּם׃ יג וְאִם־הָפֵר יָפֵר אֹתָם ׀
אִישָׁהּ בְּיוֹם שָׁמְעוֹ כָּל־מוֹצָא שְׂפָתֶיהָ לִנְדָרֶיהָ
וּלְאִסַּר נַפְשָׁהּ לֹא יָקוּם אִישָׁהּ הֲפֵרָם וַיהוָה
יִסְלַח־לָהּ׃ יד כָּל־נֵדֶר וְכָל־שְׁבֻעַת אִסָּר לְעַנֹּת
נָפֶשׁ אִישָׁהּ יְקִימֶנּוּ וְאִישָׁהּ יְפֵרֶנּוּ׃ טו וְאִם־
הַחֲרֵשׁ יַחֲרִישׁ לָהּ אִישָׁהּ מִיּוֹם אֶל־יוֹם וְהֵקִים
אֶת־כָּל־נְדָרֶיהָ אוֹ אֶת־כָּל־אֱסָרֶיהָ אֲשֶׁר עָלֶיהָ
הֵקִים אֹתָם כִּי־הֶחֱרִשׁ לָהּ בְּיוֹם שָׁמְעוֹ׃
טז וְאִם־הָפֵר יָפֵר אֹתָם אַחֲרֵי שָׁמְעוֹ וְנָשָׂא
אֶת־עֲוֺנָהּ׃ יז אֵלֶּה הַחֻקִּים אֲשֶׁר צִוָּה יְהוָה
אֶת־מֹשֶׁה בֵּין אִישׁ לְאִשְׁתּוֹ בֵּין־אָב לְבִתּוֹ
בִּנְעֻרֶיהָ בֵּית אָבִיהָ׃ פ שני לא א וַיְדַבֵּר יְהוָה
אֶל־מֹשֶׁה לֵּאמֹר׃ ב נְקֹם נִקְמַת בְּנֵי יִשְׂרָאֵל

bound for her will shall stand. 9. But if on the day that her man hears it, he obstructs her, he annuls her vow that she has [taken] upon herself and the utterance of her lips that she has bound for her will, and *God* will forgive her. 10. [As for] the vow of a widow or of a divorced woman—anything that she has bound for her will shall stand for her. 11. But if she made a vow in her husband's house, or has bound a bond for her will with an oath, 12. and her husband heard them and remained silent to her [and] did not obstruct her, then all her vows shall stand, and any bond that she has made for her will shall stand. 13. But if her husband annuls them on the day he hears them, then whatever proceeded from her lips regarding her vows and the binding of her will shall not stand. Her husband has annulled them and *God* will forgive her. 14. Every vow and every binding oath of self-denial, her husband can let it stand, and her husband can annul it. 15. But if her husband remains silent for her from one day to the next, then he has caused all her vows and all her bonds which she has [taken] upon herself to stand; he has caused them to stand because he remained silent for her on the day he heard it. 16. If he annuls them then, after he has heard them, he shall bear her iniquity." 17. These are the laws that *God* commanded Moshe, between a man and his wife, between a father and his daughter in her youth, in her father's house.

XXXI

1. *God* spoke to Moshe [saying]: 2. "Accomplish the vengeance, in order to raise the

CHAPTER XXXI

1. The text has already explained earlier (Numbers 25:16–17) that it would be necessary to break the power of Midian in order to safeguard the moral and spiritual integrity of the Jewish people, because the Midianites persisted in practicing their arts of seduction on Israel. Now the command is given to launch the war against the Midianites.

2. ***Accomplish the vengeance.*** Moses had been commanded to transmit to the people God's Law, which was founded on chastity and on loyalty to God. Now, before his death, Moses was bidden to strike a blow against the Midianites in order to safeguard these two basic pillars of his mission, to protect his people from the influences of immorality and idol worship. . . . The purpose of this war is not to take revenge upon the enemy or to overthrow him but to "raise the sons of Yisrael from the Midianites," to effect Israel's spiritual and moral liberation from the effects of Midian's intrigues.

sons of Yisrael from the Midianites; afterwards you shall be gathered to your
peoples." 3. And Moshe spoke to the
people [saying]: "Detach from your midst
men for the army, and let them be over
Midian to bring the retribution of *God* to
Midian. 4. One thousand from each
tribe, one thousand from each tribe, from all
the tribes of Yisrael shall you send to the
army." 5. And from among the thousands of Yisrael, one thousand from each
tribe were given over, twelve thousand
fitted out for the army. 6. And Moshe
sent them, one thousand from each tribe, to
the army, them and Phineḥas, son of
Eleazar the priest, to the army, with utensils
of the Sanctuary and trumpets of the *teruah*
in his hand. 7. They mounted a campaign against Midian, as *God* had commanded Moshe, and they slew all the males.
8. They slew the kings of Midian upon
their slain: Evi, Rekem, Tzur, Ḥur and
Reva, five kings of Midian; also Balaam, son
of Beor, did they slay with the sword.
9. The sons of Yisrael took captive the
women of Midian and their children, all
their livestock and all their flocks and all
their possessions did they take as booty.
10. All their cities in their dwelling places
and all their fortresses did they burn with
fire. 11. They took all the booty and all
that had been seized, of men and livestock,
12. and they brought to Moshe and to
Eleazar the priest and to the community of
the sons of Yisrael the prisoners, those that

מֵאֵת הַמִּדְיָנִים אַחַר תֵּאָסֵף אֶל־עַמֶּיךָ׃ ג וַיְדַבֵּר
מֹשֶׁה אֶל־הָעָם לֵאמֹר הֵחָלְצוּ מֵאִתְּכֶם אֲנָשִׁים
לַצָּבָא וְיִהְיוּ עַל־מִדְיָן לָתֵת נִקְמַת־יְהוָה בְּמִדְיָן׃
ד אֶלֶף לַמַּטֶּה אֶלֶף לַמַּטֶּה לְכֹל מַטּוֹת יִשְׂרָאֵל
תִּשְׁלְחוּ לַצָּבָא׃ ה וַיִּמָּסְרוּ מֵאַלְפֵי יִשְׂרָאֵל אֶלֶף
לַמַּטֶּה שְׁנֵים־עָשָׂר אֶלֶף חֲלוּצֵי צָבָא׃ ו וַיִּשְׁלַח
אֹתָם מֹשֶׁה אֶלֶף לַמַּטֶּה לַצָּבָא אֹתָם וְאֶת־
פִּינְחָס בֶּן־אֶלְעָזָר הַכֹּהֵן לַצָּבָא וּכְלֵי הַקֹּדֶשׁ
וַחֲצֹצְרוֹת הַתְּרוּעָה בְּיָדוֹ׃ ז וַיִּצְבְּאוּ עַל־מִדְיָן
כַּאֲשֶׁר צִוָּה יְהוָה אֶת־מֹשֶׁה וַיַּהַרְגוּ כָּל־זָכָר׃
ח וְאֶת־מַלְכֵי מִדְיָן הָרְגוּ עַל־חַלְלֵיהֶם אֶת־
אֱוִי וְאֶת־רֶקֶם וְאֶת־צוּר וְאֶת־חוּר וְאֶת־רֶבַע
חֲמֵשֶׁת מַלְכֵי מִדְיָן וְאֵת בִּלְעָם בֶּן־בְּעוֹר הָרְגוּ
בֶּחָרֶב׃ ט וַיִּשְׁבּוּ בְנֵי־יִשְׂרָאֵל אֶת־נְשֵׁי מִדְיָן
וְאֶת־טַפָּם וְאֵת כָּל־בְּהֶמְתָּם וְאֶת־כָּל־מִקְנֵהֶם
וְאֶת־כָּל־חֵילָם בָּזָזוּ׃ י וְאֵת כָּל־עָרֵיהֶם
בְּמוֹשְׁבֹתָם וְאֵת כָּל־טִירֹתָם שָׂרְפוּ בָּאֵשׁ׃
יא וַיִּקְחוּ אֶת־כָּל־הַשָּׁלָל וְאֵת כָּל־הַמַּלְקוֹחַ
בָּאָדָם וּבַבְּהֵמָה׃ יב וַיָּבִאוּ אֶל־מֹשֶׁה וְאֶל־
אֶלְעָזָר הַכֹּהֵן וְאֶל־עֲדַת בְּנֵי־יִשְׂרָאֵל אֶת־הַשְּׁבִי

3. ***And Moshe spoke to the people.*** אֶל הָעָם ["to the people"], not to the leaders, because the vindication of Israel's spiritual and moral integrity was to come from among the people themselves. The fact that this war was to be waged against Midian and not against Moab (which sought to weaken Israel physically but did not seek its moral and spiritual destruction) must have made the people doubly aware of the moral and spiritual motivation of this campaign. Israel's true enemy is not the one who seeks its physical destruction but the one who plots its moral and spiritual demise. . . . Any disturbance of Israel's moral and spiritual integrity tears the people away from God. That is why He Himself now sends them forth to work His retribution on Midian. By its policy of corrupting other nations, Midian has been guilty of the gravest international crime and has therefore lost its right to exist as a nation among other nations before God.

6. ***And Moshe sent them . . . and Phineḥas.*** In none of the accounts of earlier military campaigns—the wars against Siḥon, Og and the Emorites . . . is it so explicitly stressed as it is here that a priest was present, along with the Ark of the Law and the trumpets of the Sanctuary. Those other wars had been wars of self-defense or conquest, fought for material reasons. This campaign was different in that it was waged for the highest moral and spiritual purposes. It was therefore only fitting that a priest should be there, along with the Testimony of the Law and the trumpets of the Sanctuary with which to summon God's aid. . . .

had been seized, and the booty, to the camp, to the Moabite wastelands that are on the Yarden near Jericho. 13. And Moshe and Eleazar the priest and all the princes of the community went out to meet them outside the camp. 14. And Moshe was angry at the officers of the army, at the princes of the thousands and the princes of the hundreds who had returned from the army service of the war. 15. And Moshe said to them: "So you allowed all the females to live? 16. Lo! these are exactly the ones who, on Balaam's advice, were to cause the sons of Yisrael to act faithlessly against *God* in the matter of Peor, so that the plague broke out within the community of *God!* 17. And now kill every male among the children, and every female who has known a man for sexual intercourse; 18. all the children among the females who have not yet experienced sexual intercourse keep alive for yourselves. 19. You shall camp outside the camp for seven days. Everyone that has slain a person and everyone that has touched a slain person you must clear of sin for yourselves, on the third day and on the seventh day, you and your prisoners. 20. Every garment and every leather utensil and everything made out of goat's hair and every wooden utensil you must clear of sin for yourselves." 21. And Eleazar the priest said to the men of the army who had gone to the war: "This is a basic statute of the Teaching that *God* has commanded Moshe: 22. Only the gold and the silver, the copper and the iron, the tin and the lead, 23. everything that has entered [these materials] by fire you shall cause to go out [of them] by fire, and then it can become pure; however, it must clear itself of sin by the waters of separation; and everything that has not entered [it] by fire you shall cause to go out [of it] by water. 24. And you shall rinse your clothes on the seventh day and become pure; after that you may come into the camp." 25. And *God* said to Moshe: 26. "Take up the sum of the booty seized, of what was captured in human beings and in animals, you and Eleazar the priest and the heads of the fathers of the community. 27. And you shall divide the booty seized among those who took the war in hand, who went

וְאֶת־הַמַּלְק֣וֹחַ וְאֶת־הַשָּׁלָ֑ל אֶל־הַֽמַּחֲנֶ֖ה אֶל־
עַֽרְבֹ֣ת מוֹאָ֔ב אֲשֶׁ֖ר עַל־יַרְדֵּ֥ן יְרֵחֽוֹ׃ ס שלישי (שני
כשהן מחוברין) יג וַיֵּצְא֣וּ מֹשֶׁ֩ה וְאֶלְעָזָ֨ר הַכֹּהֵ֜ן וְכָל־
נְשִׂיאֵ֧י הָעֵדָ֛ה לִקְרָאתָ֖ם אֶל־מִח֥וּץ לַֽמַּחֲנֶֽה׃
יד וַיִּקְצֹ֣ף מֹשֶׁ֔ה עַ֖ל פְּקוּדֵ֣י הֶחָ֑יִל שָׂרֵ֤י הָֽאֲלָפִים֙
וְשָׂרֵ֣י הַמֵּא֔וֹת הַבָּאִ֖ים מִצְּבָ֥א הַמִּלְחָמָֽה׃
טו וַיֹּ֥אמֶר אֲלֵיהֶ֖ם מֹשֶׁ֑ה הַֽחִיִּיתֶ֖ם כָּל־נְקֵבָֽה׃
טז הֵ֣ן הֵ֜נָּה הָי֨וּ לִבְנֵ֤י יִשְׂרָאֵל֙ בִּדְבַ֣ר בִּלְעָ֔ם
לִמְסָר־מַ֥עַל בַּֽיהֹוָ֖ה עַל־דְּבַר־פְּע֑וֹר וַתְּהִ֥י
הַמַּגֵּפָ֖ה בַּֽעֲדַ֥ת יְהֹוָֽה׃ יז וְעַתָּ֕ה הִרְג֥וּ כָל־זָכָ֖ר
בַּטָּ֑ף וְכָל־אִשָּׁ֗ה יֹדַ֥עַת אִ֛ישׁ לְמִשְׁכַּ֥ב זָכָ֖ר הֲרֹֽגוּ׃
יח וְכֹל֙ הַטַּ֣ף בַּנָּשִׁ֔ים אֲשֶׁ֥ר לֹֽא־יָֽדְע֖וּ מִשְׁכַּ֣ב זָכָ֑ר
הַֽחֲי֖וּ לָכֶֽם׃ יט וְאַתֶּ֗ם חֲנ֛וּ מִח֥וּץ לַֽמַּחֲנֶ֖ה שִׁבְעַ֣ת
יָמִ֑ים כֹּל֩ הֹרֵ֨ג נֶ֜פֶשׁ וְכֹ֣ל ׀ נֹגֵ֣עַ בֶּֽחָלָ֗ל תִּֽתְחַטְּא֤וּ
בַּיּ֣וֹם הַשְּׁלִישִׁי֙ וּבַיּ֣וֹם הַשְּׁבִיעִ֔י אַתֶּ֖ם וּשְׁבִיכֶֽם׃
כ וְכָל־בֶּ֤גֶד וְכָל־כְּלִי־ע֨וֹר֙ וְכָל־מַֽעֲשֵׂ֣ה עִזִּ֔ים
וְכָל־כְּלִי־עֵ֖ץ תִּתְחַטָּֽאוּ׃ ס כא וַיֹּ֨אמֶר אֶלְעָזָ֤ר
הַכֹּהֵן֙ אֶל־אַנְשֵׁ֣י הַצָּבָ֔א הַבָּאִ֖ים לַמִּלְחָמָ֑ה זֹ֚את
חֻקַּ֣ת הַתּוֹרָ֔ה אֲשֶׁר־צִוָּ֥ה יְהֹוָ֖ה אֶת־מֹשֶֽׁה׃ כב אַ֣ךְ
אֶת־הַזָּהָ֥ב וְאֶת־הַכָּ֖סֶף אֶֽת־הַנְּחֹ֥שֶׁת אֶת־הַבַּרְזֶ֑ל
אֶֽת־הַבְּדִ֖יל וְאֶת־הָֽעֹפָֽרֶת׃ כג כָּל־דָּבָ֞ר אֲשֶׁר־
יָבֹ֣א בָאֵ֗שׁ תַּֽעֲבִ֤ירוּ בָאֵשׁ֙ וְטָהֵ֔ר אַ֕ךְ בְּמֵ֥י נִדָּ֖ה
יִתְחַטָּ֑א וְכֹ֨ל אֲשֶׁ֧ר לֹֽא־יָבֹ֛א בָּאֵ֖שׁ תַּֽעֲבִ֥ירוּ
בַמָּֽיִם׃ כד וְכִבַּסְתֶּ֧ם בִּגְדֵיכֶ֛ם בַּיּ֥וֹם הַשְּׁבִיעִ֖י
וּטְהַרְתֶּ֑ם וְאַחַ֖ר תָּבֹ֥אוּ אֶל־הַֽמַּחֲנֶֽה׃ ס רביעי
כה וַיֹּ֥אמֶר יְהֹוָ֖ה אֶל־מֹשֶׁ֥ה לֵּאמֹֽר׃ כו שָׂ֗א אֵ֣ת
רֹ֤אשׁ מַלְק֨וֹחַ֙ הַשְּׁבִ֔י בָּֽאָדָ֖ם וּבַבְּהֵמָ֑ה אַתָּה֙
וְאֶלְעָזָ֣ר הַכֹּהֵ֔ן וְרָאשֵׁ֖י אֲב֥וֹת הָֽעֵדָֽה׃ כז וְחָצִ֨יתָ֙
אֶת־הַמַּלְק֔וֹחַ בֵּ֚ין תֹּֽפְשֵׂ֣י הַמִּלְחָמָ֔ה הַיֹּֽצְאִ֖ים

forth into the army, and among the entire community.   28. And you shall levy a tribute for *God* from the men of war who went forth into the army, one out of five hundred from the men, from the cattle, from the donkeys and from the sheep. 29. Take from their half, and give to Eleazar the priest the uplifted donation of *God*.   30. And of the sons of Yisrael's half you shall take one taken out of fifty from the men, from the cattle, from the donkeys and from the sheep, from all the animals, and you shall give them to the Levites, the keepers of the charge of the Dwelling Place of *God*."   31. Moshe did and [so did] Eleazar the priest, as *God* had commanded Moshe.   32. The booty that had been seized, apart from that which the army people had plundered was: sheep: six hundred seventy-five thousand.   33. Cattle: seventy-two thousand.   34. Donkeys: sixty-one thousand.   35. Human souls: of the females who had not yet experienced sexual intercourse, all the souls: thirty-two thousand.   36. And the half, the portion of those who had gone forth into the army, the number of sheep [was] three hundred thirty-seven thousand five hundred.   37. Thus the tribute to *God* from the sheep [was] six hundred seventy-five.   38. And the cattle: thirty-six thousand, and out of these the tribute to *God* [was] seventy-two.   39. And donkeys: thirty thousand five hundred, and out of these the tribute to *God* [was] sixty-one. 40. Human souls: sixteen thousand, and out of these the tribute to *God* [was] thirty-two souls.   41. Moshe gave the tribute, the uplifted donation of *God*, to Eleazar the priest, as *God* had commanded Moshe.   42. And of the sons of Yisrael's half, which Moshe had divided off from the men who had gone into the army, 43. the community's half was, of sheep: three hundred thirty-seven thousand five hundred.   44. Cattle: thirty-six thousand. 45. Donkeys: thirty thousand five hundred. 46. Human souls: sixteen thousand. 47. And Moshe took from the sons of Yisrael's half, that which had been taken out, one out of every fifty, from the men and from the animals, and he gave it to the Levites, the keepers of the charge of

לַצָּבָ֖א וּבֵ֥ין כָּל־הָעֵדָֽה: כח וַהֲרֵמֹתָ֨ מֶ֜כֶס לַֽיהֹוָ֗ה מֵאֵ֞ת אַנְשֵׁ֤י הַמִּלְחָמָה֙ הַיֹּֽצְאִ֣ים לַצָּבָ֔א אֶחָ֣ד נֶ֔פֶשׁ מֵֽחֲמֵ֖שׁ הַמֵּא֑וֹת מִן־הָֽאָדָם֙ וּמִן־הַבָּקָ֔ר וּמִן־הַֽחֲמֹרִ֖ים וּמִן־הַצֹּֽאן: כט מִמַּֽחֲצִיתָ֖ם תִּקָּ֑חוּ וְנָֽתַתָּ֛ה לְאֶלְעָזָ֥ר הַכֹּהֵ֖ן תְּרוּמַ֥ת יְהֹוָֽה: ל וּמִמַּֽחֲצִ֨ת בְּנֵֽי־יִשְׂרָאֵ֜ל תִּקַּ֣ח ׀ אֶחָ֣ד ׀ אָחֻ֣ז מִן־הַֽחֲמִשִּׁ֗ים מִן־הָֽאָדָם֙ מִן־הַבָּקָ֤ר מִן־הַֽחֲמֹרִים֙ וּמִן־הַצֹּ֔אן מִכָּל־הַבְּהֵמָ֑ה וְנָֽתַתָּ֤ה אֹתָם֙ לַֽלְוִיִּ֔ם שֹֽׁמְרֵ֕י מִשְׁמֶ֖רֶת מִשְׁכַּ֥ן יְהֹוָֽה: לא וַיַּ֣עַשׂ מֹשֶׁ֔ה וְאֶלְעָזָ֖ר הַכֹּהֵ֑ן כַּֽאֲשֶׁ֛ר צִוָּ֥ה יְהֹוָ֖ה אֶת־מֹשֶֽׁה: לב וַיְהִי֙ הַמַּלְק֔וֹחַ יֶ֖תֶר הַבָּ֑ז אֲשֶׁ֥ר בָּֽזְז֖וּ עַ֣ם הַצָּבָ֑א צֹ֗אן שֵׁשׁ־מֵא֥וֹת אֶ֛לֶף וְשִׁבְעִ֥ים אֶ֖לֶף וַֽחֲמֵ֥שֶׁת אֲלָפִֽים: לג וּבָקָ֕ר שְׁנַ֥יִם וְשִׁבְעִ֖ים אָֽלֶף: לד וַֽחֲמֹרִ֕ים אֶחָ֥ד וְשִׁשִּׁ֖ים אָֽלֶף: לה וְנֶ֣פֶשׁ אָדָ֔ם מִן־הַ֨נָּשִׁ֔ים אֲשֶׁ֥ר לֹא־יָֽדְע֖וּ מִשְׁכַּ֣ב זָכָ֑ר כָּל־נֶ֕פֶשׁ שְׁנַ֥יִם וּשְׁלֹשִׁ֖ים אָֽלֶף: לו וַתְּהִי֙ הַמֶּֽחֱצָ֔ה חֵ֕לֶק הַיֹּֽצְאִ֖ים בַּצָּבָ֑א מִסְפַּ֣ר הַצֹּ֗אן שְׁלֹשׁ־מֵא֥וֹת אֶ֨לֶף֙ וּשְׁלֹשִׁ֣ים אֶ֔לֶף וְשִׁבְעַ֥ת אֲלָפִ֖ים וַֽחֲמֵ֥שׁ מֵאֽוֹת: לז וַיְהִ֛י הַמֶּ֥כֶס לַֽיהֹוָ֖ה מִן־הַצֹּ֑אן שֵׁ֥שׁ מֵא֖וֹת חָמֵ֥שׁ וְשִׁבְעִֽים: לח וְהַ֨בָּקָ֔ר שִׁשָּׁ֥ה וּשְׁלֹשִׁ֖ים אָ֑לֶף וּמִכְסָ֥ם לַֽיהֹוָ֖ה שְׁנַ֥יִם וְשִׁבְעִֽים: לט וַֽחֲמֹרִ֕ים שְׁלֹשִׁ֥ים אֶ֖לֶף וַֽחֲמֵ֣שׁ מֵא֑וֹת וּמִכְסָ֥ם לַֽיהֹוָ֖ה אֶחָ֥ד וְשִׁשִּֽׁים: מ וְנֶ֣פֶשׁ אָדָ֔ם שִׁשָּׁ֥ה עָשָׂ֖ר אָ֑לֶף וּמִכְסָם֙ לַֽיהֹוָ֔ה שְׁנַ֥יִם וּשְׁלֹשִׁ֖ים נָֽפֶשׁ: מא וַיִּתֵּ֣ן מֹשֶׁ֗ה אֶת־מֶ֨כֶס֙ תְּרוּמַ֣ת יְהֹוָ֔ה לְאֶלְעָזָ֖ר הַכֹּהֵ֑ן כַּֽאֲשֶׁ֛ר צִוָּ֥ה יְהֹוָ֖ה אֶת־מֹשֶֽׁה: חמישי מב וּמִֽמַּחֲצִ֖ת בְּנֵ֣י יִשְׂרָאֵ֑ל אֲשֶׁר֙ חָצָ֣ה מֹשֶׁ֔ה מִן־הָֽאֲנָשִׁ֖ים הַצֹּֽבְאִֽים: מג וַתְּהִ֛י מֶֽחֱצַ֥ת הָֽעֵדָ֖ה מִן־הַצֹּ֑אן שְׁלֹשׁ־מֵא֥וֹת אֶ֨לֶף֙ וּשְׁלֹשִׁ֣ים אֶ֔לֶף שִׁבְעַ֥ת אֲלָפִ֖ים וַֽחֲמֵ֥שׁ מֵאֽוֹת: מד וּבָקָ֕ר שִׁשָּׁ֥ה וּשְׁלֹשִׁ֖ים אָֽלֶף: מה וַֽחֲמֹרִ֕ים שְׁלֹשִׁ֥ים אֶ֖לֶף וַֽחֲמֵ֥שׁ מֵאֽוֹת: מו וְנֶ֣פֶשׁ אָדָ֔ם שִׁשָּׁ֥ה עָשָׂ֖ר אָֽלֶף: מז וַיִּקַּ֨ח מֹשֶׁ֜ה מִֽמַּחֲצִ֣ת בְּנֵֽי־יִשְׂרָאֵ֗ל אֶת־הָֽאָחֻז֙ אֶחָ֣ד מִן־הַֽחֲמִשִּׁ֔ים מִן־הָֽאָדָ֖ם וּמִן־הַבְּהֵמָ֑ה וַיִּתֵּ֨ן אֹתָ֜ם

the Dwelling Place of *God*, as *God* had commanded Moshe. 48. And the officers who were over the thousands of the army approached Moshe—the princes of the thousands and the princes of the hundreds— 49. and they said to Moshe: "Your servants have taken up the sum of the men of war who were entrusted to our hand, and not one man of us is missing. 50. Therefore we have dedicated the offering of *God*, every man who has acquired a gold article, an anklet or a bracelet, a finger ring, earring or clasp, to attain atonement for our souls before *God*." 51. And Moshe and Eleazar the priest took from them the gold, all articles wrought for [practical] use. 52. And all the gold of the uplifted donation that they had dedicated to *God* was sixteen thousand seven hundred and fifty shekels from the princes of the thousands and from the princes of the hundreds. 53. The men of the army had seized booty, each man for himself. 54. Moshe and Eleazar the priest took the gold from the princes of the thousands and of the hundreds and they brought it into the Tent of Appointed Meeting as a memorial for the sons of Yisrael before *God*.

XXXII

1. And the sons of Reuben and the sons of Gad had great wealth in herds [of cattle] in mighty measure. And they saw the land of Yaazer, and the land of Gilead, and lo! The region was a region [well suited] for herds. 2. And the sons of Gad and the sons of Reuben came and said to Moshe and to Eleazar the priest and to the princes of the community: 3. Ataroth, Dibon, Yaazer, Nimrah, Ḥeshbon, El'aleh, Sebam, Nebo and Be'on: 4. "The land that *God*

לַלְוִיִּם שֹׁמְרֵי מִשְׁמֶרֶת מִשְׁכַּן יְהֹוָה כַּאֲשֶׁר צִוָּה יְהֹוָה אֶת־מֹשֶׁה: מח וַיִּקְרְבוּ אֶל־מֹשֶׁה הַפְּקֻדִים אֲשֶׁר לְאַלְפֵי הַצָּבָא שָׂרֵי הָאֲלָפִים וְשָׂרֵי הַמֵּאוֹת: מט וַיֹּאמְרוּ אֶל־מֹשֶׁה עֲבָדֶיךָ נָשְׂאוּ אֶת־רֹאשׁ אַנְשֵׁי הַמִּלְחָמָה אֲשֶׁר בְּיָדֵנוּ וְלֹא־נִפְקַד מִמֶּנּוּ אִישׁ: נ וַנַּקְרֵב אֶת־קָרְבַּן יְהֹוָה אִישׁ אֲשֶׁר מָצָא כְלִי־זָהָב אֶצְעָדָה וְצָמִיד טַבַּעַת עָגִיל וְכוּמָז לְכַפֵּר עַל־נַפְשֹׁתֵינוּ לִפְנֵי יְהֹוָה: נא וַיִּקַּח מֹשֶׁה וְאֶלְעָזָר הַכֹּהֵן אֶת־הַזָּהָב מֵאִתָּם כֹּל כְּלִי מַעֲשֶׂה: נב וַיְהִי ׀ כָּל־זְהַב הַתְּרוּמָה אֲשֶׁר הֵרִימוּ לַיהֹוָה שִׁשָּׁה עָשָׂר אֶלֶף שְׁבַע־מֵאוֹת וַחֲמִשִּׁים שָׁקֶל מֵאֵת שָׂרֵי הָאֲלָפִים וּמֵאֵת שָׂרֵי הַמֵּאוֹת: נג אַנְשֵׁי הַצָּבָא בָּזְזוּ אִישׁ לוֹ: נד וַיִּקַּח מֹשֶׁה וְאֶלְעָזָר הַכֹּהֵן אֶת־הַזָּהָב מֵאֵת שָׂרֵי הָאֲלָפִים וְהַמֵּאוֹת וַיָּבִאוּ אֹתוֹ אֶל־אֹהֶל מוֹעֵד זִכָּרוֹן לִבְנֵי־יִשְׂרָאֵל לִפְנֵי יְהֹוָה: פ

ששי (שלישי כשהן מחוברין) לב א וּמִקְנֶה ׀ רַב הָיָה לִבְנֵי רְאוּבֵן וְלִבְנֵי־גָד עָצוּם מְאֹד וַיִּרְאוּ אֶת־אֶרֶץ יַעְזֵר וְאֶת־אֶרֶץ גִּלְעָד וְהִנֵּה הַמָּקוֹם מְקוֹם מִקְנֶה: ב וַיָּבֹאוּ בְנֵי־גָד וּבְנֵי רְאוּבֵן וַיֹּאמְרוּ אֶל־מֹשֶׁה וְאֶל־אֶלְעָזָר הַכֹּהֵן וְאֶל־נְשִׂיאֵי הָעֵדָה לֵאמֹר: ג עֲטָרוֹת וְדִיבֹן וְיַעְזֵר וְנִמְרָה וְחֶשְׁבּוֹן וְאֶלְעָלֵה וּשְׂבָם וּנְבוֹ וּבְעֹן:

---

50. **Therefore we have dedicated the offering of God.** The wording is not וַנַּקְרֵב קָרְבָּן לַד' ["therefore we have dedicated *an* offering *to God*"] but אֶת קָרְבָּן ד' ["...*the* offering *of God*"]. Thus the offering is defined as a קָרְבָּן which, as the result of such an experience, one feels the self-evident need and the duty to make, in order to express the awareness that one owed this experience solely to the nearness of God; i.e., to our relationship to God and His Law. Appropriately and deliberately, they chose for this purpose all the women's jewelry they had seized as booty. Perhaps this choice had been motivated by a dual purpose: to remove from their midst every last memory of the Midianite women, and to justify their portion in God's wonderful, protective favor by demonstrating their resolve henceforth to adhere faithfully to the dictates of morality. In Sabbath 64a and b the word קָרְבָּן as employed in this passage is interpreted in a similar vein.

has struck down before the community of Yisrael is a land for herds, and your servants have herds." 5. They said: "If we have found favor in your eyes, let this land be given to your servants as a possession; do not let us cross the Yarden." 6. And Moshe said to the sons of Gad and to the sons of Reuben: "Shall your brothers come into war and you will sit here? 7. And why do you restrain the heart of the sons of Yisrael from crossing over into the land that *God* has given them? 8. That is how your fathers acted when I sent them from Kadesh Barnea to look at the land. 9. They went up as far as the Valley of the Grapes, looked at the land and restrained the heart of the sons of Yisrael so that they should not come into the land that *God* had given them. 10. And the anger of *God* was stirred on that day and He swore: 11. The men who came up from Mitzrayim from twenty years old and upward shall not see the land that I have sworn to Abraham, Yitzhak and Yaakov, for they did not fulfill their duty [to] follow Me. 12. Except for Caleb, son of Yefunneh, the Kenizite, and Yehoshua, son of Nun, for they fulfilled their duty [by] following *God*. 13. So the anger of *God* was stirred against Yisrael, and He made them wander about in the wilderness for forty years, until that whole generation which had done what was evil in the eyes of *God* had come to an end. 14. And now you have arisen in the place of your fathers, [you] brood of sinful men, to add to the wrath of *God* that was kindled against Yisrael. 15. If you will hold back from following Him, He will make them remain in the wilderness even longer, and you will have prepared ruin for this whole people." 16. And they came up to him and said: "We want to build sheepfolds for our cattle

ד הָאָרֶץ אֲשֶׁר הִכָּה יְהֹוָה לִפְנֵי עֲדַת יִשְׂרָאֵל אֶרֶץ מִקְנֶה הִוא וְלַעֲבָדֶיךָ מִקְנֶה: ס ה וַיֹּאמְרוּ אִם־מָצָאנוּ חֵן בְּעֵינֶיךָ יֻתַּן אֶת־הָאָרֶץ הַזֹּאת לַעֲבָדֶיךָ לַאֲחֻזָּה אַל־תַּעֲבִרֵנוּ אֶת־הַיַּרְדֵּן: ו וַיֹּאמֶר מֹשֶׁה לִבְנֵי־גָד וְלִבְנֵי רְאוּבֵן הַאַחֵיכֶם יָבֹאוּ לַמִּלְחָמָה וְאַתֶּם תֵּשְׁבוּ פֹה: ז וְלָמָּה תְנוּאוּן (תניאון קרי) אֶת־לֵב בְּנֵי יִשְׂרָאֵל מֵעֲבֹר אֶל־הָאָרֶץ אֲשֶׁר־נָתַן לָהֶם יְהֹוָה: ח כֹּה עָשׂוּ אֲבֹתֵיכֶם בְּשָׁלְחִי אֹתָם מִקָּדֵשׁ בַּרְנֵעַ לִרְאוֹת אֶת־הָאָרֶץ: ט וַיַּעֲלוּ עַד־נַחַל אֶשְׁכּוֹל וַיִּרְאוּ אֶת־הָאָרֶץ וַיָּנִיאוּ אֶת־לֵב בְּנֵי יִשְׂרָאֵל לְבִלְתִּי־בֹא אֶל־הָאָרֶץ אֲשֶׁר־נָתַן לָהֶם יְהֹוָה: י וַיִּחַר־אַף יְהֹוָה בַּיּוֹם הַהוּא וַיִּשָּׁבַע לֵאמֹר: יא אִם־יִרְאוּ הָאֲנָשִׁים הָעֹלִים מִמִּצְרַיִם מִבֶּן עֶשְׂרִים שָׁנָה וָמַעְלָה אֵת הָאֲדָמָה אֲשֶׁר נִשְׁבַּעְתִּי לְאַבְרָהָם לְיִצְחָק וּלְיַעֲקֹב כִּי לֹא־מִלְאוּ אַחֲרָי: יב בִּלְתִּי כָּלֵב בֶּן־יְפֻנֶּה הַקְּנִזִּי וִיהוֹשֻׁעַ בִּן־נוּן כִּי מִלְאוּ אַחֲרֵי יְהֹוָה: יג וַיִּחַר־אַף יְהֹוָה בְּיִשְׂרָאֵל וַיְנִעֵם בַּמִּדְבָּר אַרְבָּעִים שָׁנָה עַד־תֹּם כָּל־הַדּוֹר הָעֹשֶׂה הָרַע בְּעֵינֵי יְהֹוָה: יד וְהִנֵּה קַמְתֶּם תַּחַת אֲבֹתֵיכֶם תַּרְבּוּת אֲנָשִׁים חַטָּאִים לִסְפּוֹת עוֹד עַל חֲרוֹן אַף־יְהֹוָה אֶל־יִשְׂרָאֵל: טו כִּי תְשׁוּבֻן מֵאַחֲרָיו וְיָסַף עוֹד לְהַנִּיחוֹ בַּמִּדְבָּר וְשִׁחַתֶּם לְכָל־הָעָם הַזֶּה: ס טז וַיִּגְּשׁוּ אֵלָיו וַיֹּאמְרוּ גִּדְרֹת צֹאן נִבְנֶה לְמִקְנֵנוּ פֹּה

CHAPTER XXXII

5. וַיֹּאמְרוּ [*They said*]. The reiteration of this formal introductory device indicates that the sons of Gad and the sons of Reuben are continuing their speech after a pause. It shows that they themselves were not at all sure how their proposal would be received. They needed a pause in which to compose themselves sufficiently to continue their presentation.

16. *We want to build sheepfolds for our cattle.* Our Sages in the *Midrash Rabbah* point out that the order in which the sons of Gad and Reuben phrased their proposal demonstrates the paramount importance they attached to property. Their cattle meant more to them than their children; hence, they first mentioned "sheepfolds for our cattle" and only thereafter "cities for our children." Had they not considered their livestock more important than their offspring, they would

וְעָרִ֖ים לְטַפֵּֽנוּ׃ יז וַאֲנַ֜חְנוּ נֵחָלֵ֣ץ חֻשִׁ֗ים לִפְנֵי֙ בְּנֵ֣י
יִשְׂרָאֵ֔ל עַ֛ד אֲשֶׁ֥ר אִם־הֲבִיאֹנֻ֖ם אֶל־מְקוֹמָ֑ם
וְיָשַׁ֤ב טַפֵּ֙נוּ֙ בְּעָרֵ֣י הַמִּבְצָ֔ר מִפְּנֵ֖י יֹשְׁבֵ֥י הָאָֽרֶץ׃
יח לֹ֥א נָשׁ֖וּב אֶל־בָּתֵּ֑ינוּ עַ֗ד הִתְנַחֵל֙ בְּנֵ֣י יִשְׂרָאֵ֔ל
אִ֖ישׁ נַחֲלָתֽוֹ׃ יט כִּ֣י לֹ֤א נִנְחַל֙ אִתָּ֔ם מֵעֵ֥בֶר
לַיַּרְדֵּ֖ן וָהָ֑לְאָה כִּ֣י בָ֤אָה נַחֲלָתֵ֙נוּ֙ אֵלֵ֔ינוּ מֵעֵ֥בֶר
הַיַּרְדֵּ֖ן מִזְרָֽחָה׃ פ שביעי (רביעי כשהן מחוברין)
כ וַיֹּ֤אמֶר אֲלֵיהֶם֙ מֹשֶׁ֔ה אִם־תַּעֲשׂ֖וּן אֶת־הַדָּבָ֣ר
הַזֶּ֑ה אִם־תֵּחָלְצ֛וּ לִפְנֵ֥י יְהוָ֖ה לַמִּלְחָמָֽה׃
כא וְעָבַ֨ר לָכֶ֧ם כָּל־חָל֛וּץ אֶת־הַיַּרְדֵּ֖ן לִפְנֵ֣י יְהוָ֑ה
עַ֧ד הוֹרִישׁ֛וֹ אֶת־אֹיְבָ֖יו מִפָּנָֽיו׃ כב וְנִכְבְּשָׁה֩
הָאָ֨רֶץ לִפְנֵ֤י יְהוָה֙ וְאַחַ֣ר תָּשֻׁ֔בוּ וִהְיִיתֶ֧ם נְקִיִּ֛ם
מֵיְהוָ֖ה וּמִיִּשְׂרָאֵ֑ל וְ֠הָיְתָה הָאָ֨רֶץ הַזֹּ֥את לָכֶ֛ם
לַאֲחֻזָּ֖ה לִפְנֵ֥י יְהוָֽה׃ כג וְאִם־לֹ֤א תַעֲשׂוּן֙ כֵּ֔ן הִנֵּ֥ה
חֲטָאתֶ֖ם לַיהוָ֑ה וּדְעוּ֙ חַטַּאתְכֶ֔ם אֲשֶׁ֥ר תִּמְצָ֖א
אֶתְכֶֽם׃ כד בְּנוּ־לָכֶ֤ם עָרִים֙ לְטַפְּכֶ֔ם וּגְדֵרֹ֖ת
לְצֹנַאֲכֶ֑ם וְהַיֹּצֵ֥א מִפִּיכֶ֖ם תַּעֲשֽׂוּ׃ כה וַיֹּ֤אמֶר
בְּנֵי־גָד֙ וּבְנֵ֣י רְאוּבֵ֔ן אֶל־מֹשֶׁ֖ה לֵאמֹ֑ר עֲבָדֶ֣יךָ
יַעֲשׂ֔וּ כַּאֲשֶׁ֥ר אֲדֹנִ֖י מְצַוֶּֽה׃ כו טַפֵּ֣נוּ נָשֵׁ֔ינוּ
מִקְנֵ֖נוּ וְכָל־בְּהֶמְתֵּ֑נוּ יִֽהְיוּ־שָׁ֖ם בְּעָרֵ֥י הַגִּלְעָֽד׃
כז וַעֲבָדֶ֨יךָ יַעַבְר֜וּ כָּל־חֲל֥וּץ צָבָ֛א לִפְנֵ֥י יְהוָ֖ה
לַמִּלְחָמָ֑ה כַּאֲשֶׁ֥ר אֲדֹנִ֖י דֹּבֵֽר׃ כח וַיְצַ֤ו לָהֶם֙
מֹשֶׁ֔ה אֵ֚ת אֶלְעָזָ֣ר הַכֹּהֵ֔ן וְאֵ֖ת יְהוֹשֻׁ֣עַ בִּן־נ֑וּן

[here] and cities for our children, 17. and we will go out quickly [in the vanguard] before the sons of Yisrael until we have brought them to their place. Our children can remain in the fortified cities because of the inhabitants of the land. 18. We shall not return to our homes until the sons of Yisrael have taken over every one his inheritance, 19. for we do not want to inherit with them on the other side of the Yarden and beyond, if our inheritance has already come to us on this side of the Yarden to the east." 20. And Moshe said to them: "If you will do this, if you will go forth to the war before *God* [in the vanguard], 21. and every one of you who went out into the vanguard will cross the Yarden before *God*, until He has driven out His enemies from before Him, 22. and the land is conquered before *God*, and you will return only then, and you will thus be freed from your obligation by *God* and by Yisrael, then this land shall become your property before *God*. 23. But if you will not do this, then lo! You have sinned against *God* and [you must] know very well your sin that will find you out! 24. Build yourselves cities for your children and sheepfolds for your sheep and that which has proceeded from your mouth you shall do." 25. And the sons of Gad and the sons of Reuben said to Moshe in one accord: "Your servants will do as my lord commands. 26. Our children, our wives, our herds and all our livestock shall remain there in the cities of Gilead, 27. and your servants, every one who has gone forth into the army, shall cross over before *God* to the war, just as my lord says." 28. And Moshe commanded Eleazar the priest, Yehoshua, son of Nun, and

surely have thought twice, if only for the sake of their children, before jeopardizing their spiritual contact with the rest of the nation and its Sanctuary by settling so far away from their brethren solely for the sake of the attractive pastureland. In his reply (Verse 24), Moses puts the care of the children first, and the petitioners obviously took due notice of this, because in their summation they, too, mention their children and their womenfolk before their livestock. Also, as our Sages further comment, their overrating of material wealth caused them to fare badly in the end, for even as they had requested and occupied their land before all the others, the tribes of Reuben and Gad were also to be the first to lose their possessions and their homeland. They were the first to be carried off into exile through [King] Pul and [King] Tillegath-pilneser [of Assyria]. (I Chronicles 5:26).

the heads of the tribal fathers of the sons of
Yisrael concerning them. 29. And Moshe
said to them: "If the sons of Gad and the
sons of Reuben will cross the Yarden with
you, each one who has gone forth to war
before *God,* and the land will be conquered
before you, then you shall give them the
land of Gilead as a possession. 30. But if
they will not cross with you, ready for
battle, they shall settle down among you in
the land of Canaan." 31. And the sons of
Gad and the sons of Reuben answered:
"That which *God* has spoken to your
servants, so we will do. 32. We will
cross, ready for battle, before *God,* into the
land of Canaan, and with us [shall go]
the occupancy of our inheritance on this
side of the Yarden." 33. And Moshe gave
to them—to the sons of Gad and the sons of
Reuben and the half-tribe of Menashe, son
of Yosef—the realm of Siḥon, king of the
Emorite[s], and the realm of Og, king of
the Bashan, the land according to its cities
within borders, the cities of the land round
about. 34. The sons of Gad built Dibon
and Ataroth and Aroer, 35. Atroth
Shofan, Yaazer and Yagbehah, 36. Beth
Nimrah and Beth Haran, as fortified cities
and sheepfolds. 37. The sons of Reuben
built Ḥeshbon and El'ale and Kiryataim,
38. Nebo and Baal Me'on—their names
being changed—and Sibmah; for the rest,
they retained the names of the cities that
they had constructed. 39. The sons of
Makhir, son of Menashe, went to Gilead and
conquered it, and he drove out the Emorite[s] who dwelt there. 40. And Moshe
gave the Gilead to Makhir, son of Menashe,
and he settled there. 41. Yair, son of
Menashe, went and conquered their villages
and called them "Villages of Yair."
42. Nobaḥ went and conquered Kenath
and its daughter cities and called it Nobaḥ,
after his own name.

וְאֶת־רָאשֵׁי אֲבוֹת הַמַּטּוֹת לִבְנֵי יִשְׂרָאֵל:
כט וַיֹּאמֶר מֹשֶׁה אֲלֵהֶם אִם־יַעַבְרוּ בְנֵי־גָד
וּבְנֵי־רְאוּבֵן | אִתְּכֶם אֶת־הַיַּרְדֵּן כָּל־חָלוּץ
לַמִּלְחָמָה לִפְנֵי יְהֹוָה וְנִכְבְּשָׁה הָאָרֶץ לִפְנֵיכֶם
וּנְתַתֶּם לָהֶם אֶת־אֶרֶץ הַגִּלְעָד לַאֲחֻזָּה: ל וְאִם־
לֹא יַעַבְרוּ חֲלוּצִים אִתְּכֶם וְנֹאחֲזוּ בְתֹכְכֶם
בְּאֶרֶץ כְּנָעַן: לא וַיַּעֲנוּ בְנֵי־גָד וּבְנֵי רְאוּבֵן
לֵאמֹר אֵת אֲשֶׁר דִּבֶּר יְהֹוָה אֶל־עֲבָדֶיךָ כֵּן
נַעֲשֶׂה: לב נַחְנוּ נַעֲבֹר חֲלוּצִים לִפְנֵי יְהֹוָה אֶרֶץ
כְּנָעַן וְאִתָּנוּ אֲחֻזַּת נַחֲלָתֵנוּ מֵעֵבֶר לַיַּרְדֵּן:
לג וַיִּתֵּן לָהֶם | מֹשֶׁה לִבְנֵי־גָד וְלִבְנֵי רְאוּבֵן
וְלַחֲצִי | שֵׁבֶט | מְנַשֶּׁה בֶן־יוֹסֵף אֶת־מַמְלֶכֶת
סִיחֹן מֶלֶךְ הָאֱמֹרִי וְאֶת־מַמְלֶכֶת עוֹג מֶלֶךְ
הַבָּשָׁן הָאָרֶץ לְעָרֶיהָ בִּגְבֻלֹת עָרֵי הָאָרֶץ סָבִיב:
לד וַיִּבְנוּ בְנֵי־גָד אֶת־דִּיבֹן וְאֶת־עֲטָרֹת וְאֵת
עֲרֹעֵר: לה וְאֶת־עַטְרֹת שׁוֹפָן וְאֶת־יַעְזֵר
וְיָגְבְּהָה: לו וְאֶת־בֵּית נִמְרָה וְאֶת־בֵּית הָרָן עָרֵי
מִבְצָר וְגִדְרֹת צֹאן: לז וּבְנֵי רְאוּבֵן בָּנוּ אֶת־
חֶשְׁבּוֹן וְאֶת־אֶלְעָלֵא וְאֵת קִרְיָתָיִם: לח וְאֶת־
נְבוֹ וְאֶת־בַּעַל מְעוֹן מוּסַבֹּת שֵׁם וְאֶת־שִׂבְמָה
וַיִּקְרְאוּ בְשֵׁמֹת אֶת־שְׁמוֹת הֶעָרִים אֲשֶׁר בָּנוּ:
לט וַיֵּלְכוּ בְּנֵי מָכִיר בֶּן־מְנַשֶּׁה גִּלְעָדָה וַיִּלְכְּדֻהָ
וַיּוֹרֶשׁ אֶת־הָאֱמֹרִי אֲשֶׁר־בָּהּ: מפטיר מ וַיִּתֵּן
מֹשֶׁה אֶת־הַגִּלְעָד לְמָכִיר בֶּן־מְנַשֶּׁה וַיֵּשֶׁב בָּהּ:
מא וְיָאִיר בֶּן־מְנַשֶּׁה הָלַךְ וַיִּלְכֹּד אֶת־חַוֺּתֵיהֶם
וַיִּקְרָא אֶתְהֶן חַוֺּת יָאִיר: מב וְנֹבַח הָלַךְ וַיִּלְכֹּד
אֶת־קְנָת וְאֶת־בְּנֹתֶיהָ וַיִּקְרָא לָה נֹבַח בִּשְׁמוֹ: פ

32. ***and with us [shall go] the occupancy of our inheritance.*** This probably means: Our occupancy of our inheritance on this side of the Jordan will go across with us; i.e., we cannot formally take possession of this land while we are still here, on this side of the Jordan. Only by virtue of what we will accomplish on the other side of the Jordan will we establish our occupancy of the land we requested on this side of the river.

The Haftarah for this Sidra may be found on page 904.

מסעי

MASSE

XXXIII 1. These are the
journeys of the sons
of Yisrael, who had gone out of the land of
Mitzrayim according to their organized
groups, under the guidance of Moshe
and Aharon. 2. Moshe recorded their
decampments for the continuations of
their journeys at the command of *God*, and
these are the continuations of their journeys
following their decampments. 3. They
journeyed from Raamses in the first month,
on the fifteenth day of the first month; on
the morning after the Pesaḥ offering did the
sons of Yisrael go out with a high hand
before the eyes of all the Mitzrites.
4. And the Mitzrites buried what *God*
had struck down from among them, every
first-born, and *God* had executed judgments also upon their gods. 5. The sons

לג א אֵלֶּה מַסְעֵי בְנֵי־יִשְׂרָאֵל אֲשֶׁר יָצְאוּ
מֵאֶרֶץ מִצְרַיִם לְצִבְאֹתָם בְּיַד־מֹשֶׁה וְאַהֲרֹן׃
ב וַיִּכְתֹּב מֹשֶׁה אֶת־מוֹצָאֵיהֶם לְמַסְעֵיהֶם עַל־
פִּי יְהוָה וְאֵלֶּה מַסְעֵיהֶם לְמוֹצָאֵיהֶם׃ ג וַיִּסְעוּ
מֵרַעְמְסֵס בַּחֹדֶשׁ הָרִאשׁוֹן בַּחֲמִשָּׁה עָשָׂר יוֹם
לַחֹדֶשׁ הָרִאשׁוֹן מִמָּחֳרַת הַפֶּסַח יָצְאוּ בְנֵי־
יִשְׂרָאֵל בְּיָד רָמָה לְעֵינֵי כָּל־מִצְרָיִם׃ ד וּמִצְרַיִם
מְקַבְּרִים אֵת אֲשֶׁר הִכָּה יְהוָה בָּהֶם כָּל־בְּכוֹר
וּבֵאלֹהֵיהֶם עָשָׂה יְהוָה שְׁפָטִים׃ ה וַיִּסְעוּ בְנֵי־

CHAPTER XXXIII

1–2. There could be many explanations for this listing of the journeys and stopovers made by the Children of Israel during their wanderings through the wilderness. It seems that these journeys and stopovers were associated with a whole series of events and personal experiences which were worthy of being remembered by the kinsmen, the fellow tribesmen and the descendants of those directly affected by them, but for which no room had been found in this book where the history of the nation as a whole is recorded. The memory of these events was therefore meant to be preserved by oral tradition, and this listing of the places where the Children of Israel rested and from which they journeyed forth was to serve as an aid to the memory for oral recitals of the experiences associated with these localities.

One can only surmise how many other traces of the wanderings and sojournings of our forefathers may have been preserved in these places in the wilderness for the immediate and more distant future, and what opportunities these could have offered to the sons and the grandchildren of the generation of the wilderness to visit the places where God's wondrous works became manifest. Visiting these places, future generations could contemplate, then and there, the authenticity of God's presence on earth so eloquently expressed in the history of their forebears. The very barrenness and aridity of these localities in the wilderness, a desert so vast that even those experienced in traveling with caravans must carefully count the days in order to make their provisions hold out, a desert in which an entire people, at least one million and a half souls, lived for forty years—the very sight of these places in the wilderness (as Maimonides notes in *Moreh Nebukhim*) provides ample documentation for the Divine basis of Israel's establishment as a nation. Rashi records a remark of Rabbi Moshe HaDarshan[10] that of the forty-two stages of the wanderings recorded in this register, fourteen—from Ra'amses to Rithmah—preceded the sending of the scouts, and eight—from Mount Hor to the wastelands of Moab—came during the fortieth year, after the death of Aaron. This means that only twenty such stages occurred during the thirty-eight years after the decree that the Israelites would have to wander in the wilderness for forty years. Thus it is clear that God in His mercy did not implement His decree by making the Children of Israel travel through the wilderness for four decades without stops for rest, for we can see that the average duration of Israel's rests at each stopover was nearly two years.

° ° °

[10]*Note to the English translation*: R. Moses the Preacher. French Bible commentator active in Narbonne, in the south of France, during the 10th and 11th centuries. [G.H.]

of Yisrael journeyed from Raamses and
camped in Sukkoth. 6. They journeyed
from Sukkoth and camped in Etham, which
lies at the edge of the wilderness. 7. They
journeyed from Etham, and it turned back
toward Pi HaḤiroth, which lies before Baal
Tzefon, and they camped before Migdol.
They journeyed from before HaḤiroth and
crossed through the midst of the sea toward
the wilderness. They went a three days'
journey in the wilderness of Etham and
camped in Marah. 9. They journeyed
from Marah and came to Elim, and there
were in Elim twelve springs of water and
seventy date palms; there they camped.
10. They journeyed from Elim and
camped by the Sea of Reeds; 11. they
journeyed from the Sea of Reeds and
camped in the wilderness of Sin.
12. They journeyed from the wilderness
of Sin and camped in Dofkah. 13. They
journeyed from Dofkah and camped in
Alush. 14. They journeyed from Alush
and camped in Refidim, where there was no
water for the people to drink. 15. They
journeyed from Refidim and camped in the
wilderness of Sinai. 16. They journeyed
from the wilderness of Sinai and camped in
Kibroth HaTaavah. 17. They journeyed
from Kibroth HaTaavah and camped in
Ḥatzeroth. 18. They journeyed from
Ḥatzeroth and camped in Rithmah.
19. They journeyed from Rithmah and
camped in Rimmon Peretz. 20. They
journeyed from Rimmon Peretz and
camped in Libnah. 21. They journeyed
from Libnah and camped in Rissah.
22. They journeyed from Rissah and
camped in Kehelathah. 23. They journeyed from Kehelathah and camped in Har
Shefer. 24. They journeyed from Har
Shefer and camped in Ḥaradah. 25. They
journeyed from Ḥaradah and camped in
Makheloth. 26. They journeyed from
Makheloth and camped in Taḥath.
27. They journeyed from Taḥath and

יִשְׂרָאֵ֖ל מֵרַעְמְסֵ֑ס וַֽיַּחֲנ֖וּ בְּסֻכֹּֽת׃ ו וַיִּסְע֖וּ מִסֻּכֹּ֑ת
וַיַּחֲנ֣וּ בְאֵתָ֔ם אֲשֶׁ֖ר בִּקְצֵ֥ה הַמִּדְבָּֽר׃ ז וַיִּסְעוּ֙
מֵֽאֵתָ֔ם וַיָּ֨שָׁב֙ עַל־פִּ֣י הַֽחִירֹ֔ת אֲשֶׁ֥ר עַל־פְּנֵ֖י בַּ֣עַל
צְפ֑וֹן וַֽיַּחֲנ֖וּ לִפְנֵ֥י מִגְדֹּֽל׃ ח וַיִּסְעוּ֙ מִפְּנֵ֣י הַֽחִירֹ֔ת
וַיַּֽעַבְר֥וּ בְתוֹךְ־הַיָּ֖ם הַמִּדְבָּ֑רָה וַ֠יֵּֽלְכוּ דֶּ֣רֶךְ שְׁלֹ֤שֶׁת
יָמִים֙ בְּמִדְבַּ֣ר אֵתָ֔ם וַֽיַּחֲנ֖וּ בְּמָרָֽה׃ ט וַיִּסְעוּ֙
מִמָּרָ֔ה וַיָּבֹ֖אוּ אֵילִ֑מָה וּ֠בְאֵילִם שְׁתֵּ֨ים עֶשְׂרֵ֜ה
עֵינֹ֥ת מַ֛יִם וְשִׁבְעִ֥ים תְּמָרִ֖ים וַיַּחֲנוּ־שָֽׁם׃ י וַיִּסְע֖וּ
מֵאֵילִ֑ם וַֽיַּחֲנ֖וּ עַל־יַם־סֽוּף׃ שני יא וַיִּסְע֖וּ מִיַּם־
ס֑וּף וַֽיַּחֲנ֖וּ בְּמִדְבַּר־סִֽין׃ יב וַיִּסְע֖וּ מִמִּדְבַּר־סִ֑ין
וַֽיַּחֲנ֖וּ בְּדָפְקָֽה׃ יג וַיִּסְע֖וּ מִדָּפְקָ֑ה וַֽיַּחֲנ֖וּ בְּאָלֽוּשׁ׃
יד וַיִּסְעוּ֙ מֵאָל֔וּשׁ וַֽיַּחֲנוּ֙ בִּרְפִידִ֔ם וְלֹא־הָ֨יָה שָׁ֥ם
מַ֛יִם לָעָ֖ם לִשְׁתּֽוֹת׃ טו וַיִּסְע֖וּ מֵרְפִידִ֑ם וַֽיַּחֲנ֖וּ
בְּמִדְבַּ֥ר סִינָֽי׃ טז וַיִּסְע֖וּ מִמִּדְבַּ֣ר סִינָ֑י וַֽיַּחֲנ֖וּ
בְּקִבְרֹ֥ת הַֽתַּאֲוָֽה׃ יז וַיִּסְע֖וּ מִקִּבְרֹ֣ת הַֽתַּאֲוָ֑ה
וַֽיַּחֲנ֖וּ בַּחֲצֵרֹֽת׃ יח וַיִּסְע֖וּ מֵחֲצֵרֹ֑ת וַֽיַּחֲנ֖וּ
בְּרִתְמָֽה׃ יט וַיִּסְע֖וּ מֵרִתְמָ֑ה וַֽיַּחֲנ֖וּ בְּרִמֹּ֥ן פָּֽרֶץ׃
כ וַיִּסְע֖וּ מֵרִמֹּ֣ן פָּ֑רֶץ וַֽיַּחֲנ֖וּ בְּלִבְנָֽה׃ כא וַיִּסְע֖וּ
מִלִּבְנָ֑ה וַֽיַּחֲנ֖וּ בְּרִסָּֽה׃ כב וַיִּסְע֖וּ מֵרִסָּ֑ה וַֽיַּחֲנ֖וּ
בִּקְהֵלָֽתָה׃ כג וַיִּסְע֖וּ מִקְּהֵלָ֑תָה וַֽיַּחֲנ֖וּ בְּהַר־
שָֽׁפֶר׃ כד וַיִּסְע֖וּ מֵהַר־שָׁ֑פֶר וַֽיַּחֲנ֖וּ בַּחֲרָדָֽה׃
כה וַיִּסְע֖וּ מֵחֲרָדָ֑ה וַֽיַּחֲנ֖וּ בְּמַקְהֵלֹֽת׃ כו וַיִּסְע֖וּ
מִמַּקְהֵלֹ֑ת וַֽיַּחֲנ֖וּ בְּתָֽחַת׃ כז וַיִּסְע֖וּ מִתָּ֑חַת וַֽיַּחֲנ֖וּ

7. ***and it turned.*** The subject of the verses that went before and of those that follow is "they." Hence the transition in this verse to the third person singular, "it," is in need of explanation. Might it be intended to show the unanimous trust in God with which the Children of Israel, as one, obeyed the order to retreat, an order which must certainly have seemed odd to them?

camped in Teraḥ. 28. They journeyed from Teraḥ and camped in Mithkah. 29. They journeyed from Mithkah and camped in Ḥashmonah. 30. They journeyed from Ḥashmonah and camped in Moseroth. 31. They journeyed from Moseroth and camped in B'ne Yaakan. 32. They journeyed from B'ne Yaakan and camped in Ḥor HaGidgad. 33. They journeyed from Ḥor HaGidgad and camped in Yatbathah. 34. They journeyed from Yatbathah and camped in Abronah. 35. They journeyed from Abronah and camped in Etzion Geber. 36. They journeyed from Etzion Geber and camped in the wilderness of Tzin; i.e. Kadesh. 37. They journeyed from Kadesh and camped on Mount Hor, at the edge of the land of Edom. 38. Aharon the priest went up to Mount Hor at the command of *God* and he died there, in the fortieth year after the exodus of the sons of Yisrael from the land of Mitzrayim, in the fifth month, on the first [day] of the month. 39. And Aharon was one hundred twenty-three years old when he died on Mount Hor. 40. And the Canaanite, the king of Arad—he dwelt in the south in the land of Canaan—heard that the sons of Yisrael were approaching. 41. They journeyed from Mount Hor and camped in Tzalmonah. 42. They journeyed from Tzalmonah and camped in Punon. 43. They journeyed from Punon and camped in Oboth. 44. They journeyed from Oboth and camped in the Wastelands of Transitions on the border of Moab. 45. They journeyed from the wastelands and camped in Dibon Gad. 46. They journeyed from Dibon Gad and camped in Almon-toward-Diblothayim. 47. They journeyed from Almon-toward-Diblothayim and camped in the Mountains of Transitions before Nebo. 48. They journeyed from the Mountains of Transitions and camped in the wastelands of Moab, along the Yarden near Jericho. 49. They camped along the Yarden from Beth HaYeshimoth to Abel HaShittim in the wastelands of Moab. 50. *God* spoke to Moshe in the wastelands of Moab along the Yarden before Jericho [saying]: 51. "Speak to the sons of Yisrael and say

בְּתָֽרַח׃ כח וַיִּסְע֖וּ מִתָּ֑רַח וַֽיַּחֲנ֖וּ בְּמִתְקָֽה׃
כט וַיִּסְע֖וּ מִמִּתְקָ֑ה וַֽיַּחֲנ֖וּ בְּחַשְׁמֹנָֽה׃ ל וַיִּסְע֖וּ
מֵֽחַשְׁמֹנָ֑ה וַֽיַּחֲנ֖וּ בְּמֹסֵרֽוֹת׃ לא וַיִּסְע֖וּ מִמֹּֽסֵר֑וֹת
וַֽיַּחֲנ֖וּ בִּבְנֵ֥י יַעֲקָֽן׃ לב וַיִּסְע֖וּ מִבְּנֵ֣י יַעֲקָ֑ן וַֽיַּחֲנ֖וּ
בְּחֹ֥ר הַגִּדְגָּֽד׃ לג וַיִּסְע֖וּ מֵחֹ֣ר הַגִּדְגָּ֑ד וַֽיַּחֲנ֖וּ
בְּיָטְבָֽתָה׃ לד וַיִּסְע֖וּ מִיָּטְבָ֑תָה וַֽיַּחֲנ֖וּ בְּעַבְרֹנָֽה׃
לה וַיִּסְע֖וּ מֵעַבְרֹנָ֑ה וַֽיַּחֲנ֖וּ בְּעֶצְיֹ֥ן גָּֽבֶר׃ לו וַיִּסְע֖וּ
מֵעֶצְיֹ֣ן גָּ֑בֶר וַיַּחֲנ֥וּ בְמִדְבַּר־צִ֖ן ה֥וא קָדֵֽשׁ׃
לז וַיִּסְע֖וּ מִקָּדֵ֑שׁ וַֽיַּחֲנוּ֙ בְּהֹ֣ר הָהָ֔ר בִּקְצֵ֖ה אֶ֥רֶץ
אֱדֽוֹם׃ לח וַיַּ֩עַל֩ אַהֲרֹ֨ן הַכֹּהֵ֜ן אֶל־הֹ֥ר הָהָ֛ר עַל־
פִּ֥י יְהוָ֖ה וַיָּ֣מָת שָׁ֑ם בִּשְׁנַ֣ת הָֽאַרְבָּעִ֗ים לְצֵ֤את
בְּנֵֽי־יִשְׂרָאֵל֙ מֵאֶ֣רֶץ מִצְרַ֔יִם בַּחֹ֥דֶשׁ הַחֲמִישִׁ֖י
בְּאֶחָ֥ד לַחֹֽדֶשׁ׃ לט וְאַֽהֲרֹ֔ן בֶּן־שָׁלֹ֧שׁ וְעֶשְׂרִ֛ים
וּמְאַ֖ת שָׁנָ֑ה בְּמֹת֖וֹ בְּהֹ֥ר הָהָֽר׃ ס מ וַיִּשְׁמַ֗ע
הַֽכְּנַעֲנִי֙ מֶ֣לֶךְ עֲרָ֔ד וְהֽוּא־יֹשֵׁ֥ב בַּנֶּ֖גֶב בְּאֶ֣רֶץ כְּנָ֑עַן
בְּבֹ֖א בְּנֵ֥י יִשְׂרָאֵֽל׃ מא וַיִּסְע֖וּ מֵהֹ֣ר הָהָ֑ר וַֽיַּחֲנ֖וּ
בְּצַלְמֹנָֽה׃ מב וַיִּסְע֖וּ מִצַּלְמֹנָ֑ה וַֽיַּחֲנ֖וּ בְּפוּנֹֽן׃
מג וַיִּסְע֖וּ מִפּוּנֹ֑ן וַֽיַּחֲנ֖וּ בְּאֹבֹֽת׃ מד וַיִּסְע֖וּ מֵאֹבֹ֑ת
וַֽיַּחֲנ֛וּ בְּעִיֵּ֥י הָעֲבָרִ֖ים בִּגְב֥וּל מוֹאָֽב׃ מה וַיִּסְע֖וּ
מֵעִיִּ֑ים וַֽיַּחֲנ֖וּ בְּדִיבֹ֥ן גָּֽד׃ מו וַיִּסְע֖וּ מִדִּיבֹ֣ן גָּ֑ד
וַֽיַּחֲנ֖וּ בְּעַלְמֹ֥ן דִּבְלָתָֽיְמָה׃ מז וַיִּסְע֖וּ מֵעַלְמֹ֣ן
דִּבְלָתָ֑יְמָה וַֽיַּחֲנ֛וּ בְּהָרֵ֥י הָעֲבָרִ֖ים לִפְנֵ֥י נְבֽוֹ׃
מח וַיִּסְע֖וּ מֵהָרֵ֣י הָעֲבָרִ֑ים וַֽיַּחֲנוּ֙ בְּעַרְבֹ֣ת מוֹאָ֔ב
עַ֖ל יַרְדֵּ֥ן יְרֵחֽוֹ׃ מט וַיַּחֲנ֤וּ עַל־הַיַּרְדֵּן֙ מִבֵּ֣ית
הַיְשִׁמֹ֔ת עַ֖ד אָבֵ֣ל הַשִּׁטִּ֑ים בְּעַרְבֹ֖ת מוֹאָֽב׃ ס
שלישי (חמישי כשהן מחוברין) נ וַיְדַבֵּ֥ר יְהוָ֖ה אֶל־מֹשֶׁ֑ה
בְּעַרְבֹ֥ת מוֹאָ֖ב עַל־יַרְדֵּ֥ן יְרֵח֖וֹ לֵאמֹֽר׃ נא דַּבֵּר֙

אֶל־בְּנֵי יִשְׂרָאֵל וְאָמַרְתָּ אֲלֵהֶם כִּי אַתֶּם עֹבְרִים
אֶת־הַיַּרְדֵּן אֶל־אֶרֶץ כְּנָעַן׃ נב וְהוֹרַשְׁתֶּם אֶת־
כָּל־יֹשְׁבֵי הָאָרֶץ מִפְּנֵיכֶם וְאִבַּדְתֶּם אֵת כָּל־
מַשְׂכִּיֹּתָם וְאֵת כָּל־צַלְמֵי מַסֵּכֹתָם תְּאַבֵּדוּ וְאֵת
כָּל־בָּמוֹתָם תַּשְׁמִידוּ׃ נג וְהוֹרַשְׁתֶּם אֶת־הָאָרֶץ
וִישַׁבְתֶּם־בָּהּ כִּי לָכֶם נָתַתִּי אֶת־הָאָרֶץ לָרֶשֶׁת
אֹתָהּ׃ נד וְהִתְנַחַלְתֶּם אֶת־הָאָרֶץ בְּגוֹרָל
לְמִשְׁפְּחֹתֵיכֶם לָרַב תַּרְבּוּ אֶת־נַחֲלָתוֹ וְלַמְעַט
תַּמְעִיט אֶת־נַחֲלָתוֹ אֶל אֲשֶׁר־יֵצֵא לוֹ שָׁמָּה
הַגּוֹרָל לוֹ יִהְיֶה לְמַטּוֹת אֲבֹתֵיכֶם תִּתְנֶחָלוּ׃
נה וְאִם־לֹא תוֹרִישׁוּ אֶת־יֹשְׁבֵי הָאָרֶץ מִפְּנֵיכֶם
וְהָיָה אֲשֶׁר תּוֹתִירוּ מֵהֶם לְשִׂכִּים בְּעֵינֵיכֶם
וְלִצְנִינִם בְּצִדֵּיכֶם וְצָרְרוּ אֶתְכֶם עַל־הָאָרֶץ
אֲשֶׁר אַתֶּם יֹשְׁבִים בָּהּ׃ נו וְהָיָה כַּאֲשֶׁר דִּמִּיתִי
לַעֲשׂוֹת לָהֶם אֶעֱשֶׂה לָכֶם׃ פ לד א וַיְדַבֵּר
יְהוָה אֶל־מֹשֶׁה לֵּאמֹר׃ ב צַו אֶת־בְּנֵי יִשְׂרָאֵל

to them: When you cross the Yarden into the land of Canaan, 52. you shall drive out from before you all the inhabitants of the land and destroy all their symbols; you shall destroy all their molten [metal] images and demolish all their high places. 53. You shall first clear out the land for occupancy and [only] then settle in it, for to you have I given the land to take possession of it. 54. You shall divide the land among yourselves by lot according to your families; to the numerous you shall increase his inheritance and to the fewer in numbers you shall diminish his inheritance; wherever his lot comes out, that shall be his; according to the tribes of your fathers shall you divide the possession. 55. But if you will not drive out the inhabitants of the land from before you, then those whom you will leave over will become as hedges in your eyes and thorns in your sides; they will oppress you as enemies in the land in which you dwell. 56. It will then come to pass that what I had intended to do to them I will do to you."

XXXIV

1. *God* spoke to Moshe [saying]: 2. "Command the sons of Yisrael and say

51. ***Speak.*** Already in Exodus 34:12 ff., following the reestablishment of the Divine covenant that had been broken by the sin with the golden calf, and because the alien elements among the people had succeeded only too well in their attempts to lead the nation astray, the Children of Israel were warned that when they settled in the land they must not have tolerated in their midst, or even by their side, the pagan inhabitants of the land and idolatrous shrines. . . . Here, at the border, within sight of the land, even before we learn the exact borders of the land to be dedicated to, and acquired for, the realization of the Law, this warning is reiterated as the first basic condition for Israel's possession of the land. Indeed, the statement in Joshua 4:10, that the priests stood in the midst of the Jordan, bearing the Ark of the Covenant, waiting until Joshua had finished telling the people everything that God, through Moses, had commanded him to say to them, is interpreted in Sotah 34a as referring to the warning given to the Israelites as they were about to cross the Jordan. We are told there that while they stood in the river, at the critical moment when it would be decided whether they would be drowned in the waters of the Jordan or whether they would be permitted to cross the river safely into the land, they heard this warning again, and whether or not they would be permitted to take possession of the land and to keep it depended entirely on whether or not they would heed this admonition.

55. **לְשִׂכִּים בְּעֵינֵיכֶם** ***[hedges in your eyes].*** שוך and שכך denote a hedge made of thorns. . . . The pagan inhabitants whom you will permit to remain in the land will become a hedge, as it were, around their pagan excesses, so that these outrages will be screened from your sight and your judgment. If you show tolerance toward the pagan inhabitants of the land, you will become tolerant also toward paganism (Cf. Exodus 34:15 and 16). And by showing such tolerance that gives sanction to paganism in the land of God, you will forfeit the integrity of your own bond with God, and thus also the justification and the Divine protection for your own existence in this land. Then, once God has removed His protection from you, those toward whom you have been so tolerant will become your enemies and will oppress you in your own land. The entire Book of Judges is nothing but a history of what befell the people of Israel when it disregarded this admonition.

to them: When you come to the land of Canaan, this is the land that shall fall to you as your possession, the land of Canaan according to its borders. 3. Your southernmost point shall be from the wilderness of Tzin alongside Edom, and your southern border, to the east, shall be at the edge of the Salt Sea. 4. Then your border shall turn from the south to the elevation of Akrabim; it shall pass over to Tzin, and its ends shall be in the south of Kadesh Barnea. It shall then extend to Ḥatzar Adar and over to Atzmon. 5. The border shall then turn from Atzmon to the brook Mitzrayim, and its ends shall be at the sea. 6. And the western border: it shall be for you the Great Sea and its territory. This shall be your western border. 7. And this shall be your northern border: From the Great Sea you shall draw a line extending to Mount Hor; 8. from Mount Hor you shall draw a line extending to the road [leading] to Ḥamath, and the ends of the border shall be toward Tzedad. 9. Then the border shall run out to Zifron, and its ends shall be Ḥatzar Enon. This shall be your northern border. 10. You shall then demarcate as your eastern border the territory from Ḥatzar Enon to Shefam. 11. The border shall then run down from Shefam toward the Riblah, to the east of Ayin, and run down and strike upon the shore of Lake Kinnereth eastward. 12. Then the border shall run down along the Yarden, and its ends shall be the Salt Sea. This shall be the land for you according to its borders round about." 13. And Moshe commanded the sons of Yisrael: "This is the land that you are to divide among yourselves by lot as a possession that *God* has commanded to give to the nine and one-half tribes; 14. for the tribe of the sons of Reuben according to their fathers' house and the tribe of the sons of Gad according to their fathers' house and the half-tribe of Menashe have [already] received their inheritance. 15. The two

וְאָמַרְתָּ֣ אֲלֵהֶ֔ם כִּֽי־אַתֶּ֥ם בָּאִ֖ים אֶל־הָאָ֣רֶץ כְּנָ֑עַן
זֹ֣את הָאָ֗רֶץ אֲשֶׁ֨ר תִּפֹּ֤ל לָכֶם֙ בְּנַחֲלָ֔ה אֶ֖רֶץ כְּנַ֥עַן
לִגְבֻלֹתֶֽיהָ: ג וְהָיָ֨ה לָכֶ֤ם פְּאַת־נֶ֨גֶב֙ מִמִּדְבַּר־צִ֔ן
עַל־יְדֵ֖י אֱד֑וֹם וְהָיָ֤ה לָכֶם֙ גְּב֣וּל נֶ֔גֶב מִקְצֵ֥ה יָם־
הַמֶּ֖לַח קֵֽדְמָה: ד וְנָסַ֣ב לָכֶם֩ הַגְּב֨וּל מִנֶּ֜גֶב
לְמַעֲלֵ֣ה עַקְרַבִּים֮ וְעָ֣בַר צִ֒נָה֒ וְהָיָ֕ה (והיו קרי)
תוֹצְאֹתָ֔יו מִנֶּ֖גֶב לְקָדֵ֣שׁ בַּרְנֵ֑עַ וְיָצָ֥א חֲצַר־אַדָּ֖ר
וְעָבַ֥ר עַצְמֹֽנָה: ה וְנָסַ֧ב הַגְּב֛וּל מֵעַצְמ֖וֹן נַ֣חְלָה
מִצְרָ֑יִם וְהָי֥וּ תוֹצְאֹתָ֖יו הַיָּֽמָּה: ו וּגְב֣וּל יָ֔ם וְהָ֥יָה
לָכֶ֛ם הַיָּ֥ם הַגָּד֖וֹל וּגְב֑וּל זֶֽה־יִהְיֶ֥ה לָכֶ֖ם גְּב֥וּל יָֽם:
ז וְזֶֽה־יִהְיֶ֥ה לָכֶ֖ם גְּב֣וּל צָפ֑וֹן מִן־הַיָּם֙ הַגָּדֹ֔ל
תְּתָא֥וּ לָכֶ֖ם הֹ֥ר הָהָֽר: ח מֵהֹ֣ר הָהָ֔ר תְּתָא֖וּ לְבֹ֣א
חֲמָ֑ת וְהָי֛וּ תּוֹצְאֹ֥ת הַגְּבֻ֖ל צְדָֽדָה: ט וְיָצָ֤א הַגְּבֻל֙
זִפְרֹ֔נָה וְהָי֥וּ תוֹצְאֹתָ֖יו חֲצַ֣ר עֵינָ֑ן זֶֽה־יִהְיֶ֥ה לָכֶ֖ם
גְּב֥וּל צָפֽוֹן: י וְהִתְאַוִּיתֶ֥ם לָכֶ֖ם לִגְב֣וּל קֵ֑דְמָה
מֵחֲצַ֥ר עֵינָ֖ן שְׁפָֽמָה: יא וְיָרַ֨ד הַגְּבֻ֜ל מִשְּׁפָ֣ם
הָרִבְלָ֗ה מִקֶּ֤דֶם לָעָ֨יִן֙ וְיָרַ֣ד הַגְּבֻ֔ל וּמָחָ֥ה עַל־כֶּ֛תֶף
יָם־כִּנֶּ֖רֶת קֵֽדְמָה: יב וְיָרַ֤ד הַגְּבוּל֙ הַיַּרְדֵּ֔נָה וְהָי֥וּ
תוֹצְאֹתָ֖יו יָ֣ם הַמֶּ֑לַח זֹאת֩ תִּהְיֶ֨ה לָכֶ֤ם הָאָ֨רֶץ֙
לִגְבֻלֹתֶ֖יהָ סָבִֽיב: יג וַיְצַ֣ו מֹשֶׁ֔ה אֶת־בְּנֵ֥י יִשְׂרָאֵ֖ל
לֵאמֹ֑ר זֹ֣את הָאָ֗רֶץ אֲשֶׁ֨ר תִּתְנַחֲל֤וּ אֹתָהּ֙ בְּגוֹרָ֔ל
אֲשֶׁ֨ר צִוָּ֤ה יְהֹוָה֙ לָתֵ֔ת לְתִשְׁעַ֥ת הַמַּטּ֖וֹת וַחֲצִ֥י
הַמַּטֶּֽה: יד כִּ֣י לָקְח֞וּ מַטֵּ֨ה בְנֵ֤י הָראוּבֵנִי֙ לְבֵ֣ית
אֲבֹתָ֔ם וּמַטֵּ֥ה בְנֵֽי־הַגָּדִ֖י לְבֵ֣ית אֲבֹתָ֑ם וַחֲצִי֙
מַטֵּ֣ה מְנַשֶּׁ֔ה לָקְח֖וּ נַחֲלָתָֽם: טו שְׁנֵ֣י הַמַּטּ֗וֹת

CHAPTER XXXIV

7. הֹ֥ר הָהָ֖ר ... [Mount Hor] is not to be confused with

the mountain by the same name in the southeast on which Aaron died; the mountain in the present verse lay in the extreme northwest of the land.

tribes and the half-tribe have received their inheritance on this side of the Yarden near Jericho, to the east, toward the sunrise."
16. *God* spoke to Moshe [saying]:
17. "These are the names of the men who shall take possession of the land for you: Eleazar the priest and Yehoshua, son of Nun. 18. And one prince each from a tribe shall you take, to take possession of the land. 19. These are the names of the men: for the tribe of Yehudah: Caleb, son of Yefunneh. 20. And for the tribe of the sons of Shimeon: Sh'muel, son of Ammihud. 21. For the tribe of Binyamin: Elidad, son of Kislon. 22. And for the tribe of the sons of Dan, as prince: Bukki, son of Yogli. 23. For the sons of Yosef, for the tribe of the sons of Menashe, as prince: Ḥanniel, son of Ephod. 24. And for the tribe of the sons of Ephraim, as prince: Kemuel, son of Shiftan. 25. And for the tribe of the sons of Zebulun, as prince: Elitzafan, son of Parnakh. 26. And for the tribe of the sons of Yissakhar, as prince: Paltiel, son of Azzan. 27. And for the tribe of the sons of Asher, as prince: Aḥihud, son of Shelomi. 28. And for the tribe of the sons of Naphtali, as prince: Pedahel,

וַחֲצִי הַמַּטֶּה לָקְחוּ נַחֲלָתָם מֵעֵבֶר לְיַרְדֵּן יְרֵחוֹ
קֵדְמָה מִזְרָחָה: פ רביעי (ששי כשהן מחוברין)
טז וַיְדַבֵּר יְהוָה אֶל־מֹשֶׁה לֵּאמֹר: יז אֵלֶּה
שְׁמוֹת הָאֲנָשִׁים אֲשֶׁר־יִנְחֲלוּ לָכֶם אֶת־הָאָרֶץ
אֶלְעָזָר הַכֹּהֵן וִיהוֹשֻׁעַ בִּן־נוּן: יח וְנָשִׂיא אֶחָד
נָשִׂיא אֶחָד מִמַּטֶּה תִּקְחוּ לִנְחֹל אֶת־הָאָרֶץ:
יט וְאֵלֶּה שְׁמוֹת הָאֲנָשִׁים לְמַטֵּה יְהוּדָה כָּלֵב
בֶּן־יְפֻנֶּה: כ וּלְמַטֵּה בְּנֵי שִׁמְעוֹן שְׁמוּאֵל בֶּן־
עַמִּיהוּד: כא לְמַטֵּה בִנְיָמִן אֱלִידָד בֶּן־כִּסְלוֹן:
כב וּלְמַטֵּה בְנֵי־דָן נָשִׂיא בֻּקִּי בֶּן־יָגְלִי: כג לִבְנֵי
יוֹסֵף לְמַטֵּה בְנֵי־מְנַשֶּׁה נָשִׂיא חַנִּיאֵל בֶּן־אֵפֹד:
כד וּלְמַטֵּה בְנֵי־אֶפְרַיִם נָשִׂיא קְמוּאֵל בֶּן־
שִׁפְטָן: כה וּלְמַטֵּה בְנֵי־זְבוּלֻן נָשִׂיא אֱלִיצָפָן
בֶּן־פַּרְנָךְ: כו וּלְמַטֵּה בְנֵי־יִשָּׂשכָר נָשִׂיא
פַּלְטִיאֵל בֶּן־עַזָּן: כז וּלְמַטֵּה בְנֵי־אָשֵׁר נָשִׂיא
אֲחִיהוּד בֶּן־שְׁלֹמִי: כח וּלְמַטֵּה בְנֵי־נַפְתָּלִי
נָשִׂיא פְּדַהְאֵל בֶּן־עַמִּיהוּד: כט אֵלֶּה אֲשֶׁר צִוָּה

19–28. ***These are the names of the men.*** It is worthy of note that the order in which the tribes and their representatives are listed here, in connection with the division of the land, corresponds exactly to the locations in the land, from south to north, which the tribes were assigned for settlement in the land, near one another, and one after the other. Judah, Simeon and Benjamin occupied the south; Dan, Menashe (and Ephraim in between them), the central region, and Yissakhar, Zebulun, Asher and Naphtali, the north. True, it was only afterwards that the allocation of the tribal territories, which had been made by lottery, received Divine confirmation through the אוּרִים וְתוּמִּים [Urim and Thummim] . . . but their assignment is already given in these verses, in their intended order.

Here, in the instructions for the division of the territory, each tribe is identified as—מַטֵּה בְּנֵי ["the tribe of the sons of. . ."]; e.g., לְמַטֵּה בְנֵי דָן, לְמַטֵּה בְּנֵי שִׁמְעוֹן, etc. Only the tribes of Judah and Benjamin are identified simply as לְמַטֵּה בִנְיָמִן, לְמַטֵּה יְהוּדָה. Perhaps the logic in this difference is as follows: The designation—מַטֵּה בְּנֵי ["the tribe of the sons of. . ."] characterizes the tribe as a higher entity, to which the—בְּנֵי ["sons of. . ."] subordinate themselves as individuals. But this does not apply to the tribes of Judah and Benjamin. Their territory was to be the site of the national Sanctuary. Precisely for this reason they are not to be viewed as higher entities that encompass their members, but only as parts of the national community, as "branches" of that whole which comprises the nation. Hence their designation here is not מַטֵּה בְּנֵי בִנְיָמִן, מַטֵּה בְּנֵי יְהוּדָה ["the tribe of the sons of Yehudah, the tribe of the sons of Binyamin"], but מַטֵּה בִנְיָמִן, מַטֵּה יְהוּדָה ["the tribe of Yehudah, the tribe of Binyamin"].

A similar reasoning may also explain another peculiarity in the present passage. The representatives of all the other tribes are explicitly identified by the title of נָשִׂיא ["prince"] in accordance with the position they hold within their tribe. The only tribes in which this is not the case are those of Judah, Simeon and Benjamin. If we consider that the territory of Judah and Benjamin is to be viewed as the immediate periphery of the Sanctuary of God to be erected on their land, and that in fact the territory of Simeon forms only an enclave within that of Judah, it will be clear that, since the Sanctuary represents the supreme sovereignty of God and of His Law, no one person in that territory ought to be identified in this context as a prince.

son of Ammihud.   29. These are the ones whom *God* ordered to install the sons of Yisrael in the land of Canaan in their possession."

XXXV

1. *God* spoke to Moshe in the wastelands of Moab at the Yarden before Jericho [saying]:   2. "Command the sons of Yisrael that they give to the Levites, from the inheritance of their possession, cities to dwell in, and open land round about the cities shall you give to the Levites. 3. The cities shall be for them to dwell in, and their areas of open land shall be for their livestock, for their movable property and for all the needs of their life.   4. The areas of open land of the cities that you shall give to the Levites shall extend from the wall of the city and outward one thousand cubits all around.   5. And you shall measure off outside the city, on the east side, two thousand cubits; on the south side, two thousand cubits; and on the west side, two thousand cubits; and on the north side, two thousand cubits; with the city in the middle. There shall be suburbs of the cities for them.   6. And [among] the cities that you shall give to the Levites there shall be, first of all, the six cities of reception which you shall designate so that a manslayer can flee there; and to them you shall add another forty-two cities.   7. All the cities that you will give to the Levites [shall be]: forty-eight cities, they and their areas of open land.   8. [As for] the cities that you will give from the possession of the sons of Yisrael, you shall take more from the larger and less from the smaller [holdings]. Each one shall give of his cities to the Levites according to his inheritance that is allotted to them."   9. *God* spoke to Moshe [saying]:   10. "Speak to the sons of Yisrael

יְהֹוָ֖ה לְנַחֵ֥ל אֶת־בְּנֵֽי־יִשְׂרָאֵ֖ל בְּאֶ֥רֶץ כְּנָֽעַן: פ

חמישי לה א וַיְדַבֵּ֧ר יְהֹוָ֛ה אֶל־מֹשֶׁ֖ה בְּעַֽרְבֹ֣ת מוֹאָ֑ב עַל־יַרְדֵּ֥ן יְרֵחֹ֖ו לֵאמֹֽר: ב צַו֮ אֶת־בְּנֵ֣י יִשְׂרָאֵל֒ וְנָֽתְנ֣וּ לַלְוִיִּ֗ם מִֽנַּחֲלַ֛ת אֲחֻזָּתָ֖ם עָרִ֣ים לָשָׁ֑בֶת וּמִגְרָ֗שׁ לֶֽעָרִים֙ סְבִיבֹ֣תֵיהֶ֔ם תִּתְּנ֖וּ לַלְוִיִּֽם: ג וְהָי֧וּ הֶֽעָרִ֛ים לָהֶ֖ם לָשָׁ֑בֶת וּמִגְרְשֵׁיהֶ֗ם יִהְי֤וּ לִבְהֶמְתָּם֙ וְלִרְכֻשָׁ֔ם וּלְכֹ֖ל חַיָּתָֽם: ד וּמִגְרְשֵׁי֙ הֶֽעָרִ֔ים אֲשֶׁ֥ר תִּתְּנ֖וּ לַלְוִיִּ֑ם מִקִּ֤יר הָעִיר֙ וָח֔וּצָה אֶ֥לֶף אַמָּ֖ה סָבִֽיב: ה וּמַדֹּתֶ֞ם מִח֣וּץ לָעִ֗יר אֶת־פְּאַת־קֵ֣דְמָה אַלְפַּ֣יִם בָּֽאַמָּ֗ה וְאֶת־פְּאַת־נֶ֜גֶב אַלְפַּ֣יִם בָּֽאַמָּ֗ה וְאֶת־פְּאַת־יָ֣ם ׀ אַלְפַּ֤יִם בָּֽאַמָּה֙ וְאֵ֨ת פְּאַ֥ת צָפֹ֛ון אַלְפַּ֥יִם בָּֽאַמָּ֖ה וְהָעִ֣יר בַּתָּ֑וֶךְ זֶ֚ה יִהְיֶ֣ה לָהֶ֔ם מִגְרְשֵׁ֖י הֶֽעָרִֽים: ו וְאֵ֣ת הֶֽעָרִ֗ים אֲשֶׁ֣ר תִּתְּנוּ֮ לַלְוִיִּם֒ אֵ֤ת שֵׁשׁ־עָרֵ֣י הַמִּקְלָ֔ט אֲשֶׁ֣ר תִּתְּנ֔וּ לָנֻ֥ס שָׁ֖מָּה הָֽרֹצֵ֑חַ וַֽעֲלֵיהֶ֣ם תִּתְּנ֔וּ אַרְבָּעִ֥ים וּשְׁתַּ֖יִם עִֽיר: ז כָּל־הֶֽעָרִ֗ים אֲשֶׁ֤ר תִּתְּנוּ֙ לַלְוִיִּ֔ם אַרְבָּעִ֥ים וּשְׁמֹנֶ֖ה עִ֑יר אֶתְהֶ֖ן וְאֶת־מִגְרְשֵׁיהֶֽן: ח וְהֶֽעָרִ֗ים אֲשֶׁ֤ר תִּתְּנוּ֙ מֵֽאֲחֻזַּ֣ת בְּנֵֽי־יִשְׂרָאֵ֔ל מֵאֵ֤ת הָרַב֙ תַּרְבּ֔וּ וּמֵאֵ֥ת הַמְעַ֖ט תַּמְעִ֑יטוּ אִ֗ישׁ כְּפִ֤י נַֽחֲלָתֹו֙ אֲשֶׁ֣ר יִנְחָ֔לוּ יִתֵּ֥ן מֵֽעָרָ֖יו לַלְוִיִּֽם: פ

ששי (שביעי כשהן מחוברין) ט וַיְדַבֵּ֥ר יְהֹוָ֖ה אֶל־מֹשֶׁ֥ה לֵּאמֹֽר: י דַּבֵּר֙ אֶל־בְּנֵ֣י יִשְׂרָאֵ֔ל וְאָֽמַרְתָּ֖ אֲלֵהֶ֑ם

CHAPTER XXXV

10. **When you cross. . .** The land of the Law of God exists for the sake of human beings. Its most precious product, the purpose and goal of all the blessings bestowed upon it by God, is every human soul that it nurtures and thus consecrates for the realization of God's Law. The land is given to all the people only under the condition that they will regard every human life, which is sacred to the Law, as sacred and inviolable. Even one drop of innocent blood spilled unnoticed will drop a stitch from the bond that binds the land to the nation and both the land and the nation to God (see Verses 33 and 34). This respect for the sanctity of human life is to be demonstrated [by Israel] as soon as it takes possession of the land, and when the land is divided, there shall be created that legal institution to which

and say to them: When you cross the Yarden into the land of Canaan, 11. you shall designate for yourselves cities in an accommodating location; cities of reception shall they be for you so that a manslayer who committed manslaughter can flee there. 12. The cities shall serve you as [a place of] reception from the advocate, so that the manslayer will not die until he has stood before the community for judgment. 13. The cities that you shall give them shall be for you six cities of reception. 14. Three of the cities you shall give on this side of the Yarden, and three of the cities you shall give in the land of Canaan. Cities of reception shall they be. 15. For the sons of Yisrael and for those who have entered from abroad and the settlers in their midst shall these six cities serve as [places of] reception, so that anyone who inadvertently committed manslaughter can flee there. 16. If someone strikes another with an iron instrument so that he died, then he is a murderer, and the murderer must be executed. 17. If he strikes someone with a rock that can be held in the hand, from which he may die, and he died, he is a murderer, and the murderer must be executed. 18. Or someone strikes down another with a wooden instrument that can be held in the hand, from which he may die, and he died, he is a murderer, and the murderer must be executed. 19. The blood advocate himself shall kill the murderer; wherever he meets him, he may kill him. 20. Also if he pushes him down out of hatred, or throws something at him with deliberate aim, so that he died, 21. or

כִּי אַתֶּם עֹבְרִים אֶת־הַיַּרְדֵּן אַרְצָה כְּנָעַן:
יא וְהִקְרִיתֶם לָכֶם עָרִים עָרֵי מִקְלָט תִּהְיֶינָה
לָכֶם וְנָס שָׁמָּה רֹצֵחַ מַכֵּה־נֶפֶשׁ בִּשְׁגָגָה:
יב וְהָיוּ לָכֶם הֶעָרִים לְמִקְלָט מִגֹּאֵל וְלֹא יָמוּת
הָרֹצֵחַ עַד־עָמְדוֹ לִפְנֵי הָעֵדָה לַמִּשְׁפָּט:
יג וְהֶעָרִים אֲשֶׁר תִּתֵּנוּ שֵׁשׁ־עָרֵי מִקְלָט תִּהְיֶינָה
לָכֶם: יד אֵת | שְׁלֹשׁ הֶעָרִים תִּתְּנוּ מֵעֵבֶר לַיַּרְדֵּן
וְאֵת שְׁלֹשׁ הֶעָרִים תִּתְּנוּ בְּאֶרֶץ כְּנָעַן עָרֵי
מִקְלָט תִּהְיֶינָה: טו לִבְנֵי יִשְׂרָאֵל וְלַגֵּר וְלַתּוֹשָׁב
בְּתוֹכָם תִּהְיֶינָה שֵׁשׁ־הֶעָרִים הָאֵלֶּה לְמִקְלָט
לָנוּס שָׁמָּה כָּל־מַכֵּה־נֶפֶשׁ בִּשְׁגָגָה: טז וְאִם־
בִּכְלִי בַרְזֶל | הִכָּהוּ וַיָּמֹת רֹצֵחַ הוּא מוֹת יוּמַת
הָרֹצֵחַ: יז וְאִם בְּאֶבֶן יָד אֲשֶׁר־יָמוּת בָּהּ הִכָּהוּ
וַיָּמֹת רֹצֵחַ הוּא מוֹת יוּמַת הָרֹצֵחַ: יח אוֹ בִּכְלִי
עֵץ־יָד אֲשֶׁר־יָמוּת בּוֹ הִכָּהוּ וַיָּמֹת רֹצֵחַ הוּא
מוֹת יוּמַת הָרֹצֵחַ: יט גֹּאֵל הַדָּם הוּא יָמִית אֶת־
הָרֹצֵחַ בְּפִגְעוֹ־בוֹ הוּא יְמִתֶנּוּ: כ וְאִם־בְּשִׂנְאָה
יֶהְדָּפֶנּוּ אוֹ־הִשְׁלִיךְ עָלָיו בִּצְדִיָּה וַיָּמֹת: כא אוֹ

reference has already been made in the basic outline of the social legislation (Exodus 21:13).

11. ***you shall designate for yourselves . . . in an accommodating location.*** You shall designate for yourselves cities in locations that will offer themselves, as it were, to the fugitive, without his having to go out of his way to seek them out. . . .

16. ***If . . . with an iron instrument.*** First, Verses 16–21 list the criteria defining an act of deliberate murder, subject to punishment by a court of law. Apart from subjective indications—confirmed by the presence on the scene of witnesses who warned the offender before he committed the crime (Numbers 15:33)—that the accused was aware of what he was doing and had done so with criminal intent, the text now cites objective factors; i.e., the murder instruments set in motion or employed in the killing, which must be considered to determine whether the victim died under such circumstances that, in human estimation, his death could not be judged as anything but a direct result of the act of the accused. The text lists, for the consideration of the court, such factors as the size of the weapon, the material from which the weapon was made, its properties, the amount of force exerted by the accused, the part of the victim's body that was threatened and the part actually struck, the physical condition of the victim, etc. . . .

בְאֵיבָה הִכָּהוּ בְיָדוֹ וַיָּמֹת מוֹת־יוּמַת הַמַּכֶּה
רֹצֵחַ הוּא גֹּאֵל הַדָּם יָמִית אֶת־הָרֹצֵחַ בְּפִגְעוֹ־
בוֹ׃ כב וְאִם־בְּפֶתַע בְּלֹא־אֵיבָה הֲדָפוֹ אוֹ־
הִשְׁלִיךְ עָלָיו כָּל־כְּלִי בְּלֹא צְדִיָּה׃ כג אוֹ בְכָל־
אֶבֶן אֲשֶׁר־יָמוּת בָּהּ בְּלֹא רְאוֹת וַיַּפֵּל עָלָיו
וַיָּמֹת וְהוּא לֹא־אוֹיֵב לוֹ וְלֹא מְבַקֵּשׁ רָעָתוֹ׃
כד וְשָׁפְטוּ הָעֵדָה בֵּין הַמַּכֶּה וּבֵין גֹּאֵל הַדָּם עַל
הַמִּשְׁפָּטִים הָאֵלֶּה׃ כה וְהִצִּילוּ הָעֵדָה אֶת־
הָרֹצֵחַ מִיַּד גֹּאֵל הַדָּם וְהֵשִׁיבוּ אֹתוֹ הָעֵדָה אֶל־
עִיר מִקְלָטוֹ אֲשֶׁר־נָס שָׁמָּה וְיָשַׁב בָּהּ עַד־מוֹת
הַכֹּהֵן הַגָּדֹל אֲשֶׁר־מָשַׁח אֹתוֹ בְּשֶׁמֶן הַקֹּדֶשׁ׃
כו וְאִם־יָצֹא יֵצֵא הָרֹצֵחַ אֶת־גְּבוּל עִיר מִקְלָטוֹ
אֲשֶׁר יָנוּס שָׁמָּה׃ כז וּמָצָא אֹתוֹ גֹּאֵל הַדָּם
מִחוּץ לִגְבוּל עִיר מִקְלָטוֹ וְרָצַח גֹּאֵל הַדָּם אֶת־
הָרֹצֵחַ אֵין לוֹ דָּם׃ כח כִּי בְעִיר מִקְלָטוֹ יֵשֵׁב
עַד־מוֹת הַכֹּהֵן הַגָּדֹל וְאַחֲרֵי־מוֹת הַכֹּהֵן הַגָּדֹל
יָשׁוּב הָרֹצֵחַ אֶל־אֶרֶץ אֲחֻזָּתוֹ׃ כט וְהָיוּ אֵלֶּה
לָכֶם לְחֻקַּת מִשְׁפָּט לְדֹרֹתֵיכֶם בְּכֹל
מוֹשְׁבֹתֵיכֶם׃ ל כָּל־מַכֵּה־נֶפֶשׁ לְפִי עֵדִים יִרְצַח
אֶת־הָרֹצֵחַ וְעֵד אֶחָד לֹא־יַעֲנֶה בְנֶפֶשׁ לָמוּת׃

he struck him in enmity with his hand, so that he died, the one who struck him must be executed; he is a murderer. The blood advocate may kill the murderer wherever he meets him.
22. But if he pushed him down inadvertently, without enmity, or if he threw at him some article without deliberate aim,
23. or with any rock, from which he may die—without seeing him, he threw it at him—so that he died, but he was not an enemy to him and in no manner sought his hurt,
24. then the community shall judge between the slayer and the blood advocate on the basis of these [social] ordinances.
25. And the community shall rescue the manslayer from the hand of the blood advocate, and the community shall have him brought back to his city of reception to which he had fled, and he must remain there until the death of the high priest whom he had anointed with the sacred oil.
26. But if the manslayer goes outside the boundaries of his city of reception to which he has fled,
27. and the blood advocate finds him outside the boundaries of his city of reception, the blood advocate is permitted to kill the manslayer; there is no blood guilt on his account;
28. for he has to remain in his city of reception until the death of the high priest. After the death of the high priest, the manslayer shall return to the land of his possession.
29. These regulations shall be for you a law of justice for your descendants in all your dwelling places.
30. Whoever slays another person, he may kill the murderer only on the basis of testimony from witnesses. However, one witness shall not testify against a person when the death penalty is involved.

25. ***whom he had anointed with the sacred oil.*** The high priest who died must be the one who had been כֹּהֵן גָּדוֹל at the time when the court of justice handed down its verdict. The text reads . . . "whom he had anointed with the sacred oil"; i.e., in whose anointment he, the accused, still participated. If we understand this correctly, the reference is to a high priest who had been anointed while the accused was still part of the nation at large, in whose name every high priest is appointed to office; i.e., while the accused had not yet been banished from the nation at large by the verdict passed against him; cf. "who was anointed in his day" (Makkoth 11b). If the high priest dies before the verdict is pronounced, and the verdict is pronounced only after a new high priest has been appointed, the accused may return to his home only after the new high priest, too, has died. . . .

30. ***he may kill the murderer.*** The subject of the verb יִרְצַח [kill] is the "blood advocate," who has been described throughout this chapter not only as the individual authorized to carry out the death sentence upon the murderer but also as the one permitted to kill the manslayer if the latter deliberately went outside the reception city to which he had been banished. . . .

31. You may not take ransom for the life
of a murderer who has incurred the death
penalty, for he must be executed.
32. And you may not take ransom for
one who has fled to his city of reception [to
permit him] to return to live in the land,
until the death of the priest. 33. Do not
turn the land in which you are into a
hypocrite, for the blood turns the land into a
hypocrite; and for the land, there can be no

לא וְלֹא־תִקְחוּ כֹפֶר לְנֶפֶשׁ רֹצֵחַ אֲשֶׁר־הוּא
רָשָׁע לָמוּת כִּי־מוֹת יוּמָת: לב וְלֹא־תִקְחוּ כֹפֶר
לָנוּס אֶל־עִיר מִקְלָטוֹ לָשׁוּב לָשֶׁבֶת בָּאָרֶץ עַד־
מוֹת הַכֹּהֵן: לג וְלֹא־תַחֲנִיפוּ אֶת־הָאָרֶץ אֲשֶׁר
אַתֶּם בָּהּ כִּי הַדָּם הוּא יַחֲנִיף אֶת־הָאָרֶץ וְלָאָרֶץ

33. ***Do not turn . . . into a hypocrite.*** חנף, as is clear from its use in the Books of Job and Proverbs, means, "to be a hypocrite," to "dissemble," to present an external appearance different from, and better than, the reality within. Thus, one who turns another into a hypocrite removes the other's inner core while leaving his outer appearance unchanged. . . .

If an entire country becomes a "hypocrite," it is חֲנוּפָּה [hypocrisy] in the literal sense of the term. The soil is still the same, predestined to bear abundant fruit beneath God's blessed dew and sunshine. But the soil, the dew and the sunshine are only an illusion, for no blessed seed germinates from within to give life and joy to mankind. And whatever sprouts the seeds do send forth are illusive, too, for there is no blessing in the pith of the sprouts and in the sap of the plants. We are told וְלֹא תַחֲנִיפוּ אֶת הָאָרֶץ ["do not turn the land into a hypocrite"]: If you tolerate deliberate murder and careless manslaughter in your midst, you turn the land אֲשֶׁר אַתֶּם בָּהּ, "in which you *are*" (not merely אֲשֶׁר אַתֶּם יוֹשְׁבִים בָּהּ ["the land in which you *dwell*"] as in Verse 34), the land in which your very existence on earth is rooted, the land of which you should be regarded as the most precious product, into a "hypocrite." The land will frustrate the expectations with which you normally would be justified in looking upon it; it will withhold the blessings that should emanate from it, "because it (i.e., the blood) turns the land into a hypocrite."

Blood, human blood, is the most precious sap nurtured by the land and the soil; therefore any innocent blood that is spilled turns the land into a "hypocrite." Man, endowed with free will and thus brought close to God, represents the culmination of all terrestrial forces and phenomena. Since every drop of living blood bears within it the נֶפֶשׁ [soul] of a human being, and hence is responsible for man's existence, it represents a point of contact between heaven and earth, a union of the terrestrial with the Divine. A human society that does not regard the blood of each of its members as sacred, one that does not take up the cudgel for innocent human blood that has been spilled, negates the very purpose for which the forces of earth operate. It breaks the terms under which it may possess the soil of its land and contravenes the assumptions under which the soil has made its energies available to it. Accordingly, such a society becomes a "hypocrite" that deceives its own land and at the same time turns the land into a "hypocrite" that deceives the expectations of those who are in it.

for the land, there can be no atonement for the blood that is spilled in it, except by the blood of the one who spilled it. This חֲנוּפָּה [hypocrisy] can be purged from the land only if the innocent blood that has been spilled, and the human being who has lost his life as a result, finds an advocate in the society that survives him and the murderer is made to atone for his deed by dying at the hands of that advocate, thus losing his own life, which he has forfeited by his crime. For since he has spilled the blood of his fellow man, his own blood no longer has a right to life; he has forfeited his own right to existence. And to tolerate the continued existence of one who knowingly and deliberately murdered a fellow man would be a travesty on the dignity of man, who was made in the image of God. It would constitute a breach of the contract under which God gave the earth to man and the Land to Israel.

At the moment when God allowed Noah and his sons to set foot again upon the earth, newly restored to man, and when He handed over to them the world of plants and animals to do with as they saw fit, He said to them: "But your blood which belongs to your souls I will demand. . . . Whoever sheds the blood of man, by man shall his blood be shed, for in the image of God made He man" (Genesis 9:5–6). God proclaimed the inviolability of the dignity of man, who had been created in the image of God, as a basic condition for man's use of this gift and for his freedom to do with it as he wishes. Similarly, when God handed over to Israel the land [of Canaan] as the soil which it was to develop for the purpose of translating His Law into reality, He said to them, ". . . for the land, there can be no atonement for the blood that is spilled in it, except by the blood of the one who spilled it." He thus reiterated for Israel the same declaration of the dignity of man as the basic condition for Israel's right to possess the land and to enjoy its fruits, and He extended it by establishing the institution through which atonement could be made for unpremeditated manslaughter.

atonement for the blood that is spilled in it, except by the blood of the one who spilled it. 34. And do not defile the land in which you dwell, in whose midst I am

לֹא־יְכֻפַּר לַדָּם אֲשֶׁר שֻׁפַּךְ־בָּהּ כִּי־אִם בְּדַם שֹׁפְכוֹ: לד וְלֹא תְטַמֵּא אֶת־הָאָרֶץ אֲשֶׁר אַתֶּם

34. אֲשֶׁר אַתֶּם יוֹשְׁבִים בָּהּ אֲשֶׁר אֲנִי שֹׁכֵן בְּתוֹכָהּ *[in which you dwell, in whose midst I am present].* These words express a relationship between land and people different from that expressed in Verse 33 by the words אֲשֶׁר אַתֶּם בָּהּ ["in which you are"]. In Verse 33 the land is viewed as the basis for human existence. The soil will deny this existence to men if they will stand idly by while one man destroys the existence of another. In the present verse, the land is seen as the basis for יְשִׁיבָה and שְׁכִינָה, for the human society that makes up the nation and for the presence of God on earth. It is clear that the communal welfare of the nation (which is to be founded on allegiance to God and to His Law) and the presence of God on earth (which is assured if every aspect of earthly life is uplifted toward God) (Exodus 25:8) both depend on man's awareness and acknowledgment of the fact that he and his fellow men are created in the image of God. The entire Law of God is based on justice and mercy in society and on the moral sanctification of individual life. While justice is founded on man's acknowledgment that his fellow men are created in the image of God, mercy and moral sanctification are based on man's awareness that he himself is also created in that Divine image. If man is only another species of animal, only a physical creature like all other living things in creation, then his life, too, will be motivated only by violence, selfishness and the urge to gratify his animal drives. In that case there can be no thought of justice, or mercy, or moral sanctification; in that case, the world of both man and nature will bear only the imprint of טוּמְאָה, bondage to the physical elements, and of total lack of freedom, with all its logical manifestations of violence and depravity. In that case, bestiality will be the ideal worshipped in the home and by the state, by individuals and by nations. And then God, the One sole Being Who is to be acknowledged by the practice of justice and mercy and by moral sanctification, will have no place on earth.

In the eyes of the Law, indifference on the part of the community to the spilling of innocent human blood is the most patent denial of the basic concept of man's godliness, the outright proclamation of טוּמְאָה as the basic principle of individual and national life. For this reason the Law proclaims the command for the united entity that represents the Jewish state. [Hence the change to the singular form of address:] לֹא תְטַמֵּא אֶת הָאָרֶץ אֲשֶׁר אַתֶּם יֹשְׁבִים בָּהּ ["And do not defile the land in which you dwell"]: Do not, by your indifference to the spilling of human blood, proclaim טוּמְאָה as the dominant principle in the land which has you as its inhabitants and in the midst of which God manifests His presence: "I, *God,* am present in the midst of the sons of Yisrael." For it has just been said, אֲשֶׁר אֲנִי שֹׁכֵן בְּתוֹכָהּ ["in whose midst I am present"]; i.e., that God is present in the midst of the land. Not through the land as such, but through the men who dwell in it, through the people, the sons of Israel, and through the life this nation will build up on this land, will conditions on earth become worthy of receiving the promised presence of God. And if the presence of God is to become manifest in the midst of the nation (no matter how distant the life of the nation and the lives of the individuals comprising it may still be from the goal of perfection); if God, in His love that seeks to train the nation for the eventual attainment of moral perfection, wishes to be near to every epoch of Jewish national life, then, for the sake of this ideal of perfection, and for the sake of the continued presence of God, the nation as a whole must ever hold aloft, in unequivocal terms, that standard upon which all progress toward the future attainment of this ideal depends. The human societies that rally around God must constantly activate in their lives the concept of the godliness of man. All this must be done so that the principle of טָהֳרָה, as opposed to the phenomena of טוּמְאָה, may receive the devoted allegiance to which it is entitled and that the spirit of the nation as a whole may remain worthy of Him Who said of Himself that "I, *God,* am present in the midst of the sons of Yisrael."...

Only these concluding sentences afford a full view of the concepts behind the legal institutions which relate to the manslayer and the cities of reception, and whose implementation was to be the nation's first concern after it took possession of the land. Indeed, Moses had already implemented these institutions in the Transjordanian territory of which the Israelites had taken possession. When the nation of God takes possession of its land, it is to proclaim that even the blood of its lowliest citizens is sacred and irreplaceable. This particular state is to regard the lives of its citizens as the supreme and most precious of all the earthly treasures entrusted to its care, and the nation as a whole must accept responsibility for every minute by which the life of any one of its members is prematurely curtailed. God, and man created in the image of God—these concepts, along with all their consequences, are to form the spiritual and moral basis for the existence of this state and for the private and public lives of the individuals who belong to it. Every single member of this state is guaranteed life and possession of the land only under the condition that he will respect each and every one of his fellow citizens as having been created in the image of God, that he will therefore regard the

present, for I, *God*, am present in the midst
of the sons of Yisrael."

XXXVI

1. The heads of the
fathers of the family
of the sons of Gilead, son of Makhir, the son
of Menashe, of the families of the sons of
Yosef, approached and spoke before Moshe
and before the princes, the heads of the
fathers of the sons of Yisrael. 2. They
said: "*God* has commanded my lord to give
the land, by lot, as an inheritance to the sons
of Yisrael, and my lord was commanded by
God to give the inheritance of our brother
Tzelophehad to his daughters. 3. Now if
these should become wives to any of the

יֹשְׁבִים בָּהּ אֲשֶׁר אֲנִי שֹׁכֵן בְּתוֹכָהּ כִּי אֲנִי יְהֹוָה
שֹׁכֵן בְּתוֹךְ בְּנֵי יִשְׂרָאֵל: פ שביעי **לו** א וַיִּקְרְבוּ
רָאשֵׁי הָאָבוֹת לְמִשְׁפַּחַת בְּנֵי־גִלְעָד בֶּן־מָכִיר
בֶּן־מְנַשֶּׁה מִמִּשְׁפְּחֹת בְּנֵי יוֹסֵף וַיְדַבְּרוּ לִפְנֵי
מֹשֶׁה וְלִפְנֵי הַנְּשִׂאִים רָאשֵׁי אָבוֹת לִבְנֵי
יִשְׂרָאֵל: ב וַיֹּאמְרוּ אֶת־אֲדֹנִי צִוָּה יְהֹוָה לָתֵת
אֶת־הָאָרֶץ בְּנַחֲלָה בְּגוֹרָל לִבְנֵי יִשְׂרָאֵל וַאדֹנִי
צֻוָּה בַיהֹוָה לָתֵת אֶת־נַחֲלַת צְלָפְחָד אָחִינוּ
לִבְנֹתָיו: ג וְהָיוּ לְאֶחָד מִבְּנֵי שִׁבְטֵי בְנֵי־יִשְׂרָאֵל

lives of them all as inviolable, and that he will be mindful of this concern in all his actions. The cities of *miklat*, set at equal distances from one another throughout the land, and assuming their legal functions only after all of them have been designated (see Verse 13), proclaim this principle throughout the land and to all its inhabitants, without exception. And the blood advocate who is to be authorized or, if need be, expressly appointed by the state for this purpose, acts not only in behalf of the victim and his closest kin but also on behalf of the state to uphold the principle that was violated by the murder, or the killing, of one of its members.

° ° °

The fact that the banishment of the manslayer is explicitly defined as a banishment to the cities of the Levites, or, more accurately, to one of the Levite cities, so that the manslayer is given completely to the influence of the Levites, to the "assistants in the priestly functions," should only serve to emphasize the connection of all that has gone before with the basic functions of the Levites and the priests.

The emphasis in the duties of the priests and the Levites, with the high priest as their supreme representative, is on the functions of teaching the people and of effecting atonement for them. The atonement, which is to be effected within the Sanctuary, and the educational tasks, which are to be performed outside the Sanctuary, are closely interrelated. The function of effecting atonement, which the priest must perform within the Sanctuary, relates primarily, indeed almost exclusively, to unintentional deviations from the right path. Acts committed in conscious, deliberate violation of the dictates of duty, in defiant disobedience, are not within the purview of the priests but are subject to the jurisdiction of the courts of justice.

The essential function of the priests among the people is to disseminate the spirit of knowledge and the solemn resolves by which we are to place every aspect of our lives under the sovereignty of God's Law; to ponder our every step and every action with care and circumspection, leaving no room for levity or criminal thoughtlessness; to nurture that serious view of life which will guard even against acts of unintentional wrongdoing. In cases of sin against God, where criminal thoughtlessness has led to acts of unintentional wrongdoing involving capital sins (i.e., sins subject to the penalty of being "cut off"), the atonement must be effected by the priest inside the Sanctuary. . . . By the same token, if, in sins of man against man, criminal thoughtlessness resulted in the killing of a man, which is a capital offense, that act stands as a reproach and warning to the priests, and there is a twofold connection between their highest representative, the high priest, during whose tenure the verdict was given, and the verdict itself. The banishment of the accused is regarded as a banishment from the presence of the high priest. As a result, the high priest's life becomes linked with that of the accused in that the death of the high priest at any time after the issuance of the verdict is regarded as a final atonement for the act of manslaughter. The priests (and the high priest, as the foremost exponent of the priestly functions) must awaken and nurture among the people a spirit conducive to a purposeful, ever-renewed life of duty lived under God's guidance and subject to His rule, that will cause the individual not only to let his own life run its appointed course until the end but also to refrain from doing anything to shorten the lives of others. Concomitantly, the priests must awaken and nurture among the people that spirit of conscious moral freedom of will that removes all of human life from the sphere of טוּמְאָה, of bondage to blind physical forces, and that molds all of morally free-willed human life into a bearer and instrument of God's presence on earth. . . .

° ° °

sons of the [other] tribes of the sons of Yisrael, their inheritance will be deducted from the inheritance of our fathers and will be added to the inheritance of the tribe into which they marry, and it will be deducted from the lot of our inheritance. 4. Even if the *yovel* will come for the sons of Yisrael, their inheritance will be added to the inheritance of the tribe into which they marry, and their inheritance will be deducted from the inheritance of the tribe of our fathers." 5. And Moshe commanded the sons of Yisrael according to the word of *God*: "The tribe of the sons of Yosef speaks justly. 6. This is the word that *God* has commanded concerning the daughters of Tzelophehad: Let them become wives to anyone who pleases them, but let them become wives, nevertheless, to the family of their paternal tribe. 7. So that no inheritance of the sons of Yisrael should be transferred from tribe to tribe; for the sons of Yisrael shall attach themselves, each one to the inheritance of the tribe of his fathers. 8. And every daughter who inherits an inheritance from the tribes of the sons of Yisrael shall become a wife to one from the family of her paternal tribe so that the sons of Yisrael, every man, shall inherit the inheritance of his fathers. 9. And no inheritance will be transferred from one tribe to the tribe of another; for the tribes of the sons of Yisrael, each one shall attach itself to its [own] inheritance." 10. As *God* had commanded Moshe, so did the daughters of Tzelophehad do. 11. Mahlah, Thirtzah, Hoglah, Milkah and Noa, the daughters of Tzelophehad, became wives to the sons of their uncles. 12. They became wives to [men] from the families of the sons of Menashe, son of Yosef, and so their inheritance remained in the tribe of their paternal families. 13. These are the com-

לְנָשִׁים֒ וְנִגְרְעָה֙ נַחֲלָתָ֔ן מִנַּחֲלַת֙ אֲבֹתֵ֔ינוּ וְנוֹסַ֕ף עַ֚ל נַחֲלַ֣ת הַמַּטֶּ֔ה אֲשֶׁ֥ר תִּהְיֶ֖ינָה לָהֶ֑ם וּמִגֹּרַ֥ל נַחֲלָתֵ֖נוּ יִגָּרֵֽעַ: ד וְאִם־יִהְיֶ֣ה הַיֹּבֵל֮ לִבְנֵ֣י יִשְׂרָאֵל֒ וְנֽוֹסְפָה֙ נַחֲלָתָ֔ן עַ֚ל נַחֲלַ֣ת הַמַּטֶּ֔ה אֲשֶׁ֥ר תִּהְיֶ֖ינָה לָהֶ֑ם וּמִנַּֽחֲלַת֙ מַטֵּ֣ה אֲבֹתֵ֔ינוּ יִגָּרַ֖ע נַחֲלָתָֽן: ה וַיְצַ֤ו מֹשֶׁה֙ אֶת־בְּנֵ֣י יִשְׂרָאֵ֔ל עַל־פִּ֥י יְהֹוָ֖ה לֵאמֹ֑ר כֵּ֛ן מַטֵּ֥ה בְנֵֽי־יוֹסֵ֖ף דֹּבְרִֽים: ו זֶ֣ה הַדָּבָ֞ר אֲשֶׁר־צִוָּ֣ה יְהֹוָ֗ה לִבְנ֣וֹת צְלָפְחָד֮ לֵאמֹר֒ לַטּ֨וֹב בְּעֵֽינֵיהֶ֖ם תִּהְיֶ֣ינָה לְנָשִׁ֑ים אַ֗ךְ לְמִשְׁפַּ֛חַת מַטֵּ֥ה אֲבִיהֶ֖ם תִּהְיֶ֥ינָה לְנָשִֽׁים: ז וְלֹֽא־תִסֹּ֤ב נַחֲלָה֙ לִבְנֵ֣י יִשְׂרָאֵ֔ל מִמַּטֶּ֖ה אֶל־מַטֶּ֑ה כִּ֣י אִ֗ישׁ בְּנַחֲלַת֙ מַטֵּ֣ה אֲבֹתָ֔יו יִדְבְּק֖וּ בְּנֵ֥י יִשְׂרָאֵֽל: ח וְכָל־בַּ֞ת יֹרֶ֣שֶׁת נַחֲלָ֗ה מִמַּטּוֹת֮ בְּנֵ֣י יִשְׂרָאֵל֒ לְאֶחָ֗ד מִמִּשְׁפַּ֛חַת מַטֵּ֥ה אָבִ֖יהָ תִּהְיֶ֣ה לְאִשָּׁ֑ה לְמַ֗עַן יִֽירְשׁוּ֙ בְּנֵ֣י יִשְׂרָאֵ֔ל אִ֖ישׁ נַחֲלַ֥ת אֲבֹתָֽיו: ט וְלֹֽא־תִסֹּ֤ב נַחֲלָה֙ מִמַּטֶּ֔ה לְמַטֶּ֖ה אַחֵ֑ר כִּי־אִ֗ישׁ בְּנַ֣חֲלָת֔וֹ יִדְבְּק֕וּ מַטּ֖וֹת בְּנֵ֥י יִשְׂרָאֵֽל: י כַּֽאֲשֶׁ֛ר צִוָּ֥ה יְהֹוָ֖ה אֶת־מֹשֶׁ֑ה כֵּ֣ן עָשׂ֔וּ בְּנ֖וֹת צְלָפְחָֽד: מפטיר יא וַתִּהְיֶ֜ינָה מַחְלָ֣ה תִרְצָ֗ה וְחָגְלָ֧ה וּמִלְכָּ֛ה וְנֹעָ֖ה בְּנ֣וֹת צְלָפְחָ֑ד לִבְנֵ֥י דֹֽדֵיהֶ֖ן לְנָשִֽׁים: יב מִֽמִּשְׁפְּחֹ֛ת בְּנֵֽי־מְנַשֶּׁ֥ה בֶן־יוֹסֵ֖ף הָי֣וּ לְנָשִׁ֑ים וַתְּהִי֙ נַחֲלָתָ֔ן עַל־מַטֵּ֖ה מִשְׁפַּ֥חַת אֲבִיהֶֽן: יג אֵ֣לֶּה

CHAPTER XXXVI

13. ***These are the commandments.*** The commandments and social ordinances set forth from Chapter 22 until this point deal with the following subjects: The new census of the people; regulations pertaining to the division of the land among the tribes; the appoint-

ment of Joshua [as Moses' successor]; the compulsory offerings to be made by the nation as a whole; rules pertaining to self-imposed obligations; the treatment of foods and cooking utensils taken over from a non-Jewish owner; the rights and obligations of the tribes that received land in the Transjordanian area; the purging of the land from pagan outrages; the boundarmandments and the [social] ordinances that *God* commanded through Moshe to the sons of Yisrael in the wastelands of Moab on the Yarden before Jericho.

הַמִּצְוֺת וְהַמִּשְׁפָּטִים אֲשֶׁר צִוָּה יְהוָה בְּיַד־מֹשֶׁה אֶל־בְּנֵי יִשְׂרָאֵל בְּעַרְבֹת מוֹאָב עַל יַרְדֵּן יְרֵחוֹ:

חזק

ies of the land; the *miklat* cities; temporary regulations pertaining to marriages contracted by daughters who have inherited property from their fathers. All these commandments and ordinances are connected, to a greater or lesser degree, with Israel's imminent occupancy of the land. That is why they were given when the Children of Israel had arrived at the border and had come within sight of the land, "in the wastelands of Moab on the Yarden before Jericho."

The Haftarah for this Sidra may be found on page 905.

DEVARIM דברים

[DEUTERONOMY]

—————————◦⊂◦⊃◦—————————

"The Fifth Book now records all that Moses had to tell his people because he was about to depart from their midst and they would not have his guidance to carry out their mission in the land of which they would shortly take possession. . . . Now the people are about to make the transition from constant influence by a central guiding power° into a life of individualization in which, more than ever, the Jew needs to be constantly reminded of his calling. . . . We believe we are not in error if we view this Fifth Book as a compendium of those laws that had to be particularly noted both by the authorities of the Law and by every member of the nation now that the nation was about to move from the wilderness into the Land."

—Commentaries on Chapter 1, Verses 1 and 3

° The Sanctuary that traveled in their midst while they journeyed through the wilderness.

דברים

DEVARIM

I 1. These are the words that Moshe
spoke to all of Yisrael on the far side
of the Yarden, in the wilderness, in the
wasteland, opposite Suf, between Paran and
Tofel, Laban, Ḥatzeroth and Di-Zahav.
2. Eleven days' journey from Ḥoreb, by
way of the mountain of Seir to Kadesh
Barnea. 3. It came to pass in the fortieth
year, in the eleventh month, on the first
[day] of the month, that Moshe uttered it

א א אֵ֣לֶּה הַדְּבָרִ֗ים אֲשֶׁ֨ר דִּבֶּ֤ר מֹשֶׁה֙ אֶל־כָּל־
יִשְׂרָאֵ֔ל בְּעֵ֖בֶר הַיַּרְדֵּ֑ן בַּמִּדְבָּ֡ר בָּֽעֲרָבָה֩ מ֨וֹל ס֜וּף
בֵּֽין־פָּארָ֧ן וּבֵֽין־תֹּ֛פֶל וְלָבָ֥ן וַחֲצֵרֹ֖ת וְדִ֥י זָהָֽב׃
ב אַחַ֨ד עָשָׂ֥ר יוֹם֙ מֵֽחֹרֵ֔ב דֶּ֖רֶךְ הַר־שֵׂעִ֑יר עַ֖ד
קָדֵ֥שׁ בַּרְנֵֽעַ׃ ג וַיְהִי֙ בְּאַרְבָּעִ֣ים שָׁנָ֔ה בְּעַשְׁתֵּֽי־
עָשָׂ֥ר חֹ֖דֶשׁ בְּאֶחָ֣ד לַחֹ֑דֶשׁ דִּבֶּ֤ר מֹשֶׁה֙ אֶל־בְּנֵ֣י

CHAPTER I

1. ***These are the words.*** These introductory words refer to the whole of this Fifth Book. The final chapter of the Fourth Book recorded the orders and arrangements communicated by God to Moses regarding Israel's imminent occupancy of the Land. The Fifth Book now records all that Moses had to tell his people because he was about to depart from their midst, and they would not have his guidance to carry out their mission in the land of which they would shortly take possession. It would seem that the descriptions of the localities that now follow were intended to define the precise geographical location of the places where Moses spent his final weeks on earth among his people; where the people had last seen their leader in their midst; where they had last heard Moses speak to them alive. Each word of these final orations of our leader, who had been sent by God Himself, reflects his deep-felt attachment to his people and his concern for their future welfare; indeed, his profound yearning to give his own soul and his own spirit, as it were, to his people to sustain them in the trials that awaited them. Note, too, that this part of the wilderness cannot be identified by any landmark or other unique physical feature. Thus, one can readily understand the desire that the region should be preserved in the nation's memory by precise definitions of its geographical position and boundaries. After all, Moses is about to leave us, and no monument, no memorial, no visible reminder of his life will remain with us. There will not even be a grave to serve as a concrete memorial for future generations to view. With Moses' death, all of his physical personality will depart. Only a description, recorded in the most precise terms possible, of the place where the people had heard the last of his faithful words, will be handed down to posterity so that, if some day a late descendant of the Children of Israel will come to this place, it may perhaps echo for him these words and inspire him to follow them faithfully in the midst, and for the good, of his people.

° ° °

3. ***It came to pass . . . that Moshe uttered.*** כְּכֹל וגו׳ ["how (*God* had commanded him) everything . . ."]: The text does not say כָּל אֲשֶׁר וגו׳ but כְּכֹל אֲשֶׁר צִוָּה ד׳ אֹתוֹ אֲלֵיהֶם (See Commentary on Numbers 30:1). Moses did not merely repeat everything that God had commanded, but reiterated *how*, the manner in which, God had commanded it. Moses pronounced once again, in precise, terse sentences, the basic norms of the Law, and at the same time, set forth in full detail, the manner in which these laws were to be observed. What Moses gives to his people at this point is defined in Verse 5 as בֵּאֵר, an "expounding" of the Law.

However, these reiterations and elucidations given orally by Moses are not recorded in this Fifth Book. Nor do the reiterations and elucidations of laws already recorded in the preceding Books form the substantive content of the present Book. Of the more than one hundred articles of law contained in the present Book, more than seventy are entirely new; they do not appear in the preceding Books. These topics include: "Hear, O Yisrael" (*Deut.* 6:4ff.); the prohibition against marriage to natives of the land of Canaan (*Deut.* 7:3); the prohibition against deriving benefit from idol worship or places of idol worship (*Deut.* 7:26); the commandment to give thanks to God after meals (*Deut.* 8:10); acceptance of the yoke of the commandments (*Deut.* 11:13); the blessings and the curses recited on Mount Gerizim and Mount Ebal (*Deut.* 11:26ff.); the prohibition against destroying places and objects consecrated to God (*Deut.* 12:4ff.); laws regarding the bringing of offerings to the Temple (*Deut.* 12:11); the prohibition against making offerings on "high places" and against worshipping on such elevations after the manner of the heathens (*Deut.* 12:8, 9); the prohibition against partaking of specified tithes or firstlings at a place other than that chosen by God (*Deut.* 12:17ff.); the manner of slaughtering animals (*Deut.* 12:23); laws regarding the meat and the blood of animal offerings (*Deut.* 12:27); the prohibition against adding anything to the Law of God (*Deut.* 13:1); the prohibition against eliminating any part of the Law (*Deut.* 13:1); laws regarding a false prophet (*Deut.* 13:2f.); laws regarding temptations to go astray (*Deut.* 13:7ff.); laws applicable if a whole city goes astray (*Deut.* 13:13ff.); the tithe to the poor (*Deut.* 14:22ff.); the law regarding the release of debts at the end of the seventh year (*Deut.* 15:1ff.); the laws of *tzedakah* (*Deut.* 15:8); the institution of the Sanhedrin (*Deut.* 16:18ff.); the prohibition against *asheroth* (*Deut.* 16:21); the law regarding a Jewish individual who worships idols (*Deut.* 17:3ff.); testimonies of witnesses (*Deut.* 17:6ff.); kingship (*Deut.* 17:14ff.); laws regarding the "rebellious elder" (*Deut.* 17:12); the first of the fleece of the sheep to be given to the priests (*Deut.* 18:4); the ministering duties of the priests (*Deut.* 18:5ff.); attitude toward true prophets (*Deut.* 18:15ff.); the prohibition against removing the landmark of another in the land of Canaan (*Deut.* 19:14); regarding scheming witnesses (*Deut.* 19:15ff.); regarding military service (*Deut.* 20:1ff.); regarding peace offers to be made before laying siege to a city (*Deut.* 20:10ff.); the prohibition against the wanton destruction of trees in a captured city (*Deut.* 20:19); procedure to be followed if a murder victim is discovered but the murderer is not known (*Deut.* 21:1ff.); laws regarding the treatment of women captured from the enemy (*Deut.* 21:11ff.); regarding the rights of firstborn sons (*Deut.* 21:15ff.); how to deal with a rebellious son (*Deut.* 21:18ff.); the prohibition against allowing the body of a hanged criminal to remain unburied (*Deut.* 21:22–23); the prohibition against wearing garments or accessories usually worn by the opposite sex (*Deut.* 22:5); sending away the mother bird before taking her young (*Deut.* 22:6–7); regarding the construction of a guard rail on roofs to prevent accidents (*Deut.* 22:8); the prohibition against using an ox and a donkey together in plowing (*Deut.* 22:10); casting unjustified aspersions on a woman's virginity (*Deut.* 22:13ff.); punishment for adulterous relationships (i.e., sexual relations between a married woman and a man other than her husband) (*Deut.* 22:22); punishment for sexual relations between a betrothed maiden and a man other than her betrothed (*Deut.* 22:23ff.); laws regarding rape (*Deut.* 22:25); the prohibition against sexual relations with the wife of one's father (*Deut.* 23:1); regarding a man with maimed genitals (*Deut.* 23:2); restrictions applicable to *mamzerim* (*Deut.* 23:3); restrictions in relations with Ammonites and Moabites (*Deut.* 23:4); the attitude toward an Edomite (*Deut.* 23:8); the attitude toward a Mitzrite (*Deut.* 23:8); the "holiness of the camp" (*Deut.* 23:10ff.); extradition of an escaped bondservant (*Deut.* 23:16–17); harlotry (*Deut.* 23:18–19); the prohibition against the use of a harlot's hire or the price of a dog for redeeming a pledge (*Deut.* 23:19); the right of a hired laborer to eat grapes from the vineyard he is harvesting for his employer (*Deut.* 23:25); bills of divorce (*Deut.* 24:1ff.); prohibition against a man remarrying his divorced wife after she has been married to another man (*Deut.* 24:4); legal exemptions to which a newly-married man is entitled (*Deut.* 24:5); regarding loan pledges (*Deut.* 24:10–13); fathers must not be put to death for the sins of their children, or vice versa (*Deut.* 24:16); punishment by lashes (*Deut.* 25:2–3); prohibition against muzzling an ox while it is treading grain (*Deut.* 25:4); levirate marriage (*Deut.* 25:5ff.); the commandment to remember the Amalekite sneak attack on the Israelites in the wilderness (*Deut.* 25:17ff.); regarding the offering of first fruits at the Temple (*Deut.* 26:1ff.); declaration to be pronounced when offering the tithe (*Deut.* 26:5ff.); the commandment to inscribe the Law upon stones (*Deut.* 27:2ff.); the public reading of the Law (*Deut.* 31:11ff.); the command that every Jew must have a correct *Sefer Torah* written for himself (*Deut.* 31:19).

As distinct from the laws enumerated above, the following laws in the present Book are repetitions of laws that already appear in earlier Books: the appointment of judges (*Deut.* 16:18); reference to the prohibition against making carved images (*Deut.* 4:16); the Ten Commandments (*Deut.* 5:6–18); the demolition of idols (*Deut.* 7:5, 25; 12:2, 3); the commandment to fear and love God (*Deut.* 6:2, 5); idol worship (*Deut.* 6:14, 7:4); the permission to eat meat slaughtered for the purpose of food without its having to be brought as an offering (*Deut.* 12:20, 21); the prohibition against eating blood (*Deut.* 12:23); the prohibition against eating parts of a living animal (*Deut.* 12:23); the prohibition against making cuts in one's flesh as a sign of mourning (*Deut.* 14:1); animals that must not be eaten (*Deut.* 14:3ff.); the prohibition against making a bald patch on one's head as a sign of mourning (*Deut.* 14:1); the second tithe (*Deut.* 14:28ff.); sanctification of firstlings (*Deut.* 15:19ff.); Passover (*Deut.* 16:1–8); Shevuoth (*Deut.* 16:9–12); Sukkoth (*Deut.* 16:13–15); the prohibition against setting up a "memorial stone" (*Deut.* 16:22); the prohibition against offering a blemished animal to God (*Deut.* 17:1); the prohibition against making human sacrifices (*Deut.* 18:10); the prohibitions against various forms of divination and witchcraft (*Deut.* 18:10ff.); the commandment to be wholehearted in one's integrity before God (*Deut.* 18:13); regarding the unintentional manslayer (*Deut.* 19:3ff.); return of lost property (*Deut.* 22:1–3); forbidden mixtures of wool and flax (*Deut.* 22:11); *tzitzith* (*Deut.* 22:12); the prohibition against lending at interest (*Deut.* 23:30ff.); vows (*Deut.* 23:22–24); punishment for kidnapping (*Deut.* 24:7); reference to leprous marks (*Deut.* 24:8); regarding the return of pledges (*Deut.* 24:10ff.); treatment of the day laborer (*Deut.*

again to the sons of Yisrael, how *God* had commanded him everything for them

יִשְׂרָאֵל כְּכֹל אֲשֶׁר צִוָּה יְהֹוָה אֹתוֹ אֲלֵהֶם:

24:14-15); the perversion of justice (*Deut.* 24:17); the prohibition against taking a widow's garment as a pledge (*Deut.* 24:17); "the forgotten sheaf" (*Deut.* 24:19); and fair weights (*Deut.* 25:13-15).

In order to assess the intent of this Fifth Book, one must attempt to find the answer to the questions of why the new laws listed earlier were not set down in the preceding Books and why, on the other hand, of all the laws reiterated orally by Moses at this point, precisely the laws listed immediately above should have been singled out for written reiteration in our present text.

A closer examination of one of these groups of laws that first appeared in earlier Books and are partially reiterated here may afford us a key to the answer. The laws regarding the festivals, which first occurred in Chapter 23 of Leviticus, are reiterated in Chapter 16, Verses 1-17, of Deuteronomy. But one is immediately struck by the fact that this reiteration includes only the festivals of Passover, Shevuoth and Sukkoth. The Sabbath, Rosh HaShanah, Yom Kippur and Shemini Atzereth, which are also discussed in Leviticus 23, are not mentioned in this Deuteronomy chapter. Now these last-named four festivals have one feature in common: their basic significance derives purely from our relationship to God; or, more accurately put, primarily from the relationship of the individual to God. For this reason, their basic purpose could be realized also in the wilderness, and Israel's settling in its own land will hardly make a difference in their observance. Not so Passover, Shevuoth and Sukkoth. In the case of these three festivals, one aspect of their significance, namely, their association with the soil and its seasonal cycle, will become relevant only now [when Israel dwells in a land of its own]. Indeed, the festival of Sukkoth, as a historical reminder of Israel's life in huts during its wanderings through the wilderness, will attain its full significance only after Israel has made the transition from its nomadic sojourns in huts to a settled life in town and countryside. Certainly the commandment to wave the *lulav*, for example, could hardly have been observed in the wilderness. Moreover, in the case of all three festivals, the nation as a whole is commanded to make a pilgrimage to the Sanctuary of the Law, to rally around this Sanctuary, which is its focal point. Obviously, this commandment can be observed only after the nation has dispersed throughout its land, for in the wilderness Israel was grouped around the Sanctuary at all times.

Therefore, the following assumption would suggest itself: When the entire Law was reiterated and expounded during the final weeks preceding Israel's entry into its land, it was not the Sabbath, Rosh HaShanah, Yom Kippur and Shemini Atzereth [whose observance would remain unaffected by the change in Israel's situation], but only Passover, Shevuoth and Sukkoth that were discussed again also in the written text because only the observance of these last three festivals would be directly influenced by circumstances resulting from Israel's settling on its own land.

This assumption would be supported by the two factors that are emphasized in the written reiteration of the laws regarding the observance of Passover, Shevuoth and Sukkoth: First, each of these festivals is related to a specific season of the year (indeed, the entire Jewish calendar is fixed to accommodate this relationship): "Keep the month of standing grain" (16:1); "From the time that the sickle begins (to be put) to the grain" (16:9); ". . . by gathering up [the produce] from your threshing floor and your wine press" (16:13). Secondly, the observance of all three festivals must be concentrated in one central point designated by God: "And you shall make the Pesaḥ (offering). . ." (16:2); "at the place that (*God*) will choose" (16:2); "You may not make the Pesaḥ offering within one of your gates. . ." (16:5); "but you must go to the place. . ." (16:6); "And you shall cook and eat it in the place. . ." (16:7); "And you shall rejoice before *God*, your God . . . in the place that (*God*, your God) will choose" (16:11); "For seven days you shall celebrate. . ." (16:15); "in the place. . ." (16:15); "Three times each year shall all your males appear. . ." (16:16).

If we now apply this same viewpoint to the consideration of all the other laws contained in this Book, we will note, at the outset, the obvious reason for the repeated warnings given here against idol worship and all the evils and aberrations associated with it. Such admonitions are needed at this juncture, for as soon as the people will enter the land they will be exposed to contacts with the polytheistic abominations of the Canaanite population. Hence, the laws referring to a whole city that has gone astray (*Deut.* 13:13ff.); temptations to go astray (*Deut.* 13:7ff.); the prohibition against deriving benefit from idol worship or places of idol worship (*Deut.* 7:26); the prohibition against marriage to natives of the land of Canaan (*Deut.* 7:3); the prohibition against *asheroth* (*Deut.* 16:21ff.); a Jewish individual who worships idols (*Deut.* 17:3ff.); prohibitions against various forms of divination and witchcraft (*Deut.* 18:10ff.); prohibitions against making human sacrifices (*Deut.* 18:10); the prohibition against making cuts in one's flesh as a sign of mourning (*Deut.* 14:1); regarding the demolition of idols (*Deut.* 7:5, 25; 12:2, 3); the prohibition against making carved images (*Deut.* 4:16); and the prohibition against setting up a "memorial stone" (*Deut.* 16:22).

The same logic [namely, the imminence of Israel's entry into its own land] is applicable to the creation of a national leadership that must take place after Moses' departure, and to the judicial system that is to be organized throughout the land and to center in one supreme judicial authority. Hence, there are the laws referring to the institution of the Sanhedrin (*Deut.* 16:18ff.); kingship (*Deut.* 17:14ff.); fair weights (*Deut.* 25:13–15); punishment by lashes (*Deut.* 25:2–3); false prophets (*Deut.* 13:2f.); true prophets (*Deut.* 18:15ff.); scheming witnesses (*Deut.* 19:16ff.); the "rebellious elder" (*Deut.* 17:12); the appointment of judges (*Deut.* 16:18ff.); harlotry (*Deut.*23:18–19).

Obviously, too, this is also the logical place for reiterating, in written form, the laws pertinent to warfare: peace offers to be made before laying siege to a city (*Deut.* 20:10ff.); prohibition against the wanton destruction of trees in a captured city (*Deut.* 20:19); the treatment of women captured from the enemy (*Deut.* 21:11ff.); the "holiness of the camp" (*Deut.* 23:10ff.); legal exemptions to which a newly-married man is entitled (*Deut.* 24:5); the laws relating to the inscribing of the Law upon stones (*Deut.* 27:2ff.); the blessings and the curses recited on Mount Gerizim and Mount Ebal (*Deut.* 11:26ff.), laws which must be carried out as soon as the people set foot in its land. This is the logical place, too, for the reference to meat slaughtered for the purpose of food only, which becomes permissible once the people has dispersed over its land. Under this law both the procedures of *sheḥitah* and the observance of the dietary laws are entrusted to the personal honor of each member of the nation. Thus, the fact that meat slaughtered for the purpose of food only becomes permissible once the nation has entered its land is sufficient explanation for the fact that, at this point, the text should set forth, for the first time, or by way of repetition, respectively, the law of *sheḥitah* (*Deut.* 12:21); the prohibition against eating blood (*Deut.* 12:23); the prohibition against eating parts of a living animal (*Deut.* 12:23) and the section on animals that may not be eaten (*Deut.* 14:3ff.), as well as the laws referring to the second tithe (*Deut.* 14:28ff.); the offering of first fruits at the Temple (*Deut.* 26:1ff.); the prohibition against partaking of specified tithes or firstlings at a place other than that chosen by God (*Deut.* 12:17ff.); laws regarding the bringing of offerings to the Temple (*Deut.* 12:11); the prohibition against making offerings on "high places" and against worshipping on such elevations after the manner of the heathens (*Deut.* 12:8, 9), and the declaration to be pronounced when offering the tithe (*Deut.* 26:5ff.). All these laws preserve and promote Israel's subordination to the central Sanctuary of the Law.

However, the transition from immediate Divine guidance and providence to the normal conditions of national life as a human society in a land of its own must have brought about far-reaching changes also in the nation's communal life, and this would be sufficient explanation as to why, at this point, a whole series of social laws should be set down here either for the first time or by way of reiteration. This explanation would apply to all the detailed laws of *tzedakah* (*Deut.* 15:8); the tithe to the poor (*Deut.* 14:22ff.); the law regarding the release of debts at the end of the seventh year (*Deut.* 15:1ff.) and the right of a hired laborer to eat grapes from the vineyard he is harvesting for his employer (*Deut.* 23:25), all of which are set down for the first time in the Book of Deuteronomy. It would apply also to laws reiterated in Deuteronomy, such as those referring to the "forgotten sheaf" (*Deut.* 24:19); the prohibition against borrowing at interest (*Deut.* 23:20ff.); the prohibition against taking a widow's garment as a pledge (*Deut:* 24:17); treatment of the day laborer (*Deut.* 24:14–15) and the return of pledges (*Deut.* 24:10ff.).

While the Children of Israel journeyed through the wilderness, God Himself provided them with shelter, clothing and all the other necessities of life. During that period there were no poor people, and probably also no day laborers, among the Children of Israel. Only when the people of Israel entered into the normal conditions of life, in which human existence depends on man's own productive labor and commercial activity, did differences in economic status first arise, including various degrees of poverty in which people became dependent on aid from their fellow men. In the wilderness, where everyone had everything he needed, but no more than that, there was neither the necessity for *tzedakah,* nor the possibility to practice it. Thus, it was only after the people of Israel had made the transition from immediate Divine providence to normal social and economic conditions that the male truly became the provider for his wife and home. As long as Israel journeyed through the wilderness, this essential aspect of the marital relationship was lacking. Only after Israel had entered its land did marriage receive its full social and legal basis.

The earlier Books had already recorded the laws regulating the physiological and moral aspects of sex in marriage that were relevant even to life in the wilderness; the norms regulating the contracting and dissolution of marriages; the law regarding a man with maimed genitals (*Deut.* 23:2); restrictions pertinent to *mamzerim* (*Deut.* 23:3); restrictions in relations with Ammonites and Moabites (*Deut.* 23:4); the attitude toward an Edomite (*Deut.* 23:8) and toward a Mitzrite (*Deut.* 23:8). But the law of levirate marriage and the law regarding the rights of the first-born son (*Deut.* 21:15ff.), which are closely linked to the legal and civic aspects of family life in a settled society, were not set down in writing until just before Israel was about to enter into its own land and the entire Law was reiterated. And so the reasoning that motivated the recording of these laws in the Fifth Book seems utterly clear and uncontrived, and since the laws selected for general discussion here so definitely constitute the majority of all the laws, we believe we will not be mistaken if we

4. after he had struck down Siḥon, king
of the Emorites, who dwelt in Ḥeshbon, and
Og, king of Bashan, who dwelt at Ashtaroth,
in Edrei.   5. On the other side of the
Yarden, in the land of Moab, Moshe, in
expounding this Law, began as follows:
6. *God*, our God, spoke to us at Ḥoreb

ד אַחֲרֵי הַכֹּתוֹ אֵת סִיחֹן מֶלֶךְ הָאֱמֹרִי אֲשֶׁר
יוֹשֵׁב בְּחֶשְׁבּוֹן וְאֵת עוֹג מֶלֶךְ הַבָּשָׁן אֲשֶׁר־
יוֹשֵׁב בְּעַשְׁתָּרֹת בְּאֶדְרֶעִי: ה בְּעֵבֶר הַיַּרְדֵּן
בְּאֶרֶץ מוֹאָב הוֹאִיל מֹשֶׁה בֵּאֵר אֶת־הַתּוֹרָה
הַזֹּאת לֵאמֹר: ו יְהֹוָה אֱלֹהֵינוּ דִּבֶּר אֵלֵינוּ

assume that a similar logic motivated also the inclusion
of all the other laws that appear in the Book of
Deuteronomy.

However, the introduction with which Moses, "in
expounding the Law. . .," began the repeated elucida-
tion of the Law, is set down in its entirety. For precisely
these orations that comprise the first eleven chapters of
Deuteronomy are intended to define the basic attitudes
toward God and His Law that are expected of Israel,
and the basic duties that Israel is expected to fulfill as a
result. These orations are supported by a review,
through the mouth of Moses, of a past replete with
God-revealing experiences that is now coming to a
close but that should remain forever in the hearts and
minds of the Jews, inspiring them to step forth as faithful sons of God's covenant. The desired attitudes are
fear of God, love of God and adherence to God, all three
based on an awareness, both theoretical and practical,
of the unity of God. Each member of the people is
expected personally to assume the obligation to study
the Law. Every Jewish father has the duty toward
his child to fulfill the commandment "and you shall
impress them sharply upon your sons." Moreover,
every Jew is bound by the commandment "you must
not add anything to (what God has commanded) nor
subtract anything from it" (*Deut*. 13:1); i.e., the
premise that the Law which has been handed down to
us is inviolable and immutable. At the same time, these
preambles of Moses to the Law, which in fact constitute
his testament to his people, include commandments
that are to accompany every Jewish individual even
into isolation and that to this day serve to train us
constantly for God and for our duties; e.g., the reading
of the *Shema*; the reference to the rewards for hearkening to God's commandments and obeying them (*Deut*.
11:13); the phylacteries (*Deut*. 6:8); the *mezuzah*
(*Deut*. 6:9) and giving thanks to God after meals
(*Deut*. 8:10). Also, the commandments to remember
the Exodus from Egypt every day, and the commandments concerning *tzitzith* and forbidden mixtures
of wool and flax (*Deut*. 22:11), are once again repeated in writing. For now the people are about to
make the transition from constant influence by a
central guiding power into a life of individualization in
which, more than ever, the Jew needs to be constantly
reminded of his calling Even his garments are to serve

as his preceptors in the duties of the Jewish individual
and in the moral ennoblement of the human being.

In recapitulation, we believe we are not in error if we
view this Fifth Book as a compendium of those laws
that had to be particularly noted both by the authorities
of the Law and by every member of the nation now that
the nation was about to move from the wilderness into
the Land. Some of these laws had purposely not been
put into writing until this point; others, which had
already been mentioned before, were now reiterated
because it was considered essential for the desired
objective. If, therefore, this book is usually referred to
as מִשְׁנֶה תּוֹרָה and hence construed as a "repetition of the
Law," this cannot imply that the material set down
here is merely a repetition of laws already recorded in
the earlier Books of the Law. We have seen that by far
the greater part of the laws set down in Deuteronomy
had never been put into writing before. Hence, the
term "repetition" in this case can be construed as a
"repetition" only in the sense that the Book of
Deuteronomy tells of the oral reiteration and elucida-
tion of the entire Law with which Moses ended his
work for his people on earth. It is from this oral reiteration that the laws contained in this book—some of them
appearing here for the first time, others already recorded in earlier Books—were abstracted.

5. . . . The basic purpose of the first portion of these
preambles (Chapter 1:6 through 3:22) is to use the
nation's historical experiences as a means of impressing
upon the nation that what Israel requires in order to
subdue the other nations and to take possession of the
Land is not the skills and instruments of warfare, but
dutiful devotion to God in the fulfillment of His will; and
that such obedience toward God, which constitutes
our sole task in times of peace, will be sufficient also in
times of war to overcome all the powers that oppose us.
With obedience toward God we can accomplish everything; without it, nothing. Israel is to enter upon its
path in the history of nations not as a mighty nation,
skilled in the arts of warfare, but as the people of God's
moral law. Israel's triumphs and defeats throughout its
history are ample proof of this point, in which the
development of Israel differs from that of all other
nations.

[saying]: "You have stayed long enough
at this mountain; 7. turn and journey
forth and enter into the mountains of the
Emorite[s] and to all its neighbors in the
wasteland, in the highland, in the low land,
in the south and by the seashore, in the land
of the Canaanite[s], and the Lebanon as
far as the great river, the river Perath.
8. Lo! I have set the land before you; go
in and take possession of the land that *God*
swore to your fathers, Abraham, Yitzḥak
and Yaakov, to give to them and to their
descendants after them." 9. At that time
I said to you: "I am not able to bear you by
myself; 10. *God*, your God, has multiplied you, and you are now like the stars of
heaven in multitude. 11. May *God*, the
God of your fathers, add to you another
thousand times as many as you are now, and
may He bless you, even as He has spoken
concerning yourselves. 12. How am I to
carry your trouble, your burden and your
strife by myself? 13. Give yourselves
men, wise and discerning and known to our
tribes, and I will set them at your head."
14. And you answered me and said: "The
thing that you have spoken to do is good."
15. And I took the heads of your tribes,
wise and recognized, and set them as heads
above you, princes out of thousands, princes
out of hundreds, princes out of fifties and
princes out of tens, and overseers over your
tribes. 16. At that time I charged your
judges with their duties as follows: "Hear
[disputes] between your brethren and make
right prevail through your judgment
between every man and his brother and the
one that has come to him from abroad.
17. Do not recognize a face in judgment; you must hear the small and the great

בְּחֹרֵב לֵאמֹר רַב־לָכֶם שֶׁבֶת בָּהָר הַזֶּה: ז פְּנוּ ׀
וּסְעוּ לָכֶם וּבֹאוּ הַר הָאֱמֹרִי וְאֶל־כָּל־שְׁכֵנָיו
בָּעֲרָבָה בָהָר וּבַשְּׁפֵלָה וּבַנֶּגֶב וּבְחוֹף הַיָּם אֶרֶץ
הַכְּנַעֲנִי וְהַלְּבָנוֹן עַד־הַנָּהָר הַגָּדֹל נְהַר פְּרָת:
ח רְאֵה נָתַתִּי לִפְנֵיכֶם אֶת־הָאָרֶץ בֹּאוּ וּרְשׁוּ
אֶת־הָאָרֶץ אֲשֶׁר נִשְׁבַּע יְהֹוָה לַאֲבֹתֵיכֶם
לְאַבְרָהָם לְיִצְחָק וּלְיַעֲקֹב לָתֵת לָהֶם וּלְזַרְעָם
אַחֲרֵיהֶם: ט וָאֹמַר אֲלֵכֶם בָּעֵת הַהִוא לֵאמֹר
לֹא־אוּכַל לְבַדִּי שְׂאֵת אֶתְכֶם: י יְהֹוָה אֱלֹהֵיכֶם
הִרְבָּה אֶתְכֶם וְהִנְּכֶם הַיּוֹם כְּכוֹכְבֵי הַשָּׁמַיִם
לָרֹב: יא יְהֹוָה אֱלֹהֵי אֲבוֹתֵכֶם יֹסֵף עֲלֵיכֶם כָּכֶם
אֶלֶף פְּעָמִים וִיבָרֵךְ אֶתְכֶם כַּאֲשֶׁר דִּבֶּר לָכֶם:
שני יב אֵיכָה אֶשָּׂא לְבַדִּי טָרְחֲכֶם וּמַשַּׂאֲכֶם
וְרִיבְכֶם: יג הָבוּ לָכֶם אֲנָשִׁים חֲכָמִים וּנְבֹנִים
וִידֻעִים לְשִׁבְטֵיכֶם וַאֲשִׂימֵם בְּרָאשֵׁיכֶם:
יד וַתַּעֲנוּ אֹתִי וַתֹּאמְרוּ טוֹב־הַדָּבָר אֲשֶׁר־דִּבַּרְתָּ
לַעֲשׂוֹת: טו וָאֶקַּח אֶת־רָאשֵׁי שִׁבְטֵיכֶם אֲנָשִׁים
חֲכָמִים וִידֻעִים וָאֶתֵּן אוֹתָם רָאשִׁים עֲלֵיכֶם
שָׂרֵי אֲלָפִים וְשָׂרֵי מֵאוֹת וְשָׂרֵי חֲמִשִּׁים וְשָׂרֵי
עֲשָׂרֹת וְשֹׁטְרִים לְשִׁבְטֵיכֶם: טז וָאֲצַוֶּה אֶת־
שֹׁפְטֵיכֶם בָּעֵת הַהִוא לֵאמֹר שָׁמֹעַ בֵּין־אֲחֵיכֶם
וּשְׁפַטְתֶּם צֶדֶק בֵּין־אִישׁ וּבֵין־אָחִיו וּבֵין גֵּרוֹ:
יז לֹא־תַכִּירוּ פָנִים בַּמִּשְׁפָּט כַּקָּטֹן כַּגָּדֹל

10. ***like the stars.*** When you behold the starry sky, the one impression you receive is that of vastness; it would not occur to you to count the stars, one by one. You, [O Israel] create the same impression when viewed in your totality. After all, the history of mankind has not offered many occasions to behold an entire nation, six hundred thousand men, three and a half million souls, gathered together in one place. At the same time, it seems that this comparison of the numberless multitude of the people with the uncounted multitude of stars is intended to refute, in advance, the erroneous notion that because of its multitude, this people should be regarded as an uncounted mass in which the individual has no significance. As with the countless multitude of stars, so, too, each individual member of this nation retains his significance as an independent entity; he is a "world unto himself." God has assigned him his personal mission and guides him as an individual with a personal worth all his own. . . .

alike; you have no one to fear; for the judgment is God's. The matter that is too difficult for you, you shall bring to me, and I will hear it." 18. At that time I commanded you everything that you have to do. 19. We then journeyed from Ḥoreb and went through all that great and awesome wilderness that you have seen, the way to the mountains of the Emorite[s], as *God*, our God, had commanded us, and we came as far as Kadesh Barnea. 20. And I said to you: "You have come as far as the mountains of the Emorite[s], which *God*, our God, is giving us. 21. Lo! *God*, your God, has set the land before you; go up, take possession of it, as *God*, the God of your fathers, has spoken to you; do not fear and do not be frightened." 22. And all of you approached me and said: "We would send men before us that they may spy out the land for us and bring us [an] answer regarding the way by which we are to go up and the cities to which we are to come." 23. The matter found approval in my eyes and I took twelve men from [among] you, one man each for every tribe. 24. They turned and ascended the mountain and came as far as the Valley of Grapes and scouted it. 25. They took of the fruit of the land in their hands with them, brought it down to us and brought us [an] answer and said: "Good is the land that *God*, our God, is giving us." 26. But you did not want to go up and disobeyed the utterance of *God*, your God. 27. You incited one another in your tents and said: "Because *God* hates us has He brought us out of the land of Mitzrayim, to deliver us into the hand of the Emorite[s], in order to destroy us. 28. Whither shall we go up?

תִּשְׁמָעוּן לֹא תָגוּרוּ מִפְּנֵי־אִישׁ כִּי הַמִּשְׁפָּט לֵאלֹהִים הוּא וְהַדָּבָר אֲשֶׁר יִקְשֶׁה מִכֶּם תַּקְרִבוּן אֵלַי וּשְׁמַעְתִּיו: יח וָאֲצַוֶּה אֶתְכֶם בָּעֵת הַהִוא אֵת כָּל־הַדְּבָרִים אֲשֶׁר תַּעֲשׂוּן: יט וַנִּסַּע מֵחֹרֵב וַנֵּלֶךְ אֵת כָּל־הַמִּדְבָּר הַגָּדוֹל וְהַנּוֹרָא הַהוּא אֲשֶׁר רְאִיתֶם דֶּרֶךְ הַר הָאֱמֹרִי כַּאֲשֶׁר צִוָּה יְהוָה אֱלֹהֵינוּ אֹתָנוּ וַנָּבֹא עַד קָדֵשׁ בַּרְנֵעַ: כ וָאֹמַר אֲלֵכֶם בָּאתֶם עַד־הַר הָאֱמֹרִי אֲשֶׁר־יְהוָה אֱלֹהֵינוּ נֹתֵן לָנוּ: כא רְאֵה נָתַן יְהוָה אֱלֹהֶיךָ לְפָנֶיךָ אֶת־הָאָרֶץ עֲלֵה רֵשׁ כַּאֲשֶׁר דִּבֶּר יְהוָה אֱלֹהֵי אֲבֹתֶיךָ לָךְ אַל־תִּירָא וְאַל־תֵּחָת: שלישי כב וַתִּקְרְבוּן אֵלַי כֻּלְּכֶם וַתֹּאמְרוּ נִשְׁלְחָה אֲנָשִׁים לְפָנֵינוּ וְיַחְפְּרוּ־לָנוּ אֶת־הָאָרֶץ וְיָשִׁבוּ אֹתָנוּ דָּבָר אֶת־הַדֶּרֶךְ אֲשֶׁר נַעֲלֶה־בָּהּ וְאֵת הֶעָרִים אֲשֶׁר נָבֹא אֲלֵיהֶן: כג וַיִּיטַב בְּעֵינַי הַדָּבָר וָאֶקַּח מִכֶּם שְׁנֵים עָשָׂר אֲנָשִׁים אִישׁ אֶחָד לַשָּׁבֶט: כד וַיִּפְנוּ וַיַּעֲלוּ הָהָרָה וַיָּבֹאוּ עַד־ נַחַל אֶשְׁכֹּל וַיְרַגְּלוּ אֹתָהּ: כה וַיִּקְחוּ בְיָדָם מִפְּרִי הָאָרֶץ וַיּוֹרִדוּ אֵלֵינוּ וַיָּשִׁבוּ אֹתָנוּ דָבָר וַיֹּאמְרוּ טוֹבָה הָאָרֶץ אֲשֶׁר־יְהוָה אֱלֹהֵינוּ נֹתֵן לָנוּ: כו וְלֹא אֲבִיתֶם לַעֲלֹת וַתַּמְרוּ אֶת־פִּי יְהוָה אֱלֹהֵיכֶם: כז וַתֵּרָגְנוּ בְאָהֳלֵיכֶם וַתֹּאמְרוּ בְּשִׂנְאַת יְהוָה אֹתָנוּ הוֹצִיאָנוּ מֵאֶרֶץ מִצְרָיִם לָתֵת אֹתָנוּ בְּיַד הָאֱמֹרִי לְהַשְׁמִידֵנוּ: כח אָנָה |

18.[1] **At that time.** At that time, when you were to go forth to take possession of a land inhabited by mighty men experienced in warfare, I did not drill you in the use of weapons. I did not make you study plans of war and military strategy. I did not make you replenish

your arms and other materials of war. I did not appoint captains or generals for you. Even at the moment when you are about to subdue nations and conquer lands, you should have only one concern: how to realize the Law of God in your own midst as faithfully and punctiliously as possible. The observance of God's moral law is sufficient to conquer the world. Let Israel only attain the standard set by the ideal of its Divinely-ordained purpose and leave it to God to defend its position before the world. . . .

[1]*Note to the English translation*: In the original, complete Hirsch commentary on the Pentateuch, this note appears as a commentary on Verse 9. [E.O.]

Our brethren have made us downhearted by saying: 'A population far greater and taller than ourselves, cities great and fortified up to heaven, and also descendants of Anakites have we seen there!'" 29. And I said to you: "Do not be dismayed and do not fear them! 30. *God*, your God, Who goes before you, He will fight for you, just as He did for you, standing by you, in Mitzrayim before your eyes. 31. And also in the wilderness, where you saw that *God*, your God, carried you just as a man carries his son, on all the way that you went, until you came to this place. 32. Yet in this matter you have no trust in *God*, in your God! 33. He Who goes before you upon the way to seek out for you a place for your camping, in fire by night to light your way which you go, and in a cloud by day." 34. But *God* heard the voice of your words and was angry and swore [saying]: 35. "No man among these men, this evil generation, shall see the good land that I swore to give to your fathers. 36. Only Caleb, son of Yefunneh, he shall see it and to him will I give the land in which he set foot, and to his sons, because he has faithfully fulfilled [the duty of] following *God*." 37. *God* spoke also against me in anger on your account [saying]: "You shall not come there. 38. Yehoshua, son of Nun, who stands before you, he shall come there; strengthen him, because he shall put Yisrael into possession of it. 39. And your children, concerning whom you said that they will become prey, and your sons who to this day have no knowledge of good and evil; to them will I give it, and they shall inherit it. 40. But you turn and journey into the wilderness toward the Sea of Reeds." 41. And you answered and said to me: "We have sinned against *God*; we will go up and fight, just as *God*, our God, has commanded us." You girded, every man, his weapons of war and considered this sufficient for ascending the mountain. 42. But *God* said to me: "Say to them: Do not ascend and do not fight, because I am not in your midst, so that you will not be beaten before your enemies." 43. Thus did I speak to you, but you did not listen; you rebelled against the utterance of *God*; you were presumptuous and ascended the

אֲנַחְנוּ עֹלִים אַחֵינוּ הֵמַסּוּ אֶת־לְבָבֵנוּ לֵאמֹר
עַם גָּדוֹל וָרָם מִמֶּנּוּ עָרִים גְּדֹלֹת וּבְצוּרֹת
בַּשָּׁמָיִם וְגַם־בְּנֵי עֲנָקִים רָאִינוּ שָׁם: כט וָאֹמַר
אֲלֵכֶם לֹא־תַעַרְצוּן וְלֹא־תִירְאוּן מֵהֶם: ל יְהוָה
אֱלֹהֵיכֶם הַהֹלֵךְ לִפְנֵיכֶם הוּא יִלָּחֵם לָכֶם כְּכֹל
אֲשֶׁר עָשָׂה אִתְּכֶם בְּמִצְרַיִם לְעֵינֵיכֶם:
לא וּבַמִּדְבָּר אֲשֶׁר רָאִיתָ אֲשֶׁר נְשָׂאֲךָ יְהוָה
אֱלֹהֶיךָ כַּאֲשֶׁר יִשָּׂא־אִישׁ אֶת־בְּנוֹ בְּכָל־הַדֶּרֶךְ
אֲשֶׁר הֲלַכְתֶּם עַד־בֹּאֲכֶם עַד־הַמָּקוֹם הַזֶּה:
לב וּבַדָּבָר הַזֶּה אֵינְכֶם מַאֲמִינִם בַּיהוָה
אֱלֹהֵיכֶם: לג הַהֹלֵךְ לִפְנֵיכֶם בַּדֶּרֶךְ לָתוּר לָכֶם
מָקוֹם לַחֲנֹתְכֶם בָּאֵשׁ ׀ לַיְלָה לַרְאֹתְכֶם בַּדֶּרֶךְ
אֲשֶׁר תֵּלְכוּ־בָהּ וּבֶעָנָן יוֹמָם: לד וַיִּשְׁמַע יְהוָה
אֶת־קוֹל דִּבְרֵיכֶם וַיִּקְצֹף וַיִּשָּׁבַע לֵאמֹר:
לה אִם־יִרְאֶה אִישׁ בָּאֲנָשִׁים הָאֵלֶּה הַדּוֹר הָרָע
הַזֶּה אֵת הָאָרֶץ הַטּוֹבָה אֲשֶׁר נִשְׁבַּעְתִּי לָתֵת
לַאֲבֹתֵיכֶם: לו זוּלָתִי כָּלֵב בֶּן־יְפֻנֶּה הוּא יִרְאֶנָּה
וְלוֹ־אֶתֵּן אֶת־הָאָרֶץ אֲשֶׁר דָּרַךְ־בָּהּ וּלְבָנָיו יַעַן
אֲשֶׁר מִלֵּא אַחֲרֵי יְהוָה: לז גַּם־בִּי הִתְאַנַּף יְהוָה
בִּגְלַלְכֶם לֵאמֹר גַּם־אַתָּה לֹא־תָבֹא שָׁם:
לח יְהוֹשֻׁעַ בִּן־נוּן הָעֹמֵד לְפָנֶיךָ הוּא יָבֹא שָׁמָּה
אֹתוֹ חַזֵּק כִּי־הוּא יַנְחִלֶנָּה אֶת־יִשְׂרָאֵל: רביעי
לט וְטַפְּכֶם אֲשֶׁר אֲמַרְתֶּם לָבַז יִהְיֶה וּבְנֵיכֶם
אֲשֶׁר לֹא־יָדְעוּ הַיּוֹם טוֹב וָרָע הֵמָּה יָבֹאוּ שָׁמָּה
וְלָהֶם אֶתְּנֶנָּה וְהֵם יִירָשׁוּהָ: מ וְאַתֶּם פְּנוּ לָכֶם
וּסְעוּ הַמִּדְבָּרָה דֶּרֶךְ יַם־סוּף: מא וַתַּעֲנוּ ׀
וַתֹּאמְרוּ אֵלַי חָטָאנוּ לַיהוָה אֲנַחְנוּ נַעֲלֶה
וְנִלְחַמְנוּ כְּכֹל אֲשֶׁר־צִוָּנוּ יְהוָה אֱלֹהֵינוּ וַתַּחְגְּרוּ
אִישׁ אֶת־כְּלֵי מִלְחַמְתּוֹ וַתָּהִינוּ לַעֲלֹת הָהָרָה:
מב וַיֹּאמֶר יְהוָה אֵלַי אֱמֹר לָהֶם לֹא תַעֲלוּ וְלֹא־
תִלָּחֲמוּ כִּי אֵינֶנִּי בְּקִרְבְּכֶם וְלֹא תִּנָּגְפוּ לִפְנֵי
אֹיְבֵיכֶם: מג וָאֲדַבֵּר אֲלֵיכֶם וְלֹא שְׁמַעְתֶּם
וַתַּמְרוּ אֶת־פִּי יְהוָה וַתָּזִדוּ וַתַּעֲלוּ הָהָרָה:

mountain.   44. And the Emorite who dwells upon that mountain came out to meet you, and pursued you as bees do, and struck you to the point of crushing you, in Seir as far as Ḥormah.   45. You returned and wept before *God*, but *God* did not listen to your voice and did not incline His ear toward you.   46. Thereupon you remained in Kadesh for a long time, as long as you had to stay there.

II   1. Thereupon we turned and journeyed into the wilderness, toward the Sea of Reeds, as *God* had spoken to me, and we traveled around Mount Seir for a long time.   2. And *God* said to me: 3. "You have traveled around this mountain long enough; now turn northward.   4. And command the people: You are now passing into the territory of your brethren, the sons of Esav, who dwell in Seir; they will be afraid of you; be very careful.   5. Do not let yourselves come into strife with them, for I will not give you of their land even so much as the sole of a foot can tread, for I have given to Esav the mountain of Seir as an inheritance. 6. You shall purchase food from them for money if you want to eat, and you shall obtain also water from them for money if you want to drink.   7. For *God*, your

מד וַיֵּצֵא הָאֱמֹרִי הַיֹּשֵׁב בָּהָר הַהוּא לִקְרַאתְכֶם וַיִּרְדְּפוּ אֶתְכֶם כַּאֲשֶׁר תַּעֲשֶׂינָה הַדְּבֹרִים וַיַּכְּתוּ אֶתְכֶם בְּשֵׂעִיר עַד־חָרְמָה: מה וַתָּשֻׁבוּ וַתִּבְכּוּ לִפְנֵי יְהֹוָה וְלֹא־שָׁמַע יְהֹוָה בְּקֹלְכֶם וְלֹא הֶאֱזִין אֲלֵיכֶם: מו וַתֵּשְׁבוּ בְקָדֵשׁ יָמִים רַבִּים כַּיָּמִים אֲשֶׁר יְשַׁבְתֶּם: ב א וַנֵּפֶן וַנִּסַּע הַמִּדְבָּרָה דֶּרֶךְ יַם־סוּף כַּאֲשֶׁר דִּבֶּר יְהֹוָה אֵלָי וַנָּסָב אֶת־הַר־שֵׂעִיר יָמִים רַבִּים: ס חמישי ב וַיֹּאמֶר יְהֹוָה אֵלַי לֵאמֹר: ג רַב־לָכֶם סֹב אֶת־הָהָר הַזֶּה פְּנוּ לָכֶם צָפֹנָה: ד וְאֶת־הָעָם צַו לֵאמֹר אַתֶּם עֹבְרִים בִּגְבוּל אֲחֵיכֶם בְּנֵי־עֵשָׂו הַיֹּשְׁבִים בְּשֵׂעִיר וְיִירְאוּ מִכֶּם וְנִשְׁמַרְתֶּם מְאֹד: ה אַל־תִּתְגָּרוּ בָם כִּי לֹא־אֶתֵּן לָכֶם מֵאַרְצָם עַד מִדְרַךְ כַּף־רָגֶל כִּי־יְרֻשָּׁה לְעֵשָׂו נָתַתִּי אֶת־הַר שֵׂעִיר: ו אֹכֶל תִּשְׁבְּרוּ מֵאִתָּם בַּכֶּסֶף וַאֲכַלְתֶּם וְגַם־מַיִם תִּכְרוּ מֵאִתָּם בַּכֶּסֶף וּשְׁתִיתֶם: ז כִּי יְהֹוָה אֱלֹהֶיךָ

CHAPTER II

4. *they will be afraid of you.* They will not attack you.

be very careful. But be very careful not to take even the slightest liberties with the sons of Esau. Or rather: They are afraid that they will have to suffer cruelly at your hands. They think that after such a long journey through the wilderness you will be starved and stripped of all your possessions, and that therefore, as soon as you enter an inhabited, civilized region you will seize everything upon which you can lay your hands. Therefore restrain yourselves and show them that you are not so.

5. . . . With regard to the nations in general, the Biblical text states: "When the Most High assigned property to the nations" (Deuteronomy 32:8); i.e., the many races of mankind did not find their domicile on earth without the guidance of God. But with regard to the descendants of Esau and Lot, the people descended from the family of Abraham, we are told explicitly: "I

have given to Esav . . . as an inheritance." We are told the same concerning Moab and Ammon (Deuteronomy 2:9 and 19). The fact that Israel is reminded of these things when it is about to receive its land from the hand of God would seem to have far-reaching implications. For it gives the Jewish people to understand that God's providence also reigns over the destinies of nations other than the Jewish people, and that Israel is to take its place among the nations with a God-fearing respect for their possessions. Israel must not see itself as a nation of conquerors from whom no nation on earth will henceforth be safe. Rather, Israel must limit its military actions and prowess to the task of occupying that one sole land which God has intended for it and promised to it from the very outset of its history. Thus, too, the statement "I have given to Esav . . . as an inheritance" is cited in Nazir 61a as proof that the laws of inheritance, which are among the basic factors in all social development, enjoy Divine sanction even among the rest of humanity, which is bound [only] by Noahide law.

God, has blessed you in all the works of your hands; He has had His eye upon your wandering through this great wilderness; it is now forty years that *God*, your God, has been with you; you have lacked nothing." 8. And we departed from our brethren, the sons of Esav, who dwelt in Seir, from the way of the wasteland, from Elath and Etzion-Geber, and we turned and went to the way toward the wilderness of Moab. 9. And *God* said to me: "Do not press Moab and do not let yourself come into warfare with him, for I will give you no inheritance from his land, for to the sons of Lot have I given Ar as an inheritance." 10. Formerly, the Emim dwelt there, a great and numerous people, and tall like Anakites. 11. The Rephaim are also counted like Anakites; the Moabites call them Emim. 12. The Ḥorim formerly dwelt in Seir, when the sons of Esav were to drive them away. And they destroyed them from before them and settled down in their place, just as Yisrael had already done with the land of its inheritance that *God* had given them. 13. "Now rise and cross the brook Zered!" And we crossed the brook Zered. 14. And the time during which we went from Kadesh Barnea until we crossed the brook Zered was thirty-eight years, until the entire generation, the men able to do battle, had vanished from the midst of the camp as *God* had sworn to them. 15. Also, the hand of *God* showed itself upon them, to snatch them away suddenly from the midst of the camp, until they have now died out. 16. It came to pass when all the men able to do battle had died out from the midst of the people 17. that *God* spoke to me [saying]: 18. "Today you are to cross the border of Moab, Ar, 19. and you will come near over against the sons of Ammon; do not press them and do not involve yourself in strife with them, for I will not give you any of the land of the sons of Ammon as an inheritance; for to the sons of Lot have I given it as an inheritance." 20. It is also counted to the land of the Rephaim. Rephaim formerly dwelt in it, and the Ammonites call them Zamzummim, 21. a great and numerous people, and tall like Anakites; *God* had destroyed them from before them, and they drove

בֵּרַכְךָ֙ בְּכֹל֙ מַעֲשֵׂ֣ה יָדֶ֔ךָ יָדַ֣ע לֶכְתְּךָ֔ אֶת־הַמִּדְבָּ֥ר הַגָּדֹ֖ל הַזֶּ֑ה ׀ אַרְבָּעִ֣ים שָׁנָ֗ה יְהוָ֤ה אֱלֹהֶ֨יךָ֙ עִמָּ֔ךְ לֹ֥א חָסַ֖רְתָּ דָּבָֽר: ח וַֽנַּעֲבֹ֞ר מֵאֵ֧ת אַחֵ֣ינוּ בְנֵי־עֵשָׂ֗ו הַיֹּֽשְׁבִים֙ בְּשֵׂעִ֔יר מִדֶּ֙רֶךְ֙ הָֽעֲרָבָ֔ה מֵאֵילַ֖ת וּמֵֽעֶצְיֹ֣ן גָּ֑בֶר ס וַנֵּ֙פֶן֙ וַֽנַּעֲבֹ֔ר דֶּ֖רֶךְ מִדְבַּ֥ר מוֹאָֽב: ט וַיֹּ֨אמֶר יְהוָ֜ה אֵלַ֗י אַל־תָּ֙צַר֙ אֶת־מוֹאָ֔ב וְאַל־תִּתְגָּ֥ר בָּ֖ם מִלְחָמָ֑ה כִּ֠י לֹֽא־אֶתֵּ֨ן לְךָ֤ מֵֽאַרְצוֹ֙ יְרֻשָּׁ֔ה כִּ֣י לִבְנֵי־ל֔וֹט נָתַ֥תִּי אֶת־עָ֖ר יְרֻשָּֽׁה: י הָֽאֵמִ֥ים לְפָנִ֖ים יָ֣שְׁבוּ בָ֑הּ עַ֣ם גָּד֥וֹל וְרַ֖ב וָרָ֥ם כָּֽעֲנָקִֽים: יא רְפָאִ֞ים יֵחָֽשְׁב֤וּ אַף־הֵם֙ כָּֽעֲנָקִ֔ים וְהַמֹּ֣אָבִ֔ים יִקְרְא֥וּ לָהֶ֖ם אֵמִֽים: יב וּבְשֵׂעִ֞יר יָֽשְׁב֣וּ הַֽחֹרִים֮ לְפָנִים֒ וּבְנֵ֧י עֵשָׂ֣ו יִֽירָשׁ֗וּם וַיַּשְׁמִידוּם֙ מִפְּנֵיהֶ֔ם וַיֵּֽשְׁב֖וּ תַּחְתָּ֑ם כַּֽאֲשֶׁ֧ר עָשָׂ֣ה יִשְׂרָאֵ֗ל לְאֶ֨רֶץ֙ יְרֻשָּׁת֔וֹ אֲשֶׁר־נָתַ֥ן יְהוָ֖ה לָהֶֽם: יג עַתָּ֗ה קֻ֚מוּ וְעִבְר֣וּ לָכֶ֔ם אֶת־נַ֣חַל זָ֑רֶד וַֽנַּעֲבֹ֖ר אֶת־נַ֥חַל זָֽרֶד: יד וְהַיָּמִ֞ים אֲשֶׁר־הָלַ֣כְנוּ ׀ מִקָּדֵ֣שׁ בַּרְנֵ֗עַ עַ֤ד אֲשֶׁר־עָבַ֨רְנוּ֙ אֶת־נַ֣חַל זֶ֔רֶד שְׁלֹשִׁ֥ים וּשְׁמֹנֶ֖ה שָׁנָ֑ה עַד־תֹּ֨ם כָּל־הַדּ֜וֹר אַנְשֵׁ֤י הַמִּלְחָמָה֙ מִקֶּ֣רֶב הַֽמַּחֲנֶ֔ה כַּֽאֲשֶׁ֛ר נִשְׁבַּ֥ע יְהוָ֖ה לָהֶֽם: טו וְגַ֤ם יַד־יְהוָה֙ הָ֣יְתָה בָּ֔ם לְהֻמָּ֖ם מִקֶּ֣רֶב הַֽמַּחֲנֶ֑ה עַ֖ד תֻּמָּֽם: טז וַיְהִ֨י כַֽאֲשֶׁר־תַּ֜מּוּ כָּל־אַנְשֵׁ֧י הַמִּלְחָמָ֛ה לָמ֖וּת מִקֶּ֥רֶב הָעָֽם: ס יז וַיְדַבֵּ֥ר יְהוָ֖ה אֵלַ֥י לֵאמֹֽר: יח אַתָּ֨ה עֹבֵ֥ר הַיּ֛וֹם אֶת־גְּב֥וּל מוֹאָ֖ב אֶת־עָֽר: יט וְקָֽרַבְתָּ֗ מ֚וּל בְּנֵ֣י עַמּ֔וֹן אַל־תְּצֻרֵ֖ם וְאַל־תִּתְגָּ֣ר בָּ֑ם כִּ֣י לֹֽא־אֶ֠תֵּן מֵאֶ֨רֶץ בְּנֵֽי־עַמּ֥וֹן לְךָ֛ יְרֻשָּׁ֖ה כִּ֥י לִבְנֵי־ל֖וֹט נְתַתִּ֥יהָ יְרֻשָּֽׁה: כ אֶֽרֶץ־רְפָאִ֥ים תֵּֽחָשֵׁ֖ב אַף־הִ֑וא רְפָאִ֤ים יָֽשְׁבוּ־בָהּ֙ לְפָנִ֔ים וְהָֽעַמֹּנִ֔ים יִקְרְא֥וּ לָהֶ֖ם זַמְזֻמִּֽים: כא עַ֣ם גָּד֥וֹל וְרַ֖ב וָרָ֑ם כָּֽעֲנָקִ֑ים וַיַּשְׁמִידֵ֤ם יְהוָה֙

them away and settled down in their place. 22. Just as He had done for the sons of Esav, who dwelt in Seir, before whom He destroyed the Ḥorites, so that they drove them away and settled down in their place to this very day. 23. The Avvim, too, who dwelt in open villages as far as Aza, the Caphthorim who came out of Caphthor destroyed them and settled down in their place. 24. Rise and journey on; cross the Arnon stream; lo! I have given into your hand Siḥon, the Emorite king of Ḥeshbon, and his land; begin the occupation and let yourself come into war with him. 25. Today I will begin to spread the dread of you and the fear of you upon the peoples that are beneath the whole heaven, who will hear the report of you and will tremble and be frightened because of you. 26. And I sent messengers from the wilderness of Kedemoth to Siḥon, king of Ḥeshbon, words of peace: 27. "Let me pass through your land; upon the road, only upon the road will I go, and I will not turn aside to the right or to the left. 28. You may let me purchase food for money if I want to eat, and give me water for money if I want to drink; only with my feet will I pass through: 29. —just as the sons of Esav, who dwell in Seir, and the Moabites, who dwell in Ar, did to me—until I will pass over the Yarden, to the land that *God*, our God, is giving us." 30. But Siḥon, king of Ḥeshbon, would not let us pass through, for *God*, your God, had hardened his spirit and made his heart firm so that he might deliver him into your hand, as [it is] today. 31. And *God* said to me: "Lo! I have begun to deliver up Siḥon and his land before you; begin the occupation, to take possession of his land." 32. And Siḥon came out to meet us, he and all his people, to battle, to Yahatz. 33. *God*, our God, delivered him up before us; we struck him down, and his sons, and all his people. 34. We conquered all his cities at that time and laid waste every inhabited city, women and children; we did not leave anyone remaining. 35. Only the livestock did we take as plunder for ourselves, and the spoil of the cities that we had conquered. 36. From Aroer, which is on the banks of the Arnon stream, and also the city

מִפְּנֵיהֶם וַיִּירָשֻׁם וַיֵּשְׁבוּ תַחְתָּם׃ כב כַּאֲשֶׁר
עָשָׂה לִבְנֵי עֵשָׂו הַיֹּשְׁבִים בְּשֵׂעִיר אֲשֶׁר הִשְׁמִיד
אֶת־הַחֹרִי מִפְּנֵיהֶם וַיִּירָשֻׁם וַיֵּשְׁבוּ תַחְתָּם עַד
הַיּוֹם הַזֶּה׃ כג וְהָעַוִּים הַיֹּשְׁבִים בַּחֲצֵרִים עַד־
עַזָּה כַּפְתֹּרִים הַיֹּצְאִים מִכַּפְתֹּר הִשְׁמִידֻם
וַיֵּשְׁבוּ תַחְתָּם׃ כד קוּמוּ סְּעוּ וְעִבְרוּ אֶת־נַחַל
אַרְנֹן רְאֵה נָתַתִּי בְיָדְךָ אֶת־סִיחֹן מֶלֶךְ־חֶשְׁבּוֹן
הָאֱמֹרִי וְאֶת־אַרְצוֹ הָחֵל רָשׁ וְהִתְגָּר בּוֹ
מִלְחָמָה׃ כה הַיּוֹם הַזֶּה אָחֵל תֵּת פַּחְדְּךָ וְיִרְאָתְךָ
עַל־פְּנֵי הָעַמִּים תַּחַת כָּל־הַשָּׁמָיִם אֲשֶׁר
יִשְׁמְעוּן שִׁמְעֲךָ וְרָגְזוּ וְחָלוּ מִפָּנֶיךָ׃ כו וָאֶשְׁלַח
מַלְאָכִים מִמִּדְבַּר קְדֵמוֹת אֶל־סִיחוֹן מֶלֶךְ
חֶשְׁבּוֹן דִּבְרֵי שָׁלוֹם לֵאמֹר׃ כז אֶעְבְּרָה בְאַרְצֶךָ
בַּדֶּרֶךְ בַּדֶּרֶךְ אֵלֵךְ לֹא אָסוּר יָמִין וּשְׂמֹאול׃
כח אֹכֶל בַּכֶּסֶף תַּשְׁבִּרֵנִי וְאָכַלְתִּי וּמַיִם בַּכֶּסֶף
תִּתֶּן־לִי וְשָׁתִיתִי רַק אֶעְבְּרָה בְרַגְלָי׃ כט כַּאֲשֶׁר
עָשׂוּ־לִי בְּנֵי עֵשָׂו הַיֹּשְׁבִים בְּשֵׂעִיר וְהַמּוֹאָבִים
הַיֹּשְׁבִים בְּעָר עַד אֲשֶׁר־אֶעֱבֹר אֶת־הַיַּרְדֵּן אֶל־
הָאָרֶץ אֲשֶׁר־יְהוָה אֱלֹהֵינוּ נֹתֵן לָנוּ׃ ל וְלֹא
אָבָה סִיחֹן מֶלֶךְ חֶשְׁבּוֹן הַעֲבִרֵנוּ בּוֹ כִּי־הִקְשָׁה
יְהוָה אֱלֹהֶיךָ אֶת־רוּחוֹ וְאִמֵּץ אֶת־לְבָבוֹ לְמַעַן
תִּתּוֹ בְיָדְךָ כַּיּוֹם הַזֶּה׃ ס ששי לא וַיֹּאמֶר יְהוָה
אֵלַי רְאֵה הַחִלֹּתִי תֵּת לְפָנֶיךָ אֶת־סִיחֹן וְאֶת־
אַרְצוֹ הָחֵל רָשׁ לָרֶשֶׁת אֶת־אַרְצוֹ׃ לב וַיֵּצֵא
סִיחֹן לִקְרָאתֵנוּ הוּא וְכָל־עַמּוֹ לַמִּלְחָמָה יָהְצָה׃
לג וַיִּתְּנֵהוּ יְהוָה אֱלֹהֵינוּ לְפָנֵינוּ וַנַּךְ אֹתוֹ וְאֶת־
בָּנָו (בניו קרי) וְאֶת־כָּל־עַמּוֹ׃ לד וַנִּלְכֹּד אֶת־כָּל־
עָרָיו בָּעֵת הַהִוא וַנַּחֲרֵם אֶת־כָּל־עִיר מְתִם
וְהַנָּשִׁים וְהַטָּף לֹא הִשְׁאַרְנוּ שָׂרִיד׃ לה רַק
הַבְּהֵמָה בָּזַזְנוּ לָנוּ וּשְׁלַל הֶעָרִים אֲשֶׁר לָכָדְנוּ׃
לו מֵעֲרֹעֵר אֲשֶׁר עַל־שְׂפַת־נַחַל אַרְנֹן וְהָעִיר

that is in the river bed, as far as Gilead, there was no city that would have been too strong for us. *God,* our God, delivered them all before us. 37. Only to the land of the sons of Ammon did you not come near, to the entire side of the Yabbok stream and the cities of the mountains and all that *God,* our God, commanded us [not to approach].

III

1. We then turned and went up toward the Bashan. And Og, king of the Bashan, came out to meet us, he and all his people, to battle, to Edrei. 2. And *God* said to me: "Do not fear him, for I have delivered him and all his people and his land into your hand; do to him as you did to Siḥon, king of the Emorite[s], who dwells in Ḥeshbon." 3. And *God,* our God, delivered into our hand also Og, king of the Bashan; we struck him until nothing was left remaining to him. 4. We conquered all his cities at that time; there was no city that we did not take away from them; sixty cities, the entire region of Argov, the kingdom of Og in the Bashan. 5. All these were fortified cities with high walls, gates and bars, in addition to the very many cities of the open country. 6. We laid them waste as we had done to Siḥon, king of Ḥeshbon; we laid waste every inhabited city, [destroying] women and children. 7. But all the livestock and the spoil of the city we took as plunder for ourselves. 8. And so we took the land at that time from the hand of the two kings of the Emorite[s], who dwelt on this side of the Yarden, from the Arnon stream as far as Mount Ḥermon. 9. The Tziddonim call the Ḥermon "Sirion"; among the Emorites, they call it Senir. 10. All the cities of the plain and the entire Gilead, as well as the entire Bashan as far as Salkhah and Edrei, the cities of the kingdom of Og in the Bashan. 11. For only Og, king of Bashan, had remained from the rest of the Rephaim; lo! His bedstead, an iron bedstead, is in Rabbah of the sons of Ammon; it is nine cubits long and four cubits wide, according to the cubit of a man. 12. And this land, of which we took possession at that time, from Aroer, which is on the Arnon stream, and half of the mountain of Gilead and its cities, I have given to the Reubenite[s] and

אֲשֶׁ֣ר בַּנַּ֔חַל וְעַד־הַגִּלְעָ֔ד לֹ֤א הָֽיְתָה֙ קִרְיָ֔ה אֲשֶׁ֥ר שָֽׂגְבָ֖ה מִמֶּ֑נּוּ אֶת־הַכֹּ֕ל נָתַ֛ן יְהֹוָ֥ה אֱלֹהֵ֖ינוּ לְפָנֵֽינוּ: לז רַ֛ק אֶל־אֶ֥רֶץ בְּנֵֽי־עַמּ֖וֹן לֹ֣א קָרָ֑בְתָּ כָּל־יַ֞ד נַ֤חַל יַבֹּק֙ וְעָרֵ֣י הָהָ֔ר וְכֹ֛ל אֲשֶׁר־צִוָּ֖ה יְהֹוָ֥ה אֱלֹהֵֽינוּ: ג א וַנֵּ֣פֶן וַנַּ֔עַל דֶּ֖רֶךְ הַבָּשָׁ֑ן וַיֵּצֵ֣א עוֹג֩ מֶֽלֶךְ־הַבָּשָׁ֨ן לִקְרָאתֵ֜נוּ ה֧וּא וְכָל־עַמּ֛וֹ לַמִּלְחָמָ֖ה אֶדְרֶֽעִי: ב וַיֹּ֨אמֶר יְהֹוָ֤ה אֵלַי֙ אַל־תִּירָ֣א אֹת֔וֹ כִּ֣י בְיָֽדְךָ֞ נָתַ֧תִּי אֹת֛וֹ וְאֶת־כָּל־עַמּ֖וֹ וְאֶת־אַרְצ֑וֹ וְעָשִׂ֣יתָ לּ֔וֹ כַּֽאֲשֶׁ֣ר עָשִׂ֗יתָ לְסִיחֹן֙ מֶ֣לֶךְ הָֽאֱמֹרִ֔י אֲשֶׁ֥ר יוֹשֵׁ֖ב בְּחֶשְׁבּֽוֹן: ג וַיִּתֵּן֩ יְהֹוָ֨ה אֱלֹהֵ֜ינוּ בְּיָדֵ֗נוּ גַּ֛ם אֶת־ע֥וֹג מֶֽלֶךְ־הַבָּשָׁ֖ן וְאֶת־כָּל־עַמּ֑וֹ וַנַּכֵּ֕הוּ עַד־בִּלְתִּ֥י הִשְׁאִֽיר־ל֖וֹ שָׂרִֽיד: ד וַנִּלְכֹּ֤ד אֶת־כָּל־עָרָיו֙ בָּעֵ֣ת הַהִ֔וא לֹ֤א הָֽיְתָה֙ קִרְיָ֔ה אֲשֶׁ֥ר לֹֽא־לָקַ֖חְנוּ מֵֽאִתָּ֑ם שִׁשִּׁ֥ים עִיר֙ כָּל־חֶ֣בֶל אַרְגֹּ֔ב מַמְלֶ֥כֶת ע֖וֹג בַּבָּשָֽׁן: ה כָּל־אֵ֜לֶּה עָרִ֧ים בְּצֻרֹ֛ת חוֹמָ֥ה גְבֹהָ֖ה דְּלָתַ֣יִם וּבְרִ֑יחַ לְבַ֛ד מֵֽעָרֵ֥י הַפְּרָזִ֖י הַרְבֵּ֥ה מְאֹֽד: ו וַנַּֽחֲרֵ֣ם אוֹתָ֔ם כַּֽאֲשֶׁ֣ר עָשִׂ֔ינוּ לְסִיחֹ֖ן מֶ֣לֶךְ חֶשְׁבּ֑וֹן הַֽחֲרֵם֙ כָּל־עִ֣יר מְתִ֔ם הַנָּשִׁ֖ים וְהַטָּֽף: ז וְכָל־הַבְּהֵמָ֛ה וּשְׁלַ֥ל הֶֽעָרִ֖ים בַּזּ֥וֹנוּ לָֽנוּ: ח וַנִּקַּ֞ח בָּעֵ֤ת הַהִוא֙ אֶת־הָאָ֔רֶץ מִיַּ֗ד שְׁנֵי֙ מַלְכֵ֣י הָֽאֱמֹרִ֔י אֲשֶׁ֖ר בְּעֵ֣בֶר הַיַּרְדֵּ֑ן מִנַּ֥חַל אַרְנֹ֖ן עַד־הַ֥ר חֶרְמֽוֹן: ט צִֽידֹנִ֛ים יִקְרְא֥וּ לְחֶרְמ֖וֹן שִׂרְיֹ֑ן וְהָ֣אֱמֹרִ֔י יִקְרְאוּ־ל֖וֹ שְׂנִֽיר: י כֹּ֣ל ׀ עָרֵ֣י הַמִּישֹׁ֗ר וְכָל־הַגִּלְעָד֙ וְכָל־הַבָּשָׁ֔ן עַד־סַלְכָ֖ה וְאֶדְרֶ֑עִי עָרֵ֛י מַמְלֶ֥כֶת ע֖וֹג בַּבָּשָֽׁן: יא כִּ֣י רַק־ע֞וֹג מֶ֣לֶךְ הַבָּשָׁ֗ן נִשְׁאַר֮ מִיֶּ֣תֶר הָֽרְפָאִים֒ הִנֵּ֤ה עַרְשׂוֹ֙ עֶ֣רֶשׂ בַּרְזֶ֔ל הֲלֹ֣ה הִ֔וא בְּרַבַּ֖ת בְּנֵ֣י עַמּ֑וֹן תֵּ֧שַׁע אַמּ֣וֹת אָרְכָּ֗הּ וְאַרְבַּ֥ע אַמּ֛וֹת רָחְבָּ֖הּ בְּאַמַּת־אִֽישׁ: יב וְאֶת־הָאָ֧רֶץ הַזֹּ֛את יָרַ֖שְׁנוּ בָּעֵ֣ת הַהִ֑וא מֵֽעֲרֹעֵ֞ר אֲשֶׁר־עַל־נַ֣חַל אַרְנֹ֗ן וַֽחֲצִ֤י הַֽר־הַגִּלְעָד֙ וְעָרָ֔יו נָתַ֕תִּי לָרֽאוּבֵנִ֖י

וְלַגָּדִֽי׃ יג וְיֶ֨תֶר הַגִּלְעָ֤ד וְכָל־הַבָּשָׁן֙ מַמְלֶ֣כֶת ע֔וֹג
נָתַ֕תִּי לַחֲצִ֖י שֵׁ֣בֶט הַֽמְנַשֶּׁ֑ה כֹּ֣ל חֶ֤בֶל הָֽאַרְגֹּב֙
לְכָל־הַבָּשָׁ֔ן הַה֥וּא יִקָּרֵ֖א אֶ֥רֶץ רְפָאִֽים׃ יד יָאִ֣יר
בֶּן־מְנַשֶּׁ֗ה לָקַח֙ אֶת־כָּל־חֶ֣בֶל אַרְגֹּ֔ב עַד־גְּב֥וּל
הַגְּשׁוּרִ֖י וְהַמַּֽעֲכָתִ֑י וַיִּקְרָא֩ אֹתָ֨ם עַל־שְׁמ֤וֹ אֶת־
הַבָּשָׁן֙ חַוֺּ֣ת יָאִ֔יר עַ֖ד הַיּ֥וֹם הַזֶּֽה׃ שביעי
טו וּלְמָכִ֖יר נָתַ֥תִּי אֶת־הַגִּלְעָֽד׃ טז וְלָרֽאוּבֵנִ֨י
וְלַגָּדִ֜י נָתַ֤תִּי מִן־הַגִּלְעָד֙ וְעַד־נַ֣חַל אַרְנֹ֔ן תּ֥וֹךְ
הַנַּ֖חַל וּגְבֻ֑ל וְעַד֙ יַבֹּ֣ק הַנַּ֔חַל גְּב֖וּל בְּנֵ֥י עַמּֽוֹן׃
יז וְהָעֲרָבָ֖ה וְהַיַּרְדֵּ֣ן וּגְבֻ֑ל מִכִּנֶּ֗רֶת וְעַ֨ד יָ֤ם
הָֽעֲרָבָה֙ יָ֣ם הַמֶּ֔לַח תַּ֛חַת אַשְׁדֹּ֥ת הַפִּסְגָּ֖ה מִזְרָֽחָה׃
יח וָאֲצַ֣ו אֶתְכֶ֔ם בָּעֵ֥ת הַהִ֖וא לֵאמֹ֑ר יְהוָ֣ה
אֱלֹֽהֵיכֶ֗ם נָתַ֨ן לָכֶ֜ם אֶת־הָאָ֤רֶץ הַזֹּאת֙ לְרִשְׁתָּ֔הּ
חֲלוּצִ֣ים תַּֽעַבְר֗וּ לִפְנֵ֛י אֲחֵיכֶ֥ם בְּנֵֽי־יִשְׂרָאֵ֖ל כָּל־
בְּנֵי־חָֽיִל׃ יט רַ֠ק נְשֵׁיכֶ֣ם וְטַפְּכֶם֮ וּמִקְנֵכֶם֒
יָדַ֕עְתִּי כִּֽי־מִקְנֶ֥ה רַ֖ב לָכֶ֑ם יֵֽשְׁבוּ֙ בְּעָ֣רֵיכֶ֔ם אֲשֶׁ֥ר
נָתַ֖תִּי לָכֶֽם׃ מפטיר כ עַ֠ד אֲשֶׁר־יָנִ֨יחַ יְהוָ֥ה ׀
לַאֲחֵיכֶם֮ כָּכֶם֒ וְיָרְשׁ֣וּ גַם־הֵ֔ם אֶת־הָאָ֕רֶץ אֲשֶׁ֨ר
יְהוָ֧ה אֱלֹהֵיכֶ֛ם נֹתֵ֥ן לָהֶ֖ם בְּעֵ֣בֶר הַיַּרְדֵּ֑ן וְשַׁבְתֶּ֗ם
אִ֚ישׁ לִֽירֻשָּׁת֔וֹ אֲשֶׁ֖ר נָתַ֥תִּי לָכֶֽם׃ כא וְאֶת־
יְהוֹשׁ֣וּעַ צִוֵּ֔יתִי בָּעֵ֥ת הַהִ֖וא לֵאמֹ֑ר עֵינֶ֣יךָ הָֽרֹאֹ֗ת
אֵת֩ כָּל־אֲשֶׁ֨ר עָשָׂ֜ה יְהוָ֤ה אֱלֹהֵיכֶם֙ לִשְׁנֵי֙
הַמְּלָכִ֣ים הָאֵ֔לֶּה כֵּֽן־יַעֲשֶׂ֤ה יְהוָה֙ לְכָל־
הַמַּמְלָכ֔וֹת אֲשֶׁ֥ר אַתָּ֖ה עֹבֵ֥ר שָֽׁמָּה׃ כב לֹ֖א
תִּֽירָא֑וּם כִּ֚י יְהוָ֣ה אֱלֹֽהֵיכֶ֔ם ה֖וּא הַנִּלְחָ֥ם
לָכֶֽם׃ ס

the Gaddite[s]. 13. The rest of the Gilead and the entire Bashan, the kingdom of Og, I have given to the half-tribe of Menashe. The entire Argov region toward the entire Bashan, it is called "the land of the Rephaim." 14. Yair, son of Menashe, took the entire Argov region as far as the territory of the Geshurite[s] and the Ma'akhtite[s], and he called them after his [own] name: the Bashan, the villages of Yair, until this day. 15. To Makhir I have given the Gilead. 16. To the Reubenite[s] and to the Gaddite[s] I have given [the area] from the Gilead as far as the Arnon stream, the middle of the river and the territory as far as the Yabbok stream, the border of the sons of Ammon. 17. And also the wasteland, along with the Yarden and the territory of Kinnereth, as far as the Sea of the Wasteland, the Salt Sea, beneath the rapids of the elevation to the east. 18. I commanded you at that time: "*God*, your God, has given you this land to take possession of it; you are to pass as a vanguard before your brethren, the sons of Yisrael, all the men of the army. 19. Only your wives and your young children and your stock of cattle—I know that you have a large stock of cattle—shall remain in your cities that I have given you. 20. Until *God* gives rest to your brethren even as to you, and they, too, have taken possession of the land that *God*, your God, is giving them on the other side of the Yarden; then you can return, every man, to his inheritance that I have given you." 21. And I commanded Yehoshua at that time: "Your own eyes have seen all that *God*, your God, has done to these two kings; so shall *God* do to all the kingdoms to which you will cross over. 22. Do not fear them; for *God*, your God, it is He Who fights for you."

The Haftarah for this Sidra may be found on page 908.

ואתחנן

VAETHḤANAN

23. I sought worthiness of favor with *God* at that time and said: 24. "O my Lord, *God!* Thou hast begun to give Thy servant insight into Thy greatness and Thy mighty hand; indeed, where is there any power in heaven or on earth that can perform like Thy creations and Thy almighty power? 25. Let me cross over, I pray Thee, and see the good land that is on the far side of the Yarden, that good mountain and the Lebanon." 26. And *God* turned against me in anger on your account and He would not listen to me. And *God* said to me: "You have enough; do not speak to Me any more about this matter! 27. Go up to the top of the elevation and lift up your eyes to the west and to the north, to the south and to the east, and look with your eyes; for you shall not cross this Yarden. 28. Charge Yehoshua with his duty and make him firm and strong; for he shall go before this people and shall have them take possession of the land that you see." 29. At that time we were staying in the valley opposite Beth-Peor.

IV 1. And now, O Yisrael, hearken to the statutes and to the [social] ordinances that I am teaching you to carry out, so that you may live and come and take

כג וָאֶתְחַנַּן אֶל־יְהֹוָה בָּעֵת הַהִוא לֵאמֹר:
כד אֲדֹנָי יֱהֹוִה אַתָּה הַחִלּוֹתָ לְהַרְאוֹת אֶת־עַבְדְּךָ
אֶת־גָּדְלְךָ וְאֶת־יָדְךָ הַחֲזָקָה אֲשֶׁר מִי־אֵל
בַּשָּׁמַיִם וּבָאָרֶץ אֲשֶׁר־יַעֲשֶׂה כְמַעֲשֶׂיךָ
וְכִגְבוּרֹתֶךָ: כה אֶעְבְּרָה־נָּא וְאֶרְאֶה אֶת־הָאָרֶץ
הַטּוֹבָה אֲשֶׁר בְּעֵבֶר הַיַּרְדֵּן הָהָר הַטּוֹב הַזֶּה
וְהַלְּבָנֹן: כו וַיִּתְעַבֵּר יְהֹוָה בִּי לְמַעַנְכֶם וְלֹא
שָׁמַע אֵלָי וַיֹּאמֶר יְהֹוָה אֵלַי רַב־לָךְ אַל־תּוֹסֶף
דַּבֵּר אֵלַי עוֹד בַּדָּבָר הַזֶּה: כז עֲלֵה ׀ רֹאשׁ
הַפִּסְגָּה וְשָׂא עֵינֶיךָ יָמָּה וְצָפֹנָה וְתֵימָנָה
וּמִזְרָחָה וּרְאֵה בְעֵינֶיךָ כִּי־לֹא תַעֲבֹר אֶת־
הַיַּרְדֵּן הַזֶּה: כח וְצַו אֶת־יְהוֹשֻׁעַ וְחַזְּקֵהוּ
וְאַמְּצֵהוּ כִּי־הוּא יַעֲבֹר לִפְנֵי הָעָם הַזֶּה וְהוּא
יַנְחִיל אוֹתָם אֶת־הָאָרֶץ אֲשֶׁר תִּרְאֶה: כט וַנֵּשֶׁב
בַּגָּיְא מוּל בֵּית פְּעוֹר: פ ד א וְעַתָּה יִשְׂרָאֵל
שְׁמַע אֶל־הַחֻקִּים וְאֶל־הַמִּשְׁפָּטִים אֲשֶׁר אָנֹכִי
מְלַמֵּד אֶתְכֶם לַעֲשׂוֹת לְמַעַן תִּחְיוּ וּבָאתֶם

CHAPTER III

24. ***Thou hast begun.*** All that Thou hast permitted me to experience thus far is only the beginning of an insight into Thy greatness and almighty power. . . .

25. ***Let me cross over, I pray Thee.*** The significance of the Land transcends by far even the greatness and omnipotence of which Thou hast already granted me an intimation. For the Land embodies the purpose of all Thy workings that have become known to me thus far. From there it is Thy intention to show "Thy greatness and Thy mighty hand," to perform the work of training all mankind and to win it over for the establishment of Thy kingdom on earth. Seeing this land with my own eyes would afford me additional insights into the greatness and might of Thy future world sovereignty. . . .

CHAPTER IV

1. ***And now, O Yisrael.*** "And now"—this is the appeal to the people of Israel to implement in the future, upon which they are now to embark, all the truths from their past history that Moses has set forth to them thus far. All their past experiences yield only one conclusion: that obedience to the will of God is the one sole, indispensable condition upon which their future welfare will depend. Moses is about to depart, but the laws that he transmitted to them from God and taught to them contain everything they need for building up a happy future. Therefore, Moses' last wish before his death was to impress upon the people the importance of observing these laws and to teach them the manner and the frame of mind in which they must observe them.

hearken to. "Hearkening" denotes the constant

possession of the land that *God*, the God of your fathers, is giving you. 2. Do not add anything to that which I am commanding you, and do not subtract anything from it, to keep the commandments of *God*, your God, which I am commanding you. 3. It is your own eyes that see what *God* did at Baal Peor. For everyone that followed Baal Peor, *God*, your God, has destroyed him from your midst. 4. And you who have remained firm with *God*, your God, are all alive today. 5. See! I have taught you statutes and [social] ordinances as *God*, my God, made it my duty, so that you may act accordingly in the midst of the land to

וִירִשְׁתֶּם אֶת־הָאָרֶץ אֲשֶׁר יְהֹוָה אֱלֹהֵי אֲבֹתֵיכֶם
נֹתֵן לָכֶם: ב לֹא תֹסִפוּ עַל־הַדָּבָר אֲשֶׁר אָנֹכִי
מְצַוֶּה אֶתְכֶם וְלֹא תִגְרְעוּ מִמֶּנּוּ לִשְׁמֹר אֶת־
מִצְוֹת יְהֹוָה אֱלֹהֵיכֶם אֲשֶׁר אָנֹכִי מְצַוֶּה אֶתְכֶם:
ג עֵינֵיכֶם הָרֹאוֹת אֵת אֲשֶׁר־עָשָׂה יְהֹוָה בְּבַעַל
פְּעוֹר כִּי כָל־הָאִישׁ אֲשֶׁר הָלַךְ אַחֲרֵי בַעַל־
פְּעוֹר הִשְׁמִידוֹ יְהֹוָה אֱלֹהֶיךָ מִקִּרְבֶּךָ: ד וְאַתֶּם
הַדְּבֵקִים בַּיהֹוָה אֱלֹהֵיכֶם חַיִּים כֻּלְּכֶם הַיּוֹם: שני
ה רְאֵה ׀ לִמַּדְתִּי אֶתְכֶם חֻקִּים וּמִשְׁפָּטִים
כַּאֲשֶׁר צִוַּנִי יְהֹוָה אֱלֹהָי לַעֲשׂוֹת כֵּן בְּקֶרֶב

activity of listening to something that is taught; we should not be content to perceive it only once, but should keep it clearly before us at all times, particularly when the occasion arises to translate it into reality. . . .

° ° °

that I am teaching you. Once again Moses refers to his activity of transmitting the knowledge of God's Law to his people as לְמוּד ["teaching"], not כְּתִיבָה ["writing"]. Thus we see that not the written text but the spoken word, תּוֹרָה שֶׁבְּעַל פֶּה [the Oral Law], was the medium by which the Law of God was implanted in the people. . . . לַמֵּד also means to accustom another person to a certain pattern of behavior, to train him in this behavior by practice. . . . Such teaching implies far more than merely making something understood in theory; it denotes instructions given with the intention that what is taught in theory should also be applied in practice. Thus, Moses' teaching of the Law was תַּלְמוּד in the literal sense of the term, and the Talmud is, in fact, the Law of Moses.

so that you may live and come and take possession. Free-willed obedience to the Law of God will give us life. . . . and even as such free-willed obedience is the *sine qua non* for the development of our personal existence into true life, so, too, it alone will enable us to establish and develop our life as a nation on our own soil. ". . . Hearken . . . so that you may live and come. . ."

° ° °

2. To add anything to the Law or to strike anything from it on one's own authority would mean to tamper with the Word of God, to impose human judgment upon the eternal truths of Divine thought, to drag Divinely-ordained institutions down to the level of human superficiality.

° ° °

3. ***It is your own eyes that see.*** This experience was a very recent one; the sin of Baal Peor occurred after the defeat of Siḥon and Og. Hence it was still quite fresh in the minds of the generation that was now ready to enter the Land. The fact that the commandment neither to add to, nor to subtract from, the Law of God immediately precedes this admonitory reference to the destruction of the idolators has profound instructive significance. It proclaims that any denial of the inviolable Divinity of the Law, even if it is only with reference to one single commandment—thus equating human discretion with the statutes of God—is tantamount to a complete defection to idolatry. . . .

that followed Baal Peor. This may be a reference not merely to those who actually performed the rites of the Peor cult but even to those who participated in any manner in this great sin or showed themselves partial to it in any way. In that case, it would serve only to underscore all the more impressively the warning against deviating from any one of the laws of God.

5. ***See!*** Here is one more fact that you should keep in mind as something you yourselves have experienced: "I have taught you . . . so that you may act accordingly in the midst of the land to which you are coming. . .": You see that I have taught you statutes and [social] ordinances in accordance with the Divine command given to me, so that you may observe them in the land you are about to enter. Thus you have been presented with a fact that identifies your calling and the significance of these laws, and that sets you and these laws apart from all other laws and nations: You are the only nation on earth that possessed laws before it possessed a land of its own. Furthermore, these laws that have been given to you are the only laws extant that are not intended as a *means* for building up a national existence and for achieving national independence and

which you are coming to take possession of
it. 6. So keep [it] and carry [it] out; for
that is your wisdom and your understanding
before the eyes of the nations that will hear
all these statutes and will say: "So it is, after
all, a wise and understanding nation, this
great people!" 7. For which is a great
nation? One that has a Deity near to it, as
God, our God, is, whenever we call to Him.

הָאָ֫רֶץ אֲשֶׁר אַתֶּם בָּאִים שָׁמָּה לְרִשְׁתָּהּ:
ו וּשְׁמַרְתֶּם וַעֲשִׂיתֶם כִּי הִוא חָכְמַתְכֶם
וּבִינַתְכֶם לְעֵינֵי הָעַמִּים אֲשֶׁר יִשְׁמְעוּן אֵת כָּל־
הַחֻקִּים הָאֵלֶּה וְאָמְרוּ רַק עַם־חָכָם וְנָבוֹן הַגּוֹי
הַגָּדוֹל הַזֶּה: ז כִּי מִי־גוֹי גָּדוֹל אֲשֶׁר־לוֹ אֱלֹהִים
קְרֹבִים אֵלָיו כַּיהוָה אֱלֹהֵינוּ בְּכָל־קָרְאֵנוּ אֵלָיו:

prosperity based on the possession of a land of your own. They represent, instead, the sole *end* for which you were given existence as an independent nation on your own soil. Every other nation becomes a nation solely by virtue of the fact that it has a land of its own; only after that does it create its own laws to be observed in that land. You, by contrast, became a nation solely by virtue of your Law and were given a land of your own solely for the purpose that you may observe that Law.

The laws of all the other nations are the product of national characteristics fostered by the land; they are the result of changing needs and conditions. But your lawgiver, the man from whose hands you received your Law, has never even seen your land, never set foot in it. He was merely the transmitter of the Law, and the fact that his grave is to be in the wilderness represents God's own seal upon the Law that he, Moses, communicated to you; it is the guarantee that this Law is eternal and immutable.

The Law is constant; you and the Land are the variables. The Law is not obliged to change in accordance with changes in your fortunes or in the fortunes of your land. It is your fortunes, and the fortunes of your land that will change in accordance with the extent to which you will be loyal to the Law. It is with the Law in your arms that you now stand as a nation on the border of the land you are to enter, in order that you may there observe the Law in its entirety. And even in days to come, when you will have forfeited the land, albeit temporarily, you will appear again and again as that nation which has no other calling but to live for the observance of this Law and to await the moment when you will be able once again to enter the land which was given to you so that you may observe the Law in its entirety. You are the people of the Law; *Eretz Yisrael* is the Land of the Law, but you are not [simply] the "Palestinian people," and *Eretz Yisrael* is not [unconditionally] the "Jewish land."

° ° °

6. **וּשְׁמַרְתֶּם וַעֲשִׂיתֶם** *[So keep (it) and carry (it) out].* The first prerequisite in performing the duty to "keep" the Law is to study it, as we are told again and again. "*Keep*: This means, to study" (cf. Leviticus 18:4 and 5). . . . Since, therefore, your whole existence, your calling and your future, are rooted in this Law, you have to do nothing else but study the Law and carry it out. "For that," both of them together, שְׁמִירָה and עֲשִׂיָּה, the study and the practical observance of the Law, constitutes your חָכְמָה ["wisdom"] and your בִּינָה ["understanding"] in the eyes of the other nations. חָכְמָה ["wisdom"] denotes the absorption of truths. בִּינָה ["understanding"] denotes the intelligence needed to draw the correct inferences and conclusions from what one has learned. . . . Whatever arts and sciences may characterize the heritage of other civilized nations, yours, the *Jewish* arts and sciences, are the knowledge and skills needed to build up all of personal and national life upon two foundations: your awareness of God and your awareness of your duties as human beings. These are the arts and sciences entailed in knowing the Law of God and translating it into reality, the arts and sciences of truth and of a harmonious life.

before the eyes of the nations. This, your knowledge and art of living, will be regarded by the other nations as your distinguishing feature. You will be living proof of the words of the ancient seer [Genesis 9:27]: יַפְתְּ אֱלֹהִים לְיֶפֶת וְיִשְׁכֹּן בְּאָהֳלֵי־שֵׁם ["God will open the emotions (of men) to Yapheth but He will dwell in the tents of Shem"]: If you should learn the skills needed for producing the beauty that appeals to the senses, you must go to the other nations. But if you should learn the skills needed for building homes, cities and states in which God reveals His blessed presence, you will find these only among the sons of Shem. Hence, if you [Israel] will live solely for attaining such knowledge and for observing the Law of God before the eyes of the other nations, your whole existence will serve as a means of propagating the establishment of God's kingdom on earth, built upon allegiance to the Law of God.

° ° °

7 and 8. ***For which is a great nation? One that has a Deity near to it . . . And which is a great nation? One that has righteous statutes . . .*** If this were meant to ask what other nation could compare itself to Israel, one might have expected the text to read not מִי גוֹי גָּדוֹל, but מִי גוֹי אֲשֶׁר ["Which (other) nation is it (that

ח וּמִי֙ גּ֣וֹי גָּד֔וֹל אֲשֶׁר־ל֛וֹ חֻקִּ֥ים וּמִשְׁפָּטִ֖ים
צַדִּיקִ֑ם כְּכֹל֙ הַתּוֹרָ֣ה הַזֹּ֔את אֲשֶׁ֧ר אָנֹכִ֛י נֹתֵ֥ן
לִפְנֵיכֶ֖ם הַיּֽוֹם׃ ט רַ֡ק הִשָּׁ֣מֶר לְךָ֩ וּשְׁמֹ֨ר נַפְשְׁךָ֜
מְאֹ֗ד פֶּן־תִּשְׁכַּ֨ח אֶת־הַדְּבָרִ֜ים אֲשֶׁר־רָא֣וּ עֵינֶ֗יךָ

8. And which is a great nation? One that has righteous statutes and [social] ordinances like this entire Law which I am setting before you today. 9. Only take heed and guard your soul exceedingly, so that you do not forget the facts that your [own] eyes have seen, and that they do not

has). . .''], or better still, אִי זֶה גוֹי אֲשֶׁר [''What (other) nation. . .'']. We therefore believe that אֲשֶׁר לוֹ וגו׳ is the answer to the question מִי גוֹי גָּדוֹל. We were told just before that the nations will call Israel a great nation Here we are given the reasons for this. The greatness of a nation is usually measured by two standards: its prosperity within and without, and the wisdom of its constitution. In the case of Israel, the nations are immediately struck by the presence of both these blessings. For, we read, which is a great nation? One that has deities that are close to it; i.e., a nation whose deities bestow upon it the blessings of growth and prosperity, security and victory, just as, indeed, God, the One sole God, to Whom we give our allegiance and obedience as our God, has bestowed these favors upon us whenever we are need of His help. And furthermore which is a great nation? One that has righteous statutes and ordinances, just like those that are, indeed, contained in the Teaching that Moses has brought us from God and set before us so that we may accept it. Israel's spiritual and moral greatness lies precisely in the fact that it has accepted this Law to observe it faithfully for all time to come. Nevertheless, אֱלֹקִים refers only to קָדֹשׁ [the Holy One]. For, as a matter of fact, only God is near to man; all other deities are sham and the powers attributed to them are remote from man and his concerns. Therefore אֱלֹקִים truly refers to God, and the literal interpretation of this passage is: ''Which nation is great? One that has a God as near to it as God, our God, is near to us.''

° ° °

9. . . . Everything rests upon this one basic fact: That the nation itself witnessed the Divine revelation of the Law. Thus, the nation has a direct guarantee that this Law is indeed Divine and that God is a personal and supernatural Being. Hence it is, before all else, this basic historic fact, the revelation of the Law at Sinai, proven by the evidence of our own physical senses, that must remain alive forever in our hearts and minds and must be handed down to our children so that they, too, may take it to heart and pass it on to future generations. A personal experience, perceived simultaneously by an entire nation, is an unparalleled, unique foundation for the historicity of the Revelation, and the fact that the entire nation communicated it from one generation to the next represents a similarly unique, unparalleled preservation of that experience in the basic awareness of all future generations.

. . . Non-Jews develop their approach to history and nature without these two facts that were perceived by Israel: the existence of one sole, supernatural, personal God, and the existence of a moral law proclaimed by Him. . . . As far as you [Jews] are concerned, these two facts are the most real among all the realities of nature and history. In the midst of a world caught up in notions developed from incomplete premises, you are to maintain your own spiritual independence. If you were to accept their notions, which are erroneous because they are founded on defective premises and therefore yield false conclusions, you would run the risk of forgetting that very personal experience of those realities from which alone the truths of life and existence can be derived. Therefore, take heed lest you forget the facts that your own eyes have beheld.

But above all, ''guard your soul exceedingly. . .'': The un-Jewish view of nature and history may all too easily gain a dangerous advocate within your own heart. Once God has vanished from nature, man's physical life, the sensual aspects of his existence, will be deified, and once the historic significance of God's Law is denied, the seat of sovereignty is prepared for self-seeking human brutality. Both these notions will appeal only too readily to your נֶפֶשׁ, to your sensual and intellectual nature and aspirations. They hold out the promise of liberating the sensual aspects of your life from their subordination to the standards of moral sanctity, and the historical aspects of your existence from their subordination to the demands of justice and loving-kindness that the Law has brought to you, on Mount Sinai, from God. Therefore, even as you must guard against un-Jewish influences from without, so, too, above all, guard your own inner being against insinuations that may appeal to your sensuality and your selfishness, so that you do not forget the facts that vouch for the existence of God and the authenticity of His Law. And above all, guard the spiritual aspect of your nature, so that you do not lose sight of the facts that your own eyes have beheld.

° ° °

and make them known to your children and your children's children. You must now see to it that the truths which you have come to know through your own depart from your heart all the days of your life; and make them known to your children and your children's children; 10. the day that you stood before *God*, your God, at Ḥoreb, when *God* said to me: "Assemble this people for me; I will let them hear My words so that they may learn to fear Me all the days that they live on earth, and teach their children accordingly." 11. You approached, you stood below, at the mountain; and the mountain [was] blazing in fire up to the heart of the heaven; [with] darkness, clouds and opaque darkness. 12. Then *God* spoke to you out of the midst of the fire; you heard [the] voice of words, but you saw no form; only a voice. 13. And He made known to you His

וּפֶן־יָסוּרוּ מִלְּבָבְךָ כֹּל יְמֵי חַיֶּיךָ וְהוֹדַעְתָּם לְבָנֶיךָ וְלִבְנֵי בָנֶיךָ: י יוֹם אֲשֶׁר עָמַדְתָּ לִפְנֵי יְהֹוָה אֱלֹהֶיךָ בְּחֹרֵב בֶּאֱמֹר יְהֹוָה אֵלַי הַקְהֶל־לִי אֶת־הָעָם וְאַשְׁמִעֵם אֶת־דְּבָרָי אֲשֶׁר יִלְמְדוּן לְיִרְאָה אֹתִי כָּל־הַיָּמִים אֲשֶׁר הֵם חַיִּים עַל־הָאֲדָמָה וְאֶת־בְּנֵיהֶם יְלַמֵּדוּן: יא וַתִּקְרְבוּן וַתַּעַמְדוּן תַּחַת הָהָר וְהָהָר בֹּעֵר בָּאֵשׁ עַד־לֵב הַשָּׁמַיִם חֹשֶׁךְ עָנָן וַעֲרָפֶל: יב וַיְדַבֵּר יְהֹוָה אֲלֵיכֶם מִתּוֹךְ הָאֵשׁ קוֹל דְּבָרִים אַתֶּם שֹׁמְעִים וּתְמוּנָה אֵינְכֶם רֹאִים זוּלָתִי קוֹל: יג וַיַּגֵּד לָכֶם

experience and which, by virtue of this personal experience, have become the granite foundation for all your thoughts and actions, become the "knowledge"—not merely the "belief"—of your children and your children's children. Let your children *know* what you yourself have *seen*. Hand it down to them with all the resoluteness and certainty born of personal experience, in such a manner that this experience of yours will become the basis for the knowledge attained by all your descendants. Such is the tradition received by an entire national entity and handed down by each generation to an entire national posterity. This is the only way in which historic fact can remain authentic even in the minds of your remotest descendants. For in the final analysis the authenticity even of written records rests on the fact that their contents have been handed down collectively by all the fathers to all the sons and are therefore considered true beyond doubt. . . .

Perhaps, too, we have here another thought, as follows: Only one who, as he hands down the Law to his child, becomes aware that he is now faithfully and punctiliously passing on to his child the heritage he himself once received from his own father, will truly be able to realize the living authenticity of this tradition, which goes back to Mount Sinai. He will then realize that the care and the faithfulness with which he now passes the tradition to his own child was practiced also toward him by his own father, and toward his father by *his* father before him, and so on, back to that original generation which stood at Mount Sinai. Thus the chain of tradition leads each of its links, through its own conscious loyalty to the tradition, directly back to Mount Sinai. Only when he himself passes on the tradition to the next generation does [the Jew] truly identify with those who originally received the Law at Sinai. . . .

∘   ∘   ∘

10. . . . This Jewish "fear of God" is not produced by vague moods and sentiments. The fear of God must be taught and learned. The Word of God repeatedly refers to "teaching the fear of God." In the present verse, the text reads: יִלְמְדוּן לְיִרְאָה אֹתִי ["so that they may learn to fear Me"]. Cf. also "So that you may learn to fear *God*, your God, at all times" (Deuteronomy 14:23); "So that he may learn to fear *God*, his God" (Deuteronomy 17:19); and "And learn to fear *God*, your God" (Deuteronomy 31:13). The fear of God is acquired through study and practice. it is a mental science and a moral art; both these aspects are implicit in למד. Our first lesson in this Jewish intellectual and moral skill was imparted to us by God Himself. All that follows is merely an elaboration of this instruction. He let us hear His Word without showing Himself to us; we heard Him but we did not see Him. Thus we became aware of Him, in His invisibility, through His Word; these were words of His Law, addressed to us, through which we entered into our eternal covenant with Him. This constant awareness of God, the invisible God, through his Word, the Word of His will; this constant listening to God—that is what is meant by "fearing" God. . . .

all the days that they live on earth. As long as the people are on earth, surrounded by, and caught up in, all the physical things on earth, let them look beyond all these visible things to the invisible One of Whom they became aware in the midst of this visible, physical world, so that He will remain present in their midst, and they may walk before Him even amidst the things of this world and listen to His voice from Ḥoreb.

13. . . . The Law He has made it our duty to observe is His בְּרִית [covenant]. It is the *sine qua non* for His relationship with us. It is this covenant, namely, the

covenant that He commanded you to fulfill, in the Ten Statements, and He inscribed them upon two tablets of stone. 14. And *God* commanded me at that time to teach you statutes and [social] ordinances so that you may carry them out in the land into which you are passing over to take possession of it. 15. So take heed exceedingly for [the sake of] your souls! For you have seen no [manner of] form on the day that *God* spoke to you at Ḥoreb out of the midst of the fire. 16. So that you will not become corrupt and make yourselves an image, the representation of any form whatsoever; the likeness of a male or a female; 17. the likeness of any animal on earth; the likeness of any winged bird that flies upon the heaven; 18. the likeness of any creeping thing on the ground; the likeness of any fish creature that is in the water beneath the earth— 19. and so that you will not lift up your eyes to heaven and see

אֶת־בְּרִיתוֹ אֲשֶׁר צִוָּה אֶתְכֶם לַעֲשׂוֹת עֲשֶׂרֶת
הַדְּבָרִים וַיִּכְתְּבֵם עַל־שְׁנֵי לֻחוֹת אֲבָנִים׃
יד וְאֹתִי צִוָּה יְהֹוָה בָּעֵת הַהִוא לְלַמֵּד אֶתְכֶם
חֻקִּים וּמִשְׁפָּטִים לַעֲשֹׂתְכֶם אֹתָם בָּאָרֶץ אֲשֶׁר
אַתֶּם עֹבְרִים שָׁמָּה לְרִשְׁתָּהּ׃ טו וְנִשְׁמַרְתֶּם מְאֹד
לְנַפְשֹׁתֵיכֶם כִּי לֹא רְאִיתֶם כָּל־תְּמוּנָה בְּיוֹם
דִּבֶּר יְהֹוָה אֲלֵיכֶם בְּחֹרֵב מִתּוֹךְ הָאֵשׁ׃ טז פֶּן־
תַּשְׁחִתוּן וַעֲשִׂיתֶם לָכֶם פֶּסֶל תְּמוּנַת כָּל־סָמֶל
תַּבְנִית זָכָר אוֹ נְקֵבָה׃ יז תַּבְנִית כָּל־בְּהֵמָה
אֲשֶׁר בָּאָרֶץ תַּבְנִית כָּל־צִפּוֹר כָּנָף אֲשֶׁר תָּעוּף
בַּשָּׁמָיִם׃ יח תַּבְנִית כָּל־רֹמֵשׂ בָּאֲדָמָה תַּבְנִית
כָּל־דָּגָה אֲשֶׁר־בַּמַּיִם מִתַּחַת לָאָרֶץ׃ יט וּפֶן־
תִּשָּׂא עֵינֶיךְ הַשָּׁמַיְמָה וְרָאִיתָ אֶת־הַשֶּׁמֶשׁ וְאֶת־

laws He commanded us to observe, that He has set before us in ten statements. These עֲשֶׂרֶת הַדְּבָרִים [ten statements] do not comprise everything He commanded us, but they constitute a proclamation of His covenant. They give us an idea of what He expects us to do as our part in His covenant with us. They contain the fundamentals of the entire Covenantal Law. . . .

15. ***So take heed exceedingly for [the sake of] your souls.*** Preserve your souls; do not permit any outside influence to remove you from the guiding and decisive influence exercised by the spiritual aspect of your character. As indicated by all that follows, we must not let ourselves be robbed of our clear perception and conviction that God is a supernatural Being, yet at the same time uniquely real and personal. He is the invisible One, and we must not permit anything to erase or even merely dilute this conception of Him by attempting to assign Him to the sphere of physical existence. It is therefore particularly important that we should communicate this awareness of ours to the internal tribunal represented by our souls and punctiliously observe the commandment to keep stringent watch over ourselves, so that nothing should ever estrange this internal tribunal from us. Aside from God there is only one other form of existence that is invisible, one which cannot be perceived by the physical senses, but concerning which we are certain nevertheless that it is a real and present form of existence: our soul. Because they themselves have this quality, our souls are capable of grasping also the real, personal existence of an invisible Being and are as convinced of God's existence as they are of their own. As sure as we are of our own existence, so certain are we of the existence of God. . . .

19. . . . Here is the prohibition against star worship, the deification of the heavenly bodies whose influences—both real and imagined—on earthly phenomena were probably the chief impetus to idolatry. You look upon the heavens . . . and behold upon them the sun (whose Hebrew name [שמש] identifies it as the first "servant," the "sexton," as it were, upon the great dome of God's universe), the moon and the stars, and all the vast celestial world. Despite the infinite variety of sizes and magnitudes, of distances and orbits, which they present, the thinking man will perceive all these heavenly bodies as one single host, subordinate to One sole Being, governed by His own unique consistent will.

But there is the danger that you may allow the emotional impact of this vast panorama to overwhelm you, so that instead of following the dictates of your נֶפֶשׁ [soul], you will submit to the impulses of your senses and will ascribe to these heavenly bodies powers of their own, "and cast yourself down before them." You will feel that you must prostrate yourself before them without a will of your own, "and serve them," so that you must devise some form of worship in order to win their favor. . . .

The nations have been directed to apply the gifts of

the sun and the moon and the stars and the entire host of heaven, and allow yourself to be carried away and cast yourself down before them and serve them, which *God*, your God, has assigned to all the nations beneath the whole heaven. 20. But you has *God* taken, when He led you out from the iron crucible, from Mitzrayim, so that you may remain His as a heritage nation, as on this day. 21. And *God* was angry with me because of your provocations and swore that I would not pass over the Yarden, that I would not come into the good land that *God*, your God, is giving you as an inheritance. 22. For I will die in this land; I will not pass over the Yarden. But you will pass over and will take possession of this good land. 23. Therefore take heed to yourselves so that you will not forget the covenant of *God*, your God, which He made with you, and not make yourselves an image, a representation of anything concerning which *God*, your God, has given you your duty. 24. For *God*, your God, is a consuming fire—a God Who demands [His] right. 25. When you will beget children and children's children, and you will have grown old in the Land, and you will practice corruption and make an image,

הַיָּרֵחַ וְאֶת־הַכּֽוֹכָבִים כֹּל צְבָא הַשָּׁמַיִם וְנִדַּחְתָּ וְהִשְׁתַּחֲוִיתָ לָהֶם וַעֲבַדְתָּם אֲשֶׁר חָלַק יְהֹוָה אֱלֹהֶיךָ אֹתָם לְכֹל הָעַמִּים תַּחַת כָּל־הַשָּׁמָיִם: כ וְאֶתְכֶם לָקַח יְהֹוָה וַיּוֹצִא אֶתְכֶם מִכּוּר הַבַּרְזֶל מִמִּצְרָיִם לִהְיוֹת לוֹ לְעַם נַחֲלָה כַּיּוֹם הַזֶּה: כא וַיהֹוָה הִתְאַנַּף־בִּי עַל־דִּבְרֵיכֶם וַיִּשָּׁבַע לְבִלְתִּי עָבְרִי אֶת־הַיַּרְדֵּן וּלְבִלְתִּי־בֹא אֶל־ הָאָרֶץ הַטּוֹבָה אֲשֶׁר יְהֹוָה אֱלֹהֶיךָ נֹתֵן לְךָ נַחֲלָה: כב כִּי אָנֹכִי מֵת בָּאָרֶץ הַזֹּאת אֵינֶנִּי עֹבֵר אֶת־הַיַּרְדֵּן וְאַתֶּם עֹבְרִים וִירִשְׁתֶּם אֶת־הָאָרֶץ הַטּוֹבָה הַזֹּאת: כג הִשָּׁמְרוּ לָכֶם פֶּן־תִּשְׁכְּחוּ אֶת־בְּרִית יְהֹוָה אֱלֹהֵיכֶם אֲשֶׁר כָּרַת עִמָּכֶם וַעֲשִׂיתֶם לָכֶם פֶּסֶל תְּמוּנַת כֹּל אֲשֶׁר צִוְּךָ יְהֹוָה אֱלֹהֶיךָ: כד כִּי יְהֹוָה אֱלֹהֶיךָ אֵשׁ אֹכְלָה הוּא אֵל קַנָּא: פ כה כִּי־תוֹלִיד בָּנִים וּבְנֵי בָנִים וְנוֹשַׁנְתֶּם בָּאָרֶץ וְהִשְׁחַתֶּם וַעֲשִׂיתֶם פֶּסֶל

the human intellect to the utilization of the physical powers of these heavenly bodies, so that they may serve mankind in the upbuilding and development of individual and national life on earth. It is God, your God, Who has placed these talents at the service of the nations so that they may be able to fulfill their purpose on earth. Hence it is His favor alone that men must seek by utilizing their position in the world in accordance with their moral duty. But the nations have forgotten this, and therefore they have fallen from their lofty position of free-willed world rulership to the level of non-freedom that comes of worshipping the physical forces of nature. As long as men have the correct attitude with regard to their position in the world in which they live, the forces of nature will be "their portion"; but when men go astray, it is they who become subordinate to the forces of nature.

25. **When you will beget.** Moses' fear is not that the nation will go astray immediately after it has entered the Land. But he sees the danger increasing the longer it will live in the Land. The danger of corruption will come when a second and third generation will have

been born in the Land, וְנוֹשַׁנְתֶּם בָּאָרֶץ ["and you have grown old in the Land"]—and the nation has become "old" in the Land.

יָשַׁן, as distinct from זָקֵן, is not the opposite of "young," but the opposite of "new" or "fresh." . . . Once the nation has lived in its land for two or three generations, its citizens will regard themselves as aborigines of the land, as being bound up with the land. They will no longer remember the days when they had no home and no land of their own, and they will forget their origin and Him to Whom they owe the land and the possibility to remain there. Not without good reason did God, in His statement "so that you may remember the day of your exodus from the land of Mitzrayim all the days of your life" (Deuteronomy 16:3), introduce the fact of our redemption from Egypt into our everyday thoughts. Not without good reason did He ordain His festivals and His great institutions of *shemittah* and *yovel* as national acts of recognition and avowal, to be performed at stated recurring intervals by the entire nation, so that it may remain mindful of its origin and remember that the land belongs to God. . . . Nothing would be more detrimental to our relationship a representation of anything, and you will do what is evil in the eyes of *God*, your God, to anger Him; 26. then I will appoint heaven and earth as witnesses against you today so that you will be lost, quickly lost from the land to which you are passing over the Yarden to take possession of it; you will not remain there for a longer period, for otherwise you would be utterly destroyed. 27. *God* will scatter you among the nations, and you will be left few in number

תְּמוּנַת כֹּל וַעֲשִׂיתֶם הָרַע בְּעֵינֵי יְהֹוָה־אֱלֹהֶיךָ לְהַכְעִיסוֹ: כו הַעִידֹתִי בָכֶם הַיּוֹם אֶת־הַשָּׁמַיִם וְאֶת־הָאָרֶץ כִּי־אָבֹד תֹּאבֵדוּן מַהֵר מֵעַל הָאָרֶץ אֲשֶׁר אַתֶּם עֹבְרִים אֶת־הַיַּרְדֵּן שָׁמָּה לְרִשְׁתָּהּ לֹא־תַאֲרִיכֻן יָמִים עָלֶיהָ כִּי הִשָּׁמֵד תִּשָּׁמֵדוּן: כז וְהֵפִיץ יְהֹוָה אֶתְכֶם בָּעַמִּים וְנִשְׁאַרְתֶּם מְתֵי

to God, both as individuals and as a nation, than if we "will have grown old in the Promised Land"; i.e., that our original youthful enthusiasm, engendered by the awareness that we are God's, should change to smugness when that for which we once yearned as the promised goal of our hopes and desires become "ours" [in that we are taking it for granted], and we become "old" and "stale" in our possession of it.

and you will practice corruption. Once the thought of the sole supernatural One, Who was revealed to you in your history as the sole true support of your existence—and indeed, of the entire universe—fades from your memory, the world of the senses, with its supposedly sovereign realities, will push its way to the foreground in your minds. You will then fling yourselves into the arms of heathen depravity which sees all of human existence—both personal and national—merely as a product of the physical forces that shape a land into the cradle of a nation; forces from which that nation must then wrest its fortunes.

Once this happens, it is no longer God Who blesses you in and through His Land, depending on the extent to which you subordinate your conduct to His will as it was revealed to you. You will then see this land, with all its physical potentialities, as the only power that can grant you prosperity or withhold it from you.

and make an image, a representation of anything. You will then attempt to visualize these forces by constructing physical representations of them for yourselves, and eventually you will come to a point where "you will do what is evil in the eyes of *God*, your God, to anger Him." You will regard God—along with His Law that requires you to subordinate to it the sensual aspects of your nature—not as the Giver of all your joy of living but as the one Who stands in the way of your happiness, and you will feel that in order to safeguard your personal happiness, you must, in principle, set yourselves up in opposition to His will.

26. *I will appoint . . . as witnesses.* These very heavens and earth, the entire physical universe to which the forces that you worship belong, will I appoint as witnesses to testify against you. In Jewish law, the function of witnesses is to admonish and warn a person before he commits a crime, and to indict and punish the criminal after the act. Similarly, God will appoint heaven and earth to admonish and warn you on His behalf, and finally to carry out the sentence passed against you if, instead of serving Him to the exclusion of all others, you will worship anything encompassed by heaven and earth. The world, the heavens and the earth, will not look upon you with favor if you will jeopardize God's approval in order to curry favor with them. . . .

. . . The Children of Israel are herewith warned that if their defection should attain the extent described above, they will be quickly removed from the land. . . . The statement "for otherwise you would be utterly destroyed" gives the reason why they would then be quickly removed from the land: If they were permitted to remain in the land after having reached this stage of defection, they would move toward total ruin. Hence their removal from the land will be their spiritual and moral salvation. They must lose their land and their political independence in order not to descend to the depths of depravity that caused the annihilation of the Canaanite population which dwelt in the land before them. . . . The state and the Temple were destroyed, but the nation, with that remnant of the spiritual heritage which was still within its heart, went forth to discharge its great mission in dispersion.

27. . . . You will not be allowed to remain together in exile. There will be some of you in the midst of each nation. This dispersion among the nations would seem to have a dual purpose. First, the [Jewish] nation will nowhere be able to form a solid numerical bloc; as a result, it will be protected from lapsing into that political aberration into which it fell when it had a state of its own. Secondly, it will act as God's own seed, scattered among the nations, in order that it may awaken and promote among the societies of these nations a different view of the world, a different philosophy of life. . . .

and you will be left few in number. Although you will be small in number you will remain a separate national entity among the nations. . . .

among the peoples to which *God* will lead you.   28. There you will be subjected to gods, the work of human hands, wood and stone, that neither see nor hear, nor eat, nor smell.   29. From there you will seek *God,* your God, and you will find Him; for you will seek Him with all your heart and all your soul.   30. In this distress that will befall you, and when all these decrees [of fate] will have come to you, in the end of days, you will return to *God,* your God, and listen to His voice.   31. For *God,* your God, is a merciful God; He will not turn you adrift and will not let you be destroyed, and He will not forget the covenant of your fathers that He swore to them.   32. For inquire, now, about the earlier times that were before you, from the day that God created man on earth, and from one end of heaven to the other end of heaven, whether anything such as this great [event] has ever happened, or whether anything like it has ever been heard.   33. Has any people heard the voice of God, speaking from the midst of the fire, as you have heard, and still remained alive?   34. Or has a god proven himself to come, to take a nation from the midst of a[nother] nation, with demonstrations of power, with signs and with instructive miracles, and with war, and with a strong hand and an outstretched arm, and with great terrors, comparable to all that which *God,* your God, did for you in Mitzrayim before your [own] eyes?

מִסְפָּר בַּגּוֹיִם אֲשֶׁר יְנַהֵג יְהֹוָה אֶתְכֶם שָׁמָּה: כח וַעֲבַדְתֶּם־שָׁם אֱלֹהִים מַעֲשֵׂה יְדֵי אָדָם עֵץ וָאֶבֶן אֲשֶׁר לֹא־יִרְאוּן וְלֹא יִשְׁמְעוּן וְלֹא יֹאכְלוּן וְלֹא יְרִיחֻן: כט וּבִקַּשְׁתֶּם מִשָּׁם אֶת־יְהֹוָה אֱלֹהֶיךָ וּמָצָאתָ כִּי תִדְרְשֶׁנּוּ בְּכָל־לְבָבְךָ וּבְכָל־נַפְשֶׁךָ: ל בַּצַּר לְךָ וּמְצָאוּךָ כֹּל הַדְּבָרִים הָאֵלֶּה בְּאַחֲרִית הַיָּמִים וְשַׁבְתָּ עַד־יְהֹוָה אֱלֹהֶיךָ וְשָׁמַעְתָּ בְּקֹלוֹ: לא כִּי אֵל רַחוּם יְהֹוָה אֱלֹהֶיךָ לֹא יַרְפְּךָ וְלֹא יַשְׁחִיתֶךָ וְלֹא יִשְׁכַּח אֶת־בְּרִית אֲבֹתֶיךָ אֲשֶׁר נִשְׁבַּע לָהֶם: לב כִּי שְׁאַל־נָא לְיָמִים רִאשֹׁנִים אֲשֶׁר־הָיוּ לְפָנֶיךָ לְמִן־הַיּוֹם אֲשֶׁר בָּרָא אֱלֹהִים ׀ אָדָם עַל־הָאָרֶץ וּלְמִקְצֵה הַשָּׁמַיִם וְעַד־קְצֵה הַשָּׁמָיִם הֲנִהְיָה כַּדָּבָר הַגָּדוֹל הַזֶּה אוֹ הֲנִשְׁמַע כָּמֹהוּ: לג הֲשָׁמַע עָם קוֹל אֱלֹהִים מְדַבֵּר מִתּוֹךְ־הָאֵשׁ כַּאֲשֶׁר־שָׁמַעְתָּ אַתָּה וַיֶּחִי: לד אוֹ ׀ הֲנִסָּה אֱלֹהִים לָבוֹא לָקַחַת לוֹ גוֹי מִקֶּרֶב גּוֹי בְּמַסֹּת בְּאֹתֹת וּבְמוֹפְתִים וּבְמִלְחָמָה וּבְיָד חֲזָקָה וּבִזְרוֹעַ נְטוּיָה וּבְמוֹרָאִים גְּדֹלִים כְּכֹל אֲשֶׁר־עָשָׂה לָכֶם יְהֹוָה אֱלֹהֵיכֶם בְּמִצְרָיִם:

28. ***There you will subjected to gods.*** There you will be subordinated to that idol worship which you regarded as so attractive, and you will come to know the power it wields; you will learn from your own sad experience what becomes of men when they worship gods that are "the work of human hands"—idols that men have fashioned for themselves.... Whenever a human being casts himself down before physical forces and subordinates his conduct to the commands of blind physical imperatives, he divests himself of his own spiritual dignity, and his idol worship will serve only to demoralize him.... Then the purposeless lack of freedom by which his idols are bound will become his ideal, "there you will be subjected to gods," and, thus subjected to the world of paganism, you will come to feel the full impact of this demoralizing idolatry.

29. ... All of Israel's history in exile, its triumphant perseverance to the outside and its gladsome inner quest for enlightenment and refinement, is a continuous revelation of the living God, in contrast to paganism, which is not only dead itself but also kills everything it touches.

30. ***In this distress.*** It seems that eventually this conflict will set off one final struggle, so that one final "distress" is still in store for Israel "in the end of days." Emerging from this final "distress," purified and steeled by its experiences, Israel will return in the end of days to the path of complete obedience to God, which it will then never forsake again.

35. You have been made to know by sight
that *God* alone is God; [there is] none beside
Him. 36. Out of heaven has He let you
hear His voice in order to take you up into
the bond of His discipline, and on earth He
let you see His great fire, and you heard His
words out of the fire. 37. And in their
place, because He loved your fathers, He
chose His seed that followed after Him and
led you out from Mitzrayim with His countenance in His mighty power, 38. to
drive away from before you nations greater
and mightier than you; to bring you there;
to give you their land as an inheritance, as it
is now happening today. 39. Therefore
know it today and take it to heart repeatedly
that *God* alone is God; in heaven above
and on earth below, [there is] nothing else.
40. And keep His statutes and His
commandments which I command you
today—which will do good to you and your
children after you—and so that you may
long remain upon the soil that *God*, your
God, is giving you for all time. 41. At
that time Moshe set aside three cities on the
other side of the Yarden toward sunrise,
42. so that a manslayer might flee there,
who kills his neighbor unawares and who
has not been his enemy from yesterday and
the day before; he has to flee to one of these
cities and will remain alive: 43. Betzer in
the wilderness in the land of the plain, of
the tribe of Reuben; Ramoth in Gilead, of the
tribe of Gad, and Golan in the Bashan, of
the tribe of Menashe. 44. And this is the

לְעֵינֶֽיךָ׃ לה אַתָּה֙ הָרְאֵ֣תָ לָדַ֔עַת כִּ֥י יְהֹוָ֖ה ה֣וּא
הָֽאֱלֹהִ֑ים אֵ֥ין ע֖וֹד מִלְּבַדּֽוֹ׃ לו מִן־הַשָּׁמַ֛יִם
הִשְׁמִֽיעֲךָ֥ אֶת־קֹל֖וֹ לְיַסְּרֶ֑ךָּ וְעַל־הָאָ֗רֶץ הֶרְאֲךָ֙
אֶת־אִשּׁ֣וֹ הַגְּדוֹלָ֔ה וּדְבָרָ֥יו שָׁמַ֖עְתָּ מִתּ֥וֹךְ הָאֵֽשׁ׃
לז וְתַ֗חַת כִּ֤י אָהַב֙ אֶת־אֲבֹתֶ֔יךָ וַיִּבְחַ֥ר בְּזַרְע֖וֹ
אַחֲרָ֑יו וַיּוֹצִֽאֲךָ֧ בְּפָנָ֛יו בְּכֹח֥וֹ הַגָּדֹ֖ל מִמִּצְרָֽיִם׃
לח לְהוֹרִ֗ישׁ גּוֹיִ֛ם גְּדֹלִ֧ים וַעֲצֻמִ֛ים מִמְּךָ֖ מִפָּנֶ֑יךָ
לַהֲבִיאֲךָ֗ לָתֶת־לְךָ֛ אֶת־אַרְצָ֥ם נַחֲלָ֖ה כַּיּ֥וֹם הַזֶּֽה׃
לט וְיָדַעְתָּ֣ הַיּ֗וֹם וַהֲשֵׁבֹתָ֮ אֶל־לְבָבֶךָ֒ כִּ֤י יְהֹוָה֙
ה֣וּא הָֽאֱלֹהִ֔ים בַּשָּׁמַ֣יִם מִמַּ֔עַל וְעַל־הָאָ֖רֶץ
מִתָּ֑חַת אֵ֖ין עֽוֹד׃ מ וְשָׁמַרְתָּ֞ אֶת־חֻקָּ֣יו וְאֶת־
מִצְוֺתָ֗יו אֲשֶׁ֨ר אָנֹכִ֤י מְצַוְּךָ֙ הַיּ֔וֹם אֲשֶׁר֙ יִיטַ֣ב לְךָ֔
וּלְבָנֶ֖יךָ אַחֲרֶ֑יךָ וּלְמַ֨עַן תַּאֲרִ֤יךְ יָמִים֙ עַל־
הָֽאֲדָמָ֔ה אֲשֶׁ֨ר יְהֹוָ֧ה אֱלֹהֶ֛יךָ נֹתֵ֥ן לְךָ֖ כָּל־
הַיָּמִֽים׃ פ שלישי מא אָ֚ז יַבְדִּ֣יל מֹשֶׁ֔ה שָׁלֹ֣שׁ
עָרִ֔ים בְּעֵ֖בֶר הַיַּרְדֵּ֑ן מִזְרְחָ֖ה שָֽׁמֶשׁ׃ מב לָנֻ֨ס
שָׁ֜מָּה רוֹצֵ֗חַ אֲשֶׁ֨ר יִרְצַ֤ח אֶת־רֵעֵ֙הוּ֙ בִּבְלִי־דַ֔עַת
וְה֛וּא לֹא־שֹׂנֵ֥א ל֖וֹ מִתְּמֹ֣ל שִׁלְשֹׁ֑ם וְנָ֗ס אֶל־אַחַ֛ת
מִן־הֶעָרִ֥ים הָאֵ֖ל וָחָֽי׃ מג אֶת־בֶּ֤צֶר בַּמִּדְבָּר֙
בְּאֶ֥רֶץ הַמִּישֹׁ֖ר לָרֽאוּבֵנִ֑י וְאֶת־רָאמֹ֤ת בַּגִּלְעָד֙
לַגָּדִ֔י וְאֶת־גּוֹלָ֥ן בַּבָּשָׁ֖ן לַֽמְנַשִּֽׁי׃ מד וְזֹ֖את הַתּוֹרָ֑ה

35. ***You have been made to know by sight.*** Your awareness of God is based not on belief but on knowledge, and this knowledge is not founded upon a report or even upon a conclusion derived from a logical association of ideas. Your knowledge of God is based on the certainty of personal, direct experience; an experience presented to the entire nation at one time. Your own eyes were given sufficient visual evidence to know that God, Who was revealed to you under this Name, is the sole true God, Whom the rest of mankind seek amidst such a great variety of delusive images.

[there is] none beside Him. You know that aside from Him nothing has absolute being on its own. He alone is the absolute Being; all other forms of existence are dependent upon Him alone.

40. ***And keep His statutes.*** All your knowledge of God is to have only one purpose: that in this world, filled with God—in which He reigns supreme everywhere and all things serve His will—you, too, should have only one concern—to observe punctiliously all His "statutes" and His "commandments" with which He has assigned limits and tasks for your will.

which will do good to you and your children after you. Only in this manner will you be able to win salvation for yourself and for your children.

so that you may long remain. This is the one condition under which you will be able to remain in the land that God is now giving to you for all time; a land which will remain the land of your mission for all time but which you will be permitted to possess only as long as you will prove yourself loyal to your calling.

Law that Moshe has placed before the sons of Yisrael. 45. These are the testimonies, the statutes and the [social] ordinances that Moshe uttered verbally to the sons of Yisrael when they went out from Mitzrayim, 46. on the other side of the Yarden, in the valley, opposite Beth-Peor, in the land of Siḥon, king of the Emorites, who resided in Ḥeshbon; whom Moshe and the sons of Yisrael had struck down when they went out from Mitzrayim; 47. and they took possession of his land and of the land of Og, the king of the Bashan—the two kings of the Emorite[s], that are located on the other side of the Yarden, toward [the direction of] sunrise, 48. from Aroer, which [is] on the bank of the Arnon stream, as far as Mount Sion; that is, Ḥermon— 49. and the entire wasteland on the other side of the Yarden, eastward as far as the Sea of the Wasteland beneath the rapids of the elevation.

V 1. And Moshe called to all of Yisrael and said to them: Hear, O Yisrael, the statutes and the [social] ordinances that I am presenting in your ears today; learn them and take care to observe them. 2. *God*, our God, has made a covenant with us at Ḥoreb. 3. Not with our ancestors did *God* make this covenant,

אֲשֶׁר־שָׂם מֹשֶׁה לִפְנֵי בְּנֵי יִשְׂרָאֵל: מה אֵלֶּה הָעֵדֹת וְהַחֻקִּים וְהַמִּשְׁפָּטִים אֲשֶׁר דִּבֶּר מֹשֶׁה אֶל־בְּנֵי יִשְׂרָאֵל בְּצֵאתָם מִמִּצְרָיִם: מו בְּעֵבֶר הַיַּרְדֵּן בַּגַּיְא מוּל בֵּית פְּעוֹר בְּאֶרֶץ סִיחֹן מֶלֶךְ הָאֱמֹרִי אֲשֶׁר יוֹשֵׁב בְּחֶשְׁבּוֹן אֲשֶׁר הִכָּה מֹשֶׁה וּבְנֵי יִשְׂרָאֵל בְּצֵאתָם מִמִּצְרָיִם: מז וַיִּירְשׁוּ אֶת־אַרְצוֹ וְאֶת־אֶרֶץ | עוֹג מֶלֶךְ־הַבָּשָׁן שְׁנֵי מַלְכֵי הָאֱמֹרִי אֲשֶׁר בְּעֵבֶר הַיַּרְדֵּן מִזְרַח שָׁמֶשׁ: מח מֵעֲרֹעֵר אֲשֶׁר עַל־שְׂפַת־נַחַל אַרְנֹן וְעַד־הַר שִׂיאֹן הוּא חֶרְמוֹן: מט וְכָל־הָעֲרָבָה עֵבֶר הַיַּרְדֵּן מִזְרָחָה וְעַד יָם הָעֲרָבָה תַּחַת אַשְׁדֹּת הַפִּסְגָּה: פ רביעי ה א וַיִּקְרָא מֹשֶׁה אֶל־כָּל־יִשְׂרָאֵל וַיֹּאמֶר אֲלֵהֶם שְׁמַע יִשְׂרָאֵל אֶת־הַחֻקִּים וְאֶת־הַמִּשְׁפָּטִים אֲשֶׁר אָנֹכִי דֹּבֵר בְּאָזְנֵיכֶם הַיּוֹם וּלְמַדְתֶּם אֹתָם וּשְׁמַרְתֶּם לַעֲשֹׂתָם: ב יְהֹוָה אֱלֹהֵינוּ כָּרַת עִמָּנוּ בְּרִית בְּחֹרֵב: ג לֹא אֶת־אֲבֹתֵינוּ כָּרַת יְהֹוָה אֶת־

44. וְזֹאת הַתּוֹרָה [*And this is the Law*]. The true conception of God which Israel obtained through the exodus from Egypt and the giving of the Law, and the true conception of humanity as proclaimed by the institution of the cities of refuge—these are the fundamentals of Jewish national life. And this Book, in which Moses set down these things, is the Law that Moses has placed, in writing, before the sons of Israel as the absolute standard for all their conduct.

CHAPTER V

1. . . . The purpose of the first part [of Moses' oration], Deuteronomy 1:6 to 3:22, is to make it clear to the nation, by recalling its own experiences, that its loyalty to God is the only condition under which it will be allowed to take possession of the land, and also that this loyalty in itself will be sufficient to enable it to do so. The second part, Chapters 3:23 to 4:29, is primarily devoted to the proper appreciation of the Law, of Israel's position and, above all, of God in the truth and majesty of His unique essence. This fifth chapter opens a third part, which summons the people to adopt certain general, basic attitudes—to fear, love and trust God—and intertwines with this appeal those commandments which are now to accompany the nation into the greater decentralization that awaits it, and which are to stir and cultivate these fundamental attitudes in its midst at all times.

This detailed discussion of the Law begins with one more review of the historic revelation on Mount Sinai. . . .

. . . In the present chapter, Moses' orations approach their true purpose: the repetition and explanation of the Law. Hence the introductory summons „שְׁמַע אֶת" ["Hear"]; i.e., "hearken to," not "obey."

2. . . . The revelation was not intended merely as a theoretical communication, leaving it to us to decide at some later date whether or not to give it our attention and to observe the laws set forth in it. The revelation was an act that imposed specific duties upon us; an act by which we were placed under an obligation, and by which we were enjoined to assume specific responsibilities. The revelation forged an indissoluble bond between God and ourselves.

but with us, we who are, all of us, still alive here today. 4. Face to face did *God* speak with you on the mountain out of the fire. 5. At that time I stood between *God* and yourselves, to bring toward° you the Word of *God,* because you were afraid of the fire and did not ascend the mountain for the utterance: 6. "I, ה׳, shall be your God; I, Who brought you out from the land of Mitzrayim, from the house of slaves. 7. You shall not have another God before My Presence. 8. Do not make yourself [a representation] in the form of an image, nor in the form of any [other] likeness, [of] that which is in heaven above, that which is on earth below, or that which is in the water far below the earth. 9. Do not cast yourself down before them, and do not serve them; for I, ה׳, your God, am a God Who demands His exclusive right; I remember the sin of parents for [their] children and for the third and fourth generations for those who hate Me, 10. and I practice loving-kindness upon thousands, upon those who love Me and those Who keep My commandments. 11. Do not take upon yourself the Name of ה׳, your God, in vain, for *God* will not hold guiltless one who takes His Name upon himself in vain. 12. Keep the Sabbath day to sanctify it, as *God,* your God, has commanded you. 13. Six days you shall serve and do all your [creating] work, 14. and the seventh day is a Sabbath to *God,* your God. [On it] you shall not perform any kind of [creating] work, neither you, nor your son, nor your daughter, nor your manservant, nor your handmaid, nor your ox, nor your donkey, nor any of your livestock, nor your stranger who is within your gates, so that your manservant and your handmaid may rest just like you; 15. and remember that you

הַבְּרִית הַזֹּאת כִּי אִתָּנוּ אֲנַחְנוּ אֵלֶּה פֹה הַיּוֹם
כֻּלָּנוּ חַיִּים: ד פָּנִים | בְּפָנִים דִּבֶּר יְהוָה עִמָּכֶם
בָּהָר מִתּוֹךְ הָאֵשׁ: ה אָנֹכִי עֹמֵד בֵּין־יְהוָה
וּבֵינֵיכֶם בָּעֵת הַהִוא לְהַגִּיד לָכֶם אֶת־דְּבַר יְהוָה
כִּי יְרֵאתֶם מִפְּנֵי הָאֵשׁ וְלֹא־עֲלִיתֶם בָּהָר
לֵאמֹר: ס (טעם עליון תמצא בסוף הספר)° ו אָנֹכִי יְהוָה
אֱלֹהֶיךָ אֲשֶׁר הוֹצֵאתִיךָ מֵאֶרֶץ מִצְרַיִם מִבֵּית
עֲבָדִים: ז לֹא־יִהְיֶה לְךָ אֱלֹהִים אֲחֵרִים עַל־פָּנָי:
ח לֹא־תַעֲשֶׂה לְךָ פֶסֶל כָּל־תְּמוּנָה אֲשֶׁר בַּשָּׁמַיִם
מִמַּעַל וַאֲשֶׁר בָּאָרֶץ מִתָּחַת וַאֲשֶׁר בַּמַּיִם מִתַּחַת
לָאָרֶץ: ט לֹא־תִשְׁתַּחֲוֶה לָהֶם וְלֹא תָעָבְדֵם כִּי
אָנֹכִי יְהוָה אֱלֹהֶיךָ אֵל קַנָּא פֹּקֵד עֲוֺן אָבוֹת עַל־
בָּנִים וְעַל־שִׁלֵּשִׁים וְעַל־רִבֵּעִים לְשֹׂנְאָי: י וְעֹשֶׂה
חֶסֶד לַאֲלָפִים לְאֹהֲבַי וּלְשֹׁמְרֵי מִצְוֹתָו (מצותי
קרי): ס יא לֹא תִשָּׂא אֶת־שֵׁם־יְהוָה אֱלֹהֶיךָ
לַשָּׁוְא כִּי לֹא יְנַקֶּה יְהוָה אֵת אֲשֶׁר־יִשָּׂא אֶת־
שְׁמוֹ לַשָּׁוְא: ס יב שָׁמוֹר אֶת־יוֹם הַשַּׁבָּת לְקַדְּשׁוֹ
כַּאֲשֶׁר צִוְּךָ יְהוָה אֱלֹהֶיךָ: יג שֵׁשֶׁת יָמִים תַּעֲבֹד
וְעָשִׂיתָ כָּל־מְלַאכְתֶּךָ: יד וְיוֹם הַשְּׁבִיעִי שַׁבָּת
לַיהוָה אֱלֹהֶיךָ לֹא־תַעֲשֶׂה כָל־מְלָאכָה אַתָּה |
וּבִנְךָ־וּבִתֶּךָ וְעַבְדְּךָ־וַאֲמָתֶךָ וְשׁוֹרְךָ וַחֲמֹרְךָ
וְכָל־בְּהֶמְתֶּךָ וְגֵרְךָ אֲשֶׁר בִּשְׁעָרֶיךָ לְמַעַן יָנוּחַ
עַבְדְּךָ וַאֲמָתְךָ כָּמוֹךָ: טו וְזָכַרְתָּ כִּי עֶבֶד הָיִיתָ

°*Note to the English translation*: לְהַגִּיד—Hirsch's German rendering here, *entgegenzubringen* ("to bring toward"), alludes to the relationship of the verb הגד to נגד, "against." The German language is a more felicitous vehicle than English for conveying Hirsch's thought here, because the German *gegen* can mean either "against" or "toward." [G.H.]

° For *Ta'am Ha'elyon* see page 1057.

5. ***I stood.*** The position I took up between yourselves and God at the time of the giving of the Law was not in any way that of a lawgiver. I was merely the one who transmitted the law. The Lawgiver was God Himself; He was present before you, and even as He addressed His Word directly to each and every one of you, so, too, each and every one of you was able to hear the Word addressed to him. . . .

were a slave in the land of Mitzrayim when *God*, your God, brought you out from there with a strong hand and an outstretched arm; therefore, did *God*, your God, command you to observe the Sabbath in practice. 16. Honor your father and your mother, as *God*, your God, has commanded you, so that your days may be long, and that it may go well with you upon the soil that *God*, your God, is giving you.   17. You shall not murder, and you shall not commit adultery; and you shall not steal; and you shall not testify as a worthless witness against your neighbor.   18. And you shall not covet the wife of your neighbor; and you shall not desire your neighbor's house, his field, his manservant, his hand-maid, his ox, his donkey, or anything else that belongs to your neighbor." 19. These words did *God* speak to your entire assembly upon the mountain out of the fire, the clouds and the opaque darkness—a great voice, and it reached no further—and He wrote them upon two stone tablets and gave them to me. 20. And it came to pass when you heard the voice out of the darkness, and the mountain blazed with fire, that you approached me, all the heads of your tribes and your elders,   21. and you said: "Lo! *God*, our God, has let us see His glory and His greatness, and we have heard his voice out of the fire; today we have seen that God speaks to man and he [still] remains alive. 22. And now, why should we die, that this great fire should consume us? If we will continue hearing the voice of *God*, our God, we will die.   23. For who in the flesh has heard the voice of the living God speak out of the fire as we have and has [still] remained alive?   24. You approach and hear all that *God*, our God, will say; and you

בְּאֶרֶץ מִצְרַיִם וַיֹּצִאֲךָ יְהֹוָה אֱלֹהֶיךָ מִשָּׁם בְּיָד חֲזָקָה וּבִזְרֹעַ נְטוּיָה עַל־כֵּן צִוְּךָ יְהֹוָה אֱלֹהֶיךָ לַעֲשׂוֹת אֶת־יוֹם הַשַּׁבָּת: ס טז כַּבֵּד אֶת־אָבִיךָ וְאֶת־אִמֶּךָ כַּאֲשֶׁר צִוְּךָ יְהֹוָה אֱלֹהֶיךָ לְמַעַן ׀ יַאֲרִיכֻן יָמֶיךָ וּלְמַעַן יִיטַב לָךְ עַל הָאֲדָמָה אֲשֶׁר־יְהֹוָה אֱלֹהֶיךָ נֹתֵן לָךְ: ס יז לֹא תִרְצָח ס וְלֹא תִנְאָף ס וְלֹא תִגְנֹב ס וְלֹא־תַעֲנֶה בְרֵעֲךָ עֵד שָׁוְא: ס יח וְלֹא תַחְמֹד אֵשֶׁת רֵעֶךָ ס וְלֹא תִתְאַוֶּה בֵּית רֵעֶךָ שָׂדֵהוּ וְעַבְדּוֹ וַאֲמָתוֹ שׁוֹרוֹ וַחֲמֹרוֹ וְכֹל אֲשֶׁר לְרֵעֶךָ: ס חמישי יט אֶת־הַדְּבָרִים הָאֵלֶּה דִּבֶּר יְהֹוָה אֶל־כָּל־קְהַלְכֶם בָּהָר מִתּוֹךְ הָאֵשׁ הֶעָנָן וְהָעֲרָפֶל קוֹל גָּדוֹל וְלֹא יָסָף וַיִּכְתְּבֵם עַל־שְׁנֵי לֻחֹת אֲבָנִים וַיִּתְּנֵם אֵלָי: כ וַיְהִי כְּשָׁמְעֲכֶם אֶת־הַקּוֹל מִתּוֹךְ הַחֹשֶׁךְ וְהָהָר בֹּעֵר בָּאֵשׁ וַתִּקְרְבוּן אֵלַי כָּל־רָאשֵׁי שִׁבְטֵיכֶם וְזִקְנֵיכֶם: כא וַתֹּאמְרוּ הֵן הֶרְאָנוּ יְהֹוָה אֱלֹהֵינוּ אֶת־כְּבֹדוֹ וְאֶת־גָּדְלוֹ וְאֶת־קֹלוֹ שָׁמַעְנוּ מִתּוֹךְ הָאֵשׁ הַיּוֹם הַזֶּה רָאִינוּ כִּי־יְדַבֵּר אֱלֹהִים אֶת־הָאָדָם וָחָי: כב וְעַתָּה לָמָּה נָמוּת כִּי תֹאכְלֵנוּ הָאֵשׁ הַגְּדֹלָה הַזֹּאת אִם־יֹסְפִים ׀ אֲנַחְנוּ לִשְׁמֹעַ אֶת־קוֹל יְהֹוָה אֱלֹהֵינוּ עוֹד וָמָתְנוּ: כג כִּי מִי כָל־בָּשָׂר אֲשֶׁר שָׁמַע קוֹל אֱלֹהִים חַיִּים מְדַבֵּר מִתּוֹךְ־הָאֵשׁ כָּמֹנוּ וַיֶּחִי: כד קְרַב אַתָּה וּשֲׁמָע אֵת כָּל־אֲשֶׁר יֹאמַר יְהֹוָה

---

16. The addition of the words "and that it may go well with you" to the commandment "Honor your father and your mother" is intended to tell every future generation in the land that it owes all its present good solely to the fact that it has maintained a loyal, devoted link with its past. Any generation in Israel will be granted happiness only to the extent to which it will accept from the hands of its parents, respectfully and obediently, the tradition of history and law as its heritage, to be upheld forever. . . .

19. . . . The Voice was great, yet it "reached no further." It was not audible beyond the immediate circle of the Jews. It was heard only by those to whom it had been addressed. This very limitation proved that this Voice was the free-willed, personal Word of God, thus placing it on a level loftier than that of any physical acoustic phenomenon. . . .

will speak to us faithfully all that *God*, our God, will speak to you; we will hear it and do it." 25. And *God* heard the tone of your words when you spoke to me, and *God* said to me: "I have heard the voice of the words of this people which they have spoken to you; they have meant well everything that they have spoken. 26. Would that this spirit were to remain with them, to fear Me and to keep all My commandments always, so that it may go well with them and with their children, forever. 27. Go, say to them: 'Return to your tents.' 28. And [as for] you, remain with Me so that I may speak to you all the commitment to duty, the statutes and the [social] ordinances which you are to teach them, and they are to do them in the land which I am giving them, to possess it." 29. Now therefore be careful to do just as *God*, your God, has commanded you; do not turn aside to the right or to the left. 30. Walk in all the way that *God*, your God, has commanded you, so that you may live, and it may go well with you, and you will long remain in the land of which you are taking possession.

VI 1. And now this is the commitment to duty, the statutes and the [social] ordinances which *God*, your God, has commanded to teach you, to carry out in the land into which you are passing over, to take possession of it, 2. so that

אֱלֹהֵינוּ וְאַתְּ ׀ תְּדַבֵּר אֵלֵינוּ אֵת כָּל־אֲשֶׁר יְדַבֵּר
יְהֹוָה אֱלֹהֵינוּ אֵלֶיךָ וְשָׁמַעְנוּ וְעָשִׂינוּ:
כה וַיִּשְׁמַע יְהֹוָה אֶת־קוֹל דִּבְרֵיכֶם בְּדַבֶּרְכֶם
אֵלָי וַיֹּאמֶר יְהֹוָה אֵלַי שָׁמַעְתִּי אֶת־קוֹל דִּבְרֵי
הָעָם הַזֶּה אֲשֶׁר דִּבְּרוּ אֵלֶיךָ הֵיטִיבוּ כָּל־אֲשֶׁר
דִּבֵּרוּ: כו מִי־יִתֵּן וְהָיָה לְבָבָם זֶה לָהֶם לְיִרְאָה
אֹתִי וְלִשְׁמֹר אֶת־כָּל־מִצְוֹתַי כָּל־הַיָּמִים לְמַעַן
יִיטַב לָהֶם וְלִבְנֵיהֶם לְעֹלָם: כז לֵךְ אֱמֹר לָהֶם
שׁוּבוּ לָכֶם לְאָהֳלֵיכֶם: כח וְאַתָּה פֹּה עֲמֹד עִמָּדִי
וַאֲדַבְּרָה אֵלֶיךָ אֵת כָּל־הַמִּצְוָה וְהַחֻקִּים
וְהַמִּשְׁפָּטִים אֲשֶׁר תְּלַמְּדֵם וְעָשׂוּ בָאָרֶץ אֲשֶׁר
אָנֹכִי נֹתֵן לָהֶם לְרִשְׁתָּהּ: כט וּשְׁמַרְתֶּם לַעֲשׂוֹת
כַּאֲשֶׁר צִוָּה יְהֹוָה אֱלֹהֵיכֶם אֶתְכֶם לֹא תָסֻרוּ
יָמִין וּשְׂמֹאל: ל בְּכָל־הַדֶּרֶךְ אֲשֶׁר צִוָּה יְהֹוָה
אֱלֹהֵיכֶם אֶתְכֶם תֵּלֵכוּ לְמַעַן תִּחְיוּן וְטוֹב לָכֶם
וְהַאֲרַכְתֶּם יָמִים בָּאָרֶץ אֲשֶׁר תִּירָשׁוּן:
ו א וְזֹאת הַמִּצְוָה הַחֻקִּים וְהַמִּשְׁפָּטִים אֲשֶׁר
צִוָּה יְהֹוָה אֱלֹהֵיכֶם לְלַמֵּד אֶתְכֶם לַעֲשׂוֹת בָּאָרֶץ
אֲשֶׁר אַתֶּם עֹבְרִים שָׁמָּה לְרִשְׁתָּהּ: ב לְמַעַן

CHAPTER VI

1–3. *so that you* (sing.) *may fear* **God, your God.** The form of address in Verse 1 is in the plural; in Verses 2 and 3 it changes to the singular. Whenever such a change occurs in the Scriptural text, the plural refers to the nation in its aspect of multiplicity. The singular form of address denotes the nation as one single entity. The duty to observe the Law devolves upon every single member of the nation. The Law must be observed by every individual who belongs to the nation, not just by official representatives of the national entity. In the view of Divine truth, a national entity that officially professes loyalty to the Law but whose individual members deny this loyalty by their personal conduct is an absurdity. At the same time, the happiness that results from the observance of the Law is promised in full measure only to the nation as a whole, and individual members of the nation will be able to

share in it only if all the other members of the nation, too, will observe the Law punctiliously. The community derives its collective moral character from the loyalty that its individual members show [to the Law] in their personal lives, and the individual will receive his own full measure of personal happiness only to the extent that he has done his part in securing the happiness of the community. Here the principle כָּל יִשְׂרָאֵל עֲרֵבִים זֶה לָזֶה ["all of Israel are responsible for one another"] stands out in all its far-reaching significance.

For this reason, the text here conveys ideas as follows: The components of the duty devolving upon us, the moral laws and the social ordinances commanded by God, must be studied and observed by every individual member of the nation (Verse 1), so that the nation as a whole may acquire for itself and for its posterity the character of a God-fearing entity that observes the Law punctiliously, and so that the life-span of the nation will be unlimited (Verse 2). Therefore, too, you may fear *God*, your God, to keep all His statutes and commandments which I am commanding you; you and your child and your child's child, all the days of your life, so that your days may be prolonged. 3. Hear, O Yisrael, and see to the fulfillment, so that it may go well with you and that you may increase greatly, as *God*, the God of your fathers, has promised you through that land which flows with milk and honey.   4. Hear, O Yisrael: *HaShem*, our God, is *HaShem*, the sole One. 5. And love *God*, your God, with all your

תִּירָא אֶת־יְהֹוָה אֱלֹהֶיךָ לִשְׁמֹר אֶת־כָּל־חֻקֹּתָיו
וּמִצְוֹתָיו אֲשֶׁר אָנֹכִי מְצַוֶּ֑ךָ אַתָּה וּבִנְךָ וּבֶן־בִּנְךָ
כֹּל יְמֵי חַיֶּיךָ וּלְמַעַן יַאֲרִכֻן יָמֶיךָ: ג וְשָׁמַעְתָּ
יִשְׂרָאֵל וְשָׁמַרְתָּ לַעֲשׂוֹת אֲשֶׁר יִיטַב לְךָ וַאֲשֶׁר
תִּרְבּוּן מְאֹד כַּאֲשֶׁר דִּבֶּר יְהֹוָה אֱלֹהֵי אֲבֹתֶיךָ לָךְ
אֶרֶץ זָבַת חָלָב וּדְבָשׁ: פ ששי ד שְׁמַע (ע רבתי)
יִשְׂרָאֵל יְהֹוָה אֱלֹהֵינוּ יְהֹוָה | אֶחָד(ד רבתי):
ה וְאָהַבְתָּ אֵת יְהֹוָה אֱלֹהֶיךָ בְּכָל־לְבָבְךָ וּבְכָל־

the nation as a whole can have not greater concern than to observe the Law with the utmost care, so that it may attain the greatest measure of national prosperity and the most abundant blessings possible for its individual members—as God had promised that Israel would attain through the Land, which is indeed capable of yielding the greatest measure of prosperity (Verse 3). Prosperity and an ever-increasing number of souls—these are the visible characteristics of a happy nation. But the fact that the promise of increase is stated in terms of the nation's individual members [i.e., in the second person plural] points out the true spiritual and moral value inherent in such an increase in population. It is the individual who is multiplied when he is blessed with offspring. When he rears his children, he produces multiples of his own spiritual and moral image. Thus, a large population constitutes a blessing for the nation not because an increase in population could yield a corresponding growth in the nation's military potential, but because every additional infant soul represents an increase in the sum total of the humanity that is to be realized in the nation; it is one more addition to the nation's treasure of humanity.

4. שְׁמַע [*Hear*]. This is the very first sentence of the written compendium of the Law which Moses abstracted from his oral recapitulation of the Law to guide his people as they entered a new phase of decentralization. It is the sentence which to this day acts to preserve the Jewish consciousness of every Jew, no matter how alienated he may have become from his fellow Jews. It is the first sentence every Jewish child learns as soon as he becomes aware of his surroundings; it is also the last greeting that his friends will cry after him in farewell when he passes into the other world. It is the declaration that the Jews have borne through the world as the standard of God, for His reconquest of mankind. It is the last truth that a son of Israel, mired in estrangement from his people, will discard. It is the declaration of the Jewish awareness of God's unity, and

it is logically followed by sentences intended to make the Jew aware of his life's mission, of the objectives of his education, and of the true purpose of his endeavors, personal and public. These statements encompass the basic principles that should guide his conduct, the axioms that should form the basis for all his thinking and the consecration of his domestic and communal life. They are intended to perform these functions no matter where the Jew may live and breathe, raise his children, carry on his domestic and public life; no matter where he lies down and rises up, readies his hands for action and his mind for thought; no matter where he builds his home and where he sets up his gates. That is why he must repeat all these statements to himself early and late, every day of his life.

. . . For the declaration of the אַחְדוּת [unity (of God)] set down here as the very first fundamental truth for us to bear in mind at all times is nothing but the most categorical negation of all polytheistic notions, ancient or modern. . . .

5. וְאָהַבְתָּ [*And love*]. This means: Seek the nearness of God by surrendering all your heart, all your soul and all your means to this end. All your thoughts and emotions, all your wishes and aspirations and all the things you possess are to be regarded by you only as means for winning the nearness of God; they are of value to you only insofar as they can serve to bring God closer to you. . . .

. . . The awareness of God's unity serves also to unite all the aspects of our own personality, with all its seeming disparities, physical and mental, and its responses to fate and fortune, so that all the facets of our personality become one unity of existence and will. Whatever we are, whatever we do and whatever we possess is devoted to one and the same purpose, one and the same mission, one and the same desire: to

נַפְשְׁךָ וּבְכָל־מְאֹדֶךָ: ו וְהָיוּ הַדְּבָרִים הָאֵלֶּה
אֲשֶׁר אָנֹכִי מְצַוְּךָ הַיּוֹם עַל־לְבָבֶךָ: ז וְשִׁנַּנְתָּם

heart and with all your soul and with all your means. 6. These words that I command you today shall be upon your heart,

"love" God with all the manifold aspects of our lives; to fulfill only His wishes, not our own; to remain worthy—and to make us even worthier—of His nearness. It is to God, the sole One, that man surrenders wholly; and it is this surrender to the sole One that makes his own personality one harmonious whole.

° ° °

The most significant and far-reaching result of our awareness of God's unity is that we are to love God "with all your heart"; i.e., בְּיֵצֶר טוֹב וּבְיֵצֶר רָע [with the good as well as the evil inclination]. The capacity to be attracted by things that are evil, base, ignoble and sensual—this is the source of the יֵצֶר הָרָע [evil inclination]—has been given to us by the same One sole God Who also gave us the capacity to be drawn to things that are good, noble, moral and spiritual—this is the source of the יֵצֶר הַטּוֹב [good inclination]. Both inclinations are manifestations of the same love of the One sole God. It is He Who has interwoven the former and the latter alike into our human potential.

The fact that He has made us susceptible also to the allurements of evil does not mean that He loves us any less. Indeed, this capacity to be attracted by evil represents the ultimate kiss, as it were, of His love. For in this capacity lies all our nobility and moral dignity. Without the capacity to feel drawn to evil we would not be human; there would be no morality and no virtue. All our essence would then consist merely of bodily desires and actions, like those of the animal. For that which we call "animal instinct" is simply the one-sided nature of the animal. The animal is attracted only to that which accords with its functions; everything else repels it or leaves it indifferent. Hence the intensity and the immutability that characterize the manifestations of animal life. If baseness and evil held no charms for us, if they left us indifferent or if they would repel us as things contrary to our nature; if only goodness would attract us with a powerful, irresistible magnetism; if goodness did not entail also renunciation and self-control, then we certainly would never do "evil," but then we also would never do "good." In that case, the good that we would do would not be our own doing; it would not be a morally free-willed, human act. We would only be following the physical imperatives of our nature, which would then be inexorably determined by the stimuli acting upon our nature. Thus the disappearance of the יֵצֶר הָרָע would spell also the end of all our moral dignity. . . .

As a matter of fact, none of our inclinations are "good" or "evil" in themselves. All our impulses, from the most sensual to the most spiritual, become "good" or "evil" solely by virtue of the use to which we put them; depending on whether we utilize them within the limits and for the purposes assigned by God, or whether we misuse them by exceeding these limits, neglecting these purposes, or employing them for purposes not set by God. Thus, to love God with all our hearts, with both יֵצֶר טוֹב and יֵצֶר רָע, means, to consecrate all our thoughts—along with all our proclivities, tendencies and aspirations—exclusively to the fulfillment of God's will, using them all in the service of the One sole God in such a manner that our utilization or control of them carries us forward in our endeavor to win His nearness.

° ° °

and with all your means. With all your assets: Loving God with all of one's assets is to be demonstrated not only by using all of one's fortune in the service of God, but also by foregoing any gain or possession that could be secured or retained only by transgressing the Law of God. Indeed, when there is a choice between financial sacrifice and transgressing the Law, the Law stands inviolable. One must go so far as to sacrifice all one's possessions if keeping them would necessitate the violation of even only one of the prohibitions set down in God's Law. מְאֹד does not denote only financial means, but any means that we may be given for any achievement; it thus denotes anything that the Providence of God's love sees fit to "measure out" to us.

° ° °

6. . . . In truth, the entire Law is nothing other than a disclosure of how we are to demonstrate our love of God, "with all your heart and with all your soul and with all your means." תּוֹרוֹת, the *teachings*, which make the heart and spirit free from passion and delusion, fructifying them instead with truth and noble thought, instruct us how to love God with all our hearts. חֻקִּים, the *statutes*, which limit and consecrate the development of our physical and sensual nature within the bounds of morality drawn by God, teach us how to love God with all our souls. מִשְׁפָּטִים and מִצְוֹת, the *social ordinances* and the *commandments*, which structure our communal lives upon the foundations of justice and duty, teach us how to love God with all our means. עֵדוֹת, the *testimonies*, which bring these truths and tasks to our minds by ordaining symbolic acts that avow them, and עֲבוֹדָה, the symbolic offerings that celebrate our consecration to all this service of life by which we are to seek God's nearness, engage every aspect of our personality and so teach us how to love God with all our hearts, all our souls and all our means.

7. and impress them sharply upon your sons, and speak of them when you sit in your house and when you walk upon the way; when you lie down, and when you get up. 8. And bind them as a sign upon your hand, and they shall be an ornament for your head between your eyes. 9. And write them upon the [door]posts of your house

לְבָנֶיךָ וְדִבַּרְתָּ בָּם בְּשִׁבְתְּךָ בְּבֵיתֶךָ וּבְלֶכְתְּךָ בַדֶּרֶךְ וּבְשָׁכְבְּךָ וּבְקוּמֶךָ: ח וּקְשַׁרְתָּם לְאוֹת עַל־יָדֶךָ וְהָיוּ לְטֹטָפֹת בֵּין עֵינֶיךָ: ט וּכְתַבְתָּם עַל־מְזֻזוֹת בֵּיתֶךָ וּבִשְׁעָרֶיךָ: ס י וְהָיָה כִּי

7. **when you sit in your house.** The renewal of our awareness of God's Unity (שְׁמַע [Verse 4]) and the unity of our life's task (וְאָהַבְתָּ [Verse 5]) that is its logical outgrowth; the subordination of all our thoughts and desires to these basic truths of our mission and to the resultant laws revealed by God in His Law (וְהָיוּ [Verse 6]), and hence our task to educate our children and ourselves by teaching them, and studying for ourselves these basic laws and truths (וְשִׁנַּנְתָּם וְדִבַּרְתָּ בָּם ["and impress them . . . and speak of them"])—all these concepts are to be applied in practice, at all times and wherever we may be, at home or abroad. It is with them that we must begin our night's rest and our day's work. . . .

בְּשָׁכְבְּךָ וּבְקוּמֶךָ [when you lie down, and when you get up]. . . . We are thus commanded to remember the Unity of God, and its implications for all our lives and aspirations, when we retire for the night and again when we arise to do our day's work—at night, to avow our complete trust in the One sole Guide of our destinies, and in the morning, to ready ourselves for the new day with cheerful obedience to the One sole Guide of our actions.

8. וּקְשַׁרְתָּם [And bind them]. Our allegiance to the One sole God, the surrender of all our lives and aspirations to Him with all our hearts and all our souls and all our means—these concepts are to form the total content of our life's mission, of our own studies and of the education of our children. We are to bind them upon our hands to symbolize that they are "binding upon us," and bear them upon the front of our heads to symbolize that they are to "direct our eyes."

The commandments relating to the *tefillin* are of symbolic character, and we are expected to absorb their symbolic content and meaning into our spiritual and moral selves. This is clearly indicated to us by the concepts of אוֹת [sign] and זִכָּרוֹן [reminder], terms by which the Law designates the *tefillin,* as well as the stipulation that all the components of the *tefillin* and the materials used to make them . . . must be derived from בְּהֵמָה טְהוֹרָה [clean (i.e., kosher) animals]. . . .

By binding upon our hands and upon our heads the basic truths symbolized by the *tefillin,* we "bind" our mind, the instrument of our thoughts, as well as our hands, the instruments of our physical activities, to the fulfillment of their [Divinely-ordained] duties.

9. **And write them upon the [door]posts.** All these concepts should form the basis of your every thought and action; to them you are to dedicate all of your personality and commit all of your life. You are to endeavor to understand them yourself and to transmit this knowledge also to your children. You shall concern yourself with them early and late; they shall accompany you wherever you go, so that they will place their imprint on all your thoughts and actions. These things shall be inscribed upon the entrances of your houses and upon your doorposts, thus consecrating the rooms in which your domestic and public lives unfold as places where these concepts are to be translated into reality.

The reason why the commandments relating to the *mezuzah* were not given before, but only now, in the recapitulation of the Law, as the nation is about to enter its Land, is obvious: Only after they had taken possession of the Land would the people of Israel have "houses and gates," permanent homes. . . .

The salient feature of all the laws [relating to the *mezuzah*] is that the *mezuzah* and its contents are intended to influence first and foremost the minds and spirits of the persons who live and work inside the house.

וּקְשַׁרְתָּם וּכְתַבְתָּם [And bind . . . And write]. He who puts on his *tefillin* thereby subordinates all his personal thoughts, aspirations and actions to the dictates of the will of God that form the contents of the *tefillin.* Similarly, he who places the *mezuzah* inscription upon the entrances of the rooms in which he lives thereby subordinates his home; i.e., all the lives of its occupants that unfold there, to these dictates. The *mezuzah* is to be noticed immediately by him, and by everyone else entering the house, as an admonition and as a reminder. That is why he must place the *mezuzah* upon his house and not upon his own body. The *mezuzah* is not an amulet. Only insofar as they shape their lives in

and upon your gates. 10. And it shall
come to pass, when *God*, your God, will
bring you to the land that He has sworn to
your fathers, Abraham, Yitzḥak and Yaakov,
to give to you, cities great and goodly
which you did not build; 11. houses, full
of all good things, which you did not fill;
hewn-out cisterns, which you did not hew;
vineyards and olive trees, which you did not
plant, and you will then eat and be satisfied:
12. then take heed to yourself that you
do not forget *God*, Who has brought you
out from the land of Mitzrayim, from the
home of slaves. 13. Fear *God*, your God;
Him [shall you] serve, and by His Name
[shall you] swear. 14. Do not go after
other gods from among the gods of the
peoples that surround you. 15. For *God*,
your God, is a God Who demands [His]
right, in your midst; lest the anger of *God*,
your God, will be stirred up against you, and
He will destroy you from the face of the
earth. 16. Do not put *God*, your God, to
the test, as you put Him to the test at
Massah. 17. Rather keep, yes, keep the
commandments of *God*, your God, and His
testimonies and His statutes that He has
commanded you! 18. And do that which
is [up]right and good in the eyes of *God*;
therefore it will go well with you, and you
will come and take possession of the good
land that *God* has sworn to your fathers,

יְבִֽיאֲךָ ׀ יְהוָה אֱלֹהֶיךָ אֶל־הָאָרֶץ אֲשֶׁר נִשְׁבַּע
לַאֲבֹתֶיךָ לְאַבְרָהָם לְיִצְחָק וּלְיַעֲקֹב לָתֶת לָךְ
עָרִים גְּדֹלֹת וְטֹבֹת אֲשֶׁר לֹא־בָנִיתָ׃ יא וּבָתִּים
מְלֵאִים כָּל־טוּב אֲשֶׁר לֹא־מִלֵּאתָ וּבֹרֹת
חֲצוּבִים אֲשֶׁר לֹא־חָצַבְתָּ כְּרָמִים וְזֵיתִים אֲשֶׁר
לֹא־נָטָעְתָּ וְאָכַלְתָּ וְשָׂבָעְתָּ׃ יב הִשָּׁמֶר לְךָ פֶּן־
תִּשְׁכַּח אֶת־יְהוָה אֲשֶׁר הוֹצִיאֲךָ מֵאֶרֶץ מִצְרַיִם
מִבֵּית עֲבָדִים׃ יג אֶת־יְהוָה אֱלֹהֶיךָ תִּירָא וְאֹתוֹ
תַעֲבֹד וּבִשְׁמוֹ תִּשָּׁבֵעַ׃ יד לֹא תֵלְכוּן אַחֲרֵי
אֱלֹהִים אֲחֵרִים מֵאֱלֹהֵי הָעַמִּים אֲשֶׁר
סְבִיבוֹתֵיכֶם׃ טו כִּי אֵל קַנָּא יְהוָה אֱלֹהֶיךָ
בְּקִרְבֶּךָ פֶּן־יֶחֱרֶה אַף־יְהוָה אֱלֹהֶיךָ בָּךְ
וְהִשְׁמִידְךָ מֵעַל פְּנֵי הָאֲדָמָה׃ ס טז לֹא תְנַסּוּ
אֶת־יְהוָה אֱלֹהֵיכֶם כַּאֲשֶׁר נִסִּיתֶם בַּמַּסָּה׃
יז שָׁמוֹר תִּשְׁמְרוּן אֶת־מִצְוֹת יְהוָה אֱלֹהֵיכֶם
וְעֵדֹתָיו וְחֻקָּיו אֲשֶׁר צִוָּךְ׃ יח וְעָשִׂיתָ הַיָּשָׁר
וְהַטּוֹב בְּעֵינֵי יְהוָה לְמַעַן יִיטַב לָךְ וּבָאתָ
וְיָרַשְׁתָּ אֶת־הָאָרֶץ הַטֹּבָה אֲשֶׁר־נִשְׁבַּע יְהוָה

accordance with the intended purpose of the *mezuzah* and its contents can the people within the house expect help and protection from God, the "All-Sovereign and All-Sufficing" (Whose Name [שדי] by custom adorns the outside of the *mezuzah*) in all the vicissitudes of domestic life. . . .

° ° °

10–13. The end of the preceding passage sets forth the commandment to place *mezuzoth* upon our homes and gates; i.e., the symbolic consecration and subordination of our domestic and public lives to the One sole God and to His will. We are now instructed to remember God and to remain faithful and devoted to Him in thought, word and deed. We are also warned not to follow the example of the other nations. Israel's obedience to these instructions is the result expected from the presence of these inscriptions of excerpts from the Law of God upon our houses and upon our gates.

° ° °

18–19. ***And do.*** By doing that which is "straight" or "upright" [this is the literal meaning of יָשָׁר]; namely, that which accords with your own nature and with that of your fellow men; and that which is good, that which accords only with His intentions for the world, you assure for yourself God's approval and thus also the permanent, undisturbed possession of the land whose abundance has been described above.

טוב, the good that you do, will make you worthy of the land; your יושר [uprightness] will invest you with the moral nobility before which the personal signifi-to-himsef early and late, every day of his life.

Our conduct is to be guided by the standard of "that which in God's judgment is upright and good." Our Sages interpret this statement as a principle that extends even further the demands of God's Law with regard to our social behavior, as follows: We are not to obey merely the dictates of right and duty explicitly set forth in the Law, but [we] must also let ourselves be guided by that spirit of goodness and right

19. to thrust away all your enemies from before you, as *God* has spoken. 20. When your son will ask you in time to come, "Which are the testimonies, the laws and the [social] ordinances that *God,* our God, has commanded you?" 21. Then you shall say to your son: "We were slaves to Pharaoh in Mitzrayim, and *God* brought us out from Mitzrayim with a mighty hand; 22. and *God* placed signs and convincing acts, great and painful, upon Mitzrayim, upon Pharaoh and upon all his house[hold] before our [own] eyes. 23. But us did He bring out from there so that He might bring us home, to give us the land that He swore to our fathers. 24. And *God* commanded us to fulfill all these statutes, to fear *God,* our God, for our [own] good all the days—to preserve us alive as [we are] today. 25. And it will remain to us a[n act of] righteous duty that we fulfill punctiliously this entire commandment before *God,* our God, as He has commanded us."

VII 1. When *God,* your God, will bring you to the land to

לַאֲבֹתֶיךָ: יט לַהֲדֹף אֶת־כָּל־אֹיְבֶיךָ מִפָּנֶיךָ
כַּאֲשֶׁר דִּבֶּר יְהוָה: ס כ כִּי־יִשְׁאָלְךָ בִנְךָ מָחָר
לֵאמֹר מָה הָעֵדֹת וְהַחֻקִּים וְהַמִּשְׁפָּטִים אֲשֶׁר
צִוָּה יְהוָה אֱלֹהֵינוּ אֶתְכֶם: כא וְאָמַרְתָּ לְבִנְךָ
עֲבָדִים הָיִינוּ לְפַרְעֹה בְּמִצְרָיִם וַיֹּצִיאֵנוּ יְהוָה
מִמִּצְרַיִם בְּיָד חֲזָקָה: כב וַיִּתֵּן יְהוָה אוֹתֹת
וּמֹפְתִים גְּדֹלִים וְרָעִים | בְּמִצְרַיִם בְּפַרְעֹה
וּבְכָל־בֵּיתוֹ לְעֵינֵינוּ: כג וְאוֹתָנוּ הוֹצִיא מִשָּׁם
לְמַעַן הָבִיא אֹתָנוּ לָתֶת לָנוּ אֶת־הָאָרֶץ אֲשֶׁר
נִשְׁבַּע לַאֲבֹתֵינוּ: כד וַיְצַוֵּנוּ יְהוָה לַעֲשׂוֹת אֶת־
כָּל־הַחֻקִּים הָאֵלֶּה לְיִרְאָה אֶת־יְהוָה אֱלֹהֵינוּ
לְטוֹב לָנוּ כָּל־הַיָּמִים לְחַיֹּתֵנוּ כְּהַיּוֹם הַזֶּה:
כה וּצְדָקָה תִּהְיֶה־לָּנוּ כִּי־נִשְׁמֹר לַעֲשׂוֹת אֶת־
כָּל־הַמִּצְוָה הַזֹּאת לִפְנֵי יְהוָה אֱלֹהֵינוּ כַּאֲשֶׁר
צִוָּנוּ: ס שביעי ז א כִּי יְבִיאֲךָ יְהוָה אֱלֹהֶיךָ אֶל־

which is implicit in these stipulations. This principle includes, first and foremost, the concept of fairness that commands us not to avail ourselves of a right—even if we are legally entitled to it—if the advantage we would gain from claiming that right is disproportionately small compared to the advantage the other party would gain if we were to waive our claim. . . . When there is a higher, positive and good purpose you should be ready to forego even those rights to which the law entitles you. . . .

20. ***When your son will ask you.*** In the preceding passage—Verses 16 through 19—we are reminded not to expect continuous miracles from God to reinforce our conviction that His sovereignty is indeed present in our midst. Instead, the remembrance of the miracles with which the history of our establishment as a nation is replete should serve to make us certain forever of His presence and should teach us that we can expect further manifestations of His presence only if we remain punctiliously devoted to that which is right and good in the eyes of God. This trend of thought is logically and closely linked with the concluding passages of this chapter (Verses 10 through 25), which now follow. Here we are told that transmitting to our youth the awareness of these miracles of our early history, which attest to God's sovereignty, must be the basis for all the training of our young for the Law of God. Indeed, such transmission of our historical experiences will obviate, for all time to come, the need for a constant recurrence of miracles necessitating a suspension of the normal order of nature.

° ° °

25. וּצְדָקָה ***[And it will remain to us a(n act of) righteous duty].*** (See Commentary on Genesis 15:6). This righteousness is and shall ever be our duty; we can discharge the tasks of our life's mission only if we observe all the laws, without distinction, as one מִצְוָה—one Divine commandment, our Divinely-ordained assignment to our life's station—carefully, without diminishing from it or changing it; in its entirety, in accordance with its content and with the manner in which it is meant to be observed.

this entire commandment . . . as He has commanded. We do not have the right to abrogate or to "reform" any of it.

CHAPTER VII

1. ***When God, your God, will bring you.*** The concluding section of the preceding chapter assigned us the

which you are coming to take possession of it, He will deprive many nations of their foothold before you—the Ḥittite[s] and the Girgashite[s], the Emorite[s], the Canaanite[s], the Perizzite[s], the Ḥivvite[s] and the Yebusite[s]—seven nations too great and too powerful for you.   2. *God*, your God, will place them before you, and you will strike them down; and you shall give them utterly to be annihilated; you shall make no covenant with them nor show them any favor.   3. You shall not ally yourself with them by marriage; you shall not give your daughter to his son nor take his daughter for your son.   4. For he will cause your son to deviate from following Me, and they will serve alien gods, and then *God's* indignation will be kindled against you and He will destroy you quickly.   5. Rather, you shall deal with them as follows: You shall tear down their altars, break up their pillars, cut down their sacred groves and burn their images in fire.   6. For you are a holy people to *God*, your God! It is you whom *God*, your God, has chosen to be a people belonging exclusively to Him, more than all

הָאָ֗רֶץ אֲשֶׁר־אַתָּ֥ה בָא־שָׁ֖מָּה לְרִשְׁתָּ֑הּ וְנָשַׁ֣ל גּֽוֹיִם־רַבִּ֣ים ׀ מִפָּנֶ֡יךָ הַֽחִתִּי֩ וְהַגִּרְגָּשִׁ֨י וְהָֽאֱמֹרִ֜י וְהַכְּנַעֲנִ֣י וְהַפְּרִזִּ֗י וְהַֽחִוִּי֙ וְהַיְבוּסִ֔י שִׁבְעָ֣ה גוֹיִ֔ם רַבִּ֥ים וַעֲצוּמִ֖ים מִמֶּֽךָּ: ב וּנְתָנָ֞ם יְהֹוָ֧ה אֱלֹהֶ֛יךָ לְפָנֶ֖יךָ וְהִכִּיתָ֑ם הַחֲרֵ֤ם תַּחֲרִים֙ אֹתָ֔ם לֹא־תִכְרֹ֥ת לָהֶ֛ם בְּרִ֖ית וְלֹ֥א תְחָנֵּֽם: ג וְלֹ֥א תִתְחַתֵּ֖ן בָּ֑ם בִּתְּךָ֙ לֹא־תִתֵּ֣ן לִבְנ֔וֹ וּבִתּ֖וֹ לֹא־תִקַּ֥ח לִבְנֶֽךָ: ד כִּֽי־יָסִ֤יר אֶת־בִּנְךָ֙ מֵֽאַחֲרַ֔י וְעָבְד֖וּ אֱלֹהִ֣ים אֲחֵרִ֑ים וְחָרָ֤ה אַף־יְהֹוָה֙ בָּכֶ֔ם וְהִשְׁמִֽידְךָ֖ מַהֵֽר: ה כִּ֣י אִם־כֹּ֤ה תַֽעֲשׂוּ֙ לָהֶ֔ם מִזְבְּחֹֽתֵיהֶ֣ם תִּתֹּ֔צוּ וּמַצֵּבֹתָ֖ם תְּשַׁבֵּ֑רוּ וַאֲשֵֽׁירֵהֶם֙ תְּגַדֵּע֔וּן וּפְסִילֵיהֶ֖ם תִּשְׂרְפ֥וּן בָּאֵֽשׁ: ו כִּ֣י עַ֤ם קָדוֹשׁ֙ אַתָּ֔ה לַֽיהֹוָ֖ה אֱלֹהֶ֑יךָ בְּךָ֞ בָּחַ֣ר ׀ יְהֹוָ֣ה אֱלֹהֶ֗יךָ לִהְי֥וֹת לוֹ֙ לְעַ֣ם סְגֻלָּ֔ה מִכֹּל֙

task to pass on to our children, on the basis of our own historic experience, the obligation to observe the Divine Law faithfully. This observance is to be the life's mission of every generation, present and future. However, our efforts to hand down the Law of God to the next generation, to draw our children to our eternal life's mission and to train them for it, will be frustrated from the outset if our young are born and educated under non-Jewish influences; if they are conceived in the wombs of non-Jewish mothers or dandled upon the knees of non-Jewish fathers; if their minds and characters are formed by the teachings and examples of non-Jewish fathers and mothers, and if our marriages and family lives are permeated with non-Jewish elements. The commandments that follow are intended to counter the menace to our mission at the very root of our future.

3–4. . . . Not only must you not give your daughter to a son of Gentiledom—because in so doing you are alienating your child and your grandchildren from Judaism from the very outset and giving them up to a future as non-Jews—but you must also not take a daughter of a Gentile as a wife for your son. You must not believe that your own influence and the example of your own family life will induce the non-Jewess to

enter into the Jewish spirit and into Jewish ways. You must not believe that the womb of a non-Jewish woman can bear you Jewish grandchildren amenable to training in the spirit of Judaism. Not only will the non-Jewish mother bear no children for Judaism, but even your son, who was begotten by you and born of a Jewish mother, will come under the influence of his non-Jewish father-in-law, who will draw him away from loyalty to Jewish Law and into the sphere of his own non-Jewish ideas and ways. "For he will cause your son to deviate from following Me," and both of them, one like the other, your daughter who has married a non-Jew, and your son who has married a non-Jewess, "will serve alien gods," they will fall to the non-Jewish ways of the heathen gods. . . .

○   ○   ○

6. *For you are a holy people*. You are a national entity that is holy. As for the other nations, it is they themselves that form the objective of their destiny; the supreme purpose of their national entity is their self-preservation as independent nations. But this is not the purpose of *your* national entity; your purpose lies outside yourselves. Your national entity belongs to God, and it must commit all its relationships, every aspect of its life—individual, familial and political—to the tasks

the [other] peoples that are upon the earth. 7. Not because you are more numerous than any [other] peoples did *God* take delight in you and choose you; for [in fact] you are the smallest among all the peoples; 8. but out of *God*'s love for you, and because He kept the vow that He swore to your fathers, did *God* bring you out with a mighty hand and did He free you from the home of the slaves—from the hand of Pharaoh, king of Mitzrayim. 9. Therefore you know that *God*, your God, is "God," the God Whom one can trust, Who preserves the covenant and the love for those who love Him and who keep His commandments, to the one thousandth generation. 10. He rewards also those who hate Him, but to his face, so that he may be lost! He does not postpone it for him who hates Him; He rewards him to his face. 11. Therefore keep the commandment, the statutes and the [social] ordinances which I command you today to carry them out.

הָעַמִּים אֲשֶׁר עַל־פְּנֵי הָאֲדָמָה׃ ז לֹא מֵרֻבְּכֶם
מִכָּל־הָעַמִּים חָשַׁק יְהוָה בָּכֶם וַיִּבְחַר בָּכֶם כִּי־
אַתֶּם הַמְעַט מִכָּל־הָעַמִּים׃ ח כִּי מֵאַהֲבַת יְהוָה
אֶתְכֶם וּמִשָּׁמְרוֹ אֶת־הַשְּׁבֻעָה אֲשֶׁר נִשְׁבַּע
לַאֲבֹתֵיכֶם הוֹצִיא יְהוָה אֶתְכֶם בְּיָד חֲזָקָה
וַיִּפְדְּךָ מִבֵּית עֲבָדִים מִיַּד פַּרְעֹה מֶלֶךְ־מִצְרָיִם׃
מפטיר ט וְיָדַעְתָּ כִּי־יְהוָה אֱלֹהֶיךָ הוּא הָאֱלֹהִים
הָאֵל הַנֶּאֱמָן שֹׁמֵר הַבְּרִית וְהַחֶסֶד לְאֹהֲבָיו
וּלְשֹׁמְרֵי מִצְוֺתָו (מצותיו קרי) לְאֶלֶף דּוֹר׃
י וּמְשַׁלֵּם לְשֹׂנְאָיו אֶל־פָּנָיו לְהַאֲבִידוֹ לֹא
יְאַחֵר לְשֹׂנְאוֹ אֶל־פָּנָיו יְשַׁלֶּם־לוֹ׃ יא וְשָׁמַרְתָּ
אֶת־הַמִּצְוָה וְאֶת־הַחֻקִּים וְאֶת־הַמִּשְׁפָּטִים
אֲשֶׁר אָנֹכִי מְצַוְּךָ הַיּוֹם לַעֲשׂוֹתָם׃ פ

and objectives set for it by God, its Owner and Master. Therefore it must keep out of its affairs anything that would work against these purposes: "You are a holy national entity, belonging to *God*, your God."

9. ***Therefore you know.*** From the experience of your own redemption you *know* that God, Who revealed Himself in your own history as *your* God, is the same God Whom all the nations recognize or instinctively sense to be "God," no matter what name they give Him. . . .

° ° °

10. ***He rewards.*** He rewards even the good that is done by those who hate Him; and He does so with each one "to his face." This may mean [1] "before his face": He will personally receive the reward for whatever good he has done, so that he himself will enjoy it in his lifetime. This is unlike the lot of the one who loves God, for such a person, God "preserves loving-kindness to the one thousandth generation." The earthly reward for his good deeds therefore comes [only] in the form of the happiness he has founded, by his acts of goodness, for his children and grandchildren (see Exodus 34:7); or [2] "in the direction in which he turns his face"; i.e., in accordance with the direction taken by his ideas and aspirations. His selfish mind considers as a reward only that which he can enjoy personally (Erubin 22a). . . . The good person has already acquired immortality on earth by being able to live on in his descendants who, along with his moral potential for goodness, inherit also the rewards of his virtues. The progeny of the wicked man, on the other hand, becomes extinct after the third or fourth generation if it continues in his evil ways (Exodus 20:5). . . .

° ° °

The Haftarah for this Sidra may be found on page 909.

עקב

EKEV

12. It will come to pass, as a result of your hearing these [social] ordinances and carrying them out with care, that *God*, your God, will keep for you the covenant and the love that He swore to your fathers. 13. He will love you and will bless you and will multiply you; [He] will bless the fruit of your body

יב וְהָיָה ׀ עֵקֶב תִּשְׁמְעוּן אֵת הַמִּשְׁפָּטִים הָאֵלֶּה
וּשְׁמַרְתֶּם וַעֲשִׂיתֶם אֹתָם וְשָׁמַר יְהוָה אֱלֹהֶיךָ
לְךָ אֶת־הַבְּרִית וְאֶת־הַחֶסֶד אֲשֶׁר נִשְׁבַּע
לַאֲבֹתֶיךָ׃ יג וַאֲהֵבְךָ וּבֵרַכְךָ וְהִרְבֶּךָ וּבֵרַךְ פְּרִי־

12. ***It will come to pass, as a result.*** In the preceding section it was pointed out that the truly good individual will not receive his personal reward for his good deeds while he himself is still on earth. The passages which now follow describe the blessings that will come to the community if it lives collectively in accordance with its duty. These blessings, we are told, come as the result of such a life; they are not rewards to be pursued for their own sake. That is why all the commandments of the Divine Law, the עֵדוֹת [testimonies], מִצְוֹת [commandments], חֻקִּים [statutes] and מִשְׁפָּטִים [(social) ordinances], are subsumed here under one heading, that of מִשְׁפָּטִים. Basically, they are all nothing else but legal axioms through which the many varied aspects and relationships of physical and spiritual life of both individual and nation receive their rightful due in accordance with the standard of צֶדֶק, the Divinely-set ideal state of the world. This is the spirit in which these laws are to be carried out; their observance is to be regarded as nothing more than the fulfillment of one's duty, for which one must not expect thanks or rewards.

However, all these laws accord so completely with the nature of things and the purpose of man, and are so completely in harmony with one another, that if the entire nation observes them faithfully, the result will be the greatest happiness that can possibly come to a nation on earth. This result, which is not to be sought as such, but will come of itself, as it were, is termed עֵקֶב, literally, "the heel." It represents that which follows "upon the heels" of obedience, not that upon which one should "keep an eye" when carrying out the Law of God. That is why our Sages attach to this particular verse certain detailed teachings regarding the spirit in which we are expected to observe the Law of God. We are not to weigh each commandment separately in our minds, to consider which one might yield a greater reward than the others and should therefore be given particular priority and attention. The paths of the Law form ever-widening spheres that merge into one another. We cannot, at one glance, predict the results of the observance of any one commandment. The results mesh with one another, as it were, and the very commandment that would seem to us most insignificant and least important may have the most far-reaching effects. We must therefore observe all the commandments, without exception, with equal punctiliousness; we must consider them all equally important; we must carry them out solely because it is our duty, without any thought of whether our reward for [doing so] will be great or small.

The etymological fact that עֵקֶב connotes something not deliberately sought, something that is not given consideration, motivated our Sages to admonish us as follows: "It will come to pass, as a result of your hearing. . . ." We are to give particular attention to the observance of those laws which, seen in terms of changing circumstances, might be disregarded as supposedly less important than the others; as they put it, "commandments upon which people (tend to) tread with their heels," leaving them behind as they "walk over" them because they consider them to be of little significance. From time immemorial such arbitrary differentiations between laws that are supposedly "more important," and those presumed "less important," particularly between the commandments pertaining to the relationship between man and his fellow man and those pertaining to the relationship between man and God, have had disastrous consequences for us. The end of our first happy era of political independence is ascribed particularly to our neglect of the commandments pertaining to the relationship between man and God; the collapse of our second statehood is attributed to our neglect of the commandments pertaining to the relationship between man and his fellow man. We can expect future happiness only if we will accept the Law of God as a whole and observe it in its entirety, without any distinctions. Cf. ". . . the Law of *God*, all-encompassing, responds to the soul" (Psalm 19:8): only as an all-encompassing, complete entity will the Law of God have its intended effect.

° ° °

and the fruit of your soil; your grain and your new wine and your oil; the litter of your cattle and the abundance of your sheep, upon the soil that He swore to your fathers to give to you. 14. You will be blessed more than all peoples; there will not be any sterile male or barren female among you or among your livestock. 15. *God* will keep away from you every sickness and all the evil afflictions of Mitzrayim, which you know, He will not lay upon you—[but] will lay them upon all those who hate you. 16. You will have to annihilate all the peoples that *God,* your God, is giving you; your eye shall not feel any mercy for them—so that you will not serve their gods—for this is a trap for you. 17. If you will say in your heart: "These nations are too powerful for me; how will I be able to dispossess them?," 18. then do not be afraid of them; always remember what *God,* your God, did to Pharaoh and to all of Mitzrayim; 19. the great acts of proof which your [own] eyes saw; the signs and the convincing acts; the mighty hand and the outstretched arm, with which *God,* your God, brought you out. Thus will *God,* your God, do to all the peoples of whom you are afraid. 20. *God,* your God, will send also the hornet against them until those who are left and have remained hidden from you will perish. 21. Do not be terrified of them, for *God,* your God, in your midst, is a great and awesome God. 22. Little by little will *God,* your God, deprive these peoples of their foothold before you; you will not be able to destroy them quickly, for otherwise the beast[s] of the field would

בִטְנְךָ וּפְרִי־אַדְמָתֶךָ דְּגָנְךָ וְתִירֹשְׁךָ וְיִצְהָרֶךָ
שְׁגַר־אֲלָפֶיךָ וְעַשְׁתְּרֹת צֹאנֶךָ עַל הָאֲדָמָה
אֲשֶׁר־נִשְׁבַּע לַאֲבֹתֶיךָ לָתֶת לָךְ: יד בָּרוּךְ תִּהְיֶה
מִכָּל־הָעַמִּים לֹא־יִהְיֶה בְךָ עָקָר וַעֲקָרָה
וּבִבְהֶמְתֶּךָ: טו וְהֵסִיר יְהוָה מִמְּךָ כָּל־חֹלִי וְכָל־
מַדְוֵי מִצְרַיִם הָרָעִים אֲשֶׁר יָדַעְתָּ לֹא יְשִׂימָם
בָּךְ וּנְתָנָם בְּכָל־שֹׂנְאֶיךָ: טז וְאָכַלְתָּ אֶת־כָּל־
הָעַמִּים אֲשֶׁר יְהוָה אֱלֹהֶיךָ נֹתֵן לָךְ לֹא־תָחוֹס
עֵינְךָ עֲלֵיהֶם וְלֹא תַעֲבֹד אֶת־אֱלֹהֵיהֶם כִּי־
מוֹקֵשׁ הוּא לָךְ: ס יז כִּי תֹאמַר בִּלְבָבְךָ רַבִּים
הַגּוֹיִם הָאֵלֶּה מִמֶּנִּי אֵיכָה אוּכַל לְהוֹרִישָׁם:
יח לֹא תִירָא מֵהֶם זָכֹר תִּזְכֹּר אֵת אֲשֶׁר־עָשָׂה
יְהוָה אֱלֹהֶיךָ לְפַרְעֹה וּלְכָל־מִצְרָיִם: יט הַמַּסֹּת
הַגְּדֹלֹת אֲשֶׁר־רָאוּ עֵינֶיךָ וְהָאֹתֹת וְהַמֹּפְתִים
וְהַיָּד הַחֲזָקָה וְהַזְּרֹעַ הַנְּטוּיָה אֲשֶׁר הוֹצִאֲךָ יְהוָה
אֱלֹהֶיךָ כֵּן־יַעֲשֶׂה יְהוָה אֱלֹהֶיךָ לְכָל־הָעַמִּים
אֲשֶׁר־אַתָּה יָרֵא מִפְּנֵיהֶם: כ וְגַם אֶת־הַצִּרְעָה
יְשַׁלַּח יְהוָה אֱלֹהֶיךָ בָּם עַד־אֲבֹד הַנִּשְׁאָרִים
וְהַנִּסְתָּרִים מִפָּנֶיךָ: כא לֹא תַעֲרֹץ מִפְּנֵיהֶם כִּי־
יְהוָה אֱלֹהֶיךָ בְּקִרְבֶּךָ אֵל גָּדוֹל וְנוֹרָא: כב וְנָשַׁל
יְהוָה אֱלֹהֶיךָ אֶת־הַגּוֹיִם הָאֵל מִפָּנֶיךָ מְעַט מְעָט
לֹא תוּכַל כַּלֹּתָם מַהֵר פֶּן־תִּרְבֶּה עָלֶיךָ חַיַּת

14. ***You will be blessed.*** The concluding clause "there will not be . . . among you. . ." demonstrates that the blessing which is to distinguish this nation, living under the regime of God's Law, from all the other nations, is to be construed as that of an abundant population. The Word of God knows of nothing more precious than a human soul: it regards an increase in the number of a nation's souls as the measure of that nation's true happiness and prosperity. . . .

16. ***your eye shall not feel any mercy for them.*** These repeated admonitions not to show any mercy to the Canaanite population may demonstrate how little such behavior normally accords with the character and the purpose of the Jewish people. The tendency of the Jewish people is, and always should be, to show mercy to all living things, and the Jewish people should view such merciless conduct against the Canaanite population as an exception, explicitly commanded by God and necessitated by the special circumstances described in the text.

feel any mercy. Do not show them any mercy, lest you come to serve their gods. For "this," the mercy you would show them, would become "a trap for you"; mercy on your part in such cases would lead you to defection. . . .

multiply upon you.   23. *God*, your God, will deliver them up before you; He will put them into great confusion until they are destroyed.   24. He will deliver their kings into your hand and you will eradicate their name from under heaven; no man will stand upright before you until you have destroyed them.   25. The images of their gods you shall burn in fire; do not lust after the silver and the gold that is upon them and take it for yourself, lest you be trapped thereby; for it is an abomination to *God*, your God.   26. Do not bring anything that is an abomination into your house, for, like it, you shall come under a ban. You shall feel an aversion for it and detest it because it is subject to a ban.

VIII   1. The entire commandment, which I enjoin upon you today, you shall keep to carry it out, so that you may live and multiply and come [in] and take possession of the land that *God* swore to your fathers.   2. Remember the entire path [along] which *God*, your God, has led you these forty years in the wilderness, in order to have you live in want, to test you so that you may come to know what is in your heart, whether you will keep His commandments or not.   3. He had you live in want; he let you go hungry, and then He fed you with the *manna* that you did not know and your fathers did not know, in

הַשָּׂדֶה: כג וּנְתָנָם יְהֹוָה אֱלֹהֶיךָ לְפָנֶיךָ וְהָמָם מְהוּמָה גְדֹלָה עַד הִשָּׁמְדָם: כד וְנָתַן מַלְכֵיהֶם בְּיָדֶךָ וְהַאֲבַדְתָּ אֶת־שְׁמָם מִתַּחַת הַשָּׁמָיִם לֹא־יִתְיַצֵּב אִישׁ בְּפָנֶיךָ עַד הִשְׁמִדְךָ אֹתָם: כה פְּסִילֵי אֱלֹהֵיהֶם תִּשְׂרְפוּן בָּאֵשׁ לֹא־תַחְמֹד כֶּסֶף וְזָהָב עֲלֵיהֶם וְלָקַחְתָּ לָךְ פֶּן תִּוָּקֵשׁ בּוֹ כִּי תוֹעֲבַת יְהֹוָה אֱלֹהֶיךָ הוּא: כו וְלֹא־תָבִיא תוֹעֵבָה אֶל־בֵּיתֶךָ וְהָיִיתָ חֵרֶם כָּמֹהוּ שַׁקֵּץ ׀ תְּשַׁקְּצֶנּוּ וְתַעֵב ׀ תְּתַעֲבֶנּוּ כִּי־חֵרֶם הוּא: פ ח א כָּל־הַמִּצְוָה אֲשֶׁר אָנֹכִי מְצַוְּךָ הַיּוֹם תִּשְׁמְרוּן לַעֲשׂוֹת לְמַעַן תִּחְיוּן וּרְבִיתֶם וּבָאתֶם וִירִשְׁתֶּם אֶת־הָאָרֶץ אֲשֶׁר־נִשְׁבַּע יְהֹוָה לַאֲבֹתֵיכֶם: ב וְזָכַרְתָּ אֶת־כָּל־הַדֶּרֶךְ אֲשֶׁר הוֹלִיכְךָ יְהֹוָה אֱלֹהֶיךָ זֶה אַרְבָּעִים שָׁנָה בַּמִּדְבָּר לְמַעַן עַנֹּתְךָ לְנַסֹּתְךָ לָדַעַת אֶת־אֲשֶׁר בִּלְבָבְךָ הֲתִשְׁמֹר מִצְוֹתָו (מצותיו קרי) אִם־לֹא: ג וַיְעַנְּךָ וַיַּרְעִבֶךָ וַיַּאֲכִלְךָ אֶת־הַמָּן אֲשֶׁר לֹא־יָדַעְתָּ וְלֹא

---

25. The images. These represent the antithesis of the very first tenet among all the truths that form the basis of human enlightenment and civilization. Hence images of idols for worship have no place in Jewish territory. They must be destroyed as soon as they come into the possession of a Jew. . . .

lest you be trapped thereby. We have already noted to Leviticus 19:6 that we must not leave room in our thoughts for any heathen concepts. We must therefore also keep away from our possessions and from our thoughts anything associated with idol worship. We must not expose ourselves to the danger of having such things disturb the purity of our awareness of God and of our relationship to Him, the One sole God.

for it is an abomination to God, your God. The heathen aberration symbolized by the representation of an idol, by the glorification given to that idol by men, and by heathen sacrifices and ceremonial implements—all these are in such crass contrast to the moral

and spiritual level to which the One sole God has raised you from that aberration, and to which indeed all men are summoned by virtue of their human calling, that any physical evidence of idolatry must be utterly at variance with the will of your God.

CHAPTER VIII

1. The end of the preceding chapter declared the utter nullity of heathen deities and set forth the commandment to remove from the Jewish intellectual and spiritual horizon, and from the physical property of Jews, everything even remotely related to these idols. In contrast, the present chapter stresses the supreme positive essence of God as experienced by Israel, which we are to keep before us at all times; a concept which alone is conducive to the faithful observance of His Law and thus also to our enduring salvation.

order to have you know that it is not by bread alone that man can make a life for himself, but that man can live by everything that comes from the mouth of *God*. 4. Your garment did not become worn with age upon you, neither did your foot swell, these forty years. 5. Therefore hold fast upon your heart the knowledge that,

יָדְע֣וּן אֲבֹתֶ֑יךָ לְמַ֣עַן הוֹדִיעֲךָ֗ כִּ֠י לֹ֣א עַל־הַלֶּ֤חֶם לְבַדּוֹ֙ יִחְיֶ֣ה הָֽאָדָ֔ם כִּ֛י עַל־כָּל־מוֹצָ֥א פִֽי־יְהֹוָ֖ה יִחְיֶ֥ה הָֽאָדָֽם: ד שִׂמְלָ֣תְךָ֗ לֹ֤א בָֽלְתָה֙ מֵֽעָלֶ֔יךָ וְרַגְלְךָ֖ לֹ֣א בָצֵ֑קָה זֶ֖ה אַרְבָּעִ֥ים שָׁנָֽה: ה וְיָֽדַעְתָּ֮

3. *He had you live in want.* He provided your sustenance in a manner for which you could find no parallel in your own past experience, nor in that of your forefathers.

in order to have you know. Namely, in order to allow you to form this conviction on the basis of your own experience of forty years.

that it is not by bread alone. לֶחֶם ["bread"] is the nourishment that man wrests[2] from nature, in competition with his fellow men. "Bread" is the joint product of nature and of the intelligence with which man masters the world. Thus bread is the visual manifestation of the intelligence with which man creates his own sustenance, interacting socially with his fellow men in order to gain control over nature.

But it would be erroneous to believe that this creative human power is the sole requirement for man's existence on earth. The prime factor in man's sustenance is the Providence of God; His generous care is evident in every morsel of bread with which we sustain yet another moment of our existence. To forget this would mean to fall prey to a most dangerous delusion upon which our devotion to duty on earth would founder. The task of providing our wives and children with their daily bread is in itself such a legitimate incentive for our activities that it could easily cause us to lose sight of all other considerations once we persuade ourselves that we and only we ourselves can provide our own sustenance and that of our dependents. We could then persuade ourselves that any gain wrested from nature and from our fellow men will assure our sustenance and that of our dependents regardless of the means we employ for this purpose. If this is our attitude, then we will not care whether, in so doing, we observe the Law of God, earning our "daily bread" only by means within the limits shown us by God, or whether we obtain our sustenance by skillful manipulation without considering whether God would approve of our methods. Even if the notion that we can look to human power alone for our daily bread will not cause us to stray from the paths of duty and righteousness, it may well lead our thoughts beyond the necessities of the

immediate present, further and further into the remote future, so that we will come to think that we have not done our duty unless we have assured sustenance not only for our own future but also for the future of our children and grandchildren. As a result, our normal concern for breadwinning will become an endless race, leaving us neither time nor energy for purely spiritual and moral concerns.

That is why God put us through the great training course of forty years' wandering in the wilderness. There, in the absence of all the factors that normally enable man to win his bread through a combination of natural resources and human energy, He brought out in sharp relief the one factor which under normal circumstances is only too easily ignored. Instead of nourishing us with the bread that bears the stamp of human achievement, He fed us with the *manna* that is allotted by God alone, and He had it come to us day after day, to every soul in our humble dwellings, in a manner that made it the most eloquent proof of God's personal care for every soul, both great and small. Hence, in this course of basic training for our future life, we learned the following basic truth: that human existence is not dependent solely on "bread"—or, more accurately put, on the natural and human resources represented by bread—but that man can make a life for himself with anything that is apportioned to him by God. (Even the bread that he obtains by his own skill is only another gift from God.) Therefore, man will not be lost if, for the sake of the allegiance he owes to God, he will be compelled to forego all that can be obtained from human and natural resources; indeed, man must know that even in the midst of plenty derived from the resources of man and nature, he still owes his sustenance solely to God's special care. . . .

⋅   ⋅   ⋅

5. . . . The forty years of wandering in the wilderness were nothing but a course of instruction and training: instruction about God's Providence—omnipresent, caring and ever-near—and training for serene and trusting surrender to His guidance. These two elements together form the basis for the conviction that our moral perfection, to be attained through instruction and practice, is a matter of close concern to the Divine Providence that shapes our destinies in accordance with

---

[2]*Note to the English translation:* לחם means both "to eat" and "to wage war." [G.H.]

עִם־לְבָבֶךָ כִּי כַּאֲשֶׁר יְיַסֵּר אִישׁ אֶת־בְּנוֹ יְהוָה
אֱלֹהֶיךָ מְיַסְּרֶךָּ׃ ו וְשָׁמַרְתָּ אֶת־מִצְוֺת יְהוָה
אֱלֹהֶיךָ לָלֶכֶת בִּדְרָכָיו וּלְיִרְאָה אֹתוֹ׃ ז כִּי יְהוָה
אֱלֹהֶיךָ מְבִיאֲךָ אֶל־אֶרֶץ טוֹבָה אֶרֶץ נַחֲלֵי מָיִם
עֲיָנֹת וּתְהֹמֹת יֹצְאִים בַּבִּקְעָה וּבָהָר׃ ח אֶרֶץ
חִטָּה וּשְׂעֹרָה וְגֶפֶן וּתְאֵנָה וְרִמּוֹן אֶרֶץ־זֵית שֶׁמֶן
וּדְבָשׁ׃ ט אֶרֶץ אֲשֶׁר לֹא בְמִסְכֵּנֻת תֹּאכַל־בָּהּ
לֶחֶם לֹא־תֶחְסַר כֹּל בָּהּ אֶרֶץ אֲשֶׁר אֲבָנֶיהָ בַרְזֶל
וּמֵהֲרָרֶיהָ תַּחְצֹב נְחֹשֶׁת׃ י וְאָכַלְתָּ וְשָׂבָעְתָּ
וּבֵרַכְתָּ אֶת־יְהוָה אֱלֹהֶיךָ עַל־הָאָרֶץ הַטֹּבָה

even as a man trains his son, so does *God,*
your God, train you. 6. And keep the
commandments of *God,* your God, to walk
in His ways and to fear Him. 7. For *God,*
your God, is bringing you into a good land,
to a land full of brooks of water, wellsprings
and depths, springing forth in valley and
mountain; 8. to a land of wheat and
barley, vines and figs and pomegranates; to
a land of olives and dates; 9. a land in
which you will not eat bread in parsimony,
in which you will lack for nothing; a land
whose stones are iron and from whose
mountains you will dig copper. 10. When
you eat and are satisfied, then bless *God,*
your God, for the good land that He has

the requirements of our moral training and instructs us through personal experience, training our moral strength through constant practice. . . .

7. ***For* God, *your God.*** Your training course of wandering in the wilderness has now come to an end. You are about to enter upon that future for which your anomalous situation on earth thus far was to be a preparation. Now, given a normal position as individuals and as a nation, you must demonstrate in practice the lessons which you should have learned during that singular training course, and which you must not forget if the future you are about to enter is to endure.

a land full of brooks of water. At the very outset, the contrast between the nature of the land, on the one hand, and that of the wilderness, on the other, is stated in terms of the abundance of water that characterizes the land, a natural resource which is a prerequisite for the abundance of crops and fruit that will now be described. . . .

10. . . . Whenever you have partaken of the abundance given you by God to strengthen yourself and to satisfy the requirements for your physical survival, you must remember that it is to God alone, your personal God, that you owe each restoration of your strength, each gratification of your needs. You must therefore dedicate all of your being, strengthened and uplifted by Him, to His service, to the furtherance of His purposes and to the realization of His will on earth. This vow of dedication on your part must be pronounced in the form of a בְּרָכָה [blessing]. We have here the commandment relating to the בִּרְכַּת הַמָּזוֹן, the *berakhah* that must be recited after partaking of bread. The function of this *berakhah* is to cultivate and reinforce, even under normal conditions, when you obtain nourishment by the usual means, the conviction gained through the obvious miracle of the *manna*: That God extends His direct, personal care to every individual. You will then regard every piece of bread as no less a direct gift from God than the *manna* He sent from heaven to the generation that wandered in the wilderness. . . .

° ° °

The context in which the *mitzvah* of בִּרְכַּת הַמָּזוֹן [reciting the Grace after Meals] is set forth in the Biblical text (i.e., the verses that precede it and those that follow it), along with the concept of *berakhah* as such, teaches us that the Jewish "Grace after Meals," as it is popularly known, is something more than a formal "rendering of thanks for what we have received." It is intended not only to remind us that it is to God and God alone that we owe our existence, but also to make us aware of the logical implications of this fact for the discharge of our life's mission. For this reason our בִּרְכַּת הַמָּזוֹן consists of four distinct *berakhoth,*which together subsume all the factors that, given God's guidance of the world in general and of Jewish history in particular, constitute the concept of "Jew" and should make every generation of Jews aware of its mission.

The בִּרְכַּת הַזָּן [the blessing for sustenance], the very first *berakhah,* gives expression to that verity which the *manna* has demonstrated to every Jewish soul as an inalienable truth; namely, that God (Whose very Name implies that He grants a future to every human soul) extends His special attention and care to every single individual and to his personal needs for continued survival. Therefore, every piece of bread that is eaten and every moment of survival obtained thereby is to be regarded as a gift of His goodness, regardless of whether (depending on the merits of the recipient) this goodness is manifested in the form of "favor" or "loving-kindness" or of His inalienable "compassion." These are the ideas expressed by the first *berakhah* in which we vow to devote our lives to the service of Him Who gives sustenance to all.

However, while God is near to the fate and destiny of every human being, the destinies of the Jewish individual have an additional particular relationship to God and His Providence. This relationship has been confirmed by the fact that God promised and assigned the Jewish land to the Jewish family of men for all time to come. Not only in its prosperity, but also in its temporary *ḥurban* [ruin], this Jewish land represents the pledge for Israel's unique historical position on earth. This is the idea expressed in the second *berakhah*, בִּרְכַּת הָאָרֶץ [the blessing for the land]. However, Israel must understand its historical position in terms of its purpose and of the conditions attached to this purpose. The basis for the historical position of the Jews, documented by the "Land of the Promise," is the covenant of Abraham (Genesis 17:7 and 8), in which all the physical aspects of life are consecrated to the service of God, and the purpose of Israel's place in history is that Israel should punctiliously observe the Torah. Cf. "And He gave them the lands of nations . . . so that they might keep His statutes and cherish His teachings" (Psalms 105:44 and 45). Therefore, we can conceive of the Divinely-promised land only in connection with the Covenant and the Torah. Only by upholding this covenant sealed upon our flesh and by remaining constantly devoted to the tasks set by the Torah will we receive the special care of Divine Providence that sustains us "every day, at every hour, and through all time."

The calling of the Jewish nation, which is inextricably linked with the practical realization of God's Law, was given permanent expression in the Sanctuary of the Law in Zion. Its eternal bearer is the dynasty of David, the king who secured political independence for his nation and who, at the same time, left it the echoes of his harp, as it were, to raise it to the spiritual level of its vocation. It is to these [the Sanctuary and the Davidian dynasty] that the third *berakhah* has been assigned. Jerusalem, at the foot of Mount Zion, whose summit is the site of the Sanctuary, represents the people of God, rallying around the Law of God as the spiritual center which dominates it and to which it looks for guidance. And the most noble family that is forever linked with the attainment of this lofty goal of Judaism is the dynasty of David. The stamp of spiritual calling that is impressed by Jerusalem-Zion upon the entire Jewish land is implied in Berakhoth 48b by the description הָאָרֶץ הַטּוֹבָה [the good land], even as the purpose of the land, centered on Mount Zion, is referred to in Deuteronomy 3:25: הָאָרֶץ הַטּוֹבָה וגו׳ הָהָר הַטּוֹב ["the good land . . . the goodly mountain. . ."].

The third *berakhah*, a prayer for the continued bestowal of existence and independence upon the individual, is linked to a prayer for the continued bestowal of material and spiritual welfare also upon the nation. Hence, while the Davidian kingdom and the Temple were in existence, this petition had to be expressed in the form of a prayer for the preservation of these bearers of the nation's future. Since the *ḥurban* and the *galuth* [the destruction of the land and independence of the Jews, and the exiling of the Jewish people], this petition has taken the form of a prayer for the restoration of Jerusalem; i.e. בּוֹנֵה יְרוּשָׁלָיִם ["... Who builds Jerusalem"].

These three blessings cover all the factors to be considered in the בִּרְכַּת הַמָּזוֹן [Grace after Meals] דְאוֹרַיְתָא [according to Biblical Law]. However, one addition was made by the Sages after the revolt led by Bar Kokhba during the reign of Hadrian had proven a disastrous error, and it had become necessary to admonish the Jews that they must never again attempt to restore their nationhood by their own might—but should leave their future as a nation entirely to Divine Providence. After the crushed nation had begun to recover, even welcoming, as a portent of better days to come, the permission finally granted them to bury the hundreds of thousands who had fallen at Betar, the Sages, meeting at Yavneh, composed a fourth *berakhah* to be added to the daily Grace after Meals: הַטּוֹב וְהַמֵּטִיב ["... He Who is good and bestows good"]. This blessing was intended to commemorate the unprecedented massacre at Betar in the form of a prayer of thanksgiving: Even the fact that the bodies of the fallen had remained intact until they could be buried was seen as a mark of boundless Divine favor. (Cf. "*Who is good*: In that (the bodies) did not decompose; *and Who bestows good*: In that permission was obtained to give the bodies a burial" (Berakhoth 48b). In this blessing our eyes are directed away from all human assistance and turned toward God alone, הוּא הֵטִיב וגו׳ הוּא יֵטִיב לָנוּ הוּא יִגְמְלֵנוּ וכו׳ הוּא יִמְלֹךְ וכו׳ הוּא יִשְׁבּוֹר וכו׳ ["Who is good . . . Who will do good to us . . . Who will redeem us . . . He will reign . . . He will break our yoke. . ."].

There seems to be a profound ethical significance in the *halakhah* that stresses the element of companionship in the partaking and enjoyment of food. Whenever three or more males who have attained [religious] majority sit down to break bread together, they are to put this companionship on record also in the Grace to be recited after the meal. One of the participants in the meal is invited to recite the Grace on behalf of the entire company, and he, along with the others, is to remember that it is one Provider and one Goodness that has given food to them all. נְבָרֵךְ שֶׁאָכַלְנוּ מִשֶּׁלוֹ, בָּרוּךְ שֶׁאָכַלְנוּ מִשֶּׁלוֹ ["Let us bless Him from Whose bounty we have eaten. . . . Blessed be He from Whose bounty we have eaten (and by Whose goodness we live)"]. The leader is to recite the *berakhah* on behalf of all the others, who in turn are then to make it their own by responding: אָמֵן. Nothing is more apt to throw men back to self-seeking greed, and to make one man the rival of another, than the quest for nourishment. Therefore it would seem that the stress on the element of companionship in the meal and in the recitation of the *berakhah* afterwards, which reminds us of the goodness of God, directed simultaneously and in equal measure to all, should serve to liberate us from selfish thoughts. This is the reason why the בִּרְכַּת הַמָּזוֹן [the invitation to recite the Grace together] refers essentially to בִּרְכַּת הַזָּן [the first of the three Biblically-ordained blessings; namely, the blessing for sustenance] (Tosefoth Berakhoth 46a).

The statement in the Law of God וּבֵרַכְתָּ אֶת ד׳ אֱלֹקֶיךָ וגו׳ [. . . then bless *God,* your God. . ."] has become the prototype of the great institution of *berakhoth* which the Sages, seeking to mold the spirit of the Jewish people, have woven into every aspect of our lives. Here the Law of God has made the enjoyment of the fruits of the land an occasion for directing our thoughts from the fruit itself to the One Who gave us both the land and the fruit. In this manner, the Law helps us arrive at certain conclusions for our own lives, conclusions subsumed under the concept of בְּרָכָה. Similarly, the Sages in their wisdom have turned every aspect of our lives, and all their phenomena that we may experience, into tutors, as it were, to instruct us about God and about our obligations toward Him. Each time we recite them, these *berakhoth* teach us anew to look up to God and to reiterate our pledge, as expressed by the words בָּרוּךְ אַתָּה וגו׳ ["Blessed art Thou. . ."], to serve Him with all our lives. Every pleasure we enjoy, every stirring phenomenon of nature, every significant event in our lives, any occasion to perform a *mitzvah* (e.g., בִּרְכוֹת הַנֶּהֱנִין [blessings to be recited in connection with various types of enjoyment], בִּרְכוֹת הָרְאִיָּה וְהַשְּׁמִיעָה [blessings to be recited on beholding specific sights or hearing tidings, good or bad], בִּרְכוֹת הַמִּצְוָה [blessings to be recited before performing a *mitzvah*])—afford us an opportunity to recite the pledge בָּרוּךְ אַתָּה ד׳ וגו׳, and thus to attain the correct perspective toward God, as *our* God, with regard to all these things.

Indeed, the core and fruit of our entire Divine service, the entire "service of the heart" . . . all the work which we are duty-bound to perform upon ourselves, is a consecration of our lives to the practical fulfillment of God's will on earth as expressed in the בְּרָכָה. That which the concept of the עוֹלָה [ascent offering] is in relation to the "sacrificial" service to God (symbolizing our continuous struggle to attain the high spiritual level appropriate to our life's mission and embodying this quest in our every heartbeat) is expressed in our present prayer service by the בְּרָכָה. Indeed, the idea expressed by the words בָּרוּךְ אַתָּה ד׳ ["Blessed art Thou, O *God.* . ."] epitomizes all the truths that form the basis for our moral life: the fact that God has a special relationship to every individual, that every individual is in the service of God, and that God has endowed man with a free will, thus making the fulfillment of His own will, the attainment of His purposes on earth, the "benediction [or prospering] of His work," dependent on the free will of His human creatures. Hence, the human being who dedicates himself to the service of God can express this dedication by addressing to God the word *barukh* ["blessed art Thou"].

The element of שֵׁם [the Divine Name] that is part of the commandment in the Biblical text, ד׳ אֱלֹקֶיךָ [". . . *God,* your God. . ."], is expressed in our *berakhoth* by the words ד׳ אֱלֹקֵינוּ ["*God,* our God"]. Significantly, the *berakhoth* add also the element of God's מַלְכוּת [kingship], expressed by the words מֶלֶךְ הָעוֹלָם ["King of the universe"]. The *halakhah* teaches us that "Any blessing in which (the concepts of) God's Name . . . and Kingship are not mentioned is not a blessing" (Berakhoth 40b). For the purpose of the *berakhoth* is to lead us from matters we encounter in the earthly world to Him Who is the everlasting Ruler of all earthly affairs, so that we may realize that He Whose sovereignty is proclaimed to us by every moment of our earthly existence is ה׳ אֱלֹקֵינוּ [*God,* our God], and that we must therefore render Him homage by devoting to Him all of our existence and all our aspirations. It is equally significant that while the first half of each blessing addresses God directly, in the second person singular, the second half always uses the indirect form of address, the third person. The reason for this is that, as a rule, the second half of each blessing states the specific occasion for the blessing: it points to the work of Him to Whom we have addressed our personal homage in the first half. The pleasure we have enjoyed, the natural phenomenon we have beheld, or the *mitzvah* we have performed, all of which are occasions for reciting a blessing, refer us to Him הַזָּן אֶת הָעוֹלָם כֻּלּוֹ ["Who nourishes the entire world"], שֶׁכֹּחוֹ וּגְבוּרָתוֹ מָלֵא עוֹלָם ["Whose strength and might fill the universe"], or אֲשֶׁר קִדְּשָׁנוּ בְּמִצְוֹתָיו ["Who has sanctified us by His commandments"]. It is to Him that we turn directly with the words בָּרוּךְ אַתָּה ["Blessed art Thou"]; this is our pledge to use the benefits we expect to obtain, or have already obtained, from the pleasure enjoyed or from the act to be performed in accordance with His Law, for the purpose of carrying out His will on the earth which is filled with His omnipotence.

Even as the בְּרָכוֹת in בִּרְכַּת הַמָּזוֹן [the Grace after Meals] set down by our Sages for recitation *after* the enjoyment of food have their Biblical prototype (דְאוֹרַיְתָא), so, too, many authorities hold that the blessing to be pronounced *prior to* the study of Torah (Berakhoth 21a) is also דְאוֹרַיְתָא [based on Biblical Law]. See Naḥmanides, postscript to *Sefer HaMitzvoth,* Positive Commandment #15, and *Peri Ḥadash* to *Orakh Ḥayyim* 47. . . . Thus, both these blessings would be the prototypes for the *berakhoth* ordained by the Sages for recitation before and after specified acts and occasions. Only if we resolve, as it is expressed by the *berakhah* recited prior to partaking of any pleasure, that any renewed vital energy we will gain from this pleasure will be employed by us to serve God's purposes, will we become worthy of enjoying that pleasure. As the Sages

אֲשֶׁר נָתַן־לָךְ׃ שני יא הִשָּׁמֶר לְךָ פֶּן־תִּשְׁכַּח אֶת־
יְהוָה אֱלֹהֶיךָ לְבִלְתִּי שְׁמֹר מִצְוֺתָיו וּמִשְׁפָּטָיו
וְחֻקֹּתָיו אֲשֶׁר אָנֹכִי מְצַוְּךָ הַיּוֹם׃ יב פֶּן־תֹּאכַל
וְשָׂבָעְתָּ וּבָתִּים טֹבִים תִּבְנֶה וְיָשָׁבְתָּ׃ יג וּבְקָרְךָ
וְצֹאנְךָ יִרְבְּיֻן וְכֶסֶף וְזָהָב יִרְבֶּה־לָּךְ וְכֹל אֲשֶׁר־
לְךָ יִרְבֶּה׃ יד וְרָם לְבָבֶךָ וְשָׁכַחְתָּ אֶת־יְהוָה
אֱלֹהֶיךָ הַמּוֹצִיאֲךָ מֵאֶרֶץ מִצְרַיִם מִבֵּית עֲבָדִים׃
טו הַמּוֹלִיכְךָ בַּמִּדְבָּר ׀ הַגָּדֹל וְהַנּוֹרָא נָחָשׁ ׀
שָׂרָף וְעַקְרָב וְצִמָּאוֹן אֲשֶׁר אֵין־מָיִם הַמּוֹצִיא
לְךָ מַיִם מִצּוּר הַחַלָּמִישׁ׃ טז הַמַּאֲכִלְךָ מָן
בַּמִּדְבָּר אֲשֶׁר לֹא־יָדְעוּן אֲבֹתֶיךָ לְמַעַן עַנֹּתְךָ
וּלְמַעַן נַסֹּתֶךָ לְהֵיטִבְךָ בְּאַחֲרִיתֶךָ׃ יז וְאָמַרְתָּ
בִּלְבָבֶךָ כֹּחִי וְעֹצֶם יָדִי עָשָׂה לִי אֶת־הַחַיִל הַזֶּה׃

given you. 11. Take heed to yourself that you do not forget *God,* your God, in not keeping His commandments, His [social] ordinances and His statutes which I command you today. 12. You might [then] eat and be satisfied, build goodly houses and live in them; 13. your cattle and sheep might multiply; your silver and gold might increase for you; all that you have might increase, 14. and then your spirit might become haughty, and you might forget *God,* your God, Who brought you out from the land of Mitzrayim, from the home of slaves; 15. Who led you in the great and terrible wilderness where there were snakes, *saraf* and scorpions, thirst and no water; Who gave you water out of the flinty rock; 16. Who fed you in the wilderness with *manna,* which your fathers did not know, in order to let you live in want and to test you—in order to bestow good upon you ultimately. 17. You might then say in your spirit: "It was my [own] power and the might of my [own] hand that has gotten me

put it, "If one enjoys anything of this world without reciting a benediction, he has committed a sacrilege." One who has enjoyed anything of this world without reciting a benediction is as if he had profaned one of God's holy things. Until the *berakhah* has been recited, everything in this world belongs to God; only by reciting the *berakhah* does the individual become entitled to share in the good things of this world (Berakhoth 35a).

Similarly, the purpose of reciting a *berakhah* prior to performing a *mitzvah* is to help us form the attitude with which that *mitzvah* should be carried out; i.e., that we regard the act we are about to perform as a *mitzvah,* a commandment of God, given for the purpose of "making us holy": אֲשֶׁר קִדְּשָׁנוּ בְּמִצְוֺתָיו ["Who has sanctified us by His commandments"]. For this reason *berakhoth* are recited only prior to performing *mitzvoth* designed to rectify and to enrich our thoughts and aspirations; i.e., to exercise a hallowing influence upon us (e.g., prior to שׁוֹפָר [sounding the *shofar*], מְגִלָּה [the reading of the Book of Esther], צִיצִית [the putting on of *tzitzith*]). There are no *berakhoth* for *mitzvoth* that are intended only to yield immediate, practical results (e.g., charity, restoring stolen property to its rightful owner, returning a pledge given as security for a loan; results not directly dependent on the mood or attitude with which the *mitzvah* is carried out.

We believe that we have thus found a key to the order of blessings to be recited before carrying out a *mitzvah.* The only blessing that apparently does not conform to this interpretation is the one to be recited before constructing a guardrail (Deuteronomy 22:8), see Abudraham, Chap. III. . . .

11. . . . It is significant that the מִצְוֺת [commandments] are mentioned here first, and the מִשְׁפָּטִים [(social) ordinances] and the חֻקִּים [statutes] only thereafter. Possessions and pleasures easily give rise to egotism and overweening self-confidence. This tendency is to be countered by the admonition that each new possession and each new pleasure only adds to our duty to use all that we have and enjoy solely for the service of God, Who has assigned us our "station in His kingdom," and Who has given us these good things as means for accomplishing the tasks He has set for us. This, the employment of one's means and energies for God's purposes, is the literal connotation of מִצְוֺת; מִשְׁפָּטִים and חֻקִּים state the dictates of right and morality as limits for our pursuit of wealth and pleasures.

14–17. ***and then your spirit might become haughty.*** To this the *Gemarah* (Sotah 5a) adds a general warning against all pride and arrogance and shows how closely pride borders on idolatry and the denial of God. As a matter of fact, arrogance is not merely conducive to ungodliness; it is in itself the beginning of ungodliness, for where the concept of God dwells, there can be no room for pride and arrogance. We are told in this

this wealth." 18. Therefore remember *God,* your God; that it is He Who gives you the power to get wealth in order to uphold the covenant that He swore to your fathers as [it is] this day. 19. It will come to pass if you should nevertheless forget *God,* your God, and walk after other gods, and serve them and bow to them: then I bear witness to you today that you will certainly perish. 20. Like the nations that *God* will cause to perish before you, so will you perish as a result of your not hearkening to the voice of *God,* your God.

IX 1. Hear, O Yisrael: You are now passing over the Yarden in order to go in, to take over the property of nations that are greater and mightier than you and of cities that are great and fortified up to heaven. 2. A great and towering population, sons of the Anakites, of whom you know and of whom you have heard [it said], "Who can stand up before the sons of Anak?" 3. So you shall know today that *God,* your God, is the One Who goes before you as a consuming fire; He will destroy them; that is why He will bend them before you so that you may drive them away quickly and destroy them, as *God* has spoken to you. 4. Do not say in your heart, when *God,* your God, thrusts them away from

יח וְזָכַרְתָּ֙ אֶת־יְהֹוָ֣ה אֱלֹהֶ֔יךָ כִּ֣י ה֗וּא הַנֹּתֵ֥ן לְךָ֛ כֹּ֖חַ לַעֲשׂ֣וֹת חָ֑יִל לְמַ֨עַן הָקִ֧ים אֶת־בְּרִית֛וֹ אֲשֶׁר־נִשְׁבַּ֥ע לַאֲבֹתֶ֖יךָ כַּיּ֥וֹם הַזֶּֽה: פ יט וְהָיָ֗ה אִם־שָׁכֹ֤חַ תִּשְׁכַּח֙ אֶת־יְהֹוָ֣ה אֱלֹהֶ֔יךָ וְהָֽלַכְתָּ֗ אַחֲרֵי֙ אֱלֹהִ֣ים אֲחֵרִ֔ים וַעֲבַדְתָּ֖ם וְהִשְׁתַּחֲוִ֣יתָ לָהֶ֑ם הַעִדֹ֤תִי בָכֶם֙ הַיּ֔וֹם כִּ֥י אָבֹ֖ד תֹּאבֵדֽוּן: כ כַּגּוֹיִ֗ם אֲשֶׁ֤ר יְהֹוָה֙ מַאֲבִ֣יד מִפְּנֵיכֶ֔ם כֵּ֖ן תֹּאבֵד֑וּן עֵ֚קֶב לֹ֣א תִשְׁמְע֔וּן בְּק֖וֹל יְהֹוָ֥ה אֱלֹהֵיכֶֽם: פ

ט א שְׁמַ֣ע יִשְׂרָאֵ֗ל אַתָּ֨ה עֹבֵ֤ר הַיּוֹם֙ אֶת־הַיַּרְדֵּ֔ן לָבֹא֙ לָרֶ֣שֶׁת גּוֹיִ֔ם גְּדֹלִ֥ים וַעֲצֻמִ֖ים מִמֶּ֑ךָּ עָרִ֛ים גְּדֹלֹ֥ת וּבְצֻרֹ֖ת בַּשָּׁמָֽיִם: ב עַם־גָּד֥וֹל וָרָ֖ם בְּנֵ֣י עֲנָקִ֑ים אֲשֶׁ֨ר אַתָּ֤ה יָדַ֨עְתָּ֙ וְאַתָּ֣ה שָׁמַ֔עְתָּ מִ֣י יִתְיַצֵּ֔ב לִפְנֵ֖י בְּנֵ֥י עֲנָֽק: ג וְיָדַעְתָּ֣ הַיּ֗וֹם כִּי֩ יְהֹוָ֨ה אֱלֹהֶ֜יךָ הֽוּא־הָעֹבֵ֤ר לְפָנֶ֨יךָ֙ אֵ֣שׁ אֹֽכְלָ֔ה ה֧וּא יַשְׁמִידֵ֛ם וְה֥וּא יַכְנִיעֵ֖ם לְפָנֶ֑יךָ וְהֽוֹרַשְׁתָּ֤ם וְהַֽאֲבַדְתָּם֙ מַהֵ֔ר כַּֽאֲשֶׁ֛ר דִּבֶּ֥ר יְהֹוָ֖ה לָֽךְ: שלישי ד אַל־תֹּאמַ֣ר בִּלְבָבְךָ֗ בַּהֲדֹ֤ף יְהֹוָה֙ אֱלֹהֶ֔יךָ

Gemarah that God says of the arrogant: "He and I cannot dwell together in the world."

·   ∘   ∘

19. *It will come to pass.* Constant reminders of God are needed, such as the Grace after Meals and all the other institutions set up by the Law. Man does not turn his back on God all at once; he becomes estranged from Him only by degrees, and this happens most often at times when one feels that he has everything he needs for his happiness. Hence the statement of the Sages: "Wherever you find a reference (in the Torah) to eating and being satisfied, there you will also find a warning."

CHAPTER IX

1. . . . The thoughts contained in the preceding chapter are now continued. Before all else (Verses 1 through 6), the downfall of the other nations is impressed upon [the Children of Israel] in order to teach them a twofold lesson. First: That notwithstanding their awesome power, the nations will perish as a result of their moral

degeneration as soon as "their iniquity is complete" (Genesis 15:16). It is not the bravery and superiority of the conquerors (who are, indeed, weaker and fewer in numbers that the vanquished) that will act as the "consuming fire," before which all depravity will melt away, but God, Who has ordained that His moral Law shall reign supreme over the future of His mankind. The conquerors are only the tool of God; they can conquer only that which God has already doomed to destruction. Second: That even as Israel's bravery had no significant role in the downfall of these nations, so, too, the moral merits already demonstrated by Israel are not factors in God's decree that Israel inherit the possessions of the nations which have been doomed to destruction. Hence, Israel has no reason to become smug and to imagine that its past devotion to duty is sufficient for it to gain possession of the land in the place of its former inhabitants, and that therefore Israel's past merits will be sufficient also to maintain it in possession of the land. Even if Israel is not as evil as the other nations, it is still by far not good enough to meet the requirements attaching to the possession of before you: "Because of my devotion to duty did *God* bring me there, to take possession of this land," when [in fact] it is only because of the wickedness of these nations that *God* drives them away from before you.   5. Not because of your devotion to duty and because of the uprightness of your heart are you coming there, to take possession of their land, but because of the wickedness of these nations does *God,* your God, drive them away from before you, and in order to fulfill the word that *God* swore to your fathers, Abraham, Yitzḥak and Yaakov. 6. For you must know that it is not because of your devotion to duty that *God,* your God, is giving you this good land to take possession of it, for indeed you are a stiff-necked people.   7. Remember, do not forget how you provoked *God,* your God, in the wilderness; from the day that you went out from the land of Mitzrayim until you came to this place you have rebelled against *God.*   8. Even at Horeb you provoked *God,* and God was so angry with you that He wanted to destroy you. 9. When I had ascended the mountain to receive stone tablets, tablets of the Covenant that *God* had made with you, and I

אַתֶּ֣ם ׀ מִלְּפָנֶ֗יךָ לֵאמֹר֙ בְּצִדְקָתִי֙ הֱבִיאַ֣נִי יְהֹוָ֔ה לָרֶ֜שֶׁת אֶת־הָאָ֤רֶץ הַזֹּאת֙ וּבְרִשְׁעַת֙ הַגּוֹיִ֣ם הָאֵ֔לֶּה יְהֹוָ֖ה מוֹרִישָׁ֥ם מִפָּנֶֽיךָ: ה לֹ֣א בְצִדְקָֽתְךָ֗ וּבְיֹ֙שֶׁר֙ לְבָ֣בְךָ֔ אַתָּ֥ה בָ֖א לָרֶ֣שֶׁת אֶת־אַרְצָ֑ם כִּ֞י בְּרִשְׁעַ֣ת ׀ הַגּוֹיִ֣ם הָאֵ֗לֶּה יְהֹוָ֤ה אֱלֹהֶ֙יךָ֙ מוֹרִישָׁ֣ם מִפָּנֶ֔יךָ וּלְמַ֜עַן הָקִ֣ים אֶת־הַדָּבָ֗ר אֲשֶׁ֨ר נִשְׁבַּ֤ע יְהֹוָה֙ לַֽאֲבֹתֶ֔יךָ לְאַבְרָהָ֥ם לְיִצְחָ֖ק וּֽלְיַֽעֲקֹֽב: ו וְיָ֣דַעְתָּ֗ כִּ֠י לֹ֤א בְצִדְקָֽתְךָ֙ יְהֹוָ֣ה אֱלֹהֶ֗יךָ נֹתֵ֨ן לְךָ֜ אֶת־הָאָ֧רֶץ הַטּוֹבָ֛ה הַזֹּ֖את לְרִשְׁתָּ֑הּ כִּ֥י עַם־ קְשֵׁה־עֹ֖רֶף אָֽתָּה: ז זְכֹר֙ אַל־תִּשְׁכַּ֔ח אֵ֧ת אֲשֶׁר־ הִקְצַ֛פְתָּ אֶת־יְהֹוָ֥ה אֱלֹהֶ֖יךָ בַּמִּדְבָּ֑ר לְמִן־הַיּ֣וֹם אֲשֶׁר־יָצָ֣אתָ ׀ מֵאֶ֣רֶץ מִצְרַ֗יִם עַד־בֹּֽאֲכֶם֙ עַד־ הַמָּק֣וֹם הַזֶּ֔ה מַמְרִ֥ים הֱיִיתֶ֖ם עִם־יְהֹוָֽה: ח וּבְחֹרֵ֥ב הִקְצַפְתֶּ֖ם אֶת־יְהֹוָ֑ה וַיִּתְאַנַּ֧ף יְהֹוָ֛ה בָּכֶ֖ם לְהַשְׁמִ֥יד אֶתְכֶֽם: ט בַּֽעֲלֹתִ֣י הָהָ֗רָה לָקַ֜חַת לוּחֹ֤ת הָֽאֲבָנִים֙ לוּחֹ֣ת הַבְּרִ֔ית אֲשֶׁר־כָּרַ֥ת יְהֹוָ֖ה

---

the land. Israel is to be brought into the land not because of its own merits, but solely because of the merits of its forefathers and because of the promise God made to the latter, a promise to be fulfilled for their descendants. These merits of the forefathers, and the promise that was given to them, are sufficient to give Israel the land of the other nations. But Israel will be able to keep the land only through its own merits, merits that it has not yet acquired because it is still "a stiff-necked people."

7–29.; Chapter 10:1–11 . . . Hence [the Law] must look beyond the Israel of the present, toward the Israel of the future. . . . No community and no individual, no matter how important their mission on behalf of God's purposes on earth, may be so conceited as to imagine that they are indispensable to the work of God on earth and that they may therefore sin [with impunity]. . . .

In order to achieve its purposes, God's Providence passes over whole generations and individual members of the nation, who are, after all, transient, no matter how great they may appear to be.

•   •   •

9. *for forty days.* Again and again in this review

—here, and again in Verses 11, 18 and 25 of the present chapter and in Verse 10 of Chapter 10—the text stresses the three periods of forty days and forty nights that Moses spent before God, without taking any food or drink: first, prior to the giving of the original Tablets of the Law; then, following the defection of the people with the golden calf and, finally, prior to the giving of the second Tablets.

These periods of preparation prior to the giving of the first and second Tablets, the period spent in between these two in the endeavor to regain God's full favor, and the fact that all three periods were of equal length, must have a profound significance. No one could even presume to surmise the impact that such a forty-day sojourn before God must have had upon the spirit of Moses, a period he spent in isolation from all earthly concerns and yet with all his being attuned so intensely to the most sublime of all earthly relationships. Particularly, the intermediate forty-day period that led to Moses' receiving the supreme revelation of God's sovereignty (Exodus 33:12 f.) must have elevated him to a spiritual level appropriate, perhaps, to the revelation he was given to behold. On the other hand, a more proper subject for our consideration

עִמָּכֶם וָאֵשֵׁב בָּהָר אַרְבָּעִים יוֹם וְאַרְבָּעִים
לַיְלָה לֶחֶם לֹא אָכַלְתִּי וּמַיִם לֹא שָׁתִיתִי׃ י וַיִּתֵּן
יְהוָה אֵלַי אֶת־שְׁנֵי לוּחֹת הָאֲבָנִים כְּתֻבִים
בְּאֶצְבַּע אֱלֹהִים וַעֲלֵיהֶם כְּכָל־הַדְּבָרִים אֲשֶׁר
דִּבֶּר יְהוָה עִמָּכֶם בָּהָר מִתּוֹךְ הָאֵשׁ בְּיוֹם
הַקָּהָל׃ יא וַיְהִי מִקֵּץ אַרְבָּעִים יוֹם וְאַרְבָּעִים
לַיְלָה נָתַן יְהוָה אֵלַי אֶת־שְׁנֵי לֻחֹת הָאֲבָנִים
לֻחוֹת הַבְּרִית׃ יב וַיֹּאמֶר יְהוָה אֵלַי קוּם רֵד

remained upon the mountain for forty days and forty nights—I neither ate bread nor drank water— 10. then *God* gave me the two stone tablets, written with the finger of God, and on them was [indicated] in accordance with all the words that *God* had spoken with you on the mountain out of the fire on the day of the assembly. 11. And it came to pass at the end of forty days and forty nights—*God* had already given me the two stone tablets, the Tablets of the Covenant— 12. that *God* said to me: "Arise, go down quickly from here, because

would be the impact of these preparatory periods on the people, when their leader was separated from them, and they awaited his return. These forty-day waiting periods must have impressed the hearts and minds of all the people with the lofty significance of the objectives they were to attain through Moses, and with the gap that still existed between their own condition and the goal toward which they were to aspire.

There was still a considerable interval between the giving of the Law and the receiving of the Tablets. The former event made known to the Children of Israel their duty to observe the Law; the latter, in which the Tablets were physically turned over to them, was intended to signal the appointment of the Israelite nation as the custodian, guardian and bearer of God's Law for all time. The nation was to be entrusted with the Law of God, which had been given for it and for all mankind. Such a trust presupposed, above all, that Israel itself should be most firmly and consistently rooted in the soil of the Law. We will then see how these forty-day waiting periods were intended to effect in every single member of the people a personal labor of self-refinement. During that period, each one was to allow his spirit to be permeated by what he had heard, to become confirmed in the loyalty expressed by the words נַעֲשֶׂה וְנִשְׁמַע ["we will do and we will hear"], thus attaining at least the resolve to acquire an attitude commensurate with the spiritual level presupposed by the receiving of the Tablets. We will then understand, too, how the mere fact of Moses' absence should have impelled every individual in the nation to become a guardian, in his own right, of the Law of God which he himself had heard. Accordingly, we would then understand also the motive and the significance of the "breaking of the Tablets before their eyes," after the nation had so miserably failed its first test. The breaking of the Tablets did not imply a change in Israel's obligations to observe the Law. Rather, its purpose was to make the people realize how unworthy they were to be the trustees of this Divine law.

The destruction of the golden calf, the resolute action taken by the tribe of Levi among the people, the execution of the guilty and the sense of guilt and self-condemnation expressed by the people when they divested themselves of their ornaments at Ḥoreb—these developments averted the annihilation of which the nation would have been deserving, and opened up the possibility that Israel might enter once again into a pure relationship to God and to the great future ordained for it. However, it was not enough for Israel merely to realize these things. A realization of this kind must mature into a mental attitude, which in turn must engender a solemn resolve for future devotion to duty. A mere momentary expression of repentance is never enough to expunge guilt, great or small. Work upon one's own person is required if one is to be reborn to complete purity. In order to accomplish this work and to attain the miracle of כַּפָּרָה [atonement] that buries all past guilt, the help of God is needed. And for this work, too, for the attainment of this lofty goal, God granted a period of forty days which, as we surmised in our notes to Exodus 33:9–11, Moses spent before Him not on the mountain but in his own tent, outside the camp.

Moses was given the promise, in the form of the new Tablets of the Law, that a more complete relationship would be opened between God and the nation and that the nation would re-enter upon its Divinely-ordained future on the basis of a past cleansed of sin. Once again, a period of forty days was assigned during which the nation was to pass the test of separation from Moses, and during which it was to work its way up to a level commensurate with the vocation that awaited it once more, to be the trustee of God's Law both for its own posterity and for the future of all mankind.

Whether the apportionment of forty days for each of these periods was intended to correspond to the initial phase in the development of a human embryo, and hence was meant as a symbolic period during which Israel was to "become human" again, is a question we would only dare suggest.

מַהֵר מִזֶּה כִּי שִׁחֵת עַמְּךָ אֲשֶׁר הוֹצֵאתָ
מִמִּצְרָיִם סָרוּ מַהֵר מִן־הַדֶּרֶךְ אֲשֶׁר צִוִּיתִם
עָשׂוּ לָהֶם מַסֵּכָה: יג וַיֹּאמֶר יְהֹוָה אֵלַי לֵאמֹר
רָאִיתִי אֶת־הָעָם הַזֶּה וְהִנֵּה עַם־קְשֵׁה־עֹרֶף
הוּא: יד הֶרֶף מִמֶּנִּי וְאַשְׁמִידֵם וְאֶמְחֶה אֶת־
שְׁמָם מִתַּחַת הַשָּׁמָיִם וְאֶעֱשֶׂה אוֹתְךָ לְגוֹי־
עָצוּם וָרָב מִמֶּנּוּ: טו וָאֵפֶן וָאֵרֵד מִן־הָהָר וְהָהָר
בֹּעֵר בָּאֵשׁ וּשְׁנֵי לוּחֹת הַבְּרִית עַל שְׁתֵּי יָדָי:
טז וָאֵרֶא וְהִנֵּה חֲטָאתֶם לַיהֹוָה אֱלֹהֵיכֶם
עֲשִׂיתֶם לָכֶם עֵגֶל מַסֵּכָה סַרְתֶּם מַהֵר מִן־הַדֶּרֶךְ
אֲשֶׁר־צִוָּה יְהֹוָה אֶתְכֶם: יז וָאֶתְפֹּשׂ בִּשְׁנֵי
הַלֻּחֹת וָאַשְׁלִכֵם מֵעַל שְׁתֵּי יָדָי וָאֲשַׁבְּרֵם
לְעֵינֵיכֶם: יח וָאֶתְנַפַּל לִפְנֵי יְהֹוָה כָּרִאשֹׁנָה
אַרְבָּעִים יוֹם וְאַרְבָּעִים לַיְלָה לֶחֶם לֹא אָכַלְתִּי
וּמַיִם לֹא שָׁתִיתִי עַל כָּל־חַטַּאתְכֶם אֲשֶׁר
חֲטָאתֶם לַעֲשׂוֹת הָרַע בְּעֵינֵי יְהֹוָה לְהַכְעִיסוֹ:
יט כִּי יָגֹרְתִּי מִפְּנֵי הָאַף וְהַחֵמָה אֲשֶׁר קָצַף
יְהֹוָה עֲלֵיכֶם לְהַשְׁמִיד אֶתְכֶם וַיִּשְׁמַע יְהֹוָה אֵלַי
גַּם בַּפַּעַם הַהִוא: כ וּבְאַהֲרֹן הִתְאַנַּף יְהֹוָה מְאֹד
לְהַשְׁמִידוֹ וָאֶתְפַּלֵּל גַּם־בְּעַד אַהֲרֹן בָּעֵת הַהִוא:
כא וְאֶת־חַטַּאתְכֶם אֲשֶׁר־עֲשִׂיתֶם אֶת־הָעֵגֶל
לָקַחְתִּי וָאֶשְׂרֹף אֹתוֹ | בָּאֵשׁ וָאֶכֹּת אֹתוֹ טָחוֹן
הֵיטֵב עַד אֲשֶׁר־דַּק לְעָפָר וָאַשְׁלִךְ אֶת־עֲפָרוֹ
אֶל־הַנַּחַל הַיֹּרֵד מִן־הָהָר: כב וּבְתַבְעֵרָה
וּבְמַסָּה וּבְקִבְרֹת הַתַּאֲוָה מַקְצִפִים הֱיִיתֶם אֶת־
יְהֹוָה: כג וּבִשְׁלֹחַ יְהֹוָה אֶתְכֶם מִקָּדֵשׁ בַּרְנֵעַ
לֵאמֹר עֲלוּ וּרְשׁוּ אֶת־הָאָרֶץ אֲשֶׁר נָתַתִּי לָכֶם
וַתַּמְרוּ אֶת־פִּי יְהֹוָה אֱלֹהֵיכֶם וְלֹא הֶאֱמַנְתֶּם לוֹ
וְלֹא שְׁמַעְתֶּם בְּקֹלוֹ: כד מַמְרִים הֱיִיתֶם עִם־

your people, whom you brought out from Mitzrayim, has become corrupt. They have turned aside quickly from the way that I commanded them; they have made themselves a cast image!" 13. *God* further said to me [as follows]: "I have seen this people and lo! It is a stiff-necked people. 14. Leave Me alone, that I may destroy them and blot out their name from under heaven; I will make you into a nation more numerous and mighty [than they]." 15. I turned and descended from the mountain; the mountain was still blazing with fire and the two Tablets of the Covenant were upon my two hands. 16. When I looked and lo! You had sinned against *God*, your God; you had made for yourself a cast calf; you had turned aside quickly from the way that *God* had commanded you, 17. I grasped the two Tablets and threw them down from my two hands and broke them before your eyes. 18. And I cast myself down before *God* as I had done the first time, forty days and forty nights; I neither ate bread nor drank water, because of all your sins that you committed, that which was evil in the eyes of *God*, to provoke Him. 19. For I shuddered at the anger and the indignation with which *God* was angry with you, [enough] to destroy you. And this time, too, *God* hearkened to me. 20. *God* was also very angry with Aharon, [enough] to destroy him, and I prayed also for Aharon at that time. 21. But your sin, the calf that you had made, I took [it] and burned it in fire; I crushed it and ground it until it was fine powder, and I cast its powder into the brook that descends from the mountain. 22. You likewise provoked *God* at Tabera and at Massah and in Kibroth HaTaavah. 23. And when *God* sent you from Kadesh Barnea with the order: "Go up and take possession of the land that I have given you," you rebelled against the utterance of *God*, your God, and did not believe Him and did not hearken to His voice. 24. You

20. ***with Aharon.*** But for Moses' intercession on his behalf, even Aaron would have been doomed because of his unacceptable response to the iniquitous demands of the people. That which the *kohen* is to the people [of Israel], Israel is to the other nations. The position assigned to both by God does not protect them from the consequences of their actions; it only serves to increase their burden of accountability.

have been rebellious against *God* ever since I have known you.   25. But when I threw myself down before *God* for those forty days and forty nights that I spent lying prostrate because *God* had said He would destroy you,   26. I prayed to *God* and said: "O *God*, Who practices justice with loving-kindness, My Lord! Do not decree ruin for Thy people and Thine inheritance that Thou hast redeemed with Thy greatness, which Thou hast brought out from Mitz-rayim with a mighty hand!   27. Remember Thy servants, Abraham, Yitzhak and Yaakov; turn not to the stubbornness of this people, to its lawlessness and its light-headedness,   28. so that the land from which Thou didst bring us out should not say: 'It is not in the power of *God* to bring them into the land that He promised to them, and because He hated them did He bring them out to let them die in the wilderness.'   29. And yet they are Thy people and Thine inheritance, whom Thou didst bring out with Thy great power and Thine outstretched arm.''

X   1. At that time *God* said to me: "Hew for yourself two tablets of stone like the first ones, and come up to Me to the mountain and make for yourself a wooden ark.   2. I will write upon the Tablets the words that were upon the first tablets, which you broke, and you shall

יְהֹוָה מִיּוֹם דַּעְתִּי אֶתְכֶם: כה וָאֶתְנַפַּל לִפְנֵי יְהֹוָה אֵת אַרְבָּעִים הַיּוֹם וְאֶת־אַרְבָּעִים הַלַּיְלָה אֲשֶׁר הִתְנַפָּלְתִּי כִּי־אָמַר יְהֹוָה לְהַשְׁמִיד אֶתְכֶם: כו וָאֶתְפַּלֵּל אֶל־יְהֹוָה וָאֹמַר אֲדֹנָי יֱהֹוִה אַל־תַּשְׁחֵת עַמְּךָ וְנַחֲלָתְךָ אֲשֶׁר פָּדִיתָ בְּגָדְלֶךָ אֲשֶׁר־הוֹצֵאתָ מִמִּצְרַיִם בְּיָד חֲזָקָה: כז זְכֹר לַעֲבָדֶיךָ לְאַבְרָהָם לְיִצְחָק וּלְיַעֲקֹב אַל־תֵּפֶן אֶל־קְשִׁי הָעָם הַזֶּה וְאֶל־רִשְׁעוֹ וְאֶל־חַטָּאתוֹ: כח פֶּן־יֹאמְרוּ הָאָרֶץ אֲשֶׁר הוֹצֵאתָנוּ מִשָּׁם מִבְּלִי יְכֹלֶת יְהֹוָה לַהֲבִיאָם אֶל־הָאָרֶץ אֲשֶׁר־דִּבֶּר לָהֶם וּמִשִּׂנְאָתוֹ אוֹתָם הוֹצִיאָם לַהֲמִתָם בַּמִּדְבָּר: כט וְהֵם עַמְּךָ וְנַחֲלָתֶךָ אֲשֶׁר הוֹצֵאתָ בְּכֹחֲךָ הַגָּדֹל וּבִזְרֹעֲךָ הַנְּטוּיָה: פ רביעי א בָּעֵת הַהִוא אָמַר יְהֹוָה אֵלַי פְּסָל־לְךָ שְׁנֵי־לוּחֹת אֲבָנִים כָּרִאשֹׁנִים וַעֲלֵה אֵלַי הָהָרָה וְעָשִׂיתָ לְּךָ אֲרוֹן עֵץ: ב וְאֶכְתֹּב עַל־הַלֻּחֹת אֶת־הַדְּבָרִים אֲשֶׁר הָיוּ עַל־הַלֻּחֹת הָרִאשֹׁנִים אֲשֶׁר שִׁבַּרְתָּ

---

26. אַל תַּשְׁחֵת עַמְּךָ וְגֹו׳ [*Do not decree ruin for Thy people*]. They are, after all, עַמְּךָ ["Thy people"]; they are the only national entity that is held together as one united community solely by their subordination and commitment to Thee.

וְנַחֲלָתְךָ [*and Thine inheritance*]. They are the "inheritance" that reverted to Thee, as it were, from all the heathen delusion of the rest of mankind.

אַל תַּשְׁחֵת [*Do not decree ruin*]. Do not let them go to ruin when they are already so well on their way to the goal Thou hast intended for them. . .

        °   °   °

29. . . . The third forty-day period that is recalled in the passages now following was devoted to the re-election of Israel [for its mission].

CHAPTER X

1. *At that time.* At the end of that intermediary forty-day period, during which Moses pleaded for a

restoration of the special relationship of Divine Providence to Israel (see Exodus 33:12 f. and 34:1 f.).

and make for yourself. This was an indication from God that the Tablets would never be broken again, implying the Divine assurance that, notwithstanding the shortcomings and errors which the people have yet to overcome, their ultimate calling to act as bearers and keepers of the Law of God would endure along with them.

2. *I will write.* God will not alter His Law to accommodate the lapses of men. There is always only the choice between two alternatives: to forsake the Law or to return to it in complete faithfulness. The task that will be ours for all time and at all times is not to reform the Law, but to reform ourselves in accordance with the standards set by the Law. God will write upon the new Tablets only the original Law that was written upon the old ones. The Torah is the one constant factor; it will

place them into the ark.'' 3. And I made
an ark of *shittim* wood, hewed two tablets of
stone like the first ones, ascended the
mountain, and the two tablets [were] in my
hand. 4. And He wrote upon the Tablets,
like the first writing, the Ten Statements
that *God* had spoken to you upon the
mountain from out of the midst of the fire
on the day of the assembly, and *God* gave
them to me. 5. And I turned, descended
from the mountain and placed the Tablets
into the ark that I had made; and there they
remained, as *God* had commanded me.
6. And the sons of Yisrael journeyed from
the wells of B'ne Yaakon to Moserah; there
Aharon died and was buried there, and his
son Eleazar became priest in his stead.
7. From there they journeyed to Gudgod
and from Gudgod to Yotbah, a land of
brooks of water. 8. At that time, too, *God*
had set apart the tribe of Levi to bear the
Ark of the Covenant of *God*, to stand before
God, in order to serve Him and to bless with
His Name, to this day. 9. It is for this
reason that Levi received no portion and no
inheritance among his brethren; *God* is his
inheritance, as *God*, your God, has spoken
to him. 10. And I remained upon the
mountain, just as the first time, forty days

וְשַׂמְתָּם בָּאָרוֹן: ג וָאַעַשׂ אֲרוֹן עֲצֵי שִׁטִּים
וָאֶפְסֹל שְׁנֵי־לֻחֹת אֲבָנִים כָּרִאשֹׁנִים וָאַעַל
הָהָרָה וּשְׁנֵי הַלֻּחֹת בְּיָדִי: ד וַיִּכְתֹּב עַל־הַלֻּחֹת
כַּמִּכְתָּב הָרִאשׁוֹן אֵת עֲשֶׂרֶת הַדְּבָרִים אֲשֶׁר
דִּבֶּר יְהֹוָה אֲלֵיכֶם בָּהָר מִתּוֹךְ הָאֵשׁ בְּיוֹם הַקָּהָל
וַיִּתְּנֵם יְהֹוָה אֵלָי: ה וָאֵפֶן וָאֵרֵד מִן־הָהָר וָאָשִׂם
אֶת־הַלֻּחֹת בָּאָרוֹן אֲשֶׁר עָשִׂיתִי וַיִּהְיוּ שָׁם
כַּאֲשֶׁר צִוַּנִי יְהֹוָה: ו וּבְנֵי יִשְׂרָאֵל נָסְעוּ מִבְּאֵרֹת
בְּנֵי־יַעֲקָן מוֹסֵרָה שָׁם מֵת אַהֲרֹן וַיִּקָּבֵר שָׁם
וַיְכַהֵן אֶלְעָזָר בְּנוֹ תַּחְתָּיו: ז מִשָּׁם נָסְעוּ
הַגֻּדְגֹּדָה וּמִן־הַגֻּדְגֹּדָה יָטְבָתָה אֶרֶץ נַחֲלֵי־מָיִם:
ח בָּעֵת הַהִוא הִבְדִּיל יְהֹוָה אֶת־שֵׁבֶט הַלֵּוִי
לָשֵׂאת אֶת־אֲרוֹן בְּרִית־יְהֹוָה לַעֲמֹד לִפְנֵי יְהֹוָה
לְשָׁרְתוֹ וּלְבָרֵךְ בִּשְׁמוֹ עַד הַיּוֹם הַזֶּה: ט עַל־כֵּן
לֹא־הָיָה לְלֵוִי חֵלֶק וְנַחֲלָה עִם־אֶחָיו יְהֹוָה הוּא
נַחֲלָתוֹ כַּאֲשֶׁר דִּבֶּר יְהֹוָה אֱלֹהֶיךָ לוֹ: י וְאָנֹכִי
עָמַדְתִּי בָהָר כַּיָּמִים הָרִאשֹׁנִים אַרְבָּעִים יוֹם

endure beyond the generations that forsake it and will
await that posterity which will be loyal to it.

○   ○   ○

8-9. At that time. The selection of the tribe of
Levi, too, dates from that time. This is the tribe which,
by its proven loyalty and devotion during the period of
[Israel's] error and atonement, made itself worthy of
becoming the permanent cultivator and guardian
of God's Law in the midst of the people. This selection
of an entire tribe to renounce every claim to landed
property, and to make the service of the Law of God
and of the Sanctuary of the Law its sole calling, is basic
to the securing of that future whose eventual realization
depends on the possibility that the Covenant of the
Law will be reinstated. Even as the tribe of Levi had to
serve [physically] as the bearers of the Ark of the
Covenant and of the parts of the Sanctuary, and the
Aaronide family which belonged to that tribe had to
perform before God the service symbolizing devotion to
the fire of the Law and to utter the Name of God in
order to bless the nation, so, too, the entire life of the
tribe of Levi must be devoted to the Law of God also in

practice. The function of the Levites was to teach and
to preserve the Law, to inspire hearts and minds with
devotion to the Law of God and to make the entire
nation worthy of the Name of God that had been placed
upon it. In this manner, the tribe of Levi had to secure
for the nation the blessing inherent in the Name of
God. Thus the [Tablets of the Law, the] symbolic
expression of the stipulations and objectives of the
renewed Covenant of God, had been entrusted to the
Levites so that they might make it their life's vocation
to work for the realization of the Covenant in the day-
to-day life of the people.

God had set apart. This act of setting apart the
tribe of Levi from the other components of the nation,
having the tribe of Levi, to the exclusion of all others,
become by birth the bearers and guardians of the
Sanctuary of the Law, made the rest of the people
constantly aware of the shortcomings they themselves
had yet to overcome.

10. **God had not yielded to the dictate to destroy
you.** According to the strict dictates of justice you
would have deserved to perish. However [Moses

and forty nights, and *God* hearkened to me also at that time; *God* had not yielded to the dictate to destroy you. 11. And *God* said to me: "Arise; go before the people so that they may journey forth, that they may go in and take possession of the land that I have sworn to their fathers to give to them." 12. And now, O Yisrael, what does *God*, your God, require of you? Only to fear *God*, your God; to walk in all His ways and to love Him, and to serve *God*, your God, with all your heart and with all your soul. 13. To keep the commandments of *God* and His statutes, which I command you today, for your [own] good. 14. Behold! It is to *God*, your God, that the heavens and the heaven of heavens belong, the earth and all that is upon it. 15. Only in your fathers did *God* take pleasure, to love them; and He chose their descendants after them—you—from among all people, as [it is] today. 16. Therefore circumcise the foreskin of your heart and do not stiffen your necks any more. 17. For *God*, your God, is God of gods and Lord of lords; He is the great, mighty and feared God, Who does not consider [personal] standing and accepts no bribe; 18. Who secures the right[s] of the orphan and the widow and loves the stranger, to give him bread and clothing.

וְאַרְבָּעִים לַיְלָה וַיִּשְׁמַע יְהֹוָה אֵלַי גַּם בַּפַּעַם הַהִוא לֹא־אָבָה יְהֹוָה הַשְׁחִיתֶךָ: יא וַיֹּאמֶר יְהֹוָה אֵלַי קוּם לֵךְ לְמַסַּע לִפְנֵי הָעָם וְיָבֹאוּ וְיִירְשׁוּ אֶת־הָאָרֶץ אֲשֶׁר־נִשְׁבַּעְתִּי לַאֲבֹתָם לָתֵת לָהֶם: פ חמישי יב וְעַתָּה יִשְׂרָאֵל מָה יְהֹוָה אֱלֹהֶיךָ שֹׁאֵל מֵעִמָּךְ כִּי אִם־לְיִרְאָה אֶת־יְהֹוָה אֱלֹהֶיךָ לָלֶכֶת בְּכָל־דְּרָכָיו וּלְאַהֲבָה אֹתוֹ וְלַעֲבֹד אֶת־יְהֹוָה אֱלֹהֶיךָ בְּכָל־לְבָבְךָ וּבְכָל־נַפְשֶׁךָ: יג לִשְׁמֹר אֶת־מִצְוֹת יְהֹוָה וְאֶת־חֻקֹּתָיו אֲשֶׁר אָנֹכִי מְצַוְּךָ הַיּוֹם לְטוֹב לָךְ: יד הֵן לַיהֹוָה אֱלֹהֶיךָ הַשָּׁמַיִם וּשְׁמֵי הַשָּׁמָיִם הָאָרֶץ וְכָל־אֲשֶׁר־בָּהּ: טו רַק בַּאֲבֹתֶיךָ חָשַׁק יְהֹוָה לְאַהֲבָה אוֹתָם וַיִּבְחַר בְּזַרְעָם אַחֲרֵיהֶם בָּכֶם מִכָּל־הָעַמִּים כַּיּוֹם הַזֶּה: טז וּמַלְתֶּם אֵת עָרְלַת לְבַבְכֶם וְעָרְפְּכֶם לֹא תַקְשׁוּ עוֹד: יז כִּי יְהֹוָה אֱלֹהֵיכֶם הוּא אֱלֹהֵי הָאֱלֹהִים וַאֲדֹנֵי הָאֲדֹנִים הָאֵל הַגָּדֹל הַגִּבֹּר וְהַנּוֹרָא אֲשֶׁר לֹא־יִשָּׂא פָנִים וְלֹא יִקַּח שֹׁחַד: יח עֹשֶׂה מִשְׁפַּט יָתוֹם וְאַלְמָנָה וְאֹהֵב גֵּר לָתֶת לוֹ לֶחֶם וְשִׂמְלָה: יט וַאֲהַבְתֶּם

declares], the disclosure made to me, at the time of the third response, concerning the ways of God's Providence, has taught me that already from the outset God, in His loving-kindness, seeking to train the individual and all of mankind for their Divinely-ordained future, had not intended to yield to the dictates of mere justice in your case. (The literal connotation of אבה is to yield to a demand or dictate placed upon us.) . . . .

12. According to the cantillation, לְיִרְאָה ["to fear"], לָלֶכֶת ["to walk"] and לְאַהֲבָה ["to love"] are not three separate requirements. Rather, לָלֶכֶת and לְאַהֲבָה are both logical outgrowths of לְיִרְאָה; we are to fear God in such a manner that our fear of God will lead us to walk in all His ways, which in turn will make us come to love Him. For יְרָא אֶת ד' literally means to keep God in our sight at all times in all His greatness and majesty. . . .

to walk in all His ways. And this should induce us to strive after all the goals to which He has shown us the way. Such an unfolding of all our energies in the presence of God, toward the attainment of the goals He has

set for us, will make us happy. The feeling that one is living and accomplishing his life's purpose beneath the eye of God engenders such a sense of elation that the mere act of following in this path before God will cause him to love God. The love of God knows no greater bliss than the complete surrender of self to God as a lover of God and the knowledge that one is close to Him; and to serve God, impelled by this love, to have all the emotions of one's heart and all the physical and spiritual energies of one's soul become absorbed in serving God, in accomplishing His purposes on earth.

       o   o   o

13. לִשְׁמֹר *[To keep].* יְרְאָה [fear] and אַהֲבָה [love], this God-fearing way of life, this loving service of God with all of one's heart and soul, can be put into practice only by the punctilious observance of God's laws and commandments that were communicated to us through Moses. מִצְוֹת [commandments] refer to the positive tasks assigned to us; חֻקּוֹת [statutes], to the moral limits within which we are to strive to carry them out.

19. You, too, [shall] love the stranger, for
you were strangers in the land of Mitzrayim.
20. Fear *God,* your God, in such a
manner that you will serve Him; to Him
[shall you] attach yourself, and by His
Name [shall you] swear. 21. He is your
praise, and He is your God, Who has done
with you all the great and awesome thing[s]
that your eye has seen. 22. With seventy
souls did your fathers go to Mitzrayim, and
now *God,* your God, has made you like the
stars of the heaven for multitude.

XI

1. Therefore love *God,* your
God, and keep that which He
has entrusted to you: His statutes, His
[social] ordinances and His commandments,
all the days. 2. For you do know today—
that it is not with your chidren, who have
not experienced and not seen the training of
God, your God—His greatness and His
mighty hand and His outstretched arm;
3. His signs and His acts that He did in
Mitzrayim, to Pharaoh, king of Mitzrayim,
and to all his land; 4. what He did to the
army of Mitzrayim, to its horses and its
chariots; how He made the water of the Sea
of Reeds rise over them when they pursued
you, and so *God* has annihilated them to this
day; 5. and what He did to you in the
wilderness until you came to this place;
6. and what He did to Dathan and
Abiram, the sons of Eliab, son of Reuben,
that the earth opened its mouth and swallowed them up along with their households
and their tents, and everything existing that
was in their retinue in the midst of all
Yisrael— 7. but it is your [own] eyes that
see all this great work of *God,* that He did.
8. Therefore keep the entire commandment that I command you today, so that
you may become strong and go in and
take possession of the land into which you
are passing over to take possession of it,
9. and that you may long remain upon

אֶת־הַגֵּר כִּֽי־גֵרִים הֱיִיתֶם בְּאֶרֶץ מִצְרָֽיִם׃
כ אֶת־יְהֹוָה אֱלֹהֶיךָ תִּירָא אֹתוֹ תַעֲבֹד וּבוֹ
תִדְבָּק וּבִשְׁמוֹ תִּשָּׁבֵֽעַ׃ כא הוּא תְהִלָּֽתְךָ וְהוּא
אֱלֹהֶיךָ אֲשֶׁר־עָשָׂה אִתְּךָ אֶת־הַגְּדֹלֹת וְאֶת־
הַנּֽוֹרָאֹת הָאֵלֶּה אֲשֶׁר רָאוּ עֵינֶֽיךָ׃ כב בְּשִׁבְעִים
נֶפֶשׁ יָרְדוּ אֲבֹתֶיךָ מִצְרָֽיְמָה וְעַתָּה שָֽׂמְךָ יְהֹוָה
אֱלֹהֶיךָ כְּכוֹכְבֵי הַשָּׁמַיִם לָרֹֽב׃ יא א וְאָֽהַבְתָּ
אֵת יְהֹוָה אֱלֹהֶיךָ וְשָֽׁמַרְתָּ מִשְׁמַרְתּוֹ וְחֻקֹּתָיו
וּמִשְׁפָּטָיו וּמִצְוֺתָיו כָּל־הַיָּמִֽים׃ ב וִֽידַעְתֶּם
הַיּוֹם כִּי | לֹא אֶת־בְּנֵיכֶם אֲשֶׁר לֹא־יָֽדְעוּ וַֽאֲשֶׁר
לֹא־רָאוּ אֶת־מוּסַר יְהֹוָה אֱלֹהֵיכֶם אֶת־גָּדְלוֹ
אֶת־יָדוֹ הַֽחֲזָקָה וּזְרֹעוֹ הַנְּטוּיָֽה׃ ג וְאֶת־אֹתֹתָיו
וְאֶת־מַֽעֲשָׂיו אֲשֶׁר עָשָׂה בְּתוֹךְ מִצְרָיִם לְפַרְעֹה
מֶֽלֶךְ־מִצְרַיִם וּלְכָל־אַרְצֽוֹ׃ ד וַֽאֲשֶׁר עָשָׂה לְחֵיל
מִצְרַיִם לְסוּסָיו וּלְרִכְבּוֹ אֲשֶׁר הֵצִיף אֶת־מֵי
יַם־סוּף עַל־פְּנֵיהֶם בְּרָדְפָם אַחֲרֵיכֶם וַיְאַבְּדֵם
יְהֹוָה עַד הַיּוֹם הַזֶּֽה׃ ה וַֽאֲשֶׁר עָשָׂה לָכֶם
בַּמִּדְבָּר עַד־בֹּֽאֲכֶם עַד־הַמָּקוֹם הַזֶּֽה׃ ו וַֽאֲשֶׁר
עָשָׂה לְדָתָן וְלַֽאֲבִירָם בְּנֵי אֱלִיאָב בֶּן־רְאוּבֵן
אֲשֶׁר פָּֽצְתָה הָאָרֶץ אֶת־פִּיהָ וַתִּבְלָעֵם וְאֶת־
בָּֽתֵּיהֶם וְאֶת־אָֽהֳלֵיהֶם וְאֵת כָּל־הַיְקוּם אֲשֶׁר
בְּרַגְלֵיהֶם בְּקֶרֶב כָּל־יִשְׂרָאֵֽל׃ ז כִּי עֵֽינֵיכֶם
הָֽרֹאֹת אֶת כָּל־מַֽעֲשֵׂה יְהֹוָה הַגָּדֹל אֲשֶׁר עָשָֽׂה׃
ח וּשְׁמַרְתֶּם אֶת־כָּל־הַמִּצְוָה אֲשֶׁר אָֽנֹכִי מְצַוְּךָ
הַיּוֹם לְמַעַן תֶּֽחֶזְקוּ וּבָאתֶם וִֽירִשְׁתֶּם אֶת־הָאָרֶץ
אֲשֶׁר אַתֶּם עֹֽבְרִים שָׁמָּה לְרִשְׁתָּֽהּ׃ ט וּלְמַעַן

CHAPTER XI

1. . . God has given His Law to Israel as a treasure entrusted to its care. וְחֻקֹּתָיו: the prefix *vav* [before חֻקֹּתָיו] along with what follows, implies "as well as," indicating that all the components of the Law—the moral laws, the laws of social justice and the positive commandments—are equally important parts of the treasure entrusted to us. The purpose of all that God did for us, to save, preserve, bless, teach and train us, was to create a custodian and executor for His Law among the nations. Israel must demonstrate its love for God, and its devotion to Him, by fulfilling this purpose.

תַּאֲרִיכוּ יָמִים עַל־הָאֲדָמָה אֲשֶׁר נִשְׁבַּע יְהוָה
לַאֲבֹתֵיכֶם לָתֵת לָהֶם וּלְזַרְעָם אֶרֶץ זָבַת חָלָב
וּדְבָשׁ: ס ששי י כִּי הָאָרֶץ אֲשֶׁר אַתָּה בָא־שָׁמָּה
לְרִשְׁתָּהּ לֹא כְאֶרֶץ מִצְרַיִם הִוא אֲשֶׁר יְצָאתֶם
מִשָּׁם אֲשֶׁר תִּזְרַע אֶת־זַרְעֲךָ וְהִשְׁקִיתָ בְרַגְלְךָ
כְּגַן הַיָּרָק: יא וְהָאָרֶץ אֲשֶׁר אַתֶּם עֹבְרִים שָׁמָּה
לְרִשְׁתָּהּ אֶרֶץ הָרִים וּבְקָעֹת לִמְטַר הַשָּׁמַיִם
תִּשְׁתֶּה־מָּיִם: יב אֶרֶץ אֲשֶׁר־יְהוָה אֱלֹהֶיךָ דֹּרֵשׁ
אֹתָהּ תָּמִיד עֵינֵי יְהוָה אֱלֹהֶיךָ בָּהּ מֵרֵשִׁית
הַשָּׁנָה וְעַד אַחֲרִית שָׁנָה: ס יג וְהָיָה אִם־שָׁמֹעַ
תִּשְׁמְעוּ אֶל־מִצְוֹתַי אֲשֶׁר אָנֹכִי מְצַוֶּה אֶתְכֶם
הַיּוֹם לְאַהֲבָה אֶת־יְהוָה אֱלֹהֵיכֶם וּלְעָבְדוֹ בְּכָל־
לְבַבְכֶם וּבְכָל־נַפְשְׁכֶם: יד וְנָתַתִּי מְטַר־אַרְצְכֶם
בְּעִתּוֹ יוֹרֶה וּמַלְקוֹשׁ וְאָסַפְתָּ דְגָנֶךָ וְתִירֹשְׁךָ
וְיִצְהָרֶךָ: טו וְנָתַתִּי עֵשֶׂב בְּשָׂדְךָ לִבְהֶמְתֶּךָ
וְאָכַלְתָּ וְשָׂבָעְתָּ: טז הִשָּׁמְרוּ לָכֶם פֶּן־יִפְתֶּה

the soil that *God* swore to your fathers to
give to them and to their descendants—a
land that can flow with milk and honey.
10. For the land to which you are going,
to take possession of it, is not like the land of
Mitzrayim, from which you came out, that
you sowed your seed and watered it with
your foot like a vegetable garden.
11. The land to which you are passing
over, to take possession of it, is a land of
mountains and valleys—by the rain from
heaven does it drink water— 12. a land
for which *God*, your God, cares; the eyes of
God, your God, are always upon it, from the
beginning of the year until the end of the
year. 13. And so it will come to pass
if you will hearken, hearken ever more
earnestly to My commandments that I
command you today, so that you love *God*,
your God, and serve Him with all your heart
and with all your soul; 14. then I will
give the rain of your land in its season—the
early rain and the late rain—so that you may
gather in your grain, your new wine and
your oil, 15. and I will give you herbage
on your field for your livestock; you will eat
of it and be satisfied. 16. But take heed to
yourselves that your heart does not open

10–11. Note the alternation in the form of address between the second person singular and the second person plural ["to which you (*sing.*) are going" . . . from which you (*plu.*) came out, that you (*sing.*) sowed your seed. . . . The land to which you (*plu.*) are passing over"]. The alternation between singular and plural forms of address that occurs throughout Moses' admonitions to Israel seems intended to impress upon the people that though they will disperse over the land they will still belong together as one united whole. . . .

12. . . . Whether or not this land will flourish is not simply left to the consequences of an order of nature that was once established for all time to come. It is subject to the decision of Divine Providence that has singled you out to accomplish His moral purposes for all mankind. It is He Who trains and supervises you to this end. . . . The land of the Jews bears the memorial to the revelation of God's Law and hence also the future moral salvation of all mankind, so that the Kingdom of God will ultimately be brought about by the moral law that has gone forth from Zion. It can therefore be said that the flowering of all mankind is dependent upon the flowering of Zion. . . .

13. ***And so it will come to pass.*** This thought is a continuation of what has been said before; i.e., that the flowering and prosperity of our land are dependent on our moral behavior toward "*God*, our God." . . .

° ° °

לְאַהֲבָה וגו׳ is not ["*to* love,"]; i.e., it is not the subject matter of the preceding מִצְוָה [commandment]. It is ["*so that* you love"], the result to be attained by hearkening ever more earnestly. . . . Mental and spiritual absorption of the Law will engender אַהֲבָה [love], a total loving surrender to God, which regards such devotion and the resulting nearness of God as the supreme goal of all endeavors. Such internalization should also result in עֲבוֹדָה [lit., "service"], the active furtherance of God's purposes on earth. This אַהֲבָה and this עֲבוֹדָה are both to be accomplished בְּכָל לֵבָב וּבְכָל נֶפֶשׁ [with all one's heart and soul], with single-minded devotion and, if need be, with the surrender (אַהֲבָה) of all thoughts and emotions and of all the desires and achievements in life, even as the fulfillment of God's will (עֲבוֹדָה) must be accomplished by our own work upon all our לֵב וָנֶפֶשׁ [hearts and souls] and by the utilization of all our לֵב וָנֶפֶשׁ (see notes on Chapter 6:5).

° ° °

itself to enticement, and you turn aside, and you serve other gods and cast yourselves down before them. 17. Then the anger of *God* will be kindled against you; He will hold back the heaven, and there will be no rain, and the soil will not yield its produce, and you will quickly vanish from the good land that *God* is giving you. 18. But even then you shall place these My words upon your heart and upon your soul, and bind them as a sign upon your hand, and let them be a head ornament between your eyes, 19. and teach them to your sons, to speak of them when you sit in your house and when you walk upon the way, when you lie

לְבַבְכֶם וְסַרְתֶּם וַעֲבַדְתֶּם אֱלֹהִים אֲחֵרִים
וְהִשְׁתַּחֲוִיתֶם לָהֶם: יז וְחָרָה אַף־יְהֹוָה בָּכֶם
וְעָצַר אֶת־הַשָּׁמַיִם וְלֹא־יִהְיֶה מָטָר וְהָאֲדָמָה
לֹא תִתֵּן אֶת־יְבוּלָהּ וַאֲבַדְתֶּם מְהֵרָה מֵעַל
הָאָרֶץ הַטֹּבָה אֲשֶׁר יְהֹוָה נֹתֵן לָכֶם: יח וְשַׂמְתֶּם
אֶת־דְּבָרַי אֵלֶּה עַל־לְבַבְכֶם וְעַל־נַפְשְׁכֶם
וּקְשַׁרְתֶּם אֹתָם לְאוֹת עַל־יֶדְכֶם וְהָיוּ לְטוֹטָפֹת
בֵּין עֵינֵיכֶם: יט וְלִמַּדְתֶּם אֹתָם אֶת־בְּנֵיכֶם
לְדַבֵּר בָּם בְּשִׁבְתְּךָ בְּבֵיתֶךָ וּבְלֶכְתְּךָ בַדֶּרֶךְ

16. ***and you turn aside and you serve.*** Even the slightest deviation is conducive to עֲבוֹדָה זָרָה [idolatry]; indeed, it is already עֲבוֹדָה זָרָה in principle. . . .

and you serve other gods. By subordinating the practical aspects of our lives to the influences of heathen delusions.

and cast yourselves down before them. By placing our destinies at the command of the supposed power of pagan deities.

18. . . . According to *Sifri*, this verse, interpreted in the context of the preceding verse, and the commandment (Verse 19) to teach the Law to one's children, imply that if "you will . . . vanish. . .," if we are driven out from the land which is the actual soil of the Law, our obligations with regard to תְּפִלִּין [phylacteries] and תַּלְמוּד תּוֹרָה [the study of the Law] remain in full force even in *galuth*, when we dwell outside the land, as do other personal obligations that do not relate directly to the land and its produce. . . .

If we compare these verses (18 through 20) with the parallel passage in Chapter 6:6 through 9, the purpose of the present passage becomes readily apparent. It is to stress our personal obligation to observe the Law that remains in force regardless of any situation in which we may find ourselves. The intent of the earlier passage was to teach us the unity of human life by making us aware of the unity of God. That is why we are taught there that the surrender of our total personality, with all its aspects, בְּכָל לְבָבְךָ וּבְכָל נַפְשְׁךָ וּבְכָל מְאֹדֶךָ (6:5), is our life's mission; one that should be the object of all our thoughts and emotions (6:6), the content of the education of our children and of all our own domestic and public lives, both at work and at rest (6:7). We are then commanded (6:8 and 9) to keep this self-dedication before us symbolically by means of the תְּפִלִּין [*tefillin*] and the מְזוּזָה [*mezuzah*]. In the present passage, however, the תְּפִלִּין are completely separated from the מְזוּזָה [Verse 19 comes between the two], because the former is a separate concept, focusing on the adaptation of all the thinking, aspiring and achieving aspects of the individual *personality* to the requirements of the Law. Thus the [first of these two symbols] is nothing but a symbolic expression of our personal commitment to the Law as implicit in the words וְשַׂמְתֶּם אֶת דְּבָרַי אֵלֶּה עַל לְבַבְכֶם וְעַל נַפְשְׁכֶם ["But even then you shall place these My words upon your heart and upon your soul"]. Verses 18 and 19 together express the thought that this personal commitment is the ideal which we should teach to our children and which should be the content of all our own domestic and public lives, whether we are at work or at rest. Clearly all this is meant to tell us: Even if you should be forced to leave the land and will no longer have your own soil to place at the service of the Law of God, you must take the Law of God with you wherever you may go. Your hearts and souls, the thinking, aspiring and achieving aspects of your individual personality, remain committed to the Word of God. By placing the symbol of the תְּפִלִּין upon your hand and upon your head, you constantly remind yourselves and others of your commitment to the Law. No matter where you are, you remain bearers of the Word of God; you remain the people of the Law of God, and you are duty-bound to educate your children in this spirit and to devote all your own lives, at home or outside, to this purpose. . . .

19. . . . For an explanation of the alternation in forms of address [between the second person singular and the second person plural] see note to Verse 10. In the present verse the shift [from plural to singular: "And [you (*plu.*)] teach them to your (*plu.*) sons . . . when you (*sing.*) sit in your (*sing.*) house. . ."] is of particular significance. Even in dispersion, when there is no physical bond to unify them, the people must always be mindful of the ideas taught here. The subordination of every single individual [in heart, mind,

down and when you get up. 20. Write
them upon the [door]posts of your house
and upon your gates, 21. so that your
days and the days of your children may long
endure upon the soil that *God* swore to give
to your fathers, as the day of the heaven
upon the earth. 22. For if you will keep,
and always keep, this commandment that I
command you, to carry it out, to love *God*,
your God; to walk in all His ways and to
hold fast to Him, 23. then *God* will drive
away all these people before you, and you
will take over the property of nations greater
and more powerful than you. 24. Every
place that the ball of your foot will tread
shall become yours; from the wilderness
up to the Lebanon; from the river, the
Euphrates river, up to the sea at your back,
shall be your territory. 25. No man will
remain erect before you; *God*, your God,
will place the fear and the dread of you
upon all the land on which you will tread,
even as He has spoken to you.

וּֽבְשָׁכְבְּךָ֖ וּבְקוּמֶֽךָ׃ כ וּכְתַבְתָּ֛ם עַל־מְזוּז֥וֹת
בֵּיתֶ֖ךָ וּבִשְׁעָרֶֽיךָ׃ כא לְמַ֨עַן יִרְבּ֤וּ יְמֵיכֶם֙ וִימֵ֣י
בְנֵיכֶ֔ם עַ֚ל הָאֲדָמָ֔ה אֲשֶׁ֨ר נִשְׁבַּ֧ע יְהוָ֛ה לַאֲבֹתֵיכֶ֖ם
לָתֵ֣ת לָהֶ֑ם כִּימֵ֥י הַשָּׁמַ֖יִם עַל־הָאָֽרֶץ׃ ס שביעי
ומפטיר כב כִּי֩ אִם־שָׁמֹ֨ר תִּשְׁמְר֜וּן אֶת־כָּל־
הַמִּצְוָ֣ה הַזֹּ֗את אֲשֶׁ֧ר אָנֹכִ֛י מְצַוֶּ֥ה אֶתְכֶ֖ם
לַעֲשֹׂתָ֑הּ לְאַהֲבָ֞ה אֶת־יְהוָ֧ה אֱלֹהֵיכֶ֛ם לָלֶ֥כֶת
בְּכָל־דְּרָכָ֖יו וּלְדָבְקָה־בֽוֹ׃ כג וְהוֹרִ֧ישׁ יְהוָ֛ה אֶת־
כָּל־הַגּוֹיִ֥ם הָאֵ֖לֶּה מִלִּפְנֵיכֶ֑ם וִֽירִשְׁתֶּ֣ם גּוֹיִ֔ם
גְּדֹלִ֥ים וַעֲצֻמִ֖ים מִכֶּֽם׃ כד כָּל־הַמָּק֗וֹם אֲשֶׁ֨ר
תִּדְרֹ֧ךְ כַּף־רַגְלְכֶ֛ם בּ֖וֹ לָכֶ֣ם יִהְיֶ֑ה מִן־הַמִּדְבָּ֨ר
וְהַלְּבָנ֜וֹן מִן־הַנָּהָ֣ר נְהַר־פְּרָ֗ת וְעַד֙ הַיָּ֣ם הָאַחֲר֔וֹן
יִהְיֶ֖ה גְּבֻֽלְכֶֽם׃ כה לֹא־יִתְיַצֵּ֥ב אִ֖ישׁ בִּפְנֵיכֶ֑ם
פַּחְדְּכֶ֨ם וּמוֹרַאֲכֶ֜ם יִתֵּ֣ן ׀ יְהוָ֣ה אֱלֹהֵיכֶ֗ם עַל־פְּנֵ֤י
כָל־הָאָ֨רֶץ֙ אֲשֶׁ֣ר תִּדְרְכוּ־בָ֔הּ כַּאֲשֶׁ֖ר דִּבֶּ֥ר
לָכֶֽם׃ ס

thought and deed] to the one law will weld the widely-scattered individual components of the nation into one unit that will always stand out at as one single entity. . . .

◦ ◦ ◦

The Haftarah for this Sidra may be found on page 911.

ראה

RE-EH

26. See! I am setting before you today:
Blessing and curse. 27. The blessing:
That you will hearken to the commandments of *God*, your God, which I command
you today. 28. And the curse, if you will
not hearken to the commandments of *God*,
your God, and will turn aside from the way
that I command you today, to go after other
gods, of whom you have experienced
nothing. 29. And it shall come to pass,
when *God*, your God, will bring you to the

כו רְאֵה אָנֹכִי נֹתֵן לִפְנֵיכֶם הַיּוֹם בְּרָכָה וּקְלָלָה:
כז אֶת־הַבְּרָכָה אֲשֶׁר תִּשְׁמְעוּ אֶל־מִצְוֹת יְהוָה
אֱלֹהֵיכֶם אֲשֶׁר אָנֹכִי מְצַוֶּה אֶתְכֶם הַיּוֹם:
כח וְהַקְּלָלָה אִם־לֹא תִשְׁמְעוּ אֶל־מִצְוֹת יְהוָה
אֱלֹהֵיכֶם וְסַרְתֶּם מִן־הַדֶּרֶךְ אֲשֶׁר אָנֹכִי מְצַוֶּה
אֶתְכֶם הַיּוֹם לָלֶכֶת אַחֲרֵי אֱלֹהִים אֲחֵרִים אֲשֶׁר
לֹא־יְדַעְתֶּם: ס כט וְהָיָה כִּי יְבִיאֲךָ יְהוָה אֱלֹהֶיךָ

26. רְאֵה *[See!. . .]* This marks the end of the introductory review and is the transition to the compendium of laws intended for the generation that is about to take possession of the Land. רְאֵה ["See!"]: You now understand that, by means of the Law communicated to you through Moses, God has placed it completely into your hands to choose whether your future will be one of blessings or one of curses. Understand, too, that you have formed this conviction not on the basis of "belief" of teachings you have accepted from another person, but from everything you yourselves have experienced up to this point; these are the experiences that were recalled to you in the retrospective survey just completed.

° ° °

27. ***The blessing: That.*** Significantly, the text here reads אֲשֶׁר תִּשְׁמְעוּ ["*That* you will hearken. . ."] as distinct from the קְלָלָה [curse] in the next verse, אִם לֹא תִשְׁמְעוּ ["*if* you will not hearken. . ."]. The observance of the commandments of God is in itself part of the blessing. This blessing does not come only as a reward subsequent to obedience, but already begins to materialize in the act of obedience and fulfillment of duty as such. The spiritual and moral act accomplished by every observance of the Law represents in itself a blessed progress, an advancement of our entire personality; hence, each time we carry out a *mitzvah*, we really "bless" ourselves.

° ° °

28. ***And the curse, if . . .*** קְלָלָה, the loss of all self-worth, retrogression to personal nullity, comes only as an aftermath to the act of disobedience.

and will turn aside . . . to go after. Every step away from the Law is a step toward עֲבוֹדָה זָרָה [idolatry]. We are told in *Sifri*: "From *this* it follows that every espousal of idolatry is to be considered tantamount to a denial of the entire Law, and [conversely] every denial of idolatry is to be considered tantamount to an espousal of the entire Law." We do not think it redundant to point out that this statement is the exact antithesis of the notion that "belief in one God" is sufficient to make a person a Jew in the full sense of the term, even if he turns his back on all of God's laws. It is made clear to us here that the acknowledgement of God's unity is inextricably linked with our personal acknowledgement that we are duty-bound to observe all the commandments of God. The Jewish "belief in God" is identical with "the acceptance of the kingdom of Heaven," the subordination of our destinies and our acts to the One sole God; that is why the denial of polytheism is tantamount to the espousal of the entire Law of God. To deny the Jewish belief in One sole God, to accept the existence of another deity in additon to, or beside, Him Who is One to the exclusion of all others, is literally עֲבוֹדָה זָרָה, "subordination to another," a deliberate withdrawal of our own lives and of our own sense of duty from the dictates of the One sole God. Thus the espousal of idolatry is tantamount to a denial of the entire Law of God. Indeed, the Biblical source from which these maxims are derived ("from *this* it follows. . .") does not admit the slightest doubt in this matter. For the Biblical text ". . . and will turn aside from the way . . to go after other gods . . ." equates, albeit in a negative torm, the espousal of idolatry with a denial of the Law, by showing that every deviation from the path of the Law is in fact a step on the path of idolatry. . . .

° ° °

29. . . . Mounts Gerizim and Ebal are both part of the mountain range of Ephraim, but there is a striking physical contrast between the two. Mount Gerizim, located to the south of the valley of Shekhem, is verdant and fertile, with terraced landscaping. Mount Ebal, on

land into which you are coming to take possession of it; you shall deliver the blessing on Mount Gerizim and the curse on Mount Ebal. 30. Are these not on the other side of the Yarden, further on toward sunset, in the land of the Canaanite, who lives in the wasteland, opposite Gilgal, next to the groves of Moreh? 31. For you are passing over the Yarden to come in, to take possession of the land that *God*, your God, is giving you, to take possession of it; and you will take possession of it and dwell in it, 32. and you must then punctiliously carry out all the statutes and [social] ordinances that I set before you today.

XII   1. These are the statutes and the [social] ordinances which you are to carry out punctiliously in the land that *God*, the God of your fathers, has given you to take possession of it, all the days on which you dwell upon the earth. 2. You shall utterly destroy the places where the nations whose property you are taking over served their gods upon the high mountains and upon the hills and beneath every verdant tree. 3. You shall destroy their

אֶל־הָאָ֗רֶץ אֲשֶׁר־אַתָּ֥ה בָא־שָׁ֖מָּה לְרִשְׁתָּ֑הּ וְנָתַתָּ֤ה אֶת־הַבְּרָכָה֙ עַל־הַ֣ר גְּרִזִ֔ים וְאֶת־הַקְּלָלָ֖ה עַל־הַ֥ר עֵיבָֽל: ל הֲלֹא־הֵ֜מָּה בְּעֵ֣בֶר הַיַּרְדֵּ֗ן אַֽחֲרֵי֙ דֶּ֚רֶךְ מְב֣וֹא הַשֶּׁ֔מֶשׁ בְּאֶ֙רֶץ֙ הַֽכְּנַעֲנִ֔י הַיֹּשֵׁ֖ב בָּֽעֲרָבָ֑ה מ֚וּל הַגִּלְגָּ֔ל אֵ֖צֶל אֵֽלוֹנֵ֥י מֹרֶֽה: לא כִּ֤י אַתֶּם֙ עֹֽבְרִ֣ים אֶת־הַיַּרְדֵּ֔ן לָבֹא֙ לָרֶ֣שֶׁת אֶת־הָאָ֔רֶץ אֲשֶׁר־יְהֹוָ֥ה אֱלֹֽהֵיכֶ֖ם נֹתֵ֣ן לָכֶ֑ם וִֽירִשְׁתֶּ֥ם אֹתָ֖הּ וִֽישַׁבְתֶּם־בָּֽהּ: לב וּשְׁמַרְתֶּ֣ם לַֽעֲשׂ֔וֹת אֵ֥ת כָּל־הַֽחֻקִּ֖ים וְאֶת־הַמִּשְׁפָּטִ֑ים אֲשֶׁ֧ר אָֽנֹכִ֛י נֹתֵ֥ן לִפְנֵיכֶ֖ם הַיּֽוֹם: יב א אֵ֠לֶּה הַֽחֻקִּ֣ים וְהַמִּשְׁפָּטִים֮ אֲשֶׁ֣ר תִּשְׁמְר֣וּן לַֽעֲשׂוֹת֒ בָּאָ֕רֶץ אֲשֶׁר֩ נָתַ֨ן יְהֹוָ֜ה אֱלֹהֵ֧י אֲבֹתֶ֛יךָ לְךָ֖ לְרִשְׁתָּ֑הּ כָּל־הַ֨יָּמִ֔ים אֲשֶׁר־אַתֶּ֥ם חַיִּ֖ים עַל־הָֽאֲדָמָֽה: ב אַבֵּ֣ד תְּ֠אַבְּד֠וּן אֶת־כָּל־הַמְּקֹמ֞וֹת אֲשֶׁ֧ר עָֽבְדוּ־שָׁ֣ם הַגּוֹיִ֗ם אֲשֶׁ֤ר אַתֶּם֙ יֹֽרְשִׁ֣ים אֹתָ֔ם אֶת־אֱלֹֽהֵיהֶ֑ם עַל־הֶֽהָרִ֤ים הָֽרָמִים֙ וְעַל־הַגְּבָע֔וֹת וְתַ֖חַת כָּל־עֵ֥ץ רַֽעֲנָֽן:

---

the north side, is steep and barren. Mount Ebal is about 2900 feet high, a little higher than Mount Gerizim. . . . These two mountains, located side by side, present the most striking, instructive visualization of a blessing and a curse. Both of them rise from the same soil, both are watered by the same precipitation—rain and dew. The same air passes over them both; the same pollen is blown over them both. Yet Ebal remains starkly barren, while Gerizim is covered with lush vegetation to its very top. Thus we see that blessings and curses are not dependent on external circumstances—but on the manner in which we react to these circumstances. Hence, whether we are blessed or cursed is not dependent on the superficial conditions that are imposed upon us, but on how we deal with them—on our attitude toward that which should bring us blessings.

As we cross the Jordan and take our first steps upon the soil of the Law that hallows us, the sight of these two mountains presents us with the eternal lesson that we are always faced with a choice between blessings and curses, and that we ourselves, by our own moral conduct, can decide which of the two will symbolize our own future—Mount Gerizim or Mount Ebal. . . .

* * *

31 and 32. . . . One of your first acts when you take

possession of the land should be to acknowledge that whether or not you will have a happy future there will depend on whether or not you observe the laws of God. For (כִּי) you are receiving the land only in order that you fulfill these laws. This is the only purpose for which you will be permitted to take possession of the land.

* * *

CHAPTER XII

1. *These are the statutes.* This is the actual beginning of the compendium of laws pertinent to Israel's possession of the land. . . .

2. *You shall utterly destroy.* Your very first task is to cleanse the land of every trace of polytheism. The land is to become the soil of the One sole God and His Law: it must therefore not bear any reminders of philosophies or ideologies opposed to Him.

every verdant tree. עֵץ רַעֲנָן could denote a tree that can be expected to keep its foliage *permanently*; i.e., an evergreen tree. This would indicate that the heathens favored as sites for their idolatrous practices particularly those places where the power of nature seemed especially obvious.

altars and break up their memorial stones, and you shall burn their sacred trees in fire and cut down the images of their gods; you shall obliterate their name from that place. 4. You must not do any such thing to *God,* your God;   5. but toward the place that *God,* your God, will choose from among all your tribes, to give His Name a habitation there, shall you [turn to] search for the manifestation of His Presence so that you may come there.   6. And it is there that you shall bring your ascent offerings and your meal offerings, your tithes and the uplifted donation of your hand, your pledges and dedicated things, the firstlings of your cattle and of your sheep. 7. There, before *God,* shall you eat and rejoice in all that which is at your hand's disposal; you and your households, [rejoicing] that *God,* your God, has blessed you. 8. Meanwhile, you must not do all that which we are doing here today, each individual doing only that which accords with his [own] desire.   9. For you will not yet have come to the rest and to the inheritance that *God,* your God, is giving you.   10. But once you have passed over the Yarden, and you dwell in the land that *God,* your God, is giving you as an inheritance, and He has

ג וְנִתַּצְתֶּם אֶת־מִזְבְּחֹתָם וְשִׁבַּרְתֶּם אֶת־
מַצֵּבֹתָם וַאֲשֵׁרֵיהֶם תִּשְׂרְפוּן בָּאֵשׁ וּפְסִילֵי
אֱלֹהֵיהֶם תְּגַדֵּעוּן וְאִבַּדְתֶּם אֶת־שְׁמָם מִן־
הַמָּקוֹם הַהוּא: ד לֹא־תַעֲשׂוּן כֵּן לַיהוָה
אֱלֹהֵיכֶם: ה כִּי אִם־אֶל־הַמָּקוֹם אֲשֶׁר־יִבְחַר
יְהוָה אֱלֹהֵיכֶם מִכָּל־שִׁבְטֵיכֶם לָשׂוּם אֶת־שְׁמוֹ
שָׁם לְשִׁכְנוֹ תִדְרְשׁוּ וּבָאתָ שָׁמָּה: ו וַהֲבֵאתֶם
שָׁמָּה עֹלֹתֵיכֶם וְזִבְחֵיכֶם וְאֵת מַעְשְׂרֹתֵיכֶם וְאֵת
תְּרוּמַת יֶדְכֶם וְנִדְרֵיכֶם וְנִדְבֹתֵיכֶם וּבְכֹרֹת
בְּקַרְכֶם וְצֹאנְכֶם: ז וַאֲכַלְתֶּם־שָׁם לִפְנֵי יְהוָה
אֱלֹהֵיכֶם וּשְׂמַחְתֶּם בְּכֹל מִשְׁלַח יֶדְכֶם אַתֶּם
וּבָתֵּיכֶם אֲשֶׁר בֵּרַכְךָ יְהוָה אֱלֹהֶיךָ: ח לֹא
תַעֲשׂוּן כְּכֹל אֲשֶׁר אֲנַחְנוּ עֹשִׂים פֹּה הַיּוֹם אִישׁ
כָּל־הַיָּשָׁר בְּעֵינָיו: ט כִּי לֹא־בָאתֶם עַד־עָתָּה
אֶל־הַמְּנוּחָה וְאֶל־הַנַּחֲלָה אֲשֶׁר־יְהוָה אֱלֹהֶיךָ
נֹתֵן לָךְ: י וַעֲבַרְתֶּם אֶת־הַיַּרְדֵּן וִישַׁבְתֶּם בָּאָרֶץ
אֲשֶׁר־יְהוָה אֱלֹהֵיכֶם מַנְחִיל אֶתְכֶם וְהֵנִיחַ לָכֶם

---

4. *You must not do any such thing.* Even as you must eradicate the very last traces of idolatry, so, conversely, you must not destroy even the least of anything that is associated with the Name of God or is consecrated to Him. . . .

5. *but toward.* Not only are you forbidden to destroy anything that bears the Name of your God, but the place which God will choose to bear His Name must become the central point to be honored by all of you, and to summon you as a nation to rally around God and the Law of His will. At the same time, we are told here, that contrary to the practice of the nations whose places of idol worship in the land of the Jews are now to be destroyed, the selection of the particular place that is to bear the Name of our God is not subject to our personal preferences, but solely to the express choice to be made by God Himself. It is not we who are to dedicate a place to God; it is He Who will indicate to us the site He has chosen as His holy place, the place in which we are to rally around Him and His Sanctuary.

         o   o   o

7. *There . . . shall you eat . . . and rejoice.* Such feasting and such joy of living before the Countenance of God, in the proximity of the Sanctuary—of His Law— the center for the Jewish "worship of God"—is a basic characteristic of Judaism. Judaism differs in this respect not only from ancient paganism, whose deities, creations of fear, are inimical to good cheer and to human happiness, but just as sharply from the modern perversions that attempt to split the human personality and preach that God's nearness can be attained only through the spirit, while the physical aspects of life are regarded as low and profane. . . .

that God, your God, has blessed you. The quintessence of your rejoicing lies in the fact that you are permitted to regard everything you possess as a blessing from God and thus as a sign of His favor. The feeling that one enjoys God's favor is the purest form of joy in life. It cannot be won by egoism, but only in association with the community; by the awareness that the individual can seek and find his own happiness only in conjunction with that of his entire community. Hence [the shift from the plural to the singular form of

given you rest from all your enemies round
about, and you will dwell in safety,
11. then that place which *God*, your God,
will choose, to let His Name rest there—
there shall you bring all that concerning
which I am obligating you: your ascent
offerings and your meal offerings, your
tithes and the uplifted donation of your
hand, and all the choice of your pledges that
you pledge to *God*.   12. And you will then
rejoice before *God*, your God; you, your
sons and your daughters, your manservants
and your handmaids and the Levite who
dwells within your gates, because he has
no portion and no inheritance among you.
13. Take heed to yourself that you do not
offer your ascent offerings at any place that
you see,   14. but at the place that *God*
will choose in one of your tribes; *there* you
shall offer your ascent offerings, and there
you shall carry out everything that I
command you.   15. However, you may
slaughter and eat the meat according to all
the desire of your will, according to the
blessing that *God*, your God, has given you
within all your gates; that which [both] the
unclean and the [ritually] pure may eat,
such as the deer and the doe.   16. Only
the blood you may not eat; you shall pour it
out upon the ground like water.   17. You
are not at unrestricted liberty to eat within
your gates the tithe of your grain, of your
new wine and of your oil; the firstlings of
your cattle and of your sheep, and all your
pledges you have made; your dedicated
things and the uplifted donation of your
hand.   18. But before *God*, your God,
shall you eat it in the place that *God*, your
God, will choose; you and your son and your
daughter, your manservant and your handmaid and the Levite who dwells within
your gates; and you shall rejoice before
God, your God, with all that over which
your hand has authority.   19. Take heed to

מִכָּל־אֹיְבֵיכֶם מִסָּבִיב וִישַׁבְתֶּם־בֶּֽטַח: שני
יא וְהָיָה הַמָּקוֹם אֲשֶׁר־יִבְחַר יְהוָֹה אֱלֹהֵיכֶם
בּוֹ לְשַׁכֵּן שְׁמוֹ שָׁם שָׁמָּה תָבִיאוּ אֵת כָּל־אֲשֶׁר
אָנֹכִי מְצַוֶּה אֶתְכֶם עוֹלֹתֵיכֶם וְזִבְחֵיכֶם
מַעְשְׂרֹתֵיכֶם וּתְרֻמַת יֶדְכֶם וְכֹל מִבְחַר נִדְרֵיכֶם
אֲשֶׁר תִּדְּרוּ לַֽיהֹוָה: יב וּשְׂמַחְתֶּם לִפְנֵי יְהוָֹה
אֱלֹהֵיכֶם אַתֶּם וּבְנֵיכֶם וּבְנֹתֵיכֶם וְעַבְדֵיכֶם
וְאַמְהֹתֵיכֶם וְהַלֵּוִי אֲשֶׁר בְּשַׁעֲרֵיכֶם כִּי אֵין לוֹ
חֵלֶק וְנַחֲלָה אִתְּכֶם: יג הִשָּׁמֶר לְךָ פֶּן־תַּעֲלֶה
עֹלֹתֶיךָ בְּכָל־מָקוֹם אֲשֶׁר תִּרְאֶה: יד כִּי אִם־
בַּמָּקוֹם אֲשֶׁר־יִבְחַר יְהֹוָה בְּאַחַד שְׁבָטֶיךָ שָׁם
תַּעֲלֶה עֹלֹתֶיךָ וְשָׁם תַּעֲשֶׂה כֹּל אֲשֶׁר אָנֹכִי
מְצַוֶּךָּ: טו רַק בְּכָל־אַוַּת נַפְשְׁךָ תִּזְבַּח | וְאָכַלְתָּ
בָשָׂר כְּבִרְכַּת יְהֹוָה אֱלֹהֶיךָ אֲשֶׁר נָתַן־לְךָ בְּכָל־
שְׁעָרֶיךָ הַטָּמֵא וְהַטָּהוֹר יֹאכְלֶנּוּ כַּצְּבִי וְכָאַיָּל:
טז רַק הַדָּם לֹא תֹאכֵלוּ עַל־הָאָרֶץ תִּשְׁפְּכֶנּוּ
כַּמָּיִם: יז לֹא־תוּכַל לֶאֱכֹל בִּשְׁעָרֶיךָ מַעְשַׂר
דְּגָנְךָ וְתִירֹשְׁךָ וְיִצְהָרֶךָ וּבְכֹרֹת בְּקָרְךָ וְצֹאנֶךָ
וְכָל־נְדָרֶיךָ אֲשֶׁר תִּדֹּר וְנִדְבֹתֶיךָ וּתְרוּמַת יָדֶךָ:
יח כִּי אִם־לִפְנֵי יְהוָֹה אֱלֹהֶיךָ תֹּאכְלֶנּוּ בַּמָּקוֹם
אֲשֶׁר יִבְחַר יְהוָֹה אֱלֹהֶיךָ בּוֹ אַתָּה וּבִנְךָ וּבִתֶּךָ
וְעַבְדְּךָ וַאֲמָתֶךָ וְהַלֵּוִי אֲשֶׁר בִּשְׁעָרֶיךָ וְשָׂמַחְתָּ
לִפְנֵי יְהוָֹה אֱלֹהֶיךָ בְּכֹל מִשְׁלַח יָדֶךָ: יט הִשָּׁמֶר

---

address]: וּשְׂמַחְתֶּם ["shall you (*plu.*) rejoice"], אֲשֶׁר בֵּרַכְךָ
["that *God*, your (*sing.*) God, has blessed you (*sing.*)"].

10–11. *But once you have passed over . . . and you
dwell . . . and you will dwell in safety.* The selection of
a site for the Sanctuary of God's Law, to be the nation's

stationary rallying point for all time, is cited as the
act that will crown Israel's complete occupation of the
land.

19. *Take heed to yourself.* (See Verse 12). Now
that the nation is about to settle down and disperse in

yourself that you do not forsake the Levite all your days on your soil.   20. When *God,* your God, will extend your territory as He has promised you, and you will say: "I want to eat meat," because your will craves to eat meat, then you may eat meat according to all the desire of your will,   21. because the place that *God,* your God, will choose, to give His Name a habitation there, will be far away from you; you shall slaughter of your cattle and of your sheep that *God* has given you, in the manner that I have commanded you, and you shall eat within your gates, according to all the desire of your will.   22. However, as the deer and the doe is eaten, so shall you eat it; the unclean and the pure may eat it together.   23. Only remain firm not to eat the blood; for the blood, it is the soul. Also, do not eat the soul with the flesh.   24. Do not eat it! Pour it out upon the ground like

לְךָ פֶּן־תַּעֲזֹב אֶת־הַלֵּוִי כָּל־יָמֶיךָ עַל־אַדְמָתֶךָ: ס כ כִּי־יַרְחִיב יְהוָֹה אֱלֹהֶיךָ אֶת־גְּבֻלְךָ כַּאֲשֶׁר דִּבֶּר־לָךְ וְאָמַרְתָּ אֹכְלָה בָשָׂר כִּי־תְאַוֶּה נַפְשְׁךָ לֶאֱכֹל בָּשָׂר בְּכָל־אַוַּת נַפְשְׁךָ תֹּאכַל בָּשָׂר: כא כִּי־יִרְחַק מִמְּךָ הַמָּקוֹם אֲשֶׁר יִבְחַר יְהוָֹה אֱלֹהֶיךָ לָשׂוּם שְׁמוֹ שָׁם וְזָבַחְתָּ מִבְּקָרְךָ וּמִצֹּאנְךָ אֲשֶׁר נָתַן יְהוָֹה לְךָ כַּאֲשֶׁר צִוִּיתִךָ וְאָכַלְתָּ בִּשְׁעָרֶיךָ בְּכֹל אַוַּת נַפְשֶׁךָ: כב אַךְ כַּאֲשֶׁר יֵאָכֵל אֶת־הַצְּבִי וְאֶת־הָאַיָּל כֵּן תֹּאכְלֶנּוּ הַטָּמֵא וְהַטָּהוֹר יַחְדָּו יֹאכְלֶנּוּ: כג רַק חֲזַק לְבִלְתִּי אֲכֹל הַדָּם כִּי הַדָּם הוּא הַנָּפֶשׁ וְלֹא־תֹאכַל הַנֶּפֶשׁ עִם־הַבָּשָׂר: כד לֹא תֹּאכְלֶנּוּ עַל־הָאָרֶץ תִּשְׁפְּכֶנּוּ כַּמָּיִם: כה לֹא תֹּאכְלֶנּוּ

---

its own land, the fact that the Levites will live scattered among the people is of great significance. The Levites will act as the vital nerves and arteries, as it were, emanating from the center that is the Sanctuary, maintaining the spiritual links between the members of the nation and the Sanctuary that represents the nation's brain and heart. The Levites are to be the exponents of the Sanctuary of the Law in the midst of the people. But in the midst of a population engaged in agriculture, cattle-breeding and other industries relating to these pursuits, such "unproductive" members of the community as the Levites could easily come to be neglected and despised. The people might fail to appreciate the vital role of the Levites in their spiritual and moral welfare as a nation. Hence the reiterated admonition not to neglect the Levite all your days upon your soil. How long you will be permitted to dwell upon your own soil will depend essentially on the respect you will accord to the Levites and on the extent to which you will permit the Levites to influence your own moral and spiritual development.

21. because the place ... will be far away ... you shall slaughter ... in the manner that I have commanded you. Until now, cattle and sheep could be slaughtered only in the forecourt of the Tent of Appointed Meeting, and thus under the supervision of the priests. But once the people will dwell in their land, they will be permitted to eat meat whenever they desire to do so, so that the observance of the laws pertaining to slaughter will be left to the personal conscience of each individual. Therefore, the admonition to observe the

laws of שְׁחִיטָה [ritual slaughter] quite properly belongs into this compendium of laws set forth in מִשְׁנֵה תּוֹרָה [the Book of Deuteronomy; lit., "the repetition of the Law," given to the nation as it is about to enter its land]. The regulations concerning the method of slaughter to which reference is made in the present verse are not set forth in the Written Law; they are part of those laws which remained unwritten—תּוֹרָה שֶׁבְּעַל פֶּה—and to which reference is expressly made in this verse ["in the manner that I have commanded you"]. . . .

      o   o   o

23. *Only remain firm.* This particularly impressive admonition which precedes the prohibition against eating blood attests to the great importance that the Law attaches to its observance. At the same time, it demonstrates the full extent of the peril that the eating of animal blood poses to man's spiritual nature in relation to the moral mission which the Law expects the Jewish individual to perform. . . . Now with Israel's settlement in the land, the permission to eat meat whenever one so desired was about to go into effect, and the observance of the laws pertaining to its preparation was left to the conscience of each individual. Therefore, this point in the text was considered the proper place for setting forth, once again, in all solemnity, the warning against eating blood and against the danger of falling back into the heathen lusts and superstitions associated with this practice. . . .

      o   o   o

24-25. *Pour it out upon the ground like water.* As

water.   25. Do not eat it! So that it may go
well with you and with your children after
you; for you will be doing that which is
[up]right in the eyes of *God*.   26. Only
your holy things that will be yours and your
pledges shall you take up and go to the
place that *God* will choose.   27. And you
shall offer your ascent offerings in [the form
of] the meat and the blood upon the altar of
God, your God; and the blood of your meal
offerings shall be poured out upon the altar
of *God*, your God, but you shall eat the
meat.   28. Listen with care to all these words
that I command you, so that it may go well
with you and your children after you forever; for you will be doing that which is
good and [up]right in the eyes of *God*, your
God.   29. When *God*, your God, will cut
off the nations to which you will come, to
drive them away before you, and you will
succeed them in the possession and will
dwell in their land,   30. then take heed to
yourself that you do not let yourself be
drawn to follow them, after they were
destroyed before you, and that you do not
inquire after their deities and say: "How do
these nations serve their gods? I will do
likewise."   31. You must not do so, also
not to *God*, your God; for everything that is
detested by *God*, that He hates, have they
done to their gods; for they burn even their
sons and daughters in the fire for their gods!

לְמַ֨עַן֙ יִיטַ֣ב לְךָ֔ וּלְבָנֶ֥יךָ אַחֲרֶ֖יךָ כִּֽי־תַעֲשֶׂ֥ה הַיָּשָׁ֖ר
בְּעֵינֵ֥י יְהוָֽה: כו רַ֣ק קָֽדָשֶׁ֧יךָ אֲשֶׁר־יִהְי֛וּ לְךָ֖
וּנְדָרֶ֑יךָ תִּשָּׂ֣א וּבָ֔אתָ אֶל־הַמָּק֖וֹם אֲשֶׁר־יִבְחַ֥ר
יְהוָֽה: כז וְעָשִׂ֤יתָ עֹלֹתֶ֙יךָ֙ הַבָּשָׂ֣ר וְהַדָּ֔ם עַל־
מִזְבַּ֖ח יְהוָ֣ה אֱלֹהֶ֑יךָ וְדַם־זְבָחֶ֗יךָ יִשָּׁפֵךְ֙ עַל־
מִזְבַּח֙ יְהוָ֣ה אֱלֹהֶ֔יךָ וְהַבָּשָׂ֖ר תֹּאכֵֽל: כח שְׁמֹ֣ר
וְשָׁמַעְתָּ֗ אֵ֚ת כָּל־הַדְּבָרִ֣ים הָאֵ֔לֶּה אֲשֶׁ֥ר אָנֹכִ֖י
מְצַוֶּ֑ךָּ לְמַ֨עַן֙ יִיטַ֣ב לְךָ֗ וּלְבָנֶ֤יךָ אַחֲרֶ֙יךָ֙ עַד־עוֹלָ֔ם
כִּ֤י תַעֲשֶׂה֙ הַטּ֣וֹב וְהַיָּשָׁ֔ר בְּעֵינֵ֖י יְהוָ֥ה אֱלֹהֶֽיךָ: ס
שלישי כט כִּֽי־יַכְרִ֞ית יְהוָ֤ה אֱלֹהֶ֙יךָ֙ אֶת־הַגּוֹיִ֔ם
אֲשֶׁ֨ר אַתָּ֥ה בָא־שָׁ֛מָּה לָרֶ֥שֶׁת אוֹתָ֖ם מִפָּנֶ֑יךָ
וְיָרַשְׁתָּ֣ אֹתָ֔ם וְיָשַׁבְתָּ֖ בְּאַרְצָֽם: ל הִשָּׁ֣מֶר לְךָ֗ פֶּן־
תִּנָּקֵשׁ֙ אַחֲרֵיהֶ֔ם אַחֲרֵ֖י הִשָּׁמְדָ֣ם מִפָּנֶ֑יךָ וּפֶן־
תִּדְרֹ֨שׁ לֵאלֹֽהֵיהֶ֜ם לֵאמֹ֗ר אֵיכָ֨ה יַעַבְד֜וּ הַגּוֹיִ֤ם
הָאֵ֙לֶּה֙ אֶת־אֱלֹ֣הֵיהֶ֔ם וְאֶעֱשֶׂה־כֵּ֖ן גַּם־אָֽנִי׃
לֹא־תַעֲשֶׂ֣ה כֵ֔ן לַיהוָ֖ה אֱלֹהֶ֑יךָ כִּ֣י כָל־תּֽוֹעֲבַ֣ת
יְהוָ֗ה אֲשֶׁ֤ר שָׂנֵא֙ עָשׂ֣וּ לֵֽאלֹהֵיהֶ֔ם כִּ֣י גַ֤ם אֶת־
בְּנֵיהֶם֙ וְאֶת־בְּנֹ֣תֵיהֶ֔ם יִשְׂרְפ֥וּ בָאֵ֖שׁ לֵאלֹהֵיהֶֽם:

opposed to the heathen practice, you must not ascribe
any value to blood and must not perform any
superstitious rites with it.

° ° °

29. The clearing away of every trace of pagan
excesses from the land of which Israel is about to take
possession; the total devotion of all the new inhabitants
of the land to the habitation of God, the Sanctuary of
the Law, the center that is to unite them all; the observance of the laws pertaining to ritual slaughter and the
prohibition against eating blood, which are to ensure
that both the physical and moral tendencies of all the
individual members of the nation will be directed
toward the pursuit of the goals set by the Law: these
subjects formed the content of the present chapter thus
far. Now, before the compendium of the Law intended
for the member of the nation as they are about to
disperse in their land proceeds to enumerate the
remainder of the dietary laws that belong here, we are

warned against four spiritual and social influences that
could divert the individual members of the Jewish
nation from the ways of God and His Law: reminders of
the pagan ways of the previous inhabitants of the land;
the influence of superior intellects; the influence of
family relationships and the influence of self-important
fellow citizens.

31. *You must not do so.* Not only are you forbidden to perform such rituals to worship their gods,
but it is a crime to perform these rites even before God,
the One sole God, with the intention of worshipping
Him. For the spirit in which the pagans worship their
deities is in direct opposition to the things that are
pleasing to your God, even as your God represents
the complete negation of their gods. Your God is a God
of life, while the gods of their delusion are gods of
death. The gods of their delusion gloat over death and
destruction, while your God delights in exaltation
and rejuvenation.

XIII

1. Everything that I command you, you shall carry out punctiliously; you must not add anything to it nor subtract anything from it. 2. If there arises among you a prophet or a receiver of dreams, and he gives you a sign or a convincing manifestation, 3. and the sign or the convincing manifestation comes to pass, [that] which he uttered for you, to say to you: "Let us go after other gods whom you do not know, and let us serve them," 4. then do not hearken to the words of that prophet or of that receiver of dreams, because *God,* your God, is testing you with this to know whether you truly love *God,* your God, with all your heart and with all your soul. 5. After *God,* your God, shall you walk, and Him shall you fear, and His commandments shall you keep and to His voice shall you hearken, and Him shall you serve and to Him shall you hold fast. 6. And that prophet or that receiver of dreams shall be put to death, for he has uttered untruth concerning *God,* your God, Who brought you out from the land of Mitzrayim, and Who delivered you from the home of slaves, to lead you away from the path in which *God,* your God, commanded you to walk; so shall you clear away the evil from your midst. 7. If your brother, a son of your mother, or your son, or your daughter, or the wife of your bosom, or your friend who is like your [own] soul, should try to entice you in secret [as follows]: "Let us go and serve other gods," of whom you have experienced nothing, neither you nor your parents, 8. of the gods of the peoples that are round about you, that are near to you, or that are far away from you—from [one] end of the earth to [the other] end of the earth— 9. then do not consent to him and do not hearken to him, and your eye must not cherish pity for him; neither shall you show him mercy or keep silent concerning him. 10. Rather you [yourself] must bring him to be put to death; your [own] hand shall be the first upon him to kill him, and the hand of the entire people afterwards. 11. You shall stone him so that he dies, for he sought to lead you away from *God,* your God, Who brought you out from the land of Mitzrayim, from the home of slaves. 12. And all of Yisrael shall hear it and be afraid and never again commit such wicked-

יג א אֵת כָּל־הַדָּבָר אֲשֶׁר אָנֹכִי מְצַוֶּה אֶתְכֶם אֹתוֹ תִשְׁמְרוּ לַעֲשׂוֹת לֹא־תֹסֵף עָלָיו וְלֹא תִגְרַע מִמֶּנּוּ: פ ב כִּי־יָקוּם בְּקִרְבְּךָ נָבִיא אוֹ חֹלֵם חֲלוֹם וְנָתַן אֵלֶיךָ אוֹת אוֹ מוֹפֵת: ג וּבָא הָאוֹת וְהַמּוֹפֵת אֲשֶׁר־דִּבֶּר אֵלֶיךָ לֵאמֹר נֵלְכָה אַחֲרֵי אֱלֹהִים אֲחֵרִים אֲשֶׁר לֹא־יְדַעְתָּם וְנָעָבְדֵם: ד לֹא תִשְׁמַע אֶל־דִּבְרֵי הַנָּבִיא הַהוּא אוֹ אֶל־חוֹלֵם הַחֲלוֹם הַהוּא כִּי מְנַסֶּה יְהֹוָה אֱלֹהֵיכֶם אֶתְכֶם לָדַעַת הֲיִשְׁכֶם אֹהֲבִים אֶת־יְהֹוָה אֱלֹהֵיכֶם בְּכָל־לְבַבְכֶם וּבְכָל־נַפְשְׁכֶם: ה אַחֲרֵי יְהֹוָה אֱלֹהֵיכֶם תֵּלֵכוּ וְאֹתוֹ תִירָאוּ וְאֶת־מִצְוֹתָיו תִּשְׁמֹרוּ וּבְקֹלוֹ תִשְׁמָעוּ וְאֹתוֹ תַעֲבֹדוּ וּבוֹ תִדְבָּקוּן: ו וְהַנָּבִיא הַהוּא אוֹ חֹלֵם הַחֲלוֹם הַהוּא יוּמָת כִּי דִבֶּר־סָרָה עַל־יְהֹוָה אֱלֹהֵיכֶם הַמּוֹצִיא אֶתְכֶם ׀ מֵאֶרֶץ מִצְרַיִם וְהַפֹּדְךָ מִבֵּית עֲבָדִים לְהַדִּיחֲךָ מִן־הַדֶּרֶךְ אֲשֶׁר צִוְּךָ יְהֹוָה אֱלֹהֶיךָ לָלֶכֶת בָּהּ וּבִעַרְתָּ הָרָע מִקִּרְבֶּךָ: ס ז כִּי יְסִיתְךָ אָחִיךָ בֶן־אִמֶּךָ אוֹ־בִנְךָ אוֹ־בִתְּךָ אוֹ ׀ אֵשֶׁת חֵיקֶךָ אוֹ רֵעֲךָ אֲשֶׁר כְּנַפְשְׁךָ בַּסֵּתֶר לֵאמֹר נֵלְכָה וְנַעַבְדָה אֱלֹהִים אֲחֵרִים אֲשֶׁר לֹא יָדַעְתָּ אַתָּה וַאֲבֹתֶיךָ: ח מֵאֱלֹהֵי הָעַמִּים אֲשֶׁר סְבִיבֹתֵיכֶם הַקְּרֹבִים אֵלֶיךָ אוֹ הָרְחֹקִים מִמֶּךָּ מִקְצֵה הָאָרֶץ וְעַד־קְצֵה הָאָרֶץ: ט לֹא־תֹאבֶה לוֹ וְלֹא תִשְׁמַע אֵלָיו וְלֹא־תָחוֹס עֵינְךָ עָלָיו וְלֹא־תַחְמֹל וְלֹא־תְכַסֶּה עָלָיו: י כִּי הָרֹג תַּהַרְגֶנּוּ יָדְךָ תִּהְיֶה־בּוֹ בָרִאשׁוֹנָה לַהֲמִיתוֹ וְיַד כָּל־הָעָם בָּאַחֲרֹנָה: יא וּסְקַלְתּוֹ בָאֲבָנִים וָמֵת כִּי בִקֵּשׁ לְהַדִּיחֲךָ מֵעַל יְהֹוָה אֱלֹהֶיךָ הַמּוֹצִיאֲךָ מֵאֶרֶץ מִצְרַיִם מִבֵּית עֲבָדִים: יב וְכָל־יִשְׂרָאֵל יִשְׁמְעוּ וְיִרָאוּן וְלֹא־יוֹסִפוּ לַעֲשׂוֹת כַּדָּבָר הָרָע

ness in your midst. 13. If you should hear
[it said as follows] in one of your cities that
God, your God, is giving you to dwell there:
14. "Worthless men have come forth from
your midst and have led the inhabitants
of their city astray, by saying: 'Let us go
and serve other gods, of whom you know
nothing,'" 15. then you shall inquire
and probe and question diligently, and if it
is true—if the assertion is founded on fact—
that this depravity has [indeed] occurred in
your midst, 16. then you shall strike
down the inhabitants of that city with the
edge of the sword; it, and all that is in it,
and its livestock you shall destroy with the
edge of the sword as something banned.
17. You shall pile up all its spoil in its market place, and you shall burn completely
in fire the city and all its spoil, for the sake
of *God*, your God; it shall remain an eternal
heap of rubble; never again shall it be
rebuilt. 18. Not the least of the banned
[things] shall adhere to your hand, so that
God may turn back from the fierceness of
His anger, grant you mercy, love you with
compassion and multiply you as He has
sworn to your fathers, 19. if you will
hearken to the voice of *God*, your God, to
keep all His commandments that I command
you today, to do that which is [up]right in
the eyes of *God*, your God.

XIV 1. You are sons of *God*, your
God; do not cut yourselves
and do not put a bald spot between your

הַזֶּה בְּקִרְבֶּךָ: ס יג כִּי־תִשְׁמַע בְּאַחַת עָרֶיךָ
אֲשֶׁר יְהוָה אֱלֹהֶיךָ נֹתֵן לְךָ לָשֶׁבֶת שָׁם לֵאמֹר:
יד יָצְאוּ אֲנָשִׁים בְּנֵי־בְלִיַּעַל מִקִּרְבֶּךָ וַיַּדִּיחוּ
אֶת־יֹשְׁבֵי עִירָם לֵאמֹר נֵלְכָה וְנַעַבְדָה אֱלֹהִים
אֲחֵרִים אֲשֶׁר לֹא־יְדַעְתֶּם: טו וְדָרַשְׁתָּ וְחָקַרְתָּ
וְשָׁאַלְתָּ הֵיטֵב וְהִנֵּה אֱמֶת נָכוֹן הַדָּבָר נֶעֶשְׂתָה
הַתּוֹעֵבָה הַזֹּאת בְּקִרְבֶּךָ: טז הַכֵּה תַכֶּה אֶת־
יֹשְׁבֵי הָעִיר הַהִוא לְפִי־חָרֶב הַחֲרֵם אֹתָהּ וְאֶת־
כָּל־אֲשֶׁר־בָּהּ וְאֶת־בְּהֶמְתָּהּ לְפִי־חָרֶב: יז וְאֶת־
כָּל־שְׁלָלָהּ תִּקְבֹּץ אֶל־תּוֹךְ רְחֹבָהּ וְשָׂרַפְתָּ בָאֵשׁ
אֶת־הָעִיר וְאֶת־כָּל־שְׁלָלָהּ כָּלִיל לַיהוָה אֱלֹהֶיךָ
וְהָיְתָה תֵּל עוֹלָם לֹא תִבָּנֶה עוֹד: יח וְלֹא־יִדְבַּק
בְּיָדְךָ מְאוּמָה מִן־הַחֵרֶם לְמַעַן יָשׁוּב יְהוָה
מֵחֲרוֹן אַפּוֹ וְנָתַן־לְךָ רַחֲמִים וְרִחַמְךָ וְהִרְבֶּךָ
כַּאֲשֶׁר נִשְׁבַּע לַאֲבֹתֶיךָ: יט כִּי תִשְׁמַע בְּקוֹל
יְהוָה אֱלֹהֶיךָ לִשְׁמֹר אֶת־כָּל־מִצְוֹתָיו אֲשֶׁר
אָנֹכִי מְצַוְּךָ הַיּוֹם לַעֲשׂוֹת הַיָּשָׁר בְּעֵינֵי יְהוָה
אֱלֹהֶיךָ: ס רביעי יד א בָּנִים אַתֶּם לַיהוָה
אֱלֹהֵיכֶם לֹא תִתְגֹּדְדוּ וְלֹא־תָשִׂימוּ קָרְחָה בֵּין

CHAPTER XIII

13–19. The intent of the two preceding laws is to combat those prophets, relatives or friends, who misuse their influence on you by seeking to entice you away from God. These laws are now followed by instructions for dealing with individuals who would exploit their social position to lure an entire community away from God. . . .

° ° °

CHAPTER XIV

1. The preceding chapter dealt with the adverse influence that can be exerted on us by one who has attained eminence through his intellectual gifts or his social position—a false prophet or a citizen who leads the population of an entire community astray—or by one who is as dear to us as a relative or friend, to lead us astray from our loyalty to God. Intellectual gifts, social position, ties of blood or friendship—all these must cease to exist for us if they are exploited as tools to lead us astray from God.

In close logical association with the foregoing, the present chapter opens with laws which, in essence, were already set down in the Third Book [Leviticus] (19:27, 28 and 21:5), but which are reiterated at this point because they have particular significance now that the nation is about to disperse in its land.

We have already noted variously to Leviticus that the prohibition against making a wound in one's flesh or a bald spot upon one's head as a sign of mourning is intended to preserve the respect that every individual

eyes for a dead [person]. 2. For you are a
holy people to *God*, your God, and it is you
that *God* has chosen to be a people belonging exclusively to Him, from among all the
[other] nations that are on the face of the
earth. 3. You shall not eat any abominable thing. 4. This is the livestock you
may eat: ox, lamb and kid. 5. Doe, deer
and *yaḥmur, akko, dishon, te'o* and *zemer.*

עֵינֵיכֶם לָמֵת: ב כִּי עַם קָדוֹשׁ אַתָּה לַיהוָה
אֱלֹהֶיךָ וּבְךָ בָּחַר יְהוָה לִהְיוֹת לוֹ לְעַם סְגֻלָּה
מִכֹּל הָעַמִּים אֲשֶׁר עַל־פְּנֵי הָאֲדָמָה: ס ג לֹא
תֹאכַל כָּל־תּוֹעֵבָה: ד זֹאת הַבְּהֵמָה אֲשֶׁר
תֹּאכֵלוּ שׁוֹר שֵׂה כְשָׂבִים וְשֵׂה עִזִּים: ה אַיָּל
וּצְבִי וְיַחְמוּר וְאַקּוֹ וְדִישֹׁן וּתְאוֹ וָזָמֶר: ו וְכָל־

should have for himself because of his awareness that he is bound directly to God. This is a sense of self-worth that he must maintain also in relation to all other persons, no matter how much he may love and honor them. No human being may have such a strong hold upon us or permit us to become so completely identified with him that if he ceases to exist we will feel compelled to throw away our own personality after him, because we will feel that, with his departure, we have, in fact, lost our own selves. Such an unjustifiable loss of self-esteem would be implied by our inflicting permanent injuries or bald spots upon our bodies. The preceding chapter pointed out how even our most sublime bond with God can be endangered by excessive devotion to persons who have won our love and respect.

Such a threat to our own relationship with God can arise all the more easily once the members of the nation have dispersed in their land. When they will dwell in small, scattered settlements, physically remote from the impact of the spiritual center, they will become more amenable to the influence of persons who impress them with their intellectual gifts or their social position.

It is therefore most significant that the Law at this point reiterates the prohibitions against making a wound in our flesh or a bald spot on our bodies, thus impressing upon all the people, no matter what their station, that "You are sons of *God*, your God." You are related to God before all else, and the bond that binds you to your God must take precedence over all your other spiritual and emotional ties (See note on Leviticus 19:28).

° ° °

2. כִּי עַם קָדוֹשׁ אַתָּה וגו׳ ***[For you are a holy people].*** Not גּוֹי קָדוֹשׁ ["a holy *nation*"] in terms of the unity they represent to the outside, but עַם קָדוֹשׁ ["a holy *people*"] united also within, in all their heterogeneous social structure. Each member of this national community, which is subordinate to God, is as holy as all the others, and his contact with God is as direct as that of all the others. Indeed, the very purpose for which you were chosen is that you should thus form a community of human beings belonging exclusively to God and base your communal life entirely on your subordination to Him. . . .

In Tractate Yebamoth 13b and 14a, the prohibition לֹא תִתְגֹּדְדוּ, "do not make any cuts upon your bodies," is interpreted as applicable also to the body of the nation as a whole, and we are told, "Do not cut yourselves apart into many factions." We are to remain united in the observance of the Law and not permit differences in the teaching and interpretation of the Law to "cut us apart" into dissenting communities. Note that the Hebrew term for a separate body of people, a military "detachment," is גְּדוּד. Hence לֹא תִתְגֹּדְדוּ can mean [not only, "Do not cut yourselves" but] also, "do not cut yourselves apart into factions."

° ° °

Accordingly, the purpose of the commandment set forth in this verse would be to admonish us not to permit differences of opinion in the interpretation of the Law, or in inferences to be drawn from the Law; to create schisms that would break up the community, with one faction following the exponents of one view and the other supporting the preachers of an opposing position . . . so that the one united community would be split into "many factions." Rather, all such differences of opinion should be settled in accordance with the rules provided by the Law itself for the arbitration of such disputes, and the practical observance of the Law should be kept uniform to the extent that the Law specifies these observances.

° ° °

Consider that all the preceding laws referred to the harm that can be done by the influence of certain individuals upon their immediate circles. Consider, too, that (as we believe) the prohibition against inflicting wounds upon one's flesh as a sign of mourning for the dead is intended to counteract precisely such an unjustified overvaluation of individual personalities. Finally, consider that the splitting into many factions against which the other interpretation of "do not cut yourselves" is intended symbolically to warn us, results primarily when people take the side of one or the other party in a dispute. If we consider all these factors, we believe that we will readily understand the close link between these two prohibitions, both of which are derived from לֹא תִתְגֹּדְדוּ.

6. And every animal that forms a hoof and cleaves it completely into two hooves and at the same time chews the cud among the animals, this you may eat. 7. But this you may not eat from among those that chew the cud and that are thus cloven-hoofed: the camel, the hare and the rabbit, because they chew the cud but have not formed a hoof; they are unclean to you. 8. And the pig, because it forms hooves but does not chew the cud; it is unclean to you; you shall not eat of their flesh nor touch their carcasses. 9. This you may eat of all that is in the water: whatever has fins and scales you may eat. 10. But whatever does not have fins and scales you may not eat; it is unclean to you. 11. You may eat any clean bird. 12. But this is [the grouping of] those of which you may not eat: the *nesher*, the *peres* and the *ozniyah*; 13. the *ra'ah*, the *ayah* and the *dayah*, according to their species; 14. any *orev* according to its species; 15. the *bat ha-yaanah*, the *taḥmas*, the *shaḥaf* and the *netz*, according to its species; 16. the *kos*, the *yanshuf* and the *tinshemet*; 17. the *ka'at* and the *raḥamah* and the *shalakh*; 18. the *ḥasidah* and the *anafah*, according to its species; the *dukhiphat* and the *atalef*. 19. Every winged creeping thing is unclean to you; they may not be eaten. 20. Any clean flying creature you may eat. 21. You shall not eat any carrion; you may give it to one who has come in from outside, who is within your gates, that he may eat it, or [you may] sell it to a foreigner, for you are a holy people to *God*, your God; you shall not cook a young in the milk of its mother. 22. Again and again you must

בְּהֵמָה מַפְרֶסֶת פַּרְסָה וְשֹׁסַעַת שֶׁסַע שְׁתֵּי
פְרָסוֹת מַעֲלַת גֵּרָה בַּבְּהֵמָה אֹתָהּ תֹּאכֵלוּ:
ז אַךְ אֶת־זֶה לֹא תֹאכְלוּ מִמַּעֲלֵי הַגֵּרָה
וּמִמַּפְרִיסֵי הַפַּרְסָה הַשְּׁסוּעָה אֶת־הַגָּמָל וְאֶת־
הָאַרְנֶבֶת וְאֶת־הַשָּׁפָן כִּי־מַעֲלֵה גֵרָה הֵמָּה
וּפַרְסָה לֹא הִפְרִיסוּ טְמֵאִים הֵם לָכֶם: ח וְאֶת־
הַחֲזִיר כִּי־מַפְרִיס פַּרְסָה הוּא וְלֹא גֵרָה טָמֵא
הוּא לָכֶם מִבְּשָׂרָם לֹא תֹאכֵלוּ וּבְנִבְלָתָם לֹא
תִגָּעוּ: ס ט אֶת־זֶה תֹּאכְלוּ מִכֹּל אֲשֶׁר בַּמָּיִם
כֹּל אֲשֶׁר־לוֹ סְנַפִּיר וְקַשְׂקֶשֶׂת תֹּאכֵלוּ: י וְכֹל
אֲשֶׁר אֵין־לוֹ סְנַפִּיר וְקַשְׂקֶשֶׂת לֹא תֹאכֵלוּ
טָמֵא הוּא לָכֶם: ס יא כָּל־צִפּוֹר טְהֹרָה
תֹּאכֵלוּ: יב וְזֶה אֲשֶׁר לֹא־תֹאכְלוּ מֵהֶם הַנֶּשֶׁר
וְהַפֶּרֶס וְהָעָזְנִיָּה: יג וְהָרָאָה וְאֶת־הָאַיָּה וְהַדַּיָּה
לְמִינָהּ: יד וְאֵת כָּל־עֹרֵב לְמִינוֹ: טו וְאֵת בַּת
הַיַּעֲנָה וְאֶת־הַתַּחְמָס וְאֶת־הַשָּׁחַף וְאֶת־הַנֵּץ
לְמִינֵהוּ: טז אֶת־הַכּוֹס וְאֶת־הַיַּנְשׁוּף
וְהַתִּנְשָׁמֶת: יז וְהַקָּאָת וְאֶת־הָרָחָמָה וְאֶת־
הַשָּׁלָךְ: יח וְהַחֲסִידָה וְהָאֲנָפָה לְמִינָהּ וְהַדּוּכִיפַת
וְהָעֲטַלֵּף: יט וְכֹל שֶׁרֶץ הָעוֹף טָמֵא הוּא לָכֶם
לֹא יֵאָכֵלוּ: כ כָּל־עוֹף טָהוֹר תֹּאכֵלוּ: כא לֹא
תֹאכְלוּ כָל־נְבֵלָה לַגֵּר אֲשֶׁר־בִּשְׁעָרֶיךָ תִּתְּנֶנָּה
וַאֲכָלָהּ אוֹ מָכֹר לְנָכְרִי כִּי עַם קָדוֹשׁ אַתָּה
לַיהוָה אֱלֹהֶיךָ לֹא־תְבַשֵּׁל גְּדִי בַּחֲלֵב אִמּוֹ: פ

21. ***You shall not eat any carrion . . . for you are a holy people . . . you shall not cook.*** This is the law that makes us a "holy people." We see, then, that the prohibitions against נְבֵלָה [eating "carrion"] and בָּשָׂר בְּחָלָב [cooking meat and dairy foods together] are closely interrelated and, together, convey the following thought: You shall not take as nourishment for your personality an animal that has become forfeit to the elemental world, which is strictly circumscribed. For you belong to a group of human beings that is sanctified to God; in view of your calling, you are not permitted to let any of the animal, physical aspects of your nature become subordinate to life's vegetative functions. You must, instead, elevate these aspects of your nature to the level of human morality in the service of God. Not only, therefore, are you forbidden to eat נְבֵלָה, but even when you eat or prepare such meat as is permitted to you, you must remember the sacred moral calling of the creature you wish to nourish and be mindful of what your calling requires of you.

take a tithe from all that you bring home from your seed that goes out upon the field, year after year. 23. And you shall eat before *God*, your God—in the place that He will choose to give His Name a habitation there—one tenth of your grain, of your new wine and of your oil, as well as the firstlings

חמישי כב עַשֵּׂר תְּעַשֵּׂר אֵת כָּל־תְּבוּאַת זַרְעֶךָ
הַיֹּצֵא הַשָּׂדֶה שָׁנָה שָׁנָה׃ כג וְאָכַלְתָּ לִפְנֵי ׀ יְהוָה
אֱלֹהֶיךָ בַּמָּקוֹם אֲשֶׁר־יִבְחַר לְשַׁכֵּן שְׁמוֹ שָׁם
מַעְשַׂר דְּגָנְךָ תִּירֹשְׁךָ וְיִצְהָרֶךָ וּבְכֹרֹת בְּקָרְךָ

22. ***Again and again you must take a tithe.*** The dietary laws in the preceding verses reiterated that, in selecting animals or animal products for our nourishment, we are duty-bound to remember the spiritual and moral sanctification of the human personality that this food is to nourish. We may eat only such foods (and even these only under specified conditions and prepared in a specified manner) that will not endanger our spiritual and moral integrity. Even as we prepare animal products for our nourishment, we are to keep in mind that the human being is called upon to rise, both physically and spiritually, above the animal.

The law concerning מַעֲשֵׂר שֵׁנִי [the second tithe], which now follows, is closely linked with this same purpose, for its intent is to elevate the physical enjoyment of food to a sacred duty, performed in the service of God and within sight of the Sanctuary of His Law. In this manner, "taking nourishment in the presence of God" actually becomes a means of teaching and training us to fear God all the days of our lives, cf. "so that you may learn to fear *God*, your God, at all times." This accords completely with the basic character of the worship of God and the ideal set for man in Judaism. Neither of these ideals includes elements that would equate the nearness of God and the dignity of man with the spirit only, and denigrate the physical and sensual aspects of human nature. Judaism enlists every aspect of human nature for the purpose of man's ennoblement and regards the sanctification of the physical aspects of life as the first, indispensable requirement for man's elevation to God. This idea is basic also to the institution of *milah*.

° ° °

The three purposes to be promoted by מַעֲשֵׂר רִאשׁוֹן [the first tithe], מַעֲשֵׂר שֵׁנִי [the second tithe] and מַעֲשַׂר עָנִי [the tithe for the poor] accord with the purposes that can and should be served by all our material means. These are: the cultivation of the spiritual aspects of our lives (as symbolized by the first tithe, which belongs to the Levites), attention to our physical needs (as symbolized by the second tithe, which is to be eaten by the donor in Jerusalem) and the promotion of the welfare of our fellow men (as symbolized by the tithe for the poor). But let us remember that under Biblical Law, only grain, new wine and oil are subject to the tithe, and even that only if they are intended for the landowner's personal use. They are not subject to the tithe if they were prepared for sale. In fact, they are subject to the tithe only if the landowner brought them into his house and home openly, in full public view. We therefore believe we may make the following statement: It should not be believed that the mere donation of these three types of *ma'aser*, subject to so many formal limitations, is in any wise sufficient to promote the three purposes enumerated above. The adequate promotion of these purposes requires that we devote [not only part but] all of our material assets (see note to 15:8) to this end. Now, all the fruits and other produce not liable to *ma'aser* under Biblical Law still remain part of our material assets, and we must remember that the intent of the three tithes is precisely to make us aware that we must dedicate all our means to the fulfillment of God's purposes. This thought is set forth in our chapter on the second tithe.

23. ***so that you may learn to fear* God, *your God, at all times.*** The tithe commanded by Biblical Law is an act acknowledging that man's work for his personal subsistence is to be dedicated to God. We are permitted to enjoy those of our first fruits that we have set aside for our personal use only after we have paid the tribute of our concern to the needs of the landless Levites (who cultivate the spirit of the Law), to the hallowing of all our personal pleasures (which we must learn to do in the presence of God) and, every third year, to the support of our unpropertied brethren.

Under God's Law, the observance of these procedures has been entrusted entirely to the conscience of the Jewish individual, who, presumably, is eager to perform all of God's *mitzvoth*. The landowner is given the possibility to evade these tithes under the strict letter of the Law. If he wishes to bring in his harvest in secret, "by way of roofs or enclosures," unseen by others, he is not obligated to perform this *mitzvah*. He can then use all of his harvest for his own purposes, without being legally obligated to remember the Levites and the poor or to enjoy his produce before God in physical proximity to the national Sanctuary of the Law. But if he wishes to demonstrate his rejoicing in God by bearing his harvest through the wide-open gates of his house and home, he is indeed duty-bound to perform this *mitzvah*. As a matter of fact, the Law presumes that the Jewish landowner will not enjoy his harvest if he has

וְצֹאנֶ֑ךָ לְמַ֣עַן תִּלְמַ֗ד לְיִרְאָ֛ה אֶת־יְהוָ֥ה אֱלֹהֶ֖יךָ
כָּל־הַיָּמִֽים׃ כד וְכִֽי־יִרְבֶּ֨ה מִמְּךָ֜ הַדֶּ֗רֶךְ כִּ֣י לֹ֮א
תוּכַל֮ שְׂאֵתוֹ֒ כִּֽי־יִרְחַ֤ק מִמְּךָ֙ הַמָּק֔וֹם אֲשֶׁ֤ר
יִבְחַר֙ יְהוָ֣ה אֱלֹהֶ֔יךָ לָשׂ֥וּם שְׁמ֖וֹ שָׁ֑ם כִּ֥י יְבָרֶכְךָ֖
יְהוָ֥ה אֱלֹהֶֽיךָ׃ כה וְנָתַתָּ֖ה בַּכָּ֑סֶף וְצַרְתָּ֤ הַכֶּ֙סֶף֙
בְּיָ֣דְךָ֔ וְהָלַכְתָּ֙ אֶל־הַמָּק֔וֹם אֲשֶׁ֥ר יִבְחַ֛ר יְהוָ֥ה
אֱלֹהֶ֖יךָ בּֽוֹ׃ כו וְנָתַתָּ֣ה הַכֶּ֡סֶף בְּכֹל֩ אֲשֶׁר־תְּאַוֶּ֨ה
נַפְשְׁךָ֜ בַּבָּקָ֣ר וּבַצֹּ֗אן וּבַיַּ֙יִן֙ וּבַשֵּׁכָ֔ר וּבְכֹ֛ל אֲשֶׁ֥ר
תִּֽשְׁאָלְךָ֖ נַפְשֶׁ֑ךָ וְאָכַ֣לְתָּ שָּׁ֗ם לִפְנֵי֙ יְהוָ֣ה אֱלֹהֶ֔יךָ
וְשָׂמַחְתָּ֖ אַתָּ֥ה וּבֵיתֶֽךָ׃ כז וְהַלֵּוִ֥י אֲשֶׁר־בִּשְׁעָרֶ֖יךָ
לֹ֣א תַעַזְבֶ֑נּוּ כִּ֣י אֵ֥ין ל֛וֹ חֵ֥לֶק וְנַחֲלָ֖ה עִמָּֽךְ׃ ס
כח מִקְצֵ֣ה ׀ שָׁלֹ֣שׁ שָׁנִ֗ים תּוֹצִיא֙ אֶת־כָּל־מַעְשַׂר֙
תְּבוּאָֽתְךָ֔ בַּשָּׁנָ֖ה הַהִ֑וא וְהִנַּחְתָּ֖ בִּשְׁעָרֶֽיךָ׃ כט וּבָ֣א
הַלֵּוִ֡י כִּ֣י אֵֽין־לוֹ֩ חֵ֨לֶק וְנַחֲלָ֜ה עִמָּ֗ךְ וְהַגֵּ֨ר וְהַיָּת֤וֹם
וְהָֽאַלְמָנָה֙ אֲשֶׁ֣ר בִּשְׁעָרֶ֔יךָ וְאָכְל֖וּ וְשָׂבֵ֑עוּ לְמַ֤עַן
יְבָרֶכְךָ֙ יְהוָ֣ה אֱלֹהֶ֔יךָ בְּכָל־מַעֲשֵׂ֥ה יָדְךָ֖ אֲשֶׁ֥ר
תַּעֲשֶֽׂה׃ ס ששי טו א מִקֵּ֥ץ שֶֽׁבַע־שָׁנִ֖ים תַּעֲשֶׂ֥ה

of your cattle and your sheep, so that you may learn to fear *God*, your God, at all times.
24. And if the way will be too long for you, so that you are not able to take it up because the place is too far for you, which *God*, your God will choose there to give a habitation to His Name, when *God*, your God, will bless you;
25. then you shall convert it into money and take the money tightly into your hand, and you shall go to the place that *God*, your God, will choose;
26. and you shall convert the money into anything you may desire; into cattle, into sheep, into wine, into strong drink and into anything after which your soul craves; and you shall eat [it] there before *God*, your God; and you shall rejoice, you and your household.
27. But also you must not forsake the Levite who is within your gates, because he received no portion nor inheritance beside you.
28. At the end of three years you shall put out the entire tithe of your harvest that you bring home for that year and place it within your gates.
29. And the Levite shall come, because he received no portion nor inheritance in your midst; and the stranger, and the orphan and the widow who are within your gate; and they shall eat it and be satisfied, so that *God*, your God, may bless you in all the work of your hands that you do.

XV

1. At the end of seven years you shall make a release.

circumvented this *mitzvah*. That is why a later generation looked back with longing to those better days of old, when landowners bore their harvest home through their wide-open gates in order to make the produce liable to the tithe, in sad contrast to their own day, in which the landowners brought their harvest home by circuitous routes in order to exempt it from this duty. "Observe the difference between the earlier and later generations. The earlier generations used to bring in their produce through the kitchen gardens on purpose, in order to make it liable to the tithe, whereas the later generations bring it in by way of roofs or courtyards or enclosures in order to make it exempt from the tithe." (Berakhoth 35b). And in Baba Metzia 88a, the early decline of the fruit trade [in Eretz Yisrael] is attributed to the fact that the dealers took advantage of the opportunity for circumvention given them by the Law; i.e., that those who merely purchase or sell such produce are exempt from the duty of tithing: "Why were the bazaars of Bet Hini destroyed? Because they based their actions upon [the letter of] Scripture. They used to say, 'You shall surely tithe . . . and you shall eat' [implies] 'but not if you sell it.' 'The increase of your seed,' [implies] 'but not if it is purchased.'"

Note that, according to the Law, each kind of produce must be tithed separately for each year and during each year. The intention of this stipulation apparently is to make us aware of the הַשְׁגָּחָה פְּרָטִית [personal Divine Providence] that makes the human toil of each year and every kind of produce the object of its loving concern.

CHAPTER XV

1. The preceding chapter concluded with the law pertaining to מַעְשַׂר עָנִי [the tithe for the poor]. Under this law, the tithe that, as a rule, is to be eaten with rejoicing before God, in the City of God, is replaced

2. And this is the pronouncement concerning the release: Every creditor shall release from his hand the debt [for] which he can claim [payment] from his neighbor. He may no longer exact payment from his neighbor and from his brother, because he has declared a release, for the sake of *God*. 3. From the foreigner you may exact payment; but that of yours which is with your brother, your hand shall release. 4. However, there shall be no needy among you, for *God* wishes to bless you in the land that *God*, your God, is giving you as an inheritance, to take possession of it, 5. but only if you hearken earnestly to the voice of *God*, your God, to carry out punctiliously this whole commandment that I command you today. 6. If then *God*, your God, has blessed you as He has spoken to you, you will make many nations indebted to you, but you [yourself] will not become indebted; you will be ruler over

שְׁמִטָּה׃ ב וְזֶה דְּבַר הַשְּׁמִטָּה שָׁמוֹט כָּל־בַּעַל
מַשֵּׁה יָדוֹ אֲשֶׁר יַשֶּׁה בְּרֵעֵהוּ לֹא יִגֹּשׂ אֶת־רֵעֵהוּ
וְאֶת־אָחִיו כִּי־קָרָא שְׁמִטָּה לַיהוָה׃ ג אֶת־
הַנָּכְרִי תִּגֹּשׂ וַאֲשֶׁר יִהְיֶה לְךָ אֶת־אָחִיךָ תַּשְׁמֵט
יָדֶךָ׃ ד אֶפֶס כִּי לֹא יִהְיֶה־בְּךָ אֶבְיוֹן כִּי־בָרֵךְ
יְבָרֶכְךָ יְהוָה בָּאָרֶץ אֲשֶׁר יְהוָה אֱלֹהֶיךָ נֹתֵן־לְךָ
נַחֲלָה לְרִשְׁתָּהּ׃ ה רַק אִם־שָׁמוֹעַ תִּשְׁמַע בְּקוֹל
יְהוָה אֱלֹהֶיךָ לִשְׁמֹר לַעֲשׂוֹת אֶת־כָּל־הַמִּצְוָה
הַזֹּאת אֲשֶׁר אָנֹכִי מְצַוְּךָ הַיּוֹם׃ ו כִּי־יְהוָה
אֱלֹהֶיךָ בֵּרַכְךָ כַּאֲשֶׁר דִּבֶּר־לָךְ וְהַעֲבַטְתָּ גּוֹיִם
רַבִּים וְאַתָּה לֹא תַעֲבֹט וּמָשַׁלְתָּ בְּגוֹיִם רַבִּים

every third year by the tithe for the poor. Thus, concern for the welfare of one's needy neighbor was seen as a direct result of the landowner's enjoyment of his own harvest before God, and the Jew was taught not to rejoice in his personal happiness before God without first having done everything in his power to give practical aid to his less fortunate brother. שָׂמַחְתִּי וְשִׂמַּחְתִּי, "I have rejoiced and I have given joy also to others" [Maaser Sheni 5:12] is the final statement in the avowal to be recited when giving the tithe at the end of each three-year cycle (Deuteronomy 26:14). . . .

However, the giving of the tithe for the poor does not in itself mean that we have discharged in full our duty to care for the poor and the needy. Indeed, like all the other [legally stipulated] gifts to the poor, the tithe is intended to be no more than a solemn reminder to the propertied individual, impressing upon him the importance of his full responsibilities before God. . . . This thought is made patently clear by the laws concerning the release of debts and *tzedakah*, in which our duties toward our less fortunate brethren are specified in greater detail.

° ° °

2. . . . It is in terms of רֵעֵהוּ ["his neighbor"] and אָחִיו ["his brother"] that the שְׁמִיטָה [law of release] expresses the prohibition "he may no longer exact payment. . . ." During the Sabbatical year, the Divine concept iniects itself with full legal force into the nation's social conditions. It is the intent of this law that, when the Sabbatical year is over, all of us should relate to one another once again as רֵעִים [neighbors] and אַחִים [brothers]. For this reason, the Law urges upon every individual, in the spirit implicit in the term רֵעִים,[3] the importance of striving to promote his neighbor's welfare, and to this end the Law requires that we release the debtor from the bonds that would otherwise permanently inhibit the free development of his earning capacity. At the end of each year of שְׁמִיטָה [release], the repayment of all previously contracted debts remains only as a moral obligation, which the debtor can discharge in a mode of his own choosing. Because of the trust which the Law thus places in him, the debtor, instead of feeling weighed down by the burden of his obligation, feels morally uplifted and will make it a matter of his personal honor to repay his debt, even though this repayment is no longer his obligation under the law—but is left to his own free will. The implications of the term רֵעַ teach creditors and debtors alike what is expected of them, and it is God, the Father of them all, Who wishes to see them behave accordingly, as His children, all of them אַחִים, brothers, in the household of His sovereignty. . . .

[3]*Note to the English translation*: In the latter part of his extensive notes on Leviticus 19:15 and 16 (which was omitted from this excerpted edition), Hirsch relates רֵעַ to מִרְעֶה, "pasture." This, he explains, means that your neighbor should be able to regard you as his "pasture," a source of aid for his welfare; while you, in turn, should see *his* welfare as your own "pasture," as adding to your own happiness and prosperity. [G.H.]

many nations, but they will not rule over you.   7. If there will be among you a needy [man] from among one of your brothers within one of your gates, in the land that *God,* your God, is giving you, you shall not make your heart unfeeling and not close up your hand to your brother, the needy [man].   8. Rather, you shall open, open your hand to him; and you shall also lend, lend him sufficient for his need, what

וּבְךָ֖ לֹ֣א יִמְשֹֽׁלוּ׃ ס ז כִּֽי־יִהְיֶה֩ בְךָ֨ אֶבְי֜וֹן מֵאַחַ֤ד אַחֶ֙יךָ֙ בְּאַחַ֣ד שְׁעָרֶ֔יךָ בְּאַ֨רְצְךָ֔ אֲשֶׁר־יְהֹוָ֥ה אֱלֹהֶ֖יךָ נֹתֵ֣ן לָ֑ךְ לֹ֧א תְאַמֵּ֣ץ אֶת־לְבָבְךָ֗ וְלֹ֤א תִקְפֹּץ֙ אֶת־יָ֣דְךָ֔ מֵאָחִ֖יךָ הָאֶבְיֽוֹן׃ ח כִּֽי־פָתֹ֧חַ תִּפְתַּ֛ח אֶת־יָדְךָ֖ ל֑וֹ וְהַעֲבֵט֙ תַּעֲבִיטֶ֔נּוּ דֵּ֖י מַחְסֹר֔וֹ

7. כִּי יִהְיֶה בְךָ אֶבְיוֹן [*If there will be among you (sing.) a needy man].* [The form of address is the second person singular]. But these words must be construed as being addressed to a communal entity, for one cannot say to an individual concerning himself alone, "If there is a needy man among you." On the other hand, in light of the language used, the words לֹא תְאַמֵּץ אֶת לְבָבְךָ ["you *(sing.)* shall not make your heart unfeeling"], and the statements that follow, refer primarily to the individual. Thus, the Law in this instance has in mind the community and the individual alike, and the obligation to care for the poor, which is set forth here, is incumbent equally upon the community as a whole and each one of its members separately. . . . The requirements of this law, as we shall see, cannot be met by the individual alone, or by the community alone. Each must strive to outdo the other in this respect. Both must work side by side, if the goal set by the Law is to be attained. The signs on buildings warning beggars to keep out because the occupants are already contributing to public relief funds are not products of the Jewish spirit nurtured by this law. . . .

you shall not make your heart unfeeling. Literally, "You shall not do violence to your heart." It is assumed that if Jewish hearts are permitted to give free rein to their natural impulses, they will do good, and that only cold, calculating, selfish considerations can suppress these impulses. Jewish hands, too, are by nature open to the poor; they, too, can be closed up only by such unnatural selfishness. Hence, "do not close up your hand."

Again and again in this chapter on doing good, the needy man is referred to as אָחִיךָ ["your brother"]. Every needy person, whether or not he is known to you, is your brother, a child of your Father in heaven, and when he turns to you, he does so with a letter of introduction, as it were, from Him Who is the Father of you both.

8. . . . The admonition פָּתֹחַ תִּפְתַּח ["You shall open, open. . ."], נָתוֹן תִּתֵּן ["Rather, you shall give, give. . ."] and דֵּי מַחְסֹרוֹ ["sufficient for his need"]; and conversely,

the warning, "you shall not make your heart unfeeling, and not close up your hand to your brother, the needy [man]," have produced all those wonders of Jewish charity which to this day have quietly welded the dispersed sons of the House of Jacob into one great worldwide charitable society, so that all those in distress and in need of help tend to turn to Jewish homes and Jewish hearts before seeking assistance elsewhere. The duty to satisfy the needs of the poor in every respect, cf. דֵּי מַחְסֹרוֹ ["sufficient for his need"], has made it necessary that the care of the poor should become the concern of every duly constituted Jewish community, which has the authority to enlist the efforts of its members for this purpose.

. . . At the same time, however, the Law makes it clear that the duty of the Jew does not end there by any means. Rather, it opens up unending opportunities to private charity and voluntary relief organizations for most beneficial work. The task imposed by the duty of *tzedakah* in Judaism is so great and important that only a combination of these three factors—communal, organizational and private—can even begin to do justice to it. . . .

However, there are two particular factors that determine the manner in which the Jewish concept of charity is cultivated and put into practice. Jewish thought regards the task of doing good as צְדָקָה, [lit., "righteousness"], as a duty in the most eminent sense of the term (see notes on Genesis 15:6). He who does not help the poor with all the energies at his command commits a sin and bears a heavy burden of guilt before God. The statement "and a sin would attach to you" in Verse 9 refers to such a person. This approach makes "doing good" independent of the impulses of pity that may vary with the donor's mood, and classes it, instead, as a categorical duty, thus at the same time liberating the recipient from the crushing sense of humiliation [that he is "receiving charity"]. In Judaism, the Jewish poor do not receive "alms" (from *eleemosyne,* the Greek term for "gift of mercy"). In their profound insight, our Sages, harking back to the law of מַעֲשֵׂר עָנִי [the tithe for the poor], have set the dimension of the duty of *tzedakah* at one tenth. This

אֲשֶׁר יֶחְסַר לוֹ: ט הִשָּׁמֶר לְךָ פֶּן־יִהְיֶה דָבָר
עִם־לְבָבְךָ בְלִיַּעַל לֵאמֹר קָרְבָה שְׁנַת־הַשֶּׁבַע
שְׁנַת הַשְּׁמִטָּה וְרָעָה עֵינְךָ בְּאָחִיךָ הָאֶבְיוֹן וְלֹא
תִתֵּן לוֹ וְקָרָא עָלֶיךָ אֶל־יְהוָה וְהָיָה בְךָ חֵטְא:
י נָתוֹן תִּתֵּן לוֹ וְלֹא־יֵרַע לְבָבְךָ בְּתִתְּךָ לוֹ כִּי
בִּגְלַל | הַדָּבָר הַזֶּה יְבָרֶכְךָ יְהוָה אֱלֹהֶיךָ בְּכָל־
מַעֲשֶׂךָ וּבְכֹל מִשְׁלַח יָדֶךָ: יא כִּי לֹא־יֶחְדַּל
אֶבְיוֹן מִקֶּרֶב הָאָרֶץ עַל־כֵּן אָנֹכִי מְצַוְּךָ לֵאמֹר
פָּתֹחַ תִּפְתַּח אֶת־יָדְךָ לְאָחִיךָ לַעֲנִיֶּךָ וּלְאֶבְיֹנְךָ

he lacks.
9. Take heed for yourself that the unworthy word not take root in your heart, saying: "The seventh year, the year of release, is at hand," and then your eye would look in an evil manner upon your brother, the needy [man], and you would not give him [anything]; he would then cry to *God* concerning you, and a sin would attach to you.
10. Rather, you shall give, [indeed] give, to him, and your heart shall not feel badly when you give to him; for as a result, *God*, your God, will bless you in all your work and in all that is at the command of your hand.
11. For the needy will not cease from the earth; therefore I command you: Open, open your hand to your brother, to your poor and your needy in your land.

amount must be deducted for charity from every newly-gained amount of capital and again from the yearly income yielded by the principal. In this manner, every Jew is made to regard himself as the administrator of a charity fund—large or small—that has been entrusted to his care and consecrated to God, so that he must rejoice at every opportunity to turn these assets, which are no longer his, but have been entrusted to him for appropriate disbursement to a good purpose.

11. ***For the needy will not cease.*** The text does not read מִקִּרְבֶּךָ ["... from your midst"] or מִקֶּרֶב אַרְצְךָ ["from the midst of your land"]—but מִקֶּרֶב הָאָרֶץ ["from the earth"]. It is in the natural order of human events that if things are left to develop as they will, the most extreme economic differences, destitution and plenty, poverty and wealth, will exist side by side. If from nothing else, this would result already from the fact that all men have not been endowed with equal intellectual abilities. Indeed, even assuming that two sons of the same father start out from their paternal home with equal [material and intellectual] resources, and then one of them has only one child, while the other must provide for a large family, this alone would produce a substantial disparity in their economic situation, and if, in addition, the brother with the large family will be beset with illness and other misfortunes, the generation that follows him may already be in dire want, in sharp contrast to the affluence of the other branch of the family.

It is in the nature of things that such situations should arise all over the earth. However, you must not permit them to arise בְּאַרְצְךָ, in your land. בְּאַרְצְךָ, in "your" land, in the land of God's Law, and of the special Divine Providence Whose gifts depend on your observance of this Law; the Law is to help level these natural disparities. Every less fortunate brother shall find a brother in his more affluent kinsman; in this land every poor and needy individual belongs to you; i.e., to the community, and even as we know that a [Jewish] community never dies and never becomes destitute, so, too, in a Jewish community that is aware of its duty, individual poverty and misery should be only a passing phase, to be transformed, under the egis of Divine assistance, into a decent, happy existence on earth. . . .

It is true, then, that under Jewish Law, help and support are assured to the poor who are in need of assistance. True it is, also, that in Judaism, *tzedakah* does not shame the recipient who is in need of it. Indeed, in the spirit of this law, anyone who is unable to work or is destitute but who, out of misplaced pride, deprives himself and his family of the necessities of life rather than turn to the *tzedakah* to which he is entitled, bears a heavy burden of responsibility; cf. "He who needs to take but does not take is as if he had shed blood" (Jerusalem Talmud, end of Tractate Peah). Yet, the spirit of this same Law attaches great importance also to the preservation of personal independence. An individual should be prepared to restrict himself to the barest necessities of life and accept any work, even that considered most menial in the eyes of a thoughtless world, in order to avoid having to appeal to the charity of his fellow men. In no society is honest toil for an independent living held in such high esteem as it was among the Jews of old. Some of our greatest heroes of the spirit, whose light still shines before us, and to whom not only their own contemporaries, but also all the generations that followed, have looked upon with respect and admiration to this day—Hillel, R. Joshua, R. Ḥaninah, R. Oshaya, R. Sheshet and R. Huna—were in the most straitened circumstances and eked out

12. If your brother, a Hebrew [man] or a Hebrew woman, is sold to you, he shall serve you six years, and in the seventh year you shall send him away from you to freedom. 13. When you then send him away from you to freedom, do not send him away empty-handed. 14. Rather, you shall provide him, [indeed] provide him from out of your flock, out of your barn and out of your wine press; that which *God*, your God, has blessed for you, you shall give to him. 15. Remember that you were a slave in the land of Mitzrayim, when *God*, your God, redeemed you; therefore I command you today to do so. 16. And it shall be if, nevetherless, he will say to you: "I will not go away from you," and he has grown to love you and your household because he fares well with you, 17. then you shall take an awl and pierce it into his ear, at the door, and he shall remain a bondsman to you forever. You shall do the same with your handmaid. 18. And this shall not seem excessive in your eyes, when you send him away from you to freedom, for he has served you for double the hire of a day laborer for six years, and *God*, your God, will bless you in all that you do. 19. Every firstling male that is born among your cattle and your flock you must sanctify to *God*, your God; you must not do any work with the firstling of your ox, and you must not shear the firstling of your flock. 20. Before *God*, your God, shall you eat it year by year in the place that *God* will choose, you and your household. 21. But if there is a blemish upon it—if it is lame or blind—any bad blemish, you may not offer it to *God*, your God; 22. you may eat it within your gates, the unclean and the [ritually] pure together, as the deer and the doe. 23. But its blood you may not eat. You must pour it out upon the ground like water.

XVI

1. Keep the month of the standing grain and make

בְּאַרְצֶךָ: ס יב כִּי־יִמָּכֵר לְךָ אָחִיךָ הָעִבְרִי אוֹ
הָעִבְרִיָּה וַעֲבָדְךָ שֵׁשׁ שָׁנִים וּבַשָּׁנָה הַשְּׁבִיעִת
תְּשַׁלְּחֶנּוּ חָפְשִׁי מֵעִמָּךְ: יג וְכִי־תְשַׁלְּחֶנּוּ חָפְשִׁי
מֵעִמָּךְ לֹא תְשַׁלְּחֶנּוּ רֵיקָם: יד הַעֲנֵיק תַּעֲנִיק לוֹ
מִצֹּאנְךָ וּמִגָּרְנְךָ וּמִיִּקְבֶךָ אֲשֶׁר בֵּרַכְךָ יְהוָֹה
אֱלֹהֶיךָ תִּתֶּן־לוֹ: טו וְזָכַרְתָּ כִּי עֶבֶד הָיִיתָ בְּאֶרֶץ
מִצְרַיִם וַיִּפְדְּךָ יְהוָֹה אֱלֹהֶיךָ עַל־כֵּן אָנֹכִי מְצַוְּךָ
אֶת־הַדָּבָר הַזֶּה הַיּוֹם: טז וְהָיָה כִּי־יֹאמַר אֵלֶיךָ
לֹא אֵצֵא מֵעִמָּךְ כִּי אֲהֵבְךָ וְאֶת־בֵּיתֶךָ כִּי־טוֹב
לוֹ עִמָּךְ: יז וְלָקַחְתָּ אֶת־הַמַּרְצֵעַ וְנָתַתָּה בְאָזְנוֹ
וּבַדֶּלֶת וְהָיָה לְךָ עֶבֶד עוֹלָם וְאַף לַאֲמָתְךָ
תַּעֲשֶׂה־כֵּן: יח לֹא־יִקְשֶׁה בְעֵינֶךָ בְּשַׁלֵּחֲךָ אֹתוֹ
חָפְשִׁי מֵעִמָּךְ כִּי מִשְׁנֶה שְׂכַר שָׂכִיר עֲבָדְךָ שֵׁשׁ
שָׁנִים וּבֵרַכְךָ יְהוָֹה אֱלֹהֶיךָ בְּכֹל אֲשֶׁר
תַּעֲשֶׂה: פ שביעי יט כָּל־הַבְּכוֹר אֲשֶׁר יִוָּלֵד
בִּבְקָרְךָ וּבְצֹאנְךָ הַזָּכָר תַּקְדִּישׁ לַיהוָֹה אֱלֹהֶיךָ
לֹא תַעֲבֹד בִּבְכֹר שׁוֹרֶךָ וְלֹא תָגֹז בְּכוֹר צֹאנֶךָ:
כ לִפְנֵי יְהוָֹה אֱלֹהֶיךָ תֹאכְלֶנּוּ שָׁנָה בְשָׁנָה
בַּמָּקוֹם אֲשֶׁר־יִבְחַר יְהוָֹה אַתָּה וּבֵיתֶךָ: כא וְכִי־
יִהְיֶה בוֹ מוּם פִּסֵּחַ אוֹ עִוֵּר כֹּל מוּם רָע לֹא
תִזְבָּחֶנּוּ לַיהוָֹה אֱלֹהֶיךָ: כב בִּשְׁעָרֶיךָ תֹּאכְלֶנּוּ
הַטָּמֵא וְהַטָּהוֹר יַחְדָּו כַּצְּבִי וְכָאַיָּל: כג רַק אֶת־
דָּמוֹ לֹא תֹאכֵל עַל־הָאָרֶץ תִּשְׁפְּכֶנּוּ כַּמָּיִם: פ
טז א שָׁמוֹר אֶת־חֹדֶשׁ הָאָבִיב וְעָשִׂיתָ פֶּסַח

their livelihoods as woodcutters, blacksmiths, cobblers, porters and water carriers, and by their personal example taught the maxim, "Do not live better on the Sabbath than you do during the week, and do not put yourself in need of assistance from your fellow men (Pesaḥim 113a). "Work as a day laborer at skinning carcasses in the market place, and do not say: 'I am a *kohen*, I am a scholar; such work is beneath me.'' . . . .

the Pesah offering to *God*, your God; for in the month of the standing grain did *God*,

לַיהוָה אֱלֹהֶיךָ כִּי בְּחֹדֶשׁ הָאָבִיב הוֹצִיאֲךָ יְהוָה

CHAPTER XVI

1. The chapter that now follows deals with the appointed festive seasons whose significance in the מִשְׁנֵה תּוֹרָה compendium we have already discussed in our notes to Chapter 1:3. The present chapter omits all the festivals that could be fully observed already during Israel's years in the wilderness; i.e. the Sabbath, the New Year, Yom Kippur and Shemini Atzereth. This compendium, intended for the generation that is about to enter the Land, reiterates only those festivals which (like Shevuoth and Sukkoth) can assume their true, full significance only in the Land, or those concerning which, as in the case of פֶּסַח, the intention was to stress that they had to be observed in the City of God, the center of the nation—an obligation stated also with regard to שָׁבוּעוֹת and סוּכּוֹת. These three festivals are all רְגָלִים [pilgrim festivals], whose significance as such begins only after the people have dispersed in the Land, and which are therefore grouped together in Verse 16 of the present chapter. This chapter contains also a number of essential supplements to the מוֹעֵד regulations already set forth in earlier books. It opens with the laws relating to the observance of Passover.

° ° °

We have already explained in our notes to Exodus 12:2 and Leviticus 23:2 and 4[4] how the sanctification of the New Moon and the leap year and the fixing of our festive seasons, based equally on historical and seasonal factors, serve to counteract every cult of nature worship, ancient and modern. These institutions summon us to do homage instead to the One sole God, Whose presence is proclaimed by every living thing, every change of seasons, every breath of life. His Law is almighty in the unfolding of all physical existence, but at the same time He is even more intimately close to the morally free-willed life of man, and was revealed to us through His Law as the Molder and Pilot of our destinies and the Guide of our actions.

The fact that the One sole God of nature is also the One sole God of history—this is the basis for our awareness of both God and ourselves, and this is the truth which the Law, "Keep the month of the standing grain and make the Pesaḥ offering to *God*, your God. . .," proclaims through our entire calendar cycle. The festival that commemorates our rise in history must celebrate also the revival of nature. The God Whose breath of spring bestirs nature from the death-like numbness of winter is the same God Who summoned us to life and freedom from death and enslavement. The God Who, with His call, "By your blood shall you live" (Ezekiel 16:6), burst asunder what was intended to be the Egyptian grave of our existence, is the same God Whose liberating, life-giving rule in nature is proclaimed to this very day by every sprout that breaks through the soil, every bud that bursts into bloom, every living thing that bestirs itself each spring from the frozen rigidity of winter. The fourteenth day of Nisan is the day we must honor each year by making the פֶּסַח offering that celebrates the historic moment at which the threat of death, physical and political, hovered over our heads and at which God, after careful deliberation, caused both perils to pass from us, rewarding us instead with life and freedom for the pledge of our devotion, symbolized by our offering.

That day must occur each year at the beginning of springtime, when nature reawakens, and it must be kept at this season of the year [by the intercalation of an additional month]. We now understand, therefore, the meaning of the Talmudic dictum "no other month but Adar may be intercalated" (Sanhedrin 12a); i.e., why the necessary adjustment of the calendar cycle can be made only by the intercalation of a second month of Adar, not by that of any other month. Only the intercalation of a month immediately preceding Nisan can properly draw attention to the purpose of this intercalation: that the month of Passover must always coincide with the month of springtime. . . .

However, the profound significance of this leap year institution becomes fully apparent only once the people has settled in its land. This is the reason why the specific legal institutions pertaining to it could be reserved for discussion in the present compendium of the Law. Only when men live amidst fields and farmland does springtime make the human mind truly aware of nature, with its powerful stimuli and its measured rhythm; only then is the human heart filled with the realization that there is One sole Power upon Whom the fulfillment of all human hopes depends.

At the same time, however, dwelling in the midst of fields and farmland poses a particular threat to the nation of God. For only once it is settled amidst these physical surroundings will the nation of God run the danger that it will come to worship the forces of nature and make room in its heart for Baal, giving him a sovereign throne side by side with that of the God Who guides this nation's history and its actions. At this point the Law steps in and demands that the day of the Passover offering must coincide with the beginning of spring; it demands that even as we contemplate the springtime of nature we must commemorate also the

[4] *Note to the English translation:* The notes on Lev. 23:4 are not included in this excerpted edition. [G.H.]

אֱלֹהֶ֛יךָ מִמִּצְרַ֖יִם לָֽיְלָה׃ ב וְזָבַ֥חְתָּ פֶּ֛סַח לַיהוָ֥ה
אֱלֹהֶ֖יךָ צֹ֣אן וּבָקָ֑ר בַּמָּקוֹם֙ אֲשֶׁר־יִבְחַ֣ר יְהוָ֔ה
לְשַׁכֵּ֥ן שְׁמ֖וֹ שָֽׁם׃ ג לֹא־תֹאכַ֤ל עָלָיו֙ חָמֵ֔ץ
שִׁבְעַ֥ת יָמִ֛ים תֹּֽאכַל־עָלָ֥יו מַצּ֖וֹת לֶ֣חֶם עֹ֑נִי כִּ֣י

your God, bring you out from Mitzrayim, by night. 2. And you shall make the Pesaḥ [offering] as an offertory meal to *God*, your God, from the flock and herd in the place that *God* will choose to give His Name a habitation there. 3. You shall eat no leaven together with it; rather, for seven days shall you eat together with it unleavened bread, the bread of dependence,

coming of our own springtime [as a nation]. The Law calls us away from verdant fields and blossoming meadows to that place where there dwells the Law of God, which is the wellspring of our spiritual rejuvenation, the source of our moral and political blossoming, and whose observance at the same time is the one true precondition for the fertility of our fields and meadows. Thus, in full view of the testimony of the pledge we have received from the One sole God, we are to renew our homage to Him Who, on that one spring night, led us forth from physical and political death to life and freedom.

With this one act, unique in the annals of world history, He inscribed Himself in the records of men and nations, but above all in our own minds and hearts, forever, as the One Whose hand controls both nature and history. And even as He has given and maintained the law by which the sun and the earth run their course, the seasons alternate and all living things happily and hopefully begin and eventually complete their life cycles; so, too, He gave us that Law under which we are to develop our own character and all its potential for goodness and truth. In this manner we are to become capable of attaining the even loftier, ever-young, happy and hopeful perfection of a springtime of man and nations. Hence, "keep the month of spring and, with complete devotion, make the offering of your own revival . . . to *God*, your own God, for it was in the month of spring that *God*, your own God, brought you out from Mitzrayim."

° ° °

3. ***for in haste.*** Your departure from Egypt was marked by enforced haste. The hand of God lay heavily upon the Egyptians, so that they, who earlier had refused to grant you three days' freedom from your labors—indeed, not even a moment's respite from your toil—now actually drove you out into freedom. And even as they had done during all the years of your slavery, so now, too, they did not permit you sufficient time to bake proper bread for yourselves. Thus, even at the moment of your redemption—you still were slaves. You did not achieve your freedom by your own power; you received it from God, Who moved the hand of your oppressors. Your oppressors were in haste, and so were you; your oppressors were driven by God, and you, in turn, were driven by your oppressors. Cf. "Mitzrayim used force upon the people to send them out from the land in haste, for they said: 'We are all dead men!' . . . for they had been driven out of Mitzrayim and could not linger, and they had not even prepared provisions for themselves" (Exodus 12:33 and 39). God was the sole free agent on that day in world history, and all this took place "so that you may remember the day of your going out from the land of Mitzrayim all the days of your life," because this day is to become the starting point of all your future thoughts and actions. For on this day you did not become "your own master," but made the transition from the dominion of man to become the possession of God; you left the servitude of men to enter the service of God. . . .

The words "so that you may remember. . ." state that it is our duty to remember the going out from Egypt every day. In Berakhoth 12b, "all the days of your life" is expanded to include also the nights; "the exodus from Mitzrayim must be remembered (also) during the nights." . . . Our departure from Egypt supplied the foundation for both aspects of our lives: our history and our day-to-day activities. Our historical life is to be based on trust in God; our day-to-day activities, on our sense of duty toward Him. Our trust in God must be proven above all during the dark nights of life; our sense of duty toward Him must be demonstrated during the daytime, which is to be devoted to practical activity. Superficially, one could conclude from the redemption from Egypt that one should trust in God primarily during the nights of life, and that therefore the commandment to remember the exodus from Egypt is applicable, first and foremost, to the night. Jewish thought, however, knows that it is much easier to trust in God during the nights of dire misfortune than to remain faithful to our duty in the bright daylight of our everyday endeavors. Therefore our sense of duty as Jews, as constantly reaffirmed by our remembrance of the exodus from Egypt, is infinitely more important; hence there can be no doubt that the commandment to remember the exodus from Egypt is applicable first and foremost to the daytime, both literally and figuratively. . . .

for in haste did you go out from the land of Mitzrayim, so that you may remember the day of your going out from the land of Mitzrayim all the days of your life. 4. No leaven shall be seen with you in all your territory for seven days, and nothing of the meat that you offer in the evening as a meal shall remain through the night of the first day until the morning. 5. You may not make the Pesaḥ offering within one of your gates that *God*, your God, is giving you. 6. But you must go to the place that *God*, your God, will choose to give His Name a habitation there; there you shall make the Pesaḥ meal offering in the evening, when the sun has set, at the appointed season of your going out from Mitzrayim. 7. And you shall cook and eat in the place that *God*, your God, will choose; and then you shall turn in the morning and go to your tents. 8. Then for [another] six days you shall still eat *matzoth*, and on the seventh day shall be a gathering up, for preservation directed toward *God*, your God; you may do

בְּחִפָּזוֹן יָצָאתָ מֵאֶרֶץ מִצְרַיִם לְמַעַן תִּזְכֹּר אֶת־
יוֹם צֵאתְךָ מֵאֶרֶץ מִצְרַיִם כֹּל יְמֵי חַיֶּיךָ: ד וְלֹא־יֵרָאֶה
לְךָ שְׂאֹר בְּכָל־גְּבֻלְךָ שִׁבְעַת יָמִים וְלֹא־יָלִין מִן־הַבָּשָׂר
אֲשֶׁר תִּזְבַּח בָּעֶרֶב בַּיּוֹם הָרִאשׁוֹן לַבֹּקֶר: ה לֹא תוּכַל
לִזְבֹּחַ אֶת־הַפָּסַח בְּאַחַד שְׁעָרֶיךָ אֲשֶׁר־יְהֹוָה אֱלֹהֶיךָ
נֹתֵן לָךְ: ו כִּי אִם־אֶל־הַמָּקוֹם אֲשֶׁר־יִבְחַר יְהֹוָה
אֱלֹהֶיךָ לְשַׁכֵּן שְׁמוֹ שָׁם תִּזְבַּח אֶת־הַפֶּסַח בָּעָרֶב כְּבוֹא
הַשֶּׁמֶשׁ מוֹעֵד צֵאתְךָ מִמִּצְרָיִם: ז וּבִשַּׁלְתָּ וְאָכַלְתָּ
בַּמָּקוֹם אֲשֶׁר יִבְחַר יְהֹוָה אֱלֹהֶיךָ בּוֹ וּפָנִיתָ בַבֹּקֶר
וְהָלַכְתָּ לְאֹהָלֶיךָ: ח שֵׁשֶׁת יָמִים תֹּאכַל מַצּוֹת וּבַיּוֹם
הַשְּׁבִיעִי עֲצֶרֶת לַיהֹוָה

The fact that the duty to remember the redemption from Egypt was not mentioned until this point, in the compendium intended for the generation that is about to enter the Land, should require no explanation. Up to this point, the people could still be regarded as being in the process of redemption from Egypt. Only once they had settled down in their land could the memories of their historic origin, and its consequences for our duties in theory and practice, grow dim. Hence it was only at this time, and for all times to come, that the commandment "remember the day of your going out from the land of Mitzrayim all the days of your life" would receive its full significance.

7. *And you shall cook and eat.* You have not done justice to this commandment by merely knowing how to recite prayers and make offerings in a place consecrated to God. Only when you have learned also to "cook and eat" in places consecrated to God; only when your entire being is so thoroughly infused with the spirit of the Sanctuary that even your "cooking and eating," the physical, sensual aspects of your life (borne by a sense of duty, by the awareness that these parts of your life, too, are linked to God) will be elevated to the level of moral, sanctified duty in the service of God, only when you will "cook and eat in the place that *God*, your God, will choose..."—only then will you "turn in the morning and go to your tents": Only then will you have gained at God's Sanctuary the attitude

that should accompany you as you return to your homes.

and then you shall turn in the morning and go to your tents. It is on this statement that the Halakhah bases the general dictum that any time one appears in the Sanctuary with a gift he has consecrated to God, even if it is only "birds and meal offerings of wine and incense and wood for the altar," he is not permitted to leave the City of God, the area surrounding the Sanctuary, and to go home immediately after making the offering. All authorities agree that it is obligatory to remain in the area of the Sanctuary overnight and not set out for home until the next morning (*Sifri*). Under the Law of God, the mere completion of an offering is not sufficient to accomplish the purpose for which His Sanctuary was established. We have fulfilled our duty only after we have permitted His Sanctuary and its ritual to exercise its impact upon our thoughts, our aspirations and our actions. That is why we are required to remain in the vicinity of the Sanctuary even after we have placed our offering there, to give ourselves an opportunity to gather our thoughts and, in the stillness of the night, to allow the impressions we have gathered in the Sanctuary to mature, so that, spiritually enriched by the clarity of thought that comes with the morning, we may take these impressions back with us to our homes as the true, blessed treasures we have gained from the Sanctuary.

no [creating] work.   9. Seven weeks shall
you count for yourself, from the time that
the sickle begins [to be put] to the grain
shall you begin to count seven weeks;
10. and then you shall make to *God*,
your God, the Festival of Weeks with the
tribute—with the free-will gift of your hand
that you shall give, according to [the extent]
that *God*, your God, will bless you.
11. And you shall rejoice before *God*,

אֱלֹהֶיךָ לֹא תַעֲשֶׂה מְלָאכָה: ס ט שִׁבְעָה שָׁבֻעֹת
תִּסְפָּר־לָךְ מֵהָחֵל חֶרְמֵשׁ בַּקָּמָה תָּחֵל לִסְפֹּר
שִׁבְעָה שָׁבֻעוֹת: י וְעָשִׂיתָ חַג שָׁבֻעוֹת לַיהוָה
אֱלֹהֶיךָ מִסַּת נִדְבַת יָדְךָ אֲשֶׁר תִּתֵּן כַּאֲשֶׁר
יְבָרֶכְךָ יְהוָה אֱלֹהֶיךָ: יא וְשָׂמַחְתָּ לִפְנֵי | יְהוָה

9. *Seven weeks shall you count for yourself, from
the time that the sickle ... shall you begin to
count seven weeks.* Clearly, the Law would have us
conceive of this counting of weeks in terms of two distinct aspects: (1) As a counting of weeks *for ourselves*
(תִּסְפָּר לָךְ) and (2) as a counting of weeks *from the first
stroke of the sickle* (מֵהָחֵל וגו׳). The exodus from Egypt
has made us free as individuals; it culminated in our
being granted independence also as a nation by being
given a land of our own. We are to consider both these
factors as we count the weeks during which we are to
make ourselves worthy of receiving the beginning of
the revealed Law. Without law there can be no personal freedom; without law, personal freedom turns
into anarchy. True freedom can exist only where there
is law.

Above all, it must be remembered that Israel
received personal freedom only in order that it might
become a servant of the Law. Its sole purpose is to
become the "people of the Law," and it requires all the
vigorous work of a free man upon his own personality to
burst asunder the fetters of lust and passion—to break
the defiance of obstinacy and willfulness that would
make him a slave of sensuality and a scorner of the Law.
It is an easy thing to receive one's personal freedom as a
gift of grace from the hands of God. But to make ourselves free also within, as free as we must be in order to
carry out our calling as bearers of the Law, requires a
sevenfold, continuous push of our inner forward
striving: "Seven weeks shall you count for yourself"!

Israel, the nation that owes its land solely to the
covenant made with its ancestors—a covenant that is
nothing else but בְּרִית הַתּוֹרָה—a covenant of and for the
Law, steers the course to disaster if it fails to see that
the land, and all the prosperity apparently guaranteed
by the land, is only a means to an end. If Israel were to
seek material prosperity without that spiritual enlightenment and moral ennoblement, which postulate that
the material blessings of prosperity may be used only in
the service of whatever is morally lofty, good and true;
if Israel were to seek material prosperity without God's
Teaching and Law; if Israel should wish to have the
Land of God without the Law of God—that would be
the surest way to Israel's downfall. Israel would be lost,

it would have to strike its name from the Divine record
of the history of nations if, like the other nations, it were
to view a land of its own, and the prosperity to be
gained from that land, as the one supreme goal compared to which spiritual and moral concerns have no
intrinsic value but serve only as a means to an end.
Israel would be denying its true mission among the
nations if it were not to begin to count only at that point
where all the others stop counting. And it requires
sevenfold labor upon oneself to attain the lofty level of
the ideal that contrasts so sharply with the philosophy
of other nations: that right and morality are not
valuable only insofar as they can yield and insure
material prosperity, but that rather, material prosperity
has meaning only insofar as it helps attain and maintain
right and morality—humanity in the truest sense of the
word. Therefore, "from the time that the sickle begins
(to be put) to the grain shall you begin to count seven
weeks."

In recapitulation: If you have already attained freedom and, in addition, a land of your own that will provide a physical guarantee for your freedom, you should
not think that you have thereby already reached the
goal of your destiny. On the contrary, you should consider yourself to be only at the beginning of your task
and should begin the sevenfold labor upon yourself so
that, in addition to the freedom and the land, you may
be able to accept from the hand of God, again and
again, also the Law of God, to the end that you may use
both your freedom and your land to serve the Law and
to translate the Law into reality. Only in this manner
will your freedom and your land attain their true value
and significance.

o   o   o

11. *and the Levite.* The Levite is characterized as
אֲשֶׁר בִּשְׁעָרֶיךָ ["who is within your gates"]: The Levites
dwell dispersed among the other tribes, each of which
was to receive a territory of its own.... The Levite
cities need not necessarily have been intended as places
where the Levites would be concentrated. These cities,
too, were scattered throughout the land, and the intention must have been to have the Levites dwell dispersed
among the population also outside the Levite cities.

אֱלֹהֶיךָ אַתָּה וּבִנְךָ וּבִתֶּךָ וְעַבְדְּךָ וַאֲמָתֶךָ וְהַלֵּוִי
אֲשֶׁר בִּשְׁעָרֶיךָ וְהַגֵּר וְהַיָּתוֹם וְהָאַלְמָנָה אֲשֶׁר
בְּקִרְבֶּךָ בַּמָּקוֹם אֲשֶׁר יִבְחַר יְהוָה אֱלֹהֶיךָ לְשַׁכֵּן
שְׁמוֹ שָׁם: יב וְזָכַרְתָּ כִּי־עֶבֶד הָיִיתָ בְּמִצְרָיִם
וְשָׁמַרְתָּ וְעָשִׂיתָ אֶת־הַחֻקִּים הָאֵלֶּה: פ מפטיר
יג חַג הַסֻּכֹּת תַּעֲשֶׂה לְךָ שִׁבְעַת יָמִים בְּאָסְפְּךָ
מִגָּרְנְךָ וּמִיִּקְבֶךָ: יד וְשָׂמַחְתָּ בְּחַגֶּךָ אַתָּה וּבִנְךָ
וּבִתֶּךָ וְעַבְדְּךָ וַאֲמָתֶךָ וְהַלֵּוִי וְהַגֵּר וְהַיָּתוֹם
וְהָאַלְמָנָה אֲשֶׁר בִּשְׁעָרֶיךָ: טו שִׁבְעַת יָמִים תָּחֹג
לַיהוָה אֱלֹהֶיךָ בַּמָּקוֹם אֲשֶׁר־יִבְחַר יְהוָה כִּי

your God; you, and your son and your daughter, and your manservant and your handmaid, and the Levite who is within your gates, and the stranger and the orphan and the widow that are in your midst, in the place that *God,* your God, will choose, to give His Name a habitation there.
12. Remember that you were a slave in Mitzrayim, and carry out these laws punctiliously.
13. You shall make yourself the Festival of Huts by gathering up [the produce] from your threshing floor and your wine press,
14. and you shall rejoice in your festival; you, and your son and your daughter, and your manservant and your handmaid, and the Levite and the stranger and the orphan and the widow that are within your gates.
15. For seven days shall you celebrate for *God,* your God, the festival in the place that *God* has chosen; for

The stranger, the orphan and the widow are described as being בְּקִרְבֶּךָ ["in your midst"]; since they have no family ties, they should be compensated for this loss by being accepted in your midst. That which we have already said elsewhere concerning the Levites applies also to the stranger, the widow and the orphan. The families that make the pilgrimage to the City of God during the festive seasons must take these individuals with them, for the rejoicing of these people is part of the general rejoicing that comes with the festival. The next verse, "Remember. . ." is probably intended to refer specifically to the attention we owe to those who have lost their freedom or their family ties.

12. ***Remember.*** (See Note to Verse 11). This admonition, which assures participation in the joys of life also to those who otherwise would feel abandoned, most eloquently reflects the character of the mission assigned to the nation of God, delivered from slavery. . . .

15. ***for God. . . will bless you . . . and then you shall remain only joyful.*** We believe that this motivation should be interpreted in the context of the preceding verses, as follows: You shall use the leavings of your threshing floor and of your wine press to make the huts for the observance of your festival. Dwelling in your cities, secure in your nationhood, you shall enter these flimsy dwellings that recall your wanderings, and there you shall rejoice, together with all your loved ones. At the very time of your harvest, you are to leave your fields, your threshing floor and your wine press and meet together with all the other members of your nation in the place that God has chosen, rallying around the Sanctuary of His Law. For the source of your abundance and your rejoicing is to be found neither in your cities, nor in your fields, nor on your threshing floors, nor in your wine presses. It is God, your God, Who grants you blessings from and through the habitation of His Law, if only you will gather around it in faithfulness. It is this attachment to God and to His Law, not your ties to town or countryside, to threshing floor or wine press, that should cause you to rejoice and to remain joyful always.

וְהָיִיתָ שָׂמֵחַ ["and you shall remain joyful"] means much more than merely וְשָׂמַחְתָּ ["and you shall rejoice"]. וְשָׂמַחְתָּ denotes a transient manifestation of joy. The behest וְהָיִיתָ שָׂמֵחַ ["you shall remain joyful]" turns your rejoicing into a permanent trait of your personality, and the words אַךְ שָׂמֵחַ ["*only* joyful"] mean that this joyfulness in your character will persist even under circumstances that would otherwise tend to cast a cloud over it. You will remain joyful *nevertheless,* "only" joyful. שִׂמְחָה [rejoicing] is the most sublime flower and fruit to ripen on the tree of life planted by the Law of God. In the same spirit, the joyfulness to which the present verse refers is not restricted to festivals and festive gatherings, but will extend beyond the festive seasons and accompany us back into everyday life, from the exuberance of the festive assemblies into the quiet privacy of our homes, and remain with us through all the vicissitudes of life.

However, this kind of joy will not be found "within your gates," or on your threshing floor, or at your wine press. To be sure, one can stage happy celebrations on one's threshing floor and at one's wine press, but וְהָיִיתָ

God, your God, will bless you in all your produce and in all the work of your hands, and then you shall remain only joyful. 16. Three times each year shall all your males appear in the immediate Presence of God, your God, in the place that He will choose; on the Festival of *Matzoth*, on the Festival of Weeks, and on the Festival of Huts; and he shall not appear in the immediate Presence of *God* empty-handed. 17. Every person according to the gift of his hand, in accordance with the blessing of *God*, your God, that He has given you.

יְבָרֶכְךָ֙ יְהֹוָ֣ה אֱלֹהֶ֔יךָ בְּכֹ֣ל תְּבוּאָֽתְךָ֔ וּבְכֹל֙ מַעֲשֵׂ֣ה יָדֶ֔יךָ וְהָיִ֖יתָ אַ֥ךְ שָׂמֵֽחַ׃ טז שָׁל֣וֹשׁ פְּעָמִ֣ים ׀ בַּשָּׁנָ֡ה יֵרָאֶה֩ כׇל־זְכ֨וּרְךָ֜ אֶת־פְּנֵ֣י ׀ יְהֹוָ֣ה אֱלֹהֶ֗יךָ בַּמָּקוֹם֙ אֲשֶׁ֣ר יִבְחָ֔ר בְּחַ֧ג הַמַּצּ֛וֹת וּבְחַ֥ג הַשָּׁבֻע֖וֹת וּבְחַ֣ג הַסֻּכּ֑וֹת וְלֹ֧א יֵרָאֶ֛ה אֶת־פְּנֵ֥י יְהֹוָ֖ה רֵיקָֽם׃ יז אִ֖ישׁ כְּמַתְּנַ֣ת יָד֑וֹ כְּבִרְכַּ֛ת יְהֹוָ֥ה אֱלֹהֶ֖יךָ אֲשֶׁ֥ר נָֽתַן־לָֽךְ׃ ס

שָׂמֵחַ, "to be joyful and to remain so always," is an art that can be learned only through God and His Law. Hence, in order to win this lasting joy that you will never lose, along with the material blessings received from your "threshing floor and wine press," you must leave your threshing floor and wine press and travel to the place that God will choose. This is the place where, gathering around God and His Law together with the entire community, you will gain the spirit that will enable you to attain the true, genuine joy of life that will accompany you through all your days. There you will learn not only to "rejoice," but to be "joyful

nevertheless," whatever life may bring: וְהָיִיתָ אַךְ שָׂמֵחַ. . . .

16. . . . This verse expresses the following thought: Three times each year every individual who belongs to the nation shall come forth from his isolation and perceive himself as being in the immediate presence of the nation's One God, in the periphery of the one Sanctuary which all the members of the nation cherish in common. In this manner, he will become aware of the tie that binds every individual member to all the other members of the nation, to God and to His Law.

∘   ∘   ∘

The Haftarah for this Sidra may be found on page 913.

שפטים

SHOFETIM

18. Judges and [law-]enforcing officials shall you appoint for yourself in all your gates that *God*, your God, is giving you for your tribes, so that they may judge the people according to the judgment of justice. 19. You shall not twist judgment, and you shall not recognize a face, and you shall not accept bribery, because bribery blinds the eyes of the wise and causes the words of the righteous to falter. 20. Justice, justice shall you pursue, so that you may live and take possession of the land which *God*, your God, is giving you. 21. Do not plant yourself an *asherah*, no tree at all, beside the altar of *God*, your God, which you shall make for yourself; 22. and do not erect for yourself a memorial stone, which *God*, your God, hates.

XVII 1. Do not offer to *God*, your God, an ox or a

יח שֹׁפְטִים וְשֹׁטְרִים תִּתֶּן־לְךָ בְּכָל־שְׁעָרֶיךָ
אֲשֶׁר יְהוָה אֱלֹהֶיךָ נֹתֵן לְךָ לִשְׁבָטֶיךָ וְשָׁפְטוּ
אֶת־הָעָם מִשְׁפַּט־צֶדֶק׃ יט לֹא־תַטֶּה מִשְׁפָּט לֹא
תַכִּיר פָּנִים וְלֹא־תִקַּח שֹׁחַד כִּי הַשֹּׁחַד יְעַוֵּר
עֵינֵי חֲכָמִים וִיסַלֵּף דִּבְרֵי צַדִּיקִם׃ כ צֶדֶק צֶדֶק
תִּרְדֹּף לְמַעַן תִּחְיֶה וְיָרַשְׁתָּ אֶת־הָאָרֶץ אֲשֶׁר־
יְהוָה אֱלֹהֶיךָ נֹתֵן לָךְ׃ ס כא לֹא־תִטַּע לְךָ אֲשֵׁרָה
כָּל־עֵץ אֵצֶל מִזְבַּח יְהוָה אֱלֹהֶיךָ אֲשֶׁר
תַּעֲשֶׂה־לָּךְ׃ כב וְלֹא־תָקִים לְךָ מַצֵּבָה אֲשֶׁר
שָׂנֵא יְהוָה אֱלֹהֶיךָ׃ ס יז א לֹא־תִזְבַּח לַיהוָה

18. שֹׁפְטִים ***[Judges].*** The laws set forth thus far focused on the centralizing influence that the place chosen by God as the Sanctuary of His Law should exert upon the sons of His people, who will dwell dispersed throughout the land. The laws that now follow relate to the institutions through which representatives of this Law are to be appointed from this central point, to function throughout the land, so that the effectiveness of the Sanctuary of the Law may be ensured wherever the members of the nation may dwell. . . .

• • •

20. ***Justice, justice shall you pursue.*** צֶדֶק, "Justice—"right" — the shaping of all private and communal affairs in accordance with the requirements of God's Law, is to be the one supreme goal sought purely for its own sake; a goal to which all other considerations must defer. Israel's sole task is to pursue this goal unceasingly and with single-minded devotion, "so that you may live and take possession. . . ." If Israel does this, it has done everything within its power to secure its physical and political existence (cf. תִּחְיֶה ["live"] and וְיָרַשְׁתָּ ["take possession"] respectively). Note that even now, when it clearly refers to the time when Israel has already completed its occupation of the Land, the text still uses the term וְיָרַשְׁתָּ ["and take possession"] (from יְרֻשָּׁה [inheritance]), with reference to the political security that Israel will gain if it will honor and promote justice. The use of this term makes clear the crucial fact that Israel's possession of the Land can be called in question at any time, and that Israel must take possession of its land anew at every moment, as it were, by making certain that the Jewish state will honor justice and translate it into reality throughout the land. . . .

21. ***Do not plant.*** אֲשֵׁרָה is a tree which was considered to be under the special protection of a pagan deity, so that, if this tree thrived (אשר [=luck, progress, fruitfulness]), it was considered a manifestation of the power of this deity. For this reason, this tree was regarded as sacred. This mentality accords entirely with the ideas of the pagans, who worshipped primarily the forces of nature, forces whose power the heathen mind saw manifest above all in the development and phenomena of the physical world. But such notions are diametrically opposed to the Jewish concept of God. Judaism sees not only the physical world, but on a much loftier, more direct and intimate plane, also the moral and spiritual world of man as the sphere of God's sovereignty; and only if the Jew subordinates all of his own spiritual essence, all his aspirations and actions to the authority of his God, can he expect to have a share in the abundance of the physical world. . . .

sheep on which there is a blemish, anything bad; for it is an abomination to *God,* your God.   2. If there is found in your midst, in one of your gates which *God,* your God, is giving you, a man or a woman who does that which is evil in the eyes of *God,* your God, to transgress His covenant;   3. and he went and served other gods and cast himself down before them, or to the sun or the moon or all the host of the heaven that I have not commanded;   4. and it is testified for you and you have heard it, then you shall make careful inquiry, and if it turns out to be true—if the testimony is based on fact; if such a depravity has [indeed] been perpetrated in Israel—   5. then you shall take out that man or that woman who has committed this evil thing; to your gates, the man or the woman, and you shall stone them with stones so that they die.   6. At the word of two witnesses or three witnesses

אֱלֹהֶיךָ שׁוֹר וָשֶׂה אֲשֶׁר יִהְיֶה בוֹ מוּם כֹּל דָּבָר
רָע כִּי תוֹעֲבַת יְהֹוָה אֱלֹהֶיךָ הוּא: ס ב כִּי־
יִמָּצֵא בְקִרְבְּךָ בְּאַחַד שְׁעָרֶיךָ אֲשֶׁר־יְהֹוָה
אֱלֹהֶיךָ נֹתֵן לָךְ אִישׁ אוֹ־אִשָּׁה אֲשֶׁר יַעֲשֶׂה אֶת־
הָרַע בְּעֵינֵי יְהֹוָה־אֱלֹהֶיךָ לַעֲבֹר בְּרִיתוֹ: ג וַיֵּלֶךְ
וַיַּעֲבֹד אֱלֹהִים אֲחֵרִים וַיִּשְׁתַּחוּ לָהֶם וְלַשֶּׁמֶשׁ ׀
אוֹ לַיָּרֵחַ אוֹ לְכָל־צְבָא הַשָּׁמַיִם אֲשֶׁר לֹא־
צִוִּיתִי: ד וְהֻגַּד־לְךָ וְשָׁמָעְתָּ וְדָרַשְׁתָּ הֵיטֵב וְהִנֵּה
אֱמֶת נָכוֹן הַדָּבָר נֶעֶשְׂתָה הַתּוֹעֵבָה הַזֹּאת
בְּיִשְׂרָאֵל: ה וְהוֹצֵאתָ אֶת־הָאִישׁ הַהוּא אוֹ אֶת־
הָאִשָּׁה הַהִוא אֲשֶׁר עָשׂוּ אֶת־הַדָּבָר הָרַע הַזֶּה
אֶל־שְׁעָרֶיךָ אֶת־הָאִישׁ אוֹ אֶת־הָאִשָּׁה וּסְקַלְתָּם
בָּאֲבָנִים וָמֵתוּ: ו עַל־פִּי ׀ שְׁנַיִם עֵדִים אוֹ

CHAPTER XVII

1. *Do not offer.* The present verse is the conclusion of what has gone before. We were told in the preceding chapter that our welfare, both physical and political, depends on our devotion to our duties as symbolically expressed by the offerings placed upon the altar of God. Now we are told, in addition, that this devotion of ours must encompass the whole of our personality, and that it must accord in every respect with the dictates of God's will. Nothing must be missing (מום [blemish]) from the body of the animal that is meant to symbolize our own surrender to God, and this pure expression of our devotion to duty must not be tainted by any of the violations of the Law ("anything bad") described in the Book of Leviticus. . . .

2. *If there is found.* In connection with what has gone before, we are now given the rules for the criminal proceedings to be followed by the representative authorities of the nation, or by its delegates, in carrying out their function to uphold the Law when that Law is violated. The case chosen as an illustration here involves the most serious of all crimes: עֲבוֹדָה זָרָה [idolatry]. Even in such a case, however, the prosecution must follow the same precisely detailed procedure that is specified for misdemeanors of lesser gravity. Even in the case of this, the most serious of all crimes, the prosecution, as in all of Jewish criminal law, must be based on testimony from eyewitnesses. Circumstantial evi-

dence is not admissible. Even in such a case, the court can enter into the proceedings only after charges have been brought by eyewitnesses, who must be able to produce legally acceptable evidence. Inquisitorial procedures based on mere denunciation are unlawful. The testimony of the witnesses must be subjected to the most meticulous, careful scrutiny, and a human court of law can take action against the accused only if it has been established beyond doubt that, at the moment he committed the act, the accused had been warned and had been aware of the unlawful character of his act. All these details are discussed in the case in point that follows.

•   •   •

3. *and he went and served.* (cf. Deuteronomy 13:6 and 14). The use of the expression "and he went and served," his "going" for the purpose of doing this, expresses the revulsion a Jewish individual should feel against such a crime, and at the same time stresses the audacity required for committing such a crime when one is fully aware of how repugnant such an act is to the Jewish spirit.

•   •   •

6. יוּמַת הַמֵּת [*shall the dead man be put to death*]. Note that the accused is referred to here as מֵת ["the dead man"], even before he has been executed and, in fact, even before he has been sentenced to death. The text is still discussing the hearing of testimony from eyewitnesses in the case. This verse is the basis for the

שְׁלֹשָׁה עֵדִים יוּמַת הַמֵּת לֹא יוּמַת עַל־פִּי עֵד
אֶחָד: ז יַד הָעֵדִים תִּהְיֶה־בּוֹ בָרִאשֹׁנָה לַהֲמִיתוֹ
וְיַד כָּל־הָעָם בָּאַחֲרֹנָה וּבִעַרְתָּ הָרָע מִקִּרְבֶּךָ: פ
ח כִּי יִפָּלֵא מִמְּךָ דָבָר לַמִּשְׁפָּט בֵּין־דָּם | לְדָם
בֵּין־דִּין לְדִין וּבֵין נֶגַע לָנֶגַע דִּבְרֵי רִיבֹת
בִּשְׁעָרֶיךָ וְקַמְתָּ וְעָלִיתָ אֶל־הַמָּקוֹם אֲשֶׁר יִבְחַר
יְהֹוָה אֱלֹהֶיךָ בּוֹ: ט וּבָאתָ אֶל־הַכֹּהֲנִים הַלְוִיִּם
וְאֶל־הַשֹּׁפֵט אֲשֶׁר יִהְיֶה בַּיָּמִים הָהֵם וְדָרַשְׁתָּ

---

shall the dead man be put to death; he shall not be put to death on the basis of the word of [only] one witness. 7. The hand of the witnesses shall be the first upon him to put him to death, and the hand of all the people afterwards; you are to clear away the evil from your midst. 8. If a matter is too difficult for you to decide, between blood and blood, between right and right, between damage and damage, or any [other] disputes within your gates, then you shall arise and go up to the place that *God,* your God, will choose, 9. and you shall come to the priests, the Levites, and to the judge that will be in those days, and you shall make

---

halakhah (Sanhedrin 41a), according to which the accused must have been warned, at the moment he committed the crime, not only that what he was doing was against the law, but also that this act would make him liable to the death penalty. If, despite these explicit warnings, he commited the crime, "he has delivered himself up to death." In other words, he is already under the death sentence when he first appears before the court, and the task of the court is now only to seek extenuating circumtances that might warrant his acquittal. . . .

In Bekhoroth 18b, this Biblical text is cited as the basis for the dictum that "the wicked are called dead (even) while they are (still) alive"; i.e., whereas the righteous are called "living" even after they have died, the wicked must be referred to as "dead" even while they are still alive. A sinful way of life does not accord with the concept of "living."

       ◦   ◦   ◦

8. *If a matter is too difficult.* In Verses 8 to 13 the supreme court, sitting at the central point of the nation, the Sanctuary of the Law, is appointed as the sole supreme authority responsible for the authentic transmission and interpretation of the Law and for all the dispositions required in the proper observance and implementation of that Law. The decisions handed down by this authority are not subject to appeal and must be carried out without reservations by the people as a whole, along with the functionaries that expound the Law. . . .

to the place that God, *your God, will choose.* The place as such is an essential factor in the law set down here (Sanhedrin 87a). God has chosen one place where the testimony of the revelation of His Law was to be deposited, where the demands and consequences of this Law were to be communicated to the nation in symbolic terms, and where the nation was to perform symbolic acts to express its devotion to this Law. He

has also designated this place as the sole seat of the supreme authority charged with the practical understanding and implementation of His Law. In other words, the symbolic center of the Law and the center for its practical application are to be in one and the same place. . . .

9. *and you shall come to the priests, the Levites, and to the judge.* The close link between the Sanhedrin and the Sanctuary of the Law discussed in our notes to the preceding verse is expressed also in the present verse by the juxtaposition of the priests and the supreme court (see Sanhedrin 52b). They both serve one and the same purpose and one and the same truth of life (cf. Exodus 20:22). The authentic text of the Written Law, תּוֹרָה שֶׁבִּכְתָב, was placed into the custody of the priests, side by side with the Testimony of the Law (cf. Deuteronomy 17:18 and 31:25, 26), even as the Sanhedrin was the first to possess the [Oral] Tradition of the Law, the תּוֹרָה שֶׁבְּעַל פֶּה.

True, as is clear from Leviticus 4:3, the priests and even the high priest *per se* did not possess any authority [as expounders or implementers] of the Law; indeed, as regards the dissemination of the Law, the priest is on the same level as the lowliest among the people; and the members of the first Sanhedrin, the Council of Seventy that Moses had appointed to assist him, were chosen without distinction from among all the tribes (Numbers 11:16). Nevertheless, as noted ibid., and as indicated here, it was considered a *mitzvah* to coopt Aaronides into the Sanhedrin, provided they had the necessary personal qualifications. Indeed, in the present verse, and again in Verse 18, the כֹּהֲנִים are referred to as הַכֹּהֲנִים הַלְוִיִּם ["the priests, the Levites"]; i.e., they are identified by their tribal affiliation. This was probably done not so much to stress their special position of priesthood as it was to underscore their qualities as members of the tribe of Levi, the proven, undaunted active champions of the Law. It certainly inquiry and they shall tell you the word of the judgment.   10. And you must do according to the utterance of the word that they will tell you from that place which *God* will choose; you must do with care according to all that they will teach you. 11. Upon the utterance of the teaching that they will teach you, and upon the judgment that they will say to you, must you base your [own] action; you must not turn aside from the word that they will tell you, [neither] to the right [n]or to the left. 12. But the man who will rebel in not hearkening to the priest that stands there to serve *God*, your God, or to the judge—that man shall die, and you shall clear away the evil from Yisrael.   13. And all the people shall hear it and be afraid and rebel no more.   14. When you will come to the land that *God*, your God, is giving you, and

וְהִגִּ֣ידוּ לְךָ֔ אֵ֖ת דְּבַ֥ר הַמִּשְׁפָּֽט: י וְעָשִׂ֗יתָ עַל־פִּ֤י הַדָּבָר֙ אֲשֶׁ֣ר יַגִּ֣ידֽוּ לְךָ֔ מִן־הַמָּק֣וֹם הַה֔וּא אֲשֶׁ֖ר יִבְחַ֣ר יְהֹוָ֑ה וְשָׁמַרְתָּ֣ לַעֲשׂ֔וֹת כְּכֹ֖ל אֲשֶׁ֥ר יוֹרֽוּךָ: יא עַל־פִּ֣י הַתּוֹרָ֞ה אֲשֶׁ֣ר יוֹר֗וּךָ וְעַל־הַמִּשְׁפָּ֛ט אֲשֶׁר־יֹֽאמְר֥וּ לְךָ֖ תַּעֲשֶׂ֑ה לֹ֣א תָס֗וּר מִן־הַדָּבָ֛ר אֲשֶׁר־יַגִּ֥ידֽוּ לְךָ֖ יָמִ֥ין וּשְׂמֹֽאל: יב וְהָאִ֞ישׁ אֲשֶׁר־יַעֲשֶׂ֣ה בְזָד֗וֹן לְבִלְתִּ֨י שְׁמֹ֤עַ אֶל־הַכֹּהֵן֙ הָעֹמֵ֞ד לְשָׁ֤רֶת שָׁם֙ אֶת־יְהֹוָ֣ה אֱלֹהֶ֔יךָ א֖וֹ אֶל־הַשֹּׁפֵ֑ט וּמֵת֙ הָאִ֣ישׁ הַה֔וּא וּבִֽעַרְתָּ֥ הָרָ֖ע מִיִּשְׂרָאֵֽל: יג וְכָל־הָעָ֖ם יִשְׁמְע֣וּ וְיִרָ֑אוּ וְלֹ֥א יְזִיד֖וּן עֽוֹד: ס שני יד כִּֽי־תָבֹ֣א אֶל־הָאָ֗רֶץ אֲשֶׁ֨ר יְהֹוָ֧ה אֱלֹהֶ֛יךָ

would be most desirable to have such a spirit represented in the supreme council of the Law. . . .

∘   ∘   ∘

12. . . . Jewish Law, with all its rules applicable to private and communal life, does not serve notions of justice or expediency devised by man. It represents the realization of the will of God on earth as set down in the written outline of the Law for which the Sanctuary was erected, and as expressed in further detail in the Oral Law. The Divine will, served by the Law and its implementation, is the same lawgiving will of God that endorses the decisions handed down by any supreme court convened in the precincts of His Sanctuary as the sole authority for the implementation of His Law. The implementation of these decisions represents compliance with the will and approval of God regarding the practical shaping of our affairs on earth. Any act contrary to such a decision would be contrary to the will of God—even if that decision had been made in error. This does not in any way imply that the supreme tribunal is infallible. However, it is the will of God, our Lawgiver, that His Law should be implemented by the mandate of this tribunal. . . .

14. **When you will come.** The purpose of the preceding law was to safeguard the observance of the Law against the possibility that an authority entrusted with its enforcement might not have the proper understanding of its duty. To this is now added a further safeguard: to protect the Law against the chance that an individual whom the people has vested with royal powers might misinterpret the scope of his functions. . .

When you will come to the land that God, *your* God, *is giving you, and you have taken possession of it and will dwell in it.* These words, which introduce the chapter dealing with the function of kings in Israel, unequivocally state at the very outset that the function of the Jewish king is neither to conquer the land nor to secure Israel's possession of it [by physical might]. In general, the function of the Jewish king is not to develop the nation's physical power in relationship to the world outside. It is God Who gives the Land to Israel; it is with His help that Israel will conquer the land, and only under His protection will it dwell there securely. This Divine assistance, protection and blessing have been promised to Israel again and again in the Law, and have also been stressed repeatedly by Moses, in his admonitions preparing Israel for the conquest of the land. For these purposes Israel does not need a king; all that Israel needs to do—so that God's promises may be fulfilled—is to be "Israel"; to prove that it is indeed the people loyal to the Law of God: to win a moral victory over itself from within so as to be sure of victory also against all its enemies from without. . . . Indeed, the *halakhah* (Kiddushin 37b) points out that there was need for the appointment of a king only after Israel had completed the conquest and the occupation of the land; it also categorically denies that the purpose of the Jewish monarchy was to wield warlike powers.

Nevertheless, we are told here "You will say: 'I will set a king over me, like all the nations that are around me.'"; i.e., after Israel has completed the conquest of the land and has settled down upon it, the need will be felt for a royal chief of state, and the satisfaction of this need will then not only be permitted but, in fact, you have taken possession of it and will dwell in it, you will say: "I will set a king over me, like all the nations that are around me." 15. You shall then set a king over yourself whom *God*, your God, will choose. From the midst of your brethren shall you set a king over yourself; you cannot set over yourself a foreigner who is not your brother. 16. Only he must not get himself many horses, nor cause the people to return to

נֹתֵן לָ֣ךְ וִֽירִשְׁתָּ֖הּ וְיָשַׁ֣בְתָּה בָּ֑הּ וְאָמַרְתָּ֗ אָשִׂ֤ימָה עָלַי֙ מֶ֔לֶךְ כְּכָל־הַגּוֹיִ֖ם אֲשֶׁ֥ר סְבִיבֹתָֽי׃ טו שׂ֣וֹם תָּשִׂ֤ים עָלֶ֙יךָ֙ מֶ֔לֶךְ אֲשֶׁ֥ר יִבְחַ֛ר יְהֹוָ֥ה אֱלֹהֶ֖יךָ בּ֑וֹ מִקֶּ֣רֶב אַחֶ֗יךָ תָּשִׂ֤ים עָלֶ֙יךָ֙ מֶ֔לֶךְ לֹ֣א תוּכַ֗ל לָתֵ֤ת עָלֶ֙יךָ֙ אִ֣ישׁ נָכְרִ֔י אֲשֶׁ֥ר לֹֽא־אָחִ֖יךָ הֽוּא׃ טז רַק֩ לֹא־יַרְבֶּה־לּ֨וֹ סוּסִ֜ים וְלֹֽא־יָשִׁ֤יב אֶת־הָעָם֙

according to the *halakhah* (Sanhedrin 20b), virtually commanded. It is therefore obvious that the proclamation of the commandment to appoint a king, "You shall then set a king over yourself" (Verse 15), was deferred only until the time when the need for a king could be articulated so that, emanating from these sentiments, the institution of monarchy would be interpreted in the proper manner and not be regarded as loss of independence imposed upon the people from without.

Accordingly, the purpose of the command [to appoint a king] can only be to promote the sole factor upon which God's continued protection and blessing depend: to make the nation be "Israel," the loyal people of the Law of God. Accordingly, too, it is obvious that the qualification, "like all the nations that are around me" can be interpreted only as follows: All the nations seek to unify all their national resources for the greatest good of their own nation, which in their view consists in the unfolding of the greatest possible power vis-a-vis the world outside. To this end they must subordinate themselves to one chief of state at whose command all the nation's resources must be placed for this purpose.

You, too, [O Israel,] will feel the need for national unity in order to obtain the greatest possible good for yourself, but [as distinct from the other nations,] you deem this good to lie solely in the most complete possible realization of the Law of God in your own midst. For this purpose, you, too, will feel that you need a king [but the function of your king will be different from that of the kings of other nations]. The function of your king will be to stand out as the first among all Jews loyal to the Law—to shine forth personally in all the moral nobility of this allegiance to the Law. Himself imbued with the spirit of your mission, he will deem it his task to win the hearts and minds of all his subjects for this spirit, in thought, word and deed, and to utilize the power of his word, his personal example and his personal prestige to combat anything that would violate this spirit. You are to place all your resources at his command, so that he may function as the champion and defender of your national mission. The full extent to which this should be the true vocation of the Jewish king, and the full extent to which your king must

combat the threat resulting from the nation's decentralization—i.e., the alienation of its individual segments from their one common moral task as a nation—can be seen from the moral corruption of the Jewish people as recorded in the Book of Judges: the graven image made by the man Micah, who lived in the hill country of Ephraim (Judges 17) and the Levite's concubine (Judges 19), concerning which Scripture variously laments (Judges 17:6, 18:1, 19:1 and 21:25): "In those days there was no king in Israel; every man did that which was right in his own eyes."

o   o   o

16. *Only he must not get himself many horses.* The word רַק ["only"] qualifies the commandment "you shall then set . . . ," by which [as explained in Sanhedrin 19b] the nation is commanded to give its king absolute authority, "so that his dread may be upon you." The modifying particle רַק serves as a counterweight, imposing upon the king the duty of self-restraint above all with regard to those factors that past history has shown to be the rocks upon which the virtue of kings has been wrecked, and thus the happiness of their peoples shattered. These are: the lust after military glory, after women and after wealth.

o   o   o

nor cause the people to return to Mitzrayim . . . and God has said to you. From the very beginning of Jewish history, ancient Egypt had been a land of refuge for the inhabitants of the land of Canaan. Abraham went to Egypt because there was a famine in Canaan (Genesis 12:10). Isaac was about to go there for the same reason and was kept from doing so only by a direct command from God (ibid. 26:2). Indeed, the only reason for Israel's migration to Egypt was the famine in the land of Canaan that caused the sons of Jacob to travel to that country repeatedly in order to purchase food. Hence, Egypt's agricultural wealth gave her superiority over other countries and caused those lands, particularly Canaan, to appear dependent upon her.

Consequently, the meaning of the statement "You shall henceforth return no more upon this path" would seem to be: Never again shall you go from Canaan

Mitzrayim in order to get many horses, and *God* has said to you: "You shall henceforth return no more upon this path." 17. He also must not take himself many wives, so that his heart may not go astray, and he must not amass silver and gold for himself in excess. 18. Rather, when he sits upon the throne of his sovereignty, he shall write for himself a duplicate of this Teaching in a book out of the one that is in the custody of the priests, the Levites. 19. It shall be with him; he shall read from it as long as he shall live, so that he may learn to fear *God*, his God, and to carry out punctiliously all the words of this Teaching and all these laws, 20. so that his heart may not lift itself up above his brethren and so that he may not turn aside from the commandment, to the right or to the left, so that he may long remain in his sovereignty, he and his sons, in the midst of Yisrael.

XVIII 1. The priests—the Levites—and all the tribe of Levi shall have no portion or inheritance in Yisrael; they shall eat the offerings to the fire of *God*, and that which is directed

מִצְרַ֗יְמָה לְמַ֙עַן֙ הַרְבּ֣וֹת ס֔וּס וַֽיהֹוָה֙ אָמַ֣ר לָכֶ֔ם
לֹ֣א תֹסִפ֗וּן לָשׁ֛וּב בַּדֶּ֥רֶךְ הַזֶּ֖ה ע֑וֹד: יז וְלֹ֤א
יַרְבֶּה־לּוֹ֙ נָשִׁ֔ים וְלֹ֥א יָס֖וּר לְבָב֑וֹ וְכֶ֣סֶף וְזָהָ֔ב לֹ֥א
יַרְבֶּה־לּ֖וֹ מְאֹֽד: יח וְהָיָ֣ה כְשִׁבְתּ֔וֹ עַ֖ל כִּסֵּ֣א
מַמְלַכְתּ֑וֹ וְכָ֨תַב ל֜וֹ אֶת־מִשְׁנֵ֨ה הַתּוֹרָ֤ה הַזֹּאת֙
עַל־סֵ֔פֶר מִלִּפְנֵ֖י הַכֹּֽהֲנִ֥ים הַלְוִיִּֽם: יט וְהָיְתָ֣ה
עִמּ֗וֹ וְקָ֥רָא ב֛וֹ כׇּל־יְמֵ֣י חַיָּ֑יו לְמַ֣עַן יִלְמַ֗ד לְיִרְאָה֙
אֶת־יְהֹוָ֣ה אֱלֹהָ֔יו לִ֠שְׁמֹ֠ר אֶֽת־כׇּל־דִּבְרֵ֞י הַתּוֹרָ֥ה
הַזֹּ֛את וְאֶת־הַֽחֻקִּ֥ים הָאֵ֖לֶּה לַֽעֲשֹׂתָֽם: כ לְבִלְתִּ֤י
רוּם־לְבָבוֹ֙ מֵֽאֶחָ֔יו וּלְבִלְתִּ֛י ס֥וּר מִן־הַמִּצְוָ֖ה
יָמִ֣ין וּשְׂמֹ֑אול לְמַ֨עַן יַֽאֲרִ֤יךְ יָמִים֙ עַל־מַמְלַכְתּ֔וֹ
ה֥וּא וּבָנָ֖יו בְּקֶ֥רֶב יִשְׂרָאֵֽל: ס שלישי יח א לֹֽא־
יִ֠הְיֶ֠ה לַכֹּֽהֲנִ֨ים הַלְוִיִּ֜ם כׇּל־שֵׁ֧בֶט לֵוִ֛י חֵ֥לֶק וְנַֽחֲלָ֖ה
עִם־יִשְׂרָאֵ֑ל אִשֵּׁ֥י יְהֹוָ֛ה וְנַֽחֲלָת֖וֹ יֹאכֵלֽוּן:

[Eretz Yisrael] to Egypt as you did in the past, to obtain from there the things that your nation needs but your own land does not supply. You shall not make yourselves dependent on Egypt. A Jewish king who glories in building up a mighty military force is guilty of a two-fold sin. He commits a direct transgression, because his true calling lies elsewhere. He also sins indirectly, for in this manner he makes himself and his people dependent upon Egypt, the only place from which he can obtain horses for his mounted troops. If Egypt does not allow him to have the horses, he is lost. He is therefore obliged to maintain friendly relations and constant traffic with Egypt, and so, along with the Egyptian horses, Egyptian ideas and Egyptian notions of statecraft will also be introduced into the land of Israel. In the description of the unspeakable distress and misery that lie in store for Israel if, dwelling in the land given to it so that it may perform its mission, it should break faith with that mission, Chapter 28:68 concludes with a portrayal of utmost forsakenness and despair: "Indeed, *God* will cause you to return to Mitzrayim in ships in the manner of which I said to you that you will never see it again; you will there offer yourselves for sale as manservants and maidservants to your enemies, but there will be no purchaser." God will compel the people of Israel to travel to Egypt by roundabout routes, aboard ships, as a last refuge in order to survive, there

to offer themselves for sale as slaves—but no one will want to purchase them. They should have lived contentedly in their land, prizing their independence, and should never have looked to Egypt for any of their nation's needs. But since they acted contrary to the admonition against dependence on Egypt, their own land will cease to support them, and they will find themselves in such misery that the servitude from which God liberated them will seem attractive to them. Thus, centuries after their deliverance from slavery, they will offer themselves voluntarily as slaves to their former masters, only to be scorned by them.

.   .   .

18. *Rather, when he sits.* His first act on ascending the throne shall be to write out for himself, with his own hand, a copy of the תּוֹרָה. By this act he acknowledges that the Law was given to him before all others; that he is not above the Law, but rather that the Law must be the immutable guideline for all his life; that the realization of this Law in his nation is the sum total of his mission as king and that by his own punctilious observance of the Law, and his own self-sacrificing devotion to the tasks assigned by it, he will provide a personal example to his people as the "first son of the Law."

.   .   .

to Him.   2. But he shall have no inheritance in the midst of his brethren; *God* is his inheritance, as He has spoken it to him. 3. And this shall be the right[ful due] of the priests from the people, from those that slaughter an animal fit for food, whether it be an ox or a sheep; he must give to the priest the foreleg, the two parts of the lower jaw and the maw.   4. The first of your grain, your new wine and your oil, and also the first of the shearing of your sheep shall you give to him.   5. For *God*, your God, has chosen him out of all your tribes to stand, to serve in the Name of *God*, him and his sons forever.   6. And if the Levite from one of your gates where he sojourns comes forth from the [national] entity of Yisrael, and if he comes, entirely of his own desire, to the place that *God* will choose, 7. he can serve in the Name of *God*, his God, as do all his brethren, the Levites, who stand there before *God*.   8. They shall receive the same portions to eat, except for his exchanges according to [the right of] the heads of the tribes.   9. When you come into the land that *God*, your God, is giving

ב וְנַחֲלָה לֹא־יִהְיֶה־לּוֹ בְּקֶרֶב אֶחָיו יְהֹוָה הוּא נַחֲלָתוֹ כַּאֲשֶׁר דִּבֶּר־לוֹ: ס ג וְזֶה יִהְיֶה מִשְׁפַּט הַכֹּהֲנִים מֵאֵת הָעָם מֵאֵת זֹבְחֵי הַזֶּבַח אִם־שׁוֹר אִם־שֶׂה וְנָתַן לַכֹּהֵן הַזְּרֹעַ וְהַלְּחָיַיִם וְהַקֵּבָה: ד רֵאשִׁית דְּגָנְךָ תִּירֹשְׁךָ וְיִצְהָרֶךָ וְרֵאשִׁית גֵּז צֹאנְךָ תִּתֶּן־לּוֹ: ה כִּי בוֹ בָּחַר יְהֹוָה אֱלֹהֶיךָ מִכָּל־שְׁבָטֶיךָ לַעֲמֹד לְשָׁרֵת בְּשֵׁם־יְהֹוָה הוּא וּבָנָיו כָּל־הַיָּמִים: ס רביעי ו וְכִי־יָבֹא הַלֵּוִי מֵאַחַד שְׁעָרֶיךָ מִכָּל־יִשְׂרָאֵל אֲשֶׁר־הוּא גָּר שָׁם וּבָא בְּכָל־אַוַּת נַפְשׁוֹ אֶל־הַמָּקוֹם אֲשֶׁר־יִבְחַר יְהֹוָה: ז וְשֵׁרֵת בְּשֵׁם יְהֹוָה אֱלֹהָיו כְּכָל־אֶחָיו הַלְוִיִּם הָעֹמְדִים שָׁם לִפְנֵי יְהֹוָה: ח חֵלֶק כְּחֵלֶק יֹאכֵלוּ לְבַד מִמְכָּרָיו עַל־הָאָבוֹת: ס ט כִּי אַתָּה בָּא אֶל־הָאָרֶץ אֲשֶׁר־יְהֹוָה אֱלֹהֶיךָ נֹתֵן לָךְ לֹא־

CHAPTER XVIII

7–8. *except for his exchanges according to [the right of] the heads of the tribes.* The Law assumes that in the course of time the priestly tribe will have grown to such numbers that all the priests will not be able to minister in the Temple at the same time. An agreement will then have to be made between the various priestly families under which a system of rotation will be set up, with certain priests ministering in the Temple and entitled to partake of the tribute for a specified period, after which other priests will take their place. Such a rotation is termed מִמְכָּר [''exchange''; lit. ''sale''] because of all those who have the prerogatives of performing the priestly functions, one group transfers or cedes its prerogatives to another group, with the understanding that this second group in turn will transfer its prerogatives to a third group, until every priest will have had his turn to minister as a priest and to enjoy the prerogatives of priesthood. This arrangement, then, is one based on מכר, a mutual exchange.... And it is presumed that these ministering divisions, מִשְׁמָר [lit. ''watch''], will be constituted according to family groups related by אָבוֹת, common ancestry....

9. *When you come.* Judges, kings, priests—these were the functionaries that served the nation, whose position and duties were discussed above, and whose authority was placed within prescribed limits. These three groups of functionaries, in fact, complete the political structure required for the implementation of the Law. Now there follows only a discussion of the place occupied in this structure by the prophets. This stipulation opens with negative statements, banning functionaries whom the heathen nations considered indispensable, but for whom there should be neither room nor need within the Jewish national entity, and whom the Jewish state should not tolerate in its midst: the practitioners of so-called ''divination.''

The introductory statements remind us that ''*God*, your God,'' being the sole Pilot of our destinies and Guide of our actions, gave us the Land, the basis for the development of our national welfare; and that He has given it לָךְ, *to you*—as *Sifre* repeatedly explains, בְּזָכוּתֶךָ—solely on the basis of your own moral merits, which you have already demonstrated, or which you are expected to demonstrate in the future. This, then, tells you all that needs to be said for what follows: All that you need to acquire and maintain your welfare and happiness lies within your own hands.

• • •

you, do not learn to do after the abominations of these nations.   10. There shall not
be found among you anyone who makes his
son or his daughter pass through fire, no
soothsayer, diviner of [auspicious] times,
interpreter of omens, or sorcerer;   11. no
charmer; no one who consults *ob* or *yiddoni*
and no necromancer.   12. For whoever
does these things is abominable to *God*, and
because of these abominations, *God*, your
God, is driving them away from before you.
13. Be whole[hearted] with *God*, your
God.   14. For those nations whom you are
to succeed in possession, they hearken to
soothsayers and to diviners of auspicious

תִּלְמַ֣ד לַעֲשׂ֔וֹת כְּתוֹעֲבֹ֖ת הַגּוֹיִ֥ם הָהֵֽם׃ י לֹא־
יִמָּצֵ֣א בְךָ֔ מַעֲבִ֥יר בְּנֽוֹ־וּבִתּ֖וֹ בָּאֵ֑שׁ קֹסֵ֣ם קְסָמִ֔ים
מְעוֹנֵ֥ן וּמְנַחֵ֖שׁ וּמְכַשֵּֽׁף׃ יא וְחֹבֵ֖ר חָ֑בֶר וְשֹׁאֵ֥ל
א֖וֹב וְיִדְּעֹנִ֑י וְדֹרֵ֖שׁ אֶל־הַמֵּתִֽים׃ יב כִּֽי־תוֹעֲבַ֥ת
יְהֹוָ֖ה כָּל־עֹ֣שֵׂה אֵ֑לֶּה וּבִגְלַל֙ הַתּוֹעֵבֹ֣ת הָאֵ֔לֶּה
יְהֹוָ֣ה אֱלֹהֶ֔יךָ מוֹרִ֥ישׁ אוֹתָ֖ם מִפָּנֶֽיךָ׃ יג תָּמִ֣ים
תִּֽהְיֶ֔ה עִ֖ם יְהֹוָ֥ה אֱלֹהֶֽיךָ׃ חמישי יד כִּ֣י ׀ הַגּוֹיִ֣ם
הָאֵ֗לֶּה אֲשֶׁ֤ר אַתָּה֙ יוֹרֵ֣שׁ אוֹתָ֔ם אֶל־מְעֹֽנְנִ֥ים

12. *For whoever does these things is abominable
... and because of these abominations.* We have
already explained, in our notes to relevant passages in
the Books of Exodus and Leviticus, the moral errors
inherent in these pagan practices, and the moral
depravity to which they give rise. Once man comes to
believe that his destinies, his actions, his hopes and his
fears are all under the dominion of dark, unfree forces
born of delusion, and once he gives himself up to these
forces, which are indifferent to the moral value (or
worthlessness) of his ambitions and his achievements,
he deliberately drops from his hands the scales of moral
judgment by which alone he should measure his ambitions and achievements, his fears and his hopes. And so
he falls victim to a lack of freedom that digs the grave
for all morality. The mischief wrought by the diviners
was the source and the mainstay of the corruption that
reigned among the Canaanite inhabitants of the land.

13. *Be whole[hearted].* In our notes to the Book of
Leviticus[5] concerning the requirement that the offerings, as well as the individuals who make them, must
be תָּמִים [''without blemish'' or ''whole''], we have
explained that the wholeheartedness of our devotion to
God—the surrender of the entire human personality,
with all its relationships—is the most immediate result
of our awareness of the Unity of God. It is the realization of our vocation as a nation belonging exclusively
to God.

In the present chapter, we are confronted by this
requirement in its most concrete application. We must
not detach ourselves from God with even the smallest
fiber of our lives; we must be with God in our entirety.
Consequently, the heathen excesses described in the
preceding verses are banned from the domain of

[5]*Note to the English translation*: This note is not included in
this excerpted edition. [G.H.]

Judaism. It is God—the sole Pilot of our destinies and
Guide of our actions—He, alone, that decides our
future. His approval alone can be our standard to tell us
what we may, or must not, do. It is not the *molekh* of
blind chance that rules over our lives and the lives of
our children. Neither the dead, nor a magician's
wand, nor [an animal singled out by superstition] etc.
can predict what lies in store for us. Nor can
morbidly ecstatic madness act as an oracle for our conduct, or carry any weight—not even that of a grain of
dust—in the scale of our destinies. Only of God
could we make inquiry about our future, if, indeed, a
תָּמִים [one who is ''wholehearted'' with God] would feel
the need to know what the future holds for him. And
only from God could we seek a pronouncement concerning what we should, or should not, do—if God had
not already told us these things in His Law long ago.
Actually, one who is תָּמִים is so completely engrossed in
God with every aspect of his life that he will think only
of the duties he must perform at the present moment
and will leave the consequences of his acts and his
future entirely in the hands of God. As far as he is
concerned, his actions have already attained their
supreme goal if he has done his duty. He has paid God
the tribute of duty faithfully performed, and so he is
calm and feels immune to anything beyond that.

Accordingly, the significance of the positive commandment, ''Be whole(hearted). . . ,'' transcends the
prohibition against heathen outrages cited in the preceding verse; it expects us also to refrain from any other
practice believed capable of foretelling the future. . . .

∘   ∘   ∘

14. . . . But as for you—*God*, your God, has not
given you to do such things. By entering into the most
intimate relationship with you as the sole Pilot of your
destinies and Guide of your actions, and by giving you
His Law, in written and oral form, by which to fashion

times; but as for you, *God*, your God, has not given you [thus]. 15. A prophet from your [own] midst—from among your brethren, like myself—will *God*, your God, raise up for you; to him shall you hearken. 16. Even as you requested of *God*, your God, at Ḥoreb on the day of the assembly, saying: "I cannot continue to hear the voice of *God*, my God, and cannot see this great fire anymore, lest I die." 17. Then *God* said to me: "It is good what they have spoken. 18. I will raise up for them a prophet from among their [own] brethren, like yourself, and I will put My words into his mouth, so that he may speak to them everything that I will command him. 19. And it shall be that the man who will not hearken to My words that he will speak in My Name, of him will I demand [an accounting]. 20. But a prophet who will speak wantonly in My Name a word that I did not command him to speak, or one

וְאֶל־קֹסְמִים יִשְׁמָעוּ וְאַתָּה לֹא כֵן נָתַן לְךָ יְהֹוָה אֱלֹהֶיךָ: טו נָבִיא מִקִּרְבְּךָ מֵאַחֶיךָ כָּמֹנִי יָקִים לְךָ יְהֹוָה אֱלֹהֶיךָ אֵלָיו תִּשְׁמָעוּן: טז כְּכֹל אֲשֶׁר־שָׁאַלְתָּ מֵעִם יְהֹוָה אֱלֹהֶיךָ בְּחֹרֵב בְּיוֹם הַקָּהָל לֵאמֹר לֹא אֹסֵף לִשְׁמֹעַ אֶת־קוֹל יְהֹוָה אֱלֹהָי וְאֶת־הָאֵשׁ הַגְּדֹלָה הַזֹּאת לֹא־אֶרְאֶה עוֹד וְלֹא אָמוּת: יז וַיֹּאמֶר יְהֹוָה אֵלָי הֵיטִיבוּ אֲשֶׁר דִּבֵּרוּ: יח נָבִיא אָקִים לָהֶם מִקֶּרֶב אֲחֵיהֶם כָּמוֹךָ וְנָתַתִּי דְבָרַי בְּפִיו וְדִבֶּר אֲלֵיהֶם אֵת כָּל־אֲשֶׁר אֲצַוֶּנּוּ: יט וְהָיָה הָאִישׁ אֲשֶׁר לֹא־יִשְׁמַע אֶל־דְּבָרַי אֲשֶׁר יְדַבֵּר בִּשְׁמִי אָנֹכִי אֶדְרֹשׁ מֵעִמּוֹ: כ אַךְ הַנָּבִיא אֲשֶׁר יָזִיד לְדַבֵּר דָּבָר בִּשְׁמִי אֵת אֲשֶׁר לֹא־צִוִּיתִיו לְדַבֵּר וַאֲשֶׁר יְדַבֵּר

your individual and national life, He has placed into your own hands all that you require for the successful discharge of your life's task. It is He Who fashions your future, but whether your future will be happy or unhappy is a decision He has entrusted to you through the Law which you have in your hands, and of which you are to obtain a clear understanding from the living tradition of your nation. To study this Law, to teach it in theory and to carry it out in practice—that is the sum total of your life's task. In order to discharge this task, you do not need supernatural, superhuman insights or the ability to perceive supernatural spheres veiled from the view of man. Your task is one that can be entrusted to any healthy, cogent, clear and rational human intelligence; it presumes no other qualifications. . . . Unlike the other nations, you not only are in no need of sooth-sayers or diviners of (auspicious) times, but you also do not require even purer or more authentic substitutes for such individuals.

15. The present verse, opening with the words, "A prophet from your (own) midst," promises that prophets will be sent and describes these prophets. Taking this verse in the context of the preceding verses, we believe that the purpose of our prophets is not to take the place in Israel of the diviners of (auspicious) times and soothsayers, in whom the other nations believe. For the dictum "Be whole(hearted) with *God*, your God" categorically denies that Israel should have any need for such practitioners (cf. Rashi on Verse 14).

. . . God will not send us His prophet in order that we may consult him about the expediency or feasibility of our intentions, nor that, seeking to satisfy our desire for knowledge ordinarily denied to man, we may inquire of him about anything hidden from us. God will send us His prophet not in order that we may find out through that prophet what *we* would like to know, but in order that he, the prophet, may tell us what *God* wishes us to know. The prophet is not *our* instrument; he is the instrument of God. . . .

A prophet from your [own] midst, from among your brethren, like myself. The men whom God will send to you as His prophets will be men from your own midst. They will live in your midst. They will not be surrounded by an aura of mystery. You will know how they live and the background from which they came. They will have been born and raised in your midst. They will have proven themselves in your midst. You will know who their fathers and mothers are; you will know their brothers and sisters and other relatives. They will be "from your [own] midst, from among your brethren." They will not address themselves to you with super-human pretensions; they will be ordinary human beings and not seek to be anything more than that. They will be כָּמֹנִי, "like myself," like [Moses,] the first man whom God sent to you. . . . And again, כָּמֹנִי, they will be in the same position as I [Moses] and will be sent to you for the same purpose as I was. They will be only messengers communicating to you the word of God.

who will speak in the name of other gods, that prophet shall die." 21. And if you will then say in your hearts," "How can we recognize the word that *God* has not spoken?"— 22. That which the prophet speaks in the name of *God*, and the word does not materialize and does not come [true], that is the word *God* has not spoken; the prophet has spoken it wantonly. You shall not be afraid of him.

XIX 1. When *God*, your God, has cut off the nations whose land *God*, your God, is giving you, and you have succeeded them in possession and have settled in their cities and in their houses, 2. you shall separate for yourselves three cities in the midst of your land that *God*, your God, is giving you to take possession of it. 3. You shall prepare yourself the road to these and divide the territory of your land—which *God*, your God, is giving you as an inheritance—into three parts, and it shall serve for every manslayer to flee there. 4. And this is the utterance concerning the manslayer who shall flee there and remain alive: One who kills his neighbor unintentionally and did not hate

בְּשֵׁם אֱלֹהִים אֲחֵרִים וּמֵת הַנָּבִיא הַהוּא: כא וְכִי תֹאמַר בִּלְבָבֶךָ אֵיכָה נֵדַע אֶת־הַדָּבָר אֲשֶׁר לֹא־דִבְּרוֹ יְהֹוָה: כב אֲשֶׁר יְדַבֵּר הַנָּבִיא בְּשֵׁם יְהֹוָה וְלֹא־יִהְיֶה הַדָּבָר וְלֹא יָבֹא הוּא הַדָּבָר אֲשֶׁר לֹא־דִבְּרוֹ יְהֹוָה בְּזָדוֹן דִּבְּרוֹ הַנָּבִיא לֹא תָגוּר מִמֶּנּוּ: ס יט א כִּי־יַכְרִית יְהֹוָה אֱלֹהֶיךָ אֶת־הַגּוֹיִם אֲשֶׁר יְהֹוָה אֱלֹהֶיךָ נֹתֵן לְךָ אֶת־אַרְצָם וִירִשְׁתָּם וְיָשַׁבְתָּ בְעָרֵיהֶם וּבְבָתֵּיהֶם: ב שָׁלוֹשׁ עָרִים תַּבְדִּיל לָךְ בְּתוֹךְ אַרְצֶךָ אֲשֶׁר יְהֹוָה אֱלֹהֶיךָ נֹתֵן לְךָ לְרִשְׁתָּהּ: ג תָּכִין לְךָ הַדֶּרֶךְ וְשִׁלַּשְׁתָּ אֶת־גְּבוּל אַרְצְךָ אֲשֶׁר יַנְחִילְךָ יְהֹוָה אֱלֹהֶיךָ וְהָיָה לָנוּס שָׁמָּה כָּל־רֹצֵחַ: ד וְזֶה דְּבַר הָרֹצֵחַ אֲשֶׁר־יָנוּס שָׁמָּה וָחָי אֲשֶׁר יַכֶּה אֶת־רֵעֵהוּ בִּבְלִי־דַעַת וְהוּא לֹא־

CHAPTER XIX

1. We have already discussed, in our notes on Numbers 35: 9f. and Deuteronomy 4:41[6], the profound significance of the cities of *miklat* ["reception"]. We attempted to show how the fact that these cities were to be established simultaneously with the apportionment of the land was to be the most eloquent proclamation of the great basic principle that man was created in the likeness of God. There is dignity in each human life, and for this there can be no adequate compensation. This is the second inviolable principle on which the Jewish political entity is based, immediately after the concept that God is One. That is why, after the establishment of all the instruments of the state—the judiciary, the monarchy, the priesthood and the prophets—there now follows, as the very first object of the functions of these institutions, a chapter supplementing the regulations that guarantee the security of human life in the Jewish state. This supplement includes, first and foremost, a case in point (Verse 5) to illustrate the

kind of manslaughter that would necessitate the manslayer's banishment to a city of *miklat*, and the command to set up three additional cities of *miklat* for that time in the future when the boundaries of the state will have been extended (Verses 8 and 9).

When *God*, **your God, has cut off.** (Cf. Deuteronomy 12:29): They were doomed to ruin because of their depravity. . . .

and in their houses. This phrase is added only in this particular statement, introducing the institution that is to impress upon the state the personal dignity and worth of every one of its members, without exception. It seems to convey a message of dual significance: (1) Not what happens in the land and in the cities, but what happens within the "houses"—the homes— determines the moral worth, and thus the woe or weal, of the state; hence, the nation really does not live in the land or in the cities, but only within the homes of its members, and (2) settling in homes whose former inhabitants led immoral lives does not foster morality. Hence the principle of the moral law must be doubly stressed as a shining example to all, so that the might of its spirit may wipe out even the memory of the evil example set by the previous inhabitants.

---

[6]*Note to the English translation:* The note on Deuteronomy 4:41 is not included in this excerpted edition. [G.H.]

him from yesterday and the day before.
5. And whoever goes with his neighbor
into a forest to cut down trees, and his hand
swings the ax to cut down the tree, and the
iron [head] slips off the wood[en handle]
and strikes his neighbor, and he dies: he
must then flee to one of these cities and
shall remain alive.   6. [For] the blood
advocate could pursue the murderer in the
heat of his emotion, and he could overtake
him if the road is too long, and he could
strike him down mortally, even though he
was not deserving of death because he had
not hated him from yesterday and the day
before.   7. Therefore I give you your duty
as follows: Separate for yourself three cities.
8. And if *God*, your God, will extend your
territory, as He swore to your fathers, and
will give you all the land that He promised
to give to your fathers—   9. if you carry
out carefully all this commandment that I
am giving you as your duty today, to love
God, your God, and to walk in His ways at
all times—then you shall add for yourself
three more cities to these three.   10. So that
innocent blood be not shed in the midst of
your land that *God*, your God, is giving to
you as an inheritance, and blood-guilt be
upon him and strikes him mortally, and he
his neighbor and lies in wait for him and sets
upon him and strikes him mortally and he
dies, and he flees to one of these cities,
12. the elders of his city shall send and
have him taken from there and deliver him
into the hand of the blood advocate so that
he may die.   13. Your eye must not take
pity upon him; you must put away the
blood of the innocent from Yisrael; then it
will be well with you.   14. Do not move

שֵׁנָא לוֹ מִתְּמֹל שִׁלְשֹׁם: ה וַאֲשֶׁר יָבֹא אֶת־
רֵעֵהוּ בַיַּעַר לַחְטֹב עֵצִים וְנִדְּחָה יָדוֹ בַגַּרְזֶן
לִכְרֹת הָעֵץ וְנָשַׁל הַבַּרְזֶל מִן־הָעֵץ וּמָצָא אֶת־
רֵעֵהוּ וָמֵת הוּא יָנוּס אֶל־אַחַת הֶעָרִים־הָאֵלֶּה
וָחָי: ו פֶּן־יִרְדֹּף גֹּאֵל הַדָּם אַחֲרֵי הָרֹצֵחַ כִּי יֵחַם
לְבָבוֹ וְהִשִּׂיגוֹ כִּי־יִרְבֶּה הַדֶּרֶךְ וְהִכָּהוּ נָפֶשׁ וְלוֹ
אֵין מִשְׁפַּט־מָוֶת כִּי לֹא שֹׂנֵא הוּא לוֹ מִתְּמוֹל
שִׁלְשׁוֹם: ז עַל־כֵּן אָנֹכִי מְצַוְּךָ לֵאמֹר שָׁלֹשׁ
עָרִים תַּבְדִּיל לָךְ: ח וְאִם־יַרְחִיב יְהֹוָה אֱלֹהֶיךָ
אֶת־גְּבֻלְךָ כַּאֲשֶׁר נִשְׁבַּע לַאֲבֹתֶיךָ וְנָתַן לְךָ אֶת־
כָּל־הָאָרֶץ אֲשֶׁר דִּבֶּר לָתֵת לַאֲבֹתֶיךָ: ט כִּי־
תִשְׁמֹר אֶת־כָּל־הַמִּצְוָה הַזֹּאת לַעֲשֹׂתָהּ אֲשֶׁר
אָנֹכִי מְצַוְּךָ הַיּוֹם לְאַהֲבָה אֶת־יְהֹוָה אֱלֹהֶיךָ
וְלָלֶכֶת בִּדְרָכָיו כָּל־הַיָּמִים וְיָסַפְתָּ לְךָ עוֹד
שָׁלֹשׁ עָרִים עַל הַשָּׁלֹשׁ הָאֵלֶּה: י וְלֹא יִשָּׁפֵךְ דָּם
נָקִי בְּקֶרֶב אַרְצְךָ אֲשֶׁר יְהֹוָה אֱלֹהֶיךָ נֹתֵן לְךָ
נַחֲלָה וְהָיָה עָלֶיךָ דָּמִים: פ יא וְכִי־יִהְיֶה אִישׁ
שֹׂנֵא לְרֵעֵהוּ וְאָרַב לוֹ וְקָם עָלָיו וְהִכָּהוּ נֶפֶשׁ
וָמֵת וְנָס אֶל־אַחַת הֶעָרִים הָאֵל: יב וְשָׁלְחוּ
זִקְנֵי עִירוֹ וְלָקְחוּ אֹתוֹ מִשָּׁם וְנָתְנוּ אֹתוֹ בְּיַד
גֹּאֵל הַדָּם וָמֵת: יג לֹא־תָחוֹס עֵינְךָ עָלָיו וּבִעַרְתָּ
דַם־הַנָּקִי מִיִּשְׂרָאֵל וְטוֹב לָךְ: ס ששי יד לֹא

13. **Your eye must not take pity.** One who commits a
murder with aggravating circumstances has forfeited
his own life. The same principle that hallows every drop
of human blood above all worldly goods—this same
principle upon which the institution of the *miklat* cities
is based, and which constitutes the essence of the
Jewish state—demands the execution of the intentional
murderer. This demand is just as categorical as the
institution of the *miklat* cities, which are intended to
protect not only the life of every citizen against manslaughter but also the life of an unintentional manslayer
against the victim's avenger. To spare an intentional

murderer would demonstrate not mercy upon human
blood—but only indifference to the shedding of innocent human blood. . . .

14. . . . Life and property—these are the two principal values to be placed under the protection of the Law
of God, which is to be administered by the state. The
inviolability of both in the land of God's Law was proclaimed immediately upon Israel's occupation of the
land, to be demonstrated in a manner that is concrete
and therefore enduring. The *miklat* cities, dispersed
[for easy access] throughout the land, proclaimed the

the boundary [marker] of your neighbor that those of old have set in your inheritance, which you are taking as an inheritance in the land that *God,* your God, is giving you to take possession of it. 15. The testimony of one witness shall not stand against a man with regard to any crime or with regard to any offense, in any sin that he may have committed; through the testimony of two witnesses or through the testimony of three witnesses must a case be established.   16. If a pair of witnesses, misusing their power, rise up against a man to give unfounded testimony against him, 17. both the men who raise this contention before *God,* shall stand before the priests and the judges who shall be in those

תַּסִּיג֙ גְּב֣וּל רֵֽעֲךָ֔ אֲשֶׁ֥ר גָּֽבְל֖וּ רִֽאשֹׁנִ֑ים בְּנַחֲלָֽתְךָ֙ אֲשֶׁ֣ר תִּנְחַ֔ל בָּאָ֕רֶץ אֲשֶׁר֙ יְהֹוָ֣ה אֱלֹהֶ֔יךָ נֹתֵ֥ן לְךָ֖ לְרִשְׁתָּֽהּ׃ ס טו לֹא־יָק֣וּם עֵ֣ד אֶחָ֣ד בְּאִ֗ישׁ לְכָל־ עָוֺן֙ וּלְכָל־חַטָּ֔את בְּכָל־חֵ֖טְא אֲשֶׁ֣ר יֶֽחֱטָ֑א עַל־ פִּ֣י ׀ שְׁנֵ֣י עֵדִ֗ים א֛וֹ עַל־פִּ֥י שְׁלֹשָֽׁה־עֵדִ֖ים יָק֥וּם דָּבָֽר׃ טז כִּֽי־יָק֥וּם עֵד־חָמָ֖ס בְּאִ֑ישׁ לַעֲנ֥וֹת בּ֖וֹ סָרָֽה׃ יז וְעָֽמְד֧וּ שְׁנֵֽי־הָאֲנָשִׁ֛ים אֲשֶׁר־לָהֶ֥ם הָרִ֖יב לִפְנֵ֣י יְהֹוָ֑ה לִפְנֵ֤י הַכֹּֽהֲנִים֙ וְהַשֹּׁ֣פְטִ֔ים אֲשֶׁ֥ר יִֽהְי֖וּ

sanctity of human life, while the boundary markers of the fields that were to be left untouched proclaimed the inviolability of personal property. Both these sacred values, life and property, constitute the two great spheres of the law: דִּינֵי נְפָשׁוֹת [laws regarding human life] and דִּינֵי מָמוֹנוֹת [property laws]. They constitute, first and foremost, the purview of the courts of law, which, in fact, form the subject matter of this entire portion. At the same time, they set forth the juridical categories to which the laws concerning the testimony of witnesses, which now follow, refer.

15. . . . The inviolability of life (which, in a wider sense, encompasses all the physical aspects of living) and of property can become forfeit only through a sentence passed by a court of justice. Property can be confiscated only on the basis of lawful evidence that it was acquired by unlawful means or that he who owns it is obligated to satisfy a legal claim made against him. From this principle derive the two great spheres of Jewish jurisprudence, דִּינֵי נְפָשׁוֹת and דִּינֵי מָמוֹנוֹת. In the former, the court imposes capital or corporal punishment; in the latter, the court imposes a fine or enforces the payment of a debt. In both, the underlying principle is that the individual is responsible for the lawfulness of his own conduct and for the legitimacy of his property claims. The evidence upon which every sentence relating to either must be based comes from the testimony of witnesses. This is the subject discussed in the verses that follow.

17. . . . Jewish jurisprudence knows only one kind of legal evidence: the testimony of eyewitnesses. Through the dictum that "through the testimony of two witnesses . . . must a case be established," the Law has

placed all the honor, happiness, life and property of individuals and groups of individuals into the hands of any two men who are impartial and of unblemished reputation. It is clear, of course, that the viability of this juridical procedure and of the society governed by it depends on the assumption that every individual concerned is honest unless proven otherwise. But this assumption can be based only upon the fact, and upon the awareness derived from it, that all human relationships, as well as the implementation of the laws and legal institutions ordained by God to structure and regulate them, must take place "before *God.*" They must be subject to God's own sovereignty and judgment. Probably this fact—and the implicit references to it—is nowhere more significantly evident than in the testimony of witnesses, which derives its legal effect from the circumstance that it is given "before *God.*" In the final analysis, such evidence is beyond the judgment of the human eye or the human mind. For any testimony, no matter how objective, of necessity entails an element of subjectivity. It represents a testimony by the witness concerning himself; i.e., concerning his own presence at the scene and his perceptions there.

Such testimony, which is really testimony concerning the witness' own person, has no legal force for or against the witness who gives it, except in admissions regarding property rights. And yet every testimony, the basis of the entire judicial process, rests upon it. Under the law, every witness is vested with the legal authority and legal credibility to testify concerning himself that he was present at the scene and that he personally perceived the events which are the content of his testimony. But in this manner, the Law places every witness "before *God,*" Who alone examines man's inmost thoughts and emotions and weighs every word days. 18. And the judges will then inquire carefully, and it will turn out that the pair of witnesses is a pair of false witnesses, that they testified falsely against their brother; 19. then you shall cause to happen to it what it had planned to have happen to its brother; and you clear away the evil from your midst, 20. so that those who remain shall hear it and be afraid and never again commit anything like this evil in your midst. 21. Your eye must not have pity: life for life, eye for eye, tooth for tooth, hand for hand, foot for foot.

XX 1. When you go forth to battle against your enemy and see horses and chariots, a body of men more numerous than yourself, do not be afraid of them; for *God,* your God, is with you, Who brought you out from the land of Mitzrayim. 2. And it shall be when you will

בַּיָּמִים הָהֵם: יח וְדָרְשׁוּ הַשֹּׁפְטִים הֵיטֵב וְהִנֵּה עֵד־שֶׁקֶר הָעֵד שֶׁקֶר עָנָה בְאָחִיו: יט וַעֲשִׂיתֶם לוֹ כַּאֲשֶׁר זָמַם לַעֲשׂוֹת לְאָחִיו וּבִעַרְתָּ הָרָע מִקִּרְבֶּךָ: כ וְהַנִּשְׁאָרִים יִשְׁמְעוּ וְיִרָאוּ וְלֹא־יֹסִפוּ לַעֲשׂוֹת עוֹד כַּדָּבָר הָרָע הַזֶּה בְּקִרְבֶּךָ: כא וְלֹא תָחוֹס עֵינֶךָ נֶפֶשׁ בְּנֶפֶשׁ עַיִן בְּעַיִן שֵׁן בְּשֵׁן יָד בְּיָד רֶגֶל בְּרָגֶל: ס כ א כִּי־תֵצֵא לַמִּלְחָמָה עַל־אֹיְבֶךָ וְרָאִיתָ סוּס וָרֶכֶב עַם רַב מִמְּךָ לֹא תִירָא מֵהֶם כִּי־יְהֹוָה אֱלֹהֶיךָ עִמָּךְ הַמַּעַלְךָ מֵאֶרֶץ מִצְרָיִם: ב וְהָיָה כְּקָרָבְכֶם אֶל־

and thought upon the scales of His own justice and truth. Perhaps that is why Jewish law does not place witnesses under oath, as present-day courts do. The testimony of the witnesses is in itself an invocation of God, to Whose presence and sovereignty the witness subordinates himself by the very words of his testimony.

19. . . . The Law was given to human tribunals, to be binding upon them; its scope cannot be measured by human standards. God stands above and beyond the Law and its implementation. In handing over the Law and its implementation to a human court, He gave them only part of His own judicial authority. The courts are to administer justice only as His agents and only within the framework of the mandate He has conferred upon them. Where the power and authority of the human law courts ends, the sole sovereignty of God's justice begins. Hence, as is stated in our text, judges and witnesses alike stand before God, Who alone is the Foundation and Source of conscience—that conscience which forms the granite rock for the lawful state composed of a society of men.

    °   °   °

CHAPTER XX

1. The final section dealing with the legal institution of testimony from eyewitnesses, the basis for all [Jewish] legal procedure, concludes the laws relating to the internal administration of the [Jewish] state. There now follow laws dealing with the external operations of the state. Verses 1-9 deal with compulsory military

service and mobilization in the event of war, the manner in which the nation is to arm for military action. Verses 10-20 discuss the conduct of war as such.

and see horses and chariots, a body of men more numerous than yourself. You must not imagine that your victory will depend on your having the largest possible number of warriors under arms and that, therefore, you must mobilize the largest possible contingent of fighting men. In fact, according to Verses 5 through 7, certain categories of able-bodied men are exempt from military service.

2. . . . If the leaders of the Jewish state felt that it would be necessary for them to go to battle, they had to consider as the most important factor in this serious step not the numerical size of their army, but the support of God; and they were expected, through the servants of God's Law, to stir up the same spirit in the hearts of their warriors at the moment of battle, as the sole spirit conducive to victory. . . .

. . . A priest was expressly appointed to perform this function and was consecrated for this purpose by anointment; he was therefore termed "the anointed for war". . . .

Thus it is a servant of the Sanctuary of Jewish Law, representing the nation's highest moral ideal, who must accompany the nation to battle and must utter the words assuring them that victory will be theirs. In times of war, [Israel's] confidence in victory should derive not from its military efficiency or from its knowledge of the arts of war, but from that same Law toward which the arts of peace are oriented; the Law for which the inner moral struggles of private and public life draw nearer to the battle that the priest will approach and speak to the people 3. and shall say to them: "Hear, O Yisrael, today you are drawing near to war against your enemies; let not your heart be weak, and do not be afraid, and do not run away, and do not be terrified because of them, 4. because it is *God,* your God, Who is going with you to fight for you against your enemies—to grant you victory." 5. And the officers shall speak to the people [saying]: "What man is there that has built a new home and has not yet dedicated it? Let him go and return home; he might die in the war and another man might [then] dedicate it. 6. And what man is there that has planted a vineyard and has not yet brought it to [the stage] where he may enjoy it? Let him go and return home; he might die in the war and another man might [then] enjoy it[s fruit]. 7. And what man is there that has betrothed a wife and not yet taken her [to his] home [as his wife]? Let him go and return home; he might die in the war and another man might [then] take her [to his] home [as his wife]." 8. And the officers shall continue to speak to the people and say: "What man is there who is afraid and fainthearted? Let him go and return home and not make the heart of his brothers cowardly like his [own]." 9. And it shall be when the officers have finished speaking to the people that the generals shall assume command at the head of the people. 10. When you draw near

הַמִּלְחָמָה וְנִגַּשׁ הַכֹּהֵן וְדִבֶּר אֶל־הָעָם: ג וְאָמַ֣ר אֲלֵהֶם֙ שְׁמַ֣ע יִשְׂרָאֵ֔ל אַתֶּ֨ם קְרֵבִ֥ים הַיּ֛וֹם לַמִּלְחָמָ֖ה עַל־אֹיְבֵיכֶ֑ם אַל־יֵרַ֣ךְ לְבַבְכֶ֗ם אַל־תִּֽירְא֧וּ וְאַֽל־תַּחְפְּז֛וּ וְאַל־תַּֽעַרְצ֖וּ מִפְּנֵיהֶֽם: ד כִּ֚י יְהֹוָ֣ה אֱלֹֽהֵיכֶ֔ם הַהֹלֵ֖ךְ עִמָּכֶ֑ם לְהִלָּחֵ֥ם לָכֶ֛ם עִם־אֹֽיְבֵיכֶ֖ם לְהוֹשִׁ֥יעַ אֶתְכֶֽם: ה וְדִבְּר֣וּ הַשֹּֽׁטְרִים֮ אֶל־הָעָ֣ם לֵאמֹר֒ מִֽי־הָאִ֞ישׁ אֲשֶׁ֨ר בָּנָ֤ה בַֽיִת־חָדָשׁ֙ וְלֹ֣א חֲנָכ֔וֹ יֵלֵ֖ךְ וְיָשֹׁ֣ב לְבֵית֑וֹ פֶּן־יָמוּת֙ בַּמִּלְחָמָ֔ה וְאִ֥ישׁ אַחֵ֖ר יַחְנְכֶֽנּוּ: ו וּמִֽי־הָאִ֞ישׁ אֲשֶׁ֨ר נָטַ֥ע כֶּ֨רֶם֙ וְלֹ֣א חִלְּל֔וֹ יֵלֵ֖ךְ וְיָשֹׁ֣ב לְבֵית֑וֹ פֶּן־יָמוּת֙ בַּמִּלְחָמָ֔ה וְאִ֥ישׁ אַחֵ֖ר יְחַלְּלֶֽנּוּ: ז וּמִֽי־הָאִ֞ישׁ אֲשֶׁ֨ר אֵרַ֤שׂ אִשָּׁה֙ וְלֹ֣א לְקָחָ֔הּ יֵלֵ֖ךְ וְיָשֹׁ֣ב לְבֵית֑וֹ פֶּן־יָמוּת֙ בַּמִּלְחָמָ֔ה וְאִ֥ישׁ אַחֵ֖ר יִקָּחֶֽנָּה: ח וְיָֽסְפ֣וּ הַשֹּֽׁטְרִים֮ לְדַבֵּ֣ר אֶל־הָעָם֒ וְאָֽמְר֗וּ מִֽי־הָאִ֤ישׁ הַיָּרֵא֙ וְרַ֣ךְ הַלֵּבָ֔ב יֵלֵ֖ךְ וְיָשֹׁ֣ב לְבֵית֑וֹ וְלֹ֥א יִמַּ֛ס אֶת־לְבַ֥ב אֶחָ֖יו כִּלְבָבֽוֹ: ט וְהָיָ֛ה כְּכַלֹּ֥ת הַשֹּֽׁטְרִ֖ים לְדַבֵּ֣ר אֶל־הָעָ֑ם וּפָֽקְד֛וּ שָׂרֵ֥י צְבָא֖וֹת בְּרֹ֥אשׁ הָעָֽם: ס שביעי י כִּֽי־תִקְרַ֣ב אֶל־עִ֗יר

achieve the victories of peace; the Law whose supremacy and unimpeded development are the basis for attaining the nation's objectives and its victory in a [justified] war. It is as the nation of God's Law that Israel goes to war, and the call to battle must be uttered by a servant of God's Law . . . who, as the high priest, holds aloft, both in war and in peace, a shining example to his people by his own observance of the laws pertaining to uncleanness and things forbidden to a priest. For these laws symbolize the moral ideal to which both individual and family life must aspire.

•　　•　　•

3. . . . The priest "anointed for war" is to utter the words of the Biblical text verbatim, בִּלְשׁוֹן הַקֹּדֶשׁ [in the original Hebrew form] (Sotah 32a and 42a). In this manner, the words he utters represent neither his own

thoughts nor his own assurances of victory, but the promises of God as set down in His Law for all time. In the same vein, the בִּרְכַּת הַכֹּהֲנִים [priestly blessing] must be uttered by the priests verbatim, בִּלְשׁוֹן הַקֹּדֶשׁ . . . .

שְׁמַע יִשְׂרָאֵל *[Hear, O Yisrael].* These are also the words with which every Jew bestirs himself anew each day, early and late, to do homage to the One sole God, with all the consequences deriving from this declaration of allegiance. It is this same thought and this same declaration of homage to the One sole God before which, at the moment of battle, all other concepts of greatness and power become meaningless. The awareness that one is serving His will and can therefore be sure of His support will promote strength and courage, serenity and vigor, even within the faintest of human hearts. . . .

to a city to wage war against it, you must first proclaim peace offers to it.   11. And it shall be, if it gives you an answer of peace and opens to you, that the entire population that is found in it shall be tributary to you and serve you.   12. But if it will not make peace with you, but will make war against you; and you will lay siege to it, 13. and *God*, your God, will deliver it into your hand; then you shall strike down all their males with the sword. 14. However, the women and children and the animals and everything else that is in the city, all their booty you shall take as your spoils, and you shall eat the booty of your enemies that *God*, your God, has given you.   15. Thus shall you do with all the cities that are very far from you, that are not the cities of these nations.   16. However, of the cities of these nations which *God*, your God, is giving you as an inheritance, you shall not allow a soul to remain alive; 17. you shall banish them to utter destruction: the Ḥittite, the Emorite, the Canaanite, the Perizzite, the Ḥivvite and the Yebusite, as *God*, your God, has commanded you,   18. so that they will not teach you to do according to their abominations that they practiced for their gods, and you would sin against *God*, your God. 19. When you lay siege to a city for many days to capture it by making war against it, you shall not destroy its tree, wielding an axe against it; for you shall eat of it but not cut it down. For the tree of the field is the existence of man; [hence it is also] to go into

לְהִלָּחֵם עָלֶיהָ וְקָרָאתָ אֵלֶיהָ לְשָׁלוֹם: יא וְהָיָה אִם־שָׁלוֹם תַּעַנְךָ וּפָתְחָה לָךְ וְהָיָה כָּל־הָעָם הַנִּמְצָא־בָהּ יִהְיוּ לְךָ לָמַס וַעֲבָדוּךָ: יב וְאִם־לֹא תַשְׁלִים עִמָּךְ וְעָשְׂתָה עִמְּךָ מִלְחָמָה וְצַרְתָּ עָלֶיהָ: יג וּנְתָנָהּ יְהֹוָה אֱלֹהֶיךָ בְּיָדֶךָ וְהִכִּיתָ אֶת־כָּל־זְכוּרָהּ לְפִי־חָרֶב: יד רַק הַנָּשִׁים וְהַטַּף וְהַבְּהֵמָה וְכֹל אֲשֶׁר יִהְיֶה בָעִיר כָּל־שְׁלָלָהּ תָּבֹז לָךְ וְאָכַלְתָּ אֶת־שְׁלַל אֹיְבֶיךָ אֲשֶׁר נָתַן יְהֹוָה אֱלֹהֶיךָ לָךְ: טו כֵּן תַּעֲשֶׂה לְכָל־הֶעָרִים הָרְחֹקֹת מִמְּךָ מְאֹד אֲשֶׁר לֹא־מֵעָרֵי הַגּוֹיִם־הָאֵלֶּה הֵנָּה: טז רַק מֵעָרֵי הָעַמִּים הָאֵלֶּה אֲשֶׁר יְהֹוָה אֱלֹהֶיךָ נֹתֵן לְךָ נַחֲלָה לֹא תְחַיֶּה כָּל־נְשָׁמָה: יז כִּי־ הַחֲרֵם תַּחֲרִימֵם הַחִתִּי וְהָאֱמֹרִי הַכְּנַעֲנִי וְהַפְּרִזִּי הַחִוִּי וְהַיְבוּסִי כַּאֲשֶׁר צִוְּךָ יְהֹוָה אֱלֹהֶיךָ: יח לְמַעַן אֲשֶׁר לֹא־יְלַמְּדוּ אֶתְכֶם לַעֲשׂוֹת כְּכֹל תּוֹעֲבֹתָם אֲשֶׁר עָשׂוּ לֵאלֹהֵיהֶם וַחֲטָאתֶם לַיהֹוָה אֱלֹהֵיכֶם: ס יט כִּי־תָצוּר אֶל־עִיר יָמִים רַבִּים לְהִלָּחֵם עָלֶיהָ לְתָפְשָׂהּ לֹא־תַשְׁחִית אֶת־עֵצָהּ לִנְדֹּחַ עָלָיו גַּרְזֶן כִּי מִמֶּנּוּ תֹאכֵל וְאֹתוֹ לֹא תִכְרֹת כִּי הָאָדָם עֵץ הַשָּׂדֶה לָבֹא מִפָּנֶיךָ

10–14. When you draw near. The laws preceding these verses deal with the organization of the army for open battle. Now follow the regulations concerning the procedure to be observed when laying siege to an enemy city. It is stated as Israel's duty that it must always initially make offers of peace, and if the city then surrenders of its own accord, it is forbidden to harm, even in the slightest, any person or object within it. All that Israel may compel the inhabitants of such a city to do is to pay tribute to the Israelite nation and to become its subjects. . . .

19. . . . .You must not cut down the trees in the environs of the city for the purpose of destroying them. . . .

. . . It seems to us that this verse should be interpreted as follows: You must not cut down the fruit trees of the city to which you have laid siege, because the fruit trees make human existence possible. Therefore they "go into the siege" along with everything else in the city; i.e., they are included in the objectives you are seeking to attain by laying siege to the city. Even as the purpose of your laying siege to the city must not be to destroy the city, so, too, you must not destroy the trees of the city, because they are part of the city to which you are laying siege.

20. . . . The prohibition against the wanton destruction of trees in a siege is to be interpreted as only one case in point. The legal concept of בַּל תַּשְׁחִית is defined as

the siege before you.   20. However, a tree of which you know that it does not afford nourishment, that [tree] you may destroy and cut down, and build up siege machinery against the city that is waging war against you, until it surrenders.

XXI   1. If a slain person is found upon the soil that *God,* your God, is giving you to possess it—fallen in the field, it is not known who struck him down—   2. your elders and your judges shall go out and measure to the cities that are round about the slain man.   3. And then it shall be, the city that is closest to the slain man, that the elders of that city shall take a

בַּמָּצוֹר: כ רַק עֵץ אֲשֶׁר־תֵּדַע כִּי לֹא־עֵץ מַאֲכָל הוּא אֹתוֹ תַשְׁחִית וְכָרָתָּ וּבָנִיתָ מָצוֹר עַל־הָעִיר אֲשֶׁר־הִוא עֹשָׂה עִמְּךָ מִלְחָמָה עַד רִדְתָּהּ: פ

כא א כִּי־יִמָּצֵא חָלָל בָּאֲדָמָה אֲשֶׁר יְהֹוָה אֱלֹהֶיךָ נֹתֵן לְךָ לְרִשְׁתָּהּ נֹפֵל בַּשָּׂדֶה לֹא נוֹדַע מִי הִכָּהוּ: ב וְיָצְאוּ זְקֵנֶיךָ וְשֹׁפְטֶיךָ וּמָדְדוּ אֶל־הֶעָרִים אֲשֶׁר סְבִיבֹת הֶחָלָל: ג וְהָיָה הָעִיר הַקְּרֹבָה אֶל־הֶחָלָל וְלָקְחוּ זִקְנֵי הָעִיר הַהִוא

---

a prohibition against the purposeless, wasteful destruction of any object. Thus the concept of בַּל תַּשְׁחִית becomes an all-encompassing warning to man not to misuse his assigned station in the world by destroying the things of earth capriciously, in a fit of violence, or even just thoughtlessly. When God placed the world at man's feet, bidding him to subdue the world and have dominion over it, He did so only so that man should use his power wisely.

    ∘   ∘   ∘

CHAPTER XXI

1. This entire weekly portion, שֹׁפְטִים, which deals with the authorities empowered to enforce the Law, concludes with a legal institution that is a most striking example of a summons to the authorities of the Law, calling them into God's presence, in full view of the public, so that they may publicly clear themselves of the suspicion that they were lax in the performance of their duties. We have already seen repeatedly how, of all the values entrusted to the care of the [Jewish] state and of its representatives, human life virtually takes first place. The prosperity of the entire land is made conditional upon the reverence that the nation will accord to human life. The Law now sets forth the procedure to be followed if the body of a murder victim is found lying in an open field under circumstances which, as we shall see, appear to be a downright mockery of the enforcers of the Law, virtually demanding that they justify their conduct in office.

If a slain person is found. "Not at a time when such things are usually discovered" (*Sifri*). This legal institution assumes that the incident occurred at a time when the Law was enforced in a manner making murder a rare occurrence and the discovery of the body of a murder victim a startling "find." However, this institution, like certain others, was no longer applicable at times such as the days of the decline and fall of the Second Jewish Commonwealth, when the Law had become so powerless that murder was an everyday occurrence. "When murderers multiplied," the procedure of breaking a heifer's neck was no longer to be carried out (Sotah 47a).

    ∘   ∘   ∘

that **God,** *your* **God,** *is giving you to possess it.* When God gives you the land so that you may take the place of its previous inhabitants, He does so under the assumption that you will enforce His Law wherever you may dwell. The officers of the Law in each district are answerable to you; i.e., to the representatives of your national entity, for everything that transpires in their bailiwick. . . .

    ∘   ∘   ∘

2. . . . The measuring stipulated here must be done by the members of the Supreme Court of Law in person. This fact is expressed by the use of the term וְיָצְאוּ ["(they) shall go out"]. They, whose duties of office ordinarily necessitate their constant presence in the central city, must go out to the scene of the crime. The use of the term וְיָצְאוּ makes it clear that they cannot send a deputy to perform this act. The reason why this act must be carried out by members of the Supreme Council [i.e., the Sanhedrin] in person, and not by anyone appointed by them to act on their behalf, is implicit in the nature of the case. For the crime had the effect of making precisely those acting on their behalf, the law officers subordinate to them, all of whom act only as their deputies, suspect of being remiss in their duties. The elders and the judges must now publicly clear themselves of that suspicion. The blame for negligence in such a case reflects indirectly upon the members of the Supreme Court, and that is why they must act personally to clear themselves before the public.

    ∘   ∘   ∘

עֶגְלַת בָּקָר אֲשֶׁר לֹא־עֻבַּד בָּהּ אֲשֶׁר לֹא־מָשְׁכָה
בְּעֹל: ד וְהוֹרִדוּ זִקְנֵי הָעִיר הַהִוא אֶת־הָעֶגְלָה
אֶל־נַחַל אֵיתָן אֲשֶׁר לֹא־יֵעָבֵד בּוֹ וְלֹא יִזָּרֵעַ
וְעָרְפוּ־שָׁם אֶת־הָעֶגְלָה בַּנָּחַל: ה וְנִגְּשׁוּ
הַכֹּהֲנִים בְּנֵי לֵוִי כִּי בָם בָּחַר יְהוָֹה אֱלֹהֶיךָ
לְשָׁרְתוֹ וּלְבָרֵךְ בְּשֵׁם יְהוָֹה וְעַל־פִּיהֶם יִהְיֶה
כָּל־רִיב וְכָל־נָגַע: ו וְכֹל זִקְנֵי הָעִיר הַהִוא
הַקְּרֹבִים אֶל־הֶחָלָל יִרְחֲצוּ אֶת־יְדֵיהֶם עַל־
הָעֶגְלָה הָעֲרוּפָה בַנָּחַל: מפטיר ז וְעָנוּ וְאָמְרוּ
יָדֵינוּ לֹא שָׁפְכָה (שפכו קרי) אֶת־הַדָּם הַזֶּה
וְעֵינֵינוּ לֹא רָאוּ: ח כַּפֵּר לְעַמְּךָ יִשְׂרָאֵל אֲשֶׁר־
פָּדִיתָ יְהוָֹה וְאַל־תִּתֵּן דָּם נָקִי בְּקֶרֶב עַמְּךָ
יִשְׂרָאֵל וְנִכַּפֵּר לָהֶם הַדָּם: ט וְאַתָּה תְּבַעֵר הַדָּם
הַנָּקִי מִקִּרְבֶּךָ כִּי־תַעֲשֶׂה הַיָּשָׁר בְּעֵינֵי יְהוָֹה: ס

female calf that has never been worked, that has not yet pulled the yoke. 4. And the elders of this city shall lead the calf to a valley that has been primevally rugged, that must neither be worked nor sown, and there they shall kill the calf in the valley with a cut through the neck. 5. And the priests, the sons of Levi, shall approach—because it is they whom *God*, your God, has chosen to serve Him and to pronounce blessing[s] in the Name of *God*, and according to their declaration shall every dispute and every damage be— 6. and all the elders of that city who are nearest to the slain person shall wash their hands over the calf whose neck was cut in the valley, 7. and they shall begin and say: "Our hands have not spilled this blood, and our eyes have not seen him. 8. Grant atonement to Thy people Yisrael, whom Thou hast redeemed, O *God*; and do not place innocent blood into the midst of Thy people Yisrael!" And so shall atonement be made for them for the blood. 9. But you must put away the innocent blood from your midst by doing that which is right in the eyes of *God*.

---

5. . . . That every man should be able to live out his life uninterrupted and undisturbed by his fellow men is one of the supreme goals of God's arrangements with Israel. Therefore, any murder victim struck down upon the soil of God's Law represents an act of rank defiance of that Law, a bitter reproach to the representatives of the Law and a challenge to all the ideals represented by the כֹּהֵן [priest]. . . .

6. *and all the elders of that city who are nearest to the slain person shall wash their hands.* This is obviously intended as a symbolic act to demonstrate that their hands (i.e., their deeds) are clean of all guilt, direct or indirect, in the crime, and that no blame, direct or indirect, attaches to them for the fact that no action has yet been taken against the murderer.

8. *Grant atonement to Thy people.* Whenever there would arise a generation of Jews that would feel heavily burdened by a sense of collective guilt if even one of its contemporaries were driven by poverty to commit a crime, so that the representatives of that generation could stand beside the body of a murder victim and publicly declare in good conscience before God, "our hands have not spilled this blood"; i.e., "in our society no one is compelled to turn to crime because of poverty," this would represent a momentous triumph for the laws of justice and mercy taught by God's Law of justice and loving-kindness. That triumph would be so great that, no matter how gravely the generations of the past (up to the generation of the Exodus) may have sinned, their sins would be forgiven because they would be the ancestors of such a society. The merit of a state thus based on the precepts of justice and brotherly love would be so great that it would retroactively ennoble all the past generations from whose roots that state would have sprung.

· · · ·

The Haftarah for this Sidra may be found on page 914.

כי תצא

KI THETZE

10. When you go forth to war against your enemies, and *God*, your God, delivers one [of them] into your hand, and you will take his captives, 11. and you see among the captives a woman of beautiful form, you desire her and you take her as your wife, 12. then you shall bring her home to your house, and she shall shave her head and allow her nails to grow, 13. and she shall take off the garment of her captivity and sit in your house and weep for her father and her mother for one month; only after that may you go to her and become her husband, so that she may become a wife to you. 14. But it shall be if you do not take pleasure in her, you shall let her go wherever she wishes; you must

י כִּי־תֵצֵא לַמִּלְחָמָה עַל־אֹיְבֶיךָ וּנְתָנוֹ יְהוָה
אֱלֹהֶיךָ בְּיָדֶךָ וְשָׁבִיתָ שִׁבְיוֹ: יא וְרָאִיתָ בַּשִּׁבְיָה
אֵשֶׁת יְפַת־תֹּאַר וְחָשַׁקְתָּ בָהּ וְלָקַחְתָּ לְךָ
לְאִשָּׁה: יב וַהֲבֵאתָהּ אֶל־תּוֹךְ בֵּיתֶךָ וְגִלְּחָה
אֶת־רֹאשָׁהּ וְעָשְׂתָה אֶת־צִפָּרְנֶיהָ: יג וְהֵסִירָה
אֶת־שִׂמְלַת שִׁבְיָהּ מֵעָלֶיהָ וְיָשְׁבָה בְּבֵיתֶךָ
וּבָכְתָה אֶת־אָבִיהָ וְאֶת־אִמָּהּ יֶרַח יָמִים וְאַחַר
כֵּן תָּבוֹא אֵלֶיהָ וּבְעַלְתָּהּ וְהָיְתָה לְךָ לְאִשָּׁה:
יד וְהָיָה אִם־לֹא חָפַצְתָּ בָּהּ וְשִׁלַּחְתָּהּ לְנַפְשָׁהּ

10. The weekly portion of שֹׁפְטִים dealt primarily with regulations concerning the general affairs of the nation, regulations which were needed now that the nation was about to settle as a state in its own land. The portion כִּי תֵצֵא sets forth additional groups of laws intended primarily to regulate private relationships, such as family and social life. Israel's imminent dispersion over its land and the beginning of its civic life may give occasion to various excesses. Therefore, these laws place particular emphasis upon the regulations intended to promote respect for the Law of justice, lovingkindness and moral sanctity among the individual members of the nation who will now be left on their own. Special stress is placed on family life, the relationships between the sexes, marital relations, the relationship of parents to their children and of children to their parents. On the one hand, Israel's settlement in close proximity to the indigenous neighboring populations could be expected to cause disturbances in the nation's family life. On the other hand, Israel's family life, particularly in its civic and legal aspects, could develop toward full realization only after the family's support had been transferred from the hands of direct Divine Providence to the hands of the father of the family, who will now assume a role of direct responsibility as provider for his wife and children as a result of Israel's settlement in its land.

This group of laws begins with a case that proclaims the inviolability of the female sex against wanton abuse by the passions of the male. This concept was already discussed partly in Exodus 21:2 and 7, where the personal and marital rights of the criminal and of the

most unfortunate of maidens are set forth. The verses that now follow teach the same precepts with regard to the treatment to be accorded a woman who has been taken captive in a war. In Deuteronomy, Chapter 20:19 f., the general prohibition against all wanton destructiveness is taught; in Chapter 23:10 f., the injunctions "keep away from every evil thing" and "so that He may see no nakedness in you" set forth the general commandment of chastity and modesty. These commands are binding in both theory and practice, and they are now applied to wartime conditions in which vandalism and sexual license are usually given free rein. Of course, that which even under such extreme circumstances is made a matter of duty for the conscience of the Jew, holds good in even greater measure for normal times.

. . .

12-14. *then you shall bring her home to your house.* It is then the man's duty either to marry her in accordance with the procedures set forth in Verses 12 and 13, whereby she becomes a full Jewess and his lawful wife with all the rights appertaining to that position; or, if he does not wish to marry her, then (Verse 14) he must set her free. He is forbidden to abuse her, to keep her as a slave, or to dispose of her for the benefit of another man. . . .

According to *Sifri* and Yebamoth 48a, the procedures set forth in these verses are intended to reduce her physical charms so that the man may see her for some time unadorned and unattractive in his home, where he can give himself time to search his heart and mind not sell her for money; you must have no advantage whatsoever from her, because you have violated her.　15. If a man has two wives, one beloved and the other hated, and they have borne him sons, both the beloved and the hated, and the first-born son is that of the hated one, 16. then it shall be on the day when he bequeathes to his sons that which is his property, that he is not at liberty to grant to the son of the beloved the birthright over the son of the hated, the first-born. 17. Rather, he must recognize the first-born, the son of the hated one, by giving him a double portion of all his extant possessions, because he is the first of his acquisitions; the birthright is his.　18. If a man has a son who is disobedient and recalcitrant, he does not hearken to the voice of his father and to the voice of his

וּמָכֹר לֹא־תִמְכְּרֶנָּה בַּכָּסֶף לֹא־תִתְעַמֵּר בָּהּ תַּחַת אֲשֶׁר עִנִּיתָהּ: ס טו כִּי־תִהְיֶיןָ לְאִישׁ שְׁתֵּי נָשִׁים הָאַחַת אֲהוּבָה וְהָאַחַת שְׂנוּאָה וְיָלְדוּ־לוֹ בָנִים הָאֲהוּבָה וְהַשְּׂנוּאָה וְהָיָה הַבֵּן הַבְּכֹר לַשְּׂנִיאָה: טז וְהָיָה בְּיוֹם הַנְחִילוֹ אֶת־בָּנָיו אֵת אֲשֶׁר־יִהְיֶה לוֹ לֹא יוּכַל לְבַכֵּר אֶת־בֶּן־הָאֲהוּבָה עַל־פְּנֵי בֶן־הַשְּׂנוּאָה הַבְּכֹר: יז כִּי אֶת־הַבְּכֹר בֶּן־הַשְּׂנוּאָה יַכִּיר לָתֶת לוֹ פִּי שְׁנַיִם בְּכֹל אֲשֶׁר־יִמָּצֵא לוֹ כִּי־הוּא רֵאשִׁית אֹנוֹ לוֹ מִשְׁפַּט הַבְּכֹרָה: ס יח כִּי־יִהְיֶה לְאִישׁ בֵּן סוֹרֵר וּמוֹרֶה אֵינֶנּוּ שֹׁמֵעַ בְּקוֹל אָבִיו

---

before deciding whether or not to marry her. For the Law does not sanction marriages based solely on the dictates of physical passion. The fact that this passage is followed directly by Verses 15 to 18, which relate to marital discord and to the wayward son, points out the likely consequences of a marriage based not on considerations of duty and reason—but [solely] on passion.

。　　。　　。

15. *If a man has two wives.* The law concerning the woman of "beautiful form" set forth in the preceding verses permits, by way of exception, under exceptional circumstances, the admissibility of purely sensual impressions as leading factors in the choice of a wife. However, in the way of warning, this law is now followed by laws dealing with problems raised by disturbances in relationships between spouses and between parents and children, caused by emotions of sympathy and antipathy, and by discords that can continue over generations in a family because of an inequity in the division of an inheritance. In view of the infinite variety of possible circumstantial and personal factors, the Law, as we shall see, grants the father considerable latitude in dividing his estate among his heirs. But at the same time, the Law sets definite limits to his authority, thus implying that he must be most judicious and circumspect in exercising such authority.

。　　。　　。

17. . . . The reason why this supplement to the laws of inheritance already set forth in Numbers 27:6 f. appears only now, in this compendium, is obvious. For only now, when the nation is about to settle in its land,

will wealth and disparities in economic circumstances truly assume a significance that they would scarcely have been accorded while the nation journeyed through the wilderness, and all its needs were supplied directly by Divine Providence.

18. *If a man has a son.* The law regarding the inheritance rights of the firstborn son, which stresses the important role of the son in the home and family as the legal continuator of his father's economic person, as it were, is now followed by a law concerning "the disobedient and recalcitrant son," the hopeless reprobate, in whose case the Law compels his own parents to request that he be put to death in order to save him from total depravity. . . .

According to one authority (Sanhedrin 71a) this chapter deals with a problem that in all the past and in all the future will remain purely academic, because in practice, no individual will ever fit all the criteria stated in the Law. Nevertheless, or perhaps precisely for this reason, this question affords a rich source of pedagogic truths which, if studied thoroughly, will amply reward the parents by the aid these truths will afford them in raising their children.

This law pronounces the death sentence over a youthful delinquent who is classed as irreclaimable, and it declares that his premature death will be the only way of saving him from total degeneracy. However, the law makes this sentence dependent on precisely defined factors, such as the offender's age; the nature of his offense; but particularly, on the relationship of his parents with one another and with their son. Only if the parents act together, in complete harmony, can they mother; they will chastise him but he still will not listen to them,   19. then his father and his mother shall lay hold of him and bring him out to the elders of his city

וּבְקוֹל אִמּוֹ וְיִסְּרוּ אֹתוֹ וְלֹא יִשְׁמַע אֲלֵיהֶם: יט וְתָפְשׂוּ בוֹ אָבִיו וְאִמּוֹ וְהוֹצִיאוּ אֹתוֹ אֶל־

consider that they have discharged their task as educators of their children; only then can they say that their son acted as he did because he is irreclaimable. The factors enumerated in the Law provide the most significant indications of the elements on which all successful child-rearing depends. . . .

כִּי יִהְיֶה לְאִישׁ בֵּן [*If a man has a son*]. The text does not simply state, כִּי יִהְיֶה בֵּן סוֹרֵר וּמוֹרֶה ["If *there is* a son . . . who is disobedient and recalcitrant. . ."], nor even כִּי יִהְיֶה לְאָב בֵּן ["If *a father has* a son. . ."], as in בֵּן הָיִיתִי לְאָבִי ["For I was a son to my father"] (Proverbs 4:3), in both of which cases the son would have to be viewed in general terms as the child of his parents; but כִּי יִהְיֶה לְאִישׁ בֵּן ["If *a man has* a son. . ."]. . . The son is viewed in terms of his relationship to his father as a man. He is viewed as a child whom the man would have the right to regard as his future heir and as the continuator of his male personality, as a "building brick and builder of his house after him," as is implicit in the [Hebrew] בֵּן.[7]

The significance of this idea becomes readily apparent if we consider the contrast between the "disobedient and recalcitrant son" to be discussed in the verses that follow, and the kind of son designated in the preceding law (Verse 17) as the first of his father's acquisitions. In the preceding law, the father about to die sees his son as the continuator of his own manly striving to provide for his home and family. In the present case, by contrast, the father sees his son as "a glutton and a drunkard" (cf. Verse 20), who will squander the wealth earned by his father; "in the end he will have exhausted his father's assets" (Sanhedrin 72a). The term בֵּן as such would define the son also in childhood, but in view of what has just been said, the words "if a man has a son" specifically make the law applicable only to a son who has reached the age at which his father can already recognize in him the future man, who has already come close to the father's own manhood; cf. "*If a man has a son*": A *son* implies a son near to the strength of manhood" (ibid., 68b). According to the *halakhah*, this refers to the first three months after the son has reached puberty; i.e., after he has reached the age of thirteen. [Cf. "The days of the 'stubborn and recalcitrant son' are only three months (following his attainment of puberty)" ibid. 69a.]

We believe that by this limitation the Law makes a most significant suggestion to all educators seriously concerned about the moral future of their pupils. The

Law considers the first three months after the boy's attainment of Bar Mitzvah age as the critical period that will decide his moral future. At the very time when, in the popular mind, the first stirrings of the youth's sensuality will awaken also the "evil" in him, the Law expects a decisive breakthrough of the "good" which, through its struggle with sensuality, works itself up to the moral strength of true manhood. The Creator of mankind, Who gave this period of struggle to the young man, has ordained that this period should serve also to awaken within him a spirit capable of enthusiasm for all that is morally great and noble, a spirit that will make him turn aside in outraged disgust from all things base and common. This is true above all in the case of the Jewish youth, if his parents have done their duty by him and have enabled him to grow to maturity "upon the knees of the Teaching and the duty," of תּוֹרָה and מִצְוָה; so that when he reaches the age of בַּר מִצְוָה, the "son of the duty commanded by God," they will be able to leave it to his own sense of duty to continue his education along the proper path. With regard to such a man, the statement "I (i.e., God) have created the evil inclination, but I have created the Torah as a sweet antidote to combat it" (Kiddushin 30b) holds true even more than in the case of others.

The obedience that the son shows to his parents during that initial period of his elevation to the rank of adolescence, and the extent to which he will then turn away from base sensuality and toward all things spiritual and lofty, is perceived by the Law as the power which the spirit of *mitzvah* wields over him, the *mitzvah* whose banners he must now join with the seriousness of manhood and, at the same time, with the joyous enthusiasm of youth. . . .

* * *

he does not hearken to the voice of his father and to the voice of his mother. Only if the child has both a father and a mother, and only if the father and the mother alike have sought to bring their influence to bear upon him as his educators, and only if, as stated in verse 20, "he does not hearken *to our voice*"; i.e., if both parents speak in one and the same voice, if both relate to the child with equal seriousness and dignity, and, above all, only if both parents are as one in their thoughts and desire [with regard to their child's education], can they tell themselves that they are not to blame if their child has turned out to be an irreclaimable reprobate. If even only one of these factors is absent; if, above all, the parents have not worked together in complete harmony in the education of their

---

[7]*Note to the English translation*: בֵּן = son; from the root בנה, to build. [G.H.]

and to the gate of his place,   20. and they shall say to the elders of his city: "This our son is disobedient and recalcitrant; he does not hearken to our voice; he is a glutton and a drunkard."   21. And all the people of his city shall stone him so that he will die, and [so] you will clear away the evil from your midst. And all of Yisrael shall hear it and be afraid.   22. And if there is a capital sin upon a man, and he is executed, and you hang him upon a pole, 23. you shall not allow his body to remain upon the pole overnight because you must bury even him on the same day; for one who remains suspended expresses an act of blasphemy. And you shall not defile the soil that *God*, your God, is giving you as an inheritance.

XXII

1. You shall not see your brother's ox or his sheep go astray and hold yourself back from them; rather, you must bring them back to your brother.   2. But if your brother is not near to you, or you do not know him, you must take it into your house and it shall stay with you until your brother inquires after it; then you shall restore it to him.   3. You shall do so with his donkey, you shall do so with his garment and you shall do so with any lost object of your brother's that he has lost and

זִקְנֵי עִירוֹ וְאֶל־שַׁעַר מְקֹמוֹ: כ וְאָמְרוּ אֶל־ זִקְנֵי עִירוֹ בְּנֵנוּ זֶה סוֹרֵר וּמֹרֶה אֵינֶנּוּ שֹׁמֵעַ בְּקֹלֵנוּ זוֹלֵל וְסֹבֵא: כא וּרְגָמֻהוּ כָּל־אַנְשֵׁי עִירוֹ בָאֲבָנִים וָמֵת וּבִעַרְתָּ הָרָע מִקִּרְבֶּךָ וְכָל־ יִשְׂרָאֵל יִשְׁמְעוּ וְיִרָאוּ: ס שני כב וְכִי־יִהְיֶה בְאִישׁ חֵטְא מִשְׁפַּט־מָוֶת וְהוּמָת וְתָלִיתָ אֹתוֹ עַל־עֵץ: כג לֹא־תָלִין נִבְלָתוֹ עַל־הָעֵץ כִּי־ קָבוֹר תִּקְבְּרֶנּוּ בַּיּוֹם הַהוּא כִּי־קִלְלַת אֱלֹהִים תָּלוּי וְלֹא תְטַמֵּא אֶת־אַדְמָתְךָ אֲשֶׁר יְהֹוָה אֱלֹהֶיךָ נֹתֵן לְךָ נַחֲלָה: ס כב א לֹא־תִרְאֶה אֶת־שׁוֹר אָחִיךָ אוֹ אֶת־שֵׂיוֹ נִדָּחִים וְהִתְעַלַּמְתָּ מֵהֶם הָשֵׁב תְּשִׁיבֵם לְאָחִיךָ: ב וְאִם־לֹא קָרוֹב אָחִיךָ אֵלֶיךָ וְלֹא יְדַעְתּוֹ וַאֲסַפְתּוֹ אֶל־תּוֹךְ בֵּיתֶךָ וְהָיָה עִמְּךָ עַד דְּרֹשׁ אָחִיךָ אֹתוֹ וַהֲשֵׁבֹתוֹ לוֹ: ג וְכֵן תַּעֲשֶׂה לַחֲמֹרוֹ וְכֵן תַּעֲשֶׂה לְשִׂמְלָתוֹ וְכֵן תַּעֲשֶׂה לְכָל־אֲבֵדַת אָחִיךָ אֲשֶׁר־תֹּאבַד

child, the fact that the child has become a reprobate is not in itself proof of his innate moral depravity. Perhaps if his father and mother had given him a better, more genuine education, he might have become a different person, and it is even possible that life and experience may succeed in improving him where his parents have failed.

* * *

20. ... Of all the possible moral perversions, the Law has chosen as a criterion of completely hopeless corruption the case of a Jewish youth who, having reached adolescence, a time in life when he should enthusiastically embrace every ideal of spirituality and morality, devotes himself to drink and gluttony instead. Herein lies another important hint for both the father and the mother, and also for the spirit to be cultivated in the home where young human souls are to mature toward their moral and spiritual future: If for nothing else but the sake of their children, parents should be careful not to allow "good food and drink" to assume a place of predominance in their home and among the members of their household. Only where

spiritual and moral factors are given priority over all other considerations can that atmosphere develop in which young human emotions will be protected from brutalization.

* * *

CHAPTER XXII

Chapter 22 opens with a group of laws (Verses 1 through 5) which set down three basic principles for Israel's civic and commercial life, which are now about to begin; principles by which alone the nation will be able to fashion its society in character with its calling. These three principles are: The brotherly solidarity of all for the protection of the private property of each individual (Verses 1 through 3); the brotherly solidarity of all in supporting the personal endeavors of each individual (Verse 4); and the upholding of the natural differentiation between the sexes with regard to occupation and personal way of life (Verse 5). As in similar cases throughout the text, so here, too, these principles are illustrated by practical problems and cases in point. ...

* * *

that comes into your hands; it shall not be in your power to hold yourself back. 4. You shall not see your brother's donkey or his ox lying on the way and seek to hold yourself back from them; rather, you shall raise them up with him. 5. No male article shall be on a woman, and a man shall not clothe himself in a woman's garment, for whoever does these things is an abomination to *God*, your God. 6. If a bird's nest happens to be before you on the way, in any tree or on the ground, with young ones or eggs, and the mother is sitting upon the young or

מִמֶּנּוּ וּמְצָאתָהּ לֹא תוּכַל לְהִתְעַלֵּם: ס ד לֹא־
תִרְאֶה אֶת־חֲמוֹר אָחִיךָ אוֹ שׁוֹרוֹ נֹפְלִים
בַּדֶּרֶךְ וְהִתְעַלַּמְתָּ מֵהֶם הָקֵם תָּקִים עִמּוֹ: ס
ה לֹא־יִהְיֶה כְלִי־גֶבֶר עַל־אִשָּׁה וְלֹא־יִלְבַּשׁ
גֶּבֶר שִׂמְלַת אִשָּׁה כִּי תוֹעֲבַת יְהוָה אֱלֹהֶיךָ
כָּל־עֹשֵׂה אֵלֶּה: פ ו כִּי יִקָּרֵא קַן־צִפּוֹר ׀
לְפָנֶיךָ בַּדֶּרֶךְ בְּכָל־עֵץ ׀ אוֹ עַל־הָאָרֶץ
אֶפְרֹחִים אוֹ בֵיצִים וְהָאֵם רֹבֶצֶת עַל־

4. . . . The following halakhah is set forth in Baba Metziah 32a: No compensation may be taken for restoring lost property. Likewise, no compensation may be taken for unloading an animal that has collapsed under its burden. However, it is permissible to take compensation for rendering assistance in loading an animal. The restoration of lost property and the unloading of an overburdened animal involve direct action to forestall a material loss. The act of loading an animal, on the other hand, initially entails only a furtherance of your neighbor's purposes. This may be the motivation for the legal distinction cited above.

Note that assistance rendered in loading an animal is a duty for which compensation may be demanded, and even restoration of lost property without compensation can be expected only of one who has no other employment. The Law does not obligate one otherwise employed to neglect his own livelihood without appropriate compensation. These qualifications are outstanding traits of Jewish laws pertinent to the duties of social justice. The spirit of Jewish law is far removed from that extravagant zeal which demands complete self-abnegation as a general rule in communal life, and which equates virtue with self-sacrifice. Jewish life does not accept such a philosophy because it could never become a universal standard. Indeed, if it were to be put into practice, it would spell the end of all social relationships. If such an impracticable ideal were to be accepted as the standard for everyday conduct, "practical-minded" people would feel they would have no other alternative but to adopt an attitude of rank egotism. The Jewish principles of social relations that are universally binding accord full moral validity to man's need to provide for his own existence and independence. At the same time, however, the Law demands just as categorically and impressively that, in addition to, and simultaneously with, seeing that our own needs are supplied, we concern ourselves, in a caring, helpful manner, with the preservation of our neighbor's property and with the furtherance of his endeavors.

Jewish truth . . . basically denies that any selfishness attaches to striving for one's own purposes; indeed, it views such striving as a duty commanded by God. Only thus could it truly place the stamp of God, אֲנִי ד׳ ["I, *God*"], upon its rule, "Love your neighbor as yourself." For this reason, too, the Mishnah (Baba Metziah 33a) could set forth as a general principle the rule that if both your property and that of your neighbor are in danger, and it is a question of saving the one or the other, your property comes first. The Law does not require you to neglect your own property, and R. Yehudah, in the name of Rav, explains this on the basis of the qualification in Deuteronomy 15:4, "However, there shall be no needy among you," saying, "(As far as you are concerned), your property shall take precedence over that of any other person." . . . At the same time, however, this authority hastens to add the admonition that one who will insist on adhering strictly to this principle [that he may put his own property first] will eventually fall into the very destitution he sought to avoid by behaving in this manner. For the same Law that has drawn for us שׁוּרַת הַדִּין, the "boundaries of right" with regard to all our actions (so that we do wrong if we transgress these boundaries), expects us to be sufficiently noble-minded to place restraints upon ourselves לִפְנִים מִשּׁוּרַת הַדִּין, even within the limits permitted by God; to forego our own rights for the sake of our neighbor's welfare and to do that which, under the given circumstances, we should be able to recognize as הַיָּשָׁר וְהַטּוֹב בְּעֵינֵי ד׳ ["that which is right and good in the eyes of *God*"] (See notes on Chapter 6:18). . . .

° ° °

6. ***If a bird's nest happens to be.*** The laws in the preceding verses (Verses 1–5) posit the basic principles that are to guide the nation as it is about to establish and develop its national life: (1) solidarity and brotherliness in the preservation of the property of others and in the furtherance of the endeavors of others, and (2) the maintenance of sex differentiation between male and female with regard to occupation and way of

upon the eggs, you shall not take the mother with the young. 7. You shall send the mother away free, but the young you may take for yourself; if you do this, it will be well with you, and you will live long. 8. When you build a new house, you shall make a [guard]rail for your roof and you shall not bring blood guilt upon your house if anyone falling should fall from there. 9. Do not sow your vineyard with species that exclude each other, lest the

הָאֶפְרֹחִים אוֹ עַל־הַבֵּיצִים לֹא־תִקַּח הָאֵם עַל־
הַבָּנִים: ז שַׁלֵּחַ תְּשַׁלַּח אֶת־הָאֵם וְאֶת־הַבָּנִים
תִּקַּח־לָךְ לְמַעַן יִיטַב לָךְ וְהַאֲרַכְתָּ יָמִים: ס
שלישי ח כִּי תִבְנֶה בַּיִת חָדָשׁ וְעָשִׂיתָ מַעֲקֶה
לְגַגֶּךָ וְלֹא־תָשִׂים דָּמִים בְּבֵיתֶךָ כִּי־יִפֹּל הַנֹּפֵל
מִמֶּנּוּ: ט לֹא־תִזְרַע כַּרְמְךָ כִּלְאָיִם פֶּן־תִּקְדַּשׁ

life. The first of the two constitutes the basis of all social relationships; the second forms the foundation for the home, which, after all, is the bedrock upon which all the nation's welfare is built. Already in Verse 5 the female was given first place in this respect: "No male article shall be on a woman." The woman must understand that all her personal honor and dignity are rooted in her calling as "the mother of the home." It is within these "limits" that she finds her self-respect and is, in turn, entitled to respect and protection from others as she stands, inviolate, in the midst of her people. It is on this concept of womanhood, more than on anything else, that the nation's prosperity and progress depend. The respect that a nation accords to the woman's calling is a reliable barometer of that nation's moral level.

By continuing in this manner with regulations relating predominantly to the structure of family life, the Law emphasizes a legal institution that should impress upon every member of the nation the paramount importance which the Law attaches to the domestic functions of any female creature. It extends this principle even to animal life by assuring protection for a mother bird while she performs her maternal functions, and by demanding that all men, when given an opportunity to do so, should demonstrate, by practical action, the respect due to the female as she carries out the tasks of motherhood.

· · ·

7. *if you do this, it will be well with you and you will live long.* You shall do this in the knowledge that all your happiness, present and future, depends upon the spirit that informs the *mitzvah* you are carrying out; namely, your expression of respect for the dignity of motherhood. Cf. similar Divine promises in connection with practical demonstrations of respect for one's parents (Exodus 20:12 and Deuteronomy 5:16). These similarities should serve to confirm our interpretation also of the present commandment.

· · ·

8. *When you build.* The preceding law taught the

significance of the home and of the functions of the female sex within it, ideals that are to be respected even in the case of a bird's nest and the mother bird. The group of laws beginning with the present verse now makes us aware of the higher meaning inherent in the home built by man and in man's domestic functions. In animal life, nest-building and child care are instinctive, but in man these instinctive drives are joined by the demands of moral law. The bird builds its nest only for itself and for those most closely related to it; in this endeavor it is guided solely and unfailingly by egotism, by the powerful drive of self-preservation. Not so man. In building his house, he must be motivated from the outset by consideration for the welfare not only of those people who will dwell in it at present, but also of those who may dwell there in the future. He must therefore not permit anything in his household that might cause injury to someone else (Verse 8).

In all his work of food-getting and self-support, in whatever he does as master over nature and also in his outer appearance as a human being, he must always be mindful of the great Lawgiver of the Universe, Whose creative will endowed man with the ability to obey God's Law of his own free will, even as He made animals and plants obey His Law instinctively, without a will of their own (Verses 9, 10 and 11). Above all, man must always remember that, wherever his pursuits may take him, he can prove his manly strength and dignity only by the self-discipline he shows in observing the Law (Verse 12). All these laws were already set down in earlier Books (Exodus 21:28 through 34; Leviticus 19:19 and Numbers 15:37 through 41) in terms of their implications in civil law, their significance in the hallowing of life and their earnestness of purpose, promoting manly circumspection. They are incorporated in the present compendium for those about to enter the Land, partly in order to supplement what has already been stated before, but primarily in order to address themselves directly to the agricultural and domestic activities that the nation is about to begin at this point.

· · ·

9. *Do not sow your vineyard.* When you set up your

increase, or even the seed, and the yield of
the vineyard, be forfeited as sanctified.
10. Do not plow with an ox and a donkey
together.   11. Do not clothe yourself
with *shaatnez*—wool and linen together.

הַמְלֵאָה הַזֶּרַע אֲשֶׁר תִּזְרָע וּתְבוּאַת הַכָּרֶם: ס
י לֹא־תַחֲרֹשׁ בְּשׁוֹר־וּבַחֲמֹר יַחְדָּו: יא לֹא
תִלְבַּשׁ שַׁעַטְנֵז צֶמֶר וּפִשְׁתִּים יַחְדָּו: ס

household, you must immediately think not only of
yourself, but you must remember to be careful also lest
you endanger the safety or happiness of your fellow
men. In the same spirit, when you cultivate your
ground for your nourishment and pleasure, you must be
mindful, at once, of the Lawgiver of the Universe, Who
is revealed through the entire organic world. By His law
of לְמִינוֹ [species], He has shown to every species of
living things the path it must follow in the development
of its own life and individuality. By this law He has
also engaged you, as a human being, to follow your own
particular calling as a Jewish person, so that you may
always be a man and a Jew, demonstrating your unique
vocation even when you seek your nourishment and
pleasure.

The laws pertaining to כִּלְאַיִם [forbidden mixtures]
have already been set forth in Leviticus 19:19, with
reference to cattle breeding, arboriculture and agriculture.... These laws are now supplemented by the
law pertaining to כִּלְאֵי כֶּרֶם [forbidden mixtures in
viticulture], which is embedded in the concept that the
land of the Jews is hallowed as the soil of God's Law.
This would seem to be a primary reason why this particular law should have been incorporated into the compendium given to the nation as it was about to enter
that land. The very sight of the soil cultivated under the
laws of כִּלְאַיִם should call out to anyone setting foot on
this land: "Take your shoes from your feet, because the
soil on which you are standing is soil hallowed to the
Law of God. Let the men who are nourished and borne
by this soil give their allegiance to the Law of God!"

Now there is one plant species whose cultivation, we
might imagine, should be forbidden altogether upon
the soil sanctified to God's moral law, because the
consumption of the fruit of this species, more than any
other fruit, is capable of leading man into excesses and
moral lapses unworthy of human beings. One might
expect, therefore, that viticulture should not be permitted upon the soil hallowed to the moral law of God. Yet,
the Law not only permits viticulture in the land of the
Jews but actually makes the enjoyment of the fruit of
the vine a part of the offertory ritual.... As a consequence, [however,] the Torah imposes the כִּלְאַיִם laws
upon viticulture in the land of the Jews with
even greater stringency than upon the cultivation of
other fruit. Vines may be grown only if every com-
mingling of species is avoided in their cultivation. The
seed or the fruits of any vineyard cultivated without
reference to this law must be destroyed. Through these

regulations, the Law expresses the profound truth so
characteristic of all Jewish law: the Law of God not only
permits, but in fact sanctifies, even the greatest physical pleasures, as long as he who partakes of them does
so under the control of God's Law; as long as these
pleasures do not cause him to exceed the limits drawn
by that Law for the Jewish species of man. Wine
obtained in strict observance of the Divine law of
species can even be taken into the Sanctuary of God as
an offering, to symbolize the supreme expression of joy.
On the other hand, the yield of vines planted without
regard to the Divine law of species has no justifiable
place even in man's everyday life. The fact that such
plants and their products must be destroyed by fire
symbolizes the negation of all pleasures obtained without regard for the Law, but thus, conversely, underscores the sanctity inherent in pleasures enjoyed in an
atmosphere of moral purity.

∘   ∘   ∘

10. *Do not plow*. When you build your house, you
must remember your duty toward your neighbor.
When you plant your vineyard, you must remember the
moral law. So, too, when you yoke into your service
your animals, over whom you have dominion, you are
to remember the supreme sovereignty of the One
Whose law of species confronts you also in animal life; a
law to which you are subject no less than the animal. If
you banish willfulness from your activities, and do not
place under one yoke, for your purposes, two animal
species that God has kept apart, you will be reminded
that His decree of לְמִינוֹ [species] is addressed also to you
and to all your pursuits; and that, in whatever you do,
you must prove yourself specifically as a "Jewish
person" in the service of your Master.

∘   ∘   ∘

11. *Do not clothe yourself with* **shaatnez**. Finally,
the Law turns to your outer appearance. Let your
clothing, which reflects your personality, remind you
that you must preserve the division between the animal
vitality and the vegetative instinctiveness that are both
part of your nature; that you must not subordinate the
former to the latter, but rather, the latter to the former;
and that you must subordinate them both to God. This
is the basic requirement of the human calling assigned
to you by God. And do not clothe yourself in the
"garment of distortion" made by mingling two species
of textiles that should be kept separate: the animal

12. Make yourself twisted threads on the four corners of your garment with which you cover yourself. 13. If a man takes himself a wife and he comes to her and hates her, 14. and he institutes proceedings against her and brings forth an evil name upon her and says: "I have taken myself this woman and came near to her, but I did not find any [evidence of] virginity for her"; 15. and the father of the girl and her mother take action in the matter and bring the girl's virginity to light before the elders of the city in court, 16. and the father of the girl says to the elders: "I have given my daughter to this man as a wife, and now he hates her, 17. and so he has instituted

יב גְּדִלִים תַּעֲשֶׂה־לָּךְ עַל־אַרְבַּע כַּנְפוֹת כְּסוּתְךָ אֲשֶׁר תְּכַסֶּה־בָּהּ: ס יג כִּי־יִקַּח אִישׁ אִשָּׁה וּבָא אֵלֶיהָ וּשְׂנֵאָהּ: יד וְשָׂם לָהּ עֲלִילֹת דְּבָרִים וְהוֹצִא עָלֶיהָ שֵׁם רָע וְאָמַר אֶת־הָאִשָּׁה הַזֹּאת לָקַחְתִּי וָאֶקְרַב אֵלֶיהָ וְלֹא־מָצָאתִי לָהּ בְּתוּלִים: טו וְלָקַח אֲבִי הַנַּעֲרָ (הנערה קרי) וְאִמָּהּ וְהוֹצִיאוּ אֶת־בְּתוּלֵי הַנַּעֲרָ (הנערה קרי) אֶל־זִקְנֵי הָעִיר הַשָּׁעְרָה: טז וְאָמַר אֲבִי הַנַּעֲרָ (הנערה קרי) אֶל־הַזְּקֵנִים אֶת־בִּתִּי נָתַתִּי לָאִישׁ הַזֶּה לְאִשָּׁה וַיִּשְׂנָאֶהָ: יז וְהִנֵּה־הוּא שָׂם עֲלִילֹת

---

derivative (wool) and the vegetable derivative (linen). . . .

12. **Make yourself twisted threads.** By intertwining the prohibition against כִּלְאַיִם with all our activities and our own outer appearance, the three preceding laws remind us of our calling as human beings and as Jews. Particularly the last of these laws, the prohibition against שַׁעַטְנֵז, calls our attention to these thoughts by forbidding us to use certain mixtures of textiles in our clothing. Now the Law adds to this series of "negative commandments" a positive commandment, that of the *tzitzith*, which are meant to remind us, wherever we may be, of our concept of God and of our calling as Jewish persons. While the prohibition against שַׁעַטְנֵז, a "negative commandment," has every fiber of our clothing say to us, "You *shall not* be an animal," the positive commandment relating to the *tzitzith* has our clothing admonish us, "You *shall* be a man *and* a Jew!" . . . The factors of protective covering, twisted threads and the four corners were reserved for incorporation into this compendium, given when the Jewish nation was about to disperse in its own land. These laws address themselves to every Jew who now enters the land, as follows: No matter how far away—to the east or west, to the north or south—you may settle from the center of the Sanctuary of the Law and its representatives; no matter what struggles your particular habitat may impose upon you in mastering the forces of nature on which your physical survival depends—wherever you may dwell, be your own watchman over your observance of the Law. Wherever you may dwell, bind up your physical sensuality within the powerful bond of the Divinely human and Jewishly hallowed element within you. Wherever you may go, take with you the תְּכֵלֶת [sky blue] thread as a reminder of your priestly calling as a

Jew. Wherever you may dwell, see that this thread and all the Divinely human elements connected with it shall remain firm and strong to overcome the sensual creature element within you. And you shall never tear asunder the knot that binds you, as a human being, to God and to the Sanctuary of His Law.

      °   °   °

13. **If a man takes himself a wife.** The preceding group of laws (Verses 5–12) centers on one common purpose: to call the attention of men and women alike to the lofty significance of, and the basic standards for, the function of both sexes in human domesticity; functions that are to be performed by husband and wife together, in a specified division of labor. We note that in this division of labor, particular significance and sanctity are accorded to the female sex. The preceding laws served as an introduction to the groups of laws that now follow and that relate to the practical aspects of building a home and a society upon the principles expressed by those introductory laws. Here again, we shall note the particular emphasis on the significance of the woman's role.

. . . In the eyes of the Law, the human female with the highest sexual status is the virgin who is already—or still—in the initial phase of pubescence, and who will become linked to a man only by his legal act of personal acquisition. . . . This demonstrates the truth that the nation has no more precious treasure than the virginal purity of its daughters. The greatest pride of the home lies in the virginal innocence of the children within it. Any aspersion on the innocence of a maiden is an aspersion on the honor of the home in which she was raised and on the honor of the nation whose name she bears.

      °   °   °

proceedings against her as follows: 'I did not find any [evidence of] virginity for her'; and here are the proofs of my daughter's virginity"; and they spread out that which covered the truth before the elders of the city; 18. and the elders of the city shall take the man and chastise him, 19. and they shall fine him one hundred pieces of silver and give them to the father of the girl, because he has brought forth an evil name upon a virgin of Yisrael. But she shall remain his wife; he no longer has the authority to send her away as long as he lives. 20. But if this thing was true; no [evidence of] virginity was found for the girl, 21. then they shall bring out the girl to the gate of her father's house, and the people of her city shall stone her with stones so that she dies, because she has committed a shameful act in Yisrael, to commit lewdness in her father's house; you must clear away the evil from your midst. 22. If a man is found cohabiting with a woman married to another man, both of them shall die: the man cohabiting with the woman, and [also] the woman; and you shall clear away

דְּבָרִים לֵאמֹר לֹא־מָצָאתִי לְבִתְּךָ בְּתוּלִים וְאֵלֶּה בְּתוּלֵי בִתִּי וּפָרְשׂוּ הַשִּׂמְלָה לִפְנֵי זִקְנֵי הָעִיר: יח וְלָקְחוּ זִקְנֵי הָעִיר־הַהִוא אֶת־הָאִישׁ וְיִסְּרוּ אֹתוֹ: יט וְעָנְשׁוּ אֹתוֹ מֵאָה כֶסֶף וְנָתְנוּ לַאֲבִי הַנַּעֲרָה כִּי הוֹצִיא שֵׁם רָע עַל בְּתוּלַת יִשְׂרָאֵל וְלוֹ־תִהְיֶה לְאִשָּׁה לֹא־יוּכַל לְשַׁלְּחָהּ כָּל־יָמָיו: ס כ וְאִם־אֱמֶת הָיָה הַדָּבָר הַזֶּה לֹא־נִמְצְאוּ בְתוּלִים לַנַּעֲרָ (לנערה קרי): כא וְהוֹצִיאוּ אֶת־הַנַּעֲרָ (הנערה קרי) אֶל־פֶּתַח בֵּית־אָבִיהָ וּסְקָלוּהָ אַנְשֵׁי עִירָהּ בָּאֲבָנִים וָמֵתָה כִּי־עָשְׂתָה נְבָלָה בְּיִשְׂרָאֵל לִזְנוֹת בֵּית אָבִיהָ וּבִעַרְתָּ הָרָע מִקִּרְבֶּךָ: ס כב כִּי־יִמָּצֵא אִישׁ שֹׁכֵב ׀ עִם־אִשָּׁה בְעֻלַת־בַּעַל וּמֵתוּ גַּם־שְׁנֵיהֶם הָאִישׁ הַשֹּׁכֵב עִם־הָאִשָּׁה וְהָאִשָּׁה וּבִעַרְתָּ הָרָע

---

17. . . . וּפָרְשׂוּ הַשִּׂמְלָה [and they spread out that which covered the truth]. Throughout Scripture, the term שִׂמְלָה denotes a garment in which something has been wrapped. . . . Hence in Ketuboth 46a, "They spread out that which he secretly contrived against her (they bring his underhandedness to light)." . . . The witnesses called by the girl's father confront the witnesses cited by the man, and then the whole matter is spread out [or "laid out"] for all to see, like a new garment without folds or creases.

18 and 19. *But she shall remain his wife; he no longer has the authority to send her away as long as he lives.* The original standpoint of Jewish Law, as may be seen throughout the sacred writings of Judaism . . . was to assume that a wife should always be worthy of her husband's highest regard. The Law took it for granted, therefore, that the husband would cherish her as the jewel of his heart and the joy of his life, so much so that the Law could safely leave it to the husband to decide to dissolve the marriage if he were to find out that his wife was not what he had presumed her to be. Jewish Law could assume that the kind of marriage a Jewish husband would find it in his heart to dissolve would not be one worth preserving. The fact that circumstances of time and place made it necessary for

the Law to divest the husband of this one-sided prerogative would seem to have been not an advance, but rather a step backward in the development of Jewish civilization (cf. notes on Deuteronomy 24:1). . . . A husband who took such scandalous action against his wife as is described in this text, in order to force a dissolution of the marriage, was deprived for all time of the authority to divorce his wife. As far as *he* is concerned, his wife must remain his wife forever; he will never be able to dissolve the marriage without her consent.

∘   ∘   ∘

21. *to commit lewdness in her father's house.* The enormity of this offense, this act of moral depravity, lies in the fact that here we have a girl, still in the legal custody of her parents, still living under her parents' supervision, who has committed what amounts to adultery, even though she was fully aware of the gravity of her offense. (Since she was to be stoned, there must have been eyewitnesses and warnings prior to the offense.)

22–27. *If a man is found.* The laws that now follow refer to the problem of deliberate adultery, a crime against the fundamental institution of all human society and morality. . . .

the evil from Yisrael. 23. If a virgin girl is betrothed to a man, and a man finds her in the city and cohabits with her, 24. then you shall bring them both out to the gate of this city and stone them with stones, so that they die; the girl, by reason of evidence that she did not cry out in the city, and the man, by reason of evidence that he violated his neighbor's wife; and you shall clear away the evil from your midst. 25. But if the man comes upon the betrothed girl in the field, and the man seizes her and cohabits with her, then only the man who cohabited with her shall die, 26. and to the girl you shall do nothing whatsoever; no capital sin attaches to her; for as if a man rises up against his neighbor and murders him, so is this incident; 27. for he came upon her in the field; even if the betrothed girl had cried out, there was no one to rescue her. 28. If a man finds a virgin girl who is not yet betrothed, and he lays hold of her and cohabits with her, and they are found, 29. then the man cohabiting with her shall give to the girl's father fifty pieces of silver. But she must become his wife because he has violated her; he does not have the authority to send her away as long as he lives.

XXIII

1. No man may marry his father's wife, and he also must not uncover his father's garb. 2. One who was injured by crushing [of testicles] or one with a mutilated [male] sexual organ shall not enter into the assembly of *God*. 3. A bastard [*mamzer*] shall not enter into the assembly of *God*; even the

מִיִּשְׂרָאֵל: ס כג כִּי יִהְיֶה נַעֲרָ (נערה קרי)
בְתוּלָה מְאֹרָשָׂה לְאִישׁ וּמְצָאָהּ אִישׁ בָּעִיר
וְשָׁכַב עִמָּהּ: כד וְהוֹצֵאתֶם אֶת־שְׁנֵיהֶם אֶל־
שַׁעַר ׀ הָעִיר הַהִוא וּסְקַלְתֶּם אֹתָם בָּאֲבָנִים
וָמֵתוּ אֶת־הַנַּעֲרָ (הנערה קרי) עַל־דְּבַר אֲשֶׁר
לֹא־צָעֲקָה בָעִיר וְאֶת־הָאִישׁ עַל־דְּבַר אֲשֶׁר־
עִנָּה אֶת־אֵשֶׁת רֵעֵהוּ וּבִעַרְתָּ הָרָע מִקִּרְבֶּךָ: ס
כה וְאִם־בַּשָּׂדֶה יִמְצָא הָאִישׁ אֶת־הַנַּעֲרָ (הנערה
קרי) הַמְאֹרָשָׂה וְהֶחֱזִיק־בָּהּ הָאִישׁ וְשָׁכַב
עִמָּהּ וּמֵת הָאִישׁ אֲשֶׁר־שָׁכַב עִמָּהּ לְבַדּוֹ:
כו וְלַנַּעֲרָ (ולנערה קרי) לֹא־תַעֲשֶׂה דָבָר אֵין
לַנַּעֲרָ (לנערה קרי) חֵטְא מָוֶת כִּי כַּאֲשֶׁר יָקוּם
אִישׁ עַל־רֵעֵהוּ וּרְצָחוֹ נֶפֶשׁ כֵּן הַדָּבָר הַזֶּה:
כז כִּי בַשָּׂדֶה מְצָאָהּ צָעֲקָה הַנַּעֲרָ (הנערה קרי)
הַמְאֹרָשָׂה וְאֵין מוֹשִׁיעַ לָהּ: ס כח כִּי־יִמְצָא
אִישׁ נַעֲרָ (נערה קרי) בְתוּלָה אֲשֶׁר לֹא־אֹרָשָׂה
וּתְפָשָׂהּ וְשָׁכַב עִמָּהּ וְנִמְצָאוּ: כט וְנָתַן הָאִישׁ
הַשֹּׁכֵב עִמָּהּ לַאֲבִי הַנַּעֲרָ (הנערה קרי) חֲמִשִּׁים
כָּסֶף וְלוֹ־תִהְיֶה לְאִשָּׁה תַּחַת אֲשֶׁר עִנָּהּ לֹא־
יוּכַל שַׁלְּחָהּ כָּל־יָמָיו: ס כג א לֹא־יִקַּח אִישׁ
אֶת־אֵשֶׁת אָבִיו וְלֹא יְגַלֶּה כְּנַף אָבִיו: ס
ב לֹא־יָבֹא פְצוּעַ־דַּכָּא וּכְרוּת שָׁפְכָה בִּקְהַל
יְהוָה: ס ג לֹא־יָבֹא מַמְזֵר בִּקְהַל יְהוָה גַּם דּוֹר

as if . . . so is this incident. By this juxtaposition of sexual immorality and murder, sexual immorality is categorically put into the same class as murder with regard to the offender's accountability before God. Hence, if it is self-evident that no one is permitted to save his own life by murdering someone who is not threatening his life (because the life of the other person is worth at least as much as his own) . . . then it follows also . . . that no one may attempt to save his own life by committing an act of sexual immorality. The principle (Sanhedrin 74a) that holds good in the case of idolatry is equally applicable to murder and sexual immorality. . . . "Let him be put to death rather than (commit this) sin": It is forbidden to attempt to save one's own life by committing any one of these three sins. . . .

CHAPTER XXIII

3. . . . According to a halakhah set forth in Yebamoth 49a and Kiddushin 66b (*Tosefot* ibid.), a *mamzer* is an individual born of a sexual union in which the father and the mother, under Jewish law, could each contract a marriage with another individual but are forbidden by Jewish Law to marry each other. . . .

A *mamzer* thus represents, by his very existence, an offense against the law through which God wishes to see marriage in His assembly elevated from a mere physical relationship to the moral and spiritual level expressed by קדושין [the legal act of Jewish marriage]. For this reason, a *mamzer* is excluded for life from the קְהַל ד׳ [assembly of *God*]. However, *mamzerim* may tenth generation of his shall not enter into the assembly of *God*.   4. An Ammonite or a Moabite shall not enter into the assembly of *God*; even the tenth generation of theirs shall not enter into the assembly of *God*, forever.   5. Because they did not come to meet you with bread and water on your way when you went out from Mitzrayim, and because he hired against you Balaam, son of Beor, from Pethor Aram Naharayim, to curse you.   6. And *God*, your God, would not hearken to Balaam; but *God*, your God, turned the curse into a blessing for you, because *God*, your God, loved you. 7. You shall not seek their peace nor their prosperity, all your days, forever.   8. Do not reject the Edomite entirely, because he is your brother. Do not reject the Mitzrite entirely, because you were a stranger in his land.   9. Of the children that are born to them, the third generation may enter into the assembly of *God*.   10. When you go out as a camp against your enemies, keep away from every evil thing.   11. If there is among you a man who is unclean by reason of a nocturnal occurrence, he shall go forth

עֲשִׂירִי לֹא־יָבֹא לוֹ בִּקְהַל יְהֹוָה: ס ד לֹא־יָבֹא עַמּוֹנִי וּמוֹאָבִי בִּקְהַל יְהֹוָה גַּם דּוֹר עֲשִׂירִי לֹא־יָבֹא לָהֶם בִּקְהַל יְהֹוָה עַד־עוֹלָם: ה עַל־דְּבַר אֲשֶׁר לֹא־קִדְּמוּ אֶתְכֶם בַּלֶּחֶם וּבַמַּיִם בַּדֶּרֶךְ בְּצֵאתְכֶם מִמִּצְרָיִם וַאֲשֶׁר שָׂכַר עָלֶיךָ אֶת־בִּלְעָם בֶּן־בְּעוֹר מִפְּתוֹר אֲרַם נַהֲרַיִם לְקַלְלֶךָ: ו וְלֹא־אָבָה יְהֹוָה אֱלֹהֶיךָ לִשְׁמֹעַ אֶל־בִּלְעָם וַיַּהֲפֹךְ יְהֹוָה אֱלֹהֶיךָ לְּךָ אֶת־הַקְּלָלָה לִבְרָכָה כִּי אֲהֵבְךָ יְהֹוָה אֱלֹהֶיךָ: ז לֹא־תִדְרֹשׁ שְׁלֹמָם וְטֹבָתָם כָּל־יָמֶיךָ לְעוֹלָם: ס רביעי ח לֹא־תְתַעֵב אֲדֹמִי כִּי אָחִיךָ הוּא לֹא־תְתַעֵב מִצְרִי כִּי־גֵר הָיִיתָ בְאַרְצוֹ: ט בָּנִים אֲשֶׁר־יִוָּלְדוּ לָהֶם דּוֹר שְׁלִישִׁי יָבֹא לָהֶם בִּקְהַל יְהֹוָה: ס י כִּי־תֵצֵא מַחֲנֶה עַל־אֹיְבֶיךָ וְנִשְׁמַרְתָּ מִכֹּל דָּבָר רָע: יא כִּי־יִהְיֶה בְךָ אִישׁ אֲשֶׁר לֹא־יִהְיֶה טָהוֹר מִקְּרֵה־לָיְלָה וְיָצָא אֶל־מִחוּץ

marry converts to Judaism . . . and they are not subject to any other legal disability. A *mamzer* is the legitimate son of his father in every respect and has the same rights of inheritance as individuals not classed as *mamzerim*.

      o   o   o

    8 and 9. . . . Reviewing the categories of those not permitted to enter the assembly of God, we will note that the Jewish nation is to be built upon the preservation of physical and moral integrity in sexual relationships (cf. the prohibition forbidding one with crushed or mutilated male genitals, or a *mamzer*, to enter into the assembly of God) and upon humane feelings of kindness and respect for members of other nations. (Ammonite and Moabite males were not permitted to marry Jewish women, but female members of these nationalities could marry Jewish men, and Edomites and Mitzrites were permitted to marry Jews in the third generation after embracing Judaism.)

    However, subsequent to the Assyrian and Babylonian wars of conquest, the original inhabitants of the lands of Ammon, Moab, Edom and ancient Egypt were driven out from their lands and settled among, and merged with, other nations. "Sanherib, king of Assyria, has already gone up and commingled all the nations, as

it is written (Isaiah 10:13): *In that I have removed the boundaries of the people and have robbed their treasures, and have brought down as one mighty the inhabitants*" (Tractate Yadayim, Chapter 4, Mishnah 4). As a result, the descendants of the national entities named here (Verses 4 through 9) as excluded under Jewish Law can no longer be identified. Thus, since that time, any non-Jew who has become a גֵּר [convert to Judaism], including present-day inhabitants of the territories once known as Ammon, Moab, Edom and Egypt, are "permitted to enter into the assembly"; i.e., they are permitted to marry a Jewish person in accordance with the principle that "whatever strays (from a group) is assumed to belong to the larger section (of the group)" cf. Berakhoth 28a. . . .

    10. When you go out as a camp. The laws immediately preceding were intended to ensure that personal morality and sympathetic attitudes toward other nations would become the basic character traits of the Jewish nation. Now, Verses 10–15 and 16 and 17, respectively, deal with two factors: the moral sanctity of the (Israelite) camp and the treatment to be accorded to a runaway slave, in which these two basic Jewish character traits are brought out in bold relief.

      o   o   o

outside the camp and not come within the camp. 12. Only at the turn toward evening shall he bathe himself in water, and when the sun has set, he shall come within the camp. 13. And you shall have a place outside the camp; to that place shall you go out. 14. And you shall have a trowel in your equipment, so that when you sit down outside, you shall dig with it and cover over that which you leave behind. 15. For *God*, your God, walks in the midst of your camp, to rescue you and to deliver up your enemies before you; so your camps shall be a holy thing, so that He may see no nakedness in you and restrain Himself from accompanying you. 16. You must not hand over, to his master, a slave who has taken refuge with you from his master. 17. He shall settle down with you in your midst, in the place that he will choose, within one of your gates where he feels best; you must not grieve him. 18. There shall be

לַמַּחֲנֶה לֹא יָבֹא אֶל־תּוֹךְ הַמַּחֲנֶה: יב וְהָיָה
לִפְנוֹת־עֶרֶב יִרְחַץ בַּמָּיִם וּכְבֹא הַשֶּׁמֶשׁ יָבֹא
אֶל־תּוֹךְ הַמַּחֲנֶה: יג וְיָד תִּהְיֶה לְךָ מִחוּץ
לַמַּחֲנֶה וְיָצָאתָ שָׁמָּה חוּץ: יד וְיָתֵד תִּהְיֶה לְךָ
עַל־אֲזֵנֶךָ וְהָיָה בְּשִׁבְתְּךָ חוּץ וְחָפַרְתָּה בָהּ
וְשַׁבְתָּ וְכִסִּיתָ אֶת־צֵאָתֶךָ: טו כִּי יְהוָה אֱלֹהֶיךָ
מִתְהַלֵּךְ | בְּקֶרֶב מַחֲנֶךָ לְהַצִּילְךָ וְלָתֵת אֹיְבֶיךָ
לְפָנֶיךָ וְהָיָה מַחֲנֶיךָ קָדוֹשׁ וְלֹא־יִרְאֶה בְךָ
עֶרְוַת דָּבָר וְשָׁב מֵאַחֲרֶיךָ: ס טז לֹא־תַסְגִּיר
עֶבֶד אֶל־אֲדֹנָיו אֲשֶׁר־יִנָּצֵל אֵלֶיךָ מֵעִם אֲדֹנָיו:
יז עִמְּךָ יֵשֵׁב בְּקִרְבְּךָ בַּמָּקוֹם אֲשֶׁר־יִבְחַר
בְּאַחַד שְׁעָרֶיךָ בַּטּוֹב לוֹ לֹא תּוֹנֶנּוּ: ס יח לֹא־

15. . . . You can triumph only if God is present in your midst, so that your victory will be a victory of the kingdom of God on earth. The presence of God in your camp does not depend on your strength and bravery directed to the outside, but on the bravery that you direct, first and foremost, toward yourself. The presence of God in your midst will depend on whether you will keep watch over yourself and guard yourself against all moral evil, in such a manner that all the "naked" animal elements in human nature, and everything that reminds one of it, will vanish from your environment, your appearance, your speech, your actions, you thoughts and your emotions. For God does not walk ahead of your camp; He walks *in the midst* of your camp, at the side of every single member of your society (see Sotah 3b). Therefore, let your society be morally hallowed. Let no one be able to discover in you, without or within, a "nakedness," no matter what it may be. For only on that condition will *God*, your God, walk with you, accompany you and never restrain Himself from going with you. . . .

מחניך *[your camps]*. The plural is used, probably in order to indicate that the things said here concerning our army camp should hold good also for any environment in which we may find ourselves, temporarily or permanently. Any place where we may be must bear the stamp of pure human morality. Not only our synagogues and schools, but every space within which we may dwell must be hallowed by thoughts of our life's mission, which can be understood only through the Law of God; thoughts that are to fill our minds at all times and wherever we may be. We must drive out from our dwelling places everything that recalls the animal-like aspects of human physicality. . . . Let every "nakedness" upon the human body be covered, as it were, so that we may turn our spirits, undisturbed, toward God and toward the teachings of His Law. . . . For the clear awareness that our spirit has been endowed with a unique personal essence and with the dignity of moral free will, and that, by the breath of God, this spirit has been temporarily wed to our physically fettered bodies, is the first, indispensable basis of our life's mission shown us by God.

With this awareness, all our morality and all thoughts of a dutiful life rise and fall. The laws of טומאה [uncleanness] and טָהֳרָה [purity] symbolically banish from the spheres consecrated to our moral ennoblement and sanctification the notion that we are like animals in that we, too, lack free will. Similarly, this law regarding the sanctity of the Israelite camp banishes every manifestation of animal physicality from our thoughts and actions that should be directed toward God and toward the fulfillment of our duty. In this way we will remain mindful of the dignity of our spiritual essence, which is related to God and which has been endowed with God-like freedom of will, and we will give no room to materialistic notions that would spell the grave of duty and morality. . . .

° ° °

18. ***There shall be none.*** קָדוֹשׁ denotes complete dedication to what is morally good; קָדֵשׁ denotes com-

תִהְיֶה קְדֵשָׁה מִבְּנוֹת יִשְׂרָאֵל וְלֹא־יִהְיֶה קָדֵשׁ
מִבְּנֵי יִשְׂרָאֵל׃ יט לֹא־תָבִיא אֶתְנַן זוֹנָה וּמְחִיר
כֶּלֶב בֵּית יְהוָה אֱלֹהֶיךָ לְכָל־נֶדֶר כִּי תוֹעֲבַת
יְהוָה אֱלֹהֶיךָ גַּם־שְׁנֵיהֶם׃ ס כ לֹא־תַשִּׁיךְ
לְאָחִיךָ נֶשֶׁךְ כֶּסֶף נֶשֶׁךְ אֹכֶל נֶשֶׁךְ כָּל־דָּבָר
אֲשֶׁר יִשָּׁךְ׃ כא לַנָּכְרִי תַשִּׁיךְ וּלְאָחִיךָ לֹא
תַשִּׁיךְ לְמַעַן יְבָרֶכְךָ יְהוָה אֱלֹהֶיךָ בְּכֹל מִשְׁלַח
יָדֶךָ עַל־הָאָרֶץ אֲשֶׁר־אַתָּה בָא־שָׁמָּה
לְרִשְׁתָּהּ׃ ס כב כִּי תִדֹּר נֶדֶר לַיהוָה אֱלֹהֶיךָ לֹא
תְאַחֵר לְשַׁלְּמוֹ כִּי־דָרֹשׁ יִדְרְשֶׁנּוּ יְהוָה אֱלֹהֶיךָ
מֵעִמָּךְ וְהָיָה בְךָ חֵטְא׃ כג וְכִי תֶחְדַּל לִנְדֹּר לֹא־
יִהְיֶה בְךָ חֵטְא׃ כד מוֹצָא שְׂפָתֶיךָ תִּשְׁמֹר
וְעָשִׂיתָ כַּאֲשֶׁר נָדַרְתָּ לַיהוָה אֱלֹהֶיךָ נְדָבָה
אֲשֶׁר דִּבַּרְתָּ בְּפִיךָ׃ ס חמישי כה כִּי תָבֹא בְּכֶרֶם
רֵעֶךָ וְאָכַלְתָּ עֲנָבִים כְּנַפְשְׁךָ שָׂבְעֶךָ וְאֶל־כֶּלְיְךָ
לֹא תִתֵּן׃ ס כו כִּי תָבֹא בְּקָמַת רֵעֶךָ וְקָטַפְתָּ

none dedicated to lewdness among the daughters of Yisrael, and there shall be none dedicated to lewdness among the sons of Yisrael. 19. You must not bring a harlot's wage or the price of a dog into the house of *God*, your God, for any pledge; because both of these are an abomination to *God*, your God. 20. You must not pay your brother any interest, be it interest in money or interest in food; no interest at all, nothing that could be construed in any way as interest. 21. You may pay interest to the stranger, [but] to your brother you must not pay interest, so that *God*, your God, may bless you in everything to which you may put your hand in the land to which you are coming, to take possession of it. 22. If you make a vow to *God*, your God, do not put off paying it, for *God*, your God, will demand it of you and sin would cling to you. 23. If you refrain from making vows, no sin will cling to you. 24. But that which your lips have uttered, you must keep and carry out according to that which you have vowed as a consecration to *God*, what you have spoken with your mouth. 25. When you come into your neighbor's vineyard, you may eat grapes as you desire until you have had your fill, but you must not put any into your vessel. 26. When you come into your neighbor's standing grain, you may

plete dedication to what is morally evil. An analogy is offered by the root כבד; as כָּבוֹד, it conveys the impression of spiritual and moral content, while as כָּבֵד it denotes only material, physical weight. Lewdness is defined as any sexual union not consecrated by קדושין [the legal act of Jewish marriage]. The wording of our text makes it clear that the Law demands the same modesty and morality from Israel's sons as it does from Israel's daughters. It regards the preservation of such modesty and morality as a confirmation of the good name of the Jewish people.

בְּנוֹת יִשְׂרָאֵל and בְּנֵי יִשְׂרָאֵל, "daughters of Israel" and "sons of Israel": these names shall remain pure at all times from any taint of immorality. . . .

25 and 26. This chapter closes with two rules which, like the prohibition against paying interest (Verses 20 and 21), derive from God's unlimited powers of disposition over our possessions that He reserved for Himself when our nation was founded. Under these laws, a sense of duty, founded on both justice and loving-kindness, is to be the basis for our development as a nation. The Jewish landowner is told that it is his duty to permit the workers who harvest the fruits of his field to eat as much of the harvest as they like while they are engaged in reaping his crops. At the same time, however, the worker is admonished that it is his duty to keep strictly within the limits of this right, which are explicitly set forth, and to be careful not to misuse it.

• • •

This regulation is applicable only while the worker is actually preparing for human consumption his employer's fruit, which nature has ripened. Not before and not after, but on the threshold of man's mastery over nature, so apt to engender the selfish thought, "This is my own, and mine alone," does God scatter, in both directions, the seeds of the ideal of duty, deriving from justice and loving-kindness. . . .

• • •

pluck ears with your hand, but you must not swing a sickle over your neighbor's standing grain.

XXIV

1. When a man takes himself a wife and marries her, then it shall be, if she has not found favor in his eyes because he has found in her a [moral] nakedness justifying legal proceedings, and he writes her a bill of divorce and places it in her hand, and thus dismisses her from his house;   2. and she departs from his house and goes and becomes another man's [wife],   3. and then the latter man hates her and writes her a bill of divorce and places it in her hand, and thus dismisses her from his house; or if that latter man, who took her for himself as a wife, dies,   4. then her first husband, who dismissed her, shall not have the authority to take her for himself again, to become his

מְלִילֹת בְּיָדֶךָ וְחֶרְמֵשׁ לֹא תָנִיף עַל קָמַת
רֵעֶךָ: ס כד א כִּי־יִקַּח אִישׁ אִשָּׁה וּבְעָלָהּ
וְהָיָה אִם־לֹא תִמְצָא־חֵן בְּעֵינָיו כִּי־מָצָא בָהּ
עֶרְוַת דָּבָר וְכָתַב לָהּ סֵפֶר כְּרִיתֻת וְנָתַן בְּיָדָהּ
וְשִׁלְּחָהּ מִבֵּיתוֹ: ב וְיָצְאָה מִבֵּיתוֹ וְהָלְכָה
וְהָיְתָה לְאִישׁ־אַחֵר: ג וּשְׂנֵאָהּ הָאִישׁ הָאַחֲרוֹן
וְכָתַב לָהּ סֵפֶר כְּרִיתֻת וְנָתַן בְּיָדָהּ וְשִׁלְּחָהּ
מִבֵּיתוֹ אוֹ כִי יָמוּת הָאִישׁ הָאַחֲרוֹן אֲשֶׁר־
לְקָחָהּ לוֹ לְאִשָּׁה: ד לֹא־יוּכַל בַּעְלָהּ הָרִאשׁוֹן
אֲשֶׁר־שִׁלְּחָהּ לָשׁוּב לְקַחְתָּהּ לִהְיוֹת לוֹ לְאִשָּׁה

CHAPTER XXIV

1–4. The present chapter contains laws of which some are new, others reiterate laws already set down in earlier books, and still others supplement laws discussed earlier in the Biblical text. These laws relate to the sanctity of marriage; to the duty of the state to have regard for the undisturbed domestic happiness of the individual, and to make it possible for the individual to earn an honest living; the inviolability of personal freedom; attention to God's admonition to cultivate social virtues; restrictions on the taking of security for a loan; the punctilious payment of a worker's wages; the duty to protect the rights of widows, orphans and strangers and to deal kindly with such individuals. The observance of all these laws is now urged upon the nation about to enter the land, as a duty entailed in the coexistence of its members. Now that the members of the nation are about to disperse over the land, it is incumbent on all circles in the nation to give particular attention to the observance of these rules if the land is to prosper and Israel is to prove itself as the people of God, delivered from the misery of oppression at the hands of their fellow men in Egypt.

Verses 1 through 4 contain rules governing the contracting and dissolution of marriages. The prohibition in Verse 4 against a man remarrying his divorced wife after she has been married to another man obviously represents the true object of these laws, which preface the regulations for the manner in which marriages may be contracted or dissolved. The intent of the prohibition in Verse 4 is to prevent a shameful abuse of the Law for immoral purposes, even if it seems that the

letter of the Law has not been violated. It is because of this prohibition that all these regulations for the contracting and dissolution of marriages have been reserved for inclusion in the compendium of laws given to the nation as it is about to enter the Land. For now that the members of the nation are about to disperse in this land and will be left largely on their own honor, the danger is all the greater that such abuses of the Law may occur and undermine the morality of the entire land. This thought is, in fact, implied by the concluding words of Verse 4, "and you shall not bring sin upon the land. . . ."

     °   °   °

All the regulations regarding divorce are directed to one and the same end: The written word is to be used here deliberately in place of a spoken word uttered with equal purposefulness. The concept of divorce must be set down in writing, purposely and deliberately, with the mind constantly directed to this end, so that, just as the spoken word can be used immediately to communicate what is to be said, so, too, the written law must now be made complete, ready to be turned over to the nation.

     °   °   °

Note the profound thought inherent in the fact that the law regarding divorce is immediately followed (Verse 5) by a regulation which opens with the words "When a man takes himself a new wife. . . ." This regulation, like hardly any other, manifests the great value which the Law places upon the wife and upon her husband's duty to make her happy, in a manner that hardly another society on earth could—or can—boast of to this day.

wife, since she was caused by him to cease being pure for him; for this is an abominable thing before *God,* and you shall not bring sin upon the land that *God,* your God, is giving you as an inheritance. 5. When a man takes himself a new wife, he shall not go out into the army, and he shall not be subjected to anything associated with it; he shall remain free for his home for one year and make happy his wife that he has taken himself.   6. A lower or an upper millstone must not be taken as security; for one [who does that] takes a life as security. 7. If a man is found stealing a person from among his brothers, of the sons of Yisrael, and he has availed himself of his services and has sold him, then this thief shall die, and you shall·clear away the evil from your midst.   8. Take heed concerning the leprous mark, to observe and to carry out with exceeding care, in accordance with everything that the priests, the Levites,

אַחֲרֵי֙ אֲשֶׁ֣ר הֻטַּמָּ֔אָה כִּֽי־תוֹעֵבָ֥ה הִ֖וא לִפְנֵ֣י יְהֹוָ֑ה וְלֹ֤א תַחֲטִיא֙ אֶת־הָאָ֔רֶץ אֲשֶׁר֙ יְהֹוָ֣ה אֱלֹהֶ֔יךָ נֹתֵ֥ן לְךָ֖ נַחֲלָֽה׃ ס ששי ה כִּֽי־יִקַּ֥ח אִישׁ֙ אִשָּׁ֣ה חֲדָשָׁ֔ה לֹ֤א יֵצֵא֙ בַּצָּבָ֔א וְלֹא־יַעֲבֹ֥ר עָלָ֖יו לְכָל־דָּבָ֑ר נָקִ֞י יִהְיֶ֤ה לְבֵיתוֹ֙ שָׁנָ֣ה אֶחָ֔ת וְשִׂמַּ֖ח אֶת־אִשְׁתּ֥וֹ אֲשֶׁר־לָקָֽח׃ ו לֹא־יַחֲבֹ֥ל רֵחַ֖יִם וָרָ֑כֶב כִּי־נֶ֖פֶשׁ ה֥וּא חֹבֵֽל׃ ס ז כִּֽי־יִמָּצֵ֣א אִ֗ישׁ גֹּנֵ֨ב נֶ֤פֶשׁ מֵאֶחָיו֙ מִבְּנֵ֣י יִשְׂרָאֵ֔ל וְהִתְעַמֶּר־בּ֖וֹ וּמְכָר֑וֹ וּמֵת֙ הַגַּנָּ֣ב הַה֔וּא וּבִֽעַרְתָּ֥ הָרָ֖ע מִקִּרְבֶּֽךָ׃ ס ח הִשָּׁ֧מֶר בְּנֶֽגַע־הַצָּרַ֛עַת לִשְׁמֹ֥ר מְאֹ֖ד וְלַעֲשׂ֑וֹת כְּכֹל֩ אֲשֶׁר־יוֹר֨וּ אֶתְכֶ֜ם הַכֹּהֲנִ֣ים

4. *an abominable thing before God.* Seen objectively, in the sight of man, no illegal action would have taken place[8]; yet, before God, the very possibility that His holy laws could be abused for immoral purposes represents in itself a violation of His Law. It is therefore תּוֹעֵבָה ["an abominable thing"] before Him, and so you, the Jewish community, must see to it, through your official representatives, the Beth Din [Court of Religious Law], that the moral grandeur of the Law is not violated upon the soil which God gave us, so that we might translate His Law into reality—lest the land eventually go to ruin because of the moral aberrations of its inhabitants. . . .

5. . . . The Law now proclaims the husband's solemn duty to gladden the wife he has taken for himself. He acquired his wife by pronouncing the word לִי ["to me"].[9] Let his wife not be deceived in the expectations she cherished when she consented to become "his." Let

[8]*Note to the English translation*: The woman had been divorced in conformity with Jewish Law; her second marriage had been dissolved either by her second husband's death or by divorce in conformity with Jewish Law; and the remarriage to her original husband would have been performed in a manner prescribed by Jewish Law. [G.H.]

[9]*Note to the English translation*: When the bridegroom places the wedding ring upon the finger of his bride, he pronounces the legal formula: הֲרֵי אַתְּ מְקֻדֶּשֶׁת לִי בְּטַבַּעַת זוֹ כְּדַת מֹשֶׁה וְיִשְׂרָאֵל—"Behold, you are sanctified to me with this ring in accordance with the Law of Moses and Israel." [G.H.]

her husband consider it his most important task in marriage to work for the happiness of the woman who has become *his* wife. In the eyes of the Law, this husbandly duty is of crucial significance not only for individual domestic happiness but also for the welfare of the entire nation, so much so that the Law exempts the husband from all public duties and services for one whole year after his marriage. Indeed, the Law virtually forbids him to undertake such work throughout that period—leaving him free to devote the first year of his marriage entirely to domesticity and to building the foundations for his wife's happiness.

• • •

Clearly these laws are based on the view that the state can be said to have reality only in terms of its individual members. The state cannot exist as an entity apart from its members, or even side by side with them. Consequently, the welfare of the whole can be attained only through the happiness and prosperity of its individual parts; and so the upbuilding of every new happy home contributes to the achievement of the goal that has been set for the entire nation. For this reason, the state must give protection, help and consideration to every individual household.

8. *Take heed.* Outright criminal attacks made by one man upon another, such as the attack on a man's personal freedom and dignity described in the preceding verse, are subject to the jurisdiction of human courts of justice. But never forget this and, by scrupu-

teach you; as I have commanded them, so shall you carry [it] out with care. 9. Remember what *God*, your God, did to Miriam on the way when you came out from Mitzrayim. 10. When you must assert to your neighbor your claim to a debt he owes you, you shall not go into his house to seize his security. 11. You shall stand outside, and the man on whom you have the claim shall bring the security outside to you. 12. And if he is a poor man, you shall not go to sleep with his security. 13. You must always return the security to him at sundown so that he may go to sleep in his garment and bless you. And this will stand for you as a[n act of] righteous duty before *God*, your God. 14. Do not withhold anything from a day laborer who is poor and needy, [whether he be] of your brethren or of the stranger that lives in your land, within your gates. 15. On his day shall you give him his wage, and do not let the sun go down

הַלְוִיִּם כַּאֲשֶׁר צִוִּיתִם תִּשְׁמְרוּ לַעֲשׂוֹת: ט זָכוֹר
אֵת אֲשֶׁר־עָשָׂה יְהוָה אֱלֹהֶיךָ לְמִרְיָם בַּדֶּרֶךְ
בְּצֵאתְכֶם מִמִּצְרָיִם: ס י כִּי־תַשֶּׁה בְרֵעֲךָ
מַשַּׁאת מְאוּמָה לֹא־תָבֹא אֶל־בֵּיתוֹ לַעֲבֹט
עֲבֹטוֹ: יא בַּחוּץ תַּעֲמֹד וְהָאִישׁ אֲשֶׁר אַתָּה
נֹשֶׁה בוֹ יוֹצִיא אֵלֶיךָ אֶת־הַעֲבוֹט הַחוּצָה:
יב וְאִם־אִישׁ עָנִי הוּא לֹא תִשְׁכַּב בַּעֲבֹטוֹ:
יג הָשֵׁב תָּשִׁיב לוֹ אֶת־הַעֲבוֹט כְּבוֹא הַשֶּׁמֶשׁ
וְשָׁכַב בְּשַׂלְמָתוֹ וּבֵרֲכֶךָּ וּלְךָ תִּהְיֶה צְדָקָה לִפְנֵי
יְהוָה אֱלֹהֶיךָ: ס שביעי יד לֹא־תַעֲשֹׁק שָׂכִיר עָנִי
וְאֶבְיוֹן מֵאַחֶיךָ אוֹ מִגֵּרְךָ אֲשֶׁר בְּאַרְצְךָ
בִּשְׁעָרֶיךָ: טו בְּיוֹמוֹ תִתֵּן שְׂכָרוֹ וְלֹא־תָבוֹא

lously observing all the pertinent rules, bear this in mind at all times: In the nation of God, all social relationships between men, even the words they utter or the thoughts they harbor, are subject to the jurisdiction of a higher Judge, Who can put His finger as a sign of warning and admonition upon the house, the garment, or the body of anyone who forgets to treat his brothers with brotherly love. (See notes on Leviticus 13 regarding leprous marks.)

10. ***When you must assert.*** Verses 8 and 9 recall the legal institution of *negaim* [leprous marks], which expresses the idea that the nation's whole social life is subject to the special testing and admonishing rule of God. The verses that now follow—10 through 13, 14 and 15, 17 and 18, and 19 through 22—reiterate Israel's duties toward the underprivileged and the dependent. These are duties whose fulfillment is the object of God's special attention, so much so that God's blessing upon the land is dependent on whether the people who dwell in it perform these duties faithfully. Consequently, the observance of these laws had to be urged upon the nation especially at the point, when the nation entered its land, and class distinctions based on property would first emerge.

• • •

13. ***And this will stand for you as a[n act of] righteousness.*** For a definition of צְדָקָה, see Genesis 15:6. Returning the security to the debtor for his personal use, thus allowing him to sleep in the garment he has offered you as security for his debt, is described as an act of צְדָקָה. This makes it clear that, legally speaking, the security is considered to be no longer, or at least no longer entirely the property of the debtor. In the view of the Law, it has already become the property of the creditor. Hence, by returning the security to the debtor, the creditor has performed an act of kindness with an object in his possession.

• • •

14 and 15. ***Do not withhold.*** These obligations regarding scrupulous punctuality in paying wages have already been set forth in Leviticus 19:13 in connection with the sanctification of life, and we have already explained them in detail in our notes *ibid.*[10] The reiteration of these laws in the present compendium for the nation about to settle in its land is accompanied by most impressive warnings against sinning in this respect, particularly if the worker is poor and needy. For only now that the nation is about to settle in its land can these obligations truly assume practical significance; and subsequent history has shown how, particularly, tardiness on the part of the wealthy in meeting their financial obligations toward the workers and artisans in their employ has undermined the nation's prosperity in the past.

• • •

[10]*Note to the English translation*: These explanations are not included in this excerpted edition.

upon it, because he is poor, and he sets his soul upon it. Let him not cry out to *God* against you, so that sin would cling to you. 16. Fathers shall not be put to death on account of sons, and sons shall not be put to death on account of fathers. Every man shall be put to death [only] for his own sin. 17. You also shall not twist the justice [due to] an orphaned stranger, and you shall not take a widow's garment as security. 18. You shall remember that you were a slave in Mitzrayim, when *God*, your God, delivered you from there; therefore do I command you to do this.   19. When you reap your harvest in your field, and you forget a sheaf in the field, you shall not go

עָלָיו הַשֶּׁמֶשׁ כִּי עָנִי הוּא וְאֵלָיו הוּא נֹשֵׂא
אֶת־נַפְשׁוֹ וְלֹא־יִקְרָא עָלֶיךָ אֶל־יְהֹוָה וְהָיָה בְךָ
חֵטְא: ס טז לֹא־יוּמְתוּ אָבוֹת עַל־בָּנִים וּבָנִים
לֹא־יוּמְתוּ עַל־אָבוֹת אִישׁ בְּחֶטְאוֹ יוּמָתוּ: ס
יז לֹא תַטֶּה מִשְׁפַּט גֵּר יָתוֹם וְלֹא תַחֲבֹל בֶּגֶד
אַלְמָנָה: יח וְזָכַרְתָּ כִּי עֶבֶד הָיִיתָ בְּמִצְרַיִם
וַיִּפְדְּךָ יְהֹוָה אֱלֹהֶיךָ מִשָּׁם עַל־כֵּן אָנֹכִי מְצַוְּךָ
לַעֲשׂוֹת אֶת־הַדָּבָר הַזֶּה: ס יט כִּי תִקְצֹר
קְצִירְךָ בְשָׂדֶךָ וְשָׁכַחְתָּ עֹמֶר בַּשָּׂדֶה לֹא תָשׁוּב

16. ***Fathers shall not be put to death.*** According to the Talmud (Sanhedrin 27b), this law proclaims two distinct principles; i.e., not only that "fathers shall not be put to death on account of sins committed by their sons," but also that neither the crimes nor the testimonies of close relatives such as fathers and sons should be used to harm the one or the other. Now if these sentences had been intended solely to set standards for the administration of justice, it would be odd that they should occur in this particular context. It is clear that Verse 17, with its prohibition against taking a widow's garment as security for a loan, is intended to continue the tendency of the preceding laws [Verses 6 through 15] regarding the consideration to be accorded to one's fellow men in depressed circumstances. The statement in the same verse, "You also shall not twist the justice (due to) an orphaned stranger," would bear out this interpretation. For the motivation given to both of these directives in Verse 18, "You shall remember that you were a slave in Mitzrayim," is the same as that stated in Deuteronomy 15:15, 16:12 and again in Verse 22 of the present chapter with regard to our duty toward the stranger, the orphan and the widow at harvest time.

. . . [Now, in between Verses 15 and 17, we are told that] no one shall be made to suffer—legally, politically or socially—for a crime committed by his closest kin, not even if the crime was a capital offense. . . . The universal rule regarding verdicts handed down by human courts of justice is that "every man shall be put to death (only) for his own sin." A person can become a criminal only on account of an offense he himself has committed. No matter whether the verdict of the human court of justice has been correct or in error, [innocent] children of criminals are to be regarded as untainted by crime.

In light of all the foregoing, the law that "fathers shall not be put to death on account of sons" would fit closely into the context of the entire group of laws that deals with the treatment to be accorded individuals in a vulnerable social position. For hardly anyone will be more unhappy and feel more vulnerable in society than the child or the parent of a criminal. The primary purpose of the law in Verse 16, then, is to uphold the honor—social as well as political—of such innocent persons, within the independent state of the Jewish nation.

•   •   •

19. ***When you reap your harvest in your field.*** Here the emphasis is on the concept of property ownership: it is *your* harvest, *your* field. You are now standing on your own soil, where nature has worked for you. You cultivated the soil, and yours is the abundance that you are about to reap, either by your own effort or by the labor of persons in your employ.

This proud sense of ownership is now to be modified by the מַתְּנוֹת עֲנִיִּים [gifts to the poor] specified in the laws about to be set forth. You are reminded that you must perform your duty of *tzedakah* in order to provide sustenance from your fields for those who have no land of their own. The commandments relating to leaving the corner of your field and your unripe grapes to the stranger, the orphan and the widow admonish you not to think that *all* of your field and vineyard, everything that nature, with God's blessing, has brought forth upon your land, is intended for your use alone. The commandments relating to leaving the gleanings from your field and the grape gleanings to the poor are to admonish you not to become so greedy and possessive that you will feel driven to exploit all the fruits of your labors for your own ends alone, down to the last penny. Rather, you should be willing to forego that gain which escaped your attention at harvest time. Therefore, you are commanded to leave part of the crops of your field back to take it; it shall be for the stranger, the orphan and the widow, so that *God*, your God, may bless you in all the work of your hands. 20. When you beat your olive tree, you shall not break off the crown that you have left behind; it shall be for the stranger, the orphan and the widow. 21. When you gather the grapes of your vineyard, you shall not pick the unripe grapes that you have left behind; it shall be for the stranger, the orphan and the widow. 22. Remember that you were a slave in the land of Mitzrayim; therefore do I command you to do this.

XXV

1. If there is a dispute between men, and they come before the court so that they should judge them, then they must justify the righteous and condemn the guilty. 2. But if the guilty party has incurred corporal punishment, the judge shall cause him to lie down and have him beaten in his presence,

לְקַחְתּוֹ לַגֵּר לַיָּתוֹם וְלָאַלְמָנָה יִהְיֶה לְמַעַן
יְבָרֶכְךָ יְהוָה אֱלֹהֶיךָ בְּכֹל מַעֲשֵׂה יָדֶיךָ: ס
כ כִּי תַחְבֹּט זֵיתְךָ לֹא תְפַאֵר אַחֲרֶיךָ לַגֵּר
לַיָּתוֹם וְלָאַלְמָנָה יִהְיֶה: כא כִּי תִבְצֹר כַּרְמְךָ
לֹא תְעוֹלֵל אַחֲרֶיךָ לַגֵּר לַיָּתוֹם וְלָאַלְמָנָה
יִהְיֶה: כב וְזָכַרְתָּ כִּי־עֶבֶד הָיִיתָ בְּאֶרֶץ מִצְרָיִם
עַל־כֵּן אָנֹכִי מְצַוְּךָ לַעֲשׂוֹת אֶת־הַדָּבָר הַזֶּה: ס
כה א כִּי־יִהְיֶה רִיב בֵּין אֲנָשִׁים וְנִגְּשׁוּ אֶל־
הַמִּשְׁפָּט וּשְׁפָטוּם וְהִצְדִּיקוּ אֶת־הַצַּדִּיק
וְהִרְשִׁיעוּ אֶת־הָרָשָׁע: ב וְהָיָה אִם־בִּן הַכּוֹת
הָרָשָׁע וְהִפִּילוֹ הַשֹּׁפֵט וְהִכָּהוּ לְפָנָיו כְּדֵי

and vineyard for the poor. Whatever has escaped your sickle or dropped from your hand must also be left for the poor.

Now there is added to these commandments the one regarding שִׁכְחָה [the forgotten sheaf]. This is to teach you that your thoughts and plans for your sustenance, too, must not be selfishly centered upon your welfare only; whatever escaped your attention at harvest time must be left for the poor. . . . Under the laws relating to these concepts, whatever slipped from your memory or dropped from your hands, respectively, in the harvesting process, belongs to the poor. We have already pointed out in Leviticus (ibid.) that the purpose of these obligatory gifts from the residue of your harvest is not to satisfy the poor in fact, but is merely symbolic: It is intended to remind you of your duty to provide for the needy. For the quantities entailed in לֶקֶט [gleanings from the field], שִׁכְחָה [forgotten sheaf], פֶּרֶט [grape gleanings] and even in the עוֹלֵלוֹת [unripe grapes] are a matter of chance. According to the original Biblical law, even פֵּאָה [leaving the corner of the field], which is the one sole obligatory donation, can be made with a minimum quantity. For this reason, the Law states explicitly what is to be understood by לֶקֶט, שִׁכְחָה, פֶּרֶט and עוֹלֵלוֹת. These obligatory donations represent merely acts by which we are to be reminded of certain fundamental ideas, whose truth we acknowledge when we make these symbolic gifts.

All of the laws pertaining to donations from the harvest express the same thought: Whatever God has caused to grow for us upon our fields and farmlands is intended in the first place for our own use, but immediately thereafter also for the use of our needy brethren. Therefore, according to God's Law, whatever we had dropped or left behind when we harvested our crops automatically becomes the property of the poor.

° ° °

CHAPTER XXV

1 and 2. ***If there is a dispute.*** If we were to interpret Verse 1 as an antecedent to Verse 2; i.e., if two litigants were to bring their dispute to court (Verse 1) and one of them was sentenced to corporal punishment (Verse 2), etc., this would pose a problem that would be difficult to solve. For most of the disputes that come before a court of [Jewish] law involve property or bodily injury, and in neither of these cases is מַלְקוֹת, corporal punishment, applicable. The court may impose the payment of an indemnity in cash or the equivalent thereof, or the payment of damages, as is stipulated in cases involving bodily injury (Exodus 21:18f.), but none of this entails corporal punishment. In such cases, the punishment of מַלְקוֹת is applicable only in very rare instances; e.g., if the bodily injury is so slight that the damages would amount to less than one *p'rutah*, and the court consequently cannot award an indemnity to the plaintiff (Ketuboth 32b), or if the defendant has transgressed a prohibition with regard to the taking of security for a loan, and, for some reason, this injustice cannot be redressed by the restoration of the security to the debtor (Baba Metziah 115a). It is hardly conceivable, then,

רִשְׁעָתוֹ בְּמִסְפָּר: ג אַרְבָּעִים יַכֶּנּוּ לֹא יֹסִיף
פֶּן־יֹסִיף לְהַכֹּתוֹ עַל־אֵלֶּה מַכָּה רַבָּה וְנִקְלָה
אָחִיךָ לְעֵינֶיךָ: ד לֹא־תַחְסֹם שׁוֹר בְּדִישׁוֹ: ס
ה כִּי־יֵשְׁבוּ אַחִים יַחְדָּו וּמֵת אַחַד מֵהֶם וּבֵן

according to his offense, with a fixed
number. 3. He shall not go on to give
him forty lashes; were he to go on and give
him a blow in excess of this, your brother
would be degraded before your eyes.
4. You shall not muzzle an ox when it is
treading grain. 5. When brothers are on
earth at the same time, and one of them dies,

that the Law should want to state the rule concerning מַלְקוֹת [corporal punishment] in connection with a type of dispute in which corporal punishment is imposed only in very rare cases.

Note, however, the context in which the rule concerning punishment by מַלְקוֹת has been set down. It is followed immediately by a prohibition (Verse 4) against muzzling an ox while it is treading grain. It would seem, therefore, that the intent of the law here is not so much the imposition of the מַלְקוֹת punishment as it is to stress the restraints that the Law imposes upon the administration of corporal punishment. The laws set forth earlier demand kind and considerate treatment for individuals who are in depressed circumstances and socially vulnerable. The law that follows (Verse 4) demands considerate treatment even for the animals that work for us. It would seem, then, that the laws regarding corporal punishment were placed immediately before the law demanding kindness to an animal in order to show that even if a person, by rebelling and sinning against the Law, has temporarily descended to the level of an animal and must therefore be given physical chastisement, the court must accord him humane treatment.

In view of the above, we believe that Verse 1 stands in deliberate, marked contrast to Verse 2. As is apparent from its wording, Verse 1 refers to disputes involving money matters in which both the plaintiff and the defendant come before the court for arbitration. In such cases, as has already been stated several times (Leviticus 19:15 and Deuteronomy 1:17), the court must not allow itself to be guided by personal consideration for either party. If the court finds in favor of one litigant; i.e., it "justifies the righteous," then it follows that the court's verdict is against the other party, cf. "and condemn the guilty." The court cannot practice mercy toward the one party without infringing upon the rights of the other. For this reason the judge must be most explicit and categorical in pronouncing his verdict.

On the other hand, when the case before the court involves not a legal claim of one party against another, but only the defendant's violation of the Law, a misdemeanor subject to physical disciplining. . ., then the Law does indeed impose restrictions upon the actions of the court and specifies that, in administering this punishment, consideration must be given to personal factors that vary from individual to individual [such as the offender's physical condition].

בִּן הַכּוֹת ***[has incurred corporal punishment].*** Lit., "*the son of* corporal punishment," like יְהוֹשֻׁעַ בִּן נוּן [Joshua *son of* Nun]; cf. also בֶּן מָוֶת ["he deserves to die," or, lit., "he is a son of death"] (I Samuel 20:31). It would seem that the term בֵּן [son] is used in connection with the punishment incurred by an offender in order to show that the purpose of the punishment is not to destroy the offender, but rather to ensure his moral survival, either by making him atone for his offense or by teaching him to mend his ways. [In view of this disciplinary and instructive function of punishment,] he is only a "son" of the punishment. And the fact that the Law uses this expression only in this passage, with reference to corporal punishment, would substantiate our reasoning, because, as we have already noted in Leviticus ibid.,[11] this is the only punishment that is not only disciplinary, but also makes it possible for the offender to survive physically, since, by receiving the corporal punishment, he atones for his past. . . .

3. ***your brother would be degraded before your eyes.*** "Once he has received his corporal punishment he is (to be considered) once more as your brother" (Makkoth 23a). Once he has received the lashes to which he has been sentenced, he is restored to your respect; he is then, once more, אָחִיךָ [your brother] and no longer רָשָׁע [the guilty party], as he was called before.

In this connection, the *halakhah* teaches that it is never the intention of the Law to effect a "degradation" of the offender. . . . As we have already pointed out in Leviticus *ibid.*,[12] the implementation of this law is intended not so much as physical chastisement as it is to teach the offender to mend his ways.

° ° °

5. ***When brothers are on earth.*** The preceding laws dealt with our duty to show consideration, mercy

[11] *Note to the English translation*: Hirsch discusses this in his notes on Leviticus 19:20, which are not included in this excerpted edition. [G.H.]

[12] *Note to the English translation*: This note is not included in this excerpted edition. [G.H.]

אֵין־ל֑וֹ לֹא־תִהְיֶ֧ה אֵֽשֶׁת־הַמֵּ֛ת הַח֖וּצָה לְאִ֣ישׁ
זָ֑ר יְבָמָהּ֙ יָבֹ֣א עָלֶ֔יהָ וּלְקָחָ֥הּ ל֛וֹ לְאִשָּׁ֖ה וְיִבְּמָֽהּ׃
ו וְהָיָ֗ה הַבְּכוֹר֙ אֲשֶׁ֣ר תֵּלֵ֔ד יָק֕וּם עַל־שֵׁ֥ם אָחִ֖יו
הַמֵּ֑ת וְלֹֽא־יִמָּחֶ֥ה שְׁמ֖וֹ מִיִּשְׂרָאֵֽל׃ ז וְאִם־לֹ֤א
יַחְפֹּץ֙ הָאִ֔ישׁ לָקַ֖חַת אֶת־יְבִמְתּ֑וֹ וְעָלְתָה֩ יְבִמְתּ֨וֹ
הַשַּׁ֜עְרָה אֶל־הַזְּקֵנִ֗ים וְאָֽמְרָה֙ מֵאֵ֨ן יְבָמִ֜י

and he has no child; the wife of the dead
man must not marry outside, to a strange
man. Her brother-in-law shall come to
her and perform [the duty of] levirate marriage with her. 6. And he shall be the
first-born whom she bears; he shall succeed
to the name of his dead brother, and so the
name of the latter will not be blotted out
from Yisrael. 7. But if the man does not
want to take his sister-in-law, his sister-in-
law shall go up to the gate to the elders and
say: "My brother-in-law refuses to raise up

and kindness to widows and orphans, the poor and the stranger and, finally, also to criminals and animals. This group of laws relating to various acts of loving-kindness now concludes with the loving-kindness that must be practiced even toward one who is no longer alive, so that his memory may be perpetuated among the living. . . .

The first task of the male on earth is expressed by the very first commandment given to man: פְּרוּ וּרְבוּ ["Be fruitful and multiply"]; it was for this purpose that he was bidden to exercise dominion over the earth (Genesis 1:28). He was commanded to beget children, to raise them and to acquire property in order to be able to discharge these tasks. The performance of this male duty includes the building of a home, whose true "building blocks" are בָּנִים, children. . . .

Our text now discusses the following case: A man aspired to fulfill his mission by setting up a home and by contracting a marriage. Thus, he could have hoped to discharge his task, had it been given him to beget, with his wife, children that would have survived him; children whom husband and wife together would have molded in their own spiritual and moral image; children for whose future the husband and wife would jointly have managed the resources, large or small, that God had granted them. However, it is not given to this man to achieve his goal. He departs this life without leaving a descendant to inherit his acquisitions, great or small, with which to continue in the way of life for which the father paved the way. This man would have to depart with the sad thought that, once he was gone, there would be no one left on earth to perpetuate his memory as a matter of duty. The wife he called his own would enter other family circles, completely unknown to him, and whatever material goods he might have acquired for the perpetuation of his moral and spiritual existence on earth would be divided among his more distant relations or their descendants. That is, these things would happen, had not the Law, for specified circumstances, provided a possibility for a moral and spiritual replacement in the form of יִבּוּם [levirate marriage].

If a married man who has no living children dies and is survived by a [male] blood relative who has lived during the same time and under the same influences as he (and this can only be a brother, begotten by the same father, living contemporaneously with the deceased—not a brother who was born after his death), then the Law demands that the surviving brother continue his deceased brother's marriage by marrying the latter's widow, in the spirit of יִבּוּם [the levirate marriage]; i.e., for the purpose of continuing the work of building the home which the deceased had been unable to complete. To this end, the surviving brother, upon taking his brother's widow as his wife, becomes the sole legal heir also to the material estate of the deceased. The new marriage is to be considered simply as a continuation of the deceased man's marriage; therefore, according to the original law, it did not require confirmation by קִדּוּשִׁין [the legal act of Jewish marriage]. Contracted with the intention of perpetuating the memory of the deceased, this new marriage, along with the inheritance that the kinsman assumes together with it, makes it possible for the name of the deceased to survive, so that, through this marriage and through any offspring resulting from it, his moral and spiritual influence will live on. . . .

° ° °

7. ***But if the man does not want.*** However, the commandment of levirate marriage is not absolute. . . .

° ° °

There are circumstances under which, for legal or other justifiable reasons, levirate marriage must be considered inadmissible or impracticable. For such situations, the Torah has commanded, in place of the duty of levirate marriage, the מִצְוַת חֲלִיצָה [duty of *halitzah*], which the text now describes. Under the Law, it is the function of the community's legal authorities to decide whether levirate marriage is inadmissible or impracticable in a given case. By the judgment of our legal authorities, the duty of *halitzah* [rather than levirate marriage] has become the universally applicable rule on our day. For the *halakhah* (Yebamoth 101b) for his brother a name in Yisrael; he does not want to perform [the duty of] levirate marriage with me."   8. And the elders of his city shall call him and speak to him, and if he then stands up and says: "I do not want to take her,"   9. then his sister-in-law shall approach him before the eyes of the elders, and take off his shoe from his foot and spit before his face, and then she shall begin and say: "So shall it be done to the man who does not want to build his brother's house."   10. His name shall be called in Yisrael: "The house of him whose shoe was removed."   11. If men fight together, one with the other, and the wife of the one draws near to rescue her husband from the hand of the one who strikes him, and she puts out her hand and grips his private parts,   12. you shall cut off her

לְהָקִים לְאָחִיו שֵׁם בְּיִשְׂרָאֵל לֹא אָבָה יַבְּמִי:
ח וְקָרְאוּ־לוֹ זִקְנֵי־עִירוֹ וְדִבְּרוּ אֵלָיו וְעָמַד
וְאָמַר לֹא חָפַצְתִּי לְקַחְתָּהּ: ט וְנִגְּשָׁה יְבִמְתּוֹ
אֵלָיו לְעֵינֵי הַזְּקֵנִים וְחָלְצָה נַעֲלוֹ מֵעַל רַגְלוֹ
וְיָרְקָה בְּפָנָיו וְעָנְתָה וְאָמְרָה כָּכָה יֵעָשֶׂה
לָאִישׁ אֲשֶׁר לֹא־יִבְנֶה אֶת־בֵּית אָחִיו: י וְנִקְרָא
שְׁמוֹ בְּיִשְׂרָאֵל בֵּית חֲלוּץ הַנָּעַל: ס יא כִּי־יִנָּצוּ
אֲנָשִׁים יַחְדָּו אִישׁ וְאָחִיו וְקָרְבָה אֵשֶׁת הָאֶחָד
לְהַצִּיל אֶת־אִישָׁהּ מִיַּד מַכֵּהוּ וְשָׁלְחָה יָדָהּ
וְהֶחֱזִיקָה בִּמְבֻשָׁיו: יב וְקַצֹּתָה אֶת־כַּפָּהּ לֹא

interprets the words "and (they shall) speak to him" (Verse 8) to denote not only an attempt to persuade the brother-in-law to perform the duty of levirate marriage as requested by the widow, but also an attempt to dissuade the man from performing levirate marriage, persuading him to resort to ḥalitzah instead. In other words, the implication of Verse 8 is that the elders should discuss each case and then advise what should best be done under the circumstances....

       °   °   °

11. *If men fight together.* The three preceding chapters were devoted primarily to the promotion of attitudes and behavior patterns that should form the basic character traits of the Jewish nation. Particular emphasis was placed on the commandments to exercise consideration and kindness toward anyone afflicted or suffering for any reason, and toward those particularly vulnerable because of their fate or their social position. This catalogue of social legislation now concludes with rules supplementing all the foregoing commandments with admonitions not to forget oneself and not to act brutally or dishonestly in any manner. The references are to errors a person may commit even though he practices charity and kindness in other respects. The weekly portion concludes with a reminder of the stark contrast between the character traits which the Jewish nation is expected to realize in ever-growing measure, and those of Amalek, whose elimination from the community and the annals of mankind is one of the ultimate goals of Israel's historic mission.

       °   °   °

12. ... The directive "You shall cut off her hand" is

only a figurative expression, meaning that her hand should be rendered harmless in the future by means of a fine which the court must impose upon her, just as the rule "eye for eye, tooth for tooth. . ." (Deuteronomy 19:21) in connection with scheming witnesses . . . can refer only to monetary restitution.

Moreover, in the present passage, just as in 19:21, we are bidden not to have pity. The rationale for these statements is that the woman committed the physical insult under the influence of strong emotion and with the intention of saving her husband, and also (as taught in Baba Kammah 28a) that this act can be regarded as a punishable offense only if she could have saved her husband by some other means. The case used here to illustrate the culpability of a physical insult was chosen because the incident selected should admonish us to control our strong emotions even when such emotions would seem justified, and never to stoop to brutality. This admonition is addressed, first and foremost, to women, to whom all brutality should be alien, even more so than to men. If women become caught up in a dispute between their menfolk, they should confine themselves to acting as guardians of decency and propriety.

That a case of this nature should be cited precisely at this point in the text might be explained in terms of the laws of levirate marriage and ḥalitzah that immediately precede it. A question of levirate marriage is the only occasion for which the Law bids a woman to step out into the public arena of the court of law, there to demand publicly that a certain man marry her. Both these acts would seem contrary to the modesty and reticence usually associated with Jewish womanhood. Also, under any other circumstances, the act of hand; you shall have no pity. 13. You shall not have in your bag two different stone weights, one large and one small. 14. You shall not have in your house two different measures, one large and one small. 15. You shall have perfect stone weights and just [ones], a perfect measure and a just [one]. On this account your days shall long endure upon the soil that *God,* your God, is giving you. 16. For an abomination to *God,* your God, is anyone who does such things, anyone who does wrong. 17. Remember what Amalek did to you on the way, when you went out from Mitzrayim. 18. How

תָחוֹס עֵינֶךָ: ס יג לֹא־יִהְיֶה לְךָ בְּכִיסְךָ אֶבֶן
וָאֶבֶן גְּדוֹלָה וּקְטַנָּה: יד לֹא־יִהְיֶה לְךָ בְּבֵיתְךָ
אֵיפָה וְאֵיפָה גְּדוֹלָה וּקְטַנָּה: טו אֶבֶן שְׁלֵמָה
וָצֶדֶק יִהְיֶה־לָּךְ אֵיפָה שְׁלֵמָה וָצֶדֶק יִהְיֶה־לָּךְ
לְמַעַן יַאֲרִיכוּ יָמֶיךָ עַל הָאֲדָמָה אֲשֶׁר־יְהֹוָה
אֱלֹהֶיךָ נֹתֵן לָךְ: טז כִּי תוֹעֲבַת יְהֹוָה אֱלֹהֶיךָ
כָּל־עֹשֵׂה אֵלֶּה כֹּל עֹשֵׂה עָוֶל: פ מפטיר יז זָכוֹר
אֵת אֲשֶׁר־עָשָׂה לְךָ עֲמָלֵק בַּדֶּרֶךְ בְּצֵאתְכֶם

---

halitzah, of rendering another person barefooted, would be a physical act of humiliation. Only in the case [discussed in Verses 7 through 10] does it become a moral act by virtue of the purpose for which it is performed and of the idea that it expresses under the Law.

The logical association between these ideas, and the teaching that every true physical insult is culpable and that women in particular are expected to preserve their self-control and keep away from impudence and vulgarity, would seem self-evident.

° ° °

13 and 14. . . . Even as the momentous chapter dealing with the sanctification of our lives (Leviticus 19) concludes with laws regarding honest weights and measures, so here the catalogue of social legislation for those about to enter the Land ends with a reiteration of the commandment to use only honest weights and measures and a warning against any violation of this commandment. In the Book of Leviticus we have already examined the laws of fair weights and measures in the context in which they are stated, and we have pointed out the paramount significance that the Law attaches to scrupulous honesty in business and social relationships as far as the character of the Jewish nation is concerned: the Law declares that a Jew guilty of using dishonest weights, measures or means of counting is rejected before the countenance of God. In this spirit, as we have seen, the Law places punishment for the use of dishonest measures on a par with—if not even higher than—punishment for acts of immorality, thus declaring honesty in business relationships to be the basic principle for the Jew as a social being, even as it declares morality in sexual relations to be the basic principle for the Jew as a moral being.

° ° °

15. *On this account your days shall long endure.* The duration of your political existence on your own soil will depend on the extent to which you will practice

that most punctilious honesty and fairness in your business dealings which your God requires of you, and which should be a basic trait of your national character.

16. *For an abomination to* God, *your God, is anyone who does such things.* Not only the wrongdoing itself is abominable to God. The man, the Jewish person, upon whom God has bestowed the privilege of calling Him *his* God—the Pilot of his destinies and the Guide of his actions—becomes an abomination "to *God,* his God" if he calls himself a Jew but fails to observe most scrupulously the laws of honesty in human relationships. The Jew who uses a dishonest yardstick or dishonest weights can no longer call God *his* God, "for an abomination to *God,* your God, is anyone who does such things, anyone who does wrong."

° ° °

17. זָכוֹר וגו' *[Remember].* The avoidance of any עָוֶל, any misuse of one's position of power (עוֹל [= yoke]) to the detriment of a person over whom he has control, even if that control is only temporary; the refusal to violate the trust that one human being must be able to place in another for human coexistence; the firm conviction that we may call God "*our* God" only as long as we scrupulously avoid doing even the slightest wrong to our fellow men on earth; thus, in short, the most untarnished probity in all our dealings with our fellow men — these are the final strokes of the picture drawn by the Law as a character pattern for the people that is to be guided by the Law and to call itself by its name. That nation whose character should reflect sympathy, consideration, charity and kindness toward all living things—a nation which (as repeatedly stressed in the concluding chapters of the Law of God) must be ready at all times to do good, must be prevented by the Law, first and foremost, from doing harm to anyone. This nation is to walk the earth as the most perfect incarnation of the ideal of יְשֻׁרוּן (Deuteronomy 33:26); it

he fell upon you on the way and massacred your stragglers, all those who trailed after you when you were faint and spent, and he did not fear God. 19. Therefore it shall be: when *God*, your God, will have given you rest from all your enemies round about in the land that *God*, your God, is giving you as an inheritance, to take possession of it, you shall blot out the memory of Amalek from under the heaven; do not forget this.

מִמִּצְרָיִם: יח אֲשֶׁר קָרְךָ֫ בַּדֶּ֫רֶךְ וַיְזַנֵּ֤ב בְּךָ֙ כָּל־הַנֶּחֱשָׁלִ֖ים אַֽחֲרֶ֑יךָ וְאַתָּ֖ה עָיֵ֣ף וְיָגֵ֑עַ וְלֹ֥א יָרֵ֖א אֱלֹהִֽים: יט וְהָיָ֡ה בְּהָנִ֣יחַ יְהֹוָ֣ה אֱלֹהֶ֣יךָ ׀ לְ֠ךָ֠ מִכָּל־אֹ֨יְבֶ֜יךָ מִסָּבִ֗יב בָּאָ֨רֶץ֙ אֲשֶׁ֣ר יְהֹוָ֣ה אֱלֹהֶ֗יךָ נֹתֵ֤ן לְךָ֙ נַֽחֲלָה֙ לְרִשְׁתָּ֔הּ תִּמְחֶה֙ אֶת־זֵ֣כֶר עֲמָלֵ֔ק מִתַּ֖חַת הַשָּׁמָ֑יִם לֹ֖א תִּשְׁכָּֽח: פ

should appear as the "straightest" [יָשָׁר = straight], most honest and upright of nations in its relations with others. A statement by the prophet [Zephaniah] views as שְׁאֵרִית יִשְׂרָאֵל [the (saving) remnant of Israel] those who, through all times and amidst all trials, endure and move steadily foward to the goal of ultimate perfection as seen by Judaism; men who "do no wrong, speak no deceit, and in whose mouth there is no tongue of deception—they shall find their pasture and peace on earth; they alone will have no cause to fear anything or anyone" (Zephaniah 3:13).

By contrast, as the complete antithesis of this national ethos based on justice and loving-kindness, of the nation that sees its power and future only in terms of punctilious devotion to its duty; the nation whose example will someday make this obedience to God's Law a trait common to all mankind, we see a nation such as Amalek, which measures its strength only in terms of its armed might and can slake its thirst for glory only by trampling the unarmed and the weak. When the nation of duty first entered into the history of nations triumphant (Exodus 17:8–16), Amalek attacked it at once, and from that very first attack, it was decreed that Amalek must be blotted out completely from the memory of nations. . . .

Hence, now that the nation of Israel is about to enter its land so that it may faithfully discharge its duties there, the Law once again calls attention to the contrast between Israel and Amalek. By remembering Amalek's sneak attack, Israel is to realize the contrast between the attitude of Amalek and its own national mission. In the Book of Exodus, the struggle against the principles represented by Amalek, until Amalek's complete disappearance, is described as the intent of all the workings of God in the history of mankind. In the present passage, in more positive terms, Israel is invited to regard itself, and to prove itself, as a co-worker and instrument in God's battle against Amalek. For the final leaf will drop from Amalek's sham laurels only when Amalek's sword will be broken by a mightier weapon, a national entity that flourishes only by virtue

of its loyalty to God's moral law—a nation upheld solely by its obedience to God.

•   •   •

19. *is giving you as an inheritance to take possession of it.* The land that He is now giving to you so that you may take possession of it was already promised to your fathers. You are receiving it only as an inheritance from them so that you may pass it on to your children. You did not gain possession of it by your own power. You owe the land solely to your forefathers' loyalty to their covenant with God, and only if you will transmit this same loyalty to your own children as a spiritual heritage will you be able to bequeath to them also this land as an inheritance.

•   •   •

לֹא תִשְׁכָּח *[do not forget this]*. Do not forget this if you should ever falter and, like Amalek, forget God and your duty, seeking only opportunities to use your superiority, in matters great or small, to the detriment of your fellow men.

Do not forget this if you should ever wish to forget your calling and your mission as Israel among mankind; if ever you should envy the laurel wreaths woven by a besotted world to the memory of successful wreckers of human happiness and if ever you should forget the tear-drenched soil from which such laurels grow.

Do not forget this when you yourself will have to suffer from the brutality and violence of Amalek. Remain firm! Persevere in the humanity and justice that your God has taught you. It is to these virtues that the future belongs. Justice and humanity will forever triumph over brutality and violence, and you yourself have been sent to proclaim that future by your fate and to help bring about that future by your personal example.

לֹא תִשְׁכָּח, do not forget this, and, in order that you may not forget, זָכוֹר [remember], refresh in your mind, from time to time, the memory of Amalek and what has been said to you concerning Amalek's future.

The Haftarah for this Sidra may be found on page 915.

כי תבא

KI THABO

XXVI 1. It shall be, when you come to the land that *God*, your God, is giving you as an inheritance, and you have taken possession of it and dwell in it, 2. you shall take a selection of the first of all the fruits of the soil that you bring home from your land that *God*, your God, is giving you; and you shall put it in a basket and go to the place that *God*, your God, will choose to give a habitation to His Name. 3. And you shall come to the priest who will be in those days and say to him: "I have given evidence this day to *God*, your God, that I have come to the land that *God* swore to our fathers to give to us." 4. And the priest shall take the basket from your hand to set it down before the altar of *God*, your God. 5. And you shall begin and say before the Presence of *God*, your God: "An Aramean, close to ruin, was my father; and he went to Mitzrayim

כו א וְהָיָה כִּי־תָבוֹא אֶל־הָאָרֶץ אֲשֶׁר יְהוָה
אֱלֹהֶיךָ נֹתֵן לְךָ נַחֲלָה וִירִשְׁתָּהּ וְיָשַׁבְתָּ בָּהּ:
ב וְלָקַחְתָּ מֵרֵאשִׁית ׀ כָּל־פְּרִי הָאֲדָמָה אֲשֶׁר
תָּבִיא מֵאַרְצְךָ אֲשֶׁר יְהוָה אֱלֹהֶיךָ נֹתֵן לָךְ
וְשַׂמְתָּ בַטֶּנֶא וְהָלַכְתָּ אֶל־הַמָּקוֹם אֲשֶׁר יִבְחַר
יְהוָה אֱלֹהֶיךָ לְשַׁכֵּן שְׁמוֹ שָׁם: ג וּבָאתָ אֶל־
הַכֹּהֵן אֲשֶׁר יִהְיֶה בַּיָּמִים הָהֵם וְאָמַרְתָּ אֵלָיו
הִגַּדְתִּי הַיּוֹם לַיהוָה אֱלֹהֶיךָ כִּי־בָאתִי אֶל־
הָאָרֶץ אֲשֶׁר נִשְׁבַּע יְהוָה לַאֲבֹתֵינוּ לָתֶת לָנוּ:
ד וְלָקַח הַכֹּהֵן הַטֶּנֶא מִיָּדֶךָ וְהִנִּיחוֹ לִפְנֵי מִזְבַּח
יְהוָה אֱלֹהֶיךָ: ה וְעָנִיתָ וְאָמַרְתָּ לִפְנֵי ׀ יְהוָה
אֱלֹהֶיךָ אֲרַמִּי אֹבֵד אָבִי וַיֵּרֶד מִצְרַיְמָה וַיָּגָר

CHAPTER XXVI

1. ***when you come.*** The body of laws concludes with two legal institutions: the declaration to be recited when offering the first fruits and the declaration to be recited when offering tithes. Both these declarations summarize the basic facts of the history of the Jewish nation and the basic standards for the mission assigned to that nation. These two declarations are to be recited by every Jewish man once each year, and once every three years, respectively, to remind him of his historic origin and of the laws and the mission that derive from it. Both these declarations refer to two other institutions that have already been set down elsewhere in the Law. These are the offering of the first fruits and the tithe, which are intended to express, by acts of profound ideal significance, the gratitude of the Jew for his land and for the material wealth derived from it—those two foundations of the nation's existence—and the Jew's understanding of the origin and the purpose of these gifts. As a consequence, these institutions are closely linked to the land of which the nation is about to take possession. It is therefore most appropriate that they should be discussed here, at the conclusion of the laws for whose observance the nation is to come into its land.

3. . . . By bringing the fruit of my land to you [the priest], I have given evidence that I own my field and my farmland only because I am descended from the forefathers to whom God promised, by His covenant, that He would give this land to their descendants. This has been set forth in the Teaching of the Law for which the Sanctuary that you represent has been built. My field and my farmland are upon the soil of *your* God; they are mine solely by virtue of the fact that I am a son of His covenant, and it is in witness of this fact that I have brought these fruits here.

5. ***And you shall begin and say.*** He is holding in his hand the basket of fruits which, by the symbolic act of waving, he has already consecrated to endeavors on behalf of God and mankind. As already pointed out, he is making this offering in order to express his awareness that he possesses the land only because God has fulfilled the promise of the covenant He made with his forefathers. Now, as he brings his basket of fruits before the priest, he looks back to these early beginnings of the Jewish people and, in his formal declaration, stresses the historic facts which demonstrated for all time to come that God's almighty will and power were the sole active factors in the establishment of Jewish nationhood.

• • •

The word "Aramean," which the person making the

and sojourned there as a stranger with a
small number, and there he became a great
nation, strong and numerous. 6. And the
Mitzrites treated us badly and afflicted us
and imposed hard labor upon us. 7. And
we cried out to *God*, the God of our fathers,
and *God* hearkened to our voice and saw our
affliction, our trouble and our oppression.
8. And *God* brought us out from Mitzrayim

שָׁ֖ם בִּמְתֵ֣י מְעָ֑ט וַֽיְהִי־שָׁ֕ם לְג֥וֹי גָּד֖וֹל עָצ֥וּם
וָרָֽב: ו וַיָּרֵ֧עוּ אֹתָ֛נוּ הַמִּצְרִ֖ים וַיְעַנּ֑וּנוּ וַיִּתְּנ֥וּ
עָלֵ֖ינוּ עֲבֹדָ֥ה קָשָֽׁה: ז וַנִּצְעַ֕ק אֶל־יְהוָ֖ה אֱלֹהֵ֣י
אֲבֹתֵ֑ינוּ וַיִּשְׁמַ֤ע יְהוָה֙ אֶת־קֹלֵ֔נוּ וַיַּ֧רְא אֶת־
עָנְיֵ֛נוּ וְאֶת־עֲמָלֵ֖נוּ וְאֶת־לַחֲצֵֽנוּ: ח וַיּוֹצִאֵ֤נוּ

offering uses to describe his ancestor, implies the greatest possible contrast to blessed independence in a land of one's own, to that happy state to which the fruits in the basket bear witness.

The land of Canaan was not the original home of our forefathers. Abraham was born in Aram; it was Aram that he called his country and the land of his birth. He himself had no right of domicile in the land, so that his descendants could have enjoyed that same right as his legal heirs. Our original ancestor had no home in the land that is now the homeland of his descendants. He had to consider it a special favor that he was permitted to acquire, on the soil that is now the home of his descendants, a burial plot for his wife. As for his first grandson, Jacob-Israel, whose name the nation now bears—when he journeyed back to his Aramean home as a refugee, eking out a living there by slave labor, again, his Aramean homeland had no use for him. Threatened by physical destruction, Jacob was forced to run away from his scheming father-in-law and, together with his wives and children, to return to Canaan as a fugitive. But there, too, he could find no peace. Famine struck, and once again he had to flee. He was still an "Aramean," still homeless; and because of his homelessness, combined with the most adverse blows of fate, he was "close to ruin." [אֹבֵד="one about to go to ruin," from אבד, "to go to ruin"]. According to human judgment, he had no prospects of ever attaining independence, and it was in this condition that he went down to Egypt, a foreign land even more alien to him in its language, its customs and its outlook on life than the other lands he had known.

Their forefathers had been promised a future as an independent nation on the soil of Canaan, yet it was as a family without a future, with rights of domicile only in Aram, that Jacob's clan went to Egypt. Cf. "An Aramean, close to ruin, was my father," and the Haggadah adds, "He was forced to do so, in accordance with instructions from God." According to human judgment, the migration of Jacob's family to Egypt was a move still further away from the realization of the future that had been promised to them. Notwithstanding the instantaneous splendor to which they came, their migration was a יְרִידָה, a "going down" or "descent" in the truest sense of the term. For this reason the family was in need of God's words of encouragement: "Do not fear to go down to Mitzrayim" (Genesis 46:3). For this reason, too, Joseph, all the splendor of his high office notwithstanding, departed this life convinced that a special intervention of God's sovereignty would be needed to lead the nation out of Egypt and "up" to the Promised Land (ibid. 50:24). However, they went "down"; seemingly "close to ruin"; "forced" by the pressure of circumstances and in obedience to the instructions they had received from God.

and sojourned there as a stranger. It had not been their intention to settle permanently in Egypt. They only sought permission to sojourn there as foreigners, and this permission they did indeed receive, with all the bitter consequences of dwelling in a state such as ancient Egypt as homeless strangers, without a right of domicile. "With a small number (of persons)"—with seventy souls.

and there he became. There, contrary to all reasonable expectations and united by their unique spiritual and moral qualities, which they had preserved in contrast to the indigenous population, they became a separate national entity; "they stood out (from among all the others)," a great national entity; and, by God's blessing, they became strong and numerous.

6. וַיָּרֵעוּ אֹתָנוּ ***[And (the Mitzrites) treated us badly].*** הרע is to "hurt" a person, to treat him badly.

The Haggadah, referring to the words [of Pharaoh], "Let us deal cleverly with them" (Exodus 1:10), interprets the verb וַיָּרֵעוּ to mean: They wanted to harm us, they sought to diminish our greatness and to break our strength.

וַיְעַנּוּנוּ וַיִּתְּנוּ עָלֵינוּ וגו׳ ***[and afflicted us and imposed].*** This refers to the עִנּוּי [affliction] and עַבְדוּת [servitude] resulting from their גֵּרוּת [alienhood], which, taken together, constituted the three typical aspects of the *galuth* in ancient Egypt (see Exodus 22:20).

7. ***And we cried out.*** עִנּוּי ["distress"] refers to עָנְיֵנוּ ["our affliction"]; עַבְדוּת ["servitude"] to עֲמָלֵנוּ ["our trouble"] and לַחֲצֵנוּ ["our oppression"] to the oppression and the restrictions resulting from גֵּרוּת ["alienhood"] (see Exodus 22:20).

יְהוָה֙ מִמִּצְרַ֔יִם בְּיָ֤ד חֲזָקָה֙ וּבִזְרֹ֣עַ נְטוּיָ֔ה
וּבְמֹרָ֖א גָּדֹ֑ל וּבְאֹת֖וֹת וּבְמֹפְתִֽים׃ ט וַיְבִאֵ֖נוּ
אֶל־הַמָּק֣וֹם הַזֶּ֑ה וַיִּתֶּן־לָ֙נוּ֙ אֶת־הָאָ֣רֶץ הַזֹּ֔את
אֶ֛רֶץ זָבַ֥ת חָלָ֖ב וּדְבָֽשׁ׃ י וְעַתָּ֗ה הִנֵּ֤ה הֵבֵ֙אתִי֙
אֶת־רֵאשִׁית֙ פְּרִ֣י הָאֲדָמָ֔ה אֲשֶׁר־נָתַ֥תָּה לִּ֖י יְהוָ֑ה
וְהִנַּחְתּ֗וֹ לִפְנֵי֙ יְהוָ֣ה אֱלֹהֶ֔יךָ וְהִֽשְׁתַּחֲוִ֔יתָ לִפְנֵ֖י
יְהוָ֥ה אֱלֹהֶֽיךָ׃ יא וְשָׂמַחְתָּ֣ בְכָל־הַטּ֗וֹב אֲשֶׁ֧ר
נָֽתַן־לְךָ֛ יְהוָ֥ה אֱלֹהֶ֖יךָ וּלְבֵיתֶ֑ךָ אַתָּה֙ וְהַלֵּוִ֔י

with a strong hand, with an outstretched
arm and with great awesomeness; with
instructive signs and punishing miracles;
9. and He brought us to this place and gave
us this land, a land flowing with milk and
honey. 10. And now I have brought here
the first of the fruit of the soil that Thou,
O *God*, hast given me." Then you shall
set it before the Presence of *God*, your God,
and you shall cast yourself down before the
Presence of *God*, your God. 11. And
then you shall rejoice in all the good
that *God*, your God, has given to you and
to your house[hold]; you and the Levite

8. ***And* God *brought us out.*** "With a strong hand": A hand that was stronger than that of our taskmasters, and that burst the yoke of our servitude asunder.

with an outstretched arm. An arm whose dominion extends over all the lands of the world, and which makes all men גֵּרִים ["sojourners"] with equal rights upon His earth.

and with great awesomeness. Which all those have cause to fear who misuse their power to עַנּוּי [impose affliction upon] their weaker fellow men.

with instructive signs and punishing miracles. His יָד חֲזָקָה ["strong hand"], זְרוֹעַ נְטוּיָה ["outstretched arm"] and מוֹרָא גָּדוֹל ["great awesomeness"], with which He put an end to Israel's עַבְדוּת [servitude], גֵּרוּת [alienhood] and עִנּוּי [affliction], were demonstrated by Him in the form of אוֹתוֹת וּמוֹפְתִים [instructive signs and punishing miracles] (see Exodus 4:21 and notes on 7:15).

9. ***and He brought us to this place.*** To this place, which He chose as the habitation of the Sanctuary of His Law (cf. Exodus 15:17), and as the place where the Law that reposed there should be translated into reality.

and gave us. He gave us this blessed land that encircles the Sanctuary of the Law, and whose possession at last gave us the home we never had before.

"*And He brought us to this place*: This refers to the Temple. *And He brought us to this place (and gave us)*: As a reward for our coming to this place did He give us this land" (*Sifri*).

10. ***And now.*** And now, because we have obtained the land only through Thee, and because Thou hast given us this land only for the sake of the Law to which this Sanctuary has been erected, now therefore have I brought here the first fruits of the soil that Thou, O God, hast given me.

And for this reason "you shall set it"; you shall set down the basket of fruits before God, *your* God, upon that side of the altar which is dedicated to the spirit shining forth to you from His Law; and you shall depart from His House with an act of prostration, expressing your complete surrender to God. But you are not yet permitted to leave the environs of the Sanctuary. For, as with any other occasion on which you appear in the Temple, the act of offering first fruits, too, requires that you remain in [Jerusalem], the city of the Temple, until the next morning. (Cf. Mishnah, Bikkurim II:14; Deuteronomy 16:7.)

° ° °

11. ***And then you shall rejoice.*** Then, after you have understood, from your reflection upon your past, that you have only God to thank for whatever independence and prosperity you now enjoy; and after you have expressed your renewed surrender to God based on this understanding, you shall rejoice before God in all the good things He has granted you. This is a form of rejoicing which, like the rejoicing on festivals—cf. "and you shall rejoice in your festival" (Deuteronomy 16:14)—is to be expressed in the form of זִבְחֵי שְׁלָמִים ["meal-of-peace offerings"]. Cf. וְשָׂמַחְתָּ לִפְנֵי ד׳ אֱלֹהֶיךָ: "And you shall slaughter meal-of-peace offerings and shall eat them, and you shall rejoice before *God*, your God" (Deuteronomy 27:7). And "you shall rejoice in all the good"—the goodness and the rejoicing brought you by the good things that have been granted you shall be expressed through joy and elation. According to Arakhin 11a, such expression can only be given by means of inspired song. Hence, "the offering of the first fruits requires an offering and a song" (Bikkurim II:4). In this spirit, the entire performance of the commandment relating to the בִּכּוּרִים [offering of the first fruits] was to be characterized by a mood of rejoicing.

As a rule, these offerings were not brought to Jerusalem by each individual on his own. All the people of the cities belonging to a *ma'amad* [Temple service] district would assemble in the district seat, where they and the stranger who has entered into your midst. 12. When you have finished tithing all the tithes of your produce in the third year, the year of tithing, and you give it to the Levite, the stranger, the orphan and the widow, and they eat it within your gates and are satisfied, 13. then you shall say before the Presence of *God*, your God: "I have cleared away that which is holy from the house, and I have also given it to the Levite, to the stranger, to the orphan and to the widow, entirely in accordance with the commandment that Thou hast commanded me; I have not transgressed any of Thy commandments and have forgotten nothing; 14. I have not eaten of it in my mourning; I have not consumed any of it in [a state of] uncleanness, and I have used none of it for the dead; I have hearkened to the voice of *God*, my God; I have done entirely as Thou hast commanded me: 15. O direct Thy examining look down from Thy holy place, from heaven, and bless Thy people Yisrael and the soil that Thou hast given us,

וְהַגֵּ֖ר אֲשֶׁ֥ר בְּקִרְבֶּֽךָ׃ ס שני יב כִּ֣י תְכַלֶּ֞ה לַעְשֵׂ֞ר
אֶֽת־כָּל־מַעְשַׂ֧ר תְּבוּאָתְךָ֛ בַּשָּׁנָ֥ה הַשְּׁלִישִׁ֖ת שְׁנַ֣ת
הַֽמַּעֲשֵׂ֑ר וְנָתַתָּ֣ה לַלֵּוִ֗י לַגֵּר֙ לַיָּת֣וֹם וְלָֽאַלְמָנָ֔ה
וְאָכְל֥וּ בִשְׁעָרֶ֖יךָ וְשָׂבֵֽעוּ׃ יג וְאָמַרְתָּ֡ לִפְנֵי֩ יְהוָ֨ה
אֱלֹהֶ֜יךָ בִּעַ֧רְתִּי הַקֹּ֣דֶשׁ מִן־הַבַּ֗יִת וְגַ֨ם נְתַתִּ֤יו
לַלֵּוִי֙ וְלַגֵּר֙ לַיָּת֣וֹם וְלָֽאַלְמָנָ֔ה כְּכָל־מִצְוָתְךָ֖
אֲשֶׁ֣ר צִוִּיתָ֑נִי לֹֽא־עָבַ֥רְתִּי מִמִּצְוֺתֶ֖יךָ וְלֹ֥א
שָׁכָֽחְתִּי׃ יד לֹֽא־אָכַ֨לְתִּי בְאֹנִ֜י מִמֶּ֗נּוּ וְלֹֽא־
בִעַ֤רְתִּי מִמֶּ֙נּוּ֙ בְּטָמֵ֔א וְלֹא־נָתַ֥תִּי מִמֶּ֖נּוּ לְמֵ֑ת
שָׁמַ֗עְתִּי בְּקוֹל֙ יְהוָ֣ה אֱלֹהָ֔י עָשִׂ֕יתִי כְּכֹ֖ל אֲשֶׁ֥ר
צִוִּיתָֽנִי׃ טו הַשְׁקִ֩יפָה֩ מִמְּע֨וֹן קָדְשְׁךָ֜ מִן־
הַשָּׁמַ֗יִם וּבָרֵ֤ךְ אֶֽת־עַמְּךָ֙ אֶת־יִשְׂרָאֵ֔ל וְאֵת֙

would spend the night outdoors. They would not enter any house in the town for fear of טוּמְאָה [that they might become ritually unclean and consequently unable to make the offering at the Temple]. At daybreak the leader would call out, "Arise! Let us go up to Zion, to the House of our God!" The procession was led by a band of flute players and by a steer—its horns gilded and crowned with a wreath of olive branches—that was to be used as the שְׁלָמִים [meal-of-peace offering]. And so they marched toward the outskirts of Jerusalem. When they arrived there, they sent word to the city to announce their arrival, and then they set to work decorating their baskets of בִּכּוּרִים [first fruits]. The warden of the Temple, his assistants and the Temple administrators went out to meet them. The number of greeters would correspond to the number of visitors to be welcomed. All the workers in Jerusalem stopped their work, even if it was work they were under obligation to complete, and welcomed the visitors with the words, "O brothers from Such-and-Such place, peace be to your coming!" The band of flute players at the head of the procession continued playing until the procession reached the Temple Mount. On arrival there, everyone, including the king, took his basket upon his shoulders and moved toward the antechamber of the Temple. When they arrived there, the Levites began to chant Psalm 30: "I can raise Thee on high, O *God*, for Thou hast raised me from the depth and hast not allowed my enemies to rejoice over me" (Bikkurim III:2–4).

° ° °

15. . . . The declaration of the tithe concludes the legislative section [of the Pentateuch]. Only two commandments still follow. They relate to the preservation of the now-completed Law in the minds of the people: that an assembly should be held at which the Law is to be read to the entire people (Deuteronomy 31:10 and 11), and that every individual should have a correct *Sefer Torah* written (Deuteronomy 31:19).

Note that the commandments related to מַעֲשֵׂר [tithing] are the only ones in the entire Law of God whose complete observance requires the recitation of so formal a retrospective declaration before God. Hence, the principles and attitudes to be promoted by these מַעֲשֵׂר laws and their practical application are clearly intended to play a very important role in the attainment of the objectives sought by the Law.

As we have repeatedly noted and discussed in some detail in the chapter dealing with the מַעֲשֵׂר as such (Deuteronomy 14:22f.), the three prescribed tithes are intended to teach us to employ our material resources in both theory and practice for the purposes that God has set before us, as follows: (1) מַעֲשֵׂר רִאשׁוֹן [the "first tithe"], to cultivate the spirit, which is to be enlightened by the תּוֹרָה; (2) מַעֲשֵׂר שֵׁנִי [the "second tithe"], the

as Thou hast sworn to our fathers—a land
flowing with milk and honey." 16. On
this day *God*, your God, commands you to
carry out these laws and [social] ordinances;
keep them and carry them out with all your
heart and with all your soul. 17. You have
today caused it to be said of *God* that he
shall be a God to you and that you would
walk in His ways, keep His commandments
and His [social] ordinances, and that you
would hearken to His voice. 18. And *God*
has today caused it to be said of you that you
shall be a people belonging to Him alone, as
He promised you, and that you shall keep
all His commandments; 19. He would
place you high above all the nations He has
created, as a proclamation of His acts, for
His Name and for His glory; and that you
shall be a holy people to *God*, your God, as
He has spoken.

הָֽאֲדָמָה אֲשֶׁר נָתַתָּה לָנוּ כַּאֲשֶׁר נִשְׁבַּעְתָּ
לַאֲבֹתֵינוּ אֶרֶץ זָבַת חָלָב וּדְבָשׁ: ס שלישי
טז הַיּוֹם הַזֶּה יְהוָֹה אֱלֹהֶיךָ מְצַוְּךָ לַעֲשׂוֹת
אֶת־הַחֻקִּים הָאֵלֶּה וְאֶת־הַמִּשְׁפָּטִים וְשָׁמַרְתָּ
וְעָשִׂיתָ אוֹתָם בְּכָל־לְבָבְךָ וּבְכָל־נַפְשֶׁךָ:
יז אֶת־יְהוָֹה הֶאֱמַרְתָּ הַיּוֹם לִהְיוֹת לְךָ לֵאלֹהִים
וְלָלֶכֶת בִּדְרָכָיו וְלִשְׁמֹר חֻקָּיו וּמִצְוֺתָיו
וּמִשְׁפָּטָיו וְלִשְׁמֹעַ בְּקֹלוֹ: יח וַיהוָֹה הֶאֱמִירְךָ
הַיּוֹם לִהְיוֹת לוֹ לְעַם סְגֻלָּה כַּאֲשֶׁר דִּבֶּר־לָךְ
וְלִשְׁמֹר כָּל־מִצְוֺתָיו: יט וּלְתִתְּךָ עֶלְיוֹן עַל כָּל־
הַגּוֹיִם אֲשֶׁר עָשָׂה לִתְהִלָּה וּלְשֵׁם וּלְתִפְאָרֶת
וְלִהְיֹתְךָ עַם־קָדֹשׁ לַיהוָֹה אֱלֹהֶיךָ כַּאֲשֶׁר

care of our bodies in a spirit of moral purity; and (3) מַעֲשַׂר עָנִי [the "tithe of the poor"], concern for the welfare of our fellow men, which we are to implement out of a feeling of devotion to our duty. The realization of these three objectives should encompass the sum total of our mission. The life of a nation whose material endeavors are devoted to the achievement of these objectives; a nation that has been freed of all egotism and moral corruption—should be so healthy and so close to human perfection that it may indeed presume to call upon God הַשְׁקִיפָה [to look down upon it in order to examine it] and to beseech His blessing, so that the nation may obtain the material means which it needs to continue its good endeavors.

° ° °

17. . . . Israel's pledge to God and God's promise to Israel have not remained a private matter. Both have become a matter of worldwide knowledge and have impressed themselves upon the minds of all mankind. Since that time, God has been described as the God of Israel, and Israel, as the people of God.

° ° °

18 and 19. God has promised to the people of Israel that once it has proven itself a scrupulous guardian of His Law, it will be given a place in world history far above all the other nations He has created; so that Israel's appearance on the scene of world history should serve to proclaim the acts of God, and redound to His Name and to His glory. Israel's appearance is to be תְּהִלָּה, a revelation of God's sovereignty among men; indeed, an "emanation" reflecting the Divine origin of all historical phenomena and confirming His existence and supreme sovereignty. More than that, Israel is to serve God לְשֵׁם [for His Name]; it must not convey merely a vague notion of the existence of one sole Master in the processes of nature and history. Israel is to be שֵׁם; by its wanderings among the nations with the Book of His revealed laws and teachings, the sole source of its spiritual and practical life and of its miraculous survival, Israel is to bring to the world a specific, clearly-defined conception of the existence and the will of this One God. And if, upheld by this God and by its faithful observance of His Law, the people of Israel will achieve that individual and national happiness which God promised them in His Law, then this happy state of affairs will become לְתִפְאָרֶת—a glorification of God and of His Law—outshining all else with such brilliance that "nations will walk toward that light," and Israel will become a "crown of glory in the hand of *God*, a royal diadem to its God" (Isaiah 62:3).

and that you shall be a holy people. By declaring it for all the world to know that Israel, as the people of God's Law, is to become an instrument for the enlightenment and civilization of all the nations, "He caused it to be said of you"—He made all men aware of Israel's mission and of what may be expected of Israel: Through each and every one of its members, Israel is to be עַם קָדוֹשׁ, a holy nation, one committed only to that which is morally good and pleasing to God. Thus, if Israel should ever become unfaithful to its sacred calling, even the youngest lad from any of the other nations of mankind could remind it of its mission and of its commitment.

XXVII

1. And Moshe and the elders of Yisrael commanded the people [saying]: "It is now for you to keep the entire commandment that I am commanding you today! 2. Therefore it shall be on the day when you will pass over the Yarden to the land that *God*, your God, is giving you, that you shall erect for yourself large stones and plaster them with lime, 3. and when you have passed over, you shall write upon them all the words of this Teaching, so that you may come to the land that *God*, your God, is giving you; a land flowing with milk and honey, as *God*, the God of your fathers, has promised you. 4. And when you have passed over the Yarden, you shall erect these stones, which I am now commanding you, on Mount Ebal, and you shall plaster them with lime; 5. and there you shall build an altar to *God*, your God; an altar of stones over which you must not swing [an] iron [tool]. 6. Of uncut stones shall you build the altar to *God*, your God; and you shall

דִּבֶּר: פ רביעי כז א וַיְצַו מֹשֶׁה וְזִקְנֵי יִשְׂרָאֵל אֶת־הָעָם לֵאמֹר שָׁמֹר אֶת־כָּל־הַמִּצְוָה אֲשֶׁר אָנֹכִי מְצַוֶּה אֶתְכֶם הַיּוֹם: ב וְהָיָה בַּיּוֹם אֲשֶׁר תַּעַבְרוּ אֶת־הַיַּרְדֵּן אֶל־הָאָרֶץ אֲשֶׁר־יְהֹוָה אֱלֹהֶיךָ נֹתֵן לָךְ וַהֲקֵמֹתָ לְךָ אֲבָנִים גְּדֹלוֹת וְשַׂדְתָּ אֹתָם בַּשִּׂיד: ג וְכָתַבְתָּ עֲלֵיהֶן אֶת־כָּל־ דִּבְרֵי הַתּוֹרָה הַזֹּאת בְּעָבְרֶךָ לְמַעַן אֲשֶׁר תָּבֹא אֶל־הָאָרֶץ אֲשֶׁר־יְהֹוָה אֱלֹהֶיךָ ׀ נֹתֵן לְךָ אֶרֶץ זָבַת חָלָב וּדְבַשׁ כַּאֲשֶׁר דִּבֶּר יְהֹוָה אֱלֹהֵי־ אֲבֹתֶיךָ לָךְ: ד וְהָיָה בְּעָבְרְכֶם אֶת־הַיַּרְדֵּן תָּקִימוּ אֶת־הָאֲבָנִים הָאֵלֶּה אֲשֶׁר אָנֹכִי מְצַוֶּה אֶתְכֶם הַיּוֹם בְּהַר עֵיבָל וְשַׂדְתָּ אוֹתָם בַּשִּׂיד: ה וּבָנִיתָ שָּׁם מִזְבֵּחַ לַיהֹוָה אֱלֹהֶיךָ מִזְבַּח אֲבָנִים לֹא־תָנִיף עֲלֵיהֶם בַּרְזֶל: ו אֲבָנִים שְׁלֵמוֹת תִּבְנֶה אֶת־מִזְבַּח יְהֹוָה אֱלֹהֶיךָ

CHAPTER XXVII

2. ... If you wish to cross the Jordan, you must immediately set about erecting these stones for the writing of the Law. You must begin this work before you have completed your crossing. Only by virtue of accomplishing this task will you be able to pass over the Jordan and enter the Promised Land. Only thanks to the תּוֹרָה will you have the Land; solely for the sake of the Law, for its preservation and observance, will you receive the Land; and you shall demonstrate that truth at this very moment, when you cross the river that marks the boundary of this land....

Note the alternation between the singular and plural forms of address in Verses 1 to 8.[13] This alternation would seem to express the thought that the task of observing the Law, for which the nation of Israel has been granted the Promised Land, is not only the

responsibility of the individual members of the nation, nor is it only the responsibility of the community as personified by its official representatives. It is the responsibility of the whole national entity in terms of all its components, so that the entire nation, with its members functioning as one united whole, must be answerable for it. This idea is expressed most aptly by the fact that the people themselves are to choose twelve men, one from each tribe [cf. Joshua 3:12], to erect the stones for the monument to the Law.

5-7. *and there you shall build.* Upon the bleak summit of Mount Ebal, not on verdant Mount Gerizim, shall the stones of the Law be built up to form an altar. The observance of the Law of God and the elevation of all earthly affairs toward God, which are to be sought by this observance, are not dependent on any earthly conditions. The poorest soil on earth can pro-

---

[13]*Note to the English translation:*

Verse 1: "It is now for you (*plu.*)..."

Verse 2: "... on the day when you (*plu.*) will pass over the Yarden to the land that *God*, your (*sing.*) God, is giving you (*sing.*) that you (*sing.*) shall erect for yourself..."

Verse 3: "And when you (*sing.*) have passed over..."

Verse 4: "And when you (*plu.*) have passed over the Yarden, you (*plu.*) shall erect... which I am now

commanding you (*plu.*)... and you (*sing.*) shall plaster them with lime,"

Verse 5: "And there you (*sing.*) shall build... over which you (*sing.*) must not swing..."

Verse 6: "Of uncut stones shall you (*sing.*) build... and you (*sing.*) shall make ascent offerings upon it..."

Verse 7: "And you (*sing.*) shall slaughter... and you (*sing.*) shall rejoice before *God*, your (*sing.*) God."

Verse 8: "And you (*sing.*) shall write..." [G.H.]

וְהַעֲלִ֤יתָ עָלָיו֙ עוֹלֹ֔ת לַיהוָ֖ה אֱלֹהֶֽיךָ׃ ז וְזָבַחְתָּ֥
שְׁלָמִ֖ים וְאָכַ֣לְתָּ שָּׁ֑ם וְשָׂמַחְתָּ֕ לִפְנֵ֖י יְהוָ֥ה
אֱלֹהֶֽיךָ׃ ח וְכָתַבְתָּ֣ עַל־הָאֲבָנִ֗ים אֶֽת־כָּל־דִּבְרֵ֛י
הַתּוֹרָ֥ה הַזֹּ֖את בַּאֵ֥ר הֵיטֵֽב׃ ס ט וַיְדַבֵּ֤ר מֹשֶׁה֙
וְהַכֹּהֲנִ֣ים הַלְוִיִּ֔ם אֶ֥ל־כָּל־יִשְׂרָאֵ֖ל לֵאמֹ֑ר
הַסְכֵּ֤ת ׀ וּשְׁמַע֙ יִשְׂרָאֵ֔ל הַיּ֤וֹם הַזֶּה֙ נִהְיֵ֣יתָ לְעָ֔ם
לַיהוָ֖ה אֱלֹהֶֽיךָ׃ י וְשָׁ֣מַעְתָּ֔ בְּק֖וֹל יְהוָ֣ה אֱלֹהֶ֑יךָ
וְעָשִׂ֤יתָ אֶת־מִצְוֺתָו֙ (מצותיו קרי) וְאֶת־חֻקָּ֔יו אֲשֶׁ֛ר
אָנֹכִ֥י מְצַוְּךָ֖ הַיּֽוֹם׃ ס חמישי יא וַיְצַ֤ו מֹשֶׁה֙ אֶת־
הָעָ֔ם בַּיּ֥וֹם הַה֖וּא לֵאמֹֽר׃ יב אֵ֠לֶּה יַעַמְד֞וּ לְבָרֵ֤ךְ
אֶת־הָעָם֙ עַל־הַ֣ר גְּרִזִ֔ים בְּעָבְרְכֶ֖ם אֶת־הַיַּרְדֵּ֑ן
שִׁמְעוֹן֙ וְלֵוִ֣י וִֽיהוּדָ֔ה וְיִשָּׂשכָ֖ר וְיוֹסֵ֥ף וּבִנְיָמִֽן׃
יג וְאֵ֛לֶּה יַעַמְד֥וּ עַל־הַקְּלָלָ֖ה בְּהַ֣ר עֵיבָ֑ל רְאוּבֵן֙
גָּ֣ד וְאָשֵׁ֔ר וּזְבוּלֻ֖ן דָּ֥ן וְנַפְתָּלִֽי׃ יד וְעָנ֣וּ הַלְוִיִּ֔ם

make ascent offerings upon it to *God*, your
God. 7. And you shall slaughter meal-
of-peace offerings and shall eat there, and
you shall rejoice before *God*, your God;
8. and you shall write upon the stones
all the words of this Teaching, so that
they may be adequately understood."
9. Thereupon Moshe and the priests, the
Levites, spoke to all of Yisrael [saying]:
"Pay attention and hear, O Yisrael: On this
day you have become a people to *God*, your
God! 10. Now therefore hearken to the
voice of *God*, your God, and carry out His
uniform system of commandments, and
His laws that I command you today."
11. Finally, Moshe commanded the people
on that same day [saying]: 12. "The
following shall stand upon Mount Gerizim
to bless the people when you have passed
over the Yarden: Shimeon, Levi, Yehudah,
Yissakhar, Yosef and Binyamin. 13. And
the following shall stand for the curse on
Mount Ebal: Reuben, Gad and Asher,
Zebulun and Naphtali. 14. The Levites
shall raise their voices and say to every

vide a base for God's Law and for your striving toward its lofty ideal; so that, by thus striving toward God, you may find your peace and happiness before His countenance.

° ° °

8. . . . According to Sotah 32a, בָּאֵר [to be understood] is to be interpeted here as "expounding," as in הוֹאִיל מֹשֶׁה בֵּאֵר אֶת הַתּוֹרָה הַזֹּאת ["Moshe, in expounding this Law, began as follows"] (Deuteronomy 1:5). We are taught that there was a translation, attached to this copy of the Law, so that all the other nations would be able to understand it also. Far from the exclusiveness so wrongly imputed to it, Israel was to understand from the very outset that its mission was to help bring about the spiritual and moral salvation of all mankind, and that all mankind would attain its salvation when the Law of God would enter into its midst. . . .

9. . . . On this day you have become a people! Your commitment and responsibility to the Law that has just been proclaimed for every member of your nation, without exception; your guardianship of the Law that has been assigned to all of you—these are the things that make you a nation. "This day": It is not the fact that you are about to take possession of the land, but the fact that all of you together already possess the Law today, that makes you a nation. You may lose the land, as indeed you will, but the Law and your eternal commitment to it will remain the everlasting, inalienable bond that will keep you united as a nation. This basic fact, which clearly sets Israel apart from all other national entities, holds the key to the immortality of the Jewish people, with all its implications for Israel's future. This, if we understand it correctly, is the thought conveyed by the verse, "On this day you have become a people." And the very first implication of this fact, is, of course, as follows. . . .

10. ***Now therefore hearken.*** You must henceforth be even more faithful and punctilious in observing these laws. For Israel, disloyalty to the Law will be what high treason is the other nations. . . .

11. . . . The formulation of the pronouncements that follow shows how the members of the nation that has been appointed guardian of God's Law, who are now about to disperse over the land, are to take with them into their new homes the awareness that God's sovereignty is present everywhere. He dispenses blessings and curses in all cases that are beyond human understanding; cases in which, therefore, the nation cannot act as a whole to exercise its collective responsibility as guardian of the Law.

man in Yisrael with a raised voice: 15. 'Cursed is the man who makes a graven or molten image , an abomination to *God*, the work of craftsmen's hands, and sets it up in secret!' And all the people shall raise their voices and say: 'Amen.' 16. 'Cursed is he who slights his father or mother!' And all the people shall say: 'Amen.' 17. 'Cursed is he who moves the boundary [marker] of his neighbor!' And all the people shall say: 'Amen.' 18. 'Cursed is he who misleads a blind man on the way!' And all the people shall say: 'Amen.' 19. 'Cursed is he who twists the right[ful due] of an orphaned stranger or a widow!' And all the people shall say: 'Amen.' 20. 'Cursed is he who lies with his father's wife, when he has uncovered his father's garment!' And all the people shall say: 'Amen.' 21. 'Cursed is he who lies with any animal!' And all the people shall say: 'Amen.' 22. 'Cursed is he who lies with his sister, the daughter of his father or the daughter of his mother!' And all the people

וְאָמְר֛וּ אֶל־כָּל־אִ֥ישׁ יִשְׂרָאֵ֖ל ק֥וֹל רָֽם׃ ס
טו אָר֣וּר הָאִ֡ישׁ אֲשֶׁ֣ר יַעֲשֶׂה֩ פֶ֨סֶל וּמַסֵּכָ֜ה
תּוֹעֲבַ֣ת יְהוָ֗ה מַעֲשֵׂ֛ה יְדֵ֥י חָרָ֖שׁ וְשָׂ֣ם בַּסָּ֑תֶר
וְעָנ֧וּ כָל־הָעָ֛ם וְאָמְר֖וּ אָמֵֽן׃ ס טז אָר֕וּר מַקְלֶ֥ה
אָבִ֖יו וְאִמּ֑וֹ וְאָמַ֥ר כָּל־הָעָ֖ם אָמֵֽן׃ ס יז אָר֕וּר
מַסִּ֖יג גְּב֣וּל רֵעֵ֑הוּ וְאָמַ֥ר כָּל־הָעָ֖ם אָמֵֽן׃ ס
יח אָר֕וּר מַשְׁגֶּ֥ה עִוֵּ֖ר בַּדָּ֑רֶךְ וְאָמַ֥ר כָּל־הָעָ֖ם
אָמֵֽן׃ ס יט אָר֗וּר מַטֶּ֛ה מִשְׁפַּ֥ט גֵּר־יָת֖וֹם
וְאַלְמָנָ֑ה וְאָמַ֥ר כָּל־הָעָ֖ם אָמֵֽן׃ כ אָר֗וּר שֹׁכֵב֙
עִם־אֵ֣שֶׁת אָבִ֔יו כִּ֥י גִלָּ֖ה כְּנַ֣ף אָבִ֑יו וְאָמַ֥ר כָּל־
הָעָ֖ם אָמֵֽן׃ ס כא אָר֕וּר שֹׁכֵ֖ב עִם־כָּל־בְּהֵמָ֑ה
וְאָמַ֥ר כָּל־הָעָ֖ם אָמֵֽן׃ ס כב אָר֗וּר שֹׁכֵב֙ עִם־
אֲחֹת֔וֹ בַּת־אָבִ֖יו א֣וֹ בַת־אִמּ֑וֹ וְאָמַ֥ר כָּל־הָעָ֖ם

14. ***The Levites shall raise their voices and say.*** . . . "They (the Levites) turned toward Mount Gerizim and began to recite the blessing; they [then] turned toward Mount Ebal and began to recite the curse" (Sotah 32a). The Halakhah teaches that each of the sentences beginning with אָרוּר ["cursed be"] now following was, in fact, preceded by a blessing referring to the opposite of the act that was cursed; e.g. "Blessed is the man who does *not* make a graven or molten image,"and only thereafter, "Cursed is the man who makes a graven or molten image" (Sotah 32a and 37b). This would accord with the wording of Verses 12 and 13 and Chapter 11:29, and also with the statement in the Book of Joshua (8:33): "As Moses, the servant of God, had commanded that they should first bless the people of Israel."

15–25. . . . These are the sins that, as a rule, elude the attention of human courts of justice. In Verses 15 and 24 this thought is expressed by the apposition of the word בַּסָּתֶר ["in secret"]. It is true that the other sins upon which the curse has been placed are also of a kind that, as a rule, remain secret because of their nature. But the express use of the term בַּסָּתֶר at the beginning and again at the end of this series of sins is intended to stress that the secret character of these particular offenses is considered especially deserving of a curse. Thus, the curse would affect particularly those who practice moral and social abominations beneath the cloak of outward respectability.

Seen in this context, the thought conveyed by these curses would be as follows:

ארור *[Cursed is].* All growth, prosperity and success will be withheld from the following: One who outwardly acts the pious man, devoted to God, but who privately denies that God is the sole existing Deity and that He reigns supreme to the exclusion of all else; one who shows respect to his parents in public but in reality despises them; one who cultivates a reputation for honesty but who, when he is unobserved, infringes upon the rights of his neighbor to his own advantage; one who, in the presence of men of wisdom and insight, waxes lyrical over the need to promote the welfare of others, but in fact brings misfortune upon the short-sighted and the credulous; one who grovels before the high and the mighty but removes himself from the weak and the helpless whom it would be his human duty to assist; the hypocrite who poses as a highly respectable member of society but whose private life is lewd (Verses 20–24); one who will not openly point his dagger at his neighbor, but nonetheless kills the latter's happiness, peace of mind and personal dignity by innuendos in his conversations with others; one who enjoys a position of trust in his community and abuses it

אָמֵן׃ ס כג אָרוּר שֹׁכֵב עִם־חֹתַנְתּוֹ וְאָמַר כָּל־
הָעָם אָמֵן׃ ס כד אָרוּר מַכֵּה רֵעֵהוּ בַּסָּתֶר
וְאָמַר כָּל־הָעָם אָמֵן׃ ס כה אָרוּר לֹקֵחַ שֹׁחַד
לְהַכּוֹת נֶפֶשׁ דַּם נָקִי וְאָמַר כָּל־הָעָם אָמֵן׃ ס
כו אָרוּר אֲשֶׁר לֹא־יָקִים אֶת־דִּבְרֵי הַתּוֹרָה־

shall say: 'Amen.' 23. 'Cursed is he
who lies with his mother-in-law!' And all
the people shall say: 'Amen.' 24. 'Cursed
is he who strikes down his neighbor in
secret!' And all the people shall say: 'Amen.'
25. 'Cursed is he who takes a bribe to
strike down a man, innocent blood.' And
all the people shall say: 'Amen.'
26. 'Cursed is he who does not uphold
the words of this Teaching, to carry

by undercover acts of corruption; and finally, even one who, though he himself is faithful to his duty [in his personal observance of the Law], stands idly by while loyalty to the Law declines among his contemporaries, near or far.

° ° °

who strikes down his neighbor in secret. He strikes down his neighbor without the latter being aware of it or knowing from where the blow came. This is the blow struck by an evil tongue, לְשׁוֹן הָרָע, which is beyond the reach of human courts of justice, but which undermines the happiness, peace and personal dignity of its victim. This is one offense which, like no other, can become a habitual vice, practiced any day and at any hour. Therefore, the form used in this verse is not the verb מַכֶּה, which could also denote a one-time offense, but the noun מַכֵּה [lit., "the striker"], an epithet for an individual with whom scandal-mongering has become a habit—indeed, part of his character. The word—and the curse—refers not to isolated violations of the prohibition against evil gossip, but to habitual scandal-mongering that has become the offender's second nature.

26. **אֲשֶׁר לֹא יָקִים** ***[who does not uphold].*** The text does not read אֲשֶׁר לֹא יַעֲשֶׂה ["... who does not *carry out* (the words of this Teaching)"], which already would mean that even failure to observe just one of the commandments would be subject to a curse. Rather, the text reads: "... who does *not uphold* the words of this Teaching, *to carry them out*." The curse applies to anyone who does not "uphold" the words of the תּוֹרָה; i.e., anyone who says that even so much as one word of God's Law is no longer binding. It applies to anyone who persuades himself, or allows himself to be persuaded by others, that the Law no longer "stands"; that it has lost its significance and validity (Naḥmanides). It applies also to anyone who does not do his part to uphold the Law, so that it will be observed; one who does not, wherever he can, labor with all his might that others, too, should observe the Law. A man is subject to the curse also if he himself studied and taught [the Law] and observed both the commandments and the prohibitions but failed to influence and encourage others to do likewise, although he was in a position to do so (Tosefoth Sota 37b, according to Jerusalem Talmud).

It seems conspicuous that in this list of pronouncements, the series of curses referring to social transgressions (Verses 17 through 19 and 24 through 26) is interrupted (Verses 20 through 23) by curses referring to sexual transgressions. Logically, one might have expected the curses upon "one who strikes down his neighbor" and "one who takes a bribe..." to follow immediately after the curse upon "one who twists the justice of an orphaned stranger...." It seems, however, that these secret sexual aberrations were interpolated into the series of social transgressions for a specific purpose. The intention was to show that both these types of sin are equally serious, and to disabuse us of the following two notions: That (1) while social sins such as moving one's neighbor's boundary marker, misleading a blind man and perverting the justice due to an orphaned stranger or a widow, etc., are indeed a menace to society as a whole, sexual offenses are less serious because they may, at the most, undermine the happiness of a few individuals but do not affect the public welfare; or that (2) while sexual offenses should indeed weigh heavily upon the conscience of Jews, other types of transgression, such as moving one's neighbor's boundary marker or evil gossip, etc., are not so serious. The fact that both types of transgression are intermingled in the list should effectively refute both of these notions....

As already noted, the Pentateuchal text mentions only the curses, but in fact they were preceded by blessings upon those who did not commit the sins enumerated in the text as subject to the curse. "Blessed is he who does *not* make..." Except for the last one [Verse 26], all the sins that come under the curse are active violations of prohibitions in God's Law. Thus, the promises of blessings (בָּרוּךְ) apply even to one who does nothing more than abstain from acts prohibited by the Law. Blessings and prosperity are promised to the following: one who does not cherish idolatrous notions even in secret; one who does not think of his parents in disrespectful terms even in his secret heart; one who commits no unjust or illegal act against his neighbor them out!' And all the people shall say: 'Amen.'"

XXVIII

1. And it will come to pass if you will hearken, hearken ever more earnestly to the voice of *God*, your God, punctiliously to carry out all His commandments that I command you today: *God*, your God, will set you on high, high above all the nations of the earth.   2. All these blessings will come upon you and overtake you if you will hearken to the voice of *God*, your God. 3. Blessed will you be in the city, and blessed will you be in the field.   4. Blessed

הַזֹּאת לַעֲשׂוֹת אוֹתָם וְאָמַר כָּל־הָעָם אָמֵן: פ
כח א וְהָיָה אִם־שָׁמוֹעַ תִּשְׁמַע בְּקוֹל יְהֹוָה
אֱלֹהֶיךָ לִשְׁמֹר לַעֲשׂוֹת אֶת־כָּל־מִצְוֹתָיו אֲשֶׁר
אָנֹכִי מְצַוְּךָ הַיּוֹם וּנְתָנְךָ יְהֹוָה אֱלֹהֶיךָ עֶלְיוֹן
עַל כָּל־גּוֹיֵי הָאָרֶץ: ב וּבָאוּ עָלֶיךָ כָּל־הַבְּרָכוֹת
הָאֵלֶּה וְהִשִּׂיגֻךָ כִּי תִשְׁמַע בְּקוֹל יְהֹוָה אֱלֹהֶיךָ:
ג בָּרוּךְ אַתָּה בָּעִיר וּבָרוּךְ אַתָּה בַּשָּׂדֶה:

even when he is unobserved; one who does not permit himself to commit acts of sexual immorality even in private, etc.

Herein lies a message of infinite comfort: Our prospects of receiving blessings are much greater than our chances of being cursed. We are cursed only if we actually commit an evil act. Abstention from acts deserving of a curse is sufficient to bring blessings upon us. Only the final verse, "Cursed is he who does not uphold. . ." pronounces a curse on a failure on our part to act, promising us God's blessing only if we take positive action: "Blessed is he who upholds the words of this Teaching, to carry them out." This is so because the question here is a basic one; namely, whether one is, or is not, willing and ready to acknowledge that the Law is binding upon all, and to uphold it. Under these circumstances, failure to act is a sin deserving of a curse, and God's blessing will come only if everyone actively does his share to make certain that the Law, which is everlasting, will also be recognized and observed for all time to come.

CHAPTER XXVIII

1. *And it will come to pass.* In the preceding chapter the nation was appointed as the guardian of the Law. As such, it was commanded, immediately upon its entry into the Land, and even before it would take possession of the Land and apportion it among the tribes, to inscribe the Law upon rocks that were to be used to build an altar and a memorial. The purpose of this act was to consecrate and to proclaim the Land as the soil of the Law, and to make it clear to each and every member of the nation that, even though he will now live on his own, he will still be subject to the sovereignty of God, Who will bless or curse him depending on whether or not he will fulfill the duties that have been assigned him by God's Law.

In the present chapter, Moses describes the future that awaits the entire nation if it will observe the Law,

or if it will fail to do so. He enumerates the blessings that the nation as a whole may expect if it remains faithful to the Law and, on the other hand, the curse that will befall it if it will break faith with the Law of God. A similar prediction of encouragement and admonition concerning the nation's future had already been delivered at the conclusion of the Book of Leviticus (Chapter 26). If we carefully compare these two predictions, we will note that in the first one, in Leviticus, the prosperity or adversity awaiting the nation is depicted primarily in terms of the nation as a whole, while in the present chapter—part of the compendium intended for the nation's dispersal over its land—the future is described, rather, in terms of the individuals who belong to this nation. The stress here is on the effect which the prosperity or the misfortunes of the nation will have on its individual members, so that each and every member of the national entity will clearly understand how he will be personally affected by the blessings or the curses that come upon his nation.

This approach accords entirely with the general tendency in מִשְׁנֵה תּוֹרָה [Deuteronomy; literally, "the Repetition of the Law"] to stress the collective responsibility of the individual members of the nation for one another, which was so solemnly expressed in the concluding verse of the preceding chapter: "Cursed is he who does not uphold. . . ." Thus the duty is imposed on every member of the nation not only to accept and observe the Law himself, but also to actively promote the wider observance of God's Law among his contemporaries. The formulation of the warning that now follows places added stress on this collective responsibility by impressing upon each member of the nation that whenever he promotes loyalty to the Law among the other members of his nation, he only ensures his own personal welfare, and that, conversely, whenever he is indifferent to instances of defection among his brethren, he is only contributing to his own ruin.

* * *

ד בָּר֥וּךְ פְּרִֽי־בִטְנְךָ֖ וּפְרִ֣י אַדְמָתְךָ֑ וּפְרִ֣י
בְהֶמְתֶּ֑ךָ שְׁגַ֥ר אֲלָפֶ֖יךָ וְעַשְׁתְּר֥וֹת צֹאנֶֽךָ׃ ה בָּר֥וּךְ
טַנְאֲךָ֖ וּמִשְׁאַרְתֶּֽךָ׃ ו בָּר֥וּךְ אַתָּ֖ה בְּבֹאֶ֑ךָ וּבָר֥וּךְ
אַתָּ֖ה בְּצֵאתֶֽךָ׃ ששי ז יִתֵּ֨ן יְהוָ֤ה אֶת־אֹֽיְבֶ֙יךָ֙
הַקָּמִ֣ים עָלֶ֔יךָ נִגָּפִ֖ים לְפָנֶ֑יךָ בְּדֶ֤רֶךְ אֶחָד֙ יֵצְא֣וּ
אֵלֶ֔יךָ וּבְשִׁבְעָ֥ה דְרָכִ֖ים יָנ֥וּסוּ לְפָנֶֽיךָ׃ ח יְצַ֨ו
יְהוָ֤ה אִתְּךָ֙ אֶת־הַבְּרָכָ֔ה בַּאֲסָמֶ֕יךָ וּבְכֹ֖ל מִשְׁלַ֣ח
יָדֶ֑ךָ וּבֵ֣רַכְךָ֔ בָּאָ֕רֶץ אֲשֶׁר־יְהוָ֥ה אֱלֹהֶ֖יךָ נֹתֵ֥ן לָֽךְ׃
ט יְקִֽימְךָ֨ יְהוָ֥ה לוֹ֙ לְעַ֣ם קָד֔וֹשׁ כַּאֲשֶׁ֖ר נִֽשְׁבַּֽע־
לָ֑ךְ כִּ֣י תִשְׁמֹ֗ר אֶת־מִצְוֺת֙ יְהוָ֣ה אֱלֹהֶ֔יךָ וְהָלַכְתָּ֖
בִּדְרָכָֽיו׃ י וְרָאוּ֙ כָּל־עַמֵּ֣י הָאָ֔רֶץ כִּ֛י שֵׁ֥ם יְהוָ֖ה
נִקְרָ֣א עָלֶ֑יךָ וְיָֽרְא֖וּ מִמֶּֽךָּ׃ יא וְהוֹתִֽרְךָ֤ יְהוָה֙
לְטוֹבָ֔ה בִּפְרִ֧י בִטְנְךָ֛ וּבִפְרִ֥י בְהֶמְתְּךָ֖ וּבִפְרִ֣י
אַדְמָתֶ֑ךָ עַ֚ל הָאֲדָמָ֔ה אֲשֶׁ֨ר נִשְׁבַּ֧ע יְהוָ֛ה
לַאֲבֹתֶ֖יךָ לָ֥תֶת לָֽךְ׃ יב יִפְתַּ֣ח יְהוָ֣ה ׀ לְ֠ךָ֠ אֶת־
אוֹצָר֨וֹ הַטּ֜וֹב אֶת־הַשָּׁמַ֗יִם לָתֵ֤ת מְטַר־אַרְצְךָ֙
בְּעִתּ֔וֹ וּלְבָרֵ֕ךְ אֵ֖ת כָּל־מַעֲשֵׂ֣ה יָדֶ֑ךָ וְהִלְוִ֙יתָ֙ גּוֹיִ֣ם
רַבִּ֔ים וְאַתָּ֖ה לֹ֥א תִלְוֶֽה׃ יג וּנְתָֽנְךָ֨ יְהוָ֤ה לְרֹאשׁ֙
וְלֹ֣א לְזָנָ֔ב וְהָיִ֙יתָ֙ רַ֣ק לְמַ֔עְלָה וְלֹ֥א תִהְיֶ֖ה לְמָ֑טָּה
כִּֽי־תִשְׁמַ֞ע אֶל־מִצְוֺ֣ת ׀ יְהוָ֣ה אֱלֹהֶ֗יךָ אֲשֶׁ֨ר
אָנֹכִ֧י מְצַוְּךָ֛ הַיּ֖וֹם לִשְׁמֹ֥ר וְלַעֲשֽׂוֹת׃ יד וְלֹ֣א
תָס֗וּר מִכָּל־הַדְּבָרִים֙ אֲשֶׁ֨ר אָנֹכִ֜י מְצַוֶּ֥ה אֶתְכֶ֛ם
הַיּ֖וֹם יָמִ֣ין וּשְׂמֹ֑אול לָלֶ֗כֶת אַחֲרֵ֛י אֱלֹהִ֥ים
אֲחֵרִ֖ים לְעָבְדָֽם׃ פ טו וְהָיָ֗ה אִם־לֹ֤א תִשְׁמַע֙

will be the fruit of your body and the fruit of your soil and the fruit of your livestock, the litter of your cattle and the riches of your sheep.
5. Blessed will be your basket and your [kneading] trough.
6. Blessed will you be when you come in, and blessed will you be when you go out.
7. *God* will deliver your enemies that rise up against you, beaten before you; they will march against you upon one road, and they will flee before you upon seven roads.
8. *God* will command the blessing with you in your storehouses and in everything to which you will put your hand, and He will bless you in the land that *God*, your God, is giving you.
9. Thus will *God* raise you up for Himself as a holy nation, as He swore to you, if you will keep the commandments of *God*, your God, and walk in His ways;
10. and all the peoples of the earth will see that the Name of *God* is called upon you, and they will be afraid of you.
11. *God* will mark you out for goodness in the fruit of your body, in the fruit of your livestock and in the fruit of your soil, upon the soil that *God* has sworn to your fathers to give to you.
12. *God* will open to you His best treasure, the heaven, to give to you the rain of your land in its season and to bless all the work of your hand. You will lend to many nations but you will not borrow.
13. *God* will make you a head and not a tail; you will be only above and not below, if you will hearken to the commandments of *God*, your God, which I command you today—to keep them and to carry them out—
14. and if you will not turn aside from all the words which I command you today, neither to the right nor to the left, to follow other gods to serve them.
15. But it shall come to pass

9–10. . . . God's wish is to mark you for Himself; that is, for His purposes on behalf of mankind. He wishes to have you be a holy nation, a nation belonging to Him; a nation that keeps far away from all things base and vulgar; a nation doing only what is morally good; a model nation—so that all the other nations may *see* that the Name of God has been called upon you. Let all the nations of the world see what it really means to be "the people of God"; what it means if an entire nation—all its members, great and small—subordinates its existence and its aspirations, both as individuals and as a nation, entirely to the will of God. Let them see the blessings and the power that will come to such a nation—a *tefillin*-bearing nation, as the Sages put it (Menaḥoth 35b).

and they will be afraid of you. Your moral greatness and historic splendor will shine forth to them in such majesty that all the nations will feel their own power and glory fade away before a nation of such greatness and might as yours.

° ° °

if you will not hearken to the voice of *God*, your God, to carry out punctiliously all His commandments and His laws that I command you today: then all these curses will come upon you and overtake you. 16. Cursed will you be in the city, and cursed will you be in the field. 17. Cursed will be your basket and your [kneading] trough. 18. Cursed will be the fruit of your body and the fruit of your soil, the litter of your livestock and the riches of your sheep. 19. Cursed will you be when you come in, and cursed will you be when you go out. 20. *God* will unleash against you the curse, restlessness, and a feeling of guilt in everything to which you will put your hand, so that you will be destroyed and perish quickly because of the wickedness of your doings in that you have forsaken Me. 21. *God* will make the pestilence cling to you until He wipes you out from the soil to which you are now coming to take possession of it. 22. *God* will strike you with consumption and with the heat of fever, with inflammation and with parchedness, and with a drying up of sap; with a wasting away and with chlorosis; these will pursue you until you perish. 23. Your heavens that are above your head will be brass, and the earth that is beneath you will be iron. 24. *God* will give the rainfall of your land in the form of dust and earth; it will come down upon you from heaven until you are destroyed. 25. *God* will cause you to be beaten before your enemies; you will march against him upon one road, and you will flee before him upon seven roads, so that you will become a horror to all the kingdoms of the earth. 26. Your corpse shall remain as

בְּקוֹל יְהֹוָה אֱלֹהֶיךָ לִשְׁמֹר לַעֲשׂוֹת אֶת־כָּל־מִצְוֹתָיו וְחֻקֹּתָיו אֲשֶׁר אָנֹכִי מְצַוְּךָ הַיּוֹם וּבָאוּ עָלֶיךָ כָּל־הַקְּלָלוֹת הָאֵלֶּה וְהִשִּׂיגוּךָ: טז אָרוּר אַתָּה בָּעִיר וְאָרוּר אַתָּה בַּשָּׂדֶה: יז אָרוּר טַנְאֲךָ וּמִשְׁאַרְתֶּךָ: יח אָרוּר פְּרִי־בִטְנְךָ וּפְרִי אַדְמָתֶךָ שְׁגַר אֲלָפֶיךָ וְעַשְׁתְּרֹת צֹאנֶךָ: יט אָרוּר אַתָּה בְּבֹאֶךָ וְאָרוּר אַתָּה בְּצֵאתֶךָ: כ יְשַׁלַּח יְהֹוָה בְּךָ אֶת־הַמְּאֵרָה אֶת־הַמְּהוּמָה וְאֶת־הַמִּגְעֶרֶת בְּכָל־מִשְׁלַח יָדְךָ אֲשֶׁר תַּעֲשֶׂה עַד הִשָּׁמֶדְךָ וְעַד־אֲבָדְךָ מַהֵר מִפְּנֵי רֹעַ מַעֲלָלֶיךָ אֲשֶׁר עֲזַבְתָּנִי: כא יַדְבֵּק יְהֹוָה בְּךָ אֶת־הַדָּבֶר עַד כַּלֹּתוֹ אֹתְךָ מֵעַל הָאֲדָמָה אֲשֶׁר־אַתָּה בָא־שָׁמָּה לְרִשְׁתָּהּ: כב יַכְּכָה יְהֹוָה בַּשַּׁחֶפֶת וּבַקַּדַּחַת וּבַדַּלֶּקֶת וּבַחַרְחֻר וּבַחֶרֶב וּבַשִּׁדָּפוֹן וּבַיֵּרָקוֹן וּרְדָפוּךָ עַד אָבְדֶךָ: כג וְהָיוּ שָׁמֶיךָ אֲשֶׁר עַל־רֹאשְׁךָ נְחֹשֶׁת וְהָאָרֶץ אֲשֶׁר־תַּחְתֶּיךָ בַּרְזֶל: כד יִתֵּן יְהֹוָה אֶת־מְטַר אַרְצְךָ אָבָק וְעָפָר מִן־הַשָּׁמַיִם יֵרֵד עָלֶיךָ עַד הִשָּׁמְדָךְ: כה יִתֶּנְךָ יְהֹוָה נִגָּף לִפְנֵי אֹיְבֶיךָ בְּדֶרֶךְ אֶחָד תֵּצֵא אֵלָיו וּבְשִׁבְעָה דְרָכִים תָּנוּס לְפָנָיו וְהָיִיתָ לְזַעֲוָה לְכֹל מַמְלְכוֹת הָאָרֶץ: כו וְהָיְתָה נִבְלָתְךָ

17 and 18. The blessings of God that will bring joy to those loyal to their duty will become apparent immediately, first in the flourishing of all the children and of all living things, and thereafter in an abundance of crops that will make this flourishing life possible. First, "blessed will be the fruit of your body," and thereafter "blessed will be your basket and your (kneading) trough." The reverse will be true in the adversity that will strike if the nation defects from God's Law. The curse will not immediately affect living things. It will first be felt, by way of warning, in "your basket and

your (kneading) trough." Only after that will it strike "the fruit of your body. . . ."

21. **God *will make the pestilence cling to you.*** The possibility should not be ruled out that the inner unrest and guilt feelings that would plague the nation would intensify the effects of the pestilence to a point where the disease would become devastating. Conversely, peace of mind and trust in God could bolster the nation's psychological resistance to the ravages of the disease.

food for all the fowl of the heaven and for the beast[s] of the earth, and there will be no one to frighten them away.　27. *God* will strike you with the boil[s] of Mitzrayim and with hemorrhoids, with oozing and dry scabs of which you cannot be cured. 28. *God* will strike you with insanity and with blindness and with mental confusion. 29. You will grope about at noontime as the blind man gropes in the darkness, and you will not carry your ways to a successful conclusion; you will only be cheated and robbed all the time, and there will be no one to help you.　30. You will betroth a woman and another man will cohabit with her; you will build a house, and you will not live in it; you will plant a vineyard, and you will not enjoy its first vintage.　31. Your ox will be slaughtered before your eyes, and you will not eat any of it; your donkey will be snatched from before you, and it will not return; your sheep will be given to your enemies, and there will be no one to help you.　32. Your sons and your daughters will be given to another people, and your eyes will see it and languish for them all day long, but your hand will be powerless. 33. The fruit of your soil and [that of] your toil, a people that you do not know will consume, and so you will only be cheated and crushed all the time,　34. and you will go insane from the sight of your eyes that you will see.　35. *God* will strike you with evil boil[s] on [your] knees and thighs, of which you cannot be cured, from the sole of your foot to the crown of your head. 36. *God* will lead you and your king, whom you will set above yourself, to a nation neither you nor your fathers have known, and there you will serve other gods,

לְמַאֲכָ֗ל לְכָל־ע֥וֹף הַשָּׁמַ֖יִם וּלְבֶהֱמַ֣ת הָאָ֑רֶץ וְאֵ֖ין מַחֲרִֽיד: כז יַכְּכָ֨ה יְהֹוָ֜ה בִּשְׁחִ֤ין מִצְרַ֙יִם֙ וּבַעֳפָלִ֔ים (ובטחרים קרי) וּבַגָּרָ֖ב וּבֶחָ֑רֶס אֲשֶׁ֥ר לֹא־תוּכַ֖ל לְהֵרָפֵֽא: כח יַכְּכָ֣ה יְהֹוָ֔ה בְּשִׁגָּע֖וֹן וּבְעִוָּר֑וֹן וּבְתִמְה֖וֹן לֵבָֽב: כט וְהָיִ֜יתָ מְמַשֵּׁ֣שׁ בַּֽצׇהֳרַ֗יִם כַּאֲשֶׁ֨ר יְמַשֵּׁ֤שׁ הַֽעִוֵּר֙ בָּֽאֲפֵלָ֔ה וְלֹ֥א תַצְלִ֖יחַ אֶת־דְּרָכֶ֑יךָ וְהָיִ֜יתָ אַ֣ךְ עָשׁ֤וּק וְגָזוּל֙ כָּל־ הַיָּמִ֔ים וְאֵ֖ין מוֹשִֽׁיעַ: ל אִשָּׁ֣ה תְאָרֵ֗שׂ וְאִ֤ישׁ אַחֵר֙ יִשְׁגָּלֶ֔נָּה (ישכבנה קרי) בַּ֥יִת תִּבְנֶ֖ה וְלֹא־ תֵשֵׁ֣ב בּ֑וֹ כֶּ֥רֶם תִּטַּ֖ע וְלֹ֥א תְחַלְּלֶֽנּוּ: לא שׁ֣וֹרְךָ֤ טָב֙וּחַ֙ לְעֵינֶ֔יךָ וְלֹ֥א תֹאכַ֖ל מִמֶּ֑נּוּ חֲמֹֽרְךָ֙ גָּז֣וּל מִלְּפָנֶ֔יךָ וְלֹ֥א יָשׁ֖וּב לָ֑ךְ צֹֽאנְךָ֙ נְתֻנ֣וֹת לְאֹֽיְבֶ֔יךָ וְאֵ֥ין לְךָ֖ מוֹשִֽׁיעַ: לב בָּנֶ֨יךָ וּבְנֹתֶ֜יךָ נְתֻנִ֣ים לְעַ֣ם אַחֵ֗ר וְעֵינֶ֤יךָ רֹאוֹת֙ וְכָל֣וֹת אֲלֵיהֶ֔ם כָּל־הַיּ֑וֹם וְאֵ֥ין לְאֵ֖ל יָדֶֽךָ: לג פְּרִ֤י אַדְמָֽתְךָ֙ וְכָל־יְגִיעֲךָ֔ יֹאכַ֥ל עַ֖ם אֲשֶׁ֣ר לֹא־יָדָ֑עְתָּ וְהָיִ֗יתָ רַ֛ק עָשׁ֥וּק וְרָצ֖וּץ כָּל־הַיָּמִֽים: לד וְהָיִ֖יתָ מְשֻׁגָּ֑ע מִמַּרְאֵ֥ה עֵינֶ֖יךָ אֲשֶׁ֥ר תִּרְאֶֽה: לה יַכְּכָ֨ה יְהֹוָ֜ה בִּשְׁחִ֣ין רָ֗ע עַל־הַבִּרְכַּ֙יִם֙ וְעַל־הַשֹּׁקַ֔יִם אֲשֶׁ֥ר לֹא־תוּכַ֖ל לְהֵרָפֵ֑א מִכַּ֥ף רַגְלְךָ֖ וְעַ֥ד קָדְקֳדֶֽךָ: לו יוֹלֵ֨ךְ יְהֹוָ֜ה אֹֽתְךָ֗ וְאֶֽת־מַלְכְּךָ֙ אֲשֶׁ֣ר תָּקִ֣ים עָלֶ֔יךָ אֶל־גּ֕וֹי אֲשֶׁ֥ר לֹא־יָדַ֖עְתָּ אַתָּ֣ה וַאֲבֹתֶ֑יךָ וְעָבַ֥דְתָּ שָּׁ֖ם

---

36. **and there you will serve.** As is clear from the context, this does not mean that the people of Israel will literally become idol worshippers. Rather, it is an allusion, in general terms, to the fate that will befall Israel in exile. The nations whose subjects Israel will become, and whose ideas and attitudes will determine Israel's future fate, are under the sway of paganism, so that all their lives and actions are guided by the influence they impute to their idols. Thus, Israel will become enslaved by paganism. It had defected from the service of the

One sole God; therefore it must now feel the impact of the error and corruption into which the hearts and minds of men will fall if they allow pagan ideas to influence their thoughts and emotions, their attitudes and their actions. All the bitterness of Israel's future centuries in exile resulted from the fact that Israel's fate became dependent on men to whom the truth of monotheism meant nothing, and whom monotheism, therefore, could not educate to become truly human. . . .

wood and stone.   37. But you will become a desolation, as an example and object lesson among all the peoples to which *God* will lead you.   38. You will take much seed out into the field, and you will bring little back because the locust will pick it off. 39. You will plant vineyards and work hard to cultivate them, but you will not drink the wine, nor gather [the grapes] because the worm[s] will eat it.   40. You will have olive trees throughout your territory, but you will not anoint yourself with oil because your olive tree will cast off its fruit.   41. You will beget sons and daughters, but they will not remain yours because they will go into captivity. 42. All your trees and the fruit of your soil will be possessed entirely by the swarm of locusts.   43. The stranger that dwells in your midst will rise higher and higher above you, and you will descend lower and lower.   44. He will lend to you, [but] you will have nothing to lend him; he will be the head, and you will be the tail. 45. And all these curses will come upon you and pursue you and overtake you until you are destroyed, because you did not hearken to the voice of *God,* your God, to keep His commandments and His laws that He commanded you.   46. And so they shall be upon you as a sign and as an instructive wonder, and upon your descendants, forever.   47. Since you did not serve *God,* your God, with joy and with gladness of heart, by reason of abundance in all things;   48. therefore you will serve your enemies, whom *God* will send against you, in hunger and in thirst, in nakedness and in want of all things, and He will place a yoke of iron upon your neck until He has destroyed you.   49. *God* will bring upon you a nation from afar, from the ends of the earth, swooping down like an eagle; a nation whose language you will not understand; 50. a nation of harsh countenance that has no consideration for the aged and shows no favor to the young.   51. It will eat the fruit of your livestock and the fruit of your soil until you are destroyed, because it will not leave you grain, wine or oil, nor the litter of your cattle, nor the riches of your sheep, until it has caused you to perish. 52. It will lay siege to you in all your

אֱלֹהִים אֲחֵרִים עֵץ וָאָבֶן: לז וְהָיִיתָ לְשַׁמָּה לְמָשָׁל וְלִשְׁנִינָה בְּכֹל הָעַמִּים אֲשֶׁר־יְנַהֶגְךָ יְהוָה שָׁמָּה: לח זֶרַע רַב תּוֹצִיא הַשָּׂדֶה וּמְעַט תֶּאֱסֹף כִּי יַחְסְלֶנּוּ הָאַרְבֶּה: לט כְּרָמִים תִּטַּע וְעָבָדְתָּ וְיַיִן לֹא־תִשְׁתֶּה וְלֹא תֶאֱגֹר כִּי תֹאכְלֶנּוּ הַתֹּלָעַת: מ זֵיתִים יִהְיוּ לְךָ בְּכָל־גְּבוּלֶךָ וְשֶׁמֶן לֹא תָסוּךְ כִּי יִשַּׁל זֵיתֶךָ: מא בָּנִים וּבָנוֹת תּוֹלִיד וְלֹא־יִהְיוּ לָךְ כִּי יֵלְכוּ בַּשֶּׁבִי: מב כָּל־עֵצְךָ וּפְרִי אַדְמָתֶךָ יְיָרֵשׁ הַצְּלָצַל: מג הַגֵּר אֲשֶׁר בְּקִרְבְּךָ יַעֲלֶה עָלֶיךָ מַעְלָה מָּעְלָה וְאַתָּה תֵרֵד מַטָּה מָּטָּה: מד הוּא יַלְוְךָ וְאַתָּה לֹא תַלְוֶנּוּ הוּא יִהְיֶה לְרֹאשׁ וְאַתָּה תִּהְיֶה לְזָנָב: מה וּבָאוּ עָלֶיךָ כָּל־הַקְּלָלוֹת הָאֵלֶּה וּרְדָפוּךָ וְהִשִּׂיגוּךָ עַד הִשָּׁמְדָךְ כִּי־לֹא שָׁמַעְתָּ בְּקוֹל יְהוָה אֱלֹהֶיךָ לִשְׁמֹר מִצְוֹתָיו וְחֻקֹּתָיו אֲשֶׁר צִוָּךְ: מו וְהָיוּ בְךָ לְאוֹת וּלְמוֹפֵת וּבְזַרְעֲךָ עַד־עוֹלָם: מז תַּחַת אֲשֶׁר לֹא־עָבַדְתָּ אֶת־יְהוָה אֱלֹהֶיךָ בְּשִׂמְחָה וּבְטוּב לֵבָב מֵרֹב כֹּל: מח וְעָבַדְתָּ אֶת־אֹיְבֶיךָ אֲשֶׁר יְשַׁלְּחֶנּוּ יְהוָה בָּךְ בְּרָעָב וּבְצָמָא וּבְעֵירֹם וּבְחֹסֶר כֹּל וְנָתַן עֹל בַּרְזֶל עַל־צַוָּארֶךָ עַד הִשְׁמִידוֹ אֹתָךְ: מט יִשָּׂא יְהוָה עָלֶיךָ גּוֹי מֵרָחֹק מִקְצֵה הָאָרֶץ כַּאֲשֶׁר יִדְאֶה הַנָּשֶׁר גּוֹי אֲשֶׁר לֹא־תִשְׁמַע לְשֹׁנוֹ: נ גּוֹי עַז פָּנִים אֲשֶׁר לֹא־יִשָּׂא פָנִים לְזָקֵן וְנַעַר לֹא יָחֹן: נא וְאָכַל פְּרִי בְהֶמְתְּךָ וּפְרִי־אַדְמָתְךָ עַד הִשָּׁמְדָךְ אֲשֶׁר לֹא־יַשְׁאִיר לְךָ דָּגָן תִּירוֹשׁ וְיִצְהָר שְׁגַר אֲלָפֶיךָ וְעַשְׁתְּרֹת צֹאנֶךָ עַד הַאֲבִידוֹ אֹתָךְ: נב וְהֵצַר לְךָ בְּכָל־שְׁעָרֶיךָ עַד

gates until your high and fortified walls—in which you put your trust—will come down throughout your land; it will lay siege to you in all your gates throughout your land that *God,* your God, has given you.
53. You will eat the fruit of your own body, the flesh of your own sons and daughters whom *God,* your God, has given you, in the siege and the oppression with which your enemy will oppress you.
54. The most delicate man among you and the most self-indulgent will cast a grudging eye upon his brother, upon his bosom wife, upon the remnant of his children whom he has left over,
55. so that he will not give to any one of them the flesh of his children whom he will eat because he will have nothing else left in the siege and in the oppression with which your enemy will oppress you in all your gates.
56. The most delicate woman among you and the most self-indulgent, who otherwise would not even attempt to set the sole of her foot upon the ground because of her fastidiousness and delicacy, will cast a grudging eye upon her bosom husband; upon her son and upon her daughter;
57. upon the fruit of her [own] body; upon the children that she bears, when she eats of them in secret for utter want, in the siege and in the opression with which your enemy will oppress you in all your gates.
58. If you will not be careful to carry out all the words of this Teaching that are written in this

רֶדֶת חֹמֹתֶיךָ הַגְּבֹהֹת וְהַבְּצֻרוֹת אֲשֶׁר אַתָּה
בֹּטֵחַ בָּהֵן בְּכָל־אַרְצֶךָ וְהֵצַר לְךָ בְּכָל־שְׁעָרֶיךָ
בְּכָל־אַרְצְךָ אֲשֶׁר נָתַן יְהוָה אֱלֹהֶיךָ לָךְ׃
נג וְאָכַלְתָּ פְרִי־בִטְנְךָ בְּשַׂר בָּנֶיךָ וּבְנֹתֶיךָ אֲשֶׁר
נָתַן־לְךָ יְהוָה אֱלֹהֶיךָ בְּמָצוֹר וּבְמָצוֹק אֲשֶׁר־
יָצִיק לְךָ אֹיְבֶךָ׃ נד הָאִישׁ הָרַךְ בְּךָ וְהֶעָנֹג מְאֹד
תֵּרַע עֵינוֹ בְאָחִיו וּבְאֵשֶׁת חֵיקוֹ וּבְיֶתֶר בָּנָיו
אֲשֶׁר יוֹתִיר׃ נה מִתֵּת ׀ לְאַחַד מֵהֶם מִבְּשַׂר
בָּנָיו אֲשֶׁר יֹאכֵל מִבְּלִי הִשְׁאִיר־לוֹ כֹּל בְּמָצוֹר
וּבְמָצוֹק אֲשֶׁר יָצִיק לְךָ אֹיִבְךָ בְּכָל־שְׁעָרֶיךָ׃
נו הָרַכָּה בְךָ וְהָעֲנֻגָּה אֲשֶׁר לֹא־נִסְּתָה כַף־
רַגְלָהּ הַצֵּג עַל־הָאָרֶץ מֵהִתְעַנֵּג וּמֵרֹךְ תֵּרַע
עֵינָהּ בְּאִישׁ חֵיקָהּ וּבִבְנָהּ וּבְבִתָּהּ׃
נז וּבְשִׁלְיָתָהּ הַיּוֹצֵת ׀ מִבֵּין רַגְלֶיהָ וּבְבָנֶיהָ
אֲשֶׁר תֵּלֵד כִּי־תֹאכְלֵם בְּחֹסֶר־כֹּל בַּסָּתֶר
בְּמָצוֹר וּבְמָצוֹק אֲשֶׁר יָצִיק לְךָ אֹיִבְךָ
בִּשְׁעָרֶיךָ׃ נח אִם־לֹא תִשְׁמֹר לַעֲשׂוֹת אֶת־כָּל־
דִּבְרֵי הַתּוֹרָה הַזֹּאת הַכְּתֻבִים בַּסֵּפֶר הַזֶּה

58. ***If you will not be careful.*** One thought, in the final analysis, should have deterred the nation from disobeying the Law entrusted to it in this Scripture: By virtue of His giving us the Law and our accepting it, the one sole God became ד׳ אֱלֹקֵינוּ ["*God,* our God"]. By virtue of these two acts, the One sole God—upon Whose will depends every moment of the future existence of the universe and of every creature in it—has undertaken to guide our actions and to direct our fate in a very special manner (Exodus 20:2). God therefore expects undeviating obedience from us.

This appellation, ד׳ אֱלֹקֶיךָ ["*God,* your God"] is נִכְבָּד ["to be honored"] and נוֹרָא ["to be feared"]. Its positive aspect is נִכְבָּד—weighty, full of content—even as the universe itself. God will place the world at the feet of those who will make His Name relevant to their own lives. Conversely, He will be נוֹרָא, [fear-inspiring] to those who would oppose Him. His Name ד׳ אֱלֹקֵינוּ was applied to us by virtue of the giving of the Law; we were thus placed into world history as upholders of this Name.

all the words of this Teaching that are written in this Book. Every word of this תּוֹרָה that was entrusted to each and every one of us with this Scripture teaches us nothing but how to do justice to this Name, which is to be honored and feared; a Name indelibly imprinted upon us. We must ever bear in mind the description of that nameless misery which we could call down upon our children if we should ever degrade the Name we bear. We must always remember that this Name, which is to be honored, is also to be feared, so that we will be careful to carry out all the words of this Teaching that are written in this Book, even if for no other reason but "to fear this Name (which is) to be honored and feared, the Name of *God,* your God." But even if all these warnings should be in vain; even if, unmindful of them,

Book, to fear this Name, [which is] to be
honored and feared—the Name of *God*,
your God— 59. *God*, your God, will make
your plagues and the plagues of your
descendants wondrous, sufferings great and
enduring, sicknesses evil and enduring.
60. He will bring back upon you all the
sicknesses of Mitzrayim that you dreaded,
and they will cling to you. 61. Also every
illness and every plague that is not written
down in the Book of this Teaching will *God*
bring upon you until you are destroyed.
62. And you will be left only few in
number instead [of being as] you were, like
the stars of the heaven in multitude,
because you did not hearken to the voice of
God, your God. 63. And it will come to
pass that even as *God* rejoiced over you to
do you good and to multiply you, so will
God rejoice over you to cause you to perish,
and to destroy you; and you will be snatched
from the land to which you are now going,
to take possession of it. 64. *God* will
scatter you among all the peoples, from one
end of the earth to the other end of the earth,
and there you will serve other gods whom
neither you nor your fathers have known:
wood and stone. 65. And among these
nations you will find no peace, and there
will be no place of rest for the sole of your
foot. There *God* will give you a heart full of
trembling and a languishing of the eyes and
a grieving of the soul. 66. Your life will
always hover in the balance; you will be in
terror night and day and you will have no
faith in your life. 67. In the morning you
will say: "Would that it were evening!," and
in the evening you will say: "Would that it
were morning!"—because of the terror of
your heart that will fill you, and because of
the sight of your eyes that you will see.

לְ֠יִרְאָ֞ה אֶת־הַשֵּׁ֣ם הַנִּכְבָּ֤ד וְהַנּוֹרָא֙ הַזֶּ֔ה אֵ֖ת
יְהוָ֥ה אֱלֹהֶֽיךָ׃ נט וְהִפְלָ֤א יְהוָה֙ אֶת־מַכֹּ֣תְךָ֔ וְאֵ֖ת
מַכּ֣וֹת זַרְעֶ֑ךָ מַכּ֤וֹת גְּדֹלֹת֙ וְנֶ֣אֱמָנ֔וֹת וָחֳלָיִ֥ם
רָעִ֖ים וְנֶאֱמָנִֽים׃ ס וְהֵשִׁ֣יב בְּךָ֗ אֵ֚ת כָּל־מַדְוֵ֣ה
מִצְרַ֔יִם אֲשֶׁ֥ר יָגֹ֖רְתָּ מִפְּנֵיהֶ֑ם וְדָבְק֖וּ בָּֽךְ׃ סא גַּ֤ם
כָּל־חֳלִי֙ וְכָל־מַכָּ֔ה אֲשֶׁר֙ לֹ֣א כָת֔וּב בְּסֵ֖פֶר
הַתּוֹרָ֣ה הַזֹּ֑את יַעְלֵ֤ם יְהוָה֙ עָלֶ֔יךָ עַ֖ד הִשָּׁמְדָֽךְ׃
סב וְנִשְׁאַרְתֶּם֙ בִּמְתֵ֣י מְעָ֔ט תַּ֚חַת אֲשֶׁ֣ר הֱיִיתֶ֔ם
כְּכוֹכְבֵ֥י הַשָּׁמַ֖יִם לָרֹ֑ב כִּי־לֹ֣א שָׁמַ֔עְתָּ בְּק֖וֹל
יְהוָ֥ה אֱלֹהֶֽיךָ׃ סג וְ֠הָיָה כַּאֲשֶׁר־שָׂ֨שׂ יְהוָ֜ה
עֲלֵיכֶ֗ם לְהֵיטִ֣יב אֶתְכֶם֮ וּלְהַרְבּ֣וֹת אֶתְכֶם֒ כֵּ֣ן
יָשִׂ֤ישׂ יְהוָה֙ עֲלֵיכֶ֔ם לְהַאֲבִ֥יד אֶתְכֶ֖ם וּלְהַשְׁמִ֣יד
אֶתְכֶ֑ם וְנִסַּחְתֶּם֙ מֵעַ֣ל הָאֲדָמָ֔ה אֲשֶׁר־אַתָּ֥ה בָא־
שָׁ֖מָּה לְרִשְׁתָּֽהּ׃ סד וֶהֱפִֽיצְךָ֤ יְהוָה֙ בְּכָל־הָ֣עַמִּ֔ים
מִקְצֵ֥ה הָאָ֖רֶץ וְעַד־קְצֵ֣ה הָאָ֑רֶץ וְעָבַ֨דְתָּ שָּׁ֜ם
אֱלֹהִ֤ים אֲחֵרִים֙ אֲשֶׁ֧ר לֹא־יָדַ֛עְתָּ אַתָּ֥ה וַאֲבֹתֶ֖יךָ
עֵ֥ץ וָאָֽבֶן׃ סה וּבַגּוֹיִ֤ם הָהֵם֙ לֹ֣א תַרְגִּ֔יעַ וְלֹא־
יִהְיֶ֥ה מָנ֖וֹחַ לְכַף־רַגְלֶ֑ךָ וְנָתַן֩ יְהוָ֨ה לְךָ֥ שָׁם֙ לֵ֣ב
רַגָּ֔ז וְכִלְי֥וֹן עֵינַ֖יִם וְדַאֲב֥וֹן נָֽפֶשׁ׃ סו וְהָי֣וּ חַיֶּ֔יךָ
תְּלֻאִ֥ים לְךָ֖ מִנֶּ֑גֶד וּפָֽחַדְתָּ֙ לַ֣יְלָה וְיוֹמָ֔ם וְלֹ֥א
תַאֲמִ֖ין בְּחַיֶּֽיךָ׃ סז בַּבֹּ֤קֶר תֹּאמַר֙ מִֽי־יִתֵּ֣ן עֶ֔רֶב
וּבָעֶ֥רֶב תֹּאמַ֖ר מִֽי־יִתֵּ֣ן בֹּ֑קֶר מִפַּ֤חַד לְבָֽבְךָ֙ אֲשֶׁ֣ר
תִּפְחָ֔ד וּמִמַּרְאֵ֥ה עֵינֶ֖יךָ אֲשֶׁ֥ר תִּרְאֶֽה׃

you would deny that Name by your levity and disobedience . . . then. . . .

59. **God, *your God will make your plagues . . . wondrous.*** Even then, even if you do these things, He will turn the sufferings that will strike you and your children into a פֶּלֶא [wonder], clearly demonstrating His existence and His sovereignty (see Exodus 15:11). The sufferings that will strike you will not be ordinary sufferings; they will demonstrate, in all its solemn import, "the Name (which is) to be honored and feared," but which you disregarded. Each of the extraordinary plagues that will strike you will be a sign for you that the eye of God is still upon you; a proof of the authenticity of the תּוֹרָה; an indication of the sole path that can lead to your salvation. As for the other nations of the world, your sufferings will be a sign for them of the One sole God Whom they do not know and an indication of man's duty toward Him, of which, until then, they had no idea.

68. Indeed, *God* will cause you to return to Mitzrayim in ships, in the manner of which I said to you that you will never see it again; you will there offer yourselves for sale as manservants and maidservants to your enemies, but there will be no purchaser. 69. These are the words of the Covenant which *God* commanded Moshe to establish with the sons of Yisrael in the land of Moab, besides the Covenant which He had established with them at Ḥoreb.

XXIX

1. Moshe called to all of Yisrael and said to them: You have seen all that *God* did—before your eyes in the land of Mitzrayim—to Pha-

סח וֶהֱשִׁיבְךָ֨ יְהוָ֥ה ׀ מִצְרַ֘יִם֮ בָּאֳנִיּוֹת֒ בַּדֶּ֙רֶךְ֙
אֲשֶׁ֣ר אָמַ֣רְתִּֽי לְךָ֔ לֹא־תֹסִ֥יף ע֖וֹד לִרְאֹתָ֑הּ
וְהִתְמַכַּרְתֶּ֨ם שָׁ֧ם לְאֹיְבֶ֛יךָ לַעֲבָדִ֥ים וְלִשְׁפָח֖וֹת
וְאֵ֥ין קֹנֶֽה׃ ס סט אֵלֶּה֩ דִבְרֵ֨י הַבְּרִ֜ית אֲשֶׁר־צִוָּ֧ה
יְהוָ֣ה אֶת־מֹשֶׁ֗ה לִכְרֹ֛ת אֶת־בְּנֵ֥י יִשְׂרָאֵ֖ל בְּאֶ֣רֶץ
מוֹאָ֑ב מִלְּבַ֣ד הַבְּרִ֔ית אֲשֶׁר־כָּרַ֥ת אִתָּ֖ם בְּחֹרֵֽב׃
פ שביעי כט א וַיִּקְרָ֥א מֹשֶׁ֛ה אֶל־כָּל־יִשְׂרָאֵ֖ל
וַיֹּ֣אמֶר אֲלֵהֶ֑ם אַתֶּ֣ם רְאִיתֶ֗ם אֵ֣ת כָּל־אֲשֶׁר֩
עָשָׂ֨ה יְהוָ֤ה לְעֵֽינֵיכֶם֙ בְּאֶ֣רֶץ מִצְרַ֔יִם לְפַרְעֹ֖ה

69. **אֵלֶּה** *[These].* Moses had been commanded to utter "these," the predictions of blessings and curses that comprised this entire chapter, as "words of the Covenant"; the contents of a covenant to be established with Israel "in the land of Moab," within view of the Promised Land of which they were about to take possession. This was to be a confirmation and continuation of the covenant that had already been established at Ḥoreb, the place of the giving of the Law, after the Law had been given and accepted.

Between these two covenants lay the entire period of wandering through the wilderness and the beginning of the conquest of the Land. Both these factors—Israel's forty years of wandering in the wilderness and Israel's victory over Siḥon and Og—served to complete Israel's direct experiences of God's sovereignty and presence in the destinies of men and nations in general, and of Israel in particular, beginning with the redemption from Egypt. The Children of Israel had personally experienced in their own lives God's intervention to overthrow forces of men and nature in order to save the most helpless—as He had done at crucial moments in their history, such as in the case of Egypt. But they had also seen in their own lives how He can demonstrate His most particular Providence, not only in miraculously preserving life under conditions of utter desolation, but also in guiding ordinary relations between nations, judiciously meting out victory and defeat.

These experiences were now to be applied, even before Israel entered the Land, for the purpose of renewing and confirming the covenant that had already been established for the Law. This was all the more necessary because the covenant established at Ḥoreb on the basis of the experiences of the redemption from Egypt had not been strong enough to keep the generation thus redeemed worthy of receiving the Land. By now, however, a new generation had grown up, ready to take possession of the Land — a generation which mostly knew of that redemption and that covenant only from the stories of fathers no longer alive; a generation whose own direct observations of God's workings were based only on His having led them through the wilderness and having granted them victory over Siḥon and Og.

Hence, before completing the predictions which he had been commanded to make known to the people (Deuteronomy 29:21–30:10), telling them what was in store for them because of the long periods of suffering that would be visited upon Israel, Moses now interrupts his description of the blessings and calamities, and. . . .

CHAPTER XXIX

1. ***Moshe called.*** Before continuing his description of the blessings and curses, Moses appealed to all of Israel always to bear in mind the following facts:

You have seen. Among the generation about to enter the Land there was still a large number of people who had witnessed at first hand the deliverance from Egypt. Besides the entire tribe of Levi and the women, to whom the decree of death in the wilderness had not been applicable, there were males between the ages of 40 and 60 who themselves had gone forth from Egypt. Thus there were, even in the midst of this new generation that stood before Moses, a large number of surviving eyewitnesses to the deliverance, and Moses was entirely justified in opening his address with the words "You have seen. . ."

to Pharaoh and to all his servants and to all his land. The account in the Book of Exodus relating the punishments meted out to the Egyptians specifically mentions, in addition to the king and the people, "the servants of Pharaoh," the officials of Pharaoh's court. For it is precisely such officials who, with their advice, wield the greatest influence upon the king and his decisions and, therefore, must bear prime responsibility for the right, or the wrong, that is done in the state.

raoh and to all his servants and to all his land; 2. the great acts of proof that your eyes have seen, those great signs and instructive miracles; 3. but with [all] this, *God* did not give you a heart to recognize, or eyes to see, or ears to hear, to this day. 4. Then I led you for forty years in the wilderness; your clothes did not wear out on you, and your shoes did not wear out upon your foot. 5. You neither ate bread nor drank wine and strong drink, so that you might know that אֲנִי ד׳ is your God. 6. And you came to this place, and Siḥon, king of Ḥeshbon, and Og, king of Bashan, came out against us into war, and we struck them down; 7. we took away from them their land and gave it to the Reubenite[s] and the Gaddite[s] and to half the tribe of the Menashite[s]. 8. Therefore, keep carefully the words of this Covenant and carry them out so that you may practice intelligently everything you do.

וּלְכָל־עֲבָדָיו וּלְכָל־אַרְצוֹ׃ ב הַמַּסּוֹת הַגְּדֹלֹת
אֲשֶׁר רָאוּ עֵינֶיךָ הָאֹתֹת וְהַמֹּפְתִים הַגְּדֹלִים
הָהֵם׃ ג וְלֹא־נָתַן יְהוָה לָכֶם לֵב לָדַעַת וְעֵינַיִם
לִרְאוֹת וְאָזְנַיִם לִשְׁמֹעַ עַד הַיּוֹם הַזֶּה׃ ד וָאוֹלֵךְ
אֶתְכֶם אַרְבָּעִים שָׁנָה בַּמִּדְבָּר לֹא־בָלוּ
שַׂלְמֹתֵיכֶם מֵעֲלֵיכֶם וְנַעַלְךָ לֹא־בָלְתָה מֵעַל
רַגְלֶךָ׃ ה לֶחֶם לֹא אֲכַלְתֶּם וְיַיִן וְשֵׁכָר לֹא
שְׁתִיתֶם לְמַעַן תֵּדְעוּ כִּי אֲנִי יְהוָה אֱלֹהֵיכֶם׃
מפטיר ו וַתָּבֹאוּ אֶל־הַמָּקוֹם הַזֶּה וַיֵּצֵא סִיחֹן
מֶלֶךְ־חֶשְׁבּוֹן וְעוֹג מֶלֶךְ־הַבָּשָׁן לִקְרָאתֵנוּ
לַמִּלְחָמָה וַנַּכֵּם׃ ז וַנִּקַּח אֶת־אַרְצָם וַנִּתְּנָהּ
לְנַחֲלָה לָראוּבֵנִי וְלַגָּדִי וְלַחֲצִי שֵׁבֶט הַמְנַשִּׁי׃
ח וּשְׁמַרְתֶּם אֶת־דִּבְרֵי הַבְּרִית הַזֹּאת וַעֲשִׂיתֶם
אֹתָם לְמַעַן תַּשְׂכִּילוּ אֵת כָּל־אֲשֶׁר תַּעֲשׂוּן׃ פ

4–5. . . . It required these forty years of Israel's miraculous preservation in the wilderness, "so that you might know that אֲנִי ד׳ is your God." Since Moses is the speaker, the pronoun אֲנִי ["I"] in Verse 5 cannot, of course, refer to him; therefore the words אֲנִי ד׳, together, form the subject of אֱלֹקֵיכֶם ["your God"]. . . . "So that you might know. . ." So that you might begin your future as a nation in the Land with this complete "knowledge of God.". . . .

6–7. ***And you came.*** Moreover, you have now left behind you that anomalous state of landlessness and helplessness that characterized you during your wanderings in the wilderness, and you have already begun your transition to the normal life of a people supported by its own soil. You have experienced the help of this your God, as demonstrated in the victory over the mighty kings Siḥon and Og, and in your gaining possession of their lands.

8. ***Therefore, keep carefully.*** Now, then, consider all these things that you yourselves have experienced in Egypt and in the wilderness. These experiences must have established, firmly and unshakably, your "knowledge" of God and of the almighty Providence with which He guides the fate of men and nations and brings about the fulfillment of His promises. It is in the light of these experiences that you must now consider "the words of this Covenant," the contents of this choice between prosperity and ruin that I have communicated to you as having been established by God in the same categorical manner as a בְּרִית [covenant] (Genesis 6:18). This choice is dependent solely on your conduct. Now, after all that you have experienced in your own lives, you must know that not even one word of this בְּרִית will remain unfulfilled. Therefore, "keep carefully. . .": If you know all these facts, you will never lose sight of the words of this בְּרִית, and you will use them as guidelines for everything you will do, "so that you may intelligently practice everything you do." . . . After all that you have experienced, you must indeed know that your woe or weal depends entirely on your punctilious observance of the Law.

The Haftarah for this Sidra may be found on page 917.

נצבים

NITZAVIM

9. You are standing today, all of you, before *God*, your God—your heads, your tribes, your elders and your officers; all the men of Yisrael; 10. your children, your women and he who has entered into the midst of your camps from the outside; from your woodcutter, to your water drawer— 11. so that you may pass over as one into the Covenant of *God*, your God, and into His oath that *God*, your God, makes with you today— 12. in order to raise you up today to Himself as a people, and that He may show Himself to you as a God as He promised to do, and as He swore to your fathers, Abraham, Yitzhak and Yaakov. 13. And not with you alone do I make

ט אַתֶּם נִצָּבִים הַיּוֹם כֻּלְּכֶם לִפְנֵי יְהוָה
אֱלֹהֵיכֶם רָאשֵׁיכֶם שִׁבְטֵיכֶם זִקְנֵיכֶם
וְשֹׁטְרֵיכֶם כֹּל אִישׁ יִשְׂרָאֵל׃ י טַפְּכֶם נְשֵׁיכֶם
וְגֵרְךָ אֲשֶׁר בְּקֶרֶב מַחֲנֶיךָ מֵחֹטֵב עֵצֶיךָ עַד
שֹׁאֵב מֵימֶיךָ׃ יא לְעָבְרְךָ בִּבְרִית יְהוָה אֱלֹהֶיךָ
וּבְאָלָתוֹ אֲשֶׁר יְהוָה אֱלֹהֶיךָ כֹּרֵת עִמְּךָ הַיּוֹם׃
שני יב לְמַעַן הָקִים־אֹתְךָ הַיּוֹם ׀ לוֹ לְעָם וְהוּא
יִהְיֶה־לְּךָ לֵאלֹהִים כַּאֲשֶׁר דִּבֶּר־לָךְ וְכַאֲשֶׁר
נִשְׁבַּע לַאֲבֹתֶיךָ לְאַבְרָהָם לְיִצְחָק וּלְיַעֲקֹב׃
יג וְלֹא אִתְּכֶם לְבַדְּכֶם אָנֹכִי כֹּרֵת אֶת־הַבְּרִית

9–10. ***You are standing.*** As we have noted to Chapter 28:69, Moses interrupted the predictions regarding Israel's future so that, by reminding Israel of its historical experiences, he could have the nation gain a correct understanding of the blessings and curses announced thus far. Also, he wished to add certain explanations to ensure that the nation would not misinterpret its historical experiences or its duties under the Covenant.

Verses 1 through 8 contain the facts to which Moses will make reference. The explanations then come in Verses 9 through 20. Verses 9 through 14 refute the notion that Israel's commitment to the Covenant might be limited to certain classes of the nation, to certain generations or to a certain period of time. Rather, we are told, the Covenant and the oath are applicable to each and every member of the nation and to all future generations. Verses 15 through 20 refute the notion that the predictions of blessings and curses apply only if the nation formally abandons the Law, and that therefore the individual may feel free to violate the Law in his personal life as long as the nation officially keeps faith with God and His Law. Here was the most appropriate time for dealing with this particularly dangerous error, since it was pointed out in Chapter 27 that though the members of the nation were about to disperse over the land, the nation was still bound together by ties of solidarity, so that its members were collectively responsible for the theoretical preservation and practical observance of the Law. As a consequence, no member of the nation, no matter how faithful he might be to his duty in his personal life, could consider his task fulfilled if he had not done his share also to promote the preservation and observance of the Law throughout his community.

In the same vein, as we have already noted, the blessings and curses, particularly the latter, enumerated in Chapter 28 were intended to make each and every member of the nation aware of how adversely he, too, would be affected if he were to stand idly by while the entire nation defected from the Law and was therefore threatened with collective ruin.

Conversely, there was the misinterpretation of the concept of solidarity in the opposite direction: that the individual had done enough for his personal salvation if he had duly helped preserve the Law as a communal value but had withheld his own private life from the dominion of God's Law. Such a person might be under the illusion that in this case his share in the nation's prosperity would be assured even if his personal life could not bear scrutiny by God. These illusions are destroyed in Verses 15 through 20.

° ° °

11. לְעָבְרְךָ *[so that you may pass over].* If you wish to enter into the Covenant with God, you must abandon entirely the standpoint you have held hitherto. You must pass by all other things—renounce all else—in order to enter into an exclusive relationship with God. Therefore, the text reads not לְבוֹאֲךָ ["so that you may *come*"], but לְעָבְרְךָ ["so that you may *pass over*"]. Once you have entered into the Covenant of God, your standpoint is fundamentally different from the one you held before.

this covenant and this oath,   14. but with him who is standing here with us today before *God*, our God, and with him who is not here with us today.   15. For you know how we dwelt in the land of Mitzrayim, and how we wandered through the midst of the nations through whom you passed. 16. There you saw their abominations and their depravities, wood and stone, silver and gold, that is with them.   17. Now there could be among you a man or a woman, or a family, or a tribe, whose heart turns away today from *God*, our God, to go to serve the gods of these nations; there could be among you a root that will ripen someday as a fruit of poison and wormwood. 18. Now if such a one hears the words of this oath and blesses himself in his heart, saying: "I will have happiness, even if I walk in the tenacity of my heart, so that whatever is watered will provide also for that which is [meant] to remain thirsty," 19. then *God* will not be willing to forgive him; rather, *God*'s anger and His demand for His right will become manifest in the case of this man, and the entire oath that is written in this Book will rest upon him; *God* will blot out his name from under the heaven,   20. and *God* will set him apart for evil from all the tribes of Yisrael, according to all the oaths of the Covenant that are written in this Book of the Teaching.   21. And then the later generation—your sons that will arise from those who come after you, and the stranger who comes from a distant land—

הַזֹּאת וְאֶת־הָאָלָה הַזֹּאת: יד כִּי אֶת־אֲשֶׁר יֶשְׁנוֹ פֹּה עִמָּנוּ עֹמֵד הַיּוֹם לִפְנֵי יְהֹוָה אֱלֹהֵינוּ וְאֵת אֲשֶׁר אֵינֶנּוּ פֹּה עִמָּנוּ הַיּוֹם: שלישי טו כִּי־אַתֶּם יְדַעְתֶּם אֵת אֲשֶׁר־יָשַׁבְנוּ בְּאֶרֶץ מִצְרָיִם וְאֵת אֲשֶׁר־עָבַרְנוּ בְּקֶרֶב הַגּוֹיִם אֲשֶׁר עֲבַרְתֶּם: טז וַתִּרְאוּ אֶת־שִׁקּוּצֵיהֶם וְאֵת גִּלֻּלֵיהֶם עֵץ וָאֶבֶן כֶּסֶף וְזָהָב אֲשֶׁר עִמָּהֶם: יז פֶּן־יֵשׁ בָּכֶם אִישׁ אוֹ־אִשָּׁה אוֹ מִשְׁפָּחָה אוֹ־שֵׁבֶט אֲשֶׁר לְבָבוֹ פֹנֶה הַיּוֹם מֵעִם יְהֹוָה אֱלֹהֵינוּ לָלֶכֶת לַעֲבֹד אֶת־אֱלֹהֵי הַגּוֹיִם הָהֵם פֶּן־יֵשׁ בָּכֶם שֹׁרֶשׁ פֹּרֶה רֹאשׁ וְלַעֲנָה: יח וְהָיָה בְּשָׁמְעוֹ אֶת־דִּבְרֵי הָאָלָה הַזֹּאת וְהִתְבָּרֵךְ בִּלְבָבוֹ לֵאמֹר שָׁלוֹם יִהְיֶה־לִּי כִּי בִּשְׁרִרוּת לִבִּי אֵלֵךְ לְמַעַן סְפוֹת הָרָוָה אֶת־הַצְּמֵאָה: יט לֹא־יֹאבֶה יְהֹוָה סְלֹחַ לוֹ כִּי אָז יֶעְשַׁן אַף־יְהֹוָה וְקִנְאָתוֹ בָּאִישׁ הַהוּא וְרָבְצָה בּוֹ כָּל־הָאָלָה הַכְּתוּבָה בַּסֵּפֶר הַזֶּה וּמָחָה יְהֹוָה אֶת־שְׁמוֹ מִתַּחַת הַשָּׁמָיִם: כ וְהִבְדִּילוֹ יְהֹוָה לְרָעָה מִכֹּל שִׁבְטֵי יִשְׂרָאֵל כְּכֹל אָלוֹת הַבְּרִית הַכְּתוּבָה בְּסֵפֶר הַתּוֹרָה הַזֶּה: כא וְאָמַר הַדּוֹר הָאַחֲרוֹן בְּנֵיכֶם אֲשֶׁר יָקוּמוּ מֵאַחֲרֵיכֶם וְהַנָּכְרִי אֲשֶׁר יָבֹא מֵאֶרֶץ

13–14. *And not with you alone.* Even as no limit has been placed upon the number of persons included in the covenantal oath, so, too, no limit has been set to its validity. The covenant embraces all persons that are counted among the nation of Israel, for all time to come. Thus the text unequivocally refutes the notion that the commitment to the Law is only temporary, or that anyone is ever free to withdraw from this commitment. . . .

18. . . . The idea conveyed in this verse is as follows: This person is under the illusion that the predictions of blessings and curses refer only to the conduct of the majority of the nation. He thinks, therefore, that if the nation as a whole is deserving of God's blessings

and also receives them, then no individual member of the nation will be barred from a share in the nation's prosperity. An analogous situation would be that when rain falls upon a field, the weeds, which really should not receive any water, will also benefit from the rain. רָוָה is that which is watered because it is good; צְמֵאָה refers to the weeds, which, actually, should be left to go thirsty. . . .

21–27. *And then the later generation . . . will say.* Verse 20 completes the facts and explanations interpolated so that the nation might obtain the correct understanding of the blessings or curses predicted for its future. Now Verse 21 resumes the predictions that were interrupted by Verse 69 of the preceding chapter.

רְחוֹקָה וְרָאוּ אֶת־מַכּוֹת הָאָרֶץ הַהִוא וְאֶת־
תַּחֲלֻאֶיהָ אֲשֶׁר־חִלָּה יְהוָה בָּהּ: כב גָּפְרִית
וָמֶלַח שְׂרֵפָה כָל־אַרְצָהּ לֹא תִזָּרַע וְלֹא תַצְמִחַ
וְלֹא־יַעֲלֶה בָהּ כָּל־עֵשֶׂב כְּמַהְפֵּכַת סְדֹם
וַעֲמֹרָה אַדְמָה וּצְבֹיִים (וצבוים קרי) אֲשֶׁר הָפַךְ
יְהוָה בְּאַפּוֹ וּבַחֲמָתוֹ: כג וְאָמְרוּ כָּל־הַגּוֹיִם
עַל־מֶה עָשָׂה יְהוָה כָּכָה לָאָרֶץ הַזֹּאת מֶה חֳרִי
הָאַף הַגָּדוֹל הַזֶּה: כד וְאָמְרוּ עַל אֲשֶׁר עָזְבוּ
אֶת־בְּרִית יְהוָה אֱלֹהֵי אֲבֹתָם אֲשֶׁר כָּרַת עִמָּם
בְּהוֹצִיאוֹ אֹתָם מֵאֶרֶץ מִצְרָיִם: כה וַיֵּלְכוּ
וַיַּעַבְדוּ אֱלֹהִים אֲחֵרִים וַיִּשְׁתַּחֲווּ לָהֶם אֱלֹהִים
אֲשֶׁר לֹא־יְדָעוּם וְלֹא חָלַק לָהֶם: כו וַיִּחַר־אַף
יְהוָה בָּאָרֶץ הַהִוא לְהָבִיא עָלֶיהָ אֶת־כָּל־
הַקְּלָלָה הַכְּתוּבָה בַּסֵּפֶר הַזֶּה: כז וַיִּתְּשֵׁם יְהוָה
מֵעַל אַדְמָתָם בְּאַף וּבְחֵמָה וּבְקֶצֶף גָּדוֹל
וַיַּשְׁלִכֵם (ל' רבתי) אֶל־אֶרֶץ אַחֶרֶת כַּיּוֹם הַזֶּה:
כח הַנִּסְתָּרֹת לַיהוָה אֱלֹהֵינוּ וְהַנִּגְלֹת לָנוּ
וּלְבָנֵינוּ עַד־עוֹלָם לַעֲשׂוֹת אֶת־כָּל־דִּבְרֵי
הַתּוֹרָה הַזֹּאת: ס רביעי (שני כשהן מחוברין)

will say when they see the plagues of that land and its sicknesses that *God* has brought upon it:
22. "Sulfur and salt, all the soil is burned up; it will not be sown, it will permit nothing to grow; no vegetation will rise [from] within it, as in the devastation of Sodom and Gomorrah, of Admah and Tzeboyim, which *God* devastated in His anger and indignation."
23. And then all the nations will say: "Why has *God* done thus to this land? What has caused this great anger?"
24. And then they will say: "Because they forsook the Covenant of *God*, the God of their fathers, that He established with them when He brought them out from the land of Mitzrayim;
25. and they went and served other gods and cast themselves down before them, gods of whom they had experienced nothing and whom He had not allotted to them;
26. therefore *God*'s anger was kindled against that land, to bring upon it the entire curse that is written in this Book.
27. For this reason did *God* tear them out and remove them from their soil, with anger and indignation and great outrage, and cast them into another land as it is today."
28. The secret things belong to *God*, our God, but that which has been revealed is ours and our children's forever: To carry out all the words of this Teaching.

The passage beginning with the words, "And then the later generation . . . will say. . ." is a direct continuation of the thought expressed in Verse 68. Seen in the context of the prediction already made much earlier in this Book, the catastrophe that was described up to this point and that will overtake you and your land, and the prolonged misery that will come upon both the land and the nation, will serve not only your descendants, but also all the nations of the world, as a most eloquent, spectacular proof of God and of His workings in world history (see Deuteronomy 28:46).

° ° °

that is written in this Book. The Land, the nation and this Book—these are the three factors which, inextricably linked to one another, each shedding light upon the others—are the eternal manifestations of God before the eyes of the nations to this very day.

° ° °

28. . . . In Sanhedrin 43b, the words "secret things" and "that which has been revealed" are interpreted as referring to the responsibility for the observance of the Law which, according to the solidarity established by this covenant of the Law (see Deuteronomy 27:1 and 9), devolves equally upon the entire nation and upon each one of its members. This individual and collective responsibility is expressed once again by the words "ours and our children's forever: To carry out. . . ." For these statements make every individual responsible not only for his own observance of the Law, but also for the observance of the Law throughout the nation. In the present passage, the duty of solidarity—the עֲרֵבוּת [responsibility]—the ruling that כָּל יִשְׂרָאֵל עֲרֵבִין זֶה בָּזֶה ["all Israel are responsible for one another"], is limited to "that which has been revealed," to public acts or omissions for which responsibility is shared by all those who could have used their influence to prevent violations of the Law or failure to observe a law, but did not do so; i.e., "those who would have been in a position to protest, but did not do so". . . .

XXX

1. And it will come to pass when all these words, the blessing and the curse, which I have set before you, will come upon you, that you will take it to heart in the midst of all the nations to which *God*, your God, has exiled you,   2. and you will return all the way to *God*, your God, and hearken to His voice, according to all that I command you today; you and your children, with all your heart and with all your soul.   3. And then *God*, your God, will also turn back again to seek out your exiles and have compassion upon you and will gather you together from among all the peoples to which *God*, your God, has scattered you.   4. Even if one of your exiles should be at the end of the heaven, *God*, your God, will gather you together from there and will take you to Himself from there,   5. and *God*, your God, will bring you home to the land of which your fathers once took possession; and you will take possession of it; and He will do good to you and multiply you even more than your fathers.   6. *God*, your God, will circumcise your heart and the heart of your descendants, to love *God*, your

ל א וְהָיָה כִי־יָבֹאוּ עָלֶיךָ כָּל־הַדְּבָרִים הָאֵלֶּה הַבְּרָכָה וְהַקְּלָלָה אֲשֶׁר נָתַתִּי לְפָנֶיךָ וַהֲשֵׁבֹתָ אֶל־לְבָבֶךָ בְּכָל־הַגּוֹיִם אֲשֶׁר הִדִּיחֲךָ יְהֹוָה אֱלֹהֶיךָ שָׁמָּה: ב וְשַׁבְתָּ עַד־יְהֹוָה אֱלֹהֶיךָ וְשָׁמַעְתָּ בְקֹלוֹ כְּכֹל אֲשֶׁר־אָנֹכִי מְצַוְּךָ הַיּוֹם אַתָּה וּבָנֶיךָ בְּכָל־לְבָבְךָ וּבְכָל־נַפְשֶׁךָ: ג וְשָׁב יְהֹוָה אֱלֹהֶיךָ אֶת־שְׁבוּתְךָ וְרִחֲמֶךָ וְשָׁב וְקִבֶּצְךָ מִכָּל־הָעַמִּים אֲשֶׁר הֱפִיצְךָ יְהֹוָה אֱלֹהֶיךָ שָׁמָּה: ד אִם־יִהְיֶה נִדַּחֲךָ בִּקְצֵה הַשָּׁמָיִם מִשָּׁם יְקַבֶּצְךָ יְהֹוָה אֱלֹהֶיךָ וּמִשָּׁם יִקָּחֶךָ: ה וֶהֱבִיאֲךָ יְהֹוָה אֱלֹהֶיךָ אֶל־הָאָרֶץ אֲשֶׁר־יָרְשׁוּ אֲבֹתֶיךָ וִירִשְׁתָּהּ וְהֵיטִבְךָ וְהִרְבְּךָ מֵאֲבֹתֶיךָ: ו וּמָל יְהֹוָה אֱלֹהֶיךָ אֶת־לְבָבְךָ וְאֶת־לְבַב זַרְעֶךָ

CHAPTER XXX

1-2. וַהֲשֵׁבֹתָ וגו׳ [*that you will take it to heart*]. It seems that the perception of facts outside ourselves is regarded as an outward movement of the mind. But the mental activity that brings these perceptions before the tribunal of our intelligence for the forming of judgments and conclusions is interpreted as an act of "bringing back," with the mind working inward; a "bringing back" to the inner mind of that which was observed on the outside. Hence the term הֵשִׁיב אֶל לֵב ["take it (lit. "back") to heart"] is an apt expression for this activity.... The words וְיָדַעְתָּ וגו׳ וַהֲשֵׁבֹתָ וגו׳ ["know . . . and take it to heart"], cited in Chapter 4:39 above, are a call to direct our perceptive faculties to the historical facts cited earlier (וְיָדַעְתָּ), and then וַהֲשֵׁבֹתָ אֶל לְבָבֶךָ, to bring these perceptions back to our mind, so that we may draw from them the right conclusions and, based upon them, make the right decisions for action.

So, too, we are told here: Only after all the blessings and curses foretold in this Book of the Law thousands of years in advance will actually have come true in your case, will you "bring back" to your mind for consideration the sum total of what you have experienced over these thousands of years. The result will be that you will

return to your God and to His Law with all your heart and with all your soul, and that you will win over also your children to the same loyalty to God and to His Law. For your experiences over these thousands of years will finally have convinced you for all time that God is your God and that the Law that has been given you is indeed of Divine origin.

in the midst of all the nations. Even while you are in exile in the midst of the nations among whom God has scattered you, and despite the vicissitudes of your life in exile, you will remain, through all the millennia, "the people of God with the Law of God in its hands." This, coupled with the fact that the fate predicted for you will indeed come to pass, will make possible, and bring about, your final move upward and back to God and to His Law.

2. וְשַׁבְתָּ עַד וגו׳ [*and you will return all the way*]. The text does not read וְשַׁבְתָּ אֶל ["and you will return to. . ."], which could imply merely a return movement *toward* God; i.e., only a partial return; but עַד ["*all the way* to. . ."]. You will not stop halfway; your return will be so complete that you will come back all the way to God.

God, with all your heart and with all your soul, so that you may live. 7. Then *God*, your God, will place all these curses upon your enemies and upon those who hate you, who persecuted you. 8. But you will return and hearken to the voice of *God* and carry out all His commandments that I command you today, 9. and *God*, your God, will mark you for the good in all the work of your hands— in the fruit of your body, in the fruit of your cattle and in the fruit of your soil. For *God* will rejoice over you for good, even as He rejoiced over your fathers. 10. For you will then hearken to the voice of *God*, your God, which is written in this Book of the Teaching, to keep all His commandments and His laws, for you will then return to *God*, your God, with all your heart and all your soul. 11. For this commandment that I command you today is not beyond your understanding, nor is it far away. 12. It is not in heaven so that you

לְאַהֲבָ֞ה אֶת־יְהֹוָ֤ה אֱלֹהֶ֙יךָ֙ בְּכָל־לְבָבְךָ֖ וּבְכָל־
נַפְשְׁךָ֖ לְמַ֥עַן חַיֶּֽיךָ: חמישי (שלישי כשהן מחוברין)
ז וְנָתַן֩ יְהֹוָ֨ה אֱלֹהֶ֜יךָ אֵ֣ת כָּל־הָאָל֣וֹת הָאֵ֗לֶּה
עַל־אֹיְבֶ֛יךָ וְעַל־שֹׂנְאֶ֖יךָ אֲשֶׁ֥ר רְדָפֽוּךָ: ח וְאַתָּ֣ה
תָשׁ֔וּב וְשָֽׁמַעְתָּ֖ בְּק֣וֹל יְהֹוָ֑ה וְעָשִׂ֙יתָ֙ אֶת־כָּל־
מִצְוֹתָ֔יו אֲשֶׁ֛ר אָֽנֹכִ֥י מְצַוְּךָ֖ הַיּֽוֹם: ט וְהוֹתִֽירְךָ֩
יְהֹוָ֨ה אֱלֹהֶ֜יךָ בְּכֹ֣ל | מַֽעֲשֵׂ֣ה יָדֶ֗ךָ בִּפְרִ֧י בִטְנְךָ֛
וּבִפְרִ֧י בְהֶמְתְּךָ֛ וּבִפְרִ֥י אַדְמָֽתְךָ֖ לְטֹבָ֑ה כִּ֣י |
יָשׁ֣וּב יְהֹוָ֗ה לָשׂ֤וּשׂ עָלֶ֙יךָ֙ לְט֔וֹב כַּֽאֲשֶׁר־שָׂ֖שׂ
עַל־אֲבֹתֶֽיךָ: י כִּ֣י תִשְׁמַ֗ע בְּקוֹל֙ יְהֹוָ֣ה אֱלֹהֶ֔יךָ
לִשְׁמֹ֤ר מִצְוֹתָיו֙ וְחֻקֹּתָ֔יו הַכְּתוּבָ֕ה בְּסֵ֖פֶר
הַתּוֹרָ֣ה הַזֶּ֑ה כִּ֤י תָשׁוּב֙ אֶל־יְהֹוָ֣ה אֱלֹהֶ֔יךָ בְּכָל־
לְבָבְךָ֖ וּבְכָל־נַפְשֶֽׁךָ: ס ששי יא כִּ֚י הַמִּצְוָ֣ה
הַזֹּ֔את אֲשֶׁ֛ר אָֽנֹכִ֥י מְצַוְּךָ֖ הַיּ֑וֹם לֹֽא־נִפְלֵ֥את הִוא֙
מִמְּךָ֔ וְלֹֽא־רְחֹקָ֖ה הִֽוא: יב לֹ֥א בַשָּׁמַ֖יִם הִ֑וא

8–10. *But you will return.* Verse 2 of the present chapter foretells Israel's return to the faithful observance of God's Law, to the extent that this can be accomplished in exile. But what follows now is the ultimate, complete realization of all the laws of God within that land which has been promised God's most abundant blessing in every respect. God's promise will then become a reality without our having to fear that our prosperity will cause us to fall back into our old ways—as happened in the past—and thus once again endanger our happiness (see note on Deuteronomy 31:20).

10. *which is written.* This entire "Book of the Teaching" is nothing less than the voice of God set down in writing. From it, the voice of God speaks to us for all time, teaching us all the "tasks and limitations," His commandments and statutes, for every aspect of our existence on earth. The observance of these laws will henceforth be the manifestation of our return to "*God*, our God" with all our hearts and with all our souls. This observance of the Law, not the extraordinary blessing resulting from this observance, will become the sole aim of our existence and of our aspirations. That is why the text makes reference here again to the full realization of the Law of God. . . .

Now these clear, unambiguously formulated sentences (Verses 1 through 10) have laid the immovable granite foundation upon which Judaism rests to this day and will rest for all time to come. Here we read, proclaimed in clear and unambiguous terms, the ingathering of the exiles from dispersion for the entire nation's return to the Promised Land—which we are still awaiting—and, in terms no less clear and unambiguous, the eternity of the Torah; the immutable, permanent binding force of the Law that was transmitted to us through Moses. Our dispersion among the nations will end only if we return completely to unswerving loyalty to this Law while we are still thus dispersed, and the sole objective of our future ingathering in the Land will be the final, complete realization of this Law upon the soil of the Land to which it belongs.

These clear, unambiguous pronouncements of God give the lie to any notion, preached to mislead minds and spirits, that Israel and its laws have become outdated. Neither Israel nor the Law belong to a dead past; they are part of a most vital present and of a promising future. Only if we clearly recognize and appreciate this truth, and devote ourselves joyously and unreservedly to this mission, will we be able to determine in every age what is right and pleasing in the eyes of God and see, from the vantage point of any period in history, the path to our salvation which God Himself has shown us. "The secret things belong to *God*, our God, but that which has been revealed is ours and our children's forever: To carry out all the words of this Teaching": These words were addressed to us at the conclusion of the preceding chapter to give us our bearings for the period of our exile. The revelation of the future that is in store for us forms the commentary to these words.

could say: "Who shall go up for us to
heaven and bring it to us and make us
hear it so that we may carry it out?"
13. Neither is it beyond the sea so that
you could say: "Who shall go for us to the
other side of the sea and bring it to us and
make us hear it so that we may carry it out?"
14. For the Word is very near to you, to
carry it out with your mouth and with your
heart. 15. See, I have set before you today
life and good and, also, death and evil;
16. inasmuch as I command you today to
love *God*, your God; to walk in His ways and
to keep His commandments, His statutes
and His [social] ordinances, so that you may
live and multiply, and *God*, your God, will
bless you in the land to which you are
coming in order to take possession of it.
17. But if your heart should turn in a
manner that you will not hearken, and you
will let yourself be carried away, and
you will cast yourself down before other
gods and serve them,   18. then I have
announced to you this day that you will
quickly perish; that you will not last long
upon the soil which you are now passing
over the Yarden in order to take possession
of it.   19. I have called heaven and earth
today as witnesses against you; I have set
life and death before you, blessing and
curse. Choose life, so that you may live—
you and your descendants—   20. to love
God, your God; to hearken to His voice and
to cling firmly to Him; for that is your life
and the length of your days—to dwell upon

לֵאמֹר מִי יַעֲלֶה־לָּנוּ הַשָּׁמַ֫יְמָה וְיִקָּחֶ֫הָ לָּ֫נוּ
וְיַשְׁמִעֵ֫נוּ אֹתָהּ וְנַעֲשֶֽׂנָּה: יג וְלֹא־מֵעֵ֫בֶר לַיָּם
הִוא לֵאמֹר מִי יַעֲבָר־לָ֫נוּ אֶל־עֵ֫בֶר הַיָּם וְיִקָּחֶ֫הָ
לָּ֫נוּ וְיַשְׁמִעֵ֫נוּ אֹתָהּ וְנַעֲשֶֽׂנָּה: יד כִּי־קָרוֹב אֵלֶ֫יךָ
הַדָּבָר מְאֹד בְּפִ֫יךָ וּבִלְבָבְךָ לַעֲשֹׂתֽוֹ: ס שביעי
ומפטיר (רביעי כשהן מחוברין) טו רְאֵה נָתַ֫תִּי לְפָנֶ֫יךָ
הַיּוֹם אֶת־הַחַיִּים וְאֶת־הַטּוֹב וְאֶת־הַמָּ֫וֶת וְאֶת־
הָרָע: טז אֲשֶׁר אָנֹכִי מְצַוְּךָ הַיּוֹם לְאַהֲבָה אֶת־
יְהֹוָה אֱלֹהֶ֫יךָ לָלֶ֫כֶת בִּדְרָכָיו וְלִשְׁמֹר מִצְוֺתָיו
וְחֻקֹּתָיו וּמִשְׁפָּטָיו וְחָיִ֫יתָ וְרָבִ֫יתָ וּבֵרַכְךָ יְהֹוָה
אֱלֹהֶ֫יךָ בָּאָ֫רֶץ אֲשֶׁר־אַתָּה בָא־שָׁ֫מָּה לְרִשְׁתָּֽהּ:
יז וְאִם־יִפְנֶה לְבָבְךָ וְלֹא תִשְׁמָע וְנִדַּחְתָּ
וְהִשְׁתַּחֲוִ֫יתָ לֵאלֹהִים אֲחֵרִים וַעֲבַדְתָּֽם:
יח הִגַּ֫דְתִּי לָכֶם הַיּוֹם כִּי אָבֹד תֹּאבֵדוּן לֹא־
תַאֲרִיכֻן יָמִים עַל־הָאֲדָמָה אֲשֶׁר אַתָּה עֹבֵר
אֶת־הַיַּרְדֵּן לָבוֹא שָׁ֫מָּה לְרִשְׁתָּֽהּ: יט הַעִדֹ֫תִי
בָכֶם הַיּוֹם אֶת־הַשָּׁמַ֫יִם וְאֶת־הָאָ֫רֶץ הַחַיִּים
וְהַמָּ֫וֶת נָתַ֫תִּי לְפָנֶ֫יךָ הַבְּרָכָה וְהַקְּלָלָה וּבָחַרְתָּ
בַּחַיִּים לְמַ֫עַן תִּחְיֶה אַתָּה וְזַרְעֶֽךָ: כ לְאַהֲבָה
אֶת־יְהֹוָה אֱלֹהֶ֫יךָ לִשְׁמֹעַ בְּקֹלוֹ וּלְדָבְקָה־בוֹ כִּי
הוּא חַיֶּ֫יךָ וְאֹ֫רֶךְ יָמֶ֫יךָ לָשֶׁ֫בֶת עַל־הָאֲדָמָה

---

14. **For the Word is very near to you.** The content
and subject matter of this Law are very close to you.
You yourself are its subject matter, and its contents
concern your own life on earth. In order to understand
both, you need only delve into your own inner self and
examine your material and personal position with open
eyes. As regards whatever instructions, in addition to
those already set down in the Book of the Law that has
been turned over to you, you may still need in order to
understand this Law and to observe it—these instructions are being given to you בְּפִ֫יךָ ["with your mouth"];
i.e., by the tradition that is to be passed from mouth to
mouth. Cf. עַל פִּי הַדְּבָרִים הָאֵ֫לֶּה ["according to (lit., "by the
mouth of") the living content of these words"]
(Exodus 34:27); שִׂ֫ימָה בְּפִיהֶם ["put it in their mouth"]
(Deuteronomy 31:19); לֹא יָמוּשׁ סֵ֫פֶר הַתּוֹרָה הַזֶּה מִפִּ֫יךָ ["This
Book of the Teaching shall not depart from your

mouth"] (Joshua 1:8), וּדְבָרַי אֲשֶׁר שַׂ֫מְתִּי בְּפִ֫יךָ ["and My
words which I have put in your mouth"] (Isaiah 59:21).

All this you must study, and grasp it וּבִלְבָבְךָ, with
your heart and spirit; לַעֲשֹׂתֽוֹ, in order to carry it out. To
"learn" the Book of God's Law in the light of the Oral
Tradition, with heart and mind; understand our duty
and fulfill it: that is the only path to the understanding
of the Law of God, close to us at all times, wherever we
may be, so that it may cause us to comprehend our
eternal mission on earth.

And because the subject matter of this Law is so close
to us and the path to its knowledge so obvious, the Law
will accompany us through all the changes of time, and,
after all our wanderings and trials, we will find our way
back to it in everlasting loyalty.

o   o   o

the soil that *God*, your God, swore to your
fathers, Abraham, Yitzḥak and Yaakov, to
give to them.

אֲשֶׁר נִשְׁבַּע יְהֹוָה לַאֲבֹתֶיךָ לְאַבְרָהָם לְיִצְחָק
וּלְיַעֲקֹב לָתֵת לָהֶם: פ

The Haftarah for this Sidra may be found on page 919.

וילך

VAYELEKH

XXXI 1. Thereupon Moshe went and spoke these words to all of Yisrael. 2. He said to them: "I am one hundred and twenty years old today; I will no longer be able to go out and to come in; moreover, *God* has said to me: 'You shall not pass over this Yarden.' 3. *God*, your God—it is He that will pass before you; He will destroy these nations before you so that you may succeed them in [the] possession [of the land]. Yehoshua, he will go before you, as *God* has spoken. 4. And *God* will do to them as He did to Siḥon and Og, the kings of the Emorites, and to their land, whom He destroyed. 5. *God* will deliver them up before you, and you shall deal with them entirely in accordance with the commandment to which I have committed you. 6. Be steadfast and be strong; do not fear them or be frightened of them, for *God*, your God—it is He Who is going with you; He will not let go of you, nor will He forsake you." 7. Then Moshe called Yehoshua and said to him before the eyes of all Yisrael: "Be steadfast and strong, for you are to go with this people to the land that *God* swore

לא א וַיֵּ֖לֶךְ מֹשֶׁ֑ה וַיְדַבֵּ֛ר אֶת־הַדְּבָרִ֥ים הָאֵ֖לֶּה אֶל־כָּל־יִשְׂרָאֵל: ב וַיֹּ֣אמֶר אֲלֵהֶ֗ם בֶּן־מֵאָ֨ה וְעֶשְׂרִ֤ים שָׁנָה֙ אָנֹכִ֣י הַיּ֔וֹם לֹא־אוּכַ֥ל ע֖וֹד לָצֵ֣את וְלָב֑וֹא וַֽיהֹוָה֙ אָמַ֣ר אֵלַ֔י לֹ֥א תַעֲבֹ֖ר אֶת־הַיַּרְדֵּ֥ן הַזֶּֽה: ג יְהֹוָ֨ה אֱלֹהֶ֜יךָ ה֣וּא ׀ עֹבֵ֣ר לְפָנֶ֗יךָ הֽוּא־יַשְׁמִ֞יד אֶת־הַגּוֹיִ֤ם הָאֵ֨לֶּה֙ מִלְּפָנֶ֔יךָ וִֽירִשְׁתָּ֑ם יְהוֹשֻׁ֗עַ ה֚וּא עֹבֵ֣ר לְפָנֶ֔יךָ כַּאֲשֶׁ֖ר דִּבֶּ֥ר יְהֹוָֽה: שני ד וְעָשָׂ֤ה יְהֹוָה֙ לָהֶ֔ם כַּאֲשֶׁ֣ר עָשָׂ֗ה לְסִיח֤וֹן וּלְעוֹג֙ מַלְכֵ֣י הָאֱמֹרִ֔י וּלְאַרְצָ֖ם אֲשֶׁ֥ר הִשְׁמִ֖יד אֹתָֽם: ה וּנְתָנָ֥ם יְהֹוָ֖ה לִפְנֵיכֶ֑ם וַעֲשִׂיתֶ֣ם לָהֶ֔ם כְּכָל־הַמִּצְוָ֔ה אֲשֶׁ֥ר צִוִּ֖יתִי אֶתְכֶֽם: ו חִזְק֣וּ וְאִמְצ֔וּ אַל־תִּֽירְא֥וּ וְאַל־תַּֽעַרְצ֖וּ מִפְּנֵיהֶ֑ם כִּ֣י ׀ יְהֹוָ֣ה אֱלֹהֶ֗יךָ ה֚וּא הַהֹלֵ֣ךְ עִמָּ֔ךְ לֹ֥א יַרְפְּךָ֖ וְלֹ֥א יַעַזְבֶֽךָּ: ס שלישי (חמישי כשהן מחוברין) ז וַיִּקְרָ֨א מֹשֶׁ֜ה לִֽיהוֹשֻׁ֗עַ וַיֹּ֤אמֶר אֵלָיו֙ לְעֵינֵ֣י כָל־יִשְׂרָאֵ֔ל חֲזַ֣ק וֶאֱמָ֔ץ כִּ֣י אַתָּ֗ה תָּבוֹא֙ אֶת־הָעָ֣ם הַזֶּ֔ה אֶל־הָאָ֕רֶץ אֲשֶׁ֨ר נִשְׁבַּ֤ע יְהֹוָה֙

CHAPTER XXXI

1. *Thereupon Moshe went.* The promises of blessings and curses and the epilogue that follows them complete the words that Moses had been commanded to address to the nation in the name of God. He could therefore consider his mission completed, and so could apply himself entirely to the tasks that still had to be done by him before he died: to bid farewell to the nation (Verses 1 through 6); to present to the nation his successor with words of encouragement (Verses 7 and 8); and, finally, to hand over to the priests and to the elders of the nation the written Torah, complete up to that point, with instructions to have it read to the people every seventh year on the Festival of Huts [Sukkoth], when the entire nation gathered at the site of the Sanctuary of God's Law (Verses 9 through 13).

Accordingly, Moses did not summon the whole nation to himself as he customarily did when he had a message to communicate to it in the name of God, but

וַיֵּלֶךְ—he "went" before the nation to bid farewell to it in the simple manner typical of this, the most humble among men.

7. *Then Moshe called.* חֲזַק וֶאֱמָץ ["Be steadfast and strong"]. The charge to Joshua, חֲזַק וֶאֱמָץ, summed up Joshua's task as leader of the nation. This charge is reiterated in the Book of Joshua (1:6, 7, 9): "Be steadfast and strong because you will have this people inherit.... Only be steadfast and very strong, to observe to carry out according to all the Teaching.... Have I not commanded you: 'Be steadfast and strong?'" This is interpreted in Berakhoth 32b as follows: "Be steadfast in keeping the Torah and strong in good deeds"; remain steadfast in looking to the תורה for an understanding of your tasks, and be strong in overcoming any obstacles to the fulfillment of these tasks. Be steadfast in adhering to your principles and be strong in carrying them out: these are the most important qualities required of a leader.

to their fathers to give to them; you shall
have them take possession of it, to inherit it.
8. *God*—it is He Who goes before you;
He will be with you; He will not let go of
you, nor will He forsake you; fear nothing
and do not be frightened."   9. Moshe
wrote down this Teaching and handed it
over to the priests, the sons of Levi, who
carried the Ark of the Covenant of *God*, and
to all the elders of Yisrael.   10. And Moshe
commanded them [saying]: "At the end of
seven years, at the time of appointed meeting of the year of release, on the Festival of
Huts, 11. when all Yisrael come to see
themselves directly before the Presence of
God, your God, in the place that He will
choose—you shall read this Teaching in the
presence of all Yisrael before their ears.
12. You must assemble for this purpose
the people—the men and the women and
the children and the stranger who has entered
among you, who is within your gates—so that

לַאֲבֹתָם לָתֵת לָהֶם וְאַתָּה תַּנְחִילֶנָּה אוֹתָם:
ח וַיהֹוָה הוּא ׀ הַהֹלֵךְ לְפָנֶיךָ הוּא יִהְיֶה עִמָּךְ
לֹא יַרְפְּךָ וְלֹא יַעַזְבֶךָּ לֹא תִירָא וְלֹא תֵחָת:
ט וַיִּכְתֹּב מֹשֶׁה אֶת־הַתּוֹרָה הַזֹּאת וַיִּתְּנָהּ אֶל־
הַכֹּהֲנִים בְּנֵי לֵוִי הַנֹּשְׂאִים אֶת־אֲרוֹן בְּרִית
יְהֹוָה וְאֶל־כָּל־זִקְנֵי יִשְׂרָאֵל: רביעי י וַיְצַו מֹשֶׁה
אוֹתָם לֵאמֹר מִקֵּץ ׀ שֶׁבַע שָׁנִים בְּמֹעֵד שְׁנַת
הַשְּׁמִטָּה בְּחַג הַסֻּכּוֹת: יא בְּבוֹא כָל־יִשְׂרָאֵל
לֵרָאוֹת אֶת־פְּנֵי יְהֹוָה אֱלֹהֶיךָ בַּמָּקוֹם אֲשֶׁר
יִבְחָר תִּקְרָא אֶת־הַתּוֹרָה הַזֹּאת נֶגֶד כָּל־
יִשְׂרָאֵל בְּאָזְנֵיהֶם: יב הַקְהֵל אֶת־הָעָם הָאֲנָשִׁים
וְהַנָּשִׁים וְהַטַּף וְגֵרְךָ אֲשֶׁר בִּשְׁעָרֶיךָ לְמַעַן

10-11. *And Moshe commanded.* The public reading
of the Torah commanded here is not intended as a
means for making the Law known to the people, for the
knowledge of the Law should be cultivated by each and
every member of the nation, every day, as part of
his ordinary domestic life. This is why we are told, "and
speak of them when you sit in your house and when you
walk upon the way. . ." (Deuteronomy 6:7), and "and
teach them to your sons, to speak of them. . ."
(Deuteronomy 11:19). Indeed, the public reading of
the Law commanded here is a special event that is to
recur at seven-year intervals for a very special purpose.
It is to take place בְּמוֹעֵד ["at the time of appointed
meeting"], at a season during which every Jewish soul
is invited to commune with God; שְׁנַת הַשְּׁמִטָּה ["of the
year of release"], each time the agricultural and commercial circle is resumed following the year of release;
בְּחַג הַסֻּכּוֹת ["on the Festival of Huts"}, when the Festival
of Huts unites the whole nation in recalling those days
of old, when it was neither agriculture nor commerce,
but only God's wondrous favor that kept all of them
alive in the wilderness—together with their wives and
children, under the protection of His cloud—and that
gave them His Law to prepare them for the agricultural
and commercial life they were now about to begin.

בְּבוֹא כָּל יִשְׂרָאֵל וגו׳ *[when all Yisrael come].* When the
entire people has followed the call to the place where
there is the Sanctuary—not of God, Who may be found
everywhere, but of the Law—that pledge of His omnipresence in the midst of the nation. The reading is

to take place at a time when all the members of the
nation have already appeared before the Presence of
God at the site of the Sanctuary of His Law, each with
his personal ascent offering, symbolizing his personal
appearance before God. Then, immediately after the
end of the first day of this act of appearing before
God, "you shall read"; the nation is to have this Law
read to the assembled people by its supreme representative. The purpose of this reading is that, with the
beginning of each new agricultural and commercial
cycle, the nation should proclaim anew its awareness
that the way to God can be found only upon the path to
His Law; that the covenant with God connotes a covenant with His Law; that the unity of the nation and
God's protection of the nation are both dependent on
the nation's observance of the Law; and that this
nation—under whose care the Testimony of the Law
reposes—represents and vouches for the authenticity
and the Divine origin of the Law.

∴

12. *so that they may hear.* Here, in the general
assembly of the entire nation, they shall hear proclaimed and reconfirmed again and again, by the
presence of the nation itself and of its supreme representative, the Divine origin of the Law and their
commitment to it. This is the same Law that each and
every member of the nation, no matter how remote his
dwelling place, has in his home, in his hands. Now they
all hear it read in public so that, listening to the reading together with all the other members of the nation,

they may hear and that they may learn and fear *God*, your God, and punctiliously carry out all the words of this Teaching. 13. And even their children who do not yet understand will hear and learn to fear *God*, your God, all the days that you live upon the soil which you are passing over the Yarden in order to take possession of it." 14. And *God* said to Moshe: "See, your days are approaching that you must die. Call Yehoshua, and present yourselves in the Tent of Appointed Meeting so that I may give him his duty." Moshe went and [so did] Yehoshua, and they presented themselves in the Tent of Appointed Meeting. 15. And *God* appeared in the Tent in a pillar of cloud, and the pillar of cloud stood at the entrance of the Tent. 16. And *God* said to Moshe: "You are now going to lie down beside your fathers, and then this people will rise and—straying after the deities of the excesses alien to the land, into the midst of which it is now coming—it will become unfaithful and forsake Me and break My covenant that I established with it. 17. At

יִשְׁמְע֗וּ וּלְמַ֣עַן יִלְמְד֔וּ וְיָֽרְא֖וּ אֶת־יְהֹוָ֣ה אֱלֹֽהֵיכֶ֑ם וְשָֽׁמְר֣וּ לַֽעֲשׂ֔וֹת אֶת־כָּל־דִּבְרֵ֖י הַתּוֹרָ֥ה הַזֹּֽאת: יג וּבְנֵיהֶ֞ם אֲשֶׁ֣ר לֹֽא־יָֽדְעוּ֮ יִשְׁמְעוּ֒ וְלָ֣מְד֔וּ לְיִרְאָ֖ה אֶת־יְהֹוָ֣ה אֱלֹֽהֵיכֶ֑ם כָּל־הַיָּמִ֗ים אֲשֶׁ֨ר אַתֶּ֤ם חַיִּים֙ עַל־הָ֣אֲדָמָ֔ה אֲשֶׁ֨ר אַתֶּ֜ם עֹֽבְרִ֧ים אֶת־הַיַּרְדֵּ֛ן שָׁ֖מָּה לְרִשְׁתָּֽהּ: פ חמישי (ששי כשהן מחוברין) יד וַיֹּ֨אמֶר יְהֹוָ֜ה אֶל־מֹשֶׁ֗ה הֵ֣ן קָֽרְב֣וּ יָמֶ֘יךָ֮ לָמוּת֒ קְרָ֣א אֶת־יְהוֹשֻׁ֗עַ וְהִֽתְיַצְּב֛וּ בְּאֹ֥הֶל מוֹעֵ֖ד וַֽאֲצַוֶּ֑נּוּ וַיֵּ֤לֶךְ מֹשֶׁה֙ וִֽיהוֹשֻׁ֔עַ וַיִּֽתְיַצְּב֖וּ בְּאֹ֥הֶל מוֹעֵֽד: טו וַיֵּרָ֧א יְהֹוָ֛ה בָּאֹ֖הֶל בְּעַמּ֣וּד עָנָ֑ן וַיַּֽעֲמֹ֛ד עַמּ֥וּד הֶֽעָנָ֖ן עַל־פֶּ֥תַח הָאֹֽהֶל: טז וַיֹּ֨אמֶר יְהֹוָ֜ה אֶל־מֹשֶׁ֗ה הִנְּךָ֤ שֹׁכֵב֙ עִם־אֲבֹתֶ֔יךָ וְקָם֩ הָעָ֨ם הַזֶּ֜ה וְזָנָ֣ה ׀ אַֽחֲרֵ֣י ׀ אֱלֹהֵ֣י נֵֽכַר־הָאָ֗רֶץ אֲשֶׁ֨ר ה֤וּא בָא־שָׁ֨מָּה֙ בְּקִרְבּ֔וֹ וַֽעֲזָבַ֔נִי וְהֵפֵר֙ אֶת־בְּרִיתִ֔י אֲשֶׁ֥ר כָּרַ֖תִּי אִתּֽוֹ:

they may renew their awareness, which will inspire them "that they may learn"; so that they may concern themselves more and more with the task of increasing their familiarity with the Law; "and fear": so that both the assembly and their study in their own homes, by reconfirming their perception of God as the Pilot of the nation's fate and the Guide of all its actions, may enhance their fear of God; that "they may punctiliously carry out," that they will be inspired to observe the entire Law faithfully and punctiliously. This punctilious observance of God's Law is the supreme goal of all the institutions established by the Law. . . .

13. **And even their children.** Even the children, who do not yet have so much understanding that what they hear at the public reading should move them to study and observe the Law, will benefit from attending this great assembly. The fact that they are listening to the reading of the Law together with their parents, and the impact of the reverent multitudes also listening to the reading of the Law, will be sufficient to inspire them to fear God. In the case of the children, listening, learning and fearing God are not three separate concepts, but "they will hear and learn to fear." By their activity of listening, they will learn to fear God, even though the punctilious observance of the Law is still beyond their capacity.

○   ○   ○

16. *after the deities of the excesses alien to the land.* They will regard the deities worshipped by the indigenous population as part of the land, and they will believe that no one dwelling in the land can afford to ignore these deities if he wishes to dwell there in safety and prosperity. In fact, however, this idolatry is an outrage that should remain alien to the land, since this is the land of the Jews, the land of the Law of God. . . . The nation will think that when it enters this land it enters into a territory under the dominion of local deities. As a consequence, the nation will begin to lean toward these idolatrous excesses. At first, it will do so without formally breaking the covenant with God. The people will continue to make the prescribed offerings to God in the Sanctuary, and they will probably also continue observing the regulations set down in His Law. However, at the same time they will worship the local deities upon the high places of the land. And by so doing, "it will forsake Me," the people will forsake God, "and break My covenant," and finally they will indeed break the covenant with the Law to which they had been committed through their covenant with God. And this is the Law of which God had told them, as they were about to enter the land; that their observance of it would determine whether they would receive His aid and His blessing in the land (Deuteronomy 28:69 and 29:8).

that time My anger will be stirred up against it; I will forsake them; I will hide My face from them so that it will fall prey to destruction and many evils and troubles will come upon it. At that time it will say: 'Truly because my God is not in my midst have these evils come upon me.' 18. And I, I will hide My face at that time only because of all the evil that it has done in turning to other gods. 19. And now, write down for yourselves this song and teach it to the sons of Yisrael; put it in their mouth so that this song may become a witness for Me against the sons of Yisrael. 20. When I will have brought it to the soil that I have sworn to its fathers—that flows with milk and honey—and it will eat and be satisfied, and it will become obese, and it will turn to other

יז וְחָרָה אַפִּי בוֹ בַיּוֹם־הַהוּא וַעֲזַבְתִּים
וְהִסְתַּרְתִּי פָנַי מֵהֶם וְהָיָה לֶאֱכֹל וּמְצָאֻהוּ
רָעוֹת רַבּוֹת וְצָרוֹת וְאָמַר בַּיּוֹם הַהוּא הֲלֹא
עַל כִּי־אֵין אֱלֹהַי בְּקִרְבִּי מְצָאוּנִי הָרָעוֹת
הָאֵלֶּה׃ יח וְאָנֹכִי הַסְתֵּר אַסְתִּיר פָּנַי בַּיּוֹם
הַהוּא עַל כָּל־הָרָעָה אֲשֶׁר עָשָׂה כִּי פָנָה אֶל־
אֱלֹהִים אֲחֵרִים׃ יט וְעַתָּה כִּתְבוּ לָכֶם אֶת־
הַשִּׁירָה הַזֹּאת וְלַמְּדָהּ אֶת־בְּנֵי־יִשְׂרָאֵל שִׂימָהּ
בְּפִיהֶם לְמַעַן תִּהְיֶה־לִּי הַשִּׁירָה הַזֹּאת לְעֵד
בִּבְנֵי יִשְׂרָאֵל׃ ששי (שביעי כשהן מחוברין) כ כִּי־
אֲבִיאֶנּוּ אֶל־הָאֲדָמָה ׀ אֲשֶׁר־נִשְׁבַּעְתִּי לַאֲבֹתָיו
זָבַת חָלָב וּדְבַשׁ וְאָכַל וְשָׂבַע וְדָשֵׁן וּפָנָה אֶל־

17–18. ***My anger will be stirred up . . . I will forsake them.*** I will leave them to fend for themselves.

I will hide. I will withdraw My special care from them.

so that it will fall prey to destruction. So that Israel will fall prey to the other nations. Once Israel is left to fend for itself, its political downfall will come as a natural consequence of its weakness. Israel's survival and prosperity in history is the work of God's own miraculous power.

At that time it will say . . . my God is not in my midst. The nation will ascribe its troubles not to its own defection from God but to God's defection from it. God, whom Israel believes it may call its own despite its sins; the God Who promised to defend and protect it from the other nations, has ceased to fulfill His promise, for otherwise Israel would not be suffering so greatly now. Israel believes that it has a right to blame God and forget that it has only itself to blame. It does not think to investigate why God is no longer acting toward it as its own God.

And as for Me, I will hide My face. Israel forgets that God has withdrawn His special care from it only "because of all the evil that it has done," "in turning to other gods," because it has turned to idolatry. God has forsaken Israel because Israel has forsaken Him. God will be the God of Israel only as long as Israel will be the people of God; only as long as Israel subordinates all its life and all its aspirations exclusively to God and to the fulfillment of His will. More than with any other nation, God's special relationship with Israel is dependent on Israel's exclusive and complete obedience, loyalty and devotion to Him. . . . Israel's accusation against God is unfounded. God is still "in its midst." He will never abrogate His special relationship with Israel. However, precisely because He is indeed "in its midst," none of Israel's sins will escape His attention, and the sufferings that will befall Israel as the result of its sins will cause it to descend to the moral level of the other nations—though never below that level. . . .

19. ***And now.*** The purpose of this song is to provide a cogent answer to Israel's complaint against God. Whenever troubles befall Israel because it has lost the protection of Divine Providence, causing Israel to complain: "Truly, because my God is not in my midst have these evils come upon me," Israel should have God's own answer, directing its attention to the true cause of its troubles. For this purpose, "write down for yourselves this song," so that this שִׁירָה [song] may serve as a witness in God's behalf and refute every such accusation on Israel's part with God's own countercharge.

so that this song may become a witness for Me against the sons of Yisrael. This entire שִׁירָה is nothing but an answer to the complaint arising from any one of Israel's periods of distress, that "Truly, because my God is not in my midst. . . ."

In Nedarim 38a, the stated purpose of the song, "so that this song may become a witness for Me against the sons of Yisrael" is interpreted as implying that the command "Write down for yourselves this song" applies not only to this song, but to the entire תּוֹרָה, whose epilogue the שִׁירָה constitutes. For, as is explained in *Ran*[14] (ibid.), if the command were indeed applicable

[14]*Note to the English translation*: Rabbenu Nissim ben Reuben Gerondi (ca. 1308–76), whose commentary on Tractate Nedarim is included in virtually all editions of the Talmud. [G.H.]

gods; they will serve them, mock Me, and
it will break My covenant: 21. Then it
will come to pass when many oppressive
evils have come upon them, that this song
will testify against them as a witness; for
it will not be forgotten out of the mouth of
its children. For I know its frame of mind,
which it applies even today, before I have
brought it to the land that I have sworn to
[it]." 22. And Moshe wrote down this

אֱלֹהִ֤ים אֲחֵרִים֙ וַעֲבָד֔וּם וְנִ֣אֲצ֔וּנִי וְהֵפֵ֖ר אֶת־
בְּרִיתִֽי׃ כא וְהָיָה֩ כִּֽי־תִמְצֶ֨אןָ אֹת֜וֹ רָע֣וֹת רַבּוֹת֮
וְצָרוֹת֒ וְ֠עָנְתָה הַשִּׁירָ֨ה הַזֹּ֤את לְפָנָיו֙ לְעֵ֔ד כִּ֛י
לֹ֥א תִשָּׁכַ֖ח מִפִּ֣י זַרְע֑וֹ כִּ֧י יָדַ֣עְתִּי אֶת־יִצְר֗וֹ
אֲשֶׁ֨ר ה֤וּא עֹשֶׂה֙ הַיּ֔וֹם בְּטֶ֣רֶם אֲבִיאֶ֔נּוּ אֶל־
הָאָ֖רֶץ אֲשֶׁ֥ר נִשְׁבָּֽעְתִּי׃ כב וַיִּכְתֹּ֥ב מֹשֶׁ֛ה אֶת־

only to the שִׁירָה, it would not be much of a "witness." All that the שִׁירָה does is perpetuate in general terms our awareness that our woe and weal depend on whether we perform the task God has assigned to us. But we will be able to understand the character of our task only if we are familiar with the entire Law. . . .

20–21. . . . The words "and it will eat and be satisfied, and it will become obese" (Verse 20) indicate the factor which, despite the Torah and the שִׁירָה [song], will bring about Israel's defection; so that the תּוֹרָה and the שִׁירָה will be capable of curing the defection, but not of preventing it. This factor is the self-indulgence that results from affluence. The spiritual and moral discipline with which the תּוֹרָה sets limits also to man's corporeality, in order to sanctify it, is not compatible with lush, self-indulgent sensuality. Paganism—the free and easy heathen cults that worship sensuality—is much more attractive to such a frame of mind, in comparison to which the serene happiness of the moral life found in the Covenant of God seems meaningless.

The words "it will eat and be satisfied, and it will become obese" describe the rock upon which Israel's loyalty, and hence also its happiness, has already been wrecked several times. The task which, at present, still awaits true, complete accomplishment, is: to remain loyal to God and to His Law even in the midst of affluence and good fortune. Only once the people of Israel has met this challenge will it have matured for final, permanent redemption. Only then will prosperity come to us without jeopardizing our obedience to God and to His Law; at that stage abundant blessings will only serve further to promote the realization of the tasks set by God's Law, unhindered by extraneous limitations. Therefore, in the promise of this ultimate future (Deuteronomy 30:8–10), the allusion to the return of prosperity (Verse 9) is followed by a reiteration (Verse 10) of an even more intense return, showing this return as a spiritual achievement that will not be endangered—but, in fact, will only be enhanced and perfected—by Israel's restored prosperity.

when many oppressive evils have come upon them. When, as a result of its defection, the people of Israel will be plagued by many sufferings, by "restrictions or limitations that will force it to turn its senses back upon its inner self" [as is implicit in the Hebrew term צָרוֹת, lit., "oppressions"], the תּוֹרָה that is upheld by the שִׁירָה will at last have the desired effect upon the nation. Then, under the impact of this שִׁירָה, Israel will no longer blame its God for its troubles; the contents of this שִׁירָה will come before Israel again and again as its accuser on behalf of God, causing Israel to attain a proper understanding of its fate; and thus, in due time, to return to God and to its duty toward Him.

for it will not be forgotten out of the mouth of its children. The words "and it will eat and be satisfied, and it will become obese, and it will turn to other gods" portray to us the seamy side of Israel's appearance in history, and the rock on which its national prosperity will be wrecked. Conversely, the words "for it will not be forgotten out of the mouth of its children" reveal to us the secret of Israel's eternal survival in the history of nations and explain why ultimately Israel will be able to discharge its mission. No matter how far it may fall, no matter how low it may sink as a result of its sins, it will still have one blessing to accompany it even through the darkest tunnels of its sufferings, and that is the Torah. Even if it should ever happen that Israel turns its back on the entire תּוֹרָה, it will still have the שִׁירָה of that Torah, the Word of God that attests to its calling and to its mission, and that interprets Israel's fate in terms of that mission. This inextinguishable Divine spark will be sufficient to turn Israel's spirit back to the תּוֹרָה again and again, to inspire it again with enthusiasm for the teachings and tasks set forth in the Torah. So, this Divine spark will keep awake the vital spirit which will not allow this nation to die; which will strengthen it to withstand all oppression from without; and which, in the midst of every misfortune, will enable Israel to preserve that clearsightedness, that serenity, that warm heart and that open hand by which it will survive to discharge its unique task in the history of nations. "For it will not be forgotten out of the mouth of its children." This promise guarantees that Israel will never entirely forfeit its calling, never totally forget its mission; that it will remain, until the end of time, "the people of the Bible"; that there will survive within Israel a spiritual principle, protected by God Himself,

הַשִּׁירָה הַזֹּאת בַּיּוֹם הַהוּא וַיְלַמְּדָהּ אֶת־בְּנֵי
יִשְׂרָאֵל: כג וַיְצַו אֶת־יְהוֹשֻׁעַ בִּן־נוּן וַיֹּאמֶר
חֲזַק וֶאֱמָץ כִּי אַתָּה תָּבִיא אֶת־בְּנֵי יִשְׂרָאֵל
אֶל־הָאָרֶץ אֲשֶׁר־נִשְׁבַּעְתִּי לָהֶם וְאָנֹכִי אֶהְיֶה
עִמָּךְ: כד וַיְהִי ׀ כְּכַלּוֹת מֹשֶׁה לִכְתֹּב אֶת־דִּבְרֵי
הַתּוֹרָה־הַזֹּאת עַל־סֵפֶר עַד תֻּמָּם: שביעי
כה וַיְצַו מֹשֶׁה אֶת־הַלְוִיִּם נֹשְׂאֵי אֲרוֹן בְּרִית־
יְהֹוָה לֵאמֹר: כו לָקֹחַ אֵת סֵפֶר הַתּוֹרָה הַזֶּה
וְשַׂמְתֶּם אֹתוֹ מִצַּד אֲרוֹן בְּרִית־יְהֹוָה אֱלֹהֵיכֶם
וְהָיָה־שָׁם בְּךָ לְעֵד: כז כִּי אָנֹכִי יָדַעְתִּי אֶת־
מֶרְיְךָ וְאֶת־עָרְפְּךָ הַקָּשֶׁה הֵן בְּעוֹדֶנִּי חַי עִמָּכֶם
הַיּוֹם מַמְרִים הֱיִתֶם עִם־יְהֹוָה וְאַף כִּי־אַחֲרֵי
מוֹתִי: מפטיר כח הַקְהִילוּ אֵלַי אֶת־כָּל־זִקְנֵי
שִׁבְטֵיכֶם וְשֹׁטְרֵיכֶם וַאֲדַבְּרָה בְאָזְנֵיהֶם אֵת
הַדְּבָרִים הָאֵלֶּה וְאָעִידָה בָּם אֶת־הַשָּׁמַיִם וְאֶת־

song on that day and taught it to the sons of
Yisrael. 23. And He gave Yehoshua his
duty and said: "Be steadfast and strong! For
you are to bring the sons of Yisrael to the
land that I have sworn to them, and I will be
with you." 24. It came to pass after
Moshe had finished writing down the words
of this Teaching in a Book to the very end,
25. that Moshe commanded the Levites,
the bearers of the Ark of *God*'s Covenant
[saying]: 26. "Take this Book of the
Teaching and place it by the side of the
Covenant of *God*, your God; there it shall
remain as a witness against you. 27. For
I know your disobedience and your stiff-
neckedness. See, even while I am still alive
with you, you were disobedient against
God; how much more after my death!
28. Assemble to me all the elders of
your tribes and your officials; I will speak
these words in their ears and I will call
heaven and earth as witnesses against them.
29. For I know that after my death you

through which, again and again, it will achieve spiritual revival.

° ° °

22. . . . The words addressed by God to Moses in Verses 16–21 contain the most important ideas that Moses' successor must keep in mind at all times.

These words drew Joshua's attention to the moral perils which his people would encounter. The work of combating these perils will be even more urgent than the conquest and apportionment of the Land, because both the conquest and the Land become irrelevant if Israel should waver in its loyalty to God and to His Law.

These words point out to Joshua that "learning"; i.e., the cultivation of the knowledge and understanding of the Torah in the nation, is the most important, indeed the only means, of keeping Israel faithful to God and to His Law and of bringing it back to this loyalty after each lapse. This "learning" implies not only the cultivation of the knowledge and understanding of the מִצְוֹת [commandments], but also a knowledge and understanding of the שִׁירָה [song], of the spirit that informs these מִצְוֹת. Only if Israel knows and understands both will it remain ever aware of its splendid, unique position and mission in the midst of mankind. Therefore the cultivation of this spiritual instrument, the winning and the training of all classes of the population for the knowledge of and scholarship in the Torah, shall be the primary object of Joshua's attention.

But above all, this address emphasized for Joshua the indispensable requirement that Israel's leader must never allow himself to be deterred from action when Israel breaks faith with God and strays from His Law. He must remain calm and steadfast at all times, deliberately and earnestly holding high the standard of the Law entrusted to him by God; knowing that it can never be his mission to adjust the Law of God to accommodate the deviation and vacillation that may be rife among the people at any given period. He must know that above and beyond every era of aberration there is still the Law, awaiting a future generation that will return to God and to His Law in loyalty and devotion. It is for this future generation that the leaders of every generation must preserve the authentic Law intact; keeping it alive no matter how many or how few minds he will find receptive to it at the time, because he is certain that the promise, "for it will not be forgotten out of the mouth of its children," will surely be fulfilled.

° ° °

29. . . . Now, thousands of years later, we look back upon these past millennia of that people and of that "Book of Moses." We see how everything predicted in that text has come true in the course of time. We see how, in the end, precisely during the periods of its direst suffering, this nation wedded itself so intimately to this Law that for its [the Law's] sake it endured a

הָאָרֶץ׃ כט כִּי יָדַעְתִּי אַחֲרֵי מוֹתִי כִּי־הַשְׁחֵת
תַּשְׁחִתוּן וְסַרְתֶּם מִן־הַדֶּרֶךְ אֲשֶׁר צִוִּיתִי אֶתְכֶם
וְקָרָאת אֶתְכֶם הָרָעָה בְּאַחֲרִית הַיָּמִים כִּי־
תַעֲשׂוּ אֶת־הָרַע בְּעֵינֵי יְהוָֹה לְהַכְעִיסוֹ
בְּמַעֲשֵׂה יְדֵיכֶם׃ ל וַיְדַבֵּר מֹשֶׁה בְּאָזְנֵי כָּל־קְהַל
יִשְׂרָאֵל אֶת־דִּבְרֵי הַשִּׁירָה הַזֹּאת עַד תֻּמָּם׃ פ

will become very corrupt; you will turn aside from the way that I have commanded you; and the evil will befall you in the end of days if you do that which is evil in the eyes of *God*, to anger Him with the doings of your hands." 30. Moshe spoke in the ears of the entire assembly of Yisrael the words of this song until the end:

martyrdom unparallelled in world history. This Law became the "wings of eagles" upon which Divine Providence bore Israel, beyond all trials and tribulations, from the midst of a world that offered it only hatred and scorn, misunderstanding and embitterment, into ever renewed vitality and mental vigor.

At the same time, this Law became that fountain of life and truth from which the very nations among whom God had scattered Israel—because of its defection from the Law—have drunk and still drink, to this very day. To this very day the Law has remained the Tree of Life—whose seeds have been borne by its scattered sons, both in theory and in practice, whether they realized it or not—into the fields of the future of peoples and nations, so that today these seeds are increasingly bearing fruit for the salvation of all mankind. Thus the *Israel* of flowering prosperity has indeed become a *Yizra-el*[15] of dispersion (cf. Hosea 1:4).

[15] *Note to the English translation*: *Yizra-el*—i.e., lit., "God sows." Israel is depicted as scattered into exile like seeds into a field. [G.H.]

As a consequence, the catchword of Jewish history, "and they will mingle with the nations and learn their actions" (Psalms 106:35) is applicable in a double meaning: In retrospect, the thought indeed suggests itself that precisely its dual proclivities, "you were disobedient against *God*," and "it will turn to other gods," on the one hand; and "it will not be forgotten out of the mouth of its children," on the other, made the Jewish people the best-suited instrument to fulfill God's purposes for mankind. Note that even defection and those who defect have not been entirely ineffectual agents serving God's purposes. For despite their sin, the Jewish people have carried with them into exile sparks that can spread and seeds that can germinate among all mankind. Is there a thinking man who, reading this final declaration of Moses, Verse 27–29, and reviewing the history of this nation and of this book, could refrain from acknowledging that this, precisely, is why this Law could not have been the work of Moses, the man, but only the Law of God, of which Moses was merely the messenger; so that both the nation and the Law will remain forever the finger of God showing the way to all mankind.

The Haftarah for this Sidra may be found on page 919.

האזינו

HAAZINU

XXXII

1. "Incline your ear, O heaven;
I would speak,
And let the earth hear the words of my mouth.
2. So that My Teaching may penetrate like a rain breaking up [the soil],
That My promise may flow gently like the dew,
Like rainstorms on the meadow
And like pouring rains upon the grass.
3. For it is the Name of *God* that I proclaim;
Ascribe greatness to our God!
4. The Rock, His work is perfect,
For all His ways are justice;
A God of trust and no violence,
Righteous and upright is He.

לב א הַאֲזִינוּ הַשָּׁמַיִם וַאֲדַבֵּרָה
וְתִשְׁמַע הָאָרֶץ אִמְרֵי־פִי׃
ב יַעֲרֹף כַּמָּטָר לִקְחִי
תִּזַּל כַּטַּל אִמְרָתִי
כִּשְׂעִירִם עֲלֵי־דֶשֶׁא
וְכִרְבִיבִים עֲלֵי־עֵשֶׂב׃
ג כִּי שֵׁם יְהוָה אֶקְרָא
הָבוּ גֹדֶל לֵאלֹהֵינוּ׃
ד הַצּוּר תָּמִים פָּעֳלוֹ
כִּי כָל־דְּרָכָיו מִשְׁפָּט
אֵל אֱמוּנָה וְאֵין עָוֶל
צַדִּיק וְיָשָׁר הוּא׃

CHAPTER XXXII

1. This is the appointment of heaven and earth—announced in Chapter 28—as witnesses and guarantors of God's covenant with Israel and of what will be said regarding Israel's future as a result of this relationship. . . .

האזין, to "incline one's ear," connotes a greater readiness to perceive and accept a spoken word than does the verb שמע ["hear," or "hearken"]. Words or sounds can be "heard" even if the hearer does not wish to "hearken" to them. Not so האזין. The implementation of God's covenant that is to be expected from both heaven and earth comes initially from heaven. The earth functions only indirectly to consummate it. Heaven is the immediate active factor. The role of the earth is more passive, because all the blessings and adversities in the physical development of the earth and, also, in human affairs to the extent that they depend on these terrestrial developments, are dependent on cosmic changes that take place outside the earth and are subsumed under the term שָׁמַיִם ["heaven"]. Whatever is to develop on earth must begin with activities initiated in heaven.

° ° °

2. יַעֲרֹף וגו׳ *[So that My Teaching may penetrate].* עֹרֶף is the joint of the neck, the most flexible, movable joint in the human body. Its movements are the quickest to obey any command given by the will; its antithesis is קְשֵׁה עֹרֶף [stiff-necked]. Hence, עָרַף connotes the rain's action of "breaking up" hard clods of soil, separating the soil into loose particles.

° ° °

The mission of Moses consists of two elements: The Teaching and the promise. Moses expects that the interaction of heaven and earth in shaping the future of his people will preserve both elements of his mission, so that both elements will ultimately attain their objective. Heaven and earth have been appointed by God Himself to act as witnesses and guarantors of His Covenant. Therefore, Moses expects that heaven and earth will not rest until God's תּוֹרָה will finally become לֶקַח [lit., "that which is taken up," from לקח, "take"], accepted and absorbed by the nation; breaking up the "soil" of its heart and mind that had remained hard so long; so that the seeds of warmth and light, of knowledge and life, may germinate there. Thus, too, the promises, refreshing like the dew, will revive and sustain his people amidst the difficult turns of fate that lie in store for them, and both the Teaching and the promise will cleanse the nation like rainstorms sweeping over the meadow and, finally, cause it to bear fruit, even as pouring rains fructify the grass.

4. הַצּוּר וגו׳ *[The Rock].* It is with these words that the "Song of Moses" actually begins. צור as an allegorical description of God occurs several times in this שִׁירָה and appears as a characterizing concept. . . .

With reference to Israel, the designation of God as הצור ["the Rock"] implies a twofold certainty. Israel knows that God is the everlasting support of its exist-

5. Their moral frailty has corrupted it to become non-children;
A generation persistent in crookedness, breaking away in opposition.
6. Pray ask yourselves: Is this how you would repay *God*?
O people withered, and in no way wise!

ה שִׁחֵת לוֹ לֹא בָּנָיו מוּמָם
דּוֹר עִקֵּשׁ וּפְתַלְתֹּל:
ו הַ לְיהוָֹה (ה רבתי) תִּגְמְלוּ־זֹאת
עַם נָבָל וְלֹא חָכָם

ence in history. It is God's will that Israel exist; therefore, Israel will never perish. However, it is also God's wish that Israel exist in accordance with specific ways which He revealed to Israel in His Law. Israel can never ignore these demands because they are as immutable as the existence and the will of God Himself. Whatever turns of fate Israel may have to endure, they will all serve only one purpose: To bring about the ultimate realization of God's objectives for and through Israel. They are nothing but hammer blows of God's own shaping power. Cf. Isaiah 26:4: כִּי בְּיָהּ ד׳ צוּר עוֹלָמִים ["for God is the Rock (i.e., absolute power, Creator and Molder) of all the worlds"]. . . . Hence the designation צור is the signature of שִׁירַת הַאֲזִינוּ [the song entitled "Incline Your Ear"]. It holds the key to this song, which reveals the workings of this God on, with and through Israel.

° ° °

כִּי כָל דְּרָכָיו מִשְׁפָּט ***[For all His ways are justice].*** All His ways, not only His ultimate goals, are מִשְׁפָּט; i.e., the implementation of what is right; the realization of whatever, at that given moment, is good and right for those affected by His workings. The ways of God are essentially the ways of His workings as they affect His creatures, particularly man. . . . In Psalm 145:7, we read: "*God* is just in all His ways and full of lovingkindness in all His works." Each one of God's creatures is the product of His love. No creature of God has a claim to existence on its own merits or the right to expect that its aspirations will be fulfilled. For all of its existence is a free gift of God's creative love. Nevertheless, God treats it as if indeed it had a personal right to existence and welfare.

A God of trust. He is a God Who can be trusted because He is צור ["the Rock"], always remaining the same, immutable. Even when He wields justice He does not merely follow the letter of justice but does only what is best for the individual affected by His מִשְׁפָּט [justice].

and no violence. He never wields His power over any creature merely for the sake of manifesting His power. Infinitesimal though the sum total of the world's power is compared to that of its Master and Creator, He nevertheless does not do violence even to the least of His creatures.

° ° °

6. הַ לַד׳ וגו׳ ***[Pray ask yourselves: Is this how you would repay God?]*** The particle ה is written larger than the other letters in the text, as a word in its own right. Thus: "Pray ask." Let us consider that, according to Deuteronomy 31:19 and 20, the primary purpose of the שִׁירָה [Song of Moses] is to confront the nation with the truth when, under the impact of the sufferings it has brought upon itself by its defection, it accuses God of no longer demonstrating His saving and protecting Presence in its midst, as He had done in better days.

Accordingly, we must interpret Verses 4 through 6 as follows: As the nation groans amidst its sufferings and accuses God of having changed His attitude toward it, the words of the שִׁירָה refute this accusation, declaring: הצור ["The Rock"], God, is firm as a rock, unchanging in His existence and in His will. He is always constant, and so are His workings. Just as your former good fortune, so, too, every moment of the misfortunes He has decreed for you, and now has brought upon you, constitutes a "perfect" act, based on justice and right, intended for your own good and for the good of all mankind. He has not changed; it is you who have changed. That is why your fate has changed. It no longer reveals God's wondrous saving power in your midst because you are no longer the same people; you no longer have the character traits required for ensuring God's presence in your midst. שִׁחֵת, your old failing, the intractability with which you oppose the will of God, has brought you to such a state of corruption that one could hardly know you anymore as the children of God.

הַ: Only one question is to be asked. Instead of hurling accusations at God, you should ask yourselves this question, which should always be before you in large, black letters: לַד׳ תִּגְמְלוּ זאת ["Is this how you would repay *God*?"]. Is this to be all the fruit you will allow to ripen as a reward to God for what He has done for and with you? Could you imagine that God would do, and would continue to do, such great things for you of all nations, only to have you become as morally and spiritually corrupt as all the other nations?

. . . The question הַ לַד׳ תִּגְמְלוּ זאת ["Is this how you would repay *God*?"] underscores the true connotation of the term נבל [lit., "withered"]. Both גמל [lit., "ripen"] and נבל ["withered"] in their literary meaning refer to phases of plant life. גמל is the ripe fruit; נבל connotes the withering of a plant and its consequent inability to produce fruit. All that God has done for and with Israel, both in His special guidance of its destinies and in the

Is He not your Father Who calls you His own;	הֲלוֹא־הוּא֙ אָבִ֣יךָ קָּנֶ֔ךָ
Did He not form you when He gave you your purpose?	ה֥וּא עָֽשְׂךָ֖ וַֽיְכֹנְנֶֽךָ׃ שני
7. Remember the days of old;	ז זְכֹר֙ יְמ֣וֹת עוֹלָ֔ם
Understand the years of the generations;	בִּ֖ינוּ שְׁנ֣וֹת דֹּר־וָדֹ֑ר
Ask your father so that he may tell you,	שְׁאַ֤ל אָבִ֙יךָ֙ וְיַגֵּ֔דְךָ
Your elders so that they may explain it to you:	זְקֵנֶ֖יךָ וְיֹ֥אמְרוּ לָֽךְ׃
8. When the Most High assigned property to the nations,	ח בְּהַנְחֵ֤ל עֶלְיוֹן֙ גּוֹיִ֔ם
When He separated the sons of men,	בְּהַפְרִיד֖וֹ בְּנֵ֣י אָדָ֑ם
He set the territories of peoples	יַצֵּב֙ גְּבֻלֹ֣ת עַמִּ֔ים
For the sons of Yisrael [who were] yet to be counted.	לְמִסְפַּ֖ר בְּנֵ֥י יִשְׂרָאֵֽל׃
9. For *God*'s portion is His people;	ט כִּ֛י חֵ֥לֶק יְהוָ֖ה עַמּ֑וֹ
Yaakov, the lot of His inheritance.	יַעֲקֹ֖ב חֶ֥בֶל נַחֲלָתֽוֹ׃

regulations He has given it in His Law, has only one purpose: To scatter into the mind and spirit of the nation the seeds of life and light, so that they may germinate and eventually bear fruit, in both theory and practice, in the life of the nation as a whole and in the personal lives of its members. However, the nation has become נבל, "withered" in mind and spirit; it has permitted the "seeds" planted by God, with all their many institutions, to "wither" before they could germinate into full bloom; so that, instead of having developed into a model nation, it stands here as עַם נָבָל, a people that has withered both in mind and in spirit. . . .

Is He not your Father Who calls you His own? Seeing that He calls you His own and through His Law disposes over all your energies and resources, physical and spiritual, does He not have the right to do so, and should you yourself not realize beyond the shadow of a doubt that in everything He withholds from you, He only desires what is best for you? After all, He Who has ordained all this for you is Your Father; you are literally His creation in the history of nations. All your existence as a nation is exclusively His work. Without Him you would not be here. While the other national entities were evolving around you, He alone created and trained you as a nation from the most insignificant, individual beginnings. That which other men are as individuals, only you are also as a nation: a creation of God. He therefore has an exclusive claim upon you. At the same time, your unique origin should assure you that whatever He, your Father, requires of you, the child He Himself has created, is intended solely for your own welfare.

° ° °

8. ***When the Most High assigned property to the nations.*** The reference is to the time when God, Who was then honored by the nations only as the "Most High" [among other deities], . . . allowed the nations to take possession of various territories on earth.

When He separated the sons of men. Each of these territories was physically different from all the others; therefore, each territory had its own effect on the people who settled in it. As a result, mankind, which began as a homogeneous whole (all men being descended from Adam), became diversified with regard to physical shape, mental capacity, language, occupations, customs and character. Mankind was separated into nations of many kinds, and each of these nations, being a product of its land, came to manifest different aspects of the human personality. . . .

He set the territories of peoples. At that time, He prepared the territories of the nations for the sons of Israel, who had yet to be counted. He permitted a specific territory to be occupied by several tribes. These tribes had to go through the process of acquiring dominion over the land and then of being dominated by the land in turn. Their land became territories of peoples. . . . But they would not be allowed to keep this territory because it had been set aside from the very beginning for a people that was still in the very early stages of its existence, present only as individual members of a certain family. . . .

9. ***For God's portion is His people.*** God did not permit the Children of Israel to become a nation in the land that was intended for them, to develop and grow under the impact of conditions and influences inherent in that land. Unlike all the other nations, God had the Children of Israel first become a nation without a land. Only thereafter did He cause them to take possession of

10. He sought him out in a desert land,

    In desolation, a howling wilderness;

He surrounds him, instructs him,

    Watches over him as the apple of His eye.

11. As an eagle first stirs up his nest,

    Hovering over its young,

Then spreads out its wings, takes it,

    Carrying it aloft upon its pinions,

י יִמְצָאֵ֙הוּ֙ בְּאֶ֣רֶץ מִדְבָּ֔ר

וּבְתֹ֖הוּ יְלֵ֣ל יְשִׁמֹ֑ן

יְסֹֽבְבֶ֙נְהוּ֙ יְב֣וֹנְנֵ֔הוּ

יִצְּרֶ֖נְהוּ כְּאִישׁ֥וֹן עֵינֽוֹ:

יא כְּנֶ֙שֶׁר֙ יָעִ֣יר קִנּ֔וֹ

עַל־גּֽוֹזָלָ֖יו יְרַחֵ֑ף

יִפְרֹ֤שׂ כְּנָפָיו֙ יִקָּחֵ֔הוּ

יִשָּׂאֵ֖הוּ עַל־אֶבְרָתֽוֹ:

a land especially intended for them, a land that had already been fully cultivated and built up by others . . . because "*God*'s portion is His people," because this nation, being the nation of God, belonging to Him, was to become and to remain the people of God, by virtue of its becoming a nation.

What the soil of their land is to the other nations, Israel's relationship with God is to Israel. The origin and existence of other nations are rooted in the soil of their land. By conquering the land, taking possession of it, cultivating it and developing it, they turn it into the basis for the development of their society. It is the climatic conditions of the land that then determine the physical, intellectual, moral and social evolution of their civilization. As a result, these nations come to deify what they consider to be the forces that shape their civilization; they come to worship these factors as gods on whom they think their development depends. Not so Israel. Israel is to bring into its land its *physical, intellectual, moral and social culture already fashioned by God*. It must not permit itself and its national life to be subordinated to the land; instead, it must make the land subordinate to itself and to its national life as fashioned by God. In this manner, as opposed to the aberrations and illusions of other nations, Israel's nationhood, its life and development as a nation, is to proclaim God as the sole true Power and the sole true Source of the prosperity of all nations. At the time this nation was born, amidst terrible sufferings, God first proclaimed: "I will take you to Myself as a people." Only after that did He say: "And then I will bring you into the land" (Exodus 6:7,8). Other nations are basically the "portion of their land," but Israel, by virtue of its origin and purpose, is חֵלֶק ד׳ ["*God*'s portion"]; "Yaakov, the lot of His inheritance."

For this reason, the source of this nation is not called *Yisrael* but *Yaakov*. This nation began as a family of individuals who, as יַעֲקֹב, had no home or land of their own. As such, they had to drain to the dregs the full cup of bitterness handed to people who have neither a land nor a home of their own, and who must live in the midst of a nation that glories in its land and its sovereign power, a nation that knows nothing of the innate, inalienable dignity to which every individual is entitled simply because he is a human being. In the view of the nations, a homeless, landless people has no human rights and no rights of domicile. Here was Yaakov, "hanging on to the heel of others," as it were, with regard to all the values by which other nations define their strength and greatness. Having neither soil nor power, he was inexperienced and undistinguished in the inventions, arts, sciences and skills that the human mind acquires in its struggle with nature and with other men and nations for the upbuilding of personal and national lives—achievements which these nations triumphantly equate with human greatness.

Yet "Yaakov (is) the lot of His inheritance": Rejected by the councils of the nations because of his threadbare, unprepossessing appearance, Yaakov literally "fell" to God, as it were, as His own inheritance. The other nations had no use for God and even less for His Law. They looked to other gods whose favors they believed had made them great. Above all, they defined their lives in terms of other goals and motivations than did Yaakov. In a society which launched the construction of the tower of historic fame with the triumphant cry, "Let us make a name for ourselves!," there was no room for a life built on God's dictates of hallowed morality; of truth, righteousness and loving-kindness, which in every respect was to proclaim the sole sovereignty of God on earth and over all the earth. Only Yaakov, who had nothing of his own, and who had not and could not have received anything from the forces that the nations worshipped as divine powers; Yaakov, who had received and could receive everything only from the hands of God—he was the sole instrument suited for the fulfillment of God's purposes among men on earth. Only because he was *Yaakov* could he be given the mission of being *Yisrael*, of proclaiming among men the sovereignty of God and of pledging allegiance to it by a life pursued in loyalty to his duties.

∘   ∘   ∘

12. So would *God* lead him, apart,	יב יְהֹוָה בָּדָד יַנְחֶנּוּ
And no alien god beside Him.	וְאֵין עִמּוֹ אֵל נֵכָר: שלישי
13. He made him climb the high places of the earth;	יג יַרְכִּבֵהוּ עַל-בָּמֳותֵי (במתי קרי) אָרֶץ
He ate the fruits of the fields;	וַיֹּאכַל תְּנוּבֹת שָׂדָי
He suckled him with honey from the rock	וַיֵּנִקֵהוּ דְבַשׁ מִסֶּלַע
And with the oil from the gravel of rock.	וְשֶׁמֶן מֵחַלְמִישׁ צוּר:
14. The cream of cattle and sheep's milk,	יד חֶמְאַת בָּקָר וַחֲלֵב צֹאן
With the fat of sheep,	עִם-חֵלֶב כָּרִים
And rams bred in Bashan,	וְאֵילִים בְּנֵי-בָשָׁן
And he-goats with fat from the kidneys of wheat;	וְעַתּוּדִים עִם-חֵלֶב כִּלְיוֹת חִטָּה
And the blood of the grape you drink as fermented wine!	וְדַם-עֵנָב תִּשְׁתֶּה-חָמֶר:
15. Then Yeshurun became fat and kicked—	טו וַיִּשְׁמַן יְשֻׁרוּן וַיִּבְעָט

12. בָּדָד *[apart]* is not synonymous with לְבַדּוֹ ["alone"]. It refers not to God's being alone in leading the nation, but to the isolation of that nation from all the other nations and from the powers to which they look for protection. . . .

13. . . . After God had awakened His people in the wilderness and trained them to entrust themselves entirely to the eagle's wings of His guidance, "He made him climb the high places of the earth." He permitted them to climb to the double pinnacle of earthly endeavor; i.e., to attain mental and moral accomplishments and, at the same time, physical health and material prosperity.

He ate the fruits of the fields. The nation was given, for its nourishment and its enjoyment, everything that fields cultivated by human toil had to offer. . . .

° ° °

15. ***Then Yeshurun became fat.*** Here, for the first time in Scripture, we read the name Yeshurun. It describes Israel in terms of the ideal of its moral calling, which is יָשָׁר ["straightness," "uprightness"], never deviating from the straight path of its calling. . . .

In Verse 13 we were told that God wanted Israel to ascend to the double pinnacle of earthly achievement: the peak of material prosperity and the peak of spiritual and moral perfection. For Israel was to be a shining example, demonstrating that a spiritual and moral life completely dedicated to duty does not by any means require a renunciation of all earthly pleasures. Indeed, the highest degree of morality is entirely compatible with the greatest measure of earthly happiness. In fact, the former must prove itself precisely under conditions associated with the latter, and all earthly resources and pleasures should be transposed into spiritual and moral accomplishments. However, when the people of Yeshurun, whose purpose it was to attain this moral ideal, received an abundance of material riches and pleasures; when it came out from the wilderness and into the land of milk and honey, it became fat and kicked. "Whenever you became fat, you became obese and overwhelmed by fat" is a parenthetical characterization of the nation that stood before Moses, and also of every future generation that was to read the words of his שִׁירָה [song]. It contains the quintessence of all subsequent Jewish history. As a rule, the Jewish people has proven itself splendid during periods of suffering. But it has rarely been able to endure good fortune. "Whenever it became fat, it became obese and overgrown (literally, "covered") with fat." . . .

The sense of this passage is: The more substantial and fat the food introduced into the body, the more should the body seek to transform the surplus of nourishment into energy and work. The better-nourished his body, the more active should the person be; the greater should be his output of activity and performance. In that case he will have control over his opulence; he will remain healthy in both mind and body; and his moral worth, too, will increase because of his greater moral and spiritual performance. But if he does not act in this manner, the surplus will be deposited in his body; he will become corpulent, obese and, instead of remaining in control over his substance, he—his true spiritual, active self—will be overwhelmed by the fat, and that will be his downfall. Such has been

Whenever you became fat, you became obese and overwhelmed by fat—	שָׁמַנְתָּ עָבִיתָ כָּשִׂיתָ
And he forsook God Who had made him,	וַיִּטֹּשׁ אֱלוֹהַּ עָשָׂהוּ
And regarded as worthless the Rock of his salvation.	וַיְנַבֵּל צוּר יְשֻׁעָתוֹ:
16. They impaired His rights with aliens,	טז יַקְנִאֻהוּ בְּזָרִים
Angering Him with abominations.	בְּתוֹעֵבֹת יַכְעִיסֻהוּ:
17. They made offerings to demons, non-gods,	יז יִזְבְּחוּ לַשֵּׁדִים לֹא אֱלֹהַּ
Deities of whom they knew nothing,	אֱלֹהִים לֹא יְדָעוּם
New ones that came up of late,	חֲדָשִׁים מִקָּרֹב בָּאוּ
Whom your fathers never dreaded.	לֹא שְׂעָרוּם אֲבֹתֵיכֶם:
18. The Rock had hardly borne you,	יח צוּר יְלָדְךָ תֶּשִׁי (י זעירא)
When you gave Him up to do homage to others,	

the history of the people of Israel. It failed to utilize its abundance and surplus for increased spiritual and moral performance, for a more complete discharge of its task. Its moral progress did not keep abreast of its material prosperity. It did not understand how to remain in control of its riches and its prosperity. It did not know how to use them for the achievement of its moral duties. Instead, it allowed itself to be overwhelmed by wealth and prosperity, and it allowed its better spiritual, moral self to be drowned in them.

° ° °

16. ***They impaired His rights with aliens.*** They transferred God's rightful, exclusive claim upon them to other powers completely alien to them, to whom they owe nothing and from whom they can expect nothing; who can do nothing for them and with whom, by the nature of their very essence, the people of Israel should never have established a relationship of allegiance. . . .

17. שֵׁדִים *[demons]* are invisible forces injurious to growth and prosperity. לֹא אֱלֹהַּ ["non-gods"] are forces which not even the deluded nations regard as gods.

Deities of whom they knew nothing. Of whom they had never experienced anything that could have given them cause to worship them as gods.

New ones that came up of late. The latest figments of illusion or invention.

Whom your fathers never dreaded. Whom not even your forefathers in the pagan era before the days of Abraham ever dreaded. One certainty alone—the certainty that there is One sole God, Who maintains a covenant of intimate closeness with those who do Him homage—will serve to sustain man and to lift him high above all of the other forces between heaven and earth. This conviction alone will make him free of all fear and will keep him from quaking before any power, real or imaginary, that is inimical to his prosperity. But once he leaves the service of the One sole God, man loses all inner support; and he who boasted of his wonderful freedom finds himself trembling in fear before the forces of nature and fate—which are truly more powerful than man if he is left on his own—and quaking before all the delusions born of superstition and claiming to have insight into the mysteries of nature and the universe.

Beneath the light of truth emanating from the One sole God, man sees all the world in the sunlight of the powers of wisdom and goodness, in which all things are led, even through darkness and death, grief and destruction, toward a higher state of existence and of life, strength and joy, immortality and eternity. He will see his life as a condition in which, as a child of the One sole God, leading a life devoted to Him, he is bound up with his Father even now, when he is still alive. Clinging to the hand of his One sole God, he can walk even through darkness and death in untroubled serenity toward light and life.

But if he should close his eyes to that light and that life, then the world will descend before his eyes into a dark night filled with specters, real and imaginary. In that case he has only the miners' lamp of his personal experience to guide him through the darkness in which he must wrestle with hostile demons for his life and happiness. Then every delight and joy will end for him in disgust and frustration. His life will be one he enters crying, only to depart from it with lamentations and in resignation. In such a life, man appears as the most unfortunate of all creatures, because he is aware how unfortunate he is, and because he feels an urgent desire for peace and happiness—but this claim can never be satisfied as long as he does not lead a life of devotion to duty. A descent from the bliss of a world of God to the pessimism of a world of demons: this has ever been the dismal road along which defection from God must

And forgot God while He was still forming you.	וַתִּשְׁכַּח אֵל מְחֹלְלֶךָ: רביעי
19. *God* saw this and turned away in disdain,	יט וַיַּרְא יְהוָה וַיִּנְאָץ
Because of annoyance from His sons and daughters,	מִכַּעַס בָּנָיו וּבְנֹתָיו:
20. And He said: I will hide My face from them;	כ וַיֹּאמֶר אַסְתִּירָה פָנַי מֵהֶם
I will see what their end will be;	אֶרְאֶה מָה אַחֲרִיתָם
For they are a generation of constant changes,	כִּי דוֹר תַּהְפֻּכֹת הֵמָּה
Sons in whom there is no trust.	בָּנִים לֹא־אֵמֻן בָּם:
21. They have invaded My right with non-gods;	כא הֵם קִנְאוּנִי בְלֹא־אֵל
They have angered Me with their trifles;	כִּעֲסוּנִי בְּהַבְלֵיהֶם
I will have their rights invaded by non-peoples;	וַאֲנִי אַקְנִיאֵם בְּלֹא־עָם
I will cause them grief through a withered nation.	בְּגוֹי נָבָל אַכְעִיסֵם:
22. For the fire was kindled by My anger;	כב כִּי־אֵשׁ קָדְחָה בְאַפִּי
Therefore it burned to the nethermost depths;	וַתִּיקַד עַד־שְׁאוֹל תַּחְתִּית
It consumed the land and its fruit,	וַתֹּאכַל אֶרֶץ וִיבֻלָהּ
And set the foundations of mountains ablaze.	וַתְּלַהֵט מוֹסְדֵי הָרִים:
23. I will let evil upon evil come upon them;	כג אַסְפֶּה עָלֵימוֹ רָעוֹת
I will use up My arrows against them.	חִצַּי אֲכַלֶּה־בָּם:
24. Emaciation of hunger, heat of fever	כד מְזֵי רָעָב וּלְחֻמֵי רֶשֶׁף
and bitterness of death,	וְקֶטֶב מְרִירִי
And the teeth of beasts will I send against them,	וְשֶׁן־בְּהֵמֹת אֲשַׁלַּח־בָּם
With the fury of things that creep in the dust.	עִם־חֲמַת זֹחֲלֵי עָפָר:

lead; a road to which the people of Israel must also descend if it defects from God: "And he forsook God Who had made him. . . . They impaired His rights with aliens. . . . They made offerings to demons."

° ° °

19–20. . . . If, under the impact of your sufferings, you will complain that God's help is no longer manifest in your midst as it was in days of old, here you have your answer. . . . God no longer felt bound by any considerations; He saw nothing that would have been worthy of His remaining in your midst. . . . [God says:] They think they can do without Me and My support; well, then, let them see for themselves how far they will get without Me.

I will hide My face from them. I will no longer show them My special care. . . .

21. . . . I will cause them to be robbed of their rights by nations which, even in their own societies, no longer give one another that mutual respect upon which the survival of any nation depends. They oppressed and robbed one another, so it is only natural that they should oppress and rob the Jews even more. . . .

22. . . . For the destructive power that overtook them did so as the result of My anger with them; it was My anger that endowed this power with such deep and thorough destructive force.

23. . . . I will send every kind of trouble to overtake them, but at the same time I will give them the strength to survive all these sufferings. חִצַּי כָּלִים וְהֵם אֵינָן כָּלִים [My arrows will be used up but they (the sons of Jacob) will not cease.] (*Sifri*).

25. The sword will bereave from outside,
And terror from within,
Young man and maiden,
Infant and hoary head.
26. I would say: 'I will put them in a corner;
I will make their memory disappear from among mankind,'
27. If I would not thereby amass unpleasantness from the enemy.
Their oppressors could misunderstand it;
They could say: 'Our hand is high;
It is not *God* that has caused all this!'
28. For they, too, are a nation that perishes in its own plans,
And insight is not found among them.
29. If they were wise, they would turn their mind to this;
They would discern their own end.
30. How should one pursue one thousand,
Or two put ten thousand to flight,
Had their Rock not surrendered them,
And *God* delivered them up?
31. For their rock is not like our Rock;
Our enemies themselves are judges of this.

כה מִחוּץ֙ תְּשַׁכֶּל־חֶ֔רֶב
וּמֵחֲדָרִ֖ים אֵימָ֑ה
גַּם־בָּחוּר֙ גַּם־בְּתוּלָ֔ה
יוֹנֵ֖ק עִם־אִ֥ישׁ שֵׂיבָֽה׃
כו אָמַ֖רְתִּי אַפְאֵיהֶ֑ם
אַשְׁבִּ֥יתָה מֵאֱנ֖וֹשׁ זִכְרָֽם׃
כז לוּלֵי֙ כַּ֤עַס אוֹיֵב֙ אָג֔וּר
פֶּן־יְנַכְּר֖וּ צָרֵ֑ימוֹ
פֶּן־יֹֽאמְרוּ֙ יָדֵ֣נוּ רָ֔מָה
וְלֹ֥א יְהוָ֖ה פָּעַ֥ל כָּל־זֹֽאת׃
כח כִּי־ג֛וֹי אֹבַ֥ד עֵצ֖וֹת הֵ֑מָּה
וְאֵ֥ין בָּהֶ֖ם תְּבוּנָֽה׃ חמישי
כט ל֥וּ חָכְמ֖וּ יַשְׂכִּ֣ילוּ זֹ֑את
יָבִ֖ינוּ לְאַחֲרִיתָֽם׃
ל אֵיכָ֞ה יִרְדֹּ֤ף אֶחָד֙ אֶ֔לֶף
וּשְׁנַ֖יִם יָנִ֣יסוּ רְבָבָ֑ה
אִם־לֹא֙ כִּֽי־צוּרָ֣ם מְכָרָ֔ם
וַֽיהוָ֖ה הִסְגִּירָֽם׃
לא כִּ֛י לֹ֥א כְצוּרֵ֖נוּ צוּרָ֑ם
וְאֹיְבֵ֖ינוּ פְּלִילִֽים׃

26–27. . . . [God says:] "After all this evil had come upon them, I could have placed them into a remote corner of the earth—as with the Ten Tribes—to remove them from further ill-treatment. There, left entirely to themselves, they could become sufficiently mature to engage in serious reflection, so that, ultimately, they would return to Me. I would indeed do this, were I not deterred by the thought that it might result in even greater trouble for Israel from its enemies. . . . These enemies might misunderstand such a development. They could "estrange" it from the truth [from נָכְר, "strange"]; they might interpret this development differently from what it was meant to be. . . ."

Hence, Israel must remain in the midst of a world hostile to it and to its God, among men even more sinful and corrupt than they. True, Israel will thus have to be exposed to continued ill-treatment, but this is the one way to avoid results utterly at variance with the purpose of Israel's mission. Instead of regarding Israel's disappearance from human memory as an indication of the workings of the One sole God in world history, of His will and His sovereignty, the nations would view it as a triumph of heathen delusion over the truth of Judaism. They would consider God's judgment upon Israel not as the judgment of God, but as a triumph of their own human might. Therefore, in order to disabuse the nations of such illusions, Israel must endure, suffer and, with it all, survive.

28. ***For they, too, are a nation that perishes in its own plans.*** The nations opposed to Israel will perish, together, as a result of their self-made plans and their conceited notions of their political sagacity. They lack the insight to draw the right conclusions from the events and realities they observe.

29. ***If they were wise.*** If they were receptive to wisdom, they would address their intelligence to the Divine judgment, which is being carried out against Israel before their very eyes and in which they themselves are used as an instrument. Seeing these things in their proper light, they would be able to arrive at certain conclusions about their own fate.

32. For their vine is of the vine of S'dom,

    And from the open country of Gomorrah;

Their grapes are poisonous grapes,

    Clusters of bitterness to them.

33. The fury of dragons is their wine,

    And the cruel poison of vipers.

34. Therefore it lies concealed with Me,

    Sealed up within My treasuries.

35. Mine is the office of avenger and retribution,

    At the appointed time their foot will slip.

For the day of their smoke-cloud is near,

    It rushes toward them in events to come.

36. For *God* will judge His people

    And reveal Himself in a changed decree concerning

        His servants

When He sees that all power has vanished,

    And nothing left to keep or abandon.

לב כִּי־מִגֶּפֶן סְדֹם גַּפְנָם
וּמִשַּׁדְמֹת עֲמֹרָה
עֲנָבֵמוֹ עִנְּבֵי־רוֹשׁ
אַשְׁכְּלֹת מְרֹרֹת לָמוֹ:

לג חֲמַת תַּנִּינִם יֵינָם
וְרֹאשׁ פְּתָנִים אַכְזָר:

לד הֲלֹא־הוּא כָּמֻס עִמָּדִי
חָתוּם בְּאוֹצְרֹתָי:

לה לִי נָקָם וְשִׁלֵּם
לְעֵת תָּמוּט רַגְלָם
כִּי קָרוֹב יוֹם אֵידָם
וְחָשׁ עֲתִדֹת לָמוֹ:

לו כִּי־יָדִין יְהוָה עַמּוֹ
וְעַל־עֲבָדָיו יִתְנֶחָם
כִּי יִרְאֶה כִּי־אָזְלַת יָד
וְאֶפֶס עָצוּר וְעָזוּב:

32. . . . Had they understood Israel's fate as a Divine judgment; had they considered the judgments that this God of Israel had already meted out to other nations, then, instead of oppressing and mocking Israel, they would have given thought to what their own end might be; how they themselves will fare when God will sit in judgment on them. . . .

36. . . . The nations are reminded to think of the day of judgment and retribution that will come to them also. True, we are told here, Israel, having forfeited its political independence because of its sins, has had to wander into exile and, for its own education—and that of the other nations, too—was scattered among the nations and delivered, helpless, to their mercies. Nevertheless, no matter how gravely the nation of Israel has defected from its ideal mission, it is still, as far as the other nations are concerned, "His people and His servants." They are the people of God, servants who subordinate themselves to His will, as expressed in His Law, and to the purposes of His sovereignty.

Israel has never completely broken its covenant with God and His Law, nor has it ever categorically disavowed either of these. The promise "for it will not be forgotten out of the mouth of its children" (Deuteronomy 31:21), the underlying theme of this שִׁירָה, has come true, along with the sufferings that have been foretold. Hence, though the withdrawal of God's pro-

tection from them left the people of Israel without defense against the outrages of the nations, this did not justify all the abuses to which they were subjected. Rather, this dispersion of the weak among the mighty was, at the same time, a test of the mighty, to see how much justice and humanity was within their hearts. The treatment one accords to the mighty, who presumably have means of retaliating for any wrong done to them, is not a demonstration of one's justice and humanity. The true index of the moral worth of the mighty is the sympathy and respect they show for the plight and the rights of the weak. Therefore "*God* will judge His people": He will sit in judgment on the treatment accorded to His people among the nations of the world, "and reveal Himself in a changed decree concerning His servants," when He sees that His people and servants have lost everything and have nothing left, great or small, to sustain them or to hold out any promise for their future. With the sufferings described in Verses 23, 24 and 25, the fate decreed for Israel has reached the point of greatest devastation. When Israel arrives at this stage, the words "When He sees that all power has vanished" (Verse 36) and the statement "I will see what their end will be" (Verse 20) will become relevant, and the dispersion that was inflicted on Israel, instead of their being "put in a corner" (Verse 26), will signify the beginning of Israel's deliverance and restoration. . . .

* * *

37. Then He will say: Where are their gods now,

    The rock in whom they placed their trust?

לז וְאָמַ֖ר אֵ֣י אֱלֹהֵ֑ימוֹ
צ֖וּר חָסָ֥יוּ בֽוֹ׃

38. Those who were to eat the fat of their meal offerings,

    Drink the wine of their libations?

Let them rise up and help you

    So that you may have protection!

לח אֲשֶׁ֨ר חֵ֤לֶב זְבָחֵ֙ימוֹ֙ יֹאכֵ֔לוּ
יִשְׁתּ֖וּ יֵ֣ין נְסִיכָ֑ם
יָק֙וּמוּ֙ וְיַעְזְרֻכֶ֔ם
יְהִ֥י עֲלֵיכֶ֖ם סִתְרָֽה׃

39. See now that I am indeed "I"

    And there is no god beside Me;

I kill and restore to life;

    I have inflicted wounds, and I will heal;

    Nothing can be snatched from My hand.

לט רְא֣וּ ׀ עַתָּ֗ה כִּ֣י אֲנִ֤י אֲנִי֙ ה֔וּא
וְאֵ֥ין אֱלֹהִ֖ים עִמָּדִ֑י
אֲנִ֧י אָמִ֣ית וַאֲחַיֶּ֗ה
מָחַ֙צְתִּי֙ וַאֲנִ֣י אֶרְפָּ֔א
וְאֵ֥ין מִיָּדִ֖י מַצִּֽיל׃ ששי

40. For I raise My hand to heaven

    And say: I live forever!

מ כִּֽי־אֶשָּׂ֥א אֶל־שָׁמַ֖יִם יָדִ֑י
וְאָמַ֕רְתִּי חַ֥י אָנֹכִ֖י לְעֹלָֽם׃

41. Were I to sharpen the lightning of My sword,

    Were my hand to take up justice,

Were I to turn vengeance back upon My enemies

    And repay those that hate Me,

מא אִם־שַׁנּוֹתִי֙ בְּרַ֣ק חַרְבִּ֔י
וְתֹאחֵ֥ז בְּמִשְׁפָּ֖ט יָדִ֑י
אָשִׁ֤יב נָקָם֙ לְצָרָ֔י
וְלִמְשַׂנְאַ֖י אֲשַׁלֵּֽם׃

42. I would have to make My arrows drunk with blood,

    And My sword would devour flesh

From the blood of the slain and the captive,

    From the curly heads of the enemy.

מב אַשְׁכִּ֤יר חִצַּי֙ מִדָּ֔ם
וְחַרְבִּ֖י תֹּאכַ֣ל בָּשָׂ֑ר
מִדַּ֤ם חָלָל֙ וְשִׁבְיָ֔ה
מֵרֹ֖אשׁ פַּרְע֥וֹת אוֹיֵֽב׃

43. Therefore, O nations, make His people's lot a happy one,

    For He will avenge the blood of His servants,

And He will turn back vengeance upon His enemies,

    And His people will atone for His world."

מג הַרְנִ֤ינוּ גוֹיִם֙ עַמּ֔וֹ
כִּ֥י דַם־עֲבָדָ֖יו יִקּ֑וֹם
וְנָקָם֙ יָשִׁ֣יב לְצָרָ֔יו
וְכִפֶּ֥ר אַדְמָת֖וֹ עַמּֽוֹ׃ פ שביעי

41–42. . . . Were I to deal with them as they dealt with Israel and with other defenseless human beings, My retribution would have to be bloody, savage and terrible. . . .

43. . . . Therefore, even as He disperses Israel among them, God calls out to the nations: "Make My people's lot a happy one! Do not deal inhumanly and cruelly with them!" Three motives are given for this Divine warning ("Therefore, O nations, make His people's lot a happy one"):

For He will avenge the blood of His servants. The

dispersed of Israel enter into the midst of the nations as "His servants," as bearers of the Name of God, with his imprint upon them. And in this God there lives an Avenger for every drop of their innocent blood that is shed.

He will turn back vengeance upon His enemies. God will cause each violation of the dictates of justice and humanity to "fall back" upon its perpetrators who, by denying the standards of justice and humanity, also deny His sovereignty and are therefore "His enemies." And finally,

His people will atone for His world. The function of

44. Moshe came and spoke all the words
of this song in the ears of the people, he
and Hoshea, son of Nun. 45. When
Moshe had finished speaking all these words
to all Yisrael, 46. he said to them: "Set
your mind earnestly to all the words with
which I bear witness to you today, that you
may charge your children to carry out punctiliously all the words of this Teaching.
47. For it is not a word empty of you; it
is your very life, and with it you will prolong
your days upon the soil, to which you pass
over the Yarden, to take possession of it."
48. On that same day *God* spoke to
Moshe [saying]: 49. "Go up to this
Mountain of Transitions, to Mount Nebo,
which is in the land of Moab, facing Jericho,
and see the land of Canaan, which I am
giving to the sons of Yisrael as a possession;

מד וַיָּבֹא מֹשֶׁה וַיְדַבֵּר אֶת־כָּל־דִּבְרֵי הַשִּׁירָה־
הַזֹּאת בְּאָזְנֵי הָעָם הוּא וְהוֹשֵׁעַ בִּן־נוּן: מה וַיְכַל
מֹשֶׁה לְדַבֵּר אֶת־כָּל־הַדְּבָרִים הָאֵלֶּה אֶל־כָּל־
יִשְׂרָאֵל: מו וַיֹּאמֶר אֲלֵהֶם שִׂימוּ לְבַבְכֶם לְכָל־
הַדְּבָרִים אֲשֶׁר אָנֹכִי מֵעִיד בָּכֶם הַיּוֹם אֲשֶׁר
תְּצַוֻּם אֶת־בְּנֵיכֶם לִשְׁמֹר לַעֲשׂוֹת אֶת־כָּל־דִּבְרֵי
הַתּוֹרָה הַזֹּאת: מז כִּי לֹא־דָבָר רֵק הוּא מִכֶּם
כִּי־הוּא חַיֵּיכֶם וּבַדָּבָר הַזֶּה תַּאֲרִיכוּ יָמִים
עַל־הָאֲדָמָה אֲשֶׁר אַתֶּם עֹבְרִים אֶת־הַיַּרְדֵּן
שָׁמָּה לְרִשְׁתָּהּ: פ מפטיר מח וַיְדַבֵּר יְהוָֹה
אֶל־מֹשֶׁה בְּעֶצֶם הַיּוֹם הַזֶּה לֵאמֹר: מט עֲלֵה
אֶל־הַר הָעֲבָרִים הַזֶּה הַר־נְבוֹ אֲשֶׁר בְּאֶרֶץ
מוֹאָב אֲשֶׁר עַל־פְּנֵי יְרֵחוֹ וּרְאֵה אֶת־אֶרֶץ כְּנַעַן
אֲשֶׁר אֲנִי נֹתֵן לִבְנֵי יִשְׂרָאֵל לַאֲחֻזָּה: נ וּמֻת

God's people will be to bring atonement to His world, which was given to man to rule [see notes on Genesis 2:7]. By according better treatment to His people, thus showing their obedience to God's moral law, the nations are to pay homage at last to God's dominion on earth. Then there will be an end to, and an atonement for, the sins against justice and humanity committed by those who would deny His supremacy on earth. Thus, the treatment accorded by the nations to Israel will be the barometer showing the degree to which man gives allegiance to God on earth, so that the Kingdom of God will come when the nations will cease to oppress Israel. . . .

The admonition to the nations, "Make His people's lot a happy one," suggests the following thought: It was anticipated that the Book of God's Teaching, carried to the nations by its scattered bearers, would become the common property of all nations—a preconception which indeed has come to pass. The nations, therefore, would become aware of God's warning. In addition, and in equal measure, they would come to understand, and increasingly to put into practice, the concept of the One sole God and the principles deriving from this truth: the equality and brotherhood of man and man's duty to practice justice and humanity. This assumption would include the presupposition that the Book of Books, which Israel has carried into the midst of the nations, will enlighten and civilize not only the nations, but also Israel, so that Israel will clear the path to the gateway of its own redemption.

° ° °

The divisions [observed when this portion is read in the synagogue on the Sabbath] correspond to the logical train of thought that runs through the שִׁירָה [Song of Moses]. Verses 1 through 6 speak of God and characterize the relationship of His ways to the world in general and to Israel in particular. Verses 7 through 12 deal with Israel, its destiny and its origins. Verses 13 through 18 relate Israel's prosperity and the sins committed by Israel during periods of good fortune. Verses 19 through 26 describe Israel's downfall as a result of these sins. Verses 27 through 35 explain the purpose of Israel's dispersion among the nations and also serve as an admonition to the nations. Verses 36 through 43 sing of Israel's restoration and afford an insight into the future of Israel and the nations.

47. ***For it is not a word empty of you.*** It is not a word that does not have you yourselves as its content. Hence the interpretation of this clause would be, either, "This summons you to understand the Law and to observe it. It is not a word to which you should remain indifferent, for it encompasses all of your existence and all of your aspirations"; or, "In all of this Teaching there is not one word that does not relate to you, to all of your existence and your aspirations. Not one word of the תּוֹרָה is irrelevant. Every word in it contains truths vital to all of your existence and all of your aspirations.". . .

50. and die on the mountain that you are ascending, and be gathered there to your people, even as your brother Aharon died on Mount Hor and was gathered to his people; 51. because you trespassed against Me in the midst of the sons of Yisrael at the waters of contention in Kadesh, in the wilderness of Tzin; because you did not sanctify Me in the midst of the sons of Yisrael.   52. For [only] from afar shall you see the Land; you will not come there, not to the land that I am giving to the sons of Yisrael."

בָּהָר אֲשֶׁר אַתָּה עֹלֶה שָׁמָּה וְהֵאָסֵף אֶל־עַמֶּיךָ
כַּאֲשֶׁר־מֵת אַהֲרֹן אָחִיךָ בְּהֹר הָהָר וַיֵּאָסֶף
אֶל־עַמָּיו: נא עַל אֲשֶׁר מְעַלְתֶּם בִּי בְּתוֹךְ בְּנֵי
יִשְׂרָאֵל בְּמֵי־מְרִיבַת קָדֵשׁ מִדְבַּר־צִן עַל אֲשֶׁר
לֹא־קִדַּשְׁתֶּם אוֹתִי בְּתוֹךְ בְּנֵי יִשְׂרָאֵל: נב כִּי
מִנֶּגֶד תִּרְאֶה אֶת־הָאָרֶץ וְשָׁמָּה לֹא תָבוֹא אֶל־
הָאָרֶץ אֲשֶׁר־אֲנִי נֹתֵן לִבְנֵי יִשְׂרָאֵל: פ

The Haftarah for this Sidra may be found on page 925.

ברכה

BERAKHAH

XXXIII 1. And this is the blessing with which Moshe, the man of God, blessed the sons of Yisrael before his death. 2. He said: "God entered from Sinai and had already shone forth to them from Seir; He had dawned upon them from Mount Paran and then come from the myriads of holy ones; from His right hand there was for them fire–become–law. 3. Also in order to lead peoples to duty dost Thou take all Thy holy ones into Thy hand; Thy sovereignty makes them aware of their powerlessness; however, it bears Thy words expressing Thee. 4. The Teaching that Moshe commanded us—*this* is the inheritance, O

לג א וְזֹאת הַבְּרָכָה אֲשֶׁר בֵּרַךְ מֹשֶׁה אִישׁ
הָאֱלֹהִים אֶת־בְּנֵי יִשְׂרָאֵל לִפְנֵי מוֹתוֹ:
ב וַיֹּאמַר יְהֹוָה מִסִּינַי בָּא וְזָרַח מִשֵּׂעִיר לָמוֹ
הוֹפִיעַ מֵהַר פָּארָן וְאָתָה מֵרִבְבֹת קֹדֶשׁ
מִימִינוֹ אֵשְׁדָּת (אש דת קרי) לָמוֹ: ג אַף חֹבֵב
עַמִּים כָּל־קְדֹשָׁיו בְּיָדֶךָ וְהֵם תֻּכּוּ לְרַגְלֶךָ יִשָּׂא
מִדַּבְּרֹתֶיךָ: ד תּוֹרָה צִוָּה־לָנוּ מֹשֶׁה מוֹרָשָׁה

CHAPTER XXXIII

2. מִימִינוֹ אֵשְׁדָּת לָמוֹ [*from His right hand there was for them fire–become–law*]. The two words [אֵשׁ and דָּת] are written here as one word because they form one idea. This is the only place in Scripture where the word דָּת is used with reference to the תּוֹרָה. It is the cosmic conception, as it were, of the תּוֹרָה, a designation of the תּוֹרָה's significance in God's universal scheme. אֵשׁ [fire] is the force that generates movement, change and life in all physical creations; the dark, invisible fire, as our Sages call it (in Deuteronomy Rabbah to *Parshath Ekev*), through which the eternal, God-given laws for the universe are fulfilled. These laws operate in all creatures without their being aware of them, and independently of their will. But these same laws, established and willed by God, the Supreme Consciousness and Will, and operating through the almighty power of His will, are to work differently with man, the creature called upon to exercise moral free will. In the case of man, God's Law is not to operate from within him, without his conscious will; it is to come to him from without, so that, out of his own free volition, he may absorb it in his mind and will. Such is the תּוֹרָה. It is the same Law of God which speaks out from within every other creature but which is addressed to man from without. Only by fulfilling this Law can man assume, consciously and of his own free will, that position which all other creatures must take unconsciously, without freedom of choice. It is the "fire become law." And מִימִינוֹ ["from His right hand"]: it is by the helping, sustaining right hand of God's salvation . . . that this Law was handed to them. . . .

3. . . . All Thy holy ones serve as Thy instruments to this end. Not only Israel but also the rest of mankind will benefit from the educational and moral influence of those among Israel who hallow their lives by faithfully observing this Law. These individuals tacitly serve as a light to all mankind, as models showing how man's sacred calling is to be put into practice. Though we are told above that even Seir and Paran, nations closely related to Israel, were not yet sufficiently mature to accept the Law, the revelation of the Law to Israel on Mount Sinai was intended to benefit all mankind. With and through Israel, the ground was prepared for the future gathering of all mankind to perform its duty toward God. . . . Only through the Law, whose bearer Israel became at Sinai, will the lessons imparted to the other nations by historical experience attain their purpose. . . .

4. . . . This Teaching is מוֹרָשָׁה ["the inheritance"]: This, the Teaching, not the Land and what it has to offer, constitutes the true inheritance of the nation. Land and power are only factors conditional on this spiritual heritage. . . .

The use of the terms יַעֲקֹב [Yaakov] and קְהִלָּה [assembly] in this passage is significant. יַעֲקֹב is the designation for the people of Israel implying its material insignificance. Moreover, note that the text uses a form of the word קְהִלָּה, not קָהָל. This is the only place in Scripture where the Jewish entity is called קְהִלָּה; elsewhere in Scripture, the term is always קְהַל יִשְׂרָאֵל, stressing the nation's independence. קְהִלָּה is the weaker form of קָהָל; it denotes either the entire community in a condition of weakness, or a small, weak branch of a larger community. God entrusted His

קְהִלַּת יַעֲקֹב: ה וַיְהִי בִישֻׁרוּן מֶלֶךְ בְּהִתְאַסֵּף רָאשֵׁי עָם יַחַד שִׁבְטֵי יִשְׂרָאֵל: ו יְחִי רְאוּבֵן וְאַל־יָמֹת וִיהִי מְתָיו מִסְפָּר: ס ז וְזֹאת לִיהוּדָה וַיֹּאמַר שְׁמַע יְהֹוָה קוֹל יְהוּדָה וְאֶל־עַמּוֹ תְּבִיאֶנּוּ יָדָיו רָב לוֹ וְעֵזֶר מִצָּרָיו תִּהְיֶה: פ שני ח וּלְלֵוִי אָמַר תֻּמֶּיךָ וְאוּרֶיךָ לְאִישׁ חֲסִידֶךָ אֲשֶׁר נִסִּיתוֹ בְּמַסָּה תְּרִיבֵהוּ עַל־מֵי מְרִיבָה:

assembly of Yaakov! 5. It became king in Yeshurun. Inasmuch as the heads of the people gathered around it, the tribes of Yisrael became united, all of them together. 6. So Reuben, too, will live; he shall not go under, and let his common ones always be numbered. 7. And the same is true for Yehudah, when he said: Hear, O *God*, the voice of Yehudah and bring him to his people, for with His might does he fight for them. Mayest Thou be a help against his enemies." 8. And regarding Levi he said: "Thy Thummim and Thy Urim go to the man who devotes himself to Thee, whom Thou hast tested repeatedly, and with whom Thou didst dispute at the water of conten-

Law as a heritage not to individuals, but to the community as a whole, because only the community lives forever, and only the community will always have the material resources for what it seeks to accomplish. Cf. "The community does not die, and the community does not become destitute." Also, the תּוֹרָה was not meant to be observed only during periods of prosperity, nor was it given to the larger community alone. It must be upheld and observed even when Israel is in a state implied by the term יַעֲקֹב; moreover, every *kehillah* [Jewish religious community] is responsible for the observance and transmission of the תּוֹרָה within its own circle, no matter how small that circle may be.

5. *It became king in Yeshurun.* The תּוֹרָה, the Law, became "king in Yeshurun." It alone is the reigning, commanding and governing power in Israel. Even the kings in Israel were under its dominion: the king was to be only its very first model subject. . . .

Inasmuch as the heads of the people gathered. The fact that the heads of the nation gathered around the תּוֹרָה bound all the tribes of Israel together. The Law constitutes the sole true bond that unites all the segments of the Jewish people. If the entire leadership of the nation subscribes to the Law and subordinates itself to it, then the union of the nation and the Law becomes, at the same time, the bond that binds all the tribes of the nation to one another. And when they all thus share in common this, the nation's most precious possession, each and every member of the nation will attain a position of equality as part of the whole.

6. . . . Under Jacob's last will [as pronounced in his blessing of his sons], Reuben had lost the position of leadership that normally would have come to him as the first-born. As a result, it seems that his tribe, too, did not attain any material or spiritual distinction. However, as has just been said, there is one posses-

sion—the most precious possession of all—the תּוֹרָה; the one true inheritance of the nation, which all the tribes share alike and in terms of which all the tribes are regarded as equally worthy. Hence even a tribe as undistinguished materially and spiritually as Reuben can develop to its full potential as long as it upholds and observes the Law; Reuben need not go under, and מְתָיו, those of its members that are of no consequence, will be only a numbered few, or few in number.

8. . . . Everywhere else in Scripture the אוּרִים are mentioned first. It is significant that in this passage the תֻּמִּים, which represent the highest stage of moral perfection, precede the אוּרִים, which symbolize the highest level of intellectual enlightenment. This verse speaks of the tribe that was considered worthy of bearing both these symbols. Here the first requirement is not intellectual brilliance but moral probity. The everyday life of a tribe in this position must, above all, not conflict with that moral standard which qualified it to become the bearer of the אוּרִים and תֻּמִּים in the first place. Indeed, the tribe is described not in terms of its intellectual endowments, but primarily in terms of its moral characteristics.

Thy Thummim and Thy Urim go to the man who devotes himself to Thee. Thou [God] gavest Thy Urim and Thummim to Levi because he is "the man who devotes himself to Thee." Herein lies the distinctive character of Judaism. In Judaism neither intellectual prowess nor membership in an intellectual profession constitutes a license for a relaxation of ethics and morals. On the contrary, Judaism insists that such gifted individuals must show outstanding talent also in their respect for and observance of the moral law. We have already had occasion repeatedly to point this out.

•   •   •

tion;   9. he who says of his father and
mother: 'I have not seen him,' who did not
recognize his brothers, who was not conscious of his children; for they have guarded
Thy promise, and they now watch over Thy
Covenant.   10. They teach Thy [social]
ordinances to Yaakov and Thy Teaching to
Yisrael; they place incense for Thy perception and whole offerings upon Thy altar.
11. Bless, O *God*, his substance and
accept with favor the achievement of his
hands; smash Thou the loins of those that
rise up against him, so that those that hate
him   may   not   rise   in   opposition."
12. Regarding   Binyamin   he   said:
"Beloved of *God*, he rests securely with
Him. He caused His covering to rest upon
him at all times and takes up His abode
between his high places."   13. And
regarding Yosef he said: "Blessed by *God* be
his land, with the fruit of the heaven, with
dew and with floods that rest far below;
14. with the fruit dispensed by the sun
and with the fruit driven forth by the
[linear] months;   15. with the summit of
the primeval mountains and with the fruit
of the hills eternal;   16. with the fruit of
the earth and its abundance and, at the
same time, with the favor of the One Who
took up [His] abode in the thornbush for
me—O that it may thus come to rest upon
Yosef's head, upon the crown of the most
abstinent of his brothers.   17. Glory will
come to the firstling of his bull, and the

ט הָאֹמֵר לְאָבִיו וּלְאִמּוֹ לֹא רְאִיתִיו וְאֶת־אֶחָיו
לֹא הִכִּיר וְאֶת־בָּנָו (בניו קרי) לֹא יָדָע כִּי שָׁמְרוּ
אִמְרָתֶךָ וּבְרִיתְךָ יִנְצֹרוּ: י יוֹרוּ מִשְׁפָּטֶיךָ
לְיַעֲקֹב וְתוֹרָתְךָ לְיִשְׂרָאֵל יָשִׂימוּ קְטוֹרָה
בְאַפֶּךָ וְכָלִיל עַל־מִזְבְּחֶךָ: יא בָּרֵךְ יְהֹוָה חֵילוֹ
וּפֹעַל יָדָיו תִּרְצֶה מְחַץ מָתְנַיִם קָמָיו וּמְשַׂנְאָיו
מִן־יְקוּמוּן: ס יב לְבִנְיָמִן אָמַר יְדִיד יְהֹוָה
יִשְׁכֹּן לָבֶטַח עָלָיו חֹפֵף עָלָיו כָּל־הַיּוֹם וּבֵין
כְּתֵפָיו שָׁכֵן: ס שלישי יג וּלְיוֹסֵף אָמַר מְבֹרֶכֶת
יְהֹוָה אַרְצוֹ מִמֶּגֶד שָׁמַיִם מִטָּל וּמִתְּהוֹם רֹבֶצֶת
תָּחַת: יד וּמִמֶּגֶד תְּבוּאֹת שָׁמֶשׁ וּמִמֶּגֶד גֶּרֶשׁ
יְרָחִים: טו וּמֵרֹאשׁ הַרְרֵי־קֶדֶם וּמִמֶּגֶד גִּבְעוֹת
עוֹלָם: טז וּמִמֶּגֶד אֶרֶץ וּמְלֹאָהּ וּרְצוֹן שֹׁכְנִי
סְנֶה תָּבוֹאתָה לְרֹאשׁ יוֹסֵף וּלְקָדְקֹד נְזִיר
אֶחָיו: יז בְּכוֹר שׁוֹרוֹ הָדָר לוֹ וְקַרְנֵי רְאֵם

---

11. *Bless . . . his substance.* (See notes on Exodus
18:25). Bless his intellectual and moral gifts, the intellectual and spiritual strength and abilities required for
his calling as teacher and guardian of the Law among
the people. . . .

12. *Regarding Binyamin.* First there is Judah, the
bearer of the nation's power; then, Levi, the guardian
of the Law and the Sanctuary. These are now followed
by Benjamin, in whose territory the Sanctuary, or,
more accurately, the most sacred part of the Sanctuary,
was placed. It is significant that the altar, the *hekhal*
[the Hall containing the altar] and the *d'vir* [Holy of
Holies] were not placed in the territory of the mighty
tribe of kings, but in the territory of Benjamin, the
youngest and weakest of all the tribes. . . .

· · · ·

and takes up His abode between his high places. As
explained in Zebaḥim 54b, this was not upon the
summit of the mountain where the source of the river
Etam is located, but somewhat lower on the slope; this
accords with the expression בֵּין כְּתֵפָיו, lit., "between the
shoulders," the relative height of the shoulders to
the top of the head.

17. *the firstling of his bull.* Joseph's true calling,
described in the preceding verses, is that of a peaceful
entity, devoted primarily to agriculture, for which the
appropriate simile is שׁוֹר [the bull], not the lion, as with
Judah in Genesis 49:9. However, "the firstling of his
bull," the firstborn of this tribe of peaceful pursuits;
i.e., the first member of this tribe to rise to prominence
in Israel's subsequent history, will be assigned a warrior's mission, vested with eminence. He will be given

horns of *re'em* are his horns; with them will
he push the peoples together unto the end
of the earth; these are the ten thousands of
Ephraim; and these, the thousands of
Menashe." 18. And regarding Zebulun
he said: "Rejoice, O Zebulun, when you go
out, and Yissakhar, you in your tents!
19. They summon peoples to the mountain; there they will learn to make
offerings of righteousness. For they suck the
abundance of the seas and what is hidden in
the secret treasures of the sand." 20. And
regarding Gad he said: "Blessed be He Who
granted space to Gad! Now he reposes there
like a lion and has already overpowered the
arm and the crown of the head. 21. He
saw a beginning for himself, for there lies
also the portion of the lawgiver, of him who
remains concealed. He came to the head
of the people, accomplished the beneficence
of *God* and His righteous decrees with
Yisrael." 22. And regarding Dan he said:
"Dan [is] a young lion, leaping far afield
from Bashan." 23. And regarding Naphtali he said: "But as for Naphtali—his wishes
well satisfied and full of *God*'s blessing—he
inherits the west and the south." 24. And
regarding Asher he said: "Blessed of sons
[is] Asher; He shall be the desired of his
brothers and dip his foot in oil. 25. Iron

קַרְנָיו בָּהֶם עַמִּים יְנַגַּח יַחְדָּו אַפְסֵי־אָרֶץ וְהֵם
רִבְבוֹת אֶפְרַיִם וְהֵם אַלְפֵי מְנַשֶּׁה: ס רביעי
יח וְלִזְבוּלֻן אָמַר שְׂמַח זְבוּלֻן בְּצֵאתֶךָ
וְיִשָּׂשכָר בְּאֹהָלֶיךָ: יט עַמִּים הַר־יִקְרָאוּ שָׁם
יִזְבְּחוּ זִבְחֵי־צֶדֶק כִּי שֶׁפַע יַמִּים יִינָקוּ וּשְׂפֻנֵי
טְמוּנֵי חוֹל: ס כ וּלְגָד אָמַר בָּרוּךְ מַרְחִיב גָּד
כְּלָבִיא שָׁכֵן וְטָרַף זְרוֹעַ אַף־קָדְקֹד: כא וַיַּרְא
רֵאשִׁית לוֹ כִּי־שָׁם חֶלְקַת מְחֹקֵק סָפוּן וַיֵּתֵא
רָאשֵׁי עָם צִדְקַת יְהוָה עָשָׂה וּמִשְׁפָּטָיו עִם־
יִשְׂרָאֵל: ס חמישי כב וּלְדָן אָמַר דָּן גּוּר אַרְיֵה
יְזַנֵּק מִן־הַבָּשָׁן: כג וּלְנַפְתָּלִי אָמַר נַפְתָּלִי
שְׂבַע רָצוֹן וּמָלֵא בִּרְכַּת יְהוָה יָם וְדָרוֹם
יְרָשָׁה: ס כד וּלְאָשֵׁר אָמַר בָּרוּךְ מִבָּנִים אָשֵׁר
יְהִי רְצוּי אֶחָיו וְטֹבֵל בַּשֶּׁמֶן רַגְלוֹ: כה בַּרְזֶל

the horns of a *re'em*, as it were, with which to overpower other nations. The first to perform this function
under his leadership will be the tens of thousands and
the thousands belonging to the tribe of Joseph. The
reference obviously is to Joshua, who was a member of
the tribe of Ephraim (Numbers 13:7), and who was
assigned the task of taking possession of the land, which
entailed also the expulsion of the nations [that lived
there at the time]. . . .

20. **and has already overpowered the arm and
the crown of the head.** The [arms of the] warring
nations and the leaders at their head. . . .

25. **Iron.** All the blessings up to this point refer to
their objects in the third person singular. The blessings
that now follow, until the end, are couched in general
terms, clearly referring to the community of Israel as a
total unit. That is why they are phrased in the second
person singular. Since this change already begins with
the present verse, Verse 25, it would seem that the
blessings addressed to the individual tribes conclude

with Verse 24, and that Verse 25 is a quick transition
from the specific to the general. . . .

The transition (Verse 6) from the general to the specific, to the blessings addressed to the individual tribes,
was made without a *parshah* separation. Now the blessing of Moses reverts from the specific to the general,
again without a *parshah* separation. This structural
arrangement indicates that the reference to the nation
as a total unit (Verses 2 through 5 and 25 through 29)
constitutes the true, comprehensive blessing. Only the
portion in between these two sections refers to character traits associated with individual tribes, explaining
how these blessings will apply to the special characteristics of these tribes. From Verse 13 on, the reference
is primarily to blessings associated with agricultural
abundance.

It seems to us that now, in Verse 25, these blessings
are completed with several general statements before
the address quickly turns to complete the blessing
intended for the nation as a unit. First Judah, Levi and
Benjamin were blessed as the bearers of the nation's
power, the nation's honor and the nation's Sanctuary,

and copper will be your closure and your loss of strength will accord with your days." 26. "There is none like this God, O Yeshurun! He guides heavens as your help and clouds in His majesty. 27. The God of antiquity is the Bearer of each passing moment of time; He is the support everlasting that raises up all things from the depths. He has driven away the enemy from before you; He has said: Destruction. 28. Thus did Yisrael gain a dwelling place, secure and alone, the fountain of Yaakov, for a land of grain and new wine; even the dew drips down from His heaven. 29. True progress is yours, O Yisrael; who is like you, O people saved by *God*, the Shield of your help; and Who is the sword of your eminence? Your enemies will deny themselves because of you, and you will tread upon their high places!"

XXXIV

1. Moshe went up from the wastelands of Moab to Mount Nebo, to the summit of

וּנְחֹשֶׁת מִנְעָלֶךָ וּכְיָמֶיךָ דָּבְאֶךָ: כו אֵין כָּאֵל יְשֻׁרוּן רֹכֵב שָׁמַיִם בְּעֶזְרֶךָ וּבְגַאֲוָתוֹ שְׁחָקִים: ששי כז מְעֹנָה אֱלֹהֵי קֶדֶם וּמִתַּחַת זְרֹעֹת עוֹלָם וַיְגָרֶשׁ מִפָּנֶיךָ אוֹיֵב וַיֹּאמֶר הַשְׁמֵד: כח וַיִּשְׁכֹּן יִשְׂרָאֵל בֶּטַח בָּדָד עֵין יַעֲקֹב אֶל־אֶרֶץ דָּגָן וְתִירוֹשׁ אַף־שָׁמָיו יַעַרְפוּ־טָל: כט אַשְׁרֶיךָ יִשְׂרָאֵל מִי כָמוֹךָ עַם נוֹשַׁע בַּיהֹוָה מָגֵן עֶזְרֶךָ וַאֲשֶׁר־חֶרֶב גַּאֲוָתֶךָ וְיִכָּחֲשׁוּ אֹיְבֶיךָ לָךְ וְאַתָּה עַל־בָּמוֹתֵימוֹ תִדְרֹךְ: ס שביעי לד א וַיַּעַל מֹשֶׁה מֵעַרְבֹת מוֹאָב אֶל־הַר נְבוֹ רֹאשׁ הַפִּסְגָּה

---

respectively. The blessings addressed to the other seven tribes refer to the wealth of the entire nation as produced by the special characteristics of the various tribal territories. To this description of the blessings given to the land of the Jews, Verse 25 now adds some words regarding the mineral resources and the healthy climate of the land. Thereafter, in Verse 26, the address mounts to its climax and conclusion by encompassing all that has been said before in one blessing, addressed to the entire nation.

*   °   *

26. **There is none.** כָּאֵל ["This God"]; i.e., this manifestation of God. Nothing can compare to the manner in which He manifests Himself here, in your case, יְשֻׁרוּן ["O Yeshurun"], if you remain Jeshurun; if you remain straight [יָשָׁר] and upright, pursuing your life in undeviating loyalty to your duty.

רֹכֵב שָׁמַיִם [*He guides heavens*], not הַשָּׁמַיִם ["... *the* heavens"]: In order to help you, He guides all the extraterrestrial phenomena that can influence your growth and development; i.e., He directs all the extraterrestrial forces for the purpose of helping you. . . . In all His majesty, so high above all earthly affairs, he directs even that which you, from earth, perceive as heaven—all in order to help you.

28. עֵין יַעֲקֹב [*the fountain of Yaakov*]. It is most significant that the text does not read יַעֲקֹב עַל עֵין אֶרֶץ דָּגָן וְתִירוֹשׁ, "*Yaakov* at the fountain of a richly blessed

land," but עֵין יַעֲקֹב אֶל אֶרֶץ וגו׳, literally, "the fountain of Yaakov, toward a land full of grain and new wine." This implies that it is not "*Yaakov*" who flourishes because of the land, but the land that will flourish because of "*Yaakov*." "*Yaakov*" is the source of the fountain through which the land will become rich in grain and new wine. The prosperity of the land does not come from physical factors. The moral conduct to be expected from "*Yaakov*," the manner in which he fulfills his moral calling, will be the source of the blessings his land will receive. Hence, "even the dew drips down from *His* heaven."

29. **True progress is yours, O Yisrael.** In Israel shall be realized the one principle that can ensure true and enduring progress. Israel is that society on earth to which God, the God of all the future, assures a happy existence. He aids and defends it against all dangers. It is He, too, Who bestows upon it the sword of its eminence; that is, He bestows upon Israel that eminence among the nations which all the other nations achieve by the sword.

Your enemies will deny themselves because of you. The time will come when the principle you have held aloft will shine forth so triumphantly that all your opponents will deny their past opposition to you. You will then ascend to the pinnacle of all human endeavors, which they vainly sought to accomplish by other means.

the high place, which lies before Jericho; and *God* showed him all the land: Gilead as far as Dan, 2. all of Naphtali, the land of Ephraim and Menashe and the entire land of Yehudah until the sea at your back; 3. the south and the flat valley, the plain of Jericho, the City of Dates, as far as Tzoar. 4. And *God* said to him: "This is the land regarding which I swore to Abraham, Yitzḥak and Yaakov: 'To your descendants will I give it.' I have let you see it with your eyes, [but] you will not go over there." 5. And Moshe, the servant of *God,* died there in the land of Moab, according to the utterance of *God.* 6. [And] He buried him in the valley in the land of Moab, opposite Beth-Peor; and no one has known his grave to this day. 7. Moshe was one hundred and twenty years old when he died; his eye had not become dim and his freshness had not departed. 8. The sons of Yisrael wept for Moshe in the wastelands of Moab thirty days; then the days of weeping in mourning for Moshe were at an end. 9. Yehoshua, son of Nun, was filled with the spirit of wisdom, for Moshe had laid his hands upon him; and the sons of Yisrael hearkened to him and did as *God* had commanded Moshe. 10. And no prophet has arisen in Yisrael like Moshe, whom *God* had permitted to know Him face to face; 11. in all

אֲשֶׁ֗ר עַל־פְּנֵ֣י יְרֵח֑וֹ וַיַּרְאֵ֨הוּ יְהֹוָ֤ה אֶת־כָּל־הָאָ֙רֶץ֙ אֶת־הַגִּלְעָ֖ד עַד־דָּ֑ן: ב וְאֵת֙ כָּל־נַפְתָּלִ֔י וְאֶת־אֶ֥רֶץ אֶפְרַ֖יִם וּמְנַשֶּׁ֑ה וְאֵת֙ כָּל־אֶ֣רֶץ יְהוּדָ֔ה עַ֖ד הַיָּ֥ם הָאַחֲרֽוֹן: ג וְאֶת־הַנֶּ֜גֶב וְאֶֽת־הַכִּכָּ֗ר בִּקְעַ֛ת יְרֵח֥וֹ עִ֥יר הַתְּמָרִ֖ים עַד־צֹֽעַר: ד וַיֹּ֨אמֶר יְהֹוָ֜ה אֵלָ֗יו זֹ֤את הָאָ֙רֶץ֙ אֲשֶׁ֣ר נִ֠שְׁבַּ֠עְתִּי לְאַבְרָהָ֨ם לְיִצְחָ֤ק וּֽלְיַעֲקֹב֙ לֵאמֹ֔ר לְזַרְעֲךָ֖ אֶתְּנֶ֑נָּה הֶרְאִיתִ֣יךָ בְעֵינֶ֔יךָ וְשָׁ֖מָּה לֹ֥א תַעֲבֹֽר: ה וַיָּ֨מָת שָׁ֜ם מֹשֶׁ֧ה עֶֽבֶד־יְהֹוָ֛ה בְּאֶ֥רֶץ מוֹאָ֖ב עַל־פִּ֥י יְהֹוָֽה: ו וַיִּקְבֹּ֨ר אֹת֤וֹ בַגַּי֙ בְּאֶ֣רֶץ מוֹאָ֔ב מ֖וּל בֵּ֣ית פְּע֑וֹר וְלֹֽא־יָדַ֥ע אִישׁ֙ אֶת־קְבֻ֣רָת֔וֹ עַ֖ד הַיּ֥וֹם הַזֶּֽה: ז וּמֹשֶׁ֗ה בֶּן־מֵאָ֧ה וְעֶשְׂרִ֛ים שָׁנָ֖ה בְּמֹת֑וֹ לֹֽא־כָֽהֲתָ֥ה עֵינ֖וֹ וְלֹא־נָ֥ס לֵחֹֽה: ח וַיִּבְכּ֨וּ בְנֵ֤י יִשְׂרָאֵל֙ אֶת־מֹשֶׁ֔ה בְּעַרְבֹ֥ת מוֹאָ֖ב שְׁלֹשִׁ֣ים י֑וֹם וַיִּתְּמ֔וּ יְמֵ֥י בְכִ֖י אֵ֥בֶל מֹשֶֽׁה: ט וִֽיהוֹשֻׁ֣עַ בִּן־נ֗וּן מָלֵא֙ ר֣וּחַ חָכְמָ֔ה כִּֽי־סָמַ֥ךְ מֹשֶׁ֛ה אֶת־יָדָ֖יו עָלָ֑יו וַיִּשְׁמְע֨וּ אֵלָ֤יו בְּנֵֽי־יִשְׂרָאֵל֙ וַיַּ֣עֲשׂ֔וּ כַּֽאֲשֶׁ֛ר צִוָּ֥ה יְהֹוָ֖ה אֶת־מֹשֶֽׁה: י וְלֹא־קָ֨ם נָבִ֥יא ע֛וֹד בְּיִשְׂרָאֵ֖ל כְּמֹשֶׁ֑ה אֲשֶׁר֙ יְדָע֣וֹ יְהֹוָ֔ה פָּנִ֖ים אֶל־פָּנִֽים: יא לְכָל־הָֽאֹתֹת֩

CHAPTER XXXIV

10–12. And no prophet has arisen ... before the eyes of all Yisrael. These three concluding verses place the seal of authenticity upon the Law of God that had been transmitted through Moses, and confirm the eternal inviolability and immutability of that Law. For this reason they single out only three elements of Moses' mission, those that will hold out an everlasting iron shield against any prophet who, in the future, might seek to abrogate all or part of the Law of God, and against any impudent or thoughtless disregard of any part of the Law. The statement "And no prophet has arisen" (Verse 10) refers also to the statement "in all the signs..." (Verses 11, 12). Moses stands unique in that God permitted him to know Him face to face, in the "signs and convincing deeds" God had sent him to perform in Egypt and in the "mighty hand and all the great awesomeness" which he had to perform "before the eyes of all Yisrael."

The direct contact through which God made Himself and His will known to Moses for the mission he was to fulfill ..., a purpose for which He singled him out from the rest of mankind, will never be achieved by any other prophet. No other man among Israel will ever be able to boast [of having had such encounters with God or of having been assigned such a mission by Him]. In "face to face" encounters with God did Moses receive every word regarding his mission.... No word not received [by man from God] in a similar direct manner can ever throw the slightest doubt on so much as one syllable of the Word of God that came to Moses so directly, without any intermediary. The "signs and convincing deeds" revealing God and His almighty power, with which Moses, in the course of his mission, was bidden to liberate Israel from Egypt's might for the sake of God and of His Law; "the mighty hand" and "the great awesomeness"—the mighty hand that will not permit anyone to snatch away what it possesses; the great awesomeness that must be feared by anyone who

וְהַמּוֹפְתִים אֲשֶׁר שְׁלָחוֹ יְהוָה לַעֲשׂוֹת בְּאֶרֶץ
מִצְרָיִם לְפַרְעֹה וּלְכָל־עֲבָדָיו וּלְכָל־אַרְצוֹ:
יב וּלְכֹל הַיָּד הַחֲזָקָה וּלְכֹל הַמּוֹרָא הַגָּדוֹל
אֲשֶׁר עָשָׂה מֹשֶׁה לְעֵינֵי כָּל־יִשְׂרָאֵל:
חזק

the signs and convincing deeds that *God* had sent him to perform in the land of Mitzrayim, to Pharaoh, to all his servants, and to all his land; 12. and in all of the mighty hand and all the great awesomeness that Moshe performed before the eyes of all Yisrael.

would dare disobey—These are the things that Moses had to demonstrate "before the eyes of all Yisrael" *in* Israel—and sometimes *to* Israel—for the sake of the Law he had brought to Israel, so that Israel might live to keep this Law. All this shall stand forever as a warning to any power from without and to any impudence or sin from within that would ever dare alienate Israel from its calling and thus jeopardize the work begun with the mission of Moses.

The Haftarah for this Sidra may be found on page 952.
(Haftarath Simchath Torah)

חזק
ברוך נותן ליעף כח ולאין אונים עצמה ירבה

This English translation was completed
in New York, N.Y. on י׳ מנחם אב תשמ״ג (July 20, 1983).

The editing for this work was completed
in Yerushalayim עיה״ק
on ז׳ מרחשון תשד״מ—ערב שבת קודש (November 14, '83).

„כי טל אורות טלך"
„ונתתי מטר ארצכם בעתו"

הפטרות
וחמש מגילות

HAFTAROTH
AND
THE FIVE MEGILLOTH

הפטרות
HAFTAROTH

Introductory material, instructions and translation by

Rabbi A.J. Rosenberg
Editor of the Judaica Books of the Prophets

HAFTARATH BERESHITH הפטרת בראשית
(Isaiah 42:5–43:10)
Sephardim conclude with 42:21. Should Rosh Chodesh fall on Sunday, the Haftarah
For The Day Preceding Rosh Chodesh (p. 933) is read.

The beginning of this selection mentions the Creation.

42:5. So said God the Lord, the Creator of the heavens and the One Who stretched them out, Who spread out the earth and what springs forth from it, Who gave a soul to the people upon it and a spirit to those who walk thereon. 6. I am the Lord; I called you with righteousness, and I will strengthen your hand; and I formed you, and I made you for a people's covenant, for a light to nations. 7. To open blind eyes, to bring prisoners out of a dungeon, those who sit in darkness out of a prison. 8. I am the Lord, that is My Name; and My glory I will not give to another, nor My praise to the graven images. 9. The former things, behold they have come to pass, and the new things I tell; before they sprout I will let you hear. 10. Sing to the Lord a new song, His praise from the end of the earth, those who go down to the sea and those therein, the islands and their inhabitants. 11. The desert and its cities shall raise [their voice]; Kedar shall be inhabited with villages; the rock dwellers shall exult; from the mountain peaks they shall shout. 12. They shall give glory to the Lord, and they shall recite His praise on the islands. 13. The Lord shall go out like a hero; like a warrior shall He arouse zeal; He shall shout, He shall even cry, He shall overpower His foes. 14. I was silent from time immemorial; I am still, I restrain Myself. Like a travailing woman will I cry; I will be terrified and destroy them together. 15. I will destroy mountains and hills, and all their grass I will dry out, and I will make rivers into islands and I will

ה כֹּה־אָמַר הָאֵל ׀ יְהֹוָה בּוֹרֵא הַשָּׁמַיִם
וְנוֹטֵיהֶם רֹקַע הָאָרֶץ וְצֶאֱצָאֶיהָ נֹתֵן נְשָׁמָה
לָעָם עָלֶיהָ וְרוּחַ לַהֹלְכִים בָּהּ: ו אֲנִי יְהֹוָה
קְרָאתִיךָ בְצֶדֶק וְאַחְזֵק בְּיָדֶךָ וְאֶצָּרְךָ וְאֶתֶּנְךָ
לִבְרִית עָם לְאוֹר גּוֹיִם: ז לִפְקֹחַ עֵינַיִם עִוְרוֹת
לְהוֹצִיא מִמַּסְגֵּר אַסִּיר מִבֵּית כֶּלֶא יֹשְׁבֵי חֹשֶׁךְ:
ח אֲנִי יְהֹוָה הוּא שְׁמִי וּכְבוֹדִי לְאַחֵר לֹא־אֶתֵּן
וּתְהִלָּתִי לַפְּסִילִים: ט הָרִאשֹׁנוֹת הִנֵּה־בָאוּ
וַחֲדָשׁוֹת אֲנִי מַגִּיד בְּטֶרֶם תִּצְמַחְנָה אַשְׁמִיעַ
אֶתְכֶם: י שִׁירוּ לַיהֹוָה שִׁיר חָדָשׁ תְּהִלָּתוֹ
מִקְצֵה הָאָרֶץ יוֹרְדֵי הַיָּם וּמְלֹאוֹ אִיִּים
וְיֹשְׁבֵיהֶם: יא יִשְׂאוּ מִדְבָּר וְעָרָיו חֲצֵרִים תֵּשֵׁב
קֵדָר יָרֹנּוּ יֹשְׁבֵי סֶלַע מֵרֹאשׁ הָרִים יִצְוָחוּ:
יב יָשִׂימוּ לַיהֹוָה כָּבוֹד וּתְהִלָּתוֹ בָּאִיִּים יַגִּידוּ:
יג יְהֹוָה כַּגִּבּוֹר יֵצֵא כְּאִישׁ מִלְחָמוֹת יָעִיר
קִנְאָה יָרִיעַ אַף־יַצְרִיחַ עַל־אֹיְבָיו יִתְגַּבָּר:
יד הֶחֱשֵׁיתִי מֵעוֹלָם אַחֲרִישׁ אֶתְאַפָּק כַּיּוֹלֵדָה
אֶפְעֶה אֶשֹּׁם וְאֶשְׁאַף יָחַד: טו אַחֲרִיב הָרִים
וּגְבָעוֹת וְכָל־עֶשְׂבָּם אוֹבִישׁ וְשַׂמְתִּי נְהָרוֹת

[[821]]

dry up the pools. 16. And I will lead the blind on a road they did not know; in paths they did not know I will lead them; I will make darkness into light before them, and crooked paths into straight ones. These things, I will do them and I will not forsake them. 17. They shall turn back greatly ashamed, those who trust in the graven image, who say to the molten idols, "You are our gods." 18. You deaf ones, listen, and you blind ones, look to see. 19. Who is blind but My servant, and deaf as My messenger whom I will send? He who was blind is as the one who received his payment, and he who was blind is as the servant of the Lord. 20. There is much to see but you do not observe, to open the ears but no one listens. 21. The Lord desires [this] for His righteousness' sake; He magnifies the Torah and strengthens it. (*Sephardim conclude here.*) 22. And it is a robbed and pillaged people; all their youths are grieved, and they are hidden in dungeons; they are subject to plunderers, and none rescues [them]; to pillagers, and no one says, "Return." 23. Who among you will hearken to this, will listen and hear for the future? 24. Who subjected Jacob to plunder and Israel to spoilers? Was it not the Lord? This, that we sinned against Him, and they did not want to go in His way and did not hearken to His Torah. 25. And He poured out upon them the fury of His anger and the strength of battle, and it blazed upon them all around and they did not know, and it burned among them and they did not take heed. 43:1. And now, so said the Lord, your Creator, O Jacob, and the One Who formed you, O Israel, Do not fear, for I have redeemed you, and I called by your name, you are Mine. 2. When you pass through water, I am with you, and in rivers, they shall not overflow you; when you go amidst fire, you shall not be burnt, neither shall a flame burn amongst you. 3. For I am the Lord your God, the Holy One of Israel, your Savior; I have given Egypt as your ransom, Cush and Seba in your stead. 4. Since you are dear in My eyes, you were honored and I loved you, and I give men in your stead and nations instead of your life. 5. Fear not for I am with you; from the east I will bring your

לְאִיִּים וַאֲגַמִּים אוֹבִישׁ: טז וְהוֹלַכְתִּי עִוְרִים
בְּדֶרֶךְ לֹא יָדָעוּ בִּנְתִיבוֹת לֹא־יָדְעוּ אַדְרִיכֵם
אָשִׂים מַחְשָׁךְ לִפְנֵיהֶם לָאוֹר וּמַעֲקַשִּׁים
לְמִישׁוֹר אֵלֶּה הַדְּבָרִים עֲשִׂיתִם וְלֹא עֲזַבְתִּים:
יז נָסֹגוּ אָחוֹר יֵבֹשׁוּ בֹשֶׁת הַבֹּטְחִים בַּפָּסֶל
הָאֹמְרִים לְמַסֵּכָה אַתֶּם אֱלֹהֵינוּ: יח הַחֵרְשִׁים
שְׁמָעוּ וְהַעִוְרִים הַבִּיטוּ לִרְאוֹת: יט מִי עִוֵּר כִּי
אִם־עַבְדִּי וְחֵרֵשׁ כְּמַלְאָכִי אֶשְׁלָח מִי עִוֵּר
כִּמְשֻׁלָּם וְעִוֵּר כְּעֶבֶד יְהוָֹה: כ רָאִית (ראות קרי)
רַבּוֹת וְלֹא תִשְׁמֹר פָּקוֹחַ אָזְנַיִם וְלֹא יִשְׁמָע:
כא יְהוָֹה חָפֵץ לְמַעַן צִדְקוֹ יַגְדִּיל תּוֹרָה וְיַאְדִּיר:
(כאן מסיימין הספרדים) כב וְהוּא עַם־בָּזוּז וְשָׁסוּי
הָפֵחַ בַּחוּרִים כֻּלָּם וּבְבָתֵּי כְלָאִים הָחְבָּאוּ הָיוּ
לָבַז וְאֵין מַצִּיל מְשִׁסָּה וְאֵין־אֹמֵר הָשַׁב: כג מִי
בָכֶם יַאֲזִין זֹאת יַקְשִׁב וְיִשְׁמַע לְאָחוֹר: כד מִי־
נָתַן לִמְשׁוֹסָּה (למשיסה קרי) יַעֲקֹב וְיִשְׂרָאֵל לְבֹזְזִים
הֲלוֹא יְהוָֹה זוּ חָטָאנוּ לוֹ וְלֹא־אָבוּ בִדְרָכָיו
הָלוֹךְ וְלֹא שָׁמְעוּ בְּתוֹרָתוֹ: כה וַיִּשְׁפֹּךְ עָלָיו
חֵמָה אַפּוֹ וֶעֱזוּז מִלְחָמָה וַתְּלַהֲטֵהוּ מִסָּבִיב וְלֹא
יָדָע וַתִּבְעַר־בּוֹ וְלֹא־יָשִׂים עַל־לֵב: א וְעַתָּה
כֹּה־אָמַר יְהוָֹה בֹּרַאֲךָ יַעֲקֹב וְיֹצֶרְךָ יִשְׂרָאֵל אַל־
תִּירָא כִּי גְאַלְתִּיךָ קָרָאתִי בְשִׁמְךָ לִי־אָתָּה:
ב כִּי־תַעֲבֹר בַּמַּיִם אִתְּךָ אָנִי וּבַנְּהָרוֹת לֹא
יִשְׁטְפוּךָ כִּי־תֵלֵךְ בְּמוֹ־אֵשׁ לֹא תִכָּוֶה וְלֶהָבָה
לֹא תִבְעַר־בָּךְ: ג כִּי אֲנִי יְהוָֹה אֱלֹהֶיךָ קְדוֹשׁ
יִשְׂרָאֵל מוֹשִׁיעֶךָ נָתַתִּי כָפְרְךָ מִצְרַיִם כּוּשׁ
וּסְבָא תַּחְתֶּיךָ: ד מֵאֲשֶׁר יָקַרְתָּ בְעֵינַי נִכְבַּדְתָּ
וַאֲנִי אֲהַבְתִּיךָ וְאֶתֵּן אָדָם תַּחְתֶּיךָ וּלְאֻמִּים תַּחַת
נַפְשֶׁךָ: ה אַל־תִּירָא כִּי־אִתְּךָ אָנִי מִמִּזְרָח אָבִיא

seed, and from the west I will gather you.
6. I will say to the north, "Give," and to the
south, "Do not refrain; bring My sons
from afar and My daughters from the end of
the earth." 7. Everyone that is called by My
name, and whom I created for My glory, I
formed him; yea, I made him. 8. To bring
out a blind people who have eyes and deaf
ones who have ears. 9. Were all the nations
gathered together, and kingdoms assembled, who of them would tell this or let us
know of the first events? Let them present
their witnesses, and they shall be deemed
just, and let them hear and say, "True."
10. "You are My witnesses," says the Lord,
"and My servant whom I chose," in order
that you know and believe Me, and understand that I am He; before Me no god was
formed and after Me none shall be.

זַרְעֶ֔ךָ וּמִמַּֽעֲרָ֖ב אֲקַבְּצֶֽךָּ׃ ו אֹמַ֤ר לַצָּפוֹן֙ תֵּ֔נִי
וּלְתֵימָ֖ן אַל־תִּכְלָ֑אִי הָבִ֤יאִי בָנַי֙ מֵֽרָח֔וֹק וּבְנוֹתַ֖י
מִקְצֵ֥ה הָאָֽרֶץ׃ ז כֹּ֚ל הַנִּקְרָ֣א בִשְׁמִ֔י וְלִכְבוֹדִ֖י
בְּרָאתִ֑יו יְצַרְתִּ֖יו אַף־עֲשִׂיתִֽיו׃ ח הוֹצִ֣יא עַם־
עִוֵּ֥ר וְעֵינַ֖יִם יֵ֑שׁ וְחֵֽרְשִׁ֖ים וְאָזְנַ֥יִם לָֽמוֹ׃ ט כָּל־
הַגּוֹיִ֞ם נִקְבְּצ֣וּ יַחְדָּ֗ו וְיֵאָֽסְפוּ֙ לְאֻמִּ֔ים מִ֤י בָהֶם֙
יַגִּ֣יד זֹ֔את וְרִֽאשֹׁנ֖וֹת יַשְׁמִיעֻ֑נוּ יִתְּנ֤וּ עֵֽדֵיהֶם֙
וְיִצְדָּ֔קוּ וְיִשְׁמְע֖וּ וְיֹֽאמְר֥וּ אֱמֶֽת׃ י אַתֶּ֤ם עֵדַי֙
נְאֻם־יְהֹוָ֔ה וְעַבְדִּ֖י אֲשֶׁ֣ר בָּחָ֑רְתִּי לְמַ֣עַן תֵּֽדְע֩וּ
וְתַֽאֲמִ֨ינוּ לִ֜י וְתָבִ֗ינוּ כִּֽי־אֲנִ֣י ה֔וּא לְפָנַי֙ לֹא־נ֣וֹצַר
אֵ֔ל וְאַֽחֲרַ֖י לֹ֥א יִֽהְיֶֽה׃

HAFTARATH NOAH   הפטרת נח
(Isaiah 54:1–55:5)
**Sephardim conclude with 54:10. Should Rosh Chodesh coincide with the Sabbath,
the Haftarah for Sabbath Rosh Chodesh (p. 930) is read.**

The reference to "the waters of Noah" connects this selection to the Sidra.

54.1. Sing, you barren woman who has not
borne; burst out into song and jubilate, you
who have not experienced birth pangs, for
the children of the desolate one are more
than the children of the married woman,
says the Lord. 2. Widen the place of your
tent, and let them stretch forth the curtains
of your habitations, do not spare; lengthen
your cords and strengthen your stakes.
3. For right and left shall you prevail, and
your seed shall inherit nations and repeople
desolate cities. 4. Fear not, for you shall not
be ashamed, and be not embarrassed for
you shall not be put to shame, for the shame
of your youth you shall forget, and the
disgrace of your widowhood you shall no
longer remember. 5. For your Master is
your Maker, the Lord of Hosts is His name,
and your Redeemer, the Holy One of Israel,
shall be called the God of all the earth.
6. For, like a wife who is deserted and
distressed in spirit has the Lord called you,
and a wife of one's youth who was rejected,
said your God. 7. For a small moment

א רׇנִּ֤י עֲקָרָה֙ לֹ֣א יָלָ֔דָה פִּצְחִ֥י רִנָּ֛ה וְצַֽהֲלִ֖י לֹא־
חָ֑לָה כִּֽי־רַבִּ֧ים בְּֽנֵֽי־שֽׁוֹמֵמָ֛ה מִבְּנֵ֥י בְעוּלָ֖ה אָמַ֥ר
יְהֹוָֽה׃ ב הַרְחִ֣יבִי ׀ מְק֣וֹם אׇֽהֳלֵ֗ךְ וִֽירִיע֧וֹת
מִשְׁכְּנוֹתַ֛יִךְ יַטּ֖וּ אַל־תַּחְשֹׂ֑כִי הַֽאֲרִ֨יכִי֙ מֵֽיתָרַ֔יִךְ
וִיתֵֽדֹתַ֖יִךְ חַזֵּֽקִי׃ ג כִּֽי־יָמִ֥ין וּשְׂמֹ֖אול תִּפְרֹ֑צִי
וְזַרְעֵךְ֙ גּוֹיִ֣ם יִירָ֔שׁ וְעָרִ֥ים נְשַׁמּ֖וֹת יוֹשִֽׁיבוּ׃
ד אַל־תִּֽירְאִי֙ כִּי־לֹ֣א תֵב֔וֹשִׁי וְאַל־תִּכָּֽלְמִ֖י כִּי־
לֹ֣א תַחְפִּ֑ירִי כִּ֣י בֹ֤שֶׁת עֲלוּמַ֙יִךְ֙ תִּשְׁכָּ֔חִי וְחֶרְפַּ֥ת
אַלְמְנוּתַ֖יִךְ לֹ֥א תִזְכְּרִי־עֽוֹד׃ ה כִּ֤י בֹֽעֲלַ֙יִךְ֙ עֹשַׂ֔יִךְ
יְהֹוָ֥ה צְבָא֖וֹת שְׁמ֑וֹ וְגֹֽאֲלֵךְ֙ קְד֣וֹשׁ יִשְׂרָאֵ֔ל אֱלֹהֵ֥י
כָל־הָאָ֖רֶץ יִקָּרֵֽא׃ ו כִּֽי־כְאִשָּׁ֧ה עֲזוּבָ֛ה וַֽעֲצ֥וּבַת
ר֖וּחַ קְרָאָ֣ךְ יְהֹוָ֑ה וְאֵ֧שֶׁת נְעוּרִ֛ים כִּ֥י תִמָּאֵ֖ס אָמַ֥ר
אֱלֹהָֽיִךְ׃ ז בְּרֶ֥גַע קָטֹ֖ן עֲזַבְתִּ֑יךְ וּבְרַֽחֲמִ֥ים

have I forsaken you, and with great mercy will I gather you. 8. With a little wrath did I hide My countenance for a moment from you, and with everlasting kindness will I have compassion on you, said your Redeemer, the Lord. 9. For this is to Me [as] the waters of Noah, as I swore that the waters of Noah shall never again pass over the earth, so have I sworn neither to be wroth with you nor to rebuke you. 10. For the mountains shall depart and the hills totter, but My kindness shall not depart from you, neither shall the covenant of My peace totter, says the Lord, Who has compassion on you. (*Sephardim conclude here.*) 11. O poor tempestuous one, who was not consoled, behold I will set your stones with carbuncle, and I will lay your foundations with sapphires. 12. And I will make your windows of jasper and your gates of carbuncle stones, and all your border of precious stones. 13. And all your children shall be disciples of the Lord, and your children's peace shall increase. 14. With righteousness shall you be established, go far away from oppression, for you shall not fear, and from ruin, for it will not come near you. 15. Behold, the one with whom I am not, shall fear, whoever mobilizes against you shall defect to you. 16. Behold I have created a smith, who blows on a charcoal fire and produces a weapon for his work, and I have created a destroyer to destroy [it]. 17. Any weapon whetted against you shall not succeed, and any tongue that contends with you in judgment, you shall condemn; this is the heritage of the servants of the Lord and their due reward from Me, says the Lord. 55:1. Ho! All who thirst, go to water, and whoever has no money, go, buy and eat, and go, buy without money and without a price, wine and milk. 2. Why should you weigh out money without bread and your toil without satiety? Hearken to Me and eat what is good, and your soul shall delight in fatness. 3. Incline your ear and come to Me, hearken and your soul shall live, and I will make for you an everlasting covenant, the dependable mercies of David. 4. Behold, a witness to nations have I appointed him, a ruler and a commander of nations. 5. Behold, a nation you do not know you shall call, and a nation that did

גְּדוֹלִים אֲקַבְּצֵךְ: ח בְּשֶׁצֶף קֶצֶף הִסְתַּרְתִּי פָנַי רֶגַע מִמֵּךְ וּבְחֶסֶד עוֹלָם רִחַמְתִּיךְ אָמַר גֹּאֲלֵךְ יְהֹוָה: ט כִּי־מֵי נֹחַ זֹאת לִי אֲשֶׁר נִשְׁבַּעְתִּי מֵעֲבֹר מֵי־נֹחַ עוֹד עַל־הָאָרֶץ כֵּן נִשְׁבַּעְתִּי מִקְּצֹף עָלַיִךְ וּמִגְּעָר־בָּךְ: י כִּי הֶהָרִים יָמוּשׁוּ וְהַגְּבָעוֹת תְּמוּטֶינָה וְחַסְדִּי מֵאִתֵּךְ לֹא־יָמוּשׁ וּבְרִית שְׁלוֹמִי לֹא תָמוּט אָמַר מְרַחֲמֵךְ יְהֹוָה:

(כאן מסיימין הספרדים) יא עֲנִיָּה סֹעֲרָה לֹא נֻחָמָה הִנֵּה אָנֹכִי מַרְבִּיץ בַּפּוּךְ אֲבָנַיִךְ וִיסַדְתִּיךְ בַּסַּפִּירִים: יב וְשַׂמְתִּי כַּדְכֹד שִׁמְשֹׁתַיִךְ וּשְׁעָרַיִךְ לְאַבְנֵי אֶקְדָּח וְכָל־גְּבוּלֵךְ לְאַבְנֵי־חֵפֶץ: יג וְכָל־בָּנַיִךְ לִמּוּדֵי יְהֹוָה וְרַב שְׁלוֹם בָּנָיִךְ: יד בִּצְדָקָה תִּכּוֹנָנִי רַחֲקִי מֵעֹשֶׁק כִּי־לֹא תִירָאִי וּמִמְּחִתָּה כִּי לֹא־תִקְרַב אֵלָיִךְ: טו הֵן גּוֹר יָגוּר אֶפֶס מֵאוֹתִי מִי־גָר אִתָּךְ עָלַיִךְ יִפּוֹל: טז הֵן (הנה קרי) אָנֹכִי בָּרָאתִי חָרָשׁ נֹפֵחַ בְּאֵשׁ פֶּחָם וּמוֹצִיא כְלִי לְמַעֲשֵׂהוּ וְאָנֹכִי בָּרָאתִי מַשְׁחִית לְחַבֵּל: יז כָּל־כְּלִי יוּצַר עָלַיִךְ לֹא יִצְלָח וְכָל־לָשׁוֹן תָּקוּם־אִתָּךְ לַמִּשְׁפָּט תַּרְשִׁיעִי זֹאת נַחֲלַת עַבְדֵי יְהֹוָה וְצִדְקָתָם מֵאִתִּי נְאֻם־יְהֹוָה: א הוֹי כָּל־צָמֵא לְכוּ לַמַּיִם וַאֲשֶׁר אֵין־לוֹ כָּסֶף לְכוּ שִׁבְרוּ וֶאֱכֹלוּ וּלְכוּ שִׁבְרוּ בְּלוֹא־כֶסֶף וּבְלוֹא מְחִיר יַיִן וְחָלָב: ב לָמָּה תִשְׁקְלוּ־כֶסֶף בְּלוֹא־לֶחֶם וִיגִיעֲכֶם בְּלוֹא לְשָׂבְעָה שִׁמְעוּ שָׁמוֹעַ אֵלַי וְאִכְלוּ־טוֹב וְתִתְעַנַּג בַּדֶּשֶׁן נַפְשְׁכֶם: ג הַטּוּ אָזְנְכֶם וּלְכוּ אֵלַי שִׁמְעוּ וּתְחִי נַפְשְׁכֶם וְאֶכְרְתָה לָכֶם בְּרִית עוֹלָם חַסְדֵי דָוִד הַנֶּאֱמָנִים: ד הֵן עֵד לְאוּמִּים נְתַתִּיו נָגִיד וּמְצַוֵּה לְאֻמִּים: ה הֵן גּוֹי

not know you shall run to you, for the sake of the Lord your God and for the Holy One of Israel, for He glorified you.

לֹא־תֵדַ֣ע תִּקְרָ֔א וְג֖וֹי לֹֽא־יְדָע֣וּךָ אֵלֶ֣יךָ יָר֑וּצוּ לְמַ֙עַן֙ יְהֹוָ֣ה אֱלֹהֶ֔יךָ וְלִקְד֥וֹשׁ יִשְׂרָאֵ֖ל כִּ֥י פֵאֲרָֽךְ׃

HAFTARATH LEKH-LEKHA   הפטרת לך לך
(Isaiah 40:27–41:16)

This selection deals with Abraham's slaying of the kings.

40:27. What should you say, O Jacob, and speak, O Israel, "My way has been hidden from the Lord, and from my God, my judgment passes"? 28. Do you not know — if you have not heard — an everlasting God is the Lord, the Creator of the ends of the earth; He neither tires nor wearies; there is no fathoming His understanding; 29. Who gives the tired strength, and to him who has no strength, He increases strength. 30. Now youths shall become tired and weary, and young men shall stumble. 31. But those who put their hope in the Lord shall renew [their] vigor, they shall raise wings as eagles; they shall run and not weary, they shall walk and not tire. 41:1. Be silent to Me, you islands, and kingdoms shall renew [their] strength; they shall approach, then they shall speak, together to judgment let us draw near. 2. Who aroused from the East, [the one] whom righteousness accompanied? He placed nations before him and over kings He gave him dominion; He made his sword like dust, his bow like wind-blown stubble. 3. He pursued them and passed on safely, on a path upon which he had not come with his feet. 4. Who worked and did, Who calls the generations from the beginning; I, the Lord, am first, and with the last ones I am He. 5. The islands shall see and fear; the ends of the earth shall quake; they have approached and come. 6. Each one shall aid his fellow, and to his brother he shall say, "Strengthen yourself." 7. And the craftsman strengthened the smith, the one who smooths with the hammer [strengthened] the one who wields the sledge hammer; he says of the cement, "It is good," and he strengthened it with nails that it should not move. 8. But you, Israel My servant, Jacob whom I have chosen, the seed of Abraham, who loved Me, 9. whom I

כז לָ֤מָּה תֹאמַר֙ יַעֲקֹ֔ב וּתְדַבֵּ֖ר יִשְׂרָאֵ֑ל נִסְתְּרָ֤ה דַרְכִּי֙ מֵיהֹוָ֔ה וּמֵאֱלֹהַ֖י מִשְׁפָּטִ֥י יַעֲבֽוֹר׃ כח הֲל֨וֹא יָדַ֜עְתָּ אִם־לֹ֣א שָׁמַ֗עְתָּ אֱלֹהֵ֨י עוֹלָ֤ם ׀ יְהֹוָה֙ בּוֹרֵא֙ קְצ֣וֹת הָאָ֔רֶץ לֹ֥א יִיעַ֖ף וְלֹ֣א יִיגָ֑ע אֵ֥ין חֵ֖קֶר לִתְבוּנָתֽוֹ׃ כט נֹתֵ֥ן לַיָּעֵ֖ף כֹּ֑חַ וּלְאֵ֥ין אוֹנִ֖ים עָצְמָ֥ה יַרְבֶּֽה׃ ל וְיִֽעֲפ֤וּ נְעָרִים֙ וְיִגָ֔עוּ וּבַחוּרִ֖ים כָּשׁ֥וֹל יִכָּשֵֽׁלוּ׃ לא וְקוֹיֵ֤ יְהֹוָה֙ יַחֲלִ֣יפוּ כֹ֔חַ יַעֲל֥וּ אֵ֖בֶר כַּנְּשָׁרִ֑ים יָר֙וּצוּ֙ וְלֹ֣א יִיגָ֔עוּ יֵלְכ֖וּ וְלֹ֥א יִיעָֽפוּ׃ א הַחֲרִ֤ישׁוּ אֵלַי֙ אִיִּ֔ים וּלְאֻמִּ֖ים יַחֲלִ֣יפוּ כֹ֑חַ יִגְּשׁוּ֙ אָ֣ז יְדַבֵּ֔רוּ יַחְדָּ֖ו לַמִּשְׁפָּ֥ט נִקְרָֽבָה׃ ב מִ֤י הֵעִיר֙ מִמִּזְרָ֔ח צֶ֖דֶק יִקְרָאֵ֣הוּ לְרַגְל֑וֹ יִתֵּ֨ן לְפָנָ֤יו גּוֹיִם֙ וּמְלָכִ֣ים יַ֔רְדְּ יִתֵּ֤ן כֶּֽעָפָר֙ חַרְבּ֔וֹ כְּקַ֥שׁ נִדָּ֖ף קַשְׁתּֽוֹ׃ ג יִרְדְּפֵ֖ם יַעֲב֣וֹר שָׁל֑וֹם אֹ֖רַח בְּרַגְלָ֥יו לֹ֥א יָבֽוֹא׃ ד מִֽי־פָעַ֣ל וְעָשָׂ֔ה קֹרֵ֥א הַדֹּר֖וֹת מֵרֹ֑אשׁ אֲנִ֤י יְהֹוָה֙ רִאשׁ֔וֹן וְאֶת־אַחֲרֹנִ֖ים אֲנִי־הֽוּא׃ ה רָא֤וּ אִיִּים֙ וְיִירָ֔אוּ קְצ֥וֹת הָאָ֖רֶץ יֶחֱרָ֑דוּ קָרְב֖וּ וַיֶּֽאֱתָיֽוּן׃ ו אִ֥ישׁ אֶת־רֵעֵ֖הוּ יַעְזֹ֑רוּ וּלְאָחִ֖יו יֹאמַ֥ר חֲזָֽק׃ ז וַיְחַזֵּ֤ק חָרָשׁ֙ אֶת־צֹרֵ֔ף מַחֲלִ֥יק פַּטִּ֖ישׁ אֶת־ה֣וֹלֶם פָּ֑עַם אֹמֵ֤ר לַדֶּ֙בֶק֙ ט֔וֹב וַיְחַזְּקֵ֥הוּ בְמַסְמְרִ֖ים לֹ֥א יִמּֽוֹט׃ ח וְאַתָּ֞ה יִשְׂרָאֵ֣ל עַבְדִּ֔י יַעֲקֹ֖ב אֲשֶׁ֣ר בְּחַרְתִּ֑יךָ זֶ֖רַע אַבְרָהָ֥ם

grasped from the ends of the earth, and from its nobles I called you, and I said to you, You are My servant; I chose you and I did not despise you. 10. Do not fear for I am with you; be not discouraged for I am your God; I encouraged you, I also helped you, I also supported you with My righteous hand. 11. Behold all those incensed against you shall be ashamed and confounded; those who quarreled with you shall be as nought and be lost. 12. You may seek them but not find them, those who quarrel with you; those who war with you shall be as nought and as nothing. 13. For I, the Lord your God, grasp your right hand; Who says to you, Fear not, I help you. 14. Fear not, O worm of Jacob, the number of Israel; "I have helped you," says the Lord, and your Redeemer, the Holy One of Israel. 15. Behold I have made you a new grooved threshing-sledge, with sharp points; you shall thresh the mountains and crush them fine, and you shall make hills like chaff. 16. You shall winnow them, and a wind shall carry them off, and a tempest shall scatter them, and you shall rejoice with the Lord, with the Holy One of Israel shall you praise yourself.

אֹהַבִי׃ ט אֲשֶׁר הֶחֱזַקְתִּ֫יךָ מִקְצוֹת הָאָ֫רֶץ
וּמֵאֲצִילֶ֫יהָ קְרָאתִ֫יךָ וָאֹ֫מַר לְךָ עַבְדִּי־אַ֫תָּה
בְּחַרְתִּ֫יךָ וְלֹא מְאַסְתִּ֫יךָ׃ י אַל־תִּירָא כִּי עִמְּךָ
אָ֫נִי אַל־תִּשְׁתָּע כִּי־אֲנִי אֱלֹהֶ֫יךָ אִמַּצְתִּ֫יךָ אַף־
עֲזַרְתִּ֫יךָ אַף־תְּמַכְתִּ֫יךָ בִּימִין צִדְקִי׃ יא הֵן יֵבֹ֫שׁוּ
וְיִכָּלְמוּ כֹּל הַנֶּחֱרִים בָּךְ יִהְיוּ כְאַ֫יִן וְיֹאבְדוּ
אַנְשֵׁי רִיבֶ֫ךָ׃ יב תְּבַקְשֵׁם וְלֹא תִמְצָאֵם אַנְשֵׁי
מַצֻּתֶ֫ךָ יִהְיוּ כְאַ֫יִן וּכְאֶ֫פֶס אַנְשֵׁי מִלְחַמְתֶּ֫ךָ׃
יג כִּי אֲנִי יְהֹוָה אֱלֹהֶ֫יךָ מַחֲזִיק יְמִינֶ֫ךָ הָאֹמֵר
לְךָ אַל־תִּירָא אֲנִי עֲזַרְתִּ֫יךָ׃ יד אַל־תִּֽירְאִי
תוֹלַ֫עַת יַעֲקֹב מְתֵי יִשְׂרָאֵל אֲנִי עֲזַרְתִּ֫יךָ נְאֻם־
יְהֹוָה וְגֹאֲלֵךְ קְדוֹשׁ יִשְׂרָאֵל׃ טו הִנֵּה שַׂמְתִּ֫יךְ
לְמוֹרַג חָרוּץ חָדָשׁ בַּ֫עַל פִּיפִיּוֹת תָּדוּשׁ הָרִים
וְתָדֹק וּגְבָעוֹת כַּמֹּץ תָּשִׂים׃ טז תִּזְרֵם וְרוּחַ
תִּשָּׂאֵם וּסְעָרָה תָּפִיץ אֹתָם וְאַתָּה תָּגִיל בַּיהֹוָה
בִּקְדוֹשׁ יִשְׂרָאֵל תִּתְהַלָּל׃

HAFTARATH VAYERA   הפטרת וירא
(II Kings 4:1–37)
Sephardim conclude with verse 23.

The similarity of this selection to the Sidra is in the prophet's promise, "At this time next year, when you will be alive like now, you will be embracing a son" (v. 16). This is similar to the angel's promise to Abraham.

4:1. Now a woman, of the wives of the disciples of the prophets, cried out to Elisha, saying, "Your servant, my husband, has died, and you know that your servant did fear the Lord; and the creditor has come to take my two children for himself as slaves." 2. And Elisha said to her, "What shall I do for you? Tell me what you have in the house." And she said, "Your maidservant has nothing at all in the house except a jug of oil." 3. And he said, "Borrow vessels for yourself from outside, from all your neighbors; do not borrow only a few empty vessels. 4. And you shall come and close the

א וְאִשָּׁה אַחַת מִנְּשֵׁי בְנֵי־הַנְּבִיאִים צָעֲקָה אֶל־
אֱלִישָׁע לֵאמֹר עַבְדְּךָ אִישִׁי מֵת וְאַתָּה יָדַ֫עְתָּ כִּי
עַבְדְּךָ הָיָה יָרֵא אֶת־יְהֹוָה וְהַנֹּשֶׁה בָּא לָקַ֫חַת
אֶת־שְׁנֵי יְלָדַי לוֹ לַעֲבָדִים׃ ב וַיֹּ֫אמֶר אֵלֶ֫יהָ
אֱלִישָׁע מָה אֶעֱשֶׂה־לָּךְ הַגִּ֫ידִי לִי מַה־יֶּשׁ־לָכִי
(לָךְ קרי) בַּבָּ֫יִת וַתֹּ֫אמֶר אֵין לְשִׁפְחָתְךָ כֹל בַּבַּ֫יִת
כִּי אִם־אָסוּךְ שָׁ֫מֶן׃ ג וַיֹּ֫אמֶר לְכִי שַׁאֲלִי־לָךְ
כֵּלִים מִן־הַחוּץ מֵאֵת כָּל־שְׁכֵנָ֫יכִי (שְׁכֵנַיִךְ קרי)
כֵּלִים רֵקִים אַל־תַּמְעִ֫יטִי׃ ד וּבָאת וְסָגַרְתְּ

door about yourself and about your sons,
and you shall pour upon all these vessels;
and the full one you shall carry away."
5. And she went away from him and closed
the door about herself and about her sons;
they were bringing [vessels] to her and she
was pouring. 6. And it was when the vessels
were full, that she said to her son, "Bring
me another vessel," and he said to her,
"There is no other vessel." And the oil
stopped. 7. And she came and told the man
of God; and he said, "Go sell the oil and pay
your debt; and you and your sons will live
with the remainder." 8. And it was that day
that Elisha went as far as Shumen, and there
was a prominent woman who prevailed
upon him to eat a meal; and it was, whenever he would pass, he would stop there to
eat a meal. 9. And she said to her husband,
"Behold now I know that he is a holy man of
God, who passes by us regularly. 10. Now
let us make a small walled upper chamber,
and place there for him a bed, a table, a
chair, and a lamp; and it will be that when
he comes to us, he will turn into there.
11. And it was one day that he went there,
that he turned into the upper chamber and
lay down there. 12. And he said to Gehazi
his servant, "Call this Shunemitess"; and he
called her, and she stood before him.
13. And he said to him, "Please say to her,
'Behold you have busied yourself on our
account with all this trouble. What is there
to do for you? Can we speak on your behalf
to the king or to the general of the army?'"
And she said, "I dwell in the midst of my
people." 14. And he said, "Now what can
we do for her?" And Gehazi said, "Indeed,
she has no son, and her husband is old."
15. And he said, "Summon her," and he
summoned her, and she stood at the doorway. 16. And he said, "At this time next
year, when you will be alive like now, you
will be embracing a son." And she said, "No
my lord, O man of God, do not fail your
maidservant." 17. And the woman conceived and bore a son, at this time a year
later, which Elisha had spoken to her.
18. And the child grew up; and it was one
day that he went out to his father, to the
reapers. 19. And he said to his father, "My
head! My head!" And he said to the servant,
"Carry him to his mother." 20. And he

הַדֶּ֫לֶת בַּעֲדֵךְ וּבְעַד־בָּנַ֫יִךְ וְיָצַ֫קְתְּ עַ֚ל כָּל־הַכֵּלִ֣ים
הָאֵ֑לֶּה וְהַמָּלֵ֖א תַּסִּֽיעִי: ה וַתֵּ֙לֶךְ֙ מֵֽאִתּ֔וֹ וַתִּסְגֹּ֣ר
הַדֶּ֔לֶת בַּעֲדָ֖הּ וּבְעַ֣ד בָּנֶ֑יהָ הֵ֚ם מַגִּשִׁ֣ים אֵלֶ֔יהָ
וְהִ֖יא מיצָֽקֶת (מוֹצֶ֣קֶת קרי): ו וַיְהִ֣י | כִּמְלֹ֣את
הַכֵּלִ֗ים וַתֹּ֤אמֶר אֶל־בְּנָהּ֙ הַגִּ֤ישָׁה אֵלַי֙ ע֣וֹד כֶּ֔לִי
וַיֹּ֣אמֶר אֵלֶ֔יהָ אֵ֥ין ע֖וֹד כֶּ֑לִי וַֽיַּעֲמֹ֖ד הַשָּֽׁמֶן:
ז וַתָּבֹ֗א וַתַּגֵּד֙ לְאִ֣ישׁ הָֽאֱלֹהִ֔ים וַיֹּ֙אמֶר֙ לְכִ֣י
מִכְרִ֣י אֶת־הַשֶּׁ֔מֶן וְשַׁלְּמִ֖י אֶת־נשִׁיֵּ֑כִי (נִשְׁיֵ֣ךְ קרי)
וְאַ֣תְּ בָּנַ֫יכִי (וּבָנַ֫יִךְ קרי) תִֽחְיִ֖י בַּנּוֹתָֽר: ח וַיְהִ֣י הַיּ֗וֹם
וַיַּעֲבֹ֨ר אֱלִישָׁ֜ע אֶל־שׁוּנֵ֗ם וְשָׁם֙ אִשָּׁ֣ה גְדוֹלָ֔ה
וַתַּחֲזֶק־בּ֖וֹ לֶֽאֱכָל־לָ֑חֶם וַֽיְהִי֙ מִדֵּ֣י עָבְר֔וֹ יָסֻ֥ר
שָׁ֖מָּה לֶֽאֱכָל־לָֽחֶם: ט וַתֹּ֨אמֶר֙ אֶל־אִישָׁ֔הּ הִנֵּה־
נָ֣א יָדַ֔עְתִּי כִּ֛י אִ֥ישׁ אֱלֹהִ֖ים קָד֣וֹשׁ ה֑וּא עֹבֵ֥ר
עָלֵ֖ינוּ תָּמִֽיד: י נַעֲשֶׂה־נָּ֤א עֲלִיַּת־קִיר֙ קְטַנָּ֔ה
וְנָשִׂ֨ים ל֥וֹ שָׁ֛ם מִטָּ֥ה וְשֻׁלְחָ֖ן וְכִסֵּ֣א וּמְנוֹרָ֑ה וְהָיָ֛ה
בְּבֹא֥וֹ אֵלֵ֖ינוּ יָס֥וּר שָֽׁמָּה: יא וַיְהִ֥י הַיּ֖וֹם וַיָּבֹ֣א
שָׁ֑מָּה וַיָּ֥סַר אֶל־הָעֲלִיָּ֖ה וַיִּשְׁכַּב־שָֽׁמָּה: יב וַיֹּ֙אמֶר֙
אֶל־גֵּֽחֲזִ֣י נַעֲר֔וֹ קְרָ֖א לַשּׁוּנַמִּ֣ית הַזֹּ֑את וַיִּקְרָא־
לָ֔הּ וַֽתַּעֲמֹ֖ד לְפָנָֽיו: יג וַיֹּ֣אמֶר ל֗וֹ אֱמָר־נָ֣א אֵלֶ֘יהָ֘
הִנֵּ֣ה חָרַ֣דְתְּ | אֵלֵ֘ינוּ֘ אֶת־כָּל־הַחֲרָדָ֣ה הַזֹּאת֒ מֶ֚ה
לַעֲשׂ֣וֹת לָ֔ךְ הֲיֵ֤שׁ לְדַבֶּר־לָךְ֙ אֶל־הַמֶּ֔לֶךְ א֖וֹ
אֶל־שַׂ֣ר הַצָּבָ֑א וַתֹּ֕אמֶר בְּת֥וֹךְ עַמִּ֖י אָנֹכִ֥י ישָֽׁבֶת:
יד וַיֹּ֕אמֶר וּמֶ֖ה לַעֲשׂ֣וֹת לָ֑הּ וַיֹּ֣אמֶר גֵּֽחֲזִ֗י אֲבָל֙
בֵּ֣ן אֵֽין־לָ֔הּ וְאִישָׁ֖הּ זָקֵֽן: טו וַיֹּ֖אמֶר קְרָא־לָ֑הּ
וַיִּקְרָא־לָ֔הּ וַֽתַּעֲמֹ֖ד בַּפָּֽתַח: טז וַיֹּ֗אמֶר לַמּוֹעֵ֤ד
הַזֶּה֙ כָּעֵ֣ת חַיָּ֔ה אתי (אַ֖תְּ קרי) חֹבֶ֣קֶת בֵּ֑ן וַתֹּ֗אמֶר
אַל־אֲדֹנִ֛י אִ֥ישׁ הָאֱלֹהִ֖ים אַל־תְּכַזֵּ֥ב בְּשִׁפְחָתֶֽךָ:
יז וַתַּ֥הַר הָאִשָּׁ֖ה וַתֵּ֣לֶד בֵּ֑ן לַמּוֹעֵ֙ד הַזֶּ֚ה כָּעֵ֣ת חַיָּ֔ה
אֲשֶׁר־דִּבֶּ֥ר אֵלֶ֖יהָ אֱלִישָֽׁע: יח וַיִּגְדַּ֖ל הַיָּ֑לֶד וַיְהִ֣י
הַיּ֔וֹם וַיֵּצֵ֥א אֶל־אָבִ֖יו אֶל־הַקֹּֽצְרִֽים: יט וַיֹּ֣אמֶר
אֶל־אָבִ֖יו רֹאשִׁ֣י | רֹאשִׁ֑י וַיֹּ֙אמֶר֙ אֶל־הַנַּ֔עַר
שָׂאֵ֖הוּ אֶל־אִמּֽוֹ: כ וַיִּ֨שָּׂאֵ֔הוּ וַיְבִיאֵ֖הוּ אֶל־אִמּ֑וֹ

carried him and brought him to his mother, and he sat on her knees until noon, and he died. 21. And she went up and laid him on the bed of the man of God, and she closed about him and left. 22. And she called her husband and said, "Please send me one of the servants and one of the she-asses; and I will run up to the man of God and return." 23. And he said, "Why are you going to him today; it is neither the New Moon nor the Sabbath." And she said, "It's all right." (*Sephardim conclude here.*) 24. And she saddled the she-ass, and she said to her servant, "Drive and go forward. Don't keep back from riding because of me unless I will tell you." 25. And she went and came to the man of God, to Mt. Carmel; and it was when the man of God saw her from afar, that he said to Gehazi his servant, "Here is that Shunemitess. 26. Now please run toward her, and say to her, 'Are you well? Is your husband well? Is the child well?'" And she said, "We are well." 27. And she came to the man of God to the mountain, and she took hold of his feet; and Gehazi approached to push her away. Now the man of God said, "Let her be, for her soul is bitter to her, and the Lord has hidden it from me and has not told me." 28. And she said, "Did I ask for a son from my lord? Did I not say, 'Do not mislead me?'" 29. And he said to Gehazi, "Gird your loins and take my staff in your hand and go. If you meet anyone, do not greet him, and if anyone greets you, do not answer him; and you shall place my staff on the lad's face." 30. And the lad's mother said, "As the Lord lives and by your life, I will not leave you." And he rose and went after her. 31. And Gehazi went ahead of them, and he placed the staff on the lad's face, and there was no sound nor any attention; and he returned toward him and told him saying, "The lad has not awakened." 32. And Elisha came into the house, and behold the lad was dead, laid out on his bed. 33. And he came and closed the door about both of them; and he prayed to the Lord. 34. And he went up and lay on the child, and placed his mouth on his mouth and his eyes on his eyes and his palms on his palms, and he prostrated himself upon him; and the child's flesh became warm. 35. And he returned and

וַיֵּ֨שֶׁב עַל־בִּרְכֶּ֛יהָ עַד־הַֽצָּהֳרַ֖יִם וַיָּמֹֽת: כא וַתַּ֗עַל וַתַּשְׁכִּבֵ֙הוּ֙ עַל־מִטַּ֖ת אִ֣ישׁ הָאֱלֹהִ֑ים וַתִּסְגֹּ֥ר בַּעֲד֖וֹ וַתֵּצֵֽא: כב וַתִּקְרָא֮ אֶל־אִישָׁהּ֒ וַתֹּ֗אמֶר שִׁלְחָ֨ה נָ֥א לִ֜י אֶחָ֤ד מִן־הַנְּעָרִים֙ וְאַחַ֣ת הָאֲתֹנ֔וֹת וְאָר֛וּצָה עַד־אִ֥ישׁ הָאֱלֹהִ֖ים וְאָשֽׁוּבָה: כג וַיֹּ֗אמֶר מַ֠דּוּעַ אַ֣תְּ הֹלֶ֤כֶת (את הלכת קרי) אֵלָיו֙ הַיּ֔וֹם לֹֽא־ חֹ֖דֶשׁ וְלֹ֣א שַׁבָּ֑ת וַתֹּ֖אמֶר שָׁלֽוֹם: (כאן מסיימין הספרדים) כד וַֽתַּחֲבֹשׁ֙ הָֽאָת֔וֹן וַתֹּ֥אמֶר אֶל־ נַעֲרָ֛הּ נְהַ֥ג וָלֵ֖ךְ אַל־תַּעֲצׇר־לִ֣י לִרְכֹּ֔ב כִּ֖י אִם־ אָמַ֥רְתִּי לָֽךְ: כה וַתֵּ֗לֶךְ וַתָּב֛וֹא אֶל־אִ֥ישׁ הָאֱלֹהִ֖ים אֶל־הַ֣ר הַכַּרְמֶ֑ל וַ֠יְהִי כִּרְא֨וֹת אִישׁ־הָאֱלֹהִ֤ים אֹתָהּ֙ מִנֶּ֔גֶד וַיֹּ֙אמֶר֙ אֶל־גֵּֽיחֲזִ֣י נַעֲר֔וֹ הִנֵּ֖ה הַשּׁוּנַמִּ֥ית הַלָּֽז: כו עַתָּה֮ רֽוּץ־נָ֣א לִקְרָאתָהּ֒ וֶֽאֱמָר־לָ֗הּ הֲשָׁל֥וֹם לָ֛ךְ הֲשָׁל֥וֹם לְאִישֵׁ֖ךְ הֲשָׁל֣וֹם לַיָּ֑לֶד וַתֹּ֖אמֶר שָׁלֽוֹם: כז וַתָּבֹ֞א אֶל־אִ֤ישׁ הָֽאֱלֹהִים֙ אֶל־הָהָ֔ר וַתַּחֲזֵ֖ק בְּרַגְלָ֑יו וַיִּגַּ֨שׁ גֵּֽיחֲזִ֜י לְהׇדְפָ֗הּ וַיֹּ֩אמֶר֩ אִ֨ישׁ הָאֱלֹהִ֤ים הַרְפֵּֽה־לָהּ֙ כִּֽי־ נַפְשָׁ֣הּ מָֽרָה־לָ֔הּ וַֽיהֹוָה֙ הֶעְלִ֣ים מִמֶּ֔נִּי וְלֹ֥א הִגִּ֖יד לִֽי: כח וַתֹּ֕אמֶר הֲשָׁאַ֥לְתִּי בֵ֖ן מֵאֵ֣ת אֲדֹנִ֑י הֲלֹ֣א אָמַ֔רְתִּי לֹ֥א תַשְׁלֶ֖ה אֹתִֽי: כט וַיֹּ֨אמֶר לְגֵֽיחֲזִ֜י חֲגֹ֣ר מׇתְנֶ֗יךָ וְקַ֨ח מִשְׁעַנְתִּ֣י בְיָדְךָ֮ וָלֵךְ֒ כִּֽי־תִמְצָ֨א אִישׁ֙ לֹ֣א תְבָרְכֶ֔נּוּ וְכִֽי־יְבָרֶכְךָ֥ אִ֖ישׁ לֹ֣א תַעֲנֶ֑נּוּ וְשַׂמְתָּ֥ מִשְׁעַנְתִּ֖י עַל־פְּנֵ֥י הַנָּֽעַר: ל וַתֹּ֙אמֶר֙ אֵ֣ם הַנַּ֔עַר חַי־יְהֹוָ֥ה וְחֵֽי־נַפְשְׁךָ֖ אִם־אֶעֶזְבֶ֑ךָּ וַיָּ֖קׇם וַיֵּ֥לֶךְ אַחֲרֶֽיהָ: לא וְגֵחֲזִ֞י עָבַ֣ר לִפְנֵיהֶ֗ם וַיָּ֜שֶׂם אֶת־ הַמִּשְׁעֶ֙נֶת֙ עַל־פְּנֵ֣י הַנַּ֔עַר וְאֵ֥ין ק֖וֹל וְאֵ֣ין קָ֑שֶׁב וַיָּ֣שׇׁב לִקְרָאת֗וֹ וַיַּגֶּד־ל֤וֹ לֵאמֹר֙ לֹ֥א הֵקִ֖יץ הַנָּֽעַר: לב וַיָּבֹ֥א אֱלִישָׁ֖ע הַבָּ֑יְתָה וְהִנֵּ֤ה הַנַּ֙עַר֙ מֵ֔ת מֻשְׁכָּ֖ב עַל־מִטָּתֽוֹ: לג וַיָּבֹ֕א וַיִּסְגֹּ֥ר הַדֶּ֖לֶת בְּעַ֣ד שְׁנֵיהֶ֑ם וַיִּתְפַּלֵּ֖ל אֶל־יְהֹוָֽה: לד וַיַּ֜עַל וַיִּשְׁכַּ֣ב עַל־הַיֶּ֗לֶד וַיָּ֩שֶׂם֩ פִּ֨יו עַל־פִּ֜יו וְעֵינָ֤יו עַל־עֵינָיו֙ וְכַפָּ֣יו עַל־כַּפָּ֔יו וַיִּגְהַ֖ר עָלָ֑יו וַיָּ֖חׇם בְּשַׂ֥ר הַיָּֽלֶד: לה וַיָּ֣שׇׁב

walked in the house once here and once there, and he went up and prostrated himself upon him; and the lad sneezed up to seven times, and the lad opened his eyes. 36. And he summoned Gehazi and said, "Call this Shunemitess." And he called her, and she came to him, and he said, "Pick up your son." 37. And she came and fell at his feet and bowed to the ground; and she picked up her son and departed.

וַיֵּלֶךְ בַּבַּיִת אַחַת הֵנָּה וְאַחַת הֵנָּה וַיַּעַל וַיִּגְהַר
עָלָיו וַיְזוֹרֵר הַנַּעַר עַד־שֶׁבַע פְּעָמִים וַיִּפְקַח
הַנַּעַר אֶת־עֵינָיו׃ לו וַיִּקְרָא אֶל־גֵּיחֲזִי וַיֹּאמֶר
קְרָא אֶל־הַשֻּׁנַמִּית הַזֹּאת וַיִּקְרָאֶהָ וַתָּבוֹא אֵלָיו
וַיֹּאמֶר שְׂאִי בְנֵךְ׃ לז וַתָּבֹא וַתִּפֹּל עַל־רַגְלָיו
וַתִּשְׁתַּחוּ אָרְצָה וַתִּשָּׂא אֶת־בְּנָהּ וַתֵּצֵא׃

HAFTARATH HAYYE SARAH הפטרת חיי שרה
(I Kings 1:1–31)

The similarity of this selection to the Sidra is in the first verse, "And King David was old, he came into his old age." This is similar to the verse, "And Abraham was old, coming into his old age" (Gen. 24:1).

1:1. And King David was old, he came into his old age, and they covered him with clothes, but he was not warmed. 2. And his servants said to him, "Let them seek for my lord the king a young girl, a virgin, and she shall stand before the king, and she shall be to him a warmer, and she shall lie in your lap, and it shall be warm for my lord the king." 3. And they sought a beautiful young girl throughout the borders of Israel, and found Abishag the Shunemitess and brought her to the king. 4. And the young girl was very beautiful, and she was a warmer to the king, and she ministered to him, but the king did not know her. 5. And Adoniahu the son of Haggith exalted himself saying: 'I will be king"; and he made for himself chariots and horsemen and fifty men to run before him. 6. And his father had not angered him all his days saying, "Why have you done so?" And he too was of very handsome appearance, and she bore him after Absalom. 7. And he conferred with Joab the son of Zeruiah and with Abiathar the priest, and they helped [by following] after Adoniahu. 8. And Zadok the priest and Benaiahu the son of Jehoiada, and Nathan the prophet, and Shimei and Rei and the mighty men who were with David, were not with Adoniahu. 9. And Adoniahu slew sheep and oxen and fatlings by the stone of Zoheleth, which is beside En-Rogel, and he called all his brothers, the

א וְהַמֶּלֶךְ דָּוִד זָקֵן בָּא בַּיָּמִים וַיְכַסֻּהוּ בַּבְּגָדִים
וְלֹא יִחַם לוֹ׃ ב וַיֹּאמְרוּ לוֹ עֲבָדָיו יְבַקְשׁוּ
לַאדֹנִי הַמֶּלֶךְ נַעֲרָה בְתוּלָה וְעָמְדָה לִפְנֵי הַמֶּלֶךְ
וּתְהִי־לוֹ סֹכֶנֶת וְשָׁכְבָה בְחֵיקֶךָ וְחַם לַאדֹנִי
הַמֶּלֶךְ׃ ג וַיְבַקְשׁוּ נַעֲרָה יָפָה בְּכֹל גְּבוּל יִשְׂרָאֵל
וַיִּמְצְאוּ אֶת־אֲבִישַׁג הַשּׁוּנַמִּית וַיָּבִאוּ אֹתָהּ
לַמֶּלֶךְ׃ ד וְהַנַּעֲרָה יָפָה עַד־מְאֹד וַתְּהִי לַמֶּלֶךְ
סֹכֶנֶת וַתְּשָׁרְתֵהוּ וְהַמֶּלֶךְ לֹא יְדָעָהּ׃ ה וַאֲדֹנִיָּה
בֶן־חַגִּית מִתְנַשֵּׂא לֵאמֹר אֲנִי אֶמְלֹךְ וַיַּעַשׂ לוֹ
רֶכֶב וּפָרָשִׁים וַחֲמִשִּׁים אִישׁ רָצִים לְפָנָיו׃
ו וְלֹא־עֲצָבוֹ אָבִיו מִיָּמָיו לֵאמֹר מַדּוּעַ כָּכָה
עָשִׂיתָ וְגַם־הוּא טוֹב־תֹּאַר מְאֹד וְאֹתוֹ יָלְדָה
אַחֲרֵי אַבְשָׁלוֹם׃ ז וַיִּהְיוּ דְבָרָיו עִם יוֹאָב בֶּן־
צְרוּיָה וְעִם אֶבְיָתָר הַכֹּהֵן וַיַּעְזְרוּ אַחֲרֵי אֲדֹנִיָּה׃
ח וְצָדוֹק הַכֹּהֵן וּבְנָיָהוּ בֶן־יְהוֹיָדָע וְנָתָן הַנָּבִיא
וְשִׁמְעִי וְרֵעִי וְהַגִּבּוֹרִים אֲשֶׁר לְדָוִד לֹא הָיוּ
עִם־אֲדֹנִיָּהוּ׃ ט וַיִּזְבַּח אֲדֹנִיָּהוּ צֹאן וּבָקָר
וּמְרִיא עִם אֶבֶן הַזֹּחֶלֶת אֲשֶׁר־אֵצֶל עֵין רֹגֵל
וַיִּקְרָא אֶת־כָּל־אֶחָיו בְּנֵי הַמֶּלֶךְ וּלְכָל־אַנְשֵׁי

king's sons, and all the men of Judah, the king's servants. 10. And Nathan the prophet and Benaiahu and the mighty men and his brother, Solomon, he did not call. 11. And Nathan said to Bath-Sheba, Solomon's mother, saying, "You have surely heard the Adoniahu the son of Haggith has reigned, and our lord, David, did not know [it]. 12. And now come and I shall council you with advice, and you shall save your life and the life of your son Solomon. 13. Go and come to King David, and you shall say to him, 'Surely, you, my lord the king, did swear to your maid saying that "Solomon your son will reign after me and he shall sit upon my throne." Now why did Adoniahu reign?' 14. Behold, you are talking there with the king, and I shall come in after you and I shall complete your words." 15. And Bath-Sheba came in unto the king, into the chamber: and the king was very old; and Abishag the Shunemitess ministered to the king. 16. And Bath-Sheba bowed her head, and prostrated herself unto the king, and the king said, "What is your [wish]?" 17. And she said to him, "My lord, you swore by the Lord your God to your maid that 'Solomon, your son, shall reign after me, and he shall sit on my throne.' 18. And now, behold Adoniahu has reigned, and now my lord the king, you did not know. 19. And he has slain oxen and fatlings and sheep in abundance and he called all the king's sons and Abiathar the priest and Joab the general of the army, but Solomon, your servant, he did not call. 20. And you, my lord the king, the eyes of all Israel are upon you, that you should tell them who shall sit on the throne of my lord the king after him. 21. And [otherwise] when my lord the king shall sleep with his fathers, I and my son Solomon shall be [considered] offenders." 22. And behold, she was still speaking with the king, and Nathan the prophet came. 23. And they told the king saying, "Behold, Nathan the prophet." And he came in before the king and prostrated himself unto the king upon his face, to the ground. 24. And Nathan said, "My lord, the king, did you say 'Adoniahu shall reign after me and he shall sit upon my throne?' 25. For he has gone down this day and has slain oxen and

יְהוּדָה עַבְדֵי הַמֶּלֶךְ: י וְאֶת־נָתָן הַנָּבִיא וּבְנָיָהוּ וְאֶת־הַגִּבּוֹרִים וְאֶת־שְׁלֹמֹה אָחִיו לֹא קָרָא: יא וַיֹּאמֶר נָתָן אֶל־בַּת־שֶׁבַע אֵם־שְׁלֹמֹה לֵאמֹר הֲלוֹא שָׁמַעַתְּ כִּי מָלַךְ אֲדֹנִיָּהוּ בֶן־חַגִּית וַאֲדֹנֵינוּ דָוִד לֹא יָדָע: יב וְעַתָּה לְכִי אִיעָצֵךְ נָא עֵצָה וּמַלְּטִי אֶת־נַפְשֵׁךְ וְאֶת־נֶפֶשׁ בְּנֵךְ שְׁלֹמֹה: יג לְכִי וּבֹאִי ׀ אֶל־הַמֶּלֶךְ דָּוִד וְאָמַרְתְּ אֵלָיו הֲלֹא־אַתָּה אֲדֹנִי הַמֶּלֶךְ נִשְׁבַּעְתָּ לַאֲמָתְךָ לֵאמֹר כִּי־שְׁלֹמֹה בְנֵךְ יִמְלֹךְ אַחֲרַי וְהוּא יֵשֵׁב עַל־כִּסְאִי וּמַדּוּעַ מָלַךְ אֲדֹנִיָּהוּ: יד הִנֵּה עוֹדָךְ מְדַבֶּרֶת שָׁם עִם־הַמֶּלֶךְ וַאֲנִי אָבוֹא אַחֲרַיִךְ וּמִלֵּאתִי אֶת־דְּבָרָיִךְ: טו וַתָּבֹא בַת־שֶׁבַע אֶל־הַמֶּלֶךְ הַחַדְרָה וְהַמֶּלֶךְ זָקֵן מְאֹד וַאֲבִישַׁג הַשּׁוּנַמִּית מְשָׁרַת אֶת־הַמֶּלֶךְ: טז וַתִּקֹּד בַּת־שֶׁבַע וַתִּשְׁתַּחוּ לַמֶּלֶךְ וַיֹּאמֶר הַמֶּלֶךְ מַה־לָּךְ: יז וַתֹּאמֶר לוֹ אֲדֹנִי אַתָּה נִשְׁבַּעְתָּ בַּיהוָה אֱלֹהֶיךָ לַאֲמָתֶךָ כִּי־שְׁלֹמֹה בְנֵךְ יִמְלֹךְ אַחֲרָי וְהוּא יֵשֵׁב עַל־כִּסְאִי: יח וְעַתָּה הִנֵּה אֲדֹנִיָּה מָלָךְ וְעַתָּה אֲדֹנִי הַמֶּלֶךְ לֹא יָדָעְתָּ: יט וַיִּזְבַּח שׁוֹר וּמְרִיא־ וְצֹאן לָרֹב וַיִּקְרָא לְכָל־בְּנֵי הַמֶּלֶךְ וּלְאֶבְיָתָר הַכֹּהֵן וּלְיֹאָב שַׂר הַצָּבָא וְלִשְׁלֹמֹה עַבְדְּךָ לֹא קָרָא: כ וְאַתָּה אֲדֹנִי הַמֶּלֶךְ עֵינֵי כָל־יִשְׂרָאֵל עָלֶיךָ לְהַגִּיד לָהֶם מִי יֵשֵׁב עַל־כִּסֵּא אֲדֹנִי־הַמֶּלֶךְ אַחֲרָיו: כא וְהָיָה כִּשְׁכַב אֲדֹנִי־הַמֶּלֶךְ עִם־אֲבֹתָיו וְהָיִיתִי אֲנִי וּבְנִי שְׁלֹמֹה חַטָּאִים: כב וְהִנֵּה עוֹדֶנָּה מְדַבֶּרֶת עִם־הַמֶּלֶךְ וְנָתָן הַנָּבִיא בָּא: כג וַיַּגִּידוּ לַמֶּלֶךְ לֵאמֹר הִנֵּה נָתָן הַנָּבִיא וַיָּבֹא לִפְנֵי הַמֶּלֶךְ וַיִּשְׁתַּחוּ לַמֶּלֶךְ עַל־אַפָּיו אָרְצָה: כד וַיֹּאמֶר נָתָן אֲדֹנִי הַמֶּלֶךְ אַתָּה אָמַרְתָּ אֲדֹנִיָּהוּ יִמְלֹךְ אַחֲרָי וְהוּא יֵשֵׁב עַל־כִּסְאִי: כה כִּי ׀ יָרַד הַיּוֹם וַיִּזְבַּח שׁוֹר וּמְרִיא־וְצֹאן

fatlings and sheep in abundance, and he called all the king's sons, and the officers of the army, and Abiathar the priest, and behold, they eat and drink before him, and they said, 'Long live King Adoniahu.' 26. And me, [even] me your servant, and Zadok the priest and Benaiahu the son of Yehoiada and Solomon, your servant, he did not call. 27. If this matter stems from my lord the king, [I wonder that] you have not informed your servant who should sit on the throne of my lord the king after him." 28. And King David answered and said, "Call Bath-Sheba to me." And she came before the king and stood before the king. 29. And he swore and said, "[I swear as] God lives Who redeemed my soul from all distress. 30. Indeed, as I swore to you by the Lord God of Israel saying, 'Surely Solomon, your son, shall reign after me and he shall sit on my throne in my stead'; surely, so will I do this day." 31. And Bath-Sheba bowed [her] face to the earth, and she prostrated herself to the king and said: "Let my lord King David live forever."

לָרֹב וַיִּקְרָא לְכָל־בְּנֵי הַמֶּלֶךְ וּלְשָׂרֵי הַצָּבָא וּלְאֶבְיָתָר הַכֹּהֵן וְהִנָּם אֹכְלִים וְשֹׁתִים לְפָנָיו וַיֹּאמְרוּ יְחִי הַמֶּלֶךְ אֲדֹנִיָּהוּ: כו וְלִי אֲנִי־עַבְדֶּךָ וּלְצָדֹק הַכֹּהֵן וְלִבְנָיָהוּ בֶן־יְהוֹיָדָע וְלִשְׁלֹמֹה עַבְדְּךָ לֹא קָרָא: כז אִם מֵאֵת אֲדֹנִי הַמֶּלֶךְ נִהְיָה הַדָּבָר הַזֶּה וְלֹא הוֹדַעְתָּ אֶת־עַבְדְּיךָ (עבדך קרי) מִי יֵשֵׁב עַל־כִּסֵּא אֲדֹנִי־הַמֶּלֶךְ אַחֲרָיו: כח וַיַּעַן הַמֶּלֶךְ דָּוִד וַיֹּאמֶר קִרְאוּ־לִי לְבַת־שָׁבַע וַתָּבֹא לִפְנֵי הַמֶּלֶךְ וַתַּעֲמֹד לִפְנֵי הַמֶּלֶךְ: כט וַיִּשָּׁבַע הַמֶּלֶךְ וַיֹּאמַר חַי־יְהֹוָה אֲשֶׁר־פָּדָה אֶת־נַפְשִׁי מִכָּל־צָרָה: ל כִּי כַּאֲשֶׁר נִשְׁבַּעְתִּי לָךְ בַּיהֹוָה אֱלֹהֵי יִשְׂרָאֵל לֵאמֹר כִּי־שְׁלֹמֹה בְנֵךְ יִמְלֹךְ אַחֲרַי וְהוּא יֵשֵׁב עַל־כִּסְאִי תַּחְתָּי כִּי כֵּן אֶעֱשֶׂה הַיּוֹם הַזֶּה: לא וַתִּקֹּד בַּת־שֶׁבַע אַפַּיִם אֶרֶץ וַתִּשְׁתַּחוּ לַמֶּלֶךְ וַתֹּאמֶר יְחִי אֲדֹנִי הַמֶּלֶךְ דָּוִד לְעֹלָם:

HAFTARATH TOLEDOTH הפטרת תולדת
(Malachi 1:1–2:7)
Should Rosh Chodesh fall on a Sunday, the Haftarah For The Day Preceding Rosh Chodesh (p. 933) is read.

The beginning of the selection discusses Jacob and Esau, and how God loved Jacob and hated Esau.

1:1. The prophecy of the word of the Lord to Israel through Malachi. 2. I loved you, says the Lord, but you asked, "How have You loved us?" Was not Esau Jacob's brother? says the Lord, and I loved Jacob. 3. And I hated Esau, and I made his mountains desolate and his heritage into [a habitat for] the jackals of the desert. 4. Should Edom say, "We have become impoverished, but we will rebuild the ruins"; so said the Lord of Hosts, They shall build, but I will demolish, and they shall be called the border of wickedness, and the people whom the Lord has damned forever. 5. And your eyes shall see, and you shall say, "The Lord is great beyond the border of Israel." 6. A son honors a father, and a

א מַשָּׂא דְבַר־יְהֹוָה אֶל־יִשְׂרָאֵל בְּיַד מַלְאָכִי: ב אָהַבְתִּי אֶתְכֶם אָמַר יְהֹוָה וַאֲמַרְתֶּם בַּמָּה אֲהַבְתָּנוּ הֲלוֹא־אָח עֵשָׂו לְיַעֲקֹב נְאֻם־יְהֹוָה וָאֹהַב אֶת־יַעֲקֹב: ג וְאֶת־עֵשָׂו שָׂנֵאתִי וָאָשִׂים אֶת־הָרָיו שְׁמָמָה וְאֶת־נַחֲלָתוֹ לְתַנּוֹת מִדְבָּר: ד כִּי־תֹאמַר אֱדוֹם רֻשַּׁשְׁנוּ וְנָשׁוּב וְנִבְנֶה חֳרָבוֹת כֹּה אָמַר יְהֹוָה צְבָאוֹת הֵמָּה יִבְנוּ וַאֲנִי אֶהֱרוֹס וְקָרְאוּ לָהֶם גְּבוּל רִשְׁעָה וְהָעָם אֲשֶׁר־זָעַם יְהֹוָה עַד־עוֹלָם: ה וְעֵינֵיכֶם תִּרְאֶינָה וְאַתֶּם תֹּאמְרוּ יִגְדַּל יְהֹוָה מֵעַל לִגְבוּל יִשְׂרָאֵל: ו בֵּן יְכַבֵּד אָב וְעֶבֶד אֲדֹנָיו וְאִם־אָב אָנִי אַיֵּה

כְבוֹדִ֗י וְאִם־אֲדוֹנִ֣ים אָ֘נִי֮ אַיֵּ֣ה מוֹרָאִ֗י אָמַ֣ר ׀
יְהוָ֣ה צְבָא֗וֹת לָכֶם֙ הַכֹּֽהֲנִים֙ בּוֹזֵ֣י שְׁמִ֔י וַאֲמַרְתֶּ֕ם
בַּמֶּ֥ה בָזִ֖ינוּ אֶת־שְׁמֶֽךָ׃ ז מַגִּישִׁ֤ים עַֽל־מִזְבְּחִי֙
לֶ֣חֶם מְגֹאָ֔ל וַאֲמַרְתֶּ֖ם בַּמֶּ֣ה גֵֽאַלְנ֑וּךָ בֶּאֱמָרְכֶ֕ם
שֻׁלְחַ֥ן יְהוָ֖ה נִבְזֶ֥ה הֽוּא׃ ח וְכִֽי־תַגִּשׁ֨וּן עִוֵּ֤ר
לִזְבֹּ֙חַ֙ אֵ֣ין רָ֔ע וְכִ֥י תַגִּ֛ישׁוּ פִּסֵּ֥חַ וְחֹלֶ֖ה אֵ֣ין רָ֑ע
הַקְרִיבֵ֨הוּ נָ֜א לְפֶחָתֶ֗ךָ הֲיִרְצְךָ֙ א֚וֹ הֲיִשָּׂ֣א פָנֶ֔יךָ
אָמַ֖ר יְהוָ֥ה צְבָאֽוֹת׃ ט וְעַתָּ֛ה חַלּוּ־נָ֥א פְנֵי־אֵ֖ל
וִֽיחָנֵ֑נוּ מִיֶּדְכֶם֙ הָ֣יְתָה זֹּ֔את הֲיִשָּׂ֤א מִכֶּם֙ פָּנִ֔ים
אָמַ֖ר יְהוָ֥ה צְבָאֽוֹת׃ י מִ֤י גַם־בָּכֶם֙ וְיִסְגֹּ֣ר
דְּלָתַ֔יִם וְלֹא־תָאִ֥ירוּ מִזְבְּחִ֖י חִנָּ֑ם אֵין־לִ֨י חֵ֜פֶץ
בָּכֶ֗ם אָמַר֙ יְהוָ֣ה צְבָא֔וֹת וּמִנְחָ֖ה לֹא־אֶרְצֶ֥ה
מִיֶּדְכֶֽם׃ יא כִּ֣י מִמִּזְרַח־שֶׁ֜מֶשׁ וְעַד־מְבוֹא֗וֹ גָּד֤וֹל
שְׁמִי֙ בַּגּוֹיִ֔ם וּבְכָל־מָק֗וֹם מֻקְטָ֥ר מֻגָּ֛שׁ לִשְׁמִ֖י
וּמִנְחָ֣ה טְהוֹרָ֑ה כִּֽי־גָד֤וֹל שְׁמִי֙ בַּגּוֹיִ֔ם אָמַ֖ר יְהוָ֥ה
צְבָאֽוֹת׃ יב וְאַתֶּ֖ם מְחַלְּלִ֣ים אוֹת֑וֹ בֶּאֱמָרְכֶ֗ם
שֻׁלְחַ֤ן אֲדֹנָי֙ מְגֹאָ֣ל ה֔וּא וְנִיב֖וֹ נִבְזֶ֥ה אָכְלֽוֹ׃
יג וַאֲמַרְתֶּם֩ הִנֵּ֨ה מַתְּלָאָ֜ה וְהִפַּחְתֶּ֣ם אוֹת֗וֹ אָמַר֙
יְהוָ֣ה צְבָא֔וֹת וַהֲבֵאתֶ֣ם גָּז֗וּל וְאֶת־הַפִּסֵּ֙חַ֙ וְאֶת־
הַח֣וֹלֶה וַהֲבֵאתֶ֖ם אֶת־הַמִּנְחָ֑ה הַאֶרְצֶ֥ה אוֹתָ֛הּ
מִיֶּדְכֶ֖ם אָמַ֥ר יְהוָֽה׃ יד וְאָר֣וּר נוֹכֵ֗ל וְיֵ֤שׁ בְּעֶדְרוֹ֙
זָכָ֔ר וְנֹדֵ֛ר וְזֹבֵ֥חַ מָשְׁחָ֖ת לַאדֹנָ֑י כִּי֩ מֶ֨לֶךְ גָּד֜וֹל
אָ֗נִי אָמַר֙ יְהוָ֣ה צְבָא֔וֹת וּשְׁמִ֖י נוֹרָ֥א בַגּוֹיִֽם׃
א וְעַתָּ֗ה אֲלֵיכֶ֛ם הַמִּצְוָ֥ה הַזֹּ֖את הַכֹּהֲנִֽים׃ ב אִם־
לֹ֣א תִשְׁמְע֡וּ וְאִם־לֹ֩א תָשִׂ֨ימוּ עַל־לֵ֜ב לָתֵ֧ת
כָּב֣וֹד לִשְׁמִ֗י אָמַר֙ יְהוָ֣ה צְבָא֔וֹת וְשִׁלַּחְתִּ֤י בָכֶם֙
אֶת־הַמְּאֵרָ֔ה וְאָרוֹתִ֖י אֶת־בִּרְכֽוֹתֵיכֶ֑ם וְגַם֙
אָרוֹתִ֔יהָ כִּ֥י אֵינְכֶ֖ם שָׂמִ֥ים עַל־לֵֽב׃ ג הִנְנִ֨י גֹעֵ֤ר
לָכֶם֙ אֶת־הַזֶּ֔רַע וְזֵרִ֤יתִי פֶ֙רֶשׁ֙ עַל־פְּנֵיכֶ֔ם פֶּ֖רֶשׁ
חַגֵּיכֶ֑ם וְנָשָׂ֥א אֶתְכֶ֖ם אֵלָֽיו׃ ד וִֽידַעְתֶּ֕ם כִּ֚י

slave his master. Now if I am a father, where
is My honor? And if I am a Master, where is
My fear? says the Lord of Hosts to you, the
priests, who despise My Name. But you
said, "How have we despised Your Name?"
7. You offer on My altar defiled food, yet
you say, "How have we defiled You?" By
your saying, "God's table is defiled."
8. And when you offer a blind [animal] to
sacrifice, there is nothing wrong, and when
you offer a lame or a sick one, there is
nothing wrong. Were you to offer it to your
governor, would he accept you or would he
favor you? says the Lord of Hosts. 9. And
now, pray before the Lord that He be
gracious to us. This has come from your
hand. Will He favor any of you? says the
Lord of Hosts. 10. O that there were even
one among you that would close the doors
[of the Temple] and that you would not
kindle fire on My altar in vain! I
have no desire in you, says the Lord of
Hosts, neither will I accept an offering from
your hand. 11. For, from the rising of the
sun until its setting, My Name is great
among the nations, and in every place
offerings are burnt and offered up to My
Name and a pure oblation, for My Name is
great among the nations, says the Lord of
Hosts. 12. But you are profaning it, by your
saying, "The Lord's table is defiled," and its
expression is "Its food is defiled." 13. And
you say, "Behold this is wearisome," and
you cast it down, says the Lord of Hosts, and
you brought that which was taken by
violence, and the lame and the sick; will I
accept it from your hand? says the Lord.
14. And cursed is he who deals craftily, and,
although there is a male in his flock, he
vows and sacrifices a blemished one, for I
am a great King, says the Lord of Hosts, and
My Name is feared among the nations.
2:1. And now, to you is this commandment,
O priests. 2. If you do not heed and if you
do not lay it to your heart to give honor to
My Name, says the Lord of Hosts, I will
send the curse upon you, and I will curse
your blessings; and indeed, I have [already]
cursed it, for you do not lay it to your heart.
3. Behold I rebuke the seed because of you,
and I will scatter dung upon your face, the
dung of your festive sacrifices, and it shall
take you to itself. 4. And you shall know

that I have sent you this commandment,
that My covenant be with Levi, says the
Lord of Hosts. 5. My covenant was with
him, life and peace, and I gave them to him
[with] fear, and he feared Me, and because
of My Name, he is over-awed. 6. The
teaching of the truth was in his mouth, and
injustice was not found in his lips; in peace
and equity he went with Me, and he
brought back many from iniquity. 7. For a
priest's lips shall guard knowledge, and
teaching should be sought from his mouth,
for he is a messenger of the Lord of Hosts.

שִׁלַּחְתִּי אֲלֵיכֶם אֵת הַמִּצְוָה הַזֹּאת לִהְיוֹת
בְּרִיתִי אֶת־לֵוִי אָמַר יְהוָה צְבָאוֹת: ה בְּרִיתִי ׀
הָיְתָה אִתּוֹ הַחַיִּים וְהַשָּׁלוֹם וָאֶתְּנֵם־לוֹ מוֹרָא
וַיִּירָאֵנִי וּמִפְּנֵי שְׁמִי נִחַת הוּא: ו תּוֹרַת אֱמֶת
הָיְתָה בְּפִיהוּ וְעַוְלָה לֹא־נִמְצָא בִשְׂפָתָיו
בְּשָׁלוֹם וּבְמִישׁוֹר הָלַךְ אִתִּי וְרַבִּים הֵשִׁיב
מֵעָוֺן: ז כִּי־שִׂפְתֵי כֹהֵן יִשְׁמְרוּ־דַעַת וְתוֹרָה
יְבַקְשׁוּ מִפִּיהוּ כִּי מַלְאַךְ יְהוָה־צְבָאוֹת הוּא:

HAFTARATH VAYETZE הפטרת ויצא

The generally accepted custom among Ashkenazim is to read Hosea 12:13–14:10 (which is the end of Hosea). *Chaye Adam* rules that Joel 2:26, 27 be added in order to end with a cheerful note. Chabad Chasidim read the Haftarah of the Sephardim, Hosea 11:17 to 12:12, adding the first two verses of the Haftarah of the Ashkenazim in accordance with the Rambam. According to some authorities, the custom of those following the ritual of Frankfort-on-the-Main is to read both Haftaroth.

[There are chumashim in which the Haftarah of Vayetze for Asheknazim is Hosea 11:7 to 12:12, the selection read by Sephardim, and the Haftarah of Vayishlach is 12:13 to 14:10. This is, however, deemed an error by *Levush*, since the contents match Vayetze rather than Vayishlach.]

The selection dealing with Jacob's flight to the field of Aram, where he tended Laban's flocks, relates to the narrative in the Sidra.

(*Sephardim and Chabad Chasidim commence here.*) 11:7. And My people are
wavering about the return to Me; and to the
Most High they call him; together they do
not exalt Him. 8. How can I give you over,
O Ephraim, deliver you, O Israel? How can
I make you like Admah, place you like
Zeboim? My heart has turned about within
Me; My consolations have been aroused.
9. I will not execute the kindling of My
wrath; I will not return to destroy Ephraim,
for I am God and not a man. In your midst
shall be the holy [place], and I will not enter
a[nother] city. 10. After the Lord they shall
go; like a lion He shall roar, for He shall
roar, and the children shall be gathered
from the west. 11. They shall hasten like a
bird from Egypt, and like a dove from
Assyria, and I will make them dwell securely
in their houses, says the Lord. 12:1. Ephraim has surrounded Me with lies, and the
house of Israel with deceit, but Judah is still
ruling with God, and with the Holy One he

כאן מתחילין הספרדים

ז וְעַמִּי תְלוּאִים לִמְשׁוּבָתִי וְאֶל־עַל יִקְרָאֻהוּ
יַחַד לֹא יְרוֹמֵם: ח אֵיךְ אֶתֶּנְךָ אֶפְרַיִם אֲמַגֶּנְךָ
יִשְׂרָאֵל אֵיךְ אֶתֶּנְךָ כְאַדְמָה אֲשִׂימְךָ כִּצְבֹאיִם
נֶהְפַּךְ עָלַי לִבִּי יַחַד נִכְמְרוּ נִחוּמָי: ט לֹא
אֶעֱשֶׂה חֲרוֹן אַפִּי לֹא אָשׁוּב לְשַׁחֵת אֶפְרָיִם כִּי
אֵל אָנֹכִי וְלֹא־אִישׁ בְּקִרְבְּךָ קָדוֹשׁ וְלֹא אָבוֹא
בְּעִיר: י אַחֲרֵי יְהוָה יֵלְכוּ כְּאַרְיֵה יִשְׁאָג כִּי־
הוּא יִשְׁאַג וְיֶחֶרְדוּ בָנִים מִיָּם: יא יֶחֶרְדוּ
כְצִפּוֹר מִמִּצְרַיִם וּכְיוֹנָה מֵאֶרֶץ אַשּׁוּר
וְהוֹשַׁבְתִּים עַל־בָּתֵּיהֶם נְאֻם־יְהוָה: א סְבָבֻנִי
בְכַחַשׁ אֶפְרַיִם וּבְמִרְמָה בֵּית יִשְׂרָאֵל וִיהוּדָה
עֹד רָד עִם־אֵל וְעִם־קְדוֹשִׁים נֶאֱמָן: ב אֶפְרַיִם

is faithful. 2. Ephraim joins the wind and pursues the east wind. All day, lies and plunder he increases, and they form a covenant with Assyria, and oil is brought to Egypt. 3. And the Lord has a quarrel with Judah, and to visit upon Jacob according to his ways; according to his deeds He recompenses him. 4. In the womb, he seized his brother's heel, and with his strength, he strove with an angel. 5. He strove with an angel and prevailed over him; he wept and supplicated him, "In Bethel he will find Him, and there He will speak with us." 6. And the Lord God of Hosts, the Lord is His remembrance. 7. And you, by your God you shall return; kindness and justice keep, and hope to your God always. 8. A merchant has deceitful scales in his hand; he loves to oppress. 9. And Ephraim said, "Surely I have become rich, I have found strength for myself; in all my toils, they will not find for me any iniquity that is a sin." 10. And I am the Lord your God from the land of Egypt; I will yet make you dwell in tents like the days of that time. 11. And I spoke to the prophets, and I increased vision, and I spoke to the prophets with similitudes. 12. If a calamity befalls Gilead, they were but unjust; in Gilgal they slaughtered cattle [for sacrifices to idols]. Also their altars are like heaps in the furrows of the field. (*Sephardim conclude here.* *Ashkenazim commence here.*) 13. And Jacob fled to the field of Aram, and Israel worked for a wife, and for a wife he guarded [the sheep]. 14. And with a prophet the Lord brought Israel up from Egypt, and through a prophet they were guarded. (*Chabad chasidim conclude here.*) 15. Ephraim provoked bitterly, and his blood shall be spread over him, and for his mockery, his Lord shall recompense him. 13:1. When Ephraim spoke tremblingly, he became exalted in Israel, but he became guilty with Baal and died. 2. And now they continue to sin, and they made for themselves a molten image from their silver according to their pattern, even idols, all of it the work of craftsmen; to them they say, "Those who sacrifice men are worthy to kiss the calves." 3. Therefore, they shall be like a morning cloud, and like dew that goes away early, like chaff that is carried away by a

רֹעֶ֥ה ר֙וּחַ֙ וְרֹדֵ֣ף קָדִ֔ים כָּל־הַיּ֕וֹם כָּזָ֥ב וָשֹׁ֖ד יַרְבֶּ֑ה וּבְרִית֙ עִם־אַשּׁ֣וּר יִכְרֹ֔תוּ וְשֶׁ֖מֶן לְמִצְרַ֥יִם יוּבָֽל׃ ג וְרִ֥יב לַֽיהֹוָ֖ה עִם־יְהוּדָ֑ה וְלִפְקֹ֤ד עַֽל־יַעֲקֹב֙ כִּדְרָכָ֔יו כְּמַֽעֲלָלָ֖יו יָשִׁ֥יב לֽוֹ׃ ד בַּבֶּ֖טֶן עָקַ֣ב אֶת־אָחִ֑יו וּבְאוֹנ֖וֹ שָׂרָ֥ה אֶת־אֱלֹהִֽים׃ ה וַיָּ֤שַׂר אֶל־מַלְאָךְ֙ וַיֻּכָ֔ל בָּכָ֖ה וַיִּתְחַנֶּן־ל֑וֹ בֵּֽית־אֵל֙ יִמְצָאֶ֔נּוּ וְשָׁ֖ם יְדַבֵּ֥ר עִמָּֽנוּ׃ ו וַֽיהֹוָ֖ה אֱלֹהֵ֣י הַצְּבָא֑וֹת יְהֹוָ֖ה זִכְרֽוֹ׃ ז וְאַתָּ֖ה בֵּֽאלֹהֶ֣יךָ תָשׁ֑וּב חֶ֤סֶד וּמִשְׁפָּט֙ שְׁמֹ֔ר וְקַוֵּ֥ה אֶל־אֱלֹהֶ֖יךָ תָּמִֽיד׃ ח כְּנַ֗עַן בְּיָד֛וֹ מֹֽאזְנֵ֥י מִרְמָ֖ה לַֽעֲשֹׁ֥ק אָהֵֽב׃ ט וַיֹּ֣אמֶר אֶפְרַ֔יִם אַ֣ךְ עָשַׁ֔רְתִּי מָצָ֥אתִי א֖וֹן לִ֑י כָּל־יְגִיעַ֕י לֹ֥א יִמְצְאוּ־לִ֖י עָוֺ֥ן אֲשֶׁר־חֵֽטְא׃ י וְאָֽנֹכִ֛י יְהֹוָ֥ה אֱלֹהֶ֖יךָ מֵאֶ֣רֶץ מִצְרָ֑יִם עֹ֛ד אוֹשִֽׁיבְךָ֥ בָֽאֳהָלִ֖ים כִּימֵ֥י מוֹעֵֽד׃ יא וְדִבַּ֨רְתִּי֙ עַל־הַנְּבִיאִ֔ים וְאָֽנֹכִ֖י חָז֣וֹן הִרְבֵּ֑יתִי וּבְיַ֥ד הַנְּבִיאִ֖ים אֲדַמֶּֽה׃ יב אִם־גִּלְעָ֥ד אָ֨וֶן֙ אַךְ־שָׁ֣וְא הָי֔וּ בַּגִּלְגָּ֖ל שְׁוָרִ֣ים זִבֵּ֑חוּ גַּ֤ם מִזְבְּחוֹתָם֙ כְּגַלִּ֔ים עַ֖ל תַּלְמֵ֥י שָׂדָֽי׃ (כאן מסיימין הספרדים)

(כאן מתחילין האשכנזים) יג וַיִּבְרַ֥ח יַֽעֲקֹ֖ב שְׂדֵ֣ה אֲרָ֑ם וַיַּֽעֲבֹ֤ד יִשְׂרָאֵל֙ בְּאִשָּׁ֔ה וּבְאִשָּׁ֖ה שָׁמָֽר׃ יד וּבְנָבִ֕יא הֶֽעֱלָ֧ה יְהֹוָ֛ה אֶת־יִשְׂרָאֵ֖ל מִמִּצְרָ֑יִם וּבְנָבִ֖יא נִשְׁמָֽר׃ (כאן מסיימין חסידי חב״ד) טו הִכְעִ֥יס אֶפְרַ֖יִם תַּמְרוּרִ֑ים וְדָמָיו֙ עָלָ֣יו יִטּ֔וֹשׁ וְחֶ֨רְפָּת֔וֹ יָשִׁ֥יב ל֖וֹ אֲדֹנָֽיו׃ א כְּדַבֵּ֤ר אֶפְרַ֨יִם֙ רְתֵ֔ת נָשָׂ֥א ה֖וּא בְּיִשְׂרָאֵ֑ל וַיֶּֽאְשַׁ֥ם בַּבַּ֖עַל וַיָּמֹֽת׃ ב וְעַתָּ֣ה ׀ יוֹסִ֣פוּ לַֽחֲטֹ֗א וַיַּֽעֲשׂ֣וּ לָהֶם֩ מַסֵּכָ֨ה מִכַּסְפָּ֜ם כִּתְבוּנָ֗ם עֲצַבִּים֙ מַֽעֲשֵׂ֣ה חָֽרָשִׁ֔ים כֻּלֹּ֑ה לָהֶ֗ם הֵ֚ם אֹֽמְרִ֔ים זֹֽבְחֵ֣י אָדָ֔ם עֲגָלִ֖ים יִשָּׁקֽוּן׃ ג לָכֵ֗ן יִֽהְיוּ֙ כַּֽעֲנַן־בֹּ֔קֶר וְכַטַּ֖ל מַשְׁכִּ֣ים הֹלֵ֑ךְ כְּמֹ֤ץ

storm wind from the threshing floor, and like smoke from a chimney. 4. And I am the Lord your God from the land of Egypt, and you shall know no other god besides Me, for there is no Savior except Me. 5. I knew you in the desert in a wasteland. 6. As they came to their pastureland, and they were sated; when they were sated their heart grew haughty; therefore they forgot Me. 7. And I was to them as a lion, as a leopard on the road I lurked. 8. I would strike them as a bereaving bear, and I would rend their closed up heart, and I would devour them there like a lion, the beasts of the field would rend them to pieces. 9. You have destroyed yourself, O Israel, for [you have rebelled] against Me, against your Aid. 10. I will be [forever, but] where is your king, and let him save you in all your cities, and your judges, concerning whom you said, "Give me a king and princes." 11. I gave you a king with My wrath, and I took [him away] with My anger. 12. Ephraim's iniquity is bound; his sin is hidden away. 13. The pangs of a woman in confinement will come to him; he is an unwise son, for a time will come that he will be unable to stand in the birthstool [to bear] children. 14. I would redeem them from the grave, from death I would redeem them; I will speak of you words of death, I will decree upon you a sentence of the grave, consolation shall be hidden from My eyes. 15. For he would be fruitful among the swamps; an east wind will come, a wind sent by the Lord will come up from the desert, and his source will dry up, and his spring will become arid; he will plunder the treasure of all desirable vessels. 14:1. Samaria will be shown guilty, for she has rebelled against her God; by the sword they will fall, their infants will be dashed, and their pregnant women will be ripped up. 2. Return, O Israel, to the Lord your God, for you have stumbled in your iniquity. 3. Take words with you and return to the Lord; say to Him, "Forgive all iniquity and take [our] good [deeds], and let us pay [the sacrifices of] bulls [with] our lips. 4. Assyria will not help us; we will not ride on a horse, and we will no longer say, 'our god' to the work of our hands, for through You [alone] shall an orphan find mercy." 5. I will heal their

יְסֹעֵר מִגֹּרֶן וּכְעָשָׁן מֵאֲרֻבָּה׃ ד וְאָנֹכִי יְהֹוָה
אֱלֹהֶיךָ מֵאֶרֶץ מִצְרָיִם וֵאלֹהִים זוּלָתִי לֹא תֵדָע
וּמוֹשִׁיעַ אַיִן בִּלְתִּי׃ ה אֲנִי יְדַעְתִּיךָ בַּמִּדְבָּר
בְּאֶרֶץ תַּלְאֻבוֹת׃ ו כְּמַרְעִיתָם וַיִּשְׂבָּעוּ שָׂבְעוּ
וַיָּרָם לִבָּם עַל־כֵּן שְׁכֵחוּנִי׃ ז וָאֱהִי לָהֶם כְּמוֹ־
שָׁחַל כְּנָמֵר עַל־דֶּרֶךְ אָשׁוּר׃ ח אֶפְגְּשֵׁם כְּדֹב
שַׁכּוּל וְאֶקְרַע סְגוֹר לִבָּם וְאֹכְלֵם שָׁם כְּלָבִיא
חַיַּת הַשָּׂדֶה תְּבַקְּעֵם׃ ט שִׁחֶתְךָ יִשְׂרָאֵל כִּי־בִי
בְעֶזְרֶךָ׃ י אֱהִי מַלְכְּךָ אֵפוֹא וְיוֹשִׁיעֲךָ בְּכָל־
עָרֶיךָ וְשֹׁפְטֶיךָ אֲשֶׁר אָמַרְתָּ תְּנָה־לִּי מֶלֶךְ
וְשָׂרִים׃ יא אֶתֶּן־לְךָ מֶלֶךְ בְּאַפִּי וְאֶקַּח בְּעֶבְרָתִי׃
יב צָרוּר עֲוֹן אֶפְרָיִם צְפוּנָה חַטָּאתוֹ׃ יג חֶבְלֵי
יוֹלֵדָה יָבֹאוּ לוֹ הוּא־בֵן לֹא חָכָם כִּי־עֵת לֹא־
יַעֲמֹד בְּמִשְׁבַּר בָּנִים׃ יד מִיַּד שְׁאוֹל אֶפְדֵּם
מִמָּוֶת אֶגְאָלֵם אֱהִי דְבָרֶיךָ מָוֶת אֱהִי קָטָבְךָ
שְׁאוֹל נֹחַם יִסָּתֵר מֵעֵינָי׃ טו כִּי הוּא בֵּין אַחִים
יַפְרִיא יָבוֹא קָדִים רוּחַ יְהֹוָה מִמִּדְבָּר עֹלֶה
וְיֵבוֹשׁ מְקוֹרוֹ וְיֶחֱרַב מַעְיָנוֹ הוּא יִשְׁסֶה אוֹצַר
כָּל־כְּלִי חֶמְדָּה׃ א תֶּאְשַׁם שֹׁמְרוֹן כִּי מָרְתָה
בֵּאלֹהֶיהָ בַּחֶרֶב יִפְּלוּ עֹלְלֵיהֶם יְרֻטָּשׁוּ וְהָרִיּוֹתָיו
יְבֻקָּעוּ׃ ב שׁוּבָה יִשְׂרָאֵל עַד יְהֹוָה אֱלֹהֶיךָ כִּי
כָשַׁלְתָּ בַּעֲוֹנֶךָ׃ ג קְחוּ עִמָּכֶם דְּבָרִים וְשׁוּבוּ
אֶל־יְהֹוָה אִמְרוּ אֵלָיו כָּל־תִּשָּׂא עָוֺן וְקַח־טוֹב
וּנְשַׁלְּמָה פָרִים שְׂפָתֵינוּ׃ ד אַשּׁוּר ׀ לֹא יוֹשִׁיעֵנוּ
עַל־סוּס לֹא נִרְכָּב וְלֹא־נֹאמַר עוֹד אֱלֹהֵינוּ
לְמַעֲשֵׂה יָדֵינוּ אֲשֶׁר־בְּךָ יְרֻחַם יָתוֹם׃ ה אֶרְפָּא

מְשׁוּבָתָם אֹהֲבֵם נְדָבָה כִּי שָׁב אַפִּי מִמֶּנּוּ׃
ו אֶהְיֶה כַטַּל לְיִשְׂרָאֵל יִפְרַח כַּשּׁוֹשַׁנָּה וְיַךְ
שָׁרָשָׁיו כַּלְּבָנוֹן׃ ז יֵלְכוּ יֹנְקוֹתָיו וִיהִי כַזַּיִת
הוֹדוֹ וְרֵיחַ לוֹ כַּלְּבָנוֹן׃ ח יָשֻׁבוּ יֹשְׁבֵי בְצִלּוֹ
יְחַיּוּ דָגָן וְיִפְרְחוּ כַגָּפֶן זִכְרוֹ כְּיֵין לְבָנוֹן׃
ט אֶפְרַיִם מַה־לִּי עוֹד לָעֲצַבִּים אֲנִי עָנִיתִי
וַאֲשׁוּרֶנּוּ אֲנִי כִּבְרוֹשׁ רַעֲנָן מִמֶּנִּי פֶּרְיְךָ נִמְצָא׃
י מִי חָכָם וְיָבֵן אֵלֶּה נָבוֹן וְיֵדָעֵם כִּי־יְשָׁרִים
דַּרְכֵי יְהוָה וְצַדִּקִים יֵלְכוּ בָם וּפֹשְׁעִים יִכָּשְׁלוּ
בָם׃ (החיי אדם פסק להוסיף את שני הפסוקים מספר יואל ב:
טז,יז) כו וַאֲכַלְתֶּם אָכוֹל וְשָׂבוֹעַ וְהִלַּלְתֶּם
אֶת־שֵׁם יְהוָה אֱלֹהֵיכֶם אֲשֶׁר־עָשָׂה עִמָּכֶם
לְהַפְלִיא וְלֹא־יֵבֹשׁוּ עַמִּי לְעוֹלָם׃ כז וִידַעְתֶּם כִּי
בְקֶרֶב יִשְׂרָאֵל אָנִי וַאֲנִי יְהוָה אֱלֹהֵיכֶם וְאֵין
עוֹד וְלֹא־יֵבֹשׁוּ עַמִּי לְעוֹלָם׃

perverseness, and I will love them in free-willed devotion, for My wrath has receded from him. 6. I will be like dew to Israel, he shall blossom like a rose, and his roots shall spread like the Lebanon. 7. His tender boughs shall spread and his beauty shall be like an olive tree, and he shall have a fragrance like the Lebanon. 8. Those who sat in his shadow shall return; they shall revive themselves like corn and they shall blossom like a vine; his fragrance shall be like the wine of the Lebanon. 9. Ephraim [shall say], "What more do I have with idols?" I answered and I shall see him; I am like a leafy cypress; because of Me, your fruit is found. 10. Who is wise and shall understand these, understanding and shall know them?—for the ways of the Lord are straight; and the righteous shall walk in them and the transgressors shall stumble in them. (*Chaye Adam rules that the following verses be added* (Joel 2:26–27.) 2:26. And you shall eat to satiety, and you shall praise the name of the Lord your God Who has dealt wondrously with you, and My people shall never be ashamed. 27. And you shall know that I am in the midst of Israel, and I am the Lord your God, and there is no other, and My people shall never be ashamed.

HAFTARATH VAYISHLAḤ הפטרת וישלח

(The entire prophecy of Obadiah).

Some Ashkenazic congregations read Hosea 11:7–12:2, which deals with Jacob's striving with the angel, mentioned in the Sidra. See above Haftarath Vayetze (p. 833).

This selection deals with the downfall of Edom, the nation descended from Esau. "Because of the violence done your brother Jacob" (v. 10) relates to Esau's hatred toward Jacob, as in the Sidra, when he came toward him with four hundred men.

א חֲזוֹן עֹבַדְיָה כֹּה־אָמַר אֲדֹנָי יֱהוִֹה לֶאֱדוֹם
שְׁמוּעָה שָׁמַעְנוּ מֵאֵת יְהוָה וְצִיר בַּגּוֹיִם שֻׁלָּח
קוּמוּ וְנָקוּמָה עָלֶיהָ לַמִּלְחָמָה׃ ב הִנֵּה קָטֹן
נְתַתִּיךְ בַּגּוֹיִם בָּזוּי אַתָּה מְאֹד׃ ג זְדוֹן לִבְּךְ
הִשִּׁיאֶךְ שֹׁכְנִי בְחַגְוֵי־סֶלַע מְרוֹם שִׁבְתּוֹ אֹמֵר
בְּלִבּוֹ מִי יוֹרִדֵנִי אָרֶץ׃ ד אִם־תַּגְבִּיהַּ כַּנֶּשֶׁר

1:1. The vision of Obadiah: So said the Lord God concerning Edom: We have heard a message from the Lord, and a messenger has been sent among the nations: "Arise, and let us rise up against her in battle." 2. Behold I have made you small among the nations; you are greatly despised. 3. The wickedness of your heart has enticed you, you who dwell in the clefts of the rock, whose dwelling is lofty, who says to himself, "Who will bring me down to earth?" 4. If you make [your dwelling] on high like an eagle, and even if you place your nest among stars, from there I will bring you down, says the Lord. 5. If thieves came upon you, if robbers at night, how were you silent? Would they not steal until they had enough? If grapegatherers came upon you, would they not leave over some gleaning grapes? 6. How was Esau searched out? [How] were his hidden places sought out? 7. All your confederates escorted you up to the border, those who were at peace with you tempted you and prevailed against you: [those who eat] your bread placed a snare in your place, for he has no understanding. 8. On that day, says the Lord, Will I not cause the wise to perish from Edom, and understanding from the mountain of Esau? 9. And your mighty men shall be broken, O Teman, so that every man will be cut off from the mountain of Esau by slaughter. 10. Because of the violence done to your brother Jacob, shame will cover you, and you will be cut off forever. 11. On the day you stood from afar, on the day strangers captured his possessions, and foreigners came into his gates, and upon Jerusalem they cast lots; you too shall be like one of them. 12. You should not have gazed on the day of your brother, on the day of his being given over, and you should not have rejoiced concerning the children of Judah on the day of their ruin, nor should you have spoken triumphantly on the day of distress. 13. You should not have come into My people's gate on the day of their calamity, neither should you have gazed on his affliction on the day of his calamity, nor should you have stretched forth [your hand] upon his possessions on the day of his calamity. 14. And you should not have stood at the crossroads to cut off his refugees, and you should not have delivered his survivors on the day of distress. 15. For the day of the Lord is near upon all the nations; as you have done will be done to you; your recompense shall return upon your head. 16. For, just as you drank on My Holy Mount, all the nations shall always drink, and they shall drink and become confounded, and they shall be as though they did not exist. 17. And on Mount Zion shall be a remnant, and it shall be holy, and the house of Jacob shall inherit those who

וְאִם־בֵּין כּוֹכָבִים שִׂים קִנֶּךָ מִשָּׁם אוֹרִידְךָ נְאֻם־
יְהוָֹה: ה אִם־גַּנָּבִים בָּאוּ־לְךָ אִם־שׁוֹדְדֵי לַיְלָה
אֵיךְ נִדְמֵיתָה הֲלוֹא יִגְנְבוּ דַּיָּם אִם־בֹּצְרִים בָּאוּ
לָךְ הֲלוֹא יַשְׁאִירוּ עֹלֵלוֹת: ו אֵיךְ נֶחְפְּשׂוּ עֵשָׂו
נִבְעוּ מַצְפֻּנָיו: ז עַד־הַגְּבוּל שִׁלְּחוּךָ כֹּל אַנְשֵׁי
בְרִיתֶךָ הִשִּׁיאוּךָ יָכְלוּ לְךָ אַנְשֵׁי שְׁלֹמֶךָ לַחְמְךָ
יָשִׂימוּ מָזוֹר תַּחְתֶּיךָ אֵין תְּבוּנָה בּוֹ: ח הֲלוֹא
בַּיּוֹם הַהוּא נְאֻם־יְהוָֹה וְהַאֲבַדְתִּי חֲכָמִים
מֵאֱדוֹם וּתְבוּנָה מֵהַר עֵשָׂו: ט וְחַתּוּ גִבּוֹרֶיךָ
תֵּימָן לְמַעַן יִכָּרֶת־אִישׁ מֵהַר עֵשָׂו מִקָּטֶל:
י מֵחֲמַס אָחִיךָ יַעֲקֹב תְּכַסְּךָ בוּשָׁה וְנִכְרַתָּ
לְעוֹלָם: יא בְּיוֹם עֲמָדְךָ מִנֶּגֶד בְּיוֹם שְׁבוֹת זָרִים
חֵילוֹ וְנָכְרִים בָּאוּ שְׁעָרוֹ וְעַל־יְרוּשָׁלַםִ יַדּוּ
גוֹרָל גַּם־אַתָּה כְּאַחַד מֵהֶם: יב וְאַל־תֵּרֶא
בְיוֹם־אָחִיךָ בְּיוֹם נָכְרוֹ וְאַל־תִּשְׂמַח לִבְנֵי־
יְהוּדָה בְּיוֹם אָבְדָם וְאַל־תַּגְדֵּל פִּיךָ בְּיוֹם צָרָה:
יג אַל־תָּבוֹא בְשַׁעַר־עַמִּי בְּיוֹם אֵידָם אַל־תֵּרֶא
גַם־אַתָּה בְּרָעָתוֹ בְּיוֹם אֵידוֹ וְאַל־תִּשְׁלַחְנָה
בְחֵילוֹ בְּיוֹם אֵידוֹ: יד וְאַל־תַּעֲמֹד עַל־הַפֶּרֶק
לְהַכְרִית אֶת־פְּלִיטָיו וְאַל־תַּסְגֵּר שְׂרִידָיו בְּיוֹם
צָרָה: טו כִּי־קָרוֹב יוֹם־יְהוָֹה עַל־כָּל־הַגּוֹיִם
כַּאֲשֶׁר עָשִׂיתָ יֵעָשֶׂה לָּךְ גְּמֻלְךָ יָשׁוּב בְּרֹאשֶׁךָ:
טז כִּי כַּאֲשֶׁר שְׁתִיתֶם עַל־הַר קָדְשִׁי יִשְׁתּוּ כָל־
הַגּוֹיִם תָּמִיד וְשָׁתוּ וְלָעוּ וְהָיוּ כְּלוֹא הָיוּ:
יז וּבְהַר צִיּוֹן תִּהְיֶה פְלֵיטָה וְהָיָה קֹדֶשׁ וְיָרְשׁוּ

inherited them. 18. And the house of Jacob shall be fire, and the house of Joseph a flame, and the house of Esau shall become stubble; and they shall blaze up among them and consume them, and the house of Esau shall have no survivor, for the Lord has spoken. 19. And they shall inherit the south, the mountain of Esau, and the lowlands, the [land of the] Philistines; and they shall inherit the field of Ephraim and the field of Samaria, and Benjamin [shall inherit] the [land of] Gilead. 20. And the exile of this host of the children of Israel who were with the Canaanites up to Zarephath, and the exile of Jerusalem that is in Sepharad, shall inherit the cities of the south. 21. And saviors shall ascend Mount Zion to judge the mountain of Esau, and the Lord shall have the kingdom.

בֵּית יַעֲקֹב אֵת מוֹרָשֵׁיהֶם: יח וְהָיָה בֵית־יַעֲקֹב
אֵשׁ וּבֵית יוֹסֵף לֶהָבָה וּבֵית עֵשָׂו לְקַשׁ וְדָלְקוּ
בָהֶם וַאֲכָלוּם וְלֹא־יִהְיֶה שָׂרִיד לְבֵית עֵשָׂו כִּי
יְהוָֹה דִּבֵּר: יט וְיָרְשׁוּ הַנֶּגֶב אֶת־הַר עֵשָׂו
וְהַשְּׁפֵלָה אֶת־פְּלִשְׁתִּים וְיָרְשׁוּ אֶת־שְׂדֵה
אֶפְרַיִם וְאֵת שְׂדֵה שֹׁמְרוֹן וּבִנְיָמִן אֶת־הַגִּלְעָד:
כ וְגָלֻת הַחֵל־הַזֶּה לִבְנֵי יִשְׂרָאֵל אֲשֶׁר־כְּנַעֲנִים
עַד־צָרְפַת וְגָלֻת יְרוּשָׁלִַם אֲשֶׁר בִּסְפָרַד יִרְשׁוּ
אֵת עָרֵי הַנֶּגֶב: כא וְעָלוּ מוֹשִׁעִים בְּהַר צִיּוֹן
לִשְׁפֹּט אֶת־הַר עֵשָׂו וְהָיְתָה לַיהוָֹה הַמְּלוּכָה:

HAFTARATH VAYESHEV הפטרת וישב

(Amos 2:6–3:8).

If this falls on the first Sabbath of Chanukah, the Haftarah is Zechariah 2:14–4:7 (p. 953).

The first verse of this selection speaks of selling a righteous man for silver. This is similar to the sale of Joseph narrated in the Sidra.

2:6. So says the Lord: For three transgressions of Israel, and for four I will not reverse it: Because they sell the righteous for silver and the poor in order to lock him in. 7. Those who long for the dust of the earth [that it be] on the heads of the poor, and they turn aside the way of the humble, and a man and his father go to a maid, in order to profane My holy Name. 8. And on clothes taken in pledge they lean beside every altar, and wine of those fined they drink in the house of their gods. 9. Yet I destroyed the Emorite before them, whose height was like the height of cedar trees, and he was as strong as the oaks, and I destroyed his fruit from above and his roots from below. 10. And I brought you up from the land of Egypt, and I led you in the desert forty years, to inherit the land of the Emorite. 11. And I raised up some of your sons as prophets and some of your youths as Nazirites. Is this not so, O children of Israel? says the Lord. 12. And you caused the

ו כֹּה אָמַר יְהוָֹה עַל־שְׁלֹשָׁה פִּשְׁעֵי יִשְׂרָאֵל
וְעַל־אַרְבָּעָה לֹא אֲשִׁיבֶנּוּ עַל־מִכְרָם בַּכֶּסֶף
צַדִּיק וְאֶבְיוֹן בַּעֲבוּר נַעֲלָיִם: ז הַשֹּׁאֲפִים עַל־
עֲפַר־אֶרֶץ בְּרֹאשׁ דַּלִּים וְדֶרֶךְ עֲנָוִים יַטּוּ וְאִישׁ
וְאָבִיו יֵלְכוּ אֶל־הַנַּעֲרָה לְמַעַן חַלֵּל אֶת־שֵׁם
קָדְשִׁי: ח וְעַל־בְּגָדִים חֲבֻלִים יַטּוּ אֵצֶל כָּל־
מִזְבֵּחַ וְיֵין עֲנוּשִׁים יִשְׁתּוּ בֵּית אֱלֹהֵיהֶם:
ט וְאָנֹכִי הִשְׁמַדְתִּי אֶת־הָאֱמֹרִי מִפְּנֵיהֶם אֲשֶׁר
כְּגֹבַהּ אֲרָזִים גָּבְהוֹ וְחָסֹן הוּא כָּאַלּוֹנִים
וָאַשְׁמִיד פִּרְיוֹ מִמַּעַל וְשָׁרָשָׁיו מִתָּחַת: י וְאָנֹכִי
הֶעֱלֵיתִי אֶתְכֶם מֵאֶרֶץ מִצְרָיִם וָאוֹלֵךְ אֶתְכֶם
בַּמִּדְבָּר אַרְבָּעִים שָׁנָה לָרֶשֶׁת אֶת־אֶרֶץ
הָאֱמֹרִי: יא וָאָקִים מִבְּנֵיכֶם לִנְבִיאִים
וּמִבַּחוּרֵיכֶם לִנְזִרִים הַאַף אֵין־זֹאת בְּנֵי יִשְׂרָאֵל
נְאֻם־יְהוָֹה: יב וַתַּשְׁקוּ אֶת־הַנְּזִרִים יַיִן וְעַל־

Nazirites to drink wine, and the prophets you commanded, saying, "Prophesy not." 13. Behold I bring distress in your place, as it is distressful for the wagon that is full of sheaves. 14. And flight shall fail the swift, and the strong shall not exert his strength, and the mighty shall not save himself. 15. And he who grasps the bow shall not stand, and the fleet of foot shall not escape, and the rider of the horse shall not save his life. 16. And he of courageous heart among the mighty shall flee naked on that day, says the Lord. 3:1. Hear this word that the Lord has spoken about you, O children of Israel, about all the family that I brought up from the land of Egypt, saying, 2. Only you have I known of all the families of the earth; therefore, I will visit upon you all your iniquities. 3. Will two walk together unless they have agreed? 4. Will a lion roar in the forest if he has no prey? Will a young lion give forth his voice from his den unless he has caught something? 5. Will a bird fall on a snare on the ground if there is nothing to trap it? Will a snare rise up from the earth and not catch [anything]? 6. Will a shofar be blown in a city and the people not tremble? Should evil befall a city, and the Lord has not done it? 7. For the Lord God shall do nothing unless He reveals his secret to His servants, the prophets. 8. The lion has roared; who will not fear? The Lord God has spoken; who will not prophesy?

הַנְּבִיאִים צִוִּיתֶם לֵאמֹר לֹא תִּנָּבְאוּ׃ יג הִנֵּה
אָנֹכִי מֵעִיק תַּחְתֵּיכֶם כַּאֲשֶׁר תָּעִיק הָעֲגָלָה
הַמְלֵאָה לָהּ עָמִיר׃ יד וְאָבַד מָנוֹס מִקָּל וְחָזָק
לֹא־יְאַמֵּץ כֹּחוֹ וְגִבּוֹר לֹא־יְמַלֵּט נַפְשׁוֹ׃
טו וְתֹפֵשׂ הַקֶּשֶׁת לֹא יַעֲמֹד וְקַל בְּרַגְלָיו לֹא
יְמַלֵּט וְרֹכֵב הַסּוּס לֹא יְמַלֵּט נַפְשׁוֹ׃ טז וְאַמִּיץ
לִבּוֹ בַּגִּבּוֹרִים עָרוֹם יָנוּס בַּיּוֹם־הַהוּא נְאֻם־
יְהוָה׃ א שִׁמְעוּ אֶת־הַדָּבָר הַזֶּה אֲשֶׁר דִּבֶּר יְהוָה
עֲלֵיכֶם בְּנֵי יִשְׂרָאֵל עַל כָּל־הַמִּשְׁפָּחָה אֲשֶׁר
הֶעֱלֵיתִי מֵאֶרֶץ מִצְרַיִם לֵאמֹר׃ ב רַק אֶתְכֶם
יָדַעְתִּי מִכֹּל מִשְׁפְּחוֹת הָאֲדָמָה עַל־כֵּן אֶפְקֹד
עֲלֵיכֶם אֵת כָּל־עֲוֹנֹתֵיכֶם׃ ג הֲיֵלְכוּ שְׁנַיִם יַחְדָּו
בִּלְתִּי אִם־נוֹעָדוּ׃ ד הֲיִשְׁאַג אַרְיֵה בַּיַּעַר וְטֶרֶף
אֵין לוֹ הֲיִתֵּן כְּפִיר קוֹלוֹ מִמְּעֹנָתוֹ בִּלְתִּי אִם־
לָכָד׃ ה הֲתִפֹּל צִפּוֹר עַל־פַּח הָאָרֶץ וּמוֹקֵשׁ אֵין
לָהּ הֲיַעֲלֶה־פַּח מִן־הָאֲדָמָה וְלָכוֹד לֹא יִלְכּוֹד׃
ו אִם־יִתָּקַע שׁוֹפָר בְּעִיר וְעָם לֹא יֶחֱרָדוּ אִם־
תִּהְיֶה רָעָה בְּעִיר וַיהוָה לֹא עָשָׂה׃ ז כִּי לֹא
יַעֲשֶׂה אֲדֹנָי יֱהוִה דָּבָר כִּי אִם־גָּלָה סוֹדוֹ אֶל־
עֲבָדָיו הַנְּבִיאִים׃ ח אַרְיֵה שָׁאָג מִי לֹא יִירָא
אֲדֹנָי יֱהוִה דִּבֶּר מִי לֹא יִנָּבֵא׃

HAFTARATH MIKETZ הפטרת מקץ

(I Kings 3:15–4:1)

If this is Sabbath Chanukah, the Haftarah read is Zechariah 2:14–4:7 (p. 953) even if this Sabbath falls on Rosh Chodesh or on the day preceding Rosh Chodesh. If it falls on the second Sabbath of Chanukah, the Haftarah is I Kings 7:40–50 (p. 955).

The opening verse of this selection, King Solomon's awakening from a dream, is reminiscent of the dreams of Pharaoh discussed in the Sidra.

3:15. And Solomon awoke, and behold [it was] a dream. And he came to Jerusalem, and stood before the Ark of the covenant of the Lord, and offered up burnt offerings, and offered peace offerings, and made a feast for all his servants. 16. Then came two women, harlots, to the king, and stood before him. 17. And the one woman said,

טו וַיִּקַץ שְׁלֹמֹה וְהִנֵּה חֲלוֹם וַיָּבוֹא יְרוּשָׁלַםִ
וַיַּעֲמֹד ׀ לִפְנֵי אֲרוֹן בְּרִית־אֲדֹנָי וַיַּעַל עֹלוֹת
וַיַּעַשׂ שְׁלָמִים וַיַּעַשׂ מִשְׁתֶּה לְכָל־עֲבָדָיו׃ טז אָז
תָּבֹאנָה שְׁתַּיִם נָשִׁים זֹנוֹת אֶל־הַמֶּלֶךְ וַתַּעֲמֹדְנָה
לְפָנָיו׃ יז וַתֹּאמֶר הָאִשָּׁה הָאַחַת בִּי אֲדֹנִי אֲנִי

וְהָאִשָּׁה הַזֹּאת יֹשְׁבֹת בְּבַיִת אֶחָד וָאֵלֵד עִמָּהּ
בַּבָּיִת: יח וַיְהִי בַּיּוֹם הַשְּׁלִישִׁי לְלִדְתִּי וַתֵּלֶד גַּם־
הָאִשָּׁה הַזֹּאת וַאֲנַחְנוּ יַחְדָּו אֵין־זָר אִתָּנוּ בַּבַּיִת
זוּלָתִי שְׁתַּיִם־אֲנַחְנוּ בַּבָּיִת: יט וַיָּמָת בֶּן־הָאִשָּׁה
הַזֹּאת לָיְלָה אֲשֶׁר שָׁכְבָה עָלָיו: כ וַתָּקָם בְּתוֹךְ
הַלַּיְלָה וַתִּקַּח אֶת־בְּנִי מֵאֶצְלִי וַאֲמָתְךָ יְשֵׁנָה
וַתַּשְׁכִּיבֵהוּ בְּחֵיקָהּ וְאֶת־בְּנָהּ הַמֵּת הִשְׁכִּיבָה
בְחֵיקִי: כא וָאָקֻם בַּבֹּקֶר לְהֵינִיק אֶת־בְּנִי וְהִנֵּה־
מֵת וָאֶתְבּוֹנֵן אֵלָיו בַּבֹּקֶר וְהִנֵּה לֹא־הָיָה בְנִי
אֲשֶׁר יָלָדְתִּי: כב וַתֹּאמֶר הָאִשָּׁה הָאַחֶרֶת לֹא כִי
בְּנִי הַחַי וּבְנֵךְ הַמֵּת וְזֹאת אֹמֶרֶת לֹא כִי בְּנֵךְ
הַמֵּת וּבְנִי הֶחָי וַתְּדַבֵּרְנָה לִפְנֵי הַמֶּלֶךְ:
כג וַיֹּאמֶר הַמֶּלֶךְ זֹאת אֹמֶרֶת זֶה־בְּנִי הַחַי וּבְנֵךְ
הַמֵּת וְזֹאת אֹמֶרֶת לֹא כִי בְּנֵךְ הַמֵּת וּבְנִי הֶחָי:
כד וַיֹּאמֶר הַמֶּלֶךְ קְחוּ־לִי חָרֶב וַיָּבִאוּ הַחֶרֶב
לִפְנֵי הַמֶּלֶךְ: כה וַיֹּאמֶר הַמֶּלֶךְ גִּזְרוּ אֶת־הַיֶּלֶד
הַחַי לִשְׁנָיִם וּתְנוּ אֶת־הַחֲצִי לְאַחַת וְאֶת־הַחֲצִי
לְאֶחָת: כו וַתֹּאמֶר הָאִשָּׁה אֲשֶׁר־בְּנָהּ הַחַי אֶל־
הַמֶּלֶךְ כִּי־נִכְמְרוּ רַחֲמֶיהָ עַל־בְּנָהּ וַתֹּאמֶר ׀ בִּי
אֲדֹנִי תְּנוּ־לָהּ אֶת־הַיָּלוּד הַחַי וְהָמֵת אַל־
תְּמִיתֻהוּ וְזֹאת אֹמֶרֶת גַּם־לִי גַם־לָךְ לֹא יִהְיֶה
גְּזֹרוּ: כז וַיַּעַן הַמֶּלֶךְ וַיֹּאמֶר תְּנוּ־לָהּ אֶת־הַיָּלוּד
הַחַי וְהָמֵת לֹא תְמִיתֻהוּ הִיא אִמּוֹ: כח וַיִּשְׁמְעוּ
כָל־יִשְׂרָאֵל אֶת־הַמִּשְׁפָּט אֲשֶׁר שָׁפַט הַמֶּלֶךְ
וַיִּרְאוּ מִפְּנֵי הַמֶּלֶךְ כִּי רָאוּ כִּי־חָכְמַת אֱלֹהִים
בְּקִרְבּוֹ לַעֲשׂוֹת מִשְׁפָּט: א וַיְהִי הַמֶּלֶךְ שְׁלֹמֹה
מֶלֶךְ עַל־כָּל־יִשְׂרָאֵל:

"O, my lord, I and this woman dwell in one house; and I gave birth to a child with her in the house. 18. And it came to pass the third day after I had given birth, that this woman gave birth also; and we [were] together, [there was] no stranger with us in the house, besides us two in the house. 19. And this woman's son died at night; because she had lain on him. 20. And she arose in the middle of the night and took my son from beside me, while your handmaid slept, and laid him in her bosom, and laid her dead son in my bosom. 21. And I rose in the morning to nurse my son, and behold he was dead, but I looked closely at him in the morning, and behold, it was not my son whom I had borne." 22. And the other woman said, "Not so, the living [is] my son, and the dead [is] your son." And this one said, "Not so, the dead [is] your son, and the living [is] my son." Thus they spoke before the king. 23. And the king said, "This one says, 'This [is] my son that lives, and your son [is] the dead,' and the other says, 'Not so, your son [is] the dead, and my son [is] the living.'" 24. And the king said, "Fetch me a sword." And they brought a sword before the king. 25. And the king said, "Divide the living child in two, and give half to the one and half to the other. 26. And the woman whose son [was] the live one, said to the king, for her compassion was aroused for her son, and she said, "O my lord, give her the living child, and by no means slay him." But the other said, "Let it be neither mine nor yours, divide [it]." 27. And the king answered and said, "Give her the living child, and by no means slay him; she [is] his mother." 28. And all Israel heard of the judgment which the king had judged; and they feared the king; for they saw that the wisdom of God [was] in him to do judgment. 4:1. And king Solomon was king over all Israel.

HAFTARATH VAYIGGASH הפטרת ויגש
(Ezekiel 37:15–28)

In this selection, the prophet divides Israel into two groups, headed by Judah and Joseph, as regards the redemption, just as Judah and Joseph were the main characters in the descent to Egypt described in this Sidra.

37:15. And the word of God came to me, saying: 16. And you, son of man, take for yourself one stick and write upon it, "For Judah and for the children of Israel his companions," and take one stick and write upon it, "For Joseph, the stick of Ephraim, and all the house of Israel, his companions." 17. And bring them close one to the other into one stick, and they shall be one in your hand. 18. And when the children of your people say to you, saying, "Will you not tell us what these are to you?" 19. Speak to them, "So says the Lord God, 'Behold, I will take the stick of Joseph, which is in the hand of Ephraim and the tribes of Israel his companions, and I will place them with him with the stick of Judah, and I will make them into one stick, and they shall become one in My hand.'" 20. And the sticks upon which you shall write shall be in your hand before their eyes. 21. And speak to them, "So says the Lord God, 'Behold, I will take the children of Israel from among the nations where they have gone, and I will gather them from every side, and I will bring them to their land. 22. And I will make them into one nation in the land upon the mountains of Israel, and one king shall be to them all as a king; and they shall no longer be two nations, neither shall they be divided into two kingdoms anymore. 23. And they shall no longer defile themselves with their idols nor with their detestable things nor with all their transgressions, and I will save them from all their habitations in which they have sinned, and I will purify them, and they shall be to Me as a people, and I will be to them as a God. 24. And My servant David shall be king over them, and one shepherd shall be for them all, and they shall walk in My ordinances and observe My statutes and perform them. 25. And they shall dwell on the land that I have given My servant Jacob, wherein your forefathers lived; and they

טו וַיְהִי דְבַר־יְהוָֹה אֵלַי לֵאמֹר: טז וְאַתָּה בֶן־
אָדָם קַח־לְךָ עֵץ אֶחָד וּכְתֹב עָלָיו לִיהוּדָה
וְלִבְנֵי יִשְׂרָאֵל חֲבֵרָו (חבריו קרי) וּלְקַח עֵץ אֶחָד
וּכְתוֹב עָלָיו לְיוֹסֵף עֵץ אֶפְרַיִם וְכָל־בֵּית
יִשְׂרָאֵל חֲבֵרָו (חבריו קרי): יז וְקָרַב אֹתָם אֶחָד
אֶל־אֶחָד לְךָ לְעֵץ אֶחָד וְהָיוּ לַאֲחָדִים בְּיָדֶךָ:
יח וְכַאֲשֶׁר יֹאמְרוּ אֵלֶיךָ בְּנֵי עַמְּךָ לֵאמֹר
הֲלוֹא־תַגִּיד לָנוּ מָה־אֵלֶּה לָּךְ: יט דַּבֵּר אֲלֵהֶם
כֹּה־אָמַר אֲדֹנָי יֱהוִֹה הִנֵּה אֲנִי לֹקֵחַ אֶת־עֵץ
יוֹסֵף אֲשֶׁר בְּיַד־אֶפְרַיִם וְשִׁבְטֵי יִשְׂרָאֵל חֲבֵרָו
(חבריו קרי) וְנָתַתִּי אוֹתָם עָלָיו אֶת־עֵץ יְהוּדָה
וַעֲשִׂיתִם לְעֵץ אֶחָד וְהָיוּ אֶחָד בְּיָדִי: כ וְהָיוּ
הָעֵצִים אֲשֶׁר תִּכְתֹּב עֲלֵיהֶם בְּיָדְךָ לְעֵינֵיהֶם:
כא וְדַבֵּר אֲלֵיהֶם כֹּה־אָמַר אֲדֹנָי יֱהוִֹה הִנֵּה אֲנִי
לֹקֵחַ אֶת־בְּנֵי יִשְׂרָאֵל מִבֵּין הַגּוֹיִם אֲשֶׁר הָלְכוּ־
שָׁם וְקִבַּצְתִּי אֹתָם מִסָּבִיב וְהֵבֵאתִי אוֹתָם אֶל־
אַדְמָתָם: כב וְעָשִׂיתִי אֹתָם לְגוֹי אֶחָד בָּאָרֶץ
בְּהָרֵי יִשְׂרָאֵל וּמֶלֶךְ אֶחָד יִהְיֶה לְכֻלָּם לְמֶלֶךְ
וְלֹא יִהְיֶה (יהיו קרי) ־עוֹד לִשְׁנֵי גוֹיִם וְלֹא יֵחָצוּ
עוֹד לִשְׁתֵּי מַמְלָכוֹת עוֹד: כג וְלֹא יִטַּמְּאוּ עוֹד
בְּגִלּוּלֵיהֶם וּבְשִׁקּוּצֵיהֶם וּבְכֹל פִּשְׁעֵיהֶם
וְהוֹשַׁעְתִּי אוֹתָם מִכֹּל מוֹשְׁבֹתֵיהֶם אֲשֶׁר חָטְאוּ
בָהֶם וְטִהַרְתִּי אוֹתָם וְהָיוּ־לִי לְעָם וַאֲנִי אֶהְיֶה
לָהֶם לֵאלֹהִים: כד וְעַבְדִּי דָוִד מֶלֶךְ עֲלֵיהֶם
וְרוֹעֶה אֶחָד יִהְיֶה לְכֻלָּם וּבְמִשְׁפָּטַי יֵלֵכוּ
וְחֻקּוֹתַי יִשְׁמְרוּ וְעָשׂוּ אוֹתָם: כה וְיָשְׁבוּ עַל־
הָאָרֶץ אֲשֶׁר נָתַתִּי לְעַבְדִּי לְיַעֲקֹב אֲשֶׁר יָשְׁבוּ־

shall dwell upon it, they and their children and their children's children, forever; and My servant David shall be their prince forever. 26. And I will form a covenant of peace for them, an everlasting covenant shall be with them; and I will establish them and I will multiply them, and I will place My Sanctuary in their midst forever. 27. And My Dwelling-Place shall be over them, and I will be to them for a God, and they shall be to Me as a people. 28. And the nations shall know that I am the Lord, Who sanctifies Israel, when My Sanctuary is in their midst forever.'"

בָּהּ אֲבוֹתֵיכֶם וְיָשְׁבוּ עָלֶיהָ הֵמָּה וּבְנֵיהֶם וּבְנֵי
בְנֵיהֶם עַד־עוֹלָם וְדָוִד עַבְדִּי נָשִׂיא לָהֶם
לְעוֹלָם׃ כו וְכָרַתִּי לָהֶם בְּרִית שָׁלוֹם בְּרִית
עוֹלָם יִהְיֶה אוֹתָם וּנְתַתִּים וְהִרְבֵּיתִי אוֹתָם
וְנָתַתִּי אֶת־מִקְדָּשִׁי בְּתוֹכָם לְעוֹלָם׃ כז וְהָיָה
מִשְׁכָּנִי עֲלֵיהֶם וְהָיִיתִי לָהֶם לֵאלֹהִים וְהֵמָּה
יִהְיוּ־לִי לְעָם׃ כח וְיָדְעוּ הַגּוֹיִם כִּי אֲנִי יְהֹוָה
מְקַדֵּשׁ אֶת־יִשְׂרָאֵל בִּהְיוֹת מִקְדָּשִׁי בְּתוֹכָם
לְעוֹלָם׃

HAFTARATH VAYEHI הפטרת ויחי
(I Kings 2:1–12)

The opening verse, "And the days of David drew near that he should die," is reminiscent of the verse in the Sidra (Genesis 47:29) "And the days of Israel drew near that he should die."

2:1. And the days of David drew near that he should die; and he charged Solomon, his son, saying: 2. "I go the way of all the earth; you shall be strong, therefore, and show yourself a man; 3. And keep the charge of the Lord your God to walk in His ways, to keep His statutes and His commandments and His judgments and His testimonies, as it is written in the law of Moses, that you may prosper in all that you do, and wherever you turn: 4. That the Lord may continue His word which He spoke concerning me, saying, 'If your children take heed to their way, to walk before Me in truth with all their heart and with all their soul, there shall not fail you,' said He, 'a man on the throne of Israel.' 5. Moreover, you also know what Joab the son of Zeruiah did to me, [and] what he did to the two captains of the hosts of Israel, to Abner the son of Ner and to Amasa the son of Jether, whom he slew, and shed the blood of war in peace, and put the blood of war upon his girdle [that was] about his loins, and in his shoes that [were] on his feet. 6. And you shall do according to your wisdom, and do not let his hoary head go down to the grave in peace. 7. But show kindness to the children of Barzillai the

א וַיִּקְרְבוּ יְמֵי־דָוִד לָמוּת וַיְצַו אֶת־שְׁלֹמֹה בְנוֹ
לֵאמֹר׃ ב אָנֹכִי הֹלֵךְ בְּדֶרֶךְ כָּל־הָאָרֶץ וְחָזַקְתָּ
וְהָיִיתָ לְאִישׁ׃ ג וְשָׁמַרְתָּ אֶת־מִשְׁמֶרֶת | יְהֹוָה
אֱלֹהֶיךָ לָלֶכֶת בִּדְרָכָיו לִשְׁמֹר חֻקֹּתָיו מִצְוֹתָיו
וּמִשְׁפָּטָיו וְעֵדְוֹתָיו כַּכָּתוּב בְּתוֹרַת מֹשֶׁה לְמַעַן
תַּשְׂכִּיל אֵת כָּל־אֲשֶׁר תַּעֲשֶׂה וְאֵת כָּל־אֲשֶׁר
תִּפְנֶה שָׁם׃ ד לְמַעַן יָקִים יְהֹוָה אֶת־דְּבָרוֹ אֲשֶׁר
דִּבֶּר עָלַי לֵאמֹר אִם־יִשְׁמְרוּ בָנֶיךָ אֶת־דַּרְכָּם
לָלֶכֶת לְפָנַי בֶּאֱמֶת בְּכָל־לְבָבָם וּבְכָל־נַפְשָׁם
לֵאמֹר לֹא־יִכָּרֵת לְךָ אִישׁ מֵעַל כִּסֵּא יִשְׂרָאֵל׃
ה וְגַם אַתָּה יָדַעְתָּ אֵת אֲשֶׁר־עָשָׂה לִי יוֹאָב בֶּן־
צְרוּיָה אֲשֶׁר עָשָׂה לִשְׁנֵי־שָׂרֵי צִבְאוֹת יִשְׂרָאֵל
לְאַבְנֵר בֶּן־נֵר וְלַעֲמָשָׂא בֶן־יֶתֶר וַיַּהַרְגֵם וַיָּשֶׂם
דְּמֵי־מִלְחָמָה בְּשָׁלֹם וַיִּתֵּן דְּמֵי מִלְחָמָה
בַּחֲגֹרָתוֹ אֲשֶׁר בְּמָתְנָיו וּבְנַעֲלוֹ אֲשֶׁר בְּרַגְלָיו׃
ו וְעָשִׂיתָ כְּחָכְמָתֶךָ וְלֹא־תוֹרֵד שֵׂיבָתוֹ בְּשָׁלֹם
שְׁאֹל׃ ז וְלִבְנֵי בַרְזִלַּי הַגִּלְעָדִי תַּעֲשֶׂה־חֶסֶד

Gileadite, and let them be of those that eat at your table, for so did they befriend me when I fled from Absalom your brother. 8. And, behold, there is with you Shimei the son of Gera the Benjamite of Bahurim, who cursed me with a grievous curse on the day when I went to Mahanaim, and he came down to meet me at the Jordan, and I swore to him by the Lord, saying, 'I will not put you to death with the sword.' 9. And now hold him not guiltless, for you are a wise man, and you will surely know what you ought to do to him, and you shall bring his hoary head down to the grave with blood." 10. And David slept with his fathers, and was buried in the city of David. 11. And the days that David reigned over Israel [were] forty years: seven years he reigned in Hebron, and in Jerusalem he reigned thirty-three years. 12. And Solomon sat upon the throne of David his father, and his kingdom was firmly established.

וְהָי֖וּ בְּאֹכְלֵ֣י שֻׁלְחָנֶ֑ךָ כִּי־כֵן֙ קָרְב֣וּ אֵלַ֔י בְּבָרְחִ֕י
מִפְּנֵ֖י אַבְשָׁל֥וֹם אָחִֽיךָ׃ ח וְהִנֵּ֨ה עִמְּךָ֜ שִׁמְעִ֣י בֶן־
גֵּרָ֣א בֶן־הַיְמִינִי֮ מִבַּחֻרִים֒ וְה֤וּא קִֽלְלַ֙נִי֙ קְלָלָ֣ה
נִמְרֶ֔צֶת בְּי֖וֹם לֶכְתִּ֣י מַחֲנָ֑יִם וְהוּא־יָרַ֤ד לִקְרָאתִי֙
הַיַּרְדֵּ֔ן וָאֶשָּׁ֨בַֽע ל֤וֹ בַֽיהוָה֙ לֵאמֹ֔ר אִם־אֲמִֽיתְךָ֖
בֶּחָֽרֶב׃ ט וְעַתָּה֙ אַל־תְּנַקֵּ֔הוּ כִּ֛י אִ֥ישׁ חָכָ֖ם אָ֑תָּה
וְיָֽדַעְתָּ֙ אֵ֣ת אֲשֶׁ֣ר תַּעֲשֶׂה־לּ֔וֹ וְהוֹרַדְתָּ֧ אֶת־
שֵׂיבָת֛וֹ בְּדָ֖ם שְׁאֽוֹל׃ י וַיִּשְׁכַּ֥ב דָּוִ֖ד עִם־אֲבֹתָ֑יו
וַיִּקָּבֵ֖ר בְּעִ֥יר דָּוִֽד׃ יא וְהַיָּמִ֗ים אֲשֶׁ֨ר מָלַ֤ךְ דָּוִד֙
עַל־יִשְׂרָאֵ֔ל אַרְבָּעִ֖ים שָׁנָ֑ה בְּחֶבְר֤וֹן מָלַךְ֙ שֶׁ֣בַע
שָׁנִ֔ים וּבִירוּשָׁלִַ֣ם מָלַ֔ךְ שְׁלֹשִׁ֥ים וְשָׁלֹ֖שׁ שָׁנִֽים׃
יב וּשְׁלֹמֹ֕ה יָשַׁ֕ב עַל־כִּסֵּ֖א דָּוִ֣ד אָבִ֑יו וַתִּכֹּ֥ן
מַלְכֻת֖וֹ מְאֹֽד׃

HAFTARATH SHEMOTH הפטרת שמות

(Isaiah 27:6–28:13, 29:22, 23) according to the Ashkenazim.

The first verse, "Those who came, whom Jacob caused to take root," is interpreted as alluding to the Children of Israel "who came into Egypt" (Exodus 1:1).

27:6. Those who came, whom Jacob caused to take root, Israel flourished and blossomed, and they filled the face of the world with fruitage. 7. Like the smiting of him who smote him did He smite him; like the slaying of his slain ones, was he slain? 8. In that measure, when they sent them out, it strove with it; He spoke with His harsh wind on the day of the east wind. 9. Therefore, with this shall Jacob's iniquity be atoned for, and this is all the fruit of removing his sin; by making all the altar stones like crushed chalkstones; *asherim* and sun-images shall not rise. 10. For a fortified city is solitary, a dwelling is forsaken and abandoned like a pasture; there a calf shall graze, and there he shall lie and consume its branches. 11. When its branches dry out, they shall be broken; women shall come and ignite it, for it is not a people of understanding; therefore, its Maker shall not have compassion on it, and He Who formed it shall not grant it favor.

ו הַבָּאִים֙ יַשְׁרֵ֣שׁ יַעֲקֹ֔ב יָצִ֥יץ וּפָרַ֖ח יִשְׂרָאֵ֑ל
וּמָלְא֥וּ פְנֵי־תֵבֵ֖ל תְּנוּבָֽה׃ ז הַכְּמַכַּ֥ת מַכֵּ֖הוּ
הִכָּ֑הוּ אִם־כְּהֶ֥רֶג הֲרֻגָ֖יו הֹרָֽג׃ ח בְּסַאסְּאָ֖ה
בְּשַׁלְחָ֣הּ תְּרִיבֶ֑נָּה הָגָ֛ה בְּרוּח֥וֹ הַקָּשָׁ֖ה בְּי֥וֹם
קָדִֽים׃ ט לָכֵ֗ן בְּזֹאת֙ יְכֻפַּ֣ר עֲוֺן־יַעֲקֹ֔ב וְזֶ֕ה
כָּל־פְּרִ֖י הָסִ֣ר חַטָּאת֑וֹ בְּשׂוּמ֣וֹ ׀ כָּל־אַבְנֵ֣י מִזְבֵּ֗חַ
כְּאַבְנֵי־גִר֙ מְנֻפָּצ֔וֹת לֹא־יָקֻ֥מוּ אֲשֵׁרִ֖ים וְחַמָּנִֽים׃
י כִּ֣י עִ֤יר בְּצוּרָה֙ בָּדָ֔ד נָוֶ֕ה מְשֻׁלָּ֥ח
וְנֶעֱזָ֖ב כַּמִּדְבָּ֑ר שָׁ֣ם יִרְעֶ֥ה עֵ֛גֶל וְשָׁ֥ם יִרְבָּ֖ץ וְכִלָּ֥ה
סְעִפֶֽיהָ׃ יא בִּיבֹ֤שׁ קְצִירָהּ֙ תִּשָּׁבַ֔רְנָה נָשִׁ֕ים
בָּא֖וֹת מְאִיר֣וֹת אוֹתָ֑הּ כִּ֣י לֹ֤א עַם־בִּינוֹת֙ ה֔וּא
עַל־כֵּן֙ לֹא־יְרַחֲמֶ֣נּוּ עֹשֵׂ֔הוּ וְיֹצְר֖וֹ לֹ֥א יְחֻנֶּֽנּוּ׃

12. And it shall come to pass on that day, that the Lord shall gather from the flood of the river to the stream of Egypt, and you shall be gathered one by one, O children of Israel. 13. And it shall come to pass on that day, that a great shofar shall be sounded, and those lost in the land of Assyria and those exiled in the land of Egypt shall come and they shall prostrate themselves before the Lord on the holy mount in Jerusalem. 28:1. Woe is to the crown of the pride of the drunkards of Ephraim and the young fruit of an inferior fig is the position of his glory, which is at the end of a valley of fatness, crushed by wine. 2. Behold God [has] a strong and powerful [wind], like a downpour of hail, a storm of destruction, like a stream of powerful, flooding water, He lays it on the land with [His] hand. 3. With the feet, they shall be trampled, the crown of the pride of the drunkards of Ephraim. 4. And his glorious beauty shall be the young fruit of an inferior fig, which is on the head of the valley of fatness; as a fig that ripens before the summer, which, if the seer sees it, he will swallow it while it is still in his hand. 5. On that day, the Lord of Hosts shall be for a crown of beauty and for a diadem of glory, for the rest of His people. 6. And for a spirit of justice to him who sits in judgment, and for might for those who bring back the war to the gate. 7. These, too, erred because of wine and strayed because of strong wine; priest and prophet erred because of strong wine, they became corrupt because of wine; they went astray because of strong wine, they erred against the seer, they caused justice to stumble. 8. For all tables were filled with vomit and ordure, without place. 9. Whom shall he teach knowledge and to whom shall he explain the message? To those weaned from milk, removed from breasts? 10. For a precept for a precept, a precept for a precept, a line for a line, a line for a line, a little there, a little there. 11. For with distorted speech and in another language, does he speak to this people. 12. For he said to them, "This is the rest; give rest to the weary, and this is the tranquility," but they would not listen. 13. And the word of the Lord shall be for them a precept for a precept, a precept for a precept, a line for a

יב וְהָיָה בַּיּוֹם הַהוּא יַחְבֹּט יְהוָה מִשִּׁבֹּלֶת
הַנָּהָר עַד־נַחַל מִצְרָיִם וְאַתֶּם תְּלֻקְּטוּ לְאַחַד
אֶחָד בְּנֵי יִשְׂרָאֵל׃ יג וְהָיָה ׀ בַּיּוֹם הַהוּא יִתָּקַע
בְּשׁוֹפָר גָּדוֹל וּבָאוּ הָאֹבְדִים בְּאֶרֶץ אַשּׁוּר
וְהַנִּדָּחִים בְּאֶרֶץ מִצְרָיִם וְהִשְׁתַּחֲווּ לַיהוָה בְּהַר
הַקֹּדֶשׁ בִּירוּשָׁלָם׃ א הוֹי עֲטֶרֶת גֵּאוּת שִׁכֹּרֵי
אֶפְרַיִם וְצִיץ נֹבֵל צְבִי תִפְאַרְתּוֹ אֲשֶׁר עַל־
רֹאשׁ גֵּיא־שְׁמָנִים הֲלוּמֵי יָיִן׃ ב הִנֵּה חָזָק
וְאַמִּץ לַאדֹנָי כְּזֶרֶם בָּרָד שַׂעַר קָטֶב כְּזֶרֶם מַיִם
כַּבִּירִים שֹׁטְפִים הִנִּיחַ לָאָרֶץ בְּיָד׃ ג בְּרַגְלַיִם
תֵּרָמַסְנָה עֲטֶרֶת גֵּאוּת שִׁכּוֹרֵי אֶפְרָיִם׃
ד וְהָיְתָה צִיצַת נֹבֵל צְבִי תִפְאַרְתּוֹ אֲשֶׁר עַל־
רֹאשׁ גֵּיא שְׁמָנִים כְּבִכּוּרָהּ בְּטֶרֶם קַיִץ אֲשֶׁר
יִרְאֶה הָרֹאֶה אוֹתָהּ בְּעוֹדָהּ בְּכַפּוֹ יִבְלָעֶנָּה׃
ה בַּיּוֹם הַהוּא יִהְיֶה יְהוָה צְבָאוֹת לַעֲטֶרֶת צְבִי
וְלִצְפִירַת תִּפְאָרָה לִשְׁאָר עַמּוֹ׃ ו וּלְרוּחַ
מִשְׁפָּט לַיּוֹשֵׁב עַל־הַמִּשְׁפָּט וְלִגְבוּרָה מְשִׁיבֵי
מִלְחָמָה שָׁעְרָה׃ ז וְגַם־אֵלֶּה בַּיַּיִן שָׁגוּ וּבַשֵּׁכָר
תָּעוּ כֹּהֵן וְנָבִיא שָׁגוּ בַשֵּׁכָר נִבְלְעוּ מִן־הַיַּיִן
תָּעוּ מִן־הַשֵּׁכָר שָׁגוּ בָּרֹאֶה פָּקוּ פְּלִילִיָּה׃ ח כִּי
כָּל־שֻׁלְחָנוֹת מָלְאוּ קִיא צֹאָה בְּלִי מָקוֹם׃
ט אֶת־מִי יוֹרֶה דֵעָה וְאֶת־מִי יָבִין שְׁמוּעָה
גְּמוּלֵי מֵחָלָב עַתִּיקֵי מִשָּׁדָיִם׃ י כִּי צַו לָצָו צַו
לָצָו קַו לָקָו קַו לָקָו זְעֵיר שָׁם זְעֵיר שָׁם׃ יא כִּי
בְּלַעֲגֵי שָׂפָה וּבְלָשׁוֹן אַחֶרֶת יְדַבֵּר אֶל־הָעָם
הַזֶּה׃ יב אֲשֶׁר ׀ אָמַר אֲלֵיהֶם זֹאת הַמְּנוּחָה
הָנִיחוּ לֶעָיֵף וְזֹאת הַמַּרְגֵּעָה וְלֹא אָבוּא שְׁמוֹעַ׃
יג וְהָיָה לָהֶם דְּבַר־יְהוָה צַו לָצָו צַו לָצָו קַו

line, a line for a line, a little there, a little there, in order that they go and stumble backwards and be broken, and be trapped and caught. 29:22. Therefore, so said the Lord to the House of Jacob, Who redeemed Abraham, "Now Jacob shall not be ashamed, and now his face shall not pale. 23. For, when he sees his children, the work of My hands, in his midst, who shall hallow My Name, and they shall hallow the Holy One of Jacob, and the God of Israel they shall revere."

לָקָו קַו לָקָו זְעֵיר שָׁם זְעֵיר שָׁם לְמַעַן יֵלְכוּ
וְכָשְׁלוּ אָחוֹר וְנִשְׁבָּרוּ וְנוֹקְשׁוּ וְנִלְכָּדוּ: כב לָכֵן
כֹּה־אָמַר יְהוָה אֶל־בֵּית יַעֲקֹב אֲשֶׁר פָּדָה אֶת־
אַבְרָהָם לֹא־עַתָּה יֵבוֹשׁ יַעֲקֹב וְלֹא עַתָּה פָּנָיו
יֶחֱוָרוּ: כג כִּי בִרְאוֹתוֹ יְלָדָיו מַעֲשֵׂה יָדַי
בְּקִרְבּוֹ יַקְדִּישׁוּ שְׁמִי וְהִקְדִּישׁוּ אֶת־קְדוֹשׁ
יַעֲקֹב וְאֶת־אֱלֹהֵי יִשְׂרָאֵל יַעֲרִיצוּ:

HAFTARATH SHEMOTH הפטרת שמות
(Jeremiah 1:1–2:3) according to the Sephardim.

Jeremiah's reluctant acceptance of God's mission is reminiscent of Moses' reluctance to accept God's mission to redeem the Israelites from Egyptian bondage.

1:1. The words of Jeremiah, the son of Hilkiah, of the priests that were in Anathoth, in the land of Benjamin, 2. to whom the word of the Lord came in the days of Josiah the son of Amon, king of Judah, in the thirteenth year of his reign. 3. And it [also] came in the days of Jehoiakim the son of Josiah, king of Judah, until the end of the eleventh year of Zedekiah the son of Josiah, king of Judah, until the exile of Jerusalem in the fifth month. 4. And the word of the Lord came to me, saying: 5. Before I formed you in the womb, I knew you, and before you came out of the womb I dedicated you, to be a prophet to the nations did I ordain you. 6. And I said, "Ah! O Lord God, behold I have no knowledge of speaking, for I am quite young." 7. But the Lord said to me: Say not, I am too young, for wherever I send you, you shall go, and whatever I command you, you shall speak. 8. Fear not before them, for I am with you, to save you, says the Lord. 9. And the Lord stretched out His hand and made it touch my mouth, and the Lord said to me: Behold I have placed My words in your mouth. 10. Behold I have appointed you this day over the nations and over the kingdoms, to uproot and to pull down and to destroy and to demolish, to build and to plant. 11. And the word of the

א דִּבְרֵי יִרְמְיָהוּ בֶּן־חִלְקִיָּהוּ מִן־הַכֹּהֲנִים אֲשֶׁר
בַּעֲנָתוֹת בְּאֶרֶץ בִּנְיָמִן: ב אֲשֶׁר הָיָה דְבַר־יְהוָה
אֵלָיו בִּימֵי יֹאשִׁיָּהוּ בֶן־אָמוֹן מֶלֶךְ יְהוּדָה
בִּשְׁלֹשׁ־עֶשְׂרֵה שָׁנָה לְמָלְכוֹ: ג וַיְהִי בִּימֵי
יְהוֹיָקִים בֶּן־יֹאשִׁיָּהוּ מֶלֶךְ יְהוּדָה עַד־תֹּם
עַשְׁתֵּי־עֶשְׂרֵה שָׁנָה לְצִדְקִיָּהוּ בֶן־יֹאשִׁיָּהוּ מֶלֶךְ
יְהוּדָה עַד־גְּלוֹת יְרוּשָׁלַםִ בַּחֹדֶשׁ הַחֲמִישִׁי:
ד וַיְהִי דְבַר־יְהוָה אֵלַי לֵאמֹר: ה בְּטֶרֶם
אֶצָּרְךָ (אצורך קרי) בַבֶּטֶן יְדַעְתִּיךָ וּבְטֶרֶם תֵּצֵא
מֵרֶחֶם הִקְדַּשְׁתִּיךָ נָבִיא לַגּוֹיִם נְתַתִּיךָ: ו וָאֹמַר
אֲהָהּ אֲדֹנָי יֱהוִה הִנֵּה לֹא־יָדַעְתִּי דַּבֵּר כִּי־נַעַר
אָנֹכִי: ז וַיֹּאמֶר יְהוָה אֵלַי אַל־תֹּאמַר נַעַר
אָנֹכִי כִּי עַל־כָּל־אֲשֶׁר אֶשְׁלָחֲךָ תֵּלֵךְ וְאֵת כָּל־
אֲשֶׁר אֲצַוְּךָ תְּדַבֵּר: ח אַל־תִּירָא מִפְּנֵיהֶם כִּי־
אִתְּךָ אֲנִי לְהַצִּלֶךָ נְאֻם־יְהוָה: ט וַיִּשְׁלַח יְהוָה
אֶת־יָדוֹ וַיַּגַּע עַל־פִּי וַיֹּאמֶר יְהוָה אֵלַי הִנֵּה
נָתַתִּי דְבָרַי בְּפִיךָ: י רְאֵה הִפְקַדְתִּיךָ | הַיּוֹם
הַזֶּה עַל־הַגּוֹיִם וְעַל־הַמַּמְלָכוֹת לִנְתוֹשׁ וְלִנְתוֹץ
וּלְהַאֲבִיד וְלַהֲרוֹס לִבְנוֹת וְלִנְטוֹעַ: יא וַיְהִי

Lord came to me, saying: What do you see, Jeremiah? And I said, "I see the rod of an almond tree." 12. And the Lord said to me: You have seen rightly, for [like the almond blossoms], I hasten My word to carry it out. 13. And the word of the Lord came to me a second time, saying: What do you see? And I said, "I see a boiling pot, and its bubbles are from the north side." 14. And the Lord said to me: From the north, the misfortune will break forth over all the inhabitants of the earth. 15. For lo, I will call all the families of the kingdoms of the north, says the Lord, and they will come and they will set each one his throne at the entrance of the gates of Jerusalem, and against all its walls around, and against all the cities of Judah. 16. And I will utter all My judgments against them because of all their evil, that they have forsaken Me and burned incense to other gods and prostrated themselves to the works of their hands. 17. And you shall gird your loins and arise and speak to them all that I will command you; fear them not lest I break you before them. 18. And I, behold, I have set you today as a fortified city and as an iron pillar and as copper walls over the whole land, for the kings of Judah, for its princes, for its priests and for the people of the land. 19. And they will fight against you, but they will not prevail against you, for I am with you, says the Lord, to save you. 2:1. Then the word of the Lord came to me, saying: 2. Go and proclaim in the ears of Jerusalem, saying, "Thus says the Lord: 'I remember to you the love of your youth, the attachment of your bridal state when you went after Me into the desert, into a land where nothing was sown. 3. Israel is the Lord's hallowed portion, the best of His grain; all those who would devour him shall bear guilt; evil shall come upon them,'" says the Lord.

דְּבַר־יְהֹוָה אֵלַי לֵאמֹר מָה־אַתָּה רֹאֶה יִרְמְיָהוּ וָאֹמַר מַקֵּל שָׁקֵד אֲנִי רֹאֶה: יב וַיֹּאמֶר יְהֹוָה אֵלַי הֵיטַבְתָּ לִרְאוֹת כִּי־שֹׁקֵד אֲנִי עַל־דְּבָרִי לַעֲשֹׂתוֹ: יג וַיְהִי דְבַר־יְהֹוָה אֵלַי שֵׁנִית לֵאמֹר מָה אַתָּה רֹאֶה וָאֹמַר סִיר נָפוּחַ אֲנִי רֹאֶה וּפָנָיו מִפְּנֵי צָפוֹנָה: יד וַיֹּאמֶר יְהֹוָה אֵלַי מִצָּפוֹן תִּפָּתַח הָרָעָה עַל כָּל־יֹשְׁבֵי הָאָרֶץ: טו כִּי הִנְנִי קֹרֵא לְכָל־מִשְׁפְּחוֹת מַמְלְכוֹת צָפוֹנָה נְאֻם־יְהֹוָה וּבָאוּ וְנָתְנוּ אִישׁ כִּסְאוֹ פֶּתַח שַׁעֲרֵי יְרוּשָׁלַם וְעַל כָּל־חוֹמֹתֶיהָ סָבִיב וְעַל כָּל־עָרֵי יְהוּדָה: טז וְדִבַּרְתִּי מִשְׁפָּטַי אוֹתָם עַל כָּל־רָעָתָם אֲשֶׁר עֲזָבוּנִי וַיְקַטְּרוּ לֵאלֹהִים אֲחֵרִים וַיִּשְׁתַּחֲווּ לְמַעֲשֵׂי יְדֵיהֶם: יז וְאַתָּה תֶּאְזֹר מָתְנֶיךָ וְקַמְתָּ וְדִבַּרְתָּ אֲלֵיהֶם אֵת כָּל־אֲשֶׁר אָנֹכִי אֲצַוֶּךָּ אַל־תֵּחַת מִפְּנֵיהֶם פֶּן־אֲחִתְּךָ לִפְנֵיהֶם: יח וַאֲנִי הִנֵּה נְתַתִּיךָ הַיּוֹם לְעִיר מִבְצָר וּלְעַמּוּד בַּרְזֶל וּלְחֹמוֹת נְחֹשֶׁת עַל־כָּל־הָאָרֶץ לְמַלְכֵי יְהוּדָה לְשָׂרֶיהָ לְכֹהֲנֶיהָ וּלְעַם הָאָרֶץ: יט וְנִלְחֲמוּ אֵלֶיךָ וְלֹא־יוּכְלוּ לָךְ כִּי־אִתְּךָ אֲנִי נְאֻם־יְהֹוָה לְהַצִּילֶךָ: א וַיְהִי דְבַר־יְהֹוָה אֵלַי לֵאמֹר: ב הָלֹךְ וְקָרָאתָ בְאָזְנֵי יְרוּשָׁלַם לֵאמֹר כֹּה אָמַר יְהֹוָה זָכַרְתִּי לָךְ חֶסֶד נְעוּרַיִךְ אַהֲבַת כְּלוּלֹתָיִךְ לֶכְתֵּךְ אַחֲרַי בַּמִּדְבָּר בְּאֶרֶץ לֹא זְרוּעָה: ג קֹדֶשׁ יִשְׂרָאֵל לַיהֹוָה רֵאשִׁית תְּבוּאָתֹה כָּל־אֹכְלָיו יֶאְשָׁמוּ רָעָה תָּבֹא אֲלֵיהֶם נְאֻם־יְהֹוָה:

HAFTARATH VAERA הפטרת וארא

(Ezekiel 28:25, 26; 29:1–21)

Should Rosh Chodesh coincide with the Sabbath, the Haftarah for Sabbath Rosh Chodesh (p. 929) is read.

The prophecy of the ingathering of the House of Israel is reminiscent of Israel's redemption from Egypt, and the prophecy of Pharaoh's downfall is reminiscent of the fall of another Pharaoh who kept Israel in bondage.

28:25. So says the Lord God: When I
gather the House of Israel from the peoples
among whom they have been scattered, and
I have been sanctified through them in the
eyes of the nations, then shall they dwell on
their land that I gave to My servant Jacob.
26. And they shall dwell upon it securely,
and they shall build houses and plant vineyards and dwell securely when I execute
judgments against all those who plunder
them round about them, and they shall
know that I am the Lord their God.
29:1. In the tenth year, in the tenth
[month], on the twelfth of the month, the
word of the Lord came to me, saying:
2. Son of man! Set your face against
Pharaoh, king of Egypt, and prophesy
against him, and against all Egypt. 3. Speak
and you shall say: So says the Lord God:
Behold I am upon you, O Pharaoh, king of
Egypt, you great crocodile that lies down in
the midst of its rivers, who said, "My river is
my own, and I made myself." 4. And I will
put hooks in your jaws and I will cause the
fish of your rivers to fasten onto your scales,
and I will drag you up out of the midst of
your rivers and all the fish of your rivers
shall stick to your scales. 5. And I will
scatter you in the desert, you and all the fish
of your rivers; upon the open fields shall you
fall, you shall not be brought home, nor
gathered together; to the beasts of the earth
and to the birds of the air have I given you
to be devoured. 6. And all the inhabitants
of Egypt shall know that I am the Lord,
because they have been a prop of reeds to
the House of Israel. 7. When they took hold
of you by the hand, you splintered and
pierced the whole of their shoulders, and
when they leaned upon you, you broke, and
you made all their loins stand upright.
8. Therefore, so says the Lord God: Behold
I will bring the sword over you, and I will

כה כֹּה־אָמַר אֲדֹנָי יֱהֹוִה בְּקַבְּצִי ׀ אֶת־בֵּית
יִשְׂרָאֵל מִן־הָעַמִּים אֲשֶׁר נָפֹצוּ בָם וְנִקְדַּשְׁתִּי
בָם לְעֵינֵי הַגּוֹיִם וְיָשְׁבוּ עַל־אַדְמָתָם אֲשֶׁר
נָתַתִּי לְעַבְדִּי לְיַעֲקֹב: כו וְיָשְׁבוּ עָלֶיהָ לָבֶטַח
וּבָנוּ בָתִּים וְנָטְעוּ כְרָמִים וְיָשְׁבוּ לָבֶטַח
בַּעֲשׂוֹתִי שְׁפָטִים בְּכֹל הַשָּׁאטִים אֹתָם
מִסְּבִיבוֹתָם וְיָדְעוּ כִּי אֲנִי יְהֹוָה אֱלֹהֵיהֶם:
א בַּשָּׁנָה הָעֲשִׂרִית בָּעֲשִׂרִי בִּשְׁנֵים עָשָׂר
לַחֹדֶשׁ הָיָה דְבַר־יְהֹוָה אֵלַי לֵאמֹר: ב בֶּן־אָדָם
שִׂים פָּנֶיךָ עַל־פַּרְעֹה מֶלֶךְ מִצְרָיִם וְהִנָּבֵא
עָלָיו וְעַל־מִצְרַיִם כֻּלָּהּ: ג דַּבֵּר וְאָמַרְתָּ כֹּה־
אָמַר ׀ אֲדֹנָי יֱהֹוִה הִנְנִי עָלֶיךָ פַּרְעֹה מֶלֶךְ־
מִצְרַיִם הַתַּנִּים הַגָּדוֹל הָרֹבֵץ בְּתוֹךְ יְאֹרָיו
אֲשֶׁר אָמַר לִי יְאֹרִי וַאֲנִי עֲשִׂיתִנִי: ד וְנָתַתִּי
חַחִיִּים (חחים קרי) בִּלְחָיֶיךָ וְהִדְבַּקְתִּי דְגַת־יְאֹרֶיךָ
בְּקַשְׂקְשֹׂתֶיךָ וְהַעֲלִיתִיךָ מִתּוֹךְ יְאֹרֶיךָ וְאֵת כָּל־
דְּגַת יְאֹרֶיךָ בְּקַשְׂקְשֹׂתֶיךָ תִּדְבָּק: ה וּנְטַשְׁתִּיךָ
הַמִּדְבָּרָה אוֹתְךָ וְאֵת כָּל־דְּגַת יְאֹרֶיךָ עַל־פְּנֵי
הַשָּׂדֶה תִּפּוֹל לֹא תֵאָסֵף וְלֹא תִקָּבֵץ לְחַיַּת
הָאָרֶץ וּלְעוֹף הַשָּׁמַיִם נְתַתִּיךָ לְאָכְלָה: ו וְיָדְעוּ
כָּל־יֹשְׁבֵי מִצְרַיִם כִּי אֲנִי יְהֹוָה יַעַן הֱיוֹתָם
מִשְׁעֶנֶת קָנֶה לְבֵית יִשְׂרָאֵל: ז בְּתָפְשָׂם בְּךָ
בַכַּפֶּךָ (בכף קרי) תֵּרוֹץ וּבָקַעְתָּ לָהֶם כָּל־כָּתֵף
וּבְהִשָּׁעֲנָם עָלֶיךָ תִּשָּׁבֵר וְהַעֲמַדְתָּ לָהֶם כָּל־
מָתְנָיִם: ח לָכֵן כֹּה אָמַר אֲדֹנָי יֱהֹוִה הִנְנִי
מֵבִיא עָלַיִךְ חָרֶב וְהִכְרַתִּי מִמֵּךְ אָדָם וּבְהֵמָה:

cut off from you man and beast. 9. And the land of Egypt shall be desolate and in ruins, and they shall know that I am the Lord! Because he said, "The river is mine, and I have made it." 10. Therefore, I am against you and against your rivers, and I will make the land of Egypt into ruins, ruins of desolation from Migdol till Syene and until the border of Ethiopia. 11. No foot of man shall pass through it, nor foot of beast shall pass through it, neither shall it be inhabited for forty years. 12. And I will make the land of Egypt desolate even amongst the desolate lands, and its cities, a desolation even amongst cities in ruins, forty years. 13. Yet thus has the Lord God said: At the end of forty years will I gather the Egyptians from the peoples where they have been scattered. 14. And I will return the captives of Egypt and will lead them to the land of Pathros, to the land of their habitation, and they shall be there an unimportant kingdom. 15. It shall be the lowest of the kingdoms and shall no longer exalt itself above the nations, for I will diminish their numbers so that they shall not domineer over the nations. 16. And it will no longer be confidence of the House of Israel, bringing iniquity into remembrance when they turn after them, and they shall know that I am the Lord God. 17. And it came to pass in the twenty-seventh year in the first [month], on the first of the month, the word of the Lord came to me, saying: 18. Son of man! Nebuchadrezzar, the king of Babylon, made his army serve a great work against Tyre, every head became bald and every shoulder sore, yet he had no wages nor did his army out of Tyre for the service he had served against it. 19. Therefore, thus says the Lord God: Behold I will give Nebuchadrezzar, king of Babylon, the land of Egypt, and he shall carry away its multitude, pillage its spoils, and plunder its booty, and that shall be the wages for his army. 20. For his labor wherewith he worked against it I have given him the land of Egypt, for it was for that they worked, says the Lord God. 21. On that day will I cause the horn [the strength] of the House of Israel to blossom out, and I will give you free speech in their midst, and they shall know that I am the Lord.

ט וְהָיְתָה אֶֽרֶץ־מִצְרַ֙יִם֙ לִשְׁמָמָה וְחָרְבָּה וְיָדְעוּ
כִּֽי־אֲנִי יְהוָה יַעַן אָמַר יְאֹר לִי וַאֲנִי עָשִֽׂיתִי׃
י לָכֵן הִנְנִי אֵלֶיךָ וְאֶל־יְאֹרֶיךָ וְנָתַתִּי אֶת־אֶרֶץ
מִצְרַיִם לְחָרְבוֹת֙ חֹרֶב שְׁמָמָה מִמִּגְדֹּל סְוֵנֵה
וְעַד־גְּבוּל כּֽוּשׁ׃ יא לֹא תַֽעֲבָר־בָּהּ֙ רֶגֶל אָדָם
וְרֶגֶל בְּהֵמָה לֹא תַֽעֲבָר־בָּהּ וְלֹא תֵשֵׁב אַרְבָּעִים
שָׁנָֽה׃ יב וְנָתַתִּי אֶת־אֶרֶץ מִצְרַיִם שְׁמָמָה בְּתוֹךְ
׀ אֲרָצוֹת נְשַׁמּוֹת וְעָרֶיהָ֙ בְּתוֹךְ עָרִים מָֽחֳרָבוֹת֙
תִּהְיֶיןָ שְׁמָמָה אַרְבָּעִים שָׁנָה וַהֲפִצֹתִי אֶת־
מִצְרַ֙יִם֙ בַּגּוֹיִם וְזֵרִיתִים בָּאֲרָצֽוֹת׃ יג כִּי כֹּה
אָמַר אֲדֹנָי יֱהוִה מִקֵּץ אַרְבָּעִים שָׁנָה֙ אֲקַבֵּץ
אֶת־מִצְרַיִם מִן־הָעַמִּים אֲשֶׁר־נָפֹצוּ שָֽׁמָּה׃
יד וְשַׁבְתִּי֙ אֶת־שְׁבוּת מִצְרַיִם וַהֲשִׁבֹתִי אֹתָם
אֶרֶץ פַּתְרוֹס עַל־אֶרֶץ מְכֽוּרָתָם וְהָיוּ שָׁם
מַמְלָכָה שְׁפָלָֽה׃ טו מִן־הַמַּמְלָכוֹת֙ תִּהְיֶה
שְׁפָלָה וְלֹֽא־תִתְנַשֵּׂא עוֹד עַל־הַגּוֹיִם
וְהִמְעַטְתִּים לְבִלְתִּי רְדוֹת בַּגּוֹיִֽם׃ טז וְלֹא
יִֽהְיֶה־עוֹד לְבֵית יִשְׂרָאֵל לְמִבְטָח֙ מַזְכִּיר עָוֺן
בִּפְנוֹתָם אַחֲרֵיהֶם וְיָדְעוּ כִּי אֲנִי אֲדֹנָי יֱהוִֽה׃
יז וַיְהִי בְּעֶשְׂרִים וָשֶׁבַע֙ שָׁנָה בָּרִאשׁוֹן בְּאֶחָד
לַחֹדֶשׁ הָיָה דְבַר־יְהוָה אֵלַי לֵאמֹֽר׃ יח בֶּן־אָדָם
נְבוּכַדְרֶאצַּר מֶֽלֶךְ־בָּבֶל הֶעֱבִיד אֶת־חֵילוֹ
עֲבֹדָה גְדוֹלָה֙ אֶל־צֹר כָּל־רֹאשׁ מֻקְרָח וְכָל־
כָּתֵף מְרוּטָה וְשָׂכָר לֹא־הָיָה לוֹ וּלְחֵילוֹ֙ מִצֹּר
עַל־הָעֲבֹדָה אֲשֶׁר־עָבַד עָלֶֽיהָ׃ יט לָכֵן כֹּה אָמַר֙
אֲדֹנָי יֱהוִה הִנְנִי נֹתֵן לִנְבוּכַדְרֶאצַּר מֶֽלֶךְ־בָּבֶל
אֶת־אֶרֶץ מִצְרָיִם וְנָשָׂא הֲמֹנָהּ וְשָׁלַל שְׁלָלָהּ֙
וּבָזַז בִּזָּהּ וְהָיְתָה שָׂכָר לְחֵילֽוֹ׃ כ פְּעֻלָּתוֹ֙
אֲשֶׁר־עָבַד בָּהּ נָתַתִּי לוֹ אֶת־אֶרֶץ מִצְרָיִם
אֲשֶׁר֙ עָשׂוּ לִי נְאֻם אֲדֹנָי יֱהוִֽה׃ כא בַּיּוֹם הַהוּא
אַצְמִיחַ קֶ֙רֶן֙ לְבֵית יִשְׂרָאֵל וּלְךָ אֶתֵּן פִּתְחֽוֹן־
פֶּה בְּתוֹכָם וְיָדְעוּ כִּֽי־אֲנִי יְהוָֽה׃

HAFTARATH BO   הפטרת בא
(Jeremiah 46:13–28)

The destruction wrought in the land of Egypt mentioned in this selection is reminiscent of the plagues visited on Egypt in this Sidra.

46:13. The word that the Lord spoke to Jeremiah the prophet, concerning the coming of Nebuchadrezzar, king of Babylon, to smite the land of Egypt, 14. proclaim it in Egypt and let it be heard in Migdol, and let it be heard in Noph and in Tahpanhes. Say: "Stand fast and prepare yourself, for the sword has devoured round about you." 15. Why have your mighty men been swept away? None of them stood, for the Lord pushed him down. 16. He made many to stumble; yea, they fell one against the other, and they said, "Arise, and let us go back to our own people and to the land of our birth, before the oppressing sword." 17. There they called out, "Pharaoh, king of Egypt, who made a lot of noise, has allowed the appointed time to pass by!" 18. As I live, says the King, Whose name is the Lord of Hosts, that as sure as Tabor is among the mountains, and Carmel is by the sea, it shall come about. 19. O you daughter who lives in Egypt, make for yourself equipment for exile, for Noph shall become waste and desolate without an inhabitant. 20. Egypt was a very fair heifer; a destruction from the north is coming, yea it is coming! 21. Also her mercenaries who are in her midst are like fattened calves, for they too turn around and flee together; they do not hold their ground, for the day of their calamity has come upon them, the time of their visitation. 22. Its sound shall go like the hissing of the snake, for they will march with an army and will come against her with axes as if they were hewers of wood. 23. They will cut down her forest, says the Lord, for they are innumerable, for they are more numerous than locusts, and they are uncountable. 24. The daughter of Egypt has been put to shame; she has been delivered into the hand of the people of the north. 25. The Lord of Hosts, the God of Israel, has said: Lo I visit upon Amon of No and upon Pharaoh and upon Egypt, and

יג הַדָּבָר אֲשֶׁר דִּבֶּר יְהֹוָה אֶל־יִרְמְיָהוּ הַנָּבִיא לָבוֹא נְבוּכַדְרֶאצַּר מֶלֶךְ בָּבֶל לְהַכּוֹת אֶת־אֶרֶץ מִצְרָיִם: יד הַגִּידוּ בְמִצְרַיִם וְהַשְׁמִיעוּ בְמִגְדּוֹל וְהַשְׁמִיעוּ בְנֹף וּבְתַחְפַּנְחֵס אִמְרוּ הִתְיַצֵּב וְהָכֵן לָךְ כִּי־אָכְלָה חֶרֶב סְבִיבֶיךָ: טו מַדּוּעַ נִסְחַף אַבִּירֶיךָ לֹא עָמַד כִּי יְהֹוָה הֲדָפוֹ: טז הִרְבָּה כּוֹשֵׁל גַּם־נָפַל אִישׁ אֶל־רֵעֵהוּ וַיֹּאמְרוּ קוּמָה וְנָשֻׁבָה אֶל־עַמֵּנוּ וְאֶל־אֶרֶץ מוֹלַדְתֵּנוּ מִפְּנֵי חֶרֶב הַיּוֹנָה: יז קָרְאוּ שָׁם פַּרְעֹה מֶלֶךְ־מִצְרַיִם שָׁאוֹן הֶעֱבִיר הַמּוֹעֵד: יח חַי־אָנִי נְאֻם־הַמֶּלֶךְ יְהֹוָה צְבָאוֹת שְׁמוֹ כִּי כְּתָבוֹר בֶּהָרִים וּכְכַרְמֶל בַּיָּם יָבוֹא: יט כְּלֵי גוֹלָה עֲשִׂי לָךְ יוֹשֶׁבֶת בַּת־מִצְרָיִם כִּי־נֹף לְשַׁמָּה תִהְיֶה וְנִצְּתָה מֵאֵין יוֹשֵׁב: כ עֶגְלָה יְפֵה־פִיָּה מִצְרָיִם קֶרֶץ מִצָּפוֹן בָּא בָא: כא גַּם־שְׂכִרֶיהָ בְקִרְבָּהּ כְּעֶגְלֵי מַרְבֵּק כִּי־גַם־הֵמָּה הִפְנוּ נָסוּ יַחְדָּיו לֹא עָמָדוּ כִּי יוֹם אֵידָם בָּא עֲלֵיהֶם עֵת פְּקֻדָּתָם: כב קוֹלָהּ כַּנָּחָשׁ יֵלֵךְ כִּי־בְחַיִל יֵלֵכוּ וּבְקַרְדֻּמּוֹת בָּאוּ לָהּ כְּחֹטְבֵי עֵצִים: כג כָּרְתוּ יַעְרָהּ נְאֻם־יְהֹוָה כִּי לֹא יֵחָקֵר כִּי רַבּוּ מֵאַרְבֶּה וְאֵין לָהֶם מִסְפָּר: כד הֹבִישָׁה בַּת־מִצְרָיִם נִתְּנָה בְּיַד עַם־צָפוֹן: כה אָמַר יְהֹוָה צְבָאוֹת אֱלֹהֵי יִשְׂרָאֵל הִנְנִי פוֹקֵד אֶל־אָמוֹן מִנֹּא וְעַל־פַּרְעֹה וְעַל־מִצְרַיִם וְעַל־אֱלֹהֶיהָ וְעַל־מְלָכֶיהָ וְעַל־פַּרְעֹה וְעַל

הַבֹּטְחִים בּוֹ: כו וּנְתַתִּים בְּיַד מְבַקְשֵׁי נַפְשָׁם
וּבְיַד נְבוּכַדְרֶאצַּר מֶלֶךְ־בָּבֶל וּבְיַד עֲבָדָיו
וְאַחֲרֵי־כֵן תִּשְׁכֹּן כִּימֵי־קֶדֶם נְאֻם־יְהֹוָה:
כז וְאַתָּה אַל־תִּירָא עַבְדִּי יַעֲקֹב וְאַל־תֵּחַת
יִשְׂרָאֵל כִּי הִנְנִי מוֹשִׁעֲךָ מֵרָחוֹק וְאֶת־זַרְעֲךָ
מֵאֶרֶץ שִׁבְיָם וְשָׁב יַעֲקוֹב וְשָׁקַט וְשַׁאֲנַן וְאֵין
מַחֲרִיד: כח אַתָּה אַל־תִּירָא עַבְדִּי יַעֲקֹב נְאֻם־
יְהֹוָה כִּי אִתְּךָ אָנִי כִּי אֶעֱשֶׂה כָלָה בְּכָל־הַגּוֹיִם
| אֲשֶׁר הִדַּחְתִּיךָ שָׁמָּה וְאֹתְךָ לֹא־אֶעֱשֶׂה כָלָה
וְיִסַּרְתִּיךָ לַמִּשְׁפָּט וְנַקֵּה לֹא אֲנַקֶּךָּ:

upon their gods and upon their kings, both upon Pharaoh and upon those who put their trust in him. 26. And I will deliver them into the hand of those who seek their lives and into the hand of Nebuchadrezzar, king of Babylon, and into the hand of his servants — and after that it will be inhabited again as in the days of old, says the Lord. 27. You fear not, O Jacob My servant, and be not dismayed, O Israel! for behold, I will redeem you from afar and your children from the land of their captivity, and Jacob shall return and be quiet and at ease, and there shall be none who disturbs his rest. 28. You fear not, My servant Jacob, says the Lord, for I am with you, for I will make a full end of all the nations where I have driven you; but of you I will not make a full end, but I will chastise you justly, and I will not completely destroy you.

HAFTARATH BESHALLAḤ הפטרת בשלח

(Judges 4:4–5:31 for Ashkenazim; 5:1–31 for Sephardim)

The miraculous defeat of Sisera related in Deborah's song resembles that of Pharaoh, related in Moses' song in this Sidra.

ד וּדְבוֹרָה אִשָּׁה נְבִיאָה אֵשֶׁת לַפִּידוֹת הִיא
שֹׁפְטָה אֶת־יִשְׂרָאֵל בָּעֵת הַהִיא: ה וְהִיא
יוֹשֶׁבֶת תַּחַת־תֹּמֶר דְּבוֹרָה בֵּין הָרָמָה וּבֵין
בֵּית־אֵל בְּהַר אֶפְרָיִם וַיַּעֲלוּ אֵלֶיהָ בְּנֵי יִשְׂרָאֵל
לַמִּשְׁפָּט: ו וַתִּשְׁלַח וַתִּקְרָא לְבָרָק בֶּן־אֲבִינֹעַם
מִקֶּדֶשׁ נַפְתָּלִי וַתֹּאמֶר אֵלָיו הֲלֹא־צִוָּה | יְהֹוָה
אֱלֹהֵי־יִשְׂרָאֵל לֵךְ וּמָשַׁכְתָּ בְּהַר תָּבוֹר וְלָקַחְתָּ
עִמְּךָ עֲשֶׂרֶת אֲלָפִים אִישׁ מִבְּנֵי נַפְתָּלִי וּמִבְּנֵי
זְבֻלוּן: ז וּמָשַׁכְתִּי אֵלֶיךָ אֶל־נַחַל קִישׁוֹן אֶת־
סִיסְרָא שַׂר־צְבָא יָבִין וְאֶת־רִכְבּוֹ וְאֶת־הֲמוֹנוֹ
וּנְתַתִּיהוּ בְּיָדֶךָ: ח וַיֹּאמֶר אֵלֶיהָ בָּרָק אִם־
תֵּלְכִי עִמִּי וְהָלָכְתִּי וְאִם־לֹא תֵלְכִי עִמִּי לֹא
אֵלֵךְ: ט וַתֹּאמֶר הָלֹךְ אֵלֵךְ עִמָּךְ אֶפֶס כִּי לֹא
תִהְיֶה תִּפְאַרְתְּךָ עַל־הַדֶּרֶךְ אֲשֶׁר אַתָּה הוֹלֵךְ כִּי
בְּיַד אִשָּׁה יִמְכֹּר יְהֹוָה אֶת־סִיסְרָא וַתָּקָם
דְּבוֹרָה וַתֵּלֶךְ עִם־בָּרָק קֶדְשָׁה: י וַיַּזְעֵק בָּרָק

4:4. Now Deborah was a woman prophetess, the wife of Lappidoth; she judged Israel at that time. 5. And she sat under the palm tree of Deborah, between Ramah and Beth-el, in the mountain of Ephraim; and the children of Israel came up to her for judgment. 6. And she sent and called Barak the son of Abinoam out of Kedesh-Naphtali. And she said to him, "Indeed the Lord, God of Israel, has commanded, 'Go and draw toward Mount Tabor, and take with you ten thousand men of the children of Naphtali and of the children of Zebulun. 7. And I shall draw to you, to the brook Kishon, Sisera, the chieftain of Jabin's army, with his chariots and his multitude; and I will give him into your hand.'" 8. And Barak said to her, "If you will go with me then I shall go, but if you will not go with me, I shall not go." 9. And she said, "I shall surely go with you, but your glory will not be on the way which you go, for into the hand of a woman will the Lord deliver Sisera." And Deborah rose and went with Barak to Kedesh. 10. And Barak gathered

Zebulun and Naphtali to Kedesh; and ten
thousand men went up at his feet; and
Deborah went up with him. 11. Now Heber
the Kenite had separated from the Kenites,
of the children of Hobab, the father-in-law
of Moses; and he pitched his tent as far as
Elon-bezaanannim, which is by Kedesh.
12. And they told Sisera that Barak, the son
of Abinoam, had gone up to Mount Tabor.
13. And Sisera gathered all his chariots,
nine hundred iron chariots, and all the
people that were with him from Harosheth-
goiim to the brook Kishon. 14. And
Deborah said to Barak, "Rise, for this is the
day which the Lord has given Sisera into
your hand. Did not the Lord go out before
you?" And Barak went down from Mount
Tabor, with ten thousand men after him.
15. And the Lord confused Sisera and all
the chariots and all of the camp with the
edge of the sword before Barak; and Sisera
alighted from his chariot, and fled on foot.
16. And Barak pursued the chariots and the
camp, to Harosheth-goiim; and all of
Sisera's camp fell by the edge of the sword,
not even one was left. 17. And Sisera fled
on foot to the tent of Jael, the wife of Heber
the Kenite; for there was peace between
Jabin, the king of Hazor, and the house of
Heber the Kenite. 18. And Jael went out to
meet Sisera and said to him, "Turn in, my
lord, turn in to me; fear not." And he turned
in to her into the tent, and she covered him
with a garment. 19. And he said to her,
"Give me now a little water to drink, for I
am thirsty"; and she opened the flask of
milk and gave him to drink, and covered
him. 20. And he said to her, "Stand in the
doorway of the tent; and it shall be, if any
man comes and asks you and says, 'Is a man
here?' then you shall say, 'There is not.'"
21. And Jael, the wife of Heber, took the
tent-pin, and placed the hammer in her
hand, and came to him stealthily, and thrust
the pin into his temple, and it pierced
through into the ground; and he was in a
deep sleep and weary; and he died. 22. And
behold, Barak pursued Sisera, and Jael came
out to meet him, and she said to him,
"Come and I will show you the man whom
you seek," and he came to her, and behold,
Sisera lay dead, and the pin was in his
temple. 23. And God subdued on that day

אֶת־זְבוּלֻן וְאֶת־נַפְתָּלִי קֶדְשָׁה וַיַּעַל בְּרַגְלָיו
עֲשֶׂרֶת אַלְפֵי אִישׁ וַתַּעַל עִמּוֹ דְּבוֹרָה׃
יא וְחֶבֶר הַקֵּינִי נִפְרָד מִקַּיִן מִבְּנֵי חֹבָב חֹתֵן
מֹשֶׁה וַיֵּט אָהֳלוֹ עַד־אֵלוֹן בְּצַעֲנַיִּם (בצעננים קרי)
אֲשֶׁר אֶת־קֶדֶשׁ׃ יב וַיַּגִּדוּ לְסִיסְרָא כִּי עָלָה
בָּרָק בֶּן־אֲבִינֹעַם הַר־תָּבוֹר׃ יג וַיַּזְעֵק סִיסְרָא
אֶת־כָּל־רִכְבּוֹ תְּשַׁע מֵאוֹת רֶכֶב בַּרְזֶל וְאֶת־
כָּל־הָעָם אֲשֶׁר אִתּוֹ מֵחֲרֹשֶׁת הַגּוֹיִם אֶל־נַחַל
קִישׁוֹן׃ יד וַתֹּאמֶר דְּבֹרָה אֶל־בָּרָק קוּם כִּי זֶה
הַיּוֹם אֲשֶׁר נָתַן יְהוָה אֶת־סִיסְרָא בְּיָדֶךָ הֲלֹא
יְהוָה יָצָא לְפָנֶיךָ וַיֵּרֶד בָּרָק מֵהַר תָּבוֹר
וַעֲשֶׂרֶת אֲלָפִים אִישׁ אַחֲרָיו׃ טו וַיָּהָם יְהוָה
אֶת־סִיסְרָא וְאֶת־כָּל־הָרֶכֶב וְאֶת־כָּל־הַמַּחֲנֶה
לְפִי־חֶרֶב לִפְנֵי בָרָק וַיֵּרֶד סִיסְרָא מֵעַל
הַמֶּרְכָּבָה וַיָּנָס בְּרַגְלָיו׃ טז וּבָרָק רָדַף אַחֲרֵי
הָרֶכֶב וְאַחֲרֵי הַמַּחֲנֶה עַד חֲרֹשֶׁת הַגּוֹיִם וַיִּפֹּל
כָּל־מַחֲנֵה סִיסְרָא לְפִי־חֶרֶב לֹא נִשְׁאַר עַד־
אֶחָד׃ יז וְסִיסְרָא נָס בְּרַגְלָיו אֶל־אֹהֶל יָעֵל
אֵשֶׁת חֶבֶר הַקֵּינִי כִּי שָׁלוֹם בֵּין יָבִין מֶלֶךְ־
חָצוֹר וּבֵין בֵּית חֶבֶר הַקֵּינִי׃ יח וַתֵּצֵא יָעֵל
לִקְרַאת סִיסְרָא וַתֹּאמֶר אֵלָיו סוּרָה אֲדֹנִי
סוּרָה אֵלַי אַל־תִּירָא וַיָּסַר אֵלֶיהָ הָאֹהֱלָה
וַתְּכַסֵּהוּ בַּשְּׂמִיכָה׃ יט וַיֹּאמֶר אֵלֶיהָ הַשְׁקִינִי־
נָא מְעַט־מַיִם כִּי צָמֵאתִי וַתִּפְתַּח אֶת־נֹאוד
הֶחָלָב וַתַּשְׁקֵהוּ וַתְּכַסֵּהוּ׃ כ וַיֹּאמֶר אֵלֶיהָ עֲמֹד
פֶּתַח הָאֹהֶל וְהָיָה אִם־אִישׁ יָבֹא וּשְׁאֵלֵךְ וְאָמַר
הֲיֵשׁ־פֹּה אִישׁ וְאָמַרְתְּ אָיִן׃ כא וַתִּקַּח יָעֵל
אֵשֶׁת־חֶבֶר אֶת־יְתַד הָאֹהֶל וַתָּשֶׂם אֶת־הַמַּקֶּבֶת
בְּיָדָהּ וַתָּבוֹא אֵלָיו בַּלָּאט וַתִּתְקַע אֶת־הַיָּתֵד
בְּרַקָּתוֹ וַתִּצְנַח בָּאָרֶץ וְהוּא־נִרְדָּם וַיָּעַף וַיָּמֹת׃
כב וְהִנֵּה בָרָק רֹדֵף אֶת־סִיסְרָא וַתֵּצֵא יָעֵל
לִקְרָאתוֹ וַתֹּאמֶר לוֹ לֵךְ וְאַרְאֶךָּ אֶת־הָאִישׁ
אֲשֶׁר־אַתָּה מְבַקֵּשׁ וַיָּבֹא אֵלֶיהָ וְהִנֵּה סִיסְרָא
נֹפֵל מֵת וְהַיָּתֵד בְּרַקָּתוֹ׃ כג וַיַּכְנַע אֱלֹהִים

Jabin, the king of Canaan, before the children of Israel. 24. And the hand of the children of Israel prevailed constantly harder against Jabin, the king of Canaan, until they had destroyed Jabin, king of Canaan. (*The Sephardim commence here.*) 5:1. Now Deborah and Barak the son of Abinoam sang on that day, saying. 2. "When breaches are made in Israel, when the people offer themselves willingly, bless the Lord. 3. Hear, O kings; give ear, O princes; I, to the Lord I shall sing, I shall sing to the Lord, the God of Israel. 4. Lord, when You went forth out of Seir, when You marched out of the field of Edom, the earth trembled, the heavens also dripped; also the clouds dripped water. 5. The mountains melted at the presence of the Lord, this [was at] Sinai, because of the presence of the Lord, the God of Israel. 6. In the days of Shamgar the son of Anath, in the days of Jael, caravans ceased, and travellers walked on crooked paths. 7. The open cities ceased, in Israel they ceased, until Deborah arose; I arose as a mother in Israel. 8. When they chose new gods, then there was war in the cities; was there seen a shield or a spear [when the] forty thousand [went against] Israel? 9. My heart is toward the lawgivers of Israel, that offered themselves willingly among the people, [saying], 'Bless the Lord.' 10. The riders of white donkeys, those that sit in judgment, and those that walk on the path, tell of it. 11. Instead of the noise of adversaries, between the places of drawing water, there they will tell the righteous acts of the Lord, the righteous acts of restoring open cities in Israel. Then the people of the Lord went down to the cities. 12. Praise! Praise! Deborah. Praise! Praise! Utter a song. Arise Barak, and capture your captives, son of Abinoam. 13. Then ruled a remnant among the mighty of the nations; the Lord dominated the strong for me. 14. Out of Ephraim, whose root was against Amalek; after you [will be] Benjamin with your abaters; out of Machir came down officers, and out of Zebulun they that handle the pen of the scribe. 15. And the princes of Issachar were with Deborah, as was Issachar with Barak; into the valley they rushed forth with their feet. [But] among the divisions of Reuben, [there were] great

בַּיּוֹם הַהוּא אֵת יָבִין מֶלֶךְ־כְּנַעַן לִפְנֵי בְּנֵי יִשְׂרָאֵל: כד וַתֵּלֶךְ יַד בְּנֵי־יִשְׂרָאֵל הָלוֹךְ וְקָשָׁה עַל יָבִין מֶלֶךְ־כְּנַעַן עַד אֲשֶׁר הִכְרִיתוּ אֵת יָבִין מֶלֶךְ־כְּנַעַן: (כאן מתחילין הספרדים) א וַתָּשַׁר דְּבוֹרָה וּבָרָק בֶּן־אֲבִינֹעַם בַּיּוֹם הַהוּא לֵאמֹר: ב בִּפְרֹעַ פְּרָעוֹת בְּיִשְׂרָאֵל בְּהִתְנַדֵּב עָם בָּרֲכוּ יְהֹוָה: ג שִׁמְעוּ מְלָכִים הַאֲזִינוּ רֹזְנִים אָנֹכִי לַיהֹוָה אָנֹכִי אָשִׁירָה אֲזַמֵּר לַיהֹוָה אֱלֹהֵי יִשְׂרָאֵל: ד יְהֹוָה בְּצֵאתְךָ מִשֵּׂעִיר בְּצַעְדְּךָ מִשְּׂדֵה אֱדוֹם אֶרֶץ רָעָשָׁה גַּם־שָׁמַיִם נָטָפוּ גַּם־עָבִים נָטְפוּ מָיִם: ה הָרִים נָזְלוּ מִפְּנֵי יְהֹוָה זֶה סִינַי מִפְּנֵי יְהֹוָה אֱלֹהֵי יִשְׂרָאֵל: ו בִּימֵי שַׁמְגַּר בֶּן־עֲנָת בִּימֵי יָעֵל חָדְלוּ אֳרָחוֹת וְהֹלְכֵי נְתִיבוֹת יֵלְכוּ אֳרָחוֹת עֲקַלְקַלּוֹת: ז חָדְלוּ פְרָזוֹן בְּיִשְׂרָאֵל חָדֵלּוּ עַד שַׁקַּמְתִּי דְּבוֹרָה שַׁקַּמְתִּי אֵם בְּיִשְׂרָאֵל: ח יִבְחַר אֱלֹהִים חֲדָשִׁים אָז לָחֶם שְׁעָרִים מָגֵן אִם־יֵרָאֶה וָרֹמַח בְּאַרְבָּעִים אֶלֶף בְּיִשְׂרָאֵל: ט לִבִּי לְחוֹקְקֵי יִשְׂרָאֵל הַמִּתְנַדְּבִים בָּעָם בָּרֲכוּ יְהֹוָה: י רֹכְבֵי אֲתֹנוֹת צְחֹרוֹת יֹשְׁבֵי עַל־מִדִּין וְהֹלְכֵי עַל־דֶּרֶךְ שִׂיחוּ: יא מִקּוֹל מְחַצְצִים בֵּין מַשְׁאַבִּים שָׁם יְתַנּוּ צִדְקוֹת יְהֹוָה צִדְקֹת פִּרְזוֹנוֹ בְּיִשְׂרָאֵל אָז יָרְדוּ לַשְּׁעָרִים עַם־יְהֹוָה: יב עוּרִי עוּרִי דְּבוֹרָה עוּרִי עוּרִי דַּבְּרִי־שִׁיר קוּם בָּרָק וּשֲׁבֵה שֶׁבְיְךָ בֶּן־אֲבִינֹעַם: יג אָז יְרַד שָׂרִיד לְאַדִּירִים עָם יְהֹוָה יְרַד־לִי בַּגִּבּוֹרִים: יד מִנִּי אֶפְרַיִם שָׁרְשָׁם בַּעֲמָלֵק אַחֲרֶיךָ בִנְיָמִין בַּעֲמָמֶיךָ מִנִּי מָכִיר יָרְדוּ מְחֹקְקִים וּמִזְּבוּלֻן מֹשְׁכִים בְּשֵׁבֶט סֹפֵר: טו וְשָׂרַי בְּיִשָּׂשכָר עִם־דְּבֹרָה וְיִשָּׂשכָר כֵּן בָּרָק בָּעֵמֶק שֻׁלַּח בְּרַגְלָיו בִּפְלַגּוֹת רְאוּבֵן

resolves of heart. 16. Why do you sit
between the borders, to hear the bleatings
of the flocks? At the divisions of Reuben,
[there are] great searchings of heart.
17. Gilead abides beyond the Jordan; and
Dan, why does he gather into the ships?
Asher dwelt at the shore of the seas, and by
his breaches he abides. 18. Zebulun is a
people that jeopardized their lives to die, as
did Naphtali, upon the high places of the
field. 19. The kings came and fought; then
fought the kings of Canaan in Taanach by
the waters of Megiddo; they took no gain of
money. 20. From heaven they fought; the
stars from their courses fought against
Sisera. 21. The brook Kishon swept them
away, that ancient brook, the brook Kishon;
tread down, O my soul, [their] strength.
22. Then were pounded the heels of the
horses by reason of the prancings, the
prancings of their mighty ones. 23. "Curse
you, Meroz," said the messenger of the
Lord, "curse you bitterly the inhabitants
thereof, because they came not to the aid of
the Lord, to the aid of the Lord against the
mighty." 24. Blessed above women shall
Jael, the wife of Heber the Kenite, be;
above women in the tent shall she be
blessed. 25. Water he requested, [but] milk
she gave him; in a lordly bowl she brought
him cream. 26. She put forth her hand to
the pin, and her right hand to strike the
weary; she struck Sisera, pierced his head,
and wounded and penetrated his temple.
27. At her feet he sank, fell, lay; at her feet
he sank [and] fell; where he sank, there he
fell down dead. 28. Through the window
the mother of Sisera looked forth, and
peered through the window; why is his
chariot late in coming? Why tarry the
strides of his chariots? 29. The wisest of her
princesses answer her, she too returns
answers to herself. 30. "Are they not finding [and] dividing the spoils? A damsel, two
damsels to every man; a spoil of dyed
garments to Sisera, a spoil of dyed garments
of embroidery; dyed garments of embroidery for the neck of the spoiler." 31. So may
perish all Thine enemies, O Lord; but they
that love Him [should be] as the sun when
he goes forth in his might. And the land
rested forty years.

גְּדֹלִים חִקְקֵי־לֵב: טז לָמָּה יָשַׁבְתָּ בֵּין
הַמִּשְׁפְּתַיִם לִשְׁמֹעַ שְׁרִקוֹת עֲדָרִים לִפְלַגּוֹת
רְאוּבֵן גְּדוֹלִים חִקְרֵי־לֵב: יז גִּלְעָד בְּעֵבֶר
הַיַּרְדֵּן שָׁכֵן וְדָן לָמָּה יָגוּר אֳנִיּוֹת אָשֵׁר יָשַׁב
לְחוֹף יַמִּים וְעַל־מִפְרָצָיו יִשְׁכּוֹן: יח זְבֻלוּן עַם
חֵרֵף נַפְשׁוֹ לָמוּת וְנַפְתָּלִי עַל מְרוֹמֵי שָׂדֶה:
יט בָּאוּ מְלָכִים נִלְחָמוּ אָז נִלְחֲמוּ מַלְכֵי כְנַעַן
בְּתַעְנַךְ עַל־מֵי מְגִדּוֹ בֶּצַע כֶּסֶף לֹא לָקָחוּ:
כ מִן־שָׁמַיִם נִלְחָמוּ הַכּוֹכָבִים מִמְּסִלּוֹתָם
נִלְחֲמוּ עִם סִיסְרָא: כא נַחַל קִישׁוֹן גְּרָפָם נַחַל
קְדוּמִים נַחַל קִישׁוֹן תִּדְרְכִי נַפְשִׁי עֹז: כב אָז
הָלְמוּ עִקְּבֵי־סוּס מִדַּהֲרוֹת דַּהֲרוֹת אַבִּירָיו:
כג אוֹרוּ מֵרוֹז אָמַר מַלְאַךְ יְהֹוָה אֹרוּ אָרוֹר
יֹשְׁבֶיהָ כִּי לֹא־בָאוּ לְעֶזְרַת יְהֹוָה לְעֶזְרַת יְהֹוָה
בַּגִּבּוֹרִים: כד תְּבֹרַךְ מִנָּשִׁים יָעֵל אֵשֶׁת חֶבֶר
הַקֵּינִי מִנָּשִׁים בָּאֹהֶל תְּבֹרָךְ: כה מַיִם שָׁאַל
חָלָב נָתָנָה בְּסֵפֶל אַדִּירִים הִקְרִיבָה חֶמְאָה:
כו יָדָהּ לַיָּתֵד תִּשְׁלַחְנָה וִימִינָהּ לְהַלְמוּת
עֲמֵלִים וְהָלְמָה סִיסְרָא מָחֲקָה רֹאשׁוֹ וּמָחֲצָה
וְחָלְפָה רַקָּתוֹ: כז בֵּין רַגְלֶיהָ כָּרַע נָפַל שָׁכָב
בֵּין רַגְלֶיהָ כָּרַע נָפָל בַּאֲשֶׁר כָּרַע שָׁם נָפַל
שָׁדוּד: כח בְּעַד הַחַלּוֹן נִשְׁקְפָה וַתְּיַבֵּב אֵם
סִיסְרָא בְּעַד הָאֶשְׁנָב מַדּוּעַ בֹּשֵׁשׁ רִכְבּוֹ לָבוֹא
מַדּוּעַ אֶחֱרוּ פַּעֲמֵי מַרְכְּבוֹתָיו: כט חַכְמוֹת
שָׂרוֹתֶיהָ תַּעֲנֶינָּה אַף־הִיא תָּשִׁיב אֲמָרֶיהָ לָהּ:
ל הֲלֹא יִמְצְאוּ יְחַלְּקוּ שָׁלָל רַחַם רַחֲמָתַיִם
לְרֹאשׁ גֶּבֶר שְׁלַל צְבָעִים לְסִיסְרָא שְׁלַל
צְבָעִים רִקְמָה צֶבַע רִקְמָתַיִם לְצַוְּארֵי שָׁלָל:
לא כֵּן יֹאבְדוּ כָל־אוֹיְבֶיךָ יְהֹוָה וְאֹהֲבָיו כְּצֵאת
הַשֶּׁמֶשׁ בִּגְבֻרָתוֹ וַתִּשְׁקֹט הָאָרֶץ אַרְבָּעִים שָׁנָה:

HAFTARATH YITHRO הפטרת יתרו
(Isaiah 6:1–13 for Sephardim; Ashkenazim add 7:1–6, 9:5, 6)

This selection contains the vision of the Celestial Chariot, and is therefore reminiscent of the vision the Israelites beheld at Mount Sinai.

6:1. In the year of the death of king Uzziah, I saw the Lord sitting on a high and exalted throne, and His lower extremity filled the Temple. 2. Seraphim stood above for Him, six wings, six wings to each one; with two he would cover his face, and with two he would cover his feet, and with two he would fly. 3. And one called to the other and said, "Holy, holy, holy is the Lord of Hosts; the whole earth is full of His glory." 4. And the doorposts quaked from the voice of him who called, and the House became filled with smoke. 5. And I said, "Woe is me for I am lost, for I am a man of unclean lips, and amidst a people of unclean lips I dwell, for the King, the Lord of Hosts, have my eyes seen. 6. And one of the seraphim flew to me, and in his hand was a glowing coal; with tongs he had taken it from upon the altar. 7. And he caused it to touch my mouth, and he said, "Behold, this has touched your lips; and your iniquity shall be removed, and your sin shall be atoned for." 8. And I heard the voice of the Lord, saying, "Whom shall I send, and who will go for us?" And I said, "Here I am; send me." 9. And He said, Go and say to this people, 'Indeed you hear, but you do not understand; indeed you see, but you do not know.' 10. This heart of his people is becoming fat, and their ears are becoming heavy, and their eyes are becoming sealed, lest they see with their eyes and hear with their ears, and their heart understand, repent and be healed." 11. And I said, "Until when, O Lord?" And He said: Until cities be desolate without inhabitant and houses without people, and the ground lies waste and desolate. 12. And the Lord removes the people far away, and the deserted places be many in the midst of the land. 13. And when there is yet a tenth of it, it will again be purged, like the terebinth and like the oak, which in the fall have but a trunk, the holy seed is its trunk. (*Sephardim conclude here.*) 7:1. And it came to pass in the days of Ahaz son of Jotham son of

א בִּשְׁנַת־מוֹת הַמֶּלֶךְ עֻזִּיָּהוּ וָאֶרְאֶה אֶת־אֲדֹנָי
יֹשֵׁב עַל־כִּסֵּא רָם וְנִשָּׂא וְשׁוּלָיו מְלֵאִים אֶת־
הַהֵיכָל׃ ב שְׂרָפִים עֹמְדִים ׀ מִמַּעַל לוֹ שֵׁשׁ
כְּנָפַיִם שֵׁשׁ כְּנָפַיִם לְאֶחָד בִּשְׁתַּיִם ׀ יְכַסֶּה פָנָיו
וּבִשְׁתַּיִם יְכַסֶּה רַגְלָיו וּבִשְׁתַּיִם יְעוֹפֵף׃
ג וְקָרָא זֶה אֶל־זֶה וְאָמַר קָדוֹשׁ ׀ קָדוֹשׁ קָדוֹשׁ
יְהוָה צְבָאוֹת מְלֹא כָל־הָאָרֶץ כְּבוֹדוֹ׃ ד וַיָּנֻעוּ
אַמּוֹת הַסִּפִּים מִקּוֹל הַקּוֹרֵא וְהַבַּיִת יִמָּלֵא
עָשָׁן׃ ה וָאֹמַר אוֹי־לִי כִי־נִדְמֵיתִי כִּי אִישׁ
טְמֵא־שְׂפָתַיִם אָנֹכִי וּבְתוֹךְ עַם־טְמֵא שְׂפָתַיִם
אָנֹכִי יֹשֵׁב כִּי אֶת־הַמֶּלֶךְ יְהוָה צְבָאוֹת רָאוּ
עֵינָי׃ ו וַיָּעָף אֵלַי אֶחָד מִן־הַשְּׂרָפִים וּבְיָדוֹ
רִצְפָּה בְּמֶלְקַחַיִם לָקַח מֵעַל הַמִּזְבֵּחַ׃ ז וַיַּגַּע
עַל־פִּי וַיֹּאמֶר הִנֵּה נָגַע זֶה עַל־שְׂפָתֶיךָ וְסָר
עֲוֺנֶךָ וְחַטָּאתְךָ תְּכֻפָּר׃ ח וָאֶשְׁמַע אֶת־קוֹל
אֲדֹנָי אֹמֵר אֶת־מִי אֶשְׁלַח וּמִי יֵלֶךְ־לָנוּ וָאֹמַר
הִנְנִי שְׁלָחֵנִי׃ ט וַיֹּאמֶר לֵךְ וְאָמַרְתָּ לָעָם הַזֶּה
שִׁמְעוּ שָׁמוֹעַ וְאַל־תָּבִינוּ וּרְאוּ רָאוֹ וְאַל־
תֵּדָעוּ׃ י הַשְׁמֵן לֵב־הָעָם הַזֶּה וְאָזְנָיו הַכְבֵּד
וְעֵינָיו הָשַׁע פֶּן־יִרְאֶה בְעֵינָיו וּבְאָזְנָיו יִשְׁמָע
וּלְבָבוֹ יָבִין וָשָׁב וְרָפָא לוֹ׃ יא וָאֹמַר עַד־מָתַי
אֲדֹנָי וַיֹּאמֶר עַד אֲשֶׁר אִם־שָׁאוּ עָרִים מֵאֵין
יוֹשֵׁב וּבָתִּים מֵאֵין אָדָם וְהָאֲדָמָה תִּשָּׁאֶה
שְׁמָמָה׃ יב וְרִחַק יְהוָה אֶת־הָאָדָם וְרַבָּה
הָעֲזוּבָה בְּקֶרֶב הָאָרֶץ׃ יג וְעוֹד בָּהּ עֲשִׂרִיָּה
וְשָׁבָה וְהָיְתָה לְבָעֵר כָּאֵלָה וְכָאַלּוֹן אֲשֶׁר
בְּשַׁלֶּכֶת מַצֶּבֶת בָּם זֶרַע קֹדֶשׁ מַצַּבְתָּהּ׃ (כאן
מסיימין הספרדים) א וַיְהִי בִּימֵי אָחָז בֶּן־יוֹתָם בֶּן־

Uzziah, king of Judah, that Rezin, king of Aram, and Pekah son of Remaliah, king of Israel, marched on Jerusalem to wage war against it, and he could not wage war against it. 2. And it was told to the House of David, saying, "Aram has allied itself with Ephraim," and his heart and the heart of his people trembled as the trees of the forest tremble because of the wind. 3. And the Lord said to Isaiah: Now go out toward Ahaz, you and Shear-Yashuv your son, to the edge of the conduit of the upper pool, to the road of the washer's field. 4. And you shall say to him: Feel secure and calm yourself, do not fear, and let your heart not be faint because of these two smoking stubs of firebrands, because of the raging anger of Rezin and Aram and the son of Remaliah. 5. Since Aram planned harm to you, Ephraim and the son of Remaliah, saying: 6. Let us go up against Judah and provoke it, and annex it to us; and let us crown a king in its midst, one who is good for us: 5. For a child has been born to us, a son given to us, and the authority is upon his shoulder; and the wondrous adviser, the mighty God, the everlasting Father, called his name, "the prince of peace." 6. To him who increases the authority, and for peace without end, on David's throne and on his kingdom, to establish it and to support it with justice and with righteousness; from now and to eternity, the zeal of the Lord of Hosts shall accomplish this.

עֻזִּיָּ֙הוּ מֶ֣לֶךְ יְהוּדָ֔ה עָלָ֣ה רְצִ֣ין מֶֽלֶךְ־אֲרָ֡ם וּפֶ֣קַח בֶּן־רְמַלְיָ֩הוּ מֶֽלֶךְ־יִשְׂרָאֵ֨ל יְרוּשָׁלִַ֜ם לַמִּלְחָמָ֣ה עָלֶ֗יהָ וְלֹ֥א יָכֹ֖ל לְהִלָּחֵ֥ם עָלֶֽיהָ׃ ב וַיֻּגַּ֗ד לְבֵ֤ית דָּוִד֙ לֵאמֹ֔ר נָ֥חָֽה אֲרָ֖ם עַל־אֶפְרָ֑יִם וַיָּ֤נַע לְבָבוֹ֙ וּלְבַ֣ב עַמּ֔וֹ כְּנ֥וֹעַ עֲצֵי־יַ֖עַר מִפְּנֵי־רֽוּחַ׃ ג וַיֹּ֣אמֶר יְהוָה֮ אֶֽל־יְשַׁעְיָהוּ֒ צֵא־נָא֙ לִקְרַ֣את אָחָ֔ז אַתָּ֕ה וּשְׁאָ֖ר יָשׁ֣וּב בְּנֶ֑ךָ אֶל־קְצֵ֗ה תְּעָלַת֙ הַבְּרֵכָ֣ה הָעֶלְיוֹנָ֔ה אֶל־מְסִלַּ֖ת שְׂדֵ֥ה כוֹבֵֽס׃ ד וְאָמַרְתָּ֣ אֵ֠לָיו הִשָּׁמֵ֨ר וְהַשְׁקֵ֜ט אַל־תִּירָ֗א וּלְבָבְךָ֙ אַל־יֵרַ֔ךְ מִשְּׁנֵ֨י זַנְב֧וֹת הָאוּדִ֛ים הָעֲשֵׁנִ֖ים הָאֵ֑לֶּה בׇּחֳרִי־אַ֛ף רְצִ֥ין וַאֲרָ֖ם וּבֶן־רְמַלְיָֽהוּ׃ ה יַ֗עַן כִּֽי־יָעַ֥ץ עָלֶ֛יךָ אֲרָ֖ם רָעָ֑ה אֶפְרַ֥יִם וּבֶן־רְמַלְיָ֖הוּ לֵאמֹֽר׃ ו נַעֲלֶ֤ה בִֽיהוּדָה֙ וּנְקִיצֶ֔נָּה וְנַבְקִעֶ֖נָּה אֵלֵ֑ינוּ וְנַמְלִ֥יךְ מֶ֙לֶךְ֙ בְּתוֹכָ֔הּ אֵ֖ת בֶּן־טָֽבְאַֽל׃ ה כִּי־יֶ֣לֶד יֻלַּד־לָ֗נוּ בֵּ֚ן נִתַּן־לָ֔נוּ וַתְּהִ֥י הַמִּשְׂרָ֖ה עַל־שִׁכְמ֑וֹ וַיִּקְרָ֨א שְׁמ֜וֹ פֶּ֠לֶא יוֹעֵץ֙ אֵ֣ל גִּבּ֔וֹר אֲבִי־עַ֖ד שַׂר־שָׁלֽוֹם׃ ו לְמַרְבֵּ֨ה **(לםרבה קרי)** הַמִּשְׂרָ֜ה וּלְשָׁל֣וֹם אֵֽין־קֵ֗ץ עַל־כִּסֵּ֤א דָוִד֙ וְעַ֣ל־מַמְלַכְתּ֔וֹ לְהָכִ֤ין אֹתָהּ֙ וּֽלְסַעֲדָ֔הּ בְּמִשְׁפָּ֖ט וּבִצְדָקָ֑ה מֵעַתָּה֙ וְעַד־עוֹלָ֔ם קִנְאַ֛ת יְהוָ֥ה צְבָא֖וֹת תַּעֲשֶׂה־זֹּֽאת׃

HAFTARATH MISHPATIM　הפטרת משפטים
(Jeremiah 34:8–22; 33:25, 26)
Should Parashath Shekalim fall on this Sabbath, the Haftarah for Shekalim (p. 956) is read. If Rosh Chodesh Adar I coincides with this Sabbath, the Haftarah for Sabbath Rosh Chodesh (p. 930) is read.

The command to free the slaves is the one stated in this Sidra.

34:8. The word that came to Jeremiah from the Lord after the king Zedekiah made a covenant with all the people who were in Jerusalem, to proclaim freedom to them: 9. That every man should let his manservant and every man his maidservant, a Jew and a Jewess, go free, that none should hold his Jewish brother as a slave. 10. Now when all the princes and all the people who had

ח הַדָּבָ֞ר אֲשֶׁר־הָיָ֤ה אֶֽל־יִרְמְיָ֙הוּ֙ מֵאֵ֣ת יְהוָ֔ה אַֽחֲרֵ֡י כְּרֹת֩ הַמֶּ֨לֶךְ צִדְקִיָּ֜הוּ בְּרִ֗ית אֶת־כׇּל־הָעָם֙ אֲשֶׁ֣ר בִּירֽוּשָׁלִַ֔ם לִקְרֹ֥א לָהֶ֖ם דְּרֽוֹר׃ ט לְשַׁלַּ֗ח אִ֣ישׁ אֶת־עַבְדּ֞וֹ וְאִ֧ישׁ אֶת־שִׁפְחָת֛וֹ הָעִבְרִ֥י וְהָעִבְרִיָּ֖ה חׇפְשִׁ֑ים לְבִלְתִּ֧י עֲבָד־בָּ֛ם בִּיהוּדִ֥י אָחִ֖יהוּ אִֽישׁ׃ י וַיִּשְׁמְעוּ֩ כׇל־הַשָּׂרִ֨ים וְכׇל־הָעָ֜ם

entered into the covenant heard that everyone should let his manservant and everyone
his maidservant go free, no longer hold
them in slavery, they obeyed and let them
go. 11. But afterwards they turned and
brought back the manservants and the
maidservants whom they had let free, and
forcibly made them into menservants and
maidservants. 12. Then the word of the
Lord came to Jeremiah from the Lord,
saying: 13. So says the Lord God of Israel: I
made a covenant with your fathers on the
day that I brought them forth out of the
land of Egypt, out of the house of slaves,
saying: 14. "At the end of seven years you
shall let go every man his brother Jew who
has been sold to you, and when he has
served you for six years you shall let him go
free from you''; but your fathers did not
obey Me, nor did they incline their ear.
15. And now this day you turned and did
what was right in My sight in proclaiming
liberty every man to his neighbor, and you
made a covenant before Me in the House
upon which My Name is called. 16. But
then you turned and profaned My Name,
and you brought back, each man his manservant and each man his maidservant,
whom you had let go free to themselves,
and forced them to be menservants and
maidservants to you. 17. Therefore, so says
the Lord: You have not hearkened to Me to
proclaim freedom, every one to his brother
and every one to his neighbor; behold I
proclaim freedom to the sword, to the pestilence, and to the famine to you, says the
Lord, and I will make you an object of
horror to all the kingdoms of the earth.
18. And I will deliver the men who have
transgressed My covenant, who have not
kept the words of the covenant which they
made before Me when they cut the calf in
two and passed before its parts. 19. The
princes of Judah and the princes of Jerusalem, the officers and the priests and all the
people of the land who passed between the
parts of the calf — 20. I will deliver them
into the hand of their enemies and into the
hand of those who seek their lives, and their
dead bodies shall become food for the birds
of the heavens and for the beasts of the
earth. 21. And Zedekiah, king of Judah, and
his princes I will deliver into the hand of

אֲשֶׁר־בָּ֣אוּ בַבְּרִ֔ית לְשַׁלַּ֗ח אִ֣ישׁ אֶת־עַבְדּ֞וֹ
וְאִ֣ישׁ אֶת־שִׁפְחָתוֹ֮ חָפְשִׁים֒ לְבִלְתִּ֥י עֲבָד־בָּ֖ם
ע֑וֹד וַיִּשְׁמְע֖וּ וַיְשַׁלֵּֽחוּ: יא וַיָּשׁ֜וּבוּ אַחֲרֵי־כֵ֗ן
וַיָּשִׁ֙בוּ֙ אֶת־הָ֣עֲבָדִ֔ים וְאֶת־הַשְּׁפָח֖וֹת אֲשֶׁ֣ר
שִׁלְּח֣וּ חָפְשִׁ֑ים וַֽיִּכְבְּשׁ֔וּם (ויכבשום קרי) לַעֲבָדִ֖ים
וְלִשְׁפָחֽוֹת: יב וַיְהִ֤י דְבַר־יְהוָֹה֙ אֶֽל־יִרְמְיָ֔הוּ
מֵאֵ֥ת יְהוָֹ֖ה לֵאמֹֽר: יג כֹּֽה־אָמַ֞ר יְהוָֹ֣ה אֱלֹהֵ֣י
יִשְׂרָאֵ֗ל אָֽנֹכִ֞י כָּרַ֤תִּי בְרִית֙ אֶת־אֲב֣וֹתֵיכֶ֔ם בְּי֨וֹם
הֽוֹצִאִ֤י אוֹתָם֙ מֵאֶ֣רֶץ מִצְרַ֔יִם מִבֵּ֥ית עֲבָדִ֖ים
לֵאמֹֽר: יד מִקֵּ֣ץ שֶׁ֣בַע שָׁנִ֗ים תְּשַׁלְּ֞חוּ אִ֣ישׁ אֶת־
אָחִ֣יו הָֽעִבְרִ֗י אֲשֶֽׁר־יִמָּכֵ֤ר לְךָ֙ וַעֲבָֽדְךָ֙ שֵׁ֣שׁ
שָׁנִ֔ים וְשִׁלַּחְתּ֥וֹ חָפְשִׁ֖י מֵעִמָּ֑ךְ וְלֹֽא־שָׁמְע֤וּ
אֲבֽוֹתֵיכֶם֙ אֵלַ֔י וְלֹ֥א הִטּ֖וּ אֶת־אָזְנָֽם: טו וַתָּשֻׁ֨בוּ
אַתֶּ֜ם הַיּ֗וֹם וַתַּעֲשׂ֤וּ אֶת־הַיָּשָׁר֙ בְּעֵינַ֔י לִקְרֹ֥א
דְר֖וֹר אִ֣ישׁ לְרֵעֵ֑הוּ וַתִּכְרְת֤וּ בְרִית֙ לְפָנַ֔י בַּבַּ֕יִת
אֲשֶׁר־נִקְרָ֥א שְׁמִ֖י עָלָֽיו: טז וַתָּשֻׁ֙בוּ֙ וַתְּחַלְּל֣וּ
אֶת־שְׁמִ֔י וַתָּשִׁ֗בוּ אִ֤ישׁ אֶת־עַבְדּוֹ֙ וְאִ֣ישׁ אֶת־
שִׁפְחָת֔וֹ אֲשֶׁר־שִׁלַּחְתֶּ֥ם חָפְשִׁ֖ים לְנַפְשָׁ֑ם
וַתִּכְבְּשׁ֣וּ אֹתָ֔ם לִֽהְי֣וֹת לָכֶ֔ם לַעֲבָדִ֖ים וְלִשְׁפָחֽוֹת:
יז לָכֵ֞ן כֹּֽה־אָמַ֣ר יְהוָֹ֗ה אַתֶּם֙ לֹֽא־שְׁמַעְתֶּ֣ם אֵלַ֔י
לִקְרֹ֣א דְר֔וֹר אִ֤ישׁ לְאָחִיו֙ וְאִ֣ישׁ לְרֵעֵ֔הוּ הִנְנִ֣י
קֹרֵ֩א לָכֶ֨ם דְּר֜וֹר נְאֻם־יְהוָֹ֗ה אֶל־הַחֶ֙רֶב֙ אֶל־
הַדֶּ֣בֶר וְאֶל־הָֽרָעָ֔ב וְנָתַתִּ֥י אֶתְכֶ֖ם לְזַוָֹעָ֑ה (לזעוה
קרי) לְכֹ֖ל מַמְלְכ֥וֹת הָאָֽרֶץ: יח וְנָֽתַתִּ֣י אֶת־
הָֽאֲנָשִׁ֗ים הָעֹֽבְרִים֙ אֶת־בְּרִתִ֔י אֲשֶׁ֤ר לֹֽא־הֵקִ֙ימוּ֙
אֶת־דִּבְרֵ֣י הַבְּרִ֔ית אֲשֶׁ֥ר כָּרְת֖וּ לְפָנָ֑י הָעֵ֙גֶל֙ אֲשֶׁ֣ר
כָּרְת֣וּ לִשְׁנַ֔יִם וַיַּעַבְר֖וּ בֵּ֥ין בְּתָרָֽיו: יט שָׂרֵ֨י
יְהוּדָ֜ה וְשָׂרֵ֣י יְרֽוּשָׁלִַ֗ם הַסָּֽרִסִים֙ וְהַכֹּ֣הֲנִ֔ים וְכֹ֖ל
עַ֣ם הָאָ֑רֶץ הָעֹ֣בְרִ֔ים בֵּ֖ין בִּתְרֵ֥י הָעֵֽגֶל: כ וְנָתַתִּ֤י
אוֹתָם֙ בְּיַ֣ד אֹֽיְבֵיהֶ֔ם וּבְיַ֖ד מְבַקְשֵׁ֣י נַפְשָׁ֑ם וְהָיְתָ֤ה
נִבְלָתָם֙ לְמַֽאֲכָ֔ל לְע֥וֹף הַשָּׁמַ֖יִם וּלְבֶהֱמַ֥ת הָאָֽרֶץ:
כא וְאֶת־צִדְקִיָּ֨הוּ מֶֽלֶךְ־יְהוּדָ֣ה וְאֶת־שָׂרָיו֮ אֶתֵּן֒

their enemies and into the hand of those who seek their lives, and into the hand of the army of the king of Babylon who have gone up away from you. 22. Behold I command, says the Lord, And I will return them to this city, and they shall fight against it and capture it, and burn it with fire, and the cities of Judah I will make desolate without an inhabitant. 33:25. So says the Lord: If My covenant, the sequence of day and night no longer exists, if I have not established the laws of heaven and earth, 26. also the seed of Jacob and David My servant will I reject, from taking from his seed rulers for the descendants of Abraham, Isaac, and Jacob, for I will bring back their captives and have mercy on them.

בְּיַד אֹיְבֵיהֶם וּבְיַד מְבַקְשֵׁי נַפְשָׁם וּבְיַד חֵיל מֶלֶךְ בָּבֶל הָעֹלִים מֵעֲלֵיכֶם: כב הִנְנִי מְצַוֶּה נְאֻם־יְהוָֹה וַהֲשִׁבֹתִים אֶל־הָעִיר הַזֹּאת וְנִלְחֲמוּ עָלֶיהָ וּלְכָדוּהָ וּשְׂרָפֻהָ בָאֵשׁ וְאֶת־עָרֵי יְהוּדָה אֶתֵּן שְׁמָמָה מֵאֵין יֹשֵׁב: כה כֹּה אָמַר יְהוָֹה אִם־לֹא בְרִיתִי יוֹמָם וָלָיְלָה חֻקּוֹת שָׁמַיִם וָאָרֶץ לֹא־שָׂמְתִּי: כו גַּם־זֶרַע יַעֲקוֹב וְדָוִד עַבְדִּי אֶמְאַס מִקַּחַת מִזַּרְעוֹ מֹשְׁלִים אֶל־זֶרַע אַבְרָהָם יִשְׂחָק וְיַעֲקֹב כִּי־אָשׁוּב (אשיב קרי) אֶת־שְׁבוּתָם וְרִחַמְתִּים:

HAFTARATH TERUMAH　הפטרת תרומה
(I Kings 5:26-6:13)

Should Parashath Zachor fall on this Sabbath, the Haftarah for Zachor (p. 958) is read. Should Parashath Shekalim fall on this Sabbath, the Haftarah for Shekalim (p. 956) is read. If Rosh Chodesh Adar I coincides with the Sabbath the Haftarah for Sabbath Rosh Chodesh (p. 930) is read.

The building of the Temple and the preparations for it described in this selection are a historic parallel to the erection of the Tabernacle in the wilderness, discussed in the Sidra.

5:26. And the Lord gave Solomon wisdom, as He had promised him, and there was peace between Hiram and Solomon, and they both made a league together. 27. And King Solomon raised a levy out of all Israel, and the levy was thirty thousand men. 28. And he sent them to Lebanon, ten thousand a month alternately; a month they were in Lebanon, [and] two months at home, and Adoniram [was] over the levy. 29. And Solomon had seventy thousand who bore burdens, and eighty thousand hewers in the mountains, 30. besides Solomon's chief officers that were over the work, three thousand and three hundred, who bore rule over the people that wrought in the work. 31. And the king commanded, and they quarried great stones, heavy stones, to lay the foundation of the house [with] hewn stone. 32. And Solomon's builders and Hiram's builders and the Gebalites hewed [them], and they prepared the timber and the stones to build the

כו וַיהוָֹה נָתַן חָכְמָה לִשְׁלֹמֹה כַּאֲשֶׁר דִּבֶּר־לוֹ וַיְהִי שָׁלֹם בֵּין חִירָם וּבֵין שְׁלֹמֹה וַיִּכְרְתוּ בְרִית שְׁנֵיהֶם: כז וַיַּעַל הַמֶּלֶךְ שְׁלֹמֹה מַס מִכָּל־יִשְׂרָאֵל וַיְהִי הַמַּס שְׁלֹשִׁים אֶלֶף אִישׁ: כח וַיִּשְׁלָחֵם לְבָנוֹנָה עֲשֶׂרֶת אֲלָפִים בַּחֹדֶשׁ חֲלִיפוֹת חֹדֶשׁ יִהְיוּ בַלְּבָנוֹן שְׁנַיִם חֳדָשִׁים בְּבֵיתוֹ וַאֲדֹנִירָם עַל־הַמַּס: כט וַיְהִי לִשְׁלֹמֹה שִׁבְעִים אֶלֶף נֹשֵׂא סַבָּל וּשְׁמֹנִים אֶלֶף חֹצֵב בָּהָר: ל לְבַד מִשָּׂרֵי הַנִּצָּבִים לִשְׁלֹמֹה אֲשֶׁר עַל־הַמְּלָאכָה שְׁלֹשֶׁת אֲלָפִים וּשְׁלֹשׁ מֵאוֹת הָרֹדִים בָּעָם הָעֹשִׂים בַּמְּלָאכָה: לא וַיְצַו הַמֶּלֶךְ וַיַּסִּעוּ אֲבָנִים גְּדֹלוֹת אֲבָנִים יְקָרוֹת לְיַסֵּד הַבָּיִת אַבְנֵי גָזִית: לב וַיִּפְסְלוּ בֹּנֵי שְׁלֹמֹה וּבֹנֵי חִירוֹם וְהַגִּבְלִים וַיָּכִינוּ הָעֵצִים וְהָאֲבָנִים

לִבְנ֥וֹת הַבָּֽיִת׃ א וַיְהִ֣י בִשְׁמוֹנִ֣ים שָׁנָ֣ה וְאַרְבַּ֣ע
מֵא֪וֹת שָׁנָ֟ה לְצֵ֣את בְּנֵֽי־יִשְׂרָאֵ֣ל מֵאֶֽרֶץ־מִצְרַ֡יִם
בַּשָּׁנָ֣ה הָרְבִיעִ֡ית בְּחֹ֣דֶשׁ זִ֠ו ה֚וּא הַחֹ֣דֶשׁ הַשֵּׁנִ֔י
לִמְלֹ֥ךְ שְׁלֹמֹ֖ה עַל־יִשְׂרָאֵ֑ל וַיִּ֥בֶן הַבַּ֖יִת לַיהוָֽה׃
ב וְהַבַּ֗יִת אֲשֶׁ֨ר בָּנָ֜ה הַמֶּ֤לֶךְ שְׁלֹמֹה֙ לַֽיהוָ֔ה
שִׁשִּֽׁים־אַמָּ֤ה אָרְכּוֹ֙ וְעֶשְׂרִ֣ים רָחְבּ֔וֹ וּשְׁלֹשִׁ֥ים
אַמָּ֖ה קוֹמָתֽוֹ׃ ג וְהָֽאוּלָ֗ם עַל־פְּנֵי֙ הֵיכַ֣ל הַבַּ֔יִת
עֶשְׂרִ֤ים אַמָּה֙ אָרְכּ֔וֹ עַל־פְּנֵ֖י רֹ֣חַב הַבָּ֑יִת עֶ֧שֶׂר
בָּאַמָּ֛ה רָחְבּ֖וֹ עַל־פְּנֵ֥י הַבָּֽיִת׃ ד וַיַּ֣עַשׂ לַבָּ֔יִת
חַלּוֹנֵ֖י שְׁקֻפִ֥ים אֲטֻמִֽים׃ ה וַיִּבֶן֩ עַל־קִ֨יר הַבַּ֤יִת
יָצִ֙וע (יציע קרי) סָבִ֔יב אֶת־קִיר֤וֹת הַבַּ֙יִת֙ סָבִ֔יב
לַֽהֵיכָ֖ל וְלַדְּבִ֑יר וַיַּ֥עַשׂ צְלָע֖וֹת סָבִֽיב׃ ו הַיָּצִ֨וע
(היציע קרי) הַתַּחְתֹּנָ֜ה חָמֵ֧שׁ בָּאַמָּ֣ה רָחְבָּ֗הּ
וְהַתִּֽיכֹנָה֙ שֵׁ֤שׁ בָּֽאַמָּה֙ רָחְבָּ֔הּ וְהַשְּׁלִישִׁ֕ית שֶׁ֥בַע
בָּאַמָּ֖ה רָחְבָּ֑הּ כִּ֣י מִגְרָע֗וֹת נָתַ֨ן לַבַּ֤יִת סָבִיב֙
ח֔וּצָה לְבִלְתִּ֖י אֲחֹ֥ז בְּקִירוֹת הַבָּֽיִת׃ ז וְהַבַּ֙יִת֙
בְּהִבָּ֣נֹת֔וֹ אֶ֧בֶן שְׁלֵמָ֛ה מַסָּ֖ע נִבְנָ֑ה וּמַקָּב֤וֹת
וְהַגַּרְזֶן֙ כָּל־כְּלִ֣י בַרְזֶ֔ל לֹֽא־נִשְׁמַ֥ע בַּבַּ֖יִת
בְּהִבָּנֹתֽוֹ׃ ח פֶּ֗תַח הַצֵּלָע֙ הַתִּ֣יכֹנָ֔ה אֶל־כֶּ֥תֶף
הַבַּ֖יִת הַיְמָנִ֑ית וּבְלוּלִּ֣ים יַעֲל֗וּ עַל־הַתִּ֣יכֹנָ֔ה
וּמִן־הַתִּיכֹנָ֖ה אֶל־הַשְּׁלִשִֽׁים׃ ט וַיִּ֥בֶן אֶת־הַבַּ֖יִת
וַיְכַלֵּ֑הוּ וַיִּסְפֹּ֤ן אֶת־הַבַּ֙יִת֙ גֵּבִ֣ים וּשְׂדֵרֹ֔ת
בָּאֲרָזִֽים׃ י וַיִּ֤בֶן אֶת־הַיָּצִ֙וע֙ (היציע קרי) עַל־כָּל־
הַבַּ֔יִת חָמֵ֥שׁ אַמּ֖וֹת קוֹמָת֑וֹ וַיֶּאֱחֹ֥ז אֶת־הַבַּ֖יִת
בַּעֲצֵ֥י אֲרָזִֽים׃ יא וַֽיְהִי֙ דְּבַר־יְהוָ֔ה אֶל־שְׁלֹמֹ֖ה
לֵאמֹֽר׃ יב הַבַּ֨יִת הַזֶּ֜ה אֲשֶׁר־אַתָּ֣ה בֹנֶ֗ה אִם־
תֵּלֵ֤ךְ בְּחֻקֹּתַי֙ וְאֶת־מִשְׁפָּטַ֣י תַּעֲשֶׂ֔ה וְשָׁמַרְתָּ֥
אֶת־כָּל־מִצְוֺתַ֖י לָלֶ֣כֶת בָּהֶ֑ם וַהֲקִמֹתִ֤י אֶת־דְּבָרִי֙
אִתָּ֔ךְ אֲשֶׁ֥ר דִּבַּ֖רְתִּי אֶל־דָּוִ֥ד אָבִֽיךָ׃ יג וְשָׁ֣כַנְתִּ֔י
בְּת֖וֹךְ בְּנֵ֣י יִשְׂרָאֵ֑ל וְלֹ֥א אֶעֱזֹ֖ב אֶת־עַמִּ֥י
יִשְׂרָאֵֽל׃

house. 6:1. And it was in the four hundred and eightieth year after the departure of the children of Israel from Egypt, in the fourth year of Solomon's reign over Israel, in the month Ziv, which [is] the second month, that he did [begin to] build the house of the Lord. 2. And the house which king Solomon built for the Lord, the length thereof [was] sixty cubits, and the breadth thereof twenty cubits, and the height thereof thirty cubits. 3. And the porch before the temple of the house, twenty cubits [was] the length thereof, before the breadth of the house, [and] ten cubits [was] the breadth thereof before the house. 4. And he made for the house windows broad within, and narrow without. 5. And against the wall of the house he built a chamber round about, [against] the walls of the house round about, [both] of the Temple and of the Sanctuary, and he made chambers round about. 6. The nethermost chamber [was] five cubits broad, and the middle [was] six cubits broad, and the third [was] seven cubits broad, for he made rebatements in [the wall of] the house round about on the outside, that [the beams] should not have hold in the walls of the house. 7. And the house, when it was in building, was built of stone finished at the quarry, and there was neither hammer nor axe [nor] any tool of iron heard in the house, while it was in building. 8. The door of the lowest chamber [was] in the right side of the house, and with winding stairs they went up into the middle [chamber], and from the middle into the third. 9. And he built the house, and finished it, and he covered the house with panelling and joined planks of cedar. 10. And he built the chambers against all the house, [each] five cubits high, and he covered the house with timber of cedar. 11. And the word of the Lord came to Solomon saying, 12. [Concerning] this house which you are building, if you walk in My statutes, and execute My ordinances, and keep all My commandments to walk in them; then will I establish My word with you, which I spoke to David your father. 13. And I will dwell among the children of Israel, and will not forsake My people Israel.

HAFTARATH TETZAVEH הפטרת תצוה

(Ezekiel 43:10–27)

Should Parashath Zachor fall on this Sabbath, the Haftarah for Zachor (p. 958) is read.

Here Ezekiel, the prophet of the Exile, envisions the dedication of the altar in the future Temple. This is reminiscent of the dedication of the altar of the Tabernacle, as depicted in the Sidra.

43:10. You, son of man, describe the House graphically to the house of Israel, that they may be ashamed of their iniquities; let them measure its plan. 11. And if they are ashamed of all that they have done, let them know the form of the house and its arrangement, its exits and its entrances, and all its forms, and all its laws and all its teachings, and write it down in their sight so that they keep the whole form thereof and the laws thereof, and do them. 12. This is the teaching of the House: Upon the top of the mountain, all its boundary round about shall be most holy; behold, this is the teaching of the House. 13. And these are the measurements of the altar in cubits: the cubit, one cubit and one handbreadth, but for the base one ordinary cubit, and such a cubit also for the breadth; and its border to its edge around one span, and equally so the very top of the altar. 14. And from the base on the ground to the lower edge shall be two cubits; and the breadth one cubit; and from the smaller ledge to the greater ledge, four cubits; and the breadth, one cubit. 15. And the altar hearth shall be four cubits, and from the altar hearth and above, the horns shall be four. 16. And the altar hearth shall be twelve [cubits in] length by twelve [cubits in] breadth, square to its four sides. 17. And the upper ledge, fourteen [cubits in] length by fourteen [cubits in] breadth, to its four sides, and the boundary around it half a cubit, and its base a cubit around, and its ascent shall look towards the east. 18. And He said to me: Son of man, thus says the Lord God: These are the ordinances of the altar on the day when it will be made, to offer burnt offerings thereon and to sprinkle blood thereon. 19. And you shall give it to the priests, the Levites, who are of the seed of Zadok, who are near to Me, says the Lord God, to serve Me, a young bull for

י אַתָּה בֶן־אָדָם הַגֵּד אֶת־בֵּית־יִשְׂרָאֵל אֶת־
הַבַּיִת וְיִכָּלְמוּ מֵעֲוֺנוֹתֵיהֶם וּמָדְדוּ אֶת־תָּכְנִית׃
יא וְאִם־נִכְלְמוּ מִכֹּל אֲשֶׁר־עָשׂוּ צוּרַת הַבַּיִת
וּתְכוּנָתוֹ וּמוֹצָאָיו וּמוֹבָאָיו ׀ וְכָל־צוּרֹתָו וְאֵת
כָּל־חֻקֹּתָיו וְכָל־צוּרֹתָו וְכָל־תּוֹרֹתָו הוֹדַע
אוֹתָם וּכְתֹב לְעֵינֵיהֶם וְיִשְׁמְרוּ אֶת־כָּל־צוּרָתוֹ
וְאֶת־כָּל־חֻקֹּתָיו וְעָשׂוּ אוֹתָם׃ יב זֹאת תּוֹרַת
הַבָּיִת עַל־רֹאשׁ הָהָר כָּל־גְּבֻלוֹ סָבִיב ׀ סָבִיב
קֹדֶשׁ קָדָשִׁים הִנֵּה־זֹאת תּוֹרַת הַבָּיִת׃ יג וְאֵלֶּה
מִדּוֹת הַמִּזְבֵּחַ בָּאַמּוֹת אַמָּה אַמָּה וָטֹפַח וְחֵיק
הָאַמָּה וְאַמָּה־רֹחַב וּגְבוּלָהּ אֶל־שְׂפָתָהּ סָבִיב
זֶרֶת הָאֶחָד וְזֶה גַּב הַמִּזְבֵּחַ׃ יד וּמֵחֵיק הָאָרֶץ
עַד־הָעֲזָרָה הַתַּחְתּוֹנָה שְׁתַּיִם אַמּוֹת וְרֹחַב
אַמָּה אֶחָת וּמֵהָעֲזָרָה הַקְּטַנָּה עַד־הָעֲזָרָה
הַגְּדוֹלָה אַרְבַּע אַמּוֹת וְרֹחַב הָאַמָּה׃ טו וְהַהַרְאֵל
אַרְבַּע אַמּוֹת וּמֵהָאֲרִאֵיל וּלְמַעְלָה הַקְּרָנוֹת
אַרְבַּע׃ טז וְהָאֲרִאֵיל שְׁתֵּים עֶשְׂרֵה אֹרֶךְ
בִּשְׁתֵּים עֶשְׂרֵה רֹחַב רָבוּעַ אֶל אַרְבַּעַת
רְבָעָיו׃ יז וְהָעֲזָרָה אַרְבַּע עֶשְׂרֵה אֹרֶךְ בְּאַרְבַּע
עֶשְׂרֵה רֹחַב אֶל אַרְבַּעַת רְבָעֶיהָ וְהַגְּבוּל סָבִיב
אוֹתָהּ חֲצִי הָאַמָּה וְהַחֵיק־לָהּ אַמָּה סָבִיב
וּמַעֲלֹתֵהוּ פְּנוֹת קָדִים׃ יח וַיֹּאמֶר אֵלַי בֶּן־אָדָם
כֹּה אָמַר אֲדֹנָי יֱהוִה אֵלֶּה חֻקּוֹת הַמִּזְבֵּחַ בְּיוֹם
הֵעָשׂוֹתוֹ לְהַעֲלוֹת עָלָיו עוֹלָה וְלִזְרֹק עָלָיו דָּם׃
יט וְנָתַתָּה אֶל־הַכֹּהֲנִים הַלְוִיִּם אֲשֶׁר הֵם מִזֶּרַע
צָדוֹק הַקְּרֹבִים אֵלַי נְאֻם אֲדֹנָי יֱהוִה לְשָׁרְתֵנִי

a sin-offering. 20. And you shall take of its blood and place it on its four horns and on the four corners of the upper edge and to the border around, and you shall purify it and make it fit for atonement. 21. And you shall take the bull of the sin-offering, and he shall burn it on the appointed place of the House, outside the Sanctuary. 22. And on the second day you shall offer a he-goat without blemish for a sin-offering, and they shall purify the altar as they purified it with the bull. 23. When you have completed the purification, you shall bring near a young bull without a blemish and a ram without a blemish from the flock. 24. And you shall offer them before the Lord, and the priests shall cast salt upon them, and offer them up to God as a burnt offering. 25. For seven days shall you make a he-goat for a sin-offering every day, and a young bull and a ram from the flock without blemish shall they make. 26. For seven days shall they effect atonement for the altar, and purify it and dedicate it. 27. And when they have completed these days, then it shall be that on the eighth day and thenceforth the priests shall make your burnt offerings and your peace offerings on the altar, and I will accept you with satisfaction, says the Lord God.

פַּר בֶּן־בָּקָר לְחַטָּאת: כ וְלָקַחְתָּ מִדָּמוֹ וְנָתַתָּה עַל־אַרְבַּע קַרְנוֹתָיו וְאֶל־אַרְבַּע פִּנּוֹת הָעֲזָרָה וְאֶל־הַגְּבוּל סָבִיב וְחִטֵּאתָ אוֹתוֹ וְכִפַּרְתָּהוּ: כא וְלָקַחְתָּ אֵת הַפָּר הַחַטָּאת וּשְׂרָפוֹ בְּמִפְקַד הַבַּיִת מִחוּץ לַמִּקְדָּשׁ: כב וּבַיּוֹם הַשֵּׁנִי תַּקְרִיב שְׂעִיר־עִזִּים תָּמִים לְחַטָּאת וְחִטְּאוּ אֶת־הַמִּזְבֵּחַ כַּאֲשֶׁר חִטְּאוּ בַּפָּר: כג בְּכַלּוֹתְךָ מֵחַטֵּא תַּקְרִיב פַּר בֶּן־בָּקָר תָּמִים וְאַיִל מִן־הַצֹּאן תָּמִים: כד וְהִקְרַבְתָּם לִפְנֵי יְהֹוָה וְהִשְׁלִיכוּ הַכֹּהֲנִים עֲלֵיהֶם מֶלַח וְהֶעֱלוּ אוֹתָם עֹלָה לַיהֹוָה: כה שִׁבְעַת יָמִים תַּעֲשֶׂה שְׂעִיר־חַטָּאת לַיּוֹם וּפַר בֶּן־בָּקָר וְאַיִל מִן־הַצֹּאן תְּמִימִם יַעֲשׂוּ: כו שִׁבְעַת יָמִים יְכַפְּרוּ אֶת־הַמִּזְבֵּחַ וְטִהֲרוּ אֹתוֹ וּמִלְאוּ יָדָו: כז וִיכַלּוּ אֶת־הַיָּמִים וְהָיָה בַיּוֹם הַשְּׁמִינִי וָהָלְאָה יַעֲשׂוּ הַכֹּהֲנִים עַל־הַמִּזְבֵּחַ אֶת־עוֹלוֹתֵיכֶם וְאֶת־שַׁלְמֵיכֶם וְרָצִאתִי אֶתְכֶם נְאֻם אֲדֹנָי יֱהֹוִה:

HAFTARATH KI THISSA הפטרת כי תשא
(I Kings 18:1–39 for Ashkenazim. Sephardim and the congregation of Frankfort-on-the-Main commence with verse 20.)
Should Parashath Parah fall on this Sabbath, the Haftarah for Parah (p. 960) is read.

In this selection, Elijah castigates the people for their worship of Baal. This is reminiscent of Moses' castigation of Israel after the episode of the Golden Calf.

18:1. And it was [after] many days that the word of God came to Elijah in the third year, saying, "Go, appear to Ahab and I will give rain upon the surface of the earth." 2. And Elijah went to appear to Ahab. Now the famine was severe in the land. 3. Ahab had called to Obadiah, who was over the household, and Obadiah feared of the Lord greatly. 4. And it was when Jezebel cut off the prophets of the Lord that Obadiah took one hundred prophets and his them fifty men in a cave, and he nourished them with bread and water. 5. And Ahab said to

א וַיְהִי יָמִים רַבִּים וּדְבַר יְהֹוָה הָיָה אֶל־אֵלִיָּהוּ בַּשָּׁנָה הַשְּׁלִישִׁית לֵאמֹר לֵךְ הֵרָאֵה אֶל־אַחְאָב וְאֶתְּנָה מָטָר עַל־פְּנֵי הָאֲדָמָה: ב וַיֵּלֶךְ אֵלִיָּהוּ לְהֵרָאוֹת אֶל־אַחְאָב וְהָרָעָב חָזָק בְּשֹׁמְרוֹן: ג וַיִּקְרָא אַחְאָב אֶל־עֹבַדְיָהוּ אֲשֶׁר עַל־הַבָּיִת וְעֹבַדְיָהוּ הָיָה יָרֵא אֶת־יְהֹוָה מְאֹד: ד וַיְהִי בְּהַכְרִית אִיזֶבֶל אֵת נְבִיאֵי יְהֹוָה וַיִּקַּח עֹבַדְיָהוּ מֵאָה נְבִיאִים וַיַּחְבִּיאֵם חֲמִשִּׁים אִישׁ בַּמְּעָרָה וְכִלְכְּלָם לֶחֶם וָמָיִם: ה וַיֹּאמֶר אַחְאָב

Obadiah, "Go in the land to all the wells of
water and to all the brooks, maybe we will
find grass, and we will save the lives of horse
and mule and we will not lose all our
beasts." 6. They divided the land between
them to pass through it; Ahab went on one
way by himself and Obadiah went on one
way by himself. 7. Now Obadiah was on the
road, and behold Elijah was in front of him.
He recognized him and fell on his face, and
he said, "Is this you, my master, Elijah?"
8. And he said to him, "This is I. Go and
tell your master, 'Here is Elijah.'" 9. And
he said, "What have I sinned that you have
delivered your servant into the hands of
Ahab to kill me? 10. As the Lord your God
lives, if there is a nation or a kingdom where
my master has not sent to search for you,
and they have said, 'He is not there,' and he
adjured the kingdom and nation that they
did not find you. 11. And now you say, 'Go
tell your master, Here is Elijah.' 12. And it
will be that I will go from here, and a wind
from the Lord will carry you to [a place] I
know not where, and I will come to tell
Ahab, and he will not find you, and he will
kill me; yet your servant fears the Lord from
my youth. 13. My master was surely told
what I did when Jezebel killed all the
prophets of the Lord. I hid one hundred
men of the prophets of the Lord by fifty
men in a cave, and provided them with
bread and water. 14. And now you say 'Go
tell your master, Here is Elijah'; and he
will kill me." 15. And Elijah said, "As the
Lord of Hosts before whom I have stood,
lives, I will appear to him today." 16. And
Obadiah went towards Ahab and he told
him, and Ahab went towards Elijah.
17. And it was when Ahab saw Elijah, that
Ahab said to him, "Is this you, the one who
brings trouble upon Israel?" 18. And he
said, "I have not brought trouble upon
Israel, but you and your father's house,
since you have forsaken the commandments
of the Lord, and you went after the Baalim.
19. And now, send and gather for me all of
Israel to Mount Carmel, and the prophets of
the Baal four hundred and fifty and the
prophets of the Ashera four hundred who
eat at Jezebel's table. *(Sephardim commence here as do those congregations following the ritual of Frankfort-on-the-*

אֶל־עֹבַדְיָהוּ לֵךְ בָּאָרֶץ אֶל־כָּל־מַעְיְנֵי הַמַּיִם
וְאֶל כָּל־הַנְּחָלִים אוּלַי ׀ נִמְצָא חָצִיר וּנְחַיֶּה
סוּס וָפֶרֶד וְלוֹא נַכְרִית מֵהַבְּהֵמָה: ו וַיְחַלְּקוּ
לָהֶם אֶת־הָאָרֶץ לַעֲבָר־בָּהּ אַחְאָב הָלַךְ בְּדֶרֶךְ
אֶחָד לְבַדּוֹ וְעֹבַדְיָהוּ הָלַךְ בְּדֶרֶךְ־אֶחָד לְבַדּוֹ:
ז וַיְהִי עֹבַדְיָהוּ בַּדֶּרֶךְ וְהִנֵּה אֵלִיָּהוּ לִקְרָאתוֹ
וַיַּכִּרֵהוּ וַיִּפֹּל עַל־פָּנָיו וַיֹּאמֶר הַאַתָּה זֶה אֲדֹנִי
אֵלִיָּהוּ: ח וַיֹּאמֶר לוֹ אָנִי לֵךְ אֱמֹר לַאדֹנֶיךָ
הִנֵּה אֵלִיָּהוּ: ט וַיֹּאמֶר מֶה חָטָאתִי כִּי־אַתָּה
נֹתֵן אֶת־עַבְדְּךָ בְּיַד־אַחְאָב לַהֲמִיתֵנִי: י חַי ׀
יְהֹוָה אֱלֹהֶיךָ אִם־יֶשׁ־גּוֹי וּמַמְלָכָה אֲשֶׁר לֹא־
שָׁלַח אֲדֹנִי שָׁם לְבַקֶּשְׁךָ וְאָמְרוּ אָיִן וְהִשְׁבִּיעַ
אֶת־הַמַּמְלָכָה וְאֶת־הַגּוֹי כִּי לֹא יִמְצָאֶכָּה:
יא וְעַתָּה אַתָּה אֹמֵר לֵךְ אֱמֹר לַאדֹנֶיךָ הִנֵּה
אֵלִיָּהוּ: יב וְהָיָה אֲנִי ׀ אֵלֵךְ מֵאִתָּךְ וְרוּחַ יְהֹוָה ׀
יִשָּׂאֲךָ עַל אֲשֶׁר לֹא־אֵדַע וּבָאתִי לְהַגִּיד
לְאַחְאָב וְלֹא יִמְצָאֲךָ וַהֲרָגָנִי וְעַבְדְּךָ יָרֵא אֶת־
יְהֹוָה מִנְּעֻרָי: יג הֲלֹא־הֻגַּד לַאדֹנִי אֵת אֲשֶׁר־
עָשִׂיתִי בַּהֲרֹג אִיזֶבֶל אֵת נְבִיאֵי יְהֹוָה וָאַחְבִּא
מִנְּבִיאֵי יְהֹוָה מֵאָה אִישׁ חֲמִשִּׁים חֲמִשִּׁים אִישׁ
בַּמְּעָרָה וָאֲכַלְכְּלֵם לֶחֶם וָמָיִם: יד וְעַתָּה אַתָּה
אֹמֵר לֵךְ אֱמֹר לַאדֹנֶיךָ הִנֵּה אֵלִיָּהוּ וַהֲרָגָנִי:
טו וַיֹּאמֶר אֵלִיָּהוּ חַי יְהֹוָה צְבָאוֹת אֲשֶׁר
עָמַדְתִּי לְפָנָיו כִּי הַיּוֹם אֵרָאֶה אֵלָיו: טז וַיֵּלֶךְ
עֹבַדְיָהוּ לִקְרַאת אַחְאָב וַיַּגֶּד־לוֹ וַיֵּלֶךְ אַחְאָב
לִקְרַאת אֵלִיָּהוּ: יז וַיְהִי כִּרְאוֹת אַחְאָב אֶת־
אֵלִיָּהוּ וַיֹּאמֶר אַחְאָב אֵלָיו הַאַתָּה זֶה עֹכֵר
יִשְׂרָאֵל: יח וַיֹּאמֶר לֹא עָכַרְתִּי אֶת־יִשְׂרָאֵל כִּי
אִם־אַתָּה וּבֵית אָבִיךָ בַּעֲזָבְכֶם אֶת־מִצְוֹת
יְהֹוָה וַתֵּלֶךְ אַחֲרֵי הַבְּעָלִים: יט וְעַתָּה שְׁלַח
קְבֹץ אֵלַי אֶת־כָּל־יִשְׂרָאֵל אֶל־הַר הַכַּרְמֶל
וְאֶת־נְבִיאֵי הַבַּעַל אַרְבַּע־מֵאוֹת וַחֲמִשִּׁים
וּנְבִיאֵי הָאֲשֵׁרָה אַרְבַּע מֵאוֹת אֹכְלֵי שֻׁלְחַן
אִיזָבֶל: (כאן מתחילין הספרדים וק"ק פרנקפורט ד'מיין)

Main.) 20. And Ahab sent among all of the children of Israel, and he gathered the prophets to Mount Carmel. 21. And Elijah drew near to all the people and said, "Until when are you hopping between two ideas? If the Lord is God, go after Him, and if the Baal, go after him." And the people did not answer him a word. 22. And Elijah said to the people, "I have remained a prophet to the Lord by myself, and the prophets of the Baal are four hundred and fifty men. 23. And let them give us two bulls and let them choose one bull for themselves and cut it up and place it on the wood, but fire they shall not put, and I will prepare one bull, and I will put it on the wood, and fire will I not put. 24. And you will call in the name of your deity, and I will call in the name of the Lord, and it will be the God that will answer with fire, he is God." And all of the people answered and said, "The thing is good." 25. And Elijah said to the prophets of the Baal, "Choose for yourselves the one bull and prepare it first since you are the majority, and call in the name of your deity, and fire place not." 26. They took the bull that he gave them and prepared [it]. And they called in the name of the Baal from the morning until noon, saying, "O Baal, answer us!" But there was no voice and no answer, and they hopped on the altar that they had made. 27. And it was at noon that Elijah scoffed at them, and he said, "Call with a loud voice, for he is a god. [Perhaps] he is talking or he is pursuing [enemies] or he is on a journey; perhaps he is sleeping and will awaken." 28. And they called with a loud voice and gashed themselves as was their custom, with swords and lances, until blood gushed on them. 29. And as the afternoon passed and they feined to prophesy until the time of the sacrifice of the [evening] offering, and there was no voice and no answer, and no one was listening. 30. And Elijah said to all the people, "Come near to me," and all the people came near to him and he repaired the torn down altar of the Lord. 31. Elijah took twelve stones, corresponding to the number of the tribes of the sons of Jacob, to whom the word of the Lord came, saying, "Israel shall be your name." 32. He built the stones into an altar in the name of the Lord, and he made a

כ וַיִּשְׁלַח אַחְאָב בְּכָל־בְּנֵי יִשְׂרָאֵל וַיִּקְבֹּץ אֶת־הַנְּבִיאִים אֶל־הַר הַכַּרְמֶל: כא וַיִּגַּשׁ אֵלִיָּהוּ אֶל־כָּל־הָעָם וַיֹּאמֶר עַד־מָתַי אַתֶּם פֹּסְחִים עַל־שְׁתֵּי הַסְּעִפִּים אִם־יְהֹוָה הָאֱלֹהִים לְכוּ אַחֲרָיו וְאִם־הַבַּעַל לְכוּ אַחֲרָיו וְלֹא־עָנוּ הָעָם אֹתוֹ דָּבָר: כב וַיֹּאמֶר אֵלִיָּהוּ אֶל־הָעָם אֲנִי נוֹתַרְתִּי נָבִיא לַיהֹוָה לְבַדִּי וּנְבִיאֵי הַבַּעַל אַרְבַּע־מֵאוֹת וַחֲמִשִּׁים אִישׁ: כג וְיִתְּנוּ־לָנוּ שְׁנַיִם פָּרִים וְיִבְחֲרוּ לָהֶם הַפָּר הָאֶחָד וִינַתְּחֻהוּ וְיָשִׂימוּ עַל־הָעֵצִים וְאֵשׁ לֹא יָשִׂימוּ וַאֲנִי אֶעֱשֶׂה אֶת־הַפָּר הָאֶחָד וְנָתַתִּי עַל־הָעֵצִים וְאֵשׁ לֹא אָשִׂים: כד וּקְרָאתֶם בְּשֵׁם אֱלֹהֵיכֶם וַאֲנִי אֶקְרָא בְשֵׁם־יְהֹוָה וְהָיָה הָאֱלֹהִים אֲשֶׁר־יַעֲנֶה בָאֵשׁ הוּא הָאֱלֹהִים וַיַּעַן כָּל־הָעָם וַיֹּאמְרוּ טוֹב הַדָּבָר: כה וַיֹּאמֶר אֵלִיָּהוּ לִנְבִיאֵי הַבַּעַל בַּחֲרוּ לָכֶם הַפָּר הָאֶחָד וַעֲשׂוּ רִאשֹׁנָה כִּי אַתֶּם הָרַבִּים וְקִרְאוּ בְּשֵׁם אֱלֹהֵיכֶם וְאֵשׁ לֹא תָשִׂימוּ: כו וַיִּקְחוּ אֶת־הַפָּר אֲשֶׁר־נָתַן לָהֶם וַיַּעֲשׂוּ וַיִּקְרְאוּ בְשֵׁם־הַבַּעַל מֵהַבֹּקֶר וְעַד־הַצָּהֳרַיִם לֵאמֹר הַבַּעַל עֲנֵנוּ וְאֵין קוֹל וְאֵין עֹנֶה וַיְפַסְּחוּ עַל־הַמִּזְבֵּחַ אֲשֶׁר עָשָׂה: כז וַיְהִי בַצָּהֳרַיִם וַיְהַתֵּל בָּהֶם אֵלִיָּהוּ וַיֹּאמֶר קִרְאוּ בְקוֹל־גָּדוֹל כִּי־אֱלֹהִים הוּא כִּי־שִׂיחַ וְכִי־שִׂיג לוֹ וְכִי־דֶרֶךְ לוֹ אוּלַי יָשֵׁן הוּא וְיִקָץ: כח וַיִּקְרְאוּ בְּקוֹל גָּדוֹל וַיִּתְגֹּדְדוּ כְּמִשְׁפָּטָם בַּחֲרָבוֹת וּבָרְמָחִים עַד־שְׁפָךְ־דָּם עֲלֵיהֶם: כט וַיְהִי כַּעֲבֹר הַצָּהֳרַיִם וַיִּתְנַבְּאוּ עַד לַעֲלוֹת הַמִּנְחָה וְאֵין־קוֹל וְאֵין־עֹנֶה וְאֵין קָשֶׁב: ל וַיֹּאמֶר אֵלִיָּהוּ לְכָל־הָעָם גְּשׁוּ אֵלַי וַיִּגְּשׁוּ כָל־הָעָם אֵלָיו וַיְרַפֵּא אֶת־מִזְבַּח יְהֹוָה הֶהָרוּס: לא וַיִּקַּח אֵלִיָּהוּ שְׁתֵּים עֶשְׂרֵה אֲבָנִים כְּמִסְפַּר שִׁבְטֵי בְנֵי־יַעֲקֹב אֲשֶׁר הָיָה דְבַר־יְהֹוָה אֵלָיו לֵאמֹר יִשְׂרָאֵל יִהְיֶה שְׁמֶךָ: לב וַיִּבְנֶה אֶת־הָאֲבָנִים מִזְבֵּחַ בְּשֵׁם יְהֹוָה וַיַּעַשׂ תְּעָלָה כְּבֵית

trench as great as would contain two se'ah of seed, around the altar. 33. And he arranged the wood, and he cut up the bull and placed [it] upon the wood. And he said, "Fill me four pitchers of water and pour them on the burnt offerings and on the wood." 34. And he said, "Repeat it," and they repeated it. And he said, "Do it a third time," and they did it a third time. 35. And the water went around the altar, and also the trench he filled with water. 36. And it was when the evening sacrifice was offered that Elijah the prophet came near and said, "Lord the God of Abraham, Isaac and Israel, today let it be known that You are God in Israel and that I am Your servant, and at Your word have I done all these things. 37. Answer me, O Lord, answer me, and this people shall know that You are the Lord God, and You have turned their hearts backwards." 38. And the fire of the Lord fell and consumed the burnt offerings and the wood and the stones, and the water which was in the trench it licked up. 39. And all the people saw and fell on their faces, and they said, "The Lord is God, the Lord is God."

סָאתַיִם זֶרַע סָבִיב לַמִּזְבֵּחַ׃ לג וַיַּעֲרֹךְ אֶת־
הָעֵצִים וַיְנַתַּח אֶת־הַפָּר וַיָּשֶׂם עַל־הָעֵצִים׃
לד וַיֹּאמֶר מִלְאוּ אַרְבָּעָה כַדִּים מַיִם וְיִצְקוּ
עַל־הָעֹלָה וְעַל־הָעֵצִים וַיֹּאמֶר שְׁנוּ וַיִּשְׁנוּ
וַיֹּאמֶר שַׁלֵּשׁוּ וַיְשַׁלֵּשׁוּ׃ לה וַיֵּלְכוּ הַמַּיִם סָבִיב
לַמִּזְבֵּחַ וְגַם אֶת־הַתְּעָלָה מִלֵּא־מָיִם׃ לו וַיְהִי ׀
בַּעֲלוֹת הַמִּנְחָה וַיִּגַּשׁ אֵלִיָּהוּ הַנָּבִיא וַיֹּאמַר
יְהוָה אֱלֹהֵי אַבְרָהָם יִצְחָק וְיִשְׂרָאֵל הַיּוֹם יִוָּדַע
כִּי־אַתָּה אֱלֹהִים בְּיִשְׂרָאֵל וַאֲנִי עַבְדֶּךָ
ובדבריך (ובדברך קרי) עָשִׂיתִי אֵת כָּל־הַדְּבָרִים
הָאֵלֶּה׃ לז עֲנֵנִי יְהוָה עֲנֵנִי וְיֵדְעוּ הָעָם הַזֶּה
כִּי־אַתָּה יְהוָה הָאֱלֹהִים וְאַתָּה הֲסִבֹּתָ אֶת־לִבָּם
אֲחֹרַנִּית׃ לח וַתִּפֹּל אֵשׁ־יְהוָה וַתֹּאכַל אֶת־
הָעֹלָה וְאֶת־הָעֵצִים וְאֶת־הָאֲבָנִים וְאֶת־הֶעָפָר
וְאֶת־הַמַּיִם אֲשֶׁר־בַּתְּעָלָה לִחֵכָה׃ לט וַיַּרְא
כָּל־הָעָם וַיִּפְּלוּ עַל־פְּנֵיהֶם וַיֹּאמְרוּ יְהוָה הוּא
הָאֱלֹהִים יְהוָה הוּא הָאֱלֹהִים׃

HAFTARATH VAYAKHEL הפטרת ויקהל

(I Kings 7:13–26 for Sephardim; for Ashkenazim, I Kings 7:40–50.)

Should Parashath Shekalim fall on this Sabbath, the Haftarah for Shekalim (p. 956) is read. Should Parashath Parah fall on this Sabbath, the Haftarah for Parah (p. 960) is read.

The building of the Temple is reminiscent of the building of the Tabernacle. The Ashkenazim read a selection summarizing the construction of the Temple, just as the construction of the Tabernacle is summarized in the Sidra.

7:13. And King Solomon sent and fetched Hiram out of Tyre. 14. He [was] a widow's son of the tribe of Naphtali, and his father was a man of Tyre, a coppersmith; and he was filled with the wisdom and understanding and skill, to work all works in copper; and he came to king Solomon and wrought all his work. 15. And he cast the two pillars of copper, eighteen cubits [was] the height of each pillar, and a line of twelve cubits did encompass it about, and so the other pillar. 16. And he made two chapiters, to set upon

יג וַיִּשְׁלַח הַמֶּלֶךְ שְׁלֹמֹה וַיִּקַּח אֶת־חִירָם מִצֹּר׃
יד בֶּן־אִשָּׁה אַלְמָנָה הוּא מִמַּטֵּה נַפְתָּלִי וְאָבִיו
אִישׁ־צֹרִי חֹרֵשׁ נְחֹשֶׁת וַיִּמָּלֵא אֶת־הַחָכְמָה
וְאֶת־הַתְּבוּנָה וְאֶת־הַדַּעַת לַעֲשׂוֹת כָּל־מְלָאכָה
בַּנְּחֹשֶׁת וַיָּבוֹא אֶל־הַמֶּלֶךְ שְׁלֹמֹה וַיַּעַשׂ אֶת־
כָּל־מְלַאכְתּוֹ׃ טו וַיָּצַר אֶת־שְׁנֵי הָעַמּוּדִים
נְחֹשֶׁת שְׁמֹנֶה עֶשְׂרֵה אַמָּה קוֹמַת הָעַמּוּד
הָאֶחָד וְחוּט שְׁתֵּים־עֶשְׂרֵה אַמָּה יָסֹב אֶת־
הָעַמּוּד הַשֵּׁנִי׃ טז וּשְׁתֵּי כֹתָרֹת עָשָׂה לָתֵת עַל־

the tops of the pillars, [of] molten copper; five cubits [was] the height of the one chapiter, and five cubits [was] the height of the other chapiter. 17. Nets of checker-work, wreaths of chain-work, for the chapiters which [were] upon the top of the pillars; seven for the one chapiter, and seven for the other chapiter. 18. And he made the pillars; and two rows round about upon the one network, to cover the chapiters that [were] upon the top, with pomegranates; and so he did for the other chapiter. 19. And the chapiters that [were] upon the top of the pillars [were] of lily-work in the porch, four cubits. 20. And [there were] chapiters above, also upon the two pillars, over against the belly which [was] by the network; and the pomegranates [were] two hundred in rows round about upon each chapiter. 21. And he set up the pillars in the porch of the temple; and he set up the right pillar, and called the name thereof Jachin; and he set up the left pillar, and called the name thereof Boaz. 22. And upon the top of the pillars [was] lily-work; so was the work of the pillars finished. 23. And he made the molten sea, ten cubits from brim to brim: it [was] round all about, and the height thereof [was] five cubits; and a line of thirty cubits did compass it round about. 24. And under the brim [there were] knops compassing it round about, for ten cubits, compassing the sea round about; the knops [were] cast in two rows, when it was cast. 25. It stood on twelve oxen, three looking toward the west, and three looking toward the south, and three looking toward the east; and the sea [was set] upon them above, and all their hinder parts [were] inward. 26. And it [was] a hand-breadth thick, and the brim thereof [was] wrought like the brim of a cup, with flowers of lilies; it contained two thousand measures.

(Ashkenazim read the following.)

40. And Hiram made the lavers, and the shovels, and the basins. And Hiram finished doing all the work which he did for King Solomon [in] the House of the Lord.

רָאשֵׁי הָעַמּוּדִים מֻצַק נְחֹשֶׁת חָמֵשׁ אַמּוֹת
קוֹמַת הַכֹּתֶרֶת הָאֶחָת וְחָמֵשׁ אַמּוֹת קוֹמַת
הַכֹּתֶרֶת הַשֵּׁנִית: יז שְׂבָכִים מַעֲשֵׂה שְׂבָכָה
גְּדִלִים מַעֲשֵׂה שַׁרְשְׁרוֹת לַכֹּתָרֹת אֲשֶׁר עַל־
רֹאשׁ הָעַמּוּדִים שִׁבְעָה לַכֹּתֶרֶת הָאֶחָת וְשִׁבְעָה
לַכֹּתֶרֶת הַשֵּׁנִית: יח וַיַּעַשׂ אֶת־הָעַמּוּדִים וּשְׁנֵי
טוּרִים סָבִיב עַל־הַשְּׂבָכָה הָאֶחָת לְכַסּוֹת אֶת־
הַכֹּתָרֹת אֲשֶׁר עַל־רֹאשׁ הָרִמֹּנִים וְכֵן עָשָׂה
לַכֹּתֶרֶת הַשֵּׁנִית: יט וְכֹתָרֹת אֲשֶׁר עַל־רֹאשׁ
הָעַמּוּדִים מַעֲשֵׂה שׁוּשַׁן בָּאוּלָם אַרְבַּע אַמּוֹת:
כ וְכֹתָרֹת עַל־שְׁנֵי הָעַמּוּדִים גַּם־מִמַּעַל
מִלְּעֻמַּת הַבֶּטֶן אֲשֶׁר לְעֵבֶר הַשְּׂבָכָה וְהָרִמּוֹנִים
מָאתַיִם טֻרִים סָבִיב עַל הַכֹּתֶרֶת הַשֵּׁנִית:
כא וַיָּקֶם אֶת־הָעַמֻּדִים לְאֻלָם הַהֵיכָל וַיָּקֶם
אֶת־הָעַמּוּד הַיְמָנִי וַיִּקְרָא אֶת־שְׁמוֹ יָכִין וַיָּקֶם
אֶת־הָעַמּוּד הַשְּׂמָאלִי וַיִּקְרָא אֶת־שְׁמוֹ בֹּעַז:
כב וְעַל רֹאשׁ הָעַמּוּדִים מַעֲשֵׂה שׁוֹשָׁן וַתִּתֹּם
מְלֶאכֶת הָעַמּוּדִים: כג וַיַּעַשׂ אֶת־הַיָּם מוּצָק
עֶשֶׂר בָּאַמָּה מִשְּׂפָתוֹ עַד־שְׂפָתוֹ עָגֹל ׀ סָבִיב
וְחָמֵשׁ בָּאַמָּה קוֹמָתוֹ וְקָו שְׁלֹשִׁים בָּאַמָּה יָסֹב
אֹתוֹ סָבִיב: כד וּפְקָעִים מִתַּחַת לִשְׂפָתוֹ ׀ סָבִיב
סֹבְבִים אֹתוֹ עֶשֶׂר בָּאַמָּה מַקִּפִים אֶת־הַיָּם
סָבִיב שְׁנֵי טוּרִים הַפְּקָעִים יְצֻקִים בִּיצֻקָתוֹ:
כה עֹמֵד עַל־שְׁנֵי עָשָׂר בָּקָר שְׁלֹשָׁה פֹנִים ׀
צָפוֹנָה וּשְׁלֹשָׁה פֹּנִים ׀ יָמָּה וּשְׁלֹשָׁה ׀ פֹּנִים
נֶגְבָּה וּשְׁלֹשָׁה פֹּנִים מִזְרָחָה וְהַיָּם עֲלֵיהֶם
מִלְמָעְלָה וְכָל־אֲחֹרֵיהֶם בָּיְתָה: כו וְעָבְיוֹ טֶפַח
וּשְׂפָתוֹ כְּמַעֲשֵׂה שְׂפַת־כּוֹס פֶּרַח שׁוֹשָׁן
אַלְפַּיִם בַּת יָכִיל:

(כמנהג האשכנזים)

מ וַיַּעַשׂ חִירוֹם אֶת־הַכִּיֹּרוֹת וְאֶת־הַיָּעִים
וְאֶת־הַמִּזְרָקוֹת וַיְכַל חִירָם לַעֲשׂוֹת אֶת־כָּל־
הַמְּלָאכָה אֲשֶׁר עָשָׂה לַמֶּלֶךְ שְׁלֹמֹה בֵּית יְהוָה:

41. The two pillars and the two bowls of the chapiters that [were] on the top of the pillars; and the two networks, to cover the two bowls of the chapiters that [were] on the top of the pillars. 42. And the four hundred pomegranates for the two networks, two rows of pomegranates for each network, to cover the two bowls of the chapiters that [were] upon the pillars. 43. And the ten bases, and the ten lavers on the bases. 44. And the one sea, and the twelve oxen under the sea. 45. And the pots, and the shovels, and the basins, and all these vessels, which Hiram made for King Solomon [in] the House of the Lord, [were] of bright copper. 46. In the plain of the Jordan did the king cast them, in the thick clay, between Succoth and Tsarethan. 47. And Solomon left all the vessels [unweighed], because [there were] very very many; [therefore] the weight of the copper was not found out. 48. And Solomon made all the vessels that [were] in the house of the Lord; the altar of gold, and the table whereupon the showbread [was], of gold. 49. And the candlesticks, five on the right [side] and five on the left before the Sanctuary, of pure gold; and the flowers, and the lamps, and the tongs, of gold. 50. And the bowls, and the musical instruments, and the basins, and the spoons, and the censers, of pure gold; and the hinges, for the doors of the inner house, the most holy [place], [and] for the doors of the House, [that is] of the Temple, of gold.

מא עַמֻּדִ֣ים שְׁנַ֔יִם וְגֻלֹּ֧ת הַכֹּתָרֹ֛ת אֲשֶׁר־עַל־
רֹ֥אשׁ הָֽעַמּוּדִ֖ים שְׁתָּ֑יִם וְהַשְּׂבָכ֣וֹת שְׁתַּ֔יִם
לְכַסּ֗וֹת אֶת־שְׁתֵּי֙ גֻּלּ֣וֹת הַכֹּתָרֹ֔ת אֲשֶׁ֖ר עַל־
רֹ֥אשׁ הָֽעַמּוּדִֽים׃ מב וְאֶת־הָרִמֹּנִ֥ים אַרְבַּ֛ע
מֵא֖וֹת לִשְׁתֵּ֣י הַשְּׂבָכ֑וֹת שְׁנֵי־טוּרִ֨ים רִמֹּנִ֜ים
לַשְּׂבָכָ֣ה הָאֶחָ֗ת לְכַסּ֞וֹת אֶת־שְׁתֵּי֙ גֻּלֹּ֣ת הַכֹּתָרֹ֔ת
אֲשֶׁ֖ר עַל־פְּנֵ֥י הָֽעַמּוּדִֽים׃ מג וְאֶת־הַמְּכֹנ֖וֹת
עֶ֑שֶׂר וְאֶת־הַכִּיֹּרֹ֥ת עֲשָׂרָ֖ה עַל־הַמְּכֹנֽוֹת׃
מד וְאֶת־הַיָּ֖ם הָאֶחָ֑ד וְאֶת־הַבָּקָ֥ר שְׁנֵים־עָשָׂ֖ר
תַּ֥חַת הַיָּֽם׃ מה וְאֶת־הַסִּיר֨וֹת וְאֶת־הַיָּעִ֜ים
וְאֶת־הַמִּזְרָק֗וֹת וְאֵת֙ כָּל־הַכֵּלִ֣ים הָאֹ֔הֶל (האלה
קרי) אֲשֶׁ֨ר עָשָׂ֥ה חִירָ֛ם לַמֶּ֥לֶךְ שְׁלֹמֹ֖ה בֵּ֣ית
יְהוָ֑ה נְחֹ֖שֶׁת מְמֹרָֽט׃ מו בְּכִכַּ֤ר הַיַּרְדֵּן֙ יְצָקָ֣ם
הַמֶּ֔לֶךְ בְּמַעֲבֵ֖ה הָאֲדָמָ֑ה בֵּ֥ין סֻכּ֖וֹת וּבֵ֥ין צָרְתָֽן׃
מז וַיַּנַּ֤ח שְׁלֹמֹה֙ אֶת־כָּל־הַכֵּלִ֔ים מֵרֹ֖ב מְאֹ֣ד
מְאֹ֑ד לֹ֥א נֶחְקַ֖ר מִשְׁקַ֥ל הַנְּחֹֽשֶׁת׃ מח וַיַּ֣עַשׂ
שְׁלֹמֹ֔ה אֵ֚ת כָּל־הַכֵּלִ֔ים אֲשֶׁ֖ר בֵּ֣ית יְהוָ֑ה אֵ֚ת
מִזְבַּ֣ח הַזָּהָ֔ב וְאֶת־הַשֻּׁלְחָ֗ן אֲשֶׁ֥ר עָלָ֛יו לֶ֥חֶם
הַפָּנִ֖ים זָהָֽב׃ מט וְאֶת־הַ֠מְּנֹרוֹת חָמֵ֨שׁ מִיָּמִ֜ין
וְחָמֵ֧שׁ מִשְּׂמֹ֛אל לִפְנֵ֥י הַדְּבִ֖יר זָהָ֣ב סָג֑וּר וְהַפֶּ֧רַח
וְהַנֵּרֹ֛ת וְהַמֶּלְקַחַ֖יִם זָהָֽב׃ נ וְ֠הַסִּפּוֹת וְהַֽמְזַמְּר֧וֹת
וְהַמִּזְרָק֛וֹת וְהַכַּפּ֥וֹת וְהַמַּחְתּ֖וֹת זָהָ֣ב סָג֑וּר
וְהַפֹּת֞וֹת לְדַלְתוֹת֙ הַבַּ֣יִת הַפְּנִימִ֗י לְקֹ֙דֶשׁ֙
הַקֳּדָשִׁ֔ים לְדַלְתֵ֥י הַבַּ֖יִת לַֽהֵיכָ֑ל זָהָֽב׃

HAFTARATH PEKUDE הפטרת פקודי

(I Kings 7:51–8:21 for Ashkenazim. Sephardim read the Haftarah read by Ashkenazim with the Sidra Vaykhel.)

This Haftarah is read whether Pekudey is read alone or together with Vayakhel. Should Sabbath Shekalim coincide with the reading of Vayakhel, many congregations read ויעש חירום for Pekudey followed by the two verses of ותשלם. Should Parashath Shekalim fall on *this* Sabbath, the Haftarah for Shekalim (p. 954) is read. (This can occur if Pekudey is read separately. Should Parashath HaChodesh fall on this Sabbath, whether Pekudey is read separately or together with Vayakhel, Haftarath HaChodesh (p. 962) supersedes.

This selection depicts the completion of the Temple, when it was filled with the glory of God. This is reminiscent of the completion of the construction of the Tabernacle.

7:51. And all the work that King Solomon had wrought in the house of the Lord was finished. And Solomon brought in the things which David his father had dedicated: the silver and the gold and the vessels, [and] put them in the treasuries of the House of the Lord. 8:1. Then Solomon assembled the elders of Israel, and all the heads of the tribes, the princes of the fathers' [houses] of the children of Israel, unto King Solomon in Jerusalem, to bring up the ark of the covenant of the Lord out of the city of David, which is Zion. 2. And all the men of Israel assembled themselves unto King Solomon at the feast in the month Ethanim, which [is] the seventh month. 3. And all the elders of Israel came, and the priests took up the ark. 4. And they brought up the ark of the Lord, and the Tabernacle of Meeting, and all the holy vessels which [were] in the Tabernacle, and the priests and the Levites did bring them up. 5. And King Solomon and all the congregation of Israel that were assembled unto him [were] with him before the ark, sacrificing sheep and oxen, that could not be counted nor numbered for multitude. 6. And the priests brought in the ark of the covenant of the Lord to its place, into the Sanctuary of the House, to the most holy [place], under the wings of the cherubim. 7. For the cherubim spread forth [their] wings over the place of the ark, and the cherubim covered the ark and the staves thereof above. 8. And the staves were so long that the ends of the staves were seen from the holy [place] before the Sanctuary, and they were not seen without; and they are there unto this day. 9. There was nothing in the ark save

נא וַתִּשְׁלַם֙ כָּל־הַמְּלָאכָ֔ה אֲשֶׁ֥ר עָשָׂ֖ה הַמֶּ֣לֶךְ
שְׁלֹמֹ֑ה בֵּ֣ית יְהוָ֑ה וַיָּבֵ֨א שְׁלֹמֹ֜ה אֶת־קָדְשֵׁ֣י ׀
דָּוִ֣ד אָבִ֗יו אֶת־הַכֶּ֤סֶף וְאֶת־הַזָּהָב֙ וְאֶת־הַכֵּלִ֔ים
נָתַ֕ן בְּאֹצְר֖וֹת בֵּ֥ית יְהוָֽה׃ א אָ֣ז יַקְהֵ֣ל שְׁלֹמֹ֣ה
אֶת־זִקְנֵ֣י יִשְׂרָאֵ֡ל אֶת־כָּל־רָאשֵׁ֣י הַמַּטּוֹת֩
נְשִׂיאֵ֨י הָאָב֜וֹת לִבְנֵ֧י יִשְׂרָאֵ֛ל אֶל־הַמֶּ֥לֶךְ שְׁלֹמֹ֖ה
יְרֽוּשָׁלִָ֑ם לְהַעֲל֞וֹת אֶת־אֲר֧וֹן בְּרִית־יְהוָ֛ה מֵעִ֥יר
דָּוִ֖ד הִ֥יא צִיּֽוֹן׃ ב וַיִּקָּ֨הֲל֜וּ אֶל־הַמֶּ֤לֶךְ שְׁלֹמֹה֙
כָּל־אִ֣ישׁ יִשְׂרָאֵ֔ל בְּיֶ֥רַח הָאֵתָנִ֖ים בֶּחָ֑ג ה֖וּא
הַחֹ֥דֶשׁ הַשְּׁבִיעִֽי׃ ג וַיָּבֹ֕אוּ כֹּ֖ל זִקְנֵ֣י יִשְׂרָאֵ֑ל
וַיִּשְׂא֥וּ הַכֹּהֲנִ֖ים אֶת־הָאָרֽוֹן׃ ד וַיַּעֲל֞וּ אֶת־אֲר֤וֹן
יְהוָה֙ וְאֶת־אֹ֣הֶל מוֹעֵ֔ד וְאֶת־כָּל־כְּלֵ֥י הַקֹּ֖דֶשׁ
אֲשֶׁ֣ר בָּאֹ֑הֶל וַיַּעֲל֣וּ אֹתָ֔ם הַכֹּהֲנִ֖ים וְהַלְוִיִּֽם׃
ה וְהַמֶּ֣לֶךְ שְׁלֹמֹ֗ה וְכָל־עֲדַ֤ת יִשְׂרָאֵל֙ הַנּוֹעָדִ֣ים
עָלָ֔יו אִתּ֖וֹ לִפְנֵ֣י הָאָר֑וֹן מְזַבְּחִים֙ צֹ֣אן וּבָקָ֔ר
אֲשֶׁ֛ר לֹֽא־יִסָּפְר֥וּ וְלֹ֥א יִמָּנ֖וּ מֵרֹֽב׃ ו וַיָּבִ֣אוּ
הַכֹּהֲנִ֡ים אֶת־אֲר֣וֹן בְּרִית־יְהוָ֧ה אֶל־מְקוֹמ֛וֹ
אֶל־דְּבִ֥יר הַבַּ֖יִת אֶל־קֹ֣דֶשׁ הַקֳּדָשִׁ֑ים אֶל־תַּ֖חַת
כַּנְפֵ֥י הַכְּרוּבִֽים׃ ז כִּ֤י הַכְּרוּבִים֙ פֹּרְשִׂ֣ים כְּנָפַ֔יִם
אֶל־מְק֖וֹם הָאָר֑וֹן וַיָּסֹ֧כּוּ הַכְּרֻבִ֛ים עַל־הָאָר֥וֹן
וְעַל־בַּדָּ֖יו מִלְמָֽעְלָה׃ ח וַיַּאֲרִ֘כוּ֮ הַבַּדִּים֒ וַיֵּרָא֨וּ
רָאשֵׁ֤י הַבַּדִּים֙ מִן־הַקֹּ֙דֶשׁ֙ עַל־פְּנֵ֣י הַדְּבִ֔יר וְלֹ֥א
יֵרָא֖וּ הַח֑וּצָה וַיִּ֣הְיוּ שָׁ֔ם עַ֖ד הַיּ֥וֹם הַזֶּֽה׃ ט אֵ֣ין

the two tablets of stone which Moses put there at Horeb, when the Lord made [a covenant] with the children of Israel, when they came out of the land of Egypt. 10. And it came to pass when the priests came out of the holy [place] and the cloud filled the House of the Lord. 11. And the priests could not stand to minister because of the cloud; for the glory of the Lord filled the House of the Lord. 12. Then Solomon said, "The Lord said that He would dwell in the thick darkness. 13. I have surely built You a house to dwell in; a settled place for You to dwell in forever." 14. And the king turned his face about, and blessed all the congregation of Israel, and all the congregation of Israel stood. 15. And he said, "Blessed [be] the Lord, the God of Israel Who spoke with His mouth unto David my father, and has fulfilled it with His hand, saying: 16. Since the day that I brought forth my people Israel out of Egypt, I chose no city out of all the tribes of Israel to build a house, that my name might be therein; but I chose David to be over my people Israel. 17. And it was in the heart of David my father to build a house for the Name of the Lord, the God of Israel. 18. And the Lord said to David my father, since it was in your heart to build a house unto my name, you did well that it was in your heart. 19. Nevertheless, you shall not build the House; but your son that shall come forth out of your loins, he shall build the House for My Name. 20. And the Lord has established His word that he spoke, and I have risen up in the place of David my father, and sit on the throne of Israel, as the Lord spoke, and have built a house for the Name of the Lord, the God of Israel. 21. And I have set there a place for the ark, wherein [is] the covenant of the Lord, which He made with our fathers when He brought them out of the land of Egypt.''

בָּאָרוֹן רַק שְׁנֵי לֻחוֹת הָאֲבָנִים אֲשֶׁר הִנִּחַ שָׁם מֹשֶׁה בְּחֹרֵב אֲשֶׁר כָּרַת יְהֹוָה עִם־בְּנֵי יִשְׂרָאֵל בְּצֵאתָם מֵאֶרֶץ מִצְרָיִם: י וַיְהִי בְּצֵאת הַכֹּהֲנִים מִן־הַקֹּדֶשׁ וְהֶעָנָן מָלֵא אֶת־בֵּית יְהֹוָה: יא וְלֹא־יָכְלוּ הַכֹּהֲנִים לַעֲמֹד לְשָׁרֵת מִפְּנֵי הֶעָנָן כִּי־מָלֵא כְבוֹד־יְהֹוָה אֶת־בֵּית יְהֹוָה: יב אָז אָמַר שְׁלֹמֹה יְהֹוָה אָמַר לִשְׁכֹּן בָּעֲרָפֶל: יג בָּנֹה בָנִיתִי בֵּית זְבֻל לָךְ מָכוֹן לְשִׁבְתְּךָ עוֹלָמִים: יד וַיַּסֵּב הַמֶּלֶךְ אֶת־פָּנָיו וַיְבָרֶךְ אֵת כָּל־קְהַל יִשְׂרָאֵל וְכָל־קְהַל יִשְׂרָאֵל עֹמֵד: טו וַיֹּאמֶר בָּרוּךְ יְהֹוָה אֱלֹהֵי יִשְׂרָאֵל אֲשֶׁר דִּבֶּר בְּפִיו אֵת דָּוִד אָבִי וּבְיָדוֹ מִלֵּא לֵאמֹר: טז מִן־הַיּוֹם אֲשֶׁר הוֹצֵאתִי אֶת־עַמִּי אֶת־יִשְׂרָאֵל מִמִּצְרַיִם לֹא־בָחַרְתִּי בְעִיר מִכֹּל שִׁבְטֵי יִשְׂרָאֵל לִבְנוֹת בַּיִת לִהְיוֹת שְׁמִי שָׁם וָאֶבְחַר בְּדָוִד לִהְיוֹת עַל־עַמִּי יִשְׂרָאֵל: יז וַיְהִי עִם־לְבַב דָּוִד אָבִי לִבְנוֹת בַּיִת לְשֵׁם יְהֹוָה אֱלֹהֵי יִשְׂרָאֵל: יח וַיֹּאמֶר יְהֹוָה אֶל־דָּוִד אָבִי יַעַן אֲשֶׁר הָיָה עִם־לְבָבְךָ לִבְנוֹת בַּיִת לִשְׁמִי הֱטִיבֹתָ כִּי הָיָה עִם־לְבָבֶךָ: יט רַק אַתָּה לֹא תִבְנֶה הַבָּיִת כִּי אִם־בִּנְךָ הַיֹּצֵא מֵחֲלָצֶיךָ הוּא־יִבְנֶה הַבַּיִת לִשְׁמִי: כ וַיָּקֶם יְהֹוָה אֶת־דְּבָרוֹ אֲשֶׁר דִּבֵּר וָאָקֻם תַּחַת דָּוִד אָבִי וָאֵשֵׁב | עַל־כִּסֵּא יִשְׂרָאֵל כַּאֲשֶׁר דִּבֶּר יְהֹוָה וָאֶבְנֶה הַבַּיִת לְשֵׁם יְהֹוָה אֱלֹהֵי יִשְׂרָאֵל: כא וָאָשִׂם שָׁם מָקוֹם לָאָרוֹן אֲשֶׁר־שָׁם בְּרִית יְהֹוָה אֲשֶׁר כָּרַת עִם־אֲבֹתֵינוּ בְּהוֹצִיאוֹ אֹתָם מֵאֶרֶץ מִצְרָיִם:

HAFTARATH VAYIKRA הפטרת ויקרא

(Isaiah 43:21–44:23)

Should Parashath Zachor fall on this Sabbath, the Haftarah for Zachor (p. 956) is read. Should Parashath HaChodesh fall on this Sabbath, the Haftarah for Parashath HaChodesh is read (p. 962).

The prophet rebukes Israel, declaring that it is better to obey the word of God than to sin and atone for sins with the offerings described in the Sidra.

43:21. This people I formed for Myself; they shall recite My praise. 22. But you did not call Me, O Jacob, for you wearied of Me, O Israel. 23. You did not bring Me the lambs of your burnt offerings, nor did you honor Me with your sacrifices; neither did I overwork you with meal-offerings nor did I weary you with frankincense. 24. Neither did you purchase cane for Me with money, nor have you sated Me with the fat of your sacrifices. But you have burdened Me with your sins; you have wearied Me with your iniquities. 25. I, yea I erase your transgressions for My sake, and your sins I will not remember. 26. Remind Me, let us stand in judgment; you tell, in order that you be accounted just. 27. Your first father sinned, and your intercessors transgressed against Me. 28. And I profane the holy princes, and I deliver Jacob to destruction and Israel to revilings. 44:1. And now, hearken, Jacob My servant, and Israel whom I have chosen. 2. So said the Lord your Maker, and He Who formed you from the womb shall aid you. Fear not, My servant Jacob, and Jeshurun whom I have chosen. 3. As I will pour water on the thirsty and running water on dry land, I will pour My spirit on your seed and My blessing on your offspring. 4. And they shall sprout among the grass like willows on rivulets of water. 5. This one shall say, "I am the Lord's," and this one shall call himself by the name of Jacob, and this one shall write [with] his hand, "To the Lord," and adopt the name Israel. 6. So said the Lord, the King of Israel and his Redeemer, the Lord of Hosts: I am first and I am last, and besides Me there is no God. 7. And who will call [that he is] like Me and will tell it and arrange it for Me, since My placing the ancient people; and the signs and those that will come, let them tell for themselves. 8. Fear not and be not dis-

כא עַם־זוּ יָצַרְתִּי לִי תְּהִלָּתִי יְסַפֵּרוּ: כב וְלֹא־
אֹתִי קָרָאתָ יַעֲקֹב כִּי־יָגַעְתָּ בִּי יִשְׂרָאֵל:
כג לֹא־הֵבֵיאתָ לִּי שֵׂה עֹלֹתֶיךָ וּזְבָחֶיךָ לֹא
כִבַּדְתָּנִי לֹא הֶעֱבַדְתִּיךָ בְּמִנְחָה וְלֹא הוֹגַעְתִּיךָ
בִּלְבוֹנָה: כד לֹא־קָנִיתָ לִּי בַכֶּסֶף קָנֶה וְחֵלֶב
זְבָחֶיךָ לֹא הִרְוִיתָנִי אַךְ הֶעֱבַדְתַּנִי בְּחַטֹּאותֶיךָ
הוֹגַעְתַּנִי בַּעֲוֺנֹתֶיךָ: כה אָנֹכִי אָנֹכִי הוּא מֹחֶה
פְשָׁעֶיךָ לְמַעֲנִי וְחַטֹּאתֶיךָ לֹא אֶזְכֹּר: כו הַזְכִּירֵנִי
נִשָּׁפְטָה יָחַד סַפֵּר אַתָּה לְמַעַן תִּצְדָּק: כז אָבִיךָ
הָרִאשׁוֹן חָטָא וּמְלִיצֶיךָ פָּשְׁעוּ בִי: כח וַאֲחַלֵּל
שָׂרֵי קֹדֶשׁ וְאֶתְּנָה לַחֵרֶם יַעֲקֹב וְיִשְׂרָאֵל
לְגִדּוּפִים: א וְעַתָּה שְׁמַע יַעֲקֹב עַבְדִּי וְיִשְׂרָאֵל
בָּחַרְתִּי בוֹ: ב כֹּה־אָמַר יְהוָה עֹשֶׂךָ וְיֹצֶרְךָ
מִבֶּטֶן יַעְזְרֶךָּ אַל־תִּירָא עַבְדִּי יַעֲקֹב וִישֻׁרוּן
בָּחַרְתִּי בוֹ: ג כִּי אֶצָּק־מַיִם עַל־צָמֵא וְנֹזְלִים
עַל־יַבָּשָׁה אֶצֹּק רוּחִי עַל־זַרְעֶךָ וּבִרְכָתִי עַל־
צֶאֱצָאֶיךָ: ד וְצָמְחוּ בְּבֵין חָצִיר כַּעֲרָבִים עַל־
יִבְלֵי־מָיִם: ה זֶה יֹאמַר לַיהוָה אָנִי וְזֶה יִקְרָא
בְשֵׁם־יַעֲקֹב וְזֶה יִכְתֹּב יָדוֹ לַיהוָה וּבְשֵׁם
יִשְׂרָאֵל יְכַנֶּה: ו כֹּה־אָמַר יְהוָה מֶלֶךְ־יִשְׂרָאֵל
וְגֹאֲלוֹ יְהוָה צְבָאוֹת אֲנִי רִאשׁוֹן וַאֲנִי אַחֲרוֹן
וּמִבַּלְעָדַי אֵין אֱלֹהִים: ז וּמִי־כָמוֹנִי יִקְרָא
וְיַגִּידֶהָ וְיַעְרְכֶהָ לִי מִשּׂוּמִי עַם־עוֹלָם וְאֹתִיּוֹת
וַאֲשֶׁר תָּבֹאנָה יַגִּידוּ לָמוֹ: ח אַל־תִּפְחֲדוּ וְאַל־

mayed; did I not let you hear it from them, and I told [it], and you are My witnesses: Is there a God besides Me? And there is no rock I did not know. 9. Those who form idols are all of them vanity, and their treasures are of no avail, and they are their witnesses; they neither see nor hear, nor do they know, so that they be ashamed. 10. Who formed a god or molded an image, being of no avail? 11. Behold, all his colleagues shall be ashamed, and they are smiths — of man. Let all of them gather, let them stand, they shall fear, they shall be ashamed together. 12. The ironsmith [makes] an axe, and he works with coal, and with sledge hammers he fashions it; and he made it with his strong arm; yea, he is hungry, and he has no strength; he did not drink water, and he becomes faint. 13. The carpenter stretched out a line; he beautifies it with a saw; he fixes it with planes, and with a compass he rounds it, and he made it in the likeness of a man, like the beauty of man to sit [in] the house. 14. To hew for himself cedars, and he took an ilex and an oak and he reinforced it with forest trees; he planted a sapling, and rain makes it grow. 15. And it was for man to ignite, and he took from them and warmed himself; he even heated [the oven] and baked bread; he even made a god and prostrated himself: he made a graven image and bowed to them. 16. Half of it he burnt with fire; on half of it he ate meat; he roasted a roast and became sated; he even warmed himself and said, "Aha, I am warm, I see fire." 17. And what is left over from it he made for a god, for his graven image; he kneels to it and prostrates himself and prays to it, and he says, "Save me, for you are my god." 18. Neither do they know nor do they understand, for their eyes are bedaubed from seeing, their hearts from understanding. 19. And he does not give it thought, and he has neither knowledge nor understanding to say, "Half of it I burnt with fire, and I even baked bread on its coals, I roasted meat and ate. And what was left over from it, shall I make for an abomination? Shall I bow to rotten wood?" 20. [To] a provider [made] of ashes, a deceived heart has perverted him, and he shall not save his soul, and he shall not say, "Is there not falsehood in my right hand?"

תִּרְהוּ הֲלֹא מֵאָז הִשְׁמַעְתִּיךָ וְהִגַּדְתִּי וְאַתֶּם עֵדָי
הֲיֵשׁ אֱלוֹהַּ מִבַּלְעָדַי וְאֵין צוּר בַּל־יָדָעְתִּי׃
ט יֹצְרֵי־פֶסֶל כֻּלָּם תֹּהוּ וַחֲמוּדֵיהֶם בַּל־יוֹעִילוּ
וְעֵדֵיהֶם הֵמָּה בַּל־יִרְאוּ וּבַל־יֵדְעוּ לְמַעַן יֵבֹשׁוּ׃
י מִי־יָצַר אֵל וּפֶסֶל נָסָךְ לְבִלְתִּי הוֹעִיל׃ יא הֵן
כָּל־חֲבֵרָיו יֵבֹשׁוּ וְחָרָשִׁים הֵמָּה מֵאָדָם יִתְקַבְּצוּ
כֻלָּם יַעֲמֹדוּ יִפְחֲדוּ יֵבֹשׁוּ יָחַד׃ יב חָרַשׁ בַּרְזֶל
מַעֲצָד וּפָעַל בַּפֶּחָם וּבַמַּקָּבוֹת יִצְּרֵהוּ וַיִּפְעָלֵהוּ
בִּזְרוֹעַ כֹּחוֹ גַּם־רָעֵב וְאֵין כֹּחַ לֹא־שָׁתָה מַיִם
וַיִּיעָף׃ יג חָרַשׁ עֵצִים נָטָה קָו יְתָאֲרֵהוּ בַשֶּׂרֶד
יַעֲשֵׂהוּ בַּמַּקְצֻעוֹת וּבַמְּחוּגָה יְתָאֳרֵהוּ וַיַּעֲשֵׂהוּ
כְּתַבְנִית אִישׁ כְּתִפְאֶרֶת אָדָם לָשֶׁבֶת בָּיִת׃
יד לִכְרָת־לוֹ אֲרָזִים וַיִּקַּח תִּרְזָה וְאַלּוֹן וַיְאַמֶּץ־
לוֹ בַּעֲצֵי־יָעַר נָטַע אֹרֶן וְגֶשֶׁם יְגַדֵּל׃ טו וְהָיָה
לְאָדָם לְבָעֵר וַיִּקַּח מֵהֶם וַיָּחָם אַף־יַשִּׂיק וְאָפָה
לָחֶם אַף־יִפְעַל־אֵל וַיִּשְׁתָּחוּ עָשָׂהוּ פֶסֶל
וַיִּסְגָּד־לָמוֹ׃ טז חֶצְיוֹ שָׂרַף בְּמוֹ־אֵשׁ עַל־חֶצְיוֹ
בָּשָׂר יֹאכֵל יִצְלֶה צָלִי וְיִשְׂבָּע אַף־יָחֹם וְיֹאמַר
הֶאָח חַמּוֹתִי רָאִיתִי אוּר׃ יז וּשְׁאֵרִיתוֹ לְאֵל
עָשָׂה לְפִסְלוֹ יִסְגּוֹד־ (יסגד קרי) לוֹ וְיִשְׁתַּחוּ
וְיִתְפַּלֵּל אֵלָיו וְיֹאמַר הַצִּילֵנִי כִּי אֵלִי אָתָּה׃
יח לֹא יָדְעוּ וְלֹא יָבִינוּ כִּי טַח מֵרְאוֹת עֵינֵיהֶם
מֵהַשְׂכִּיל לִבֹּתָם׃ יט וְלֹא־יָשִׁיב אֶל־לִבּוֹ וְלֹא
דַעַת וְלֹא־תְבוּנָה לֵאמֹר חֶצְיוֹ שָׂרַפְתִּי בְמוֹ־
אֵשׁ וְאַף אָפִיתִי עַל־גֶּחָלָיו לֶחֶם אֶצְלֶה בָשָׂר
וְאֹכֵל וְיִתְרוֹ לְתוֹעֵבָה אֶעֱשֶׂה לְבוּל עֵץ אֶסְגּוֹד׃
כ רֹעֶה אֵפֶר לֵב הוּתַל הִטָּהוּ וְלֹא־יַצִּיל אֶת־
נַפְשׁוֹ וְלֹא יֹאמַר הֲלוֹא שֶׁקֶר בִּימִינִי׃ כא זְכָר־

21. Remember these, O Jacob; and Israel, for you are My servant; I formed you that you be a servant to Me, Israel; do not forget Me. 22. I erased your transgressions like a thick cloud, and like a cloud have I erased your sins; return to Me for I have redeemed you. 23. Sing, ye heavens, for the Lord has done [this]! Shout, ye lowest parts of the earth! Ye mountains, burst out in song, the forest and all trees therein! For the Lord has redeemed Jacob, and with Israel shall He be glorified.

אֵ֣לֶּה יַֽעֲקֹ֣ב וְיִשְׂרָאֵ֔ל כִּ֥י עַבְדִּי־אָ֖תָּה יְצַרְתִּ֥יךָ עֶֽבֶד־לִ֣י אַ֔תָּה יִשְׂרָאֵ֖ל לֹ֥א תִנָּשֵֽׁנִי: כב מָחִ֤יתִי כָעָב֙ פְּשָׁעֶ֔יךָ וְכֶעָנָ֖ן חַטֹּאותֶ֑יךָ שׁוּבָ֥ה אֵלַ֖י כִּ֥י גְאַלְתִּֽיךָ: כג רָנּ֤וּ שָׁמַ֨יִם֙ כִּֽי־עָשָׂ֣ה יְהֹוָ֔ה הָרִ֖יעוּ תַּֽחְתִּיּ֣וֹת אָ֑רֶץ פִּצְח֧וּ הָרִ֣ים רִנָּ֗ה יַ֛עַר וְכָל־עֵ֖ץ בּ֑וֹ כִּֽי־גָאַ֤ל יְהֹוָה֙ יַֽעֲקֹ֔ב וּבְיִשְׂרָאֵ֖ל יִתְפָּאָֽר:

HAFTARATH TZAV הפטרת צו
(Jeremiah 7:21–8:3; 9:22, 23)
Usually this Sidra is read on Shabbath Hagadol, the Sabbath preceding Passover. Then the specially designated Haftarah for that Sabbath is read (p. 965). Should Parashath Zachor fall on this Sabbath, the Haftarah for Zachor (p. 958) is read. Should Parashath Parah fall on this Sabbath the Haftarah for Parah (p. 960) is read.

The theme of this selection, too, is that it is better not to sin than to have to resort to the sin offerings and guilt offerings which are discussed in detail in this Sidra.

7:21. So says the Lord of Hosts, the God of Israel: Add your burnt offerings to your sacrifices and eat meat. 22. For I spoke not to your fathers nor commanded them on the day that I brought them out of the land of Egypt, for the purpose of burnt offerings or sacrifices. 23. But this thing did I command them: Obey Me so that I am God to you and you are a people to Me, and you walk in all the ways that I command you, so that it may be well with you. 24. But they did not obey nor inclined their ear, but walked according to [their] own counsels and in the stubbornness of their evil heart and belonged to retrogression and not to progress. 25. Since the day that your fathers came forth out of the land of Egypt until this day, I sent to you all My servants, the prophets, sent them day after day with every fresh morn. 26. Yet they hearkened not to Me nor inclined their ear, but stiffened their neck; they did worse than their fathers. 27. And when you will speak all these words to them, and they will not hearken to you, and you call to them and they will not answer you, 28. then say to them: This is the nation that does not obey

כא כֹּ֤ה אָמַר֙ יְהֹוָ֣ה צְבָא֔וֹת אֱלֹהֵ֖י יִשְׂרָאֵ֑ל עֹלֽוֹתֵיכֶ֛ם סְפ֥וּ עַל־זִבְחֵיכֶ֖ם וְאִכְל֥וּ בָשָֽׂר: כב כִּ֣י לֹֽא־דִבַּ֗רְתִּי אֶת־אֲב֥וֹתֵיכֶ֛ם וְלֹ֣א צִוִּיתִ֗ים בְּי֛וֹם הוֹצִיא (הוֹצִיאִי קרי) אוֹתָ֖ם מֵאֶ֣רֶץ מִצְרָ֑יִם עַל־דִּבְרֵ֥י עוֹלָ֖ה וָזָֽבַח: כג כִּ֣י אִם־אֶת־הַדָּבָ֣ר הַ֠זֶּ֠ה צִוִּ֨יתִי אוֹתָ֤ם לֵאמֹר֙ שִׁמְע֣וּ בְקוֹלִ֔י וְהָיִ֤יתִי לָכֶם֙ לֵֽאלֹהִ֔ים וְאַתֶּ֖ם תִּֽהְיוּ־לִ֣י לְעָ֑ם וַהֲלַכְתֶּ֗ם בְּכָל־הַדֶּ֨רֶךְ֙ אֲשֶׁ֣ר אֲצַוֶּ֣ה אֶתְכֶ֔ם לְמַ֖עַן יִיטַ֥ב לָכֶֽם: כד וְלֹ֤א שָֽׁמְעוּ֙ וְלֹֽא־הִטּ֣וּ אֶת־אָזְנָ֔ם וַיֵּ֣לְכ֗וּ בְּמֹֽעֵצ֤וֹת בִּשְׁרִרוּת֙ לִבָּ֣ם הָרָ֔ע וַיִּֽהְי֥וּ לְאָח֖וֹר וְלֹ֥א לְפָנִֽים: כה לְמִן־הַיּ֗וֹם אֲשֶׁ֨ר יָֽצְא֜וּ אֲב֤וֹתֵיכֶם֙ מֵאֶ֣רֶץ מִצְרַ֔יִם עַ֖ד הַיּ֣וֹם הַזֶּ֑ה וָֽאֶשְׁלַ֤ח אֲלֵיכֶם֙ אֶת־כָּל־עֲבָדַ֣י הַנְּבִיאִ֔ים י֖וֹם הַשְׁכֵּ֥ם וְשָׁלֹֽחַ: כו וְל֤וֹא שָֽׁמְעוּ֙ אֵלַ֔י וְלֹ֥א הִטּ֖וּ אֶת־אָזְנָ֑ם וַיַּקְשׁוּ֙ אֶת־עָרְפָּ֔ם הֵרֵ֖עוּ מֵֽאֲבוֹתָֽם: כז וְדִבַּרְתָּ֤ אֲלֵיהֶם֙ אֶת־כָּל־הַדְּבָרִ֣ים הָאֵ֔לֶּה וְלֹ֥א יִשְׁמְע֖וּ אֵלֶ֑יךָ וְקָרָ֥אתָ אֲלֵיהֶ֖ם וְלֹ֥א יַֽעֲנֽוּכָה: כח וְאָֽמַרְתָּ֣ אֲלֵיהֶ֗ם זֶ֤ה הַגּוֹי֙ אֲשֶׁ֣ר לֽוֹא־שָֽׁמְעוּ֙

בְּקוֹל יְהוָה אֱלֹהָיו וְלֹא לָקְחוּ מוּסָר אָבְדָה
הָאֱמוּנָה וְנִכְרְתָה מִפִּיהֶם׃ כט גָּזִּי נִזְרֵךְ
וְהַשְׁלִיכִי וּשְׂאִי עַל־שְׁפָיִם קִינָה כִּי מָאַס יְהוָה
וַיִּטֹּשׁ אֶת־דּוֹר עֶבְרָתוֹ׃ ל כִּי־עָשׂוּ בְנֵי־יְהוּדָה
הָרַע בְּעֵינַי נְאֻם־יְהוָה שָׂמוּ שִׁקּוּצֵיהֶם בַּבַּיִת
אֲשֶׁר־נִקְרָא שְׁמִי־עָלָיו לְטַמְּאוֹ׃ לא וּבָנוּ בָּמוֹת
הַתֹּפֶת אֲשֶׁר בְּגֵיא בֶן־הִנֹּם לִשְׂרֹף אֶת־בְּנֵיהֶם
וְאֶת־בְּנֹתֵיהֶם בָּאֵשׁ אֲשֶׁר לֹא צִוִּיתִי וְלֹא
עָלְתָה עַל־לִבִּי׃ לב לָכֵן הִנֵּה יָמִים בָּאִים נְאֻם־
יְהוָה וְלֹא־יֵאָמֵר עוֹד הַתֹּפֶת וְגֵיא בֶן־הִנֹּם כִּי
אִם־גֵּיא הַהֲרֵגָה וְקָבְרוּ בְתֹפֶת מֵאֵין מָקוֹם׃
לג וְהָיְתָה נִבְלַת הָעָם הַזֶּה לְמַאֲכָל לְעוֹף
הַשָּׁמַיִם וּלְבֶהֱמַת הָאָרֶץ וְאֵין מַחֲרִיד׃
לד וְהִשְׁבַּתִּי ׀ מֵעָרֵי יְהוּדָה וּמֵחֻצוֹת יְרוּשָׁלִַם
קוֹל שָׂשׂוֹן וְקוֹל שִׂמְחָה קוֹל חָתָן וְקוֹל כַּלָּה
כִּי לְחָרְבָּה תִּהְיֶה הָאָרֶץ׃ א בָּעֵת הַהִיא נְאֻם־
יְהוָה ויוצִיאו (יוציאו קרי) אֶת־עַצְמוֹת מַלְכֵי־
יְהוּדָה וְאֶת־עַצְמוֹת שָׂרָיו וְאֶת־עַצְמוֹת
הַכֹּהֲנִים וְאֵת ׀ עַצְמוֹת הַנְּבִיאִים וְאֵת עַצְמוֹת
יוֹשְׁבֵי־יְרוּשָׁלִָם מִקִּבְרֵיהֶם׃ ב וּשְׁטָחוּם לַשֶּׁמֶשׁ
וְלַיָּרֵחַ וּלְכֹל ׀ צְבָא הַשָּׁמַיִם אֲשֶׁר אֲהֵבוּם
וַאֲשֶׁר עֲבָדוּם וַאֲשֶׁר הָלְכוּ אַחֲרֵיהֶם
וַאֲשֶׁר דְּרָשׁוּם וַאֲשֶׁר הִשְׁתַּחֲווּ לָהֶם לֹא
יֵאָסְפוּ וְלֹא יִקָּבֵרוּ לְדֹמֶן עַל־פְּנֵי הָאֲדָמָה
יִהְיוּ׃ ג וְנִבְחַר מָוֶת מֵחַיִּים לְכֹל הַשְּׁאֵרִית
הַנִּשְׁאָרִים מִן־הַמִּשְׁפָּחָה הָרָעָה הַזֹּאת בְּכָל־
הַמְּקֹמוֹת הַנִּשְׁאָרִים אֲשֶׁר הִדַּחְתִּים שָׁם נְאֻם
יְהוָה צְבָאוֹת׃ כב כֹּה ׀ אָמַר יְהוָה אַל־יִתְהַלֵּל
חָכָם בְּחָכְמָתוֹ וְאַל־יִתְהַלֵּל הַגִּבּוֹר בִּגְבוּרָתוֹ
אַל־יִתְהַלֵּל עָשִׁיר בְּעָשְׁרוֹ׃ כג כִּי אִם־בְּזֹאת

the Lord their God, and has not accepted correction, out of their mouth faithfulness has disappeared, yea, rooted out! 29. So tear off your diadem and throw it away, and let lamentation sound out over the hillocks, for the Lord has spurned and abandoned the generation of His wrath. 30. For the sons of Judah have done that which is evil in My eyes, says the Lord; they have set their abominations in the House which is called by My Name, to pollute it. 31. And they have built the high places of Topheth, which are in the valley of Ben-Hinnom, to burn their sons and their daughters in the fire, which I did not command and which did not come into My mind. 32. Behold, therefore, the days come, says the Lord, when it shall no longer be called Topheth, nor the Valley of Ben-Hinnom, but the Valley of Slaughter, and they bury in Topheth until there be no more place. 33. And the carcasses of this people shall be food for the birds of the heaven and the beasts of the earth, and none shall fray them away. 34. Then will I cause to cease from the cities of Judah and from the streets of Jerusalem the voice of joy and the voice of gladness, the voice of the bridegroom and the voice of the bride, for the land shall be desolate. 8:1. At that time, says the Lord, they shall bring the bones of the kings of Judah and the bones of his princes, and the bones of the priests and the bones of the prophets and the bones of the inhabitants of Jerusalem, out of their graves, 2. and spread them to the sun and to the moon, and to the whole host of the heavens whom they have loved, and whom they served, and whom they have followed, and from whom they have enquired, and before whom they have prostrated themselves; they shall not be gathered up nor be buried; they shall be for dung on the surface of the ground. 3. And death shall be preferable to life for all the residue that remain of this evil family, which remain in all the places whither I have cast them out — says the Lord of Hosts. 9:22. So says the Lord: Let not the wise man glorify himself in his wisdom, neither let the mighty glorify himself in his strength; let not the rich man glorify himself in his riches. 23. But let him

that would glorify himself glorify himself in
this: that he understands and knows Me, for
I, the Lord, exercise kindness, justice, and
righteousness on the earth; for these things I
desire, says the Lord.

יִתְהַלֵּל הַמִּתְהַלֵּל הַשְׂכֵּל וְיָדֹעַ אוֹתִי כִּי אֲנִי
יְהֹוָה עֹשֶׂה חֶסֶד מִשְׁפָּט וּצְדָקָה בָּאָרֶץ כִּי־
בְאֵלֶּה חָפַצְתִּי נְאֻם־יְהֹוָה:

HAFTARATH SHEMINI הפטרת שמיני
(II. Sam. 6:1–7:17)

**Sephardim conclude with 6:19, with some congregations adding 7:16,17. Jews
following the Italian ritual conclude with 7:3. Should Parashath Parah fall on this
Sabbath the Haftarah for Parah (p. 960) is read. Should Parashath HaChodesh fall on
this Sabbath the Haftarah for Parashath HaChodesh (p. 962) is read. Should Rosh
Chodesh Iyar fall on Sunday, the Haftarah For The Day Preceding Rosh Chodesh
(p. 933) is read.**

This selection includes the account of the breach of Uzzah, who came too close to the
Holy Ark. This story is reminiscent of the incident involving Nadab and Abihu, told in
this Sidra, who died when they brought "strange fire" into the Sanctuary.

6:1. And David continued [to gather] all
the chosen of Israel, thirty thousand. 2. And
David arose and went with all the people
that were with him, from Baale-Judah, to
bring up from there the ark of God, which is
called a Name: the Name of the Lord of
Hosts, Who dwells upon the cherubim
[being] upon it. 3. And they set the ark of
God upon a new cart, and they carried it
from the house of Avinadav, which was on
the hill; and Uzzah and Ahio, the sons of
Avinadav, drove the new cart. 4. And they
brought it out of the house of Avinadav,
which was on the hill, with the ark of God;
and Ahio went before the ark. 5. And David
and all the house of Israel made merry with
all [manner of instruments of] cypress wood,
and with harps, and with psalteries, and
with timbrels, and with sistra, and with
cymbals. 6. And they came to Goren-
nachon, and Uzzah put forth [his hand] to
the ark of God, and grasped hold of it, for
the oxen swayed it. 7. And the anger of the
Lord was kindled against Uzzah; and God
struck him down there for his error; and
there he died by the ark of God. 8. And
David was angered, because the Lord had
made a breach upon Uzzah; and he called
that place Peretz-Uzzah, unto this day.
9. And David was afraid of the Lord that
day, and he said: "How can the ark of the
Lord come to me?" 10. And David did not
want to remove unto him the ark of the

א וַיֹּסֶף עוֹד דָּוִד אֶת־כָּל־בָּחוּר בְּיִשְׂרָאֵל
שְׁלֹשִׁים אָלֶף: ב וַיָּקָם ׀ וַיֵּלֶךְ דָּוִד וְכָל־הָעָם
אֲשֶׁר אִתּוֹ מִבַּעֲלֵי יְהוּדָה לְהַעֲלוֹת מִשָּׁם אֵת
אֲרוֹן הָאֱלֹהִים אֲשֶׁר־נִקְרָא שֵׁם שֵׁם יְהֹוָה
צְבָאוֹת יֹשֵׁב הַכְּרֻבִים עָלָיו: ג וַיַּרְכִּבוּ אֶת־
אֲרוֹן הָאֱלֹהִים אֶל־עֲגָלָה חֲדָשָׁה וַיִּשָּׂאֻהוּ
מִבֵּית אֲבִינָדָב אֲשֶׁר בַּגִּבְעָה וְעֻזָּא וְאַחְיוֹ בְּנֵי
אֲבִינָדָב נֹהֲגִים אֶת־הָעֲגָלָה חֲדָשָׁה: ד וַיִּשָּׂאֻהוּ
מִבֵּית אֲבִינָדָב אֲשֶׁר בַּגִּבְעָה עִם אֲרוֹן
הָאֱלֹהִים וְאַחְיוֹ הֹלֵךְ לִפְנֵי הָאָרוֹן: ה וְדָוִד ׀
וְכָל־בֵּית יִשְׂרָאֵל מְשַׂחֲקִים לִפְנֵי יְהֹוָה בְּכֹל
עֲצֵי בְרוֹשִׁים וּבְכִנֹּרוֹת וּבִנְבָלִים וּבְתֻפִּים
וּבִמְנַעַנְעִים וּבְצֶלְצֱלִים: ו וַיָּבֹאוּ עַד־גֹּרֶן נָכוֹן
וַיִּשְׁלַח עֻזָּה אֶל־אֲרוֹן הָאֱלֹהִים וַיֹּאחֶז בּוֹ כִּי
שָׁמְטוּ הַבָּקָר: ז וַיִּחַר־אַף יְהֹוָה בְּעֻזָּה וַיַּכֵּהוּ
שָׁם הָאֱלֹהִים עַל־הַשַּׁל וַיָּמָת שָׁם עִם אֲרוֹן
הָאֱלֹהִים: ח וַיִּחַר לְדָוִד עַל אֲשֶׁר פָּרַץ יְהֹוָה
פֶּרֶץ בְּעֻזָּה וַיִּקְרָא לַמָּקוֹם הַהוּא פֶּרֶץ עֻזָּה עַד
הַיּוֹם הַזֶּה: ט וַיִּרָא דָוִד אֶת־יְהֹוָה בַּיּוֹם הַהוּא
וַיֹּאמֶר אֵיךְ יָבוֹא אֵלַי אֲרוֹן יְהֹוָה: י וְלֹא־אָבָה
דָוִד לְהָסִיר אֵלָיו אֶת־אֲרוֹן יְהֹוָה עַל־עִיר דָּוִד

Lord, into the city of David; and David took it aside to the house of Oved-Edom the Gittite. 11. And the ark of the Lord dwelled in the house of Oved-Edom the Gittite three months; and the Lord blessed Oved-Edom and all his household. 12. And it was told to King David saying: "The Lord has blessed the house of Oved-Edom, and all that belongs to him, because of the ark of the Lord." And David went and brought up the ark of God from the house of Oved-Edom into the city of David with joy. 13. And it was when the bearers of the ark of God had trodden six paces, he sacrificed an ox and a fatling. 14. And David danced with all his might before the Lord; and David was girded with a linen ephod. 15. And David and all the house of Israel brought up the ark of the Lord with shouting and with the sound of [the] shofar. 16. And [as] the ark of the Lord came [into] the city of David, Michal the daughter of Saul peered through the window, and she saw King David hopping and dancing before the Lord; and she loathed him in her heart. 17. And they brought the ark of the Lord, and they set it in its place, inside the tent that David had pitched for it; and David offered burnt offerings before the Lord and peace offerings. 18. And David finished offering the burnt offering and the peace offerings, and he blessed the people in the name of the Lord of Hosts. 19. And he distributed to all the people, to the whole multitude of Israel, both to men and women, to each individual, a loaf of bread and a portion of meat and a barrel of wine. And all the people departed, every one to his home. (*Sephardim conclude here; some add the last two verses.*) 20. And David returned to bless his household. And Michal the daughter of Saul came out to meet David, and she said, "How honored was today the king of Israel, who exposed himself today in the eyes of the handmaids of his servants, as would expose himself one of the idlers." 21. And David said unto Michal: "Before the Lord, who chose me above your father, and above all his house, to appoint me prince over the people of the Lord, over Israel; therefore I have made merry before the Lord. 22. And if I be demeaned more than this, and be abased in

וַיַּטֵּהוּ דָוִד בֵּית עֹבֵד־אֱדֹם הַגִּתִּי׃ יא וַיֵּשֶׁב
אֲרוֹן יְהוָֹה בֵּית עֹבֵד אֱדֹם הַגִּתִּי שְׁלֹשָׁה
חֳדָשִׁים וַיְבָרֶךְ יְהוָֹה אֶת־עֹבֵד אֱדֹם וְאֶת־כָּל־
בֵּיתוֹ׃ יב וַיֻּגַּד לַמֶּלֶךְ דָּוִד לֵאמֹר בֵּרַךְ יְהוָֹה
אֶת־בֵּית עֹבֵד אֱדֹם וְאֶת־כָּל־אֲשֶׁר־לוֹ בַּעֲבוּר
אֲרוֹן הָאֱלֹהִים וַיֵּלֶךְ דָּוִד וַיַּעַל אֶת־אֲרוֹן
הָאֱלֹהִים מִבֵּית עֹבֵד אֱדֹם עִיר דָּוִד בְּשִׂמְחָה׃
יג וַיְהִי כִּי צָעֲדוּ נֹשְׂאֵי אֲרוֹן־יְהוָֹה שִׁשָּׁה
צְעָדִים וַיִּזְבַּח שׁוֹר וּמְרִיא׃ יד וְדָוִד מְכַרְכֵּר
בְּכָל־עֹז לִפְנֵי יְהוָֹה וְדָוִד חָגוּר אֵפוֹד בָּד׃
טו וְדָוִד וְכָל־בֵּית יִשְׂרָאֵל מַעֲלִים אֶת־אֲרוֹן
יְהוָֹה בִּתְרוּעָה וּבְקוֹל שׁוֹפָר׃ טז וְהָיָה אֲרוֹן
יְהוָֹה בָּא עִיר דָּוִד וּמִיכַל בַּת־שָׁאוּל נִשְׁקְפָה ׀
בְּעַד הַחַלּוֹן וַתֵּרֶא אֶת־הַמֶּלֶךְ דָּוִד מְפַזֵּז
וּמְכַרְכֵּר לִפְנֵי יְהוָֹה וַתִּבֶז לוֹ בְּלִבָּהּ׃ יז וַיָּבִאוּ
אֶת־אֲרוֹן יְהוָֹה וַיַּצִּגוּ אֹתוֹ בִּמְקוֹמוֹ בְּתוֹךְ
הָאֹהֶל אֲשֶׁר נָטָה־לוֹ דָּוִד וַיַּעַל דָּוִד עֹלוֹת לִפְנֵי
יְהוָֹה וּשְׁלָמִים׃ יח וַיְכַל דָּוִד מֵהַעֲלוֹת הָעוֹלָה
וְהַשְּׁלָמִים וַיְבָרֶךְ אֶת־הָעָם בְּשֵׁם יְהוָֹה
צְבָאוֹת׃ יט וַיְחַלֵּק לְכָל־הָעָם לְכָל־הֲמוֹן
יִשְׂרָאֵל לְמֵאִישׁ וְעַד־אִשָּׁה לְאִישׁ חַלַּת לֶחֶם
אַחַת וְאֶשְׁפָּר אֶחָד וַאֲשִׁישָׁה אֶחָת וַיֵּלֶךְ כָּל־
הָעָם אִישׁ לְבֵיתוֹ׃ (כאן מסיימין הספרדים. ויש מוסיפים
את שני הפסוקים האחרונים: „ונאמן ביתך וגו׳") כ וַיָּשָׁב
דָּוִד לְבָרֵךְ אֶת־בֵּיתוֹ וַתֵּצֵא מִיכַל בַּת־שָׁאוּל
לִקְרַאת דָּוִד וַתֹּאמֶר מַה־נִּכְבַּד הַיּוֹם מֶלֶךְ
יִשְׂרָאֵל אֲשֶׁר נִגְלָה הַיּוֹם לְעֵינֵי אַמְהוֹת עֲבָדָיו
כְּהִגָּלוֹת נִגְלוֹת אַחַד הָרֵקִים׃ כא וַיֹּאמֶר דָּוִד
אֶל־מִיכַל לִפְנֵי יְהוָֹה אֲשֶׁר בָּחַר־בִּי מֵאָבִיךְ
וּמִכָּל־בֵּיתוֹ לְצַוֹּת אֹתִי נָגִיד עַל־עַם יְהוָֹה עַל־
יִשְׂרָאֵל וְשִׂחַקְתִּי לִפְנֵי יְהוָֹה׃ כב וּנְקַלֹּתִי עוֹד

mine own eyes, [yet] of the maidservants of which you have spoken, with them will I get me honor.'' 23. And Michal the daughter of Saul had no child until the day of her death. 7:1. And it came to pass, when the king dwelt in his house, and the Lord had given him rest round about from all his enemies. 2. That the king said unto Nathan the prophet: "See now, I dwell in a house of cedar, but the ark of God dwells within the curtains." 3. And Nathan said to the king: "All that is in your heart go do; for the Lord is with you." (*Congregations following the Italian ritual conclude here.*) 4. And it came to pass on the same night, that the word of God was to Nathan, saying: 5. Go and say to My servant, to David: So says the Lord: Shall you build Me a house for My dwelling? 6. For I have not dwelt in a house from the day that I brought up the children of Israel out of Egypt, to this day, but have walked in a tent and in a tabernacle. 7. In all [the places] wherein I have walked with all the children of Israel, did I speak a word with any of the rulers of Israel, whom I commanded to shepherd My people Israel, saying: Why do you not build for me a house of cedar? 8. And now, so shall you say to My servant, to David: Thus says the Lord of Hosts: I took you from the sheepcote, from following the sheep, to be a leader over My people Israel. 9. And I have been with you wherever you have gone, and I have cut off all your enemies from before you, and have made for you a great name, like the name of the great ones that are in the earth. 10. And I will appoint a place for My people, for Israel, and I will plant them, and they will dwell in their own place, and be disturbed no more; and the wicked people shall not continue to afflict them as formerly. 11. And even from the day that I commanded judges to be over My people Israel; and I will give you rest from all your enemies. And the Lord has told you that the Lord will make for you a house. 12. When your days are finished and you shall lie with your forefathers, then I will raise up your seed that shall proceed from your body after you, and I will establish his kingdom. 13. He shall build a house for My Name, and I will establish the throne of his king-

מִזֹּאת וְהָיִיתִי שָׁפָל בְּעֵינַי וְעִם־הָאֲמָהוֹת אֲשֶׁר אָמַרְתְּ עִמָּם אִכָּבֵדָה: כג וּלְמִיכַל בַּת־שָׁאוּל לֹא־הָיָה לָהּ יָלֶד עַד יוֹם מוֹתָהּ: א וַיְהִי כִּי־יָשַׁב הַמֶּלֶךְ בְּבֵיתוֹ וַיהֹוָה הֵנִיחַ־לוֹ מִסָּבִיב מִכָּל־אֹיְבָיו: ב וַיֹּאמֶר הַמֶּלֶךְ אֶל־נָתָן הַנָּבִיא רְאֵה נָא אָנֹכִי יוֹשֵׁב בְּבֵית אֲרָזִים וַאֲרוֹן הָאֱלֹהִים יֹשֵׁב בְּתוֹךְ הַיְרִיעָה: ג וַיֹּאמֶר נָתָן אֶל־הַמֶּלֶךְ כֹּל אֲשֶׁר בִּלְבָבְךָ לֵךְ עֲשֵׂה כִּי יְהֹוָה עִמָּךְ: ד (כאן מסיימין האיטליאנים) וַיְהִי בַּלַּיְלָה הַהוּא וַיְהִי דְּבַר־יְהֹוָה אֶל־נָתָן לֵאמֹר: ה לֵךְ וְאָמַרְתָּ אֶל־עַבְדִּי אֶל־דָּוִד כֹּה אָמַר יְהֹוָה הַאַתָּה תִּבְנֶה־לִּי בַיִת לְשִׁבְתִּי: ו כִּי לֹא יָשַׁבְתִּי בְּבַיִת לְמִיּוֹם הַעֲלֹתִי אֶת־בְּנֵי יִשְׂרָאֵל מִמִּצְרַיִם וְעַד הַיּוֹם הַזֶּה וָאֶהְיֶה מִתְהַלֵּךְ בְּאֹהֶל וּבְמִשְׁכָּן: ז בְּכֹל אֲשֶׁר־הִתְהַלַּכְתִּי בְּכָל־בְּנֵי יִשְׂרָאֵל הֲדָבָר דִּבַּרְתִּי אֶת־אַחַד שִׁבְטֵי יִשְׂרָאֵל אֲשֶׁר צִוִּיתִי לִרְעוֹת אֶת־עַמִּי אֶת־יִשְׂרָאֵל לֵאמֹר לָמָּה לֹא־בְנִיתֶם לִי בֵּית אֲרָזִים: ח וְעַתָּה כֹּה־תֹאמַר לְעַבְדִּי לְדָוִד כֹּה אָמַר יְהֹוָה צְבָאוֹת אֲנִי לְקַחְתִּיךָ מִן־הַנָּוֶה מֵאַחַר הַצֹּאן לִהְיוֹת נָגִיד עַל־עַמִּי עַל־יִשְׂרָאֵל: ט וָאֶהְיֶה עִמְּךָ בְּכֹל אֲשֶׁר הָלַכְתָּ וָאַכְרִתָה אֶת־כָּל־אֹיְבֶיךָ מִפָּנֶיךָ וְעָשִׂתִי לְךָ שֵׁם גָּדוֹל כְּשֵׁם הַגְּדֹלִים אֲשֶׁר בָּאָרֶץ: י וְשַׂמְתִּי מָקוֹם לְעַמִּי לְיִשְׂרָאֵל וּנְטַעְתִּיו וְשָׁכַן תַּחְתָּיו וְלֹא יִרְגַּז עוֹד וְלֹא־יֹסִיפוּ בְנֵי־עַוְלָה לְעַנּוֹתוֹ כַּאֲשֶׁר בָּרִאשׁוֹנָה: יא וּלְמִן־הַיּוֹם אֲשֶׁר צִוִּיתִי שֹׁפְטִים עַל־עַמִּי יִשְׂרָאֵל וַהֲנִיחֹתִי לְךָ מִכָּל־אֹיְבֶיךָ וְהִגִּיד לְךָ יְהֹוָה כִּי־בַיִת יַעֲשֶׂה־לְּךָ יְהֹוָה: יב כִּי יִמְלְאוּ יָמֶיךָ וְשָׁכַבְתָּ אֶת־אֲבֹתֶיךָ וַהֲקִימֹתִי אֶת־זַרְעֲךָ אַחֲרֶיךָ אֲשֶׁר יֵצֵא מִמֵּעֶיךָ וַהֲכִינֹתִי אֶת־מַמְלַכְתּוֹ: יג הוּא יִבְנֶה־בַיִת לִשְׁמִי וְכֹנַנְתִּי אֶת־כִּסֵּא מַמְלַכְתּוֹ עַד־עוֹלָם:

dom forever. 14. I will be to him a Father,
and he shall be to Me a son; so that when he
goes astray I will chasten him with the rod
of men, and with the stripes of the sons of
Adam. 15. But My mercy shall not depart
from him as I withdrew it from Saul, whom
I removed from before you. 16. And your
house and your kingdom shall be confirmed
forever before you; your throne shall be
established forever. 17. According to all
these words, and according to all this vision,
so did Nathan speak to David.

יד אֲנִי אֶהְיֶה־לּוֹ לְאָב וְהוּא יִהְיֶה־לִּי לְבֵן
אֲשֶׁר בְּהַעֲוֺתוֹ וְהֹכַחְתִּיו בְּשֵׁבֶט אֲנָשִׁים וּבְנִגְעֵי
בְּנֵי אָדָם: טו וְחַסְדִּי לֹא־יָסוּר מִמֶּנּוּ כַּאֲשֶׁר
הֲסִרֹתִי מֵעִם שָׁאוּל אֲשֶׁר הֲסִרֹתִי מִלְּפָנֶיךָ:
טז וְנֶאְמַן בֵּיתְךָ וּמַמְלַכְתְּךָ עַד־עוֹלָם לְפָנֶיךָ
כִּסְאֲךָ יִהְיֶה נָכוֹן עַד־עוֹלָם: יז כְּכֹל הַדְּבָרִים
הָאֵלֶּה וּכְכֹל הַחִזָּיוֹן הַזֶּה כֵּן דִּבֶּר נָתָן אֶל־דָּוִד:

HAFTARATH THAZRIA   הפטרת תזריע
(II Kings 4:42–5:19)
Should Parashath HaChodesh fall on this Sabbath the Haftarah for Parashath
HaChodesh (p. 962) is read.

The prophet's curing of Naaman's leprosy resembles this Sidra which deals with the
purification of lepers.

4:42. And a man came from Baal-
Shalishah, and he brought to the man of
God bread of the first fruits, twenty loaves
of barley bread and sheaves of fresh grain in
their shells; and he said, "Give to the people
and let them eat." 43. And his servant said,
"How will I give this before one hundred
men?" And he said, "Give the people and
let them eat, for so has the Lord said, 'They
shall eat and leave over.'" 44. And he
placed it before them, and they ate and left
over, according to the word of the Lord.
5:1. Now Naaman, the general of the king
of Aram, was a prominent man before his
lord and respected, for through him had the
lord given victory to Aram; and the man was
a great warrior, and he was a *mezora*.
2. Now the Arameans went out in bands
and captured from the land of Israel a
young girl, who ministered to Naaman's
wife. 3. And she said to her mistress, "The
supplications for my master should be that
he go before the prophet who is in Samaria;
then he would cure him of his *zaraath*."
4. And he came and told his master, saying,
"In the following manner has the girl from
the land of Israel spoken." 5. And the king
of Aram said, "Come, go, and I will send a
letter to the king of Israel." He went and
took in his possession ten talents of silver

מב וְאִישׁ בָּא מִבַּעַל שָׁלִשָׁה וַיָּבֵא לְאִישׁ
הָאֱלֹהִים לֶחֶם בִּכּוּרִים עֶשְׂרִים־לֶחֶם שְׂעֹרִים
וְכַרְמֶל בְּצִקְלֹנוֹ וַיֹּאמֶר תֵּן לָעָם וְיֹאכֵלוּ:
מג וַיֹּאמֶר מְשָׁרְתוֹ מָה אֶתֵּן זֶה לִפְנֵי מֵאָה
אִישׁ וַיֹּאמֶר תֵּן לָעָם וְיֹאכֵלוּ כִּי כֹה אָמַר
יְהֹוָה אָכֹל וְהוֹתֵר: מד וַיִּתֵּן לִפְנֵיהֶם וַיֹּאכְלוּ
וַיּוֹתִרוּ כִּדְבַר יְהֹוָה: א וְנַעֲמָן שַׂר־צְבָא מֶלֶךְ־
אֲרָם הָיָה אִישׁ גָּדוֹל לִפְנֵי אֲדֹנָיו וּנְשֻׂא פָנִים
כִּי־בוֹ נָתַן־יְהֹוָה תְּשׁוּעָה לַאֲרָם וְהָאִישׁ הָיָה
גִּבּוֹר חַיִל מְצֹרָע: ב וַאֲרָם יָצְאוּ גְדוּדִים
וַיִּשְׁבּוּ מֵאֶרֶץ יִשְׂרָאֵל נַעֲרָה קְטַנָּה וַתְּהִי לִפְנֵי
אֵשֶׁת נַעֲמָן: ג וַתֹּאמֶר אֶל־גְּבִרְתָּהּ אַחֲלַי אֲדֹנִי
לִפְנֵי הַנָּבִיא אֲשֶׁר בְּשֹׁמְרוֹן אָז יֶאֱסֹף אֹתוֹ
מִצָּרַעְתּוֹ: ד וַיָּבֹא וַיַּגֵּד לַאדֹנָיו לֵאמֹר כָּזֹאת
וְכָזֹאת דִּבְּרָה הַנַּעֲרָה אֲשֶׁר מֵאֶרֶץ יִשְׂרָאֵל:
ה וַיֹּאמֶר מֶלֶךְ־אֲרָם לֶךְ בֹּא וְאֶשְׁלְחָה סֵפֶר
אֶל־מֶלֶךְ יִשְׂרָאֵל וַיֵּלֶךְ וַיִּקַּח בְּיָדוֹ עֶשֶׂר כִּכְּרֵי־

and six thousand gold pieces, and ten suits of clothes. 6. And the letter came to the king of Israel, saying, "And now, when this letter comes to you, behold I have sent Naaman my servant to you, and you shall cure him of his *zaraath.*" 7. And it was when the king of Israel read the letter, that he rent his garments and said, "Do I have the power from God to put to death and to bring to life, that this one sends to me to cure a man of his *zaraath*? Just know now and see that he is looking for a pretext against me." 8. And it was when Elisha the man of God heard that the king of Israel had rent his garments, that he sent to the king, saying, "Why have you rent your garments? Let him come to me now, and let him know that there is a prophet in Israel." 9. And Naaman came with his horses and with his chariots, and he stood at the doorway of Elisha's house. 10. And Elisha dispatched a messenger to him, saying, "Go and immerse yourself seven times in the Jordan, and your flesh will be restored to you, and you will become clean." 11. Now Naaman became incensed, and he went away, and he said, "Here I thought that he would come out to see me, and he would stand and call in the name of YHVH his God, and he would raise his hand toward the spot and cure the *mezora.* 12. Are not Amanah and Parpar, the rivers of Damascus, better than all the waters of Israel? Will I not immerse myself in them and become clean?" And he turned and went away in anger. 13. And his servants approached and spoke to him and said, "Master, if the prophet spoke to you to do a difficult thing, would you not do it? And surely since he said to you, 'Immerse yourself and become clean.'" 14. And he went down and immersed himself in the Jordan seven times according to the word of the man of God; and his flesh was restored like the flesh of a young lad, and he became clean. 15. And he returned to the man of God, he and his entire camp; and he came and stood before him; and he said, "Behold, now I know that there is no God in all the earth except in Israel. And now, accept a gift from your servant." 16. And he said, "As the Lord, before Whom I have stood, lives, I will not accept." And he urged him to accept, but he refused. 17. And Naaman

כֶּ֣סֶף וְשֵׁ֤שֶׁת אֲלָפִים֙ זָהָ֔ב וְעֶ֖שֶׂר חֲלִיפ֥וֹת בְּגָדִֽים: ו וַיָּבֵ֣א הַסֵּ֔פֶר אֶל־מֶ֖לֶךְ יִשְׂרָאֵ֣ל לֵאמֹ֑ר וְעַתָּ֗ה כְּב֨וֹא הַסֵּ֤פֶר הַזֶּה֙ אֵלֶ֔יךָ הִנֵּ֨ה שָׁלַ֤חְתִּי אֵלֶ֨יךָ֙ אֶֽת־נַעֲמָ֣ן עַבְדִּ֔י וַאֲסַפְתּ֖וֹ מִצָּֽרַעְתּֽוֹ: ז וַיְהִ֡י כִּקְרֹא֩ מֶֽלֶךְ־יִשְׂרָאֵ֨ל אֶת־הַסֵּ֜פֶר וַיִּקְרַ֣ע בְּגָדָ֗יו וַיֹּ֨אמֶר֙ הַֽאֱלֹהִ֣ים אָ֔נִי לְהָמִ֖ית וּֽלְהַחֲי֑וֹת כִּֽי־זֶ֤ה שֹׁלֵ֨חַ֙ אֵלַ֔י לֶאֱסֹ֥ף אִ֖ישׁ מִצָּֽרַעְתּ֑וֹ כִּ֣י אַךְ־דְּעֽוּ־נָא֙ וּרְא֔וּ כִּֽי־מִתְאַנֶּ֥ה ה֖וּא לִֽי: ח וַיְהִ֡י כִּשְׁמֹ֣עַ ׀ אֱלִישָׁ֣ע אִֽישׁ־הָאֱלֹהִ֗ים כִּֽי־קָרַ֤ע מֶֽלֶךְ־יִשְׂרָאֵל֙ אֶת־בְּגָדָ֔יו וַיִּשְׁלַ֤ח אֶל־הַמֶּ֨לֶךְ֙ לֵאמֹ֔ר לָ֥מָּה קָרַ֖עְתָּ בְּגָדֶ֑יךָ יָֽבֹא־נָ֣א אֵלַ֔י וְיֵדַ֕ע כִּ֛י יֵ֥שׁ נָבִ֖יא בְּיִשְׂרָאֵֽל: ט וַיָּבֹ֥א נַֽעֲמָ֖ן בְּסוּסָ֣ו (בסוסיו קרי) וּבְרִכְבּ֑וֹ וַיַּֽעֲמֹ֥ד פֶּֽתַח־הַבַּ֖יִת לֶֽאֱלִישָֽׁע: י וַיִּשְׁלַ֥ח אֵלָ֛יו אֱלִישָׁ֖ע מַלְאָ֣ךְ לֵאמֹ֑ר הָל֗וֹךְ וְרָֽחַצְתָּ֤ שֶֽׁבַע־פְּעָמִים֙ בַּיַּרְדֵּ֔ן וְיָשֹׁ֧ב בְּשָֽׂרְךָ֛ לְךָ֖ וּטְהָֽר: יא וַיִּקְצֹ֥ף נַֽעֲמָ֖ן וַיֵּלַ֑ךְ וַיֹּ֨אמֶר֙ הִנֵּ֤ה אָמַ֨רְתִּי֙ אֵלַ֔י ׀ יֵצֵ֤א יָצוֹא֙ וְעָמַ֔ד וְקָרָא֙ בְּשֵׁם־יְהֹוָ֣ה אֱלֹהָ֔יו וְהֵנִ֥יף יָד֛וֹ אֶל־הַמָּק֖וֹם וְאָסַ֥ף הַמְּצֹרָֽע: יב הֲלֹ֡א טוֹב֩ אֲבָנָ֨ה (אמנה כתיב) וּפַרְפַּ֜ר נַֽהֲר֣וֹת דַּמֶּ֗שֶׂק מִכֹּל֙ מֵימֵ֣י יִשְׂרָאֵ֔ל הֲלֹֽא־אֶרְחַ֥ץ בָּהֶ֖ם וְטָהָ֑רְתִּי וַיִּ֥פֶן וַיֵּ֖לֶךְ בְּחֵמָֽה: יג וַיִּגְּשׁ֣וּ עֲבָדָיו֮ וַיְדַבְּר֣וּ אֵלָיו֒ וַיֹּֽאמְר֗וּ אָבִי֙ דָּבָ֣ר גָּד֗וֹל הַנָּבִ֛יא דִּבֶּ֥ר אֵלֶ֖יךָ הֲל֣וֹא תַֽעֲשֶׂ֑ה וְאַ֛ף כִּֽי־אָמַ֥ר אֵלֶ֖יךָ רְחַ֥ץ וּטְהָֽר: יד וַיֵּ֗רֶד וַיִּטְבֹּ֤ל בַּיַּרְדֵּן֙ שֶׁ֣בַע פְּעָמִ֔ים כִּדְבַ֖ר אִ֣ישׁ הָֽאֱלֹהִ֑ים וַיָּ֣שָׁב בְּשָׂר֗וֹ כִּבְשַׂ֛ר נַ֥עַר קָטֹ֖ן וַיִּטְהָֽר: טו וַיָּשָׁב֩ אֶל־אִ֨ישׁ הָֽאֱלֹהִ֜ים ה֣וּא וְכָֽל־מַֽחֲנֵ֗הוּ וַיָּבֹא֙ וַיַּֽעֲמֹ֣ד לְפָנָ֔יו וַיֹּ֗אמֶר הִנֵּה־נָ֤א יָדַ֨עְתִּי֙ כִּ֣י אֵ֤ין אֱלֹהִים֙ בְּכָל־הָאָ֔רֶץ כִּ֖י אִם־בְּיִשְׂרָאֵ֑ל וְעַתָּ֛ה קַח־נָ֥א בְרָכָ֖ה מֵאֵ֥ת עַבְדֶּֽךָ: טז וַיֹּ֕אמֶר חַי־יְהֹוָ֛ה אֲשֶׁר־עָמַ֥דְתִּי לְפָנָ֖יו אִם־אֶקָּ֑ח וַיִּפְצַר־בּ֥וֹ לָקַ֖חַת וַיְמָאֵֽן:

said, "Now, if only your servant be given a
load of earth as carried by a team of mules,
for your servant will no longer offer up a
burnt offering or a sacrifice to other deities,
but to the Lord. 18. For this thing may the
Lord forgive your servant; when my master
comes to Beth-Rimmon to prostrate himself
there, and he leans on my hand, and I will
prostrate myself in Beth-Rimmon; when I
bow in Beth-Rimmon, may the Lord forgive your servant for this thing." 19. And
he said to him, "Go in peace"; and he went
some distance away from him.

יז וַיֹּאמֶר נַעֲמָן וָלֹא יֻתַּן־נָא לְעַבְדְּךָ מַשָּׂא
צֶמֶד־פְּרָדִים אֲדָמָה כִּי לוֹא־יַעֲשֶׂה עוֹד עַבְדְּךָ
עֹלָה וָזֶבַח לֵאלֹהִים אֲחֵרִים כִּי אִם־לַיהוָה:
יח לַדָּבָר הַזֶּה יִסְלַח יְהוָה לְעַבְדֶּךָ בְּבוֹא אֲדֹנִי
בֵית־רִמּוֹן לְהִשְׁתַּחֲוֹת שָׁמָּה וְהוּא ׀ נִשְׁעָן עַל־
יָדִי וְהִשְׁתַּחֲוֵיתִי בֵּית רִמֹּן בְּהִשְׁתַּחֲוָיָתִי בֵּית
רִמֹּן יִסְלַח־נָא (כתיב ולא קרי)־יְהוָה לְעַבְדְּךָ בַּדָּבָר
הַזֶּה: יט וַיֹּאמֶר לוֹ לֵךְ לְשָׁלוֹם וַיֵּלֶךְ מֵאִתּוֹ
כִּבְרַת־אָרֶץ:

HAFTARATH METZORA   הפטרת מצרע
(II Kings 7:3–20)

**This Haftarah is also read when Thazria and Metzora are read together. Should
Shabbath Hagadol fall on this Sabbath, the Haftarah for Shabbath Hagadol (p. 965)
is read. Should Rosh Chodesh coincide with the Sabbath, the Haftarah for Shabbath
Rosh Chodesh (p. 930) is read.**

The narrative of the four leprous men closely resembles the Sidra with the purification
of the *metzora*.

7:3. Now there were four men, stricken
with *zaraath*, [at] the entrance of the gate.
And they said to each other, "Why are we
sitting here until we die? 4. If we say that
we will come into the city, with the famine
in the city, we will die there; and if we stay
here, we will die. So now, let us go, and let
us defect to the Aramean camp. If they
spare us, we will live; and if they kill us, we
will die." 5. And they arose in the evening
to come to the Aramean camp. And they
came to the edge of the Aramean camp, and
behold, no one was there. 6. Now the Lord
had caused the Aramean camp to hear the
sound of chariots and the sound of horses,
the sound of a great army. And they said to
one another, "Behold, the king of Israel has
hired for us the kings of the Hittites and the
kings of the Egyptians to attack us." 7. And
they picked themselves up and fled at dusk,
leaving behind their tents, their horses, and
their donkeys, the camp as it was, and they
fled for their lives. 8. Now these *mezoraim*
came up to the edge of the camp, entered
one tent, ate and drank, and carried off from
there silver, gold, and clothing, and they
went and hid [them]. And they returned

ג וְאַרְבָּעָה אֲנָשִׁים הָיוּ מְצֹרָעִים פֶּתַח הַשָּׁעַר
וַיֹּאמְרוּ אִישׁ אֶל־רֵעֵהוּ מָה אֲנַחְנוּ יֹשְׁבִים פֹּה
עַד־מָתְנוּ: ד אִם־אָמַרְנוּ נָבוֹא הָעִיר וְהָרָעָב
בָּעִיר וָמַתְנוּ שָׁם וְאִם־יָשַׁבְנוּ פֹה וָמָתְנוּ וְעַתָּה
לְכוּ וְנִפְּלָה אֶל־מַחֲנֵה אֲרָם אִם־יְחַיֻּנוּ נִחְיֶה
וְאִם־יְמִיתֻנוּ וָמָתְנוּ: ה וַיָּקֻמוּ בַנֶּשֶׁף לָבוֹא
אֶל־מַחֲנֵה אֲרָם וַיָּבֹאוּ עַד־קְצֵה מַחֲנֵה אֲרָם
וְהִנֵּה אֵין־שָׁם אִישׁ: ו וַאדֹנָי הִשְׁמִיעַ ׀ אֶת־
מַחֲנֵה אֲרָם קוֹל רֶכֶב קוֹל סוּס קוֹל חַיִל גָּדוֹל
וַיֹּאמְרוּ אִישׁ אֶל־אָחִיו הִנֵּה שָׂכַר־עָלֵינוּ מֶלֶךְ
יִשְׂרָאֵל אֶת־מַלְכֵי הַחִתִּים וְאֶת־מַלְכֵי מִצְרַיִם
לָבוֹא עָלֵינוּ: ז וַיָּקוּמוּ וַיָּנוּסוּ בַנֶּשֶׁף וַיַּעַזְבוּ
אֶת־אָהֳלֵיהֶם וְאֶת־סוּסֵיהֶם וְאֶת־חֲמֹרֵיהֶם
הַמַּחֲנֶה כַּאֲשֶׁר־הִיא וַיָּנֻסוּ אֶל־נַפְשָׁם: ח וַיָּבֹאוּ
הַמְצֹרָעִים הָאֵלֶּה עַד־קְצֵה הַמַּחֲנֶה וַיָּבֹאוּ אֶל־
אֹהֶל אֶחָד וַיֹּאכְלוּ וַיִּשְׁתּוּ וַיִּשְׂאוּ מִשָּׁם כֶּסֶף
וְזָהָב וּבְגָדִים וַיֵּלְכוּ וַיַּטְמִנוּ וַיָּשֻׁבוּ וַיָּבֹאוּ אֶל־

אֹהֶל אַחֵר וַיִּשְׂאוּ מִשָּׁם וַיֵּלְכוּ וַיַּטְמִנוּ׃
ט וַיֹּאמְרוּ אִישׁ אֶל־רֵעֵהוּ לֹא־כֵן ׀ אֲנַחְנוּ
עֹשִׂים הַיּוֹם הַזֶּה יוֹם־בְּשֹׂרָה הוּא וַאֲנַחְנוּ
מַחְשִׁים וְחִכִּינוּ עַד־אוֹר הַבֹּקֶר וּמְצָאָנוּ עָווֹן
וְעַתָּה לְכוּ וְנָבֹאָה וְנַגִּידָה בֵּית הַמֶּלֶךְ׃ י וַיָּבֹאוּ
וַיִּקְרְאוּ אֶל־שֹׁעֵר הָעִיר וַיַּגִּידוּ לָהֶם לֵאמֹר
בָּאנוּ אֶל־מַחֲנֵה אֲרָם וְהִנֵּה אֵין־שָׁם אִישׁ
וְקוֹל אָדָם כִּי אִם־הַסּוּס אָסוּר וְהַחֲמוֹר אָסוּר
וְאֹהָלִים כַּאֲשֶׁר הֵמָּה׃ יא וַיִּקְרָא הַשֹּׁעֲרִים
וַיַּגִּידוּ בֵּית הַמֶּלֶךְ פְּנִימָה׃ יב וַיָּקָם הַמֶּלֶךְ
לַיְלָה וַיֹּאמֶר אֶל־עֲבָדָיו אַגִּידָה־נָּא לָכֶם אֵת
אֲשֶׁר־עָשׂוּ לָנוּ אֲרָם יָדְעוּ כִּי־רְעֵבִים אֲנַחְנוּ
וַיֵּצְאוּ מִן־הַמַּחֲנֶה לְהֵחָבֵה בְהַשָּׂדֶה (בשדה קרי)
לֵאמֹר כִּי־יֵצְאוּ מִן־הָעִיר וְנִתְפְּשֵׂם חַיִּים וְאֶל־
הָעִיר נָבֹא׃ יג וַיַּעַן אֶחָד מֵעֲבָדָיו וַיֹּאמֶר
וְיִקְחוּ־נָא חֲמִשָּׁה מִן־הַסּוּסִים הַנִּשְׁאָרִים אֲשֶׁר
נִשְׁאֲרוּ־בָהּ הִנָּם כְּכָל־הֶהָמוֹן (המון קרי) יִשְׂרָאֵל
אֲשֶׁר נִשְׁאֲרוּ־בָהּ הִנָּם כְּכָל־הֲמוֹן יִשְׂרָאֵל
אֲשֶׁר־תָּמּוּ וְנִשְׁלְחָה וְנִרְאֶה׃ יד וַיִּקְחוּ שְׁנֵי
רֶכֶב סוּסִים וַיִּשְׁלַח הַמֶּלֶךְ אַחֲרֵי מַחֲנֵה־אֲרָם
לֵאמֹר לְכוּ וּרְאוּ׃ טו וַיֵּלְכוּ אַחֲרֵיהֶם עַד־
הַיַּרְדֵּן וְהִנֵּה כָל־הַדֶּרֶךְ מְלֵאָה בְגָדִים וְכֵלִים
אֲשֶׁר־הִשְׁלִיכוּ אֲרָם בְּהֵחָפְזָם (בחפזם קרי) וַיָּשֻׁבוּ
הַמַּלְאָכִים וַיַּגִּדוּ לַמֶּלֶךְ׃ טז וַיֵּצֵא הָעָם וַיָּבֹזּוּ
אֵת מַחֲנֵה אֲרָם וַיְהִי סְאָה־סֹלֶת בְּשֶׁקֶל
וְסָאתַיִם שְׂעֹרִים בְּשֶׁקֶל כִּדְבַר יְהֹוָה׃ יז וְהַמֶּלֶךְ
הִפְקִיד אֶת־הַשָּׁלִישׁ אֲשֶׁר נִשְׁעָן עַל־יָדוֹ עַל־
הַשַּׁעַר וַיִּרְמְסֻהוּ הָעָם בַּשַּׁעַר וַיָּמֹת כַּאֲשֶׁר
דִּבֶּר אִישׁ הָאֱלֹהִים אֲשֶׁר דִּבֶּר בְּרֶדֶת הַמֶּלֶךְ
אֵלָיו׃ יח וַיְהִי כְּדַבֵּר אִישׁ הָאֱלֹהִים אֶל־הַמֶּלֶךְ
לֵאמֹר סָאתַיִם שְׂעֹרִים בְּשֶׁקֶל וּסְאָה־סֹלֶת
בְּשֶׁקֶל יִהְיֶה כָּעֵת מָחָר בְּשַׁעַר שֹׁמְרוֹן׃
יט וַיַּעַן הַשָּׁלִישׁ אֶת־אִישׁ הָאֱלֹהִים וַיֹּאמַר
וְהִנֵּה יְהֹוָה עֹשֶׂה אֲרֻבּוֹת בַּשָּׁמַיִם הֲיִהְיֶה כַּדָּבָר

and entered another tent and carried off from there, and they went and hid [them]. 9. Now one said to another, "We are not doing right. This day is a day of good news, yet we are keeping quiet. If we wait until daybreak, we will incur guilt. Now, let us go and come and relate this in the king's palace." 10. And they came and called to the gatekeepers of the city and told them, saying, "We came to the Aramean camp, and behold there is no man there nor the sound of a human, but the horses are tethered and the donkeys are tethered, and the tents are as they were." 11. And he called the gatekeepers, and they related it to the king's palace inside. 12. And the king arose at night and said to his servants, "Now I will tell you what the Arameans have done to us. They know that we are hungry. So they left the camp to hide in the field, saying, 'When they come out of the city, we will seize them alive and enter the city.'" 13. Now one of his servants called out and said, "Let them take now five of the remaining horses that are left there. Behold, they are like all the multitude of Israel that are left there, behold, they are like all the multitude of Israel that have perished; and let us send, and we will see." 14. So they took two riders of horses, and the king sent them after the Aramean camp, saying, "Go and see." 15. And they followed them up to the Jordan, and behold all the way was full of garments and vessels that the Arameans had cast off in their haste; and the messengers returned and related it to the king. 16. And the people went out and plundered the Aramean camp; and a *se'ah* of fine flour was sold for a shekel, and two *se'ahs* of barley were sold for a shekel, according to the word of the Lord. 17. Now the king appointed the officer upon whose hand he leaned, over the gate, and the people trampled him and he died, as the man of God had spoken, which he spoke when the king had come down to him. 18. And it was when the man of God had spoken to the king, saying, "Two *se'ahs* of barley will be sold for a shekel and a *se'ah* of fine flour will be sold at this time tomorrow in the gate of Samaria," 19. that the officer answered the man of God and said, "And behold, if God makes windows in the sky, will this thing come about?"

And he said, "Behold you will see it with your own eyes, yet you shall not eat therefrom." 20. And so it happened to him, that the people trampled him in the gate, and he died.

הַזֶּה וַיֹּאמֶר הִנְּךָ רֹאֶה בְּעֵינֶיךָ וּמִשָּׁם לֹא תֹאכֵל: כ וַיְהִי־לוֹ כֵּן וַיִּרְמְסוּ אֹתוֹ הָעָם בַּשַּׁעַר וַיָּמֹת:

HAFTARATH AḤARAY MOTH FOR ASHKENAZIM הפטרת אחרי מות
(Amos 9:7–15)

This selection is generally accepted by Ashkenazim as the Haftarah for the Sidra Acharey Moth. This Haftarah is also read on a Sabbath when the Sidroth Acharey Moth and Kedoshim are read together. If the Sabbath on which Acharey Moth is read is one of the Sabbaths calling for another Haftarah (e.g., the day before Rosh Chodesh or Shabbath Hagadol, the Sabbath immediately preceding Passover), this Haftarah is read with the Sidra Kedoshim. According to *Levush*, the Haftarah to be read when Acharey Moth and Kedoshim are read together is the one ordinarily read with Kedoshim. Should Shabbath Hagadol fall on this Sabbath see p. 965. Should this be the day before Rosh Chodesh, see p. 933.

This selection makes reference to the Exile, as does the Sidra (Leviticus 28:28).

9:7. Are you not like the children of the **Cushites** to Me, O children of Israel? says the Lord. Did I not bring Israel up from the land of Egypt, and the Philistines out of Caphtor and the Aram out of Kir? 8. Behold, the eyes of the Lord God are upon the sinful kingdom, and I will destroy it from off the face of the earth; nevertheless, I will in no wise destroy the house of Jacob, says the Lord. 9. For, lo, I will command, and I will sift the house of Israel through all the nations as something is sifted in a sieve, yet no pebble falls to the ground. 10. By the sword shall the sinful of My people die—those who say, "Through us the misfortune does not come any nearer or any earlier." 11. On that day I will set up the fallen tabernacle of David, and I will close up their breaches, and I will raise up his ruins and build it up as in the days of old. 12. So that they may inherit the remainder of Edom and of all the nations upon whom My Name is called, says the Lord, Who does this. 13. Behold, days are coming, says the Lord, when the plowman will overtake the reaper and the treader of grapes him that sows the seed, and the mountains shall drip with sweet wine, and all the hills shall melt. 14. And I will return the captivity of My people Israel, and they shall build the waste cities and inhabit

ז הֲלוֹא כִבְנֵי כֻשִׁיִּים אַתֶּם לִי בְּנֵי יִשְׂרָאֵל נְאֻם־יְהֹוָה הֲלוֹא אֶת־יִשְׂרָאֵל הֶעֱלֵיתִי מֵאֶרֶץ מִצְרַיִם וּפְלִשְׁתִּיִּים מִכַּפְתּוֹר וַאֲרָם מִקִּיר: ח הִנֵּה עֵינֵי | אֲדֹנָי יֱהֹוִה בַּמַּמְלָכָה הַחַטָּאָה וְהִשְׁמַדְתִּי אֹתָהּ מֵעַל פְּנֵי הָאֲדָמָה אֶפֶס כִּי לֹא הַשְׁמֵיד אַשְׁמִיד אֶת־בֵּית יַעֲקֹב נְאֻם־יְהֹוָה: ט כִּי־הִנֵּה אָנֹכִי מְצַוֶּה וַהֲנִעוֹתִי בְכָל־הַגּוֹיִם אֶת־בֵּית יִשְׂרָאֵל כַּאֲשֶׁר יִנּוֹעַ בַּכְּבָרָה וְלֹא־ יִפּוֹל צְרוֹר אָרֶץ: י בַּחֶרֶב יָמוּתוּ כֹּל חַטָּאֵי עַמִּי הָאֹמְרִים לֹא־תַגִּישׁ וְתַקְדִּים בַּעֲדֵינוּ הָרָעָה: יא בַּיּוֹם הַהוּא אָקִים אֶת־סֻכַּת דָּוִיד הַנֹּפֶלֶת וְגָדַרְתִּי אֶת־פִּרְצֵיהֶן וַהֲרִסֹתָיו אָקִים וּבְנִיתִיהָ כִּימֵי עוֹלָם: יב לְמַעַן יִירְשׁוּ אֶת־ שְׁאֵרִית אֱדוֹם וְכָל־הַגּוֹיִם אֲשֶׁר־נִקְרָא שְׁמִי עֲלֵיהֶם נְאֻם־יְהֹוָה עֹשֶׂה זֹּאת: יג הִנֵּה יָמִים בָּאִים נְאֻם־יְהֹוָה וְנִגַּשׁ חוֹרֵשׁ בַּקֹּצֵר וְדֹרֵךְ עֲנָבִים בְּמֹשֵׁךְ הַזָּרַע וְהִטִּיפוּ הֶהָרִים עָסִיס וְכָל־הַגְּבָעוֹת תִּתְמוֹגַגְנָה: יד וְשַׁבְתִּי אֶת־שְׁבוּת עַמִּי יִשְׂרָאֵל וּבָנוּ עָרִים נְשַׁמּוֹת וְיָשָׁבוּ וְנָטְעוּ

them, and plant vineyards and drink their wine, and lay out gardens and eat their fruit. 15. And I will plant them upon their land, and they shall no more be uprooted out of their land which I have given them, says the Lord your God.

כְּרָמִים וְשָׁתוּ אֶת־יֵינָם וְעָשׂוּ גַנּוֹת וְאָכְלוּ אֶת־פְּרִיהֶם: טו וּנְטַעְתִּים עַל־אַדְמָתָם וְלֹא יִנָּתְשׁוּ עוֹד מֵעַל אַדְמָתָם אֲשֶׁר־נָתַתִּי לָהֶם אָמַר יְהֹוָה אֱלֹהֶיךָ:

HAFTARATH AḤARAY MOTH FOR SEPHARDIM הפטרת אחרי מות
(Ezekiel 22:1–19 according to the Ashkenazim in the Holy Land and all Sephardim.)
The latter conclude with verse 16, as do congregations following the ritual of Frankfort-on-the-Main, which read this Haftarah with Kedoshim.

This selection castigates the immoral practices mentioned at the end of the Sidra.

22:1. And the word of the Lord came to me, saying: 2. And you, son of man, will you judge the city of bloodshed and let her know all her abominations? 3. Then you shall say: So says the Lord God: O city that sheds blood in her midst, even now, when her time is approaching, and makes idols over her to defile herself. 4. By the blood that you have shed you have become laden with guilt, and by your idols that you have made have you become defiled; and you have made your days draw near, and you have come into your years; therefore have I put you to shame to the nations and ridicule to all the lands. 5. Those that are near and those that are far from you shall mock you—you—whose name is so befouled, in whom the turmoil is so great. 6. Behold, the princes of Israel were in you, each one for his own arm in order to shed blood. 7. Father and mother are held light in you; they have dealt against the stranger with oppression in your midst; orphan and widow have they wronged in you. 8. My holy things have you despised, and My Sabbaths have you profaned. 9. Talebearers have been in you in order to shed blood, and in you they have eaten upon the mountains; in your midst they have committed lewdness. 10. In you they uncovered their fathers' nakedness; in you they have afflicted the woman that was unclean because of her period of separation. 11. In you one man committed an abomination with his neighbor's wife; another incestuously defiled his daughter-in-law, and another afflicted his sister, the

א וַיְהִי דְבַר־יְהֹוָה אֵלַי לֵאמֹר: ב וְאַתָּה בֶן־ אָדָם הֲתִשְׁפֹּט הֲתִשְׁפֹּט אֶת־עִיר הַדָּמִים וְהוֹדַעְתָּהּ אֵת כָּל־תּוֹעֲבוֹתֶיהָ: ג וְאָמַרְתָּ כֹּה אָמַר אֲדֹנָי יֱהֹוִה עִיר שֹׁפֶכֶת דָּם בְּתוֹכָהּ לָבוֹא עִתָּהּ וְעָשְׂתָה גִלּוּלִים עָלֶיהָ לְטָמְאָה: ד בְּדָמֵךְ אֲשֶׁר־שָׁפַכְתְּ אָשַׁמְתְּ וּבְגִלּוּלַיִךְ אֲשֶׁר־עָשִׂית טָמֵאת וַתַּקְרִיבִי יָמַיִךְ וַתָּבוֹא עַד־שְׁנוֹתָיִךְ עַל־כֵּן נְתַתִּיךְ חֶרְפָּה לַגּוֹיִם וְקַלָּסָה לְכָל־ הָאֲרָצוֹת: ה הַקְּרֹבוֹת וְהָרְחֹקוֹת מִמֵּךְ יִתְקַלְּסוּ־ בָךְ טְמֵאַת הַשֵּׁם רַבַּת הַמְּהוּמָה: ו הִנֵּה נְשִׂיאֵי יִשְׂרָאֵל אִישׁ לִזְרֹעוֹ הָיוּ בָךְ לְמַעַן שְׁפָךְ־דָּם: ז אָב וָאֵם הֵקַלּוּ בָךְ לַגֵּר עָשׂוּ בַעֹשֶׁק בְּתוֹכֵךְ יָתוֹם וְאַלְמָנָה הוֹנוּ בָךְ: ח קָדָשַׁי בָּזִית וְאֶת־ שַׁבְּתֹתַי חִלָּלְתְּ: ט אַנְשֵׁי רָכִיל הָיוּ בָךְ לְמַעַן שְׁפָךְ־דָּם וְאֶל־הֶהָרִים אָכְלוּ בָךְ זִמָּה עָשׂוּ בְתוֹכֵךְ: י עֶרְוַת־אָב גִּלָּה־בָךְ טְמֵאַת הַנִּדָּה עִנּוּ־בָךְ: יא וְאִישׁ אֶת־אֵשֶׁת רֵעֵהוּ עָשָׂה תּוֹעֵבָה וְאִישׁ אֶת־כַּלָּתוֹ טִמֵּא בְזִמָּה וְאִישׁ אֶת־ אֲחֹתוֹ בַת־אָבִיו עִנָּה־בָךְ: יב שֹׁחַד לָקְחוּ־בָךְ

daughter of his father. 12. In you they have taken bribes to shed blood; usury and increased pay have you taken, and robbed your neighbor by withholding his dues — but Me have you entirely forgotten, says the Lord God. 13. And behold, I clap My hands together over your dishonest gain which you have made and over your blood-guilt that is in you. 14. Will your heart endure, or will your hands remain strong in the days that I will deal with you? I, the Lord, have said it, and I will do it. 15. I will scatter you among the nations and fling you out into the countries and will make your impurity completely disappear out of you. 16. And you shall be profaned in yourself before the eyes of the nations, and you shall know that I am the Lord. (*The Sephardim and the congregation of Frankfort-on-the-Main conclude here.*) 17. And the word of the Lord came to me, saying: 18. Son of man! The house of Israel has become base metal to Me; all of them are copper and tin and iron and lead in the midst of the furnace; dross of silver have they become. 19. Therefore, as says the Lord God: Because you have all become dross, therefore, behold, I gather you together in the midst of Jerusalem.

לְמַעַן שְׁפָךְ־דָּם נֶשֶׁךְ וְתַרְבִּית לָקַחַתְּ וַתְּבַצְּעִי
רֵעַיִךְ בַּעֹשֶׁק וְאֹתִי שָׁכַחַתְּ נְאֻם אֲדֹנָי יֱהֹוִה:
יג וְהִנֵּה הִכֵּיתִי כַפִּי אֶל־בִּצְעֵךְ אֲשֶׁר עָשִׂית
וְעַל־דָּמֵךְ אֲשֶׁר הָיוּ בְּתוֹכֵךְ: יד הֲיַעֲמֹד לִבֵּךְ
אִם־תֶּחֱזַקְנָה יָדַיִךְ לַיָּמִים אֲשֶׁר אֲנִי עֹשֶׂה אוֹתָךְ
אֲנִי יְהֹוָה דִּבַּרְתִּי וְעָשִׂיתִי: טו וַהֲפִיצוֹתִי אוֹתָךְ
בַּגּוֹיִם וְזֵרִיתִיךְ בָּאֲרָצוֹת וַהֲתִמֹּתִי טֻמְאָתֵךְ
מִמֵּךְ: טז וְנִחַלְתְּ בָּךְ לְעֵינֵי גוֹיִם וְיָדַעַתְּ כִּי־אֲנִי
יְהֹוָה: יז וַיְהִי דְבַר־יְהֹוָה אֵלַי לֵאמֹר: יח בֶּן־
אָדָם הָיוּ־לִי בֵית־יִשְׂרָאֵל לְסוּג (לסיג קרי) כֻּלָּם
נְחֹשֶׁת וּבְדִיל וּבַרְזֶל וְעוֹפֶרֶת בְּתוֹךְ כּוּר סִיגִים
כֶּסֶף הָיוּ: יט לָכֵן כֹּה אָמַר אֲדֹנָי יֱהֹוִה יַעַן הֱיוֹת
כֻּלְּכֶם לְסִגִים לָכֵן הִנְנִי קֹבֵץ אֶתְכֶם אֶל־תּוֹךְ
יְרוּשָׁלָ͏ִם:

HAFTARATH KEDOSHIM FOR ASHKENAZIM הפטרת קדשים

(Ezekiel 22:1–19 for Ashkenazim.)

As stated above, Ashkenazim read with Kedoshim the Haftarah that Sephardim read with Acharey Moth. This Haftarah is read only if Acharey Moth and Kedoshim are read on separate Sabbaths, and neither Haftarah is replaced by a special Haftarah, such as the one For the Day Preceding Rosh Chodesh. Otherwise, הלא כבני כשיים is read, and התשפוט is omitted entirely. As mentioned above, according to *Levush*, this Haftarah is read when both Sidroth are read together. Ashkenazim in the Holy Land read this Haftarah for Acharey Moth and הלא כבני כשיים for Kedoshim. They, too, omit this Haftarah if the two Sidroth are read together or if one Haftarah is superseded.

HAFTARATH KEDOSHIM FOR SEPHARDIM הפטרת קדשים

(Ezekiel 20:1–20 according to the Sephardim.)

Congregations following the Yemenite and Italian rituals commence with verse 1; other Sephardim commence with verse 2.

The prophet foretells the impending destruction of Jerusalem due to Israel's disobedience of the laws of God, such as those described in the Sidra.

20:1. And it came to pass in the seventh year, in the fifth [month], on the tenth of the month, that certain men of the elders of Israel came to inquire of the Lord and sat

א וַיְהִי ׀ בַּשָּׁנָה הַשְּׁבִיעִית בַּחֲמִשִׁי בֶּעָשׂוֹר
לַחֹדֶשׁ בָּאוּ אֲנָשִׁים מִזִּקְנֵי יִשְׂרָאֵל לִדְרֹשׁ אֶת־

before me. (*Sephardim commence here.*) 2. Then came the word of the Lord to me, saying: 3. Son of man, speak to the elders of Israel and say to them: So says the Lord God: Have you come to inquire of Me? As true as I live, I will not be inquired of by you! says the Lord God. 4. Will you debate with them? Will you debate, O son of man? Let them know the abominations of their fathers. 5. And you shall say to them: So says the Lord God: On the day when I chose Israel, then I lifted up My hand to the seed of the house of Jacob, and made Myself known to them in the land of Egypt, when I lifted My hand to them, saying: I am the Lord your God. 6. On that day I lifted up My hand to them to bring them out of the land of Egypt, to a land that I had sought out for them, flowing with milk and honey, which is the glory of all the lands. 7. And I said to them: Cast away every man the despicable idols from before his eyes, and pollute not yourselves with the idols of Egypt; I am the Lord your God. 8. But they rebelled against Me and would not consent to hearken to Me; they did not cast away every man the despicable idols from before their eyes, neither did they forsake the idols of Egypt; and I said to pour out My wrath over them, to give My anger full rein over them in the midst of the land of Egypt. 9. But I wrought for the sake of My Name so that it should not be desecrated before the eyes of the nations in whose midst they were, before whose eyes I made Myself known to them, to bring them out of the land of Egypt. 10. And I brought them out of the land of Egypt, and I brought them into the wilderness. 11. And I gave them My statutes, and My ordinances I made known to them, which, if a man keep, he will live through them. 12. Moreover, I gave them My Sabbaths to be for a sign between Me and them, to know that I, the Lord, make them holy. 13. But the house of Israel rebelled against Me in the wilderness; they walked not in My statutes, and they despised My ordinances, which, if a man keep, he will live through them, and My Sabbaths they desecrated exceedingly. Then I said to pour out My wrath upon them in the wilderness, to make an end to them. 14. And I wrought for the sake of My

יְהוָה וַיֵּשְׁבוּ לְפָנָי׃ ב וַיְהִי דְבַר־יְהוָה אֵלַי
לֵאמֹר׃ ג בֶּן־אָדָם דַּבֵּר אֶת־זִקְנֵי יִשְׂרָאֵל
וְאָמַרְתָּ אֲלֵהֶם כֹּה אָמַר אֲדֹנָי יֱהוִה הֲלִדְרֹשׁ
אֹתִי אַתֶּם בָּאִים חַי־אָנִי אִם־אִדָּרֵשׁ לָכֶם נְאֻם
אֲדֹנָי יֱהוִה׃ ד הֲתִשְׁפֹּט אֹתָם הֲתִשְׁפּוֹט בֶּן־
אָדָם אֶת־תּוֹעֲבֹת אֲבוֹתָם הוֹדִיעֵם׃ ה וְאָמַרְתָּ
אֲלֵיהֶם כֹּה־אָמַר אֲדֹנָי יֱהוִה בְּיוֹם בָּחֳרִי
בְיִשְׂרָאֵל וָאֶשָּׂא יָדִי לְזֶרַע בֵּית יַעֲקֹב וָאִוָּדַע
לָהֶם בְּאֶרֶץ מִצְרָיִם וָאֶשָּׂא יָדִי לָהֶם לֵאמֹר
אֲנִי יְהוָה אֱלֹהֵיכֶם׃ ו בַּיּוֹם הַהוּא נָשָׂאתִי יָדִי
לָהֶם לְהוֹצִיאָם מֵאֶרֶץ מִצְרָיִם אֶל־אֶרֶץ אֲשֶׁר־
תַּרְתִּי לָהֶם זָבַת חָלָב וּדְבַשׁ צְבִי הִיא לְכָל־
הָאֲרָצוֹת׃ ז וָאֹמַר אֲלֵהֶם אִישׁ שִׁקּוּצֵי עֵינָיו
הַשְׁלִיכוּ וּבְגִלּוּלֵי מִצְרַיִם אַל־תִּטַּמָּאוּ אֲנִי
יְהוָה אֱלֹהֵיכֶם׃ ח וַיַּמְרוּ־בִי וְלֹא אָבוּ לִשְׁמֹעַ
אֵלַי אִישׁ אֶת־שִׁקּוּצֵי עֵינֵיהֶם לֹא הִשְׁלִיכוּ
וְאֶת־גִּלּוּלֵי מִצְרַיִם לֹא עָזָבוּ וָאֹמַר לִשְׁפֹּךְ
חֲמָתִי עֲלֵיהֶם לְכַלּוֹת אַפִּי בָּהֶם בְּתוֹךְ אֶרֶץ
מִצְרָיִם׃ ט וָאַעַשׂ לְמַעַן שְׁמִי לְבִלְתִּי הֵחֵל
לְעֵינֵי הַגּוֹיִם אֲשֶׁר־הֵמָּה בְתוֹכָם אֲשֶׁר נוֹדַעְתִּי
אֲלֵיהֶם לְעֵינֵיהֶם לְהוֹצִיאָם מֵאֶרֶץ מִצְרָיִם׃
י וָאוֹצִיאֵם מֵאֶרֶץ מִצְרָיִם וָאֲבִאֵם אֶל־
הַמִּדְבָּר׃ יא וָאֶתֵּן לָהֶם אֶת־חֻקּוֹתַי וְאֶת־
מִשְׁפָּטַי הוֹדַעְתִּי אוֹתָם אֲשֶׁר יַעֲשֶׂה אוֹתָם
הָאָדָם וָחַי בָּהֶם׃ יב וְגַם אֶת־שַׁבְּתוֹתַי נָתַתִּי
לָהֶם לִהְיוֹת לְאוֹת בֵּינִי וּבֵינֵיהֶם לָדַעַת כִּי אֲנִי
יְהוָה מְקַדְּשָׁם׃ יג וַיַּמְרוּ־בִי בֵית־יִשְׂרָאֵל
בַּמִּדְבָּר בְּחֻקּוֹתַי לֹא־הָלָכוּ וְאֶת־מִשְׁפָּטַי
מָאָסוּ אֲשֶׁר יַעֲשֶׂה אֹתָם הָאָדָם וָחַי בָּהֶם
וְאֶת־שַׁבְּתֹתַי חִלְּלוּ מְאֹד וָאֹמַר לִשְׁפֹּךְ חֲמָתִי
עֲלֵיהֶם בַּמִּדְבָּר לְכַלּוֹתָם׃ יד וָאֶעֱשֶׂה לְמַעַן

Name, so it should not be desecrated before the eyes of the nations before whose eyes I had brought them out. 15. But I also lifted up My hand to them in the wilderness, that I would not bring them into the land which I had given them, flowing with milk and honey, which is the glory of all lands. 16. Because they despised My ordinances, and in My statutes they did not walk, and My Sabbaths they desecrated — for their heart went constantly after their idols. 17. Nevertheless, My eye looked pityingly upon them, not to destroy them, and I did not make an end to them in the wilderness. 18. But I said to their children in the wilderness: Do not walk in the statutes of your fathers, and do not observe their ordinances, and do not defile yourselves with their idols. 19. I am the Lord your God; walk in My statutes, and keep My ordinances and fulfill them. 20. And keep My Sabbaths holy so that they be a sign between Me and you, that you may know that I am the Lord your God.

שְׁמִי לְבִלְתִּי הֵחֵל לְעֵינֵי הַגּוֹיִם אֲשֶׁר
הוֹצֵאתִים לְעֵינֵיהֶם: טו וְגַם־אֲנִי נָשָׂאתִי יָדִי
לָהֶם בַּמִּדְבָּר לְבִלְתִּי הָבִיא אֹתָם אֶל־הָאָרֶץ
אֲשֶׁר־נָתַתִּי זָבַת חָלָב וּדְבַשׁ צְבִי הִיא לְכָל־
הָאֲרָצוֹת: טז יַעַן בְּמִשְׁפָּטַי מָאָסוּ וְאֶת־חֻקּוֹתַי
לֹא־הָלְכוּ בָהֶם וְאֶת־שַׁבְּתוֹתַי חִלֵּלוּ כִּי אַחֲרֵי
גִלּוּלֵיהֶם לִבָּם הֹלֵךְ: יז וַתָּחָס עֵינִי עֲלֵיהֶם
מִשַּׁחֲתָם וְלֹא־עָשִׂיתִי אוֹתָם כָּלָה בַּמִּדְבָּר:
יח וָאֹמַר אֶל־בְּנֵיהֶם בַּמִּדְבָּר בְּחוּקֵּי אֲבוֹתֵיכֶם
אַל־תֵּלֵכוּ וְאֶת־מִשְׁפְּטֵיהֶם אַל־תִּשְׁמֹרוּ
וּבְגִלּוּלֵיהֶם אַל־תִּטַּמָּאוּ: יט אֲנִי יְהֹוָה אֱלֹהֵיכֶם
בְּחֻקּוֹתַי לֵכוּ וְאֶת־מִשְׁפָּטַי שִׁמְרוּ וַעֲשׂוּ אֹתָם:
כ וְאֶת־שַׁבְּתוֹתַי קַדֵּשׁוּ וְהָיוּ לְאוֹת בֵּינִי
וּבֵינֵיכֶם לָדַעַת כִּי אֲנִי יְהֹוָה אֱלֹהֵיכֶם:

HAFTARATH EMOR   הפטרת אמר
(Ezekiel 44:15–31)

This selection discusses the laws of the priesthood, as does the Sidra.

44:15. But the priests, the Levites, the sons of Zadok, who kept the charge of My Sanctuary when the children of Israel went astray from Me, they shall come near to Me to minister to Me, and they shall stand before Me to offer to Me fat and blood, says the Lord God. 16. They shall enter My Sanctuary, and they shall approach My Table to minister to Me, and they shall keep My charge. 17. And it shall be, when they enter the gates of the inner court, they shall be clothed with linen garments, and no wool shall be upon them when they minister the gates of the inner court and within. 18. Linen hats shall be upon their heads, and linen breeches shall be upon their loins; they shall not gird themselves in a place that sweats. 19. But when they go out into the outer court, into the outer court to the people, they shall put off their garments

טו וְהַכֹּהֲנִים הַלְוִיִּם בְּנֵי צָדוֹק אֲשֶׁר שָׁמְרוּ
אֶת־מִשְׁמֶרֶת מִקְדָּשִׁי בִּתְעוֹת בְּנֵי־יִשְׂרָאֵל
מֵעָלַי הֵמָּה יִקְרְבוּ אֵלַי לְשָׁרְתֵנִי וְעָמְדוּ לְפָנַי
לְהַקְרִיב לִי חֵלֶב וָדָם נְאֻם אֲדֹנָי יֱהֹוִה:
טז הֵמָּה יָבֹאוּ אֶל־מִקְדָּשִׁי וְהֵמָּה יִקְרְבוּ אֶל־
שֻׁלְחָנִי לְשָׁרְתֵנִי וְשָׁמְרוּ אֶת־מִשְׁמַרְתִּי:
יז וְהָיָה בְּבוֹאָם אֶל־שַׁעֲרֵי הֶחָצֵר הַפְּנִימִית
בִּגְדֵי פִשְׁתִּים יִלְבָּשׁוּ וְלֹא־יַעֲלֶה עֲלֵיהֶם צֶמֶר
בְּשָׁרְתָם בְּשַׁעֲרֵי הֶחָצֵר הַפְּנִימִית וָבָיְתָה:
יח פַּאֲרֵי פִשְׁתִּים יִהְיוּ עַל־רֹאשָׁם וּמִכְנְסֵי
פִשְׁתִּים יִהְיוּ עַל־מָתְנֵיהֶם לֹא יַחְגְּרוּ בַּיָּזַע:
יט וּבְצֵאתָם אֶל־הֶחָצֵר הַחִיצוֹנָה אֶל־הֶחָצֵר
הַחִיצוֹנָה אֶל־הָעָם יִפְשְׁטוּ אֶת־בִּגְדֵיהֶם אֲשֶׁר

wherein they minister and lay them down in rooms belonging to the Sanctuary and clothe themselves with other garments, and they shall not make the people appear holy through their garments. 20. And the hair of their heads they are not to shave, but also not to let it grow wild; carefully are they to trim the hair of their heads. 21. And wine may no priest drink when they come into the inner court. 22. Neither a widow nor a divorced woman may they take for their wives, but they shall take virgins from the descendants of the house of Israel; also the widow who is only a widow, some of the priests may marry. 23. And My people shall they teach the difference between holy and profane, and cause them to discern between the impure and the pure. 24. And in dispute they shall stand in judgment, according to My ordinances shall they decide it; and My teachings and My statutes shall they keep on all My times appointed for meeting, and My Sabbaths shall they sanctify. 25. To no human corpse shall they come to defile themselves, except to father and to mother and to son and daughter, to brother and to a sister who has had no husband have they to defile themselves. 26. And after he has become purified, they shall count seven days for him. 27. And on the day that he enters the Sanctuary, into the inner court, to minister in the Sanctuary, he shall offer his sin-offering, says the Lord God. 28. Their inheritance shall be: — I am their inheritance! You shall give them no possession in Israel; I am their possession. 29. The meal-offering and the sin-offering and the guilt-offering are they to eat, and everything that is vowed to be banned in Israel shall belong to them. 30. And the first of all the first fruits of everything, and every heave-offering; everything from every sort of your heave-offerings shall belong to the priests; also the first out of your kneading-troughs shall you give to the priest, to bring enduring blessing into your home. 31. Anything that has died of itself or is fatally wounded, whether it be bird or beast, the priests may not eat.

הֵמָּה מְשָׁרְתִם בָּם וְהִנִּיחוּ אוֹתָם בְּלִשְׁכֹת
הַקֹּדֶשׁ וְלָבְשׁוּ בְּגָדִים אֲחֵרִים וְלֹא־יְקַדְּשׁוּ
אֶת־הָעָם בְּבִגְדֵיהֶם: כ וְרֹאשָׁם לֹא יְגַלֵּחוּ
וּפֶרַע לֹא יְשַׁלֵּחוּ כָּסוֹם יִכְסְמוּ אֶת־רָאשֵׁיהֶם:
כא וְיַיִן לֹא־יִשְׁתּוּ כָּל־כֹּהֵן בְּבוֹאָם אֶל־הֶחָצֵר
הַפְּנִימִית: כב וְאַלְמָנָה וּגְרוּשָׁה לֹא־יִקְחוּ לָהֶם
לְנָשִׁים כִּי אִם־בְּתוּלֹת מִזֶּרַע בֵּית יִשְׂרָאֵל
וְהָאַלְמָנָה אֲשֶׁר־תִּהְיֶה אַלְמָנָה מִכֹּהֵן יִקָּחוּ:
כג וְאֶת־עַמִּי יוֹרוּ בֵּין קֹדֶשׁ לְחֹל וּבֵין־טָמֵא
לְטָהוֹר יוֹדִעֻם: כד וְעַל רִיב הֵמָּה יַעַמְדוּ
לְ. שְׁפֹּט (למשפט קרי) בְּמִשְׁפָּטַי וְשְׁפְּטֻהוּ (ישפטהו
קרי) וְאֶת־תּוֹרֹתַי וְאֶת־חֻקֹּתַי בְּכָל־מוֹעֲדַי
יִשְׁמֹרוּ וְאֶת־שַׁבְּתוֹתַי יְקַדֵּשׁוּ: כה וְאֶל־מֵת
אָדָם לֹא יָבוֹא לְטָמְאָה כִּי אִם־לְאָב וּלְאֵם
וּלְבֵן וּלְבַת לְאָח וּלְאָחוֹת אֲשֶׁר־לֹא־הָיְתָה
לְאִישׁ יִטַּמָּאוּ: כו וְאַחֲרֵי טָהֳרָתוֹ שִׁבְעַת יָמִים
יִסְפְּרוּ־לוֹ: כז וּבְיוֹם בֹּאוֹ אֶל־הַקֹּדֶשׁ אֶל־
הֶחָצֵר הַפְּנִימִית לְשָׁרֵת בַּקֹּדֶשׁ יַקְרִיב חַטָּאתוֹ
נְאֻם אֲדֹנָי יֱהֹוִה: כח וְהָיְתָה לָהֶם לְנַחֲלָה אֲנִי
נַחֲלָתָם וַאֲחֻזָּה לֹא־תִתְּנוּ לָהֶם בְּיִשְׂרָאֵל אֲנִי
אֲחֻזָּתָם: כט הַמִּנְחָה וְהַחַטָּאת וְהָאָשָׁם הֵמָּה
יֹאכְלוּם וְכָל־חֵרֶם בְּיִשְׂרָאֵל לָהֶם יִהְיֶה:
ל וְרֵאשִׁית כָּל־בִּכּוּרֵי כֹל וְכָל־תְּרוּמַת כֹּל
מִכֹּל תְּרוּמֹתֵיכֶם לַכֹּהֲנִים יִהְיֶה וְרֵאשִׁית
עֲרִיסוֹתֵיכֶם תִּתְּנוּ לַכֹּהֵן לְהָנִיחַ בְּרָכָה אֶל־
בֵּיתֶךָ: לא כָּל־נְבֵלָה וּטְרֵפָה מִן־הָעוֹף וּמִן־
הַבְּהֵמָה לֹא יֹאכְלוּ הַכֹּהֲנִים:

HAFTARATH BEHAR הפטרת בהר
(Jeremiah 32:6–27)

This selection tells how Jeremiah's cousin Hanamel sold him a field. This account is an implementation of the laws discussed in the Sidra. Jeremiah refers to the Babylonian exile, which came about, in part, because Israel failed to observe the Sabbatical and Jubilee years discussed in the Sidra.

32:6. And Jeremiah said: "The word of the
Lord came to me, saying: 7. 'Behold,
Hanamel the son of Shallum your uncle
will come to you, saying: Buy for yourself
my field that is in Anathoth, for the right of
redemption is yours to buy it.' 8. Then
Hanamel, my uncle's son, came to me in
the courtyard of the prison, according to the
word of the Lord, and said to me: 'Please
buy my field that is in Anathoth, that is in
the country of Benjamin, for the right of
inheritance is yours, and you have the right
of redemption; buy it for yourself.' But I
knew that this was a word of the Lord. 9. So
I bought the field of Hanamel my uncle's
son, which was in Anathoth, and weighed
him the money, seven shekels and ten
pieces of silver. 10. And I wrote a bill of sale
and signed it and took witnesses, and
weighed the silver on a scale. 11. And I took
the deed of the purchase, that which was
signed according to the law and the conditions, and that which was open. 12. And I
gave the deed of the purchase to Baruch the
son of Neriah the son of Mahseiah in the
presence of Hanamel my uncle's son and in
the presence of the witnesses who signed the
deed of purchase, in the presence of all the
Jews who sat in the courtyard of the prison.
13. And I charged Baruch in their presence,
saying: 14. So says the Lord of Hosts, the
God of Israel: Take these scrolls, this deed of
purchase and the signed one and this open
scroll, and put them into an earthen vessel
so that they remain many years. 15. For so
says the Lord of Hosts, the God of Israel:
Houses and fields and vineyards shall be
purchased again in this land. 16. And I
prayed to the Lord after I had delivered the
deed of purchase into the hand of Baruch
the son of Neriah, saying: 17. 'O Lord
God, behold, You have made the heaven
and the earth by Your great power and Your

ו וַיֹּאמֶר יִרְמְיָהוּ הָיָה דְּבַר־יְהֹוָה אֵלַי לֵאמֹר:
ז הִנֵּה חֲנַמְאֵל בֶּן־שַׁלֻּם דֹּדְךָ בָּא אֵלֶיךָ לֵאמֹר
קְנֵה לְךָ אֶת־שָׂדִי אֲשֶׁר בַּעֲנָתוֹת כִּי לְךָ מִשְׁפַּט
הַגְּאֻלָּה לִקְנוֹת: ח וַיָּבֹא אֵלַי חֲנַמְאֵל בֶּן־דֹּדִי
כִּדְבַר יְהֹוָה אֶל־חֲצַר הַמַּטָּרָה וַיֹּאמֶר אֵלַי קְנֵה
נָא אֶת־שָׂדִי אֲשֶׁר־בַּעֲנָתוֹת אֲשֶׁר | בְּאֶרֶץ
בִּנְיָמִין כִּי לְךָ מִשְׁפַּט הַיְרֻשָּׁה וּלְךָ הַגְּאֻלָּה
קְנֵה־לָךְ וָאֵדַע כִּי דְבַר־יְהֹוָה הוּא: ט וָאֶקְנֶה
אֶת־הַשָּׂדֶה מֵאֵת חֲנַמְאֵל בֶּן־דֹּדִי אֲשֶׁר
בַּעֲנָתוֹת וָאֶשְׁקְלָה־לּוֹ אֶת־הַכֶּסֶף שִׁבְעָה
שְׁקָלִים וַעֲשָׂרָה הַכָּסֶף: י וָאֶכְתֹּב בַּסֵּפֶר
וָאֶחְתֹּם וָאָעֵד עֵדִים וָאֶשְׁקֹל הַכֶּסֶף בְּמֹאזְנָיִם:
יא וָאֶקַּח אֶת־סֵפֶר הַמִּקְנָה אֶת־הֶחָתוּם
הַמִּצְוָה וְהַחֻקִּים וְאֶת־הַגָּלוּי: יב וָאֶתֵּן אֶת־
הַסֵּפֶר הַמִּקְנָה אֶל־בָּרוּךְ בֶּן־נֵרִיָּה בֶּן־מַחְסֵיָה
לְעֵינֵי חֲנַמְאֵל דֹּדִי וּלְעֵינֵי הָעֵדִים הַכֹּתְבִים
בְּסֵפֶר הַמִּקְנָה לְעֵינֵי כָּל־הַיְּהוּדִים הַיֹּשְׁבִים
בַּחֲצַר הַמַּטָּרָה: יג וָאֲצַוֶּה אֶת־בָּרוּךְ לְעֵינֵיהֶם
לֵאמֹר: יד כֹּה־אָמַר יְהֹוָה צְבָאוֹת אֱלֹהֵי
יִשְׂרָאֵל לָקוֹחַ אֶת־הַסְּפָרִים הָאֵלֶּה אֵת סֵפֶר
הַמִּקְנָה הַזֶּה וְאֵת הֶחָתוּם וְאֵת סֵפֶר הַגָּלוּי
הַזֶּה וּנְתַתָּם בִּכְלִי־חָרֶשׂ לְמַעַן יַעַמְדוּ יָמִים
רַבִּים: טו כִּי כֹה אָמַר יְהֹוָה צְבָאוֹת אֱלֹהֵי
יִשְׂרָאֵל עוֹד יִקָּנוּ בָתִּים וְשָׂדוֹת וּכְרָמִים
בָּאָרֶץ הַזֹּאת: טז וָאֶתְפַּלֵּל אֶל־יְהֹוָה אַחֲרֵי
תִתִּי אֶת־סֵפֶר הַמִּקְנָה אֶל־בָּרוּךְ בֶּן־נֵרִיָּה
לֵאמֹר: יז אֲהָהּ אֲדֹנָי יֱהֹוִה הִנֵּה | אַתָּה עָשִׂיתָ
אֶת־הַשָּׁמַיִם וְאֶת־הָאָרֶץ בְּכֹחֲךָ הַגָּדוֹל וּבִזְרֹעֲךָ

outstretched arm, and nothing is too wonderful for You, 18. Who exercises lovingkindness to thousands and requites the iniquity of the fathers in the bosom of the children who follow them; O Great and Mighty God, the Lord of Hosts is His Name, 19. Who is great in counsel and mighty in carrying it out, for Your eyes are open to all the ways of mankind, to give everyone in accordance with his ways and in accordance with the fruits of his doings; 20. Who made signs and wonders in the land of Egypt until this day, and in Israel and in mankind, and have made a name for Yourself as at this day. 21. And You have brought forth Your people Israel out of the land of Egypt, with signs and with wonders and with a strong hand and with an outstretched arm and with great fearfulness. 22. And You have given them this land which You did swear to their fathers to give them, a land flowing with milk and honey. (*Many congregations conclude here.*) 23. And they came in and took possession of it, but they did not obey You, nor did they walk in Your teachings, all that You commanded them to do they did not do; then You did cause all this evil to come upon them. 24. Behold the mounds, they have come to the city to take it; by the sword and the famine and the pestilence the city is already given into the hands of the Chaldeans who are fighting against it, and what You have proclaimed has come to pass, and lo! You see it. 25. And You did say to me, O Lord God, 'Buy yourself the field for money and appoint witnesses!' Yet the city is given into the hands of the Chaldeans!" 26. Then the word of the Lord came to Jeremiah, saying: 27. "Behold, I am the Lord, the God of all flesh. Is anything too wonderful for Me?"

הַנְּטוּיָה לֹא־יִפָּלֵא מִמְּךָ כָּל־דָּבָר: יח עֹשֶׂה חֶסֶד לַאֲלָפִים וּמְשַׁלֵּם עֲוֺן אָבוֹת אֶל־חֵיק בְּנֵיהֶם אַחֲרֵיהֶם הָאֵל הַגָּדוֹל הַגִּבּוֹר יְהֹוָה צְבָאוֹת שְׁמוֹ: יט גְּדֹל הָעֵצָה וְרַב הָעֲלִילִיָּה אֲשֶׁר־עֵינֶיךָ פְקֻחוֹת עַל־כָּל־דַּרְכֵי בְּנֵי אָדָם לָתֵת לְאִישׁ כִּדְרָכָיו וְכִפְרִי מַעֲלָלָיו: כ אֲשֶׁר שַׂמְתָּ אֹתוֹת וּמֹפְתִים בְּאֶרֶץ מִצְרַיִם עַד־הַיּוֹם הַזֶּה וּבְיִשְׂרָאֵל וּבָאָדָם וַתַּעֲשֶׂה־לְּךָ שֵׁם כַּיּוֹם הַזֶּה: כא וַתֹּצֵא אֶת־עַמְּךָ אֶת־יִשְׂרָאֵל מֵאֶרֶץ מִצְרָיִם בְּאֹתוֹת וּבְמוֹפְתִים וּבְיָד חֲזָקָה וּבְאֶזְרוֹעַ נְטוּיָה וּבְמוֹרָא גָּדוֹל: כב וַתִּתֵּן לָהֶם אֶת־הָאָרֶץ הַזֹּאת אֲשֶׁר־נִשְׁבַּעְתָּ לַאֲבוֹתָם לָתֵת לָהֶם אֶרֶץ זָבַת חָלָב וּדְבָשׁ: (בהרבה קהלות מסיימין כאן) כג וַיָּבֹאוּ וַיִּרְשׁוּ אֹתָהּ וְלֹא־שָׁמְעוּ בְקוֹלֶךָ וּבְתֹרוֹתְךָ (ובתורתך קרי) לֹא־הָלָכוּ אֵת כָּל־אֲשֶׁר צִוִּיתָה לָהֶם לַעֲשׂוֹת לֹא עָשׂוּ וַתַּקְרֵא אֹתָם אֵת כָּל־הָרָעָה הַזֹּאת: כד הִנֵּה הַסֹּלְלוֹת בָּאוּ הָעִיר לְלָכְדָהּ וְהָעִיר נִתְּנָה בְּיַד הַכַּשְׂדִּים הַנִּלְחָמִים עָלֶיהָ מִפְּנֵי הַחֶרֶב וְהָרָעָב וְהַדָּבֶר וַאֲשֶׁר דִּבַּרְתָּ הָיָה וְהִנְּךָ רֹאֶה: כה וְאַתָּה אָמַרְתָּ אֵלַי אֲדֹנָי יְהֹוִה קְנֵה־לְךָ הַשָּׂדֶה בַּכֶּסֶף וְהָעֵד עֵדִים וְהָעִיר נִתְּנָה בְּיַד הַכַּשְׂדִּים: כו וַיְהִי דְּבַר־יְהֹוָה אֶל־יִרְמְיָהוּ לֵאמֹר: כז הִנֵּה אֲנִי יְהֹוָה אֱלֹהֵי כָּל־בָּשָׂר הֲמִמֶּנִּי יִפָּלֵא כָּל־דָּבָר:

HAFTARATH BEHUKKOTHAI הפטרת בחקתי

(Jeremiah 16:19–17:14)

This Haftarah is read also on Sabbaths when Behukkothai is read with Behar. Congregations following the Italian ritual read it as the Haftarah of Behar.

This selection contains warnings concerning the exile similar to those found in the Sidra (Leviticus 26).

16:19. O Lord, Who is my power and my
strength and my refuge in the day of
trouble, to You nations will come from the
ends of the earth and say, "Only lies have
our fathers handed down to us, emptiness in
which there is nothing of any avail! 20. Can
a man make gods for himself, and they are
no gods?" 21. Therefore, behold I let them
know; at this time, I will let them know My
power and My might, and they shall know
that My Name is the Lord. 17:1. The sin of
Judah is written with a pen of iron, with a
diamond point, engraved on the tablet of
their heart and on the horns of your altars.
2. As they remember their children, [so do
they remember] their altars, and their
asherim by the green trees upon the high
hillocks. 3. You, who sit upon the mountain
in the field, I will give your substance, all
your treasures for a spoil; your high places
are made for sin within all your borders.
4. And you, even of yourself, shall release
your heritage that I gave you, and I will
make you serve your enemies in the land
that you did not know, for you have kindled
fire in My nostrils that shall burn forever.
5. So says the Lord: Cursed is the man who
trusts in mankind and makes mortal muscle
his power, and turns his heart away from the
Lord. 6. He shall be like a lonely tree in the
desert, and he will not see when good
comes, and he will dwell on parched land in
the desert, on salt-sodden soil that is not
habitable. 7. Blessed is the man who trusts
in the Lord, and to whom the Lord is his
confidence. 8. For he shall be like a tree
planted by water, and by a rivulet he
spreads his roots, and he will not see when
heat comes, and his leaves shall be green,
and in the year of drought he will not be
anxious, neither shall he cease from bearing
fruit. 9. The heart is deceitful above all
things, and when it is sick, who will recog-

יט יְהֹוָה עֻזִּי וּמָעֻזִּי וּמְנוּסִי בְּיוֹם צָרָה אֵלֶיךָ
גּוֹיִם יָבֹאוּ מֵאַפְסֵי־אָרֶץ וְיֹאמְרוּ אַךְ־שֶׁקֶר
נָחֲלוּ אֲבוֹתֵינוּ הֶבֶל וְאֵין־בָּם מוֹעִיל:
כ הֲיַעֲשֶׂה־לּוֹ אָדָם אֱלֹהִים וְהֵמָּה לֹא אֱלֹהִים:
כא לָכֵן הִנְנִי מוֹדִיעָם בַּפַּעַם הַזֹּאת אוֹדִיעֵם
אֶת־יָדִי וְאֶת־גְּבוּרָתִי וְיָדְעוּ כִּי־שְׁמִי יְהֹוָה:
א חַטַּאת יְהוּדָה כְּתוּבָה בְּעֵט בַּרְזֶל בְּצִפֹּרֶן
שָׁמִיר חֲרוּשָׁה עַל־לוּחַ לִבָּם וּלְקַרְנוֹת
מִזְבְּחוֹתֵיכֶם: ב כִּזְכֹּר בְּנֵיהֶם מִזְבְּחוֹתָם
וַאֲשֵׁרֵיהֶם עַל־עֵץ רַעֲנָן עַל גְּבָעוֹת הַגְּבֹהוֹת:
ג הֲרָרִי בַּשָּׂדֶה חֵילְךָ כָל־אוֹצְרוֹתֶיךָ לָבַז אֶתֵּן
בָּמֹתֶיךָ בְּחַטָּאת בְּכָל־גְּבוּלֶיךָ: ד וְשָׁמַטְתָּה וּבְךָ
מִנַּחֲלָתְךָ אֲשֶׁר נָתַתִּי לָךְ וְהַעֲבַדְתִּיךָ אֶת־
אֹיְבֶיךָ בָּאָרֶץ אֲשֶׁר לֹא־יָדָעְתָּ כִּי־אֵשׁ קְדַחְתֶּם
בְּאַפִּי עַד־עוֹלָם תּוּקָד: ה כֹּה | אָמַר יְהֹוָה
אָרוּר הַגֶּבֶר אֲשֶׁר יִבְטַח בָּאָדָם וְשָׂם בָּשָׂר
זְרֹעוֹ וּמִן־יְהֹוָה יָסוּר לִבּוֹ: ו וְהָיָה כְּעַרְעָר
בָּעֲרָבָה וְלֹא יִרְאֶה כִּי־יָבוֹא טוֹב וְשָׁכַן חֲרֵרִים
בַּמִּדְבָּר אֶרֶץ מְלֵחָה וְלֹא תֵשֵׁב: ז בָּרוּךְ הַגֶּבֶר
אֲשֶׁר יִבְטַח בַּיהֹוָה וְהָיָה יְהֹוָה מִבְטַחוֹ:
ח וְהָיָה כְּעֵץ | שָׁתוּל עַל־מַיִם וְעַל־יוּבַל
יְשַׁלַּח שָׁרָשָׁיו וְלֹא יִרְאֶ (יראה קרי) כִּי־יָבֹא חֹם
וְהָיָה עָלֵהוּ רַעֲנָן וּבִשְׁנַת בַּצֹּרֶת לֹא יִדְאָג וְלֹא
יָמִישׁ מֵעֲשׂוֹת פֶּרִי: ט עָקֹב הַלֵּב מִכֹּל וְאָנֻשׁ

nize it? 10. I, the Lord, search the heart, test the kidneys, to give everyone according to his ways, according to the fruit of his deeds. 11. The cuckoo calls but has not laid, so is he who gathers riches but not by right; he shall leave them in the midst of his days, and at his end he stands there dishonored. 12. As a Throne of Glory, exalted from the beginning, so is the place of our Sanctuary. 13. The Lord is the source of the hopes of Israel, all that forsake You shall be shamed; and they who turn away from Me shall be marked out on earth that they have forsaken the source of living waters, the Lord. 14. Heal me, O Lord, then shall I be healed; help me, then I shall be helped, for You are my praise!

הָ֑וּא מִ֖י יֵדָעֶֽנּוּ׃ י אֲנִ֧י יְהֹוָ֛ה חֹקֵ֥ר לֵ֖ב בֹּחֵ֣ן
כְּלָי֑וֹת וְלָתֵ֤ת לְאִישׁ֙ כִּדְרָכָ֔ו (כדרכיו קרי) כִּפְרִ֖י
מַעֲלָלָֽיו׃ יא קֹרֵ֤א דָגַר֙ וְלֹ֣א יָלָ֔ד עֹ֥שֶׂה עֹ֖שֶׁר
וְלֹ֣א בְמִשְׁפָּ֑ט בַּחֲצִ֤י יָמָו֙ (ימיו קרי) יַֽעַזְבֶ֔נּוּ
וּבְאַחֲרִית֖וֹ יִהְיֶ֥ה נָבָֽל׃ יב כִּסֵּ֣א כָב֔וֹד מָר֖וֹם
מֵרִֽאשׁ֑וֹן מְק֖וֹם מִקְדָּשֵֽׁנוּ׃ יג מִקְוֵ֤ה יִשְׂרָאֵל֙
יְהֹוָ֔ה כָּל־עֹזְבֶ֖יךָ יֵבֹ֑שׁוּ יְסוּרַי֙ (וסורי קרי) בָּאָ֣רֶץ
יִכָּתֵ֔בוּ כִּ֥י עָזְב֛וּ מְק֥וֹר מַֽיִם־חַיִּ֖ים אֶת־יְהֹוָֽה׃
יד רְפָאֵ֤נִי יְהֹוָה֙ וְאֵ֣רָפֵ֔א הוֹשִׁיעֵ֖נִי וְאִוָּשֵׁ֑עָה כִּ֥י
תְהִלָּתִ֖י אָֽתָּה׃

HAFTARATH BAMIDBAR הפטרת במדבר

(Hosea 2:1–22)

Should Rosh Chodesh fall on Sunday, the Haftarah for The Day Preceding Rosh Chodesh (p. 933) is read.

The prophecy in the opening verse of this selection, that "the number of the children of Israel shall be as the sand of the sea," corresponds to the census discussed in the Sidra, when the people numbered more than 600,000, as they had been blessed.

2:1. The number of the children of Israel shall be as the sand of the sea, which is neither measured nor counted, and it shall come to pass that instead of what is being said of them: "You are not My people!" it shall be said of them: "[They are] the children of the living God." 2. Then the sons of Judah and the sons of Israel shall be gathered together and appoint one head for themselves and will come up out of the world, for great will be the day of "God's scattered ones." 3. Say to your brothers: "My people," and to your sisters, "She who obtains compassion." 4. Contend against your mother, take up the cause, for she is not my wife, and I am not her Husband; let her put away her whoredoms from her face and her adulteries from between her breasts. 5. Lest I strip her naked and set her as in the day of her birth, and make her as a wilderness and like a dried up land, and let her die of thirst. 6. And for her children will I have no compassion, for they are children of

א וְֽהָיָ֞ה מִסְפַּ֤ר בְּנֵֽי־יִשְׂרָאֵל֙ כְּח֣וֹל הַיָּ֔ם אֲשֶׁ֥ר
לֹֽא־יִמַּ֖ד וְלֹ֣א יִסָּפֵ֑ר וְֽהָיָ֡ה בִּמְק֞וֹם אֲשֶׁר־יֵאָמֵ֤ר
לָהֶם֙ לֹֽא־עַמִּ֣י אַתֶּ֔ם יֵאָמֵ֥ר לָהֶ֖ם בְּנֵ֥י אֵל־חָֽי׃
ב וְֽנִקְבְּצ֞וּ בְּנֵֽי־יְהוּדָ֤ה וּבְנֵֽי־יִשְׂרָאֵל֙ יַחְדָּ֔ו
וְשָׂמ֥וּ לָהֶ֛ם רֹ֥אשׁ אֶחָ֖ד וְעָל֣וּ מִן־הָאָ֑רֶץ כִּ֥י
גָד֖וֹל י֥וֹם יִזְרְעֶֽאל׃ ג אִמְר֥וּ לַאֲחֵיכֶ֖ם עַמִּ֑י
וְלַאֲחֽוֹתֵיכֶ֖ם רֻחָֽמָה׃ ד רִ֤יבוּ בְאִמְּכֶם֙ רִ֔יבוּ כִּי־
הִיא֙ לֹ֣א אִשְׁתִּ֔י וְאָנֹכִ֖י לֹ֣א אִישָׁ֑הּ וְתָסֵ֤ר זְנוּנֶ֙יהָ֙
מִפָּנֶ֔יהָ וְנַאֲפוּפֶ֖יהָ מִבֵּ֥ין שָׁדֶֽיהָ׃ ה פֶּן־
אַפְשִׁיטֶ֣נָּה עֲרֻמָּ֔ה וְהִ֨צַּגְתִּ֔יהָ כְּי֖וֹם הִוָּֽלְדָ֑הּ
וְשַׂמְתִּ֣יהָ כַמִּדְבָּ֗ר וְשַׁתִּ֙הָ֙ כְּאֶ֣רֶץ צִיָּ֔ה וַהֲמִתִּ֖יהָ
בַּצָּמָֽא׃ ו וְאֶת־בָּנֶ֖יהָ לֹ֣א אֲרַחֵ֑ם כִּֽי־בְנֵ֥י זְנוּנִ֖ים

whoredoms. 7. For their mother has played the harlot, she who conceived them has dealt shamefully, for she said: "I will follow my lovers, those who give me my bread and my water, my wool and my flax, my oil and my drinks." 8. Therefore, behold I will hedge your way with thorns, and build up its wall so that she shall not find her paths. 9. Then she will run after her lovers but she will not overtake them, and she will seek them but not find them, and then she will say, "I would go and return to my first Husband, for then was it better with me than now." 10. For she did not know that I had given her the corn, the new wine, and the oil, and given her silver and gold in abundance —which they ascribed to Baal! 11. Therefore will I return, and I will take away My corn in its time and My new wine in its appointed time, and I will save My wool and My flax to cover her nakedness. 12. But now I will disclose her shame before the eyes of her lovers, and no man will save her from My hand. 13. And I will make all her mirth cease, her feast days, her new moons, and her Sabbaths, all her festival days. 14. And I will lay waste her vines and her fig trees, of which she said, "They are my wages, which my lovers have given me." I will make them into a forest, and the beasts of the field shall eat them. 15. And I will visit upon her the days of the Baal-gods, wherein she offered incense to them and bedecked herself with her rings and her jewelry, and went after her lovers, but Me she had forgotten, says the Lord. 16. Therefore, behold I will allure her, lead her out to the wilderness, and speak to her heart. 17. And from there will I give her her vineyards and the Vale of Sadness make into the Gate of Hope, and she shall sing there as the days of her youth and as the day she came up out of the land of Egypt. 18. And it shall be, on that day, says the Lord, you shall call "Ishi" (my Husband), and no longer shall you call Me "Baali" (my master, resembling Baal). 19. And I will remove the names of the Baal-gods from her mouth, and they shall no longer be mentioned by their name. 20. And on that day I will make a cove- nant for them with the beasts of the field

הֵֽמָּה: ז כִּי זָנְתָה֙ אִמָּ֔ם הֹבִ֖ישָׁה הֽוֹרָתָ֑ם כִּ֣י אָמְרָ֗ה אֵֽלְכָ֞ה אַחֲרֵ֤י מְאַֽהֲבַי֙ נֹֽתְנֵ֤י לַחְמִי֙ וּמֵימַ֔י צַמְרִ֣י וּפִשְׁתִּ֔י שַׁמְנִ֖י וְשִׁקּוּיָֽי: ח לָכֵ֛ן הִנְנִי־שָׂ֥ךְ אֶת־דַּרְכֵּ֖ךְ בַּסִּירִ֑ים וְגָֽדַרְתִּי֙ אֶת־גְּדֵרָ֔הּ וּנְתִֽיבוֹתֶ֖יהָ לֹ֥א תִמְצָֽא: ט וְרִדְּפָ֤ה אֶת־ מְאַֽהֲבֶ֨יהָ֙ וְלֹֽא־תַשִּׂ֣יג אֹתָ֔ם וּבִקְשָׁ֖תַם וְלֹ֣א תִמְצָ֑א וְאָֽמְרָ֗ה אֵֽלְכָ֤ה וְאָשׁ֨וּבָה֙ אֶל־אִישִׁ֣י הָֽרִאשׁ֔וֹן כִּ֣י ט֥וֹב לִ֛י אָ֖ז מֵֽעָֽתָּה: י וְהִיא֙ לֹ֣א יָֽדְעָ֔ה כִּ֤י אָֽנֹכִי֙ נָתַ֣תִּי לָ֔הּ הַדָּגָ֖ן וְהַתִּיר֣וֹשׁ וְהַיִּצְהָ֑ר וְכֶ֨סֶף֙ הִרְבֵּ֣יתִי לָ֔הּ וְזָהָ֖ב עָשׂ֥וּ לַבָּֽעַל: יא לָכֵ֣ן אָשׁ֗וּב וְלָֽקַחְתִּ֤י דְגָנִי֙ בְּעִתּ֔וֹ וְתִירוֹשִׁ֖י בְּמֽוֹעֲד֑וֹ וְהִצַּלְתִּי֙ צַמְרִ֣י וּפִשְׁתִּ֔י לְכַסּ֖וֹת אֶת־ עֶרְוָתָֽהּ: יב וְעַתָּ֛ה אֲגַלֶּ֥ה אֶת־נַבְלֻתָ֖הּ לְעֵינֵ֣י מְאַֽהֲבֶ֑יהָ וְאִ֖ישׁ לֹֽא־יַצִּילֶ֥נָּה מִיָּדִֽי: יג וְהִשְׁבַּתִּי֙ כָּל־מְשׂוֹשָׂ֔הּ חַגָּ֖הּ חָדְשָׁ֣הּ וְשַׁבַּתָּ֑הּ וְכֹ֖ל מֽוֹעֲדָֽהּ: יד וַֽהֲשִׁמֹּתִ֗י גַּפְנָהּ֙ וּתְאֵ֣נָתָ֔הּ אֲשֶׁ֣ר אָֽמְרָ֗ה אֶתְנָ֥ה הֵ֨מָּה֙ לִ֔י אֲשֶׁ֥ר נָֽתְנוּ־לִ֖י מְאַֽהֲבָ֑י וְשַׂמְתִּ֣ים לְיַ֔עַר וַֽאֲכָלָ֖תַם חַיַּ֥ת הַשָּׂדֶֽה: טו וּפָֽקַדְתִּ֣י עָלֶ֗יהָ אֶת־ יְמֵ֤י הַבְּעָלִים֙ אֲשֶׁ֣ר תַּקְטִ֣יר לָהֶ֔ם וַתַּ֤עַד נִזְמָהּ֙ וְחֶלְיָתָ֔הּ וַתֵּ֖לֶךְ אַֽחֲרֵ֣י מְאַֽהֲבֶ֑יהָ וְאֹתִ֥י שָֽׁכְחָ֖ה נְאֻם־יְהֹוָֽה: טז לָכֵ֗ן הִנֵּ֤ה אָֽנֹכִי֙ מְפַתֶּ֔יהָ וְהֹֽלַכְתִּ֖יהָ הַמִּדְבָּ֑ר וְדִבַּרְתִּ֖י עַל־לִבָּֽהּ: יז וְנָתַ֨תִּי לָ֤הּ אֶת־כְּרָמֶ֨יהָ֙ מִשָּׁ֔ם וְאֶת־עֵ֥מֶק עָכ֖וֹר לְפֶ֣תַח תִּקְוָ֑ה וְעָ֤נְתָה שָּׁ֨מָּה֙ כִּימֵ֣י נְעוּרֶ֔יהָ וּכְי֖וֹם עֲלוֹתָ֥הּ מֵאֶֽרֶץ־מִצְרָֽיִם: יח וְהָיָ֤ה בַיּֽוֹם־הַהוּא֙ נְאֻם־יְהֹוָ֔ה תִּקְרְאִ֖י אִישִׁ֑י וְלֹֽא־תִקְרְאִי־לִ֥י ע֖וֹד בַּעְלִֽי: יט וַֽהֲסִֽרֹתִ֛י אֶת־שְׁמ֥וֹת הַבְּעָלִ֖ים מִפִּ֑יהָ וְלֹֽא־יִזָּֽכְר֥וּ ע֖וֹד בִּשְׁמָֽם: כ וְכָֽרַתִּ֨י לָהֶ֤ם בְּרִית֙ בַּיּ֣וֹם הַה֔וּא עִם־חַיַּ֤ת הַשָּׂדֶה֙ וְעִם־ע֣וֹף הַשָּׁמַ֔יִם

and with the birds of the heavens and the creeping creatures of the ground, and bow and sword and war will I destroy from the earth, and I will make you repose in security. 21. And I will betroth you to Me forever! Yea, I will betroth you to Me with righteousness, and with justice and with lovingkindness and with pity. 22. And I will betroth you to Me with faith, and you shall know the Lord.

וְרֶמֶשׂ הָאֲדָמָה וְקֶשֶׁת וְחֶרֶב וּמִלְחָמָה אֶשְׁבּוֹר
מִן־הָאָרֶץ וְהִשְׁכַּבְתִּים לָבֶטַח׃ כא וְאֵרַשְׂתִּיךְ לִי
לְעוֹלָם וְאֵרַשְׂתִּיךְ לִי בְּצֶדֶק וּבְמִשְׁפָּט וּבְחֶסֶד
וּבְרַחֲמִים׃ כב וְאֵרַשְׂתִּיךְ לִי בֶּאֱמוּנָה וְיָדַעַתְּ
אֶת־יְהֹוָה׃

HAFTARATH NASO הפטרת נשא
(Judges 13:2–25)

This selection tells the story of the birth of Samson the Nazirite, and hence corresponds to the Sidra which (in Numbers 6) discusses the laws pertaining to Naziriteship.

13:2. And there was one man from Zorah, from the family of the Danites, whose name was Manoah; and his wife was barren and had not borne. 3. And an angel of the Lord appeared to the woman and said to her, "Behold now, you are barren and have not borne, and you shall conceive and bear a son. 4. Consequently, beware now, and do not drink wine or strong drink, and do not eat any unclean thing. 5. Because you shall conceive and bear a son; and a razor shall not come upon his head, for a Nazirite to God shall the lad be from the womb; and he will begin to save Israel from the hand of the Philistines." 6. And the woman came and said to her husband, saying, "A man of God came to me, and his appearance was like the appearance of an angel of God, very awesome; and I did not ask him from where he was, and his name he did not tell me. 7. And he said to me, 'Behold, you shall conceive and bear a son; and now do not drink wine and strong drink, and do not eat any unclean [thing], for a Nazirite to God shall the lad be, from the womb until the day of his death.'" 8. And Manoah entreated the Lord and said, "Please, O Lord, the man of God whom You sent, let him come now again to us, and teach us what we shall do to the lad that will be born." 9. And God hearkened to the voice of Manoah, and the angel of God came again to the woman;

ב וַיְהִי אִישׁ אֶחָד מִצָּרְעָה מִמִּשְׁפַּחַת הַדָּנִי
וּשְׁמוֹ מָנוֹחַ וְאִשְׁתּוֹ עֲקָרָה וְלֹא יָלָדָה׃ ג וַיֵּרָא
מַלְאַךְ־יְהֹוָה אֶל־הָאִשָּׁה וַיֹּאמֶר אֵלֶיהָ הִנֵּה־נָא
אַתְּ־עֲקָרָה וְלֹא יָלַדְתְּ וְהָרִית וְיָלַדְתְּ בֵּן׃
ד וְעַתָּה הִשָּׁמְרִי נָא וְאַל־תִּשְׁתִּי יַיִן וְשֵׁכָר
וְאַל־תֹּאכְלִי כָּל־טָמֵא׃ ה כִּי הִנָּךְ הָרָה וְיֹלַדְתְּ
בֵּן וּמוֹרָה לֹא־יַעֲלֶה עַל־רֹאשׁוֹ כִּי־נְזִיר
אֱלֹהִים יִהְיֶה הַנַּעַר מִן־הַבָּטֶן וְהוּא יָחֵל
לְהוֹשִׁיעַ אֶת־יִשְׂרָאֵל מִיַּד פְּלִשְׁתִּים׃ ו וַתָּבֹא
הָאִשָּׁה וַתֹּאמֶר לְאִישָׁהּ לֵאמֹר אִישׁ הָאֱלֹהִים
בָּא אֵלַי וּמַרְאֵהוּ כְּמַרְאֵה מַלְאַךְ הָאֱלֹהִים
נוֹרָא מְאֹד וְלֹא שְׁאִלְתִּיהוּ אֵי־מִזֶּה הוּא וְאֶת־
שְׁמוֹ לֹא־הִגִּיד לִי׃ ז וַיֹּאמֶר לִי הִנָּךְ הָרָה
וְיֹלַדְתְּ בֵּן וְעַתָּה אַל־תִּשְׁתִּי ׀ יַיִן וְשֵׁכָר וְאַל־
תֹּאכְלִי כָּל־טֻמְאָה כִּי־נְזִיר אֱלֹהִים יִהְיֶה הַנַּעַר
מִן־הַבֶּטֶן עַד־יוֹם מוֹתוֹ׃ ח וַיֶּעְתַּר מָנוֹחַ אֶל־
יְהֹוָה וַיֹּאמַר בִּי אֲדוֹנָי אִישׁ הָאֱלֹהִים אֲשֶׁר
שָׁלַחְתָּ יָבוֹא־נָא עוֹד אֵלֵינוּ וְיוֹרֵנוּ מַה־נַּעֲשֶׂה
לַנַּעַר הַיּוּלָּד׃ ט וַיִּשְׁמַע הָאֱלֹהִים בְּקוֹל מָנוֹחַ
וַיָּבֹא מַלְאַךְ הָאֱלֹהִים עוֹד אֶל־הָאִשָּׁה וְהִיא

and she was sitting in the field, and Manoah her husband was not with her. 10. And the woman hurried and ran, and told to her husband, and she said to him, "Behold there has appeared to me the man that came to me on that day." 11. And Manoah arose and went after his wife; and he came to the man and said to him, "Are you the man that spoke to the woman?" And he said, "I am." 12. And Manoah said, "Now your words will come forth; what shall be the rule for the lad, and his doing?" 13. And the angel of the Lord said to Manoah, "Of all that I said to the woman shall she beware. 14. From all that comes out of the grapevine she shall not eat, and wine or strong drink she may not drink, and any unclean [thing] she may not eat; all that I commanded her, shall she observe." 15. And Manoah said to the angel of the Lord, "Let us take you in now, and prepare for you a kid goat." 16. And the angel of the Lord said to Manoah, "If you take me in I will not eat of your bread, and if you will make a burnt offering, you must offer it to the Lord," for Manoah did not know that he was an angel of the Lord. 17. And Manoah said to the angel of the Lord, "What is your name, that when your word will come we may do you honor?" 18. And the angel of the Lord said to him, "Why do you presently ask for my name; since it is hidden?" 19. And Manoah took the kid goat and the meal-offering and offered it upon the rock to the Lord; and [the angel] did wondrously, and Manoah and his wife looked on. 20. And it was, when the flame went up from upon the altar toward heaven, that the angel of the Lord ascended in the flame of the altar. And Manoah and his wife looked on, and they fell on their faces to the ground. 21. And the angel of the Lord did not continue to appear to Manoah and to his wife. Then Manoah knew that he was an angel of the Lord. 22. And Manoah said to his wife, "We shall surely die, because we have seen God." 23. But his wife said to him, "If the Lord wanted to kill us, He would not have accepted from our hand a burnt offering and a meal-offering, and He would not have shown us all these things;

יוֹשֶׁבֶת בַּשָּׂדֶה וּמָנוֹחַ אִישָׁהּ אֵין עִמָּהּ:
י וַתְּמַהֵר הָאִשָּׁה וַתָּרָץ וַתַּגֵּד לְאִישָׁהּ וַתֹּאמֶר
אֵלָיו הִנֵּה נִרְאָה אֵלַי הָאִישׁ אֲשֶׁר־בָּא בַיּוֹם
אֵלָי: יא וַיָּקָם וַיֵּלֶךְ מָנוֹחַ אַחֲרֵי אִשְׁתּוֹ וַיָּבֹא
אֶל־הָאִישׁ וַיֹּאמֶר לוֹ הַאַתָּה הָאִישׁ אֲשֶׁר־
דִּבַּרְתָּ אֶל־הָאִשָּׁה וַיֹּאמֶר אָנִי: יב וַיֹּאמֶר מָנוֹחַ
עַתָּה יָבֹא דְבָרֶיךָ מַה־יִּהְיֶה מִשְׁפַּט הַנַּעַר
וּמַעֲשֵׂהוּ: יג וַיֹּאמֶר מַלְאַךְ יְהוָה אֶל־מָנוֹחַ
מִכֹּל אֲשֶׁר־אָמַרְתִּי אֶל־הָאִשָּׁה תִּשָּׁמֵר: יד מִכֹּל
אֲשֶׁר־יֵצֵא מִגֶּפֶן הַיַּיִן לֹא תֹאכַל וְיַיִן וְשֵׁכָר
אַל־תֵּשְׁתְּ וְכָל־טֻמְאָה אַל־תֹּאכַל כֹּל אֲשֶׁר־
צִוִּיתִיהָ תִּשְׁמֹר: טו וַיֹּאמֶר מָנוֹחַ אֶל־מַלְאַךְ
יְהוָה נַעְצְרָה־נָּא אוֹתָךְ וְנַעֲשֶׂה לְפָנֶיךָ גְּדִי
עִזִּים: טז וַיֹּאמֶר מַלְאַךְ יְהוָה אֶל־מָנוֹחַ אִם־
תַּעְצְרֵנִי לֹא־אֹכַל בְּלַחְמֶךָ וְאִם־תַּעֲשֶׂה עֹלָה
לַיהוָה תַּעֲלֶנָּה כִּי לֹא־יָדַע מָנוֹחַ כִּי־מַלְאַךְ
יְהוָה הוּא: יז וַיֹּאמֶר מָנוֹחַ אֶל־מַלְאַךְ יְהוָה
מִי שְׁמֶךָ כִּי־יָבֹא דְבָרֶיךָ (דברך קרי) וְכִבַּדְנוּךָ:
יח וַיֹּאמֶר לוֹ מַלְאַךְ יְהוָה לָמָּה זֶּה תִּשְׁאַל
לִשְׁמִי וְהוּא־פֶלִאי: יט וַיִּקַּח מָנוֹחַ אֶת־גְּדִי
הָעִזִּים וְאֶת־הַמִּנְחָה וַיַּעַל עַל־הַצּוּר לַיהוָה
וּמַפְלִא לַעֲשׂוֹת וּמָנוֹחַ וְאִשְׁתּוֹ רֹאִים: כ וַיְהִי
בַעֲלוֹת הַלַּהַב מֵעַל הַמִּזְבֵּחַ הַשָּׁמַיְמָה וַיַּעַל
מַלְאַךְ־יְהוָה בְּלַהַב הַמִּזְבֵּחַ וּמָנוֹחַ וְאִשְׁתּוֹ
רֹאִים וַיִּפְּלוּ עַל־פְּנֵיהֶם אָרְצָה: כא וְלֹא יָסַף
עוֹד מַלְאַךְ יְהוָה לְהֵרָאֹה אֶל־מָנוֹחַ וְאֶל־
אִשְׁתּוֹ אָז יָדַע מָנוֹחַ כִּי־מַלְאַךְ יְהוָה הוּא:
כב וַיֹּאמֶר מָנוֹחַ אֶל־אִשְׁתּוֹ מוֹת נָמוּת כִּי
אֱלֹהִים רָאִינוּ: כג וַתֹּאמֶר לוֹ אִשְׁתּוֹ לוּ חָפֵץ
יְהוָה לַהֲמִיתֵנוּ לֹא־לָקַח מִיָּדֵנוּ עֹלָה וּמִנְחָה

and at this time He would not let us hear [such things] as these." 24. And the woman bore a son and called his name Samson; and the lad grew, and the Lord blessed him. 25. And the spirit of the Lord began to come to him at times in the camp of Dan, between Zorah and Eshtaol.

וְלֹא הֶרְאָנוּ אֶת־כָּל־אֵלֶּה וְכָעֵת לֹא הִשְׁמִיעָנוּ כָּזֹאת: כד וַתֵּלֶד הָאִשָּׁה בֵּן וַתִּקְרָא אֶת־שְׁמוֹ שִׁמְשׁוֹן וַיִּגְדַּל הַנַּעַר וַיְבָרְכֵהוּ יְהֹוָה: כה וַתָּחֶל רוּחַ יְהֹוָה לְפַעֲמוֹ בְּמַחֲנֵה־דָן בֵּין צָרְעָה וּבֵין אֶשְׁתָּאֹל:

HAFTARATH BEHA'ALOTHEKHA   הפטרת בהעלתך
(Zechariah 2:14–4:7)

This selection includes Zechariah's vision of the menorah and its seven lamps. This is appropriate to the opening verses of the Sidra, in which Aaron is instructed how to light the menorah in the Tabernacle, and the menorah itself is briefly described.

2:14. Sing and rejoice, O daughter of Zion, for, lo, I enter, and I will dwell in your midst, says the Lord. 15. And many nations will attach themselves to the Lord on that day and will become My people, and I will dwell in your midst, and you will know that the Lord of Hosts has sent me to you. 16. And the Lord will take Judah into His possessions as His portion on the holy soil and will choose Jerusalem forever. 17. Be silent, all flesh, before the Lord, for He is aroused out of His Holy Habitation. 3:1. Then He showed me Joshua, the high-priest, standing before the angel of the Lord, and the hinderer standing at his right hand to hinder him. 2. And the Lord said to the hinderer: "The Lord repulse you, O hinderer, the Lord Who has chosen Jerusalem repulse you. For is not this a brand plucked out of the fire?" 3. Now Joshua was clothed with soiled garments and standing before the angel. 4. And he [the angel] lifted his voice and said to those that stood before him, saying, "Remove the soiled garments from upon him." Then he said to him, "Behold, I have caused your iniquity to pass from you, now clothe yourself with pure garments." 5. Then I said, "Let them set a pure miter on his head." And they set the pure miter upon his head and invested him with garments. But the angel of the Lord remained standing. 6. The angel of the Lord warned Joshua, saying: 7. "So says the Lord of Hosts: If you will walk in My ways and if you will keep My charge, and you will also judge My House, and you

יד רָנִּי וְשִׂמְחִי בַּת־צִיּוֹן כִּי הִנְנִי־בָא וְשָׁכַנְתִּי בְתוֹכֵךְ נְאֻם־יְהֹוָה: טו וְנִלְווּ גוֹיִם רַבִּים אֶל־יְהֹוָה בַּיּוֹם הַהוּא וְהָיוּ לִי לְעָם וְשָׁכַנְתִּי בְתוֹכֵךְ וְיָדַעַתְּ כִּי־יְהֹוָה צְבָאוֹת שְׁלָחַנִי אֵלָיִךְ: טז וְנָחַל יְהֹוָה אֶת־יְהוּדָה חֶלְקוֹ עַל אַדְמַת הַקֹּדֶשׁ וּבָחַר עוֹד בִּירוּשָׁלָם: יז הַס כָּל־בָּשָׂר מִפְּנֵי יְהֹוָה כִּי נֵעוֹר מִמְּעוֹן קָדְשׁוֹ: א וַיַּרְאֵנִי אֶת־יְהוֹשֻׁעַ הַכֹּהֵן הַגָּדוֹל עֹמֵד לִפְנֵי מַלְאַךְ יְהֹוָה וְהַשָּׂטָן עֹמֵד עַל־יְמִינוֹ לְשִׂטְנוֹ: ב וַיֹּאמֶר יְהֹוָה אֶל־הַשָּׂטָן יִגְעַר יְהֹוָה בְּךָ הַשָּׂטָן וְיִגְעַר יְהֹוָה בְּךָ הַבֹּחֵר בִּירוּשָׁלָם הֲלוֹא זֶה אוּד מֻצָּל מֵאֵשׁ: ג וִיהוֹשֻׁעַ הָיָה לָבֻשׁ בְּגָדִים צוֹאִים וְעֹמֵד לִפְנֵי הַמַּלְאָךְ: ד וַיַּעַן וַיֹּאמֶר אֶל־הָעֹמְדִים לְפָנָיו לֵאמֹר הָסִירוּ הַבְּגָדִים הַצֹּאִים מֵעָלָיו וַיֹּאמֶר אֵלָיו רְאֵה הֶעֱבַרְתִּי מֵעָלֶיךָ עֲוֹנֶךָ וְהַלְבֵּשׁ אֹתְךָ מַחֲלָצוֹת: ה וָאֹמַר יָשִׂימוּ צָנִיף טָהוֹר עַל־רֹאשׁוֹ וַיָּשִׂימוּ הַצָּנִיף הַטָּהוֹר עַל־רֹאשׁוֹ וַיַּלְבִּשֻׁהוּ בְּגָדִים וּמַלְאַךְ יְהֹוָה עֹמֵד: ו וַיָּעַד מַלְאַךְ יְהֹוָה בִּיהוֹשֻׁעַ לֵאמֹר: ז כֹּה־אָמַר יְהֹוָה צְבָאוֹת אִם־בִּדְרָכַי תֵּלֵךְ וְאִם אֶת־מִשְׁמַרְתִּי תִּשְׁמֹר וְגַם־אַתָּה תָּדִין אֶת־

will also guard My courtyards, then I will give you free access among those that are standing still here. 8. Hear now, O Joshua the high-priest! For you and your companions who sit before you are men worthy of miracles, for, behold, I bring My servant the Shoot. 9. For, behold, the stone that I have placed before Joshua, on this one stone seven eyes are directed; behold I engrave its engraving, says the Lord of Hosts, and I will make the iniquity of that land disappear in one day. 10. On that day, says the Lord of Hosts, every man will invite his neighbor beneath his vine and beneath his fig tree."4:1. Then the angel that talked with me came again and awakened me as a man who is awakened from his sleep. 2. And he said to me, "What do you see?" And I said, "I have looked, and behold a candelabrum all of gold, with its oil-bowl upon the top of it and its seven lamps thereon and seven tubes to the seven lamps which were upon its top. 3. And two olive trees by it, one upon the right side of the bowl, and the other on the left side thereof." 4. So I answered and spoke to the angel who talked with me, saying, "What do these mean, my lord?" 5. Then the angel that talked with me answered to me, "Have you not understood what these mean?" And I said, "No, my lord." 6. Then he answered and spoke to me, saying, "This is the word of the Lord to Zerubbabel, saying, 'Not by military force and not by physical strength, but by My Spirit,' says the Lord of Hosts. 7. Who are you, O great mountain? Before Zerubbabel you sink to a plain! He will bring out the best stone, with shoutings of grace, grace, to it."

בֵּיתִי וְגַם תִּשְׁמֹר אֶת־חֲצֵרָי וְנָתַתִּי לְךָ
מַהְלְכִים בֵּין הָעֹמְדִים הָאֵלֶּה׃ ח שְׁמַע־נָא
יְהוֹשֻׁעַ ׀ הַכֹּהֵן הַגָּדוֹל אַתָּה וְרֵעֶיךָ הַיֹּשְׁבִים
לְפָנֶיךָ כִּי־אַנְשֵׁי מוֹפֵת הֵמָּה כִּי־הִנְנִי מֵבִיא
אֶת־עַבְדִּי צֶמַח׃ ט כִּי ׀ הִנֵּה הָאֶבֶן אֲשֶׁר נָתַתִּי
לִפְנֵי יְהוֹשֻׁעַ עַל־אֶבֶן אַחַת שִׁבְעָה עֵינָיִם הִנְנִי
מְפַתֵּחַ פִּתֻּחָהּ נְאֻם יְהוָה צְבָאוֹת וּמַשְׁתִּי אֶת־
עֲוֺן הָאָרֶץ־הַהִיא בְּיוֹם אֶחָד׃ י בַּיּוֹם הַהוּא
נְאֻם יְהוָה צְבָאוֹת תִּקְרְאוּ אִישׁ לְרֵעֵהוּ
אֶל־תַּחַת גֶּפֶן וְאֶל־תַּחַת תְּאֵנָה׃ א וַיָּשָׁב
הַמַּלְאָךְ הַדֹּבֵר בִּי וַיְעִירֵנִי כְּאִישׁ אֲשֶׁר־יֵעוֹר
מִשְּׁנָתוֹ׃ ב וַיֹּאמֶר אֵלַי מָה אַתָּה רֹאֶה וַיֹּאמֶר
(ואמר קרי) רָאִיתִי וְהִנֵּה מְנוֹרַת זָהָב כֻּלָּהּ וְגֻלָּהּ
עַל־רֹאשָׁהּ וְשִׁבְעָה נֵרֹתֶיהָ עָלֶיהָ שִׁבְעָה
וְשִׁבְעָה מוּצָקוֹת לַנֵּרוֹת אֲשֶׁר עַל־רֹאשָׁהּ׃
ג וּשְׁנַיִם זֵיתִים עָלֶיהָ אֶחָד מִימִין הַגֻּלָּה וְאֶחָד
עַל־שְׂמֹאלָהּ׃ ד וָאַעַן וָאֹמַר אֶל־הַמַּלְאָךְ הַדֹּבֵר
בִּי לֵאמֹר מָה־אֵלֶּה אֲדֹנִי׃ ה וַיַּעַן הַמַּלְאָךְ
הַדֹּבֵר בִּי וַיֹּאמֶר אֵלַי הֲלוֹא יָדַעְתָּ מָה־הֵמָּה
אֵלֶּה וָאֹמַר לֹא אֲדֹנִי׃ ו וַיַּעַן וַיֹּאמֶר אֵלַי
לֵאמֹר זֶה דְּבַר־יְהוָה אֶל־זְרֻבָּבֶל לֵאמֹר לֹא
בְחַיִל וְלֹא בְכֹחַ כִּי אִם־בְּרוּחִי אָמַר יְהוָה
צְבָאוֹת׃ ז מִי־אַתָּה הַר־הַגָּדוֹל לִפְנֵי זְרֻבָּבֶל
לְמִישֹׁר וְהוֹצִיא אֶת־הָאֶבֶן הָרֹאשָׁה תְּשֻׁאוֹת
חֵן ׀ חֵן לָהּ׃

HAFTARATH SHELAḤ LEKHA הפטרת שלח לך

(Joshua 2:1–24)

This selection tells how Joshua sent spies to reconnoiter the land of Canaan. It thus parallels the account of this Sidra (Numbers 13) of Moses' sending spies from the wilderness to explore the Promised Land.

2:1. And Joshua the son of Nun sent two men out of Shittim to spy secretly, saying, "Go see the land and Jericho." And they went, and came to the house of a harlot

א וַיִּשְׁלַח יְהוֹשֻׁעַ בִּן־נוּן מִן־הַשִּׁטִּים שְׁנַיִם
אֲנָשִׁים מְרַגְּלִים חֶרֶשׁ לֵאמֹר לְכוּ רְאוּ אֶת־
הָאָרֶץ וְאֶת־יְרִיחוֹ וַיֵּלְכוּ וַיָּבֹאוּ בֵּית אִשָּׁה

named Rahab, and they lay there. 2. And it was told to the king of Jericho, saying, "Behold, men have come here this night from the children of Israel to search the land." 3. And the king of Jericho sent to Rahab, saying, "Bring forth the men who have come to you, that have entered your house, for they have come to search out the entire land." 4. Now the woman had taken the two men, and had hidden them, and she said, "Indeed the men came to me, but I did not know from where they were. 5. And it was time to close the gate, at darkness, that the men went out. I do not know where they went. Pursue them quickly, for you will overtake them." 6. And she had brought them up to the roof, and she hid them with the stalks of flax that she had laid arranged upon the roof. 7. And the men pursued them in the direction of the Jordan, to the fords; and as soon as the pursuers had gone out, they shut the gate. 8. And before they were asleep, she came up to them upon the roof. 9. And she said to the men, "I know that the Lord has given you the land, and that your terror is fallen upon us, and that all the inhabitants of the land have melted away because of you. 10. For we have heard how the Lord dried up the water of the Red Sea for you when you came out of Egypt; and what you did to the two kings of the Emorites that were on the other side of the Jordan, Sihon and Og, whom you completely destroyed. 11. And as soon as we heard, our hearts melted, nor did there remain anymore spirit in any man because of you, for the Lord your God, He is God in heaven above and on the earth below. 12. And now, I pray, swear to me by the Lord, since I have shown you kindness, that you will also show kindness to my father's house and give me a true token. 13. And you shall preserve alive my father and my mother and my brothers and my sisters and all they have, and you shall deliver our lives from death." 14. And the men answered her, "Our life for yours, if you will not tell this, our discussion. And it shall be, when the Lord gives us the land, that we will deal

זוֹנָה וּשְׁמָהּ רָחָב וַיִּשְׁכְּבוּ־שָׁמָּה׃ ב וַיֵּאָמַר
לְמֶלֶךְ יְרִיחוֹ לֵאמֹר הִנֵּה אֲנָשִׁים בָּאוּ הֵנָּה
הַלַּיְלָה מִבְּנֵי יִשְׂרָאֵל לַחְפֹּר אֶת־הָאָרֶץ׃
ג וַיִּשְׁלַח מֶלֶךְ יְרִיחוֹ אֶל־רָחָב לֵאמֹר הוֹצִיאִי
הָאֲנָשִׁים הַבָּאִים אֵלַיִךְ אֲשֶׁר־בָּאוּ לְבֵיתֵךְ כִּי
לַחְפֹּר אֶת־כָּל־הָאָרֶץ בָּאוּ׃ ד וַתִּקַּח הָאִשָּׁה
אֶת־שְׁנֵי הָאֲנָשִׁים וַתִּצְפְּנוֹ וַתֹּאמֶר כֵּן בָּאוּ
אֵלַי הָאֲנָשִׁים וְלֹא יָדַעְתִּי מֵאַיִן הֵמָּה׃ ה וַיְהִי
הַשַּׁעַר לִסְגּוֹר בַּחֹשֶׁךְ וְהָאֲנָשִׁים יָצָאוּ לֹא
יָדַעְתִּי אָנָה הָלְכוּ הָאֲנָשִׁים רִדְפוּ מַהֵר
אַחֲרֵיהֶם כִּי תַשִּׂיגוּם׃ ו וְהִיא הֶעֱלָתַם הַגָּגָה
וַתִּטְמְנֵם בְּפִשְׁתֵּי הָעֵץ הָעֲרֻכוֹת לָהּ עַל־הַגָּג׃
ז וְהָאֲנָשִׁים רָדְפוּ אַחֲרֵיהֶם דֶּרֶךְ הַיַּרְדֵּן עַל
הַמַּעְבְּרוֹת וְהַשַּׁעַר סָגָרוּ אַחֲרֵי כַּאֲשֶׁר יָצְאוּ
הָרֹדְפִים אַחֲרֵיהֶם׃ ח וְהֵמָּה טֶרֶם יִשְׁכָּבוּן
וְהִיא עָלְתָה עֲלֵיהֶם עַל־הַגָּג׃ ט וַתֹּאמֶר אֶל־
הָאֲנָשִׁים יָדַעְתִּי כִּי־נָתַן יְהוָה לָכֶם אֶת־הָאָרֶץ
וְכִי־נָפְלָה אֵימַתְכֶם עָלֵינוּ וְכִי נָמֹגוּ כָּל־יֹשְׁבֵי
הָאָרֶץ מִפְּנֵיכֶם׃ י כִּי שָׁמַעְנוּ אֵת אֲשֶׁר־
הוֹבִישׁ יְהוָה אֶת־מֵי יַם־סוּף מִפְּנֵיכֶם
בְּצֵאתְכֶם מִמִּצְרָיִם וַאֲשֶׁר עֲשִׂיתֶם לִשְׁנֵי מַלְכֵי
הָאֱמֹרִי אֲשֶׁר בְּעֵבֶר הַיַּרְדֵּן לְסִיחֹן וּלְעוֹג אֲשֶׁר
הֶחֱרַמְתֶּם אוֹתָם׃ יא וַנִּשְׁמַע וַיִּמַּס לְבָבֵנוּ וְלֹא־
קָמָה עוֹד רוּחַ בְּאִישׁ מִפְּנֵיכֶם כִּי יְהוָה
אֱלֹהֵיכֶם הוּא אֱלֹהִים בַּשָּׁמַיִם מִמַּעַל וְעַל־
הָאָרֶץ מִתָּחַת׃ יב וְעַתָּה הִשָּׁבְעוּ־נָא לִי בַּיהוָה
כִּי־עָשִׂיתִי עִמָּכֶם חָסֶד וַעֲשִׂיתֶם גַּם־אַתֶּם עִם־
בֵּית אָבִי חֶסֶד וּנְתַתֶּם לִי אוֹת אֱמֶת׃
יג וְהַחֲיִתֶם אֶת־אָבִי וְאֶת־אִמִּי וְאֶת־אַחַי וְאֶת־
אַחוֹתַי (אחיותי קרי) וְאֵת כָּל־אֲשֶׁר לָהֶם וְהִצַּלְתֶּם
אֶת־נַפְשֹׁתֵינוּ מִמָּוֶת׃ יד וַיֹּאמְרוּ לָהּ הָאֲנָשִׁים
נַפְשֵׁנוּ תַחְתֵּיכֶם לָמוּת אִם לֹא תַגִּידוּ אֶת־
דְּבָרֵנוּ זֶה וְהָיָה בְּתֵת יְהוָה לָנוּ אֶת־הָאָרֶץ

with you with kindness and truth." 15. And she let them down by a rope through the window, for her house was in the town wall, and she dwelt in the wall. 16. And she said to them, "Go to the mountain lest the pursuers meet you; and hide there three days until the pursuers return, and afterwards you will go your way." 17. And the men said to her, "We will be blameless of this, your oath, which you made us swear: 18. Behold, when we come into the land, you shall bind this line of scarlet thread in the window by which you let us down; and you shall bring your father and your mother, and your brothers and all your father's household home to you. 19. And it shall be that whosoever shall go out of the doors of your house outside, his blood shall be upon his head, and we will be blameless; and whosoever shall be with you in the house, his blood shall be upon our head if any hand be upon him. 20. And if you tell this, our discussion, then we will be blameless of your oath, which you have made us swear." 21. And she said, "According to your words, so be it." And she sent them away, and they departed; and she bound the scarlet line in the window. 22. And they went and came to the mountain and stayed there three days, until the pursuers returned; and the pursuers sought them throughout all the way, but they did not find them. 23. And the two men returned and descended from the mountain and crossed over and came to Joshua the son of Nun and told him all that had happened to them. 24. And they said to Joshua, "For the Lord has delivered into our hands all the land, and also the inhabitants of the country have melted away because of us."

וְעָשִׂינוּ עִמָּךְ חֶסֶד וֶאֱמֶת׃ טו וַתּוֹרִדֵם בַּחֶבֶל
בְּעַד הַחַלּוֹן כִּי בֵיתָהּ בְּקִיר הַחוֹמָה וּבַחוֹמָה
הִיא יוֹשָׁבֶת׃ טז וַתֹּאמֶר לָהֶם הָהָרָה לֵּכוּ פֶּן־
יִפְגְּעוּ בָכֶם הָרֹדְפִים וְנַחְבֵּתֶם שָׁמָּה שְׁלֹשֶׁת
יָמִים עַד שׁוֹב הָרֹדְפִים וְאַחַר תֵּלְכוּ לְדַרְכְּכֶם׃
יז וַיֹּאמְרוּ אֵלֶיהָ הָאֲנָשִׁים נְקִיִּם אֲנַחְנוּ
מִשְּׁבֻעָתֵךְ הַזֶּה אֲשֶׁר הִשְׁבַּעְתָּנוּ׃ יח הִנֵּה אֲנַחְנוּ
בָאִים בָּאָרֶץ אֶת־תִּקְוַת חוּט הַשָּׁנִי הַזֶּה
תִּקְשְׁרִי בַּחַלּוֹן אֲשֶׁר הוֹרַדְתֵּנוּ בוֹ וְאֶת־אָבִיךְ
וְאֶת־אִמֵּךְ וְאֶת־אַחַיִךְ וְאֵת כָּל־בֵּית אָבִיךְ
תַּאַסְפִי אֵלַיִךְ הַבָּיְתָה׃ יט וְהָיָה כֹּל אֲשֶׁר־יֵצֵא
מִדַּלְתֵי בֵיתֵךְ ׀ הַחוּצָה דָּמוֹ בְרֹאשׁוֹ וַאֲנַחְנוּ
נְקִיִּם וְכֹל אֲשֶׁר יִהְיֶה אִתָּךְ בַּבַּיִת דָּמוֹ
בְרֹאשֵׁנוּ אִם־יָד תִּהְיֶה־בּוֹ׃ כ וְאִם־תַּגִּידִי אֶת־
דְּבָרֵנוּ זֶה וְהָיִינוּ נְקִיִּם מִשְּׁבֻעָתֵךְ אֲשֶׁר
הִשְׁבַּעְתָּנוּ׃ כא וַתֹּאמֶר כְּדִבְרֵיכֶם כֶּן־הוּא
וַתְּשַׁלְּחֵם וַיֵּלֵכוּ וַתִּקְשֹׁר אֶת־תִּקְוַת הַשָּׁנִי
בַּחַלּוֹן׃ כב וַיֵּלְכוּ וַיָּבֹאוּ הָהָרָה וַיֵּשְׁבוּ שָׁם
שְׁלֹשֶׁת יָמִים עַד־שָׁבוּ הָרֹדְפִים וַיְבַקְשׁוּ
הָרֹדְפִים בְּכָל־הַדֶּרֶךְ וְלֹא מָצָאוּ׃ כג וַיָּשֻׁבוּ
שְׁנֵי הָאֲנָשִׁים וַיֵּרְדוּ מֵהָהָר וַיַּעַבְרוּ וַיָּבֹאוּ אֶל־
יְהוֹשֻׁעַ בִּן־נוּן וַיְסַפְּרוּ־לוֹ אֵת כָּל־הַמֹּצְאוֹת
אוֹתָם׃ כד וַיֹּאמְרוּ אֶל־יְהוֹשֻׁעַ כִּי־נָתַן יְהוָה
בְּיָדֵנוּ אֶת־כָּל־הָאָרֶץ וְגַם־נָמֹגוּ כָּל־יֹשְׁבֵי
הָאָרֶץ מִפָּנֵינוּ׃

HAFTARATH KORAḤ הפטרת קרח

(I Samuel 11:14–12:22)

Should Rosh Chodesh coincide with the Sabbath, the Haftarah for Sabbath Rosh Chodesh (p. 930) is read.

Samuel appeals to the people to testify that he has never wronged or mistreated them. This story parallels a similar declaration by Moses, at the time of Korach's rebellion, which is described in the Sidra.

11:14. And Samuel said to the people, "Come, and let us go to Gilgal, and renew there the kingdom." 15. And all the people

יד וַיֹּאמֶר שְׁמוּאֵל אֶל־הָעָם לְכוּ וְנֵלְכָה הַגִּלְגָּל
וּנְחַדֵּשׁ שָׁם הַמְּלוּכָה׃ טו וַיֵּלְכוּ כָל־הָעָם

went to Gilgal, and there they made Saul king before the Lord in Gilgal, and there they slaughtered peace offerings before the Lord, and Saul and all the people rejoiced greatly. 12:1. And Samuel said to all Israel, "Behold, I have hearkened to your voice, to everything which you have said to me, and I have made a king to reign over you. 2. And now, behold, the king is walking before you; and I have become old and hoary, and my sons are here with you, and I have walked before you from my youth and until this day. 3. Here I am; bear witness against me before the Lord and before His anointed; whose ox did I take, or whose ass did I take, or whom did I rob; or whom did I oppress, or from whose hand did I take a ransom, that I hide my eyes therewith, and I shall restore [it] to you." 4. And they said, "You did not rob us, nor did you oppress us, neither did you take anything from anyone's hand." 5. And he said to them, "The Lord is a witness against you, and His anointed is witness this day, that you have not found anything in my hand; and they said, "[He is] witness." 6. And Samuel said to the people, "[It is] the Lord Who made Moses and Aaron, and Who brought your forefathers up from the land of Egypt. 7. And now, stand and I shall reason with you before the Lord concerning all the righteous acts which He did to you and to your forefathers. 8. When Jacob came to Egypt, and your forefathers cried out to the Lord, the Lord sent Moses and Aaron, and they brought your forefathers out of Egypt, and they made them dwell in this place. 9. And they forgot the Lord their God, and He delivered them into the hand of Sisera, the commander of the army of Hazor, and into the hand of the Philistines, and into the hand of the king of Moab, and they waged war with them. 10. And they cried out to the Lord and said, 'We have sinned, for we have forsaken the Lord, and have served the Baalim and Ashtaroth. Now, save us from the hand of our enemies, and we shall serve You.' 11. And the Lord sent Jerubaal and Bedan and Jephthah and Samuel, and He saved you from the hand of your enemies round about, and you dwelt in safety. 12. And when you saw that Nahash, the

הַגִּלְגָּל וַיַּמְלִכוּ שָׁם אֶת־שָׁאוּל לִפְנֵי יְהֹוָה בַּגִּלְגָּל וַיִּזְבְּחוּ־שָׁם זְבָחִים שְׁלָמִים לִפְנֵי יְהֹוָה וַיִּשְׂמַח שָׁם שָׁאוּל וְכָל־אַנְשֵׁי יִשְׂרָאֵל עַד־ מְאֹד: א וַיֹּאמֶר שְׁמוּאֵל אֶל־כָּל־יִשְׂרָאֵל הִנֵּה שָׁמַעְתִּי בְקֹלְכֶם לְכֹל אֲשֶׁר־אֲמַרְתֶּם לִי וָאַמְלִיךְ עֲלֵיכֶם מֶלֶךְ: ב וְעַתָּה הִנֵּה הַמֶּלֶךְ | מִתְהַלֵּךְ לִפְנֵיכֶם וַאֲנִי זָקַנְתִּי וָשַׂבְתִּי וּבָנַי הִנָּם אִתְּכֶם וַאֲנִי הִתְהַלַּכְתִּי לִפְנֵיכֶם מִנְּעֻרַי עַד־ הַיּוֹם הַזֶּה: ג הִנְנִי עֲנוּ בִי נֶגֶד יְהֹוָה וְנֶגֶד מְשִׁיחוֹ אֶת־שׁוֹר | מִי לָקַחְתִּי וַחֲמוֹר מִי לָקַחְתִּי וְאֶת־מִי עָשַׁקְתִּי אֶת־מִי רַצּוֹתִי וּמִיַּד־ מִי לָקַחְתִּי כֹפֶר וְאַעְלִים עֵינַי בּוֹ וְאָשִׁיב לָכֶם: ד וַיֹּאמְרוּ לֹא עֲשַׁקְתָּנוּ וְלֹא רַצּוֹתָנוּ וְלֹא־ לָקַחְתָּ מִיַּד־אִישׁ מְאוּמָה: ה וַיֹּאמֶר אֲלֵיהֶם עֵד יְהֹוָה בָּכֶם וְעֵד מְשִׁיחוֹ הַיּוֹם הַזֶּה כִּי לֹא מְצָאתֶם בְּיָדִי מְאוּמָה וַיֹּאמֶר עֵד: ו וַיֹּאמֶר שְׁמוּאֵל אֶל־הָעָם יְהֹוָה אֲשֶׁר עָשָׂה אֶת־מֹשֶׁה וְאֶת־אַהֲרֹן וַאֲשֶׁר הֶעֱלָה אֶת־אֲבוֹתֵיכֶם מֵאֶרֶץ מִצְרָיִם: ז וְעַתָּה הִתְיַצְּבוּ וְאִשָּׁפְטָה אִתְּכֶם לִפְנֵי יְהֹוָה אֵת כָּל־צִדְקוֹת יְהֹוָה אֲשֶׁר־עָשָׂה אִתְּכֶם וְאֶת־אֲבֹתֵיכֶם: ח כַּאֲשֶׁר־בָּא יַעֲקֹב מִצְרָיִם וַיִּזְעֲקוּ אֲבוֹתֵיכֶם אֶל־יְהֹוָה וַיִּשְׁלַח יְהֹוָה אֶת־מֹשֶׁה וְאֶת־אַהֲרֹן וַיּוֹצִיאוּ אֶת־ אֲבֹתֵיכֶם מִמִּצְרַיִם וַיֹּשִׁבוּם בַּמָּקוֹם הַזֶּה: ט וַיִּשְׁכְּחוּ אֶת־יְהֹוָה אֱלֹהֵיהֶם וַיִּמְכֹּר אֹתָם בְּיַד סִיסְרָא שַׂר־צְבָא חָצוֹר וּבְיַד־פְּלִשְׁתִּים וּבְיַד מֶלֶךְ מוֹאָב וַיִּלָּחֲמוּ בָּם: י וַיִּזְעֲקוּ אֶל־ יְהֹוָה וַיֹּאמֶר (ויאמרו קרי) חָטָאנוּ כִּי עָזַבְנוּ אֶת־ יְהֹוָה וַנַּעֲבֹד אֶת־הַבְּעָלִים וְאֶת־הָעַשְׁתָּרוֹת וְעַתָּה הַצִּילֵנוּ מִיַּד אֹיְבֵינוּ וְנַעַבְדֶךָּ: יא וַיִּשְׁלַח יְהֹוָה אֶת־יְרֻבַּעַל וְאֶת־בְּדָן וְאֶת־יִפְתָּח וְאֶת־ שְׁמוּאֵל וַיַּצֵּל אֶתְכֶם מִיַּד אֹיְבֵיכֶם מִסָּבִיב וַתֵּשְׁבוּ בֶּטַח: יב וַתִּרְאוּ כִּי נָחָשׁ מֶלֶךְ בְּנֵי־

king of Ammon, came upon you, you said to me, 'No, but a king shall rule over us,' when the Lord your God was your King. 13. And now, behold the king whom you have chosen, whom you have requested, and behold, the Lord has appointed a king over you. 14. If you will fear the Lord and serve Him and hearken to His voice, and you will not rebel against the commandments of the Lord, both you and the king who reigns over you will be after the Lord your God. 15. But, if you will not hearken to the voice of the Lord, and you will rebel against the commandments of the Lord, the Lord's hand will be against you and against your fathers. 16. Even now, stand and see this great thing which the Lord will do before your eyes. 17. Is it not wheat harvest today? I shall call to the Lord, and He will send thunder and rain, and you shall know and see, that your evil is great, which you have done in the eyes of the Lord, to ask for yourselves a king.'' 18. And Samuel called to the Lord, and the Lord sent thunder and rain on that day, and all the people greatly feared the Lord and Samuel. 19. And all the people said to Samuel, ''Pray for your servants to the Lord your God and let us not die, for we have added evil to all our sins, to ask for ourselves a king.'' 20. And Samuel said to the people, ''Fear not. You have done all this evil, but do not turn aside from following the Lord, and you shall serve the Lord with all your heart. 21. And you shall not turn aside, for then [you would go] after vain things which cannot profit or deliver, for they are vain. 22. For the Lord will not forsake His people for His great name's sake; for the Lord has sworn to make you a people for Himself.''

עָמוֹן בָּא עֲלֵיכֶם וַתֹּאמְרוּ לִי לֹא כִּי־מֶלֶךְ
יִמְלֹךְ עָלֵינוּ וַיהוָֹה אֱלֹהֵיכֶם מַלְכְּכֶם: יג וְעַתָּה
הִנֵּה הַמֶּלֶךְ אֲשֶׁר בְּחַרְתֶּם אֲשֶׁר שְׁאֶלְתֶּם וְהִנֵּה
נָתַן יְהוָֹה עֲלֵיכֶם מֶלֶךְ: יד אִם־תִּירְאוּ אֶת־
יְהוָֹה וַעֲבַדְתֶּם אֹתוֹ וּשְׁמַעְתֶּם בְּקוֹלוֹ וְלֹא
תַמְרוּ אֶת־פִּי יְהוָֹה וִהְיִתֶם גַּם־אַתֶּם וְגַם־
הַמֶּלֶךְ אֲשֶׁר מָלַךְ עֲלֵיכֶם אַחַר יְהוָֹה אֱלֹהֵיכֶם:
טו וְאִם־לֹא תִשְׁמְעוּ בְּקוֹל יְהוָֹה וּמְרִיתֶם אֶת־
פִּי יְהוָֹה וְהָיְתָה יַד־יְהוָֹה בָּכֶם וּבַאֲבֹתֵיכֶם:
טז גַּם־עַתָּה הִתְיַצְּבוּ וּרְאוּ אֶת־הַדָּבָר הַגָּדוֹל
הַזֶּה אֲשֶׁר יְהוָֹה עֹשֶׂה לְעֵינֵיכֶם: יז הֲלוֹא
קְצִיר־חִטִּים הַיּוֹם אֶקְרָא אֶל־יְהוָֹה וְיִתֵּן קֹלוֹת
וּמָטָר וּדְעוּ וּרְאוּ כִּי־רָעַתְכֶם רַבָּה אֲשֶׁר
עֲשִׂיתֶם בְּעֵינֵי יְהוָֹה לִשְׁאוֹל לָכֶם מֶלֶךְ:
יח וַיִּקְרָא שְׁמוּאֵל אֶל־יְהוָֹה וַיִּתֵּן יְהוָֹה קֹלֹת
וּמָטָר בַּיּוֹם הַהוּא וַיִּירָא כָל־הָעָם מְאֹד אֶת־
יְהוָֹה וְאֶת־שְׁמוּאֵל: יט וַיֹּאמְרוּ כָל־הָעָם אֶל־
שְׁמוּאֵל הִתְפַּלֵּל בְּעַד־עֲבָדֶיךָ אֶל־יְהוָֹה אֱלֹהֶיךָ
וְאַל־נָמוּת כִּי־יָסַפְנוּ עַל־כָּל־חַטֹּאתֵינוּ רָעָה
לִשְׁאֹל לָנוּ מֶלֶךְ: כ וַיֹּאמֶר שְׁמוּאֵל אֶל־הָעָם
אַל־תִּירָאוּ אַתֶּם עֲשִׂיתֶם אֵת כָּל־הָרָעָה הַזֹּאת
אַךְ אַל־תָּסוּרוּ מֵאַחֲרֵי יְהוָֹה וַעֲבַדְתֶּם אֶת־
יְהוָֹה בְּכָל־לְבַבְכֶם: כא וְלֹא תָּסוּרוּ כִּי ׀ אַחֲרֵי
הַתֹּהוּ אֲשֶׁר לֹא־יוֹעִילוּ וְלֹא יַצִּילוּ כִּי־תֹהוּ
הֵמָּה: כב כִּי לֹא־יִטֹּשׁ יְהוָֹה אֶת־עַמּוֹ בַּעֲבוּר
שְׁמוֹ הַגָּדוֹל כִּי הוֹאִיל יְהוָֹה לַעֲשׂוֹת אֶתְכֶם לוֹ
לְעָם:

HAFTARATH HUKKATH הפטרת חקת

(Judges 11:1–33)

Read when Ḥukkath is read separately. Should Rosh Chodesh coincide with this Sabbath, the Haftarah for Sabbath Rosh Chodesh (p. 930) is read.

This selection tells the story of Jephthah's war with the Ammonites, in which much of the story of the Sidra is repeated.

11:1. Now Jephthah the Gileadite was a mighty man of valor, and he was the son of a woman harlot, and Gilead begot Jephthah. 2. And Gilead's wife bore him sons; and his wife's sons grew up and drove Jephthah out, and they said to him, "You shall not inherit in our father's house, for you are the son of another woman." 3. And Jephthah fled from his brothers, and he dwelt in the land of Tob; and idle men were gathered to Jephthah, and they went out with him. 4. And it was after many days that the children of Ammon made war with Israel. 5. And it was when the children of Ammon fought with Israel, and the elders of Gilead went to take Jephthah from the land of Tob. 6. And they said to Jephthah, "Come and become our chief, and we will fight with the children of Ammon." 7. And Jephthah said to the elders of Gilead, "Did you not hate me, and drive me from my father's house? So why have you come to me now when you are in distress?" 8. And the elders of Gilead said to Jephthah, "Therefore we returned to you now, and you shall go with us, and you will fight with the children of Ammon, and you shall become our head, over all the inhabitants of Gilead." 9. And Jephthah said to the elders of Gilead, "If you bring me back to fight with the children of Ammon, and the Lord delivers them before me, I will become your head." 10. And the elders of Gilead said to Jephthah, "The Lord shall hear between us, if not according to your word, so will we do." 11. And Jephthah went with the elders of Gilead, and the people appointed him a head and chief over them; and Jephthah spoke all his words before the Lord in Mizpah. 12. And Jephthah sent messengers to the king of the children of Ammon, saying, "What is [between] me and you, that you have come to me to fight in my land?" 13. And the king of the children of Ammon said to the

א וְיִפְתָּח הַגִּלְעָדִי הָיָה גִּבּוֹר חַיִל וְהוּא בֶּן־
אִשָּׁה זוֹנָה וַיּוֹלֶד גִּלְעָד אֶת־יִפְתָּח׃ ב וַתֵּלֶד
אֵשֶׁת־גִּלְעָד לוֹ בָּנִים וַיִּגְדְּלוּ בְנֵי־הָאִשָּׁה
וַיְגָרְשׁוּ אֶת־יִפְתָּח וַיֹּאמְרוּ לוֹ לֹא־תִנְחַל
בְּבֵית־אָבִינוּ כִּי בֶן־אִשָּׁה אַחֶרֶת אָתָּה׃
ג וַיִּבְרַח יִפְתָּח מִפְּנֵי אֶחָיו וַיֵּשֶׁב בְּאֶרֶץ טוֹב
וַיִּתְלַקְּטוּ אֶל־יִפְתָּח אֲנָשִׁים רֵיקִים וַיֵּצְאוּ
עִמּוֹ׃ ד וַיְהִי מִיָּמִים וַיִּלָּחֲמוּ בְנֵי־עַמּוֹן עִם־
יִשְׂרָאֵל׃ ה וַיְהִי כַּאֲשֶׁר־נִלְחֲמוּ בְנֵי־עַמּוֹן עִם־
יִשְׂרָאֵל וַיֵּלְכוּ זִקְנֵי גִלְעָד לָקַחַת אֶת־יִפְתָּח
מֵאֶרֶץ טוֹב׃ ו וַיֹּאמְרוּ לְיִפְתָּח לְכָה וְהָיִיתָה
לָּנוּ לְקָצִין וְנִלָּחֲמָה בִּבְנֵי עַמּוֹן׃ ז וַיֹּאמֶר
יִפְתָּח לְזִקְנֵי גִלְעָד הֲלֹא אַתֶּם שְׂנֵאתֶם אוֹתִי
וַתְּגָרְשׁוּנִי מִבֵּית אָבִי וּמַדּוּעַ בָּאתֶם אֵלַי עַתָּה
כַּאֲשֶׁר צַר לָכֶם׃ ח וַיֹּאמְרוּ זִקְנֵי גִלְעָד אֶל־
יִפְתָּח לָכֵן עַתָּה שַׁבְנוּ אֵלֶיךָ וְהָלַכְתָּ עִמָּנוּ
וְנִלְחַמְתָּ בִּבְנֵי עַמּוֹן וְהָיִיתָ לָּנוּ לְרֹאשׁ לְכֹל
יֹשְׁבֵי גִלְעָד׃ ט וַיֹּאמֶר יִפְתָּח אֶל־זִקְנֵי גִלְעָד
אִם־מְשִׁיבִים אַתֶּם אוֹתִי לְהִלָּחֵם בִּבְנֵי עַמּוֹן
וְנָתַן יְהוָה אוֹתָם לְפָנָי אָנֹכִי אֶהְיֶה לָכֶם
לְרֹאשׁ׃ י וַיֹּאמְרוּ זִקְנֵי־גִלְעָד אֶל־יִפְתָּח יְהוָה
יִהְיֶה שֹׁמֵעַ בֵּינוֹתֵינוּ אִם־לֹא כִדְבָרְךָ כֵּן
נַעֲשֶׂה׃ יא וַיֵּלֶךְ יִפְתָּח עִם־זִקְנֵי גִלְעָד וַיָּשִׂימוּ
הָעָם אוֹתוֹ עֲלֵיהֶם לְרֹאשׁ וּלְקָצִין וַיְדַבֵּר
יִפְתָּח אֶת־כָּל־דְּבָרָיו לִפְנֵי יְהוָה בַּמִּצְפָּה׃
יב וַיִּשְׁלַח יִפְתָּח מַלְאָכִים אֶל־מֶלֶךְ בְּנֵי־עַמּוֹן
לֵאמֹר מַה־לִּי וָלָךְ כִּי־בָאתָ אֵלַי לְהִלָּחֵם
בְּאַרְצִי׃ יג וַיֹּאמֶר מֶלֶךְ בְּנֵי־עַמּוֹן אֶל־מַלְאֲכֵי

messengers of Jephthah, "Because Israel took away my land, when they came out of Egypt, from Arnon and up to the Jabbok, and up to the Jordan; and now restore them peacefully." 14. And Jephthah continued, and sent messengers to the king of the children of Ammon. 15. And he said to him, "So said Jephthah, 'Israel did not take the land of Moab and the land of the children of Ammon, 16. because when they came up from Egypt, and Israel went through the wilderness up to the Red Sea, and they came to Kadesh; 17. and Israel sent messengers to the king of Edom, saying, 'Let me pass now through your land,' and the king of Edom did not listen, and also to the king of Moab he sent, and he was unwilling; and Israel abode in Kadesh. 18. And they went through the wilderness and went around the land of Edom and the land of Moab, and they came to the east of the land of Moab; and they encamped on the other side of the Arnon, and they did not come within the border of Moab, for [the] Arnon [was] the border of Moab. 19. And Israel sent messengers to Sichon, king of the Emorites, the king of Heshbon; and Israel said to him, 'Please let us pass through your land up to my place.' 20. And Sichon did not trust Israel to pass through his border, and Sichon gathered all his people, and they encamped in Jahaz, and he fought with Israel. 21. And the Lord, the God of Israel, delivered Sichon and all his people into the hand of Israel, and they struck them; and Israel possessed all the land of the Emorites, the inhabitants of that land. 22. And they possessed all the border of the Emorites, from the Arnon up to the Jabbok and from the wilderness up to the Jordan. 23. And now the Lord, the God of Israel, has driven out the Emorites from before His people Israel, and you want to possess it? 24. Is it not that which Chemosh, your god, gives you to possess, that you may possess; so all that which the Lord our God has driven out from before us, that we shall possess. 25. And now, are you any better than Balak the son of Zippor, king of Moab? Did he ever strive with Israel, [or] did he ever fight against them? 26. When Israel dwelt in Heshbon and its towns, and in Aroer and its towns, and in all the cities that are along

יִפְתָּח כִּי־לָקַח יִשְׂרָאֵל אֶת־אַרְצִי בַּעֲלוֹתוֹ
מִמִּצְרַיִם מֵאַרְנוֹן וְעַד־הַיַּבֹּק וְעַד־הַיַּרְדֵּן וְעַתָּה
הָשִׁיבָה אֶתְהֶן בְּשָׁלוֹם: יד וַיּוֹסֶף עוֹד יִפְתָּח
וַיִּשְׁלַח מַלְאָכִים אֶל־מֶלֶךְ בְּנֵי עַמּוֹן: טו וַיֹּאמֶר
לוֹ כֹּה אָמַר יִפְתָּח לֹא־לָקַח יִשְׂרָאֵל אֶת־אֶרֶץ
מוֹאָב וְאֶת־אֶרֶץ בְּנֵי עַמּוֹן: טז כִּי בַּעֲלוֹתָם
מִמִּצְרָיִם וַיֵּלֶךְ יִשְׂרָאֵל בַּמִּדְבָּר עַד־יַם־סוּף
וַיָּבֹא קָדֵשָׁה: יז וַיִּשְׁלַח יִשְׂרָאֵל מַלְאָכִים ׀ אֶל־
מֶלֶךְ אֱדוֹם ׀ לֵאמֹר אֶעְבְּרָה־נָּא בְאַרְצֶךָ וְלֹא
שָׁמַע מֶלֶךְ אֱדוֹם וְגַם אֶל־מֶלֶךְ מוֹאָב שָׁלַח
וְלֹא אָבָה וַיֵּשֶׁב יִשְׂרָאֵל בְּקָדֵשׁ: יח וַיֵּלֶךְ
בַּמִּדְבָּר וַיָּסָב אֶת־אֶרֶץ אֱדוֹם וְאֶת־אֶרֶץ מוֹאָב
וַיָּבֹא מִמִּזְרַח־שֶׁמֶשׁ לְאֶרֶץ מוֹאָב וַיַּחֲנוּן
בְּעֵבֶר אַרְנוֹן וְלֹא־בָאוּ בִּגְבוּל מוֹאָב כִּי אַרְנוֹן
גְּבוּל מוֹאָב: יט וַיִּשְׁלַח יִשְׂרָאֵל מַלְאָכִים אֶל־
סִיחוֹן מֶלֶךְ־הָאֱמֹרִי מֶלֶךְ חֶשְׁבּוֹן וַיֹּאמֶר לוֹ
יִשְׂרָאֵל נַעְבְּרָה־נָּא בְאַרְצְךָ עַד־מְקוֹמִי:
כ וְלֹא־הֶאֱמִין סִיחוֹן אֶת־יִשְׂרָאֵל עֲבֹר בִּגְבֻלוֹ
וַיֶּאֱסֹף סִיחוֹן אֶת־כָּל־עַמּוֹ וַיַּחֲנוּ בְּיָהְצָה
וַיִּלָּחֶם עִם־יִשְׂרָאֵל: כא וַיִּתֵּן יְהֹוָה אֱלֹהֵי־
יִשְׂרָאֵל אֶת־סִיחוֹן וְאֶת־כָּל־עַמּוֹ בְּיַד יִשְׂרָאֵל
וַיַּכּוּם וַיִּירַשׁ יִשְׂרָאֵל אֵת כָּל־אֶרֶץ הָאֱמֹרִי
יוֹשֵׁב הָאָרֶץ הַהִיא: כב וַיִּירְשׁוּ אֵת כָּל־גְּבוּל
הָאֱמֹרִי מֵאַרְנוֹן וְעַד־הַיַּבֹּק וּמִן־הַמִּדְבָּר וְעַד־
הַיַּרְדֵּן: כג וְעַתָּה יְהֹוָה ׀ אֱלֹהֵי יִשְׂרָאֵל הוֹרִישׁ
אֶת־הָאֱמֹרִי מִפְּנֵי עַמּוֹ יִשְׂרָאֵל וְאַתָּה תִּירָשֶׁנּוּ:
כד הֲלֹא אֵת אֲשֶׁר יוֹרִישְׁךָ כְּמוֹשׁ אֱלֹהֶיךָ אוֹתוֹ
תִירָשׁ וְאֵת כָּל־אֲשֶׁר הוֹרִישׁ יְהֹוָה אֱלֹהֵינוּ
מִפָּנֵינוּ אוֹתוֹ נִירָשׁ: כה וְעַתָּה הֲטוֹב טוֹב אַתָּה
מִבָּלָק בֶּן־צִפּוֹר מֶלֶךְ מוֹאָב הֲרוֹב רָב עִם־
יִשְׂרָאֵל אִם־נִלְחֹם נִלְחַם בָּם: כו בְּשֶׁבֶת
יִשְׂרָאֵל בְּחֶשְׁבּוֹן וּבִבְנוֹתֶיהָ וּבְעַרְעוֹר
וּבִבְנוֹתֶיהָ וּבְכָל־הֶעָרִים אֲשֶׁר עַל־יְדֵי אַרְנוֹן

Arnon, three hundred years—why did you not recover them at that time? 27. And I have not sinned against you, and you do wrong with me by fighting against me; may the Lord, the Judge, decide this day between the children of Israel and between the children of Ammon." 28. And the king of the children of Ammon did not listen to the words of Jephthah which he had sent him. 29. And a spirit of the Lord was upon Jephthah, and he passed over Gilead and Menasseh, and he passed over Mizpeh of Gilead, and from Mizpeh of Gilead he passed over (to) the children of Ammon. 30. And Jephthah vowed a vow to the Lord, and said, "If You will indeed deliver the children of Ammon into my hand, 31. and it will be whatever comes forth that shall come forth from the doors of my house towards me, when I return in peace from the children of Ammon, shall be to the Lord, and I will offer him up for a burnt-offering." 32. And Jephthah passed over to the children of Ammon to fight against them; and the Lord delivered them into his hand. 33. And he struck them from Aroer until you come to Minnith, twenty cities, and up to Abel Cheramim, a very great slaughter. And the children of Ammon were subdued before the children of Israel.

שְׁלֹ֤שׁ מֵאוֹת֙ שָׁנָ֔ה וּמַדּ֗וּעַ לֹֽא־הִצַּלְתֶּ֛ם בָּעֵ֥ת הַהִֽיא: כז וְאָֽנֹכִי֙ לֹֽא־חָטָ֣אתִי לָ֔ךְ וְאַתָּ֞ה עֹשֶׂ֤ה אִתִּי֙ רָעָ֔ה לְהִלָּ֖חֶם בִּ֑י יִשְׁפֹּ֨ט יְהֹוָ֤ה הַשֹּׁפֵט֙ הַיּ֔וֹם בֵּ֚ין בְּנֵ֣י יִשְׂרָאֵ֔ל וּבֵ֖ין בְּנֵ֣י עַמּֽוֹן: כח וְלֹ֣א שָׁמַ֔ע מֶ֖לֶךְ בְּנֵ֣י עַמּ֑וֹן אֶל־דִּבְרֵ֣י יִפְתָּ֔ח אֲשֶׁ֥ר שָׁלַ֖ח אֵלָֽיו: כט וַתְּהִ֤י עַל־יִפְתָּח֙ ר֣וּחַ יְהֹוָ֔ה וַיַּֽעֲבֹ֥ר אֶת־הַגִּלְעָ֖ד וְאֶת־מְנַשֶּׁ֑ה וַיַּֽעֲבֹר֙ אֶת־מִצְפֵּ֣ה גִלְעָ֔ד וּמִמִּצְפֵּ֣ה גִלְעָ֔ד עָבַ֖ר בְּנֵ֥י עַמּֽוֹן: ל וַיִּדַּ֨ר יִפְתָּ֥ח נֶ֛דֶר לַיהֹוָ֖ה וַיֹּאמַ֑ר אִם־נָת֥וֹן תִּתֵּ֛ן אֶת־בְּנֵ֥י עַמּ֖וֹן בְּיָדִֽי: לא וְהָיָ֣ה הַיּוֹצֵ֗א אֲשֶׁ֨ר יֵצֵ֜א מִדַּלְתֵ֤י בֵיתִי֙ לִקְרָאתִ֔י בְּשׁוּבִ֥י בְשָׁל֖וֹם מִבְּנֵ֣י עַמּ֑וֹן וְהָיָה֙ לַֽיהֹוָ֔ה וְהַֽעֲלִיתִ֖הוּ עוֹלָֽה: לב וַיַּֽעֲבֹ֥ר יִפְתָּ֛ח אֶל־בְּנֵ֥י עַמּ֖וֹן לְהִלָּ֣חֶם בָּ֑ם וַיִּתְּנֵ֥ם יְהֹוָ֖ה בְּיָדֽוֹ: לג וַיַּכֵּ֡ם מֵֽעֲרוֹעֵר֩ וְעַד־בּֽוֹאֲךָ֙ מִנִּ֜ית עֶשְׂרִ֣ים עִ֗יר וְעַד֙ אָבֵ֣ל כְּרָמִ֔ים מַכָּ֖ה גְּדוֹלָ֣ה מְאֹ֑ד וַיִּכָּֽנְעוּ֙ בְּנֵ֣י עַמּ֔וֹן מִפְּנֵ֖י בְּנֵ֥י יִשְׂרָאֵֽל:

HAFTARATH BALAK הפטרת בלק
(Micah 5:6-6:8)
Read whether Balak is read separately or together with Ḥukkath.

This selection contains a reference to Balak and Balaam, the protagonists of the Sidra.

5:6. And the remnant of Jacob will be in the midst of many peoples like dew sent by the Lord, like torrents of rain upon vegetation that has not to hope for any man and does not wait for the sons of men. 7. But amongst the nations, the remnant of Jacob [scattered] in the midst of these peoples will be like a lion among the beasts of the forest, as a young lion amongst flocks of sheep, which if it passes through, it treads down and tears in pieces and none saves anything. 8. Your hand will be raised above your oppressors, and all your enemies will be destroyed. 9. On that day, says the Lord, I

ו וְהָיָ֣ה | שְׁאֵרִ֣ית יַֽעֲקֹ֗ב בְּקֶ֨רֶב֙ עַמִּ֣ים רַבִּ֔ים כְּטַל֙ מֵאֵ֣ת יְהֹוָ֔ה כִּרְבִיבִ֖ים עֲלֵי־עֵ֑שֶׂב אֲשֶׁ֤ר לֹֽא־יְקַוֶּה֙ לְאִ֔ישׁ וְלֹ֥א יְיַחֵ֖ל לִבְנֵ֥י אָדָֽם: ז וְהָיָ֣ה שְׁאֵרִ֣ית יַֽעֲקֹ֗ב בַּגּוֹיִם֙ בְּקֶ֨רֶב֙ עַמִּ֣ים רַבִּ֔ים כְּאַרְיֵה֙ בְּבַֽהֲמ֣וֹת יַ֔עַר כִּכְפִ֖יר בְּעֶדְרֵי־צֹ֑אן אֲשֶׁ֧ר אִם־עָבַ֛ר וְרָמַ֥ס וְטָרַ֖ף וְאֵ֥ין מַצִּֽיל: ח תָּרֹ֥ם יָֽדְךָ֖ עַל־צָרֶ֑יךָ וְכָל־אֹֽיְבֶ֖יךָ יִכָּרֵֽתוּ: ט וְהָיָ֤ה בַיּֽוֹם־הַהוּא֙ נְאֻם־יְהֹוָ֔ה וְהִכְרַתִּ֥י סוּסֶ֖יךָ

will have cut off your horses out of your
midst and destroyed your chariots. 10. And
I will have destroyed the cities of your land
and broken down all your fortresses.
11. And I will have destroyed witchcraft
out of your hand, and you shall have no
more soothsayers. 12. And I will have
destroyed your graven images and your
monuments out of your midst, and you will
no longer bow down to the work of your
hands. 13. And I will have uprooted your
sacred groves from out of your midst and
have destroyed your enemies. 14. And I will
exercise in anger and fury on the nations
who have paid no attention [thereto].
6:1. Hear now what the Lord says: Rise,
contend with the mountains, and may the
hills hearken to your voice. 2. Hear ye, O
mountains, the Lord's controversy, and you
enduring rocks, the foundations of the
earth, for the Lord has a controversy with
His people and will set Himself to rights
with Israel. 3. O, My people, what have I
done to you, and wherein have I wearied
you? Testify against Me. 4. For I brought
you up out of the land of Egypt and
redeemed you from the house of slavery,
and I sent before you Moses, Aaron and
Miriam. 5. O, My people, I pray you, what
plan Balak, king of Moab, devised, and
what Balaam the son of Beor answered him;
from Shittim to Gilgal, that you may recognize the Lord's righteous acts. 6. With what
shall I propitiate the Lord, bow myself more
deeply down before the Most High God?
Shall I propitiate Him with burnt offerings,
with one-year-old calves? Will the Lord be
pleased with thousands of rams, with ten
thousands of streams of oil? Shall I give my
first-born for my transgression, the fruit of
my body and for the sin of my soul? 8. He
has told you, man, what is good and what
the Lord requires of you: only to do justly,
**to love lovingkindness, and to walk modest-
ly with your God.**

מִקִּרְבֶּ֖ךָ וְהַאֲבַדְתִּ֥י מַרְכְּבֹתֶֽיךָ׃ י וְהִכְרַתִּ֖י עָרֵ֣י
אַרְצֶ֑ךָ וְהָרַסְתִּ֖י כָּל־מִבְצָרֶֽיךָ׃ יא וְהִכְרַתִּ֤י
כְשָׁפִים֙ מִיָּדֶ֔ךָ וּמְעֽוֹנְנִ֖ים לֹ֥א יִֽהְיוּ־לָֽךְ׃
יב וְהִכְרַתִּ֧י פְסִילֶ֛יךָ וּמַצֵּבוֹתֶ֖יךָ מִקִּרְבֶּ֑ךָ וְלֹֽא־
תִשְׁתַּֽחֲוֶ֥ה ע֖וֹד לְמַֽעֲשֵׂ֥ה יָדֶֽיךָ׃ יג וְנָֽתַשְׁתִּ֥י
אֲשֵׁירֶ֖יךָ מִקִּרְבֶּ֑ךָ וְהִשְׁמַדְתִּ֖י עָרֶֽיךָ׃ יד וְעָשִׂ֜יתִי
בְּאַ֧ף וּבְחֵמָ֛ה נָקָ֖ם אֶת־הַגּוֹיִ֑ם אֲשֶׁ֖ר לֹ֥א שָׁמֵֽעוּ׃
א שִׁמְעוּ־נָ֕א אֵ֥ת אֲשֶׁר־יְהֹוָ֖ה אֹמֵ֑ר ק֚וּם רִ֣יב
אֶת־הֶֽהָרִ֔ים וְתִשְׁמַ֖עְנָה הַגְּבָע֥וֹת קוֹלֶֽךָ׃
ב שִׁמְע֤וּ הָרִים֙ אֶת־רִ֣יב יְהֹוָ֔ה וְהָאֵֽתָנִ֖ים מֹֽסְדֵי
אָ֑רֶץ כִּ֣י רִ֤יב לַֽיהֹוָה֙ עִם־עַמּ֔וֹ וְעִם־יִשְׂרָאֵ֖ל
יִתְוַכָּֽח׃ ג עַמִּ֛י מֶה־עָשִׂ֥יתִי לְךָ֖ וּמָ֣ה הֶלְאֵתִ֑יךָ
עֲנֵ֥ה בִּֽי׃ ד כִּ֤י הֶעֱלִתִ֙יךָ֙ מֵאֶ֣רֶץ מִצְרַ֔יִם וּמִבֵּ֥ית
עֲבָדִ֖ים פְּדִיתִ֑יךָ וָֽאֶשְׁלַ֣ח לְפָנֶ֔יךָ אֶת־מֹשֶׁ֖ה
אַֽהֲרֹ֥ן וּמִרְיָֽם׃ ה עַמִּ֗י זְכׇר־נָא֙ מַה־יָּעַ֗ץ בָּלָק֙
מֶ֣לֶךְ מוֹאָ֔ב וּמֶה־עָנָ֥ה אֹת֖וֹ בִּלְעָ֣ם בֶּן־בְּע֑וֹר
מִן־הַשִּׁטִּים֙ עַד־הַגִּלְגָּ֔ל לְמַ֕עַן דַּ֖עַת צִדְק֥וֹת
יְהֹוָֽה׃ ו בַּמָּה֙ אֲקַדֵּ֣ם יְהֹוָ֔ה אִכַּ֖ף לֵֽאלֹהֵ֣י מָר֑וֹם
הַֽאֲקַדְּמֶ֣נּוּ בְעוֹל֔וֹת בַּֽעֲגָלִ֖ים בְּנֵ֥י שָׁנָֽה׃
ז הֲיִרְצֶ֤ה יְהֹוָה֙ בְּאַלְפֵ֣י אֵילִ֔ים בְּרִֽבְב֖וֹת נַֽחֲלֵי־
שָׁ֑מֶן הַֽאֶתֵּ֤ן בְּכוֹרִי֙ פִּשְׁעִ֔י פְּרִ֥י בִטְנִ֖י חַטַּ֥את
נַפְשִֽׁי׃ ח הִגִּ֥יד לְךָ֛ אָדָ֖ם מַה־טּ֑וֹב וּמָֽה־יְהֹוָ֞ה
דּוֹרֵ֣שׁ מִמְּךָ֗ כִּ֣י אִם־עֲשׂ֤וֹת מִשְׁפָּט֙ וְאַ֣הֲבַת חֶ֔סֶד
וְהַצְנֵ֥עַ לֶ֖כֶת עִם־אֱלֹהֶֽיךָ׃

HAFTARATH PINḤAS הפטרת פינחס

(I Kings 18:46–19:21)

This Haftarah is read only if the Sidra Pinḥas is read on the Sabbath preceding the Fast of the Seventeenth Day of Tammuz. Otherwise, we read Jeremiah 1–2:3, the first of the תְּלָת דְּפֻרְעֲנוּתָא, "The Three Haftaroth of Divine Retribution," otherwise read as the Haftarah for Parashath Mattoth.

This selection, describing Elijah's zeal on behalf of God, is appropriate to the Sidra, which describes the zeal of Phinehas. The Rabbis have a saying, "Phinehas is Elijah."

18:46. And a spirit of strength from the Lord was with Elijah, and he girded his loins and ran before Ahab until coming to Jezreel. 19:1. And Ahab told Jezebel all that Elijah had done, and all that he had killed all of the prophets with the sword. 2. Jezebel sent a messenger to Elijah, saying, "So may the gods do, and so may they continue, unless at this time tomorrow I will make your life like the life of one of them." 3. And he saw, and he arose and went for his life, and he came to Beer Sheba which belonged to Judah. And he left his servant there. 4. He went to the desert, a distance of one day's travel, and he came and sat under a juniper and requested that his soul die. He said, "Enough; now, Lord, take my soul, as I am not better than my forefathers." 5. He lay and slept underneath one juniper, and behold an angel touched him and said to him: "Rise and eat." 6. And he looked, and at his head there was a cake baked on hot coals, and a flask of water. He ate and drank, and again he lay down. 7. And the angel of the Lord returned to him again and touched him and said: "Arise and eat, as the journey is too much for you." 8. And he arose and ate and drank, and he went with the strength of this meal forty days and forty nights up to the mountain of the Lord, Horeb. 9. And he came there to the cave, and he lodged there, and behold! The word of the Lord came to him. And He said to him: "What are you doing here, Elijah?" 10. And he said: "I have been zealous for the Lord, the God of Hosts, for the children of Israel have forsaken Your covenant. They have torn down Your altars, and they have killed Your prophets by the sword, and I have remained alone, and they seek my life to take it." 11. And He said: "Go out and stand in the mountain before

מו וְיַד יְהוָה הָיְתָה אֶל־אֵלִיָּהוּ וַיְשַׁנֵּס מָתְנָיו
וַיָּרָץ לִפְנֵי אַחְאָב עַד־בֹּאֲכָה יִזְרְעֶאלָה: א וַיַּגֵּד
אַחְאָב לְאִיזֶבֶל אֵת כָּל־אֲשֶׁר עָשָׂה אֵלִיָּהוּ וְאֵת
כָּל־אֲשֶׁר הָרַג אֶת־כָּל־הַנְּבִיאִים בֶּחָרֶב:
ב וַתִּשְׁלַח אִיזֶבֶל מַלְאָךְ אֶל־אֵלִיָּהוּ לֵאמֹר
כֹּה־יַעֲשׂוּן אֱלֹהִים וְכֹה יוֹסִפוּן כִּי־כָעֵת מָחָר
אָשִׂים אֶת־נַפְשְׁךָ כְּנֶפֶשׁ אַחַד מֵהֶם: ג וַיַּרְא
וַיָּקָם וַיֵּלֶךְ אֶל־נַפְשׁוֹ וַיָּבֹא בְּאֵר שֶׁבַע אֲשֶׁר
לִיהוּדָה וַיַּנַּח אֶת־נַעֲרוֹ שָׁם: ד וְהוּא־הָלַךְ
בַּמִּדְבָּר דֶּרֶךְ יוֹם וַיָּבֹא וַיֵּשֶׁב תַּחַת רֹתֶם אֶחָת
(אחד קרי) וַיִּשְׁאַל אֶת־נַפְשׁוֹ לָמוּת וַיֹּאמֶר ׀ רַב
עַתָּה יְהוָה קַח נַפְשִׁי כִּי לֹא־טוֹב אָנֹכִי
מֵאֲבֹתָי: ה וַיִּשְׁכַּב וַיִּישַׁן תַּחַת רֹתֶם אֶחָד
וְהִנֵּה־זֶה מַלְאָךְ נֹגֵעַ בּוֹ וַיֹּאמֶר לוֹ קוּם אֱכוֹל:
ו וַיַּבֵּט וְהִנֵּה מְרַאֲשֹׁתָיו עֻגַת רְצָפִים וְצַפַּחַת
מָיִם וַיֹּאכַל וַיֵּשְׁתְּ וַיָּשָׁב וַיִּשְׁכָּב: ז וַיָּשָׁב מַלְאַךְ
יְהוָה ׀ שֵׁנִית וַיִּגַּע־בּוֹ וַיֹּאמֶר קוּם אֱכֹל כִּי רַב
מִמְּךָ הַדָּרֶךְ: ח וַיָּקָם וַיֹּאכַל וַיִּשְׁתֶּה וַיֵּלֶךְ בְּכֹחַ
׀ הָאֲכִילָה הַהִיא אַרְבָּעִים יוֹם וְאַרְבָּעִים לַיְלָה
עַד הַר הָאֱלֹהִים חֹרֵב: ט וַיָּבֹא־שָׁם אֶל־
הַמְּעָרָה וַיָּלֶן שָׁם וְהִנֵּה דְבַר־יְהוָה אֵלָיו
וַיֹּאמֶר לוֹ מַה־לְּךָ פֹה אֵלִיָּהוּ: י וַיֹּאמֶר קַנֹּא
קִנֵּאתִי לַיהוָה ׀ אֱלֹהֵי צְבָאוֹת כִּי־עָזְבוּ בְרִיתְךָ
בְּנֵי יִשְׂרָאֵל אֶת־מִזְבְּחֹתֶיךָ הָרָסוּ וְאֶת־נְבִיאֶיךָ
הָרְגוּ בֶחָרֶב וָאִוָּתֵר אֲנִי לְבַדִּי וַיְבַקְשׁוּ אֶת־
נַפְשִׁי לְקַחְתָּהּ: יא וַיֹּאמֶר צֵא וְעָמַדְתָּ בָהָר

the Lord. Behold the Lord passes, and a great and strong wind splitting mountains and shattering boulders before the Lord, but the Lord was not in the wind. And after the wind an earthquake; not in the earthquake was the Lord. 12. After the earthquake; fire; not in the fire was the Lord, and after the fire, a still small sound. 13. And as Elijah heard, he wrapped his face in his mantle, and he went out and stood at the entrance to the cave, and behold a Voice came to him and said: What are you doing here, Elijah? 14. And he said, "I have been zealous for the Lord, the God of Hosts, for the children of Israel have forsaken Your covenant; they have torn down Your altars, and they have killed Your prophets by the sword; and I alone remain, and they seek my soul to take it." 15. And the Lord said to him: "Go; return to your way to the desert of Damascus, and you shall come and anoint Hazael to be king over Aram. 16. And Jehu the son of Nimshi you shall anoint as king over Israel, and Elisha the son of Shafat from Abel Meholah, you shall anoint to be prophet in your stead. 17. And it will be: those who escape the sword of Hazael, Jehu will kill, and those who escape the sword of Jehu, Elisha will kill. 18. And I will leave over in Israel seven thousand, all the knees that did not kneel to the Baal and every mouth that did not kiss him." 19. And he went from there, and he found Elisha the son of Shafat as he was plowing; twelve yoke were before him, and he was with the twelfth; and Elijah went over to him and threw his mantle over him. 20. And he left the oxen and ran after Elijah and said: "Let me please kiss my father and my mother, and I will go after you"; and he said to him, "Go, return, for what have I done to you?" 21. And he returned from after him, and he took the yoke of oxen and slaughtered them; and with the gear of the oxen he cooked the meat for them, and he gave the people and they ate; and he rose and followed Elijah and ministered to him.

לִפְנֵי יְהֹוָה וְהִנֵּה יְהֹוָה עֹבֵר וְרוּחַ גְּדוֹלָה וְחָזָק מְפָרֵק הָרִים וּמְשַׁבֵּר סְלָעִים לִפְנֵי יְהֹוָה לֹא בָרוּחַ יְהֹוָה וְאַחַר הָרוּחַ רַעַשׁ לֹא בָרַעַשׁ יְהֹוָה: יב וְאַחַר הָרַעַשׁ אֵשׁ לֹא בָאֵשׁ יְהֹוָה וְאַחַר הָאֵשׁ קוֹל דְּמָמָה דַקָּה: יג וַיְהִי ׀ כִּשְׁמֹעַ אֵלִיָּהוּ וַיָּלֶט פָּנָיו בְּאַדַּרְתּוֹ וַיֵּצֵא וַיַּעֲמֹד פֶּתַח הַמְּעָרָה וְהִנֵּה אֵלָיו קוֹל וַיֹּאמֶר מַה־לְּךָ פֹה אֵלִיָּהוּ: יד וַיֹּאמֶר קַנֹּא קִנֵּאתִי לַיהֹוָה ׀ אֱלֹהֵי צְבָאוֹת כִּי־עָזְבוּ בְרִיתְךָ בְּנֵי יִשְׂרָאֵל אֶת־מִזְבְּחֹתֶיךָ הָרָסוּ וְאֶת־נְבִיאֶיךָ הָרְגוּ בֶחָרֶב וָאִוָּתֵר אֲנִי לְבַדִּי וַיְבַקְשׁוּ אֶת־נַפְשִׁי לְקַחְתָּהּ: טו וַיֹּאמֶר יְהֹוָה אֵלָיו לֵךְ שׁוּב לְדַרְכְּךָ מִדְבַּרָה דַמָּשֶׂק וּבָאתָ וּמָשַׁחְתָּ אֶת־חֲזָאֵל לְמֶלֶךְ עַל־אֲרָם: טז וְאֵת יֵהוּא בֶן־נִמְשִׁי תִּמְשַׁח לְמֶלֶךְ עַל־יִשְׂרָאֵל וְאֶת־אֱלִישָׁע בֶּן־שָׁפָט מֵאָבֵל מְחוֹלָה תִּמְשַׁח לְנָבִיא תַּחְתֶּיךָ: יז וְהָיָה הַנִּמְלָט מֵחֶרֶב חֲזָאֵל יָמִית יֵהוּא וְהַנִּמְלָט מֵחֶרֶב יֵהוּא יָמִית אֱלִישָׁע: יח וְהִשְׁאַרְתִּי בְיִשְׂרָאֵל שִׁבְעַת אֲלָפִים כָּל־הַבִּרְכַּיִם אֲשֶׁר לֹא־כָרְעוּ לַבַּעַל וְכָל־הַפֶּה אֲשֶׁר לֹא־נָשַׁק לוֹ: יט וַיֵּלֶךְ מִשָּׁם וַיִּמְצָא אֶת־אֱלִישָׁע בֶּן־שָׁפָט וְהוּא חֹרֵשׁ שְׁנֵים־עָשָׂר צְמָדִים לְפָנָיו וְהוּא בִּשְׁנֵים הֶעָשָׂר וַיַּעֲבֹר אֵלִיָּהוּ אֵלָיו וַיַּשְׁלֵךְ אַדַּרְתּוֹ אֵלָיו: כ וַיַּעֲזֹב אֶת־הַבָּקָר וַיָּרָץ אַחֲרֵי אֵלִיָּהוּ וַיֹּאמֶר אֶשְּׁקָה־נָּא לְאָבִי וּלְאִמִּי וְאֵלְכָה אַחֲרֶיךָ וַיֹּאמֶר לוֹ לֵךְ שׁוּב כִּי מֶה עָשִׂיתִי לָךְ: כא וַיָּשָׁב מֵאַחֲרָיו וַיִּקַּח אֶת־צֶמֶד הַבָּקָר וַיִּזְבָּחֵהוּ וּבִכְלִי הַבָּקָר בִּשְּׁלָם הַבָּשָׂר וַיִּתֵּן לָעָם וַיֹּאכֵלוּ וַיָּקָם וַיֵּלֶךְ אַחֲרֵי אֵלִיָּהוּ וַיְשָׁרְתֵהוּ:

HAFTARATH MATTOTH הפטרת מטות

(Jeremiah 1:1–2:3)

This is the first of "The Three Haftaroth of Divine Retribution." If the Sidra Mattoth is read by itself, then this Haftarah is read for Mattoth, since then it comes after the Fast of the Seventeenth Day of Tammuz. If Mattoth is read together with Massei, this Haftarah is read for the Sidra Pinḥas, and the Haftarah of the Sidra Massei is read for Mattoth-Massei.

Jeremiah prophesies the Babylonian invasion.

1:1. The words of Jeremiah the son of Hilkiah, of the priests that were in Anathoth, in the land of Benjamin, 2. to whom the word of the Lord came in the days of Josiah the son of Amon, king of Judah, in the thirteenth year of his reign. 3. And it [also] came in the days of Jehoiakim the son of Josiah, king of Judah, until the end of the eleventh year of Zedekiah the son of Josiah, king of Judah, until the exile of Jerusalem in the fifth month. 4. And the word of the Lord came to me, saying: 5. Before I formed you in the womb I knew you, and before you came out of the womb I dedicated you; to be a prophet to the nations did I ordain you. 6. And I said, "Ah! O Lord God, behold I have no knowledge of speaking, for I am quite young." 7. But the Lord said to me: Say not, I am too young, for wherever I send you you shall go, and whatever I command you you shall speak. 8. Fear not before them, for I am with you, to save you, says the Lord. 9. And the Lord stretched out His hand and made it touch my mouth, and the Lord said to me: Behold, I have placed My words in your mouth. 10. Behold, I have appointed you this day over the nations and over the kingdoms, to uproot and to pull down and to destroy and to demolish, to build and to plant. 11. And the word of the Lord came to me, saying, What do you see, Jeremiah? And I said, "I see the rod of an almond tree." 12. And the Lord said to me, You have seen rightly, for [like the almond blossoms], I hasten My word to carry it out. 13. And the word of the Lord came to me a second time, saying: What do you see? And I said, "I see a boiling pot, and its bubbles are from the north side." And the Lord said to me: From the north the misfortune will break forth over all the inhabitants of the earth. 15. For lo, I will call all the families

א דִּבְרֵי יִרְמְיָהוּ בֶּן־חִלְקִיָּהוּ מִן־הַכֹּהֲנִים אֲשֶׁר
בַּעֲנָתוֹת בְּאֶרֶץ בִּנְיָמִן׃ ב אֲשֶׁר הָיָה דְבַר־יְהוָה
אֵלָיו בִּימֵי יֹאשִׁיָּהוּ בֶן־אָמוֹן מֶלֶךְ יְהוּדָה
בִּשְׁלֹשׁ־עֶשְׂרֵה שָׁנָה לְמָלְכוֹ׃ ג וַיְהִי בִּימֵי
יְהוֹיָקִים בֶּן־יֹאשִׁיָּהוּ מֶלֶךְ יְהוּדָה עַד־תֹּם
עַשְׁתֵּי־עֶשְׂרֵה שָׁנָה לְצִדְקִיָּהוּ בֶן־יֹאשִׁיָּהוּ מֶלֶךְ
יְהוּדָה עַד־גְּלוֹת יְרוּשָׁלַםִ בַּחֹדֶשׁ הַחֲמִישִׁי׃
ד וַיְהִי דְבַר־יְהוָה אֵלַי לֵאמֹר׃ ה בְּטֶרֶם
אֶצָּורְךָ (אצרך קרי) בַבֶּטֶן יְדַעְתִּיךָ וּבְטֶרֶם תֵּצֵא
מֵרֶחֶם הִקְדַּשְׁתִּיךָ נָבִיא לַגּוֹיִם נְתַתִּיךָ׃ ו וָאֹמַר
אֲהָהּ אֲדֹנָי יֱהוִה הִנֵּה לֹא־יָדַעְתִּי דַּבֵּר כִּי־נַעַר
אָנֹכִי׃ ז וַיֹּאמֶר יְהוָה אֵלַי אַל־תֹּאמַר נַעַר
אָנֹכִי כִּי עַל־כָּל־אֲשֶׁר אֶשְׁלָחֲךָ תֵּלֵךְ וְאֵת כָּל־
אֲשֶׁר אֲצַוְּךָ תְּדַבֵּר׃ ח אַל־תִּירָא מִפְּנֵיהֶם כִּי־
אִתְּךָ אֲנִי לְהַצִּלֶךָ נְאֻם־יְהוָה׃ ט וַיִּשְׁלַח יְהוָה
אֶת־יָדוֹ וַיַּגַּע עַל־פִּי וַיֹּאמֶר יְהוָה אֵלַי הִנֵּה
נָתַתִּי דְבָרַי בְּפִיךָ׃ י רְאֵה הִפְקַדְתִּיךָ ׀ הַיּוֹם
הַזֶּה עַל־הַגּוֹיִם וְעַל־הַמַּמְלָכוֹת לִנְתוֹשׁ וְלִנְתוֹץ
וּלְהַאֲבִיד וְלַהֲרוֹס לִבְנוֹת וְלִנְטוֹעַ׃ יא וַיְהִי
דְבַר־יְהוָה אֵלַי לֵאמֹר מָה־אַתָּה רֹאֶה
יִרְמְיָהוּ וָאֹמַר מַקֵּל שָׁקֵד אֲנִי רֹאֶה׃ יב וַיֹּאמֶר
יְהוָה אֵלַי הֵיטַבְתָּ לִרְאוֹת כִּי־שֹׁקֵד אֲנִי עַל־
דְּבָרִי לַעֲשֹׂתוֹ׃ יג וַיְהִי דְבַר־יְהוָה ׀ אֵלַי שֵׁנִית
לֵאמֹר מָה אַתָּה רֹאֶה וָאֹמַר סִיר נָפוּחַ אֲנִי
רֹאֶה וּפָנָיו מִפְּנֵי צָפוֹנָה׃ יד וַיֹּאמֶר יְהוָה אֵלָי
מִצָּפוֹן תִּפָּתַח הָרָעָה עַל כָּל־יֹשְׁבֵי הָאָרֶץ׃
טו כִּי ׀ הִנְנִי קֹרֵא לְכָל־מִשְׁפְּחוֹת מַמְלְכוֹת

of the kingdoms of the north, says the Lord,
and they will come and they will set each
one his throne at the entrance of the gates of
Jerusalem, and against all its walls around,
and against all the cities of Judah. 16. And I
will utter all My judgments against them
because of all their evil, that they have
forsaken Me and burned incense to other
gods and prostrated themselves to the works
of their hands. 17. And you shall gird your
loins and arise and speak to them all that I
will command you; fear them not, lest
I break you before them. 18. And I, behold
I have set you today as a fortified city and as
an iron pillar and as copper walls over the
whole land, for the kings of Judah, for its
princes, for its priests, and for the people of
the land. 19. And they will fight against
you, but they will not prevail against you,
for I am with you, says the Lord, to save
you. 2:1. Then the word of the Lord came
to me, saying: 2. Go and proclaim in the
ears of Jerusalem, saying, Thus says the
Lord: I remember to you the love of your
youth, the attachment of your bridal state,
when you went after Me into the desert,
into a land where nothing was sown.
3. Israel is the Lord's hallowed portion, the
best of His grain; all those who would
devour him shall bear guilt; evil shall come
upon them, says the Lord.

צְפוֹנָה נְאֻם־יְהֹוָה וּבָאוּ וְנָתְנוּ אִישׁ כִּסְאוֹ
פֶּתַח ׀ שַׁעֲרֵי יְרוּשָׁלַםִ וְעַל כָּל־חוֹמֹתֶיהָ סָבִיב
וְעַל כָּל־עָרֵי יְהוּדָה: טז וְדִבַּרְתִּי מִשְׁפָּטַי
אוֹתָם עַל כָּל־רָעָתָם אֲשֶׁר עֲזָבוּנִי וַיְקַטְּרוּ
לֵאלֹהִים אֲחֵרִים וַיִּשְׁתַּחֲווּ לְמַעֲשֵׂי יְדֵיהֶם:
יז וְאַתָּה תֶּאְזֹר מָתְנֶיךָ וְקַמְתָּ וְדִבַּרְתָּ אֲלֵיהֶם
אֵת כָּל־אֲשֶׁר אָנֹכִי אֲצַוֶּךָּ אַל־תֵּחַת מִפְּנֵיהֶם
פֶּן־אֲחִתְּךָ לִפְנֵיהֶם: יח וַאֲנִי הִנֵּה נְתַתִּיךָ הַיּוֹם
לְעִיר מִבְצָר וּלְעַמּוּד בַּרְזֶל וּלְחֹמוֹת נְחֹשֶׁת
עַל־כָּל־הָאָרֶץ לְמַלְכֵי יְהוּדָה לְשָׂרֶיהָ לְכֹהֲנֶיהָ
וּלְעַם הָאָרֶץ: יט וְנִלְחֲמוּ אֵלֶיךָ וְלֹא־יוּכְלוּ לָךְ
כִּי־אִתְּךָ אֲנִי נְאֻם־יְהֹוָה לְהַצִּילֶךָ: א וַיְהִי דְבַר־
יְהֹוָה אֵלַי לֵאמֹר: ב הָלֹךְ וְקָרָאתָ בְאָזְנֵי
יְרוּשָׁלַםִ לֵאמֹר כֹּה אָמַר יְהֹוָה זָכַרְתִּי לָךְ חֶסֶד
נְעוּרַיִךְ אַהֲבַת כְּלוּלֹתָיִךְ לֶכְתֵּךְ אַחֲרַי בַּמִּדְבָּר
בְּאֶרֶץ לֹא זְרוּעָה: ג קֹדֶשׁ יִשְׂרָאֵל לַיהֹוָה
רֵאשִׁית תְּבוּאָתֹה כָּל־אֹכְלָיו יֶאְשָׁמוּ רָעָה
תָּבֹא אֲלֵיהֶם נְאֻם־יְהֹוָה:

HAFTARATH MASSEI הפטרת מסעי

(Jeremiah 2:4–28. Ashkenazim add 3:4; Sephardim add 4:1,2.)

This is the second of "The Three Haftaroth of Divine Retribution," read whether Massei is read separately or together with Mattoth. According to prevalent custom, this selection is read even if Sidrath Massei falls on Shabbath Rosh Chodesh.

The prophet continues to castigate the people for their sins, which ultimately led to the destruction of the Temple and the exile.

2:4. Hear ye the word of the Lord, O house
of Jacob, and all the families of the house of
Israel. 5. So says the Lord: What wrong did
your fathers find in Me that they went far
away from Me, and went after futility and
became themselves futile? 6. And they did
not say, "Where is the Lord Who brought
us up out of the land of Egypt and led us
through the wilderness, through a land of

ד שִׁמְעוּ דְבַר־יְהֹוָה בֵּית יַעֲקֹב וְכָל־מִשְׁפְּחוֹת
בֵּית יִשְׂרָאֵל: ה כֹּה ׀ אָמַר יְהֹוָה מַה־מָּצְאוּ
אֲבוֹתֵיכֶם בִּי עָוֶל כִּי רָחֲקוּ מֵעָלָי וַיֵּלְכוּ אַחֲרֵי
הַהֶבֶל וַיֶּהְבָּלוּ: ו וְלֹא אָמְרוּ אַיֵּה יְהֹוָה הַמַּעֲלֶה
אֹתָנוּ מֵאֶרֶץ מִצְרָיִם הַמּוֹלִיךְ אֹתָנוּ בַּמִּדְבָּר

desert and pits, through a land of waste and the shadow of death, through a land which no man had traveled, and where no man had ever dwelt?" 7. And I brought you into a fruitful country to eat the fruit thereof and the goodness thereof, but you came therein and defiled My land and made My heritage into an abomination. 8. The priests said not, "Where is the Lord?" And those who study the Torah knew Me not, and the leaders rebelled against Me, and the prophets prophesied by Baal and walked after things that do not avail. 9. That is why I contend with you for yet a long time, says the Lord, and with your children's children will I [still] contend. 10. For pass over the isles of Chittim and see, and send to Kedar and bring it diligently to your consideration and see: has there been anything like this? 11. Has ever a nation exchanged its gods and yet they are no gods! But My people has exchanged His glory for something that avails not. 12. Stand astonished thereat, you heavens, and rage in storms and devastate greatly, says the Lord. 13. For two wrongs have My people committed: they have forsaken Me, the Fount of living waters, to dig out for themselves cisterns, broken cisterns which do not hold the water. 14. Is then Israel a slave or born in slavery? Why then has it become a prey? 15. Young lions roared against it; they had made their voices heard, and they made its land to a waste; its cities, devastated without an inhabitant. 16. Even the men of Noph and Tahpanhes smash the crown of your head! 17. Is it not that you have forsaken the Lord your God even at the time when He wishes to lead you on the right path, that has brought this on you? 18. And now, what are you doing on the road to Egypt, is it to drink the waters of Shihor? And what are you doing on the road to Assyria, is it to drink the waters of the river [Euphrates]? 19. Your evil shall chastise you, and your backslidings shall bring you to reason, and know and see that it is bad and bitter that you have forsaken your God, and that the fear of Me is not before you, says the Lord God of Hosts. 20. Forever have I broken your yoke and burst your chains, but you said, "I will not transgress"; but on every

בְּאֶרֶץ עֲרָבָה וְשׁוּחָה בְּאֶרֶץ צִיָּה וְצַלְמָוֶת
בְּאֶרֶץ לֹא־עָבַר בָּהּ אִישׁ וְלֹא־יָשַׁב אָדָם שָׁם׃
ז וָאָבִיא אֶתְכֶם אֶל־אֶרֶץ הַכַּרְמֶל לֶאֱכֹל פִּרְיָהּ
וְטוּבָהּ וַתָּבֹאוּ וַתְּטַמְּאוּ אֶת־אַרְצִי וְנַחֲלָתִי
שַׂמְתֶּם לְתוֹעֵבָה׃ ח הַכֹּהֲנִים לֹא אָמְרוּ אַיֵּה
יְהֹוָה וְתֹפְשֵׂי הַתּוֹרָה לֹא יְדָעוּנִי וְהָרֹעִים
פָּשְׁעוּ בִי וְהַנְּבִיאִים נִבְּאוּ בַבַּעַל וְאַחֲרֵי לֹא־
יוֹעִלוּ הָלָכוּ׃ ט לָכֵן עֹד אָרִיב אִתְּכֶם נְאֻם־
יְהֹוָה וְאֶת־בְּנֵי בְנֵיכֶם אָרִיב׃ י כִּי עִבְרוּ אִיֵּי
כִתִּיִּים וּרְאוּ וְקֵדָר שִׁלְחוּ וְהִתְבּוֹנְנוּ מְאֹד וּרְאוּ
הֵן הָיְתָה כָּזֹאת׃ יא הַהֵימִיר גּוֹי אֱלֹהִים וְהֵמָּה
לֹא אֱלֹהִים וְעַמִּי הֵמִיר כְּבוֹדוֹ בְּלוֹא יוֹעִיל׃
יב שֹׁמּוּ שָׁמַיִם עַל־זֹאת וְשַׂעֲרוּ חָרְבוּ מְאֹד
נְאֻם־יְהֹוָה׃ יג כִּי־שְׁתַּיִם רָעוֹת עָשָׂה עַמִּי אֹתִי
עָזְבוּ מְקוֹר ׀ מַיִם חַיִּים לַחְצֹב לָהֶם בֹּארוֹת
בֹּארֹת נִשְׁבָּרִים אֲשֶׁר לֹא־יָכִלוּ הַמָּיִם׃
יד הַעֶבֶד יִשְׂרָאֵל אִם־יְלִיד בַּיִת הוּא מַדּוּעַ
הָיָה לָבַז׃ טו עָלָיו יִשְׁאֲגוּ כְפִרִים נָתְנוּ קוֹלָם
וַיָּשִׁיתוּ אַרְצוֹ לְשַׁמָּה עָרָיו נִצְּתָה (נצתו קרי)
מִבְּלִי יֹשֵׁב׃ טז גַּם־בְּנֵי־נֹף וְתַחְפְּנֵס (ותחפנחס
קרי) יִרְעוּךְ קָדְקֹד׃ יז הֲלוֹא־זֹאת תַּעֲשֶׂה־לָּךְ
עָזְבֵךְ אֶת־יְהֹוָה אֱלֹהַיִךְ בְּעֵת מוֹלִכֵךְ בַּדָּרֶךְ׃
יח וְעַתָּה מַה־לָּךְ לְדֶרֶךְ מִצְרַיִם לִשְׁתּוֹת מֵי
שִׁחוֹר וּמַה־לָּךְ לְדֶרֶךְ אַשּׁוּר לִשְׁתּוֹת מֵי נָהָר׃
יט תְּיַסְּרֵךְ רָעָתֵךְ וּמְשֻׁבוֹתַיִךְ תּוֹכִחֻךְ וּדְעִי
וּרְאִי כִּי־רַע וָמָר עָזְבֵךְ אֶת־יְהֹוָה אֱלֹהָיִךְ וְלֹא
פַחְדָּתִי אֵלַיִךְ נְאֻם־אֲדֹנָי יֱהֹוִה צְבָאוֹת׃ כ כִּי
מֵעוֹלָם שָׁבַרְתִּי עֻלֵּךְ נִתַּקְתִּי מוֹסְרוֹתַיִךְ

high hill and under every leafy tree you wander, playing the harlot. 21. Yet I planted you a noble vine stock, throughout of right seed; how then have you turned yourself into the degenerate plant of a wild vine to Me? 22. For though you wash yourself with nitre and take ever so much soap, your sin stands stained before Me, says the Lord God. 23. How can you say, "I have not defiled myself, I have not gone after the Baalim"? Look at your wandering in the valley! Recognize what you have done, you swift young camel clinging to her ways! 24. A wild ass, accustomed to the desert, that in the avidity of its desire snuffs up the wind; in its mourning, who can influence it to return? All those who seek it will not weary; in its month they will find it. 25. But spare your foot from being bare and your throat from thirst. But then you said, "I am sick of it. No! For I have loved strangers and after them will I go." 26. As a thief is ashamed when he is found, so has the House of Israel been ashamed; they, their kings, their princes, their priests and their prophets. 27. Saying to wood, "You are my father," and to stone, "You bore us." For they have turned their back and not their face to Me, but in the time of their trouble they will say, "Arise and save us!" 28. Where then are your gods that you have made for yourself? Let them arise if they can save you in the time of your trouble, for the number of your cities were your gods, O Judah. (*Ashkenazim add the following:*) 3:4. Assuredly, henceforth will you cry to Me, "My Father, You are the Guide of my youth." (*Sephardim add the following:*) 4:1. If you will return, O Israel, return to Me; and if you remove your abominations out of My sight, you will not falter. 2. And if you swear in truth, in exercising justice and righteousness, "As true as the Lord lives," then the nations will bless themselves by Him and in Him shall they glory.

וַתֹּאמְרִי לֹא אֶעֱבוֹד (אעבור קרי) כִּי עַל־כָּל־
גִּבְעָה גְּבֹהָה וְתַחַת כָּל־עֵץ רַעֲנָן אַתְּ צֹעָה
זֹנָה: כא וְאָנֹכִי נְטַעְתִּיךְ שׂוֹרֵק כֻּלֹּה זֶרַע אֱמֶת
וְאֵיךְ נֶהְפַּכְתְּ לִי סוּרֵי הַגֶּפֶן נָכְרִיָּה: כב כִּי
אִם־תְּכַבְּסִי בַּנֶּתֶר וְתַרְבִּי־לָךְ בֹּרִית נִכְתָּם
עֲוֺנֵךְ לְפָנַי נְאֻם אֲדֹנָי יֱהֹוִה: כג אֵיךְ תֹּאמְרִי
לֹא נִטְמֵאתִי אַחֲרֵי הַבְּעָלִים לֹא הָלַכְתִּי רְאִי
דַרְכֵּךְ בַּגַּיְא דְּעִי מֶה עָשִׂית בִּכְרָה קַלָּה
מְשָׂרֶכֶת דְּרָכֶיהָ: כד פֶּרֶה ׀ לִמֻּד מִדְבָּר בְּאַוַּת
נַפְשׁוֹ (נפשה קרי) שָׁאֲפָה רוּחַ תַּאֲנָתָהּ מִי
יְשִׁיבֶנָּה כָּל־מְבַקְשֶׁיהָ לֹא יִיעָפוּ בְּחָדְשָׁהּ
יִמְצָאוּנְהָ: כה מִנְעִי רַגְלֵךְ מִיָּחֵף וּגְרוֹנֵךְ (וגרונך
קרי) מִצִּמְאָה וַתֹּאמְרִי נוֹאָשׁ לוֹא כִּי־אָהַבְתִּי
זָרִים וְאַחֲרֵיהֶם אֵלֵךְ: כו כְּבֹשֶׁת גַּנָּב כִּי יִמָּצֵא
כֵּן הֹבִישׁוּ בֵּית יִשְׂרָאֵל הֵמָּה מַלְכֵיהֶם שָׂרֵיהֶם
וְכֹהֲנֵיהֶם וּנְבִיאֵיהֶם: כז אֹמְרִים לָעֵץ אָבִי
אַתָּה וְלָאֶבֶן אַתְּ יְלִדְתָּנִי (ילדתנו קרי) כִּי־פָנוּ אֵלַי
עֹרֶף וְלֹא פָנִים וּבְעֵת רָעָתָם יֹאמְרוּ קוּמָה
וְהוֹשִׁיעֵנוּ: כח וְאַיֵּה אֱלֹהֶיךָ אֲשֶׁר עָשִׂיתָ לָּךְ
יָקוּמוּ אִם־יוֹשִׁיעוּךָ בְּעֵת רָעָתֶךָ כִּי מִסְפַּר
עָרֶיךָ הָיוּ אֱלֹהֶיךָ יְהוּדָה: (האשכנזים מוסיפים)
ד הֲלוֹא מֵעַתָּה קָרָאתי (קראת קרי) לִי אָבִי אַלּוּף
נְעֻרַי אָתָּה: (הספרדים מוסיפים) א אִם־תָּשׁוּב
יִשְׂרָאֵל ׀ נְאֻם־יְהֹוָה אֵלַי תָּשׁוּב וְאִם־תָּסִיר
שִׁקּוּצֶיךָ מִפָּנַי וְלֹא תָנוּד: ב וְנִשְׁבַּעְתָּ חַי־יְהֹוָה
בֶּאֱמֶת בְּמִשְׁפָּט וּבִצְדָקָה וְהִתְבָּרְכוּ בוֹ גּוֹיִם
וּבוֹ יִתְהַלָּלוּ:

HAFTARATH DEVARIM הפטרת דברים

(Isaiah 1:1–27)

This is the third of "The Three Haftaroth of Divine Retribution;" it is always read on the Sabbath preceding the Fast of the Ninth of Av.

This Haftarah, read on the Sabbath preceding the Ninth of Av, contains the expression אֵיכָה הָיְתָה לְזוֹנָה, which is reminiscent of Jeremiah's lament, אֵיכָה יָשְׁבָה בָדָד, which is read on the Ninth of Av.

1:1. The vision of Isaiah the son of Amoz, which he saw concerning Judah and Jerusalem, in the days of Uzziah, Jotham, Ahaz [and] Hezekiah, kings of Judah. 2. Hear, O heavens, and give ear, O earth, for the Lord has spoken: Children I have raised and exalted, yet they have rebelled against Me. 3. An ox knows his owner and a donkey his master's crib; Israel does not know, My people does not consider. 4. Woe to a sinful nation, a people heavy with iniquity, evildoing seed, corrupt children. They forsook the Lord; they provoked the Holy One of Israel; they drew backwards. 5. Why are you beaten when you still continue to rebel? Every head is [afflicted] with illness and every heart with malaise. 6. From the sole of the foot until the head there is no soundness — wounds and contusions and lacerated sores; they have not sprinkled, neither have they been bandaged, nor was it softened with oil. 7. Your land is desolate; your cities burnt with fire. Your land — in your presence, strangers devour it; and it is desolate as that turned over to strangers. 8. And the daughter of Zion shall be left like a hut in the vineyard, like a lodge in a cucumber field, like a besieged city. 9. Had not the Lord of Hosts left us a remnant, we would soon be like Sodom; we would resemble Gomorrah. 10. Hear the word of the Lord, O rulers of Sodom; give ear to the law of our God, O people of Gomorrah! 11. Of what use are your many sacrifices to Me? says the Lord. I am sated with the burnt offerings of rams and the fat of fattened cattle; and the blood of bulls and sheep and he-goats I do not want. 12. When you come to appear before Me, who requested this of you, to trample My courts? 13. You shall no longer bring vain meal offerings, it is smoke of abomination to Me; New Moons and Sabbaths, calling convocations, I cannot [bear] iniquity with assembly. 14. Your New Moons and your

א חֲזוֹן יְשַׁעְיָהוּ בֶן־אָמוֹץ אֲשֶׁר חָזָה עַל־
יְהוּדָה וִירוּשָׁלָםִ בִּימֵי עֻזִּיָּהוּ יוֹתָם אָחָז
יְחִזְקִיָּהוּ מַלְכֵי יְהוּדָה׃ ב שִׁמְעוּ שָׁמַיִם
וְהַאֲזִינִי אֶרֶץ כִּי יְהוָה דִּבֵּר בָּנִים גִּדַּלְתִּי
וְרוֹמַמְתִּי וְהֵם פָּשְׁעוּ בִי׃ ג יָדַע שׁוֹר קֹנֵהוּ
וַחֲמוֹר אֵבוּס בְּעָלָיו יִשְׂרָאֵל לֹא יָדַע עַמִּי לֹא
הִתְבּוֹנָן׃ ד הוֹי | גּוֹי חֹטֵא עַם כֶּבֶד עָוֺן זֶרַע
מְרֵעִים בָּנִים מַשְׁחִיתִים עָזְבוּ אֶת־יְהוָה נִאֲצוּ
אֶת־קְדוֹשׁ יִשְׂרָאֵל נָזֹרוּ אָחוֹר׃ ה עַל־מֶה תֻכּוּ
עוֹד תּוֹסִיפוּ סָרָה כָּל־רֹאשׁ לָחֳלִי וְכָל־לֵבָב
דַּוָּי׃ ו מִכַּף־רֶגֶל וְעַד־רֹאשׁ אֵין־בּוֹ מְתֹם פֶּצַע
וְחַבּוּרָה וּמַכָּה טְרִיָּה לֹא־זֹרוּ וְלֹא חֻבָּשׁוּ וְלֹא
רֻכְּכָה בַּשָּׁמֶן׃ ז אַרְצְכֶם שְׁמָמָה עָרֵיכֶם
שְׂרֻפוֹת אֵשׁ אַדְמַתְכֶם לְנֶגְדְּכֶם זָרִים אֹכְלִים
אֹתָהּ וּשְׁמָמָה כְּמַהְפֵּכַת זָרִים׃ ח וְנוֹתְרָה בַת־
צִיּוֹן כְּסֻכָּה בְכָרֶם כִּמְלוּנָה בְמִקְשָׁה כְּעִיר
נְצוּרָה׃ ט לוּלֵי יְהוָה צְבָאוֹת הוֹתִיר לָנוּ שָׂרִיד
כִּמְעָט כִּסְדֹם הָיִינוּ לַעֲמֹרָה דָּמִינוּ׃ י שִׁמְעוּ
דְבַר־יְהוָה קְצִינֵי סְדֹם הַאֲזִינוּ תּוֹרַת אֱלֹהֵינוּ
עַם עֲמֹרָה׃ יא לָמָּה לִּי רֹב־זִבְחֵיכֶם יֹאמַר
יְהוָה שָׂבַעְתִּי עֹלוֹת אֵילִים וְחֵלֶב מְרִיאִים וְדַם
פָּרִים וּכְבָשִׂים וְעַתּוּדִים לֹא חָפָצְתִּי׃ יב כִּי
תָבֹאוּ לֵרָאוֹת פָּנָי מִי־בִקֵּשׁ זֹאת מִיֶּדְכֶם רְמֹס
חֲצֵרָי׃ יג לֹא תוֹסִיפוּ הָבִיא מִנְחַת־שָׁוְא
קְטֹרֶת תּוֹעֵבָה הִיא לִי חֹדֶשׁ וְשַׁבָּת קְרֹא
מִקְרָא לֹא־אוּכַל אָוֶן וַעֲצָרָה׃ יד חָדְשֵׁיכֶם

appointed seasons My soul hates, they are a
burden to Me; I am weary of bearing
[them]. 15. And when you spread out your
hands, I will hide My eyes from you, even
when you pray at length, I do not hear; your
hands are full of blood. 16. Wash, cleanse
yourselves, remove the evil of your deeds
from before My eyes, cease to do evil.
17. Learn to do good, seek justice, strength-
en the robbed, perform justice for the
orphan, plead the case of the widow.
18. Come now, let us debate, says the Lord.
If your sins prove to be like crimson, they
will become white as snow; if they prove to
be as red as crimson dye, they shall become
as wool. 19. If you be willing and obey, you
shall eat the best of the land. 20. But if you
refuse and rebel, you shall be devoured by
the sword, for the mouth of the Lord spoke.
21. How has she become a harlot, a faithful
city, full of justice, in which righteousness
would lodge—but now murderers. 22. Your
silver has become dross; your wine is diluted
with water. 23. Your princes are rebellious
and companions of thieves; everyone loves
bribes and runs after payments; the orphan
they do not judge, and the quarrel of the
widow does not come to them. 24. Therefore, says the Master, the Lord of Hosts, the
Mighty One of Israel, "Oh, I will console
Myself from My adversaries, and I will
avenge Myself of My foes. 25. And I will
return My hand upon you and purge away
your dross as with lye, and remove all your
tin. 26. And I will restore your judges as at
first and your counsellors as in the beginning; afterwards you shall be called City of
Righteousness, Faithful City. 27. Zion shall
be redeemed through justice, and her
penitent through righteousness.

וּמוֹעֲדֵיכֶם שָׂנְאָה נַפְשִׁי הָיוּ עָלַי לָטֹרַח
נִלְאֵיתִי נְשֹׂא: טו וּבְפָרִשְׂכֶם כַּפֵּיכֶם אַעְלִים
עֵינַי מִכֶּם גַּם כִּי־תַרְבּוּ תְפִלָּה אֵינֶנִּי שֹׁמֵעַ
יְדֵיכֶם דָּמִים מָלֵאוּ: טז רַחֲצוּ הִזַּכּוּ הָסִירוּ רֹעַ
מַעַלְלֵיכֶם מִנֶּגֶד עֵינָי חִדְלוּ הָרֵעַ: יז לִמְדוּ
הֵיטֵב דִּרְשׁוּ מִשְׁפָּט אַשְּׁרוּ חָמוֹץ שִׁפְטוּ יָתוֹם
רִיבוּ אַלְמָנָה: יח לְכוּ־נָא וְנִוָּכְחָה יֹאמַר יְהֹוָה
אִם־יִהְיוּ חֲטָאֵיכֶם כַּשָּׁנִים כַּשֶּׁלֶג יַלְבִּינוּ אִם־
יַאְדִּימוּ כַתּוֹלָע כַּצֶּמֶר יִהְיוּ: יט אִם־תֹּאבוּ
וּשְׁמַעְתֶּם טוּב הָאָרֶץ תֹּאכֵלוּ: כ וְאִם־תְּמָאֲנוּ
וּמְרִיתֶם חֶרֶב תְּאֻכְּלוּ כִּי פִּי יְהֹוָה דִּבֵּר:
כא אֵיכָה הָיְתָה לְזוֹנָה קִרְיָה נֶאֱמָנָה מְלֵאֲתִי
מִשְׁפָּט צֶדֶק יָלִין בָּהּ וְעַתָּה מְרַצְּחִים:
כב כַּסְפֵּךְ הָיָה לְסִיגִים סָבְאֵךְ מָהוּל בַּמָּיִם:
כג שָׂרַיִךְ סוֹרְרִים וְחַבְרֵי גַּנָּבִים כֻּלּוֹ אֹהֵב
שֹׁחַד וְרֹדֵף שַׁלְמֹנִים יָתוֹם לֹא יִשְׁפֹּטוּ וְרִיב
אַלְמָנָה לֹא־יָבוֹא אֲלֵיהֶם: כד לָכֵן נְאֻם הָאָדוֹן
יְהֹוָה צְבָאוֹת אֲבִיר יִשְׂרָאֵל הוֹי אֶנָּחֵם מִצָּרַי
וְאִנָּקְמָה מֵאוֹיְבָי: כה וְאָשִׁיבָה יָדִי עָלַיִךְ
וְאֶצְרֹף כַּבֹּר סִיגָיִךְ וְאָסִירָה כָּל־בְּדִילָיִךְ:
כו וְאָשִׁיבָה שֹׁפְטַיִךְ כְּבָרִאשֹׁנָה וְיֹעֲצַיִךְ
כְּבַתְּחִלָּה אַחֲרֵי־כֵן יִקָּרֵא לָךְ עִיר הַצֶּדֶק קִרְיָה
נֶאֱמָנָה: כז צִיּוֹן בְּמִשְׁפָּט תִּפָּדֶה וְשָׁבֶיהָ
בִּצְדָקָה:

HAFTARATH VAETHHANAN   הפטרת ואתחנן
(Isaiah 40:1-26)

**This is the first of "The Seven Haftaroth of Consolation" that are read from the Sab-
bath after the Fast of the Ninth of Av until the Sabbath preceding Rosh Hashanah.**

God commands the prophet to console the people of Israel.

40:1. "Console, console My people," says
your God. 2. Speak to the heart of Jerusalem and call to her, for she has become full
[from] her host, for her iniquity has been
appeased, for she has taken from the hand

א נַחֲמוּ נַחֲמוּ עַמִּי יֹאמַר אֱלֹהֵיכֶם: ב דַּבְּרוּ
עַל־לֵב יְרוּשָׁלַ͏ִם וְקִרְאוּ אֵלֶיהָ כִּי מָלְאָה צְבָאָהּ
כִּי נִרְצָה עֲוֺנָהּ כִּי לָקְחָה מִיַּד יְהֹוָה כִּפְלַיִם

of the Lord double for all her sins. 3. A voice calls, "In the desert, clear the way of the Lord, straighten out in the wilderness, a highway for our God." 4. Every valley shall be raised, and every mountain and hill shall be lowered, and the crooked terrain shall become a plain, and the close mountains a champaign. 5. And the glory of the Lord shall be revealed, and all flesh together shall see that the mouth of the Lord spoke. 6. A voice says, "Call!" and it says, "What shall I call?" "All flesh is grass, and all its kindness is like the blossom of the field. 7. The grass shall dry out, the blossom shall wilt, for a wind from the Lord has blown upon it; behold, the people is grass. 8. The grass shall dry out, the blossom shall wilt, but the word of our God shall last forever. 9. Upon a lofty mountain ascend O herald of Zion, raise your voice with strength, O herald of Jerusalem; raise [your voice], fear not; say to the cities of Judah, "Behold your God!" 10. Behold the Lord God shall come with a strong [hand], and His arm rules for Him; behold His reward is with Him, and His recompense is before Him. 11. Like a shepherd [who] tends his flock, with his arm he gathers lambs, and in his bosom he carries [them]; the nursing ones he leads. 12. Who measured water with his gait, and measured the heavens with his span, and measured by thirds the dust of the earth, and weighed mountains with a scale and hills with a balance? 13. Who meted the spirit of the Lord, and His adviser who informs Him? 14. With whom did He take counsel and give him to understand, and teach him in the way of justice, and teach him knowledge, and the way of understandings did He let him know? 15. Behold the nations are like a drop from a bucket, and like dust on a balance are they counted; behold the islands are like fine [dust] that blows away. 16. And the Lebanon,— there is not enough to burn, and its beasts,—there not enough for burnt offerings. 17. All the nations are as nought before Him; as things of nought and vanity are they regarded by Him. 18. And to whom do you compare God, and what likeness do you arrange for Him? 19. The graven image, the craftsman has melted, and the smith plates it with gold, and chains of silver he attaches.

בְּכָל־חַטֹּאתֶיהָ: ג קוֹל קוֹרֵא בַּמִּדְבָּר פַּנּוּ דֶּרֶךְ יְהֹוָה יַשְּׁרוּ בָּעֲרָבָה מְסִלָּה לֵאלֹהֵינוּ: ד כָּל־גֶּיא יִנָּשֵׂא וְכָל־הַר וְגִבְעָה יִשְׁפָּלוּ וְהָיָה הֶעָקֹב לְמִישׁוֹר וְהָרְכָסִים לְבִקְעָה: ה וְנִגְלָה כְּבוֹד יְהֹוָה וְרָאוּ כָל־בָּשָׂר יַחְדָּו כִּי פִּי יְהֹוָה דִּבֵּר: ו קוֹל אֹמֵר קְרָא וְאָמַר מָה אֶקְרָא כָּל־הַבָּשָׂר חָצִיר וְכָל־חַסְדּוֹ כְּצִיץ הַשָּׂדֶה: ז יָבֵשׁ חָצִיר נָבֵל צִיץ כִּי רוּחַ יְהֹוָה נָשְׁבָה בּוֹ אָכֵן חָצִיר הָעָם: ח יָבֵשׁ חָצִיר נָבֵל צִיץ וּדְבַר אֱלֹהֵינוּ יָקוּם לְעוֹלָם: ט עַל הַר־גָּבֹהַּ עֲלִי־לָךְ מְבַשֶּׂרֶת צִיּוֹן הָרִימִי בַכֹּחַ קוֹלֵךְ מְבַשֶּׂרֶת יְרוּשָׁלַ‍ִם הָרִימִי אַל־תִּירָאִי אִמְרִי לְעָרֵי יְהוּדָה הִנֵּה אֱלֹהֵיכֶם: י הִנֵּה אֲדֹנָי יֱהֹוִה בְּחָזָק יָבוֹא וּזְרֹעוֹ מֹשְׁלָה לוֹ הִנֵּה שְׂכָרוֹ אִתּוֹ וּפְעֻלָּתוֹ לְפָנָיו: יא כְּרֹעֶה עֶדְרוֹ יִרְעֶה בִּזְרֹעוֹ יְקַבֵּץ טְלָאִים וּבְחֵיקוֹ יִשָּׂא עָלוֹת יְנַהֵל: יב מִי־מָדַד בְּשָׁעֳלוֹ מַיִם וְשָׁמַיִם בַּזֶּרֶת תִּכֵּן וְכָל בַּשָּׁלִשׁ עֲפַר הָאָרֶץ וְשָׁקַל בַּפֶּלֶס הָרִים וּגְבָעוֹת בְּמֹאזְנָיִם: יג מִי־תִכֵּן אֶת־רוּחַ יְהֹוָה וְאִישׁ עֲצָתוֹ יוֹדִיעֶנּוּ: יד אֶת־מִי נוֹעָץ וַיְבִינֵהוּ וַיְלַמְּדֵהוּ בְּאֹרַח מִשְׁפָּט וַיְלַמְּדֵהוּ דַעַת וְדֶרֶךְ תְּבוּנוֹת יוֹדִיעֶנּוּ: טו הֵן גּוֹיִם כְּמַר מִדְּלִי וּכְשַׁחַק מֹאזְנַיִם נֶחְשָׁבוּ הֵן אִיִּים כַּדַּק יִטּוֹל: טז וּלְבָנוֹן אֵין דֵּי בָּעֵר וְחַיָּתוֹ אֵין דֵּי עוֹלָה: יז כָּל־הַגּוֹיִם כְּאַיִן נֶגְדּוֹ מֵאֶפֶס וָתֹהוּ נֶחְשְׁבוּ־לוֹ: יח וְאֶל־מִי תְּדַמְּיוּן אֵל וּמַה־דְּמוּת תַּעַרְכוּ־לוֹ: יט הַפֶּסֶל נָסַךְ חָרָשׁ וְצֹרֵף בַּזָּהָב יְרַקְּעֶנּוּ וּרְתֻקוֹת כֶּסֶף

20. He who is accustomed to select, chooses a tree that does not rot; he seeks for himself a skilled craftsman, to prepare a graven image which will not move. 21. Do you not know, have you not heard, has it not been told to you from the beginning? Do you not understand the foundations of the earth? 22. It is He Who sits above the circle of the earth and whose inhabitants are like grasshoppers, Who stretches out the heaven like a curtain, and He spread them out like a tent to dwell; 23. Who brings princes to nought; judges of the land He made like a thing of nought. 24. Even [as though] they were not planted, even [as though] they were not sown, even [as though] their trunk was not rooted in the earth; and also He blew on them, and they dried up, and a tempest shall carry them away like straw. 25. "Now, to whom will you compare Me that I should be equal?" says the Holy One. 26. Lift up your eyes on high and see who created these, who takes out their host by number; all of them He calls by name; because of His great might and because He is strong in power, no one is missing.

צוֹרֵף: כ הַמְסֻכָּן תְּרוּמָה עֵץ לֹא־יִרְקַב יִבְחָר
חָרָשׁ חָכָם יְבַקֶּשׁ־לוֹ לְהָכִין פֶּסֶל לֹא יִמּוֹט:
כא הֲלוֹא תֵדְעוּ הֲלוֹא תִשְׁמָעוּ הֲלוֹא הֻגַּד
מֵרֹאשׁ לָכֶם הֲלוֹא הֲבִינוֹתֶם מוֹסְדוֹת הָאָרֶץ:
כב הַיֹּשֵׁב עַל־חוּג הָאָרֶץ וְיֹשְׁבֶיהָ כַּחֲגָבִים
הַנּוֹטֶה כַדֹּק שָׁמַיִם וַיִּמְתָּחֵם כָּאֹהֶל לָשָׁבֶת:
כג הַנּוֹתֵן רוֹזְנִים לְאָיִן שֹׁפְטֵי אֶרֶץ כַּתֹּהוּ
עָשָׂה: כד אַף בַּל־נִטָּעוּ אַף בַּל־זֹרָעוּ אַף בַּל־
שֹׁרֵשׁ בָּאָרֶץ גִּזְעָם וְגַם נָשַׁף בָּהֶם וַיִּבָשׁוּ
וּסְעָרָה כַּקַּשׁ תִּשָּׂאֵם: כה וְאֶל־מִי תְדַמְּיוּנִי
וְאֶשְׁוֶה יֹאמַר קָדוֹשׁ: כו שְׂאוּ־מָרוֹם עֵינֵיכֶם
וּרְאוּ מִי־בָרָא אֵלֶּה הַמּוֹצִיא בְמִסְפָּר צְבָאָם
לְכֻלָּם בְּשֵׁם יִקְרָא מֵרֹב אוֹנִים וְאַמִּיץ כֹּחַ
אִישׁ לֹא נֶעְדָּר:

HAFTARATH EKEV הפטרת עקב

(Isaiah 49:14–51:3)

This is the second of "The Seven Haftaroth of Consolation."

Israel complains, "The Lord has forsaken me," because He commanded the prophets to console His people instead of consoling them Himself.

49:14. And Zion said, "The Lord has forsaken me, and the Lord has forgotten me." 15. Shall a woman forget her sucking child, from having mercy on the child of her womb? These too shall forget, but I will not forget you. 16. Behold, on [My] hands have I engraved you; your walls are before Me always. 17. Your sons have hastened; those who destroy you and those who lay you waste shall go forth from you. 18. Lift your eyes around and see, all of them have gathered, have come to you; as I live, says the Lord, that you shall wear all of them as jewelry, and you shall tie them as a bride. 19. For your ruins and your desolate places and your land that has been destroyed, for now you shall be crowded by the inhabitants, and those who would destroy you shall be far away. 20. Your children, of whom you were bereaved, shall yet say in

יד וַתֹּאמֶר צִיּוֹן עֲזָבַנִי יְהוָה וַאדֹנָי שְׁכֵחָנִי:
טו הֲתִשְׁכַּח אִשָּׁה עוּלָהּ מֵרַחֵם בֶּן־בִּטְנָהּ גַּם־
אֵלֶּה תִשְׁכַּחְנָה וְאָנֹכִי לֹא אֶשְׁכָּחֵךְ: טז הֵן עַל־
כַּפַּיִם חַקֹּתִיךְ חוֹמֹתַיִךְ נֶגְדִּי תָּמִיד: יז מִהֲרוּ
בָּנָיִךְ מְהָרְסַיִךְ וּמַחֲרִבַיִךְ מִמֵּךְ יֵצֵאוּ: יח שְׂאִי־
סָבִיב עֵינַיִךְ וּרְאִי כֻּלָּם נִקְבְּצוּ בָאוּ־לָךְ חַי־אָנִי
נְאֻם־יְהוָה כִּי כֻלָּם כָּעֲדִי תִלְבָּשִׁי וּתְקַשְּׁרִים
כַּכַּלָּה: יט כִּי חָרְבֹתַיִךְ וְשֹׁמְמֹתַיִךְ וְאֶרֶץ
הֲרִסֻתֵךְ כִּי עַתָּה תֵּצְרִי מִיּוֹשֵׁב וְרָחֲקוּ
מְבַלְּעָיִךְ: כ עוֹד יֹאמְרוּ בְאָזְנַיִךְ בְּנֵי שִׁכֻּלָיִךְ

צַר־לִ֥י הַמָּק֖וֹם גְּשָׁה־לִּ֥י וְאֵשֵֽׁבָה׃ כא וְאָמַ֣רְתְּ
בִּלְבָבֵ֗ךְ מִ֤י יָֽלַד־לִי֙ אֶת־אֵ֔לֶּה וַאֲנִ֥י שְׁכוּלָ֖ה
וְגַלְמוּדָ֑ה גֹּלָ֣ה ׀ וְסוּרָ֗ה וְאֵ֙לֶּה֙ מִ֣י גִדֵּ֔ל הֵ֤ן אֲנִי֙
נִשְׁאַ֣רְתִּי לְבַדִּ֔י אֵ֖לֶּה אֵיפֹ֥ה הֵֽם׃ כב כֹּֽה־אָמַ֞ר
אֲדֹנָ֣י יֱהֹוִ֗ה הִנֵּ֨ה אֶשָּׂ֤א אֶל־גּוֹיִם֙ יָדִ֔י וְאֶל־עַמִּ֖ים
אָרִ֣ים נִסִּ֑י וְהֵבִ֤יאוּ בָנַ֙יִךְ֙ בְּחֹ֔צֶן וּבְנֹתַ֖יִךְ
עַל־כָּתֵ֥ף תִּנָּשֶֽׂאנָה׃ כג וְהָי֨וּ מְלָכִ֜ים אֹמְנַ֗יִךְ
וְשָׂרֽוֹתֵיהֶם֙ מֵינִיקֹתַ֔יִךְ אַפַּ֗יִם אֶ֚רֶץ יִשְׁתַּ֣חֲווּ־לָ֔ךְ
וַעֲפַ֥ר רַגְלַ֖יִךְ יְלַחֵ֑כוּ וְיָדַ֙עַתְּ֙ כִּֽי־אֲנִ֣י יְהֹוָ֔ה אֲשֶׁ֥ר
לֹֽא־יֵבֹ֖שׁוּ קֹוָֽי׃ כד הֲיֻקַּ֥ח מִגִּבּ֖וֹר מַלְק֑וֹחַ וְאִם־
שְׁבִ֥י צַדִּ֖יק יִמָּלֵֽט׃ כה כִּי־כֹ֣ה ׀ אָמַ֣ר יְהֹוָ֗ה גַּם־
שְׁבִ֤י גִבּוֹר֙ יֻקָּ֔ח וּמַלְק֥וֹחַ עָרִ֖יץ יִמָּלֵ֑ט וְאֶת־
יְרִיבֵךְ֙ אָנֹכִ֣י אָרִ֔יב וְאֶת־בָּנַ֖יִךְ אָנֹכִ֥י אוֹשִֽׁיעַ׃
כו וְהַאֲכַלְתִּ֤י אֶת־מוֹנַ֙יִךְ֙ אֶת־בְּשָׂרָ֔ם וְכֶעָסִ֖יס
דָּמָ֣ם יִשְׁכָּר֑וּן וְיָדְע֣וּ כָל־בָּשָׂ֗ר כִּ֣י אֲנִ֤י יְהֹוָה֙
מֽוֹשִׁיעֵ֔ךְ וְגֹאֲלֵ֖ךְ אֲבִ֥יר יַעֲקֹֽב׃ א כֹּ֣ה ׀ אָמַ֣ר
יְהֹוָ֗ה אֵ֣י זֶ֜ה סֵ֣פֶר כְּרִית֤וּת אִמְּכֶם֙ אֲשֶׁ֣ר
שִׁלַּחְתִּ֔יהָ א֚וֹ מִ֣י מִנּוֹשַׁ֔י אֲשֶׁר־מָכַ֥רְתִּי אֶתְכֶ֖ם
ל֑וֹ הֵ֤ן בַּעֲוֺנֹֽתֵיכֶם֙ נִמְכַּרְתֶּ֔ם וּבְפִשְׁעֵיכֶ֖ם שֻׁלְּחָ֥ה
אִמְּכֶֽם׃ ב מַדּ֨וּעַ בָּ֜אתִי וְאֵ֣ין אִ֗ישׁ קָרָ֙אתִי֙ וְאֵ֣ין
עוֹנֶ֔ה הֲקָצ֨וֹר קָצְרָ֤ה יָדִי֙ מִפְּד֔וּת וְאִם־אֵין־בִּ֥י
כֹ֖חַ לְהַצִּ֑יל הֵ֣ן בְּגַעֲרָתִ֞י אַחֲרִ֣יב יָ֗ם אָשִׂ֤ים
נְהָרוֹת֙ מִדְבָּ֔ר תִּבְאַ֤שׁ דְּגָתָם֙ מֵאֵ֣ין מַ֔יִם וְתָמֹ֖ת
בַּצָּמָֽא׃ ג אַלְבִּ֥ישׁ שָׁמַ֖יִם קַדְר֑וּת וְשַׂ֖ק אָשִׂ֥ים
כְּסוּתָֽם׃ ד אֲדֹנָ֣י יֱהֹוִ֗ה נָ֤תַן לִי֙ לְשׁ֣וֹן לִמּוּדִ֔ים
לָדַ֛עַת לָע֥וּת אֶת־יָעֵ֖ף דָּבָ֑ר יָעִ֣יר ׀ בַּבֹּ֣קֶר בַּבֹּ֗קֶר
יָעִ֥יר לִי֙ אֹ֔זֶן לִשְׁמֹ֖עַ כַּלִּמּוּדִֽים׃ ה אֲדֹנָ֤י יֱהֹוִה֙
פָּֽתַח־לִ֣י אֹ֔זֶן וְאָנֹכִ֖י לֹ֣א מָרִ֑יתִי אָח֖וֹר לֹ֥א
נְסוּגֹֽתִי׃ ו גֵּוִי֙ נָתַ֣תִּי לְמַכִּ֔ים וּלְחָיַ֖י לְמֹרְטִ֑ים

your ears, "The place is too narrow for me;
move over for me so that I will dwell."
21. And you shall say to yourself, "Who
begot these for me, seeing that I am
bereaved and solitary, exiled and rejected,
and who raised these? Behold, I was left
alone; these — [from] where are they?"
22. So said the Lord God, "Behold, I will
raise My hand to the nations, and to the
peoples will I raise My standard, and they
shall bring your sons in their armpits, and
your daughters shall be borne on their
shoulder[s]. 23. And kings shall be your
nursing fathers and their princesses your
wet nurses; they shall prostrate themselves
to you with their face on the ground, and
they shall lick the dust of your feet, and you
shall know that I am the Lord, for those who
wait for Me shall not be ashamed. 24. Shall
prey be taken from a mighty warrior, or
shall the captives of the righteous escape?"
25. For so said the Lord, "Even the captives of a mighty warrior can be taken
and the prey of a tyrant shall escape, and
with your contender will I contend, and
your sons I will save. 26. And those who
taunt you — I will feed their flesh, and as
with sweet wine they shall become drunk
[from] their blood; and all flesh shall know
that I am the Lord Who saves you, and your
Redeemer, the Mighty One of Jacob."
50:1. So said the Lord, "Where is your
mother's bill of divorce, that I sent her
away? Or, who is it of My creditors to whom
I sold you? Behold, for your iniquities you
were sold, and for your transgressions your
mother was sent away. 2. Why have I come
and there is no man? [Why] have I called
and no one answers? Is My hand too short to
redeem, or do I have no strength to save?
Behold, with My rebuke I dry up the sea, I
make rivers into a desert; their fish become
foul because there is no water, and die
because of thirst. 3. I clothe the heavens
with darkness, and I make sackcloth their
raiment." 4. The Lord God gave me a
tongue for teaching, to know to establish
times for the faint [for His] word; He
awakens me every morning; He awakens
My ear, to hear according to the teachings.
5. The Lord God opened my ear, and I did
not rebel; I did not turn away backwards.
6. I gave my back to smiters and my cheeks
to them that plucked off the hair; I did not

hide my face from embarrassments and spitting. 7. But the Lord God helps me; therefore, I was not embarrassed; therefore, I made my face like flint, and I knew that I would not be ashamed. 8. He Who vindicates me is near, whoever wishes to quarrel with me — let us stand together; whoever is my contender shall approach me. 9. Behold, the Lord God shall help me. Who is he that will condemn me? Behold, all of them shall wear out like a garment, a moth shall consume them. 10. Who among you is God-fearing, who hearkens to the voice of His servant, who went in darkness and who has no light? Let him trust in the name of the Lord and lean on his God. 11. Behold, all of you who kindle fire, who give power to flames; go in the flame of your fire and in the flames you have kindled; from My hand has this come to you, in grief you shall lie down. 51:1. Hearken to Me, you pursuers of righteousness, you seekers of the Lord; look at the rock whence you were hewn and at the hole of the pit whence you were dug. 2. Look at Abraham your father and at Sarah who bore you, for when he was but one I called him, and I blessed him and made him many. 3. For the Lord shall console Zion, He shall console all its ruins, and He shall make its desert like a paradise and its wasteland like the garden of the Lord; joy and happiness shall be found therein, thanksgiving and a voice of song.

פָּנַי֙ לֹ֣א הִסְתַּ֔רְתִּי מִכְּלִמּ֖וֹת וָרֹֽק: ז וַאדֹנָ֤י יֱהֹוִה֙ יַֽעֲזָר־לִ֔י עַל־כֵּ֖ן לֹ֣א נִכְלָ֑מְתִּי עַל־כֵּ֞ן שַׂ֤מְתִּי פָנַי֙ כַּֽחַלָּמִ֔ישׁ וָֽאֵדַ֖ע כִּי־לֹ֥א אֵבֽוֹשׁ: ח קָר֨וֹב מַצְדִּיקִ֜י מִֽי־יָרִ֤יב אִתִּי֙ נַֽעַמְדָ֣ה יָּ֔חַד מִי־בַ֥עַל מִשְׁפָּטִ֖י יִגַּ֥שׁ אֵלָֽי: ט הֵ֣ן אֲדֹנָ֤י יֱהֹוִה֙ יַֽעֲזָר־לִ֔י מִי־ה֖וּא יַרְשִׁיעֵ֑נִי הֵ֤ן כֻּלָּם֙ כַּבֶּ֣גֶד יִבְל֔וּ עָ֖שׁ יֹֽאכְלֵֽם: י מִ֤י בָכֶם֙ יְרֵ֣א יְהֹוָ֔ה שֹׁמֵ֖עַ בְּק֣וֹל עַבְדּ֑וֹ אֲשֶׁ֣ר | הָלַ֣ךְ חֲשֵׁכִ֗ים וְאֵ֥ין נֹ֨גַהּ֙ ל֔וֹ יִבְטַח֙ בְּשֵׁ֣ם יְהֹוָ֔ה וְיִשָּׁעֵ֖ן בֵּֽאלֹהָֽיו: יא הֵ֧ן כֻּלְּכֶ֣ם קֹ֣דְחֵי אֵ֗שׁ מְאַזְּרֵ֖י זִיק֑וֹת לְכ֣וּ | בְּא֣וּר אֶשְׁכֶ֗ם וּבְזִיקוֹת֙ בִּֽעַרְתֶּ֔ם מִיָּדִי֙ הָֽיְתָה־זֹּ֣את לָכֶ֔ם לְמַֽעֲצֵבָ֖ה תִּשְׁכָּבֽוּן: א שִׁמְע֤וּ אֵלַי֙ רֹ֣דְפֵי צֶ֔דֶק מְבַקְשֵׁ֖י יְהֹוָ֑ה הַבִּ֨יטוּ֙ אֶל־צ֣וּר חֻצַּבְתֶּ֔ם וְאֶל־מַקֶּ֥בֶת בּ֖וֹר נֻקַּרְתֶּֽם: ב הַבִּ֨יטוּ֙ אֶל־אַבְרָהָ֣ם אֲבִיכֶ֔ם וְאֶל־שָׂרָ֖ה תְּחֽוֹלֶלְכֶ֑ם כִּֽי־אֶחָ֣ד קְרָאתִ֔יו וַֽאֲבָרְכֵ֖הוּ וְאַרְבֵּֽהוּ: ג כִּֽי־נִחַ֨ם יְהֹוָ֜ה צִיּ֗וֹן נִחַם֙ כָּל־חָרְבֹתֶ֔יהָ וַיָּ֤שֶׂם מִדְבָּרָהּ֙ כְּעֵ֔דֶן וְעַרְבָתָ֖הּ כְּגַן־יְהֹוָ֑ה שָׂשׂ֤וֹן וְשִׂמְחָה֙ יִמָּ֣צֵא בָ֔הּ תּוֹדָ֖ה וְק֥וֹל זִמְרָֽה:

HAFTARATH RE'EH הפטרת ראה
(Isaiah 54:11–55:5)

This is the third of "The Seven Haftaroth of Consolation." Sephardim read this Haftarah even if Rosh Chodesh Elul falls on this Sabbath, but add the opening and closing verses of the Haftarah of Shabbath Rosh Chodesh (p. 930). Ashkenazim read the Haftarah of Shabbath Rosh Chodesh. In that case, this Haftarah is read on the Sabbath of Ki Thetze, following the Haftarah of that Sabbath. Should Rosh Chodesh fall on Sunday, the Haftarah usually read on that occasion, I Sam. 20:18–42 (p. 933) is completely superseded. The Sephardim, however, read the first and last verses of that Haftarah (p. 933) after the Haftarath Re'eh. Congregations following the custom of Frankfort read the Haftarah of the day preceding Rosh Chodesh (I Samuel 20:18–42) and make up the Haftarah for this Sabbath on the Sabbath of Ki Thetze, following the Haftarah for that Sabbath.

The prophet reports to God that Israel is not yet consoled.

54:11. O poor tempestuous one, who was not consoled, behold I will set your stones with carbuncle, and I will lay your foundations with sapphires. 12. And I will make

יא עֲנִיָּ֥ה סֹֽעֲרָ֖ה לֹ֣א נֻחָ֑מָה הִנֵּ֨ה אָֽנֹכִ֜י מַרְבִּ֤יץ בַּפּוּךְ֙ אֲבָנַ֔יִךְ וִֽיסַדְתִּ֖יךְ בַּסַּפִּירִֽים: יב וְשַׂמְתִּ֤י

your windows of jasper and your gates of carbuncle stones, and all your border of precious stones. 13. And all your children shall be disciples of the Lord, and your children's peace shall increase. 14. With **righteousness** shall you be established; go far away from oppression, for you shall not fear, and from ruin, for it will not come near you. 15. Behold, the one with whom I am not shall fear; whoever mobilizes against you shall defect to you. 16. Behold I have created a smith, who blows on a charcoal fire and produces a weapon for his work, and I have created a destroyer to destroy [it]. 17. Any weapon whetted against you shall not succeed, and any tongue that contends with you in judgment, you shall condemn; this is the heritage of the servants of the Lord and their due reward from Me, says the Lord. 55:1. Ho! All who thirst, go to water, and whoever has no money, go, buy and eat, and go, buy without money and without a price, wine and milk. 2. Why should you weigh out money without bread and your toil without satiety? Hearken to Me and eat what is good, and your soul shall delight in fatness. 3. Incline your ear and come to Me, hearken and your soul shall live, and I will make for you an everlasting covenant, the dependable mercies of David. 4. Behold, a witness to nations have I appointed him, a ruler and a commander of nations. 5. Behold, a nation you do not know you shall call, and a nation that did not know you shall run to you, for the sake of the Lord your God and for the Holy One of Israel, for He glorified you.

כַּדְכֹד שִׁמְשֹׁתַיִךְ וּשְׁעָרַיִךְ לְאַבְנֵי אֶקְדָּח וְכָל־
גְּבוּלֵךְ לְאַבְנֵי־חֵפֶץ: יג וְכָל־בָּנַיִךְ לִמּוּדֵי יְהֹוָה
וְרַב שְׁלוֹם בָּנָיִךְ: יד בִּצְדָקָה תִּכּוֹנָנִי רַחֲקִי
מֵעֹשֶׁק כִּי־לֹא תִירָאִי וּמִמְּחִתָּה כִּי לֹא־תִקְרַב
אֵלָיִךְ: טו הֵן גּוֹר יָגוּר אֶפֶס מֵאוֹתִי מִי־גָר
אִתָּךְ עָלַיִךְ יִפּוֹל: טז הֵן_(הנה קרי) אָנֹכִי בָּרָאתִי
חָרָשׁ נֹפֵחַ בְּאֵשׁ פֶּחָם וּמוֹצִיא כְלִי לְמַעֲשֵׂהוּ
וְאָנֹכִי בָּרָאתִי מַשְׁחִית לְחַבֵּל: יז כָּל־כְּלִי יוּצַר
עָלַיִךְ לֹא יִצְלָח וְכָל־לָשׁוֹן תָּקוּם־אִתָּךְ
לַמִּשְׁפָּט תַּרְשִׁיעִי זֹאת נַחֲלַת עַבְדֵי יְהֹוָה
וְצִדְקָתָם מֵאִתִּי נְאֻם־יְהֹוָה: א הוֹי כָּל־צָמֵא
לְכוּ לַמַּיִם וַאֲשֶׁר אֵין־לוֹ כָּסֶף לְכוּ שִׁבְרוּ
וֶאֱכֹלוּ וּלְכוּ שִׁבְרוּ בְּלוֹא־כֶסֶף וּבְלוֹא מְחִיר
יַיִן וְחָלָב: ב לָמָּה תִשְׁקְלוּ־כֶסֶף בְּלוֹא־לֶחֶם
וִיגִיעֲכֶם בְּלוֹא לְשָׂבְעָה שִׁמְעוּ שָׁמוֹעַ אֵלַי
וְאִכְלוּ־טוֹב וְתִתְעַנַּג בַּדֶּשֶׁן נַפְשְׁכֶם: ג הַטּוּ
אָזְנְכֶם וּלְכוּ אֵלַי שִׁמְעוּ וּתְחִי נַפְשְׁכֶם
וְאֶכְרְתָה לָכֶם בְּרִית עוֹלָם חַסְדֵי דָוִד
הַנֶּאֱמָנִים: ד הֵן עֵד לְאוּמִּים נְתַתִּיו נָגִיד
וּמְצַוֵּה לְאֻמִּים: ה הֵן גּוֹי לֹא־תֵדַע תִּקְרָא וְגוֹי
לֹא־יְדָעוּךָ אֵלֶיךָ יָרוּצוּ לְמַעַן יְהֹוָה אֱלֹהֶיךָ
וְלִקְדוֹשׁ יִשְׂרָאֵל כִּי פֵאֲרָךְ:

HAFTARATH SHOFETIM הפטרת שפטים
(Isaiah 51:12–52:12)
This is the fourth of "The Seven Haftaroth of Consolation."

Here, God Himself consoles Israel.

51:12. I, yea I am He Who consoles you; who are you that you fear man who will die, and the son of man, who shall be made [as] grass? 13. And you forgot the Lord your Maker, Who spread out the heavens and founded the earth, and you fear constantly the whole day because of the wrath of the

יב אָנֹכִי אָנֹכִי הוּא מְנַחֶמְכֶם מִי־אַתְּ וַתִּירְאִי
מֵאֱנוֹשׁ יָמוּת וּמִבֶּן־אָדָם חָצִיר יִנָּתֵן:
יג וַתִּשְׁכַּח יְהֹוָה עֹשֶׂךָ נוֹטֶה שָׁמַיִם וְיֹסֵד אָרֶץ
וַתְּפַחֵד תָּמִיד כָּל־הַיּוֹם מִפְּנֵי חֲמַת הַמֵּצִיק

oppressor when he prepared to destroy. Now where is the wrath of the oppressor? 14. What must be poured out hastened to be opened, and he shall not die of destruction, and his bread shall not be wanting. 15. I am the Lord your God, Who wrinkles the sea and its waves stir; the Lord of Hosts is His name. 16. And I placed My words into your mouth, and with the shadow of My hand I covered you, to plant the heavens and to found the earth and to say to Zion [that] you are My people. 17. Awaken, awaken, arise, Jerusalem, for you have drunk from the hand of the Lord the cup of His wrath; the dregs of the cup of weakness you have drained. 18. She has no guide of all the sons she bore, and she has no one who takes her by the hand out of all the sons she raised. 19. These two things have befallen you; who will lament for you? Plunder and destruction, and famine and sword. [With] whom will I console you? 20. Your sons have fainted, they lie at the entrance of all streets like a wild ox in a net, full of the wrath of the Lord, the rebuke of your God. 21. Therefore, hearken now to this, you poor one, and who is drunk but not from wine. 22. So said your Master, the Lord, and your God Who shall judge His people, "Behold, I took from you the cup of weakness; the dregs of the cup of My wrath — you shall no longer continue to drink it. 23. And I will place it into the hand of those who cause you to wander, who said to your soul, 'Bend down and let us cross,' and you made your body like the earth and like the street for those who cross." 52:1. Awaken, awaken, put on your strength, O Zion; put on the garments of your beauty, Jerusalem the Holy City, for no longer shall the uncircumcised or the unclean continue to enter you. 2. Shake yourselves from the dust, arise, sit down, O Jerusalem; free yourself of the bands of your neck, O captive daughter of Zion. 3. For so said the Lord, "You were sold for nought, and you shall not be redeemed for money." 4. For so said the Lord God, "My people first went down to Egypt to sojourn there, but Assyria oppressed them for nothing." 5. And now, what have I here, says the Lord, that My people has been taken for nothing. "His rulers boast," says the Lord, "and constant-

כַּאֲשֶׁר כּוֹנֵן לְהַשְׁחִית וְאַיֵּה חֲמַת הַמֵּצִיק׃
יד מִהַר צֹעֶה לְהִפָּתֵחַ וְלֹא־יָמוּת לַשַּׁחַת וְלֹא
יֶחְסַר לַחְמוֹ׃ טו וְאָנֹכִי יְהוָה אֱלֹהֶיךָ רֹגַע הַיָּם
וַיֶּהֱמוּ גַּלָּיו יְהוָה צְבָאוֹת שְׁמוֹ׃ טז וָאָשִׂם
דְּבָרַי בְּפִיךָ וּבְצֵל יָדִי כִּסִּיתִיךָ לִנְטֹעַ שָׁמַיִם
וְלִיסֹד אָרֶץ וְלֵאמֹר לְצִיּוֹן עַמִּי אָתָּה׃
יז הִתְעוֹרְרִי הִתְעוֹרְרִי קוּמִי יְרוּשָׁלַםִ אֲשֶׁר
שָׁתִית מִיַּד יְהוָה אֶת־כּוֹס חֲמָתוֹ אֶת־קֻבַּעַת
כּוֹס הַתַּרְעֵלָה שָׁתִית מָצִית׃ יח אֵין־מְנַהֵל לָהּ
מִכָּל־בָּנִים יָלָדָה וְאֵין מַחֲזִיק בְּיָדָהּ מִכָּל־בָּנִים
גִּדֵּלָה׃ יט שְׁתַּיִם הֵנָּה קֹרְאֹתַיִךְ מִי יָנוּד לָךְ
הַשֹּׁד וְהַשֶּׁבֶר וְהָרָעָב וְהַחֶרֶב מִי אֲנַחֲמֵךְ׃
כ בָּנַיִךְ עֻלְּפוּ שָׁכְבוּ בְּרֹאשׁ כָּל־חוּצוֹת כְּתוֹא
מִכְמָר הַמְלֵאִים חֲמַת־יְהוָה גַּעֲרַת אֱלֹהָיִךְ׃
כא לָכֵן שִׁמְעִי־נָא זֹאת עֲנִיָּה וּשְׁכֻרַת וְלֹא
מִיָּיִן׃ כב כֹּה־אָמַר אֲדֹנַיִךְ יְהוָה וֵאלֹהַיִךְ יָרִיב
עַמּוֹ הִנֵּה לָקַחְתִּי מִיָּדֵךְ אֶת־כּוֹס הַתַּרְעֵלָה
אֶת־קֻבַּעַת כּוֹס חֲמָתִי לֹא־תוֹסִיפִי לִשְׁתּוֹתָהּ
עוֹד׃ כג וְשַׂמְתִּיהָ בְּיַד מוֹגַיִךְ אֲשֶׁר־אָמְרוּ
לְנַפְשֵׁךְ שְׁחִי וְנַעֲבֹרָה וַתָּשִׂימִי כָאָרֶץ גֵּוֵךְ
וְכַחוּץ לַעֹבְרִים׃ א עוּרִי עוּרִי לִבְשִׁי עֻזֵּךְ צִיּוֹן
לִבְשִׁי ׀ בִּגְדֵי תִפְאַרְתֵּךְ יְרוּשָׁלַםִ עִיר הַקֹּדֶשׁ
כִּי לֹא יוֹסִיף יָבֹא־בָךְ עוֹד עָרֵל וְטָמֵא׃
ב הִתְנַעֲרִי מֵעָפָר קוּמִי שְׁבִי יְרוּשָׁלָםִ
הִתְפַּתְּחוּ (התפתחי קרי) מוֹסְרֵי צַוָּארֵךְ שְׁבִיָּה
בַּת־צִיּוֹן׃ ג כִּי־כֹה אָמַר יְהוָה חִנָּם נִמְכַּרְתֶּם
וְלֹא בְכֶסֶף תִּגָּאֵלוּ׃ ד כִּי כֹה אָמַר אֲדֹנָי יֱהוִה
מִצְרַיִם יָרַד־עַמִּי בָרִאשֹׁנָה לָגוּר שָׁם וְאַשּׁוּר
בְּאֶפֶס עֲשָׁקוֹ׃ ה וְעַתָּה מַה־לִּי־פֹה נְאֻם־יְהוָה
כִּי־לֻקַּח עַמִּי חִנָּם מֹשְׁלָו (משליו קרי) יְהֵילִילוּ

ly all day My name is blasphemed. 6. Therefore, My people shall know My name; therefore, on that day, for I am He Who speaks, here I am." 7. How beautiful are the feet of the herald on the mountains, announcing peace, heralding good tidings, announcing salvation, saying to Zion, "Your God has manifested His kingdom." 8. The voice of your watchmen — they raised a voice; together they shall sing, for eye to eye they shall see when the Lord returns to Zion. 9. Burst out in song, sing together, O ruins of Jerusalem, for the Lord has consoled his people; He has redeemed Jerusalem. 10. The Lord has revealed His holy arm before the eyes of all the nations, and all the ends of the earth shall see the salvation of our God. 11. Turn away, turn away, get out of there; touch no unclean one, get out of its midst; purify yourselves, you who bear the Lord's vessels. 12. For not with haste shall you go forth, and not in a flurry of flight shall you go, for the Lord goes before you, and your rear guard is the God of Israel.

נְאֻם־יְהוָֹה וְתָמִיד כָּל־הַיּוֹם שְׁמִי מִנֹּאָץ: ו לָכֵן
יֵדַע עַמִּי שְׁמִי לָכֵן בַּיּוֹם הַהוּא כִּי־אֲנִי־הוּא
הַמְדַבֵּר הִנֵּנִי: ז מַה־נָּאווּ עַל־הֶהָרִים רַגְלֵי
מְבַשֵּׂר מַשְׁמִיעַ שָׁלוֹם מְבַשֵּׂר טוֹב מַשְׁמִיעַ
יְשׁוּעָה אֹמֵר לְצִיּוֹן מָלַךְ אֱלֹהָיִךְ: ח קוֹל צֹפַיִךְ
נָשְׂאוּ קוֹל יַחְדָּו יְרַנֵּנוּ כִּי עַיִן בְּעַיִן יִרְאוּ
בְּשׁוּב יְהוָֹה צִיּוֹן: ט פִּצְחוּ רַנְּנוּ יַחְדָּו חָרְבוֹת
יְרוּשָׁלָם כִּי־נִחַם יְהוָֹה עַמּוֹ גָּאַל יְרוּשָׁלָם:
י חָשַׂף יְהוָֹה אֶת־זְרוֹעַ קָדְשׁוֹ לְעֵינֵי כָּל־
הַגּוֹיִם וְרָאוּ כָּל־אַפְסֵי־אָרֶץ אֵת יְשׁוּעַת
אֱלֹהֵינוּ: יא סוּרוּ סוּרוּ צְאוּ מִשָּׁם טָמֵא אַל־
תִּגָּעוּ צְאוּ מִתּוֹכָהּ הִבָּרוּ נֹשְׂאֵי כְּלֵי יְהוָֹה:
יב כִּי לֹא בְחִפָּזוֹן תֵּצֵאוּ וּבִמְנוּסָה לֹא תֵלֵכוּן
כִּי־הֹלֵךְ לִפְנֵיכֶם יְהוָֹה וּמְאַסִּפְכֶם אֱלֹהֵי
יִשְׂרָאֵל:

HAFTARATH KI THETZE הפטרת כי תצא

(Isaiah 54:1–10)

This is the fifth of "The Seven Haftaroth of Consolation." In the event that the Haftarah of Re'eh (p. 913) was not read on its proper Sabbath it is now read following this Haftarah.

Since God himself is consoling Israel, He urges her to rejoice.

54:1. "Sing, you barren woman who has not borne; burst out into song and jubilate, you who have not experienced birth pangs, for the children of the desolate one are more than the children of the married woman," says the Lord. 2. Widen the place of your tent, and let them stretch forth the curtains of your habitations, do not spare; lengthen your cords and strengthen your stakes. 3. For right and left shall you prevail, and your seed shall inherit nations and repeople desolate cities. 4. Fear not, for you shall not be ashamed, and be not embarrassed for you shall not be put to shame, for the shame of your youth you shall forget, and the disgrace of your widowhood you shall no longer remember. 5. For your Master is

א רָנִּי עֲקָרָה לֹא יָלָדָה פִּצְחִי רִנָּה וְצַהֲלִי לֹא־
חָלָה כִּי־רַבִּים בְּנֵי־שׁוֹמֵמָה מִבְּנֵי בְעוּלָה אָמַר
יְהוָֹה: ב הַרְחִיבִי | מְקוֹם אָהֳלֵךְ וִירִיעוֹת
מִשְׁכְּנוֹתַיִךְ יַטּוּ אַל־תַּחְשֹׂכִי הַאֲרִיכִי מֵיתָרַיִךְ
וִיתֵדֹתַיִךְ חַזֵּקִי: ג כִּי־יָמִין וּשְׂמֹאול תִּפְרֹצִי
וְזַרְעֵךְ גּוֹיִם יִירָשׁ וְעָרִים נְשַׁמּוֹת יוֹשִׁיבוּ:
ד אַל־תִּירְאִי כִּי־לֹא תֵבוֹשִׁי וְאַל־תִּכָּלְמִי כִּי־
לֹא תַחְפִּירִי כִּי בֹשֶׁת עֲלוּמַיִךְ תִּשְׁכָּחִי וְחֶרְפַּת
אַלְמְנוּתַיִךְ לֹא תִזְכְּרִי־עוֹד: ה כִּי בֹעֲלַיִךְ

your Maker, the Lord of Hosts is His name; and your Redeemer, the Holy One of Israel, shall be called the God of all the earth. 6. For, like a wife who is deserted and distressed in spirit has the Lord called you, and a wife of one's youth who was rejected, said your God. 7. "For a small moment have I forsaken you, and with great mercy will I gather you. 8. With a little wrath did I hide My countenance for a moment from you, and with everlasting kindness will I have compassion on you," said your Redeemer, the Lord. 9. "For this is to Me [as] the waters of Noah, as I swore that the waters of Noah shall never again pass over the earth, so have I sworn neither to be wroth with you nor to rebuke you. 10. For the mountains shall depart and the hills totter, but My kindness shall not depart from you, neither shall the covenant of My peace totter," says the Lord, Who has compassion on you.

עֹשַׂ֔יִךְ יְהֹוָ֥ה צְבָא֖וֹת שְׁמ֑וֹ וְגֹֽאֲלֵךְ֙ קְד֣וֹשׁ
יִשְׂרָאֵ֔ל אֱלֹהֵ֥י כָל־הָאָ֖רֶץ יִקָּרֵֽא: ו כִּֽי־כְאִשָּׁ֧ה
עֲזוּבָ֛ה וַעֲצ֥וּבַת ר֖וּחַ קְרָאָ֣ךְ יְהֹוָ֑ה וְאֵ֧שֶׁת
נְעוּרִ֛ים כִּ֥י תִמָּאֵ֖ס אָמַ֥ר אֱלֹהָֽיִךְ: ז בְּרֶ֥גַע קָטֹ֖ן
עֲזַבְתִּ֑יךְ וּבְרַחֲמִ֥ים גְּדוֹלִ֖ים אֲקַבְּצֵֽךְ: ח בְּשֶׁ֣צֶף
קֶ֗צֶף הִסְתַּ֨רְתִּי פָנַ֥י רֶ֙גַע֙ מִמֵּ֔ךְ וּבְחֶ֥סֶד עוֹלָ֖ם
רִחַמְתִּ֑יךְ אָמַ֥ר גֹּאֲלֵ֖ךְ יְהֹוָֽה: ט כִּי־מֵ֥י נֹ֙חַ֙ זֹ֣את
לִ֔י אֲשֶׁ֣ר נִשְׁבַּ֗עְתִּי מֵעֲבֹ֥ר מֵי־נֹ֛חַ ע֖וֹד עַל־
הָאָ֑רֶץ כֵּ֥ן נִשְׁבַּ֛עְתִּי מִקְּצֹ֥ף עָלַ֖יִךְ וּמִגְּעָר־בָּֽךְ:
י כִּ֤י הֶֽהָרִים֙ יָמ֔וּשׁוּ וְהַגְּבָע֖וֹת תְּמוּטֶ֑ינָה וְחַסְדִּ֞י
מֵאִתֵּ֣ךְ לֹֽא־יָמ֗וּשׁ וּבְרִ֤ית שְׁלוֹמִי֙ לֹ֣א תָמ֔וּט
אָמַ֥ר מְרַחֲמֵ֖ךְ יְהֹוָֽה:

HAFTARATH KI THAVO הפטרת כי תבוא

(Isaiah 60)

This is the sixth of "The Seven Haftaroth of Consolation."

God urges Israel to arise and shine for His light has shone upon them.

60:1. Arise, shine, for your light has come, and the glory of the Lord has shone upon you. 2. For behold, darkness shall cover the earth, and a gross darkness, the kingdoms, and the Lord shall shine upon you, and His glory shall appear over you. 3. And nations shall go by your light and kings by the brilliance of your shine. 4. Lift up your eyes all around and see, they all have gathered, they have come to you; your sons shall come from afar, and your daughters shall be raised on [their] side. 5. Then you shall see and be radiant, and your heart shall be startled and become enlarged, for the abundance of the west shall be turned over to you, the wealth of the nations that will come to you. 6. A multitude of camels shall cover you, the young camels of Midian and Ephah, all of them shall come from Sheba; gold and frankincense they shall carry, and the praises of the Lord they shall report. 7. All the sheep of Kedar shall be gathered to you; the rams of Nebaioth shall serve

א ק֥וּמִי א֖וֹרִי כִּ֣י בָ֣א אוֹרֵ֑ךְ וּכְב֥וֹד יְהֹוָ֖ה עָלַ֥יִךְ
זָרָֽח: ב כִּֽי־הִנֵּ֤ה הַחֹ֙שֶׁךְ֙ יְכַסֶּה־אֶ֔רֶץ וַעֲרָפֶ֖ל
לְאֻמִּ֑ים וְעָלַ֙יִךְ֙ יִזְרַ֣ח יְהֹוָ֔ה וּכְבוֹד֖וֹ עָלַ֥יִךְ יֵרָאֶֽה:
ג וְהָלְכ֥וּ גוֹיִ֖ם לְאוֹרֵ֑ךְ וּמְלָכִ֖ים לְנֹ֥גַהּ זַרְחֵֽךְ:
ד שְׂאִֽי־סָבִ֤יב עֵינַ֙יִךְ֙ וּרְאִ֔י כֻּלָּ֖ם נִקְבְּצ֣וּ בָֽאוּ־לָ֑ךְ
בָּנַ֙יִךְ֙ מֵרָח֣וֹק יָבֹ֔אוּ וּבְנֹתַ֖יִךְ עַל־צַ֥ד תֵּאָמַֽנָה:
ה אָ֤ז תִּרְאִי֙ וְנָהַ֔רְתְּ וּפָחַ֥ד וְרָחַ֖ב לְבָבֵ֑ךְ כִּֽי־
יֵהָפֵ֤ךְ עָלַ֙יִךְ֙ הֲמ֣וֹן יָ֔ם חֵ֥יל גּוֹיִ֖ם יָבֹ֥אוּ לָֽךְ:
ו שִֽׁפְעַ֨ת גְּמַלִּ֜ים תְּכַסֵּ֗ךְ בִּכְרֵ֤י מִדְיָן֙ וְעֵיפָ֔ה
כֻּלָּ֖ם מִשְּׁבָ֣א יָבֹ֑אוּ זָהָ֤ב וּלְבוֹנָה֙ יִשָּׂ֔אוּ וּתְהִלּ֥וֹת
יְהֹוָ֖ה יְבַשֵּֽׂרוּ: ז כָּל־צֹ֤אן קֵדָר֙ יִקָּ֣בְצוּ לָ֔ךְ אֵילֵ֥י

you; they shall be offered up with acceptance upon My altar, and I will glorify My glorious house. 8. Who are these that fly like a cloud and like doves to their cotes? 9. For the isles will hope for Me, and the ships of Tarshish [as] in the beginning, to bring your sons from afar, their silver and their gold with them, in the name of the Lord your God and for the Holy One of Israel, for He has glorified you. 10. And foreigners shall build your walls, and their kings shall serve you, for in My wrath I struck you, and in My grace have I had mercy on you. 11. And they shall open your gates always; day and night they shall not be closed, to bring to you the wealth of the nations and their kings in procession. 12. For the nation and the kingdom that shall not serve you shall perish, and the nations shall be destroyed. 13. The glory of the Lebanon shall come to you—box trees, firs, and cypresses together—to glorify the place of My Sanctuary, and the place of My feet I will honor. 14. And the children of your oppressors shall go to you bent over, and those who despised you shall prostrate themselves at the soles of your feet, and they shall call you "the city of the Lord, Zion of the Holy One of Israel." 15. Instead of your being forsaken and hated without a passerby, I will make you an everlasting pride, the joy of every generation. 16. And you shall suck the milk of nations, and the breast of kings you shall suck, and you shall know that I am the Lord, your Savior and your Redeemer, the Mighty One of Jacob. 17. Instead of the copper I will bring gold, and instead of the iron I will bring silver, and instead of the wood, copper, and instead of the stones, iron, and I will make your officers peace and your rulers righteousness. 18. Violence shall no longer be heard in your land, neither robbery nor destruction within your borders, and you shall call salvation your walls and your gates praise. 19. You shall no longer have the sun for light by day, and for brightness, the moon shall not give you light, but the Lord shall be to you for an everlasting light, and your God for your glory. 20. Your sun shall no longer set, neither shall your moon be gathered in, for the Lord shall be to you for an everlasting light, and the days of your

נְבָיוֹת יְשָׁרְתוּנֶךְ יַעֲלוּ עַל־רָצוֹן מִזְבְּחִי וּבֵית תִּפְאַרְתִּי אֲפָאֵר: ח מִי־אֵלֶּה כָּעָב תְּעוּפֶינָה וְכַיּוֹנִים אֶל־אֲרֻבֹּתֵיהֶם: ט כִּי־לִי ׀ אִיִּים יְקַוּוּ וָאֳנִיּוֹת תַּרְשִׁישׁ בָּרִאשֹׁנָה לְהָבִיא בָנַיִךְ מֵרָחוֹק כַּסְפָּם וּזְהָבָם אִתָּם לְשֵׁם יְהוָה אֱלֹהַיִךְ וְלִקְדוֹשׁ יִשְׂרָאֵל כִּי פֵאֲרָךְ: י וּבָנוּ בְנֵי־נֵכָר חֹמֹתַיִךְ וּמַלְכֵיהֶם יְשָׁרְתוּנֶךְ כִּי בְקִצְפִּי הִכִּיתִיךְ וּבִרְצוֹנִי רִחַמְתִּיךְ: יא וּפִתְּחוּ שְׁעָרַיִךְ תָּמִיד יוֹמָם וָלַיְלָה לֹא יִסָּגֵרוּ לְהָבִיא אֵלַיִךְ חֵיל גּוֹיִם וּמַלְכֵיהֶם נְהוּגִים: יב כִּי־הַגּוֹי וְהַמַּמְלָכָה אֲשֶׁר לֹא־יַעַבְדוּךְ יֹאבֵדוּ וְהַגּוֹיִם חָרֹב יֶחֱרָבוּ: יג כְּבוֹד הַלְּבָנוֹן אֵלַיִךְ יָבוֹא בְּרוֹשׁ תִּדְהָר וּתְאַשּׁוּר יַחְדָּו לְפָאֵר מְקוֹם מִקְדָּשִׁי וּמְקוֹם רַגְלַי אֲכַבֵּד: יד וְהָלְכוּ אֵלַיִךְ שְׁחוֹחַ בְּנֵי מְעַנַּיִךְ וְהִשְׁתַּחֲווּ עַל־כַּפּוֹת רַגְלַיִךְ כָּל־מְנַאֲצָיִךְ וְקָרְאוּ לָךְ עִיר יְהוָה צִיּוֹן קְדוֹשׁ יִשְׂרָאֵל: טו תַּחַת הֱיוֹתֵךְ עֲזוּבָה וּשְׂנוּאָה וְאֵין עוֹבֵר וְשַׂמְתִּיךְ לִגְאוֹן עוֹלָם מְשׂוֹשׂ דּוֹר וָדוֹר: טז וְיָנַקְתְּ חֲלֵב גּוֹיִם וְשֹׁד מְלָכִים תִּינָקִי וְיָדַעַתְּ כִּי אֲנִי יְהוָה מוֹשִׁיעֵךְ וְגֹאֲלֵךְ אֲבִיר יַעֲקֹב: יז תַּחַת הַנְּחֹשֶׁת אָבִיא זָהָב וְתַחַת הַבַּרְזֶל אָבִיא כֶסֶף וְתַחַת הָעֵצִים נְחֹשֶׁת וְתַחַת הָאֲבָנִים בַּרְזֶל וְשַׂמְתִּי פְקֻדָּתֵךְ שָׁלוֹם וְנֹגְשַׂיִךְ צְדָקָה: יח לֹא־יִשָּׁמַע עוֹד חָמָס בְּאַרְצֵךְ שֹׁד וָשֶׁבֶר בִּגְבוּלָיִךְ וְקָרָאת יְשׁוּעָה חוֹמֹתַיִךְ וּשְׁעָרַיִךְ תְּהִלָּה: יט לֹא־יִהְיֶה־לָּךְ עוֹד הַשֶּׁמֶשׁ לְאוֹר יוֹמָם וּלְנֹגַהּ הַיָּרֵחַ לֹא־יָאִיר לָךְ וְהָיָה־לָךְ יְהוָה לְאוֹר עוֹלָם וֵאלֹהַיִךְ לְתִפְאַרְתֵּךְ: כ לֹא־יָבוֹא עוֹד שִׁמְשֵׁךְ וִירֵחֵךְ לֹא יֵאָסֵף כִּי יְהוָה יִהְיֶה־לָּךְ לְאוֹר עוֹלָם וְשָׁלְמוּ יְמֵי אֶבְלֵךְ:

כא וְעַמֵּךְ כֻּלָּם צַדִּיקִים לְעוֹלָם יִירְשׁוּ אָרֶץ
נֵצֶר מַטָּעַו (מטעי קרי) מַעֲשֵׂה יָדַי לְהִתְפָּאֵר:
כב הַקָּטֹן יִהְיֶה לָאֶלֶף וְהַצָּעִיר לְגוֹי עָצוּם אֲנִי
יְהֹוָה בְּעִתָּהּ אֲחִישֶׁנָּה:

mourning shall be completed. 21. And your people, all of them righteous, shall inherit the land forever, a scion of My planting, the work of My hands in which I will glory. 22. The smallest shall become a thousand and the least a mighty nation; I am the Lord, in its time I will hasten it.

HAFTARATH NITZAVIM הפטרת נצבים
(Isaiah 61:10–63:9)

This is the last of "The Seven Haftaroth of Consolation." This Haftarah is always read on the Sabbath preceding Rosh Hashanah, regardless of whether or not the next Sidra, Vayelech, is read together with this Sidra.

Israel replies: "I will rejoice with the Lord. . . ."

י שׂוֹשׂ אָשִׂישׂ בַּיהֹוָה תָּגֵל נַפְשִׁי בֵּאלֹהַי כִּי
הִלְבִּישַׁנִי בִּגְדֵי־יֶשַׁע מְעִיל צְדָקָה יְעָטָנִי כֶּחָתָן
יְכַהֵן פְּאֵר וְכַכַּלָּה תַּעְדֶּה כֵלֶיהָ: יא כִּי כָאָרֶץ
תּוֹצִיא צִמְחָהּ וּכְגַנָּה זֵרוּעֶיהָ תַצְמִיחַ כֵּן |
אֲדֹנָי יֱהֹוִה יַצְמִיחַ צְדָקָה וּתְהִלָּה נֶגֶד כָּל־
הַגּוֹיִם: א לְמַעַן צִיּוֹן לֹא אֶחֱשֶׁה וּלְמַעַן
יְרוּשָׁלַ͏ִם לֹא אֶשְׁקוֹט עַד־יֵצֵא כַנֹּגַהּ צִדְקָהּ
וִישׁוּעָתָהּ כְּלַפִּיד יִבְעָר: ב וְרָאוּ גוֹיִם צִדְקֵךְ
וְכָל־מְלָכִים כְּבוֹדֵךְ וְקֹרָא לָךְ שֵׁם חָדָשׁ אֲשֶׁר
פִּי יְהֹוָה יִקֳּבֶנּוּ: ג וְהָיִיתְ עֲטֶרֶת תִּפְאֶרֶת בְּיַד־
יְהֹוָה וּצְנוֹף (וצניף קרי) מְלוּכָה בְּכַף־אֱלֹהָיִךְ:
ד לֹא־יֵאָמֵר לָךְ עוֹד עֲזוּבָה וּלְאַרְצֵךְ לֹא־
יֵאָמֵר עוֹד שְׁמָמָה כִּי לָךְ יִקָּרֵא חֶפְצִי־בָהּ
וּלְאַרְצֵךְ בְּעוּלָה כִּי־חָפֵץ יְהֹוָה בָּךְ וְאַרְצֵךְ
תִּבָּעֵל: ה כִּי־יִבְעַל בָּחוּר בְּתוּלָה יִבְעָלוּךְ בָּנָיִךְ
וּמְשׂוֹשׂ חָתָן עַל־כַּלָּה יָשִׂישׂ עָלַיִךְ אֱלֹהָיִךְ:
ו עַל־חוֹמֹתַיִךְ יְרוּשָׁלַ͏ִם הִפְקַדְתִּי שֹׁמְרִים כָּל־
הַיּוֹם וְכָל־הַלַּיְלָה תָּמִיד לֹא יֶחֱשׁוּ הַמַּזְכִּרִים
אֶת־יְהֹוָה אַל־דֳּמִי לָכֶם: ז וְאַל־תִּתְּנוּ דֳמִי לוֹ
עַד־יְכוֹנֵן וְעַד־יָשִׂים אֶת־יְרוּשָׁלַ͏ִם תְּהִלָּה

61:10. I will rejoice with the Lord; my soul shall exult with my God, for He has attired me with garments of salvation, with a robe of righteousness He has enwrapped me; like a bridegroom, who, priestlike, dons garments of glory, and like a bride, who adorns herself with her jewelry. 11. For, like the earth, which gives forth its plants, and like a garden that causes its seeds to grow, so shall the Lord God cause righteousness and praise to grow opposite all the nations. 62:1. For the sake of Zion, I will not be silent, and for the sake of Jerusalem I will not rest, until her righteousness comes out like brilliance, and her salvation burns like a torch. 2. And nations shall see your righteousness, and all kings your glory, and you shall be called a new name, which the mouth of the Lord shall pronounce. 3. And you shall be a crown of glory in the hand of the Lord and a kingly diadem in the hand of your God. 4. No longer shall "forsaken" be said of you, and "desolate" shall no longer be said of your land, for you shall be called "My desire is in her," and your land, "inhabited," for the Lord desires you, and your land shall be inhabited. 5. As a young man lives with a virgin, so shall your children live in you, and the rejoicing of a bridegroom over a bride shall your God rejoice over you. 6. On your walls, O Jerusalem, I have appointed watchmen; all day and all night, they shall never be silent; those who remind the Lord, be not silent. 7. And give Him no rest, until He establishes and until He makes Jerusalem a praise in the land. 8. The Lord swore by His right hand and by the arm of His strength; I will no longer give your grain to your enemies, and foreigners shall no longer drink your wine for which you have toiled. 9. But its gatherers shall eat it, and they shall praise the Lord; and its gatherers shall drink it in My holy courts. 10. Pass, pass through the portals, clear the way of the people, pave the highway, clear it of stones, lift up a banner over the peoples. 11. Behold, the Lord announced to the end of the earth, "Say to the daughter of Zion, 'Behold your salvation has come.'" Behold His reward is with Him, and His wage is before Him. 12. And they shall call them the holy people, those redeemed by the Lord, and you shall be called "sought, a city not forsaken." 63:1. Who is this coming from Edom, with soiled garments, from Bozrah, this one [Who was] stately in His apparel, girded with the greatness of His strength? "I speak with righteousness, great to save." 2. Why is Your clothing red, and Your attire like [that of] one who trod in a wine press? 3. "A wine press I trod alone, and from the peoples, none was with Me; and I trod them with My wrath, and I trampled them with My fury, and their life blood sprinkled on My garments, and all My clothing I soiled. 4. For a day of vengeance was in My heart, and the year of My redemption has arrived. 5. And I looked, and there was no one helping, and I was astounded, and there was no one supporting; and My arm saved for Me, and My fury — that supported Me. 6. And I trod peoples with My wrath, and I intoxicated them with My fury, and I brought their power down to the earth." 7. The kind acts of the Lord I will mention, the praises of the Lord, according to all that the Lord bestowed upon us, and much good to the house of Israel, which He bestowed upon them according to His mercies and according to His many kind acts. 8. And He said, "They are but My people, children who will not deal falsely." And He became their Savior. 9. In all their trouble, He did not trouble [them], and the angel of His Presence saved them; with His love and with His pity He redeemed them, and He bore them, and He carried them all the days of old.

בָּאָרֶץ׃ ח נִשְׁבַּע יְהֹוָה בִּימִינוֹ וּבִזְרוֹעַ עֻזּוֹ
אִם־אֶתֵּן אֶת־דְּגָנֵךְ עוֹד מַאֲכָל לְאֹיְבַיִךְ וְאִם־
יִשְׁתּוּ בְנֵי־נֵכָר תִּירוֹשֵׁךְ אֲשֶׁר יָגַעַתְּ בּוֹ׃ ט כִּי
מְאַסְפָיו יֹאכְלֻהוּ וְהִלְלוּ אֶת־יְהֹוָה וּמְקַבְּצָיו
יִשְׁתֻּהוּ בְּחַצְרוֹת קָדְשִׁי׃ י עִבְרוּ עִבְרוּ
בַּשְּׁעָרִים פַּנּוּ דֶּרֶךְ הָעָם סֹלּוּ סֹלּוּ הַמְסִלָּה
סַקְּלוּ מֵאֶבֶן הָרִימוּ נֵס עַל־הָעַמִּים׃ יא הִנֵּה
יְהֹוָה הִשְׁמִיעַ אֶל־קְצֵה הָאָרֶץ אִמְרוּ לְבַת־
צִיּוֹן הִנֵּה יִשְׁעֵךְ בָּא הִנֵּה שְׂכָרוֹ אִתּוֹ וּפְעֻלָּתוֹ
לְפָנָיו׃ יב וְקָרְאוּ לָהֶם עַם־הַקֹּדֶשׁ גְּאוּלֵי יְהֹוָה
וְלָךְ יִקָּרֵא דְרוּשָׁה עִיר לֹא נֶעֱזָבָה׃ א מִי־זֶה ׀
בָּא מֵאֱדוֹם חֲמוּץ בְּגָדִים מִבָּצְרָה זֶה הָדוּר
בִּלְבוּשׁוֹ צֹעֶה בְּרֹב כֹּחוֹ אֲנִי מְדַבֵּר בִּצְדָקָה רַב
לְהוֹשִׁיעַ׃ ב מַדּוּעַ אָדֹם לִלְבוּשֶׁךָ וּבְגָדֶיךָ
כְּדֹרֵךְ בְּגַת׃ ג פּוּרָה ׀ דָּרַכְתִּי לְבַדִּי וּמֵעַמִּים
אֵין־אִישׁ אִתִּי וְאֶדְרְכֵם בְּאַפִּי וְאֶרְמְסֵם
בַּחֲמָתִי וְיֵז נִצְחָם עַל־בְּגָדַי וְכָל־מַלְבּוּשַׁי
אֶגְאָלְתִּי׃ ד כִּי יוֹם נָקָם בְּלִבִּי וּשְׁנַת גְּאוּלַי
בָּאָה׃ ה וְאַבִּיט וְאֵין עֹזֵר וְאֶשְׁתּוֹמֵם וְאֵין
סוֹמֵךְ וַתּוֹשַׁע לִי זְרֹעִי וַחֲמָתִי הִיא סְמָכָתְנִי׃
ו וְאָבוּס עַמִּים בְּאַפִּי וַאֲשַׁכְּרֵם בַּחֲמָתִי
וְאוֹרִיד לָאָרֶץ נִצְחָם׃ ז חַסְדֵי יְהֹוָה ׀ אַזְכִּיר
תְּהִלֹּת יְהֹוָה כְּעַל כֹּל אֲשֶׁר־גְּמָלָנוּ יְהֹוָה וְרַב־
טוּב לְבֵית יִשְׂרָאֵל אֲשֶׁר־גְּמָלָם כְּרַחֲמָיו וּכְרֹב
חֲסָדָיו׃ ח וַיֹּאמֶר אַךְ־עַמִּי הֵמָּה בָּנִים לֹא
יְשַׁקֵּרוּ וַיְהִי לָהֶם לְמוֹשִׁיעַ׃ ט בְּכָל־צָרָתָם ׀
לֹא (לו קרי) צָר וּמַלְאַךְ פָּנָיו הוֹשִׁיעָם בְּאַהֲבָתוֹ
וּבְחֶמְלָתוֹ הוּא גְאָלָם וַיְנַטְּלֵם וַיְנַשְּׂאֵם כָּל־יְמֵי
עוֹלָם׃

HAFTARATH VAYELEKH הפטרת וילך

(Hosea 14:2–10; Micah 7:18–20; Joel 2:11–27)

If this Sidra is read on the Sabbath before Rosh Hashanah together with Nitzavim, the Haftarah for Nitzavim is read instead of this one. However, if Vayelekh is read separately, after Rosh Hashanah, the custom prevailing among both Ashkenazim and Sephardim is to read *Shuvah Yisrael* (Hosea 14:2–10).

As regards the selections from Micah and Joel, there is some controversy. These selections were added to the Haftarah because the passage from Hosea ends on a sad note, and it was considered proper to conclude the Haftarah on a more cheerful note. The addition of the verses from Micah originates from Abudraham, and the addition from Joel dates from the Tosafists. It appears that originally, the verses from Micah were added by Sephardim, and those from Joel by Ashkenazim. In fact, the present-day custom among Sephardim, as well as among Chabad Chassidim, is to add only the verses from Micah. Similarly, in the Roedelheim Chumash, and also in *Noheg Katzon Yosef*, we find only the verses from Joel. According to the 18th-century work, *Eliyah Rabbah*, the custom in Prague was to read both Micah and Joel. But *Dagul Merevavah*, by R. Ezekiel Landau, questions the necessity for reading both passages, pointing out that either one of these suffices to end the Haftarah on a positive note. The author of this work states that the verses from Micah should be read if Vayyelech is read on the Sabbath between Rosh Hashanah and Yom Kippur (Shabbbath Shuvah), and the verses from Joel, if the Sidra on that Sabbath is Ha'azinu. *Iggroth Moshe*, the treatise by R. Moshe Feinstein (*Orach Chaim* Vol. I, 174) states that if the Haftarah is read from a printed book or a parchment scroll containing only the Haftaroth, only the passage from Micah should be read, since it is briefer than that from Joel, and would entail less trouble for the congregation. However, if the Haftarah is read from a scroll containing the entire book of the Twelve Prophets, only the passage of Joel should be read. The passage from Micah is to be omitted since the book of Micah is at some distance in sequence from Hosea and Joel, and the rolling of the scroll would cause an unseemly interruption in the reading. The custom in the Holy Land is to read the passage from Joel first and the passage from Micah thereafter. However, the prevalent custom is to read the Haftarah in the order printed here, as it is stated in Eliyah Rabbah 603.

This Haftarah deals with repentance; suitable for the Sabbath between Rosh Ha-Shanah and Yom Kippur.

14:2. Return, O Israel, to the Lord your God, for you have stumbled in your iniquity. 3. Take words with you and return to the Lord; say to Him, "Forgive all iniquity and take [our] good [deeds], and let us pay [the sacrifices of] bulls [with] our lips." 4. Assyria will not help us; we will not ride on a horse, and we will no longer say, "our god" to the work of our hands, for through You [alone] shall an orphan find mercy. 5. I will heal their perverseness, and I will love them in free-willed devotion, for My wrath has receded from him. 6. I will be like dew to Israel, he shall blossom like a rose, and his roots shall spread like the Lebanon. 7. His tender boughs shall spread, and his beauty

שׁוּבָה יִשְׂרָאֵל עַד יְהוָה אֱלֹהֶיךָ כִּי כָשַׁלְתָּ
עֲוֺנֶךָ: ג קְחוּ עִמָּכֶם דְּבָרִים וְשׁוּבוּ אֶל־יְהוָה
מְרוּ אֵלָיו כָּל־תִּשָּׂא עָוֺן וְקַח־טוֹב וּנְשַׁלְּמָה
רִים שְׂפָתֵינוּ: ד אַשּׁוּר ׀ לֹא יוֹשִׁיעֵנוּ עַל־
וּס לֹא נִרְכָּב וְלֹא־נֹאמַר עוֹד אֱלֹהֵינוּ
מַעֲשֵׂה יָדֵינוּ אֲשֶׁר־בְּךָ יְרֻחַם יָתוֹם: ה אֶרְפָּא
שׁוּבָתָם אֹהֲבֵם נְדָבָה כִּי שָׁב אַפִּי מִמֶּנּוּ:
אֶהְיֶה כַטַּל לְיִשְׂרָאֵל יִפְרַח כַּשּׁוֹשַׁנָּה וְיַךְ
שָׁרָשָׁיו כַּלְּבָנוֹן: ז יֵלְכוּ יֹנְקוֹתָיו וִיהִי כַזַּיִת

shall be like an olive tree, and he shall have a fragrance like the Lebanon. 8. Those who sat in his shadow shall return; they shall revive themselves like corn, and they shall blossom like a vine; his fragrance shall be like the wine of the Lebanon. 9. Ephraim [shall say], "What more do I have with idols?" I answered and I shall see him; I am like a leafy cypress; because of Me, your fruit is found. 10. Who is wise and shall understand these, understanding and shall know them? For the ways of the Lord are straight; and the righteous shall walk in them, and the transgressors shall stumble in them. (*The following is added by Sephardim and by many Ashkenazim:*) Micah 7:18. Who is a God like You, forgiving iniquity and passing over transgression of the remnant of His heritage; He does not retain His wrath forever, for He desires kindness. 19. He shall return to grant us mercy; He shall subdue our iniquities; and You shall cast into the depths of the sea all their sins. 20. You shall give truth to Jacob, kindness to Abraham, as You swore to our forefathers from days of old. (*Some Ashkenazim commence here:*) Joel 2:11. And the Lord gave forth His voice before His host, for His camp is very great; those who do His will are very strong, for the day of the Lord is great and very awesome, who can contain it? 12. And even now, says the Lord, return to Me with all your heart and with fasting and weeping and lamenting. 13. And rend your heart and not your clothing, and return to the Lord your God, for He is gracious and merciful, slow to anger and with much kindness, and retracting evil. 14. Whoever knows shall return and regret, and he shall leave after him blessing, meal offering and oblation to the Lord your God. (*Some Ashkenazim commence here:*) 15. Sound the shofar in Zion, proclaim a fast, call an assembly. 16. Gather the people, prepare the congregation, assemble the elders, gather the small children and the babes at the breast; let the bridegroom leave his chamber, and the bride, her bridal closet. 17. Between the porch and the altar, the priests, the ministers of the Lord, shall weep, and they shall say, "O Lord, pity

הוֹדוֹ וְרֵיחַ לוֹ כַּלְּבָנוֹן: ח יָשֻׁבוּ יֹשְׁבֵי בְצִלּוֹ יְחַיּוּ דָגָן וְיִפְרְחוּ כַגָּפֶן זִכְרוֹ כְּיֵין לְבָנוֹן: ט אֶפְרַיִם מַה־לִּי עוֹד לָעֲצַבִּים אֲנִי עָנִיתִי וַאֲשׁוּרֶנּוּ אֲנִי כִּבְרוֹשׁ רַעֲנָן מִמֶּנִּי פֶּרְיְךָ נִמְצָא: י מִי חָכָם וְיָבֵן אֵלֶּה נָבוֹן וְיֵדָעֵם כִּי־יְשָׁרִים דַּרְכֵי יְהֹוָה וְצַדִּקִים יֵלְכוּ בָם וּפֹשְׁעִים יִכָּשְׁלוּ בָם: (הספרדים, וכן הרבה אשכנזים, מוסיפים) יח מִי־אֵל כָּמוֹךָ נֹשֵׂא עָוֹן וְעֹבֵר עַל־פֶּשַׁע לִשְׁאֵרִית נַחֲלָתוֹ לֹא־הֶחֱזִיק לָעַד אַפּוֹ כִּי־חָפֵץ חֶסֶד הוּא: יט יָשׁוּב יְרַחֲמֵנוּ יִכְבֹּשׁ עֲוֹנֹתֵינוּ וְתַשְׁלִיךְ בִּמְצֻלוֹת יָם כָּל־חַטֹּאתָם: כ תִּתֵּן אֱמֶת לְיַעֲקֹב חֶסֶד לְאַבְרָהָם אֲשֶׁר־נִשְׁבַּעְתָּ לַאֲבֹתֵינוּ מִימֵי קֶדֶם: (מקצת אשכנזים מתחילין כאן) יא וַיהֹוָה נָתַן קוֹלוֹ לִפְנֵי חֵילוֹ כִּי רַב מְאֹד מַחֲנֵהוּ כִּי עָצוּם עֹשֵׂה דְבָרוֹ כִּי־גָדוֹל יוֹם־יְהֹוָה וְנוֹרָא מְאֹד וּמִי יְכִילֶנּוּ: יב וְגַם־עַתָּה נְאֻם־יְהֹוָה שֻׁבוּ עָדַי בְּכָל־לְבַבְכֶם וּבְצוֹם וּבִבְכִי וּבְמִסְפֵּד: יג וְקִרְעוּ לְבַבְכֶם וְאַל־בִּגְדֵיכֶם וְשׁוּבוּ אֶל־יְהֹוָה אֱלֹהֵיכֶם כִּי־חַנּוּן וְרַחוּם הוּא אֶרֶךְ אַפַּיִם וְרַב־חֶסֶד וְנִחָם עַל־הָרָעָה: יד מִי יוֹדֵעַ יָשׁוּב וְנִחָם וְהִשְׁאִיר אַחֲרָיו בְּרָכָה מִנְחָה וָנֶסֶךְ לַיהֹוָה אֱלֹהֵיכֶם: (מקצת אשכנזים מתחילין כאן) טו תִּקְעוּ שׁוֹפָר בְּצִיּוֹן קַדְּשׁוּ־צוֹם קִרְאוּ עֲצָרָה: טז אִסְפוּ־עָם קַדְּשׁוּ קָהָל קִבְצוּ זְקֵנִים אִסְפוּ עוֹלָלִים וְיֹנְקֵי שָׁדָיִם יֵצֵא חָתָן מֵחֶדְרוֹ וְכַלָּה מֵחֻפָּתָהּ: יז בֵּין הָאוּלָם וְלַמִּזְבֵּחַ יִבְכּוּ הַכֹּהֲנִים מְשָׁרְתֵי יְהֹוָה וְיֹאמְרוּ חוּסָה יְהֹוָה

Your people, and let not Your heritage be disgraced, that nations should rule over them; why should it be said among the peoples, "Where is their God?" 18. And the Lord was jealous for His land, and He pitied His people. 19. And the Lord replied and said to His people, "Behold I send you the corn and the wine and the oil, and you shall be sated therefrom, and I will no longer make you a disgrace among the nations. 20. And the northern one I will remove far from you, and I will exile him to a land of waste and desolation—his beginning into the eastern sea and his end into the western sea—and his stench shall rise, and his decay shall come up, for he has done great [evils]. 21. Fear not, O land, rejoice and be happy, for the Lord has done great things. 22. Fear not, O beasts of the field, for the pastures of the desert have grown verdant, for the tree has borne its fruit, the fig tree and the vine have given forth their strength. 23. And you children of Zion, rejoice and be happy with the Lord your God, for He has given you the teacher of righteousness, and He has brought down for you the former rain and the latter rain in the first month. 24. And the threshing floors shall be filled with pure grain, and the pits shall sound with wine and oil. 25. And I will restore to you the years that the numerous locusts, the nibbling locusts, the destroying locusts, and the punishing locusts have eaten—My great host that I have sent against you. 26. And you shall eat to satiety, and you shall praise the name of the Lord your God Who has dealt wondrously with you, and My people shall never be ashamed. 27. And you shall know that I am in the midst of Israel, and I am the Lord your God, and there is no other, and My people shall never be ashamed.

עַל־עַמֶּ֔ךָ וְאַל־תִּתֵּ֨ן נַחֲלָתְךָ֤ לְחֶרְפָּה֙ לִמְשָׁל־בָּ֣ם גּוֹיִ֔ם לָ֚מָּה יֹאמְר֣וּ בָֽעַמִּ֔ים אַיֵּ֖ה אֱלֹֽהֵיהֶֽם: יח וַיְקַנֵּ֥א יְהֹוָ֖ה לְאַרְצ֑וֹ וַיַּחְמֹ֖ל עַל־עַמּֽוֹ: יט וַיַּ֨עַן יְהֹוָ֜ה וַיֹּ֣אמֶר לְעַמּ֗וֹ הִנְנִ֨י שֹׁלֵ֤חַ לָכֶם֙ אֶת־הַדָּגָן֙ וְהַתִּיר֣וֹשׁ וְהַיִּצְהָ֔ר וּשְׂבַעְתֶּ֖ם אֹת֑וֹ וְלֹא־אֶתֵּ֨ן אֶתְכֶ֥ם ע֛וֹד חֶרְפָּ֖ה בַּגּוֹיִֽם: כ וְאֶת־הַצְּפוֹנִ֞י אַרְחִ֣יק מֵֽעֲלֵיכֶ֗ם וְהִדַּחְתִּיו֘ אֶל־אֶ֣רֶץ צִיָּ֣ה וּשְׁמָמָה֒ אֶת־פָּנָ֗יו אֶל־הַיָּם֙ הַקַּדְמֹנִ֔י וְסֹפ֖וֹ אֶל־הַיָּ֣ם הָאַֽחֲר֑וֹן וְעָלָ֣ה בָאְשׁ֗וֹ וְתַ֙עַל֙ צַֽחֲנָת֔וֹ כִּ֥י הִגְדִּ֖יל לַֽעֲשֽׂוֹת: כא אַל־תִּֽירְאִ֖י אֲדָמָ֑ה גִּ֣ילִי וּשְׂמָ֔חִי כִּֽי־הִגְדִּ֥יל יְהֹוָ֖ה לַֽעֲשֽׂוֹת: כב אַל־תִּֽירְאוּ֙ בַּֽהֲמ֣וֹת שָׂדַ֔י כִּ֥י דָֽשְׁא֖וּ נְא֣וֹת מִדְבָּ֑ר כִּי־עֵץ֙ נָשָׂ֣א פִרְי֔וֹ תְּאֵנָ֥ה וָגֶ֖פֶן נָֽתְנ֥וּ חֵילָֽם: כג וּבְנֵ֣י צִיּ֗וֹן גִּ֚ילוּ וְשִׂמְחוּ֙ בַּֽיהֹוָ֣ה אֱלֹֽהֵיכֶ֔ם כִּֽי־נָתַ֥ן לָכֶ֛ם אֶת־הַמּוֹרֶ֖ה לִצְדָקָ֑ה וַיּ֣וֹרֶד לָכֶ֗ם גֶּ֚שֶׁם מוֹרֶ֣ה וּמַלְק֔וֹשׁ בָּרִאשֽׁוֹן: כד וּמָֽלְא֥וּ הַגֳּרָנ֖וֹת בָּ֑ר וְהֵשִׁ֥יקוּ הַיְקָבִ֖ים תִּיר֥וֹשׁ וְיִצְהָֽר: כה וְשִׁלַּמְתִּ֤י לָכֶם֙ אֶת־הַשָּׁנִ֔ים אֲשֶׁר֙ אָכַ֣ל הָֽאַרְבֶּ֔ה הַיֶּ֖לֶק וְהֶֽחָסִ֣יל וְהַגָּזָ֑ם חֵילִי֙ הַגָּד֔וֹל אֲשֶׁ֥ר שִׁלַּ֖חְתִּי בָּכֶֽם: כו וַֽאֲכַלְתֶּ֤ם אָכוֹל֙ וְשָׂב֔וֹעַ וְהִלַּלְתֶּ֗ם אֶת־שֵׁ֤ם יְהֹוָה֙ אֱלֹ֣הֵיכֶ֔ם אֲשֶׁר־עָשָׂ֥ה עִמָּכֶ֖ם לְהַפְלִ֑יא וְלֹֽא־יֵבֹ֥שׁוּ עַמִּ֖י לְעוֹלָֽם: כז וִֽידַעְתֶּ֗ם כִּ֣י בְקֶ֤רֶב יִשְׂרָאֵל֙ אָ֔נִי וַֽאֲנִ֛י יְהֹוָ֥ה אֱלֹֽהֵיכֶ֖ם וְאֵ֣ין ע֑וֹד וְלֹֽא־יֵבֹ֥שׁוּ עַמִּ֖י לְעוֹלָֽם:

HAFTARATH VAYELEKH הפטרת וילך

(Isaiah 55:6–56:8)

According to some authorities, if Vayelekh is read by itself between Rosh Hashanah and Yom Kippur, the following Haftarah is read. Then "Shuvah Yisrael" is read after Yom Kippur, for Ha'azinu. These two Haftaroth form "The Two Haftaroth of Repentance." The prevalent custom is not in accordance with these authorities, however; rather this Haftarah is read on the Fast of Gedaliah at minchah, as it is on other fast days, and "Shuvah" is read for Vayelekh.

This Haftarah is read during the Ten Days of Pentenance, in accordance with the Rabbinic maxim that its opening phrase, "Seek the Lord when He is found. . . .," refers to this period.

55:6. Seek the Lord when He is found; call Him when He is near. 7. The wicked shall give up his way, and the man of iniquity his thoughts, and he shall return to the Lord, Who shall have mercy upon him, and to our God, for He will freely pardon. 8. "For My thoughts are not your thoughts, neither are your ways My ways," says the Lord. 9. "As the heavens are higher than the earth, so are My ways higher than your ways, and My thoughts, [higher] than your thoughts. 10. For, just as the rain and the snow fall from the heavens, and it does not return there, unless it has satiated the earth and fructified it and furthered its growth, and has given seed to the sower and bread to the eater, 11. so shall be My word that emanates from My mouth; it shall not return to Me empty, unless it has done what I desire and has made prosperous the one to whom I sent it. 12. For with joy shall you go forth, and with peace shall you be brought; the mountains and the hills shall burst into song before you, and all the trees of the field shall clap hands. 13. Instead of the briar, a cypress shall rise, and instead of the nettle, a myrtle shall rise, and it shall be for the Lord as a name, as an everlasting sign, which shall not be discontinued." 56:1. So says the Lord, "Keep justice and practice righteousness, for My salvation is near to come, and My benevolence, to be revealed. 2. Fortunate is the man who will do this and the person who will hold fast to it, he who keeps the Sabbath from profaning it and guards his hand from doing any evil. 3. Now let not the foreigner who joined the Lord say, "The Lord will surely separate me from His people"; and let not the eunuch

ו דִּרְשׁוּ יְהוָה בְּהִמָּצְאוֹ קְרָאֻהוּ בִּהְיוֹתוֹ קָרוֹב:
ז יַעֲזֹב רָשָׁע דַּרְכּוֹ וְאִישׁ אָוֶן מַחְשְׁבֹתָיו וְיָשֹׁב
אֶל־יְהוָה וִירַחֲמֵהוּ וְאֶל־אֱלֹהֵינוּ כִּי־יַרְבֶּה
לִסְלוֹחַ: ח כִּי לֹא מַחְשְׁבוֹתַי מַחְשְׁבוֹתֵיכֶם
וְלֹא דַרְכֵיכֶם דְּרָכָי נְאֻם יְהוָה: ט כִּי־גָבְהוּ
שָׁמַיִם מֵאָרֶץ כֵּן גָּבְהוּ דְרָכַי מִדַּרְכֵיכֶם
וּמַחְשְׁבֹתַי מִמַּחְשְׁבֹתֵיכֶם: י כִּי כַּאֲשֶׁר יֵרֵד
הַגֶּשֶׁם וְהַשֶּׁלֶג מִן־הַשָּׁמַיִם וְשָׁמָּה לֹא יָשׁוּב כִּי
אִם־הִרְוָה אֶת־הָאָרֶץ וְהוֹלִידָהּ וְהִצְמִיחָהּ וְנָתַן
זֶרַע לַזֹּרֵעַ וְלֶחֶם לָאֹכֵל: יא כֵּן יִהְיֶה דְבָרִי
אֲשֶׁר יֵצֵא מִפִּי לֹא־יָשׁוּב אֵלַי רֵיקָם כִּי אִם־
עָשָׂה אֶת־אֲשֶׁר חָפַצְתִּי וְהִצְלִיחַ אֲשֶׁר
שְׁלַחְתִּיו: יב כִּי־בְשִׂמְחָה תֵצֵאוּ וּבְשָׁלוֹם
תּוּבָלוּן הֶהָרִים וְהַגְּבָעוֹת יִפְצְחוּ לִפְנֵיכֶם רִנָּה
וְכָל־עֲצֵי הַשָּׂדֶה יִמְחֲאוּ־כָף: יג תַּחַת הַנַּעֲצוּץ
יַעֲלֶה בְרוֹשׁ וְתַחַת הַסִּרְפַּד יַעֲלֶה הֲדַס וְהָיָה
לַיהוָה לְשֵׁם לְאוֹת עוֹלָם לֹא יִכָּרֵת: א כֹּה
אָמַר יְהוָה שִׁמְרוּ מִשְׁפָּט וַעֲשׂוּ צְדָקָה כִּי־
קְרוֹבָה יְשׁוּעָתִי לָבוֹא וְצִדְקָתִי לְהִגָּלוֹת:
ב אַשְׁרֵי אֱנוֹשׁ יַעֲשֶׂה־זֹּאת וּבֶן־אָדָם יַחֲזִיק
בָּהּ שֹׁמֵר שַׁבָּת מֵחַלְּלוֹ וְשֹׁמֵר יָדוֹ מֵעֲשׂוֹת
כָּל־רָע: ג וְאַל־יֹאמַר בֶּן־הַנֵּכָר הַנִּלְוָה אֶל־
יְהוָה לֵאמֹר הַבְדֵּל יַבְדִּילַנִי יְהוָה מֵעַל עַמּוֹ

say, "Behold, I am a dry tree." 4. For so says the Lord to the eunuchs who will keep My Sabbaths and will choose what I desire and hold fast to My covenant, 5. "I will give them in My house and in My walls a place and a name, better than sons and daughters; an everlasting name I will give him, which will not be discontinued. 6. And the foreigners who join with the Lord to serve Him and to love the name of the Lord, to be His servants—everyone who observes the Sabbath from profaning it and who holds fast to My covenant— 7. I will bring them to My holy mount, and I will cause them to rejoice in My house of prayer; their burnt offerings and their sacrifices shall be acceptable upon My altar, for My house shall be called a house of prayer for all peoples. 8. So says the Lord God, Who gathers in the dispersed of Israel, "I will yet gather others to him, together with his gathered ones."

וְאַל־יֹאמַר֙ הַסָּרִ֔יס הֵ֥ן אֲנִ֖י עֵ֥ץ יָבֵֽשׁ: ד כִּי־כֹ֣ה ׀ אָמַ֣ר יְהֹוָ֗ה לַסָּֽרִיסִים֙ אֲשֶׁ֣ר יִשְׁמְרוּ֙ אֶת־שַׁבְּתוֹתַ֔י וּבָ֣חֲר֔וּ בַּֽאֲשֶׁ֖ר חָפָ֑צְתִּי וּמַֽחֲזִיקִ֖ים בִּבְרִיתִֽי: ה וְנָֽתַתִּ֨י לָהֶ֜ם בְּבֵיתִ֤י וּבְחֽוֹמֹתַי֙ יָ֣ד וָשֵׁ֔ם ט֖וֹב מִבָּנִ֣ים וּמִבָּנ֑וֹת שֵׁ֤ם עוֹלָם֙ אֶתֶּן־ל֔וֹ אֲשֶׁ֖ר לֹ֥א יִכָּרֵֽת: ו וּבְנֵ֣י הַנֵּכָ֗ר הַנִּלְוִ֤ים עַל־יְהֹוָה֙ לְשָׁ֣רְת֔וֹ וּֽלְאַֽהֲבָה֙ אֶת־שֵׁ֣ם יְהֹוָ֔ה לִֽהְי֥וֹת ל֖וֹ לַֽעֲבָדִ֑ים כָּל־שֹׁמֵ֤ר שַׁבָּת֙ מֵֽחַלְּל֔וֹ וּמַֽחֲזִיקִ֖ים בִּבְרִיתִֽי: ז וַֽהֲבִֽיאוֹתִ֞ים אֶל־הַ֣ר קָדְשִׁ֗י וְשִׂמַּחְתִּים֙ בְּבֵ֣ית תְּפִלָּתִ֔י עֽוֹלֹֽתֵיהֶ֥ם וְזִבְחֵיהֶ֖ם לְרָצ֣וֹן עַל־מִזְבְּחִ֑י כִּ֣י בֵיתִ֔י בֵּית־תְּפִלָּ֥ה יִקָּרֵ֖א לְכָל־הָֽעַמִּֽים: ח נְאֻם֙ אֲדֹנָ֣י יֱהֹוִ֔ה מְקַבֵּ֖ץ נִדְחֵ֣י יִשְׂרָאֵ֑ל ע֛וֹד אֲקַבֵּ֥ץ עָלָ֖יו לְנִקְבָּצָֽיו:

HAFTARATH HAAZINU   הפטרת האזינו
(II Samuel 22:1-51)

This Haftarah is read only if the Sidra Haazinu is read after Yom Kippur. If the Sidra Haazinu is read on Shabbath Shuvah, the Haftarah is Hosea 14:2-10 (p. 921). Congregations that read Isaiah 55:6-56:8 (p. 924) with Vayelekh read the portion from Hosea with Haazinu—if it is read after Yom Kippur.

The Song of David is reminiscent of the Song of Moses in the Sidra Haazinu.

22:1. And David spoke to the Lord the words of this song, on the day that the Lord delivered him from the hand of all his enemies and from the hand of Saul. 2. And he said, "The Lord is my Rock and my Fortress, and a Rescuer to me. 3. God is my Rock, under whom I take cover; My Shield and the Horn of my salvation, my Support and my Refuge; [He is] my Savior, Who saves me from violence. 4. With praise I call to the Lord, for from my enemies I shall be saved. 5. For the pains of death have encompassed me; streams of scoundrels would affright me. 6. Bands of [those that shall inherit] the nether world have surrounded me; the snares of death confronted me. 7. When I am in distress, I call upon the Lord, yea, I call upon my God; and out of His abode He hears my voice, and my cry

א וַיְדַבֵּ֤ר דָּוִד֙ לַֽיהֹוָ֔ה אֶת־דִּבְרֵ֖י הַשִּׁירָ֣ה הַזֹּ֑את בְּיוֹם֩ הִצִּ֨יל יְהֹוָ֥ה אֹת֛וֹ מִכַּ֥ף כָּל־אֹֽיְבָ֖יו וּמִכַּ֥ף שָׁאֽוּל: ב וַיֹּאמַ֑ר יְהֹוָ֥ה סַֽלְעִ֛י וּמְצֻֽדָתִ֖י וּמְפַלְטִי־לִֽי: ג אֱלֹהֵ֥י צוּרִ֖י אֶֽחֱסֶה־בּ֑וֹ מָֽגִנִּ֞י וְקֶ֣רֶן יִשְׁעִ֗י מִשְׂגַּבִּי֙ וּמְנוּסִ֔י מֹֽשִׁעִ֕י מֵֽחָמָ֖ס תֹּֽשִׁעֵֽנִי: ד מְהֻלָּ֖ל אֶקְרָ֣א יְהֹוָ֑ה וּמֵאֹֽיְבַ֖י אִוָּשֵֽׁעַ: ה כִּ֥י אֲפָפֻ֖נִי מִשְׁבְּרֵי־מָ֑וֶת נַֽחֲלֵ֥י בְלִיַּ֖עַל יְבַֽעֲתֻֽנִי: ו חֶבְלֵ֥י שְׁא֖וֹל סַבֻּ֑נִי קִדְּמֻ֖נִי מֹ֥קְשֵׁי־מָֽוֶת: ז בַּצַּר־לִ֣י אֶקְרָ֣א יְהֹוָ֔ה וְאֶל־אֱלֹהַ֖י אֶקְרָ֑א

וַיִּשְׁמַע מֵהֵיכָלוֹ קוֹלִי וְשַׁוְעָתִי בְּאָזְנָיו׃
ח וַ תְגָּעַשׁ (ויתגעש קרי) וַתִּרְעַשׁ הָאָרֶץ מוֹסְדוֹת
הַשָּׁמַיִם יִרְגָּזוּ וַיִּתְגָּעֲשׁוּ כִּי־חָרָה לוֹ׃ ט עָלָה
עָשָׁן בְּאַפּוֹ וְאֵשׁ מִפִּיו תֹּאכֵל גֶּחָלִים בָּעֲרוּ
מִמֶּנּוּ׃ י וַיֵּט שָׁמַיִם וַיֵּרַד וַעֲרָפֶל תַּחַת רַגְלָיו׃
יא וַיִּרְכַּב עַל־כְּרוּב וַיָּעֹף וַיֵּרָא עַל־כַּנְפֵי־רוּחַ׃
יב וַיָּשֶׁת חֹשֶׁךְ סְבִיבֹתָיו סֻכּוֹת חַשְׁרַת־מַיִם
עָבֵי שְׁחָקִים׃ יג מִנֹּגַהּ נֶגְדּוֹ בָּעֲרוּ גַּחֲלֵי־אֵשׁ׃
יד יַרְעֵם מִן־שָׁמַיִם יְהוָה וְעֶלְיוֹן יִתֵּן קוֹלוֹ׃
טו וַיִּשְׁלַח חִצִּים וַיְפִיצֵם בָּרָק וַיָּהֹמם (ויהם
קרי)׃ טז וַיֵּרָאוּ אֲפִקֵי יָם יִגָּלוּ מֹסְדוֹת תֵּבֵל
בְּגַעֲרַת יְהוָה מִנִּשְׁמַת רוּחַ אַפּוֹ׃ יז יִשְׁלַח
מִמָּרוֹם יִקָּחֵנִי יַמְשֵׁנִי מִמַּיִם רַבִּים׃ יח יַצִּילֵנִי
מֵאֹיְבִי עָז מִשֹּׂנְאַי כִּי אָמְצוּ מִמֶּנִּי׃ יט יְקַדְּמֻנִי
בְּיוֹם אֵידִי וַיְהִי יְהוָה מִשְׁעָן לִי׃ כ וַיֹּצֵא
לַמֶּרְחָב אֹתִי יְחַלְּצֵנִי כִּי־חָפֵץ בִּי׃ כא יִגְמְלֵנִי
יְהוָה כְּצִדְקָתִי כְּבֹר יָדַי יָשִׁיב לִי׃ כב כִּי
שָׁמַרְתִּי דַּרְכֵי יְהוָה וְלֹא רָשַׁעְתִּי מֵאֱלֹהָי׃
כג כִּי כָל־מִשְׁפָּטָו (משפטיו קרי) לְנֶגְדִּי וְחֻקֹּתָיו
לֹא־אָסוּר מִמֶּנָּה׃ כד וָאֶהְיֶה תָמִים לוֹ
וָאֶשְׁתַּמְּרָה מֵעֲוֺנִי׃ כה וַיָּשֶׁב יְהוָה לִי כְּצִדְקָתִי
כְּבֹרִי לְנֶגֶד עֵינָיו׃ כו עִם־חָסִיד תִּתְחַסָּד עִם־
גִּבּוֹר תָּמִים תִּתַּמָּם׃ כז עִם־נָבָר תִּתָּבָר וְעִם־
עִקֵּשׁ תִּתַּפָּל׃ כח וְאֶת־עַם עָנִי תּוֹשִׁיעַ וְעֵינֶיךָ
עַל־רָמִים תַּשְׁפִּיל׃ כט כִּי־אַתָּה נֵירִי יְהוָה
וַיהוָה יַגִּיהַּ חָשְׁכִּי׃ ל כִּי בְכָה אָרוּץ גְּדוּד

enters His ears. 8. Then the earth shook and quaked, the [very] foundations of heaven did tremble; and they were shaken when He was angered. 9. Smoke went up in His nostrils, and fire out of His mouth did devour; coals flamed forth from Him. 10. And He bent the heavens, and He came down; and thick darkness was under His feet. 11. And He rode upon a cherub and did fly; He was seen upon the wings of the wind. 12. And He fixed darkness about Him as booths; gathering of waters, thick clouds of the skies. 13. From the brightness before Him flamed forth coals of fire. 14. The Lord thundered from heaven; and the Most High gave forth His voice. 15. And He sent out arrows, and He scattered them, lightning and He discomfited them. 16. And the depths of the sea appeared; the foundations of the world were laid bare, by the rebuke of the Lord and the blast of the breath of His nostrils. 17. He sent from on high, [and] He took me; He drew me out of many waters. 18. He delivered me from my mighty enemy; from them that hated me; for they were too powerful for me. 19. They confronted me on the day of my calamity, but the Lord was a support to me. 20. And He brought me forth into a wider place; He delivered me because He took delight in me. 21. The Lord rewarded me according to my righteousness; according to the cleanness of my hands He recompensed me. 22. For I have kept the ways of the Lord and have not wickedly departed from [the commandments of] my God. 23. For all His ordinances were before me; and [as for] His statutes, I did not depart from it. 24. And I was single-hearted toward Him, and I kept myself from my iniquity. 25. And the Lord has recompensed me according to my righteousness; according to my cleanness before His eyes. 26. With a kind man, You show Yourself kind. With an upright man, You show Yourself upright. 27. With a pure man, You show Yourself pure; but with a perverse man, You deal crookedly. 28. And the humble people You do deliver; but Your eyes are upon the haughty [in order] to humble them. 29. For You are my lamp, O Lord; and the Lord does light my darkness. 30. For by You do I run upon a troop; by my God I scale a wall. 31. [He is] the God Whose way is perfect; the word of the Lord is tried; He is a Shield unto all them that trust in Him. 32. For who is God, save the Lord? And who is a Rock, save our God? 33. God is He Who has fortified me with strength; and He looses perfectly my path. 34. He makes my feet like hinds, and sets me upon my high places. 35. He trains my hand for war, so that mine arms do bend a brass bow. 36. And You have given me the shield of Your salvation; and You have increased Your modesty for me. 37. You have enlarged my step[s] beneath me, and my ankles have not slipped. 38. I have pursued my enemies and have destroyed them, never turning back until they were consumed. 39. And I have consumed them, and I have crushed them that they cannot rise; yes, they are fallen under my feet. 40. For You have girded me with strength for the battle; You have subdued under me those that rose up against me. 41. And of my enemies, You have given me the back of their necks; them that hate me, that I may cut them off. 42. They looked about, but there was no one to save them; [even] to the Lord, but He answered them not. 43. Then I ground them as the dust of the earth, as the mud of the streets I did tread upon them; I did stamp them down. 44. And You have allowed me to escape from the contenders amongst my people; You shall keep me as head of nations; a people whom I have not known serve me. 45. Strangers lie to me; as soon as their ears hear, they obey me. 46. The strangers will wilt and become lame from their bondage. 47. The Lord lives, and blessed be my Rock; and exalted be the God [Who is] my Rock of salvation. 48. The God who takes vengence for me, and brings down peoples under me. 49. and that brings me forth from my enemies; and above those that rise against me, You have lifted me; from the violent man You deliver me. 50. Therefore, I will give thanks to You, O Lord, among the nations, and to Your Name will I sing praises. 51. He gives great salvation to His king, and He performs kindness to His anointed; to David and to his seed, forevermore.

בֵּאלֹהַי אֲדַלֶּג־שׁוּר׃ לא הָאֵל תָּמִים דַּרְכּוֹ
אִמְרַת יְהוָֹה צְרוּפָה מָגֵן הוּא לְכֹל הַחֹסִים בּוֹ׃
לב כִּי מִי־אֵל מִבַּלְעֲדֵי יְהוָֹה וּמִי צוּר מִבַּלְעֲדֵי
אֱלֹהֵינוּ׃ לג הָאֵל מָעוּזִּי חָיִל וַיַּתֵּר תָּמִים דַּרְכּוֹ
(דרכי קרי)׃ לד מְשַׁוֶּה רַגְלָיו (רגלי קרי) כָּאַיָּלוֹת
וְעַל־בָּמֹתַי יַעֲמִידֵנִי׃ לה מְלַמֵּד יָדַי לַמִּלְחָמָה
וְנִחַת קֶשֶׁת־נְחוּשָׁה זְרֹעֹתָי׃ לו וַתִּתֶּן־לִי מָגֵן
יִשְׁעֶךָ וַעֲנֹתְךָ תַּרְבֵּנִי׃ לז תַּרְחִיב צַעֲדִי תַּחְתֵּנִי
וְלֹא מָעֲדוּ קַרְסֻלָּי׃ לח אֶרְדְּפָה אֹיְבַי וָאַשְׁמִידֵם
וְלֹא אָשׁוּב עַד־כַּלּוֹתָם׃ לט וָאֲכַלֵּם וָאֶמְחָצֵם
וְלֹא יְקוּמוּן וַיִּפְּלוּ תַּחַת רַגְלָי׃ מ וַתַּזְרֵנִי חַיִל
לַמִּלְחָמָה תַּכְרִיעַ קָמַי תַּחְתֵּנִי׃ מא וְאֹיְבַי תַּתָּה
לִּי עֹרֶף מְשַׂנְאַי וָאַצְמִיתֵם׃ מב יִשְׁעוּ וְאֵין
מֹשִׁיעַ אֶל־יְהוָֹה וְלֹא עָנָם׃ מג וְאֶשְׁחָקֵם
כַּעֲפַר־אָרֶץ כְּטִיט־חוּצוֹת אֲדִקֵּם אֶרְקָעֵם׃
מד וַתְּפַלְּטֵנִי מֵרִיבֵי עַמִּי תִּשְׁמְרֵנִי לְרֹאשׁ גּוֹיִם
עַם לֹא־יָדַעְתִּי יַעַבְדֻנִי׃ מה בְּנֵי נֵכָר יִתְכַּחֲשׁוּ־
לִי לִשְׁמוֹעַ אֹזֶן יִשָּׁמְעוּ לִי׃ מו בְּנֵי נֵכָר יִבֹּלוּ
וְיַחְגְּרוּ מִמִּסְגְּרוֹתָם׃ מז חַי־יְהוָֹה וּבָרוּךְ צוּרִי
וְיָרֻם אֱלֹהֵי צוּר יִשְׁעִי׃ מח הָאֵל הַנֹּתֵן נְקָמֹת לִי
וּמֹרִיד עַמִּים תַּחְתֵּנִי׃ מט וּמוֹצִיאִי מֵאֹיְבָי
וּמִקָּמַי תְּרוֹמְמֵנִי מֵאִישׁ חֲמָסִים תַּצִּילֵנִי׃
נ עַל־כֵּן אוֹדְךָ יְהוָֹה בַּגּוֹיִם וּלְשִׁמְךָ אֲזַמֵּר׃
נא מִגְדִּיל (מגדול קרי) יְשׁוּעוֹת מַלְכּוֹ וְעֹשֶׂה־חֶסֶד
לִמְשִׁיחוֹ לְדָוִד וּלְזַרְעוֹ עַד־עוֹלָם׃

ALTERNATIVE HAFTARATH HAAZINU הפטרת האזינו

(Ezekiel 17:22–24, 18:1–32)

Alternative custom followed by some congregations.

17:22. So says the Lord God: I will take from the lofty top of the cedar, and I will place [it]; I will crop off from the topmost of its young twigs a tender one, and I will plant it upon a high and lofty mountain. 23. In the mountain of the height of Israel I will plant it, and it will bear boughs and bring forth fruit and become a beautiful cedar, and under it shall dwell all birds of every feather; in the shade of the branches thereof shall they dwell. 24. And all the trees of the field will recognize that I, the Lord, have lowered the high tree, have raised aloft the low tree; that I have dried up the green tree, and have made the dry tree blossom. I, the Lord, have spoken; and I will accomplish it. 18:1. And the word of the Lord came to me, saying: 2. What do you mean that you use this parable over the land of Israel, saying, "The fathers have eaten sour grapes and the children's teeth are set on edge?" 3. As truly as I live, says the Lord God, you shall no longer use this parable in Israel. 4. Behold, all souls are Mine. Like the soul of the father, like the soul of the son they are Mine; the soul that sins, it shall die. 5. So a man who is righteous and practices justice and righteousness, 6. and does not eat [offerings of meals] to the mountains, and does not lift up his eyes to the idols of the house of Israel; neither defiles his fellowman's wife nor approaches a woman in her period of separation, 7. and wrongs no man; what has been pledged for a debt he returns, has committed no robbery, gives his bread to the hungry, and clothes the naked with garments, 8. does not lend on interest, nor does he accept any increase on a loan, keeps his hand back from wrong, executes true judgment between man and man, 9. has walked in My laws, and has kept My ordinances to deal truly—he is a righteous man; he shall surely live, says the Lord God. 10. If he beget a profligate son, a shedder of blood, and he commits to his brother any of these [crimes]; 11. and he does not do all these [good deeds], but has even eaten [offerings of a meal] to the mountains and defiled his fellow-man's

כב כֹּה אָמַר֮ אֲדֹנָ֣י יֱהֹוִה֒ וְלָקַ֣חְתִּי אָ֗נִי מִצַּמֶּ֛רֶת
הָאֶ֥רֶז הָרָמָ֖ה וְנָתָ֑תִּי מֵרֹ֣אשׁ יֹנְקוֹתָ֗יו רַ֚ךְ אֶקְטֹ֔ף
וְשָׁתַ֣לְתִּי אָ֔נִי עַ֥ל הַר־גָּבֹ֖הַּ וְתָלֽוּל׃ כג בְּהַ֨ר
מְר֤וֹם יִשְׂרָאֵל֙ אֶשְׁתֳּלֶ֔נּוּ וְנָשָׂ֤א עָנָף֙ וְעָ֣שָׂה פֶ֔רִי
וְהָיָ֖ה לְאֶ֣רֶז אַדִּ֑יר וְשָׁכְנ֣וּ תַחְתָּ֗יו כֹּ֚ל צִפּ֣וֹר
כָּל־כָּנָ֔ף בְּצֵ֥ל דָּלִיּוֹתָ֖יו תִּשְׁכֹּֽנָּה׃ כד וְיָדְע֞וּ כָּל־
עֲצֵ֣י הַשָּׂדֶ֗ה כִּ֣י אֲנִ֣י יְהֹוָה֮ הִשְׁפַּ֣לְתִּי ׀ עֵ֣ץ גָּבֹ֗הַּ
הִגְבַּ֙הְתִּי֙ עֵ֣ץ שָׁפָ֔ל הוֹבַ֙שְׁתִּי֙ עֵ֣ץ לָ֔ח וְהִפְרַ֖חְתִּי
עֵ֣ץ יָבֵ֑שׁ אֲנִ֥י יְהֹוָ֖ה דִּבַּ֥רְתִּי וְעָשִֽׂיתִי׃ א וַיְהִ֥י
דְבַר־יְהֹוָ֖ה אֵלַ֥י לֵאמֹֽר׃ ב מַה־לָּכֶ֗ם אַתֶּם֙
מֹֽשְׁלִים֙ אֶת־הַמָּשָׁ֣ל הַזֶּ֔ה עַל־אַדְמַ֥ת יִשְׂרָאֵ֖ל
לֵאמֹ֑ר אָבוֹת֙ יֹ֣אכְלוּ בֹ֔סֶר וְשִׁנֵּ֥י הַבָּנִ֖ים
תִּקְהֶֽינָה׃ ג חַי־אָ֕נִי נְאֻ֖ם אֲדֹנָ֣י יֱהֹוִ֑ה אִם־יִֽהְיֶ֨ה
לָכֶ֜ם ע֗וֹד מְשֹׁ֛ל הַמָּשָׁ֥ל הַזֶּ֖ה בְּיִשְׂרָאֵֽל׃ ד הֵ֤ן
כָּל־הַנְּפָשׁוֹת֙ לִ֣י הֵ֔נָּה כְּנֶ֧פֶשׁ הָאָ֛ב וּכְנֶ֥פֶשׁ הַבֵּ֖ן
לִי־הֵ֑נָּה הַנֶּ֥פֶשׁ הַחֹטֵ֖את הִ֥יא תָמֽוּת׃ ה וְאִ֖ישׁ
כִּֽי־יִהְיֶ֣ה צַדִּ֑יק וְעָשָׂ֥ה מִשְׁפָּ֖ט וּצְדָקָֽה׃ ו אֶל־
הֶֽהָרִים֙ לֹ֣א אָכָ֔ל וְעֵינָיו֙ לֹ֣א נָשָׂ֔א אֶל־גִּלּוּלֵ֖י
בֵּ֣ית יִשְׂרָאֵ֑ל וְאֶת־אֵ֤שֶׁת רֵעֵ֙הוּ֙ לֹ֣א טִמֵּ֔א וְאֶל־
אִשָּׁ֥ה נִדָּ֖ה לֹ֥א יִקְרָֽב׃ ז וְאִישׁ֙ לֹ֣א יוֹנֶ֔ה חֲבֹלָת֥וֹ
חוֹב֙ יָשִׁ֔יב גְּזֵלָ֖ה לֹ֣א יִגְזֹ֑ל לַחְמוֹ֙ לְרָעֵ֣ב יִתֵּ֔ן
וְעֵירֹ֖ם יְכַסֶּה־בָּֽגֶד׃ ח בַּנֶּ֣שֶׁךְ לֹֽא־יִתֵּ֗ן וְתַרְבִּית֙
לֹ֣א יִקָּ֔ח מֵעָ֖וֶל יָשִׁ֣יב יָד֑וֹ מִשְׁפַּ֤ט אֱמֶת֙ יַעֲשֶׂ֔ה
בֵּ֥ין אִ֖ישׁ לְאִֽישׁ׃ ט בְּחֻקּוֹתַ֧י יְהַלֵּ֛ךְ וּמִשְׁפָּטַ֥י
שָׁמַ֖ר לַעֲשׂ֣וֹת אֱמֶ֑ת צַדִּ֥יק הוּא֙ חָיֹ֣ה יִֽחְיֶ֔ה נְאֻ֖ם
אֲדֹנָ֥י יֱהֹוִֽה׃ י וְהוֹלִ֥יד בֵּן־פָּרִ֖יץ שֹׁ֣פֵךְ דָּ֑ם
וְעָ֣שָׂה אָ֔ח מֵאַחַ֖ד מֵאֵֽלֶּה׃ יא וְה֕וּא אֶת־כָּל־
אֵ֖לֶּה לֹ֣א עָשָׂ֑ה כִּ֣י גַ֤ם אֶל־הֶֽהָרִים֙ אָכַ֔ל וְאֶת־

wife; 12. wronged the poor and the needy, practiced robberies, did not return pledges, lifted up his eyes to the idols, committed abomination; 13. gave out on interest, accepted increase on loans—and shall he then live? He shall not live! He has done all these abominations; he shall surely die; his blood falls back on himself! 14. And behold, if he beget a son, who sees all the sins of his father which he has done, he sees and does not do likewise; 15. he did not eat to the mountains and did not lift up his eyes to the idols of the house of Israel, did not defile his fellowman's wife, 16. wronged no man; did not retain any pledge, and committed no robbery; his bread he gave to the hungry and the naked he covered with clothes; 17. from the poor he kept his hand back, interest and increase he did not take; My ordinances he kept, in My laws did he walk—he shall not die for the sins of his father; he shall surely live. 18. [But] his father, because he illegally suppressed, committed robbery against his brother and did that which is not good among his people, behold, he shall die for his iniquity. 19. Yet you say, "Why does the son not bear with the sin of the father?" But the son has practiced justice and righteousness, he has kept all My laws and he carries them out, he shall surely live. 20. The soul that sins, it shall die; a son shall not bear the iniquity of the father, and a father shall not bear the iniquity of the son; the righteousness of the righteous shall be upon himself, and the wickedness of the wicked upon himself. 21. And if the wicked man repent of all his sins that he has committed and keeps all My laws and executes justice and righteousness, he shall surely live, he shall not die. 22. All his transgressions that he has committed shall not be remembered to him; in his righteousness that he has done he shall live. 23. Do I desire the death of the wicked? says the Lord God. Is it not rather in his repenting of his ways that he may live? 24. But when the righteous repents of his righteousness and does wrong, and does like all the abominations that the wicked man did, shall he live? All his righteousness that he has done shall not be remembered; in his treachery that he has perpetrated and in his sin that he has

אֵשֶׁת רֵעֵהוּ טִמֵּא׃ יב עָנִי וְאֶבְיוֹן הוֹנָה גְּזֵלוֹת
גָּזָל חֲבֹל לֹא יָשִׁיב וְאֶל־הַגִּלּוּלִים נָשָׂא עֵינָיו
תּוֹעֵבָה עָשָׂה׃ יג בַּנֶּשֶׁךְ נָתַן וְתַרְבִּית לָקַח וָחָי
לֹא יִחְיֶה אֵת כָּל־הַתּוֹעֵבוֹת הָאֵלֶּה עָשָׂה מוֹת
יוּמָת דָּמָיו בּוֹ יִהְיֶה׃ יד וְהִנֵּה הוֹלִיד בֵּן וַיַּרְא
אֶת־כָּל־חַטֹּאת אָבִיו אֲשֶׁר עָשָׂה וַיִּרְאֶה וְלֹא
יַעֲשֶׂה כָּהֵן׃ טו עַל־הֶהָרִים לֹא אָכָל וְעֵינָיו לֹא
נָשָׂא אֶל־גִּלּוּלֵי בֵּית יִשְׂרָאֵל אֶת־אֵשֶׁת רֵעֵהוּ
לֹא טִמֵּא׃ טז וְאִישׁ לֹא הוֹנָה חֲבֹל לֹא חָבָל
וּגְזֵלָה לֹא גָזָל לַחְמוֹ לְרָעֵב נָתָן וְעֵרוֹם כִּסָּה־
בָגֶד׃ יז מֵעָנִי הֵשִׁיב יָדוֹ נֶשֶׁךְ וְתַרְבִּית לֹא
לָקָח מִשְׁפָּטַי עָשָׂה בְּחֻקּוֹתַי הָלָךְ הוּא לֹא
יָמוּת בַּעֲוֺן אָבִיו חָיֹה יִחְיֶה׃ יח אָבִיו כִּי־עָשַׁק
עֹשֶׁק גָּזַל גֵּזֶל אָח וַאֲשֶׁר לֹא־טוֹב עָשָׂה בְּתוֹךְ
עַמָּיו וְהִנֵּה־מֵת בַּעֲוֺנוֹ׃ יט וַאֲמַרְתֶּם מַדֻּעַ לֹא־
נָשָׂא הַבֵּן בַּעֲוֺן הָאָב וְהַבֵּן מִשְׁפָּט וּצְדָקָה
עָשָׂה אֵת כָּל־חֻקּוֹתַי שָׁמַר וַיַּעֲשֶׂה אֹתָם חָיֹה
יִחְיֶה׃ כ הַנֶּפֶשׁ הַחֹטֵאת הִיא תָמוּת בֵּן לֹא־
יִשָּׂא ׀ בַּעֲוֺן הָאָב וְאָב לֹא יִשָּׂא בַּעֲוֺן הַבֵּן
צִדְקַת הַצַּדִּיק עָלָיו תִּהְיֶה וְרִשְׁעַת הָרָשָׁע עָלָיו
תִּהְיֶה׃ כא וְהָרָשָׁע כִּי יָשׁוּב מִכָּל־חַטֹּאתָו
אֲשֶׁר עָשָׂה וְשָׁמַר אֶת־כָּל־חֻקּוֹתַי וְעָשָׂה
מִשְׁפָּט וּצְדָקָה חָיֹה יִחְיֶה לֹא יָמוּת׃ כב כָּל־
פְּשָׁעָיו אֲשֶׁר עָשָׂה לֹא יִזָּכְרוּ לוֹ בְּצִדְקָתוֹ
אֲשֶׁר־עָשָׂה יִחְיֶה׃ כג הֶחָפֹץ אֶחְפֹּץ מוֹת רָשָׁע
נְאֻם אֲדֹנָי יֱהֹוִה הֲלוֹא בְּשׁוּבוֹ מִדְּרָכָיו וְחָיָה׃
כד וּבְשׁוּב צַדִּיק מִצִּדְקָתוֹ וְעָשָׂה עָוֶל כְּכֹל
הַתּוֹעֵבוֹת אֲשֶׁר־עָשָׂה הָרָשָׁע יַעֲשֶׂה וָחָי כָּל־
צִדְקָתוֹ אֲשֶׁר־עָשָׂה לֹא תִזָּכַרְנָה בְּמַעֲלוֹ אֲשֶׁר־
מָעַל וּבְחַטָּאתוֹ אֲשֶׁר־חָטָא בָּם יָמוּת׃

sinned, in them shall he die. 25. Yet you say, "The way of the Lord is not right!" Hear now, O house of Israel, is it My way that is not right? Is it not rather your ways that are not right? 26. When a righteous man repents of his righteousness and does wrong and dies on that account; for the wrong that he has done he dies. 27. And when a wicked man repents of his wickedness that he has done, and does justice and righteousness, he will keep his soul alive. 28. And he sees and repents of all his transgressions that he has committed—he shall surely live; he shall not die. 29. And yet the house of Israel say, "The way of the Lord is not right!" Is it My ways that are not right, O house of Israel? Is it not rather your ways that are not right? 30. Therefore, I will judge you, O house of Israel, every one according to his ways, says the Lord God; repent and cause others to repent of all your transgressions, and let it not be for you as a stumbling block of iniquity. 31. Cast away from you all your transgressions whereby you have transgressed, and make yourselves a new heart and a new spirit, for why should you die, O house of Israel! 32. For I do not desire the death of him who dies, says the Lord God; so cause others to repent, and live!

כה וַאֲמַרְתֶּם לֹא יִתָּכֵן דֶּרֶךְ אֲדֹנָי שִׁמְעוּ־נָא
בֵּית יִשְׂרָאֵל הֲדַרְכִּי לֹא יִתָּכֵן הֲלֹא דַרְכֵיכֶם
לֹא יִתָּכֵנוּ: כו בְּשׁוּב־צַדִּיק מִצִּדְקָתוֹ וְעָשָׂה
עָוֶל וּמֵת עֲלֵיהֶם בְּעַוְלוֹ אֲשֶׁר־עָשָׂה יָמוּת:
כז וּבְשׁוּב רָשָׁע מֵרִשְׁעָתוֹ אֲשֶׁר עָשָׂה וַיַּעַשׂ
מִשְׁפָּט וּצְדָקָה הוּא אֶת־נַפְשׁוֹ יְחַיֶּה:
כח וַיִּרְאֶה וַיָּשׁב מִכָּל־פְּשָׁעָיו אֲשֶׁר עָשָׂה חָיוֹ
יִחְיֶה לֹא יָמוּת: כט וְאָמְרוּ בֵּית יִשְׂרָאֵל לֹא
יִתָּכֵן דֶּרֶךְ אֲדֹנָי הַדְּרָכַי לֹא יִתָּכֵנוּ בֵּית יִשְׂרָאֵל
הֲלֹא דַרְכֵיכֶם לֹא יִתָּכֵן: ל לָכֵן אִישׁ כִּדְרָכָיו
אֶשְׁפֹּט אֶתְכֶם בֵּית יִשְׂרָאֵל נְאֻם אֲדֹנָי יְהוִֹה
שׁוּבוּ וְהָשִׁיבוּ מִכָּל־פִּשְׁעֵיכֶם וְלֹא־יִהְיֶה לָכֶם
לְמִכְשׁוֹל עָוֹן: לא הַשְׁלִיכוּ מֵעֲלֵיכֶם אֶת־כָּל־
פִּשְׁעֵיכֶם אֲשֶׁר פְּשַׁעְתֶּם בָּם וַעֲשׂוּ לָכֶם לֵב
חָדָשׁ וְרוּחַ חֲדָשָׁה וְלָמָּה תָמֻתוּ בֵּית יִשְׂרָאֵל:
לב כִּי לֹא אֶחְפֹּץ בְּמוֹת הַמֵּת נְאֻם אֲדֹנָי יְהוִֹה
וְהָשִׁיבוּ וִחְיוּ:

HAFTARATH SHABBATH ROSH CHODESH   הפטרת שבת ראש חדש
(Sabbath and New Moon)
(Isaiah 66)
Additional Torah reading: Numbers 28:9–15. Should Rosh Chodesh fall on the Sabbath and Sunday, many congregations add the opening and closing verses of the Haftarah For The Day Preceding Rosh Chodesh. (p. 933)

The verse repeated at the end mentions the New Moon.

66:1. So says the Lord, "The heavens are My throne, and the earth is My footstool; which is the house that you will build for Me, and which is the place of My rest? 2. And all these My hand made, and all these have become," says the Lord. "But to this one will I look, to one poor and of crushed spirit, who hastens to do My bidding. 3. Whoever slaughters an ox has slain a man; he who slaughters a lamb is as though he beheads a dog; he who offers up a

א כֹּה אָמַר יְהוָֹה הַשָּׁמַיִם כִּסְאִי וְהָאָרֶץ הֲדֹם
רַגְלָי אֵי־זֶה בַיִת אֲשֶׁר תִּבְנוּ־לִי וְאֵי־זֶה מָקוֹם
מְנוּחָתִי: ב וְאֶת־כָּל־אֵלֶּה יָדִי עָשָׂתָה וַיִּהְיוּ
כָל־אֵלֶּה נְאֻם־יְהוָֹה וְאֶל־זֶה אַבִּיט אֶל־עָנִי
וּנְכֵה־רוּחַ וְחָרֵד עַל־דְּבָרִי: ג שׁוֹחֵט הַשּׁוֹר
מַכֵּה־אִישׁ זוֹבֵחַ הַשֶּׂה עֹרֵף כֶּלֶב מַעֲלֶה מִנְחָה

meal-offering is [like] swine blood; he who burns frankincense brings a gift of violence; they, too, chose their ways, and their soul desired their abominations. 4. I, too, will choose their mockeries, and their fears I will bring to them, since I called and no one answered, I spoke, and they did not hearken, and they did what was evil in My eyes, and what I did not wish they chose. 5. Hearken to the word of the Lord, who quake at His word, Your brethren who hate you, who cast you out, said, "For the sake of my name, the Lord shall be glorified," but we will see your joy, and they shall be ashamed. 6. There is a sound of stirring from the city, a sound from the Temple, the voice of the Lord, recompensing His enemies. 7. When she has not yet travailed, she has given birth; when the pang has not yet come to her, she has been delivered of a male child. 8. Who heard [anything] like this? Who saw [anything] like these? Is a land born in one day? Is a nation born at once, that Zion both experienced birth pangs and bore her children? 9. "Will I bring to the birth stool and not cause to give birth?" says the Lord. "Am I not He who causes to give birth, now should I shut the womb?" says your God. 10. Rejoice with Jerusalem and exult in her all those who love her; rejoice with her a rejoicing, all who mourn over her. 11. In order that you suck and become sated from the breast of her consolations—in order that you drink deeply and delight from her approaching glory. 12. For so says the Lord, "Behold, I will extend peace to you like a river, and like a flooding stream the wealth of the nations, and you shall suck thereof; on the side you shall be borne, and on knees you shall be dandled. 13. Like a man whose mother consoles him, so will I console you; and in Jerusalem, you shall be consoled. 14. And you shall see, and your heart shall rejoice, and your bones shall bloom like grass, and the hand of the Lord shall be known to His servants, and He shall be wroth with His enemies. 15. For, behold, the Lord shall come with fire, and like a tempest, His chariots, to render His anger with fury, and His rebuke with flames of fire. 16. For with fire will the Lord contend, and with His sword with all flesh, and those slain by the

דַּם־חֲזִיר מַזְכִּיר לְבֹנָה מְבָרֵךְ אָוֶן גַּם־הֵמָּה
בָּחֲרוּ בְּדַרְכֵיהֶם וּבְשִׁקּוּצֵיהֶם נַפְשָׁם חָפֵצָה׃
ד גַּם־אֲנִי אֶבְחַר בְּתַעֲלוּלֵיהֶם וּמְגוּרֹתָם אָבִיא
לָהֶם יַעַן קָרָאתִי וְאֵין עוֹנֶה דִּבַּרְתִּי וְלֹא
שָׁמֵעוּ וַיַּעֲשׂוּ הָרַע בְּעֵינַי וּבַאֲשֶׁר לֹא־חָפַצְתִּי
בָּחָרוּ׃ ה שִׁמְעוּ דְּבַר־יְהֹוָה הַחֲרֵדִים אֶל־דְּבָרוֹ
אָמְרוּ אֲחֵיכֶם שֹׂנְאֵיכֶם מְנַדֵּיכֶם לְמַעַן שְׁמִי
יִכְבַּד יְהֹוָה וְנִרְאֶה בְשִׂמְחַתְכֶם וְהֵם יֵבֹשׁוּ׃
ו קוֹל שָׁאוֹן מֵעִיר קוֹל מֵהֵיכָל קוֹל יְהֹוָה
מְשַׁלֵּם גְּמוּל לְאֹיְבָיו׃ ז בְּטֶרֶם תָּחִיל יָלָדָה
בְּטֶרֶם יָבוֹא חֵבֶל לָהּ וְהִמְלִיטָה זָכָר׃ ח מִי־
שָׁמַע כָּזֹאת מִי רָאָה כָּאֵלֶּה הֲיוּחַל אֶרֶץ בְּיוֹם
אֶחָד אִם־יִוָּלֵד גּוֹי פַּעַם אֶחָת כִּי־חָלָה גַּם־
יָלְדָה צִיּוֹן אֶת־בָּנֶיהָ׃ ט הַאֲנִי אַשְׁבִּיר וְלֹא
אוֹלִיד יֹאמַר יְהֹוָה אִם־אֲנִי הַמּוֹלִיד וְעָצַרְתִּי
אָמַר אֱלֹהָיִךְ׃ י שִׂמְחוּ אֶת־יְרוּשָׁלַםִ וְגִילוּ בָהּ
כָּל־אֹהֲבֶיהָ שִׂישׂוּ אִתָּהּ מָשׂוֹשׂ כָּל־הַמִּתְאַבְּלִים
עָלֶיהָ׃ יא לְמַעַן תִּינְקוּ וּשְׂבַעְתֶּם מִשֹּׁד תַּנְחֻמֶיהָ
לְמַעַן תָּמֹצּוּ וְהִתְעַנַּגְתֶּם מִזִּיז כְּבוֹדָהּ׃ יב כִּי־
כֹה ׀ אָמַר יְהֹוָה הִנְנִי נֹטֶה־אֵלֶיהָ כְּנָהָר שָׁלוֹם
וּכְנַחַל שׁוֹטֵף כְּבוֹד גּוֹיִם וִינַקְתֶּם עַל־צַד
תִּנָּשֵׂאוּ וְעַל־בִּרְכַּיִם תְּשָׁעֳשָׁעוּ׃ יג כְּאִישׁ אֲשֶׁר
אִמּוֹ תְּנַחֲמֶנּוּ כֵּן אָנֹכִי אֲנַחֶמְכֶם וּבִירוּשָׁלַםִ
תְּנֻחָמוּ׃ יד וּרְאִיתֶם וְשָׂשׂ לִבְּכֶם וְעַצְמוֹתֵיכֶם
כַּדֶּשֶׁא תִפְרַחְנָה וְנוֹדְעָה יַד־יְהֹוָה אֶת־עֲבָדָיו
וְזָעַם אֶת־אֹיְבָיו׃ טו כִּי־הִנֵּה יְהֹוָה בָּאֵשׁ יָבוֹא
וְכַסּוּפָה מַרְכְּבֹתָיו לְהָשִׁיב בְּחֵמָה אַפּוֹ וְגַעֲרָתוֹ
בְּלַהֲבֵי־אֵשׁ׃ טז כִּי בָאֵשׁ יְהֹוָה נִשְׁפָּט וּבְחַרְבּוֹ
אֶת־כָּל־בָּשָׂר וְרַבּוּ חַלְלֵי יְהֹוָה׃ יז הַמִּתְקַדְּשִׁים

Lord shall be many. 17. "Those who prepare themselves and purify themselves to the gardens, [one] after another in the middle, those who eat the flesh of the swine and the detestable thing and the rodent, shall perish together," says the Lord. 18. "And I—their deeds and their thoughts have come to gather all the nations and the tongues, and they shall come, and they shall see My glory. 19. And I will place a sign upon them, and I will send from them refugees to the nations, Tarshish, Pul, and Lud, who draw the bow; to Tubal and Javan, the distant islands, who did not hear of My fame and did not see My glory; and they shall recount My glory among the nations. 20. And they shall bring all your brethren from all the nations as a tribute to the Lord, with horses and with chariots, and with covered wagons and with mules and with joyous songs upon My holy mount, Jerusalem," says the Lord, "as the children of Israel bring the offering in a pure vessel to the house of the Lord. 21. And from them, too, will I take for priests and for Levites," says the Lord. 22. "For, as the new heavens and the new earth that I am making stand before Me," says the Lord, "so shall your seed and your name stand. 23. And it shall be from new moon to new moon and from Sabbath to Sabbath, that all flesh shall come to prostrate themselves before Me," says the Lord. 24. And they shall go out and see the corpses of the people who rebelled against Me, for their worm shall not die, and their fire shall not be quenched, and they shall be an abhorrance for all flesh." ["And it shall be from new moon to new moon, and from Sabbath to Sabbath, that all flesh shall come to prostrate themselves before Me," says the Lord.]

וְהַמִּטַּהֲרִים אֶל־הַגַּנּוֹת אַחַר אַחַד (אחת קרי)
בַּתָּוֶךְ אֹכְלֵי בְּשַׂר הַחֲזִיר וְהַשֶּׁקֶץ וְהָעַכְבָּר
יַחְדָּו יָסֻפוּ נְאֻם־יְהוָה: יח וְאָנֹכִי מַעֲשֵׂיהֶם
וּמַחְשְׁבֹתֵיהֶם בָּאָה לְקַבֵּץ אֶת־כָּל־הַגּוֹיִם
וְהַלְּשֹׁנוֹת וּבָאוּ וְרָאוּ אֶת־כְּבוֹדִי: יט וְשַׂמְתִּי
בָהֶם אוֹת וְשִׁלַּחְתִּי מֵהֶם ׀ פְּלֵיטִים אֶל־הַגּוֹיִם
תַּרְשִׁישׁ פּוּל וְלוּד מֹשְׁכֵי קֶשֶׁת תֻּבַל וְיָוָן
הָאִיִּים הָרְחֹקִים אֲשֶׁר לֹא־שָׁמְעוּ אֶת־שִׁמְעִי
וְלֹא־רָאוּ אֶת־כְּבוֹדִי וְהִגִּידוּ אֶת־כְּבוֹדִי בַּגּוֹיִם:
כ וְהֵבִיאוּ אֶת־כָּל־אֲחֵיכֶם ׀ מִכָּל־הַגּוֹיִם ׀
מִנְחָה ׀ לַיהוָה בַּסּוּסִים וּבָרֶכֶב וּבַצַּבִּים
וּבַפְּרָדִים וּבַכִּרְכָּרוֹת עַל הַר קָדְשִׁי יְרוּשָׁלַ͏ִם
אָמַר יְהוָה כַּאֲשֶׁר יָבִיאוּ בְנֵי יִשְׂרָאֵל אֶת־
הַמִּנְחָה בִּכְלִי טָהוֹר בֵּית יְהוָה: כא וְגַם־מֵהֶם
אֶקַּח לַכֹּהֲנִים לַלְוִיִּם אָמַר יְהוָה: כב כִּי כַאֲשֶׁר
הַשָּׁמַיִם הַחֲדָשִׁים וְהָאָרֶץ הַחֲדָשָׁה אֲשֶׁר אֲנִי
עֹשֶׂה עֹמְדִים לְפָנַי נְאֻם־יְהוָה כֵּן יַעֲמֹד
זַרְעֲכֶם וְשִׁמְכֶם: כג וְהָיָה מִדֵּי־חֹדֶשׁ בְּחָדְשׁוֹ
וּמִדֵּי שַׁבָּת בְּשַׁבַּתּוֹ יָבוֹא כָל־בָּשָׂר לְהִשְׁתַּחֲוֺת
לְפָנַי אָמַר יְהוָה: כד וְיָצְאוּ וְרָאוּ בְּפִגְרֵי
הָאֲנָשִׁים הַפֹּשְׁעִים בִּי כִּי תוֹלַעְתָּם לֹא תָמוּת
וְאִשָּׁם לֹא תִכְבֶּה וְהָיוּ דֵרָאוֹן לְכָל־בָּשָׂר:

[כג וְהָיָה מִדֵּי־חֹדֶשׁ בְּחָדְשׁוֹ וּמִדֵּי שַׁבָּת בְּשַׁבַּתּוֹ יָבוֹא
כָל־בָּשָׂר לְהִשְׁתַּחֲוֺת לְפָנַי אָמַר יְהוָה:]

הפטרת מחר חדש

HAFTARAH FOR THE DAY PRECEDING ROSH CHODESH

(Eve of the New Moon)

(I Samuel 20:18–42)

This selection is read when Rosh Chodesh occurs on Sunday. If Rosh Chodesh falls on the Sabbath and Sunday, many congregations add the opening and closing verses of this Haftarah after reading the Haftarah for Sabbath Rosh Chodesh.

The first verse mentions, "Tomorrow is the new moon."

יח וַיֹּאמֶר־ל֥וֹ יְהוֹנָתָ֖ן מָחָ֣ר חֹ֑דֶשׁ וְנִפְקַ֕דְתָּ כִּ֥י
יִפָּקֵ֖ד מוֹשָׁבֶֽךָ׃ יט וְשִׁלַּשְׁתָּ֙ תֵּרֵ֣ד מְאֹ֔ד וּבָאתָ֙
אֶל־הַמָּק֔וֹם אֲשֶׁר־נִסְתַּ֥רְתָּ שָּׁ֖ם בְּי֣וֹם הַֽמַּעֲשֶׂ֑ה
וְיָשַׁבְתָּ֔ אֵ֖צֶל הָאֶ֥בֶן הָאָֽזֶל׃ כ וַאֲנִ֕י שְׁלֹ֥שֶׁת
הַחִצִּ֖ים צִדָּ֣ה אוֹרֶ֑ה לְשַֽׁלַּֽח־לִ֖י לְמַטָּרָֽה׃
כא וְהִנֵּה֙ אֶשְׁלַ֣ח אֶת־הַנַּ֔עַר לֵ֖ךְ מְצָ֣א אֶת־
הַחִצִּ֑ים אִם־אָמֹ֨ר אֹמַ֜ר לַנַּ֗עַר הִנֵּ֤ה הַחִצִּ֣ים ׀
מִמְּךָ֙ וָהֵ֙נָּה֙ קָחֶ֣נּוּ וָבֹ֗אָה כִּֽי־שָׁל֥וֹם לְךָ֛ וְאֵ֥ין דָּבָ֖ר
חַי־יְהוָֽה׃ כב וְאִם־כֹּ֤ה אֹמַר֙ לָעֶ֔לֶם הִנֵּ֥ה
הַחִצִּ֖ים מִמְּךָ֣ וָהָ֑לְאָה לֵ֕ךְ כִּ֥י שִֽׁלַּחֲךָ֖ יְהוָֽה׃
כג וְהַ֨דָּבָ֔ר אֲשֶׁ֥ר דִּבַּ֖רְנוּ אֲנִ֣י וָאָ֑תָּה הִנֵּ֧ה יְהוָ֛ה
בֵּינִ֥י וּבֵינְךָ֖ עַד־עוֹלָֽם׃ כד וַיִּסָּתֵ֥ר דָּוִ֖ד בַּשָּׂדֶ֑ה
וַיְהִ֣י הַחֹ֔דֶשׁ וַיֵּ֧שֶׁב הַמֶּ֛לֶךְ עַל־ (אל קרי) הַלֶּ֖חֶם
לֶאֱכֽוֹל׃ כה וַיֵּ֣שֶׁב הַ֠מֶּלֶךְ עַל־מ֨וֹשָׁב֜וֹ כְּפַ֣עַם ׀
בְּפַ֗עַם אֶל־מוֹשַׁב֙ הַקִּ֔יר וַיָּ֙קָם֙ יְה֣וֹנָתָ֔ן וַיֵּ֥שֶׁב
אַבְנֵ֖ר מִצַּ֣ד שָׁא֑וּל וַיִּפָּקֵ֖ד מְק֥וֹם דָּוִֽד׃ כו וְלֹֽא־
דִבֶּ֥ר שָׁא֛וּל מְא֖וּמָה בַּיּ֣וֹם הַה֑וּא כִּ֤י אָמַר֙
מִקְרֶ֣ה ה֔וּא בִּלְתִּ֥י טָה֛וֹר ה֖וּא כִּֽי־לֹ֥א טָהֽוֹר׃
כז וַיְהִ֗י מִֽמָּחֳרַ֤ת הַחֹ֙דֶשׁ֙ הַשֵּׁנִ֔י וַיִּפָּקֵ֖ד מְק֣וֹם
דָּוִ֑ד וַיֹּ֤אמֶר שָׁאוּל֙ אֶל־יְהוֹנָתָ֣ן בְּנ֔וֹ מַדּ֜וּעַ לֹא־
בָ֧א בֶן־יִשַׁ֛י גַּם־תְּמ֥וֹל גַּם־הַיּ֖וֹם אֶל־הַלָּֽחֶם׃
כח וַיַּ֥עַן יְהוֹנָתָ֖ן אֶת־שָׁא֑וּל נִשְׁאֹ֨ל נִשְׁאַ֥ל דָּוִ֛ד
מֵעִמָּדִ֖י עַד־בֵּ֥ית לָֽחֶם׃ כט וַיֹּ֡אמֶר שַׁלְּחֵ֣נִי נָ֡א
כִּ֣י זֶבַח֩ מִשְׁפָּחָ֨ה לָ֜נוּ בָּעִ֗יר וְה֤וּא צִוָּֽה־לִי֙ אָחִ֔י
וְעַתָּ֗ה אִם־מָצָ֤אתִי חֵן֙ בְּעֵינֶ֔יךָ אִמָּ֥לְטָה נָּ֖א
וְאֶרְאֶ֣ה אֶת־אֶחָ֑י עַל־כֵּ֣ן לֹא־בָ֔א אֶל־שֻׁלְחַ֖ן
הַמֶּֽלֶךְ׃ ל וַיִּֽחַר־אַ֤ף שָׁאוּל֙ בִּיה֣וֹנָתָ֔ן וַיֹּ֣אמֶר ל֔וֹ

20:18. And Jonathan said to him, "Tomorrow is the new moon, and you will be remembered, for your seat will be vacant. 19. And for three days, you shall hide very well, and you shall come to the place where you hid on the day of work, and you shall stay beside the traveler's stone. 20. And I shall shoot three arrows to the side, as though I shot at a mark. 21. And behold, I shall send the youth, (saying,) 'Go, find the arrows.' If I say to the youth, 'Behold, the arrows are on this side of you,' take it and come, for it is well with you, and there is nothing the matter, as the Lord lives. 22. But, if I say thus to the youth, 'Behold, the arrows are beyond you,' go! For the Lord has sent you away. 23. And [concerning] the matter which we have spoken, I and you, behold, the Lord is between me and you forever." 24. And David hid in the field, and when it was the new moon, Saul sat down to the meal to eat. 25. And the king sat upon his seat, as at other times, upon the seat by the wall, and Jonathan arose, and Abner sat down beside Saul, and David's place was vacant. 26. And Saul did not say anything on that day, for he thought, "It is an incident; he is not clean, for he is not clean." 27. And it was, on the morrow of the new moon, the second [day of the month], that David's place was vacant, and Saul said to Jonathan, his son, "Why has not the son of Jesse come to the meal either yesterday or today?" 28. And Jonathan answered Saul, "David asked leave of me [to go] to Bethlehem. 29. And he said, 'Let me go away now, for we have a family sacrifice in the city, and he, my brother, commanded me, and now, if I have found favor in your eyes, let me slip away now, and see my brothers.' He, therefore, did not come to the king's table." 30. And Saul's wrath was kindled against Jonathan, and he said to him, "You son of a straying woman deserving of punishment! Did I not know that you choose the son of Jesse, to your shame and to the shame of your mother's nakedness? 31. For all the days that the son of Jesse is living on the earth, you and your kingdom will not be established. And now, send and take him to me, for he is condemned to death." 32. And Jonathan answered Saul his father, and said to him, "Why should he be put to death? What has he done?" 33. And Saul cast the spear upon him to strike him; and Jonathan knew that it had been decided upon by his father, to put David to death. 34. And Jonathan arose from the table in fierce anger; and he did not eat any food on the second day of the new moon, for he was grieved concerning David, for his father had put him to shame. 35. And it was in the morning that Jonathan went out at David's appointed time, and a small boy was with him. 36. And he said to his boy, "Run, find now the arrows which I shoot." The boy ran; and he shot the arrow to cause it to go beyond him. 37. And the lad came up to the place of the arrow that Jonathan had shot. And Jonathan called after the lad and said, "Isn't the arrow beyond you?" 38. And Jonathan called after the lad, "Quickly, hasten, do not stand!" And Jonathan's lad gathered up the arrows and came to his master. 39. And the lad knew nothing; only Jonathan and David knew the matter. 40. And Jonathan gave his weapons to his boy, and said to him, "Go, bring [them] to the city." 41. The lad departed, and David arose from [a place] toward the south; and he fell upon his face to the ground three times, and prostrated himself three times. And they kissed one another, and wept one with the other, until David exceeded. 42. And Jonathan said to David, "Go in peace! [And bear in mind] that we have sworn both of us in the name of the Lord, saying, 'May the Lord be between me and you, and between my descendants and your descendants forever.'"

בֶּן־נַעֲוַת הַמַּרְדּוּת הֲלוֹא יָדַעְתִּי כִּי־בֹחֵר אַתָּה לְבֶן־יִשַׁי לְבָשְׁתְּךָ וּלְבֹשֶׁת עֶרְוַת אִמֶּךָ: לא כִּי כָל־הַיָּמִים אֲשֶׁר בֶּן־יִשַׁי חַי עַל־הָאֲדָמָה לֹא תִכּוֹן אַתָּה וּמַלְכוּתֶךָ וְעַתָּה שְׁלַח וְקַח אֹתוֹ אֵלַי כִּי בֶן־מָוֶת הוּא: לב וַיַּעַן יְהוֹנָתָן אֶת־שָׁאוּל אָבִיו וַיֹּאמֶר אֵלָיו לָמָּה יוּמַת מֶה עָשָׂה: לג וַיָּטֶל שָׁאוּל אֶת־הַחֲנִית עָלָיו לְהַכֹּתוֹ וַיֵּדַע יְהוֹנָתָן כִּי־כָלָה הִיא מֵעִם אָבִיו לְהָמִית אֶת־דָּוִד: לד וַיָּקָם יְהוֹנָתָן מֵעִם הַשֻּׁלְחָן בָּחֳרִי־אָף וְלֹא־אָכַל בְּיוֹם־הַחֹדֶשׁ הַשֵּׁנִי לֶחֶם כִּי נֶעְצַב אֶל־דָּוִד כִּי הִכְלִמוֹ אָבִיו: לה וַיְהִי בַבֹּקֶר וַיֵּצֵא יְהוֹנָתָן הַשָּׂדֶה לְמוֹעֵד דָּוִד וְנַעַר קָטֹן עִמּוֹ: לו וַיֹּאמֶר לְנַעֲרוֹ רֻץ מְצָא נָא אֶת־הַחִצִּים אֲשֶׁר אָנֹכִי מוֹרֶה הַנַּעַר רָץ וְהוּא־יָרָה הַחֵצִי לְהַעֲבִרוֹ: לז וַיָּבֹא הַנַּעַר עַד־מְקוֹם הַחֵצִי אֲשֶׁר יָרָה יְהוֹנָתָן וַיִּקְרָא יְהוֹנָתָן אַחֲרֵי הַנַּעַר וַיֹּאמֶר הֲלוֹא הַחֵצִי מִמְּךָ וָהָלְאָה: לח וַיִּקְרָא יְהוֹנָתָן אַחֲרֵי הַנַּעַר מְהֵרָה חוּשָׁה אַל־תַּעֲמֹד וַיְלַקֵּט נַעַר יְהוֹנָתָן אֶת־הַחֵצִי (החצים קרי) וַיָּבֹא אֶל־אֲדֹנָיו: לט וְהַנַּעַר לֹא־יָדַע מְאוּמָה אַךְ יְהוֹנָתָן וְדָוִד יָדְעוּ אֶת־הַדָּבָר: מ וַיִּתֵּן יְהוֹנָתָן אֶת־כֵּלָיו אֶל־הַנַּעַר אֲשֶׁר־לוֹ וַיֹּאמֶר לוֹ לֵךְ הָבֵיא הָעִיר: מא הַנַּעַר בָּא וְדָוִד קָם מֵאֵצֶל הַנֶּגֶב וַיִּפֹּל לְאַפָּיו אַרְצָה וַיִּשְׁתַּחוּ שָׁלֹשׁ פְּעָמִים וַיִּשְּׁקוּ ׀ אִישׁ אֶת־רֵעֵהוּ וַיִּבְכּוּ אִישׁ אֶת־רֵעֵהוּ עַד־דָּוִד הִגְדִּיל: מב וַיֹּאמֶר יְהוֹנָתָן לְדָוִד לֵךְ לְשָׁלוֹם אֲשֶׁר נִשְׁבַּעְנוּ שְׁנֵינוּ אֲנַחְנוּ בְּשֵׁם יְהֹוָה לֵאמֹר יְהֹוָה יִהְיֶה ׀ בֵּינִי וּבֵינֶךָ וּבֵין זַרְעִי וּבֵין זַרְעֲךָ עַד־עוֹלָם:

HAFTARAH FOR THE FIRST DAY OF ROSH HASHANAH

(I Samuel 1–2:10)

Torah reading: Genesis 21, Numbers 29:1–6

This selection relates the story of Hannah, her prayer for offspring, the subsequent birth and infancy of Samuel, and Hannah's prayer of thanksgiving. According to tradition, Hannah conceived her son on Rosh Hashanah.

1:1. And there was one man from Ramathaim Zophim, from Mt. Ephraim, and his name was Elkanah, the son of Jeroham, the son of Elihu, the son of Tohu, the son of Zuph, an Ephraimite. 2. And he had two wives; the name of the one was Hannah, and the name of the second was Peninnah; and Peninnah had children, but Hannah had no children. 3. And that man was wont to go up from his city from appointed time to appointed time, to prostrate himself and to slaughter (peace offerings) to the Lord of Hosts in Shiloh, and there the two sons of Eli, Hophni and Phinhas, were serving the Lord. 4. And when it was the day, and Elkanah slaughtered (peace offerings), and he would give to Peninnah his wife and to all her sons and daughters portions. 5. And to Hannah he would give one choice portion, for he loved Hannah, and the Lord had shut up her womb. 6. And her rival would frequently anger her, in order to make her complain, for the Lord had shut up her womb. 7. And so he would do year by year, as often as she went up to the house of the Lord, so she would anger her, and she wept and would not eat. 8. And Elkanah, her husband, said to her, "Hannah, why do you weep? And why do you not eat? And why is your heart sad? Am I not better to you than ten sons?" 9. And Hannah arose after eating and after drinking, and Eli the priest was sitting on the chair beside the doorpost of the Temple of the Lord. 10. And she was bitter in spirit, and she prayed to the Lord, and wept. 11. And she vowed a vow, and said: "O Lord of Hosts, if You will look upon the affliction of Your bondswoman, and You will remember me, and You will not forget Your bondswoman, and You will give Your bondswoman a man-child, and I shall give him to the Lord all the days of his life, and no razor shall come upon his head." 12. And it was, as she prayed long before

א וַיְהִי אִישׁ אֶחָד מִן־הָרָמָתַיִם צוֹפִים מֵהַר
אֶפְרָיִם וּשְׁמוֹ אֶלְקָנָה בֶּן־יְרֹחָם בֶּן־אֱלִיהוּא
בֶּן־תֹּחוּ בֶן־צוּף אֶפְרָתִי׃ ב וְלוֹ שְׁתֵּי נָשִׁים
שֵׁם אַחַת חַנָּה וְשֵׁם הַשֵּׁנִית פְּנִנָּה וַיְהִי לִפְנִנָּה
יְלָדִים וּלְחַנָּה אֵין יְלָדִים׃ ג וְעָלָה הָאִישׁ הַהוּא
מֵעִירוֹ מִיָּמִים ׀ יָמִימָה לְהִשְׁתַּחֲוֺת וְלִזְבֹּחַ
לַיהוָה צְבָאוֹת בְּשִׁלֹה וְשָׁם שְׁנֵי בְנֵי־עֵלִי חָפְנִי
וּפִנְחָס כֹּהֲנִים לַיהוָה׃ ד וַיְהִי הַיּוֹם וַיִּזְבַּח
אֶלְקָנָה וְנָתַן לִפְנִנָּה אִשְׁתּוֹ וּלְכָל־בָּנֶיהָ
וּבְנוֹתֶיהָ מָנוֹת׃ ה וּלְחַנָּה יִתֵּן מָנָה אַחַת אַפָּיִם
כִּי אֶת־חַנָּה אָהֵב וַיהוָה סָגַר רַחְמָהּ׃
ו וְכִעֲסַתָּה צָרָתָהּ גַּם־כַּעַס בַּעֲבוּר הַרְּעִמָהּ
כִּי־סָגַר יְהוָה בְּעַד רַחְמָהּ׃ ז וְכֵן יַעֲשֶׂה שָׁנָה
בְשָׁנָה מִדֵּי עֲלֹתָהּ בְּבֵית יְהוָה כֵּן תַּכְעִסֶנָּה
וַתִּבְכֶּה וְלֹא תֹאכַל׃ ח וַיֹּאמֶר לָהּ אֶלְקָנָה
אִישָׁהּ חַנָּה לָמֶה תִבְכִּי וְלָמֶה לֹא תֹאכְלִי
וְלָמֶה יֵרַע לְבָבֵךְ הֲלוֹא אָנֹכִי טוֹב לָךְ מֵעֲשָׂרָה
בָּנִים׃ ט וַתָּקָם חַנָּה אַחֲרֵי אָכְלָה בְשִׁלֹה
וְאַחֲרֵי שָׁתֹה וְעֵלִי הַכֹּהֵן יֹשֵׁב עַל־הַכִּסֵּא עַל־
מְזוּזַת הֵיכַל יְהוָה׃ י וְהִיא מָרַת נָפֶשׁ וַתִּתְפַּלֵּל
עַל־יְהוָה וּבָכֹה תִבְכֶּה׃ יא וַתִּדֹּר נֶדֶר וַתֹּאמַר
יְהוָה צְבָאוֹת אִם־רָאֹה תִרְאֶה ׀ בָּעֳנִי אֲמָתֶךָ
וּזְכַרְתַּנִי וְלֹא־תִשְׁכַּח אֶת־אֲמָתֶךָ וְנָתַתָּה
לַאֲמָתְךָ זֶרַע אֲנָשִׁים וּנְתַתִּיו לַיהוָה כָּל־יְמֵי
חַיָּיו וּמוֹרָה לֹא־יַעֲלֶה עַל־רֹאשׁוֹ׃ יב וְהָיָה כִּי

the Lord, that Eli watched her mouth. 13. But Hannah, she was speaking in her heart, only her lips were moving, and her voice was not heard, and Eli thought her to be a drunken woman. 14. And Eli said to her: "Until when will you be drunk? Throw off your wine from upon yourself." 15. And Hannah answered and said: "No, my lord, I am a woman of sorrowful spirit, and neither new wine nor old wine have I drunk, and I poured out my soul before the Lord. 16. Deliver not your bondswoman before the unscrupulous woman, for out of the abundance of my complaint and my vexation have I spoken until now." 17. And Eli answered and said: "Go in peace, and the God of Israel will grant your request which you have asked of Him." 18. And she said: "May your bondswoman find favor in your eyes." And the woman went on her way and ate, and her face was not [sad] anymore. 19. And they arose early in the morning, and prostrated themselves before the Lord; and they returned and came to their house, to Ramah, and Elkanah knew Hannah, his wife, and the Lord remembered her. 20. And it was, when the time came about, after Hannah had conceived, that she bore a son, and she called his name Samuel, because [she said]: "I asked him of the Lord." 21. And the man, Elkanah, and his entire household, went up to slaughter to the Lord, the sacrifice of the days and his vow. 22. But Hannah did not go up, for she said to her husband: "Until the child is weaned, then I shall bring him, and he shall appear before the Lord, and abide there forever." 23. And Elkanah, her husband, said to her: "Do what seems good to you. Stay until you have weaned him, only, may the Lord fulfill His word." And the woman stayed and nursed her son, until she weaned him. 24. And she brought him with her when she had weaned him, with three bulls, and one ephah of meal and an earthenware jug of wine, and she brought him to the house of the Lord, to Shiloh, and the child was young. 25. And they slaughtered the bull, and they brought the child to Eli. 26. And she said, "Please, my lord! As surely as your soul lives, my lord, I am the woman who was standing here with you, to pray to the Lord. 27. For this child did I

הִרְבְּתָה לְהִתְפַּלֵּל לִפְנֵי יְהוָה וְעֵלִי שֹׁמֵר אֶת־
פִּיהָ: יג וְחַנָּה הִיא מְדַבֶּרֶת עַל־לִבָּהּ רַק
שְׂפָתֶיהָ נָּעוֹת וְקוֹלָהּ לֹא יִשָּׁמֵעַ וַיַּחְשְׁבֶהָ עֵלִי
לְשִׁכֹּרָה: יד וַיֹּאמֶר אֵלֶיהָ עֵלִי עַד־מָתַי
תִּשְׁתַּכָּרִין הָסִירִי אֶת־יֵינֵךְ מֵעָלָיִךְ: טו וַתַּעַן
חַנָּה וַתֹּאמֶר לֹא אֲדֹנִי אִשָּׁה קְשַׁת־רוּחַ אָנֹכִי
וְיַיִן וְשֵׁכָר לֹא שָׁתִיתִי וָאֶשְׁפֹּךְ אֶת־נַפְשִׁי לִפְנֵי
יְהוָה: טז אַל־תִּתֵּן אֶת־אֲמָתְךָ לִפְנֵי בַּת־בְּלִיָּעַל
כִּי־מֵרֹב שִׂיחִי וְכַעְסִי דִּבַּרְתִּי עַד־הֵנָּה: יז וַיַּעַן
עֵלִי וַיֹּאמֶר לְכִי לְשָׁלוֹם וֵאלֹהֵי יִשְׂרָאֵל יִתֵּן
אֶת־שֵׁלָתֵךְ אֲשֶׁר שָׁאַלְתְּ מֵעִמּוֹ: יח וַתֹּאמֶר
תִּמְצָא שִׁפְחָתְךָ חֵן בְּעֵינֶיךָ וַתֵּלֶךְ הָאִשָּׁה
לְדַרְכָּהּ וַתֹּאכַל וּפָנֶיהָ לֹא־הָיוּ־לָהּ עוֹד:
יט וַיַּשְׁכִּמוּ בַבֹּקֶר וַיִּשְׁתַּחֲווּ לִפְנֵי יְהוָה וַיָּשֻׁבוּ
וַיָּבֹאוּ אֶל־בֵּיתָם הָרָמָתָה וַיֵּדַע אֶלְקָנָה אֶת־
חַנָּה אִשְׁתּוֹ וַיִּזְכְּרֶהָ יְהוָה: כ וַיְהִי לִתְקֻפוֹת
הַיָּמִים וַתַּהַר חַנָּה וַתֵּלֶד בֵּן וַתִּקְרָא אֶת־שְׁמוֹ
שְׁמוּאֵל כִּי מֵיְהוָה שְׁאִלְתִּיו: כא וַיַּעַל הָאִישׁ
אֶלְקָנָה וְכָל־בֵּיתוֹ לִזְבֹּחַ לַיהוָה אֶת־זֶבַח
הַיָּמִים וְאֶת־נִדְרוֹ: כב וְחַנָּה לֹא עָלָתָה כִּי־
אָמְרָה לְאִישָׁהּ עַד יִגָּמֵל הַנַּעַר וַהֲבִאֹתִיו
וְנִרְאָה אֶת־פְּנֵי יְהוָה וְיָשַׁב שָׁם עַד־עוֹלָם:
כג וַיֹּאמֶר לָהּ אֶלְקָנָה אִישָׁהּ עֲשִׂי הַטּוֹב
בְּעֵינַיִךְ שְׁבִי עַד־גָּמְלֵךְ אֹתוֹ אַךְ יָקֵם יְהוָה
אֶת־דְּבָרוֹ וַתֵּשֶׁב הָאִשָּׁה וַתֵּינֶק אֶת־בְּנָהּ עַד־
גָּמְלָהּ אֹתוֹ: כד וַתַּעֲלֵהוּ עִמָּהּ כַּאֲשֶׁר גְּמָלַתּוּ
בְּפָרִים שְׁלֹשָׁה וְאֵיפָה אַחַת קֶמַח וְנֵבֶל יַיִן
וַתְּבִאֵהוּ בֵית־יְהוָה שִׁלוֹ וְהַנַּעַר נָעַר:
כה וַיִּשְׁחֲטוּ אֶת־הַפָּר וַיָּבִאוּ אֶת־הַנַּעַר אֶל־
עֵלִי: כו וַתֹּאמֶר בִּי אֲדֹנִי חֵי נַפְשְׁךָ אֲדֹנִי אֲנִי
הָאִשָּׁה הַנִּצֶּבֶת עִמְּכָה בָּזֶה לְהִתְפַּלֵּל אֶל־יְהוָה:

pray, and the Lord granted me my request, which I asked of Him. 28. And I also have lent him to the Lord; all the days which he will be [alive], he is borrowed by the Lord." And he prostrated himself there to the Lord. 2:1. And Hannah prayed and said: "My heart has rejoiced through the Lord; my horn has been raised by the Lord. My mouth is opened wide against my enemies, for I have rejoiced in Your salvation. 2. There is none as holy as the Lord, for there is none besides You; and there is no Rock like our God. 3. Do not increasingly speak haughtily; let not arrogance come out of your mouth, for the Lord is a God of thoughts, and to Him are deeds counted. 4. The bows of the mighty are broken; and those who stumbled are girded with strength. 5. Those who were satiated have hired themselves out for bread, while the hungry have ceased. While the barren woman has born seven, she that had many children has been bereaved. 6. The Lord kills and makes alive; He brings down to the grave and raises up. 7. The Lord impoverishes and makes rich. He humbles; He also exalts. 8. He lifts the poor from the dust; from the dunghill He raises the pauper to seat them with princes, and a seat of honor He causes them to inherit, for the pillars of the earth are the Lord's, and He placed the world upon them. 9. The feet of His pious ones He will guard, and the wicked shall be cut off in darkness, for not by strength will man prevail. 10. Those who strive with the Lord will be broken; upon him will He thunder in Heaven; the Lord will judge the ends of the earth. And He will grant strength to his king, and raise the horn of his anointed one."

כז אֶל־הַנַּעַר הַזֶּה הִתְפַּלָּלְתִּי וַיִּתֵּן יְהֹוָה לִי אֶת־שְׁאֵלָתִי אֲשֶׁר שָׁאַלְתִּי מֵעִמּוֹ: כח וְגַם אָנֹכִי הִשְׁאִלְתִּהוּ לַיהֹוָה כָּל־הַיָּמִים אֲשֶׁר הָיָה הוּא שָׁאוּל לַיהֹוָה וַיִּשְׁתַּחוּ שָׁם לַיהֹוָה: א וַתִּתְפַּלֵּל חַנָּה וַתֹּאמַר עָלַץ לִבִּי בַּיהֹוָה רָמָה קַרְנִי בַּיהֹוָה רָחַב פִּי עַל־אוֹיְבַי כִּי שָׂמַחְתִּי בִּישׁוּעָתֶךָ: ב אֵין־קָדוֹשׁ כַּיהֹוָה כִּי־אֵין בִּלְתֶּךָ וְאֵין צוּר כֵּאלֹהֵינוּ: ג אַל־תַּרְבּוּ תְדַבְּרוּ גְּבֹהָה גְבֹהָה יֵצֵא עָתָק מִפִּיכֶם כִּי אֵל דֵּעוֹת יְהֹוָה וְלֹא (ולו קרי) נִתְכְּנוּ עֲלִלוֹת: ד קֶשֶׁת גִּבֹּרִים חַתִּים וְנִכְשָׁלִים אָזְרוּ חָיִל: ה שְׂבֵעִים בַּלֶּחֶם נִשְׂכָּרוּ וּרְעֵבִים חָדֵלּוּ עַד־עֲקָרָה יָלְדָה שִׁבְעָה וְרַבַּת בָּנִים אֻמְלָלָה: ו יְהֹוָה מֵמִית וּמְחַיֶּה מוֹרִיד שְׁאוֹל וַיָּעַל: ז יְהֹוָה מוֹרִישׁ וּמַעֲשִׁיר מַשְׁפִּיל אַף־מְרוֹמֵם: ח מֵקִים מֵעָפָר דָּל מֵאַשְׁפֹּת יָרִים אֶבְיוֹן לְהוֹשִׁיב עִם־נְדִיבִים וְכִסֵּא כָבוֹד יַנְחִלֵם כִּי לַיהֹוָה מְצֻקֵי אֶרֶץ וַיָּשֶׁת עֲלֵיהֶם תֵּבֵל: ט רַגְלֵי חֲסִידָו (חסידיו קרי) יִשְׁמֹר וּרְשָׁעִים בַּחֹשֶׁךְ יִדָּמּוּ כִּי־לֹא בְכֹחַ יִגְבַּר־אִישׁ: י יְהֹוָה יֵחַתּוּ מְרִיבָו (מריביו קרי) עָלָו (עליו קרי) בַּשָּׁמַיִם יַרְעֵם יְהֹוָה יָדִין אַפְסֵי־אָרֶץ וְיִתֶּן־עֹז לְמַלְכּוֹ וְיָרֵם קֶרֶן מְשִׁיחוֹ:

הפטרת יום ב׳ דראש השנה

HAFTARAH FOR THE SECOND DAY OF ROSH HASHANAH

(Jeremiah 31:1–19)

Torah reading: Genesis 22, Numbers 29:1–6

The closing verse of this selection mentions God's remembrance of His people; hence it is an appropriate reading for Rosh Hashanah, the "Day of Remembrance." One of the obligations of the day is to mention God's remembrances.

31:1. So says the Lord: In the wilderness, the people who had escaped the sword found favor; He therefore went to give Israel their resting place. 2. From long ago, the Lord appeared to me: With everlasting love have I loved you; therefore have I drawn you to Me with lovingkindness. 3. Yet again will I rebuild you, then you will be built, O virgin of Israel; yet again shall you be adorned with your taborets, and you shall go out with the dances of those who make merry. 4. Yet again shall you plant vineyards on the mountains of Samaria; indeed, planters had once planted them, but now they will redeem them. 5. For there is a day the watchers shall call on the mountains of Ephraim: Rise! Let us go up to Zion, to the Lord, our God. 6. For so says the Lord to Jacob: Sing with joy and shout at the head of the nations, make it heard, praise, and say, "O Lord, help Your people, the remnant of Israel!" 7. Behold I bring them from the north country and gather them from the uttermost ends of the earth, the blind and the lame amongst them, the woman with child and her who travails with child all together; a great company shall they return here. 8. With weeping will they come, and with supplications will I lead them; along brooks of water will I make them go, on a straight road upon which they will not stumble, for I have become a Father to Israel, and Ephraim is My firstborn. 9. Hear the word of the Lord, O nations, and declare it on the islands from afar, and say, He Who scattered Israel will gather them together and watch them as a shepherd his flock. 10. For the Lord has redeemed Jacob and has saved him out of the hand of him who is stronger than he. 11. And they shall come and jubilate on the height of Zion, and they will stream to the goodness of the Lord over corn, wine, and oil, and over

א כֹּה אָמַר יְהֹוָה מָצָא חֵן בַּמִּדְבָּר עַם שְׂרִידֵי
חָרֶב הָלוֹךְ לְהַרְגִּיעוֹ יִשְׂרָאֵל: ב מֵרָחוֹק יְהֹוָה
נִרְאָה לִי וְאַהֲבַת עוֹלָם אֲהַבְתִּיךְ עַל־כֵּן
מְשַׁכְתִּיךְ חָסֶד: ג עוֹד אֶבְנֵךְ וְנִבְנֵית בְּתוּלַת
יִשְׂרָאֵל עוֹד תַּעְדִּי תֻפַּיִךְ וְיָצָאת בִּמְחוֹל
מְשַׂחֲקִים: ד עוֹד תִּטְּעִי כְרָמִים בְּהָרֵי שֹׁמְרוֹן
נָטְעוּ נֹטְעִים וְחִלֵּלוּ: ה כִּי יֶשׁ־יוֹם קָרְאוּ
נֹצְרִים בְּהַר אֶפְרָיִם קוּמוּ וְנַעֲלֶה צִיּוֹן אֶל־
יְהֹוָה אֱלֹהֵינוּ: ו כִּי־כֹה | אָמַר יְהֹוָה רָנּוּ
לְיַעֲקֹב שִׂמְחָה וְצַהֲלוּ בְּרֹאשׁ הַגּוֹיִם הַשְׁמִיעוּ
הַלְלוּ וְאִמְרוּ הוֹשַׁע יְהֹוָה אֶת־עַמְּךָ אֵת
שְׁאֵרִית יִשְׂרָאֵל: ז הִנְנִי מֵבִיא אוֹתָם מֵאֶרֶץ
צָפוֹן וְקִבַּצְתִּים מִיַּרְכְּתֵי־אָרֶץ בָּם עִוֵּר וּפִסֵּחַ
הָרָה וְיֹלֶדֶת יַחְדָּו קָהָל גָּדוֹל יָשׁוּבוּ הֵנָּה:
ח בִּבְכִי יָבֹאוּ וּבְתַחֲנוּנִים אוֹבִילֵם אוֹלִיכֵם
אֶל־נַחֲלֵי מַיִם בְּדֶרֶךְ יָשָׁר לֹא יִכָּשְׁלוּ בָּהּ כִּי־
הָיִיתִי לְיִשְׂרָאֵל לְאָב וְאֶפְרַיִם בְּכֹרִי הוּא:
ט שִׁמְעוּ דְבַר־יְהֹוָה גּוֹיִם וְהַגִּידוּ בָאִיִּים
מִמֶּרְחָק וְאִמְרוּ מְזָרֵה יִשְׂרָאֵל יְקַבְּצֶנּוּ וּשְׁמָרוֹ
כְּרֹעֶה עֶדְרוֹ: י כִּי־פָדָה יְהֹוָה אֶת־יַעֲקֹב וּגְאָלוֹ
מִיַּד חָזָק מִמֶּנּוּ: יא וּבָאוּ וְרִנְּנוּ בִמְרוֹם־צִיּוֹן
וְנָהֲרוּ אֶל־טוּב יְהֹוָה עַל־דָּגָן וְעַל־תִּירֹשׁ וְעַל־

יִצְהָר וְעַל־בְּנֵי־צֹאן וּבָקָר וְהָיְתָה נַפְשָׁם כְּגַן
רָוֶה וְלֹא־יוֹסִיפוּ לְדַאֲבָה עוֹד: יב אָז תִּשְׂמַח
בְּתוּלָה בְּמָחוֹל וּבַחֻרִים וּזְקֵנִים יַחְדָּו וְהָפַכְתִּי
אֶבְלָם לְשָׂשׂוֹן וְנִחַמְתִּים וְשִׂמַּחְתִּים מִיגוֹנָם:
יג וְרִוֵּיתִי נֶפֶשׁ הַכֹּהֲנִים דָּשֶׁן וְעַמִּי אֶת־טוּבִי
יִשְׂבָּעוּ נְאֻם־יְהוָה: יד כֹּה | אָמַר יְהוָה קוֹל
בְּרָמָה נִשְׁמָע נְהִי בְּכִי תַמְרוּרִים רָחֵל מְבַכָּה
עַל־בָּנֶיהָ מֵאֲנָה לְהִנָּחֵם עַל־בָּנֶיהָ כִּי אֵינֶנּוּ:
טו כֹּה | אָמַר יְהוָה מִנְעִי קוֹלֵךְ מִבֶּכִי וְעֵינַיִךְ
מִדִּמְעָה כִּי יֵשׁ שָׂכָר לִפְעֻלָּתֵךְ נְאֻם־יְהוָה
וְשָׁבוּ מֵאֶרֶץ אוֹיֵב: טז וְיֵשׁ־תִּקְוָה לְאַחֲרִיתֵךְ
נְאֻם־יְהוָה וְשָׁבוּ בָנִים לִגְבוּלָם: יז שָׁמוֹעַ
שָׁמַעְתִּי אֶפְרַיִם מִתְנוֹדֵד יִסַּרְתַּנִי וָאִוָּסֵר כְּעֵגֶל
לֹא לֻמָּד הֲשִׁבֵנִי וְאָשׁוּבָה כִּי אַתָּה יְהוָה אֱלֹהָי:
יח כִּי־אַחֲרֵי שׁוּבִי נִחַמְתִּי וְאַחֲרֵי הִוָּדְעִי
סָפַקְתִּי עַל־יָרֵךְ בֹּשְׁתִּי וְגַם־נִכְלַמְתִּי כִּי
נָשָׂאתִי חֶרְפַּת נְעוּרָי: יט הֲבֵן יַקִּיר לִי אֶפְרַיִם
אִם יֶלֶד שַׁעֲשֻׁעִים כִּי־מִדֵּי דַבְּרִי בּוֹ זָכֹר
אֶזְכְּרֶנּוּ עוֹד עַל־כֵּן הָמוּ מֵעַי לוֹ רַחֵם
אֲרַחֲמֶנּוּ נְאֻם־יְהוָה:

sheep and cattle, and their soul shall be like a well-watered garden, and they shall have no further worry at all. 12. Then shall the virgin rejoice in the round dance with music, and the young men and the old men together, and I will turn their mourning into joy and will comfort them and make them rejoice from their sorrow. 13. And I will refresh the soul of the priests with fat, and My people, they will be satisfied with My goodness, is the word of the Lord. 14. So says the Lord: A voice is heard on high, lamentation, bitter weeping, Rachel weeping for her children; she refuses to be comforted for her children for they are not. 15. So says the Lord: Refrain your voice from weeping and your eyes from tears, for there is reward for your work, says the Lord, and they shall come back from the land of the enemy. 16. And there is hope for your future, says the Lord, and the children shall return to their own border. 17. I have indeed heard Ephraim complaining, [saying,] "You have chastised me, and I was chastised as an ungoaded calf, O lead me back, and I will return, for You are the Lord, my God. 18. For after my return I have completely changed my mind, and after I had been brought to know myself, I smote upon my thigh; I was ashamed, yea, I stood confounded, for I bore the reproach of my youth. 19. "Is Ephraim a son who is dear to me? Is he a child who is dandled? For whenever I speak of him, I still remember him; therefore, My very innards are agitated for him; I will surely have compassion on him," says the Lord.

HAFTARATH YOM KIPPUR SHACHARITH הפטרת יום כפור שחרית

Haftarah for Yom Kippur Morning Service

(Isaiah 57:14–58:14)

Torah reading: Leviticus 16, Numbers 29:7–11

This selection deals with fasting and repentance.

יד וְאָמַר סֹלּוּ־סֹלּוּ פַּנּוּ־דָרֶךְ הָרִימוּ מִכְשׁוֹל
מִדֶּרֶךְ עַמִּי: טו כִּי כֹה אָמַר רָם וְנִשָּׂא שֹׁכֵן עַד
וְקָדוֹשׁ שְׁמוֹ מָרוֹם וְקָדוֹשׁ אֶשְׁכּוֹן וְאֶת־דַּכָּא
וּשְׁפַל־רוּחַ לְהַחֲיוֹת רוּחַ שְׁפָלִים וּלְהַחֲיוֹת לֵב

57:14. And he shall say, "Pave, pave, clear the way; remove the obstacles from the way of My people." 15. For so said the High and Exalted One—Who dwells to eternity, and His name is Holy,—With the lofty and the holy ones I dwell, and with the crushed and humble in spirit, to revive the spirit of the humble and to revive the heart of the crushed. 16. For I will not contend forever, neither will I be wroth to eternity, when a spirit from before Me humbles itself, and souls [which] I have made. 17. For the iniquity of his thievery I became wroth, and I smote him; I hid Myself and became wroth, for he went rebelliously in the way of his heart. 18. I saw his ways, and I will heal him, and I will lead him and requite with consolations him and his mourners. 19. "[I] create the speech of the lips; peace, peace to the far and to the near," says the Lord, "and I will heal him." 20. But the wicked are like the turbulent sea, for it cannot rest, and its waters cast up mud and dirt. 21. "There is no peace," says my God, "for the wicked." 58:1. Call with a [full] throat—do not spare—like a shofar raise your voice, and relate to My people their transgression, and to the house of Jacob their sins. 2. Yet they seek Me daily and they wish to know My ways, like a nation that performed righteousness and did not forsake the ordinance of its God; they ask Me ordinances of righteousness; they desire nearness to God. 3. "Why have we fasted, and You did not see; we have afflicted our soul, and You do not know?" Behold, on the day of your fast you pursue business, and [from] all your debtors you exact [payment]. 4. Behold, for quarrel and strife you fast, and to strike with a fist of wickedness. Do not fast like this day, to make your voice heard on high. 5. Will such be the fast I will choose, a day of man's afflicting his soul? Is it to bend his head like a fishhook and spread out sackcloth and ashes? Will you call this a fast and an acceptable day to the Lord? 6. Is this not the fast I will choose? To undo the fetters of wickedness, to untie the bands of perverseness, and to let out the oppressed free, and all perverseness you shall eliminate. 7. Is it not to share your bread with the hungry, and moaning poor you shall bring home; when you see a naked one, you shall clothe him, and from your flesh you shall not hide. 8. Then your light shall break forth as the dawn, and your healing shall quickly sprout, and your righteousness shall go before you; the glory of the Lord shall gather you in. 9. Then you shall call, and the Lord shall answer; you shall cry, and He shall say,

נִדְכָּאִים: טז כִּי לֹא לְעוֹלָם אָרִיב וְלֹא לָנֶצַח אֶקְצוֹף כִּי־רוּחַ מִלְּפָנַי יַעֲטוֹף וּנְשָׁמוֹת אֲנִי עָשִׂיתִי: יז בַּעֲוֹן בִּצְעוֹ קָצַפְתִּי וְאַכֵּהוּ הַסְתֵּר וְאֶקְצֹף וַיֵּלֶךְ שׁוֹבָב בְּדֶרֶךְ לִבּוֹ: יח דְּרָכָיו רָאִיתִי וְאֶרְפָּאֵהוּ וְאַנְחֵהוּ וַאֲשַׁלֵּם נִחֻמִים לוֹ וְלַאֲבֵלָיו: יט בּוֹרֵא נִוב (ניב קרי) שְׂפָתָיִם שָׁלוֹם | שָׁלוֹם לָרָחוֹק וְלַקָּרוֹב אָמַר יְהוָה וּרְפָאתִיו: כ וְהָרְשָׁעִים כַּיָּם נִגְרָשׁ כִּי הַשְׁקֵט לֹא יוּכָל וַיִּגְרְשׁוּ מֵימָיו רֶפֶשׁ וָטִיט: כא אֵין שָׁלוֹם אָמַר אֱלֹהַי לָרְשָׁעִים: א קְרָא בְגָרוֹן אַל־תַּחְשֹׂךְ כַּשּׁוֹפָר הָרֵם קוֹלֶךָ וְהַגֵּד לְעַמִּי פִּשְׁעָם וּלְבֵית יַעֲקֹב חַטֹּאתָם: ב וְאוֹתִי יוֹם יוֹם יִדְרֹשׁוּן וְדַעַת דְּרָכַי יֶחְפָּצוּן כְּגוֹי אֲשֶׁר־צְדָקָה עָשָׂה וּמִשְׁפַּט אֱלֹהָיו לֹא עָזָב יִשְׁאָלוּנִי מִשְׁפְּטֵי־ צֶדֶק קִרְבַת אֱלֹהִים יֶחְפָּצוּן: ג לָמָּה צַּמְנוּ וְלֹא רָאִיתָ עִנִּינוּ נַפְשֵׁנוּ וְלֹא תֵדָע הֵן בְּיוֹם צֹמְכֶם תִּמְצְאוּ־חֵפֶץ וְכָל־עַצְּבֵיכֶם תִּנְגֹּשׂוּ: ד הֵן לְרִיב וּמַצָּה תָּצוּמוּ וּלְהַכּוֹת בְּאֶגְרֹף רֶשַׁע לֹא־תָצוּמוּ כַיּוֹם לְהַשְׁמִיעַ בַּמָּרוֹם קוֹלְכֶם: ה הֲכָזֶה יִהְיֶה צוֹם אֶבְחָרֵהוּ יוֹם עַנּוֹת אָדָם נַפְשׁוֹ הֲלָכֹף כְּאַגְמֹן רֹאשׁוֹ וְשַׂק וָאֵפֶר יַצִּיעַ הֲלָזֶה תִּקְרָא־צוֹם וְיוֹם רָצוֹן לַיהוָה: ו הֲלוֹא זֶה צוֹם אֶבְחָרֵהוּ פַּתֵּחַ חַרְצֻבּוֹת רֶשַׁע הַתֵּר אֲגֻדּוֹת מוֹטָה וְשַׁלַּח רְצוּצִים חָפְשִׁים וְכָל־ מוֹטָה תְּנַתֵּקוּ: ז הֲלוֹא פָרֹס לָרָעֵב לַחְמֶךָ וַעֲנִיִּים מְרוּדִים תָּבִיא בָיִת כִּי־תִרְאֶה עָרֹם וְכִסִּיתוֹ וּמִבְּשָׂרְךָ לֹא תִתְעַלָּם: ח אָז יִבָּקַע כַּשַּׁחַר אוֹרֶךָ וַאֲרֻכָתְךָ מְהֵרָה תִצְמָח וְהָלַךְ לְפָנֶיךָ צִדְקֶךָ כְּבוֹד יְהוָה יַאַסְפֶךָ: ט אָז תִּקְרָא וַיהוָה יַעֲנֶה תְּשַׁוַּע וְיֹאמַר הִנֵּנִי אִם־תָּסִיר

"Here I am," if you remove perverseness from your midst, putting forth the finger and speaking wickedness. 10. And you draw out your soul to the hungry, and an afflicted soul you sate, then your light shall shine in the darkness, and your darkness shall be like noon. 11. And the Lord shall always lead you, and He shall satisfy your soul in drought and strengthen your bones; and you shall be like a well-watered garden and like a spring of water whose water does not fail. 12. And [those coming] from you shall build ancient ruins; foundations of generations you shall erect, and you shall be called the repairer of the breaches, restorer of the paths to dwell in. 13. If you restrain your foot because of the Sabbath, from performing your affairs on My holy day, and you call the Sabbath a delight, the holy of the Lord honored; and you honor it by not doing your wonted ways, by not pursuing your affairs and speaking words. 14. Then you shall delight with the Lord, and I will cause you to ride on the high places of the land, and I will give you to eat the heritage of Jacob your father, for the mouth of the Lord has spoken.

מִתּוֹכְךָ֙ מוֹטָ֔ה שְׁלַ֥ח אֶצְבַּ֖ע וְדַבֶּר־אָֽוֶן: י וְתָפֵ֧ק לָרָעֵ֣ב נַפְשֶׁ֗ךָ וְנֶ֤פֶשׁ נַעֲנָה֙ תַּשְׂבִּ֔יעַ וְזָרַ֤ח בַּחֹ֙שֶׁךְ֙ אוֹרֶ֔ךָ וַאֲפֵלָתְךָ֖ כַּֽצָּהֳרָֽיִם: יא וְנָחֲךָ֣ יְהֹוָה֮ תָּמִיד֒ וְהִשְׂבִּ֤יעַ בְּצַחְצָחוֹת֙ נַפְשֶׁ֔ךָ וְעַצְמֹתֶ֖יךָ יַחֲלִ֑יץ וְהָיִ֙יתָ֙ כְּגַ֣ן רָוֶ֔ה וּכְמוֹצָ֣א מַ֔יִם אֲשֶׁ֥ר לֹא־יְכַזְּב֖וּ מֵימָֽיו: יב וּבָנ֤וּ מִמְּךָ֙ חָרְב֣וֹת עוֹלָ֔ם מוֹסְדֵ֥י דוֹר־וָד֖וֹר תְּקוֹמֵ֑ם וְקֹרָ֤א לְךָ֙ גֹּדֵ֣ר פֶּ֔רֶץ מְשֹׁבֵ֥ב נְתִיב֖וֹת לָשָֽׁבֶת: יג אִם־תָּשִׁ֤יב מִשַּׁבָּת֙ רַגְלֶ֔ךָ עֲשׂ֥וֹת חֲפָצֶ֖ךָ בְּי֣וֹם קָדְשִׁ֑י וְקָרָ֨אתָ לַשַּׁבָּ֜ת עֹ֗נֶג לִקְד֤וֹשׁ יְהֹוָה֙ מְכֻבָּ֔ד וְכִבַּדְתּוֹ֙ מֵעֲשׂ֣וֹת דְּרָכֶ֔יךָ מִמְּצ֥וֹא חֶפְצְךָ֖ וְדַבֵּ֥ר דָּבָֽר: יד אָ֗ז תִּתְעַנַּג֙ עַל־ יְהֹוָ֔ה וְהִרְכַּבְתִּ֖יךָ עַל־בָּמֳתֵי (במתי קרי) אָ֑רֶץ וְהַאֲכַלְתִּ֗יךָ נַחֲלַת֙ יַעֲקֹ֣ב אָבִ֔יךָ כִּ֛י פִּ֥י יְהֹוָ֖ה דִּבֵּֽר:

HAFTARATH YOM KIPPUR MINCHAH   הפטרת יום כפור מנחה
Haftarah for Yom Kippur Afternoon Service
(The Book of Jonah and Micah 7:18-20)
Torah reading: Leviticus 18

This selection is appropriate for the spirit of Yom Kippur because it speaks of the repentance of the people of Nineveh and how God forgave them.

1:1. And the word of the Lord came to Jonah the son of Amittai, saying: 2. Arise; go to Nineveh, the great city, and proclaim over it, for their wickedness has come up before Me. 3. Then Jonah rose up to flee to Tarshish, away from the presence of the Lord, and he went down to Joppa and found a ship going home to Tarshish, so he paid the fare thereof and went down into it to go with them to Tarshish, away from the presence of the Lord. 4. But the Lord had sent a strong wind out to sea, and it became a mighty tempest in the sea, so that the ship threatened to split. 5. Then the sailors were afraid and prayed each man to his god, and they cast away the wares that were in the ship into the sea to lighten it for them. But

א וַֽיְהִי֙ דְּבַר־יְהֹוָ֔ה אֶל־יוֹנָ֥ה בֶן־אֲמִתַּ֖י לֵאמֹֽר: ב ק֠וּם לֵ֧ךְ אֶל־נִֽינְוֵ֛ה הָעִ֥יר הַגְּדוֹלָ֖ה וּקְרָ֣א עָלֶ֑יהָ כִּֽי־עָלְתָ֥ה רָעָתָ֖ם לְפָנָֽי: ג וַיָּ֤קָם יוֹנָה֙ לִבְרֹ֣חַ תַּרְשִׁ֔ישָׁה מִלִּפְנֵ֖י יְהֹוָ֑ה וַיֵּ֨רֶד יָפ֜וֹ וַיִּמְצָ֥א אֳנִיָּ֣ה ׀ בָּאָ֣ה תַרְשִׁ֗ישׁ וַיִּתֵּ֥ן שְׂכָרָהּ֙ וַיֵּ֣רֶד בָּ֔הּ לָב֤וֹא עִמָּהֶם֙ תַּרְשִׁ֔ישָׁה מִלִּפְנֵ֖י יְהֹוָֽה: ד וַֽיהֹוָ֗ה הֵטִ֤יל רֽוּחַ־גְּדוֹלָה֙ אֶל־הַיָּ֔ם וַיְהִ֥י סַֽעַר־גָּד֖וֹל בַּיָּ֑ם וְהָ֣אֳנִיָּ֔ה חִשְּׁבָ֖ה לְהִשָּׁבֵֽר: ה וַיִּֽירְא֣וּ הַמַּלָּחִ֗ים וַֽיִּזְעֲקוּ֮ אִ֣ישׁ אֶל־אֱלֹהָיו֒ וַיָּטִ֨לוּ אֶת־ הַכֵּלִ֜ים אֲשֶׁ֤ר בָּֽאֳנִיָּה֙ אֶל־הַיָּ֔ם לְהָקֵ֖ל מֵעֲלֵיהֶ֑ם

Jonah had gone down into the innermost parts of the ship, and he lay down and was fast asleep. 6. Then the shipmaster came to him and said to him, "What do you mean that you sleep so soundly? Get up, call upon your God; perchance God will allow Himself to be entreated for us so that we do not perish." 7. And they said one to the other, "Come, and let us cast lots that we may know on whose account this misfortune is upon us. So they cast lots, and the lot fell on Jonah. 8. Then they said to him, "Tell us then, as being the one through whom this misfortune is upon us, what is your occupation, and from where do you come; what is your country, and of what people are you?" 9. And he said to them, "I am a Hebrew, and the Lord, the God of the heavens, do I fear, Who made the sea and the dry land." 10. Then the men were seized with great terror, and they said to him, "What is this then that you have done?" For the men knew that he was fleeing from being before the Lord, for he had told them. 12. And he said to them, "Take me up and cast me forth into the sea so that the sea shall become quiet from threatening you. For I know that it is on my account that this great tempest is upon you." 13. Then the men rowed to get back to the land but were unable to do so, for the sea grew more and more tempestuous against them. 14. [Therefore,] they cried to the Lord and said, "We beseech You, O Lord, let us not perish for this man's life, and reckon it not to us as shedding innocent blood, for You, O Lord, have done as it pleased You." 15. So they took up Jonah and cast him into the sea, and the sea ceased from its raging. 16. Then the men were filled with deep fear of the Lord, and they offered a sacrifice to the Lord and made vows. 2:1. And the Lord prepared a great fish to swallow up Jonah, and Jonah was in the belly of the fish three days and three nights. 2. Then Jonah prayed to the Lord his God out of the belly of the fish. 3. And he said, "Out of the distress that came to me did I call to the Lord, and He answered me; out of the belly of the grave did I cry, and You heard my voice. 4. Then You cast me into the depths in the midst of the sea, and a river encompassed me; all Your breakers and Your waves passed over

וְיוֹנָה יָרַד אֶל־יַרְכְּתֵי הַסְּפִינָה וַיִּשְׁכַּב וַיֵּרָדַם׃
ו וַיִּקְרַב אֵלָיו רַב הַחֹבֵל וַיֹּאמֶר לוֹ מַה־לְּךָ
נִרְדָּם קוּם קְרָא אֶל־אֱלֹהֶיךָ אוּלַי יִתְעַשֵּׁת
הָאֱלֹהִים לָנוּ וְלֹא נֹאבֵד׃ ז וַיֹּאמְרוּ אִישׁ אֶל־
רֵעֵהוּ לְכוּ וְנַפִּילָה גוֹרָלוֹת וְנֵדְעָה בְּשֶׁלְּמִי
הָרָעָה הַזֹּאת לָנוּ וַיַּפִּלוּ גּוֹרָלוֹת וַיִּפֹּל הַגּוֹרָל
עַל־יוֹנָה׃ ח וַיֹּאמְרוּ אֵלָיו הַגִּידָה־נָּא לָנוּ
בַּאֲשֶׁר לְמִי־הָרָעָה הַזֹּאת לָנוּ מַה־מְּלַאכְתְּךָ
וּמֵאַיִן תָּבוֹא מָה אַרְצֶךָ וְאֵי־מִזֶּה עַם אָתָּה׃
ט וַיֹּאמֶר אֲלֵיהֶם עִבְרִי אָנֹכִי וְאֶת־יְהוָֹה אֱלֹהֵי
הַשָּׁמַיִם אֲנִי יָרֵא אֲשֶׁר־עָשָׂה אֶת־הַיָּם וְאֶת־
הַיַּבָּשָׁה׃ י וַיִּירְאוּ הָאֲנָשִׁים יִרְאָה גְדוֹלָה
וַיֹּאמְרוּ אֵלָיו מַה־זֹּאת עָשִׂיתָ כִּי־יָדְעוּ
הָאֲנָשִׁים כִּי־מִלִּפְנֵי יְהוָֹה הוּא בֹרֵחַ כִּי הִגִּיד
לָהֶם׃ יא וַיֹּאמְרוּ אֵלָיו מַה־נַּעֲשֶׂה לָּךְ וְיִשְׁתֹּק
הַיָּם מֵעָלֵינוּ כִּי הַיָּם הוֹלֵךְ וְסֹעֵר׃ יב וַיֹּאמֶר
אֲלֵיהֶם שָׂאוּנִי וַהֲטִילֻנִי אֶל־הַיָּם וְיִשְׁתֹּק הַיָּם
מֵעֲלֵיכֶם כִּי יוֹדֵעַ אָנִי כִּי בְשֶׁלִּי הַסַּעַר הַגָּדוֹל
הַזֶּה עֲלֵיכֶם׃ יג וַיַּחְתְּרוּ הָאֲנָשִׁים לְהָשִׁיב אֶל־
הַיַּבָּשָׁה וְלֹא יָכֹלוּ כִּי הַיָּם הוֹלֵךְ וְסֹעֵר עֲלֵיהֶם׃
יד וַיִּקְרְאוּ אֶל־יְהוָֹה וַיֹּאמְרוּ אָנָּה יְהוָֹה אַל־נָא
נֹאבְדָה בְּנֶפֶשׁ הָאִישׁ הַזֶּה וְאַל־תִּתֵּן עָלֵינוּ דָּם
נָקִיא כִּי־אַתָּה יְהוָֹה כַּאֲשֶׁר חָפַצְתָּ עָשִׂיתָ׃
טו וַיִּשְׂאוּ אֶת־יוֹנָה וַיְטִלֻהוּ אֶל־הַיָּם וַיַּעֲמֹד
הַיָּם מִזַּעְפּוֹ׃ טז וַיִּירְאוּ הָאֲנָשִׁים יִרְאָה גְדוֹלָה
אֶת־יְהוָֹה וַיִּזְבְּחוּ־זֶבַח לַיהוָֹה וַיִּדְּרוּ נְדָרִים׃
א וַיְמַן יְהוָֹה דָּג גָּדוֹל לִבְלֹעַ אֶת־יוֹנָה וַיְהִי
יוֹנָה בִּמְעֵי הַדָּג שְׁלֹשָׁה יָמִים וּשְׁלֹשָׁה לֵילוֹת׃
ב וַיִּתְפַּלֵּל יוֹנָה אֶל־יְהוָֹה אֱלֹהָיו מִמְּעֵי הַדָּגָה׃
ג וַיֹּאמֶר קָרָאתִי מִצָּרָה לִי אֶל־יְהוָֹה וַיַּעֲנֵנִי
מִבֶּטֶן שְׁאוֹל שִׁוַּעְתִּי שָׁמַעְתָּ קוֹלִי׃ ד וַתַּשְׁלִיכֵנִי
מְצוּלָה בִּלְבַב יַמִּים וְנָהָר יְסֹבְבֵנִי כָּל־מִשְׁבָּרֶיךָ

וְגַלֶּ֖יךָ עָלַ֥י עָבָֽרוּ׃ ה וַאֲנִ֣י אָמַ֔רְתִּי נִגְרַ֖שְׁתִּי מִנֶּ֣גֶד
עֵינֶ֑יךָ אַ֚ךְ אוֹסִ֣יף לְהַבִּ֔יט אֶל־הֵיכַ֖ל קָדְשֶֽׁךָ׃
ו אֲפָפ֤וּנִי מַ֙יִם֙ עַד־נֶ֔פֶשׁ תְּה֖וֹם יְסֹבְבֵ֑נִי ס֖וּף
חָב֥וּשׁ לְרֹאשִֽׁי׃ ז לְקִצְבֵ֤י הָרִים֙ יָרַ֔דְתִּי הָאָ֛רֶץ
בְּרִחֶ֥יהָ בַעֲדִ֖י לְעוֹלָ֑ם וַתַּ֧עַל מִשַּׁ֛חַת חַיַּ֖י יְהוָ֥ה
אֱלֹהָֽי׃ ח בְּהִתְעַטֵּ֤ף עָלַי֙ נַפְשִׁ֔י אֶת־יְהוָ֖ה זָכָ֑רְתִּי
וַתָּב֤וֹא אֵלֶ֙יךָ֙ תְּפִלָּתִ֔י אֶל־הֵיכַ֖ל קָדְשֶֽׁךָ׃
ט מְשַׁמְּרִ֖ים הַבְלֵי־שָׁ֑וְא חַסְדָּ֖ם יַעֲזֹֽבוּ׃ י וַאֲנִ֗י
בְּק֤וֹל תּוֹדָה֙ אֶזְבְּחָה־לָּ֔ךְ אֲשֶׁ֥ר נָדַ֖רְתִּי אֲשַׁלֵּ֑מָה
יְשׁוּעָ֖תָה לַיהוָֽה׃ יא וַיֹּ֥אמֶר יְהוָ֖ה לַדָּ֑ג וַיָּקֵ֥א
אֶת־יוֹנָ֖ה אֶל־הַיַּבָּשָֽׁה׃ א וַיְהִ֧י דְבַר־יְהוָ֛ה אֶל־
יוֹנָ֖ה שֵׁנִ֥ית לֵאמֹֽר׃ ב ק֛וּם לֵ֥ךְ אֶל־נִֽינְוֵ֖ה הָעִ֣יר
הַגְּדוֹלָ֑ה וּקְרָ֤א אֵלֶ֙יהָ֙ אֶת־הַקְּרִיאָ֔ה אֲשֶׁ֥ר אָנֹכִ֖י
דֹּבֵ֥ר אֵלֶֽיךָ׃ ג וַיָּ֣קָם יוֹנָ֗ה וַיֵּ֛לֶךְ אֶל־נִֽינְוֶ֖ה כִּדְבַ֣ר
יְהוָ֑ה וְנִֽינְוֵ֗ה הָיְתָ֤ה עִיר־גְּדוֹלָה֙ לֵֽאלֹהִ֔ים מַהֲלַ֖ךְ
שְׁלֹ֥שֶׁת יָמִֽים׃ ד וַיָּ֤חֶל יוֹנָה֙ לָב֣וֹא בָעִ֔יר מַהֲלַ֖ךְ
י֣וֹם אֶחָ֑ד וַיִּקְרָא֙ וַיֹּאמַ֔ר ע֚וֹד אַרְבָּעִ֣ים י֔וֹם
וְנִֽינְוֵ֖ה נֶהְפָּֽכֶת׃ ה וַיַּאֲמִ֛ינוּ אַנְשֵׁ֥י נִֽינְוֵ֖ה
בֵּאלֹהִ֑ים וַיִּקְרְאוּ־צוֹם֙ וַיִּלְבְּשׁ֣וּ שַׂקִּ֔ים מִגְּדוֹלָ֖ם
וְעַד־קְטַנָּֽם׃ ו וַיִּגַּ֤ע הַדָּבָר֙ אֶל־מֶ֣לֶךְ נִֽינְוֵ֔ה וַיָּ֙קָם֙
מִכִּסְא֔וֹ וַיַּעֲבֵ֥ר אַדַּרְתּ֖וֹ מֵעָלָ֑יו וַיְכַ֣ס שַׂ֔ק וַיֵּ֖שֶׁב
עַל־הָאֵֽפֶר׃ ז וַיַּזְעֵ֗ק וַיֹּ֙אמֶר֙ בְּנִֽינְוֵ֔ה מִטַּ֧עַם
הַמֶּ֛לֶךְ וּגְדֹלָ֖יו לֵאמֹ֑ר הָאָדָ֨ם וְהַבְּהֵמָ֜ה הַבָּקָ֣ר
וְהַצֹּ֗אן אַל־יִטְעֲמוּ֙ מְא֔וּמָה אַל־יִרְע֕וּ וּמַ֖יִם
אַל־יִשְׁתּֽוּ׃ ח וְיִתְכַּסּ֣וּ שַׂקִּ֗ים הָֽאָדָם֙ וְהַבְּהֵמָ֔ה
וְיִקְרְא֥וּ אֶל־אֱלֹהִ֖ים בְּחָזְקָ֑ה וְיָשֻׁ֗בוּ אִ֚ישׁ
מִדַּרְכּ֣וֹ הָרָעָ֔ה וּמִן־הֶחָמָ֖ס אֲשֶׁ֥ר בְּכַפֵּיהֶֽם׃
ט מִֽי־יוֹדֵ֣עַ יָשׁ֔וּב וְנִחַ֖ם הָאֱלֹהִ֑ים וְשָׁ֛ב מֵחֲר֥וֹן
אַפּ֖וֹ וְלֹ֥א נֹאבֵֽד׃ י וַיַּ֤רְא הָאֱלֹהִים֙ אֶת־
מַ֣עֲשֵׂיהֶ֔ם כִּי־שָׁ֖בוּ מִדַּרְכָּ֣ם הָרָעָ֑ה וַיִּנָּ֣חֶם

me. 5. I had already said, 'I am entirely driven away from before Your eyes,' but still I will continue to gaze towards Your holy Temple. 6. The waters surrounded me even to my very soul; then the deep sea whirled around me, seaweed was wrapped around my head. 7. To the bottom of mountains I sank down; the earth had already its bolts on me forever; then You raised my life out of the nethermost pit, O Lord, my God. 8. When my soul fainted within me, I remembered the Lord, and my prayer came to You, into Your Holy Temple. 9. Vanities that come to nothing they carefully guard, but the kindness bestowed upon them they forsake! 10. But I will sacrifice to You with a voice of thanksgiving; that which I vowed I will pay, because my deliverance depends on the Lord.'' 11. Then the Lord spoke to the fish, and it vomited Jonah out upon the dry land. 3:1. And the word of the Lord came to Jonah a second time, saying: 2. Arise; go to Nineveh, that great city, and proclaim to it the proclamation that I will bid you. 3. So Jonah arose and went to Nineveh according to the word of the Lord. Now Nineveh was a great city for God, of three days' journey. 4. But Jonah had only commenced to enter one day's journey into the city, when he called out and said, "In another forty days Nineveh will be overturned." 5. And the people of Nineveh believed in God, and they proclaimed a fast and put on sackcloth, from the greatest of them even to the least of them. 6. And the tidings reached the king of Nineveh, and he arose from his throne and took off his robe, covered himself with sackcloth, and sat in ashes. 7. And he had it called out and proclaimed in Nineveh by the decree of the king and his nobles, saying, "Man and beast, herd and flock, are not to taste anything, are not to feed and not to drink water. 8. And they are to cover themselves with sackcloth, both men and beasts, and let them cry mightily to God, and every man is to turn back from his evil way, and from what is wrongfully in their hands. 9. He who comes to understanding shall repent, and God will alter His Mind and turn away from His burning wrath, so that we perish not." 10. And God saw their deeds, that they had repented of their evil way, and

God altered His decision of the calamity which He said He would do to them, and He did not do it. 4:1. But this seemed to Jonah a great misfortune, and it upset him. 2. And he prayed to the Lord and said, "I beseech You, O Lord, was not this what I said when I was still in my country? That was why I fled beforehand to Tarshish, for I knew that You are a gracious and compassionate God, slow to anger, and plenteous in lovingkindness, and ready to alter His Mind regarding the catastrophe. 3. Therefore, now, O Lord, take my life from me, I beseech You, for it is better for me that I die than that I live." 4. And the Lord said, "Are you greatly upset?" 5. Then Jonah went out of the city and remained on the east side of the city and made himself a booth there and sat under it in the shade till he might see what would become of the city. 6. And the Lord God prepared a *kikayon*, that it should grow above Jonah to be a shade over his head, to deliver him from his evil plight. Then Jonah rejoiced with great joy over the *kikayon*. 7. But God prepared a worm, when the day dawned on the morrow, which attacked the *kikayon*, and it withered. 8. And it came to pass when the sun shone that God prepared a deafening east wind, and the sun beat upon Jonah's head, and he became faint and wished death for himself and said, "It is better for me to die than to live." 9. Then God said to Jonah, "Are you greatly upset over the *kikayon*?" And he said, "I am greatly upset, even to death!" 10. Then the Lord said, "You have pity on the *kikayon*, for which you have not labored neither have you made it grow up, which, as the product of one night came into existence, and, as the product of one night, perished. 11. And should I not have pity on Nineveh, that great city, wherein are more than twelve times ten thousand persons who cannot discern between their right hand and their left, and [added thereto] many animals?" *(Most congregations, except for those that follow the ritual of Frankfort-on-the-Main, add the following passage:)* Micah 7:18. Who, O God, is like You, Who pardons iniquity and even passes over willful transgression to the remnant of His heritage? He retains not His anger forever,

הָאֱלֹהִים עַל־הָרָעָה אֲשֶׁר־דִּבֶּר לַעֲשׂוֹת־לָהֶם וְלֹא עָשָׂה: א וַיֵּרַע אֶל־יוֹנָה רָעָה גְדוֹלָה וַיִּחַר לוֹ: ב וַיִּתְפַּלֵּל אֶל־יְהֹוָה וַיֹּאמַר אָנָּה יְהֹוָה הֲלוֹא־זֶה דְבָרִי עַד־הֱיוֹתִי עַל־אַדְמָתִי עַל־כֵּן קִדַּמְתִּי לִבְרֹחַ תַּרְשִׁישָׁה כִּי יָדַעְתִּי כִּי אַתָּה אֵל־חַנּוּן וְרַחוּם אֶרֶךְ אַפַּיִם וְרַב־חֶסֶד וְנִחָם עַל־הָרָעָה: ג וְעַתָּה יְהֹוָה קַח־נָא אֶת־נַפְשִׁי מִמֶּנִּי כִּי טוֹב מוֹתִי מֵחַיָּי: ד וַיֹּאמֶר יְהֹוָה הַהֵיטֵב חָרָה לָךְ: ה וַיֵּצֵא יוֹנָה מִן־הָעִיר וַיֵּשֶׁב מִקֶּדֶם לָעִיר וַיַּעַשׂ לוֹ שָׁם סֻכָּה וַיֵּשֶׁב תַּחְתֶּיהָ בַּצֵּל עַד אֲשֶׁר יִרְאֶה מַה־יִּהְיֶה בָּעִיר: ו וַיְמַן יְהֹוָה־אֱלֹהִים קִיקָיוֹן וַיַּעַל ׀ מֵעַל לְיוֹנָה לִהְיוֹת צֵל עַל־רֹאשׁוֹ לְהַצִּיל לוֹ מֵרָעָתוֹ וַיִּשְׂמַח יוֹנָה עַל־הַקִּיקָיוֹן שִׂמְחָה גְדוֹלָה: ז וַיְמַן הָאֱלֹהִים תּוֹלַעַת בַּעֲלוֹת הַשַּׁחַר לַמָּחֳרָת וַתַּךְ אֶת־הַקִּיקָיוֹן וַיִּיבָשׁ: ח וַיְהִי ׀ כִּזְרֹחַ הַשֶּׁמֶשׁ וַיְמַן אֱלֹהִים רוּחַ קָדִים חֲרִישִׁית וַתַּךְ הַשֶּׁמֶשׁ עַל־רֹאשׁ יוֹנָה וַיִּתְעַלָּף וַיִּשְׁאַל אֶת־נַפְשׁוֹ לָמוּת וַיֹּאמֶר טוֹב מוֹתִי מֵחַיָּי: ט וַיֹּאמֶר אֱלֹהִים אֶל־יוֹנָה הַהֵיטֵב חָרָה־לְךָ עַל־הַקִּיקָיוֹן וַיֹּאמֶר הֵיטֵב חָרָה־לִי עַד־מָוֶת: י וַיֹּאמֶר יְהֹוָה אַתָּה חַסְתָּ עַל־הַקִּיקָיוֹן אֲשֶׁר לֹא־עָמַלְתָּ בּוֹ וְלֹא גִדַּלְתּוֹ שֶׁבִּן־לַיְלָה הָיָה וּבִן־לַיְלָה אָבָד: יא וַאֲנִי לֹא אָחוּס עַל־נִינְוֵה הָעִיר הַגְּדוֹלָה אֲשֶׁר יֶשׁ־בָּהּ הַרְבֵּה מִשְׁתֵּים־עֶשְׂרֵה רִבּוֹ אָדָם אֲשֶׁר לֹא־יָדַע בֵּין־יְמִינוֹ לִשְׂמֹאלוֹ וּבְהֵמָה רַבָּה: יח מִי־אֵל כָּמוֹךָ נֹשֵׂא עָוֹן וְעֹבֵר עַל־פֶּשַׁע לִשְׁאֵרִית נַחֲלָתוֹ לֹא־הֶחֱזִיק לָעַד אַפּוֹ

for He desires lovingkindness. 19. He will turn again and have compassion and will subdue our iniquities, and then You will cast all our sins into the depths of the sea. 20. You will give the truth to Jacob, the lovingkindness to Abraham, that You have sworn to our fathers from the days of old.

כִּֽי־חָפֵ֥ץ חֶ֖סֶד הֽוּא׃ יט יָשׁ֣וּב יְרַחֲמֵ֔נוּ יִכְבֹּ֖שׁ
עֲוֺנֹתֵ֑ינוּ וְתַשְׁלִ֛יךְ בִּמְצֻל֥וֹת יָ֖ם כָּל־חַטֹּאתָֽם׃
כ תִּתֵּ֤ן אֱמֶת֙ לְיַֽעֲקֹ֔ב חֶ֖סֶד לְאַבְרָהָ֑ם אֲשֶׁר־
נִשְׁבַּ֥עְתָּ לַאֲבֹתֵ֖ינוּ מִ֥ימֵי קֶֽדֶם׃

HAFTARAH FOR THE FIRST DAY OF SUKKOTH הפטרת יום א׳ דסוכות

(Zechariah 14)

Torah reading: Leviticus 22:26–23:44, Numbers 29:12–16

In this selection, Zechariah envisions the celebration of the Festival of Sukkoth in the Messianic era.

14:1. Behold a day is coming which will be for the Lord, when all that of which you have been despoilt will be shared in your midst. 2. For I will gather all nations against Jerusalem to battle, and the city will be taken and the houses plundered and the women ravished, and half the city will go out into exile, but a remnant of the people will not be cut off from the city. 3. And the Lord will go forth and fight against those nations as He has always fought on the day of battle. 4. And on that day His feet will stand on the Mount of Olives, which is before Jerusalem to the east, and the Mount of Olives will split from its center towards the east and towards the west to a very great valley, and then half the mount will move to the north and its other half to the south. 5. And then you shall flee into this valley which the mountains have formed, for the valley formed by the mountains will reach Azal, and you will flee as you fled from before the earthquake in the days of Uzziah, king of Judah; and the Lord, my God, will come, all the holy ones with You. 6. And it will come to pass that on that day there will be no light, only heavy clouds and thick. 7. And there shall be one day, known [only] to the Lord, not day and not night, but it shall come to pass that at eventide there will be light. 8. And it shall come to pass that on that day living waters will flow out of Jerusalem, one half towards the eastern sea and the other half towards the western sea, in summer and in winter will it last. 9. And the Lord will be King over all the earth; on that day the Lord will be One and His name

א הִנֵּ֥ה יוֹם־בָּ֖א לַֽיהוָ֑ה וְחֻלַּ֥ק שְׁלָלֵ֖ךְ בְּקִרְבֵּֽךְ׃
ב וְאָסַפְתִּ֨י אֶת־כָּל־הַגּוֹיִ֥ם ׀ אֶל־יְרוּשָׁלַ֘͏ִם֮
לַמִּלְחָמָה֒ וְנִלְכְּדָ֣ה הָעִ֗יר וְנָשַׁ֙סּוּ֙ הַבָּתִּ֔ים
וְהַנָּשִׁ֖ים תִּשָּׁגַ֑לְנָה (תשכבנה קרי) וְיָצָ֞א חֲצִ֤י הָעִיר֙
בַּגּוֹלָ֔ה וְיֶ֣תֶר הָעָ֔ם לֹ֥א יִכָּרֵ֖ת מִן־הָעִֽיר׃ ג וְיָצָ֣א
יְהוָ֔ה וְנִלְחַ֖ם בַּגּוֹיִ֣ם הָהֵ֑ם כְּי֥וֹם הִֽלָּחֲמ֖וֹ בְּי֥וֹם
קְרָֽב׃ ד וְעָמְד֣וּ רַגְלָיו֩ בַּיּוֹם־הַה֨וּא עַל־הַ֜ר
הַזֵּיתִ֗ים אֲשֶׁ֨ר עַל־פְּנֵ֣י יְרוּשָׁלַ֘͏ִם֮ מִקֶּדֶם֒ וְנִבְקַע֩
הַ֨ר הַזֵּיתִ֤ים מֵֽחֶצְיוֹ֙ מִזְרָ֣חָה וָיָ֔מָּה גֵּ֖יא גְּדוֹלָ֣ה
מְאֹ֑ד וּמָ֨שׁ חֲצִ֥י הָהָ֛ר צָפ֖וֹנָה וְחֶצְי֥וֹ נֶֽגְבָּה׃
ה וְנַסְתֶּ֣ם גֵּיא־הָרַ֗י כִּֽי־יַגִּ֣יעַ גֵּי־הָרִים֮ אֶל־אָצַל֒
וְנַסְתֶּ֗ם כַּאֲשֶׁ֤ר נַסְתֶּם֙ מִפְּנֵ֣י הָרַ֔עַשׁ בִּימֵ֖י עֻזִּיָּ֣ה
מֶֽלֶךְ־יְהוּדָ֑ה וּבָא֙ יְהוָ֣ה אֱלֹהַ֔י כָּל־קְדֹשִׁ֖ים
עִמָּֽךְ׃ ו וְהָיָ֖ה בַּיּ֣וֹם הַה֑וּא לֹא־יִהְיֶ֣ה א֔וֹר
יְקָר֖וֹת יְקִפָּאֽוֹן (וקפאון קרי)׃ ז וְהָיָ֣ה יוֹם־אֶחָ֗ד
ה֛וּא יִוָּדַ֥ע לַֽיהוָ֖ה לֹא־י֣וֹם וְלֹא־לָ֑יְלָה וְהָיָ֥ה
לְעֵֽת־עֶ֖רֶב יִֽהְיֶה־אֽוֹר׃ ח וְהָיָ֣ה ׀ בַּיּ֣וֹם הַה֗וּא
יֵצְא֤וּ מַֽיִם־חַיִּים֙ מִיר֣וּשָׁלַ֔͏ִם חֶצְיָ֗ם אֶל־הַיָּם֙
הַקַּדְמוֹנִ֔י וְחֶצְיָ֖ם אֶל־הַיָּ֣ם הָאַחֲר֑וֹן בַּקַּ֥יִץ
וּבָחֹ֖רֶף יִֽהְיֶֽה׃ ט וְהָיָ֧ה יְהוָ֛ה לְמֶ֖לֶךְ עַל־כָּל־
הָאָ֑רֶץ בַּיּ֣וֹם הַה֗וּא יִהְיֶ֧ה יְהוָ֛ה אֶחָ֖ד וּשְׁמ֥וֹ

One. 10. And the whole earth will then be changed round about like a plain, from Geba to Rimmon in the south of Jerusalem, but it will be elevated high and remain in its old place, from the gate of Benjamin to the place of the first gate until the corner gate, and from the Tower of Hananel until the king's wine-cellars. 11. And they shall dwell therein, and there shall be no more destruction, but Jerusalem shall dwell in safety. 12. And this will be the plague wherewith the Lord will smite all the nations who besieged Jerusalem; his flesh will waste away while he still stands on his feet, his eyes will waste away in their sockets, and his tongue will waste away in his mouth. 13. And it will come to pass on that day that there will be great consternation sent by the Lord, each one will support the hand of the other, and his hand shall rise up against the hand of the other. 14. Yea, even Judah will fight against Jerusalem! And the wealth of all the nations round about, gold and silver and apparel will be gathered in very great abundance. 15. And there will be the plague of the horses, the mules, the camels, the asses, and all the animals that are in those camps, similar to this plague. 16. And it will come to pass that everyone that is left of the nations that came up against Jerusalem will go up from year to year to prostrate himself to the King, the Lord of Hosts, and to celebrate the festival of Tabernacles. 17. And it shall be that whoever of all the families of the earth does not go up to Jerusalem to prostrate himself to the King, the Lord of Hosts, upon them there will be no rain. 18. And if the family of Egypt does not go up and does not come, for [it does not rain] upon them, the same plague will be wherewith the Lord will plague the nations who do not go up to celebrate the Festival of Tabernacles. 19. Such will be the guilt of Egypt and the guilt of all the nations who do not go up to celebrate the Festival of Tabernacles. 20. On that day there will be upon the bells of the horses "holy to the Lord," and the pots in the House of the Lord will be like the sprinkling bowls before the altar. 21. Yea, every pot in Jerusalem and in Judah will be holy to the Lord of Hosts, and all they who sacrifice will come and take of

אֶחָֽד: י יִסּ֨וֹב כָּל־הָאָ֤רֶץ כָּֽעֲרָבָה֙ מִגֶּ֣בַע לְרִמּ֔וֹן נֶ֖גֶב יְרֽוּשָׁלָ֑͏ִם וְֽרָאֲמָ֞ה וְיָֽשְׁבָ֣ה תַחְתֶּ֗יהָ לְמִשַּׁ֤עַר בִּנְיָמִן֙ עַד־מְק֞וֹם שַׁ֤עַר הָֽרִאשׁוֹן֙ עַד־שַׁ֣עַר הַפִּנִּ֔ים וּמִגְדַּ֣ל חֲנַנְאֵ֔ל עַ֖ד יִקְבֵ֥י הַמֶּֽלֶךְ: יא וְיָ֣שְׁבוּ בָ֔הּ וְחֵ֖רֶם לֹ֣א יִֽהְיֶה־ע֑וֹד וְיָֽשְׁבָ֥ה יְרֽוּשָׁלַ֖͏ִם לָבֶֽטַח: יב וְזֹ֣את ׀ תִּֽהְיֶ֣ה הַמַּגֵּפָ֗ה אֲשֶׁ֨ר יִגֹּ֤ף יְהֹוָה֙ אֶת־כָּל־הָ֣עַמִּ֔ים אֲשֶׁ֥ר צָֽבְא֖וּ עַל־יְרֽוּשָׁלָ֑͏ִם הָמֵ֣ק ׀ בְּשָׂר֗וֹ וְהוּא֙ עֹמֵ֣ד עַל־רַגְלָ֔יו וְעֵינָיו֙ תִּמַּ֣קְנָה בְחֹֽרֵיהֶ֔ן וּלְשׁוֹנ֖וֹ תִּמַּ֥ק בְּפִיהֶֽם: יג וְהָיָה֙ בַּיּ֣וֹם הַה֔וּא תִּֽהְיֶ֧ה מְהֽוּמַת־יְהֹוָ֛ה רַבָּ֖ה בָּהֶ֑ם וְהֶֽחֱזִ֗יקוּ אִ֚ישׁ יַ֣ד רֵעֵ֔הוּ וְֽעָֽלְתָ֥ה יָד֖וֹ עַל־יַ֥ד רֵעֵֽהוּ: יד וְגַ֨ם־יְהוּדָ֔ה תִּלָּחֵ֖ם בִּירֽוּשָׁלָ֑͏ִם וְאֻסַּף֩ חֵ֨יל כָּל־הַגּוֹיִ֜ם סָבִ֗יב זָהָ֥ב וָכֶ֛סֶף וּבְגָדִ֖ים לָרֹ֥ב מְאֹֽד: טו וְכֵ֨ן תִּֽהְיֶ֜ה מַגֵּפַ֣ת הַסּ֗וּס הַפֶּ֙רֶד֙ הַגָּמָ֣ל וְהַֽחֲמ֔וֹר וְכָ֨ל־הַבְּהֵמָ֔ה אֲשֶׁ֥ר יִֽהְיֶ֖ה בַּֽמַּֽחֲנ֣וֹת הָהֵ֑מָּה כַּמַּגֵּפָ֖ה הַזֹּֽאת: טז וְהָיָ֗ה כָּל־הַנּוֹתָר֙ מִכָּל־הַגּוֹיִ֔ם הַבָּאִ֖ים עַל־יְרֽוּשָׁלָ֑͏ִם וְעָל֞וּ מִדֵּ֧י שָׁנָ֣ה בְשָׁנָ֗ה לְהִֽשְׁתַּֽחֲוֺת֙ לְמֶ֙לֶךְ֙ יְהֹוָ֣ה צְבָא֔וֹת וְלָחֹ֖ג אֶת־חַ֥ג הַסֻּכּֽוֹת: יז וְֽהָיָ֡ה אֲשֶׁר֩ לֹֽא־יַֽעֲלֶ֨ה מֵאֵ֜ת מִשְׁפְּח֣וֹת הָאָ֗רֶץ אֶל־יְרֽוּשָׁלַ֙͏ִם֙ לְהִֽשְׁתַּֽחֲוֺת֙ לְמֶ֙לֶךְ֙ יְהֹוָ֣ה צְבָא֔וֹת וְלֹ֥א עֲלֵיהֶ֖ם יִֽהְיֶ֥ה הַגָּֽשֶׁם: יח וְאִם־מִשְׁפַּ֣חַת מִצְרַ֩יִם֩ לֹֽא־תַֽעֲלֶ֨ה וְלֹ֜א בָאָ֗ה וְלֹ֤א עֲלֵיהֶם֙ תִּֽהְיֶ֣ה הַמַּגֵּפָ֔ה אֲשֶׁ֨ר יִגֹּ֤ף יְהֹוָה֙ אֶת־הַגּוֹיִ֔ם אֲשֶׁר֙ לֹ֣א יַֽעֲל֔וּ לָחֹ֖ג אֶת־חַ֥ג הַסֻּכּֽוֹת: יט זֹ֥את תִּֽהְיֶ֖ה חַטַּ֣את מִצְרָ֑יִם וְחַטַּאת֙ כָּל־הַגּוֹיִ֔ם אֲשֶׁר֙ לֹ֣א יַֽעֲל֔וּ לָחֹ֖ג אֶת־חַ֥ג הַסֻּכּֽוֹת: כ בַּיּ֣וֹם הַה֗וּא יִֽהְיֶה֙ עַל־מְצִלּ֣וֹת הַסּ֔וּס קֹ֖דֶשׁ לַֽיהֹוָ֑ה וְהָיָ֤ה הַסִּירוֹת֙ בְּבֵ֣ית יְהֹוָ֔ה כַּמִּזְרָקִ֖ים לִפְנֵ֥י הַמִּזְבֵּֽחַ: כא וְהָיָ֡ה כָּל־סִ֣יר בִּירֽוּשָׁלַ֙͏ִם֙ וּבִ֣יהוּדָ֔ה קֹ֖דֶשׁ לַֽיהֹוָ֣ה צְבָא֑וֹת וּבָ֙אוּ֙ כָּל־הַזֹּ֣בְחִ֔ים וְלָֽקְח֥וּ מֵהֶ֖ם וּבָֽשְׁל֣וּ

them and cook in them, and there will no longer be a trafficker in the House of the Lord of Hosts on that day.

בָּהֶם וְלֹא־יִהְיֶה כְנַעֲנִי עוֹד בְּבֵית־יְהֹוָה צְבָאוֹת בַּיּוֹם הַהוּא:

HAFTARAH FOR THE SECOND DAY OF SUKKOTH הפטרת יום ב׳ דסוכות
(I Kings 8:2–21)
Torah reading: Leviticus 22:26–23:44, Numbers 29:12–16

This selection describes the dedication of Solomon's Temple, which took place during the Sukkoth festival.

8:2. And all the men of Israel assembled themselves unto King Solomon at the feast in the month Ethanim, which [is] the seventh month. 3. And all the elders of Israel came, and the priests took up the ark. 4. And they brought up the ark of the Lord and the tabernacle of meeting and all the holy vessels which [were] in the tabernacle, and the priests and the Levites did bring them up. 5. And King Solomon and all the congregation of Israel that were assembled unto him [were] with him before the ark, sacrificing sheep and oxen, that could not be counted nor numbered for multitude. 6. And the priests brought in the ark of the covenant of the Lord to its place, into the Sanctuary of the house, to the most holy [place], under the wings of the cherubim. 7. For the cherubim spread forth [their] wings over the place of the ark, and the cherubim covered the ark and the staves thereof above. 8. And the staves were so long that the ends of the staves were seen from the holy [place] before the Sanctuary, and they were not seen without; and they are there unto this day. 9. There was nothing in the ark save the two tablets of stone which Moses put there at Horeb, when the Lord made [a covenant] with the children of Israel, when they came out of the land of Egypt. 10. And it came to pass when the priests came out of the holy [place], and the cloud filled the House of the Lord, 11. and the priests could not stand to minister because of the cloud; for the glory of the Lord filled the House of the Lord. 12. Then Solomon said, "The Lord said that He would dwell in the thick darkness. 13. I have surely built You a house to dwell in; a settled place for You to dwell in forever." 14. And the king turned his face

ב וַיִּקָּהֲלוּ אֶל־הַמֶּלֶךְ שְׁלֹמֹה כָּל־אִישׁ יִשְׂרָאֵל בְּיֶרַח הָאֵתָנִים בֶּחָג הוּא הַחֹדֶשׁ הַשְּׁבִיעִי: ג וַיָּבֹאוּ כֹּל זִקְנֵי יִשְׂרָאֵל וַיִּשְׂאוּ הַכֹּהֲנִים אֶת־הָאָרוֹן: ד וַיַּעֲלוּ אֶת־אֲרוֹן יְהֹוָה וְאֶת־אֹהֶל מוֹעֵד וְאֶת־כָּל־כְּלֵי הַקֹּדֶשׁ אֲשֶׁר בָּאֹהֶל וַיַּעֲלוּ אֹתָם הַכֹּהֲנִים וְהַלְוִיִּם: ה וְהַמֶּלֶךְ שְׁלֹמֹה וְכָל־עֲדַת יִשְׂרָאֵל הַנּוֹעָדִים עָלָיו אִתּוֹ לִפְנֵי הָאָרוֹן מְזַבְּחִים צֹאן וּבָקָר אֲשֶׁר לֹא־יִסָּפְרוּ וְלֹא יִמָּנוּ מֵרֹב: ו וַיָּבִאוּ הַכֹּהֲנִים אֶת־אֲרוֹן בְּרִית־יְהֹוָה אֶל־מְקוֹמוֹ אֶל־דְּבִיר הַבַּיִת אֶל־קֹדֶשׁ הַקֳּדָשִׁים אֶל־תַּחַת כַּנְפֵי הַכְּרוּבִים: ז כִּי הַכְּרוּבִים פֹּרְשִׂים כְּנָפַיִם אֶל־מְקוֹם הָאָרוֹן וַיָּסֹכּוּ הַכְּרֻבִים עַל־הָאָרוֹן וְעַל־בַּדָּיו מִלְמָעְלָה: ח וַיַּאֲרִכוּ הַבַּדִּים וַיֵּרָאוּ רָאשֵׁי הַבַּדִּים מִן־הַקֹּדֶשׁ עַל־פְּנֵי הַדְּבִיר וְלֹא יֵרָאוּ הַחוּצָה וַיִּהְיוּ שָׁם עַד הַיּוֹם הַזֶּה: ט אֵין בָּאָרוֹן רַק שְׁנֵי לֻחוֹת הָאֲבָנִים אֲשֶׁר הִנִּחַ שָׁם מֹשֶׁה בְּחֹרֵב אֲשֶׁר כָּרַת יְהֹוָה עִם־בְּנֵי יִשְׂרָאֵל בְּצֵאתָם מֵאֶרֶץ מִצְרָיִם: י וַיְהִי בְּצֵאת הַכֹּהֲנִים מִן־הַקֹּדֶשׁ וְהֶעָנָן מָלֵא אֶת־בֵּית יְהֹוָה: יא וְלֹא־יָכְלוּ הַכֹּהֲנִים לַעֲמֹד לְשָׁרֵת מִפְּנֵי הֶעָנָן כִּי־מָלֵא כְבוֹד־יְהֹוָה אֶת־בֵּית יְהֹוָה: יב אָז אָמַר שְׁלֹמֹה יְהֹוָה אָמַר לִשְׁכֹּן בָּעֲרָפֶל: יג בָּנֹה בָנִיתִי בֵּית זְבֻל לָךְ מָכוֹן לְשִׁבְתְּךָ עוֹלָמִים: יד וַיַּסֵּב הַמֶּלֶךְ אֶת־פָּנָיו וַיְבָרֶךְ אֵת כָּל־קְהַל

יִשְׂרָאֵל וְכָל־קְהַל יִשְׂרָאֵל עֹמֵד׃ טו וַיֹּאמֶר
בָּרוּךְ יְהוָה אֱלֹהֵי יִשְׂרָאֵל אֲשֶׁר דִּבֶּר בְּפִיו אֵת
דָּוִד אָבִי וּבְיָדוֹ מִלֵּא לֵאמֹר׃ טז מִן־הַיּוֹם אֲשֶׁר
הוֹצֵאתִי אֶת־עַמִּי אֶת־יִשְׂרָאֵל מִמִּצְרַיִם לֹא־
בָחַרְתִּי בְעִיר מִכֹּל שִׁבְטֵי יִשְׂרָאֵל לִבְנוֹת בַּיִת
לִהְיוֹת שְׁמִי שָׁם וָאֶבְחַר בְּדָוִד לִהְיוֹת עַל־עַמִּי
יִשְׂרָאֵל׃ יז וַיְהִי עִם־לְבַב דָּוִד אָבִי לִבְנוֹת בַּיִת
לְשֵׁם יְהוָה אֱלֹהֵי יִשְׂרָאֵל׃ יח וַיֹּאמֶר יְהוָה
אֶל־דָּוִד אָבִי יַעַן אֲשֶׁר הָיָה עִם־לְבָבְךָ לִבְנוֹת
בַּיִת לִשְׁמִי הֱטִיבֹתָ כִּי הָיָה עִם־לְבָבֶךָ׃ יט רַק
אַתָּה לֹא תִבְנֶה הַבָּיִת כִּי אִם־בִּנְךָ הַיֹּצֵא
מֵחֲלָצֶיךָ הוּא־יִבְנֶה הַבַּיִת לִשְׁמִי׃ כ וַיָּקֶם
יְהוָה אֶת־דְּבָרוֹ אֲשֶׁר דִּבֵּר וָאָקֻם תַּחַת דָּוִד
אָבִי וָאֵשֵׁב ׀ עַל־כִּסֵּא יִשְׂרָאֵל כַּאֲשֶׁר דִּבֶּר
יְהוָה וָאֶבְנֶה הַבַּיִת לְשֵׁם יְהוָה אֱלֹהֵי יִשְׂרָאֵל׃
כא וָאָשִׂם שָׁם מָקוֹם לָאָרוֹן אֲשֶׁר־שָׁם בְּרִית
יְהוָה אֲשֶׁר כָּרַת עִם־אֲבֹתֵינוּ בְּהוֹצִיאוֹ אֹתָם
מֵאֶרֶץ מִצְרָיִם׃

about and blessed all the congregation of Israel, and all the congregation of Israel stood. 15. And he said, "Blessed [be] the Lord, the God of Israel, Who spoke with His mouth unto David my father, and has fulfilled it with His hand, saying: 16. 'Since the day that I brought forth My people Israel out of Egypt, I chose no city out of all the tribes of Israel to build a house, that My Name might be therein; but I chose David to be over My people Israel.' 17. And it was in the heart of David my father to build a house for the name of the Lord, the God of Israel. 18. And the Lord said to David my father, 'Since it was in your heart to build a house unto My Name, you did well that it was in your heart. 19. Nevertheless, you shall not build the house; but your son that shall come forth out of your loins, he shall build the house for My Name.' 20. And the Lord has established His word that He spoke, and I have risen up in the place of David my father, and sit on the throne of Israel, as the Lord spoke, and have built a house for the Name of the Lord, the God of Israel. 21. And I have set there a place for the ark, wherein [is] the covenant of the Lord, which He made with our fathers when He brought them out of the land of Egypt."

הפטרת שבת חול המועד סוכות

HAFTARAH FOR THE INTERMEDIATE SABBATH OF SUKKOTH

(Ezekiel 38:18–39:16)

Torah reading: Exodus 33:12–34:26, Numbers 29:17–31. Many congregations read Koheleth (p. 1039) prior to the Torah reading.

This selection refers to the war of Gog and Magog, which, according to tradition, will take place in the month of Tishri.

יח וְהָיָה ׀ בַּיּוֹם הַהוּא בְּיוֹם בּוֹא גוֹג עַל־
אַדְמַת יִשְׂרָאֵל נְאֻם אֲדֹנָי יֱהֹוִה תַּעֲלֶה חֲמָתִי
בְּאַפִּי׃ יט וּבְקִנְאָתִי בְאֵשׁ־עֶבְרָתִי דִּבַּרְתִּי אִם־
לֹא ׀ בַּיּוֹם הַהוּא יִהְיֶה רַעַשׁ גָּדוֹל עַל אַדְמַת
יִשְׂרָאֵל׃ כ וְרָעֲשׁוּ מִפָּנַי דְּגֵי הַיָּם וְעוֹף
הַשָּׁמַיִם וְחַיַּת הַשָּׂדֶה וְכָל־הָרֶמֶשׂ הָרֹמֵשׂ עַל־
הָאֲדָמָה וְכֹל הָאָדָם אֲשֶׁר עַל־פְּנֵי הָאֲדָמָה

38:18. And it will come to pass on that day, when Gog comes against the land of Israel, declares the Lord God, that My blazing indignation will blaze in My nostrils. 19. For in My jealousy and in the fire of My wrath I have spoken: Surely there shall be a great earthquake on that day in the land of Israel. 20. And at My Presence, the fishes of the sea and the birds of the heaven and the beasts of the field and all the creeping things that creep upon the earth and all the men who are upon the surface of the earth shall quake, and the mountains shall be thrown down, and the cliffs shall fall, and every wall shall fall to the ground. 21. And I will call the sword against him upon all My mountains, says the Lord God; every man's sword shall be against his brother. 22. And I will plead against him with pestilence and with blood, and rain bringing floods, and great hailstones, fire and brimstone will I rain down upon him and upon his hordes and upon the many peoples that are with him. 23. And I will reveal Myself in My greatness and in My holiness and will be recognized in the eyes of many nations, and they will know that I am the Lord. 39:1. And you, son of man, prophesy about Gog, and say: So says the Lord God: Lo! I am against you, O Gog, prince and head of Meshech and Tubal. 2. And I will turn you about and leave a sixth of your camp and lead you up from the uttermost parts of the north and bring you upon the mountains of Israel. 3. And I will smite the bow out of your left hand and make your arrows fall from your right hand. 4. Upon the mountains of Israel shall you fall, you and all your hordes, and the peoples that are with you; to the birds of prey, to all the winged creatures and the beasts of the field have I given you to be devoured. 5. Upon the open field shall you fall, for I have spoken, says the Lord God. 6. And I will send fire on Magog and on those who dwell in safety in the distant coastlands, and they will know that I am the Lord. 7. And I will make known My Holy Name in the midst of My people Israel, and I will no longer cause My Holy Name to be profaned, and the nations shall know that I, the Lord, am holy in Israel. 8. Behold it is coming, and it will be, says the Lord God; that is the day whereof I have spoken. 9. Then the inhabitants of the cities of Israel will go forth and make fires and heat up with the weapons, the shields and the bucklers, the bows and the arrows and the handstaves and the spears, and burn them as fires for seven years. 10. So that they shall carry no wood from the fields nor cut down any from the forests, for they shall make fires from the weapons, thus will they spoil those who spoiled them and plunder those who plundered them, says the Lord God. 11. And it shall come to pass on that day that I will

וְנֶהֶרְסוּ הֶהָרִים וְנָפְלוּ הַמַּדְרֵגוֹת וְכָל־חוֹמָה
לָאָרֶץ תִּפּוֹל׃ כא וְקָרָאתִי עָלָיו לְכָל־הָרַי חֶרֶב
נְאֻם אֲדֹנָי יֱהֹוִה חֶרֶב אִישׁ בְּאָחִיו תִּהְיֶה׃
כב וְנִשְׁפַּטְתִּי אִתּוֹ בְּדֶבֶר וּבְדָם וְגֶשֶׁם שׁוֹטֵף
וְאַבְנֵי אֶלְגָּבִישׁ אֵשׁ וְגָפְרִית אַמְטִיר עָלָיו
וְעַל־אֲגַפָּיו וְעַל־עַמִּים רַבִּים אֲשֶׁר אִתּוֹ׃
כג וְהִתְגַּדִּלְתִּי וְהִתְקַדִּשְׁתִּי וְנוֹדַעְתִּי לְעֵינֵי גּוֹיִם
רַבִּים וְיָדְעוּ כִּי־אֲנִי יְהֹוָה׃ א וְאַתָּה בֶן־אָדָם
הִנָּבֵא עַל־גּוֹג וְאָמַרְתָּ כֹּה אָמַר אֲדֹנָי יֱהֹוִה
הִנְנִי אֵלֶיךָ גּוֹג נְשִׂיא רֹאשׁ מֶשֶׁךְ וְתֻבָל׃
ב וְשֹׁבַבְתִּיךָ וְשִׁשֵּׁאתִיךָ וְהַעֲלִיתִיךָ מִיַּרְכְּתֵי
צָפוֹן וַהֲבִאוֹתִךָ עַל־הָרֵי יִשְׂרָאֵל׃ ג וְהִכֵּיתִי
קַשְׁתְּךָ מִיַּד שְׂמֹאולֶךָ וְחִצֶּיךָ מִיַּד יְמִינְךָ אַפִּיל׃
ד עַל־הָרֵי יִשְׂרָאֵל תִּפּוֹל אַתָּה וְכָל־אֲגַפֶּיךָ
וְעַמִּים אֲשֶׁר אִתָּךְ לְעֵיט צִפּוֹר כָּל־כָּנָף וְחַיַּת
הַשָּׂדֶה נְתַתִּיךָ לְאָכְלָה׃ ה עַל־פְּנֵי הַשָּׂדֶה תִּפּוֹל
כִּי אֲנִי דִבַּרְתִּי נְאֻם אֲדֹנָי יֱהֹוִה׃ ו וְשִׁלַּחְתִּי־
אֵשׁ בְּמָגוֹג וּבְיֹשְׁבֵי הָאִיִּים לָבֶטַח וְיָדְעוּ כִּי־
אֲנִי יְהֹוָה׃ ז וְאֶת־שֵׁם קָדְשִׁי אוֹדִיעַ בְּתוֹךְ עַמִּי
יִשְׂרָאֵל וְלֹא־אַחֵל אֶת־שֵׁם־קָדְשִׁי עוֹד וְיָדְעוּ
הַגּוֹיִם כִּי־אֲנִי יְהֹוָה קָדוֹשׁ בְּיִשְׂרָאֵל׃ ח הִנֵּה
בָאָה וְנִהְיָתָה נְאֻם אֲדֹנָי יֱהֹוִה הוּא הַיּוֹם אֲשֶׁר
דִּבַּרְתִּי׃ ט וְיָצְאוּ יֹשְׁבֵי ׀ עָרֵי יִשְׂרָאֵל וּבִעֲרוּ
וְהִשִּׂיקוּ בְּנֶשֶׁק וּמָגֵן וְצִנָּה בְּקֶשֶׁת וּבְחִצִּים
וּבְמַקֵּל יָד וּבְרֹמַח וּבִעֲרוּ בָהֶם אֵשׁ שֶׁבַע
שָׁנִים׃ י וְלֹא־יִשְׂאוּ עֵצִים מִן־הַשָּׂדֶה וְלֹא
יַחְטְבוּ מִן־הַיְּעָרִים כִּי בַנֶּשֶׁק יְבַעֲרוּ־אֵשׁ
וְשָׁלְלוּ אֶת־שֹׁלְלֵיהֶם וּבָזְזוּ אֶת־בֹּזְזֵיהֶם נְאֻם
אֲדֹנָי יֱהֹוִה׃ יא וְהָיָה בַיּוֹם הַהוּא אֶתֵּן לְגוֹג ׀

give Gog a place that a grave be there in Israel, the valley of them who pass along the east side of the sea, and it will then stop those who pass along. And there shall they bury Gog and all his hordes, and they shall call it the Valley of Hamon Gog [the masses of Gog]. 12. And seven months will the House of Israel be burying them in order to purify the land. 13. Yea, all the people of the land shall bury them, and they will be renowned; it is a day when I will be glorified, says the Lord God. 14. And they shall separate men of continuous employment who pass through the land, burying those who are left on the surface of the land with those who pass through, in order to purify it, at the end of seven months shall they search. 15. And when they that pass through shall pass and see a human bone, they shall build a sign next to it until the buriers bury it in the Valley of Hamon Gog. 16. And also the name of the city shall be Hamonah. Thus they shall purify the land.

מְקוֹם־שָׁ֠ם קֶ֨בֶר בְּיִשְׂרָאֵ֜ל גֵּ֣י הָעֹֽבְרִים֮ קִדְמַ֣ת הַיָּם֒ וְחֹסֶ֥מֶת הִ֖יא אֶת־הָעֹֽבְרִ֑ים וְקָ֣בְרוּ שָׁ֗ם אֶת־גּוֹג֙ וְאֶת־כָּל־הֲמוֹנֹ֔ה וְקָ֣רְא֔וּ גֵּ֖יא הֲמ֥וֹן גּֽוֹג: יב וּקְבָרוּם֙ בֵּ֣ית יִשְׂרָאֵ֔ל לְמַ֖עַן טַהֵ֣ר אֶת־הָאָ֑רֶץ שִׁבְעָ֖ה חֳדָשִֽׁים: יג וְקָֽבְרוּ֙ כָּל־עַ֣ם הָאָ֔רֶץ וְהָיָ֥ה לָהֶ֖ם לְשֵׁ֑ם י֚וֹם הִכָּ֣בְדִ֔י נְאֻ֖ם אֲדֹנָ֥י יֱהֹוִֽה: יד וְאַנְשֵׁ֨י תָמִ֤יד יַבְדִּ֙ילוּ֙ עֹֽבְרִ֣ים בָּאָ֔רֶץ מְקַבְּרִ֣ים אֶת־הָעֹֽבְרִ֗ים אֶת־הַנּֽוֹתָרִ֛ים עַל־פְּנֵ֥י הָאָ֖רֶץ לְטַֽהֲרָ֑הּ מִקְצֵ֥ה שִׁבְעָֽה־חֳדָשִׁ֖ים יַחְקֹֽרוּ: טו וְעָֽבְר֤וּ הָעֹֽבְרִים֙ בָּאָ֔רֶץ וְרָאָה֙ עֶ֣צֶם אָדָ֔ם וּבָנָ֥ה אֶצְל֖וֹ צִיּ֑וּן עַ֣ד קָֽבְר֤וּ אֹתוֹ֙ הַֽמְקַבְּרִ֔ים אֶל־גֵּ֖יא הֲמ֥וֹן גּֽוֹג: טז וְגַ֥ם שֶׁם־עִ֖יר הֲמוֹנָ֑ה וְטִֽהֲר֖וּ הָאָֽרֶץ:

HAFTARATH SHEMINI ATZERET הפטרת שמיני עצרת
(I Kings 8:54–66) Most congregations add 9:1.
Torah reading: Those following the German and Sephardic rituals read Deuteronomy 15:19–16:17 if Shemini Atzereth falls on a weekday, and Deuteronomy 14:22–16:17 if it falls on a Sabbath. Congregations following the Polish ritual read Deuteronomy 14:22–16:17 in both instances.
Additional Torah reading: Numbers 29:35–39. If Shemini Atzereth falls on a Sabbath many congregations read Koheleth (p. 1039) prior to the Torah reading.

This selection deals with the conclusion of the dedication of the Temple, when Solomon sent the people away. This took place on the eighth day of the Sukkoth festival, Shemini Atzeret.

8:54. And it was as Solomon finished praying all this prayer and supplication to the Lord, that he arose from before the altar of the Lord, from kneeling on his knees with his hands spread out toward heaven. 55. And he stood, and blessed the entire congregation of Israel [with] a loud voice, saying, 56. "Blessed [be] the Lord, Who has given rest to His people Israel, according to all that He spoke; there has not failed one word of all his good word, that He spoke through Moses His servant. 57. May the Lord our God be with us, as He was with our forefathers; let Him not leave us nor forsake us. 58. That He may incline our hearts to Him, to go in all His ways and to

נד וַיְהִ֣י | כְּכַלּ֣וֹת שְׁלֹמֹ֗ה לְהִתְפַּלֵּל֙ אֶל־יְהֹוָ֔ה אֵ֚ת כָּל־הַתְּפִלָּ֣ה וְהַתְּחִנָּ֣ה הַזֹּ֔את קָ֖ם מִלִּפְנֵ֣י מִזְבַּ֣ח יְהֹוָ֔ה מִכְּרֹ֖עַ עַל־בִּרְכָּ֑יו וְכַפָּ֖יו פְּרֻשׂ֥וֹת הַשָּׁמָֽיִם: נה וַֽיַּעֲמֹ֕ד וַיְבָ֕רֶךְ אֵ֖ת כָּל־קְהַ֣ל יִשְׂרָאֵ֑ל ק֥וֹל גָּד֖וֹל לֵאמֹֽר: נו בָּר֣וּךְ יְהֹוָ֗ה אֲשֶׁ֨ר נָתַ֤ן מְנוּחָה֙ לְעַמּ֣וֹ יִשְׂרָאֵ֔ל כְּכֹ֖ל אֲשֶׁ֣ר דִּבֵּ֑ר לֹֽא־נָפַ֞ל דָּבָ֣ר אֶחָ֗ד מִכֹּל֙ דְּבָר֣וֹ הַטּ֔וֹב אֲשֶׁ֣ר דִּבֶּ֔ר בְּיַ֖ד מֹשֶׁ֥ה עַבְדּֽוֹ: נז יְהִ֨י יְהֹוָ֤ה אֱלֹהֵ֙ינוּ֙ עִמָּ֔נוּ כַּֽאֲשֶׁ֥ר הָיָ֖ה עִם־אֲבֹתֵ֑ינוּ אַל־יַֽעַזְבֵ֖נוּ וְאַֽל־יִטְּשֵֽׁנוּ: נח לְהַטּ֥וֹת לְבָבֵ֖נוּ אֵלָ֑יו לָלֶ֣כֶת בְּכָל־דְּרָכָ֗יו

keep His commandments and His statutes and His judgments, which He commanded our forefathers. 59. And may these words of mine, with which I have made supplication before the Lord, be close to the Lord our God, day and night, that He sustain the cause of His servant and the cause of His people Israel, each day's need granted on its day, 60. so that all the peoples of the earth may know that the Lord is God; there is none else. 61. Let your heart, [therefore,] be whole with the Lord our God, to follow His statutes and to keep His precepts as of this day." 62. And the King and all Israel with him slaughtered sacrifices before the Lord. 63. And Solomon slaughtered the peace-offerings that he slaughtered to the Lord, twenty-two thousand oxen and one hundred and twenty thousand sheep. [With this] the King and all the children of Israel inaugurated the Temple of the Lord. 64. On that day the King consecrated the middle of the court that was before the Temple of the Lord, for there he offered the burnt-offerings [and] the meal-offerings and the fat of the peace-offerings, for the copper altar that was before the Lord was too small to contain the burnt-offerings [and] the meal-offerings and the fat of the peace-offerings. 65. Now Solomon observed the Feast at that time and all Israel with him, a great assemblage from the entrance of Hamath to the brook of Egypt, before the Lord our God, seven days and seven days, [totalling] fourteen days. 66. On the eighth day he dismissed the people, and they blessed the King and went to their homes, rejoicing and delighted of heart for all the goodness that the Lord had wrought for David His servant and for Israel His people. (*Most congregations add:*) 9:1. And it was when Solomon had finished building the Temple of the Lord and the King's palace and all Solomon's desire that he wished to make.

וְלִשְׁמֹר מִצְוֺתָיו וְחֻקָּיו וּמִשְׁפָּטָיו אֲשֶׁר צִוָּה
אֶת־אֲבֹתֵינוּ: נט וְיִהְיוּ דְבָרַי אֵלֶּה אֲשֶׁר
הִתְחַנַּנְתִּי לִפְנֵי יְהֹוָה קְרֹבִים אֶל־יְהֹוָה אֱלֹהֵינוּ
יוֹמָם וָלָיְלָה לַעֲשׂוֹת | מִשְׁפַּט עַבְדּוֹ וּמִשְׁפַּט
עַמּוֹ יִשְׂרָאֵל דְּבַר־יוֹם בְּיוֹמוֹ: ס לְמַעַן דַּעַת
כָּל־עַמֵּי הָאָרֶץ כִּי יְהֹוָה הוּא הָאֱלֹהִים אֵין
עוֹד: סא וְהָיָה לְבַבְכֶם שָׁלֵם עִם יְהֹוָה אֱלֹהֵינוּ
לָלֶכֶת בְּחֻקָּיו וְלִשְׁמֹר מִצְוֺתָיו כַּיּוֹם הַזֶּה:
סב וְהַמֶּלֶךְ וְכָל־יִשְׂרָאֵל עִמּוֹ זֹבְחִים זֶבַח לִפְנֵי
יְהֹוָה: סג וַיִּזְבַּח שְׁלֹמֹה אֵת זֶבַח הַשְּׁלָמִים
אֲשֶׁר זָבַח לַיהֹוָה בָּקָר עֶשְׂרִים וּשְׁנַיִם אֶלֶף
וְצֹאן מֵאָה וְעֶשְׂרִים אָלֶף וַיַּחְנְכוּ אֶת־בֵּית
יְהֹוָה הַמֶּלֶךְ וְכָל־בְּנֵי יִשְׂרָאֵל: סד בַּיּוֹם הַהוּא
קִדַּשׁ הַמֶּלֶךְ אֶת־תּוֹךְ הֶחָצֵר אֲשֶׁר לִפְנֵי בֵית־
יְהֹוָה כִּי־עָשָׂה שָׁם אֶת־הָעֹלָה וְאֶת־הַמִּנְחָה
וְאֵת חֶלְבֵי הַשְּׁלָמִים כִּי־מִזְבַּח הַנְּחֹשֶׁת אֲשֶׁר
לִפְנֵי יְהֹוָה קָטֹן מֵהָכִיל אֶת־הָעֹלָה וְאֶת־
הַמִּנְחָה וְאֵת חֶלְבֵי הַשְּׁלָמִים: סה וַיַּעַשׂ שְׁלֹמֹה
בָעֵת־הַהִיא | אֶת־הֶחָג וְכָל־יִשְׂרָאֵל עִמּוֹ קָהָל
גָּדוֹל מִלְּבוֹא חֲמָת | עַד־נַחַל מִצְרַיִם לִפְנֵי
יְהֹוָה אֱלֹהֵינוּ שִׁבְעַת יָמִים וְשִׁבְעַת יָמִים
אַרְבָּעָה עָשָׂר יוֹם: סו בַּיּוֹם הַשְּׁמִינִי שִׁלַּח
אֶת־הָעָם וַיְבָרְכוּ אֶת־הַמֶּלֶךְ וַיֵּלְכוּ לְאָהֳלֵיהֶם
שְׂמֵחִים וְטוֹבֵי לֵב עַל כָּל־הַטּוֹבָה אֲשֶׁר עָשָׂה
יְהֹוָה לְדָוִד עַבְדּוֹ וּלְיִשְׂרָאֵל עַמּוֹ: (רוב קהלות
מוסיפים) א וַיְהִי כְּכַלּוֹת שְׁלֹמֹה לִבְנוֹת אֶת־
בֵּית־יְהֹוָה וְאֶת־בֵּית הַמֶּלֶךְ וְאֵת כָּל־חֵשֶׁק
שְׁלֹמֹה אֲשֶׁר חָפֵץ לַעֲשׂוֹת:

(Joshua 1. Sephardim conclude with verse 9.)

Torah reading: Deuteronomy 23:24, Genesis 1–2:3, Numbers 29:35–39.

This selection takes up the Scriptural narrative from the death of Moses.

1:1. And it was after the death of Moses, the servant of the Lord, that the Lord said to Joshua the son of Nun, Moses' minister, saying. 2. "Moses my servant has died; and now arise cross this Jordan, you and all this nation, to the land which I give the children of Israel. 3. Every place on which the soles of your feet will tread I have given to you, as I have spoken to Moses. 4. From this desert and Lebanon to the great river, the Euphrates, all the land of the Hittites to the great sea westward shall be your boundary. 5. No man shall stand up before you all the days of your life; as I was with Moses, so shall I be with you. I will not weaken My grasp on you nor will I abandon you. 6. Be strong and have courage; for you will cause this nation to inherit the land that I have sworn to their ancestors to give to them. 7. Just be strong and very courageous to observe and do in accordance with all of the Torah that Moses My servant has commanded you. Do not stray therefrom right or left, in order that you succeed wherever you go. 8. This book of the Torah shall not leave your mouth; you shall meditate therein day and night in order that you observe to do all that is written in it, for then will you succeed in all your ways, and then will you prosper. 9. Did I not command you, be strong and have courage, do not fear and do not be dismayed, for the Lord your God is with you wherever you go." (*Sephardim conclude here.*) 10. And Joshua commanded the officers of the nation, saying: 11. "Go through the midst of the camp and command the nation, saying: 'Prepare provision for yourselves, for in another three days you will cross this Jordan to come and inherit the land that the Lord your God is giving you to inherit.'" 12. And to the Reubenites and the Gadites and the half tribe of Manasseh, Joshua said, saying: 13. "Remember the word that Moses, the servant of the Lord, commanded you,

א וַיְהִי אַחֲרֵי מוֹת מֹשֶׁה עֶבֶד יְהוָה וַיֹּאמֶר
יְהוָה אֶל־יְהוֹשֻׁעַ בִּן־נוּן מְשָׁרֵת מֹשֶׁה לֵאמֹר:
ב מֹשֶׁה עַבְדִּי מֵת וְעַתָּה קוּם עֲבֹר אֶת־הַיַּרְדֵּן
הַזֶּה אַתָּה וְכָל־הָעָם הַזֶּה אֶל־הָאָרֶץ אֲשֶׁר
אָנֹכִי נֹתֵן לָהֶם לִבְנֵי יִשְׂרָאֵל: ג כָּל־מָקוֹם
אֲשֶׁר תִּדְרֹךְ כַּף־רַגְלְכֶם בּוֹ לָכֶם נְתַתִּיו כַּאֲשֶׁר
דִּבַּרְתִּי אֶל־מֹשֶׁה: ד מֵהַמִּדְבָּר וְהַלְּבָנוֹן הַזֶּה
וְעַד־הַנָּהָר הַגָּדוֹל נְהַר־פְּרָת כֹּל אֶרֶץ הַחִתִּים
וְעַד־הַיָּם הַגָּדוֹל מְבוֹא הַשָּׁמֶשׁ יִהְיֶה גְּבוּלְכֶם:
ה לֹא־יִתְיַצֵּב אִישׁ לְפָנֶיךָ כֹּל יְמֵי חַיֶּיךָ כַּאֲשֶׁר
הָיִיתִי עִם־מֹשֶׁה אֶהְיֶה עִמָּךְ לֹא אַרְפְּךָ וְלֹא
אֶעֶזְבֶךָּ: ו חֲזַק וֶאֱמָץ כִּי אַתָּה תַּנְחִיל אֶת־
הָעָם הַזֶּה אֶת־הָאָרֶץ אֲשֶׁר־נִשְׁבַּעְתִּי לַאֲבוֹתָם
לָתֵת לָהֶם: ז רַק חֲזַק וֶאֱמַץ מְאֹד לִשְׁמֹר
לַעֲשׂוֹת כְּכָל־הַתּוֹרָה אֲשֶׁר צִוְּךָ מֹשֶׁה עַבְדִּי
אַל־תָּסוּר מִמֶּנּוּ יָמִין וּשְׂמֹאול לְמַעַן תַּשְׂכִּיל
בְּכֹל אֲשֶׁר תֵּלֵךְ: ח לֹא־יָמוּשׁ סֵפֶר הַתּוֹרָה
הַזֶּה מִפִּיךָ וְהָגִיתָ בּוֹ יוֹמָם וָלַיְלָה לְמַעַן
תִּשְׁמֹר לַעֲשׂוֹת כְּכָל־הַכָּתוּב בּוֹ כִּי־אָז תַּצְלִיחַ
אֶת־דְּרָכֶךָ וְאָז תַּשְׂכִּיל: ט הֲלוֹא צִוִּיתִיךָ חֲזַק
וֶאֱמָץ אַל־תַּעֲרֹץ וְאַל־תֵּחָת כִּי עִמְּךָ יְהוָה
אֱלֹהֶיךָ בְּכֹל אֲשֶׁר תֵּלֵךְ: (כאן מסיימין הספרדים)
י וַיְצַו יְהוֹשֻׁעַ אֶת־שֹׁטְרֵי הָעָם לֵאמֹר:
יא עִבְרוּ | בְּקֶרֶב הַמַּחֲנֶה וְצַוּוּ אֶת־הָעָם
לֵאמֹר הָכִינוּ לָכֶם צֵידָה כִּי בְּעוֹד | שְׁלֹשֶׁת
יָמִים אַתֶּם עֹבְרִים אֶת־הַיַּרְדֵּן הַזֶּה לָבוֹא
לָרֶשֶׁת אֶת־הָאָרֶץ אֲשֶׁר יְהוָה אֱלֹהֵיכֶם נֹתֵן
לָכֶם לְרִשְׁתָּהּ: יב וְלָראוּבֵנִי וְלַגָּדִי וְלַחֲצִי שֵׁבֶט
הַמְנַשֶּׁה אָמַר יְהוֹשֻׁעַ לֵאמֹר: יג זָכוֹר אֶת־
הַדָּבָר אֲשֶׁר צִוָּה אֶתְכֶם מֹשֶׁה עֶבֶד־יְהוָה

saying: 'The Lord your God is giving you rest and has given you this land. 14. Your wives, your children, and your cattle shall settle in the land that Moses gave you on this side of the Jordan, and you, all the warriors, shall cross over armed before your brothers, and you shall help them. 15. Until the Lord gives your brothers rest as He has given you, and they too shall inherit the land that the Lord your God gives them. You will then return to the land of your inheritance, which Moses, the servant of the Lord, gave you on this side of the Jordan towards the rising of the sun, and you will inherit it.'" 16. And they answered Joshua saying: "All that you have commanded us we shall do and wherever you send us we shall go. 17. Just as we obeyed Moses in everything, so shall we obey you. Only that the Lord your God be with you as He was with Moses. 18. Every man that shall rebel against your words and will not listen to your commands in all that you order him shall be put to death. Only be strong and have courage."

לֵאמֹ֑ר יְהוָ֤ה אֱלֹֽהֵיכֶם֙ מֵנִ֣יחַ לָכֶ֔ם וְנָתַ֥ן לָכֶ֖ם
אֶת־הָאָ֥רֶץ הַזֹּֽאת׃ יד נְשֵׁיכֶ֣ם טַפְּכֶם֮ וּמִקְנֵיכֶם֒
יֵשְׁב֕וּ בָּאָ֕רֶץ אֲשֶׁ֨ר נָתַ֥ן לָכֶ֛ם מֹשֶׁ֖ה בְּעֵ֣בֶר
הַיַּרְדֵּ֑ן וְאַתֶּם֩ תַּעַבְר֨וּ חֲמֻשִׁ֜ים לִפְנֵ֣י אֲחֵיכֶ֗ם כֹּ֚ל
גִּבּוֹרֵ֣י הַחַ֔יִל וַעֲזַרְתֶּ֖ם אוֹתָֽם׃ טו עַ֠ד אֲשֶׁר־יָנִ֨יחַ
יְהוָ֥ה ׀ לַאֲחֵיכֶם֮ כָּכֶם֒ וְיָרְשׁ֣וּ גַם־הֵ֔מָּה אֶת־
הָאָ֕רֶץ אֲשֶׁר־יְהוָ֥ה אֱלֹהֵיכֶ֖ם נֹתֵ֣ן לָהֶ֑ם וְשַׁבְתֶּ֞ם
לְאֶ֤רֶץ יְרֻשַּׁתְכֶם֙ וִֽירִשְׁתֶּ֣ם אוֹתָ֔הּ אֲשֶׁ֣ר ׀ נָתַ֣ן
לָכֶ֗ם מֹשֶׁה֙ עֶ֣בֶד יְהוָ֔ה בְּעֵ֥בֶר הַיַּרְדֵּ֖ן מִזְרַ֥ח
הַשָּֽׁמֶשׁ׃ טז וַֽיַּעֲנ֔וּ אֶת־יְהוֹשֻׁ֖עַ לֵאמֹ֑ר כֹּ֤ל
אֲשֶׁר־צִוִּיתָ֙נוּ֙ נַעֲשֶׂ֔ה וְאֶל־כָּל־אֲשֶׁ֥ר תִּשְׁלָחֵ֖נוּ
נֵלֵֽךְ׃ יז כְּכֹ֤ל אֲשֶׁר־שָׁמַ֙עְנוּ֙ אֶל־מֹשֶׁ֔ה כֵּ֖ן נִשְׁמַ֣ע
אֵלֶ֑יךָ רַ֠ק יִֽהְיֶ֞ה יְהוָ֤ה אֱלֹהֶ֙יךָ֙ עִמָּ֔ךְ כַּאֲשֶׁ֥ר הָיָ֖ה
עִם־מֹשֶֽׁה׃ יח כָּל־אִ֞ישׁ אֲשֶׁר־יַמְרֶ֣ה אֶת־פִּ֗יךָ
וְלֹֽא־יִשְׁמַ֧ע אֶת־דְּבָרֶ֛יךָ לְכֹ֥ל אֲשֶׁר־תְּצַוֶּ֖נּוּ
יוּמָ֑ת רַ֖ק חֲזַ֥ק וֶאֱמָֽץ׃

HAFTARATH SHABBATH CHANUKAH הפטרת שבת חנוכה

(Zechariah 2:14–4:7)

Additional Torah reading: First day of Chanukah, Numbers 7:1–17. On other days, the section dealing with the Prince's offering for that day is read. See Numbers 7:18–53 for appropriate reading.

If the new moon coincides with the Sabbath, three Torah Scrolls are taken out of the Ark. In the first, we call six people to the reading of the Sidra of the week; in the second, we read the selection for Rosh Chodesh (Numbers 28:9–15), and in the third, the Maftir, we read the section dealing with the Prince's offering for the sixth day (Numbers 7:42–47).

This Haftarah is read on the first Sabbath of Chanukah replacing the Haftarah ordinarily read with the Sidra of that week, the Haftarah of Shabbath Rosh Chodesh as well as if that Sabbath happens to coincide with the new moon of Teveth, or the Haftarah for the Day Preceding Rosh Chodesh.

This Haftarah describes Zechariah's vision of the Menorah and its lamps.

2:14. Sing and rejoice, O daughter of Zion, for, lo, I enter, and I will dwell in your midst, says the Lord. 15. And many nations will attach themselves to the Lord on that day and will become My people, and I will dwell in your midst, and you will know that the Lord of Hosts has sent me to you. 16. And the Lord will take Judah into His possessions as His portion on the holy soil and will choose Jerusalem forever. 17. Be

יד רָנִּ֥י וְשִׂמְחִ֖י בַּת־צִיּ֑וֹן כִּ֧י הִנְנִי־בָ֛א וְשָׁכַנְתִּ֥י
בְתוֹכֵ֖ךְ נְאֻם־יְהוָֽה׃ טו וְנִלְווּ֩ גוֹיִ֨ם רַבִּ֤ים אֶל־
יְהוָה֙ בַּיּ֣וֹם הַה֔וּא וְהָ֥יוּ לִ֖י לְעָ֑ם וְשָׁכַנְתִּ֣י בְתוֹכֵ֔ךְ
וְיָדַ֕עַתְּ כִּֽי־יְהוָ֥ה צְבָא֖וֹת שְׁלָחַ֥נִי אֵלָֽיִךְ׃ טז וְנָחַ֨ל
יְהוָ֤ה אֶת־יְהוּדָה֙ חֶלְק֔וֹ עַ֖ל אַדְמַ֣ת הַקֹּ֑דֶשׁ וּבָחַ֥ר
ע֖וֹד בִּירוּשָׁלִָֽם׃ יז הַ֥ס כָּל־בָּשָׂ֖ר מִפְּנֵ֣י יְהוָ֑ה כִּ֥י

נֵעוֹר מִמְּעוֹן קָדְשׁוֹ׃ א וַיַּרְאֵנִי אֶת־יְהוֹשֻׁעַ
הַכֹּהֵן הַגָּדוֹל עֹמֵד לִפְנֵי מַלְאַךְ יְהוָה וְהַשָּׂטָן
עֹמֵד עַל־יְמִינוֹ לְשִׂטְנוֹ׃ ב וַיֹּאמֶר יְהוָה אֶל־
הַשָּׂטָן יִגְעַר יְהוָה בְּךָ הַשָּׂטָן וְיִגְעַר יְהוָה בְּךָ
הַבֹּחֵר בִּירוּשָׁלָםִ הֲלוֹא זֶה אוּד מֻצָּל מֵאֵשׁ׃
ג וִיהוֹשֻׁעַ הָיָה לָבֻשׁ בְּגָדִים צוֹאִים וְעֹמֵד
לִפְנֵי הַמַּלְאָךְ׃ ד וַיַּעַן וַיֹּאמֶר אֶל־הָעֹמְדִים
לְפָנָיו לֵאמֹר הָסִירוּ הַבְּגָדִים הַצֹּאִים מֵעָלָיו
וַיֹּאמֶר אֵלָיו רְאֵה הֶעֱבַרְתִּי מֵעָלֶיךָ עֲוֺנֶךָ
וְהַלְבֵּשׁ אֹתְךָ מַחֲלָצוֹת׃ ה וָאֹמַר יָשִׂימוּ צָנִיף
טָהוֹר עַל־רֹאשׁוֹ וַיָּשִׂימוּ הַצָּנִיף הַטָּהוֹר עַל־
רֹאשׁוֹ וַיַּלְבִּשֻׁהוּ בְּגָדִים וּמַלְאַךְ יְהוָה עֹמֵד׃
ו וַיָּעַד מַלְאַךְ יְהוָה בִּיהוֹשֻׁעַ לֵאמֹר׃ ז כֹּה־
אָמַר יְהוָה צְבָאוֹת אִם־בִּדְרָכַי תֵּלֵךְ וְאִם אֶת־
מִשְׁמַרְתִּי תִשְׁמֹר וְגַם־אַתָּה תָּדִין אֶת־בֵּיתִי וְגַם
תִּשְׁמֹר אֶת־חֲצֵרָי וְנָתַתִּי לְךָ מַהְלְכִים בֵּין
הָעֹמְדִים הָאֵלֶּה׃ ח שְׁמַע־נָא יְהוֹשֻׁעַ ׀ הַכֹּהֵן
הַגָּדוֹל אַתָּה וְרֵעֶיךָ הַיֹּשְׁבִים לְפָנֶיךָ כִּי־אַנְשֵׁי
מוֹפֵת הֵמָּה כִּי־הִנְנִי מֵבִיא אֶת־עַבְדִּי צֶמַח׃
ט כִּי ׀ הִנֵּה הָאֶבֶן אֲשֶׁר נָתַתִּי לִפְנֵי יְהוֹשֻׁעַ עַל־
אֶבֶן אַחַת שִׁבְעָה עֵינָיִם הִנְנִי מְפַתֵּחַ פִּתֻּחָהּ
נְאֻם יְהוָה צְבָאוֹת וּמַשְׁתִּי אֶת־עֲוֺן הָאָרֶץ־
הַהִיא בְּיוֹם אֶחָד׃ י בַּיּוֹם הַהוּא נְאֻם יְהוָה
צְבָאוֹת תִּקְרְאוּ אִישׁ לְרֵעֵהוּ (בס"א אל־רעהו כתיב)
אֶל־תַּחַת גֶּפֶן וְאֶל־תַּחַת תְּאֵנָה׃ א וַיָּשָׁב
הַמַּלְאָךְ הַדֹּבֵר בִּי וַיְעִירֵנִי כְּאִישׁ אֲשֶׁר־יֵעוֹר
מִשְּׁנָתוֹ׃ ב וַיֹּאמֶר אֵלַי מָה אַתָּה רֹאֶה וָיֹּאמַר
(ואמר קרי) רָאִיתִי וְהִנֵּה מְנוֹרַת זָהָב כֻּלָּהּ וְגֻלָּהּ
עַל־רֹאשָׁהּ וְשִׁבְעָה נֵרֹתֶיהָ עָלֶיהָ שִׁבְעָה
וְשִׁבְעָה מוּצָקוֹת לַנֵּרוֹת אֲשֶׁר עַל־רֹאשָׁהּ׃
ג וּשְׁנַיִם זֵיתִים עָלֶיהָ אֶחָד מִימִין הַגֻּלָּה וְאֶחָד
עַל־שְׂמֹאלָהּ׃ ד וָאַעַן וָאֹמַר אֶל־הַמַּלְאָךְ הַדֹּבֵר

silent, all flesh, before the Lord, for He is aroused out of His Holy Habitation. 3:1. Then He showed me Joshua, the High-priest, standing before the angel of the Lord, and the hinderer standing at his right hand to hinder him. 2. And the Lord said to the hinderer: The Lord repulse you, O hinderer, the Lord Who has chosen Jerusalem repulse you. For is not this a brand plucked out of the fire? 3. Now Joshua was clothed with soiled garments and standing before the angel. 4. And he (the angel) lifted his voice and said to those that stood before him, saying, "Remove the soiled garments from upon him." Then he said to him, "Behold, I have caused your iniquity to pass from you, now clothe yourself with pure garments." 5. Then I said, "Let them set a pure miter on his head," and they set the pure miter upon his head and invested him with garments. But the angel of the Lord remained standing. 6. The angel of the Lord warned Joshua, saying: 7. So says the Lord of Hosts: If you will walk in My ways, and if you will keep My charge, and you will also judge My House, and you will also guard My court-yards, then I will give you free access among those that are standing still here. 8. Hear now, O Joshua the high-priest! For you and your companions who sit before you are men worthy of miracles; for, behold, I bring My servant the shoot. 9. For, behold the stone that I have placed before Joshua, on this one stone seven eyes are directed; behold, I engrave its engraving, says the Lord of Hosts, and I will make the iniquity of that land disappear in one day. 10. On that day, says the Lord of Hosts, every man will invite his neighbor beneath his vine and beneath his fig tree. 4:1. Then the angel that talked within me came again and awakened me up as a man who is awakened from his sleep. 2. And he said to me, "What do you see?" And I said, "I have looked, and behold a candelabrum all of gold, with its oil-bowl upon the top of it and its seven lamps thereon and seven tubes to the seven lamps which were upon its top. 3. And two olive trees by it, one upon the right side of the bowl, and the other on the left side thereof." 4. So I answered and spoke to the angel who talked within me, saying, "What do these mean, my lord?" 5. Then the angel that talked within me answered to me, "Have you not understood what these mean?" And I said, "No, my lord." 6. Then he answered and spoke to me, saying, "This is the word of the Lord to Zerubbabel, saying, 'Not by military force and not by physical strength, but by My spirit,' says the Lord of Hosts. 7. Who are you, O great mountain? Before Zerubbabel you sink to a plain! He will bring up the best stone, with shoutings of Grace, grace, to it."

כִּי לֵאמֹר מָה־אֵלֶּה אֲדֹנִי: ה וַיַּעַן הַמַּלְאָךְ
הַדֹּבֵר בִּי וַיֹּאמֶר אֵלַי הֲלוֹא יָדַעְתָּ מָה־הֵמָּה
אֵלֶּה וָאֹמַר לֹא אֲדֹנִי: ו וַיַּעַן וַיֹּאמֶר אֵלַי לֵאמֹר
זֶה דְּבַר־יְהוָה אֶל־זְרֻבָּבֶל לֵאמֹר לֹא בְחַיִל וְלֹא
בְכֹחַ כִּי אִם־בְּרוּחִי אָמַר יְהוָה צְבָאוֹת: ז מִי־
אַתָּה הַר־הַגָּדוֹל לִפְנֵי זְרֻבָּבֶל לְמִישֹׁר וְהוֹצִיא
אֶת־הָאֶבֶן הָרֹאשָׁה תְּשֻׁאוֹת חֵן | חֵן לָהּ:

HAFTARATH SHABBATH CHANUKAH II הפטרת שבת שניה דחנוכה

(I Kings 7:40–50)

Additional Torah reading: Numbers 7:54–8:4. This Haftarah replaces the Haftarah ordinarily read with the Sidra of that week.

This selection includes a reference to the preparation of the candlesticks for the First Temple.

7:40. And Hiram made the lavers and the shovels and the basins. And Hiram finished doing all the work which he did for king Solomon [in] the house of the Lord. 41. The two pillars and the two bowls of the chapiters that [were] on the top of the pillars; and the two networks, to cover the two bowls of the chapiters which [were] on the top of the pillars. 42. And the four hundred pomegranates for the two networks, two rows of pomegranates for each network, to cover the two bowls of the chapiters that [were] upon the pillars. 43. And the ten bases, and the ten lavers on the bases. 44. And the one sea, and the twelve oxen under the sea. 45. And the pots, and the shovels, and the basins, and all these vessels, which Hiram made for king Solomon [in] the house of the Lord, [were] of bright copper. 46. In the plain of the Jordan did the king cast them, in the thick clay, between Succoth and Tsarethan. 47. And Solomon left all the vessels [unweighed], because [there were] very very many; [therefore] the weight of the copper was not found out. 48. And Solomon made all the vessels that [were] in the house of the Lord; the altar of gold and the table whereupon the showbread [was], of gold. 49. And the candlesticks, five on the right [side] and five on the left, before the Sanctuary, of pure gold; and the flowers

מ וַיַּעַשׂ חִירוֹם אֶת־הַכִּיֹּרוֹת וְאֶת־הַיָּעִים וְאֶת־
הַמִּזְרָקוֹת וַיְכַל חִירָם לַעֲשׂוֹת אֶת־כָּל־
הַמְּלָאכָה אֲשֶׁר עָשָׂה לַמֶּלֶךְ שְׁלֹמֹה בֵּית יְהוָה:
מא עַמֻּדִים שְׁנַיִם וְגֻלֹּת הַכֹּתָרֹת אֲשֶׁר־עַל־
רֹאשׁ הָעַמּוּדִים שְׁתָּיִם וְהַשְּׂבָכוֹת שְׁתַּיִם לְכַסּוֹת
אֶת־שְׁתֵּי גֻּלּוֹת הַכֹּתָרֹת אֲשֶׁר עַל־רֹאשׁ
הָעַמּוּדִים: מב וְאֶת־הָרִמֹּנִים אַרְבַּע מֵאוֹת
לִשְׁתֵּי הַשְּׂבָכוֹת שְׁנֵי־טוּרִים רִמֹּנִים לַשְּׂבָכָה
הָאֶחָת לְכַסּוֹת אֶת־שְׁתֵּי גֻּלּוֹת הַכֹּתָרֹת אֲשֶׁר
עַל־פְּנֵי הָעַמּוּדִים: מג וְאֶת־הַמְּכֹנוֹת עֶשֶׂר
וְאֶת־הַכִּיֹּרֹת עֲשָׂרָה עַל־הַמְּכֹנוֹת: מד וְאֶת־הַיָּם
הָאֶחָד וְאֶת־הַבָּקָר שְׁנֵים־עָשָׂר תַּחַת הַיָּם:
מה וְאֶת־הַסִּירוֹת וְאֶת־הַיָּעִים וְאֶת־הַמִּזְרָקוֹת
וְאֵת כָּל־הַכֵּלִים הָאֹהֶל (האלה קרי) אֲשֶׁר עָשָׂה
חִירָם לַמֶּלֶךְ שְׁלֹמֹה בֵּית יְהוָה נְחֹשֶׁת מְמֹרָט:
מו בְּכִכַּר הַיַּרְדֵּן יְצָקָם הַמֶּלֶךְ בְּמַעֲבֵה הָאֲדָמָה
בֵּין סֻכּוֹת וּבֵין צָרְתָן: מז וַיַּנַּח שְׁלֹמֹה אֶת־כָּל־
הַכֵּלִים מֵרֹב מְאֹד מְאֹד לֹא נֶחְקַר מִשְׁקַל
הַנְּחֹשֶׁת: מח וַיַּעַשׂ שְׁלֹמֹה אֵת כָּל־הַכֵּלִים אֲשֶׁר
בֵּית יְהוָה אֵת מִזְבַּח הַזָּהָב וְאֶת־הַשֻּׁלְחָן אֲשֶׁר
עָלָיו לֶחֶם הַפָּנִים זָהָב: מט וְאֶת־הַמְּנֹרוֹת חָמֵשׁ

and the lamps and the tongs, of gold.
50. And the bowls and the musical instruments, and the basins and the spoons, and the censers, of pure gold; and the hinges, for the doors of the inner house, the most holy [place], [and] for the doors of the house, [that is] of the temple, of gold.

מִיָּמִין וְחָמֵשׁ מִשְּׂמֹאל לִפְנֵי הַדְּבִיר זָהָב סָגוּר וְהַפֶּרַח וְהַנֵּרֹת וְהַמֶּלְקָחַיִם זָהָב: נ וְהַסִּפּוֹת וְהַמְזַמְּרוֹת וְהַמִּזְרָקוֹת וְהַכַּפּוֹת וְהַמַּחְתּוֹת זָהָב סָגוּר וְהַפֹּתוֹת לְדַלְתוֹת הַבַּיִת הַפְּנִימִי לְקֹדֶשׁ הַקֳּדָשִׁים לְדַלְתֵי הַבַּיִת לַהֵיכָל זָהָב:

HAFTARATH SHEKALIM הפטרת שקלים
(Sephardim read: II Kings 11:17–12:17; Ashkenazim begin 12:1)
Additional Torah reading: Exodus 30:11–16

If the new moon coincides with the Sabbath, three Torah Scrolls are taken out of the Ark. In the first one, we call six people to the reading of the Sidra of the week; in the second, we read the selection for Rosh Chodesh (Numbers 28:9–15), and in the third, we read Parashath Shekalim for the Maftir. This selection is read on the Sabbath preceding Rosh Chodesh Adar or on Rosh Chodesh Adar itself, if it coincides with the Sabbath. This Haftarah replaces the Haftarah ordinarily read with the Sidra of that week, the Haftarah of Rosh Chodesh or the Haftarah for the Day Preceding Rosh Chodesh.

This selection refers to the donations received for the renovation of the Temple during the reign of Jehoash, king of Judah. It thus parallels the additional Torah reading for this Sabbath, which discusses the collection of half-shekels for the sacrificial services and for the building of the Tabernacle in the wilderness.

11:17. And Jehoiada enacted the covenant between the Lord and between the king and [between] the people, to be the people of the Lord, and between the king and between the people. 18. And all the people of the land came to the temple of the Baal and tore it down; its altars and its images they smashed, and Mattan the priest of the Baal they slew before the altars; and the priest set up appointees over the house of the Lord. 19. And he took the officers of the hundreds and the mighty warriors and the couriers and all the people of the land, and they brought the king down from the house of the Lord and they came by way of the gate of the couriers to the king's palace; and he sat on the throne of the kings. 20. And all the people of the land rejoiced, and the city quieted down, and Athaliah they had dispatched by the sword in the royal palace. (Ashkenazim commence here.) 12:1. Jehoash was seven years old when he became king. 2. Jehoash became king in the seventh year of Jehu, and he reigned in Jerusalem for forty years; and his mother's name was Zibiah from Beersheba. 3. And Jehoash did what was proper in the eyes of

יז וַיִּכְרֹת יְהוֹיָדָע אֶת־הַבְּרִית בֵּין יְהֹוָה וּבֵין הַמֶּלֶךְ וּבֵין הָעָם לִהְיוֹת לְעָם לַיהֹוָה וּבֵין הַמֶּלֶךְ וּבֵין הָעָם: יח וַיָּבֹאוּ כָל־עַם הָאָרֶץ בֵּית־הַבַּעַל וַיִּתְּצֻהוּ אֶת־מִזְבְּחֹתָו (מזבחתיו קרי) וְאֶת־צְלָמָיו שִׁבְּרוּ הֵיטֵב וְאֵת מַתָּן כֹּהֵן הַבַּעַל הָרְגוּ לִפְנֵי הַמִּזְבְּחוֹת וַיָּשֶׂם הַכֹּהֵן פְּקֻדֹּת עַל־בֵּית יְהֹוָה: יט וַיִּקַּח אֶת־שָׂרֵי הַמֵּאוֹת וְאֶת־הַכָּרִי וְאֶת־הָרָצִים וְאֵת | כָּל־עַם הָאָרֶץ וַיֹּרִידוּ אֶת־הַמֶּלֶךְ מִבֵּית יְהֹוָה וַיָּבוֹאוּ דֶּרֶךְ־שַׁעַר הָרָצִים בֵּית הַמֶּלֶךְ וַיֵּשֶׁב עַל־כִּסֵּא הַמְּלָכִים: כ וַיִּשְׂמַח כָּל־עַם־הָאָרֶץ וְהָעִיר שָׁקָטָה וְאֶת־עֲתַלְיָהוּ הֵמִיתוּ בַחֶרֶב בֵּית _ מֶלֶךְ (המלך קרי): (כאן מתחילים האשכנזים) א בֶּן־שֶׁבַע שָׁנִים יְהוֹאָשׁ בְּמָלְכוֹ: ב בִּשְׁנַת־שֶׁבַע לְיֵהוּא מָלַךְ יְהוֹאָשׁ וְאַרְבָּעִים שָׁנָה מָלַךְ בִּירוּשָׁלָ͏ִם וְשֵׁם אִמּוֹ צִבְיָה מִבְּאֵר שָׁבַע: ג וַיַּעַשׂ יְהוֹאָשׁ

the Lord all his days, what Jehoiada the priest instructed him. 4. However, the high places were not removed. The people were still slaughtering sacrifices and burning incense on the high places. 5. And Jehoash said to the priests, "All money of the hallowed things which is brought to the house of the Lord, the money of anyone who passes [the numbering], each one the money of the value of the people [whose value he vows to donate,] all money which comes upon a man's heart to bring to the house of the Lord.—6. the priests shall take for themselves each one from his acquaintance, and they shall strengthen the damage of the house, wherever damage is found." 7. And it was that in the twenty-third year of King Jehoash, the priests did not strengthen the damages of the house. 8. And King Jehoash summoned Jehoiada the priest and the priests and said to them, "Why are you not repairing the damage of the house? Now, take no money from your acquaintances, but give it for the damage of the house." 9. And the priests agreed not to take money from the people and not to repair the damage of the house. 10. And Jehoiada the priest took one chest and bored a hole in its door; and he placed it near the altar on the right, where a person enters the house of the Lord; and the priests, the guards of the threshold, would put all the money that was brought into the house of the Lord, into there. 11. And it was when they saw that there was much money in the chest that the king's scribe and the high priest went up and packed and counted the money which was brought into the house of the Lord. 12. And they would give the counted money into the hands of the foremen of the work who were appointed in the house of the Lord; and they spent it for the carpenters and for the builders who work in the house of the Lord. 13. And for the masons and for the stonecutters and to buy wood and quarried stones to repair the damage of the house of the Lord, and for everything which would be spent for the house to strengthen it. 14. However, there would not be made for the house of the Lord silver pitchers, musical instruments, basins, trumpets, or any golden or silver utensils, from the money brought into the

הַיָּשָׁ֛ר בְּעֵינֵ֥י יְהֹוָ֖ה כָּל־יָמָ֑יו אֲשֶׁ֣ר הוֹרָ֔הוּ יְהוֹיָדָ֖ע הַכֹּהֵֽן: ד רַ֥ק הַבָּמ֖וֹת לֹא־סָ֑רוּ ע֣וֹד הָעָ֗ם מְזַבְּחִ֥ים וּֽמְקַטְּרִ֖ים בַּבָּמֽוֹת: ה וַיֹּ֨אמֶר יְהוֹאָ֜שׁ אֶל־הַכֹּ֣הֲנִ֗ים כֹּל֩ כֶּ֨סֶף הַקֳּדָשִׁ֜ים אֲשֶׁר־ יוּבָ֣א בֵית־יְהֹוָה֮ כֶּ֣סֶף עוֹבֵר֒ אִ֗ישׁ כֶּ֤סֶף נַפְשׁוֹת֙ עֶרְכּ֔וֹ כָּל־כֶּ֕סֶף אֲשֶׁ֥ר יַעֲלֶ֖ה עַ֣ל לֶב־אִ֑ישׁ לְהָבִ֖יא בֵּ֥ית יְהֹוָֽה: ו יִקְח֤וּ לָהֶם֙ הַכֹּ֣הֲנִ֔ים אִ֖ישׁ מֵאֵ֣ת מַכָּר֑וֹ וְהֵ֗ם יְחַזְּקוּ֙ אֶת־בֶּ֣דֶק הַבַּ֔יִת לְכֹ֛ל אֲשֶׁר־יִמָּצֵ֥א שָׁ֖ם בָּֽדֶק: ז וַיְהִ֗י בִּשְׁנַ֨ת עֶשְׂרִ֧ים וְשָׁלֹ֛שׁ שָׁנָ֖ה לַמֶּ֣לֶךְ יְהוֹאָ֑שׁ לֹֽא־חִזְּק֥וּ הַכֹּ֣הֲנִ֖ים אֶת־בֶּ֥דֶק הַבָּֽיִת: ח וַיִּקְרָא֩ הַמֶּ֨לֶךְ יְהוֹאָ֜שׁ לִיהוֹיָדָ֤ע הַכֹּהֵן֙ וְלַכֹּ֣הֲנִ֔ים וַיֹּ֣אמֶר אֲלֵהֶ֗ם מַדּ֛וּעַ אֵינְכֶ֥ם מְחַזְּקִ֖ים אֶת־בֶּ֣דֶק הַבָּ֑יִת וְעַתָּ֗ה אַל־תִּקְחוּ־כֶ֙סֶף֙ מֵאֵ֣ת מַכָּֽרֵיכֶ֔ם כִּֽי־לְבֶ֥דֶק הַבַּ֖יִת תִּתְּנֻֽהוּ: ט וַיֵּאֹ֖תוּ הַכֹּֽהֲנִ֑ים לְבִלְתִּ֤י קְחַת־כֶּ֙סֶף֙ מֵאֵ֣ת הָעָ֔ם וּלְבִלְתִּ֥י חַזֵּ֖ק אֶת־בֶּ֥דֶק הַבָּֽיִת: י וַיִּקַּ֞ח יְהוֹיָדָ֤ע הַכֹּהֵן֙ אֲר֣וֹן אֶחָ֔ד וַיִּקֹּ֥ב חֹ֖ר בְּדַלְתּ֑וֹ וַיִּתֵּ֣ן אֹת֠וֹ אֵ֣צֶל הַמִּזְבֵּ֤חַ בַּיָּמִין֙ (מימין קרי) בְּבֽוֹא־אִישׁ֙ בֵּ֣ית יְהֹוָ֔ה וְנָתְנוּ־שָׁ֨מָּה הַכֹּ֣הֲנִ֜ים שֹֽׁמְרֵ֣י הַסַּ֗ף אֶֽת־כָּל־הַכֶּ֛סֶף הַמּוּבָ֖א בֵית־יְהֹוָֽה: יא וַיְהִ֗י כִּרְאוֹתָם֙ כִּֽי־רַ֤ב הַכֶּ֙סֶף֙ בָּֽאָר֔וֹן וַיַּ֨עַל סֹפֵ֤ר הַמֶּ֙לֶךְ֙ וְהַכֹּהֵ֣ן הַגָּד֔וֹל וַיָּצֻ֙רוּ֙ וַיִּמְנ֔וּ אֶת־ הַכֶּ֖סֶף הַנִּמְצָ֥א בֵית־יְהֹוָֽה: יב וְנָתְנוּ֙ אֶת־הַכֶּ֣סֶף הַֽמְתֻכָּ֔ן עַל־יַ֣ד (ידי קרי) עֹשֵׂ֖י הַמְּלָאכָ֑ה הַפְקֻדִ֖ים (המפקדים קרי) בֵּ֣ית יְהֹוָ֑ה וַיּוֹצִיאֻ֗הוּ לְחָרָשֵׁ֤י הָעֵץ֙ וְלַבֹּנִ֔ים הָעֹשִׂ֖ים בֵּ֥ית יְהֹוָֽה: יג וְלַגֹּֽדְרִים֙ וּלְחֹצְבֵ֣י הָאֶ֔בֶן וְלִקְנ֤וֹת עֵצִים֙ וְאַבְנֵ֣י מַחְצֵ֔ב לְחַזֵּ֖ק אֶת־בֶּ֣דֶק בֵּית־יְהֹוָ֑ה וּלְכֹ֛ל אֲשֶׁר־יֵצֵ֥א עַל־הַבַּ֖יִת לְחָזְקָֽה: יד אַ֣ךְ לֹ֧א יֵעָשֶׂ֛ה בֵּ֣ית יְהֹוָ֗ה סִפּ֥וֹת כֶּ֙סֶף֙ מְזַמְּר֤וֹת מִזְרָקוֹת֙ חֲצֹ֣צְר֔וֹת כָּל־כְּלִ֥י זָהָ֖ב וּכְלִי־כָ֑סֶף מִן־הַכֶּ֖סֶף

הַמּוּבָא בֵּית־יְהֹוָה: טו כִּֽי־לְעֹשֵׂי הַמְּלָאכָה
יִתְּנֻהוּ וְחִזְּקוּ־בוֹ אֶת־בֵּית יְהֹוָה: טז וְלֹא
יְחַשְּׁבוּ אֶת־הָאֲנָשִׁים אֲשֶׁר יִתְּנוּ אֶת־הַכֶּסֶף
עַל־יָדָם לָתֵת לְעֹשֵׂי הַמְּלָאכָה כִּי בֶאֱמֻנָה הֵם
עֹשִׂים: יז כֶּסֶף אָשָׁם וְכֶסֶף חַטָּאוֹת לֹא יוּבָא
בֵּית יְהֹוָה לַכֹּהֲנִים יִהְיוּ:

house of the Lord. 15. But they would give it to the foremen over the work, and they would repair therewith the house of the Lord. 16. And they would not reckon with the men into whose hand they would give the money to give the foremen over the work, for they did [the work] honestly. 17. The money for guilt-offerings and the money for sin-offerings would not be brought to the house of the Lord; they would go to the priests.

HAFTARATH ZACHOR הפטרת זכור

(Sephardim read I Samuel 15:1–34; Ashkenazim commence with verse 2.)
Additional Torah reading: Deuteronomy 24:17–19, read on the Sabbath preceding Purim.

This selection deals with Saul's battle against Amalek, in which Agag, King of Amalek, was spared. Agag was a remote ancestor of the wicked Haman.

א וַיֹּאמֶר שְׁמוּאֵל אֶל־שָׁאוּל אֹתִי שָׁלַח יְהֹוָה
לִמְשָׁחֳךָ לְמֶלֶךְ עַל־עַמּוֹ עַל־יִשְׂרָאֵל וְעַתָּה
שְׁמַע לְקוֹל דִּבְרֵי יְהֹוָה: (כאן מתחילין האשכנזים)
ב כֹּה אָמַר יְהֹוָה צְבָאוֹת פָּקַדְתִּי אֵת אֲשֶׁר־עָשָׂה
עֲמָלֵק לְיִשְׂרָאֵל אֲשֶׁר־שָׂם לוֹ בַּדֶּרֶךְ בַּעֲלֹתוֹ
מִמִּצְרָיִם: ג עַתָּה לֵךְ וְהִכִּיתָה אֶת־עֲמָלֵק
וְהַחֲרַמְתֶּם אֶת־כָּל־אֲשֶׁר־לוֹ וְלֹא תַחְמֹל עָלָיו
וְהֵמַתָּה מֵאִישׁ עַד־אִשָּׁה מֵעֹלֵל וְעַד־יוֹנֵק
מִשּׁוֹר וְעַד־שֶׂה מִגָּמָל וְעַד־חֲמוֹר: ד וַיְשַׁמַּע
שָׁאוּל אֶת־הָעָם וַיִּפְקְדֵם בַּטְּלָאִים מָאתַיִם
אֶלֶף רַגְלִי וַעֲשֶׂרֶת אֲלָפִים אֶת־אִישׁ יְהוּדָה:
ה וַיָּבֹא שָׁאוּל עַד־עִיר עֲמָלֵק וַיָּרֶב בַּנָּחַל:
ו וַיֹּאמֶר שָׁאוּל אֶל־הַקֵּינִי לְכוּ סֻּרוּ רְדוּ מִתּוֹךְ
עֲמָלֵקִי פֶּן־אֹסִפְךָ עִמּוֹ וְאַתָּה עָשִׂיתָה חֶסֶד
עִם־כָּל־בְּנֵי יִשְׂרָאֵל בַּעֲלוֹתָם מִמִּצְרָיִם וַיָּסַר
קֵינִי מִתּוֹךְ עֲמָלֵק: ז וַיַּךְ שָׁאוּל אֶת־עֲמָלֵק
מֵחֲוִילָה בּוֹאֲךָ שׁוּר אֲשֶׁר עַל־פְּנֵי מִצְרָיִם:
ח וַיִּתְפֹּשׂ אֶת־אֲגַג מֶלֶךְ־עֲמָלֵק חָי וְאֶת־כָּל־
הָעָם הֶחֱרִים לְפִי־חָרֶב: ט וַיַּחְמֹל שָׁאוּל וְהָעָם
עַל־אֲגָג וְעַל־מֵיטַב הַצֹּאן וְהַבָּקָר וְהַמִּשְׁנִים

15:1. And Samuel said to Saul, "The Lord sent me to anoint you to be king over His people, over Israel; and now hearken to the voice of the words of the Lord. (*Ashkenazim commence here:*) 2. "So said the Lord of Hosts, 'I remember that which Amalek did to Israel, how he laid [wait] for him on the way, when he came up out of Egypt. 3. Now, go, and you shall smite Amalek, and you shall utterly destroy all that is his, and you shall not have pity on him; and you shall slay both man and woman, infant and suckling, ox and sheep, camel and ass.'" 4. And Saul called the people together, and he counted them in Telaim: two hundred thousand footmen, and ten thousand, the men of Judah. 5. And Saul came as far as the city of Amalek, and he fought in the valley. 6. And Saul said to the Kenite, "Turn away and go down from among the Amalekites, lest I destroy you with them, and you did kindness with all the children of Israel, when they went up out of Egypt." And the Kenites turned away from amidst Amalek. 7. And Saul smote Amalek, from Havilah until you come to Shur, which is in front of Egypt. 8. And he seized Agag, the king of Amalek, alive; and he completely destroyed all the people with the edge of the sword. 9. And Saul and the people had pity on Agag, and on the best of the sheep and the cattle and the fatlings, and on the fattened sheep and on all that was good; and they did not want to destroy them; but everything which was vile and feeble, that they utterly destroyed. 10. And the word of the Lord came to Samuel, saying, 11. "I regret that I have made Saul king, for he has turned back from following Me, and he has not fulfilled My words." And it distressed Samuel, and he cried out to the Lord all night. 12. And Samuel arose early in the morning to meet Saul; and it was told to Samuel, saying, "Saul has come to Carmel, and behold, he is setting up a place for himself, and he passed and went down to Gilgal." 13. And Samuel came to Saul, and Saul said to him, "May you be blessed of the Lord; I have fulfilled the word of the Lord." 14. And Samuel said, "What then is this bleating of the sheep in my ears and the lowing of the oxen which I hear?" 15. And Saul said, "They brought them from the Amalekites, for the people had pity on the best of the sheep and the oxen, in order to sacrifice to the Lord your God; and the rest we have utterly destroyed." 16. And Samuel said to Saul, "Desist, and I shall tell you what the Lord spoke to me last night." And he said to him, "Speak." 17. And Samuel said, "Even if you are small in your own eyes, are you not the head of the tribes of Israel? And the Lord anointed you as king over Israel. 18. And the Lord sent you on a mission, and said, 'Go, and you shall utterly destroy the sinners, the Amalekites, and you shall wage war against them until they destroy them.' 19. Now, why did you not hearken to the voice of the Lord, but you flew upon the spoil, and you did what was evil in the eyes of the Lord?" 20. And Saul said to Samuel, "Yes, I did hearken to the voice of the Lord. I did go on the mission on which the Lord sent me, and I brought Agag, the king of Amalek, alive and have utterly destroyed the Amalekites. 21. And the people took from the spoil, sheep and oxen, the best of the ban, to sacrifice to your God in Gilgal." 22. And Samuel said, "Has the Lord [as much] desire in burnt-offerings and peace-offerings, as in obeying the voice of the Lord? Behold, to obey is better than a peace-offering; to hearken [is better] than the fat of rams. 23. For rebellion is as the sin of divination, and stubbornness is as

וְעַל־הַכָּרִים֙ וְעַל־כָּל־הַטּוֹב֒ וְלֹא אָב֖וּ הַחֲרִימָ֑ם וְכָל־הַמְּלָאכָ֛ה נְמִבְזָ֥ה וְנָמֵ֖ס אֹתָ֥הּ הֶחֱרִֽימוּ: י וַֽיְהִי֙ דְּבַר־יְהֹוָ֔ה אֶל־שְׁמוּאֵ֖ל לֵאמֹֽר: יא נִחַ֗מְתִּי כִּֽי־הִמְלַ֤כְתִּי אֶת־שָׁאוּל֙ לְמֶ֔לֶךְ כִּֽי־שָׁ֤ב מֵאַֽחֲרַי֙ וְאֶת־דְּבָרַ֖י לֹ֣א הֵקִ֑ים וַיִּ֙חַר֙ לִשְׁמוּאֵ֔ל וַיִּזְעַ֥ק אֶל־יְהֹוָ֖ה כָּל־הַלָּֽיְלָה: יב וַיַּשְׁכֵּ֧ם שְׁמוּאֵ֛ל לִקְרַ֥את שָׁא֖וּל בַּבֹּ֑קֶר וַיֻּגַּ֨ד לִשְׁמוּאֵ֜ל לֵאמֹ֗ר בָּֽא־שָׁא֤וּל הַכַּרְמֶ֙לָה֙ וְהִנֵּ֨ה מַצִּ֥יב לוֹ֙ יָ֔ד וַיִּסֹּב֙ וַֽיַּעֲבֹ֔ר וַיֵּ֖רֶד הַגִּלְגָּֽל: יג וַיָּבֹ֥א שְׁמוּאֵ֖ל אֶל־שָׁא֑וּל וַיֹּ֧אמֶר ל֣וֹ שָׁא֗וּל בָּר֤וּךְ אַתָּה֙ לַֽיהֹוָ֔ה הֲקִימֹ֖תִי אֶת־דְּבַ֥ר יְהֹוָֽה: יד וַיֹּ֣אמֶר שְׁמוּאֵ֔ל וּמֶ֛ה קֽוֹל־הַצֹּ֥אן הַזֶּ֖ה בְּאָזְנָ֑י וְק֣וֹל הַבָּקָ֔ר אֲשֶׁ֥ר אָֽנֹכִ֖י שֹׁמֵֽעַ: טו וַיֹּ֨אמֶר שָׁא֜וּל מֵֽעֲמָֽלֵקִ֣י הֱבִיא֗וּם אֲשֶׁ֨ר חָמַ֤ל הָעָם֙ עַל־מֵיטַ֤ב הַצֹּאן֙ וְהַבָּקָ֔ר לְמַ֥עַן זְבֹ֖חַ לַֽיהֹוָ֣ה אֱלֹהֶ֑יךָ וְאֶת־הַיּוֹתֵ֖ר הֶחֱרַֽמְנוּ: טז וַיֹּ֣אמֶר שְׁמוּאֵל֮ אֶל־שָׁאוּל֒ הֶ֗רֶף וְאַגִּ֤ידָה לְּךָ֙ אֵת֩ אֲשֶׁ֨ר דִּבֶּ֤ר יְהֹוָה֙ אֵלַ֔י הַלָּ֑יְלָה וַיֹּ֥אמְרֽוּ (ויאמר קרי) ל֖וֹ דַּבֵּֽר: יז וַיֹּ֣אמֶר שְׁמוּאֵ֔ל הֲל֗וֹא אִם־קָטֹ֤ן אַתָּה֙ בְּעֵינֶ֔יךָ רֹ֛אשׁ שִׁבְטֵ֥י יִשְׂרָאֵ֖ל אָ֑תָּה וַיִּמְשָֽׁחֲךָ֧ יְהֹוָ֛ה לְמֶ֖לֶךְ עַל־יִשְׂרָאֵֽל: יח וַיִּשְׁלָֽחֲךָ֥ יְהֹוָ֖ה בְּדָ֑רֶךְ וַיֹּ֗אמֶר לֵ֣ךְ וְהַֽחֲרַמְתָּ֞ה אֶת־הַֽחַטָּאִים֙ אֶת־עֲמָלֵ֔ק וְנִלְחַמְתָּ֣ ב֔וֹ עַ֥ד כַּלּוֹתָ֖ם אֹתָֽם: יט וְלָ֛מָּה לֹֽא־שָׁמַ֖עְתָּ בְּק֣וֹל יְהֹוָ֑ה וַתַּ֙עַט֙ אֶל־הַשָּׁלָ֔ל וַתַּ֥עַשׂ הָרַ֖ע בְּעֵינֵ֥י יְהֹוָֽה: כ וַיֹּ֨אמֶר שָׁא֜וּל אֶל־שְׁמוּאֵ֗ל אֲשֶׁ֤ר שָׁמַ֙עְתִּי֙ בְּק֣וֹל יְהֹוָ֔ה וָֽאֵלֵ֕ךְ בַּדֶּ֖רֶךְ אֲשֶׁר־שְׁלָחַ֣נִי יְהֹוָ֑ה וָֽאָבִ֗יא אֶת־אֲגַג֙ מֶ֣לֶךְ עֲמָלֵ֔ק וְאֶת־עֲמָלֵ֖ק הֶֽחֱרַֽמְתִּי: כא וַיִּקַּ֨ח הָעָ֧ם מֵֽהַשָּׁלָ֛ל צֹ֥אן וּבָקָ֖ר רֵאשִׁ֣ית הַחֵ֑רֶם לִזְבֹּ֛חַ לַֽיהֹוָ֥ה אֱלֹהֶ֖יךָ בַּגִּלְגָּֽל: כב וַיֹּ֣אמֶר שְׁמוּאֵ֗ל הַחֵ֤פֶץ לַֽיהֹוָה֙ בְּעֹל֣וֹת וּזְבָחִ֔ים כִּשְׁמֹ֖עַ בְּק֣וֹל יְהֹוָ֑ה הִנֵּ֤ה שְׁמֹ֙עַ֙ מִזֶּ֣בַח ט֔וֹב לְהַקְשִׁ֖יב מֵחֵ֥לֶב אֵילִֽים: כג כִּ֤י חַטַּאת־קֶ֙סֶם֙ מֶ֔רִי וְאָ֥וֶן

idolatry and *teraphim.* Since you rejected the word of the Lord, He has rejected you from [being] a king." 24. And Saul said to Samuel, "I have sinned, for I transgressed the Lord's command and your words, for I feared the people, and I hearkened to their voice. 25. And now, forgive now my sin, and return with me, and I shall prostrate myself to the Lord." 26. And Samuel said to Saul, "I shall not return with you, for you have rejected the word of the Lord, and the Lord has rejected you from being a king over Israel." 27. And Samuel turned to go, and he seized the skirt of his robe, and it tore. 28. And Samuel said to him, "The Lord has torn the kingdom of Israel from you, today, and has given it to your fellow who is better than you. 29. And also, the Strength of Israel will neither lie nor repent, for He is not a man to repent." 30. And he said, "I have sinned. Now, honor me now in the presence of the elders of my people, and in the presence of Israel, and return with me, and I shall prostrate myself to the Lord your God." 31. And Samuel returned after Saul, and Saul prostrated himself to the Lord. 32. And Samuel said, "Bring Agag, the king of Amalek, near to me." And Agag went to him delicately. And Agag said, "Surely, the bitterness of death has turned." 33. And Samuel said, "As your sword bereaved women, so will your mother be bereaved among women." And Samuel hewed Agag in pieces before the Lord in Gilgal. 34. And Samuel went to Ramah, and Saul went up to his house in Gibeah of Saul.

וּתְרָפִים הַפְצַר יַעַן מָאַסְתָּ אֶת־דְּבַר יְהֹוָה וַיִּמְאָסְךָ מִמֶּלֶךְ: כד וַיֹּאמֶר שָׁאוּל אֶל־שְׁמוּאֵל חָטָאתִי כִּי־עָבַרְתִּי אֶת־פִּי־יְהֹוָה וְאֶת־דְּבָרֶיךָ כִּי יָרֵאתִי אֶת־הָעָם וָאֶשְׁמַע בְּקוֹלָם: כה וְעַתָּה שָׂא נָא אֶת־חַטָּאתִי וְשׁוּב עִמִּי וְאֶשְׁתַּחֲוֶה לַיהֹוָה: כו וַיֹּאמֶר שְׁמוּאֵל אֶל־שָׁאוּל לֹא אָשׁוּב עִמָּךְ כִּי מָאַסְתָּה אֶת־דְּבַר יְהֹוָה וַיִּמְאָסְךָ יְהֹוָה מִהְיוֹת מֶלֶךְ עַל־יִשְׂרָאֵל: כז וַיִּסֹּב שְׁמוּאֵל לָלֶכֶת וַיַּחֲזֵק בִּכְנַף־מְעִילוֹ וַיִּקָּרַע: כח וַיֹּאמֶר אֵלָיו שְׁמוּאֵל קָרַע יְהֹוָה אֶת־מַמְלְכוּת יִשְׂרָאֵל מֵעָלֶיךָ הַיּוֹם וּנְתָנָהּ לְרֵעֲךָ הַטּוֹב מִמֶּךָּ: כט וְגַם נֵצַח יִשְׂרָאֵל לֹא יְשַׁקֵּר וְלֹא יִנָּחֵם כִּי לֹא אָדָם הוּא לְהִנָּחֵם: ל וַיֹּאמֶר חָטָאתִי עַתָּה כַּבְּדֵנִי נָא נֶגֶד־זִקְנֵי עַמִּי וְנֶגֶד יִשְׂרָאֵל וְשׁוּב עִמִּי וְהִשְׁתַּחֲוֵיתִי לַיהֹוָה אֱלֹהֶיךָ: לא וַיָּשָׁב שְׁמוּאֵל אַחֲרֵי שָׁאוּל וַיִּשְׁתַּחוּ שָׁאוּל לַיהֹוָה: לב וַיֹּאמֶר שְׁמוּאֵל הַגִּישׁוּ אֵלַי אֶת־אֲגַג מֶלֶךְ עֲמָלֵק וַיֵּלֶךְ אֵלָיו אֲגַג מַעֲדַנֹּת וַיֹּאמֶר אֲגָג אָכֵן סָר מַר־הַמָּוֶת: לג וַיֹּאמֶר שְׁמוּאֵל כַּאֲשֶׁר שִׁכְּלָה נָשִׁים חַרְבֶּךָ כֵּן־תִּשְׁכַּל מִנָּשִׁים אִמֶּךָ וַיְשַׁסֵּף שְׁמוּאֵל אֶת־אֲגָג לִפְנֵי יְהֹוָה בַּגִּלְגָּל: לד וַיֵּלֶךְ שְׁמוּאֵל הָרָמָתָה וְשָׁאוּל עָלָה אֶל־בֵּיתוֹ גִּבְעַת שָׁאוּל:

HAFTARATH PARAH הפטרת פרה
(Ezekiel 36:16–38. Sephardim conclude with verse 36)
Additional Torah reading: Numbers 19:1–22, read on the Sabbath preceding Parashath Hachodesh, (see p. 962).

The verse "And I will sprinkle clean water upon you" alludes to the water of purification mentioned in the additional Torah reading.

36:16. And the word of the Lord came to me, saying: 17. "Son of man! The house of Israel, as long as they lived on their own land, they defiled it by their way and by their misdeeds, like the uncleanness of a woman in the period of her separation was

טז וַיְהִי דְבַר־יְהֹוָה אֵלַי לֵאמֹר: יז בֶּן־אָדָם בֵּית יִשְׂרָאֵל יֹשְׁבִים עַל־אַדְמָתָם וַיְטַמְּאוּ אוֹתָהּ בְּדַרְכָּם וּבַעֲלִילוֹתָם כְּטֻמְאַת הַנִּדָּה

their way before Me. 18. Wherefore I poured My wrath upon them for the blood that they had shed in the land, because they had defiled it with their idols. 19. And I scattered them among the nations, and they were dispersed through the countries, according to their way and their misdeeds did I judge them. 20. And they entered the nations where they came, and they profaned My Holy Name, inasmuch as it was said of them, 'These are the people of the Lord, and they have come out of His land.' 21. But I had pity on My Holy Name, which the house of Israel had profaned among the nations from where they had come. 22. Therefore, say to the house of Israel: So says the Lord God: Not for your sake do I do this, O house of Israel, but for My Holy Name, which you have profaned among the nations to which they have come. 23. And I will sanctify My great Name, which was profaned among the nations, which you have profaned in their midst; and the nations shall know that I am the Lord—is the declaration of the Lord God—when I will be sanctified through you before their eyes. 24. For I will take you from among the nations and gather you from all countries, and I will bring you to your land. 25. And I will sprinkle clean water upon you, and you will be clean; from all your impurities and from all your abominations will I cleanse you. 26. And I will give you a new heart, and a new spirit will I put within you, and I will take away the heart of stone out of your flesh, and I will give you a heart of flesh. 27. And I will put My spirit within you and bring it about that you will walk in My statutes and you will keep My ordinances and do [them]. 28. Then will you dwell in the land that I gave your fathers, and you will be a people to Me, and I will be to you as a God. 29. And I will save you from all your uncleannesses, and I will call to the corn and will multiply it, and I will not decree famine again over you. 30. And I will multiply the fruit of the tree and the produce of the field, so that you shall no more have to accept the shame of famine among the nations. 31. And you shall remember your evil ways and your deeds that were not good, and you will loathe

הָיְתָה דַרְכָּם לְפָנָי: יח וָאֶשְׁפֹּךְ חֲמָתִי עֲלֵיהֶם עַל־הַדָּם אֲשֶׁר־שָׁפְכוּ עַל־הָאָרֶץ וּבְגִלּוּלֵיהֶם טִמְּאוּהָ: יט וָאָפִיץ אֹתָם בַּגּוֹיִם וַיִּזָּרוּ בָּאֲרָצוֹת כְּדַרְכָּם וְכַעֲלִילוֹתָם שְׁפַטְתִּים: כ וַיָּבוֹא אֶל־הַגּוֹיִם אֲשֶׁר־בָּאוּ שָׁם וַיְחַלְּלוּ אֶת־שֵׁם קָדְשִׁי בֶּאֱמֹר לָהֶם עַם־יְהֹוָה אֵלֶּה וּמֵאַרְצוֹ יָצָאוּ: כא וָאֶחְמֹל עַל־שֵׁם קָדְשִׁי אֲשֶׁר חִלְּלֻהוּ בֵּית יִשְׂרָאֵל בַּגּוֹיִם אֲשֶׁר־בָּאוּ שָׁמָּה: כב לָכֵן אֱמֹר לְבֵית־יִשְׂרָאֵל כֹּה אָמַר אֲדֹנָי יֱהֹוִה לֹא לְמַעַנְכֶם אֲנִי עֹשֶׂה בֵּית יִשְׂרָאֵל כִּי אִם־לְשֵׁם־קָדְשִׁי אֲשֶׁר חִלַּלְתֶּם בַּגּוֹיִם אֲשֶׁר־בָּאתֶם שָׁם: כג וְקִדַּשְׁתִּי אֶת־שְׁמִי הַגָּדוֹל הַמְחֻלָּל בַּגּוֹיִם אֲשֶׁר חִלַּלְתֶּם בְּתוֹכָם וְיָדְעוּ הַגּוֹיִם כִּי־אֲנִי יְהֹוָה נְאֻם אֲדֹנָי יֱהֹוִה בְּהִקָּדְשִׁי בָכֶם לְעֵינֵיהֶם (בספרים אחרים: לעיניכם): כד וְלָקַחְתִּי אֶתְכֶם מִן־הַגּוֹיִם וְקִבַּצְתִּי אֶתְכֶם מִכָּל־הָאֲרָצוֹת וְהֵבֵאתִי אֶתְכֶם אֶל־אַדְמַתְכֶם: כה וְזָרַקְתִּי עֲלֵיכֶם מַיִם טְהוֹרִים וּטְהַרְתֶּם מִכֹּל טֻמְאוֹתֵיכֶם וּמִכָּל־גִּלּוּלֵיכֶם אֲטַהֵר אֶתְכֶם: כו וְנָתַתִּי לָכֶם לֵב חָדָשׁ וְרוּחַ חֲדָשָׁה אֶתֵּן בְּקִרְבְּכֶם וַהֲסִרֹתִי אֶת־לֵב הָאֶבֶן מִבְּשַׂרְכֶם וְנָתַתִּי לָכֶם לֵב בָּשָׂר: כז וְאֶת־רוּחִי אֶתֵּן בְּקִרְבְּכֶם וְעָשִׂיתִי אֵת אֲשֶׁר־בְּחֻקַּי תֵּלֵכוּ וּמִשְׁפָּטַי תִּשְׁמְרוּ וַעֲשִׂיתֶם: כח וִישַׁבְתֶּם בָּאָרֶץ אֲשֶׁר נָתַתִּי לַאֲבֹתֵיכֶם וִהְיִיתֶם לִי לְעָם וְאָנֹכִי אֶהְיֶה לָכֶם לֵאלֹהִים: כט וְהוֹשַׁעְתִּי אֶתְכֶם מִכֹּל טֻמְאוֹתֵיכֶם וְקָרָאתִי אֶל־הַדָּגָן וְהִרְבֵּיתִי אֹתוֹ וְלֹא־אֶתֵּן עֲלֵיכֶם רָעָב: ל וְהִרְבֵּיתִי אֶת־פְּרִי הָעֵץ וּתְנוּבַת הַשָּׂדֶה לְמַעַן אֲשֶׁר לֹא תִקְחוּ עוֹד חֶרְפַּת רָעָב בַּגּוֹיִם: לא וּזְכַרְתֶּם אֶת־דַּרְכֵיכֶם הָרָעִים וּמַעַלְלֵיכֶם אֲשֶׁר לֹא־טוֹבִים וּנְקֹטֹתֶם

yourselves in your own eyes on account of
your sins and on account of your abominations. 32. Not for your sake do I do it," says
the Lord God, "may it be known to you; be
ashamed and confounded for your ways, O
house of Israel." 33. So says the Lord God:
On the day that I will have cleansed you
from all your iniquities, and I will resettle
the cities, and the ruins shall be built up.
34. And the desolate land shall be worked,
instead of its lying desolate in the sight of all
that pass by. 35. And they shall say, 'This
land that was desolate has become like the
Garden of Eden, and the cities that were
destroyed and desolate and pulled down
have become settled as fortified [cities].'
36. And the nations that are left round
about you shall know that I, the Lord, have
built up the ruined places and have planted
the desolate ones; I, the Lord, have spoken,
and I will do [it]." (*The Sephardim conclude here.*) 37. So says the Lord God: "I will
yet for this be inquired of by the house of
Israel to do for them: I will multiply them
like a flock of sheep, as men. 38. Like the
flocks appointed for the holy offerings, like
the flocks of Jerusalem on its festivals, so
will these cities now laid waste be filled with
flocks of men, and they shall know that I am
the Lord."

בִּפְנֵיכֶ֗ם עַ֤ל עֲוֺנֹֽתֵיכֶם֙ וְעַ֖ל תּוֹעֲבֹֽתֵיכֶ֑ם: לב לֹ֣א
לְמַעַנְכֶ֤ם אֲנִֽי־עֹשֶׂה֙ נְאֻם֙ אֲדֹנָ֣י יֱהֹוִ֔ה יִוָּדַ֖ע לָכֶ֑ם
בּ֤וֹשׁוּ וְהִכָּֽלְמוּ֙ מִדַּרְכֵיכֶ֔ם בֵּ֖ית יִשְׂרָאֵֽל: לג כֹּ֤ה
אָמַר֙ אֲדֹנָ֣י יֱהֹוִ֔ה בְּיוֹם֙ טַהֲרִ֣י אֶתְכֶ֔ם מִכֹּ֖ל
עֲוֺנֽוֹתֵיכֶ֑ם וְהֽוֹשַׁבְתִּי֙ אֶת־הֶ֣עָרִ֔ים וְנִבְנ֖וּ
הֶחֳרָבֽוֹת: לד וְהָאָ֥רֶץ הַנְּשַׁמָּ֖ה תֵּֽעָבֵ֑ד תַּ֣חַת
אֲשֶׁ֣ר הָֽיְתָ֣ה שְׁמָמָ֔ה לְעֵינֵ֖י כָּל־עוֹבֵֽר:
לה וְאָֽמְר֗וּ הָאָ֤רֶץ הַלֵּ֨זוּ֙ הַנְּשַׁמָּ֔ה הָֽיְתָ֖ה כְּגַן־עֵ֑דֶן
וְהֶֽעָרִ֧ים הֶֽחֳרֵב֛וֹת וְהַֽנְשַׁמּ֥וֹת וְהַנֶּֽהֱרָס֖וֹת
בְּצוּר֥וֹת יָשָֽׁבוּ: לו וְיָֽדְע֣וּ הַגּוֹיִ֗ם אֲשֶׁ֣ר יִֽשָּֽׁאֲרוּ֮
סְבִיבֽוֹתֵיכֶם֒ כִּ֣י | אֲנִ֣י יְהֹוָ֗ה בָּנִ֨יתִי֙ הַנֶּֽהֱרָס֔וֹת
נָטַ֖עְתִּי הַנְּשַׁמָּ֑ה אֲנִ֥י יְהֹוָ֛ה דִּבַּ֖רְתִּי וְעָשִֽׂיתִי: (כאן
מסיימין הספרדים) לז כֹּ֤ה אָמַר֙ אֲדֹנָ֣י יֱהֹוִ֔ה ע֗וֹד
זֹ֚את אִדָּרֵ֣שׁ לְבֵית־יִשְׂרָאֵ֔ל לַֽעֲשׂ֥וֹת לָהֶ֑ם אַרְבֶּ֥ה
אֹתָ֛ם כַּצֹּ֖אן אָדָֽם: לח כְּצֹ֣אן קָֽדָשִׁ֗ים כְּצֹ֣אן
יְרֽוּשָׁלַ֨͏ִם֙ בְּמֽוֹעֲדֶ֔יהָ כֵּ֤ן תִּֽהְיֶ֨ינָה֙ הֶֽעָרִ֣ים
הֶֽחֳרֵב֔וֹת מְלֵא֖וֹת צֹ֣אן אָדָ֑ם וְיָֽדְע֖וּ כִּֽי־
אֲנִ֥י יְהֹוָֽה:

HAFTARATH HACHODESH   הפטרת החדש
(Ezekiel 45:16–46:18. Sephardim read 45:18–46:15)
Additional Torah reading: Exodus 12:1–20.

If the New Moon coincides with the Sabbath, three Torah Scrolls are taken out of
the Ark. In the first one, we call six people to the reading of the Sidra of the week, in
the second, we read the selection for Rosh Chodesh (Numbers 28:9–15), and in the
third, we read Parashath Hachodesh for the Maftir.

This Haftarah is read on the Sabbath preceding Rosh Chodesh Nissan, or on Rosh
Chodesh itself if it coincides with the Sabbath. In either instance, this Haftarah
replaces the Haftarah ordinarily read with the Sidra of that week, the Haftarah of
Shabbath Rosh Chodesh, or the Haftarah for the Day Preceding Rosh Chodesh.

"The first month, on the first of the month" (verse 18) refers to Rosh Chodesh Nissan.

45:16. It shall be incumbent on all the
people of the land to give this oblation to
the prince in Israel. 17. And the burnt-
offerings and the meal-offerings and the
libations on the Festivals and on the New
Moons and on the Sabbaths and on the
times fixed for meetings of the house of

טז כֹּ֚ל הָעָ֣ם הָאָ֔רֶץ יִֽהְי֖וּ אֶל־הַתְּרוּמָ֣ה הַזֹּ֑את
לַנָּשִׂ֖יא בְּיִשְׂרָאֵֽל: יז וְעַל־הַנָּשִׂ֣יא יִֽהְיֶ֗ה הָֽעוֹל֣וֹת
וְהַמִּנְחָה֙ וְהַנֵּ֔סֶךְ בַּֽחַגִּ֥ים וּבֶֽחֳדָשִׁ֖ים וּבַשַּׁבָּת֑וֹת
בְּכָל־מֽוֹעֲדֵ֖י בֵּ֣ית יִשְׂרָאֵ֑ל הֽוּא־יַֽעֲשֶׂ֣ה אֶת־

Israel shall devolve on the prince; he shall prepare the sin-offering and the meal-offering, and the burnt-offering and the peace-offering, to effect atonement for the house of Israel. (*Sephardim commence here:*) 18. So says the Lord God: "In the first month, on the first of the month, you shall take a young bullock without blemish, and you shall purify the altar. 19. And the priest shall take of the blood of the sin-offering and put it on the doorposts of the House, and on the four corners of the ledge of the altar and on the doorposts of the gate of the inner court. 20. And so shall you do on seven [days] in the month, because of mistaken and simple-minded men, and expiate the House. 21. In the first, on the fourteenth day of the month, shall you have the Passover, a festival of seven days; unleavened bread shall be eaten. 22. And the prince shall bring on that day for himself and for all the people of Israel a bullock for a sin-offering. 23. On the seven days of the Festival he shall bring as a burnt-offering to the Lord seven bullocks and seven rams without blemish daily for seven days, and a sin offering, a he-goat daily. 24. And a meal-offering he shall bring, an ephah for a bullock and an ephah for a ram, and for each ephah one hin of oil. 25. In the seventh [month] on the fifteenth day of the month on the Festival, he shall bring quite the same on the seven days, a similar sin-offering, a similar burnt-offering, similar meal-offering and similar oil." 46:1. So says the Lord God: "The gate of the inner court that faces toward the east shall remain closed the six working days, but on the Sabbath day it shall be opened, and on the New Moon day it shall be opened. 2. And the prince shall enter by way of the vestibule of the gate without, and he shall stand at the doorposts of the gate, and the priests shall offer his burnt-offering and his peace-offering, and he shall prostrate himself at the threshold of the gate, then he shall go out, but the gate shall not be closed until the evening. 3. And the people of the land shall [also] prostrate themselves at the entrance of this gate on the Sabbaths and on the New Moons, before the Lord. 4. But the burnt-offering which the prince offers to the Lord: On the Sabbath day shall be six

הַחַטָּאת וְאֶת־הַמִּנְחָה וְאֶת־הָעוֹלָה֙ וְאֶת־
הַשְּׁלָמִ֔ים לְכַפֵּ֖ר בְּעַ֥ד בֵּֽית־יִשְׂרָאֵֽל׃ (כאן מתחילין
הספרדים) יח כֹּֽה־אָמַר֮ אֲדֹנָ֣י יֱהוִה֒ בָּרִאשׁוֹן֙
בְּאֶחָ֣ד לַחֹ֔דֶשׁ תִּקַּ֥ח פַּר־בֶּן־בָּקָ֖ר תָּמִ֑ים וְחִטֵּאתָ֖
אֶת־הַמִּקְדָּֽשׁ׃ יט וְלָקַ֨ח הַכֹּהֵ֜ן מִדַּ֣ם הַחַטָּ֗את
וְנָתַן֙ אֶל־מְזוּזַ֣ת הַבַּ֔יִת וְאֶל־אַרְבַּ֛ע פִּנּ֥וֹת הָעֲזָרָ֖ה
לַמִּזְבֵּ֑חַ וְעַ֨ל־מְזוּזַ֔ת שַׁ֖עַר הֶחָצֵ֥ר הַפְּנִימִֽית׃
כ וְכֵ֤ן תַּֽעֲשֶׂה֙ בְּשִׁבְעָ֣ה בַחֹ֔דֶשׁ מֵאִ֥ישׁ שֹׁגֶ֖ה
וּמִפֶּ֑תִי וְכִפַּרְתֶּ֖ם אֶת־הַבָּֽיִת׃ כא בָּ֠רִאשׁוֹן
בְּאַרְבָּעָ֨ה עָשָׂ֥ר יוֹם֙ לַחֹ֔דֶשׁ יִהְיֶ֥ה לָכֶ֖ם הַפָּ֑סַח חָ֕ג
שְׁבֻע֣וֹת יָמִ֔ים מַצּ֖וֹת יֵאָכֵֽל׃ כב וְעָשָׂ֤ה הַנָּשִׂיא֙
בַּיּ֣וֹם הַה֔וּא בַּעֲד֕וֹ וּבְעַ֖ד כָּל־עַ֣ם הָאָ֑רֶץ פַּ֖ר
חַטָּֽאת׃ כג וְשִׁבְעַ֨ת יְמֵי־הֶחָ֜ג יַעֲשֶׂ֧ה עוֹלָ֣ה
לַיהוָ֗ה שִׁבְעַ֣ת פָּ֠רִים וְשִׁבְעַ֨ת אֵילִ֤ים תְּמִימִם֙
לַיּ֔וֹם שִׁבְעַ֖ת הַיָּמִ֑ים וְחַטָּ֕את שְׂעִ֥יר עִזִּ֖ים לַיּֽוֹם׃
כד וּמִנְחָ֗ה אֵיפָ֥ה לַפָּ֛ר וְאֵיפָ֥ה לָאַ֖יִל יַעֲשֶׂ֑ה וְשֶׁ֖מֶן
הִ֥ין לָאֵיפָֽה׃ כה בַּשְּׁבִיעִ֡י בַּחֲמִשָּׁה֩ עָשָׂ֨ר י֜וֹם
לַחֹ֨דֶשׁ֙ בֶּחָ֔ג יַעֲשֶׂ֥ה כָאֵ֖לֶּה שִׁבְעַ֣ת הַיָּמִ֑ים
כַּחַטָּאת֙ כָּעֹלָ֔ה וְכַמִּנְחָ֖ה וְכַשָּֽׁמֶן׃ א כֹּֽה־אָמַר֮
אֲדֹנָ֣י יֱהוִה֒ שַׁ֜עַר הֶחָצֵ֤ר הַפְּנִימִית֙ הַפֹּנֶ֣ה קָדִ֔ים
יִהְיֶ֣ה סָג֔וּר שֵׁ֖שֶׁת יְמֵ֣י הַֽמַּעֲשֶׂ֑ה וּבְי֤וֹם הַשַּׁבָּת֙
יִפָּתֵ֔חַ וּבְי֥וֹם הַחֹ֖דֶשׁ יִפָּתֵֽחַ׃ ב וּבָ֣א הַנָּשִׂ֡יא דֶּ֩רֶךְ֩
אוּלָ֨ם הַשַּׁ֜עַר מִח֗וּץ וְעָמַד֙ עַל־מְזוּזַ֣ת הַשַּׁ֔עַר
וְעָשׂ֣וּ הַכֹּהֲנִ֗ים אֶת־עוֹלָתוֹ֙ וְאֶת־שְׁלָמָ֔יו
וְהִֽשְׁתַּחֲוָ֛ה עַל־מִפְתַּ֥ן הַשַּׁ֖עַר וְיָצָ֑א וְהַשַּׁ֥עַר לֹֽא־
יִסָּגֵ֖ר עַד־הָעָֽרֶב׃ ג וְהִשְׁתַּחֲו֣וּ עַם־הָאָ֗רֶץ פֶּ֚תַח
הַשַּׁ֣עַר הַה֔וּא בַּשַּׁבָּת֖וֹת וּבֶחֳדָשִׁ֑ים לִפְנֵ֖י יְהוָֽה׃
ד וְהָעֹלָ֕ה אֲשֶׁר־יַקְרִ֥ב הַנָּשִׂ֖יא לַֽיהוָ֑ה בְּי֣וֹם

lambs without blemish and a ram without blemish. 5. And as a meal-offering: one ephah for the ram; and for the lambs, a meal-offering: one ephah for the ram, and for the lambs a meal-offering as he is able to give, and a hin of oil to an ephah. 6. But on the New Moon Day: a young bullock from those without blemish, and six lambs and a ram, without blemish are they to be. 7. And an ephah for the bullock and an ephah for the ram he shall bring as a meal-offering, but for the lambs as much as he can afford, but of oil a hin to an ephah. 8. And whenever the prince goes in, he shall go in by way of the vestibule, and by the same way shall he go out. 9. But when the people of the land come before the Lord on the times fixed for meeting, he who enters by way of the north gate to prostrate himself shall go out by way of the south gate, and he that enters by way of the south gate shall go out by way of the north gate; he shall not return by way of the gate whereby he came in, but he shall go out by that which is opposite to him. 10. The prince also [then] goes in in their midst there where they go in, and when they go out, they [prince and people together] go out. 11. And on the Festivals and on the times fixed for meeting, the meal-offering shall consist of an ephah for a bullock and an ephah for a ram, but for the lambs a gift which is in accordance with his means, and oil, a hin to an ephah. 12. But when the prince brings a freewill-offering, a burnt-offering or a peace-offering as a freewill-offering to the Lord, one shall then open for him the gate that faces the east, and he shall bring his burnt-offering and his peace-offering as he will do on the Sabbath day, and after he has gone out, one shall close the gate. 13. And a lamb of the first year shall you bring as a burnt-offering daily to the Lord, every morning shall you bring it. 14. And as a meal-offering you shall bring for it every morning a sixth of an ephah and a third of a hin to stir with the fine flour, a meal-offering to the Lord, according to the perpetual ordinance constantly. 15. Thus shall they bring the lamb and the meal-offering and the oil every morning, a continual burnt-offering." (*Sephardim conclude here.*) 16. So says the Lord God: "If the prince give a gift to any

הַשַּׁבָּת שִׁשָּׁה כְבָשִׂים תְּמִימִם וְאַיִל תָּמִים: ה וּמִנְחָה אֵיפָה לָאַיִל וְלַכְּבָשִׂים מִנְחָה מַתַּת יָדוֹ וְשֶׁמֶן הִין לָאֵיפָה: ו וּבְיוֹם הַחֹדֶשׁ פַּר בֶּן־בָּקָר תְּמִימִם וְשֵׁשֶׁת כְּבָשִׂים וָאַיִל תְּמִימִם יִהְיוּ: ז וְאֵיפָה לַפָּר וְאֵיפָה לָאַיִל יַעֲשֶׂה מִנְחָה וְלַכְּבָשִׂים כַּאֲשֶׁר תַּשִּׂיג יָדוֹ וְשֶׁמֶן הִין לָאֵיפָה: ח וּבְבוֹא הַנָּשִׂיא דֶּרֶךְ אוּלָם הַשַּׁעַר יָבוֹא וּבְדַרְכּוֹ יֵצֵא: ט וּבְבוֹא עַם־הָאָרֶץ לִפְנֵי יְהֹוָה בַּמּוֹעֲדִים הַבָּא דֶּרֶךְ שַׁעַר צָפוֹן לְהִשְׁתַּחֲוֺת יֵצֵא דֶּרֶךְ־שַׁעַר נֶגֶב וְהַבָּא דֶּרֶךְ־שַׁעַר נֶגֶב יֵצֵא דֶּרֶךְ־שַׁעַר צָפוֹנָה לֹא יָשׁוּב דֶּרֶךְ הַשַּׁעַר אֲשֶׁר־בָּא בוֹ כִּי נִכְחוֹ יֵצֵאוּ (יצא קרי): י וְהַנָּשִׂיא בְּתוֹכָם בְּבוֹאָם יָבוֹא וּבְצֵאתָם יֵצֵאוּ: יא וּבַחַגִּים וּבַמּוֹעֲדִים תִּהְיֶה הַמִּנְחָה אֵיפָה לַפָּר וְאֵיפָה לָאַיִל וְלַכְּבָשִׂים מַתַּת יָדוֹ וְשֶׁמֶן הִין לָאֵיפָה: יב וְכִי־יַעֲשֶׂה הַנָּשִׂיא נְדָבָה עוֹלָה אוֹ־שְׁלָמִים נְדָבָה לַיהֹוָה וּפָתַח לוֹ אֶת־הַשַּׁעַר הַפֹּנֶה קָדִים וְעָשָׂה אֶת־עֹלָתוֹ וְאֶת־שְׁלָמָיו כַּאֲשֶׁר יַעֲשֶׂה בְּיוֹם הַשַּׁבָּת וְיָצָא וְסָגַר אֶת־הַשַּׁעַר אַחֲרֵי צֵאתוֹ: יג וְכֶבֶשׂ בֶּן־שְׁנָתוֹ תָּמִים תַּעֲשֶׂה עוֹלָה לַיּוֹם לַיהֹוָה בַּבֹּקֶר בַּבֹּקֶר תַּעֲשֶׂה אֹתוֹ: יד וּמִנְחָה תַעֲשֶׂה עָלָיו בַּבֹּקֶר בַּבֹּקֶר שִׁשִּׁית הָאֵיפָה וְשֶׁמֶן שְׁלִישִׁית הַהִין לָרֹס אֶת־הַסֹּלֶת מִנְחָה לַיהֹוָה חֻקּוֹת עוֹלָם תָּמִיד: טו וְעָשׂוּ (יעשו קרי) אֶת־הַכֶּבֶשׂ וְאֶת־הַמִּנְחָה וְאֶת־הַשֶּׁמֶן בַּבֹּקֶר בַּבֹּקֶר עוֹלַת תָּמִיד: (כאן מסיימין הספרדים) טז כֹּה־אָמַר אֲדֹנָי יֱהֹוִה כִּי־

of his sons, it is his inheritance and remains in his sons' possession; it is their property by inheritance. 17. But if he gives a gift from his inheritance to one of his servants, then it shall be his until the year of liberty, and then it comes back to the prince; only to his sons shall his inheritance belong. 18. But the prince may not take of the people's inheritance to force them out of their possessions, only from his own possessions shall he give his sons inheritance, so that My people be not scattered each man from his inheritance."

יִתֵּן הַנָּשִׂיא מַתָּנָה לְאִישׁ מִבָּנָיו נַחֲלָתוֹ הִיא לְבָנָיו תִּהְיֶה אֲחֻזָּתָם הִיא בְּנַחֲלָה: יז וְכִי־יִתֵּן מַתָּנָה מִנַּחֲלָתוֹ לְאַחַד מֵעֲבָדָיו וְהָיְתָה לּוֹ עַד־שְׁנַת הַדְּרוֹר וְשָׁבַת לַנָּשִׂיא אַךְ נַחֲלָתוֹ בָּנָיו לָהֶם תִּהְיֶה: יח וְלֹא־יִקַּח הַנָּשִׂיא מִנַּחֲלַת הָעָם לְהוֹנֹתָם מֵאֲחֻזָּתָם מֵאֲחֻזָּתוֹ יַנְחִל אֶת־בָּנָיו לְמַעַן אֲשֶׁר לֹא־יָפֻצוּ עַמִּי אִישׁ מֵאֲחֻזָּתוֹ:

HAFTARATH SHABBATH HAGADOL   הפטרת שבת הגדול
(Malachi 3:4–24)

Most congregations read this Haftarah on the Sabbath preceding Pesaḥ, regardless of the day of the week on which the festival begins. Many congregations, however, read the Haftarah that usually accompanies the Sidra of that particular Sabbath, and read this special Haftarah only when Shabbath Hagadol is the eve of Pesaḥ. The latter custom is followed by congregations adhering to the ritual of Frankfort-on-the-Main, Prague, and by Chabad and Munkacs Chassidim. Many congregations that adhere to the Lithuanian ritual follow the ruling of Rabbi Elijah, the Gaon of Vilna, according to which this Haftarah should be read only when Shabbath Hagadol does not fall on the Eve of Pesaḥ.

There are many reasons for reading this Haftarah before Pesaḥ. Rabbi Jacob Ashkenazi of Emden (1691–1776) offers one. He explains this custom with the rabbinic maxim that on Pesaḥ God judges the world to determine whether it is worthy of a good grain harvest. The blessing of the grain is mentioned in this Haftarah.

3:4. And then the offerings of Judah and Jerusalem shall be pleasant to the Lord, as in the days of old and former years. 5. And I will approach you for judgment, and I will be a swift witness against the sorcerers and against the adulterers and against those who swear falsely, and also against those who keep back the wages of the day-laborers, of the widow and fatherless, and who pervert the rights of the stranger, and fear Me not, says the Lord of Hosts. 6. For I, the Lord, have not changed, and you, the sons of Jacob, have not reached the end. 7. From the days of your fathers you have departed from My laws and have not kept [them]: "Return to Me, and I will return to you," said the Lord of Hosts, but you said, "With what have we to return?" 8. Will a man rob God? Yet you rob Me, and you say, "With what have we robbed You?" With tithes and with the terumah-levy. 9. You are cursed with a curse, but you rob Me, the whole

ד וְעָרְבָה לַיהֹוָה מִנְחַת יְהוּדָה וִירוּשָׁלָ͏ִם כִּימֵי עוֹלָם וּכְשָׁנִים קַדְמֹנִיּוֹת: ה וְקָרַבְתִּי אֲלֵיכֶם לַמִּשְׁפָּט וְהָיִיתִי ׀ עֵד מְמַהֵר בַּמְכַשְּׁפִים וּבַמְנָאֲפִים וּבַנִּשְׁבָּעִים לַשָּׁקֶר וּבְעֹשְׁקֵי שְׂכַר־שָׂכִיר אַלְמָנָה וְיָתוֹם וּמַטֵּי־גֵר וְלֹא יְרֵאוּנִי אָמַר יְהֹוָה צְבָאוֹת: ו כִּי אֲנִי יְהֹוָה לֹא שָׁנִיתִי וְאַתֶּם בְּנֵי־יַעֲקֹב לֹא כְלִיתֶם: ז לְמִימֵי אֲבֹתֵיכֶם סַרְתֶּם מֵחֻקַּי וְלֹא שְׁמַרְתֶּם שׁוּבוּ אֵלַי וְאָשׁוּבָה אֲלֵיכֶם אָמַר יְהֹוָה צְבָאוֹת וַאֲמַרְתֶּם בַּמֶּה נָשׁוּב: ח הֲיִקְבַּע אָדָם אֱלֹהִים כִּי אַתֶּם קֹבְעִים אֹתִי וַאֲמַרְתֶּם בַּמֶּה קְבַעֲנוּךָ הַמַּעֲשֵׂר וְהַתְּרוּמָה: ט בַּמְּאֵרָה אַתֶּם נֵאָרִים

nation! 10. Bring the whole of the tithes into the treasury so that there may be nourishment in My House and test Me now therewith, says the Lord of Hosts, if I will not open for you the sluices of heaven and pour down for you blessing until there be no room to suffice for it. 11. And I will rebuke the devourer [the locusts] for your sake, and he will not destroy the fruits of your land, neither shall your vine cast its fruit before its time in the field, says the Lord of Hosts. 12. And then all the nations shall praise you, for you shall be a desirable land, says the Lord of Hosts. 13. "Still harder did your words strike Me," says the Lord, but you say, "What have we spoken against You?" 14. You have said, "It is futile to serve God, and what profit do we get that we have kept His charge and that we have gone about in anxious worry because of the Lord of Hosts?" 15. And now we praise the bold transgressors; yea, those who work wickedness are built up; yea, those tempt God, and they are nevertheless saved. 16. Then the God-fearing men spoke to one another, and the Lord hearkened and heard it, and a book of remembrance was written before Him for those who feared the Lord and for those who valued His Name highly. 17. "And they shall be Mine," says the Lord of Hosts, "for that day when I form that which belongs exclusively to Me, and I will have compassion on them as a man has compassion on his son who serves him. 18. And you shall return and discern between the righteous and the wicked, and between him who serves God and him who has not served Him. 19. For lo, the day comes, glowing like a furnace, and all the audacious sinners and all the perpetrators of wickedness will be dry stubble, and the day that comes shall burn them up so that neither root nor branch will it leave them," says the Lord of Hosts. 20. And for you who fear My Name, shall the sun of mercy rise with healing in its wings, then will you go forth and be fat as fatted calves. 21. And you shall crush the wicked, for they shall be as ash under the soles of your feet on the day that I will prepare, says the Lord of Hosts. 22. Keep in remembrance the teaching of Moses, My servant, which I commanded him in Horeb for all Israel, laws and ordi-

וְאֹתִי אַתֶּם קֹבְעִים הַגּוֹי כֻּלּוֹ: י הָבִיאוּ אֶת־
כָּל־הַמַּעֲשֵׂר אֶל־בֵּית הָאוֹצָר וִיהִי טֶרֶף בְּבֵיתִי
וּבְחָנוּנִי נָא בָּזֹאת אָמַר יְהֹוָה צְבָאוֹת אִם־לֹא
אֶפְתַּח לָכֶם אֵת אֲרֻבּוֹת הַשָּׁמַיִם וַהֲרִיקֹתִי
לָכֶם בְּרָכָה עַד־בְּלִי־דָי: יא וְגָעַרְתִּי לָכֶם בָּאֹכֵל
וְלֹא־יַשְׁחִת לָכֶם אֶת־פְּרִי הָאֲדָמָה וְלֹא־תְשַׁכֵּל
לָכֶם הַגֶּפֶן בַּשָּׂדֶה אָמַר יְהֹוָה צְבָאוֹת:
יב וְאִשְּׁרוּ אֶתְכֶם כָּל־הַגּוֹיִם כִּי־תִהְיוּ אַתֶּם
אֶרֶץ חֵפֶץ אָמַר יְהֹוָה צְבָאוֹת: יג חָזְקוּ עָלַי
דִּבְרֵיכֶם אָמַר יְהֹוָה וַאֲמַרְתֶּם מַה־נִּדְבַּרְנוּ
עָלֶיךָ: יד אֲמַרְתֶּם שָׁוְא עֲבֹד אֱלֹהִים וּמַה־בֶּצַע
כִּי שָׁמַרְנוּ מִשְׁמַרְתּוֹ וְכִי הָלַכְנוּ קְדֹרַנִּית מִפְּנֵי
יְהֹוָה צְבָאוֹת: טו וְעַתָּה אֲנַחְנוּ מְאַשְּׁרִים זֵדִים
גַּם־נִבְנוּ עֹשֵׂי רִשְׁעָה גַּם בָּחֲנוּ אֱלֹהִים
וַיִּמָּלֵטוּ: טז אָז נִדְבְּרוּ יִרְאֵי יְהֹוָה אִישׁ אֶל־
רֵעֵהוּ וַיַּקְשֵׁב יְהֹוָה וַיִּשְׁמָע וַיִּכָּתֵב סֵפֶר זִכָּרוֹן
לְפָנָיו לְיִרְאֵי יְהֹוָה וּלְחֹשְׁבֵי שְׁמוֹ: יז וְהָיוּ לִי
אָמַר יְהֹוָה צְבָאוֹת לַיּוֹם אֲשֶׁר אֲנִי עֹשֶׂה סְגֻלָּה
וְחָמַלְתִּי עֲלֵיהֶם כַּאֲשֶׁר יַחְמֹל אִישׁ עַל־בְּנוֹ
הָעֹבֵד אֹתוֹ: יח וְשַׁבְתֶּם וּרְאִיתֶם בֵּין צַדִּיק
לְרָשָׁע בֵּין עֹבֵד אֱלֹהִים לַאֲשֶׁר לֹא
עֲבָדוֹ: יט כִּי־הִנֵּה הַיּוֹם בָּא בֹּעֵר כַּתַּנּוּר וְהָיוּ
כָל־זֵדִים וְכָל־עֹשֵׂה רִשְׁעָה קַשׁ וְלִהַט אֹתָם
הַיּוֹם הַבָּא אָמַר יְהֹוָה צְבָאוֹת אֲשֶׁר לֹא־יַעֲזֹב
לָהֶם שֹׁרֶשׁ וְעָנָף: כ וְזָרְחָה לָכֶם יִרְאֵי שְׁמִי
שֶׁמֶשׁ צְדָקָה וּמַרְפֵּא בִּכְנָפֶיהָ וִיצָאתֶם וּפִשְׁתֶּם
כְּעֶגְלֵי מַרְבֵּק: כא וְעַסּוֹתֶם רְשָׁעִים כִּי־יִהְיוּ
אֵפֶר תַּחַת כַּפּוֹת רַגְלֵיכֶם בַּיּוֹם אֲשֶׁר אֲנִי
עֹשֶׂה אָמַר יְהֹוָה צְבָאוֹת: כב זִכְרוּ (ז' רבתי)
תּוֹרַת מֹשֶׁה עַבְדִּי אֲשֶׁר צִוִּיתִי אוֹתוֹ בְחֹרֵב

nances. 23. Lo, I will send you Elijah the Prophet before the coming of the great and awesome day of the Lord, 24. that he may turn the mind of the fathers back to the children, and the mind of the children back to their fathers, so that I do not come and smite the earth with utter destruction. [Lo, I will send you Elijah the Prophet before the coming of the great and awesome day of the Lord.]

עַל־כָּל־יִשְׂרָאֵל חֻקִּים וּמִשְׁפָּטִים׃ כג הִנֵּה אָנֹכִי
שֹׁלֵחַ לָכֶם אֵת אֵלִיָּה הַנָּבִיא לִפְנֵי בּוֹא יוֹם יְהוָה
הַגָּדוֹל וְהַנּוֹרָא׃ כד וְהֵשִׁיב לֵב־אָבוֹת עַל־בָּנִים
וְלֵב בָּנִים עַל־אֲבוֹתָם פֶּן־אָבוֹא וְהִכֵּיתִי אֶת־
הָאָרֶץ חֵרֶם׃ [הִנֵּה אָנֹכִי שֹׁלֵחַ לָכֶם אֵת אֵלִיָּה הַנָּבִיא
לִפְנֵי בּוֹא יוֹם יְהוָה הַגָּדוֹל וְהַנּוֹרָא׃]

HAFTARAH FOR THE FIRST DAY OF PESAḤ הפטרת יום א׳ דפסח

(Joshua 3:5–7, 5:2–6:1 and 27. Sephardim omit the first selection.)
Torah reading: Exodus 12:21–51, Numbers 28:16–25.

This selection speaks of the first Pesaḥ offering made by the children of Israel in Eretz Yisrael.

3:5. And Joshua said to the people: Prepare yourselves, for tomorrow the Lord will do wonders among you. 6. And Joshua said to the priests, saying: "Carry the Ark of the covenant, and pass before the people." And they carried the Ark of the covenant, and went before the people. 7. And the Lord said to Joshua: This day I will begin to make you great in the sight of all Israel, that they may know that as I was with Moses, so will I be with you. (*Sephardim and those following the ritual of Frankfort-on-the-Main commence here.*) 5:2. At that time the Lord said to Joshua, "Make for yourself sharp knives, and circumcise again the children of Israel the second time." 3. And Joshua made for himself sharp knives, and circumcised the children of Israel at the hill of the foreskins. 4. And this is the reason that Joshua did circumcise: All the people that came out of Egypt, that were males, all the men of war, had died in the desert by the way [after] they came out of Egypt. 5. For all the people that came out were circumcised, but all the people that were born in the wilderness by the way as they came forth out of Egypt, they had not circumcised. 6. For the children of Israel walked forty years in the wilderness, until all the people, the men of war that came out of Egypt, were consumed; those who did not listen to the voice of the Lord, to whom the Lord had sworn that He would not show them the land which the Lord had sworn to

ה וַיֹּאמֶר יְהוֹשֻׁעַ אֶל־הָעָם הִתְקַדָּשׁוּ כִּי מָחָר
יַעֲשֶׂה יְהוָה בְּקִרְבְּכֶם נִפְלָאוֹת׃ ו וַיֹּאמֶר
יְהוֹשֻׁעַ אֶל־הַכֹּהֲנִים לֵאמֹר שְׂאוּ אֶת־אֲרוֹן
הַבְּרִית וְעִבְרוּ לִפְנֵי הָעָם וַיִּשְׂאוּ אֶת־אֲרוֹן
הַבְּרִית וַיֵּלְכוּ לִפְנֵי הָעָם׃ ז וַיֹּאמֶר יְהוָה אֶל־
יְהוֹשֻׁעַ הַיּוֹם הַזֶּה אָחֵל גַּדֶּלְךָ בְּעֵינֵי כָּל־
יִשְׂרָאֵל אֲשֶׁר יֵדְעוּן כִּי כַּאֲשֶׁר הָיִיתִי עִם־
מֹשֶׁה אֶהְיֶה עִמָּךְ׃ (כאן מתחילין הספרדים וק"ק
פרנקפורט ד'מיין) ב בָּעֵת הַהִיא אָמַר יְהוָה אֶל־
יְהוֹשֻׁעַ עֲשֵׂה לְךָ חַרְבוֹת צֻרִים וְשׁוּב מֹל אֶת־
בְּנֵי־יִשְׂרָאֵל שֵׁנִית׃ ג וַיַּעַשׂ־לוֹ יְהוֹשֻׁעַ חַרְבוֹת
צֻרִים וַיָּמָל אֶת־בְּנֵי יִשְׂרָאֵל אֶל־גִּבְעַת
הָעֲרָלוֹת׃ ד וְזֶה הַדָּבָר אֲשֶׁר־מָל יְהוֹשֻׁעַ כָּל־
הָעָם הַיֹּצֵא מִמִּצְרַיִם הַזְּכָרִים כֹּל ׀ אַנְשֵׁי
הַמִּלְחָמָה מֵתוּ בַמִּדְבָּר בַּדֶּרֶךְ בְּצֵאתָם
מִמִּצְרָיִם׃ ה כִּי־מֻלִים הָיוּ כָּל־הָעָם הַיֹּצְאִים
וְכָל־הָעָם הַיִּלֹּדִים בַּמִּדְבָּר בַּדֶּרֶךְ בְּצֵאתָם
מִמִּצְרַיִם לֹא־מָלוּ׃ ו כִּי ׀ אַרְבָּעִים שָׁנָה הָלְכוּ
בְנֵי־יִשְׂרָאֵל בַּמִּדְבָּר עַד־תֹּם כָּל־הַגּוֹי אַנְשֵׁי
הַמִּלְחָמָה הַיֹּצְאִים מִמִּצְרַיִם אֲשֶׁר לֹא־שָׁמְעוּ
בְּקוֹל יְהוָה אֲשֶׁר נִשְׁבַּע יְהוָה לָהֶם לְבִלְתִּי
הַרְאוֹתָם אֶת־הָאָרֶץ אֲשֶׁר נִשְׁבַּע יְהוָה

לַאֲבוֹתָם֙ לָ֣תֶת לָ֔נוּ אֶ֛רֶץ זָבַ֥ת חָלָ֖ב וּדְבָֽשׁ׃
ז וְאֶת־בְּנֵיהֶם֙ הֵקִ֣ים תַּחְתָּ֔ם אֹתָ֖ם מָ֣ל יְהוֹשֻׁ֑עַ
כִּֽי־עֲרֵלִ֣ים הָי֔וּ כִּ֛י לֹא־מָ֥לוּ אוֹתָ֖ם בַּדָּֽרֶךְ׃
ח וַיְהִ֛י כַּאֲשֶׁר־תַּ֥מּוּ כָל־הַגּ֖וֹי לְהִמּ֑וֹל וַיֵּשְׁב֤וּ
תַחְתָּם֙ בַּֽמַּחֲנֶ֔ה עַ֖ד חֲיוֹתָֽם׃ ט וַיֹּ֤אמֶר יְהוָה֙
אֶל־יְהוֹשֻׁ֔עַ הַיּ֗וֹם גַּלּ֛וֹתִי אֶת־חֶרְפַּ֥ת מִצְרַ֖יִם
מֵעֲלֵיכֶ֑ם וַיִּקְרָ֞א שֵׁ֣ם הַמָּק֤וֹם הַהוּא֙ גִּלְגָּ֔ל עַ֖ד
הַיּ֥וֹם הַזֶּֽה׃ י וַיַּחֲנ֥וּ בְנֵֽי־יִשְׂרָאֵ֖ל בַּגִּלְגָּ֑ל וַיַּעֲשׂ֣וּ
אֶת־הַפֶּ֡סַח בְּאַרְבָּעָה֩ עָשָׂ֨ר י֥וֹם לַחֹ֛דֶשׁ בָּעֶ֖רֶב
בְּעַֽרְב֥וֹת יְרִיחֽוֹ׃ יא וַיֹּ֨אכְל֜וּ מֵעֲב֥וּר הָאָ֛רֶץ
מִמָּחֳרַ֥ת הַפֶּ֖סַח מַצּ֣וֹת וְקָל֑וּי בְּעֶ֖צֶם הַיּ֥וֹם הַזֶּֽה׃
יב וַיִּשְׁבֹּ֨ת הַמָּ֜ן מִֽמָּחֳרָ֗ת בְּאָכְלָם֙ מֵעֲב֣וּר הָאָ֔רֶץ
וְלֹא־הָ֥יָה ע֛וֹד לִבְנֵ֥י יִשְׂרָאֵ֖ל מָ֑ן וַיֹּאכְל֗וּ
מִתְּבוּאַת֙ אֶ֣רֶץ כְּנַ֔עַן בַּשָּׁנָ֖ה הַהִֽיא׃ יג וַיְהִ֗י
בִּֽהְי֣וֹת יְהוֹשֻׁעַ֮ בִּירִיחוֹ֒ וַיִּשָּׂ֤א עֵינָיו֙ וַיַּ֔רְא
וְהִנֵּה־אִישׁ֙ עֹמֵ֣ד לְנֶגְדּ֔וֹ וְחַרְבּ֥וֹ שְׁלוּפָ֖ה בְּיָד֑וֹ
וַיֵּ֨לֶךְ יְהוֹשֻׁ֤עַ אֵלָיו֙ וַיֹּ֣אמֶר ל֔וֹ הֲלָ֥נוּ אַתָּ֖ה אִם־
לְצָרֵֽינוּ׃ יד וַיֹּ֣אמֶר ׀ לֹ֗א כִּ֛י אֲנִ֥י שַׂר־צְבָֽא־יְהוָ֖ה
עַתָּ֣ה בָ֑אתִי וַיִּפֹּל֩ יְהוֹשֻׁ֨עַ אֶל־פָּנָ֥יו אַ֛רְצָה
וַיִּשְׁתָּ֖חוּ וַיֹּ֣אמֶר ל֔וֹ מָ֥ה אֲדֹנִ֖י מְדַבֵּ֥ר אֶל־עַבְדּֽוֹ׃
טו וַיֹּ֩אמֶר֩ שַׂר־צְבָ֨א יְהוָ֜ה אֶל־יְהוֹשֻׁ֗עַ שַׁל־
נַֽעַלְךָ֙ מֵעַ֣ל רַגְלֶ֔ךָ כִּ֣י הַמָּק֔וֹם אֲשֶׁ֥ר אַתָּ֛ה עֹמֵ֥ד
עָלָ֖יו קֹ֣דֶשׁ ה֑וּא וַיַּ֥עַשׂ יְהוֹשֻׁ֖עַ כֵּֽן׃ א וִירִיחוֹ֙
סֹגֶ֣רֶת וּמְסֻגֶּ֔רֶת מִפְּנֵ֖י בְּנֵ֣י יִשְׂרָאֵ֑ל אֵ֥ין יוֹצֵ֖א
וְאֵ֥ין בָּֽא׃ כז וַיְהִ֥י יְהוָ֖ה אֶת־יְהוֹשֻׁ֑עַ וַיְהִ֥י
שָׁמְע֖וֹ בְּכָל־הָאָֽרֶץ׃

their forefathers that He would give us, a land that flows with milk and honey. 7. And their children, whom he raised up in their stead, them Joshua circumcised, for they had not circumcised them by the way. 8. And it was, when all the people were finished being circumcised, that they remained in their places in the camp until they recovered. 9. And the Lord said to Joshua, "This day have I rolled away the reproach of Egypt from you." And he called the name of the place Gilgal to this day. 10. And the children of Israel encamped in Gilgal, and they made the Passover sacrifice on the fourteenth day of the month at evening, in the plains of Jericho. 11. And they ate of the grain of the land on the morrow of the Passover, unleavened cakes and parched grain on this very day. 12. And the manna ceased on the morrow when they ate of the grain of the land; neither had the children of Israel manna anymore; and they ate of the produce of the land of Canaan that year. 13. And it was when Joshua was in Jericho, that he lifted up his eyes and saw, and, behold, a man was standing opposite him with his sword drawn in his hand; and Joshua went to him, and said to him, "Are you for us, or for our adversaries?" 14. And he said, "No, but I am the captain of the host of the Lord; I have now come." And Joshua fell on his face to the earth and prostrated himself, and said to him, "What does my lord say to his servant?" 15. And the captain of the Lord's host said to Joshua, "Remove your shoe from your foot, for the place upon which you stand is holy." And Joshua did so. 6:1. And Jericho had shut its gates and was barred because of the children of Israel: none went out and none came in. 27. So the Lord was with Joshua, and his fame was throughout the entire land.

HAFTARAH FOR THE SECOND DAY OF PESAḤ הפטרת יום ב׳ דפסח

(II Kings 23:1–9, 21–25)

Torah reading: Leviticus 22:26–23:44, Numbers 28:16–25.

This selection tells of the Pesaḥ sacrifice offered by King Josiah.

א וַיִּשְׁלַ֖ח הַמֶּ֑לֶךְ וַיַּאַסְפ֣וּ אֵלָ֔יו כָּל־זִקְנֵ֥י יְהוּדָ֖ה
וִירוּשָׁלִָֽם׃ ב וַיַּ֣עַל הַמֶּ֣לֶךְ בֵּית־יְהוָ֡ה וְכָל־אִ֣ישׁ

23:1. And the king summoned, and they assembled before him all the elders of Judah and Jerusalem. 2. And the king went up to the house of the Lord, and all the people of Judah and all the inhabitants of Jerusalem were with him, and the priests and the prophets, and all the people from small to great, and he read within their hearing all the words of the scroll of the covenant that was found in the house of the Lord. 3. And the king stood on his place and enacted the covenant before the Lord, to follow the Lord and to observe His commandments and His testimonies and His statutes with all their heart and soul, to fulfill the words of this covenant, which are written in this scroll. And all the people were steadfast in their acceptance of the covenant. 4. And the king commanded Hilkiah the high priest and the priests of the second rank and the guards of the threshold to take out of the Temple of the Lord all the utensils that were made for the Baal and for the *asherah*, and for the entire host of the heaven, and he burnt them outside Jerusalem in the plains of Kidron, and he carried their ashes to Bethel. 5. And he abolished the pagan priests whom the kings of Judah had appointed and who had burnt incense on the high places in the cities of Judah and the environs of Jerusalem, and those who burnt incense to the Baal, to the sun, to the moon, and to the constellations, and to all the host of heaven. 6. And he took the *asherah* out of the house of the Lord to the outside of Jerusalem, to the Kidron Valley, and he burnt it in the Kidron Valley, and he pulverized it into dust; and he threw its dust on the graves of the members of the people. 7. And he demolished the houses devoted to pagan worship that were in the house of the Lord, where the women weave enclosures for the *asherah*. 8. And he brought all the priests from the cities of Judah, and he defiled the high places where the priests had burnt incense, from Geba as far as Beersheba, and he demolished the high places near the gates, the one that was at the entrance of the gate of Joshua, the mayor of the city, which is on a person's left in the gate of the city. 9. However, the priests of the high places would not go up to the Lord's altar in Jerusalem, but they would eat unleavened cakes among their brethren. 21. And the king commanded all the people, saying, ''Perform a Passover sacri-

יְהוּדָה וְכָל־יֹשְׁבֵי יְרוּשָׁלַ͏ִם אִתּוֹ וְהַכֹּהֲנִים וְהַנְּבִיאִים וְכָל־הָעָם לְמִקָּטֹן וְעַד־גָּדוֹל וַיִּקְרָא בְאָזְנֵיהֶם אֶת־כָּל־דִּבְרֵי סֵפֶר הַבְּרִית הַנִּמְצָא בְּבֵית יְהוָֹה: ג וַיַּעֲמֹד הַמֶּלֶךְ עַל־הָעַמּוּד וַיִּכְרֹת אֶת־הַבְּרִית ׀ לִפְנֵי יְהוָֹה לָלֶכֶת אַחַר יְהוָֹה וְלִשְׁמֹר מִצְוֺתָיו וְאֶת־עֵדְוֺתָיו וְאֶת־חֻקֹּתָיו בְּכָל־לֵב וּבְכָל־נֶפֶשׁ לְהָקִים אֶת־דִּבְרֵי הַבְּרִית הַזֹּאת הַכְּתֻבִים עַל־הַסֵּפֶר הַזֶּה וַיַּעֲמֹד כָּל־הָעָם בַּבְּרִית: ד וַיְצַו הַמֶּלֶךְ אֶת־חִלְקִיָּהוּ הַכֹּהֵן הַגָּדוֹל וְאֶת־כֹּהֲנֵי הַמִּשְׁנֶה וְאֶת־שֹׁמְרֵי הַסַּף לְהוֹצִיא מֵהֵיכַל יְהוָֹה אֵת כָּל־הַכֵּלִים הָעֲשׂוּיִם לַבַּעַל וְלָאֲשֵׁרָה וּלְכֹל צְבָא הַשָּׁמָיִם וַיִּשְׂרְפֵם מִחוּץ לִירוּשָׁלַ͏ִם בְּשַׁדְמוֹת קִדְרוֹן וְנָשָׂא אֶת־עֲפָרָם בֵּית־אֵל: ה וְהִשְׁבִּית אֶת־הַכְּמָרִים אֲשֶׁר נָתְנוּ מַלְכֵי יְהוּדָה וַיְקַטֵּר בַּבָּמוֹת בְּעָרֵי יְהוּדָה וּמְסִבֵּי יְרוּשָׁלָ͏ִם וְאֶת־הַמְקַטְּרִים לַבַּעַל לַשֶּׁמֶשׁ וְלַיָּרֵחַ וְלַמַּזָּלוֹת וּלְכֹל צְבָא הַשָּׁמָיִם: ו וַיֹּצֵא אֶת־הָאֲשֵׁרָה מִבֵּית יְהוָֹה מִחוּץ לִירוּשָׁלַ͏ִם אֶל־נַחַל קִדְרוֹן וַיִּשְׂרֹף אֹתָהּ בְּנַחַל קִדְרוֹן וַיָּדֶק לְעָפָר וַיַּשְׁלֵךְ אֶת־עֲפָרָהּ עַל־קֶבֶר בְּנֵי הָעָם: ז וַיִּתֹּץ אֶת־בָּתֵּי הַקְּדֵשִׁים אֲשֶׁר בְּבֵית יְהוָֹה אֲשֶׁר הַנָּשִׁים אֹרְגוֹת שָׁם בָּתִּים לָאֲשֵׁרָה: ח וַיָּבֵא אֶת־כָּל־הַכֹּהֲנִים מֵעָרֵי יְהוּדָה וַיְטַמֵּא אֶת־הַבָּמוֹת אֲשֶׁר קִטְּרוּ־שָׁמָּה הַכֹּהֲנִים מִגֶּבַע עַד־בְּאֵר שָׁבַע וְנָתַץ אֶת־בָּמוֹת הַשְּׁעָרִים אֲשֶׁר־פֶּתַח שַׁעַר יְהוֹשֻׁעַ שַׂר־הָעִיר אֲשֶׁר־עַל־שְׂמֹאול אִישׁ בְּשַׁעַר הָעִיר: ט אַךְ לֹא יַעֲלוּ כֹּהֲנֵי הַבָּמוֹת אֶל־מִזְבַּח יְהוָֹה בִּירוּשָׁלָ͏ִם כִּי אִם־אָכְלוּ מַצּוֹת בְּתוֹךְ אֲחֵיהֶם: כא וַיְצַו הַמֶּלֶךְ אֶת־כָּל־הָעָם לֵאמֹר עֲשׂוּ פֶסַח לַיהוָֹה

אֱלֹהֵיכֶם כַּכָּתוּב עַל סֵפֶר הַבְּרִית הַזֶּה: כב כִּי
לֹא נַעֲשָׂה כַּפֶּסַח הַזֶּה מִימֵי הַשֹּׁפְטִים אֲשֶׁר
שָׁפְטוּ אֶת־יִשְׂרָאֵל וְכֹל יְמֵי מַלְכֵי יִשְׂרָאֵל
וּמַלְכֵי יְהוּדָה: כג כִּי אִם־בִּשְׁמֹנֶה עֶשְׂרֵה שָׁנָה
לַמֶּלֶךְ יֹאשִׁיָּהוּ נַעֲשָׂה הַפֶּסַח הַזֶּה לַיהוָה
בִּירוּשָׁלָם: כד וְגַם אֶת־הָאֹבוֹת וְאֶת־הַיִּדְּעֹנִים
וְאֶת־הַתְּרָפִים וְאֶת־הַגִּלֻּלִים וְאֵת כָּל־הַשִּׁקֻּצִים
אֲשֶׁר נִרְאוּ בְּאֶרֶץ יְהוּדָה וּבִירוּשָׁלַם בִּעֵר
יֹאשִׁיָּהוּ לְמַעַן הָקִים אֶת־דִּבְרֵי הַתּוֹרָה
הַכְּתֻבִים עַל־הַסֵּפֶר אֲשֶׁר מָצָא חִלְקִיָּהוּ הַכֹּהֵן
בֵּית יְהוָה: כה וְכָמֹהוּ לֹא־הָיָה לְפָנָיו מֶלֶךְ
אֲשֶׁר־שָׁב אֶל־יְהוָה בְּכָל־לְבָבוֹ וּבְכָל־נַפְשׁוֹ
וּבְכָל־מְאֹדוֹ כְּכֹל תּוֹרַת מֹשֶׁה וְאַחֲרָיו לֹא־קָם
כָּמֹהוּ:

fice to the Lord your God, as it is written in this scroll of the covenant." 22. For such a Passover sacrifice had not been performed since the time of the judges who judged Israel, and all the days of the kings of Israel and the kings of Judah. 23. Except in the eighteenth year of King Josiah, this Passover sacrifice was performed to the Lord, in Jerusalem. 24. And also the necromancers and those who divine by the Jidoa bone and the *teraphim* and the idols and all the abominations that were seen in the land of Judah and in Jerusalem, Josiah abolished, in order to fulfill the words of the Torah which were written in the scroll that Hilkiah the priest had found in the house of the Lord. 25. Now, before him there was no king like him, who returned to the Lord with all his heart and with all his soul and with all his possessions, according to the entire Torah of Moses, and after him no one arose.

הפטרת שבת חול המועד פסח

HAFTARAH FOR THE INTERMEDIATE SABBATH OF PESAḤ

(Ezekiel 37:1–14)

Some congregations read 36:37–37:17.

Torah reading: Exodus 33:12–34:26, Numbers 28:19–25.

Many congregations read the Song of Songs (p. 1007) prior to the Torah reading.

This Haftarah is Ezekiel's renowned vision of the dry bones that were resurrected. According to tradition, the resurrection of the dead will take place during the month of Nissan.

(יש קהלות שמתחילין כאן:) לז כֹּה אָמַר אֲדֹנָי יֱהוִה עוֹד
זֹאת אִדָּרֵשׁ לְבֵית־יִשְׂרָאֵל לַעֲשׂוֹת לָהֶם אַרְבֶּה
אֹתָם כַּצֹּאן אָדָם: לח כְּצֹאן קָדָשִׁים כְּצֹאן
יְרוּשָׁלַםִ בְּמוֹעֲדֶיהָ כֵּן תִּהְיֶינָה הֶעָרִים הֶעָרִים
הֶחֳרֵבוֹת מְלֵאוֹת צֹאן אָדָם וְיָדְעוּ כִּי־אֲנִי יְהוָה:
(ספרדים ורוב אשכנזים מתחילין כאן:) א הָיְתָה עָלַי יַד־
יְהוָה וַיּוֹצִיאֵנִי בְרוּחַ יְהוָה וַיְנִיחֵנִי בְּתוֹךְ
הַבִּקְעָה וְהִיא מְלֵאָה עֲצָמוֹת: ב וְהֶעֱבִירַנִי
עֲלֵיהֶם סָבִיב ׀ סָבִיב וְהִנֵּה רַבּוֹת מְאֹד עַל־פְּנֵי
הַבִּקְעָה וְהִנֵּה יְבֵשׁוֹת מְאֹד: ג וַיֹּאמֶר אֵלַי בֶּן־
אָדָם הֲתִחְיֶינָה הָעֲצָמוֹת הָאֵלֶּה וָאֹמַר אֲדֹנָי

(Some congregations begin here:) 36:37. So says the Lord God: I will yet for this be inquired of by the house of Israel to do for them: I will multiply them like a flock of sheep, as men. 38. Like the flocks appointed for the holy offerings, like the flocks of Jerusalem on its festivals, so will these cities now laid waste be filled with flocks of men, and they shall know that I am the Lord. (*Sephardim and most Ashkenazim commence here:*) 37:1. The hand of the Lord came upon me, and carried me out in the spirit of the Lord, and set me down in the midst of the valley, and that was full of bones. 2. And He made me pass by them round about, and lo! They were exceedingly many on the surface of the valley, and lo! They were exceedingly dry. 3. Then He said to me: "Son of man, can these bones become alive?" And I

answered, "O Lord God, You [alone] know." 4. And He said to me, "Prophesy over these bones, and say to them, 'O dry bones, hear the word of the Lord.' 5. So says the Lord God to these bones, 'Behold, I will cause spirit to enter into you, and you shall live! 6. And I will lay ligaments upon you, and I will make flesh grow over you and cover you with skin and put breath into you, and you will live, and you will then know that I am the Lord.'" 7. So I prophesied as I was commanded, and there arose a noise when I prophesied, and behold a commotion, and the bones came together, bone to its bone! 8. And I looked, and lo! Ligaments were upon them, and flesh came up on them, and skin covered them from above, but there was still no spirit in them. 9. Then He said to me, "Prophesy to the spirit, prophesy, O son of man, and say to the spirit, 'So says the Lord God: From four sides, come, O spirit, and breathe into these slain ones that they may live.'" 10. And I prophesied as He had commanded me, and the spirit came into them, and they lived and stood on their feet, a very exceedingly great army. 11. Then He said to me, "son of man, these bones are the whole house of Israel. Behold, they say, 'Our bones have become dried up, our hope is lost, we are clean cut off to ourselves.' 12. Therefore, prophesy and say to them, So says the Lord God, 'Lo! I open your graves and cause you to come up out of your graves as My people, and bring you home to the Land of Israel. 13. Then you shall know that I am the Lord, when I open your graves and lead you up out of your graves as My people. 14. And I will put My spirit in you, and you shall live, and I will set you on your land, and you shall know that I, the Lord, have spoken it and have performed it,'" says the Lord. (*Some congregations add:*) 15. And the word of the Lord came to me, saying: 16. And you, son of man, take for yourself one stick and write upon it, "For Judah and for the children of Israel his companions"; and take one stick and write upon it, "For Joseph, the stick of Ephraim and all the house of Israel, his companions." 17. And bring them close, one to the other into one stick, and they shall be one in your hand.

יְהֹוָ֖ה אַתָּ֣ה יָדָֽעְתָּ: ד וַיֹּ֣אמֶר אֵלַ֔י הִנָּבֵ֖א עַל־הָעֲצָמ֣וֹת הָאֵ֑לֶּה וְאָמַרְתָּ֣ אֲלֵיהֶ֔ם הָעֲצָמוֹת֙ הַיְבֵשׁ֔וֹת שִׁמְע֖וּ דְּבַר־יְהֹוָֽה: ה כֹּ֤ה אָמַר֙ אֲדֹנָ֣י יֱהֹוִ֔ה לָעֲצָמ֖וֹת הָאֵ֑לֶּה הִנֵּ֨ה אֲנִ֜י מֵבִ֥יא בָכֶ֛ם ר֖וּחַ וִחְיִיתֶֽם: ו וְנָתַתִּי֩ עֲלֵיכֶ֨ם גִּדִ֜ים וְהַעֲלֵתִ֧י עֲלֵיכֶ֣ם בָּשָׂ֗ר וְקָרַמְתִּ֤י עֲלֵיכֶם֙ ע֔וֹר וְנָתַתִּ֤י בָכֶם֙ ר֔וּחַ וִחְיִיתֶ֑ם וִידַעְתֶּ֖ם כִּֽי־אֲנִ֥י יְהֹוָֽה: ז וְנִבֵּ֖אתִי כַּֽאֲשֶׁ֣ר צֻוֵּ֑יתִי וַֽיְהִי־ק֤וֹל כְּהִנָּֽבְאִי֙ וְהִנֵּה־רַ֔עַשׁ וַתִּקְרְב֣וּ עֲצָמ֔וֹת עֶ֖צֶם אֶל־עַצְמֽוֹ: ח וְרָאִ֜יתִי וְהִנֵּֽה־עֲלֵיהֶ֤ם גִּדִים֙ וּבָשָׂ֣ר עָלָ֔ה וַיִּקְרַ֧ם עֲלֵיהֶ֛ם ע֖וֹר מִלְמָ֑עְלָה וְר֖וּחַ אֵ֥ין בָּהֶֽם: ט וַיֹּ֣אמֶר אֵלַ֔י הִנָּבֵ֖א אֶל־הָר֑וּחַ הִנָּבֵ֣א בֶן־אָדָ֗ם וְאָמַרְתָּ֣ אֶל־הָר֘וּחַ֒ כֹּֽה־אָמַ֣ר ׀ אֲדֹנָ֣י יֱהֹוִ֗ה מֵאַרְבַּ֤ע רוּחוֹת֙ בֹּ֣אִי הָר֔וּחַ וּפְחִ֛י בַּֽהֲרוּגִ֥ים הָאֵ֖לֶּה וְיִֽחְיֽוּ: י וְהִנַּבֵּ֨אתִי֙ כַּֽאֲשֶׁ֣ר צִוָּ֔נִי וַתָּבוֹא֩ בָהֶ֨ם הָר֜וּחַ וַיִּֽחְי֗וּ וַיַּֽעַמְדוּ֙ עַל־רַגְלֵיהֶ֔ם חַ֖יִל גָּד֥וֹל מְאֹֽד־מְאֹֽד: יא וַיֹּאמֶר֮ אֵלַי֒ בֶּן־אָדָ֔ם הָעֲצָמ֣וֹת הָאֵ֔לֶּה כָּל־בֵּ֥ית יִשְׂרָאֵ֖ל הֵ֑מָּה הִנֵּ֣ה אֹֽמְרִ֗ים יָֽבְשׁ֧וּ עַצְמוֹתֵ֛ינוּ וְאָֽבְדָ֥ה תִקְוָתֵ֖נוּ נִגְזַ֥רְנוּ לָֽנוּ: יב לָכֵן֩ הִנָּבֵ֨א וְאָֽמַרְתָּ֜ אֲלֵיהֶ֗ם כֹּֽה־אָמַר֮ אֲדֹנָ֣י יֱהֹוִה֒ הִנֵּה֩ אֲנִ֨י פֹתֵ֜חַ אֶת־קִבְרֽוֹתֵיכֶ֗ם וְהַֽעֲלֵיתִ֥י אֶתְכֶ֛ם מִקִּבְרֽוֹתֵיכֶ֖ם עַמִּ֑י וְהֵֽבֵאתִ֥י אֶתְכֶ֖ם אֶל־אַדְמַ֥ת יִשְׂרָאֵֽל: יג וִֽידַעְתֶּ֖ם כִּֽי־אֲנִ֣י יְהֹוָ֑ה בְּפִתְחִ֣י אֶת־קִבְרֽוֹתֵיכֶ֗ם וּבְהַֽעֲלוֹתִ֥י אֶתְכֶ֛ם מִקִּבְרֽוֹתֵיכֶ֖ם עַמִּֽי: יד וְנָֽתַתִּ֨י רוּחִ֤י בָכֶם֙ וִֽחְיִיתֶ֔ם וְהִנַּחְתִּ֥י אֶתְכֶ֖ם עַל־אַדְמַתְכֶ֑ם וִֽידַעְתֶּ֞ם כִּֽי־אֲנִ֧י יְהֹוָ֛ה דִּבַּ֥רְתִּי וְעָשִׂ֖יתִי נְאֻם־יְהֹוָֽה: (בקצת קהלות מוסיפים:) טו וַֽיְהִ֥י דְבַר־יְהֹוָ֖ה אֵלַ֥י לֵאמֹֽר: טז וְאַתָּ֣ה בֶן־אָדָ֗ם קַח־לְךָ֙ עֵ֣ץ אֶחָ֔ד וּכְתֹ֤ב עָלָיו֙ לִֽיהוּדָ֔ה וְלִבְנֵ֥י יִשְׂרָאֵ֖ל חֲבֵרָ֑ו (חבריו קרי) וּלְקַח֙ עֵ֣ץ אֶחָ֔ד וּכְת֣וֹב עָלָ֗יו לְיוֹסֵף֙ עֵ֣ץ אֶפְרַ֔יִם וְכָל־בֵּ֥ית יִשְׂרָאֵ֖ל חֲבֵרָֽו (חבריו קרי): יז וְקָרַ֨ב אֹתָ֜ם אֶחָ֧ד אֶל־אֶחָ֛ד לְךָ֖ לְעֵ֣ץ אֶחָ֑ד וְהָי֥וּ לַֽאֲחָדִ֖ים בְּיָדֶֽךָ:

HAFTARAH FOR THE SEVENTH DAY OF PESAḤ הפטרת שביעי של פסח

(II Samuel 22:1–51)

Torah reading: Exodus 13:17–15:26, Numbers 28:19–25. On the Sabbath, many congregations read the Song of Songs (p. 1007) prior to the Torah reading.

David's song of thanksgiving for his deliverance from his enemies parallels the song that Moses and the children of Israel sang after their deliverance at the Red Sea, which is read on the seventh day of Pesaḥ.

22:1. And David spoke to the Lord the words of this song, on the day that the Lord delivered him from the hand of all his enemies, and from the hand of Saul; 2. and he said: "The Lord is my rock and my fortress, and a rescuer to me. 3. God is my rock, under whom I take cover; my shield and the horn of my salvation, my support and my refuge; [He is] my Savior, Who saves me from violence. 4. With praise I call to the Lord, for from my enemies I shall be saved. 5. For the pains of death have encompassed me; streams of scoundrels would affright me. 6. Bands of [those that shall inherit] the nether world have surrounded me; the snares of death confronted me. 7. When I am in distress, I call upon the Lord; yea, I call upon my God; and out of His abode He hears my voice, and my cry enters His ears. 8. Then the earth shook and quaked, the [very] foundations of heaven did tremble; and they were shaken when He was angered. 9. Smoke went up in His nostrils, and fire out of His mouths did devour; coals flamed forth from Him. 10. And He bent the heavens, and He came down; and thick darkness was under His feet. 11. And He rode upon a cherub and did fly; He was seen upon the wings of the wind. 12. And He fixed darkness about Him as booths, gathering of waters, thick clouds of the skies. 13. From the brightness before Him flamed forth coals of fire. 14. The Lord thundered from heaven, and the Most High gave forth His voice. 15. And He sent out arrows, and He scattered them—lightning—and He discomfited them. 16. And the depths of the sea appeared; the foundations of the world were laid bare by the rebuke of the Lord and the blast of the breath of His nostrils. 17. He sent from on high, [and] He took me; He drew me out of many waters.

א וַיְדַבֵּר דָּוִד לַיהוָה אֶת־דִּבְרֵי הַשִּׁירָה הַזֹּאת
בְּיוֹם הִצִּיל יְהוָה אֹתוֹ מִכַּף כָּל־אֹיְבָיו וּמִכַּף
שָׁאוּל׃ ב וַיֹּאמַר יְהוָה סַלְעִי וּמְצֻדָתִי
וּמְפַלְטִי־לִי׃ ג אֱלֹהֵי צוּרִי אֶחֱסֶה־בּוֹ מָגִנִּי
וְקֶרֶן יִשְׁעִי מִשְׂגַּבִּי וּמְנוּסִי מֹשִׁעִי מֵחָמָס
תֹּשִׁעֵנִי׃ ד מְהֻלָּל אֶקְרָא יְהוָה וּמֵאֹיְבַי אִוָּשֵׁעַ׃
ה כִּי אֲפָפֻנִי מִשְׁבְּרֵי־מָוֶת נַחֲלֵי בְלִיַּעַל
יְבַעֲתֻנִי׃ ו חֶבְלֵי שְׁאוֹל סַבֻּנִי קִדְּמֻנִי מֹקְשֵׁי־
מָוֶת׃ ז בַּצַּר־לִי אֶקְרָא יְהוָה וְאֶל־אֱלֹהַי אֶקְרָא
וַיִּשְׁמַע מֵהֵיכָלוֹ קוֹלִי וְשַׁוְעָתִי בְּאָזְנָיו׃
ח וַ תִּגְעַשׁ (ויתגעש קרי) וַתִּרְעַשׁ הָאָרֶץ מוֹסְדוֹת
הַשָּׁמַיִם יִרְגָּזוּ וַיִּתְגָּעֲשׁוּ כִּי־חָרָה לוֹ׃ ט עָלָה
עָשָׁן בְּאַפּוֹ וְאֵשׁ מִפִּיו תֹּאכֵל גֶּחָלִים בָּעֲרוּ
מִמֶּנּוּ׃ י וַיֵּט שָׁמַיִם וַיֵּרַד וַעֲרָפֶל תַּחַת רַגְלָיו׃
יא וַיִּרְכַּב עַל־כְּרוּב וַיָּעֹף וַיֵּרָא עַל־כַּנְפֵי־רוּחַ׃
יב וַיָּשֶׁת חֹשֶׁךְ סְבִיבֹתָיו סֻכּוֹת חַשְׁרַת־מַיִם
עָבֵי שְׁחָקִים׃ יג מִנֹּגַהּ נֶגְדּוֹ בָּעֲרוּ גַּחֲלֵי־אֵשׁ׃
יד יַרְעֵם מִן־שָׁמַיִם יְהוָה וְעֶלְיוֹן יִתֵּן קוֹלוֹ׃
טו וַיִּשְׁלַח חִצִּים וַיְפִיצֵם בָּרָק וַיָּהֹמם (ויהם
קרי)׃ טז וַיֵּרָאוּ אֲפִקֵי יָם יִגָּלוּ מֹסְדוֹת תֵּבֵל
בְּגַעֲרַת יְהוָה מִנִּשְׁמַת רוּחַ אַפּוֹ׃ יז יִשְׁלַח
מִמָּרוֹם יִקָּחֵנִי יַמְשֵׁנִי מִמַּיִם רַבִּים׃ יח יַצִּילֵנִי

18. He delivered me from my mighty enemy; from them that hated me; for they were too powerful for me. 19. They confronted me on the day of my calamity but the Lord was a support to me, 20. and He brought me forth into a wide place; He delivered me because He took delight in me. 21. The Lord rewarded me according to my righteousness; according to the cleanness of my hands He recompensed me. 22. For I have kept the ways of the Lord and have not wickedly departed from [the commandments of] my God. 23. For all His ordinances were before me, and [as for] His statutes, I did not depart from it. 24. And I was single-hearted toward Him, and I kept myself from my iniquity. 25. And the Lord has recompensed me according to my righteousness, according to my cleanness before His eyes. 26. With a kind one, You show Yourself kind; with an upright man, You show Yourself upright. 27. With a pure one, You show Yourself pure; but with a perverse one, You deal crookedly. 28. And the humble people You do deliver; but Your eyes are upon the haughty [in order] to humble them. 29. For You are my lamp, O Lord, and the Lord does light my darkness. 30. For by You I run upon a troop; by my God I scale a wall. 31. [He is] the God Whose way is perfect; the word of the Lord is tried; He is a shield unto all them that trust in him. 32. For who is God, save the Lord? And who is a rock, save our God? 33. God is He Who has fortified me with strength, and He looses perfectly my path. 34. He makes my feet like hinds, and sets me upon my high places. 35. He trains my hand for war, so that my arms do bend a brass bow. 36. And You have given me the shield of Your salvation, and You have increased Your modesty for me. 37. You have enlarged my step[s] beneath me, and my ankles have not slipped. 38. I have pursued my enemies and have destroyed them, never turning back until they were consumed. 39. And I have consumed them, and I have crushed them that they cannot rise; yea, they are fallen under my feet. 40. For You have girded me with strength for the battle; You have subdued under me those that rose up against me. 41. And of my enemies, You have given me the back of

מֵאֹיְבִי עָז מִשֹּׂנְאַי כִּי אָמְצוּ מִמֶּנִּי: יט יְקַדְּמֻנִי בְיוֹם אֵידִי וַיְהִי יְהֹוָה מִשְׁעָן לִי: כ וַיֹּצֵא לַמֶּרְחָב אֹתִי יְחַלְּצֵנִי כִּי־חָפֵץ בִּי: כא יִגְמְלֵנִי יְהֹוָה כְּצִדְקָתִי כְּבֹר יָדַי יָשִׁיב לִי: כב כִּי שָׁמַרְתִּי דַּרְכֵי יְהֹוָה וְלֹא רָשַׁעְתִּי מֵאֱלֹהָי: כג כִּי כָל־מִשְׁפָּטָו (משפטיו קרי) לְנֶגְדִּי וְחֻקֹּתָיו לֹא־אָסוּר מִמֶּנָּה: כד וָאֶהְיֶה תָמִים לוֹ וָאֶשְׁתַּמְּרָה מֵעֲוֹנִי: כה וַיָּשֶׁב יְהֹוָה לִי כְּצִדְקָתִי כְּבֹרִי לְנֶגֶד עֵינָיו: כו עִם־חָסִיד תִּתְחַסָּד עִם־גִּבּוֹר תָּמִים תִּתַּמָּם: כז עִם־נָבָר תִּתָּבָר וְעִם־עִקֵּשׁ תִּתַּפָּל: כח וְאֶת־עַם עָנִי תּוֹשִׁיעַ וְעֵינֶיךָ עַל־רָמִים תַּשְׁפִּיל: כט כִּי־אַתָּה נֵירִי יְהֹוָה וַיהֹוָה יַגִּיהַּ חָשְׁכִּי: ל כִּי בְכָה אָרוּץ גְּדוּד בֵּאלֹהַי אֲדַלֶּג־שׁוּר: לא הָאֵל תָּמִים דַּרְכּוֹ אִמְרַת יְהֹוָה צְרוּפָה מָגֵן הוּא לְכֹל הַחֹסִים בּוֹ: לב כִּי מִי־אֵל מִבַּלְעֲדֵי יְהֹוָה וּמִי צוּר מִבַּלְעֲדֵי אֱלֹהֵינוּ: לג הָאֵל מָעוּזִּי חָיִל וַיַּתֵּר תָּמִים דַּרְכּוֹ (דרכי קרי): לד מְשַׁוֶּה רַגְלָיו (רגלי קרי) כָּאַיָּלוֹת וְעַל־בָּמֹתַי יַעֲמִידֵנִי: לה מְלַמֵּד יָדַי לַמִּלְחָמָה וְנִחַת קֶשֶׁת־נְחוּשָׁה זְרֹעֹתָי: לו וַתִּתֶּן־לִי מָגֵן יִשְׁעֶךָ וַעֲנֹתְךָ תַּרְבֵּנִי: לז תַּרְחִיב צַעֲדִי תַּחְתֵּנִי וְלֹא מָעֲדוּ קַרְסֻלָּי: לח אֶרְדְּפָה אֹיְבַי וָאַשְׁמִידֵם וְלֹא אָשׁוּב עַד־כַּלּוֹתָם: לט וָאֲכַלֵּם וָאֶמְחָצֵם וְלֹא יְקוּמוּן וַיִּפְּלוּ תַּחַת רַגְלָי: מ וַתַּזְרֵנִי חַיִל לַמִּלְחָמָה תַּכְרִיעַ קָמַי תַּחְתֵּנִי: מא וְאֹיְבַי תַּתָּה לִּי עֹרֶף מְשַׂנְאַי וָאַצְמִיתֵם: מב יִשְׁעוּ וְאֵין

מֹשִׁיעַ אֶל־יְהוָה וְלֹא עָנָם׃ מג וְאֶשְׁחָקֵם
כַּעֲפַר־אָרֶץ כְּטִיט־חוּצוֹת אֲדִקֵּם אֶרְקָעֵם׃
מד וַתְּפַלְּטֵנִי מֵרִיבֵי עַמִּי תִּשְׁמְרֵנִי לְרֹאשׁ גּוֹיִם
עַם לֹא־יָדַעְתִּי יַעַבְדֻנִי׃ מה בְּנֵי נֵכָר יִתְכַּחֲשׁוּ־
לִי לִשְׁמוֹעַ אֹזֶן יִשָּׁמְעוּ לִי׃ מו בְּנֵי נֵכָר יִבֹּלוּ
וְיַחְגְּרוּ מִמִּסְגְּרוֹתָם׃ מז חַי־יְהוָה וּבָרוּךְ צוּרִי
וְיָרֻם אֱלֹהֵי צוּר יִשְׁעִי׃ מח הָאֵל הַנֹּתֵן נְקָמֹת לִי
וּמוֹרִיד עַמִּים תַּחְתֵּנִי׃ מט וּמוֹצִיאִי מֵאֹיְבָי
וּמִקָּמַי תְּרוֹמְמֵנִי מֵאִישׁ חֲמָסִים תַּצִּילֵנִי׃
נ עַל־כֵּן אוֹדְךָ יְהוָה בַּגּוֹיִם וּלְשִׁמְךָ אֲזַמֵּר׃
נא מִגְדִּיל (מגדול קרי) יְשׁוּעוֹת מַלְכּוֹ וְעֹשֶׂה־חֶסֶד
לִמְשִׁיחוֹ לְדָוִד וּלְזַרְעוֹ עַד־עוֹלָם׃

their necks; them that hate me, that I may cut them off. 42. They looked about, but there was no one to save them; [even] to the Lord, but He answered them not. 43. Then I ground them as the dust of the earth, as the mud of the streets I did tread upon them, I did stamp them down. 44. And You have allowed me to escape from the contenders amongst my people; You shall keep me as head of nations; a people whom I have not known serve me. 45. Strangers lie to me; as soon as their ears hear, they obey me. 46. The strangers will wilt and become lame from their bondage. 47. The Lord lives, and blessed be my rock; and exalted be the God [Who is] my rock of salvation, 48. the God Who takes vengeance for me and brings down peoples under me. 49. and Who brings me forth from my enemies; and above those that rise against me, You have lifted me; from the violent man You deliver me. 50. Therefore, I will give thanks to You, O Lord, among the nations, and to Your name I will sing praises. 51. He gives great salvation to His king, and He performs kindness to His anointed—to David and to his seed—forevermore.

HAFTARAH FOR THE EIGHTH DAY OF PESAḤ הפטרת אחרון של פסח

(Isaiah 10:32–12:6)

Torah reading: Deuteronomy 15:19–16:17. On the Sabbath we read: Deuteronomy 14:22–16:17.

Additional Torah reading: Numbers 28:19–25

On the Sabbath, many congregations read the Song of Songs (p. 1007) prior to the Torah reading.

According to tradition, the fall of Sennacherib, with which this selection is concerned, occurred on Pesaḥ. This selection also makes reference to the exodus from Egypt.

לב עוֹד הַיּוֹם בְּנֹב לַעֲמֹד יְנֹפֵף יָדוֹ הַר בֵּית־
(בת קרי) צִיּוֹן גִּבְעַת יְרוּשָׁלִָם׃ לג הִנֵּה הָאָדוֹן
יְהוָה צְבָאוֹת מְסָעֵף פֻּארָה בְּמַעֲרָצָה וְרָמֵי
הַקּוֹמָה גְּדֻעִים וְהַגְּבֹהִים יִשְׁפָּלוּ׃ לד וְנִקַּף
סִבְכֵי הַיַּעַר בַּבַּרְזֶל וְהַלְּבָנוֹן בְּאַדִּיר יִפּוֹל׃
א וְיָצָא חֹטֶר מִגֵּזַע יִשָׁי וְנֵצֶר מִשָּׁרָשָׁיו יִפְרֶה׃

10:32. Still today, [he intends] to stand in Nob; he waves his hand toward the mount of the daughter of Zion, the hill of Jerusalem. 33. Behold the Master, the Lord of Hosts, lops off the branches with a saw, and those of lofty height are hewn down, and the tall ones shall be humbled. 34. And the thickets of the forests shall be cut off with iron, and the Lebanon shall fall through a mighty one. 11:1. And a shoot shall spring forth from the stem of Jesse, and a twig shall sprout from his roots. 2. And the spirit of the Lord shall rest upon him—a spirit of wisdom and understanding, a spirit of counsel and heroism, a spirit of knowledge and fear of the Lord. 3. And he shall be animated by the fear of the Lord, and neither with the sight of his eyes shall he judge, nor with the hearing of his ears shall he chastise. 4. And he shall judge the poor justly, and he shall chastise with equity the humble of the earth, and he shall smite the earth with the rod of his mouth, and with the breath of his lips he shall put the wicked to death. 5. And righteousness shall be the girdle of his loins and faith the girdle of his loins. 6. And a wolf shall live with a lamb, and a leopard shall lie with a kid; and a calf and a lion cub and a fatling [shall lie] together, and a small child shall lead them. 7. And a cow and a bear shall graze together, their children shall lie; and a lion, like cattle, shall eat straw. 8. And an infant shall play over the hole of an old snake and over the eyeball of an adder, a weaned child shall stretch forth his hand. 9. They shall neither harm nor destroy on all My holy mount, for the land shall be full of knowledge of the Lord, as water covers the sea bed. 10. And it shall come to pass on that day, that the root of Jesse, which stands as a banner for peoples, to him shall the nations inquire, and his peace shall be [with] honor. 11. And it shall come to pass that on that day, the Lord shall continue to apply His hand a second time to acquire the rest of His people, that will remain from Assyria and from Egypt and from Pathros and from Cush and from Elam and from Sumeria and from Hamath and from the islands of the sea. 12. And He shall raise a banner to the nations, and He shall gather the lost of Israel, and the scattered ones of Judah He shall gather from the four corners of the earth. 13. And the envy of Ephraim shall cease, and the adversaries of Judah shall be cut off; Ephraim shall not envy Judah, nor shall Judah vex Ephraim. 14. And they shall fly of one accord against the Philistines in the west; together they shall plunder the children of the east; upon Edom and Moab shall they stretch forth their hand, and the children of Ammon

ב וְנָחָה עָלָיו רוּחַ יְהֹוָה רוּחַ חָכְמָה וּבִינָה רוּחַ עֵצָה וּגְבוּרָה רוּחַ דַּעַת וְיִרְאַת יְהֹוָה: ג וַהֲרִיחוֹ בְּיִרְאַת יְהֹוָה וְלֹא־לְמַרְאֵה עֵינָיו יִשְׁפּוֹט וְלֹא־לְמִשְׁמַע אָזְנָיו יוֹכִיחַ: ד וְשָׁפַט בְּצֶדֶק דַּלִּים וְהוֹכִיחַ בְּמִישׁוֹר לְעַנְוֵי־אָרֶץ וְהִכָּה־אֶרֶץ בְּשֵׁבֶט פִּיו וּבְרוּחַ שְׂפָתָיו יָמִית רָשָׁע: ה וְהָיָה צֶדֶק אֵזוֹר מָתְנָיו וְהָאֱמוּנָה אֵזוֹר חֲלָצָיו: ו וְגָר זְאֵב עִם־כֶּבֶשׂ וְנָמֵר עִם־גְּדִי יִרְבָּץ וְעֵגֶל וּכְפִיר וּמְרִיא יַחְדָּו וְנַעַר קָטֹן נֹהֵג בָּם: ז וּפָרָה וָדֹב תִּרְעֶינָה יַחְדָּו יִרְבְּצוּ יַלְדֵיהֶן וְאַרְיֵה כַּבָּקָר יֹאכַל־תֶּבֶן: ח וְשִׁעֲשַׁע יוֹנֵק עַל־חֻר פָּתֶן וְעַל מְאוּרַת צִפְעוֹנִי גָּמוּל יָדוֹ הָדָה: ט לֹא־יָרֵעוּ וְלֹא־יַשְׁחִיתוּ בְּכָל־הַר קָדְשִׁי כִּי־מָלְאָה הָאָרֶץ דֵּעָה אֶת־יְהֹוָה כַּמַּיִם לַיָּם מְכַסִּים: י וְהָיָה בַּיּוֹם הַהוּא שֹׁרֶשׁ יִשַׁי אֲשֶׁר עֹמֵד לְנֵס עַמִּים אֵלָיו גּוֹיִם יִדְרֹשׁוּ וְהָיְתָה מְנֻחָתוֹ כָּבוֹד: יא וְהָיָה | בַּיּוֹם הַהוּא יוֹסִיף אֲדֹנָי | שֵׁנִית יָדוֹ לִקְנוֹת אֶת־שְׁאָר עַמּוֹ אֲשֶׁר יִשָּׁאֵר מֵאַשּׁוּר וּמִמִּצְרַיִם וּמִפַּתְרוֹס וּמִכּוּשׁ וּמֵעֵילָם וּמִשִּׁנְעָר וּמֵחֲמָת וּמֵאִיֵּי הַיָּם: יב וְנָשָׂא נֵס לַגּוֹיִם וְאָסַף נִדְחֵי יִשְׂרָאֵל וּנְפֻצוֹת יְהוּדָה יְקַבֵּץ מֵאַרְבַּע כַּנְפוֹת הָאָרֶץ: יג וְסָרָה קִנְאַת אֶפְרַיִם וְצֹרְרֵי יְהוּדָה יִכָּרֵתוּ אֶפְרַיִם לֹא־יְקַנֵּא אֶת־יְהוּדָה וִיהוּדָה לֹא־יָצֹר אֶת־אֶפְרָיִם: יד וְעָפוּ בְכָתֵף פְּלִשְׁתִּים יָמָּה יַחְדָּו יָבֹזּוּ אֶת־בְּנֵי־קֶדֶם אֱדוֹם וּמוֹאָב מִשְׁלוֹחַ

shall obey them. 15. And the Lord shall dry up the tongue of the Egyptian Sea, and He shall lift His hand over the river with the strength of His wind, and He shall beat it into seven streams, and He shall lead [the exiles] with shoes. 16. And there shall be a highway for the remnant of His people who remain from Assyria, as there was for Israel on the day they went up from the land of Egypt. 12:1. And you shall say on that day, "I will thank You, O Lord, for You were wroth with me; may Your wrath turn away and may You comfort me. 2. Here is the God of my salvation, I shall trust and not fear; for the strength and praise of the Eternal the Lord was my salvation." 3. And you shall draw water with joy from the fountains of the salvation. 4. And you shall say on that day, "Thank the Lord, call in His Name, publicize His deeds among the peoples; keep it in remembrance, for His Name is exalted. 5. Sing to the Lord for He has performed mighty deeds; this is known throughout the land. 6. Shout and praise, O dwellers of Zion, for great in your midst is the Holy One of Israel.

יָדָם וּבְנֵי עַמּוֹן מִשְׁמַעְתָּם: טו וְהֶחֱרִים יְהֹוָה אֵת לְשׁוֹן יָם־מִצְרַיִם וְהֵנִיף יָדוֹ עַל־הַנָּהָר בַּעְיָם רוּחוֹ וְהִכָּהוּ לְשִׁבְעָה נְחָלִים וְהִדְרִיךְ בַּנְּעָלִים: טז וְהָיְתָה מְסִלָּה לִשְׁאָר עַמּוֹ אֲשֶׁר יִשָּׁאֵר מֵאַשּׁוּר כַּאֲשֶׁר הָיְתָה לְיִשְׂרָאֵל בְּיוֹם עֲלֹתוֹ מֵאֶרֶץ מִצְרָיִם: א וְאָמַרְתָּ בַּיּוֹם הַהוּא אוֹדְךָ יְהֹוָה כִּי אָנַפְתָּ בִּי יָשֹׁב אַפְּךָ וּתְנַחֲמֵנִי: ב הִנֵּה אֵל יְשׁוּעָתִי אֶבְטַח וְלֹא אֶפְחָד כִּי־עָזִּי וְזִמְרָת יָהּ יְהֹוָה וַיְהִי־לִי לִישׁוּעָה: ג וּשְׁאַבְתֶּם־מַיִם בְּשָׂשׂוֹן מִמַּעַיְנֵי הַיְשׁוּעָה: ד וַאֲמַרְתֶּם בַּיּוֹם הַהוּא הוֹדוּ לַיהֹוָה קִרְאוּ בִשְׁמוֹ הוֹדִיעוּ בָעַמִּים עֲלִילֹתָיו הַזְכִּירוּ כִּי נִשְׂגָּב שְׁמוֹ: ה זַמְּרוּ יְהֹוָה כִּי גֵאוּת עָשָׂה מְיֻדַּעַת (מוֹדַעַת קרי) זֹאת בְּכָל־הָאָרֶץ: ו צַהֲלִי וָרֹנִּי יוֹשֶׁבֶת צִיּוֹן כִּי־גָדוֹל בְּקִרְבֵּךְ קְדוֹשׁ יִשְׂרָאֵל:

HAFTARAH FOR THE FIRST DAY OF SHAVUOTH הפטרת יום א' דשבועות
(Ezekiel 1 and 3:12)
Torah reading: Exodus 19–20, Numbers 28:26–31

This is Ezekiel's vision of the Divine Chariot. It is most appropriate for reading on Shavuoth, for, according to tradition, all of Israel was granted the gift of prophecy on the day of the Giving of the Law. They were permitted to gaze into the heavens and perceive the camps of the angels. This vision is not meant to be interpreted literally, however. It has been variously interpreted by the mystics of the Kabbalah.

1:1. Now it came to pass in the thirtieth year, in the fourth month, on the fifth of the month, as I was among the exiles by the river Chebar, the heavens opened, and I saw visions of God. 2. On the fifth of the month, that is the fifth year of King Jehoiachin's exile. 3. The word of the Lord came to Ezekiel the son of Buzi, the priest, in the land of the Chaldeans, by the river Chebar, and the hand of the Lord came upon him there. 4. And I saw, and behold, a tempest was coming from the north, a huge cloud and a flaming fire, with a brightness around

א וַיְהִי | בִּשְׁלֹשִׁים שָׁנָה בָּרְבִיעִי בַּחֲמִשָּׁה לַחֹדֶשׁ וַאֲנִי בְתוֹךְ־הַגּוֹלָה עַל־נְהַר־כְּבָר נִפְתְּחוּ הַשָּׁמַיִם וָאֶרְאֶה מַרְאוֹת אֱלֹהִים: ב בַּחֲמִשָּׁה לַחֹדֶשׁ הִיא הַשָּׁנָה הַחֲמִישִׁית לְגָלוּת הַמֶּלֶךְ יוֹיָכִין: ג הָיֹה הָיָה דְבַר־יְהֹוָה אֶל־יְחֶזְקֵאל בֶּן־בּוּזִי הַכֹּהֵן בְּאֶרֶץ כַּשְׂדִּים עַל־נְהַר־כְּבָר וַתְּהִי עָלָיו שָׁם יַד־יְהֹוָה: ד וָאֵרֶא וְהִנֵּה רוּחַ סְעָרָה בָּאָה מִן־הַצָּפוֹן עָנָן גָּדוֹל וְאֵשׁ מִתְלַקַּחַת וְנֹגַהּ לוֹ סָבִיב וּמִתּוֹכָהּ

כְּעֵ֥ין הַחַשְׁמַ֖ל מִתּ֥וֹךְ הָאֵֽשׁ׃ ה וּמִ֨תּוֹכָ֔הּ דְּמ֖וּת
אַרְבַּ֣ע חַיּ֑וֹת וְזֶה֙ מַרְאֵיהֶ֔ן דְּמ֥וּת אָדָ֖ם לָהֵֽנָּה׃
ו וְאַרְבָּעָ֥ה פָנִ֖ים לְאֶחָ֑ת וְאַרְבַּ֥ע כְּנָפַ֖יִם לְאַחַ֥ת
לָהֶֽם׃ ז וְרַגְלֵיהֶ֖ם רֶ֣גֶל יְשָׁרָ֑ה וְכַ֣ף רַגְלֵיהֶ֗ם כְּכַף֙
רֶ֣גֶל עֵ֔גֶל וְנֹ֣צְצִ֔ים כְּעֵ֖ין נְחֹ֥שֶׁת קָלָֽל׃ ח וִידֵ֣ו (וידי
קרי) אָדָ֗ם מִתַּ֙חַת֙ כַּנְפֵיהֶ֔ם עַ֖ל אַרְבַּ֣עַת רִבְעֵיהֶ֑ם
וּפְנֵיהֶ֥ם וְכַנְפֵיהֶ֖ם לְאַרְבַּעְתָּֽם׃ ט חֹֽבְרֹ֛ת אִשָּׁ֥ה
אֶל־אֲחוֹתָ֖הּ כַּנְפֵיהֶ֑ם לֹֽא־יִסַּ֣בּוּ בְלֶכְתָּ֔ן אִ֛ישׁ
אֶל־עֵ֥בֶר פָּנָ֖יו יֵלֵֽכוּ׃ י וּדְמ֣וּת פְּנֵיהֶם֮ פְּנֵ֣י אָדָם֒
וּפְנֵ֨י אַרְיֵ֤ה אֶל־הַיָּמִין֙ לְאַרְבַּעְתָּ֔ם וּפְנֵי־שׁ֥וֹר
מֵהַשְּׂמֹ֖אול לְאַרְבַּעְתָּ֑ן וּפְנֵי־נֶ֖שֶׁר לְאַרְבַּעְתָּֽן׃
יא וּפְנֵיהֶ֕ם וְכַנְפֵיהֶ֥ם פְּרֻד֖וֹת מִלְמָ֑עְלָה לְאִ֗ישׁ
שְׁתַּ֙יִם֙ חֹבְר֣וֹת אִ֔ישׁ וּשְׁתַּ֣יִם מְכַסּ֔וֹת אֵ֖ת
גְּוִיֹתֵיהֶֽנָה׃ יב וְאִ֛ישׁ אֶל־עֵ֥בֶר פָּנָ֖יו יֵלֵ֑כוּ אֶ֣ל
אֲשֶׁ֣ר יִֽהְיֶה־שָׁ֨מָּה הָר֤וּחַ לָלֶ֙כֶת֙ יֵלֵ֔כוּ לֹ֥א יִסַּ֖בּוּ
בְּלֶכְתָּֽן׃ יג וּדְמ֨וּת הַחַיּ֜וֹת מַרְאֵיהֶ֣ם כְּגַחֲלֵי־אֵ֗שׁ
בֹּֽעֲרוֹת֙ כְּמַרְאֵ֣ה הַלַּפִּדִ֔ים הִ֕יא מִתְהַלֶּ֖כֶת בֵּ֣ין
הַחַיּ֑וֹת וְנֹ֣גַהּ לָאֵ֔שׁ וּמִן־הָאֵ֖שׁ יוֹצֵ֥א בָרָֽק׃
יד וְהַחַיּ֖וֹת רָצ֣וֹא וָשׁ֑וֹב כְּמַרְאֵ֖ה הַבָּזָֽק׃
טו וָאֵ֖רֶא הַחַיּ֑וֹת וְהִנֵּה֩ אוֹפַ֨ן אֶחָ֥ד בָּאָ֛רֶץ אֵ֥צֶל
הַחַיּ֖וֹת לְאַרְבַּ֥עַת פָּנָֽיו׃ טז מַרְאֵ֨ה הָאוֹפַנִּ֤ים
וּמַעֲשֵׂיהֶם֙ כְּעֵ֣ין תַּרְשִׁ֔ישׁ וּדְמ֥וּת אֶחָ֖ד
לְאַרְבַּעְתָּ֑ן וּמַרְאֵיהֶם֙ וּמַ֣עֲשֵׂיהֶ֔ם כַּאֲשֶׁ֛ר יִהְיֶ֥ה
הָאוֹפַ֖ן בְּת֥וֹךְ הָאוֹפָֽן׃ יז עַל־אַרְבַּ֣עַת רִבְעֵיהֶ֔ן
בְּלֶכְתָּ֖ם יֵלֵ֑כוּ לֹ֥א יִסַּ֖בּוּ בְּלֶכְתָּֽן׃ יח וְגַ֨בֵּיהֶ֔ן
וְגֹ֥בַהּ לָהֶ֖ם וְיִרְאָ֣ה לָהֶ֑ם וְגַבֹּתָ֗ם מְלֵאֹ֥ת עֵינַ֛יִם
סָבִ֖יב לְאַרְבַּעְתָּֽן׃ יט וּבְלֶ֙כֶת֙ הַחַיּ֔וֹת יֵלְכ֥וּ
הָאוֹפַנִּ֖ים אֶצְלָ֑ם וּבְהִנָּשֵׂ֤א הַחַיּוֹת֙ מֵעַ֣ל הָאָ֔רֶץ

it, and from its midst, it was like the color of
the *hashmal* from the midst of the fire.
5. And from its midst was the likeness of
four living creatures, and this is their
appearance, they had the likeness of a man.
6. And each one had four faces, and each
one had four wings. 7. And their feet were
straight feet, and the soles of their feet
were like a calf's hoof, and they sparkled
like the color of burnished copper. 8. And
human hands were beneath their wings on
their four sides, and their faces and their
wings were the same with all four of them.
9. Their wings joined one to the other; they
did not turn when they walked; each one
went to the direction of his face. 10. And
the likeness of their faces was the face of a
man, and the four of them had the face of
a lion to their right, and the four of them
had the face of an ox to their left, and the
four of them had the face of an eagle.
11. And so were their faces, and their wings
were extended upward; each one had two
wings, joined to each other, and two covering their bodies. 12. Now each one would
go toward the direction of his face; to the
place where there would be a will to
go, they would go; they would not turn
when they would go. 13. And the likeness
of the living creatures, their appearance
was like fiery coals, burning like the appearance of firebrands; that was going among
the living creatures; and the fire had brightness, and from the fire came forth lightning.
14. And the living creatures would run and
return, like the appearance of the lightning.
15. And I saw the living creatures, and
behold one wheel on the ground beside the
living creatures for its four faces. 16. The
appearance of the wheels and their work
was like the appearance of crystal, and the
four of them had one likeness, and their
appearance and their works were as a wheel
would be within a wheel. 17. When they
went, they went toward their four sides;
they did not turn when they went. 18. And
they had backs, and they were very high,
and they were dreadful, and their backs
were full of eyes round about to the four of
them. 19. And when the living creatures
would go, the wheels would go beside them;
and when the living creatures would lift
themselves off the earth, the wheels would

יִנָּשְׂאוּ הָאוֹפַנִּים: כ עַל אֲשֶׁר יִהְיֶה־שָּׁם הָרוּחַ
לָלֶכֶת יֵלֵכוּ שָׁמָּה הָרוּחַ לָלֶכֶת וְהָאוֹפַנִּים
יִנָּשְׂאוּ לְעֻמָּתָם כִּי רוּחַ הַחַיָּה בָּאוֹפַנִּים:
כא בְּלֶכְתָּם יֵלֵכוּ וּבְעָמְדָם יַעֲמֹדוּ וּבְהִנָּשְׂאָם
מֵעַל הָאָרֶץ יִנָּשְׂאוּ הָאוֹפַנִּים לְעֻמָּתָם כִּי רוּחַ
הַחַיָּה בָּאוֹפַנִּים: כב וּדְמוּת עַל־רָאשֵׁי הַחַיָּה
רָקִיעַ כְּעֵין הַקֶּרַח הַנּוֹרָא נָטוּי עַל־רָאשֵׁיהֶם
מִלְמָעְלָה: כג וְתַחַת הָרָקִיעַ כַּנְפֵיהֶם יְשָׁרוֹת
אִשָּׁה אֶל־אֲחוֹתָהּ לְאִישׁ שְׁתַּיִם מְכַסּוֹת לָהֵנָּה
וּלְאִישׁ שְׁתַּיִם מְכַסּוֹת לָהֵנָּה אֵת גְּוִיֹּתֵיהֶם:
כד וָאֶשְׁמַע אֶת־קוֹל כַּנְפֵיהֶם כְּקוֹל מַיִם רַבִּים
כְּקוֹל־שַׁדַּי בְּלֶכְתָּם קוֹל הֲמֻלָּה כְּקוֹל מַחֲנֶה
בְּעָמְדָם תְּרַפֶּינָה כַנְפֵיהֶן: כה וַיְהִי־קוֹל מֵעַל
לָרָקִיעַ אֲשֶׁר עַל־רֹאשָׁם בְּעָמְדָם תְּרַפֶּינָה
כַנְפֵיהֶן: כו וּמִמַּעַל לָרָקִיעַ אֲשֶׁר עַל־רֹאשָׁם
כְּמַרְאֵה אֶבֶן־סַפִּיר דְּמוּת כִּסֵּא וְעַל דְּמוּת
הַכִּסֵּא דְּמוּת כְּמַרְאֵה אָדָם עָלָיו מִלְמָעְלָה:
כז וָאֵרֶא | כְּעֵין חַשְׁמַל כְּמַרְאֵה־אֵשׁ בֵּית־לָהּ
סָבִיב מִמַּרְאֵה מָתְנָיו וּלְמָעְלָה וּמִמַּרְאֵה
מָתְנָיו וּלְמַטָּה רָאִיתִי כְּמַרְאֵה־אֵשׁ וְנֹגַהּ לוֹ
סָבִיב: כח כְּמַרְאֵה הַקֶּשֶׁת אֲשֶׁר יִהְיֶה בֶעָנָן
בְּיוֹם הַגֶּשֶׁם כֵּן מַרְאֵה הַנֹּגַהּ סָבִיב הוּא מַרְאֵה
דְּמוּת כְּבוֹד־יְהֹוָה וָאֶרְאֶה וָאֶפֹּל עַל־פָּנַי
וָאֶשְׁמַע קוֹל מְדַבֵּר: יב וַתִּשָּׂאֵנִי רוּחַ וָאֶשְׁמַע
אַחֲרַי קוֹל רַעַשׁ גָּדוֹל בָּרוּךְ כְּבוֹד־יְהֹוָה
מִמְּקוֹמוֹ:

lift themselves. 20. Wherever there was a will to go, they would go; there was the will to go, and the wheels would lift themselves opposite them, for the will of the living creature was in the wheels. 21. When they [the living creatures] would go, they [the wheels] would go, and when they would stand, they would stand, and when they would lift themselves up from the ground, the wheels would lift themselves opposite them, for the will of the living creature is in the wheels. 22. And there was a likeness over the heads of the living creatures, of an expanse, like the color of the frightful ice, inclined over their heads above. 23. And below the expanse, their wings were straight, one towards the other, this one of them had two that covered, and that one of them had two that covered, their bodies. 24. And I heard the sound of their wings, like the sound of many waters, like the sound of the Almighty, when they went, the sound of stirring, like the sound of a camp; when they would stand, they would let down their wings. 25. And there was a sound above the expanse that was over their heads; when they stood still, they would let down their wings. 26. And above the expanse that was over their heads, like the appearance of a sapphire stone, was the likeness of a throne, and on the likeness of the throne, was a likeness like the appearance of a man upon it above. 27. And I saw like the color of *hashmal* like the appearance of fire within it round about, from the appearance of his loins and above, and from the appearance of his loins and below, I saw [a thing] like the appearance of fire, and it had a brightness round about. 28. Like the appearance of the rainbow that is in the cloud on a rainy day, so was the appearance of the brightness around; that is the appearance of the likeness of the glory of the Lord, and when I saw, I fell on my face, and I heard a voice speaking. 3:12. And a wind lifted me up, and heard behind me the sound of a great noise, "Blessed is the glory of the Lord from His place."

HAFTARAH FOR THE SECOND DAY OF SHAVUOTH הפטרת יום ב׳ דשבועות

(Habakkuk 2:20–3:19)

Torah reading: Deuteronomy 15:19–16:17; if the second day of Shavuoth falls on a Sabbath: Deuteronomy 14:22–16:17.

Additional reading: Numbers 28:26–31

Many congregations read the Book of Ruth (p. 1017) prior to the Torah reading.

In this selection, the prophet alludes to the giving of the Torah.

כ וַיהוָה בְּהֵיכַל קָדְשׁוֹ הַס מִפָּנָיו כָּל־הָאָרֶץ:

(ברוב קהלות אשכנז ואיטליא מתחילין כאן:) א תְּפִלָּה

לַחֲבַקּוּק הַנָּבִיא עַל שִׁגְיֹנוֹת:

2:20. But the Lord is in His Holy Temple; let all the world be silent before Him. (*Most congregations following the German and Italian rituals commence here.*) 3:1. A prayer of Habakkuk the prophet concerning the errors.

At this point, many congregations recite the following hymn, which was originally composed as an **introduction** *to the Aramaic translation of the Haftarah:*

(בהרבה קהלות מוסיפים:)

יְצִיב פִּתְגָּם, לְאָת וּדְגָם, בְּרִבּוֹ רִבְבָן עִי רִין:

This word is true, for Him Who is a sign and a signal among the myriads of angels.

עֲנֵי אֲנָא, בְּמִנְיָנָא, דְפָסְלִין, אַרְבְּעָה טוּ רִין:

I proclaim His praise among the number of scholars who hew four mountains (alluding to the four orders of the Mishnah that have Gemara).

קֳדָמוֹהִי, לְגוֹ מוֹהִי, נְגִיד וְנָפִיק, נְהַר דְּנוּ רִין:

בְּטוּר תַּלְגָּא, נְהוֹר שְׁרַגָּא, וְזִיקִין דְּנוּר וּבָעוּ רִין:

Before Him, into the water, a river of fire flows in and out. On a mountain of snow shines a lamp, and sparks of fire and flames are there.

בְּרָא וּסְכָא, מַה בַּחֲשׁוֹכָא, וְעִמֵּהּ שַׁרְיָן נְהוֹ רִין:

He created and views what is in the darkness, for light dwells with Him.

רְחִיקִין צְפָא, בְּלָא שִׁטְפָא, וְגַלְיָן לֵהּ דְּמִטַּמְ רִין:

He sees distant things without hindrance, and the hidden things are revealed to Him.

בְּעֵית מִנֵּיהּ, יָת הוּרְמָנֵהּ, וּבַתְרוֹהִי עֲדֵי גוּבְ רִין:

יָדְעֵי הִלְכְתָא, וּמַתְנִיתָא, וְתוֹסֶפְתָּא סִפְרָא וְסִפְ רִין:

I ask of Him His permission, and after Him, that of men, well versed in law, in the Mishnah, the Tosefta, Sifra, and Sifrei.

מֶלֶךְ חַיָּא, לְעָלְמַיָּא, יְמַגֵּן עָם לְהוֹן מְשַׁחֲ רִין:

May the King Who lives forever save the people who engage therein.

אֲמִיר עֲלֵיהוֹן, כְּחָלָא יְהוֹן, וְלָא יִתְמְנוּן הֵיךְ עַפְרִין:

Of whom it is said that they shall be numerous as dust.

יַחֲוְרוּן כְּעָן, לְהוֹן בִּקְעָן, יְטוּפוּן נַעֲוֹהִי חַמְ רִין:

May their valleys be white with flocks of sheep, and may their vats flow with wine.

רְעוּתְהוֹן הַב, וְאַפֵּיהוֹן צְהַב, יְנַהֲרוּן כִּנְהַר צַפְ רִין:

Grant their desires and make their faces shine; may they shine like the light of dawn.

לִי הַב תְּקוֹף, וְעֵינָךְ זְקוֹף, חֲזֵי עָרָךְ דְּבָךְ כַּפְ רִין:

Grant me strength, and lift Your eyes to see Your foes who deny You.

And let them be as straw inside a brick; like stones let them be dumb in their shame.

Jonathan, a meek man, let us bestow thanks upon him.

2. O Lord! When I heard tidings of You, then I feared. O Lord! Your work, in the midst of the years; revive it, in the midst of the years, make it known; in wrath, remember compassion. 3. God came from Teman, and the forever Holy One from Mt. Paran; His glory covered the heavens, and His praise filled the earth. 4. And a brightness was like the light; rays of light came to them from His hand, and there was the hiding of His power. 5. Pestilence went before Him, and fiery angels went forth at His feet. 6. He stood and meted out justice to the world; He saw and scattered nations, and the everlasting mountains were shattered; the everlasting hills were humbled, the proceedings of the world are His. 7. Because of the iniquity, I saw the tents of Cushan; the curtains of Midian quaked. 8. Was the Lord incensed against the rivers? Was Your wrath against the rivers? Was Your anger against the sea? That You rode on Your horses, and through Your chariots You wrought salvation. 9. Naked was Your bow uncovered; the oaths made to the tribes remain an everlasting word; with rivers You cleft the earth. 10. When they saw You, the mountains trembled, the surging waters passed, the deep made its voice heard, the exaltation of His hand was raised on high. 11. The sun and the moon stood in their habitation; at the light of Your arrows they went, at the shining of Your glittering spear. 12. You strode through the earth with wrath; in anger You trod down nations. 13. You went forth for the salvation of Your people, for the salvation of Your anointed; You severed every head of the house of the wicked, forever baring the foundation even to the neck. 14. You pierced with his staves the heads of his armies, they storm to scatter me; their shouts of joy were as if to devour a poor man stealthily. 15. You trod the sea with Your chargers, a gathering of many waters. 16. When I heard, my innards trembled; my lips quivered at the sound; decay entered my bones, and in my place I quake, where I should rest quietly on the

וִיהוֹן כְּתִבְנָא, בְּגוֹ לִבְנָא, כְּאַבְנָא יִשְׁתְּקוּן חַפְ רִין:

יְהוֹנָתָן, גְּבַר עִנְוְתָן, בְּכֵן נַמְטֵי לֵהּ אַפְּ רִין:

ב יְהוָה שָׁמַעְתִּי שִׁמְעֲךָ יָרֵאתִי יְהוָה פָּעָלְךָ
בְּקֶרֶב שָׁנִים חַיֵּיהוּ בְּקֶרֶב שָׁנִים תּוֹדִיעַ בְּרֹגֶז
רַחֵם תִּזְכּוֹר: ג אֱלוֹהַּ מִתֵּימָן יָבוֹא וְקָדוֹשׁ
מֵהַר־פָּארָן סֶלָה כִּסָּה שָׁמַיִם הוֹדוֹ וּתְהִלָּתוֹ
מָלְאָה הָאָרֶץ: ד וְנֹגַהּ כָּאוֹר תִּהְיֶה קַרְנַיִם
מִיָּדוֹ לוֹ וְשָׁם חֶבְיוֹן עֻזֹּה: ה לְפָנָיו יֵלֶךְ דָּבֶר
וְיֵצֵא רֶשֶׁף לְרַגְלָיו: ו עָמַד ׀ וַיְמֹדֶד אֶרֶץ רָאָה
וַיַּתֵּר גּוֹיִם וַיִּתְפֹּצְצוּ הַרְרֵי־עַד שַׁחוּ גִּבְעוֹת
עוֹלָם הֲלִיכוֹת עוֹלָם לוֹ: ז תַּחַת אָוֶן רָאִיתִי
אָהֳלֵי כוּשָׁן יִרְגְּזוּן יְרִיעוֹת אֶרֶץ מִדְיָן:
ח הֲבִנְהָרִים חָרָה יְהוָה אִם בַּנְּהָרִים אַפֶּךָ אִם־
בַּיָּם עֶבְרָתֶךָ כִּי תִרְכַּב עַל־סוּסֶיךָ מַרְכְּבֹתֶיךָ
יְשׁוּעָה: ט עֶרְיָה תֵעוֹר קַשְׁתֶּךָ שְׁבֻעוֹת מַטּוֹת
אֹמֶר סֶלָה נְהָרוֹת תְּבַקַּע־אָרֶץ: י רָאוּךָ יָחִילוּ
הָרִים זֶרֶם מַיִם עָבָר נָתַן תְּהוֹם קוֹלוֹ רוֹם
יָדֵיהוּ נָשָׂא: יא שֶׁמֶשׁ יָרֵחַ עָמַד זְבֻלָה לְאוֹר
חִצֶּיךָ יְהַלֵּכוּ לְנֹגַהּ בְּרַק חֲנִיתֶךָ: יב בְּזַעַם
תִּצְעַד־אָרֶץ בְּאַף תָּדוּשׁ גּוֹיִם: יג יָצָאתָ לְיֵשַׁע
עַמֶּךָ לְיֵשַׁע אֶת־מְשִׁיחֶךָ מָחַצְתָּ רֹּאשׁ מִבֵּית
רָשָׁע עָרוֹת יְסוֹד עַד־צַוָּאר סֶלָה: יד נָקַבְתָּ
בְמַטָּיו רֹאשׁ פְּרָזָו יִסְעֲרוּ לַהֲפִיצֵנִי עֲלִיצֻתָם
כְּמוֹ־לֶאֱכֹל עָנִי בַּמִּסְתָּר: טו דָּרַכְתָּ בַיָּם סוּסֶיךָ
חֹמֶר מַיִם רַבִּים: טז שָׁמַעְתִּי ׀ וַתִּרְגַּז בִּטְנִי
לְקוֹל צָלֲלוּ שְׂפָתַי יָבוֹא רָקָב בַּעֲצָמַי וְתַחְתַּי

day of trouble, to repulse therefrom a
people that will retreat with its troops.
17. For the fig tree will not blossom, nor is
there any fruit in the vines; the work of the
olive trees fails, and the fields yield no food;
the sheep are cut off from the fold, and
there is no herd in the stalls. 18. And I will
joyfully exult with the Lord; I will rejoice in
the God of my salvation. 19. God the Lord
is my strength, He makes my feet like hinds,
and upon my high places He causes me to
tread. This is for the chief musician to sing
with my melodies.

אֶרְגַּז אֲשֶׁר אָנוּחַ לְיוֹם צָרָה לַעֲלוֹת לְעַם
יְגוּדֶנּוּ: יז כִּי־תְאֵנָה לֹא־תִפְרָח וְאֵין יְבוּל
בַּגְּפָנִים כִּחֵשׁ מַעֲשֵׂה־זַיִת וּשְׁדֵמוֹת לֹא־עָשָׂה
אֹכֶל גָּזַר מִמִּכְלָה צֹאן וְאֵין בָּקָר בָּרְפָתִים:
יח וַאֲנִי בַּיהוָה אֶעְלוֹזָה אָגִילָה בֵּאלֹהֵי יִשְׁעִי:
יט יְהוִֹה אֲדֹנָי חֵילִי וַיָּשֶׂם רַגְלַי כָּאַיָּלוֹת וְעַל־
בָּמוֹתַי יַדְרִכֵנִי לַמְנַצֵּחַ בִּנְגִינוֹתָי:

הפטרת תשעה באב שחרית
HAFTARAH FOR TISHA B'AV MORNING SERVICE
(Jeremiah 8:13–9:23)
Torah reading: Deuteronomy 4:25–40
For the Haftarah to be read at the afternoon service, see Haftarah For Fast Days
(p. 984).

This selection is appropriate for Tisha b'Av because it describes the conditions leading
to the destruction of the First Temple.

8:13. "I will utterly consume them," says
the Lord, "there shall be no grapes on the
vine, nor figs on the fig tree; even the leaves
will be withered, and what I gave them shall
pass away from them." 14. Why do we sit
still? Gather together, and let us go to the
fortified cities, and there let us meet our
doom! For the Lord our God has doomed us
[to death] and has given us poisoned water
to drink because we have sinned against the
Lord. 15. We hoped for peace, but no good
came; for a time of healing, but behold,
terror. 16. From Dan is heard the snorting
of their horses, at the sound of the neighing
of their stallions the whole land quakes;
they come and devour the land and its produce, the city and those that dwell therein.
17. "For behold, I am sending among you
serpents, adders which cannot be charmed,
and they shall bite you," says the Lord.
18. My grief is beyond healing; my
heart is sick within me. 19. Hark the voice
from a distant land, the cry of the daughter
of my people; is the Lord not in Zion? Is not
her King therein? Why have they provoked Me with their graven images, with
their strange vanities? 20. The harvest is
past, the summer is ended; and we are not

יג אָסֹף אֲסִיפֵם נְאֻם־יְהוָֹה אֵין עֲנָבִים בַּגֶּפֶן
וְאֵין תְּאֵנִים בַּתְּאֵנָה וְהֶעָלֶה נָבֵל וָאֶתֵּן לָהֶם
יַעַבְרוּם: יד עַל־מָה אֲנַחְנוּ יֹשְׁבִים הֵאָסְפוּ
וְנָבוֹא אֶל־עָרֵי הַמִּבְצָר וְנִדְּמָה־שָּׁם כִּי יְהוָֹה
אֱלֹהֵינוּ הֲדִמָּנוּ וַיַּשְׁקֵנוּ מֵי־רֹאשׁ כִּי חָטָאנוּ
לַיהוָֹה: טו קַוֵּה לְשָׁלוֹם וְאֵין טוֹב לְעֵת מַרְפֵּה
וְהִנֵּה בְעָתָה: טז מִדָּן נִשְׁמַע נַחְרַת סוּסָיו
מִקּוֹל מִצְהֲלוֹת אַבִּירָיו רָעֲשָׁה כָּל־הָאָרֶץ
וַיָּבוֹאוּ וַיֹּאכְלוּ אֶרֶץ וּמְלוֹאָהּ עִיר וְיֹשְׁבֵי בָהּ:
יז כִּי הִנְנִי מְשַׁלֵּחַ בָּכֶם נְחָשִׁים צִפְעֹנִים אֲשֶׁר
אֵין־לָהֶם לָחַשׁ וְנִשְּׁכוּ אֶתְכֶם נְאֻם־יְהוָֹה:
יח מַבְלִיגִיתִי עֲלֵי יָגוֹן עָלַי לִבִּי דַוָּי: יט הִנֵּה־
קוֹל שַׁוְעַת בַּת־עַמִּי מֵאֶרֶץ מַרְחַקִּים הַיהוָֹה
אֵין בְּצִיּוֹן אִם־מַלְכָּהּ אֵין בָּהּ מַדּוּעַ הִכְעִסוּנִי
בִּפְסִלֵיהֶם בְּהַבְלֵי נֵכָר: כ עָבַר קָצִיר כָּלָה קַיִץ

saved. 21. For the wound of the daughter of my people I am wounded [with grief]; I mourn, [and] dismay has taken hold of me. 22. Is there no balm in Gilead? Is there no physician there? Why then has the health of the daughter of my people not been restored? 23. O that my head were [full of] waters and my eyes a fountain of tears; that I might weep day and night for the slain of the daughter of my people! 9:1. "O that I had in the desert a wayfarers' lodging-place, that I might leave My people and go away from them! For they are all adulterers, a company of traitors! 2. They have directed their tongue treacherously [as] their bows, and they have grown strong in the land not for the sake of truth; for they proceed from evil to evil, and they do not know Me," says the Lord. 3. "Let each one beware of his neighbor, and do not trust any brother; for every brother forges plans, and every neighbor spreads slander. 4. Indeed, they deceive one another and do not speak the truth; they have taught their tongue to speak lies; they commit iniquity [until] they are weary. 5. Your habitation is in the midst of deceit; through deceit they refuse to know Me," says the Lord. 6. Therefore, thus says the Lord of hosts: "Behold, because of the [wickedness of the] daughter of My people, I will refine them and test them, for what else can I do? 7. Their tongue is a deadly arrow, it speaks deceit; each one speaks peaceably with his mouth to his neighbor, but in his heart he lays a trap for him. 8. Shall I not punish them for these things," says the Lord, "shall I not avenge myself on a nation such as this? 9. I will take up weeping and wailing for the mountains, and a lamentation for the pastures of the wilderness, because they are withered and without any one passing through, and the lowing of the cattle is not heard; both the fowl of the heavens and the beast have fled and are gone. 10. And I will make Jerusalem heaps [of ruins], a lair of jackals; and I will make the cities of Judah a desolation, without inhabitant." 11. Who is the man so wise that he can understand this? And who is he to whom the mouth of the Lord has spoken, that he may declare it? Why is the land ruined [and] withered like a wilderness,

וַאֲנַ֖חְנוּ ל֥וֹא נוֹשָֽׁעְנוּ: כא עַל־שֶׁ֥בֶר בַּת־עַמִּ֖י הָשְׁבָּ֑רְתִּי קָדַ֕רְתִּי שַׁמָּ֖ה הֶחֱזִקָֽתְנִי: כב הַצֳרִ֞י אֵ֣ין בְּגִלְעָ֗ד אִם־רֹפֵ֖א אֵ֣ין שָׁ֑ם כִּ֗י מַדּ֙וּעַ֙ לֹ֣א עָֽלְתָ֔ה אֲרֻכַ֖ת בַּת־עַמִּֽי: כג מִֽי־יִתֵּ֤ן רֹאשִׁי֙ מַ֔יִם וְעֵינִ֖י מְק֣וֹר דִּמְעָ֑ה וְאֶבְכֶּה֙ יוֹמָ֣ם וָלַ֔יְלָה אֵ֖ת חַֽלְלֵ֥י בַת־עַמִּֽי: א מִֽי־יִתְּנֵ֣נִי בַמִּדְבָּ֗ר מְלוֹן֙ אֹֽרְחִ֔ים וְאֶֽעֶזְבָה֙ אֶת־עַמִּ֔י וְאֵֽלְכָ֖ה מֵֽאִתָּ֑ם כִּ֤י כֻלָּם֙ מְנָ֣אֲפִ֔ים עֲצֶ֖רֶת בֹּֽגְדִֽים: ב וַֽיַּדְרְכ֤וּ אֶת־לְשׁוֹנָם֙ קַשְׁתָּ֣ם שֶׁ֔קֶר וְלֹ֥א לֶאֱמוּנָ֖ה גָּבְר֣וּ בָאָ֑רֶץ כִּי֩ מֵרָעָ֨ה אֶל־רָעָ֤ה ׀ יָצָ֙אוּ֙ וְאֹתִ֣י לֹֽא־יָדָ֔עוּ נְאֻם־יְהֹוָֽה: ג אִ֤ישׁ מֵֽרֵעֵ֙הוּ֙ הִשָּׁמֵ֔רוּ וְעַל־כָּל־אָ֖ח אַל־תִּבְטָ֑חוּ כִּ֤י כָל־אָח֙ עָק֣וֹב יַעְקֹ֔ב וְכָל־רֵ֖עַ רָכִ֥יל יַהֲלֹֽךְ: ד וְאִ֤ישׁ בְּרֵעֵ֙הוּ֙ יְהָתֵ֔לּוּ וֶֽאֱמֶ֖ת לֹ֣א יְדַבֵּ֑רוּ לִמְּד֧וּ לְשׁוֹנָ֛ם דַּבֶּר־שֶׁ֖קֶר הַֽעֲוֵ֥ה נִלְאֽוּ: ה שִׁבְתְּךָ֖ בְּת֣וֹךְ מִרְמָ֑ה בְּמִרְמָ֖ה מֵֽאֲנ֥וּ דַֽעַת־אוֹתִ֖י נְאֻם־יְהֹוָֽה: ו לָכֵ֗ן כֹּ֤ה אָמַר֙ יְהֹוָ֣ה צְבָא֔וֹת הִנְנִ֥י צֽוֹרְפָ֖ם וּבְחַנְתִּ֑ים כִּי־אֵ֣יךְ אֶֽעֱשֶׂ֔ה מִפְּנֵ֖י בַּת־עַמִּֽי: ז חֵ֥ץ שָׁחֵ֖ט (שחוט קרי) לְשׁוֹנָ֛ם מִרְמָ֥ה דִבֵּ֑ר בְּפִ֗יו שָׁל֤וֹם אֶת־רֵעֵ֙הוּ֙ יְדַבֵּ֔ר וּבְקִרְבּ֖וֹ יָשִׂ֥ים אָרְבּֽוֹ: ח הַעַל־אֵ֥לֶּה לֹֽא־אֶפְקָד־בָּ֖ם נְאֻם־יְהֹוָ֑ה אִ֚ם בְּג֣וֹי אֲשֶׁר־כָּזֶ֔ה לֹ֥א תִתְנַקֵּ֖ם נַפְשִֽׁי: ט עַל־הֶֽהָרִ֗ים אֶשָּׂ֤א בְכִי֙ וָנֶ֔הִי וְעַל־נְא֤וֹת מִדְבָּר֙ קִינָ֔ה כִּ֤י נִצְּתוּ֙ מִבְּלִי־אִ֣ישׁ עֹבֵ֔ר וְלֹ֥א שָֽׁמְע֖וּ ק֣וֹל מִקְנֶ֑ה מֵע֤וֹף הַשָּׁמַ֙יִם֙ וְעַד־בְּהֵמָ֔ה נָֽדְד֖וּ הָלָֽכוּ: י וְנָתַתִּ֧י אֶת־יְרֽוּשָׁלַ֛͏ִם לְגַלִּ֖ים מְע֣וֹן תַּנִּ֑ים וְאֶת־עָרֵ֧י יְהוּדָ֛ה אֶתֵּ֥ן שְׁמָמָ֖ה מִבְּלִ֥י יוֹשֵֽׁב: יא מִֽי־הָאִ֤ישׁ הֶֽחָכָם֙ וְיָבֵ֣ן אֶת־זֹ֔את וַֽאֲשֶׁ֨ר דִּבֶּ֧ר פִּֽי־יְהֹוָ֛ה אֵלָ֖יו וְיַגִּדָ֑הּ עַל־מָ֤ה אָֽבְדָה֙ הָאָ֔רֶץ נִצְּתָ֥ה כַמִּדְבָּ֖ר מִבְּלִ֥י

without anyone passing through? 12. And
the Lord said: "[It is] because they have
forsaken My Law, which I set before them,
and have not hearkened to My voice, nor
walked by it, 13. but have followed the
stubbornness of their own heart and after
the Baalim, which their fathers taught them
[to worship]." 14. Therefore thus said the
Lord of hosts, the God of Israel: "Behold, I
will feed them — this people — with wormwood, and will give them poisonous water to
drink. 15. I will scatter them among the
nations, whom neither they nor their fathers
have known; and I will send the sword after
them, until I have consumed them."
16. Thus said the Lord of hosts: "Consider
and call for the [hired] women mourners
that they may come; and send for the skillful women, and let them come." 17. O let
them make haste and raise a wailing over us,
so that our eyes may shed tears, and our
eyelids gush with water. 18. For a sound of
wailing is heard from Zion: 'O how we are
ruined! We are very much ashamed,
because we have left the land, because they
have cast down our dwelling!' 19. Indeed
hear, O women, the word of the Lord, and
let your ear receive the word of his mouth;
teach your daughters a lamentation, and
each to her neighbor a dirge. 20. For death
has penetrated our windows, it has entered
our palaces; to cut off the infants from the
streets, and the young men from the
squares. 21. "Speak, thus" says the Lord:
"Indeed, the carcasses of men shall fall like
dung on the open field, and like sheaves
after the reaper, with none to gather them!"
22. Thus says the Lord: "Let not the wise
man boast of his wisdom, nor the strong
man boast of his strength, nor the rich man
boast of his riches. 23. But let him that
boasts exult in this, that he understands and
knows Me, that I am the Lord Who practices kindness, justice and righteousness
on the earth; for in these things I delight,"
says the Lord.

עֹבֵר: יב וַיֹּאמֶר יְהֹוָה עַל־עָזְבָם אֶת־תּוֹרָתִי
אֲשֶׁר נָתַתִּי לִפְנֵיהֶם וְלֹא־שָׁמְעוּ בְקוֹלִי וְלֹא־
הָלְכוּ בָהּ: יג וַיֵּלְכוּ אַחֲרֵי שְׁרִרוּת לִבָּם וְאַחֲרֵי
הַבְּעָלִים אֲשֶׁר לִמְּדוּם אֲבוֹתָם: יד לָכֵן כֹּה־
אָמַר יְהֹוָה צְבָאוֹת אֱלֹהֵי יִשְׂרָאֵל הִנְנִי
מַאֲכִילָם אֶת־הָעָם הַזֶּה לַעֲנָה וְהִשְׁקִיתִים מֵי־
רֹאשׁ: טו וַהֲפִצוֹתִים בַּגּוֹיִם אֲשֶׁר לֹא יָדְעוּ
הֵמָּה וַאֲבוֹתָם וְשִׁלַּחְתִּי אַחֲרֵיהֶם אֶת־הַחֶרֶב
עַד כַּלּוֹתִי אוֹתָם: טז כֹּה אָמַר יְהֹוָה צְבָאוֹת
הִתְבּוֹנְנוּ וְקִרְאוּ לַמְקוֹנְנוֹת וּתְבוֹאֶינָה וְאֶל־
הַחֲכָמוֹת שִׁלְחוּ וְתָבוֹאנָה: יז וּתְמַהֵרְנָה
וְתִשֶּׂנָה עָלֵינוּ נֶהִי וְתֵרַדְנָה עֵינֵינוּ דִּמְעָה
וְעַפְעַפֵּינוּ יִזְּלוּ־מָיִם: יח כִּי קוֹל נְהִי נִשְׁמַע
מִצִּיּוֹן אֵיךְ שֻׁדָּדְנוּ בֹּשְׁנוּ מְאֹד כִּי־עָזַבְנוּ אָרֶץ
כִּי הִשְׁלִיכוּ מִשְׁכְּנוֹתֵינוּ: יט כִּי־שְׁמַעְנָה נָשִׁים
דְּבַר־יְהֹוָה וְתִקַּח אָזְנְכֶם דְּבַר־פִּיו וְלַמֵּדְנָה
בְנוֹתֵיכֶם נֶהִי וְאִשָּׁה רְעוּתָהּ קִינָה: כ כִּי־עָלָה
מָוֶת בְּחַלּוֹנֵינוּ בָּא בְּאַרְמְנוֹתֵינוּ לְהַכְרִית
עוֹלָל מִחוּץ בַּחוּרִים מֵרְחֹבוֹת: כא דַּבֵּר כֹּה
נְאֻם־יְהֹוָה וְנָפְלָה נִבְלַת הָאָדָם כְּדֹמֶן עַל־פְּנֵי
הַשָּׂדֶה וּכְעָמִיר מֵאַחֲרֵי הַקֹּצֵר וְאֵין מְאַסֵּף:
כב כֹּה אָמַר יְהֹוָה אַל־יִתְהַלֵּל חָכָם בְּחָכְמָתוֹ
וְאַל־יִתְהַלֵּל הַגִּבּוֹר בִּגְבוּרָתוֹ אַל־יִתְהַלֵּל
עָשִׁיר בְּעָשְׁרוֹ: כג כִּי אִם־בְּזֹאת יִתְהַלֵּל
הַמִּתְהַלֵּל הַשְׂכֵּל וְיָדֹעַ אוֹתִי כִּי אֲנִי יְהֹוָה
עֹשֶׂה חֶסֶד מִשְׁפָּט וּצְדָקָה בָּאָרֶץ כִּי־בְאֵלֶּה
חָפַצְתִּי נְאֻם־יְהֹוָה:

HAFTARAH FOR FAST DAYS הפטרת תענית צבור
(Isaiah 55:6–56:8)
Torah reading (morning and afternoon): Exodus 32:11–14, 34:1–10.
The Haftarah is read at the afternoon service only.

This selection deals with repentance, appropriate for a fast day. It is one of "The Two Haftaroth of Repentance."

55:6. Seek the Lord when He is found, call Him when He is near. 7. The wicked shall give up his way, and the man of iniquity his thoughts, and he shall return to the Lord, Who shall have mercy upon him, and to our God, for He will freely pardon. 8. "For My thoughts are not your thoughts, neither are your ways My ways," says the Lord. 9. "As the heavens are higher than the earth, so are My ways higher than your ways and My thoughts [higher] than your thoughts. 10. For, just as the rain and the snow fall from the heavens, and it does not return there, unless it has satiated the earth and fructified it and furthered its growth, and has given seed to the sower and bread to the eater, 11. so shall be My word that emanates from My mouth; it shall not return to Me empty, unless it has done what I desire and has made prosperous the one to whom I sent it. 12. For with joy shall you go forth, and with peace shall you be brought; the mountains and the hills shall burst into song before you, and all the trees of the field shall clap hands. 13. Instead of the briar, a cypress shall rise, and instead of the nettle, a myrtle shall rise, and it shall be for the Lord as a name, as an everlasting sign, which shall not be discontinued." 56:1. So says the Lord, "Keep justice and practice righteousness, for My salvation is near to come, and My benevolence to be revealed." 2. Fortunate is the man who will do this and the person who will hold fast to it, he who keeps the Sabbath from profaning it and guards his hand from doing any evil. 3. Now let not the foreigner who joined the Lord, say, "The Lord will surely separate me from His people"; and let not the eunuch say, "Behold, I am a dry tree." 4. For so says the Lord to the eunuchs who will keep My Sabbaths and will choose what I desire and hold fast to My covenant, 5. "I will give them in My house and in My walls a place and a name, better than sons and

ו דִּרְשׁ֥וּ יְהֹוָ֖ה בְּהִמָּצְא֑וֹ קְרָאֻ֖הוּ בִּֽהְיוֹת֥וֹ קָרֽוֹב׃
ז יַעֲזֹ֤ב רָשָׁע֙ דַּרְכּ֔וֹ וְאִ֥ישׁ אָ֖וֶן מַחְשְׁבֹתָ֑יו וְיָשֹׁ֤ב אֶל־יְהֹוָה֙ וִֽירַחֲמֵ֔הוּ וְאֶל־אֱלֹהֵ֖ינוּ כִּֽי־יַרְבֶּ֥ה לִסְלֽוֹחַ׃ ח כִּ֣י לֹ֤א מַחְשְׁבוֹתַי֙ מַחְשְׁב֣וֹתֵיכֶ֔ם וְלֹ֥א דַרְכֵיכֶ֖ם דְּרָכָ֑י נְאֻ֖ם יְהֹוָֽה׃ ט כִּֽי־גָבְה֥וּ שָׁמַ֖יִם מֵאָ֑רֶץ כֵּ֣ן גָּבְה֤וּ דְרָכַי֙ מִדַּרְכֵיכֶ֔ם וּמַחְשְׁבֹתַ֖י מִמַּחְשְׁבֹתֵיכֶֽם׃ י כִּ֡י כַּאֲשֶׁ֣ר יֵרֵד֩ הַגֶּ֨שֶׁם וְהַשֶּׁ֜לֶג מִן־הַשָּׁמַ֗יִם וְשָׁ֙מָּה֙ לֹ֣א יָשׁ֔וּב כִּ֚י אִם־הִרְוָ֣ה אֶת־הָאָ֔רֶץ וְהוֹלִידָ֖הּ וְהִצְמִיחָ֑הּ וְנָ֤תַן זֶ֙רַע֙ לַזֹּרֵ֔עַ וְלֶ֖חֶם לָאֹכֵֽל׃ יא כֵּ֣ן יִֽהְיֶ֤ה דְבָרִי֙ אֲשֶׁ֣ר יֵצֵ֣א מִפִּ֔י לֹֽא־יָשׁ֥וּב אֵלַ֖י רֵיקָ֑ם כִּ֤י אִם־עָשָׂה֙ אֶת־אֲשֶׁ֣ר חָפַ֔צְתִּי וְהִצְלִ֖יחַ אֲשֶׁ֥ר שְׁלַחְתִּֽיו׃ יב כִּֽי־בְשִׂמְחָ֣ה תֵצֵ֔אוּ וּבְשָׁל֖וֹם תּֽוּבָל֑וּן הֶֽהָרִ֣ים וְהַגְּבָע֗וֹת יִפְצְח֤וּ לִפְנֵיכֶם֙ רִנָּ֔ה וְכָל־עֲצֵ֥י הַשָּׂדֶ֖ה יִמְחֲאוּ־כָֽף׃ יג תַּ֤חַת הַֽנַּעֲצוּץ֙ יַעֲלֶ֣ה בְר֔וֹשׁ תַּ֥חַת (ותחת קרי) הַסִּרְפַּ֖ד יַעֲלֶ֣ה הֲדַ֑ס וְהָיָ֤ה לַֽיהֹוָה֙ לְשֵׁ֔ם לְא֥וֹת עוֹלָ֖ם לֹ֥א יִכָּרֵֽת׃ א כֹּ֚ה אָמַ֣ר יְהֹוָ֔ה שִׁמְר֥וּ מִשְׁפָּ֖ט וַעֲשׂ֣וּ צְדָקָ֑ה כִּֽי־קְרוֹבָ֤ה יְשֽׁוּעָתִי֙ לָב֔וֹא וְצִדְקָתִ֖י לְהִגָּלֽוֹת׃ ב אַשְׁרֵ֤י אֱנוֹשׁ֙ יַעֲשֶׂה־זֹּ֔את וּבֶן־אָדָ֖ם יַחֲזִ֣יק בָּ֑הּ שֹׁמֵ֤ר שַׁבָּת֙ מֵֽחַלְּל֔וֹ וְשֹׁמֵ֥ר יָד֖וֹ מֵעֲשׂ֥וֹת כָּל־רָֽע׃ ג וְאַל־יֹאמַ֣ר בֶּן־הַנֵּכָ֗ר הַנִּלְוָ֤ה אֶל־יְהֹוָה֙ לֵאמֹ֔ר הַבְדֵּ֧ל יַבְדִּילַ֛נִי יְהֹוָ֖ה מֵעַ֣ל עַמּ֑וֹ וְאַל־יֹאמַר֙ הַסָּרִ֔יס הֵ֥ן אֲנִ֖י עֵ֥ץ יָבֵֽשׁ׃ ד כִּי־כֹ֣ה ׀ אָמַ֣ר יְהֹוָ֗ה לַסָּֽרִיסִים֙ אֲשֶׁ֤ר יִשְׁמְרוּ֙ אֶת־שַׁבְּתוֹתַ֔י וּבָֽחֲר֖וּ בַּאֲשֶׁ֣ר חָפָ֑צְתִּי וּמַחֲזִיקִ֖ים בִּבְרִיתִֽי׃ ה וְנָתַתִּ֨י לָהֶ֜ם בְּבֵיתִ֣י וּבְחֽוֹמֹתַ֗י יָ֚ד וָשֵׁ֣ם ט֔וֹב מִבָּנִ֖ים וּמִבָּנ֑וֹת שֵׁ֤ם עוֹלָם֙ אֶתֶּן־ל֔וֹ

[[984]]

daughters; an everlasting name I will give him, which will not be discontinued. 6. And the foreigners who join with the Lord to serve Him and to love the Name of the Lord, to be His servants, everyone who observes the Sabbath from profaning it and who holds fast to My Covenant. 7. I will bring them to My holy mount, and I will cause them to rejoice in My house of prayer; their burnt-offerings and their sacrifices shall be acceptable upon My altar, for My house shall be called a house of prayer for all peoples." 8. So says the Lord God, Who gathers in the dispersed of Israel, "I will yet gather others to him, together with his gathered ones."

אֲשֶׁר לֹא יִכָּרֵת: ו וּבְנֵי הַנֵּכָר הַנִּלְוִים עַל־
יְהֹוָה לְשָׁרְתוֹ וּלְאַהֲבָה אֶת־שֵׁם יְהֹוָה לִהְיוֹת
לוֹ לַעֲבָדִים כָּל־שֹׁמֵר שַׁבָּת מֵחַלְּלוֹ וּמַחֲזִיקִים
בִּבְרִיתִי: ז וַהֲבִיאוֹתִים אֶל־הַר קָדְשִׁי
וְשִׂמַּחְתִּים בְּבֵית תְּפִלָּתִי עוֹלֹתֵיהֶם וְזִבְחֵיהֶם
לְרָצוֹן עַל־מִזְבְּחִי כִּי בֵיתִי בֵּית־תְּפִלָּה יִקָּרֵא
לְכָל־הָעַמִּים: ח נְאֻם אֲדֹנָי יֱהֹוִה מְקַבֵּץ נִדְחֵי
יִשְׂרָאֵל עוֹד אֲקַבֵּץ עָלָיו לְנִקְבָּצָיו:

חמש מגילות
THE FIVE MEGILLOTH

Introductory material, instructions and translation by

Rabbi A.J. Rosenberg
Editor of the Judaica Books of the Prophets

MEGILLATH ESTHER מגילת אסתר

[BOOK OF ESTHER]

BLESSINGS BEFORE READING THE BOOK OF ESTHER

Before reading the Megillah, the following blessings are said.

Blessed are You, O Lord our God, King of the universe, Who has hallowed us by His commandments, and has commanded us concerning the reading of the Megillah.

בָּרוּךְ אַתָּה יְהוָֹה, אֱלֹהֵינוּ מֶלֶךְ הָעוֹלָם, אֲשֶׁר
קִדְּשָׁנוּ, בְּמִצְוֹתָיו, וְצִוָּנוּ עַל־מִקְרָא מְגִלָּה:

Blessed are You, O Lord our God, King of the universe, Who performed miracles for our fathers in days of old, at this season.

בָּרוּךְ אַתָּה יְהוָֹה, אֱלֹהֵינוּ מֶלֶךְ הָעוֹלָם, שֶׁעָשָׂה
נִסִּים לַאֲבוֹתֵינוּ, בַּיָּמִים הָהֵם, בַּזְּמַן הַזֶּה:

Blessed are You, O Lord our God, King of the universe, Who has kept us in life, and has preserved us, and has enabled us to reach this season.

בָּרוּךְ אַתָּה יְהוָֹה, אֱלֹהֵינוּ מֶלֶךְ הָעוֹלָם,
שֶׁהֶחֱיָנוּ, וְקִיְּמָנוּ, וְהִגִּיעָנוּ לַזְּמַן הַזֶּה:

THE BOOK OF ESTHER מגילת אסתר

The Book of Esther, traditionally known as the "Megillah" (lit. "Scroll"), is the most beloved book of the Bible. It tells the story of the miraculous rescue of the Jews of Persia from the evil plot of Haman, prime minister of the simple-minded King Ahasuerus. Esther, the Jewish maiden who becomes Ahasuerus's queen, and her cousin Mordecai, become the instruments of Divine Providence in the downfall of wicked Haman and the preservation of the Jews.

The Book of Esther is read on the joyous holiday of Purim, which was instituted by the Men of the Great Assembly to commemorate this historic event. The reading takes place on the eve of Purim, and again at morning services the next day. The holiday is celebrated in accordance with the instructions given in the text of the Book, by feasting and by sending gifts to friends and to the needy.

CHAPTER I

1. And it came to pass in the days of Ahasuerus — he [was the] Ahasuerus who reigned from Hodu to Cush, one hundred twenty-seven provinces. 2. In those days, when King Ahasuerus sat on the throne of his kingdom, which was in Shushan the capital, 3. in the third year of his reign, he made a banquet for all his princes and his servants, the army of Persia and Media, the nobles, and the princes of the provinces [who were] before him. 4. When he showed the riches of his glorious kingdom, and the splendor of his excellent majesty, many days, yea, one hundred and eighty days. 5. And when these days were over, the king made for all the people found in Shushan the capital, for [everyone,] both great and small, a banquet for seven days, in the court of the garden of the king's orchard. 6. [There were hangings of] white, fine cotton, and blue, held with cords of linen and purple, on silver rods and marble columns; couches of gold and silver, on a pavement of green, white, shell, and onyx marble. 7. And they gave them to drink in golden vessels, and the vessels differed from one another, and royal wine was plentiful, according to the bounty of the king. 8. And the drinking was according to the law [with] no one coercing, for so had the king ordained upon every steward of his house, to do according to every man's wish. 9. Also Vashti the queen made a banquet for the women, in the royal house of King Ahasuerus. 10. On the seventh day, when the king's heart was merry with wine, he ordered Mehuman, Bizzetha, Harbona,

א א וַיְהִי בִּימֵי אֲחַשְׁוֵרוֹשׁ הוּא אֲחַשְׁוֵרוֹשׁ
הַמֹּלֵךְ מֵהֹדּוּ וְעַד־כּוּשׁ שֶׁבַע וְעֶשְׂרִים וּמֵאָה
מְדִינָה: ב בַּיָּמִים הָהֵם כְּשֶׁבֶת ׀ הַמֶּלֶךְ
אֲחַשְׁוֵרוֹשׁ עַל כִּסֵּא מַלְכוּתוֹ אֲשֶׁר בְּשׁוּשַׁן
הַבִּירָה: ג בִּשְׁנַת שָׁלוֹשׁ לְמָלְכוֹ עָשָׂה מִשְׁתֶּה
לְכָל־שָׂרָיו וַעֲבָדָיו חֵיל ׀ פָּרַס וּמָדַי הַפַּרְתְּמִים
וְשָׂרֵי הַמְּדִינוֹת לְפָנָיו: ד בְּהַרְאֹתוֹ אֶת־עֹשֶׁר
כְּבוֹד מַלְכוּתוֹ וְאֶת־יְקָר תִּפְאֶרֶת גְּדוּלָּתוֹ יָמִים
רַבִּים שְׁמוֹנִים וּמְאַת יוֹם: ה וּבִמְלוֹאת ׀ הַיָּמִים
הָאֵלֶּה עָשָׂה הַמֶּלֶךְ לְכָל־הָעָם הַנִּמְצְאִים
בְּשׁוּשַׁן הַבִּירָה לְמִגָּדוֹל וְעַד־קָטָן מִשְׁתֶּה
שִׁבְעַת יָמִים בַּחֲצַר גִּנַּת בִּיתַן הַמֶּלֶךְ: ו חוּר ׀
כַּרְפַּס וּתְכֵלֶת אָחוּז בְּחַבְלֵי־בוּץ וְאַרְגָּמָן עַל־
גְּלִילֵי כֶסֶף וְעַמּוּדֵי שֵׁשׁ מִטּוֹת ׀ זָהָב וָכֶסֶף עַל
רִצְפַת בַּהַט־וָשֵׁשׁ וְדַר וְסֹחָרֶת: ז וְהַשְׁקוֹת
בִּכְלֵי זָהָב וְכֵלִים מִכֵּלִים שׁוֹנִים וְיֵין מַלְכוּת רָב
כְּיַד הַמֶּלֶךְ: ח וְהַשְּׁתִיָּה כַדָּת אֵין אֹנֵס כִּי־כֵן ׀
יִסַּד הַמֶּלֶךְ עַל כָּל־רַב בֵּיתוֹ לַעֲשׂוֹת כִּרְצוֹן
אִישׁ־וָאִישׁ: ס ט גַּם וַשְׁתִּי הַמַּלְכָּה עָשְׂתָה
מִשְׁתֵּה נָשִׁים בֵּית הַמַּלְכוּת אֲשֶׁר לַמֶּלֶךְ
אֲחַשְׁוֵרוֹשׁ: י בַּיּוֹם הַשְּׁבִיעִי כְּטוֹב לֵב־הַמֶּלֶךְ
בַּיָּיִן אָמַר לִמְהוּמָן בִּזְּתָא חַרְבוֹנָא בִּגְתָא
וַאֲבַגְתָא זֵתַר וְכַרְכַּס שִׁבְעַת הַסָּרִיסִים

Bigtha, and Abagtha, Zethar, and Carcas,
the seven chamberlains who ministered in
the presence of King Ahasuerus,   11. to
bring Vashti the queen before the king with
the royal crown, to show the peoples and the
princes her beauty, for she was of comely
appearance.   12. But Queen Vashti
refused to come at the king's behest which
was [brought] by the hand of the chamberlains, and the king became very wroth, and
his fury burnt within him.   13. And the
king said to the wise men who knew the
times—for so was the king's custom, [to
present the case] before all who know law
and judgment—   14. and the nearest to
him were Carshena, Shethar, Admatha,
Tarshish, Meres, Marsena, and Memucan,
the seven princes of Persia and Media, who
saw the king's face, who sat first in the kingdom,   15. "According to the law, what [is
there] to do to Queen Vashti, because she
did not comply with the order of the king,
[brought] by the hand of the chamberlains?"   16. Then Memucan declared
before the king and the princes, "Not
against the king alone has Vashti the queen
done wrong, but against all the princes and
all the peoples that are in all King
Ahasuerus's provinces.   17 For the conduct of the queen will spread to all the
women, to make their husbands contemptible in their eyes, when they say, 'King
Ahasuerus ordered to bring Vashti the
queen before him, but she did not come.'
18. And this day, the princesses of Persia
and Media who heard the conduct of the
queen will say [the like] to all the princes of
the king, and [there will be] much contempt
and wrath.   19. If it please the king, let a
royal edict go forth from before him, and let
it be inscribed in the laws of Persia and
Media, that it be not revoked, that Vashti
shall not come before the king, and let the
king give her royal position to her peer who
is better than she.   20. And let the verdict
of the king be heard throughout his entire
kingdom, for it is great, and all the women
shall give honor to their husbands, both
great and small."   21. And the matter
pleased the king and the princes, and the
king did according to the word of
Memucan.   22. And he sent letters to all
the king's provinces, to every province

הַמְשָׁרְתִים אֶת־פְּנֵי הַמֶּלֶךְ אֲחַשְׁוֵרוֹשׁ:
יא לְהָבִיא אֶת־וַשְׁתִּי הַמַּלְכָּה לִפְנֵי הַמֶּלֶךְ
בְּכֶתֶר מַלְכוּת לְהַרְאוֹת הָעַמִּים וְהַשָּׂרִים אֶת־
יָפְיָהּ כִּי־טוֹבַת מַרְאֶה הִיא: יב וַתְּמָאֵן הַמַּלְכָּה
וַשְׁתִּי לָבוֹא בִּדְבַר הַמֶּלֶךְ אֲשֶׁר בְּיַד הַסָּרִיסִים
וַיִּקְצֹף הַמֶּלֶךְ מְאֹד וַחֲמָתוֹ בָּעֲרָה בוֹ: ס
יג וַיֹּאמֶר הַמֶּלֶךְ לַחֲכָמִים יֹדְעֵי הָעִתִּים כִּי־כֵן
דְּבַר הַמֶּלֶךְ לִפְנֵי כָּל־יֹדְעֵי דָּת וָדִין: יד וְהַקָּרֹב
אֵלָיו כַּרְשְׁנָא שֵׁתָר אַדְמָתָא תַרְשִׁישׁ מֶרֶס
מַרְסְנָא מְמוּכָן שִׁבְעַת שָׂרֵי | פָּרַס וּמָדַי רֹאֵי
פְּנֵי הַמֶּלֶךְ הַיֹּשְׁבִים רִאשֹׁנָה בַּמַּלְכוּת: טו כְּדָת
מַה־לַּעֲשׂוֹת בַּמַּלְכָּה וַשְׁתִּי עַל | אֲשֶׁר לֹא־
עָשְׂתָה אֶת־מַאֲמַר הַמֶּלֶךְ אֲחַשְׁוֵרוֹשׁ בְּיַד
הַסָּרִיסִים: ס טז וַיֹּאמֶר מְמוּכָן (ממוכן קרי) לִפְנֵי
הַמֶּלֶךְ וְהַשָּׂרִים לֹא עַל־הַמֶּלֶךְ לְבַדּוֹ עָוְתָה
וַשְׁתִּי הַמַּלְכָּה כִּי עַל־כָּל־הַשָּׂרִים וְעַל־כָּל־
הָעַמִּים אֲשֶׁר בְּכָל־מְדִינוֹת הַמֶּלֶךְ אֲחַשְׁוֵרוֹשׁ:
יז כִּי־יֵצֵא דְבַר־הַמַּלְכָּה עַל־כָּל־הַנָּשִׁים
לְהַבְזוֹת בַּעְלֵיהֶן בְּעֵינֵיהֶן בְּאָמְרָם הַמֶּלֶךְ
אֲחַשְׁוֵרוֹשׁ אָמַר לְהָבִיא אֶת־וַשְׁתִּי הַמַּלְכָּה
לְפָנָיו וְלֹא־בָאָה: יח וְהַיּוֹם הַזֶּה תֹּאמַרְנָה |
שָׂרוֹת פָּרַס־וּמָדַי אֲשֶׁר שָׁמְעוּ אֶת־דְּבַר
הַמַּלְכָּה לְכֹל שָׂרֵי הַמֶּלֶךְ וּכְדַי בִּזָּיוֹן וָקָצֶף:
יט אִם־עַל־הַמֶּלֶךְ טוֹב יֵצֵא דְבַר־מַלְכוּת
מִלְּפָנָיו וְיִכָּתֵב בְּדָתֵי פָרַס־וּמָדַי וְלֹא יַעֲבוֹר
אֲשֶׁר לֹא־תָבוֹא וַשְׁתִּי לִפְנֵי הַמֶּלֶךְ אֲחַשְׁוֵרוֹשׁ
וּמַלְכוּתָהּ יִתֵּן הַמֶּלֶךְ לִרְעוּתָהּ הַטּוֹבָה מִמֶּנָּה:
כ וְנִשְׁמַע פִּתְגָם הַמֶּלֶךְ אֲשֶׁר־יַעֲשֶׂה בְּכָל־
מַלְכוּתוֹ כִּי רַבָּה הִיא וְכָל־הַנָּשִׁים יִתְּנוּ יְקָר
לְבַעְלֵיהֶן לְמִגָּדוֹל וְעַד־קָטָן: כא וַיִּיטַב הַדָּבָר
בְּעֵינֵי הַמֶּלֶךְ וְהַשָּׂרִים וַיַּעַשׂ הַמֶּלֶךְ כִּדְבַר
מְמוּכָן: כב וַיִּשְׁלַח סְפָרִים אֶל־כָּל־מְדִינוֹת

according to its script, and to every nationality according to its language, that every man dominate over his household and speak according to the language of his nationality.

CHAPTER II

1. After these events, when King Ahasuerus's fury subsided, he remembered Vashti and what she had done, and what had been decreed upon her.   2. And the king's young men, his servants, said, "Let young virgins of comely appearance be sought for the king.   3. And let the king appoint commissioners in all the provinces of his kingdom, and let them gather every young virgin of comely appearance to Shushan the capital, to the house of the women, to the custody of Hege, the king's chamberlain, the keeper of the women, and let their ointments be given them.   4. And let the maiden who pleases the king reign in Vashti's stead"; and the matter pleased the king, and he did so.   5. There was a Judean man in Shushan the capital, whose name was Mordecai the son of Jair the son of Shimei the son of Kish, a Benjamite, 6. who had been exiled from Jerusalem with the exile that had been exiled with Jeconiah, king of Judah, which Nebuchadnezzar, king of Babylon, had exiled. 7. And he had brought up Hadassah, that is Esther, his uncle's daughter, for she had neither father nor mother, and the maiden was of comely form and of comely appearance, and when her father and mother died, Mordecai took her to himself for a daughter. 8. And it came to pass, when the king's order and his decree were heard, and when many maidens were gathered to Shushan the capital, to the custody of Hegai, that Esther was taken to the king's house, to the custody of Hegai, keeper of the women. 9. And the maiden pleased him, and she won his favor, and he hastened her ointments and her portions to give [them] to her, and the seven maidens fitting to give her from the king's house, and he changed her and her maidens to the best [portions in] the house of the women. 10. Esther did not tell of her nationality or her lineage, for Mordecai had ordered

הַמֶּ֨לֶךְ֙ אֶל־מְדִינָ֤ה וּמְדִינָה֙ כִּכְתָבָ֔הּ וְאֶל־עַ֥ם וָעָ֖ם כִּלְשׁוֹנ֑וֹ לִהְי֤וֹת כָּל־אִישׁ֙ שֹׂרֵ֣ר בְּבֵית֔וֹ וּמְדַבֵּ֖ר כִּלְשׁ֥וֹן עַמּֽוֹ׃ ס

ב א אַחַר֙ הַדְּבָרִ֣ים הָאֵ֔לֶּה כְּשֹׁ֕ךְ חֲמַ֖ת הַמֶּ֣לֶךְ אֲחַשְׁוֵר֑וֹשׁ זָכַ֣ר אֶת־וַשְׁתִּ֗י וְאֵ֤ת אֲשֶׁר־עָשָׂ֔תָה וְאֵ֥ת אֲשֶׁר־נִגְזַ֖ר עָלֶֽיהָ׃ ב וַיֹּאמְר֥וּ נַעֲרֵֽי־הַמֶּ֖לֶךְ מְשָׁרְתָ֑יו יְבַקְשׁ֥וּ לַמֶּ֛לֶךְ נְעָר֥וֹת בְּתוּל֖וֹת טוֹב֥וֹת מַרְאֶֽה׃ ג וְיַפְקֵ֨ד הַמֶּ֜לֶךְ פְּקִידִ֗ים בְּכָל־מְדִינ֣וֹת מַלְכוּת֒וֹ וְיִקְבְּצ֣וּ אֶת־כָּל־נַעֲרָֽה־בְ֠תוּלָה טוֹבַ֨ת מַרְאֶ֜ה אֶל־שׁוּשַׁ֤ן הַבִּירָה֙ אֶל־בֵּ֣ית הַנָּשִׁ֔ים אֶל־יַ֥ד הֵגֶ֛א סְרִ֥יס הַמֶּ֖לֶךְ שֹׁמֵ֣ר הַנָּשִׁ֑ים וְנָת֖וֹן תַּמְרֻקֵיהֶֽן׃ ד וְהַֽנַּעֲרָ֗ה אֲשֶׁ֤ר תִּיטַב֙ בְּעֵינֵ֣י הַמֶּ֔לֶךְ תִּמְלֹ֖ךְ תַּ֣חַת וַשְׁתִּ֑י וַיִּיטַ֧ב הַדָּבָ֛ר בְּעֵינֵ֥י הַמֶּ֖לֶךְ וַיַּ֥עַשׂ כֵּֽן׃ ס ה אִ֣ישׁ יְהוּדִ֗י הָיָ֖ה בְּשׁוּשַׁ֣ן הַבִּירָ֑ה וּשְׁמ֣וֹ מָרְדֳּכַ֗י בֶּ֣ן יָאִ֧יר בֶּן־שִׁמְעִ֛י בֶּן־קִ֖ישׁ אִ֥ישׁ יְמִינִֽי׃ ו אֲשֶׁ֤ר הָגְלָה֙ מִירֽוּשָׁלַ֔יִם עִם־הַגֹּלָה֙ אֲשֶׁ֣ר הָגְלְתָ֔ה עִ֖ם יְכָנְיָ֣ה מֶֽלֶךְ־יְהוּדָ֑ה אֲשֶׁ֣ר הֶגְלָ֔ה נְבֽוּכַדְנֶאצַּ֖ר מֶ֥לֶךְ בָּבֶֽל׃ ז וַיְהִ֨י אֹמֵ֜ן אֶת־הֲדַסָּ֗ה הִ֤יא אֶסְתֵּר֙ בַּת־דֹּד֔וֹ כִּ֛י אֵ֥ין לָ֖הּ אָ֣ב וָאֵ֑ם וְהַנַּעֲרָ֤ה יְפַת־תֹּ֙אַר֙ וְטוֹבַ֣ת מַרְאֶ֔ה וּבְמ֤וֹת אָבִ֙יהָ֙ וְאִמָּ֔הּ לְקָחָ֧הּ מָרְדֳּכַ֛י ל֖וֹ לְבַֽת׃ ח וַיְהִ֗י בְּהִשָּׁמַ֤ע דְּבַר־הַמֶּ֙לֶךְ֙ וְדָת֔וֹ וּֽבְהִקָּבֵ֞ץ נְעָר֥וֹת רַבּ֛וֹת אֶל־שׁוּשַׁ֥ן הַבִּירָ֖ה אֶל־יַ֣ד הֵגָ֑י וַתִּלָּקַ֤ח אֶסְתֵּר֙ אֶל־בֵּ֣ית הַמֶּ֔לֶךְ אֶל־יַ֥ד הֵגַ֖י שֹׁמֵ֥ר הַנָּשִֽׁים׃ ט וַתִּיטַ֨ב הַנַּעֲרָ֣ה בְעֵינָיו֮ וַתִּשָּׂ֣א חֶ֣סֶד לְפָנָיו֒ וַ֠יְבַהֵל אֶת־תַּמְרוּקֶ֤יהָ וְאֶת־מָנוֹתֶ֙הָ֙ לָתֵ֣ת לָ֔הּ וְאֵת֙ שֶׁ֣בַע הַנְּעָר֔וֹת הָרְאֻי֥וֹת לָֽתֶת־לָ֖הּ מִבֵּ֣ית הַמֶּ֑לֶךְ וַיְשַׁנֶּ֧הָ וְאֶת־נַעֲרוֹתֶ֛יהָ לְט֖וֹב בֵּ֥ית הַנָּשִֽׁים׃ י לֹא־הִגִּ֣ידָה אֶסְתֵּ֔ר אֶת־עַמָּ֖הּ וְאֶת־מֽוֹלַדְתָּ֑הּ כִּ֧י מָרְדֳּכַ֛י צִוָּ֥ה עָלֶ֖יהָ אֲשֶׁ֥ר לֹא־תַגִּֽיד׃ יא וּבְכָל־י֣וֹם וָי֔וֹם

her not to tell. 11. And every day, Mordecai would walk about in front of court of the house of the women, to learn of Esther's welfare and what would be done to her. 12. And when each maiden's turn arrived to go to King Ahasuerus, after having been treated according to the practice prescribed for the women, for twelve months, for so were the days of their ointments completed, six months with myrrh oil, and six months with perfumes, and with the ointments of the women. 13. Then with this the maiden would come to the king; all that she would request would be given to her to come with her from the house of the women to the king's house. 14. In the evening she would go, and in the morning she would return to the second house of the women, to the custody of Shaashgaz, the king's chamberlain, the guard of the concubines; she would no longer come to the king unless the king wanted her, and she was called by name. 15. Now upon the arrival of the turn of Esther, the daughter of Abihail, Mordecai's uncle, to come to the king, she requested nothing, except what Hegai the king's chamberlain, the guard of the women, would say, and Esther obtained grace in the eyes of all who saw her. 16. So Esther was taken to King Ahasuerus, to his royal house in the tenth month, which is the month of Tebeth, in the seventh year of his reign. 17. And the king loved Esther more than all the women, and she won more grace and favor before him than all the virgins, and he placed the royal crown on her head and made her queen instead of Vashti. 18. And the king made a great banquet for all his princes and his vassals, the banquet of Esther, and he granted a release for the provinces and gave gifts according to the bounty of the king. 19. And when the virgins were gathered a second time, and Mordecai was sitting in the king's gate — 20. Esther would not tell her lineage or her nationality as Mordecai had commanded her, for Esther kept Mordecai's orders as she had done when she was raised by him. 21. In those days, when Mordecai was sitting in the king's gate, Bigthan and Teresh, two of the king's chamberlains, of the guards of the threshold, became angry and sought to lay a hand on King Ahasue-

מָרְדֳּכַי מִתְהַלֵּךְ לִפְנֵי חֲצַר בֵּית־הַנָּשִׁים לָדַעַת אֶת־שְׁלוֹם אֶסְתֵּר וּמַה־יֵּעָשֶׂה בָּהּ: יב וּבְהַגִּיעַ תֹּר נַעֲרָה וְנַעֲרָה לָבוֹא ׀ אֶל־הַמֶּלֶךְ אֲחַשְׁוֵרוֹשׁ מִקֵּץ הֱיוֹת לָהּ כְּדָת הַנָּשִׁים שְׁנֵים עָשָׂר חֹדֶשׁ כִּי כֵּן יִמְלְאוּ יְמֵי מְרוּקֵיהֶן שִׁשָּׁה חֳדָשִׁים בְּשֶׁמֶן הַמֹּר וְשִׁשָּׁה חֳדָשִׁים בַּבְּשָׂמִים וּבְתַמְרוּקֵי הַנָּשִׁים: יג וּבָזֶה הַנַּעֲרָה בָּאָה אֶל־הַמֶּלֶךְ אֵת כָּל־אֲשֶׁר תֹּאמַר יִנָּתֵן לָהּ לָבוֹא עִמָּהּ מִבֵּית הַנָּשִׁים עַד־בֵּית הַמֶּלֶךְ: יד בָּעֶרֶב ׀ הִיא בָאָה וּבַבֹּקֶר הִיא שָׁבָה אֶל־בֵּית הַנָּשִׁים שֵׁנִי אֶל־יַד שַׁעַשְׁגַז סְרִיס הַמֶּלֶךְ שֹׁמֵר הַפִּילַגְשִׁים לֹא־תָבוֹא עוֹד אֶל־הַמֶּלֶךְ כִּי אִם־חָפֵץ בָּהּ הַמֶּלֶךְ וְנִקְרְאָה בְשֵׁם: טו וּבְהַגִּיעַ תֹּר־אֶסְתֵּר בַּת־אֲבִיחַיִל ׀ דֹּד מָרְדֳּכַי אֲשֶׁר לָקַח־לוֹ לְבַת לָבוֹא אֶל־הַמֶּלֶךְ לֹא בִקְשָׁה דָּבָר כִּי אִם אֶת־אֲשֶׁר יֹאמַר הֵגַי סְרִיס־הַמֶּלֶךְ שֹׁמֵר הַנָּשִׁים וַתְּהִי אֶסְתֵּר נֹשֵׂאת חֵן בְּעֵינֵי כָּל־רֹאֶיהָ: טז וַתִּלָּקַח אֶסְתֵּר אֶל־הַמֶּלֶךְ אֲחַשְׁוֵרוֹשׁ אֶל־בֵּית מַלְכוּתוֹ בַּחֹדֶשׁ הָעֲשִׂירִי הוּא־חֹדֶשׁ טֵבֵת בִּשְׁנַת־שֶׁבַע לְמַלְכוּתוֹ: יז וַיֶּאֱהַב הַמֶּלֶךְ אֶת־אֶסְתֵּר מִכָּל־הַנָּשִׁים וַתִּשָּׂא־חֵן וָחֶסֶד לְפָנָיו מִכָּל־הַבְּתוּלוֹת וַיָּשֶׂם כֶּתֶר־מַלְכוּת בְּרֹאשָׁהּ וַיַּמְלִיכֶהָ תַּחַת וַשְׁתִּי: יח וַיַּעַשׂ הַמֶּלֶךְ מִשְׁתֶּה גָדוֹל לְכָל־שָׂרָיו וַעֲבָדָיו אֵת מִשְׁתֵּה אֶסְתֵּר וַהֲנָחָה לַמְּדִינוֹת עָשָׂה וַיִּתֵּן מַשְׂאֵת כְּיַד הַמֶּלֶךְ: יט וּבְהִקָּבֵץ בְּתוּלוֹת שֵׁנִית וּמָרְדֳּכַי יֹשֵׁב בְּשַׁעַר־הַמֶּלֶךְ: כ אֵין אֶסְתֵּר מַגֶּדֶת מוֹלַדְתָּהּ וְאֶת־עַמָּהּ כַּאֲשֶׁר צִוָּה עָלֶיהָ מָרְדֳּכָי וְאֶת־מַאֲמַר מָרְדֳּכַי אֶסְתֵּר עֹשָׂה כַּאֲשֶׁר הָיְתָה בְאָמְנָה אִתּוֹ: ס כא בַּיָּמִים הָהֵם וּמָרְדֳּכַי יוֹשֵׁב בְּשַׁעַר־הַמֶּלֶךְ קָצַף בִּגְתָן וָתֶרֶשׁ שְׁנֵי־סָרִיסֵי הַמֶּלֶךְ מִשֹּׁמְרֵי הַסַּף וַיְבַקְשׁוּ לִשְׁלֹחַ יָד בַּמֶּלֶךְ

rus. 22. And the matter became known to Mordecai, and he told [it] to Esther the queen, and Esther told [it] to the king in Mordecai's name. 23. Now the matter was investigated and found [to be so], and they both were hanged on a gallows, and it was written in the diary [that was read] before the king.

CHAPTER III

1. After these events, King Ahasuerus promoted Haman son of Hammedatha the Agagite and advanced him, and he placed his seat above all the princes who were with him. 2. And all the king's servants who were in the king's gate would kneel and prostrate themselves before Haman, for so had the king commanded concerning him, but Mordecai would neither kneel nor prostrate himself. 3. Then the king's servants, who were in the king's gate, said to Mordecai, "Why do you disobey the king's orders?" 4. Now it came to pass when they said [this] to him daily, and he did not heed them, that they told [this] to Haman, to see whether Mordecai's words would stand up, for he had told them that he was a Jew. 5. And when Haman saw that Mordecai would neither kneel nor prostrate himself before him, Haman became full of wrath. 6. But it seemed contemptible to him to lay hands on Mordecai alone, for they had told him Mordecai's nationality, and Haman sought to destroy all the Jews who were throughout Ahasuerus's entire kingdom, Mordecai's people. 7. In the first month — that is the month of Nisan — in the twelfth year of King Ahasuerus, one cast *pur* — that is the lot — before Haman from day to day and from month [to month], to the twelfth month, which is the month of Adar. 8. And Haman said to King Ahasuerus, "There is one people scattered yet separate among the peoples throughout all the provinces of your kingdom, and their laws differ from [those of] every people, and they do not keep the king's laws; it is [therefore] no use for the king to let them be. 9. If it pleases the king, let it be written to destroy them, and I will weigh out ten thousand silver talents into the hands of those who perform

אֲחַשְׁוֵרֽוֹשׁ: כב וַיִּוָּדַ֤ע הַדָּבָר֙ לְמָרְדֳּכַ֔י וַיַּגֵּ֖ד לְאֶסְתֵּ֣ר הַמַּלְכָּ֑ה וַתֹּ֧אמֶר אֶסְתֵּ֛ר לַמֶּ֖לֶךְ בְּשֵׁ֥ם מָרְדֳּכָֽי: כג וַיְבֻקַּ֤שׁ הַדָּבָר֙ וַיִּמָּצֵ֔א וַיִּתָּל֥וּ שְׁנֵיהֶ֖ם עַל־עֵ֑ץ וַיִּכָּתֵ֗ב בְּסֵ֛פֶר דִּבְרֵ֥י הַיָּמִ֖ים לִפְנֵ֥י הַמֶּֽלֶךְ: ס

ג א אַחַ֣ר ׀ הַדְּבָרִ֣ים הָאֵ֗לֶּה גִּדַּל֩ הַמֶּ֨לֶךְ אֲחַשְׁוֵר֜וֹשׁ אֶת־הָמָ֧ן בֶּֽן־הַמְּדָ֛תָא הָאֲגָגִ֖י וַֽיְנַשְּׂאֵ֑הוּ וַיָּ֙שֶׂם֙ אֶת־כִּסְא֔וֹ מֵעַ֕ל כָּל־הַשָּׂרִ֖ים אֲשֶׁ֥ר אִתּֽוֹ: ב וְכָל־עַבְדֵ֨י הַמֶּ֜לֶךְ אֲשֶׁר־בְּשַׁ֣עַר הַמֶּ֗לֶךְ כֹּרְעִ֤ים וּמִֽשְׁתַּחֲוִים֙ לְהָמָ֔ן כִּי־כֵ֖ן צִוָּה־ל֣וֹ הַמֶּ֑לֶךְ וּמָ֨רְדֳּכַ֔י לֹ֥א יִכְרַ֖ע וְלֹ֥א יִֽשְׁתַּחֲוֶֽה: ג וַיֹּ֨אמְר֜וּ עַבְדֵ֥י הַמֶּ֛לֶךְ אֲשֶׁר־בְּשַׁ֥עַר הַמֶּ֖לֶךְ לְמָרְדֳּכָ֑י מַדּ֙וּעַ֙ אַתָּ֣ה עוֹבֵ֔ר אֵ֖ת מִצְוַ֥ת הַמֶּֽלֶךְ: ד וַיְהִ֗י בְּאָמְרָ֤ם (כאמרם קרי) אֵלָיו֙ י֣וֹם וָי֔וֹם וְלֹ֥א שָׁמַ֖ע אֲלֵיהֶ֑ם וַיַּגִּ֣ידוּ לְהָמָ֗ן לִרְאוֹת֙ הֲיַֽעַמְדוּ֙ דִּבְרֵ֣י מָרְדֳּכַ֔י כִּֽי־הִגִּ֥יד לָהֶ֖ם אֲשֶׁר־ה֥וּא יְהוּדִֽי: ה וַיַּ֣רְא הָמָ֔ן כִּי־אֵ֣ין מָרְדֳּכַ֔י כֹּרֵ֥עַ וּמִֽשְׁתַּחֲוֶ֖ה ל֑וֹ וַיִּמָּלֵ֥א הָמָ֖ן חֵמָֽה: ו וַיִּ֣בֶז בְּעֵינָ֗יו לִשְׁלֹ֤חַ יָד֙ בְּמָרְדֳּכַ֣י לְבַדּ֔וֹ כִּֽי־הִגִּ֥ידוּ ל֖וֹ אֶת־עַ֣ם מָרְדֳּכָ֑י וַיְבַקֵּ֣שׁ הָמָ֗ן לְהַשְׁמִ֧יד אֶת־כָּל־הַיְּהוּדִ֛ים אֲשֶׁ֛ר בְּכָל־מַלְכ֥וּת אֲחַשְׁוֵר֖וֹשׁ עַ֥ם מָרְדֳּכָֽי: ז בַּחֹ֤דֶשׁ הָֽרִאשׁוֹן֙ הוּא־חֹ֣דֶשׁ נִיסָ֔ן בִּשְׁנַת֙ שְׁתֵּ֣ים עֶשְׂרֵ֔ה לַמֶּ֖לֶךְ אֲחַשְׁוֵר֑וֹשׁ הִפִּ֣יל פּוּר֩ ה֨וּא הַגּוֹרָ֜ל לִפְנֵ֣י הָמָ֗ן מִיּ֧וֹם ׀ לְי֛וֹם וּמֵחֹ֛דֶשׁ לְחֹ֥דֶשׁ שְׁנֵים־עָשָׂ֖ר הוּא־חֹ֥דֶשׁ אֲדָֽר: ס ח וַיֹּ֤אמֶר הָמָן֙ לַמֶּ֣לֶךְ אֲחַשְׁוֵר֔וֹשׁ יֶשְׁנ֣וֹ עַם־אֶחָ֗ד מְפֻזָּ֤ר וּמְפֹרָד֙ בֵּ֣ין הָֽעַמִּ֔ים בְּכֹ֖ל מְדִינ֣וֹת מַלְכוּתֶ֑ךָ וְדָתֵיהֶ֣ם שֹׁנ֤וֹת מִכָּל־עָ֔ם וְאֶת־דָּתֵ֤י הַמֶּ֙לֶךְ֙ אֵינָ֣ם עֹשִׂ֔ים וְלַמֶּ֖לֶךְ אֵין־שֹׁוֶ֥ה לְהַנִּיחָֽם: ט אִם־עַל־הַמֶּ֣לֶךְ ט֔וֹב יִכָּתֵ֖ב לְאַבְּדָ֑ם וַעֲשֶׂ֨רֶת אֲלָפִ֜ים כִּכַּר־כֶּ֗סֶף אֶשְׁקוֹל֙ עַל־

the work, to bring [it] into the king's treasuries." 10. And the king took his ring off his hand and gave it to Haman son of Hammedatha the Agagite, the adversary of the Jews. 11. Said the king to Haman, "The silver is given to you, and the people — to do to them as it pleases you." 12. The king's scribes were summoned in the first month, on the thirteenth day thereof, and it was written according to everything that Haman had ordained to the king's satraps and to the governors who were over every province, and to the princes of every people, each province according to its script and each people according to its tongue; it was written in the name of King Ahasuerus, and it was sealed with the king's ring. 13. And letters were sent by the hand of the couriers to all the king's provinces, to destroy, kill, and cause to perish all the Jews, both young and old, little children and women, on one day, on the thirteenth of the twelfth month, that is the month of Adar, and their spoils to be taken as prey. 14. The copy of the writ for an edict to be given in every province, published to all the peoples, to be ready for that day. 15. The couriers went forth in all haste by the king's order, and the edict was given in Shushan the capital; and the king and Haman sat down to drink, and the city of Shushan was perplexed.

CHAPTER IV

1. And Mordecai knew all that had transpired, and Mordecai rent his clothes and put on sackcloth and ashes, and he went out into the midst of the city and cried [with] a loud and bitter cry. 2. And he came up as far as the king's gate, for one may not enter the king's gate dressed in sackcloth. 3. And in every province, wherever the king's orders and his edict reached, there was great mourning for the Jews, and fasting and weeping and lamenting; sackcloth and ashes were laid out for the most prominent. 4. And Esther's maidens and her chamberlains came and told her, and the queen was extremely terrified, and she sent clothing to dress Mordecai and to take off his sackcloth, but he did not accept [it]. 5. Then Esther summoned Hathach, [one]

יְדֵי עֹשֵׂי הַמְּלָאכָה לְהָבִיא אֶל־גִּנְזֵי הַמֶּלֶךְ׃
י וַיָּסַר הַמֶּלֶךְ אֶת־טַבַּעְתּוֹ מֵעַל יָדוֹ וַיִּתְּנָהּ
לְהָמָן בֶּן־הַמְּדָתָא הָאֲגָגִי צֹרֵר הַיְּהוּדִים׃
יא וַיֹּאמֶר הַמֶּלֶךְ לְהָמָן הַכֶּסֶף נָתוּן לָךְ וְהָעָם
לַעֲשׂוֹת בּוֹ כַּטּוֹב בְּעֵינֶיךָ׃ יב וַיִּקָּרְאוּ סֹפְרֵי
הַמֶּלֶךְ בַּחֹדֶשׁ הָרִאשׁוֹן בִּשְׁלוֹשָׁה עָשָׂר יוֹם בּוֹ
וַיִּכָּתֵב כְּכָל־אֲשֶׁר־צִוָּה הָמָן אֶל אֲחַשְׁדַּרְפְּנֵי־
הַמֶּלֶךְ וְאֶל־הַפַּחוֹת אֲשֶׁר ׀ עַל־מְדִינָה וּמְדִינָה
וְאֶל־שָׂרֵי עַם וָעָם מְדִינָה וּמְדִינָה כִּכְתָבָהּ וְעַם
וָעָם כִּלְשׁוֹנוֹ בְּשֵׁם הַמֶּלֶךְ אֲחַשְׁוֵרֹשׁ נִכְתָּב
וְנֶחְתָּם בְּטַבַּעַת הַמֶּלֶךְ׃ יג וְנִשְׁלוֹחַ סְפָרִים בְּיַד
הָרָצִים אֶל־כָּל־מְדִינוֹת הַמֶּלֶךְ לְהַשְׁמִיד לַהֲרֹג
וּלְאַבֵּד אֶת־כָּל־הַיְּהוּדִים מִנַּעַר וְעַד־זָקֵן טַף
וְנָשִׁים בְּיוֹם אֶחָד בִּשְׁלוֹשָׁה עָשָׂר לְחֹדֶשׁ
שְׁנֵים־עָשָׂר הוּא־חֹדֶשׁ אֲדָר וּשְׁלָלָם לָבוֹז׃
יד פַּתְשֶׁגֶן הַכְּתָב לְהִנָּתֵן דָּת בְּכָל־מְדִינָה
וּמְדִינָה גָּלוּי לְכָל־הָעַמִּים לִהְיוֹת עֲתִדִים לַיּוֹם
הַזֶּה׃ טו הָרָצִים יָצְאוּ דְחוּפִים בִּדְבַר הַמֶּלֶךְ
וְהַדָּת נִתְּנָה בְּשׁוּשַׁן הַבִּירָה וְהַמֶּלֶךְ וְהָמָן יָשְׁבוּ
לִשְׁתּוֹת וְהָעִיר שׁוּשָׁן נָבוֹכָה׃ ס

ד א וּמָרְדֳּכַי יָדַע אֶת־כָּל־אֲשֶׁר נַעֲשָׂה וַיִּקְרַע
מָרְדֳּכַי אֶת־בְּגָדָיו וַיִּלְבַּשׁ שַׂק וָאֵפֶר וַיֵּצֵא בְּתוֹךְ
הָעִיר וַיִּזְעַק זְעָקָה גְדוֹלָה וּמָרָה׃ ב וַיָּבוֹא עַד
לִפְנֵי שַׁעַר־הַמֶּלֶךְ כִּי אֵין לָבוֹא אֶל־שַׁעַר הַמֶּלֶךְ
בִּלְבוּשׁ שָׂק׃ ג וּבְכָל־מְדִינָה וּמְדִינָה מְקוֹם
אֲשֶׁר דְּבַר־הַמֶּלֶךְ וְדָתוֹ מַגִּיעַ אֵבֶל גָּדוֹל
לַיְּהוּדִים וְצוֹם וּבְכִי וּמִסְפֵּד שַׂק וָאֵפֶר יֻצַּע
לָרַבִּים׃ ד וַתָּבוֹאינָה (ותבואנה קרי) נַעֲרוֹת אֶסְתֵּר
וְסָרִיסֶיהָ וַיַּגִּידוּ לָהּ וַתִּתְחַלְחַל הַמַּלְכָּה מְאֹד
וַתִּשְׁלַח בְּגָדִים לְהַלְבִּישׁ אֶת־מָרְדֳּכַי וּלְהָסִיר
שַׂקּוֹ מֵעָלָיו וְלֹא קִבֵּל׃ ה וַתִּקְרָא אֶסְתֵּר לַהֲתָךְ

מִסָּרִיסֵי הַמֶּלֶךְ אֲשֶׁר הֶעֱמִיד לְפָנֶיהָ וַתְּצַוֵּהוּ
עַל־מָרְדֳּכָי לָדַעַת מַה־זֶּה וְעַל־מַה־זֶּה: ו וַיֵּצֵא
הֲתָךְ אֶל־מָרְדֳּכָי אֶל־רְחוֹב הָעִיר אֲשֶׁר לִפְנֵי
שַׁעַר־הַמֶּלֶךְ: ז וַיַּגֶּד־לוֹ מָרְדֳּכַי אֵת כָּל־אֲשֶׁר
קָרָהוּ וְאֵת | פָּרָשַׁת הַכֶּסֶף אֲשֶׁר אָמַר הָמָן
לִשְׁקוֹל עַל־גִּנְזֵי הַמֶּלֶךְ בַּיְּהוּדִיִּים (ביהודים קרי)
לְאַבְּדָם: ח וְאֶת־פַּתְשֶׁגֶן כְּתָב־הַדָּת אֲשֶׁר־נִתַּן
בְּשׁוּשָׁן לְהַשְׁמִידָם נָתַן לוֹ לְהַרְאוֹת אֶת־אֶסְתֵּר
וּלְהַגִּיד לָהּ וּלְצַוּוֹת עָלֶיהָ לָבוֹא אֶל־הַמֶּלֶךְ
לְהִתְחַנֶּן־לוֹ וּלְבַקֵּשׁ מִלְּפָנָיו עַל־עַמָּהּ: ט וַיָּבוֹא
הֲתָךְ וַיַּגֵּד לְאֶסְתֵּר אֵת דִּבְרֵי מָרְדֳּכָי: י וַתֹּאמֶר
אֶסְתֵּר לַהֲתָךְ וַתְּצַוֵּהוּ אֶל־מָרְדֳּכָי: יא כָּל־עַבְדֵי
הַמֶּלֶךְ וְעַם מְדִינוֹת הַמֶּלֶךְ יֹדְעִים אֲשֶׁר כָּל־
אִישׁ וְאִשָּׁה אֲשֶׁר־יָבוֹא אֶל־הַמֶּלֶךְ אֶל־הֶחָצֵר
הַפְּנִימִית אֲשֶׁר לֹא־יִקָּרֵא אַחַת דָּתוֹ לְהָמִית
לְבַד מֵאֲשֶׁר יוֹשִׁיט־לוֹ הַמֶּלֶךְ אֶת־שַׁרְבִיט
הַזָּהָב וְחָיָה וַאֲנִי לֹא נִקְרֵאתִי לָבוֹא אֶל־הַמֶּלֶךְ
זֶה שְׁלוֹשִׁים יוֹם: יב וַיַּגִּידוּ לְמָרְדֳּכָי אֵת דִּבְרֵי
אֶסְתֵּר: יג וַיֹּאמֶר מָרְדֳּכַי לְהָשִׁיב אֶל־אֶסְתֵּר
אַל־תְּדַמִּי בְנַפְשֵׁךְ לְהִמָּלֵט בֵּית־הַמֶּלֶךְ מִכָּל־
הַיְּהוּדִים: יד כִּי אִם־הַחֲרֵשׁ תַּחֲרִישִׁי בָּעֵת
הַזֹּאת רֶוַח וְהַצָּלָה יַעֲמוֹד לַיְּהוּדִים מִמָּקוֹם
אַחֵר וְאַתְּ וּבֵית־אָבִיךְ תֹּאבֵדוּ וּמִי יוֹדֵעַ אִם־
לְעֵת כָּזֹאת הִגַּעַתְּ לַמַּלְכוּת: טו וַתֹּאמֶר אֶסְתֵּר
לְהָשִׁיב אֶל־מָרְדֳּכָי: טז לֵךְ כְּנוֹס אֶת־כָּל־
הַיְּהוּדִים הַנִּמְצְאִים בְּשׁוּשָׁן וְצוּמוּ עָלַי וְאַל־
תֹּאכְלוּ וְאַל־תִּשְׁתּוּ שְׁלֹשֶׁת יָמִים לַיְלָה וָיוֹם
גַּם־אֲנִי וְנַעֲרֹתַי אָצוּם כֵּן וּבְכֵן אָבוֹא אֶל־
הַמֶּלֶךְ אֲשֶׁר לֹא־כַדָּת וְכַאֲשֶׁר אָבַדְתִּי אָבָדְתִּי:
יז וַיַּעֲבֹר מָרְדֳּכָי וַיַּעַשׂ כְּכֹל אֲשֶׁר־צִוְּתָה עָלָיו
אֶסְתֵּר:

ה א וַיְהִי | בַּיּוֹם הַשְּׁלִישִׁי וַתִּלְבַּשׁ אֶסְתֵּר
מַלְכוּת וַתַּעֲמֹד בַּחֲצַר בֵּית־הַמֶּלֶךְ הַפְּנִימִית

of the king's chamberlains, whom he had appointed before her, and she commanded him concerning Mordecai, to know what this was and why this was.   6. So Hathach went forth to Mordecai, to the city square, which is before the king's gate. 7. And Mordecai told him all that had befallen him, and the full account of the silver that Haman had proposed to weigh out into the king's treasuries on the Jews' account, to cause them to perish.   8. And the copy of the writ of the decree that was given in Shushan he gave him, to show Esther and to tell her, and to order her to come before the king to beseech him and to beg him for her people.   9. And Hathach came, and he told Esther what Mordecai had said.   10. And Esther said to Hathach, and ordered him to [tell] Mordecai,   11. "All the king's servants and the people of the king's provinces know that any man or woman who comes to the king, into the inner court, who is not summoned, there is but one law for him, to be put to death, except the one to whom the king extends the golden scepter, that he may live, but I have not been summoned to come to the king these thirty days."   12. And they told Esther's words to Mordecai.   13. And Mordecai ordered to reply to Esther, "Do not think to escape in the king's house from among all the Jews.   14. For, if you remain silent at this time, relief and rescue will arise for the Jews from somewhere else, and you and your father's household will perish; and who knows whether [it was] for a time such as this [that] you attained the kingdom."   15. Then Esther ordered to reply to Mordecai,   16. "Go, assemble all the Jews who are found in Shushan and fast on my behalf, and neither eat nor drink for three days, day and night; also I and my maidens will do so; then I will go to the king contrary to the law, and if I perish, I perish."   17. So Mordecai went his way and did according to all that Esther had ordered him.

CHAPTER V

1. Now it came to pass on the third day, that Esther clothed herself regally, and she stood in the inner court of the king's house,

opposite the king's house, and the king was sitting on his royal throne in the royal palace, opposite the entrance of the house. 2. And it came to pass when the king saw Esther the queen standing in the court, that she won favor in his eyes, and the king extended to Esther the golden scepter that was in his hand, and Esther approached and touched the end of the scepter. 3. And the king said to her, "What concerns you, Esther the queen, and what is your petition? Even to half the kingdom, it will be given you." 4. And Esther said, "If it pleases the king, let the king and Haman come today to the banquet that I have made for him." 5. And the king said, "Rush Haman to do the bidding of Esther," and the king and Haman came to the banquet that Esther had made. 6. Now the king said to Esther during the wine banquet, "What is your petition? It shall be granted you. And what is your request? Even up to half the kingdom, it shall be fulfilled." 7. Then Esther replied and said, "My petition and my request are [as follows]: 8. If I have found favor in the king's eyes, and if it pleases the king to grant my petition and to fulfill my request, let the king and Haman come to the banquet that I will make for them, and tomorrow I will do the king's bidding." 9. And Haman went out on that day, happy and with a cheerful heart, and when Haman saw Mordecai in the king's gate, and he neither rose nor stirred because of him, Haman was filled with wrath against Mordecai. 10. And Haman restrained himself, and he came home, and he sent and brought his friends and Zeresh his wife. 11. And Haman recounted to them the glory of his riches and the multitude of his sons, and all [the ways] that the king had promoted him and that he had exalted him over the princes and the king's slaves. 12. And Haman said, "Esther did not even bring [anyone] to the party that she made, but me, and tomorrow, too, I am invited by her with the king. 13. But all this is worth nothing to me; every time I see Mordecai the Jew sitting in the king's gate." 14. And Zeresh his wife and all his friends said, "Let them make a gallows fifty cubits high, and in the morning

נֹכַח בֵּית הַמֶּלֶךְ וְהַמֶּלֶךְ יוֹשֵׁב עַל־כִּסֵּא מַלְכוּתוֹ בְּבֵית הַמַּלְכוּת נֹכַח פֶּתַח הַבָּיִת: ב וַיְהִי כִרְאוֹת הַמֶּלֶךְ אֶת־אֶסְתֵּר הַמַּלְכָּה עֹמֶדֶת בֶּחָצֵר נָשְׂאָה חֵן בְּעֵינָיו וַיּוֹשֶׁט הַמֶּלֶךְ לְאֶסְתֵּר אֶת־שַׁרְבִיט הַזָּהָב אֲשֶׁר בְּיָדוֹ וַתִּקְרַב אֶסְתֵּר וַתִּגַּע בְּרֹאשׁ הַשַּׁרְבִיט: ג וַיֹּאמֶר לָהּ הַמֶּלֶךְ מַה־לָּךְ אֶסְתֵּר הַמַּלְכָּה וּמַה־בַּקָּשָׁתֵךְ עַד־חֲצִי הַמַּלְכוּת וְיִנָּתֵן לָךְ: ד וַתֹּאמֶר אֶסְתֵּר אִם־עַל־הַמֶּלֶךְ טוֹב יָבוֹא הַמֶּלֶךְ וְהָמָן הַיּוֹם אֶל־הַמִּשְׁתֶּה אֲשֶׁר־עָשִׂיתִי לוֹ: ה וַיֹּאמֶר הַמֶּלֶךְ מַהֲרוּ אֶת־הָמָן לַעֲשׂוֹת אֶת־דְּבַר אֶסְתֵּר וַיָּבֹא הַמֶּלֶךְ וְהָמָן אֶל־הַמִּשְׁתֶּה אֲשֶׁר־עָשְׂתָה אֶסְתֵּר: ו וַיֹּאמֶר הַמֶּלֶךְ לְאֶסְתֵּר בְּמִשְׁתֵּה הַיַּיִן מַה־שְּׁאֵלָתֵךְ וְיִנָּתֵן לָךְ וּמַה־ בַּקָּשָׁתֵךְ עַד־חֲצִי הַמַּלְכוּת וְתֵעָשׂ: ז וַתַּעַן אֶסְתֵּר וַתֹּאמַר שְׁאֵלָתִי וּבַקָּשָׁתִי: ח אִם־מָצָאתִי חֵן בְּעֵינֵי הַמֶּלֶךְ וְאִם־עַל־הַמֶּלֶךְ טוֹב לָתֵת אֶת־ שְׁאֵלָתִי וְלַעֲשׂוֹת אֶת־בַּקָּשָׁתִי יָבוֹא הַמֶּלֶךְ וְהָמָן אֶל־הַמִּשְׁתֶּה אֲשֶׁר אֶעֱשֶׂה לָהֶם וּמָחָר אֶעֱשֶׂה כִּדְבַר הַמֶּלֶךְ: ט וַיֵּצֵא הָמָן בַּיּוֹם הַהוּא שָׂמֵחַ וְטוֹב לֵב וְכִרְאוֹת הָמָן אֶת־מָרְדֳּכַי בְּשַׁעַר הַמֶּלֶךְ וְלֹא־קָם וְלֹא־זָע מִמֶּנּוּ וַיִּמָּלֵא הָמָן עַל־ מָרְדֳּכַי חֵמָה: י וַיִּתְאַפַּק הָמָן וַיָּבוֹא אֶל־בֵּיתוֹ וַיִּשְׁלַח וַיָּבֵא אֶת־אֹהֲבָיו וְאֶת־זֶרֶשׁ אִשְׁתּוֹ: יא וַיְסַפֵּר לָהֶם הָמָן אֶת־כְּבוֹד עָשְׁרוֹ וְרֹב בָּנָיו וְאֵת כָּל־אֲשֶׁר גִּדְּלוֹ הַמֶּלֶךְ וְאֵת אֲשֶׁר נִשְּׂאוֹ עַל־הַשָּׂרִים וְעַבְדֵי הַמֶּלֶךְ: יב וַיֹּאמֶר הָמָן אַף לֹא־הֵבִיאָה אֶסְתֵּר הַמַּלְכָּה עִם־הַמֶּלֶךְ אֶל־ הַמִּשְׁתֶּה אֲשֶׁר־עָשָׂתָה כִּי אִם־אוֹתִי וְגַם־לְמָחָר אֲנִי קָרוּא־לָהּ עִם־הַמֶּלֶךְ: יג וְכָל־זֶה אֵינֶנּוּ שֹׁוֶה לִי בְּכָל־עֵת אֲשֶׁר אֲנִי רֹאֶה אֶת־מָרְדֳּכַי הַיְּהוּדִי יוֹשֵׁב בְּשַׁעַר הַמֶּלֶךְ: יד וַתֹּאמֶר לוֹ זֶרֶשׁ אִשְׁתּוֹ וְכָל־אֹהֲבָיו יַעֲשׂוּ־עֵץ גָּבֹהַּ חֲמִשִּׁים

say to the king that they should hang Mordecai on it, and come with the king to the banquet joyfully." The matter pleased Haman, and he made the gallows.

CHAPTER VI

1. On that night, the king's sleep was disturbed, and he ordered to bring the book of the records, the chronicles, and they were read before the king. 2. And it was found written, that Mordecai had reported about Bigthana and Teresh, the two chamberlains of the king, of the guards of the threshold, who had sought to lay a hand on King Ahasuerus. 3. Said the king, "What honor and greatness was done for Mordecai on that account?" And the king's servants who minister before him said, "Nothing was done for him." 4. And the king said, "Who is in the court?" And Haman had come to the outside court of the king's house, to petition the king to hang Mordecai on the gallows that he had prepared for him. 5. And the king's servants said to him, "Behold: Haman is standing in the yard." And the king said, "Let him enter." 6. And Haman entered, and the king said to him, "What should be done to the man whom the king wishes to honor?" And Haman said to himself, "Whom would the king wish to honor more than me?" 7. And Haman said to the king, "A man whom the king wishes to honor — 8. Let them bring the royal raiment that the king wore, and the horse upon which the king rode when the royal crown was placed on his head. 9. And he should give the raiment and the horse into the hand of a man of the king's princes, the nobles, and let them dress the man whom the king wishes to honor, and let them parade him on the horse in the city square and announce before him, 'So shall be done to the man whom the king wishes to honor.'" 10. And the king said to Haman, "Hurry, take the raiment and the horse as you have spoken, and do so to Mordecai the Jew who sits in the king's gate; let nothing fail of all that you have spoken." 11. And Haman took the raiment and the horse, and he dressed Mordecai, and he paraded him in

אִמָּהּ וּבַבֹּקֶר ׀ אֱמֹר לַמֶּלֶךְ וְיִתְלוּ אֶת־מָרְדֳּכַי
עָלָיו וּבֹא עִם־הַמֶּלֶךְ אֶל־הַמִּשְׁתֶּה שָׂמֵחַ וַיִּיטַב
הַדָּבָר לִפְנֵי הָמָן וַיַּעַשׂ הָעֵץ: ס

ו א בַּלַּיְלָה הַהוּא נָדְדָה שְׁנַת הַמֶּלֶךְ וַיֹּאמֶר
לְהָבִיא אֶת־סֵפֶר הַזִּכְרֹנוֹת דִּבְרֵי הַיָּמִים וַיִּהְיוּ
נִקְרָאִים לִפְנֵי הַמֶּלֶךְ: ב וַיִּמָּצֵא כָתוּב אֲשֶׁר
הִגִּיד מָרְדֳּכַי עַל־בִּגְתָנָא וָתֶרֶשׁ שְׁנֵי סָרִיסֵי
הַמֶּלֶךְ מִשֹּׁמְרֵי הַסַּף אֲשֶׁר בִּקְשׁוּ לִשְׁלֹחַ יָד
בַּמֶּלֶךְ אֲחַשְׁוֵרוֹשׁ: ג וַיֹּאמֶר הַמֶּלֶךְ מַה־נַּעֲשָׂה
יְקָר וּגְדוּלָּה לְמָרְדֳּכַי עַל־זֶה וַיֹּאמְרוּ נַעֲרֵי
הַמֶּלֶךְ מְשָׁרְתָיו לֹא־נַעֲשָׂה עִמּוֹ דָּבָר: ד וַיֹּאמֶר
הַמֶּלֶךְ מִי בֶחָצֵר וְהָמָן בָּא לַחֲצַר בֵּית־הַמֶּלֶךְ
הַחִיצוֹנָה לֵאמֹר לַמֶּלֶךְ לִתְלוֹת אֶת־מָרְדֳּכַי
עַל־הָעֵץ אֲשֶׁר־הֵכִין לוֹ: ה וַיֹּאמְרוּ נַעֲרֵי הַמֶּלֶךְ
אֵלָיו הִנֵּה הָמָן עֹמֵד בֶּחָצֵר וַיֹּאמֶר הַמֶּלֶךְ יָבוֹא:
ו וַיָּבוֹא הָמָן וַיֹּאמֶר לוֹ הַמֶּלֶךְ מַה־לַּעֲשׂוֹת
בָּאִישׁ אֲשֶׁר הַמֶּלֶךְ חָפֵץ בִּיקָרוֹ וַיֹּאמֶר הָמָן
בְּלִבּוֹ לְמִי יַחְפֹּץ הַמֶּלֶךְ לַעֲשׂוֹת יְקָר יוֹתֵר
מִמֶּנִּי: ז וַיֹּאמֶר הָמָן אֶל־הַמֶּלֶךְ אִישׁ אֲשֶׁר
הַמֶּלֶךְ חָפֵץ בִּיקָרוֹ: ח יָבִיאוּ לְבוּשׁ מַלְכוּת
אֲשֶׁר לָבַשׁ־בּוֹ הַמֶּלֶךְ וְסוּס אֲשֶׁר רָכַב עָלָיו
הַמֶּלֶךְ וַאֲשֶׁר נִתַּן כֶּתֶר מַלְכוּת בְּרֹאשׁוֹ
ט וְנָתוֹן הַלְּבוּשׁ וְהַסּוּס עַל־יַד־אִישׁ מִשָּׂרֵי
הַמֶּלֶךְ הַפַּרְתְּמִים וְהִלְבִּשׁוּ אֶת־הָאִישׁ אֲשֶׁר
הַמֶּלֶךְ חָפֵץ בִּיקָרוֹ וְהִרְכִּיבֻהוּ עַל־הַסּוּס בִּרְחוֹב
הָעִיר וְקָרְאוּ לְפָנָיו כָּכָה יֵעָשֶׂה לָאִישׁ אֲשֶׁר
הַמֶּלֶךְ חָפֵץ בִּיקָרוֹ: י וַיֹּאמֶר הַמֶּלֶךְ לְהָמָן מַהֵר
קַח אֶת־הַלְּבוּשׁ וְאֶת־הַסּוּס כַּאֲשֶׁר דִּבַּרְתָּ
וַעֲשֵׂה־כֵן לְמָרְדֳּכַי הַיְּהוּדִי הַיּוֹשֵׁב בְּשַׁעַר
הַמֶּלֶךְ אַל־תַּפֵּל דָּבָר מִכֹּל אֲשֶׁר דִּבַּרְתָּ: יא וַיִּקַּח
הָמָן אֶת־הַלְּבוּשׁ וְאֶת־הַסּוּס וַיַּלְבֵּשׁ אֶת־

the city square and announced before him, "So shall be done to the man whom the king wishes to honor." 12. And Mordecai returned to the king's gate, and Haman was rushed to his house, mourning and with his head covered. 13. And Haman recounted to Zeresh his wife and to all his friends all that had befallen him, and his wise men and Zeresh his wife said to him, "If Mordecai, before whom you have started to fall, is of Jewish stock, you will not prevail against him, but you will surely fall before him." 14. While they were still talking to him, the king's chamberlains arrived, and they hastened to bring Haman to the banquet that Esther had made.

CHAPTER VII

1. And the king and Haman came to drink with Esther the queen. 2. And the king said to Esther also on the second day during the wine feast, "What is your petition, Esther the queen? And it shall be given to you. And what is your request? Even up to half the kingdom, and it shall be granted." 3. And Esther the queen replied and said, "If I have found favor in your eyes, O king, and if it pleases the king, may my life be given me in my petition and my people in my request. 4. For we have been sold, I and my people, to be destroyed, to be slain, and to perish; now had we been sold for slaves and bondswomen, I would be silent, for the adversary has no consideration for the king's loss." 5. And King Ahasuerus said, and he said to Esther the queen, "Who is this and where is he, who dared to do this?" 6. And Esther said, "An adversary and an enemy, this evil Haman!" And Haman became terrified from before the king and the queen. 7. Now the king arose in his fury from the wine feast to the orchard garden, and Haman stood to beg for his life of Esther the queen, for he saw that evil was determined against him by the king. 8. Then the king returned from the orchard garden to the house of the wine feast, and Haman was falling on the couch upon which Esther was, and the king said, "Will you even force the queen with me in the house?" The word came out of the king's mouth, and they

מָרְדֳּכַי וַיַּרְכִּיבֵהוּ בִּרְחוֹב הָעִיר וַיִּקְרָא לְפָנָיו כָּכָה יֵעָשֶׂה לָאִישׁ אֲשֶׁר הַמֶּלֶךְ חָפֵץ בִּיקָרוֹ: יב וַיָּשָׁב מָרְדֳּכַי אֶל־שַׁעַר הַמֶּלֶךְ וְהָמָן נִדְחַף אֶל־בֵּיתוֹ אָבֵל וַחֲפוּי רֹאשׁ: יג וַיְסַפֵּר הָמָן לְזֶרֶשׁ אִשְׁתּוֹ וּלְכָל־אֹהֲבָיו אֵת כָּל־אֲשֶׁר קָרָהוּ וַיֹּאמְרוּ לוֹ חֲכָמָיו וְזֶרֶשׁ אִשְׁתּוֹ אִם מִזֶּרַע הַיְּהוּדִים מָרְדֳּכַי אֲשֶׁר הַחִלּוֹתָ לִנְפֹּל לְפָנָיו לֹא־תוּכַל לוֹ כִּי־נָפוֹל תִּפּוֹל לְפָנָיו: יד עוֹדָם מְדַבְּרִים עִמּוֹ וְסָרִיסֵי הַמֶּלֶךְ הִגִּיעוּ וַיַּבְהִלוּ לְהָבִיא אֶת־הָמָן אֶל־הַמִּשְׁתֶּה אֲשֶׁר־עָשְׂתָה אֶסְתֵּר:

ז א וַיָּבֹא הַמֶּלֶךְ וְהָמָן לִשְׁתּוֹת עִם־אֶסְתֵּר הַמַּלְכָּה: ב וַיֹּאמֶר הַמֶּלֶךְ לְאֶסְתֵּר גַּם בַּיּוֹם הַשֵּׁנִי בְּמִשְׁתֵּה הַיַּיִן מַה־שְּׁאֵלָתֵךְ אֶסְתֵּר הַמַּלְכָּה וְתִנָּתֵן לָךְ וּמַה־בַּקָּשָׁתֵךְ עַד־חֲצִי הַמַּלְכוּת וְתֵעָשׂ: ג וַתַּעַן אֶסְתֵּר הַמַּלְכָּה וַתֹּאמַר אִם־מָצָאתִי חֵן בְּעֵינֶיךָ הַמֶּלֶךְ וְאִם־עַל־הַמֶּלֶךְ טוֹב תִּנָּתֶן־לִי נַפְשִׁי בִּשְׁאֵלָתִי וְעַמִּי בְּבַקָּשָׁתִי: ד כִּי נִמְכַּרְנוּ אֲנִי וְעַמִּי לְהַשְׁמִיד לַהֲרוֹג וּלְאַבֵּד וְאִלּוּ לַעֲבָדִים וְלִשְׁפָחוֹת נִמְכַּרְנוּ הֶחֱרַשְׁתִּי כִּי אֵין הַצָּר שֹׁוֶה בְּנֵזֶק הַמֶּלֶךְ: ס ה וַיֹּאמֶר הַמֶּלֶךְ אֲחַשְׁוֵרוֹשׁ וַיֹּאמֶר לְאֶסְתֵּר הַמַּלְכָּה מִי הוּא זֶה וְאֵי־זֶה הוּא אֲשֶׁר מְלָאוֹ לִבּוֹ לַעֲשׂוֹת כֵּן: ו וַתֹּאמֶר אֶסְתֵּר אִישׁ צַר וְאוֹיֵב הָמָן הָרָע הַזֶּה וְהָמָן נִבְעַת מִלִּפְנֵי הַמֶּלֶךְ וְהַמַּלְכָּה: ז וְהַמֶּלֶךְ קָם בַּחֲמָתוֹ מִמִּשְׁתֵּה הַיַּיִן אֶל־גִּנַּת הַבִּיתָן וְהָמָן עָמַד לְבַקֵּשׁ עַל־נַפְשׁוֹ מֵאֶסְתֵּר הַמַּלְכָּה כִּי רָאָה כִּי־כָלְתָה אֵלָיו הָרָעָה מֵאֵת הַמֶּלֶךְ: ח וְהַמֶּלֶךְ שָׁב מִגִּנַּת הַבִּיתָן אֶל־בֵּית מִשְׁתֵּה הַיַּיִן וְהָמָן נֹפֵל עַל־הַמִּטָּה אֲשֶׁר אֶסְתֵּר עָלֶיהָ וַיֹּאמֶר הַמֶּלֶךְ הֲגַם לִכְבּוֹשׁ אֶת־הַמַּלְכָּה עִמִּי בַּבָּיִת הַדָּבָר יָצָא מִפִּי הַמֶּלֶךְ וּפְנֵי הָמָן חָפוּ:

covered Haman's face.   9. Then said Harbonah, one of the chamberlains before the king, "Also, behold the gallows that Haman has made for Mordecai who spoke well for the king, standing in Haman's house, fifty cubits high!" And the king said, "Hang him on it!"   10. And they hanged Haman on the gallows that he had prepared for Mordecai, and the king's anger abated.

CHAPTER VIII

1. On that day, King Ahasuerus gave to Esther the queen the house of Haman, the adversary of the Jews, and Mordecai came before the king, for Esther had told him what he was to her.   2. Now the king took off his ring, which he had removed from Haman, and gave it to Mordecai, and Esther placed Mordecai in charge of the house of Haman.   3. And Esther resumed speaking before the king, and she fell before his feet; she wept and beseeched him to avert the harm of Haman the Agagite and his device that he had plotted against the Jews.   4. Then the king extended the golden scepter to Esther, and Esther arose and stood before the king.   5. And she said, "If it please the king, and if I have found favor before him, and the matter is proper before the king, and I am good in his sight, let it be written to rescind the letters, the device of Haman the son of Hammedatha, the Agagite, which he wrote to destroy the Jews who are in all the king's provinces.   6. For, how can I see the evil that will befall my people, and how can I see the destruction of my kindred?"   7. Then King Ahasuerus said to Esther the queen and to Mordecai the Jew, "Behold the house of Haman I have given to Esther, and they have hanged him on the gallows because he laid a hand on the Jews. And you — write about the Jews as you see fit, in the name of the king, and seal [it] with the king's ring, for a writ that is written in the name of the king and sealed with the king's ring may not be rescinded.   9. And the king's scribes were summoned at that time, in the third month — that is the month of Sivan — on the twenty-third day thereof, and it was written according to all that Mordecai commanded, to the Jews and to the satraps

ט וַיֹּאמֶר חַרְבוֹנָה אֶחָד מִן־הַסָּרִיסִים לִפְנֵי הַמֶּלֶךְ גַּם הִנֵּה־הָעֵץ אֲשֶׁר־עָשָׂה הָמָן לְמָרְדֳּכַי אֲשֶׁר דִּבֶּר־טוֹב עַל־הַמֶּלֶךְ עֹמֵד בְּבֵית הָמָן גָּבֹהַּ חֲמִשִּׁים אַמָּה וַיֹּאמֶר הַמֶּלֶךְ תְּלֻהוּ עָלָיו: י וַיִּתְלוּ אֶת־הָמָן עַל־הָעֵץ אֲשֶׁר־הֵכִין לְמָרְדֳּכָי וַחֲמַת הַמֶּלֶךְ שָׁכָכָה: ס

ח א בַּיּוֹם הַהוּא נָתַן הַמֶּלֶךְ אֲחַשְׁוֵרוֹשׁ לְאֶסְתֵּר הַמַּלְכָּה אֶת־בֵּית הָמָן צֹרֵר הַיְּהוּדִיִּים (הַיְּהוּדִים קרי) וּמָרְדֳּכַי בָּא לִפְנֵי הַמֶּלֶךְ כִּי־הִגִּידָה אֶסְתֵּר מַה הוּא־לָהּ: ב וַיָּסַר הַמֶּלֶךְ אֶת־טַבַּעְתּוֹ אֲשֶׁר הֶעֱבִיר מֵהָמָן וַיִּתְּנָהּ לְמָרְדֳּכָי וַתָּשֶׂם אֶסְתֵּר אֶת־מָרְדֳּכַי עַל־בֵּית הָמָן: ס ג וַתּוֹסֶף אֶסְתֵּר וַתְּדַבֵּר לִפְנֵי הַמֶּלֶךְ וַתִּפֹּל לִפְנֵי רַגְלָיו וַתֵּבְךְּ וַתִּתְחַנֶּן־לוֹ לְהַעֲבִיר אֶת־רָעַת הָמָן הָאֲגָגִי וְאֵת מַחֲשַׁבְתּוֹ אֲשֶׁר חָשַׁב עַל־הַיְּהוּדִים: ד וַיּוֹשֶׁט הַמֶּלֶךְ לְאֶסְתֵּר אֵת שַׁרְבִט הַזָּהָב וַתָּקָם אֶסְתֵּר וַתַּעֲמֹד לִפְנֵי הַמֶּלֶךְ: ה וַתֹּאמֶר אִם־עַל־הַמֶּלֶךְ טוֹב וְאִם־מָצָאתִי חֵן לְפָנָיו וְכָשֵׁר הַדָּבָר לִפְנֵי הַמֶּלֶךְ וְטוֹבָה אֲנִי בְּעֵינָיו יִכָּתֵב לְהָשִׁיב אֶת־הַסְּפָרִים מַחֲשֶׁבֶת הָמָן בֶּן־הַמְּדָתָא הָאֲגָגִי אֲשֶׁר כָּתַב לְאַבֵּד אֶת־הַיְּהוּדִים אֲשֶׁר בְּכָל־מְדִינוֹת הַמֶּלֶךְ: ו כִּי אֵיכָכָה אוּכַל וְרָאִיתִי בָּרָעָה אֲשֶׁר־יִמְצָא אֶת־עַמִּי וְאֵיכָכָה אוּכַל וְרָאִיתִי בְּאָבְדַן מוֹלַדְתִּי: ס ז וַיֹּאמֶר הַמֶּלֶךְ אֲחַשְׁוֵרֹשׁ לְאֶסְתֵּר הַמַּלְכָּה וּלְמָרְדֳּכַי הַיְּהוּדִי הִנֵּה בֵית־הָמָן נָתַתִּי לְאֶסְתֵּר וְאֹתוֹ תָּלוּ עַל־הָעֵץ עַל אֲשֶׁר־שָׁלַח יָדוֹ בַּיְּהוּדִיִּים (בַּיְּהוּדִים קרי): ח וְאַתֶּם כִּתְבוּ עַל־הַיְּהוּדִים כַּטּוֹב בְּעֵינֵיכֶם בְּשֵׁם הַמֶּלֶךְ וְחִתְמוּ בְּטַבַּעַת הַמֶּלֶךְ כִּי־כְתָב אֲשֶׁר־נִכְתָּב בְּשֵׁם־הַמֶּלֶךְ וְנַחְתּוֹם בְּטַבַּעַת הַמֶּלֶךְ אֵין לְהָשִׁיב: ט וַיִּקָּרְאוּ סֹפְרֵי־הַמֶּלֶךְ בָּעֵת־הַהִיא בַּחֹדֶשׁ הַשְּׁלִישִׁי הוּא־חֹדֶשׁ סִיוָן בִּשְׁלוֹשָׁה וְעֶשְׂרִים בּוֹ וַיִּכָּתֵב כְּכָל־אֲשֶׁר־צִוָּה מָרְדֳּכַי אֶל־הַיְּהוּדִים

and the governors, and the princes of the provinces that were from Hodu to Cush, one hundred twenty-seven provinces; every province according to its script and every nationality according to its tongue, and to the Jews according to their script and according to their tongue. 10. And he wrote in the name of King Ahasuerus and sealed with the king's ring, and he sent letters by the couriers on horseback, the riders of the king's steeds—the mules, offspring of the mares— 11. that the king had given to the Jews who are in every city, to assemble and to protect themselves; to destroy, to slay, and to cause to perish the entire host of every people and province that oppress them, women and small children, and to take their spoils for a prey, 12. in one day, in all the provinces of King Ahasuerus, on the thirteenth of the twelfth month, that is the month of Adar. 13. The copy of the writ was that an edict be given in every province, published before all the peoples, and that the Jews be ready for that day, to avenge themselves upon their enemies. 14. The couriers, those who ride the king's steeds, the mules, went out hastened and pressed by the king's order, and the edict was given in Shushan the capital. 15. And Mordecai left the king's presence with royal raiment, blue and white, and a huge golden crown, and a wrap of linen and purple, and the city of Shushan shouted and rejoiced. 16. The Jews had light and joy, and cheer and honor. 17. And in every province and in every city, wherever the king's order and his edict reached, [there was] joy and cheer for the Jews, a banquet and a festive day, and many of the peoples of the land became Jews, for the fear of the Jews was upon them.

CHAPTER IX

1. Now in the twelfth month — that is the month of Adar — on the thirteenth day thereof, when the king's order and his edict drew near to be put in execution, on the day that the Jews' enemies looked forward to ruling over them, it was reversed, that the Jews should rule over their enemies. 2. The Jews assembled in their cities, in all the provinces of King Ahasuerus, to lay hand on those who sought to harm them,

וְאֶל הָאֲחַשְׁדַּרְפְּנִים וְהַפַּחוֹת וְשָׂרֵי הַמְּדִינוֹת
אֲשֶׁר ׀ מֵהֹדּוּ וְעַד־כּוּשׁ שֶׁבַע וְעֶשְׂרִים וּמֵאָה
מְדִינָה מְדִינָה וּמְדִינָה כִּכְתָבָהּ וְעַם וָעָם כִּלְשֹׁנוֹ
וְאֶל־הַיְּהוּדִים כִּכְתָבָם וְכִלְשׁוֹנָם: י וַיִּכְתֹּב
בְּשֵׁם הַמֶּלֶךְ אֲחַשְׁוֵרֹשׁ וַיַּחְתֹּם בְּטַבַּעַת הַמֶּלֶךְ
וַיִּשְׁלַח סְפָרִים בְּיַד הָרָצִים בַּסּוּסִים רֹכְבֵי
הָרֶכֶשׁ הָאֲחַשְׁתְּרָנִים בְּנֵי הָרַמָּכִים: יא אֲשֶׁר
נָתַן הַמֶּלֶךְ לַיְּהוּדִים ׀ אֲשֶׁר ׀ בְּכָל־עִיר וָעִיר
לְהִקָּהֵל וְלַעֲמֹד עַל־נַפְשָׁם לְהַשְׁמִיד לַהֲרֹג
וּלְאַבֵּד אֶת־כָּל־חֵיל עַם וּמְדִינָה הַצָּרִים אֹתָם
טַף וְנָשִׁים וּשְׁלָלָם לָבוֹז: יב בְּיוֹם אֶחָד בְּכָל־
מְדִינוֹת הַמֶּלֶךְ אֲחַשְׁוֵרוֹשׁ בִּשְׁלוֹשָׁה עָשָׂר
לְחֹדֶשׁ שְׁנֵים־עָשָׂר הוּא־חֹדֶשׁ אֲדָר: יג פַּתְשֶׁגֶן
הַכְּתָב לְהִנָּתֵן דָּת בְּכָל־מְדִינָה וּמְדִינָה גָּלוּי
לְכָל־הָעַמִּים וְלִהְיוֹת הַיְּהוּדִיִּים עֲתוּדִים (היהודים
עתידים קרי) לַיּוֹם הַזֶּה לְהִנָּקֵם מֵאֹיְבֵיהֶם:
יד הָרָצִים רֹכְבֵי הָרֶכֶשׁ הָאֲחַשְׁתְּרָנִים יָצְאוּ
מְבֹהָלִים וּדְחוּפִים בִּדְבַר הַמֶּלֶךְ וְהַדָּת נִתְּנָה
בְּשׁוּשַׁן הַבִּירָה: ס טו וּמָרְדֳּכַי יָצָא ׀ מִלִּפְנֵי
הַמֶּלֶךְ בִּלְבוּשׁ מַלְכוּת תְּכֵלֶת וָחוּר וַעֲטֶרֶת זָהָב
גְּדוֹלָה וְתַכְרִיךְ בּוּץ וְאַרְגָּמָן וְהָעִיר שׁוּשָׁן
צָהֲלָה וְשָׂמֵחָה: טז לַיְּהוּדִים הָיְתָה אוֹרָה
וְשִׂמְחָה וְשָׂשֹׂן וִיקָר: יז וּבְכָל־מְדִינָה וּמְדִינָה
וּבְכָל־עִיר וָעִיר מְקוֹם אֲשֶׁר דְּבַר־הַמֶּלֶךְ וְדָתוֹ
מַגִּיעַ שִׂמְחָה וְשָׂשׂוֹן לַיְּהוּדִים מִשְׁתֶּה וְיוֹם טוֹב
וְרַבִּים מֵעַמֵּי הָאָרֶץ מִתְיַהֲדִים כִּי־נָפַל פַּחַד־
הַיְּהוּדִים עֲלֵיהֶם:

ט א וּבִשְׁנֵים עָשָׂר חֹדֶשׁ הוּא־חֹדֶשׁ אֲדָר
בִּשְׁלוֹשָׁה עָשָׂר יוֹם בּוֹ אֲשֶׁר הִגִּיעַ דְּבַר־הַמֶּלֶךְ
וְדָתוֹ לְהֵעָשׂוֹת בַּיּוֹם אֲשֶׁר שִׂבְּרוּ אֹיְבֵי
הַיְּהוּדִים לִשְׁלוֹט בָּהֶם וְנַהֲפוֹךְ הוּא אֲשֶׁר
יִשְׁלְטוּ הַיְּהוּדִים הֵמָּה בְּשֹׂנְאֵיהֶם: ב נִקְהֲלוּ
הַיְּהוּדִים בְּעָרֵיהֶם בְּכָל־מְדִינוֹת הַמֶּלֶךְ
אֲחַשְׁוֵרוֹשׁ לִשְׁלֹחַ יָד בִּמְבַקְשֵׁי רָעָתָם וְאִישׁ

and no one stood up before them, for their
fear had fallen upon all the peoples.
3. And all the princes of the provinces
and the satraps and the governors and those
that conduct the king's affairs elevated the
Jews, for the fear of Mordecai fell upon
them. 4. For Mordecai was great in the
king's house, and his fame went forth
throughout all the provinces, for the man
Mordecai waxed greater and greater.
5. And the Jews smote all of their
enemies with the stroke of the sword and
with slaying and destruction, and they did
to their enemies as they wished. 6. And
in Shushan the capital, the Jews slew
and destroyed five hundred men, 7. and
Parshandatha, and Dalphon, and Aspatha,
8. and Poratha, and Adalia, and Ari-
datha, 9. and Parmashta, and Arisai, and
Aridai, and Vaizatha, 10. the ten sons of
Haman, the son of Hammedatha, the adversary of the Jews, they slew, but on the spoil
they did not lay their hand. 11. On that
day, the number of those slain in Shushan
the capital came before the king. 12. And
the king said to Esther the queen, "In
Shushan the capital the Jews slew and
destroyed five hundred men, and the ten
sons of Haman; in the rest of the provinces
of the king what have they done! Now what
is your petition, and it shall be granted you,
and what is your request, and it shall be
done." 13. And Esther said, "If it please
the king, let tomorrow too be granted to the
Jews to do as today's decree, and let them
hang Haman's ten sons on the gallows."
14. Now the king ordered that it be done
so, and a decree was given in Shushan, and
they hanged Haman's ten sons. 15. Now
the Jews who were in Shushan assembled
on the fourteenth day of Adar as well, and
they slew in Shushan three hundred men,
and upon the spoils they did not lay their
hands. 16. And the rest of the Jews who
were in the king's provinces assembled and
protected themselves and had relief from
their enemies and were slaying among their
foes, seventy-five thousand; but upon the
spoil they did not lay their hand, 17. on
the thirteenth of the month of Adar; and
they had relief on the fourteenth thereof,
and made it a day of feasting and joy.
18. And the Jews who were in Shushan

לֹא־עָמַד בִּפְנֵיהֶם כִּי־נָפַל פַּחְדָּם עַל־כָּל־
הָעַמִּים׃ ג וְכָל־שָׂרֵי הַמְּדִינוֹת וְהָאֲחַשְׁדַּרְפְּנִים
וְהַפַּחוֹת וְעֹשֵׂי הַמְּלָאכָה אֲשֶׁר לַמֶּלֶךְ מְנַשְּׂאִים
אֶת־הַיְּהוּדִים כִּי־נָפַל פַּחַד־מָרְדֳּכַי עֲלֵיהֶם׃
ד כִּי־גָדוֹל מָרְדֳּכַי בְּבֵית הַמֶּלֶךְ וְשָׁמְעוֹ הוֹלֵךְ
בְּכָל־הַמְּדִינוֹת כִּי־הָאִישׁ מָרְדֳּכַי הוֹלֵךְ וְגָדוֹל׃
ה וַיַּכּוּ הַיְּהוּדִים בְּכָל־אֹיְבֵיהֶם מַכַּת־חֶרֶב
וְהֶרֶג וְאַבְדָן וַיַּעֲשׂוּ בְשֹׂנְאֵיהֶם כִּרְצוֹנָם׃
ו וּבְשׁוּשַׁן הַבִּירָה הָרְגוּ הַיְּהוּדִים וְאַבֵּד חֲמֵשׁ
מֵאוֹת אִישׁ׃ ז וְאֵת ׀ פַּרְשַׁנְדָּתָא וְאֵת ׀ דַּלְפוֹן
וְאֵת ׀ אַסְפָּתָא׃ ח וְאֵת ׀ פּוֹרָתָא וְאֵת ׀ אֲדַלְיָא
וְאֵת ׀ אֲרִידָתָא׃ ט וְאֵת ׀ פַּרְמַשְׁתָּא וְאֵת ׀ אֲרִיסַי
וְאֵת ׀ אֲרִידַי וְאֵת ׀ וַיְזָתָא׃ י עֲשֶׂרֶת בְּנֵי הָמָן
בֶּן־הַמְּדָתָא צֹרֵר הַיְּהוּדִים הָרָגוּ וּבַבִּזָּה לֹא
שָׁלְחוּ אֶת־יָדָם׃ יא בַּיּוֹם הַהוּא בָּא מִסְפַּר
הַהֲרוּגִים בְּשׁוּשַׁן הַבִּירָה לִפְנֵי הַמֶּלֶךְ׃
יב וַיֹּאמֶר הַמֶּלֶךְ לְאֶסְתֵּר הַמַּלְכָּה בְּשׁוּשַׁן
הַבִּירָה הָרְגוּ הַיְּהוּדִים וְאַבֵּד חֲמֵשׁ מֵאוֹת אִישׁ
וְאֵת עֲשֶׂרֶת בְּנֵי־הָמָן בִּשְׁאָר מְדִינוֹת הַמֶּלֶךְ מֶה
עָשׂוּ וּמַה־שְּׁאֵלָתֵךְ וְיִנָּתֵן לָךְ וּמַה־בַּקָּשָׁתֵךְ עוֹד
וְתֵעָשׂ׃ יג וַתֹּאמֶר אֶסְתֵּר אִם־עַל־הַמֶּלֶךְ טוֹב
יִנָּתֵן גַּם־מָחָר לַיְּהוּדִים אֲשֶׁר בְּשׁוּשָׁן לַעֲשׂוֹת
כְּדָת הַיּוֹם וְאֵת עֲשֶׂרֶת בְּנֵי־הָמָן יִתְלוּ עַל־הָעֵץ׃
יד וַיֹּאמֶר הַמֶּלֶךְ לְהֵעָשׂוֹת כֵּן וַתִּנָּתֵן דָּת
בְּשׁוּשָׁן וְאֵת עֲשֶׂרֶת בְּנֵי־הָמָן תָּלוּ׃ טו וַיִּקָּהֲלוּ
הַיְּהוּדִיים (היהודים קרי) אֲשֶׁר־בְּשׁוּשָׁן גַּם בְּיוֹם
אַרְבָּעָה עָשָׂר לְחֹדֶשׁ אֲדָר וַיַּהַרְגוּ בְשׁוּשָׁן שְׁלֹשׁ
מֵאוֹת אִישׁ וּבַבִּזָּה לֹא שָׁלְחוּ אֶת־יָדָם׃
טז וּשְׁאָר הַיְּהוּדִים אֲשֶׁר בִּמְדִינוֹת הַמֶּלֶךְ
נִקְהֲלוּ ׀ וְעָמֹד עַל־נַפְשָׁם וְנוֹחַ מֵאֹיְבֵיהֶם וְהָרוֹג
בְּשֹׂנְאֵיהֶם חֲמִשָּׁה וְשִׁבְעִים אָלֶף וּבַבִּזָּה לֹא
שָׁלְחוּ אֶת־יָדָם׃ יז בְּיוֹם־שְׁלוֹשָׁה עָשָׂר לְחֹדֶשׁ
אֲדָר וְנוֹחַ בְּאַרְבָּעָה עָשָׂר בּוֹ וְעָשֹׂה אֹתוֹ יוֹם
מִשְׁתֶּה וְשִׂמְחָה׃ יח וְהַיְּהוּדִיים (והיהודים קרי)

assembled on the thirteenth thereof and on the fourteenth thereof, and had relief on the fifteenth thereof, and made it a day of feasting and joy. 19. Therefore, the Jewish villagers, who live in the open towns, make the fourteenth day of the month of Adar [a day of] joy and feasting and a festive day, and of sending portions one to another. 20. And Mordecai inscribed these things, and sent letters to all the Jews who were in all the provinces of King Ahasuerus, both near and far, 21. to enjoin them to make the fourteenth day of the month of Adar and the fifteenth day thereof, every year, 22. as the days when the Jews rested from their enemies, and the month that was reversed for them from grief to joy and from mourning to a festive day—to make them days of feasting and joy, and sending portions one to another, and gifts to the poor. 23. And the Jews took upon themselves what they had commenced to do, and what Mordecai had written to them. 24. For Haman the son of Hammedatha, the Agagite, the adversary of all the Jews, had devised against the Jews to cause them to perish, and he cast *pur* — that is the lot — to confuse them and to destroy them. 25. And when she came before the king, he said concerning the letter, "Let his evil device that he devised against the Jews return upon his own head, and let them hang him and his sons on the gallows." 26. Therefore, they called these days Purim after the name of Pur; therefore, because of all the words of this letter, and what they saw concerning this and what happened to them. 27. The Jews ordained and took upon themselves and upon their seed and upon all those who joined them, that it is not to be revoked, to make these two days according to their writing and according to their time, every year. 28. And these days shall be mentioned and celebrated throughout every generation, every family, every province, and every city, and these Purim days shall not be revoked from amidst the Jews, and their memory shall not end from their seed. 29. Now Esther the queen, the daughter of Abihail, and Mordecai the Jew wrote

אֲשֶׁר־בְּשׁוּשָׁן נִקְהֲלוּ בִּשְׁלוֹשָׁה עָשָׂר בּוֹ
וּבְאַרְבָּעָה עָשָׂר בּוֹ וְנוֹחַ בַּחֲמִשָּׁה עָשָׂר בּוֹ
וְעָשֹׂה אֹתוֹ יוֹם מִשְׁתֶּה וְשִׂמְחָה׃ יט עַל־כֵּן
הַיְּהוּדִים הַפְּרָוזִים (הפרזים קרי) הַיֹּשְׁבִים בְּעָרֵי
הַפְּרָזוֹת עֹשִׂים אֵת יוֹם אַרְבָּעָה עָשָׂר לְחֹדֶשׁ
אֲדָר שִׂמְחָה וּמִשְׁתֶּה וְיוֹם טוֹב וּמִשְׁלֹחַ מָנוֹת
אִישׁ לְרֵעֵהוּ׃ כ וַיִּכְתֹּב מָרְדֳּכַי אֶת־הַדְּבָרִים
הָאֵלֶּה וַיִּשְׁלַח סְפָרִים אֶל־כָּל־הַיְּהוּדִים אֲשֶׁר
בְּכָל־מְדִינוֹת הַמֶּלֶךְ אֲחַשְׁוֵרוֹשׁ הַקְּרוֹבִים
וְהָרְחוֹקִים׃ כא לְקַיֵּם עֲלֵיהֶם לִהְיוֹת עֹשִׂים אֵת
יוֹם אַרְבָּעָה עָשָׂר לְחֹדֶשׁ אֲדָר וְאֵת יוֹם־חֲמִשָּׁה
עָשָׂר בּוֹ בְּכָל־שָׁנָה וְשָׁנָה׃ כב כַּיָּמִים אֲשֶׁר־נָחוּ
בָהֶם הַיְּהוּדִים מֵאֹיְבֵיהֶם וְהַחֹדֶשׁ אֲשֶׁר נֶהְפַּךְ
לָהֶם מִיָּגוֹן לְשִׂמְחָה וּמֵאֵבֶל לְיוֹם טוֹב לַעֲשׂוֹת
אוֹתָם יְמֵי מִשְׁתֶּה וְשִׂמְחָה וּמִשְׁלֹחַ מָנוֹת אִישׁ
לְרֵעֵהוּ וּמַתָּנוֹת לָאֶבְיֹנִים׃ כג וְקִבֵּל הַיְּהוּדִים
אֵת אֲשֶׁר־הֵחֵלּוּ לַעֲשׂוֹת וְאֵת אֲשֶׁר־כָּתַב
מָרְדֳּכַי אֲלֵיהֶם׃ כד כִּי הָמָן בֶּן־הַמְּדָתָא הָאֲגָגִי
צֹרֵר כָּל־הַיְּהוּדִים חָשַׁב עַל־הַיְּהוּדִים לְאַבְּדָם
וְהִפִּל פּוּר הוּא הַגּוֹרָל לְהֻמָּם וּלְאַבְּדָם׃
כה וּבְבֹאָהּ לִפְנֵי הַמֶּלֶךְ אָמַר עִם־הַסֵּפֶר יָשׁוּב
מַחֲשַׁבְתּוֹ הָרָעָה אֲשֶׁר־חָשַׁב עַל־הַיְּהוּדִים עַל־
רֹאשׁוֹ וְתָלוּ אֹתוֹ וְאֶת־בָּנָיו עַל־הָעֵץ׃ כו עַל־כֵּן
קָרְאוּ לַיָּמִים הָאֵלֶּה פוּרִים עַל־שֵׁם הַפּוּר
עַל־כֵּן עַל־כָּל־דִּבְרֵי הָאִגֶּרֶת הַזֹּאת וּמָה־רָאוּ
עַל־כָּכָה וּמָה הִגִּיעַ אֲלֵיהֶם׃ כז קִיְּמוּ וְקִבְּלֻ
(וקבלו קרי) הַיְּהוּדִים | עֲלֵיהֶם | וְעַל־זַרְעָם וְעַל
כָּל־הַנִּלְוִים עֲלֵיהֶם וְלֹא יַעֲבוֹר לִהְיוֹת עֹשִׂים
אֶת־שְׁנֵי הַיָּמִים הָאֵלֶּה כִּכְתָבָם וְכִזְמַנָּם בְּכָל־
שָׁנָה וְשָׁנָה׃ כח וְהַיָּמִים הָאֵלֶּה נִזְכָּרִים וְנַעֲשִׂים
בְּכָל־דּוֹר וָדוֹר מִשְׁפָּחָה וּמִשְׁפָּחָה מְדִינָה
וּמְדִינָה וְעִיר וָעִיר וִימֵי הַפּוּרִים הָאֵלֶּה לֹא
יַעַבְרוּ מִתּוֹךְ הַיְּהוּדִים וְזִכְרָם לֹא־יָסוּף
מִזַּרְעָם׃ ס כט וַתִּכְתֹּב אֶסְתֵּר הַמַּלְכָּה בַת־

down all [the acts of] power, to confirm this second Purim letter. 30. And he sent letters to all the Jews, to one hundred twenty-seven provinces, the realm of Ahasuerus, words of peace and truth, 31. to confirm these Purim days in their times, as Mordecai the Jew and Esther the queen had enjoined them, and as they had ordained for themselves and for their seed, the matters of the fasts and their cry. 32. Now Esther's order confirmed these matters of Purim, and it was written in the book.

אֲבִיחַיִל וּמָרְדֳּכַי הַיְּהוּדִי אֶת־כָּל־תֹּקֶף לְקַיֵּם
אֶת־אִגֶּרֶת הַפֻּרִים הַזֹּאת הַשֵּׁנִית: ל וַיִּשְׁלַח
סְפָרִים אֶל־כָּל־הַיְּהוּדִים אֶל־שֶׁבַע וְעֶשְׂרִים
וּמֵאָה מְדִינָה מַלְכוּת אֲחַשְׁוֵרוֹשׁ דִּבְרֵי שָׁלוֹם
וֶאֱמֶת: לא לְקַיֵּם אֶת־יְמֵי הַפֻּרִים הָאֵלֶּה
בִּזְמַנֵּיהֶם כַּאֲשֶׁר קִיַּם עֲלֵיהֶם מָרְדֳּכַי הַיְּהוּדִי
וְאֶסְתֵּר הַמַּלְכָּה וְכַאֲשֶׁר קִיְּמוּ עַל־נַפְשָׁם וְעַל־
זַרְעָם דִּבְרֵי הַצּוֹמוֹת וְזַעֲקָתָם: לב וּמַאֲמַר
אֶסְתֵּר קִיַּם דִּבְרֵי הַפֻּרִים הָאֵלֶּה וְנִכְתָּב
בַּסֵּפֶר: ס

CHAPTER X

1. And King Ahasuerus imposed tribute on the land and on the isles of the sea. 2. And all the acts of his power and his might and the full account of Mordecai's greatness — are they not written in book of the chronicles of the kings of Media and Persia? 3. For Mordecai the Jew was King Ahasuerus's viceroy, and great among the Jews and accepted by most of his brethren, seeking the good of his people and speaking peace to all his seed.

י א וַיָּשֶׂם הַמֶּלֶךְ אֲחַשְׁרֵשׁ (אחשורוש קרי) | מַס
עַל־הָאָרֶץ וְאִיֵּי הַיָּם: ב וְכָל־מַעֲשֵׂה תָקְפּוֹ
וּגְבוּרָתוֹ וּפָרָשַׁת גְּדֻלַּת מָרְדֳּכַי אֲשֶׁר גִּדְּלוֹ
הַמֶּלֶךְ הֲלוֹא־הֵם כְּתוּבִים עַל־סֵפֶר דִּבְרֵי
הַיָּמִים לְמַלְכֵי מָדַי וּפָרָס: ג כִּי | מָרְדֳּכַי
הַיְּהוּדִי מִשְׁנֶה לַמֶּלֶךְ אֲחַשְׁוֵרוֹשׁ וְגָדוֹל
לַיְּהוּדִים וְרָצוּי לְרֹב אֶחָיו דֹּרֵשׁ טוֹב לְעַמּוֹ
וְדֹבֵר שָׁלוֹם לְכָל־זַרְעוֹ:

חזק

BLESSINGS AFTER READING THE BOOK OF ESTHER

After reading the Megillah, the reader says:

Blessed are You, O Lord our God, King of the universe, Who champions our cause, and judges our claim, and Who wreaks vengeance for us, and Who metes out retribution upon all our mortal enemies, and Who punishes our oppressors for us. Blessed are You, O Lord, Who punishes for His people Israel all their oppressors, O redeeming God.

בָּרוּךְ אַתָּה יְהוָה, אֱלֹהֵינוּ מֶלֶךְ הָעוֹלָם, הָרָב
אֶת רִיבֵנוּ, וְהַדָּן אֶת דִּינֵנוּ, וְהַנּוֹקֵם אֶת
נִקְמָתֵנוּ, וְהַמְשַׁלֵּם גְּמוּל לְכָל־אֹיְבֵי נַפְשֵׁנוּ,
וְהַנִּפְרָע לָנוּ מִצָּרֵינוּ. בָּרוּךְ אַתָּה יְהוָה, הַנִּפְרָע
לְעַמּוֹ יִשְׂרָאֵל, מִכָּל צָרֵיהֶם, הָאֵל הַמּוֹשִׁיעַ:

The following paragraph is said in the evening only.

Who foiled the counsel of the nations and frustrated the plans of the cunning. When a wicked man arose against us, a scion of wickedness of the seed of Amalek. He was haughty with his wealth and dug himself a

אֲשֶׁר הֵנִיא עֲצַת גּוֹיִם, וַיָּפֶר מַחְשְׁבוֹת
עֲרוּמִים: בְּקוּם עָלֵינוּ אָדָם רָשָׁע, נֵצֶר זָדוֹן
מִזֶּרַע עֲמָלֵק: גָּאָה בְעָשְׁרוֹ, וְכָרָה לוֹ בּוֹר,

pit, and his own greatness ensnared him. He designed to trap but was himself trapped; he sought to destroy but was quickly destroyed. Haman displayed the hatred of his forefathers, and the brotherly hatred upon the children. He did not remember Saul's compassion, for thanks to his pity on Agag the foe was born. The wicked planned to cut off the righteous, and the unclean was trapped by the hands of the pure. Kindness overcame the father's error, but the wicked one added sin upon his sins. In his heart he hid his cunning thoughts and devoted himself to commit evil. He stretched forth his hand against G-d's holy ones, he gave his money to cut off their remembrance. When Mordecai saw that wrath had gone forth, and that Haman's decree were issued in Shushan, He donned sackcloth and bound himself in mourning, decreed a fast and sat down in ashes. Who will rise up to atone for error, to gain pardon for our fathers' iniquity? A blossom from a palm branch; behold! Hadassah stood up to arouse the sleeping. Her servants hastened Haman, to give him to drink the venom of serpents. He rose by his wealth and fell by his wickedness; he made himself a gallows and was hanged on it. All the dwellers of the earth opened their mouth, for Haman's lot was turned in our favor. The righteous was extricated from the hand the wicked, the enemy was substituted for him. They undertook to celebrate Purim, to rejoice every year. You noted the prayer of Mordecai and Esther; Haman and his sons You hanged on the gallows.

וּגְדֻלָּתוֹ יָקְשָׁה לּוֹ לָכֶד: דָּמָה בְנַפְשׁוֹ לִלְכֹּד, וְנִלְכָּד. בִּקֵּשׁ לְהַשְׁמִיד, וְנִשְׁמַד מְהֵרָה: הָמָן הוֹדִיעַ אֵיבַת אֲבוֹתָיו, וְעוֹרֵר שִׂנְאַת אַחִים לַבָּנִים: וְלֹא זָכַר רַחֲמֵי שָׁאוּל, כִּי בְחֶמְלָתוֹ עַל־אֲגָג נוֹלַד אוֹיֵב: זָמַם רָשָׁע לְהַכְרִית צַדִּיק, וְנִלְכַּד טָמֵא, בִּידֵי טָהוֹר: חֶסֶד גָּבַר עַל שִׁגְגַת אָב, וְרָשָׁע הוֹסִיף חֵטְא עַל־חֲטָאָיו: טָמַן בְּלִבּוֹ מַחְשְׁבוֹת עֲרוּמָיו, וַיִּתְמַכֵּר לַעֲשׂוֹת רָעָה: יָדוֹ שָׁלַח בִּקְדוֹשֵׁי אֵל, כַּסְפּוֹ נָתַן לְהַכְרִית זִכְרָם: כִּרְאוֹת מָרְדְּכַי, כִּי יָצָא קֶצֶף, וְדָתֵי הָמָן נִתְּנוּ בְשׁוּשָׁן: לָבַשׁ שַׂק וְקָשַׁר מִסְפֵּד, וְגָזַר צוֹם, וַיֵּשֶׁב עַל הָאֵפֶר: מִי זֶה יַעֲמֹד לְכַפֵּר שְׁגָגָה, וְלִמְחֹל חַטַּאת עֲוֹן אֲבוֹתֵינוּ: נֵץ פָּרַח מִלּוּלָב, הֵן הֲדַסָּה עָמְדָה לְעוֹרֵר יְשֵׁנִים: סָרִיסֶיהָ הִבְהִילוּ לְהָמָן, לְהַשְׁקוֹתוֹ יֵין חֲמַת תַּנִּינִים: עָמַד בְּעָשְׁרוֹ, וְנָפַל בְּרִשְׁעוֹ, עָשָׂה לוֹ עֵץ, וְנִתְלָה עָלָיו: פִּיהֶם פָּתְחוּ כָּל יוֹשְׁבֵי תֵבֵל, כִּי פּוּר הָמָן נֶהְפַּךְ לְפוּרֵנוּ: צַדִּיק נֶחֱלַץ מִיַּד רָשָׁע, אוֹיֵב נִתַּן תַּחַת נַפְשׁוֹ: קִיְּמוּ עֲלֵיהֶם לַעֲשׂוֹת פּוּרִים, וְלִשְׂמֹחַ בְּכָל שָׁנָה וְשָׁנָה: רָאִיתָ אֶת תְּפִלַּת מָרְדְּכַי וְאֶסְתֵּר, הָמָן וּבָנָיו עַל הָעֵץ תָּלִיתָ:

The following is said both in the evening and in the morning.

The Jews of Shushan shouted and rejoiced, when together they saw Mordecai's blue robes. You were their salvation forever and their hope throughout all generations, to let know that all who hope for You will not be ashamed forever, neither will those who take shelter in You be humiliated to eternity. Cursed be Haman, who sought to destroy me; blessed be Mordecai the Jew. Cursed be Zeresh, the wife of him who frightened me; Blessed be Esther, my protectress, and may Harbonah, too, be remembered for good.

שׁוֹשַׁנַּת יַעֲקֹב, צָהֲלָה וְשָׂמֵחָה, בִּרְאוֹתָם יַחַד תְּכֵלֶת מָרְדְּכַי: תְּשׁוּעָתָם הָיִיתָ לָנֶצַח, וְתִקְוָתָם בְּכָל דּוֹר וָדוֹר: לְהוֹדִיעַ, שֶׁכָּל־קֹוֶיךָ לֹא יֵבוֹשׁוּ, וְלֹא־יִכָּלְמוּ לָנֶצַח כָּל הַחוֹסִים בָּךְ: אָרוּר הָמָן, אֲשֶׁר בִּקֵּשׁ לְאַבְּדִי, בָּרוּךְ מָרְדְּכַי הַיְּהוּדִי: אֲרוּרָה זֶרֶשׁ, אֵשֶׁת מַפְחִידִי, בְּרוּכָה אֶסְתֵּר בַּעֲדִי, וְגַם חַרְבוֹנָה זָכוּר לַטוֹב:

SHIR HASHIRIM שיר השירים

[SONG OF SONGS]

Proclaimed by the Rabbis the most sacred of all the Holy Writings, the "Song of Songs, which is Solomon's," is an allegory depicting Israel's yearning to return to its God. God is depicted as the husband who has left his wayward wife, but will return to her when the proper time has come.

What seems to be a song of love surveys, in allegorical terms, the whole history of the Jewish people, from its journeys through the wilderness at the time of the Exodus, its early settlement in the Promised Land, the period of the First Temple, the Babylonian exile, the period of the Second Temple, the exile in which we still find ourselves today—to a vision of our ultimate deliverance in the Messianic era.

According to the Midrashic interpretation, King Solomon, who in this book is portrayed as seeking to take a maiden from the shepherd with whom she is in love, is actually the "King to whom all peace (*shalom*) belongs"; i.e., God Himself.

M.L. Malbim (1809–79), the great modern Bible commentator, equates the maiden with the soul of King Solomon, which struggles to merge with the Almighty.

It is customary to read the Song of Songs every Friday before mincha. Many congregations read this book on the intermediate Shabbath of Pesaḥ prior to the reading of the Torah. Should there be no intermediate Shabbath, this book is read on either the seventh or eighth day of Pesaḥ whichever falls on Shabbath.

This beautiful song of love is read on Pesaḥ because it allegorically pertains to the Exodus.

CHAPTER I

1. The song of songs, which is Solomon's. 2. "Let him kiss me with the kisses of his mouth, for your love is better than wine. 3. Because of your goodly oils, your name is 'Oil poured forth.' Therefore, the maidens loved you. 4. Draw me, we will run after you; the king brought me to his chambers. We will rejoice and be glad with you. We will find your love more fragrant than wine; they have loved you sincerely. 5. I am black but comely, O daughters of Jerusalem! Like the tents of Kedar, like the curtains of Solomon. 6. Do not look upon me disdainfully because I am swarthy, for the sun has gazed upon me; my mother's sons were incensed against me; they made me a keeper of the vineyards; I did not keep my own vineyard. 7. Tell me, you whom my soul loves, where do you feed, where do you rest the flocks at noon, for why should I be like one who veils herself beside the flocks of your companions?" 8. "If you do not know, O fairest of women, go your way in the footsteps of the flocks and pasture your kids beside the shepherds' dwellings. 9. To a mare in Pharaoh's

א א שִׁיר הַשִּׁירִים אֲשֶׁר לִשְׁלֹמֹה׃ ב יִשָּׁקֵנִי
מִנְּשִׁיקוֹת פִּיהוּ כִּי־טוֹבִים דֹּדֶיךָ מִיָּיִן׃ ג לְרֵיחַ
שְׁמָנֶיךָ טוֹבִים שֶׁמֶן תּוּרַק שְׁמֶךָ עַל־כֵּן עֲלָמוֹת
אֲהֵבוּךָ׃ ד מָשְׁכֵנִי אַחֲרֶיךָ נָּרוּצָה הֱבִיאַנִי הַמֶּלֶךְ
חֲדָרָיו נָגִילָה וְנִשְׂמְחָה בָּךְ נַזְכִּירָה דֹדֶיךָ מִיַּיִן
מֵישָׁרִים אֲהֵבוּךָ׃ ס ה שְׁחוֹרָה אֲנִי וְנָאוָה בְּנוֹת
יְרוּשָׁלָםִ כְּאָהֳלֵי קֵדָר כִּירִיעוֹת שְׁלֹמֹה׃ ו אַל־
תִּרְאוּנִי שֶׁאֲנִי שְׁחַרְחֹרֶת שֶׁשְּׁזָפַתְנִי הַשָּׁמֶשׁ בְּנֵי
אִמִּי נִחֲרוּ־בִי שָׂמֻנִי נֹטֵרָה אֶת־הַכְּרָמִים כַּרְמִי
שֶׁלִּי לֹא נָטָרְתִּי׃ ז הַגִּידָה לִּי שֶׁאָהֲבָה נַפְשִׁי
אֵיכָה תִרְעֶה אֵיכָה תַּרְבִּיץ בַּצָּהֳרָיִם שַׁלָּמָה
אֶהְיֶה כְּעֹטְיָה עַל עֶדְרֵי חֲבֵרֶיךָ׃ ח אִם־לֹא
תֵדְעִי לָךְ הַיָּפָה בַּנָּשִׁים צְאִי־לָךְ בְּעִקְבֵי הַצֹּאן
וּרְעִי אֶת־גְּדִיֹּתַיִךְ עַל מִשְׁכְּנוֹת הָרֹעִים׃ ס

chariots have I compared you, my beloved. 10. Your cheeks are comely with circlets, your neck with necklaces. 11. We will make you circlets of gold with studs of silver." 12. "While the king was still at his table, my spikenard gave forth its fragrance. 13. A bundle of myrrh is my beloved to me; between my breasts he shall lie. 14. A cluster of henna is my beloved to me, in the vineyards of En-Gedi.' 15. "Behold, you are comely, my beloved; behold, you are comely; your eyes are like doves. 16. Behold, you are comely, my beloved; yea, pleasant; also our couch is leafy. 17. The beams of our houses are cedars, our corridors are cypresses.

CHAPTER II

1. "I am a rose of Sharon, a rose of the valleys." 2. "As a rose among thorns, so is my beloved among the daughters." 3. "As an apple tree among the trees of the forest, so is my beloved among the sons; in his shade I delighted and sat, and his fruit was sweet to my palate. 4. He brought me to the banquet hall, and his banner over me was [symbolic of his] love. 5. Sustain me with flagons of wine, spread my bed with apples, for I am lovesick. 6. His left hand was under my head, and his right hand would embrace me. 7. I adjure you, O daughters of Jerusalem, by the gazelles or by the hinds of the field, that you awaken not nor stir up the love until it is desirous. 8. The sound of my beloved! Behold, he is coming, skipping over the mountains, jumping over the hills. 9. My beloved resembles a gazelle or a fawn of the hinds; behold, he is standing behind our wall, looking from the windows, peering from the lattices. 10. My beloved spoke up and said to me, 'Arise, my beloved, my fair one, and come away. 11. For behold, the winter has passed, the rain is over and has gone away. 12. The blossoms have appeared in the land, the time of singing has arrived, and the voice of the turtledove is heard in our land. 13. The fig tree has put forth its green figs, and the vines with their tiny grapes have given forth their fragrance; come, my beloved, my fair one, and come away. 14. My dove, in the

ט לְסֻסָתִי בְּרִכְבֵי פַרְעֹה דִּמִּיתִיךְ רַעְיָתִי׃
י נָאווּ לְחָיַיִךְ בַּתֹּרִים צַוָּארֵךְ בַּחֲרוּזִים׃
יא תּוֹרֵי זָהָב נַעֲשֶׂה־לָּךְ עִם נְקֻדּוֹת הַכָּסֶף׃
יב עַד־שֶׁהַמֶּלֶךְ בִּמְסִבּוֹ נִרְדִּי נָתַן רֵיחוֹ׃
יג צְרוֹר הַמֹּר ׀ דּוֹדִי לִי בֵּין שָׁדַי יָלִין׃
יד אֶשְׁכֹּל הַכֹּפֶר ׀ דּוֹדִי לִי בְּכַרְמֵי עֵין גֶּדִי׃ ס
טו הִנָּךְ יָפָה רַעְיָתִי הִנָּךְ יָפָה עֵינַיִךְ יוֹנִים׃
טז הִנְּךָ יָפֶה דוֹדִי אַף נָעִים אַף־עַרְשֵׂנוּ רַעֲנָנָה׃
יז קֹרוֹת בָּתֵּינוּ אֲרָזִים רַחִיטֵנוּ (רהיטנו קרי)
בְּרוֹתִים׃
ב א אֲנִי חֲבַצֶּלֶת הַשָּׁרוֹן שׁוֹשַׁנַּת הָעֲמָקִים׃
ב כְּשׁוֹשַׁנָּה בֵּין הַחוֹחִים כֵּן רַעְיָתִי בֵּין הַבָּנוֹת׃
ג כְּתַפּוּחַ בַּעֲצֵי הַיַּעַר כֵּן דּוֹדִי בֵּין הַבָּנִים
בְּצִלּוֹ חִמַּדְתִּי וְיָשַׁבְתִּי וּפִרְיוֹ מָתוֹק לְחִכִּי׃
ד הֱבִיאַנִי אֶל־בֵּית הַיָּיִן וְדִגְלוֹ עָלַי אַהֲבָה׃
ה סַמְּכוּנִי בָּאֲשִׁישׁוֹת רַפְּדוּנִי בַּתַּפּוּחִים כִּי־
חוֹלַת אַהֲבָה אָנִי׃ ו שְׂמֹאלוֹ תַּחַת לְרֹאשִׁי
וִימִינוֹ תְּחַבְּקֵנִי׃ ז הִשְׁבַּעְתִּי אֶתְכֶם בְּנוֹת
יְרוּשָׁלַםִ בִּצְבָאוֹת אוֹ בְּאַיְלוֹת הַשָּׂדֶה אִם־
תָּעִירוּ ׀ וְאִם־תְּעוֹרְרוּ אֶת־הָאַהֲבָה עַד
שֶׁתֶּחְפָּץ׃ ס ח קוֹל דּוֹדִי הִנֵּה־זֶה בָּא מְדַלֵּג עַל־
הֶהָרִים מְקַפֵּץ עַל־הַגְּבָעוֹת׃ ט דּוֹמֶה דוֹדִי
לִצְבִי אוֹ לְעֹפֶר הָאַיָּלִים הִנֵּה־זֶה עוֹמֵד אַחַר
כָּתְלֵנוּ מַשְׁגִּיחַ מִן־הַחַלֹּנוֹת מֵצִיץ מִן־הַחֲרַכִּים׃
י עָנָה דוֹדִי וְאָמַר לִי קוּמִי לָךְ רַעְיָתִי יָפָתִי
וּלְכִי־לָךְ׃ יא כִּי־הִנֵּה הַסְּתָו עָבָר הַגֶּשֶׁם חָלַף
הָלַךְ לוֹ׃ יב הַנִּצָּנִים נִרְאוּ בָאָרֶץ עֵת הַזָּמִיר
הִגִּיעַ וְקוֹל הַתּוֹר נִשְׁמַע בְּאַרְצֵנוּ׃ יג הַתְּאֵנָה
חָנְטָה פַגֶּיהָ וְהַגְּפָנִים ׀ סְמָדַר נָתְנוּ רֵיחַ קוּמִי
לָכִי (לך קרי) רַעְיָתִי יָפָתִי וּלְכִי־לָךְ׃ ס יד יוֹנָתִי

clefts of the rock, in the coverture of the cliff, show me your appearance, let me hear your voice, for your voice is pleasant, and your appearance is comely.' 15. Seize for us the foxes, the little foxes, who destroy the vineyards, for our vineyards are with tiny grapes. 16. My beloved is mine, and I am his, who grazes among the roses. 17. Until the day blows, and the shadows flee, go around; liken yourself to a gazelle or to a fawn of the hinds, on distant mountains."

CHAPTER III

1. On my bed at night, I sought him whom my soul loves; I sought him but I did not find him. 2. I will arise now and go about the city, in the market places and in the city squares. I will seek him whom my soul loves; I have sought him, but I have not found him. 3. The watchmen who patrol the city found me; "Have you seen him whom my soul loves?" 4. I had just passed them by, when I found him whom my soul loves; I held him and would not let him go, until I brought him into my mother's house and into the chamber of her who had conceived me. 5. I adjure you, O daughters of Jerusalem, by the gazelles or by the hinds of the field, that you awaken not nor stir up the love until it is desirous. 6. Who is this coming up from the desert, like columns of smoke, perfumed with myrrh and frankincense, of all the powders of the cosmetic peddler? 7. Behold, the litter of Solomon; sixty mighty men are around it, of the mighty men of Israel. 8. They all hold the sword, skilled in warfare; each one with his sword on his thigh because of fear at night. 9. King Solomon made himself a palanquin of the trees of the Lebanon. 10. Its pillars he made of silver, its couch of gold, its curtain of purple, its interior inlaid with love, from the daughters of Jerusalem. 11. Go out, O daughters of Zion, and gaze upon King Solomon, upon the crown with which his mother crowned him on the day of his nuptials and on the day of the joy of his heart.

CHAPTER IV

1. Behold, you are fair, my beloved; behold, you are fair; your eyes are [like] doves, from within your veil; your hair is like a flock of goats streaming down from Mount Gilead. 2. Your teeth are like a flock

בְּחַגְוֵי הַסֶּלַע בְּסֵתֶר הַמַּדְרֵגָה הַרְאִינִי אֶת־
מַרְאַיִךְ הַשְׁמִיעִינִי אֶת־קוֹלֵךְ כִּי־קוֹלֵךְ עָרֵב
וּמַרְאֵיךְ נָאוֶה: ס טו אֶחֱזוּ־לָנוּ שׁוּעָלִים שֻׁעָלִים
קְטַנִּים מְחַבְּלִים כְּרָמִים וּכְרָמֵינוּ סְמָדַר:
טז דּוֹדִי לִי וַאֲנִי לוֹ הָרֹעֶה בַּשּׁוֹשַׁנִּים: יז עַד
שֶׁיָּפוּחַ הַיּוֹם וְנָסוּ הַצְּלָלִים סֹב דְּמֵה־לְךָ דוֹדִי
לִצְבִי אוֹ לְעֹפֶר הָאַיָּלִים עַל־הָרֵי בָתֶר: ס
ג א עַל־מִשְׁכָּבִי בַּלֵּילוֹת בִּקַּשְׁתִּי אֵת שֶׁאָהֲבָה
נַפְשִׁי בִּקַּשְׁתִּיו וְלֹא מְצָאתִיו: ב אָקוּמָה נָּא
וַאֲסוֹבְבָה בָעִיר בַּשְּׁוָקִים וּבָרְחֹבוֹת אֲבַקְשָׁה
אֵת שֶׁאָהֲבָה נַפְשִׁי בִּקַּשְׁתִּיו וְלֹא מְצָאתִיו:
ג מְצָאוּנִי הַשֹּׁמְרִים הַסֹּבְבִים בָּעִיר אֵת
שֶׁאָהֲבָה נַפְשִׁי רְאִיתֶם: ד כִּמְעַט שֶׁעָבַרְתִּי מֵהֶם
עַד שֶׁמָּצָאתִי אֵת שֶׁאָהֲבָה נַפְשִׁי אֲחַזְתִּיו וְלֹא
אַרְפֶּנּוּ עַד־שֶׁהֲבֵיאתִיו (שהבאתיו קרי) אֶל־בֵּית
אִמִּי וְאֶל־חֶדֶר הוֹרָתִי: ה הִשְׁבַּעְתִּי אֶתְכֶם בְּנוֹת
יְרוּשָׁלִַם בִּצְבָאוֹת אוֹ בְּאַיְלוֹת הַשָּׂדֶה אִם־
תָּעִירוּ | וְאִם־תְּעוֹרְרוּ אֶת־הָאַהֲבָה עַד
שֶׁתֶּחְפָּץ: ס ו מִי זֹאת עֹלָה מִן־הַמִּדְבָּר
כְּתִימְרוֹת עָשָׁן מְקֻטֶּרֶת מֹר וּלְבוֹנָה מִכֹּל
אַבְקַת רוֹכֵל: ז הִנֵּה מִטָּתוֹ שֶׁלִּשְׁלֹמֹה שִׁשִּׁים
גִּבֹּרִים סָבִיב לָהּ מִגִּבֹּרֵי יִשְׂרָאֵל: ח כֻּלָּם אֲחֻזֵי
חֶרֶב מְלֻמְּדֵי מִלְחָמָה אִישׁ חַרְבּוֹ עַל־יְרֵכוֹ
מִפַּחַד בַּלֵּילוֹת: ס ט אַפִּרְיוֹן עָשָׂה לוֹ הַמֶּלֶךְ
שְׁלֹמֹה מֵעֲצֵי הַלְּבָנוֹן: י עַמּוּדָיו עָשָׂה כֶסֶף
רְפִידָתוֹ זָהָב מֶרְכָּבוֹ אַרְגָּמָן תּוֹכוֹ רָצוּף אַהֲבָה
מִבְּנוֹת יְרוּשָׁלִָם: יא צְאֶינָה | וּרְאֶינָה בְּנוֹת צִיּוֹן
בַּמֶּלֶךְ שְׁלֹמֹה בָּעֲטָרָה שֶׁעִטְּרָה־לּוֹ אִמּוֹ בְּיוֹם
חֲתֻנָּתוֹ וּבְיוֹם שִׂמְחַת לִבּוֹ: ס
ד א הִנָּךְ יָפָה רַעְיָתִי הִנָּךְ יָפָה עֵינַיִךְ יוֹנִים
מִבַּעַד לְצַמָּתֵךְ שַׂעְרֵךְ כְּעֵדֶר הָעִזִּים שֶׁגָּלְשׁוּ
מֵהַר גִּלְעָד: ב שִׁנַּיִךְ כְּעֵדֶר הַקְּצוּבוֹת שֶׁעָלוּ

of uniformly shaped [ewes] that came up from the washing, all of whom are paired, and there is no blemish on them. 3. Your lips are like a scarlet thread, and your speech is comely; your temple is like a split pomegranate from beneath your veil. 4. Your neck is like the tower of David, built as a model; a thousand shields hanging on it, all the armor of the mighty men. 5. Your two breasts are like two fawns, the twins of a gazelle, who graze among the roses. 6. Until the day blows and the shadows flee, I will go away to the mountain of myrrh and to the hill of frankincense. 7. You are all fair, my beloved, and there is no blemish in you. 8. With me from Lebanon, my bride, with me from Lebanon shall you come; you shall look from the peak of Amanah, from the peak of Senir and Hermon, from lions' dens, from mountains of leopards. 9. You have captivated my heart, my sister, [my] bride; you have captivated my heart with one of your eyes, with one link of your necklaces. 10. How fair is your love, my sister, [my] bride; how much better is your love than wine, and the fragrance of your oils than all spices! 11. Your lips drip honey, O bride; honey and milk are under your tongue, and the fragrance of your garments is like the fragrance of Lebanon. 12. A locked up garden is my sister, [my] bride; a locked up spring, a sealed fountain. 13. Your shoots are a pomegranate orchard with sweet fruit, henna with spikenard. 14. Spikenard and saffron, calamus and cinnamon, with all frankincense trees, myrrh and aloes, with all the chief spices. 15. A garden fountain, a well of living waters and flowing streams from Lebanon. 16. Awake, O north wind and come O south wind; blow upon my garden, let its spices flow; let my beloved come to his garden and eat his sweet fruit.

CHAPTER V

1. I have come to my garden, my sister, [my] bride; I have gathered my myrrh with my spice, I have eaten my honeycomb with my honey, I have drunk my wine with my milk; eat, friends, drink; yea, drink abundantly, beloved ones. 2. I sleep, but my heart is awake. Hark! My beloved is knocking: "Open for me, my sister, my

מִן־הָרַחְצָה שֶׁכֻּלָּם מַתְאִימוֹת וְשַׁכֻּלָה אֵין
בָּהֶם: ג כְּחוּט הַשָּׁנִי שִׂפְתוֹתַיִךְ וּמִדְבָּרֵךְ נָאוֶה
כְּפֶלַח הָרִמּוֹן רַקָּתֵךְ מִבַּעַד לְצַמָּתֵךְ: ד כְּמִגְדַּל
דָּוִיד צַוָּארֵךְ בָּנוּי לְתַלְפִּיּוֹת אֶלֶף הַמָּגֵן תָּלוּי
עָלָיו כֹּל שִׁלְטֵי הַגִּבֹּרִים: ה שְׁנֵי שָׁדַיִךְ כִּשְׁנֵי
עֳפָרִים תְּאוֹמֵי צְבִיָּה הָרוֹעִים בַּשּׁוֹשַׁנִּים: ו עַד
שֶׁיָּפוּחַ הַיּוֹם וְנָסוּ הַצְּלָלִים אֵלֶךְ לִי אֶל־הַר
הַמּוֹר וְאֶל־גִּבְעַת הַלְּבוֹנָה: ז כֻּלָּךְ יָפָה רַעְיָתִי
וּמוּם אֵין בָּךְ: ס ח אִתִּי מִלְּבָנוֹן כַּלָּה אִתִּי
מִלְּבָנוֹן תָּבוֹאִי תָּשׁוּרִי | מֵרֹאשׁ אֲמָנָה מֵרֹאשׁ
שְׂנִיר וְחֶרְמוֹן מִמְּעֹנוֹת אֲרָיוֹת מֵהַרְרֵי נְמֵרִים:
ט לִבַּבְתִּנִי אֲחֹתִי כַלָּה לִבַּבְתִּנִי בְּאַחַד (באחת קרי)
מֵעֵינַיִךְ בְּאַחַד עֲנָק מִצַּוְּרֹנָיִךְ: י מַה־יָּפוּ דֹדַיִךְ
אֲחֹתִי כַלָּה מַה־טֹּבוּ דֹדַיִךְ מִיַּיִן וְרֵיחַ שְׁמָנַיִךְ
מִכָּל־בְּשָׂמִים: יא נֹפֶת תִּטֹּפְנָה שִׂפְתוֹתַיִךְ כַּלָּה
דְּבַשׁ וְחָלָב תַּחַת לְשׁוֹנֵךְ וְרֵיחַ שַׂלְמֹתַיִךְ כְּרֵיחַ
לְבָנוֹן: ס יב גַּן | נָעוּל אֲחֹתִי כַלָּה גַּל נָעוּל מַעְיָן
חָתוּם: יג שְׁלָחַיִךְ פַּרְדֵּס רִמּוֹנִים עִם פְּרִי
מְגָדִים כְּפָרִים עִם־נְרָדִים: יד נֵרְדְּ | וְכַרְכֹּם
קָנֶה וְקִנָּמוֹן עִם כָּל־עֲצֵי לְבוֹנָה מֹר וַאֲהָלוֹת
עִם כָּל־רָאשֵׁי בְשָׂמִים: טו מַעְיַן גַּנִּים בְּאֵר מַיִם
חַיִּים וְנֹזְלִים מִן־לְבָנוֹן: טז עוּרִי צָפוֹן וּבוֹאִי
תֵימָן הָפִיחִי גַנִּי יִזְּלוּ בְשָׂמָיו יָבֹא דוֹדִי לְגַנּוֹ
וְיֹאכַל פְּרִי מְגָדָיו:

ה א בָּאתִי לְגַנִּי אֲחֹתִי כַלָּה אָרִיתִי מוֹרִי עִם־
בְּשָׂמִי אָכַלְתִּי יַעְרִי עִם־דִּבְשִׁי שָׁתִיתִי יֵינִי עִם־
חֲלָבִי אִכְלוּ רֵעִים שְׁתוּ וְשִׁכְרוּ דּוֹדִים: ס ב אֲנִי
יְשֵׁנָה וְלִבִּי עֵר קוֹל | דּוֹדִי דוֹפֵק פִּתְחִי־לִי

beloved, my dove, my perfect one, for
my head is full of dew, my locks with the
drops of the night." 3. "I have taken off
my chemise; how can I put it on? I have
bathed my feet; how can I soil them?"
4. My beloved stretched forth his hand
from the hole, and my insides stirred
because of him. 5. I arose to open for my
beloved, and my hands dripped with myrrh,
and my fingers with flowing myrrh, upon
the handles of the lock. 6. I opened for
my beloved, but my beloved had hidden
and was gone; my soul went out when he
spoke; I sought him, but found him not; I
called him, but he did not answer me.
7. The watchmen who patrol the city
found me, they smote me and wounded me;
the watchmen of the walls took my veil off
me. 8. "I adjure you, O daughters of
Jerusalem, if you find my beloved, what will
you tell him? That I am lovesick."
9. "What is your beloved more than
another beloved, O fairest of women?
What is your beloved more than another
beloved, that you have so adjured us?"
10. "My beloved is white and ruddy,
surrounded by myriads. 11. His head is
[as] finest gold; his locks are curled, black as
a raven. 12. His eyes are like doves
beside rivulets of water, bathing in milk,
fitly set. 13. His cheeks are like a bed of
spice, growths of aromatic plants; his lips
are [like] roses, dripping with flowing
myrrh. 14. His hands are [like] rods of
gold, set with chrysolite; his abdomen is [as]
a block of ivory, overlaid with sapphires.
15. His legs are [as] pillars of marble,
founded upon sockets of fine gold; his
appearance is like the Lebanon, excellent
as the cedars. 16. His palate is sweet,
and he is altogether desirable; this is my
beloved, and this is my friend, O daughters
of Jerusalem."

אֲחֹתִי רַעְיָתִי יוֹנָתִי תַמָּתִי שֶׁרֹּאשִׁי נִמְלָא־טָל
קְוֻצּוֹתַי רְסִיסֵי לָיְלָה׃ ג פָּשַׁטְתִּי אֶת־כֻּתָּנְתִּי
אֵיכָכָה אֶלְבָּשֶׁנָּה רָחַצְתִּי אֶת־רַגְלַי אֵיכָכָה
אֲטַנְּפֵם׃ ד דּוֹדִי שָׁלַח יָדוֹ מִן־הַחֹור וּמֵעַי הָמוּ
עָלָיו׃ ה קַמְתִּי אֲנִי לִפְתֹּחַ לְדוֹדִי וְיָדַי נָטְפוּ־
מוֹר וְאֶצְבְּעֹתַי מוֹר עֹבֵר עַל כַּפּוֹת הַמַּנְעוּל׃
ו פָּתַחְתִּי אֲנִי לְדוֹדִי וְדוֹדִי חָמַק עָבָר נַפְשִׁי
יָצְאָה בְדַבְּרוֹ בִּקַּשְׁתִּיהוּ וְלֹא מְצָאתִיהוּ
קְרָאתִיו וְלֹא עָנָנִי׃ ז מְצָאֻנִי הַשֹּׁמְרִים הַסֹּבְבִים
בָּעִיר הִכּוּנִי פְצָעוּנִי נָשְׂאוּ אֶת־רְדִידִי מֵעָלַי
שֹׁמְרֵי הַחֹמוֹת׃ ח הִשְׁבַּעְתִּי אֶתְכֶם בְּנוֹת
יְרוּשָׁלָםִ אִם־תִּמְצְאוּ אֶת־דּוֹדִי מַה־תַּגִּידוּ לוֹ
שֶׁחוֹלַת אַהֲבָה אָנִי׃ ט מַה־דּוֹדֵךְ מִדּוֹד הַיָּפָה
בַּנָּשִׁים מַה־דּוֹדֵךְ מִדּוֹד שֶׁכָּכָה הִשְׁבַּעְתָּנוּ׃
י דּוֹדִי צַח וְאָדוֹם דָּגוּל מֵרְבָבָה׃ יא רֹאשׁוֹ
כֶּתֶם פָּז קְוֻצּוֹתָיו תַּלְתַּלִּים שְׁחֹרוֹת כָּעוֹרֵב׃
יב עֵינָיו כְּיוֹנִים עַל־אֲפִיקֵי מָיִם רֹחֲצוֹת בֶּחָלָב
יֹשְׁבוֹת עַל־מִלֵּאת׃ יג לְחָיָו כַּעֲרוּגַת הַבֹּשֶׂם
מִגְדְּלוֹת מֶרְקָחִים שִׂפְתוֹתָיו שׁוֹשַׁנִּים נֹטְפוֹת
מוֹר עֹבֵר׃ יד יָדָיו גְּלִילֵי זָהָב מְמֻלָּאִים
בַּתַּרְשִׁישׁ מֵעָיו עֶשֶׁת שֵׁן מְעֻלֶּפֶת סַפִּירִים׃
טו שׁוֹקָיו עַמּוּדֵי שֵׁשׁ מְיֻסָּדִים עַל־אַדְנֵי־פָז
מַרְאֵהוּ כַּלְּבָנוֹן בָּחוּר כָּאֲרָזִים׃ טז חִכּוֹ
מַמְתַקִּים וְכֻלּוֹ מַחֲמַדִּים זֶה דוֹדִי וְזֶה רֵעִי בְּנוֹת
יְרוּשָׁלָםִ׃

CHAPTER VI

1. "Where has your beloved gone, O fairest
of women? Where has your beloved gone,
that we may seek him with you?" 2. "My
beloved has gone down to his garden, to the
spice beds, to graze in the gardens and to
gather roses. 3. I am my beloved's, and
my beloved is mine, who grazes among the

ו א אָנָה הָלַךְ דּוֹדֵךְ הַיָּפָה בַּנָּשִׁים אָנָה פָּנָה
דוֹדֵךְ וּנְבַקְשֶׁנּוּ עִמָּךְ׃ ב דּוֹדִי יָרַד לְגַנּוֹ לַעֲרוּגוֹת
הַבֹּשֶׂם לִרְעוֹת בַּגַּנִּים וְלִלְקֹט שׁוֹשַׁנִּים׃ ג אֲנִי
לְדוֹדִי וְדוֹדִי לִי הָרֹעֶה בַּשּׁוֹשַׁנִּים׃ פ ד יָפָה

roses."   4. "You are fair, my beloved, as Tirzah, comely as Jerusalem, awesome as the bannered legions.   5. Turn away your eyes from me, for they have made me haughty; your hair is like a flock of goats that streamed down from Gilead.   6. Your teeth are like a flock of ewes that came up from the washing, all of whom are paired, and there is no blemish on them.   7. Your temple is like a split pomegranate from beneath your veil.   8. There are sixty queens and eighty concubines, and innumerable maidens.   9. My dove, my perfect one, is but one; she is one to her mother, she is the pure one of her who bore her; daughters saw her and praised her, queens and concubines, and they lauded her.   10. Who is this who looks forth like the dawn, fair as the moon, clear as the sun, awesome as the bannered legions?   11. I went down to the nut garden to see the green plants of the valley, to see whether the vine had blossomed, the pomegranates were in flower.   12. I did not know; my soul made me chariots for the princes of a people.

CHAPTER VII

1. "Return, return, O Shulammite; return, return, and let us gaze upon you." "What will you see in the Shulammite as in the dance of the two camps?"   2. How fair are your steps in sandals, O daughter of nobles! The curves of your thighs are like jewels, the handiwork of a craftsman.   3. Your navel is [like] a round basin, where no mixed wine is lacking; your belly is like a stack of wheat, fenced in with roses.   4. Your two breasts are like two fawns, the twins of a gazelle. 5. Your neck is like an ivory tower; your eyes are [like] pools in Heshbon, by the gate of Bath-rabbim; your nose is as [straight as] the tower of Lebanon, overlooking the face of Damascus.   6. Your head upon you is like Carmel, and the braided locks of your head are like purple; the king is bound in the tresses.   7. How fair and how pleasant are you, a love with delights!   8. This your stature is like a palm tree, and your breasts are like clusters [of grapes].   9. I said, "Let me climb up the palm tree, let me seize its boughs, and let your breasts be now

אַתְּ רַעְיָתִי כְּתִרְצָה נָאוָה כִּירוּשָׁלָ֖ם אֲיֻמָּ֖ה
כַּנִּדְגָּלֽוֹת: ה הָסֵ֣בִּי עֵינַ֙יִךְ֙ מִנֶּגְדִּ֔י שֶׁהֵ֖ם הִרְהִיבֻ֑נִי
שַׂעְרֵךְ֙ כְּעֵ֣דֶר הָֽעִזִּ֔ים שֶׁגָּֽלְשׁ֖וּ מִן־הַגִּלְעָֽד:
ו שִׁנַּ֙יִךְ֙ כְּעֵ֣דֶר הָֽרְחֵלִ֔ים שֶׁעָל֖וּ מִן־הָֽרַחְצָ֑ה
שֶׁכֻּלָּם֙ מַתְאִימ֔וֹת וְשַׁכֻּלָ֖ה אֵ֥ין בָּהֶֽם: ז כְּפֶ֤לַח
הָֽרִמּוֹן֙ רַקָּתֵ֔ךְ מִבַּ֖עַד לְצַמָּתֵֽךְ: ח שִׁשִּׁ֥ים הֵ֙מָּה֙
מְלָכ֔וֹת וּשְׁמֹנִ֖ים פִּֽילַגְשִׁ֑ים וַֽעֲלָמ֖וֹת אֵ֥ין מִסְפָּֽר:
ט אַחַ֥ת הִיא֙ יֽוֹנָתִ֣י תַמָּתִ֔י אַחַ֥ת הִיא֙ לְאִמָּ֔הּ
בָּרָ֥ה הִ֖יא לְיֽוֹלַדְתָּ֑הּ רָא֤וּהָ בָנוֹת֙ וַֽיְאַשְּׁר֔וּהָ
מְלָכ֥וֹת וּפִֽילַגְשִׁ֖ים וַֽיְהַלְלֽוּהָ: ס י מִי־זֹ֣את
הַנִּשְׁקָפָ֖ה כְּמוֹ־שָׁ֑חַר יָפָ֣ה כַלְּבָנָ֗ה בָּרָה֙ כַּֽחַמָּ֔ה
אֲיֻמָּ֖ה כַּנִּדְגָּלֽוֹת: יא אֶל־גִּנַּ֤ת אֱגוֹז֙ יָרַ֔דְתִּי
לִרְא֖וֹת בְּאִבֵּ֣י הַנָּ֑חַל לִרְאוֹת֙ הֲפָֽרְחָ֣ה הַגֶּ֔פֶן הֵנֵ֖צוּ
הָֽרִמֹּנִֽים: יב לֹ֣א יָדַ֔עְתִּי נַפְשִׁ֣י שָׂמַ֔תְנִי מַרְכְּב֖וֹת
עַמִּ֥י נָדִֽיב:

ז א שׁ֤וּבִי שׁ֙וּבִי֙ הַשּׁ֣וּלַמִּ֔ית שׁ֥וּבִי שׁ֖וּבִי וְנֶֽחֱזֶה־
בָּ֑ךְ מַֽה־תֶּֽחֱזוּ֙ בַּשּׁ֣וּלַמִּ֔ית כִּמְחֹלַ֖ת הַֽמַּֽחֲנָֽיִם:
ב מַה־יָּפ֧וּ פְעָמַ֛יִךְ בַּנְּעָלִ֖ים בַּת־נָדִ֑יב חַמּוּקֵ֣י
יְרֵכַ֔יִךְ כְּמ֣וֹ חֲלָאִ֔ים מַֽעֲשֵׂ֖ה יְדֵ֥י אָמָּֽן: ג שָׁרְרֵךְ֙
אַגַּ֣ן הַסַּ֔הַר אַל־יֶחְסַ֖ר הַמָּ֑זֶג בִּטְנֵךְ֙ עֲרֵמַ֣ת חִטִּ֔ים
סוּגָ֖ה בַּשּֽׁוֹשַׁנִּֽים: ד שְׁנֵ֥י שָׁדַ֖יִךְ כִּשְׁנֵ֣י עֳפָרִ֑ים
תָּֽאֳמֵ֖י צְבִיָּֽה: ה צַוָּארֵ֖ךְ כְּמִגְדַּ֣ל הַשֵּׁ֑ן עֵינַ֜יִךְ
בְּרֵכ֣וֹת בְּחֶשְׁבּ֗וֹן עַל־שַׁ֙עַר֙ בַּת־רַבִּ֔ים אַפֵּךְ֙
כְּמִגְדַּ֣ל הַלְּבָנ֔וֹן צוֹפֶ֖ה פְּנֵ֥י דַמָּֽשֶׂק: ו רֹאשֵׁ֤ךְ
עָלַ֙יִךְ֙ כַּכַּרְמֶ֔ל וְדַלַּ֥ת רֹאשֵׁ֖ךְ כָּֽאַרְגָּמָ֑ן מֶ֖לֶךְ אָס֥וּר
בָּֽרְהָטִֽים: ז מַה־יָּפִית֙ וּמַה־נָּעַ֔מְתְּ אַֽהֲבָ֖ה
בַּתַּֽעֲנוּגִֽים: ח זֹ֤את קֽוֹמָתֵךְ֙ דָּֽמְתָ֣ה לְתָמָ֔ר
וְשָׁדַ֖יִךְ לְאַשְׁכֹּלֽוֹת: ט אָמַ֙רְתִּי֙ אֶֽעֱלֶ֣ה בְתָמָ֔ר
אֹֽחֲזָ֖ה בְּסַנְסִנָּ֑יו וְיִֽהְיוּ־נָ֤א שָׁדַ֙יִךְ֙ כְּאֶשְׁכְּל֣וֹת

like clusters of the vine and the fragrance of your countenance like [that of] apples. 10. And your palate is like the best wine, that glides down smoothly to my beloved, making the lips of the sleeping speak. 11. I am my beloved's, and his desire is upon me. 12. Come, my beloved, let us go out of the field, let us lodge in the villages. 13. Let us arise early to the vineyards; let us see whether the vine has blossomed, the tiny grapes have developed, the pomegranates are in bloom; there I will give you my love. 14. The mandrakes have given forth [their] fragrance, and on our doorways are all manner of sweet fruits, both new and old, which I have laid up for you, my beloved."

CHAPTER VIII

1. O, that you were like my brother, who sucked my mother's breasts! I would find you outside, I would kiss you, and they would not despise me. 2. I would lead you, I would bring you to the house of my mother, who instructed me; I would give you to drink some spiced wine, some juice of my pomegranate. 3. His left hand would be under my head, and his right hand would embrace me. 4. I adjure you, O daughters of Jerusalem; why should you awaken, and why should you stir up the love until it is desirous? 5. "Who is this coming up from the desert, longing for her beloved?" "Under the apple tree I aroused you; there your mother was in travail with you; there she that bore you was in travail. 6. Place me like a seal on your heart, like a seal on your arm, for love is as strong as death, jealousy is as harsh as the grave; its coals are coals of fire, yea, a great flame! 7. Many waters cannot quench the love, nor can rivers flood it; should a man give all the property of his house for love, they would despise him. 8. We have a little sister who has no breasts; what shall we do for our sister on the day she is spoken for? 9. If she be a wall, we will build upon her a silver turret, but if she be a door, we will enclose her with cedar boards. 10. I am a wall, and my breasts are like towers; then I was in his eyes as one who finds peace. 11. Solomon had a vineyard in Baal-

הַגֶּפֶן וְרֵיחַ אַפֵּךְ כַּתַּפּוּחִים: י וְחִכֵּךְ כְּיֵין הַטּוֹב
הוֹלֵךְ לְדוֹדִי לְמֵישָׁרִים דּוֹבֵב שִׂפְתֵי יְשֵׁנִים:
יא אֲנִי לְדוֹדִי וְעָלַי תְּשׁוּקָתוֹ: יב לְכָה דוֹדִי נֵצֵא
הַשָּׂדֶה נָלִינָה בַּכְּפָרִים: יג נַשְׁכִּימָה לַכְּרָמִים
נִרְאֶה אִם־פָּרְחָה הַגֶּפֶן פִּתַּח הַסְּמָדַר הֵנֵצוּ
הָרִמּוֹנִים שָׁם אֶתֵּן אֶת־דֹּדַי לָךְ: יד הַדּוּדָאִים
נָתְנוּ־רֵיחַ וְעַל־פְּתָחֵינוּ כָּל־מְגָדִים חֲדָשִׁים גַּם־
יְשָׁנִים דּוֹדִי צָפַנְתִּי לָךְ:

ח א מִי יִתֶּנְךָ כְּאָח לִי יוֹנֵק שְׁדֵי אִמִּי אֶמְצָאֲךָ
בַחוּץ אֶשָּׁקְךָ גַּם לֹא־יָבֻזוּ לִי: ב אֶנְהָגֲךָ אֲבִיאֲךָ
אֶל־בֵּית אִמִּי תְּלַמְּדֵנִי אַשְׁקְךָ מִיַּיִן הָרֶקַח
מֵעֲסִיס רִמֹּנִי: ג שְׂמֹאלוֹ תַּחַת רֹאשִׁי וִימִינוֹ
תְּחַבְּקֵנִי: ד הִשְׁבַּעְתִּי אֶתְכֶם בְּנוֹת יְרוּשָׁלָם
מַה־תָּעִירוּ | וּמַה־תְּעֹרְרוּ אֶת־הָאַהֲבָה עַד־
שֶׁתֶּחְפָּץ: ס ה מִי זֹאת עֹלָה מִן־הַמִּדְבָּר
מִתְרַפֶּקֶת עַל־דּוֹדָהּ תַּחַת הַתַּפּוּחַ עוֹרַרְתִּיךָ
שָׁמָּה חִבְּלַתְךָ אִמֶּךָ שָׁמָּה חִבְּלָה יְלָדַתְךָ:
ו שִׂימֵנִי כַחוֹתָם עַל־לִבֶּךָ כַּחוֹתָם עַל־זְרוֹעֶךָ
כִּי־עַזָּה כַמָּוֶת אַהֲבָה קָשָׁה כִשְׁאוֹל קִנְאָה
רְשָׁפֶיהָ רִשְׁפֵּי אֵשׁ שַׁלְהֶבֶתְיָה: ז מַיִם רַבִּים לֹא
יוּכְלוּ לְכַבּוֹת אֶת־הָאַהֲבָה וּנְהָרוֹת לֹא יִשְׁטְפוּהָ
אִם־יִתֵּן אִישׁ אֶת־כָּל־הוֹן בֵּיתוֹ בָּאַהֲבָה בּוֹז
יָבוּזוּ לוֹ: ס ח אָחוֹת לָנוּ קְטַנָּה וְשָׁדַיִם אֵין לָהּ
מַה־נַּעֲשֶׂה לַאֲחוֹתֵנוּ בַּיּוֹם שֶׁיְּדֻבַּר־בָּהּ: ט אִם־
חוֹמָה הִיא נִבְנֶה עָלֶיהָ טִירַת כָּסֶף וְאִם־דֶּלֶת
הִיא נָצוּר עָלֶיהָ לוּחַ אָרֶז: י אֲנִי חוֹמָה וְשָׁדַי
כַּמִּגְדָּלוֹת אָז הָיִיתִי בְעֵינָיו כְּמוֹצְאֵת שָׁלוֹם:
יא כֶּרֶם הָיָה לִשְׁלֹמֹה בְּבַעַל הָמוֹן נָתַן אֶת־

hamon; he gave the vineyard to the keepers; each one brought for the fruit thereof one thousand pieces of silver.   12. My vineyard, which is mine, is before me; you, O Solomon, shall have the thousand, and those who watch the fruit two hundred. 13. You, who sit in the gardens, the friends hearken to your voice; let me hear [it].   14. Flee, my beloved, and liken yourself to a gazelle or to a fawn of the hinds on the spice mountains."

הַכֶּרֶם לַנֹּטְרִים אִישׁ יָבִא בְּפִרְיוֹ אֶלֶף כָּסֶף:
יב כַּרְמִי שֶׁלִּי לְפָנָי הָאֶלֶף לְךָ שְׁלֹמֹה וּמָאתַיִם
לְנֹטְרִים אֶת־פִּרְיוֹ: יג הַיּוֹשֶׁבֶת בַּגַּנִּים חֲבֵרִים
מַקְשִׁיבִים לְקוֹלֵךְ הַשְׁמִיעִנִי: יד בְּרַח | דּוֹדִי
וּדְמֵה־לְךָ לִצְבִי אוֹ לְעֹפֶר הָאַיָּלִים עַל הָרֵי
בְשָׂמִים:

RUTH רות

RUTH רות

The Book of Ruth is the moving story of Ruth, the Moabite, who cast her lot with the Jewish people and eventually became the progenitor of the dynasty of David. Ruth, the widow of Maḥlon, a Jew who had settled in Moab, leaves her native land for the land of Judah with her widowed mother-in-law, Naomi: "Do not urge me to leave you, to return from following you," Ruth tells Naomi when the latter suggests that she remain in Moab. "Wherever you go, I will go . . . your people shall be my people, and your God my God." Naomi brings about Ruth's marriage to the family's kinsman, Boaz. The son of this marriage, Obed, becomes the father of Jesse, the father of David, King of Israel.

The Book of Ruth is read on Shavuoth, the season of the giving of the Torah, when Israel, like Ruth, chose of its own free will to accept the Law of God, regardless of the trials and sacrifices such acceptance would entail.

According to tradition, Shavuoth is the date of the birth, as well as the death of King David.

CHAPTER I

1. Now it came to pass in the days of the judging of the judges, that there was a famine in the land, and a man went from Bethlehem of Judah to sojourn in the fields of Moab, he and his wife and his two sons. 2. And the man's name was Elimelech, and his wife's name was Naomi, and his two sons' names were Mahlon and Chilion, Ephrathites, from Bethlehem of Judah, and they came to the fields of Moab and remained there. 3. Now Elimelech, Naomi's husband, died, and she was left with her two sons. 4. And they married Moabite women, one named Orpah, and the other named Ruth, and they dwelt there for about ten years. 5. Now both Mahlon and Chilion also died, and the woman was left [bereft] of her two children and of her husband. 6. Now she arose with her daughters-in-law and returned from the fields of Moab, for she had heard in the field of Moab that the Lord had remembered His people to give them bread. 7. Then she went forth from the place where she had been, her two daughters-in-law with her, and they went on the road to return to the land of Judah. 8. And Naomi said to her daughters-in-law, "Go, return, each woman to her mother's house. May the Lord deal kindly with you as you have dealt with the deceased and with me. 9. May the Lord grant you that you find rest, each woman in her husband's house," and she kissed them, and they raised their

א א וַיְהִ֗י בִּימֵי֙ שְׁפֹ֣ט הַשֹּׁפְטִ֔ים וַיְהִ֥י רָעָ֖ב בָּאָ֑רֶץ וַיֵּ֨לֶךְ אִ֜ישׁ מִבֵּ֧ית לֶ֣חֶם יְהוּדָ֗ה לָגוּר֙ בִּשְׂדֵ֣י מוֹאָ֔ב ה֥וּא וְאִשְׁתּ֖וֹ וּשְׁנֵ֥י בָנָֽיו: ב וְשֵׁ֣ם הָאִ֣ישׁ אֱ‍ֽלִימֶ֡לֶךְ וְשֵׁם֩ אִשְׁתּ֨וֹ נָֽעֳמִ֜י וְשֵׁ֥ם שְׁנֵֽי־בָנָ֣יו ׀ מַחְל֤וֹן וְכִלְיוֹן֙ אֶפְרָתִ֔ים מִבֵּ֥ית לֶ֖חֶם יְהוּדָ֑ה וַיָּבֹ֥אוּ שְׂדֵֽי־מוֹאָ֖ב וַיִּֽהְיוּ־שָֽׁם: ג וַיָּ֥מָת אֱלִימֶ֖לֶךְ אִ֣ישׁ נָֽעֳמִ֑י וַתִּשָּׁאֵ֥ר הִ֖יא וּשְׁנֵ֥י בָנֶֽיהָ: ד וַיִּשְׂא֣וּ לָהֶ֗ם נָשִׁים֙ מֹֽאֲבִיּ֔וֹת שֵׁ֤ם הָֽאַחַת֙ עָרְפָּ֔ה וְשֵׁ֥ם הַשֵּׁנִ֖ית ר֑וּת וַיֵּ֥שְׁבוּ שָׁ֖ם כְּעֶ֥שֶׂר שָׁנִֽים: ה וַיָּמֻ֥תוּ גַם־שְׁנֵיהֶ֖ם מַחְל֣וֹן וְכִלְי֑וֹן וַתִּשָּׁאֵר֙ הָֽאִשָּׁ֔ה מִשְּׁנֵ֥י יְלָדֶ֖יהָ וּמֵֽאִישָֽׁהּ: ו וַתָּ֤קָם הִיא֙ וְכַלֹּתֶ֔יהָ וַתָּ֖שָׁב מִשְּׂדֵ֣י מוֹאָ֑ב כִּ֤י שָֽׁמְעָה֙ בִּשְׂדֵ֣ה מוֹאָ֔ב כִּֽי־פָקַ֤ד יְהֹוָה֙ אֶת־עַמּ֔וֹ לָתֵ֥ת לָהֶ֖ם לָֽחֶם: ז וַתֵּצֵ֗א מִן־הַמָּקוֹם֙ אֲשֶׁ֣ר הָֽיְתָה־שָׁ֔מָּה וּשְׁתֵּ֥י כַלֹּתֶ֖יהָ עִמָּ֑הּ וַתֵּלַ֣כְנָה בַדֶּ֔רֶךְ לָשׁ֖וּב אֶל־אֶ֥רֶץ יְהוּדָֽה: ח וַתֹּ֤אמֶר נָֽעֳמִי֙ לִשְׁתֵּ֣י כַלֹּתֶ֔יהָ לֵ֣כְנָה שֹּׁ֔בְנָה אִשָּׁ֖ה לְבֵ֣ית אִמָּ֑הּ יַ֣עֲשֶׂ֪ה (יעש קרי) יְהֹוָ֤ה עִמָּכֶם֙ חֶ֔סֶד כַּֽאֲשֶׁ֧ר עֲשִׂיתֶ֛ם עִם־הַמֵּתִ֖ים וְעִמָּדִֽי: ט יִתֵּ֤ן יְהֹוָה֙ לָכֶ֔ם וּמְצֶ֣אןָ מְנוּחָ֔ה אִשָּׁ֖ה בֵּ֣ית אִישָׁ֑הּ וַתִּשַּׁ֣ק לָהֶ֔ן וַתִּשֶּׂ֥אנָה קוֹלָ֖ן וַתִּבְכֶּֽינָה:

voices and wept. 10. And they said to her, "[No,] but we will return with you to your land." 11. And Naomi said, "Return, my daughters; why should you go with me? Have I yet sons in my womb, that they should be your husbands? 12. Return, my daughters, go, for I have become too old to marry, that I should say that I have hope. Even if I would marry tonight, and even if I would have already borne sons, 13. would you wait for them until they grow up? Would you shut yourselves off for them and not marry? No, my daughters, for it is much more bitter for me than for you, for the hand of the Lord has gone forth against me." 14. And they raised their voices and wept again; and Orpah kissed her mother-in-law, but Ruth clung to her. 15. And she said, "Lo, your sister-in-law has returned to her people and to her god; return after your sister-in-law." 16. And Ruth said, "Do not urge me to leave you, to return from following you, for wherever you go, I will go, and wherever you lodge, I will lodge; your people shall be my people and your God my God. 17. Where you die I will die, and there I will be buried. So may the Lord do to me and so may He continue, if anything but death separate me and you." 18. Now Naomi saw that she was determined to go with her, so she stopped speaking to her. 19. And they both went on until they arrived at Bethlehem. And it came to pass when they arrived at Bethlehem, that the entire city was astir on their account, and they said, "Is this Naomi?" 20. And she said to them, "Do not call me Naomi[1]; call me Marah,[2] for the Almighty has dealt very bitterly with me. 21. I went away full, and the Lord has brought me back empty. Why [then] should you call me Naomi, seeing that the Lord has testified against me, and the Almighty has dealt harshly with me?" 22. So Naomi returned, and Ruth the Moabite, her daughter-in-law, with her, and they returned from the fields of Moab — and they came to Bethlehem in the beginning of the barley harvest.

1. i.e. *pleasant.*
2. i.e. *bitter.*

י וַתֹּאמַרְנָה־לָּהּ כִּי־אִתָּךְ נָשׁוּב לְעַמֵּךְ׃
יא וַתֹּאמֶר נָעֳמִי שֹׁבְנָה בְנֹתַי לָמָּה תֵלַכְנָה עִמִּי
הַעוֹד־לִי בָנִים בְּמֵעַי וְהָיוּ לָכֶם לַאֲנָשִׁים׃
יב שֹׁבְנָה בְנֹתַי לֵכְןָ כִּי זָקַנְתִּי מִהְיוֹת לְאִישׁ כִּי
אָמַרְתִּי יֶשׁ־לִי תִקְוָה גַּם הָיִיתִי הַלַּיְלָה לְאִישׁ
וְגַם יָלַדְתִּי בָנִים׃ יג הֲלָהֵן ׀ תְּשַׂבֵּרְנָה עַד אֲשֶׁר
יִגְדָּלוּ הֲלָהֵן תֵּעָגֵנָה לְבִלְתִּי הֱיוֹת לְאִישׁ אַל
בְּנֹתַי כִּי־מַר־לִי מְאֹד מִכֶּם כִּי־יָצְאָה בִי יַד־
יְהוָה׃ יד וַתִּשֶּׂנָה קוֹלָן וַתִּבְכֶּינָה עוֹד וַתִּשַּׁק
עָרְפָּה לַחֲמוֹתָהּ וְרוּת דָּבְקָה בָּהּ׃ טו וַתֹּאמֶר
הִנֵּה שָׁבָה יְבִמְתֵּךְ אֶל־עַמָּהּ וְאֶל־אֱלֹהֶיהָ שׁוּבִי
אַחֲרֵי יְבִמְתֵּךְ׃ טז וַתֹּאמֶר רוּת אַל־תִּפְגְּעִי־בִי
לְעָזְבֵךְ לָשׁוּב מֵאַחֲרָיִךְ כִּי אֶל־אֲשֶׁר תֵּלְכִי אֵלֵךְ
וּבַאֲשֶׁר תָּלִינִי אָלִין עַמֵּךְ עַמִּי וֵאלֹהַיִךְ אֱלֹהָי׃
יז בַּאֲשֶׁר תָּמוּתִי אָמוּת וְשָׁם אֶקָּבֵר כֹּה יַעֲשֶׂה
יְהוָה לִי וְכֹה יֹסִיף כִּי הַמָּוֶת יַפְרִיד בֵּינִי
וּבֵינֵךְ׃ יח וַתֵּרֶא כִּי־מִתְאַמֶּצֶת הִיא לָלֶכֶת אִתָּהּ
וַתֶּחְדַּל לְדַבֵּר אֵלֶיהָ׃ יט וַתֵּלַכְנָה שְׁתֵּיהֶם עַד־
בּוֹאָנָה בֵּית לָחֶם וַיְהִי כְּבוֹאָנָה בֵּית לֶחֶם וַתֵּהֹם
כָּל־הָעִיר עֲלֵיהֶן וַתֹּאמַרְנָה הֲזֹאת נָעֳמִי׃
כ וַתֹּאמֶר אֲלֵיהֶן אַל־תִּקְרֶאנָה לִי נָעֳמִי קְרֶאןָ
לִי מָרָא כִּי־הֵמַר שַׁדַּי לִי מְאֹד׃ כא אֲנִי מְלֵאָה
הָלַכְתִּי וְרֵיקָם הֱשִׁיבַנִי יְהוָה לָמָּה תִקְרֶאנָה לִי
נָעֳמִי וַיהוָה עָנָה בִי וְשַׁדַּי הֵרַע לִי׃ כב וַתָּשָׁב
נָעֳמִי וְרוּת הַמּוֹאֲבִיָּה כַלָּתָהּ עִמָּהּ הַשָּׁבָה מִשְּׂדֵי
מוֹאָב וְהֵמָּה בָּאוּ בֵּית לֶחֶם בִּתְחִלַּת קְצִיר
שְׂעֹרִים׃

CHAPTER II

1. Now Naomi had a kinsman of her husband, a mighty man of valor, of the family
of Elimelech, and his name was Boaz.
2. And Ruth the Moabite said to Naomi, "I
will go now to the field, and I will
glean among the ears of grain, after some
one whom I will please." And she said, "Go,
my daughter." 3. And she went, and she
came, and she gleaned in the field after the
reapers, and her chance was [to come to] the
portion of the field that [belonged] to Boaz,
who was of Elimelech's family. 4. And
behold, Boaz came from Bethlehem, and he
said to the reapers, "May the Lord be with
you!" And they said to him, "The Lord
bless you." 5. Then Boaz said to his
servant, who stood over the reapers, "To
whom does this maiden belong?" 6. And
the servant in charge of the reapers
answered and said, "She is a Moabite
maiden, who returned with Naomi from the
fields of Moab. 7. And she said, 'I will
glean now and gather from among the
sheaves after the reapers.' And she came
and stood even from the morning until now,
except for her sitting a little in the house."
8. And Boaz said to Ruth, "Haven't you
heard, my daughter? Do not go to glean in
another field, neither shall you go away
from here, and here you shall stay with my
maidens. 9. Your eyes shall be on the
field that they reap, and you shall follow
them; have I not ordered the youths not to
touch you? And [if] you are thirsty, you may
go to the vessels and drink from what the
youths draw." 10. And she fell on her
face and prostrated herself to the ground,
and she said to him, "Why have I pleased
you that you should recognize me, seeing
that I am a foreigner?" 11. And Boaz
replied and said to her, "It has been told to
me all that you did for your mother-in-law
after your husband's death; and you left
your father and your mother and your
native land, and you went to a land that you
did not know before. 12. May the Lord
reward your deeds, and may your reward be
full, from the Lord God of Israel, under
Whose wings you have come to take
shelter." 13. And she said, "Let me find
favor in your sight, my lord, for you have

ב א וּלְנָעֳמִי מְיֻדָּע (מודע קרי) לְאִישָׁהּ אִישׁ גִּבּוֹר
חַיִל מִמִּשְׁפַּחַת אֱלִימֶלֶךְ וּשְׁמוֹ בֹּעַז: ב וַתֹּאמֶר
רוּת הַמּוֹאֲבִיָּה אֶל־נָעֳמִי אֵלְכָה־נָּא הַשָּׂדֶה
וַאֲלַקֳטָה בַשִּׁבֳּלִים אַחַר אֲשֶׁר אֶמְצָא־חֵן בְּעֵינָיו
וַתֹּאמֶר לָהּ לְכִי בִתִּי: ג וַתֵּלֶךְ וַתָּבוֹא וַתְּלַקֵּט
בַּשָּׂדֶה אַחֲרֵי הַקֹּצְרִים וַיִּקֶר מִקְרֶהָ חֶלְקַת
הַשָּׂדֶה לְבֹעַז אֲשֶׁר מִמִּשְׁפַּחַת אֱלִימֶלֶךְ:
ד וְהִנֵּה־בֹעַז בָּא מִבֵּית לֶחֶם וַיֹּאמֶר לַקּוֹצְרִים
יְהוָה עִמָּכֶם וַיֹּאמְרוּ לוֹ יְבָרֶכְךָ יְהוָה: ה וַיֹּאמֶר
בֹּעַז לְנַעֲרוֹ הַנִּצָּב עַל־הַקּוֹצְרִים לְמִי הַנַּעֲרָה
הַזֹּאת: ו וַיַּעַן הַנַּעַר הַנִּצָּב עַל־הַקּוֹצְרִים
וַיֹּאמַר נַעֲרָה מוֹאֲבִיָּה הִיא הַשָּׁבָה עִם־נָעֳמִי
מִשְּׂדֵה מוֹאָב: ז וַתֹּאמֶר אֲלַקֳטָה־נָּא וְאָסַפְתִּי
בָעֳמָרִים אַחֲרֵי הַקּוֹצְרִים וַתָּבוֹא וַתַּעֲמוֹד מֵאָז
הַבֹּקֶר וְעַד־עַתָּה זֶה שִׁבְתָּהּ הַבַּיִת מְעָט:
ח וַיֹּאמֶר בֹּעַז אֶל־רוּת הֲלוֹא שָׁמַעַתְּ בִּתִּי אַל־
תֵּלְכִי לִלְקֹט בְּשָׂדֶה אַחֵר וְגַם לֹא תַעֲבוּרִי מִזֶּה
וְכֹה תִדְבָּקִין עִם־נַעֲרֹתָי: ט עֵינַיִךְ בַּשָּׂדֶה
אֲשֶׁר־יִקְצֹרוּן וְהָלַכְתְּ אַחֲרֵיהֶן הֲלוֹא צִוִּיתִי
אֶת־הַנְּעָרִים לְבִלְתִּי נָגְעֵךְ וְצָמִת וְהָלַכְתְּ אֶל־
הַכֵּלִים וְשָׁתִית מֵאֲשֶׁר יִשְׁאֲבוּן הַנְּעָרִים:
י וַתִּפֹּל עַל־פָּנֶיהָ וַתִּשְׁתַּחוּ אָרְצָה וַתֹּאמֶר אֵלָיו
מַדּוּעַ מָצָאתִי חֵן בְּעֵינֶיךָ לְהַכִּירֵנִי וְאָנֹכִי
נָכְרִיָּה: יא וַיַּעַן בֹּעַז וַיֹּאמֶר לָהּ הֻגֵּד הֻגַּד לִי כֹּל
אֲשֶׁר־עָשִׂית אֶת־חֲמוֹתֵךְ אַחֲרֵי מוֹת אִישֵׁךְ
וַתַּעַזְבִי אָבִיךְ וְאִמֵּךְ וְאֶרֶץ מוֹלַדְתֵּךְ וַתֵּלְכִי
אֶל־עַם אֲשֶׁר לֹא־יָדַעַתְּ תְּמוֹל שִׁלְשׁוֹם:
יב יְשַׁלֵּם יְהוָה פָּעֳלֵךְ וּתְהִי מַשְׂכֻּרְתֵּךְ שְׁלֵמָה
מֵעִם יְהוָה אֱלֹהֵי יִשְׂרָאֵל אֲשֶׁר־בָּאת לַחֲסוֹת
תַּחַת־כְּנָפָיו: יג וַתֹּאמֶר אֶמְצָא־חֵן בְּעֵינֶיךָ

comforted me, and because you have spoken to the heart of your handmaid, but I am not [as worthy] as one of your handmaids."
14. And Boaz said to her at mealtime, "Come over here and partake of the bread, and dip your morsel in the vinegar." So she sat down beside the reapers, and he handed her parched grain, and she ate and was sated and left over. 15. And she rose to glean, and Boaz ordered his servants, saying, "Let her glean also among the sheaves, and do not embarrass her. 16. And also let some of the bundles fall for her, and leave it that she may glean, and do not scold her." 17. And she gleaned in the field until evening, and she beat out what she had gleaned, and it was about an ephah of barley. 18. And she carried [it] and came to the city, and her mother-in-law saw what she had gleaned. And she took [it] out and gave her what she had left over after being sated. 19. And her mother-in-law said to her, "Where have you gleaned today and where have you worked? May he who recognized you be blessed." So she told her mother-in-law with whom she had worked, and she said, "The name of the man with whom I worked today is Boaz. 20. And Naomi said to her daughter-in-law, "Blessed be he of the Lord, who did not leave off his kindness with the living and with the deceased." And Naomi said to her, "The man is our kinsman; he is one of our near kinsmen." 21. And Ruth the Moabite said, "Also, he said to me, 'You shall stay with my youths until they finish all my harvest.'" 22. And Naomi said to Ruth, her daughter-in-law, "It is good, my daughter, that you go out with his maidens, and so that they do not molest you in another field." 23. And she stayed with Boaz's maidens to glean until the completion of the barley harvest and the wheat harvest, and she dwelt with her mother-in-law.

CHAPTER III

1. And Naomi her mother-in-law said to her, "My daughter, shall I not seek rest for you, that it be good for you? 2. And now, is there not Boaz our kinsman, with whose maidens you were? Behold, he is winnowing the threshing-floor of the barley tonight.

אֲדֹנִי כִּי נִחַמְתָּנִי וְכִי דִבַּרְתָּ עַל־לֵב שִׁפְחָתֶךָ וְאָנֹכִי לֹא אֶהְיֶה כְּאַחַת שִׁפְחֹתֶךָ: יד וַיֹּאמֶר לָהּ בֹעַז לְעֵת הָאֹכֶל גֹּשִׁי הֲלֹם וְאָכַלְתְּ מִן־הַלֶּחֶם וְטָבַלְתְּ פִּתֵּךְ בַּחֹמֶץ וַתֵּשֶׁב מִצַּד הַקֹּצְרִים וַיִּצְבָּט־לָהּ קָלִי וַתֹּאכַל וַתִּשְׂבַּע וַתֹּתַר: טו וַתָּקָם לְלַקֵּט וַיְצַו בֹּעַז אֶת־נְעָרָיו לֵאמֹר גַּם בֵּין הָעֳמָרִים תְּלַקֵּט וְלֹא תַכְלִימוּהָ: טז וְגַם שֹׁל־ תָּשֹׁלּוּ לָהּ מִן־הַצְּבָתִים וַעֲזַבְתֶּם וְלִקְּטָה וְלֹא תִגְעֲרוּ־בָהּ: יז וַתְּלַקֵּט בַּשָּׂדֶה עַד־הָעָרֶב וַתַּחְבֹּט אֵת אֲשֶׁר־לִקֵּטָה וַיְהִי כְּאֵיפָה שְׂעֹרִים: יח וַתִּשָּׂא וַתָּבוֹא הָעִיר וַתֵּרֶא חֲמוֹתָהּ אֵת אֲשֶׁר־לִקֵּטָה וַתּוֹצֵא וַתִּתֶּן־לָהּ אֵת אֲשֶׁר־ הוֹתִרָה מִשָּׂבְעָהּ: יט וַתֹּאמֶר לָהּ חֲמוֹתָהּ אֵיפֹה לִקַּטְתְּ הַיּוֹם וְאָנָה עָשִׂית יְהִי מַכִּירֵךְ בָּרוּךְ וַתַּגֵּד לַחֲמוֹתָהּ אֵת אֲשֶׁר־עָשְׂתָה עִמּוֹ וַתֹּאמֶר שֵׁם הָאִישׁ אֲשֶׁר עָשִׂיתִי עִמּוֹ הַיּוֹם בֹּעַז: כ וַתֹּאמֶר נָעֳמִי לְכַלָּתָהּ בָּרוּךְ הוּא לַיהוָה אֲשֶׁר לֹא־עָזַב חַסְדּוֹ אֶת־הַחַיִּים וְאֶת־הַמֵּתִים וַתֹּאמֶר לָהּ נָעֳמִי קָרוֹב לָנוּ הָאִישׁ מִגֹּאֲלֵנוּ הוּא: כא וַתֹּאמֶר רוּת הַמּוֹאֲבִיָּה גַּם כִּי־אָמַר אֵלַי עִם־הַנְּעָרִים אֲשֶׁר־לִי תִּדְבָּקִין עַד אִם־כִּלּוּ אֵת כָּל־הַקָּצִיר אֲשֶׁר־לִי: כב וַתֹּאמֶר נָעֳמִי אֶל־ רוּת כַּלָּתָהּ טוֹב בִּתִּי כִּי תֵצְאִי עִם־נַעֲרוֹתָיו וְלֹא יִפְגְּעוּ־בָךְ בְּשָׂדֶה אַחֵר: כג וַתִּדְבַּק בְּנַעֲרוֹת בֹּעַז לְלַקֵּט עַד־כְּלוֹת קְצִיר־הַשְּׂעֹרִים וּקְצִיר הַחִטִּים וַתֵּשֶׁב אֶת־חֲמוֹתָהּ:

ג א וַתֹּאמֶר לָהּ נָעֳמִי חֲמוֹתָהּ בִּתִּי הֲלֹא אֲבַקֶּשׁ־לָךְ מָנוֹחַ אֲשֶׁר יִיטַב־לָךְ: ב וְעַתָּה הֲלֹא בֹעַז מֹדַעְתָּנוּ אֲשֶׁר הָיִית אֶת־נַעֲרוֹתָיו הִנֵּה־ הוּא זֹרֶה אֶת־גֹּרֶן הַשְּׂעֹרִים הַלָּיְלָה: ג וְרָחַצְתְּ |

3. And you shall bathe, and anoint yourself, and put on your clothes and go down to the threshing-floor; do not make yourself known to the man until he has finished eating and drinking. 4. And it shall be when he lies down, that you shall know where he will lie, and you shall come and uncover his feet and lie down, and he will tell you what you shall do." 5. And she said to her, "All that you say to me I will do." 6. And she went down to the threshing-floor, and she did all that her mother-in-law had charged her. 7. Now Boaz ate and drank, and his heart was merry, and he came to lie at the edge of the stack, and she came softly and uncovered his feet and lay down. 8. And it came to pass at midnight, that the man quaked and was taken around, and behold a woman was lying at his feet. 9. And he said, "Who are you?" And she said, "I am Ruth, your handmaid, and you shall spread your skirt over your handmaid, for you are a near kinsman." 10. And he said, "May you be blessed of the Lord, my daughter; your latest act of kindness is greater than the first, not to follow the young men, whether poor or rich. 11. And now, my daughter, do not fear, all you say I will do for you, for the entire gate of my people knows that you are a valiant woman. 12. And now, indeed, I am a near kinsman, but there is a nearer kinsman than I. 13. Stay over tonight, and it will come to pass in the morning, that if he redeem you, good, let him redeem you, but if he does not wish to redeem you, I will redeem you, as the Lord lives; lie until morning." 14. And she lay at his feet until morning, and she rose before one could recognize his fellow, and he said, "Let it not be known that the woman came to the threshing-floor." 15. And he said, "Ready the shawl you are wearing and hold it," and she held it, and he measured out six barleys and placed it upon her, and he came to the city. 16. And she came to her mother-in-law, and she said, "Who are you, my daughter?" And she told her all that the man had done to her. 17. And she said, "He gave me these six barleys, for he said to me, 'Do not come empty-handed to your mother-in-law.'" 18. And she said,

וָסַ֗כְתְּ וְשַׂמְתְּ (ושמת קרי) שִׂמְלֹתֵ֙ךְ (שמלתיך קרי)
עָלַ֔יִךְ וְיָרַ֖דְתְּ (וירדת קרי) הַגֹּ֑רֶן אַל־תִּוָּדְעִ֣י לָאִ֔ישׁ
עַ֚ד כַּלֹּת֔וֹ לֶאֱכֹ֖ל וְלִשְׁתּֽוֹת: ד וִיהִ֣י בְשָׁכְב֗וֹ
וְיָדַ֙עַתְּ֙ אֶת־הַמָּקוֹם֙ אֲשֶׁ֣ר יִשְׁכַּב־שָׁ֔ם וּבָ֛את
וְגִלִּ֥ית מַרְגְּלֹתָ֖יו וְשָׁכָ֑בְתִּי (ושכבת קרי) וְהוּא֙ יַגִּ֣יד
לָ֔ךְ אֵ֖ת אֲשֶׁ֥ר תַּעֲשִֽׂין: ה וַתֹּ֖אמֶר אֵלֶ֑יהָ כֹּ֛ל
אֲשֶׁר־תֹּאמְרִ֖י ._.. (אלי קרי ולא כתיב) אֶֽעֱשֶֽׂה:
ו וַתֵּ֖רֶד הַגֹּ֑רֶן וַתַּ֕עַשׂ כְּכֹ֥ל אֲשֶׁר־צִוַּ֖תָּה חֲמוֹתָֽהּ:
ז וַיֹּ֨אכַל בֹּ֤עַז וַיֵּשְׁתְּ֙ וַיִּיטַ֣ב לִבּ֔וֹ וַיָּבֹ֕א לִשְׁכַּ֕ב
בִּקְצֵ֖ה הָעֲרֵמָ֑ה וַתָּבֹ֣א בַלָּ֔ט וַתְּגַ֥ל מַרְגְּלֹתָ֖יו
וַתִּשְׁכָּֽב: ח וַיְהִי֙ בַּחֲצִ֣י הַלַּ֔יְלָה וַיֶּחֱרַ֥ד הָאִ֖ישׁ
וַיִּלָּפֵ֑ת וְהִנֵּ֣ה אִשָּׁ֔ה שֹׁכֶ֖בֶת מַרְגְּלֹתָֽיו: ט וַיֹּ֖אמֶר
מִי־אָ֑תְּ וַתֹּ֗אמֶר אָנֹכִי֙ ר֣וּת אֲמָתֶ֔ךָ וּפָרַשְׂתָּ֤ כְנָפֶ֙ךָ֙
עַל־אֲמָ֣תְךָ֔ כִּ֥י גֹאֵ֖ל אָֽתָּה: י וַיֹּ֗אמֶר בְּרוּכָ֨ה אַ֤תְּ
לַֽיהֹוָה֙ בִּתִּ֔י הֵיטַ֛בְתְּ חַסְדֵּ֥ךְ הָאַחֲר֖וֹן מִן־הָֽרִאשׁ֑וֹן
לְבִלְתִּי־לֶ֗כֶת אַחֲרֵי֙ הַבַּ֣חוּרִ֔ים אִם־דַּ֖ל וְאִם־
עָשִֽׁיר: יא וְעַתָּ֣ה בִּתִּי֮ אַל־תִּ֣ירְאִי֒ כֹּ֛ל אֲשֶׁר־
תֹּאמְרִ֖י אֶֽעֱשֶׂה־לָּ֑ךְ כִּ֣י יוֹדֵ֗עַ כָּל־שַׁ֣עַר עַמִּ֔י כִּ֛י
אֵ֥שֶׁת חַ֖יִל אָֽתְּ: יב וְעַתָּה֙ כִּ֣י אׇמְנָ֔ם כִּ֥י אם (אם
כתיב ולא קרי) גֹאֵ֖ל אָנֹ֑כִי וְגַ֛ם יֵ֥שׁ גֹּאֵ֖ל קָר֥וֹב מִמֶּֽנִּי:
יג לִ֣ינִי ׀ הַלַּ֗יְלָה וְהָיָ֤ה בַבֹּ֙קֶר֙ אִם־יִגְאָלֵ֥ךְ טוֹב֙
יִגְאָ֔ל וְאִם־לֹ֨א יַחְפֹּ֤ץ לְגׇאֳלֵךְ֙ וּגְאַלְתִּ֣יךְ אָנֹ֔כִי
חַי־יְהֹוָ֖ה שִׁכְבִ֥י עַד־הַבֹּֽקֶר: יד וַתִּשְׁכַּ֤ב
מַרְגְּלוֹתָו֙ עַד־הַבֹּ֔קֶר וַתָּ֕קׇם בְּטֶ֛רֶם (בטרם קרי)
יַכִּ֥יר אִ֖ישׁ אֶת־רֵעֵ֑הוּ וַיֹּ֙אמֶר֙ אַל־יִוָּדַ֔ע כִּי־בָ֥אָה
הָאִשָּׁ֖ה הַגֹּֽרֶן: טו וַיֹּ֗אמֶר הָ֠בִי הַמִּטְפַּ֧חַת אֲשֶׁר־
עָלַ֛יִךְ וְאֶחֳזִי־בָ֖הּ וַתֹּ֣אחֶז בָּ֑הּ וַיָּ֤מׇד שֵׁשׁ־שְׂעֹרִים֙
וַיָּ֣שֶׁת עָלֶ֔יהָ וַיָּבֹ֖א הָעִֽיר: טז וַתָּבוֹא֙ אֶל־חֲמוֹתָ֔הּ
וַתֹּ֖אמֶר מִי־אַ֣תְּ בִּתִּ֑י וַתַּ֨גֶּד־לָ֔הּ אֵ֛ת כָּל־אֲשֶׁ֥ר
עָֽשָׂה־לָ֖הּ הָאִֽישׁ: יז וַתֹּ֕אמֶר שֵׁשׁ־הַשְּׂעֹרִ֥ים
הָאֵ֖לֶּה נָ֣תַן לִ֑י כִּ֚י אָמַ֣ר אֵלַ֔י (אלי קרי ולא כתיב) אַל־
תָּב֥וֹאִי רֵיקָ֖ם אֶל־חֲמוֹתֵֽךְ: יח וַתֹּ֙אמֶר֙ שְׁבִ֣י בִתִּ֔י

"Sit still, my daughter, until you know how the thing will fall, for the man will not rest until he has finished the matter today."

CHAPTER IV

1. And Boaz went up to the gate and sat down there, and behold, the near kinsman of whom Boaz had spoken was passing, and he said, "Turn aside, sit down here, So-and-so," and he turned aside and sat down. 2. And he took ten men of the elders of the city and said, "Sit down here," and they sat down. 3. And he said to the near kinsman, "The portion of the field that belonged to our brother, to Elimelech, Naomi, who has returned from the field of Moab, is selling." 4. And I said, "I will let you know, saying, 'Buy [it] in the presence of those seated and in the presence of the elders of my people; if you will redeem, redeem; and if he will not redeem, tell me, and I will know that there is nobody besides you to redeem, and I am after you.'" And he said, "I will redeem." 5. And Boaz said, "On the day you buy the field from the hand of Naomi and from Ruth the Moabite, the wife the deceased you have bought [it], to preserve the name of the deceased on his heritage." 6. And the near kinsman said, "I cannot redeem [it] for myself, lest I mar my heritage. You redeem my redemption for yourself for I cannot redeem [it]." 7. Now this was the custom in former times in Israel concerning redemption and exchange, to confirm anything, one would remove his shoe and give [it] to his fellow, and this was the attestation in Israel. 8. And the near kinsman said to Boaz, "Buy for yourself," and he removed his shoe. 9. And Boaz said to the elders and to the entire people, "You are witnesses today that I have bought all that was Elimelech's and all that was Mahlon's and Chilion's from Naomi. 10. And also, Ruth, Mahlon's wife, have I acquired for myself for a wife, to preserve the name of the deceased on his heritage, and so that the name of the deceased be not obliterated from his brethren and from the gate of his place, you are witnesses today." 11. And all the people who were in the gate and the

עַד אֲשֶׁר תֵּדְעִין אֵיךְ יִפֹּל דָּבָר כִּי לֹא יִשְׁקֹט הָאִישׁ כִּי אִם־כִּלָּה הַדָּבָר הַיּוֹם:

ד א וּבֹעַז עָלָה הַשַּׁעַר וַיֵּשֶׁב שָׁם וְהִנֵּה הַגֹּאֵל עֹבֵר אֲשֶׁר דִּבֶּר־בֹּעַז וַיֹּאמֶר סוּרָה שְׁבָה־פֹּה פְּלֹנִי אַלְמֹנִי וַיָּסַר וַיֵּשֵׁב: ב וַיִּקַּח עֲשָׂרָה אֲנָשִׁים מִזִּקְנֵי הָעִיר וַיֹּאמֶר שְׁבוּ־פֹה וַיֵּשֵׁבוּ: ג וַיֹּאמֶר לַגֹּאֵל חֶלְקַת הַשָּׂדֶה אֲשֶׁר לְאָחִינוּ לֶאֱלִימֶלֶךְ מָכְרָה נָעֳמִי הַשָּׁבָה מִשְּׂדֵה מוֹאָב: ד וַאֲנִי אָמַרְתִּי אֶגְלֶה אָזְנְךָ לֵאמֹר קְנֵה נֶגֶד הַיֹּשְׁבִים וְנֶגֶד זִקְנֵי עַמִּי אִם־תִּגְאַל גְּאָל וְאִם־לֹא יִגְאַל הַגִּידָה לִּי וְאֵדְעָ (וְאֵדְעָה קרי) כִּי אֵין זוּלָתְךָ לִגְאוֹל וְאָנֹכִי אַחֲרֶיךָ וַיֹּאמֶר אָנֹכִי אֶגְאָל: ה וַיֹּאמֶר בֹּעַז בְּיוֹם־קְנוֹתְךָ הַשָּׂדֶה מִיַּד נָעֳמִי וּמֵאֵת רוּת הַמּוֹאֲבִיָּה אֵשֶׁת־הַמֵּת קָנִיתִי (קָנִיתָ קרי) לְהָקִים שֵׁם־הַמֵּת עַל־נַחֲלָתוֹ: ו וַיֹּאמֶר הַגֹּאֵל לֹא אוּכַל לִגְאוֹל־ (לִגְאָל קרי) לִי פֶּן־אַשְׁחִית אֶת־נַחֲלָתִי גְּאַל־לְךָ אַתָּה אֶת־גְּאֻלָּתִי כִּי לֹא־אוּכַל לִגְאֹל: ז וְזֹאת לְפָנִים בְּיִשְׂרָאֵל עַל־הַגְּאוּלָּה וְעַל־הַתְּמוּרָה לְקַיֵּם כָּל־דָּבָר שָׁלַף אִישׁ נַעֲלוֹ וְנָתַן לְרֵעֵהוּ וְזֹאת הַתְּעוּדָה בְּיִשְׂרָאֵל: ח וַיֹּאמֶר הַגֹּאֵל לְבֹעַז קְנֵה־לָךְ וַיִּשְׁלֹף נַעֲלוֹ: ט וַיֹּאמֶר בֹּעַז לַזְּקֵנִים וְכָל־הָעָם עֵדִים אַתֶּם הַיּוֹם כִּי קָנִיתִי אֶת־כָּל־אֲשֶׁר לֶאֱלִימֶלֶךְ וְאֵת כָּל־אֲשֶׁר לְכִלְיוֹן וּמַחְלוֹן מִיַּד נָעֳמִי: י וְגַם אֶת־רוּת הַמֹּאֲבִיָּה אֵשֶׁת מַחְלוֹן קָנִיתִי לִי לְאִשָּׁה לְהָקִים שֵׁם־הַמֵּת עַל־נַחֲלָתוֹ וְלֹא־יִכָּרֵת שֵׁם־הַמֵּת מֵעִם אֶחָיו וּמִשַּׁעַר מְקוֹמוֹ עֵדִים אַתֶּם הַיּוֹם: יא וַיֹּאמְרוּ כָּל־הָעָם אֲשֶׁר־בַּשַּׁעַר וְהַזְּקֵנִים

elders declared, "[We are] witnesses! May
the Lord make this woman, who is entering
your house, like Rachel and like Leah, both
of whom built up the house of Israel, and
prosper in Ephrathah and be famous in
Bethlehem. 12. And may your house be
like the house of Perez, whom Tamar bore to
Judah, from the seed that the Lord shall
give you from this maiden." 13. And
Boaz took Ruth, and she became his wife,
and he was intimate with her, and the Lord
gave her conception, and she bore a son.
14. And the women said to Naomi,
"Blessed is the Lord, Who did not deprive
you of a redeemer today, and may his name
be famous in Israel. 15. And may he be to
you as a restorer of life and to sustain your
old age, for your daughter-in-law who loves
you bore him, who is better to you than
seven sons." 16. And Naomi took the
child and placed him in her bosom, and
became his nurse. 17. And the neighbor
women gave it a name, saying, "A son has
been born to Naomi," and they called his
name Obed — he is the father of Jesse, the
father of David. 18. And these are the
generations of Perez: Perez begot Hezron.
19. And Hezron begot Ram, and Ram
begot Amminadab. 20. And Amminadab
begot Nahshon, and Nahshon begot
Salmah. 21. And Salmon begot Boaz, and
Boaz begot Obed. 22. And Obed begot
Jesse, and Jesse begot David.

עֵדִ֑ים יִתֵּן֩ יְהוָ֨ה אֶת־הָאִשָּׁ֜ה הַבָּאָ֣ה אֶל־בֵּיתֶ֗ךָ
כְּרָחֵ֤ל ׀ וּכְלֵאָה֙ אֲשֶׁ֨ר בָּנ֤וּ שְׁתֵּיהֶם֙ אֶת־בֵּ֣ית
יִשְׂרָאֵ֔ל וַעֲשֵׂה־חַ֣יִל בְּאֶפְרָ֔תָה וּקְרָא־שֵׁ֖ם בְּבֵ֥ית
לָֽחֶם׃ יב וִיהִ֤י בֵֽיתְךָ֙ כְּבֵ֣ית פֶּ֔רֶץ אֲשֶׁר־יָלְדָ֥ה
תָמָ֖ר לִֽיהוּדָ֑ה מִן־הַזֶּ֗רַע אֲשֶׁ֨ר יִתֵּ֤ן יְהוָה֙ לְךָ֔ מִן־
הַנַּעֲרָ֖ה הַזֹּֽאת׃ יג וַיִּקַּ֨ח בֹּ֤עַז אֶת־רוּת֙ וַתְּהִי־ל֣וֹ
לְאִשָּׁ֔ה וַיָּבֹ֖א אֵלֶ֑יהָ וַיִּתֵּ֨ן יְהוָ֥ה לָ֛הּ הֵרָי֖וֹן וַתֵּ֥לֶד
בֵּֽן׃ יד וַתֹּאמַ֤רְנָה הַנָּשִׁים֙ אֶל־נָעֳמִ֔י בָּר֣וּךְ יְהוָ֔ה
אֲשֶׁ֨ר לֹ֣א הִשְׁבִּ֥ית לָ֛ךְ גֹּאֵ֖ל הַיּ֑וֹם וְיִקָּרֵ֥א שְׁמ֖וֹ
בְּיִשְׂרָאֵֽל׃ טו וְהָ֤יָה לָךְ֙ לְמֵשִׁ֣יב נֶ֔פֶשׁ וּלְכַלְכֵּ֖ל
אֶת־שֵׂיבָתֵ֑ךְ כִּ֣י כַלָּתֵ֣ךְ אֲשֶׁר־אֲהֵבַ֗תֶךְ יְלָדַ֔תּוּ
אֲשֶׁר־הִיא֙ ט֣וֹבָה לָ֔ךְ מִשִּׁבְעָ֖ה בָּנִֽים׃ טז וַתִּקַּ֨ח
נָעֳמִ֤י אֶת־הַיֶּ֙לֶד֙ וַתְּשִׁתֵ֣הוּ בְחֵיקָ֔הּ וַתְּהִי־ל֖וֹ
לְאֹמֶֽנֶת׃ יז וַתִּקְרֶאנָה֩ ל֨וֹ הַשְּׁכֵנ֥וֹת שֵׁם֙ לֵאמֹ֔ר
יֻלַּד־בֵּ֖ן לְנָעֳמִ֑י וַתִּקְרֶ֤אנָה שְׁמוֹ֙ עוֹבֵ֔ד ה֥וּא אֲבִֽי־
יִשַׁ֖י אֲבִ֥י דָוִֽד׃ פ יח וְאֵ֙לֶּה֙ תּוֹלְד֣וֹת פָּ֔רֶץ פֶּ֖רֶץ
הוֹלִ֥יד אֶת־חֶצְרֽוֹן׃ יט וְחֶצְרוֹן֙ הוֹלִ֣יד אֶת־רָ֔ם
וְרָ֖ם הוֹלִ֥יד אֶת־עַמִּֽינָדָֽב׃ כ וְעַמִּֽינָדָב֙ הוֹלִ֣יד
אֶת־נַחְשׁ֔וֹן וְנַחְשׁ֖וֹן הוֹלִ֥יד אֶת־שַׂלְמָֽה׃
כא וְשַׂלְמוֹן֙ הוֹלִ֣יד אֶת־בֹּ֔עַז וּבֹ֖עַז הוֹלִ֥יד אֶת־
עוֹבֵֽד׃ כב וְעֹבֵד֙ הוֹלִ֣יד אֶת־יִשָׁ֔י וְיִשַׁ֖י הוֹלִ֥יד
אֶת־דָּוִֽד׃

EKHAH   איכה

[LAMENTATIONS]

The Book of Lamentations, a work of the prophet Jeremiah, transports us back in time to the siege of Jerusalem and its destruction by Nebuzaradan, chief executioner at the court of Nebuchadnezzar, king of Babylon.

This book is appropriately read on the Fast of the Ninth of Av, which commemorates the fall of Jerusalem, and of the Temple, first to the Babylonians in the year 588 before the Common Era, and six centuries later, in the year 70 of the Common Era, to the Roman legions.

The prophet gives a heartrending description of the siege and the lot of its hapless victims. Because of his frank chastisement of the Jewish people for its sins, which lead to the loss of the Temple and of Jerusalem, Jeremiah and his scribe and disciple, Baruch, were persecuted by Jehoiakim, the wicked king of Judah, who had the book burned. Eventually, Jehoiakim met an ignominious death while being carried off in captivity to Babylonia.

The Book of Lamentations ends on a note of hope, a plea to God to "renew our days as of old."

Prior to the reading of this book the congregation is seated on the ground or on a low seat as a sign of mourning. The Book of Lamentations is read on the evening of the ninth of Av, and in some congregations, after the morning service as well.

CHAPTER I

1. O how the city that was once so populous remained lonely like a widow! She that was great among nations, a princess among the provinces, has become tributary.
2. She weeps bitterly in the night, and her tears are on her cheeks; she has no comforter among all her lovers; all her friends have betrayed her, they have become her enemies.
3. Judah went into exile because of affliction and great servitude, she settled among heathens, [and] finds no rest; her pursuers have all overtaken her in the midst of her distress.
4. The roads of Zion mourn because none come to the appointed season, all her gates are desolate, her priests moan; her maidens grieve while she herself suffers bitterly.
5. Her adversaries have become the head, her enemies are at ease; her young children went into captivity before the enemy, for the Lord has afflicted her because of the multitude of her sins.
6. And from the daughter of Zion has gone all her splendour, her princes have departed exhausted before her pursuers, like harts that find no pasture.
7. Jerusalem recalls [in] the days of her affliction and her miseries, all her precious things that were hers of old; when her people fell into the

א א אֵיכָה ׀ יָשְׁבָה בָדָד הָעִיר רַבָּתִי עָם הָיְתָה
כְּאַלְמָנָה רַבָּתִי בַגּוֹיִם שָׂרָתִי בַּמְּדִינוֹת הָיְתָה
לָמַס׃ ב בָּכוֹ תִבְכֶּה בַּלַּיְלָה וְדִמְעָתָהּ עַל לֶחֱיָהּ
אֵין־לָהּ מְנַחֵם מִכָּל־אֹהֲבֶיהָ כָּל־רֵעֶיהָ בָּגְדוּ בָהּ
הָיוּ לָהּ לְאֹיְבִים׃ ג גָּלְתָה יְהוּדָה מֵעֹנִי וּמֵרֹב
עֲבֹדָה הִיא יָשְׁבָה בַגּוֹיִם לֹא מָצְאָה מָנוֹחַ כָּל־
רֹדְפֶיהָ הִשִּׂיגוּהָ בֵּין הַמְּצָרִים׃ ד דַּרְכֵי צִיּוֹן
אֲבֵלוֹת מִבְּלִי בָּאֵי מוֹעֵד כָּל־שְׁעָרֶיהָ שׁוֹמֵמִין
כֹּהֲנֶיהָ נֶאֱנָחִים בְּתוּלֹתֶיהָ נוּגוֹת וְהִיא מַר־לָהּ׃
ה הָיוּ צָרֶיהָ לְרֹאשׁ אֹיְבֶיהָ שָׁלוּ כִּי־יְהוָה הוֹגָהּ
עַל־רֹב פְּשָׁעֶיהָ עוֹלָלֶיהָ הָלְכוּ שְׁבִי לִפְנֵי־צָר׃
ו וַיֵּצֵא מִן בַּת־ (מבת קרי) צִיּוֹן כָּל־הֲדָרָהּ הָיוּ
שָׂרֶיהָ כְּאַיָּלִים לֹא־מָצְאוּ מִרְעֶה וַיֵּלְכוּ בְלֹא־
כֹחַ לִפְנֵי רוֹדֵף׃ ז זָכְרָה יְרוּשָׁלַםִ יְמֵי עָנְיָהּ
וּמְרוּדֶיהָ כֹּל מַחֲמֻדֶיהָ אֲשֶׁר הָיוּ מִימֵי קֶדֶם

hand of the oppressor, the enemies gazed,
gloating on her desolation, and there was
none to help her. 8. Jerusalem sinned
grievously, therefore she became impure;
all who honored her despised her, for they
have seen her shame; moreover, she herself
moans and turns away. 9. Her unclean-
liness she made public, she was not mindful
of her end, and she fell astonishingly with
none to comfort her; behold, O Lord, my
affliction, for the enemy has become
increased. 10. The enemy has laid his
hands upon all her pleasant things; indeed,
she has seen heathens enter her Sanctuary,
whom You did command not to enter
into Your assembly. 11. All her people
are moaning; [as] they search for bread
they gave away their treasures for food to
revive the soul; see, O Lord, and behold,
how I have become worthless. 12. All of
you who pass along the road, let it not
happen to you. Behold, and see, if there is
any pain like my pain, which has been dealt
out to me; which the Lord inflicted on the
day of His fierce anger. 13. From above
He has hurled fire in my bones, and caused
it to become master; He has spread a net for
my feet, He has turned me back, He has
made me desolate [and] faint all day long.
14. The yoke of my transgression became
bent in his hand, they have come up
interwoven upon my neck [and] caused my
strength to fail; the Lord delivered me into
the hands of those whom I cannot withstand. 15. The Lord flouted all my
mighty men in my midst, He summoned an
assembly against me to crush my young
men; the Lord has trodden as in a wine
press, the virgin daughter of Judah.
16. For these things I weep, my eyes
shed tears, for the comforter to restore my
soul is removed from me; my children are
desolate, for the enemy has prevailed.
17. Zion spreads out her hands [for help],
but there is none to comfort her;
the Lord has commanded concerning Jacob
[that] his oppressors shall be round about
him; Jerusalem has become as [a woman]
unclean among them. 18. The Lord is
righteous, for I have rebelled against His
word; hear, I pray, all you peoples, and
behold my pain; my maidens and youths
have gone into captivity. 19. I called to
my allies, [but] they deceived me; my

בִּנְפֹל עַמָּהּ בְּיַד־צָר וְאֵין עוֹזֵר לָהּ רָאוּהָ צָרִים
שָׂחֲקוּ עַל־מִשְׁבַּתֶּהָ׃ ח חֵטְא חָטְאָה יְרוּשָׁלַםִ
עַל־כֵּן לְנִידָה הָיָתָה כָּל־מְכַבְּדֶיהָ הִזִּילוּהָ כִּי־
רָאוּ עֶרְוָתָהּ גַּם־הִיא נֶאֶנְחָה וַתָּשָׁב אָחוֹר׃
ט טֻמְאָתָהּ בְּשׁוּלֶיהָ לֹא זָכְרָה אַחֲרִיתָהּ וַתֵּרֶד
פְּלָאִים אֵין מְנַחֵם לָהּ רְאֵה יְהוָה אֶת־עָנְיִי כִּי
הִגְדִּיל אוֹיֵב׃ י יָדוֹ פָּרַשׂ צָר עַל כָּל־מַחֲמַדֶּיהָ
כִּי־רָאֲתָה גוֹיִם בָּאוּ מִקְדָּשָׁהּ אֲשֶׁר צִוִּיתָה לֹא־
יָבֹאוּ בַקָּהָל לָךְ׃ יא כָּל־עַמָּהּ נֶאֱנָחִים מְבַקְּשִׁים
לֶחֶם נָתְנוּ מַחֲמַוֹדֵּיהֶם (מחמדיהם קרי) בְּאֹכֶל
לְהָשִׁיב נָפֶשׁ רְאֵה יְהוָה וְהַבִּיטָה כִּי הָיִיתִי
זוֹלֵלָה׃ יב לוֹא (ל זעירא) אֲלֵיכֶם כָּל־עֹבְרֵי דֶרֶךְ
הַבִּיטוּ וּרְאוּ אִם־יֵשׁ מַכְאוֹב כְּמַכְאֹבִי אֲשֶׁר
עוֹלַל לִי אֲשֶׁר הוֹגָה יְהוָה בְּיוֹם חֲרוֹן אַפּוֹ׃
יג מִמָּרוֹם שָׁלַח־אֵשׁ בְּעַצְמֹתַי וַיִּרְדֶּנָּה פָּרַשׂ
רֶשֶׁת לְרַגְלַי הֱשִׁיבַנִי אָחוֹר נְתָנַנִי שֹׁמֵמָה כָּל־
הַיּוֹם דָּוָה׃ יד נִשְׂקַד עֹל פְּשָׁעַי בְּיָדוֹ יִשְׂתָּרְגוּ
עָלוּ עַל־צַוָּארִי הִכְשִׁיל כֹּחִי נְתָנַנִי אֲדֹנָי בִּידֵי
לֹא־אוּכַל קוּם׃ טו סִלָּה כָל־אַבִּירַי ׀ אֲדֹנָי
בְּקִרְבִּי קָרָא עָלַי מוֹעֵד לִשְׁבֹּר בַּחוּרָי גַּת דָּרַךְ
אֲדֹנָי לִבְתוּלַת בַּת־יְהוּדָה׃ טז עַל־אֵלֶּה ׀ אֲנִי
בוֹכִיָּה עֵינִי ׀ עֵינִי יֹרְדָה מַּיִם כִּי־רָחַק מִמֶּנִּי
מְנַחֵם מֵשִׁיב נַפְשִׁי הָיוּ בָנַי שׁוֹמֵמִים כִּי גָבַר
אוֹיֵב׃ יז פֵּרְשָׂה צִיּוֹן בְּיָדֶיהָ אֵין מְנַחֵם לָהּ צִוָּה
יְהוָה לְיַעֲקֹב סְבִיבָיו צָרָיו הָיְתָה יְרוּשָׁלַםִ לְנִדָּה
בֵּינֵיהֶם׃ יח צַדִּיק הוּא יְהוָה כִּי פִיהוּ מָרִיתִי
שִׁמְעוּ־נָא כָל־עַמִּים (העמים קרי) וּרְאוּ מַכְאֹבִי
בְּתוּלֹתַי וּבַחוּרַי הָלְכוּ בַשֶּׁבִי׃ יט קָרָאתִי
לַמְאַהֲבַי הֵמָּה רִמּוּנִי כֹּהֲנַי וּזְקֵנַי בָּעִיר גָּוָעוּ

priests and elders perished in the city, when they sought food for themselves to revive their souls.   20. Behold, O Lord, for I am in distress, my spirits are troubled, my heart is turned within me, for I have grievously rebelled; in the street the sword bereaves, in the house it is like death.   21. They hear how I moan, [and] there is none to comfort me, all my enemies have heard of my trouble [and] are glad that You have done it; may You bring the day which You did proclaim [upon] me and let them be as I am. 22. Let all their wickedness come before You, and deal with them as You have dealt with me for all my transgressions; for my sighs are many and my heart is faint.

CHAPTER II

1. How the Lord in His anger brought darkness upon the daughter of Zion! He has cast down from heaven to earth the glory of Israel, and has not remembered His footstool in the day of His anger.   2. The Lord has destroyed and has had no pity; He has broken down in His wrath all the habitations of Jacob, He has struck to the ground the strongholds of Judah; He has profaned the kingdom and its princes.   3. He has cut down in fierce anger all the strength of Israel; He has withdrawn His right hand [that shielded Israel] from the enemy, and He has burned through Jacob like a flaming fire, consuming all around.   4. He has bent His bow like an enemy, standing [with] His right hand as an adversary, and He has slain all the notables; in the tent of the daughter of Zion He has poured out His fury like fire.   5. The Lord has become like an enemy; He has destroyed Israel; He has destroyed all its palaces, laid in ruins its strongholds, and He increased mourning and lamentation on the daughter of Judah. 6. He stripped His Tabernacle like that of a garden, and laid in ruins His Meeting-place; the Lord has caused to be forgotten in Zion the Festival and Shabbath [offerings], and in His fierce indignation has spurned king and priest.   7. The Lord has rejected His altar, He has abhorred His Sanctuary, He has delivered into the hand of the enemy the walls of her palaces; they raised a clamor in the House of the Lord, as

כִּֽי־בִקְשׁ֤וּ אֹ֙כֶל֙ לָ֔מוֹ וְיָשִׁ֖יבוּ אֶת־נַפְשָֽׁם: כ רְאֵ֨ה
יְהֹוָ֤ה כִּֽי־צַר־לִי֙ מֵעַ֣י חֳמַרְמָ֔רוּ נֶהְפַּ֤ךְ לִבִּי֙
בְּקִרְבִּ֔י כִּ֥י מָר֖וֹ מָרִ֑יתִי מִח֥וּץ שִׁכְּלָה־חֶ֖רֶב בַּבַּ֥יִת
כַּמָּֽוֶת: כא שָֽׁמְע֞וּ כִּ֧י נֶאֱנָחָ֣ה אָ֗נִי אֵ֤ין מְנַחֵם֙ לִ֔י
כָּל־אֹ֨יְבַ֜י שָֽׁמְע֤וּ רָֽעָתִי֙ שָׂ֔שׂוּ כִּ֥י אַתָּ֖ה עָשִׂ֑יתָ
הֵבֵ֛אתָ יוֹם־קָרָ֖אתָ וְיִֽהְי֥וּ כָמֹֽנִי: כב תָּבֹ֧א כָל־
רָֽעָתָ֣ם לְפָנֶ֗יךָ וְעוֹלֵ֤ל לָמוֹ֙ כַּֽאֲשֶׁ֣ר עוֹלַ֣לְתָּ לִ֔י עַ֖ל
כָּל־פְּשָׁעָ֑י כִּֽי־רַבּ֥וֹת אַנְחֹתַ֖י וְלִבִּ֥י דַוָּֽי: פ

ב א אֵיכָה֩ יָעִ֨יב בְּאַפּ֤וֹ | אֲדֹנָי֙ אֶת־בַּת־צִיּ֔וֹן
הִשְׁלִ֤יךְ מִשָּׁמַ֙יִם֙ אֶ֔רֶץ תִּפְאֶ֖רֶת יִשְׂרָאֵ֑ל וְלֹא־זָכַ֥ר
הֲדֹם־רַגְלָ֖יו בְּי֥וֹם אַפּֽוֹ: ב בִּלַּ֨ע אֲדֹנָ֜י לֹ֤א (ולא
קרי) חָמַל֙ אֵ֣ת כָּל־נְא֣וֹת יַֽעֲקֹ֔ב הָרַ֧ס בְּעֶבְרָת֛וֹ
מִבְצְרֵ֥י בַת־יְהוּדָ֖ה הִגִּ֣יעַ לָאָ֑רֶץ חִלֵּ֥ל מַמְלָכָ֖ה
וְשָׂרֶֽיהָ: ג גָּדַ֣ע בָּֽחֳרִי־אַ֗ף כֹּ֚ל קֶ֣רֶן יִשְׂרָאֵ֔ל
הֵשִׁ֥יב אָח֛וֹר יְמִינ֖וֹ מִפְּנֵ֣י אוֹיֵ֑ב וַיִּבְעַ֤ר בְּיַֽעֲקֹב֙
כְּאֵ֣שׁ לֶֽהָבָ֔ה אָֽכְלָ֖ה סָבִֽיב: ד דָּרַ֨ךְ קַשְׁתּ֜וֹ כְּאוֹיֵ֗ב
נִצָּ֤ב יְמִינוֹ֙ כְּצָ֔ר וַֽיַּהֲרֹ֔ג כֹּ֖ל מַֽחֲמַדֵּי־עָ֑יִן בְּאֹ֙הֶל֙
בַּת־צִיּ֔וֹן שָׁפַ֥ךְ כָּאֵ֖שׁ חֲמָתֽוֹ: ה הָיָ֨ה אֲדֹנָ֤י |
כְּאוֹיֵב֙ בִּלַּ֣ע יִשְׂרָאֵ֔ל בִּלַּע֙ כָּל־אַרְמְנוֹתֶ֔יהָ שִׁחֵ֖ת
מִבְצָרָ֑יו וַיֶּ֙רֶב֙ בְּבַת־יְהוּדָ֔ה תַּֽאֲנִיָּ֖ה וַֽאֲנִיָּֽה:
ו וַיַּחְמֹ֤ס כַּגַּן֙ שֻׂכּ֔וֹ שִׁחֵ֖ת מֹֽעֲד֑וֹ שִׁכַּ֣ח יְהֹוָ֣ה |
בְּצִיּ֗וֹן מוֹעֵד֙ וְשַׁבָּ֔ת וַיִּנְאַ֥ץ בְּזַֽעַם־אַפּ֖וֹ מֶ֥לֶךְ
וְכֹהֵֽן: ז זָנַ֨ח אֲדֹנָ֤י | מִזְבְּחוֹ֙ נִאֵ֣ר מִקְדָּשׁ֔וֹ הִסְגִּיר֙
בְּיַד־אוֹיֵ֔ב חוֹמֹ֖ת אַרְמְנוֹתֶ֑יהָ ק֛וֹל נָֽתְנ֥וּ בְּבֵית־

on a day of a festival. 8. The Lord determined to destroy the wall of the daughter of Zion; He stretched out a line, [but] He did not restrain His hand from destroying; indeed, He caused rampart and wall to mourn, [and] they languish together. 9. Her gates are sunk into the ground; He has ruined and broken her bars; her kings and princes are [exiled] among the heathens, [and] there is no more teaching; moreover, her prophets obtain no vision from the Lord. 10. The elders of the daughter of Zion sit on the ground in silence, they laid dust on their heads [and] put on sackcloth; the maidens of Jerusalem have bowed their heads to the ground. 11. My eyes are spent with tears, my spirits are troubled; my heart is poured out in grief over the destruction of the daughter of my people, while infants and babes faint in the streets of the city. 12. They say to their mothers: "Where is bread and wine?" as they faint like one wounded in the streets of the city, while their soul ebbs away on their mothers' bosom. 13. What shall I testify for you? To what shall I compare you, O daughter of Jerusalem? To what can I liken you, that I may comfort you, O virgin daughter of Zion? For your ruin is as vast as the sea—who can repair you? 14. Your prophets have seen false and deceptive visions, and they have not exposed your iniquity to bring you back in repentance; but have prophesied for you false and misleading oracles. 15. All who passed along the road clapped their hands at you, they hissed and wagged their heads at the daughter of Jerusalem: "Is this the city that was called the perfection of beauty, the joy of all the earth?" 16. All your enemies have opened their mouth wide against you, they hissed and gnashed their teeth [and] said: "We have engulfed [her]! Indeed, this is the day we longed for, we have found it; we have seen it!" 17. The Lord has done what He devised, He has carried out his word, which He decreed long ago, [and] has devastated without pity; He has caused the enemy to rejoice over you, and exalted the might of your adversaries. 18. Their heart cries out to the Lord: "O Protector of the daughter of Zion! Let tears stream down like a torrent day and night, give yourself no respite, let

יְהֹוָה כְּיוֹם מוֹעֵד: ח חָשַׁב יְהֹוָה ׀ לְהַשְׁחִית
חוֹמַת בַּת־צִיּוֹן נָטָה קָו לֹא־הֵשִׁיב יָדוֹ מִבַּלֵּעַ
וַיַּאֲבֶל־חֵל וְחוֹמָה יַחְדָּו אֻמְלָלוּ: ט טָבְעוּ (ט
זעירא) בָאָרֶץ שְׁעָרֶיהָ אִבַּד וְשִׁבַּר בְּרִיחֶיהָ
מַלְכָּהּ וְשָׂרֶיהָ בַגּוֹיִם אֵין תּוֹרָה גַּם־נְבִיאֶיהָ לֹא
מָצְאוּ חָזוֹן מֵיְהֹוָה: י יֵשְׁבוּ לָאָרֶץ יִדְּמוּ זִקְנֵי
בַת־צִיּוֹן הֶעֱלוּ עָפָר עַל־רֹאשָׁם חָגְרוּ שַׂקִּים
הוֹרִידוּ לָאָרֶץ רֹאשָׁן בְּתוּלֹת יְרוּשָׁלָם: יא כָּלוּ
בַדְּמָעוֹת עֵינַי חֳמַרְמְרוּ מֵעַי נִשְׁפַּךְ לָאָרֶץ
כְּבֵדִי עַל־שֶׁבֶר בַּת־עַמִּי בֵּעָטֵף עוֹלֵל וְיוֹנֵק
בִּרְחֹבוֹת קִרְיָה: יב לְאִמֹּתָם יֹאמְרוּ אַיֵּה דָּגָן
וָיָיִן בְּהִתְעַטְּפָם כֶּחָלָל בִּרְחֹבוֹת עִיר בְּהִשְׁתַּפֵּךְ
נַפְשָׁם אֶל־חֵיק אִמֹּתָם: יג מָה־אֲעוֹדֵךְ (אעידך
קרי) מָה אֲדַמֶּה־לָּךְ הַבַּת יְרוּשָׁלַם מָה אַשְׁוֶה־
לָּךְ וַאֲנַחֲמֵךְ בְּתוּלַת בַּת־צִיּוֹן כִּי־גָדוֹל כַּיָּם
שִׁבְרֵךְ מִי יִרְפָּא־לָךְ: יד נְבִיאַיִךְ חָזוּ לָךְ שָׁוְא
וְתָפֵל וְלֹא־גִלּוּ עַל־עֲוֹנֵךְ לְהָשִׁיב שְׁבִיתֵךְ (שבותך
קרי) וַיֶּחֱזוּ לָךְ מַשְׂאוֹת שָׁוְא וּמַדּוּחִים: טו סָפְקוּ
עָלַיִךְ כַּפַּיִם כָּל־עֹבְרֵי דֶרֶךְ שָׁרְקוּ וַיָּנִעוּ רֹאשָׁם
עַל־בַּת יְרוּשָׁלָם הֲזֹאת הָעִיר שֶׁיֹּאמְרוּ כְּלִילַת
יֹפִי מָשׂוֹשׂ לְכָל־הָאָרֶץ: טז פָּצוּ עָלַיִךְ פִּיהֶם
כָּל־אֹיְבַיִךְ שָׁרְקוּ וַיַּחַרְקוּ־שֵׁן אָמְרוּ בִּלָּעְנוּ אַךְ
זֶה הַיּוֹם שֶׁקִּוִּינֻהוּ מָצָאנוּ רָאִינוּ: יז עָשָׂה יְהֹוָה
אֲשֶׁר זָמָם בִּצַּע אֶמְרָתוֹ אֲשֶׁר צִוָּה מִימֵי־קֶדֶם
הָרַס וְלֹא חָמָל וַיְשַׂמַּח עָלַיִךְ אוֹיֵב הֵרִים קֶרֶן
צָרָיִךְ: יח צָעַק לִבָּם אֶל־אֲדֹנָי חוֹמַת בַּת־צִיּוֹן
הוֹרִידִי כַנַּחַל דִּמְעָה יוֹמָם וָלַיְלָה אַל־תִּתְּנִי

your eyes not rest! 19. Arise, cry out in the night, at the beginning of the watches! Pour out your heart like water before the presence of the Lord; lift up your hands to Him [and pray] for the lives of your infants, who faint because of hunger at the head of every street." 20. See, O Lord, and behold, to whom [else] have You done thus! Whether it be women devouring their own offspring, children that are petted, or priest and prophet slain in the Sanctuary of the Lord. 21. In the streets, on the [bare] ground lie [both] young and old, my maidens and my young men have fallen by the sword; You have slain them in the day of their anger, You have slaughtered [them] without mercy. 22. You have proclaimed my terrors on every side, as though it were a feast day, and on the day of the Lord's anger there was none that escaped or survived; those whom I dandled and reared, my enemy exterminated.

פּוּגַת לָךְ אַל־תִּדֹּם בַּת־עֵינֵךְ: יט קוּמִי ׀ רֹנִּי
בַלַּיְלָ (בלילה קרי) לְרֹאשׁ אַשְׁמֻרוֹת שִׁפְכִי כַמַּיִם
לִבֵּךְ נֹכַח פְּנֵי אֲדֹנָי שְׂאִי אֵלָיו כַּפַּיִךְ עַל־נֶפֶשׁ
עוֹלָלַיִךְ הָעֲטוּפִים בְּרָעָב בְּרֹאשׁ כָּל־חוּצוֹת:
כ רְאֵה יְהוָה וְהַבִּיטָה לְמִי עוֹלַלְתָּ כֹּה אִם־
תֹּאכַלְנָה נָשִׁים פִּרְיָם עֹלְלֵי טִפֻּחִים אִם־יֵהָרֵג
בְּמִקְדַּשׁ אֲדֹנָי כֹּהֵן וְנָבִיא: כא שָׁכְבוּ לָאָרֶץ
חוּצוֹת נַעַר וְזָקֵן בְּתוּלֹתַי וּבַחוּרַי נָפְלוּ בֶחָרֶב
הָרַגְתָּ בְּיוֹם אַפֶּךָ טָבַחְתָּ לֹא חָמָלְתָּ: כב תִּקְרָא
כְיוֹם מוֹעֵד מְגוּרַי מִסָּבִיב וְלֹא הָיָה בְּיוֹם אַף־
יְהוָה פָּלִיט וְשָׂרִיד אֲשֶׁר־טִפַּחְתִּי וְרִבִּיתִי אֹיְבִי
כִלָּם: פ

CHAPTER III

1. I am the man who has seen affliction by the rod of His wrath. 2. He has led me and made me walk [in] darkness and not [in] light. 3. Only against me would He repeatedly turn His hand the whole day long. 4. He has made my flesh and my skin waste away [and] broken my bones. 5. He has built up [camps of siege] against me, and encompassed [me with] bitterness and travail. 6. He has made me dwell in darkness like those who are forever dead. 7. He has fenced me in, He has made my chains heavy, so that I cannot get out. 8. Though I call and cry for help, He shuts out my prayer. 9. He has walled up my roads with hewn stones, He has made my paths crooked. 10. He is to me a bear lying in wait, a lion in hiding. 11. He led me off my ways, tore me to pieces, and made me desolate. 12. He bent his bow and set me up as a target for the arrow. 13. He has caused the arrows of His quiver to enter into my heart. 14. I have become the laughing stock of all peoples, their song [of derision] all day long. 15. He has filled me with bitterness; He has sated me with wormwood. 16. Indeed, He has made my teeth grind

ג א אֲנִי הַגֶּבֶר רָאָה עֳנִי בְּשֵׁבֶט עֶבְרָתוֹ:
ב אוֹתִי נָהַג וַיֹּלַךְ חֹשֶׁךְ וְלֹא־אוֹר: ג אַךְ בִּי
יָשֻׁב יַהֲפֹךְ יָדוֹ כָּל־הַיּוֹם: ד בִּלָּה בְשָׂרִי וְעוֹרִי
שִׁבַּר עַצְמוֹתָי: ה בָּנָה עָלַי וַיַּקַּף רֹאשׁ וּתְלָאָה:
ו בְּמַחֲשַׁכִּים הוֹשִׁיבַנִי כְּמֵתֵי עוֹלָם: ז גָּדַר
בַּעֲדִי וְלֹא אֵצֵא הִכְבִּיד נְחָשְׁתִּי: ח גַּם כִּי אֶזְעַק
וַאֲשַׁוֵּעַ שָׂתַם תְּפִלָּתִי: ט גָּדַר דְּרָכַי בְּגָזִית
נְתִיבֹתַי עִוָּה: י דֹּב אֹרֵב הוּא לִי אֲרִיה (ארי קרי)
בְּמִסְתָּרִים: יא דְּרָכַי סוֹרֵר וַיְפַשְּׁחֵנִי שָׂמַנִי
שֹׁמֵם: יב דָּרַךְ קַשְׁתּוֹ וַיַּצִּיבֵנִי כַּמַּטָּרָא לַחֵץ:
יג הֵבִיא בְּכִלְיוֹתָי בְּנֵי אַשְׁפָּתוֹ: יד הָיִיתִי שְּׂחֹק
לְכָל־עַמִּי נְגִינָתָם כָּל־הַיּוֹם: טו הִשְׂבִּיעַנִי
בַמְּרוֹרִים הִרְוַנִי לַעֲנָה: טז וַיַּגְרֵס בֶּחָצָץ שִׁנָּי

on gravel, and made me cower in ashes. 17. And my soul is far removed from peace, I have forgotten [what] happiness is. 18. So I said: "Gone is my strength, and my expectation from the Lord." 19. Remember my affliction and my misery, wormwood and gall. 20. My soul well remembers and is bowed down within me. 21. This I recall to my mind, therefore I have hope. 22. Verily, the kindnesses of the Lord never cease! Indeed, His mercies never fail! 23. They are new every morning; great is Your faithfulness. 24. "The Lord is my portion," says my soul: "Therefore I will hope in Him." 25. The Lord is good to those who wait for Him, to the soul that seeks Him. 26. It is good that one should wait quietly for the salvation of the Lord. 27. It is good for a man that he bear the yoke in his youth. 28. Let him sit solitary and keep silence, for he has laid it upon him. 29. Let him drop his head in submission; there may yet be hope. 30. Let him offer his cheek to the smiter, [and] let him be filled with reproach. 31. For the Lord will not cast him off forever. 32. Though He cause grief, He will yet have compassion according to the abundance of his kindness. 33. For He does not willingly afflict, nor grieve the sons of men. 34. [Nor] crush under foot all the prisoners of the earth. 35. [Nor] turn aside the right of a man in the presence of the Most High. 36. To subvert a man in his cause, the Lord does not approve. 37. Who has commanded and it came to pass, unless the Lord ordained it? 38. Is it not by command of the Most High, that good and evil come? 39. Why should a living man complain, a man for [the punishment] of his sins? 40. Let us search and examine our ways, and return to the Lord. 41. Let us lift up our heart and hands to God in heaven. 42. We have transgressed and rebelled, [this we confess, but] You have not forgiven. 43. You have enveloped Yourself with anger and pursued us; You have slain without mercy. 44. You have enveloped Yourself in a cloud, so that no prayer can pass through. 45. You have made us [as] scum and refuse among the people. 46. All our enemies have opened wide

הִכְפִּישַׁנִי בָּאֵפֶר: יז וַתִּזְנַח מִשָּׁלוֹם נַפְשִׁי
נָשִׁיתִי טוֹבָה: יח וָאֹמַר אָבַד נִצְחִי וְתוֹחַלְתִּי
מֵיְהֹוָה: יט זְכָר־עָנְיִי וּמְרוּדִי לַעֲנָה וָרֹאשׁ:
כ זָכוֹר תִּזְכּוֹר וְתָשִׁיחַ (ותשוח קרי) עָלַי נַפְשִׁי:
כא זֹאת אָשִׁיב אֶל־לִבִּי עַל־כֵּן אוֹחִיל:
כב חַסְדֵי יְהֹוָה כִּי לֹא־תָמְנוּ כִּי לֹא־כָלוּ
רַחֲמָיו: כג חֲדָשִׁים לַבְּקָרִים רַבָּה אֱמוּנָתֶךָ:
כד חֶלְקִי יְהֹוָה אָמְרָה נַפְשִׁי עַל־כֵּן אוֹחִיל לוֹ:
כה טוֹב יְהֹוָה לְקוָֹו לְנֶפֶשׁ תִּדְרְשֶׁנּוּ: כו טוֹב
וְיָחִיל וְדוּמָם לִתְשׁוּעַת יְהֹוָה: כז טוֹב לַגֶּבֶר כִּי־
יִשָּׂא עֹל בִּנְעוּרָיו: כח יֵשֵׁב בָּדָד וְיִדֹּם כִּי נָטַל
עָלָיו: כט יִתֵּן בֶּעָפָר פִּיהוּ אוּלַי יֵשׁ תִּקְוָה:
ל יִתֵּן לְמַכֵּהוּ לֶחִי יִשְׂבַּע בְּחֶרְפָּה: לא כִּי לֹא
יִזְנַח לְעוֹלָם אֲדֹנָי: לב כִּי אִם־הוֹגָה וְרִחַם כְּרֹב
חֲסָדָו (חסדיו קרי): לג כִּי לֹא עִנָּה מִלִּבּוֹ וַיַּגֶּה בְּנֵי־
אִישׁ: לד לְדַכֵּא תַּחַת רַגְלָיו כֹּל אֲסִירֵי אָרֶץ:
לה לְהַטּוֹת מִשְׁפַּט־גָּבֶר נֶגֶד פְּנֵי עֶלְיוֹן:
לו לְעַוֵּת אָדָם בְּרִיבוֹ אֲדֹנָי לֹא רָאָה: לז מִי זֶה
אָמַר וַתֶּהִי אֲדֹנָי לֹא צִוָּה: לח מִפִּי עֶלְיוֹן לֹא
תֵצֵא הָרָעוֹת וְהַטּוֹב: לט מַה־יִּתְאוֹנֵן אָדָם חָי
גֶּבֶר עַל־חֲטָאָו (חטאיו קרי): מ נַחְפְּשָׂה דְרָכֵינוּ
וְנַחְקֹרָה וְנָשׁוּבָה עַד־יְהֹוָה: מא נִשָּׂא לְבָבֵנוּ
אֶל־כַּפָּיִם אֶל־אֵל בַּשָּׁמָיִם: מב נַחְנוּ פָשַׁעְנוּ
וּמָרִינוּ אַתָּה לֹא סָלָחְתָּ: מג סַכֹּתָה בָאַף
וַתִּרְדְּפֵנוּ הָרַגְתָּ לֹא חָמָלְתָּ: מד סַכּוֹתָה בֶעָנָן לָךְ
מֵעֲבוֹר תְּפִלָּה: מה סְחִי וּמָאוֹס תְּשִׂימֵנוּ בְּקֶרֶב
הָעַמִּים: מו פָּצוּ עָלֵינוּ פִּיהֶם כָּל־אֹיְבֵינוּ:

their mouth against us. 47. Desolation
and destruction brought upon us terror and
pitfall. 48. My eyes shed torrents of
water over the downfall of the daughter of
my people. 49. My eyes stream without
intermission, without respite. 50. While
the Lord looks down from the heavens, and
beholds. 51. My eyes cause me pain
because of all the daughters of my city.
52. I have been hunted like a bird [by]
my enemies without cause. 53. They
have cut off my life in the pit and have cast
stones upon me. 54. Water flowed over
my head, I thought: "I am lost." 55. I
called on Your name, O Lord, from the
depths of the pit. 56. You did hear my
voice; hide not Your ear from my sighing
[and] from my crying. 57. You did draw
near when I called on You, [and] You did
say: "Do not fear." 58. You did plead my
cause, O Lord, You did redeem my life.
59. You have seen wrong done to me; O
Lord, judge my cause. 60. You have seen
all their [acts of] vengeance, all their devices
against me. 61. You have heard their
insults, O Lord, all their plots against me.
62. The utterances of my assailants and
their thoughts are against me all day long.
63. Behold their sitting down and their
rising; I am their song [of derision].
64. Requite them, O Lord, according to
the work of their hands. 65. Give them a
weakness of heart; may Your curse be upon
them. 66. Pursue them in anger and
destroy them from under the heavens, O
Lord!

CHAPTER IV

1. How dim the gold has become, [how]
changed is the pure gold; the holy stones lie
scattered at the head of every street.
2. The precious children of Zion, [worth]
their weight in fine gold; how they are
regarded as earthen pitchers, the work of a
potter's hands. 3. Even the sea-monsters
offer the breast [and] suckle their young;
the daughter of my people [was left] to the
cruel, like the ostriches in the wilderness.
4. The tongue of the suckling child
cleaves to his palate through thirst; the
young children beg [for] food, [but] no one
gives it to them. 5. Those that used to eat

מז פַּחַד וָפַחַת הָיָה לָנוּ הַשֵּׁאת וְהַשָּׁבֶר׃
מח פַּלְגֵי־מַיִם תֵּרַד עֵינִי עַל־שֶׁבֶר בַּת־עַמִּי׃
מט עֵינִי נִגְּרָה וְלֹא תִדְמֶה מֵאֵין הֲפֻגוֹת׃ נ עַד־
יַשְׁקִיף וְיֵרֶא יְהֹוָה מִשָּׁמָיִם׃ נא עֵינִי עוֹלְלָה
לְנַפְשִׁי מִכֹּל בְּנוֹת עִירִי׃ נב צוֹד צָדוּנִי כַּצִּפֹּר
אֹיְבַי חִנָּם׃ נג צָמְתוּ בַבּוֹר חַיָּי וַיַּדּוּ־אֶבֶן בִּי׃
נד צָפוּ־מַיִם עַל־רֹאשִׁי אָמַרְתִּי נִגְזָרְתִּי׃
נה קָרָאתִי שִׁמְךָ יְהֹוָה מִבּוֹר תַּחְתִּיּוֹת׃ נו קוֹלִי
שָׁמָעְתָּ אַל־תַּעְלֵם אָזְנְךָ לְרַוְחָתִי לְשַׁוְעָתִי׃
נז קָרַבְתָּ בְּיוֹם אֶקְרָאֶךָּ אָמַרְתָּ אַל־תִּירָא׃
נח רַבְתָּ אֲדֹנָי רִיבֵי נַפְשִׁי גָּאַלְתָּ חַיָּי׃ נט רָאִיתָה
יְהֹוָה עַוָּתָתִי שָׁפְטָה מִשְׁפָּטִי׃ ס רָאִיתָה כָּל־
נִקְמָתָם כָּל־מַחְשְׁבֹתָם לִי׃ סא שָׁמַעְתָּ חֶרְפָּתָם
יְהֹוָה כָּל־מַחְשְׁבֹתָם עָלָי׃ סב שִׂפְתֵי קָמַי
וְהֶגְיוֹנָם עָלַי כָּל־הַיּוֹם׃ סג שִׁבְתָּם וְקִימָתָם
הַבִּיטָה אֲנִי מַנְגִּינָתָם׃ סד תָּשִׁיב לָהֶם גְּמוּל
יְהֹוָה כְּמַעֲשֵׂה יְדֵיהֶם׃ סה תִּתֵּן לָהֶם מְגִנַּת־לֵב
תַּאֲלָתְךָ לָהֶם׃ סו תִּרְדֹּף בְּאַף וְתַשְׁמִידֵם מִתַּחַת
שְׁמֵי יְהֹוָה׃

ד א אֵיכָה יוּעַם זָהָב יִשְׁנֶא הַכֶּתֶם הַטּוֹב
תִּשְׁתַּפֵּכְנָה אַבְנֵי־קֹדֶשׁ בְּרֹאשׁ כָּל־חוּצוֹת׃
ב בְּנֵי צִיּוֹן הַיְקָרִים הַמְסֻלָּאִים בַּפָּז אֵיכָה
נֶחְשְׁבוּ לְנִבְלֵי־חֶרֶשׂ מַעֲשֵׂה יְדֵי יוֹצֵר׃ ג גַּם־
תַּנִּין (תנים קרי) חָלְצוּ שַׁד הֵינִיקוּ גּוּרֵיהֶן בַּת־
עַמִּי לְאַכְזָר כִּי עֲנִים (כיענים קרי) בַּמִּדְבָּר׃ ד דָּבַק
לְשׁוֹן יוֹנֵק אֶל־חִכּוֹ בַּצָּמָא עוֹלָלִים שָׁאֲלוּ לֶחֶם
פֹּרֵשׂ אֵין לָהֶם׃ ה הָאֹכְלִים לְמַעֲדַנִּים נָשַׁמּוּ

dainties are perishing in the streets; they that were reared amid purple clasp the heaps [of dust]. 6. Indeed, the iniquity of the daughter of my people is greater than the sin of Sodom, which was overthrown as in a moment, and no [mortal] hands fell on her. 7. Her princes were purer than snow, they were whiter than milk; their bodies were ruddier than coral, [and] sapphire was their outline. 8. [But now] their appearance has become blacker than coal, they are not recognized in the streets; their skin is shrivelled on their bones; it has become as dry as a stick. 9. Better off were the victims of the sword than the victims of hunger, for they, the stricken ones, are pining away for [want] of the fruits of the field. 10. The hands of the compassionate women have boiled their own children; they became their food at the destruction of the daughter of my people. 11. The Lord has spent His fury, he has poured out His fierce anger, and He has kindled a fire in Zion that has consumed her foundation. 12. The kings of the earth did not believe, nor any of the inhabitants of the world, that the foe or enemy could enter the gates of Jerusalem. 13. [It was] for the sins of her [false] prophets, [and] the iniquities of her priests, who shed in her midst the blood of the righteous. 14. They stagger blindly through the streets; they are defiled with blood, and none can touch their garments. 15. They called out to them: "Depart, unclean! Depart, depart, do not touch!," for they are fugitives, even wanderers; they said: "They shall no more sojourn among the nations." 16. The presence of the Lord divided them; He will regard them no longer; they respected no more the presence of the priests, they favored not the elders. 17. Our eyes still strain in vain [for the promise] "to help us"; in our expectations we hoped for a nation that cannot save [us]. 18. They dogged our steps [and prevented us] from walking in the streets; our end drew near, our days were fulfilled, for our end had come. 19. Our pursuers were swifter than the eagles of the heavens; they chased us on the mountains, they lay in wait for us in the wilderness. 20. The breath of our nostrils, the Lord's anointed, was cap-

בַּחוּצ֑וֹת הָאֱמֻנִים֙ עֲלֵ֣י תוֹלָ֔ע חִבְּק֖וּ אַשְׁפַּתּֽוֹת׃
ו וַיִּגְדַּל֙ עֲוֺ֣ן בַּת־עַמִּ֔י מֵחַטַּ֖את סְדֹ֑ם הַֽהֲפוּכָ֣ה
כְמוֹ־רָ֔גַע וְלֹא־חָ֥לוּ בָ֖הּ יָדָֽיִם׃ ז זַכּ֤וּ נְזִירֶ֙יהָ֙
מִשֶּׁ֔לֶג צַח֖וּ מֵחָלָ֑ב אָ֤דְמוּ עֶ֙צֶם֙ מִפְּנִינִ֔ים סַפִּ֖יר
גִּזְרָתָֽם׃ ח חָשַׁ֤ךְ מִשְּׁחוֹר֙ תָּֽאֳרָ֔ם לֹ֥א נִכְּר֖וּ
בַּחוּצ֑וֹת צָפַ֤ד עוֹרָם֙ עַל־עַצְמָ֔ם יָבֵ֖שׁ הָיָ֥ה כָעֵֽץ׃
ט טוֹבִ֤ים הָיוּ֙ חַלְלֵי־חֶ֔רֶב מֵחַלְלֵ֖י רָעָ֑ב שֶׁ֣הֵ֔ם
יָז֣וּבוּ֙ מְדֻקָּרִ֔ים מִתְּנוּבֹ֖ת שָׂדָֽי׃ י יְדֵ֗י נָשִׁים֙
רַחֲמָ֣נִיּ֔וֹת בִּשְּׁל֖וּ יַלְדֵיהֶ֑ן הָי֤וּ לְבָרוֹת֙ לָ֔מוֹ בְּשֶׁ֖בֶר
בַּת־עַמִּֽי׃ יא כִּלָּ֤ה יְהוָֹה֙ אֶת־חֲמָת֔וֹ שָׁפַ֖ךְ חֲר֣וֹן
אַפּ֑וֹ וַיַּצֶּת־אֵ֣שׁ בְּצִיּ֔וֹן וַתֹּ֖אכַל יְסוֹדֹתֶֽיהָ׃ יב לֹ֤א
הֶאֱמִ֙ינוּ֙ מַלְכֵי־אֶ֔רֶץ וכֹ֖ל (כל קרי) יֹ֖שְׁבֵי תֵבֵ֑ל כִּ֤י
יָבֹא֙ צַ֣ר וְאוֹיֵ֔ב בְּשַׁעֲרֵ֖י יְרוּשָׁלִָֽם׃ יג מֵחַטֹּ֣את
נְבִיאֶ֔יהָ עֲוֺנ֖וֹת כֹּהֲנֶ֑יהָ הַשֹּׁפְכִ֥ים בְּקִרְבָּ֖הּ דַּ֥ם
צַדִּיקִֽים׃ יד נָע֤וּ עִוְרִים֙ בַּחוּצ֔וֹת נְגֹֽאֲל֖וּ בַּדָּ֑ם
בְּלֹ֣א יוּכְל֔וּ יִגְּע֖וּ בִּלְבֻשֵׁיהֶֽם׃ טו ס֣וּרוּ טָמֵ֞א
קָ֣רְאוּ לָ֗מוֹ ס֤וּרוּ ס֙וּרוּ֙ אַל־תִּגָּ֔עוּ כִּ֥י נָצ֖וּ גַּם־נָ֑עוּ
אָֽמְרוּ֙ בַּגּוֹיִ֔ם לֹ֥א יוֹסִ֖פוּ לָגֽוּר׃ טז פְּנֵ֤י יְהוָֹה֙
חִלְּקָ֔ם לֹ֥א יוֹסִ֖יף לְהַבִּיטָ֑ם פְּנֵ֤י כֹהֲנִים֙ לֹ֣א נָשָׂ֔אוּ
זְקֵנִ֖ים (וזקנים קרי) לֹ֥א חָנָֽנוּ׃ יז עוֹדֶ֙ינָה֙ (עודינו קרי)
תִּכְלֶ֣ינָה עֵינֵ֔ינוּ אֶל־עֶזְרָתֵ֖נוּ הָ֑בֶל בְּצִפִּיָּתֵ֣נוּ
צִפִּ֔ינוּ אֶל־גּ֖וֹי לֹ֥א יוֹשִֽׁעַ׃ יח צָד֣וּ צְעָדֵ֔ינוּ מִלֶּ֖כֶת
בִּרְחֹבֹתֵ֑ינוּ קָרַ֥ב קִצֵּ֛נוּ מָלְא֥וּ יָמֵ֖ינוּ כִּי־בָ֥א
קִצֵּֽנוּ׃ יט קַלִּ֤ים הָיוּ֙ רֹֽדְפֵ֔ינוּ מִנִּשְׁרֵ֖י שָׁמָ֑יִם עַל־
הֶֽהָרִ֣ים דְּלָקֻ֔נוּ בַּמִּדְבָּ֖ר אָ֥רְבוּ לָֽנוּ׃ כ ר֤וּחַ אַפֵּ֙ינוּ֙
מְשִׁ֣יחַ יְהוָֹ֔ה נִלְכַּ֖ד בִּשְׁחִיתוֹתָ֑ם אֲשֶׁ֣ר אָמַ֔רְנוּ

tured in their pits, of whom we had said: "Under his protection we shall live among the nations." 21. Rejoice and be glad, O Daughter of Edom, that dwells in the land of Uz; to you also shall the cup pass, you shall become drunk and strip yourself bare. 22. [The punishment of] your iniquity is complete, O daughter of Zion; He will no longer send you into exile; [but] your iniquity, O daughter of Edom, He will punish—He will reveal your sins.

CHAPTER V

1. Recall, O Lord, what has befallen us; behold, and see our disgrace. 2. Our heritage has been turned over to strangers, our homes to aliens. 3. We have become orphans and fatherless, our mothers are like widows. 4. Our [own] water we have drunk for payment, our wood must needs come by purchase. 5. We are pursued [with a yoke] on our necks; we toil and are given no rest. 6. We have stretched out our hands to Egypt [and to] Assyria to get enough food. 7. Our fathers have sinned and are no more, and we have borne their iniquities. 8. Slaves rule over us, [and] there is none to deliver [us] from their hand. 9. With [the peril of] our lives we win our bread, because of the sword of the wilderness. 10. Our skin is parched as by a furnace because of the heat of hunger. 11. They have outraged women in Zion [and] maidens in the cities of Judah. 12. Princes are hanged by their hands, elders are shown no respect. 13. Young men carry the millstones, [and] youths stumble under [loads of] wood. 14. The elders have ceased from the [city] gate, the young men from their music. 15. The joy of our heart has ceased, our dancing has been turned into mourning. 16. The crown of our head has fallen, woe to us, for we have sinned. 17. For this our heart has become faint, for these things our eyes have grown dim. 18. For Mount Zion which [lies] desolate, foxes prowl over it. 19. But You, O Lord, remain forever; Your throne endures throughout the generations. 20. Why do You forget us forever, forsake us so long? 21. Restore us to You, O Lord, that we may be restored!

בְּצִלּוֹ נִחְיֶה בַגּוֹיִם׃ כא שִׂישִׂי וְשִׂמְחִי בַּת־אֱדוֹם
יוֹשֶׁבְתִּי (יושבת קרי) בְּאֶרֶץ עוּץ גַּם־עָלַיִךְ תַּעֲבָר־
כּוֹס תִּשְׁכְּרִי וְתִתְעָרִי׃ כב תַּם־עֲוֺנֵךְ בַּת־צִיּוֹן
לֹא יוֹסִיף לְהַגְלוֹתֵךְ פָּקַד עֲוֺנֵךְ בַּת־אֱדוֹם גִּלָּה
עַל־חַטֹּאתָיִךְ׃ פ

ה א זְכֹר יְהוָה מֶה־הָיָה לָנוּ הַבִּיטָ (הביטה קרי)
וּרְאֵה אֶת־חֶרְפָּתֵנוּ׃ ב נַחֲלָתֵנוּ נֶהֶפְכָה לְזָרִים
בָּתֵּינוּ לְנָכְרִים׃ ג יְתוֹמִים הָיִינוּ אֵין (ואין קרי)
אָב אִמֹּתֵינוּ כְּאַלְמָנוֹת׃ ד מֵימֵינוּ בְּכֶסֶף שָׁתִינוּ
עֵצֵינוּ בִּמְחִיר יָבֹאוּ׃ ה עַל צַוָּארֵנוּ נִרְדָּפְנוּ
יָגַעְנוּ לֹא (ולא קרי) הוּנַח־לָנוּ׃ ו מִצְרַיִם נָתַנּוּ יָד
אַשּׁוּר לִשְׂבֹּעַ לָחֶם׃ ז אֲבֹתֵינוּ חָטְאוּ אֵינָם
(ואינם קרי) אֲנַחְנוּ (ואנחנו קרי) עֲוֺנֹתֵיהֶם סָבָלְנוּ׃
ח עֲבָדִים מָשְׁלוּ בָנוּ פֹּרֵק אֵין מִיָּדָם׃
ט בְּנַפְשֵׁנוּ נָבִיא לַחְמֵנוּ מִפְּנֵי חֶרֶב הַמִּדְבָּר׃
י עוֹרֵנוּ כְּתַנּוּר נִכְמָרוּ מִפְּנֵי זַלְעֲפוֹת רָעָב׃
יא נָשִׁים בְּצִיּוֹן עִנּוּ בְּתֻלֹת בְּעָרֵי יְהוּדָה׃
יב שָׂרִים בְּיָדָם נִתְלוּ פְּנֵי זְקֵנִים לֹא נֶהְדָּרוּ׃
יג בַּחוּרִים טְחוֹן נָשָׂאוּ וּנְעָרִים בָּעֵץ כָּשָׁלוּ׃
יד זְקֵנִים מִשַּׁעַר שָׁבָתוּ בַּחוּרִים מִנְּגִינָתָם׃
טו שָׁבַת מְשׂוֹשׂ לִבֵּנוּ נֶהְפַּךְ לְאֵבֶל מְחֹלֵנוּ׃
טז נָפְלָה עֲטֶרֶת רֹאשֵׁנוּ אוֹי־נָא לָנוּ כִּי חָטָאנוּ׃
יז עַל־זֶה הָיָה דָוֶה לִבֵּנוּ עַל־אֵלֶּה חָשְׁכוּ
עֵינֵינוּ׃ יח עַל הַר־צִיּוֹן שֶׁשָּׁמֵם שׁוּעָלִים
הִלְּכוּ־בוֹ׃ יט אַתָּה יְהוָה לְעוֹלָם תֵּשֵׁב כִּסְאֲךָ
לְדֹר וָדוֹר׃ כ לָמָּה לָנֶצַח תִּשְׁכָּחֵנוּ תַּעַזְבֵנוּ
לְאֹרֶךְ יָמִים׃ כא הֲשִׁיבֵנוּ יְהוָה ׀ אֵלֶיךָ וְנָשׁוּבָ

(ונשובה קרי) חַדֵּ֥שׁ יָמֵ֖ינוּ כְּקֶֽדֶם׃ כב כִּ֚י אִם־מָאֹ֣ס
מְאַסְתָּ֔נוּ קָצַ֥פְתָּ עָלֵ֖ינוּ עַד־מְאֹֽד׃ הקהל חוזר לומר
השיבנו ואח"כ החזן: הֲשִׁיבֵ֨נוּ יְהֹוָ֤ה ׀ אֵלֶ֙יךָ֙ וְנָשׁ֔וּבָה חַדֵּ֥שׁ
יָמֵ֖ינוּ כְּקֶֽדֶם׃

Renew our days as of old. 22. For if You have utterly rejected us, You have [already] been exceedingly wroth against us.

Restore us to You, O Lord, that we may be restored! Renew our days as of old.

KOHELETH קהלת

[ECCLESIASTES]

ECCLESIASTES קהלת

King Solomon, referring to himself as *Koheleth,* "the preacher," seeks the true meaning of life in the Book of Ecclesiastes. He begins with the thesis that "all is vanity," and comes to the conclusion that "the end of the matter" is that man should "fear God and keep His commandments, for this is the entire man."

Ecclesiastes is read on the Festival of Sukkoth, the season when, in ancient times, all of Israel would assemble to hear the reading of the Torah and exhortations to lead lives of justice and morality.

King Solomon's wisdom was highly respected also among Israel's gentile neighbors. Many thinkers and philosophers from other lands came to Jerusalem to listen to his discourses and to hear the Jewish king cite the Word of God in refutation of godless philosophies.

At one time, the Book of Ecclesiastes was considered controversial, since many of the statements contained in it seemed contradictory at first glance. Eventually, however, the Rabbis came to the conclusion that this Book was genuine, sacred, and fit for inclusion in the Holy Writ.

It is customary to read Ecclesiastes on the intermediate Shabbath of Sukkoth. Should there be no intermediate Shabbath, it is read on Shemini Atzereth.

This Book is reflective of Solomon's addresses to the people assembled in the Temple on the Festival of Sukkoth.

CHAPTER I

1. The words of Koheleth son of David, king in Jerusalem. 2. Vanity of vanities, said Koheleth; vanity of vanities, all is vanity. 3. What profit has man in all his toil that he toils under the sun? 4. A generation goes and a generation comes, but the earth endures forever. 5. The sun rises and the sun sets, and to its place it yearns and rises there. 6. It goes to the south and goes around to the north; the wind goes around and around, and the wind returns to its circuits. 7. All the rivers run into the sea, yet the sea is not full; to the place where the rivers flow, there they repeatedly go. 8. All things are wearisome; no one can utter it; the eye shall not be sated from seeing, nor shall the ear be filled from hearing. 9. That which has been is the same as that which will be, and that which has been done is the same as that which will be done, and there is nothing new under the sun. 10. There is a thing of which [someone] will say, "See this, it is new." It has already been for ages which were before us. 11. [But] there is no remembrance of former [generations],

א א דִּבְרֵי קֹהֶלֶת בֶּן־דָּוִד מֶלֶךְ בִּירוּשָׁלָם: ב הֲבֵל הֲבָלִים אָמַר קֹהֶלֶת הֲבֵל הֲבָלִים הַכֹּל הָבֶל: ג מַה־יִּתְרוֹן לָאָדָם בְּכָל־עֲמָלוֹ שֶׁיַּעֲמֹל תַּחַת הַשָּׁמֶשׁ: ד דּוֹר הֹלֵךְ וְדוֹר בָּא וְהָאָרֶץ לְעוֹלָם עֹמָדֶת: ה וְזָרַח הַשֶּׁמֶשׁ וּבָא הַשָּׁמֶשׁ וְאֶל־מְקוֹמוֹ שׁוֹאֵף זוֹרֵחַ הוּא שָׁם: ו הוֹלֵךְ אֶל־דָּרוֹם וְסוֹבֵב אֶל־צָפוֹן סוֹבֵב ׀ סֹבֵב הוֹלֵךְ הָרוּחַ וְעַל־סְבִיבֹתָיו שָׁב הָרוּחַ: ז כָּל־הַנְּחָלִים הֹלְכִים אֶל־הַיָּם וְהַיָּם אֵינֶנּוּ מָלֵא אֶל־מְקוֹם שֶׁהַנְּחָלִים הֹלְכִים שָׁם הֵם שָׁבִים לָלָכֶת: ח כָּל־הַדְּבָרִים יְגֵעִים לֹא־יוּכַל אִישׁ לְדַבֵּר לֹא־תִשְׂבַּע עַיִן לִרְאוֹת וְלֹא־תִמָּלֵא אֹזֶן מִשְּׁמֹעַ: ט מַה־שֶּׁהָיָה הוּא שֶׁיִּהְיֶה וּמַה־שֶּׁנַּעֲשָׂה הוּא שֶׁיֵּעָשֶׂה וְאֵין כָּל־חָדָשׁ תַּחַת הַשָּׁמֶשׁ: י יֵשׁ דָּבָר שֶׁיֹּאמַר רְאֵה־זֶה חָדָשׁ הוּא כְּבָר הָיָה לְעֹלָמִים אֲשֶׁר הָיָה מִלְּפָנֵנוּ: יא אֵין זִכְרוֹן לָרִאשֹׁנִים וְגַם

neither will the later ones that will be have any remembrance among those that will be afterwards. 12. I, Koheleth, was king over Israel in Jerusalem. 13. And I applied my heart to inquire and to search with wisdom all that was done under the heaven. That is a sore task that God has given to the sons of men with which to occupy themselves. 14. I saw all the deeds that were done under the sun, and everything is vanity and frustration. 15. What is crooked cannot be straightened, and what is missing cannot be counted. 16. I spoke to myself, saying, "Look, I have acquired great wisdom, and I have increased more than all who were before me over Jerusalem"; and my heart saw much wisdom and knowledge. 17. And I applied my heart to know wisdom and to know madness and folly; I know that this too is a frustration. 18. For in much wisdom is much vexation, and he who increases knowledge, increases pain.

CHAPTER II

1. I said to myself, "Come now, I will test you with joy and experience pleasure"; and behold, this too was vanity. 2. Concerning laughter, I said, "[It is] mad"; and concerning joy, "What does this accomplish?" 3. I searched in my heart to indulge my body with wine, and my heart conducting itself with wisdom and holding onto folly, until I would see which is better for the children of men that they should do under the heavens the number of the days of their lives. 4. I made myself great works; I built myself houses, and I planted vineyards for myself. 5. I made for myself gardens and orchards, and I planted in them all sorts of fruit trees. 6. I made for myself pools of water, to water from them a forest sprouting with trees. 7. I acquired male and female slaves, and I have those born in my house; also I had possession of cattle and flocks, more than all who were before me in Jerusalem. 8. I accumulated for myself also silver and gold, and the treasures of the kings and the provinces; I acquired for myself men singers and women singers, the delights of the sons of men, wagons and coaches. 9. So I was great,

לָאַחֲרֹנִים שֶׁיִּהְיוּ לֹא־יִהְיֶה לָהֶם זִכָּרוֹן עִם
שֶׁיִּהְיוּ לָאַחֲרֹנָה: פ יב אֲנִי קֹהֶלֶת הָיִיתִי מֶלֶךְ
עַל־יִשְׂרָאֵל בִּירוּשָׁלָם: יג וְנָתַתִּי אֶת־לִבִּי
לִדְרוֹשׁ וְלָתוּר בַּחָכְמָה עַל כָּל־אֲשֶׁר נַעֲשָׂה
תַּחַת הַשָּׁמָיִם הוּא ׀ עִנְיַן רָע נָתַן אֱלֹהִים לִבְנֵי
הָאָדָם לַעֲנוֹת בּוֹ: יד רָאִיתִי אֶת־כָּל־הַמַּעֲשִׂים
שֶׁנַּעֲשׂוּ תַּחַת הַשָּׁמֶשׁ וְהִנֵּה הַכֹּל הֶבֶל וּרְעוּת
רוּחַ: טו מְעֻוָּת לֹא־יוּכַל לִתְקֹן וְחֶסְרוֹן לֹא־
יוּכַל לְהִמָּנוֹת: טז דִּבַּרְתִּי אֲנִי עִם־לִבִּי לֵאמֹר
אֲנִי הִנֵּה הִגְדַּלְתִּי וְהוֹסַפְתִּי חָכְמָה עַל כָּל־
אֲשֶׁר־הָיָה לְפָנַי עַל־יְרוּשָׁלָם וְלִבִּי רָאָה הַרְבֵּה
חָכְמָה וָדָעַת: יז וָאֶתְּנָה לִבִּי לָדַעַת חָכְמָה וְדַעַת
הֹלֵלוֹת וְשִׂכְלוּת יָדַעְתִּי שֶׁגַּם־זֶה הוּא רַעְיוֹן
רוּחַ: יח כִּי בְּרֹב חָכְמָה רָב־כָּעַס וְיוֹסִיף דַּעַת
יוֹסִיף מַכְאוֹב:

ב א אָמַרְתִּי אֲנִי בְּלִבִּי לְכָה־נָּא אֲנַסְּכָה
בְשִׂמְחָה וּרְאֵה בְטוֹב וְהִנֵּה גַם־הוּא הָבֶל:
ב לִשְׂחוֹק אָמַרְתִּי מְהוֹלָל וּלְשִׂמְחָה מַה־זֹּה
עֹשָׂה: ג תַּרְתִּי בְלִבִּי לִמְשׁוֹךְ בַּיַּיִן אֶת־בְּשָׂרִי
וְלִבִּי נֹהֵג בַּחָכְמָה וְלֶאֱחֹז בְּסִכְלוּת עַד אֲשֶׁר־
אֶרְאֶה אֵי־זֶה טוֹב לִבְנֵי הָאָדָם אֲשֶׁר יַעֲשׂוּ
תַּחַת הַשָּׁמַיִם מִסְפַּר יְמֵי חַיֵּיהֶם: ד הִגְדַּלְתִּי
מַעֲשָׂי בָּנִיתִי לִי בָּתִּים נָטַעְתִּי לִי כְּרָמִים:
ה עָשִׂיתִי לִי גַּנּוֹת וּפַרְדֵּסִים וְנָטַעְתִּי בָהֶם עֵץ
כָּל־פֶּרִי: ו עָשִׂיתִי לִי בְּרֵכוֹת מָיִם לְהַשְׁקוֹת
מֵהֶם יַעַר צוֹמֵחַ עֵצִים: ז קָנִיתִי עֲבָדִים
וּשְׁפָחוֹת וּבְנֵי־בַיִת הָיָה לִי גַּם מִקְנֶה בָקָר
וָצֹאן הַרְבֵּה הָיָה לִי מִכֹּל שֶׁהָיוּ לְפָנַי
בִּירוּשָׁלָם: ח כָּנַסְתִּי לִי גַּם־כֶּסֶף וְזָהָב וּסְגֻלַּת
מְלָכִים וְהַמְּדִינוֹת עָשִׂיתִי לִי שָׁרִים וְשָׁרוֹת
וְתַעֲנוּגוֹת בְּנֵי הָאָדָם שִׁדָּה וְשִׁדּוֹת: ט וְגָדַלְתִּי

and I increased more than all who were before me in Jerusalem; also my wisdom remained with me.   10. And [of] all that my eyes desired, I did not deprive them; I did not deprive my heart of any joy, but my heart rejoices from all my toil, and this was my portion from all my toil.   11. Then I turned [to look] at all my deeds that my hands had wrought and upon the toil that I had toiled to do, and behold, everything is vanity and frustration, and there is no profit under the sun.   12. And I turned to see wisdom and madness and folly, for what is the man who will come after the king, that which they have already done?   13. And I saw that wisdom has an advantage over folly, as the advantage of light over darkness.   14. The wise man has his eyes in his head, and the fool goes in the darkness, and I too knew that one event happens to them all.   15. And I said to myself, "As it happens to the fool, so will it happen to me too, so why then did I become wiser?" And I said to myself that this too is vanity. 16. For there is no remembrance of the wise man with the fool forever, for seeing that in the coming days, all is forgotten. And how shall the wise man die with the fool?   17. So I hated life, for the deed that was done under the sun grieved me, for everything is vanity and frustration. 18. And I hated all my toil that I toil under the sun, that I should leave it to the man who will be after me.   19. And who knows whether he will be wise or foolish? And he will rule over all my toil that I have toiled and that I have gained wisdom under the sun; this too is vanity.   20. And I turned about to cause my heart to despair concerning all the toil that I have toiled under the sun.   21. For there is a man whose toil is with wisdom and with knowledge and with honesty, and to a man who did not toil for it he will give it as his portion; this too is vanity and a great evil. 22. For what has a man out of all his toil and the breaking of his heart that he toils under the sun?   23. For all his days are pains and his occupation is vexation; even at night his heart does not rest; this too is vanity.   24. Is it not good for a man that he eat and drink and show himself enjoyment in his toil; this too have I seen, that it

וְהוֹסַפְתִּי מִכֹּל שֶׁהָיָה לְפָנַי בִּירוּשָׁלָ͏ִם אַף חָכְמָתִי עָמְדָה לִּי: י וְכֹל אֲשֶׁר שָׁאֲלוּ עֵינַי לֹא אָצַלְתִּי מֵהֶם לֹא־מָנַעְתִּי אֶת־לִבִּי מִכָּל־שִׂמְחָה כִּי־לִבִּי שָׂמֵחַ מִכָּל־עֲמָלִי וְזֶה־הָיָה חֶלְקִי מִכָּל־עֲמָלִי: יא וּפָנִיתִי אֲנִי בְּכָל־מַעֲשַׂי שֶׁעָשׂוּ יָדַי וּבֶעָמָל שֶׁעָמַלְתִּי לַעֲשׂוֹת וְהִנֵּה הַכֹּל הֶבֶל וּרְעוּת רוּחַ וְאֵין יִתְרוֹן תַּחַת הַשָּׁמֶשׁ: יב וּפָנִיתִי אֲנִי לִרְאוֹת חָכְמָה וְהוֹלֵלוֹת וְסִכְלוּת כִּי ׀ מֶה הָאָדָם שֶׁיָּבוֹא אַחֲרֵי הַמֶּלֶךְ אֵת אֲשֶׁר־כְּבָר עָשׂוּהוּ: יג וְרָאִיתִי אָנִי שֶׁיֵּשׁ יִתְרוֹן לַחָכְמָה מִן־הַסִּכְלוּת כִּיתְרוֹן הָאוֹר מִן־הַחֹשֶׁךְ: יד הֶחָכָם עֵינָיו בְּרֹאשׁוֹ וְהַכְּסִיל בַּחֹשֶׁךְ הוֹלֵךְ וְיָדַעְתִּי גַם־אָנִי שֶׁמִּקְרֶה אֶחָד יִקְרֶה אֶת־כֻּלָּם: טו וְאָמַרְתִּי אֲנִי בְּלִבִּי כְּמִקְרֵה הַכְּסִיל גַּם־אֲנִי יִקְרֵנִי וְלָמָּה חָכַמְתִּי אֲנִי אָז יֹתֵר וְדִבַּרְתִּי בְלִבִּי שֶׁגַּם־זֶה הָבֶל: טז כִּי אֵין זִכְרוֹן לֶחָכָם עִם־הַכְּסִיל לְעוֹלָם בְּשֶׁכְּבָר הַיָּמִים הַבָּאִים הַכֹּל נִשְׁכָּח וְאֵיךְ יָמוּת הֶחָכָם עִם־הַכְּסִיל: יז וְשָׂנֵאתִי אֶת־הַחַיִּים כִּי רַע עָלַי הַמַּעֲשֶׂה שֶׁנַּעֲשָׂה תַּחַת הַשָּׁמֶשׁ כִּי־הַכֹּל הֶבֶל וּרְעוּת רוּחַ: יח וְשָׂנֵאתִי אֲנִי אֶת־כָּל־עֲמָלִי שֶׁאֲנִי עָמֵל תַּחַת הַשָּׁמֶשׁ שֶׁאַנִּיחֶנּוּ לָאָדָם שֶׁיִּהְיֶה אַחֲרָי: יט וּמִי יוֹדֵעַ הֶחָכָם יִהְיֶה אוֹ סָכָל וְיִשְׁלַט בְּכָל־עֲמָלִי שֶׁעָמַלְתִּי וְשֶׁחָכַמְתִּי תַּחַת הַשָּׁמֶשׁ גַּם־זֶה הָבֶל: כ וְסַבּוֹתִי אֲנִי לְיַאֵשׁ אֶת־לִבִּי עַל כָּל־הֶעָמָל שֶׁעָמַלְתִּי תַּחַת הַשָּׁמֶשׁ: כא כִּי־יֵשׁ אָדָם שֶׁעֲמָלוֹ בְּחָכְמָה וּבְדַעַת וּבְכִשְׁרוֹן וּלְאָדָם שֶׁלֹּא עָמַל־בּוֹ יִתְּנֶנּוּ חֶלְקוֹ גַּם־זֶה הֶבֶל וְרָעָה רַבָּה: כב כִּי מֶה־הֹוֶה לָאָדָם בְּכָל־עֲמָלוֹ וּבְרַעְיוֹן לִבּוֹ שֶׁהוּא עָמֵל תַּחַת הַשָּׁמֶשׁ: כג כִּי כָל־יָמָיו מַכְאֹבִים וָכַעַס עִנְיָנוֹ גַּם־בַּלַּיְלָה לֹא־שָׁכַב לִבּוֹ גַּם־זֶה הֶבֶל הוּא: כד אֵין־טוֹב בָּאָדָם שֶׁיֹּאכַל וְשָׁתָה וְהֶרְאָה אֶת־נַפְשׁוֹ טוֹב בַּעֲמָלוֹ גַּם־זֹה

is from the hand of God. 25. For who will eat, and who will hasten [to swallow it] except me? 26. For to a man who is good in His sight, He has given wisdom and knowledge and joy, and to the sinner He has given a task to gather and to accumulate, to give to him who is good in God's sight; this too is vanity and frustration.

CHAPTER III

1. Everything has an appointed season, and there is a time for every matter under the sun. 2. A time to be born and a time to die, a time to plant and a time to uproot what is planted. 3. A time to kill and a time to heal, a time to break and a time to build. 4. A time to weep and a time to laugh, a time of wailing and a time of dancing. 5. A time to cast stones and a time to gather stones, a time to embrace and a time to refrain from embracing. 6. A time to seek and a time to lose, a time to keep and a time to cast away. 7. A time to rend and a time to sew, a time to be silent and a time to speak. 8. A time to love and a time to hate, a time for war and a time for peace. 9. What profit has the one who works in what he toils? 10. I have seen the task that God gave to the sons of men with which to occupy themselves. 11. He has made everything in its time; also the [wisdom of] the world He put into their hearts, save that man should not find the deed which God did, from beginning to end. 12. I knew that there is no good in them except to rejoice and to do good during his lifetime. 13. And also, every man who eats and drinks and enjoys what is good in all his toil, it is a gift of God. 14. I knew that everything that God did, that will be forever; we cannot add to it, nor can we subtract from it; and God made it so that they fear Him. 15. That which is already done, and that which is [destined] to be, already was, and God seeks the pursued. 16. And moreover, I saw under the sun, the place of justice, there is wickedness, and the place of righteousness, there is wickedness. 17. I said to myself, "God will judge the righteous and the wicked, for there is a time for every matter and for every deed there." 18. I said to myself, concerning

רָאִיתִי אָנִי כִּי מִיַּד הָאֱלֹהִים הִיא: כה כִּי מִי
יֹאכַל וּמִי יָחוּשׁ חוּץ מִמֶּנִּי: כו כִּי לְאָדָם שֶׁטּוֹב
לְפָנָיו נָתַן חָכְמָה וְדַעַת וְשִׂמְחָה וְלַחוֹטֶא נָתַן
עִנְיָן לֶאֱסֹף וְלִכְנוֹס לָתֵת לְטוֹב לִפְנֵי הָאֱלֹהִים
גַּם־זֶה הֶבֶל וּרְעוּת רוּחַ:

ג א לַכֹּל זְמָן וְעֵת לְכָל־חֵפֶץ תַּחַת הַשָּׁמָיִם:
ב עֵת לָלֶדֶת וְעֵת לָמוּת עֵת לָטַעַת וְעֵת לַעֲקוֹר
נָטוּעַ: ג עֵת לַהֲרוֹג וְעֵת לִרְפּוֹא עֵת לִפְרוֹץ
וְעֵת לִבְנוֹת: ד עֵת לִבְכּוֹת וְעֵת לִשְׂחוֹק עֵת
סְפוֹד וְעֵת רְקוֹד: ה עֵת לְהַשְׁלִיךְ אֲבָנִים וְעֵת
כְּנוֹס אֲבָנִים עֵת לַחֲבוֹק וְעֵת לִרְחֹק מֵחַבֵּק:
ו עֵת לְבַקֵּשׁ וְעֵת לְאַבֵּד עֵת לִשְׁמוֹר וְעֵת
לְהַשְׁלִיךְ: ז עֵת לִקְרוֹעַ וְעֵת לִתְפּוֹר עֵת לַחֲשׁוֹת
וְעֵת לְדַבֵּר: ח עֵת לֶאֱהֹב וְעֵת לִשְׂנֹא עֵת
מִלְחָמָה וְעֵת שָׁלוֹם: ט מַה־יִּתְרוֹן הָעוֹשֶׂה
בַּאֲשֶׁר הוּא עָמֵל: י רָאִיתִי אֶת־הָעִנְיָן אֲשֶׁר
נָתַן אֱלֹהִים לִבְנֵי הָאָדָם לַעֲנוֹת בּוֹ: יא אֶת־הַכֹּל
עָשָׂה יָפֶה בְעִתּוֹ גַּם אֶת־הָעֹלָם נָתַן בְּלִבָּם
מִבְּלִי אֲשֶׁר לֹא־יִמְצָא הָאָדָם אֶת־הַמַּעֲשֶׂה
אֲשֶׁר־עָשָׂה הָאֱלֹהִים מֵרֹאשׁ וְעַד־סוֹף:
יב יָדַעְתִּי כִּי אֵין טוֹב בָּם כִּי אִם־לִשְׂמוֹחַ
וְלַעֲשׂוֹת טוֹב בְּחַיָּיו: יג וְגַם כָּל־הָאָדָם שֶׁיֹּאכַל
וְשָׁתָה וְרָאָה טוֹב בְּכָל־עֲמָלוֹ מַתַּת אֱלֹהִים
הִיא: יד יָדַעְתִּי כִּי כָּל־אֲשֶׁר יַעֲשֶׂה הָאֱלֹהִים
הוּא יִהְיֶה לְעוֹלָם עָלָיו אֵין לְהוֹסִיף וּמִמֶּנּוּ אֵין
לִגְרוֹעַ וְהָאֱלֹהִים עָשָׂה שֶׁיִּרְאוּ מִלְּפָנָיו: טו מַה־
שֶּׁהָיָה כְּבָר הוּא וַאֲשֶׁר לִהְיוֹת כְּבָר הָיָה
וְהָאֱלֹהִים יְבַקֵּשׁ אֶת־נִרְדָּף: טז וְעוֹד רָאִיתִי
תַּחַת הַשָּׁמֶשׁ מְקוֹם הַמִּשְׁפָּט שָׁמָּה הָרֶשַׁע
וּמְקוֹם הַצֶּדֶק שָׁמָּה הָרָשַׁע: יז אָמַרְתִּי אֲנִי
בְּלִבִּי אֶת־הַצַּדִּיק וְאֶת־הָרָשָׁע יִשְׁפֹּט הָאֱלֹהִים
כִּי־עֵת לְכָל־חֵפֶץ וְעַל כָּל־הַמַּעֲשֶׂה שָׁם:
יח אָמַרְתִּי אֲנִי בְּלִבִּי עַל־דִּבְרַת בְּנֵי הָאָדָם

the children of men, concerning that which God chose them, and to see that they are like their beasts. 19. For that which happens to the children of men and that which happens to a beast—and they have one happening—like the death of this one is the death of this one, and all have one spirit, and the superiority of man over beast is nought, for all is vanity. 20. Everything goes to one place; everything became from the dust, and everything returns to the dust. 21. Who knows that the spirit of the children of men is that which ascends on high and the spirit of the beast is that which descends below to the earth? 22. And I saw that there is nothing better than that man rejoice with his deeds, for that is his portion, for who will bring him to see what will be after him?

CHAPTER IV

1. But I returned and saw all the oppressions that are done under the sun, and behold, the tears of the oppressed, and they have no consoler, and from the hand of their oppressors there is power, yet they have no consoler. 2. And I praised the dead who had already died, more than the living who are still alive. 3. And better than both of them is he who has not yet been, who did not see the evil work that is done under the sun. 4. And I saw all the toil and all the excellence of work, for it is one man's envy of his friend; this too is vanity and frustration. 5. The fool folds his hands and eats his own flesh. 6. Better is a handful of ease than two handfuls of toil and frustration. 7. And I returned and saw vanity under the sun. 8. There is one, and there is no second; yea, he has neither son nor brother, and there is no end to all his toil; his eye is not even sated from wealth; now for whom do I toil and deprive my soul of pleasure? This too is vanity and an unhappy affair. 9. Two are better than one, since they have good reward for their toil. 10. For, if they fall, one will lift up his friend, but woe to the *one* who falls and has no second one to lift him up. 11. Moreover, if two lie down, they will have warmth, but how will one have warmth? 12. And if a man prevails

לְבָרָם הָאֱלֹהִים וְלִרְאוֹת שְׁהֶם־בְּהֵמָה הֵמָּה
לָהֶם׃ יט כִּי מִקְרֶה בְנֵי־הָאָדָם וּמִקְרֶה הַבְּהֵמָה
וּמִקְרֶה אֶחָד לָהֶם כְּמוֹת זֶה כֵּן מוֹת זֶה וְרוּחַ
אֶחָד לַכֹּל וּמוֹתַר הָאָדָם מִן־הַבְּהֵמָה אָיִן כִּי
הַכֹּל הָבֶל׃ כ הַכֹּל הוֹלֵךְ אֶל־מָקוֹם אֶחָד הַכֹּל
הָיָה מִן־הֶעָפָר וְהַכֹּל שָׁב אֶל־הֶעָפָר׃ כא מִי
יוֹדֵעַ רוּחַ בְּנֵי הָאָדָם הָעֹלָה הִיא לְמָעְלָה וְרוּחַ
הַבְּהֵמָה הַיֹּרֶדֶת הִיא לְמַטָּה לָאָרֶץ׃ כב וְרָאִיתִי
כִּי אֵין טוֹב מֵאֲשֶׁר יִשְׂמַח הָאָדָם בְּמַעֲשָׂיו כִּי־
הוּא חֶלְקוֹ כִּי מִי יְבִיאֶנּוּ לִרְאוֹת בְּמֶה שֶׁיִּהְיֶה
אַחֲרָיו׃

ד א וְשַׁבְתִּי אֲנִי וָאֶרְאֶה אֶת־כָּל־הָעֲשׁוּקִים
אֲשֶׁר נַעֲשִׂים תַּחַת הַשָּׁמֶשׁ וְהִנֵּה ׀ דִּמְעַת
הָעֲשׁוּקִים וְאֵין לָהֶם מְנַחֵם וּמִיַּד עֹשְׁקֵיהֶם כֹּחַ
וְאֵין לָהֶם מְנַחֵם׃ ב וְשַׁבֵּחַ אֲנִי אֶת־הַמֵּתִים
שֶׁכְּבָר מֵתוּ מִן־הַחַיִּים אֲשֶׁר הֵמָּה חַיִּים עֲדֶנָה׃
ג וְטוֹב מִשְּׁנֵיהֶם אֵת אֲשֶׁר־עֲדֶן לֹא הָיָה אֲשֶׁר
לֹא־רָאָה אֶת־הַמַּעֲשֶׂה הָרָע אֲשֶׁר נַעֲשָׂה תַּחַת
הַשָּׁמֶשׁ׃ ד וְרָאִיתִי אֲנִי אֶת־כָּל־עָמָל וְאֵת כָּל־
כִּשְׁרוֹן הַמַּעֲשֶׂה כִּי הִיא קִנְאַת־אִישׁ מֵרֵעֵהוּ
גַּם־זֶה הֶבֶל וּרְעוּת רוּחַ׃ ה הַכְּסִיל חֹבֵק אֶת־
יָדָיו וְאֹכֵל אֶת־בְּשָׂרוֹ׃ ו טוֹב מְלֹא כַף נָחַת
מִמְּלֹא חָפְנַיִם עָמָל וּרְעוּת רוּחַ׃ ז וְשַׁבְתִּי אֲנִי
וָאֶרְאֶה הֶבֶל תַּחַת הַשָּׁמֶשׁ׃ ח יֵשׁ אֶחָד וְאֵין
שֵׁנִי גַּם בֵּן וָאָח אֵין־לוֹ וְאֵין קֵץ לְכָל־עֲמָלוֹ
גַּם־עֵינָיו (עינו קרי) לֹא־תִשְׂבַּע עֹשֶׁר וּלְמִי ׀ אֲנִי
עָמֵל וּמְחַסֵּר אֶת־נַפְשִׁי מִטּוֹבָה גַּם־זֶה הֶבֶל
וְעִנְיַן רָע הוּא׃ ט טוֹבִים הַשְּׁנַיִם מִן־הָאֶחָד
אֲשֶׁר יֵשׁ־לָהֶם שָׂכָר טוֹב בַּעֲמָלָם׃ י כִּי אִם־
יִפֹּלוּ הָאֶחָד יָקִים אֶת־חֲבֵרוֹ וְאִילוֹ הָאֶחָד
שֶׁיִּפּוֹל וְאֵין שֵׁנִי לַהֲקִימוֹ׃ יא גַּם אִם־יִשְׁכְּבוּ
שְׁנַיִם וְחַם לָהֶם וּלְאֶחָד אֵיךְ יֵחָם׃ יב וְאִם־

against the one, the two will stand up against him, but a three-strand cord is not quickly broken. 13. Better a poor and wise child than an old and foolish king, who knows not to receive admonition anymore. 14. For, out of the prison he has come to reign, for even in his kingdom he has become humble. 15. I saw all the living who walk under the sun, with the second child who will rise in his stead. 16. There is no end to all the people, to all that were before them; also the last ones will not rejoice with him, for this too is vanity and frustration. 17. Watch your foot when you go to the House of God, and be ready to obey rather than fools should give sacrifice, for they know not that they do evil.

CHAPTER V

1. Be not rash with your mouth, and let your heart be not hasty to utter a word before God, for God is in heaven, and you are on the earth; therefore, let your words be few. 2. For a dream comes with much concern, and the voice of the fool with many words. 3. When you pronounce a vow to God, do not delay paying it, for He has no pleasure in fools; what you vow, pay. 4. It is better that you vow not, than that you vow and do not pay. 5. Do not allow your mouth to cause sin to your flesh, and say not before the messenger that it is an error; why should God be wroth with your voice and destroy the work of your hands? 6. For only many dreams and vanities and many words, fear God. 7. If oppression of the poor and deprivation of justice and righteousness you see in the province, wonder not about the matter, for the highest over the high waits, and there are higher ones over them. 8. And the advantage of the land is in everything; even the king will be subservient to the land. 9. Whoever loves silver will not be sated with silver, and he who loves a multitude will have no abundance; this too is vanity. 10. With the increase of good, its eaters increase, and what is the advantage to its master except seeing [with] his eyes? 11. The sleep of the laborer is sweet, whether he eat little or much, but the satiety to the rich will not allow him to

יִתְקְפוֹ הָאֶחָד הַשְּׁנַיִם יַעַמְדוּ נֶגְדּוֹ וְהַחוּט
הַמְשֻׁלָּשׁ לֹא בִמְהֵרָה יִנָּתֵק׃ יג טוֹב יֶלֶד מִסְכֵּן
וְחָכָם מִמֶּלֶךְ זָקֵן וּכְסִיל אֲשֶׁר לֹא־יָדַע לְהִזָּהֵר
עוֹד׃ יד כִּי־מִבֵּית הָסוּרִים יָצָא לִמְלֹךְ כִּי גַּם
בְּמַלְכוּתוֹ נוֹלַד רָשׁ׃ טו רָאִיתִי אֶת־כָּל־הַחַיִּים
הַמְהַלְּכִים תַּחַת הַשָּׁמֶשׁ עִם הַיֶּלֶד הַשֵּׁנִי אֲשֶׁר
יַעֲמֹד תַּחְתָּיו׃ טז אֵין־קֵץ לְכָל־הָעָם לְכֹל
אֲשֶׁר־הָיָה לִפְנֵיהֶם גַּם הָאַחֲרוֹנִים לֹא יִשְׂמְחוּ־
בוֹ כִּי־גַם־זֶה הֶבֶל וְרַעְיוֹן רוּחַ׃ יז שְׁמֹר רַגְלֶיךָ
(רגלך קרי) כַּאֲשֶׁר תֵּלֵךְ אֶל־בֵּית הָאֱלֹהִים וְקָרוֹב
לִשְׁמֹעַ מִתֵּת הַכְּסִילִים זָבַח כִּי־אֵינָם יוֹדְעִים
לַעֲשׂוֹת רָע׃

ה א אַל־תְּבַהֵל עַל־פִּיךָ וְלִבְּךָ אַל־יְמַהֵר
לְהוֹצִיא דָבָר לִפְנֵי הָאֱלֹהִים כִּי הָאֱלֹהִים
בַּשָּׁמַיִם וְאַתָּה עַל־הָאָרֶץ עַל־כֵּן יִהְיוּ דְבָרֶיךָ
מְעַטִּים׃ ב כִּי בָּא הַחֲלוֹם בְּרֹב עִנְיָן וְקוֹל כְּסִיל
בְּרֹב דְּבָרִים׃ ג כַּאֲשֶׁר תִּדֹּר נֶדֶר לֵאלֹהִים אַל־
תְּאַחֵר לְשַׁלְּמוֹ כִּי אֵין חֵפֶץ בַּכְּסִילִים אֵת
אֲשֶׁר־תִּדֹּר שַׁלֵּם׃ ד טוֹב אֲשֶׁר לֹא־תִדֹּר
מִשֶּׁתִּדּוֹר וְלֹא תְשַׁלֵּם׃ ה אַל־תִּתֵּן אֶת־פִּיךָ
לַחֲטִיא אֶת־בְּשָׂרֶךָ וְאַל־תֹּאמַר לִפְנֵי הַמַּלְאָךְ
כִּי שְׁגָגָה הִיא לָמָּה יִקְצֹף הָאֱלֹהִים עַל־קוֹלֶךָ
וְחִבֵּל אֶת־מַעֲשֵׂה יָדֶיךָ׃ ו כִּי בְרֹב חֲלֹמוֹת
וַהֲבָלִים וּדְבָרִים הַרְבֵּה כִּי אֶת־הָאֱלֹהִים יְרָא׃
ז אִם־עֹשֶׁק רָשׁ וְגֵזֶל מִשְׁפָּט וָצֶדֶק תִּרְאֶה
בַמְּדִינָה אַל־תִּתְמַהּ עַל־הַחֵפֶץ כִּי גָבֹהַּ מֵעַל
גָּבֹהַּ שֹׁמֵר וּגְבֹהִים עֲלֵיהֶם׃ ח וְיִתְרוֹן אֶרֶץ בַּכֹּל
הִיא (הוא קרי) מֶלֶךְ לְשָׂדֶה נֶעֱבָד׃ ט אֹהֵב כֶּסֶף
לֹא־יִשְׂבַּע כֶּסֶף וּמִי־אֹהֵב בֶּהָמוֹן לֹא תְבוּאָה
גַּם־זֶה הָבֶל׃ י בִּרְבוֹת הַטּוֹבָה רַבּוּ אוֹכְלֶיהָ
וּמַה־כִּשְׁרוֹן לִבְעָלֶיהָ כִּי אִם־רְאִית (ראות קרי)
עֵינָיו׃ יא מְתוּקָה שְׁנַת הָעֹבֵד אִם־מְעַט וְאִם־
הַרְבֵּה יֹאכֵל וְהַשָּׂבָע לֶעָשִׁיר אֵינֶנּוּ מַנִּיחַ לוֹ

sleep. 12. There is a grievous evil that I saw under the sun; riches kept by their owner for his harm. 13. And those riches are lost through an evil design, and he will beget a son who will have nothing in his hand. 14. As he left his mother's womb, naked shall he return to go as he came, and he will carry nothing with his toil, that he will take in his hand. 15. This too is a grievous evil, that just as he came so shall he go, and what advantage does he have that he toil for the wind? 16. Also all his days he eats in the dark, and he has much vexation and sickness and wrath. 17. Behold what I saw: it is good, yea it is beautiful to eat and to drink and to experience pleasure in all his toil that he toils under the sun, the number of the days of his life that God gave him, for that is his portion. 18. Also every man whom God has given riches and property and has given him power to eat thereof and to take his portion and to rejoice with his toil; this is a gift of God. 19. For let him remember that the days of his life are not many, for God testifies of the joy of his heart.

CHAPTER VI

1. There is an evil that I have seen under the sun, and it is prevalent among men. 2. A man whom God gives riches and property and honor, and his soul lacks nothing of all he desires, and God gives him no power to eat of it, but a strange man eats it; this is vanity and a grievous sickness. 3. Should a man beget one hundred [children] and live many years, and he will have much throughout the days of his years, and his soul will not be sated from all the good, neither did he have burial I said [that] the stillborn is better than he. 4. For he comes in vanity and goes in darkness, and in darkness his name is covered. 5. Moreover, he did not see the sun nor did he know [it]; this one has more gratification than that one. 6. And if he had lived a thousand years twice and experienced no pleasure, does not everything go to one place? 7. All of a person's toil is for his mouth, yet the appetite is not sated? 8. For what is the advantage of the wise over the fool? What [less] has the poor man who knows how to go along with the

לִישׁוֹן׃ יב יֵשׁ רָעָה חוֹלָה רָאִיתִי תַּחַת הַשָּׁמֶשׁ
עֹשֶׁר שָׁמוּר לִבְעָלָיו לְרָעָתוֹ׃ יג וְאָבַד הָעֹשֶׁר
הַהוּא בְּעִנְיַן רָע וְהוֹלִיד בֵּן וְאֵין בְּיָדוֹ מְאוּמָה׃
יד כַּאֲשֶׁר יָצָא מִבֶּטֶן אִמּוֹ עָרוֹם יָשׁוּב לָלֶכֶת
כְּשֶׁבָּא וּמְאוּמָה לֹא־יִשָּׂא בַעֲמָלוֹ שֶׁיֹּלֵךְ בְּיָדוֹ׃
טו וְגַם־זֹה רָעָה חוֹלָה כָּל־עֻמַּת שֶׁבָּא כֵּן יֵלֵךְ
וּמַה־יִּתְרוֹן לוֹ שֶׁיַּעֲמֹל לָרוּחַ׃ טז גַּם כָּל־יָמָיו
בַּחֹשֶׁךְ יֹאכֵל וְכָעַס הַרְבֵּה וְחָלְיוֹ וָקָצֶף׃ יז הִנֵּה
אֲשֶׁר־רָאִיתִי אָנִי טוֹב אֲשֶׁר־יָפֶה לֶאֱכוֹל
וְלִשְׁתּוֹת וְלִרְאוֹת טוֹבָה בְּכָל־עֲמָלוֹ ׀ שֶׁיַּעֲמֹל
תַּחַת־הַשֶּׁמֶשׁ מִסְפַּר יְמֵי־חַיָּו אֲשֶׁר־נָתַן־לוֹ
הָאֱלֹהִים כִּי־הוּא חֶלְקוֹ׃ יח גַּם כָּל־הָאָדָם אֲשֶׁר
נָתַן־לוֹ הָאֱלֹהִים עֹשֶׁר וּנְכָסִים וְהִשְׁלִיטוֹ לֶאֱכֹל
מִמֶּנּוּ וְלָשֵׂאת אֶת־חֶלְקוֹ וְלִשְׂמֹחַ בַּעֲמָלוֹ זֹה
מַתַּת אֱלֹהִים הִיא׃ יט כִּי לֹא הַרְבֵּה יִזְכֹּר אֶת־
יְמֵי חַיָּיו כִּי הָאֱלֹהִים מַעֲנֶה בְּשִׂמְחַת לִבּוֹ׃
ו א יֵשׁ רָעָה אֲשֶׁר רָאִיתִי תַּחַת הַשָּׁמֶשׁ וְרַבָּה
הִיא עַל־הָאָדָם׃ ב אִישׁ אֲשֶׁר יִתֶּן־לוֹ הָאֱלֹהִים
עֹשֶׁר וּנְכָסִים וְכָבוֹד וְאֵינֶנּוּ חָסֵר לְנַפְשׁוֹ ׀ מִכֹּל
אֲשֶׁר־יִתְאַוֶּה וְלֹא־יַשְׁלִיטֶנּוּ הָאֱלֹהִים לֶאֱכֹל
מִמֶּנּוּ כִּי אִישׁ נָכְרִי יֹאכְלֶנּוּ זֶה הֶבֶל וָחֳלִי רָע
הוּא׃ ג אִם־יוֹלִיד אִישׁ מֵאָה וְשָׁנִים רַבּוֹת
יִחְיֶה וְרַב ׀ שֶׁיִּהְיוּ יְמֵי־שָׁנָיו וְנַפְשׁוֹ לֹא־תִשְׂבַּע
מִן־הַטּוֹבָה וְגַם־קְבוּרָה לֹא־הָיְתָה לּוֹ אָמַרְתִּי
טוֹב מִמֶּנּוּ הַנָּפֶל׃ ד כִּי־בַהֶבֶל בָּא וּבַחֹשֶׁךְ יֵלֵךְ
וּבַחֹשֶׁךְ שְׁמוֹ יְכֻסֶּה׃ ה גַּם־שֶׁמֶשׁ לֹא־רָאָה וְלֹא
יָדָע נַחַת לָזֶה מִזֶּה׃ ו וְאִלּוּ חָיָה אֶלֶף שָׁנִים
פַּעֲמַיִם וְטוֹבָה לֹא רָאָה הֲלֹא אֶל־מָקוֹם אֶחָד
הַכֹּל הוֹלֵךְ׃ ז כָּל־עֲמַל הָאָדָם לְפִיהוּ וְגַם־
הַנֶּפֶשׁ לֹא תִמָּלֵא׃ ח כִּי מַה־יּוֹתֵר לֶחָכָם מִן־
הַכְּסִיל מַה־לֶּעָנִי יוֹדֵעַ לַהֲלֹךְ נֶגֶד הַחַיִּים׃

living? 9. It is better for him what he sees with his eyes than what goes to sate his appetite; this too is vanity and frustration. 10. What was, its name was already called, and it is known that he was a man, and he will not be able to judge with him that is stronger than he. 11. For there are many things that increase vanity; what advantage has a man? 12. For who knows what is good for a man in his lifetime, the number of the days of his life of vanity, that he do them like a shadow, for who will tell man what will be after him under the sun?

CHAPTER VII

1. A [good] name is better than good oil, and the day of death than the day of one's birth. 2. It is better to go to a house of mourning than to go to a house of feasting, for that is the end of every man, and the living shall lay it to his heart. 3. Vexation is better than laughter, for with a stern countenance the heart will rejoice. 4. The heart of the wise is in a house of mourning, whereas the heart of the fools is in a house of joy. 5. It is better to hear the rebuke of a wise man than for a man to hear the song of the fools. 6. For as the sound of the thorns under the pot, so is the laughter of the fool, and this too is vanity. 7. For the taunt makes the wise foolish, and it destroys the understanding which is a gift. 8. The end of a thing is better than its beginning; better a patient one than a haughty one. 9. Be not hasty with your spirit to become wroth, for wrath lies in the bosom of fools. 10. Do not say, "How was it that the former days were better than these?" For not out of wisdom have you asked concerning this. 11. Wisdom is good with a heritage, and it is a profit to those who see the sun. 12. For whoever is in the shade of wisdom is in the shade of money, and the advantage of knowledge is that the wisdom gives life to its possessor. 13. See God's work, for who can straighten out what He made crooked? 14. On a day of good fortune, be happy, and on a day of adversity, ponder: God has made one corresponding to the other, to the end that man will find nothing after Him. 15. I have seen everything in the days of my vanity; there is a righteous man who per-

ט טוֹב מַרְאֵה עֵינַיִם מֵהֲלָךְ־נָפֶשׁ גַּם־זֶה הֶבֶל וּרְעוּת רוּחַ: י מַה־שֶּׁהָיָה כְּבָר נִקְרָא שְׁמוֹ וְנוֹדָע אֲשֶׁר־הוּא אָדָם וְלֹא־יוּכַל לָדִין עִם שֶׁהַתַּקִּיף (שתקיף קרי) מִמֶּנּוּ: יא כִּי יֵשׁ־דְּבָרִים הַרְבֵּה מַרְבִּים הָבֶל מַה־יֹּתֵר לָאָדָם: יב כִּי מִי־יוֹדֵעַ מַה־טּוֹב לָאָדָם בַּחַיִּים מִסְפַּר יְמֵי־חַיֵּי הֶבְלוֹ וְיַעֲשֵׂם כַּצֵּל אֲשֶׁר מִי־יַגִּיד לָאָדָם מַה־יִּהְיֶה אַחֲרָיו תַּחַת הַשָּׁמֶשׁ: ס

ז א טוֹב שֵׁם מִשֶּׁמֶן טוֹב וְיוֹם הַמָּוֶת מִיּוֹם הִוָּלְדוֹ: ב טוֹב לָלֶכֶת אֶל־בֵּית־אֵבֶל מִלֶּכֶת אֶל־בֵּית מִשְׁתֶּה בַּאֲשֶׁר הוּא סוֹף כָּל־הָאָדָם וְהַחַי יִתֵּן אֶל־לִבּוֹ: ג טוֹב כַּעַס מִשְּׂחוֹק כִּי־בְרֹעַ פָּנִים יִיטַב לֵב: ד לֵב חֲכָמִים בְּבֵית אֵבֶל וְלֵב כְּסִילִים בְּבֵית שִׂמְחָה: ה טוֹב לִשְׁמֹעַ גַּעֲרַת חָכָם מֵאִישׁ שֹׁמֵעַ שִׁיר כְּסִילִים: ו כִּי כְקוֹל הַסִּירִים תַּחַת הַסִּיר כֵּן שְׂחֹק הַכְּסִיל וְגַם־זֶה הָבֶל: ז כִּי הָעֹשֶׁק יְהוֹלֵל חָכָם וִיאַבֵּד אֶת־לֵב מַתָּנָה: ח טוֹב אַחֲרִית דָּבָר מֵרֵאשִׁיתוֹ טוֹב אֶרֶךְ־רוּחַ מִגְּבַהּ רוּחַ: ט אַל־תְּבַהֵל בְּרוּחֲךָ לִכְעוֹס כִּי כַעַס בְּחֵיק כְּסִילִים יָנוּחַ: י אַל־תֹּאמַר מֶה הָיָה שֶׁהַיָּמִים הָרִאשֹׁנִים הָיוּ טוֹבִים מֵאֵלֶּה כִּי לֹא מֵחָכְמָה שָׁאַלְתָּ עַל־זֶה: יא טוֹבָה חָכְמָה עִם־נַחֲלָה וְיֹתֵר לְרֹאֵי הַשָּׁמֶשׁ: יב כִּי בְּצֵל הַחָכְמָה בְּצֵל הַכָּסֶף וְיִתְרוֹן דַּעַת הַחָכְמָה תְּחַיֶּה בְעָלֶיהָ: יג רְאֵה אֶת־מַעֲשֵׂה הָאֱלֹהִים כִּי מִי יוּכַל לְתַקֵּן אֵת אֲשֶׁר עִוְּתוֹ: יד בְּיוֹם טוֹבָה הֱיֵה בְטוֹב וּבְיוֹם רָעָה רְאֵה גַּם אֶת־זֶה לְעֻמַּת זֶה עָשָׂה הָאֱלֹהִים עַל־דִּבְרַת שֶׁלֹּא יִמְצָא הָאָדָם אַחֲרָיו מְאוּמָה: טו אֶת־הַכֹּל רָאִיתִי בִּימֵי הֶבְלִי

ishes in his righteousness, and there is a wicked man who lives long in his wickedness. 16. Be not overly righteous, and be not overly wise; why should you bring desolation upon yourself? 17. Be not overly alarmed, yet be not a fool; why should you die before your time? 18. It is good that you should take hold of this, and also from this you shall not withdraw your hand, for he who fears God will discharge himself of them all. 19. Wisdom affords strength to the wise more than ten rulers who were in the city. 20. For there is no righteous man on the earth who does good and sins not. 21. Also, take no heed of all the words that they speak, lest you hear your servant curse you. 22. For your heart knows that many times you too cursed others. 23. All this I tested with wisdom; I said, "I will become wise," but it was far from me. 24. That which was is far off, and it is very deep, who can find it? 25. I turned about with my heart to know and to search out and to seek wisdom and the reason of things, and to know the wickedness of folly and the folly of madness. 26. And I find more bitter than death the woman whose heart is snares and nets, her hands are bands; whoever is good in God's sight will escape from her, and a sinner will be taken by her. 27. See, this have I found, says Koheleth, adding one to another to find out the account. 28. Which my soul sought yet, but I did not find; one man out of a thousand I found, but a woman among all these I did not find. 29. See, only this I found, that God made man straight, but they sought many intrigues.

CHAPTER VIII

1. Who is like the wise man, and who knows the meaning of a thing? A man's wisdom makes his face shine, and the boldness of his face is changed. 2. I [admonish you]: observe the commandment of the king, and concerning the oath of God. 3. Hasten not to go away from before him; stay not in an evil thing, for all that he wishes, he will do. 4. Inasmuch as the king's word is the rule, and who will say to him, "What are you doing?" 5. Whoever keeps the commandment shall know no evil thing, and the heart of a wise man knows time and justice. 6. For every

יֵ֣שׁ צַדִּ֗יק אֹבֵד֙ בְּצִדְק֔וֹ וְיֵ֣שׁ רָשָׁ֔ע מַאֲרִ֖יךְ
בְּרָעָתֽוֹ׃ טז אַל־תְּהִ֤י צַדִּיק֙ הַרְבֵּ֔ה וְאַל־תִּתְחַכַּ֖ם
יוֹתֵ֑ר לָ֖מָּה תִּשּׁוֹמֵֽם׃ יז אַל־תִּרְשַׁ֥ע הַרְבֵּ֖ה וְאַל־
תְּהִ֣י סָכָ֑ל לָ֥מָּה תָמ֖וּת בְּלֹ֥א עִתֶּֽךָ׃ יח ט֚וֹב אֲשֶׁ֣ר
תֶּאֱחֹ֣ז בָּזֶ֔ה וְגַם־מִזֶּ֖ה אַל־תַּנַּ֣ח אֶת־יָדֶ֑ךָ כִּֽי־יְרֵ֥א
אֱלֹהִ֖ים יֵצֵ֥א אֶת־כֻּלָּֽם׃ יט הַֽחָכְמָ֖ה תָּעֹ֣ז לֶחָכָ֑ם
מֵֽעֲשָׂרָה֙ שַׁלִּיטִ֔ים אֲשֶׁ֥ר הָי֖וּ בָּעִֽיר׃ כ כִּ֣י אָדָ֔ם
אֵ֥ין צַדִּ֖יק בָּאָ֑רֶץ אֲשֶׁ֥ר יַעֲשֶׂה־טּ֖וֹב וְלֹ֥א יֶחֱטָֽא׃
כא גַּ֤ם לְכָל־הַדְּבָרִים֙ אֲשֶׁ֣ר יְדַבֵּ֔רוּ אַל־תִּתֵּ֖ן לִבֶּ֑ךָ
אֲשֶׁ֛ר לֹֽא־תִשְׁמַ֥ע אֶֽת־עַבְדְּךָ֖ מְקַלְלֶֽךָ׃ כב כִּ֛י גַּם־
פְּעָמִ֥ים רַבּ֖וֹת יָדַ֣ע לִבֶּ֑ךָ אֲשֶׁ֥ר גַּם־אַ֖תְּ (אתה קרי)
קִלַּ֥לְתָּ אֲחֵרִֽים׃ כג כָּל־זֹ֖ה נִסִּ֣יתִי בַֽחָכְמָ֑ה
אָמַ֣רְתִּי אֶחְכָּ֔מָה וְהִ֖יא רְחוֹקָ֥ה מִמֶּֽנִּי׃ כד רָח֖וֹק
מַה־שֶּֽׁהָיָ֑ה וְעָמֹ֥ק ׀ עָמֹ֖ק מִ֥י יִמְצָאֶֽנּוּ׃ כה סַבּ֨וֹתִי
אֲנִ֤י וְלִבִּי֙ לָדַ֣עַת וְלָת֔וּר וּבַקֵּ֥שׁ חָכְמָ֖ה וְחֶשְׁבּ֑וֹן
וְלָדַ֙עַת֙ רֶ֣שַׁע כֶּ֔סֶל וְהַסִּכְל֖וּת הוֹלֵלֽוֹת׃
כו וּמוֹצֶ֨א אֲנִ֜י מַ֣ר מִמָּ֗וֶת אֶת־הָֽאִשָּׁה֙ אֲשֶׁר־
הִ֛יא מְצוֹדִ֥ים וַחֲרָמִ֖ים לִבָּ֑הּ אֲסוּרִ֣ים יָדֶ֔יהָ ט֞וֹב
לִפְנֵ֤י הָֽאֱלֹהִים֙ יִמָּלֵ֣ט מִמֶּ֔נָּה וְחוֹטֵ֖א יִלָּ֥כֶד בָּֽהּ׃
כז רְאֵה֙ זֶ֣ה מָצָ֔אתִי אָמְרָ֖ה קֹהֶ֑לֶת אַחַ֥ת לְאַחַ֖ת
לִמְצֹ֥א חֶשְׁבּֽוֹן׃ כח אֲשֶׁ֛ר עוֹד־בִּקְשָׁ֥ה נַפְשִׁ֖י וְלֹ֣א
מָצָ֑אתִי אָדָ֞ם אֶחָ֤ד מֵאֶ֙לֶף֙ מָצָ֔אתִי וְאִשָּׁ֥ה בְכָל־
אֵ֖לֶּה לֹ֥א מָצָֽאתִי׃ כט לְבַד֙ רְאֵה־זֶ֣ה מָצָ֔אתִי
אֲשֶׁ֨ר עָשָׂ֧ה הָאֱלֹהִ֛ים אֶת־הָאָדָ֖ם יָשָׁ֑ר וְהֵ֥מָּה
בִקְשׁ֖וּ חִשְּׁבֹנ֥וֹת רַבִּֽים׃

ח א מִ֚י כְּהֶ֣חָכָ֔ם וּמִ֥י יוֹדֵ֖עַ פֵּ֣שֶׁר דָּבָ֑ר חָכְמַ֤ת
אָדָם֙ תָּאִ֣יר פָּנָ֔יו וְעֹ֥ז פָּנָ֖יו יְשֻׁנֶּֽא׃ ב אֲנִי֙ פִּי־
מֶ֣לֶךְ שְׁמֹ֔ר וְעַ֕ל דִּבְרַ֖ת שְׁבוּעַ֥ת אֱלֹהִֽים׃ ג אַל־
תִּבָּהֵ֤ל מִפָּנָיו֙ תֵּלֵ֔ךְ אַל־תַּעֲמֹ֖ד בְּדָבָ֣ר רָ֑ע כִּ֛י כָּל־
אֲשֶׁ֥ר יַחְפֹּ֖ץ יַעֲשֶֽׂה׃ ד בַּאֲשֶׁ֥ר דְּבַר־מֶ֖לֶךְ שִׁלְט֑וֹן
וּמִ֥י יֹֽאמַר־ל֖וֹ מַה־תַּעֲשֶֽׂה׃ ה שׁוֹמֵ֣ר מִצְוָ֔ה לֹ֥א
יֵדַ֖ע דָּבָ֣ר רָ֑ע וְעֵ֣ת וּמִשְׁפָּ֔ט יֵדַ֖ע לֵ֥ב חָכָֽם׃ ו כִּ֛י

matter has time and judgment, for the evil of man is great upon him. 7. For he knows not what will be, for how it will be, who will tell him? 8. No man controls the will [of God's messenger] to retain the spirit, and there is no ruling on the day of death; neither is there discharge in war, nor will wickedness save the one who practices it. 9. I saw all this, and I laid my heart to all the work that is done under the sun, a time that a man ruled over [another] man for his [own] harm. 10. And so I saw the wicked buried, and they came [in the person of their children], and [those] from the place of the Holy One will go away, and they will be forgotten in the city that they dealt justly; this too is vanity. 11. Since the sentence of the deed of evil is not executed swiftly; therefore, the heart of the children of men is encouraged to do evil. 12. For a sinner does evil a hundred [times], and He grants him an extension; for I know too that it will be good for those who fear God because they fear Him. 13. But it will not be well for the wicked, and he will not prolong [his] days, like a shadow, because he does not fear before God. 14. There is vanity that is done on the earth, that there are righteous men to whom it happens according to the deed of the wicked, and there are wicked men to whom it happens according to the deed of the righteous; I said that this too is vanity. 15. And I praised joy, for there is nothing better for man under the sun than to eat and to drink and to be merry, and that will accompany him in his toil the days of his life that God gave him under the sun. 16. When I applied my heart to know wisdom and to see the conduct that is done upon the earth, for neither by day nor by night does it see sleep with its eyes. 17. And I saw all the deed of God, for a person will not be able to find the deed that is done under the sun, because though a man toils to find, he will not find [it], and even if the wise man claims to know [it], he will be unable to find [it].

CHAPTER IX

1. For all this I laid to my heart and to clarify all this, that the righteous and the wise and their works are in God's hand;

לְכָל־חֵ֔פֶץ יֵ֖שׁ עֵ֣ת וּמִשְׁפָּ֑ט כִּֽי־רָעַ֥ת הָאָדָ֖ם רַבָּ֥ה
עָלָֽיו׃ ז כִּֽי־אֵינֶ֥נּוּ יֹדֵ֖עַ מַה־שֶּׁיִּֽהְיֶ֑ה כִּ֚י כַּאֲשֶׁ֣ר
יִֽהְיֶ֔ה מִ֖י יַגִּ֥יד לֽוֹ׃ ח אֵ֣ין אָדָ֞ם שַׁלִּ֤יט בָּר֙וּחַ֙
לִכְל֣וֹא אֶת־הָר֔וּחַ וְאֵ֤ין שִׁלְטוֹן֙ בְּי֣וֹם הַמָּ֔וֶת וְאֵ֥ין
מִשְׁלַ֖חַת בַּמִּלְחָמָ֑ה וְלֹֽא־יְמַלֵּ֥ט רֶ֖שַׁע אֶת־
בְּעָלָֽיו׃ ט אֶת־כָּל־זֶ֣ה רָאִ֔יתִי וְנָת֣וֹן אֶת־לִבִּ֔י
לְכָל־מַעֲשֶׂ֔ה אֲשֶׁ֥ר נַעֲשָׂ֖ה תַּ֣חַת הַשָּׁ֑מֶשׁ עֵ֗ת
אֲשֶׁ֨ר שָׁלַ֧ט הָאָדָ֛ם בְּאָדָ֖ם לְרַ֥ע לֽוֹ׃ י וּבְכֵ֡ן
רָאִיתִי֩ רְשָׁעִ֨ים קְבֻרִ֜ים וָבָ֗אוּ וּמִמְּק֤וֹם קָדוֹשׁ֙
יְהַלֵּ֔כוּ וְיִֽשְׁתַּכְּח֥וּ בָעִ֖יר אֲשֶׁ֣ר כֵּן־עָשׂ֑וּ גַּם־זֶ֖ה
הָֽבֶל׃ יא אֲשֶׁר֙ אֵין־נַעֲשָׂ֣ה פִתְגָ֔ם מַעֲשֵׂ֥ה הָרָעָ֖ה
מְהֵרָ֑ה עַל־כֵּ֡ן מָלֵ֞א לֵ֧ב בְּנֵֽי־הָאָדָ֛ם בָּהֶ֖ם לַעֲשׂ֥וֹת
רָֽע׃ יב אֲשֶׁ֣ר חֹטֶ֗א עֹשֶׂ֥ה רָ֛ע מְאַ֖ת וּמַאֲרִ֣יךְ ל֑וֹ
כִּ֚י גַּם־יוֹדֵ֣עַ אָ֔נִי אֲשֶׁ֤ר יִֽהְיֶה־טּוֹב֙ לְיִרְאֵ֣י
הָֽאֱלֹהִ֔ים אֲשֶׁ֥ר יִֽירְא֖וּ מִלְּפָנָֽיו׃ יג וְטוֹב֙ לֹא־
יִהְיֶ֣ה לָֽרָשָׁ֔ע וְלֹא־יַאֲרִ֥יךְ יָמִ֖ים כַּצֵּ֑ל אֲשֶׁ֛ר אֵינֶ֥נּוּ
יָרֵ֖א מִלִּפְנֵ֥י אֱלֹהִֽים׃ יד יֶשׁ־הֶ֘בֶל֮ אֲשֶׁ֣ר נַעֲשָׂ֣ה
עַל־הָאָרֶץ֒ אֲשֶׁ֣ר ׀ יֵ֣שׁ צַדִּיקִ֗ים אֲשֶׁ֨ר מַגִּ֤יעַ
אֲלֵהֶם֙ כְּמַעֲשֵׂ֣ה הָרְשָׁעִ֔ים וְיֵ֣שׁ רְשָׁעִ֔ים שֶׁמַּגִּ֥יעַ
אֲלֵהֶ֖ם כְּמַעֲשֵׂ֣ה הַצַּדִּיקִ֑ים אָמַ֕רְתִּי שֶׁגַּם־זֶ֖ה
הָֽבֶל׃ טו וְשִׁבַּ֤חְתִּֽי אֲנִי֙ אֶת־הַשִּׂמְחָ֔ה אֲשֶׁ֨ר אֵין־
ט֤וֹב לָֽאָדָם֙ תַּ֣חַת הַשֶּׁ֔מֶשׁ כִּ֛י אִם־לֶאֱכֹ֥ל
וְלִשְׁתּ֖וֹת וְלִשְׂמ֑וֹחַ וְהוּא֙ יִלְוֶ֣נּוּ בַעֲמָל֔וֹ יְמֵ֥י חַיָּ֛יו
אֲשֶׁר־נָֽתַן־ל֥וֹ הָאֱלֹהִ֖ים תַּ֥חַת הַשָּֽׁמֶשׁ׃ טז כַּאֲשֶׁ֨ר
נָתַ֤תִּי אֶת־לִבִּי֙ לָדַ֣עַת חָכְמָ֔ה וְלִרְאוֹת֙ אֶת־הָ֣עִנְיָ֔ן
אֲשֶׁ֥ר נַעֲשָׂ֖ה עַל־הָאָ֑רֶץ כִּ֣י גַ֤ם בַּיּוֹם֙ וּבַלַּ֔יְלָה
שֵׁנָ֕ה בְּעֵינָ֖יו אֵינֶ֥נּוּ רֹאֶֽה׃ יז וְרָאִיתִי֮ אֶת־כָּל־
מַעֲשֵׂ֣ה הָאֱלֹהִים֒ כִּי֩ לֹ֨א יוּכַ֜ל הָאָדָ֗ם לִמְצוֹא֙
אֶת־הַֽמַּעֲשֶׂה֙ אֲשֶׁ֣ר נַעֲשָׂ֣ה תַֽחַת־הַשֶּׁ֔מֶשׁ בְּשֶׁ֡ל
אֲשֶׁ֨ר יַעֲמֹ֧ל הָאָדָ֛ם לְבַקֵּ֖שׁ וְלֹ֣א יִמְצָ֑א וְגַ֨ם אִם־
יֹאמַ֤ר הֶֽחָכָם֙ לָדַ֔עַת לֹ֥א יוּכַ֖ל לִמְצֹֽא׃
ט א כִּ֣י אֶת־כָּל־זֶ֞ה נָתַ֣תִּי אֶל־לִבִּ֗י וְלָב֤וּר אֶת־
כָּל־זֶ֔ה אֲשֶׁ֨ר הַצַּדִּיקִ֧ים וְהַחֲכָמִ֛ים וַעֲבָדֵיהֶ֖ם בְּיַ֣ד

even love, even hate, man does not know; everything is before them. 2. Everything [comes to them] as [it comes] to all; [there is] one occurrence for the righteous and for the wicked, for the good, and for the pure, and for the unclean, and for him who sacrifices and for him who does not sacrifice; like the good, so is the sinner; he who swears is like him who fears an oath. 3. This is the most evil in all that is done under the sun, that all have one occurrence, and also the heart of the children of men is full of evil, and there is madness in their heart in their lifetime, and after that they go to the dead. 4. Because for anyone who is joined to all the living there is hope, for a live dog is better than a dead lion. 5. For the living know that they will die, but the dead know nothing, and they have no more reward, for their remembrance is forgotten. 6. Also their love, as well as their hate, as well as their envy has already been lost, and they have no more share forever in all that is done under the sun. 7. Go, eat your bread joyfully and drink your wine with a merry heart, for God has already accepted your deeds. 8. At all times, let your garments be white, and let oil not be wanting on your head. 9. Enjoy life with the wife you love all the days of the life of your vanity, that He gave you under the sun all the days of your vanity, for that is your portion in life and in your toil that you toil under the sun. 10. Whatever your hand attains to do [as long as you are] with your strength, do; for there is neither deed nor reckoning, neither knowledge nor wisdom in the grave where you are going. 11. I returned and saw under the sun, that the race does not belong to the swift, nor the war to the mighty; neither do the wise have bread, nor do the understanding have riches, nor the knowledgeable, favor, for time and fate will overtake them all. 12. For a person does not even know his time, like the fish that are caught in an evil net, and like the birds that are caught in the snare; like them, the children of men are trapped at the time of evil, when it falls upon them suddenly. 13. This also have I seen as wisdom under the sun, and it seemed great to me. 14. [There was] a small city, with few people in it, and a great

הָאֱלֹהִים גַּם־אַהֲבָה גַם־שִׂנְאָה אֵין יוֹדֵעַ הָאָדָם
הַכֹּל לִפְנֵיהֶם: ב הַכֹּל כַּאֲשֶׁר לַכֹּל מִקְרֶה אֶחָד
לַצַּדִּיק וְלָרָשָׁע לַטּוֹב וְלַטָּהוֹר וְלַטָּמֵא וְלַזֹּבֵחַ
וְלַאֲשֶׁר אֵינֶנּוּ זֹבֵחַ כַּטּוֹב כַּחֹטֶא הַנִּשְׁבָּע כַּאֲשֶׁר
שְׁבוּעָה יָרֵא: ג זֶה ׀ רָע בְּכֹל אֲשֶׁר־נַעֲשָׂה תַּחַת
הַשֶּׁמֶשׁ כִּי־מִקְרֶה אֶחָד לַכֹּל וְגַם לֵב בְּנֵי־הָאָדָם
מָלֵא־רָע וְהוֹלֵלוֹת בִּלְבָבָם בְּחַיֵּיהֶם וְאַחֲרָיו
אֶל־הַמֵּתִים: ד כִּי־מִי אֲשֶׁר יְבֻחַר (יחבר קרי) אֶל
כָּל־הַחַיִּים יֵשׁ בִּטָּחוֹן כִּי־לְכֶלֶב חַי הוּא טוֹב
מִן־הָאַרְיֵה הַמֵּת: ה כִּי הַחַיִּים יוֹדְעִים שֶׁיָּמֻתוּ
וְהַמֵּתִים אֵינָם יוֹדְעִים מְאוּמָה וְאֵין־עוֹד לָהֶם
שָׂכָר כִּי נִשְׁכַּח זִכְרָם: ו גַּם אַהֲבָתָם גַּם־
שִׂנְאָתָם גַּם־קִנְאָתָם כְּבָר אָבָדָה וְחֵלֶק אֵין־לָהֶם
עוֹד לְעוֹלָם בְּכֹל אֲשֶׁר־נַעֲשָׂה תַּחַת הַשָּׁמֶשׁ:
ז לֵךְ אֱכֹל בְּשִׂמְחָה לַחְמֶךָ וּשֲׁתֵה בְלֶב־טוֹב
יֵינֶךָ כִּי כְבָר רָצָה הָאֱלֹהִים אֶת־מַעֲשֶׂיךָ:
ח בְּכָל־עֵת יִהְיוּ בְגָדֶיךָ לְבָנִים וְשֶׁמֶן עַל־
רֹאשְׁךָ אַל־יֶחְסָר: ט רְאֵה חַיִּים עִם־אִשָּׁה
אֲשֶׁר־אָהַבְתָּ כָּל־יְמֵי חַיֵּי הֶבְלֶךָ אֲשֶׁר נָתַן־לְךָ
תַּחַת הַשֶּׁמֶשׁ כֹּל יְמֵי הֶבְלֶךָ כִּי הוּא חֶלְקְךָ
בַּחַיִּים וּבַעֲמָלְךָ אֲשֶׁר־אַתָּה עָמֵל תַּחַת הַשָּׁמֶשׁ:
י כֹּל אֲשֶׁר תִּמְצָא יָדְךָ לַעֲשׂוֹת בְּכֹחֲךָ עֲשֵׂה כִּי
אֵין מַעֲשֶׂה וְחֶשְׁבּוֹן וְדַעַת וְחָכְמָה בִּשְׁאוֹל אֲשֶׁר
אַתָּה הֹלֵךְ שָׁמָּה: יא שַׁבְתִּי וְרָאֹה תַחַת־הַשֶּׁמֶשׁ
כִּי לֹא לַקַּלִּים הַמֵּרוֹץ וְלֹא לַגִּבּוֹרִים הַמִּלְחָמָה
וְגַם לֹא לַחֲכָמִים לֶחֶם וְגַם לֹא לַנְּבֹנִים עֹשֶׁר
וְגַם לֹא לַיֹּדְעִים חֵן כִּי־עֵת וָפֶגַע יִקְרֶה אֶת־
כֻּלָּם: יב כִּי גַּם לֹא־יֵדַע הָאָדָם אֶת־עִתּוֹ כַּדָּגִים
שֶׁנֶּאֱחָזִים בִּמְצוֹדָה רָעָה וְכַצִּפֳּרִים הָאֲחֻזוֹת
בַּפָּח כָּהֵם יוּקָשִׁים בְּנֵי הָאָדָם לְעֵת רָעָה
כְּשֶׁתִּפּוֹל עֲלֵיהֶם פִּתְאֹם: יג גַּם־זֹה רָאִיתִי
חָכְמָה תַּחַת הַשָּׁמֶשׁ וּגְדוֹלָה הִיא אֵלָי: יד עִיר
קְטַנָּה וַאֲנָשִׁים בָּהּ מְעָט וּבָא־אֵלֶיהָ מֶלֶךְ גָּדוֹל

and surrounded it and built against it great bulwarks. 15. And there was found therein a poor wise man, and he extricated the city through his wisdom, but no man remembered that poor man. 16. And I said, "Wisdom is better than might, but the wisdom of the poor man is despised, and his words are not heard." 17. The words of the wise are heard [when spoken] softly, more than the shout of a ruler over fools. 18. Wisdom is better than weapons, and one sinner destroys much good.

CHAPTER X

1. Dying flies make putrid the oil of a perfumer; so does a little folly outweigh wisdom and honor. 2. The heart of the wise man is at his right, whereas the heart of a fool is at his left. 3. Also on the road, when a fool walks, his understanding is lacking, and he says to all that he is a fool. 4. If the spirit of the ruler rises up against you, do not leave your place, for gentleness assuages great sins. 5. There is an evil that I saw under the sun, like an error that goes forth from before the ruler. 6. Folly was set at great heights, and the rich sit in a low place. 7. I saw slaves on horses and princes walking like slaves on the ground. 8. Whoever digs a pit shall fall therein, and whoever breaks a fence — a snake will bite him. 9. He who quarries stones shall be hurt by them; who hews wood will be endangered by it. 10. If the iron is dull, and he did not sharpen the edge, he must strengthen the armies, but wisdom has a greater advantage. 11. If the snake bites because he was not charmed, so is there no advantage to one who can speak. 12. The words of a wise man's mouth are gracious, and a fool's lips will destroy him. 13. The beginning of the words of his mouth is foolishness, and the end of his speech is grievous madness. 14. And the fool increases words, a man does not know what will be, and what will be after him, who will tell him? 15. The toil of the fools wearies him, for he does not know to go to the city. 16. Woe to you, O land that your king is a boy, and your princes eat in the morning. 17. Fortunate are you, that your king is a son of nobles, and your princes eat at the

וְסָבַ֣ב אֹתָ֔הּ וּבָנָ֣ה עָלֶ֔יהָ מְצוֹדִ֖ים גְּדֹלִֽים׃
טו וּמָ֣צָא בָ֗הּ אִ֤ישׁ מִסְכֵּן֙ חָכָ֔ם וּמִלַּט־ה֥וּא אֶת־
הָעִ֖יר בְּחָכְמָת֑וֹ וְאָדָם֙ לֹ֣א זָכַ֔ר אֶת־הָאִ֥ישׁ
הַמִּסְכֵּ֖ן הַהֽוּא׃ טז וְאָמַ֣רְתִּי אָ֔נִי טוֹבָ֥ה חָכְמָ֖ה
מִגְּבוּרָ֑ה וְחָכְמַ֤ת הַמִּסְכֵּן֙ בְּזוּיָ֔ה וּדְבָרָ֖יו אֵינָ֥ם
נִשְׁמָעִֽים׃ יז דִּבְרֵ֣י חֲכָמִ֔ים בְּנַ֖חַת נִשְׁמָעִ֑ים
מִזַּֽעֲקַ֥ת מוֹשֵׁ֖ל בַּכְּסִילִֽים׃ יח טוֹבָ֥ה חָכְמָ֖ה
מִכְּלֵ֣י קְרָ֑ב וְחוֹטֶ֣א אֶחָ֔ד יְאַבֵּ֖ד טוֹבָ֥ה הַרְבֵּֽה׃
י א זְב֣וּבֵי מָ֔וֶת יַבְאִ֥ישׁ יַבִּ֖יעַ שֶׁ֣מֶן רוֹקֵ֑חַ יָקָ֛ר
מֵחָכְמָ֥ה מִכָּב֖וֹד סִכְל֥וּת מְעָֽט׃ ב לֵ֤ב חָכָם֙
לִֽימִינ֔וֹ וְלֵ֥ב כְּסִ֖יל לִשְׂמֹאלֽוֹ׃ ג וְגַם־בַּדֶּ֛רֶךְ
כְּשֶׁהַסָּכָ֥ל (כשסכל קרי) הֹלֵ֖ךְ לִבּ֣וֹ חָסֵ֑ר וְאָמַ֥ר לַכֹּ֖ל
סָכָ֥ל הֽוּא׃ ד אִם־ר֤וּחַ הַמּוֹשֵׁל֙ תַּעֲלֶ֣ה עָלֶ֔יךָ
מְקוֹמְךָ֖ אַל־תַּנַּ֑ח כִּ֚י מַרְפֵּ֔א יַנִּ֖יחַ חֲטָאִ֥ים
גְּדוֹלִֽים׃ ה יֵ֣שׁ רָעָ֔ה רָאִ֖יתִי תַּ֣חַת הַשָּׁ֑מֶשׁ
כִּשְׁגָגָ֕ה שֶׁיֹּצָ֖א מִלִּפְנֵ֥י הַשַּׁלִּֽיט׃ ו נִתַּ֣ן הַסֶּ֔כֶל
בַּמְּרוֹמִ֖ים רַבִּ֑ים וַעֲשִׁירִ֖ים בַּשֵּׁ֥פֶל יֵשֵֽׁבוּ׃
ז רָאִ֥יתִי עֲבָדִ֖ים עַל־סוּסִ֑ים וְשָׂרִ֛ים הֹלְכִ֥ים
כַּעֲבָדִ֖ים עַל־הָאָֽרֶץ׃ ח חֹפֵ֥ר גּוּמָּ֖ץ בּ֣וֹ יִפּ֑וֹל
וּפֹרֵ֥ץ גָּדֵ֖ר יִשְּׁכֶ֥נּוּ נָחָֽשׁ׃ ט מַסִּ֣יעַ אֲבָנִ֔ים יֵעָצֵ֖ב
בָּהֶ֑ם בּוֹקֵ֥עַ עֵצִ֖ים יִסָּ֥כֶן בָּֽם׃ י אִם־קֵהָ֣ה הַבַּרְזֶ֔ל
וְהוּא֙ לֹא־פָנִ֣ים קִלְקַ֔ל וַחֲיָלִ֖ים יְגַבֵּ֑ר וְיִתְר֥וֹן
הַכְשֵׁ֖יר חָכְמָֽה׃ יא אִם־יִשֹּׁ֥ךְ הַנָּחָ֖שׁ בְּלוֹא־לָ֑חַשׁ
וְאֵ֣ין יִתְר֔וֹן לְבַ֖עַל הַלָּשֽׁוֹן׃ יב דִּבְרֵ֥י פִי־חָכָ֖ם חֵ֑ן
וְשִׂפְת֥וֹת כְּסִ֖יל תְּבַלְּעֶֽנּוּ׃ יג תְּחִלַּ֥ת דִּבְרֵי־פִ֖יהוּ
סִכְל֑וּת וְאַחֲרִ֣ית פִּ֔יהוּ הוֹלֵל֖וּת רָעָֽה׃ יד וְהַסָּכָ֖ל
יַרְבֶּ֣ה דְבָרִ֑ים לֹא־יֵדַ֤ע הָאָדָם֙ מַה־שֶׁיִּֽהְיֶ֔ה וַאֲשֶׁ֣ר
יִהְיֶה֙ מֵאַחֲרָ֔יו מִ֖י יַגִּ֥יד לֽוֹ׃ טו עֲמַ֥ל הַכְּסִילִ֖ים
תְּיַגְּעֶ֑נּוּ אֲשֶׁ֛ר לֹֽא־יָדַ֖ע לָלֶ֥כֶת אֶל־עִֽיר׃ טז אִֽי־
לָ֣ךְ אֶ֔רֶץ שֶׁמַּלְכֵּ֖ךְ נָ֑עַר וְשָׂרַ֖יִךְ בַּבֹּ֥קֶר יֹאכֵֽלוּ׃
יז אַשְׁרֵ֣יךְ אֶ֔רֶץ שֶׁמַּלְכֵּ֖ךְ בֶּן־חוֹרִ֑ים וְשָׂרַ֙יִךְ֙ בָּעֵ֣ת

proper time, with strength and not with drunkenness. 18. Through laziness the rafter sinks, and with idleness of the hands the house leaks. 19. On joyous occasions, we make a feast, and wine gladdens the healthy, and money answers everything. 20. Even in your thought, do not curse a king, nor in your bedroom shall you curse a wealthy man, for the fowl of the heaven carries the voice, and the winged creature will tell the word.

CHAPTER XI

1. Cast your bread upon the face of the water, for after many days you will find it. 2. Give a portion to seven and even to eight, for you do not know what evil will be on the earth. 3. If the clouds are full of rain, they will empty it upon the earth, and if a tree fall in the south or in the north, the place where the tree falls, there it will be. 4. He who waits for the wind will not sow, and he who looks at the clouds will not reap. 5. Just as you do not know what is the way of the wind, as bones in the womb of the pregnant woman, so you will not know God's work, Who does everything. 6. In the morning, sow your seed, and in the evening, do not withhold your hand, for you know not which one will succeed, this one or that one, or whether both of them will be equally good. 7. And the light is sweet, and it is good for the eyes to see the sun. 8. For, if a man lives many years, let him rejoice in them all, and let him remember the days of darkness, for they will be many; all that befalls [him] is vanity. 9. Rejoice, O youth, in your childhood, and let your heart bring you cheer in the days of your youth, and go in the ways of your heart, and in the sight of your eyes, but know that for all these God will bring you to judgment. 10. And remove anger from your heart, and take evil away from your flesh, for childhood and youth are vanity.

CHAPTER XII

1. And remember your Creator in the days of your youth, before the days of evil come, and years arrive, about which you will say, "I have no desire in them." 2. Before the sun and the light and the moon and the stars

יֹאכֵלוּ בִּגְבוּרָה וְלֹא בַשְּׁתִי: יח בַּעֲצַלְתַּיִם יִמַּךְ
הַמְּקָרֶה וּבְשִׁפְלוּת יָדַיִם יִדְלֹף הַבָּיִת:
יט לִשְׂחוֹק עֹשִׂים לֶחֶם וְיַיִן יְשַׂמַּח חַיִּים
וְהַכֶּסֶף יַעֲנֶה אֶת־הַכֹּל: כ גַּם בְּמַדָּעֲךָ מֶלֶךְ אַל־
תְּקַלֵּל וּבְחַדְרֵי מִשְׁכָּבְךָ אַל־תְּקַלֵּל עָשִׁיר כִּי
עוֹף הַשָּׁמַיִם יוֹלִיךְ אֶת־הַקּוֹל וּבַעַל הַכְּנָפַיִם
(כנפים קרי) יַגֵּיד דָּבָר:

יא א שַׁלַּח לַחְמְךָ עַל־פְּנֵי הַמָּיִם כִּי־בְרֹב
הַיָּמִים תִּמְצָאֶנּוּ: ב תֶּן־חֵלֶק לְשִׁבְעָה וְגַם
לִשְׁמוֹנָה כִּי לֹא תֵדַע מַה־יִּהְיֶה רָעָה עַל־
הָאָרֶץ: ג אִם־יִמָּלְאוּ הֶעָבִים גֶּשֶׁם עַל־הָאָרֶץ
יָרִיקוּ וְאִם־יִפּוֹל עֵץ בַּדָּרוֹם וְאִם בַּצָּפוֹן מְקוֹם
שֶׁיִּפּוֹל הָעֵץ שָׁם יְהוּא: ד שֹׁמֵר רוּחַ לֹא יִזְרָע
וְרֹאֶה בֶעָבִים לֹא יִקְצוֹר: ה כַּאֲשֶׁר אֵינְךָ יוֹדֵעַ
מַה־דֶּרֶךְ הָרוּחַ כַּעֲצָמִים בְּבֶטֶן הַמְּלֵאָה כָּכָה
לֹא תֵדַע אֶת־מַעֲשֵׂה הָאֱלֹהִים אֲשֶׁר יַעֲשֶׂה אֶת־
הַכֹּל: ו בַּבֹּקֶר זְרַע אֶת־זַרְעֶךָ וְלָעֶרֶב אַל־תַּנַּח
יָדֶךָ כִּי אֵינְךָ יוֹדֵעַ אֵי זֶה יִכְשַׁר הֲזֶה אוֹ־זֶה
וְאִם־שְׁנֵיהֶם כְּאֶחָד טוֹבִים: ז וּמָתוֹק הָאוֹר
וְטוֹב לַעֵינַיִם לִרְאוֹת אֶת־הַשָּׁמֶשׁ: ח כִּי אִם־
שָׁנִים הַרְבֵּה יִחְיֶה הָאָדָם בְּכֻלָּם יִשְׂמָח וְיִזְכֹּר
אֶת־יְמֵי הַחֹשֶׁךְ כִּי־הַרְבֵּה יִהְיוּ כָּל־שֶׁבָּא הָבֶל:
ט שְׂמַח בָּחוּר בְּיַלְדוּתֶךָ וִיטִיבְךָ לִבְּךָ בִּימֵי
בְחוּרוֹתֶיךָ וְהַלֵּךְ בְּדַרְכֵי לִבְּךָ וּבְמַרְאֵי (ובמראה
קרי) עֵינֶיךָ וְדָע כִּי עַל־כָּל־אֵלֶּה יְבִיאֲךָ
הָאֱלֹהִים בַּמִּשְׁפָּט: י וְהָסֵר כַּעַס מִלִּבֶּךָ וְהַעֲבֵר
רָעָה מִבְּשָׂרֶךָ כִּי־הַיַּלְדוּת וְהַשַּׁחֲרוּת הָבֶל:

יב א וּזְכֹר אֶת־בּוֹרְאֶיךָ בִּימֵי בְּחוּרֹתֶיךָ עַד
אֲשֶׁר לֹא־יָבֹאוּ יְמֵי הָרָעָה וְהִגִּיעוּ שָׁנִים אֲשֶׁר
תֹּאמַר אֵין־לִי בָהֶם חֵפֶץ: ב עַד אֲשֶׁר לֹא־
תֶחְשַׁךְ הַשֶּׁמֶשׁ וְהָאוֹר וְהַיָּרֵחַ וְהַכּוֹכָבִים וְשָׁבוּ

darken, and the clouds return after the rain.
3. On the day that the keepers of the
house shall tremble, and the mighty men
shall stoop, and the grinders cease since
they have become few, and those who look
out of the windows shall become darkened.
4. And the doors shall be shut in the
street when the sound of the mill is low, and
one shall rise at the voice of a bird, and all
the songsters shall be brought low.
5. Also from the high places they will
fear, and terrors on the road; and the
almond tree shall blossom, and the grass-
hopper shall drag himself along, and the
sexual desire will fail, for man goes to his
everlasting home, and the mourners go
about in the street. 6. Before the silver
cord snaps, and the golden bowl is shattered, and the pitcher breaks at the fountain, and the wheel falls shattered into the
pit. 7. And the dust returns to the earth
as it was, and the spirit returns to God, Who
gave it. 8. "Vanity of vanities," said
Koheleth, "all is vanity." 9. And more
than Koheleth was wise, he also taught
knowledge to the people; he listened and
sought out, he established many proverbs.
10. Koheleth sought to find words of
delight and words of truth recorded
properly. 11. The words of the wise are
like goads, and like well-fastened nails with
large heads, given from one shepherd.
12. And more than they, my son, beware:
making many books has no end, and studying much is a weariness of the flesh.
13. The end of the matter, everything
having been heard, fear God and keep His
commandments, for this is the entire man.
14. For every deed God will bring to
judgment—for every hidden thing, whether
good or bad.

The end of the matter, everything having been heard, fear God and keep His commandments, for this is the entire man.

הֶעָבִים אַחַר הַגָּשֶׁם: ג בַּיּוֹם שֶׁיָּזֻעוּ שֹׁמְרֵי
הַבַּיִת וְהִתְעַוְּתוּ אַנְשֵׁי הֶחָיִל וּבָטְלוּ הַטֹּחֲנוֹת כִּי
מִעֵטוּ וְחָשְׁכוּ הָרֹאוֹת בָּאֲרֻבּוֹת: ד וְסֻגְּרוּ
דְלָתַיִם בַּשּׁוּק בִּשְׁפַל קוֹל הַטַּחֲנָה וְיָקוּם לְקוֹל
הַצִּפּוֹר וְיִשַּׁחוּ כָּל־בְּנוֹת הַשִּׁיר: ה גַּם מִגָּבֹהַּ
יִירָאוּ וְחַתְחַתִּים בַּדֶּרֶךְ וְיָנֵאץ הַשָּׁקֵד וְיִסְתַּבֵּל
הֶחָגָב וְתָפֵר הָאֲבִיּוֹנָה כִּי־הֹלֵךְ הָאָדָם אֶל־בֵּית
עוֹלָמוֹ וְסָבְבוּ בַשּׁוּק הַסֹּפְדִים: ו עַד אֲשֶׁר לֹא־
יֵרָחֵק (ירתק קרי) חֶבֶל הַכֶּסֶף וְתָרֻץ גֻּלַּת הַזָּהָב
וְתִשָּׁבֶר כַּד עַל־הַמַּבּוּעַ וְנָרֹץ הַגַּלְגַּל אֶל־הַבּוֹר:
ז וְיָשֹׁב הֶעָפָר עַל־הָאָרֶץ כְּשֶׁהָיָה וְהָרוּחַ תָּשׁוּב
אֶל־הָאֱלֹהִים אֲשֶׁר נְתָנָהּ: ח הֲבֵל הֲבָלִים אָמַר
הַקּוֹהֶלֶת הַכֹּל הָבֶל: ט וְיֹתֵר שֶׁהָיָה קֹהֶלֶת חָכָם
עוֹד לִמַּד־דַּעַת אֶת־הָעָם וְאִזֵּן וְחִקֵּר תִּקֵּן
מְשָׁלִים הַרְבֵּה: י בִּקֵּשׁ קֹהֶלֶת לִמְצֹא דִּבְרֵי־
חֵפֶץ וְכָתוּב יֹשֶׁר דִּבְרֵי אֱמֶת: יא דִּבְרֵי חֲכָמִים
כַּדָּרְבֹנוֹת וּכְמַשְׂמְרוֹת נְטוּעִים בַּעֲלֵי אֲסֻפּוֹת
נִתְּנוּ מֵרֹעֶה אֶחָד: יב וְיֹתֵר מֵהֵמָּה בְּנִי הִזָּהֵר
עֲשׂוֹת סְפָרִים הַרְבֵּה אֵין קֵץ וְלַהַג הַרְבֵּה יְגִעַת
בָּשָׂר: יג סוֹף דָּבָר הַכֹּל נִשְׁמָע אֶת־הָאֱלֹהִים
יְרָא וְאֶת־מִצְוֺתָיו שְׁמוֹר כִּי־זֶה כָּל־הָאָדָם:
יד כִּי אֶת־כָּל־מַעֲשֶׂה הָאֱלֹהִים יָבִא בְמִשְׁפָּט
עַל כָּל־נֶעְלָם אִם־טוֹב וְאִם־רָע:

סוֹף דָּבָר הַכֹּל נִשְׁמָע אֶת־הָאֱלֹהִים יְרָא וְאֶת־מִצְוֺתָיו
שְׁמוֹר כִּי־זֶה כָּל־הָאָדָם:

ברכות התורה וההפטרה

BLESSINGS FOR THE READING OF
THE TORAH AND THE HAFTARAH

BLESSINGS AT THE READING OF THE TORAH

Each person called to the reading of the Torah says the following:

Bless the Lord, Who is blessed.

בָּרְכוּ אֶת־יְהֹוָה, הַמְבֹרָךְ:

The congregation responds:

Blessed be the Lord, Who is blessed forever and ever.

בָּרוּךְ יְהֹוָה, הַמְבֹרָךְ לְעוֹלָם וָעֶד:

The person called to the reading of the Torah, repeats:

Blessed be the Lord, Who is blessed forever and ever.

בָּרוּךְ יְהֹוָה, הַמְבֹרָךְ לְעוֹלָם וָעֶד:

The person then says:

Blessed are You, O Lord our God, King of the universe, Who has chosen us from all peoples, and has given us His Torah. Blessed are You, O Lord, Giver of the Torah.

בָּרוּךְ אַתָּה יְהֹוָה, אֱלֹהֵינוּ, מֶלֶךְ הָעוֹלָם, אֲשֶׁר בָּחַר־בָּנוּ מִכָּל הָעַמִּים, וְנָתַן לָנוּ אֶת תּוֹרָתוֹ. בָּרוּךְ אַתָּה יְהֹוָה, נוֹתֵן הַתּוֹרָה:

After the reading of a section of the Torah, he says:

Blessed are You, O Lord our God, King of the universe, Who has given us the Torah of truth, and has planted everlasting life in our midst. Blessed are You, O Lord, Giver of the Torah.

בָּרוּךְ אַתָּה יְהֹוָה, אֱלֹהֵינוּ, מֶלֶךְ הָעוֹלָם, אֲשֶׁר נָתַן־לָנוּ תּוֹרַת אֱמֶת, וְחַיֵּי עוֹלָם נָטַע בְּתוֹכֵנוּ. בָּרוּךְ אַתָּה יְהֹוָה, נוֹתֵן הַתּוֹרָה:

BLESSINGS AT THE READING OF THE HAFTARAH

Before reading the haftarah, the person called for maftir says:

Blessed are You, O Lord our God, King of the universe, Who has chosen good prophets, and desired their words, which were spoken in truth. Blessed are You, O Lord, Who has chosen the Torah, and Moses His servant, and Israel His people, and prophets of truth and righteousness.

בָּרוּךְ אַתָּה יְהֹוָה אֱלֹהֵינוּ מֶלֶךְ הָעוֹלָם אֲשֶׁר בָּחַר בִּנְבִיאִים טוֹבִים וְרָצָה בְדִבְרֵיהֶם הַנֶּאֱמָרִים בֶּאֱמֶת: בָּרוּךְ אַתָּה יְהֹוָה הַבּוֹחֵר בַּתּוֹרָה וּבְמֹשֶׁה עַבְדּוֹ וּבְיִשְׂרָאֵל עַמּוֹ וּבִנְבִיאֵי הָאֱמֶת וָצֶדֶק:

Sephardim conclude each haftarah with the words:

Our Redeemer, Lord of Hosts is His Name, Holy of Israel.

גֹּאֲלֵנוּ יְהֹוָה צְבָאוֹת שְׁמוֹ קְדוֹשׁ יִשְׂרָאֵל

After reading the haftarah, the maftir says:

Blessed are You, O Lord our God, King of the universe, Rock of all worlds, righteous through all generations; O faithful God, Who says and does, Who speaks and fulfills, all of Whose words are truth and righteousness.

בָּרוּךְ אַתָּה יְהֹוָה, אֱלֹהֵינוּ, מֶלֶךְ הָעוֹלָם, צוּר כָּל־הָעוֹלָמִים, צַדִּיק בְּכָל־הַדּוֹרוֹת, הָאֵל הַנֶּאֱמָן, הָאוֹמֵר וְעוֹשֶׂה, הַמְדַבֵּר וּמְקַיֵּם, שֶׁכָּל־דְּבָרָיו אֱמֶת וָצֶדֶק:

You are faithful, O Lord our God, and Your words are faithful, and not one of Your words returns unfulfilled, for You are a faithful (and merciful) God and King. Blessed are You, O Lord God, Who is faithful in all His words.

נֶאֱמָן, אַתָּה הוּא, יְהוָֹה אֱלֹהֵינוּ, וְנֶאֱמָנִים דְּבָרֶיךָ, וְדָבָר אֶחָד מִדְּבָרֶיךָ אָחוֹר לֹא־יָשׁוּב רֵיקָם, כִּי אֵל, מֶלֶךְ, נֶאֱמָן (וְרַחֲמָן), אָתָּה: בָּרוּךְ אַתָּה יְהוָֹה, הָאֵל הַנֶּאֱמָן בְּכָל־דְּבָרָיו:

Have mercy upon Zion, for it is the seat of our life, and save the one of miserable spirit speedily, even in our days. Blessed are You, O Lord, Who makes Zion rejoice through her children.

רַחֵם עַל־צִיּוֹן, כִּי הִיא בֵּית חַיֵּינוּ, וְלַעֲלוּבַת נֶפֶשׁ תּוֹשִׁיעַ בִּמְהֵרָה בְיָמֵינוּ: בָּרוּךְ אַתָּה יְהוָֹה, מְשַׂמֵּחַ צִיּוֹן, בְּבָנֶיהָ:

Gladden us, O Lord our God, with Elijah the prophet, Your servant, and with the kingdom of the house of David, Your anointed. Soon may he come and make our hearts rejoice. Let no stranger sit upon his throne, nor let others inherit his glory any longer; for Your Holy Name have You sworn him, that his light shall never be extinguished. Blessed are You, O Lord, the Shield of David.

שַׂמְּחֵנוּ, יְהוָֹה אֱלֹהֵינוּ, בְּאֵלִיָּהוּ הַנָּבִיא, עַבְדֶּךָ, וּבְמַלְכוּת בֵּית דָּוִד, מְשִׁיחֶךָ, בִּמְהֵרָה יָבֹא, וְיָגֵל לִבֵּנוּ, עַל כִּסְאוֹ לֹא יֵשֶׁב זָר, וְלֹא יִנְחֲלוּ עוֹד אֲחֵרִים אֶת כְּבוֹדוֹ, כִּי בְשֵׁם קָדְשְׁךָ נִשְׁבַּעְתָּ לּוֹ, שֶׁלֹּא יִכְבֶּה נֵרוֹ לְעוֹלָם וָעֶד: בָּרוּךְ אַתָּה יְהוָֹה, מָגֵן דָּוִד:

On fast days, as well as at minḥah on Yom Kippur, the haftarah blessings end here.

On Shabbath, including the Intermediate Shabbath of Pesaḥ, say:

For the Torah, for the divine service, for the Prophets, and for this Shabbath Day, which You, O Lord our God, have given us for holiness and for rest, for honor and for glory—

For all these we thank and bless You, O Lord our God; blessed be Your Name by the mouth of every living being, constantly and forever. Blessed are You, O Lord, Who hallows the Shabbath.

עַל־הַתּוֹרָה, וְעַל־הָעֲבוֹדָה, וְעַל־הַנְּבִיאִים, וְעַל־יוֹם הַשַּׁבָּת הַזֶּה, שֶׁנָּתַתָּ לָּנוּ, יְהוָֹה אֱלֹהֵינוּ, לִקְדֻשָּׁה וְלִמְנוּחָה, לְכָבוֹד וּלְתִפְאָרֶת: עַל־הַכֹּל, יְהוָֹה אֱלֹהֵינוּ, אֲנַחְנוּ מוֹדִים לָךְ וּמְבָרְכִים אוֹתָךְ, יִתְבָּרַךְ שִׁמְךָ בְּפִי כָּל־חַי תָּמִיד לְעוֹלָם וָעֶד: בָּרוּךְ אַתָּה יְהוָֹה, מְקַדֵּשׁ הַשַּׁבָּת:

On the Three Festivals (Pesaḥ, Shavuoth and Sukkoth) and on the Intermediate Shabbath of Sukkoth, say:

For the Torah, for the divine service, for the Prophets; (*On Shabbath add*: for this Shabbath Day), and for this

עַל הַתּוֹרָה, וְעַל הָעֲבוֹדָה, וְעַל הַנְּבִיאִים, וְעַל יוֹם (הַשַּׁבָּת הַזֶּה, וְעַל יוֹם)

On Pesaḥ:	*On Shavuoth:*	*On Sukkoth:*	*On Shemini Atzereth:*
חַג הַמַּצּוֹת הַזֶּה:	חַג הַשָּׁבוּעוֹת הַזֶּה:	חַג הַסֻּכּוֹת הַזֶּה:	הַשְּׁמִינִי חַג הָעֲצֶרֶת הַזֶּה:
day of the Feast of Unleavened Bread,	day of the Feast of Weeks,	day of the Feast of Tabernacles,	Eighth Day feast of Atzereth,

which You, O Lord our God, has given us (*On Shabbath add*: for holiness and for

שֶׁנָּתַתָּ לָּנוּ, יְהוָֹה אֱלֹהֵינוּ, (לִקְדֻשָּׁה וְלִמְנוּחָה),

rest,) for joy and gladness, for honor and glory—for all these we thank and bless You, O Lord our God; blessed be Your Name by the mouth of every living being, constantly and forever. Blessed are You, O Lord, Who hallows (*On Shabbath add*: the Shabbath,) Israel and the Festivals.

לְשָׂשׂוֹן וּלְשִׂמְחָה, לְכָבוֹד וּלְתִפְאָרֶת: עַל־הַכֹּל,
יְהֹוָה אֱלֹהֵינוּ, אֲנַחְנוּ מוֹדִים לָךְ וּמְבָרְכִים
אוֹתָךְ, יִתְבָּרַךְ שִׁמְךָ בְּפִי כָּל־חַי תָּמִיד לְעוֹלָם
וָעֶד: בָּרוּךְ אַתָּה יְהֹוָה, מְקַדֵּשׁ (הַשַּׁבָּת
וְ)יִשְׂרָאֵל וְהַזְּמַנִּים:

On Rosh Hashanah, say:

For the Law, for the divine service, for the Prophets (*On Shabbath add*: and for this Shabbath Day), and for this Day of Remembrance which You, O Lord our God, have given us (*On Shabbath add*: for holiness and for rest,) for honor and glory—for all these we thank and bless You, O Lord our God; blessed be Your Name by the mouth of every living being, constantly and forever; Your word is true and endures forever. Blessed are You, O Lord, King over the whole earth, Who hallows (*On Shabbath add*: the Shabbath,) Israel and the Day of Remembrance.

עַל הַתּוֹרָה, וְעַל הָעֲבוֹדָה, וְעַל הַנְּבִיאִים, וְעַל
יוֹם (הַשַּׁבָּת הַזֶּה, וְעַל יוֹם) הַזִּכָּרוֹן הַזֶּה, שֶׁנָּתַתָּ
לָּנוּ, יְהֹוָה אֱלֹהֵינוּ, (לִקְדֻשָּׁה וְלִמְנוּחָה), לְכָבוֹד
וּלְתִפְאָרֶת: עַל־הַכֹּל, יְהֹוָה אֱלֹהֵינוּ, אֲנַחְנוּ
מוֹדִים לָךְ וּמְבָרְכִים אוֹתָךְ, יִתְבָּרַךְ שִׁמְךָ בְּפִי
כָּל־חַי תָּמִיד לְעוֹלָם וָעֶד, וּדְבָרְךָ אֱמֶת וְקַיָּם
לָעַד: בָּרוּךְ אַתָּה יְהֹוָה, מֶלֶךְ עַל־כָּל־הָאָרֶץ,
מְקַדֵּשׁ (הַשַּׁבָּת וְ) יִשְׂרָאֵל, וְיוֹם הַזִּכָּרוֹן:

On Yom Kippur, say:

For the Torah, for the divine service, for the Prophets (*On Shabbath add*: for this Shabbath Day,) and for this Day of Atonement, which You, O Lord our God, have given us (*On Shabbath add*: for holiness and for rest,) for forgiveness, pardon and atonement, for honor and glory—for all these we thank and bless You, O Lord our God; blessed be Your Name by the mouth of every living being, constantly and forever; Your word is true and endures forever. Blessed are You, O Lord, O King, Who pardons and forgives our iniquities and the iniquities of Your people, the house of Israel, and removes our guilt year by year; King over the whole earth, Who hallows (*On Shabbath add*: the Shabbath,) Israel and the Day of Atonement.

עַל הַתּוֹרָה, וְעַל הָעֲבוֹדָה, וְעַל הַנְּבִיאִים, וְעַל
יוֹם (הַשַּׁבָּת הַזֶּה, וְעַל) הַכִּפֻּרִים הַזֶּה, שֶׁנָּתַתָּ
לָּנוּ, יְהֹוָה אֱלֹהֵינוּ, (לִקְדֻשָּׁה וְלִמְנוּחָה),
לִמְחִילָה, וְלִסְלִיחָה, וּלְכַפָּרָה וְלִמְחָל בּוֹ אֶת כָּל
עֲוֹנוֹתֵינוּ, לְכָבוֹד וּלְתִפְאָרֶת: עַל־הַכֹּל, יְהֹוָה
אֱלֹהֵינוּ, אֲנַחְנוּ מוֹדִים לָךְ וּמְבָרְכִים אוֹתָךְ,
יִתְבָּרַךְ שִׁמְךָ, בְּפִי כָּל־חַי תָּמִיד לְעוֹלָם וָעֶד,
וּדְבָרְךָ אֱמֶת וְקַיָּם לָעַד: בָּרוּךְ אַתָּה יְהֹוָה, מֶלֶךְ,
מוֹחֵל וְסוֹלֵחַ לַעֲוֹנוֹתֵינוּ, וְלַעֲוֹנוֹת עַמּוֹ בֵּית
יִשְׂרָאֵל, וּמַעֲבִיר אַשְׁמוֹתֵינוּ, בְּכָל שָׁנָה וְשָׁנָה,
מֶלֶךְ עַל־כָּל־הָאָרֶץ, מְקַדֵּשׁ (הַשַּׁבָּת וְ) יִשְׂרָאֵל,
וְיוֹם הַכִּפֻּרִים:

Cantillation Signs

The following symbols are the cantillation signs used for chanting the Torah readings, the Haftaroth, and the Five Megilloth. Although the melodies for these readings are varied, the identical cantillation signs are used and applied to each melody in similar fashion.

These notes do not appear in the Torah scroll, but were transmitted orally over the generations, until they were finally committed to writing. In the Talmud (*Nedarim* 37b), there was a controversy whether these notes were transmitted from Sinai, along with the Torah itself, or whether they were instituted by the Sages. Some claim that Ezra read the Torah to the people with these notes. This is intimated by Scripture in Nehemiah 8:8: "And they read in the Book, in the Torah of God, distinctly and giving the sense, and they caused them to understand the reading." "Giving the sense" alludes to the cantillation signs, which serve as punctuation marks as well, thereby shedding light on the sense of the verse, which can often be understood in various ways, depending on the punctuation.

Although the Ashkenazim have no melody for other Books of the Bible, these signs appear in all Books as punctuation marks, with the exception of the Books of Job, Proverbs, and Psalms, which have their own set of cantillation signs, known as טַעֲמֵי אֱמֶ״ת (איוב משלי תהלים). The Sephardim, however, use the cantillation signs for melodious readings throughout all the Books of the Bible.

The symbols are known by different names in the various communities. The following names are those used by Ashkenazic, Sephardic and Italian Jews.

Cantillation signs according to the Ashkenazic rite

זַרְקָא֮ סֶגּוֹל֒ מֻנַּח ׀ מֻנַּח֣ רְבִ֗יעַ פָּזֵ֡ר תְּלִישָׁא֠ גְדוֹלָה֩ תְּלִישָׁא֠ קְטַנָּה֠
קַדְמָ֨א וְאַזְלָ֜א מַהְפַּ֤ךְ פַּשְׁטָא֙ זָקֵף֔ קָטֹ֔ן זָקֵף֕ גָּד֕וֹל דַּרְגָּ֧א תְּבִ֛יר מֵרְכָ֦א
טִפְּחָ֖א אֶתְנַחְתָּ֑א אַזְלָ֜א גֵּ֝רֵשׁ גֵּרְשַׁ֞יִם יְתִ֚יב פְּסִיק ׀ שַׁלְשֶׁ֓לֶת יֶרַח֪ בֶּן־
יוֹמ֫וֹ קַרְנֵי־פָרָ֟ה מֵרְכָא־כְפוּלָ֦ה טִפְּחָ֖א מֶֽתֶג מַקַּף־ סוֹף פָּסֽוּק׃

Cantillation signs according to the Sephardic rite

זַרְקָא֮ מַקַּף־שׁוֹפָ֣ר הוֹלֵ֣ךְ סְגוֹלְתָּא֒ פָּזֵ֡ר גָּד֟וֹל יָרֵ֪חַ בֶּן יוֹמ֫וֹ קַרְנֵ֟י פָרָ֟ה
גַּעְיָא תַּלְשָׁא֠ אַזְלָ֜א גְּרִ֝ישׁ פָּסֵק ׀ רְבִ֗יעַ שׁוֹפָ֤ר מְהוּפָּ֤ךְ קַדְמָא֙ תְּרֵ֨י
קַדְמִ֨ין זָקֵף֔ קָטֹ֔ן זָקֵף֕ גָּד֕וֹל שַׁלְשֶׁ֓לֶת שְׁנֵי גְרִישִׁ֞ין תְּרֵ֨י טַעְמֵ֨י דַּרְגָּ֧א
תְּבִ֛יר מַאֲרִ֥יךְ טַרְחָ֖א אַתְנָ֑ח רָפֵֿא דָּגֵשׁ יְתִ֚יב תַּרְצָ֙א שְׁבוּלֶת שְׁבוּלֶת
מַפִּיק בְּהֵ֑א שְׁבָ֑א גַּעְיָ֑א שְׁבָ֑א סוֹף פָּסֽוּק׃

Cantillation signs according to the Italian rite

זַרְקָא֮ שְׂרֵ֨י פָּזֵ֡ר גָּד֟וֹל קַרְנֵ֟י פָרָ֟ה תַּלְשָׁא֠ תַּרְסָא֩ לְגַרְמֵ֣יהּ ׀ רְבִ֗יעַ פְּסִיק
שַׁלְשֶׁ֓לֶת קַדְמָ֨א אַזְלָ֜א זָקֵף֔ גָּד֕וֹל זָקֵף֕ קָטֹ֔ן שְׁנֵי גְרִישִׁ֞ין תְּרֵ֨ין חוּטְרִ֨ין
דַּרְגָּ֧א תְּבִ֛יר טַרְחָ֖א מַאֲרִ֥יךְ שׁוֹפָ֣ר עִלּ֤וּי שׁוֹפָ֤ר הָפ֤וּךְ שׁוֹפָ֣ר יְתִ֚יב שְׁנֵ֨י
פַּשְׁטִין֙ סְמִ֣יךְ־אַתְנָ֑ח יָרֵ֪חַ בֶּן־יוֹמ֫וֹ גֵּ֝רֵשׁ סוֹף פָּסֽוּק׃

Ta'am Ha'elyon (The Upper Mode)

When reading the Ten Commandments in public, we do not use the conventional cantillation signs which divide the text into verses. Instead, a special set of cantillation signs is used which makes each commandment a seperate verse. The first two commandments, however, are read as one verse. This is reminiscent of the giving of the Torah when these two commandments were given without any interruption.

Originally, this set of notes was used only on *Shavuoth*. The present custom, however, is to use it whenever the Ten Commandments are read from the Torah in public, viz. when the weekly portions of *Yithro* and *Va'ethhanan* are read, and on *Shavuoth*.

For the antecendents of this custom, see *Havanath Hamikra*, end of *Shemoth*, by Wolf Heidenheim.

For the portion of Yithro and Shavuoth טעם העליון לפרשת יתרו וחג השבועות

אָנֹכִי֙ יְהֹוָ֣ה אֱלֹהֶ֔יךָ אֲשֶׁ֧ר הוֹצֵאתִ֛יךָ מֵאֶ֥רֶץ מִצְרַ֖יִם מִבֵּ֣ית עֲבָדִ֑ים לֹ֣א
יִֽהְיֶ֣ה לְךָ֩ אֱלֹהִ֨ים אֲחֵרִ֜ים עַל־פָּנַ֗י לֹ֣א תַֽעֲשֶׂ֨ה־לְךָ֥ פֶ֣סֶל ׀ וְכָל־תְּמוּנָ֡ה
אֲשֶׁ֣ר בַּשָּׁמַ֣יִם ׀ מִמַּ֡עַל וַאֲשֶׁר֩ בָּאָ֨רֶץ מִתַּ֜חַת וַאֲשֶׁ֥ר בַּמַּ֣יִם ׀ מִתַּ֣חַת לָאָ֗רֶץ
לֹֽא־תִשְׁתַּחֲוֶ֥ה לָהֶ֛ם וְלֹ֥א תָעָבְדֵ֖ם כִּ֣י אָנֹכִ֞י יְהֹוָ֤ה אֱלֹהֶ֙יךָ֙ אֵ֣ל קַנָּ֔א פֹּ֠קֵד
עֲוֺ֨ן אָבֹ֧ת עַל־בָּנִ֛ים עַל־שִׁלֵּשִׁ֥ים וְעַל־רִבֵּעִ֖ים לְשֹֽׂנְאָ֑י וְעֹ֤שֶׂה חֶ֙סֶד֙
לַאֲלָפִ֔ים לְאֹהֲבַ֖י וּלְשֹׁמְרֵ֥י מִצְוֺתָֽי׃ ס לֹ֥א תִשָּׂ֛א אֶת־שֵֽׁם־יְהֹוָ֥ה אֱלֹהֶ֖יךָ
לַשָּׁ֑וְא כִּ֣י לֹ֤א יְנַקֶּה֙ יְהֹוָ֔ה אֵ֛ת אֲשֶׁר־יִשָּׂ֥א אֶת־שְׁמ֖וֹ לַשָּֽׁוְא׃ פ זָכ֛וֹר֩ אֶת־
י֨וֹם הַשַּׁבָּ֜ת לְקַדְּשׁ֗וֹ שֵׁ֤שֶׁת יָמִים֙ תַּעֲבֹד֙ וְעָשִׂ֣יתָ כָל־מְלַאכְתֶּ֔ךָ וְי֙וֹם֙
הַשְּׁבִיעִ֜י שַׁבָּ֣ת ׀ לַיהֹוָ֣ה אֱלֹהֶ֗יךָ לֹ֣א תַעֲשֶׂ֣ה כָל־מְלָאכָ֡ה אַתָּ֣ה וּבִנְךָֽ־וּ֠בִתֶּךָ
עַבְדְּךָ֨ וַאֲמָתְךָ֜ וּבְהֶמְתֶּ֗ךָ וְגֵרְךָ֙ אֲשֶׁ֣ר בִּשְׁעָרֶ֔יךָ כִּ֣י שֵֽׁשֶׁת־יָמִים֩ עָשָׂ֨ה יְהֹוָ֜ה
אֶת־הַשָּׁמַ֣יִם וְאֶת־הָאָ֗רֶץ אֶת־הַיָּם֙ וְאֶת־כָּל־אֲשֶׁר־בָּ֔ם וַיָּ֖נַח בַּיּ֣וֹם
הַשְּׁבִיעִ֑י עַל־כֵּ֗ן בֵּרַ֧ךְ יְהֹוָ֛ה אֶת־י֥וֹם הַשַּׁבָּ֖ת וַֽיְקַדְּשֵֽׁהוּ׃ ס כַּבֵּ֥ד אֶת־אָבִ֖יךָ
וְאֶת־אִמֶּ֑ךָ לְמַ֙עַן֙ יַאֲרִכ֣וּן יָמֶ֔יךָ עַ֚ל הָאֲדָמָ֔ה אֲשֶׁר־יְהֹוָ֥ה אֱלֹהֶ֖יךָ נֹתֵ֥ן
לָֽךְ׃ ס לֹ֖א תִּרְצָֽח׃ ס לֹ֖א תִּנְאָֽף׃ ס לֹ֖א תִּגְנֹֽב׃ ס לֹֽא־תַעֲנֶ֥ה בְרֵעֲךָ֖ עֵ֥ד
שָֽׁקֶר׃ ס לֹ֥א תַחְמֹ֖ד בֵּ֣ית רֵעֶ֑ךָ ס לֹ֥א תַחְמֹ֞ד אֵ֣שֶׁת רֵעֶ֗ךָ וְעַבְדּ֤וֹ וַאֲמָתוֹ֙
וְשׁוֹר֣וֹ וַחֲמֹר֔וֹ וְכֹ֖ל אֲשֶׁ֥ר לְרֵעֶֽךָ׃

For the portion of Va'ethhanan טעם העליון לפרשת ואתחנן

אָנֹכִי֙ יְהֹוָ֣ה אֱלֹהֶ֔יךָ אֲשֶׁ֧ר הוֹצֵאתִ֛יךָ מֵאֶ֥רֶץ מִצְרַ֖יִם מִבֵּ֣ית עֲבָדִ֑ים לֹ֣א
יִֽהְיֶ֣ה לְךָ֩ אֱלֹהִ֨ים אֲחֵרִ֜ים עַל־פָּנַ֗י לֹ֣א תַֽעֲשֶׂה־לְךָ֥ פֶ֣סֶל ׀ כָּל־תְּמוּנָ֡ה אֲשֶׁ֣ר
בַּשָּׁמַ֣יִם ׀ מִמַּ֡עַל וַאֲשֶׁר֩ בָּאָ֨רֶץ מִתַּ֜חַת וַאֲשֶׁ֥ר בַּמַּ֣יִם ׀ מִתַּ֣חַת לָאָ֗רֶץ לֹֽא־
תִשְׁתַּחֲוֶ֥ה לָהֶ֛ם וְלֹ֥א תָעָבְדֵ֖ם כִּ֣י אָנֹכִ֞י יְהֹוָ֤ה אֱלֹהֶ֙יךָ֙ אֵ֣ל קַנָּ֔א פֹּ֠קֵד עֲוֺ֨ן
אָב֧וֹת עַל־בָּנִ֛ים וְעַל־שִׁלֵּשִׁ֥ים וְעַל־רִבֵּעִ֖ים לְשֹֽׂנְאָ֑י וְעֹ֤שֶׂה חֶ֙סֶד֙ לַאֲלָפִ֔ים
לְאֹהֲבַ֖י וּלְשֹׁמְרֵ֥י מִצְוֺתָֽו (מצותי קרי)׃ ס לֹ֥א תִשָּׂ֛א אֶת־שֵֽׁם־יְהֹוָ֥ה אֱלֹהֶ֖יךָ

לַשָּׁ֑וְא כִּ֣י לֹ֤א יְנַקֶּה֙ יְהֹוָ֔ה אֵ֛ת אֲשֶׁר־יִשָּׂ֥א אֶת־שְׁמ֖וֹ לַשָּֽׁוְא׃ ס שָׁמ֛וֹר
אֶת־י֥וֹם֩ הַשַּׁבָּ֖ת לְקַדְּשׁ֑וֹ כַּאֲשֶׁ֥ר צִוְּךָ֣ ׀ יְהֹוָ֣ה אֱלֹהֶ֗יךָ שֵׁ֤שֶׁת יָמִים֙ תַּעֲבֹ֔ד
וְעָשִׂ֖יתָ כָּל־מְלַאכְתֶּֽךָ וְי֙וֹם֙ הַשְּׁבִיעִ֔י שַׁבָּ֖ת ׀ לַיהֹוָ֣ה אֱלֹהֶ֑יךָ לֹ֣א תַעֲשֶׂ֣ה
כָל־מְלָאכָ֡ה אַתָּ֣ה וּבִנְךָ־וּבִתֶּ֣ךָ וְעַבְדְּךָ־וַ֠אֲמָתֶ֠ךָ וְשׁוֹרְךָ֨ וַחֲמֹרְךָ֜ וְכָל־
בְּהֶמְתֶּ֗ךָ וְגֵרְךָ֙ אֲשֶׁ֣ר בִּשְׁעָרֶ֔יךָ לְמַ֗עַן יָנ֛וּחַ עַבְדְּךָ֥ וַאֲמָתְךָ֖ כָּמ֑וֹךָ וְזָכַרְתָּ֞
כִּי־עֶ֣בֶד הָיִ֣יתָ ׀ בְּאֶ֣רֶץ מִצְרַ֗יִם וַיֹּצִ֨אֲךָ֜ יְהֹוָ֤ה אֱלֹהֶ֙יךָ֙ מִשָּׁם֙ בְּיָ֤ד חֲזָקָה֙
וּבִזְרֹ֣עַ נְטוּיָ֔ה עַל־כֵּ֗ן צִוְּךָ֙ יְהֹוָ֣ה אֱלֹהֶ֔יךָ לַעֲשׂ֖וֹת אֶת־י֥וֹם הַשַּׁבָּֽת׃ ס
כַּבֵּ֤ד אֶת־אָבִ֙יךָ֙ וְאֶת־אִמֶּ֔ךָ כַּאֲשֶׁ֥ר צִוְּךָ֖ יְהֹוָ֣ה אֱלֹהֶ֑יךָ לְמַ֣עַן ׀ יַאֲרִיכֻ֣ן
יָמֶ֗יךָ וּלְמַ֙עַן֙ יִ֣יטַב לָ֔ךְ עַ֚ל הָאֲדָמָ֔ה אֲשֶׁר־יְהֹוָ֥ה אֱלֹהֶ֖יךָ נֹתֵ֥ן לָֽךְ׃ ס לֹ֖א
תִּרְצָֽח׃ ס וְלֹ֖א תִּנְאָֽף׃ ס וְלֹ֖א תִּגְנֹֽב׃ ס וְלֹא־תַעֲנֶ֥ה בְרֵעֲךָ֖ עֵ֥ד שָֽׁוְא׃ ס
וְלֹ֥א תַחְמֹ֖ד אֵ֣שֶׁת רֵעֶ֑ךָ ס וְלֹ֨א תִתְאַוֶּ֜ה בֵּ֣ית רֵעֶ֗ךָ שָׂדֵ֙הוּ֙ וְעַבְדּ֣וֹ וַאֲמָתוֹ֙
שׁוֹר֣וֹ וַחֲמֹר֔וֹ וְכֹ֖ל אֲשֶׁ֥ר לְרֵעֶֽךָ׃